Dictionary of World Biography

The 19th Century

Dictionary of World Biography

The Ancient World
The Middle Ages
The Renaissance
The 17th and 18th Centuries
The 19th Century, 2 volumes
The 20th Century, 3 volumes
Index

Dictionary of World Biography

Volume 5
The 19th Century
A–J

Frank N. Magill, *editor*

Christina J. Moose, *managing editor*

Alison Aves, *researcher and bibliographer*

Mark Rehn, *acquisitions editor*

FITZROY DEARBORN PUBLISHERS
CHICAGO • LONDON

SALEM PRESS
PASADENA • HACKENSACK, NJ

Dictionary of World Biography is a copublication of Salem Press, Inc. and Fitzroy Dearborn Publishers

For information, write to:

SALEM PRESS, INC.
P.O. Box 50062
Pasadena, California 91115

or

FITZROY DEARBORN PUBLISHERS
919 North Michigan Avenue, Suite 760
Chicago, Illinois 60611
USA

or

FITZROY DEARBORN PUBLISHERS
310 Regent Street
London W1R 5AJ
England

The paper used in this volume conforms to the American National Standard for Permanence of Paper for Printed Library Materials, Z39.48-1992.

Library of Congress Cataloging-in-Publication Data
Dictionary of world biography / editor, Frank N. Magill ; managing editor, Christina J. Moose ; researcher and bibliographer, Alison Aves ; acquisitions editor, Mark Rehn.
    v. cm.
    A revision and reordering, with new entries added, of the material in the thirty vols. comprising the various subsets designated "series" published under the collective title: Great lives from history, 1987-1995.
    Includes bibliographical references and indexes.
    Contents: v.5. The nineteenth century, entries A–J.
    ISBN 0-89356-318-8 (v. 5: alk. paper)
    ISBN 0-89356-317-X (v. 5-6 set: alk. paper)
    ISBN 0-89356-273-4 (v. 1-10 set: alk paper)
    1. Biography. 2. World history. I. Magill, Frank Northen, 1907-1997. II. Moose, Christina J., 1952- . III. Aves, Alison. IV. Great lives from history.
CT104.D54 1998
920.02—dc21
                                                97-51154
                                                  CIP

British Library Cataloguing-in-Publication Data is available.
Fitzroy Dearborn ISBN 1-57958-044-0
First Published in the U.K. and U.S., 1999
    Printed by Braun-Brumfield, Inc.

Cover design by Peter Aristedes.

First Printing

CONTENTS

Publishers' Note vii

Contributing Essayists ix

List of Entrants xix

DICTIONARY OF WORLD BIOGRAPHY: The Nineteenth Century: A–J 1

K–Z 1255

Indices

Area of Achievement 2427

Geographical Location 2439

Name Index 2447

Photography Credits 2455

PUBLISHERS' NOTE

The *Dictionary of World Biography, Volumes V and VI: The Nineteenth Century* are the fifth and sixth installments in a projected ten-volume series covering the lives of important personages from the ancient world through the twentieth century. This new series is a revision and reordering of Salem Press's thirty-volume *Great Lives from History* series. The contents of the various *Great Lives from History* sets have been integrated and then rearranged from a geographical perspective into a chronological one, combining biographies of important people from all over the world into individual titles, each covering an era. The existing essays are enhanced by the addition of new entries, updated bibliographies, a new page design, and illustrations.

The Nineteenth Century, volumes 5 and 6 of the dictionary, gathers 544 essays from the *Great Lives from History* series and adds 69 new biographies, creating a total of 613 essays covering important figures who flourished between 1801 and 1900. Those dates divide the focus of this volume from those of the preceding and succeeding ones, which are devoted to the seventeenth and eighteenth centuries and to the twentieth century, respectively. Biographies spanning two centuries were moved into the period that best encompassed the subject's life's work or major accomplishments.

The articles in this series range from two thousand to three thousand words in length and follow a standard format. Each article begins with ready-reference listings, including a brief statement summarizing the individual's contribution to his or her society and to later ages. The body of the article is divided into three parts. "Early Life," the first section, provides facts about the individual's upbringing and the environment in which he or she was reared, setting the stage for the heart of the article, entitled "Life's Work." This section consists of a straightforward account of the period during which the individual's most significant achievements were made. The concluding section, the "Summary," is not a recapitulation of what has been discussed but rather an overview of the individual's place in history. Each essay is supplemented by an annotated, evaluative bibliography, a starting point for further research.

The temporal and geographical scope of *The Nineteenth Century* is broad. Represented are figures as remote as English author Jane Austen, whose realistic novels of upper-class life in late eighteenth and early nineteenth century England continue to provide an understanding of human nature, and as near to us as Thomas Edison, the American inventor who ushered in the age of electricity; the selection spans the Eastern and Western hemispheres. The editors have sought to provide coverage that is broad in area of achievement as well as geography while at the same time including the recognized shapers of history, including major world leaders, giants of religious faith, scholars, philosophers, scientists, explorers, and artists—all of them architects of today's civilization.

While each volume in the *Dictionary of World Biography* has its distinctive qualities, several features distinguish this series as a whole from other biographical reference works. The articles combine breadth of coverage with a format that offers the user quick access to the particular information needed. For convenience of reference, this volume is indexed by area of achievement and by geographical location as well as by name. The tenth volume of the series will provide a comprehensive index to all previous volumes, allowing users access to the biographies of all the figures covered, from the ancient world through the twentieth century.

We would like to extend our appreciation to all those involved in development and production of this series. Each essay has been written by an academician who specializes in the area of discussion; without their expert contribution, a project of this nature would not be possible. A full list of contributors and their affiliations appears at the beginning of this volume.

CONTRIBUTING ESSAYISTS

Michael Adams
Wagner College, New York

Beverley Allix
University of Toronto

Arthur L. Alt
College of Great Falls

Eleanor B. Amico
Independent scholar

Richard J. Amundson
Columbus College

John D. Anderson, Jr.
University of Maryland at College Park

Nancy Fix Anderson
Loyola University, New Orleans

Andrew J. Angyal
Elon College, North Carolina

Stanley Archer
Texas A&M University

James A. Arieti
Hampden-Sydney College, Virginia

Stephen M. Ashby
Bowling Green State University, Ohio

Bryan Aubrey
Independent scholar

Tom L. Auffenberg
Ouachita Baptist University, Arkansas

Ann Marie B. Bahr
South Dakota State University

Brian S. Baigrie
University of Calgary, Alberta

John W. Bailey
Carthage College, Wisconsin

Ann Stewart Balakier
University of South Dakota

John W. Barker
University of Wisconsin—Madison

Jeffrey G. Barlow
Lewis and Clark College, Oregon

Dan Barnett
California State University, Chico

David Barratt
Independent scholar

Thomas F. Barry
University of Southern California

Iraj Bashiri
University of Minnesota at Minneapolis St. Paul

Christopher Bassford
Purdue University, West Lafayette, Indiana

Erving E. Beauregard
University of Dayton, Ohio

S. Carol Berg
College of Saint Benedict, Minnesota

Martin Berger
Youngstown State University, Ohio

Milton Berman
University of Rochester, New York

Robert L. Berner
University of Wisconsin—Oshkosh

Robert E. Bieder
Indiana University at Bloomington

Terry D. Bilhartz
Sam Houston State University, Texas

Donald S. Birn
State University of New York, College at Albany

Margaret Boe Birns
New York University

Carol Bishop
Indiana University, Southeast

Brian L. Blakeley
Texas Tech University

Wayne M. Bledsoe
University of Missouri at Rolla

Arnold Blumberg
Towson State University, Maryland

David Warren Bowen
Livingston University, Alabama

Keith Bowen
Southern Oregon State College

Newell D. Boyd
Houston Baptist University, Texas

John Braeman
University of Nebraska at Lincoln

Harold Branam
Temple University, Pennsylvania

Gerhard Brand
California State University, Los Angeles

Jeff R. Bremer
California State University, Bakersfield

J. R. Broadus
University of North Carolina at Chapel Hill

Celeste Williams Brockington
Independent scholar

Judit Brody
Independent scholar

Jerry H. Brookshire
Middle Tennessee State University

Keith H. Brower
Salisbury State University, Maryland

Alan Brown
Livingston University, Alabama

Norman D. Brown
University of Texas at Austin

Philip C. Brown
University of North Carolina at Charlotte

Anthony Brundage
California State Polytechnic University, Pomona

David D. Buck
University of Wisconsin—Milwaukee

David L. Bullock
Kansas State University

William H. Burnside
John Brown University, Arkansas

D. Burrill
California State University, Los Angeles

Larry W. Burt
University of Utah

Stephen Burwood
State University of New York, College at Binghamton

Charles J. Bussey
Western Kentucky University

Andrew J. Butrica
Cité des Sciences et de l'Industrie, Paris

John R. Bylsma
Augustana College, South Dakota

Joseph Byrne
Belmont University, Tennessee

John A. Calabrese
Texas Woman's University

Susanna Calkins
Purdue University, Indiana

Byron D. Cannon
University of Utah

Jack J. Cardoso
State University of New York, College at Buffalo

W. Bernard Carlson
University of Virginia at Charlottesville

John Carpenter
University of Michigan at Ann Arbor

James A. Casada
Winthrop College, South Carolina

Thomas J. Cassidy
South Carolina State University

Elisabeth A. Cawthon
University of Texas at Arlington

Allan D. Charles
University of South Carolina

Deborah Charlie
California State University, Northridge

Victor W. Chen
Chabot College, California

Ellen Clark
Independent scholar

Walter Aaron Clark
University of California, Los Angeles

Martin B. Cohen
George Mason University, Virginia

William Condon
University of Michigan at Ann Arbor

Raymond M. Cooke
Northwest Nazarene College, Idaho

Richard G. Cormack
Independent scholar

Albert Costa
Duquesne University, Pennsylvania

Dennis Costanzo
State University of New York, College at Plattsburgh

David A. Crain
South Dakota State University

Lee B. Croft
Arizona State University

Carol Crowe-Carraco
Western Kentucky University

E. R. Crowther
Adams State College, Colorado

LouAnn Faris Culley
Kansas State University

Light Townsend Cummins
Austin College, Texas

J. D. Daubs
University of Illinois at Urbana-Champaign

Abraham A. Davidson
Temple University, Pennsylvania

Ronald W. Davis
Western Michigan University

Frank Day
Clemson University, South Carolina

Tom Dewey II
University of Mississippi

Reidar Dittmann
Saint Olaf College, Minnesota

Charles A. Dranguet, Jr.
Southeastern Louisiana University

Steven L. Driever
University of Missouri at Kansas City

Ian Duffy
Lehigh University, Pennsylvania

Frederick Dumin
Washington State University

Charles Duncan
Atlanta University, Georgia

Kathleen E. Dunlop
East Carolina University

William E. Eagan
Moorhead State University, Minnesota

Wilton Eckley
Colorado School of Mines

Bruce L. Edwards
Bowling Green State University, Ohio

Harry J. Eisenman
University of Missouri at Rolla

Thomas J. Elliott
California State Polytechnic University

Mark R. Ellis
University of Nebraska at Lincoln

Robert P. Ellis
Independent scholar

Paul H. Elovitz
Ramapo College of New Jersey

Linda Eikmeier Endersby
Massachusetts Institute of Technology

Thomas L. Erskine
Salisbury State University, Maryland

Paul F. Erwin
University of Cincinnati, Ohio

Kimberly K. Estep
Wesleyan College, Georgia

Peter R. Faber
United States Air Force Academy, Colorado

Dean Fafoutis
Salisbury State University, Maryland

Norman B. Ferris
Middle Tennessee State University

James E. Fickle
Memphis State University, Tennessee

Donald M. Fiene
University of Tennessee at Knoxville

Paul Finkelman
State University of New York, College at Binghamton

Roy E. Finkenbine
Florida State University

Edward Fiorelli
St. John's University

David Marc Fischer
Independent scholar

Michael S. Fitzgerald
Purdue University, West Lafayette, Indiana

Dale L. Flesher
University of Mississippi

Bonnie Ford
Sacramento City College, California

Kirk Ford, Jr.
Mississippi College

Margot K. Frank
Randolph-Macon Women's College, Virginia

C. E. Frazier
Sam Houston State University, Texas

Richard G. Frederick
University of Pittsburgh at Bradford, Pennsylvania

C. George Fry
Lutheran College

Gloria Fulton
Humboldt State University, California

Jean C. Fulton
Maharishi International University

John G. Gallaher
Southern Illinois University at Edwardsville

Keith Garebian
Independent scholar

K. Fred Gillum
Colby College, Maine

Juana Goergen
De Paul University, Illinois

Joseph A. Goldenberg
Virginia State University

Nancy M. Gordon
Independent scholar

Lewis L. Gould
University of Texas at Austin

C. L. Grant
Georgia State University

Lloyd J. Graybar
Eastern Kentucky University

William C. Griffin
Appalachian State University, North Carolina

Christopher E. Guthrie
Tarleton State University

D. Harland Hagler
North Texas State University

Gavin R. G. Hambly
University of Texas at Dallas

William S. Haney II
Maharishi International University, Iowa

Elizabeth Harris
National Museum of Natural History

Fred R. van Hartesveldt
Fort Valley State College, Georgia

John Harty
University of Florida

Albert A. Hayden
Wittenberg University, Ohio

David S. Heidler
Salisbury State College, Maryland

John A. Heitmann
University of Dayton, Ohio

Terry Heller
Coe College, Iowa

Michael F. Hembree
Florida State University

Carlanna Hendrick
Governors School for Science and Mathematics

Erwin Hester
East Carolina University

Richard L. Hillard
University of Arkansas, Pine Bluff

James R. Hofmann
California State University, Fullerton

Hal Holladay
Simon's Rock College of Bard, Massachusetts

Authur B. Holmes
West Virginia Wesleyan College

Ari Hoogenboom
City University of New York, Brooklyn College

Allen Horstman
Albion College, Michigan

Ronald Howard
Mississippi College

Tonya Huber
Wichita State University, Kansas

E. D. Huntley
Appalachian State University, North Carolina

Mary Hurd
East Tennessee State University

John Quinn Imholte
University of Minnesota at Morris

Carlton Jackson
Western Kentucky University

Duncan R. Jamieson
Ashland University, Ohio

George Javor
Northern Michigan University

Shakuntala Jayaswal
University of New Haven, Connecticut

Sheila Golburgh Johnson
Independent scholar

Eileen T. Johnston
United States Naval Academy, Maryland

Jonathan M. Jones
University of Memphis, Tennessee

Michelle L. Jones
Muskingum College, Ohio

Philip Dwight Jones
Bradley University, Illinois

Marcella Joy
Independent scholar

Charles L. Kammer
College of Wooster, Ohio

Paul Kane
Yale University, Connecticut

Anand Karnad
Boston City Hospital

Cynthia Lee Katona
Ohlone College

Anne Kearney
Jefferson Community College

Jeanette Keith
Vanderbilt University, Tennessee

Steven G. Kellman
University of Texas at San Antonio

W. P. Kenney
Manhattan College, New York

Karen A. Kildahl
South Dakota State University

Kenneth F. Kiple
Bowling Green State University, Ohio

Kenneth F. Kitchell, Jr.
Louisiana State University

Wm. Laird Kleine-Ahlbrandt
Purdue University, West Lafayette, Indiana

Dwight A. Klett
Rutgers University, New Jersey

Phillip E. Koerper
Jacksonville State University, Alabama

Gregory C. Kozlowski
De Paul University, Illinois

Carl E. Kramer
Indiana University, Southeast

Charles Kraszewski
Pennsylvania State University

Henry Kratz
University of Tennessee at Knoxville

Marjorie Kratz
Maryville College, Tennessee

Abraham D. Kriegel
Memphis State University, Tennessee

Lynn C. Kronzek
Independent scholar

David W. Krueger
Arkansas Tech University

Neil Kunze
Northern Arizona University

David Z. Kushner
University of Florida

Pavlin Lange
Independent scholar

Ralph L. Langenheim, Jr.
University of Illinois at Urbana-Champaign

Karl G. Larew
Towson State University, Maryland

J. C. Larrabee
Case Western Reserve University, Ohio

Eugene S. Larson
Pierce College, Washington

Jack M. Lauber
University of Wisconsin—Eau Claire

Harry Lawton
University of California, Santa Barbara

Leon Lewis
Appalachian State University, North Carolina

Victor Lindsey
East Central University, Oklahoma

Monroe H. Little, Jr.
Indiana University—Purdue University at Indianapolis

James D. Lockett
Stillman College, Alabama

Rey M. Longyear
University of Kentucky, Lexington

John L. Loos
Louisiana State University, Baton Rouge

Rita E. Loos
Framingham State College, Massachusetts

Reinhart Lutz
University of California, Santa Barbara

Richard B. McCaslin
Independent scholar

Sandra C. McClain
Georgia Southern University

Robert McColley
University of Illinois at Urbana-Champaign

C. S. McConnell
University of Calgary, Alberta

Philip McDermott
Independent scholar

Kathryne S. McDorman
Texas Christian University

Barry McGill
Oberlin College, Ohio

James E. McGoldrick
Cedarville College, Ohio

William McGucken
University of Akron, Ohio

Jennifer McLeod
California State University, Chico

Robert J. McNutt
Independent scholar

Kerrie L. MacPherson
University of Hong Kong

David K. McQuilkin
Bridgewater College, Virginia

Paul Madden
Hardin-Simmons University, Texas

Claudette R. Mainzer
University of Georgia, Athens

Richard L. Mallery
Independent scholar

E. Deanne Malpass
Stephen F. Austin State University, Texas

Nancy Farm Mannikko
Michigan Technological University

Jo Manning
Independent scholar

Carl Henry Marcoux
University of California, Riverside

Marsha Kass Marks
Alabama Agricultural and Mechanical University

Joss Marsh
University of California, Santa Barbara

John F. Marszalek
Mississippi State University

Paul Marx
University of New Haven, Connecticut

Thomas Matchie
North Dakota State University

Elaine Mathiasen
Independent scholar

Jeffrey J. Matthews
University of Kentucky

Anne Laura Mattrella
Southeastern University, D.C.

Charles E. May
California State University, Long Beach

Laurence W. Mazzeno
United States Naval Academy, Maryland

Patrick Meanor
State University of New York College at Oneonta

Deborah T. Meem
University of Cincinnati, Ohio

Linda J. Meyers
Pasadena City College, California

Rose Ethel Althaus Meza
Queensborough Community College, New York

Norton Mezvinsky
Central Connecticut State University

Sara Joan Miles
Wheaton College

Michele L. Mock
University of Pittsburgh at Johnstown, Pennsylvania

Ronald O. Moore
University of Tennessee at Chattanooga

William V. Moore
College of Charleston, South Carolina

Robert A. Morace
Daemen College, New York

Gordon R. Mork
Purdue University, West Lafayette, Indiana

Raymond Lee Muncy
Harding University, Arkansas

B. Keith Murphy
Fort Valley State University, Georgia

D. Gosselin Nakeeb
Pace University, New York

William Nelles
Northwestern State University, Louisiana

Brian J. Nichelson
United States Air Force Academy, Colorado

Glenn O. Nichols
Anderson College, South Carolina

Michael R. Nichols
Texas Christian University

Roger L. Nichols
University of Arizona

Frank Nickell
Southeast Missouri State University

Richard L. Niswonger
John Brown University, Arkansas

Helen Jean M. Nugent
Franklin College of Indiana

Parker Bradley Nutting
Framingham State College, Massachusetts

Robert H. O'Connor
North Dakota State University

James W. Oberly
University of Wisconsin—Eau Claire

Maurice R. O'Connell
Fordham University, New York

Patricia Okker
University of Missouri at Columbia

Paul Michael O'Shea
University of Oregon

Gary B. Ostrower
Alfred University, New York

Robert J. Paradowski
Rochester Institute of Technology, New York

Harold M. Parker, Jr.
Western State College of Colorado

Judith A. Parsons
Sul Ross State University, Texas

D. G. Paz
Clemson University, South Carolina

Martha E. Pemberton
Independent scholar

Robert C. Petersen
Middle Tennessee State University

R. Craig Philips
Michigan State University

Hugh J. Phillips
Independent scholar

John Phillips
University of California, Riverside

Donald K. Pickens
North Texas State University

Evelyne L. Pickett
University of Nevada at Reno

Leslie Todd Pitre
Louisiana State University

George R. Plitnik
Frostburg State University, Maryland

Dorothy T. Potter
Lynchburg College

Clifton W. Potter, Jr.
Lynchburg College, Virginia

Annette Potts
Monash University, Victoria, Australia

E. Daniel Potts
Monash University, Victoria, Australia

William S. Pretzer
Henry Ford Museum and Greenfield Village

Charles H. Pullen
Queen's University, Kingston, Ontario

Edna B. Quinn
Salisbury State University, Maryland

John Ranlett
State University of New York, College at Potsdam

Eugene L. Rasor
Emory and Henry College, Virginia

William G. Ratliff
Georgia Southern College

James A. Rawley
University of Nebraska at Lincoln

John D. Raymer
Indiana University at South Bend

Christel Reges
Independent scholar

Dennis Reinhartz
University of Texas at Arlington

Rosemary M. Canfield Reisman
Charleston Southern University, South Carolina

Clark G. Reynolds
Independent scholar

Victoria Reynolds
Southeastern Louisiana University

Vivian L. Richardson
Central Missouri State University

Edward A. Riedinger
Ohio State University

St. John Robinson
Montana State University at Billings

Vicki Robinson
State University of New York at Farmingdale

Carl Rollyson
Bernard M. Baruch College, City University of New York

Paul Rosefeldt
University of New Orleans, Louisiana

Joseph Rosenblum
University of North Carolina at Greensboro

Marc Rothenberg
Smithsonian Institution, D.C.

Bruce A. Rubenstein
University of Michigan at Flint

Emanuel D. Rudolph
Ohio State University

J. Edmund Rush
Write Away Now

Wendy Sacket
Independent scholar

Mary Wilson Sage
Duquesne University, Pennsylvania

Hilel B. Salomon
University of South Carolina

Daniel C. Scavone
University of Southern Indiana

William J. Scheick
University of Texas at Austin

Per Schelde
York College, Pennsylvania

Roger Sensenbaugh
Indiana University at Bloomington

Patricia Sharpe
Simon's Rock College of Bard, Massachusetts

David Shayt
Smithsonian Institution, D.C.

Melvin Shefftz
State University of New York, College at Binghamton

J. Lee Shneidman
Adelphi University, New York

Steven W. Shrader
University of the South

R. Baird Shuman
University of Illinois at Urbana-Champaign

Anne W. Sienkewicz
Independent scholar

L. Moody Simms, Jr.
Illinois State University

David Curtis Skaggs
Bowling Green State University, Ohio

C. Edward Skeen
Memphis State University, Tennessee

Genevieve Slomski
Independent scholar

Dale Edwyna Smith
Washington University, Missouri

Harold L. Smith
University of Houston-Victoria, Texas

Roger Smith
Independent scholar

Ira Smolensky
Monmouth College, Illinois

Valerie Snyder
Independent scholar

Norbert C. Soldon
West Chester University of Pennsylvania

Katherine R. Sopka
Four Corners Analytic Science

James E. Southerland
Brenan College

Richard Francis Spall, Jr.
Ohio Wesleyan University

Robert M. Spector
Worcester State College, Massachusetts

Joseph L. Spradley
Wheaton College

Brian Stableford
Independent scholar

James Stanlaw
Illinois State University

S. J. Stearns
City University of New York, College of Staten Island

David L. Sterling
University of Cincinnati, Ohio

Diane Prenatt Stevens
Indiana University at Bloomington

John Knox Stevens
Indiana University at Bloomington

James Brewer Stewart
Macalester College, Minnesota

Paul Stuewe
Independent scholar

James Sullivan
California State University, Los Angeles

Joseph E. Suppiger
Limestone College, South Carolina

Roy Arthur Swanson
University of Wisconsin—Milwaukee

Patricia E. Sweeney
Independent scholar

Roy Talbert, Jr.
University of South Carolina—Coastal Carolina College

Alice Taylor
Shorter College, Georgia

Nicholas C. Thomas
Auburn University at Montgomery, Alabama

J. A. Thompson
University of Kentucky, Lexington

Thomas John Thomson
Limestone College, South Carolina

Kenneth William Townsend
Coastal Carolina University, South Carolina

Judith Ann Trolander
University of Minnesota at Duluth

Eileen Tess Tyler
United States Naval Academy, Maryland

Ronald D. Tyler
Independent scholar

David Underdown
Yale University, Connecticut

George W. Van Devender
Hardin-Simmons University, Texas

Diane C. Vecchio
University of Wisconsin—Whitewater

Abraham Verghese
East Tennessee State University

Charles L. Vigue
University of New Haven, Connecticut

Mary E. Virginia
Independent scholar

Vernon L. Volpe
Texas A&M University

LeRoy J. Votto
Urban School of San Francisco, California

Paul R. Waibel
Trinity College

Harry M. Ward
University of Richmond, Virginia

Brent Waters
University of Redlands, California

Duncan Waterson
Macquarie University, New South Wales, Australia

Dover C. Watkins
University of Texas at Arlington

Sharon B. Watkins
Western Illinois University

Robert P. Watson
University of Hawaii at Hilo

Donald V. Weatherman
Arkansas College

Stewart A. Weaver
University of Rochester, New York

Henry Weisser
Colorado State University

Allen Wells
Bowdoin College, Maine

Mary B. Wickwire
University of Massachusetts at Amherst

Barbara Wiedemann
University of Alabama at Huntsville

Lance Williams
University of Missouri at Rolla

David B. Wilson
Iowa State University

David L. Wilson
Southern Illinois University at Carbondale

John Wilson
University of Hawaii at Manoa

Major L. Wilson
Memphis State University, Tennessee

John D. Windhausen
Saint Anselm College, New Hampshire

George Wise
*General Electric Company, Corporate Research
and Development*

Michael Witkoski
Independent scholar

Ken Wolf
Murray State University, Kentucky

Donald Yacovone
Florida State University

Clifton K. Yearley
State University of New York at Buffalo

Irwin Yellowitz
City University of New York, City College

William M. Zanella
Hawaii Loa College

LIST OF ENTRANTS

Abdelkader, 1
'Abduh, Muhammad, 4
Abel, Niels Henrik, 7
Acton, Lord, 10
Adams, Henry, 15
Adams, John Quincy, 20
Adler, Felix, 26
Agassiz, Louis, 30
Ahmad Khan, Sir Sayyid, 34
Alcott, Bronson, 37
Alcott, Louisa May, 40
Alexander I, 44
Alexander II, 48
Alger, Horatio, 51
Altgeld, John Peter, 54
Andersen, Hans Chrsitian, 58
Anthony, Susan B., 61
Appleseed, Johnny, 66
Arnold, Matthew, 69
Arnold, Thomas, 74
Arthur, Chester A., 77
Astor, John J., 82
Audubon, John James, 86
Austen, Jane, 90
Austin, Stephen Fuller, 94
Avogardo, Amedeo, 98

Babbage, Charles, 101
Baden-Powell, Sir Robert Stephenson Smyth, 105
Baer, Karl Ernst von, 109
Bakunin, Mikhail, 112
Baldwin, Robert, 116
Balzac, Honoré de, 120
Bancroft, Geroge, 124
Barnard, Henry, 130
Barnum, P. T., 133
Barry, Sir Charles, 138
Barton, Clara, 142
Barton, Sir Edmund, 147
Baudelaire, Charles, 150
Baum, L. Frank, 154
Beale, Dorothea, 157
Beardsley, Aubrey, 161
Becquerel Family, The, 166
Beecher, Catharine, 170
Beecher, Henry Ward, 174
Beethoven, Ludwig van, 178
Behring, Emil von, 182
Bell, Alexander Graham, 185

Bennett, James Gordon, 190
Benton, Thomas Hart, 195
Benz, Carl, 199
Berlioz, Hector, 202
Bernard, Claude, 207
Besant, Annie, 211
Bessel, Friedrich Wilhelm, 215
Bessemer, Sir Henry, 218
Beust, Friedrich von, 222
Biddle, Nicholas, 225
Bierce, Ambrose, 230
Bierstadt, Albert, 233
Bingham, George Caleb, 236
Bismarck, Otto von, 240
Bizet, Georges, 244
Black Hawk, 247
Blackwell, Elizabeth, 251
Blaine, James G., 255
Blanc, Louis, 259
Blücher, Gebhard Leberecht von, 263
Bolívar, Simón, 267
Booth, Edwin, 271
Booth, William, 275
Borah, William E., 279
Borden, Lizzie, 283
Borodin, Aleksandr, 286
Bradley, F. H., 290
Brady, Matthew B., 294
Brahms, Johannes, 299
Braille, Louis, 303
Bright, John, 306
Brontë Sisters, 310
Brougham, Henry, 314
Brown, George, 318
Brown, John, 321
Browning, Elizabeth Barrett, 327
Bruckner, Anton, 331
Brunel, Isambard Kingdom, 335
Brunel, Marc Isambard, 339
Bryant, William Cullen, 343
Buchanan, James, 346
Bulfinch, Charles, 349
Burbank, Luther, 353
Burckhardt, Jacob, 358
Burnett, Frances Hodgson, 361
Burnham, Daniel Hudson, 365
Burr, Aaron, 369
Burton, Sir Richard Francis, 374
Buxton, Sir Thomas Fowell, 378
Byron, Lord, 381

Cabrini, Frances Xavier, 386
Calamity Jane, 390
Calhoun, John C., 394
Cambacérès, Jean-Jacques-Régis de, 398
Campbell, Alexander, 401
Canning, George, 405
Canova, Antonio, 408
Carlos, Don, 413
Carlyle, Thomas, 416
Carnegie, Andrew, 420
Carroll, Lewis, 425
Carson, Kit, 429
Cassatt, Mary, 434
Castlereagh, Viscount, 438
Catlin, George, 443
Cavour, Count, 446
Cayley, Sir George, 450
Cézanne, Paul, 453
Chadwick, Edwin, 457
Chamberlain, Joseph, 462
Chang Chih-tung, 466
Channing, William Ellery, 470
Charles XIV John, 474
Chase, Salmon P., 477
Chateaubriand, 481
Chekhov, Anton, 485
Child, Lydia Maria, 489
Chopin, Frédéric, 493
Chopin, Kate, 497
Christophe, Henri, 501
Clausewitz, Carl von, 503
Clay, Henry, 507
Cleveland, Grover, 512
Clinton, DeWitt, 517
Cobbett, William, 522
Cobden, Richard, 526
Cody, William Frederick, 530
Cohn, Ferdinand Julius, 534
Coleridge, Samuel Taylor, 537
Colt, Samuel, 540
Comte, Auguste, 543
Constable, John, 547
Cooke, Jay, 551
Cooke, William Fothergill, and Charles Wheatstone, 555
Cooper, James Fenimore, 560
Courbet, Gustave, 565
Crane, Stephen, 569
Crazy Horse, 573
Crockett, David, 578
Cushing, Caleb, 581
Custer, George A., 585

Cuvier, Georges, 589

Daguerre, Jacques, 592
Daimler, Gottlieb, 597
Dalhousie, First Marquess of, 600
Dalton, John, 602
Darwin, Charles, 606
David, Jacques-Louis, 610
Davis, Jefferson, 614
Davy, Sir Humphry, 621
Deák, Ferenc, 625
Deakin, Alfred, 630
Decatur, Stephen, 634
Dedekind, Richard, 638
Degas, Edgar, 641
Delacroix, Eugène, 645
Delibes, Léo, 649
Derby, Fourteenth Earl of, 652
Dewey, George, 656
Dewey, Melvil, 660
Dickens, Charles, 663
Dickinson, Emily, 667
Diesel, Rudolf, 672
Disraeli, Benjamin, 675
Dix, Dorothea, 680
Donizetti, Gaetano, 684
Dostoevski, Fyodor, 687
Douglas, Stephen A., 692
Douglass, Frederick, 695
Doyle, Sir Arthur Conan, 700
Duke, James Buchanan, 704
Dumas, Alexandre, *père*, 708
Dunant, Jean-Henri, 711
Dunbar, Paul Laurence, 714
Du Pont, Eleuthère Irénée, 718
Durham, First Earl of, 721
Dvořák, Antonín, 725

Eads, James Buchanan, 729
Eakins, Thomas, 732
Earp, Wyatt, 735
Eddy, Mary Baker, 738
Edison, Thomas Alva, 743
Eliot, Charles William, 748
Eliot, George, 751
Emerson, Ralph Waldo, 755
Engels, Friedrich, 760

Faidherbe, Louis, 763
Faraday, Michael, 767
Farragut, David G., 772
Fawcett, Dame Millicent Garrett, 776

Fechner, Gustav Theodor, 780
Field, Marshall, 783
Field, Stephen J., 787
Fillmore, Millard, 792
Flaubert, Gustave, 796
Forrest, Edwin, 800
Forster, William Edward, 804
Forten, Charlotte, 807
Foster, Stephen Collins, 810
Fourier, Charles, 814
Fourier, Joseph, 819
Fowler, Lydia Folger, 822
France, Anatole, 825
Francis Joseph I, 829
Franck, César, 832
Frege, Gottlob, 836
Frémont, John C., 839
Froebel, Friedrich, 845
Fuller, Margaret, 849
Fulton, Robert, 854

Gadsden, James, 858
Gallatin, Albert, 861
Galois, Èvariste, 864
Galton, Francis, 867
Gambetta, Léon, 871
Garfield, James A., 875
Garibaldi, Guiseppe, 879
Garrison, William Lloyd, 883
Gauguin, Paul, 888
Gauss, Carl Friedrich, 893
Gay-Lussac, Joseph-Louis, 897
George IV, 902
George, Henry, 906
Géricault, Théodore, 910
Geronimo, 915
Gibbons, James, 919
Gibbs, Josiah Willard, 923
Gilbert, W. S., and Sir Arthur Sullivan, 927
Gioberti, Vincenzo, 932
Gladstone, William Ewart, 935
Gneisenau, August von, 940
Gogh, Vincent van, 944
Gogol, Nikolai, 949
Goldie, Sir George, 953
Gompers, Samuel, 956
Goodyear, Charles, 960
Gordon, Charles George, 964
Gounod, Charles, 967
Grace, William Gilbert, 971
Grant, Ulysses S., 975
Gray, Asa, 979

Greeley, Horace, 982
Green, Thomas Hill, 987
Greenway, Francis, 990
Grey, Second Earl, 994
Grey, Sir George Edward, 998
Grieg, Edvard, 1002
Grimm, Jacob and Wilhelm, 1006
Grove, Sir William Robert, 1010

Hadfield, Sir Robert Abbott, 1015
Haeckel, Ernst, 1018
Hale, Sarah Josepha, 1022
Hamilton, Sir William Rowan, 1025
Hanna, Marcus A., 1029
Hardenberg, Karl von, 1033
Hardie, James Keir, 1036
Hardy, Thomas, 1040
Harper, William Rainey, 1044
Harris, Joel Chandler, 1049
Harrison, Benjamin, 1053
Harrison, Frederic, 1057
Harrison, William Henry, 1061
Hawthrone, Nathaniel, 1064
Hay, John, 1068
Hayden, Ferdinand Vandeveer, 1072
Hayes, Rutherford B., 1075
Hegel, Georg Wilhelm Friedrich, 1080
Heine, Heinrich, 1085
Helmholtz, Hermann von, 1089
Henry, Joseph, 1093
Henry, O., 1096
Herzen, Aleksandr, 1099
Herzl, Theodor, 1102
Hickok, Wild Bill, 1107
Higginson, Thomas Wentworth, 1110
Hill, Octavia, 1113
Hiroshige, 1117
Hokusai, 1120
Holland, John Philip, 1123
Holmes, Oliver Wendell, 1126
Holstein, Friedrich von, 1130
Homer, Winslow, 1133
Houston, Sam, 1137
Howe, Elias, 1141
Howe, Julia Ward, 1145
Howe, Samuel Gridley, 1150
Hugo, Victor, 1154
Humboldt, Alexander von, 1159
Humperdinck, Engelbert, 1162
Hung Hsui-ch'üan, 1165
Hunt, William Holman, 1168
Huxley, Thomas Henry, 1172

Ibsen, Henrik, 1175
Ii Naosuke, 1180
Ingres, Jean-Auguste-Dominique, 1183
Irving, Henry, 1187
Irving, Washington, 1192

Jackson, Andrew, 1196
Jackson, Helen Hunt, 1200
Jackson, Stonewall, 1204
Jamāl al-Dīn al-Afghānī, 1207
James, Henry, 1211
James, William, 1216
Jaurès, Jean, 1221
Jeffrey, Lord, 1224
Jewett, Sarah Orne, 1228
Johnson, Andrew, 1232
Joplin, Scott, 1239
Joseph, Chief, 1242
Joséphine, 1246
Juárez, Benito, 1250

Kamehameha I, 1255
Kean, Edmund, 1259
Keats, John, 1264
Kelvin, Lord, 1269
Kemble, Fanny, 1273
Kent, James, 1277
Key, Francis Scott, 1281
Kierkegaard, Søren, 1284
Kipling, Rudyard, 1288
Kleist, Heinrich von, 1294
Koch, Robert, 1297
Krupp, Alfred, 1301
Kutuzov, Mikhail Illarionovich, 1305

Lancaster, Joseph, 1309
Langley, Samuel Pierpont, 1313
Lankester, Sir Edwin Ray, 1316
Laplace, Pierre-Simon, 1319
Lassalle, Ferdinand, 1323
Latrobe, Benjamin Henry, 1327
Lawrence, First Baron, 1331
Lazarus, Emma, 1334
Lee, Robert E., 1338
Lenoir, Étienne, 1343
Leo XIII, 1347
Lermontov, Mikhail, 1351
Lesseps, Ferdinand de, 1355
Lewis, Meriwether, and William Clark, 1358
Li Hung-chang, 1362
Liebig, Justus von, 1366
Liebknecht, Wilhelm, 1369

Liliuokalani, 1372
Lin Tse-hsü, 1376
Lincoln, Abraham, 1380
Lind, Jenny, 1385
Lister, Joseph, 1388
Liszt, Franz, 1391
Liverpool, Second Earl of, 1395
Livingstone, David, 1399
Lobachevsky, Nikolay Ivanovich, 1403
Lockwood, Belva A., 1406
Lockyer, Sir Joseph Norman, 1410
Longfellow, Henry Wadsworth, 1414
Lyell, Sir Charles, 1418
Lyon, Mary, 1423

Macaulay, Thomas Babington, 1427
McCormick, Cyrus Hall, 1431
Macdonald, Sir John Alexander, 1435
McGuffey, William Holmes, 1440
Machado de Assis, Joaquim Maria, 1444
Mackenzie, William Lyon, 1447
McKinley, William, 1453
Macmillan, Daniel and Alexander, 1457
Macready, William Charles, 1460
Madison, Dolley, 1464
Malthus, Thomas Robert, 1467
Manet, Édouard, 1471
Manning, Henry Edward, 1476
Mannix, Daniel, 1480
Manzoni, Alessandro, 1483
Marshall, John, 1487
Marx, Karl, 1492
Massey, Vincent, 1496
Maupassant, Guy de, 1500
Maurice, Frederick Denison, 1503
Maury, Matthew Fontaine, 1507
Maxwell, James Clerk, 1511
Mazzini, Giuseppe, 1514
Melbourne, Second Viscount, 1517
Melville, Herman, 1520
Mendel, Gregor Johann, 1526
Mendeleyev, Dmitry Ivanovich, 1529
Mendelssohn, Felix, 1534
Menelik II, 1537
Mergenthaler, Ottmar, 1541
Metternich, 1544
Michelet, Jules, 1548
Michelson, Albert A., 1551
Mill, James, 1556
Mill, John Stuart, 1559
Mommsen, Theodor, 1566
Monroe, James, 1570

Moody, Dwight L., 1575
Morgan, J. P., 1579
Morgan, Lewis Henry, 1584
Morris, William, 1588
Morse, Samuel F. B., 1592
Morton, William Thomas Green, 1596
Mott, Lucretia, 1600
Muhammad 'Alī Pasha, 1604
Muir, John, 1608
Mussorgsky, Modest, 1611

Napoleon I, 1616
Napoleon III, 1620
Nasmyth, James, 1624
Nast, Thomas, 1627
Nation, Carry, 1630
Nelson, Lord, 1634
Newcomb, Simon, 1638
Newman, John Henry, 1641
Ney, Michel, 1646
Nicholas I, 1650
Niebuhr, Barthold Georg, 1654
Niépce, Nicéphore, 1657
Nietzsche, Friedrich Wilhelm, 1662
Nightingale, Florence, 1667
Nobel, Alfred, 1673

Oakley, Annie, 1677
O'Connell, Daniel, 1680
Offenbach, Jacques, 1684
O'Higgins, Bernardo, 1688
Olmsted, Frederick Law, 1691
Osceola, 1695
Osler, Sir William, 1698
Otto, Nikolaus August, 1702
Outram, Sir James, 1705
Owen, Robert, 1708

Paganini, Niccolò, 1711
Palmer, Alice Freeman, 1715
Palmerston, Lord, 1719
Park, Mungo, 1723
Parker, Theodore, 1727
Parkes, Sir Henry, 1731
Parkman, Francis, 1735
Parnell, Charles Stewart, 1740
Pasteur, Louis, 1744
Pater, Walter, 1749
Peel, Sir Robert, 1752
Peirce, Charles Sanders, 1756
Perry, Matthew C., 1760
Perry, Oliver Hazard, 1764

Pestalozzi, Johann Heinrich, 1767
Phillips, Wendell, 1771
Pierce, Franklin, 1775
Pissarro, Camille, 1779
Pius IX, 1782
Place, Francis, 1786
Pobedonostsev, Konstantin Petrovich, 1790
Poe, Edgar Allan, 1794
Poincaré, Henri, 1798
Polk, James K., 1801
Popov, Aleksandr Stepanovich, 1806
Powell, John Wesley, 1810
Prescott, William Hickling, 1814
Proudhon, Pierre-Joseph, 1817
Pugin, Augustus Welby Northmore, 1821
Pulitzer, Joseph, 1825
Pusey, E. B., 1828
Pushkin, Alexander, 1832

Raeburn, Sir Henry, 1836
Ranke, Leopold von, 1839
Rasputin, Grigori Yefimovich, 1842
Ray, Rammohan, 1846
Red Cloud, 1850
Redon, Odilon, 1854
Reed, Walter, 1857
Remington, Frederic, 1861
Renan, Ernest, 1865
Renoir, Pierre-Auguste, 1869
Rhodes, Cecil, 1873
Ricardo, David, 1878
Richardson, Henry Hobson, 1882
Rimbaud, Arthur, 1886
Rimsky-Korsakov, Nikolay, 1889
Ritschl, Albrecht, 1892
Rockefeller, John D., 1896
Rodin, Auguste, 1900
Roebling, John Augustus, 1904
Ross, Sir James Clark, 1907
Ross, John, 1910
Rossini, Gioacchino, 1913
Rothschild Family, The, 1916
Rousseau, Henri, 1921
Ruskin, John, 1925
Russell, Lord John, 1930

Sacagawea, 1933
Saigō Takamori, 1936
Saint-Gaudens, Augustus, 1940
Salisbury, Third Marquess of, 1943
San Martín, José de, 1947
Sand, George, 1951

Santa Anna, Antonio López de, 1955
Saragossa, La, 1958
Sargent, John Singer, 1961
Savigny, Friedrich Karl von, 1966
Scharnhorst, Gerhard Johann David von, 1969
Schelling, Friedrich Wilhelm Joseph, 1972
Schleiermacher, Friedrich, 1976
Schliemann, Heinrich, 1980
Schopenhauer, Arthur, 1984
Schubert, Franz, 1988
Schumann, Robert, 1992
Schurz, Carl, 1996
Scott, Dred, 1999
Scott, Sir George Gilbert, 2002
Scott, Sir Walter, 2005
Scott, Winfield, 2009
Scripps, Edward Wyllis, 2014
Seddon, Richard John, 2017
Semmelweis, Ignaz Philipp, 2021
Sequoyah, 2025
Seton, Saint Elizabeth Ann Bayley, 2029
Seurat, Georges, 2033
Seward, William H., 2037
Shaka, 2041
Shaw, Anna Howard, 2044
Shelley, Mary Wollstonecraft, 2048
Shelley, Percy Bysshe, 2052
Sherman, William Tecumseh, 2057
Sidgwick, Henry, 2062
Siemens Family, The, 2066
Sitting Bull, 2070
Slater, Samuel, 2074
Smith, Jedediah Strong, 2077
Smith, Joseph, 2080
Speke, John Hanning, 2083
Spencer, Herbert, 2086
Speransky, Mikhail Mikhaylovich, 2089
Staël, Madame de, 2092
Stanford, Leland, 2096
Stanley, Henry Morton, 2101
Stanton, Edwin M., 2106
Stanton, Elizabeth Cady, 2110
Stein, Freiherr vom, 2115
Steiner, Jakob, 2118
Steinmetz, Charles Proteus, 2121
Stendhal, 2125
Stephens, Alexander H., 2129
Stephenson, George, 2132
Stevens, Thaddeus, 2136
Stevenson, Robert Louis, 2139
Stone, Lucy, 2143
Story, Joseph, 2147

Stowe, Harriet Beecher, 2151
Strauss, Johann, 2155
Street, George Edmund, 2160
Sucre, Antonio José de, 2164
Sullivan, Louis, 2167
Sumner, Charles, 2170
Suttner, Bertha von, 2175
Swan, Joseph Wilson, 2179

Taine, Hippolyte-Adolphe, 2182
Talleyrand, 2185
Taney, Roger Brooke, 2189
Taylor, Zachary, 2194
Tchaikovsky, Peter Ilich, 2198
Tecumseh, 2203
Telford, Thomas, 2207
Tennyson, Alfred, Lord, 2211
Terry, Ellen, 2215
Tesla, Nikola, 2219
Thayer, Sylvanus, 2223
Thiers, Adolphe, 2226
Thomas, Theodore, 2230
Thoreau, Henry David, 2234
Tocqueville, Alexis de, 2238
Tolstoy, Leo, 2242
Toulouse-Lautrec, Henri de, 2247
Trevithick, Richard, 2251
Truth, Sojourner, 2255
Tseng Kuo-fan, 2260
Tubman, Harriet, 2264
Turgenev, Ivan, 2268
Turner, J. M. W., 2272
Turner, Nat, 2276
Twain, Mark, 2279
Tweed, William Marcy, 2284
Tyler, John, 2288

Van Buren, Martin, 2292
Vanderbilt, Cornelius, 2296
Verdi, Giuseppe, 2299
Verne, Jules, 2303
Victoria, Queen, 2307
Virchow, Rudolf, 2312

Wagner, Richard, 2316
Wakefield, Edward Gibbon, 2321
Walter, John, II, 2324
Ward, Lester Frank, 2328
Ward, Montgomery, 2331
Washington, Booker T., 2335
Weber, Carl Maria von, 2340
Webster, Daniel, 2344

Weismann, August, 2348
Wellington, Duke of, 2351
Wentworth, W. C., 2355
Westinghouse, George, 2358
Whistler, James McNeill, 2363
Whitman, Walt, 2368
Whittier, John Greenleaf, 2374
Wilde, Oscar, 2377
Wilkes, Charles, 2381
Willard, Emma, 2384
Willard, Frances, 2388

William IV, 2392
Williams, George Washington, 2396
Wise, Isaac Mayer, 2400
Wöhler, Friedrich, 2403
Wordsworth, William, 2406
Workman, Fanny Bullock, 2410

Young, Brigham, 2414
Ypsilanti, Alexander and Demetrios, 2417

Zola, Émile, 2420

ABDELKADER
'Abd al-Qādirdir

Born: September 26, 1807; Guetna, Ottoman Empire

Died: May 26, 1883; Damascus, Ottoman Empire

Areas of Achievement: Government, politics, and the military

Contribution: After the French landed in Algiers in 1830, Abdelkader carved a semiautonomous state out of the remnants of the former Turkish possessions in Algeria. He achieved lasting fame for his various campaigns against the French, whom he fought until his surrender in 1847.

Early Life

The first son of Zurah, the second wife of the Islamic holy man Muhi al-Din, who traced his ancestry as far back as the prophet Muhammad, Abdelkader was born on September 26, 1807, in the small town of Guetna, near Mascara in modern Algeria. There his grandfather had founded a religious school of the Sufi Order, and Muhi al-Din had followed him as leader and himself taught his son reading, writing, and the Koran. Abdelkader's mother was learned and venerated by the people as a marabout, or holy person, as well; for a woman to accomplish this was quite extraordinary and could have helped Abdelkader to surpass his half brother, the son of his father's first wife, in the affection of his father.

As a boy, Abdelkader's handsome features and his remarkable intellectual gifts endeared him to his parents and to the people of Guetna. Throughout his life, Abdelkader would be quite aware of the potential impressiveness of his well-made body and keep himself in condition so as to command maximum respect. His dark eyes, together with the clear features of his well-formed face and full beard, conveyed an image of Oriental nobility that would prove to affect friend and foe alike.

A fine horseman and a quick learner, Abdelkader soon developed the qualities of a leader. When his father sent him to the coastal city of Oran as a student of religion in 1821, the boy became a classmate of the scions of the ruling Turks. He observed at first hand how even while the country suffered from famine and plague its Turkish masters continued to levy taxes and luxuriate in a life of debauchery and neglect of Islamic moral principles. In reaction, Arabs gathered around their holy men and led several unsuccessful revolts in the 1820's against the Turks, who repressed upheaval and summarily executed suspicious subjects. As a marabout, Muhi al-din was spared execution and placed under house arrest with his son in Oran for two years, before the two set out on a pilgrimage to Mecca in 1826. Traveling further widened Abdelkader's experience.

Two years after Abdelkader's return to Guetna, the French captured Algiers on July 5, 1830, thus ending three hundred years of Turkish rule. When the neighboring Moroccans tried to assume power in Algeria, Muhi al-Din accepted their mandate and became the leader of a jihad, or holy war, against the French infidels. The Moroccans withdrew, but Abdelkader commanded a force of ten thousand men for his father and, in the Battle of Oran from May 3 to 8, 1832, fought courageously but was defeated.

Life's Work

On November 22, 1832, tribes of the Oran Province gathered to witness the proclamation of Abdelkader as emir al-mu'minin, or commander of the believers, on the plain of Eghris. Thus, the twenty-five-year-old man was made leader of a movement to scourge the land of the French. Rather than fighting in open attacks, which his weak forces were sure to lose, Abdelkader began his jihad with a boycott against French-held Oran; Arabs who traded with the infidels were mutilated or hanged. In his dealings with Muslim tribes, Abdelkader soon strove for political recognition as emir and even tried to win the support of the Sultan of Morocco. As emir, Abdelkader wielded a power that was legitimated by religion and used it to the fullest. From the believers, he collected both new and traditional taxes to finance the jihad and used these monies to build a strong force of his own. Thus, from 1832 to 1834, he was able to subjugate most people in the Oran Province, and the sporadic French attacks were too limited to threaten seriously his nascent power; further, French blunders such as the humiliation of Turks and local leaders played into his hands.

In January, 1834, the French general Louis Alexis Desmichels, whose troops had defeated Abdelkader's without achieving a lasting effect, negotiated a bilingual treaty, complete with a secret codicil. Officially, Abdelkader would rule the Oran Province under the French, with the exception of three coastal cities; however, both Desmichels and Abdelkader told their people that the other had completely submitted to him.

For more than a year, Abdelkader enjoyed the valuable support of Desmichels, who helped him to build an army with which to defeat his indigenous enemies. The replacement of the general brought new fighting with the French, who prevented Abdelkader from forcefully relocating two tribes who had placed themselves under French protection. At the onset of his second jihad in June, 1835, Abdelkader ambushed a French force at Macta and killed 210 of their men; however, the French were able to occupy temporarily two of his cities.

While the blockade of Oran continued, General Thomas Robert Bugeaud organized a mobile French force and delivered Abdelkader a stinging blow at the Battle of Sikkak on July 6, 1836. Yet Bugeaud knew that he could not occupy the whole country. In the Treaty of Tafna, ratified on June 21, 1837, Bugeaud conceded and placed most of Algeria under Abdelkader's immediate rule. In return, Abdelkader promised peace, free trade, and, secretly, 180,000 gold francs for Bugeaud; however, only twenty-five thousand francs were delivered, as the clause was discovered. Now, Abdelkader could even buy rifles through the French, and he established a firm rule over two-thirds of Algeria. There, he established an Islamic government and consolidated his rule by placing strong emphasis on the one factor that united his subjects against the Europeans: the Muslim religion.

In the summer of 1839, it became clear that France and Abdelkader would soon clash over Algeria. On July 3, Abdelkader declared a conditional jihad, which became fully effective November 3, after the French crown prince had marched through Abdelkader's territory. The warriors of the jihad scored a first victory when they attacked a European settlement on the Mitidja plains near Algiers on November 20 and succeeded in massacring or chasing away its colonists. Until the return of Bugeaud, Abdelkader maintained the military initiative.

In May, 1841, however, Tagdempt, Abdelkader's capital, fell to Bugeaud, whose forces had razed most of his cities by October 12. In turn, Abdelkader moved to a tent city, the Zmalah, and continued to harass the enemy throughout the next year. Yet on May 16, 1843, a surprise attack on the Zmalah led to its destruction, the capture of three thousand of Abdelkader's people, and the loss of his treasury. With the French following on his heels and devastating the land of his tribes after the fashion of local warfare, Abdelkader was forced to flee into Morocco late in 1843.

From his exile, Abdelkader saw Bugeaud's defeat of the Moroccan army at the Battle of Isly in August, 1844, and the French military begin to control Algeria. Yet the harshness of their rule led to a popular uprising and agitation for a new jihad. Until he returned in September, 1845, Abdelkader had wielded no influence, but now people followed him. Yet his renewed campaign culminated in a failed attempt at capturing Algiers in January, 1846; thereafter, Abdelkader was again chased into Morocco. While the war wound down with heavy civilian casualties, Morocco grew hostile to Abdelkader. On December 21, 1847, he surrendered himself to General Christophe de Lamoricière, who had promised that he could stay in Africa. Instead, the French government kept the rebel leader under arrest in France for four years before Napoleon III released him in 1852.

From 1855 on, Abdelkader stayed in Damascus as a philosopher and religious man. During an uprising there in 1860, he saved the lives of thousands of Christians, and, when unrest returned to Algeria in 1871, he disowned one of his sons who took sides with the rebels. Abdelkader died in Damascus on May 26, 1883; in 1968, his remains were transferred to Algeria.

Summary

As an exile in Damascus, Abdelkader was seen by the French as a prime example of the beneficial effects of their rule, which had transformed a fiery Muslim fanatic and hero of desert warfare into an elder statesman of the French empire; the French government even had plans to establish a throne for him somewhere in the Middle East. With the coming of another bitter war in Algeria after 1945, Algerian interest turned to Abdelkader, who was idolized as an early protagonist of independence; the French quickly discovered that his legend had been kept alive. In 1962, after independence, Abdelkader was declared a national hero, and in Algiers his statue soon replaced the toppled one of Bugeaud.

A final historical assessment can only stress the charisma of Abdelkader and his profound impact on the history of two countries. Abdelkader's qualities as a leader of men who venerated him for his religious conviction enabled him to build an indigenous state in defiance of the French-controlled cities on the coast. When open warfare erupted, Abdelkader achieved lasting fame through his never-ending zeal and military prowess, a combination that led him into battle as long as there was a chance to reverse fortunes and prevent French rule over Algeria.

Bibliography

Abun-Nasr, Jamil N. "The Emergence of French Algeria." In *A History of the Maghrib*. 2d ed. Cambridge and New York: Cambridge University Press, 1975. Briefly describes Abdelkader's accomplishments and places him in the context of the overall history of the region. Presents an Arab point of view. Contains only brief information on Abdelkader but is an interesting complement to European and American historiography.

Alby, François Antoine. *The Prisoners of Abd-el-Kader: Or, Five Month's Captivity Among the Arabs in the Autumn of 1836*. Translated by R. F. Porter. London: Smith, Elder, 1838. An account of the ordeal of a French sailor who was captured in Algeria in 1836, delivered to Abdelkader, and released five months later. An intimate description of Abdelkader, his people, and their actions; shows what the common man in Paris or London believed about them.

Blunt, Wilfrid. *Desert Hawk: Abd el Kader and the French Conquest of Algeria*. London: Methuen, 1947. A descriptive account of Abdelkader's life and his campaigns. Takes a great interest in his military strategies, tactics, and triumphs, and in his adversaries. Admires Abdelkader's position against the French. A readable and interesting work.

Churchill, Charles Henry. *The Life of AbdelKader: Ex-Sultan of the Arabs of Algeria*. London: Chapman and Hall, 1867. This is the oldest biography of Abdelkader in English. Invaluable because it exemplifies the popular European reaction to Abdelkader during his lifetime.

Clayton, Vista. *The Phantom: Or, Abd el Kader, Emir of Algeria (1808-1883)*. Hicksville, N.Y.: Exposition Press, 1975. An analysis of the life and warfare strategies of Abdelkader. Examines French and indigenous military, logistics, and politics. Presents Abdelkader's life against the background of his region. Emphasizes the charisma of Abdelkader and gives a detailed account of his military exploits.

Danziger, Raphael. *Abd al-Qadir and the Algerians: Resistance to the French and Internal Consolidation*. New York: Holmes and Meier, 1977. A detailed account of Abdelkader's struggle for power and consolidation of his rule, and his dealings with the French. Deals primarily with the time period before 1839. This is a sympathetic view, written for both a scholarly and a general audience; useful exploitation of French sources. Contains a fine bibliography and a rare reproduction of pages of treaties in Arabic.

Sullivan, Antony Thrall. *Thomas-Robert Bugeaud, France and Algeria 1784-1849: Politics, Power, and the Good Society*. Hamden, Conn.: Archon, 1983. A fascinating portrait of Abdelkader's great adversary; room is given to a description of their relationship. Illuminates the historical background of the actions of Abdelkader's enemies by providing an explanation for the French interest in Algeria and the methods of warfare employed. For a general audience.

Reinhart Lutz

MUHAMMAD 'ABDUH

Born: c. 1849; Mahallat Nasr, Gharbiyyah Province, Egypt

Died: July 11, 1905; Alexandria, Egypt

Areas of Achievement: Education, journalism, and government

Contribution: 'Abduh was a major figure in the articulation of modern political, ethical, and social values in an Islamic context. His writings were a major stimulus to the development of Egyptian nationalism and, in a wider sense, to the elaboration of social and political thought throughout Islam.

Early Life

Muhammad 'Abduh was the child of Egyptian peasants of the Nile delta. His family life appears to have been serene and his father highly respected in his village. Although without formal education themselves, 'Abduh's parents went to considerable effort, and no doubt sacrificed much, to ensure his receiving educational opportunities. 'Abduh was trained in basic literary skills and, when ten years of age, went to learn recitation of the Koran with a professional. Few other educational opportunities were available to Egyptian peasants at the time.

'Abduh shortly became restless with Koranic memorization and Arabic grammar. Instead, he became enamored of the teachings of a number of Sufi mystics. From them, 'Abduh first perceived the relationship between the true practice of and devotion to Islam, and the pursuit of morality and ethical conduct. He gravitated toward Cairo and the great theological center of Al Azhar, where he continued his education and increasingly rigorous Sufi practices.

'Abduh's mentor at Al Azhar was the famed Jamāl al-Dīn al-Afghānī, perhaps the most important Muslim intellectual figure in the nineteenth century. Although equally devoted to Sufism, Jamāl, a dynamic reformer and pan-Islamic advocate, turned 'Abduh from the internal contemplation that had absorbed nearly all of his energies to more worldly avenues of learning and social involvement. With Jamāl's encouragement, many of his students, 'Abduh included, began writing articles for newspapers on a host of subjects related to the state of Egypt at the time and the challenge of modernization.

Despite his outstanding academic work, 'Abduh's outspoken opinions on Egyptian society and the suspicion that he meant to revive the skeptical philosophical movements characteristic of earlier periods in Islam drew the wrath of conservative clerics at Al Azhar. It required the intervention of the more liberal rector for 'Abduh to receive passing marks on his examinations and his teaching certificate in 1877.

Life's Work

Although he held numerous positions throughout his life in addition to his explicitly educational ones, 'Abduh always regarded himself as a teacher. The essence of his teachings is first a concern for the state of Egypt. He and fellow intellectuals deplored their country's drift in the 1870's toward financial chaos and foreign intervention. They understood that only internal reforms could change Egypt's fortunes. 'Abduh's experience at Al Azhar convinced him that the most essential reform must come in education. At a time when European economic and technological forces were closing in on Egypt, its greatest academic institution was still under the control of rigidly conservative theologians who resisted curricular innovation. ('Abduh had been obliged to seek instruction in mathematics and natural sciences in the streets, among unofficial, black market classes held outside the walls of Al Azhar.)

Yet it was not merely these additions to curriculum that concerned 'Abduh. He also argued that the study of religion itself must be subject to the same rigor and philosophical scrutiny that attended the sciences and other secular studies. Further, he believed that leading institutions such as Al Azhar must, in their own reforms, assume leadership in rebuilding and expanding the entire Egyptian educational system. 'Abduh's ideas and teaching methods generated much controversy at Al Azhar but also earned for him support from the reform-minded prime minister Riad Pasha, who in 1878 appointed him to the experimental school Dar al-'Ulum, founded as a pilot institution for educational reform.

In 1879, the Egyptian ruler Khedive Ismail, who had been intent on modernizing Egypt but unfortunately went far beyond the country's limited financial means, under European pressure abdicated in favor of his son, Tawfiq. The new khedive expelled Jamāl from the country and fired 'Abduh, placing him under virtual house arrest. 'Abduh was rescued from potential oblivion by Riad Pasha, who appointed him to the editorial staff of the official Egyptian government gazette *Al-Waka'i' al-Misriyyah*. 'Abduh quickly turned this rather stodgy publication into a vibrant, reformist organ, with contributions from many Egyptian intellectuals and government critics. In his own editorials, 'Abduh continually returned to the need for educational reform and his campaign to cast Egyptian national consciousness in a new Islamic mold. Islam, he argued, should return to its basic simplicity and revive the spirit of inquiry and pursuit of knowledge characteristic of its early history.

In 1881, Egyptian army officers, led by the nationalist firebrand Colonel Ahmed 'Arabi, mutinied. The uprising sparked a general confrontation between the government and its critics. Alarmed at the prospect of violence against Europeans, British troops landed in Egypt in May, 1882. 'Abduh, though opposed to 'Arabi's methods, spoke out as usual in favor of national revival and reform. In September, a government tribunal ordered him expelled from Egypt.

'Abduh went first to Syria and later to Paris, where he was reunited with Jamāl. In exile, he continued to speak and publish actively. The wide venue of his travels led 'Abduh to perceive the potential vitality of a unified Islam and the cultural renaissance of all Muslims. Increasingly he drew on the early history of Islam as a source of inspiration. On the other hand, his experiences in Syria, a country rife with ethnic and religious factionalism, led him to question whether Islam was a suitable rubric for the expression of modern Arab national aspirations. 'Abduh's reservations about pan-Islamic agitation caused him to part ways with Jamāl, who was disposed to intrigue and political maneuvering. 'Abduh insisted that his role should be educational and instructive rather than activist.

In 1886, having received a government pardon, 'Abduh returned to Egypt a national hero. He was now able to use this influence to implement his earlier ideas of curricular and institutional reform at Al Azhar, in order to make it a model of education in Islam. In 1895, the new khedive, Abbas II, at 'Abduh's instigation created an administrative committee for Al Azhar, dominated by 'Abduh and other reformists.

In an effort to enlist faculty support for curriculum changes, the government provided significant new sums for salaries, to be distributed according to a merit system rather than at the discretion of the rector. Students, many of whom lived under appalling conditions, received double their previous board allowance. New dormitories with running water and suitable furniture appeared. The committee significantly lengthened the academic year, organized it according to European standards, and eliminated many disruptive holidays. It also established modern administrative systems for the university's finances and organized its library collections.

Fears that these changes would turn students away from theology and ancient history disappeared when the student success rate on examinations increased by nearly an order of magnitude in the first two years of reform. 'Abduh himself produced statistics that he claimed proved that students who studied modern subjects along with the traditional ones performed better in both areas on examinations.

The climax of 'Abduh's career came with his appointment as Mufti of Egypt in 1899, from which post he was the final arbiter of questions of shari'a, or Muslim canon law. In this position 'Abduh had to confront, more than ever before, his own ambivalence about the relationship between Islam and modern nationalism. His arguments with respect to interpretation of shari'a generated more controversy than anything else in his career. Like many other Muslim scholars, particularly in Egypt, 'Abduh regarded shari'a as possessing a divinely inspired core of behavior and values to which all Muslims are expected to adhere. The community, however, by consensus might accept amendations to shari'a pertinent to its own experience and circumstances.

'Abduh perceived the emerging Egyptian nation as the logical outgrowth of this sense of community in Islam. Yet he believed that the nation, because it contained citizens who were Christian or Jewish rather than Muslim, and because it aspired to a role in a secular world not anticipated by shari'a, should exercise a consensus of its own. Thus 'Abduh decided that Muslims could eat animal flesh killed by Christians or Jews. Despite the ban on usury, in shari'a Egyptians could, and should, make use of modern postal savings and banking systems opposed by traditional clergy on the grounds that their strength contributed to the welfare of the nation. These positions 'Abduh regarded not as a repudiation of Islam but as an act of defense of Islam, in that they reconstituted Islam as an open and tolerant culture capable of meeting the demands of a changing world.

Summary

When Muhammad 'Abduh died in July, 1905, he received the equivalent of a state funeral. The public demonstration of respect and reverence from all political factions and religious communities was unprecedented in Egypt. The country sensed that it had lost a singular patriot and scholar, and one of the most important figures in Egypt's transformation. Later generations have borne out this assessment. Because of 'Abduh's reforms and the new intellectual environment they created, Al Azhar, and other large Egyptian universities, remain in the forefront of higher education in Islam and are recognized as among the world's major institutions of higher learning.

In all of his teachings, 'Abduh struggled to articulate an Egyptian sense of identity that reconciled the inconsistencies and often conflicting perceptions of Islam, the Islamic community, the modern nation and its role in a European-dominated world, and the tensions between modernity and tradition.

'Abduh is most fairly regarded, perhaps, as one who, rather than answering the multitude of questions arising from these issues, helped to air the issues and suggest ways in which they could be addressed satisfactorily. 'Abduh is a symbol, rather than a model, for the contemporary, educated Egyptian. His intellectual journey represents what each Egyptian individually—and the nation as a whole—must consider in the process of finding satisfying and rewarding identity in the modern world.

Bibliography

Adams, Charles C. *Islam and Modernism in Egypt: A Study of the Modern Reform Movement Inaugurated by Muhammad 'Abduh*. London: Oxford University Press, 1933; New York: Russell and Russell, 1968. Includes one of the most extensive biographical accounts of 'Abduh and attempts to analyze his personality and ideas in the light of his life experience.

Ahmed, Jamal Mohammed. *The Intellectual Origins of Egyptian Nationalism*. London and New York: Oxford University Press, 1960. A survey of the varied sources of inspiration for Egyptian nationalism. Stresses how this variety contributes to the often conflicting roles of issues such as Egyptian ethnic identity, pan-Arabism, Ottomanism, and Islamic and pan-Islamic values.

Badawi, Muhammad Zaki. *The Reformers of Egypt*. London: Croom Helm, 1978. Treats 'Abduh as a product of the same circumstances that produced other Egyptian nationalists and intellectuals, and attempts to draw comparisons among the careers of these figures.

Fadel, Mohammad. "Two Women, One Man: Knowledge, Power, and Gender in Medieval Sunni Legal Thought." *International Journal of Middle East Studies* 29, no. 2 (May, 1997). Discusses Islamic legal discrimination against women and 'Abduh's thought on the subject. His beliefs supported a woman's ability to testify but suggested that they remember things differently than men and led to the establishment of normative speech where gender is not a concern.

Jankowski, James. "Ottomanism and Arabism in Egypt, 1860-1914." *Muslim World* 70 (1980): 226-259. In the late nineteenth century, many Egyptians regarded the Ottoman Empire—to the extent that it stood for Islam as a whole—as a more legitimate outlet than identifying with the Arabs. This article shows how Ottomanism provided a more vigorous environment for the growth of Egyptian ethnic nationalism.

Kedourie, Elie. *Afghani and 'Abduh: An Essay on Religious Unbelief and Political Activism in Modern Islam*. London: Cass, and New York: Humanities Press, 1966. A brief but very controversial essay when it appeared. Argues that 'Abduh was an atheist and subverter of Islam, and a Machiavellian who behaved as a Muslim only to advance his career.

Kerr, Malcolm. *Islamic Reform: The Political and Legal Theories of Muhammad 'Abduh and Rashīd Ridā*. Berkeley: University of California Press, 1966. Considers the impact of the many influences acting on 'Abduh and his generation in the matter of articulating the nature of the state and the rationale required for a legitimate legal system supported by the citizenry.

Livingston, John W. "Muhammad 'Abduh on Science." *The Muslim World* 85, no. 3-4 (July-October, 1995). Examines 'Abduh's attempts to modernize Arab education by advocating the teaching of Western science in Islamic institutions.

Ronald W. Davis

NIELS HENRIK ABEL

Born: August 5, 1802; Finnöy, Norway

Died: April 6, 1829; Froland, Norway

Area of Achievement: Mathematics

Contribution: Abel was instrumental in the evolution of modern mathematics, especially in the field of algebra. Regarded as one of the foremost analysts of his time, he insisted on a rigorous approach to mathematical proof which was critical for the further development of abstract mathematics.

Early Life

Niels Henrik Abel was the second child of Søren Georg Abel, a second-generation Lutheran minister, and Anne Marie Simonsen, a daughter of a successful merchant and shipowner. Soon after his birth in Finnöy, his father was transferred to the parish of Gjerstad, in southeastern Norway, about 250 kilometers from Oslo, where Abel spent his childhood with his five brothers and sisters. Abel was an attractive youth, with light ash-brown hair and blue eyes.

Although his father's earnings were never adequate to provide for the large family, the emphasis on educational stimulation in the Abel household was an important formative influence on the young boy. Although his early education was conducted at home, it was sufficient to allow him to attend the Cathedral School at Oslo when he was thirteen years old. It was there that his talent in mathematics was discovered, although his initial efforts were somewhat unpromising.

The Cathedral School had once been quite good, but many positions had been filled by inexperienced or inadequate teachers because their predecessors had been recruited to join the faculty of the newly formed University of Oslo. Indeed, Abel's first mathematics instructor was dismissed abruptly after beating a student to death. Fortunately, the replacement in that position was Bernt Michael Holmboe, who was the first to recognize Abel's talent and who later edited the first edition of his work. Holmboe also assisted Christopher Hansteen, a professor at the university; this connection would prove valuable to Abel.

When Holmboe first arrived at the school, he noticed Abel's ability in mathematics and suggested that the two of them study some of the contemporary mathematics works together. Abel soon outpaced Holmboe and began developing a general solution for the quintic equation, that is, an equation of the fifth degree ($ax5 + bx4 + cx3 + dx2 + ex + f = 0$). When Abel believed that the work was complete, Holmboe and Hansteen sensed that no one in Norway, including themselves, could review the work capably. They forwarded the paper to Ferdinand Degen of the Danish Academy, who carefully reviewed the work. Before publication, Degen helped Abel discover that his solution was flawed, but he steered Abel into the field of elliptic functions, which Degen believed would be more fruitful.

At about this time, Abel discovered that several of his predecessors, particularly Leonhard Euler and Joseph-Louis Lagrange, had not completed the reasoning required to prove some of their work. Abel diligently supplied rigorous proofs where they were missing; a noted case is his proof of the general binomial theorem, which had been stated previously in part by Sir Isaac Newton and Euler. The mathematics community later was to find his meticulous treatment of the works he studied in-

valuable. Unfortunately for his personal life and his financial situation, Abel's father, who had served two terms in the *Storting* (congress), was impeached and disgraced. His father died in 1829, leaving his family in even more desperate financial straits than ever before.

Life's Work

The nineteen-year-old Abel entered the University of Oslo in 1821. While this entering age would not normally denote a prodigy, the fact that the university granted him a free room and that several professors donated funds for his support does. Abel completed the preliminary requirements for a degree in a single year. He was then free to study mathematics on his own, as he had no peers among the faculty. He developed a love for the theater at this time, which lasted throughout his short life. A modest person, he made many lasting friendships.

In addition to studying all available work, he began writing papers, the first of which were published in the journal *Magazin for Naturvidenskaberne* begun by Hansteen. In 1823, Abel's first important paper, "Oplösning afet Par Opgaver ved bjoelp af bestemte Integraler" ("Solution of Some Problems by Means of Definite Integrals"), was published, containing the first published solutions of integral equations. During 1822 and 1823, he also developed a longer paper discussing the integration of functions. This work is recognized as very significant in the evolution of that field of study.

At this time, Abel's work was largely ignored by the international mathematics community because Abel was from Norway and wrote in Norwegian, and the focal point of the mathematics community of the day was Paris, with the language of the learned being French. By applying himself diligently, Abel learned French and began to publish work in that language. The quintic equation still held his attention, and, as he thought of possibilities for its solution, he also considered that there might be no solution that could be found for all such equations. In time, he was able to prove this result. Yet still the mathematicians whose approval he desired so fervently, those in Paris, ignored his work.

He began to press for the opportunity to go to Paris, but penniless as he was he was forced to rely on grants. After his first application, it was decided that he needed to study more foreign languages before going abroad. Although it meant delaying his dream for nearly two years, Abel applied himself to learning various languages. Meanwhile, he became engaged to Christine (Krelly) Kemp before he finally received a royal grant to travel abroad in 1825.

This trip was unsuccessful in many ways. When he arrived at Copenhagen, he discovered that Degen had died. Instead of going on to Paris, Abel decided to go to Berlin because several of his friends were there. The time in Berlin was invaluable, for he met and befriended August Leopold Crelle, who became his strongest supporter and mentor. When Abel met him, Crelle was preparing to begin publication of a new journal, *Journal für die reine und angewandte Mathematik*. Crelle was so taken by Abel's ability that much of the first few issues was devoted to Abel's work in an attempt to win recognition for the young mathematician.

For a variety of reasons, Abel did not proceed to Paris until the spring of 1826. By this time, he had spent most of his grant and was physically tired, and the Parisian mathematicians he had hoped to convince were nearly all on holiday. Yet his masterwork, *Mémoire sur une propriété générale d'une classe très-étendue de fonctions transcendantes* (memoir on a general property of a very extensive class of transcendental functions), was presented to the Academy of Sciences on October 30, 1826. The paper was left in the keeping of Augustin-Louis Cauchy, a prominent mathematician, and Cauchy and Adrien-Marie Legendre were to be the referees. Whether the paper was illegible, as Cauchy claimed, or was misplaced, as most historians believe, no judgment was issued until after Abel's death.

Abel felt a great sense of failure, for many young mathematicians had been established by recognition from the academy. He returned first to Berlin and finally to Oslo in May, 1827. His prospects were bleak: He had contracted tuberculosis, there was no prospect for a mathematical position in Norway, and he was in debt. Abel began tutoring and lecturing at the university on a substitute basis in order to support himself.

Another young mathematician, Carl Gustav Jacob Jacobi, soon began publishing work in Abel's foremost field, the theory of elliptic functions and integrals. The rivalry created between them dominated the rest of Abel's life. He worked furiously to prove his ideas, and his efforts were spurred by his correspondence with Legendre. As he finally began to be recognized in Europe, many mathematicians, led by Crelle, attempted to secure a patronage for him. He succumbed, however, to tuberculosis on April 6, 1829, two days before Crelle wrote to inform him that such financial support had been found. In June, 1830, he and Jacobi were awarded the Grand Prix of the French Academy of Sciences for their work in elliptic integrals. Abel's original manuscript was found and finally published in 1841.

Summary

Although Niels Henrik Abel's life was short and his work was unrecognized for most of his life, he has exercised a great influence on modern mathematics. His primary work with elliptic functions and integrals led to interest in what became one of the great research topics of his century. Without his preliminary findings, many of the developments in mathematics and, consequently, science, may not have been made. One example of this is his theory of elliptic functions, much of which was developed very quickly during his race with Jacobi. In addition, his proof that there is no general solution to the quintic equation is quite important, as are his other findings in equation theory.

His theory of solutions using definite integrals, including what is now called Abel's theorem, is also widely used in engineering and the physical sciences and provided a foundation for the later work of others. Abelian (commutative) groups, Abelian functions, and Abelian equations are but three of the ideas which commonly carry his name. Given Abel's short life span and his living in Norway, a definite academic backwater at the time, his prolific achievements are amazing.

Abel is also significant because his writing and mathematical styles, which were easily comprehended, made his discoveries available to his contemporaries and successors. Abel's insistence that ideas should be demonstrated in such a way that the conclusions would be supported by clear and easily comprehended arguments, that is, proved rigorously, is the cornerstone of modern mathematics. It is in this regard that Abel is most often remembered.

Bibliography

Abel, Niels Henrik. "From a Memoir on Algebraic Equations, Proving the Impossibility of a Solution of the General Equation of the Fifth Degree." In *Classics of Mathematics*, edited by Ronald Calinger. Oak Park, Ill.: Moore, 1982. This extract of Abel's paper on the general quintic equation demonstrates Abel's style. Although it is too technical for the casual reader, it is of interest to mathematicians. The excerpt is preceded by a brief biography. This work also demonstrates how Abel fits into the overall development of mathematics.

Bell, Eric T. "Genius and Poverty: Abel." In *Men of Mathematics*. London: Gollancz, and New York: Simon and Schuster, 1937. This book is a compilation of brief biographies of the most famous mathematicians throughout recorded history. The emphasis is more on the subject's life than the mathematics produced.

Boyer, Carl B. *A History of Mathematics*. 2d ed. New York: Wiley, 1989. This general history of mathematics will aid the reader in placing Abel within the general development of mathematics.

Kline, Morris. *Mathematical Thought from Ancient to Modern Times*. New York: Oxford University Press, 1972. Kline includes both a brief biography of Abel and discussions of his most important work in this history of mathematics.

Ore, Øystein. *Niels Henrik Abel: Mathematician Extraordinary*. Minneapolis: University of Minnesota Press, 1957. This standard English-language biography gives a detailed account of Abel's life without requiring specialized knowledge of mathematics.

Celeste Williams Brockington

LORD ACTON

Born: January 10, 1834; Naples, Italy
Died: June 19, 1902; Tegernsee, Bavaria, Germany
Area of Achievement: Historiography
Contribution: Although he never succeeded in finishing his planned monumental "History of Liberty," Acton was one of the most learned scholars and probing intellects of his time. While a devout Roman Catholic, he was for much of his life at odds with the church hierarchy because of what he saw as its authoritarian tendencies. Acton was first and foremost a moralist, and his most passionate commitment was to the defense of individual freedom.

Early Life

John Emerich Edward Dalberg Acton, or Lord Acton as he was known after his elevation to the peerage in 1869, was born at Naples, Italy, on January 10, 1834, the only child of Sir Ferdinand Richard Edward Acton, seventh baronet, and the former Marie Louise Pelline de Dalberg. The Actons were an old Shropshire family, the first baronet having received his title (conferred in 1643) in reward for his loyalty to Charles I. Acton's paternal grandfather had been Prime Minister of the Kingdom of the Two Sicilies; his mother belonged to one of Germany's oldest noble families. His family heritage—on both sides—was staunchly Roman Catholic. Acton attended the Roman Catholic St. Mary's School at Oscott, near Oxford, and then studied under a private tutor. The turning point in his intellectual development was his study, from 1850 to 1858, with Johann Joseph Ignaz von Döllinger of the University of Munich, the leading Roman Catholic theologian and church historian of the time. The close ties that were forged between the two men had a decisive influence in shaping Acton's most salient values. Döllinger was a champion of the Rankean scientific approach to the study of history, based upon exacting research into the primary sources. He simultaneously aspired to make Roman Catholicism intellectually and theologically respectable by opening the Church to modern philosophical and scientific thought. Most important, Döllinger taught that Christian dogma was not fixed but underwent change and development. The test of any doctrine thus lay in historical evidence. The revolutionary implications of this position first became apparent when Döllinger protested the 1854 proclamation of the Immaculate Conception of Mary because of its lack of historical status.

Life's Work

Acton's social position gave him the opportunity to travel widely and provided him with access to the leading political and intellectual figures in England and on the Continent. An avid book collector, he built up a personal library of approximately fifty-nine thousand volumes that would, after his death, become part of the University of Cambridge collection. He was a prodigious reader, reputed to read, annotate, and memorize an average of two volumes per day. Fluent in English, German, French, and Italian, he was a brilliant conversationalist. "If the gods granted me the privilege of recalling to life for half an hour's conversation some of the great men of the past I have had the good fortune to know," politician and historian John Morley remarked, "I should say Acton." Acton's father died when he was three, and he succeeded to

the title as the eighth baronet. His mother in 1840 married Granville George Leveson-Gower (who would become the second Earl Granville), a power in the British Liberal Party. His stepfather arranged for Acton's election to the House of Commons in 1859, but he was not temperamentally cut out for the rough-and-tumble of politics and remained during his six years in the Commons an unimportant backbencher. His personal inclinations and talents lay in journalism and scholarship. In 1858, he became part-owner and an editor of the "liberal" Roman Catholic monthly, the *Rambler*, which in 1862 was converted into a quarterly under the name *Home and Foreign Review*. After worsening conflict with the church hierarchy led to its termination in 1864, Acton became associated with two other short-lived journals of liberal Catholic opinion—the weekly *Chronicle* (1867-1868) and the quarterly *North British Review* (1869-1872).

Acton's difficulties with the Roman Catholic church hierarchy grew out of his hostility to its ultramontanism. In its narrower meaning, ultramontanism stood for the centralization of power within the Church in the Papacy. More broadly, the ultramontanist position—most explicitly summarized by Pope Pius IX in the *Syllabus Errorum* appended to his 1864 encyclical *Quanta Cura*—repudiated "progress, Liberalism, and modern civilization." Among the heresies condemned in the *Syllabus Errorum* were separation of church and state, freedom of worship, and free intellectual inquiry in science, philosophy, and history. On the opposite side, Acton affirmed that faith could be reconciled with reason and science. Second, he called for a free church in a free state. Relying upon the force of the state would inevitably subordinate the Church to mere political expediency; alternately, an absolutist state could not tolerate an independent Church. Most important, Acton regarded individual liberty not as the antithesis of Christianity but as its product. In contrast with the theocracy of the Jews and the ancient Greek states, the Christian distinction between what was due to God and what was due to Caesar introduced the new conception of the individual conscience immune from political interference. When ultramontanists glorified the Inquisition, Acton replied that murder was no less murder because it was sanctioned by the Pope. He even published in 1869 a painstakingly researched article, "The Massacre of St. Bartholomew," showing papal complicity in the bloody 1572 attack upon the Huguenots.

The high point of Acton's conflict with the church hierarchy came over the doctrine of papal infallibility that Pius IX pushed through a tightly managed general council in 1870. Acton was in Rome during the meeting of the council, working behind the scenes as an adviser to the minority of prelates opposed to the promulgation of the doctrine. He even made an unsuccessful attempt to organize a protest from all the major European powers. In the aftermath of the council, he publicly marshaled the historical evidence in support of the anti-infallibilist position. His old mentor Döllinger was excommunicated because of his refusal to accept the new doctrine. For a time, it appeared that Acton would suffer the same fate. Such action was not taken, however, partly because Acton was a layman rather than a priest as was Döllinger, partly because of the political difficulties that his excommunication would have raised for the Church in England, and partly because of Acton's tactfulness in keeping his distance from Rome while still avoiding open defiance. Shrinking from a break with the Church, Acton adopted the face-saving formula "I have yielded obedience." He squared this acquiescence with his conscience by personally adopting a minimalist interpretation of the doctrine's meaning. Regarding the Church as a holy body transcending the shortcomings of its official leaders, he took refuge in his faith that time—or what he termed "God's providence in His government of the Church"—would undo the damage. While upholding the right of others to disbelieve, he never doubted that membership in the Church was the necessary means for his own personal salvation.

Acton appears to have begun working upon what he envisaged as his masterwork, the "History of Liberty," in the 1870's. Although rather sarcastically described as "the greatest book that never was written," its broad outlines can be reconstructed from his essays and manuscript notes. Acton's starting point was his definition of liberty as the freedom of the individual to follow the dictates of his conscience. Liberty, in turn, depended upon the existence of the rule of law; its antithesis was the exercise of arbitrary power untrammeled by any limitation. Although Acton found glimmerings of that conception in antiquity, despotism was the norm: "In religion, morality, and politics there was only one legislator and one authority." The Middle Ages represented a major advance in the growth of liberty. One reason was its corporatist social organization, whereby each class and interest had defined rights and privileges. Even more important was the belief in the existence of a higher law to which temporal rulers were subject and which the Church in theory, if not always in practice, was charged with upholding. The Renaissance, however, saw the emergence of the absolute state that accepted no law outside itself and followed the Machiavellian principle that the end justified the means. After first paying lip service to liberty, the Protestant reformers ended up in a marriage of convenience with royal absolutism. Meanwhile, the Roman Catholic church copied the Protestant enemy by joining in an alliance with monarchical power that ended in the monarchies' subjection to church power.

The liberating promise of the English revolution of the seventeenth century was successfully blunted. The result of the 1688 settlement was simply to replace the divine right of kings with the divine right of property. The American Revolution was for Acton the epochal turning point in modern history. He eulogized the revolutionaries' philosophy of natural rights and their denial of the legitimacy of all authority not derived from the people, but what he most admired was how the framers of the United States Constitution had built into their plan of government a set of checks and balances to prevent unrestrained majority rule. By contrast, the disastrous flaw in the French Revolution was its acceptance of a doctrine of unlimited popular sovereignty that substituted for monarchical absolutism the despotism of the majority. The result was the most dangerous threat to liberty yet:

> The true democratic principle, that none shall have power over the people, is taken to mean that none shall be able to restrain or to elude its power. The true democratic principle, that the people shall not be made to do what it does not like, is taken to mean that it shall never be required to tolerate what it does not like. The true democratic principle, that every man's free will shall be as unfettered as possible, is taken to mean the free will of the collective people shall be fettered in nothing.

Aggravating the situation was the accompanying rise of nationalism. Domestically, nationalism fostered a centralization of authority that swept away all intermediate institutions between the isolated individual and the omnipotent state; internationally, nationalism meant rule by force of the strong over the weak. Acton summed up his indictment in an epigram: "The nations aim at power, and the world at freedom."

Acton's hero among contemporary political leaders was British Liberal Party leader William Ewart Gladstone. He was attracted partly by Gladstone's own tendency to define issues in moral terms, even more by what he saw as Gladstone's commitment to striking a balance between democracy and liberty. While the propertied minority had rights that must be respected, the majority simultaneously had a right to social legislation that would improve the lot of the masses. Gladstone's "Little Englandism," his opposition to the imperialism of the national state run amok, was even more attractive. Deep ties of affection and mutual respect joined the two men. Gladstone submitted for Acton's criticism nearly everything he wrote. Acton, in turn, influenced Gladstone in his politics—most important, his espousal of disestablishment of the Irish (Anglican) church and Irish home rule. Gladstone was responsible for Acton's elevation to the peerage in 1869 as Baron Acton of Aldenham, his election as honorary Fellow of All Souls, Oxford, in 1891, and his appointment as lord-in-waiting to Queen Victoria in 1892. Acton had been one of the founders of the *English Historical Review* in 1886, himself contributing to the first issue an impressively learned survey of nineteenth century German historians and philosophers of history. As early as 1872, the University of Munich awarded him an honorary doctorate of philosophy. Cambridge followed with an honorary LL.D. in 1888; Oxford, with an honorary D.C.L. the year after. In 1895, Acton was named Regius Professor of Modern History at Cambridge. Along with the professorship came election as an honorary Fellow of Trinity College.

Acton's six years at Cambridge were probably the happiest of his life. Although he lectured on the French Revolution for the historical tripos, the greater part of his energy was devoted to the editorship of the *Cambridge Modern History* (1899-1912). While only the first volume and half of the second were in type at his death, he was largely responsible for the planning of the full twelve volumes and the selection of most of the individual contributors. Unfortunately, the burden of handling the manifold details of so large an undertaking badly strained his already poor health. In 1901, Acton suffered a stroke that forced him to leave Cambridge. He died on June 19, 1902, at a villa owned by his wife's family at Tegernsee in Bavaria. He was survived by his wife, Countess Maria von Arco-Valley (whom he had married in 1865), and four children—one son and three daughters.

Acton's publication during his lifetime consisted mostly of periodical contributions and reprinted lectures. After his death, however, his more important writings were collected in four volumes edited by John N. Figgis and Reginald V. Laurence: *Lectures on Modern History* (1906), *The History of Freedom and Other Essays* (1907), *Historical Essays and Studies* (1908), and *Lectures on the French Revolution* (1910). The years since World War II have witnessed a resurgence of interest in Acton's work, resulting in the appearance of four new anthologies: *Essays on Freedom and Power* (1948; edited by Gertrude Himmelfarb), *Essays on Church and State* (1952; edited by Douglas Woodruff), *Essays in the Liberal Interpretation of History* (1967; edited by William H. McNeill), and *Lord Acton on Papal Power* (1973; edited by H. A. MacDougall).

Summary

Lord Acton's strength as a historian lay in his painstaking research in and analysis of the primary sources. Yet his high scholarly standards were simultaneously a weakness. He could not bring himself to stop until he had explored everything remotely pertaining to the subject. His papers in the Cambridge University Library are filled with pages of notes for projects that were never finished. Even his planned opening chapter for the first volume of the *Cambridge Modern History*, "The Legacy of the Middle Ages," was left in too fragmentary shape for inclusion. This weakness was aggravated by the breadth of his interests, which kept him from focusing his energies upon any single period or topic. Nor was he an outstanding literary stylist. His importance as a historian lies in his broader philosophy of history. For Acton, ideas were the forces that moved the world. Therein lay the source of his conception of the historian's role. The historian's task was not the Rankean ideal of the impartial chronicler of what had actually happened. Even worse was the moral relativism that explained away—even excused—wrongdoing in terms of the values of the time. The historian's duty to the present and to the future was to judge the past by the canons of eternal justice. His judgment that murder is still murder no matter what its ostensible noble justification has a special resonance for the late twentieth century. "If we lower our standard in History," he admonished in his inaugural lecture as Regius Professor, "we cannot uphold it in Church or State."

Part of the reason for the renewed interest in Acton is his championship of what is now called "political pluralism"—his argument that the preservation of individual liberty depends upon the widest possible dispersion of power. Underlying his commitment to pluralism was his awareness of the corruptibility of human nature. "Most assuredly, now as heretofore," he explained to a friend, "the Men of the Time are, in most cases, unprincipled, and act from motives of interest, of passion, of prejudice, cherished and unchecked, of selfish hope or unworthy fear." The most dangerous temptation to which men succumbed was ambition for power. In that recognition, Acton belonged more to the present age than to his own. Only those generations that have witnessed the horrors of the twentieth century can fully appreciate his prophetic warning:

> Power tends to corrupt and absolute power corrupts absolutely. Great men are almost always bad men, even when they exercise influence and not authority: still more when you superadd the tendency or the certainty of corruption by authority. There is no worse heresy than that the office sanctifies the holder of it. . . . The inflexible authority of the moral code is, to me, the secret of the authority, the dignity, the utility of history. If we may debase the currency for the sake of genius, or success or rank, or reputation, we may debase it for the sake of a man's influence, of his religion, of his party, of the good cause which prospers by his credit and suffers by his disgrace. Then history ceases to be a science, an arbiter of controversy, a guide of the wanderer. . . . It serves where it ought to reign; and it serves the worst cause better than the purest.

Bibliography

Altholz, Josef L. *The Liberal Catholic Movement in England: The Rambler and Its Contributors, 1848-1864*. London: Burns and Oates, 1962. An excellent account of the controversy over ultramontanism in England.

Butterfield, Herbert. *Lord Acton*. London: Philip, 1948. A brief, though astute, sketch of Acton's intellectual development.

Fasnacht, George E. *Acton's Political Philosophy*. London: Hollis and Carter, 1952; New York: Viking Press, 1953. A detailed examination of Acton as a political theorist.

Himmelfarb, Gertrude. *Lord Acton: A Study in Conscience and Politics*. Chicago: University of Chicago Press, and London: Routledge, 1952. An insightful and perceptive intellectual biography that did much to stimulate renewed interest in Acton.

———. *Victorian Minds*. London: Weidenfeld and Nicolson, and New York: Knopf, 1968. Although the chapter on Acton is basically a summary of Himmelfarb's 1952 study, the volume's broader scope contributes to clarifying Acton's place within the spectrum of Victorian thought.

Kochan, Lionel. *Acton on History*. London: Deutsch, 1954; Porth Washington, N.Y.: Kennikat Press, 1971. A rather abstract analysis of Acton as historian and philosopher of history.

Mathew, David. *Acton: The Formative Years*. London: Eyre and Spottiswoode, 1946; Westport, Conn.: Greenwood Press, 1974. Informative on the world of nineteenth century Catholicism but superficial and at times even unreliable on Acton himself.

Schuettinger, Robert L. *Lord Acton: Historian of Liberty*. LaSalle, Ill.: Open Court, 1976. Includes more personal details than Himmelfarb's works, but thinner analysis.

Watson, George. *Lord Acton's History of Liberty*. Aldershot, Hampshire: Scolar Press, and Brookfield, Vt.: Ashgate, 1994. Watson has written the first full-length study of Acton's unpublished *History of Liberty* based on the author's personal notes. Includes a full account of Acton's books and papers.

Zagorin, Perez. "Lord Acton's Ordeal: The Historian and Moral Judgement." *The Virginia Quarterly Review* 74, no. 1 (Winter 1998). Examines Lord Acton's life and beliefs regarding moral judgement by historians. Discusses the feelings of isolation and his unpublished work, *The History of Liberty*.

John Braeman

HENRY ADAMS

Born: February 16, 1838; Boston, Massachusetts
Died: March 27, 1918; Washington, D.C.
Areas of Achievement: History and literature
Contribution: Adams was a first-rate historian who wrote several biographies and the monumental nine-volume *History of the United States of America* (1889-1891), covering the administrations of Thomas Jefferson and James Madison. His two most famous works are interconnected and autobiographical: *Mont-Saint-Michel and Chartres* (1904) and *The Education of Henry Adams* (1907).

Early Life

Henry Brooks Adams was born February 16, 1838, the fourth of five children of Charles Francis Adams and Abigail Brown Brooks. His father was a cold and distant figure, and it was to his mother that he looked for affection. It is not surprising that Henry would always feel out of place. His elite Brahmin heritage both paved the way for his future and controlled it. A kinsman, Samuel Adams, had become involved in the American Revolution as a manipulator of mobs. His great-grandfather John Adams helped draft the Declaration of Independence, was the first vice president, and the second president. Henry's grandfather John Quincy Adams served as secretary of state and then as president. Henry's father served as ambassador to England during the crucial diplomatic period of the Civil War and was later elected to Congress.

In addition to his distinguished heritage, Henry's immediate family was one of the wealthiest in Boston, based on the mercantile fortune of his mother, Abigail Brooks. Adams' full name appears to sum up his life—"Henry" betokening the scholar rather than the man of action; "Brooks" the moneyed inheritance that was his by birth; and "Adams" the line of blue-blooded forefathers who had taken such an active part in the creation of the United States. Henry's dilemma was to live a successful life in the shadow of such eminence.

Adams attended Harvard from 1854 through 1858. In *The Education of Henry Adams*, he later stated that he had learned nothing while there. Upon graduation, in typical patrician fashion, he set out on a tour of Europe. He studied law and learned to speak German while at the University of Berlin, from 1858 to 1860. While in Europe, he also began his efforts in journalism, which he would continue throughout his life.

In 1861, as the Civil War broke out in the United States, President Abraham Lincoln appointed Adams' father minister to England, a critical position, since the South was attempting to gain recognition from England. At age twenty-three, Adams accompanied his father and acted as his private secretary. While there, Adams continued his journalism, working anonymously for *The New York Times*, and he also began his historical work by writing articles for the *North American Review.*

Life's Work

In 1868, Adams returned to Washington. He and his brothers decided that politics had done nothing but bring sorrow to the family. Adams' worldview might be broken into two segments: his philosophical speculations about the world, especially the United States, and what he was going to do with the remainder of his life. As it turned out, Adams spent the remainder of his life looking for answers to both questions through an interaction of the two. In a way, Adams became an intellectual dilettante, one of the best America has ever produced.

Adams did not spend his whole life behind a desk. He enjoyed parties, people, and friendships immensely, and his family fame brought him into contact with the celebrities of the time. Although short in stature, he was handsome, and he became known as one of the three best dancers in Washington.

From 1868 until 1870, Adams was a free-lance journalist, serving as a correspondent for *The Nation* and other leading journals as he plunged into both the social and the political worlds of Washington. His primary interest was the reconstruction of a war-shattered nation. He fought for civil service reform and the retention of the gold standard. He wrote articles exposing political corruption and warning against economic monopolies, especially within the railroads.

In 1870, Charles W. Eliot, the famous Harvard president, asked Adams to become assistant professor of medieval history. Out of tune with the world for which he was destined, Adams accepted. Despite having one of the best minds in the country, Adams was ill-trained to be a teacher. He threw himself furiously into his new task, often staying only one lecture ahead of his class. Without planning it, Adams was preparing the groundwork for what would become one of his masterpieces, *Mont-Saint-Michel and Chartres*. Adams also became the first American to employ the seminar method in his classes.

Adams' work at Harvard became his first step toward studying the American past. In 1877, he resigned from Harvard to complete two biographies, *The Life of Albert Gallatin* (1879) and *John Randolph* (1882). This research increased his interest in the early American period, and hoping to understand the nature of an evolving American democracy, he began what was to become his nine-volume *History of the United States of America*.

In 1872, Adams married Marian "Clover" Hooper, a woman with impeccable family connections, great intelligence, and a solid income. The two took a yearlong wedding trip which included a tour of Europe and boating up the Nile. Henry and Clover made a complementary couple, and Adams would later speak of their years together as years of happiness. Their union produced no children.

Adams published two novels anonymously, *Democracy: An American Novel* (1880) and *Esther: A Novel* (1884). Neither novel was a success, since Adams did not possess the artistic talents necessary to produce fiction. Of the two, *Democracy* was the more popular and the superior. *Democracy* was a *roman á clef*, which accounted for its initial demand. Mrs. Lightfoot Lee is the heroine through the eyes of whom Washington is revealed. She becomes a confidante of a Midwestern senator, and she is introduced to the processes of democracy. She meets the president and other high-ranking figures, only to find them all to be vacuous. She represents Adams' alter ego; indeed, both came up with much the same summation of Washington: After an initial attraction for the cause, they both reject it in the end because of the emptiness and moral ambiguity they find there. *Democracy* served Adams as a trial run for *The Education of Henry Adams*.

Adams' second novel, *Esther*, is less interesting. It is similar in that it also has a woman as its main character, this one based on Adams' wife. As a novel of ideas, *Esther* investigates the relationship between religion and modern science, a theme that Adams pursued throughout his life. As the novel ends, the heroine, in her quest for meaning, stares at and listens to Niagara Falls, Adams' overpowering symbol for the life force. The roar symboliz-

es a natural representation of the dynamo Adams was to make so much of and of the eternal law of history.

In 1885, Adams was stunned when his wife of thirteen years took potassium cyanide and killed herself. There was no discernible motive for her suicide except that she feared madness, which existed in her family. Strangely, Adams had a sculpture of a mysterious, cloaked woman placed on her grave. At the time of her death, Adams had been working on his *History of the United States of America*. He set the manuscript aside and began a period of restless traveling that included Japan.

As time passed, Adams narrowed his travel to winters in Washington and summers in Paris. He eventually returned to his *History of the United States of America* and completed it in September, 1888. The work was published in nine volumes between 1889 and 1891. Initially, it was met by apathy, but eventually it would be considered of the highest order, second only to the work of Francis Parkman.

Adams' best-known works, *Mont-Saint-Michel and Chartres* and *The Education of Henry Adams*, were privately printed and distributed to friends and only later were published for general use. The two works are interconnected and are based on thoughts that Adams spent a lifetime trying to untangle.

Mont-Saint-Michel and Chartres is a work of history, aesthetics, philosophy, and theology. The book is like a Symbolist poem, with one event flowing into another and all rules of chronology and reason being defied.

Adams' starting point for *Mont-Saint-Michel and Chartres* can be found in his travels to France and his visits to the thirteenth century cathedrals. Adams was in search of a fixed point from which to measure motion down to his own time, and that point became the medieval worldview as expressed especially in the cathedrals. Adams believed that their monumental structures expressed the deepest emotions that man ever felt. For Adams, an entire age could be said to have unity, purpose, mission, and fullness of experience toward an ideological unity represented by the Blessed Virgin Mary.

The Education of Henry Adams was not finished until Adams was sixty-eight years old. It remains his single best-known work and one of the most distinguished autobiographies of all time, compared by some to St. Augustine's *Confessions* (c. 1397). Whereas the Virgin had been the center for

Mont-Saint-Michel and Chartres, the symbol for the twentieth century became the dynamo, one of which Adams had seen at the Chicago World's Fair. Adams found the twentieth century to be incomprehensible. Under the impact of the alarming growth of science and technology, historical forces had accelerated, leading to what Adams called the "multiverse" of the modern world.

Adams died on March 27, 1918, in Washington, D.C., the city from which he could not separate himself. World War I was still raging, and the breakup of the modern, civilized world, which Adams had predicted, had become reality. Adams was buried next to his wife in the Rock Creek Cemetery. At his direction, the grave was unmarked.

Summary

Henry Adams' life situation allowed him the freedom to be rebellious. He scornfully accepted the mantle of responsibility that destiny had given him. He became America's first modern historian. He briefly shared his enormous intellect with students and then resigned permanently from teaching, undertaking full-time the completion of his research and compiling his *magnum opus*, the nine-volume *History of the United States of America*.

Adams also made his mark on the historical and literary world with his *Mont-Saint-Michel and Chartres* and his *The Education of Henry Adams*. These two works, especially *The Education of Henry Adams*, are still widely read by students and the general public. One central connection between the two is the juxtaposition Adams proposed between the Virgin of the thirteenth century and the dynamo of the twentieth. Adams was interested in power—religious power, political power, and scientific power.

Adams was almost as good a prophet as he was a historian. He believed that the twentieth century was heading toward chaos; mankind was being swept away by seemingly uncontrollable technology, represented by the dynamo. Ahead of his time and unable to comprehend modern man, Adams foresaw the ultimate possibility of man's self-destruction.

Bibliography

Adams, Henry Brooks. *The Education of Henry Adams*. Edited with an introduction by Ernest Samuels. Boston: Houghton Mifflin, 1974. One of the most distinguished autobiographies of the twentieth century. Adams' best-known work.

———. *The Letters of Henry Adams*. 3 vols. Edited by J. C. Levenson et al. Cambridge, Mass.: Belknap Press of Harvard University Press, 1982. Includes bibliographical references and index. Adams' letters are valuable in that they reveal his thoughts and reflect the times in which he lived.

———. *Mont-Saint-Michel and Chartres*. With an introduction by Ernest Samuels. Boston: Houghton Mifflin, 1904; London: Constable, 1913. The best starting point for a study of Adams would be the above works, especially *The Education of Henry Adams*, one of the greatest autobiographies of all time.

Byrnes, Joseph F. *The Virgin of Chartres: An Intellectual and Psychological History of the Work of Henry Adams*. Rutherford, N.J.: Fairleigh Dickinson University Press, and London: Associated University Presses, 1981. Discusses Adams' relationships with women. Concentrates mainly on *Mont-Saint-Michel and Chartres* and Adams' thoughts concerning the Virgin Mary.

Harbert, Earl N., ed. *Critical Essays on Henry Adams*. Boston: Hall, 1981. The editor has compiled essays on Adams by R. P. Blackmur, H. S. Commager, Ernest Samuels, Charles Anderson, Howard Mumford, J. C. Levenson, and others. The essays cover various matters, including Adams' fiction and his two autobiographical works. Other matters covered include Gene Koretz's essay, which concludes that *The Education of Henry Adams* is very nearly the equivalent of Augustine's *Confessions*. Levenson compares Adams with William Shakespeare's famous character Prince Hamlet. Earl Harbert has two essays, one of which examines the autobiographical aspects of *The Education of Henry Adams* and another which contains details concerning Adams' trip to Asia.

———, ed. *Henry Adams: A Reference Guide*. Boston: Hall, 1978. This ninety-six-page annotated bibliography contains Adams' major writings and critical work about him from 1879 to 1975. The introduction contains a compact discussion of Adams' reputation and major works, a brief survey of important critical articles and books, and a short discussion about the methods used to compile the bibliography and its major contents.

Levenson, J. C. *The Mind and Art of Henry Adams*. Boston: Houghton Mifflin, 1957. This critical work concentrates on Adams' life and on his enormous distinction as a writer. Levenson examines Adams' monumental achievement as an interpretive scholar and connects the historical research with the artistic talent. Major concepts associated with Adams, such as modern man existing within a "multiverse" and Adams' thesis concerning the Unity found in *Mont-Saint-Michel and Chartres*, are developed and discussed in detail.

Rowe, John C., ed. *New Essays on the Education of Henry Adams*. Cambridge and New York: Cambridge University Press, 1996. A collection of essays on Adams' autobiography which approach the book from early twentieth-century perspectives on issues such as gender and education.

Samuels, Ernest. *The Young Henry Adams*. London: Harvard University Press, and Cambridge, Mass.: Belknap Press of Harvard University Press, 1948.

———. *Henry Adams: The Middle Years*. Cambridge, Mass.: The Belknap Press of Harvard University Press, 1958.

———. *Henry Adams: The Major Phase*. Cambridge, Mass.: The Belknap Press of Harvard University Press, 1964. The above three works constitute the standard biography of Henry Adams. Samuels examines the pattern of failure and futility which Adams experienced during his attempts at education, his observations of others' efforts, and his perplexities with language itself. The works are comprehensive and distinguished.

John Harty

JOHN QUINCY ADAMS

Born: July 11, 1767; Braintree, Massachusetts
Died: February 23, 1848; Washington, D.C.
Areas of achievement: Government and politics
Contribution: As diplomat, secretary of state, president, and member of the House of Representatives, in a career spanning the early national period to nearly the time of the Civil War, John Quincy Adams helped to shape America's major foreign and domestic policies, always in the direction of strengthening the nation as a unified whole.

Early Life

John Quincy Adams was born in Braintree (later Quincy), Massachusetts, on July 11, 1767, the second child and first son of John and Abigail (Smith) Adams. At such a time and in such a family, he was a child of both the Revolution and the Enlightenment, nurtured as well with a strong Puritan sense of duty and destiny, directed throughout his life toward politics (and its attendant sacrifices), always striving to fulfill the expectations and retain the approbation of his parents, especially the redoubtable Abigail. His unorthodox and irregular education was to produce both a scholar and a nationalist, unswerving in his principles and forever unsatisfied with his performance, always striving to increase his learning and improve his habits, and never able to mingle easily with others or develop satisfying personal relationships.

As a boy, John Quincy imbibed patriotism in the midst of the Revolution and then spent a number of years in Europe while his father was engaged in the nation's diplomatic business; in France, Holland, and Russia he learned languages, associated with important men of the time, studied sporadically, and began what was to be a lifelong diary. Returning to America in 1785 (while his father remained as minister to England), he became again a schoolboy and was graduated from Harvard in 1787. In his commencement address, he referred to this time as a "critical period." He then studied law in Newburyport with Theophilus Parsons until his admission to the bar in 1790. Uninterested in the legal profession yet reluctant to be drawn into the hardships of public service, John Quincy entered the newspaper battles with essays on the French Revolution (against Thomas Paine's *Rights of Man*, 1791) and the Genêt affair. His arguments in favor of American neutrality won for him the attention of President George Washington and the post of minister resident at The Hague, in 1794. He took up his position at this excellent listening post during the Napoleonic expansion over Europe, reporting in detail to Washington and to the secretary of state on its course, his ideas influencing Washington's foreign policy statements in the Farewell Address.

John Quincy Adams' appointment as minister to Portugal was changed before he took it up, and he and his wife, Louisa, whom he had married in 1797, traveled to Berlin, where the new minister plenipotentiary to Prussia negotiated a treaty, saw his wife successfully enter court society, and began a volume of descriptive letters about a visit to Silesia. Recalled by his father, John Adams, who had lost reelection to the presidency, Adams brought his wife and son (George Washington Adams, born April 12, 1801) to an America they had never seen in order to renew an interrupted law practice. Drawn inevitably to public service, Adams was elected to the Massachusetts Senate in April, 1802, and to the United States Senate in February, 1803. He immediately demonstrated the qualities that were to characterize and frustrate his political career: commitment to the nation rather than to any party, consistency of principle and attention to detail, and the inability to deal effectively with varied personalities and the social demands of the Washington political scene.

The young senator was five feet, seven inches tall, balding, with rather sharp and expressive features; he had always been careless in his dress, and despite his lifelong habit of exercise frequently suffered from dizziness, insomnia, stomach trouble, and attacks of anxiety and depression. Always introspective and self-critical, he was reserved and humorless; formally a Unitarian, he was well versed in the Bible, classical literature, science, and the humanities.

Although Adams opposed the Republican administration's acquisition of Louisiana for constitutional reasons, he soon demonstrated his differences from the Federalists on the important issues of the Aaron Burr intrigue, Judge John Pickering's impeachment, and the *Chesapeake* incident and embargo policy. His nationalism and independence in supporting Republican policies provoked Federalist hostility in both political and personal relations; he resigned his Senate seat before his Federalist replacement took over, and he experienced problems even in his lectures as Boylston Professor of Oratory and Rhetoric at Harvard. Without consulting Louisa, he accepted President James Madison's appointment as minister plenipotentiary to Russia; the two older boys remained with their grandparents in Quincy, and Adams, Louisa, and Charles Francis (born August 18, 1807) arrived in St. Petersburg late in 1809.

Despite inadequate funds, both Adamses established themselves with the diplomatic community and at the extravagant court of Czar Alexander I. John Quincy was able to achieve some diplomatic successes with the Russian government, attend to his youngest son, and maintain a correspondence with his older sons filled with stern expectations for their education and achievements—expectations which neither was ever able to fulfill.

As Alexander and Napoleon Bonaparte fell out over the Continental System and the War of 1812 opened, Adams was an obvious choice for the commission to negotiate peace with Great Britain. When its five members met finally in Ghent in 1814, they achieved a satisfactory treaty based on the prewar status quo. Adams then journeyed to Paris to meet Louisa, who had, by herself, wound up their affairs in Russia and traversed Europe with young Charles in the aftermath of war and during the Hundred Days. The Adamses then spent the next two years happily in London, as John Quincy had been appointed by President James Monroe as minister plenipotentiary to Great Britain. It became apparent that Great Britain was willing to negotiate and arbitrate the points still at issue after the Treaty of Ghent.

Adams' appointment as Monroe's secretary of state brought the family back to the United States late in 1817 and renewed the pattern of separation (the parents in Washington, the boys educated elsewhere) and family problems. Adams, at fifty, reentered domestic politics by becoming embroiled with the new generation of politicians. He was still and always a nationalist and an independent in a time of growing partisanship and sectional controversy and reserved and scholarly during the development of popular sovereignty and anti-intellectualism. For the rest of his long life, despite personal tragedy and bitter political disappointments, he was to shape much of America's domestic and foreign policy.

Life's Work

Adams became secretary of state as the Era of Good Feelings began to dissolve in personal and

partisan contention for the presidency, and at a time when the State Department conducted both foreign and domestic affairs with one chief clerk and seven assistant clerks. Adams organized the department and its papers, did much of the office work himself during long days and nights (even cutting down on his reading), and attended to the census, congressional printing, extraditions, and commissions. He had, early in his career as a Federalist, demonstrated his political independence; he had received his appointments from Republican administrations; as secretary of state and son of John Adams, he was inevitably a presidential candidate. His foreign policy positions therefore developed as much in response to domestic political concerns as to the international situation. Yet his early principles dominated: He was a nationalist and an expansionist, cautious but determined to develop a hemispheric role for the United States.

Attempting to defend and expand American trade interests, Adams concentrated on the problem of discriminatory British customs duties in the West Indies trade. British interests and disturbed world conditions, however, meant the retention of those duties. Boundary problems with Great Britain and Russia in the Northwest presented less difficulty than those with Spain in Florida. The Treaty of 1818 settled United States-Canadian boundary and fisheries problems and provided for joint United States-British occupation of Oregon for ten years (the northern boundary fixed with Russia at 54°40' in the Convention of 1824). When General Andrew Jackson's sensational raid into Florida threatened an international incident, Adams alone in the Cabinet supported the general and used the uncontrolled Florida situation as an effective point in the negotiations that led to the 1819 Adams-Onís (Transcontinental) Treaty. Acquisition of Florida and the demarcation of a clear southwestern boundary to the Pacific represented major gains for the United States, even though Adams' opponents then and later attacked him on certain details (in which he had been uncharacteristically careless) and charged him with deliberately giving up Texas. Although he was not directly involved in the Missouri Compromise, Adams was against slavery and fearful that the sectional controversy had the potential to dissolve the Union. Even more immediately threatening was the possibility of European powers acting in the Western Hemisphere to regain newly independent colonies. Adams urged a unilateral American statement and greatly influenced the formulation of the basic policies of nonintervention and noncolonization, and American noninvolvement in Europe, points which President Monroe incorporated into his December, 1823, message, later known as the Monroe Doctrine.

A presidential nominating system still in flux made social events crucial for politics: Protocol for formal calls was subject matter for Senate resolutions and cabinet papers; Louisa Adams' entertaining was vital for the cold, unsocial, and ambitious John Quincy, who furthermore refused to pursue the nomination actively, preferring it unsought as recognition of his ability and service. Throughout his political career he was to spurn the idea of active campaigning directed at the mass of voters, seeing public service as properly in the hands of the dedicated and qualified rather than the "popular" politicians.

In the election of 1824, Adams received eighty-four electoral votes to Jackson's ninety-nine, but as there was no majority, the House was to decide between Jackson, Adams, and Henry Clay, the third runner-up. While Adams actively swayed some Federalists, it was Clay's influence that turned the tide; "Harry of the West" feared the rash general more than a fellow nationalist, and the two rivals realized their basic agreement on major issues. With Clay's influence added, the House chose Adams to be president; Adams' appointment of Clay as secretary of state (and therefore a potential next president) led the Jacksonians to open their presidential campaign almost immediately, based on the charge of "bargain and corruption." The accusation of an Adams-Clay collusion continued to affect American politics for many years.

President like his father, and like his father a single-term executive facing the more popular candidate, Adams was a minority president in a period of great partisan pressures, a nationalist in an era of deepening sectionalism, and an executive with a program at a time of legislative dominance. He never really controlled the National Republicans, nor could he prevent the development of the Democratic Republican Party. Determined to avoid party considerations in appointments, he kept many in his cabinet and other offices (such as Postmaster General John McLean) who worked actively against him. He proposed large-scale national government action for general improvement in both learning and scientific activity (a national university, national observatories) and in the specifics of the "American System," usually identified as Clay's program, but which Adams claimed as his own. Not surprisingly, Adams considered foreign affairs very important; he had a Jeffersonian view of developing American world trade, with an emphasis on reciprocity and neutral rights. The Administration's diplomatic failures, particularly Great Britain's closure of West Indies trade, were often a result of domestic politics and sectional interests. The same was true of Adams' concept of the United States' democratic mission vis-à-vis Latin America: Any possibility of United States leadership in the Western Hemisphere was broken on the reefs of partisan opposition. The Panama Congress and the sensitive status of Cuba overshadowed negotiations and consultations which often laid the foundations for later administrations' successes.

Adams delegated much domestic policy to his cabinet and was therefore not deeply involved in the sectional maneuvering which produced the Tariff of Abominations. He strongly supported internal improvements, regarded the public lands as a long-term national resource, and backed off from a confrontation with Georgia over states' rights stemming from the Indian removal policy. Despite his concept of interdependent sectional interests producing national unity, Adams was usually identified with the economic interests of the Northeast.

A large antiadministration majority in Congress after the 1826 midterm elections left Adams a lame-duck president, depressed, ill, and socially isolated in the White House, mourning his father (who had died on July 4, 1826) and attempting to come to terms with his wife's depression and illness and the total disappointment of his hopes for his two elder sons, George, a debt-ridden depressive, and John, something of a rake. A developing interest in botany was a diverting hobby, although the live-oak plantation he established in Florida (to benefit naval construction) was abandoned by the next administration. All of Adams' personal difficulties, combined with his political ineptitude, helped ensure his isolation in the campaign of 1828, one of the most bitter and vicious ever waged.

Adams was politically inept for a variety of reasons. The Adams family considered its members to be different from the general public, more principled and determined and therefore doomed to popular misunderstanding and lack of support. Adams preferred not to respond to public criticism or to explain and justify his actions; he refused to "electioneer," and his public speeches were scholarly, elaborate, and open to ridicule. His handling of the patronage (a difficult field complicated by factions within the parties) alienated his supporters and gave aid and comfort to his political enemies. He had not been able to rally support for a nonpartisan federal government program of wide-ranging improvements for the national benefit; he could not develop an effective party organization or even meld Federalists and nationalistic Republicans into a politically supportive bloc. His administration ignored the developing labor movement and the broadening popular base of voters and played into Jacksonian egalitarian propaganda. The well-organized Jacksonians easily set the cold Yankee aristocrat against the man of the people, concentrating on Jackson's personal popularity rather than his positions on issues (such as the tariff and internal improvements), which would alienate his disparate supporters.

John Quincy Adams, like his father before him, felt his defeat deeply, taking it as his country's repudiation, refusing (also like his father) to attend his successor's inauguration and moving into regular routines, exercise, and writing in order to make the transition to private life. On April 30, 1829, George Washington Adams jumped or fell from a steamboat and drowned in Long Island Sound, leaving a mass of debts and an illegitimate child. Adams at sixty-two was a failed president with his eldest son dead; nevertheless, mutual guilt brought him and Louisa closer (they had left George with others to rear; they had pushed him too hard) and helped them to concentrate on their two grandchildren and their youngest and favorite son. The latter soon married a wealthy and passive wife and began to produce a large family (Louisa Catherine II, John Quincy II, Charles Francis, Jr., Henry, Arthur, Mary, and Brooks). Political ambition (which Adams regarded as his chief character flaw) led him to agree (as usual, without consulting his wife) to represent his district in the House of Representatives. In 1831, he was elected by a large popular majority, a victory he regarded as the most satisfying of his entire political career. He missed politics and needed the salary, and for seventeen years and eight elections he carved out another and even more effective position in the service of the nation.

Still short, stout, and bald except for a fringe, Adams, as he had done all of his life, rose early, read his Bible and classical works regularly, swam, and walked; he developed into a connoisseur of wine and mellowed socially. He accepted Anti-Masonic support for a presidential nomination in 1832 (which did not eventuate) and lost the election for governor of Massachusetts in 1833 and Massachusetts (Whig) senator in 1835; none of this lessened his commitment to his House career. The House chamber had bad acoustics, as a result of which Adams at his desk could hear whispers from everywhere; his own high-pitched voice was to become a feared instrument in the coming House debates. After he spoke against Daniel Webster in connection with the "French Question" (of treaty payments) in 1836, he began to be called "Old Man Eloquent."

In the Nullification controversy, Adams recognized again the divisive potential of sectionalism, but in the next few years he focused more on the slavery issue as the greatest threat to the Union. He was neither an egalitarian nor an abolitionist per se; while Louisa began to acquaint herself with the problem, associating with the Grimkés and other abolitionists and coming to see the parallels between black slavery and the oppression of women, Adams viewed slavery in terms of principle: as morally reprehensible and politically dangerous to the continued existence of the nation. It was fitting, therefore, that he reacted first to the House's vote, in May of 1836, to table without reading all petitions dealing with slavery. The long battle against the "gag rule" invigorated Adams; the issue of the rights of petition and free speech gave him a broad ground on which to stand and aided him in debate when he dealt with slavery as a threat to the Union, a possible provocation of war with Mexico, a politically divisive question, and the source of the denial of basic rights of citizens. In this period also he began to examine the question of slavery in a broader context. Reading his mother's papers (Abigail Adams had died on October 28, 1818) and reacting to his wife's growing involvement with feminism, Adams came to support the concept of women's political rights, although without endorsing specific issues or deflecting his emphasis on the slavery question.

Always a political independent, Adams supported many of the Jackson Administration's policies, disagreeing, however, on bank policy. As an independent and a skilled parliamentarian, he was able in 1839 to effect the necessary organization of the House committees despite paralyzing partisan divisions. Southern members frequently opposed his actions and called for resolutions of censure. Although his early ponderous and erudite *Report on Weights and Measures* (1821) had never had any direct influence, Adams was able, from 1838 to 1846, to direct the use of the fund that established the Smithsonian Institution.

Despite bitter opposition, Adams maintained his battle in the House on all issues connected with slavery, although he believed that he could only begin what must be a long struggle. He opposed the 1838 attempt to annex Texas for constitutional reasons and because he believed that it would lead to a free-land policy to gain Western political support, thus dissipating a national resource. In 1841, he argued for the defense in the *Amistad* case before the Supreme Court, never submitting a bill for his legal services. In 1842, demonstrating great intellectual resources and physical stamina, he conducted a six-day, successful defense against a House resolution to censure him. He now received and enjoyed public adulation, and in December of 1844, on his resolution, the House rescinded the gag rule.

Feebler and somewhat absentminded, Adams continued to oppose the Mexican War, being reelected as a Conscience Whig in November of 1846. Nearing eighty, he had had to discontinue his daily early morning swims in the Potomac, and on November 20, 1846, he suffered a stroke but was able to resume his seat in early February, 1847. He spoke only once, in opposition to indemnifying the *Amistad* owners, and on February 21, 1848, had another stroke in the House. Carried to the Speaker's room in the Capitol, he died two days later without having regained consciousness. The national mourning ceremonies were like none since Washington's death. John Quincy Adams was buried in the family plot in Quincy. Louisa remained in Washington, keeping in touch with politics, buying and freeing a woman slave, and for much of the time suffering from ill health; she died on May 15, 1852.

Summary

President of a disintegrating party, politically impotent halfway into his only term, his personal life marred by an unsatisfying relationship with his wife and bitter disappointments with his two elder sons, Adams left—almost fled—the nation's highest political office, the lifelong goal of his great ambition and dynastic sense of duty and destiny. He seemed to be facing a lifetime in the ebb tide of politics and the treacherous shoals of financial insecurity and family disappointment. Even as his personal tragedy deepened with the death of his eldest son, he entered into a new phase, a time nearly as long as his life until then. He experienced a growing satisfaction, a greater harmony in relationships and decision-making within his own family: his remaining son, his growing brood of grandchildren, and his wife, finding her way to her own identity and a political role which could afford her a long-delayed satisfaction in contributing to and participating in the real life of the nation, rather than the confined, ornamental, subservient place expected by contemporary society.

During the course of his "two careers," John Quincy Adams contributed mightily to the basic elements of American foreign policy, influenced domestic issues, and stood as a beacon in the sectional controversy which, as he foresaw, was to lead the Union into civil war.

Bibliography

Bemis, Samuel Flagg. *John Quincy Adams and the Foundations of American Foreign Policy.* New York: Knopf, 1949. A detailed, scholarly, analytical work by a major authority on diplomatic history. Focuses on Adams' "first career" as diplomat and continentalist.

————. *John Quincy Adams and the Union.* New York: Knopf, 1956. A companion volume, completing the biography, dealing with Adams' "second career." As effective as the preceding work; lacks details of Adams' personal life.

Clark, Bennett Champ. *John Quincy Adams: "Old Man Eloquent."* Boston: Little Brown, 1932. A rather popularized biography, not a panegyric but somewhat filiopietistic. Accurate and adequate; reads well.

East, Robert A. *John Quincy Adams: The Critical Years, 1785-1794.* New York: Bookman Associates, 1962. Deals with the early period of Adams' life, vital for shaping his basic concepts. Fulsome in spots; may read too much importance into the early years.

Falkner, Leonard. *The President Who Wouldn't Retire.* New York: Coward-McCann, 1967. Based on Bemis and various primary documents but chiefly on secondary works. Popularized; emphasizes Adams' congressional career.

Hargreaves, Mary W. M. *The Presidency of John Quincy Adams.* Lawrence: University Press of Kansas, 1985. Detailed and scholarly examination of Adams' presidency, including the political and economic background. Concludes that Adams' term was more positive in goals and action than many historians have judged it. Dense but readable.

Hecht, Marie B. *John Quincy Adams: A Personal History of an Independent Man.* New York: Macmillan, 1972. Provides political background, with good attention to various personalities. Admires John Quincy, but is rather critical of Louisa. Lengthy but not dull.

Lipsky, George A. *John Quincy Adams: His Theory and Ideas.* New York: Crowell, 1950. A good biographical chapter, but mainly concerned with Adams' intellectual system. Good analysis but a rather convoluted style. Unbounded admiration for a cold intellect. Adams seems a sanctimonious prig in some of the author's admiring references, somewhat more than he probably was.

Morse, John T., Jr. *John Quincy Adams.* Boston: Houghton Mifflin, 1882. Written in 1882 for and by the editor of the "American Statesmen" series. Brief (three hundred small pages), basic narrative.

Nagel, Paul C. *John Quincy Adams: A Public Life, a Private Life.* New York: Knopf, 1997. Nagel provides a thought-provoking look at Adams with emphasis on the psychological elements that affected his life. The author's examination is based largely on Adams' diary, which spanned seventy years.

Oliver, Andrew. *Portraits of John Quincy Adams and His Wife.* Cambridge, Mass.: Belknap Press of Harvard University Press, 1970. Portraits, busts, silhouettes, including the later daguerreotypes. Accompanying text informative.

Parsons, Lynn H. *John Quincy Adams: A Bibliography.* Westport, Conn.: Greenwood Press, 1993. Presents a comprehensive guide to literature on Adams' time as president, politician, and diplomat and lists his published writings.

Shepherd, Jack. *Cannibals of the Heart: A Personal Biography of Louisa Catherine and John Quincy Adams.* New York: McGraw-Hill, 1980. Extensive research in the primary sources. An insightful view of the private life of a very public man, with equal attention to the lives of his wife and children. Well written; the psychological analysis is not intrusive. Good blend also of political and social background.

Marsha Kass Marks

FELIX ADLER

Born: August 13, 1851; Alzey, Hesse-Darmstadt
(now Germany)
Died: April 24, 1933; New York, New York
Areas of Achievement: Education and social reform
Contribution: Adler founded the Ethical Culture
Society, whose goal was to overcome the divisions created by religious creeds and unite all
people in ethical deeds.

Early Life

Felix Adler was born in Alzey, Hesse-Darmstadt
(now Germany), on August 13, 1851. He moved to
the United States at age six when his father, Rabbi
Samuel Adler, accepted the country's most prestigious Reform pulpit at Temple Emanu-El in New
York City. Samuel had been active in Europe in
both secular struggles for freedom and religious reform. His passion for social justice was wedded to
a love of scholarship. The Adler home was filled
with books. Indeed, one of the best collections of
Judaica in New York was to be found there. Felix's
mother engaged in the works of charity characteristic of the life of the Jewish community. Felix accompanied her as she visited the poor and the sick.
She was no doubt one of Felix's earliest examples
of the power of the good deed.

The young Adler saw the socioeconomic problems that accompanied industrialization. In the
second half of the nineteenth century, immigrants
were swelling the populations of U.S. cities and
crowding into slum areas, where they were exploited by industrialists and politicians.

Adler's boyhood was punctuated by the sounds
of the Civil War. When he was fourteen years old,
President Abraham Lincoln was assassinated;
Adler later said that this occasion was the first time
that he had seen tears in his father's eyes. His adolescence paralleled the post-Civil War era, when
the calls to abolish slavery gave way to Jim Crow
laws and the Ku Klux Klan.

Adler entered Columbia College at fifteen years
of age and graduated in 1870, after which he was
sent to Germany to study with Abraham Geiger in
preparation for a career in the Reform rabbinate.
When a lengthy delay in the school's opening undercut that plan, Adler turned to university studies
in Berlin and Heidelberg; he received a doctorate
in Semitics from Heidelberg in 1873.

Upon returning to the United States, Adler was
expected to succeed his father as chief rabbi at
Emanu-El, but his university studies in Germany
precipitated a break with Judaism. After being exposed to historical and critical studies of the Bible,
evolutionary theory, anthropology, and neo-Kantianism, Adler could no longer maintain his former
beliefs. He rejected the idea of a personal God and
concentrated instead on a universal moral good,
which he saw as a metaphysical reality. Since he
had not followed his expected career track, Adler
needed a new vocation. He inaugurated a Sunday
lecture movement on May 15, 1876. In February of
the following year, this movement was incorporated as the New York Society for Ethical Culture.

Life's Work

After the New York Society for Ethical Culture
was incorporated, Adler was employed as its lecturer. In Adler's mind, the society was a religious
organization that transcended creeds and united
people in ethical deeds. Its philosophic linchpin
was a belief in the inherent worth of each individual, a belief that Adler had drawn from German philosopher Immanuel Kant's assertion that all human
beings were ends in themselves. Members of the
society were to abide by three basic goals: sexual
purity for males as well as females, donation of
surplus income to the improvement of the working
classes, and continued intellectual development.

The society included among its members workers and housewives, businesspeople and teachers,
professionals and tradespeople. Among its most influential members were Joseph Seligman, a
founder of the banking house of J. and W. Seligman and Co., and one of the wealthiest men in the
country; Samuel Gompers, founder of the American Federation of Labor; and Henry Morgenthau,
who assisted in establishing the Ethical Culture
School and in securing the site for the meeting
house of the New York Society for Ethical Culture
on Central Park Avenue West in New York City at
the beginning of the twentieth century.

As important as Adler's weekly lectures were in
laying the philosophic bases of the society, they
were obviously not sufficient for a movement centered on the importance of performing ethical
deeds. Adler and his followers did not shirk the responsibilities of their commitment to such ethical
action. In the late 1870's, they founded the first
free kindergarten east of the Mississippi River in
New York City, established a district nursing pro-

gram (forerunner of the Visiting Nurse Service), and launched a tenement house building company. The Workingman's School was organized in 1880. In 1882, Adler became a member of the New York State Tenement Housing Commission. In 1883, he and Edmond Kelly founded the Good Government Club to oppose political corruption in the city.

In the 1880's, Adler and his followers established Ethical Culture Societies in Philadelphia, Chicago, and St. Louis. These societies worked toward the reform of faith through active participation in modern communities, the reconstruction of society through ethical religion, and the moral growth of the individual through interaction with other people in the process of "ethicizing" society.

After 1890, Adler became better known in the international arena. He founded the *International Journal of Ethics* in 1890 (still published today as *Ethics: An International Journal of Social, Political and Legal Philosophy* by the University of Chicago). The ethical culture movement also became international with the founding of societies in most of the countries of Western Europe as well as in Japan. In 1896, an International Ethical Union was established through which Adler helped to develop the International Moral Education Congresses in 1908. In 1911, he and Gustave Spiller established the first International Races Congress. In 1923, he gave the Hibbert Lectures at Oxford, which were published as *The Reconstruction of the Spiritual Ideal* in 1924. He also gave another series of talks at Oxford on the reconstruction of education.

Even as the European setting was pushing Adler toward new endeavors, events in the United States were raising troubling questions in his mind. Adler moved to the forefront of those who, in the name of American ideals, were increasingly critical of U.S. imperialism. From 1898 onward, he began to raise the issue of what he came to call the "national crisis." Adler saw Central and Latin American adventurism as the beginning of the crisis and World War I as the climax. The problem lay in the incompatibility of two American myths: manifest destiny and spiritual democracy. If the United States was to become an ethical model, the nation had to first set itself right. Illusions of American self-righteousness had to be revealed for what they were, and a clear commitment needed to be made to spiritual democracy and against the imperialism of manifest destiny.

As the twentieth century dawned, increasing attention to minority rights began to characterize Adler's thought. Labor and child labor in particular had interested him for a long time. The influence of the Civil War and Lincoln reappeared in his concern with the question of racial justice. While he opposed the popular movement for equal rights for women, he did so on the grounds that the problem could not be dealt with merely by a superficial adjustment of social forms such as voting. He did support the rights of women to have careers but also saw in motherhood a vocation equal in its claims to other vocations.

From about 1890 until the end of his life in 1933, Adler developed a philosophy of industrial culture. The struggle for the rights of labor was meeting with violent repression. Economic depression was joined with political unwillingness to deal with the problems. In this setting, Adler, together with Crawford Howell Toy of Harvard University and Henry Carter Adams of Michigan, founded the Summer School of Applied Ethics at Plymouth, Massachusetts, in 1891. William James, Josiah Royce, and Jane Addams taught courses there, among others. In 1894, Adler gave a series of twelve lectures on the labor question. The clue to the reconstruction of industrial society, Adler believed, was the development of vocational opportunities for every member of society. Vocation, the commitment of a person to meaningful work, was the way in which the attribute of inalienable human worth gained realistic content in an industrial society.

As Adler thought through his philosophy of industrial democracy, he was led inevitably to a reconsideration of schooling. His interest in education had manifested itself as early as the founding of the Workingman's School in 1880. In the 1890's, a concept of "organic" education was germinating in his mind, which led to a curriculum that integrated classical studies, modern science, industrial arts, and ethics. In the 1920's, Adler began to dream more dramatically about a major new step in education, and in 1926 he formulated his ideals for the new school as one in which values were preeminent and specifically brought into the realm of commerce and business. The result was the Fieldston School, launched in 1928. On April 24, 1933, Adler died after a long struggle with cancer.

Summary

The potential relevance of Felix Adler for modern times is great. In his own life, he overcame the perennial tension between the life of thought and the life of action, and his struggle to point out an ethical path in a world that was becoming increasingly

pluralistic and increasingly secular is, if anything, even more timely now than it was during his lifetime. Sadly, however, Adler has been largely ignored by history. While the Ethical Culture Societies still exist, the knowledge that most members have of Adler is limited to the bare fact that he was their founder. His penetrating and original philosophy has seldom been studied or even referenced by more recent philosophers. The reforms in social welfare, politics, and labor relations in which he played such an important role continue, but their benefactors are largely unaware of Adler's part in their development.

Perhaps his life was simply too well rounded for specialists to notice him. Philosophers considered him suspicious because he did not hold himself aloof from social reform efforts or religion. Activists, on the other hand, thought he was too much of a thinker. Perhaps he has suffered the fate of being considered irrelevant to later time periods because he was so immersed in the issues of his own historical period. For example, even his relatively well-known work in the field of education is perceived as being too unattuned to modern psychologized education to be totally acceptable. Among religionists, he has suffered a similar fate, being neither absolute enough for the neoorthodox nor sufficiently disdainful of absolutes to find a place among situation ethicists. However, this man who was known as an exceptionally gifted pedagogue while he was alive still has much to teach later generations. Both his life and his thought deserve to be resurrected.

Bibliography

Beard, Annie E. S. *Our Foreign-Born Citizens*. 6th ed. New York: Crowell, 1968. The chapter on Adler gives a very simple introduction to his thought. The narrative is peppered with some excellent quotations from Adler's works, but the sources of the citations are not given, frustrating any serious scholar of Adler.

Friess, Horace L. *Felix Adler and Ethical Culture*. New York: Columbia University Press, 1981. This book, written by Adler's son-in-law, gives personal memories of Adler in addition to more objective biographical information and also offers an insightful analysis of Adler's intellectual evolution.

Guttchen, Robert S. *Felix Adler*. New York: Twayne, 1974. Guttchen analyzes Adler's ethical and educational philosophies, with Adler's concept of human worth being presented as the linchpin of his entire philosophy. The philosophical analysis is preceded by a very useful chronology and a fine biographical sketch.

Kraut, Benny. *From Reform Judaism to Ethical Culture: The Religious Evolution of Felix Adler*. Cincinnati: Hebrew Union College Press, 1979. Kraut analyzes Adler's religious evolution and the Jewish reaction to Adler and the Ethical Culture Society. This very useful study focuses on the early evolution of Adler's thought up until about 1880.

Neumann, Henry. *Spokesmen for Ethical Religion*. Boston: Beacon Press, 1951. This book provides a simple introduction to Adler as the founder of Ethical Culture and to the leaders who followed in his footsteps. Neumann attempts to give both a history of the movement through the lives of its leaders and a sympathetic (if not evangelistic) explanation of the movement's purpose and worth.

Ann Marie B. Bahr

LOUIS AGASSIZ

Born: May 28, 1807; Motier-en-Vuly, Switzerland
Died: December 14, 1873; Cambridge, Massachusetts
Areas of Achievement: Natural history and education
Contribution: Agassiz created an awareness of the importance of the study of natural history in the United States with his founding of the Museum of Comparative Zoology at Harvard University. He was an early pioneer in making scientific studies an integral part of the curriculum at American colleges and universities.

Early Life

Jean Louis Rodolphe Agassiz was born May 28, 1807, in Motier-en-Vuly, Canton Fribourg, Switzerland. The son of a Protestant clergyman, Agassiz was one of four children. At the age of ten, Agassiz was sent to school at Bienne, where he spent much of his time observing freshwater fish, which fascinated him. In 1822, he entered the Academy of Lausanne. Upon graduation, out of deference to his parents, he enrolled in the school of medicine at the University of Zurich. After two years of studies in medicine, he enrolled in the University of Heidelberg, where he developed a special interest in natural history. The following year, he transferred to the University of Munich to study under Ignaz von Döllinger, a pioneer embryologist whom Agassiz credited as the source of his scientific training.

In 1829, he received a doctorate in philosophy at Erlanger and returned to Munich to complete his studies in medicine. The following year, he received a doctorate in medicine and thereafter never examined a patient; his mind was set on pursuing studies in ichthyology, paleontology, and glacial geology.

While Agassiz was enrolled in Munich, Lorenz Oken, one of his professors, presented a paper on Agassiz's discovery of a new species of carp. In 1829, Agassiz published his first book on this species of Brazilian fish based on his study of a collection of specimens from the Amazon brought to Munich in 1821 by J. B. Spix and K. F. Philip von Martius. The book was written with such beauty and clarity that it was soon evident that Agassiz would become not only a man of science but also a man of letters.

Agassiz married Cecile Braun, sister of the eminent botanist Alexander Braun. There were three children born to the union, a son and two daughters. Cecile was a natural history artist whose drawings of fossil and freshwater fish forms appeared in several of Agassiz's books. She died of tuberculosis in 1848.

Agassiz was a large, robust man, slightly above medium height, who had keen brown eyes which could light up with enthusiasm. He had chestnut brown hair that gradually thinned with age but retained its color into his declining years.

Life's Work

The professional life of Agassiz is clearly divided into two chapters: his work as a research scientist in Europe, in the course of which he made significant advances in the fields of ichthyology and glacial geology, and his teaching career in the United States, during which he dedicated himself to making science an integral and respected part of the curriculum of higher education in his adopted country.

Upon completion of his formal schooling, Agassiz went to Paris to continue his studies in medicine. While there, he spent much of his time at the museum of natural history at the Jardin des Plantes, where he met Georges Cuvier, the master of comparative anatomy. The aging Cuvier willingly turned over much of his unfinished work to the young naturalist to complete. Agassiz also met the naturalist Friedrich Humbolt, who in 1832 secured for him an appointment as professor in natural history at the University of Neuchâtel.

While at Neuchâtel, Agassiz formed a natural history society and took scientists on excursions into the Alps to study and observe flora and fauna. Agassiz turned Neuchâtel into a research center, and over the course of fifteen years he published more than two hundred works, including twenty substantial volumes illustrated with more than two thousand plates. Before Agassiz began his research, only eight generic types of fossil fish had been named in formal publications. Agassiz identified 340 new genera, many of them in his books *History of the Fresh Water Fishes of Central Europe* (1839-1842) and *Monograph on the Fossil Fishes of the Old Red or Devonian of the British Isles and Russia* (1844-1845).

While at Neuchâtel, Agassiz's attention was drawn to the nearby glacier of the great median moraine of the lower Aar valley, and this sent his scientific investigations in a new direction, that of glacial geology. He concluded from his observations that gravity controls glacial movements and that glaciers travel faster in the middle and at the surface, disproving the commonly held theory that glaciers are pushed along by water freezing underneath. He published his findings in *Études sur les glaciers* (1840; studies on glaciers) and *Systèmes glaciaires* (1846; glacial systems). Agassiz came to accept Karl Schimper's "ice age" thesis and added that Europe had been subjected once to a period of extreme cold from the North Pole to the Mediterranean and Caspian seas in a widespread Pleistocene ice age. He studied earth surfaces all over Europe and concluded that drift material and polished and striated boulders gave evidence of earlier glacial movements.

A gift from the King of Prussia in 1846 enabled Agassiz to pursue his work in the United States. Sir Charles Lyell had arranged for him to participate in a course of lectures at the Lowell Institute in Boston. Agassiz's life took another turn. His intense research gave way to teaching and campaigning on behalf of natural history as a legitimate academic endeavor.

Agassiz continued to write of his discoveries with verbal precision and lucid description. He could devote fifty pages of unmatched prose describing the interior of an egg. He set about to produce a twelve-volume series entitled *Contributions to the Natural History of the United States*. More than twenty-five hundred advance subscriptions were taken, but only four volumes were ever produced (1857-1862). These four volumes represented a triumph of thought and scholarship and contributed to the nature-consciousness of the American public.

In 1848, Agassiz accepted the chair of natural history of the new Lawrence Scientific School at Harvard University, and the same year he published his popular *Principles of Zoology*. When he visited Washington, D.C., he was disappointed to find so little scientific activity in the nation's capital. At the time, the Smithsonian Institution had not begun to function. Agassiz was later made a member of the Smithsonian Board of Regents, and the institution's natural history division was developed.

In 1850, Agassiz married Elizabeth Cary, and the following year he accepted a teaching appointment

at the Medical College of Charleston, South Carolina. After two years, he resigned because he found the climate unsuitable and returned to Harvard. He and his wife opened a school for young women in Cambridge which became the precursor of Radcliffe College.

Agassiz was quite disappointed with Harvard's science department and claimed that the chemistry laboratory at Cambridge High School was better equipped; he often did his work there. In 1859, Agassiz founded the Museum of Comparative Zoology at Harvard and helped to create a new era in American higher education. He emphasized advanced and original works as factors in mental training and stressed the direct, hands-on study of nature. Ralph Waldo Emerson complained that something ought to be done to check this rush toward natural history at Harvard. Agassiz countered that the rest of the curriculum should be brought up to the standards he had set for the zoology laboratories. Agassiz found a kindred soul in Henry David Thoreau and often visited Walden Pond. At a dinner hosted by Emerson, Thoreau and Agassiz once talked of mating turtles, to the disgust of Emerson. From Walden, Thoreau sent Agassiz varieties of fish, turtles, and snakes, and was paid handsomely for them.

The same year that Agassiz opened the museum at Harvard, Charles Darwin published his *On the Origin of Species by Means of Natural Selection* (1859). The theory of evolution did not begin with Darwin, and Agassiz was thoroughly acquainted with the works of Georges-Louis Leclerc Buffon, Jean Baptiste de Monet de Lamarck, Charles Darwin's own grandfather, Erasmus Darwin, and their ideas of the gradual, continuous progress of species which contributed to the theory of evolution. Also, much of the knowledge of embryology which is integral to Darwin's theory was originally discovered by Agassiz. Agassiz once admitted that he had been on the verge of anticipating Darwinism when he found that the highest fishes were those that came first, and therefore he rejected the theory. Sharks, one of the most primitive species, had the largest brains and the most specialized teeth and muscular systems. Two years before Darwin's theory was published, Agassiz wrote "An Essay on Classification," in which he asserted that the plan of creation was the "free conception" of an all-powerful intelligence in accordance with a predetermined pattern for each of the species, which, he argued, were destined to remain changeless.

Agassiz became Darwin's most formidable opponent in the United States. His studies of fossils led him to conclude that the changes which animals undergo during their embryonic growth coincide with the order of succession of the fossils of the same type in past geological ages. He believed that all species had been immutable since their creation. From time to time, the Creator may have annihilated old species and created new ones. His exhibits at the Harvard museum were intended to reflect the permanence of the species.

Agassiz regarded himself as the "librarian of the works of God," but he was not a theologian and gave no support to those ministers who parroted his responses to Darwin. He claimed that in Europe he was accused of deriving his scientific ideas from the Church and in the United States he was regarded as an infidel because he would not let churchmen pat him on the head. Agassiz believed that there was a creator and even went so far as to posit a multiple creation theory. He claimed that blacks were created separately and were a different species from whites, an argument which gave great comfort to the defenders of slavery in the South.

Only a few American scientists, such as his Harvard colleague Asa Gray, dared to take open issue with the erudite and popular Agassiz before his death. Gray argued that the species had originated in a single creative act and that their variations were the result of causes such as climate, geographical isolation, and the phenomena described by the same glacial theory that Agassiz had done so much to establish.

Agassiz became an American citizen in 1861 and continued his opposition to Darwinism. He fought a losing battle for fifteen years with the Darwinists and went to his grave denying the reality of evolution. His last article, published posthumously in the *Atlantic Monthly* (1874), was entitled "Evolution and the Permanence of Type."

Agassiz was appointed a visiting professor at Cornell in 1868, but the following year he suffered a stroke. Although this slowed him considerably, he continued his strenuous schedule of speaking and writing. In 1872, he sailed on board a coastal survey ship from Boston around the horn to San Francisco. The trip was disappointing, since Agassiz was unable to make the scientific progress he had hoped on the voyage. In 1873, John Anderson of New York deeded the island of Penikese in Buzzards Bay off the coast of Massachusetts and gave fifty thousand dollars to help Agassiz create a summer school for science teachers. The Anderson School of Natural History became the forerunner of the Woods Hole Biological Institute.

Summary

Louis Agassiz was the man who made America nature-conscious. He was a major figure in American nineteenth century culture, in the fields of both literature and science. He assumed that the organization of nature was everyone's concern and that each community should collect and identify the elements of its own zoology and botany.

Agassiz would appear to have been the most likely to champion the theory of evolution, particularly with his vast knowledge of paleontology and embryology. Instead, he chose to do battle with the evolutionists and to maintain stoutly his belief in the unchanging forms of created species. In his *Methods of Study in Natural History* (1863), Agassiz wrote: "I have devoted my whole life to the study of Nature, and yet a single sentence may express all that I have done. I have shown that there is a correspondence between the succession of Fishes in geological times and the different stages of their growth in the egg,—this is all."

Agassiz had done much more than he modestly claimed. In the age of Chautauqua speakers, he was a spellbinder. Above all, he was a teacher who was not only a dedicated scholar but also a friend to his students. With all of his talents as lecturer and author, he might have been a wealthy man, but he remained in debt all of his life and even mortgaged his house to support the museum at Harvard.

Agassiz wished above all to be remembered as a teacher. When he died in 1873, an unshaped boulder brought from the glacier of the Aar marked his grave at Boston's Mount Auburn Cemetery. On it were carved the words he had requested: "Agassiz the Teacher."

Bibliography

Agassiz, Louis. *Studies on Glaciers: Preceded by the Discourses of Neuchatel.* Translated and edited by Albert V. Carozzi. New York: Hafner, 1967. Carozzi's introduction is excellent. Included is a reprint of the atlas which Agassiz used.

Agassiz, Louis. *The Intelligence of Agassiz: A Specimen Book of Scientific Writings.* Edited by Guy Davenport. Boston: Beacon Press, 1963. The foreword by Alfred Romer is an excellent overview of the work of Agassiz. Davenport has selected Agassiz's most incisive works and introduces each with a skill which makes this slim volume invaluable.

Baird, Spencer Fullerton. *Correspondence Between Spencer Fullerton Baird and Louis Agassiz—Two Pioneer American Naturalists.* Edited by Elmer Charles Herber. Washington, D.C.: Smithsonian, 1963. Baird was the editor of the papers of the Smithsonian Institution and carried on extensive correspondence with Agassiz. The letters contained the latest news on discoveries in natural history.

Cooper, Lane. *Louis Agassiz as a Teacher.* Ithaca, N.Y.: Comstock, 1917. An excellent account of Agassiz's expertise as a teacher. Included are many anecdotes of classroom experiences, told by students.

Croce, Jerome. "Probalistic Darwinism: Louis Agassiz v. Asa Gray on Science, Religion, and Certainty." *Journal of Religious History* 22, no. 1 (February, 1998). Discusses Agassiz's views on Darwinism and its interface with Christianity.

Lurie, Edward. *Louis Agassiz: A Life in Science.* Chicago: University of Chicago Press, 1960. A persuasive interpretation of Agassiz and an exhaustive study of his papers. Lurie acknowledges Agassiz's weaknesses and pictures a genius with faults.

Marcou, Jules. *Life, Letters, and Works of Louis Agassiz.* 2 vols. New York and London: Macmillan, 1896. Valuable for range and accuracy of details, including an annotated list of American and European publications concerning Agassiz. Also included is a complete catalog of his 425 scientific papers.

Tharp, Louise Hall. *Adventurous Alliance: The Story of the Agassiz Family of Boston.* Boston: Little Brown, 1959. An account of the personal lives of Agassiz and his second wife, Elizabeth. An interesting story which relates something of the background of late nineteenth century Boston society. Also a treatise on education.

Walls, Laura Dassow. "Textbooks and Texts from the Brooks: Inventing Scientific Authority in America." *American Quarterly* 49, no.1 (March, 1997). Discusses Agassi's contribution to the development of the institution of science through innovative teaching and exacting laboratory techniques.

Raymond Lee Muncy

SIR SAYYID AHMAD KHAN

Born: October 17, 1817; Delhi, India
Died: March 27, 1898; Alīgarh, India
Areas of Achievement: Education, literature, and religion
Contribution: Sayyid Ahmad's theological writings summarized a number of important trends within Islamic thought and attempted to redirect religious thinking to meet the challenges of the modern, European-dominated, world. His religious views were, however, too controversial to be widely influential. Yet in the field of education he founded the Muhammadan Anglo-Oriental College, and in literature he created modern Urdu prose.

Early Life

Sir Sayyid Ahmad Khan was an exceptional man born into an exceptional family. While custom in well-to-do families dictated that a bride moved in with her husband's parents, Sayyid Ahmad's mother was the favorite daughter of a wealthy and distinguished man who wanted her to remain in his home. Sayyid Ahmad's father enjoyed high status as a descendant of the prophet Muhammad, a sayyid, but he was relatively poor. Moving into his wife's home gave him the leisure to pursue his interest in archery and swimming. In that way Sayyid Ahmad came to be reared in his maternal grandfather's house.

The careers of grandfather and grandson resembled each other in many ways. The grandfather, Khwajah Farid ud-din Ahmad, not only held the post of chief minister in the much reduced Mughal court but also had the trust of the British, who sent him on a number of diplomatic missions. During an extended stay in Calcutta, he acted as superintendent of that city's premier Muslim educational establishment, the Calcutta Madrasah. He enjoyed a reputation as a mathematician and astronomer.

Sayyid Ahmad's early education took place in Khwajah Farid's home. It involved learning the Koran and the rudiments of Persian grammar. One of his maternal uncles instructed him in mathematics. He then went to study Greek medicine (*Yunani Tibb*) with one of Delhi's prominent physicians. Apart from this training, Sayyid Ahmad educated himself prodigiously in theology and history, while retaining a lifelong interest in the sciences. In addition to that small amount of formal learning, Sayyid Ahmad absorbed a deep religious seriousness. Both his mother's and his father's families were connected to the noted spiritual reformers of the seventeenth and eighteenth centuries: Ahmad Sirhindī and Shah Walliullah. These men and their disciples stressed a rational approach to Islam that avoided miracle-mongering and criticized the lax behavior of the Muslim masses. They also emphasized a moral earnestness that especially affected Sayyid Ahmad's mother. He saw dedication to high moral values as her chief legacy to him.

Life's Work

In 1838, the year of his father's death, Sayyid Ahmad began attending the office of an uncle who worked as a subordinate judge for the British. Before the latter instituted examinations and educational qualifications for government employees, this was the most common way of securing appointment as an official. Sayyid Ahmad soon began ascending through the ranks of the East India Company's judiciary. He served as a magistrate in a number of north Indian district towns before retiring in 1876.

Sayyid Ahmad's literary career began in the 1840's. He wrote a number of religious tracts encouraging the reform of Muslim social customs. He contributed to a newspaper published by his brother and edited a number of Persian works, such as the memoirs of the Mughal emperor Jahāangīr. In 1846, he published a unique book, *Āthār assanadīd* (*Asar-oos-sunnadeed: A History of Old and New Rules, or Governments and of Old and New Buildings, in the District of Delhi,* 1854), which described some of the famous buildings and personalities of Old Delhi. Though his early style of Urdu imitated the flowery diction and indirect discourse of Persian, throughout his life his writing became more vigorous and straightforward. Later writers considered him a model of clarity and acknowledged him as the creator of Urdu political rhetoric. His collected writings and speeches occupied nineteen volumes.

The Mutiny of 1857 had a lasting impact on Sayyid Ahmad's activity and thought. During the conflict, he remained loyal to the British, even risking his own life to save a number of Englishmen as well as the Bijnor district's cash box. After the uprising, a number of British officials blamed

Muslims for fomenting the rebellion. Sayyid Ahmad spent the rest of his life refuting that notion, constantly reminding the government that many of India's Muslims stood firmly for the Empire. To his fellow Muslims, he repeated the message that the failure of the revolt proved that England's way was the way of the future and that Muslims need not abandon their religion in order to adapt to the new order. He argued that in following the "new light," they were being faithful to Islam's highest ideals. After all, Islam's advanced civilization had influenced that of Europe and made the Renaissance possible. The decline of his own day Sayyid Ahmad attributed to superstitions that had become commonplace only in the century or so before. Until then, Islam had been in the vanguard of human progress.

Sayyid Ahmad's loyalty to the British and his liberal opinions about Islam brought him honors from the imperial government. In 1869, he became a commander in the Order of the Star of India and in 1888 received a knighthood in that fraternity. He became a member of the Viceroy's Legislative Council in 1878 and sat on this largely advisory body until 1883. When he visited England in 1869-1870, he was presented to Queen Victoria and the Prince of Wales while mixing with London's literary notables.

More tangible support came from a number of Sayyid Ahmad's British friends. They encouraged his educational projects both in spirit and in various forms of government aid. When he founded a translation society to render English books, especially mathematics and science texts, into Urdu, the provincial education bureau supported the effort by buying most of the books published. At this stage of his career, Sayyid Ahmad's efforts were not solely devoted to India's Muslims. The Mughal gentry of his youth had many non-Muslim members. Hindus counted in their number masters of Persian and Urdu whose talents were equal or even superior to those of Muslims. Sayyid Ahmad was concerned that this entire class, the north Indian Urdu-speaking elite, was in danger of annihilation.

With the founding of the Muhammadan Anglo-Oriental College at Aligarh in 1875, Sayyid Ahmad labored increasingly for Muslims. He envisioned the Muhammadan Anglo-Oriental College to be a residential school on the model of Eton. He thought it essential that young boys be removed from the easy discipline of their homes and taught the virtues of diligence. In place of the intensely personal, but seemingly slipshod, educational methods of his own youth, Sayyid Ahmad installed the classroom and the fixed daily schedule of study, prayer, and sport, and regular academic examinations.

Many of the school's first students came from families that combined landowning and government service. By the 1870's, posts in the imperial bureaucracy increasingly required modern educational qualifications. The Muhammadan Anglo-Oriental College provided the training in English, history, and the sciences that helped in obtaining those appointments. The majority of the school's earliest graduates became officials or lawyers.

Throughout the latter years of his life, Sayyid Ahmad spent countless hours requesting contributions to the Muhammadan Anglo-Oriental College. Often his political stands were influenced by his belief that he should utter the sentiments most likely to ensure continued government support for the college. On the surface at least, his thinking became increasingly communal, urging Muslims to develop a separate political agenda. At the same time, Sayyid Ahmad was responding to an ever more assertive Hindu nationalism. When these groups demanded democracy, Sayyid Ahmad became fearful since the Muslim minority was bound to be overwhelmed by the majority community in any strictly representative system.

While pursuing his educational and political work, Sayyid Ahmad remained a social critic and theological controversialist. As publisher of the Urdu journal *Tahzib ul-Akhlaq* (moral reform), he had a forum in which to publicize his views on religious and moral subjects. Many religious scholars hotly opposed him, finding his thought dangerously close to pure rationalism. Many of the gentry attached to the accustomed ways in religion considered him too rational. Sayyid Ahmad held on tenaciously to his approach, but his opinions did not receive a hearing even in his own college. Many of his financial backers insisted that Sayyid Ahmad have no influence over religious instruction at the Muhammadan Anglo-Oriental College. Less controversial men took charge of introducing the young to their faith.

The affairs of the college on which he lavished such great care made the last years of Sayyid Ahmad's life miserable. In 1895, his chief clerk was caught embezzling considerable sums from the college's funds. This led to confrontations between Sayyid Ahmad and one of his sons, who wanted to acquire more control over the college. On two occasions, the son ordered Sayyid Ahmad out of his own home. For a short period, he stayed in a dormitory but finally moved to the house of a longtime friend, where he died a discouraged and embittered man.

Summary

Within Sir Sayyid Ahmad Khan's lifetime, the last shadows of Mughal glory disappeared and India became the brightest diamond in Great Britain's imperial diadem. While his family had been attached to the Mughal court, Sayyid Ahmad's achievements depended, in part, on his close association with the British. While his early education had been conducted along traditional lines, he founded a college with a curriculum and discipline modeled on Great Britain's public schools. He somehow found time to write extensively on religious and social matters, presenting a bold theological program that incorporated elements from Islam's classical tradition and European sources. In the realm of politics, he encouraged Muslims to develop a renewed self-confidence. The Muhammadan Anglo-Oriental College went on to become a university that would attract thousands of students not only from India but also from Africa and the Middle East. This university, with its many buildings clustered around Sayyid Ahmad's grave, is his most obvious and fitting memorial.

Bibliography

Ahmad, Aziz. *Islamic Modernism in India and Pakistan, 1857-1964*. London and New York: Oxford University Press, 1967. This work provides an important discussion of Sayyid Ahmad and his critics. Tends to concentrate on Sayyid Ahmad's political thought and work to the exclusion of his theology.

Ahmad, Aziz, and G. E. von Grunebaum, eds. *Muslim Self-Statement in India and Pakistan*. Weisbaden, Germany: Otto Harrassowitz, 1970. Since very little of the writings of India's Muslims has been translated into English, this is a valuable anthology of their work. It contains selections from the writings of Sayyid Ahmad and a number of his contemporaries.

Brown, Daniel W. "Islamic Modernism in South Asia: A Reassessment." *Muslim World* 87, no. 3/4 (July-October, 1997). Discusses modernist Muslim thinkers and Khan's influence, in particular.

Hardy, Peter. *The Muslims of British India*. Cambridge: Cambridge University Press, 1972. This is a fine overview of the political, social, and religious history of Muslims in the British period. Readers will find all the basic interpretive themes employed by contemporary scholars—both Euro-Americans and South Asians—introduced here. The chapter "The Medieval Legacy" is a good summary of the governmental style of the Mughals.

Lelyveld, David. *Aligarh's First Generation: Muslim Solidarity in British India*. Princeton, N.J.: Princeton University Press, 1978. This brilliantly written book evokes the lives of Muslims from the period of Sayyid Ahmad's birth to the early years of the college. Not only is its scholarship first rate, but also it is written with a literary flair that makes it easily accessible to the nonspecialist.

Metcalf, Barbara D. *Islamic Revival in British India*. Princeton, N.J.: Princeton University Press, 1982. While focusing on the school of theology founded at the town of Deoband in the 1860's, Metcalf does a masterful job of describing the various groups of Muslim scholars and their divergent opinions. Covers the intellectual atmosphere of the period of Sayyid Ahmad's maturity and provides accounts of a number of debates between him and theologians connected with the Deoband movement.

Robinson, Francis. *Separatism Among Indian Muslims: The Politics of the United Provinces' Muslims, 1860-1923*. London: Cambridge University Press, 1974; New York: Oxford University Press, 1993. An encyclopedic treatment of individual Muslims, including Sayyid Ahmad, and the issues that concerned them in the nineteenth and twentieth centuries. Contains a good description of the interplay between British imperial policy and Muslim politics.

Troll, Christian. *Sayyid Ahmad Khan: A Reinterpretation of Muslim Theology*. Atlantic Highlands, N.J.: Humanities Press, 1978. Written by a trained theologian, this book reemphasizes the importance of Sayyid Ahmad's theology. The author has a fund of knowledge of classical Islamic thought, and he connects Sayyid Ahmad's views with it. He frequently refers to Sayyid Ahmad's writings and provides in an appendix a translation of one of his most important works.

Gregory C. Kozlowski

BRONSON ALCOTT

Born: November 29, 1799; Wolcott, Connecticut
Died: March 4, 1888; Concord, Massachusetts
Areas of Achievement: Education and philosophy
Contributions: Alcott was a teacher and a prominent member of New England's Transcendental community. His educational methods focused on moral, spiritual, and imaginative development and encouraged independent thought. He also founded a short-lived utopian community called Fruitlands. He is perhaps most famous as the father of author Louisa May Alcott.

Early Life

Amos Bronson Alcott, the eldest of eight children, was born into a farming family near Wolcott, Connecticut. He attended the local district school, and displayed, from the start, a fondness for literature and elegant rhetoric. His father sent him at the age of thirteen to study with his mother's brother, the Reverend Tillotson Bronson, who was principle of the Cheshire Academy. It was hoped that Alcott might enter the academy and eventually become a clergyman, but, overcome by homesickness, he returned home within a month.

The following year, Alcott was sent to nearby Plymouth, Massachusetts, to learn clock making. Again he was unhappy, this time depressed by the monotony of the work, and again he returned home. A few months' study with the local pastor completed his formal education, but his trade was still unsettled. The idea of teaching appealed to him, and he received a license to teach. However, he was not hired by any of the local schools, so he became a peddler. Alcott enjoyed the life of an itinerant salesman, which allowed him to set his own hours. Furthermore, the changing landscapes and the people he met both stimulated and educated him. Alcott stated years later that peddling had been his university.

After initially working the New England countryside, Alcott embarked on a southerly trek. In Virginia, the planters who gave him lodging were charmed by his good looks and civilized speech. Alcott was likewise taken by the southerners' elegance and easygoing warmth, which was a far cry from the austerity of New England. They opened their homes and libraries to the intellectual young peddler, and it was from them that Alcott (who, around this time, began going by the name Bron-

son Alcott) acquired one of his most remarked-upon characteristics: an elegant, royal manner that some would later refer to as his princely air. On a more substantial level, he also gained the vision of a way of life that valued ideas and pleasures as much as pious hard work.

Further south, in North Carolina, Alcott found himself trading among Quakers. These people were certainly less pleasure-loving and flashy than the Virginia planters, but their ideas—at least as contrasted with New England Calvinism—were radical. The Quakers emphasized the essential goodness of the human soul and the primacy of a personal relationship to God. Their libraries yielded William Penn, Robert Barclay, and George Fox, whose ideas would form the basis of Alcott's budding Transcendentalism. The Quakers also gave Alcott his first brief taste of school teaching. At the age of twenty-four, Alcott returned out of this "university" to Connecticut. He was transformed not only in name but also in philosophy and was determined to be a teacher.

Life's Work

Over the next five years, Alcott taught in the areas around his native Wolcott. His cousin William was already an established teacher in the region and served as a mentor to the younger Alcott. William was intelligent and hardworking and was known for the absolute discipline he maintained in his classrooms. Alcott also insisted on complete silence and attention in his classroom (this was by no means the norm in rural nineteenth century schools), but the two young men, while congenial, had very different emphases. While William had a reputation as a "smart" teacher, Alcott was emerging as a visionary—and a heretic.

Alcott's aims were lofty: an education that addressed not only the intellectual but also the physical, emotional, and moral aspects of each child. Believing that a child learned better in a beautiful environment than in a plain one, he decorated his classrooms with fine art and busts of great thinkers and philosophers. His curriculums incorporated organized games and calisthenics, singing, and group discussions; they were contrived to make learning fun, not arduous. He rarely resorted to corporal punishment, as he did not want any of his students to associate learning with pain. His classes operat-

ed largely on an honor system. Such radical restructurings were enough in themselves to create distrust. To exacerbate matters, Alcott's spiritual beliefs were also suspect.

To his earlier philosophic pastiche Alcott had added the ideas of English poet Samuel Taylor Coleridge and Plato. His Transcendental beliefs were becoming more pronounced. Alcott believed, as did most Transcendentalists, that physical reality—including human souls—was an emanation of the mind of God and that physical, intellectual, and spiritual principles operated by congruent laws. He also espoused a belief in the preexistence of the soul. While he declared himself a staunch admirer of the tenets of Christianity, he stopped short of calling himself a Christian. This amounted, in nineteenth century New England, to a declaration of moral war. Despite his talents, he repeatedly lost teaching posts—he was either let go or simply not rehired.

On May 23, 1830, Alcott married Abigail May, a clergyman's sister. The union produced four daughters (the second-born was Louisa May Alcott, who would become a well-known children's author) and complicated the young philosopher-

teacher's lot: He was the sole and inadequate support of a growing family.

These mounting responsibilities drove Alcott to try teaching once again, and, in 1834, he leased a room in the Masonic Temple in Boston and opened the Temple School. Its form and philosophy—a strong emphasis on moral and religious inquiry—were even more radical than anything Alcott had tried before. Sharp public censure ensued. When two books—*The Record of a School, Exemplifying the General Principles of Spiritual Culture* (1835) and *Conversations with Children on the Gospels* (two volumes, 1836 and 1837)—published by Alcott revealed that the topics under discussion included religion and human reproduction, he was declared a public menace in more than one respected newspaper. Alcott still garnered praise for his visionary methods (from James Freeman Clark and Ralph Waldo Emerson, among others), and the school struggled on in one location or another and in the face of failing enrollments and mounting debts for several more years. It closed in 1839 when Alcott's attempt to racially integrate the school met with overpowering resistance.

In 1842, Alcott, in search of direction and inspiration, decamped from his struggling family and sailed to England, where a group of fellow Transcendentalists had opened a school founded on his principles and named after him: Alcott House. He stayed in England for six months; when he returned to the United States, he brought three of the British mystics with him: Henry Wright, Charles Lane, and Lane's son, William.

Cooperative agrarian communities were not uncommon in the mid-nineteenth century. Many of these were fueled by a revulsion against the increasing industrialization that was quickly transforming social and economic landscapes. Alcott combined his slim resources with those of his compatriots, and together they acquired a one-hundred-acre farm near the village of Harvard. They named their enterprise Fruitlands and, in June, 1844, moved themselves, Alcott's wife and children, and several followers onto the land.

Most of the communal experiments of Alcott's time failed, but the failure of Fruitlands was on a scale comparable to the genius of its founders. Fruitlands' heroic principles clashed with the pragmatics of survival: No animals were used for either food or labor, and the Fruitlanders subsisted on a diet of fruit, grain, vegetables, and water. Alcott and his friends were well meaning but dilatory.

They loved talk more than labor, and theory more than action. A disproportionate part of the actual running of the place devolved upon the capable but increasingly Protestant Abigail Alcott and her daughters. Winter came, starvation threatened, and by January of 1845, Fruitlands was abandoned.

Thereafter, from 1845 until 1868, when Louisa May's literary success improved her family's fortunes, the Alcotts were supported by the women of the family, who variously taught, mended, and went out as servants. Alcott eventually developed a series of lectures that he plied with some popular (as opposed to monetary) success throughout the Northwest. In 1859, he was appointed superintendent of the dozen schools in Concord, Massachusetts, where he was at last able to apply many of his earlier innovations on a larger scale, albeit in diluted form. In 1879, he founded the Concord Summer School of Philosophy and Literature, which was dedicated to the furthering of Transcendental thought. Alcott was directly involved with this school until 1882, when he was stricken with paralysis while writing. He never fully recovered and died in 1888.

Summary

The central puzzle of Bronson Alcott's career is how, with such talent, intelligence, and capability at his command, he managed to make so much trouble for himself and so little money: He was usually in debt and was often the object of public censure. The trouble seems to have lain in his idealistic inflexibility. His educational philosophies were radical, and he was seemingly unable to temper them no matter how much it upset the parents of his pupils. Thus, although talented and capable, he was often unemployed. Alcott's imprint upon educational theory and practice, however, is considerable. Most of his reforms that were rejected by his contemporaries— physical education, sex education, flexible classroom design, free discussion, and racial integration—are now standard practice.

Ironically, even Alcott's impracticality and improvidence may have proved, in the end, unexpectedly influential. It was in good part the want of money and a fierce determination to lighten her mother's burdens that fueled Louisa May Alcott's literary ambitions and may have helped assure her success.

Bibliography

Baker, Carlos. *Emerson Among the Eccentrics: A Group Portrait*. London and New York: Viking Press, 1996. Baker provides an indispensable overview (with in-depth individual portraits of Alcott, Emerson, Henry David Thoreau, and others) of the complex and shifting intellectual community in which Alcott moved.

McCuskey, Dorothy. *Bronson Alcott, Teacher*. New York: Arno Press, 1969. This is a sympathetic and subjective look at Alcott that focuses on his teaching career and contains numerous excerpts from his journals and notebooks.

Sears, Clara Endicott. *Bronson Alcott's Fruitlands*. Boston: Houghton Mifflin, 1915. This book contains a fascinating account of Alcott's short-lived utopian community that includes journal accounts by Louisa May Alcott and many others associated with Fruitlands, correspondence, photographs, and a fictionalized account of Fruitlands by Louisa May called "Transcendental Wild Oats."

Shepard, Odell. *Pedlar's Progress: The Life of Bronson Alcott*. Boston: Little Brown, 1937; London: Williams and Norgate, 1938. Perhaps the most comprehensive biography of Alcott to date, this volume contains a detailed look at the man and his times.

Stoehr, Taylor. *Nay-Saying in Concord: Emerson, Alcott, and Thoreau*. Hamden, Conn.: Archon Books, 1979. Stoehr focuses on the political, philosophical, and personal relationships between Alcott and his two most august comrades in Transcendental rabble-rousing and the impact they had on their times. The author argues a comparison between the Transcendental movement and the counterculture movements of the 1960's.

Christel Reges

LOUISA MAY ALCOTT

Born: November 29, 1832; Germantown, Pennsylvania

Died: March 6, 1888; Boston, Massachusetts

Area of Achievement: Literature

Contribution: Assuming financial responsibility for the support of her family, Louisa May Alcott launched a literary career as a prolific writer of works for both adult and juvenile audiences. Her writing reveals the vitality of everyday life, with the family being her most frequent subject.

Early Life

Louisa May Alcott was devoted to her family throughout her life. Her father, Bronson Alcott, was an educator who struggled to earn a decent living for his family. Soon after Louisa's birth, her father moved the family to Boston. During the years preceding Louisa's success at writing, her family lived in poverty. This poverty forced the young Alcott daughters to work in order to contribute to the family funds. The family moved frequently, covering the areas from Boston to Concord. The four sisters, Anna, Louisa, Elizabeth, and Abba May, were reared by their father and their mother, Abigail (Abba) May.

As a result of their frequent relocations, the Alcotts came into contact with a variety of people. Through contact with Quaker neighbors, Louisa was exposed to Quaker notions of simplicity, which emphasized family relationships, rather than materialistic acquisitions. The Alcott family's admiration for this ideal of simplicity made their poverty more bearable. Louisa was also exposed to Transcendentalism by her father, a serious philosopher who believed that honesty, sincerity, unselfishness, and other spiritual characteristics were more important to acquire and practice than the material pursuit of wealth and comfort. Bronson Alcott launched a utopian communal experiment on a farm known as Fruitlands in Harvard, Massachusetts, where the girls maintained the family garden and worked in the barley fields. During this time, the family was influenced by their close proximity to the Shakers, who owned property in common and who worked together to complete tasks.

Because her father was interested in philosophy and education, Louisa and her family were acquainted with many of the great minds of the time.

Bronson Alcott was a close friend of Ralph Waldo Emerson and Henry David Thoreau, and these men greatly influenced Louisa, who had little formal education. After Thoreau's death, Louisa wrote a poem, entitled "Thoreau's Flute," which was published in *Atlantic* in May, 1863.

In Concord, at the age of thirteen, Louisa began to write and produce little dramatic plays in the barn. At age sixteen, she decided to accept a job as teacher to Emerson's children so that she could contribute to her family's earnings. During these years of teaching, Louisa wrote stories for Ellen Emerson. These stories were later compiled into a book, entitled *Flower Fables*, published by George W. Briggs in 1855.

As a child, Louisa was deeply affected by contrabands, runaway slaves who had escaped from the South and fled to northern towns for protection. She was filled with compassion for the slaves and later wrote a poem for John Brown, the radical abolitionist who led the raid on Harpers Ferry. When the Civil War broke out, Louisa volunteered as a

nurse and went to Georgetown Hospital in Washington, D.C. During her experiences in the hospital, she wrote a series of "Hospital Sketches" which were printed serially in *Commonwealth* and later published as a book in 1863. Her volunteer service as a nurse was terminated after only a month because Louisa came down with typhoid and had to return to Concord.

In 1865, Louisa sailed to Europe as a nurse and companion to a family friend's invalid daughter. During this year-long trip, Louisa met Ladislas Wisniewski, who became a close friend. Ladislas would later serve as the model for the character Laurie in *Little Women*.

Life's Work

A wide range of experiences gave Louisa May Alcott the opportunity to observe many different people. She knew farmers, Quakers, Shakers, and people of Boston society. She knew poverty, but she was also exposed to a rich intellectual world by her father, and by Emerson and Thoreau. Her travels to Europe gave her further perspectives on people, but when it came time to write, she wrote of what she knew best—her family.

Little Women, Alcott's most popular book, was published by Roberts Brothers in Boston. The book was published in two parts: part 1 (1868) and part 2 (1869). *Little Women* was Alcott's story of her life as one of four sisters. Family members and family friends were at the core of her writing. Daughters, mothers, and grandmothers across the country loved this book written by a female author who understood their experiences. With the success of *Little Women*, Alcott's works were in demand, and she wasted no time in producing more books.

In 1870, Alcott began work on *An Old-Fashioned Girl*, which was published in March of the same year. Many readers praised the story for offering an accurate picture of life in Boston society during that time period. Alcott's observations of life in Boston were particularly keen because she drew upon her own rural background to offer a point of comparison.

Alcott's next book, *Little Men*, was published in June, 1871. Although it was a fictional work, the book drew upon the real life experiences of Alcott's sister Anna, who reared two sons alone following her husband's death. Louisa May Alcott wrote *Little Men* in three weeks while staying at an

apartment in Rome. Her description of the death of the character based on her brother-in-law John Pratt is a fine illustration of how she translated intimate personal experiences into literature.

Eight Cousins was written within six to eight weeks and was published in 1875. By this time, Alcott had been labeled as a writer for children, so when Henry James read a copy of this book, he was puzzled by its content. The satirical tone used in describing elders and social mysteries seemed out of place. Nevertheless, Alcott's many juvenile readers seemed eager to accept *Eight Cousins* as a mirror of reality.

The book's sequel, *Rose in Bloom* (1876), was written in three weeks while Alcott stayed at Orchard House in Concord. Just as *Eight Cousins* revealed something of Alcott's social theory, *Rose in Bloom* reflected her views on love and morality. In *Rose in Bloom*, Alcott combines reason with emotion in warning readers to look closely at potential marriage partners before commitment. She advises that no person is completely perfect; all humans have their flaws. The story of Rose and Mac is a rational approach to love and was written for a public that used common sense to control the extremes of romance.

Alcott abandoned her customary juvenile subject matter in 1877, when she wrote *A Modern Mephistopheles*, a story inspired by Goethe's Faust. Critics claimed that this novel of emotion was similar to the romances Alcott had written at age fifteen, but this story lacked the vitality of her earlier material. The book met with an indifferent reception and was called by some, "her middle-aged folly."

Louisa May Alcott went on to write additional stories, but they came out of a life that was increasingly more difficult. In her 1938 biography on Alcott, Katharine Anthony aptly described how Alcott translated her life into writing: "Out of such flights into loneliness, restlessness, and emptiness she made her rich, breathing, ardent stories of home." When Alcott's life was touched by the tragedy of losing family members and close family friends, she concealed her grief over their deaths and wrote cheerful, lively tales. Although she enjoyed literary celebrity and financial security as a result of her publications, Alcott suffered from a variety of illnesses during her later years. After visiting her dying father in Boston on March 4, 1888, she herself fell unconscious and died in her sleep two days later at the age of fifty-five.

Summary

Louisa May Alcott was a born storyteller who could deliver realistic plots and maintain a compelling point of view. She wrote of the life she saw in Boston and Concord and also offered simple reforms to improve American society. Honing her writing skills in her early sentimental stories and Gothic thrillers for magazine readers, she was most popular as a children's writer who captured family life during a particular time in history. Although many critics admired her skill in portraying affectionate and intelligent American families, some questioned her literary art. Some claimed she wrote of a simplicity that was common rather than intelligent; others claimed that her stories were too coldly rational, mercenary, and didactic. Nevertheless, admirers praised Alcott's importance as a writer of childhood tragedy and melodrama whose popularity with young readers stemmed from her ability to depict the ups and downs of childhood from a sympathetic point of view. Her stories were read widely by daughters, mothers, and grandmothers who admired Alcott's writing because they perceived themselves in her stories.

Alcott's concern for women went beyond her stories of family and relationships. With her interests in philanthropy, abolitionism, and other aspects of the reform movements that flourished during her era, Alcott was concerned with social issues. She was particularly interested in the right of women to work to support themselves economically. Having grown up in a family of poverty, she recognized the need for women to be respected in the work place. In the early years, Alcott concentrated her efforts in gaining recognition for women workers and in striving for economic equality for women.

Later, however, she became more active in her support of political rights for women. She edited a suffrage magazine and led a procession to gain delegates for woman suffrage. She also convinced her chief publisher, Thomas Niles, to publish a history of the suffrage movement. In addition, Alcott was interested in other reforms concerning education, temperance, housing, and prisons. Realizing that because she paid a poll-tax, she was entitled to vote, Alcott encouraged several other women to follow her example. Although she took a stance on these issues, her primary interest in life was storytelling. While instructing her readers on the nature of democracy, simplicity, and affection, Alcott also created stories that convey a strong and picturesque image of life in the United States during the late nineteenth century.

Bibliography

Alcott, Louisa May. *A Double Life: Newly Discovered Thrillers of Louisa May Alcott*. Edited by Madeleine B. Stern. Boston: Little Brown, 1988; London: Macmillan, 1989. This book contains tales of mystery and melodrama that were published anonymously in weeklies before Alcott wrote her tales of social realism. These stories reveal a side of Alcott that is little known by the general public.

————. *Louisa May Alcott: Selected Fiction*. Edited by Daniel Shealy, Madeleine B. Stern, and Joel Myerson. Boston: Little Brown, 1990. A collection of stories that cover the romances Alcott wrote during her teens and the thrillers and Gothic novels she wrote before turning to realism. In these stories, Alcott's rebellious spirit is reflected as a supporter of abolition and women's rights.

————. *The Selected Letters of Louisa May Alcott*. Edited by Joel Myerson and Daniel Shealy. Boston: Little Brown, 1987; London: University of Georgia Press, 1995. Many of Alcott's unpublished journals are housed in the Houghton Library at Harvard University. This book, however, offers a personal look at the experiences and responses that she wrote in letters to family members and friends throughout her life.

Anthony, Katharine S. *Louisa May Alcott*. London and New York: Knopf, 1938. Reveals the social influence of Alcott's writing as she kept alive the ideals of the Victorian period. Anthony's biography discusses the misrepresentation of Alcott by the literary world, which consistently categorizes her as a children's writer. Includes an excellent bibliography on Alcott and her entire family.

Elbert, Sarah. *A Hunger for Home: Louisa May Alcott and Little Women*. Philadelphia: Temple University Press, 1984. A feminist study of Alcott, this critical biography analyzes the connections between Alcott's family life and her work, and places Alcott squarely within the reform tradition of the nineteenth century and the debate over the proper role of women.

Meigs, Cornelia. *Invincible Louisa*. Boston: Little Brown, 1933. This biography emphasizes Alcott's work with young people and her belief that children must have the opportunity to earn independence. Meigs also discusses Alcott's assistance to soldiers during the Civil War and her trip to Europe. Contains a fine chronology of Alcott's life.

Showalter, Elaine. *Sister's Choice: Traditions and Change in American Women's Writing.* New York: Oxford University Press, and Oxford: Clarendon Press, 1991. Showalter discusses the links between and development of women writers and feminist literary theory in the postcolonial period. The author concentrates on three classics, including *Little Women,* and follows the development of themes in these works.

Stern, Madeleine B. *Louisa May Alcott: From Blood and Thunder to Heart and Home.* Boston: Northeastern University Press, 1998. A collection of essays spanning the author's fifty years of interest in, and analysis of Alcott's work including an assessment of the writer's development over time.

Strickland, Charles. *Victorian Domesticity: Families in the Life and Art of Louisa May Alcott.* University: University of Alabama Press, 1985. Like the work by Elbert above, Strickland's study surveys the range of Alcott's ideas about domestic life and considers Alcott's literary treatment of women, families, and children within the various fictional forms in which she chose to work.

Linda J. Meyers

ALEXANDER I

Born: December 23, 1777; St. Petersburg, Russia
Died: December 1, 1825; Taganrog, Russia
Areas of Achievement: Government and politics
Contribution: As czar of Russia, Alexander I initiated a series of educational, social, and political reforms early in his reign. He was instrumental in forming the coalition that defeated Napoleon I and played a major role in the Congress of Vienna following the Napoleonic Wars.

Early Life

Alexander's birth in the Winter Palace of St. Petersburg marked his destiny to occupy the Russian throne. He was the first child of Grand Duke Pavel Petrovich (later Paul I) and Grand Duchess Maria Fyodorovna. Shortly after his birth, Alexander was taken from his parents by his grandmother, Empress Catherine II (Catherine the Great), to be reared under her careful supervision. It was Catherine's intent to disinherit her son, Pavel, because she believed that he was mentally unstable and unfit to inherit her throne. Alexander would be trained to succeed her directly. A number of outstanding tutors were brought to the imperial court by Catherine to provide an education that would prepare her grandson to be czar. The most notable tutor was Frédéric-César de La Harpe, a Swiss republican, who used classical and Enlightenment texts to inspire many of the future czar's liberal ideals. In his adolescence, Alexander was also allowed an extended visit with his father at Gatchina, where he received his military training. Alexander's formal education ended at the age of sixteen, when his grandmother arranged his marriage to Princess Louise of Baden-Durlach (later Grand Duchess and Empress Elizabeth) in 1793.

Three years later, Catherine died suddenly on November 17. She had written a manifesto disinheriting her son and naming Alexander her heir. Since the document had not been released, however, her son assumed the title of Czar Paul I. His reign was characterized by a fanatical tyranny and an irrational foreign policy. A small group of nobles and military officers formed a conspiracy to remove Paul from the throne. Alexander reluctantly agreed to the plot on the condition that his father's life be spared. Paul, however, was assassinated on the night of March 23, 1801. The next day, Alexander was proclaimed the new czar.

At the age of twenty-three, Alexander became the leader of the most populous as well as one of the most backward and troubled nations of Europe. He was a handsome young man known for his intelligence and charm, but some worried that he did not have the necessary courage to fulfill his new duties. On the night that his father was murdered, he reportedly sobbed: "I cannot go on with it. I have no strength to reign. Let someone else take my place." To which Count Peter von der Pahlen, the chief conspirator, replied: "You have played the child long enough; go reign."

Life's Work

Upon assuming his new responsibilities, Alexander I rescinded Paul's tyrannical laws. He also formed a private committee composed of four liberal friends from noble families to advise him on a variety of domestic issues. They urged him to pursue a series of educational, social, and political reforms. A comprehensive educational system was proposed by Alexander's private committee. Public and parish schools were opened to all Russians. In addition, a number of specialized and college preparatory schools were established. Existing universities received increased support, and three new ones were built during Alexander's reign.

The social institution of serfdom had long been a problem. Nearly three-quarters of the population was owned by the nobility. Alexander detested this widespread slavery among his subjects, but he moved cautiously to avoid alienating the nobility whose wealth and support depended upon this slave labor. In 1803, however, the Free Cultivator's Law was enacted which permitted the nobility to free their serfs under certain highly restricted conditions. Although its success was extremely limited—only thirty-seven thousand serfs out of ten million were freed during Alexander's reign—the new law did prompt a national debate on serfdom leading to its abolition in 1861.

Alexander also reformed the corrupt and inept bureaucracy he inherited from Catherine and Paul. The senate and state council were relieved of administrative duties, and their role was limited to offering advice and comment on proposed legislation. Administration of the czar's laws would be the responsibility of a "collegium," or cabinet, of eight ministers who reported directly to Alexander. Measures to ensure greater control over the imperial treasury and to limit expenditures by the court were also implemented. The most ambitious proposal was for a constitution that would limit the czar's autocracy. Although Alexander supported a constitution in principle—he granted constitutions to the Ionian Islands in 1803, to Finland in 1809, and to Poland in 1815—the document was never made public for fear that such rapid change would be opposed by reactionary elements in the nobility.

At the height of his reforming zeal, however, Alexander suddenly and unexpectedly turned his attention to foreign affairs. Initially his foreign policy was based on his hope for a peaceful and unified Europe. He reestablished an alliance with England that had been broken by his father, while at the same time he pursued good relations with France. A treaty of friendship was signed with Prussia, and relations with Austria were improved. Alexander believed that these alliances and overtures not only would moderate Napoleon I's aggressive ambitions but also would eventually lead to a European federation of nations.

Alexander's idealistic hopes were shattered with Napoleon's conquests and with his coronation as Emperor of France, forcing Russia to declare war in 1804. The czar assumed the role of field commander, and, along with the Austrians, suffered a bitter defeat at the Battle of Austerlitz in 1805. The following year, Napoleon invaded Prussia. Against the advice of his ministers, Alexander again intervened against the French, losing a series of battles in eastern Prussia.

Following these defeats, Alexander and Napoleon met at the village of Tilsit (now Sovetsk) on June 25, 1807. The czar used his charm to flatter the French emperor and to gain a favorable peace treaty. Russia agreed to break all relations with England and to recognize the newly created Grand Duchy of Warsaw. In exchange, Alexander would be allowed to expand his empire at the expense of Persia, Sweden, and Turkey. Napoleon left Tilsit believing that in Alexander he had a new friend and ally, and that they would conquer and divide Europe between them. The czar, however, was deceptive; his flattery and acceptance of the peace treaty were designed to buy time.

When Alexander returned to St. Petersburg, his popularity quickly declined. The Tilsit Alliance was perceived as a humiliation, and the trade restrictions with England hurt the economy. Partly in

response to this criticism, Alexander backed away from any of his earlier reforms and increasingly aligned himself with reactionary forces among the nobility. He imposed his autocratic prerogatives to ensure domestic stability in order to reorganize the army and to devise a strategy that once again would challenge the French emperor.

Alexander's public break with Napoleon came slowly. Trade with England was secretly resumed, and Russia failed to aid France in its war with Austria in 1809. Napoleon retaliated by annexing the Grand Duchy of Oldenburg (territory controlled by the czar's brother-in-law) and threatened to establish an independent kingdom of Poland. Relations between the two nations steadily deteriorated as both sides prepared for war.

On June 24, 1812, Napoleon's grand army invaded Russia. Although Alexander had been rebuilding his army for a number of years, the Russians were still outnumbered by nearly three to one. Given these odds, the Russian army quickly retreated until it faced the French at the Battle of Borodino. The two armies fought to a stalemate, but, as a result of their inferior strength, the Russians were again forced to retreat. Napoleon entered a burning Moscow that had already been torched by its citizens. The French pitched their winter camp in a burned-out city. Disease and lack of supplies took their toll forcing a retreat. Constant raids by Russian soldiers and partisans during the retreat inflicted heavy casualties. Napoleon escaped from Russia with a decimated army.

Throughout the invasion Alexander provided forceful and inspirational leadership. Even in the darkest days of the campaign, the Russian people rallied behind their czar and vowed never to surrender. The burning of Moscow had reportedly "illuminated his soul," and Alexander swore that he would defeat Napoleon. Alexander's resolve was contagious. He rallied the leaders of Europe to join his crusade against Napoleon. Along with the Prussians and Austrians, he won the decisive Battle of Nations, near Leipzig, in October, 1813. Five months later, Alexander triumphantly entered Paris, forcing Napoleon's abdication and restoring Louis XVIII to the French throne.

Alexander was now the most powerful monarch in Europe. He annexed Poland over the objections of other leaders, but none could challenge his strength. He helped convene and was a dominant figure at the Congress of Vienna, which restored European political stability following the unrest of the Napoleonic era. Even with Napoleon's brief return from exile in 1815, Alexander was still the premier monarch in establishing a new era of European peace that lasted until 1871. With the defeat of his archenemy, Alexander had achieved his dream of becoming the arbiter of Europe.

Summary

Alexander I never exploited his position of power. During the last ten years of his life, he largely withdrew from public life both in terms of foreign affairs and in terms of domestic reforms. His last foray into international politics was an unsuccessful attempt to form the Holy Alliance. The purpose of this alliance was to unite European leaders by using the principles of Christian love, peace, and justice as a common basis for their political activities. In practice, it was used to justify reactionary policies against revolutionaries. Alexander's domestic policies became increasingly autocratic and repressive because of his fear of conspiracies and revolts. The czar retreated into a private religious mysticism and piety, and, shortly before his death, he indicated a desire to abdicate.

Alexander displayed contradictory attitudes that helped shape the future of Russia and Europe. He was deeply influenced by liberal ideals, yet at crucial moments he backed away from specific reforms. Had he resolved the serfdom issue and enacted a constitution, the numerous Russian revolts of the nineteenth century and the Revolution of 1917 perhaps could have been avoided. With the defeat of Napoleon, Alexander reached the pinnacle of political power only to retreat into a private world of religious devotion, leaving the future of Europe primarily in the hands of Austria's Prince Metternich. Despite this inconsistent behavior, Alexander was both a progressive, though paternalistic, reformer and the driving force that rid Europe of Napoleon's tyranny.

Bibliography

Almedingen, Edith M. *The Emperor Alexander I.* New York: Vanguard Press, and London: Bodley Head, 1964. A sympathetic biography of Alexander and his court. Provides much personal information about the czar and his relations with family, friends, and colleagues.

Glover, Michael. *The Napoleonic Wars: An Illustrated History, 1792-1815.* New York: Hippocrene Books, 1978; London: Batsford, 1979. A general summary of the major military battles and campaigns during the Napoleonic era. Its principal value is the numerous illustrations reproduced from the nineteenth century.

Grimsted, Patricia Kennedy. *The Foreign Ministers of Alexander I: Political Attitudes and the Conduct of Russian Diplomacy, 1801-1825.* Berkeley: University of California Press, 1969. An indepth study of the various foreign ministers who served during Alexander's reign. Provides some insight on the development of Russia's foreign policy as well as on the influence of liberal and reactionary ideas on Alexander's thinking.

Hartley, Janet M. *Alexander I.* London and New York: Addison Wesley Longman, 1994. Hartley presents a comprehensive summary of the contemporary writings on the reign of Alexander I with conclusions regarding his success in achieving goals both in Russia and in Europe. Useful for students as a clearly organized and well-written text with a detailed chronology, index, and a number of maps.

Holt, Lucius Hudson, and Alexander Wheeler Chilton. *A Brief History of Europe from 1789 to 1815.* New York: Macmillan, 1919. This text offers a general historical summary of major Europeans events during this period. Provides good background material for placing Alexander in a larger context during the time of his greatest achievements.

Martin, Alexander M. *Romantics, Reformers, Reactionaries: Russian Conservative Thought and Politics in the Reign of Alexander I.* Dekalb: Northern Illinois University Press, 1997. The first work on the subject to examine the forces of conservatism in nineteenth-century Russia. Martin includes discussions on issues such as government policies, the shaping and influence of public opinion, Russian conservatives (Glinka, Karamzin), and Napoleon's invasion, making use of Russian archives and published collections of writings.

McConnell, Allen. *Tsar Alexander I: Paternalistic Reformer.* New York: Crowell, 1970. Provides a critical review of Alexander's foreign and domestic policies. The author's interest is primarily to evaluate the czar's political career and to influence rather than to provide biographical information.

Nicolson, Harold. *The Congress of Vienna: A Study in Allied Unity, 1812-1822.* London: Constable, and New York: Harcourt Brace Jovanovich, 1946. Beginning with Napoleon's retreat from Moscow, this book offers a detailed overview of European politics from 1812 to 1822.

Tarle, Eugene. *Napoleon's Invasion of Russia, 1812.* London: Allen and Unwin, and New York: Oxford University Press, 1942. A detailed account of Napoleon's invasion, campaign, and retreat from Russia.

Brent Waters

ALEXANDER II

Born: April 29, 1818; Moscow, Russia
Died: March 13, 1881; St. Petersburg, Russia
Area of Achievement: Government
Contribution: Called the czar liberator, Alexander emancipated the serfs in 1861, the first of political and legal reforms designed to quicken the pace of modernization in Russia. Despite the reforms, rising expectations caused dissidents to become radicalized. Hence, Alexander's life was ended by political assassins, and reforms were suspended by his successor.

Early Life

Born in the Chudov Monastery in the Moscow kremlin on April 29, 1818, during Easter week, Alexander Nikolayevich Romanov was the oldest son of Czar Nicholas I (reigned 1825-1855), then Grand Duke, and Charlotte, daughter of King Frederick William III of Prussia and sister of future German emperor Wilhelm I. Alexander had five siblings: Nicholas, Michael, Maria, Olga, and Alexandra. After their father became czar in 1825 they lived in the royal Russian residence, the Winter Palace, and in a royal palace at Tsarskoe Selo.

The heir to the throne was given two tutors: Captain Karl Karlovich Merder and the poet Vasily Andreyevich Zhukovsky. The former was hired when Alexander was six years old, and he stressed martial values and discipline; the latter emphasized history, letters, and the cultivation of humane sentiments. Both teachers believed in autocracy. A model soldier, throughout his life Alexander expressed excitement at watching and participating in military drills and parades. In 1837, after completing his formal education, Alexander was sent on a seven-month tour through thirty provinces of the empire. Accompanied by Zhukovsky, he received his first acquaintance with poverty. A year later Alexander took his grand tour of Western Europe, where he fell in love with fourteen-year-old Princess Wilhelmina of Hesse-Darmstadt. His father reluctantly accepted the proposed match, and the girl arrived in Russia in 1840 to be rebaptized in the Orthodox church as Maria Alexandrovna. They were married on April 16, 1841. Among their eight children the first two, Alexandra and Nicholas, died in 1849 and 1865, respectively; the third child, the future Alexander III, was born in 1845.

Czar Nicholas I carefully prepared his son for governance by appointing him to numerous positions such as chancellor of Alexander University in Finland, member of the Holy Synod and several imperial councils, and, in his father's absence, chairman of the state council. Several times Alexander participated in diplomatic missions, including one to Vienna in 1849 to persuade the Austrian Emperor Franz Joseph to pardon the Hungarian rebel generals. Although frightened by the European revolutions in 1849 and reminded by Zhukovsky about the irresponsibility of rapid reforms, Alexander would launch a movement for widespread changes after his accession.

Life's Work

Alexander came to power on February 19, 1855, during the Crimean War before the fall of Sebastopol to the French and English. Although he reminded his generals of the victory after the fall of Moscow in 1812, he was soon persuaded to negotiate for

peace. The czar was compelled to accept defeat and sign the Treaty of Paris on March 30, 1856. His coronation did not occur until the 26th of August. It is unclear to what extent Russia's weak performance in the war led him to embark upon reforms. Since his background did not portend such a reign, historians are divided by what occurred. Furthermore, since his policies were not uniformly progressive, his goals are difficult to assess. Less dictatorial than his predecessors, he freely accepted advice.

In matters of foreign affairs, he relied upon his chief aide, General Aleksandr Mikhailovich Gorchakov, who agreed with the czar that foreign affairs must be subordinated to domestic developments. Together they forged a rapprochement with Napoleon III of France, only to see it fail when the French extended sympathy to the Polish rebels in 1863. Thereafter, Alexander II drew closer to his German relatives, whom he supported during the creation of the German Empire in 1871. By that year Alexander dared to violate the terms of the Treaty of Paris by sailing warships on the Black Sea. Russia also joined with Germany and Austria-Hungary in the Three Emperors' League, but it fell apart when Alexander succumbed to Pan-Slavic pressures and to a war with the Ottoman Empire on April 24, 1877. Victorious Russian armies forced the sultan to sign a peace at San Stephano the following year, allowing Russia significant gains in Bessarabia and the lower Caucasus. Western powers compelled the Russians to scale back their gains at a congress in Berlin later that year. That event damaged Russian-German ties, but Otto von Bismarck managed to assuage the czar's feelings somewhat. The end of German-Russian cooperation came in the following reign.

Meanwhile, Russian expansion in the Far East and Central Asia was impressive. Although Alaska was sold to the United States in 1867, and Gorchakov tried to restrain commanders from conquests in Asia, the czar was pleased with their acquisitions. From 1859 to 1861 China ceded territory to Russia in the Amur-Ussuri district, and Japan yielded Sakhalin Island for the remaining Kurile Islands in 1875. Between 1865 and 1876, Alexander's empire reached Kokand, Bokhara, and Khiva in Central Asia; in 1881, other lands east of the Caspian Sea were added. Such gains in the East, however, were little appreciated.

The centerpiece of the reign was the emancipation of about twenty-five million serfs on February 19, 1861. Not only did this measure fulfill a goal which had baffled previous rulers such as Alexander I, it also made possible free labor that was so indispensable for later industrial programs and a free citizenry that was a precondition for further reforms. Alexander opened discussions for serf reform in his state council after the Crimean War and urged that the deliberations of the matter be removed from secret negotiations. He indicated that he wanted the obstacles to solution of this question overcome. Hence, the gentry accepted its inevitability and joined the czar in realizing the edict. The decree gave peasants immediate legal freedoms with lands to buy from the state. Although the terms allowed concessions to the gentry, many people agreed with Aleksandr Ivanovich Herzen that official society had moved in a progressive direction. Much of the credit was attributed to Alexander. Peasants, however, were bewildered by the requirement to purchase their lands.

Despite the uprising in Poland in 1863, Alexander forged ahead with decrees in 1864 to reform the legal administration. Reforms that were introduced were trial by jury in civil cases, equal access to the courts for all, life tenure for judges, and measures to protect due process. Also that year, local government was reorganized and newly elected assemblies called zemstvos were given wide control over local education, fire fighting, veterinary medicine, road and bridge construction, hospital care, and other matters in the thirty-four provinces of the empire. Members were elected on the all-class principle, removing the monopoly of local authority from the gentry. Alexander eased censorship in 1865 and disbanded the secret police. Similar elective bodies were introduced in 1870 in urban administration. In the 1870's, military reforms drawn up by D. A. Miliutin incorporated many principles of civil law into military law, and the penal environment of the soldier was changed to a dignified profession for national defense. Hence the brutality of military training was largely eliminated, and terms of active service were reduced from fifteen to six years.

Alexander's reforming zeal was tempered by firm measures to protect his regime. In 1862 he ordered the arrest of radical journalist Nikolay Guvrilovich Chernyshevsky for inciting violence, and he ordered Russification of the Poles after 1863. On April 4, 1866, while Alexander was walking through the Summer Gardens, an inept attempt on his life was made by a deranged nihilist, Dmitry V. Karakazov. Although the attempt failed, Alexander was shaken by the incident and appointed reactionary minister Dmitry Andreyevich Tolstoy to preside over the ministry of education. When the populist intelligentsia failed to arouse the peasantry by talking about socialism in the earlier 1870's, some turned to violence. Alexander responded with strong measures of his own, and the nation witnessed several treason trials which gave exposure to the radical cause and undermined respect for the czar. Eventually, a faction of radicals decided upon the ultimate act of terrorism—the killing of the czar.

Members of the People's Will Party believed that the assassination of the czar would bring peasants to the point of national rebellion. Their single-minded devotion to this end was realized on the morning of March 13, 1881, as Alexander was riding through the streets of the capital after addressing a meeting. When a bomb was thrown at this coach, wounding his coachmen, the czar alighted from the carriage to attend to the victims; a second bomb then killed him. On that spot was constructed the Church of the Spilt Blood.

Summary

Despite relapses into conservative policies, Alexander II authored the most significant reforms in czarist history. Designed to modernize Russian life so that the nation could better compete internationally, the reforms also fulfilled Alexander's own desires for the improvement of the commonwealth. Unfortunately, they were not effective in stemming the tide of radical politics. Some regard the reforms as too little, too late; others believe that they were meant simply to strengthen the old structures in order to make additional reforms unnecessary; and yet others believe that they were too much, too soon. The most radical intelligentsia feared that the reforms might defuse the public's desire for revolution.

The czar's popularity waned in his last years, partly through his own doing. The moving of his second family into the Winter Palace under the same roof as the empress, his hasty marriage to Princess Catherine E. Dolgoruka on the fortieth day after his wife died in 1880, and his replacement of progressive ministers with conservative ministers obscured the fact that he was, at the end, considering a major step toward representative government, having commissioned Count Mikhail Tariyelovich Loris-Melikov to draw up a plan for a national consultative assembly. Alexander's assassination came just before the plan was unveiled; the new czar dismissed the proposal and began measures to undo the work of his father.

Bibliography

Almedingen, E. M. *The Emperor Alexander II.* London: Bodley Head, 1962; New York: Vanguard Press, 1966. This work, by a writer who specializes in biographies of Russian figures, contains the most extensive account of Alexander's personal life. Despite Alexander's vacillations, the author laments that what his reign began was not pursued by his successors.

Billington, James H. *The Icon and the Axe: An Interpretive History of Russian Culture.* London: Weidenfeld and Nicolson, and New York: Knopf, 1966. The author divides Alexander's reign into a period of reform followed by a period of reaction, while brilliantly exploring the sociopolitical dimensions of art and literature in this era.

Kornilov, Alexander. *Modern Russian History from the Age of Catherine the Great to the End of the Nineteenth Century.* New York: Knopf, 1952. This classic view of the age demonstrates with keen insight the political machinations of the czar and his court.

Mosse, W. E. *Alexander II and the Modernization of Russia.* London: English Universities Press, and New York: Macmillan, 1958. A short but scholarly synopsis of the reign that traces much of the czar's troubles to his alienation of society and even of the police in the 1870's.

Pereira, N. G. O. *Tsar-Liberator: Alexander II of Russia, 1818-1881.* Newtonville, Mass.: Oriental Research Partners, 1983. Despite modest claims to the contrary by the author, this is the best biographical study of the czar's reign. Pereira, an academic historian, clearly lauds Alexander's imperial policies in the East.

Pushkarev, Sergei. *The Emergence of Modern Russia, 1801-1917.* Translated by Robert H. McNeal and Tova Yedlin. New York: Holt Rinehart, 1963. Herein are the views of a modern liberal historian who maximizes the changes at the beginning of the century and minimizes those in the 1860's.

Seton-Watson, Hugh. *The Decline of Imperial Russia, 1855-1914.* New York: Praeger, and London: Methuen, 1952. In part 1, "The Tsar Liberator 1855-1881," the author discovers the roots of the collapse of the old regime in this era.

John D. Windhausen

HORATIO ALGER

Born: January 13, 1832; Chelsea, Massachusetts
Died: July 18, 1899; Natick, Massachusetts
Area of Achievement: Literature
Contribution: Alger was a writer of books for juveniles who popularized business as a career for young boys, while at the same time motivating the poor to work hard in hopes of success. Because of the popularity of his books, the story of anyone who became successful in real life became known as a "Horatio Alger story."

Early Life

Horatio Alger, Jr., traced his ancestry to Puritans who came to Plymouth, Massachusetts, in 1621. His father, Horatio Alger, Sr., was a graduate of the Harvard Theological School and the minister at the First Congregational Church in Chelsea, Massachusetts. His mother, Olive Augusta Fenno, had married his father just ten months before the birth of Horatio, Jr. The ministerial stipend was not large; thus, the family was usually in debt. In 1844, when Horatio, Jr., was twelve, his father went bankrupt. For a time his father turned to farming but eventually went back into the ministry and later served in the Massachusetts state legislature.

Alger was a sickly child; he was nearsighted and had asthma. In 1848, at the age of sixteen, he was admitted to Harvard College. The first publication for which he received payment came in 1849 when a Boston magazine bought a poem he had penned. During his senior year, he was elected to Phi Beta Kappa, and he graduated in 1852. Although he immediately planned to enter the Harvard Divinity School, a writing job arose, and he decided to become a journalist—a career he was to follow for five years. In the fall of 1857, he entered the Harvard Divinity School, from which he graduated in 1860. Alger was soon named to the pulpit of the Unitarian Church in Brewster, Massachusetts. Because his church duties were often light, he spent a great deal of time writing stories for children, which was not a popular sideline in the eyes of his parishioners.

Unfortunately, Alger apparently had a homosexual relationship with one or more of the young boys in his church. Once this came to light in 1866, he was forced not only to resign his church but also to resign the ministry. The Unitarians agreed to keep the situation quiet if Alger agreed to never again

serve as a minister. He then moved to New York, where he became a full-time writer. His personal relations with boys never again came into question. Many authors, however, have speculated that Alger's love for boys was a vicarious motivation that surfaced in his writing. From the event, Alger learned discretion and was never again accused of a homosexual relationship, but he also never allowed himself to be in the public eye. His books and short stories were all that people ever really knew about the man during the remainder of his lifetime.

Life's Work

In middle age, at a time when he had been relatively unsuccessful in other endeavors, Alger began writing books for juveniles. He was best known as a writer of books in which the heroes started out poor and ended up wealthy. Among his more popular titles were *Ragged Dick* (1867), *Luck and Pluck* (1869), and *Tattered Tom* (1871). His heroes were typically newsboys, shoe shiners, match sellers, farmers, or luggage carriers who rose to fame and fortune via their own efforts, bravery, and courage. His young entrepreneurs earned and spent their wealth honestly. His books were particularly popular during the Progressive Era because they satisfied the Progressives' desire to reform business and government through a return to morality.

Alger's adult life was essentially dull: He did nothing but write. In addition to writing more than 120 books, he published hundreds of short stories and over one hundred poems. Many of his short stories were written under pseudonyms. His writing was not particularly difficult in that it was formulaic fiction that required little research. Short stories were turned into serials, and serials were turned into books. In one sense, Alger was a self-plagiarizer because he used the same work over and over. His first book, *Bertha's Christmas Vision*, was published in 1856. His fourth book, and first financially successful volume, was *Paul Prescott's Charge* in 1865.

Alger's writings captured the spirit of the United States. In his books, the reader could hear the turmoil of the city streets and the rattle of the milk pails on the farms. He portrayed the ambitious soul of the nation. Manly forbearance was an important part of Alger's writings; it was okay to fight or even shoot someone, but only after Alger had made it clear that there was no other possibility. Money, contracts, and instruments such as mortgages were often discussed in detail—usually with the hero eventually paying off the mortgage for his widowed mother.

Alger has been criticized at times because the event that moves the hero from destitution to wealth is often somewhat fortuitous, such as a gift arriving in the mail from a long-lost aunt, an inheritance from a little-known relative, or a payment received for an invention that had not been discussed previously in the book. Despite these criticisms, the message was that hard work and pluck on the part of the hero was the key to prosperity.

Alger's books, although popular, were not huge sellers during his lifetime. He had few assets at his death. It was only after his death, when the books were reissued in inexpensive editions, that he became a household name. His books remained popular until about 1920. A total of at least seventy different publishers issued Alger's books, some of which were first editions and some of which were reprints. Alger was so prolific that one or two publishers could not handle all of his work. Approximately forty different publishers issued reprints of his books during the first two decades of the twentieth century. The reprints sold, in hardcover, for as low as ten cents each—a price that allowed almost every child to have access to Alger's work. It has been estimated that more than 400 million copies of his novels have been sold.

It was not until 1926 that the term "Horatio Alger hero" first appeared in print as a synonym for someone who had gone from rags to riches. During the Great Depression of the 1930's, Alger's plots were again hailed as the way out of hard times. Alger's thesis was that virtue and hard work were always rewarded, and newspapers often published articles to the effect that if Americans would work harder, the Depression would cease to exist. In 1939, on the fortieth anniversary of Alger's death, New York governor Herbert Lehman essentially prescribed Alger as a home remedy for the economic ills afflicting the nation. In 1947, a *New York Times* editorial attributed America's disdain for communism and socialism to Alger; because so many Americans believed that every poor boy had a chance to succeed, they would not fall for the rantings of the anarchists and socialists who saw nothing but evil in capitalism. Readers of Alger, however, knew better; every newsboy had the potential to become rich and famous. Perhaps the fol-lowing review from *Publishers Weekly* is an overstatement, but it indicates the mind-set with which Alger is remembered: "To Call Horatio Alger, Jr., America's most influential writer may seem like an overstatement . . . but . . . only Benjamin Franklin meant as much to the formation of the American popular mind."

Summary

Horatio Alger was a private person who shunned publicity throughout his life, perhaps fearing that his reputation would be harmed if an unsavory incident from his early adulthood were to be exposed. Thus, he was one of the most widely read writers in the United States during his lifetime, yet he was unknown. To deter future biographers, he even ordered his sister to destroy all of his personal papers following his death, which she did. Even some documents in the hands of others mysteriously disappeared in the years following his death.

Other writers adapted Alger's fiction formula for their own uses. Edward Stratemeyer, who dominated the juvenile fiction market between 1910 and 1930 (and who finished eleven of Alger's book manuscripts that were left unfinished at Alger's death), also used moral heroism and economic success in his books. Owen Wister, the author of *The Virginian* (1902), applied the technique to Western stories.

One century after his death, Alger's name stands as a symbol for America's central values. It is not because his books are still widely known and read but because his name has entered the language as a substitute for a success story. His books have been lampooned and maligned, but as symbols they are so pervasive in American culture that they have far outlived what was undoubtedly nothing more than a hack writer.

In 1940, authors Nathanael West and Boris Ingster summarized Alger's life by writing, "only fools laugh at Horatio Alger, and his poor boys who make good. The wiser man who thinks twice about that sterling author will realize that Alger is to America what Homer was to the Greeks." Indeed, Alger's stories may not have been based on fact, but they told about the way Americans wanted life to be. Today, Alger would probably be a motivational speaker or writer of some sort who would encourage people to be the best that they could be and promising that success would follow. He has been called one of the great mythmakers of the modern world. There is even an award for successful individuals named the Horatio Alger Award. Henry Steele Commager stated that Alger probably exerted more influence on the national character than any other writer except perhaps Mark Twain.

Bibliography

Mayes, Herbert R. *A Biography Without a Hero.* New York: Macy- Masius, 1928. This work is a complete fabrication. When Mayes discovered that there was insufficient information to write a true biography, he decided, with the approval of his publisher, to write a parody of Alger's life based on nonexistent diaries and letters. Surprisingly, his parody was not recognized as such and was viewed as a legitimate biography for several decades. Reviews were generally favorable. Alger's surviving friends and relatives apparently did not reveal the truth, probably because they were happy that the truth had not been revealed. Many subsequent biographers unwittingly used this book as a source of factual information on Alger's life.

Nackenoff, Carol. *The Fictional Republic: Horatio Alger and American Political Discourse.* New York: Oxford University Press, 1994. The emphasis is on Alger's social leanings and his influence on politics.

Scharnhorst, Gary, and Jack Bales. *The Lost Life of Horatio Alger, Jr.* Bloomington: Indiana University Press, 1985. This is the best work on the life of Alger. It was the first to fully unmask the faulty, fictionalized biography of Herbert R. Mayes.

Tebbel, John. *From Rags to Riches: Horatio Alger and the American Dream.* New York: Macmillan, 1963. Although based on the fictional work of Mayes, this volume does contain a complete bibliography of Alger's works.

Weiss, Richard. *The American Myth of Success: From Horatio Alger to Norman Vincent Peale.* New York: Basic Books, 1969. This volume analyzes the work of popular writers who portray the ease with which Americans can become successful.

Dale L. Flesher

JOHN PETER ALTGELD

Born: December 30, 1847; Niederselters, Prussia
Died: March 12, 1902; Joliet, Illinois
Areas of Achievement: Government and politics
Contribution: Altgeld furnished American political life with a high standard of moral courage and, during a crucial historical period, helped to establish the principle that maintenance of the welfare society is an obligation of government.

Early Life

John Peter Altgeld was born December 30, 1847, in Niederselters, in the Prussian province of Nassau, the eldest son of a wagon-maker, also named John Peter Altgeld, and his wife, Mary Lanehart. The family came to the United States in the spring of the following year, and Altgeld grew up on farms near Mansfield, Ohio. Because his father was against the idea of education for his children, Altgeld attended country schools for only three terms. When he was sixteen, he enlisted in an Ohio militia regiment and was sent to Virginia. There, he contracted a fever which permanently damaged his health, but he refused to be sent home and finished out the hundred days for which the regiment had been mustered.

When he returned to Ohio, Altgeld, much against his father's wishes, attended high school in Mansfield and a teacher-training school in Lexington, Ohio, and taught school for a time. Until he was twenty-one, he turned over all of his wages to his father, but in the spring of 1869, perhaps because the parents of Emma Ford would not permit her to marry him, he headed west on foot, working on farms as he went. He arrived finally in St. Louis with only fifteen cents, worked there for a time in a chemical plant, and later worked on a railroad that was being built in southern Kansas. When a recurrence of his fever forced him to quit, he went to northwestern Missouri, most of the way on foot. Dressed in rags, he collapsed at a farm near Savannah, Missouri, and was taken in by a farmer who restored him to health and gave him work. Later, he taught school and read law, and in April, 1871, was admitted to the bar and began legal practice in Savannah. He had not revealed any interest in politics until this time, beyond a devotion to the ideals of Thomas Jefferson, but he served as city attorney for Savannah for a year and ran successfully as the Populist candidate for prosecuting attorney of Andrew County in 1874.

For reasons which remain obscure, Altgeld resigned this office after a year and, with only one hundred dollars, moved to Chicago. There he established a law practice, and in 1877, on a visit to his parents in Ohio, he married Emma Ford. During the next years, Altgeld achieved great success investing in Chicago real estate and in 1890 held property valued at a million dollars.

Life's Work

In 1884, Altgeld was the unsuccessful Democratic candidate for Congress in the traditionally Republican Fourth District. At this time, he was an apparent conservative in politics and part of the Chicago economic establishment. In the same year, however, he published *Our Penal Machinery and Its Victims*, which revealed many of the ideas for reform that he sought to implement later in his political career. The book pleaded for the elimination of the causes of crime and the rehabilitation of criminals, and it condemned police brutality against vagrants. In 1886, in the immediate wake of the Haymarket Riot, he wrote a newspaper article in which he argued for the compulsory arbitration of strikes.

That year, he ran successfully for judge of the Cook County Superior Court, serving for five years. Apparently Altgeld regarded the judgeship as the first step toward his ultimate goal—a seat in the United States Senate, the highest office possible for him because of his foreign birth. When he resigned his judgeship and failed to win election to the Senate, he embarked on his greatest project in real estate—the construction of the sixteen-story Unity Block, at that time one of Chicago's greatest buildings.

In 1892, he was nominated by the Democrats for the Illinois governorship, probably more for his success as a businessman than for any stand he had taken on social issues. In this campaign, he revealed the strict ethics and liberal instincts for which his followers admired him, mixed with a real hunger for power and an occasional tendency to political chicanery. As the first Democratic governor of Illinois in forty years, Altgeld cleared out all the Republicans in state government, and though many of his replacements were brilliant, he fired some able Republicans and appointed some incompetent Democrats.

In the aftermath of the Haymarket Riot, when a bomb killed several policemen, eight anarchists had been sentenced to death; one of them committed suicide in prison, and four others were hanged. The sentences of the other three—Samuel Fielden, Michael Schwab, and Oscar Neebe—had been commuted to life imprisonment. Altgeld's supporters expected him to pardon these three men and assumed that he would be motivated only by feelings of mercy. Yet when the pardons were issued on June 26, 1893, it was clear that though he detested anarchism, he was convinced that the eight men had been convicted not for their deeds but for their opinions, that the jury had been impaneled improperly, that the judge was prejudiced, and that five of the accused were, in effect, the victims of judicial murder. Altgeld issued a pamphlet of eighteen thousand words in which he presented his arguments with great clarity and logic, but this explanation could not allay the storm of abuse which fell upon him for his act. Those who had favored the sentences now raged at him in virtually every newspaper in the country, and those who had favored a pardon were angered that he had issued an absolute pardon and that the pamphlet exposed the errors of the judicial system itself. Altgeld was accused of being an anarchist; this was said by many editorialists to be the result of his foreign birth.

The charge that he was an anarchist seems absurd when one considers his use of the Illinois militia during the labor troubles of his term as governor. Only two weeks before he issued the pardons, he sent the militia to Lemont in response to a plea from local authorities that they could not maintain order in a labor dispute. In June, 1894, he sent the militia to Mount Olive, where striking miners were interfering with mail trains. These affirmations of the power of the state did not satisfy his enemies, because, unlike his predecessors, Altgeld used the militia only to maintain order, not to break the strikes.

This was one of several issues that led to Altgeld's break with President Grover Cleveland. In July, 1894, when the Pullman Company had locked out its employees and federal troops had been dispatched by Cleveland to break the "strike," Altgeld, in a letter to the president, condemned his action on the grounds that sufficient Illinois militia were available on the scene to preserve order. The Chicago newspapers, still harping on Altgeld's supposed anarchism, wildly denounced him for this protest, but in fact violence did not occur until the federal troops arrived, and then Chicago police and the state militia put it down. In fact, the disorder actual-

ly ended when a company of Altgeld's militia killed seven men by firing point-blank into a mob.

This dispute was only one of Altgeld's quarrels with the president. Altgeld saw Cleveland as an unquestioning supporter of "government by injunction," the use of the courts to rule strikes illegal, and he condemned the Supreme Court when it struck down the federal income tax in 1894, in an opinion written by Cleveland's appointee, Chief Justice Melville Fuller. Altgeld saw little difference between Republicans and Cleveland Democrats on the tariff question or on the silver issue. By thorough study, he made himself the outstanding authority on the latter question in American public life, and he embraced the silver issue in 1895, calling for the coinage of silver to increase the money supply. By this time, in spite of the campaign of vilification against him in the press for the Haymarket pardons and his stand on the Pullman dispute, Altgeld was the most influential Democrat in the country. With the laboring class throughout the country, he enjoyed an affection which verged on idolatry, and his stand on silver gave him a large following in the West and South. As a result, there is little reason to doubt that, had it not been for his foreign birth, he would have been the Democratic nominee for president in 1896.

As it was, he was clearly the master of the Democratic convention of that year. The platform reflected his views—free coinage of silver and gold at a ratio of sixteen to one, opposition to government by injunction, arbitration of labor disputes involving interstate commerce, protection of the rights of labor, and an income tax. While he did not favor the nomination of William Jennings Bryan, Altgeld worked mightily for his election, even at the expense of his own reelection campaign. He did not want another term as governor—his finances had suffered from the economic depression of the time, and his health was bad—but he bowed to the party's wishes. The Republican strategy, in the face of a national trend away from the gold standard, was to depict Bryan as the tool of the "anarchist" and communist Altgeld. Not for the last time in the nation's history, political profit was made from calling an opponent a communist. On October 17, 1896, in a great speech at Cooper Union, Altgeld took the fight to the enemy, arguing against government by injunction and against federal interference in the rights of states to maintain order within their own borders. Throughout the campaign, he literally rose from a sickbed to speak, sometimes seven or eight times a day.

In the Bryan debacle, Altgeld's defeat for reelection was probably inevitable, and he was defeated in the legislature as a candidate for the United States Senate. He returned to Chicago to attempt to rebuild his shattered finances, but he lost control of the Unity Building and returned to the practice of law. As governor, he had rejected a bribe of a half-million dollars from the Chicago traction magnate Charles Yerkes, and he had always favored public ownership of monopolies. On this platform, he ran unsuccessfully as an independent for mayor in 1899.

In the 1900 presidential campaign, Altgeld was still a powerful influence, as was evident in the Democratic Party's repetition of its 1896 stand on the silver issue, and he campaigned with great energy for Bryan. At this time, he was also condemning American policy in the Philippines. He died suddenly on March 12, 1902, a few hours after making a speech which condemned the treatment of Boer women and children in British concentration camps in South Africa.

Summary

During his governorship, John Peter Altgeld achieved much for Illinois in the improvement of existing state institutions and the building of others, and his use of the state's police power to preserve order reflected a deep conservative respect for the rights of property, contrary to the charge of anarchism leveled against him by journalistic hacks and by politicians who must have known better. His pardoning of Samuel Fielden, Michael Schwab, and Oscar Neebe, an act of courage with few parallels in American political life, was consistent with his stands on social and economic issues—stands which have been vindicated by history. In 1896, he forced the Democratic Party to commit itself for the first time to social reform, and the achievements of the Progressive era and the New Deal were the fruits of the seeds he planted. Indeed, it is an irony of history that Altgeld is forgotten by most Americans, while Theodore Roosevelt, who once in a foolish speech called him an apologist for wholesale murder, is a hero of American Progressivism because he enacted much of Altgeld's program. Altgeld remains what Vachel Lindsay called the "wise man, that kindled the flame."

Bibliography

Barnard, Harry. *Eagle Forgotten: The Life of John Peter Altgeld.* Indianapolis: Bobbs-Merrill, 1938. The definitive biography of Altgeld, not likely to be superseded, and the basic source for information on his early years.

Browne, Waldo R. *Altgeld of Illinois.* New York: Huebsch, 1924. The first biography of Altgeld, written out of profound respect for its subject and informed by a deep sense of social justice. Lacks a thorough account of Altgeld's pre-Chicago years. Valuable, though superseded by Barnard's biography.

Christman, Henry M., ed. *The Mind and Spirit of John Peter Altgeld.* Urbana: University of Illinois Press, 1960. Includes a useful though brief biographical account and a representative selection of Altgeld's writings, including the Cooper Union speech of 1896 and "Reasons for Pardoning Fielden, Neebe, and Schwab."

Ginger, Ray. *Altgeld's America.* New York: Funk and Wagnall, 1958. A thorough study of Altgeld's achievements in developing a progressivism which would adapt American political idealism to modern industrial conditions.

Whitlock, Brand. *Forty Years of It.* New York and London: Appleton, 1914. Whitlock served in the Illinois government during Altgeld's governorship and was his close associate. This autobiography provides a firsthand account of events surrounding the Haymarket pardons and the Pullman dispute.

Wish, Harvey. "Altgeld and the Progressive Tradition." *American Historical Review* 46 (July, 1941): 813-831. Emphasizes the progressivism of Altgeld's social and economic beliefs. Puts his career in perspective which is frequently lacking in those accounts which concentrate on his role in the Haymarket case.

Robert L. Berner

HANS CHRISTIAN ANDERSEN

Born: April 2, 1805; Odense, Denmark

Died: August 4, 1875; Rolighed, near Copenhagen, Denmark

Area of Achievement: Literature

Contribution: Andersen is the most well-known Danish writer. His greatest achievement was as the author of universally beloved fairy tales.

Early Life

Hans Christian Andersen was the first notable Danish writer of proletarian origins. He grew up with little education and in extreme poverty, and his great personal charm and exceptional talent earned him the affection and regard of both the common people and the artistic and social aristocracies of his time. Andersen's father was a shoemaker but was well read; he took his son to the theater, introduced him to books, and even built a little puppet theater for him. Andersen's mother, who eventually became a washerwoman, came from a world of hardship and penury. Illiterate and superstitious, she was one of three illegitimate daughters raised in an atmosphere of poverty and promiscuity; she turned to drink in her old age. While he received little formal education, Andersen developed performing skills that brought him to the attention of Prince Christian at Odense Castle. In spite of this distinction, he received little encouragement and was pressured to enter a conventional trade. Reluctant to give up his dream of becoming an actor and living a life of adventure, Andersen left for Copenhagen in 1819 with the blessings of his mother, who had been told by a fortune-teller that the entire town would one day be illuminated to celebrate her son's great achievements.

In Copenhagen, Andersen found little success in the theater but made friends among the most prominent members of society as well as among poets and scientists. Particularly important was his friendship with Jonas Collin, a senior civil servant and principal adviser to the king who supervised Andersen's return to school to acquire a passable education and who acted as a second father. Andersen demonstrated that in spite of his strange appearance—a lanky body, loosely swinging arms, enormous feet, and a face with a long nose and broad cheekbones—he possessed a charismatic personality that led many important people to help him succeed as an artist. By the early 1830's, he had won favor with the public, critics, and fellow poets with his poetry and, despite his unpromising origins, had been welcomed into the upper echelons of Danish society. It was in 1830 that he also fell in love for the first time with Riborg Voigt, the sister of an old school friend. His despondency over her rejection of him, combined with his restless nature, led him to begin a lifetime of almost incessant travel.

Life's Work

By 1831, Andersen had realized his dream of world fame, having made a name for himself as a lyric poet, dramatist, and travel writer. His greatest achievements came, however, in 1835 with the publication of his first fairy tales and his first novel, *Improvisatoren* (1835; *The Improvisatore*, 1845), the somewhat autobiographical story of a Danish boy who goes from rags to riches. Succeeding novels, *O.T.* (1836; English translation, 1845) and *Kun en Spillemand* (1837; *Only a*

Fiddler, 1845), were also based on his own life, depicting the bleak conditions of the poor and warning that Danish society was failing to recognize underprivileged artists. Favorably compared with Walter Scott and Victor Hugo, Andersen's novels were at the forefront of contemporary European fiction.

Although his novels were important and successful, Andersen's literary reputation has come to rest largely on his fairy tales, a short and unassuming form of fiction in which Andersen demonstrated his true genius. His first collection, *Eventyr* (1835; wonder tales), included stories of his own invention along with stories from his childhood and from the folklore of other countries. Unlike the scholarly collections of the folklorists Jacob and Wilhelm Grimm, however, Andersen's fairy tales were essentially creative and of high literary quality. Like the Brothers Grimm, however, Andersen's tales were the product of the romantic movement, which inspired a new interest in the world of the common people and the child. In this regard, Andersen had the advantage of being from the common people himself. Never disguising the fact that he was the son of a poor shoemaker and a washerwoman, Andersen was perfectly capable of calling attention to the shortcomings of the upper classes. Andersen also retained a childlike quality that made it easy for him to speak to children on their level. At the same time, however, his stylistically sophisticated and even philosophical approach to his stories also drew an adult readership.

Andersen's stories include such well-known favorites as "The Princess and The Pea," "Thumbelina," "The Little Mermaid," "The Tinder Box," and "The Emperor's New Clothes." These stories are notable for their strong romantic feeling and open sentimentality, for which Andersen is sometimes brought to task. His stories are also witty and playful, with a refreshing absence of obvious moralizing. Andersen continued to publish collections of fairy tales over the years, and the 1840's were an especially productive decade during which he perfected a style that discarded conventional literary diction in favor of everyday, colloquial speech. Of special note is "The Ugly Duckling," in which a gawky and peculiar duckling turns into a beautiful swan, a tale that is very much the story of Andersen's own life. Another important story from this period, "The Nightingale," is a tribute to the celebrated singer Jenny Lind, known as the Swedish Nightingale, with whom Andersen fell in love in 1840; he unsuccessfully courted her in the years to come. Other notable stories of this period include "The Fir Tree," "The Snow Queen," "The Red Shoes," and "The Little Match Girl." In 1850 Andersen rounded off this rich decade with stories such as "The Shadow," "The Ice Maiden," "Auntie Toothache," and "Clod-Hans."

All in all, Andersen published 156 tales, which were eventually collected under the title *Eventyr og Historier* (1874; *The Complete Andersen*, 1949; also, *Fairy Tales*, 1950-1958; also, *The Complete Fairy Tales and Stories*, 1974). These stories were translated into more languages than almost any book except the Bible. Although humorous and entertaining, Andersen's stories have become classics because they also treat serious issues such as the struggle for love and recognition as well as the realities of loss, deprivation, and death. In addition, his stories affirmed the liberal and social humanism of the European Enlightenment and had a strong spiritual component, reflective of Andersen's belief that he was always under the protection of higher powers.

Andersen's gift for writing for children was the product of his own character, which remained childlike. Andersen was also emotionally fragile, with a thin skin and a nervous, irritable temperament. At times he could be a trying companion. Of particular note in this regard was his friendship with English novelist Charles Dickens, which began amid mutual admiration and affection but ended abruptly in 1856 when the eccentric Andersen overstayed his welcome as Dickens' houseguest. On the whole, however, Andersen had a remarkable gift for friendship. Poets and men of letters flocked around him wherever he went, and among his friends were an impressive number of outstanding European writers such as Heinrich Heine, Honoré de Balzac, and Victor Hugo; composers such as Felix Mendelssohn, Robert Schumann, and Franz Liszt; and numerous painters and performers. In addition, one of his closest friends was the Grand Duke Carl Alexander of Weimar. In fact, his universal fame led Andersen to be favored by the ruling classes all over Europe, a prerogative Andersen sought and felt he not only deserved but also desperately needed.

Although given accolades and surrounded by friends, Andersen was often a sad and lonely man. He never married, even though he fell in love at least twice, once with Riborg Voigt and later with Jenny Lind. In each case, his love was ultimately unrequited. To some extent, however, Andersen seems to have made a calculated renunciation of women in order to devote himself tirelessly to his creative life and to protect his sensitive temperament from the pressures of love and marriage. In spite of his gift for friendship, Andersen was always something of an outsider, and his travels were in part an escape from a lonely life. His nomadic wanderings, however, served also as voyages of self-discovery that fed his artistic temperament. As Andersen said in his autobiography *Mit Livs Eventyr* (1855; *The Story of My Life*, 1871), to travel was to live. In spite of his notorious phobias and general hypochondria, Andersen's strong sense of curiosity and need to explore led him on many intrepid journeys. By the end of his life, Andersen had gone abroad thirty times in all, traveling all over Europe, especially to Italy, France, and Germany, and by all means available, including carriage, horseback, stagecoach, steamship, and railroad. He even ventured into North Africa and Asia Minor and wrote many books about his travels, the best of which is *En digters bazar* (1842; *The Poet's Bazaar*, 1846). By the end of his life, Andersen had become Denmark's greatest storyteller and greatest travel writer.

Summary

In his later years, Hans Christian Andersen continued to write novels, plays, stories, and travelogues. It was the great achievement of his fairy tales, however, that gave Andersen literary immortality. As the product of both Andersen's genius and the romantic movement that welcomed the fairy tale as a viable source of wisdom and aesthetic merit, his tales have spread throughout the world. It is important to note that by 1843, Andersen had removed the phrase "told for children" from his tales even though various poor and spurious English translations of his tales in the nineteenth century consigned him to the nursery. In fact, it is likely that only adults may really understand his tales, especially his later ones.

With his impoverished origins and his strange personality, it seemed highly unlikely that Andersen would one day be found dining at the table of Danish king Christian VIII or receiving a knighthood from the king of Prussia. There were those who felt that his guiding motive as a writer was to be admired and loved by the upper crust of society. Be that as it may, his literary merit is unquestionable. He spent his old age not merely as a celebrat-

ed bohemian but also as a national institution. In 1867, he was made an honorary citizen of Odense, and, taking its cue from the fortune-teller's prediction that Andersen had recorded in his autobiography, the entire town was illuminated in his honor. When he died in 1875, his funeral service in the cathedral in Copenhagen was crowded with mourners, including members of the Danish royal family.

Bibliography

Andersen, Hans Christian. *The Fairy Tale of My Life*. Translated by W. Glyn Jones. New York: British Book Centre, 1954. Andersen's autobiography depicts his life as a beautiful fairy tale that affirmed the existence of a loving God who directed all things for the best. This translation features color illustrations.

Bredsdorff, Elias. *Hans Christian Andersen, The Story of His Life and Work (1805-75)*. London: Phaidon Press, and New York: Scribner, 1975. This is an indispensable, highly readable, and well-researched biography by a major Andersen scholar. A special section examines the fairy tales as works of great artistic merit that contribute to the mainstream of European literature. Among the photographs and drawings are some of Andersen's own illustrations.

Gronbech, Bo. *Hans Christian Andersen*. Boston: Twayne, 1980. Grobech provides a solid introduction to Andersen's life told in entertaining narrative style. The book includes studies of Andersen's fairy tales, his international influence, and his influence in the twentieth century. It can be read by the general reader as well as literary specialists.

Rossel, Sven Hakon, ed. *Hans Christian Andersen: Danish Writer and Citizen of the World*. Amsterdam: Rodopi, 1996. This scholarly collection of essays establishes Andersen as a major European writer of the nineteenth century. Special attention is given to his biography as well as his travel writing and fairy tales.

Spink, Reginald. *Hans Christian Andersen and His World*. London: Thames and Hudson, and New York: Putnam, 1972. This basic introduction to Andersen's life and times is written in a simple readable style and with considerable psychological acumen. The book contains many charming photographs and drawings, including some of Andersen's own art work.

Margaret Boe Birns

SUSAN B. ANTHONY

Born: February 15, 1820; Adams, Massachusetts
Died: March 13, 1906; Rochester, New York
Area of Achievement: Women's rights
Contribution: A gifted and relentless worker for feminist causes, Anthony was for five decades the preeminent voice and inspiration of the women's suffrage movement.

Early Life

Susan Brownwell Anthony was born on February 15, 1820, in Adams, Massachusetts, the second child of Daniel and Lucy Read Anthony. Her mother, a sullen, withdrawn woman, grudgingly accepted her domestic role as housewife and mother of six. The girl loved but pitied her mother, and learned from her more what to avoid than emulate. Her father, in contrast, always loomed large in his daughter's eyes. A radical Quaker, Daniel Anthony was liberal in creed and illiberal toward those who tolerated the social evils that he so adamantly despised. Strong-willed and independent of mind, Daniel Anthony taught his children to be firm in their convictions and to demonstrate their love for God by working for human betterment.

As an owner of a small cotton mill, Daniel Anthony had the means to provide for his daughter's education. A precocious child, Anthony took full advantage of her opportunities, first attending the village school and later receiving private instruction from a tutor hired by her father. At age seventeen, Anthony left with her older sister Guelma for a Quaker boarding school in Philadelphia. Anthony's seminary training, however, was cut short by the Panic of 1837. With mounting business debts, Daniel Anthony was forced to auction his cotton mill, homestead, furniture, and even his personal belongings, and to relocate as a dirt farmer on a small tract of land outside Rochester, New York.

In response to the family crisis, Susan Anthony left boarding school, secured a teaching position, and began sending half of her two-dollar weekly salary home to the family. For the next decade, Anthony remained in the classroom, instructing her pupils in the three R's, even as she augmented her own education with extensive reading and study. Intelligent yet unpretentious, Anthony matured into an athletic, tall, and slender woman with thick brown hair and warm blue eyes. Hardly the ugly, unsexed "battle-axe" her future enemies portrayed

her to be, Anthony was courted by several suitors and remained single largely because none of her admirers, in her opinion, equaled her father in character or conviction.

Like her father, Anthony was a reformer who yearned for a society free from the evils of slavery and alcoholism. An idealist but not a dreamer, Anthony worked actively in these reform efforts, serving during her twenties as president of the Canajoharie Daughters of Temperance. In 1849, at her father's request, Anthony resigned from teaching to take over management of the family farm near Rochester. This relocation enabled Daniel Anthony to devote his full attention to a new business venture (an insurance agency that eventually made him prosperous again). The move also allowed Anthony to commit herself more fully to reform activity.

Life's Work

While still a teacher in Canajoharie, Anthony read a newspaper account of a meeting in nearby Seneca Falls, where a group of sixty-eight women and thirty-two men issued a Declaration of Women's Rights. This declaration demanded free education, equality of economic opportunity, free speech, the right to participate in public affairs, and the right to vote. As a schoolteacher making only one-third the salary of her male colleagues, Anthony sympathized with many of these demands for equal rights. Her Quaker upbringing, however, had convinced her that no person should participate in a government that waged war or condoned slavery, and she was thus not yet ready to take up the cause of women's suffrage.

In 1851, while attending an antislavery lecture in Seneca Falls, Anthony met the renowned Elizabeth Cady Stanton. The two women developed an instant friendship which led to a strong partnership in reform work. Together they organized the Woman's State Temperance Society of New York and petitioned the state legislature for a prohibition law. On numerous occasions during the 1850's, Anthony left Rochester for Seneca Falls to care for Stanton's children while their mother was away on speaking tours.

While agreeing with Stanton on most issues, Anthony for several years refrained from embracing Stanton's call for women's suffrage. Gradually, however, the arrogance and disregard of many male reformers for the rights of women altered Anthony's view. Finally, in 1853, after the male delegates of the New York Woman's Temperance Society monopolized the annual convention and rudely ousted Stanton as president, Anthony declared her full allegiance to the women's crusade for equal rights and political equality.

Anthony's political conversion brought new life to the fledgling women's movement. An experienced worker willing to assume the time-consuming chores that no one else wanted, Anthony labored around the clock for feminist causes, organizing women into local associations, scheduling conventions and arranging speakers, seeking contributions, and paying administrative expenses. During the winter of 1854-1855, Anthony personally visited fifty-four of the sixty New York counties, collecting signatures in support of legal rights for married women. When the legislature failed to act, Anthony promised to return with petitions every year until the inequities were rectified. For five years the tireless Anthony kept her promise, and in 1860, following a stirring address by coworker Stanton, the New York legislature granted property and guardian rights to married women. Much to Anthony's and Stanton's dismay, however, two years later the same body repealed portions of the marriage reform bill. This setback confirmed what Anthony had been saying for a decade: Benevolent legislation alone was insufficient; women would be fully protected only when they enjoyed full political powers.

For Anthony and her associates, the decade of the 1860's was eventful but largely disappointing. Before the Civil War, Anthony campaigned hard for the American Anti-Slavery Society, and during the war she helped establish the Women's Loyalty League to lobby for a constitutional amendment that would abolish slavery and guarantee civil and political rights for all Americans. Yet, despite her lifelong commitment to black rights, after the war Anthony opposed both the wording of the Fourteenth Amendment, because it inserted the word "male" in reference to citizen's rights, and the Fifteenth Amendment, for its failure to include the word "sex" in protecting voting rights for all citizens. Berated by her former allies, who insisted that women must not endanger the long-awaited liberation of blacks with additional demands for women's rights, Anthony countered the accusations by asserting that if reformers linked these two great causes, then the moment in history called by some "the Negro's hour" could be the woman's hour as well. This controversy ultimately split the women's

movement. Following an explosive Equal Rights Association convention in 1869, Anthony and Stanton organized the National Woman Suffrage Association (a "for women only" organization committed to the passage of a national woman's suffrage amendment), while the more conservative reformers established the American Woman Suffrage Association (a rival body that focused its efforts at the state rather than the national level).

At this time, Anthony's commitment to feminist goals did not deter her from other reform activities. In 1868, Anthony organized the Working Woman's Association in a futile attempt to unionize woman workers and build female solidarity across class lines. In the same year, Anthony and Stanton allied themselves with the eccentric millionaire George Francis Train and began publishing a radical newspaper entitled *The Revolution*. On its masthead was the motto: "Principle, not policy; justice, not favors. Men, their rights, and nothing more: Women, their rights and nothing less." This paper, which opened its columns to editorials on greenback currency, divorce laws, prostitution, and a variety of other controversial issues, survived only two years, and left Anthony with a debt of ten thousand dollars. It took six years, but Anthony ultimately repaid the entire debt from income she gained delivering suffrage lectures on the Lyceum circuit. Following this experience, Anthony determined to disassociate herself from other controversial reforms and focus all of her energy on the crusade for woman's suffrage.

In 1872, Anthony gained national media attention when she registered and voted in the presidential election. Several weeks later, a federal marshal issued her an arrest warrant for illegal voting. While awaiting trial, Anthony went on a whirlwind tour delivering the lecture, "Is It a Crime for a U.S. Citizen to Vote?" Her defense was that the Fourteenth Amendment made her a citizen, and citizenship carried with it the right to vote. During her trial, the judge refused to allow her to testify on her own behalf, demanded the jury to render a guilty verdict, and fined her one hundred dollars. Outraged by this travesty of justice, thousands sent contributions to the NWSA treasury. Although she lost the trial, Anthony (who never paid the fine) won added respect for herself and her cause.

Anthony spent the last three decades of her life recruiting and training a new generation of suffragist leaders, including, among many others, Anna Howard Shaw and Carrie Chapman Catt. In 1889, at age sixty-nine, Anthony worked to secure a

merger of the rival NWSA and AWSA. Three years later, she accepted the presidency of the unified National American Woman Suffrage Association, and served in this capacity until 1900, when she passed her mantle of leadership onto her hand-picked successors. As honorary president emeritus, Anthony remained the dominant figure in the movement until the time of her death in 1906.

Summary

When Anthony joined the women's rights movement at age thirty-three, women held little social, professional, or educational standing. They were denied the right to vote, to hold office, or to be tried by their peers. As wives, they lost their legal individuality, having no rights to inherit property, keep earnings, sign contracts, or claim more than one-third of their husbands' estates. As mothers, they lacked legal custody or control over their own children. By the time of Anthony's death, however, eighty percent of American colleges, universities, and professional schools admitted women. In many states women had legal control over their own earnings and property and, in case of divorce, generally were awarded custody of their children. Although much discrimination remained, reform legislation along with advances in the medical treatment of women had increased the life expectancy of women from forty to fifty-one years. In four states, women enjoyed full suffrage rights, and in the majority of the remaining states, women voted in school or municipal elections.

Many of these changes were in part a consequence of the Industrial Revolution, which freed many women from a portion of their domestic chores, created new opportunities for employment, and provided increasing numbers with the wealth and leisure to sponsor reform work. The improved status of American women, however, was also a result of the heroic efforts of individuals who endured decades of hardship and ridicule in their quest for equal rights. For more than half a century, Anthony campaigned tirelessly for feminist goals. A radical visionary, the "Napoleon of Feminism" was also a shrewd, practical politician who did more than any other reformer to change the minds of men toward women, and of women toward themselves. Although vilified throughout much of her career, by the time of her death Anthony was the heroine of a second generation of suffragists, who in 1920 would win the victory she had fought so hard to achieve.

Bibliography

Anthony, Katharine S. *Susan B. Anthony: Her Personal History and Her Era*. New York: Doubleday, 1954. A detailed, although somewhat tedious, account of Anthony's career, with lengthy descriptions of her family ancestry in England, her parentage, and her many friends in the battle for women's rights.

Bryan, Florence H. *Susan B. Anthony: Champion of Women's Rights*. New York: Julian Messner, 1947. The best of the many biographies of Anthony geared for younger readers. Not overly fictionized.

Buhle, Mary Jo, and Paul Bulhe. *A Concise History of Woman Suffrage: Selections from the Classic Works of Stanton, Anthony, Gage and Harper*. Urbana: University of Illinois Press, 1978. An abridged volume of the basic sources of the women's suffrage movement. Provides useful selections from the writings of Anthony and other eminent suffrage leaders.

Dorr, Rheta L. *Susan B. Anthony: The Woman Who Changed the Mind of a Nation*. New York: Stokes, 1928. A dated, warmly partisan, and undocumented biography that portrays Anthony as a radical heroine. Weak coverage of Anthony's latter years. Despite its shortcomings, its lively prose makes this entertaining book worth reading.

Flexner, Eleanor. *Century of Struggle: The Woman's Rights Movement in the United States*. Rev. ed. Cambridge, Mass.: Harvard University Press, 1975. An overview of the women's rights movement that offers insights into the intellectual origins of American feminism. It remains the standard history of the suffrage crusade.

Harper, Ida H. *The Life and Work of Susan B. Anthony*. 3 vols. Indianapolis: Bowen-Merrill, 1898-1908. The authoritative biography, written with Anthony's assistance. The only source for numerous Anthony papers that were destroyed after its publication.

Kugler, Israel. "The Trade Union Career of Susan B. Anthony." *Labor History* 6 (Winter, 1961): 90-100. An interesting and informative account of a little-known aspect of Anthony's career as a reformer.

Lutz, Alma. *Susan B. Anthony: Rebel, Crusader, Humanitarian*. Boston: Beacon Press, 1959. A well-documented, straightforward biography. Informative, but like the other dated biographies, it makes no attempt to penetrate beyond the surface record of events.

Riegel, Robert. *American Feminists*, Lawrence: University of Kansas Press, 1963. This collection of biographical essays on pioneer feminists attempts to analyze the factors that contributed to the rise of American feminism. The sketch on Anthony accentuates her shortcomings, portraying her as physically, mentally, and historically inferior to Elizabeth Cady Stanton.

Sherr, Lynn. *Failure is Impossible: Susan B. Anthony in Her Own Words.* New York: Times Books, 1995. By examining interviews, diaries, personal letters, and scrapbooks, Sherr presents a personal look into Anthony's thoughts and motivations. Provides insight into the plans and strategies employed by Anthony to level the playing field for the "other half" of society.

Stanton, Elizabeth Cady, and Susan B. Anthony. *The Selected Papers of Elizabeth Cady Stanton and Susan B. Anthony, vol. 1: In the School of Anti-Slavery, 1840-1866.* Ann D. Gordon, ed. New Brunswick, N.J.: Rutgers University Press, 1997. First in a planned six-volume set documenting the interface between Stanton and Anthony. This volume covers their early interests in temperance, women's rights, and antislavery. Useful primary source for those interested in nineteenth-century reform movements.

Truman, Margaret. *Women of Courage.* New York: Morrow, 1976. A collection of biographical sketches of noted American women. The Anthony essay concentrates on her arrest and conviction for illegal voting in the 1872 presidential election.

Terry D. Bilhartz

JOHNNY APPLESEED

Born: September 26, 1774; Leominster, Massachusetts

Died: March 18 (?), 1845; Allen County, near Fort Wayne, Indiana

Area of Achievement: Horticulture

Contribution: By planting apple seeds at new settlements in Ohio and Indiana, Johnny Appleseed laid the foundation for orchards as part of agricultural development of the Midwest.

Early Life

Johnny Appleseed, born John Chapman, was the son of Nathaniel and Elizabeth Chapman, modest inhabitants of the Worcester County, Massachusetts, town of Leominster. Chapman's mother died when he was two, and his father served in the American Revolution and remarried when he returned from the army. He then moved his family to the vicinity of Springfield, Massachusetts.

As soon as he was grown, Chapman yielded to a deep-seated urge to wander, on foot, through the frontier regions of the new republic. He headed first for western Pennsylvania, where he was listed in the 1801 census as a resident of Venango County.

Once the conflict with American Indians in the Ohio territory was resolved by the victory of General Anthony Wayne at the Battle of Fallen Timbers in 1794 and the Greenville Treaty of 1795, settlers began to pour into the area. Chapman was far from the first to settle there, but he had made forays into Ohio—mostly to the valley of the Muskingum River—in the early years of the nineteenth century. By 1809 he had already moved his base to Ohio, where he bought two town lots in the town of Mount Vernon, which was to be his base for the next twenty years.

Life's Work

Around the beginning of the nineteenth century, Chapman had the notion of gathering apple seeds from the cider presses that were ubiquitous in every frontier community and planting them on uninhabited land along the banks of a stream or a river. Wherever he found a productive plot, he planted apple seeds and created nurseries from which he later offered seedlings to the surrounding settlers. Most of his nurseries were located on the floodplains of the many streams that flowed southward toward the Muskingum River, which, in turn,

flowed farther southward until it reached the Ohio River. Chapman's methodology consisted of locating a suitable planting site in the early spring and planting the seeds that he carried with him in a sack. Before moving on, he would locate a nearby settler and arrange for that individual to keep an eye on his new nursery and to arrange for the subsequent transplantation of seedlings to the clearings of the new settlements.

It has often been objected that because apples do not "grow true" from seed but can only be properly propagated by grafting scions or new twigs from an existing tree onto the "root stock" of a smaller tree, Chapman's efforts were those of an itinerant rustic. There were, however, both practical and ideological reasons for Chapman's methodology. According to legend, when someone tried to convince Chapman of the superiority of grafting, he replied, "They can improve the apple in that way but that is only a device of man, and it is wicked to cut up trees that way. The correct method is to select good seeds and plant them in good ground and

God only can improve the apples." For Chapman, then, grafting was artificial, and planting seeds was the natural way to expand orchards.

On the practical level, securing and carrying scions from established orchards on the East Coast over frontier roads posed real problems. Keeping the scions moist and viable over the long periods needed to make the trek was difficult, and they required far more space than seeds. It had, however, been done. In the first years of the nineteenth century, General Rufus Putnam had brought scions from the famous Putnam Orchards of Connecticut and developed a substantial quantity of grafted trees at the mouth of the Muskingum River near Marietta, Ohio. By 1808 the area boasted 774 acres of apple orchards composed largely of grafted trees.

Despite the criticism, there was still practical merit in Chapman's technique. Most apples in the frontier settlements wound up as cider, and the apples produced by ordinary seedlings were perfectly adequate for this purpose. Cider was drunk in huge quantities by the early settlers. Some of it went on to become hard cider, or apple brandy, which also enjoyed widespread popularity. For such purposes, wild apples—the kind produced by trees grown from seed—were fully adequate, and occasionally the throw of the genetic dice would produce a tree bearing outstanding apples.

The result of Chapman's efforts was that an apple orchard existed on virtually every new farm created in the Ohio wilderness. The apples were used for cider, dried to make fruit that could last through the winter, or turned into apple butter. Those who had cold cellars could keep some apples fresh through the winter. The part of the crop that wound up as apple brandy was drunk throughout the region, and some even found its way down the Ohio River to New Orleans, Louisiana, where it had commercial value.

After the war of 1812, Chapman became an itinerant peddler of his seedlings, for he had nurseries throughout central Ohio. He had also become a convert to the religious philosophy of Emanuel Swedenborg, who stressed the reality of the spirit as opposed to its bodily incarnation. This philosophy appealed to such a fervent lover of nature as Chapman, and he combined peddling his seedlings with pushing Swedenborg's ideas. Thanks in large part to his missionary efforts, a number of Swedenborgian communities arose in the area, and Chapman occasionally preached at such gatherings. He distributed tracts at every isolated farmhouse and often discussed the ideas they contained with the inhabitants.

Also after the war, when settlement of Ohio resumed, Chapman began buying land in sizeable pieces rather than just the town lots of Mount Vernon. He began leasing school lots for ninety-nine years, with no rent due for the first three, during which the lessee had to clear three acres and build a cabin. The rent that became due, annually, after the first three years was supposed to provide funding for schools. At one time or another, Chapman had leases on at least five parcels of 160 acres each. Although he eventually lost all these leases through failure to pay the annual rent, he did clear the necessary three acres and build a cabin on several, and he planted a nursery on at least one. A major reason that Chapman was unable to retain ownership of the school-lot leases was the depression that hit the country in the early 1820's. The experience caused him to scale back his acquisitions and occasionally lease a small, one-half acre plot from a settler in order to plant a nursery on the site.

At the same time, sensing that the frontier had moved westward, Chapman began to explore the section of northwestern Ohio that had previously been reserved for American Indians. In this region, the Maumee River flows northward, while across the border in Indiana the Wabash River flows southward; the watersheds of the two rivers are separated by only a small ridge of land. By 1834 Chapman had again begun to purchase land in large blocks in the Fort Wayne, Indiana, area. In that year he purchased one forty-two-acre plot and one ninety-nine-acre plot. In 1836 he was back at the Fort Wayne Land Office to purchase two more parcels, one of eighteen acres and another of seventy-four. In 1838 he bought forty acres northwest of Fort Wayne. Much of the remainder of his life was spent developing these Indiana holdings with the assistance of his brother-in-law, William Broom, who, with his wife Persis, had followed Chapman first to Ohio and then to Indiana.

Chapman first ventured into Indiana only in the spring and summer. In the fall he would return to Ohio, often staying with his sister and brother-in-law, the Brooms, over the winter. By the late 1830's, however, he had transferred his activities almost wholly to Indiana, returning only occasionally and briefly to Ohio. It was in Fort Wayne that he died in March of 1845.

Summary

The legend of Johnny Appleseed began during Chapman's lifetime but ballooned after his death. A major boost to the legend, hitherto largely an oral tradition, was the publication, in 1871, of an article in *Harper's Magazine*. After the article, many people came forward to add anecdotes to the legend. Prior to that time, Chapman had been largely remembered in horticultural circles. T. S. Humerickhouse published an article praising Chapman as a nurseryman in *Hovey's Magazine of Horticulture* in 1846. In the same year, Henry Howe, an author of local histories, began producing a history of Ohio's counties in which Chapman figured. In 1858 the first fictional account of Chapman appeared in James F. McGaw's novel *Philip Seymour*. In 1904 a novel entitled *The Quest of John Chapman* by Newell Dwight Hillis ascribed Chapman's itinerant lifestyle to blighted love. Johnny Appleseed has also appeared in a number of poems, the most famous of which is Vachel Lindsay's "In Praise of Johnny Appleseed."

Various memorials to Johnny Appleseed have been erected over the years. Fort Wayne created a Johnny Appleseed Commission, and its secretary, Robert C. Harris, researched some of the historical details of his life. In 1935 the Optimist Club of Fort Wayne erected a monument at the site where Chapman is believed to have been buried. His career in Ohio is memorialized by monuments in Ashland, Mansfield, and the vicinity of Mifflin. The city of Leominster, whose public librarian, Florence Wheeler, uncovered the details of Chapman's birth there, set up a monument (later taken down to prevent vandalism) and now has a large sign proclaiming Leominster as the "birthplace of Johnny Appleseed." Commemorative celebrations have been held in both Fort Wayne and Leominster.

Bibliography

Hurt, Douglas. *The Ohio Frontier: Crucible of the Old Northwest, 1726-1830*. Bloomington: Indiana University Press, 1996. Hurt, author of other scholarly books on American agriculture, provides a comprehensive account of the early days of settlement in Ohio. The book provides the setting for Chapman's early nurseries and gives some account of Chapman's career.

Jones, Robert Leslie. *History of Agriculture in Ohio*. Kent, Ohio: Kent State University Press, 1983. Jones places Chapman's work in the context of agricultural development in Ohio.

Lindsay, Vachel. *Johnny Appleseed and Other Poems*. New York: Macmillan, 1928. This book contains Lindsay's poetic tribute to Johnny Appleseed.

Price, Robert. *Johnny Appleseed, Man and Myth*. Bloomington: Indiana University Press, 1954. Price devoted many years to searching out the historical truth about Johnny Appleseed, and it is reported in this book. Price separates truth from myth and reviews the documentary records of Chapman's life, notably his numerous land purchases. Indispensable for a historical appreciation of Johnny Appleseed.

Thoreau, Henry David. *Wild Apples*. Boston: Houghton Mifflin, 1923. Another lover of the wilderness explains the potential of the wild apple trees that still dot the landscape.

Nancy M. Gordon

MATTHEW ARNOLD

Born: December 24, 1822; Laleham, England
Died: April 15, 1888; Dingle Bank, Liverpool, England
Area of Achievement: Literature
Contribution: One of the finest elegiac poets in the English language, Arnold was also Victorian Great Britain's greatest literary and cultural critic.

Early Life

Matthew Arnold was born on December 24, 1822, in Laleham, England, a small town on the Thames near London. His father, Thomas Arnold, conducted a school there; his mother, Mary Penrose Arnold, was an Anglican clergyman's daughter. The Arnolds were a closely knit family; Matthew, the second of nine children, was especially devoted to his older sister Jane. He had a close relationship with his mother until her death in 1873, and his father's influence on him was crucial. In 1828, the Arnold family moved to Rugby, and in the years that followed, Thomas Arnold became famous as an educational and religious leader. As Headmaster of Rugby School, Thomas Arnold instituted reforms designed to regenerate his students' moral, spiritual, and intellectual lives and to prepare them to become responsible leaders in a rapidly changing society. A notable writer on the religious and political issues of the day, Thomas Arnold was a proponent of a broadly Christian and unified national Church. Throughout his career, Thomas Arnold also devoted himself to the study and teaching of history. This devotion, along with his ethical seriousness, his activity as an educational reformer, and his engagement in religious controversies, helped to shape his son Matthew's interests and thinking throughout his adult life.

In his boyhood and youth, however, Matthew Arnold did not prove to be a particularly devoted or distinguished student. Because he failed to progress under private tutorship at home, he was sent away for two years (1831-1832) to his uncle's strict school at Laleham. There, he felt exiled from his family. When he returned home to study with a private tutor, he became a somewhat more conscientious—though certainly not brilliant—student, and he began to develop a love of poetry. His family and his environment helped this love to grow. In 1831, the Arnolds had begun to make summer trips to the Lake District, where the poets Robert Southey and William Wordsworth lived, and in

1833-1834, they built a summer residence at Fox How, near Wordsworth's home. Thus the Wordsworths and the Arnolds became friends. Wordsworth's poetry eventually was to influence Arnold's at least as much as any other English poet's; many of Arnold's poems directly echo or respond to Wordsworth. A significant part of the drama of Arnold's career as a poet and critic, in fact, arises from his sad realization that, whether for personal or cultural reasons, he was unable to speak to the Victorian age as Wordsworth had to the Romantic: "But where will Europe's latter hour/ Again find Wordsworth's healing power?"

After spending a year at Winchester, the public school his father had attended, Arnold came back to Rugby School, where he studied from 1837 to 1841. There, in 1840, he met Arthur Hugh Clough (1819-1861), a brilliant scholar and accomplished poet who was to become his close friend at Oxford. This important friendship continued until Clough's death. In his conversations and correspondence with Clough, Arnold began to develop and articulate many of his ideas, feelings, and values relating to poetry and modern life. In his letters, Arnold criticized Clough's poetry as overly topical and intellectual, but he also found fault with his own poems. His chief target, however, was his age: "Reflect too, as I cannot but do here more and more, in spite of all the nonsense some people talk, how deeply *unpoetical* the age and all one's surroundings are. Not unprofound, not ungrand, not unmoving:—but *unpoetical*." Arnold wrote these words in 1849, and in much of his later work as a critic, he would proceed from that point of view.

A decade earlier, however, when he was still a student at Rugby, no one would have predicted such concern on his part, least of all his father, who worried constantly about Arnold's apparent carelessness about his studies. A normal adolescent, Arnold chose to react against his father's high seriousness by devoting much time to fishing, hunting, enjoying himself with casual acquaintances, and dressing in elegant clothes. He adopted the insouciant air of a dandy at Rugby, but his mask of sophistication slipped occasionally. Beneath the mask one could find, on the one hand, a prankster: During his final year at Rugby, having been asked to stand behind his father's chair, he decided to take advantage of the occasion by making faces at the other students. On the other hand, he managed

to write a fair amount of poetry at Rugby, to win a prize for his long poem "Alaric at Rome" in 1840, and, ultimately, to win a scholarship to Balliol College at Oxford, where he began his studies on October 15, 1841.

During his university years, Arnold continued much in the same pattern he had set at Rugby. Elegant and lively, he enjoyed himself immensely and took a casual attitude toward his studies: "The life of Oxford," he wrote in 1851, was "the *freest* and most delightful part, perhaps, of my life, when . . . I shook off all the bonds and formality of the place." At this time, however, several people and events helped move him toward a steadier, more purposeful course in life. He was influenced by the thinking of John Henry Newman and by his father's opposition to the Oxford Movement, through which Newman and his intellectual party seemed to be leading the Church of England toward Roman Catholicism. Thomas Arnold, appointed to a professorship of history at Oxford in 1841, died suddenly in June, 1842, and Matthew Arnold felt the loss deeply. His friendship with Clough strengthened after his father's death, and together

they read and were impressed by the social thought of Thomas Carlyle. In 1843, Arnold won the prestigious Newdigate Prize for his poem "Cromwell," which reflected his feelings about his father's death. This award led him to decide that he wanted seriously to be a poet. He began writing the poems that would eventually appear in 1849 in his first volume of verse, *The Strayed Reveller and Other Poems*.

Arnold's intensified focus on writing poetry did not lead him to amend his careless study habits. He left Oxford in 1844 with a second-class degree after a mediocre performance on his final examinations. His second-class degree embarrassed him and disappointed his family; he redeemed himself after a year of teaching and study at Rugby by winning, as his father had done years before, a fellowship at Oriel College, Oxford. There, he read widely in philosophy and literature and developed broad intellectual interests: He read extensively in German literature and philosophy, admired the novels of George Sand, whom he called upon during a trip to France and Switzerland in the summer of 1846, and read the *Bhagavadgita* and other Oriental writings.

In April, 1847, Arnold moved to London to become the private secretary to Lord Landsdowne, then president of council in the Liberal government. In 1848 and 1849, he was devoted to the beautiful and gifted Mary Claude, whom he fictionalized as "Marguerite" in "Switzerland," a sequence of lyrics tracing the course of a failed love affair.

Life's Work

The twenty-seven poems in Arnold's first published collection, *The Strayed Reveller and Other Poems*, strike a note that is predominantly melancholy, lonely, and introspective. Arnold's family and friends were very surprised, because they had heretofore known him as a debonair, lighthearted, worldly young man. Revealing through these poems a radical split between his outward behavior and inner feelings, Arnold himself exemplified one of the major themes of his poetry: the divided self.

In most of his major works, whether in poetry or prose, in fact, Arnold addresses questions of separation and division. His poems tend to define breaches; his critical prose defines, analyzes, and attempts to heal them. His poems articulate the loneliness, the confusion, the sense of disintegration that occurs when individuals feel alienated from nature, from their personal or cultural pasts, from God, or from other people—whether through conflicting aims and values, failed attempts at love, or death.

Yet neither his poems nor his prose were written in a vacuum. In 1851, Arnold became an inspector of schools, and for the next thirty-five years, he was intensely occupied with his travels in England and on the Continent, visiting schools and teacher-training colleges, administering oral and written examinations, and writing reports for the government on school conditions. This work was very demanding: In a single year (1855), for example, he visited 280 schools and institutions and examined 465 teachers and twenty thousand students. At the same time, he was building a family, to which he was deeply devoted: His appointment as inspector of schools made it economically feasible for him to marry Frances Lucy Wightman, a judge's daughter, in 1851; they had four sons and two daughters between 1852 and 1866.

Arnold wrote most of his major poetry between 1847 and 1853. His most important volume of poetry, *Empedocles on Etna*, appeared in 1852. Its title poem is now regarded by many as his major poetic achievement, although "Dover Beach" is his most well-known poem. *Empedocles on Etna* dramatizes a Greek philosopher of the fifth century B.C. who chose to take his own life rather than face depression and spiritual death as a result of the split between his skeptical intellect and his feelings. Arnold decided to exclude this work from the new edition of his poems published in 1853, and in his famous preface to that volume, he explained his reasons for doing so. Arnold asserted that poetry must not only interest but also "inspirit and rejoice the reader"; it must "convey a charm, and infuse delight." By depicting "suffering that finds no vent in action," *Empedocles on Etna*, he found, produced not joy but pain. Arnold went on in his preface to theorize about the nature of poetry, to discuss the shortcomings of the poetry of his day, and to recommend ways of addressing these defects—most notably through the study of classical Greek literature and the adoption of its principles.

The 1853 preface marks a watershed in Arnold's career as a writer. From this point onward, most of his major work was in the form of critical prose on literary, cultural, and religious topics. "Poetry," he wrote, "is a criticism of life"; it expresses what is best in human beings and helps to civilize them. Crucial to poetry's important office is the cultivation of the critical spirit, which Arnold defined as "a disinterested endeavor to learn and propagate the best that is known and thought in the world, and thus to establish a current of fresh and true ideas." Arnold himself became his century's finest exemplar of that spirit. In works such as *On Translating Homer* (1861) and the two series of *Essays in Criticism* (1865 and 1888), Arnold attempted, in witty and lucid prose, to persuade his readers to combat their British insularity and contemporary narrowness by reading the literature of other places and times. He opposed the contemporary tendencies toward transitory topicality, subjectivity, vulgar shallowness, and concern with decorative fragments and advocated the classical values of universality, objectivity, moral depth, wholeness, and stylistic restraint. He was a great comparative critic, and was aware, as his father before him had been, of the need to reevaluate constantly the present in the light of the past, and the past in the light of the present.

A number of Arnold's essays on literary topics were first delivered as lectures at Oxford University, where he was appointed for two five-year terms as professor of poetry. Among these works, "On the Modern Element in Literature" is of special note. He was required to deliver three lectures a year, and he was the first to give the lectures in English rather than Latin.

At the same time, Arnold continued his grueling career as a school inspector, and this work lent experiential authority to his criticism on educational, social, and political topics. His central achievement in that area is *Culture and Anarchy* (1869), a series of lectures on British political, social, and cultural life. In these lectures, he presented his idea of culture as "Sweetness and Light," a classical ideal of human perfection balancing beauty and intelligence; he criticized the British upper, middle, and lower classes ("Barbarians, Philistines and Populace"); he contrasted and called for a proper balance of the two human tendencies of "Hebraism" (moral awareness and strictness of conscience) and "Hellenism" (the critical urge to "see things as they really are"); and he attacked the idea that freedom consists merely in "Doing As One Likes." Although a number of his contemporaries chafed at Arnold's strictures in his cultural criticism (one reviewer called him an "elegant Jeremiah") he became increasingly influential in his day. *Culture and Anarchy* has also had an important influence on twentieth century social thinkers.

Arnold turned next to writing and lecturing about religion. He published his thoughts in four books: *St. Paul and Protestantism* (1870), *Literature and Dogma* (1873), *God and the Bible* (1875), and *Last Essays on Church and Religion* (1877). The inquiries of nineteenth century biologists and geologists, rationalist philosophers, and biblical scholars had helped create a crisis of religious faith in the minds of many Christians. The Bible no longer appeared to be literally true, and much religious dogma had been called into question. In the light of these developments, Arnold's effort in his writings on religion was to define an intellectually honest approach to Christian faith, to preserve the spirit, if not adhere strictly to the letter (codified dogma and biblical fundamentalism), of Christianity, and to reassert the vital connection between faith and morality: "Religion is that which binds and holds us to the practice of righteousness."

In the late 1870's and early 1880's, Arnold wrote more essays about politics and literature; "The Study of Poetry," one of his most famous essays on literature, appeared in 1880. He made two visits to the United States: a lecture tour in 1883-1884 and a visit to his daughter, who had married an American, in the summer of 1886, just after he retired from school inspecting. Of all of his prose writings, the one he wanted most to be remembered for was *Discourses in America* (1885), three lectures from his tour: "Numbers: Or, The Majority and the Remnant," "Literature and Science," and "Emerson."

Arnold died of a heart attack in a suburb of Liverpool on April 15, 1888, at the age of sixty-five. He was buried at Laleham, the town where he was born, next to the graves of three sons who had died early. He was survived by his wife, Fanny Lucy, who died in 1901, and by two daughters and a son.

Summary

In an 1859 letter, Matthew Arnold wrote:

> My poems represent . . . the main movement of mind of the last quarter of a century. . . . It might be fairly urged that I have less poetical sentiment than Tennyson, and less intellectual vigour and abundance than Browning; yet, because I have perhaps more of a fusion of the two than either of them, and have more regularly applied that fusion to the main line of modern development, I am likely enough to have my turn, as they have had theirs.

Arnold's self-estimate was prescient. His poetry articulates the problems and feelings of an age that is modern, and much of it is remarkably relevant to twentieth century society. Among Victorian poets,

his importance is surpassed only by that of Alfred Tennyson and Robert Browning.

Arnold's legacy as a critic is even more significant. More than anyone else in the nineteenth century, he helped shape the course of literary studies and values in the modern university. His cultural and religious criticism has also been very influential. It continues to foster intellectual curiosity, a humanistic outlook, and deep moral awareness. His lucid and urbane style and tone have established him as one of the great masters of English prose.

Bibliography

Arnold, Matthew. *The Complete Prose Works of Matthew Arnold*. Edited by R. H. Super. 11 vols. Ann Arbor: University of Michigan Press, 1960-1977. The standard edition of Arnold's prose. Includes comprehensive critical and explanatory notes.

———. *Letters of Matthew Arnold, 1848-1888*. Edited by G. W. E. Russell. 2 vols. London and New York: Macmillan, 1895. The standard edition of Arnold's letters. It is not complete, however, and many of the letters are abridged.

———. *The Letters of Matthew Arnold to Arthur Hugh Clough*. Edited by Howard F. Lowry. London: Oxford University Press, and New York: Milford, 1932. These letters are an important record of Arnold's friendship with Clough; in them Arnold develops many of his ideas about poetry and life in the nineteenth century.

———. *The Poems of Matthew Arnold*. Edited by Kenneth Allott. 2d ed. London and New York: Longman, 1979. The second edition is the first fully annotated edition of Arnold's poems. Includes previously unpublished material. The poems are arranged by order of composition, and the editor includes informative headnotes about the composition, publication, and historical and biographical backgrounds of each poem.

Bush, Douglas. *Matthew Arnold: A Survey of His Poetry and Prose*. New York and London: Macmillan, 1971. A very good introduction to Arnold's life and works.

Culler, A. Dwight. *Imaginative Reason: The Poetry of Matthew Arnold*. New Haven, Conn.: Yale University Press, 1966. The best study of Arnold's poetry.

Honan, Park. *Matthew Arnold: A Life*. London: Weidenfeld and Nicolson, and New York: McGraw-Hall, 1981. The most comprehensive biography of Arnold. Includes much heretofore unpublished information about Arnold and his family drawn from unpublished letters, journals, and diaries.

Neff, D. S. "The Times, the Crimean War, and 'Stanzas from the Grande Chartreuse.' " *Papers on Language and Literature* 33, no. 2 (Spring 1997). Theorizes that Arnold's use of Achilles in his "Stanzas from the Grande Chartreuse" was an allusion to the British commander (Crimean War), Lord Fitzroy James Henry Somerset Raglan who, like Achilles, Arnold apparently viewed as the victim of unjust public perceptions.

Stone, Donald D. *Communications with the Future: Matthew Arnold in Dialogue.* Ann Arbor: University of Michigan Press, 1997. The author argues Arnold's relevance in contemporary times as a proponent of open-mindedness, as opposed to his customary labeling as an elitist. Stone's fresh approach engages Arnold in conversation with a number of important modern individuals such as Henry James, Friedrich Nietzsche, Hans-Georg Gadamer, and William James.

———. "Matthew Arnold and the Pragmatics of Hebraism and Hellenism." *Poetics Today 19,* no. 2 (Summer 1998). Discusses Arnold's views on the Hellenic (or critical) spirit, including its emphasis on objectivity and lack of bias.

Tinker, C. B., and H. F. Lowry. *The Poetry of Matthew Arnold: A Commentary.* London and New York: Oxford University Press, 1940. A useful companion to Arnold's poems, including interpretation and information on sources and backgrounds.

Trilling, Lionel. *Matthew Arnold.* London: Allen and Unwin, and New York: Norton, 1939. Trilling calls his study "a biography of Arnold's mind." It is the best account of Arnold's ideas and career.

Eileen T. Johnston

THOMAS ARNOLD

Born: June 13, 1795; Cowes, Isle of Wight, England

Died: June 12, 1842; Rugby, Warwickshire, England

Areas of Achievement: Education and history

Contribution: Arnold changed British education by his reforms at Rugby School.

Early Life

Thomas Arnold was born in 1795 at Cowes, on the Isle of Wight. He was educated at home in his early years and was then sent to the school in Warminster, Wiltshire, and later to the great public school at Winchester. Arnold did very well in these schools, although he did display a youthful rebelliousness. In 1810, he began his university education at Corpus Christi College, Oxford. Arnold was enchanted by Oxford, and after three years of intense study, he received a first class degree in humane letters in 1814 at the age of nineteen. His success at Oxford was followed by a fellowship at Oriel College, Oxford, and Arnold looked forward to a career as a don. At twenty-four, however, he fell in love, and with a professorship many years away, he had to resign himself to becoming a schoolmaster, taking in private pupils at Laleham. The school was a success, and Arnold was happy with the school and the large family surrounding him. In 1827, Arnold's great opportunity came when he was elected headmaster at Rugby School. His application for the position was supported by Dr. Edward Hawkins, the provost of Oriel, who predicted in a letter that Arnold would "change the face of education all through the public schools of England." The public schools (the equivalent of private schools in the United States) at that time were notorious for floggings by the masters and the lawlessness of the pupils; they were described by the Reverend Mr. Bowlder as "the very seats and nurseries of vice." As Dr. Hawkins suggested, Arnold was to change all that.

Arnold was a young man, only thirty-two, when he became headmaster at Rugby. Yet he was a man who had boundless energy and the assurance that he could transform the former nurseries of vice into places where a "really Christian education" was the aim. Arnold experienced moments of doubt about Christianity in his early years, just as he had been a rebel earlier, but those doubts and that rebelliousness were put aside as he confidently began to take charge at Rugby. Lytton Strachey describes the Arnold of this period as a man whose "outward appearance was the index of his inward character: everything about him denoted energy, earnestness, and the best intentions."

Life's Work

Rugby School had declined from a high of 381 pupils to a low of 123 when Arnold became headmaster. He planned to reverse that trend and put his educational ideas into practice. The first thing that he did was to make the whole sixth form (seniors) praepositors (prefects). The school became a republic, and the boys were to be responsible for their own government. In addition, Arnold cultivated the boys in the sixth form and through them changed the tone of the school. The former rowdiness was replaced by a mood of piety and respectability. In addition, Arnold's sermons and presence made the boys both fear and respect him, and they tried to live up to the ideal he set for them. Nothing less than total commitment would do.

Arnold's next major reform was to raise the status and salary of the undermasters. By this move, he turned them into a professional corps and replaced the earlier brutality and carelessness with dedication. The annual salaries of the undermasters rose from about 125 to five hundred pounds, so Arnold attracted some of the most skilled and effective teachers to Rugby. As a result, Rugby boys began impressing others by their serious demeanor and their success in the Schools exams at Oxford and Cambridge. In turn, Rugby became more popular and the decline in the number of students was reversed.

Arnold did not, however, make major reforms in the curriculum of the school. He maintained the emphasis on Latin and Greek texts and resisted any attempt to add science to the curriculum. He stated his educational ideal succinctly: "Surely, the one thing needful for a Christian and an Englishman to study is Christian and moral and political philosophy." That aim was achieved by the study of the Greek and Roman classics, not science or modern languages; Arnold even taught English history through those Greek and Roman texts. The study of science might be suitable, even useful, for the masses, but Greek and Latin remained the one thing needful for the future governors of the country and its far-flung empire. Arnold did, however, help to standardize the teaching of Latin and Greek by proposing a headmasters' conference and uniform textbooks.

Arnold did not approve of the incessant flogging which took place in the public schools of the time. He believed that it degraded both pupil and master, and he preferred to expel a boy rather than flog him. He did not, however, eliminate flogging altogether at Rugby. In a letter, he was proud to announce that he had flogged only seven boys during half of one school year. Arnold had few illusions about young boys, and he did not believe that they were "innocent." They were victims of Original Sin, and the evil within them had to be exorcised in order to make them display "a more manly and Christian standard of duty." This sense of duty was extended from the classroom to the playing fields, as can be seen in a novel written by a Rugby "old boy," Thomas Hughes: *Tom Brown's School Days* (1857).

Arnold had a strong belief in social reform and progress, and these views led to some conflicts with the more conservative parents of the boys at Rugby. Although Arnold's belief in the necessity of an established Church and an aristocracy was hardly radical, his approval of the Reform Bill of 1832 and his essays and sermons disturbed many of the parents. As T. W. Bamford has noted: "Inevitably, one of them was moved to write a letter of protest to the local paper claiming that Arnold, as a Headmaster, ought to be non-political." That letter was followed by many others, and a campaign against Arnold began to gather supporters. Arnold survived this campaign but continued to have strong opposition to his rule at Rugby.

The next controversy in which Arnold became involved was the Oxford movement. The movement began with the writings of John Keble, who wished to challenge the right of the state to appoint bishops in the Anglican Church. Keble saw the Church as an Apostolic institution rather than one controlled by the secular arm. E. B. Pusey and John Henry Newman joined the Oxford movement and published a number of tracts supporting this position. Arnold's Christianity was rooted in the life and example of Jesus Christ, and the Oxford movement struck at his first principles. As he said in a letter to one of his pupils, "The moral fault . . . is in the idolatry—the setting up some idea . . . and then putting it in place of Christ." Arnold, therefore, felt compelled to oppose the movement in

print, and he published "The Oxford Malignants" in *The Edinburgh Review*. In that essay, he described those in the Oxford movement as "malignant fanatics" and accused them of "moral wickedness." Because of Arnold's tone as much as his content, he was attacked by the conservative press; one newspaper asked if the trustees would appoint a headmaster who wrote "in such a style as this." One of the trustees did ask Arnold if he were the author of such an article, but Arnold refused to answer and said that his private life and opinions were his own business. There was even a vote by the trustees on retaining Arnold, but the tie vote was not enough to oust him, and he remained headmaster. He did lose a bishopric, however, because of this incident; he was the top man on the list, but after the prime minister read Arnold's essay, he believed that Arnold was too controversial a figure to be appointed a bishop.

Arnold found relief from the burdens of his position as headmaster in the Lake Country of northern England, which has been celebrated by William Wordsworth. In fact, Arnold's summer home, Fox How, was close to Wordsworth's home, and they often met and talked. Arnold often invited his sixth form students to visit him at Fox How, and while they were there, they saw not the stern headmaster but the nature-loving human being. Arnold's teaching function did not stop in the Lake Country. He spoke of showing his students "the mountains and dales, a great point in education . . . to those who only know the central or southern counties of England."

Arnold was also involved in scholarly work while he was headmaster. He published a three-volume edition of Thucydides and a three-volume (the third volume, however, was left unfinished) *History of Rome* (1838-1843). Arnold wanted to write a Roman history that would oppose the anti-Christian attitude in Edward Gibbon's great *History of the Decline and Fall of the Roman Empire* (1776-1788). For these scholarly achievements and his Liberal politics, Arnold was appointed Regius Professor of Modern History in 1841. He continued as headmaster of Rugby and lectured at Oxford when he could arrange it. He returned to Rugby full-time in 1842 and was pleased to see that the school had continued to increase in reputation and enrollment. He fell ill, however, in June of that year and died on June 12, 1842, at the early age of forty-seven. His reputation did not decline as a result of his early death; his pupils and disciples continued and enhanced the Arnold legend. Essays in the *Quarterly Review* and Arthur Penrhyn Stanley's *Life and Correspondence of Dr. Arnold* (1844) gave support to the earlier claim of Dr. Hawkins, and it became clear to all that Arnold had reformed not only Rugby School but also the whole public school system.

Summary

Thomas Arnold's specific reforms did change and improve the public schools in England. Yet Arnold's insistence that a Rugby education be Christian and emphasize a sense of duty was, perhaps, even more important. The whole tone of the school was altered, as was the relationship of student and master. After Arnold's death, new public schools such as Marlborough and Wellington were founded on Arnoldian principles. Older schools such as Repton and Winchester also changed their tone and became more like Rugby. In addition, several of Arnold's old praepositors became headmasters at such prestigious public schools as Harrow. The Arnold model became the model for nearly all the public schools in England and for many of the most important preparatory schools and universities in the United States.

Arnold was very much a man of his age. He believed, as many Victorians did, in progress. All that was needed to create progress was to reform certain institutions in the society. Arnold died too young to see his concept of reform and an ideal Christian state be dashed by the discoveries of Charles Darwin and the doubt and cynicism that plagued many Victorians, including his famous son, Matthew. What Arnold attempted and partially achieved, however, remains impressive. Matthew Arnold's poem on the death of his father, "Rugby Chapel," says it best:

But thou would'st not *alone* Be saved, my father! *alone* Conquer and come to thy goal, Leaving the rest

in the wild. We were weary, and we Fearful, and we in our march Fain to drop down and die. Still thou turnedst, and still Beckonedst the trembler, and still-Gavest the weary thy hand.

Bibliography

Arnold, Thomas. *Thomas Arnold on Education*. Edited by T. W. Bamford. Cambridge: Cambridge University Press, 1970. A very good brief introduction to Arnold's religious, social, and educational views with a fine selection of Arnold's writings on education.

Bamford, T. W. *The Rise of the Public Schools*. London: Nelson, 1967. A detailed study of public schools since 1837; especially good on Rugby and Arnold.

———. *Thomas Arnold*. London: Cresset Press, 1960. The best available intellectual biography of Arnold. Critically surveys his ideas and the controversies in which he engaged.

Strachey, Lytton. *Eminent Victorians*. New York: Putnam, and London: Chatto and Windus, 1918. An amusing if somewhat inaccurate study of Arnold's life; the insights are marred by the sarcasm.

Willey, Basil. "Thomas Arnold." In *Nineteenth Century Studies*. London: Chatto and Windus, and New York: Columbia University Press, 1949. A sensitive essay on various aspects of Arnold, including his love for the Lake Country.

Wymer, Norman. *Dr. Arnold of Rugby*. London: Hale, 1953; Westport, Conn.: Greenwood Press, 1970. An uncritical examination of Arnold's life and influence; the best book on Arnold the man.

Zemka, Sue. "Spiritual authority and the Life of Thomas Arnold." *Victorian Studies 38,* no. 3 (Spring 1995). Discusses the negative results of Arnold's attempts to establish the Bible's importance and historical significance.

James Sullivan

CHESTER A. ARTHUR

Born: October 5, 1829; Fairfield, Vermont
Died: November 18, 1886; New York, New York
Areas of Achievement: Education, law, and politics
Contribution: Arthur's presidency, virtually free of corruption, comforted a nation grieving over the death of President James A. Garfield, maintained peace and order, promoted economic growth, and demonstrated the stability and adaptability of the American political system, particularly during emergencies.

Early Life

Chester Alan Arthur was born October 5, 1829, in Fairfield, Franklin County, Vermont, the oldest of seven children. His mother, Malvina Stone, was a Canadian whose ancestors immigrated from England and were Baptist; his father, William Arthur, was an Irish immigrant turned Baptist minister as well as a respectable scholar. Under the tutorship of his father, Arthur showed an intense interest in learning and a high aptitude in the subjects he studied, matriculating at Union College in Schenectady, New York (at that time, one of the best known colleges in the East), on September 5, 1845, at the age of fifteen. He became a member of the Psi Upsilon Society, taught in the local schools to help defray the cost of his education, and in July, 1848, at the age of eighteen, was graduated with high honors, including membership in the Phi Beta Kappa honor society.

After his graduation from college, Arthur pursued his ambition to become a lawyer by enrolling in the law school at Ballston Springs, New York, where he studied for a few months, continuing his studies at home and teaching. In 1851, he became principal and teacher at the North Pownal Academy in Bennington County, Vermont, ten miles from his family across the border in Hoosick, New York. During Arthur's tenure as principal there, James A. Garfield served for a time as a faculty member, teaching business and penmanship—a circumstance that was to be fully exploited in the presidential campaign of 1880. In 1852, Arthur became principal of an academy at Cohoes, New York; in 1853, he continued his legal studies in the office of the prestigious firm of Erastus D. Culver.

On May 4, 1854, after having been certified to the Supreme Court of New York by the Culver firm that he had satisfactorily completed his studies, Arthur was admitted to the bar. He joined Culver's firm and began practicing law. In 1856, upon becoming a judge of the Civil Court of Brooklyn, Arthur formed a partnership with an old friend, Henry D. Gardiner. For three months, Arthur and his friend tried to establish a practice out West but returned to New York City after becoming disillusioned by widespread lawlessness. Two of Arthur's first and most celebrated cases involved the Fugitive Slave Law and discrimination against black people on New York City streetcars. As a staunch abolitionist, Arthur found in these two cases an opportunity to make a significant contribution to the antislavery movement.

As a Whig delegate from Brooklyn, dedicated to the abolitionist movement, Arthur participated in the convention that met at Saratoga in August of 1854, for the purpose of developing methods for combating the Kansas-Nebraska Act, which repealed the Missouri Compromise of 1820. The action of the convention led to the birth of the Republican Party. In the party's first campaign for the presidency, Arthur wholeheartedly supported and campaigned for the first presidential nominee of the Republican Party, John C. Frémont. During the campaign, Arthur served on an executive committee that worked for the election of Frémont. On election day, Arthur served as an inspector of elections at the polls.

In October, 1859, Arthur married Ellen Lewis Herndon, a member of a distinguished Virginia family and sister of a good friend, Dabney Herndon. Their union produced two sons (one son died at the age of four) and one daughter. Arthur's wife died in January, 1881.

Life's Work

After joining the state's militia, Arthur gained extensive knowledge of military science especially concerning strategy and logistics. His highly rated performance led to his appointment as Judge Advocate-General of the Second Brigade of the New York Militia. Having fully assisted him in his bid for reelection, the governor of New York appointed Arthur as engineer-in-chief and charged him with the responsibility of drawing plans to protect the state. After the Civil War began, the governor promoted Arthur to the position of inspector general of New York troops in the field. Later, he was appointed assistant quartermaster general, then quartermaster general of New York, responsible for raising regiments to fight on the battlefields and maintaining the troops. While serving in the post of quartermaster general, Arthur got his long-awaited chance to participate in direct combat on the battlefields; on two occasions, he was elected first by the Ninth Regiment of the New York Militia and, second, by the Metropolitan Brigade of New York City to lead them in battle. Both times, the governor successfully dissuaded Arthur, convincing him to remain in his post as quartermaster general, wherein he ably carried out his responsibilities for the cause of the Union.

After he resigned his position following the election of a Democrat as governor of the Empire State, Arthur spent much time in Albany and Washington working on war claims and drafting important bills that required quick action, soon becoming one of the best lawyers in New York. In 1866, Arthur helped Roscoe Conkling get elected to the United States Senate, then became his chief henchman until he became president.

In 1867, Arthur was elected to the Century Club, a prestigious intellectual and social organization, and was elected chairman of the executive committee of the New York Republican Party. In 1871, Arthur established one of the most outstanding law firms in New York; in the same year, President Ulysses S. Grant appointed him collector of the Port of New York—the most important political position outside Washington, D.C. Impressed with Arthur's management of the Port of New York, Grant reappointed him to the collectorship, and the Senate confirmed the reappointment unanimously.

In 1878, however, President Rutherford B. Hayes dismissed Arthur from the collectorship on the grounds that his positions in the government and the Republican Party were incompatible with respect to civil service reforms. The outrageous scandals of Grant's two administrations had convinced Hayes of the dire need for an appreciable reform program in government designed to take politics out of the bureaucracy. The removal of Arthur was therefore not based on his competence but on the fact that, as a consummate politician, he had manipulated his position in a way that made him the undisputed "boss" of the Republican Party of New York City as well as chairman of the Central Committee of the Republican Party of the state. Upon his removal, a petition signed by some of the most reputable persons of the time, asking that Arthur be retained, was suppressed by Arthur. Like Garfield, Arthur never sought a position; he

wished to retain the collectorship on his own merit, but as a result of a bitter struggle between the Hayes Administration and the Conkling machine, he chose to return to practicing law.

In 1879, as chairman of the Republican Central Committee, Arthur worked hard to strengthen the Republican Party of his state—particularly the Stalwarts (1869-1880), the "regular" or machine wing of his party, who were opposed to the reform program of Hayes's administration—and, disregarding the two-term tradition honored by all the presidents since George Washington, strongly advocated and worked to secure a third term for Grant. In Chicago in June, 1880, at the Republican National Nominating Convention, destiny brought Garfield and Arthur together again as it had twenty-six years earlier at the North Pownal Academy in Vermont. This time their relationship was reversed: Arthur worked under Garfield. The nomination of Garfield and Arthur as candidates for president and vice president of the Republican Party startled the nation, including the candidates themselves.

Both men went to Chicago to do everything within their power to help get the leader of their wing nominated. A bitter struggle was expected between the Stalwarts and the Half-Breeds (a wing of the Republican Party, 1876-1884, which supported Hayes's conciliatory policy toward the South, opposed a third term for Grant, and supported the nomination of Garfield), but there were those who believed that the leaders would find a way to resolve the struggle with some kind of compromise. Finally, in order to end the deadlocked convention, the Half-Breeds turned to Garfield on the thirty-sixth ballot and nominated him to lead the Republican Party to victory in 1880. Because they knew that they had no chance of winning the presidency without the support of the Stalwarts, they offered the nomination for vice president to the second most powerful boss of the New York political machine, Chester A. Arthur.

Arthur's nomination was based on political strategy designed to produce some semblance of unity within the Republican Party. On the basis of his experiences of all the candidates available in 1880, Arthur was one of the least qualified to serve as vice president and had no qualifications that would have justified his nomination for the office of the president. Arthur was chosen because he was Conkling's right-hand man. Without the support of the New York political machine, the Republican Party

could not win the election. At the outset, Conkling squawked at Arthur's decision to join the Garfield forces, but before the campaign ended, he gave some support.

As the campaign got under way in 1880, the jockeying by the various factions for control left the Republican Party in a state of disarray, and consequently, the opposing forces expediently closed ranks. One of the most thrilling national political conventions in American history produced one of the most unusual tickets in the history of presidential nominating conventions: The presidential candidate thoroughly qualified, with seventeen years of yeoman's service in the House of Representatives on behalf of the people of his district and the nation; the vice presidential candidate was a skilled politician deeply tied to a powerful political machine, with all of his work experience limited to his home state, and with no experience that equipped him to serve as president. The ticket that had surprised the party, the nation, and the candidates themselves succeeded in achieving a narrow victory at the polls in November.

Only a few months after his inauguration, however—on July 2, 1881—Garfield was shot by a deranged office-seeker, Charles J. Guiteau, in a Washington railroad station. Eighty days later, Garfield died, and the agonizing wait of the people who had prayed so hard for his recovery came to an end. Arthur remained extremely apprehensive throughout the lingering death struggle, hoping that somehow Garfield would survive, recover, and resume his duties as president. When Arthur accepted the invitation to run on the ticket with Garfield, he did so on the basis that it would give him the opportunity to escape the continual and perplexing problems associated with his management of the political machine. After his removal from his position as collector of the New York Customhouse by the outgoing President Hayes, Arthur regarded his selection as vice presidential candidate as a vindication of his integrity.

Garfield's tragic death cast the nation into a state of shock that for a while quelled the political discord that to an appreciable degree remained constant in the wake of the presidential campaign of the previous year. As the shock gradually subsided, however, consternation gripped the nation, for the office and power of the president had devolved on the second most powerful political boss in the country, who himself was the chief lieutenant of the most powerful boss in America. To allay such fears, Arthur gradually dissolved his relationship with Conkling and his machine.

During his term as president, Arthur fought hard for a canal in Nicaragua, owned and operated by the United States; advocated a program of reciprocal trade agreements; developed America's first modern steel navy; prosecuted those who defrauded the Post Office Department; and vetoed the Chinese Exclusion Act, changing the suspension of Chinese immigration from twenty to ten years. Possibly Arthur's greatest achievement was his strong support of the act that became the foundation of civil service reform—the Pendleton Act of 1883.

In addition, Arthur recognized the significance of issues which, while not resolved during his presidency, were later to confirm the soundness of his judgment. Among the recommendations Arthur proposed were statehood for Alaska, a building for the Library of Congress, a law determining who should count the electoral votes in order to avoid the type of dispute that occurred in 1876, and the regulation of interstate commerce. In order to avoid another presidential succession crisis, Arthur strongly recommended a constitutional amendment that would provide for the expedient resolution of questions pertaining to presidential succession. Arthur's proposal concerning presidential succession was ultimately realized with the ratification of the Twenty-fifth Amendment to the Constitution on February 10, 1967.

Arthur's long bout with Bright's disease (he had it at the time he assumed the presidency) failed to affect his administration significantly; it did, however, to a large extent, prevent him from succeeding himself, which was an eventuality he very much desired. After his unsuccessful efforts to obtain the nomination of his party in 1884, his supporters in the Republican Party of New York tried to urge him for a seat in the United States Senate in their efforts to repair their badly damaged "machine." Because of his infirmity and lack of interest (after having been president, he considered campaigning for the Senate to be improper), he rejected the idea. He attended ceremonies opening the Brooklyn Bridge in May, 1883. Just before his term expired, Arthur dedicated the Washington Monument, on February 22, 1885.

After Arthur left office, he was elected president of his fraternity, Psi Upsilon, and elected the forerunner of the subway system of New York City, the New York Arcade Railway. Arthur died on November 18, 1886, at his home in New York City.

Summary

Arthur showed that the aura of the office and power of the presidency can transform a politician wedded to a political machine into a president who dissociates himself from the machine and bases his policies and programs on what he deems best for the people and the nation. Under the leadership of President Arthur, the intense perturbation of the American people caused by the assassination of Garfield was greatly alleviated. Arthur demonstrated that a man of limited experience could be inspired by prestige, office, and authority of the presidency to exploit his talents and experience to the fullest extent possible, to become an effective president.

When the leading historians in the United States were polled to rate the presidents, they evaluated their subjects as great, near great, above average, average, or below average, with a final slot reserved for outright failures. The historians assigned Arthur to the average class, along with seven other presidents: William McKinley, William Howard Taft, Martin Van Buren, Rutherford B. Hayes, Benjamin Harrison, Zachary Taylor, and Jimmy Carter. Arthur's rating indicates that he overcame his political handicaps and commendably performed his responsibilities as president.

Bibliography

Brisbin, James S. *From the Tow-path to the White House: The Early Life and Public Career of James A. Garfield, Including Also a Sketch of the Life of Honorable Chester A. Arthur.* Philadelphia: Hubbard, 1880. A classic work containing a readable story of the life of Arthur.

Doenecke, Justus D. *The Presidencies of James A. Garfield and Chester A. Arthur.* Lawrence: Regents Press of Kansas, 1981. This is a revisionist work inspired by the renewed examination occurring during the centennial of the Gilded Age (1870-1896). Includes brilliant notes and bibliographical essays.

Howe, George Frederick. *Chester A. Arthur: A Quarter-Century of Machine Politics.* New York: Dodd, Mead, 1934. One of the most significant biographical studies of Arthur. This was the only major scholarly biography of Arthur until the publication of Thomas C. Reeves's study in 1975 (see below). Howe's major thesis is that Arthur filled a place of power and responsibility far above his aspirations, bravely and adequately, if not with greatness.

Levin, Peter R. *Seven by Chance: Accidental Presidents.* New York: Farrar, Straus, 1948. This work is a study of the seven men who became president because of the death of a president. The most valuable section of Levin's work is that in which the author assesses the method of choosing a vice-presidential candidate. The author mentions a number of ways to improve the vice presidency. An erudite work that provides an excellent source for studying the vice presidency.

Reeves, Thomas C. *Gentleman Boss: The Life of Chester Alan Arthur.* New York: Knopf, 1975. The author covers Arthur's career in New York politics before he became president, showing that Arthur was a more skillful political organizer and manager than previous accounts indicate. Reeves's work provides a fresh view of Arthur and has become the standard biography.

Sievers, Harry J., ed. *Six Presidents from the Empire State.* Tarrytown, N.Y.: Sleepy Hollow Restorations, 1974. This volume is a scholarly study of the impact on the presidency of the six presidents from New York. They are divided into three pairs whose terms in office correspond broadly to three major eras in the history of the presidency: Martin Van Buren and Millard Fillmore, pre-Civil War; Chester A. Arthur and Grover Cleveland, the Gilded Age; and Theodore Roosevelt and Franklin Delano Roosevelt, the modern presidency. Includes the Schlesinger polls on presidential greatness, a selected bibliography of the Empire State presidents and their contemporaries, splendid illustrations of the six presidents, and sketches of the thirteen outstanding contributors and the editor.

James D. Lockett

JOHN J. ASTOR

Born: July 17, 1763; Waldorf, near Heidelberg, Germany

Died: March 29, 1848; New York, New York

Area of Achievement: Business

Contribution: Combining a shrewd eye for profits with relentless determination, Astor became in turn America's first monopolist, its leading fur trader, its leading trader to China, and "landlord of New York." When he died, he was by far the richest man in the United States.

Early Life

John Jacob Astor was born July 17, 1763, in the village of Waldorf near the ancient city of Heidelberg, Germany. Information concerning the origins of his family is not completely clear, but it seems certain that the Astors (or Ashdoers) were not originally German. The first Astor in Germany arrived in either the sixteenth or the eighteenth century, was either Italian or Spanish, a religious refugee or a soldier, depending on which story is preferred. In any case, the Astor family was not a wealthy one. Astor's father was a butcher who had very little aptitude for business. His mother, fortunately, was methodical and frugal, qualities she passed on to her four sons. John Jacob was the youngest.

With the death of his mother and the arrival of a stepmother, John Jacob became very unhappy and discontented. He left home at the age of sixteen or seventeen and worked his passage down the River Rhine to join an older brother in London. For two or three years, John Jacob worked in his brother's piano manufacturing company, learning English and saving money to travel to America, where a second brother was established as a butcher in New York.

In November, 1783, Astor set sail bound for Baltimore with money enough to tide him over, a stock of German flutes to trade, and a berth in steerage for the trip. The ship arrived in the Chesapeake in January but remained icebound for two months, unable to reach its destination. During that time, Astor became acquainted with a young German returning to America, where he had previously been a fur trapper and trader. Once aroused to the potential for fabulous profits, Astor inquired into the minutest details of the trade and determined to enter the fur business himself. In March, 1784, Astor arrived in New York and soon obtained a job with an old Quaker fur trader. His marriage to Sarah Todd in 1785 brought him a handsome dowry of three hundred dollars, connections with the upper classes of New York City and with various sea captains, and a wife with great business ability of her own. The following year, Astor was able to set up business on his own account as a fur trader and agent for the sale of imported musical instruments.

Life's Work

John Jacob Astor quickly became affluent. To be truly successful as a fur trader, Astor had to compete with the giant Hudson's Bay Company and the Northwest Company, both based in Montreal, and which, between them, dominated much of the trade. With a secure financial base from the music shop run by his wife Sarah, he was able to spend the time to gain the confidence of trappers and Indians in upstate New York through personal contact and by offering a better price than his enormous rivals.

In 1789, Astor was invited to attend the annual meeting of the Northwest Company at Fort William on Lake Superior. What he saw convinced him that if he was ever to compete seriously, he had to develop trade in volume. Consequently, Astor began to develop a regular trade in furs between Montreal and London, and between London and New York (direct trade between Canada and the newly independent United States was illegal until 1796). At the same time, he continued to develop his contacts and agents in the woods in anticipation of the day when he could replace the two great Canadian fur companies.

As his income soared, Astor took his brother's advice and began to invest in real estate. To further his financial interests, John Jacob began to frequent the meeting places of powerful city merchants and became a member of the Masons. By the time of Jay's Treaty in 1796, by which Great Britain agreed to leave the rich hunting grounds south of the Great Lakes and to end the trade ban on goods from Canada to the United States, Astor was in a good position to attempt to rival the great fur companies. He was, by then, one of the leading merchants of New York, estimated to be worth fifty thousand dollars.

In 1800, Astor invested in a cargo of furs bound for China. His share of the profit from this one voyage was estimated at fifty-five thousand dollars and was reinvested in the China trade. By 1803, he had ships of his own built and was becoming

America's leading merchant in the China trade. All the while, Astor continued to invest several thousand dollars per year in Manhattan real estate, trading in anything that would bring a good profit from the return journeys of his fur ships, and extending his contacts among fur trappers in the woods.

In 1808, Astor was ready to exploit the possibilities opened up by the Louisiana Purchase. He founded the American Fur Company to monopolize the fur trade west of the Mississippi. The company was capitalized at one million dollars, all of it supplied by Astor himself, and was blessed by the American government, which was full of Astor's business acquaintances and clients. The key to Astor's scheme was to establish a settlement at the mouth of the Columbia River on the Pacific coast—to be called Astoria—as a clearing-house for furs caught in the region; they could then be sent directly to China, the world's best market. Never before had the merchant taken such a big gamble. The venture was accompanied by great suspicion between Americans hired to run the settlement and the Scots-Canadians hired for their expertise. It was a suspicion shared by Astor himself and was compounded by his assignment of responsibilities. The result was the complete failure of an overland expedition sent to set up trading posts on its way to Astoria and the subsequent loss of the ship that Astor sent out to build the settlement. Worse yet, the War of 1812 allowed the Northwest Company to send an armed ship to Astoria to claim it for Great Britain. Astor's Scots-Canadians sold the settlement to their former employers, the Northwest Company, for a fraction of its real value. It was Astor's greatest setback, one of remarkably few. The nearly one-million-dollar loss sustained by Astor was subsequently made up from profits derived from his investment in American war bonds.

After the war, Astor was in a strong position. He had been able to buy several ships at cheap rates and had invested in real estate and mortgages, both at low prices as a result of wartime depression and a British blockade. Also, despite the Astoria catastrophe, the American Fur Company after 1815 was able to drive out or take over all rivals in the rich Missouri country and around the Great Lakes. It achieved a complete monopoly by 1822.

During the decade of the 1820's, Astor wound down his interests in the China trade as commodities such as tea glutted the market. He shifted his investments to transportation, insurance companies, banks, federal and state securities, and, most heavily, to real estate. In the 1830's, returns from land and property in Manhattan were so great that Astor decided to liquidate all of his interests in commerce and concentrate instead on his investments, particularly real estate. By this time, the fur trade was in decline and so was Astor, now in his seventies.

To perpetuate his name, Astor built the finest hotel in New York, Astor House, and commissioned the writing of a novel defending his actions in the Pacific Northwest. Both Astor House and *Astoria*, by Washington Irving, were completed in 1836. Both were immediate and conspicuous successes.

The Panic of 1837 drove many businessmen to ruin, but not Astor. His great wealth cushioned him and, indeed, he took advantage of the economic depression to extend his investments in Manhattan real estate. With recovery came a huge influx of immigrants, all desperately in need of housing. The value of Astor's investments soared as New York expanded as never before.

John Jacob Astor died on March 29, 1848, having suffered for several years from palsy, extremely poor circulation, and painful stomach disorders. To his son, William Backhouse Astor, he left the bulk of his fortune.

Summary

John Jacob Astor's career spanned the period from the infancy of the young American republic to the early years of its industrial revolution. It was a time of great commercial opportunity. No other single individual was able to capitalize on the possibilities with such singular success. His drive and determination to make money dominated all those with whom he did business. It mattered little to Astor in what branch of commerce or finance he made money; profit margins were all that counted. Astor is principally remembered, however, for his achievement in building the first private monopoly in United States history. It was his American Fur Company which, over the course of fifteen years, attained almost total control over the fur trade in the United States. His purchase of large tracts of Manhattan and the dispersal of investments in banking, insurance, and government stocks secured Astor's fortune for his family and ensured that it would thrive.

Bibliography

Chittenden, Hiram M. *The American Fur Trade of the Far West*. New York: Harper, 1902. A comprehensive examination of the complex structure and pattern which existed before and during the establishment of the American Fur Company. It follows the policies and actions by which independent trappers and companies were driven out of business or incorporated into Astor's company, the ways in which the Indians were dealt with, the employees kept in line, and the trade rationalized.

Gebhard, Elizabeth L. *The Life and Ventures of the Original John Jacob Astor*. Hudson, N.Y.: Bryan, 1915. A highly colored and favorable account of the great man, written by a descendant of Astor's friend and fellow German immigrant, John Gabriel Gebhard. Full of detail.

Irving, Pierre M. *The Life and Letters of Washington Irving*. 4 vols. New York: Putnam, 1863; London: Bentley, 1864. An account of the great literary figure by his nephew. Washington Irving was a longtime friend of Astor, which was why he was commissioned to write *Astoria*. Pierre and his uncle lived in Astor's house for two years preparing materials for the novel. There are a number of revealing letters and episodes concerning Astor.

Irving, Washington. *Astoria*. Edited by Richard Dilworth Rust. Boston: Twayne, 1976. This is the authorized version of Astor's astounding career, written by a longtime friend and literary client. It is the most detailed version of Astor's early career and serves as the main reference point for all later accounts, though some of its facts have been questioned, since Irving seems to have accepted many of the myths propagated about, and by, Astor. The book was a best-seller when it appeared.

Minnigerode, Meade. *Certain Rich Men*. London and New York : Putnam, 1927. Of the seven men studied, Astor merits the second chapter, following his friend Stephen Girard the banker. This is a balanced account that stresses Astor's ruthless business practice and his love of family.

Porter, Kenneth Wiggins. *John Jacob Astor: Business Man*. 2 vols. Cambridge, Mass.: Harvard University Press, 1931. Easily the most detailed and informative account of Astor's career. Porter questions some of Irving's assumptions. The author was a research assistant in the Graduate School of Business Administration at Harvard at the time and concentrates largely on Astor's financial interests. He does not, however, neglect the personal aspects in interesting asides and in the first two and last two chapters of the work.

Sinclair, David. *Dynasty: The Astors and Their Times*. London: Dent, 1983; New York: Beauford, 1984. A book primarily about the fortune bequeathed by John Jacob Astor. The elder Astor fills the first part of a four-part work. It is an iconoclastic view which subjects Astor in places to biting criticism and which, throughout, is informed by a skepticism about business practices and "great men." A good corrective to some of the other, favorable, accounts cited above.

Stephen Burwood

JOHN JAMES AUDUBON

Born: April 26, 1785; Les Cayes, Saint-Domingue
  (near Haiti)
Died: January 27, 1851; New York, New York
Areas of Achievement: Ornithology and art
Contribution: A gifted artist with a love of nature
  and a passion for discovery, Audubon became
  the greatest painter of birds of his time, an important natural scientist, and an inspiration to
  conservationists.

Early Life

John James Audubon, American naturalist, was
born in Haiti on April 26, 1785, the illegitimate son
of Jean Audubon, a French naval officer, and
Jeanne Rabin, a French servant girl from Brittany.
After his mother's death, Audubon's father took
him and a younger half sister to France, where he
legally adopted his children in 1794. In school, Audubon early revealed his talents for drawing and
music. He learned to play the violin and flute and
by age fifteen had begun drawing birds and collecting birds' eggs. After he proved unfit for a naval
career, the elder Audubon sent him to Mill Grove,
his farm near Valley Forge, Pennsylvania. In 1808,
following a four-year engagement, Audubon married Lucy Bakewell, a girl of English descent who
lived on a neighboring estate. Of their four children, two sons—Victor Gifford and John Wood-
house—survived to adulthood and provided significant help to their father in his painting and
publishing projects.

In the United States, Audubon formed a partnership with Ferdinand Rozier, an older Frenchman whom his father had sent to look after him.
They became frontier merchants, with stores in
Kentucky, first in Louisville, then in Henderson,
and finally in Ste. Genevieve, Missouri. Yet Audubon preferred to trek the forests, observing and
painting birds and other wildlife. Finding business irksome, he dissolved the partnership and entered into an ill-fated trade arrangement with his
brother-in-law, Thomas Bakewell. In 1813, Audubon and a group of associates built a combination
sawmill and gristmill in Henderson, Kentucky. It
proved far too ambitious a project to be sustained
by the local economy, and its failure left him
bankrupt. After being imprisoned for debt, he
worked as a taxidermist for the Western Museum
in Cincinnati, receiving additional income from

portrait painting. In 1820, he set out for New Orleans to continue work as an artist, but, more important, to add to his portfolio of bird paintings.
His wife worked as a tutor to support the family,
and the two endured many months apart before
she joined him in Louisiana.

Life's Work

For Audubon, an avocation developed into a vocation, though it is not known precisely when the
change occurred. In 1810, while he and Rozier
were in their Louisville store, Alexander Wilson,
the pioneer American ornithologist, showed them
his bird paintings and sought a subscription to support publication of his nine-volume *American Ornithology* (1808-1814). After seeing Wilson's
work, Rozier remarked that his partner's paintings
were better. By allowing Audubon to realize that
his amateur work surpassed the work of a professional, this incident probably served as a catalyst to
his fertile imagination.

He gradually developed the idea for *The Birds of America* (1827-1838), an ambitious portfolio of all American species, life-size, in their natural habitats. In its scope, scale, and fidelity to nature, Audubon's work would eclipse that of his predecessors. In order to include all the known species, he would rely upon the discoveries and observations of others for some of his paintings, not limiting the work to his own observations as Wilson had done. By the time he left for New Orleans in late 1820, the outlines of the work, which would require almost two decades to complete, were formed.

An experienced hunter and skilled woodsman, Audubon combined an intense interest in nature with a sharp eye and essential survival skills. He was equally comfortable alone or in company, and equally ingratiating to Indians or European noblemen. At five feet ten and a half inches tall, he was a man of almost regal appearance, with smooth facial lines, long brown hair, somewhat receding, and blue eyes. A contemporary, Mrs. Nathaniel Wells Pope, described him as "one of the handsomest men I ever saw. . .tall and slender. . . . His bearing was courteous and refined, simple and unassuming."

In Audubon's time, a naturalist needed to collect specimens (usually by shooting), to record his observations in a journal, and to sketch or paint all that he found interesting. To collect specimens, he shot thousands of birds on his expeditions. The collecting, however, did not stop there: He obtained insects, reptiles, and mammals for many other scientists throughout the world. In his lengthy journals, often romantic and even grandiloquent in tone, he made detailed notes about bird sightings and behavior. An almost compulsive painter, he sometimes began sketching a bird by placing its body on a sheet of paper and drawing an outline. Although Audubon occasionally painted live birds, his normal mode was to paint dead ones, which he wired into positions that suited him.

After his efforts to interest New York and Philadelphia publishers in his work failed, Audubon embarked in 1826 for England, where he attempted to attract wealthy patrons for his project by exhibiting his paintings. There, where he was regarded as a natural untaught genius, he became something of a celebrity, being named a fellow of the Royal Society. For *The Birds of America* he sought two hundred subscribers willing to pay one thousand dollars each; he eventually obtained 161, about half of them from the United States. Subscribers paid for a set of five prints at a time, with eighty sets, or four hundred prints, projected.

The publication, requiring eleven years, began in 1827, in Edinburgh, under the engraver William Lizars. Audubon quickly changed to Robert Havell and Company in London, after Havell impressed the painter with his ability to reproduce color tones. The images were etched on copper plates using aquatint, producing shades of gray and black on a light background. They were engraved on sheets measuring thirty-nine and a half by twenty-six and a half inches, forming the Double Elephant Folio, one of the largest books ever printed. After the engraving, artists colored the prints professionally by hand to match Audubon's original paintings.

When completed, the work included life-size color prints of 489 species on 435 pages. The total number of bird paintings was 1,065, for Audubon attempted to illustrate different color phases of each species, and for birds of varied coloration he often produced several poses to reveal the colors more effectively. One of his own favorite paintings, that of the wood duck, includes four birds so positioned as to reveal the rich coloration of the species. His painting of the little blue heron shows a full-size adult in the foreground and, at a distance, standing in a marsh, the white immature representative of the species.

During the production of his major work, Audubon returned to the United States three times to collect more specimens and to complete his paintings, leaving publication in the hands of his son Victor and Havell. In the United States, he mounted extended expeditions into the interior of the country, along the Gulf of Mexico, and to Labrador. Meanwhile, with the assistance of the gifted Scottish ornithologist William MacGillivray, he prepared and issued five volumes of commentaries as companion volumes to the paintings, *Ornithological Biography* (1831-1839). The work names and describes each species, provides an account of its behavior and habitats, and often includes vivid narration of Audubon's experience with the species, the primary source being his unpublished journals.

After completing *The Birds of America*, Audubon issued the work in a smaller and less expensive edition. He then turned to a new project, this time concerning North American mammals, *Viviparous Quadrupeds of North America* (1846-1854; plates, 1842-1845), in collaboration with his friend John Bachman. Seeking specimens to paint, he organized his last great expedition in 1843, traveling up the Missouri River to the mouth of the Yellowstone in North Dakota. After age sixty, he suffered a rapid decline in health, marked by a loss of mental powers. He died quietly at his New York home, Minnie's Land, on January 27, 1851, leaving completion of his work on the mammals to his sons and to Bachman.

Summary

In ornithology, art, and conservation, Audubon's fame and influence have endured. During his time, taxonomy was in its early stages, and science developed largely through observation and compilation. Vast areas of the world lay unexplored and unstudied. To discover new species of flora or fauna was an obvious route to achievement, possibly even to fame. Never a theorist and little inclined toward experimentation, Audubon possessed intense curiosity about nature, keen eyes, and a questing, somewhat romantic nature. He discovered a dozen subspecies, more than twenty species, and one genus of American birds. The list, though impressive, is shorter than he believed, because he mistook several variant color phases for new species and unwittingly claimed some prior discoveries of others.

The artistic quality of *The Birds of America* surpassed that of its predecessors, and the work has not been equaled since in its scale, scope, and aesthetic appeal. Although he occasionally painted with oils, Audubon achieved his best effects using watercolors with an overlay of pastels to enhance color and sharpen detail. Critics, however, have called attention to his limitations as an artist. He sometimes posed his subjects in unnatural positions and uncharacteristic settings, gave some birds human expressions, and could not sustain a uniformly high aesthetic level throughout the long project. Yet he succeeded in arousing widespread interest in ornithology and made the birds of the New World familiar to the Old.

In the twentieth century, his name has become synonymous with conservation of wildlife, a legacy not without irony considering the number of birds he felled with his gun. Still, toward the end of his life, he spoke out against egg collecting as a threat to bird populations. During his final Western expedition, he was troubled by the indiscriminate slaughter of bison. He genuinely loved the primitive frontier and feared that it might disappear under the pressure of civilization. In 1886, his protégé and admirer, George Bird Grinnell, organized the first Audubon Society to preserve some of the natural beauty and living creatures of the land Audubon loved.

Bibliography

Audubon, John J. *The 1826 Journal of John James Audubon*. Edited by Alice Ford. Norman: University of Oklahoma Press, 1967. Careful editing and extensive commentary supplement this important surviving Audubon journal. It reveals Audubon as a careful observer of birds from shipboard during his journey to England.

Chancellor, John. *Audubon: A Biography*. London: Weidenfeld and Nicholson, and New York: Viking Press, 1978. A readable brief biography of Audubon, with a judicious assessment of his achievement. Rich in illustrations.

Ford, Alice. *John James Audubon*. Norman: University of Oklahoma Press, 1964. Now the standard biography, it gives a carefully researched account of Audubon's origins and early life, adding extensive details about his early life in France.

Fries, Waldemar H. *The Double Elephant Folio: The Story of Audubon's Birds of America*. Chicago: American Library Association, 1973. A scholarly historical and bibliographic account of the production and distribution of Audubon's greatest work. Traces the location and provides description of all extant copies.

Harwood, Michael. "Mr. Audubon's Last Hurrah." *Audubon* 87 (November, 1985): 80-117. A lengthy account of Audubon's journey to North Dakota in 1843, the article provides numerous excerpts from his journals and those of contemporaries.

Harwood, Michael, and Mary Durant. "In Search of the Real Mr. Audubon." *Audubon* 87 (May, 1985): 58-119. This article traces Audubon's career in detail, assesses the many myths that surround him, and provides a critique of his biographers. Generously and judiciously illustrated, with numerous reproductions.

Herrick, Francis Hobart. *Audubon the Naturalist: A History of His Life and Time*. 2 vols. 2d ed. New York and London: Appleton, 1938. Although somewhat dated in its research, the biography remains a valuable resource for its comprehensive treatment and its inclusion of many original letters, papers, official records, and documents.

Irmscher, Christoph. "Violence and Artistic Representation in John James Audubon." *Raritan: A*

Quarterly Review 15, no. 2 (Fall 1995). Compares the work of Audubon and Mark Catesby with respect to balancing impartial depictions of nature with artistic subjectivity.

Lindsey, Alton A. *The Bicentennial of John James Audubon.* Bloomington: Indiana University Press, 1985. A collection of essays by various hands, the book assesses Audubon's character, his contributions to science and art, and his influence on conservation.

Partridge, Linda Dugan. "By the Book: Audubon and the Tradition of Ornithological Illustration." *The Huntington Library Quarterly 59,* no. 2-3 (Spring-Summer 1997). Examines the myth concerning Audubon's use of live birds in their natural habitat as subjects and provides evidence that he often used the work of other ornithologists as a basis for his art.

Stanley Archer

JANE AUSTEN

Born: December 16, 1775; Steventon, Hampshire, England

Died: July 18, 1817; Winchester, Hampshire, England

Area of Achievement: Literature

Contribution: Austen's realistic rendering of dialogue and her satirical accuracy make her novels a matchless re-creation of upper-class English society in the late eighteenth and early nineteenth centuries. Her novels owe their lasting popularity, however, to Austen's understanding of human nature as it operates in everyday life.

Early Life

Jane Austen was born December 16, 1775, in Steventon, Hampshire, England, the seventh child and second daughter of George Austen and Cassandra Leigh Austen. Her father was the reactor of Steventon and nearby Deane. A member of an old but poor family, he had been reared by a wealthy uncle, who educated him at St. John's College, Oxford, where he was later a fellow. Austen's mother was the daughter of a clergyman of noble ancestry, also an Oxford graduate and also a former fellow.

Although Jane and her older sister, Cassandra Austen, spent several years in schools in Southampton and Reading, their real education took place at home. The Austens loved words and books. The children could roam at will through George Austen's impressive library. As they grew older, they staged amateur theatricals. The environment stimulated their curiosity, whether they were observing their mother's experiments in farming or hearing their aristocratic French cousin talk about life in prerevolutionary France. With an ever-increasing family and a wide circle of friends, the Austen children had ample opportunity to analyze human motivations and relationships; it is not surprising that two of Jane's brothers and her sister Cassandra all did some writing at one time or another.

The Austens also shared in remarkable good looks; Jane and Cassandra were sometimes called the best-looking girls in England. However flattering such comments may have been, it is true that Jane was a tall, slender brunette with brown, curly hair, hazel eyes, a good complexion, and a sweet voice. Although neither Jane nor Cassandra was ever married, it was not for lack of prospects. Indeed, both were engaged, Cassandra for some time,

to a young clergyman who died in the West Indies, and Jane only overnight, to a family friend whom she rejected in the morning. There was evidently at least one other serious relationship for Jane, a holiday romance which was not pursued and which terminated when that young man, too, died.

Because Jane never left the family circle, her life has often been called uneventful. In fact, it was so busy that Jane had to snatch time to write. In addition to the normal social activities of her class, there were frequent visits to and from the brothers and their families, including lengthy stays by their children, several of whom were very close to their Aunt Jane. There were births, deaths, marriages, and remarriages; there was anxiety about Jane's cousin, whose husband was executed in the French Revolution, and about two brothers, who were British naval officers. Thus, Jane was immersed in life, grieving and rejoicing with family members and friends, mothering nieces and nephews, worrying about the effect of her unstable times on those she loved. As one may note from her letters, she was also a perceptive observer of human behavior, unimpressed by pomposity, unfooled by pretense, and always alert to the comic dimension of human relationships.

It was this comic sense which first led Austen to writing. Her three notebooks collect jokes, skits, and rudimentary character sketches dating from the time she was eleven or twelve, along with a later comic history of England and a brief, unfinished novel named "Catherine." By 1795, when she was twenty, Austen had produced "Elinor and Marianne" (which was later revised and published in 1811 as *Sense and Sensibility*). By 1797, she had completed "First Impressions," which the publisher Cadell refused even to read but which, revised, became her most famous novel, *Pride and Prejudice* (1813). Although none of her novels was to be published until 1811 (six years before her death, when *Sense and Sensibility* made its public appearance), Austen was thus involved in her mature work before her twenty-first birthday. No longer a superficially amusing girl, she had become a serious woman of letters.

Life's Work

Austen's literary reputation rests on six novels, four of which were published during the last years of her life and two posthumously. Because she revised and retitled her early works before she was able to find a publisher for them, it is difficult to trace her development. Evidently, after a work was rejected, she would put it aside, begin another work, and then later revise the earlier one. Her most famous work, *Pride and Prejudice*, for example, was the product of twelve or fourteen years; *Sense and Sensibility* took at least sixteen years and two revisions between conception and publication.

Austen's creative maturity can be divided into two major periods. During the first, she wrote three novels and vainly attempted to get them published. During the second, she revised, completed, and published two of her early novels and wrote three more, two of which were published before her death. It was only during the last half dozen years of her life, then, that she received the recognition which her genius merited.

During her years at Steventon, Austen wrote the first version of what was to be her first published work. "Elinor and Marianne" was the story of two sisters whose lives were governed by two different principles. In every crisis, one tried to be sensible, while the other gave way to uncontrolled emotion. The theme was reflected in Austen's revision a year or two later, when she changed the title to *Sense and Sensibility*. It was under the second title that the novel, again revised, was finally published in 1811.

During 1797, Austen completed "First Impressions," which pointed out how foolish rash assessments of other people may be. Like *Sense and Sensibility*, this work told the love stories of two sisters; in this case, however, the prejudiced sister, with all of her faults, captures the reader, who can hardly wait for her to capture the proud nobleman. Tentatively, Austen's father offered the manuscript to a publisher, but the publisher refused even to read it. Austen put it away. In 1809, she revised it, and in 1813, it was published as *Pride and Prejudice*, which is still one of England's best-known and best-loved novels.

The third novel of the Steventon period, *Northanger Abbey* (1818; originally titled "Susan"), began as a satire of the gothic and sentimental novels which were so popular in the late eighteenth century. Like a gothic heroine, the central character is determined to find a murderer in the country house which she visits; her curiosity is interpreted as bad manners, however, and she very

nearly loses the eligible man who had invited her. Yet Austen's genius could not be confined in a mere literary satire, and like her other works, *Northanger Abbey* is a full-fledged commentary on morals and manners.

Northanger Abbey is also interesting because it was the first novel actually sold for publication. The publisher who bought it in 1803, however, evidently changed his plans, and six years later Austen paid him for its return. It was published the year after her death.

In 1801, George Austen suddenly decided to retire and to move his household to Bath, where he and his family lived until his death in 1805. Despite her reluctance to leave Steventon, Austen was fascinated with the famous watering place, which was the setting both for *Northanger Abbey* and for *Persuasion* (1818). Whether her inability to publish discouraged her or she continued to work on her earlier manuscripts is a matter of conjecture; at any rate, *The Watsons*, begun in 1804, was never completed (although its fragment was published in 1871 in J. E. Austen-Leigh's *Memoir of Jane Austen*). In 1809, Jane, Cassandra, and their mother moved back to Hampshire, to a house in the village of Chawton, which had been made available to them by Jane's brother Edward Knight. There Jane spent the remaining years of her life, years which at last brought her success. In 1809, Jane revised *Sense and Sensibility* and *Pride and Prejudice*. Probably with the encouragement and help of her brother Henry Austen, who lived in London, in 1811 she found a publisher for *Sense and Sensibility*. Like all of her novels printed during her lifetime, it was anonymous. It was also highly successful. In 1813, it was followed by *Pride and Prejudice*.

Henry was too proud of his sister to keep her secret any longer, and in 1813 Jane had to acknowledge that she was known to be the author. By this point in time she had written another novel, *Mansfield Park* (1814), a serious work which deals with religious and ethical issues, particularly as they relate to clerical life. After its publication, she wrote *Emma* (1815), thought by many to be her best novel, even though Jane worried that her readers might dislike the spoiled, snobbish heroine. Drawing from the world of her naval officer brothers, Jane then wrote her final completed novel, *Persuasion*, whose noble but misled heroine had once rejected her true love, a navy captain. Tragicomic in tone, *Persuasion* has often been considered to be Austen's most moving book.

Happy in her Chawton home, surrounded by family and friends, admired by public and critics alike, and inspired with her ideas for another novel, at the end of 1816 Austen seemed destined for years of happiness. She was struck down, however, with a debilitating and crippling illness. By March, 1817, she put aside her novel; by May, she had moved to nearby Winchester, where her physician lived; on July 18, she died. She was buried in Winchester Cathedral.

Summary

Jane Austen has often been praised because of what she did not do: She did not write about characters or scenes with which she was unfamiliar; she did not attempt a scope which might have been above her powers; she did not indulge in self-conscious digressions, as did Henry Fielding and his imitator William Makepeace Thackeray, which displayed the author and delayed the novel; and she did not permit herself errors in plotting.

The genius of this restraint has become even more fully appreciated with time. A child of the neoclassical period, she was determined to point out the virtues of moderation in a period which was increasingly infatuated with excess, the need for reason at a time when emotion was increasingly enthroned. She had observed life; she had found that only the classical standards, combined with Christian virtues, could direct one toward happiness. She also had observed that the real dramas of life were played out in the everyday world of ordinary people. People were annihilated as hopelessly at Bath as in battle; families were destroyed as suddenly by foolish marriages as by the guillotine. Therefore, her themes were as profound as human life itself.

That restraint which Austen counseled was exemplified in her work. Every character she introduced was essential to her plot and theme. Every scene and every authorial comment were so carefully pruned that no word could be omitted. Thus, perhaps more than any previous novelist, she understood the artistic heights to which the novel could rise, and while in theme she reflected the age of Samuel Johnson, in technique she anticipated the twentieth century.

Bibliography

Austen-Leigh, William, and Richard Arthur Austen-Leigh. *Jane Austen, Her Life and Letters: A Family Record*. London: Smith, Elder, and New York: Dutton, 1913. This work by family members has been considerably augmented as later materials have become available. The seminal work of Austen biography, it includes a useful appendix with textual comments and a detailed genealogical chart.

Cecil, David. *A Portrait of Jane Austen*. London: Constable, 1978; New York: Hill and Wang, 1979. One of the most readable introductions to Jane Austen's life and work. Cecil integrates biographical data, Austen's own letters, and historical details in an attempt to place the writer within the society about which she is writing. Contains numerous color illustrations, including watercolors by Jane's sister Cassandra.

Fritzer, Penelope J. *Jane Austen and Eighteenth-Century Courtesy Books*. Westport, Conn.: Greenwood Press, 1997. Fritzer argues that Austen's works and characters rely heavily on popular eighteenth-century courtesy books (written at the time to depict the best in manners and deportment).

Gill, Richard. *Happy Rural Seat: The English Country House and the Literary Imagination*.

New Haven, Conn.: Yale University Press, 1972; London: Yale University Press, 1973. Although specifically a study of the English country house in early twentieth century fiction, Gill's book includes an appendix on earlier literature which deals extensively with the works of Austen, particularly *Mansfield Park*. An essential work for anyone who wishes to understand the viewpoint of Austen and later English writers of her class.

Pinion, F. B. *A Jane Austen Companion: Critical Survey and Reference Book*. London: Macmillan, and New York: St. Martin's Press, 1973. Useful brief biography and separate analyses of the six completed novels, along with a commentary on *Sanditon*. Contains also an alphabetical listing of characters and places in the novels, a glossary of unusual words, appendixes, maps, and a number of black-and-white illustrations. A thorough, careful book.

Sherry, Norman. *Jane Austen*. London: Evans, 1966; New York: Arno Press, 1969. A brief, simple study for the nonacademic reader, Sherry's book includes a short biography and critical generalizations on Austen's work as a whole and specifically on each of the six completed novels. While the comments on her work are fairly standard, Sherry provides helpful illustrations drawn from the novels to support his points. Convenient for a beginning student of the novel form.

Teachman, Debra. *Understanding Pride and Prejudice: A Student Casebook to Issues, Sources, and Historical Documents*. Westport, Conn.: Greenwood Press, 1997. Teachman combines analysis and primary documentation from Austen's period to assist readers of *Pride and Prejudice* in understanding the book and its place in societal context. The author includes information on issues such as marriage, women's roles, and inheritance and uses eighteenth-century letters, newspapers, histories, and other materials.

Tomalin, Claire. *Jane Austen: A Life*. New York: Knopf, and London: Viking, 1997. A fresh look at Austen and the situations that influenced her writings, including her family background, the competitive English society in which she lived, and her decision to forgo marriage to pursue her career as a writer.

Wagenknecht, Edward. *Cavalcade of the English Novel*. New York: Holt Rinehart, 1943. A widely available survey which has useful chapters on the predecessors of the novel and brief but sound discussions of major writers. Reflects earlier attitudes toward Austen as a writer who was above all a lady and whose limitations should be stressed. Comments interestingly on her grotesque characters.

Wilks, Brian. *Jane Austen*. London and New York: Hamlyn, 1978. A large, lavishly illustrated volume which depends heavily on quotations from the Austen letters for a rather rambling, episodic account of the writer's life. Although, as the index indicates, Wilks's work incorporates all of the major biographical details, his digressions are confusing for a reader who is looking for a clear chronology.

Rosemary M. Canfield-Reisman

STEPHEN FULLER AUSTIN

Born: November 3, 1793; Wythe County, Virginia
Died: December 27, 1836; Columbia, Texas
Areas of Achievement: Colonization and politics
Contribution: Austin established the first Anglo-American colony in Texas and played a significant role in the Texas Revolution, which resulted in that province securing independence from Mexico.

Early Life

Stephen Fuller Austin was born on November 3, 1793, in Wythe County, Virginia. His father, Moses Austin, was a mine owner who came from a family of Connecticut merchants. His mother, née Maria Brown, had a New Jersey Quaker heritage. The Austin family moved to the province of Spanish Louisiana in 1798 to seek better lead deposits for mining. Moses established and operated a lead mine south of St. Louis. There young Stephen passed his childhood until the age of eleven years. In 1804, his family sent him to Connecticut to begin his formal education. He spent several years as a pupil at Bacon Academy and then entered Transylvania University in Kentucky. In 1810, the youth returned to Missouri, which had become part of the United States because of the Louisiana Purchase. The young man worked at a bank in St. Louis and, for a time, engaged in storekeeping. In 1814, his neighbors elected him as a delegate to the Missouri Territorial Legislature, a post he held until 1820.

In 1817, Austin took charge of the financially troubled family mining operation at Potosi. He was, however, unable to make it a profitable business. In 1820, he therefore followed his brother-in-law James Perry to the Arkansas Territory. There he established a farm near Long Prairie on the Red River. The governor of Arkansas appointed him a district judge in July of 1820.

By early adulthood, it had become obvious that Austin had natural leadership ability. He had a pleasing personality along with a mature outlook. He was a physically small person of slight build, only five feet, six inches in height. Dark haired and fine featured, Stephen was no doubt a handsome youth who inspired confidence in all whom he met. His greatest strengths, however, were his moderate personal habits. A well-educated man, he was charitable, tolerant, and loyal in his relationships with others. Also, although he never married, he seldom lacked companionship from the many friends he made throughout his life. It is not surprising, therefore, that Austin decided upon the practice of law as his career. In 1821, he went to New Orleans to study for the bar.

Events set in motion about this time by his father, however, changed forever the course of Austin's life. Moses Austin decided to found a colony in the Spanish province of Texas. The fertile and unsettled land there had rich agricultural potential. Many Anglo-Americans from the United States, especially cotton farmers from the South, would probably be glad to immigrate to Texas. They would exploit the land, something the Spanish had never done. Moses went to San Antonio, where he secured a colonization career from the Spanish governor in 1821. This grant permitted him to settle three hundred families in the province. These immigrants would agree to become Spanish subjects in return for grants of land. Moses Austin, however, died in 1821, before he could begin his colonization venture. With his dying breath, he asked that Austin carry through this enterprise and bring it to successful conclusion. This his son agreed to do.

Life's Work

The summer of 1821 found Austin in San Antonio. There he secured a reconfirmation of his father's colonization grant from the Spanish authorities. Unfortunately, however, Mexico became independent from Spain in early 1822, and, consequently, the grant was no longer valid. Austin, who could not secure a renewal from the incoming Mexican authorities in Texas, decided to travel to Mexico City to speak about his grant directly with the newly independent government. He arrived there on April 29, 1822, in the hope that meeting with the Mexican leaders would restore his concession. In the meantime, various Anglo-American farmers began moving to Texas in anticipation of Austin's success in Mexico City.

Austin remained in Mexico for a year while he witnessed the turmoils and instabilities of the new Mexican government. Because of problems related to establishing a workable form of government, Austin could not immediately secure a confirmation of his Texas concession. He did use this time in Mexico City to personal advantage, however, learning to speak and write Spanish with marked fluency.

He also made many friends among the Mexican leaders, including Miguel Ramos Arispe, who authored the Mexican Constitution of 1824. Austin furnished Arispe with a translated copy of the United States Constitution and made recommendations concerning the contents of the Mexican document.

The Mexican government confirmed the Austin grant in early 1823. Austin returned to Texas and assumed direction of the colony, which grew rapidly. By the end of 1824, almost all three hundred colonists permitted by the colonization charter had received grants. The Austin colony centered along the rich land of the Brazos River. Most colonists settled in a region called "the bottom," several leagues inland from the Gulf coast. The small town of San Felipe became its chief settlement. A formal census of the colony taken in 1825 showed eighteen hundred residents, of whom 443 were slaves.

During the summer of 1824, the Mexican government approved the establishment of additional Anglo colonies in Texas. Any prospective colonizer could apply for an *empresario* contract, the Spanish term used to describe these concessions. In all, Mexico issued several dozen such contracts to various individuals during the following decade. Most of them did not enjoy success, although Austin continued to do so. His original contract fulfilled, he applied for additional colonial grants under the *empresario* provisions. The additional settlements which he sponsored brought hundreds of families into Texas. By 1830, Austin had attracted some five thousand people into Texas. This influx, added to the families who came under the leadership of the other *empresarios*, resulted in a considerable Anglo population in the province by the end of the 1820's.

Austin became involved in Mexican politics which, during this period, was chaotic and complicated by factions. The Anglo-Texans increasingly came to identify with the Federalists, a Mexican political group whose beliefs seemed similar to their own. The Centralists, the opposing faction, thus began to identify Austin and the Anglo-Texans as members of the Federalists by the early 1830's. Therein lay one of the causes of the Texas Revolution.

In addition, the Mexican government was concerned that too many Anglo-Americans had immigrated to Texas. As a result, it passed the law of April 6, 1830, which (among other restrictions) ended all future immigration into Texas from the United States. Austin worked hard to secure a re-

peal of this law. He once again went to Mexico City to lobby for measures favorable to Texas. Although he failed to secure all the concessions he wanted, he did convince the government to repeal some of the most objectionable aspects of the law. By the time he returned to Texas in late 1831, events during his absence had made it increasingly difficult for Anglo-Texans to reconcile themselves to continued Mexican rule.

The actions of the post commander at Anahuac on the Texas coast had caused great dissatisfaction among Anglo residents. During the summer of 1832, the colonists took to arms to force his removal. The military commander in Texas eventually removed the offensive garrison commander at Anahuac. For a time, this forestalled additional armed confrontations with the increasingly unhappy Anglo population. By then, however, the crisis had begun. The town council of San Felipe issued a call for a convention of Anglo colonists to discuss common problems and desires. The fifty-eight delegates who composed this group assembled in October, 1832, and elected Austin the presiding officer.

This Convention of 1832, as it subsequently came to be called, drafted a long list of concessions which the Anglo-Texans wanted from the Mexican government. It also created a standing committee of correspondence in each area of Texas for the purpose of monitoring additional problems with Mexico. The delegates also agreed that another convention would be held the following year. This second convention met in 1833 and drafted a provincial constitution for Texas as a separate state within the Mexican government. The Convention of 1833 delegated Austin to deliver this document to the central government. Austin left Texas in May, 1833, on a journey which would result in a two-year absence from Texas. He spent much of this time in a Mexican prison.

Austin arrived in Mexico City, where he presented the proposed constitution to government officials. He also wrote a letter to the town council in San Antonio which complained about the political situation in Mexico. A government official intercepted this letter en route to Texas and believed that it contained treason. Austin, arrested for this in early January of 1834, remained in prison until December of that year. He did not return to Texas until July 11, 1835. Austin's confinement in Mexico City, much of it in the harsh Prison of the Inquisition, permanently ruined his health. During his absence from Texas, dissatisfaction there with Mexico continued. By late 1835, many Anglo-Texans, including Austin, had come to favor a break with Mexico.

The Texas Revolution began on October 2, 1835, with a skirmish between Anglo and Mexican troops near Gonzales, Texas. A committee of colonists issued a call for a provincial convention which appointed Austin commander of the revolutionary army. He held this position for only a few months. The Texas government then appointed him as an agent to the United States, charged with finding materials and supplies for the revolt. Austin spent much of the Texas Revolution in the United States, visiting Washington, D.C., Richmond, Philadelphia, and other cities. He returned to Texas during the summer of 1836 after the Texas Revolution had ended in an Anglo-American victory. Austin permitted his supporters to place his name in candidacy as president of the Republic of Texas. When Sam Houston won election to this office, Austin looked forward to retiring to private life. Houston, however, prevailed upon him to become secretary of state in the new government, which Austin reluctantly agreed to do. He served only a few months. His health broken by the imprisonment in Mexico, Austin died on December 27, 1836.

Summary

Stephen Fuller Austin played a significant role in the westward expansion of the United States. Although credit for the Anglo colonization of Hispanic Texas belongs to his father, Austin carried out the dream, and its success belongs to him. He approached the colonization of Texas with a single-minded determination which consumed all of his efforts. In fact, he had time for little else from 1821 until the events of the Texas Revolution. Although he initially believed that Texas should remain a part of Mexico, Austin had become a vocal advocate of independence by 1835. His activities during the revolt materially assisted the Texan victory. It had been his intention to retire from public life after the success of the revolt. He had earlier selected a picturesque, unsettled location—on the lower Colorado River in Texas—as the site for his home. It is fitting that the modern city of Austin, the state capital, occupies that location. It is there Stephen Fuller Austin rests, in the State Cemetery.

Bibliography

Barker, Eugene C. *The Life of Stephen F. Austin, Founder of Texas, 1793-1836: A Chapter in the Westward Movement of the Anglo-American People*. Nashville: Cokesbury Press, 1925. Standard scholarly biography from original sources, mainly the Austin family papers. This is the most detailed and complete study of Austin and his impact on American history. It is the only full-length biography and provides a solid history of the entire Austin colony.

———. "Stephen F. Austin." In *Handbook of Texas*, vol. 1, edited by Walter P. Webb. Austin: University of Texas Press, 1952. Provides highlights of Austin's career in a short biography. It offers a concise, short treatment of Austin's life in a factual manner.

———, ed. *The Austin Papers*. 3 vols. Washington, D.C.: American Historical Association, 1919-1926. Collection of personal papers and letters of Moses and Stephen F. Austin. Covers the early years of the Austin family in Missouri, with the major part of the collection dealing with the period from 1822 to 1836.

Cantrell, Gregg. "The Partnership of Stephen F. Austin and Joseph H. Hawkins." *Southwestern Historical Quarterly* 99, no. 1 (July, 1995).

Glasscock, Sallie. *Dreams of Empire: The Story of Stephen Fuller Austin and His Colony in Texas.* San Antonio, Tex.: Naylor, 1951. Well-written biography designed for the general reader or for young readers. Good starting place for those unfamiliar with Austin's life.

Holley, Mary Austin. *Texas: Observations, Historical, Geographical, and Descriptive.* Baltimore: Armstrong and Plaskitt, 1833. Holley was Austin's cousin. Provides a firsthand account of life and events in the colony and useful insights into the Austin settlement.

Tracy, Milton, and Richard Havelock-Bailie. *The Colonizer: A Saga of Stephen F. Austin.* El Paso, Tex.: Guynes, 1941. Concentrates on the *empresario* career. Makes few improvements on the Barker biography of Austin but is a solid, general assessment of Austin's life, placing him in historical perspective.

Light Townsend Cummins

AMEDEO AVOGADRO

Born: August 9, 1776; Turin, Kingdom of Sardinia (now Italy)

Died: July 9, 1856; Turin, Kingdom of Sardinia (now Italy)

Areas of Achievement: Chemistry and physics

Contribution: Avogadro was the first scientist to distinguish between atoms and molecules. Avogadro's law, a hypothesis that relates the volume of a gas to the number of particles present, greatly advanced the understanding of chemical reactions and resolved many chemical problems.

Early Life

Amedeo Avogadro was born in Turin in the Kingdom of Sardinia about one hundred kilometers southwest of Milan in what is now Italy. He was one of four sons born to Count Filippo Avogadro and Anna Maria Vercellone. Count Avogadro was a distinguished lawyer and civil servant who came from a prominent family in the region that had produced many generations of Italian military and civil administrative leaders. The name Avogadro possibly is derived from the Italian word *avvocato* (barrister). As a young child, Avogadro likely received his first education at home from the local priests; he later attended secondary schools in Turin. Between 1792 and 1796 he studied law at the University of Turin with the intention of following his father in a legal career. For some years after graduating from law school, he held several government positions. Around 1800 he began to show an interest in natural philosophy, undertook private study of physics and mathematics, and attended physics lectures at the university. His interest in science seems likely to have been stimulated by the recent research on electricity by fellow Italian Alessandro Volta, who came from neighboring Lombardy.

After 1806, Avogadro abandoned his interest in a legal career to concentrate on science and, with one of his brothers, began working on electricity experiments. He was soon appointed as a demonstrator at the Academy of Turin. In 1809 he became professor of natural philosophy at the Royal College of Vercelli. Within one decade, Avogadro was elected as a full member of the Turin Academy of Sciences and one year later was appointed to the first Italian chair of mathematical physics at Turin. His salary was six hundred lire per year.

Life's Work

Avogadro was a prolific writer and published articles in many areas of the physical sciences throughout his life. His name appears in most modern chemistry and physics textbooks, although he has often been misrepresented as being a chemist since his work had a profound influence on the development of chemical theories. His name is usually associated with two important aspects of chemistry: Avogadro's law, which describes the relationship between the volume and number of particles of a gas, and the Avogadro number, which represents the number of particles in one mole of a substance. The concept of the mole as a unit for the measurement of atomic particles was unknown in Avogadro's time, and the term was not introduced until the 1900's.

In many ways it is quite remarkable that Avogadro had a successful scientific career. He received no formal training in science and made a dramatic career change when he was thirty years old. The former was not particularly unusual in the eighteenth and nineteenth centuries, as some of the

greatest scientists of the period were self-educated, including Humphry Davy and Michael Faraday). Others (for example, Nicolas Lémery and Jakob Berzelius) had received their early training in a related field such as pharmacy or medicine before concentrating on a career in the physical sciences. It was very surprising that Avogadro made the transition from law to science so effortlessly, and it was an obvious testament to his good mind and dedicated spirit of discovery. However, Avogadro was not a good experimentalist and had a poor reputation as such among his colleagues. He preferred to interpret the experimental results of others using a mathematical approach. Much of his work was translated and published, but it generally appeared in obscure journals. In addition, Turin was geographically isolated from the world centers of scientific research, which were generally considered to be in Germany and France. Finally Avogadro was, by nature, modest and reserved, and he never actively sought fame. He never traveled to other countries and rarely corresponded or met with other scientists outside of his region. It was not until after his death that the world really comprehended and recognized his contributions to science.

In the early 1800's, chemists began serious attempts to understand the nature of matter and chemical reactions. John Dalton measured the mass ratios of elements in compounds and found these ratios to always be simple whole numbers. For the first time, he demonstrated that the elements must exist as discrete units, or atoms. The nature of one particular form of matter, gases, had always been difficult for early scientists to understand. In 1808, Joseph Gay-Lussac published studies on the combining volumes of gases. He showed that gases always combined in simple whole number ratios. For example, 200 cubic centimeters of hydrogen always combined with 100 cubic centimeters of oxygen to form 200 cubic centimeters of water vapor (a 2:1:2 ratio). Although these types of observations suggested that equal volumes of gases contained equal numbers of atoms, Dalton rejected this hypothesis, believing that Gay-Lussac's experiments were inaccurate. Dalton and others argued that one volume of oxygen gas contained a specific number of oxygen atoms and therefore must produce the same volume of water vapor with an equivalent number of water atoms. It should be remembered that at the time, it was still generally believed that water had a chemical formula of HO and was composed of HO atoms.

Like Dalton, most chemists of the day believed that common gaseous elements such as hydrogen, oxygen, nitrogen, and chlorine existed as individual atoms. Avogadro's explanation appeared in his 1811 article *Essai d'une manière de déterminer les masses relatives des molécules élémentaires des corps et les proportions selon lesquelles elles entrent dans ces combinaisons* (essay on a manner of determining the relative masses of the elementary molecules of bodies and the proportions in which they enter into combinations), in which he attempted to explain the inconsistencies with existing theories by assuming that equal volumes of all gases contained equal numbers of molecules rather than atoms, provided conditions of temperature and pressure were kept constant. Avogadro's hypothesis (also known as the molecular hypothesis) would later become known as Avogadro's law. During a chemical reaction, therefore, Avogadro proposed that molecules could split into half-molecules (atoms) and combine with other half-molecules to form the observed product compounds. By contrast, Dalton viewed the combination of two gases such as hydrogen and oxygen as involving individual atoms. It is now known, thanks to Avogadro's insight, that this reaction involves molecules that are composed of two atoms each (diatomic molecules), which is consistent with Gay-Lussac's experimental results on combining volumes in which two volumes of hydrogen react with one volume of oxygen to generate two volumes of water vapor. According to Avogadro, each molecule of water must contain one molecule of hydrogen ($H2$) and one half-molecule of oxygen (one O atom). It followed from this that the correct chemical formula for water was $H2O$ and not HO has Dalton and others believed. It should be noted that Avogadro never used the modern system of chemical formulas that are shown in the previous equations. If he had, his theory may have been more understandable and therefore readily accepted sooner.

Avogadro's hypothesis also explained discrepancies in the measured densities of gases and resulted in more accurate determinations of atomic weights. Water vapor was known to have a lower density than oxygen, but this fact was difficult to explain if the latter existed as single atoms. The occurrence of diatomic oxygen molecules easily explained why oxygen had a greater density than water vapor. In Dalton's early table of atomic weights, which were a measurement of the relative weights of atoms, hydrogen was assigned a value of 1 and oxygen a value of 7.5. When viewed as diatomic molecules, the value of hydrogen became 2 and oxygen 15. In other words, Dalton's atomic weights had to be doubled for diatomic molecules. This eventually led to a more accurate table of atomic weights.

Avogadro's molecular hypothesis was largely ignored during his lifetime. His theory did have the support of a fellow Italian chemist Stanislao Cannizzaro, who was one of the few who seemed to grasp the significance of Avogadro's idea, but only after Avogadro's death. Most scientists, however, failed to distinguish between atoms and molecules, and Avogadro, isolated in Turin and largely unknown in Europe, never witnessed the universal acceptance of his theory. Cannizzaro showed that Avogadro's theory could be used for determining molecular size and accurate chemical formulas. His enthusiasm for the molecular hypothesis had a profound influence on the German chemist Lothar Meyer. In his 1864 textbook, Meyer employed Avogadro's hypothesis to develop his ideas on theoretical chemistry. This book had considerable influence on other chemists who applied Avogadro's ideas to many other aspects of physical chemistry.

Avogadro held his position as the chair of mathematical physics at Turin from 1820 until 1822, when it was abolished because of regional political turmoil. The position was reestablished in 1832, and Avogadro was reappointed in 1834. He held this post until his retirement in 1850 at the age of seventy-four. He spent the last six years of his life continuing with his scientific studies.

Summary

It was not until around 1870 that the term "Avogadro's law" first appeared in print; by the 1880's it had received universal recognition. The realization that common elemental gases existed as diatomic units had an enormous influence on obliterating chemical inconsistencies and linking the chemical and physical properties of substances. Accurate density determinations and atomic and molecular weight measurements for gases also became possible, which aided the rapidly developing area of organic chemistry in the nineteenth century. Once Avogadro's law was understood, a new era in the development of chemical theories and molecular composition became possible. The Dutch chemist Jacobus van't Hoff showed that Avogadro's law could be applied to solutions as well as gases, for which he was awarded the first Nobel Prize in Chemistry in 1901. For chemists, a significant consequence of Avogadro's law was the realization that one mole of all substances (that is, the atomic or molecular weight of a substance expressed in grams) contains the same number of particles. This quantity, equal to 6.02252×10^{23}, is now known as the Avogadro number in honor of a great scientist who was not recognized in his own lifetime.

Bibliography

Causey, Robert J. "Avogadro's Hypothesis and the Duhemian Pitfall." *Journal of Chemical Education* 48 (June, 1971): 365-367. This short article looks at the role of certain chemists in the history of the delayed acceptance of Avogadro's hypothesis.

Fisher, Nicholas. "Avogadro's Hypothesis: Why Did the Chemists Ignore It?" Parts 1 and 2. *History of Science* 20, nos. 2 and 3 (1982): 77-102, 212-231. Fisher examines the reasons why it took so long for Avogadro's ideas to become widely accepted.

Holmyard, E. J. *Makers of Chemistry.* Oxford; Clarendon Press, 1931. Section 52 discusses Avogadro's work in the context of its historical importance. Contains a sample of his handwriting.

Ihde, Aaron J. *The Development of Modern Chemistry.* New York: Harper & Row, 1964. Ihde gives a good account of the Avogadro story in one of the classic texts on chemical history.

Jaffe, Bernard. *Crucibles: The Story of Chemistry.* New York: Dover, 1976. This is one of the most delightful and easy to read accounts of the history of chemistry. Chapter 9 is devoted to Avogadro.

Morselli, Mario. *Amedeo Avogadro.* Boston: Kluwer, 1984. This is the most thorough account of Avogadro's life. Morselli describes most of his major contributions to science, not just the molecular hypothesis. Includes bibliographies for each chapter.

Nicholas C. Thomas

CHARLES BABBAGE

Born: December 26, 1791; in or near London, England

Died: October 18, 1871; London, England

Areas of Achievement: Mathematics, invention, and computer science

Contribution: Babbage conceptually anticipated many of the developments realized in twentieth century computation science. He contributed to the mathematics of his time and invented several practical devices.

Early Life

Charles Babbage, the first child of Benjamin and Elizabeth (Teape) Babbage, was born on December 26, 1791. The exact location of his birth is not known, but it was in the vicinity of London, where his father was a well-to-do banker. The family, on both sides, had been comfortably established in the nearby countryside for several generations. Two more sons were born but died in early childhood. A daughter, Mary Anne, outlived her brother Charles, with whom she had a lifelong close relationship.

As a young child, Charles was subject to fevers, which were naturally of great concern to his parents; when it came time for some formal education, he was placed under the tutelage of a clergyman with the admonition "to attend to his health, but not to press too much knowledge upon him." He later attended school in Enfield, where he was instructed in the classics. Charles's natural aptitude for mathematics in particular, and logical, systematic thinking in general, manifested itself early. As a schoolboy he discovered algebra and, for several months, arose at 3 A.M. for self-instruction along with a similarly precocious classmate.

As he grew older, Charles became more robust, and as an adult he was full-figured and rather handsome. When he was twelve years old his parents moved back to Totnes, where they had lived before going to London. That was Charles's home until he entered Cambridge University in 1810.

By that time his mathematical self-instruction had progressed into differential and integral calculus. He was very disappointed to find himself far in advance of the mathematical instruction available at the university.

At Cambridge his social nature developed. He had many friends and joined in numerous nonacademic activities. In addition, Babbage's liberal political consciousness emerged, curiously manifesting itself, in part, by his espousal of Gottfried Wilhelm Leibnitz's calculus notation over that of England's Isaac Newton. With a group of like-minded fellow undergraduates, he formed the Analytical Society to study the mathematical developments being made on the Continent.

He was graduated from Cambridge University in 1814. Soon thereafter, against his father's wishes, he was married to Georgiana Whitmore. The young newlyweds settled in London, but Charles continued his studies, receiving his M.A. degree in 1817. He had no income-producing position at that time, but family moneys allowed the couple to live quite comfortably in London society. Charles was accepted in scientific circles and was elected to the Royal Society in 1816.

Life's Work

The only professional appointment that Babbage ever held was to the Lucasian Chair of Mathematics

at Cambridge University (1828-1839), an appointment that had few formal duties. Consequently, and by virtue of his private wealth, he was free to pursue his own interests from his home in London.

For a dozen years after he and Georgiana settled there, he thoroughly enjoyed the social and intellectual atmosphere of the city. Eight children were born to them. Only four survived infancy, and Georgiana died in childbirth with the eighth in 1827. Babbage, devastated by the loss, became an increasingly bitter and sharply critical man. He spent the year following his wife's death traveling on the Continent. He never remarried or had a normal home life again. His surviving children were reared by relatives living outside London. Of the four, the only daughter, also named Georgiana, died as a young girl. Only after they had reached adulthood did Babbage get to know his sons well.

Nevertheless, Babbage, a gregarious man of great vitality, traveled widely and associated with a broad circle of contemporaries such as Charles Darwin and Charles Dickens as well as with fellow scientists at home and abroad. He was a great admirer of the scientific developments in Germany and France and of their associated educational institutions and professional societies. He was a significant force in establishing in England the Cambridge Philosophical Society, the Astronomical Society, the Statistical Society of London, and the British Association for the Advancement of Science. In 1830, he wrote *Reflections on the Decline of Science in England and on Some of Its Causes*, deploring the sad state of the Royal Society in England at the time.

Babbage continued to pursue his mathematical interests beyond his university days, publishing a number of significant papers in the areas of the calculus of functions, algebraic analysis, probability, and geometry. Since this was at a time when British mathematics had reached a dismally low level, Babbage's mathematical work was held in especially high regard on the Continent.

One of the important mathematical needs of that time was for tables of trigonometric, logarithmic, and other functions. Those in existence had been laboriously generated by human calculators and were not without error. About 1821, Babbage, impressed by the potential of machines to carry out fixed operations and recognizing that successive entries in such tables could be expressed in terms of finite differences, conceived of an infallible calculating machine to replace fallible human calcula-

tors. The calculated results would be automatically printed out to eliminate transcribing errors.

In constructing his first mechanical calculator, the "Difference Engine," Babbage was assisted by sizable funding from the British government, which recognized the importance of accurate tables for use in navigation, for example. He designed the engine and personally supervised its construction by a skilled, hired engineer. In connection with this activity Babbage devised some new machine tooling techniques and an unambiguous method of Mechanical Notation for parts drawings to aid in communication between designer and engineer. A working model was built which may be seen in the British Museum of South Kensington.

The upset associated with his wife's death interrupted further developments for the machine planned by Babbage. After his return to England he faced difficulties with his engineer and with obtaining further government funding. No more work was done on the Difference Engine after 1832. By that time, however, Babbage had conceived of a much more sophisticated and versatile "Analytical Engine," one which embodied many ideas now familiar in the world of electronic computers.

The Analytical Engine had a storage unit for holding numerical input data, a mill for working on them, and a separate operations control section, and he used punched-card systems for input and operation. The rest of Babbage's life—and much of his private fortune—was devoted to improving and refining these basic ideas. Only a modified version of the Analytical Engine was ever built, but detailed plans for several versions of it were carefully drawn up which show the soundness of Babbage's ideas.

In England, Babbage was widely regarded as an eccentric, irascible genius, but he was much respected abroad. In 1840, he traveled to Italy, where he gave a series of lectures on his Analytical Engine that was especially well received. A member of the audience, L. F. Menabrea, wrote up those lectures and published them in French. Subsequently, they were translated into English and provided with a lengthy commentary by Countess Ada Lovelace, the daughter of the poet Lord Byron. She was a mathematically precocious teenager when she first met Charles Babbage in 1833. He was pleased with her interest in and appreciation of his calculating machines, and the warm friendship which developed between them lasted throughout her sadly short lifetime.

Babbage was a prolific writer on social, political, economic, religious, as well as technical topics. He was the outstanding cryptologist of his time, using mathematical techniques to decipher the codes devised by others. In addition, he invented many practical devices, such as an occulting light which could be used to send messages and an ophthalmoscope for studying the eye. The American scientist Joseph Henry, who visited Babbage on two occasions, wrote of him:

> Hundreds of mechanical appliances in the factories and workshops of Europe and America, scores of ingenious expedients in mining and architecture, the construction of bridges and boring of tunnels, and a world of tools by which labor benefited and the arts improved—all the overflowings of a mind so rich that its very waste became valuable—came from Charles Babbage. He more, perhaps, than any man who ever lived, narrowed the chasm separating science and practical mechanics.

Summary

Charles Babbage enjoys higher and more widespread esteem today than he ever did during his lifetime. Many of his ideas regarding computing machines have been realized only in the late twentieth century, with the advent of modern electronic devices. In his time he was the leading advocate of the systematic application of science to industry and commerce and of statistical methods to economic and social problems—what would today be called "operations research."

Babbage was a man born ahead of his time. Disappointed with the current state of affairs in England, unappreciated, even snubbed at times in his home country, he nevertheless looked forward with optimism to the future which could be made by the application of scientific principles. He has been quoted as saying that he would willingly give up the rest of his life to be able to return five hundred years hence with a guide to explain the intervening advances that he believed were sure to come.

Bibliography

Ashworth, William J. "Memory, Efficiency, and Symbolic Analysis: Charles Babbage, John Herschel, and the Industrial Mind. *Isis* 87, no. 4 (December 1996). Discusses the influence of changes in British industry on the use of the analytical method by Babbage and Herschel. Technology and its effect on production are compared to the analytical method and its effect on mental efficiency.

Babbage, Charles. *Passages from the Life of a Philosopher.* London: Longman, 1864; New York: Kelley, 1969. Thirty-six autobiographical fragments of very uneven quality and style.

Babbage, Henry P., ed. *Babbage's Calculating Engines, a Collection of Papers Relating to Them: Their History, and Construction.* London: Spon, 1889; Los Angeles: Tomash Publishers, 1982. Recently made available as volume 2 of the Reprint Series for the History of Computing under the auspices of the Charles Babbage Institute at the University of Minnesota. Includes a new introduction by Allan G. Bromley. Contains thirty-three items, most of them assembled by Charles Babbage before his death. Additions and editing provided by his youngest son.

Dolan, Brian P. "Representing Novelty: Charles Babbage, Charles Lyell, and Experiments in Early Victorian Geology." *History of Science* 36, no. 3 (September 1998). Discusses the theories on land elevation and change developed by Babbage and Lyell and the ultimate influence of Babbage's theory on Lyell's work.

Dubbey, J. M. *The Mathematical Work of Charles Babbage.* Cambridge: Cambridge University Press, 1978. A critique of the mathematical work of Babbage with extended commentary on the calculus of functions, mathematical notation, and the mathematical basis of the operation of his calculating engines. Includes a list of all of Babbage's mathematical books and papers.

Goldstine, Herman H. *The Computer from Pascal to Von Neumann.* Princeton, N.J.: Princeton University Press, 1972. Chapter 2, "Charles Babbage and His Analytical Engine," describes the concepts developed by Babbage that are inherent in modern computing. Shows how Babbage built upon what previously had been accomplished by others and introduced significant conceptual advances.

Hyman, Anthony. *Charles Babbage: Pioneer of the Modern Computer.* Oxford: Oxford University Press, and Princeton, N.J.: Princeton University Press, 1982. Full-length biography based on the author's extended research on published works and archival materials. Analyzes the social and political climate of Babbage's time and his involvement aside from his technical achievement. Lists all Babbage's published works. Mathematical discussion of Babbage's engines placed at end of text as appendices.

Merz, John Theodore. *A History of European Scientific Thought in the Nineteenth Century.* 2 vols. New York: Dover, 1965. Republication of a work originally published between 1904 and 1912. Chapters 1-3 of volume 1 compare and contrast the scientific spirit in France, Germany, and England during the lifetime of Charles Babbage; includes several references to Babbage.

Morrison, Philip, and Emily Morrison, eds. *Charles Babbage on the Principles and Development of the Calculator.* New York: Dover, 1961. Selections from the Babbage volumes listed above with an insightful introduction by the editors summarizing the life and works of Babbage.

Moseley, Maboth. *Irascible Genius: A Life of Charles Babbage, Inventor.* London: Hutchinson, 1964; New York: Kelley, 1965. Focuses on personal details of Babbage's life. Quotes extensively from correspondence deposited in archives.

Stein, Dorothy. *Ada: A Life and a Legacy.* Cambridge, Mass.: MIT Press, 1985. Biography of Augusta Ada Byron, later Countess of Lovelace, with extensive discussion of her relationship with Charles Babbage.

Katherine R. Sopka

SIR ROBERT STEPHENSON SMYTH BADEN-POWELL

Born: February 22, 1857; London, England

Died: January 8, 1941; Nyeri, Kenya

Areas of Achievement: Military affairs and social reform

Contribution: A celebrated hero of the Boer War, Baden-Powell gained universal and lasting fame as the founder of the Boy Scouts and the Girl Guides. He was revered as the "chief scout" of the movement, shaped its ideals, and provided its essential literature.

Early Life

Robert Stephenson Smyth Baden-Powell was the sixth son of an ordained professor of geometry at Oxford University. His mother, his father's third wife, was the daughter of an admiral. Because Baden-Powell's father died when he was three, his mother, whom he always admired greatly, had to raise a family of ten children with extremely limited financial resources. She encouraged the study of natural history and took her children on holidays that featured camping and boating. Nevertheless, Baden-Powell was sent to a famous private school, Charterhouse, where he was very happy. He participated intensely in school activities, and while he did not make a mark as a scholar or as an athlete, he excelled in theatrical performances and cartooning. He also spent much time learning woodcraft. Later he would borrow much from the principles and practices of his exclusive education for the mass movement that scouting became. Denied admission to Oxford because of his scholarly weaknesses, Baden-Powell took the open examination for direct commission in the army and scored so high that he did not have to attend Sandhurst, the British equivalent of West Point.

He was commissioned as an officer in the Thirteenth Hussars, a cavalry regiment that was stationed in India at the time. He proved to be particularly skillful on reconnaissance missions, which enabled him to develop various scouting techniques. In the military sense, scouting meant sneaking up to spy in order to find out where the enemy was, where they stationed their forces, what their regular routines were, how many men they had, and what kind of equipment they used. The first of his many books were on scouting and boar hunting. He was also a noted polo player.

Baden-Powell's skills were augmented as he fulfilled various military assignments in the empire. He scouted the lesser-known passes of the Drakensberg Mountains of Natal in South Africa disguised as a reporter. He took part in the southern African campaigns in Zululand and Matabeleland, later to become Zimbabwe. He also took part in the West African campaign against the Ashanti in the area that later became Ghana. Adroit scouting of enemy positions, particularly at night, became one of his special talents. While stationed once again in India, he sought to institute training in scouting as a regular feature of soldiers' preparation.

Life's Work

Baden-Powell was slender and of medium height for his day. He was sandy haired, mustached, and freckled and liked to wear American Western-style hats. He was a warm, friendly, and modest person who nonetheless had a gift for advertising his activities. Before the Anglo-Afrikaner War in South

Africa, commonly known as the Boer War, Baden-Powell was a colonel with a good reputation but no particular fame. He emerged from that war as the youngest major general in the British army and famous throughout the world as a legendary hero. The queen of England honored him, and the public revered him.

Baden-Powell was sent to South Africa as war threatened to break out between the British and the descendants of Dutch settlers, the Afrikaners, who were strongest in the Afrikaner republics of the Transvaal and the Orange Free State. His mission was to organize two regiments of local forces to defend the British colonies of Bechuanaland (which became Botswana) and Matabeleland. He became the commander in charge during the siege of the small but strategic southern African town of Mafeking for 217 days in 1899 and 1900. Throughout the early stages of the war, while the British suffered a string of defeats, Mafeking held out and would not surrender despite the constant bombardment, the horde of enemies surrounding it, and dwindling supplies. Baden-Powell distinguished himself by holding up the morale of his troops and the inhabitants. He did so by keeping everybody busy and providing entertainment designed to promote cheerfulness. The defenders enjoyed theatrical productions and cricket games in between bouts of fending off attacks by the numerically superior enemy, often by cleverly outsmarting them. Throughout the siege, Baden-Powell was brave, resourceful, and optimistic and expressed himself in the style of confident understatement so loved by the British public. Since mail could get out, the siege was followed very closely in Britain, and its importance was exaggerated in the press. Therefore, there were massive celebrations when the siege was lifted, and Baden-Powell found that he had been made into a hero.

One particular aspect of the siege of Mafeking led to the creation of the scouting movement and thereby determined Baden-Powell's whole future. Baden-Powell organized the young cadets in the town to carry on routine work and thereby free older men for defense. They were so useful that they inspired Baden-Powell to try to organize youth for peaceful pursuits after the war. Another significant accomplishment at this time was the publication of *Aids to Scouting for N.C.O.s and Men* (1899). Noncommissioned officers (NCOs) were subordinate officers, while the "men" in the title were ordinary enlisted soldiers. Baden-Powell was surprised to learn that the book was widely used by teachers and read by boys in Britain.

Baden-Powell's military career continued after Mafeking. He was selected to raise and train a police force, called a constabulary, for South Africa. After that he became inspector general of the cavalry. He established a cavalry school and a journal to aid training. He also commanded a division of the Territorial Army, which was similar to a division of the National Guard in the United States. Lieutenant General Baden-Powell retired from the army in 1910 at the age of fifty-three so that he could devote himself full time to the scouting movement.

Baden-Powell was impressed by the religiously oriented Boy's Brigade movement and sought to create a program that would involve masses of boys from all backgrounds and creeds. To this end he rewrote his popular *Aids to Scouting for N.C.O.s and Men*, which became the enormously popular *Scouting for Boys* (1908), a book that changed through many editions published over decades. The book led to the sprouting of Boy Scout troops all over Britain and then in Canada, New Zealand, Australia, the United States, and, finally, throughout the world. Rallies, called jamborees, brought together scouts from all over the world. Girls demanded a similar organization; with the help of his sister, Agnes, Baden-Powell established the Girl Guides (called the Girl Scouts in the United States). Several other variations of the movement appeared to satisfy different age groups and interest areas.

As with any large organization, there were dissensions about strong leadership at the center, public recriminations, and forced resignations over various issues. Baden-Powell's reputation survived all of the confrontations. One contentious issue for modern scholars about Baden-Powell's leadership of the Boy Scouts centers on the question of militarism. Since he was a military man, critics perceived militaristic indoctrination as one of the goals of the movement and thought its aim was to strengthen the pool of able-bodied and obedient young men available for British forces. On the other hand, other writers cite the helpfulness, kindness, and generosity advocated in *Scouting for Boys* as well as the clear emphasis on peacetime pursuits. Baden-Powell himself brushed aside the matter by saying that the movement was aimed at developing qualities that served the nation best in peace or war.

Baden-Powell married at age fifty-five and had one son and two daughters. His wife, Olave, came to preside over the Girl Guide movement in place of Agnes. Baden-Powell always enjoyed sketching and was able to illustrate many of the books he wrote. He was a prolific and accomplished writer who produced thirty-five books from 1883 to 1940. Some were histories of his campaigns, some were accounts of his travel adventures, and the most widely circulated were about scouting. *Scouting for Boys* was his most famous work.

Baden-Powell was named chief scout of the whole world at one international jamboree. This was perhaps one of the greatest of the many honors of his life. Baden-Powell received nearly forty significant medals, the freedom of eleven cities in the United Kingdom, and six honorary doctorates. Nevertheless, he was a man who shied away from the hero worship he inspired and enjoyed the solitude that the hobby of fishing provided.

Summary

Since it began, the scouting movement has attracted approximately 500 million members and become the most successful and most enduring scheme for training youth ever known. It has had an enormously positive influence on youth through the organized practice of its ideals of loyalty, duty, honesty, kindness, helpfulness, self-reliance, and love of adventure and the outdoors. It was intended to be an inclusive movement, indifferent to class, creed, or ethnic background. It sought to incorporate boys who suffered from bad environments and excite them with adventures in the outdoors and romantic, noble ideals from knights and American Indians. Baden-Powell was the person who started this movement, sustained it, and provided its attractive ideology. From the creation of the scouts in 1908 until his death in 1941, it absorbed all of his energies. The movement is his enduring legacy. He was also one of the most prolific and popular writers of this century. He wrote over fifty books and pamphlets, gave countless addresses, and wrote countless articles.

Baden-Powell was a kind and cheerful person who shunned the hero worship he inspired. Yet he was a military man and an imperialist who fought in several colonial wars and made a name for himself by his very heroic and very colorful defense of Mafeking. In the first half of the twentieth century, he was usually revered as a selfless, secular saint. Some recent writers have been quite critical, pointing out how he naturally reflected some of the less pleasant ideas and assumptions of his background and time, such as militarism, racism, nationalism, and self-advertising. Yet even the sharpest critics cannot deny the complexity of his character, his charisma, and his enduring influence throughout the world.

Bibliography

Baden-Powell of Gilwell, Robert Stephenson Smyth Baden-Powell, Baron. *Scouting for Boys*. London: Pearson, 1908. This book has gone through many editions and gives good insight into the ideology of the movement and how it evolved over the years. One author claimed that this book made Baden-Powell the most read of all British authors with the single exception of William Shakespeare.

Brendon, Piers. *Eminent Edwardians*. London: Penguin, 1979; Boston: Houghton Mifflin, 1980. An essay on Baden-Powell concludes this book, which examines several of the revered figures of the age with a critical eye. Brendon raises questions about Baden-Powell's treatment of the natives at Mafeking and unsubstantiated questions about his sexual orientation.

Churchill, Winston S. *Great Contemporaries*. London: Butterworth, and New York: Putnam, 1937. This is a collection of Churchill's sharp and witty character sketches that appeared in various magazines and newspapers. Churchill included a sketch of Baden-Powell in this collection. Always an admirer of men of action who upheld the British Empire, Churchill uses his considerable literary skills to present a kind and heroic depiction of Baden-Powell.

Jeal, Tim. *The Boy-Man: The Life of Lord Baden-Powell*. New York: Morrow, 1990. This modern biography is well written and sympathetic toward Baden-Powell. With a total of 670 pages, it chronicles every known episode of the subject's life in considerable detail. Both sides of controversies are given.

Reynolds, Ernest Edwin. *Baden-Powell: A Biography of Lord Baden-Powell of Gilwell, O.M., G.C.M.G., G.C.V.O., K.C.B.* London and New York: Oxford University Press, 1942. This early biography was written shortly after Baden-Powell's death and tends toward hero worship and an uncritical view of Baden-Powell's shortcomings. Nevertheless, it gives a good idea of the tremendously high esteem in which Baden-Powell was held by nearly all contemporaries.

Rosenthal, Michael. *The Character Factory: Baden-Powell and the Origins of the Boy Scout Movement*. London: Collins, and New York: Pantheon, 1986. This is a work of sharp revisionism that seeks to knock the hero from his pedestal. The very worst things Baden-Powell said and did are highlighted, particularly his hypocrisy on racial matters. The book is more about the origins of the scouting movement than a biography, and it puts emphasis on the usefulness of the scouting movement for British military ends.

Henry Weisser

KARL ERNST VON BAER

Born: February 29, 1792; Piep, near Jerwen, Estonia
Died: November 28, 1876; Dorpat, Estonia
Areas of Achievement: Biology, anthropology, and geology
Contribution: Baer gained his greatest fame early in his career through his discovery of the mammalian egg and his contributions to the understanding of embryological development. In his later years, Baer would turn his attention to anthropological investigations, including the state of primitiveness of various races, and to geological studies, especially in Russia.

Early Life

In the mid-sixteenth century, an ancestor of Karl Ernst von Baer emigrated from Prussia to Livonia, and one of that ancestor's descendants bought an estate in Estonia during the mid-seventeenth century. He was made a member of the Prussian nobility, and by the time of Karl's father, Magnus Johann von Baer, the estate at Piep was of modest size. Karl's father was trained in law and served as a public official. Karl's parents were first cousins, and they had seven daughters and three sons. Because of the large size of the family, Karl was sent to live with his father's childless brother and wife on a nearby estate. It was there that Karl began to cultivate his love of botany and natural history.

He entered medical school at the University of Dorpat in 1810 but apparently never planned on a medical career. Instead, upon graduation, he continued his studies in Berlin, Vienna, and finally Würzburg. There he studied under the anatomist Ignaz Döllinger, a disciple of the German Romantic Friedrich Schelling, and was inspired to devote himself to the study of comparative embryology. In 1819, Baer finally received an appointment as an anatomy professor at Königsberg, where he stayed until 1834. That allowed him to marry Auguste von Medem, a resident of Königsberg, on January 1, 1820. They had five sons, of whom one died in childhood and a second of typhus at the age of twenty-one, and one daughter.

During Baer's tenure at Königsberg, he established himself as a brilliant embryologist and made his initial discoveries of the mammalian egg. His initial contributions are found in the first two volumes of Karl Friedrich Burdach's *Die Physiologie als Erfahrungswissenschaft* (1826-1828; physiolo-

gy as empirical science). A small brochure entitled *De ovi mammalium et hominis genesis epistola* (1827; *The Discovery of the Mammalian Egg*, 1956) appeared at about the same time. In 1834, he left Königsberg for the Academy of Sciences in St. Petersburg, and in 1837 the still-unfinished second volume of his animal embryology was published, with the two volumes now entitled *Über Entwickelungsgeschichte der Thiere* (1828-1837; on the developmental history of animals). A portion of the missing material for this volume was published posthumously in 1888.

Life's Work

While at the University of Würzburg, Baer was encouraged by Döllinger and Christian Heinrich Pander to continue the largely unknown work of Caspar Friedrich Wolff concerning the detailed development of the hen's egg. Baer expanded that research to include a wide range of organisms, and the results of his studies virtually assured the epigeneticists of victory in their battle with the preformationists. He was the first to discover and describe the mammalian egg (first found in Burdach's house dog), and he concluded that "every animal which springs from the coition of male and female is developed from an ovum, and none from a simple formative liquid." This important theoretical statement, although based on German *Naturphilosophie* and rejected by later embryologists in the vitalistic terms understood by Baer, allowed for reproductive and embryological studies to continue on a doctrinally unified basis and hence permitted the development of comparative embryology as a discipline.

In addition to describing mammalian and other vertebrate ova, Baer described the developing embryo. One of his major conceptual innovations was that he could see the individual organism as a historical entity which underwent a developmental process. He thus examined organisms at various stages of development, and he was one of the first to describe the process in terms of the formation of germ layers and the gradual production of organs and body parts. Conducting research for the second volume of his monumental work, he examined and compared the developmental processes of different organisms. In the process, he discovered the notochord (the flexible supportive rod ventral to the nerve chord, which is characteristic of all chor-

parative anatomy for classifying animals. Baer's method for classifying organisms was based on the fact that all animal embryos begin as a single fertilized egg. According to Baer, they diverged immediately into one of four types of development. Vertebrate embryos can be distinguished from the annulate embryos (essentially worms), which in turn are different from the embryos of the mollusks, and all of which differ from the radiata (echinoderms).

In addition, Baer argued that the more general traits of the group of animals to which an embryo belongs appear earlier in individual development than the specialized characteristics, that the more general form always precedes a more specialized form, that every embryo of a given form, rather than passing through the stages of other forms, instead diverges more and more from them, and that, as a result, the embryo of a higher form never resembles the adult of lower animals but only the embryonic form of those animals. He concluded that development takes place from homogeneous and general to heterogeneous and special and that ontological development reflects divergence from other forms rather than parallelism or recapitulation. With this latter conclusion, he thus argued against Johann Meckel's law of parallel development and against Ernst Haeckel's biogenetic law of ontogeny recapitulating phylogeny.

With the publication of the second volume of *Über Entwickelungsgeschichte der Thiere* in 1837, Baer had transformed embryology into a modern laboratory science. Moreover, he had produced a theoretical framework that would greatly influence evolutionary thought even though he would strongly maintain a lifelong antievolutionary position. Charles Darwin, for example, used embryological evidence to support his theory and noted that he agreed with Baer's view of divergence rather than the competing doctrine of recapitulation. Darwin also used Baer's standard for judging an organism to be "higher" than another as being related to the degree of differentiation of parts and specialization of function.

By the time the second volume of his great embryological work was published, Baer had left Königsberg for reasons that are not well understood and had settled in St. Petersburg, working at the Academy of Sciences. In 1846, he took a position with the academy in comparative anatomy and physiology, a decision that was related to his long-term interest in anthropology. Under the academy's auspices, he made a number of expeditions to such

dates) in the chicken embryo, explained the significance of the gill slits and gill arches, which Martin Rathke had earlier discovered in the embryo, and then explained the cause of the amnion formation. Finally, he described the development of the urogenital system, the formation of the lungs, the development of the digestive canal, and the formation of the nervous system. These findings are detailed and commented on in his pioneering *Über Entwickelungsgeschichte der Thiere*.

Baer is best known for his remarks in the fifth scholium of this work, in which he argued against a single *scala naturae* (chain of being), presented a parody of Jean-Baptiste de Monet, chevalier de Lamarck, rejected evolution in any form as well as the idea that embryos of higher animals pass through the adult forms of the lower animals, and proposed his own laws of individual development. His comparative embryology had led him to the same conclusions that Georges Cuvier's comparative anatomy had produced, that is, that instead of a single chain of being, there were essentially four animal types. He further argued that comparative embryology actually provided better data than did complaces as Novaya Zemlya, Lapland, the North Cape, and other regions of Russia as well as England and continental Europe. He collected specimens and made a number of geological discoveries. Although none of his work in these areas was as significant as his embryological achievements, he was instrumental in the founding of the Society of Geography and Ethnology of St. Petersburg and became a cofounder of the German Anthropological Society.

Baer retired from the academy in St. Petersburg in 1862 because of increasing problems with his vision and hearing. In 1867, he went to Dorpat, where he continued his studies and writing until 1876, when he died at the age of eighty-four.

Summary

Karl Ernst von Baer's contributions to the fledgling science of embryology in the nineteenth century were immeasurable. Methodologically and conceptually he provided the basis for further research. Yet apart from his empirical findings, little remains in modern biology of Baer's embryology. His adherence to German Idealism and *Naturphilosophie*, including the use of vitalistic explanations in embryological development, and his fervent antievolutionary position caused many scientists in the latter part of the century to ignore him. Nevertheless, his contributions were viewed as monumental during his time. He published more than three hundred papers on topics ranging from embryology and entomology to anthropology, Russian fisheries, and the routes of Odysseus' voyage. He was honored and respected by scientists throughout the world, and admired and loved for his loyalty and wit by his Estonian neighbors.

Bibliography

Baer, Karl Ernst von. *Autobiography of Karl Ernst von Baer.* Edited by Jane Oppenheimer. Translated by H. Schneider. Canton, Mass.: Science History, 1986. This relatively long autobiography was first published by the Estonian Knights in 1864 on the golden jubilee of Baer's doctorate. Oppenheimer provides a very helpful preface. An extensive bibliography and an index make this work a valuable tool for the serious student.

Coleman, William. *Biology in the Nineteenth Century: Problems of Form, Function, and Transformation.* New York: Wiley, 1971; Cambridge: Cambridge University Press, 1977. Chapter 3 provides an excellent context for Baer's embryological work as it details the advances in cytology, explains the arguments between preformationists and epigeneticists, and describes the contributions that Baer made to the understanding of ontogeny.

Lovejoy, Arthur O. "Recent Criticism of the Darwinian Theory of Recapitulation: Its Grounds and Its Initiator." In *Forerunners of Darwin, 1745-1859*, edited by Bentley Glass et al. Baltimore: Johns Hopkins University Press, 1968. Lovejoy tries to explain why so many misread Baer. Explains Baer's four embryological laws, including what is and what is not affirmed. Examines Darwin's misreading of Baer and Baer's fallacies in his criticism of Darwin's theory. The notes provide helpful explanations.

Oppenheimer, Jane. "An Embryological Enigma in the *Origin of Species*." In *Forerunners of Darwin, 1745-1859*, edited by Bentley Glass et al. Baltimore: Johns Hopkins University Press, 1968. Oppenheimer explores the professional relationship between Darwin and Baer. She examines the various ideas that each developed independently of the other and the diverse ways in which each incorporated these ideas into a total system. As a result, one understands how Darwin can use many of Baer's findings while rejecting his conclusion, and why Baer is unable to support Darwin's evolutionary position.

Ospovat, Dov. "The Influence of Karl Ernst von Baer's Embryology, 1828-1859." *Journal of the History of Biology* 9 (Spring, 1976): 1-28. This article discusses the degree of influence that Baer's embryological explanations had during his own life, especially in terms of their ability to dislodge the earlier theory of recapitulation. In the process, it clarifies the content of Baer's theories and shows the similarities to other theories then available as well as describes the essential points of difference between them. Ospovat also explains why he disagrees with some of the Baerean scholarship, including the articles by Oppenheimer and Lovejoy cited above.

Winsor, Mary P. *Starfish, Jellyfish, and the Order of Life: Issues in Nineteenth Century Science.* New Haven, Conn.: Yale University Press, 1976. While this book is not specifically about Baer, it is concerned with the issues and debates which surrounded his work and the work of other embryologists, comparative anatomists, taxonomists, and proponents of evolution. For that reason, it provides the scientific and philosophical context for understanding Baer.

Sara Joan Miles

MIKHAIL BAKUNIN

Born: May 30, 1814; Premukhino, Russia

Died: July 1, 1876; Bern, Switzerland

Areas of Achievement: Philosophy and social reform

Contribution: Bakunin was the foremost anarchist of his time. A relentless revolutionary agitator, he wrote prolifically and inspired a political movement which survived well into the twentieth century.

Early Life

Mikhail Aleksandrovich Bakunin was born into a noble Russian family in 1814. The oldest male child in a large family, Bakunin enjoyed an especially close relationship with his four sisters, born between 1811 and 1816. His parents' marriage seems to have been a good one, and Bakunin's childhood, by all accounts, was outwardly happy. A small landowner, Bakunin's father had become a doctor of philosophy at the University of Padua in Italy. He instilled in Bakunin an appreciation of the encyclopedists and the ideas of Jean-Jacques Rousseau. Ultimately, Bakunin would retain traces of both of these influences, elevating reason over faith and advocating a social philosophy which carried Rousseau's emphasis on individual consent to radical lengths.

Bakunin was sent to artillery school in St. Petersburg at the age of fourteen. He eventually was granted a commission and was posted to a military unit on the Polish frontier. The military life was not for Bakunin, and in 1835, he bolted from his unit, narrowly avoiding arrest and certain disgrace for desertion. His disdain for authority now established, Bakunin began the study of German philosophers such as Johann Gottlieb Fichte and Georg Wilhelm Friedrich Hegel and spent time in Moscow, where he became acquainted with Vissarion Grigoryevich Belinsky, advocate of the poor, and Aleksandr Herzen, a reform-minded journalist. In 1840, Bakunin journeyed to Berlin to continue his education. There, he was further influenced toward political radicalism by his contact with some of the Young Hegelians.

This atmosphere of unlimited potential for change fastened Bakunin into a career of revolutionary activism. In 1842, having moved to Dresden, Bakunin published his first theoretical work in a radical journal, concluding it with what remains his most famous aphorism: "The passion for destruction is also a creative passion." A vigorous young man with a charismatic presence, Bakunin had come of age. His education continued as he journeyed to Paris, where he met Pierre-Joseph Proudhon and Karl Marx. Bakunin's concerns would expand to include everything from national liberation for the Slavic peoples to social revolution on a global scale.

Life's Work

Bakunin began his revolutionary career in earnest during the Revolution of 1848, a series of uprisings by workers which took place in a number of European cities. Bakunin took part in street fighting during the Paris uprising, which began in February. He then traveled to Germany and Poland in an effort to aid the Revolution's spread. In June of 1848, he was present at the Slav congress in Prague, which was brought to an unceremonious end by Austrian troops. Later that year, Bakunin produced his first major manifesto, *An Appeal to the Slavs*. In it, Bakunin cited the tradition of peasant insurrections in Russia as the model for more far-reaching social revolution throughout Europe.

In May, 1849, Bakunin took part in the Dresden insurrection. He was arrested by German authorities and imprisoned until 1851, when he was sent back to Russia. There, after six more years of imprisonment, Bakunin was released to live in Siberia. Prison life had weakened his health and perhaps even dampened his revolutionary spirit temporarily. In 1857, Bakunin married Antonia Kwiatkowski, the daughter of a Polish merchant. The marriage was curious in a number of ways. Antonia was in her teens, Bakunin in his mid-forties at the time of the marriage. Troubled by impotence, Bakunin reportedly never consummated the marriage. Antonia displayed no interest in politics and disliked Bakunin's revolutionary associates. She also appears to have been unfaithful to Bakunin. Yet the marriage lasted nearly twenty years. During that time, Antonia endured embarrassing financial straits, dislocation, and a variety of other disappointments, apparently serving as a comfort to her husband until his death.

In 1861, Bakunin managed to escape his exile in Siberia and traveled to London via Japan and the United States. In London, he renewed his acquaintance with Herzen. Herzen, however, was alienated both by Bakunin's political extremism and by his nearly complete disregard for the dictates of financial responsibility. In 1863, Bakunin tried to take part in the Polish insurrection, but got only as far as Sweden. The next year, Bakunin established himself in Italy, surrounding himself with a band of disciples and organizing a largely illusory network of secret revolutionary societies across Europe. In 1868, Bakunin relocated to Geneva, where he joined the First International, a federation of various working-class parties for world socialism. It was during this period that Bakunin quarreled with Marx, also a powerful member of the International. Though ideological disparities were undoubtedly a factor, much of the conflict was personal, with neither Marx nor Bakunin inclined to share power or the spotlight. In 1872, Marx managed to have Bakunin and his followers expelled from the International. The move ultimately destroyed the International and divided the revolutionary movement in Europe for decades.

Prior to this split, the Paris Commune was formed as a result of the Revolution of 1870. Bakunin played no direct role in bringing the Commune into existence, and its success was brief. Nevertheless, the Paris Commune constituted the peak of revolutionary achievement during the nineteenth century. In its rejection of conventional political organization, the Commune lent credibility to Bakunin's ideal of an anarchistic order based on voluntary compliance rather than obedience to laws, no matter how democratically they might be derived.

The last years of Bakunin's life, spent in Switzerland, were marred by his brief association with Sergey Gennadiyevich Nechayev, an unscrupulous opportunist and nihilist, who gained Bakunin's favor. This association did little to improve the image of anarchists, and common usage often finds the words anarchist and nihilist treated as synonyms. Otherwise, Bakunin continued to work on a variety of projects, attracted disciples, and wrote. His health and financial situation grew worse, but Bakunin continued working, convinced that the Revolution, though it must wait a decade or two, would triumph eventually.

At the time of his death, Bakunin had written enough to fill volumes, but he never finished a single major work. The fragments that he left behind were ill organized and often unfocused. Thus, where Bakunin far surpassed his rival Marx in terms of direct political action, Marx clearly won the battle of theory, leaving an unfinished but nevertheless impressive body of written work that

would inspire successful revolutionary movements as well as a broad array of scholars. Bakuninism also survived but was based more on legend than on the written word.

For Bakunin, the very essence of humanity lay in thought and rebellion. Thought, or science, allowed human beings to understand the world around them in a way that other animals could never approach. Rebellion, or freedom, allowed human beings to exercise thought rather than blindly follow external authorities. To accept religious or political authority was, for Bakunin, to be less than fully human. The full development of humanity, in turn, demanded thoroughgoing social revolution, which would erase all manner of legal tyranny, class domination, and privilege, opening the way for true community.

This mandated not only exposing the bogus foundations of religion and the state but also using mass violence to overthrow established governments once they had been discredited. Bakunin disagreed with Marx on the use of political power to consolidate the gains of revolution. Marx believed that a dictatorship of the proletariat would be needed temporarily (though just how temporarily he did not say) in order to avoid counterrevolution. Bakunin's principled anarchism would not allow this compromise: All political power was tyrannical in Bakunin's eyes, even that exercised in the name of the working class. Bakunin's was a social or communitarian anarchism: Freedom and authority would no longer be at odds with each other. The result, according to Bakunin, would be a splendid harmony, featuring spontaneous cooperation rather than coercion.

Summary

During his lifetime, Mikhail Bakunin established himself as a charismatic and energetic figure, one who can truly be said to have devoted himself to social revolution. This involved extraordinary hardships. Bakunin risked his life repeatedly, spent years in prison, and, except for his highly sporadic efforts to please Antonia, disregarded material possessions. He was thoroughly impoverished at the end of his life, dependent on friends for his survival. In addition to this life of direct revolutionary action and the sacrifices it entailed, Bakunin wrote tirelessly, producing thousands of pages of treatises, polemics, and letters.

Yet, for all of this, Bakunin has left behind a rather small footprint. Though anarchist movements remained a force in Italy and Spain through the 1930's, they rarely achieved major status and never achieved victory. Bakuninism never came to rival Marxism. Both have been overshadowed by nationalism, the greatest anathema of all to Bakunin's prescriptions regarding political authority.

Why has Bakunin's influence faded so completely? One reason is that he never achieved the theoretical depth or clarity that Marx did. Marx raised questions, in a systematic way, about history, economics, sociology, and politics which have remained vitally interesting to ideologues as well as to scholars. Bakunin's fragmentary and undisciplined writings could not do the same.

Still, Bakunin's accomplishments were considerable. He transformed a polite, drawing-room philosophy into a notable historical movement, raised pertinent questions about the unlimited power of revolutionary parties and regimes that have come to haunt twentieth century Marxists, and produced written work rich in imagery and ideas. Though they may strike many people as bizarre, these images and ideas reflect commonly held values extrapolated to uncommon lengths. Bakunin valued personal freedom, and he carried this value to a logical extreme. He also tried to honor his beliefs with a life devoted to unflinching action. In this respect, too, Bakunin was uncommon.

Bibliography

Avrich, Paul. *The Russian Anarchists*. Princeton, N.J.: Princeton University Press, 1967. Focuses on the fate of the Russian anarchists, Bakunin's closest political heirs, from the Revolution of 1905 to the movement's dissolution shortly after the triumph of Bolshevism in 1917.

Bakunin, Mikhail A. *The Political Philosophy of Bakunin: Scientific Anarchism*. Edited by G. P. Maksimov. Glencoe, Ill.: Free Press, 1953. Maksimov has carefully assembled a selection of Bakunin's written work, organizing sections according to topic. The result is more coherent and comprehensive than anything produced by Bakunin during his lifetime. Includes a helpful preface, an introduction, and a biographical sketch by three different Bakunin scholars.

Billingsley, Philip. "Bakunin in Yokohama: The Dawning of the Pacific Era." *The International History Review* 20, no. 3 (September 1998). Discusses Bakunin's escape from Siberia and his resulting dialog with Karl Marx.

Carr, E. H. *Michael Bakunin*. London: Macmillan, 1937; New York: Vintage, 1961. A straightforward biography, innocent of any discernible ideological agenda. Provides a balanced account of the conflict between Bakunin and Marx. Carr does not examine Bakunin's political philosophy in any detail.

Cutler, Robert M. "A Rediscovered Source on Bakunin in 1861: The Diary of F.P. Koe and (excerpts from the diary of F.P. Koe)." *Canadian Slavonic Papers* 35, no. 1-2 (March-June 1993). Examines the diary of English cleric Frederick Pemberton Koe and its data on Bakunin's personality and beliefs.

Kelly, Aileen. *Mikhail Bakunin: A Study in the Psychology and Politics of Utopianism*. Oxford: Clarendon Press, and New York: Oxford University Press, 1982. Kelly tries to reconcile the polar images of Bakunin as champion of liberty, on one hand, and dictatorial confederate of the cynical and despotic Nechayev, on the other. She does so by showing the psychological link between absolute liberty and absolute dictatorship.

Masters, Anthony. *Bakunin: The Father of Anarchism*. New York: Saturday Review Press, and London: Sidgwick and Jackson, 1974. A sympathetic view of Bakunin's life and work. Includes a chapter on the fate of Bakuninism in the hundred years or so following Bakunin's death.

Mendel, Arthur P. *Michael Bakunin: Roots of Apocalypse*. New York: Praeger, 1981. A haunting psychohistory, which reveals the dark side of Bakunin's revolutionary zeal, linking it to some very personal details in his life as well as the notion of Christian Apocalypse. Impassioned and controversial.

Pyziur, Eugene. *The Doctrine of Anarchism of Michael A. Bakunin*. Milwaukee: Gateway Press, 1955. Provides a clear and undoctrinaire exposition of Bakunin's political and social philosophy.

Wolff, Robert Paul. *In Defense of Anarchism*. New York: Harper, 1970. Coming from a perspective far different from that of Bakunin, Wolff contends that, philosophically speaking, anarchism is defensible, since the authority of even a democratic state must come at the expense of individual autonomy. Most critics have considered the book subversively clever rather than profound, partly because Wolff lacks Bakunin's commitment to action.

Ira Smolensky

ROBERT BALDWIN

Born: May 12, 1804; York, Ontario, Canada

Died: December 9, 1858; Toronto, Canada

Areas of Achievement: Government and politics

Contribution: Baldwin worked for reform policies which led to responsible government in Upper Canada and, as part of the "Great Ministry" (1848-1851), with Louis Hippolyte La Fontaine, upheld the idea of biculturalism in forging the eventual responsible government established in Canada.

Early Life

The Baldwin family was of English origin, but they were established members of the Church of Ireland in Cork before emigrating to Upper Canada in 1799. The emigrant Robert (grandfather of the subject of this sketch) was a widower; two sons and four daughters arrived in Canada with him, while one daughter and two sons remained in Ireland.

The eldest son, William Warren Baldwin, had earned a degree in medicine from the University of Edinburgh and opted to relocate in the capital, York, rather than remain on his father's sizable acreage. When his medical practice did not prove sufficiently absorbing, Baldwin pursued the study of law. In 1803, he received his license to practice law and that same year he opened a school and married Margaret Phoebe Willcocks, daughter of an old family friend who had also emigrated from Cork. In 1804, the couple gave birth to their first child, Robert. All told, four Baldwin sons were born to William and Phoebe, but only Robert and William Augustus lived to adulthood.

Through the next several years, William Baldwin acquired considerable wealth and acreage through his legal practice, several fortuitous bequests, and even some architectural undertakings. Following the War of 1812, he continued to prosper in all of his endeavors; in 1818, he built an elegant country home, Spadina House.

William's son Robert was educated by the noted Anglican rector John Strachan, and, in 1820, Robert became a clerk in his father's law office. Soon, he was assuming considerable responsibility during William's frequent absences, and when he was admitted to the bar in 1825, he became a full partner; the firm became W. W. Baldwin and Son. All this success, however, was secondary to Robert's deep and abiding love for his cousin, Augusta Eliz-

abeth Sullivan, daughter of William's sister, Barbara, who had remained in Ireland until after the War of 1812. During a two-year separation, Robert wrote passionate and emotional letters to Eliza, revealing an affection that would remain undimmed to the end of his life.

Although the Baldwin family had the wealth, property, and connections to be a secure part of the Family Compact of Upper Canada, an oligarchical body which cooperated with the British governor, William Baldwin thoroughly rejected that association. By 1824, partly because of his Irish heritage, which excluded him from the largely Scottish clique that dominated the Family Compact, and partly because of the influence of Robert the Emigrant, an Irish Whig supporter of parliamentary reform, William had become influential in the reform movement. Young Robert was also active in the movement, although not as active as two of his friends, Marshall Bidwell or John Rolph.

Robert's personal life took a blissful turn when he married his beloved Eliza in 1827. The following year political controversies made his professional life more adventurous. Libel charges against Francis Collins, publisher of the radical *Canadian Freeman*, and the subsequent dismissal of Judge John Walpole Willis brought Baldwin and Rolph into the midst of the reform agitation which was raging against Lieutenant Governor Sir Peregrine Maitland.

Life's Work

The increased interest in the reform movement led both William and Robert to seek seats in the parliament of Upper Canada in the general election of 1828. Although William gained the seat in Norfolk County, Robert lost the riding of York, where two other, more avid reformers, William Lyon Mackenzie and Jesse Ketchum, were elected. Robert remained active in the reform movement, however, and gained the riding of the town of York in 1829, in an election held when John Beverly Robinson resigned to become chief justice. His incumbency was brief, since Parliament was dissolved when George IV died in June of 1830, and both Baldwins fell victim, in the next election, to a lessening of reform interest.

For the next few years both Baldwins were preoccupied with their law practices, property management, and architectural concerns. When the large home at Spadina burned in 1834, William built a new mansion in Toronto and rebuilt Spadina as a country home, completing both by 1836. Meanwhile, Robert was engaged in estate planning and legal activities, and was occupied with a growing family. Two sons and two daughters were born during a six-year period: Phoebe Maria (1828), William Willcocks (1830), Augusta Elizabeth (1831), and Robert (1834). The last birth was difficult for Eliza and left her in a weakened condition.

Although the reform movement had regained favor, neither of the Baldwins sought election in 1834. The radical element of the party, led by Mackenzie, seemed to have embraced a republican philosophy more compatible with American interests than with British. This was entirely unsatisfactory to the Baldwins, who still sought a system of responsible cabinet government.

In January of 1836, just before a new lieutenant governor, Sir Francis Bond Head, arrived in Upper Canada, Eliza Baldwin died. Robert was emotionally devastated by her death; always reserved and introspective, he suffered from severe depression for the rest of his life.

Less than two weeks after Eliza's death, Bond Head recognized the need to extend the Executive Council beyond the Family Compact and offered seats to John Rolph and to Robert. Although his personal desire was to decline, Robert heeded the advice of his father, Rolph, and Bidwell, and accepted the position in February of 1836. The appointment was short-lived, as differences between Bond Head and the Council led to the resignation of all six councillors on March 12. The action was significant, however, because they were functioning according to the Baldwin idea—performing in unison as a responsible cabinet.

Neither Robert nor William stood for election in 1836, and in the hope that a change of scene might lessen his deep depression, Robert left, in June, for an extended stay in England and Ireland. The trip had some political ramifications as he spent time in London trying to persuade the Colonial Office that responsible government, with the Executive Council functioning as a parliamentary cabinet, was feasible for Upper Canada. He found little knowledge of, or interest in, Canada at the Colonial Ministry, although some Whig sympathies did exist. After a sentimental sojourn in Ireland, he returned home in February to find Tory control being angrily challenged by the radical Mackenzie, who was perceived to hold Yankee-type republican tendencies.

Moderate voices went unheeded as economic depression and a bank crisis brought on calls for forceful rebellions in both Upper and Lower Canada. The Mackenzie Rebellion rose out of this unrest in 1837 but was suppressed by the British militia.

The crisis prompted Lord Durham's arrival in Upper Canada from England. William Baldwin outlined for him Upper Canada's problems while Robert had drawn up a succinct plan for responsible government. This information formed the core of Durham's 1839 report, which enumerated the wrongs in Canada and recommended responsible government and a union of the two Canadas.

Union took precedence under Durham's successor, Governor Sydenham, and was implemented by imperial authority in 1840. The underlying intent was to demonstrate to the French Canadians the benefits of their assimilation into Anglo-Canadian society. The bait was the possibility that the French could share in controlling public affairs if and when responsible government became a reality.

William Baldwin expected that responsible government would be immediately forthcoming, but major emphasis was put upon realigning the Executive Council. Reluctantly, Robert accepted the position of solicitor general in the new government without a council seat.

After the union became effective in 1841, reformers began to question the wisdom of Robert Baldwin remaining as solicitor general. The March, 1841, election demonstrated that corruption and intimidation could still return a nonreformist majority to Upper Canada. Only Baldwin and five other dedicated reformers were elected. After refusing the oath of supremacy because he denied the position of a foreign prelate, Baldwin demanded from Sydenham that French Canadians be given four cabinet posts. Thoroughly irritated with Baldwin, Sydenham accepted a resignation which Baldwin had offered only as a threat.

In the ensuing session of Parliament, which met in Kingston, Baldwin continued to insist upon the rights of the French Canadians. His popularity in Upper Canada was threatened as even Francis Hincks became sympathetic to the Sydenham ministry. Even though Baldwin assisted Louis Hippolyte La Fontaine, the French party leader, in gaining the seat from fourth York, he was unsuccessful in attempting to push total bicultural institutions. The sincerity of his endeavors was illustrated by the fact that all Robert Baldwin's children were sent to French schools in order that they never be embarrassed, as he was, by the handicap of monolingualism.

Baldwin continued his relentless drive for responsible government against Sydenham's adamant opposition. When Sydenham died in September of 1841, the new governor, Sir Charles Bagot, was persuaded by his advisers that the French Canadian leaders and Robert Baldwin must be brought into the ministry. In September of 1842, both La Fontaine and Baldwin entered the ministry. In November, Bagot became ill and Baldwin and La Fontaine functioned as copremiers of the province. Relations with Bagot's successor, Sir Charles Metcalfe, deteriorated steadily. In November of 1843, the Executive Council resigned and the reformers carried only twelve seats, including Baldwin, in Upper Canada.

For Robert, the party's defeat followed a period of depression which had come with the death of his father. Having rejected the idea of permanently retiring from politics, Robert rallied for a strong session in the 1844-1845 parliament. The tendencies toward depression, which had been evident since his wife's death in 1836, were growing increasingly troublesome and eventually became incapacitating. His frequent mentions of resignation were not idle threats, but honestly expressed doubts of his own capabilities.

Baldwin dedicated himself in the 1844-1845 session, however, to the cause of responsible government as a constitutional system which would allow Canadians to manage their own affairs. The reform party was too divided to challenge effectively the weak Tory leadership, even though Metcalfe was terminally ill and his replacement, Charles Murray Cathcart, was far less partisan than Metcalfe had been. Not until after the general election of 1848 could the reformers summon the strength to challenge the Tories on a confidence vote. In March of 1848, a vote of nonconfidence brought down the government, and Lord Elgin (who had succeeded Cathcart in January of 1847) called on La Fontaine, whose alliance with Baldwin created the so-called Great Ministry of 1848-1851.

The Ministry was plagued by difficulties within the reform party, as well as by questions over provincial finances, brutality in Kingston Penitentiary, compensation for losses in the 1837 rebellions, and trade relations with both the Maritimes and the United States. Nevertheless, the reputation of the Great Ministry was well earned when responsible government was confirmed, when the Municipal Corporations Act passed, and when Canadian nationalism affirmed both actions by rejecting discussions of annexation with the United States, and by recognition of the bicultural aspect of Canadian society. In addition, Baldwin himself can be credited with the creation of the University of Toronto as a government-controlled, rather than church-controlled, institution.

In January of 1851, while Baldwin was under attack from both the Tories and the Clear Grits from within his own party, his mother died. Once more he was overwhelmed with deep depression, becoming seriously ill in the late spring of that year. On June 30, he announced his resignation. La Fontaine did the same, and the Great Ministry was ended. In the ensuing general election, Baldwin stood for reelection in North York but was soundly defeated.

Never again was Robert Baldwin an active participant in political affairs, although he remained important as a perennial potential candidate. Gradually he withdrew into a very private existence, obsessed by the memory of his wife and troubled with the problems of his children. In December of

1858, his wearied body finally gave out, and Robert Baldwin died at Spadina, leaving a puzzling personal legacy but a solid, secure foundation for responsible government and French rights in Canada.

Summary

Throughout his life, Robert Baldwin was devoted to family responsibility, dedicated to Christian duty, and consumed by self-doubt. In his own view, he always came up short when he compared his accomplishments to those of his father—when he considered what he himself should have done, and what needed to be done for God and country. Early in life he thought he had found perfect happiness in marrying his cousin, Elizabeth. Her death, after only nine years of marriage, heightened his sense of failure and contributed to the melancholy bouts of depression which often left him dysfunctional.

Despite his self-perceived inadequacies, Baldwin persevered in obtaining a foothold for Dominion status for Canada and a degree of recognition for biculturalism which have since matured into the reality of Canadian identity.

Bibliography

Baldwin is mentioned in all histories dealing with the period in Ontario or Canadian history as well as in the papers of the prominent men of the time. The papers of Robert Baldwin and his father, W. W. Baldwin, are located in the Metropolitan Toronto Central Library.

Baldwin, Robert Macqueen, and Joyce Baldwin. *The Baldwins and the Great Experiment.* Don Mills, Ontario: Longman, 1969. Helpful work detailing the work of Robert and his father, William, toward responsible government for Upper Canada.

Careless, J. M. S. "Robert Baldwin." In *The Pre-Confederation Premiers: Ontario Government Leaders, 1841-1867.* Toronto: University of Toronto Press, 1980. Well-researched and well-written account utilizing Careless' extensive familiarity with manuscript collections, personal papers, and histories of the period. The complex personality of Baldwin and interfamily relationships are well treated.

Cross, Michael, and Robert L. Fraser. "'The Waste That Lies Before Me': The Public and Private Worlds of Robert Baldwin." In *Canadian Historical Association Historical Papers*, 1983. Sensitive and insightful comparison of Baldwin the politician and Baldwin the family man. The title is taken from Baldwin's own view of his remaining years after the death of his wife. Cross and Fraser relate Baldwin's personal tragedy to his public difficulties.

Leacock, Stephen Butler. *Baldwin, LaFontaine, Hincks: Responsible Government.* Toronto: Morang, and London: Jack, 1907.

Wilson, George E. *The Life of Robert Baldwin: A Study in the Struggle for Responsible Government.* Toronto: Ryerson Press, 1933. Both of the above are interesting earlier works which focus on the role of Baldwin during the years following the Union Act.

Helen Jean M. Nugent

HONORÉ DE BALZAC

Born: May 20, 1799; Tours, France
Died: August 18, 1850; Paris, France
Area of Achievement: Literature
Contribution: Balzac's novels, assembled under the collective title *The Human Comedy*, form a literary monument composed of some ninety-five works, with more than two thousand characters, which provides a comprehensive survey and analysis of French society and culture at all levels during the first half of the nineteenth century.

Early Life

The son of a peasant, Bernard-François Balzac had risen in society to become the head of the hospital administration and deputy mayor of the town of Tours. His wife, Anne Laure Sallambier, was the daughter of an affluent merchant. At the time of their arranged marriage, he was fifty-one and she was nineteen. Perhaps understandably, the eccentric elderly husband and romantic (but soon bitter) young wife both engaged in extramarital affairs and were not always devoted parents. When their son Honoré was born in 1799, he was sent to a wet nurse and was joined two years later by his sister Laure. After spending the first four years of his life away from his mother, he lived at home until he was seven (though even during this period he attended boarding school and was only brought home on Sundays). At the age of eight, he was sent to the Collège de Vendôme for five years, partly to get him out of the way while his mother had a child by another man, during which time he later claimed never to have been visited by his parents. Many of his biographers see his perception of this early neglect, especially on the part of his mother, as one of the reasons that several of his early love affairs were with older women. These relationships, many of which developed into friendships that lasted for decades, may in turn account for the many portraits of strong, intelligent women in his novels.

Balzac studied law for three years, a knowledge of which later became useful to him as a novelist, but after passing his law examinations in 1819 he announced to his family his determination to become a writer. Despite their apparent coldness, his parents generously agreed to support him for a two-year trial period, during which he lived in a fifth-floor attic in Paris and wrote a five-act verse tragedy on Oliver Cromwell. The experiment was a failure, never produced or even published during his lifetime, but Balzac was committed to his new vocation and merely resolved to turn from the theater to journalism and novel writing to support himself.

He produced a series of novels under various pseudonyms over the next several years, all written in haste and many in collaboration with other hack writers. During this time he also borrowed large sums of money, much of it from his mother and mistress, to establish himself in business, first as a printer, then as a publisher, and eventually as a typefounder, the beginning of a lifelong series of business failures. As a result of these speculative ventures as well as of an always extravagant lifestyle, he was heavily in debt throughout his life, despite a considerable income from his writing in later years.

Life's Work

In 1829, Balzac published *Les Chouans* (English translation, 1890), the first of his novels to have lasting merit and, significantly, the first published under his own name. Indeed, for his next novel, *La Peau de chagrin* (1831; *The Magic Skin*, 1888), the first of his masterpieces, he even embellished his name by the addition, before his surname, of the particle "de," a sign of nobility to which he was not entitled by law or birth. It is a sign of the esteem of posterity that his name has since been written invariably, if technically inaccurately, as "Honoré de Balzac."

As a result of the pressure to earn money created by his constant condition of indebtedness, Balzac's literary output reached staggering proportions. In the twenty years between 1830 and 1850, the period of his maturity as a writer, he produced some ninety-five novels, featuring more than two thousand characters, as well as several hundred short stories, essays, reviews, and plays. Even more remarkable than the sheer quantity of his work is its remarkably high quality. All but a handful of his novels are of the first rank. Balzac was able to produce so much good work only by virtue of his tremendous physical and mental vitality.

Balzac would begin a typical working day at midnight, when his servant would knock on his door to wake him. He always worked in a long white robe, similar to a monk's, at a table with candles, blank paper (of a slightly blue tinge—so as to tire his eyes less rapidly—and with an especially smooth surface that would allow him to write as quickly and effortlessly as possible), an inkwell, and several raven's quill pens. He never used any notes or books, having already fixed everything in his mind before writing. Balzac would then write for eight hours with no interruptions except for preparing and drinking large quantities of strong black coffee. At eight, he would have a light breakfast and a bath and send the night's work to the printer.

The composition of a novel had only just begun for Balzac at this stage. At about nine o'clock he would begin revising the proofs of the pages he had written the night before. His emendations and additions were often much longer than the text he was correcting, and he therefore required that his galleys be printed on large sheets, with the text occupying only a small square in the middle. After he had completely filled all the margins with scribbled changes, he would send them back to be reset. Even experienced compositors had difficulty deciphering these corrections, and even at double wages they would refuse to work more than an hour at a time on his proof sheets. When Balzac received the second revised galleys he would repeat the process, sometimes entirely rewriting a book in this manner fifteen or twenty times. Often the exorbitant cost of these typesetting charges would come out of his own fees, but his effort to make all of his work as nearly perfect as possible could never be compromised. He kept a copy of each of his books together with all the successive revisions, and these would often total two thousand pages for a two-hundred-page novel. Finally, toward five in the afternoon, he would finish the day's writing. He would then eat, perhaps see a friend, and plan the next night's writing. At eight he would go to bed, to be awakened again at midnight for another sixteen to eighteen hours of continuous labor.

Only a powerful constitution allowed him to carry out such a demanding work schedule, and Balzac was not the stereotypical delicate poet. Though only five feet, two or three inches tall, he was very strongly built, with a thick, muscular neck, broad shoulders, and a huge chest. His bulk made him an easy target for caricaturists, and most of the likenesses of Balzac that remain are caricatures, not only because of his build but also because he always insisted on attempting to dress in the latest, and invariably the least flattering, fashions, frequently carrying one of his famous gem-studded

walking sticks. Despite his lack of what would normally be thought good looks and his absurd manner of dressing, Balzac was quite attractive to women because of his depth of understanding and the intensity of his personality, which immediately dominated any gathering at which he was present, an intensity that even his enemies admitted.

Balzac's workload certainly played a part in shortening his life—he died at the age of fifty-one—but in any given year or two he produced more lasting work than many of his contemporaries did in their entire careers. The huge scale of his achievement makes it impossible to represent or judge his work on the basis of one or two, or even a dozen, examples. Although *Le Père Goriot* (1835; *Father Goriot*, 1844) and *Eugénie Grandet* (1833; English translation, 1859) might be singled out as his best-known works, there are literally dozens of others of the same caliber. It is doubtful that any other writer has produced so much work of such consistent quality, a consistency that extends over the full twenty years of his maturity. Early novels such as *La Peau de chagrin* and late novels such as *La Cousine Bette* (1846; *Cousin Bette*, 1888) are equally likely to be chosen as examples of his best work. Whereas some critics have noticed certain types of development over this period, for example a tendency toward greater realism, exceptions can be found to every rule. Balzac seems to have reached his full development almost at one stroke, at age thirty, and to have continued at full power until a year or two before his death, with few pauses between masterpieces.

When Balzac began the program for *La Comédie humaine* (1829-1848; *The Comedy of Human Life*, 1885-1893, 1896; also known as *The Human Comedy*), he set himself the task of writing the gigantic work in three sections: the "Studies of Manners," which would depict every kind of character and every way of living for every stratum of society; the "Philosophical Studies," which would analyze the motivating causes behind all of this social behavior; and the "Analytical Studies," which would outline the principles behind these various effects and causes. While his project was never to be finished (at his death he left some fifty titles of works to be written in order to complete the structure of the whole), the novels he did write are usually grouped according to these categories, with the "Studies of Manners" further subdivided into scenes of private, provincial, Parisian, political, military, and country life.

In 1842, Balzac signed a contract to issue a collected edition of his works, a massive undertaking requiring the collaboration of three publishers. Believing that "Collected Works" was too commonplace a title for the edition, they asked Balzac to find another title. He chose *The Human Comedy* by way of contrasting his work with Dante's *La divina commedia* (c. 1320; *The Divine Comedy*, 1802) and also to suggest its comprehensive scope, announcing in his preface to the edition his intention to present a history and criticism of the whole of society.

Summary

Although Honoré de Balzac lived to write "only" 95 of the 144 novels he had planned for the structure of *The Human Comedy*, the completed sections constitute one of the greatest achievements ever produced by the literary imagination, a series of explorations not only of French society of the first half of the nineteenth century but also of an unparalleled range of human types. Balzac was, in his time, France's most popular writer and, internationally, France's most respected author. Since that time, his prestige has steadily grown. As André Maurois has asserted, "It has been said that the works of Balzac, of Shakespeare, and of Tolstoy constitute the three great monuments raised by humanity to humanity. That is true and moreover *The Human Comedy* is the vastest and most complete of the three."

Bibliography

Bertault, Philippe. *Balzac and the Human Comedy.* Translated by Richard Monges. New York: New York University Press, 1963. Primarily a study of *The Human Comedy* rather than of its author, but it does include analysis of the effects of Balzac's life on his work, and features a convenient ten-page biographical sketch at the beginning of the text.

Gerson, Noel B. *The Prodigal Genius: The Life and Times of Honoré de Balzac.* New York: Doubleday, 1972. Written by a best-selling author for a general audience. Despite occasional sensationalism, an absorbing and well-researched account and a very good introduction for the nonspecialist.

Guenther, Beatrice M. *The Poetics of Death: The Short Prose of Kleist and Balzac.* Albany: State University of New York Press, 1996. Assessment of the use of death by Balzac and Kleist by placing their writings in historical context.

Hunt, Herbert J. *Honoré de Balzac: A Biography.* London: Athlone Press, 1957; New York: Greenwood Press, 1969. A straightforward historical narration of the major events of Balzac's life, competent and concise, though superseded by more recent works. Hunt's running commentary on the literary works is often still interesting. Many passages quoted in French are not translated.

Marceau, Félicien. *Balzac and His World.* Translated by Derek Coltman. New York: Orion Press, 1966; London: Allen, 1967. More a study of Balzac's characters than of his life, but interspersed with much relevant biographical information.

Maurois, André. *Prometheus: The Life of Balzac.* Translated by Norman Denny. New York: Harper, 1965; London: Bodley Head, 1966. The definitive biography by France's premier literary biographer. Primarily aimed at an audience already knowledgeable about the subject. A thorough and usually objective account of the facts of Balzac's life, clarifying many previously obscure details. Despite its close attention to specifics, however, Maurois' book is also a highly readable and entertaining narrative.

Oliver, E. J. *Balzac, the European.* London and New York: Sheed and Ward, 1959. An overview of both the life and the novels, organized around a variety of thematic emphases such as "Women of Letters," "Religion," and "The Absolute." Provides a usefully condensed survey.

Pritchett, V. S. *Balzac.* London: Chatto and Windus, and New York: Knopf, 1973. Includes more than two hundred valuable illustrations of Balzac, his contemporaries, and his environment, among them forty high-quality color plates. Extremely valuable for orienting the reader unfamiliar with Balzac and his time and place.

Zweig, Stefan. *Balzac.* Edited by Richard Friedenthal. Translated by William Rose and Dorothy Rose. New York: Viking Press, 1946; London: Cassell, 1947. After Maurois, Zweig is the best biographer of Balzac. Although slightly dated, this fascinating book reads almost like a novel about his life. Zweig's tendency to offer his own interpretations of events makes his work more subjective than Maurois', and perhaps less reliable in some particulars, but it remains the best introduction for the nonspecialist.

William Nelles

GEORGE BANCROFT

Born: October 3, 1800; Worcester, Massachusetts
Died: January 17, 1891; Washington, D.C.
Areas of Achievement: Historical scholarship, politics, and diplomacy
Contribution: Contributing greatly to both scholarly and popular thought in the nineteenth century United States, George Bancroft explained the transformation of the British Colonies into the United States in terms of the growth and development of liberty, democracy, and nationalism.

Early Life

George Bancroft was born on October 3, 1800, in Worcester, Massachusetts. He was the eighth of thirteen children produced by the union of Aaron Bancroft and Lucretia Chandler, both of whom came from old-stock New England families. Lucretia Chandler, the daughter of Judge John Chandler, known as "Tory John" because he had opposed independence, was a good-natured and spirited woman, unlettered, but devoted to her husband and and children. Aaron Bancroft was a struggling Congregational minister who played a leading role in the early Unitarian movement. Devoted to education as the basis for personal and social reform, he introduced young George to the classics, emphasized the virtues of self-discipline and obedience, and passed on to his offspring the conviction that mankind is essentially good, but not without sin, and flawed by ignorance and misunderstanding. George attended Phillips Exeter Academy, entered Harvard College at thirteen, and became a favorite of President John Thornton Kirkland. Moral philosophy dominated the Harvard curriculum at that time, and like his father before him, Bancroft found that particular mixture of Lockean rationalism and Scottish common sense captivating. It clearly categorized knowledge, stressed the importance of faith as well as reason, and acknowledged divine law as the driving force of the universe. In fact, moral philosophy provided the intellectual and theological perspective that would stay with Bancroft all of his life.

Taking his A.B. degree in 1817, Bancroft continued at Harvard for another year as a graduate student in divinity before continuing his education at the University of Gottingen in Germany. He was encouraged to go to Gottingen by Edward Everett, Joseph Green Cogswell, and George Ticknor, three young Harvard teachers who had done graduate work there and confirmed its reputation as the leading university in Europe. Thanks to President Kirkland, Bancroft got financial support from Harvard and began his studies at Gottingen in the fall of 1818. For the next two years, he rose early and studied late, immersed himself in German literature, and took courses in philosophy, biblical criticism, and history from some of the leading scholars in Europe. His hard work allowed him to take the grueling doctoral examinations early. In September, 1820, he successfully defended his thesis and was awarded the degree of Doctor of Philosophy and Master of Arts. After six more months of study at the University of Berlin, Bancroft traveled Europe and the British Isles for the next year. He met and talked with Johann Wolfgang von Goethe, George Gordon, Lord Byron, the Marquis de Lafayette, and Alexander von Humboldt, to mention the most prominent personages whom he sought out. Bancroft grew up, both intellectually and psychologically, during his four years in Europe.

When he returned to America in 1822, Bancroft was still thinking in terms of either teaching or preaching. He was an engaging young man, known for his social grace and dignified bearing. He was shorter than average and slight in build, rather handsome, and distinguished by clear-cut facial features which included a prominent nose, strikingly alert eyes, and carefully trimmed hair and beard. Some of his former Harvard teachers were put off by his foreign manners, his suggested reforms for the college, and his pompous request that he be given a professorship. President Kirkland remained a faithful ally, however, and secured for him an appointment as tutor in Greek. Though the opportunity hardly offered him the status he had had in mind, Bancroft decided to make the most of it. He added new rigor to his Greek courses and drove his students to the brink of rebellion, though they reportedly were far ahead of other Greek students. During the year of his rather unsuccessful tutorship, he also tried his hand at preaching in various churches on several occasions. He seems to have pleased few people with his sermons, not even his father, and certainly not himself. In early 1823, disheartened by his failure to reform Harvard and by the resistance of the students, Bancroft joined with Joseph Cogswell to set up the Round Hill School for Boys at Northampton. For the next eight years, he labored to adapt the educational methods of the German gymnasium to the United States. Round Hill was ahead of its time and widely praised, but it had financial problems, and Bancroft, the primary teacher, contributed to them with his demanding academic standards and less than cordial relations with students. In 1831, he sold his interest in Round Hill to Cogswell and put classroom teaching behind him.

Bancroft married Sarah Dwight in 1827. Her family was involved in various business enterprises in Springfield, Massachusetts, and Bancroft became an agent for the Dwight banking interests. To the chagrin of his young wife, who stayed home and often felt neglected, he traveled much of the time on business. He also embarked upon a literary career. His first published work had been a pedestrian volume of poetry (*Poems*, 1823), whose existence he later found embarrassing. While teaching at Round Hill, he translated several German works on Latin and Greek grammar and three volumes of history by Arnold H. L. Heeren, one of the distinguished professors who had taught him at Gottingen. Under the encouragement of editor Jared Sparks, he became a regular contributor of book reviews and essays on finance, politics, and scholarly topics to the *North American Review*. Sparks was much involved in collecting documents and writing history and may well have influenced Bancroft to embark upon his own work in American history. Bancroft was ambitious—so much so that Lillian Handlin, one of his biographers, maintains that he was rather insensitive toward his first wife and never very sympathetic toward his children. Sickly and morose, Sarah Bancroft died in 1837, shortly after the death of an infant daughter. Thereafter, relations between Bancroft and his three surviving children—Louise, John, and George—were seldom harmonious and often very strained.

Life's Work

While achieving a measure of success in business, Bancroft became even more committed to the notion that a man of letters could and should play an important part in improving society. That conviction increasingly shaped his political involvement and scholarly ambitions. In an oration that he delivered on July 4, 1826, at Northampton, Bancroft had made it clear that he was a Jeffersonian Democrat, favoring the dispersion of property and the removal of voting restrictions. His views were in sympathy with the emerging Jacksonian Party. Writing in the *North American Review* in 1831, he analyzed the National Bank in terms that pleased Jacksonians and shocked his Whig associates. His Harvard friends as well as the Dwights were almost solidly against Andrew Jackson, and Massachusetts itself was completely dominated by the Whigs. The Jacksonians in the state were badly divided, as Bancroft himself found out when the Northampton Workingmen nominated him for the General Court but failed to line up the other elements of the fragmented Democratic coalition in the election of 1834. Viciously attacked by the Whigs in the press and distrusted by many Jacksonians, Bancroft got few votes. Nevertheless, he was attracted to politics, and Jacksonian leaders recognized his talents and cultivated him.

Rebuffed politically, Bancroft experienced considerable scholarly acclaim in 1834 with the publication of the first volume of his history of the United States. He may have acquired an interest in history from his father, who had written a modestly successful popular biography of George Washington years before. At Gottingen, he studied history under Hereen. While at Round Hill, he had worked up an outline of American history for a proposed world history course at Round Hill. By the early 1830's, he had decided that there was a real need for a "critical history" of the United States and believed himself superbly equipped to write it. The first volume, which carried development of the American Colonies to 1650, was popular with both the literary critics and the general public. "You have written a work which will last while the memory of America lasts," wrote Edward Everett, still a good friend despite diverging politics. It was a classic, Everett continued, "full of learning, information, common sense, and philosophy; full of taste and eloquence; full of life and power." Ralph Waldo Emerson was equally complimentary, writing that the grandeur of the work made him weep. Emerson proclaimed it "the most valuable and splendid piece of historical composition, not only in English, but in any tongue."

Heady praise indeed, calculated to encourage the masterful young scholar, and it did. Two other volumes, the second published in 1837 and the third in 1840, followed the development of the Colonies to 1748. The central theme was clear enough. From the beginning of English settlement, America had progressively expanded the twin realms of economic and political liberty. Indeed, political and economic monopoly gave way to the rise of representative politics and free enterprise economics in Colonial America. According to Bancroft, this burgeoning freedom nurtured an emerging American nationality. It was a grand and inspiring story, and Bancroft told it with an eloquence and appreciation for drama that appealed not only to Emerson but also to thousands of his countrymen disturbed by growing sectional tensions which threatened national unity in the 1830's. By 1841, his annual income from sales of the three volumes reached $4,350. Bancroft was almost unique among scholars; he made scholarship pay, and pay handsomely.

Political success came upon the heels of scholarly recognition. In 1837, as a reward for Bancroft's efforts on behalf of the Democratic Party in Massachusetts, President Martin Van Buren appointed the budding historian collector of the Port of Boston, a most important patronage position. Over the next few years, Bancroft emerged as the leader of the Democratic Party in Massachusetts and edited its leading newspaper. He was the Democratic nominee for governor in 1844, and though he lost that election, his efforts on behalf of James K. Polk secured for him a place in the new president's cab-

inet as secretary of the navy (1845-1846). While serving in that position, Bancroft endorsed Polk's expansionist plans and the Mexican War, tied promotion in the navy more to merit than to seniority, and founded the Naval Academy at Annapolis. What he wanted most, however, was a diplomatic assignment, and Polk obligingly appointed him ambassador to England in 1846, where he served for the next two years and relished every minute. He moved in the highest political and literary circles, gained access to collections of documents in both England and France, and made friends with the English historians Thomas Macaulay, Henry Milman, and Henry Hallam and the French historians François Guizot and Louis Adolphe Thiers. He hired clerks to copy significant documents and undoubtedly had more information available to him than any previous American historian. His tenure as minister to the Court of St. James certainly enriched subsequent volumes of his history of the United States.

Returning to the United States in 1849, Bancroft decided to make his home in cosmopolitan New York. His first wife having died in 1837, he had remarried in 1838, taking as his second wife Mrs. Elizabeth (Davis) Bliss, a Boston widow with two sons of her own. Her first husband had been a law partner of Daniel Webster. She was bright, witty, and urbane; Bancroft found her the perfect mate and reveled in their marriage. He and his three children, however, remained on less than cordial terms, despite the efforts of Elizabeth to heal the breach. From 1849 to 1867, Bancroft devoted himself to writing his history and participating in the intellectual and social life of New York City and Newport, Rhode Island, where he maintained a summer home. He wrote six more volumes that brought his *History of the United States* to the year 1782. These volumes recounted American nationalism being forged by the fires of protest and revolution. They were quite popular and sold well, though the critics were less laudatory than before. Bancroft provoked a minor storm when he dared to question the military decisions of certain American generals in the Revolution; the descendants of the generals responded with vehemence in what became known as the War of the Grandfathers.

Much more troubling to him was the talk of nullification and secession that increasingly threatened the nation by the late 1840's. Bancroft took refuge in his work as the nation drifted toward civil war. As a politician and as a historian, he showed little concern regarding slavery, though he privately deplored the peculiar institution and the threat it posed to the Union. Once the war began, though still a states' rights Democrat, Bancroft came to appreciate Abraham Lincoln's leadership, subsequently advised President Johnson during Reconstruction, and was rewarded by appointment as ambassador to Prussia, where he served from 1867 to 1874. Once again, he took advantage of diplomatic service to search for American materials in European archives. He became an ardent supporter of Prince Otto von Bismarck and German unification and made friends with Leopold von Ranke and other German scholars. His public statement praising the Germans during the Franco-Prussian War enraged the French, but President Grant retained him as ambassador to Germany because of his intimacy with Bismarck and the Prussian elite.

Returning to the United States in 1874, Bancroft lived the remainder of his life in Washington, D.C., usually spending the summers in Newport. That same year, he finished the tenth volume of his history, focusing on the closing years of the American Revolution. Two years later, he published the "Centenary Edition" of his *History of the United States* in six volumes. In 1882, he brought out two volumes entitled *History of the Formation of the Constitution of the United States of America*, apparently inspired by recent Supreme Court decisions which, in his opinion, violated the principles of the Founding Fathers. Interestingly, he portrayed the Constitution as enshrining democratic ideas which ought not to be tampered with either by the Supreme Court or by legislative majorities. His last published work was a biography, *Martin Van Buren to the End of His Political Career* (1889), which he had begun in the early 1840's but put aside when Van Buren did not run in 1844. During his last years, Bancroft, still as charming and urbane as ever and wearing a flowing white beard, was the acknowledged patriarch of Washington literary and social circles. After his wife died in 1886, a daughter of his eldest son, George, stayed with him for a few years, and he then lived with his youngest son, John Chandler Bancroft. He died in Washington in 1891.

Summary

Upon his death, George Bancroft was eulogized as the Father of American History. His contribution was truly profound. It is sometimes forgotten that Bancroft pioneered the collection of American documents from foreign archives. He joined Jared Sparks and Peter Force in collecting and encouraging others to preserve early American documents scattered throughout the United States. In 1869, Bancroft estimated that he had spent between $50,000 and $75,000 in paying copyists, collecting, and researching. By the time of his death, that figure was well over $100,000. As a diplomat in England and later Germany, he had unparalleled access to both public and private archives in Europe and exploited his privileges to the fullest; his several hundred volumes of collected documents, located now in the New York Public Library, bear eloquent testimony to his industry. Whatever his shortcomings as a historian, Bancroft recognized that the sources were all important, and he must be credited with doing much to make sure that subsequent generations would have access to them.

Bancroft believed that his writing of American history accurately reflected the sources. He was not a little offended when the great von Ranke told him that "his history" was the best ever written from the democratic point of view. The fact is, though, that Bancroft projected his own patriotism and politics into his interpretation of American history. As J. Franklin Jameson put it, Bancroft voted for Jackson throughout his historical writing. He also had a tendency to quote material rather loosely, leaving himself open to the charge of manipulating the sources. By the time of his death, academic historians were dismissing his work as simply not adequate in terms of the canons of critical scholarship. Yet Bancroft was zealous, not dishonest, and his shortcomings were no worse than those of most other gentlemanly scholars of his day. Like his peers, he slighted economics and social factors, emphasizing instead politics, military affairs, and religion. Despite his knowledge of the English sources, he virtually neglected the British point of view of the American Revolution and constantly equated Catholicism with corruption and tyranny.

In the late twentieth century, Bancroft's writings have not been widely read because of his unabashed nationalism. Much of his basic interpretation has been retained, however, by scholars of the so-called Consensus School of American history, and that interpretation, though considerably more complex than Bancroft's limited point of view, still dominates American historiography. Yet Bancroft did more than simply write history. He explained

American nationalism in terms of heroic deeds, economic and political freedom, and the inevitable triumph of goodness and justice over abusive tyranny. His popular history reinforced a national mythology that brought comfort to nineteenth century Americans stunned by civil war, the Industrial Revolution, and political turmoil. He found a unity of purpose and experience in early American history that continues to appeal to the pluralistic America of the late twentieth century. George Bancroft's legacy has proven to be a lasting one. He shaped the past in terms of the dreams and aspirations of his generation. If any historian deserves to be called the Herodotus of the American people, Bancroft is surely the one.

Bibliography

Bassett, John Spencer. *The Middle Group of American Historians.* New York: Macmillan, 1917. A fine study of those nineteenth century historians known loosely as the Patriotic School, with special emphasis on leading figures such as Jeremy Belknap, George Bancroft, Jared Sparks, William Hickling Prescott, John Lothrop Motley, and Peter Force. Critical of Bancroft's methods and political bias, it is excellent for placing his life and work in its cultural context. Credits Bancroft for his literary style and ability to reflect the nationalistic aspirations of his generation of Americans.

Bush, Harold K., Jr. "Re-Inventing the Puritan Fathers: George Bancroft, Nathaniel Hawthorne, and the Birth of Endicott's Ghost." *The American Transcendental Quarterly* 9, no. 2 (June 1995). Compares Puritan portrayals by Bancroft and Hawthorne.

Fisher, Sidney George. "Legendary and Mythmaking Process in Histories of the American Revolution." *Proceedings of the American Philosophical Society* 51 (April 1912): 53-75. An incisive critique of the Patriotic School, Fisher's attack reflects the reaction of the rising generations of academic historians who thought of themselves as "scientific" scholars. Especially harsh judgment of Bancroft's methods and style.

Handlin, Lilian. *George Bancroft: The Intellectual as Democrat.* New York: Harper, 1984. The most recent and perhaps best biography of Bancroft in terms of integrating the personality of the man himself, his scholarship, and his politics. Emphasis is given to the influence of moral philosophy in his thinking and writing. Chal-lenges the notion that either German Romanticism or egalitarian politics primarily influenced his work.

Howe, M. A. DeWolf. *The Life and Letters of George Bancroft.* 2 vols. New York: Scribner, and London: Hodder and Stoughton, 1908. The authorized biography of Bancroft, this work is exceptionally detailed, filled with extensive quotations from his correspondence. Bancroft literally speaks for himself here. Not analytical, but tells much about the man and his time.

Kraus, Michael. *The Writing of American History.* Norman: University of Oklahoma Press, 1953. Dated for historical trends after the 1950's, this is one of the best historiographical works ever written. It places Bancroft in relationship to minor and other major historians of the nineteenth century. Very good for the broad perspective. Contains a most judicious evaluation of him as a historian.

Nye, Russel B. *George Bancroft: Brahmin Rebel.* New York: Knopf, 1944. Beautifully written biography that focuses on the intellectual forces which shaped Bancroft as a historian. It portrays him as a political rebel but part of the mainstream of New England thought, very much in the Emerson tradition and significantly influenced by German Romanticism. Although modified by Handlin's researches, this is in many ways the most insightful biography of Bancroft.

Sloane, William M. "George Bancroft—in Society, in Politics, in Letters." *The Century Magazine* 33 (January 1887): 473-487. Written by Bancroft's friend and former assistant, this small essay is filled with intimate details about the aging scholar. It captures Bancroft as he was seen by his friends, the sage historian who succeeded in politics, diplomacy, and scholarship.

Vitzthum, Richard C. *The American Compromise: Theme and Method in the Histories of Bancroft, Parkman, and Adams.* Norman: University of Oklahoma Press, 1974. A fascinating study that relates Bancroft and his work to the effort of two other popular nineteenth century historians. Vitzthum claims that all three were guided by the belief that Americans were driven by the struggle between separatist forces on the one hand and unifying forces on the other. Very nationalistic, they saw progress in terms of union and a strong central government.

Wood, Kirk. "George Bancroft." In *Dictionary of Literary Biography: American Historians, 1607-*

1865, vol. 30, edited by Clyde Wilson. Detroit, Mich.: Gale Research, 1984. A concise but analytical study of Bancroft as a historian and the differing views scholars have taken of him. Wood summarizes Bancroft's history and explains it in terms of the quest for American nationality and union before the Civil War.

Ronald Howard

HENRY BARNARD

Born: January 24, 1811; Hartford, Connecticut
Died: July 5, 1900; Hartford, Connecticut
Area of Achievement: Education
Contribution: Combining a high regard for learning and a strong sense of civic responsibility, Barnard stimulated and directed the development of public education during its formative years.

Early Life

Henry Barnard was born January 24, 1811, in Hartford, Connecticut. Barnard's mother, Elizabeth Andrus, died when Henry was four years old; his father, Chauncey Barnard, was a former sailor and prosperous farmer-businessman. Hartford was little more than a small country town during Barnard's childhood, but its status as one of Connecticut's capitals meant that he grew up in an atmosphere of politics and public service.

Ironically, the man who would later be hailed as a father of the public school so hated his first encounter with that institution that he conspired with a classmate to run away to sea. His father overheard them and the following day offered Henry a choice of leaving the district school and going to either sea or boarding school. Barnard chose the latter alternative and enrolled in Monson Academy, Monson, Massachusetts. Barnard was no bookworm, but he enjoyed his studies at Monson and developed an interest in literature and debating. Returning to Hartford, he received private tutoring and attended the Hopkins Grammar School in preparation for college. In 1826, Barnard entered Yale University, where he not only enhanced his writing and speaking skills, but also was suspended briefly for participating in a student food protest.

Having been graduated with distinction from Yale in 1830, Barnard resolved to devote his life to public service. He taught for a year, but appears at first to have given little thought of devoting himself exclusively to the field of education. Instead, he became involved in Whig politics and studied law. Barnard was admitted to the bar in 1835, but before beginning his legal practice he spent a year in Europe, where he met and talked with prominent European intellectuals and educators.

A year after Barnard's return to the United States, Hartford voters elected him to the Connecticut legislature, where he served from 1837 to 1840. He was active in promoting a broad range of social reform legislation, his most notable legislative achievement occurring in 1838, when he wrote and secured passage of a bill creating a state board of school commissioners and a secretary to supervise public education. This event proved to have a decisive influence on his life.

Life's Work

In 1838, Barnard was appointed one of the board's eight commissioners. He campaigned for his friend Thomas Gallaudet, a pioneering advocate of education for the deaf, to become secretary of the board. Gallaudet declined the position, however, and Barnard himself was urged to take it. At first he hesitated, partly because the office had been created through his efforts, and partly because he had been offered a partnership in a prestigious law firm. Yet in the end, he accepted the position.

As Connecticut's first secretary of education, Barnard attempted to develop widespread support for school and library reform. He wrote a letter to the people outlining the plans of the new board, distributed questionnaires, and personally visited hundreds of school districts. He presented data on schools to the legislature and the public, founded and edited the *Connecticut Common School Journal*, and lobbied for changes in school laws. Barnard also emphasized the need for trained teachers and established teachers' institutes which were among the first, if not the first, in the nation.

Yet events in Connecticut did not go well for Barnard. His campaign to improve public education awakened public opposition in the state to school reform and disturbed local politicians. In 1842, the Democrats came to power in the state and, in a move aimed at gaining support among voters, called for an end to direct state supervision of schools. Furthermore, Barnard's past affiliation with the opposition Whig Party did not help matters. After only four years of operation, the State Board of School Commissioners was abolished.

Barnard's Connecticut experience soured him on politics, but it did not dampen his enthusiasm for school reform. In 1843, he was appointed state school commissioner in Rhode Island. Predictably, Barnard engaged in a whirlwind of activity and in a relatively short time had developed popular support for public education in that state. At his urging, the Rhode Island Institute of Instruction was established in 1845. In that same year, he also secured passage of legislation to support a public education system in the state; when he resigned in 1849 for health reasons, he had already put it into successful operation. Barnard arranged for educational supplements to appear in state almanacs and caused the proceedings of school meetings to be reported in the press. In addition, he edited the state's school journal, published a book on teachers' colleges, and completed a volume on school architecture.

By the time of his marriage in 1847, Barnard was widely known and in great demand as a speaker. He was offered at least two professorships and four city school superintendencies, all of which he declined. When his home state of Connecticut again sought his leadership, however, he could not refuse. During his term of service as Connecticut's superintendent of common schools, Barnard drew up a revised code of school legislation, prepared a history of public school legislation in the state, and served as delegate to the International Exposition of Educational Methods in London, England. Still plagued by ill health, Barnard resigned as superintendent in 1855 to edit and publish the *American Journal of Education*, a monumental work that eventually comprised thirty-two volumes of more than eight hundred pages each.

Although the journal received most of Barnard's attention during the remainder of his life, he briefly held three additional administrative posts. From 1858 to 1860, he was chancellor of the University of Wisconsin and agent of the board of regents of the normal school fund. In 1866, Barnard was named president of St. John's College, resigning the following year to become the first commissioner of the newly created United States Department of Education. From the outset, Barnard's tenure as commissioner was plagued with problems. In 1868, growing criticism of the Department of Education and Barnard led Congress to downgrade it to a bureau (later, office) within the Department of the Interior. Two years later, he was unceremoniously removed from office by President Ulysses S. Grant.

Photographs of Barnard in the latter years of his life reveal a man perfectly suited for the role of reformer. His long white beard, white hair, and benign facial features gave him a patriarchal appearance. Deeply humiliated at his dismissal by Grant, he left Washington and returned to Hartford, where he continued to edit the *American Journal of Education* until 1881. Barnard lectured frequently,

continued a voluminous correspondence and in countless other ways attempted to keep busy until his death in the same house where he was born on July 5, 1900. Such activities, however, belied his true feelings. Despite the accolades he received from citizens and friends for his contribution to school reform, Barnard died doubting that his labors were sufficiently appreciated.

Summary

Barnard's contribution to the development of American education was manifold. The changes he introduced to public education in Connecticut and Rhode Island were of lasting importance and, in some degree, served as models for school reform in other states. He was always willing to offer advice and encouragement to fellow school reformers. His chief service, however, was rendered as a publicist and propagandist for education. As editor and publisher of the *American Journal of Education*, he not only furthered educational scholarship, but also helped create the necessary preconditions for the emergence of the modern teaching profession.

Undeniably, Barnard exemplified the best and the worst in nineteenth century American reform. A genuine idealist, he believed in the ability of people properly informed to make the right decision. At the same time, however, confidence in his own moral excellence could deteriorate into a brass-bolted certitude that denied any sense of rightness in other men. Indeed, at times Barnard's methods suggest that he thought the average citizen deserved little voice in school reform, except to rubber-stamp his own ideas.

The transformation which Barnard helped bring to American education is evident everywhere. It is most visible in older school-building architecture, public school systems, and schools of education throughout the United States. Less obvious, but equally important, is his role in supplying a professional literature and raising professional standards for the whole field of education.

Bibliography

Barnard, Henry. *Henry Barnard: American Educator.* Edited and introduced by Vincent P. Lannie. New York: Teacher's College Press, 1974. This collection of Barnard's writings contains excerpts from his personal correspondence, from an annual report of 1841 on public education in Connecticut, and from the *American Journal of Education.* Of particular note is the introduction by Lannie, which provides a concise biographical sketch of Barnard.

————. *Henry Barnard on Education.* Edited by John S. Brubacher. New York: McGraw-Hill, 1931. Comprising some of Barnard's most important writings, this book presents his thoughts on a variety of educational issues ranging from public interest in education to educational administration. It includes an introductory chapter that discusses Barnard's life and work.

Brickman, William W. "Early Development of Research and Writing of Educational History in the United States." *Paedagogica Historica* 19 (June 1979): 41-76. Traces early nineteenth century developments in educational historiography and discusses the work of Barnard and others in this area. Includes an examination of European influences and the impact of teachers' college curricula on writing about the history of American education.

MacMullen, Edith N. *In the Cause of True Education: Henry Barnard and Nineteenth-Century School Reform.* London and New Haven, Conn.: Yale University Press, 1991. The author focuses on Barnard's public life in education and his love of publishing, but also provides information on his personal life, which, in most cases suffered in favor of his public and career pursuits.

Rothfork, John. "Transcendentalism and Henry Barnard's School Architecture." *Journal of General Education* 29 (Fall, 1977): 173-187. Discusses the intellectual and social climate that led Barnard to advocate Greek Revival architecture for school buildings. Examines the reasons for which this style and its implicit values were popular in the nineteenth century.

Thursfield, Richard Emmons. *Henry Barnard's American Journal of Education.* Baltimore, Md.: Johns Hopkins University Press, 1945. Somewhat dated, this book nevertheless remains indispensable. It not only presents information on the journal's founding and financing, but also attempts to assess the significance of its content and its influence on readers.

Tyack, David B. *The One Best System: A History of American Urban Education.* Cambridge, Mass.: Harvard University Press, 1974. This well-documented study mentions Barnard only in passing but provides a detailed account of the social milieu in which he worked and the ideology that guided him and other educational reformers.

Warren, Donald R. *To Enforce Education: A History of the Founding Years of the United States Office of Education.* Detroit, Mich.: Wayne State University Press, 1974. Examines issues surrounding the founding of the Department of Education. Discusses the attempt by Barnard and other reformers to establish a federal bureau of education.

Monroe H. Little, Jr.

P. T. BARNUM

Born: July 5, 1810; Bethel, Connecticut

Died: April 7, 1891; Bridgeport, Connecticut

Areas of Achievement: Showmanship, politics, and writing

Contribution: With a strong business sense and the ability to take huge risks, P. T. Barnum created the modern museum and the musical concert, converted the tent carnival into the three-ring circus, and ran for a variety of political offices, serving for two terms on the Connecticut legislature and for one as a mayor of Bridgeport.

Early Life

Phineas Taylor Barnum was born on July 5, 1810, in Bethel, Connecticut. Throughout his life, Barnum always regretted that he had not been born on the Fourth of July, the perfect birth date for the man who would become one of America's first showmen. He was the sixth child of Philo and Irene Barnum, Philo's second wife. Barnum was named for his maternal grandfather, Phineas (a biblical name meaning "brazen mouth") Taylor. As Barnum's life progressed, it turned out that the name fit him and that the ancestor he was named for would influence Barnum unlike anyone else in his life.

As a boy, Barnum looked to his grandfather Phineas for amusement. Phineas Taylor, a great practical joker whose antics helped liven up the harsh New England winters, would go further than most to create his little jokes and hoaxes that he concocted to weather the stern Calvinism of his day. When Barnum was christened, grandfather Phineas deeded to him five acres of land called Ivy Island. Phineas liked to brag to others in Barnum's presence that, because of that land, Barnum would one day be wealthy, and Barnum believed this throughout his childhood. At the age of four, he began begging his father to see his inheritance; finally, when Barnum was ten, his father acquiesced. The boy was led to an ivy-infested swamp, and even at that young age he knew that he had been the butt of a long-running hoax and that his inheritance was worthless. (Ironically, later in life Barnum put Ivy Island up for collateral.) P. T. Barnum, who loved his grandfather Phineas, ended up getting the last laugh by naming his illegitimate son Phineas Taylor.

The young P. T. Barnum, who would one day prudently know when to cut his losses, excelled in mathematics. While in grammar school (high school), Barnum helped his father out on the family farm; like thinkers down through the ages, however, he detested menial work and began planning for a different life. Philo's farm was a disappointment, and so, with a partner, he bought a general store and put Barnum in charge. In that position Barnum learned much about people, about bartering, and about business. By chance, he was being trained and goaded toward his future.

Barnum's father died when Barnum was only fifteen. In charge of the family, Barnum liquidated the store only to discover that the family was bankrupt. Quickly he obtained a similar job in another store. Tiring of that, he moved to Brooklyn to clerk at a better store.

Barnum's influential grandfather, Phineas, wanted Barnum to return to Bethel and offered to set him up in business if he would come home. That was all the encouragement Barnum needed, and he returned to set up a profitable business in half of his grandfather's carriage house.

On November 8, 1829, at the age of nineteen, Barnum eloped with Charity Hallett, a twenty-one-year-old Bethel woman. One of Barnum's daughters, Frances, died before her second birthday; his surviving daughters were Caroline, Helen, and Pauline. Like King Lear, Barnum suffered much from the actions of his daughters, who let their father down innumerable times, disappointing him by their various divorce scandals and their eagerness to divide up their father's estates while he was still alive.

Barnum, disappointed that his wife never had sons, left twenty-five thousand dollars and a yearly three percent of his enterprises to his eldest grandson, Clinton H. Seeley. To receive the inheritance, Seeley was required to change his middle name to Barnum in order to perpetuate Barnum's name. Clinton Barnum Seeley accepted the bequest but dishonored Barnum by conducting licentious parties, one of which included a nude Little Egypt in the center ring.

Life's Work

P. T. Barnum's life is almost inseparable from the freaks, the oddities, the hoaxes, the hokum, the sheer entertainment that he presented to the world, from the "sucker" on the street to Queen Victoria and the president. This six-foot-two man with

curly, receding hair, blue eyes, a cleft chin, a bulbous nose, and a high voice was a pitchman *par excellence* and might almost be said to have invented the art of mass publicity.

After an apprenticeship spent selling hats, working in grocery stores, running lotteries, and maintaining a boardinghouse, Barnum found his métier. The catalyst was his discovery and purchase of Joice Heth, a black woman with legal documents that proved she was 161 years old and had served as George Washington's nurse. Barnum quit his grocery job and gambled both borrowed money and his life savings to make his break from convention.

In 1835, a Mr. Lindsay showed Barnum documents on the old woman and sold her to him for one thousand dollars. Barnum hired a hall by promising the owner half the gross, and he employed several people to help him launch a publicity campaign. At her shows, Joice Heth sang hymns and told her story of rearing Washington. The newspaper helped to spread the story, and eventually the show was a success, with Barnum splitting the weekly gross of fifteen hundred dollars with his partner.

Finally the dreaded event occurred: Joice Heth died. Barnum had given Dr. David Rogers permission to perform an autopsy, which in the end proved that Joice Heth was not more than eighty years old. Thus, the hoax was exposed and the newspapers made Barnum even more famous.

Barnum continued to collect and display oddities, both human and otherwise. He needed a central stage for his show and in 1841 acquired a dilapidated museum at Broadway and Ann Street in New York City which became known as Barnum's American Museum. For the admission fee, one could see the Feejee Mermaid (which was nothing more than a female monkey torso joined to a large stuffed fish tail), midgets, beauty contests, a bearded lady (she went to court to prove she was not a man), a tattooed man, the world's tallest woman, the Woolly Horse, the authentic Siamese twins Chang and Eng, and countless other abnormalities.

Barnum was always in search of another main attraction, and one materialized for him in 1842 when he discovered a five-year-old midget named Charles Stratton. Barnum taught him to sing and dance, to tell jokes, and to perform other stunts, all while wearing several different military uniforms. Stratton was thus converted into General Tom Thumb, one of Barnum's biggest entertainment successes.

To gain greater fame, Barnum took Tom Thumb on tour in Europe. There he was a hugh success before five million people (according to Barnum's own count), and Barnum connived to make headlines when the General performed for Queen Victoria, who presented Tom with a court uniform. When Barnum and Tom Thumb returned to the United States, the clamor was great, and even President Polk requested and got a private show at the White House.

Barnum's next big success was the signing of the famous Swedish singer Jenny Lind, whom he had neither seen nor heard, to perform on a concert tour. To finance the tour, he was forced to mortgage both his $150,000 home and his museum, as well as borrow heavily from friends. The risk paid off; Jenny Lind's tour was both a critical and a financial success. The Swedish Nightingale opened in New York City on September 11, 1850, and after ninety-five concerts in nineteen cities, Barnum had cleared profits in excess of $500,000.

In 1855, however, Barnum's time for high-risk profits had run out. As he had in the past, he became obsessed with an investment, this one with the Jerome Clock Company. Through his own bad management, Barnum carelessly invested more than $500,000 in the company, only to watch it go bankrupt. Barnum contemplated suicide, but instead, this religious man concluded that the Almighty Himself wished to teach him that there was something higher in life than money. Except for Charity's nineteen thousand dollars a year from the museum lease, all was lost. "Without Charity," he quipped, "I am nothing." This may have simply been a clever pun, however, since his financial recovery had begun immediately after the losses.

At forty-six, Barnum began his long climb toward repaying his debts. He turned to his standby, General Tom Thumb; he also realized that he himself was a viable commodity and began lecturing to packed houses. Capitalizing, as always, on a good thing, he turned his lecture notes into a best-selling pamphlet, *The Art of Money Getting*, and reused the notes a second time in his autobiography.

Fire seemed to follow Barnum around like a demon. His home, Iranistan, was lost in a fire. The Barnum American Museum burned to the ground (miraculously, the freaks with their immobile bodies all escaped). The museum loss was calculated at $400,000, with insurance covering only forty thousand dollars. Many precious objects, including irreplaceable relics of the Revolutionary War, were lost. Barnum, with his typical verve, rebuilt the museum.

One of Barnum's greatest claims to fame began when he was sixty. He joined forces with James Anthony Bailey to created "The Greatest Show on Earth." Barnum's London Zoo purchase of Jumbo the Elephant (who had given rides to some five million British children, including Winston Churchill) became one of his most famous and most disputed purchases. Queen Victoria and others in England wanted the famous elephant back. By the time Jumbo reached the American shores, the elephant was an international *cause célèbre* and had generated much free publicity. The elephant act was an instant success: The purchase price of thirty thousand dollars was recouped in six weeks, with a box-office of $336,000.

In 1873, Charity died, and in the following year Barnum married Nancy Fish, an English woman forty years his junior. Barnum and his second wife had no children.

In 1891, Barnum was eighty-one and in poor health. After a lifetime of financial reversals, he was surrounded by wealth. He remarked to a friend that he wondered how his obituary would read. Word of this got back to the New York *Evening Sun*, and the newspaper asked for and got permission to print Barnum's obituary before he died. On April 7, 1891, this American folk hero died at his home in Bridgeport.

Summary

According to Bartlett's *Familiar Quotations*, the expression "There's a sucker born every minute" is attributed to P. T. Barnum. Researchers have stated repeatedly that Barnum never said this. Indeed, in his own life he was often a "sucker." He assumed as a child that Ivy Island would make him wealthy, and as an adult he thought that he could get rich quick through his Jerome Clock investment.

Barnum knew many secrets about human nature, one of which was that although no one enjoys being duped, if the game is all in good fun, people do enjoy becoming "suckers" to an extent—so much so that they are willing to pay for the honor. Another secret Barnum learned was that of the publicist: In his pre-"global village" age, Barnum might be said to have invented the high-pressure sales campaign, creating the "hype" that sold his wares.

Barnum himself became a household name and an original American folk hero. His life was filled with contradictions. He was a good family man, yet he fathered an illegitimate son, the only son he was ever to have. He was reared in an anti-entertainment age yet believed devoutly that each person deserved to be entertained. He made a great amount of money; he lost all of his money; he made more money. He sustained spectacular triumphs unmatched by rivals. Living a long life, he experienced many personal tragedies, including the death of a daughter, the death of his wife Charity, the loss of property and money, and the divisiveness and greed of his surviving three daughters.

Barnum became an archetype of American Dream merchants such as Walt Disney, Samuel Goldwyn, Oscar Hammerstein I, John Ringling, Mike Todd, Cecil B. DeMille, Billy Rose, the brothers Shubert, Florenz Ziegfeld, Steven Spielberg, George Lucas, and hundreds of others. A lively musical, *Barnum*, and the circus that bears his name reintroduces Barnum to thousands each year.

"To the Egress," a sign in the Barnum's American Museum once read. Expecting to find another oddity, people entered and found themselves outside the museum, on the street.

Bibliography

Adams, Bluford. *E Pluribus Barnum: The Great Showman and the Making of U.S. Popular Culture.* Minneapolis: University of Minnesota Press, 1997. Discusses Barnum's influence on nineteenth-century culture and his continued influence today, providing information on his early career and his approach to such societal issues as women's rights, slavery, temperance, immigration, and capitalism.

Barnum, Phineas T. *Barnum's Own Story: Autobiography.* Edited by Waldo R. Browne. Magnolia, Mass.: Peter Smith, 1962. As of August 1986, this is the only autobiography in print. Browne's editing makes it less clumsy.

———. *Selected Letters of P. T. Barnum.* Edited by A. H. Saxon. New York: Columbia University Press, 1983. The only published collection of Barnum's letters.

———. *Struggles and Triumphs: Or, Forty Years' Recollections of P. T. Barnum.* Edited by Carl Bode. London and New York: Penguin, 1981. Good starting point for research. Barnum wrote three versions of this book, which Bode condenses into one readable volume. Bode has written an excellent introduction and has included a short, annotated bibliography.

Benton, Joel. *Life of Honorable Phineas T. Barnum.* Philadelphia: Edgewood, 1891. This book largely paraphrases (in the third person) Barnum's own autobiography. Benton knew Barnum, and he includes some of his own recollections.

Desmond, Alice Curtis. *Barnum Presents: General Tom Thumb.* New York: Macmillan, 1954. The story of one of the most famous midgets in the world and how he became a gigantic drawing card for Barnum.

Harris, Neil. *Humbug: The Art of P. T. Barnum.* Boston: Little Brown, 1973. The most reliable biography. Sound scholarship is used to place Barnum in his own cultural setting.

Kunhardt, Philip B., III, and Peter W. Kunhardt. *P. T. Barnum: America's Greatest Showman.* New York: Knopf, 1995. Deals with Barnum's life and career with emphasis on his friendships with and treatment of his performers. Many illustrations, 260 in color.

Root, Harvey W. *The Unknown Barnum.* New York and London: Harper, 1927. Provides source material on Barnum's publishing and political careers.

Sutton, Felix. *Master of Ballyhoo: The Story of P. T. Barnum.* New York: Putnam, 1968. A Literary Guild edition with large print for juveniles.

Wallace, Irving. *The Fabulous Showman: The Life and Times of P. T. Barnum.* New York: Knopf, 1959; London: Hutchinson, 1960. One of the best introductions available on Barnum, covering all the major events. Well researched with an excellent bibliography and sixteen pages of photographs.

Werner, Morris Robert. *Barnum.* London: Cape, and New York: Doubleday, 1923. This was the first biography to offer a researched, objective view of Barnum's life.

John Harty

SIR CHARLES BARRY

Born: May 23, 1795; London, England
Died: May 12, 1860; London, England
Area of Achievement: Architecture
Contribution: The chief architect of the most famous buildings in England, Barry designed the Houses of Parliament, one of the finest examples of the Victorian Gothic Revival.

Early Life

Charles Barry's father was a successful merchant in the city of London, the owner of a stationery business. At the age of fifteen, Barry was articled to a London firm of architects and surveyors, and he remained with them until his father died six years later. At the age of twenty-one, he used his inheritance to finance a Grand Tour of the Continent, intent on studying the architecture. Over a three-year period, he traveled through France, Italy, Greece, and the Near East, accumulating the firsthand knowledge of the architectural styles which he was to use with such facility in his professional life.

A personable, genial young man of considerable confidence, he set himself up as a practicing architect upon his return to England. Shortly after settling into business, he entered a government competition which was to provide churches in newly developed suburbs in cities throughout England. Barry, despite his modest experience, was awarded contracts for churches in the Islington district of London, in Manchester, and in Brighton. The Neo-Gothic style in public buildings (particularly church buildings) was popular at the time, and Barry was able to adapt his skills to it easily, if not with any particular brilliance. He showed himself able to work within modest budgets and to deal sensibly with the complications of government contracts. The churches were aesthetically interesting, built of brick with Gothic detail added in stone, but they showed little depth of artistic power.

The fact is that Barry was not a fully committed adherent to the Gothic revival. He could, and often did, work in other styles, providing his clients with what they wanted. He seemed most at home, and most engaging, in designing nineteenth century British versions of the Italian Renaissance palazzo. In Rome or Florence such buildings were combinations of the town house and the palace of the great family. Barry put them to use in the first in-

stance as havens for the English clubmen. His first important commission for such a building was the Travellers' Club in Pall Mall, which he began in 1829 (finishing it in 1832) and which is one of the best examples of how he could adopt models from another culture and time, without self-consciousness, to the needs of Victorian London. The Travellers' Club still possesses the dignity and charm which make it one of the handsomest buildings on that famous street. Its success established Barry as a designer of distinction.

Life's Work

Barry's ability to manipulate different styles, to adapt himself to the taste and enthusiasms of his patrons, made him a popular architect not only in the city but also in the country, where he gained commissions to reproduce a version of the Italianized country house. He was also willing and able to renovate and add to houses which in one way or another had become boring or unsuitable to their owners, and there are several great houses throughout England which have additions by Barry, sometimes in his Italian style, sometimes in his Gothic style, occasionally in Tudor imitation.

Architecture, perhaps of all the arts, is the one most inclined to allow imitation, and it was not considered invalid for owners to request the renovation of buildings which had come down through the family and through several centuries. Often, such renovations, such demands for additions from other historical styles, could make for the unfortunate destruction of original masterpieces. Occasionally, such messing about with the buildings not only made them more civilized but also added to their aesthetic value. At Harewood House in Yorkshire, Barry's façade, grand outer staircase, and some interior work in the library seem to have been successful, but his addition of an Italianate tower to Georgian Bowood in Wiltshire is, in the eyes of Nikolaus Pevsner, the architectural historian, "incongruous."

Such limitations seemed to work best if they were all of a piece, and Barry's Reform Club, a return to the Renaissance Italian urban palace, was set immediately west of his former success, the Travellers' Club. There is some considerable opinion that the Reform Club (begun in 1837) is not only a finer building but also his greatest work in the Renaissance style. Weightier, somewhat grander than the Travellers', both inside and out, it displays the growing maturity of his work, and his ability to go back to the same model with sufficient variation and imagination to allow it to be put side by side with his older building without fear of cloying the appetite, despite the basic similarity of the two structures. It was the mark of an architect of breadth and some considerable courage.

Barry's greatest fame, however, was not to come from tour de force juxtapositions of buildings in the same style. Indeed, it was not to come from his practice in the neo-Renaissance Italian mode at all, but from that style with which his career had begun, with the city church commissions—from answering, once again, the English allegiance to the Gothic, the style which was always before their eyes in the great cathedrals. The English Baroque architects of the late seventeenth century and the early eighteenth century, Christopher Wren, Sir John Vanbrugh, and Nicholas Hawksmoor, in their sometimes eccentric eclecticism, had managed to use Gothic motifs in a mix with classical and Renaissance ideas, but the Palladians, who came into vogue in the period after 1715, deprecated such barbarism for the high, fastidious purity of neoclassicism. The result was some of the finest architecture in the history of Great Britain, but it was not to last out the century unchallenged.

If the Gothic was unfashionable at the higher levels of aesthetic decision, it retained its hold on the affection of less sophisticated provincials, and the local church was often constructed with Gothic models in mind. Aside from these residual traces, however, Gothic came to mean, first, in the literary arts, a world of imagination, of teasing fantasy, of escape from the high rationality of the eighteenth century into the mysterious, into personal feeling. Horace Walpole not only invented the horror story (*The Castle of Otranto*, 1764), but also shared in the antiquarian enthusiasm about which he wrote; he assiduously collected examples of Gothic design and built himself a Gothic play-palace, Strawberry Hill. The pointed arch, the delicate tracery, the machicolated profile that reeked of fortified castles, the rich plethora of motif caught the late eighteenth century imagination in letters and was to lead to the Romantic movement, but architecture was also to be gradually influenced. If some wanted to live in the grandeur of Renaissance Italy, others wanted the frisson of an idealized medievalism.

Barry's early churches had been five-finger exercises in satisfying that desire to link the new, industrialized England with its roots in antiquity. The opportunity for a project on an entirely different scale came in 1834, when the House of Parliament burned down. It was decided that the new buildings should be either "Gothic" or "Elizabethan"; Barry chose to enter the competition with a plan which was basically classical in form, but dressed from head to toe (right down to the inkwells) in Gothic detail. To achieve this, he brought in as his assistant Augustus Pugin, who, despite his youth, was already a master of the Gothic mode. Barry provided the overall plan, and Pugin did the drawings, adding the details which were to turn the buildings into the best example of the Gothic Revival in Britain. While the overall conception of the project was Barry's, Pugin's contribution was central to their success in winning the commission. Years later, after both men were dead, their children were to engage in a public quarrel over who really was the major contributor. It is true that Barry was somewhat less generous than he might have been in sharing the praise, but Pugin admitted that he could not have led the project. He believed that he had nothing like Barry's organizing ability or stubbornness in fighting back the onslaughts of the bureaucrats, the public, and the envious architectural community, all of whom threw themselves singly and collectively into thwarting Barry, who exhausted himself in making the buildings such a success. Whether the Parliament complex is a major work of art is questionable—Pugin himself considered it somewhat fraudulent, a classic shape decked out in Gothic trappings—but there is no doubt that it is the most famous seat of government in the world, and that its Thames-side profile, punctuated by the Big Ben Tower, has appeared on more labels for English products than perhaps any other object in the history of art.

The success of this massive project fully established Barry's reputation and was to do the same for Pugin in later years when the extent of his contribution was fully known. So ambitious was this undertaking that Barry was not to be free of it during his lifetime, and the project was finally completed by his son. Meanwhile, however, Barry worked on other contracts as well. The Reform Club was designed after he had begun the Parliament project; in Birmingham, he designed the King Edward Grammar School in the Tudor style; in Manchester, he used his Italian palazzo plan for the Atheneum. He provided the ground plan for Parliament Square in London, and he also had a hand in laying out Trafalgar Square. Both have been altered since, but his terrace on the north side of Trafalgar Square is extant.

Perhaps the finest example of Barry's use of the Italian palazzo for a residence (although it is now a corporate head office) is Bridgewater House in Cleveland Row, facing onto Green Park. Built quite late in his career (1847-1849), it is a longer, lower, richer variation on the model which he used just down the street in the Reform Club. The long side is to the park, a quite splendidly arrogant display of architectural sonority, floating slightly above the park level, crowned by a richly detailed cornice topped by his favorite device, the ornamental urn.

Summary

If it is understood that art need not necessarily be original, that it can just as well be memory of that which has preceded it, the history of architecture and of some architects can be better appreciated. Sir Charles Barry was an imitator in the best sense of the word, just as Palladio was, and as Burlington was of Palladio. It is probably true that Barry was not quite as great an architect as either of these men, but he produced individual buildings of some considerable merit, whose aesthetic worth lies not in their originality but in the way in which the style of established merit has been made to work again, in another place at another time.

Barry also showed that it was possible to satisfy the public, to give them what they wanted, without necessarily destroying artistic integrity or merit. On several occasions, it must be admitted, Barry's additions to already established buildings did not quite work, but he was often able to solve problems of mixed styles in ways which showed how technically ingenious he was, how able to manipulate the highly difficult art of design and execution in order to make architecture which had some lasting value. He never forgot the obligation of the architect to make art which was also useful. He was not a great artist, but he was often close to being so, even when he was obliged to give his patrons what were, in fact, copies of something long ago and far away.

Bibliography

Barry, Alfred. *The Life and Works of Sir Charles Barry*. London: Murray, 1867. A family bias, aggravated by the fight between the Pugins and the Barrys, should be remembered in reading this work, but it does give a strong sense of the Victorian sensibility.

Clark, Kenneth. *The Gothic Revival: An Essay in the History of Taste*. London: Constable, 1928; New York: Schribner, 1929. The most popular, readily available essay on the peculiar zest for making everything old that seized the Victorians and turned their architectural landscape and all its trappings into the new Middle Ages. Enormously readable and scholarly in its careful development of the movement in the eighteenth century. The ramifications of the movement are fully explored, not only in architecture but also in literature and life.

Dixon, Roger, and Stefan Muthesius. *Victorian Architecture*. London: Thames and Hudson, and New York: Oxford University Press, 1978. One of those handsome, easily read, popular books on the period. Generous illustration. Some care taken to avoid technical mystery. Barry turns up quite often but is most carefully discussed in the chapters on public and religious architecture.

Ferriday, Peter, ed. *Victorian Architecture*. London: Cape, 1963; Philadelphia: Lippincott, 1964. Barry is best understood in the full context of Victorian architecture in general. This book is a collection of essays by leading experts. There is a sweet-natured essay by Sir John Betjeman, poet laureate and defender of Victoriana, and essays on the architectural profession, the home, and the public building. Peter Fleetwood-Hesketh, one of the best commentators on Barry, provides an essay. There is also an essay on Pugin that provides some sense of the collaboration between the two men.

Goodhart-Rendel, H. S. *English Architecture Since the Regency*. London: Constable, 1953; St. Clair Shores, Mich.: Scholary Press, 1977. This author provides the essay on the country house in Ferriday's *Victorian Architecture* (see above). In this book, he meets the problem of the originality of nineteenth century English architecture, given its dependence upon prior models. It is densely argued and deeply attached to the idea that architecture is part of the social history of ideas and must be judged in context.

Little, Bryan. *English Historic Architecture*. London: Batsford, and New York: Hastings House, 1964. Puts the great public buildings into the context of English history. The last five chapters, beginning with the eighteenth century, are very good for setting the Gothic movement clearly in the mind as something more than a fad.

Pevsner, Nikolaus. *London: The Cities of London and Westminster*. London: Penguin, 1957. Pevsner's magnificent feat of door-to-door criticism and description of England's buildings concentrates, in this volume, on that area in which Barry's greatest buildings stand. The best detailed look that can be had of Parliament, the Pall Mall clubs, and Bridgewater House. An education in how to look at a building, and how to talk about it.

Service, Alastair. *The Architects of London*. London: Architectural Press, and New York: Architectural Book Publishing, 1979. For all his roaming around in the country, Barry's best work is to be found in the city of London, and the short, informed chapter on him in this work, putting him in the context of his contemporaries, is very good.

Charles H. Pullen

CLARA BARTON

Born: December 25, 1821; North Oxford, Massachusetts

Died: April 12, 1912; Glen Echo, Maryland

Areas of Achievement: Education, nursing, and social reform

Contribution: After half a lifetime devoted to humanitarian pursuits, Barton became the key figure in establishing the American Red Cross.

Early Life

Clarissa Harlowe Barton (known as Clara) was influenced by her parents' liberal political attitudes. The youngest child, Clara had identity problems which worsened when she showed interests in academic and other pursuits considered masculine. Farm work and nursing relatives who were ill, however, led her increasingly to connect approval and praise to helping others.

In 1836, Barton began teaching school. She was a gifted teacher who chose to enforce discipline through kindness and persuasion at a time when physical force was the standard. During the next decade, Barton developed quite a reputation as she moved from town to town, taming obstreperous students and leaving for another challenge. As she gained self-confidence, she began to have an active social life, though she never married. Tired of teaching and concerned that her own education was inadequate, she enrolled at the Clinton Liberal Institute in Clinton, New York, at the end of 1850. She studied for a year, but as an older student, she felt out of place and made few friends.

Unable to afford more school and unwilling to be dependent on her family, Barton went to live with friends in New Jersey. In 1852, she convinced authorities to offer free public education by allowing her to open a free school. Although she was initially unpaid, Barton eventually made the school such a success that she was offered a salary and the opportunity to expand her program. As the school grew, however, the school board decided that a man should be placed in charge and paid more than any women involved. Frustrated and angry, Barton moved to Washington, D.C., in search of new opportunities in 1854.

She found work as a clerk in the Patent Office, where the commissioner was willing to give women positions. For several years Barton made good money and earned respect for her efficiency despite the resentment of her male colleagues. Shifting political fortunes forced Barton to leave her post in 1857. For three years, she lived at home in Massachusetts before returning to the Patent Office in 1860.

Life's Work

With the outbreak of the Civil War in 1861, Clara Barton began the humanitarian work that would occupy the rest of her life. Federal troops were arriving in Washington without baggage or food. She began to gather and distribute supplies to ease their distress. Her efforts quickly grew to include battlefield assistance in helping the wounded at the beginning of the war. Because the military had badly underestimated medical needs, Barton's individual effort gathering supplies and caring for the wounded at battles such as Fredericksburg proved immensely valuable. By the end of 1862, however, the army was becoming better organized and the work of amateurs was no longer significant. Barton also had problems getting official support and recognition because, unlike Barton, most volunteers were more harm than help. The army could not accept one volunteer while denying others. Barton, as she often did, became defensive, taking every rebuke, regardless of the source, personally.

After the war, Barton undertook a project to identify missing soldiers and inform their families of their fates. Her efforts included a trip to Andersonville prison where, with the help of a former inmate who had kept the death roll, Barton supervised the identification and marking of some 13,000 graves. Despite some success, Barton's work in tracing missing soldiers resulted in identification of less than ten percent of the missing. During her pursuit of these activities, Barton confronted two difficulties of a sort typical of her career. One problem arose because the army was also attempting to find missing soldiers. Barton sought sole control of the whole effort, but this control was not granted and she feuded with the officer in charge. Barton possessed a zeal for efficiency that made her reluctant to share responsibility or credit. This attitude prevented her from delegating authority and provoked hostility among many people who actually wanted to help her. The second problem was a result of poor accounting. She could not provide details of expenses, leaving herself open to charges of malfeasance. Although she was always more interested in field work than administration, Barton was unwilling to share power with someone who would handle paperwork. She paid little attention to tracking the disbursement of donated funds and poured her own limited resources into her projects even though she could produce no receipts. There is no evidence that she sought personal gain. Nevertheless, her poor accounting resulted in repeated complaints that ultimately came back to haunt her during her work with the Red Cross.

Barton's involvement with the Red Cross began in Europe, where she met some of the organization's leaders and learned that the United States had not ratified the Treaty of Geneva (1864) that had created the organization. Barton was invited to assist in the work of the International Red Cross during the Franco-Prussian War of 1870-1871. Her experiences gave her a new perspective on the suffering of civilians during war—she had worked almost entirely on behalf of soldiers in the Civil War. Friendship with Grand Duchess Louise of Baden, a Red Cross leader, resulted in Barton working six months in Strasbourg. She was convinced of the value of the Red Cross and determined that supporting self-help was better than handouts. She held these convictions the rest of her life.

In 1872, Barton returned to the United States, after suffering a nervous breakdown that some regarded as partially psychosomatic. Retiring from public life to stay in a sanatorium eventually improved her health. In 1877, she decided to form an American Red Cross society to gather funds to help victims of the Russo-Turkish War. She received permission from the International Red Cross, and began a campaign to secure American ratification of the Treaty of Geneva. U.S. government officials, however, insisted that since the country observed the tenets of the treaty, there was no reason for a formal alliance.

Barton lobbied diligently for ratification. She sought help from friends in Washington, D.C., cultivated the press, and relied upon her friendship with members of the Grand Army of the Republic, a Civil War veterans group that had honored her. To increase awareness of the work of the Red Cross, Barton made peacetime disaster relief a priority. Progress was slow, but the treaty was ratified in 1882. Her group was officially recognized by the government, paving the way for it to be associated with the International Red Cross. This recognition helped Barton launch her next campaign: to make the American Association of the Red Cross the central relief agency in the United States.

The 1880's and 1890's were times of heroic effort for Barton. Her labor was certainly greatly increased by her refusal to yield any share of control, and, during the decades of her presidency, she and the Red Cross were essentially synonymous. She wanted the national agency to be the center of a network of state groups, but she was frequently drawn away from organizing to oversee field work and was hampered by continual shortages of funds. She also spent much of 1883 running a women's prison at the request of Benjamin Butler, the former Union general who had become governor of Massachusetts. Assisting Butler with his political problems concerning the funding of the progressive prison, Barton established that the costs were mostly appropriate, despite sloppy administrative work. Unfortunately, her efforts on Butler's behalf diverted Barton's attention from the urgent demands of Red Cross work.

For the rest of her life, however, Barton devoted herself almost exclusively to Red Cross work. She traveled, seeking funds and public support—sometimes for herself as well as her cause—and attended annual meetings of the International Red Cross, where she was accepted as a delegate when no other woman was even allowed on the convention floor. She was a hero to feminists, whose cause she supported, although never so vigorously as to cause hostility toward the Red Cross. Field work continued to beckon, including relief efforts in the wake of floods in the Ohio and Mississippi River valleys in 1884 and an earthquake in Charleston, South Carolina, in 1886. She allowed the head of the New Orleans chapter to lead an effort in a yellow fever epidemic around Jacksonville, Florida, only to find that the nurses he took resembled camp followers more than care-givers. This incident confirmed her determination to do everything herself.

Barton received praise from the press for relief efforts in the wake of the 1889 Johnstown flood, but she was later greatly criticized for not keeping track of expenditures. Some of the expenses appear to have been inappropriate, though not fraudulent, but her lack of receipts made defense against such criticism almost impossible. Barton hoped to parlay the Johnstown success into government funding for the Red Cross as the official agency for coordinating wartime relief. This effort stalled, however, and she turned her attention to efforts to alleviate a Russian famine.

By the mid-1890's, relief funds were at a low ebb and criticism of her poor accounting hampered the

activities of both the American and international organizations. Although Barton was in her seventies and her energy was beginning to decline, she repudiated every criticism, attacked critics, and continued. In 1896, she went to Turkey to aid Armenians suffering from Turkish atrocities. She secured permission from the Turkish sultan to send Dr. Julian Hubbell, one of her most loyal collaborators, into Armenia, where he had significant success.

Back in the United States, she found appeals from Cuban civilians suffering in the struggle against Spain. Since the United States government wanted to keep out of the situation, little was being done to provide relief. Eventually, Barton went to survey the situation with a committee of relief agencies. When the head of another agency criticized her work and tried to supplant her, Barton returned to the United States and got her rival discredited. By the time she returned to Cuba, however, the Spanish-American War had begun. The New York Red Cross chapter, which, along with several others, had been acting almost autonomously, provided necessary assistance to stateside military hospitals, and the California chapter sent aid to the Pacific front in the Philippines. Barton headed for Cuba, eventually leaving without official sanction. Although intending to help civilians, her team stumbled into a battle fought by the Rough Riders. To her delight, Barton found herself nursing soldiers again. Important work with civilians followed, and the Red Cross proved its value.

The organization's efforts during the Spanish-American War and its aftermath did lead to legislation granting a federal charter to the American Red Cross in 1900. In the end, however, this success was also Barton's downfall. Concerned that donations were in decline, some members of the Red Cross organized independent efforts during Barton's absence and were reluctant to relinquish control to her. The crisis came after a hurricane in Galveston, Texas, in September of 1900. Barton launched relief efforts without consulting the organization's new board of directors, and her bookkeeping was so lackadaisical that the national treasurer resigned rather than defend her expenditures. The struggle went on for several years, becoming more acrimonious because Barton came to regard her critics as personal foes. Finally, Barton was forced to resign all ties to the Red Cross in 1904. She did retain quarters at a house in Maryland that had been built largely with her own money and had served as Red Cross headquarters during the final years of her presidency. Continuing to support public health efforts and the woman's rights movement, Barton alternated living in Maryland and in North Oxford, Massachusetts, until her death in 1912.

Summary

Clara Barton established the American Red Cross almost singlehandedly. Earlier efforts to do so had failed, and the nation lacked a major disaster relief agency. Rival organizations did arise, but most were launched later in imitation of Barton's efforts. Barton's prodigious labor and self-sacrifice on behalf of establishing the American Red Cross ultimately earned for her the recognition she desired, yet she never allowed her ego to prevent her from giving unstintingly of her work and wealth to those who needed help.

That ego did, however, cause problems. The combination of childhood insecurity and individual success in the Civil War rendered Barton incapable of working equally with others. She preferred to work with trusted aides who deferred to her authority, and she seemed to interpret any initiative outside her control as a personal affront. This caused Barton much disquiet and slowed the growth of the Red Cross. Although most if not all the charges made against her personally were without merit, it cannot be denied that had she shared leadership with someone who was willing to do the vital paperwork much more progress could have been made. Furthermore, Barton's reputation would not have been sullied. Nevertheless, her crusading spirit on behalf of nursing reform created for Barton an impressive legacy.

Bibliography

Barton, Clara. *The Story of My Childhood.* New York: Atwater, 1924. Although it was intended to be the first chapter of an autobiography and hence covers only Barton's first years, this work is a valuable source given the influence of her childhood on her character.

Barton, William E. *The Life of Clara Barton.* 2 vols. Boston: Houghton Mifflin, 1922. An old-fashioned and uncritical biography, but filled with details and information often missing in modern studies.

Burton, David H. *Clara Barton: In the Service of Humanity.* Westport, Conn.: Greenwood Press, 1995. Examines Barton's life, her heroism in the Civil War, and her founding of the Red Cross. Barton is portrayed as a generous, yet self-centered person unable to deal with criticism. The author provides a sympathetic story that remains honest in its reporting.

Dulles, Foster Rhea. *The American Red Cross.* New York: Harper, 1950. Written by an excellent historian, this valuable work provides background on Barton and her work with the Red Cross.

Oates, Stephen B. *A Woman of Valor: Clara Barton and the Civil War.* New York: Free Press, 1994. Best known for his biographies of Abraham Lincoln, Oates provides a vivid account of Clara Barton's early career during the Civil War years. While revealing Barton's drive to succeed and her skill in generating public support for her relief efforts, Oates's detailed narrative also sheds light on her difficult personality and strained emotional life, thus providing a welcome corrective to older, less critical accounts.

Pryor, Elizabeth B. *Clara Barton: Professional Angel.* Philadelphia: University of Pennsylvania Press, 1987. Although informed by the author's research into numerous primary sources, this biography suffers somewhat from a lack of critical distance in its approach, as suggested by its subtitle.

Ross, Ishbel. *Angel of the Battlefield: The Life of Clara Barton.* New York: Harper, 1956. A reasonable biography, though somewhat dated. Like most of the work on Barton, this volume is adulatory in its approach.

Speigel, Allan D. "The Role of Gender, Phrenology, Discrimination and Nervous Prostration in Clara Barton's Career." *Journal of Community Health* 20, no. 6 (December 1995). Speigel discusses his view that Barton was influenced by three issues: phrenology's philosophical guidelines, sex discrimination as a result of her early experiences in employment, and "psychohygienic therapy," which changed her views on illness and life.

Fred R. van Hartesveldt

SIR EDMUND BARTON

Born: January 18, 1849; Sydney, Australia
Died: January 7, 1920; Medlow Bath, Australia
Areas of Achievement: Government, law, and politics
Contribution: Barton was the leader of the movement to form a federated Australian Commonwealth and was one of the authors of the new nation's constitution. He served as Australia's first prime minister and on the first High Court of Australia.

Early Life

Edmund Barton was born in Sydney, Australia, on January 18, 1849. He was the second youngest of eleven children born to William and Mary Louisa Barton. William Barton was the younger son of a London merchant who had come to the colony of New South Wales as an agent for an agricultural company. Although a notable figure in the commercial life of Sydney—he was its first stockbroker—William Barton did not become a wealthy man. At one stage, his wife conducted a girls' school to assist in supporting the family.

Edmund, who was often known as "Ted" or "Toby," was a healthy young man, in many ways typical of the new breed of Australian-born youth. The Sydney of his time was a bustling colonial community, still somewhat wild, and very aware of itself as one of several coastal toeholds on a vast continent waiting to be developed. The young Barton was first sent to the government school at Fort Street, often known as the "Model School." He then went to Sydney Grammar School. There he met Richard O'Connor, with whom he was to form a lifelong friendship and who was to be his partner in later political life. Twice school captain of Sydney Grammar School, Barton took the classics prize and went on to Sydney University.

At the university, Barton took several prizes and scholarships, culminating in first-class honors in classics. He also fell under the influence of the noted English classical scholar and humanist Dr. Charles Badham, who brought Barton to a wide appreciation of culture. In 1870, he completed his university education with a master of arts degree. There were few opportunities in commercially minded Sydney for a classical scholar, even one of Barton's ability, and he took to the law. He started out as an articled clerk in the firm of Burton Brade-

ly, a Sydney solicitor (a lawyer in the lower courts), and later studied under G. C. Davis, a barrister. He was called to the New South Wales bar in 1872.

As a young man, Barton was large, more than six feet tall, and in his middle age he became quite stout. His features were always handsome, and he was described as dignified and well dressed. Throughout his life he was criticized for indolence, a charge difficult to support in the light of his achievements. There is no doubt that he loved the pleasures of the cultured gentleman: good company, intelligent conversation, fine wine and food. These he often found in the Athenaeum Club in Sydney, which from 1880 to 1920 was frequented by many of Australia's most prominent lawyers, politicians, and men of letters. Although once described as Australia's greatest orator, the power of his speeches came not from thundering tones or emotional rhetoric, but rather from carefully chosen phrases, which slowly and methodically established his position.

In 1876, Barton was visiting Newcastle with the Sydney cricket team, of which he was a member. There he met Jean Mason Ross, the daughter of a Scottish engineer who had emigrated to New South Wales. Their courtship lasted a year, and they were married on December 28, 1877. Together they had six children.

Life's Work

Barton was first elected to the New South Wales Legislative Assembly in 1879, as the representative of the graduates of the University of Sydney. Within a year his somewhat unusual constituency was abolished, and he ran for the Sydney seat of Wellington and was returned to office without opposition. He was described as a moderate free-trader and supporter of the government of Sir Henry Parkes. He spoke to all the issues of the day, particularly the questions of public instruction and the laws governing the opening up of the lands in the interior. The period 1879-1883 was marked by instability in the governments of New South Wales. No less than seven ministries were formed and dissolved, and, not surprisingly, little legislative progress was made. Barton's equanimity and grasp of parliamentary procedure were recognized early, and on January 3, 1883, he was elected as the youngest Speaker of the Legislative Assembly.

Barton's four-year tenure as Speaker brought him to great prominence in colonial affairs, helping to establish his reputation as a leader of deliberative assemblies. Shortly after he resigned as Speaker, he was appointed to the upper house, the Legislative Council, where he was to serve until 1894. He was attorney general in Sir George Richard Dibbs's government, which included his friend Richard O'Connor. This government saw New South Wales through some of its stormiest times, including the great strikes of 1890 and 1891 and the constant controversy over protectionism.

New South Wales was the most densely populated and most commercial of the Australian colonies. The other colonies, particularly Victoria, favored intercolonial tariffs, for the protection of their local industries. One of the arguments for federating the Australian states was the removal of such tariffs and their replacement with national customs and excise. Barton first became interested in the issue when, as acting premier of New South Wales, he attended a conference on Asian immigration, in 1888. After a conference to consider the problems of colonial defense, Sir Henry Parkes stopped at Tenterfield in northern New South Wales to deliver what became known as the "Tenterfield Oration," one of the earliest calls for a Federated Australia by a prominent figure. Barton, who by this time was in the camp opposite Parkes in New South Wales politics, wrote to him and pledged his support for the federal cause.

A few days later, on November 3, 1889, Barton made his first public speech in support of federation, at a meeting of the Australian Natives Association at Sydney's town hall. As a member of the protectionist party led by Dibbs, Barton's support for the free-trader Parkes brought much criticism. Barton worked hard with Parkes, O'Connor, and others to secure support for a National Australasian Convention, the first meeting of which was held in Sydney in March of 1891. At this gathering of the most prominent men in the colonies, Barton distinguished himself as a speaker and member of the Drafting Committee. He, Sir Samuel Griffith of Queensland, and Sir Charles Kingston of South Australia are noted for having retired to the Queensland government yacht, called the *Lucinda*, cruising the Hawkesbury River, on March 27. On March 29, they emerged with a finished constitution, which formed the basis for all further debate.

The draft bill passed by the convention had then to be accepted by the colonial parliaments. This process and the accompanying referenda were to take until 1900 and involved Barton in his greatest work. He was embarrassed, after the defeat of Parkes in 1892, by having served in the protectionist Dibbs ministry, whose leader was opposed to federation. During these difficult times, he was faced with a parliament concerned with local issues and, at best, indifferent to the cause to which Barton had devoted himself.

Eventually Barton's position in the Dibbs government became untenable, and he resigned in 1894. Having been instrumental in the founding of the populist group the Federation League, he now became a missionary for the federalist cause. During the next three years, it is recorded that he addressed three hundred meetings in New South Wales alone and, despite the difficulties of intercolonial travel, visited the other colonies and spoke at a total of a thousand meetings. Whether speaking to the profederation Australian Natives Association or the Federation League, or addressing hostile antifederalist businessmen or trade unionists, Barton stated his case simply and forcefully.

Other colonial politicians responded to the growing popularity of federation and a second Australasian National Convention met in Adelaide on March 22, 1897. Barton, despite holding no political office, was elected first to represent New South Wales, ahead of the premier, George Reid. Barton was almost unanimously elected to the Leadership of the convention and faced his greatest test within the first week, when the issue of representation and powers for the Senate, the state's house, was hotly contested. His speech on the morning of April 14, 1897, is said to have been his greatest, and the division shortly afterward approved the draft for the Senate, which has remained as the compromise between the smaller and larger states in the Australian Commonwealth.

Once again, a draft bill was passed and Barton worked tirelessly for its acceptance by all the colonies. On June 3, 1898, the bill was put to a referendum in four of the six colonies and failed by eight thousand votes to achieve the requisite majority. There are tales of Barton traveling through the bush to address a small meeting and of taking fresh horses for the drive through the night to the next town. When the bill was again put to a vote, this time in all six colonies, in 1899 (1900 in Western Australia), it passed in each colony.

Barton now faced the task of leading the colonial delegation to the imperial parliament at Westminster. Although not opposed to federating the Australian colonies, the powerful colonial secretary, Joseph Chamberlain, insisted that the Privy Council in London remain as the highest court of appeal. Barton realized that the Constitution Bill must be passed in its original form if it was to retain support in Australia. After much negotiation, he secured a compromise amendment, retaining the right of appeal to the Privy Council but making such an appeal dependent on a certificate of the High Court of Australia. The bill was passed and given royal assent on July 9, 1900.

Despite his acknowledged leadership of the movement for federation, Barton almost did not become the first prime minister of the Commonwealth he did so much to create. Lord Hopetoun, the first governor-general, was so much impressed by the premier of New South Wales, Sir William Lyne, that on December 19, 1900, he commissioned him to form the first Commonwealth government. Lyne, who had been an active opponent of federation, failed to attract men of sufficient standing to form a successful government. On December 24, therefore, he returned his commission, and the next day Barton was asked to form a ministry which was sworn in when the new parliament was opened in 1901 by the Duke of York. The elections held three months later confirmed Barton's place as prime minister.

As the leader of the new Commonwealth, Barton's principal task was the establishment of the organs of government, particularly the High Court. He attended the coronation of Edward VII in 1902 and was knighted by the new king. Upon his return, after the Imperial Conference, Barton's government addressed itself to the questions of immigration, defense, and the setting up of seven new departments. After thirty-three months in office, Barton resigned to take a seat on the first bench of the High Court of Australia.

Although himself a successful lawyer (he had been a King's Counsel since 1889) Barton recommended the Chief Justice of Queensland, Sir Samuel Griffith, rather than himself, to be the first Chief Justice of the Commonwealth of Australia. Critics have commented on the number of times he concurred with Griffith rather than publish his own judgment. It may be pointed out that on these occasions he had often written his own reasons, but concurred in order to clarify judicial precedent. His

years on the Court were marked by appreciation of his wisdom and courtesy from the bench. On the morning of January 7, 1920, he collapsed after a bath and died immediately. Barton was given a state funeral and was buried at South Head Cemetery, Sydney.

Summary

To attribute the creation of the Commonwealth of Australia solely to Sir Edmund Barton is unrealistic. There were many others who worked for federation. Barton's role was, however, pivotal. A man not normally known for passionate commitment, he threw himself into what he considered the great cause of his time. His parliamentary skills, urbanity, and capacity for advantageous compromise were essential to the success of the constitutional conventions, made up, as they were, of strong-minded, colonially interested politicians. The respect he commanded as prime minister was important for a smooth start for the fledgling Commonwealth. In his own words, the establishment of the Commonwealth of Australia saw for the first time in history "a continent for a nation and a nation for a continent."

Bibliography

Martin, A. W. *Essays in Australian Federation*. Melbourne: Melbourne University Press, 1969. Barton's role is discussed extensively in the chapters on the Australian Natives Association and the New South Wales referendum.

Norris, R. *The Emergent Commonwealth*. Melbourne: Melbourne University Press, 1975. Gives great detail of the proceedings at the constitutional conventions and of Barton's tenure as prime minster.

Quick, John, and Robert Garran. *The Annotated Constitution of the Australian Commonwealth*. Sydney: Angus and Robertson, 1901. Written by two convention participants, this is the most authoritative work on the Australian constitution. The chapter "Historical Introduction" deals, not uncritically, with Barton's role.

Reynolds, John. *Edmund Barton*. Sydney: Angus and Robertson, 1948. One of the only detailed accounts of Barton's life. Scholarly, though dated, it treats him well. The forewords in the 1979 edition are worth reading.

Paul Michael O'Shea

CHARLES BAUDELAIRE

Born: April 9, 1821; Paris, France
Died: August 31, 1867; Paris, France
Area of Achievement: Literature
Contribution: Baudelaire was instrumental in the transformation from a classical conception of poetry, which concentrated on the subject, to the Romantic focus on the self and presented in his own poetry a heightened sensitivity to the dark dimensions of the beautiful, which served as a consolation for his own awareness of the human inclination toward self-destruction.

Early Life

Charles Baudelaire was born in Paris in 1821. His father, a member of the senate during the reign of Napoleon I, died in 1827 at the age of sixty-eight, and his mother was married to a successful career officer twenty months later. In 1830, Baudelaire entered the Collège Royal, a boarding school in Lyons, where his stepfather was stationed, and remained there until his family returned to Paris in 1836. He loathed the routine and the excessively strict code of discipline at the Collège Louis-le-Grand and was expelled in 1839. To satisfy his stepfather, who hoped that he would follow a career in law, Baudelaire continued his studies at the Collège Saint-Louis and passed the examination for his baccalaureate later that year.

Between 1839 and 1841, Baudelaire lived as a sort of idle protodandy in the Latin Quarter while he tried to pursue a literary career. One of his closest friends, Ernest Praround, described him:

> . . . coming down a staircase in the Baily house, slim, a low collar, an extremely long waistcoat, detached cuffs, carrying a light cane with a small gold head, walking with a supple, almost rhythmic step . . . Baudelaire had a somewhat yellow and even complexion, which had a little color on the cheekbones, a delicate beard which he didn't clip, and which did not smother his face.

> His expression, sharpened sometimes by genuine malice, sometimes by irony, would relax when he stopped talking or listening to withdraw into himself.

Théodore de Banville remarked on his "long, dense, and silk-black hair," while others noted that he presented himself with a painterly regard for appearance, a reflection of his growing commitment to art as a means of enhancing every aspect of life. His stepfather believed that he could find "better sources of inspiration" than "the sewers of Paris," and, to separate him from his "abominable friends," convinced him to sail to India. The trip lasted eight months, giving Baudelaire a taste for the exotic.

In 1842, having returned to France, Baudelaire took possession of his inheritance, a small fortune equivalent to $100,000. He settled in the expensive Quai de Bethune area, the first of fourteen addresses he maintained in Paris during the next fourteen years, and with the resources to cultivate his public presentation of himself, he moved with a crowd that valued the shocking remark and the outrageous gesture. His experiments with hashish began at about this time, as did his liaison with Jeanne Duval, a beautiful actress of mixed racial descent—the "Black Venus" of *Les Fleurs du Mal* (1857, 1861, 1868; *Flowers of Evil*, 1909). His stepfather was so alarmed by Baudelaire's style of living that he appointed a guardian to handle his monetary affairs, an act which irritated Baudelaire for the remainder of his life and may have contributed to a halfhearted attempt at suicide in 1845.

Baudelaire's spirits were revived by his first real success as a writer, his review of the 1845 exhibition at the Louvre, which blended the emotional responsiveness of the poet with the critical acuity of the trained art critic. His "Salon de 1846" ("Salon of 1846," 1964) was similarly successful, and on its last pages there was an announcement for a book of poems to be titled "Les Lesbiennes"—a title designed for its effect. This was the first public reference to *Flowers of Evil*, which in fact would not be published for another decade. In 1847, Baudelaire published *La Fanfarlo*, an extended short story with a protagonist who served as a semisatiric reflection on his inclinations toward the sensational and began to suffer from the periodic onslaughts of syphilis, which eventually led to his death. His gradually declining health caused a radical change in his appearance, the dandy now transposed into a prematurely aged flaneur with an almost-grim visage, high forehead, and piercing eyes.

Life's Work

In 1846 or 1847, Baudelaire read Edgar Allan Poe and remarked, "The first time I opened a book of his, I saw, with horror and delight, not just subjects I had dreamt of, but *sentences* I had thought of."

He began to publish translations of Poe in 1848 and was also placing some poetry in *Revue de Paris*, a journal edited by Théophile Gautier and other friends. In 1857, the first edition of *Flowers of Evil* appeared. The title was proposed by Hippolyte Babou; Baudelaire liked its suggestion that beauty could be born of evil and that the seemingly perverse could be recast into poetic grace. Baudelaire knew that the book might be considered obscene, but a critic in *Le Figaro* may have exceeded his expectations by saying, "The book is a hospital open to all forms of mental derangements and emotional putrefaction." The government agreed and brought an indictment which compelled the confiscation of the book on July 17, three weeks after it had gone on sale. Baudelaire was found not guilty of blasphemy at the resulting hearing, but the charge of offending public morality stood, and six poems were banned. When asked if he expected to be acquitted, Baudelaire replied, "Acquitted! I was hoping for a public apology."

The prosecution of his masterwork diminished whatever remained of an optimistic outlook, and in 1860 he published *Les Paradis artificiels: Opium et haschisch* (partial translation as *Artificial Paradises: On Hashish and Wine as a Means of Expanding Individuality*, 1971). The book condemned hallucinogenic agents as providers of an illusion of the paradisiacal and described opium as a sapper of the will, which made it impossible to work. The essay, however, was misread as a celebration of decadence. Baudelaire knew that this was likely, but his imp of the perverse compelled him to continue. In 1861, he completed his definitive edition of *Flowers of Evil* (although an uncensored version did not appear in France until the twentieth century) and briefly considered applying for election to the French Academy. From 1862 to 1864, the twin plagues of poor health and poverty continued to unsettle him, but he was able to focus his mood into his final collection of poetry, *Le Spleen de Paris* (1869; *Paris Spleen, 1869*, 1905), a volume that dealt with the unreal city of T. S. Eliot's vision. He attempted to capitalize on his notoriety by scheduling a lecture tour of Belgium, and when this failed he remained in Europe until July, 1866, suffering from the effects of a stroke. His health worsened steadily, and he died in Paris in 1867.

Summary

Along with his transoceanic double, his brother in letters Edgar Allan Poe, Charles Baudelaire was the model for the nineteenth century archetype of the doomed artist, driven by an implacable destiny while struggling against his own self-destructive tendencies, an ignorant public, and a reactionary literary establishment. Underrated and misunderstood in his own time, Baudelaire—like Poe—had mythic aspects of his life that have a perverse allure that captures the imagination; but—like Poe—the perfected originality of his art, and the intensity and seriousness of his approach to his profession (which he listed as "lyric poet" on a passport application), have ultimately been recognized as the real attributes of his genius.

Baudelaire was one of the inventors of the Romantic attitude which has shaped and influenced the manner in which artists see themselves in relation to their work to this day. As Victor Brombert notes, Baudelaire's poetry defined Romantic sensibility in some of its most crucial aspects. The obsessive fascination with "erotic exoticism"; the urge to escape from the world while, in turn, being lured into its debauchery; the urge to follow the imagination to the furthest ranges of the conceivable; the sense of the artist as simultaneous victim and tyrant; the inclination toward prophetic affirmation of poetic destiny; a pervasive sense of sadness leading to strange beauty and an expression of the artist's awareness that he is damned by a kind of hyperconsciousness are some of the elements of the Romantic vision which Baudelaire fashioned.

On the other hand, as T. S. Eliot's well-known essay "Tradition and the Individual Talent" argues, Baudelaire had other attributes that are ordinarily included under the rubric of classical constraint. Baudelaire's background and early formal education enabled him to use the French language with subtlety, elegance, and precision. His command of traditional poetic technique permitted him to employ a philosophy of composition that called for the accumulation of effect through a mastery of poetic means that would overcome or transform the ugly into the beautiful, the evil into the potentially divine. Even as Baudelaire's life and work projected a counterstrain to classical aesthetics which has become a permanent part of modern artistic thinking, his ability to use the resources of language with a meticulous awareness of linguistic traditions demonstrates that placing the self at the center of experience does not mean that a refinement of craft is obsolete. The power of art, he believed, could enable mankind to transcend the limits of an inherently evil world and a fundamentally sinful human condition. This belief was based on his Catholic background, but Baudelaire's real religion was poetry, and his own work was its truest sacrament.

As Peter Quennel observes, Baudelaire was "the chief accuser of the modern world, yet he is also its most patriotic citizen." Baudelaire never felt really comfortable in his world, but he knew how to make the most of his life there. "One must always be drunk," he advised. "To escape being the martyred slaves of time, be continually drunk. On wine, poetry, or virtue, whatever you fancy." For Baudelaire himself, an intoxication with art was the only form of addiction that provided true satisfaction.

Bibliography

Baudelaire, Charles. *The Flowers of Evil*. London: Routledge, and New York: New Directions, 1955. A complete bilingual edition which includes the work of many translators. The best single source for Baudelaire's poetry in English.

———. *Selected Poems*. New York: Grove Press, 1974. A collection of translations by Geoffrey Wagner which concentrate chiefly on the erotic poetry, including some of the poems banned from the 1857 edition of *Flowers of Evil*. Includes an excellent introduction by Enid Starkie, which covers Baudelaire's life and work.

Bernstein, Susan. *Virtuosity of the Nineteenth Century: Performing Music and Language in Heine, Liszt, and Baudelaire*. Stanford, Calif.: Stanford University Press, 1998. Studies the relationship between music and language in the nineteenth century.

Blood, Susan. *Baudelaire and the Aesthetics of Bad Faith*. Stanford, Calif.: Stanford University Press, 1997. Blood focuses on Baudelaire's canonization in the critical debates of the twentieth century.

Brombert, Victor. *The Hidden Reader*. Cambridge, Mass.: Harvard University Press, 1988. Described as "a close reading of a high order," Brombert places Baudelaire within the context of Romanticism in "an uncommonly thoughtful commentary on the greatest of all ages of French literature."

Butor, Michel. *Histoire Extraordinaire: Essay on a Dream of Baudelaire*. Translated by Richard Howard. London: Cape, 1969. An approach to Baudelaire from the underside. Written in a very contemporary, somewhat fragmented style, this is a most perceptive psychoanalytic study. Speculative, daring, and sympathetic, it covers Baudelaire's life and his relationship with Poe, and captures the spirit of Baudelaire's work.

de Jonge, Alex. *Baudelaire: Prince of Clouds*. New York: Paddington Press, 1976. Probably the best biography of Baudelaire in English. De Jonge is an intelligent and understanding biographer and translator, who has utilized the best biographical work prior to his own book and included many of Baudelaire's own letters to substantiate his observations.

Poulet, Georges. *Exploding Poetry: Baudelaire/ Rimbaud*. Translated by Françoise Meltzer. Chicago: University of Chicago Press, 1984. A study of the affinities between two poets from the perspective of a critic who is firmly located in the cerebral realm of contemporary French literary criticism. Much arcane terminology combined with much critical insight. Tends toward the philosophical but offers some quite worthwhile conjectures for the advanced student.

Ruff, Marcel A. *Baudelaire*. Translated by Agnes Kertesz. London: University of London Press, and New York: New York University Press, 1966. An extremely thorough but very readable biography, based on sound scholarship, sympathetic understanding, and an appealing basic decency. A good companion to de Jonge's more dramatic presentation, with a list of all Baudelaire's publications, including dates and other important annotations.

Sartre, Jean-Paul. *Baudelaire*. Translated by Martin Turnell. London: Horizon, 1949; Norfolk, Conn.: New Directions, 1954. One brilliant, quirky, singular genius regarding another. Sometimes incisive, sometimes wrongheaded, almost always fascinating if not always reliable.

Starkie, Enid. *Baudelaire*. London: Gollancz, and New York: Putnam, 1933. Accurately described as the "foremost modern English authority on Baudelaire's life and work," Starkie writes a groundbreaking work which has provided an essential foundation for all Baudelaire studies in the United States and the United Kingdom. Still unsurpassed for breadth of coverage and intelligent commentary on the poetry and its sources in Baudelaire's life.

Leon Lewis

L. FRANK BAUM

Born: May 15, 1856; Chittenango, New York
Died: May 6, 1919; Hollywood, California
Area of Achievement: Literature
Contribution: Baum is best known for creating the marvelous land of Oz, a utopian fantasy world chronicled in a series of children's books beginning with the publication of *The Wonderful Wizard of Oz* in 1900. Through his Oz series, Baum created a unique American version of the standard fairy tale.

Early Life

Lyman Frank Baum was the seventh of nine children born to German immigrants Cynthia and Benjamin Baum. The Baum family immigrated to the United States seeking religious freedom. Frank's grandfather was a Methodist circuit rider. His father was a cooper who later became wealthy in the oil skimming business. Born with a weak heart, Frank is said to have suffered from bouts of angina throughout his entire life and was tutored at home until age twelve, when his parents decided he was healthy enough to attend the prestigious Peerskill Academy, a military boarding school in Peerskill, New York. Baum left Peerskill after two years and finished his education at home.

Baum's writing career began when his father bought him a small, foot-powered printing press for his fourteenth birthday. Within a year, in May of 1871, Frank and his younger brother Harry were publishing *The Rose Lawn Home Journal*, a neighborhood newspaper. In 1872 Baum began publishing *The Stamp Collector*, a monthly magazine for philatelists. In 1873, Baum purchased a new press and, along with Thomas G. Alford, founded *The Empire*.

When Baum turned nineteen, he put his writing and publishing career on hold to become an actor and a breeder of Hamburg chickens. After winning awards from several poultry associations, Baum started a new magazine, *The Poultry Record*. Poultry was to remain one of Baum's preoccupations. In 1886 he wrote his first book, *The Book of the Hamburgs*, a complete guide to Hamburg husbandry.

Through his late teens, Baum wandered through numerous jobs ranging from salesman to oil worker. Born with good looks, a strong stage presence, and a strong baritone voice, Baum seemed to be a natural for the stage. He attempted to fulfill his desire to act by joining up with traveling theater troupes. After being fleeced by a number of troupes, he turned to theater management when his father purchased a small chain of opera houses in New York and Pennsylvania. In 1881 Baum published the successful musical melodrama *The Maid of Arran*, which was based on the Scottish novel *A Princess of Thule* by William Black. One year later, Baum married Maude Gage, daughter of Matilda Joslyn Gage, a prominent figure in the women's suffrage movement.

In 1887, after the death of his father and the loss of most of the family fortune, Baum followed members of the Gage family to Aberdeen in the Dakota Territory. Baum opened a store called Baum's Bazaar. It was on the bazaar's sidewalks that Baum spent hours telling stories to his own children and children from the neighborhood. The bazaar failed in 1890, forcing Baum to return to journalism as he took the job of running the *Aberdeen Saturday Pioneer*, a weekly newspaper. While in this position, Baum published editorials that ranged from vehement support for the women's suffragist movement to advocating the "extermination of the [Sioux] Indians." By March, 1891, the *Aberdeen Saturday Pioneer* had gone bankrupt, and the Baum family, which now included four sons, headed to Chicago, Illinois.

Once in Chicago, Baum quickly landed a job as a reporter for the *Evening Post*. To make ends meet, Baum also became a traveling salesman for Pitkin and Brooks, a company that sold china. Baum used the traveling time as an opportunity to devise characters and story lines for the tales he told his sons. Baum's china sales were remarkably high because he took the time to teach his customers how to construct effective window displays for the products. Baum turned these lessons into a successful magazine called *The Window Dresser*, a professional organization of window trimmers, and a book, *The Art of Decorating Dry Good Windows and Interiors* (1900).

Baum continued to spend a great deal of his free time telling stories to children. When his sons had difficulty understanding the Mother Goose verses, Baum developed prose explanations of the stories. Baum's mother-in-law, Matilda Gage, urged him to submit these explanations to a publisher. Way and Williams publishers teamed Baum with artist Maxfield Parrish to produce *Mother Goose in*

Prose (1897). The modest sales of *Mother Goose* led to *Father Goose, His Book* (1899), with color illustrations (a radical idea for the day) by William Wallace Denslow. *Father Goose, His Book* was an instant success and became the best-selling children's book of 1899.

Life's Work

Denslow and Baum soon began work on their second book, tentatively titled *The Emerald City*. Because of a publishing superstition about using jewels as part of titles, the name was changed to *The Wonderful Wizard of Oz*. Denslow and Baum again insisted on color illustrations. In this case, the color of the plates referred to Oz geography: For example, blue was used for color illustrations of Munchkin Country. At first, publishers rejected the book because of the expense of reproducing color plates. Eventually George M. Hill published the book in the fall of 1900.

In the introduction to *The Wonderful Wizard of Oz*, Baum wrote, "The time has come for a series of newer 'wonder tales' in which the stereotyped genie, dwarf and fairy are eliminated, together with all the horrible and blood-curdling incidents devised by their authors to point a fearsome moral to each tale." With Oz, Baum created a utopia that, for the first time, urged American children to see the wonder of the world around them. For the first time, a fairyland was constructed from American ideals and materials. *The Wonderful Wizard of Oz* became the best-selling children's book for 1900. Its cast of characters began their journey toward becoming an integral part of the American consciousness.

Baum did not want to write sequels to *The Wonderful Wizard of Oz*, but he continued to produce a variety of children's books. In 1902, a non-Oz work, *Dot and Tot of Merryland*, also illustrated by Denslow, failed to match the commercial success of the previous two releases. In the early 1900's, Baum wrote numerous non-Oz books under his own name and under pseudonyms. As Edith Van Dyne, Baum penned *Aunt Jane's Nieces*, a highly successful series of books that targeted teenage girls and was as commercially successful as the Oz books.

Baum's love for the theater led to a collaboration with Denslow and composer Paul Tietjens to produce a musical stage play of *The Wonderful Wizard of Oz*. The production was an enormous hit and ran for 293 nights on Broadway between 1902 and 1911.

In 1904 publisher Reilly and Britton convinced Baum to continue the Oz series. Refusing to return Dorothy to Oz, Baum created the gender-changing character "Tip/Ozma" as the protagonist for *The Marvelous Land of Oz*. Tip starts as a young boy, but readers eventually discover that the witch Mombi had turned Ozma, the rightful ruler of Oz, into Tip to hide her from the wizard.

Baum attempted to capture the same theatrical success with *The Marvelous Land of Oz* that he had garnered with his musical adaptation of *The Wonderful Wizard of Oz*. *The Woggle-Bug*, Baum's adaptation of *The Marvelous Land of Oz*, opened in Chicago in 1905. While critics liked Frederic Chapman's score for the play, the show was a financial disaster and closed in one month.

Baum's readers and publisher continued to request more adventures in Oz. In 1907 Baum relented to the pressure and, in *Ozma of Oz*, Dorothy returned to Oz. *Ozma of Oz* proved to be a critical and commercial success. One of the book's characters was a mechanical being who could talk and think called Tik-Tok, one of the first artificially intelligent robots to appear in fiction. *Ozma of Oz* was quickly followed with the fourth Oz book, *Dorothy and the Wizard of Oz*, in 1908. The success of the third and fourth Oz books convinced Baum to take his Oz stories back to the stage. He financed the creation of *Fairylogue and Radio-Plays* in 1908. The show was a travelogue narrated by Baum. Hand-colored silent films displayed the action, and child actors portraying Oz characters stepped from a huge book onto the stage. The work was a critical and popular success, but it was prohibitively expensive to produce and closed after only three months, leading, in part, to Baum's bankruptcy in 1911.

Baum continued to write Oz books. In 1909, *The Road to Oz* was released to commercial success, but sales were not enough to pay the bills left by *Fairylogue and Radio-Plays*. In the sixth Oz book, *The Emerald City of Oz* (1910), Baum tried to end the series by claiming that the coming of airships led the residents of Oz to fear that they would be overrun by tourists. Glinda the Good cast a spell to render Oz invisible. The spell lasted only three years. In the introduction to the seventh Oz book, *The Patchwork Girl* (1913), Baum explained that a child wrote him to suggest that he communicate with Oz using wireless telegraphy. With that, Baum, who now called himself the Royal Historian of Oz, continued his chronicles. Baum tried the stage again with *The Tik-Tok Man* in 1913. He formed the Oz Film Company in 1914 and produced a number of Oz-related films. Distribution problems plagued the Oz Film Company, and the company was sold to Universal in 1914.

In 1915, Baum released *The Scarecrow of Oz*. Baum's health began to get increasingly worse, yet he continued to write, releasing at least one additional Oz book each year from 1915 to 1919. On May 5, 1919, Baum suffered a stroke. He died the next day. His last words were reported to have been in reference to Oz: "Now we can cross the Shifting Sands."

The final Baum-authored Oz book, *Glinda of Oz*, was released in 1920. Maud Baum, after she was promised royalties from any future Oz books, allowed publisher Reilly and Britton to find a new Royal Historian. They chose established children's writer Ruth Plumly Thompson. Thompson would write eighteen Oz books (five more than Baum) before retiring in 1939.

Summary

Oz remained a part of the American consciousness thanks to radio shows, silent film adaptations, and a steady string of new Oz books. In 1939 Metro-Goldwyn-Mayer released their film adaptation of *The Wonderful Wizard of Oz*, starring Judy Garland as Dorothy. Yearly showings of the film have made it an American classic. The film was named a national treasure under the National Film Preservation Act of 1988.

Despite the fact that Baum's work was considered "hack" work by many librarians and scholars until the 1960's, Baum established a truly American form of fairy tale. During the last nineteen years of his life, he wrote and published sixty-two books, yet it was the thirteen Oz books that created an iconic cast of characters and an archetypal story that became a permanent part of American mythology.

The marvelous land of Oz and its inhabitants are known worldwide. The concepts Baum created have become such an integral part of the growing global culture that the characters and ideas created in the books and perpetuated by the film appear in advertisements, editorial cartoons, and political speeches around the world.

Bibliography

Baum, Frank Joslyn, and Russell P. MacFall. *To Please a Child: A Biography of L. Frank Baum, Royal Historian of Oz*. Chicago: Reilly, 1961. Cowritten by L. Frank Baum's son, Frank Joslyn, this work, while continuing to perpetuate some of the more mythic aspects of the Baum legend, provides unique insights into the more private histories of Baum and Oz.

Baum, L. Frank. *The Wonderful Wizard of Oz*. New York: Oxford University Press, 1997. This edition of Baum's most significant work is prefaced with a history of the author as well as cultural and literary analysis of Baum and Oz.

Carpenter, Angelica Shirley, and Jean Shirley. *L. Frank Baum: Royal Historian of Oz*. Minneapolis, Minn.: Lerner, 1992. A detailed history of Baum's life and works and their continuing impact.

Gardner, Martin, and Russell B. Nye. *The Wizard of Oz and Who He Was*. East Lansing: Michigan State University Press, 1957. Provides a scholarly and literary approach to understanding the history and impact of Baum's works.

Harmetz, Aljean. *The Making of the Wizard of Oz*. New York: Knopf, 1977. Provides insight into the making of the film that placed Oz firmly in the American consciousness.

B. Keith Murphy

DOROTHEA BEALE

Born: March 21, 1831; Bishopsgate, London, England

Died: November 9, 1906; Cheltenham, England

Areas of Achievement: Education and social reform

Contribution: Combining business acumen, reform enthusiasm, and mystical idealism, Beale shaped an educational breakthrough with her advocacy of intellectual training for girls.

Early Life

Born on March 21, 1831, in Bishopsgate, London, England, one of eleven children, Dorothea Beale owed some of her success as a pioneer in the field of women's education to familial tradition. Her mother, Dorothea Margaret Complin, came from a family of literary women who included feminist writer Caroline Francis Cornwallis. Her father, Miles Beale, a surgeon, displayed a keen interest in contemporary social and educational issues and believed that his daughters should have every opportunity to cultivate their minds and to pursue whatever vocation they chose. In addition, Dorothea Beale possessed the traits of severe self-discipline, a driving desire to succeed, and a sense of divinely directed destiny. Religion was a potent factor in the Beale household, and Dorothea felt the pull of mysticism, expressing a strong affinity with St. Hilda of Whitby, an erudite seventh century abbess.

From early childhood, Beale wanted to be an educator, and while still small, she often created an imaginary world in which she would preside over a girls' school. Grave, quiet, and slight of stature, she did not care for outdoor activities and spent her leisure hours studying, believing that teaching carried a sacred trust. Despite this dedication, her early education was disjointed and incomplete, a result of a succession of incompetent governesses and brief stays at an English boarding school and at a Parisian finishing school. Nurturing an aptitude for mathematics, she attended lectures at London's Gresham College and Crosby Hall Institution.

In 1848, Beale and her sisters began classes at the newly established Queen's College, Harley Street. The institution's roster also included another student, Frances Mary Buss, although the two women did not meet at this time. Subsequently Beale and Buss became warm personal and professional friends, and their names and unmarried status were frozen together in time because of the rhyme, "Miss Buss and Miss Beale/ Cupid's darts do not feel;/ How different from us,/ Miss Beale and Miss Buss."

In 1849, Queen's College awarded eighteen-year-old Dorothea Beale certificates in six subjects—mathematics, geography, English, Latin, French, and German—and offered her a position on the staff. She accepted and became the college's first woman faculty member. Appointed mathematics tutor, then Latin tutor, and finally head teacher in the school connected to the college, she remained on the staff for seven years. Long chafing at the limited authority given to women faculty and the lowering of standards for student admission, Beale resigned in 1856.

In January, 1857, Beale accepted the position of head teacher in the Clergy Daughters School at Casterton. This institution, immortalized as Lowood by Charlotte Brontë's *Jane Eyre* (1847), proved to be ugly and rigid in architecture as well as philosophy and demanded that Beale teach Scripture; ancient, modern, and Church history; physical and political geography; English literature; grammar and composition; and Latin, French, German, and Italian. Beale disliked the school and requested reforms, suggesting that unless changes occurred she would resign. The school authorities accepted the challenge and dismissed her. After this humiliating blow to her pride, she returned home, did some part-time teaching, and wrote two books, *The Student's Text-book of English and General History from B.C. 100 to the Present Time* (1858) and *Self-Examination* (1858). This period also offered Beale time for introspection. She had failed in her chosen profession not once but twice. Never again, she determined, would she accept a post which did not provide her the measure of authority she desired.

Life's Work

In the summer of 1858, after the series of unhappy teaching interludes, the twenty-seven-year-old Beale, attired in a borrowed blue silk dress instead of her usual black wool, sought a position at England's oldest proprietary girls' school. Defeating fifty other candidates, she became the principal of Cheltenham Ladies' College, where she reigned for nearly fifty years. Her initial task was to ensure the school's survival, for students numbered only sixty-nine and total capital came to a mere four hundred pounds. Within four years she reversed the decline, almost doubled enrollment, and placed the institution on firm financial footing.

Equally important she began a slow but steady crusade for public acceptance of intellectual training for young ladies from upper- and upper-middle-class homes. Guided by what she thought female students needed, she curtailed the emphasis on needlework and piano exercises and encouraged greater attention to English history and the German language. Because contemporaries considered even simple arithmetic useless for women, Beale ignored her personal preference for geometry and introduced scientific reasoning in the guise of physical geography. The inclusion of an earth science in the curriculum of a girls' school did not attract attention as few males studied geography. Beale also experimented with the school day and introduced a nine to one o'clock schedule, keeping afternoons free for individual music, drawing, and needlework lessons.

At the national level, the status of girls' education gained attention when the government's School Inquiry Commission included it as part of a mid-1860's investigation. Asked to testify, Beale provided a vivid picture of the abysmal ignorance of England's upper- and middle-class young women. An examination of the entrance tests of one hundred fifteen-year-olds revealed that not one of the students understood fractions, only four could conjugate the French verb "to be," and one girl insisted that Geoffrey Chaucer lived during the reign of George III. Beale refused to make any comparisons between the mental abilities of boys and girls and insisted that she desired to educate young marriageable ladies for their subordinate role in society. She argued that well-educated women became better wives and mothers than those who were poorly educated. Her testimony, along with that of other female educators, gave impetus to much-needed improvements in education. In 1869, Beale published, with a personal introduction, an edited version of the Commission's findings, entitled *Reports on the Education of Girls, with Extracts from the Evidence* (1869).

The next three decades saw Beale's Ladies' College make great strides. Curriculum offerings expanded and the school's physical plant grew. By the turn of the century, there were more than one thousand students, fourteen boardinghouses, a secondary and kindergarten department called St. Hilda's College, a library of seven thousand volumes,

and fifteen acres of grounds. In order to provide a link between alumni and students, Beale founded *The Cheltenham Ladies' College Magazine* in 1882 and the Guild of the Cheltenham Ladies' College in 1884.

In addition to her administrative and teaching duties at Ladies' College, Beale maintained an active professional career with close ties to other female educators, especially Frances Mary Buss of the North London Collegiate School. She held life membership in the Head Mistress Association and served as president from 1895 to 1897, she testified frequently on educational issues to various royal commissions, and she introduced the concept of an annual teachers' retreat, Quiet Days. She also wrote a number of educational treatises: *Home-Life in Relation to Day Schools* (1879); *A Few Words to Those Who Are Leaving* (1881); *Work and Play in Girls Schools* (1898; with Lucy H. M. Soulsby and Jane F. Dove); *Literary Studies of Poems, New and Old* (1902); *Addresses to Teachers* (1909); and her labor of love, *History of the Cheltenham Ladies' College, 1853-1901* (1904).

With the advent of the new century more accolades came Beale's way. In 1901, the freedom of the borough of Cheltenham was conferred upon her and in 1902 she received an honorary doctorate from the University of Edinburgh. Despite deafness and infirmity, she continued to work until a few weeks before her death from cancer on November 9, 1906. After cremation, her ashes were placed in Gloucester Cathedral's Lady Chapel. A week later in memorial services at St. Paul's Cathedral, an honor accorded to very few women, the future Archbishop of Canterbury Cosmo Lang detailed her successes and piety, calling her "great."

Summary

For most of her seventy-five years, Dorothea Beale devoted her energy to the cause of girls' education. In maturity the robust spinster, dressed always in black with a white fichu, appeared aloof and unapproachable, yet she had a disarming sense of humor and often teased visitors by referring to Cheltenham Ladies' College as her husband. As a teacher, she tried to instill a hunger for knowledge rather than simply to impart information, and she proved equally adept at providing instruction in the humanities and the sciences. She also believed that a teacher's personality and mental outlook, including religious devotion, contribute greatly to the overall education process. As a school administrator, her innovations included direct supervision of the institution's boardinghouses, the inception of a rule of silence among pupils, the absence of competition and prizes, and the weekly evaluation of every student by the principal. Open-minded and willing to experiment, Beale successfully combined business acumen, reform enthusiasm, and mystical idealism.

Beale ruled Cheltenham Ladies' College as a benevolent despot and expected her own energy and sense of duty to be mirrored in her staff and students. Her associates accepted and propagated her intense belief that the education of women was a holy gift. Yet Beale was a product of her times, and her educational horizons, unlike those of Buss and other contemporary female educators, were bound by conventional notions concerning gender roles. She did not insist that girls' and boys' education programs be the same but accepted the prevailing view of alternate preparation for different roles. Very much an elitist, she had no interest in universal education for all girls.

Although England's evolving system of girls' public schools did not model itself after Cheltenham Ladies' College, the staffs of the various institutions were often graduates of the Cheltenham establishment, and thus the influence continued. Through her dedication, insight, and hard work, Dorothea Beale opened the portals of education to future generations of women.

Bibliography

Archer, Richard Lawrence. *Secondary Education in the Nineteenth Century.* Cambridge: Cambridge University Press, 1921. A dated, general overview of nineteenth century education in England and Wales. Devoid of in-depth analysis and stilted in style. Contains passing references to Beale along with anecdotal, and perhaps suspect, materials.

Digby, Anne, and Peter Searby. *Children, School, and Society in Nineteenth Century England.* London and New York: Macmillan, 1981. A pertinent analysis of the problems and perspectives of schools and schooling in nineteenth century England. Contains approximately two hundred pages of contemporary documents and includes an extract of Beale's "Girls' Schools Past and Present," which appeared in the journal *Nineteenth Century* (1888).

Gathorne-Hardy, Jonathan. *The Old School Tie: The Phenomenon of the English Public School.* New York: Viking, 1978. A comprehensive yet readable account of all facets of the English public school system. Author acknowledges limits of materials on girls' school, but work contains a sparkling examination of Beale's character and work. Follows the development of Cheltenham Ladies' College from its founding to the 1970's.

Gorham, Deborah. *The Victorian Girl and the Feminine Ideal.* London: Croom Helm, and Bloomington: Indiana University Press, 1982. A thoughtful and thought-provoking examination of the place of women and girls in Victorian England. Uses biographical evidence to examine the childhood and adolescence of a number of Victorian women. Although there are few references to Beale, the milieu in which she lived and worked is thoroughly explored.

Kamm, Josephine. *Hope Deferred: Girls' Education in English History.* London: Methuen, 1965. A general survey of the status of girls' education in England from the Anglo-Saxon period to the reign of Queen Elizabeth II. Contains a comprehensive overview of Beale's career and a critical evaluation of her impact upon nineteenth century educational reforms. Title indicates author's viewpoint.

———. *How Different from Us: A Biography of Miss Buss and Miss Beale.* London: Bodley Head, 1958. Definitive biography of two of England's most noted female education pioneers. Cleverly written and objective in analysis of motivations, successes, and failures of both Beale and Buss. For Beale study, Kamm relies heavily upon source material found in Raikes (see below).

———. *Indicative Past: A Hundred Years of the Girls' Public School Trust.* London: Allen and Unwin, 1971. Seminal study of the growth of educational opportunities for English girls, set against a background of changing social attitudes and ideas; contains photographs of Trust's founders and cooperating institutions. Comprehensive, balanced material on Beale is well researched and drawn from author's biographical study.

Raikes, Elizabeth. *Dorothea Beale of Cheltenham.* London: Constable, 1909. Official biography and intimate portrait, with extracts from correspondence, manuscript autobiography, and private diary, by a colleague. Stilted in style, not objective, long out of print and difficult to find, the work remains an indispensable source since primary materials have been destroyed. All subsequent biographies draw upon it.

Steadman, Florence Cecily. *In the Days of Miss Beale: A Study of Her Work and Influence*. London: Burrow, 1931. Greatly dependent upon Raikes (see above). Pedantic in style and far from objective, it should be used with caution and only if Raikes's work cannot be obtained.

Carol Crowe-Carraco

AUBREY BEARDSLEY

Born: August 21, 1872; Brighton, England
Died: March 16, 1898; Menton, France
Area of Achievement: Art
Contribution: Assimilating diverse artistic influences, Beardsley produced black-and-white illustrations for magazines and books that epitomize the achievement of the English Aesthetic movement of the 1890's.

Early Life

Born in Brighton, England, on August 21, 1872, Aubrey Beardsley was the son of Vincent Paul Beardsley, himself the son of a London goldsmith, and Ellen Agnus Pitt. He was educated in Brighton, the home of his maternal grandfather, Surgeon-Major William Pitt, but left Brighton Grammar School in 1888 to work in the District Surveyor's Office, Clerkenwell and Islington, London. In January, 1889, Beardsley started as a clerk at the Guardian Life and Fire Insurance office in London, where he was employed until late 1892. He left the firm when the publisher J. M. Dent gave him a commission to produce illustrations for an edition of Sir Thomas Malory's *Le Morte d'Arthur* (1485). For the rest of his short life, Beardsley worked as an illustrator and as art editor for various periodicals.

Beardsley's career was brief but meteoric, especially for an artist without much formal training. He had drawn since childhood, copying the work of the illustrator Kate Greenaway at first and then developing a style reflecting the various influences of William Morris, Edward Burne-Jones, and the Pre-Raphaelite Brotherhood. Beardsley and his older sister, Mabel, soon to begin her career as an actress, called upon Burne-Jones in 1891. The older artist encouraged Beardsley to take classes, so for a time he studied with the painter Frederick Brown at the Westminster School of Art. That, however, was the extent of his academic training as an artist. Beardsley's real education came from his observation of the work of others. He spent time with Mabel in the National Gallery and saw exhibitions in various London and Paris galleries, and he adapted for his own work motifs and techniques from the work he saw.

In filling his commission from J. M. Dent for illustrations, chapter headings, and page borders for an edition of *Le Morte d'Arthur*, Beardsley drew upon stylistic elements from the work of Burne-Jones and Morris. It took him eighteen months to produce the nearly six hundred individual designs that went into the edition Dent began publishing serially in 1893; from the first installment, however, it was clear that Beardsley had met Dent's expectation that his pseudomedieval designs would recall work printed by hand at Morris' Kelmscott Press. While working on these drawings, Beardsley was also producing sixty "grotesques" for Dent's three-volume series of *Bon-Mots* (1893, 1894) by various English writers. These pieces are not in the style derived from Burne-Jones and Morris; rather, they reflect the graphic styles of Walter Crane and James McNeill Whistler: In them Beardsley allowed himself to explore a vein of fantasy not found in the drawings for *Le Morte d'Arthur.*

One of the motifs unique to Beardsley in the *Bon-Mots* series is the figure of a fetus, perhaps a miscarried or an aborted child but treated humorously. While Beardsley's biographers disagree concerning the psychological significance of this figure, one inference drawn is that it represents the artist himself and reflects his reaction to the tuberculosis that eventually killed him. Beardsley was seven when his lungs first became a problem, and he lost time to illness while employed by the insurance company. His physical appearance signaled the presence of his disease. Tall and almost skeletally thin, as shown in a portrait done by Walter Sickert in 1894, Beardsley had piercing eyes and a shock of reddish-brown hair worn in a bang over his forehead. He kept his feelings about his illness largely to himself, frequently casting himself in the role expected by his associates. Even his letters are not very revealing of his emotions. The two people to whom Beardsley was closest throughout his life were his mother Ellen and sister Mabel.

Life's Work

Beardsley began to do drawings for periodicals as well as the books to be published by J. M. Dent, and he prepared the cover and ten pictures for the first issue of *The Studio* in April, 1893. For this issue, the editor C. Lewis Hind commissioned from Joseph Pennell, an American graphic artist, an essay entitled "A New Illustrator: Aubrey Beardsley," and the combination of article and illustrations gave Beardsley his first taste of fame. One of the drawings for *The Studio* is of the climax of Oscar Wilde's play *Salomé*, published in Paris (and in French) in 1893, the scene in which Salomé kisses the severed head of John the Baptist. Given public reaction to this startling drawing, John Lane and Elkin Mathews (of the Bodley Head publishers) asked Beardsley to do the illustrations for the English edition of the play, translated by Wilde's male lover Lord Alfred Douglas and published in 1894. The *Salomé* illustrations contain motifs from Japanese prints and the etchings of Whistler, but they are not derivative at all. In their use of black and white and in their reliance on elongated forms and sinuous lines, Beardsley's drawings prefigure the Art Nouveau style they helped to create.

Publication of the Bodley Head's *Salomé* (1894) by Lane and Mathews preceded by two months the April appearance of the first volume of *The Yellow Book*, a magazine of literature and art conceived and edited by Henry Harland and Beardsley. It, too, was printed at the Bodley Head in the form of a hardback volume. Beardsley served as art editor for the first four quarterly issues (those published in April, July, and October, 1894, and in January, 1895) designing covers, bindings, and title pages for each volume, selecting graphic materials from other artists, and providing additional illustrations himself. The hardbound quarterly magazine was a novelty, and Beardsley's contributions, given his recently published work in *Le Morte d'Arthur, Bon-Mots,* and *Salomé,* attracted both praise and negative criticism. Those who saw his work as eccentric, too frankly sexual in focus, and even morally corrupt cited Beardsley's association with Wilde as proof of the artist's decadence. When Wilde was arrested in April, 1895, after losing his libel suit against the Marquess of Queensberry, the father of Lord Alfred Douglas, he was carrying a yellow volume widely reported to be *The Yellow Book*. It was not, and indeed one of the conditions Beardsley had given Lane when he assumed the art editorship was that Wilde not be accepted as a contributor. Nevertheless, the damage to Beardsley's reputation was done, and Lane, by this time the sole publisher of *The Yellow Book,* bowed to pressure from various authors, removed Beardsley's work from volume 5 of the magazine, and terminated his service as art editor. Wilde was tried and sentenced to two years' hard labor for sexual offenses involving other men.

Beardsley's biographers agree that he was not actively homosexual, but in the public mind the association with Wilde made him suspect. For many people, he became the artist who drew the sexually suggestive illustrations for Wilde's *Salomé,* and that was evidence enough to persuade some critics that Beardsley had an unhealthy interest in sexuality. This assessment ignores the work he did between 1895 and 1898, which matured in style and moved beyond Beardsley's earlier need to shock the bourgeoisie. When his arrangements with Lane ended, Beardsley turned to the publisher Leonard Smithers for backing for a new magazine called *The Savoy.* The first issue was published in January, 1896, with Beardsley as art editor and Arthur Symons, a friend of the poet William Butler Yeats, as literary editor. A quarterly for its January, April, and July issues, the magazine became a monthly in August, 1896, and ended publication with the eighth issue in December. Part of the problem was financial. Smithers did not have the capital to back a monthly printing schedule. Another part of the difficulty was Beardsley's health. By the middle of 1896, he was experiencing symptoms of advanced tuberculosis, and he started the series of moves from one supposedly healthy location in England and France to another that ended with his death in Menton on March 16, 1898.

The quality of the work Beardsley was able to do, and the amount of it, given the state of his health, is remarkable. There is the beautifully crafted set of illustrations he produced for Smithers' edition in 1896 of Alexander Pope's mock-heroic poem *The Rape of the Lock* (1712). The use of close-laid and dotted lines, for example, to achieve the effects of the textures of fabrics is remarkable, and while the Baroque and Rococo style of the drawings is not historically appropriate for Pope's poem, Beardsley manages to make each convey a single dramatic and satiric moment in the text. The tone of the illustrations he produced for an edition (also in 1896) of Aristophanes' *Lysistrata* (411 B.C.), which was also for Smithers, is more broadly satiric than that of the drawings for *The Rape of the Lock.* Prompted by the play's fifth century B.C. origins, Beardsley turned to the style of figure drawing found on classical Greek vases, but he exaggerated the distortion of the figures to reflect the satire of Aristophanes' text. The lines are heavy and definite. In style, the *Lysistrata* illustrations have little in common with those for *The Rape of the Lock* or for an edition of Ben Jonson's *Volpone: Or, The Fox* (1606), on which Beardsley was at work at the time of his death. In these drawings, he sought to recapture the effects of seventeenth century en-

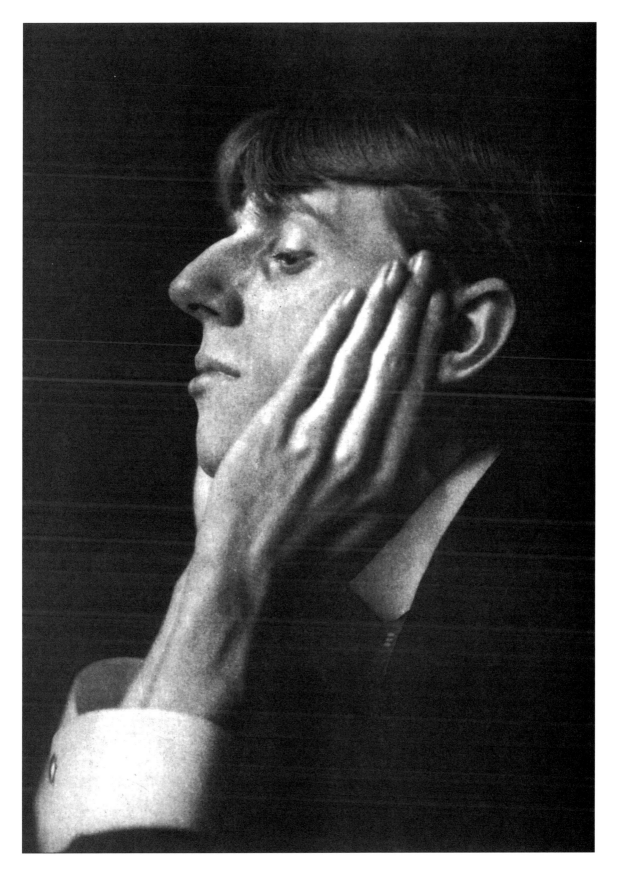

graving. They rely less on outline than Beardsley's earlier work and more on highlighting to give them a three-dimensional effect.

Summary

Since Aubrey Beardsley died so young, and had a career as a professional artist that lasted only seven years, it is hard to say how his work might have developed if he had lived longer. The variety of styles he used, the rapidity with which one gave way to another, and the fact that he sought to match his style to that of the text he was illustrating all suggest that Beardsley might have continued to mature as an artist. His actual accomplishment was so singular, however, that contemporary artists William Rothenstein and Max Beerbohm both saw him as the chief artist in the black-and-white medium of the 1890's. A generation later, Osbert Burdett suggested in *The Beardsley Period: An Essay in Perspective* (1925) that he epitomized the sense of identity and the accomplishment of his generation. While later commentators do not make so large a claim, they do see Beardsley as influencing the development of Art Nouveau in Europe. They claim, further, that his graphic work continues to appeal to each new viewing generation.

In various ways, Beardsley's work reflects both the end of nineteenth century European Romanticism and the development of modernism in the twentieth century. His unfinished *The Story of Venus and Tannhäuser: A Romantic Novel* (1967), for which he produced both text and illustrations, is a case in point. Like so much of Beardsley's work, it satirizes the conventions of romantic love. The mixture of cloying sentimentality and overt sexuality, however, in his description of the encounter of his central characters, drawn from the opera by Richard Wagner, becomes something close to a case study in sexual obsession. It invites psychoanalytic analysis, and Beardsley's biographers have mined *The Story of Venus and Tannhäuser* for evidence of the artist's real sexual nature. They are equally interested in Beardsley's conversion to Roman Catholicism in 1897, debating the genuineness of his faith in the light of his financial dependence on André Raffalovich, whose influence led to Beardsley's decision.

While Aubrey Beardsley's art can be examined in this light, stressing its affinities with so much late nineteenth century literature and art in its obsession with the irrational elements of human personality, such an emphasis obscures the grace of so much of his accomplishment. In drawings, playbills, bookplates, and bindings, there is so much vital experimentation in design that Beardsley sparked a revolution in the way fine editions are printed and illustrated. That some of this work was overtly, even morbidly, sexual in emphasis does not detract from this accomplishment. Beardsley's imagination was sparked by literary subject matter, both the texts he read and the men and women who, as authors and performers, brought the words on the page to life. His finest drawings also serve to bring words to life and to comment, at times sardonically, on them. Beardsley delighted in paradox. Appropriately, therefore, he is buried, a Roman Catholic convert, in the Protestant section of a cemetery in Menton.

Bibliography

Beardsley, Aubrey. *The Letters of Aubrey Beardsley*. Edited by Henry Maas, J. L. Duncan, and W. G. Good. London: Cassell, and Rutherford, N.J.: Fairleigh Dickinson University Press, 1970. The most complete edition of Beardsley's letters.

Benkovitz, Miriam J. *Aubrey Beardsley: An Account of His Life*. London: Hamilton, and New York: Putnam, 1981. This book benefits from later research into Beardsley's life and artistic output.

Brophy, Brigid. *Beardsley and His World*. London: Thames and Hudson, and New York: Harmony, 1976. While this book is essentially a pictorial introduction to Beardsley, it is reliable and easy to read.

Burdett, Osbert. *The Beardsley Period: An Essay in Perspective*. London: Bodley Head, and New York: Boni and Liveright, 1925. A useful introduction to the 1890's.

Easton, Malcolm. *Aubrey and the Dying Lady: A Beardsley Riddle*. London: Secker and Warburg, and Boston: Godine, 1972. Challenging accepted interpretations, Easton provides analysis of the psychosexual elements in Beardsley's life and art.

Lasner, Samuel. *A Selective Checklist of the Published Work of Aubrey Beardsley*. Boston: Thomas G. Boss, 1995. Essential book for students of Beardsley or the 1890's. Focuses on 244 of Beardley's published works spanning the twelve years between the tale "The Valient" to the Volpone illustrations done only weeks before his death.

MacFall, Haldane. *Aubrey Beardsley: The Man and His Work*. London: Bodley Head, 1928; Freeport, N.Y.: Books for Libraries Press, 1972. The first biography of the artist, Macfall's book contains plenty of anecdotal evidence collected from contemporaries.

Reade, Brian. *Aubrey Beardsley*. London: H.M.S.O., 1966; New York: Viking Press, 1967. The most complete catalog of Beardsley's work; Reade's annotations are invaluable. Includes an introduction by John Rothenstein.

Snodgrass, Chris. *Aubrey Beardsley: Dandy of the Grotesque*. New York: Oxford University Press, 1995. Snodgrass examines the bewildering quality of Beardsley's drawings based on a three-pronged approach to the issues influencing the artist.

Weintraub, Stanley. *Aubrey Beardsley: Imp of the Perverse*. University Park: Pennsylvania State University Press, 1976. This is the most complete, and easily the most readable, of the Beardsley biographies.

Robert C. Petersen

THE BECQUEREL FAMILY

Antoine-César Becquerel

Born: March 8, 1788; Châtillon-Coligny   *Died:* January 18, 1878; Paris, France

Alexandre-Edmond Becquerel

Born: March 24, 1820; Paris, France   *Died:* May 11, 1891; Paris, France

Antoine-Henri Becquerel

Born: December 15, 1852; Paris, France   *Died:* August 25, 1908; Le Croisic, France

Areas of Achievement: Physics and chemistry
Contribution: The remarkable Becquerel family spans four generations of science, with several of its members making important discoveries in physics and chemistry, particularly in the realms of electrochemistry, electromagnetic radiation, and radioactive decay physics.

Early Lives

Little is known of Antoine-César Becquerel's early life. He is known to have served in the French army as an officer in the engineering corps until 1815. In 1837, he was appointed a professor at the Museum of National History in Paris, where he began work on numerous projects in physics and chemistry.

Alexandre-Edmond Becquerel was the second son of Antoine, the family's founder. He did not attend a university but instead became assistant to his father at the Museum of Natural History at the age of eighteen. He later collaborated with his distinguished father on several important treatises. On the basis of his work, he received the doctor's degree in 1840 from the University of Paris.

Antoine-Henri Becquerel spent his early years at the Lycée-Louis-le-Grand. Already showing his brilliance, in 1872 he entered l'École Polytechnique, transferring two years later to l'École des Ponts et Chaussées, where he would later work for ten years as chief engineer. From 1875 onward, he researched various aspects of optics and engineering, obtaining his doctorate in 1888. Appointed under his father at the museum, he became professor of physics there in 1892, gaining the chair both his father and grandfather had held. In 1895, he also earned the physics professorship at l'École Polytechnique, where he had started. In 1899, he was elected to the French Academy of Sciences, continuing in the family tradition.

Life's Work

Antoine spent his life at the Museum of Natural His-

tory in Paris. His works, in the early 1800's, were devoted to research on phosphorescence, fluorescence, thermoelectricity, the magnetic properties of materials, crystal optics, the theory of primary cells, and the electrical conductivity of matter. He is best known for his work in 1829, when he invented a primary cell with weak polarization.

After receiving his doctorate in 1840, Alexandre-Edmond became professor of physics at the Agronomy Institute of Versailles. While there, he became deeply involved in investigations of electricity and magnetism. His most significant discovery was the magnetic property of liquid oxygen. He was able to show that light, through the action of inducing chemical reactions, could cause the flow of an electric current. He invented an instrument that measured light intensity by determining the electric current intensity produced. As a by-product, he determined a means of measuring the heat radiated by objects hot enough to be emitting visible light by establishing the intensity of that light. He also originated the platinum-palladium thermocouple, which is used for high-temperature measurements.

Alexandre-Edmond's interests became centered on fluorescence and phosphorescence phenomena. He was the first to discriminate between these ideas and used them for the study of ultraviolet and infrared radiation from 1857 to 1878. The problems where certain chemical materials absorbed light of one wavelength and then reemitted light of another wavelength fascinated him, particularly the circumstances in which substances were seen to glow in the dark. In 1859, he invented the phosphoroscope for doing detailed studies of light-emission intensity. As a side interest, he made the first complete solar spectrum photograph. His 1872 studies of the phosphorescence spectra or uranium compounds are considered the beginning of the path that led his son, Henri, to discover radioactivity.

Henri was involved, for most of his researches, with the phenomena of light. He had coauthored a series of memoirs with his father, Alexandre-

Edmond, on the temperature of Earth, but his real interest was in light interactions in materials. Henri was the first physicist to observe rotatory magnetic polarization in gases. Expanding the experiment, he discovered the magnetic rotation of the plane of polarized light by Earth's magnetic field. From 1886 to 1890, he performed experiments on the absorption of light by crystals, particularly investigating the anomalies of light passage along different axes within the crystal body. He then utilized that work to devise a new method of spectral analysis.

Fascinated by phosphorescence, he continued his father's research. By determined and careful investigations, he discovered the laws relating to the emission of radiation by materials being bombarded by light waves. He also showed how the emitted phosphorescence decreased with time, and why it did so. The work for which Henri is best known involved his discovery in 1896 that uranium compounds emitted some type of invisible but highly penetrating radiation, a type of light wave that would contaminate photographic plates and greatly influence the electrical conductivity in gases. He had been researching the idea that fluorescing materials might be emitting X rays (which had recently been discovered by Wilhelm Conrad Röntgen). With the aid of potassium uranyl sulfate, a fluorescent material, wrapped photographic negatives, and a fortuitous series of cloudy days, he discovered that the fogging of plates by the chemical did not depend on sunlight or phosphorescence but instead was a result of something's being emitted by the compound itself. Ignoring the sun and the fluorescence process, he studied the radiation and showed that it was quite like X rays, particularly in causing air to ionize. The radiation was emitted continuously in an unending, uninterrupted stream, heading in all directions. At his suggestion, Madame Marie Curie undertook the study of those radiations for a large number of minerals. For a brief period, the radiation was called "Becquerel rays," but in 1898, at Curie's suggestion, the phenomenon was renamed "radioactivity."

Henri's observations were announced at the French Academy of Sciences meeting on February 24, 1896, in his article entitled "Émission de radiations nouvelles par l'uranium métallique." He confirmed his studies with detailed work on the materials emitting the rays and on the properties of the rays themselves in "Sur diverses propriétés des rayons uraniques" (1896). By 1899, he had discovered that the radiation could be deflected by a mag-

Antoine-Henri Becquerel

netic field, so that at least some part of it had to be tiny charged particles: "Sur le rayonnement des corps radio-actifs" (1899). On the basis of further investigations, in 1900 he was able to announce that the part that was influenced by the field was negatively charged speeding electrons, identical to those identified in cathode-ray tubes by Sir Joseph John Thomson. After identifying the uranium atoms as the radioactive portion of the compound in 1901, he concluded that the electrons radiated had to be coming from within the uranium atoms themselves. This was, in the physics world, the first real indication that the atom was not a featureless sphere, that it had an internal structure. For all of his illustrious work, but particularly for the discovery of radioactivity, Henri Becquerel was awarded, along with Pierre and Marie Curie, the 1903 Nobel Prize in Physics.

Members of the family continued achievements into the twentieth century. Henri's son, Jean-Antoine-Édouard-Marie, also a member of the Paris

Academy of Sciences, concentrated his work on the interactions of electromagnetic energy with solid materials. Notably, he studied the propagation of circularly polarized waves in various magnetic media. In addition, he did work on the anomalous dispersion of light by sodium vapors, the Zeeman effect in pleochroic crystals, and (with Heike Kamerlingh Onnes) the phenomena occurring in a substance placed in a magnetic field at the temperatures of liquid air and liquid hydrogen.

Summary

The Becquerels are outstanding examples of a family whose members distinguished themselves in science. Of its members, Alexandre-Edmond and Antoine-Henri played the grandest roles in the history of physics. Antoine-César, a pioneer in the development of electrochemistry, set a precedent by gaining the professorship of physics at the Paris Museum of Natural History—a position which was passed on through succeeding generations. Alexandre-Edmond's discoveries on light, particularly its transmission in materials and its interactions with magnetic fields in minerals, laid the foundation for modern optical mineralogy and crystallography, vastly important in the fields of geophysical exploration and ore identification. His works, along with his father's, on phosphorescence and fluorescence, paved the way for modern chemical studies on reaction rates, mechanisms, and complex formations. Henri, the best known of the family members, founded the field of radioactivity and furthered the use of light-magnetic-field interactions, particularly important in geology, optics, and electromagnetism. Moreover, his experiments helped to refute the belief, widely held in the late nineteenth century, that physics had produced all that it ever would. The idea of radioactivity, coupled with X rays, new elements, and quantum and relativity ideas, heralded the new age of modern physics.

Bibliography

Abro, A. d'. *The Rise of the New Physics: Its Mathematical and Physical Theories*. New York: Dover, 1951. This work covers all the major ideas and experiments that have led to modern quantum physics. Besides the topic of radioactivity, it deals with the people who worked with the Becquerels to extend the realms of physics. Contains chapters for readers with mathematical background, which can be skipped. In-depth and difficult.

Badash, Lawrence. "The Discovery of Radioactivity." *Physics Today* 49, no. 2 (February 1996). Examines how Henri Becquerel's experiments with photographic plates led to the discovery of radioactivity.

Chown, Marcus. "What's Logic Got to Do with It?" *New Scientist* 151, no. 2040 (July 27, 1996). Discusses the accidental discovery of radioactivity by Henri Becquerel and details his experiments.

Curie, Marie. *Radioactive Substances*. New York: Philosophical Library, 1961. This work deals with the researches of Marie Curie and her husband, Pierre Curie, based on the discoveries of Henri Becquerel on radioactivity. Details their experiments, their hardships, and the discoveries they made. Tedious in spots, but presents a true picture of science at work.

Holmyard, Eric. *Makers of Chemistry*. Oxford: Clarendon Press, 1931. A history of chemistry from its obscure beginnings to the modern science of the 1900's. Details the explosion of chemistry programs in the nineteenth and twentieth centuries. Extensive pictures help tell the story of who did what of importance.

Ihde, Aaron. *The Development of Modern Chemistry*. New York: Harper, 1964. This book covers the history of chemistry from ancient concepts of matter to present technology. Chapters on electrochemistry and radioactivity deal with the materials on which the Becquerels worked, including discoveries and interrelationships between physics and chemistry. Extensive references and pictures of the proponents of many theories.

Magie, William. *A Source Book in Physics*. New York and London: McGraw-Hill, 1935. This is a collection of the most important abstracts from physics in the last three centuries, from Galileo to Max Planck. Henri Becquerel's discovery of radioactivity from uranium is presented, along with numerous articles on his predecessors. Allows the reader to see the high points of physics.

Ronan, Colin A. *The Atlas of Scientific Discovery*. London: Quill, and New York: Crescent Books, 1983. Surveys the march of science, tracing the development of new fields of study and the new techniques they demanded. Excellent pictures; accurate and easy to read.

Taton, René. *History of Science*. Vol. 4, *Science in the Twentieth Century*. London: Thames and Hudson, and New York: Basic Books, 1966. This work covers science from the Renaissance to the present, including astronomy, physics, chemistry, biology, and mathematics. All the major finds and their discoverers are included from Europe and North America. Numerous illustrations are provided, as are some asides on other areas of the world. Detailed reading; does not flow well.

Toulmin, Stephen, and June Goodfield. *The Architecture of Matter*. London: Hutchinson, and New York: Harper, 1962. This reference work deals with the evolution of the scientific ideas of animate and inanimate matter in terms of chemistry and physics. Various theories of matter are presented to illustrate turning points and breakthroughs. Covers significant experiments and ideas through time. Good references, lively exposition.

Arthur L. Alt

CATHARINE BEECHER

Born: September 6, 1800; East Hampton, Long Island, New York

Died: May 12, 1878; Elmira, New York

Areas of Achievement: Education and women's rights

Contribution: In pursuit of higher status and influence for women in the domestic arena, Beecher promoted women's education, urging professionalization and appreciation of women's traditional roles.

Early Life

Catharine Esther Beecher was born on September 6, 1800, in East Hampton, Long Island, New York. The eldest of nine children, Catharine was influenced most deeply by her father, Lyman Beecher, a Presbyterian minister descended from a long line of Calvinist colonial ancestors. Her mother, Roxana Ward Beecher, also from a prominent family, was reared traditionally and passed many of her domestic skills to her children. Catharine resisted these domestic tasks initially, preferring intellectual and outdoor activities.

Lyman Beecher played a major role in the Second Great Awakening, an evangelical movement that spread throughout the United States during the early 1800's. He used revivals to seek conversion and social cohesion in his communities. As a child, Catharine was enveloped by her father's dominant personality and religious zeal, and all of her life she struggled with her faith, never completely embracing it or completely deserting it.

In 1809, the Beecher family moved to Litchfield, Connecticut, a conservative town and site of a renowned law school as well as a celebrated school for young ladies. Catharine entered Miss Pierce's school in 1810, keeping a journal which reveals not only the school's emphasis on the social graces but also on the development of a social consciousness. She flourished in those years, exercising leadership and other social skills.

After Roxana died in 1816, Catharine left school to take on domestic duties, supervising her younger siblings, cooking, and sewing. Her father remarried in late 1817, but Catharine lived at home for a while longer, the ties between father and daughter remaining very strong. At the age of eighteen, she left Litchfield to teach in New London, Connecticut.

In 1822, Catharine became engaged to Alexander Fisher, a Yale professor in natural philosophy. Her father approved of Fisher wholeheartedly, but Catharine was uncertain about his potential as a husband, finding him somewhat lacking in affection. In April of 1822, Fisher died at sea when his ship crashed into cliffs on the west coast of Ireland. Catharine remained single throughout her life, devoting herself to the education of women.

Life's Work

In 1823, Catharine Beecher opened a school in Hartford, Connecticut; it flourished, allowing her to exert social, religious, and intellectual leadership. The Hartford Female Seminary offered courses in rhetoric, logic, chemistry, history, philosophy, Latin, and algebra. As principal, Beecher's status rose, and she socialized with Hartford's most respected citizens of both genders. Her self-confidence grew along with her competence as an educator. She began expanding and expounding her ideas of good pedagogy.

Beecher placed great emphasis on molding the moral character of her students. In 1829, she published an essay entitled "Suggestions Respecting Improvements in Education." In it, she stated that the most important objective of education was "the foundation of the conscience, and the direction of the moral character and habits." To accomplish such training, Beecher tried to hire an associate principal to direct the religious teaching but she was unsuccessful. Suffering a nervous collapse, she took several months rest away from Hartford while her sister, Harriet Beecher, filled in for her at the school. Upon her return to Hartford, Catharine herself gave moral instruction.

During the 1830's, Beecher became focused on women's roles and the need for more professionalism. She clearly expected women to exercise power in the home as mothers and outside it as schoolteachers. The means for enhancing this power would be a better-crafted education. Beecher viewed teaching as a noble profession, enabling women to have influence, respectability, and independence while maintaining themselves within the accepted boundaries of femininity. The time was ripe for such thinking.

The 1830's and 1840's were decades of dramatic population growth in the United States. This growing population called for more teachers. Although men had dominated the profession, fewer males were available to teach, since many of them chose to go into industrial or commercial careers. Tax-supported schools, a leisured female middle class, and the emphasis on women's nurturing qualities all aided Beecher as she began to focus on teacher training.

Resigning her position in September of 1831, Beecher left Hartford to be with her father, who had accepted the presidency of Cincinnati's Lane Theological Seminary. They arrived in Cincinnati in the spring of 1832. Within a year, Catharine Beecher founded the Western Female Institute, dedicated to both the acquisition of knowledge and moral development.

Choosing not to be fully employed in the school, Beecher busied herself with social activities and some writing. She spoke to a group of women in New York in 1835 and her lecture, "An Essay on the Education of Female Teachers," was published in New York and Cincinnati. She presented a plan for women to educate the children of immigrants and working-class families in the West.

Beecher noted that one-third of Ohio's children were without schools and that thousands of teachers would be needed to staff new schools. She envisioned her Western Female Institute as the model seminary for a national system whereby women would be trained and, in turn, would train others to educate American children and youth. She began a fund-raising campaign, appealing to Cincinnati's wealthy citizens to endow the seminary and others like it. The Cincinnati elite did not contribute, however, in part because Catharine Beecher and her father were regarded as troublemakers. Some members of Cincinnati society were angered by what they believed was a certain cultural snobbery expressed by Catharine Beecher. Further antagonism was generated by the Beechers' strong support for abolition in a city much divided over the issue even before their arrival.

The Western Female Institute closed in 1837 because of low enrollment and Beecher's alienation of her constituency. Some of Cincinnati's aristocratic families saw her as an "intellectual and social upstart." That same year, Beecher began developing a new constituency as she urged a broader image of women's role in American society. Her "Essay on Slavery and Abolition with Reference to the Duty of American Females" attempted to shape a unified consciousness in American women.

Unlike social reformers such as Sarah and Angelina Grimké, Beecher believed that female influence could best be utilized within the traditional family hierarchy and that this influence was at the core of national morals. Women would exemplify domestic virtues and by their superior moral sensibility would be a stabilizing force in the nation. The foundation of her future work was laid in this essay and Beecher turned to what she hoped would be a lucrative literary career.

Beecher wrote copiously, but only one book, published in Boston in 1841, gave her the financial base she craved. By 1843, her *Treatise on Domestic Economy* was in its fourth printing and it gave her access to a national audience. Her book intended to give women a sense of purpose, of mission: the formation of the moral and intellectual character of the young. Beecher saw that women needed specialized training for this mission. She stressed that, because of their service to others, women needed more education that would be specially tailored to prepare them for this responsibility.

Glorifying domesticity, Beecher assured women that they were engaged in "the greatest work that was ever committed to human responsibility." Women's subordinate status, Beecher stated, was not imposed by nature; rather, it was necessary to promote the general welfare. Domesticity knew no boundaries and therefore could be a focus for a new, unified national identity. Beecher intended to transcend divisions between women of different social classes by emphasizing the universality of domestic values as she built on traditional distinctions between the sex roles.

Women were uniquely able to be constructive agents of social change. The home, therefore, was not a place of isolation but rather a base from which to influence all of society. Beecher's reasoning was particularly comforting to a nation undergoing dramatic changes, as it did not require elimination of the traditional male prerogatives.

Beecher's treatise was published by Harper and Brothers after 1842, ensuring it national distribution. Reprinted almost every year from 1841 to 1856, it became Beecher's best-selling work. Previously, women had to read separate books on health, childcare, cooking, and general well-being. The treatise pulled together all the domestic arts, giving simple rules for resolving the contradictions and ambiguities of daily life.

With the continuing popularity of the treatise, Beecher's career entered a second phase in which she founded and directed the American Woman's Education Association which was to aid in the establishment of numerous women's schools. Traveling widely during the 1840's and 1850's, she helped define women's potential both within and outside the home, though primarily the former.

The last two decades of Beecher's life were given to extensive travel, fund-raising, promotion of her books, and publicizing women's education. A major focus was the founding of colleges in the West to train women for professions as teachers and homemakers. The American Women's Education Association (founded in New York in 1852) was a source of educational funding; although it helped raise respectable sums of money, the association did not meet all of Beecher's needs or expectations. For this she relied on private help, especially from well-to-do relatives and longtime friends. Beecher continued her efforts on behalf of women's education until her death in 1878.

Summary

Catharine Beecher's last years were active ones, attending teachers' conventions, keeping up a wide correspondence, and giving public lectures. Based in the East again, Beecher lived with her siblings' families on and off, becoming closest to Harriet Beecher Stowe. She continued to travel and write on behalf of women teachers, even after the disbanding of the American Woman's Educational Association in 1862.

With Harriet, Catharine coauthored *The American Woman's Home* in 1869, a sequel to the *Treatise on Domestic Economy*. It repeated much of that first book while emphasizing the family as a model of how society should function: in harmonious social interdependence. The post-Civil War years saw an urgent need for such a model since society was experiencing much change at a rapid pace. Catharine Beecher argued that an expanding democracy needed the stability provided by families supporting one another—parents and children sacrificing themselves for the good of all. In her schema, men were also tied into domesticity, although women were to be the chief ministers.

Above all, the *Treatise on Domestic Economy* assured Beecher's reputation and place in history. In it she asserted women's active role in society, according them a greater degree of dignity and respect than had been theirs. The keystone of her programs and policies was the promotion of a superior education for all females. She helped enlarge the world and role of women, offering strategies for autonomous growth. Catharine Beecher's vision of strong womanhood added much to the expansion of nineteenth century feminism.

Bibliography

Barker-Benfield, Graham J., and Catherine Clinton. *Portraits of American Women*. New York: St. Martin's Press, 1991; London: Oxford University Press, 1998. A history of gender roles and relations from the period of early settlement to the 1980's. Gives a broad scope of social history. One succinct chapter on Catharine Beecher.

Flexner, Eleanor. *Century of Struggle: The Woman's Rights Movement in the United States*. Rev. ed. Cambridge, Mass.: Belknap Press of Harvard University Press, 1975. An excellent overview of the women's rights movement. Chapter 11, "Early Stages Toward Equal Education," is very helpful. Extensive chapter notes and an index.

Kerber, Linda K., and Jane S. DeHart, eds. *Women's America*. 4th ed. New York: Oxford University Press, 1995. A collection of essays on women and their roles from 1600-1990. Selections in part 2 provide excellent background for Beecher's thinking and experiences. One essay on Beecher's educational efforts in the West. Chapter notes, bibliography, and an index.

Parker, Gail T., ed. *The Oven Birds: American Women on Womanhood, 1820-1920*. New York: Anchor, 1972. An anthology of women's writings. A lengthy excellent introduction, situating each woman in her era, relating themes and experiences. Two excerpts are included from Beecher's *Woman Suffrage* and *Woman's Profession*, published in 1871.

Preston, Jo Anne. "Domestic Ideology, School Reformers, and Female Teachers: School Teaching becomes Women's Work . . ." *New England Quarterly* 66, no. 4 (December 1993). Examines the profession of school teaching in nineteenth century New England, Beecher's contributions to women's education, and her advocacy of teaching as a vocation for women.

Sklar, Kathryn Kish. *Catharine Beecher: A Study in American Domesticity*. New Haven, Conn.: Yale University Press, 1973. An analytical study of Beecher and her times. Very thorough on her writings. Detailed chapter notes, a bibliography, and an index.

Tyler, Alice Felt. *Freedom's Ferment: Phases of American Social History to 1860*. Minneapolis:

University of Minnesota Press, 1944. Traces the crusades, reforms, and reformers in U.S. society from colonial times to the Civil War. Especially helpful are chapter 2 on "Evangelical Religion," and chapter 10 on "Education and the American Faith." Bibliography, chapter notes, and index.

Woloch, Nancy. *Women and the American Experience*. 2d ed. New York: McGraw-Hill, 1994. Examines main themes of women's history in given eras by reference to particular lives. Connects public and private spheres and women's strategies, individual and collective, as agents of change. Chapter 6, "Promoting Women's Sphere, 1800-1860," is particularly useful. Contains suggested sources for each chapter and an index.

S. Carol Berg

HENRY WARD BEECHER

Born: June 24, 1813; Litchfield, Connecticut
Died: March 8, 1887; Brooklyn, New York
Area of Achievement: The ministry
Contribution: As pastor of Plymouth Church, in Brooklyn, New York, for forty years, Beecher rapidly became one of the most articulate ministers in the United States, breaking with traditional methods of preaching in both style and content. He ushered in a new age of homiletic expertise which went far beyond his podium.

Early Life

Henry Ward Beecher was born June 24, 1813, in Litchfield, Connecticut, one of thirteen children. His father, the Reverend Lyman Beecher, was descended from Colonial settlers dating back to the 1630's. The elder Beecher was one of the leading lights in the American pulpit, as well as an outstanding theologian and educator. His mother, Roxana Foote, whose lineage could be traced back to seventeenth century England, died of consumption when Henry was three years old. Many of the elder Beecher's children later became preachers, and one of his daughters, Harriet Beecher Stowe, became a writer, philanthropist, and abolitionist.

Because there were so many children, there was little time for each one to receive personal attention. Henry's stepmother, Harriett Porter, however, engendered in them at least a sense of awe, if not affection. Yet, for the most part, Henry was a loner, growing up somewhat aloof in disposition and self-centered in outlook.

At the age of ten, he was sent away to school but had little success in his studies. Later, he went to a school conducted by his sister Catharine in Hartford—the only boy among some forty girls. He then enrolled in Mount Pleasant Classical Institute in Amherst, Massachusetts, where, for the first time, he had contact with boys his own age. There, Beecher attained some measure of popularity and encountered teachers who taught him to study and to express himself.

In 1830, Beecher entered Amherst College, where he read English classics and began writing for one of the college publications. Yet his spiritual life languished. Since his father expected all of his sons to follow him into the ministry, Beecher, following his graduation from Amherst, matriculated

at Lane Theological Seminary, Cincinnati, where his father was president. Beecher's time was about equally divided between his studies and extracurricular activities, particularly writing. Theology held no charm for him, and his father's Calvinism repelled him. One May morning, alone in the Ohio woods, however, Beecher underwent a religious experience which shaped his ideas about God and provided the structure for his spiritual life, providing a broad area for preaching which conformed to his own temperament and lifestyle.

Life's Work

After his graduation from Lane Seminary in 1837, Beecher became minister at the Presbyterian Church at Lawrenceburg, Indiana. There, he married Eunice White Bullard, with whom he would have ten children. On November 9, 1838, Beecher was ordained by the New School Presbytery of Cincinnati. The following July, he moved to the Second Presbyterian Church in Indianapolis, where he remained until October, 1848, when he went to Plymouth Church, Brooklyn, a Congregational church.

In appearance, Beecher was imposing. It has been said that he was one of the most striking figures in Brooklyn. A man of medium height and large girth, his broad shoulders accorded a resting place for his hair and a foundation for his lionesque head. His voice was responsive to every shade of emotion.

During the decade of his first two pastorates, Beecher had gradually developed his principles and his style of preaching, which was intended to bring about a moral change in his listeners. His sermons began to be published—sermons that dealt with moral renewal. Certain of these were gathered into a book, *Seven Lectures to Young Men*, published in 1844.

Like all the Beechers, he was opposed to slavery, but his thoughts on the subject were complicated and perhaps contradictory. In 1860, he announced a six-point creed on slavery: First a man may hold a slave and do no wrong; second, immediate emancipation is impossible; third, a slaveholder may still be considered a good Christian; fourth, the influence of slavery is not always evil; fifth, some slaveholders are doing more for the cause of freedom than some violent reformers; finally, antislavery bigotry is worse than the Papacy. His position on this issue probably evolved from his desire to present the Gospel to as many and as varied a group of people as possible.

Plymouth Church had only recently been organized and built when Beecher arrived. Soon afterward, the edifice burned. A new structure was then built, a large auditorium that could accommodate more than three thousand people. From his platform—he did not desire a pulpit—he gained fame as a man of eloquence and high ideals and was widely considered to be the best preacher of the age. Even after 1874, when he was accused of committing adultery with one of his parishioners, he continued to be seen almost as a national saint. This veneration was a measure of the degree to which his message had captured the spirit of popular Protestantism of the time.

Beecher's messages were frequently directed at relieving the anxieties of his affluent Brooklyn suburban audience, who sensed a conflict between their new wealth and the stern Puritan morality in which they had been reared. He preached a gospel of "virtuous wealth" as a commendable moral example to the poor, providing relief from traditional Calvinistic theological anxieties with a general liberalism that gradually unfolded as his sensibilities developed along with those of his national audience.

Beecher urged that American preaching strive for unassailable goals which would "inspire men with an idea of manhood" and kindle the "nobility of a heart opened when God has touched it." The Brooklyn preacher had discovered a formula that would, for many years, allay the apprehensions of the respectable, evangelical Americans concerning the new science and learning. He commented, "While we are taught by the scientists in truths that belong to sensual nature, while we are taught by the economists of things that belong to the social nature, we need the Christian ministry to teach us those things which are invisible." He was among the first American preachers to accept Charles Darwin's theory of evolution, by which he sought to reinterpret essential Christian convictions "in terms congenial with the assured convictions of the latest scientific theories." Beecher's acceptance of evolution had a tremendous impact on the American Protestant community. The theory of evolution, coupled with biblical criticism coming out of Germany, produced the dominant Protestant theology of the late nineteenth century, a position which was in ascendance until the rise of neoorthodoxy in the 1930's.

In 1861, Beecher became editor of the *Independent*, a Congregational journal; from 1870 to 1881, he was editor of the nondenominational *Christian Union*, which he founded. In this latter position he wrote what were considered some of the strongest editorials in the American press. His sermons were reproduced in weekly columns; others were published as pamphlets.

Beecher launched attacks against slavery, but he was not an abolitionist. He opposed the Fugitive Slave Law and the Compromise of 1850. He urged Northerners to emigrate to Kansas, using force to make it free soil. At the same time, he decried bitterness toward the South. When the Civil War erupted, he pushed for a strong prosecution by the North. In his orations, Beecher skillfully equated Christian redemptive meaning with the spirit of the Union. In 1863, he visited England, where he boldly presented the position of the North. It is questionable whether his speeches accomplished much, but they did no harm to his popularity. When hostilities ceased, Beecher went to Fort Sumter to give the oration celebrating the fourth anniversary of that fort's fall. Beecher favored Andrew Johnson's position regarding Reconstruction; he longed to see the Union reunited and the military government in the South brought to a speedy end. Indeed, he was so sympathetic to Reconstruction that he brought down upon himself the wrath of his congregation and was forced to recant.

Neither a scholar nor an original thinker, Beecher was often very impetuous in enunciating his position on various topics before thoroughly considering the logical ramifications of such pronouncements. Uninterested in theory so much as in practical application, he abhorred theological controversy, probably because his father had so delighted in it.

Summary

Beecher possessed the ability to present the most advanced thought of his generation in easily understood language and to stamp it indelibly, by means of word pictures, upon the minds of his listeners. Those who heard him were mesmerized by his delivery; those who read him were tantalized by his clarity. Many twentieth century Protestant preachers employ the same approach in their preaching, unaware that, a century earlier, Beecher was in the vanguard of those who employed such a method. Similarly, his *Yale Lectures on Preaching* (1872-1874) still rank as the apogee of instruction in the entire field of the ministry.

Henry Ward Beecher continued to be, as long as he lived, the most prominent preacher in the United States. Through a continuous stream of published sermons, in pamphlets as well as collected volumes, he preached to a whole country as completely as had any man before the coming of the radio. Beecher strongly influenced the style of delivery, worship, music, and content that has become the standard in the modern pulpit. Further, his social conscience and oratorical skill made him a spiritual and moral force in his time.

Bibliography

Abbott, Lyman. *Henry Ward Beecher.* Boston: Houghton Mifflin, 1903. A sympathetic biography of Beecher, written by one who was converted by his preaching and who succeeded him at Plymouth Church. Contains Beecher's 1882 theological statement, which resulted in his leaving the Congregational Church.

Beecher, Henry Ward. *Yale Lectures on Preaching.* New York: Ford., and London: Dickinson, 1872-1874. Probably the best material on Beecher's art of preaching and pastoral work.

Clark, Clifford E., Jr. *Henry Ward Beecher: Spokesman for Middle-Class America.* Urbana: University of Illinois Press, 1978. Interprets Beecher as one who defended the middle-class ethics and ethos of Plymouth Church, particularly during the Panic of 1873.

Garrison, Winfred Ernest. *The March of Faith: The Story of Religion in America Since 1865.* New York and London: Harper, 1933. This survey includes a sympathetic account of Beecher, placing him in the context of his times.

Hibben, Paxton. *Henry Ward Beecher: An American Portrait.* New York: Doran, 1927. This essentially negative biographical study asserts that Beecher was not a pioneer in the great work of liberalizing American theology and religion, but rather was able to present modern ideas in a form that the masses could grasp. Hibben argues that Beecher's personal development, moving from a rejection of his father's Calvinism to embrace religious liberalism, mirrored a transformation in American society.

McLoughlin, William G. *The Meaning of Henry Ward Beecher: An Essay on the Shifting Values of Mid-Victorian America, 1840-1870.* New York: Knopf, 1970. Claims that the meaning of Beecher's life lies in the story of the great shift between the Age of Jackson and the Gilded Age. Like Hibben, it points out how the development of Beecher's theological views corresponded to the major social, economic, political, and religious shifts in American society between 1840 and 1875.

Marsden, George M. *Fundamentalism and American Culture: The Shaping of Twentieth-Century Evangelicalism, 1870-1925.* New York: Oxford University Press, 1980; Oxford: Oxford University Press, 1982. Places Beecher in the forefront of those who viewed progress in science and morality as the coming of the Kingdom of God.

Rugoff, Milton. *The Beechers: An American Family in the Nineteenth Century.* New York: Harper, 1981. Places Henry Ward Beecher in the family context of the Beechers, beginning with Lyman, and extending to Henry's brothers and sisters. Four chapters give a fairly objective biography of Beecher, including a succinct presentation and appraisal of Beecher's trial for adultery. Based on extensive documents.

Ryan, Halford R. *Henry Ward Beecher: Peripatetic Preacher.* Westport, Conn.: Greenwood Press, 1990. Focuses on Beecher as a preacher and orator. Provides critique of the rhetoric in many of his important speeches. Based on extensive research of the Beecher family papers.

Wallach, Glenn. "A Depraved Taste for Publicity: The Press and Private Life in the Gilded Age." *American Studies* 39, no. 1 (Spring 1998). Discusses the expanded role of newspapers in society, which resulted from the reporting of Beecher's sex scandal in the 1870s.

Harold M. Parker, Jr.

LUDWIG VAN BEETHOVEN

Born: December 17, 1770 (baptized); Bonn
Died: March 26, 1827; Vienna, Austria
Area of Achievement: Music
Contribution: Beethoven contributed greatly to Western classical music. Clearly reflecting the transition from the classical tradition in music to the Romantic, he made numerous innovations in the piano sonata, the string quartet, and the symphony.

Early Life

Born in Bonn in 1770, Ludwig van Beethoven did not enjoy the happiest of childhoods. His father, a minor musician in the court of the archbishop-elector of Cologne, was generally more interested in drinking than in making music and was often a trial to his family. He knew well enough, however, that his son had a talent for music. Hoping that the boy might be a wunderkind, another Wolfgang Amadeus Mozart, he pushed him into a severe musical training that left little time for the pleasures of childhood. Beethoven's playmates were the piano, the organ, and the viola.

Not another Mozart, the young Beethoven nevertheless began to develop his musical abilities slowly but surely. By his thirteenth year, he was composing and was serving as an assistant to his teacher Christian Gottlob Neefe, the court organist, with the result that he began to gain notice from members of the aristocracy, people who, throughout the rest of his life, were to be patrons and friends. The family of Emanuel Joseph Breuning, for example, welcomed the boy, and he spent much time with them.

With the help of Neefe, the Breunings, and the archbishop-elector, Beethoven, at the age of seventeen, journeyed to Vienna, the preeminent musical city of Europe. It was for him a dream come true. There, he met Mozart, then at the peak of his career, and impressed him, moreover, with his own extemporaneous pieces on the piano. His stay in Vienna, however, was to be cut short. Upon hearing of his mother's illness, he hurried back to Bonn to find that she had died. He lost not only a mother but also, in his words, his "best and most faithful friend."

Shortly after his return to Bonn, Beethoven suffered another blow—the death of his younger sister. His father's drinking, moreover, had reached the point at which he could no longer support the family, and that task now fell to Beethoven. With the same indomitable spirit that marked his whole life, he accepted the challenge and cared for his two younger brothers. He also met the challenge of his musical talent and continued to increase his social and intellectual contacts among both young and old in Bonn.

When Joseph Haydn passed through Bonn in 1790, he encouraged Beethoven to come to Vienna to study with him. It took two years for Beethoven to complete the arrangements, but in 1792, he journeyed once again to Vienna, the city that was to be his permanent home. Although his relationship with Haydn lasted only two years, Beethoven began building a reputation that was to become only stronger as the years passed.

Life's Work

In Vienna, Beethoven studied counterpoint with Haydn, but the relationship between them was not a positive one. Beethoven thought that Haydn's teaching was perfunctory, and Haydn was displeased by his student's slow development—particularly in contrast to the genius of Mozart—and by his personal mannerisms and his audacious compositions. The result was that Beethoven found a new teacher of counterpoint. The young composer was, however, in the right place at the right time, because Vienna was a city rich in musical tradition and alive with the spirit of revolution.

Like so many artists and intellectuals, Beethoven was caught up in the fervor of the political changes sweeping America and Europe, and he no doubt saw a clear relationship between such changes and those occurring in the world of music. Although composers still found their main employment in the Church, the court, and the opera house, new possibilities of support were being introduced. Public concert halls, for example, offered sources of income, as did increased patronage from an aristocracy that was becoming more interested in the arts. Not content with the somewhat demeaning position to which artists and composers were relegated in relationships with their patrons, Beethoven, through his own strength of personality, worked to define a new kind of relationship that enabled him to be the careful creator and craftsman he was. Indeed, the Viennese aristocrats were eager not only to give Beethoven the support he demanded but also to gain his friendship.

While it is a general custom to approach the works of a composer, writer, or painter in terms of periods such as style and chronology, one must remember that the works themselves do not necessarily fall neatly into such divisions. As for Beethoven, most musicologists see his work falling into three distinct periods. The first period ends at 1802 or 1803 and includes the Op. 18 string quartets, the early piano sonatas, and the first two symphonies. The compositions of this period show the singular influences of Mozart and Haydn. The second period covers approximately the next ten years and may well be considered Beethoven's most productive, with 1814 being his peak year. This second period includes the third symphony (*Eroica*) through the eighth symphony, the opera *Fidelio*, the Op. 59 string quartets, some piano sonatas, and two piano concertos. The last period includes the last piano sonatas and quartets and the powerful ninth symphony (*Choral*).

While Beethoven was fulfilling his early promise as a composer, he discovered in his late twenties that his hearing was gradually getting weaker. With the devastating realization that he was going deaf, he contemplated suicide. "But how humbled I feel when someone near me hears the distant sound of a flute, and I hear *nothing*; when someone hears a shepherd singing, and I hear nothing!" he wrote to his brother. His faith in his art, however, was stronger than his desire for death, and, despite this cruel blow, he prepared to go on with his life and his music.

Stone-deaf at thirty-two, Beethoven became more depressed and eccentric in his daily living; in his music, however, he sought hope amid despair. His third symphony, the *Eroica*, was dedicated to Napoleon I and was meant to celebrate the heroic ideals of revolutionary leaders. The symphony itself was revolutionary, representing a distinct break with the classical past. Its length and complexity caused consternation among some critics, but through the years it has become one of the most widely performed of Beethoven's works.

Following the *Eroica* and the opera *Fidelio*, Beethoven concentrated primarily on the symphony, and between 1806 and 1808 he completed his fourth, fifth, and sixth symphonies. The fourth symphony is light and jovial and seems to be an effort on the composer's part to capture in music the joy that he was unable to realize in life. The powerful fifth symphony, on the other hand, is generally seen as symbolic of Beethoven's struggle against, and victory over, fate. The sixth symphony (*Pastoral*) expresses the romantic feelings and moods aroused by a walk through the Vienna woods.

Having accepted his silent world, one in which he could hear music only in his mind, Beethoven turned meditative in his later work. Two works dominate this third period—the mass in D (*Missa Solemnis*) and the *Choral*. The former, which Beethoven himself believed to be his greatest work, is a complex vocal and instrumental piece that owes much to George Frideric Handel. More a symphony than a mass, it is considered both a personal and a universal confession of faith. The *Choral*, whose outlines developed over eight years, was first performed on May 7, 1824, with Beethoven sharing in the conducting. The occasion was the composer's public farewell, and a tumultuous one it was as the audience applauded and waved handkerchiefs in appreciation not only for the *Choral* but also for a glorious career of musical creativity.

Summary

Each lover of classical music has his own favorite or favorites among the many great composers who have made the music of the Western world what it is. No one, however, can dismiss the tremendous contributions to that music made by Ludwig van Beethoven. A bridge between the classical tradition and the Romantic in music, he did much to transform a number of musical forms. His innovations included expanding the length of the symphony and of the piano concerto and increasing the number of movements in the string quartet from four to seven. His experiments in harmony and rhythm brought a new dimension to the symphony, as did his expansion of the orchestra itself. Introducing the trombone, the contrabassoon, and the piccolo, he sought to give the orchestra a broader range through which to reflect the breadth and depth of his compositions. In regard to his own instrument, the piano, he did much to bring it from its status as a relatively new invention (1710) to one in which it was seen to become the dominant and versatile instrument it is today.

Surely the greatest testament to Beethoven's power of creativity and to his overall contribution to the world of music is the universal and lasting popularity of so many of his works. His symphonies—particularly the third, fifth, sixth, and ninth—are performed regularly by virtually all orchestras. The

same is true for the fourth and fifth piano concertos and the violin concerto in D. The opera *Fidelio* is also widely performed, as are the *Missa Solemnis* and the piano sonatas and string quartets.

Beethoven had his arrogance and his uncompromising character. He also had pain and tragedy in his life. Most of all, however, he had genius—and the strength of spirit to bring that genius to the highest level of accomplishment. Some twenty thousand admirers attended his funeral. They were saying goodbye to the man. The genius, however, lives on in the music.

Bibliography

Adorno, Theodor W. *Beethoven: The Philosophy of Music.* Rolk Tiedemann, ed. Edmund Jephcott, trans. Stanford, Calif.: Stanford University Press, and Cambridge: Polity Press, 1998. Translation of Adorno's study of Beethoven, which began in 1937. The editor has organized Adorno's work in a logical manner and has included texts that the author was able to complete. There are voluminous notes and a valuable index.

Albrecht, Theodore, ed. and trans. *Letters to Beethoven and Other Correspondence: Volumes 1-3.* Lincoln: University of Nebraska Press, 1996. This collection is a significant contribution to the body of work on Beethoven. It includes 430 letters and other materials written to Beethoven between 1770 and 1827, and 70 of his own letters, all of which provide information on his compositions, performance practices, criticism of other composers, and much more.

Comini, Alessandra. *The Changing Image of Beethoven: A Study in Mythmaking.* New York: Rizzoli, 1987. Examines the image of Beethoven and the mythmaking process that began even during his lifetime. Attempts to analyze the interior image of Beethoven held by those who contributed to the mythmaking process. A solid study that places Beethoven very clearly in his time.

Jones, David W. *The Life of Beethoven.* Cambridge and New York: Cambridge University Press, 1998. This biography places Beethoven's work in context with respect to the changing nature of musical patronage in the eighteenth and early nineteenth centuries. Presents a multifaceted picture of Beethoven with attention to the effects of his deafness and difficult relationships in his life.

Landon, H. C. Robbins. *Beethoven: A Documentary Study.* London: Thames and Hudson, and New York: Macmillan, 1970. Provides a good picture of many members of the aristocracy and ruling class who were close to Beethoven. Includes excerpts from diaries and letters that provide an insight not only into Beethoven himself but also into those who knew him well.

Matthews, Denis. *Beethoven.* London: Dent, 1985; New York: Vintage, 1988. One of a series of books on great musicians. A revision of an earlier number and a reassessment of Beethoven. Covers his life in the first five chapters and his music in the next eight. Finally, attempts to place Beethoven in the world of music.

Solomon, Maynard. *Beethoven.* 2d ed. New York: Schirmer, and London: Prentice Hall, 1998. A standard biography that divides Beethoven's life into four basic phases—the Bonn years, the early Vienna years, the period of heightened creativity, and the declining years. Good introduction to Beethoven. A good essay on the music closes the book.

Thayer, Alexander Wheelock. *Thayer's Life of Beethoven.* Rev. ed. Princeton, N.J.: Princeton University Press, 1967. Revised and edited by Elliot Forbes. One of the basic studies of Beethoven that attempts to correct errors and to add new material. Good treatment of the facts of Beethoven's life, but no analytical interpretation of the music.

Valentin, Erich. *Beethoven and His World.* London: Thames and Hudson, and New York: Viking Press, 1958. Focuses more on Beethoven's life than on the music. Presents an excellent picture of Vienna in the early nineteenth century and of the politics of the period. Good introductory work.

Wilton Eckley

EMIL VON BEHRING

Born: March 15, 1854; Hansdorf, Prussia (now Germany)

Died: March 31, 1917; Marburg, Germany

Area of Achievement: Medicine

Contribution: Behring developed vaccinations against tetanus and diphtheria, thereby saving great numbers of lives. He also did important work in bacteriology that led to the modern understanding of infectious disease.

Early Life

August George Behring had four children from his first marriage. Emil Adolf von Behring was the eldest of the nine additional children he had from his second marriage to Augustine Zech, the daughter of a teacher. Teaching was a family tradition on both sides of Emil's family. His great-grandfather had been appointed as a teacher by Frederick the Great, and his grandfather and father had followed the same profession. Emil stood out as the best student among the village children in Hansdorf, prompting his father to seek a better education for him than was locally available. Emil attended the City School of Eylau (now in Poland), and a local minister tutored him for free in preparation for his admission to the *Gymnasium* in Hohenstein, which was later renamed in his honor.

Unfortunately, Behring's parents ran out of money before he completed his course of instruction at the *Gymnasium*, but the faculty members were so impressed with his abilities as a science student that they insisted he continue, although he could not pay the tuition. Financial difficulties continued to be an obstacle, and he determined that he could not pursue the career in medicine that he had hoped for. He was on the point of leaving for the University of Königsberg to begin a course as a prospective minister when one of his teachers sent for him to come and discuss another option. The teacher's nephew, a military doctor, was visiting and had become interested in the story of the poor but brilliant student. He helped Behring receive an appointment at the Friedrich Wilhelms Institute in Berlin as a medical student in 1874. The appointment meant that Behring was committing himself to ten years of service as a military doctor after he received his degree, but it was the only way he could achieve his ambition.

Behring received his medical doctorate in 1878 and was licensed in 1880. After a brief period as an intern at the Charité hospital in Berlin, he began service with the Fifty-ninth Fusilier Battalion in Wohlau in June, 1880. In 1881 he was transferred to the Second Hussars in Posen. During the same year, he wrote his first paper on sepsis and antisepsis in theory and practice, but it was not published. His next paper was on the use of iodoform, which had been adopted as a disinfectant for wounds in 1880. He had the idea that taking iodoform internally might be more effective as a disinfectant than applying it externally. However, he was forced to conclude that the poisonous effect produced by taking iodoform internally was too great to make any disinfecting it might do worthwhile. This line of inquiry seemed to be a dead end, but it was to bear significant results, as it led to his interest in antitoxins and subsequent successes.

Life's Work

In 1887 Behring was promoted to captain and sent to the Pharmacological Institute in Bonn, but his military career was nearing an end. He was already studying for the civil service medical exam because he intended to apply to the Prussian Public Health Service as soon as his ten-year military obligation was over. His duties at the Pharmacological Institute changed the direction of his life, and he turned from the life of a practicing physician with an interest in research to that of a full-time researcher. While at the institute, Behring acquired the necessary skills for a life in research and continued his work on the disinfecting effects of iodoform and acetylene. In 1888 he served at the Academy for Military Medicine in Berlin and established a working relationship with Robert Koch at the Institute of Hygiene at the Berlin University. When his term of military service was over in 1889, he went to work as Koch's assistant.

Behring's first serious research as a civilian was in partnership with Japanese scientist Shibasaburo Kitasato. They were trying to discover what made serum extracted from white rats that were immune to tetanus neutralize anthrax toxins. Their work finally led to the publication of a paper in late 1890 in which they suggested that antitoxins formed in the blood against particular diseases and that these antitoxins could be transferred to other organisms to fight the same disease. This led to some controversy with other scientists who proposed different mechanisms and explanations for the way bacteria cause disease. The basic argument centered on the question of whether all disease-producing bacteria produce the same harmful substance, which is more or less virulent depending on the quantity present, or whether each type of bacteria produce a unique toxin. Paul Ehrlich, who was a colleague of Behring at the Institute of Hygiene, showed in 1891 that Behring and Kitasato were correct by proving that organisms could form antitoxins to vegetable poisons in addition to bacteria. The vegetable poisons could not have the protein produced by bacteria that Behring's opponents believed caused disease.

Behring seems to have had a rather irritating personality. He was constantly involved in controversy about his theories and attacked others who claimed to have made some of his discoveries before he did. Many of his addresses and papers contained harsh words for his opponents. One of the pamphlets he published was titled "Streitschrift und Verteidigungsschrift gegenuber meinen medizinischen Gegnem" (attack and defense in response to my medical opponents). He made few friends and did not warm up to people very readily. His reputation for arrogance and coldness is illustrated by an encounter with a young assistant on his staff who saw him in a café and approached to ask if he could sit at his table. Behring's response was a harsh "No!" The assistant recalled the incident with bitterness for the rest of his life. When some of his claims appeared to be exaggerated, his lack of personal charm probably increased the number of his critics. By 1894, he was not getting along very well with his employer, Koch, and he accepted a position on the faculty of the University of Halle. He was not well received there and obtained a professorship at the Marburg University with the help of a friend in the Prussian Ministry of Education, despite the objections of the faculty at Marburg.

Behring is best known for his work on diphtheria. He was a significant, if not the most important, developer of the serum used to treat the disease and later produced the vaccine to prevent it. Popular accounts suggested that he first used the serum on Christmas Eve of 1891 in the surgical clinic of Berlin University, but there is some doubt that he had enough serum to use that early. He collected serum from guinea pigs and, later, from sheep, which he then used to treat the disease in other animals. His friends Andre Martin and Émile Roux successfully immunized horses against diphtheria

in 1894, and Behring extended their work to humans. Many others were involved in the development of the serum. Albrecht Kossel reported that serum therapy had reduced the mortality rate in diphtheria cases from 52 to 25 percent. In both England and the United States, further experiments were under way when Behring published two books on infectious disease; his work brought him international attention.

Behring had less success with his attempt to apply the methods used to develop a diphtheria serum to finding a serum that would be effective against tuberculosis. From 1899 to 1900, he devoted much of his time to the effort. Although he was unsuccessful, his work had important results when he showed that milk was a major vehicle for the transmission of the disease to infants. He suggested several ways to kill the tuberculosis bacillus in milk, but none proved practical. A major obstacle in his work on tuberculosis was his mistaken belief that the same bacillus produced the disease in both humans and cattle. This led him down so many dead-end lines of investigation that finally, in 1900, he announced he was giving up on the project.

Behring ultimately achieved success and lasting fame with a diphtheria preventative vaccination in 1913. His view of "serum therapy" was that low levels of a toxin could lead to the production of antitoxins in an organism, and this led him to the diphtheria vaccination. During World War I, he applied the theory to tetanus and developed a successful tetanus vaccine. Even before these accomplishments, he had received a number of honors and awards for his work. This vaccine was almost as important in saving the lives of German soldiers during World War I as the diphtheria vaccine had been in saving the lives of children.

All of his work brought him a considerable amount of recognition. The French awarded him the Legion of Honor in 1895 as well as 100,000 francs, which he shared with Roux. In 1901 he received the first Nobel Prize in Physiology or Medicine. Within his own country, he was made a German hereditary noble. He used his wealth and position to lead a comfortable life. In 1896 he married Else Spinola, the daughter of a physician. They had six sons, and their house in Marburg became a center for local society. Behring enjoyed visiting his other house on the island of Capri, but he suffered from bouts of depression that required him to be institutionalized in Switzerland from time to time. A broken thigh led to complications that weakened him, and he died of pneumonia in Marburg in 1917.

Summary

Together with Louis Pasteur, Robert Koch, and Paul Ehrlich, Emil Behring was one of the most important people in the story of human success against infectious disease in the late nineteenth and twentieth centuries. Even more important than their development of treatments for use against individual diseases were their discoveries about the mechanism of bacterial disease. Often working against the conventional wisdom of the day, they established ways of thinking about and dealing with microorganisms that continue to form the basis of the understanding of disease and its causes.

In addition to his fundamental theoretical and laboratory scientific work, Behring saved millions of lives and showed the way to save millions more with his vaccines and serum therapy. His difficult and contentious personality notwithstanding, his contributions to humanity and medical science are indisputable. The knowledge of the way antitoxins work and are formed is one of the most valuable discoveries in all of medical science, and Behring played an important role in that discovery. Toward the end of his life, he was described as "The Children's Savior." If he had accomplished nothing else, his development of the diphtheria vaccine was enough to assure him of a place among the most honored of medical researchers.

Bibliography

Behring, Emil von. *Gesammelte Abhandlungen zur ätiologischen Therapie von ansteckenden Krankenheiten.* Leipzig: Thieme, 1893. This book contains most of Behring's scientific papers to 1893.

_____. *Gesammelte Abhandlungen. Neue Folge.* Bonn: Marcus and Webers, 1915. This volume contains the scientific papers that Behring wrote between 1893 and 1915.

De Kruif, Paul. *Microbe Hunters.* New York: Harcourt Brace, and London: Cape, 1926. In a very enthusiastic and easy-to-read manner, De Kruif describes the scientific adventures of twelve men who played significant roles in the war on disease. One chapter deals specifically with diphtheria (Roux and Behring), and others give important supporting information.

Satter, Heinrich. *Emil von Behring.* Bad Godesberg, Germany: Inter Nationes, 1967. Written fifty years after Behring's death, this short (fifty-page), very readable biography provides a wealth of detail about his life and work. The author clearly had access to a considerable amount of original material.

Unger, Hellmuth. *Emil von Behring, sein Lebenswerk als unvergangliches Erbe.* Hamburg: Hoffman und Campe, 1948. This is an interesting biographical novel.

Zeiss, Heinz, and Richard Bieling. *Behring, Gestalt und Werk.* Berlin: B. Schultz, 1940. Other accounts of Behring depend on this standard biography, although the style is a bit dated and flowery.

Philip Dwight Jones

ALEXANDER GRAHAM BELL

Born: March 3, 1847; Edinburgh, Scotland
Died: August 2, 1922; Baddeck, Nova Scotia
Areas of Achievement: Invention, science, and education
Contribution: One of the major inventive geniuses of modern times, Bell created and perfected the telephone and greatly advanced the teaching of the deaf.

Early Life

The second of three boys, Alexander Graham Bell was born into a Scottish family prominent in the field of elocution. Both his grandfather Alexander Bell and his father, Alexander Melville Bell, taught the subject. The former invented a technique to check stammering, while the latter became a major innovator and author in corrective speech. His mother, Eliza Grace Symonds Bell, a portrait painter and musician, educated her son until his tenth year. After three years of formal schooling, he spent a year in London with his grandfather, who inspired the young Bell with his deep commitment to the study of the science of sound. Bell then taught music and elocution as a student teacher in Elgin, in the midst of which he spent a year at the University of Edinburgh. During 1866-1867, he taught at a college in Bath, England. Thus, he was largely family-taught and self-taught; his black, penetrating eyes and intense, though modest, manner attested his inquiring mind.

Life's Work

Bell's genius had begun to reveal itself in 1864, when, at the age of seventeen, he undertook his first experiments in the science of sound, followed the next year by initial work in the application of electricity to transmitting speech via sound waves. Upon the death of his grandfather, Bell's father replaced the former in London and published his major tract *Visible Speech: The Science of Universal Alphabetics* in 1867, the year that young Alexander became his assistant. From his father, Bell had inherited the notion of visible speech—that is, a visual-symbolic alphabet for use in producing spoken sounds—and therefore also his father's dedication to improving methods for teaching the deaf to talk. During 1868-1870, father and son established an equal partnership, even as Bell studied anatomy and physiology at University College, London, and applied his fa-

ther's techniques of visible speech at a school for the deaf at Kensington.

Such a heavy work load began to undermine Bell's health, alarming his parents, inasmuch as they had recently lost both their other sons to tuberculosis. In 1870, they emigrated to Canada, settling in the countryside near Brantford, Ontario. There, Bell's health was quickly restored, and he resumed his work in Boston, tutoring and teaching at schools for the deaf, opening his own school for other teachers, continuing his experiments in sound, and making an improvement in the system of visible speech that has remained a standard technique ever since. He also invented an audiometer. Formal recognition came early in 1873 when Boston University made him professor of vocal physiology and the mechanics of speech, a post he held for four years.

During 1873-1876, Bell brought together his disparate studies of the science of sound and its electrical telegraphic transmission. Ever since his first experiments with the latter in 1865, Bell spent whatever spare time he had in attempting to invent a device by which oral sounds could be transmitted via electrical wires: the telephone. Concurrently, he studied the human ear to discover the importance of the membrane for such a device, and he learned to transmit multiple electrical messages over a single wire. In applying the key element of acoustics to telegraphy, Bell sought and received the counsel and encouragement of the venerable experimental physicist Joseph Henry, who had worked along similar lines. Basically a scientist, Bell was fortunate to hire as his technical assistant Thomas A. Watson, an adept mechanic who shared his long nights of experiments on electrical sound transmission. Unable to fund this work himself, Bell found two patrons in the fathers of deaf children he was teaching. These men were Thomas Sanders and Gardiner G. Hubbard. Only rest, however, could restore Bell's physical strength from occasional fatigue resulting from these considerable labors, and Bell obtained it at his parents' home in Canada.

The first, though unintelligible, human sounds, Bell's to Watson, came through their wire in June, 1875, but it was not until the following March 10 that a twenty-foot-long wire carried the monumental, though unanticipated, first message: "Mr. Watson, come here; I want to see you." The two men rapidly improved their invention, and Bell astounded the scientific world with his first public demonstration of the telephone at the International Centennial Exposition at Philadelphia in June, 1876. The following spring, he demonstrated the first long-distance telephone conversation, between Boston and New York. In July, 1877, Bell, Hubbard, and Sanders created the Bell Telephone Company. Having patented all the related inventions, Bell finally began to enjoy the resulting financial rewards, although some six hundred lawsuits ensued, with rivals claiming credit—until 1888, when the Supreme Court ruled in Bell's favor as sole inventor of the telephone.

Though his fame was assured through his epic creation, Bell remained equally dedicated to the education of the deaf, especially after he married Hubbard's daughter Mabel, one of his deaf students, in July, 1877. She became an important source of encouragement and inspiration for the rest of his life and gave him two daughters. During their subsequent trip to Europe, where he introduced the telephone, Bell lectured on the teaching of the deaf at Oxford University. After settling in Washington in 1878, Bell enlarged his study of the physical nature of deafness and in 1880 founded the Volta Laboratory upon receiving the French Volta Prize of fifty thousands francs (about ten thousand dollars). He used the Volta Laboratory in the spirit of scientific philanthropy; instead of patenting new discoveries made there, he allowed their general use for the public good. Most important were the photophone to send words by light ray and an induction balance or electric probe to locate metal objects in the human body, the latter first used to find the assassin's bullet that mortally wounded President James A. Garfield.

Bell became an American citizen in 1882 and soon thereafter built a summer home and research laboratory at Baddeck, Cape Breton Island, Nova Scotia. Among many honors he received from European countries was a Ph.D., awarded by the University of Würzburg in Bavaria.

Bell's restless, inquisitive mind seemed to accelerate as he grew older, and his black hair, beard, and sideburns turned a striking, billowy white. At the Volta Laboratory, he improved upon Thomas Alva Edison's phonograph in the mid-1880's; proceeds from the sale of some of the patents were used to transform the Laboratory into the Volta Bureau for the Increase and Diffusion of Knowledge relating to the Deaf. His prize pupil the next decade became Helen Keller. In 1890, he founded

and became first president of the American Association to Promote Teaching of Speech to the Deaf (renamed the Alexander Graham Bell Association for the Deaf in 1956). An early study of marriage among the deaf led into eugenics and the problems of longevity, research which emerged as a major book in 1918. He also supported Albert A. Michelson's first measurements of the speed of light. Bell continued to improve upon the telephone, and he and Watson inaugurated the first transcontinental phone call when, in 1915, they conversed between San Francisco and New York.

The possibilities of manned powered flight held the greatest fascination for Bell from before 1891, when he supported the pioneering work of Samuel P. Langley, until the end of his life. Bell believed that tetrahedron-shaped cells could be joined for lift, and experimented with them in immense kites. During 1907-1909, he teamed up with aviation pioneer Glenn H. Curtiss and three other young men in the Aerial Experiment Association (AEA), the brainstorm of his wife, who also funded its work. Among the aircraft the five men created at Bell's Nova Scotia laboratory and Curtiss' facility at Hammondsport, New York, was Bell's own tetrahedral plane. Though it finally flew in 1912, it proved too unwieldy, but where the tetrahedron failed as an aeronautical device, it eventually proved highly successful in architecture (as, for example, in R. Buckminster Fuller's geodesic dome). In 1916, Bell advocated American preparedness in military air power, and inasmuch as the AEA operated their craft from the water and the ice, Bell during and after World War I developed a high-speed hydrofoil motorboat for riding above the water at speeds of up to seventy miles per hour.

At his Nova Scotia laboratory and in Washington, Bell carried on his manifold experiments, which also included a home air-cooling unit, an artificial respirator, the breeding of sheep, improved methods of lithography and sonar detection, and a vertical-propelled, aircraft-type engine which anticipated the helicopter and jet propulsion. His extensive notebooks were filled with other ideas which he never had time to develop; he was working on a means to distill saltwater when he died. His chief fame, however, rests on the invention of the telephone, of which thirteen million existed worldwide at the time of his death. On the day of his funeral, August 4, 1922, all telephones in the United States and Canada fell silent for one minute in tribute to him.

Summary

Alexander Graham Bell typified the remarkable generation of American inventor-scientists of the late nineteenth century whose ability to apply scientific discoveries to everyday practical technological uses played a major part in the rise of contemporary urban civilization. Driven by an insatiable curiosity and endowed with sheer experimental (though not theoretical) genius—and perfect pitch—Bell was able to focus his many interests on two or three projects simultaneously, often complementing one another. Thus, his humanitarian work on helping the deaf to learn to speak was wedded early to his efforts to invent the practical telephone. He never lost interest in either project, although aviation commanded equal attention the second half of his life. This was a fascination shared by many prominent peers in the scientific and technological worlds, among them, for example, explorer Robert Edwin Peary, yacht designer W. Starling Burgess, and naval inventor Bradley A. Fiske.

An immensely generous person, Bell was completely selfless in his devotion to the deaf, to whose improvement he committed many of the profits from the telephone. Because he championed the diffusion of scientific knowledge, he became a major catalyst in the cause of popular science. With Hubbard, in 1883, he founded and operated for eleven years *Science* magazine, subsequently taken over by the American Association for the Advancement of Science. In 1888, Bell was a founder of the National Geographic Society, ten years later succeeding Hubbard as its president, until 1904. Under his presidency, in 1899, the *National Geographic* magazine began publication. One of his daughters married the editor Gilbert H. Grosvenor; Bell's grandson, Melville Bell Grosvenor, succeeded to the editorship half a century later. In 1891, Bell funded the creation of the Astrophysical Observatory of the Smithsonian Institution and seven years after that became a regent of the Smithsonian, a post he held the rest of his life. Largely through Bell's efforts, the remains of James Smithson were returned from Genoa, Italy, to Washington, D.C., in 1904.

Like other major inventors of his day, Bell had to protect his patents from challengers, and did so by keeping copious notes and having numerous photographs taken. His love of nature was embodied in his summer home and laboratory, named Beinn Bhreagh, the commanding view of the Bras d'Or Lakes in this "New Scotland" (Nova Scotia) re-minding him of his native land. Such an idyllic environment proved especially conducive to his experiments over the last thirty-five years of his life. There he died, and there—in a mountainside—he was buried. He had shared the wonders of nature with the world at large through the pages of the *National Geographic*. The full legacy of Alexander Graham Bell is beyond measure.

Bibliography

Bruce, Robert V. *Bell: Alexander Graham Bell and the Conquest of Solitude.* Boston: Little Brown, and London: Gollancz, 1973. The standard biography, this heavily annotated work focuses on the development of the telephone but gives good general treatments of Bell's life before and after its invention.

Casey, Louis S. *Curtiss: The Hammondsport Era, 1907-1915.* New York: Crown, 1981. Though a biography of pioneer aviator and manufacturer Glenn H. Curtiss in his early years of aviation, the book discusses Bell's role in the AEA, utilizing among its sources the AEA *Bulletin.*

Costain, Thomas B. *Chord of Steel.* New York: Doubleday, 1960. A popular account of the invention of the telephone.

Grosvenor, Edwin S., and Morgan Wesson. *Alexander Graham Bell: The Life and Times of the Man Who Invented the Telephone.* New York: Abrams, 1997. Grosvenor, a great-grandson of Bell, provides a clear account of the inventor's life through family stories and touches on the almost eerie gift Bell had for foreseeing future scientific occurrences.

Mackay, James A. *Alexander Graham Bell: A Life.* New York: Wiley, 1997. Mackay's book fully handles both the humanitarian and scientific sides of this inventor who, in addition to his work in telecommunications, also made contributions in phonetics, aviation, genetics, and several other areas.

Mackenzie, Catherine Dunlap. *Alexander Graham Bell: The Man Who Contracted Space.* Boston: Houghton Mifflin, 1928. This early biography is a sound, though dated work.

Parkin, J. H. *Bell and Baldwin.* Toronto: University of Toronto Press, 1964. Centers on the association of Bell with the Canadian F. W. "Casey" Baldwin during the AEA period with Glenn Curtiss.

Waite, Helen E. *Make a Joyful Sound: The Romance of Mabel Hubbard and Alexander Graham Bell.* Philadelphia: MacRae Smith, 1961. A moving account of the relationship between Bell and his wife, who, though twelve years his junior, emerges as a key figure in her own right and proof positive of Bell's success in overcoming the handicap of deafness. She died in 1923.

Watson, Thomas A. *Exploring Life*. New York and London: Appleton, 1926. This autobiography by Bell's main assistant (1854-1934) sheds light on the great inventor's character and methods.

Clark G. Reynolds

JAMES GORDON BENNETT

Born: September 1, 1795; Newmill, Keith, Banff-
shire, Scotland

Died: June 1, 1872; New York, New York

Areas of Achievement: Journalism and publishing

Contribution: Bennett made the American newspaper an independent enterprise and established
the foundations of the profession of journalism.

Early Life

James Gordon Bennett was born on September 1,
1795, in Scotland, the first son of landholding Roman Catholic parents who abided by the teachings
of the Church. At the time of Bennett's birth, there
were perhaps fewer than forty thousand Catholics
in all of Scotland, but his parents were steadfast in
the faith and in their determination to have a son
join the priesthood. Two sisters and a close younger brother named Cosmo completed the Bennett
family. James Gordon in later life became embittered by the Church, blaming it for mistreatment of
his brother, who died in seminary.

In the strict, Presbyterian-dominated public
school system of the time, the Bible was regarded
as central to education and to the development of
good manners and industry. Latin, Greek, some
English, mathematics, history, and a large dosage
of the doctrines of John Knox constituted the curriculum, which continued until the child reached
the early teens. Bennett's formal education was reinforced at home by his parents, who read the
Scriptures regularly and discussed the colloquial
history of the family, the region, and Scotland.
Bennett attributed his later success as a newspaperman to this early training. At fifteen, he was taken
to the Catholic Seminary at Aberdeen, which was
some sixty miles from his home. He attended
Blair's College, the smallest of three schools which
would eventually combine to form the University
of Aberdeen. There, he was steeped in the study of
classical literature and philosophy and the criticism
of the great journal the *Edinburgh Review.*

Rejecting the priesthood, training for which was
to follow college, Bennett spent the years from
1814 to 1819 traveling extensively in Scotland and
living for a time in Glasgow, which had replaced
Edinburgh in size and economic importance. Glasgow was also the embarkation port for emigrants
to the West, and literature about America was in
great demand. Bennett read Benjamin Franklin's
autobiography (recently reprinted in Glasgow),

with which he was much impressed; twenty-five
years old and at a crossroads in his life, Bennett
set his sights on America.

In 1819, Bennett set sail for Halifax, Nova
Scotia, with only twenty-five dollars and a classical education to his name. Halifax was little more
than an English loyalist outpost, and Bennett—
having inherited a Scot's hatred and fear of the English—taught bookkeeping for a time in that town
and then moved on to Portland, Maine. Looking
for the America he had read about in Scotland,
Bennett found more of it in Maine, where he was
impressed with the self-confidence of the people
and saw in them something of the children of
equality and liberty. He took a teaching job in the
village of Addison and then continued on to Boston, where he discovered the reasons for which the
people of Maine had expressed dislike of that city:
Boston was a snob's town, and Bennett was quickly reminded of Edinburgh, with its arrogance and
presumption as a center of learning and culture. In
Boston, he did, however, find a position as a clerk
with a well-known bookseller and printer. He was
made a proofreader in the print shop, where he
learned something more of the rudiments of the
trade that was to make him famous. He took what
he could from Boston before moving farther south
to New York.

In New York, he was once again a new arrival
with little money and even smaller prospects. The
city excited him, however, as it seemed to be a microcosm of America: It was more representative of
the nation about which he had read. He did some
bookkeeping and proofreading, and fortune smiled
on him in the person of Aaron Willington, the owner
of the *Charleston Courier,* who eventually hired him
to translate Spanish and French news and dispatches
for his paper. In Charleston, South Carolina, Bennett
enjoyed the experience of working with well-educated and intelligent associates, men who enjoyed
all that Charleston and its culture offered. The shy
and withdrawn Bennett mixed only on the job, however, and then sparingly. He was aware early that appearances rather than ideas and wit counted the most
in social gatherings, and in the former he was always lacking. After ten months in Charleston, he returned to New York. Bennett set about determining
which were the best newspapers in New York, but
he found that none of them was interested in a still-
uncouth immigrant. He finally gained a job with the

National Advocate, a moribund publication underwritten by the New York General Republican Committee, which was connected to the Tammany Hall political machine. The original editor was Mordecai Noah, who had large political aspirations for himself and even larger aspirations for creation of a Jewish colony on Grant (modern Grand) Island in the Niagara River, some fifteen miles west of Niagara Falls. The agitation provoked by this scheme led to Noah's dismissal, but he was soon brought back. Bennett, meanwhile, became known in the newspaper world as a bright and industrious young man with a flair for writing. He was soon getting free-lance work with other papers, and in 1825 he took over ownership of a struggling weekly called the *New York Courier*, the first Sunday paper in the United States. It was a doomed project, and Bennett soon found himself working for Noah, who had changed his paper's name to the *New York Enquirer.*

When Bennett offered to write some light and humorous sketches for the *New York Enquirer*, Noah accepted, and on April 27, 1827, an article entitled "Shaking Hands" appeared. It dealt with alternatives to shaking hands as a form of greeting, with examples ranging from the Philippines to Africa. Noah was amazed at the increase in the paper's circulation following the publication of this article. Bennett followed up the piece with one called "Intemperance," which was a portent of his later tactic of using a subject to take a competing newspaper to task by making fun of it. In this case, it was *The New York Times* and its claim that New York was a very moral city that came in for a spoofing. As a result, a new excitement took hold over journalism in New York, despite the fact that disgruntled competing editors were already complaining that Bennett's work was degrading the profession.

Bennett was promoted to the position of assistant editor on the death of the incumbent in a duel. Bennett asked to go to Washington to report on Congress and the Adams Administration. In a short time, he became the first full-fledged Washington correspondent in American journalism. For four years, he was everywhere politicians traveled, submitting comment on legislation, on speeches and idiosyncrasies, on merchants, bankers, and stock hustlers. He listened for tips and rumors and followed up leads to confirm information and otherwise mastered the techniques of journalism, techniques which seemed to be lost on his contemporaries. In the meantime, his paper com-

bined with James Watson Webb's *Morning Courier* under Webb's control as publisher of the new *Morning Courier and New York Enquirer*. Bennett contributed greatly to the success of the paper, but Webb never granted him recognition by name. Like Noah, Webb took credit for Bennett's pieces or attributed them to the rewriting of others. This experience later encouraged Bennett to allow reporters their own bylines when writing for his papers. During his stay with the *Morning Courier and New York Enquirer*, the paper became perhaps the most influential in New York, though it printed only thirty-five hundred copies daily and took in an average of less than fifty dollars per issue. In 1832, the paper joined the side of the National Bank and Nicholas Biddle in its fight against the Jacksonians (though the paper had been an organ of the Democratic Party), and Bennett resigned rather than work for the opposition. The compromising of the paper's independence grated on Bennett, who now turned again to starting his own daily.

Bennett started the *Globe*, which failed to gain political support. He then went to Philadelphia, where he published the *Pennsylvanian*, which also failed. Needing capital, he appealed to Martin Van Buren and the Democrats for financing, only to be rejected. Returning to New York, he visited Horace Greeley with the hope of starting a partnership. Greeley referred Bennett to two printers with whom he had worked. The penny daily was enjoying marked success via Benjamin Day's New York *Sun*, from which spun the Philadelphia *Public Ledger* and the Baltimore *Sun*, both of which were begun by former associates of Day. With the barest of capital and a promise to print, Bennett grabbed the opportunity to create an independent newspaper.

Life's Work

Bennett started his newspaper in a basement room at 20 Wall Street with only planks and barrels for furniture. He called it the *New York Herald*. It was the traditional size for such papers—four pages with four columns to the page—and sold for one penny. The first issue appeared on May 6, 1835. Bennett worked sixteen-hour days, carefully structuring his time for each facet of publication. He spent three hours writing editorials before arriving at his office at eight o'clock and continued until he retired to his single room on Nassau Street at 10:00 P.M. Originality was his byword. Unlike his competition, he used few reprints. Fresh news flowed constantly. He sought to provide a view of the city and its people by creating scenarios, conversations, relating anecdotes with a social point of view, and delivering humorous accounts of manners, fashion, and the foibles of people generally. He brought to public view the *demi-monde;* often he relegated politicians to this realm, all to the delight of his supporters and to the rage of his growing list of enemies and competitors. Women, religion, abolitionists, bankers, speculators, and merchant hustlers all came in for a fair share of Bennett's gibes. Reformers were left to rail against his ridiculing columns. He cultivated rumor and gossip, and his coy exposition of events often of his own invention but attributable to unnamed sources foreshadowed the use of the "informed source."

Bennett took to the street to gain information firsthand and then to exploit it to its fullest. He covered an infamous murder case involving a fashionable house of prostitution to the point of questioning the guilt of the prime suspect, thereby influencing the jury's decision to acquit. He viewed the body of the dead woman, describing her in intimate detail. He also interviewed the keeper of the house in the first use of the didactic question-answer interview by a newspaper. The financial panic of 1836 and the huge fire of the same period encouraged Bennett to print the first financial news, which became an instant hit among a new business readership. He visited the fire area as well, talked to owners of properties that were burned, and interviewed displaced tenants. He printed a sketch of the burned-over area and again outdistanced his rivals.

Since the public generally bought one paper only, the one with the latest news was the one in demand, and the *New York Herald* was the paper of choice. Bennett, encouraged, hired a police reporter and expanded the size of his publication, moving the paper's offices to Broadway and Ann streets. He found more time for leisure, though he was still irascible in print. Threatened with lawsuits for libel and slander, pummeled and horsewhipped for his writings, he never wavered in his attacks. His pen was his sword. Over six feet in height and sturdy in build, he was uncoordinated in his movement and hopelessly cross-eyed; although he was always courteous and polite, he was reserved and shy.

In 1838, his wealth allowed him time to go to Europe, where he was crushed to learn of his brother Cosmo's death. Two years later, he announced his marriage to Henrietta Agnes Crean in St. Peter's Roman Catholic Church, after which they went on to Niagara Falls on their honeymoon. His declaration of his love and the description of his bride in the *New York Herald* enraged his competitors, who attacked him unmercifully. When their son, James Gordon, Jr., was born on May 10, 1841, whispers abounded as to the true father. His former associate Mordecai Noah printed the rumors, which caused Bennett to bring suit; it was successful and cost Noah a $250 fine. The Bennetts had three other children: a girl who died at eight months; a boy, Cosmo Gordon, who died within a year; and Jeanette, who married Isaac Bell and lived a long life.

Bennett enjoyed all the luxuries money could buy, but because of the harassment by his enemies, his wife spent much of her time traveling abroad or sailing. The children were taught by private tutor, and the son was especially pampered. Bennett even traded a family sailing sloop complete with cannon in return for a lieutenancy for his son in the Union navy in 1862. When the ship was put out of service in 1864, the youth promptly resigned his commission. In 1866, he was installed as managing editor of the *New York Herald* and, within two years, his father gave him ownership of the enterprise, which had grown to five hundred employees.

Bennett always put profits back into the paper by keeping a battery of reporters in Washington and as many as sixty-five in the field during the Civil War. His people were in all parts of the world. His paper was the only one Abraham Lincoln read daily because of its influence. Lincoln tried to coopt Bennett by offering him an ambassadorship to France, but to no avail. Independence had come too hard for Bennett for him to give it up so easily. Even after his retirement in 1867, he continued to visit the offices and make suggestions. His wife visited briefly in May, 1872, and he promised to join her in Europe, but he was overcome by a stroke which paralyzed his lower body and caused his death on June 1, 1872. No family members were present, though he had asked the Catholic archbishop John McCloskey to take his confession and administer the Sacraments. His son attended his funeral, accompanied by Bennett's lifelong friends and adversaries.

The *New York Herald* did not print a lengthy obituary of its own, choosing instead to reprint those of other New York papers. Every significant editor in the city had served as a pallbearer. The service was held at Bennett's home on Fifth Avenue, and he was buried in the nonsectarian Greenwood Cemetery in Brooklyn. His will left the paper to his son and his properties to his wife. His daughter's wherewithal was guaranteed in the estate. His wife did not live long after. Dying of cancer, she prevented her children from seeing her. She died in the company of strangers in Sachsen, Germany, on March 28, 1873. The *New York Tribune* was first to carry news of her death.

Summary

James Gordon Bennett was one of the three giants of journalism and publishing in America in the nineteenth century. Of the three, Horace Greeley and Charles Dana being the others, Bennett alone mastered every facet of journalism, from getting the story to editing to proofreading to printing to total management of advertising, distribution, and marketing. His public was his power. His ideas—for example, that advertisers and distributors pay cash for copy and papers—flourished and multiplied as sound practice. The byline and feature articles on styles, theater, books, business, and so on all became part of the *New York Herald* style. Bennett's organization was a model of efficiency,

with meetings of the key staff held each day to plan the day's production and assign future stories and leads.

Bennett had to survive a vicious, competitive struggle for success, and he was not above using his paper to pull down his competition. Neither money nor institutional power frightened him when he believed in a principle. His sardonic wit and sophisticated interplay of scenes and anecdotes sorely tried his enemies, and he was not reluctant to exploit the frailties inherent in the pompous and the fatuous. He instinctively knew the power he could wield with his readers, who were legion.

Bibliography

Anthony, David. "The Helen Jewett Panic: Tabloids, Men, and the Sensational Public Sphere in Antebellum New York." *American Literature* 69, no. 3 (September 1997). Examines the reporting of the murder of a prostitute in Bennet's *New York Herald* newspaper and the sensationalism associated with it.

Carlson, Oliver. *The Man Who Made the News: James Gordon Bennett*. New York: Duell, Sloan, 1942. This is the only complete biography of James Gordon Bennett. Though impressionistic and containing no illustrations, it is nevertheless very useful.

Croffut, William A. *An American Procession: A Personal Chronicle of Famous Men*. Boston: Little Brown, 1931. This is a collection of personal views and portraits of famous Americans and puts the work of Isaac Pray (see below) in perspective, showing that Pray actually tried to get Bennett to authorize his biography, which came out the same year as James Parton's biography of Horace Greeley.

Gordon, John Steele. "The Man who Invented Mass Media." *St. Louis Journalism Review* 26, no. 184 (March 1996). Discusses Bennet's founding of the *New York Herald* in the 1830s and his approach to journalism.

Herd, Harold. *Seven Editors*. London: Allen and Unwin, 1955; Westport, Conn.: Greenwood Press, 1977. This work recognizes Bennett's journalistic achievements and puts them in context.

Hudson, Frederic. *Journalism in the United States from 1690 to 1872*. New York: Harper, 1873. This is a very useful book by Bennett's confidant and the last managing editor of the *New York Herald* during his tenure, which ended in

1867. It contains great amounts of detail about newspaper development and the personalities surrounding it.

Mott, Frank Luther. *American Journalism: 1690-1960*. New York: Macmillan, 1962. Any overview of the growth of journalism in the United States owes something to this work.

Pray, Isaac Clark. *Memoirs of James Gordon Bennett and His Times*. New York: Stringer and Townsend, 1855. This work was written without the cooperation of Bennett and is taken largely from the columns of the *New York Herald* and from hearsay gathered by a man who had once worked for the Bennett paper as a theater critic. Pray was also a successful playwright and managed several theaters.

Seitz, Don C. *The James Gordon Bennetts: Father and Son, Proprietors of the "New York Herald."* Indianapolis: Bobbs-Merrill, 1928. This is a useful introduction to Bennett in a breezy, journalistic style. It shows a heavy relationship to Pray (above) but contains some useful illustrations and photographic material.

Starr, Louis M. "James Gordon Bennett: Beneficent Rascal." *American Heritage* 6 (February 1955): 32-37. A brief account of the personality of Bennett and something of his style.

Stewart, Kenneth, and John Tebbell. *Makers of Modern Journalism*. New York: Prentice-Hall, 1952. This book contains some useful material on the importance of Bennett on the shaping of modern newspapers.

Tebbel, John, and Sarah Miles Watts. *The Press and the Presidency*. New York: Oxford University Press, 1985. This has some interesting material relating to Bennett's considerable influence, most notably on Abraham Lincoln, who was always a reader of the *New York Herald* and ever-concerned with that paper's editorial thrust, which was never more than lukewarm toward the Republican Party.

Jack J. Cardoso

THOMAS HART BENTON

Born: March 14, 1782; near Hillsboro, North Carolina

Died: April 10, 1858; Washington, D.C.

Areas of Achievement: Government and politics

Contribution: A prominent United States senator from 1821 to 1851, Benton was a great champion of Western expansion, public land distribution, and "hard money." He was a leading supporter of President Andrew Jackson and his policies.

Early Life

Thomas Hart Benton, the son of Jesse and Ann Gooch Benton, was born near Hillsboro, North Carolina, in 1782. His father was a lawyer who had been a secretary to the British governor of Colonial North Carolina, a member of that state's legislature, and a speculator in Western lands. His mother was reared by her uncle, Thomas Hart, a prominent Virginia political and military leader with extensive wealth in land. Another uncle of Ann Gooch had been a British governor of Virginia.

Although his father died when he was eight, Benton's mother was able to keep the large family together. He attended local grammar schools and in 1798 enrolled at the recently established University of North Carolina, but was forced to leave in disgrace after one year when he was expelled for having stolen money from his three roommates. When he was nineteen, his mother moved the family of eight children and several slaves to a large tract of land south of Nashville, Tennessee, which had been claimed by Jesse Benton prior to his death. After three years on the family farm, young Benton left to teach school and study law. In 1806, he was admitted to the Tennessee bar and rather quickly became a successful attorney whose philosophy and practice reflected the rural frontier environment. Benton specialized in land cases, and he began to pursue the reform of the Tennessee judicial system, an issue that helped him to a seat in the state senate and wide recognition.

During the War of 1812, Benton joined Andrew Jackson in raising volunteers for the military effort against England. For this work he received an appointment as a colonel of a regiment, but Jackson apparently did not trust him enough to place him in a field command, and Benton therefore saw no action in the war. In 1813, Benton's relationship with Jackson was interrupted by a wild tavern fight in which his brother, Jesse Benton, was severely stabbed, Jackson was shot, and Thomas Benton was cut with a knife and either pushed or thrown down a flight of stairs.

In the fall of 1815, when Benton was thirty-three years of age, he moved to Missouri Territory, settling in the small riverfront village of St. Louis. He rapidly involved himself in the affairs of the city. Between 1815 and 1820, he established an active law practice, ran for local political offices, bought a house and property to which he relocated his mother and family, killed another St. Louis attorney in a duel, and for two years served as the editor of the *St. Louis Enquirer*. At this point in his life, he was clearly an imposing figure who seldom backed away from a quarrel or a fight. He was a large and physically powerful person with a wide and muscular upper body, a large head, a short, thick neck, and wide shoulders. He possessed a long nose, high forehead, and dark, wavy hair which was often worn long in the back and at the temples.

Benton used the pages of the *St. Louis Enquirer* to address current political issues. He concentrated upon the development of the West, banking and currency, and national land distribution policies, and he vigorously advanced Missouri statehood. By 1820, he was clearly established as a leader in Missouri politics. When Missouri entered the Union as a result of the great compromise of 1820, David Barton and Thomas Hart Benton were selected to represent the new state in the United States Senate.

Life's Work

After a four-week horseback ride from St. Louis, Benton reached Washington, D.C., in mid-November of 1820 to begin a celebrated thirty-year career in the Senate. En route to the capital, he stopped at the Cherry Grove Plantation, near Lexington, Virginia, and proposed marriage to Elizabeth McDowell, whom he had met in 1815. She accepted the offer and the marriage took place in March of 1821.

Once in the Senate, Benton moved quickly to an active involvement in national issues. He first pressed forward those items with a Missouri base and about which he had written in the *St. Louis Enquirer*: the opening of government mineral lands, the development of the Oregon country, federal support of the Western fur trade, and the revision of the

national land distribution policy. In the early months of 1824, he introduced two proposals which became closely identified with him and which he would continue to promote throughout his senatorial career: the elimination of the electoral college and the graduated land distribution system. In the former, his goal was to amend the Constitution so that the president and vice president could be directly elected by the people; in the latter, he pursued legislation to reduce the price of public lands by twenty-five cents per acre per year until the land was available at no cost. This practice, he argued, not only would broaden the base of the new democratic system but also would effectively serve to increase the prosperity of the entire nation.

As a result of the controversies surrounding the presidential election of 1824, Benton and Jackson established a close personal and political relationship as a result of which the Missouri senator was elevated to a leadership position in the Democratic Party. When Jacksonian Democracy carried Jackson into the presidency in 1828, Benton became the leading Jacksonian in the Senate and one of the most powerful men in American government in the

first half of the nineteenth century. He was often mentioned as a possible candidate for the presidency himself, but he quickly rejected such promotion. As a member of Jackson's famous Kitchen Cabinet, he led the fight to oppose the rechartering of the Bank of the United States and successfully expunged from the record the Senate resolution censuring Jackson for his role in the famous bank struggle. Benton also became the most ardent champion of hard-money policies—that is, those favoring a money system based upon the circulation of gold and silver only. It was his view that such a policy would best serve the common people, as paper currency was too easily manipulated by people of privilege. To this end, he prepared Jackson's famous 1836 Specie Circular, which required that public land purchases be made only with gold or silver coin. Because of his dedication to this issue, he received the nickname "Old Bullion."

Benton also played a key role in the Texas and Oregon annexation controversies. Although he was an ardent expansionist and Westerner, he opposed the acquisition of Texas in 1845 out of concern that it was unfair to Mexico and would lead to war between the two new nations. He was successful in his efforts to establish the northern boundary of Oregon at the forty-ninth latitude rather than the 54-40 line favored by many Americans in 1844 and 1845. His position on these two issues lost him much support in his home state, and he only narrowly won reelection to the Senate in 1844. In spite of his opposition to the Texas annexation and resulting war with Mexico, Benton supported the American war effort and served as chairman of the Senate Military Affairs Committee and as an important military adviser to President James K. Polk. In fact, Polk, who was suspicious of the leading field generals who were members of the Whig Party, extended to Benton the unprecedented position of joint military-diplomatic leader of the American war effort with a rank of major general. Benton considered the offer but rejected it when he could not receive from Polk the pledge of authority that he believed should cohere to such a position.

The American victory in the Mexican War and the subsequent annexation of vast new territories raised the issue of slavery to the forefront of the national political scene in 1848-1850. Although Benton was a slaveholder all of his adult life, he opposed slavery's expansion and expressed contempt for both secessionists and abolitionists. He reacted vigorously to John C. Calhoun's resolutions for noninterference with slavery in the new territories and was angered by the Missouri legislature's 1849 endorsement of the action. The Missouri resolutions assumed a strong proslavery position and directed the two Missouri senators to act accordingly. Benton spent most of 1849 in Missouri campaigning against this legislative policy and directive, and conducted a statewide speaking tour in an effort to reverse the action. This was a turbulent affair marked by name-calling, charges, countercharges, and threats of violence.

The 1850 session of the United States Senate was one of the most famous in its history. For Thomas Hart Benton, it was one of the most crucial. He was a vigorous opponent of the slavery sections of the great compromise of that year as he believed there was too much sympathy for proslavery interests and secessionist threats. His rhetoric of opposition to Henry Clay's resolutions was direct and critical and elicited a strong response from Southern senators. On one occasion, Senator Henry S. Foote of Mississippi drew and aimed a loaded revolver at the Missouri senator on the Senate floor. Benton's strong and highly publicized opposition to sections of the 1850 compromise left him with a severely weakened political base at home, and when the Missouri legislature in January of 1851 moved to the senatorial election, Benton lost to the Whig and anti-Benton candidate Henry S. Geyer, bringing his thirty-year Senate career to a close.

Frustrated by his defeat in the Missouri legislature for reelection to the Senate, the sixty-nine-year-old Benton launched a campaign for election to the House of Representatives. Few people have ever pursued a House of Representatives seat with as much to prove as Benton did in 1852—and, for the moment, victory was his. From 1853 to 1854, he returned to Congress as a member of the House of Representatives, where he took the lead in opposing the Kansas-Nebraska Act as well as all other attempts to extend slavery into the territories. Because of his determined position on this issue, he lost further support in his home state, and his effort to win reelection to the House seat failed in 1854. Undaunted by this reversal, he developed an unsuccessful campaign for the governorship of Missouri in 1856 and worked nationally for the election of James Buchanan and the Democratic Party, refusing to vote for John C. Frémont, who headed the newly formed and sectional Republican Party, even though Frémont was his son-in-law, having married his daughter, Jessie.

With his political defeats in 1854 and 1856 and the death of his wife in 1854, Benton retired to his Washington, D.C., home to work on a number of writing projects. He continued an active schedule of appearances at political rallies and public speeches. He published a large two-volume summary of his thirty-year Senate career in 1854-1856, a sixteen-volume *Abridgement of the Debates of Congress from 1789 to 1856* (1857-1861), and a historical and legal examination of the Dred Scott decision, *Examination of the Dred Scott Case* (1857). His work in this direction was hampered by the increasing pain and complications of cancer and a fire that destroyed his home and personal records. The final page of his collection of the debates in Congress was completed on April 9, 1858. He died early the next morning, April 10, 1858, at the age of seventy-six. His wife and two sons had preceded him in death; four daughters survived.

Summary

Thomas Hart Benton reflects, in many ways, the character and nature of America in the first half of the nineteenth century. An Easterner who became a Westerner, he was tough, bold, aggressive, egotistical, talkative, shrewd, self-educated, and fiercely independent. He found his career and gained a reputation on the frontier. He moved easily into law, banking, land investment, newspapers, the military, and politics. He extolled the strength and virtues of the common man in a society struggling with the issue of whether the elite or the common man should govern. As a leading proponent of Jacksonian democracy, Benton became the voice of union, a supporter of nationalism in an age of nationalism, and a builder of the nation in an era of change.

Benton believed that the great American West held the promise of the American future. He pressed for the development of the area from Missouri to Oregon and California and believed this region would provide unparalleled opportunity for the common man and unparalleled prosperity for the nation. To this end, more than anyone in American history, Benton stands as the champion of cheap land, developing policies and procedures that anticipated the great homestead movement later in the century.

To remove the benefits of privilege in a democratic society, he fought vigorously against the use of paper currency. It was his view that a financial system based upon the use of specie would protect "the people" from exploitation by people of influence. He was, thus, the leader of Jackson's war against the Bank of the United States and was the author of Jackson's famous and controversial Specie Circular.

In order to advance the cause of Union and American nationalism, Benton sought to suppress the issue of slavery on the national political scene. He believed that this could best be accomplished by preventing the extension of slavery into the territories. His great emphasis upon this may have had much to do with keeping Missouri in the Union when the great crisis of nationalism came in 1861.

Bibliography

Benton, Thomas Hart. *Thirty Years' View: Or, A History of the Working of the American Government for Thirty Years, from 1820 to 1850.* 2 vols. New York and London: Appleton, 1854-1856. An autobiographical summary of Benton's senatorial career. A valuable political commentary for insight into Benton and all American politics of the era.

Chambers, William Nisbet. *Old Bullion Benton: Senator from the New West.* Boston: Little Brown, 1956. A well-researched biography of Benton based upon extensive manuscript material. Follows Benton's life in chronological order and provides numerous quotations from his speeches and writings. This is the most widely used biography of Benton.

Kennedy, John F. *Profiles in Courage.* New York: Harper, 1956. This well-known book contains a laudatory chapter on Benton, clearly emphasizing his great individualism and political independence. Kennedy finds Benton's opposition to the extension of slavery in the face of Missouri's perspective to be a courageous act of principle.

Meigs, William M. *The Life of Thomas Hart Benton.* Philadelphia: Lippincott, 1904. An early biography of Benton that depends much upon Benton's autobiography and the memoirs of his brilliant daughter, Jessie, and her husband, John C. Frémont. Now outdated by the research of Chambers and Smith.

Oliver, Robert T. *History of Public Speaking in America.* Boston: Allyn and Bacon, 1965. A good analysis of Benton's oratorical skills with several examples of his most striking comments and most famous speeches. Incorporates the observations from several doctoral and masters' analyses of Benton's speaking methods.

Roosevelt, Theodore. *Thomas Hart Benton.* Boston: Houghton Mifflin, 1900. A biography in the American Statesmen series. Badly dated but reflects the interpretation of Benton held at the end of the nineteenth century. Roosevelt viewed Benton not as a great intellect but as a person unique for his hard work, determination, and speaking abilities.

Smith, Elbert B. *Francis Preston Blair.* New York: Macmillan, 1933. An excellent biography of Francis Blair, who was a Jacksonian editor and close personal friend of Benton. Provides good insight into Benton from the perspective of his closest friend and friendly biographer.

———. *Magnificent Missourian: The Life of Thomas Hart Benton.* Philadelphia: Lippincott, 1958. A very well-written biography of Benton based exclusively upon manuscript and original sources. Provides excellent coverage of Benton's senatorial career and his role on the national political scene. Especially good coverage of Benton's role in the bank war.

Frank Nickell

CARL BENZ

Born: November 25, 1844; Karlsruhe, Germany
Died: April 4, 1929; Ladenburg, Germany
Areas of Achievement: Invention and technology
Contribution: As one of the earliest inventors of a
    practical automobile, Benz made contributions
    of great importance to the modern way of life.
    He developed several features essential to auto-
    mobile design and function.

Early Life

When Carl Benz was only two years old, his father, a railroad engineer, died of pneumonia. His
widowed mother was left with only a small income for the support of her family. Benz was able
to contribute to the family finances by profiting
from his interest in technical matters. While still a
child, he repaired clocks and watches for the
neighbors and had his own darkroom. He used the
darkroom to develop pictures he took for the visitors to the area of the Black Forest around
Karlsruhe, where he lived.

At secondary school he remained interested in
technical subjects and became an assistant to the
physics instructor. After attending Karlsruhe Polytechnic, he gained valuable experience by working
for a manufacturer of engines. Even at this time, he
had in mind the construction of a horseless carriage
and spent evenings drawing plans for it. In 1871,
he went to Mannheim to work for a firm that made
wagons, pumps, and cranes. Soon thereafter, in
1872, he opened his own shop to produce engines.
He was apparently confident of success, as he was
married to Berta Ringer, whom he had met on a job
in Pforzheim, just before starting out on his own.

Benz's confidence was not misplaced. His engines sold well, and he found investors who provided funds for him to establish the Mannheim Gas
Engine Manufacturing Company. The new company employed forty people and was profitable. The
venture lasted only a short time, however, as his
shareholders were more interested in profits than in
experimentation. They refused to allow him to use
any of the profits for work on a horseless carriage,
and he withdrew from the company, losing his investment after only three months of operations.

A man with Benz's experience, ability, and money-making record could not fail to attract sympathetic investors for long, and on October 1, 1883,
Benz and Company was founded. Two Mannheim

businessmen, Max Caspar Rose and Friedrich Wilhelm Esslinger, were the investors in the new company for the production of "internal combustion
engines after the plans of Carl Benz." While his
new partners were not enthusiastic about his experiments with horseless carriages, they were willing
to tolerate them as long as he attended to the primary business of the company—the production of
stationary gas engines. They were not to regret
their indulgence.

Life's Work

It is difficult to maintain that Benz was the first to
invent the automobile because of the difficulty in
establishing the definition of an automobile. Self-
propelled, steam-driven vehicles had been in operation since the early nineteenth century. An Austrian, Siegfried Marcus, designed handcarts propelled
by internal-combustion engines in the 1860's, and
French experimenters constructed similar vehicles.
In these circumstances it cannot be maintained that
Benz was the first to produce an automobile, but
his vehicles were the earliest practical, marketable
horseless carriages.

The plans that Benz had been developing for
nearly two decades quickly bore fruit once he had
the necessary resources at his disposal. Probably
the most important feature of the motorized tricycle he produced in 1885 was the engine. This is not
surprising given his years of experience in designing and building engines. It was a four-cycle, or
Otto-cycle, engine that burned gasoline. The Otto-
cycle engine had existed since the late 1870's, and
its principle of operation had been established in
the 1860's. It is called a four-cycle engine because
the explosion of gasoline in the combustion chamber occurs only on every fourth stroke of the piston. During the first stroke, as the piston moves
downward, atmospheric pressure forces the gaseous fuel into the piston cylinder through a valve.
When the piston reaches the end of its downward
movement, a spring closes the valve to prevent the
gas from escaping as the piston makes its return, or
second stroke. At the top of the second stroke the
gas is compressed in the combustion chamber
above the piston to about one-third of its normal
volume. The gas is then ignited, and its expansion
as it burns forces the piston down in its third, or
power, stroke. When the power rises on its fourth

stroke, it forces the burned gas out through an exhaust valve that is opened mechanically.

In order to convert the liquid gasoline to a gaseous state, a carburetor is necessary. The carburetor used by Benz was very simple. He routed the hot exhaust gases through a pipe that passed through a chamber containing liquid gasoline, thus warming it. Air admitted through holes in an outer container flowed over the evaporating gasoline, and the mixture of air and gasoline proceeded on to the combustion chamber. The mixture could be left rich in gasoline or leaned by the addition of air as required by means of a pipe with holes between the carburetor and combustion chamber. A sliding cover allowed more, or less, air to enter the holes.

The innovation that made the Benz engine particularly important was the ignition system. For the most part, previous engines had used a heated tube for ignition. This system left much to be desired. Benz used an electrical ignition system consisting of a four-volt battery connected to an induction coil wrapped around an iron core. In the circuit was a flat spring that was magnetically attracted to the iron core when current flowed through the coil. The attraction of the spring, known as a trembler, broke the circuit, allowing the spring to return to its original position and to reestablish the circuit. The result was a rapid vibration of the trembler and the production of a series of charges to the spark plug, which sparked and ignited the gas in the combustion chamber. The spark had to be produced at the correct time. To achieve the correct timing, a rotor made of insulating material with a metal chip in its circumference was introduced into the circuit. The rotor was connected mechanically to the piston-driven shaft in such a way that the metal chip closed the circuit to the spark plug when the piston was at the top of the compression stroke. A switch allowed the circuit to be opened to stop the engine. This ignition system was the basis for all others from that time to the present.

Other features of his motorized tricycle included elliptical rear springs, rack-and-pinion steering, and water cooling. Belts and chains transmitted power from the engine to the solid rear axle. Benz later claimed that he had driven the tricycle in the spring of 1885, and many consider this to have been the first automobile powered by an internal-combustion engine. In the autumn of 1885, he tested the vehicle before witnesses. The test was a short one. In fact, Benz never made it to the road outside his workshop yard: He ran into a brick wall, but he and his passenger—his wife—escaped injury. There were other tests as he developed his design, but his first public notice came on June 4, 1886, when the *Neue Badische Landeszeitung* printed a description of the vehicle, followed on July 3, 1886, by a favorable report of a test-drive.

Benz continued to improve his invention by adding a sun and planet gear which provided a second gear. He applied for a patent for this feature in April, 1887. Further improvements included a larger engine (three horsepower instead of one horsepower), better springs, and more effective brakes. By 1887, the vehicle had reached such a stage of development that it was possible to market it.

The first customer for a Benz automobile was a Frenchman named Émile Roger, who saw one demonstrated at the Paris Exhibition of 1887. In the following year, Benz won a gold medal at the Imperial Exhibition in Munich. The publicity from these exhibitions apparently stimulated a number of orders. In 1889, the Benz Company employed fifty workers. Business was so brisk that Benz was able to find new partners who financed a move to a larger factory where the company began producing vehicles with four wheels in 1890.

The addition of a fourth wheel was one of the few concessions Benz was to make to those who wanted him to maintain an up-to-date design. He appears to have regarded the design of 1890 as final and refused to make changes in it. Even when he consented to the addition of a hood to the front of the car, it was only an empty shell added for the sake of appearance. He insisted on keeping the engine at the rear. In 1905, he finally bowed to pressure from his colleagues and allowed sweeping design changes, but he and his wife continued to drive their older models.

Photographs of Benz posing as driver of his automobiles show a man of medium stature, dark hair, and constantly changing facial hair. He always wore a large mustache, but his goatees came and went presumably in accord with fashions of the day. Pictures of him in later life indicate that he became thinner and the hair and mustache turned white. The later photographs are of a man with a prominent, sharp nose and deep-set eyes.

Benz was not alone in the attempt to build a horseless carriage. His most significant German rival was Gottlieb Daimler. Many argue that Daimler should be regarded as the inventor of a practical, engine-driven vehicle with internal combustion. His engine was better in many respects and his patent of August, 1885, predates Benz's by five months. Benz's adherents concede these points but note that Daimler's work involved a motorcycle rather than a three- or four-wheeled vehicle. Competition between the two involved more than mere claims to priority. The two companies vied for sales, especially in France and Germany. It was for the sake of the French market that the Daimler product became known as the Mercedes. The French distributor suggested the name of his daughter, Mercedes, as sounding more French than Daimler and, therefore, more acceptable to the French buying public. Rivalry between Benz and Daimler was strictly on a commercial basis; they had never met when Daimler died in 1900.

During the economic depression that followed World War I in Germany, both the Daimler and Benz companies faltered. That led to their merger to form Mercedes-Benz in 1926. By that time Benz had little to do with the active management of the company that he had founded nearly forty years before.

Summary

The inventive genius of Carl Benz was considerable. Working independently, he managed to invent the necessary components for an automobile and combine them in a practical machine. The fact that Daimler and others produced better engines and made wider use of them in boats and for other applications does not detract from his accomplishments. Whether a motorized tricycle actually qualifies as the first automobile and whether it deserves such a title more than a motorcycle are less important concerns in assessing Benz's career than his status as a pioneer in the marketing of automobiles. His contributions were certainly recognized as significant during his lifetime. Early examples of his cars were in museums, and two days before his death a procession of several hundred automobiles drove from Heidelberg to his house in Ladenburg, where dignitaries delivered a number of speeches acclaiming him as the inventor of the automobile.

As shown by the earlier inventions of Siegfried Marcus, it is one thing to produce a self-propelled vehicle but quite another to turn it into something that people will buy in significant numbers. It was to take the mass production techniques of Henry Ford and others to make the automobile into more than a plaything of the rich, but Benz and his rivals brought the idea of automobile ownership and its practicality into the minds of the buying public.

Bibliography

Nevins, Allan. *Ford: The Times, the Man, and the Company.* New York: Scribner, 1954. Although devoted to Henry Ford, the first volume of this work contains considerable discussion of the development of the early automobile in general and of the contributions of Benz in particular. It also contains a useful bibliography for use in further research on the early development of the automobile.

Nixon, St. John C. *The Invention of the Automobile.* London: Country Life, 1936. This book is the story of Benz and Daimler and the creation of their company. Most of it is devoted to Benz, and it gives him the lion's share of credit for the invention of the automobile. In fact, it proclaims him as its inventor. Contains helpful illustrations and photographs of several Daimler cars as well as a comparative chronology of Daimler's and Benz's lives.

Poole, Lynn, and Gray Poole. *Men Who Pioneered Inventions.* New York: Dodd, Mead, 1969. A book intended for juvenile readers. Gives considerable credit to Benz and boldly recognizes him as the inventor of the automobile.

Roberts, Peter. *Veteran and Vintage Cars.* London: Hamlyn, 1963. One of the more readily available picture books dealing with early automobiles. Contains a descriptive text as well as color photographs and reproductions of advertisements. Covers the period to 1914 and has illustrations of the Benz products.

Singer, Charles, et al., eds. *A History of Technology.* Vol. 5, *The Late Nineteenth Century, c. 1850 to c. 1900.* Oxford; Clarendon Press, and New York: Oxford University Press, 1958. A useful work for more detailed explanations of the technical aspects of the work of Benz and the other early designers of internal-combustion engines. The authors do not enter into the discussion of priority in the invention of the automobile.

Philip Dwight Jones

HECTOR BERLIOZ

Born: December 11, 1803; La Côte-Saint-André, France

Died: March 8, 1869; Paris, France

Area of Achievement: Music

Contribution: Berlioz, one of the foremost exponents of Romanticism, extended the art of orchestration in compositions of striking originality. In his writings, which include a treatise on orchestration and a colorful memoir of his life, he made contributions both to musical craft and cultural history. During his lifetime Berlioz's music attained more popularity outside France than within it, where the eccentric notoriety of the man often overshadowed his genius.

Early Life

Louis-Hector Berlioz was born on the morning of December 11, 1803, in the town of La Côte-Saint-André, about fifty-five kilometers northwest of Grenoble, France. Hector was the first of six children born to Louis-Joseph and Marie Antoinette Berlioz; his family, which had prospered over generations from tanning and other enterprises, could be traced on his father's side to the beginning of the seventeenth century. Louis Berlioz was a kindly but serious man, who had received his medical degree in Paris only months after Hector's birth; though culturally and intellectually refined far beyond the custom of his provincial locale, he came to be loved by the peasants he served. Hector's mother figures in his life much less prominently than her husband. As a devout Roman Catholic, she provided him with a religious upbringing, but it seems not to have had a lasting impact.

After briefly attending school in La Côte, Berlioz's education was directed with great success by his father at home. His studies included mathematics, history, and French literature, but geography became his favorite topic. At an early age, he also came to love Vergil's *Aeneid* (c. 29-19 B.C.), learning to read the Roman author in the original Latin. At age twelve, on a family holiday in nearby Meylan, he experienced his first feelings of romantic love, a passion for a young woman of eighteen named Estelle Deboeuf. This brief, one-sided experience only slowly lost its hold upon his imagination.

Part of Berlioz's education at home consisted of lessons in practical music making; Hector had learned to play the flageolet, a form of recorder, af-ter finding one in a bureau drawer at home; in his teens, he was given a flute, which he soon learned to play capably. Later, he learned the guitar, but there was no piano in his home, and he never learned the instrument aside from picking out harmonies on its keys. Hector was not a child prodigy, but his natural musical gifts soon led him to compose short instrumental and vocal works, which he would play with family and friends. At the age of fifteen, he was naïvely offering his pieces to a well-known publisher.

Louis Berlioz had determined that his son should follow a medical career and set about preparing Hector and a young friend for medical studies, which commenced in Paris in 1821. Hector's intellectual interest in his subjects was sincere, and he later praised some of the lecturers, but, when the course of study turned to the dissection of human cadavers, he recoiled violently from the work.

By 1824, Berlioz no longer pretended that he was studying medicine. Since the previous year, he had been a student in the classes of the composer Jean-François Le Sueur, who took a warm interest in him, and much of his time was devoted to attending opera performances, reading scores in the library of the music conservatory, and composing. This development was viewed with dismay by Berlioz's parents, who had hoped that a few disappointments with music would convince him to abandon his plans for a musical career. Despite occasional modest successes in the performance of his works, his failure to pass a music examination in 1826 caused his father to demand his return to La Côte. Louis persuaded his son to attempt once more to pass the examination; if he failed, he would choose a different profession.

By living extremely frugally and giving lessons in singing, flute, and guitar, Belioz was repaying a loan given by an acquaintance to finance a concert, when the thoughtless creditor requested the balance owing from Berlioz's father. Enraged by Hector's improvidence, Louis paid the debt but terminated Hector's allowance, and the twenty-three-year-old composer was thrown into virtual poverty, surviving only by taking a job in a theater chorus. Disciplining mind and body, however, he continued his studies. After a period of months, he passed the examination qualifying him to compete for the Prix de Rome, a lucrative award of the Academy of Fine Arts of the Institute of France. Soon after, his father restored his allowance, and Berlioz was able to continue his operagoing on a grand scale. His favorite composers at the time were Christoph Gluck and Gaspare Spontini, but he despised the popular Gioacchino Rossini.

Like many of his contemporaries who regarded themselves as Romantic artists, Berlioz embraced the experience and display of emotion. In 1827, a company of actors arrived from England to present a season of performances of plays by William Shakespeare. This was Berlioz's overwhelming introduction to Shakespeare on the stage, and it was also the beginning of his love for the actress Harriet Smithson, who played Ophelia on opening night. Berlioz's involved and somewhat ostentatious passion for Henriette (as she is called in his memoirs) was to play a large part in the inspiration for his *Symphonie fantastique* (1830) and its sequel, *Le Retour à la vie* (1831), or *Lélio*, as it was later known. Unsuccessful attempts to get Henriette's attention, including public concerts of his own work, were finally abandoned, but the beautiful and talented Henriette had already left her mark on Hector's imagination.

Berlioz continued his musical studies at the conservatoire and began, around 1829, to write articles on music for the Paris press. Literary work, which he generally undertook to relieve his strained finances, often seemed to Berlioz to be a curse, but he had a natural capacity for writing and his contributions to music criticism are substantial. His literary experience also led him to compose music to poems by Victor Hugo and others, and the first composition to which Berlioz gave an opus number, *Huit Scènes de Faust* (1828), was based upon Johann Wolfgang von Goethe's *Faust: Eine Tragödie* (1808). In 1830, *The Death of Sardanapalus* was the subject of a composition that won for him the Prix de Rome on his fourth attempt. The fictional but grotesque story of *Sardanapalus* had been broached only three years before by the painter Eugène Delacroix, partly relieving Berlioz of the reputation for excess that had dogged his previous competition efforts.

In the spring of 1830, Berlioz again fell in love, this time with a nineteen-year-old pianist, Marie Moke. They were soon engaged, despite the prospect of being separated by Berlioz's impending year-long stay in Rome, a condition of the Prix de Rome stipend. Sensing that his absence would be a kind of spiritual imprisonment, he tried to gain an exemption from the requirement, but the authorities would not agree to it. His fiancée's family was similarly unyielding, making the engagement conditional both upon his absence and upon the success of a pending performance of his *Symphonie fantastique*. After the work was successfully presented in December, Berlioz left for Rome, stopping to visit his family at La Côte early in the new year.

In residence at the French Academy in Rome for only a few weeks, growing fears about his engagement drove him to abandon the academy. Soon he learned in a letter from Marie's mother that his fiancée was to marry a prosperous man of fifty-eight. Berlioz, enraged, became intent upon murder and suicide, and got as far as Nice before thinking better of his plan. Berlioz was allowed to return to the academy, but he was often moody, bored, and distracted in Rome, which was to him little more than a museum. Preferring nature to city life, he toured the surrounding countryside on foot, gathering impressions of its landscape and inhabitants that later inspired the symphonic work *Harold in Italy* (1834), a musical essay evoking the atmosphere of Lord Byron's poem *Childe Harold's Pilgrimage* (1812-1818, 1819). After more than a year in Italy, Berlioz returned to Paris, arriving in the capital on November 6, 1832. On the eve of his thirtieth year, he had been well seasoned by artistic struggles and by painful episodes in his personal life.

Life's Work

The professional difficulties of Berlioz's career were often concerned with finances or with the quality of performances that could be extracted from the French orchestras of the day. Sometimes these circumstances met to produce concerts that were financial as well as artistic failures, but more often Berlioz, an excellent conductor, fared well with Parisian audiences. A concert of December 9, 1832, designed to reintroduce himself to the public, featured the *Symphonie fantastique* and *Lélio*. Harriet Smithson, his unrequited love of four years past, was in the audience, doubtless uneasily aware that the two works had grown out of the composer's passion for her in 1827-1828. The following day they met for the first time, and after months of fervent but strained courtship they were married. In August, 1834, their only child, Louis, was born.

The two works of that fateful December concert were conceived as a spiritual autobiography in music. From the moment Berlioz discovered his tragic muse in Henriette's portrayals of Ophelia and Juli-

et, he had been immersed in a painful rapture which for a time had made creative activity almost impossible, and *Symphonie fantastique* was both a fulfillment and an exorcism of the composer's torment. It is a "program symphony," evoking "an episode in the life of an artist," and follows a novelistic scenario including a ball, a march to execution, and a witches' Sabbath. For all of its eccentricities and weaknesses, it is an influential landmark in music. *Lélio*, however, is generally regarded as a gratuitous, provocatively egotistic, and somewhat incoherent sequel. The true artistic sequel to the *Symphonie fantastique* is Berlioz's *Harold in Italy*, featuring a solo viola part which gives the symphony something of the nature of a concerto.

The German poet Heinrich Heine, who was a friend of the composer, described Berlioz as "an immense nightingale, or a lark the size of an eagle," whose music "causes me to dream of fabulous empires with fabulous sins." This characterization encompasses something of the spirit of the man as well as his appearance: The composer's artistic soul was both lyric and violent, as his appearance could seem either wistful or dramatic in turn.

He was of medium height and angular, with a pronounced beaklike nose framed by intense, deep-set eyes and a great mass of hair.

The decade of 1835 through 1845 brought Berlioz fame both as composer and as conductor, but his successes were punctuated by the same kind of difficulties he had faced in previous years. He seems to have been a difficult man and was rarely at peace with the official cultural apparatus or with his colleagues. Financial problems continued and were intensified by the failure of Henriette's career following a leg injury (by 1842, Berlioz had separated from her, though his affection survived to her death in 1854). His journalistic work and his need continually to promote his own compositions strained his health, which was not robust. Nevertheless, these were the years in which he composed some of his greatest works, including the *Messe de morts*, or *Requiem* (1837), the opera *Benvenuto Cellini* (1834-1838), the symphony *Roméo et Juliette* (1839), and the dramatic cantata *La Damnation de Faust* (1846), derived in part from his early *Huit Scènes de Faust*.

The *Requiem*, commissioned by the government for a civic funeral, shows Berlioz in full command both of his musical materials and of his sense of public occasion. Berlioz specified for the work 190 instruments and 210 voices, not including timpani and brass choirs to be heard at a distance. Certain passages achieve a great acoustical and emotional effect, but other parts of the mass are models of delicacy. Berlioz's reputation for colossal effect is only partly justified, for he knew how to use large musical forces with restraint.

In 1842, Berlioz began a series of trips abroad which were to bring him many artistic triumphs and, not incidentally, a further source of income. He was in demand both as composer and conductor, and the accounts he gives in his memoirs of his travels in England, Germany, Austria, Hungary, and Russia show him directing his own works as well as those of Gluck, Ludwig van Beethoven, and others. His journeys also gave him an opportunity to meet many of the leading performers and composers of Europe, including Franz Liszt, Robert Schumann, and Richard Wagner, with whom he had a long-standing but ambivalent relationship.

In his forties, Berlioz's musical style began to show signs of retreat from the adventurous Romanticism of his youth. Official honors had already come his way: In 1839, he was made a member of the Legion of Honor and was given a modest salary as an official of the conservatory library. His treatise on orchestration and his *Voyage musical en Allemagne et en Italie* (a musical voyage in Germany and Italy) were published in 1844. Beyond these signs of increasing acceptance, however, the subtle moderation of his artistic outlook can be traced to other circumstances. He was drained by work undertaken for the sake of paying for two households—Henriette's and his own; his son, Louis, who had become a sailor, was often troublesome. More important, though, the melancholy streak in his character came to overrule his penchant for ostentation and experimentation. Berlioz turned more and more to the poetry of Vergil, which had stirred him as a child; a current of classicism emerged in his musical thought, expressing a conception of beauty that had perhaps lain dormant in him since youth. From this sensibility emerged much of Berlioz's late work: *L'Enfance du Christ*, first performed in December, 1854, belongs to this late phase of his career; *Les Troyens* (1856-1858), with a libretto by the composer, is its culmination.

Berlioz's musical work might well have ended with the staging of *Les Troyens*—he was suffering increasingly from an ill-defined internal malady—but a final commission, the two-act opera *Béatrice et Bénédict* occupied him during 1860-1862. Based upon Shakespeare's *Much Ado About Nothing* (1598-1599), it is a gracious comedy which Berlioz found to be a relaxation after the immense labors of *Les Troyens*.

Berlioz's last years brought him personal loss; in 1862, his second wife, Marie Recio, died suddenly. Her mother selflessly continued to look after the composer. In 1867, he was shattered by the news of his son's death in Havana from a fever. Their relationship had been a close one, marked on the father's side by patience and on the son's by intense devotion. In his grief and physical suffering, Berlioz told a close friend that he hardly knew how he managed to continue living. Yet in the winter of 1867-1868, he made a successful last tour to Russia on the invitation of the Grand Duchess Helena. To this evidence of his undiminished artistic renown, he is said to have exclaimed "Why am I so old and feeble?" In fact, he was to survive only one more year. In March, 1868, he suffered a serious fall while visiting the rocky coast near Nice; although by August he had recovered enough to attend a musical festival in Grenoble, he was unwell and began to experience loss of memory. Returning to Paris, he died on March 8, 1869.

Summary

Hector Berlioz was an artist whose career was formed to a great extent by the era into which he was born, the extraordinary period of upheaval when Napoleon I sought to subjugate Europe. The military conflicts of the period from 1805 to 1815 were followed in France by a reactionary politics which robbed the nation of economic and cultural vitality. Although Berlioz was, by most standards, not a political person, he was obliged to struggle against the cultural environment produced by politics. The soil on which his artistic genius had to take root was shallow and impoverished, and throughout his life—even discounting his contrary personality and his own exaggerations of his trials—he had to struggle against many odds, though they were perhaps more persistent than they were overwhelming.

The factor of temperament in Berlioz was undoubtedly strong. His precocious affinity for Vergil's poetry is shown in an anecdote from his memoirs, where he recalls bursting into tears while reciting to his father the episode of the death of Dido in the *Aeneid*. Sensitivity to landscape—a legacy both of his formative environment and early literary experiences—become bonded, in the encounter with Estelle, to an enduring conception of ideal love. Around all of these circumstances lingers an echo of classical myth with a primitive accent, which the young provincial carried with him to Paris. Berlioz's innate depth of sensibility was to be both a strength and a burden: It was a source of creative vitality which made him steadfast in the face of mediocre convention, but it also caused conflict in his professional relationships and probably narrowed his musical sympathies beyond necessity.

In his early years in Paris, Berlioz became a leading figure of the Romantic movement, acquiring a reputation as a somewhat rebellious genius. His unquestioned originality in certain spheres of musical composition was countered by a frequent lack of judgment in others. As an orchestrator he charted new territory, but his harmony and rhythm have often been criticized. Berlioz's sense of melody has also had many detractors, but in fact he was a fine and original melodist at times and was capable of great delicacy of feeling. His reputation as a seeker after effects is not unjustified, but many of the effects are astonishingly impressive—as in the offstage brass choirs of the *Requiem*, for example.

Berlioz's defiance of authority, his artistic daring, and the vigor of his journalistic rhetoric closely harmonize with the modern image of the Romantic artist, but the view of life he evoked in many of his major works exceeds the usual bounds of Romantic darkness. His capacity for despair, as man and artist, contrasts with more resilient figures such as Victor Hugo and Eugène Delacroix, who were his contemporaries. Though he gravitated toward classical ideals in his later music, clarity and harmony were never his secure possessions, either in art or in life.

Bibliography

Barzun, Jacques. *Berlioz and the Romantic Century.* 2 vols. Boston: Little Brown, 1950; London: Gollancz, 1951. Barzun's massive study was conceived in the spirit of the poet W. H. Auden's remark that "whoever wants to know about the nineteenth century must know about Berlioz." The author succeeds in being charming as well as thorough, and he provides an unmatched bibliography.

———. *Berlioz and His Century: An Introduction to the Age of Romanticism.* New York: Meridian, 1956. This condensation of Barzun's two-volume work on Berlioz concentrates on the composer's life rather than his music. It has no sense of being a mere editing of the earlier books, but it is an introduction to Romanticism only in the most oblique way; as such, it will not mislead the reader, but it cannot be substituted for a true survey of the period of Berlioz's life.

Berlioz, Hector. *The Memoirs of Hector Berlioz, Member of the French Institute, Including His Travels in Italy, Germany, Russia, and England, 1803-1865.* Edited and translated by David Cairns. London: Gollancz, and New York: Knopf, 1969. One of the great documents of nineteenth century European culture, but one that often has to be read skeptically. Apart from some portions of the book that provide details of Berlioz's concerts abroad, it is highly entertaining. Berlioz declined to write an autobiography in the manner of Jean-Jacques Rousseau, but there is a quantity of intense self-revelation nevertheless.

Bloom, Peter. *The Life of Berlioz.* Cambridge and New York: Cambridge University Press, 1998. Bloom's familiarity with archival materials and access to recently available writings has created a biography that veers from the standard Berlioz stereotype and provides a vision of the composer within the French musical culture in which he lived.

Bloom, Peter, ed. *Berlioz Studies.* Cambridge and New York: Cambridge University Press, 1992. Presents nine essays by premiere Berlioz scholars on the composer's life and works and includes pieces on individual works, the composer as a young man, obscure manuscripts, and Berlioz's metronome marks.

Elliot, J. H. *Berlioz.* London: Dent, and New York: Dutton, 1938. A volume in the Master Musicians series, it efficiently fulfills all the standard requirements of biography, description, and analysis. Its perspective, however, though intelligently critical, appears inordinately fastidious. Excellent appendices—a calendar, list of works, and the like—redeem the author's somewhat limited enthusiasm for his subject.

Rushton, Julian. *The Musical Language of Berlioz.* Cambridge and New York: Cambridge University Press, 1983. A work of critical scholarship rather than biography, this book may be consulted by the general reader for its introductory and concluding chapters and for its bibliography.

Wotton, Tom S. *Hector Berlioz.* London: Oxford University Press, 1935; New York: Johnson Reprint Corporation, 1969. Barzun honored Wotton as the foremost Berlioz scholar of his time, but the style and diction of the book are rather antiquated.

C. S. McConnell

CLAUDE BERNARD

Born: July 12, 1813; Saint-Julien, France
Died: February 10, 1878; Paris, France
Areas of Achievement: Physiology and medicine
Contribution: Bernard is called the "father of physiology," having developed the experimental methods and conceptual framework needed to change physiology from a primarily deductive science based on statistics to one which could discover empirical data using procedures borrowed from chemistry.

Early Life

Claude Bernard's parents were vineyard workers, and Bernard retained a lifelong attachment to the vineyards, returning there each fall to relax and help with the grape harvest and, later, to make his own wine. In the fields of his boyhood, he learned to observe nature and developed the manual dexterity and precision necessary for both wine making and scientific research. His father apparently died while Bernard was still a youth, though little is known concerning him. It is known, however, that Bernard adored his pious mother.

His early schooling was in the Jesuit school at Villefranche and later at the Collège de Thoissey, where he studied the humanities but little science or philosophy. When he finished this education, he became a pharmacy apprentice and during his evenings attended the theater and wrote a light comedy, *La Rose du Rhône*, and a five-act drama, *Arthur de Bretagne* (1887). His goal of becoming a playwright was shattered when the well-known literary critic Saint-Marc Girardin judged his drama as lacking merit and the author as without literary promise. The critic urged him to study medicine instead.

Bernard entered medical school in 1834 but divided his time between attending lectures and studying and giving lessons at a girls' school to help his mother pay the bills. His grades were only average, and when he took the internship examination in 1839, he ranked twenty-sixth out of twenty-nine. He began his internship, which was split between two hospitals. At one of these, the Hôtel Dieu, he became an unpaid assistant to a clinician and professor of physiology at the Collège de France, François Magendie. This experience had a life-changing effect on Bernard, for Magendie was an outspoken devotee of both experimentation and skepticism. Magendie recognized Bernard's talents in the labo-

ratory and in 1841 hired him as an assistant on several projects. Bernard was granted his medical degree on December 7, 1843, on the basis of his thesis, *Du suc gastrique et de son rôle dans la nutrition* (1843; gastric juice and its role in metabolism). Earlier the same year, his first publication had appeared, *Recherches anatomiques et physiologiques sur la corde du tympan, pour servir à l'histoire de l'hémiplegie faciale* (1843; anatomical and physiological research on the chorda tympani).

In 1844, Bernard failed the examination for a teaching position with the faculty of medicine. Disheartened, he resigned his position with Magendie and considered becoming a country doctor in his home village. A colleague suggested that he find a wife with a good dowry instead, and in July, 1845, he married the daughter of a Parisian doctor. His marriage to Marie Françoise Martin was a matter of financial convenience, allowing him to continue his research, but it was also to be the source of much unhappiness in the years ahead. His wife obtained a legal separation from him in 1870, partly because of her opposition to his vivisectionist experiments. Both sons born to the marriage died in infancy, and the two daughters, like their mother, renounced him and apparently refused to be reconciled with him even on his deathbed.

Between 1843 and 1845, he made discoveries on the chemical and nerve control of the gastric juices and on the role of bile and began experiments with curare and on the innervation of the vocal cords and the functions of the cranial nerves. With the money from the dowry, he was able to continue this research as well as initiate others, and he published a number of papers on various subjects through the mid-1840's.

Life's Work

The year 1848 is generally taken to be the year from which Bernard's mature work dates. In December, 1847, he became an assistant to Magendie at the Collège de France, and the following year began teaching the course on experimental medicine during the winter terms. He also became a charter member and the first vice president of the Société de Biologie, which indicates his growing stature within the scientific community. In 1848, his research led him to two discoveries which were to provide not only new facts but also new ways of conceptualizing bodily functions. First, in his observations on the differences between the urine of carnivores and herbivores, he discovered the part played by the pancreas in the digestion of fats. He published the results of this discovery in *Du suc pancréatique, et de son rôle dans les phénomènes de la digestion* (1848; pancreatic juice and its role in the phenomena of digestion). Second, he discovered the glycogenous function of the liver. Formerly it was believed that the body could not produce sugars and was therefore dependent upon plants for their source. Bernard's discovery explained the constancy of sugar in the body and was instrumental in leading Bernard to a concept, which he first articulated in the late 1850's, of *milieu intérieur*, or internal environment.

Between the time that he first described this condition of a constant interior environment and his death, Bernard developed and extended the idea until it became the generalized and widely accepted biological notion of homeostasis. In his last comments about it, published in 1878, he explained that the organism does not exist in the *milieu extérieur* (the external environment of air or water) but rather in a liquid *milieu intérieur*, which is made of all the intracellular liquids of the organism. These liquids are the bases of all forms of cellular metabolism and the common factor of all simple chemical or physiological exchanges. The body's task is to maintain the stability of the *milieu intérieur;* hence, the task of the physiologist is to discover how this regulation occurs.

Bernard's work in the 1850's and 1860's was directed precisely to this task. In 1851, he discovered the control of local skin temperature by sympathetic nerves, and later he showed the importance of the nervous system in regulating the vascular system. In 1856, he demonstrated that curare blocks motor nerve endings, and the following year he reported that the toxic effect of carbon monoxide resulted from blocked respiration in the erythrocytes. He was finally able to isolate glycogen in a pure form in 1857.

He started teaching in the early 1850's, and in his lectures he argued against vitalism in favor of what he called experimental determinism. He contended that the laws governing the functioning of the organism were precise and rigorous, with the laws of physics and chemistry being fundamental for understanding living phenomena. By varying conditions, the experimental biologists could make the organism respond in a strictly determined manner.

In 1865, Bernard had more time to work on his philosophical ideas, for he became too ill to teach or to conduct research. He retired to the vineyards and wrote his most famous work, *Introduction à l'étude de la médecine expérimentale* (1865; *An Introduction to the Study of Experimental Medicine*, 1927), which for many years was his only work translated into English. In this work, he showed his indebtedness to his mentor, Magendie, and to Auguste Comte's positivism; both stressed the necessity of making observations and determining facts from the evidence. Bernard was unwilling to be shackled by their strict Baconianism, and, against current opinion, he argued that the forming of hypotheses was an essential and necessary part of the scientific process.

The following year, the minister of public education asked Bernard to prepare a report on the state of physiology in France to be published on the occasion of the World Exposition of 1867. Instead of the objective, factual, historical report that was commissioned, Bernard wrote an ideological tract that continued his philosophical thinking. In his *Rapport sur les progrès et la marche de la physiologie générale en France* (1867; report on the progress and course of general physiology in France), he described his vision of a new brand of physiology founded on the concept of the *milieu intérieur* and the elucidation of regulatory functions. This report demonstrated what Bernard hoped physiology would become—not what it was.

In later years, Bernard continued to pursue his interests in the phenomena characteristic of all living organisms. He had begun to explore this issue in his lessons at the Sorbonne in 1864, and, when offered the chair of comparative physiology at the Musée d'Histoire Naturelle in 1868, he insisted that the chair be renamed "general physiology." This willingness to treat general biological problems instead of strictly medical ones not only restructured the way in which questions about living material, life processes, and the properties of living beings were framed and studied but also freed physiology from its subservience to medicine and established it as an independent discipline.

In 1869, Bernard returned to his teaching duties at the Collège de France. He attracted a large and diverse audience, including, at times, Louis Pasteur, and entertained them with demonstrations to support both his physiological and philosophical views. Bernard's ideas were publicized through ten works, the best known being *Leçons sur les pro-*

priétés des tissus vivants (1866; lessons on the properties of living tissues) and *Leçons sur les phénomènes de la vie communs aux animaux et aux végétaux* (1878-1879; lessons on the phenomena of life common to animals and plants).

Summary

The painting *Claude Bernard's Lesson in the Laboratory* by Léon Lhermitte delineates one of the most important aspects of Claude Bernard's work—his teaching and mentoring of younger scientists. In this picture, Bernard, with dark hair and eyes, is dressed in a white gardener's apron and wears a metal pince-nez around his neck. Near him are several of his disciples, including the electro-physiologist Arsène d'Arsonval; Bernard's most famous student, Paul Bert; and Louis Ranvier, the founder of histophysiology. Not all of Bernard's students agreed with him, but the discussions furthered the understanding of science in general and physiology in particular. As a teacher, Bernard ensured the continuation and independence of the new discipline of physiology.

During his lifetime, Bernard showed that general biological laws could be derived from specific experimental data; incorporated the latest techniques and findings of physics and chemistry into biology; developed the concepts of homeostasis, internal secretions, and organismic self-regulation; demonstrated the unity between physiology and medicine; and provided a philosophical basis for experimental biology. These contributions defined modern physiology, and current work in regulatory biology and much neurophysiology is the outgrowth of Bernard's scientific and philosophical initiatives.

In recognition of his work and status, he was given a chair in physiology at the University of Paris in 1854 and elected to the Academy of Medicine in 1861. In 1867, he was made a commander of the Legion of Honor and served as president of the Société de Biologie. In 1868, he was elected to the Académie Française and served as its president in 1869. In 1870, he was appointed to the senate by Napoleon III and barely escaped from Paris before the Prussian army arrived.

After his illness-enforced retirement in 1865, Bernard never fully recovered his health, although he was able to do some teaching and research. His mind was ever active, and it is reported in many sources that as he grew older, he repeated more and more often, "My mind abounds with things I want to finish." He became seriously ill in early January, 1878, and died on February 10, 1878, probably of kidney disease. He was the first scientist upon whom France bestowed the honor of a public funeral.

Bibliography

Bernard, Claude. *An Introduction to the Study of Experimental Medicine.* Translated by Henry Copley Green. New York: Macmillan, 1927. This classic by Bernard has been widely read. Bernard's purpose in writing it was to describe the basic principles of scientific research, that is, to outline and explain his philosophy of science. For a philosophical treatise, this book is remarkably clear and easy to follow.

Hall, Thomas S. *Ideas of Life and Matter, 600 B.C. to A.D. 1900.* Vol 2. Chicago: University of Chicago Press, 1969. Hall succinctly describes Bernard's answer to four questions: How is the organism constituted? What part or parts of it appear to be alive? By what sign does one recognize "living"? and What does "life" mean?

Holmes, Frederic L. *Claude Bernard and Animal Chemistry: The Emergence of a Scientist.* Cambridge, Mass.: Harvard University Press, 1974. This work focuses on Bernard's early research period (1842-1848), during which he began to develop his views on experimentation, which in turn would lead him to one of his most famous discoveries—the role and function of the liver. Holmes also describes the scientific environment within which Bernard worked to provide a context for his thought and activities.

―――. "Claude Bernard, the *Milieu Intérieur,* and Regulatory Physiology." *History and Philosophy of the Life Sciences* 8 (1986): 3-25. Holmes explains the intellectual context in which Bernard developed the concept of *milieu intérieur* and shows how twentieth century physiologists have reinterpreted Bernard's original ideas to fit the concept of homeostasis. This article demonstrates the problems involved in understanding a scientist-philosopher in his own period instead of trying to make him say what is currently believed to be true.

Olmsted, J. M. D. *Claude Bernard, Physiologist.* New York and London: Harper, 1938. This is probably the best-known biography of Bernard and is very good despite the pre-World War II date of publication.

Roll-Hansen, Nils. "Critical Teleology: Immanuel Kant and Claude Bernard on the Limitations of

Experimental Biology." *Journal of the History of Biology* 9 (Spring, 1979): 55-91. Kant and Bernard proposed similar methodologies for biology. This article examines those methodologies, compares them, and shows how Kant's program had ethical and moral implications, while Bernard's approach was related to questions of science policy. The article describes the similarities and differences between Bernard and many of the natural historians and physicians of his period.

Sullivan, Mark D. "Reconsidering the Wisdom of the Body: An Epistemological Critique of Claude Bernard's Concept of the Internal Environment." *The Journal of Medicine and Philosophy* 15, no. 5 (October 1990). Discusses Bernard's concept of the body's internal environment and its effect on the development of experimental physiology.

Wasserstein, Alan G. "Death and the Internal Milieu: Claude Bernard and the Origins of Experimental Medicine." *Perspectives in Biology and Medicine* 39, no. 3 (Spring, 1996). Discusses Bernard's biomedical paradigm of determinism.

Sara Joan Miles

ANNIE BESANT

Born: October 1, 1847; London, England

Died: September 20, 1933; Adyar, India

Areas of Achievement: Social reform, religion, and politics

Contribution: After her early work promoting radical reform in England, Besant became leader of the Theosophical Society and was active in the nationalist movement in India.

Early Life

Annie Wood Besant was born on October 1, 1847, in London, England, the second of three children of William and Emily Morris Wood. Despite her English birth, Besant had a strong sense of Irish heritage, because her mother was Irish and her father half Irish. William Wood, although trained as a physician, engaged in commerce in London. He died when Besant was five, a loss the trauma of which was compounded by the death several months later of her baby brother.

When Besant was eight, her impoverished widowed mother moved the family to Harrow so that her ten-year-old son Henry could more cheaply attend that prestigious public school. Shortly after the move, Miss Ellen Marryat, youngest sister of the novelist Frederick Marryat, offered to take Annie into her home in Devon to educate her. Although heartsick to be separated from her adored mother for the eight years she spent with Miss Marryat, Besant received excellent training, especially in literary skills, which enabled her to produce throughout her life a prodigious volume of writings for her many causes. During these adolescent years, she was intensely religious. Reading stories of early Christian martyrs, she longed to follow in their steps. She fasted regularly, tortured herself with self-flagellation, and engaged in other extremist behavior, a pattern which became characteristic of her personality. A person of deep if changing beliefs, she would always commit herself enthusiastically and wholeheartedly to her convictions, with the ever-present, self-proclaimed wish for martyrdom.

At age sixteen, Besant returned to her mother's home. She was a beautiful young woman, of small stature, with brown hair and eyes. She had, however, no romantic fantasies, for her emotional life was absorbed by her passionate love for Jesus Christ and for her mother. She nevertheless married, in 1867, the Reverend Frank Besant, younger brother of the essayist Walter Besant, because she believed that she could best serve God as a clergyman's wife.

The marriage was a disaster. Annie, who married with no knowledge of sex, was shocked by her wedding night. Self-willed and rebellious, she also resented submitting to her domineering husband's authority. Her unhappiness was only somewhat alleviated by her success in selling several stories to the *Family Herald* and by the births of her son Digby, in 1869, and daughter Mabel, in 1870. She also found satisfaction in parish work when Frank Besant became vicar at Sibsey, a village in Lincolnshire. The marriage ended when Annie lost her religious faith after the grave illness of her children, whose sufferings made her doubt her belief in a loving and merciful God. The Besants were legally separated in 1873. She moved to London to make her way on her own with her daughter, while her son remained in the custody of the Reverend Mr. Besant.

Life's Work

Annie Besant's public career went through many distinct stages. After her loss of Christian faith and separation from her husband, she came under the influence of England's leading freethinker, Charles Bradlaugh. In 1874, she joined the National Secular Society and soon became one of its vice presidents. She edited with Bradlaugh the freethinking *National Reformer*, and, from 1883 to 1889, she also edited the magazine *Our Corner*. In these journals, she wrote in support of atheism, women's rights, Irish Home Rule, land-tenure reform, and against British imperialism. Besant propagated her beliefs not only in written form but also as a public speaker, an activity not considered respectable for women at that time. Her rich, vibrant voice made her a great success, and she took intense pleasure in the power she had over her audiences. Ever eager to absorb new knowledge, the energetic Besant also found time to enroll in courses in science at London University.

Besant's most controversial work with Bradlaugh was their republication in 1877 of Charles Knowlton's 1832 treatise on birth control, *Fruits of Philosophy*. They were arrested, and, in a sensational trial, they were convicted of publishing obscene literature, although their conviction was dismissed on appeal on a technicality. The defiant Besant then pub-

lished her own birth-control pamphlet, *Law of Population: Its Consequence and Its Bearing upon Human Conduct and Morals* (1881). She was the first English woman to advocate publicly the use of birth-control methods. Even though she was not prosecuted for her pamphlet, the controversy did cause her to lose custody of her daughter.

Besant's humanitarian concerns led her in 1885 to become a Socialist. Joining the moderate Fabian Society, she contributed an article to the influential 1889 *Fabian Essays in Socialism*, edited by her close friend George Bernard Shaw. She later also joined the revolutionary Marxist Social Democratic Federation. Ever concerned with theatrical display, she began to dress in proletarian garb and always wore a piece of red clothing to show her Socialist affiliation. This latest cause separated her from Bradlaugh, who was a strong anti-Socialist individualist. They remained personal friends, but she resigned as coeditor of the *National Reformer*.

As a Socialist, Besant fought tirelessly to help working people, especially in trade-union activity. Her most significant achievement was her organization of match-girl workers into a union, after helping them in a successful strike against the Bryant and May Match Company in 1888. The Matchmaker's Union, considered the beginning of the new unionism of unskilled labor, was moreover the first successful effort to organize women workers, who had been ignored by the Trades Union Council. Besant also worked for Socialist causes as a member of the London School Board, to which she was elected in 1889.

Despite her advocacy of atheism, Besant felt increasingly unsatisfied by it and later spoke of her desperate hunger for spiritual ideals. This need was fulfilled by Theosophy, to which she, to the shock of her friends and associates, converted in 1889 after reading Mme Helena Blavatsky's *The Secret Doctrine* (1888). A charismatic Russian émigrée, Mme Blavatsky founded the Theosophical Society in 1875 along with the American lawyer Colonel Henry Olcott. The society, which remains active, aims at fostering bonds among all humanity; studying comparative religions and philosophies, especially those from ancient Eastern civilizations; and investigating and communicating with the world of the occult. Although not identified with any specific religion, Theosophists accept the Hindu and Buddhist belief in Karma and reincarnation.

Committing herself fully to her new faith, Besant withdrew from the National Secular Society and the Socialist organizations. She became editor of the Theosophist publication *Lucifer* and the leader of the Theosophical Society in England after Mme Blavatsky's death in 1891. In 1907, she was elected President of the Theosophical Society worldwide, a position she held for the rest of her life. As a Theosophist, in 1891 she renounced Malthusianism and withdrew her *Law of Population* from circulation. Although anguished at the effect this might have on the lives of poor women, she accepted Mme Blavatsky's view that humans must rise above animal passion through self-control and ascetic self-denial. Besant later returned to a qualified endorsement of birth control.

Besant traveled extensively throughout the world, organizing and lecturing for the Theosophical Society. After her first trip to India in 1893, she thought of that country as her home and believed that in earlier incarnations she had been Indian. She adopted Indian dress and in public always wore a white sari, which matched her now-white hair. Strongly drawn toward Hinduism, she learned Sanskrit and in 1895 translated the *Bhagavad-Gita* (first or second century A.D.).

Always the reformer, Besant was concerned to revitalize Indian civilization, to restore pride and self-respect in a people who had been made to feel inferior by British imperialists. She condemned child marriage, the seclusion of women, and eventually the caste system, but otherwise opposed efforts to westernize India. Disavowing at first political activity, Besant worked primarily for educational reform. Her major accomplishment was the establishment of the Central Hindu College in Benares in 1898, a college for Hindu boys based on ancient Indian religion and culture as well as modern Western science. In 1904, she established the Central Hindu Girls' School, an important step in the emancipation of Indian women. The Hindu University, which absorbed the Central Hindu College in 1916, granted Besant an honorary degree in 1921, and thereafter she always styled herself Dr. Besant.

Besant eventually came to believe that efforts to strengthen Indian cultural pride were impossible as long as India was under British domination. In 1913, therefore, she entered the political arena by working actively for Indian home rule. As a vehicle for her campaign, she bought a Madras newspaper and renamed it *New India*. Founding the Home Rule for India League in 1916, she campaigned for self-government within the British Empire, which she envisioned as a partnership among equal nations. Her agitation against the British caused the government to intern her briefly during World War I, which only increased her popularity among Indians. In 1917, after her release, she was elected President of the Indian National Congress. She did not, however, remain long as leader of the Indian nationalists. She was soon eclipsed by the rise of the Mahatma Gandhi, with whose tactic of civil disobedience she disagreed, for fear that it would lead to violence. Considered too conservative in her insistence on law and order, she lost much of her political following in India.

Besant continued working for Indian home rule, and in 1925 she had an abortive Commonwealth of India Bill introduced into the English House of Commons. Her primary focus in the last part of her life, however, was in the promotion of her Hindu protégé, Jiddu Krishnamurti, as the new Messiah. Believing that in times of world crisis the Divine Spirit enters a human body to help humankind toward higher spiritual consciousness, she was convinced that Krishnamurti was the chosen vehicle. He ultimately disappointed her by renouncing his role in the divine plan. Besant nevertheless continued working for her beliefs almost until her death on September 20, 1933, in Adyar, India, the international headquarters of the Theosophical Society. A portion of her ashes was sprinkled in the holy Ganges River, the rest deposited in a Garden of Remembrance at Adyar.

Summary

An enthusiast for many causes, the leader of diverse movements, Annie Besant remained throughout her life committed to the principles of compassion, freedom, tolerance, and human equality. As a young woman, she had the courage to challenge such icons of Victorian respectability as the Church, patriarchy, propriety, capitalism, and imperialism. Although ultimately unsuccessful in her later years as a leader of the Indian home rule movement, she nevertheless made a significant contribution to Indian nationalism in helping to restore the pride of Indians in their own cultural heritage and in sensitizing the British to the narrowness and bigotry of their attitude of superiority toward India.

In her work as a Theosophist, to which she gave her most loyal and lasting allegiance, she incorporated the humanitarian concerns that had informed her other campaigns. Through her leadership she enabled the society to survive scandals, power struggles, and schisms. Although professing beliefs that the conventional world considered bizarre, she remained a personage of influence and respect and left as her legacy the vision of one world, seen and unseen, undivided by race, class, or sex, and bound together by love.

Bibliography

Besant, Annie. *An Autobiography.* London: Unwin, and Philadelphia: Altemus, 1893. A passionate, frank account of her life up to 1891. A revision of her 1885 *Autobiographical Sketches.*

———. *A Selection of the Social and Political Pamphlets of Annie Besant.* New York: Kelley, 1970. A collection of twenty-seven of Besant's pamphlets on English radical reform, published from 1874 to 1889, with a preface and bibliographical notes by John Saville.

Besant, Annie, and Charles Knowlton. *"A Dirty, Filthy Book": The Writings of Charles Knowlton and Annie Besant on Reproductive Physiology and Birth Control and an Account of the Bradlaugh-Besant Trial.* Edited by Sripati Chandrasekhar. Berkeley and London: University of California Press, 1981. Includes Besant's *Law of Population* and her recantation, *Theosophy and the Law of Population* (1891), as well as Knowlton's *Fruits of Philosophy*. The texts are prefaced by a useful introduction.

Nethercot, Arthur H. *The First Five Lives of Annie Besant*. Chicago: University of Chicago Press, 1960; London: Hart-Davis, 1961. A balanced, detailed life of Besant up to 1893. Although relying sometimes too uncritically on Besant's autobiographical writings, it, along with the second volume (below), is the most complete and reliable biography.

———. *The Last Four Lives of Annie Besant*. Chicago: University of Chicago Press, and London: Hart-Davis, 1963. Besant's life and work in India from 1893 to her death. Based on extensive research in archives of the Theosophical Society and on interviews with Besant's family members and associates. An indispensable source.

Oppenheim, J. "Prophets without Honour? The Odyssey of Annie Besant." *History Today* (September 1989). Discusses Besant's progression from Christian to atheist and belief in theosophy and includes information on her efforts in women's rights and social issues.

West, Geoffrey. *The Life of Annie Besant*. London: Howe, 1929. A lively, opinionated biography, written by a contemporary who admired Besant's achievements but was skeptical of Theosophy.

Williams, Gertrude Marvin. *The Passionate Pilgrim: A Life of Annie Besant*. New York: Coward-McCann, 1931; London: Hamilton, 1932. A readable popular biography. No footnotes, but a good bibliography.

Nancy Fix Anderson

FRIEDRICH WILHELM BESSEL

Born: July 22, 1784; Minden, Westphalia

Died: March 17, 1846; Königsberg, Prussia

Areas of Achievement: Astronomy and mathematics

Contribution: Bessel greatly increased the accuracy of the measurements of stellar positions both by using more advanced instruments and by developing methods to account for instrument and observer error. The most famous discovery resulting from these observations was the first accurate determination of the distance to a star.

Early Life

Friedrich Wilhelm Bessel was born to a civil servant and a minister's daughter. One of nine children, he went to the local *Gymnasium* but left after only four years to become a merchant's apprentice. He showed no particular talent at school. At the age of fifteen, he began his unpaid seven-year apprenticeship to a merchant firm in Bremen. He excelled at his accounting job and received a small salary after one year. He spent his spare time teaching himself geography and languages because of his interest in foreign trade. He also learned about ships and practical navigation through self-study. Determining the position of a ship at sea—a long-standing problem in navigation—intrigued him. He therefore began to study astronomy and mathematics to understand the theory behind the existing methods.

Bessel began to make observations of stars on his own, which he was able to compare to observations reported in numerous professional journals of astronomy. One of his earliest tasks was to determine the orbit of Halley's Comet based on several observations of its position. He studied existing methods to determine the easiest way to do this, and he used observations made in 1607 to supplement his own. The precision of his observations and the scrupulous care given to minimizing or correcting for observational errors would characterize his professional work throughout his life. He made the observations, adjusted (or reduced) the 1607 data to make them directly comparable to his own, and submitted the results to Wilhelm Olbers in 1804. Olbers, a physician and highly esteemed amateur astronomer, was impressed with the agreement between Bessel's observations and Edmond Halley's calculation of the orbit. He urged Bessel to improve it further with more observations. Ol-

bers was impressed enough to recommend Bessel in 1806 for a position as assistant at a private observatory near Bremen. Bessel made further observations of the comet and published the results in 1807 to wide acclaim.

Life's Work

In 1809, Bessel was appointed director of the new observatory at Königsberg, where he remained for the rest of his life. His early fame came from his reduction of the earlier observations of James Bradley. Bradley's measurement of the apparent position of stars had to be corrected for the motion of Earth, the bending of starlight as it passes through the air, and instrument errors. With sufficient care, any observation can be reduced to a universal coordinate system.

While waiting for the construction of the observatory, Bessel worked on reducing Bradley's observations of more than thirty-two hundred stars with the goal of producing a reference system for

measuring the positions of other stars. Bessel received the Lalande Prize of the Institute of France for his production of tables of refraction based on these observations. In 1818, he completed the reduction and published the results in his work, *Fundamenta astronomiae* (1818; fundamental astronomy). This work provided the most accurate positions of a chosen set of stars. Accurate positions of a few stars are required to form the basis for extremely accurate measurements of positions for all other stars. This work has been said to mark the birth of modern astrometry. Bessel also provided accurate proper motions of many stars. (The so-called fixed stars actually move a very small amount over the centuries. When all perturbing effects are removed, the motion that is left to the star is called its proper motion.)

Bessel's next important contribution was to increase the accuracy of the measurement of stellar positions and motions. In 1820, he determined the position of the vernal equinox with great accuracy. The equinox is employed as the origin of the coordinate system used to record a star's position. He further improved accuracy in his work *Tabulae regiomontanae* (1830; *Refraction Tables*, 1855), in which he published the mean positions for thirty-eight stars for the period 1750-1850. In 1821, he noticed a systematic error in observation that was peculiar to each observer and called it the personal equation. This systematic error was reduced as each observer became more experienced, but it never disappeared. Bessel devised a method to remove the error.

Identifying and measuring the proper motion of stars was crucial in producing an important contribution to astronomy. The slight but periodic variation in proper motion of a few stars was not accountable by considering the motion of Earth or instrumental factors. In making the observations which later appeared in the *Refraction Tables*, Bessel suggested that the variations in proper motion of the stars Sirius and Procyon could be explained by the existence of an as-yet-unseen companion star. More than a century later, the companions to these stars were observed, as well as companions to many others.

Bessel also made important contributions to mathematics. Prior to Bessel, it was common for observers of the heavens to record their data and only later, if ever, reduce that data. Bradley, whose observations Bessel used extensively, carefully noted any possible perturbing effects in his obser-

vations. Nevertheless, reduction of the data for the positions of the stars was put aside in favor of recording lunar data. Bessel emphasized the need for the data reduction to be done immediately by the observer. Such reduction required extensive manipulation of complicated equations. In the process of developing ways to remove errors, Bessel noticed that he could use a class of functions which solved problems involving the perturbing influence of one planet on the orbit of another. He systematically investigated and described this class of functions in 1824. These functions, which bear Bessel's name, are not restricted to astronomy: They are used in the solution of a wide variety of problems in physics, mathematics, and engineering.

Another direct benefit of increased accuracy in stellar positions was Bessel's determination of the distance to a star, which is his most important contribution to astronomy. Although many astronomers had earlier claimed to have measured stellar distance using methods based on questionable assumptions, and although two of Bessel's contemporaries also correctly determined such distances, Bessel's comprehensive treatment of the data and his high accuracy of observations were convincing to his contemporaries.

As Earth moves in its annual orbit around the sun, the stars appear to move across the dome of the sky. By determining the location of a star at opposite ends of Earth's orbit and using some simple trigonometry, the distance to a star can be measured. Yet this so-called parallax (the apparent motion of an object caused by the motion of the observer) was small because the stars are very far away. The parallax had therefore never been measured. Indeed, some opponents of the heliocentric theory, according to which Earth revolves around the sun, used this failure to measure parallax as an argument against the theory. Astronomers had a rough figure for the radius of Earth's orbit and some idea of the extent of the solar system, but there did not seem to be a way to determine stellar distances that did not require the assumption that all stars had the same intrinsic brightness.

Earlier attempts at measuring parallax involved circumventing the problem of the immeasurably small parallax by looking at two stars that appeared to be very near to each other but were of different brightnesses. It was thought that the dimmer star would be farther away and that observing the relative change of position could lead to a determination of stellar distances. This method did not work, because not all stars are of the same intrinsic brightness. Most stars that appear near to each other are in fact binary stars and really are near each other.

Bessel used a different approach: He assumed that stars with large proper motions are closer than stars with small proper motions. He chose the star known as 61 Cygni, because it had the largest proper motion known. He used a new measuring device called the Fraunhofer heliometer (after Joseph von Fraunhofer, a nineteenth century optician), which was designed to measure the angular diameter of the sun and the planets. Its manner of comparing the images from two objects to determine angular diameter was more accurate than earlier instruments. Using nearby stars for comparison and observing for eighteen months, Bessel was able to measure a parallax of slightly under one-third of a second of arc, which is equal to the width of a dime viewed from twenty miles. From this amount of parallax, Bessel calculated that 61 Cygni was 10.9 light years or seventy trillion miles away. He completed his calculations and published the results in 1838.

The last six years of Bessel's life were marked by deteriorating health, but he managed to complete a number of works before his death from cancer in 1846.

Summary

Friedrich Wilhelm Bessel made important contributions to astronomy, mathematics, and geodesy. His work marks the turning point from a concern with planetary, solar, and lunar observations to investigations of the stars. His measurement of the distance to a star is noteworthy because it settled the centuries-old question of whether stars exhibited parallax. The care he took in his observations set much higher standards for the science of astronomy. Bessel's goal was to observe the stars accurately enough to predict their motion and to establish a reference system for their positions. As part of that plan, he developed methods for the careful determination of instrument and observer error, conducted years of observations himself, and de-

veloped the mathematical techniques to reduce the data. Bessel's lasting achievement was to raise the science of observing, reducing, and correcting astronomical data to an art.

Bibliography

Clerke, Agnes. *A Popular History of Astronomy During the Nineteenth Century.* New York: Macmillan, 1887; London: Black, 1893. Although written during the period it was supposed to cover, this work has several redeeming qualities. Expressly written for a general audience, the book's language is clear and precise. A valuable record of what near-contemporaries thought of Bessel.

Herrmann, Dieter B. *The History of Astronomy from Herschel to Hertzsprung.* Translated by Kevin Krisciunos. Cambridge and New York: Cambridge University Press, 1984. Traces the history of astronomy from 1780 to 1930. Written from a Marxist perspective.

Hoskin, Michael A. *Stellar Astronomy: Historical Studies.* Chalfont, England: Science History Publications, 1982. A collection of material published in *Journal for the History of Astronomy*, with the addition of some new material. Attempts a synthesis of existing scholarship on the history of stellar (as opposed to planetary) astronomy as of the early 1980's.

Pannekoek, Anton. *A History of Astronomy.* London: Allen and Unwin, and New York: Interscience, 1961. Traces the history of astronomy from antiquity to the present. Part 3, "Astronomy Surveying the Universe," contains information on Bessel and places him in the historical context of nineteenth century astronomy.

Williams, Henry Smith. *The Great Astronomers.* New York: Simon and Schuster, 1930. Book 5 deals with Bessel, among other subjects. Concerns parallax and Bessel's contributions to measuring the distance to 61 Cygni. Describes the work of Bessel's contemporaries who measured the parallax of other stars at about the same time.

Roger Sensenbaugh

SIR HENRY BESSEMER

Born: January 19, 1813; Charlton, Hertfordshire, England

Died: March 15, 1898; London, England

Areas of Achievement: Invention and technology

Contribution: Bessemer developed and patented the Bessemer process for purifying molten iron. As a result, steel production increased and its cost was cut in half within the next dozen years, ushering in the "Age of Steel."

Early Life

Henry Bessemer was born on January 19, 1813, in Charlton in Hertfordshire, just north of London, where his father, Anthony Bessemer, was an engineer and typefounder. Young Bessemer grew up in his father's shops and, aside from an elementary education in local schools, soon demonstrated the initiative, inventiveness, and artistic talent that had characterized his parent. Anthony had moved to Holland from London as a young engineer, helping to erect the first steam pumping engine there, and went on to Paris to become a member of the French Academy of Sciences because of his skills, including engraving, die-sinking, and the invention of a copying machine. The French Revolution forced the family to flee to England, where the elder Bessemer started a firm making gold chains and then with William Caslon turned to manufacturing in the more profitable line of typefounding. Until the age of seventeen, Henry labored in his father's workshop in Charlton; in 1830, his family moved to London, where he began his own trade in artwork of white metal.

At the age of twenty, in 1833, Bessemer married Anne Allen, daughter of Richard Allen of Amersham, in London; their marriage proved to be a long and happy one; she lived until June, 1897, less than a year before he died. They had two sons and a daughter who lived into the twentieth century. Anne's three brothers joined her husband in his bronze and steel enterprises: John and Richard Allen managed the secret operations of the bronze works which Henry eventually turned over to Richard; William D. Allen aided in the steel experiments and then ran the steelworks at Sheffield. The Bessemers spent most of their lives in three homes: first the Baxter House, at St. Pancras, to which were added large buildings for Bessemer's experimental work and the bronze factory; then Charlton,

a country house and grounds; and finally, Denmark Hill, a home he enlarged with spacious grounds and gardens.

Photographs of Bessemer depict a man with a stern countenance, a short neck, and heavy eyebrows and side whiskers beneath a balding crown.

Life's Work

Three major inventions occupied most of Bessemer's active life. His first activities in artwork in white metal led him into copper-coating castings and then embossing metals, cards, and fabrics. He showed some of his work at exhibitions of the Royal Academy at Somerset House. There, Sir Charles Presley accepted his suggestion that forging and reusing old stamps on deeds and documents could be permanently halted by use of a perforated die with a date so that each parchment or paper would be pierced by the application of the government stamp. Bessemer was promised a government job in return for his invention, which was to save the British government an estimated 100,000 pounds annually. Months passed, however, and Bessemer was never rewarded for the new government stamp, which was installed by an act of Parliament on August 29, 1833. Years later, when the British ambassador refused him permission to accept the Grand Cross of the French Legion of Honor, Bessemer sought and received recognition for his invention. He was granted a knighthood in 1879.

During the 1830's, Bessemer also worked successfully on compressing plumbago dust into marking material for cheaper black-lead pencils. He then designed a machine to make type for printers and later created a type-composing machine with a pianolike keyboard for James Young, who patented the device. He also created a device and method for stamping or embossing on Utrecht velvet.

Bessemer's second great invention he dared not patent, but kept as a family secret for more than thirty-five years at great profit to himself and his brothers-in-law, who ran a plant for making bronze powder from solid brass. Replacing the secret pounding process of the German and Oriental suppliers of these "gold" powders—used to tint paints of all kinds—Bessemer devised a way of cutting tiny flakes from a solid bar of brass on a lathe, polishing and tinting them, and finally blowing them into graded sizes. What was most impressive about his bronze-powder project was the extreme secrecy essential to designing the entire series of shop machines and equipment for the bronze manufacturing process. To prevent anyone from learning about the secret process, Bessemer had to design each part of each machine personally, then send each part to be manufactured to different firms in four different cities. Later, he and his relatives assembled the entire lot in the closed buildings erected behind his Baxter House. With only a few modifications, the entire plant was started without trouble, and the tiny bottles of various colored bronze powder were sold for high profits by the family. Bessemer's income alone was large enough to finance his experiments for the rest of his career.

In 1849, the British inventor met a Jamaican sugar-planter who told him of the problems involved in crushing sugar juices from the stocks of cane. When the Society of Arts and Prince Albert offered a gold medal for the person who could effect the greatest improvement in sugarcane production, Bessemer began a serious effort to solve those problems. Instead of the traditional rolling action of sugar mills, he developed a lightweight, movable press with hydraulic pressure that compressed six-inch lengths of cane, producing a higher percentage of sugar than any other sugar mill. He patented the first of thirteen sugar-related inventions in 1849 and won the Gold Medal the next year.

At the London Crystal Palace International Exhibition in 1851, Bessemer exhibited his version of an early centrifugal pump, which he had patented two years earlier. He spent many hours each week as a consultant to other inventors and manufacturers who came to his office for advice.

The famous Bessemer process for making steel was his most important invention, for which the Patent Office of Great Britain granted him patent number 356, dated February 12, 1856. Between 1853 and 1883, Bessemer won more than seventy-five patents in England for making iron and steel, for construction of the Bessemer converter, and for numerous soft steel products that evolved from his extensive experimentation.

In the 1850's, already a well-established inventor, Bessemer turned his attention to finding a cheaper way to make malleable iron. Cast-iron (twelve-pounder) cannon used in the Crimean War were not strong enough to fire the twenty-four-pound and thirty-pound revolving projectiles which Bessemer had presented to the French government. Yet Bessemer's projectile had proven itself; he came home

with a burning desire to develop metal to build stronger cannon. While testing his small open-hearth furnace (some ten years before the Siemens-Martin patent on the open-hearth method of steel-making), Bessemer accidentally discovered what he thought were two unmelted pieces of pig iron at the mouth of the furnace. Examination of them indicated that "they were merely thin shells of decarburized iron . . . showing that atmospheric air alone was capable of wholly decarburizing grey pig iron, and converting it into malleable iron without puddling or any other manipulation." Further trials led Bessemer to create a new style "Bessemer Converter," with a movable furnace that tipped on its side while loading hot pig iron or pouring molten steel but which turned upright during the thirty-minute heating process. Air was forced into the furnace from the bottom below the melted pig iron, gradually consuming the silicon. As the carbon in the iron was burned, it created a much-intensified heat which purified the iron into steel. That first successful melting of pig iron into steel was exciting to the British inventor, and he reflected the wonderment of that event in his autobiography: "All this was a revelation to me, as I had in no way anticipated such violent results." His friend George Rennie, an engineer, was invited to see the process and persuaded Bessemer to present his discovery to the British Association for the Advancement of Science, meeting at Cheltenham, Gloucestershire, on August 13, 1856. The complete address, titled "The Manufacture of Iron Without Fuel," was published in *The Times* of London on August 14, and within a few weeks Bessemer sold licenses to British ironmasters worth more than twenty-seven thousand pounds. This money repaid much of his costs and contributed to further research that gradually made the process commercially viable.

Within the next several years, Bessemer overcame many serious problems still plaguing his steelmaking process. Obtaining quantities of phosphorous-free iron for British steel manufacturers forced him to import Swedish ore until he could get pig iron from British mines refined sufficiently to make mild steel. He learned to add ferromanganese or spiegeleisen to remove excess oxygen, a technique patented by Robert Forester Mushet in 1856 in England (Bessemer claimed that he had previously developed the process but later granted Mushet an annual allowance as partial settlement of his claims). Eventually, Bessemer furnaces were lined with a special fire brick that aided in the removal of phosphorous; after 1878, the more widely available phosphorous iron ores expanded the tonnage of Bessemer steel production.

Much like Thomas Edison, Bessemer quickly turned many of his inventions into commercial enterprises, thereby accumulating a small fortune. In 1858, he founded his own steel plant at Sheffield. There, he designed all the supplementary equipment to support the Bessemer furnaces; in 1860, he was granted a patent on his movable converter with hydraulic controls. The five partners, including Bessemer and his brother-in-law William D. Allen, who ran the works, eventually sold the plant after fourteen years "for exactly twenty-four times the amount of the whole subscribed capital of the firm, notwithstanding that we had divided in profits during the partnership a sum equal to fifty-seven times the gross capital." As production increased in the 1860's and 1870's, the price of Bessemer steel dropped rapidly. The transportation industries were the first to benefit.

The first steel rail, laid down as a test between two iron rails, was installed on May 9, 1862, at the busy Camden Goods Station of the London and North-

Western Railway; it outlasted iron rails by seven times in two years and was only slightly worn when exhibited at a trade show. The railroad industry of Europe and the United States soon adopted the new steel rails at great savings and with added safety.

While boiler plate made from steel soon became an important use of the more durable metal in steam locomotives and steamships, the development of steel for shipbuilding, particularly for the rise of new naval vessels with protective armor plate, consumed millions of tons of steel. In 1863, at the age of fifty, Bessemer saw the first Bessemer steel used in the construction of a steel steamship.

At the end of the Civil War, the first Bessemer works built in the United States were opened by A. L. Holley at Troy, New York, in 1865. He had gone to England in 1864 and purchased the license to make steel under the Bessemer process and the right to use the Bessemer converter and machinery. A Michigan firm, however, had obtained the Mushet patent rights for the United States to use along with the Kelly Pneumatic Process, patented by the American inventor of a similar steel process. Consolidation of the two firms led to the construction of the Wyandotte Iron Works near Detroit, which made the steel rolled into rails by the North Chicago Rolling Mill on November 24, 1865, for track of the Chicago and Northwestern Railroad.

William Kelly in Eddyville, Kentucky, had worked seven or more years near the Ohio River making malleable iron for sugar kettles for farmers and boiler plate for Cincinnati steamboat builders. After 1851, he erected a series of converters and learned that the carbon in pig iron could be burned out by air alone, since the carbon itself acted as a fuel if heated enough. When he learned that Bessemer had been granted a United States patent on November 11, 1856, Kelly quickly filed his own claim and on July 23, 1857, he was awarded a patent and an interference that placed his claim ahead of Bessemer. Unfortunately, in the Panic of 1857, Kelly went bankrupt and eventually lost all chance of income from his pioneering work.

Summary

At the age of fifty-nine, Sir Henry Bessemer retired from all business enterprises and devoted nearly a quarter of a century to four new pursuits: construction of an observatory and telescope, experiments with a solar furnace, installation of a diamond-polishing factory for his grandson, and his autobiography.

Many honors and awards were presented to Bessemer in his lifetime. Perhaps the highest was also the longest in coming, for on June 26, 1879, he was knighted by Queen Victoria at Windsor Castle for his unpatented invention of a stamp for dating government documents and deeds. The French government offered Bessemer the Legion of Honor award in 1856, but he was not allowed to accept it by his own nation. The Society of Arts conferred upon him its Albert Gold Medal in 1872 for his achievements in steel manufacturing. He was one of the founders of the Iron and Steel Institute and served for a time as its president; he established the Bessemer Gold Medal of that body to be granted to distinguished metallurgists of the world thereafter. In 1877, Bessemer was elected to the Institution of Civil Engineers; in 1879, he was made a Fellow in the Royal Society of London. Many other societies made him an honorary member for his inventions; at least six steelmaking towns and counties in the United States were named for him.

Within fifty-six years he was awarded 114 patents by the British Patent office, a record of achievement which reflects the ingenuity of the man and the spirit of inquiry that motivated him far beyond any monetary rewards.

Bibliography

Bessemer, Sir Henry, *Sir Henry Bessemer, F.R.S.: An Autobiography.* London: Offices of "Engineering," 1905; Brookfield, Vt.: Institute of Metals, 1989. This autobiography, with a concluding chapter by Bessemer's son, is a rambling collection of the inventor's reminiscences and letters about his unique experiments, discoveries, patents, and manufacturing ventures. Development of the Bessemer process for making steel is related in 200 of the 380 pages of text; numerous illustrations and fifty plates help make this volume the major source of all that has been written about the process and the inventor.

Boucher, John N. *William Kelly: A True History of the So-called Bessemer Process.* Greensburg, Pa.: Private printing, 1924. This biography presents an American counterclaim that William Kelly of Eddyville, Kentucky, a native of Pittsburgh, discovered and used the "pneumatic process" successfully in converting molten pig iron into malleable iron (steel) at least seven years before Bessemer patented his process. The United States Patent Office upheld Kelly's claim and granted him a patent in 1857, but the British exports of Bessemer rails and Bessemer converters swamped the American market and Kelly's bankruptcy prevented him from gaining any financial rewards for his achievements in the Ohio Valley.

Derry, T. K., and Trevor I. Williams. *A Short History of Technology: From the Earliest Times to A.D. 1900.* Oxford: Clarendon Press, 1960; New York: Oxford University Press, 1961. This text is a sequel to the five-volume *A History of Technology* (see below). Good coverage of the Industrial Revolution, and a chapter on "Coal and the Metals" includes developments in the making of inexpensive steel. Comparative tables showing chronological events of technological achievements in Great Britain, the Continent, and the United States, along with a selected bibliography for each chapter enhance this introductory study.

Singer, Charles, ed. *A History of Technology.* 5 vols. Oxford: Clarendon Press, and New York: Oxford University Press, 1954-1958. Volume 5 covers the late nineteenth century, 1850 to 1900. Chapter 3, on the steel industry, is especially useful. The impact of Bessemer's inventions in the steel industry is best seen in histories of the railroads, steamshipping, and structural steel industries, which burgeoned as a result of the manufacture of low-priced steel. The Bessemer process dominated the production of steel until the turn of the century; after 1900, the Siemens-Martin open-hearth process outstripped both the tonnage and cost of the Bessemer process steel.

Paul F. Erwin

FRIEDRICH VON BEUST

Born: January 13, 1809; Dresden, Saxony

Died: October 24, 1886; Altenberg Castle, Austro-Hungarian Empire

Areas of Achievement: Diplomacy, government, and politics

Contribution: Beust played a leading role from his position in the Saxon government in suppressing the Revolutions of 1848 in the German states and in formulating reactionary policies adopted by the governments of those states over the following two decades. First in the Saxon government, then in the Austrian, he was Otto von Bismarck's most formidable opponent during the Prussian chancellor's attempt to unify the small German states under the leadership of Prussia. Beust was also the architect of the political settlement in 1868 which created the Austro-Hungarian Empire.

Early Life

Friedrich Ferdinand von Beust was the scion of an aristocratic Saxon family whose members had served the Saxon monarchy for more than three centuries by the time he was born in Dresden on January 13, 1809. His father, an officer in the Saxon court, married the daughter of a Saxon government official just prior to the Napoleonic Wars, which formed the backdrop to Beust's early life.

When the Napoleonic Wars ended in 1815, the diplomats representing all the nations of Europe gathered in Vienna to establish a new political order in Europe, or, more accurately, to restore insofar as possible the old order that had been destroyed by the French Revolution and Napoleon I. Although there was widespread popular support in the German states for the creation of a nation which would include all German-speaking people, nationalist hopes were frustrated through the machinations of the Austrian representative at the Congress of Vienna, Metternich. The German universities remained hotbeds of support for the unification of the small German states under a liberal, constitutional government until 1819, when Metternich convinced the leaders of all the German states to suppress the *Burchenschaften*, the student fraternities in the universities which had been among the most enthusiastic and sometimes violent organizations calling for the unification of Germany. By the time Beust entered the University of Leipzig, the voices of liberalism and nationalism had been legally silenced on German campuses.

Beust's parents determined that he should pursue the traditional career of his family and sent him to the Universities of Leipzig and Göttingen to study law and government. Accordingly, he entered the University of Leipzig in 1826, when the repressive policies imposed on the German states by Metternich in 1819 were effectively stifling liberal and nationalist ideas. The professors who lectured in Beust's classes were largely champions of the status quo and critical of liberalism and nationalism. His own opposition to those two powerful forces of the nineteenth century formed during his university years and determined the course of his life.

After completing his studies, Beust entered the Saxon bureaucracy in 1830 and married a Bavarian heiress chosen for him by his parents. He served in various diplomatic capacities in Berlin, Paris, Munich, and London, where he gained a reputation as a capable spokesman for conservatism before assuming the post of Saxon foreign minister in 1849.

Life's Work

Beust immediately became the most influential member of the Saxon ministry and was primarily responsible for its reactionary policies in 1849. On Beust's advice, the Saxon king rejected the constitution proclaimed by the Frankfurt Parliament. The parliament, composed of elected representatives from all the German states, came into being as a result of the Revolutions of 1848, which convulsed most of Europe. In 1849, it attempted to promulgate a constitution which would have established a union of all the German states. The government of the new nation would have been a constitutional monarchy with a parliament elected by universal manhood suffrage. The rejection of the Frankfurt constitution in Saxony led to the outbreak of revolution in the capital city of Dresden. Beust's first act as foreign minister was to request military assistance from Prussia to suppress the revolutionaries, who included among their numbers Mikhail Bakunin and Richard Wagner. Both men gained considerable prominence in later years and were among Beust's most outspoken critics. The assistance was quickly forthcoming. Consequently, Beust fell into disrepute with German liberals and nationalists but became the hero of conservatives and reactionaries throughout the German states.

Upon the successful suppression of the revolt, Beust assumed the ministry of education and public worship in addition to his duties as foreign minister. For the next decade and a half, he was the dominant force in the Saxon government. He reorganized the police and used them to crush resistance to the monarchy, including especially student demonstrations at the university. The next year, he overthrew the liberal constitution adopted in Saxony in 1848 and restored the full powers and prerogatives of the monarchy. In 1851, he sided with Austria in that country's successful effort diplomatically to defeat an effort by Frederick William IV of Prussia to unify the small German states under Prussian leadership. In 1853, Beust assumed the Ministry of Internal Affairs and the post of Minister-President of Saxony in addition to his other duties, making him by far the most powerful individual in the country.

With the domestic situation well in hand, Beust devoted most of his attention to foreign affairs after 1853. He became the leader of the aristocratic faction in the German states which opposed a political or economic unification of Germany. He took the lead in proposing at the Bamberg Conference in 1854 that the small German states should form a closer union among themselves to make them better able to resist pressure from the two great monarchies, Austria and Prussia. Largely through Beust's efforts, the unification of Germany was delayed for yet another decade.

In 1864, Beust's policies led him into a direct conflict with the Chancellor of Prussia, Otto von Bismarck, who was intent on territorially aggrandizing the state of Prussia at the expense of the small German states. At Bismarck's urging, the Prussian press began vitriolic denunciations of Beust in that year, condemning him as a "particularist" (one who wished to preserve the independence of the small states within the Germanic Confederation). When Bismarck's policies of expansion led to war with Austria in 1866, Beust convinced the Saxon king to side with the Austrians. Beust tried to rescue a disastrous situation after the Austrian defeat at Hradec Kralové by traveling to France and seeking aid from Napoleon III, but his mission failed. He then resigned his post when Bismarck refused to negotiate with him at the ensuing peace conference. It appeared that Beust's public career was over, but events proved otherwise.

Unexpectedly, Austrian Emperor Franz Joseph asked Beust to assume the duties of Austrian foreign minister in December, 1866 (he became Minister-President of Austria the following year). The Hungarians had used the opportunity presented by Austria's defeat at the hands of Prussia to pursue their ancient dream of independence. Beust's primary responsibility when he assumed his new post was somehow to pacify the Hungarians and preserve the empire intact. The result of Beust's efforts was the creation of the so-called dual monarchy of Austria-Hungary which in effect granted the Hungarians control of their own domestic affairs but left their foreign policy in the hands of the Habsburg monarchy.

In 1868, Beust was appointed Chancellor of the Empire and awarded the title of count. He continued to direct the foreign policy of his adopted empire. Initially, he remained adamantly opposed to Bismarck's ambitions and consequently sought close relations with France. Even after the defeat of the French at the hands of Prussia in 1870-1871 and the proclamation by Bismarck of the German Empire, Beust was unwilling to accept the idea of a unified Germany. When it became obvious that there was nothing he could do to reverse the decision of the war, Beust reluctantly sought a détente with Bismarck, who accepted eagerly, since it meant Austrian recognition of the new German Empire. In July, 1871, Beust announced the agreement to his governments and consummated it with a personal meeting with Bismarck at Gastein the next month.

Later that year, Beust managed to dissuade Franz Joseph from instating a plan to grant greater local autonomy to the various ethnic groups within the empire. Very shortly thereafter, he was relieved of his post as chancellor without explanation. He requested and received appointment as Austrian ambassador to England, in which capacity he served for seven years. In 1878, he was transferred to Paris, where he retired from public life four years later. Beust died at his villa at Altenberg (near Vienna) on October 24, 1886.

Summary

Friedrich von Beust was a leading spokesman for those aristocratic elements in the Germanic Confederation that successfully prevented the democratic unification of the German states in 1848-1849. He was also instrumental in preventing a more authoritarian but still peaceful unification in 1851. Taken together, his successes prepared the way for the creation of the German Empire by force of arms completed under Bismarck's leadership and the distinctly Prussian and militarist nature of the new state which resulted. In addition, the delaying tactics adopted by Beust and those he represented against the installation of representative, constitutional government exacerbated the class conflicts that convulsed the German states throughout the latter half of the nineteenth century and contributed both to the coming of World War I and to the eventual triumph of National Socialism in the first half of the twentieth century.

The opposition of Beust and those he represented to pluralism in the Austrian Empire also had disastrous consequences long after Beust died. The struggle of the various ethnic groups within and without the empire for autonomy or self-determination led directly to the events at Sarajevo in June of 1914 that sparked the outbreak of World War I, with calamitous results for all nations involved. Beust alone did not bring about the apocalyptic events of the first half of the twentieth century. He was, however, a clever and effective champion of the policies that led directly to the catastrophic events that befell the generations of Germans that came after him.

An ancient proverb holds that the road to Hell is paved with good intentions. Beust's intentions from his own perspective were good. He intended to preserve intact the institutions of pre-1848 Europe and to crush the twin threats of liberalism and nationalism which would destroy those institutions. His very success paved the road to the modern hell of total war.

Bibliography

Beust, Friedrich von. *Memoirs of Friedrich Ferdinand, Count von Beust*. Translated by Henry de Worms. 2 vols. London: Remington, 1887; St. Clair Shores, Mich.: Scholary Press, 1972. Beust's memoirs offer a wealth of information about the man and his policies but must be used with great caution because of Beust's tendencies toward self-glorification and magnification of his own importance in the unfolding of historical events.

Ellis, William Ashton. *1849*. London: Remington, 1892. This is the only book-length treatment of the Saxon revolution available in English. Ellis is very critical of Beust's role in the events of 1849, describing him as the chief culprit in the crushing of liberal democracy in Saxony.

Kann, Robert A. *The Multinational Empire: Nationalism and National Reform in the Habsburg Monarchy 1848-1918*. 2 vols. New York: Columbia University Press, 1950. Kann's book is the most complete account of Beust's career in the Austrian government. Kann treats Beust kindly and is especially complimentary concerning Beust's role in the formation of the dual monarchy.

May, Arthur J. *The Hapsburg Monarchy, 1867-1914*. Cambridge, Mass.: Harvard University Press, 1951. May offers a balanced account of Beust's career in the Austrian government. Beust emerges from May's pages as an egotistical but competent statesman.

Taylor, A. J. P. *The Habsburg Monarchy, 1809-1918: A History of the Austrian Empire and Austria-Hungary*. Rev. ed. London: Hamilton, 1948; Chicago: University of Chicago Press, 1976. An outstanding account of Beust's foreign and domestic policies during his career in the Austrian government, including especially his duel with Bismarck.

Paul Madden

NICHOLAS BIDDLE

Born: January 8, 1786; Philadelphia, Pennsylvania
Died: February 27, 1844; Philadelphia, Pennsylvania
Areas of Achievement: Finance and banking
Contribution: Combining superb managerial skills and a keen understanding of finance and banking, Biddle developed the Bank of the United States into a prototype of the modern central banking system.

Early Life

Nicholas Biddle, born January 8, 1786, in Philadelphia, Pennsylvania, was descended from one of the most distinguished families in Pennsylvania. His father, Charles Biddle, was a successful merchant and had become vice president of the Supreme Executive Council of Pennsylvania. His mother, Hannah Shepard Biddle, was the daughter of a North Carolina merchant. Nicholas was extremely precocious and was admitted at the age of ten to the University of Pennsylvania. His parents transferred him before he was graduated, and he was entered in Princeton as a sophomore at the age of thirteen. Nicholas was graduated in September, 1801, at the age of fifteen, as the valedictorian.

Biddle began the study of law, but his personal interests seemed to mark him for a literary career. He contributed two pieces to Joseph Dennie's literary magazine, *The Port Folio*, which showed considerable talent. Then, in the fall of 1804, Biddle went with General John Armstrong, Jr. who had been appointed minister to France, as his secretary. He assisted ably in the duties of handling claims authorized in the Louisiana Purchase, gaining valuable insights into the problems and techniques of international finance. After a year, he departed on a grand tour of Europe, including a visit to Greece. He served briefly as secretary for James Monroe in London, and he finally returned to the United States in September, 1807.

Biddle had reached his adult height of five feet, seven inches. He had a handsome oval face, a high forehead, and chestnut eyes and hair. He had a serious and dignified demeanor and an aristocratic bearing. He decided to practice law, but he also found time to make contributions to Dennie's *The Port Folio*. In 1810, he was persuaded by William Clark to edit the journals of the Lewis and Clark Expedition. Biddle did most of the work, but the journals were eventually published under another editor's name.

In October, 1810, he was elected to the Pennsylvania legislature. The highlight of this service was an eloquent defense of the first Bank of the United States. He displayed a knowledge of finance that impressed all listeners. Biddle declined renomination. One reason was that he had met and later married Jane Craig, whose father's estate was one of the largest in Philadelphia. During the War of 1812, he returned to the Pennsylvania legislature and vigorously supported the war effort, parting company with his fellow Federalists.

Secure financially, Biddle spent the next few years managing his country estate, "Andalusia," and engaging in civic and philanthropic activities. In 1818, he was defeated in a race for Congress, in part because his republicanism was still suspect and because of internal splits in Pennsylvania. President Monroe, although a good friend, hesitated to appoint Biddle to office. When mismanagement occurred in the operation of the second Bank of the United States, however, and the president of the bank, William Jones, was removed early in 1819, Biddle was one of the directors chosen by the government. For the next twenty years, his life revolved around the bank.

Life's Work

Langdon Cheves of South Carolina, who replaced Jones as president of the bank, followed a policy of retrenchment. "The bank was saved," as they said in the Southwestern part of the United States, "but the people were ruined." When Cheves resigned in 1822, Biddle was chosen as the bank's third president. The position he assumed was one of the most important in the United States. The bank was in sound financial condition, but Cheves's policies had alienated many. Biddle gradually dropped many of the restrictions imposed upon the operations of the branch banks. Enlargement of the credit operations stimulated the economy, which was still suffering from the effects of the Panic of 1819. He also increased the profits of the bank and gradually gained complete control over its operations.

From his splendid Greek Revival building on Chestnut Street in Philadelphia, Biddle controlled the operations of eventually twenty-nine branches, from New Hampshire to New Orleans. He used the power of the bank to expand and contract the credit and money supply according to the fluctuations in business activity. He was a superb administrator.

The result was a sound banking system and a stable currency that greatly benefited the country.

Biddle's success won for him many friends and growing support for the bank. He sought to avoid involving the bank in politics and tried to remain neutral in the presidential race between President John Quincy Adams and Andrew Jackson in 1828. Biddle was well aware that there were still many powerful people who were hostile toward the bank, and that one was Jackson himself.

After Jackson's election, some members of his party attempted to gain control of the bank. Allegations were made that some branches had exercised an improper influence in the past election by refusing loans to Jacksonians. Biddle was overly sensitive about bank operations. He tended to be defensive rather than to investigate fully charges of mismanagement. Nor did Bidde at first appreciate the depth of President Jackson's hostility to the Bank of the United States. Jackson had a prejudice against all banks based on little more than economic ignorance and some bad personal experiences with bank notes. A large number of voters also believed that the bank, with one-fifth of the country's loans and bank notes in circulation, and one-third of the total bank deposits and specie (gold and silver), had too much money and power for the safety of the Republic. The bank was further opposed by a group who believed that it unfairly restricted loans and denied them economic opportunities, and by yet another group of state bankers and their stockholders who resented the size, wealth, and controlling influence of the bank. Despite this opposition, a substantial majority of the American people supported the bank and favored its recharter.

Jackson's attitude and the hostility of many of the advisers around him toward the bank made Biddle uncertain about the prospect of rechartering the bank. Despite conflicting advice, he chose to ask for the rechartering in 1832, four years early, basically because it was an election year and Biddle believed that Jackson would not oppose the bank for fear of losing popularity.

The recharter bill passed both houses in the summer of 1832 by comfortable margins. Biddle had miscalculated: Jackson was not easily intimidated. He responded with a veto and denounced the Bank of the United States as a monopoly, under too much foreign influence, and unconstitutional, and he asserted that it was an institution of the rich and powerful. The message was blatantly misleading,

but it was undeniably a powerful and cleverly written polemic, well calculated to appeal to the prejudices of the mass of American people. Despite the goodwill that Biddle had built up for the bank, Jackson successfully changed the debate from the utility of the bank to whether it was a bastion of aristocratic privilege. He portrayed himself as saving the Republic from the "monster."

Although his victory was more a personal triumph than approval of his stand against the bank, Jackson resolved to destroy the bank. He directed the removal of government deposits, which would be placed in state banks, dubbed "pet banks" by opponents. Biddle responded by curtailing loans. While this action may have been necessary to protect the bank from a reduction of funds (and almost ten million dollars in government deposits were withdrawn), the effect of this restriction on credit staggered commercial and manufacturing interests. Business failures and bankruptcies multiplied, and wages and prices declined. Biddle was not entirely to blame; in fact, he thought that it would ultimately force Jackson to restore the deposits. Neither man was willing to budge. Public opinion, initially anti-Jackson, slowly turned against Biddle. Jackson was unrelenting. He administered a final blow to the Bank of the United States, declaring that the government would no longer accept branch drafts for the payment of taxes.

With the death of the bank imminent, in 1836 Biddle secured a charter from the Pennsylvania legislature to operate as a state bank. There was no longer a central bank to keep the state banks in order by calling upon them for specie or refusing to receive their bills. Moreover, the American economy was overheating as a result of speculation in large measure stimulated by government deposits in pet banks, which then numbered approximately ninety. The country was inundated with paper money. The frenzy of speculation was brought to an abrupt end by the Panic of 1837. The United States Bank (as it had become known) was forced in May, 1837, to suspend payment of specie for the redemption of notes, as did all other banks in the country. Biddle was still the most prominent banker in the country, and he played an important role in trying to shore up the nation's banking system and restore specie payments. Biddle also intervened massively in the cotton market exchange, thus preventing the collapse of that important part of the American economy. He also turned a profit for his bank.

Resumption of specie payments began again in August, 1838. The economy seemed to be recovering, and Biddle, in March, 1839, intending to devote his remaining years to leisure, resigned. In the summer of 1839, however, largely because of the operations of the Bank of England, the United States and the remainder of the world was plunged again into depression. Biddle may have had the grim satisfaction of knowing that the lack of a national bank only made the situation worse, but it was small consolation, since it was also the source of the bank's and Biddle's ruin. Falling cotton prices and mismanagement by the bank's directors led to a second suspension of specie payments in October, 1839. The bank continued to operate, but its situation grew steadily worse, and the bank closed its doors forever in February, 1841.

Biddle's personal fortune, as well as the bank's, collapsed. In his last years, he was harassed by law suits, and at one point in 1842, he was arrested on charges of criminal conspiracy, but he was exonerated. Other litigations followed and were only brought to an end by his death on February 27, 1844, from complications arising from bronchitis accompanied by dropsy.

Summary

Despite his failures, Biddle was an imposing figure in American history. He had the qualities of a statesman who saw the potential of the American economy and formulated the means for realizing it. He wanted to establish American prosperity and to make the country stronger and more secure. His views were guided by a considerable intelligence, but by inclination he displayed more the traits of the idealist and the romantic than the hardheaded, pragmatic businessman. He showed a preference more for what ought to be than the situation as it was. His naïveté, even arrogance, that reason and truth would prevail in his battle with Jackson proved disastrous for the bank.

Biddle was a brilliant administrator who maintained complete control over the Bank of the United States; yet he also gave an aristocratic tone to the bank and lent credibility to the charge of its having excessive power. Because he saw the value of the bank to the nation's economy, he believed that all men of reason must see it as well. Jackson, he assumed, could not possibly destroy an institution that was in the best interest of the country. Even at the end, his actions were still guided by a larger view of the good of the country rather than the practicalities of sound business.

Perhaps, in retrospect, the country needed the *laissez-faire* economics that dominated the United States for the next three quarters of a century. The exuberant economic growth, however, was characterized by wild speculation and the persistence of monetary evils. The Bank of the United States offered a more "managed" economic growth and a more stable currency, but it might have dampened the enterprising spirit of American business. When the abuses of the "robber barons" brought on a reform movement in the early twentieth century, one reform was to reestablish a central banking system very similar to Biddle's bank.

Bibliography

Barth, Gunter. "Timeless Journals: Reading Lewis and Clark with Nicholas Biddle's Help." *Pacific Historical Review* 63, no. 4 (November 1994). Examines the most important discoveries made by Biddle in his reading of the journals of Lewis and Clark.

Catterall, Ralph C. H. *The Second Bank of the United States.* Chicago: University of Chicago Press, 1903. Although dated both in content and interpretation, this classic work is still the most comprehensive study of the bank.

Govan, Thomas Payne. *Nicholas Biddle: Nationalist and Public Banker, 1786-1844.* Chicago: University of Chicago Press, 1959. The only satisfactory biography of Biddle. The author is partial to his subject and presents a sensitive portrayal of Biddle's role in running the bank. The book is well researched and well written.

Hammond, Bray. *Banks and Politics in America from the Revolution to the Civil War.* Princeton, N.J.: Princeton University Press, 1957; Oxford: Princeton University Press, 1991. A Pulitzer Prize-winning book that is not simply about banking. Hammond pays particular attention to Biddle and gives a fair appraisal of him. Hammond's interpretation of the Bank War, while controversial, broke new ground.

McFaul, John M. *The Politics of Jacksonian Finance.* Ithaca, N.Y.: Cornell University Press, 1972. A good general study of the issues involved in the Bank War. The positions of probank and antibank forces are carefully analyzed.

McNeal, R. A. "Nicholas Biddle and the Literature of Greek Travel." *Classical Antiquity* 12, no. 1 (April 1993). As was customary for young men at the time, Biddle spent time in Greece. His experiences as recorded in his "Bildungsroman" are examined here, expanding the understanding of his biographical information and the travel literature of his day.

Remini, Robert V. *Andrew Jackson and the Bank War.* New York: Norton, 1968. A good, short introduction to the Bank War. Remini is partial to Jackson, but his account is generally a fair, succinct exposition of the issues.

Temin, Peter. *The Jacksonian Economy.* New York: Norton, 1969. Temin presents a provocative, revisionary interpretation of the sources of the Panic of 1837. While his analysis is not entirely convincing, he adds a new dimension to the study of the Bank War.

Wilburn, Jean Alexander. *Biddle's Bank: The Crucial Years.* New York: Columbia University Press, 1967. Wilburn refutes the Jacksonian allegation of the unpopularity of the bank. She shows the support for the bank's services from the people, their congressional representatives, and many local bankers.

C. Edward Skeen

AMBROSE BIERCE

Born: June 24, 1842; Horse Cave Creek, Ohio
Died: 1914 (?); Mexico (?)
Areas of Achievement: Journalism and literature
Contribution: A legendary cynic and social satirist, Bierce won local fame in San Francisco, California, as a newspaper and magazine columnist and secured a place in American literature with his nonrealist short stories, many of which are set against the backdrop of the American Civil War.

Early Life

Ambrose Gwinett Bierce was born in Horse Cave Creek, Ohio, the tenth of thirteen children born to Laura and Marcus Aurelius Bierce. When Bierce was four, the family moved to Indiana, where young Ambrose was raised among books and religion. At the age of fifteen, Bierce began work as a printer's devil for a local newspaper, and at seventeen he entered the Kentucky Military Institute. Soon after he left the institute, the Civil War broke out, and Bierce enlisted in the Ninth Regiment of the Indiana Volunteers. During his three years with the volunteers, Bierce was wounded in the head, won numerous citations for bravery, and rose to the rank of lieutenant.

After the war, Bierce recovered confiscated Confederate cotton for the federal government and then participated in a mapping expedition in the far West. This trip took Bierce to San Francisco, California, where he would make his home for most of his adult life and earn his name as a writer. Bierce worked as a columnist for a newspaper called the *News-Letter*, where, as the "Town Crier," he used biting satire and blatant sarcasm, as well as a strong dose of tall-tale humor, to attack public figures and institutions he considered guilty of hypocrisy. As he would throughout his career, Bierce angered many of those about whom he wrote and made numerous enemies, but his column quickly won a loyal following among readers. Bierce was not content with his local reputation in journalism, however. He sought literary respectability and national fame and began publishing poems, short stories, and essays in various publications. Literary success, however, was still far in the future.

Bierce married Molly Day in 1871, and a honeymoon trip took the couple to London, England, where Bierce wrote for the publications *Fun* and *Figaro* under the pen name Dod Grile. He also published three collections of columns, sketches, and fiction while in London: *The Fiend's Delight* (1873), *Nuggets and Dust Panned in California* (1873), and *Cobwebs from an Empty Skull* (1874). The cynicism expressed in these collections, as well as in the articles he wrote for London papers, earned him the nickname "Bitter Bierce."

Bierce reluctantly returned to San Francisco in 1875, thinking that his literary future lay in England. His career, both as a social satirist and as a short-story writer, however, was just about to flourish. Soon working again as a columnist, he became a mentor for several aspiring writers, and he appears to have loved the attention. He lived apart from his wife and family, frequently hosting literary discussions with his followers and writing through the night. His marriage would eventually fail, but Bierce the writer and man of letters was just hitting his stride.

Life's Work

Bierce won local fame—some might even say infamy—as a newspaper and magazine columnist, and the egotistical and cynical personality expressed through this writing has helped make Bierce a legendary figure in American letters. Bierce's most enduring legacy as a writer, however, is found in his short stories, two of which are among the most anthologized stories in American literature.

Between 1877, two years after his return from England, and 1913, when he would attach himself to Pancho Villa's army in the Mexican Revolution and never be heard from again (also part of his legend), Bierce continued his work as a columnist almost nonstop, even after his career as a short-story writer took off. He loved journalistic writing, particularly his brand of it, and he relished the attention, both good and bad, that it brought him. He was also never satisfied with the level of national attention he received for his fiction; thus Bierce the acid-tongued columnist never fully gave way to Bierce the fiction writer.

The most enduring work from Bierce's newspaper and magazine writing is a book entitled *The Devil's Dictionary* (1906), a collection of definitions published by Bierce in his columns over the years. It is Bierce the cynic at his very best, or worst, depending on one's point of view. Bierce defines "happiness" as "an agreeable sensation arising from contemplating the misery of another." A "dentist" is "a prestidigitator who, putting metal into your mouth, pulls coins out of your pocket," while a "lawyer" is "one skilled in circumvention of the law." "Alone" is an adjective meaning "in bad company," and Bierce defines "once" as "enough." Though *The Devil's Dictionary* has not proved as popular as his short stories over the years, Bierce's cynical definitions continue to delight many readers.

Bierce's career as a short story-writer blossomed in 1891 with the publication of *Tales of Soldiers and Civilians*, better known as *In the Midst of Life* (the title of the London edition). The stories of this one collection, with their bizarre, frequently supernatural, violent, and ironic nature, are what has earned Bierce his place in American literature. They are stories that clearly do not fit in with the realist, local-color literature of their time.

This last point is key to understanding why Bierce did not earn great fame with his fiction during his lifetime. Though he wrote almost all of his fiction during the realist movement in American literature, Bierce was blatantly nonrealist. Bierce believed that fiction should be *fiction*, that it should make use of the author's imagination and engage the reader's imagination. It should take the improbable, perhaps even the impossible, and make it seem real, rather than simply document the social reality of the time. It was this belief, which Bierce stubbornly held, that placed Bierce clearly outside the mainstream of American literature during his lifetime. It was also this belief, however, that made many of the stories of *In the Midst of Life* seem ahead of their time and therefore more appealing to later readers than to readers of Bierce's own time.

In the Midst of Life contains the author's most popular stories, two of which, "An Occurrence at Owl Creek Bridge" and "Chickamauga," rank among the most anthologized stories in American literature. Set against the backdrop of the American Civil War, as are so many of Bierce's stories, "An Occurrence at Owl Creek Bridge" relates the apparently bungled execution of a Southern conspirator who escapes the hangman's noose, flees downriver, and eventually makes it home to his waiting wife. Just as he is about to reach her, he feels a blow to the back of his neck. He is not home, but instead hangs dead below the Owl Creek bridge. His escape has been nothing more than an illusion played out in the mind of the about-to-be executed spy. Also set during the Civil War, "Chickamauga" tells of a small boy playing soldier with a wooden sword by himself in the woods. He gets lost and falls asleep on the ground for several hours. When he awakens, he sees the macabre sight of hundreds of wounded and dying soldiers retreating, almost zombielike, over where he lies. Rather than be frightened, he attempts to play with them. Eventually they reach the boy's plantation, which is immersed in flames. The boy finds his mother, who is mortally and grotesquely wounded about the head. He tries to scream out in horror, but he is a deaf mute, which explains how so much has happened around him as he slept. The chief irony of the story may be the one played on the reader, who, perhaps having read other Bierce stories or because of the dreamlike quality of the story once the boy wakes up, expects the graphic war scenes to be only a dream; they are, however, reality, which Bierce has presented in a most nonrealistic manner.

Other stories in *In the Midst of Life* that show Bierce's flare for everything from cruel irony to improbable reality to supernatural events include

"The Affair at Coulter's Notch," in which a Civil War artillery officer fires on his own plantation; "The Man and the Snake," in which a man literally dies of fright of what turns out to be a stuffed snake with shoe buttons for eyes; and "The Suitable Surroundings," in which a man dies after reading a ghost story in a haunted house.

More collections of creative writing followed *In the Midst of Life*. Bierce published *Black Beetles in Amber*, a book of satirical poems, in 1892, and *Can Such Things Be?*, a collection of stories, in 1893, but his career as a fiction writer had clearly peaked with *In the Midst of Life*. His fame, though more limited at the time than he had hoped, had been made as well. He moved to Washington, D.C., in 1896, and between 1896 and 1913 he continued to write for the *San Francisco Examiner* and later for the magazine *Cosmopolitan*, all the while assembling his complete works for publication. His *Devil's Dictionary* came out in 1906 under the title *The Cynic's Word Book*.

In 1913, Bierce left Washington and headed to Mexico to observe the Mexican Revolution. Except for a letter he wrote in December of 1913 regarding his experiences with Pancho Villa, he was never heard from again. It is not certain when, where, or how Bierce died.

Summary

Ambrose Bierce is one of the true rogue characters of American letters, as well as one of the most enigmatic ones. As a journalist, he was loved by his readers and despised in many cases by those who became the targets of his bitter wit, from railroad executives and political leaders to literary contemporaries. As cruel as he was in his newspaper column, he was also the mentor to many fledgling writers in his beloved San Francisco. Still, his cynical view of the world went so far as to manifest itself in an alternative lexicon—*The Devil's Dictionary*—for the language he manipulated first as a teenage typesetter and then later as an acclaimed fiction writer. That acclaim was less than he had hoped for, however, and it made "Bitter Bierce" clearly envious of the likes of Stephen Crane, whom he considered an inferior writer, and other more mainstream authors of his time.

Writing *when* he did rather than *what* he did was precisely Bierce's problem as a fiction writer hoping for wide critical and popular acceptance. As he did in so many areas of his life, Bierce the short-story writer chose to go against the grain, and this cost him; however, he was, as always, true to himself. Though he did not live to know it, the short-story writer who disappeared into revolutionary Mexico in 1913 actually would have been right at home in the nonrealist, psychological, post-Freudian fiction of the twentieth century as practiced by writers ranging from Franz Kafka to Jorge Luis Borges. It would be with the readers of this generation and beyond that Bierce would find a more accepting reading public for his stories.

Bibliography

Davidson, Cathy N. *The Experimental Fictions of Ambrose Bierce: Structuring the Ineffable*. Lincoln: University of Nebraska Press, 1984. Contends that Bierce served as a direct influence for three twentieth century writers, among them Argentines Jorge Luis Borges and Julio Cortázar. In-depth literary analysis for serious readers.

Grenander, M. E. *Ambrose Bierce*. New York: Twayne, 1971. Excellent and highly readable overview of Bierce's life and career with literary analysis. Includes chronology, annotated bibliography, and index. Part of Twayne's United States Authors Series.

Morris, Roy, Jr. *Ambrose Bierce: Alone in Bad Company*. New York: Crown, 1995. The definitive biography of Bierce. Includes some literary commentary, but it is not intended as a critical study of Bierce's works. Contains an extensive, though unannotated, secondary bibliography and a comprehensive index.

Saunders, Richard. *Ambrose Bierce: The Making of a Misanthrope*. San Francisco: Chronicle, 1985. Another insightful biography, though not as exhaustive as Morris. Includes a brief, unannotated bibliography and an index. Part of the Literary West Series.

Wiggins, Robert A. *Ambrose Bierce*. University of Minnesota Pamphlets on American Writers 37. Minneapolis: University of Minnesota Press, 1964. An excellent thumbnail sketch of Bierce's life and career that provides a good starting point for student readers. Includes some literary commentary.

Keith H. Brower

ALBERT BIERSTADT

Born: January 7, 1830; Solingen, Germany
Died: February 18, 1902; New York, New York
Area of Achievement: Art
Contribution: Using an exaggerated, romantic style, Bierstadt painted giant landscapes of spectacular Western vistas that helped to shape the myth of the American West, establish the Rocky Mountain School of art, and interest Easterners in preservation of Western scenic areas as national parks.

Early Life

Albert Bierstadt was born in 1830 at Solingen, Germany, near the city of Düsseldorf, which was a mecca for émigré American artists. He migrated to the United States with his parents at the age of two and was reared amid the maritime atmosphere in the whaling town of New Bedford, Massachusetts. He exhibited his first painting in Boston at the age of twenty-one but returned to Europe for further training at Düsseldorf and in Rome. On the Continent, he was attracted to pastoral scenes, sketching castles along the Rhine and taking hiking expeditions among the Alps. Bierstadt returned to the United States in 1857 and painted in New England. The following year the bearded, sharp-featured artist seized the opportunity to see the trans-Mississippi regions for the first time, when he joined Colonel Frederick W. Lander on a survey party that set out for the West from St. Louis. This expedition literally opened new vistas for Bierstadt and shaped the rest of his artistic career, establishing his place in the history of both the American West and American art.

The explorer, scientist, and artist traveled hand in hand and contributed jointly to the opening of the trans-Mississippi West and in the shaping of its image in the national consciousness. Prior to the exploration of the region, most American painters had slavishly imitated the themes and styles of their European counterparts and mentors. It was almost inevitable, however, that the rising tide of nationalism would find artistic expression, as the United States sought to establish its own and unique cultural identity. Two traditions, the scientific and the artistic, were eventually conjoined in that search.

The artistic tradition established its roots in the eastern part of the country during the 1820's and 1830's as several artists, including Thomas Cole and Asher B. Durand, honed the vision and produced the work that established the Hudson River School. They grappled with the balance between civilization and wilderness and focused upon the vistas of the Hudson River, the White Mountains, Niagara Falls, and other northeastern features as expressions of truth, beauty, and eternal laws and values. Their appreciation of and emphasis upon landscape and nature would shape the perceptions of later artists, including Bierstadt, who spent time at the emerging artists' colony at North Conway, New Hampshire, on the Saco River in the White Mountain region.

In the meantime, following the historic expedition of Meriwether Lewis and William Clark, explorers and scientists were beginning to penetrate the great unknown of the trans-Mississippi West. Their expeditions often enlisted artists who traveled along and sketched the plants, animals, people, and lands they encountered both for artistic purposes and to document visually the information acquired. They traveled and worked under primitive conditions foreign to the overwhelming majority of their artistic colleagues past and present, and

233

they were virtually to a man overwhelmed and deeply impressed by what they saw and recorded.

First were two Philadelphians, Samuel Seymour and Titian Ramsay Peale, who accompanied the Stephen Long expedition to the Rockies in 1820. They were soon followed by George Catlin, who made several trips up the Missouri River in the 1830's and produced pictorial records of the Plains Indians prior to extensive contact with white civilization. Later came the Swiss artist Karl Bodmer, who produced extremely accurate depictions of the Indians and painted landscapes of the American interior as well. In the late 1830's, Baltimore artist Alfred Jacob Miller traveled the Oregon Trail and depicted the world of the mountain man, and within a few more years John James Audubon was at work painting the animals along the Missouri River. These and other artists created the scientific-artistic tradition which was part of Albert Bierstadt's milieu.

Life's Work
After his return from Europe, Bierstadt learned of Colonel Frederick W. Lander's proposed expedition to prepare a survey for a railroad route from the Mississippi River, across the north fork of the Platte, through Nebraska Territory, across South Pass, and connecting with San Francisco and Puget Sound. Bierstadt and photographer F. S. Frost joined the party and in 1858-1859 journeyed as far as the Wasatch range on the western slope of the Rockies. They then returned on their own, traveling through the Wind River range and the land of the Shoshone, producing sketches and photographic images of the scenery and people they encountered. Bierstadt was thus the first artist to utilize photography to supplement his own sketches and watercolors while on a journey of Western exploration. Bierstadt and Frost paid their own way and none of their work from this expedition survives, but the artist had been captivated by what he had seen.

Upon returning to the East, Bierstadt relocated his studio from New Bedford to New York City, where in 1860 the first of his paintings went on public display. Among them was *The Base of the Rocky Mountains, Laramie Peak* which measured some four and a half by nine feet. This canvas was prototypical of the Bierstadt style, which the public enthusiastically applauded. It was characterized by a seeming realism, which in fact presented a romanticized and even falsified depiction of a Western scene on a grandiose scale. It reflected both the

romanticization of nature and the cultural nationalism which were to be representative of the Rocky Mountain School.

Bierstadt was soon getting higher prices in Europe for his paintings than any other American artist had ever received, and with his new wealth he built a large house on the Hudson River at Irvington and a second studio in San Francisco, which served as a base for further excursions into the Western regions. He traveled through the Colorado Rockies, the Great Salt Lake region, the Pacific Northwest, and in 1863 into California's Yosemite and Hetch Hetchy valleys, sketching the vistas which became the subjects for some of his most commercially successful paintings. A series of paintings of grandiose dimension, produced in the mid-1860's, sold for the highest sums ever earned by an American artist. Featuring towering mountains, shimmering waters, and dark forests, these canvases carried the romantic concepts of nature to their apex of grandeur. While some critics scoffed, the public loved the huge size and detail of the Bierstadt canvases.

The giant paintings were done in Bierstadt's studio, based on his field sketches, photographs, stereoscopic views, and watercolors. The artist rearranged the features, gave names to nonexistent locales, and generally falsified his portrayals, even as the public praised his "realism." It is not accidental that the growing interest of the American people in the spectacular land features of the West and their preservation coincided chronologically with the popularity of Bierstadt and Thomas Moran, whose paintings of Yellowstone would contribute to the creation of the national park in 1872.

Ironically, at the height of Bierstadt's popularity two trends were developing which would relegate his large canvases to relative obscurity and general critical disdain by the turn of the century. First, with the rise of the Impressionist style in Europe, realistic painters of the Romantic school fell out of fashion. Second, those who were interested in literal depictions of the West could now examine the striking photographs of William Henry Jackson and others who were elevating photography to the status of an art form.

Bierstadt continued to paint, and his elevated reputation secured large commissions, as in the late 1870's, when he received fifteen thousand dollars from the Earl of Dunraven to paint a large landscape of Estes Park, Colorado, and Long's Peak. Bierstadt's sales and commissions steadily diminished, however, even as his critical reputation continued to decline. By the time he died in 1902, fashion and popularity had passed him by.

Summary

Although not considered a great artist by most critics, Albert Bierstadt remains a major figure in the history of both American art and the trans-Mississippi West. A founder of the Rocky Mountain School, Bierstadt's giant landscapes of the American West—its mountains, forests, waterfalls, and spectacular landforms—brought romantic appreciation of nature to a new artistic peak in nineteenth century America. Although he took numerous liberties with fact in his larger works, the general public regarded Bierstadt's paintings as quite realistic, and he thus helped to generate the mythic perception of the American West and its landscapes that contributed to the movement for preservation of spectacular landforms in national parks. Ironically, although not as well-known as his large canvases, Bierstadt's smaller pieces and sketches, done during or immediately following journeys in the field, have retained a much higher critical standing. Bierstadt's works are found in major collections across the United States and have enjoyed constant popularity among those interested in the West and its history.

Bibliography

Anderson, N. "The European Roots of Albert Bierstadt's Views of the American West." *Magazine Antiques* 139, no. 1 (January 1991). Study of Bierstadt's landscapes of the American West and his techniques.

Hassrick, Peter. *The Way West: Art of Frontier America*. New York: Abrams, 1977. A profusely illustrated introduction to the work of major artists of the nineteenth century West, including Bierstadt.

Hendricks, Gordon. *Albert Bierstadt: Painter of the American West*. New York: Abrams, 1973. The standard biography. Makes extensive use of Bierstadt's letters. Of the 428 illustrations, sixty-three are in color. Includes a catalog of Bierstadt's paintings and a bibliography.

Hine, Robert V. *The American West: An Interpretive History*. 2d ed. Boston: Little Brown, 1984. An excellent survey of Western history, with a first-rate chapter, "The Image of the West in Art."

Huth, Hans. *Nature and the American: Three Centuries of Changing Attitudes*. Berkeley: University of California Press, 1957. Evaluates the developments and factors that shaped the conservation movement in the United States. The contributions of artists, including Bierstadt, are an important part of the story.

Kernan, M. "Showing the West in Paintings as Big as All Outdoors." *Smithsonian* 21, no. 11 (February 1991). Biographical profile of Bierstadt and his landscapes, including his development as an artist and his art and sales techniques.

McCracken, Harold. *Portrait of the Old West*. New York: McGraw-Hill, 1952. A scholarly account with material on Bierstadt's early career.

Nash, Roderick. *Wilderness and the American Mind*. 3d ed. New Haven, Conn., and London: Yale University Press, 1982. While Bierstadt is mentioned only in passing, this is the standard work on the evolution of American attitudes toward wilderness.

Runte, Alfred. *National Parks: The American Experience*. Lincoln: University of Nebraska Press, 1997. Assesses Bierstadt's importance as part of a discussion of cultural nationalism as a significant factor in the establishment of the national parks.

James E. Fickle

GEORGE CALEB BINGHAM

Born: March 20, 1811; Augusta County, Virginia
Died: July 7, 1879; Kansas City, Missouri
Area of Achievement: Art
Contribution: Bingham was the first American artist to record life on the mid-nineteenth century frontier in paintings of sensitive social commentary and high aesthetic quality.

Early Life

Known throughout his career as "the Missouri Artist," Bingham was, in fact, born into a long-established Southern family. Henry Vest Bingham, his father, whose ancestors probably came from England in the latter half of the seventeenth century, married Mary Amend, of German and French Huguenot descent, and they started their married life farming tobacco in Virginia. George, born on the farm, which was just west of Charlottesville, Virginia, was one of eight children. In 1819, Bingham's father got into financial difficulties, lost his business, and went west with his family to Franklin, Missouri. In 1820, he opened an inn and dealt in tobacco as a sideline. On his death in 1823, the family moved to a farm outside town, where Mrs. Bingham ran a small school.

There is some biographical evidence that Bingham was interested in drawing, but there is no proof that he ever had any formal training. Apprenticed to a cabinetmaker at sixteen, he may have worked as such, and perhaps as a sign painter, and there is some suggestion that he planned to study law. In 1833, he was a professional portrait painter. His early work is awkward and somewhat primitive, and seems to indicate that he was self-taught. Nevertheless, he was able to make a living at it, moving around the Columbia, Missouri, area, and in 1836, he was sufficiently confident to offer his services in St. Louis. In that year, he married Sarah Elizabeth Hutchinson of Boonville.

In the late spring of 1838, he went to Philadelphia, evidently to study. There is no record of him entering any art school, but he did buy a collection of old master engravings and some antique sculpture casts, both of which were commonly used for art instruction at the time. The city itself was rich in examples of international art, and Bingham must have seen some of it. He may have gone on to New York also, since a painting of his, one of his first genre pieces, *Western Boatmen*

Ashore, was shown at the Apollo Gallery in New York in the autumn.

In 1840, he exhibited six paintings at the National Academy of Design in New York. By that time he was technically much more accomplished; already evident in these works is the flair for genre subjects, simple incidents of everyday life, which was to become his distinctive mark as an artist. He also decided to move to Washington, District of Columbia, ambitious to try his skills painting federal politicians. He spent four years, off and on, in the capital, during which he painted portraits of important figures including John Quincy Adams and Daniel Webster. By this time, he was a painter of some modest reputation, but he had not produced any works of serious moment. Looking at his *Self-Portrait of the Artist*, which he had painted a few years earlier, it would be hard to guess that this square-jawed young man with the wide brow and the slight curl in his forelock, rather tentatively painted, would suddenly in the mid-1840's produce paintings of considerable importance.

Life's Work

It is, in the main, the painting which Bingham did roughly in the ten years between 1845 and 1855 that has given him his reputation as one of America's foremost artists. After that time, for several reasons, the quality of his art fell back into competent professionalism, with occasional paintings reminding the art world of his heights in what is called his "great genre period." During this period, he continued to paint portraits, but his best work was in studies of simple life in Missouri, with special emphasis placed upon the world of the flatboatmen plying their hard trade on the Missouri River. He had anticipated the theme in his *Western Boatmen Ashore* in the late 1830's, and in the 1840's he found a market for the theme, rather surprisingly in New York.

The celebration of the simple life of the American plainsman, trapper, and boatman had already been prepared for in literature in the writing of Washington Irving, James Fenimore Cooper, John Greenleaf Whittier, and Henry Wadsworth Longfellow. Bingham, in a sense, was following the Eastern painter William Sidney Mount in putting that growing admiration for the muscle and sweat of American frontier life into pictorial terms, but in his own way.

The American Art-Union in New York City was dedicated to supporting American artists through purchase, sale, and reproduction of their paintings, and in a seven-year period it purchased twenty paintings by Bingham, all of them examples of his genre themes.

Fur Traders Descending the Missouri was one of the first paintings so purchased, and it stunningly reveals the power of Bingham as a painter, which had never been revealed in his portrait work. It is, at one and the same time, his most powerful painting and the most representative of his studies of those singular men who, in working the river, seem to exemplify an admirable truth about American life. Variations on the theme were to occupy Bingham through the next ten years, and occasionally the theme was to catch the popular imagination in ways which Bingham could hardly have imagined.

If *Fur Traders Descending the Missouri* has a focused intensity that reminds viewers of Le Nain and slightly awes on sight, Bingham also had the ability to use the theme charmingly. *The Jolly Flatboatmen*, showing its simple subjects in a moment of dance and song, was engraved by the Art-Union and eighteen thousand copies were sent out to American homes. Part of the secret lay, undoubted-

ly, in Bingham's fastidious choice of how he saw the humble boatmen. He eschewed the real vulgarity of their lives, the hard toil, the danger, for gentle, often humorous scenes of cardplaying or quiet moments of rest. He did not patronize them, but he did not tell all the story. The paintings of lively, unsentimental masculinity framed by the beauty of the western riverscapes brought out the best in Bingham, both as an artist and as a recorder of an aspect of American frontier life.

In the early 1850's, he carried the taste for paintings of Missouri life a step further in his "Election" series. These were quite as popular as his studies of the working Westerners, and he spent considerable time not only in painting them but also in promoting the sales of the originals and of engravings of the same. As in his first series, he avoided adverse comment. William Hogarth's famous election works may be seen as an influence, but while Hogarth was intent on satire, Bingham never was. Although the characters in these technically complicated paintings of speech-making, polling, and post-voting celebration may sometimes be less than proper, they are never savaged. A cheerful, sensitive appreciation of the democratic process in action, however makeshift it might be in the rural fastness of Missouri, was the dominant tone in these works, which brought Bingham praise for his appreciation of the American way of choosing their legislators.

However modest the topics of this period were, Bingham's use of them was not unsophisticated. He displayed a strong sense of composition, a considerable talent for marshaling large groups of people, and a use of light and shadow which complemented the mood succinctly. His drawing was confident, and his settings appropriate and sometimes charming. He was no longer merely a journeyman painter.

Despite the support of the Art-Union, he was never as popular in the East as he was out West. There was constant sniping at his rude subjects and at his use of color. He quarreled with the Art-Union administrators over criticism of his work printed in their house journal and became dissatisfied with the prices they paid him for his paintings.

By the mid-1850's, Bingham, dissatisfied with his career, was determined to move on to more important work. He had painted a Daniel Boone subject a few years earlier, and he saw the historical painting as the kind of theme that he wanted to pursue. He hoped to convince Washington of the appropriateness of having a Boone painting, of major proportions, commissioned for the Capitol. A step in that direction came in the form of a commission from the state of Missouri to provide paintings of George Washington and Thomas Jefferson, and in 1856, Bingham went to Europe to work on those paintings. He visited Paris but settled in Düsseldorf, then a center for painters and sculptors, and he completed his Washington and Jefferson there. Unfortunately, in the eyes of some critics, Düsseldorf, with its emphasis on high technical polish in painting, influenced Bingham adversely, and there is some informed opinion which sees a decline in the quality of his work dating from the Düsseldorf experience.

Bingham returned to Missouri with his commissions and was asked to provide two further paintings, one of Henry Clay and one of Andrew Jackson. Yet the hoped-for major commission from Washington did not come, and he kept busy doing portraits until the Civil War broke out. Always interested and sometimes involved in politics as a Whig (Republican) supporter, he served from 1862 until 1865 as the state treasurer, painting as time permitted. Although an active supporter of the war against the South, he split with the party after the war over the excessive zeal with which Republicans conducted themselves; his painting *Order 11*, not a particularly good example of his talents, got him into a continuing battle, since it illustrated the arrogance of the military during the war. It was one of the few occasions on which he used his talent to make political comment, and it did him little good.

He continued to paint portraits, landscapes (which had always been least interesting to him), and genre topics, and to take a hand in Missouri politics. There was some desultory talk at one time of standing for governor, and he served as adjutant general in the 1870's. In 1877, the University of Missouri made him its first professor of art, a post which seems to have been largely honorary; he had a studio on the campus but spent little time there. When he died in 1879, he was almost totally forgotten in the East but honored in Missouri as the state's own painter, the "Missouri Artist."

Summary

Despite the length of his career, the amount of work produced, the constant comings and goings between Missouri and the East, and the sales of his engravings and paintings, Bingham's reputation in the main was confined principally to the Midwest, and he was patronized as a competent portraitist and a sometime regional genre artist.

After his death he remained relatively unknown until 1917, when an article in *Art World* suggested that he was more than a simple hack. The first important confirmation of that idea came in 1933, when the Metropolitan Museum of Art purchased *Fur Traders Descending the Missouri*. In 1934, the City Art Museum in St. Louis mounted the first major show of his works, and in 1935, the Museum of Modern Art in New York exhibited his work.

Since then his reputation has been secure, but it is based, in the main, not upon his entire life's work as a painter but on the output of that ten-year period between 1845 and 1855 when he was principally concerned with recording the working, social, and political lives of the native Missourians. He is recognized as the first master painter of the American West, and his political paintings are a vivid record of the brash, lively vitality of a world which he knew so well—not only as an artist but also as a participant.

His reputation as a painter of serious quality, however, is centered on those brilliantly evocative paintings of trappers, flatboatmen, river people, and other simple citizens of the West, whom he sees with a stunningly poetic clarity that transcends the particularity of detail which he was so determined to record. Some critics have seen in this aesthetic aura touches of an American "luminism," that quality which gives great paintings a universal ideality and connection with the "oneness" of all things. In those paintings, the truth of Bingham's record of simple life goes beyond its factuality.

Bibliography

Baigell, Matthew. *A History of American Painting*. London: Thames and Hudson, and New York: Praeger, 1971. This book is theoretically less adventurous than the Novak work, but it does, in a genial way, put Bingham into the American tradition, and that is where it is easiest to understand and appreciate him.

Bingham, George Caleb. *An Address to the Public, Vindicating a Work of Art Illustrative of the Federal Military Policy in Missouri During the Late Civil War*. Kansas City, Mo., 1871. Expresses Bingham's conviction that it is the duty of the artist to make political use of his gift.

———. "Art, the Ideal of Art and the Utility of Art." In *Public Lectures Delivered in the Chap-*

el of the University of the State of Missouri, Columbia, Missouri, by Members of the Faculty, 1878-79, course 2, vol. 1, 311-324. Columbia, Mo.: Statesman Book and Job Print, 1879. One of Bingham's rare statements about art and the role of the artist.

Bloch, E. Maurice. *George Caleb Bingham*. 2 vols. Berkeley: University of California Press, 1967. The major study of Bingham's work. Excellent illustration. Very careful discussion of his major paintings.

Klingenborg, Verlyn. "His Art Brought Us Face-to-Face with Our Land and Ourselves." *Smithsonian* 20, no. 12 (March 1990). Discusses one of Bingham's river paintings, "Raftsmen," and the artist himself, who remains one of the least familiar to us. Comments on his original career as a lawyer and his political leanings.

Larkin, Lew. *Bingham, Fighting Artist: The Story of Missouri's Immortal Painter, Patriot, Soldier and Statesman*. Kansas City, Mo.: Burton, 1954. The title of the book may seem a bit fulsome, but Bingham was much more than simply a painter, and something less than a statesman. This book tries to bring the multiple lives of the man into context.

Maine, Barry. "The Authenticity of American Realism: Samuel Clemens and George Caleb Bingham 'On the River.' " *Prospects* 21 (Annual 1996). Discusses the similarities in the portrayals of nineteenth century Mississippi River life by Samuel Clemens and Bingham. Argues that both used representational approaches rather than striving for historical authenticity.

McDermott, John Francis. *George Caleb Bingham: River Portraitist*. Norman: University of Oklahoma Press, 1959. The title of this full-scale critical biography is misleading. It does, in fact, cover Bingham's entire career, using specific paintings or groups of paintings as a critical focus in the chapters but filling out his career and life around them. Good illustrations.

Novak, Barbara. *American Painting of the Nineteenth Century: Realism, Idealism, and the American Experience*. New York: Praeger, and London: Pall Mall, 1969. This book is helpful in putting Bingham in the tradition of American painting in interesting ways. He has a chapter to himself, and his connections, implicit and explicit, to other painters are explored with much grace.

Charles H. Pullen

OTTO VON BISMARCK

Born: April 1, 1815; Schönhausen, Prussia
Died: July 30, 1898; Friedrichsruh, Germany
Areas of Achievement: Government and politics
Contribution: Bismarck, known as the "blood and iron chancellor," occasioned the unification of the several German states into the German Empire of 1871-1918. Though his image is that of the aristocrat in a spiked helmet, he was above all a diplomat and a politician, skillfully manipulating the forces at work within Germany and among the European states to achieve his goals.

Early Life

Young Otto von Bismarck was influenced both by his father's and his mother's heritages. His father was a Prussian Junker, an aristocrat of proud lineage but modest financial means. The family estates were not particularly large or productive, but provided a setting of paternalistic rule over peasants long accustomed to serve. From his mother and her family, Bismarck learned the sophistication of the upper bourgeoisie, the cosmopolitanism of city life and foreign languages, and something of the ideals of the Enlightenment. Both sides of the family took pride in service to the Prussian state and its ruling dynasty, the Hohenzollern. The Junker aristocrats often served in the military, while the upper bourgeoisie chose the civil service.

Bismarck received a rigorous classical education and attended Göttingen and Berlin universities. He tried his hand at a career in the Prussian diplomatic and civil service. Though his excellent family connections and quick mind should have assured his success, his early career was a disaster. He was temperamentally unsuited to the discipline of a subordinate position, and he alienated his supervisors time after time. "I want to play the tune the way it sounds good to me," he commented, "or not at all. . . . My pride bids me command rather than obey." Like all young men of his class, Bismarck served a few months in the army and remained a reserve officer throughout his life, but he never considered a military career. At age twenty-four, he resigned from the Prussian bureaucracy and took charge of one of the family's estates. Then his life changed under the influence of pietist Lutheran families; he married Johanna von Puttkamer, a woman from one such family, in 1847, and settled down to the domesticity of country life.

The revolutions of 1848 roused him from the country and brought Bismarck into politics. He quickly made a name for himself as a champion of the Hohenzollern monarchy against the liberal and democratic revolutionaries, and, after the failure of the revolution, the grateful King Frederick William IV appointed him to a choice position in the diplomatic corps. He represented Prussia at the German Diet at Frankfurt am Main and then at the courts of Czar Alexander II of Russia and Emperor Napoleon III of France, making a name for himself as a shrewd negotiator and a vigorous advocate of Prussian interests.

Life's Work

Bismarck was recalled to Berlin by King William I of Prussia in 1862 to solve a political and constitutional crisis. The Prussian Diet was refusing to pass the royal budget, because it disagreed with military reforms instituted by the king and his government. To break the deadlock, Bismarck told parliament

that "great questions will not be settled by speeches and majority decisions—that was the great mistake of 1848 and 1849—but by blood and iron," and he went ahead with the royal policies in spite of parliamentary opposition. In spite of his reputation as an old-fashioned Prussian monarchist, Bismarck was making an attempt to attract middle-class German nationalists to the support of the Prussian monarchy and its military establishment. When the newly reformed Prussian armies proved their effectiveness by defeating Denmark in 1864 and Austria in 1866 and by setting Prussia on the pathway toward a united Germany, Bismarck was a hero.

Now only France could block German unity. Through a masterful (if rather deceitful) set of diplomatic maneuvers, Bismarck forced the hand of Napoleon III, causing him to declare war on Prussia. Faced by the apparent aggression of a new Napoleon, the southern German states (except for Austria) joined with Prussian-dominated northern Germany. In the Franco-Prussian War which followed, France was defeated and the German Empire was proclaimed. Its capital was Berlin, and its reigning monarch was simultaneously the King of Prussia, William I; but the triumph was Bismarck's.

Even his old enemies among the German liberals were forced to recognize his genius. Yet, under the leadership of the Prussian-Jewish National Liberal politician Eduard Lasker, they pressured Bismarck to create a constitutional government for the newly formed empire. Bismarck's constitution was a masterful manipulation of the political power structure of the age. It contained a popularly elected parliament to represent the people (the *Reichstag*), an aristocratic upper house to represent the princely German states (the *Bundesrat*), and a chancellor as the chief executive—himself. Only the emperor could appoint or dismiss the chancellor, and as long as Bismarck held the ear of William I, his position was secure. As a further means of controlling power, Bismarck retained the positions of Prussian prime minister and Prussian foreign minister throughout most of the period.

Bismarck was a man of great physical stature, who enjoyed the outdoor life of the country squire, riding horses and hunting game. He indulged himself in eating, drinking, and smoking, and, though he fell ill from time to time, he revived again and again with great vigor. He was an eloquent speaker, though with an amazingly high-pitched voice, and he was a master of the German language. He loved the domestic haven of his family life, and he was capable of bitter hatred of his political opponents, at home and abroad. For a statesman famed for his cool exploitation of realistic politics, he showed surprisingly irrational passion when faced with determined opposition.

Bismarck continued to face both domestic and foreign challenges throughout his tenure as chancellor. He opposed the power of the Catholic Center Party in the so-called *Kulturkampf*, the German version of the struggle between the Catholic church and the modern state. He sought to limit the growth of the Social Democratic Party by a combination of social legislation and limits on the political freedoms of left-wing parties. He exploited the forces of anti-Semitism and economic nationalism to undermine the German liberal and progressive parties. He made many political enemies, but he was able to retain power by balancing forces against one another and shifting coalitions among political groups.

In foreign affairs, Bismarck used the talents he had once displayed in causing three wars to keep the peace once he had achieved his major goal of German unity. He caused great bitterness in France by taking Alsace-Lorraine in 1871. Yet he simultaneously wooed Austria and Russia, establishing a "Three Emperors' League" among the three conservative states to preserve the status quo. Bismarck organized the Congress of Berlin of 1878 to settle conflicts in the Balkans, and when it was successful he chose for himself the title of the "honest broker." As nationalism in Eastern Europe and colonial rivalries overseas continued to threaten the peace of the world, Bismarck skillfully sailed the German ship of state on the safest course he could.

In 1890, however, the seventy-five-year-old Bismarck clashed with his new sovereign, the thirty-one-year-old Emperor William II. When the young man wanted to do things his own way and forced Bismarck to resign, the British magazine *Punch* published one of the most famous cartoons in history, entitled "Dropping the Pilot." Bismarck retired to his estates, where he was the object of honors from the great and powerful and much adulation from the public. Yet he loved the reality of power, not mere applause, and he died a frustrated and embittered man in his eighty-third year.

Summary

Otto von Bismarck is known to history as the "blood and iron chancellor" and the practitioner of realpolitik. He was no sentimental humanitarian, and military power always figured strongly in his calculations. Yet he was not a single-minded dictator or heavy-handed militarist as he is sometimes portrayed.

Above all, Bismarck was a diplomat and a politician. He kept open several options as long as possible before choosing a final course of action. His shift from a parliamentary alliance with the liberals in the 1870's to an alliance with the Catholics and the conservatives in the 1880's was designed to achieve a single goal: the perpetuation of the power of the traditional elites of feudal and monarchical Germany and the emerging elites of business and industry. Prior to Bismarck, liberalism and nationalism seemed inevitably linked, and those movements were opposed by the aristocratic establishment; Bismarck broke that link and attached German nationalism to the Prussian conservatism that he valued.

For all of his skill, walking the tightropes of domestic and foreign policy as Prussian prime minister and German chancellor for twenty-eight years, he could not create a system that would endure. The forces of liberalism and socialism continued to grow, pushing Germany toward either democracy or revolution, and the Hohenzollern monarchs were swept away in 1918. The forces of radical nationalism and pan-German racism were not checked by the new republic, and Adolf Hitler's Nazism led Germany to disaster between 1933 and 1945. The German unity which Bismarck created lasted only twenty years after his death, and the map of the German-speaking states of Europe after 1945 bears little resemblance to that of Bismarckian Germany. Yet in a country that has seen so much political instability and military defeat in the twentieth century, the figure of Bismarck still looms large and continues to fascinate practitioners of statecraft and writers of history.

Bibliography

Crankshaw, Edward. *Bismarck*. London: Macmillan, and New York: Viking Press, 1981. A standard volume for the general reader, colorfully written by an Englishman with a flair for political biography. Crankshaw is critical of Bismarck but does not see in him the roots of Nazism.

Gall, Lothar. *Bismarck: The White Revolutionary*. Translated by J. A. Underwood. 2 vols. London and Boston: Allen and Unwin, 1986. Though no biography of so controversial a figure as Bismarck will ever be accepted as definitive, this one by a German historian comes close. Gall ar-

gues that Bismarck was a conservative who revolutionized German politics and European international affairs.

Hamerow, Theodore S., ed. *Otto von Bismarck: A Historical Assessment*. 2d ed. Lexington, Mass.: Heath, 1972. An anthology on Bismarck drawn from German, English, and American authors, introduced and edited by a knowledgeable American professor. Several of the pieces are unavailable in English except in this volume.

Kent, George O. *Bismarck and His Times*. Carbondale: Southern Illinois University Press, 1978. A brief and lucid account of Bismarck and his age, suitable for American college students and the general reader. Kent is familiar with the primary and secondary sources, and his excellent notes provide a springboard for further reading.

Pflanze, Otto. *Bismarck and the Development of Germany*. Princeton, N.J.: Princeton University Press, 1963. The first volume of a life's work on Bismarck by the acknowledged American scholarly master of the subject. It takes the story through German unification in 1871.

Stern, Fritz. *Gold and Iron: Bismarck, Bleichroeder, and the Building of the German Empire*. London: Allen and Unwin, and New York: Knopf, 1977. A study of Bismarck and his Jewish banker, Gerson von Bleichroeder, which sheds important light on both the personal and the economic aspects of the men and their time.

Taylor, A. J. P. *Bismarck: The Man and the Statesman*. London: Hamilton, and New York: Knopf, 1955. A cleverly written portrait of Bismarck by an Oxford don famous for his acid commentaries on German history. He sees the chancellor as a man interested only in his personal power, who simply used the persons and institutions around him for his own aggrandizement.

Waller, Bruce. *Bismarck*. 2d ed. Oxford and Malden, Mass.: Blackwell, 1997. Updated and expanded, Waller provides a study of Bismarck's personality and work as the force behind German unification. The author has expanded his focus to include Bismarck's approach to the military and militarism and his period as German chancellor.

Wehler, Hans-Ulrich. *The German Empire, 1871-1918*. Translated by Kim Traynor. Leamington Spa, Warwickshire, and Dover, N.H.: Berg, 1985. A leading West German historian, who emphasizes the social and economic aspects of the Bismarck era, summarizes his argument in this useful book. Wehler sees Bismarck as representing the traditional elites of Prussia, whose "fatal successes" contributed to the German disasters of the twentieth century.

Williamson, D. G. *Bismarck and Germany, 1862-1890.* 2d ed. London and New York: Longman, 1998. An up-to-date account of Bismarck's place in modern German history focusing on defeats in Austria and France, the Germany of 1871 following these defeats, and the foreign and domestic problems he faced.

Gordon R. Mork

GEORGES BIZET

Born: October 25, 1838; Paris, France
Died: June 3, 1875; Bougival, near Paris, France
Area of Achievement: Music
Contribution: Bizet is one of the foremost French composers of the nineteenth century and the author of one of the most popular operas of all time, *Carmen.*

Early Life

Georges Bizet was an only child of musically inclined parents. His father, Adolphe Arnaud Bizet, was a teacher of voice and a composer. His mother, Aimée Marie Louise Léopoldine Joséphine Delsarte, was a gifted pianist. Bizet began informal music studies with his mother at age four. Groomed for a musical career, at age eight he began piano lessons with the celebrated teacher Antoine François Marmontel and was admitted to the Paris Conservatoire shortly before his tenth birthday. A brilliant student, Bizet excelled in his courses, winning the Premier Prix in *solfège* (sight-singing) and in Marmontel's piano class. His virtuosity was such that he could easily have launched a concert career in his late teens, had he wished to do so. The young Bizet, however, had his heart set on becoming a composer.

His first attempts in composition date from 1850, when he was twelve years old. His early works consist of virtuosic piano pieces, choruses, and a one-act comic opera. Bizet's first major work, the Symphony in C, was composed when he was seventeen. Aside from an abundance of charming themes, this work displays a mastery of orchestration unusual in a composer at any age.

In 1857, Bizet won the prestigious Prix de Rome for his cantata *Clovis et Clotilde.* That enabled him to travel to Rome, where he remained for three years, imbibing Italian culture and refining his skills as a composer. During this time, his attitude toward composition changed drastically. Always a composer of immense natural gifts, he decided to adopt a more rational approach to writing music. This, however, produced an identity crisis that resulted in a creeping paralysis of his creative powers and a series of projected and abandoned works.

Bizet's problems in Rome were compounded when the Académie des Beaux-Arts, under whose aegis the Prix de Rome was offered, refused to accept his opera *Don Procopio* (1859) in place of the mass he had originally been obliged to write according to the stipulations of the prize. Bizet, for whom the Christian faith held little appeal, was reluctant to write religious music. An ode-symphony, *Vasco de Gama* (1860), was brought to completion and accepted by the Académie.

Life's Work

In 1860, Bizet returned to Paris, where he persisted in his desire to forge a career as a composer, even in the face of tempting offers to teach and make concert appearances. In 1861, he presented his third submission to the Académie in the form of the *Scherzo et marche funèbre* and an overture entitled *La Chasse d'Ossian,* both of which were well received. His final submission, in 1862, was a one-act comic opera, *La Guzla de l'émir.* Though the music for this opera has disappeared, much of it was incorporated into Bizet's first important stage work, *Les Pêcheurs de perles.* Premiered in 1863, it was received coolly by the critics, who criticized its apparent imitation of Richard Wagner and Giuseppe Verdi in orchestration, harmony, and dynamics.

By 1863, Bizet's Rome pension had run out, and he was compelled to earn a living making transcriptions and arrangements for the publishers Choudens and Heugel. The sixteen-hour days he often worked affected his health, which had never been good. Since childhood, he had suffered from a chronic ulceration of the throat which continued to bother him and which would eventually prove fatal. He was also afflicted with articular rheumatism. Nevertheless, he found the time to begin a new operatic endeavor, *Ivan IV,* which, though finished in 1865, was never produced. His next opera, composed in 1866, was *La Jolie Fille de Perth,* based on the 1828 novel *The Fair Maid of Perth* by Sir Walter Scott. It premiered in December of the following year and was reviewed enthusiastically by the press, the only one of his operas to be so received. During the period 1865-1868, Bizet wrote a considerable amount of piano music, most of which, though published, remains obscure. Full of effects in imitation of the orchestra, these pieces also reveal the composer's ongoing fascination with Lisztian virtuosity as well as with the works of Ludwig van Beethoven and Robert Schumann. He also composed a number of songs, the finest of which is "Adieux de l'hôtesse arabe" (1866).

In 1868, Bizet underwent another period of soul-searching as a composer, resulting again in a series of aborted projects. He also endured a severe bout of quinsy. Adding to his despair was the rejection of a new opera, *La Coupe du Roi de Thulé*, which he had submitted in a competition sponsored by the Paris Opéra. In the following year, at the age of thirty-one, Bizet married Geneviève Halévy, the daughter of his former composition teacher at the Paris Conservatoire. Their union was not a harmonious one, as she came from a family with a history of mental illness and was herself emotionally unstable. Their only child, Jacques, born in 1872, inherited this trait and committed suicide when he was fifty.

At the outbreak of the Franco-Prussian War, Bizet enlisted in the National Guard and remained with his wife in Paris. After the war, Bizet resumed work on two operas, *Clarissa Harlowe* and *Grisélidis*, neither of which reached completion. These were followed, however, by his opera *Djamileh*, a one-act work with a libretto by Louis Gallet, which was premiered in May, 1872. Bizet's highly original harmonies bewildered audiences and annoyed the critics. As a result, the opera was a complete failure. Among his most engaging works for orchestra is the incidental music to Alphonse Daudet's *L'Arléssienne*, a melodrama produced at the Théâtre du Vaudeville in October, 1872. Once again, the production was ill-fated, and Bizet's music was not well received. Nevertheless, the individual numbers, twenty-seven in all, are brilliant studies in orchestration. Four of them were arranged by Bizet for full orchestra (the original scoring having been for a small ensemble of twenty-six performers), and the resulting suite, premiered the following month, was greeted with approval by audiences and critics alike.

It was in the year 1872 as well that Bizet began work on his most important opera, one that would elevate him, though posthumously, to greatness. He was offered the services of Henri Meilhac and Ludovic Halévy as librettists and chose Prosper Mérimée's novel *Carmen* (1845; English translation, 1878) as his subject. Already by 1873 the first act was completed, and in the summer of 1874 the score was finished. Some aspects of the opera were controversial from the outset, especially its conclusion with a murder, which was unprecedented at the Opéra-Comique. Bizet's realistic portrayal of the seamier aspects of Merimée's *Carmen*, as well as his highly original and difficult music, caused considerable consternation among the proprietors of the theater. The opera's initial reception in the spring of

1875 seemed to confirm their worst fears. It was dismissed as obscene and Wagnerian, though it ran for forty-eight performances in its first year. It was successfully staged in Vienna in October, 1875, and this led directly to its worldwide popularity.

Bizet's brilliant musical characterization of the principal characters, José and Carmen, his exploitation of exotic musical material and colorful orchestration, and his depiction of violent human emotion imbue the opera with a sensual vitality and pathos that continue to enthrall modern audiences. It is worth noting, however, that Bizet never set foot in Spain. Nor did he utilize Spanish musical folklore extensively, though he did resort to quoting a few popular songs of the day.

Bizet, dejected at the poor reception of *Carmen* and suffering from a bout of quinsy, became seriously ill in May, 1875. His condition worsened when he contracted rheumatism and a high fever. That was followed by a heart attack on June 1, and he died in the early morning of his wedding anniversary. After a funeral ceremony attended by four thousand people, he was buried in Père Lachaise cemetery in Paris.

Summary

Although he lived for the relatively short span of thirty-seven years, Georges Bizet produced a sizable body of work. His output—encompassing some twenty-seven operas, ten orchestral works, more than fifteen choral works, and dozens of songs and pieces for piano—was prodigious but uneven. He showed scant interest in writing chamber music, solos for instruments other than piano, or concerti. The love for literature that he displayed early in life probably dictated his preference for writing music that had some dramatic or literary connection. Bizet is an example of a composer who has suffered from his own success. The enormous popularity of a few of his works, such as *Carmen* and *L'Arléssienne*, has tended to overshadow the rest of his oeuvre. Though not all of his music is of the same quality and many pieces were left unfinished, much beautiful music awaits discovery by anyone willing to probe beneath the surface of his accomplishments.

Posterity's judgment of Bizet has fluctuated between extremes of adulation and disdain. Only in the latter half of the twentieth century has a clearer image of his achievements begun to emerge. Though he was receptive to forward-looking trends in the music of his own time, his style was highly original and not easily imitated. As a result, his influence on succeeding generations is difficult to gauge and is not necessarily commensurate with his intrinsic stature as a composer. Yet he must be counted among the greatest musical geniuses of nineteenth century Europe.

Bibliography

Curtiss, Mina. *Bizet and His World*. New York: Knopf, 1958; London: Secker and Warburg, 1959. A singular biography that sheds much light on Bizet's personal life. Progressing in chronological fashion, the discussion focuses on Bizet's relationship to such figures as Charles Gounod, Ludovic Halévy, and many others. Little emphasis is placed on analysis and critique of Bizet's music, and the text includes no musical examples. In addition to a selected bibliography and an index, the appendices include translations of Bizet's unpublished correspondence, a list of the contents of Bizet's music library, a catalog of his works, and accounts of their posthumous presentations.

Dean, Winton. *Bizet*. London: Dent, 1948; New York: Collier, 1962. A standard biography by the preeminent Bizet scholar, writing in the English language. In addition to a carefully researched biographical discussion interspersed with musical examples, the author includes valuable appendices: a catalog of Bizet's works, a calendar of Bizet's life, and a list of individuals associated with Bizet and short biographies on them. Includes an extensive bibliography and an index.

———. "Bizet's *Ivan IV*." In *Fanfare for Ernest Newman*, edited by Herbert Van Thal. London: Barker, 1955. Documents the history of Bizet's opera *Ivan IV*, which was never performed in his lifetime. Discusses the probable chronology of its composition and treats the problems involved in its posthumous productions. Presents an act-by-act critical examination of the music and the drama and establishes Bizet's use of ideas from *Ivan IV* in his later operas, especially *Carmen*.

———. *Carmen*. London: Folio Society, 1949. For devotees of the opera, an invaluable work that is divided into three parts. Part 1 presents an English translation (by Lady Mary Lloyd) of Mérimée's *Carmen*. Part 2 discusses the genesis of the libretto by Halévy and Meilhac. Part 3 treats the music of the opera and emphasizes the relationship of the music to the dramatic action.

McClary, Susan. *Georges Bizet: "Carmen."* Cambridge and New York: Cambridge University Press, 1992. McClary explores Bizet's well-known opera from a number of perspectives, which include controversy over race, class, and gender. The author focuses on conditions in nineteenth century France that affected the story, discusses the opera's development, and concludes with a bibliography and synopsis.

Shanet, Howard. "Bizet's Suppressed Symphony." *The Musical Quarterly* 54 (October 1958): 461-476. Seeks to explain the mystery of Bizet's Symphony in C, a masterpiece written when the composer was only seventeen years old but which waited eighty years for its first performance. Why did Bizet never have it performed, and why did his widow forbid its performance or publication? An engaging article that appeals to layperson and scholar alike.

Walter Aaron Clark

BLACK HAWK
Ma-ka-tai-me-she-kia-kiak

Born: 1767; Rock River, Illinois

Died: October 3, 1838; near the Des Moines River, Iowa

Areas of Achievement: Indian leadership and literature

Contribution: Black Hawk was a leader in the last Indian war of the old Northwest; he also dictated one of the most interesting Indian autobiographies, *Life of Ma-ka-tai-me-she-kia-kiak, or Black Hawk* (1834).

Early Life

Black Hawk (or Ma-ka-tai-me-she-kia-kiak) was the adopted brother of a chief of the Foxes and was brought up by the Sauk (Sacs)—"Sac" was the original French spelling. The Sauk and Foxes were small tribes which formed an alliance, sometimes including the Potawatomi and Winnebago, to defend themselves against larger neighboring nations. Black Hawk was already a warrior and a leader among his people at the age of fifteen. In his autobiography he described how he became chief at the death of his father when they were fighting together against the Cherokee near the Meramec River, a short distance below modern St. Louis. Black Hawk fell heir to the chieftainship but was obliged to mourn, pray, and fast for five years in what he called a "civil capacity," hunting and fishing. When he was twenty-one he became head chief of the Sauk and Foxes. The two tribes were united and lived together as a single group.

Black Hawk's early years were spent in warfare against neighbors, primarily the Osage, Kaskaskia (a member of the Illinois Confederacy), and Chippewa. According to Black Hawk, there were two major reasons for warfare among the Indians: the preservation of hunting grounds and revenge for the deaths of relatives. Despite Black Hawk's renown as a warrior, there was a highly developed ethical and spiritual side of his character, and he tried to do what the Supreme Spirit directed.

Life's Work

Black Hawk's personality was complex, and it would be a mistake to over-simplify the main events in his life. Probably he should not be considered a great leader. He was highly individualistic, often impulsive, colorful, and emotional. His policies did not significantly help his nation, and other Indian leaders such as Pontiac and Crazy Horse were greater than he. It could be argued that his leadership was shortsighted and brought disaster on his people. The Black Hawk War could have been avoided.

Black Hawk never liked the American settlers, and for this he may be easily forgiven—during his lifetime the Sauk continually suffered from white armies, white officials, white traders, and white settlers. His adopted son was murdered by white American settlers. He liked the British. He was on good terms with a British trader and with Robert Dixon, British agent in the War of 1812, during which Black Hawk took an active role against the Americans. Most of Black Hawk's life prior to his capture in 1832 was marked by his dislike of Americans. The experience that contributed to this attitude more than any other was the St. Louis treaty of 1804, which Black Hawk rejected. In his own words, "It has been the origin of all our difficulties."

Napoleon sold Louisiana to the United States in 1803; soon after, United States officials arrived in St. Louis to claim control and sign treaties with Indian tribes in the area. According to Black Hawk, the treaty with the Sauk was fraudulent. The Sauk had sent four representatives to St. Louis to obtain the release of a Sauk imprisoned there for killing an American—these were negotiators with a specific mission, not diplomats or chiefs. Much later they returned dressed in fine coats and wearing medals, and they could not remember much of what had happened. They were drunk most of the time they were in St. Louis. They also signed a treaty ceding all the Sauk lands east of the Mississippi to the United States. Black Hawk and the rest of the Sauk were indignant. Not long after, a United States Army detachment came to erect Fort Madison near the Sauk villages. Black Hawk was scandalized by the treaty, asserting that the Sauk and Fox signers of the treaty had no authority from their nations. Twentieth century historian Milo Quaife, however, claims that "no more than the usual cajolery of the Indians was indulged in by the white representatives in securing the cession." The rejection of this treaty by the Indians, and the acceptance of its legality by the United States, says much about the quality of American law during this period.

The second major event in Black Hawk's life prior to his battles in the 1830's against the Illinois militia and the United States Army was his rivalry with another Sauk chief, Keokuk. Although not a chief by birth, Keokuk rose by the exercise of political talents to a position of leadership in his tribe. He was more of a realist than Black Hawk, and although he may not have liked the Americans any more than Black Hawk did, he tried not to antagonize them. As a nation the Sauk were divided, some favoring Black Hawk and others, Keokuk. In 1819, Keokuk and other members of the nation were persuaded by American authorities to leave the Sauk home on Rock Island and go to the western side of the Mississippi. Keokuk ultimately triumphed over Black Hawk after the war of 1832, which placed Black Hawk under the governance of Keokuk.

The rivalry between Black Hawk and Keokuk had a long history. Throughout the 1820's, Black Hawk resisted the encroachments of white settlers, and he tried to hold on to the Sauk's ancestral home on Rock Island. At first Black Hawk favored negotiation with the white Americans no less than Keokuk. Eventually, however, having exhausted all means of peaceful resistance, Black Hawk took up arms and tried to recruit allies among the Potawatomi. He led his entire nation—warriors, women, and children—on a long anabasis from Rock Island to Bad Axe River, winning some battles and losing others, culminating in the final attempt to reach the safety of the western bank of the Mississippi. The most pitiful aspect of the tragedy was the fate of the Sauk women and children. In the words of one historian, Reuben Thwaites,

> Some of the fugitives succeeded in swimming to the west bank of the Mississippi, but many were drowned on the way, or cooly picked off by sharpshooters, who exercised no more mercy towards squaws and children than they did towards braves—treating them all as though they were rats instead of human beings.

Black Hawk led the last great war between Indians and whites on the eastern side of the Mississippi; if it terrified numerous white settlers in the frontier regions of the old Northwest—what is now Illinois and Wisconsin—it should be stressed that the Indian civilian populations living on ancestral lands had been terrorized by whites for a far longer period of time. Although Black Hawk initiated the battle, the final tragedy was not his doing. The deliberate killing of noncombatants was an act of the United States, not an Indian act. A few Sauk managed to reach the western bank only to be attacked by a war party of Sioux Indians under the orders of General Atkinson. Black Hawk would have been the first to condemn these military practices, and he fully expressed his indignation in his autobiography. These massacres went far beyond his conception of the conduct of war. Some historians have been hasty to blame him, failing to consider the requirements of defensive warfare at the time. Although the Indians received few favorable settlements in their negotiations with the whites, those who suffered the most were perhaps the most pacific—those who, because they never fought the whites, never signed treaties with them either, and consequently never received rights or privileges. Most of these nations have completely disappeared, leaving no survivors. One of Black Hawk's most telling critiques of Keokuk is the following: "I conceived that the *peaceable disposition* of Keokuk and his people had been, in a great measure, the cause of our having been driven from our village."

Black Hawk had a quixotic, romantic temperament. He could be impulsively emotional and also ethical, courageous, even idealistic and chivalrous in battle. Some of these traits might surprise a modern reader accustomed to clichés about Indians. Repeatedly Black Hawk complimented the braver of his adversaries, whether enemy Indians or whites. If he encountered an enemy group that had less than half his number, he declined to do battle. He admired both determination and heroism in war, and the traits he came to admire in his white conquerors after 1832 were largely military virtues. It was probably not a coincidence that he struck up a spontaneous friendship with Lieutenant Jefferson Davis in 1832; these two leaders of rebellion had traits in common. Jefferson Davis was to repeat Black Hawk's act of defiance against superior military forces twenty-five years later as president of the Confederate States, and the results would be comparable.

Black Hawk's autobiography was dictated and translated on the spot in 1833; there is no extant text in the Sauk language. The book has a seemingly childish quality that is probably more attributable to the interpreter and editor than to Black Hawk himself. There are many exclamation points, underlinings, and expressions of delight, and much reveling in the good fight. Nevertheless, the document gives an ample, three-dimensional portrait of a man spontaneously describing his thoughts and feelings, trying to account for what he has done and what has happened to him.

Black Hawk died a broken man on an Indian reservation in Iowa in 1838. A decade later, his rival Keokuk died a wealthy man in Kansas, where he had moved after selling the Sauk and Fox lands in Iowa.

Summary

After the Black Hawk War, the combined population of the Sauk and Foxes was greatly diminished. They were finally resettled in an area west of the Mississippi in a segment of what was known as "the Permanent Indian Frontier of 1840." It adjoined the Potawatomi to the west, the Sioux to the north, and the Winnebago to the northeast. The Sauk and Foxes would still need military virtues as well as diplomacy when they jostled with these Indians and, later, with whites in their new habitat. Military abilities did not immediately become obsolete—far from it. Soon, however, the Indians' greatest adversaries were to become alcoholism, diseases such as cholera, and starvation.

Black Hawk's major weakness was probably diplomacy. In his war against the whites he did not secure the adherence of a significant number of other Indian nations, nor did he spend much time or effort in attempting it. Seventy years earlier, Pontiac had been more successful in forging an antiwhite alliance. Whether Black Hawk could have been more successful if he had put more effort into negotiations, especially with other Indian nations, is a matter of speculation. Black Hawk thought in broad ethical categories. He believed the Great Spirit would reward him if he fought for justice. Patient diplomacy, with its concomitant drudgery and uncertainty, was not for him.

Bibliography

Black Hawk. *Life of Ma-ka-tai-me-she-kia-kiak, or Black Hawk*. Boston: Russell, Odiorne, and Metcalf, 1834. Black Hawk's autobiography is a fascinating document; at the same time, it has many inaccuracies and biases, and should be read with critical skepticism. His account of the British is naïve, as is his description of the "prophet," White Cloud. Black Hawk grossly understates his own losses in the battles of 1832. Still, a vivid picture of an admirable human being emerges from the pages of his autobiography.

Drake, Benjamin. *The Life and Adventures of Black Hawk*. Cincinnati: Conclin, 1844. Half history and half fiction, written shortly after the events described.

Eby, Cecil. *"That Disgraceful Affair," the Black Hawk War*. New York: Norton, 1973. Perhaps the best book about the Black Hawk War. Very thoroughly documented and at the same time a readable narrative; also an incisive critique of the major actors in the war.

Quaife, Milo Milton. *Chicago and the Old Northwest, 1673-1833*. Chicago: University of Chicago Press, 1913. Well-documented and thorough general history that draws somewhat specious conclusions.

Slotkin, Richard. *Regeneration Through Violence: The Mythology of the American Frontier, 1600-1860*. Middletown, Conn.: Wesleyan University Press, 1973. A critical or "revisionist" account of the frontier; a welcome antidote to earlier sentimental accounts of the frontier wars, but obsessively overstated.

Stevens, Frank E. *The Black Hawk War*. Chicago: Stevens, 1903. A thorough account, still useful.

Thwaites, Reuben G. *Story of the Black Hawk War*. Madison: Wisconsin State Historical Society, 1892. A narrative by one of the best American historians of the period; Thwaites combines great erudition with a keen critical spirit.

Whitney, Ellen M., ed. *The Black Hawk War, 1831-1832*. Springfield: Illinois Historical Collections, 1970-1973. Documents and lists.

John Carpenter

ELIZABETH BLACKWELL

Born: February 3, 1821; Counterslip, England

Died: May 31, 1910; Hastings, England

Area of Achievement: Medicine

Contribution: The first woman ever to receive a degree from an American medical school, Elizabeth Blackwell became a leading figure in the drive to open the field of medicine to women.

Early Life

Elizabeth Blackwell was born on February 3, 1821, in a small town near Bristol, England. The third of nine surviving children of Samuel and Hannah Blackwell, Elizabeth joined a family heavily influenced by the progressive and reformist values held by her father. In addition to being a successful sugar refiner, Samuel Blackwell was an outspoken member of his community, having wedded the practice of his Puritan faith with the support of various liberal causes, such as women's rights, temperance, and the abolition of slavery.

The destruction of his refinery by fire in 1832 led Samuel Blackwell to move his family to America. After a few years spent in New York and New Jersey, the Blackwells came to settle in Cincinnati, Ohio, in May, 1838. Pursued to the end by his monetary troubles, Samuel Blackwell died in August of that year, leaving Hannah, her two eldest daughters, and Elizabeth responsible for providing for the family. They were able to do so by opening what would become a successful boarding school, where Elizabeth spent the first four of her seven years as a teacher.

It was during these seven years, which also included one year in Kentucky and two more in North and South Carolina, that Elizabeth Blackwell began to grow frustrated at the limits of the teaching profession, both in its poor remuneration and its low social status. She also became aware of her growing aversion to the idea of marriage, an institution which, at the time, imposed even greater restrictions than did teaching on the women who entered into it. These realizations became important factors in Elizabeth Blackwell's decision to pursue a career in the highly respected field of medicine, a field so utterly dominated by men that no woman had ever before received a diploma from an American medical school.

Life's Work

It was during her final two years teaching in the Carolinas that Elizabeth Blackwell, within the personal libraries of the distinguished physicians John and Samuel Dickson, began her study of medicine. These years of self-education served to prepare Blackwell for her move, in May of 1847, to Philadelphia, the home of several well-respected medical schools to which she would subsequently apply. This application process forced Blackwell to confront the institutional prejudices of the day. Although they were often supported by sympathetic faculty members, her applications were rejected by every medical school in Philadelphia and New York as well as by several rural colleges of much less stellar reputations. It was only when the administration of Geneva Medical College in upstate New York put her application up for review by the all-male student body that Elizabeth Blackwell's determination won her a chance for a legitimate education. Presented with a woman's name, the students had thought the submission was a joke and passed it unanimously.

Immediately upon beginning her studies, Elizabeth Blackwell experienced the scorn of both townspeople and fellow students alike. Even the women within the community were taken aback by what they perceived as brash and unfeminine behavior by Blackwell in her pursuit of medical training, and she was often made aware that the idea of a woman physician upset many of those who would one day benefit from the course of action she was endeavoring to take. Gradually, however, Blackwell's intelligence and doggedness won her great measures of respect from important faculty members and the other students with whom she worked. After completing an internship in 1848 at the Philadelphia Hospital and writing a thesis based on her experiences there, Blackwell emerged from her course work with a focus that would last throughout her professional career: the importance of preventative care in the form of improved personal hygiene. With this focus established and her studies complete, Elizabeth Blackwell received her medical degree from Geneva Medical College on January 23, 1849. She became the first woman in the United States to ever earn such an honor and was ranked first in her graduating class.

Before she was to begin her career in earnest in New York in August of 1851, Elizabeth Blackwell spent a year and a half abroad, in both England and France, with the intention of enhancing her education. Though received graciously by the medical community in England and invited by prominent staff members of several hospitals to tour their grounds, Elizabeth Blackwell found that in France the only kind of advanced training available to her was as a midwife. This period in Blackwell's life is most notable for the eye disease she contracted from a patient during her midwives' course at La Maternité in Paris, the resulting loss of sight in one eye dashed her hopes of ever becoming a surgeon. Through these trials, Blackwell's strength of character enabled her to overcome adversity. Toward the end of her stay in Europe, she returned to England and gained valuable clinical experience under the supervision of Dr. James Paget at St. Bartholomew's Hospital. In retrospect, the setbacks she experienced in this interlude abroad helped steel Blackwell for the resistance she encountered in her attempts to establish herself as a practicing physician in New York.

For a woman doctor during the 1850's, merely finding a place in which to practice proved a near impossibility. Blackwell's applications to city dispensaries for positions in the pediatric wards were flatly rejected, as were her requests to visit the female wards of a city hospital. These rejections were handed down despite her rather impressive array of degrees and recommendations. Even more indicative of this era's prejudice was Blackwell's inability even to rent a space of her own for private practice. No landlord would lease a space for such a disreputable practice, knowing that every other tenant who might be sharing a building with a "female physician" (the contemporary euphemism for "abortionist") would be forced to move or be shamed. While overcoming these obstacles and patiently awaiting the growth of her practice, she succeeded in publishing a series of lectures on hygiene in 1852. Later, in 1853, Blackwell opened a dispensary for the poor, supported by funds she raised herself. Four years later, her dispensary became the New York Infirmary for Women and Children, the first hospital completely organized and operated by women. Outside her professional life, Blackwell in 1853 took on the responsibility of adopting a seven-year-old orphan named Katherine Barry who would remain her closest relation for the rest of her days.

In her battle to open the infirmary in 1857, Elizabeth Blackwell was joined by two other women doctors: her younger sister, Emily, who had followed Elizabeth into the profession, and Marie Zakrzewska, a Polish émigré who had been educated at Western Reserve College (later Case Western Reserve University) and who would become the resident physician at the infirmary until 1859. Once this hospital was established, Blackwell's next major goal was to create a medical college for women with a commitment to rigorous preparation and to the cause of good hygiene. Before this goal was to materialize, however, Blackwell departed in August of 1858 for a one-year stay in Great Britain, where she both practiced medicine and lectured, and also made the acquaintance of such admirers as Dr. Elizabeth Garrett and Florence Nightingale. Upon her return to the United States, Blackwell's plans were interrupted by the outbreak of the Civil War, during which she became involved in a committee concerned with the status of care for soldiers and also helped to select and train nurses going out into the field. Finally, in 1868, Elizabeth Blackwell brought her quest to fruition as she founded the Woman's Medical College of the New York Infirmary and served as the first chair of hygiene at the college. (The college eventually became part of Cornell's medical school in

1899, after the university decided to grant admission to women.)

In 1869, Elizabeth Blackwell left the United States to live and work in Great Britain. At first, she took up residence in London, where she practiced privately until she accepted a position at the New Hospital and London School of Medicine for Women in 1875. As a result of her ill health, Blackwell was forced to retire after just one year. Leaving London, she moved with Katherine Barry to Hastings, where Blackwell spent most of her last thirty years. Never one to remain idle for long, Elizabeth Blackwell spent these days writing books, essays and articles addressing a wide variety of topics, but especially focusing upon the issues of medicine and morality. She also visited the continent and traveled to the United States in 1906. In 1907, she suffered injuries as a result of falling down some stairs at her summer house in the Scottish highlands. Blackwell died at her seaside home in Hastings in 1910 and was buried in Scotland.

Summary

It would not be difficult to present Elizabeth Blackwell's achievements as a list of breakthroughs in the process of opening the field of medicine to women. As the first woman to ever receive a degree from an American medical school, the founder of the first hospital run solely by women, and the founder of one of the earliest medical colleges for women, Blackwell stands as a distinguished pioneer in the fight for a woman's right to become a practicing physician. To focus on her breakthroughs alone, however, would unfairly limit the scope of Blackwell's contribution. From the moment she decided to pursue her degree, Blackwell committed herself to more than mere medicine. Desiring a greater status than was afforded by traditional feminine pursuits and seeking a level of freedom that she could find nowhere else, Blackwell chose to challenge the various obstacles that hindered women from pursuing professional careers. Medicine was the avenue she selected in order to accomplish her ultimate goal of advancing the opportunities available to women. Immersed in her era's atmosphere of social activism, Blackwell dedicated her work and her writings to causes of morality and equality. The breadth of Elizabeth Blackwell's influence is amply illustrated by the names of those individuals—people as various as Herbert Spencer and Florence Nightingale, as Dante Gabriel Rossetti and George Eliot—who came to admire and respect Blackwell's ideas and accomplishments.

Bibliography

Abram, Ruth J., ed. *"Send Us a Lady Physician": Women Doctors in America, 1835-1920*. New York: Norton, 1985. Compiled to accompany a museum exhibit, this collection of essays celebrates the pioneering spirit of early women physicians and describes the experience of women in the health professions during the nineteenth and early twentieth centuries.

Blackwell, Elizabeth. *Pioneer Work in Opening the Medical Profession to Women*. London and New York: Longman, 1895. This work consists of autobiographical sketches which delineate the enormous struggle Blackwell had to endure in order to enter and graduate from medical school. That she was fully conscious of her historical role is clear.

Brown, Jordan. *Elizabeth Blackwell*. New York: Chelsea House, 1989. This biography is part of the publisher's American Women of Achievement series. Although primarily intended for young adult readers, this work provides an excellent introduction to Blackwell's life and examines the various issues that confronted her in her quest for providing opportunities for women in the medical profession.

Buckmaster, Henrietta. *Women Who Shaped History*. New York: Collier, 1966. Six remarkable women of the nineteenth century are the subject of this group biography. Elizabeth Blackwell's life is included with those of Prudence Crandall, Dorothea Dix, Mary Baker Eddy, Elizabeth Cady Stanton, and Harriet Tubman.

Hume, Ruth Fox. *Great Women of Medicine*. New York: Random House, 1964. Hume devotes her first chapter to Blackwell and offers the reader a compact biography that emphasizes Blackwell's early life and career in the United States and ends with her retirement to England.

Krug, Kate. "Women Ovulate, Men Spermate: Elizabeth Blackwell as a Feminist Physiologist." *Journal of the History of Sexuality* 7, no. 1 (July 1996). Discusses Blackwell's single-body model, which considered the female body the basic form and stressed the physiological similarities between men and women.

Morantz-Sanchez, Regina. "Feminist Theory and Historical Practice: Rereading Elizabeth Blackwell." *History and Theory* 31 (December 1992):

51-69. A scholar analyzes Blackwell's writings in order to demonstrate how the discussion of scientific topics in these works reflected Blackwell's feminist concerns. Morantz-Sanchez also notes that the growing predominance of laboratory-based treatment of disease and the rigorous application of scientific methodology moved the practice of medicine away from many of the nurturing, feminine aspects of health care championed by Blackwell and her colleagues.

Ross, Ishbel. *Child of Destiny: The Life Story of the First Woman Doctor.* New York: Harper, 1949; London: Gollancz, 1950. Ross wrote a full-length biography of Blackwell with the aid of interviews with family members. Full of fasci-nating detail, the book chronicles Blackwell's work as well as her personal life and her many associations with major figures of the nineteenth century. It places her within the swell of reform characteristic of the era.

Wilson, Dorothy Clarke. *Lone Woman: The Story of Elizabeth Blackwell, the First Woman Doctor.* Boston: Little Brown, and London: Hodder and Stoughton, 1970. Novelist, dramatist and biographer, Dorothy Clarke Wilson brings her dramatic skills to enliven the solid biography, which is based on family reminiscences and papers as well as extensive research in primary sources.

Bonnie L. Ford

Born: January 31, 1830; West Brownsville, Pennsylvania

Died: January 27, 1893; Washington, D.C.

Areas of Achievement: Government and politics

Contribution: Blaine was the most popular Republican politician of the late nineteenth century. Through his personal appeal and his advocacy of the protective tariff, he laid the basis for the emergence of the Republican Party as the majority party in the 1890's.

Early Life

James Gillespie Blaine was born January 31, 1830, in West Brownsville, Pennsylvania. His father, Ephraim Lyon Blaine, came from a Scotch-Irish and Scotch-Presbyterian background. Blaine's mother, Maria Louise Gillespie, was an Irish Catholic. Blaine was reared a Presbyterian, as were his brothers, while his sisters followed their mother's faith. In later life, Blaine became a Congregationalist but was tolerant of all creeds and avoided the religious issue in politics. Blaine's maternal background gave him an electoral appeal to Irish-Catholic voters.

Ephraim Blaine was a lawyer who was elected to a county clerk position in Washington County, Pennsylvania, in 1842. His son entered Washington and Jefferson College, a small school in the area, and was graduated in 1847. Blaine then taught at the Western Military Institute in Georgetown, Kentucky, from 1848 to 1851. He admired the policies of Henry Clay, the Whig leader, during his stay in the state. He also found time to court and then marry a teacher at a woman's seminary, Harriet Stanwood, on June 30, 1850. Leaving Kentucky in late 1851, Blaine taught at the Pennsylvania Institute for the Blind from 1852 to 1854. He also pursued legal studies while in Philadelphia.

Mrs. Blaine's family had connections in Maine. When a vacancy occurred for editor of the *Kennebec Journal* in 1853, her husband was asked to take over the management of this Whig newspaper. Money from his brothers-in-law helped this arrangement succeed. By November, 1854, Blaine was at work in Augusta, Maine, as a newspaperman, not a lawyer. His growing family eventually reached seven children, four of whom outlived their father. From this point onward, he became known as Blaine of Maine.

Over the next decade, Blaine became identified with the young Republican Party in his adopted state. He was elected to the Maine legislature in 1858, was reelected three times, and became Speaker of the House of Representatives during his last two terms. He was named chairman of the Republican State Committee in 1859, a post he held for two decades. Blaine attended the Republican National Convention in 1860 as a delegate. In 1862, he was elected to the United States Congress and took his seat in the House of Representatives in 1863.

As he entered the national scene at the age of thirty-three, Blaine had already shown himself to be a gifted politician. He had a charismatic quality that caused some who knew him to be loyal to him for life, becoming "Blainiacs." His speeches were received enthusiastically in an age that admired oratory. Blaine knew American politics intimately and could remember faces and election results with uncanny accuracy. Yet there was another side to him. His health and temperament were uncertain,

and his illnesses often came at moments of crisis. In his private affairs, Blaine gained wealth without having a secure income, and he would not reveal information about his finances to the public. Enemies said that he was corrupt. That went too far, but he lacked, as did many of his contemporaries, a clear sense of what constituted a conflict of interest. In fact, James G. Blaine was a diverse blend of good and bad qualities—a truth reflected in the Gilded Age quip that men went insane about him in pairs, one for, and one against.

Life's Work

Blaine spent thirteen years in the House of Representatives, serving as its Speaker between 1869 and 1875. He was a moderate on the issues of the Civil War and Reconstruction, endorsing black suffrage and a strong policy toward the South without being labeled as a "radical." He became known as a "Half-Breed" in contrast to such "Stalwarts" as New York's Roscoe Conkling. Blaine and Conkling clashed on the House floor in April, 1866. His description of Conkling as having a "majestic, supereminent turkey-gobbler strut" opened a personal and political wound that never healed for the egotistic Conkling. His opposition proved disastrous to Blaine's presidential chances in 1876 and 1880.

By 1876, Blaine had left the House of Representatives to serve in the Senate. He was a leading candidate for the Republican presidential nomination in that year. Then a public controversy arose over whether Blaine had acted corruptly in helping to save a land grant for an Arkansas railroad in 1869. The facts about favors done and favors repaid were allegedly contained in a packet of documents known as the Mulligan Letters, named for the man who possessed them. The letters came into Blaine's hands, he read from them to the House, and his friends said that he had vindicated himself. Enemies charged that the papers proved his guilt, and the reform element of the time never forgave him.

Shortly before the Republican convention, Blaine fell ill. Nevertheless, his name was placed in nomination as Robert G. Ingersoll called him the "Plumed Knight" of American politics. The Republican delegates decided that Blaine was too controversial to win, and they turned instead to Rutherford B. Hayes of Ohio. Four years later, after Hayes's single term, Blaine led the opposition to a third term for Ulysses S. Grant and again was seen as a contender for the nomination. Blaine was more interested in his party's success than in his own advancement in 1880, and he was pleased when James A. Garfield of Ohio became the compromise nominee. In the fall campaign, Blaine stumped widely for the national ticket and developed the arguments for the protective tariff that he would advance in the 1880's.

After Garfield's narrow victory, he asked Blaine to be his secretary of state. In his first brief tenure at the State Department, Blaine pursued his concern for a canal across Central America, the fostering of Pan-American sentiment, and greater trade for the nation. Garfield's assassination in the summer of 1881 ended his presidency and led to Blaine's resignation at the end of the year. The administration of Chester A. Arthur that followed did not cut into Blaine's popularity with the Republican rank and file. He received the Republican nomination on the first ballot in 1884. John A. Logan of Illinois was his running mate.

Blaine wanted to make the protective tariff the central theme of his race against the nominee of the Democrats, Grover Cleveland, the governor of New York. Instead the campaign turned on the personal character of the two candidates. Republicans stressed Cleveland's admission that he had had an affair with a woman who had given birth to an illegitimate son. Democrats attacked the legal validity of Blaine's marriage and revived the charges of the Mulligan Letters. These sensational aspects overshadowed Blaine's campaign tour, one of the first by a presidential aspirant. The election was close as the voting neared. All accounts of the election of 1884 note that on October 29, Blaine heard the Reverend Samuel Burchard say in New York that the Democrats were the party of "rum, Romanism, and rebellion." These words supposedly alienated Catholic voters, swung New York to the Democrats, and thus cost Blaine the victory. This episode, however, has been given too much importance. In fact, Blaine improved on Garfield's vote in the state and ran stronger than his party. The significance of 1884 was not that Blaine lost in a Democratic year but that he revived the Republicans and laid the groundwork for the party's victory in 1888.

Over the next four years, Blaine continued to speak out for the tariff. He set the keynote for the 1888 campaign when he responded publicly to Cleveland's attacks on tariff protection in his 1887 annual message to Congress. "The Democratic

Party in power is a standing menace to the prosperity of the country," he told an interviewer. Blaine stayed out of the presidential race and supported strongly the party's nominee, Benjamin Harrison of Indiana. After Harrison defeated Cleveland, it was logical that Blaine should again serve as secretary of state.

Blaine faced a variety of diplomatic issues, including Canadian fisheries and a running argument with Great Britain over fur seals in Alaska. He summoned the initial Pan-American Conference to Washington in October, 1889, sought to achieve the annexation of Hawaii, and was instrumental in obtaining reciprocal trade authority in the McKinley Tariff of 1890. In many ways Blaine foreshadowed the overseas expansion of the United States that occurred later in the decade. His working relationship with President Harrison deteriorated as the Administration progressed and Blaine's own health faltered. The death of two children in 1890 added to his personal troubles. Shortly before the Republican convention, on June 4, 1892, Blaine resigned as secretary of state. It is not clear whether Blaine was actually a candidate for the presidency this last time. He received some support when the Republican delegates met, but the incumbent Harrison easily controlled the convention and was renominated on the first ballot. Blaine made one speech for the Republicans in the 1892 race as Harrison lost to Grover Cleveland. In the last months of his life, Blaine gradually wasted away. He died of Bright's disease and a weakened heart on January 27, 1893.

Summary

When Blaine died, a fellow Republican said, "His is a fame that will grow with time." In fact, he is now largely a forgotten historical figure who is remembered only for a vague connection with "rum, Romanism, and rebellion." That impression does an injustice to one of the most popular and charismatic political leaders of the Gilded Age. Blaine embodied the diverse tendencies of the Republican Party in the formative stages of its development. In his advocacy of economic nationalism and growth, he spoke for a generation that wanted both to preserve the achievements of the Civil War and to move on to the fresh issues of industrial development. He was an important participant in the affairs of the House of Representatives in the early 1870's, and his tenure as Speaker contributed to the growing professionalism of that branch of government.

Blaine also symbolized the popular unease about the ethical standards that public servants should observe. In the Mulligan Letters episode and in his own affairs, he raised issues about conflict of interest and propriety that clouded his historical reputation. He became the epitome of the "spoilsman" who lived on patronage and influence. Blaine correctly understood these attacks as being to some degree partisan, but he failed to recognize the legitimacy of the questions that they posed.

Despite these failings, Blaine was a central figure in the evolution of the Republican Party during the 1870's and 1880's. His conviction that tariff protection offered both the hope of party success and an answer to the issue of economic growth laid the foundation for the emergence of the Republican Party as the majority party in the 1890's. In the 1884 presidential race, he improved the Republican performance and prepared the party for later success. As secretary of state, he was a constructive spokesman for the national interest. He educated his party on the tariff issue and, in so doing, fulfilled the essential function of a national political leader. For a generation of Republican leaders and voters, James G. Blaine came to stand for inspiration and commitment in politics. Although he failed to reach the presidency, Blaine was the most significant American politician of his era.

Bibliography

Blaine, James G. *Twenty Years of Congress: From Lincoln to Garfield*. 2 vols. Norwich, Conn.: Henry Bill, 1884-1886. Blaine's memoir of his service in Congress does not contain any striking personal revelations.

Dodge, Mary Abigail. *The Biography of James G. Blaine*. Norwich, Conn.: Henry Bill, 1895. A family biography that is most useful for the many private letters of Blaine that it contains.

Morgan, H. Wayne. *From Hayes to McKinley: National Party Politics, 1877-1896*. Syracuse, N.Y.: Syracuse University Press, 1969. The best analytic treatment of American politics during the heyday of Blaine's career. Morgan is sympathetic and perceptive about Blaine's role as a Republican leader.

Muzzey, David S. *James G. Blaine: A Political Idol of Other Days*. New York: Dodd, Mead, 1934. The best and most objective biography of Blaine. Argues that he was not consumed with the desire to be president.

Stanwood, Edward. *James Gillespie Blaine*. Boston: Houghton Mifflin, 1905. A short biography by a scholar who was related to Blaine.

Thompson, Margaret Susan. *The "Spider Web": Congress and Lobbying in the Age of Grant*. Ithaca, N.Y.: Cornell University Press, 1985. An innovative and interesting treatment of the House of Representatives and the Senate in the years when Blaine was Speaker. Reveals much about the political system in which he operated.

Tyler, Alice Felt. *The Foreign Policy of James G. Blaine*. Minneapolis: University of Minnesota Press, 1927. An older but still helpful examination of Blaine as a diplomat and shaper of American foreign policy.

Lewis L. Gould

LOUIS BLANC

Born: October 29, 1811; Madrid, Spain
Died: December 6, 1882; Cannes, France
Areas of Achievement: Politics and philosophy
Contribution: The founder of humanitarian social-ism, Blanc developed his dissatisfaction with the misery of the French people into an imperative to transform the basic governmental and eco-nomic system to end forever the capitalist ex-ploitation of the working class.

Early Life

Louis Blanc was born in Madrid during the clos-ing, turbulent days of the Napoleonic Empire. His father served King Joseph Bonaparte as an inspec-tor general of Spanish finances. The French hold over Spain, however, was never secure. Joseph, al-ready forced out of his capital several times by the successes of the British army under Sir Arthur Wellesley, finally left the country in 1813. The French bureaucrats, officials, and advisers departed with him. This exodus split the Blanc family. The father abandoned his wife after the birth of a sec-ond son, and Louis, the elder, was sent to live with his maternal grandmother in Corsica. Only after 1815, with the establishment of the Restoration Monarchy, did life become more settled. The father returned, managing to secure a royal pension, and Louis was reunited with his family. In 1821, he and his younger brother, Charles, were enrolled in the Royal College at Rodez, which they attended on scholarship. The school was run by the Catholic clergy, who instructed their pupils in the truth of Bourbon Legitimism and Scholastic theology. The Enlightenment and the Revolution were denigrat-ed, if mentioned at all. Louis was a dedicated stu-dent. He won prizes in philosophy and rhetoric and excelled at biblical study, from which he derived a sense of obligation to work for the betterment of society. He completed his formal education in 1830 when he was nineteen years of age.

Blanc left Rodez to find work in Paris and ar-rived there in August, soon after the revolution which had replaced the Bourbon Dynasty with the Orleanist monarchy of Louis-Philippe. Trained as a gentleman, Blanc had difficulty finding work, es-pecially with the new government, which looked with suspicion on all of those associated with the previous regime. To support himself, therefore, Blanc took a variety of part-time jobs such as tutor-ing, house cleaning, and clerking. He received some money from an uncle but spent much time visiting museums, palaces, and public monuments. In 1832, the prospect of more steady employment led him to leave the capital to accept a post as a tu-tor with a family in Arras.

While in Arras, he met Frédéric Degeorge, a newspaper editor and champion of democratic re-publicanism, who introduced him to political jour-nalism and prompted his admiration of one of Arras' most famous native sons, Robespierre. The associa-tion with Degeorge heightened Blanc's desire to re-turn to Paris and to begin a real career as a writer. He returned in 1834, armed with a letter of introduction, and began work on *Bon Sense* (common sense), a paper founded two years earlier by a group of men who feared the growing power of Louis-Philippe. In 1836, Blanc became the journal's editor-in-chief. He was only twenty-four years of age.

Journalism had become his way to right wrongs and to pave the way for the establishment of a more just society. He wanted to inspire men of goodwill to cooperate in a common program to safeguard individual freedom and to exact reform through evolutionary, but decisive, change. He be-came involved in election politics and, in 1837, was instrumental in forming a committee to present qualified voters with a slate of progressive candidates in the forthcoming elections. This group failed to form an effective coalition out of the various opposition groups, however, and had little practical effect on the results. The govern-ment list was returned with a large majority. The failure did not shake Blanc's faith that government power could be made responsive to the general need. Therefore, he believed it should not be limit-ed but used as the instrument of progress. Such ac-tive *étatism* put Blanc at odds with his newspaper's conservative ownership. He insisted, however, that a man should follow his convictions rather than his position and, in 1838, resigned. His entire editorial staff quit with him.

Blanc wanted to create a new kind of newspaper, one committed to the transformation of society, and one which would become a rallying point for all of those who were dedicated to democratic change and who believed in the need for the reorganization of work. This newspaper, *Revue de progrès poli-tique, social et littéraire,* (review of political, social, and literary progress), began publication in Janu-ary, 1839. In the following year, its pages contained

a series of Blanc's articles which formed the key to his own thought and the basis upon which his subsequent political and intellectual career rested.

Life's Work

Blanc believed that society was divided into two classes, the bourgeois and the people, or the oppressors and the oppressed, and that only through political action could the oppressed achieve liberation and the ability to develop their true nature. Blanc asserted that exploitation was endemic to the system of his time where not only the rich exploit the poor but also the poor exploit one another and the father exploits his family. Daughters, to earn money for survival, are often driven to prostitution. Thus, capitalist society leads to the breakdown of the family, to the enslavement of women, to the increase of crime, and to moral decay. Only if the forces of the people succeed in capturing the state can the state be used to liberate man from the horrors of poverty.

This new government must be popularly elected and run by energetic deputies who will serve the interests of the mass of the voters, not the special interests of the capitalists whose oppression will end only after they are absorbed fraternally into a classless society. Blanc hoped that this process of fraternalization could be accomplished peacefully. He suggested that this could be done through the manipulation of the credit system, controlled by the state, which would force the capitalists to transfer money into state banks to be directed toward investments in public enterprises. Thus, the capitalists would be induced to participate in their own destruction. The economic sector would then be organized into ateliers, or social workshops, a production unit of men of the same craft or profession working together at the local level. The bosses would be elected by the workers and would oversee the distribution of earnings. Each man would produce according to his aptitude and strength and would be awarded wages according to his need. The production from the local ateliers would be adjusted to overall production through central organizations that would establish general principles and policies.

The heart of his concern for human welfare lay in his early religious training which taught him the value of charity. Blanc's God, however, was hardly Roman Catholic. Blanc believed in a pantheistic deity which existed in all beings and bound them together in a sacred spirit of fraternity. The perfect society was one with collective ownership of property and complete unity of objective. People would live communally with competition being replaced by cooperation. Blanc envisaged this transformation as being accomplished peacefully through proper education.

His Utopian vision, however, stood in stark contrast to the society in which he lived. The July Monarchy preserved the Napoleonic laws forbidding workers to engage in common action to establish wages and conditions of work. The government, dominated by a strict laissez-faire ideology, made no attempt to improve the standard of living of the working class; nor did many individual employers concern themselves with bettering the lot of their workers. Indeed, many capitalists believed that, since poverty was inevitable, it would not help to call attention to it. Strikes almost never succeeded because the authorities called out the soldiers and the police to suppress the malcontents and jail their leaders.

Thus, the Revolution of 1848, which overthrew the regime of Louis-Philippe, became an opportunity for deliverance. Blanc and other social reformers viewed the advent of the Second Republic as the beginning of the economic transformation of society. Blanc, however, had developed no clear idea of how to put his concepts into practice, nor did there exist any organized political party to support him. The moderate republicans viewed the Revolution as essentially political and were not interested in an economic agenda. Nevertheless, some deference had to be made to the demands of the workers, whose power had formed the backbone of the rebellion. Consequently, the provisional government recognized the socialist principle that the workers could demand government intervention in the industrial life of the nation, and it proclaimed the principle of the right to work. It also established a system of national workshops to guarantee each citizen a job.

Blanc was made president of a special commission to study the improvement of the status of workers. He intended to use his power to enact legislation in accord with his socialist principles. He wanted the people to produce according to their ability and to consume according to their need. Competition would be replaced with workers' associations. Workers would unite like brothers and receive comparable wages. He wanted the state to provide medical insurance and old-age pensions. His commission, he hoped, would assume an active role in the settling of wage disputes. Finally, he wanted to pave the way for the nationalization of the railroads, the factories, the insurance companies, and the banks. His success, however, was limited.

The Luxembourg Commission managed to push the government into passing a law that reduced the workday from eleven hours to ten hours in Paris, and from twelve hours to eleven hours in the provinces. It also had some success in wage disputes. Blanc's schemes, however, for the most part, received a cool reception by the provisional government, whose leadership viewed them as a threat to society. While these social reforms antagonized the middle class, they raised the hopes of the workers and added to the growing class tension. The national workshops scheme ended badly. Blanc had hoped for a plan to help workers become established in a particular profession, but the scheme had never been more than a program of unemployment relief—workers being thrown together without any distinction for their trade and receiving the wages of indigents. Blanc disavowed all connection with it.

The workshops had been established only as a temporary expedient to stall the dangerous masses, and, when the situation in Paris was deemed less volatile, the government began disbanding the groups. In June, a decree was issued that drafted all unwed workers into the army and sent all others connected with the program into the provinces, where they would become less threatening. This outrage sparked six days of street fighting, which left Paris in ruins and the army in control. Blanc's dream of a new France lay in the smoldering wreckage.

Blanc fled to England, where he remained until 1871. During the early days of the Third Republic, he served as a representative to the Chamber of Deputies from Marseilles, but his years of exile had put him out of touch with the new generation of leftist leaders. The Marxists scorned his nonrevolutionary approach. His last days were lonely. He had outlived most of his friends, his wife died in 1876, and his younger brother, Charles, died in January, 1882. Blanc himself was to die within the year. France gave him a state funeral, and the city of Paris named a street after him. One hundred and fifty thousand people were present for his interment at Père Lachaise cemetery. Suddenly in death, he received the recognition that he had once enjoyed in his days of power.

Summary

Like many of his countrymen, Louis Blanc tried to give definition to the revolutionary slogans of Liberty, Equality, and Fraternity. He began his attempt with two main assumptions, both of them drawn from Jean-Jacques Rousseau—that man is basically good, and that this goodness can emerge in a proper society. The conclusion was, therefore, inescapable: Injustice exists because of a bad environment, and the fault lies in institutions not in human nature. Upon such Cartesian assumptions, Blanc built his entire system. His basic dedication to social justice, however, flowed more naturally from a belief that human concern was a logical extension of the teachings of Christ.

Though his ideas formed the basis of modern French humanitarian socialism (as well as influencing the writings of Karl Marx), their application during his lifetime was nonexistent. The Luxembourg Commission was a practical failure. Nevertheless, it furnished an important precedent for state involvement in regulating conditions of work and in collective bargaining mediation. Blanc's system was hopelessly Utopian, but he had made it clear that political liberty is closely related to a society's standard of living and that without significant popular enjoyment of the nation's wealth real democracy is impossible.

Bibliography

Berenson, Edward. *Populist Religion and Left-Wing Politics in France, 1830-1852*. Princeton, N.J.: Princeton University Press, 1984. The first in-depth study of the coalition of democrats and republicans who tried to build social reform on political democracy. Focuses on the interaction of politics and ideology at the national and local levels. Particularly valuable discussion of the diversity of the Montagnard coalition of the Second Republic, of which Blanc was one of the main leaders.

Blanc, Louis. *The History of Ten Years, 1830-1840*. London: Chapman and Hall, 1845; Philadelphia: Lea and Blanchard, 1848. A survey of the first crucial decade of the reign of Louis-Philippe, focusing largely on political events. Valuable for Blanc's partisan descriptions, complete with appropriate moralizing.

Duveau, Georges. *1848: The Making of a Revolution*. Translated by Anne Carter. New York: Pantheon Books, and London: Routledge, 1967. Disdains formal analysis in favor of a narrative re-creating events through vivid episodes and colorful portraits of the main participants. Contains a lengthy portrait of Blanc, as well as other leaders, in the book's concluding chapters. Blanc's role as head of the Luxembourg Commission is presented side by side with the deliberations of the Provisional Government. Limited almost exclusively to Paris.

Loubère, Leo A. *Louis Blanc, His Life and His Contribution to the Rise of French Jacobin-Socialism*. Evanston, Ill.: Northwestern University Press, 1961. A descriptive approach to the thought of Blanc, relating it to the circumstances of the times. Main thrust is on Blanc's intellectual development as fashioned by public experience. Shows how principal events were responsible for the change and growth of Blanc's socialist philosophy.

Price, Roger. *The French Second Republic: A Social History*. London: Batsford, and Ithaca, N.Y.: Cornell University Press, 1972. A graphic re-creation of the wretched working-class conditions and the structure of French society that led to the collapse of the July Monarchy.

Soltau, Roger Henry. *French Political Thought in the Nineteenth Century*. New Haven, Conn.: Yale University Press, and London: Benn, 1931. A competent survey of the leading political thinkers of the age. Blanc's social ideas are all the more extraordinary when placed in the context of his more conservative contemporaries.

Wm. Laird Kleine-Ahlbrandt

GEBHARD LEBERECHT VON BLÜCHER

Born: December 16, 1742; Rostock, Mecklenburg-Schwerin

Died: September 12, 1819; Krieblowitz, Silesia

Area of Achievement: The military

Contribution: Blücher served the cause of Prussia well throughout his life, especially during the French revolutionary and Napoleonic periods. Although he was not a great strategist, his considerable and undisputed ability as a leader of men and his strong support for military reforms following defeat at Jena in 1806 enabled Prussia to play a major role in the final victory over France, thereby contributing to Prussia's subsequent rise as a major power.

Early Life

Gebhard Leberecht von Blücher was born the son of a former cavalry officer who had served in the armies of the Duke of Mecklenburg-Schwerin and the *Landgraf* of Hesse-Cassell. The family was of old but poor East Elbian nobility and, at the time of Blücher's birth, was nearly penniless. The young Blücher entered Swedish military service at age fifteen. He had been sent to live with his married sister on the island of Rügen, then a part of Sweden. Early during the Seven Years' War, Blücher joined a Swedish regiment of hussars as a cadet. Cavalry service was a well-established tradition in the family. In 1760, Blücher was captured by the Prussians, and, when he was offered a commission in the Prussian army, he joined the regiment which had captured him, after obtaining a formal release from Swedish service. Such shifts of allegiance were neither uncommon nor dishonorable prior to the age of nationalism.

In 1773, when Blücher was passed over for promotion in favor of a person of higher nobility, he resigned his commission. He was in part passed over because of his so-called wild life, primarily gambling, drinking, and reckless displays of horsemanship. For Blücher, gambling was a substitute for the excitement of war, and he frequently compared the skills of gambling to the skills of war. For the next fifteen years, Blücher pursued the life of a noble landlord, first in Prussian Poland and then on his own estate in Pomerania. He married and became the father of five children by his first wife. After her death, he married a second time. At heart, however, he continued to long for the life of a soldier and repeatedly requested reinstatement.

Life's Work

Blücher's efforts to return to military life finally succeeded in 1787, when King Frederick William II commissioned him as a major in his old regiment. In 1790, Blücher was promoted to colonel of his regiment. He saw action after the Battle of Valmy (September, 1792) and distinguished himself repeatedly in the 1793 and 1794 campaigns against revolutionary France. In 1795, he was promoted to major general (one star), and in 1801, to lieutenant general (two stars). During the period of peace, Blücher, though primarily a soldier, served successfully as administrator of Münster, which had been annexed to Prussia in 1802. In this capacity, he worked together with Freiherr vom Stein, and the two developed respect for each other. Blücher was among those who advocated war against Napoleon I in 1805 and 1806, despite the fact that he recognized serious shortcomings in the

263

Prussian army. "The army is good," he told a friend, "but the leaders are not well chosen. They include too many princes and old wigs who have outlived their usefulness." Blücher was also motivated by an ever-growing dislike for the French in general (he referred to them as "parlez-vous") and Napoleon in particular.

When Prussia finally joined the war, though belatedly, Blücher participated in the disastrous Battle of Auerstedt (October, 1806). During the inglorious retreat following the humiliating defeat at Jena and Auerstedt, Blücher distinguished himself as commander of the rear guard, covering the flight of the army. While the bulk of the Prussian forces was captured by the pursuing French, Blücher's troops finally retreated northward toward Lübeck, where he was forced to surrender, having run out of ammunition and provisions. Following the disastrous defeat of 1806 and the institution of military reforms, all Prussian officers who had been captured had to justify their action before a commission of inquiry. Blücher was the only one of the field commanders who had surrendered to pass that scrutiny. The commission concluded that "this surrender belongs to the very few which were justified."

Blücher was soon exchanged and appointed governor general of Pomerania, a position in which he again held civil as well as military duties. The king was forced to dismiss him, however, in 1811, under French pressure. Napoleon had become fearful of Blücher's proven ability and undisguised hatred for the French. As early as 1805, having come under the influence of the Prussian military reformers, Blücher advocated the establishment of a national army based on conscription according to the French revolutionary model, in place of the moribund army of unpatriotic mercenaries and impressed peasant boys. He also advocated more humane treatment of the soldiers, better pay, the establishment of self-contained divisions consisting of infantry, cavalry, and artillery, and other military reforms which the French had introduced early in the Revolution.

In 1809, Blücher and other progressive officers attempted to persuade Frederick William III to join Austria's anti-French uprising, but they were unable to convince the cautious and timid king to give the order. The king not only feared defeat but also was extremely distrustful of his subjects, and he did not like the idea of arming the masses. Blücher even considered leaving Prussian service and offering his sword to the Austrians. He spoke of form-

ing a Prussian legion under Austrian command. As Napoleon's empire began to weaken, Blücher and General August Neithardt von Gneisenau, though not the Prussian military establishment, again advocated a popular uprising and guerrilla war, taking their inspiration from the successful Spanish uprising. In 1808, Blücher wrote to a friend, "I don't know why we cannot display as much respect for ourselves as the Spanish do."

In 1812, Blücher was forced into temporary hiding because Napoleon, preparing his Russian campaign, wanted to arrest him. During this period, Blücher suffered from a serious mental illness, which was a recurring problem, though it usually found expression only in depression and hypochondria. In 1813, Blücher was recalled to active duty, only one of two generals of the 142 in the Prussian army in 1806 who retained troop command. He commanded the joint Prussian-Russian "Army of Silesia" as a three-star general. In the summer of 1813, his army invaded Saxony and defeated the French in a series of engagements, including the Battle of Wahlstatt, and played a major role in the decisive allied victory in the Battle of the Nations (Leipzig), in October, 1813. For his part in this significant victory, he was promoted to field marshal. His impetuous and aggressive leadership earned for him the title "Marshal Forward" (*Vorwärts*), bestowed upon him by the Russians.

Blücher, in keeping with the new concepts of warfare, urged a continuous and unorthodox winter pursuit of Napoleon and with his forces crossed the Rhine River during New Year's night of 1814. The Austrians, on the other hand, wanted to negotiate with Napoleon, their emperor's son-in-law, and retain him on the throne of a reduced and chastened France as a counterweight to growing Russian power. Blücher, however, had no understanding of political considerations, seeing all matters solely from the military viewpoint. Though the allies still suffered some defeats, Blücher urged them to maintain the pressure until the final capture of Paris and Napoleon's abdication in March, 1814. Throughout this period, Gneisenau served as Blücher's capable chief of staff, complementing Blücher's daring and courage with competent staff work, the value of which Blücher fully and publicly recognized. Blücher, celebrated, decorated, and rewarded for his services, was always quick to praise others and give them credit. While accompanying the victorious monarchs during a visit to Britain, he received an honorary doctorate from the

University of Oxford and later accepted a similar honor from the University of Berlin.

Ill health and his strong disagreement with the victorious coalition's lenient treatment of defeated France caused him to retire from military service. He was, however, immediately recalled as Prussia's field commander when Napoleon returned from Elba in 1815. Blücher joined forces with the British under the Duke of Wellington in the southern Netherlands (modern Belgium), moving his forces dangerously close to the French frontier. On June 16, 1815, the Prussian forces, on Wellington's left flank at Ligny, were defeated by Napoleon's surprise attack, which was designed to separate the two allied forces. Napoleon then turned northward against Wellington, hoping to force him to retire to England. Blücher, though severely injured when he was pinned under his horse, which was killed during a French charge, managed to rally most of his disheveled army; instead of retreating along his line of communication toward Germany as conventional military doctrine would have dictated and as Napoleon expected him to do, Blücher retreated northward, slipped away from the pursuing Marshal Michel Ney, and joined Wellington at Waterloo on the evening of June 18. His timely arrival to assist the exhausted British turned a stalemate, or possibly a French victory, into a total French rout. For this victory, Blücher received a unique award, the "Blücher Star"—the Iron Cross superimposed on a golden star. Blücher had already received the Grand Cross of the Iron Cross in 1813 (awarded only seven times during the war). Following this final contribution to the allied cause, Blücher retired again and returned to his Silesian estates, where he devoted much time to his passion for gambling. He died in 1819 after a short illness, and his funeral became an occasion for great praise and more honors.

Summary

Gebhard Leberecht von Blücher was a man of limited formal education, a fact he clearly recognized and often lamented. Although he did not understand the essence of the French Revolution—the emphasis on democratic reforms—he recognized the benefits that a national, patriotic army offered. Though he is not considered to have been a military genius or even a capable strategist, he did join others in promoting reforms that led to the creation of the *Landwehr* (Prussian militia) and a national conscript army, so important in subsequent German history. Blücher is frequently described as being impatient with maps but able and willing to delegate authority, accept advice, and make quick and sound decisions under the pressure of battle. "Gneisenau stirs and I move forward," he said in reference to his chief of staff. Blücher was one of the few German officers of the old order to make the transition from the organizational and strategic concepts of classical (limited) warfare to the new concepts of revolutionary-national warfare. His most important contributions to victory over Napoleon were his insistence on aggressive action, close pursuit, and, above all, his folksy manner and sincere feeling for his troops. His soldiers in turn repaid him with steadfast loyalty, devotion, and obedience, even when his demands were excessive. He saw matters only from the military viewpoint and was greatly opposed to the lenient postwar diplomatic settlement.

Blücher was also firmly convinced that the army, as well as the Prussian nobility, should occupy privileged positions within the state, though he demonstrated none of the arrogance so common among his fellow aristocrats. At no time did he accept military subordination to civilian authority. His forthright, honest, and earthy character and his physical attractiveness made him a natural, charismatic leader and war hero, much admired by the German population; he is probably the most popular hero in German military history. Blücher, along with Gneisenau, is considered by Marxists to have been among the progressive Prussian officers of the War of Liberation. Karl Marx described him as "the model of a soldier."

Bibliography

Craig, Gordon A. *The Politics of the Prussian Army, 1640-1945*. Oxford: Clarendon Press, and New York: Oxford University Press, 1955. A general history, placing Prussian reforms into a broader context. Includes an index and a general bibliography.

Henderson, Ernest F. *Blücher and the Uprising of Prussia Against Napoleon, 1806-1815*. London and New York: Putnam, 1911. A critical and balanced history of the period with primary emphasis on Blücher's contributions to the allied victory. Some original sources are listed in the text. Very little is included on his early life and career.

Paret, Peter. *Clausewitz and the State*. Oxford; Clarendon Press, and New York: Oxford University Press, 1976. Emphasizes military and civil reforms in Prussia with numerous references to Blücher. Includes a very comprehensive listing of primary sources and an extensive index.

————. *Yorck and the Era of Prussian Reforms, 1807-1815*. Princeton, N.J.: Princeton University Press, 1966. After an introduction to warfare under the old order, this work concentrates on reforms and reorganization of the state and army after Jena. Includes several appendices pertaining to the reform movement, an index, and an extensive bibliography.

Parkinson, Roger. *Clausewitz: A Biography*. London: Wayland, 1970; New York: Stein and Day, 1971. A balanced treatment of Clausewitz's life and work with detailed description of the battles and frequent references to Blücher as a military leader and a supporter of reforms. Includes a bibliography, an index, and illustrations.

Frederick Dumin

SIMÓN BOLÍVAR

Born: July 24, 1783; Caracas, Venezuela

Died: December 17, 1830; Villa of San Pedro Alejandrino, near Santa Marta, Colombia

Areas of Achievement: Government, politics, and the military

Contribution: The liberator of northern South America, Bolívar epitomized the struggle against Spanish colonial rule. His most lasting contributions include his aid in the liberation of Bolivia, Colombia, Ecuador, Peru, and Venezuela, and his farsighted proposals for hemispheric solidarity among Latin American nations.

Early Life

Simón José Antonio de la Santisima Trinidad Bolívar was born the son of wealthy Creole parents in 1783. Orphaned at the age of nine (his father had died when Simón was three), the young aristocrat, who was to inherit one of the largest fortunes in the West Indies, was cared for by his maternal uncle, who managed the extensive Bolívar urban properties, agricultural estates, cattle herds, and copper mines. Appropriate to his class, Bolívar had a number of private tutors, including an eccentric disciple of the French philosophe Jean-Jacques Rousseau, Simón Rodríguez. The tutor schooled the impressionable Bolívar in Enlightenment ideas that would later indelibly mark his political thinking.

When Bolívar was sixteen, he went to Spain, ostensibly to further his education, although his actions suggested that he was much more interested in ingratiating himself with the Spanish royal court. While at the court, he met, fell in love with, and married María Teresa Rodríguez, the daughter of a Caracas-born nobleman. During his three-year stay in Madrid, Bolívar came to see the Spanish monarchy as weak and corrupt; moreover, he felt slighted because of his Creole status. He returned home at the age of nineteen. His wife died six months after they returned to Caracas, and Bolívar, although he enjoyed female companionship, never remarried.

Bolívar returned to Europe. In Paris, he read the works of the Enlightenment feverishly and watched with disillusionment the increasingly dictatorial rule of Napoleon I. He also met one of the most prominent scientists of his day, Alexander von Humboldt, who had recently returned from an extended visit to the New World. Humboldt was convinced that independence was imminent for the Spanish colonies. While in Paris, the five-foot, six-inch, slender, dark-haired Bolívar also joined a freemasonry lodge. There he met radicals who espoused similar views. After Paris, Bolívar went to Italy, where he vowed to liberate his native land from Spanish rule. This second trip to Europe, which culminated in 1807, would play a pivotal role in shaping the transformation of this young aristocrat into a firebrand revolutionary.

Life's Work

After he returned from the Old World, Bolívar spent the better part of the next twenty years in various military campaigns until in 1825, after many defeats, hardships, and bouts of self-imposed exile, Bolívar and his patriot army drove the Spanish royal forces from the continent. In the early years of the conflict against Spain, he vied for leadership of the revolutionary movement with Francisco de Miranda, an expatriate Venezuelan who viewed with suspicion Bolívar's enormous ego and his insatiable lust for glory. After a bitter dispute between the two, Bolívar, believing that Miranda had absconded with the patriot treasury, turned Miranda over to Spanish authorities. Miranda was subsequently taken to Spain in chains and died in a Spanish prison several years later.

As a commander of the patriot forces, Bolívar demonstrated an uncanny ability to adapt his strategy to the particular circumstances. Faced with poorly trained and poorly equipped troops, Bolívar compensated by using the mountainous terrain of the Andes to his advantage, by delegating responsibility to exceptional field commanders, and by using his persuasive powers to attract new troops. Bolívar endured all the hardships and privations of the military campaigns alongside his soldiers. Moreover, the sheer force of his personality and his single-minded dedication to the goal of a liberated continent inspired his troops.

Despite his military prowess, Bolívar suffered a number of difficult defeats from 1810 to 1818. On two separate occasions during this early phase of the struggle, Royalist forces dealt the rebels serious setbacks and Bolívar was forced to flee South America. He used those occasions to raise funds, secure arms and soldiers, and make alliances with other states that might provide aid for the upcoming campaigns.

Bolívar also demonstrated the ability to unite conflicting ethnic groups and classes of Venezuelans and Colombians into an improvised army. He co-opted as many different sectors of South American society as possible during the seemingly interminable war years. A perfect illustration of this penchant for compromise was his visit to Haiti during one of his exiles. There Bolívar extracted much-needed aid from Haitian president Alexandre Pétion. The Haitian president, the leader of a nation where a successful rebellion had liberated the slaves, insisted that Bolívar abolish slavery when he returned to Venezuela. Bolívar, who had set his own slaves free in 1811, agreed to do so, knowing that the Creole elite's economic viability was dependent on slave labor.

Another ethnic group which Bolívar courted were the *llaneros*. Led by their fierce regional chieftain (caudillo), José Antonio Páez, these mobile horsemen dominated the Orinoco River basin and initially supported the Royalist cause. Páez derived his power from control of local resources, especially nearby haciendas, which gave him access to men and provisions. Caudillos such as Páez formed pa-

tron-client relationships with their followers, who pledged their loyalty to their commander in return for a share of the spoils. As the abolition of slavery infuriated the Creole elite, the inclusion of Páez and other caudillos in the patriot army also upset members of the upper class, since their property often was ravaged by overzealous guerrilla bands. Bolívar's charisma enabled him to hold this fragile coalition together. After victory was achieved, however, that consensus would be lost, the fissures and fault lines of class and ethnicity would reassert themselves, and the edifice of unity would come tumbling down.

Because of Bolívar's ability to bring together people of diverse ethnic and class interests into a formidable army, the tide of the war changed. Bolívar's army was helped in its efforts to end colonial rule by South America's other liberator, José de San Martín, who began his campaign in the viceroyalty of Rio de la Plata (modern Argentina) and defeated Royalist forces in what is modern Chile and Peru. The two liberators met at an epochal meeting in Guayaquil, Ecuador, in 1822 to plan the final campaign against the Spanish forces in Peru. By 1825, five new nations were created from the Spanish colonial viceroyalties of Peru and New Granada: Venezuela, Colombia, Ecuador, Peru, and Bolivia.

The liberation of the continent was only one of Bolívar's many objectives. A human dynamo who thrived on constant activity, Bolívar also wanted to ensure that the fledgling republics of South America made a successful transition from colonies to nations. A man of words as well as action, Bolívar wrote prolifically amid his grueling military campaigns on almost every conceivable topic of his day. His main political writings—*La Carta de Jamaica* (1815; *The Jamaica Letter*, c. 1888), *Discurso pronunciado por el general Bolívar al congreso general de Venezuela en el aeto de su instalacion* (1819; *Speech of His Excellency, General Bolívar at the Installation of the Congress of Venezuela*, 1819), and his constitution for the new nation of Bolivia (1825)—demonstrate the evolution of his political thinking (and its growing conservatism) over time.

Although Bolívar fervently believed in democracy, he understood that Latin Americans lacked the political experience to adopt the model of democracy found in the United States. The colonial legacy of three centuries of autocratic rule would not be eclipsed overnight, and a transitional period was needed, during which the people had to be educated for democracy. His primary model, roughly sketched in *The Jamaica Letter*, was along the lines of the British constitutional monarchy.

Bolívar's first well-developed theory of government was presented to the Colombian Congress of Angostura in 1819. There, his eclectic mixture of individual rights and centralized government was described in detail. Many of the basic rights and freedoms articulated in the French Declaration of the Rights of Man and Citizen and the United States Bill of Rights were contained in his Angostura Address. Faithful to his promise to Pétion of Haiti, he asked that the congress of Great Colombia abolish slavery. To diminish the popular voice, he limited suffrage and asked for indirect elections. Moreover, the heart of Bolívar's political system was a hereditary senate, selected by a military aristocracy, the Order of Liberators. A strong executive would oversee the government, but his power was checked by his ministers, the senate, and a lower house which oversaw financial matters. Bolívar was elected the new nation's first president in 1821.

Bolívar preferred ideas to administration, opting to delegate responsibility for the day-to-day management of government to his vice president. Bolívar grew increasingly skeptical that a workable democracy could be implemented. His last political treatise, the constitution he wrote for the new nation of Bolivia (named for Bolívar) demonstrates this skepticism. This document included a three-house congress and a president elected for a life term with the power to choose a successor. This latest political creation was nothing more than a poorly disguised monarchy. The constitution pleased no one. When Bolívar tried to convince Great Colombia—a nation which Bolívar had fashioned, composed of Venezuela, Colombia, and Ecuador—to adopt the new constitution, his plea fell on deaf ears. To enact the goals of his administration, Bolívar then did in practice what his constitution permitted on paper: He ruled as a dictator.

Not only did Bolívar meet resistance in implementing his political agenda but he also was frustrated with his farsighted proposals for hemispheric cooperation and solidarity. Convinced that the newly formed Latin American states individually were powerless to withstand outside attack by a European power, he advocated a defensive alliance of Hispanic American states, which would provide military cooperation to defend the hemisphere from invasion. Bolívar invited all the Hispanic American countries, as well as the United States, Great Britain, and other European nations, to send delegates to a congress in Panama in 1826. It was hoped that the Panama Congress would create a league of Hispanic American states, provide for military cooperation, negotiate an alliance with Great Britain, and settle disputes among the nations. Bolívar even articulated the hope for the creation of an international peace-keeping organization. Unfortunately, few nations sent official delegates and Bolívar's visionary internationalist ideas remained dreams for more than a century.

Bolívar's last years were difficult. The new nations he had helped create were racked with internal dissension and violence. After a serious dispute with his vice president Francisco Santander in 1827, a weary Bolívar, suffering from tuberculosis, ruled as a dictator. A year later, an attempt on his life was narrowly averted. Finally, Bolívar was driven from office, when it was discovered that his cabinet had concocted a plan to search for a European monarch to rule after he stepped down. Although he knew nothing of the scheme, he suffered the political consequences. Bolívar resigned from office in 1830, almost penniless. He died on the coast near Santa Marta, Colombia, in 1830. He had asked to be buried in his home city of Caracas, but Bolívar had so many political enemies that his family feared for the safety of his remains. In 1842, his body was finally taken home.

Summary

Not until the wounds of the independence period were healed by time were the accomplishments of Simón Bolívar put in their proper perspective. In retrospect, his successes and his visionary ideas more than compensated for his egocentrism and the defeats he suffered. As a committed revolutionary and a military general, he had few peers. By sheer force of his dynamic persona and his tireless efforts, he ended colonialism and ushered in a new era of nationhood for South America.

On the political front, his successes were tempered by the political realities of the times. Bolívar knew that the new nations were not ready for independence and a long period of political maturation was needed before democracy could be achieved. His dictatorial actions in his last few years betrayed his own republican ideals, but Bolívar, ever the pragmatist, was convinced that the end justified the means. What Bolívar could not foresee was how elusive democracy would be for South America.

Similarly, his ideas for hemispheric solidarity were not accepted. Not until the creation of the Organization of American States and the signing of the Rio Pact in 1947 would the first halting steps toward pan-Americanism be taken. Bolívar's fears of the growing power of the United States and its potentially damaging effects on Hispanic America proved prophetic. One hundred fifty years after his death, Bolívar is lionized throughout Latin America not only for what he accomplished but also for what he dreamed.

Bibliography

Bolívar, Simón. *Selected Writings*. Edited by Harold A. Bierck, Jr. Translated by Lewis Bertrand. Compiled by Vicente Lecuna. 2 vols. New York: Colonial Press, 1951. A brief, complimentary biographical essay by Bierck introduces this solid collection of Bolívar's most significant political writings.

Bushnell, David. *The Santander Regime in Gran Colombia*. Newark: University of Delaware Press, 1954. A thorough academic monograph on the Santander regime, which examines Bolívar's increasingly despotic measures in his last years.

Hispanic American Historical Review 63 (February 1983). To celebrate the bicentennial of Bolívar's birth, editor John J. Johnson dedicated an entire issue of the preeminent journal in the field to a reappraisal of Bolívar. Four essays by independence period specialists reexamine and reassess both the man and his place in history. Includes John Lynch's "Bolívar and the Caudillos," Simon Collier's "Nationality, Nationalism, and Supranationalism in the Writings of Simón Bolívar," David Bushnell's "The Last Dictatorship: Betrayal or Consummation?" and Germán Carrera Damas' "Simón Bolívar, El Culto Heroico y la Nación."

Hodgson, Bryan, et al. "El Libertador: Simón Bolívar." *National Geographic* 185, no. 3 (March 1994). Bolívar is thought to be the force behind the nineteenth century move toward South American liberation. This piece debates whether he fostered democracy or dictatorship.

Johnson, John J. *Simón Bolívar and Spanish American Independence, 1783-1830*. New York: Van Nostrand, 1968. An excellent analytical overview of Bolívar's life and times. This book includes an abbreviated sample of some of the most important political writings by Bolívar.

Lynch, John. *The Spanish American Revolutions, 1808-1862*. 2d ed. New York: Norton, 1986. One of the best one-volume syntheses of the revolutionary era. Lynch's adroit analysis provides an overview of the internal and external factors that impinged on the struggle for independence. Includes a good examination of the personalities involved in the fighting.

Masur, Gerhard. *Simón Bolívar*. 2d ed. Albuquerque: University of New Mexico Press, 1948. One of the best biographies in English of Bolívar. Masur's even-handed narrative is generally sympathetic and conveys an appreciation for the difficulties that Bolívar faced in reconciling the divergent factions that threatened to divide the movement for independence.

Millington, Thomas. *Colombia's Military and Brazil's Monarchy: Undermining the Republican Foundations of South American Independence*. Westport, Conn.: Greenwood Press, 1996. A study of the relationship between the failure of republican politics in Brazil and the rise of monarchic rule.

Allen Wells

EDWIN BOOTH

Born: November 13, 1833; near Bel Air, Maryland
Died: June 7, 1893; New York, New York
Area of Achievement: Acting
Contribution: The most talented member of a family of actors, Edwin Booth suffered greatly from identity with his younger brother, the assassin John Wilkes Booth, but came to be admired for his art and his role in advancing the profession of acting in the United States.

Early Life

Edwin Thomas Booth was born November 13, 1833, on the family farm near Bel Air, Harford County, Maryland. His mother and father emigrated from London, England. She was the former Mary Ann Holmes, and he was the celebrated but temperamental actor Junius Brutus Booth. Ten children were born to the Booths, but only six of these survived early childhood. Edwin's older brother was Junius Brutus, Jr., and his older sister was Rosalie; his younger sister was Asia, and his younger brothers were John Wilkes and Joseph Adrian. Most of them, like Edwin, were short, slim, dark, and sensitive.

Edwin's formal education was cursory, but he was highly intelligent and a quick learner. Traveling with his alcoholic and unstable father as a boy, he determined to become an actor. He made his formal debut in Boston in a minor role in William Shakespeare's *Richard III* (1592-1593); two years later, in 1851, he played the lead for the first time in the same play in New York when his father refused to go on. In 1852, Edwin played the California gold camps. Junius Brutus Booth died later that year, and "Booth the Younger" was heralded in San Francisco as a worthy successor; still, it took several more years before Edwin equaled, and then exceeded, the reputation of his father.

In 1854, Booth joined a troupe headed for Australia, headlined by the distinguished actress Laura Keene; they performed in Sydney and Melbourne. Booth parted company with the troupe in Hawaii, following an argument, but while in Honolulu he was able to perform *Richard III* before King Kamehameha IV, using the king's throne for a prop. Then, in Sacramento, California, Booth proved that he could play romantic as well as tragic roles with remarkable skill when he played Raphael in a new melodrama by Charles Selby, *The Marble Heart: Or, The Sculptor's Dream* (1854). By the time he

returned to his family at last in 1856, he had the wide experience of a versatile actor.

Life's Work

Between 1857 and 1859, Booth triumphed upon the stage in Boston and New York, and became so celebrated in these and other cities for his portrayal of Richard III that both his father's version and that of his namesake, Edwin Forrest, were almost forgotten. Booth's voice was resonant and beautiful, and his gestures and looks were expressive and penetrating. No Shakespearean character was beyond him, but his Richard, Iago, Mark Anthony, Macbeth, and Hamlet were especially well received.

Admired by many, the young Edwin Booth had few close friends, among them journalist Adam Badeau and actor David Anderson. They knew better than most of his independent nature and penchant for drinking, and were surprised when he married an actress on July 7, 1860. This was the charming young Mary Devlin, daughter of a bankrupt Troy Devlin, a New York merchant. The Reverend Mr. Samuel Osgood, an Episcopalian clergyman, officiated at the ceremony in his home in New York City. On December 9, 1861, Mary gave birth to their only child, Edwina, but the mother grew ill and died on February 21, 1863. In 1869, Booth married Mary McVicker, stepdaughter of the proprietor of McVicker's Theater in Chicago; the only child of his second marriage, Edgar, died shortly after birth, and his second Mary became insane before her death in 1881.

Making his home in New York in the 1860's, Edwin played opposite Charlotte Cushman in a Philadelphia run of *Macbeth* (1606) and starred in *The Merchant of Venice* (1596-1597) and several other plays in London. In England, however, he was not as satisfied with his performances and their reception as he was in New York. The outbreak of the Civil War in the spring of 1861 also convinced him to stay close to home. Edwin, like most of the Booths, but certainly unlike John Wilkes, was supportive of the Union.

After becoming comanager of New York's Winter Garden Theatre, Edwin was able to produce his favorite Shakespearean plays and star in them as well. Obviously one of these favorites was singularly popular, as his production of *Hamlet, Prince of Denmark* (c. 1600-1601) ran for one hundred consecutive performances. Then, too, his produc-

tion of *Julius Caesar* (c. 1599-1600) with Edwin as Brutus and his brothers Junius as Cassius and John Wilkes as Mark Anthony, was very well received. The assassination of President Lincoln, however, by the latter brother five months later, in April, 1865, disgraced the family and forced Edwin to suffer an almost nine-month retirement from the public view.

Having been performing in Boston, Edwin returned to New York for his self-confinement. There he received several death threats, and the *New York Herald* treated him savagely. At first he expected never to perform again, but debts mounted and the *New York Tribune* appealed to him in print that he not waste his considerable talent. At last, on January 3, 1866, a nervous Booth appeared at New York's Winter Garden as Hamlet. The theater was packed, and the audience rose as one to applaud him at the opening curtain.

On January 22, 1867, Booth received a much-delayed gold medal for his unparalleled achievement two years before in the first hundred-night run of *Hamlet*. His popularity was such now that theatergoers in almost every major city in North America

asked to see him. A renewed *Hamlet* was followed by a production of Lord Lytton's *Richelieu: Or, The Conspiracy* (1839), then *The Merchant of Venice*, and then *Brutus: Or, The Fall of Tarquin*, by John Howard Payne. All were well received, but in *Brutus* fire was used to portray the burning of Rome, and it burned out of control one day in March to engulf the theater. With the destruction of the Winter Garden, Booth lost his finest costumes and was compelled to play benefit performances in Chicago and Baltimore.

Upon the advice of friends such as William Bispham, Booth built his own, superior, theater at the corner of Twenty-third Street and Sixth Avenue. Richard A. Robertson, a Boston businessman, was taken in as a partner. The Booth Theatre opened February 3, 1869, with a lackluster performance of *Romeo and Juliet* (c. 1595-1596). The critics felt that Booth and Mary McVicker were unconvincing in their romantic, title roles, yet they were married soon thereafter.

The excellent building, new costumes, props, and actors made the Booth Theatre the outstanding showplace for Shakespearean drama in America. Charlotte Cushman and others were coaxed out of retirement when given the opportunity to perform there. The great Edwin Forrest, however, refused to play in Booth's theater.

Booth's productions followed the Shakespearean texts rather than later adaptations, and historians were consulted to gain authenticity for the sets. Still, Booth was a poor businessman, and when he quarreled with Robertson the latter sold out to Booth, leaving the actor-manager heavily in debt. Booth's brother Junius tried to straighten out his affairs, but the Panic of 1873 destroyed their hopes. Early in 1874, Edwin Booth filed for bankruptcy, owing almost $200,000.

Repayment came, however, after Booth made a comeback in New York in October, 1875, when he played his unassailable Hamlet at Augustin Daly's Fifth Avenue Theater. A budding star in his own right also in the cast then was Maurice Barrymore, father of Ethel, Lionel, and John. In desperation, Booth now dared even to play Richard II and King Lear, although the former was new to him and the latter role had long been thought the special property of Edwin Forrest. These performances too won him much credit. He also played to packed houses in the South, although he had formerly refused to go there. In 1876, Booth performed with distinction at the California Theater in San Francisco.

Although his debts were paid off within two years of his bankruptcy and he was becoming more popular than ever, he still received threats on his life. On April 23, 1879, a madman named Mark Gray shot at him, twice, from the audience while Booth was acting the role of Richard II at McVicker's Theater in Chicago. Both shots went wild, and a composed Booth strode to the footlights so that he might point out the culprit to the police.

In the 1880's, Booth performed in Europe: in London (with Henry Irving) and elsewhere in the British Isles, in Berlin and other German cities, and in Vienna. Everywhere, but especially in Berlin, he was lauded for his Shakespearean roles, and invitations were extended from France, Spain, Italy, and Russia. Booth declined these offers; his dream was semiretirement in New England, and he returned to build a cottage called "Boothden" on the Rhode Island coast near Newport. He also acquired a larger house in Boston.

In 1888, Booth founded and served as first president of New York's club, The Players. When he performed in his later years, he liked to costar with accomplished younger actors such as Tommaso Salvini, Helena Modjeska, and Otis Skinner, and especially with another "old trouper;" Lawrence Barrett. After Barrett's death in 1891, Booth, in ill health, gave fewer and less inspired performances. His last effort was as Hamlet on April 4, 1891, at the Brooklyn Academy of Music. He weakened, suffered a brain hemorrhage, and died in New York on June 7, 1893, at the age of fifty-nine.

Summary

Booth, in his prime, was probably the world's preeminent tragedian. His performance as Hamlet moved even Germans unfamiliar with English to tears. His apt movements and the quiet but perfect modulation of his voice, its timbre and clarity, seemed to late nineteenth century audiences much more natural and refined than the loud, forced theatrics of a previous generation. Like Forrest's, Booth's King Lear was considered exquisite, but almost all the other tragic characters in Shakespeare's plays were also his meat.

Unfortunately, Booth's private life echoed the tragedy he played out upon the stage. His actor-brother's assassination of Lincoln, his father's and his own bouts with alcoholism, the failure of the Booth Theatre, the early deaths of his two Marys, and his own rapid aging were truly components of a tragic life. At last he lost heart and almost seemed to will his own death.

While the solid structure of the Booth Theatre was torn down in his lifetime, the subtle delicacy of his acting technique remains in the better theatrical performances of today. In his lifetime, he was forever compared, usually unfavorably, to his father, but Edwin Booth is universally recognized today as the greater actor of the two, and by far superior to Junius, Jr., and John Wilkes. Yet it is the continuing tragedy of the Booths that the best known of their number is the one who killed Abraham Lincoln.

Bibliography

Goodale, Katherine. *Behind the Scenes with Edwin Booth*. Boston: Houghton Mifflin, 1931. This is a charming and lively account of Booth's professional life during the years when the author knew him (after 1870). Goodale, who performed under the stage name Kitty Molony, makes excellent observations relating to Booth's mastery of his craft and is one of several authors to suggest that, despite his personal tragedies, he led a "charmed life."

Grossman, Edwina Booth. *Edwin Booth: Recollections by His Daughter*. New York: Century, 1894. Booth's sole surviving child was especially close to him during the years of his greatest success. His letters to her and some of his letters to friends such as David Anderson and William Bispham give this eulogy added strength and research value.

Kimmel, Stanley. *The Mad Booths of Maryland*. 2d ed. New York: Dover, 1969. One of the best and most readable books ever written about the Booth family, this one does much to explain the strained relationship between Edwin Booth and his brother, John Wilkes. All the Booth family members are dealt with here and treated with balance and fairness.

Lockridge, Richard. *Darling of Misfortune*. New York: Century, 1932. This is a sound enough biography, but one that was superseded by Ruggles' work (see below). It is, perhaps, most valuable on the brief life span of the Booth Theatre.

Oggel, L. Terry. *Edwin Booth: A Bio-Bibliography*. New York: Greenwood Press, 1992. A full analysis and extensive documentation of Booth's career as America's foremost nineteenth century Shakespearean actor. Includes over 1,000 annotated entries and a section on Booth's writings and manuscript materials whose locations in the United States and England are identified.

Ruggles, Eleanor. *Prince of Players: Edwin Booth*. London: Peter Davies, and New York: Norton, 1953. At this writing still the definitive biography of Booth, the book reflects the author's exhaustive research. While sympathetic toward her tragic subject, Ruggles does not hesitate to reveal the extent of his early struggle with alcoholism, which she believes to have been quieted only by the shock of his first wife's death.

Skinner, Otis. *The Last Tragedian*. New York: Dodd, Mead, 1939. Skinner, the father of the re-nowned actress Cornelia Otis Skinner, based this insider's account of Booth on their performances together, also making effective use of selected Booth letters.

Winter, William. *Life and Art of Edwin Booth*. London and New York: Macmillan, 1893. The celebrated drama critic of the *New York Tribune* was a longtime friend and confidant of Booth; he was also a prolific author, many of whose other works refer to the celebrated actor. This book contains much of value on the ups and downs of a remarkable career.

Joseph E. Suppiger

WILLIAM BOOTH

Born: April 10, 1829; Nottingham, England
Died: August 20, 1912; London, England
Areas of Achievement: Religion and social reform
Contribution: Compelled by his deep Christian faith to seek ways of serving his fellowman, Booth founded the international religious service organization, the Salvation Army, which became established in the United States fifteen years after the Civil War.

Early Life

William Booth was born in Nottingham, England, on April 10, 1829, the son of a humble builder, and was left fatherless at the age of thirteen. Determined to help support his family after his father's death, he served as an apprentice to a pawnbroker. At the age of fifteen, he underwent a dramatic Christian conversion, at which time he began his career as a preacher, eventually pursuing formal theological education through private tutors.

In 1849, Booth moved to London, where he worked on the side at a pawnbroker's shop, disliking the work but needing the income. It was during this time that he met the person who would become perhaps the single most important influence on his life and on his view of Christian service: Catherine Mumford, whom he would marry six years later and who would encourage him in his dream of becoming a full-time Christian minister.

By 1852, Booth had become entrenched in a respectable and established Methodist church, dutifully pastoring the congregation but vaguely yearning for a ministry that would bring him into contact with those who needed the assurance of God's care the most, the "street people" of Victorian London: the alcoholics, the orphans and widows, those abandoned by society. Increasingly uncomfortable with the isolation inherent in the life of a located minister, Booth left this pastorate after nine years. The Booths launched careers as independent revivalists; unattached to any particular denomination, they were free to speak their consciences.

The key event in their lives occurred in July, 1865, when they established a mission outpost at Whitechapel in London, an outreach of the "East London Revival Society," which came to be known as the Christian Mission. In typical revivalist rhetoric, Booth preached salvation from eternal punishment through belief in Christ, but he also offered a different, more immediate salvation from drunkenness, hunger, lack of clothing, and lack of shelter. By 1878, this mission was called the Salvation Army and had become a controversial yet effective means of taking Christianity out of the churches and into the streets; the Booths and their coworkers embraced the words of Jesus to the effect that "the healthy have no need of a physician; therefore, we must go to those who are sick."

Life's Work

Booth's genius was to employ a central military metaphor in organizing and conceptualizing his missionary work. Many historians of religion would argue that Booth was the first to recognize the need for and value of "packaging" religion in symbols and contexts that would arrest the attention of the public and associate his faith in the minds of adherents with something memorable and concrete. In founding the Salvation Army, Booth took the role of general and created ranks, uniforms, flags, rules of order, and even a military band.

The years between 1878 and 1890 saw the Army grow astoundingly successful in attracting other Christian workers and in assisting delinquents and lifelong ne'er-do-wells in reforming their lives and becoming respectable citizens within Victorian society. Booth's increasingly rigid, authoritarian manner, however, alienated many within Army ranks during this period, and his growing public power alarmed many outside the Army. These fears and objections came to a climax in 1890, when Booth published what was to be the most celebrated and defamed manifesto of his stormy career. Booth's *In Darkest England and the Way Out* proclaimed an elaborate plan for reforming Victorian society so that the poor would no longer be exploited and victimized by the cruelty of industrialized England.

At this time, the Victorian intelligentsia were buoyantly trumpeting the "survival-of-the-fittest" mentality arising from Charles Darwin's work on evolution and equally busily exploring and reporting upon the exotic lifestyles in "Darkest Africa." Their morbid fascination with the sordid tales of slavery and primitive worldviews angered Booth, whose book mocked their affluence and offered a ten-point plan for ridding society of poverty, including the creation of employment bureaus, farm colonies, state-provided legal assistance, and a missing-persons' agency. Progressive as it may

seem to a twentieth century readership, the book outraged Victorian society and was denounced by churchgoers and social critics as a form of reckless socialism; biologist Thomas Huxley, champion of Darwinism and opponent of religion, felt compelled to launch an unprecedented public attack on Booth and his social agenda.

Essentially, Booth's public image was never rehabilitated after the book's publication, and he lived out the remainder of his years in fervent but quiet service to the Army, assisting its formation and growth around the world until his final days in August, 1912. Only after his death did the prescience of his work and vision begin to receive the acclaim and respect it warranted.

Summary

In his time, William Booth was feared by some, loathed by others, but respected by all for his fierce determination to help the less fortunate, to prove that religion had application in this world as well as in the world to come. He succeeded admirably where others had failed in focusing the attention of the upper and middle classes on the plight of the indigent and destitute in an industrialized, capitalist culture.

Directly in England and indirectly in the United States, Booth appealed to the conscience of a wide range of church members, moving them to recognize their duty to reach the souls of men and women by first feeding and clothing them. While not the first to articulate the social dimensions of the Christian gospel, Booth as much as anyone in the early twentieth century was responsible for linking belief with action, faith with social responsibility.

The Army he started in the British Isles probably has its strongest presence in North America and is one of the most respected and responsible religious service organizations in operation. Indeed, in the minds of many, Booth's Salvation Army is more associated with relief efforts and noble self-sacrifice than it is with any specifically religious orientation or dogma. The Army's survival and health—more than a century removed from its origins and in a time more than skeptical about service institutions—is a greater tribute to General Booth's tenacity, faith, and love of mankind than any physical monument could be.

Bibliography

Begbie, Harold. *The Life of General William Booth.* 2 vols. New York: Macmillan, 1920. The standard, nearly exhaustive biography of Booth, which chronicles his childhood, adolescence, and eventful adulthood. This biography is written unabashedly as a tribute to a man whom the author regards as a "hero." While this quaintness wears thin very early, the two volumes contain the basic facts about the Booth family and their formation of the Salvation Army. Contains especially valuable excerpts from journals and letters that Booth wrote to his wife, Catherine, and others which illuminate the motivations of this driven man.

Bishop, Edward. *Blood and Fire! The Story of General William Booth and the Salvation Army.* London: Longmans, 1964; Chicago: Moody Press, 1965. A succinct narrative of the life and times of the Booth family and the Salvation Army. Helpful as it is as a brief overview of the main outlines of Booth's life and his program for reforming Victorian England, overall it is quite derivative of the earlier biographies of Booth and the Army.

Chesham, Sallie. *Born to Battle: The Salvation Army in America.* Chicago: Rand McNally, 1965. Though written primarily as a history of the Army in the United States, the early chapters of this volume provide a useful summary of Booth's life and the impact of the Salvation Army in the United States in the twenty years before the turn of the century.

Collier, Richard. *General Next to God: The Story of William Booth and the Salvation Army.* London: Collins, and New York: Dutton, 1965. A biography that updates and presents more concisely the information available in the sprawling two-volume opus of Begbie. Much less hagiographical than Begbie's work, but still disarming in its undisguised admiration for Booth and his work. The reader will not find a critical assessment of Booth's life or social agenda here.

Horridge, Glenn K. "William Booth's Officers." *Christian History* 9, no. 2 (1990). Examines how Booth encouraged young people to become Salvation Army members. Includes training strategies, Booth's organization, and the reasons young people joined and resigned.

Huxley, Thomas H. *Evolution and Ethics.* London and New York: Macmillan, 1893. Huxley, the Victorian social critic and popularizer of evolution, wrote a series of scathing attacks on Booth, which are collected in this volume under the chapter "Social Diseases and Worse Remedies." Huxley's remarks provide an interesting secularist counterpoint within Victorian England to Booth's ambitious social reform programs.

McKinley, E. H. *Somebody's Brother: A History of the Salvation Army Men's Social Services Department, 1891-1985*. Lewiston, N.Y.: Edwin Mellen Press, 1986. This volume examines in great detail the social activism of Booth that motivated him to link evangelism uniquely with feeding, clothing, and housing the poor and destitute.

Spence, Clark. *The Salvation Army Farm Colonies*. Tucson: University of Arizona Press, 1985. An interesting examination of the controversy surrounding Booth's initial call for state donation of farmland to be used for raising food for the poor. Spence chronicles the Victorian opposition to what appeared to many as "mere autocratic socialism."

Tisdale, Sallie. "Good Soldiers." *New Republic* 210, no. 1 (January 3, 1994). Overview of Booth, the Salvation Army, its membership, and its history of humanitarian work.

Wisbey, Herbert A. *Soldiers Without Swords*. New York: Macmillan, 1955. Another chronicle of the beginnings of the Salvation Army in the United States. Wisbey explains some of the reasons Booth initially refused to endorse the formal introduction of the Army in the United States.

Bruce L. Edwards

WILLIAM E. BORAH

Born: June 29, 1865; Jasper Township, Illinois
Died: January 19, 1940; Washington, D.C.
Areas of Achievement: Government and politics
Contribution: For more than three decades in the United States Senate, Borah was a leading nationalist who spoke and voted courageously for his idealistic view of American democracy.

Early Life

William Edgar Borah was born on June 29, 1865, in Wayne County in southern Illinois. The seventh child in a family of ten, he grew up in a household where hard work and religious devotion were stressed. His father, William Nathan Borah, was a strict disciplinarian and lay preacher at the local Presbyterian church. His mother, Elizabeth, moderated her husband's sternness. Grammar school, reading at home, and the tedium of farm chores marked the early life of young Borah. He attended the Cumberland Presbyterian Academy at nearby Enfield but left after only one year, largely because of insufficient family finances.

At the invitation of his sister, Sue Lasley, Borah moved to Kansas to continue his education, entering the University of Kansas in the fall of 1885. He left in 1887, after contracting tuberculosis, but not before developing an interest in the history and economics courses of Professor James H. Canfield and demonstrating proficiency at debate. He studied law in the office of his brother-in-law, Ansel Lasley, passed the bar examination in September, 1887, and entered practice with Lasley in Lyons, Kansas. Both men found the legal profession less profitable as poverty spread throughout Kansas in the late 1880's; when the Lasleys moved to Chicago in 1890, Borah set out for the developing West to make his mark.

Although associated with Idaho for his entire political career, he landed in the state almost by accident. He allegedly traveled to the Northwest until his money ran out, near Boise, which he saw as a fertile area for a young lawyer. He quickly built a solid reputation there. At the age of twenty-five, Borah was powerfully built, with a thick neck, a broad face, and a deeply cleft chin which denoted honesty and forthrightness; these physical attributes, combined with his oratorical abilities and a capacity for hard work, made him a forceful figure in the courtroom. He built a large practice and a statewide reputation as a criminal lawyer before 1900; thereafter, he mainly practiced corporate law, which earned for him an annual income of thirty thousand dollars.

Borah entered Boise politics in 1891 and was chairman of the Republican State Central Committee the next year. In 1895, Borah married Mary McConnell, the daughter of the state's Republican governor, William J. McConnell, for whom Borah worked as secretary. Following his bolt from the Republican Party for William Jennings Bryan and "free silver" in 1896, Borah returned to lead Idaho's Progressive Republicans to statewide victories in 1901-1902. He campaigned for the United States Senate in 1906, as a vigorous supporter of President Theodore Roosevelt, and was selected by the state legislature early in 1907.

Before taking his seat in the Senate later that year, Borah was involved in two significant trials in Idaho; the first helped establish him as a national figure of importance, while the second threatened to end his public career as it was beginning. In the

earlier case, Borah was appointed special prosecutor against William D. Haywood and two other leaders of the Western Federation of Miners, who were charged with conspiracy in the bombing death of former Governor Frank Steunenberg. While the jury voted to acquit the three, Borah was nevertheless outstanding in the fairness and clarity of his nine-hour summation for the prosecution. Borah was himself the defendant in the second case, in which he was charged with timber fraud while serving as attorney for the Barber Lumber Company. Although the incident was an ordeal for Borah, the evidence presented against him at the trial was flimsy, substantiating his charge that the affair was devised by his enemies to kill his political future. The jury acquitted him after less than fifteen minutes of deliberation. He was now free to assume the office in Washington which he would hold through five more elections, until he died.

Life's Work

Borah entered the Senate at a favorable time. The Progressive viewpoint was ascendant in national political affairs, and Borah was closely aligned with the Senate Progressive bloc on a number of issues. Furthermore, he was especially fortunate in being in a position to act, since Senate leader Nelson W. Aldrich assumed that Borah's former position as a corporate attorney meant that he shared Aldrich's pro-business, anti-labor outlook; consequently, Aldrich assigned Borah to choice committee appointments, including the chairmanship of the Committee on Education and Labor.

It was mainly during his first term that Borah earned his reputation for Progressive leadership. He sponsored bills for the creation of the Department of Labor and a Children's Bureau, and pushed for an eight-hour day for government-contracted labor. In addition, he was a mainstay in the fight for the direct election of United States Senators (which became the Seventeenth Amendment in 1913) and for the income tax (the Sixteenth Amendment, 1913). In the latter struggle, his major early contribution was his effective argument for the constitutionality of the income tax, contrary to the Supreme Court's finding in an 1895 case.

Borah also proved to be an effective representative of Idaho and other Western states on several key issues. He favored President William Howard Taft's proposal for a reciprocal trade agreement between the United States and Canada, involving free trade in some raw materials and agricultural products, an agreement favored by Western farmers. (The agreement passed in Congress but failed in the Canadian legislature.) He successfully promoted a plan for government-issued reclamation bonds, mainly used to finance irrigation projects in the Western states. He was the cosponsor of the Borah-Jones Act (1912), which reduced, from five years to three years, the period required for residence before homesteaders could acquire patents to the land they claimed. Finally, he managed to free, for private development, some Western land which the federal government had set aside for conservation.

Borah was not included in the roll call of other Progressives on all these issues, especially in regard to conservation matters. He was critical of the federal government's administration of conservation policy, believing that the individual states should play a greater role. In the *cause célèbre* over Interior Secretary Richard Ballinger's removal of Chief Forester Gifford Pinchot, Borah broke with the Progressives in supporting Ballinger and the Taft Administration; he also supported the Administration on the controversial Payne-Aldrich Tariff. In the election of 1912, Borah led the Theodore Roosevelt forces in the National Republican Convention but refused to bolt from the Republican Party when Roosevelt's followers formed the Progressive Party. During Woodrow Wilson's first term, Borah continued to be a selective Progressive, as he voted against legislation such as the Federal Trade Commission Act, the Clayton Antitrust Act, and the creation of the Federal Reserve system. Although opposition to some of these bills was based on partisan political considerations, Borah generally opposed federal centralization and often referred to states' rights in explaining his votes against measures supported by other Progressives.

Borah began to change the focus of his interests to international affairs with the onset of World War I; in the decades following the war, he became the acknowledged Senate spokesman on foreign policy for his party. He supported preparation for war in 1916, backed Wilson's breaking of diplomatic relations with Germany in February, 1917, and voted for the declaration of war in April. Like other Progressives, however, he became disillusioned with the war effort, which severely limited reform achievements, and stated that, if it were possible, he would change the vote he had cast in favor of war. At the end of World War I, he led the Senate irreconcilables in the fight against the Treaty of Versailles and the League of Nations, stating that it was not in the best interests of the United States to become entangled in the affairs of Europe.

As a nationalist in foreign affairs, Borah opposed any international agreements that would restrict the country's freedom of choice to act in world affairs. While he opposed American membership in the World Court as well as in the League of Nations, he was a strong proponent of disarmament plans. He was instrumental in organizing the Washington conference on disarmament in 1921 and, as Chairman of the Senate Committee on Foreign Relations after 1924, he supported plans for the international outlawry of war, which culminated in the Kellogg-Briand Pact of 1928. In the face of the international crises of the 1930's, Borah became increasingly isolationist, favoring the restriction of American trade and diplomatic involvement abroad.

Borah differed with the Republican Party on major political issues during the 1920's, but he refused to leave the party in 1924 to support his long-time political ally, Robert M. LaFollette, the Progressive Party candidate for president. He was a leading campaigner for Herbert Hoover in 1928, although he became a consistent critic of Hoover policies after the election. He supported most of the major legislation of the New Deal, with the exception of the National Industrial Recovery Act, which he criticized for its suspension of antitrust laws. Following his sixth consecutive election to the Senate, in 1936, he concentrated most of his energy on opposing the foreign policies of Franklin D. Roosevelt's administration. In January, 1940, he suffered a cerebral hemorrhage and died three days later. Following a funeral in the Senate chamber, he was buried in Boise.

Summary

In 1936, journalist Walter Lippmann wrote a trenchant description of Senator Borah as "an individualist who opposes all concentration of power, who is against private privilege and private monopoly, against political bureaucracy and centralized government." Lippmann was describing Borah the Jeffersonian Democrat, who believed in an ideal vision of the United States, with a relatively uncomplicated political system based on direct democracy, with guarantees for the freewheeling expression of rights by the individual, and without favoritism for special interests. These were the essential beliefs of Borah's political life, formed in his youth by family guidance and by reading authors such as Ralph Waldo Emerson, reinforced by his rural environment in Illinois, Kansas, and Idaho, and forged by his contacts with the Populists in the 1890's. Such beliefs formed the underpinnings of Borah's Progressive leadership.

Borah attempted to apply these principles throughout his public career. In his speeches and actions, he made it clear that his conscience and convictions served as his guide on major national issues, rather than considerations of party loyalty or personal popularity. In writing to a constituent about his religious ideals in opposition to the Ku Klux Klan, Borah averred, "If the time ever comes when I shall have to sacrifice my office for these principles, I shall unhesitatingly do so."

Borah's idealistic conception of the United States, while not always based on a realistic appraisal of modern conditions, influenced the nation during his career in the Senate because of his brilliance as an orator. He shared the belief of many other Progressives in the power of public opinion as a moral force and sought to mobilize that force through scores of well-researched and well-rehearsed addresses in Congress and the nation. His oratorical abilities, as well as the courageous pursuit of his convictions, placed him in the front rank of public men of his time.

Bibliography

Ashby, LeRoy. *The Spearless Leader: Senator Borah and the Progressive Movement in the 1920's.* Urbana: University of Illinois Press, 1972. Treats Borah's involvement in domestic affairs from 1920 to 1928, while most other accounts concentrate only on his foreign policy views as chairman of the Senate Committee on Foreign Relations. Valuable not only for Borah's viewpoints but also as a consideration of the fate of Progressivism in the 1920's.

Borah, William Edgar. *Bedrock: Views on Basic National Problems.* Washington, D.C.: National Home Library Foundation, 1936. Includes speeches and a few articles from 1909 to 1936, organized by topic. Introduces the reader to the flavor of Borah's speeches on a wide range of topics and presents Borah's viewpoints on what he considered to be paramount issues.

Cooper, John M., Jr. "William E. Borah, Political Thespian." *Pacific Northwest Quarterly* 56 (October 1965): 145-153. A stimulating discussion of Borah's career, in which the author maintains that Borah's decision to deliver moral exhortations on issues, rather than to take bolder actions in the Senate, limited his effectiveness in public life. The article is followed with comments by two other Borah scholars and a reply by Cooper.

Johnson, Claudius O. *Borah of Idaho*. New York: Longman, 1936. Based largely on interviews with Borah, as well as the Borah papers, the book is thorough (to 1936) but often partial in its advocacy of Borah's views.

McKenna, Marian C. *Borah*. Ann Arbor: University of Michigan Press, 1961. The most complete and balanced biography of Borah. A well-written book, it is based, in part, on papers relating to Borah's early career, which the Idaho State Historical Society received in 1956.

Maddox, Robert James. *William E. Borah and American Foreign Policy*. Baton Rouge: Louisiana State University Press, 1969. Evaluates Borah's positions on major foreign policy issues from World War I until the eve of World War II. Maddox asserts that Borah's seemingly paradoxical (for an isolationist) interest in international conferences and treaties was actually a smoke screen for obstructing meaningful United States involvement in international organizations.

Vinson, John Chalmers. *William E. Borah and the Outlawry of War*. Athens: University of Georgia Press, 1957. Treats Borah's growing interest, from 1917, in the movement to "outlaw" war, which resulted in the 1928 Kellogg-Briand Pact. A thoroughly documented account based primarily on Borah's papers in the Library of Congress.

Richard G. Frederick

LIZZIE BORDEN

Born: July 19, 1860; Fall River, Massachusetts

Died: June 1, 1927; Fall River, Massachusetts

Area of Achievement: Law

Contribution: The legend of Lizzie Borden, axe murderer, endures despite the fact that Borden was acquitted of the August 4, 1892, murder of her father, Andrew Jackson Borden, and stepmother, Abby Durfee Gray Borden.

Early Life

Born on July 19, 1860, Lizzie Andrew Borden and her older sister, Emma Lenora, were raised by their stepmother, Abby, and their father, Andrew. Lizzie's mother, Sarah Morse, died when Lizzie was an infant; two years later, Andrew married Abby Durfee Gray, who cared for the Borden girls for thirty years. By 1892, Lizzie was thirty-two and Emma was forty-two years of age. Unmarried, both sisters continued to live in the Borden house on 92 Second Street, one of the busiest streets in Fall River, Massachusetts.

The Borden name was influential in Fall River. The eighth generation of Bordens in the town, Andrew owned numerous properties, served as bank president, sat on the board of directors of three other banks, and was the director of several businesses. He was worth a half-million dollars (a multimillionaire by contemporary standards) and was a man of high social standing, known for his considerable wealth as well as for his penurious nature.

Lizzie was an active member of her church, a Sunday school teacher, a participant in a variety of women's groups, a leader of the town's Christian Endeavor Society, and a member of the Women's Christian Temperance Union (WCTU). At only twenty years of age, Lizzie was named to the board of the Fall River Hospital. She devoted herself to community work and was recognized for her efforts.

Life's Work

On Thursday, August 4, 1892, there were five people in the Borden's small house on Second Street: Andrew, Abby, Lizzie, Bridget Sullivan (the family servant), and John Vinnicum Morse (Lizzie and Emma's maternal uncle). Morse had unexpectedly arrived the prior evening; he brought no valise but intended to spend several nights. Emma had been staying in Fairhaven, Massachusetts, visiting friends.

Members of the Borden household had been ill, supposedly from eating spoiled meat. Abby seldom left the house but had visited family physician Seabury Bowen on Wednesday, August 3, with a story about an anonymous note; she believed someone was poisoning the family. Lizzie also told friend Alice Russell that she thought that the family's milk was being poisoned. During the inquest that followed the murders of Abby and Andrew, the prosecution brought forth Eli Bence, a druggist who claimed that Lizzie unsuccessfully attempted to purchase prussic acid in his pharmacy the day before the murders. Lizzie denied Bence's claims, stating that she remained home all day Wednesday, leaving only briefly that evening to visit Russell, who would later testify that on Wednesday night a distraught Lizzie predicted that an ominous event would soon transpire in the Borden house.

By 9:30 or 10:00 Thursday morning, Abby lay face down on the floor of the upstairs guest bedroom, mortally wounded by nineteen axe or hatchet wounds delivered to the back of the scalp. By all accounts, Lizzie was the only individual in the house between 9:30 and 10:45. Lizzie testified that she saw no one and heard nothing. Sullivan indicated that she was outside the home, washing windows at Abby's request. Morse told authorities that he left the house that morning around 8:45 to visit another niece in town and returned approximately forty-five minutes after the murders were discovered.

Lizzie alleged that early that morning Abby claimed to receive a note asking her to visit a sick friend; however, no note was ever discovered, nor did anyone come forward with information about the note despite a $5,000 reward posted by the Borden sisters.

Andrew reportedly returned home around 10:45 that morning. He greeted his daughter and reclined on a sofa in the sitting room. Shortly before 11:00 A.M., Sullivan retired to her third-floor room to rest. Lizzie testified that, supposing her stepmother had left the house, she wandered to the barn and searched the second story of the building for lead for a sinker for Monday's possible fishing excursion. She also ate some pears in the barn, remaining there for a span of fifteen or twenty minutes. Upon her return to the house, she discovered her father's prone body in the sitting room. He had been struck by eleven axe or hatchet wounds and was so disfigured by the blows that he was virtually unrecognizable to Dr. Bowen. The time was approximately 11:00 or 11:15 A.M. Lizzie cried for Bridget, asking her to find Bowen. Attracted by the commotion, neighbor Adelaide B. Churchill ran to the house at Lizzie's request and stayed with her until the doctor arrived. Shortly after Bowen's arrival, Abby's bludgeoned body was discovered upstairs.

Four legal hearings ensued: the inquest (the only proceeding in which Borden testified), the grand jury hearing, a preliminary hearing, and the murder trial itself. Denied counsel, Lizzie testified without representation at the inquest and, at the conclusion of this testimony, was arrested and held without bail in Taunton Jail for ten months awaiting trial. George D. Robinson and Andrew J. Jennings, friends of the Bordens, represented her. Robinson, former governor of Massachusetts, was hired for a fee of $25,000.

The trial began on June 7, 1893. Charged with first-degree murder, Lizzie, if found guilty, faced death by hanging. William H. Moody and Hosea M. Knowlton prosecuted for the state. (Moody would later be appointed by President Theodore Roosevelt to serve on the U.S. Supreme Court in 1906.) Three justices of the Massachusetts Supreme Court presided at the trial, one of whom faced criticism for his charge to the jurors in what many suggest was a prodefense bias. The jury comprised white, middle- to upper-class men. (Working-class men, many of them foreign-born immigrants who worked in Fall River factories, were excluded from serving on the jury despite the fact that they were naturalized citizens. Women were also excluded.) Lizzie did not testify in her defense, and her inquest testimony was excluded from the trial's proceedings.

The prosecution claimed that Lizzie's motive had been both avarice and hatred, arguing that she had committed parricide not only out of loathing for her stepmother but also to prevent Andrew from changing his will to Abby's favor. The prosecution pointed to one event as representative of the tension between Lizzie and Abby. Five years prior to the murder, Andrew bought half of a two-dwelling home in Abby's name for her sister. Lizzie's own testimony at the inquest indicated that both daughters took umbrage at their father's generosity, particularly as it was directed toward his wife's family rather than his daughters. Lizzie testified that she ceased calling Abby "mother" about that time but noted that their relationship was cordial.

The defense referred to Lizzie's stellar reputation in Fall River society to refute the prosecution's claims. The defense also noted that the Borden home had been burglarized twelve months before the murders and that the barn had been broken into twice, thus introducing the possibility of an anonymous assailant. The defense continued to stress that Lizzie was not capable of such a fiendish deed.

The prosecution argued that Lizzie, alone in the house with the victims, had ample opportunity to commit patricide. The defense refuted the prosecution's claims, pointing to the lack of blood on the accused. Churchill testified that when she arrived at the Borden house, no blood spotted Borden's dress nor was her hair disheveled. However, contradicting testimonies surfaced regarding Lizzie's attire during the time of the murder as well as which articles of clothing were turned over to the police. Russell complicated matters by testifying for the prosecution that three days after the murders, Lizzie burned a skirt in Emma and Russell's presence, complaining of irremovable paint stains. Lizzie denied that the burned skirt was the one worn during the murders.

The defense refuted the claim that Lizzie had the opportunity to commit the murders by questioning the actions of the police who interviewed her after the crimes. The defense also questioned the lack of a murder weapon, which was never found but was believed to be a handleless hatchet smeared with dust or ash that was found in the Borden basement. However, a microscopic examination of the blade revealed no traces of blood. The handle was never recovered.

After only one hour of deliberation, the jury declared Lizzie "not guilty." Newspaper reports claimed that jurors needed only ten or fifteen minutes to decide but waited another forty-five minutes to inform the court out of respect to the prosecution. Accounts also reported that prosecutor Knowlton, a reluctant litigator, clapped at the verdict.

Because Andrew died intestate, Lizzie and Emma inherited nearly a half-million dollars in cash and real estate. With this considerable wealth, the Borden sisters bought a large new house in a fashionable section of Fall River. Lizzie called the house Maplecroft and renamed herself Lizbeth. She traveled widely, associated with popular actor Nance O'Neal, and continued to live in Fall River until her death on June 1, 1927. The murders of Andrew and Abby Borden remain unsolved.

Summary

Lizzie Borden has become a part of American legend. For over a century, verses, songs, stories, dramas, and a ballet have been devoted to her. There is an enduring interest in Lizzie and the Fall River murders because she was such an unlikely murderer. The story of a dutiful daughter and Sunday school teacher brutally murdering her wealthy parents with an axe commanded much attention in the press during her legal proceedings.

Lizzie has retained legendary status perhaps in part because of widespread media coverage. The murder of Fall River's socially prominent Bordens was startling, and the arrest of their daughter was even more shocking. The advent of yellow journalism encouraged media attention. Over forty newspapers exploited the case; all of them devoted their attention to the gruesome details of the brutal double murder, and all of them questioned jurisprudence in the United States. Many, including the *Boston Herald*, *The New York Times*, and the *New York Herald*, portrayed Lizzie as a defenseless woman victimized by an inept police department. Only the Fall River *Globe*, condemning the Bordens as elite oppressors, consistently depicted Lizzie as guilty.

After her acquittal, Lizzie's image as a helpless woman maltreated by Fall River police was countered to such a degree that the name of Lizzie Borden eventually became synonymous with a female axe murderer. Children, blissfully unaware of Lizzie's acquittal, continue to sing, "Lizzie Borden took an ax/ And gave her mother forty whacks;/ When she saw what she had done/ She gave her father forty-one!"

Bibliography

Brown, Arnold R. *Lizzie Borden: The Legend, The Truth, The Final Chapter.* Nashville, Tenn.: Rutledge Hill Press, 1991. Brown argues that the Bordens were murdered by Andrew's illegitimate son. The appendix contains Lizzie's testimony at the inquest.

Kent, David. *Forty Whacks: New Evidence in the Life and Legend of Lizzie Borden.* Emmaus, Pa.: Yankee Books, 1992. Kent demystifies myths surrounding Borden and attempts to provide a balanced treatment of the Borden case.

_____, ed. *Lizzie Borden Sourcebook.* Boston: Branden, 1992. This book contains clippings from forty-three newspapers and shows the images of Lizzie generated by the media.

Lincoln, Victoria. *A Private Disgrace: Lizzie Borden by Daylight.* New York: Putnam, 1967; London: Gollancz, 1969. The author suggests that Lizzie committed the murders during an epileptic seizure initiated by her menstrual period.

Pearson, Edmund. *Trial of Lizzie Borden.* London: Heinemann, and New York: Doubleday, 1937. Pearson argues that Borden was guilty of the murders.

Porter, Edwin H. *The Fall River Tragedy: A History of the Borden Murders.* Fall River, Mass.: Buffinton, 1893. This book was the first book about the Lizzie Borden case. Porter was a reporter for the *Globe* and was present at the trial.

Radin, Edward D. *Lizzie Borden: The Untold Story.* London: Gollancz, and New York: Simon and Schuster, 1961. Radin theorizes that Bridget Sullivan committed the murders.

Schuetz, Janice. *The Logic of Women on Trial: Case Studies of Popular American Trials.* Carbondale: Southern Illinois University Press, 1994. This book contains a chapter on the Borden trial and argues that class and gender informed Borden's acquittal despite compelling evidence against her.

Spiering, Frank. *Lizzie.* New York: Random House, 1984. Spiering claims that Emma committed the murders in order to avoid being disinherited and that Lizzie stood trial for her sister.

Michele L. Mock

ALEKSANDR BORODIN

Born: November 12, 1833; St. Petersburg, Russia
Died: February 27, 1887; St. Petersburg, Russia
Area of Achievement: Music
Contribution: Borodin made a significant contribution to the repertory of Russian national music, with particular excellence in the domains of opera, symphonic music, chamber music, and song.

Early Life

Aleksandr Porfiryevich Borodin was born out of wedlock to Prince Luka Stepanovitch Gedianov and Avdotya Konstantinova Antinova. Following Aleksandr's birth, his father had him registered as the legal son of Porfiry Borodin, one of his servants, in accordance with a custom of the time and arranged for his mistress to marry Christian Ivanovitch Kleinecke, a retired army medical practitioner. Aleksandr was educated by private tutors, with emphasis placed on foreign languages (German, French, and English). Prior to his death, Luka granted freedom to his son. Avdotya, after her husband's death, bore another son, Dmitry, through another liaison, and bought a house near the Semyonov Parade Ground, which is where Aleksandr spent his youth and adolescence.

Aleksandr composed a Polka in D Minor that he entitled "Hélène." Piano study, attendance at symphonic concerts at the university during the winter and at Joseph Gungl's concerts at Pavlovsk in the summer, and self-instruction on the cello moved the youth toward serious creativity; indeed, in 1847, he composed a Trio in G Major on a theme from Giacomo Meyerbeer's *Robert le diable*, and a concert for flute and piano. There followed, in quick succession, two piano compositions, a fantasy on a theme by Johann Nepomuk Hummel, and a study, *Le Courant*. While developing his emerging musical talent, Borodin evinced an equally strong interest in chemistry.

In the fall of 1850, Borodin was an external student at the Academy of Physicians. By 1855, he completed his course of study with distinction. Borodin moved up the ladder of academic success with alacrity. He gained experience as a surgeon but came to realize that he was ill-suited for this calling. On May 5, 1858, he was awarded the doctor of medicine degree. After travels to Western Europe connected with his scientific career, he corresponded in the fall of 1859 with Modest Mussorgsky, from whom he acquired an appreciation for the music of Robert Schumann. Later that year, his teacher Nikolai Zinin arranged for Borodin to work in Heidelberg so as to gain the kind of experience that would enable him to assume a professorial position in chemistry upon his return.

Life's Work

The Heidelberg period, which extended to 1862, proved to be a turning point in Borodin's life. It was here that he developed a friendship with the Russian chemist Dmitry Mendeleyev and attended lectures by such luminaries as Hermann Helmholtz and Gustav Robert Kirchhoff, the latter a pioneer with Robert Wilhelm Bunsen in the field of spectrum analysis. Travel to Freiburg (where he heard the famed organ there), Italy, and the Netherlands turned the once-sheltered Borodin into a cosmopolite.

In May, 1861, Borodin met his future wife, the twenty-nine-year-old Ekaterina Sergeyevna Proto-

popova. He traveled with her to Mannheim to hear such Wagnerian epics as *Tannhäuser* (1845) and *Lohengrin* (1848), and settled with her in Pisa. In terms of composition, he produced in this period a Sonata in C Minor for cello and piano (a three-movement work based on the fugue theme from Johann Sebastian Bach's Sonata in G Minor for violin), a Scherzo in E Major for piano duet, several incomplete chamber works, and, most significantly, a Sextet in D Minor for strings. This last composition was written, according to its creator, to please the Germans. Its two movements reflect Mendelssohnian traits, as, for example, in the lively sonata-allegro first movement with its "feminine" second subject and in the theme and variation second movement based on the song "How Did I Grieve Thee?" employed previously by the composer. Particularly interesting is the pizzicato variation, a technique that came to be identified with the Russian as it had been with Mendelssohn. The four-movement Quintet in F Minor for strings establishes Borodin as a master of the early Romantic style associated with the German school, notably in the use of classical forms, lyrical and evocative melodic lines, excellence in part-writing, and elfinlike scherzo movements. In addition, there is present a nostalgic yearning for the homeland, an awareness of the contributions of Mikhail Glinka in particular, and a Russian imprint on the Germanic fabric.

Borodin returned to St. Petersburg in September, 1862, and by December he was actively engaged in the world of academia. Apart from lecturing and translating scientific books, he gravitated again toward musical creativity, especially after meeting Mily Balakirev, mentor of the so-called Russian Five. After hearing the incipient works by this quintet of nationalists, the groundwork was laid for a shift from mainstream German Romanticism to Russian nationalism. Despite a fitful approach to large-scale composition, necessitated by his vocation, Borodin, under Balakirev's guidance, produced his First Symphony in 1867; it was premiered under Balakirev's direction on March 7, 1868, before the Russian Musical Society's directorate and, on January 16, 1869, it received its first public hearing. Encouraged by Balakirev, Borodin acquired the confidence to pursue his creative avocation on a surer footing. Although the opera-farce *Bogatiri* was a dismal failure at its premiere on November 18, 1867, the songs, which include "Pesnya tyomnovo lesa"

(song of the dark forest) and "Falshivaya nota" (the false note) were more successful.

Borodin's personal life was solidified with his marriage to Ekaterina on April 17, 1863, in St. Petersburg. That fall, the couple moved to an apartment in a building owned by the Academy of Military Medicine, and, except for occasional travel, it was the composer's abode until his death. Throughout his life, the composer-scientist was found attractive by adoring young women; however, with the adoption of seven-year-old Liza Bolaneva, his marriage was established on solid footing.

In April, 1869, the critic Vladimir Stasov suggested that Borodin begin the opera that would be named *Prince Igor*, which was based on a twelfth century epic. By March, 1870, however, when his original interest in the project waned, he adopted some of the music he had already committed to paper for use in his Symphony No. 2 in B Minor. During the early 1870's, professional responsibilities created continuing impediments to uninterrupted musical achievement. In addition to lecturing on chemistry and supervising student work, Borodin became a leading advocate for medical courses for women. During 1874-1875, the "Polovtsian Dances" and other segments of *Prince Igor* were completed, and between 1874 and 1879 he finished the String Quartet in A Major. On March 10, 1877, Eduard Napravnik conducted the completed Second Symphony with limited success. After some revision, the work was accorded a more favorable response when it was conducted on March 4, 1879, by Nikolay Rimsky-Korsakov. The four-movement work is notable for its coloristic treatment of the orchestra, particularly for the passages for winds and harp, for its rhythmic drive and meter changes, and for its juxtaposition of long-breathed, folkloric melody and exciting, Tartarlike abandon.

Having achieved the succor that comes after so arduous an experience as seeing his Second Symphony through to a public performance, Borodin visited various German universities with a view toward gaining a better understanding of their laboratories. On one such trip, he called on Franz Liszt at Weimar (July, 1877) and met with the Hungarian master on five different occasions over a three-week period. A few more numbers were added to *Prince Igor*, but a streak of procrastination prevented the opera from moving forward to completion; it was left to Rimsky-Korsakov and Aleksandr Glazunov to orchestrate much of it after Borodin's death. Ironically, Borodin squandered much of the little time he had dallying with musical jokes, such as a polka contrived to be performed with "Chopsticks" as the accompaniment. While other composers contributed their talents to compositions on this motif, among them Rimsky-Korsakov and Anatoly Lyadov, and saw the entire set published in 1880 under the title *Paraphrases*, Balakirev rebuked the perpetrators of this farce for wasting time and effort on such trifles. Meanwhile, through Liszt's influence, Borodin's music obtained a hearing in Western Europe. The Symphony No. 1 was performed in Baden-Baden, Germany, on May 20, 1880, the year in which the composer wrote his symphonic poem, *In the Steppes of Central Asia* (dedicated to Liszt).

A setting of Alexander Pushkin's poem "Dlya beregov otchizni dalnoy" (for the shores of thy far native land) was prompted by the death from alcoholism of Mussorgsky on March 28, 1881. The String Quartet No. 2 in D Major, dedicated to Borodin's wife, suggests an evocation of the idyllic period in Heidelberg. It is best known today for its third movement, the *Nocturne*, in which the cello is given a soaring melodic line of incomparable beauty. Although Ekaterina's health was always precarious, it was Borodin who suffered an attack of cholera in June, 1885, leading, eventually, to the heart disease that took his life.

The European taste for Borodin's music spread to France and Belgium, and, in appreciation of her efforts on his behalf, the composer dedicated to the Belgian Countess of Mercy-Argenteau his six-movement *Petite Suite* for piano (1885). With César Cui, he enjoyed huge successes in Liège and Brussels. In 1886, despite the illnesses of his wife and mother-in-law, Borodin collaborated with Rimsky-Korsakov, Lyadov, and Glazunov on a string quartet in honor of the publisher, M.P. Balaiev. Two movements of his Third Symphony were completed, the second of which is a scherzo whose material is drawn from *Prince Igor*. Although interest in the opera was revived in 1887, only an overture and several additional numbers were actually completed. On the evening of February 27, 1887, at a lavish ball for the families and friends of the faculty of the Medical Academy, Borodin, attired in red shirt and high boots, and in apparent good spirits, succumbed suddenly to heart failure and died instantly. His beloved Ekaterina survived him by five months.

Summary

Of Aleksandr Borodin, Sir William Hadow said: "No musician has ever claimed immortality with so slender an offering. Yet, if there be, indeed, immortalities in music, his claim is incontestable." It is assuredly a phenomenal achievement when an individual rises to a position of eminence in fields as diverse as music and science, the one so intuitive and subjective but requiring the utmost discipline, the other so measured and objective. Borodin was somehow able to bring his analytical mind to bear on his creative impulses.

Borodin was a remarkable creative artist, a respected scientist, and a human being of the utmost sensibility and refinement. That he found the time and the inclination to cofound the School of Medicine for Women in St. Petersburg and to teach chemistry there from 1872 until his death, bespeaks of a man well ahead of his time. Borodin's compassion for humankind, his life of industry, and his zeal in the pursuit of excellence serve as reminders to a skeptical world that a job worth doing is a job worth doing well. When his music was adapted for use in the box-office triumph *Kismet*, which opened at New York's Ziegfeld Theatre on December 3, 1953, American audiences were introduced to Borodin's art in popularized format, and they were touched. Since that time, these treasures, in the original versions and touchups, have earned an honored place in the concert halls of the world. Borodin's is a music that contains a civility that transcends national boundaries.

Bibliography

Abraham, Gerald. *Borodin: The Composer and His Music*. London: Reeves, 1927; New York: AMS Press, 1974. A very thorough traversal of Borodin's life and works. Contains musical analyses.

———. *On Russian Music*. New York: Scribner, and London: Reeves, 1939. Two of the book's chapters deal expressly with Borodin and his music. One is devoted to "The History of Prince Igor," while the other deals with "Borodin's Songs."

Abraham, Gerald, and David Lloyd-Jones. "Alexander Porfir'yevich Borodin." In *The New Grove Dictionary of Music and Musicians*, edited by Stanley Sadie, vol. 3. London: Macmillan, and Washington, D.C.: Grove's Dictionaries of Music, 1980. An outstanding encyclopedia entry covering the salient biographical data and providing a clear-cut overview of Borodin's music according to genre. Contains a catalog of works and a fine bibliography.

Asafev, B. V. *Russian Music from the Beginning of the Nineteenth Century.* Translated by Alfred J. Swan. Ann Arbor, Mich.: J. W. Edwards for the American Council of Learned Societies, 1953. This influential work treats Borodin's music in the context of broad categories of subject matter. The approach allows the reader to see the composer's contributions via-à-vis those of his principal contemporaries and in the light of the aesthetic trends then prevalent in Russia.

Calvocoressi, Michel D., and Gerald Abraham. *Masters of Russian Music.* New York: Knopf, and London: Duckworth, 1936. Presents a fine traversal of the major events in the composer's life and touches on the high points of representative compositions.

Dianin, Sergei. *Borodin.* Translated by Robert Lord. London and New York: Oxford University Press, 1963. This is a major life and works study of Borodin, with very important coverage of his ancestry, his childhood, and his adolescence. The music is discussed according to genre. Includes a chronological catalog of works and a genealogical table. A first-rate piece of scholarship.

Habets, Alfred. *Borodin and Liszt.* Translated by Rosa Newmarch. London: Digby, Long, 1895; New York: AMS Press, 1977. Part 1 covers Borodin's life and works, touching on significant biographical details. A chapter entitled "The Scientist" presents insight into this major aspect of the artist's dual allegiances.

Lloyd-Jones, David. "Borodin in Heidelberg." *Musical Quarterly* 46 (1960): 500. A thorough account of Borodin's stay in Heidelberg. Emphasizes his development as a composer, offers succinct comments and insights into specific compositions, and places the musical contributions in the context of his personal life and his scientific career.

Robinson, Harlow. "If You're Afraid of Wolves, Don't Go into the Forest: On the History of Borodin's 'Prince Igor.' " *The Opera Quarterly* 7, no. 4 (Winter 1990). Discussion of Borodin's opera, "Prince Igor."

David Z. Kushner

F. H. BRADLEY

Born: January 30, 1846; Clapham, Surrey, England
Died: September 18, 1924; Oxford, England
Area of Achievement: Philosophy
Contribution: In the history of British philosophy, Bradley represents a point of view that is fundamentally Idealist. He was a vigorous, gifted, brooding critic of England's empirical philosophers.

Early Life

Francis Herbert Bradley was the fourth child of the Reverend Charles Bradley, an Evangelical minister, and Emma Linton Bradley. Little is known about his early life. He was educated at Cheltenham (1856-1861) and Marlborough (1861-1863), and in 1865 he attended University College, Oxford. In 1870, at the age of twenty-four, he became a Fellow at Merton College, Oxford, where he remained until his death in 1924. A year after arriving at Oxford, he contracted a kidney disease which disabled him and left him sick and suffering, sardonic and sometimes bitter. Fortunately, his fellowship allowed him to pursue scholarships without the added burden of teaching or lecturing, tasks which his disability would never permit. His illness made him something of a recluse, and, in some measure, this accounts for his biting, often cruel prose.

Life's Work

Bradley's frail constitution frequently forced him to take shelter from Oxford's severe winters on the southern coast of England or on the French Riviera. On one sojourn to Saint-Raphael in the winter of 1911, he became friends with Elinor Glyn, who was later to depict him as "the sage of Cheiron," in her book *Halcyone* (1912).

In appearance Bradley was erect, with a thin face, fine eyes, and a long nose. Fastidious in his habits, he was affable, courteous, and a good conversationalist, although it was said that he did not suffer fools gladly. He is said to have had a small shooting gallery constructed above his living quarters where he practiced routinely. By his own claim he was a good marksman, known to employ his skill on cats.

Bradley had strong political opinions. He was a conservative, perhaps even reactionary, with a lifelong dislike for the English Liberal Party and a specific disgust for its famous leader Prime Minister William Ewart Gladstone. In particular, he was angry at Gladstone for, as he said, betraying General Charles Gordon at Khartoum in the Egyptian Sudan in 1885. For Bradley, Gladstone represented what Bradley characterized as a degrading social sentimentality, an inviolate pacifism, and a false humanitarian notion of the natural equality of persons.

Almost nothing is known about Bradley's private life, except that he dedicated all of his books to "E. R.," an American woman named Mrs. Radcliffe who lived in France. Bradley met her while on holiday in Egypt, and although she had absolutely no literary or philosophical interests, he laid out for her, voluminously, his complete metaphysical system in a series of letters, which she later destroyed.

Although his philosophical system had its roots in German soil (specifically in the ideas of G. W. F. Hegel, Johann Friedrich Herbart, and Arthur Schopenhauer), he had little time or sympathy for the greatest of all German philosophers, Immanuel Kant.

Bradley died of blood poisoning on September 18, 1924, the same year that he was recipient of England's highest literary award, the Order of Merit. Little can be marked of the external events in Bradley's life—primarily because as a philosopher the events of moment were internal and mental—yet there can be no understanding of Bradley the man apart from Bradley the philosopher.

Richard Wollheim has called Bradley a man of caustic epigrams and poetic metaphors. Nevertheless, he was also Great Britain's finest philosopher of metaphysics in the nineteenth century. He wrote numerous articles and reviews but only four book-length pieces are of major importance: *Ethical Studies* (1876), *Principles of Logic* (1883), *Appearance and Reality* (1893), and *Essays on Truth and Reality* (1914). His *Aphorisims* appeared posthumously in 1930, and his *Collected Essays* was published in 1935. Throughout these volumes there is an obsessive criticism of empiricism, or what he refers to as that English philosophy's devotion to "sense experience." Empiricism is, Bradley argues, a shallow, surface view of the world with two rather "contemptible" qualities: first, a naïve devotion to the idea that raw sense data is philosophically significant, and second, a pedestrian attachment to the doctrine of Utilitarianism. Utilitarianism, he insists, is the inevitable philosophical result of the ill-conceived dogmas of empiricism. When Bradley was at the height of his powers, his two most illustrious adversaries were the Englishman Bertrand Russell and the American William James. Both men were empiricists and Utilitarians.

Here, too, one runs into difficulty, for an analysis of Bradley's thought is difficult because so much of what he writes is enigmatic and obscure. A primary question for Bradley was that of how one obtains knowledge. Bradley rejected as contradictory the notion that knowledge can be obtained from the senses, as was claimed by the empiricist philosophers John Locke and David Hume. For Bradley, knowledge should begin and end with an analysis of meaning. The proper role of philosophical investigation is understanding the use and meaning of the language. This powerful redirection of philosophy from an analysis of sensate ideas in the mind to an analysis of the structure and meaning of language has become the dominant theme in Anglo-American philosophy and owes much to Bradley's initial critical assessment of empiricism.

For Bradley, proper philosophical study is the examination of rationality; that is, it is understanding the "internal connection" that mental ideas have to one another, the internal relations of species, kind, and class (in more contemporary terminology, the investigation into conceptual elements of signs, symbols, and semantics). In other words, the primary interest of philosophy should be in the laws of intelligibility, rather than in particular physical facts or specific sensations as the empiricists had believed. Universal understanding transcends empirical sensations; it requires absolute knowledge. Such knowledge should embrace the logical possibilities of past, present, and future, the real and the imagined. Further, all conceptual worlds are internal and theoretically complete. Thus, rather than identifying information about an object, such as a lemon, by collecting sense data, Bradley would begin with the proposition that the lemon exists—in particular, that it possesses qualities. More important, the object, for Bradley, is more than the sum of these qualities. John Locke had recognized that there is more to things than the sum of their parts, and he called this nonsensed element underlying the sensory ideas "substance." Yet for Locke, substance is unknowable precisely because it is not sensed, a conclusion that leaves those who sense in a state of skepticism about the reality of substance—a position that was acceptable to almost no one except Locke's philosophical heir, David Hume.

Bradley argues that the confusion fostered by this notion of substance ends in a rational contradiction. Ostensibly, when one says that a lemon is yellow, one never means that "lemon" and "yellow" mean the same thing, that they are equivalent terms, as $(2 + 3)$ and $(4 + 1)$ are equivalent sets. Yellow is a quality of lemon, but lemon is more than the color yellow. The empiricists would add that the lemon is also ellipsoid in shape. Yet this, for Bradley, leads to confusion, for to say that being an ellipsoid is identical with being a lemon is contradictory, because it means that a lemon is identical with that which is yellow, which it is not, and with that which is ellipsoid, which it is not; finally, it means that that which is yellow is identical with that which is ellipsoid, which it is not. Thus, the empiricist must argue that a lemon is the sum of all its sensed qualities, not merely one of them in contradiction to some others. Hence, the "substance" of a lemon, for the empiricist, must be the collection of all of these discrete qualities taken together: yellow, elliptical, sour, and so forth. A collective relationship of these qualities constitutes the lemon's substance.

It is at this point that Bradley declares empiricism worthless. Suppose, for example, that a lemon is defined as a yellow object that is elliptical and sour. Then yellow is the subject of the proposition declaring it so, and elliptical and sour are predicates of this proposition. Yet it is as possible to define a lemon with sour as the subject and yellow and elliptical as its predicates. These combinations are, in other words, interchangeable. What this demonstrates, Bradley argues, is that these qualities are interchangeable as subjects and predicates, and hence, it is the relationship in which people think and talk about these qualities that properly establishes the meaning of "lemon." Thus, a lemon is something more than the sum of its sensed qualities; it is a cognitive entity. Yet one should not assume that there is a kind of Lockean substance underlying the sensed qualities, because this only sustains the contradictions that the limits of sense perceptions produce.

For Bradley, there is an Archimedean point upon which any definition of reality is to be balanced: That point is freedom from contradiction. In order to escape contradiction, all qualities must be internally related to all other elements of experience in a single conceptual system. This "transcendent" view of reality, however, requires Bradley to employ the language of the European

Idealists, most particularly the discourse of the post-Hegelians. Therefore, reality, the "substance behind" appearances, is not material, it is mental. In Bradley's words, it is a conceptual "unity of all multiplicity." Human knowledge is filled with contradictions; nevertheless, it is also a part of a wider and higher relation: It is part of "absolute experience." Thus, appearances (sense-data) are manifestations in lesser degree of something conceptually truer, morally higher, and aesthetically more beautiful. Collectively for society, idealized experience is nearer to the heart of things. Higher idealized experience draws society closer to ideals of perfection, closer to its historical myths about God. Reality, thus, is idealized experience, not sensible experience. Bradley thus changed the focus in philosophy from observation of phenomena to an examination of pure reality, which is mental.

Summary

Oxford philosopher Gilbert Ryle has observed that when F. H. Bradley began his career the burning issues in philosophy were between theologians and antitheologians. They were issues of faith and doubt. When he died in 1924, philosophical energies had turned to ratiocinative technique and rigor. Transcendental dicta had lost their influence, and the technicalities of logical theory, linguistic meaning, and the investigation of scientific methodology had changed the tone and temperament of philosophers. Theologians had withdrawn from the battle with scientists, claiming that their endeavors were conducted in different domains: Religion spoke to the needs, aspirations, and hopes of supplicants, while science was searching for explanations of the world's operations. Theology thus maintained a certain immunity from the restrictive, austere propositions of science, enabling theological language to become more subjective and introspective. It became the language of feeling and aspirations, a verbal instrument of communal persuasion and solidarity. Within these limits, only the most literal believers would fear the quantitative onslaught of science.

Bradley, however, had no sympathy with this verbal compromise. He believed it to be a futile, crippling solution. Scientific knowledge is not in another domain; it is, rather, an attempt to understand reality—theology and metaphysics should do no less, according to Bradley. Transcendental philosophy had been abandoned because it was unable to withstand the inexorable successes of science.

For more than two centuries, English philosophy had attempted to imitate the method of science with a philosophy of "mental science," a science of sense experience. This method failed. In fact, it produced only circumlocutions and contradictions. Bradley led philosophy into the realm of logical and semantical discourse, where its primary task was a search for meaning and understanding. Thought and judgment became the primary function of conceptual inquiry. Bradley's philosophical method begins and ends with the premise that truth is the systematic application of self-consistent coherent propositions that are derivatively appropriate, in a rationally unifying fashion, to all aspects of human experience. He envisioned a rationally coherent metaphysics that would replace an antiquated theology and supplant the spiritually bereft notions of science.

Bibliography

Bradley, F. H. *Appearance and Reality*. London: Sonnenschein, and New York: Macmillan, 1893. This is Bradley's account of metaphysics, his most famous and enduring work. In it he is concerned to show why the world is monistic and not pluralistic, and why logic is necessary for a theory of metaphysics. His principal theme is that a sensory view of things, persons, and qualities is a surface of appearances, while the proper view of reality is embodied in coherent conceptual propositions generated by logical thought.

———. *Essays on Truth and Reality*. Oxford: Clarendon Press, 1914. Bradley is concerned here to demonstrate that the theory of truth goes together with the theory of reality. Answering questions about truth entails answering questions about the nature of things. Explanations of reality must be free from conceptual contradictions, which means that truth is neither derivable nor doubtable; it is self-confirming.

———. *Ethical Studies*. London: King, 1876; New York: Stechert, 1904. Bradley produced four major books. This was the first. There is a fresh version published in 1927, which contains additional, important material. This volume includes the essay, "My Station and Its Duties," perhaps the single most widely read piece he wrote.

———. *The Principles of Logic*. Rev. ed. Oxford: Oxford University Press, and New York: Stechert, 1922. This is Bradley's text on the meaning of logical arguments. For him, logic includes both judgments and inferences. Much of this volume is devoted to refuting John Stuart Mill's claim that logic is a derivative of sense experience.

Mander, W. J. *An Introduction to Bradley's Metaphysics.* Oxford: Clarendon Press, and New York: Oxford University Press, 1994. The author analyzes Bradley, focusing on his theories on logic and metaphysics, which the author feels have been misunderstood.

Manser, A., and Guy Stock, eds. *The Philosophy of F. H. Bradley.* Oxford and New York: Clarendon Press, 1984. This is an attempt to show the relation of Bradley's thought to contemporary philosophy. The editors' desire is to demonstrate the greatness of Bradley, even though he has not been the center of philosophical discussion for more than half a century. They have succeeded. This is a collection of first-rate papers, by first-rate philosophical writers.

Muirhead, John. *The Platonic Tradition in Anglo-Saxon Philosophy.* London: Allen and Unwin, and New York: Macmillan, 1931. This is a good, although brief, account of Bradley's philosophical development. Detailed analysis of Bradley's thought is difficult to find or understand. Some of the blame is Bradley's, but much of the reason for his obscurity stems from the fact that he was a speculative philosopher writing in an analytic tradition. Muirhead's work is somewhat informal but still accurate and worthwhile.

Stock, Guy, ed. *Appearance vs. Reality: New Essays on Bradley's Metaphysics.* Oxford: Clarendon Press, and New York: Oxford University Press, 1998. A collection of essays and studies on Bradley's works, which show that his work was instrumental in the development of twentieth century philosophy and highlight contemporary debate on a number of subjects.

Wollheim, Richard. *F. H. Bradley.* London and Baltimore: Penguin, 1959. This excellent book is the most accessible today. Wollheim discusses Bradley's theory of logic and rejection of empiricism, contradiction in the notion of "facts," the relation of thought to truth, and his view of morality and God. He makes it clear why Bradley nearly dominated British philosophy in the latter part of the nineteenth century and why he has little influence today.

D. Burrill

MATHEW B. BRADY

Born: c. 1823; Warren County, New York
Died: January 15, 1896; New York, New York
Area of Achievement: Photography
Contribution: Brady brought to the American public a panorama of personalities and scenes through the photographic medium, and he was instrumental in creating a pictorial record of the Civil War.

Early Life

Mathew B. Brady's birth date is not known other than that he was born about 1823 near Lake George in Warren County, New York. The year is that given by Brady. Little is known about his parents, though his father was probably an Irish immigrant. The death certificate for Brady, which was completed in 1896, lists his father's name as Andrew and his mother's name as Julia. Brady's wife had preceded him in death, and he was therefore listed as a widower, with no name given for his spouse. This contributes to a problem surrounding Brady, because his wife, Juliet Elizabeth Handy, was apparently called "Julia," too. The literature about Brady does not deal with this matter of his parents' names, perhaps because there are so many unknowns about the man. Even the odd spelling of his given name, with a single "t," has no explanation, and as for the middle initial, Brady said it meant nothing. What is known of him comes from the sparest materials. There are no letters, notebooks, diaries, or other written matter. Despite his large enterprise, there are no wills, real estate transactions with his personal signature, or anything that is written by him. He was probably illiterate, though it has been suggested that he could read if not write. Yet this is improbable, as there is no evidence to support the claim; indeed, some historians even doubt that the signatures on his photographs are by his hand.

There is no record or account of Brady's education. Considering that all of his life seemed to be spent promoting himself in society and cultivating the prominent and the wealthy, he may have chosen to be mysterious about his humble background. His basic education was practical, beginning when he spent time in Saratoga, New York, where he met a William Page, who was a painter. Saratoga, located just south of Lake George, has a long history as a popular resort and vacation area for prominent Americans. Because of its natural hot springs and attractive setting, as well as its location close to Albany and New York City, it was already an important health spa when Brady arrived. Page became his first mentor, encouraging the young man from the lake country to sketch and draw. The life-styles of the wealthy on their summer vacations and perhaps the work ethic of the artist Page, who, like most artists, placed himself in close proximity to potential clients, must have affected Brady. He moved with Page to New York City, where he did odd jobs and came in contact with Samuel F. B. Morse, a professor at the University of New York, which later became New York University. Morse, who later became famous for the invention of the telegraph, was experimenting with the daguerreotype reproduction process. He and a colleague, John William Draper, taught some young men the process; Brady was among them. Brady also learned the rudiments of photography from Morse and Draper.

As early as 1843, Brady was listed in the New York *Doggett's* directory as a manufacturer of jewelry cases specializing in making miniature boxes with embossed tops. He also made cases for surgical instruments and storage and presentation boxes for daguerreotypes. It was shortly thereafter that Brady combined case-making with the production of daguerreotypes, setting up a gallery in a building just off Fulton Street and Broadway, directly across from P. T. Barnum's popular American Museum and a block from the famed Astor House. This location was in the center of potential commercial traffic and in close proximity to the people of power who frequented the Astor House. Brady was quite successful, charging between three and five dollars for a sitting, with posing hours from ten o'clock to three o'clock. During those early years, he maintained his association with Page, Draper, Morse, and other men who were experimenting with new technology.

Brady had adopted the costume and style of his artistic and academic associates. A quick, nervous man of five feet, seven inches in height, he allowed his hair to grow long and frame his face. He later grew a mustache and goatee and took a fancy to bright scarves and a flat-topped, broad-brimmed hat. Sometimes he wore a cape and a cavalier-type hat graced with a feather. By 1855, his eyes were failing him, and he wore increasingly thick-lensed wire-framed glasses. In the prime of life, he was virtually blind.

The United States of the 1840's rewarded technology and industry more than anything else, and Brady quickly prospered, expanded his operations, gave up his case-making business, and increasingly concentrated on a grand project: to photograph and publish pictures of every distinguished American. The newly formed American Institute of Photography held contests, and Brady won medals each year from 1844 to 1850. "Brady of Broadway" was what he was called, and in 1849 he received the first gold medal awarded for a picture taken using the daguerreotype process. He worked with reproductions on porcelain and ivory, with tinting and various exposures and light diffusion. Competition in the business was intense, all shops offering something unique to gain customers' attention. Brady pursued the great and the wealthy to complete his grand plan. It was not unusual for him to pick up the work of others and simply attach his name to it. He began to take on and quickly train a number of "operators" to take the pictures, as he could no longer focus the camera himself. He also branched out, establishing an office in Washington, D. C. There the Anthonys, Edward and Henry, had already set up a gallery and were attracting public officials and foreign dignitaries as subjects. They also set up a prosperous photography supply business on Broadway, which became the foundation for the Ansco company. Many of their pictures were sent to be put on display in their Broadway studio. It is believed that Brady, when frustrated in attempts to attract subjects for his great project, simply purchased the photographs he wanted from men such as the Anthonys.

Life's Work

Brady's ambitious project was designed to meet the growing competition from studios which stood side by side along Broadway. Camera operators rushed to open their own shops once they learned the rudiments of the craft. Physically unable to operate the equipment alone, Brady sought the grand idea that would sustain him. His master volume, *Gallery of Illustrious Americans* (1850), was a critical success but a financial failure at thirty dollars a copy. Undaunted, Brady hoped to bring out another volume and purchased the lithographic stones at one hundred dollars each. The project had caused him to neglect the paying part of his business. Brady also contributed to his own losses by mimicking the life-style of the rich in his choice of colognes, brandy, clothes, hats and scarves, and res-

taurants. Many of his prestigious clients he photographed free, ignoring the ordinary public which had sustained him. At twenty-eight, he was already well-known, but still not financially secure.

During this period, Brady married Juliet Elizabeth Handy, a woman from Maryland whom he seems to have met when he was in Washington soliciting sittings. Though there is considerable speculation about her family's status and wealth as well as her ostensible beauty, there is no support for the former, and Brady's pictures of his wife do not flatter her. The date of the wedding is not known, but it had to be prior to his planning for a trip to London in 1851. Brady's new idea was to enter a collection of forty-eight pictures in the London exposition that was being sponsored by Prince Albert. He won a prize for his entry, traveled through parts of Europe, again attaching himself to influential people, and supposedly took their pictures and purchased others for sale in his New York studio.

Returning home, he immediately embarked on the revitalization of his business. He won a prize in the New York World's Fair competition in 1853, but he was never accepted into the community of craftsmen who were moving ahead in technology. He planned a bold move at this time—establishing a permanent Washington studio and hiring Alexander Gardner to manage it. Located on Pennsylvania Avenue between Sixth and Seventh streets, the studio was ideally situated to attract important people. Brady had also moved his New York studio farther uptown, to 359 Broadway. He experimented with skylights to bring greater illumination to his work, as well as blue glass. The future really lay with the collodion wet plate method of photography, but Brady was still infatuated with the primitive daguerreotype. Photography had come of age and Brady rushed to catch up, but the technical skills that would make him famous in history belonged to others.

Stock companies to promote various new techniques and products—Crystalotype, Ambrotype, Melaintype, and tintype—were formed with the most creative inventors as principals. Brady was not among them. A development of which Brady took advantage to his profit, however, was the creation of life-size portraits which, when touched up and tinted with colors, rivaled oil paintings and commanded a high price. They consumed great amounts of time for exposure, however, and tied up studio facilities that were needed for other works. In 1857, the new rage, *cartes de visite*, captivated the nation and the world. The small portrait-bearing calling cards, printed on thin cardboard, were cheaply produced and very profitable. Brady and others saw the demand increase as immigrants wanted pictures to send abroad, Easterners wanted pictures for relatives moving to the West, and the newly married wanted pictures for family and friends. The collecting of cards was another demand that had to be satisfied, and Brady leaped into the competition, offering fees to actors, statesmen, outlaws, and others to sit for the cards, which were then peddled throughout the country. Despite a lull in sales after a few years, the Civil War revived the market for the cards as servicemen rushed to the studios.

Brady was never close to those who were on the cutting edge of photographic innovation. He was more a promoter than an operator-photographer, and the fact that he was known to appropriate the work of others and attach his own name to it did not sit well with his competitors. He picked competitive shows very selectively, such as the 1854 New York Crystal Palace show, in which he drew top honors for his daguerreotypes.

He was concentrating on his new gallery and studio, the most ornate in New York. In Washington, he placed Alexander Gardner in charge. Gardner was exactly what he needed, as the man had mastered the Archer wet-glass process in England before coming to the United States in 1856. Gardner later was to break from Brady and go on to film the history of the American West, but his experience as Brady's photographer of the Civil War projected them both to early prominence. Business was booming, and Brady again moved his New York studio further uptown in 1860, a location where his name became indelibly linked with that of Abraham Lincoln, who had come to give his celebrated Cooper Institute address.

The election of Lincoln and the advent of the Civil War encouraged all serious photographers to plan the filming of the dramatic times. Brady's early mentor, John W. Draper, formed a committee to approach the secretary of war with a project to photograph events. They were put off, however, and it was now Brady who seized the initiative. Lincoln again sat for a formal picture, this time with beard (he had previously been photographed clean-shaven), and Brady's Washington contingent also took pictures of both the inauguration and the Tyler Peace Commission. Two more photographers were sent to Washington to join Gardner as Brady gained presidential clearance to underwrite privately the photographing of the impending crisis.

More than three hundred photographers were involved in covering the Union during the Civil War, many in the direct employ of the War Department, who were not commercial people such as Brady's men. Countless others, most unknown, filmed Confederate exploits as well. Few, however, had the elaborate laboratories on wheels that Brady put in the field. His black wagons, called "what's its" by the troops, were at Bull Run to catch the first disaster of the long war.

After that debacle, Brady had seen enough of the war to realize that New York was the place for him. Keeping eighteen people in the field demanded money, and the studio in New York had to cover expenses that included his own high-toned lifestyle. The burdens of salaries, rent, transport, chemicals, and the like soon overwhelmed him, precipitating his collapse. His practice of filming dignitaries at no charge eroded his resources, and after Appomattox he drifted into virtual seclusion. He closed down his field operations and missed such events as the huge fire at P. T. Barnum's

American Museum, in the same neighborhood as his studio. It was Gardner who persevered in capturing dramatic events in Washington.

Brady soon found that the market was saturated with war pictures. He stored thousands of plates and turned others over to satisfy debts that caused him to go bankrupt in 1873. America was exhausted by war and the bloody-shirt politics which followed it. The new excitement lay in the promise of the West, but Brady stayed home while a new army of photographers followed the sun. He sought to interest the government in his collections, to no avail. Ironically, the government was a successful bidder for thousands of wartime plates when he could not pay a storage bill of $2,840. Brady got nothing, and many pictures were destroyed in moving. A petition on his behalf was drawn up by General Benjamin Butler and James A. Garfield in 1875 to reward Brady with twenty-five thousand dollars for full title to his collection. The money was appropriated too late; the collection passed to the Anthony supply firm in lieu of payment on his debts. Although Brady had fallen on hard times, he won a bronze medal for his entry in a competition of photographs at the Centennial Exposition in Philadelphia. Still, he desperately needed money.

Sporadic interest continued in the 1880's, as aging veterans' groups made inquiries about his pictures. The government called in Albert Bierstadt, the famous painter and photographer, to make an assessment of their holdings. The pieces held by the Anthony firm changed hands several times until some seven thousand glass negatives were recovered and turned over to the government by John C. Taylor of Connecticut. The prohibitive cost of making prints meant that the negatives would remain in storage. Brady nevertheless persevered in the Washington gallery at 627 Pennsylvania Avenue, working with his wife's nephew, Levin Handy. His wife, Juliet, had died of a heart condition on May 20, 1887, leaving him childless. In 1891, a newspaperman was startled to find Brady alive, wiry, and vigorous, with white hair and white mustache and goatee and wearing blue-tinted spectacles. In a revealing comment at that time, Brady suggested that he might have better spent his time becoming a craftsman instead of seeking out personalities to photograph.

He continued to struggle to keep his studio going. On April 16, 1895, however, he was struck by a carriage and suffered a broken leg. This came when he was planning a new exhibition of his personal war slides: 128 pieces to be shown in New York on January 30, 1896. Still ailing, Brady went to the city alone to confirm details with officials of the Seventh Regiment organization. He stayed in a rooming house on East Tenth Street but soon took ill with a kidney ailment. A friend took him to Presbyterian Hospital, where he died in the indigent ward on January 15, 1896. His remains were shipped to Washington, where he was buried, most probably at Congressional Cemetery.

Summary

Mathew Brady was a man possessed of vision and a passion for greatness. He was an indefatigable worker and promoter, as well as a believer in the dream of success. He believed in himself and committed his resources to photographing history. The horror and carnage of the war recorded by Brady's men will forever haunt American history. Brady was not a historian with a camera; he was the entrepreneur who put cameramen in the field to make as much of a record as they could. His pictures do not interpret events as history does; rather, they present scenes, many of which would be indescribable in words.

As with many great figures in history, there is much that was not admirable in Mathew Brady. He might have been more humble and less self-serving. He might have better stayed abreast of technology. He might have been less enamoured of great men and women and more conscious of that large constituency which he ignored to the detriment of history. He might have been kinder to those who did the photography, which is the only durable vestige of his glory. He might have been a better businessman. Nevertheless, Brady's initiative in the use of the craft of photography has provided an irreplaceable record of critical times in the history of the United States.

Bibliography

Hood, Robert E. *Twelve at War: Great Photographers Under Fire.* New York: Putnam, 1967. This volume has a short essay that establishes Brady as the first of the leading war photographers.

Horan, James D. *Mathew Brady: Historian with a Camera.* New York: Crown, 1955. This is a confounding but necessary book, which must be read very carefully as the author plays loose with dates and historical evidence and often passes off conjecture as reality. With regard to Brady, it is adulatory to a fault.

Kunhardt, Dorothy Meserve, and Philip B. Kunhardt, Jr. *Mathew Brady and His World.* Alexandria, Va.: Time-Life Books, 1977. This work grew from the collections of Frederick Meserve and, though published as a picture book for popular consumption, is clear, well-developed, and more historically correct than most works on Brady. The book also provides what has been a universal weakness in books dealing with Brady: a critique of the photographs and real effort into determining who actually took the picture.

Kunhardt, Philip B., Jr. "Mathew Brady," Parts 1, 2. *Smithsonian* 8 (July, August 1977): 24-35, 58-67. Some of this material can be found in the book by Dorothy and Philip Kunhardt, which developed from the research done for these articles.

Meredith, Roy. *Mathew Brady's Portrait of an Era.* New York: Norton, 1982.

―――. *Mr. Lincoln's Camera Man.* New York: Scribner, 1946. These are large-format picture books much like that of James Horan, though they weave a narrative around the illustrations. *Mathew Brady's Portrait of an Era* has considerable information concerning the activities of Brady at various times in his career, although much of the book seems to cry out for reexamination, especially since the object of the work is to tell a good story.

Panzer, Mary, et al. *Mathew Brady and the Image of History.* Washington, D.C.: Smithsonian Institution Press, 1997. An extensively illustrated catalog including the few known facts about Brady's life. Panzer discusses the relationship between photography and the other arts and focuses on Brady's desire to view his work as art.

Shumard, Ann. "Famous Faces by 19th Century Photographer Mathew Brady." *USA Today* 121, no. 2547 (March 1993). Discusses Brady's life as a portrait photographer in the mid-1800s and the effect the Civil War had on him professionally and financially. Lists the locations of his collections.

Townsend, G. A. "Still Taking Pictures." *World* (New York). April 12, 1891: 23. This is a newspaper reporter's interview with the elderly Brady, which, because of the dearth of material directly relating to the man, is exploited in many accounts of his life.

Jack J. Cardoso

JOHANNES BRAHMS

Born: May 7, 1833; Hamburg

Died: April 3, 1897; Vienna, Austro-Hungarian Empire

Area of Achievement: Music

Contribution: One of the greatest composers of his century, Brahms left an enduring corpus of works. He demonstrated that the forms and genres of Viennese classicism continued to have artistic validity in the late nineteenth century and that they were not incompatible with the ethos of Romanticism.

Early Life

Johannes Brahms was the son of Johann Jakob Brahms, a double bassist in the municipal orchestra of Hamburg, and Johanna Henrika Christiane Nissen, a small, crippled woman who was seventeen years her husband's senior. Though romantic biographers often exaggerated the humble origins of their subjects, accounts of Brahms's childhood in a Dickensian tenement in Hamburg are largely accurate, and it appears true that Brahms was required at an early age to play the piano in dockside taverns and dance halls in order to augment the family income. Certainly Brahms's childhood was not altogether wretched: It seems clear that his parents offered considerable affection (Brahms worshiped his mother throughout her life) and did what could be done, given their straitened circumstances, to develop their son's gifts.

Brahms's remarkable musical talent was discovered at an early age by his father. He was given competent instruction at the piano by Otto F. W. Cossel and distinguished, if conservative, instruction in composition by Eduard Marxsen. Though Brahms was not a prodigy on the order of Wolfgang Amadeus Mozart or Felix Mendelssohn, his talent developed rapidly. In the 1848-1849 season, he gave two public piano recitals, performing works as formidable as Ludwig van Beethoven's *Waldstein* Sonata, Op. 53. He was also composing prolifically, though the works from this period are no longer extant; Brahms, ever self-critical, later destroyed these "youthful indiscretions" by the trunkful.

In 1853, Brahms seized an opportunity to participate in a concert tour with the flamboyant Hungarian violinist Eduard Reményi. The tour proved to be a turning point in Brahms's life. Through Reményi's offices, Brahms was introduced first to Franz Liszt in Weimar and then to Robert and Clara Schumann in Düsseldorf. The initial meeting with the Schumanns—he the leading spirit in the German Romantic musical movement and she the greatest female pianist of the century—took place on September 30, 1853. The three immediately experienced a remarkable personal and musical communion, and Brahms became virtually a member of the Schumann household. At this time, Brahms was twenty years old, small, slightly built, blond, unbearded, and androgynously fair of face (not the bearded, well-fleshed, cigar-smoking doyen of later photographs), and he seems to have exercised a complex fascination on both the Schumanns. So impressed by Brahms's playing and compositions was Robert Schumann that he was moved to issue a review in the prestigious *New Journal for Music* declaring Brahms to be a "young eagle" who had sprung forth "fully armed." Schumann had, in effect, anointed Brahms as his musical heir; the younger man's public career had begun.

Life's Work

The first works which Brahms allowed posterity to see date from the period of the first meeting with the Schumanns. It is easy to see why Robert Schumann admired the three piano sonatas (Opp. 1, 2, and 5) which Brahms presented to him. Though the shadow of Beethoven looms over these works, they display an emerging individuality, a formal mastery, and a seriousness of purpose which justify Schumann's description of Brahms as already "fully armed." The Sonata in F Minor, Op. 5 is particularly impressive: It is a big-boned work in five movements whose carefully organized ideas are alternately fiery and lyrical. Brahms's unique, thick-textured, robust, and occasionally awkward keyboard idiom, doubtless deriving from his own idiosyncratic piano technique, is already fully present.

The years from 1854 to 1856 were years of personal turmoil for Brahms. Early in 1854, Robert Schumann suffered a nervous collapse which required his institutionalization and which led ultimately to his death in 1856. Brahms devoted much of his energy during this time of trial to the emotional support of Clara. There is no doubt that Brahms believed himself to be in love with Clara at this time. The degree of intimacy to which Brahms and Clara progressed is not known. Shortly after Robert's death, the two evidently agreed to maintain their friendship on a purely platonic basis.

The years of Schumann's illness had not been productive ones for Brahms. Shortly before Schumann's collapse, Brahms had completed his first major chamber work: the Piano Trio in B Major, Op. 8. It was an auspicious beginning. The next large works date from the end of the decade. In 1857, Brahms accepted a post as pianist and choral conductor at the small court of Detmold. There he had an opportunity to work with the court's forty-piece orchestra. In 1859, Brahms completed his first work employing full orchestra, the Concerto No. 1 in D Minor, Op. 15. The work had a complicated genesis: Brahms had first intended to write a symphony, and the work lacks the surface brilliance of most Romantic concertos. Though it was not well received at first, it is a great, if somewhat austere, work. The piano part is in some respects ungracefully written, and the work was long considered unplayable.

Though Brahms was by no means a reactionary, he found himself increasingly allied in the 1850's and 1860's with musical conservatives such as the Schumanns and violinist Joseph Joachim in opposition to radical Romantics such as Franz Liszt and Richard Wagner. Brahms himself had little interest in critical polemics of any sort, but in 1860 he allowed his name to be placed on a manifesto decrying the so-called music of the future of Liszt and his cohorts. Ultimately, Brahms was made to suffer for this gesture: He became the *bête noire* of radical critics and was the victim of critical vituperation for the remainder of his life. To these thrusts, Brahms appeared stoically indifferent; on later occasions, he expressed admiration for the works of Wagner, the leader of the opposing camp.

In 1863, Brahms accepted a post as director of the Vienna *Singakademie* (choral society) and for the remainder of his life resided chiefly in Vienna. The city of the Habsburgs, with its *Gemütlichkeit* and its memories of Franz Schubert, Mozart, and Beethoven, thus became the backdrop for Brahms's supreme achievements as a composer. The move was probably a healthy one for Brahms: The sunniness of the Viennese doubtless helped to mitigate Brahms's North German dourness and enabled the composer to show on occasion a more genial and charming face. As Brahms aged, he seemed in some respects to personify the aging of the century itself; his works increasingly assumed that cast which generations of critics have called "autumnal." Brahms's late works are indeed the Indian summer of Romanticism, warmed by a low sun whose rays shine obliquely.

Brahms's great work of the 1860's, and the work which firmly established his international reputation, was the *German Requiem*, Op. 45, for chorus, soloists, and orchestra. Despite its title, this is not a liturgical mass. Brahms assembled his own text from the German Bible, and as Karl Geiringer has observed, Brahms's requiem is not so much a prayer for the dead as an attempt to comfort and reassure the living who mourn. The occasion which gave rise to this work was the death of Brahms's mother in 1865; the great seven-movement edifice which he constructed in her memory was completed in 1868. Brahms's compositional technique was by this time completely assured in both choral and orchestral idioms, and the *German Requiem* shows Brahms working at a sustained level of inspiration throughout.

Among numerous other works which Brahms composed in his fourth decade, mention should be made of the Piano Quintet in F Minor, Op. 34 (1864), the Horn Trio in E-flat Major, Op. 40 (1865), and the orchestral *Variations on a Theme by Haydn*, Op. 56a (1873). The quintet for piano and strings began life as a duet for two pianos but is heard to greatest effect as a quintet. The trio Op. 40 was written for the unusual combination of violin, French horn, and piano; in its euphony and elegiac quality, it is purest Brahms. The Haydn variations show Brahms in his highest spirits; although the theme was not original with Haydn, a measure of his good humor pervades the work.

As Brahms entered his forties, he had not yet completed a symphony. It is part of the lore of the composer that he shrank from comparison with Beethoven in this genre. It is ironic, then, that his Symphony No. 1 in C Minor, Op. 68 (1876) was promptly dubbed "Beethoven's Tenth," and it is revealing that Brahms was not displeased by the nickname. The work borrows the key of Beethoven's Fifth Symphony and appropriates some of the emotional world of the Ninth as well, but these borrowings are not the result of a nullity on the part of Brahms; rather, they reveal the composer emboldened by the sureness of his own voice. Brahms was to write three more symphonies in 1877, 1883, and 1885; each is the product of consummate craftsmanship, and each has become a repertory staple.

Brahms's productivity did not diminish in his later years. Among the notable works of his last two decades are the Violin Concerto in D, Op. 77 (1878), the Piano Concerto No. 2 in B-flat, Op. 83 (perhaps his greatest utterance in concerto form), the second and third piano trios (1882 and 1886), the *Four Serious Songs*, Op. 121 (1896), and the miniatures for piano entitled variously *Intermezzo*, *Capriccio*, and *Ballade*, Opp. 116-119 (1892). These works for piano are an anthology of gems and have a valedictory quality; in some cases, they are an exquisite sort of sublimated café music.

The event which hastened Brahms's end shortly before his sixty-fourth birthday was the death of his great friend and artistic companion Clara Schumann in 1896. Shortly thereafter, Brahms was found to be suffering from cancer of the liver, to which he succumbed in April of 1897.

Summary

It was fashionable in progressive circles at the turn of the century to disparage Johannes Brahms. Hugo Wolf railed against Brahms's vacuousness and "hypocrisy"; George Bernard Shaw declared his style to be "euphuistic," and quipped that "his *Requiem* is patiently borne only by the corpse." These views seem today to be quaint at best and monuments to critical vanity at worst. A remarkable percentage of Brahms's works have remained in the active repertory, and they seem to appeal equally to the learned and the casual listener. Though the formulation may be simplistic, it can be said that Brahms—like Beethoven—speaks both to the intellect and to the heart. As a builder, Brahms was masterful both in design and in execution, and admirers of craftsmanship will not fail to respond to this. Brahms kindly supplied enough recondite features in his works to subsidize a large corps of scholars. At the same time, Brahms had the courage to speak directly and ingenuously to his listeners on an emotional level. This combination of sophistication and directness is the stamp of a great artist.

Bibliography

Brahms, Johannes. *Johannes Brahms: His Life and Letters*. Edited by Styra Avins. Oxford and New York: Oxford University Press, 1998. A unique approach to biography based on the first comprehensive collection of Brahms's letters to appear in English. Includes over 550 letters, ranging from 1848 until his death, some published for the first time anywhere in any language. The editor provides commentary tying the letters together into an absorbing biography.

Gál, Hans. *Johannes Brahms: His Work and Personality*. Translated by Joseph Stein. London: Weidenfeld and Nicolson, and New York: Knopf, 1977. Gál, a composer as well as a musicologist, was coeditor of the collected works of Brahms; his study is informed by an exhaustive knowledge of Brahms's works.

Geiringer, Karl. *Brahms: His Life and Work*. 3d ed. London: Allen and Unwin, and New York: Da Capo Press, 1982. Geiringer's work remains the standard study in English of Brahms's life and creative achievement. The book is divided into two parts: a chronological account of Brahms's life and a critique of his works organized by genre. Offers an appendix containing an interesting sampling of Brahms's correspondence.

Latham, Peter. *Brahms*. London: Dent, 1948; New York: Pellegrini, 1949. A valuable shorter appraisal of Brahms in a two-part life-and-works format. Contains vivid, epigrammatic descriptions of major works.

Musgrave, Michael. *The Music of Brahms*. Oxford: Clarendon Press, and New York: Oxford University Press, 1994. The author concentrates on the composer's music, providing only a brief biography in the introduction. Brahms's work is discussed in phases and by genre and includes recent discoveries.

Newman, William S. *The Sonata Since Beethoven.* 3d ed. New York: Norton, 1983. Newman's study of the sonata principle contains a section of generous dimensions discussing Brahms's affinity for the sonata form, in general, and his sonatas for violin, piano, and clarinet, in particular.

Ostwald, Peter. *Schumann: The Inner Voices of a Musical Genius.* Boston: Northeastern University Press, 1985. Contains a well-documented and thoughtful account of the relationship between Brahms and Schumann. Essential for the student who would understand the Johannes Brahms-Robert Schumann-Clara Schumann triangle. Ostwald, a practicing psychiatrist, bases much of his presentation on previously inaccessible documents.

Schauffler, Robert H. *The Unknown Brahms: His Life, Character, and Works.* New York: Dodd, Mead, 1933. An anecdotal account of Brahms's personal life, Schauffler's work is based in large part on interviews with actual acquaintances of Brahms, and herein lies its chief value. In his attempt to unravel the enigma of Brahms's sexuality, Schauffler provides an early specimen of the so-called psychobiography. Schauffler's discussion of the works is old-fashioned and florid but not altogether exiguous.

Schönberg, Arnold. "Brahms the Progressive." In *Style and Idea.* New York: Philosophical Library, 1950; London: Williams and Norgate, 1951. An essay by the influential atonal composer demonstrating the progressive aspects (rhythmic complexity and subtlety of motivic manipulation) of Brahms's art. A useful counterpoint to the prevailing view of Brahms as an autumnal composer.

Steven W. Shrader

LOUIS BRAILLE

Born: January 4, 1809; Coupvray, near Paris, France

Died: January 6, 1852; Paris, France

Areas of Achievement: Invention, technology, and social reform

Contribution: Braille was responsible for the invention of what has become a worldwide system for teaching the blind to read and write.

Early Life

Louis Braille was born in 1809 in Coupvray, France. His mother, Constance Braille, was the daughter of a farming family in the countryside near Coupvray. His father, who also bore the name Louis, was a harness-maker. While playing in his father's workshop, the three-year-old Louis suffered an accident which would lead, first to sympathetic ophthalmia, and then to total blindness. Because there were no special educational facilities for the blind in the provincial areas of France at that time, the child spent the next seven years of his life in a state of relative solitude. Then, in 1819, when Braille was ten years old, he received a scholarship that enabled him to go to the Royal Institute for the Blind in Paris. It was there that, at the age of fifteen, Braille helped develop a new system of tactile coded impressions that could be used by the blind both to read and to write. This work represented a vast improvement over earlier methods. Although some time passed before this invention gained widespread acceptance, Braille was such a model student at the institute that, once he earned his completion certificate, when he was seventeen, he was appointed as a teacher in the Institute for the Blind.

Life's Work

As his career as a teacher progressed, Braille played a role in several of the changes that affected not only the organization but also the philosophy of education for the blind in France and other countries. Before 1784, when Valentin Haüy founded what would eventually become the National Institute for the Blind in Paris, few, if any, institutional provisions had existed for special assistance to the blind either in France or elsewhere in Europe or in the United States. This is not to say that the blind had not been the focus of considerable popular attention during prior generations. Indeed, Haüy and others associated with the new institute tried immediately to address some of the most important public-image questions that both he and, ultimately, Braille would face throughout their careers as educators of the blind.

One of these was the task of counteracting traditional prejudices, ranging from innocent pity or emotional compassion to open fear, visibly present among the majority of the population in their attitudes toward the blind. In Haüy's generation, the methods used to achieve this end were not always effective. In some cases, for example, arguments were introduced that underlined special characteristics of the blind. When these had to do with presumed extraordinary talents possessed by the blind by dint of one missing sense (heightened capacities of sense perception through touch or hearing), educators of the blind could emphasize certain positive points. To a certain extent, this was being done at the institute when Braille began there as a student: Many blind children were given training in music, so they could "prove" to society that they had talents worthy of recognition and praise.

On the other hand, there was another stream of literature, supported in part by Haüy, that suggested that the blind possessed a distinct inner nature that touched the realm of the mysterious. Anyone with a tendency to react negatively to obvious differences between the blind and persons with normal vision might also have been tempted to interpret suggestions of this special characteristic more in negative than in positive terms.

Even before Braille came to the Institute for the Blind in Paris, a debate had already challenged the Société Philanthropique (the founding inspiration behind the institute) for offering only charitable assistance to the blind children who came under its care. Some argued that more practical attention needed to be given to preparing blind children for life as participating members of society. In Haüy's generation, such pressures tended to focus on a list of so-called suitable occupations for which the blind could be trained. Most of these were simple manual trades that could be learned through the sense of touch.

In practical terms, the members of the institute knew that, in order for the transmission of intellectual knowledge to occur, some technical method needed to be found to enable the blind both to read the same texts that were available to the literate majority population and to write without assis-

tance. The most obvious method—one that was already in use by the time Braille became a student at the institute—was to print texts with raised letters. Although the blind could thus follow any printed text by tactile progression, there were two disadvantages in this early system. First, the method was rather slow, since the full form of each letter was fairly complicated and difficult to feel. Second, because of the relative complexity of the forms of the letters, the likelihood of errors in reading, particularly if one tried to move rapidly, was fairly high.

On the other hand, those who insisted that fuller integration into so-called normal society would be a desirable by-product of educating the blind to read had also to keep other, less practical, considerations in mind. Prejudices against presumed special inner moral and psychological characteristics of the blind might rise if a communications system were devised for or by them that was not as immediately accessible to the "normal" majority as simple raised letters were. Haüy himself discovered, well before Braille made his contribution, that controversy would rise over any form of innovation that went further than the simple method of raised

letters: Representation of sounds by raised symbols rather than letters (the Haüy method), for example, never became an established technique for teaching the blind to read.

There are several reasons why the work of Braille—which was technologically rather commonplace—needs to be placed in the wider context of the time and society in which he lived. Braille's system of printing writing by means of a "code" of dots rather than actual letters was obviously meant to simplify the reading process for the blind. Because knowledge of what eventually came to be known as Braille involved mastery of a "secret" code, however, some of Braille's contemporaries believed that the new system ran counter to the normal integrationist objectives that education for the blind was meant to serve. As a consequence, Braille techniques did not spread as rapidly or as widely as the modern observer, more accustomed to practical criteria for judging the effectiveness of technological innovations, might imagine.

Despite its rather slow start (Braille was not used, even in the institute where Braille taught, until 1829), progress toward the official adoption of the six-dot reading code was made gradually. By the mid- to late 1830's, Braille's insistence on the fact of increased teaching efficiency through the use of his system gained important recognition. A special school was founded on the outskirts of Paris (at Maisons Alfort), in which Braille was used exclusively. Later, as the success of the Maisons Alfort program became obvious, the school moved to the center of Paris, on the rue Bagnolet.

By the late 1840's, the use of Braille was enhanced considerably by two new developments. First, in 1847 the first Braille printing press was invented and used in France, soon to be exported for use throughout Europe and the United States. Second, the French government decided to establish a series of branch schools for the blind that would use the same Braille methods as the Paris Institute to provide elementary levels of instruction through reading, as well as manual trade training at the departmental level. From the mid-nineteenth century onward, the most qualified graduates of these provincial elementary schools would qualify to continue their education in full academic subjects at the National Institute for the Blind in Paris.

Braille himself did not live to see the full effects of the application of his reading code for the blind. Because of health complications caused by tuberculosis, he was forced to retire from teaching at the institute in 1837. At the time of his death in 1852, Braille lived in seclusion and was a nearly forgotten man. His reputation as an important contributor to modern education came only in stages. In 1887, the town of Coupvray, Braille's birthplace and the site of his grave, erected a monument to his memory in the center of the town square. In 1952, one century after his death, and at a time when the techniques he had pioneered were in use throughout the world, Braille's remains were transferred from Coupvray to a place of national prestige in the Panthéon in Paris.

Summary

The life of Louis Braille is more representative in many respects of the history of an issue than the history of an individual personality. Before Braille's time, both in France and elsewhere in Europe or the United States, institutions that cared for the blind functioned more as asylums than as places where useful trades could be taught. Intellectual stimuli, and even basic educational instruction, remained even more remote than possibilities for simple vocational training. Until an effective means of communication had been found, learning was restricted to areas concentrating on the senses of touch and/or hearing.

The importance of the contribution of Braille, therefore, should be considered not only in practical terms (development of a simplified system of representing the letters of the alphabet by means of a code of raised dots) but also for its effect on attitudes toward the types of schooling that have since become possible for the blind. Even though the use of Braille to teach reading was initially limited to special schools for the blind, an important difference was in the making: Those who had formerly had no access to normal texts, be they in literature or the sciences, were now able to prepare themselves for interaction with society. Eventually, as Braille became more common and less expensive as a system of printing, this movement in the direction of fuller social and intellectual integration of the blind went further. By the early stages of the twentieth century, the blind were able to attend regular schools and follow the same academic curricula as their fellow classmates, using the same books, printed in Braille for their special use.

Bibliography

Davidson, Margaret. *Louis Braille*. New York: Scholastic Book Services, 1971. A work of historical fiction, designed mainly for young readers, recounting the life of Braille. In addition to Braille himself, the author portrays the people who influenced him, both as a youth in Coupvray and later, during his adult years.

Hampshire, Barry. *Working with Braille*. Lausanne, Switzerland: UNESCO, 1981. This book updates the 1954 United Nations Educational, Scientific, and Cultural Organization (UNESCO) analysis of methods of adapting Braille for international use. It is particularly important for its discussion of the impact of technological changes that have facilitated rapid communication beyond the imagination of original inventors of the Braille system.

Kugelmass, J. Alvin. *Louis Braille: Windows for the Blind*. New York: Messner, 1951. Although this biography was designed for a popular reading audience, it is the result of fairly extensive research into relevant resources in French and other languages. These lend an impression of historical accuracy, as well as some sense of the technical details of Braille's system, to what is otherwise a simple account of Braille's life.

Mackenzie, Sir Clutha. *World Braille Usage*. Paris: UNESCO, 1954. Provides a historical review of the processes that were followed over a century's time to alter the original system of Braille in order to meet the needs of blind readers and writers of Asian and African languages. It includes a brief review of Braille's life and work as well as a history of the World Braille Council.

Paulson, William R. *Enlightenment, Romanticism, and the Blind in France*. Princeton, N.J.: Princeton University Press, 1987. A scholarly historical study of changing cultural values that affected French attitudes toward the blind from the mid-eighteenth through to the mid-nineteenth centuries. It is in Paulson's book that the question of prejudices, particularly toward the presumed mystical inner nature of the blind, is developed most fully.

Byron D. Cannon

JOHN BRIGHT

Born: November 16, 1811; Rochdale, Lancashire, England

Died: March 27, 1889; Rochdale, Lancashire, England

Areas of Achievement: Politics and government

Contribution: Combining moral courage and personal integrity, Bright was instrumental in bringing about many liberal reforms in nineteenth century Great Britain.

Early Life

John Bright was the second, but oldest-surviving, of eleven children born to Jacob and Martha Wood Bright. Both of his parents came from old, established Society of Friends (Quaker) families. As a boy, Bright attended several Friends schools, until the age of fifteen, when he entered his father's business. Although his formal education ended, he continued his education through reading and travel. He traveled throughout the British Isles, the Continent, and the Mediterranean before he was thirty, and he continued traveling throughout his life. At age twenty-two, he and a number of friends organized the Rochdale Literary and Philosophical Society.

Jacob Bright, along with two friends, had founded a cotton mill in 1809. By 1823, he was the sole owner of the mill. Eventually, the firm had six mills, and in the 1850's it added a carpet manufacturing business. Jacob took his sons into the business and it provided a comfortable living for John throughout his life.

John Bright entered public life in 1830, when he began making temperance speeches in Rochdale. In 1834, he joined the Rochdale resistance to paying church rates. His involvement in these public causes led to difficulties when he proposed marriage to Elizabeth Priestman, also a member of the Society of Friends. Before she would marry him, she wanted his assurance that he would not become overly involved in politics. They were married in November, 1839. One daughter, Helen was born to them. Bright was devastated when his wife died in September, 1841. In June, 1847, he married another Friend, Margaret Leatham. They had four sons and three daughters. She died in May, 1878.

Life's Work

The issue which thrust Bright onto the national stage was his involvement in the Anti-Corn Law League. The Corn Law imposed a duty on imported corn and, according to the League, kept the cost of food artificially high to the advantage of the landed class and to the detriment of the rest of society. Bright had joined the local branch of the League in 1838. Through the League, he became associated with one of its founders, Richard Cobden. Cobden visited Bright three days after Bright's first wife died and convinced him to forget his melancholy through work. The two men pledged not to rest until the Corn Law was repealed.

Bright and Cobden became the two most visible agitators for the repeal of the Corn Law. Bright brought to the League his marvelous oratorical ability. He had a voice with a bell-like tone which could be heard with clarity at the large outdoor meetings. He used few gestures while speaking but could portray a variety of emotions solely through the use of his voice. His self-assured speaking style was reinforced by his impressive head and stocky body.

In 1842, the Rochdale voters chose Bright to represent them in the House of Commons. Bright

now gave speeches opposing the Corn Law both in the House and in the country. His speeches earned for him the enmity of the landed class: He accused them of being an oligarchy of the worst sort, one which legislated only for its own good. Not only did it maintain the Corn Law, but the landed class also maintained an established church, opposed electoral reform, and kept the poor from having enough to eat through the game laws.

In 1846, the Conservative prime minister, Sir Robert Peel, pressured both by the League and by famine in Ireland, repealed the Corn Law. Bright and Cobden hoped that other countries would follow Great Britain's lead and move toward free trade. Free trade, they believed, would lead to international harmony among the European nations as they became economically interdependent. As a result of the repeal, both Bright and Cobden were very popular among the middle and lower classes. Bright, much to his delight, was chosen to represent Manchester in the 1847 election.

Although the working class supported Bright's position on the Corn Law, they did not support his position on factory legislation. Bright opposed the 1847 Ten Hours' Act on the principle that the proper role of government did not include regulating conditions of work or wages. Even though Bright recognized that some working conditions needed improvement, he thought that they should be the subject of negotiation between the owners and workers, not government regulation.

The proper role of government intervention concerned Bright not only in domestic affairs but also in foreign affairs. He opposed an interventionist foreign policy throughout his life. The reason for intervention was generally the concept of balance of power. Since the balance of power was always shifting, Bright argued that it was fruitless to intervene and that intervention wasted resources which could much better be used to solve domestic problems. Therefore, when the Aberdeen government became embroiled in the Crimean War in 1854, Bright, along with Cobden, was one of the leading critics of the war.

The immediate cause of the Crimean War was the quarrel between Russia and Turkey over Russia's demands that Turkey recognize its proprietary role as protector of the Greek Orthodox subjects in the Turkish Empire. Turkey refused, and war broke out between Turkey and Russia. Great Britain and France came to Turkey's defense. Bright argued that British interests were not involved in the dispute and that the aim of preserving Turkish integrity or preventing Russian expansion was beyond Great Britain's ability to accomplish. Since the war was very popular in the beginning, those such as Bright and Cobden who opposed the war were vilified on all sides. Nevertheless, Bright's speeches in the House of Commons always drew large audiences. In his most famous speech against the war, he stated that "the angel of death has been abroad throughout the land; you may almost hear the beating of his wings."

Bright's exertions during the war contributed to his physical breakdown early in 1856. When the prescribed rest did not seem to help much, a change of scenery was advised. Bright traveled in England, Scotland, and Wales and then to North Africa, France, and Italy. His loneliness was reduced when his daughter Helen joined him. He was still traveling when Manchester rejected him in March, 1857. He returned to England in June, however, and was elected to represent Birmingham in August. He continued to represent Birmingham until his death. In February, 1858, he was sufficiently recovered to resume his parliamentary activity.

During the controversy over the Crimean War, Bright was often viewed as someone who believed in peace at any price. This view was not true during the Crimean War, and Bright's position during the American Civil War clearly demonstrated that it was not. Many of the British, including William Ewart Gladstone, were sympathetic toward the American South because of the protectionism of the North and the reliance of the textile industry upon cotton from the South. Bright thought that the key issue was a moral one, slavery, and he therefore approved of the war and championed the cause of the North. His many speeches were instrumental in keeping Great Britain neutral during the conflict. At the end of the war, many Americans, including President Abraham Lincoln, expressed their gratitude for the role which Bright had played.

The reform of the electoral system was a major concern throughout Bright's life. He advocated franchise extension, the secret ballot, and the redistribution of parliamentary seats. During the 1850's and most of the 1860's, he had little success, but he did keep the reform issue alive. His agitation contributed to the 1867 and 1884 reform bills and the Ballot Act of 1872.

His positions on the American Civil War and reform having restored his popularity, Bright joined the Gladstone cabinet as the president of the Board of Trade in 1868. He was not to enjoy his position in the cabinet for long, because in 1870 he had another breakdown. He resigned from the cabinet in November, 1870, partially because of his health and partially because he disagreed with Gladstone's resistance to Russia's desire to be a Black Sea power. He remained on the sidelines recovering until February, 1873, when he returned to Commons and the cabinet as Chancellor of the Duchy of Lancaster.

The electoral victory of the Conservatives under Benjamin Disraeli in 1874 horrified Bright, since he believed that their primary goal was to block necessary reforms. During the six years of the Disraeli government, he spent a great amount of time with his family in Rochdale and often protested the more aggressive Disraeli foreign policy. The death of his wife in 1878 was a loss from which Bright never completely recovered.

When the Liberals regained the majority in 1880, Bright again joined the Gladstone cabinet as the Chancellor of the Duchy of Lancaster. He remained in the cabinet until 1882, when he resigned over the British shelling of Alexandria. Bright thought that Great Britain had no more business meddling in the affairs of Egypt than it had had in meddling in the affairs of Turkey nearly thirty years earlier.

During his last years, the public issue upon which he spent most of his time and energy was opposing Gladstone's attempt to grant home rule to Ireland. Bright had long urged reform rather than repression as the way to treat Ireland. He had supported Gladstone's disestablishment of the Irish Church (1869) and the Irish Land Acts of 1870 and 1881, which recognized that tenants as well as landlords had rights. Bright thought, however, that home rule would be a step toward Irish independence, which he thought unacceptable because it would threaten the security of Great Britain—the only justification for meddling in the affairs of another country. His opposition to home rule lost the popularity in Ireland that his previous support of reform had gained for him.

Summary

The dominant political creed during the nineteenth century was liberalism. Liberalism supported free trade, reforms which eroded the power of the landed class, and the freedom of the individual. Liberalism found its support primarily among the middle class, and for some Liberals, liberalism did not extend beyond those reforms which benefited the middle class. John Bright personified nineteenth century liberalism but applied its principles beyond middle-class advantage. He wanted to extend the right to vote to include most of the working class. His belief in the freedom of the individual led him to oppose factory legislation, which appears to be very self-serving, but he also supported freedom of the individual when it was in his interest to oppose it. For example, he was a temperance advocate, but he opposed attempts to legislate temperance because of his conviction that the government had no right to curtail the freedom to choose or to reject temperance.

The growing influence of the middle class fundamentally changed Great Britain during the nineteenth century. Bright, a middle-class manufacturer, was a proud representative of his class, even though he was not always comfortable with all elements of it. He detested those parts of the middle class which practiced conspicuous consumption or were deferential toward the landed class.

Bright's position on foreign affairs was not shared by any large segment of nineteenth century British society. He advocated nonintervention and arbitration when most politicians and the public favored intervention and force. He regarded his inability to change the British foreign policy as a major failure on his part.

In 1883, when celebrations were held to recognize his twenty-five years as Birmingham's representative, praise came from all segments of British society, from both friends and foes, and from the United States and Latin America. Bright was praised for his humanity, earnestness, consistency, trustworthiness, courage, independence, fidelity to principle, love of freedom and justice, and trust in the people. Although he acknowledged his role in accomplishing many reforms, he thought that there was much reform yet to be accomplished. He advocated the curtailment of the power of the House of Lords, disestablishment of the Church, economic and political reform in India to prepare for its eventual independence, tax and military cuts, and educational reform.

Despite his many successes and the general approbation in which he was held, Bright remained a modest person. When he died, he requested that he be buried in the graveyard of the Friends Meeting House in Rochdale. The legacy he left was the model of a principled and moral individual who had, at great personal cost, spent his life working to improve the conditions of life in Great Britain and its dependencies.

Bibliography

Andrews, James R. "Assaulting the English Governing Classes: Strategy and Radical Ideology in John Bright's 'Trent Affair' Speech." *Western Journal of Communications* 62, no. 2 (Spring 1998). Analysis of Bright's 1861 speech on the "Trent Affair."

Ausubel, Herman. *John Bright, Victorian Reformer.* New York: Wiley, 1966. A well-written, relatively short biography which concentrates almost exclusively on Bright's public life. Ausubel argues that Bright was less self-confident than his public image portrayed. Illustrated by several cartoons from *Punch.*

Briggs, Asa. *Victorian People: A Reassessment of Persons and Themes, 1851-1867.* Chicago: University of Chicago Press, 1955. Chapter 8, "John Bright and the Creed of Reform," discusses Bright's reform activity between the 1840's and the 1867 Reform Bill. It places Bright within the context of both the "Manchester School" and middle-class politics.

Bright, John. *Diaries of John Bright.* Edited by R. A. J. Walling. New York: Morrow, 1931. Bright's entries were intended as an aid to his memory, not publication. This edited volume provides valuable insights into Bright's character and his evaluation of contemporaries.

Joyce, Patrick. *Democratic Subjects: The Self and the Social in Nineteenth-Century England.* Cambridge and New York: Cambridge University Press, 1994. Original study examining the nature of class identity through analysis of Bright and Edwin Waugh who, herein, represent the lower- and middle-working classes in nineteenth century England.

McCord, Norman. *The Anti-Corn Law League.* London: Allen and Unwin, 1958. An excellent analysis of the origin, development, and activities of the League as a political pressure group. Bright's role in the League is evaluated.

Read, Donald. *Cobden and Bright: A Victorian Political Partnership.* London: Arnold, 1967; New York: St. Martin's Press, 1968. A good discussion of both the similarities and the differences between the two men. Argues that Cobden was the more important and more radical—an assessment that other historians dispute.

Robbins, Keith. *John Bright.* London and Boston: Routledge, 1979. A good chronological discussion of Bright's life which emphasizes an analysis of his intellectual and personal characteristics as well as his contributions. Robbins regards Bright as "the most successful political figure of the Victorian Age."

Sturgis, James L. *John Bright and the British Empire.* London: Athlone Press, 1969. A topical discussion of Bright's attitude toward Ireland, India, and the colonies. There is almost no discussion of foreign affairs.

Trevelyan, George Macaulay. *The Life of John Bright.* London: Constable, and Boston: Houghton Mifflin, 1913. A descriptive biography with many quotations from Bright's journals, letters and speeches. Despite Trevelyan's tendency to overpraise his father's friend, this is still a very readable and interesting biography.

John R. Bylsma

BRONTË SISTERS

Charlotte Brontë

Born: April 21, 1816; Thornton, Yorkshire, England

Died: March 31, 1855; Haworth, Yorkshire, England

Emily Brontë

Born: July 30, 1818; Thornton, Yorkshire, England

Died: December 19, 1848; Haworth, Yorkshire, England

Anne Brontë

Born: January 17, 1820; Thornton, Yorkshire, England

Died: May 28, 1849; Scarborough, England

Area of Achievement: Literature

Contribution: One of the major English writers of the Victorian era, Charlotte Brontë wrote four novels, the first of which, *Jane Eyre* (1847), made her instantly famous. A poet and novelist, Emily Brontë's book *Wuthering Heights* (1847) remains a favorite of both readers and filmmakers. Anne Brontë published two novels, *Agnes Grey* (1847) and *The Tenant of Wildfell Hall* (1848), during her short life but died before she reached her full potential as a writer.

Early Lives

Patrick Brontë was a powerful force in his family's personal and creative life. He was born in Ireland in 1777 and overcame poverty to attend Cambridge University in England. The self-disciplined, hard-working young man became a minister in the Church of England and married Maria Branwell in 1812. They had six children in seven years: Maria, Elizabeth, Charlotte, Patrick Branwell, Emily Jane, and Anne. In 1820 Patrick moved his family to Haworth, England, where he was appointed minister for life. Maria died of cancer in 1821 at age thirty-eight, leaving Patrick with six small children.

Even after they became adults, the Brontë sisters seldom ventured far from Haworth, the center of their creative lives. The Brontë home was cold and damp, and the town suffered from the effects of open sewers and industrial pollution. Cholera and tuberculosis were common, and the average life expectancy in Haworth was only twenty-six years. It was a rough provincial town, and the family, while respected and well liked, had little social contact with townsfolk. The Brontë children turned to each other for companionship and entertainment. Although early Brontë scholarship portrayed Patrick as a tyrannical father, later research presented him more favorably. Defying the patriarchal values of his day, he educated his daughters and encouraged them in their creative efforts.

After Maria died, Patrick sent his four oldest daughters to the Clergy Daughters' School at Cowan Bridge, probably the model for Charlotte's vivid portrayal of the harsh conditions in Jane Eyre's boarding school. After the two oldest girls became ill, Patrick brought his daughters home. Within a five-week period in 1825, Maria and Elizabeth died from tuberculosis. During the next six years Patrick educated the children himself.

The children found the outside world intimidating. In 1831 Charlotte went to Roe Head, a private school that she first attended as a student and then later returned to briefly as a teacher. Emily and Anne attended Roe Head for a short time but were unhappy away from home. In 1842 Charlotte and Emily attended a private school in Belgium, where Charlotte remained until 1844. The three sisters sometimes worked as governesses, which enriched their writing by exposing them to diverse social situations and giving them insights into aspects of human nature from which they were sheltered in Haworth.

Lives' Work

While the young Brontë women found their ventures out into the world emotionally trying, their intellectual and creative lives blossomed in Haworth. In 1826 Patrick gave Branwell twelve toy soldiers. Each child chose a soldier and named it after a personal hero and then wrote and performed plays about the character. They set their stories in an imaginary African kingdom called Angria; later Emily and Anne created their own realm, which they named Gondal, and located it on an island in the Pacific Ocean. Their fantasy worlds satisfied their emotional needs more than their bleak surroundings did. Charlotte did not free herself from

her obsession with Angria until 1839, and Anne and Emily were still writing about Gondal in 1845. Angria and Gondal served as a deep well for the Brontës' creative lives. They populated their kingdoms with people from history and from contemporary society pages. They laid out cities, devised geographies and drew maps, wrote their kingdoms' histories, and incorporated the social and political controversies of their own day into Angria and Gondal. They painted and wrote poetry, drama, prose, and historical narrative.

Charlotte had a wider audience in mind. In 1845, she convinced Emily and Anne to join her in publishing a collection of their poetry, entitled *Poems by Currer, Ellis, and Acton Bell* (1846). Since the patriarchal Victorian society seldom took female writers seriously, they published their book under male-sounding pseudonyms: Currer (Charlotte), Ellis (Emily), and Acton (Anne) Bell. Even before the poems appeared, the three sisters decided that each, using their pseudonyms, would publish a novel, to be published jointly in a three-volume work. Anne wrote *Agnes Grey* (1847),

which drew on her experiences as a governess. Emily contributed *Wuthering Heights* (1847), whose dramatic characters and emotionally charged plot derived from her Gondal writings. Charlotte's *The Professor* (1857) was enriched by her work as a teacher, especially from her years in Belgium.

Publisher Thomas Cautley Newby refused *The Professor* but published Anne's and Emily's novels. Anne's book was warmly accepted by the public. She was concerned with incorporating morality and religion into daily life. *Agnes Grey* provided trenchant criticism of a society that allowed mediocrity to triumph over excellence and that tolerated an ignorant and insensitive upper class that had little understanding of the hard-working, decent people that surrounded and served them.

The first reaction to *Wuthering Heights* was that it was powerful but coarse and disturbing. In the novel, Heathcliff, a wild, abandoned child, is brought into the home—Wuthering Heights—of Mr. Earnshaw, a member of the local gentry, who has two children, Hindley and Cathy. Heathcliff and Cathy form a deep bond, but Hindley and other members of the local gentry scorn and abuse Heathcliff. Through a misunderstanding he thinks Cathy has turned against him as well; he flees, promising to avenge himself on his tormenters. He returns as a rich man and carries out his vow of revenge, destroying his own happiness and the lives of the people around him. In images that disturbed many conventional Christians, Heathcliff and Cathy find peace after their deaths, reunited as spirits wandering the moors they had loved.

Charlotte put *The Professor* aside (it was not published until after her death) and began work on *Jane Eyre* (1847). Jane Eyre, intelligent and self-reliant but poor, becomes the governess at Thornfield, the home of Edward Rochester. Her courage and intelligence attracts the aggressive, restless Rochester, who defies class distinctions by asking Eyre to marry him. At the altar Jane learns the secret of Thornfield's mysterious locked tower. As a young man Rochester had been tricked into marrying a hopelessly insane woman, now locked in the tower and cared for by a companion. Eyre, despite her love for Rochester, refuses to compromise her morality and flees. She later returns, summoned mysteriously by Rochester's voice. She finds him blinded after trying in vain to save his wife when she set fire to Thornfield. Eyre marries Rochester and both find peace and love.

Jane Eyre went into its third printing within months of its publication, and Charlotte's remarkable success as Currer Bell fueled interest in Acton and Ellis Bell. When critics began to speculate that all three books were written by one person, Charlotte and Anne went to London to prove to their publisher that they had separate identities. Emily's name became known to the outside world after her death.

People wanted more books from the young writers, but tragedy struck, leaving readers to wonder what the Brontës could have accomplished if they had lived into maturity. Branwell, a dissipated youth weakened from drinking and drugs, died in September, 1848. At his funeral, Emily, probably suffering from tuberculosis, caught a cold and died suddenly on December 19, 1848. In January, 1849, Anne, after finishing *The Tenant of Wildfell Hall* (1848), was diagnosed with tuberculosis and died on May 28, 1849.

Charlotte was devastated by these deaths, but she found relief in writing. Some critics believed that Charlotte intended *Shirley* (1849) as a tribute to Emily as she might have been had she lived. The novel deals with industrial conflict and advocates giving women the opportunity to develop their potential and exercise some control over their lives. Charlotte also wrote *Villette* (1853), which explored some of the themes she dealt with in *The Professor*.

On June 29, 1854, Charlotte married her father's curate, Arthur Bell Nicholls. She became pregnant, and, already physically frail, her health quickly deteriorated. She died on March 31, 1855. Arthur stayed on to care for Patrick until Patrick's death in 1861 and then returned to his native Ireland and remarried in 1864.

Summary

The Brontës achieved their place in literary history by overcoming the obstacles of genteel poverty, a rough provincial community, and the bleak landscape of the Yorkshire moors. The artistic and intelligent children lost themselves in fantasy realms that seemed richer and more vivid than the reality of their surroundings. Although the sisters found the outside world intimidating, they were bold and challenging in their creative lives. They believed in moral courage and, like Jane Eyre, in confronting and surmounting all obstacles, including patriarchal restraints on women. Their novels provided exemplary models of strong women confronting emotionally charged situations and dealing successfully with the pains and pleasures of everyday life.

A twentieth century critic called Anne Brontë's *Agnes Grey* English literature's most perfect prose narrative and believed that Anne would have ranked with Jane Austen had she lived another ten years. She died at age thirty, however, and has continued to be overshadowed by her famous sisters.

For many years Charlotte Brontë's critical and popular success outshone Emily, whose *Wuthering Heights* troubled many readers. Emily's book challenged conventional morality and religious beliefs. Its twisted hero, Heathcliff, a moral monster, has disturbing appeal and turns a story of cruelty and revenge into a passionate love story. Its gothic overtones provided lasting images of ghostly lovers wandering the moors, images with great appeal to twentieth century readers and filmmakers.

Since its publication, Charlotte Brontë's *Jane Eyre* has retained its important place in the British literary canon and has stood as an inspiring story of a plain woman's moral courage, as one of the great tragic love stories of literary history, and as an early and powerful plea for women's liberation. It was a major source for the literary realism that became dominant later in the nineteenth century.

Bibliography

Barker, Juliet. *The Brontës*. London: Weidenfeld and Nicolson, and New York: St. Martin's Press, 1994. This well-researched and clearly written book covers the entire Brontë family and carefully dispels the many myths and misunderstandings that have grown up around them.

Benvenuto, Richard. *Emily Brontë*. Boston: Twayne, 1982. A brief biography of the Brontë sister whose life remains most obscure. Only three of her letters survive, but Benvenuto stayed within the documentary record to provide a convincing portrait of her life and personality.

Chitham, Edward. *A Life of Anne Brontë*. Oxford and Cambridge, Mass.: Blackwell, 1991. This book covers Anne's short life and shows that although she continues to be overshadowed by her famous sisters, she was developing her own voice when she died.

Gaskell, Elizabeth Cleghorn. *The Life of Charlotte Brontë*. London: Smith, Elder, and New York: Appleton, 1857. An invaluable source because Gaskell, a friend of Charlotte Brontë, interviewed the author's father, husband, and friends and had access to Charlotte's correspondence. Despite its importance, it has also been the source of some of the misconceptions of Patrick's role in the family.

Hopkins, Annette B. *The Father of the Brontës*. Baltimore: Johns Hopkins University Press, 1958. A good description of Patrick Brontë's life and personality as he changed from an outgoing young man to a reclusive elder. He strikes people today as a stern, authoritarian figure, but he gave his daughters remarkable freedom to develop as artists.

Martha E. Pemberton

HENRY BROUGHAM

Born: September 19, 1778; Edinburgh, Scotland
Died: May 7, 1868; Cannes, France
Areas of Achievement: Education, law, and politics
Contribution: Known as a reform politician, Brougham helped in the reformation of the law and began the spread of universal education.

Early Life

Henry Peter Brougham was born September 19, 1778, in Edinburgh. His father, Henry, a squire from Westmoreland in England, had married Eleanor Syme, the widow of a Scottish minister and niece of the noted historian William Robertson. His mother's connections led the young Henry—a boy of tremendous talent who spoke clearly in his eighth month and read by the age of two years—to be reared and educated in Edinburgh, which was then still basking in the glow of the Scottish Enlightenment of the eighteenth century. Brougham remained a man of that background all of his life. He left Edinburgh High School at the head of his class in 1791, and while attending the University of Edinburgh, the best in Great Britain at the time, displayed an interest and ability in mathematics and the natural sciences; throughout his life he studied mathematics for relaxation. While at university and for the decade after he left in 1795, he and a group of talented and like-minded friends explored all topics and discussed new ideas.

In the Scotland of the day, young men of talent and ambition who lacked connections with the dominant Tory Party had few chances, and Brougham, an excellent speaker, chose law as the career least affected by this problem, though his heart was never fully in it. Though he passed the bar in 1800, he did not prosper. With his friends and during the time his languishing legal career gave him, he founded *The Edinburgh Review,* a quarterly periodical devoted to the topics of the day and reviews of books. As a result of Brougham's connection, which lasted his lifetime, and an article he later contributed in 1808, *The Edinburgh Review* became the leading Whig journal of the nineteenth century. His wide-ranging interests led him to be a cofounder of the Edinburgh Academy of Physics and a leading member of the Speculative Society, a debating group. He also wrote *An Inquiry into the Colonial Policy of the European Powers* (1803), which, because of the section condemning slavery, brought him to the attention of British politicians.

Lacking progress in his legal career, Brougham joined his friends and, as had many Scots both before and since, made the journey to London to seek his fortune. Though enrolled at Lincoln's Inn to study English law and later working in the office of a future judge, Brougham still could not put his heart into the law and never was well versed in it. Rather, his interests turned to politics. The two political parties of his day—Whigs and Tories—often resembled separate connections of aristocratic and gentry families more than groups pursuing policies flowing from principles, though the Whigs had a tradition of defending various liberties which could be traced back to the troubles of the seventeenth century and progressives could be found in the generally conservative Tory Party. Brougham spent the first few years in London working with William Wilberforce's Tory circle in the campaign for the abolition of slavery, and it appeared that Brougham, the radical and future lord chancellor of a reforming government, was headed for the ranks of the Tories. Nevertheless, by 1806 Brougham was more often found in Whig circles and received the first tangible sign of Whig favor when he was appointed secretary to a special mission to Portugal.

Back in England, Brougham represented certain Liverpool merchants before the House of Commons in an effort to change the government's policy interfering with trade with neutral nations as part of the Napoleonic Wars; though unsuccessful, he displayed his brilliant oratory, making him known to the political nation. This event cemented his connection with the commercial and industrial classes in England, a connection which provided the backbone of the reform movements in politics for the rest of his life. Brougham became the point at which the Whig defense of ancient liberties joined with these increasingly powerful groups. Brougham, unfortunately, threw his lot in with the Whigs at just the moment they were losing power, finding themselves out of office from 1807 to 1830. Nevertheless, as an opposition, the Whigs badly needed to have an effective speaker in the House of Commons, and in 1810 Brougham was found a seat at Camelford through the patronage of the Duke of Bedford.

Upon entering Parliament, Brougham, a tall, thin man with long limbs, prominent cheekbones, and dark hair, was not impressive in appearance. Two characteristics stood out to contemporaries: his piercing eyes, which he used to good effect in his speeches, and his turned-up nose, which *Punch* used to good effect in its caricatures of him. In conversation, as opposed to public orations, friends found his sharp tongue bearable because of his amiable nature and obvious goodwill. Of his personal life little is known. He married Mary Ann Spalding, a rich widow, in 1819, and they had two daughters, neither of whom survived to adulthood; she predeceased him in 1865.

Life's Work

With his election to the House of Commons, Brougham entered into the arena where his talents as a knowledgeable orator could best be displayed, but his parliamentary life, legal career, and reforming interests were all of a piece. As a lawyer, Brougham had several moments of brilliance and fame. In 1811, with the events of the French Revolution and the Napoleonic Wars in mind, the Tory government determined to suppress any efforts within England which smacked of reform or revolution and prosecuted for seditious libel Leigh and John Hunt for a publication attacking military discipline. Brougham's successful defense brought the support of various radicals to the Whigs, as well as enhancing the Whig tradition of defending traditional liberties. His reputation was firmly established by his relationship with Queen Caroline. Caroline, partner in a disastrous and broken marriage with the Prince Regent, the future George IV, took advice from Brougham as well as naming him her attorney general when she became queen in 1820. When George tried to divorce her, Brougham's defense before the House of Lords brought him enormous popularity in the kingdom for opposing the "corruption" of an extravagant king with notorious morals and helped the Whigs in their pose as the party of reform.

As the spokesman for reform and the defender of liberties, Brougham was perhaps the most popular politician in England, a popularity culminating in 1830. Since his entrance into the House of Commons, he had represented first Camelford, next Winchelsea, then Knaresborough—all small boroughs under the control of Whig magnates. In 1829, his reputation as a reformer led to an electoral victory in Yorkshire, the largest and least controlled constituency in England. Brougham's victory justified him in his belief that he was the spokesman for all reformers.

As a parliamentarian he brought his Scottish background, utilitarian perspectives, and critical eye to bear on the confused and confusing jungle of English law, and reforming that jungle occupied much of his life. During a famous six-hour speech in the House of Commons in 1828, he rehearsed an enormous litany of problems, most of which were eliminated within the next generation.

Universal education, another of Brougham's goals, he pursued both within and without Parliament. In 1816, he succeeded in getting the House of Commons to appoint a committee to examine education of the poor, and, during the investigations, Brougham uncovered that endowments were often misused. Brougham helped establish mechanics' institutes for the education of working people, a scheme he furthered by forming the Society for the Diffusion of Useful Knowledge to produce inexpensive pamphlets. Brougham also helped set up London University in the late 1820's. He submitted several bills to Parliament in the 1830's to establish a system of national education, something not accomplished until the twentieth century.

Though a brilliant and effective speaker in the House of Commons, Brougham came to have a reputation which prevented colleagues from trusting him. He made speeches in which he claimed his party's support when no such support existed. He changed positions, intrigued for power (and sometimes profit), and always sought to garner all the limelight. As a critic of Tory government, he was without equal, but the Whigs, either in or out of government, could not give him their full confidence. Within six months of his great triumph in the election for Yorkshire, the "tribune of the people" had accepted a patent of nobility and abandoned any realistic claim to be able to speak for the people. Contemporaries saw him as unsteady and untrustworthy, too argumentative and superficial, an intriguer without moral fiber, a man whose character had fatal flaws.

In 1830, the long period of Tory government ended and the Whigs, under Lord Grey, prepared to assume office, but what should have been Brougham's greatest moment never occurred. First offered the office of attorney general in the new government, he declined and threatened to ruin the Whigs' opportunity to govern. The Whig leadership knew that Brougham was too unsteady in his party loyalty to be their spokesman in the House of Commons and too vain to serve under another there, so, after a tense week of discussions, Brougham was made Lord Chancellor and raised to the peerage as Baron Brougham and Vaux, which meant that he sat in the House of Lords and could cause no trouble to the government in the more important House of Commons. With this decision to accept a peerage, Brougham removed himself from his natural arena, the House of Commons, and never, then or later, could play the role in government which he had long imagined and anticipated.

In his four years in government, he worked diligently to clean up the backlog of cases in the Chancery and to streamline its procedures, a task he largely accomplished. In matters of law reform, he established the Judicial Committee of the Privy Council—his major reform accomplishment—which heard appeals from throughout the vast British Empire.

Following the end of the Whig ministry in 1834 (his intriguing helped to bring about that end), Brougham continued in public life for nearly three decades but without the influence he had enjoyed earlier. For several years he sought greater power within Whig circles, but his reputation for ambition and intrigue dogged him in all of his parliamentary efforts at organization or leadership. He was not, however, as one of his enemies stated, "a political Ishmael." As a member of the House of Lords he lacked a constituency and, though he often opposed the Whigs in the 1830's, by the 1840's he settled into the role of an active and informed lord taking an interest in selected parliamentary business. He was active as a judge in the House of Lords and especially in the Judicial Committee of the Privy Council. He maintained an interest in other legal reforms, as, for example, divorce, where in the House of Lords he continually brought in evidence and asked for statistics, activities which kept the issue alive until Lord Palmerston's government passed the Matrimonial Causes Act in 1857. He served as president of the Law Amendment Association, founded in 1844, and as first president from 1857 until 1865 of the National Association for Promotion of Social Science, an organization of reformers interested in all aspects of English life. Articles and reviews on the wide range of topics which had always interested him continued to pour forth, though nothing of lasting value materialized. He spent increasing amounts of time at his house in Cannes, and there he died and was buried in 1868.

Summary

Henry Brougham was one of many reformers disgusted with an England which had altered little in a century and a half despite the growth of its world power and industrial life. His criticisms helped end that England. Being a critic and almost always out of political power meant that many accomplishments were negative—bad laws not enacted, administrative decisions abandoned—but Brougham also brought about significant change. The structure of politics being fluid, ministers often adopted his proposals in order to stop his criticisms. His work for the abolition of slavery well represents the moral tone of the nineteenth century, and he spoke for the desires of the growing business classes for a society based on merit, restricted government, and respect for the individual. By uniting this moral tone and these classes to the aristocratic Whigs, he contributed to what would become the Liberal Party. Neither law nor education was a glamorous area in which to make a reputation, but Brougham, nevertheless, ridiculed the abuses and suggested alternatives, laying a foundation in both subjects upon which others could build. As a result of Brougham's efforts, formal education was no longer limited to the Anglican landowning class, and the way to universal education was charted, certainly his most lasting contribution to British life. On a different level, a small carriage designed for him became very popular, and his name became attached to it. All of this contributed to making him the most popular man in England in the 1820's, a popularity he used well. As a founder of *The Edinburgh Review* and as a master of parliamentary debate in a century that valued such, Brougham stands in that select circle that made public life, and Parliament in particular, the focus of attention by most of the kingdom and led the British to seek change through peaceful politics, not violent revolution.

Bibliography

Aspinall, Arthur. *Lord Brougham and the Whig Party.* Manchester: Manchester University Press, and New York: Longman, 1927. A political study of Brougham, which assumes much knowledge of the period and places less emphasis on reforms of law and education. Brougham's relationship with the Whigs is seen as erratic.

Bagehot, Walter. "The Character of Lord Brougham." In *The English Constitution and Other Political Essays.* New York: Appleton, 1884; London: Appleton, 1930. Written late in Brougham's life by a leading political commentator, who does a fine job of catching the spirit of the times and Brougham's challenges to that spirit.

Ford, Trowbridge H. "Brougham as a Barrister: Courtroom Dilemmas of a Notorious Radical." *Journal of Legal History* 5 (1984): 108-129. A study of several of Brougham's cases in the early years of his legal career.

————. "Lord Brougham Among His Critics." *Tijdschrift voor Rechtsgeschiedenis* 49 (1981): 389-410. An article examining how writers have viewed Brougham as a function of their view of political change. Brougham's importance in effecting change, even after 1835, is exaggerated, but this is a useful corrective to many other works.

Hawes, Frances. *Henry Brougham.* New York: St. Martin's Press, 1956; London: Cape, 1957. Well-written popular biography covering important events but little detail of political struggles. Good in overall interpretation.

Levy, Robert H. "On the Pleasures of Forensic Rhetoric: Brougham and Gibbs in Rex. *v.* John and Leigh Hunt." *Renaissance and Modern Studies* 15 (1971): 85-102. A study of the rhetoric used in the arguments of Brougham and his legal opponent, the attorney general, in the trial of the Hunts for their article about flogging in the British army.

New, Chester W. *The Life of Henry Brougham to 1830.* Oxford: Clarendon Press, 1961. Stops at 1830 because of author's death. In-depth, factual study of major events but fails to catch Brougham's personality or reputation. A list of Brougham's contributions to *The Edinburgh Review* is included.

Pearce, Colin D. "Lord Brougham's Neo-Paganism." *Journal of the History of Ideas* 55, no. 4 (October 1994). Discusses Brougham's belief in reason and how it affected his views on religion and politics.

Sockwell, W. D. "Contributions of Henry Brougham to Classical Political Economy." *History of Political Economy* 23, no. 4 (Winter 1991). Examines Brougham's influence on economic education and his contributions to classical economics.

Stewart, Robert. *Henry Brougham, 1778-1868: His Public Career.* London: Bodley Head, 1985. A well-written and full-scale life of Brougham, which also uses political background well. Discusses all major and many minor events of Brougham's life and does an excellent job of describing Brougham's energy and reputation.

Swinfen, D. B. "Henry Brougham and the Judicial Committee of the Privy Council." *Law Quarterly Review* 90 (1974): 396-411. A detailed study of Brougham's greatest achievement, the court that brought uniform justice to the Empire. Brougham's role in the creation of the court as well as its early development is given good treatment.

Allen Horstman

GEORGE BROWN

Born: November 29, 1818; Alloa, Scotland
Died: May 9, 1880; Toronto, Canada
Areas of Achievement: Journalism, publishing, and politics
Contribution: In 1844, Brown became publisher of the Toronto *Globe* and eventually turned it into a leading Canadian newspaper that backed political reform. Brown became a member of the Canadian Parliament in 1851 and continued to be active in both publishing and politics until his death in 1880.

Early Life

George Brown was the third of Peter and Marianne Mackenzie Brown's nine children, three of whom died in infancy. The Browns were a closely knit family that had grown prosperous with the increasing success of Peter Brown's draper's business. The family's country home was near the Firth of Forth in Alloa, twenty miles west of Edinburgh, Scotland. It was there that George was born. The family also occupied a succession of increasingly impressive homes in Edinburgh's Hope End Park, Buccleuch Place, and Nicholson Square as George grew up. The genealogy on Marianne Brown's side of the family included such luminaries as John Baliol, John of Gaunt, and King Edward I of England.

After 1825, Brown spent most of his early life in Edinburgh. When he was old enough, he attended Edinburgh's renowned high school, where he had classmates who figured prominently in his later life in the New World, among them William and Thomas Nelson, sons of a prominent publisher, who were to become his brothers-in-law. Daniel Wilson, who later became president of the University of Toronto and a political supporter of Brown, and David Christie, who was politically active as a senator in Canada, were also among his classmates in the Edinburgh High School.

George, however, was not happy in the high school, and, using the persuasive powers for which he was noted throughout his lifetime, he convinced his father that he should transfer to the Southern Academy of Edinburgh, a new school that he thought would suit him better than the more traditional high school. He became the top student in his class at Southern Academy and was designated to make the farewell speech for his graduating class. His mentor, Dr. William Gunn, introduced him on this occasion by saying that Brown not only had great enthusiasm himself but also possessed the ability to inspire enthusiasm in others.

Brown's father envisioned a professional career for his son and presumed that he would attend university. Brown, however, had different ideas. He was quick at mathematics, and he reveled in the excitement of the business world, so he convinced his father to employ him in his draper's business, which was prospering. This turn in his career allowed Brown to go to London for a time to work with his father's agents there.

The red-headed and blue-eyed youth had just turned eighteen and was already more than six feet tall. Brown quickly became indispensable to his father, becoming a virtual partner with him in the business. Peter Brown was a man of refined sensibilities and enjoyed the company of numerous literary friends, including J. A. Lockhart (Sir Walter Scott's son-in-law), who became editor of the *Quarterly Review.*

George Brown had barely begun to make his mark in the family business when disaster struck. Shortly after the Reform Act of 1832, which Peter Brown had been active in supporting, the elder Brown was appointed Collector of Assessments for the reformed municipal administration of Edinburgh. In 1836, he was involved in the loss of twenty-eight hundred pounds of public funds, a huge amount of money in its day. The loss was attributed to bad management rather than dishonesty, but the elder Brown faced financial ruin. Friends and relatives came to his aid and enabled him to cover the loss, but he then was in their debt. When the financial panic of 1837 followed hot on the heels of this first calamity, Brown believed that his only choice was to leave Edinburgh and try to make his fortune in the New World.

The closeness that Peter Brown and his son shared made it logical for George to accompany his father to the New World, and on April 30, 1837, they set sail aboard the *Eliza Warwick* for New York, arriving on June 10, after nearly six harrowing weeks at sea. It was a year before Peter Brown could establish in New York a residence sufficient to accommodate his wife and five other children. By that time, he and George had opened a modest draper's shop on Broadway. Peter had assiduously saved his money to bring his family to New York and to repay those who had helped him meet his obligations before he left Scotland.

As Peter's business grew, George became its representative in outlying districts and managed to get as far as Canada on some of his business trips north of New York City. Peter Brown had by now begun to write political articles for the *Albion*, a weekly aimed at British emigrants. He soon wrote regularly for the paper and published a book, *The Fame and Glory of England Vindicated* (1842), which gained for him considerable celebrity. This literary success led directly to his decision to give up his draper's shop and begin the *British Chronicle*, an enterprise in which George was to share fully and enthusiastically. The success of this newspaper encouraged the family to emigrate from the United States to Canada in 1843 to begin publication of the *Banner*. The following year, Peter and George Brown began the Toronto *Globe*, a reform party newspaper published weekly. The *Globe* became a daily in 1853, and George Brown spent the rest of his life as the publisher of this important and widely influential newspaper, a career that catapulted him into politics.

Life's Work

The *Globe* reached a ready audience. It advocated separation of church and state and opposed the French separatist movement that was then current. By 1845, Brown was able to launch a second newspaper, the *Western Globe*, which would reach people in the remote areas of Ontario north and west of Toronto.

Because both of Brown's newspapers were unequivocal in their political stands, it was inevitable that Brown himself would be drawn into politics. Finally, in 1851, he stood for election as an independent liberal candidate from the county of Kent to the Canadian Parliament, which did not meet until August of the following year. Brown, who had served reform causes well, was elected handily and was to be a force in Canadian politics from that time forth.

Brown's attempts to curtail the political power of the Roman Catholic Church in Canada won for him considerable support from Canada West (modern Ontario), which was largely Protestant. Canada East (modern Quebec), however, opposed his attempts to weaken the hold the Church was gaining in the country. Although Brown succeeded in bringing about the secularization of the land that the Crown had granted as preserves for Protestant clergymen in Canada, he was unable to put into effect his plan to have Parliament secularize all Canadian schools, largely because of concerted opposition from the Roman Catholic forces that would be affected by such legislation.

Brown sought to overturn the provisions of the 1840 Act of Union that gave each province an equal number of representatives. He supported proportional representation and, on that platform, rebuilt the Liberal Party of Canada's sprawling West. Lack of consolidation and general political upheaval led to considerable political instability in Canada during the late 1850's. In 1858, Brown served as prime minister for two days. The French separatists were strong enough to force him from office almost immediately.

Brown did not marry until he was in his forty-fifth year. Anne, his bride, was the accomplished daughter of Thomas Nelson, the London publisher. She returned from Great Britain to Canada with him in 1862 following their wedding on November 27, at Abden House, Edinburgh, where her family lived.

Brown continued his efforts on behalf of the federal union of Canada as an active participant in the important Charlottestown and Quebec conferences of 1864. When a deadlock seemed imminent, Brown had no choice but to form a coalition with his old political rival, Prime Minister John Macdonald. Brown was willing now to bury old political grievances in order to secure the dream, original with him, of a unified Canada. Although his dream of unification was achieved, Brown disliked the terms of a renewed reciprocity treaty with the United States and, in 1865, resigned from government service to devote himself full-time to his newspaper interests, through which he could continue to be an effective and influential spokesman for the views he espoused.

Brown was never to sit in the House of Commons again. He stood for election in 1867 and was defeated. He worked tirelessly to bring about Canada's acquisition of the valuable Northwest Territories. In 1873, he became a senator. His chief contribution as a senator was in his renegotiation of a reciprocity treaty with the United States to replace the one to which he had so strenuously objected in 1865.

In his later years, Brown declined to serve as governor of Ontario and twice declined knighthood. He continued to be active in newspaper work until March 25, 1880, when a disgruntled former employee, George Bennett, whom Brown had never met, barged into his office and, obviously drunk, pulled a gun on Brown. In the ensuing struggle, the gun discharged, wounding Brown in the leg. The wound appeared superficial. After it was treated,

Brown was able to walk to his carriage and go home, where he remained in seclusion, visiting with his family and doing newspaper work.

The wound, however, turned gangrenous, and after lingering for six weeks, George Brown ultimately died of gangrene on May 9, 1880. His assailant was tried and found guilty of premeditated murder. He was eventually hanged. Anne Nelson Brown returned permanently to Edinburgh after her husband's death.

Summary

George Brown will long be remembered as a pioneer in the Canadian newspaper business. He was influential through both his newspaper work and his political career in bringing about the unification of Canada, a country of vast distances and far-flung outposts. Brown also fought a strenuous battle to assure the separation of church and state in Canada, a difficult task given the factionalism that was rife in the country at the time of his greatest political activity.

A polished debater from his high school days, Brown was to use this skill with astonishing effectiveness throughout his lifetime to win opposing elements to his side and to help those at opposite ends of the political spectrum to work together for the greater good of Canada through confederation.

During his lifetime, Brown came to represent the voice of reform and of liberal politics in Canada. Never one to refuse compromise if it was for the good of his country, Brown was a major force in Canadian politics for nearly forty years. His political opponents as well as his political supporters mourned his passing because they realized that the good Brown worked for was one that transcended party politics.

Bibliography

Brebner, John Bartlet. *Canada: A Modern History.* Rev. ed. Ann Arbor: University of Michigan Press, 1970. Although this broad history offers only slight coverage of Brown directly, it is valuable for the background it provides for the political stands that Brown took throughout his public life.

Careless, J. M. S. *Brown of "The Globe."* 2 vols. Toronto: Macmillan, 1959. The only thorough-going biography of Brown, this two-volume work is exhaustively and accurately researched and is the definitive biography of its subject.

———. *Canada: A Story of Challenge.* Cambridge: Cambridge University Press, 1953; New York: St. Martin's Press, 1964. This history of the development of Canada as a nation presents pertinent information about Brown as a publisher and as a politician who crusaded for a united Canada.

Creighton, Donald. *The Road to Confederation: The Emergence of Canada.* Boston: Houghton Mifflin, 1965. This book focuses on the movement that Brown spearheaded and presents extensive material about Brown's continued leadership of that movement both as a newspaper publisher and as a politician.

McInnis, Edgar. *Canada: A Political and Social History.* 3d ed. Toronto: Holt Rinehart, 1969. McInnis provides extensive direct coverage of Brown and a thorough discussion of the political arena of which he was a part.

McNaught, Kenneth. *The History of Canada.* London: Heinemann, and New York: Praeger, 1970. Chapter 8 of this book, "Problems of Destiny," presents extensive coverage of Brown, whom McNaught also mentions in salient ways elsewhere in the volume.

Morton, Desmond. *A Short History of Canada.* 3d ed. Toronto: McClelland and Stewart, 1997. This book provides extensive treatment of Brown and of the reform movement in Canada with which he was so crucially affiliated.

R. Baird Shuman

JOHN BROWN

Born: May 9, 1800; Torrington, Connecticut
Died: December 2, 1859; Charlestown, West Virginia
Area of Achievement: Abolitionism
Contribution: Brown has come to symbolize the struggle over the abolition of slavery in the United States. He was the catalyst for change from polite debate and parliamentary maneuvering aimed at modification of the institution to physical violence and a direct onslaught on Southern territory and the supporters of slavery.

Early Life

John Brown was born in a state that, like many others in New England in 1800, was agriculturally exhausted and in religious turmoil. His parents, Owen and Ruth (Mills) Brown, were affected by both problems at his birth. Economically, the Brown family was barely at the subsistence level. John's father moved from job to job: farmer, carpenter, handyman. Though the family descended from the early Mayflower settlers, they were never able to capitalize on their ancestry. Religiously, Owen Brown was a harsh practitioner of the piety of his Puritan forebears, and he instilled in his son a lifelong fear and adoration of a militant and volatile God.

The elder Brown had been married twice and fathered sixteen children. His first wife, John's mother, suffered from mental disease as did others in her family. According to some accounts, John did not take well to his stepmother, but there is little evidence to support this conjecture. The peripatetic life of the family was probably more disturbing to him. When John was five, his father moved to Hudson, Ohio, following the line of the moving frontier. Again, the family was without the necessary capital to take advantage of the opportunities available in the rich Ohio Valley. His father became a herdsman and then a tanner, a vocation that the son quickly mastered. His father had some plans for his son which included sending him to Plainsfield, Massachusetts, to study for the ministry. John did not stay long, however, either because of poor preparation or because of his poor eyesight.

John Brown returned to Hudson to help his father with the cattle and the tanning shop. At the age of twenty, he married Dianthe Lusk, who bore him seven children in twelve years of married life. She, like his mother, had mental problems. Dianthe Brown died in 1831, and within a year of her passing,

Brown married Mary Anne Day, then sixteen, who bore him thirteen more children in twenty-one years. Brown, possessing a modicum of education in a frontier region, became a surveyor as well as a tanner like his father. Also like his father, Brown was a mover. In 1825, he moved to Pennsylvania, cleared land, and set up what was to become a successful farm and tannery. He also became a postmaster, but still he was unsatisfied. Quick fortunes were being made in land and business speculation, and Brown sold off his holdings and moved back to Ohio. There he hoped to take advantage of land speculation and canal building contracts. He lost heavily and began pyramiding debt while turning to cattle and sheep selling. His creditors moved in on him and he was compelled to declare bankruptcy.

Life's Work

Brown's work in the woolen business brought him a partnership with another man, Simon Perkins, to establish a wool brokerage in Springfield, Massachusetts. Fluctuating prices and market instability, however, confounded his efforts to make a success of the business. He was also accused of "weighting" the packs of hides, which were sold by weight to English markets. The collapse of this last business venture was followed by numerous lawsuits, one involving sixty thousand dollars for breach of contract. Brown settled his affairs as best he could. He was fifty years old and virtually penniless, with a large family to support.

Even as a young man, Brown had learned from his father the biblical precept that it was sinful to earn one's living from the sweat of others and that slavery was wrong. In Ohio both he and his father had lent their resources to aiding the underground movement of runaway slaves. John Brown's barn at his farm in Pennsylvania was a station in that movement, and he formed a League of Gileadites among blacks in Springfield to encourage them to defend both themselves and fugitive slaves. Brown's activity in New England brought him in touch with men whose lives would never be the same after meeting him. Gerrit Smith, a New York benefactor of abolitionism who owned much of the Adirondack Mountains, was attracted to Brown. He had given land for use by runaway slaves in a small community known as North Elba. He gave Brown a farm from which he could train and educate the former slaves. Given the severe climate, short growing season, and lack of arable land in the region, not to mention Brown's spotty record as a farmer, problems developed. Brown himself declared that he felt "omnipotent" in his new role as guide and exemplar to the blacks in his charge.

Within two years, however, he was in Akron, Ohio. His mind was turned to developing a grand plan for an attack on slavery. As early as 1847, he had talked about gathering a band of men from the free states to make forays into slave territory to rescue blacks from bondage. He talked of setting up a mountain stronghold as a base of terrorist activity, but the ideas did not take coherent form until the Fugitive Slave Act, part of the Compromise of 1850, was passed. The Kansas-Nebraska Act, four years later, further agitated him and his sons, five of whom moved to the territory to help make Kansas a free state. In May, 1855, John Brown, Jr., wrote a mournful letter to his father explaining the conditions and imploring him to send arms to battle proslavery forces. Brown dispatched his family to North Elba again and set out for Kansas with a wagonload of guns and ammunition.

He found his sons impoverished and ill when he arrived at Osawatomie. Though he was to join the colony as a surveyor, he quickly assumed leadership of the local militia and made Free Soil a vengeance-wreaking crusade. His group fought in the ineffectual Wakarusa War and then, after the sacking of Lawrence by proslavery forces, he and his party, which included four sons and two others, ritually slaughtered five settlers at Pottawatomie. He had reached a personal turning point, viewing himself as an instrument in the hands of an angry god. His own colony was overrun and burned and one of his boys killed in retaliation. Brown now was gray in hair and features, with a bent back and glittering gray-blue eyes; he had grown a full beard that was streaked with gray, which made him appear older than his fifty-six years. His fervent attitude toward slavery fired his listeners, many of whom, such as Franklin Sanborn, Thomas W. Higginson, Theodore Parker, Gerrit Smith, G. L. Stearns, and Samuel Gridley Howe, were ripe for the leadership which Brown promised. He met with these members of the Massachusetts State Kansas Committee, and they responded with some arms and ammunition and money to take with him to Kansas again.

Kansas had no stomach for bloodshed in 1857 as it moved closer to voting the issue of free or slave, and Brown now thought of a daring plan to liberate slaves in the South itself. In the spring of 1858, he visited the colony of runaway slaves in Catham, Canada, to gain volunteers. His money gone, he turned again to Smith and the Massachusetts group. They argued for a delay, gave him some money and supplies, and Brown again headed for Kansas, this time under the name of Shubel Morgan. There he led a raid on some plantations in Missouri in which one planter was killed and some slaves liberated. Brown was now a wanted man with a bounty on his head. He headed for Canada with the slaves in tow and then proceeded east, making speeches in Cleveland and Rochester to solicit funds. Again the old group came through with thirty-eight hundred dollars, knowing full well that Brown was bent on violence.

It was Harpers Ferry that became fixed in Brown's mind; to the commander in chief of a provisional army for liberation it was an ideal objective. The federal arsenal in the town was noted for the quality of arms and its technology since its creation in 1798. The complex of forges, shops, tool and die works, and assembly areas turned out rifles and handguns in an assembly line process that foretold mass production. John Hall of Maine had gained a contract in 1819 to turn out breech-loading rifles using his idea of interchangeable parts, and his contract was renewed yearly until 1844, when a totally new rifle plant was built to produce the Standard United States Model military rifle. The skilled workers were mostly transplanted Northerners who were regarded as "foreigners" by local Southerners. A canal and a railroad as well as a macadam road led to the town of three thousand, which included 1,250 freed blacks and some eighty-eight slaves.

The Brown contingent of fourteen whites and five blacks established themselves in a farm five miles from the Ferry to lay plans for their attack. On Sunday, October 16, 1859, they marched by night down the dirt road leading to the town. By mid-morning, the men had taken both the town and its leading citizens.

Brown did not know what to do with his victory. He had control of the engine house, the federal armory, the railroad, and the town of Harpers Ferry, and the very magnitude of his success overwhelmed and confused him. He let a train continue, certainly with the knowledge that the passengers would alarm state and federal officials. He did nothing about searching out possible followers from the town population or the countryside. He had guns, powder and shells, and a well-situated

natural fortress, as well as a small though very devout band of followers. Brown lost his revolutionary compass at this critical moment. His willingness to fight was not in question. Shots were fired and lives were taken until Lee's troops stormed the engine house and cut Brown down. Though he was not severely wounded, there was little recourse for his men but to surrender. The military quickly restored order and moved Brown to prison while dispatching squads to investigate the farm which had been the band's headquarters. There they found letters and documentation which implicated Brown's Northern associates in the Harpers Ferry venture. Why Brown had kept, let alone brought with him, these damning materials is uncertain. He certainly treasured his association with successful and influential men, and given his life on the margin of society, this connection was important enough to be sustained with physical evidence. Furthermore, Brown was concerned about the shifting commitment of antislavery reformers and therefore by keeping documentation he could hold them to the course. The discovery of these materials, however, proved the conspiracy case against Brown and his men and threw fear into those who had aided them.

Of the twenty-one men who had followed him to Harpers Ferry on October 16, only eleven remained alive. Brown had seen two of his sons killed in the melee that followed the arrival of the militia from Charlestown (modern Charles Town, West Virginia) and Lee's marines. On October 18, he was jailed in Charlestown to await indictment, which came a week later.

Brown, Aaron Stevens, Edwin Coppoc, Shields Green (the black who had chosen to go with Brown despite the admonition and concerns of Frederick Douglass), and John Copeland were all indicted on October 25 for treason against Virginia, for conspiring with slaves to rebel, and for murder. All of them pleaded not guilty and requested separate trials. The court agreed and determined that Brown would be tried first. The prosecution was headed by Charles Harding, state attorney for Jefferson County, and Andrew Hunter, a seasoned Charlestown attorney. The court was presided over by Judge Richard Parker, who had just begun the semiannual term of his circuit court and already had a grand jury seated. Turner had just gaveled the court to order when Brown's defense attorney read a telegram from one A. H. Lewis of Akron, Ohio, declaring that Brown's family was suffering from hereditary insanity. It proceeded to list the people

on his mother's side who were known to have severe mental problems. The inference was that Brown himself was insane and therefore not fit for trial. His attorney had shown Brown the telegram and Brown admitted to his mother's death by insanity and the fact that his first wife and two of his sons were afflicted. Brown, however, rejected the plea of insanity on his behalf, though he apparently gave his attorney permission to use the document. The judge ruled out the plea on the basis that the evidence was in unreliable form. He also rejected a delay to enable Brown to get a new attorney.

Brown's trial began on October 27, 1859, and lasted for less than four days. He was carried to the court each day in a litter, and with each day, he became more irritated with his court-appointed attorneys. They had been joined by a twenty-one-year-old Boston attorney, George Hoyt, who had been retained by some Brown supporters who hoped to learn more about the case on behalf of the group of backers who were facing possible indictment as coconspirators. Botts and Green gratefully withdrew from the defense team, leaving the inexperienced Hoyt alone. Legal help soon came in the form of Samuel Chilton of Washington and Hiram Griswold of Cleveland, who were persuaded to take up what Brown himself realized was a lost cause.

The prosecution's case was devastating. Brown's request that he be tried as commander in chief of a provisional army, according to the laws governing warfare, was rejected. Brown's vision of himself as a messianic leader of a noble crusade against slavery was ignored. On October 31, at 1:45 P.M., the case went to the jury, which, after only forty-five minutes, declared Brown guilty on all counts. The verdict cast a pall on the audience, which days before had been vociferous in its rage against Brown. Brown himself said nothing as he lay quietly on his cot. The sentence of death by hanging was passed on November 2, with the date for execution set for December 2. The coconspirators captured with Brown were tried as well and all sentenced to the same fate. Brown had visited with them in jail, calling on them to be firm and resolute and to implicate no one. Friends of Brown had sought to bring his wife from North Elba, but Brown insisted that she remain at home. Only on the afternoon before his execution did she visit with him and then stand by to claim his body.

Governor Henry Wise was besieged with demands for clemency, threats, and warnings of plots to free Brown. Martial law was proclaimed in

Charlestown, and fifteen hundred soldiers, including a company of cadets from Virginia Military Institute commanded by Thomas "Stonewall" Jackson, ringed the gallows.

John Brown's death on a rope in Charlestown was but the end of a beginning. The larger crisis that Brown had foreshadowed soon came with a character of violence and death that would have perhaps given even Osawatomie pause. The South, by insisting on dealing with Brown's case, had arrogated to itself police authority over what was a crime against federal property. It thereby threw down a gauntlet of defiant sectionalism and states' rights.

None of this was lost on Brown's supporters in the North, who, after suffering gag rules in Congress blocking their petitions against slavery, after almost thirty years of relentless electioneering, pamphleteering, lecturing, haranguing, debating, and propagandizing against slavery, and after suffering dismaying defeats at the hands of every branch of government and in virtually every attempt to work within the system, were ready to exploit John Brown's fateful end. Antislavery reformers took charge of the body, and by wagon, train, and steamer they took it to the hills where Brown had felt "omnipotent." It was a cortege that would be duplicated six years later on the death of Abraham Lincoln—a slow, somber taking of martyred remains home. Through Lake Placid and on to the little village of North Elba they took Brown, and near his little home they buried him. Gerrit Smith, the man who had given him the land, was not with him at the burial. Smith had become mentally deranged after Brown's capture and was institutionalized. Others who were closely involved with Brown, such as Frederick Douglass, found it convenient to flee to Canada or travel abroad. Brown, the guerrilla fighter and terrorist who had taken the struggle against slavery beyond rhetoric, had made clear that the approaching confrontation would be violent.

Summary

John Brown was a tragic figure central to the great tragedy of Civil War America. Whether he was a hero in that era is, at best, controversial. There seems little doubt that had his earlier ventures been successful, he would have melded with other entrepreneurs of the moving frontier and probably been lost as another subject representing an enterprising nation. A failure as a businessman, he turned all of his energies to what became for him a holy mission: rooting out the evil of slavery. Social, economic, and political displacement encouraged many in his region to seek redress. Brown, however, personalized these conflicts to an extreme degree and placed himself at a point from which there was no turning back.

Bibliography

Boyer, Richard O. *The Legend of John Brown: A Biography and a History.* New York: Knopf, 1972. This is a fine piece of biography that takes the story of Brown up to his arrival in Kansas in 1855. Boyer died before he could complete the second volume.

Malin, James C. *John Brown and the Legend of Fifty-six.* Philadelphia: American Philosophical Society, 1942. Malin's work is highly critical of Brown's activities in Kansas and of Brown personally. It is useful, however, for its detail of that period of Brown's life.

McGlone, Robert E. "Forgotten Surrender: John Brown's Raid and the Cult of Martial Virtues." *Civil War History* 40, no. 3 (September 1994). Discusses the altered perceptions of witnesses following Brown's raid on Harper's Ferry and how their ideals of heroism and honor made it difficult to accept that Brown had offered to surrender.

National Park Service. *John Brown's Raid.* Washington, D.C.: Superintendent of Documents, 1974. Here is an outstanding piece of work based on reports by William C. Everhart and Arthur L. Sullivan that gives sweep and substance to Brown and his men at Harpers Ferry in the space of sixty-eight pages.

Oates, Stephen B. *To Purge This Land with Blood: A Biography of John Brown.* New York: Harper, 1970. Oates's book is the most modern full biography of Brown and establishes the point of view that Brown's puritanical heritage was at the base of his thought and action. See also his article: "John Brown and His Judges: A Critique of the Historical Literature." In *Civil War History* 17 (1971).

Renehan, Edward J. *The Secret Six: The True Tale of the Men Who Conspired with John Brown.* New York: Crown, 1995. The little-known story of the six Northern aristocrats who assisted Brown in his efforts to force a nationwide slave revolt. Identifies these influential men, outlines the reasons for their actions, and discusses their desire to cover their association with Brown including acts of perjury in the congressional investigation that followed Brown's failed raid.

Sanborn, Franklin B., ed. *The Life and Letters of John Brown*. Boston: Roberts, and London: Sampson Low, Marston, 1885. This is a book to be used carefully as it is biased toward Brown; the gathering of Brown's letters makes this a valuable resource.

Villard, Oswald Garrison. *John Brown, 1800-1859: A Biography Fifty Years After*. Boston: Houghton Mifflin, 1910. Villard's biography is still a standard work on Brown and his time. It cannot be ignored in any study.

Jack J. Cardoso

ELIZABETH BARRETT BROWNING

Born: March 6, 1806; Coxhoe Hall, County
  Durham, England
Died: June 29, 1861; Florence, Italy
Area of Achievement: Literature
Contribution: Browning was the most respected
  woman poet of the Victorian age. Her work is
  known for its formal iconoclasm, impetuosity of
  tone, and political content.

Early Life

Elizabeth Barrett was the eldest of the eleven children of Edward Moulton Barrett and Mary Graham Clarke. She grew up at Hope End, a large country house in Herefordshire. Both parents, but especially her father, encouraged her to read widely; unlike most privileged girls of her time, she was allowed free use of her father's library and shared her brothers' classical tuition. Her father arranged for her epic poem *The Battle of Marathon* (1820) to be privately published when she was fourteen.

In 1821 Elizabeth suffered a severe but unexplained illness that affected her spine and lungs and left her a semi-invalid for the rest of her life. During the 1830's, she produced her first successful poetry: *The Seraphim and Other Poems* (1838) was well received and gained its author considerable notice. At about the same time, her health broke down, and she traveled from London to the milder climate of Torquay to recover. During her convalescence, she begged her favorite brother Edward ("Bro") to visit her in Torquay; while there, he drowned on a sailing excursion. Elizabeth's grief and guilt were so overwhelming that for the rest of her life she could never speak or write of the event.

Somewhat recovered but still very much an invalid, Elizabeth returned to London in 1841 and plunged into literary work. In 1844 her popular two-volume *Poems, by Elizabeth Barrett Browning* appeared. One poem in this collection, "Lady Geraldine's Courtship," referred favorably to the work of then little-known poet Robert Browning. He wrote to thank her, and they began a correspondence that led to their first meeting four months later. For over a year they wrote to each other daily (sometimes twice daily). Elizabeth's father had forbidden any of his children to marry, so Elizabeth and Robert married secretly and left for Italy in 1846. They settled in Florence, in Casa Guidi, where their son Pen was born in 1849 and where they lived for the rest of Elizabeth's life.

Life's Work

During the 1840's and 1850's, Elizabeth Barrett Browning's major works appeared, and her poetic reputation reached its height. Her 1844 *Poems, by Elizabeth Barrett Browning* contain multiple voices, styles, and subjects. She experiments boldly with form, especially half-rhymes, metrical irregularities, neologisms, compound words, and lacunae. These experiments at once pleased, intrigued, infuriated, and disturbed her contemporary readers. More recently, they have been seen (by Virginia Woolf and others) as formative influences on later poets and harbingers of literary modernism.

In 1850 Browning published a collection of her poetry, including the 1844 poems plus some new material such as the famous *Sonnets from the Portuguese*, written secretly to her husband during their courtship. These poems are by far her most well known, less for any intrinsic artistic excellence than for their abiding romantic and psychological portrait of developing love. They trace the emotional state of the poet—a thirty-nine-year-old invalid wooed by a younger man—from surprise, reluctance, and confusion to passion, trust, and hope for the future.

In addition to the sonnets, the 1850 *Poems* includes two poems focused on social issues. "The Runaway Slave at Pilgrim's Point" is an impassioned first-person poem in which a slave murders her own child, who was conceived as a result of rape by her white master. "The Cry of the Children" protests the inhumane conditions for child laborers in British coal mines and factories. Not only did these poems provoke a powerful response from socially conscious readers, but they also anticipated the overtly political concerns of Browning's next book of poetry.

Browning's next book, *Casa Guidi Windows* (1851), revealed her interest in the politics of the Italian Risorgimento. *Casa Guidi Windows* is "A Poem, in Two Parts," the first written in 1848 and filled with the optimism attendant upon the abortive Italian revolution of that year. Part 2 was written in 1851 after the crushing defeat of the patriots at Novara in 1849 and is decidedly more pessimistic. The poem's confident approach is noteworthy, particularly since it was unusual in Browning's time for a woman poet to venture onto political terrain, which was considered reserved for men. *Casa Guidi Windows* is written in a modified terza rima,

and some of its vivid ironic characterizations are reminiscent of Robert Browning's poetry and have led critics to assume that Elizabeth was influenced by her husband.

Throughout the 1850's, Elizabeth and Robert traveled widely in Europe and visited England three times, in 1851, 1855, and 1856. Upon their return to Italy after the last trip, Browning, after ten years of work, published what she and generations of readers after her have considered to be her masterpiece, *Aurora Leigh* (1857). *Aurora Leigh* is a novel in verse, an epic poem in nine books inspired in part by the novels of George Sand and Charlotte Brontë but also by the long, reflective *Prelude* (1850) of William Wordsworth. It tells the story of the eponymous poet-heroine Aurora Leigh, her lover-cousin Romney Leigh, and their turbulent and finally successful romance.

Aurora Leigh is described as a successful but lonely and dissatisfied poet. Early in the poem she rejects the marriage proposal of her cousin Romney, a dedicated philanthropist. At that point in the story, Romney is simply too overbearing for the self-consciously feminist Aurora, who believes that human betterment must come through individual inspiration; Romney, by contrast, believes in organized progress by and for large groups of people. Aurora secludes herself and writes, while Romney embarks on several idealistic but hare-brained schemes (such as building a phalanstery on his ancestral estate and proposing marriage to a poor seamstress). After Romney's plans fail—the poor people he has installed in the phalanstery burn it down, he is blinded in the fire, and his intended wife is tricked into prostitution—he and Aurora can finally get together. The poem ends with their marriage, as Romney realizes that social betterment must involve the soul as well as the body, and Aurora realizes that a true artist must not separate herself utterly from the world she hopes to influence. Ironically, for all its stated concern for the poor, *Aurora Leigh*'s "moral" is a conservative one: The "mob" is to be feared, and poetry makes a greater impact on society than philanthropic activities.

Aurora Leigh contains Browning's highest convictions on life and art, particularly the responsibilities of the poet. She believed fervently that a poet must bear truthful witness to the values of her society, must "represent the age" and never "flinch from modern varnish, coat, or flounce." Thus her most poignant critique of both Aurora and Romney is that they are overly theoretical. Aurora chides Romney that his "social theory" is a better wife to him than she could ever be; she little realizes how greatly she herself is "wedded" to poetic theories.

In *Aurora Leigh*, Browning comes closest to integrating the idea "woman" with the idea "poet." In an important sense, it is about being or becoming a poet in a world that imagines the poet as male. By positioning herself at the center of her own story, the poet Aurora disrupts objectifying male discourse about women; she transforms herself from the object of Romney's gaze to the subject of her own vision and thereby enacts her liberation. Browning has taken a quintessentially male form, the extended blank-verse epic poem, and put it to the service of women's concerns. At age twenty, Aurora is aware of herself as "Woman and artist, —either incomplete." By the end of the epic, ten years have passed, and Aurora has learned that true fulfillment comes from finding completion as both woman *and* artist.

Browning's father had not seen or spoken to his daughter since she had left England in 1846. At one point, he sent her a package returning all the unread letters that she had written to him over the years. In 1857, he died unreconciled. In 1860 Browning published *Poems Before Congress*, the last volume to appear in her lifetime. Most English readers found this book to be a disappointment, too imbued with its author's often faulty judgments on contemporary French and Italian politics. Browning herself described it as "a very thin and wicked brochure" and fully expected that its pro-Italian, anti-English tone would lead to a negative public reaction.

In 1861, after a long struggle with failing health and weak lungs, Browning died in her husband's arms on the night of June 29. The following year, Browning's *Last Poems* were published. This volume included a variety of poems left uncollected at the time of her death: several on the Italian political scene, one ("De Profundis") written after Bro's drowning in 1840 but never published, and several passionate and lyrical poems in the author's rich mature voice.

Summary

After the death of William Wordsworth, Elizabeth Barrett Browning was seriously considered to replace him as England's poet laureate. Though she was not finally chosen—Alfred, Lord Tennyson was—the mere suggestion that she might fill that position and speak with that "national" voice was extraordinary in 1850. It reveals how well-known and well-respected Browning was among her peers.

In the decades following her death, her poetry was nearly forgotten. By 1932, Virginia Woolf was complaining that in the "mansion of literature" Browning had been relegated to the "servants' quarters." The revival of interest in her work that Woolf had called for did not take place until the advent of feminist literary criticism in the 1960's and 1970's. Since that time, readers have focused on Browning not simply as a poet but as a woman poet. The very characteristics of her work that were seen as most problematic by earlier generations—intense passion, interest in politics, feminist concerns—are now seen as the greatest strengths of her poetry.

Browning's work is critical to understanding the ways in which a woman poet empowers herself to speak. Browning's career provides a paradigm for the relationship of a woman poet to a poetic tradition that privileges the male voice. Moreover, she has represented a poetic "foremother" for generations of women poets after her—a figure she herself lacked and for whom she longed. Browning has typically been envisioned as a ringleted Victorian invalid living out an unlikely romantic legend. It is important to remember that she was first and foremost a technician devoted to the craft of poetry.

Bibliography

Brown, Sarah Annes. "*Paradise Lost* and *Aurora Leigh*." *Studies in English Literature 1500-1900* 37 (Autumn, 1997): 723-740. Brown examines Browning's epic novel as a stylistic and subjective rewriting of John Milton's epic.

Cooper, Helen. *Elizabeth Barrett Browning, Woman and Artist*. Chapel Hill: North Carolina University Press, 1988. Cooper discusses Browning's career as an extended effort to bring about a felicitous union of her femaleness with her art. The book deals cogently with all the major work.

Forster, Margaret. *Elizabeth Barrett Browning: A Biography*. London: Chatto and Windus, 1988; New York: Doubleday, 1989. This is the best critical biography of the poet. It includes generous selections from the letters as well as discussion of the poet's life and work.

Hayter, Alethea. "Elizabeth Barrett Browning (1806-1861)." In *British Writers*. Edited by Ian Scott-Kilvert. Vol. 4. New York: Scribner, 1981. This useful overview of the life of the poet includes an excellent six-page discussion of Browning's poetic imagery and style.

Mermin, Dorothy. *Elizabeth Barrett Browning: The Origins of a New Poetry*. Chicago: University of Chicago Press, 1989. This book is a frequently cited extended discussion of Browning's poetics.

Tucker, Herbert F. "*Aurora Leigh*: Epic Solutions to Novel Ends." In *Famous Last Words: Changes in Gender and Narrative Closure*. Edited by Alison Booth. Charlottesville: University Press of Virginia, 1993. Tucker analyzes *Aurora Leigh* in light of traditional epic form, stressing its relationship to conventional Victorian fiction and poetry.

Zonana, Joyce. "The Embodied Muse: Elizabeth Barrett Browning's *Aurora Leigh* and Feminist Poetics." *Tulsa Studies in Women's Literature* 8 (Fall 1989): 240-262. In this interesting essay, Zonana considers the problematic subject-object issue surrounding the idea of the poetic muse in Browning's epic novel. The author explores this idea in relation to previous feminist criticism.

Deborah T. Meem

ANTON BRUCKNER

Born: September 4, 1824; Ansfelden, Austro-Hungarian Empire

Died: October 11, 1896; Vienna, Austro-Hungarian Empire

Area of Achievement: Music

Contribution: ʻRising from modest rural origins, Bruckner first established himself as one of the leading organists of his time, then persevered in his creative work to produce a great series of choral and symphonic works. Musically eloquent and possessing a unique sense of spiritual aspiration, the finest of Bruckner's large-scale compositions belong to the essential repertoire of nineteenth century music.

Early Life

Anton Bruckner was born to Anton and Theresa Bruckner on September 4, 1824, in the village of Ansfelden, in the Austro-Hungarian Empire. His family was for generations engaged in modest occupations such as broom-making and innkeeping, but both Bruckner's father and his grandfather had become schoolteachers, a position of modest status but substantial responsibilities. One of the tasks of a schoolteacher in those days was to oversee the basic musical education of his students. Thus, it was Bruckner's father who first instructed him in singing and in the playing of various instruments. Though young Anton seems to have played a child's violin as early as age four, he showed no special talent until the age of ten, when his godfather and cousin, Johann Weiss, took him into his own home in the nearby town of Hörsching to instruct him in the playing of the organ. One likely cause for Anton's move may have been the crowded Bruckner household; he was the first of eleven children, though only five survived to maturity.

Under his cousin's guidance, Anton studied the rudiments of music theory and continued his organ studies. In 1836, he composed his first organ work, a prelude which suggests that Bruckner knew some of the music of Franz Joseph Haydn and Wolfgang Amadeus Mozart, the foremost Austrian composers of the late eighteenth century. Later, Bruckner was to be influenced by the music of Johann Sebastian Bach and the Counter-Reformation master Giovanni Palestrina, but his months of study in his cousin's home were cut short when Anton was needed at home to deputize for his ailing father in the schoolroom. In 1837, the elder Bruckner died, leaving Anton nominally the head of the family.

With surprising resourcefulness, Anton's mother immediately arranged for him to become a student and choirboy at the Augustinian monastery of St. Florian, which boasted a splendid Baroque church containing one of the finest organs of the time. The young student flourished in the environment of the monastery and was able to continue his mustical studies with the church organist. His progress as an instrumentalist was rapid, and although little is known of his intellectual growth it is likely that Bruckner was a diligent student, for in October, 1840, he left St. Florian to enter the preparatory course for public school teachers in Linz and was graduated from it the following year without having to repeat the course, as was usually necessary. In Linz, Bruckner was exposed to an increasing range of musical influences. It was there that he heard for the first time a symphony by Ludwig van Beethoven, but he did not record the impression it made upon him.

Upon completing the preparatory course for teachers, Bruckner was assigned as an assistant teacher to the small town of Windhaag, where he endured appalling conditions of employment. Living in the teacher's house, he had to eat his meals with the servant girl. In addition to classroom duties, he was required to ring the church bells at 4:00 A.M., help the village priest dress for services, and work in the fields during the harvest. After fifteen months in Windhaag, an understanding school inspector transferred Bruckner to nearby Kronstorf. At this time, his only stated ambition was to become a schoolteacher, despite evidence that he was capable of either a religious or a musical vocation. Bruckner's need for financial security and his sense of responsibility toward his needy family were undoubtedly factors in his reluctance to declare an interest in a career as a performing musician; even his appointment as assistant organist at St. Florian in 1849 did not quell his insecurity about abandoning a steady, if ill-paying, job as public school teacher. After assuming the permanent post of organist at St. Florian in 1851, Bruckner was still reluctant to entrust his future to music, and he continued to enroll in preparatory courses in order to be qualified for high school teaching. He even applied, unsuccessfully, for a routine clerical position in 1853.

Despite his insecurity about finances, Bruckner's growth as a musician was steady. In 1856, while living in Linz, where he had recently been appointed cathedral organist, Bruckner began studying with the noted Viennese musician Simon Sechter. This elderly organist and conservatory professor was the author of a treatise on musical composition which codified rigorous rules of harmony and counterpoint based upon the musical practices of past centuries.

In accepting private students, Sechter requested that they set aside creative work in composition during their period of study with him, and Bruckner largely complied with this condition for the six years of Sechter's rigid but benevolent instruction. Bruckner's sacrifice was perhaps less significant than it was for other musicians, since he continued improvising at the organ, in itself a creative experience akin to composition. Music historians have regretted that Bruckner seems always to have been indifferent to writing down even the outlines of his acclaimed organ improvisations, and Bruckner himself once remarked upon this fact by saying "One does not write as one plays."

Life's Work

After completing his study with Sechter—which was carried on by mail and in occasional vists to Vienna—Bruckner's creative output increased remarkably, but at age thirty-nine he continued to seek instruction from established musicians. His next teacher was an opera conductor, Otto Kitzler, who introduced Bruckner to the work of Richard Wagner, the German composer of monumental "music-dramas" such as *Tristan und Isolde* (1859) and *Der Ring des Nibelungen* (1874). The influence of Wagner's music and personality upon Bruckner is as unquestionable as it difficult to assess. Wagner's music released powerful forces in Bruckner's creative personality, but it is clear that the younger composer did not comprehend the literary and ideological content of Wagner's work, even after making Wagner's acquaintance in 1865. Wagner was a sophisticated, cosmopolitan personality, while Bruckner was a man with country schooling and manners; it is a testimony to the unique genius of each that they were able to appreciate each other. Bruckner's formal, even obsequious manner may well have been a source of concealed amusement to the self-possessed Wagner.

Bruckner's career as a composer had blossomed in the early 1860's with the composition of a Mass in D Minor and two symphonies. The second of these symphonies, long forgotten by the composer, was later acknowledged by him as "only an attempt," and numbered as "Symphony 0." The composition of Bruckner's great chain of nine symphonies began in 1865 with the Symphony No. 1 in C Minor. Two more masses followed in the years 1866-1868 before the completion of the Symphony No. 2 in C Minor in 1872. This work begins the first of two great creative waves in Bruckner's mature career, encompassing work on the second, third, fourth, and fifth symphonies between 1871 and 1876. By all standards, this first period of mastery occurred very late in the composer's life; at the time of the completion of Symphony No. 4 in E-flat Major, he had just passed his fiftieth birthday, and although he was enjoying professional success as an organist, choral composer, and, to a lesser extent, choral director, his life was a lonely one. In 1867, he had suffered a nervous breakdown and spent three months recovering at a hydropathic establishment in Bad Kreuzen, where he was assailed by thoughts of suicide and a mania for numbers. It is reported that he would count the stars or the leaves on a tree and was possessed by the idea that he had to bail out the Danube River. Though simple overwork contributed to Bruckner's depression, his inherently solitary and often-melancholy disposition magnified his sense of his life's disappointments. On the personal side, his utter inability to find a partner in marriage weighed unusually heavily upon him. Bruckner was a very religious man, even by the standards of his time, and he would not countenance a sexual relationship outside marriage. Since his romantic interests were rather ineffectually aimed at young women aged sixteen to nineteen, Bruckner's search for a mate seemed almost designed to fail.

Later, Bruckner was unable to take professional disappointments in stride. While the opposition to his music by powerful critics such as Eduard Hanslick was often malicious, the occasional incomprehension of his scores by conductors and orchestral players was essentially a transitory problem, and much of his music was well received. The episode of mental collapse he experienced in 1867-1868 was fortunately not to be repeated, but Bruckner continued to be plagued by doubts about his work, which he sought to resolve by repeated and often ill-advised revision of his scores. The creative period of the early 1870's was followed by a period of revision in 1876 through 1879. He regained his confidence and composed a series of masterpieces in the years 1879 through 1887, including his *Te Deum* (1883-1884) and the magisterial Symphony No. 8 (1884-1886), but another period of revisions ensued in 1887, lasting until 1891.

The most frequently reproduced photographs of Bruckner show him in later life as a dignified and remote man, posing rather formally in his studio—often seated next to the great Bösendorfer grand piano that was left to him by a friend of earlier years. With close-cropped hair and baggy trousers (said to aid an organist's foot-pedalling), Bruckner had nothing of the appearance of a typical artist of his era. He seemed to his friends almost completely unaware of the effect of his awkward appearance and manners, and he was once admonished to take care in dressing so as not to disadvantage himself in his professional life.

Bruckner's formative years occurred during the reign of the Austrian Emperor Franz Josef, a period of unrelieved political conservatism and social rigidity; reflecting this background, Bruckner approached most relationships in an archaic and servile manner that irritated many of his acquaintances. Nevertheless, as a professor of music theory at the University of Vienna and as a private teacher, he gained the love and respect of his students not only by his competence but also by his humanity, which must have been all but invisible to the public.

The growing recognition given Bruckner's music in the 1880's was a partial consolation for the relative neglect he had suffered, which can be measured by reference to the fact that his main rival in the field of symphonic composition, Johannes Brahms, received enormous sums for the publication of his four symphonies, while few of Bruckner's works were published in his lifetime, and then only with subsidies from friends and admirers. The burden of Bruckner's many professional responsibilities seems to have had little effect on his ability to complete massive compositions. By 1890, however, in declining health, he gave up the last of his teaching positions to devote his full efforts to the completion of his Ninth Symphony. This work was intended to bear the dedication, *Dem lieben Gott . . .*, "To the dear Lord, if he will accept it," revealing a faith that is perhaps as naïve as it is profound. The first three movements of the Ninth Symphony were composed during the period 1891 through 1894, and the fourth was begun in late 1894. By that time, Bruckner had accepted the emperor's offer of accommodation in an annex of the Belvedere Palace, where he labored

on the finale of the symphony until days before his death on October 11, 1896. Although speculative completions of the finale have been recorded, the symphony has been performed for generations as a complex but unified work of three movements, concluding with an adagio that embodies, in its final passages, a profound and valedictory innocence.

Summary

Anton Bruckner's great works were composed after a long musical apprenticeship, and they display a technical and expressive consistency which makes possible a degree of generalization about them. A Bruckner symphony tends to be expansive, developing on a scale where the formal logic of late eighteenth and early nineteenth century music is of limited use as an organizing principle. The grandeur of Bruckner's musical thought was often expressed in compositions of demanding length which some listeners perceive as formless. In reality, Bruckner's music is highly organized, but it is unusually complex and polymorphous, and seldom adheres to familiar forms. Many of Bruckner's obvious structural ideas, such as periodicity within movements, dramatic contrast of blocks of thematic material, and complete rests within movements (which the composer compared, perhaps only half seriously, to pausing to take a deep breath before saying something important), were novel in their time and were often remarked upon disparagingly.

Bruckner's harmony became increasingly daring in his mature compositions, but in this he was not out of step with contemporary trends. His harmonic practice has been often attributed to the influence of Wagner's music, but it might also be regarded as Bruckner's inevitable victory over the rigidity of Sechter's rules. Similarly, Bruckner was able to turn a conventional mastery of contrapuntal technique into a creative resource, achieving remarkable powers of thematic metamorphosis and large-scale integration. In all areas of endeavor, Bruckner blended orthodoxy with inspired inventiveness. Many of his contemporaries, acknowledging his idiosyncrasies but not his inspiration, thought him to be a naïve musician, but the more discerning of his colleagues, such as Gustav Mahler, knew the stature of the man from their earliest experience of his music. The public was soon to follow in its appreciation of Bruckner's singular genius. He is recognized as the composer of a magisterial body of music that stands somewhat outside its time, looking as much to the past as to the future, but which forms part of the great continuity of European music.

Bibliography

Barford, Philip. *Bruckner Symphonies.* London: British Broadcasting Corporation, and Seattle: University of Washington Press, 1978. One of the BBC Music Guides, this slim volume discusses the symphonies in terms understandable to the layperson and with a minimum of musical examples. A brief concluding section, "Understanding Bruckner: A Personal View," is excellent.

Botstein, Leon. "Music and Ideology: Thoughts on Bruckner." *Musical Quarterly* 80, no. 1 (Spring 1996). Discusses the ongoing debate as to the use of Bruckner's original manuscripts or his revisions for performance purposes. Many feel the originals were better than the revisions on which his fame is based.

Doernberg, Erwin. *The Life and Symphonies of Anton Bruckner.* London: Barrie and Rockliff, 1960; New York: Dover, 1968. This solid study, divided into independent sections dealing first with the composer's life and then with his symphonies, frees Bruckner from many of the character stereotypes that for so long created an almost unbridgeable gap between perceptions of the man and his music. Excerpts from Bruckner's letters are provided in sufficient quantity for the reader to imagine something of his personal trials and his musical triumphs.

Howie, Crawford. "Bruckner Scholarship in the Last Ten Years (1987-1996)." *Music and Letters* 77, no. 4 (November 1996). Argues that recent research on Bruckner's life shows that he was not, as historically believed, unrecognized outside his native Austria.

Schönzeler, Hans-Hubert. *Bruckner.* London: Calder and Boyars, and New York: Grossman, 1970. The author is a musicologist as well as a conductor who has been an advocate of Bruckner's music, and his account of the composer is notably sympathetic to Bruckner's cause. The book stands apart from others in its quanity of useful illustrations. There is no bibliography, but a chronological list of works is provided.

Simpson, Robert. *The Essence of Bruckner.* 3d ed. London: Gollancz, 1992. This book is the product of twenty-five years of reflection upon Bruckner's symphonies by a noted British composer. Each work is examined in detail, satisfying the most exacting analytical standard. A concluding chapter, "Reflections," is essential for the nonspecialist reader.

Watson, Derek. *Bruckner.* London: Dent, 1975; New York: Oxford University Press, 1996. The growth of interest in Bruckner's music in the English-speaking world brought about the publication of this new account of the composer in the Master Musicians series. Readable. The many appendices are very useful.

Wolff, Werner. *Anton Bruckner: Rustic Genius.* New York: Dutton, 1942. The author, whose father was the founder of the Berlin Philharmonic Orchestra, met Bruckner in the early 1890's, when the composer was invited to dinner. As conductor, author, and lecturer, Wolff later championed Bruckner's cause. The bibliography consists almost exclusively of German-language entries.

C. S. McConnell

ISAMBARD KINGDOM BRUNEL

Born: April 9, 1806; Portsmouth, England
Died: September 15, 1859; London, England
Area of Achievement: Engineering
Contribution: Brunel was the most important developer of iron and steamship construction and the guiding force in the building of the Great Western Railway. Perhaps more important, he continued the tradition begun by his father, Marc Isambard Brunel, of capturing the imagination of the public with great engineering projects. Thus he symbolized the budding age of technology.

Early Life

Perhaps the most famous English engineer, Isambard Kingdom Brunel was born in Portsmouth, England, on April 9, 1806. His mother, Sophie Kingdom, was the daughter of a Plymouth naval contractor. His father, Marc Brunel, was a French engineer who had fled the Terror for America in 1793. After considerable success as an engineer in New York, the elder Brunel went to England in 1799 and married Sophie Kingdom, whom he had met earlier in France. Isambard was the youngest of their three children and their only son.

In 1823, after attending private schools in England and the Henri Quatre College in Paris, the young Brunel entered his father's business to serve his apprenticeship as an engineer. By that time, Marc Brunel was on the verge of beginning the project that would establish him and his son as the most famous engineers of their day: the Thames Tunnel.

Life's Work

The tunnel was intended to relieve the pressure of traffic on London Bridge. It was obviously desirable, but also a difficult and dangerous undertaking. The younger Brunel, although only nineteen years old when the work began, soon became the superintendent in fact and finally in name. He was involved in two serious accidents that were fully reported in the press. On the first occasion, he was aboveground when the river broke into the tunnel. He had himself lowered by rope into the tunnel to rescue a drowning man. No one was killed then, but eighteen months later, in January, 1828, a second breakthrough resulted in the deaths of three men. Two of them and Brunel were actually at the face of the tunnel when the water burst through. He managed to survive but with internal injuries se-

vere enough to prevent him from returning to the project. After several other accidents and financial crises, Marc Brunel saw the tunnel to completion in 1843 but without the active assistance of his son.

The younger Brunel's fame rested on his accomplishments in three areas: ship construction, the building of the Great Western Railway, and bridge construction. His involvement with shipping began in Bristol, where he designed dock improvements. In later years, he continued the design of docks at other places, but the immediate consequence of the Bristol contract was to bring him into contact with railway promoters and investors interested in building a line between London and Bristol. From this association, there developed a scheme to build the most advanced ship of the day, and the results were the most important basis of his fame.

Steam engines had been used before as auxiliary power, but no ship had crossed the Atlantic solely under steam power. The problem was that a ship could not carry enough coal to make the crossing and leave enough room for freight to make the crossing profitable. Conventional wisdom held that bigger ships would not solve the problem, because they would require bigger engines using more coal. Brunel reasoned that bigger ships would work. As water resistance would be proportional to the cross section of the ship, greater length would not cause greater resistance. In 1836, the largest ship then in existence was 208 feet long. Brunel's backers in the Great Western Railway Company formed the Great Western Steam Ship Company to build a ship 236 feet long, displacing twenty-three hundred tons—the biggest ship of the time. After one year, the *Great Western* was afloat, and one year later it was ready to depart for New York. In the meantime, competitors had entered the race. In fact, a modified sailing vessel steamed into New York harbor a few hours before the *Great Western* arrived in the afternoon of April 23, 1838. The *Great Western* was twice the size of its rival, had two hundred tons of coal left rather than the fifteen tons of the other ship, and made the voyage three days faster.

The *Great Britain* was an even greater innovation. As soon as the *Great Western* had completed its voyage, Brunel proposed a much larger ship, but size was not as important as its other features. It was the first ship constructed entirely of iron, and it was the first ship intended for commercial use to employ a screw propeller instead of side-mounted

paddle wheels. After its maiden voyage in July, 1845, it continued in service until it was damaged in a storm in 1886 and stopped in the Falkland Islands, where it remained until rescued in 1970 and returned to Bristol.

In 1854, work began on the *Great Eastern*—the last of Brunel's great ships. None of these ships enjoyed commercial success, and the Great Western Steam Ship Company had already failed, but another company was formed to execute the new design. At 680 feet long, this ship was gigantic for its day, but again, its significance lay not so much in its size as in its innovative features. The double-hull design with watertight compartments is still a standard feature in shipbuilding. Brunel claimed that the ship could break in two and both halves would float independently. No openings were allowed in the hull below the waterline, and the design included a modern-style bridge with a variety of instruments. Construction took five years to complete because of problems with contractors, workers, and critics. The problems did not end even after construction was complete. No one knew how to launch such a huge ship, and men were killed in the attempt, but it

finally entered the water in September, 1859—ten days before its designer's death. It was used in laying the transatlantic cable and in other notable enterprises, but it, too, failed commercially and was broken up in the 1890's.

As engineer for the Great Western Railway, Brunel surveyed its route in 1833 and determined its technical aspects for as long as he lived. He specified the type of rolling stock, engines, rails, and stations it was to have. His name became associated with a number of remarkable tunnels and other engineering feats along the line, but his railway activities were best known in connection with two controversies rather than those successes. The first was the debate over narrow versus broad-gauge rails.

No one knows how the rail gauge of four feet, eight and one-half inches became standard, but Brunel disapproved of it. He wanted wider spacing of the tracks so that rolling stock would be carried inside the wheels rather than hanging over them. Much larger wheels could then be used, as they no longer had to stay under the vehicles they were carrying. These large wheels meant a reduction in loss of power attributable to friction. From the beginning, the Great Western tracks were seven feet apart, and Brunel remained the most influential champion of the "broad" gauge throughout his life. Whatever the advantages of the broad gauge, the system caused great difficulty where the lines that served the southwest of England met those in the rest of the country. Brunel devised a variety of plans to accommodate the difference and insisted on maintaining the broad gauge on any extension of the Great Western lines. Interestingly, he did not use the broad gauge on the two Italian railways he designed. The controversy reached a climax in the late 1840's as a parliamentary gauge commission held hearings on the issue. The "Gauge War," as it came to be known, ended with no standard being set, but the broad-gauge lines were converted soon after Brunel's death.

Somewhat less controversial was the "atmospheric" railway that operated for about six months in 1848 from Exeter to Newton Abbot. Trains operated on this line without benefit of locomotives. A tube fifteen inches in diameter ran between the tracks, and stationary steam engines located along the tracks maintained a partial vacuum in it. Pistons on the underside of the railway carriages fit into the tube by means of a leather flap valve, and atmospheric pressure drove the trains. The system failed for several technical reasons. Most of the controversy involved Brunel's failure to forecast accurately the cost of the project. He grossly underestimated construction costs, and the cost of maintenance proved astronomical. Detractors accused him of being impractical, the ultimate insult for an engineer, and too fanciful in his designs.

Brunel's reputation as a builder of bridges is closely related to his activities in constructing the Great Western Railway, but he was interested in bridge design before the railway. In fact, his first important independent contract was in 1829 for the Clifton Bridge, near Bristol. Lack of funds prevented completion of the bridge until after his death, but the project brought him into contact with the Bristolians who were so important to the rest of his career. There were numerous others, but the Saltash Bridge crossing the Tamar on the Great Western line probably did the most to enhance his reputation with fellow engineers and the public.

The pier footings for this bridge had to be sunk eighty feet through water and mud. The task was accomplished by pumping and digging out the material inside an iron casing thirty-five feet in diameter that had been placed in the river. The two central spans of the bridge, each 455 feet long, were floated to the piers when they had reached above water level. As the stonework extended upward, the spans went up with them by means of two of three jacks located on each pier. Each span was in the form of a truss made with tubular arches, from which were suspended bridge chains, resulting in a shape resembling an oval on its side. It was complete in 1858.

Brunel seemed to attract attention even when he was not involved with such grand projects. He received press coverage for building a prefabricated hospital used in the Crimean War, improvements on large guns, a floating gun carriage also used in the Crimean War, his membership on the building committee of the Great Exhibition of 1851, and his testimony before numerous parliamentary committees. His testimony was nearly always the subject of debate in the press, both because of the importance of the issues involved and because of the force of his convictions. For example, he was a staunch opponent of patent laws, which he believed hindered progress.

He was so well-known that an accident that befell him became the subject of a story in R. H. Barham's *The Ingoldsby Legends: Or, Mirth and Marvels, by Thomas Ingoldsby, Esquire* (1837). On April 3, 1843, he was playing with his children by pretending to make a coin go from his ear to his mouth. In the course of performing the trick he swallowed the coin, which lodged in one of his bronchial tubes. The efforts of the surgeons failed, and Brunel constructed a device to invert and shake him. Forty days after the mishap, the inverter finally worked. Brunel was so famous and the incident so well-known that when word spread that "it was out," Londoners knew what was out of whom without having to be told.

Brunel seemed to be accident-prone. As mentioned, he suffered severe internal injuries in the flooding of the Thames Tunnel, and one might speculate that these injuries contributed to the kidney failure which killed him at a relatively early age. During the trials of the *Great Western*, a fire broke out, and he tried to climb down a ladder to investigate. A fall of eighteen feet knocked him unconscious, and it took him some time to recover from his injuries.

In July, 1836, Brunel married Mary Horsley. They had two sons and a daughter. The Brunels combined office and home in a rather lavish London residence. Mary kept separate carriages for morning and afternoon use, and the servants, clerks, and apprentices, who paid one thousand pounds each for the privilege of observing Brunel at work, gave the impression of a very important establishment. Brunel seems to have had little time for anything but his work. He was traveling much of the time in order to attend to his many projects. Photographs and descriptions depict him as a rather small, energetic man with a dark complexion. He had several bouts with kidney disease in the last years of his life and finally succumbed to it on September 15, 1859.

Summary

The Brunels were not the only famous father and son team of engineers in the early nineteenth century. George and Robert Stephenson were much in the public view. There were also other famous individual engineers, such as Thomas Telford and Richard Trevithick, but the Brunels, more than any others, established the professional engineer as a hero of the Industrial Revolution.

Isambard Kingdom Brunel used his tremendous engineering abilities to improve communications both within England and between England and North America. He oversaw construction of more than one thousand miles of railway tracks in central and western England, in Ireland, and in Wales, and he built two railroads in Italy as well. His innovations in shipbuilding made the transatlantic passage both cheaper and less time-consuming, and his ship the *Great Eastern* laid the first transatlantic cable. Finally, both directly and indirectly, Brunel increased the number of bridges linking England's roadways.

Bibliography

Brunel, Isambard Kingdom. *The Life of Isambard Kingdom Brunel, Civil Engineer*. London: Longman, 1870; Rutherford, N.J.: Fairleigh Dickinson University Press, 1972. This biography was written by Brunel's son. It is not an intimate family portrait, but rather a traditional nineteenth century formal biography. It contains information available nowhere else.

Gooch, Sir Daniel. *The Diaries of Sir Daniel Gooch*. London: Kegan Paul, 1892. Gooch was one of Brunel's colleagues in the construction of the Great Western Railway. His memoir, therefore, deals mostly with that aspect of Brunel's career.

Hadfield, Charles. *Atmospheric Railways*. Newton Abbot: David and Charles, 1967; New York: Kelley, 1968. Although this book deals with the general subject of atmospheric railways, there is fairly extensive treatment of Brunel's involvement with them.

Hay, Peter. *Brunel, Engineering Giant*. London and North Pomfret, Vt.: Batsford, 1985. A short paperback giving the essential details of its subject's life. It has thirty-three useful black-and-white illustrations and is probably the best choice for someone desiring a brief account. No notes or other scholarly apparatus.

Pudney, John. *Brunel and His World*. London: Thames and Hudson, and Albuquerque, N. Mex.: Transatlantic Arts, 1974. Another popular account without footnotes. Pudney's work relies mainly on its 140 illustrations. The thesis is that Brunel surpassed contemporary engineers because of his ability to get public attention through grand projects.

Rolt, L.T.C. *Isambard Kingdom Brunel*. London and New York: Longman, 1957. The closest thing to a standard account. Rolt is the best-known modern scholar dealing with Brunel.

———. *The Story of Brunel*. London: Methuen, 1965; New York: Abelard-Schuman, 1968. A book for juveniles written in a style comprehensible to elementary school students.

Rowland, K.T. *The Great Britain*. Newton Abbot: David and Charles, 1971. An account of the construction and career of the ship that was one of Brunel's best-known creations.

Philip D. Jones

MARC ISAMBARD BRUNEL

Born: April 25, 1769; Hacqueville, France
Died: December 12, 1849; London, England
Area of Achievement: Engineering
Contribution: Brunel was one of the leaders in mechanizing production during the early nineteenth century. He was also the most famous civil engineer of his day.

Early Life

Marc Isambard Brunel was born April 25, 1769, in Hacqueville, near Gisors, France. His family had been tenant farmers in Normandy for generations. As a younger son, he was intended for the Church by his family. Consequently, he entered the seminary of St. Nicaise at Rouen in 1780. Even at the age of eleven, Brunel showed a strong interest in drawing and mathematics. For the classics, however, he had no interest whatsoever. The Superior of the seminary advised the elder Brunel against forcing the boy into a profession for which he was obviously unsuited.

In 1782, the Brunel family decided on a naval career for young Marc, and he went to live with the Carpentier family in Rouen to prepare for entrance into the navy. There, he studied mathematics, drawing, and other technical subjects. This academic regimen must have suited him, as he was appointed a cadet on a corvette headed for the West Indies in 1786. Little is known of his naval career, which ended in 1792 when his ship returned to France. The Revolution had occurred in his absence, and by 1793, Paris was a dangerous place for royalist officers. Brunel must have been particularly outspoken or politically active, since he soon fled from Paris to Rouen in some danger. While visiting the Carpentier family in Rouen, he met his future wife, Sophie Kingdom, an English girl who was staying with the Carpentiers for a few months in order to learn French. The danger for Brunel was considerable. Not even love could detain him, and he managed to obtain a passport from the American vice consul at Le Havre. He arrived in New York on September 6, 1793.

Life's Work

In America, Brunel first began to practice his profession. He obtained an appointment to survey a tract of land near Ontario, and subsequently he surveyed the route for a canal to connect the Hudson River with Lake Champlain. During these operations, he showed so much ability that he became director of the canal construction. His success in that position won numerous commissions for him. He designed several buildings and finally became chief engineer of New York in 1796. This appointment gave him an opportunity to display his skills as a mechanical engineer, since his duties included construction of an arsenal including an arms manufactory. During the construction, Brunel introduced a number of devices to improve both the boring and casting of cannon.

Brunel became an American citizen in 1796. This fact in combination with such promising prospects for a young man of twenty-nine make it rather surprising that he should have left the United States for England in January, 1799. There were, however, two compelling reasons for his departure. The first was Sophie Kingdom, who had returned to England from France in 1795 after several months of detention by French authorities. The second was his hopes for selling plans for block-making machinery to the Royal Navy.

The navy required 100,000 blocks every year for sets of blocks and tackles. On shipboard and in the shipyards, the block and tackle was the main source of motive power. Brunel believed that his machines could make better blocks with great savings in labor costs. He intended to convince the firm that had the contract for blocks, Fox and Taylor of Southampton, by means of models made for him by the London toolmaker, Henry Maudslay—virtually the founder of the machine-tool industry. The block contractors were not convinced either by his plans or by his models, but their contract was soon due to expire. Brunel made use of letters of introduction from no less a personage than Alexander Hamilton to gain access to the authorities at the Admiralty. He found them easier to convince, and the government agreed to begin its own production in May, 1803, using machines of his design.

During this period of selling and negotiations, Brunel had invented several machines for use in textile mills and a writing machine. He had also wasted little time in his pursuit of Sophie Kingdom. They were married in November, 1799. She was six years younger than he. Over the next six years, they had three children—two daughters and, in 1806, a son who was himself to become a great engineer, Isambard Kingdom Brunel.

The block-making machinery was eminently successful. As Brunel had predicted, the blocks not only were much better made but also reduced the number of workers required to produce them to less than one-tenth the number formerly employed. Brunel had been so confident in his invention that his contract with the government stipulated that his fee would be the amount of money saved in one full year of production. Although the saving in the first year amounted to twenty-four thousand pounds, he actually received seventeen thousand pounds, and that only after considerable delay.

Brunel continued to patent various machines, but his interests were increasingly entrepreneurial. Between 1805 and 1812, he built a sawmill and supplied wood to the navy. In conjunction with this activity, he designed a number of woodworking machines. As his business contacts and interests expanded, he became involved in the manufacture of boots for the army, and by 1810 he had built machinery for producing boots.

All these enterprises came to a bad end. Brunel had chosen partners to run the business side of his affairs so that he could concentrate on invention. His

choices were poor. Their lack of ability in combination with a series of disasters led to his financial ruin. The sawmill burned down in 1814. Soon thereafter, in 1815, the war with France came to an end, and he was left holding a large quantity of boots, which the government refused to buy. He still managed to survive financially, until his bankers failed in 1821. That was the final blow. Unable to pay his creditors, he and Sophie were imprisoned for debt between May and August, 1821. Their release apparently came about through the czar of Russia, who was interested in Brunel's plan for building a tunnel under the river at St. Petersburg so that communication could be maintained when the river was frozen. The influence of the czar and other prominent people led the British government to award Brunel five thousand pounds for the payment of his debts. This period was referred to as "the Misfortune" by the family, and it had the effect of spoiling his taste for independent business ventures. Thereafter Brunel remained strictly an engineer.

As usual for Brunel, he was busily turning out inventions and schemes even during this time of trouble. He invented a knitting machine and two types of tinfoil, and he made improvements in printing machinery. If his business acumen had been greater, he might have solved his financial problems with these inventions, but they brought him little profit. He also designed several bridges. In fact, his proposed solution to the ice problem at St. Petersburg was ultimately a bridge design. Only a few of his bridges were built—all by the French government on the Island of Bourbon.

After his release from jail, Brunel spent the next three years working on plans for floating piers and swing bridges that were built at the Liverpool docks. He also made improvements in paddle wheels and marine steam engines. This interest in steam engines may have led him to the design of a new engine called the gas engine. It was based on the principle that increasing the temperature of liquified gas in a confined space will increase the pressure. He hoped to operate the engine by alternately raising and lowering the temperature of such a gas, but the design never succeeded, despite the expenditure of much time and money.

In 1824, Brunel began his best-known project, the Thames Tunnel. No one had ever built a tunnel large enough for traffic to use that ran under a river, though it had been attempted under the Thames around the turn of the century. A small one could be built but not a large one, because the timbers normally used in mines could not support the great weight of a large expanse of roof with the even greater weight of water above it. Brunel's solution to the problem came to him in 1818 as he watched a beetle boring through a rotten timber. The creature ate the wood and then excreted waste to form a lining for its tunnel. It occurred to Brunel that an iron shield pressed against the face of a tunnel by hydraulic rams could keep the water from bursting through. The shield would have a wide rim extending back into the tunnel to support the walls and ceiling. As it moved forward, workers would construct brick or masonry walls behind it. He patented the idea in 1818.

Traffic congestion at London Bridge made the desirability of a tunnel under the Thames obvious, and by 1824, Brunel had convinced a number of investors to form a company, endorsed by the Duke of Wellington, for the purpose of digging a tunnel from Rotherhithe to Wapping. This time, Brunel was an employee with a salary of one thousand pounds per year. Digging began at Rotherhithe on February 16, 1825. A shaft fifty feet in diameter and seventy feet deep had to be dug before the tunnel could begin. In order to keep water out and prevent caving-in, Brunel built an iron casing for the shaft, about thirty-five feet high, aboveground. As digging proceeded inside the casing, it sank into the ground, forming the walls of the shaft. He added the rest of the casing as it continued to sink. The shield was then lowered and the tunnel begun. As completed, the tunnel was thirty-seven and one-half feet wide by twenty-two and one-quarter feet high. It was rectangular in cross section with two arches inside containing the two roadways. The shield was a grid of cells stacked three high and twelve wide. Inside each of the thirty-six cells thus formed were fourteen horizontal planks pressed against the face of the tunnel by means of large screws bracing each against the sides of the cell. Workmen removed the planks one at a time and dug nine inches from the face of the tunnel. After all the planks had been removed and replaced in this fashion, hydraulic rams forced the entire shield forward. Masons then extended the walls to cover the gap between the rim of the shield and the finished wall. The gap was the weak point in the operation. Even such a small exposure of unsupported earth and water could and did result in disaster.

The tunnel drew enormous attention from the public. Over Brunel's objections, the directors of the company allowed sightseers into the work area for a fee. Parliament, the press, the public, and friends of the directors all had ideas about how the project should be completed, but Brunel managed to retain control despite numerous battles among the directors. By 1826, his son, Isambard Kingdom Brunel, had become his second in command and actually oversaw the work. On May 18, 1827, the river broke into the tunnel. No one was killed and workmen managed to stop the flow of water by pouring clay into the hole from the river bed. After the tunnel was pumped dry, the Coldstream Guards played at a celebration dinner for fifty held inside the tunnel. On January 12, 1828, a second breakthrough occurred. This time, three men were killed and Isambard Brunel was severely injured. Such disasters in combination with strikes, panics, and strife within the company finally led to the abandonment of the undertaking for seven years in August, 1828. The public simply would not invest any more money in the company.

The company wanted a loan from the government to continue the work, but no loan was possible until the directors could end their quarrels. Finally, in 1832, the directors who questioned Brunel's management were defeated and resigned. A government loan allowed the work to begin again in 1835. Despite the incursion of the river on three more occasions, the tunnel reached completion in November, 1841. Brunel was knighted in March, 1841, and appeared as a hero at the official opening ceremony on March 25, 1843. Contemporaries suggested that the strain of building the tunnel had ruined his health. The portrait of him in the National Portrait Gallery shows a bald, bespectacled man of slight build with a serene expression. Appropriately, if incongruously, he is shown seated at a desk located inside the Thames Tunnel. He obviously considered it the great work of his life, and it may indeed have taken its toll on his health.

He had already suffered his first stroke shortly before the opening ceremony. His productive life was over. He had another stroke in 1845 and died four years later on December 12, 1849.

Summary

Marc Isambard Brunel was one of the first to popularize the notion of professional civil engineering. The Thames Tunnel and the story of his block machinery captured the public imagination to an unparalleled extent. He and, to an even greater extent, his son, Isambard Brunel, came to stand almost as symbols for technical achievement in the Industrial Revolution. The fact that he was knighted for his accomplishments as an engineer not only indicated the importance of his activities to his contemporaries but also emphasized the changing spirit of the age. When he was born, in 1769, the idea of knighting someone for engineering accomplishments would hardly have been countenanced.

Bibliography

Beamish, Richard. *Memoir of the Life of Sir Marc Isambard Brunel*. London: Longman, 1862. Most later accounts are based on this one. It is still probably the most useful source of information about Brunel's professional life.

Clements, Paul. *Marc Isambard Brunel*. London: Longman, 1970. Most of this book is devoted to a discussion of the Thames Tunnel construction.

Lampe, David. *The Tunnel*. London: Harrap, 1963. As the title indicates, this book is devoted exclusively to the construction of the Thames Tunnel. The account is much the same as that given in Clements' book.

Noble, Lady Celia Brunel. *The Brunels, Father and Son*. London: Cobden Sanderson, 1938. The author was Isambard Brunel's granddaughter and, therefore, great-granddaughter of Marc Brunel. She provides information about their family life that is available no place else.

Philip D. Jones

WILLIAM CULLEN BRYANT

Born: November 3, 1794; Cummington, Massachusetts

Died: June 12, 1878; New York, New York

Areas of Achievement: Poetry and journalism

Contribution: As a poet, Bryant is often described as a transitional figure because of his fluency in exploiting Romantic themes drawn from nature in conventional neoclassical verse forms. In his half-century as an editor for the New York *Evening Post*, he was a vigorous spokesman for American liberal thought.

Early Life

William Cullen Bryant was born November 3, 1794, in Cummington, Massachusetts. His father, Dr. Peter Bryant, was a physician who left Cummington to escape his debts soon after Bryant was born. When he returned two years later, the precocious child had already begun to read the Bible under the tutelage of his mother, née Sarah Snell, and her father, who was a noted deacon in the Congregationalist church. The child was reared in an atmosphere of Calvinist piety and sober devotion to literature.

Bryant wrote his first notable poem when he was ten years old, a fifty-four-line celebration of American education composed for the commencement exercises at his school. In 1808, when the Embargo Act was creating a violent national controversy, he wrote a twelve-page poem, "The Embargo," attacking Thomas Jefferson—a piece of youthful invective that the mature Bryant, a Jeffersonian Democrat, came to regret. Bryant continued to write verses and to study under tutors, and, in 1810, he entered Williams College. By then, Bryant was already known as a poet, a reputation romantically enhanced by his tall, slender physique crowned with a shock of brown hair. He left Williams after two years, disappointed by the instruction and in the hope of attending Yale.

Family finances, however, prohibited study at Yale, and, in 1811, Bryant went to Worthington to study law under Samuel Howe; in 1814, he moved again to Bridgewater to undertake his office training. In 1815, he was admitted to law practice. He continued to write verse, and, in 1817, five of his poems, including the first version of "Thanatopsis," appeared in the *North American Review*, to which they had been submitted by his father. Over the next few years, Bryant published more poems and essays in the *North American Review*. In 1821, firmly established in his legal practice in Great Barrington, Massachusetts, Bryant married Frances Fairchild, read "The Ages" as the Phi Beta Kappa poem at Harvard College's commencement ceremony, and published his first book of poetry. *Poems* was published through the efforts of three friends—Edward T. Channing, Richard Henry Dana, and Willard Phillips—and included such well-known works as "To a Waterfowl," "Inscription for the Entrance to a Wood," and the final version of "Thanatopsis." This successful year marked the beginning of his adult career as a stable husband and father and as a national man of letters.

Life's Work

The ambitious Bryant was not to be confined for long to the drudgery of practicing law in a small town, and, in 1825, he moved to New York City and assumed editorship of the *New York Review*. The new journal had circulation problems right

from the beginning, however, and, in 1829, Bryant abandoned efforts to give it life and became part owner and editor-in-chief of the New York *Evening Post*. This crucial change shaped the remainder of his life, for he was able to turn the *Evening Post* into both a personal and a commercial success. Under his direction and often through his own editorials, the *Evening Post* became a major organ of democratic principles in American journalism.

The political quarrels in which Bryant involved the *Evening Post* became acrimonious at times. In one contretemps with the *Commercial Advertiser*, Bryant ended up beating William Stone, one of its editors, with a cowhide whip on Broadway. Although he was suspicious of William Lloyd Garrison and the abolitionists, fearing that they would cause terrible harm to the Union, he defended eloquently the rights of antislavery writers. His outrage at the murder in Alton, Illinois, of the Reverend Elijah Lovejoy for his anti-slavery editorials produced a splendid defense of free speech:

> The right to discuss freely and openly, by speech, by the pen, by the press, all political questions, and to examine and animadvert upon all political institutions, is a right so clear and certain, so interwoven with our other liberties, so necessary, in fact to their existence, that without it we must fall at once into despotism or anarchy. To say that he who holds unpopular opinions must hold them at the peril of his life, and that, if he expresses them in public, he has only himself to blame if they who disagree with him should rise and put him to death, is to strike at all rights, all liberties, all protection of the laws, and to justify or extenuate all crimes.

Bryant expressed his humanitarianism in many ways. In 1857, he attacked the Dred Scott decision, fearing that it would make slavery a national institution. He was a fervent supporter of reform in the country's prisons and printed several editorials denouncing flogging and capital punishment. He was especially critical of the policy of imprisoning young people with veteran criminals, lamenting the corruption to which the practice led.

Bryant frequently wrote in the interest of civic reforms in New York City. He scrutinized both police and fire departments, urging that the police be given uniforms and that a paid fire department be organized. He editorialized in 1860 about the city's deplorable slum housing, demanding government regulation of tenement construction and rental. He conducted a long campaign to create a park in Manhattan, and when Central Park was planned, he fought the entrepreneurs who wanted to build apartments in the park. He was an enthusiastic friend of American dramatists and artists, lauding their efforts to produce truly American art. Aware of the lack of satisfactory copyright laws, Bryant sought the establishment of an international copyright law.

Over the years, Bryant had read such eighteenth century economists as Adam Smith, and their influence probably stood behind his swing from Federalism to Jacksonian democracy. Yet Bryant was never a completely faithful adherent of party politics and could be independent when he believed that individual liberties were being threatened. Thus, in one editorial, he attacked the practice of burning abolitionist propaganda by Southern justices of the peace. In 1839, he assailed the Democratic Administration for ruling that a group of slaves who mutinied on the *Amistad* should be returned to their owners. Bryant described the mutineers as "heroes not malefactors."

As a result of the respect he commanded for his forthrightness, Bryant achieved some influence in politics. When the Civil War broke out, Bryant urged that the slaves be quickly freed and that the war be brought to an end. He supported Abraham Lincoln, apparently influenced him in his cabinet choices, and wrote to him concerning political issues.

The man of practical affairs continued to write poetry. A devoted traveler, Bryant visited Illinois in 1832 and wrote one of his most famous poems, "The Prairies," as a result. His later volumes of verse included *The Fountain and Other Poems* (1842), *The White-Footed Deer* (1844), and *Thirty Poems* (1864). In 1870-1872, Bryant published his translations of Homer's *Iliad* (c. 800 B.C.) and *Odyssey* (c. 800 B.C.).

Bryant's poems of nature celebrate the opening up of the new nation: its topography and its flora and fauna. Famous poems such as "A Forest Hymn" and "Inscription for the Entrance to a Wood" are infused with a religious feeling that makes them confessions of personal faith. Although he did not embrace the Transcendentalism of Walt Whitman and Ralph Waldo Emerson, his poems often express a deep piety toward nature, an attitude that is essentially spiritual. Thus, in "A Forest Hymn" he sees in a "delicate forest flower,"

> An emanation of the indwelling Life, A visible token of the upholding Love, That are the soul of this great universe.

Summary

Bryant was certainly one of the giants of nineteenth century journalism. He has been praised for introducing culture to American newspapers, as well as for his important championing of free trade, civic consciousness, and the virtues of a rational liberalism. He was respected by his contemporaries as a man of high moral standards and varied literary accomplishments, and he proved to be a hardheaded businessman who made a substantial success of the New York *Evening Post*. He was tireless in his role as a public figure, and his brief final illness was precipitated by his delivery, in Central Park, of an address honoring the Italian patriot Giuseppe Mazzini.

Although his poetry was extremely popular in his own day and was praised by Edgar Allan Poe and Emerson, he has not been accorded the highest honors by posterity. Such memorable poems as "Thanatopsis" and "To a Waterfowl" are moving dramatizations of universal emotions couched in simple language, but most of his works lack the complexity and richness associated with great poetry. Scholars have judged Bryant an able student of prosody, who influenced other poets both in his theory and in his practice, and he has been praised as the first American poet to respond sensitively to the literature of Latin America.

Bryant earned an honorable place in American history for his journalistic eloquence as an advocate of democratic principles, and he has given pleasure to many readers by his lyrical power in stating a true piety and idealism in smooth verse and assuring sentiments. He will be remembered for these accomplishments.

Bibliography

Bigelow, John. *William Cullen Bryant*. Boston: Houghton Mifflin, 1890. Bigelow was a close friend and business partner of Bryant. His book lacks critical depth but is important for its firsthand account of Bryant's life and character.

Branch, Michael P. "William Cullen Bryant: The Nature Poet as Environmental Journalist." *The American Transcendental Quarterly* 12, no. 3 (September 1998). Focuses on Bryant's journalistic work and his advocacy of environmental protection.

Brown, Charles H. *William Cullen Bryant*. New York: Scribner, 1971. A well-written, comprehensive, and reliable account of Bryant's life. The study of Bryant's long career at the New York *Evening Post* is excellent. Little literary analysis.

Bryant, William Cullen, II. "Painting and Poetry: A Love Affair of Long Ago." *American Quarterly* 22 (Winter 1970): 859-882. Traces Bryant's involvement with painters such as Thomas Cole and his help in establishing the National Academy of the Arts.

Donovan, Alan B. "William Cullen Bryant: Father of American Song." *New England Quarterly* 41 (December 1968): 505-520. Identifies the importance of Calvinism and neoclassicism in shaping Bryant's Romantic verses. Finds in Bryant's work "the first native articulation of the art of poetry."

McLean, Albert F., Jr. *William Cullen Bryant*. New York: Twayne, 1964. A thorough and sensitive study of Bryant's poetry, divided into three main sections: "The Poems of Nature," "The Poems of Death," and "The Poems of Progress." Sees Bryant as a poet who "could never make the basic decision which Emerson was to formulate as the choice between self-reliance and conformity."

Morris, Timothy. "Bryant and the American Poetic Tradition." *The American Transcendental Quarterly* 8, no. 1 (March 1994). Examines Bryant's influence on poetry during his life and beyond.

Nevins, Allan. *The Evening Post: A Century of Journalism*. New York: Boni and Liveright, 1922. Includes a long account of Bryant's accomplishments as an editor, praising his business judgment, his cultural influence, and his liberal stance on social issues.

Parrington, Vernon L. "William Cullen Bryant: Puritan Liberal." In *Main Currents in American Thought*. Vol. 2, 238-246. New York: Harcourt Brace, 1927. Explicates Bryant's liberal politics and describes him as "the father of nineteenth-century journalism."

Phair, Judith Turner. *A Bibliography of William Cullen Bryant and His Critics: 1808-1972*. Troy, N.Y.: Whitston, 1975. An extremely useful annotated bibliography of critical commentary on Bryant.

Ringe, Donald A. "Kindred Spirits: Bryant and Cole." *American Quarterly* 6 (Fall 1954): 233-244. Compares Bryant's aesthetics with those of the painter Thomas Cole, finding that Bryant had much in common with Cole and the other artists of the Hudson River School.

Frank Day

JAMES BUCHANAN

Born: April 23, 1791; Mercerburg, Pennsylvania
Died: June 1, 1868; Lancaster, Pennsylvania
Areas of Achievement: Government and politics
Contribution: Buchanan worked hard to preserve the Union. His presidency was devoted to trying to maintain the Democratic Party's North-South coalition.

Early Life

James Buchanan was the second child of James and Mary Buchanan, both of whom were from strong Northern Irish-Scottish Presbyterian families. The year James was born, his elder sister died, so, understandably, James received an unusual amount of attention and affection. After James, the Buchanans had nine more children: five girls followed by four boys. One of the girls and one of the boys did not live to be one year old. The arrival of so many brothers and sisters, however, did not diminish the special place James held in the Buchanan household.

James's formal education began at the Old Stone Academy in Mercerburg. In the autumn of 1807, he entered the junior class at Dickinson College. Although he was expelled once for disorderly conduct, he still managed to be graduated in 1809. James's personality was the source of most of his difficulties in college: He had a high opinion of himself and was quite obnoxious at times.

Buchanan's self-confidence was at least partially justified. He was an able student who became an extremely successful lawyer. Along with his intellectual ability, Buchanan was distinguished in appearance. He was tall with broad shoulders, had wavy blond hair, blue eyes, and fine features. He walked in a distinctive manner, with his head tilted slightly forward. His size, appearance, and mannerisms made him stand out, even in large crowds. After college, Buchanan studied law in the office of James Hopkins of Lancaster and was admitted to the Pennsylvania bar in 1812. He quickly established a successful law practice. The two main ingredients of his success were his knowledge of the law and his talent for oral presentation.

Life's Work

The political career of James Buchanan began with his election to the Pennsylvania House of Representatives in 1813. As a Federalist, he opposed the war with England, but once war was declared, he became a volunteer in a company of dragoons. In 1815, he was reelected. During this period, he spent considerable time and energy trying to delay the return of specie payment to protect the United States Bank.

Buchanan emerged on the national political scene in 1820, as a member of the United States House of Representatives. In 1824, with the demise of the Federalist Party, he found himself increasingly at odds with President John Quincy Adams. By 1826, Buchanan was working on a new Amalgamation Party in Pennsylvania, a mixture of Federalist Congressmen and old-line Democrats. What held the group together was its desire for a new political party and its support of Andrew Jackson. The main result of the creation of this new, vaguely defined party was that Buchanan became the primary dispenser of patronage in Pennsylvania.

After ten successful years in the House of Representatives, Buchanan was offered and accepted the ministry to Russia. Before taking this post, he had

been giving serious thought to leaving public life and returning to private law practice.

Buchanan stayed in St. Petersburg (now Leningrad) until August of 1833, returning home to run for the United States Senate. By that time, Buchanan was clearly identified with the Democratic Party, and he realized that this meant supporting President Jackson, which included following Vice President Martin Van Buren's lead in the Senate.

Buchanan was quickly recognized as a loyal and principled partisan. Although the United States Bank was located in his home state, Buchanan remained true to the Jackson Administration's commitment to getting the federal government out of the banking business. Everyone knew that destroying the bank would move the United States' financial center from Philadelphia to New York; still, Buchanan believed that the interests of the nation should come before the interests of his home state. Buchanan's ability to place the nation's interests above those of his state or region were motivated, at least in part, by his political ambitions. In 1838, many of his friends encouraged him to run for the office of governor of Pennsylvania; he chose instead to remain in the Senate and focus his attention on national issues.

President James K. Polk appointed Buchanan to serve as his secretary of state in 1844. Buchanan shared Polk's desire to expand the territory of the United States, but negotiating treaties for the rigid Polk was difficult at times. Buchanan's skills at settling disputes and striking compromises were perfected during his tour of duty at the State Department.

Buchanan's friends were surprised to learn that he was considering retirement as the 1848 presidential race approached. Whether it was the bitter division in the Democratic Party or the heightened concern over sectional rivalry, Buchanan sensed that 1848 would not be a good year for the Democratic Party. His instincts were correct. Buchanan's retirement from the State Department left him time to take care of some private affairs. He purchased his country estate, Wheatland, and began the groundwork for the 1852 presidential race. Buchanan's four years of retirement were some of the happiest he had known: He pursued the life of a gentleman farmer and spent time with the niece and nephew he was rearing. Unfortunately, his presidential ambitions were not well served by his temporary retirement.

The 1852 Democratic Convention was greatly divided. After some political maneuvering, much heated debate, and many caucuses, Franklin Pierce received the party's nomination. Pierce defeated Winfield Scott in the general election and then persuaded Buchanan to end his political retirement and serve as minister to Great Britain. Though Buchanan accepted this assignment reluctantly, it proved to be a good decision for him politically.

The Kansas-Nebraska Act was passed in 1854, repealing the Missouri Compromise and leaving both the nation and the Democratic Party bitterly divided. Buchanan's chief rivals for the 1856 Democratic presidential nomination were damaged by the sectional strife. When Buchanan returned home from London, many believed that he was the only candidate who could mend the Democratic Party's wounds and save the Union.

The 1856 party nomination did not come easily. Only after Stephen A. Douglas withdrew from the race was Buchanan able to acquire the sixty percent of the vote needed for the nomination. Fortunately for Buchanan, it was a transitional year for those who opposed the Democratic Party. Buchanan did not get a majority of the popular votes but was able to secure enough electoral college votes to win the presidency.

Buchanan's long journey to the White House was over. His quest for the presidency had been difficult, and so were his years in the White House. Buchanan's administration was haunted by the question of slavery in the United States territories. He hoped that the Supreme Court's Dred Scott decision would settle the issue once and for all, but his hopes were in vain. In many respects the Court's decision complicated the issue. Stephen Douglas found the Court's ruling to be a thorn in his side throughout the Lincoln-Douglas debates of 1858. The battle raging within the Democratic Party was over the same issue. Douglas believed that "popular sovereignty" was the solution to the slavery controversy. Buchanan, like Abraham Lincoln, did not accept Douglas' solution. Unlike Lincoln, Buchanan believed that the Dred Scott decision denied the federal government authority over the institution of slavery in the territories and that only states had the authority to prohibit slavery within their boundaries. The end result was that Buchanan, the great compromiser and diplomat, could not settle the controversy.

Buchanan believed that the Democratic Party had held the Union together for the past decade; as president, he believed that it was his job to unite the party before 1860. Yet Buchanan was unable to unify his party, and the Democrats lost the 1860 presidential campaign; then, as he expected, the Union came to face its greatest threat ever: civil war.

Summary

Buchanan realized that the nation's strength was its ability to strike a compromise among conflicting interests. The Constitutional Convention of 1787 succeeded because it was able to forge a consensus among the different groups represented at the Convention. The Democratic Party's success had been built upon its ability to rise above sectional disputes and focus on national issues. The United States, according to Buchanan, was a compromise republic that had succeeded in bending when necessary so that it would not break. Buchanan's unswerving commitment to the Union kept him from seeing that many Americans were tired of compromises. The old North-South coalition had been pushed to the breaking point, and the westward expansion had given the North a decided advantage. Those in the North knew this; those in the South knew this; but Buchanan seemed not to know.

What are often interpreted as Buchanan's Southern sympathies were really little more than his sense of fair play coupled with his sincere desire to preserve the Union. One of the nation's great compromisers had the misfortune of being president at a time when compromise was no longer possible. Unfortunately, James Buchanan is remembered not for his thirty-eight successful years in politics but for his four unsuccessful years. Buchanan, like most other politicians in the United States, is remembered for what he did last.

Bibliography

Auchampaugh, Philip G. *James Buchanan and His Cabinet: On the Eve of Secession.* Lancaster, Pa.: Author, 1926. As the title indicates, this work deals with the Buchanan Administration. Special emphasis is placed on Buchanan's handling of the slavery issue.

Binder, Frederick M. *James Buchanan and the American Empire.* Selinsgrove, Pa.: Susquehanna University Press, and London: Associated University Presses, 1994. Extensive research in Buchanan's manuscripts provides the basis for a part biography, part analysis of nineteenth century U.S. diplomatic history. Looks at the period from the perspectives of U.S. and British foreign policy makers and argues that Buchanan resisted foreign powers in order to preserve the Union.

Birkner, Michael J. ed. *James Buchanan and the Political Crisis of the 1850s.* Selinsgrove, Pa.: Susquehanna University Press, 1996. A collection of essays from a group of distinguished historians who met in 1991 at Gettysburg College to establish a more balanced view of the beleaguered Buchanan than has historically been presented.

Curtis, George Ticknor. *The Life of James Buchanan.* 2 vols. New York: Harper, 1883. By far the most comprehensive work on the life of James Buchanan.

Jaffa, Harry. *Crisis of the House Divided.* New York: Doubleday, 1959; London: University of Chicago Press, 1982. The best work on the theoretical issues involved in the Lincoln-Douglas Debates of 1858. Provides a good perspective for the issues that dominated American politics at that time.

Klein, Philip. *President James Buchanan: A Biography.* University Park: Pennsylvania State University Press, 1962. A comprehensive study that covers some secondary literature that was not available to Curtis.

Moore, John Bassett, ed. *The Works of James Buchanan.* 12 vols. Philadelphia: Lippincott, 1908; London: Lippincott, 1911. A complete collection of Buchanan's public addresses and selected private papers. Includes a fine biographical essay by Moore.

Nichols, Roy F. *The Disruption of American Democracy.* New York: Macmillan, 1948; London: Macmillan, 1967. A careful examination of the Democratic Party from 1856 to 1861. Deals extensively with the differences between Douglas and Buchanan.

Smith, Elbert B. *The Presidency of James Buchanan.* Lawrence: University Press of Kansas, 1975. This work argues that Buchanan's actions were motivated by strong Southern sympathies.

Donald V. Weatherman

CHARLES BULFINCH

Born: August 8, 1763; Boston, Massachusetts
Died: April 4, 1844; Boston, Massachusetts
Areas of Achievement: Architecture and government
Contribution: One of the first American architects to have used drawings extensively for the construction of buildings, Bulfinch exercised a wide influence on the architecture of the early national period of American history, especially in his native New England.

Early Life

The son of Thomas and Susan Apthorp Bulfinch, well-to-do and socially prominent Bostonians, Charles Bulfinch was born at the family home on Bowdoin Street on August 8, 1763. One of the first American architects to complete a college education, he was graduated from Harvard in 1781, though not in architecture. Bulfinch's interest in architecture appears to have been awakened in 1785-1787, during a leisurely tour of England and the Continent. In Paris, where Bulfinch lingered for a time, Thomas Jefferson, the American ambassador to the French court, took a friendly interest in the young man. It was at Jefferson's suggestion that Bulfinch continued his travels through southern France and Italy. After spending three weeks in Rome studying the city's ancient monuments, Bulfinch revisited Paris and London on his homeward journey. Upon his return to Boston, he took a position in the accounting office of a local merchant. In his spare time, he studied architectural works and, as did other gentleman-architects of the day, dabbled in design and construction.

Soon after his return from Europe, Bulfinch pointed toward his future dedication to architecture as a profession by submitting plans for a new Massachusetts statehouse, a project which eluded him until 1795, when he was chosen to design the building. Though he designed other important buildings during these early years, he continued to be only casually involved with architecture until he went bankrupt in 1796. On November 20, 1788, he married his cousin Hannah Apthorp, by whom he would have eleven children, including the author Thomas Bulfinch. In the spring of 1789, he visited Philadelphia and New York; his observations on this tour proved to be as influential in forming his style as those he had made while abroad.

Like most other early American architects, Bulfinch was self-taught. Nevertheless, he did not wish to design buildings simply by adapting various elements of architecture chosen from books. As did later architects, he tried to understand buildings, their materials and functions, and the methods by which they were built. He was concerned about how buildings related to their surroundings, about the connections between buildings and streets, walks, parks, other structures in the vicinity, and the city as a whole.

It has been said that between about 1790 and 1825, Bulfinch practically rebuilt Boston, transforming it from a provincial town with few buildings and meandering streets into a tasteful city of well-designed buildings set amid trees, plantings, and parks. One reason for his success was the excellence of his buildings. Another was his involvement in the affairs of Boston through his civic work. He would come to understand thoroughly the city and its needs by serving as a member, and chairman, of the board of selectmen.

Life's Work

Though his later buildings are of the classical revival style, which came to be preferred by such architects as Benjamin Latrobe and Jefferson, Bulfinch's early work was Georgian in character, by way of the brothers Adam (Robert, John, James, and William) in England. In 1788, the Hollis Street Church in Boston was constructed from his plans. Representing Bulfinch's initial attempt at church design, it was followed by plans for churches in Taunton and Pittsfield, Massachusetts, and during a later period, others in Boston. His classical interests were exhibited in his triumphal arch, built in 1789 in Boston for George Washington's reception, and in his Beacon Hill Memorial Column, of Doric order, constructed in 1790-1791. More ambitious in scale than anything previously attempted in New England, the statehouse in Hartford, Connecticut, was begun from Bulfinch's plans in 1793. The same year, he provided the plans for the Boston Theatre. Erected at the corner of Franklin and Federal streets, it burned in 1798 and was rebuilt by Bulfinch in the same year.

Bulfinch was elected to Boston's board of selectmen in 1791; he would serve on the board, with only one break, for twenty-six years. He was active on the board committees which lighted Boston's streets for the first time in 1792 and admitted both male and female children to the city's public schools. For the

last eighteen of these years, he chaired the board, a position similar to that of a mayor.

During the early 1790's, Bulfinch began a reformation of New England's architecture as he introduced the delicate detail of the Adam style. Many of his designs were built on or around Beacon Hill in Boston. It has been argued that their impact on the city was even stronger than that of his churches and public buildings because the houses and their settings established an atmosphere of beauty and charm long preserved in the Beacon Hill area. His first houses were for Joseph Coolidge, Sr. (1791-1792), and Joseph Barrell (1792-1793), both of which contained the first circular staircases in New England. The Barrell house in Somerville, Massachusetts, had an oval parlor projecting from the garden side beneath a semicircular portico with tall columns. Its layout was soon used in the Elias Hasket Derby mansion (1795-1799) in Salem, which was designed by Bulfinch, then modified and executed by Samuel McIntire.

Bulfinch joined with others in the mid-1790's in planning a block of sixteen houses in Boston known as the Tontine Crescent. Work on this project was partially completed when trouble with England brought unsettled business conditions to Boston. During the ensuing financial crisis, Bulfinch's partners withdrew, leaving him to assume the cost of completing the work. Losing both his own fortune and that of his wife, he was adjudged bankrupt in January of 1796. About the time of his bankruptcy, he resigned from the board of selectmen. Previously regarded as a scholar and gentleman of fortune but an amateur in architecture, Bulfinch was now faced with earning a livelihood. He turned his talent and full attention to the practice of architecture, with most successful results. In 1796, Bulfinch designed a house for the prominent and powerful Boston politician Harrison Gray Otis. He followed it with two others for Otis: the second in 1800, usually considered the finest of the three, and the third in 1805.

The Massachusetts statehouse (1795-1797) on Boston's Beacon Hill represents the crowning achievement of Bulfinch's early work. Though by the twentieth century it became only a part of a much larger complex—having been added on to a number of times—it has survived in good condition. A simple rectangular structure in plan and exterior, it is two stories high with a basement and a portico in front. The whole is crowned by a dome made of wooden planks, matched to fit tightly against one another. With its elegant proportions, the relationship of the dome to other elements, and its richly ornamented and spacious interiors, Bulfinch's Massachusetts statehouse was immediately hailed as a masterpiece.

In 1799, Bulfinch was returned to the Boston board of selectmen, serving as its chairman until his departure for Washington in 1817. He soon found himself deeply involved in all the financial, commercial, and governmental affairs of the city. The time of his chairmanship marked the years of the great development of old Boston. Its form would be attributable largely to Bulfinch in his dual capacity as city official and architect. During this period, his architecture and civic work complemented each other. In addition to designing theaters, hospitals, churches, schools, government buildings, markets, prisons, wharves, warehouses, multifamily houses, and numerous single-family dwellings, he planned several portions of Boston. The neglected Common was turned into a park; three sides were fronted with fine buildings of uniform character: Park Street, in 1803-1804; Colonade Row on Tremont Street, in 1810-1812; and Beacon Street, from about 1800. Bulfinch laid out plans for the lands on Boston Neck, in South Boston, and on the site of the Mill Pond. He also inaugurated the development of Franklin Street and certain changes in the city's street system.

Of Bulfinch's five churches in Boston, four were built after 1800. It is said that he followed the schemes of Christopher Wren's churches in London, paying great attention to the varieties of the type. Bulfinch designed the first Roman Catholic church in Boston, the Church (later Cathedral) of the Holy Cross (1800-1803) at the corner of Franklin and Federal streets. Contemporary sources describe it as in the Italian Renaissance style. Completed in 1804, the New North Church (later St. Stephen's Catholic Church) is the only surviving example of Bulfinch's Boston churches. It has been much modified and is not considered one of his best designs. The Federal Street Church of 1809 represents Bulfinch's first and only Gothic work. The New South Church was completed in 1814. Generally considered Bulfinch's most beautiful church, it was the first stone church erected in Boston since Bulfinch's grandfather, Charles Apthorp, got Peter Harrison to design King's Chapel. The distinctive features of the New South Church were an octagonal ground plan and a Doric portico of freestanding columns. One of the two surviving Bulfinch churches is the Church of Christ in Lancaster, Massachusetts, which was built in 1816. Its most prominent feature, the triple coeval arches in the portico, is an unexplained "improvement" by the master builder sent out from Boston to supervise the work.

Bulfinch's public buildings in Boston completed after 1800 include the almshouse (1799-1801); the admirable warehouses of India Wharf (1803-1807); the Boylston Hall and Market (1809), later occupied as the city's first public library; the Suffolk County Court House (1810-1812); and the first and central unit of the Massachusetts General Hospital (1818-1823). Among the public buildings built outside Boston from Bulfinch's plans, the best known are the state prison at Charlestown, Massachusetts (1804-1805), University Hall at Harvard (1813-1814), and the statehouse in Augusta, Maine (1829-1832). The private houses Bulfinch designed after 1800 were built mainly in Boston, typical examples being those at 85 Mount Vernon Street, 45 Beacon Street, and numbers 13, 15, and 17 on Chestnut Street.

In 1817, President James Monroe appointed Bulfinch to succeed Latrobe as architect in charge of rebuilding the United States Capitol, which had been burned by the British in 1814. Moving his family to Washington, Bulfinch remained in this position until 1830. Essentially, he was called upon to complete the wings and construct the central part along lines established by the Capitol's earlier architects. Bulfinch joined the two wings with a central dome. His principal contribution was the detailed form of the western front, a portico with steps and terrace forming an approach to it. Though his dome was later replaced by a larger and grander one, the west front remains. In addition to completing the Capitol, Bulfinch designed a church in Washington and acted as a consultant for several other government buildings. Returning to Boston at the age of sixty-seven, he lived in retirement, with occasional visits elsewhere, until his death in 1844.

Summary

During and before Bulfinch's day, American architects generally fell into one of two groups: amateur gentleman-architects who pursued some other career while designing buildings as an avocation, or architect-builders who were more concerned with construction than design. Though he began as one of the former, Bulfinch soon became totally involved with architecture. Unlike the architect-builders who actually worked on their buildings, Bulfinch saw his role—much in the same vein as later professionals—as that of supervising construction to ensure the proper implementation of designs and quality of workmanship.

Bulfinch's American practice of architecture combined his New England background with his European tastes. Appropriately, the site of his remains in Cambridge's Mount Auburn Cemetery is marked by the Franklin Urn, which Bulfinch placed in front of the Tontine Crescent in 1795 as a symbol of his plans to remake Boston in the image of neoclassical London. Early in his career, Bulfinch's city honored him for his architecture and his civic work, showing an appreciation which continued to grow. Over the years, his architecture came to belong not only to Boston and New England but also to the country as a whole.

Bibliography

Bailey, Eleanor. "Charles Bulfinch." *Old House Journal* 22, no. 6 (September-October 1994). Examines the education and career of Bulfinch. Provides an overview of the first urban housing development and his contributions to the rebuilding of Boston.

Brown, Glenn. *History of the United States Capitol*. 2 vols. Washington, D.C.: Government Printing Office, 1901-1904. Relates the story of Bulfinch's long and sometimes frustrating assignment in Washington.

Bulfinch, Charles. *The Life and Letters of Charles Bulfinch*. Edited by Ellen Susan Bulfinch. Boston: Houghton Mifflin, 1896. The major source for biographical information. Bulfinch's granddaughter provides a good treatment of the forces which shaped his ultimate professional commitment.

Kimball, Fiske. *Mr. Samuel McIntire, Carver: The Architect of Salem*. Portland, Me.: Essex Institute, 1940. Details Bulfinch's work for the Derby family of Salem.

Kirker, Harold. *The Architecture of Charles Bulfinch*. Cambridge, Mass.: Harvard University Press, 1969. Concentrates on the works themselves. Bulfinch's commissions are arranged chronologically; each is treated separately. One of the appendices deals with "minor commissions and attributions." Well illustrated.

Kirker, Harold, and James Kirker. *Bulfinch's Boston, 1787-1817*. New York: Oxford University Press, 1964. Deals largely with the social and cultural history of Boston during the period. Bulfinch's architectural work is subordinated to his public career.

Morison, Samuel Eliot. *The Maritime History of Massachusetts, 1783-1860*. Boston: Houghton Mifflin, 1921; London: Heinemann, 1923. Provides a good summary treatment of Bulfinch's architecture as well as a picture of the Boston merchants who were his chief clients.

Place, Charles A. *Charles Bulfinch: Architect and Citizen*. Boston: Houghton Mifflin, 1925. A biographical treatment that focuses on Bulfinch as a citizen and Christian gentleman.

L. Moody Simms, Jr.

LUTHER BURBANK

Born: March 7, 1849; Lancaster, Massachusetts
Died: April 11, 1926; Santa Rosa, California
Area of Achievement: Horticulture
Contribution: As a plant breeder, Burbank introduced more than eight hundred new plants and gave the world a lesson in the value of horticultural science: Make plants work for the benefit of man.

Early Life

Luther Burbank was the thirteenth child of Samuel Walton Burbank, a farmer and brickmaker and a descendant of seventeenth century English stock. Luther's mother, Olive Ross, a strong-featured and strong-willed woman of Scottish and French descent, was Samuel's third wife. Luther Burbank was born on March 7, 1849, in Lancaster, Massachusetts, thirty miles from Boston.

Burbank was a shy youngster seldom disciplined by his parents. His siblings included a brother and sister as well as three half-brothers and two half-sisters. He received an elementary school education near his home but was never comfortable with oral recitation. At the age of fifteen, he entered Lancaster Academy, a preparatory school for Harvard and Yale, and studied the basic curriculum of Latin, Greek, French, geometry, algebra, arithmetic, philosophy, drawing, and English. Burbank was apparently a good student, ranking eighth out of the top ten students in his class in 1867. He was an avid reader, as is evidenced by his early familiarity with the works of Charles Darwin, Alexander von Humboldt, and Henry David Thoreau. The writings of these naturalists were to have a lasting impact on young Burbank, but the most important influence in developing his scientific curiosity was his cousin Levi Sumner Burbank, the curator of geology at the Boston Society of Natural History.

As a young man, Burbank was five feet, eight inches tall, about 125 pounds, with sparkling blue eyes. After his school experience, he attempted two nonacademic careers. The first was a job in the Worcester branch factory of the Ames Plow Works. Burbank had gone to the factory for three or four summers to learn the trade of a mechanic. After high school, he worked at the Ames Plow Works turning plow rounds on a lathe at a wage of three dollars a week. He soon designed an improvement in his machine that increased productivity, and his piecework wages rose significantly. He was not able to keep this job very long, however, since his health suffered because of the sawdust in the air.

Burbank next studied medicine under a local doctor for several months. He gave this up when his father died, in 1868. Burbank was not interested in farming at this time, although as a young boy he had shown some interest in gardening. (To the dismay of his father, Burbank transplanted weeds into the family garden plot to see if they would grow.)

In 1870, the young Burbank, always afflicted with a frail constitution, decided to take a sea voyage to improve his health. The schooner was wrecked, and he almost lost his life.

Life's Work

In 1871, Burbank made a decision that would change his life dramatically: He resolved to try his hand at truck-gardening. At the age of twenty-one, he bought seventeen acres of land adjoining his mother's home in Lunenburg, Massachusetts. He pursued this profession for about five years, but he was more interested in experimenting with plants than in growing them for market. In 1872, Luther found a seed ball on the plant of a potato containing twenty-three seeds, a rare occurrence. He planted the seeds and discovered one good potato (later named the "Burbank") of attractive shape with a white skin. The tuber was destined later to become a huge commercial success. Burbank sold sixty bushels of the potatoes to James J. H. Gregory, a seedsman of Marblehead, Massachusetts, for $150. With this money, Burbank left for California in October, 1875, as the climate there was better suited for the horticultural work that he had decided to pursue. (His mother packed him a nine-day box lunch for the long train trip.) He arrived in San Francisco on October 29, 1875. Burbank was shocked at the amount of liquor consumed in the city and he vowed never to drink it. On October 31, 1875, Burbank reached Santa Rosa, a frontier town blessed with a temperate climate. The plants he saw there grew larger than any he had ever seen, since the area had no frost.

Burbank lived for a short time with his brother Alfred and another bachelor in an eight-foot by ten-foot cabin. To earn money, Burbank did carpentry work and odd jobs in the area. In the winter of 1876, Burbank went to work in Petaluma, California, at the large nursery of W. H. Pepper. He saved his money and soon returned to Santa Rosa.

In the summer of 1877, Burbank's mother and sister Emma came to Santa Rosa and bought a house with four acres of adjacent land. Burbank rented the land and started his own nursery. Within ten years, the quality of his fruit and shade trees was famous, and he was making sixteen thousand dollars annually with his plants. His skill in plant-breeding was to assure his commercial success. In the spring of 1881, he received an order for twenty thousand prune trees for delivery in the fall. According to other nurserymen, it would take eighteen months to fill such a large order, but Burbank used the technique of "force budding" to deliver the trees on schedule.

Burbank was interested in cross-breeding domestic plant stock with foreign material, so in 1885, he imported plum seedlings from Yokohama, Japan. One of these seedlings became the famous "Burbank plum" that is still popular today. That same year, Luther bought eighteen acres at Sebastopol near Santa Rosa to use for experimental growing. By 1888, he was committed to the development of new varieties of plants, so he sold part of his retail nursery business (the fruit and shade tree segment) to his partner, R. W. Bell. Burbank could now concentrate on the creation of new or unusual plant materials to sell at wholesale to other nurserymen.

On September 23, 1890, the forty-one-year-old horticulturist married a domineering young widow, Helen A. Coleman, from Denver, Colorado. Almost immediately, conflicts developed between Helen and Burbank's mother and sister. The marriage, which lasted six years, caused Burbank much mental and physical aggravation, partly because of Helen's violent temper.

By 1893, Burbank had developed enough different varieties of walnuts, berries, plums, prunes, roses, lilies, potatoes, and quinces to list them in his nursery catalog, *New Creations in Fruits and Flowers* (1893). Stark Brothers' Nurseries of Missouri and several large Eastern retail nurseries made significant purchases from this catalog, thereby assuring Burbank's future financial success. As the years passed, Burbank attracted a large clientele of professional nurserymen both in the United States and abroad. By 1900, Burbank's products were being grown throughout the world, and his reputation as the "wizard of horticulture" was well established. There was no magical formula, however, to the Burbank success story, only hard work, perseverance, and a keen intuition as to

what plants would prove a commercial success. At this time, Burbank developed the Shasta daisy, a perennial favorite of home gardeners. His breeding method consisted of choosing American wild daisies as breeding stock, introducing pollen from European daisies, and crossing the resultant hybrids with a Japanese species. Any plant in any part of the world was fair game in Burbank's search for marketable products.

Burbank was to come increasingly under the criticism of other horticulturists, particularly those attached to university experiment stations. (Burbank did not have the formal college education in the plant sciences that some university-trained experts thought necessary, although he did receive an honorary doctor of science degree from Tufts College in 1905.) It was true that he did not keep proper records of his experimental crossings or always guard against self-pollination in his work, but he was more interested in the results of experimentation, not the theory. He gave the impression at times of being a consummate egotist; he was the most famous plant breeder in America, and none too modest about this reputation. He allowed others to exaggerate the merits of his products, and because of the sheer volume of the materials he was turning out, he did not take as much time to prove the reliability of those creations as he had been able to earlier in his career.

The Carnegie Institute became interested in Burbank's techniques and plants and, between 1905 and 1909, awarded him a grant of ten thousand dollars annually with the stipulation that a representative from the Institute would observe Burbank's methods and write a report on them. (The report on the observations was never compiled by the Institute, in part because of the difficulty of interpreting Burbank's experimental notes.)

Burbank had been working on the development of a spineless cactus for use as cattle food, and in 1906, he introduced this cactus to the nursery trade. It proved to be a disappointment since it was not completely spineless, and the resultant unfavorable publicity damaged Burbank's reputation. Other products that did not live up to the claims of his catalog included the "Winter rhubarb" and a hybrid berry which Burbank called the "Sunberry." These failures called into question his credibility, particularly among those horticulturists and breeders who may have felt resentful of his fame.

In 1912, the Luther Burbank Society and the Luther Burbank Press were formed for the purpose of promoting and selling a multivolume work on the man and his accomplishments, *Luther Burbank: His Methods and Discoveries and Their Practical Applications* (1915). Unfortunately, the promotional tactics and "hype" associated with marketing the twelve-volume set cast a further shadow upon his reputation, although the color photographs and illustrations in them were quite unusual for that time.

That same year, 1912, saw the organization of the Luther Burbank Company, another vehicle used by exploiters, with Burbank's unwitting consent, to promote his name in association with the marketing of his horticultural creations. Rollo J. Hough and W. Garner Smith received the exclusive rights to sell Burbank's products. These financiers, however, knew very little about the nursery business. Soon quality control grew lax, and Burbank's reputation suffered accordingly. By 1916, the Luther Burbank Press went out of business, and many investors lost their money in the enterprise. That same year the Luther Burbank Company declared bankruptcy and Burbank resumed control of his nursery and seed business. These failures suggest that Burbank was not a very good businessman in his later years, but in spite of these failures, he still prospered financially.

In 1916, at the age of sixty-seven, Burbank married his young secretary, Elizabeth Jane Waters. International affairs were to involve the United States in World War I by the next year, and although Burbank was a pacifist, he was to support the American war effort. During the war he introduced a wheat, "Quality," which turned out to be a previously bred Australian variety. His credibility as a cereal breeder was called into question, although he initially believed that he had developed a new hybrid.

For all the criticisms arising from the professional horticultural ranks, Burbank's popular image remained intact. His health, however, never robust, grew worse. During the first few years of the 1920's, a series of illnesses beset him that were to undermine further his already failing constitution. On March 24, 1926, Burbank suffered a heart attack; on April 11, he died. He was buried in the yard of his old home in Santa Rosa, under a cedar of Lebanon that he had grown from a seed years before.

Summary

In order to evaluate the work of Luther Burbank it is necessary to evaluate the man. Born into a strict New England Puritanical background, he changed his religion to that of the Baptist faith, then to Unitarianism. He believed that he had psychic powers, a conviction which may have contributed to his high-strung, nervous personality. Something of a hypochondriac and diet faddist, he ascribed in his latter years to the practice of Yoga.

Burbank the man was always different from those around him, as is so often the case with those who might be labeled "creative." He saw things differently from the way most of his peers did, and because of his outspoken opinions, he often became the center of controversy, both in his professional and personal life. The maverick in Burbank dictated his unique approaches to horticulture. He dared to experiment, to attempt the new and untried, and sometimes to fail. These failures were difficult for a man who needed the approval and praise of his colleagues and adoring supporters.

It was among the general gardening public that Burbank was to have the greatest appeal. He popularized horticulture as a science among those amateur gardeners who wanted something new, something different, something unique. It is for this spirit of seeking the unknown that Burbank should best be remembered: He was a pioneer unafraid to reach for the unreachable. Burbank epitomized that spirit of discovery coupled with the hope of success that so characterized early twentieth century America.

Bibliography

Burbank, Luther, with Wilbur Hall. *The Harvest of the Years.* London: Constable, and Boston: Houghton Mifflin, 1927. This alleged autobiography was ghostwritten by Wilbur Hall and published the year after Burbank's death. An introductory biography gives no real background to his life. The volume in general is a laudatory account of Burbank's work. Not documented, but Burbank does attempt to dispel the aura of mystery surrounding his plant developments.

———. *Partner of Nature.* Edited by Wilbur Hall. New York and London: Appleton, 1939. This book, ghostwritten and published after Burbank's death, is a single-volume condensation of the twelve-volume work by Burbank, *Luther Burbank: His Methods and Discoveries and Their Practical Application*, which was edited by John Whitson, Robert John, and Henry Smith Williams and published in New York by the Luther Burbank Press between 1914 and 1915. The condensed volume is aimed at a general audience interested in gardening rather than in the technical aspects of plant breeding.

Dreyer, Peter. *A Gardener Touched with Genius: The Life of Luther Burbank.* Rev. ed. Berkeley: University of California Press, 1985. This revised edition of the original 1975 work is still the definitive biography of Luther Burbank. Incorporating the correspondence of his friend Edward J. Wickson and the papers of the plant scientist George H. Shull, this book expands and refines the previous 1945 biography of Burbank by Walter L. Howard and the unpublished critical work of the plant geneticist Donald Jones. Well documented, but no separate bibliography is included.

Gould, S. J. "Does the Stoneless Plum Instruct the Thinking Reed?" *Natural History* 101, no. 4 (April 1992). Focuses on the development of Burbank's theory of a genetically superior American race and the eugenics movement of the late nineteenth century.

Harwood, W. S. *New Creations in Plant Life: An Authoritative Account of the Life and Work of Luther Burbank.* 2d ed. New York: Grosset and Dunlap, 1907; London: Macmillan, 1916. An exaggerated account of Burbank's achievements.

Misleading statements abound in this work, giving Burbank the status of a miracle worker with almost supernatural powers. This was, however, the first complete account of Burbank's plant breeding techniques.

Howard, Walter L. "Luther Burbank: A Victim of Hero Worship." *Chronica Botanica* 9 (Winter 1945): 299-506. Written by an emeritus professor of pomology at the University of California, this book-length article is a successful effort at portraying the real Burbank beneath the exaggerated facade that the general public knew. Points out the controversial episodes in Burbank's life and brings him "down to earth." Supplies the honest facts about Burbank's work without prejudice or judgmental rhetoric.

Kraft, Ken, and Pat Kraft. *Luther Burbank: The Wizard and the Man.* New York: Meredith Press, 1967. The first of the modern biographies of Burbank that dared to point out some of his faults and omissions. This well-written, readable work contains one particularly interesting chapter on Burbank's attitudes on diet and health. Generally informative, balanced account of the "plant wizard."

Charles A. Dranguet, Jr.

JACOB BURCKHARDT

Born: May 25, 1818; Basel, Switzerland
Died: August 8, 1897; Basel, Switzerland
Area of Achievement: Historiography
Contribution: Burckhardt, a uniquely gifted historian and literary artist, was a pioneer in the development of modern *Kulturgeschichte*, the study of nonpolitical aspects of civilization. His lasting contribution was in Renaissance historiography, where his work became a model for the treatment of culture in the study of civilization.

Early Life

Part of an influential, aristocratic Swiss family, Jacob Burckhardt recalled his early childhood in Basel as being very happy. For three centuries, Jacob's ancestors utilized their financial abilities to amass a considerable fortune in the silk industry and international trade, which they parlayed into political power. The Burckhardts held one of the two burgomaster positions in the city for nearly two centuries, while other members of the family served the community as professors and clergymen. Jacob's own father, one of the less affluent Burckhardts, studied theology in Heidelberg and was pastor of the Basel ministry at the time of his son's birth. In 1838, the senior Burckhardt became the administrative head of the Reformed church in the Basel canton. Jacob recalled his father as being pleasant, a good scholar, and a capable artist. It was his father's artistic ability that first stimulated the youth's enduring love for art.

The joys of early childhood turned to sorrow with the unexpected death of his mother in 1830. This experience made a lasting impression on twelve-year-old Jacob, as he became painfully aware of the transitoriness of all living things. Throughout his adult life, Jacob experienced difficulty in establishing lasting relationships, and it may well have been memories of his mother's death that influenced his decision to remain a bachelor.

Burckhardt's patrician heritage instilled in him an aristocratic prejudice, a sensitivity to beauty and form, a deep, abiding respect for the dignity of mankind, and a Protestant morality, all of which would be reflected in his life as a teacher and scholar. As he matured into adulthood, however, his personal appearance seemed to belie his conservative nature. As a young man, he was notable for his uniquely stylish clothes, distinct coiffure,

finger rings, and excessive taste for red wine and cigars. In later years, he dropped the foppish airs but retained his taste for wine and cigars.

The public school in Basel provided Burckhardt with an excellent primary education in the classics but left him undecided as to a vocation. After a brief stay in French-speaking Neuchâtel, where he wrote an essay on Gothic architecture, he entered the University of Basel in 1837 to study theology. Eighteen months later, he experienced a prolonged religious crisis that resulted in his abandoning his orthodox religious beliefs and rejecting the ministry. Because of the support and encouragement of his father, Burckhardt attended the University of Berlin from 1839 to 1843 to pursue his historical interests. While there, Burckhardt was praised by the renowned classical scholars August Boeckh and Johann Gustav Droysen for his extensive knowledge of antiquity, but Burckhardt ultimately took his degree in 1843 under the eminent scientific historian Leopold von Ranke. Burckhardt greatly admired Ranke and his seminars, but the two never established a close relationship. Although master and student have been used to illustrate two diametrically different approaches to historiography, it should be noted that Ranke had praise for his student, and in 1872 Burckhardt was offered the chair of history at the University of Berlin as Ranke's successor—an offer that he refused because of his abhorrence of German politics.

Burckhardt's closest association in Berlin was with the pioneer art historian Franz Kugler, who encouraged Burckhardt to combine his love for history with his love for art and directed the attention of the fledgling student to Italy and the Renaissance.

Life's Work

In 1843, the University of Basel awarded Burckhardt a Ph.D. in absentia and the following year invited him to become a lecturer on history and art—a position he held with distinction for nearly fifty years. Because the university did not have an official vacancy until 1858, Burckhardt had to supplement his lecturing income with a variety of other jobs. For two years, he was the editor of the conservative *Basler Zeitung*, and he taught at the local grammar school for most of his career. In 1846, Burckhardt was given permission by the author to revise Kugler's text on art history, which brought in some revenue, and he was offered a lucrative position at the Academy of Art in Berlin. Burckhardt had no desire to return to Berlin but did so out of friendship to Kugler. For the next twelve years, Burckhardt taught at Basel, Berlin, and Zurich, with lengthy visits to Italy in 1847, 1848, and 1853. Despite his excessive work load and extensive travels, he was able to publish two important works during this period. His first major work, *Die Zeit Konstantins des Grossen* (1853; *The Age of Constantine the Great*, 1949), attested his love for ancient civilization. Although the study showed the important role Christianity played in the cultural life of the Middle Ages, Burckhardt's sympathies lay clearly with the decaying ancient world. His second publication, *Der Cicerone* (1855; *The Cicerone*, 1873), was a detailed study of Italian art, and it became the most popular travel guide to Italy in Europe. In 1855, Burckhardt accepted a teaching position at the new polytechnical institute in Zurich, not only to increase his earnings but also to gain access to the rich collection of Renaissance materials housed there. Three years later, there was a vacancy at the University of Basel, and Burckhardt readily accepted that university's only chair of history.

Family influence, formal education, work experience, and foreign travel provided Burckhardt with the inspiration for his life's work. After observing at first hand the political turmoil in Germany, the quiet, freedom-loving Swiss was repulsed by those scholars who saw history as past politics or a chronology of state development. It was the nonpolitical past, more specifically, the moral and mental past, that fascinated Burckhardt. His objective was to undertake a meticulous study of thought and conduct, religion and art, scholarship and speculation in an attempt to penetrate the *Kultur* of the people and discover what he called "the spirit of the age." Thus, in 1842 he announced that it was to *Kulturgeschichte* that he intended to devote his life, and the fulfillment of this self-established goal is represented par excellence in *Die Kultur der Renaissance in Italien* (1860; *The Civilization of the Renaissance in Italy*, 1878).

Burkhardt divided this book into six sections, each of which discussed a specific aspect of Italian *Kultur*. The section on the state as a work of art provided the political framework, as it emphasized the conflict between emperors and popes, but it was not political history in the traditional sense. His intent was to demonstrate how the state became free of outside control and, in the process, produced what Burckhardt called the modern "state-spirit." This phenomenon had its counterpart in the evolution of modern individualism, which was explained in the second section of the book. The development of the individual was characterized primarily by the rebirth of secularism and the perception of the Italian Humanists as independent entities, free of any corporate structure, such as the Church. While rebirth was the general theme of the entire work, it was of specific concern in the third section on the revival of antiquity. Here, Burckhardt argued that while the rebirth of Humanism complemented the newly emerging spirit of secular individualism, it was the result of what was happening in Italy and not the cause. Individualism and secularity would have evolved without the rebirth of antiquity. The last three sections of the work provided evidence of how the new secular individualism operated in society and how it influenced the culture and moral life of the age.

Summary

After more than a century, Jacob Burckhardt's history of the Italian Renaissance remains one of the most controversial works ever published. With justification, critics have stated that the work is too static and that it exaggerates the creativeness of Italy. It is too sharply delimited in time and space, as it neglects the other European countries and fails to consider the creative forces at work in the late Middle Ages. Burckhardt overemphasizes individualism, immorality, and irreligion in Italy and exaggerates the rediscovery of the classical world. Furthermore, Burckhardt's work is limited to a study of the upper class, is devoid of any economic analysis, and is based on the debatable assumption that there was a common spirit of the age that characterized all Italy for two hundred years.

Yet even the most ardent critics regard the book as a penetrating analysis of history and civilization. Burckhardt's work was unique in that he was one of the first to interpret the psychology of an epoch with power and insight. His methodology was highly original, as he employed a topical approach that permitted him to study what he termed "cross sections in history" from a variety of directions. His work treated civilization as a unit in a series of parallel discussions, each approaching the central problem from a different point of view. Critics of Burckhardt should also remember that he approached history as an artist, not as a philosopher, and with regard to written history he always considered himself an "arch dilettante," whose vocation was teaching.

Though Burckhardt lived another forty years after completing his history of the Renaissance, he never again published. With his health waning, Burckhardt requested to be relieved of his position in art history in 1885, and in 1893, suffering from acute asthmatic troubles, he surrendered his chair of history. Four years later, he died in his small two-room apartment over the local bakery in Basel. Although Burckhardt never published again, three of his major historical works were published posthumously: *Griechische Kulturgeschichte* (1898-1902; *History of Greek Culture*, abridged 1963), *Weltgeschichtliche Betrachtungen* (1905; *Force and Freedom: Reflections on History*, 1943), and *Historische Fragmente* (1929; translated in *Gesamtausgabe: Judgments on History and Historians*, 1958).

Bibliography

Burckhardt, Jacob. *The Civilization of the Renaissance in Italy*. Translated by S. G. C. Middlemore with an introduction by Benjamin Nelson and Charles Trinkaus. Vol. 1. New York: Harper, 1958. The introduction contains an excellent summary and response to the critics of Burckhardt. Discusses what Burckhardt intended to do with his work as opposed to what others would have liked him to have done.

———. *Letters*. Selected, edited, and translated by Alexander Dru. London: Routledge, and New York: Pantheon Books, 1955. With none of Burckhardt's biographies having been translated, this introduction contains the best biographical information available in English. Also included is a bibliography of all the principal editions of Burckhardt's letters.

Ferguson, Wallace K. *The Renaissance in Historical Thought*. Boston: Houghton Mifflin, 1948. The most scholarly coverage of Burckhardt in English. Contains little on his early life but gives detailed information on his place in Renaissance historiography. Good synopsis of his major works.

Gooch, G. P. *History and Historians in the Nineteenth Century*. 2d ed. London and New York: Longman, 1913. The best work on nineteenth century historiography. Attempts to establish Burckhardt's place among nineteenth century scholars. Apologetic in nature, containing little criticism of Burckhardt.

Hinde, John R. "Jacob Burckhardt and Nineteenth-Century Realist Art." *Journal of European Studies* 27, no. 3 (December, 1997). Analysis of Burkhardt's views on nineteenth century realist art.

Thompson, James Westfall. *A History of Historical Writing*. Vol. 2. New York: Macmillan, 1942. A good first source of Burckhardt. Brief, chronological, and factual, with little attempt at analysis. Must be supplemented by one of the other sources, as Thompson's omissions can be misleading.

Tonsor, Stephen, J. "Jacob Burckhardt: Tradition and the Crisis of Western Culture." *Modern Age* 39, no. 1 (Winter 1997). Argues that Burkhardt's work supports the theory that art and literature prosper during periods of crisis.

Weintraub, Karl Joachim. "Jacob Burckhardt: The Historian Among the Philologists." *The American Scholar* 57 (Spring 1988): 273-282. A concise, readable discussion of Burckhardt's posthumously published history of Greek culture. Taking as his point of departure the harshly critical response to this work among scholars of Burckhardt's time, Weintraub illumines Burckhardt's conception of cultural history.

———. *Visions of Culture*. Chicago: University of Chicago Press, 1966. Second only to Ferguson in scholarly analysis of Burckhardt's history of the Renaissance. Surpasses Ferguson in biographical information and concentrates on Burckhardt's contribution to *Kulturgeschichte*.

Wayne M. Bledsoe

FRANCES HODGSON BURNETT

Born: November 24, 1849; Manchester, England

Died: October 29, 1924; Plandome, Long Island, New York

Areas of Achievement: Literature, and theater and entertainment

Contribution: Burnett's immensely popular stories and dramatizations brought pleasure and hope to many people and bridged divides between British and American audiences, the rich and the poor, and children and adults.

Early Life

Frances Eliza Hodgson was born into the family of a relatively prosperous hardware merchant who ran a store in Manchester, England, one of the foremost cities of the Industrial Revolution. Frances had two older brothers and two younger sisters. She had few memories of her father, Edwin, who died in 1853, leaving her mother, Eliza, to run the business. Financial constraints forced them to move to an inexpensive house in Islington Square, Salford, a little island of "respectable" houses in a sea of poor housing inhabited by cotton mill operatives. Frances was not encouraged to play with their children or speak the local Lancashire dialect. With a quick ear, however, she was able to precisely reproduce it.

Frances was an imaginative child, describing herself as having "a positively wolfish appetite for books," and from three years old began "a lifelong chase after the story." She also described how she discovered the delights of her father's library, especially a shelf of *Blackwood's Magazine* periodicals, which the Brontë sisters had also found influential in developing a taste for Romantic stories and poetry. Frances soon found an eager audience for her own first efforts at story telling at the small private school she attended.

Frances described her mother as a gentle person who instilled into her the moral priority of kindness and the need to be "always the little lady." Eliza continued to run the family business until the depression caused by the American Civil War and the slow drying up of the supply of raw cotton. Eliza's brother had previously emigrated to Eastern Tennessee, and he wrote to Eliza about the opportunities available in the United States; in 1865, the nearly destitute Hodgsons decided to join him in the small township of New Market, Tennessee. Unfortunately, postwar depression had affected business in the United States as well, and there was little work. Despite this, Frances described these as her "Dryad days," especially when they moved to the outskirts Knoxville, Tennessee. For a city girl, the abundance of forests and mountains was overwhelming. However, the desperate need for income finally induced her to write a short story for one of the popular women's magazines of the day. After a request for a second story, she had them both accepted by *Gody's Lady's Book* for the sum of thirty-five dollars, with an invitation to write more. She was eighteen years old.

Life's Work

Frances had stated in the cover letter sent with her first story that "my object is remuneration." After Eliza's death in 1870, this became even more vital. Frances began writing five or six stories per month at ten or twelve dollars each. These early stories were stylized romances of the period. In 1871 she tried a realistic story written in the Lancashire dialect called "Surly Tim," which was accepted by *Scribner's Magazine*, a literary magazine. This began a long association with the Charles Scribner's Sons publishing house.

At this time Frances was being courted by Swan Burnett, the son of a doctor in New Market. He too was training to be a doctor. Frances was reluctant to marry, preferring to return to England for fifteen months in 1872, the second of her thirty-three transatlantic crossings. On her return, however, they did marry and lived in Knoxville, where their first son, Lionel, was born in 1874. Burnett wanted to further his medical studies in ophthalmology and also wanted Frances to get away from the South. A stay in Paris, France, was arranged with advances from Frances' publishers. While there, the couple's second son, Vivian, was born at the same time that Frances was writing her first novel, *That Lass o' Lowrie's*, a story of a Lancashire mining girl, in the style of Elizabeth Gaskell's *Mary Barton* (1848). Serialization began in 1876 and complete publication came in 1877, to much acclaim.

After some financial hardship upon their return to the United States, they managed to settle in Washington, D.C., still supported by Frances' writings. Frances became a society hostess and boasted President James Garfield among her acquaintances. Sales of *That Lass o' Lowrie's* soared, as did a collection of short stories, *Surly Tim and Other*

in the strange mix of childish and adult language given to the seven-year-old hero.

Now in her thirties, Frances was famous. She was described as being plump and short with a square, projecting forehead and possessing large, soulful eyes and luxurious hair. Some accounts depicted her as being animated in talk and affable in manners. She also enjoyed excellent health during this period. As the need to write lessened, the urge to travel grew. Leaving her boys behind, she stayed longer and longer in Europe. While in Rome, Italy, during the winter of 1889-1890, she heard that her son Lionel was ill. Frances returned to Washington, D.C., and found that the diagnosis was tuberculosis. She refused to tell him, and went everywhere looking for cures and nursing him devotedly. Lionel died in Paris in December, 1890.

Little Lord Fauntleroy had been her first book to have a child hero; thereafter followed a series of books about children, including *The Pretty Sister of José* (1889). In 1896 she returned to adult heroines, most notably in *In Connection with the De Willoughby Claim* (1899) and *The Making of a Marchioness* (1901). By now Frances was reunited with her sister Edith, was based in London, and was involved in the theater and philanthropic work. She moved in high society and adopted an increasingly expensive lifestyle. She met the novelist Henry James frequently. She had also met Stephen Townesend, a doctor ten years younger than herself and a would-be actor who became her personal assistant. In 1898 she officially divorced Swan and then, to everyone's surprise, married Townesend in 1900. He had a volatile temper and was often possessive and bullying. The marriage only lasted two years. Parts of this tempestuous marriage are reflected in her novel *The Shuttle* (1907).

Another autobiographical detail reflected in *The Shuttle* was Maytham Hall, an old country mansion in southern England that Frances leased from 1898 to 1907. During this time she took up her previous children's story *Sara Crewe* (1888) and dramatized it as *Little Princess* (1903). The extra material generated was then rewritten into an enlarged novel of the same name, which was published in 1905. Although not immediately as popular as *Little Lord Fauntleroy*, *Little Princess* has since become much more so. The heroine showed the same qualities of *gentillesse* as had the hero of *Little Lord Fauntleroy*, but she also demonstrated courage in adversity, a development of Frances' favorite Cinderella theme. A surge of

Stories (1877). *Haworth's*, also set in Lancashire, followed in 1879. Some twelve novels and five collections of stories were published at this time, climaxing with her novel of Washington life, *Through One Administration* (1883). Signs of an unhappy marriage showed through, however: The book was one of her few novels without a happy ending.

In 1885, Frances wrote the novel that was to make her name, *Little Lord Fauntleroy* (1886), published with illustrations by Reginald Birch. The story was based on her own son Vivian, who never quite threw off the image constructed by the book throughout his life. It was one of the three bestsellers of the year, and over one million copies sold in Britain alone. The novel was also dramatized, a process that involved a court case over the copyright laws of the day. Much of the later criticism that the book was sickly sentimental was misplaced: Compared to other popular late Victorian fiction, *Little Lord Fauntleroy* was filled with political and psychological insights, and the "lost heir" motif was used for moral purposes in a focused storyline. Sentimentalities arose out of Frances' self-projection as "Dearest," the ideal mother, and other children's books followed, the most popular being *Racketty Packetty House* (1906).

My Robin (1912) recorded Frances' last visit to Maytham Hall and also provided a clue to the setting of her greatest novel, *The Secret Garden* (1910). *The Secret Garden*'s real genesis was probably an incident recorded in a memoir of finding an abandoned garden in a Manchester house and, by sheer force of imagination, seeing it as intensely alive. The development of her rose garden at Maytham Hall and her observation of a robin combined with this memory. The Cinderella motif was reversed, for neither the heroine nor the hero of *The Secret Garden* possessed any moral qualities. Both were neglected, unloved, and unlovely children. The novel avoided much of Frances' earlier sentimentality, and the psychological realism was completely convincing. Its structure and movement demonstrated her storytelling abilities at their best.

In 1905 Frances became a U.S. citizen and, after 1908, never leased an English property again. Instead, she bought land in Plandome, Long Island, New York, and built an ornate Italianate house and gardens. She continued to write popular works such as *The Dawn of a Tomorrow* (1906; dramatization, 1909), which contained elements of fashionable Christian Science thinking. Her final children's book was *The Lost Prince* (1915), based on a meeting with exiled Serbian aristocracy during her last visit to Europe early in 1914. By then, the cinema had begun to attract Frances, and she gained the interest of Mary Pickford, who starred in four films based on Frances' books, including *Little Lord Fauntleroy*. No less than three other motion picture versions of this book were made. After World War I, public taste turned against Frances' Victorian style, and her last books received poor reviews. In 1921 she became ill in Bermuda and then recovered. In constant ill health, she commuted between summers at Plandome and winters in New York hotels. She died in Plandome in 1924 and was buried in Roslyn, Long Island.

Summary

The New York Times obituary suggesting that Frances' greatest successes were her work to bring about the 1911 Copyright Act and her book *Little Lord Fauntleroy* merely recorded the reaction against her at the time of her death. Biographer Ann Thwaite cites the claim that *Little Lord Fauntleroy* changed "relationships between America and Britain" as well as the dress styles and even the emotional health of countless young boys of the day. To this must be added Frances' own claim that she "tried to write more happiness into the world," especially with regard to the books that have now become classics of children's literature. Her understanding of childhood and her ability to recreate it have certainly helped develop modern children's literature. *The Secret Garden* still stands as a pinnacle of Romance literature that holds realism and fantasy in perfect tension.

As a career writer, Frances Hodgson Burnett was at the forefront of defining "the new woman" as she balanced traditional views of motherhood with those of emancipation and the liberty to develop her own career. The role of wife was the one role she could not fit into the equation, though she was an excellent breadwinner, combining this with a "fairy godmother" role of philanthropist. Thwaite suggests that what she cared for most was "the invincibility of the human spirit . . . the acceptance of all experience, courage born of adversity." This was precisely what Frances portrayed in her best fiction.

Bibliography

Bixler, Phyllis. *Frances Hodgson Burnett*. Boston: Twayne, 1984. The first chapter surveys Burnett's life and writings. Successive chapters deal with the three main periods of her writing career. The final chapter seeks to define her achievement. Includes a selective bibliography and index.

Burnett, Frances Hodgson. *The One I Knew the Best of All*. London: Warne, and New York: Scribner, 1893. Burnett's only attempt at autobiography. Written for children, the book follows her life as far as her first publication.

Burnett, Vivian. *The Romantick Lady: The Life Story of an Imagination*. New York and London: Scribner, 1927. An invaluable memoir by Burnett's son Vivian and the only source for some of her correspondence.

Dusinberre, Juliet. *Alice to the Lighthouse*. London: Macmillan, and New York: St. Martin's Press, 1987. An invaluable study of the link between children's and adult literature from Lewis Carroll to Virginia Woolf. Includes an excellent chapter on *The Secret Garden* and a bibliography.

Laski, Marghanita. *Mrs Ewing, Mrs Molesworth and Mrs Hodgson Burnett*. London: Barker, 1950; New York: Oxford University Press, 1951. One of the earliest critical studies of Burnett's writings; Laski sets her in the context of late Victorian children's fiction, especially by women authors.

Thwaite, Ann. *Waiting for the Party: The Life of Frances Hodgson Burnett*. London: Secker and Warburg, and New York: Scribner, 1974. This is the definitive biography even though its thesis that Burnett never quite succeeded in achieving her ideals or her need to be loved can be questioned. Includes a complete list of all her writings and dramatic pieces.

David Barratt

DANIEL HUDSON BURNHAM

Born: September 4, 1846; near Henderson, New York

Died: June 1, 1912; Heidelberg, Germany

Areas of Achievement: Architecture and urban planning

Contribution: Energetic and practical, Burnham was master of the utilitarian, technical, and financial aspects of architecture. He made important contributions to the development of the American skyscraper form, the organization of the modern architectural office, and the encouragement of comprehensive urban and regional planning.

Early Life

The son of Edwin Burnham, later a wholesale merchant of drugs, and Elizabeth Weeks Burnham, the daughter of a Swedenborgian minister, Daniel Hudson Burnham was born on September 4, 1846, near Henderson, New York. He moved to Chicago with his family when he was nine years old. An indifferent student, he received his education in the city schools, excelling only in freehand drawing. Burnham was then sent to Bridgewater, Massachusetts, to study with a private tutor. There, his interest in architecture and his talent for drawing became increasingly apparent.

After failing the entrance examinations of both Harvard and Yale, Burnham returned to Chicago in 1868. For short periods, he tried one thing after another—clerking in a Chicago retail store, mining for gold in Nevada, and running unsuccessfully for a seat in the Illinois senate. Burnham's dissatisfactions with these undertakings led his father to seek advice from William Le Baron Jenney (1832-1907), one of Chicago's leading architects. Shortly thereafter, Burnham became an apprentice in Jenney's architectural office. He gained further experience by working with John Val Osdel and Gustav Laureau.

In 1872, at the age of twenty-six, Burnham joined the firm of Carter, Drake and Wight. Working as a draftsman under Peter Bonnett Wight, he acquired a deeper appreciation of architectural scholarship and broadened the scope of his training. Among his fellow draftsmen was a young Georgian, John Wellborn Root (1850-1891). Their friendship led to a new partnership in an architectural office of their own in 1873. Root was inventive, romantic, and versatile; Burnham was businesslike and practical, bringing to the partnership a keen understanding of the points that make an office building a profitable enterprise. One of the firm's first draftsmen was William Holabird (1854-1923), who later established his own reputation as an architect. After a slow start, the partnership's practice grew rapidly; between 1873 and 1891, the firm designed 165 private homes and seventy-five buildings of various types.

Life's Work

In 1874, Burnham and Root completed a large and fashionable house for their first important client, John B. Sherman, a wealthy Chicago stockyard executive. Two years later, Burnham married Sherman's daughter, Margaret. Three sons and two daughters were born to Daniel and Margaret Burnham during the first decade of their marriage. Two of the sons—Hubert and Daniel, Jr.—eventually became architects and joined their father's firm.

Burnham and Root concentrated on house design during the partnership's first few years. Their first big commission was the Montauk Building (1882, since demolished), followed by the Calumet Building (1884). Both in Chicago, they were composed of masonry with cast-iron columns. The term "skyscraper" is said to have been applied first to the Montauk Building, which, at ten stories in height, was the first distinctly tall building in Chicago. Its commercial success made it the forerunner of tall, fireproof buildings throughout the country.

Other masonry buildings in Chicago followed, the most notable being the Rookery (1886) and the Monadnock Building (1891). Austere and subtly proportioned, the latter structure was sixteen stories high, with brick bearing walls. It demonstrated Burnham's belief that architecture should express the uses intended for a building. In 1890 came the Rand-McNally Building (since demolished), the first all-steel, skeleton-framed building. The firm did several other metal, skeleton-framed buildings which were designed before and constructed after Root's death. Among these were the Masonic Temple (1892, since demolished), with a steel frame, and the Great Northern Hotel (1892, since demolished), with a wrought-iron and steel skeleton. Twenty stories in height, the Masonic Temple was, at the time, the tallest building in the world.

The Reliance Building is considered by many to represent the partnership's finest design. Planning for the structure had begun before Root's death and

was finished by the head of the firm's design department, Charles B. Atwood (1849-1895). The design of the Chicago skyscraper is said to have reached its logical conclusion in the Reliance Building, with its steel skeleton, its glass and terracotta walls (revealing the structure underneath), and its skillfully balanced proportions and details.

With Root and landscape architect Frederick Law Olmsted, Burnham worked out the master plan for the World's Columbian Exposition in Chicago. Jackson Park, then a sandy waste, was selected as the location; improvements were designed to fit the area ultimately for use as a city park. Five outside and five local firms of architects were selected to design the principal buildings. Root died during the first meeting of the architects in January, 1891. Burnham, as chief of construction and then chief consulting architect, assumed the responsibility of maintaining the teamwork necessary to accomplish an opening date for the exposition in 1893.

The eastern architects had already determined that the buildings surrounding the exposition's Court of Honor should be classical in design. Although no building of classical design had been erected previously in Chicago, their plan was adopted. It is commonly argued that things would have been different had Root lived. Supposedly, his authority and predilection for the romantic would have given the exposition an altogether different appearance. It should be noted, however, that the classical design of the Court of Honor had been decided upon before Root's death, with both his and Burnham's assent. Moreover, the minds of both men were already attuned to the classical notes struck in the East, especially those of the firm of McKim, Mead and White. In addition, Burnham found attractive the sense of orderliness and the largeness of conception in a series of related public buildings.

To Burnham, the World's Columbian Exposition not only represented an opportunity to express American prowess in invention, manufactures, and production, but also gave Americans a vehicle for demonstrating the capacity of the country in such areas as architecture, painting, and sculpture. Burnham found great satisfaction in the associations created and cultivated during the two years of the exposition's construction period. His management and leadership style allowed for an opportunity for individual creative activity, and his generous nature led him to give full credit to those who worked under him.

Immediate results of the exposition's success were honorary degrees bestowed on Burnham by Harvard and Yale, election to the presidency of the American Institute of Architects, and membership in New York's Century Club. Burnham was now the best-known architect in the United States. Yet the exposition's conclusion also left him with an architectural practice broken by the death of Root and two years of interrupted work. In 1896, he took on three new partners, Ernest R. Graham, Edward C. Shankland, and Charles B. Atwood, all associates at the exposition.

As early as 1897, Burnham had begun thinking about a plan for the development of the Chicago lakefront. Later, working with Jens Jensen (1860-1951) as the landscape architect, he would see this planning result in the construction of Grant Park and other Chicago parks, beginning in 1904. It would also lead to his widely acclaimed Chicago Plan of 1909.

Burnham was called to Washington, D. C., in 1901, to become chairman of a commission to plan the enlargement and extension of the L'Enfant plan for the District of Columbia. To assist him, Burnham chose Charles McKim, a leading New York architect, and Olmsted. He insisted that studies be made of those European capitols which had furnished precedents for L'Enfant's plan. The unity of the Mall was to be restored. Burnham obtained the consent of the Pennsylvania Railroad to remove its tracks from the Mall. The Union Station and the adjoining Post Office Building were planned to be subordinate to the Capitol. In this subordination and in the monumental nature of these buildings, Burnham secured results which marked his desire for teamwork and his sense of proportion.

Among Burnham's more notable later buildings are the Fisher Building (1896), the Field Museum of Natural History (1900), and the Railway Exchange Building (1904)—all in Chicago. In 1902, his Flatiron Building, New York's first skyscraper, became the tallest building in the world. Nevertheless, with the Washington project, Burnham embarked on a new phase of his career, city planning, which occupied much of his time and thought for the remainder of his life. A number of large city governments— San Francisco, Cleveland, Detroit, and Chicago— sought his aid in developing comprehensive city plans. He used these plans for civic development to express his own ideas of dignity, orderliness, and beauty. In 1904, at the request of William Howard Taft, the secretary of war, Burnham served as head of a commission to undertake the rebuilding and modernization of Manila in the Philippine Islands. There, the French idea of turning outgrown fortifications into boulevards was carried out successfully.

In 1910, President Taft appointed Burnham to head a newly organized National Commission of Fine Arts. One of the first important pieces of business for the commission was the location of the proposed Lincoln Memorial and the selection of an architect and sculptor. Early in 1912, Burnham's health began to fail. To the very end a keen student, he died during a trip to Europe in Heidelberg, Germany, on June 1, 1912.

After Burnham's death, Ernest Robert Graham (1868-1936), who had administered the company since 1900, continued the firm in partnership with Burnham's sons, Hubert and Daniel, Jr. The firm continued later as Graham, Anderson, Probst, and White.

Summary

By the late 1920's and early 1930's, as Louis Sullivan's critical writings became more widely known and as European modernist architects spread their message, the derivative neoclassicism of Burnham's day came increasingly under attack in the architectural community. Recent historians and critics have tried to redress the fashionable practice of attacking the Burnham school—a revisionist movement long overdue.

Burnham was as important as his contemporaries believed, and as great as he knew himself to be. Above all others, Burnham made distinguished and original contributions in four areas: first, in the creation of the large, modern architectural office, a hierarchical system of specialists working together in various departments; second, in the development of the skyscraper form, in the perfection of the internal arrangement and layout of tall office-building systems; third, in his early call for comprehensive planning, which included entire urban and geographical regions; and, fourth, in his work as an architectural philanthropist and cultural entrepreneur who organized and encouraged the cultivation of both the public and the private arts in the United States.

Bibliography

Condit, Carl W. *The Chicago School of Architecture: A History of Commercial and Public Building in the Chicago Area, 1875-1925*. Chicago: University of Chicago Press, 1964. The definitive treatment of the Chicago School and its influence. Any recent work on Chicago architecture during the latter part of the nineteenth century and the early part of the twentieth century is in debt to Condit's study.

Hines, Thomas S. *Burnham of Chicago: Architect and Planner*. New York: Oxford University Press, 1974; London: University of Chicago Press, 1979. The standard biography of Burnham. Solid on architectural criticism. "On Sources" is a particularly valuable section.

Hitchcock, Henry Russell. *Architecture: Nineteenth and Twentieth Centuries*. 4th ed. London and New York: Penguin, 1977. The classic one-volume history of modern architecture which deals with Burnham and his contemporaries judiciously and intelligently, if sometimes briefly.

Hoffmann, Donald. *The Architecture of John Wellborn Root*. Baltimore: Johns Hopkins University Press, 1973. The standard study of Root's work. Good on Root's relations with Burnham.

Moore, Charles. *Daniel H. Burnham, Architect, Planner of Cities*. 2 vols. Boston: Houghton Mifflin, 1921. A valuable source of an almost primary nature. Moore knew Burnham well and had access to friends, relatives, and associates.

Reps, John W. *The Making of Urban America: A History of City Planning in the United States*. Princeton, N.J.: Princeton University Press, 1965; Oxford: Princeton University Press, 1992. A helpful overview of American urban planning. Brief text but extensive illustrations.

Schuyler, Montgomery. *American Architecture and Other Writings*. Edited by William Jordy and Ralph Coe. Cambridge, Mass.: Belknap Press of Harvard University Press, 1961. Writings of the best contemporary architectural critic, who wrote extensively about Burnham and the Chicago School.

L. Moody Simms, Jr.

AARON BURR

Born: February 6, 1756; Newark, New Jersey
Died: September 14, 1836; Port Richmond, Staten Island, New York
Areas of Achievement: Politics and law
Contribution: Burr developed the political organization which assured the presidential victory of Thomas Jefferson, and was the force behind the liberalization of New York's penal codes and political process.

Early Life

Aaron Burr was born February 6, 1756, in Newark, New Jersey. His mother, Esther Edwards Burr, was the daughter of the Reverend Mr. Jonathan and Sarah Edwards; his father, the Reverend Mr. Aaron Burr, was pastor of the Newark Presbyterian Congregation and president of the College of New Jersey, which, within the year, moved to Princeton. When Burr was nineteen months old, his father died. Within the year, his mother and grandparents died as well, leaving Burr and his older sister Sarah wards of their twenty-year-old uncle, Timothy Edwards.

After graduation from Princeton at age seventeen, Burr completed his study for the ministry but decided to become a lawyer. His preparations were interrupted by the Revolution. After serving with distinction at the battles of Quebec, New York, and Monmouth and commanding American forces in Westchester, Colonel Burr's health forced him to resign (he was about five feet, two inches in height, thin, and always looked frail), and he returned to the study of law.

In 1782, he was admitted to the New York Bar and then was married to Theodosia Bartow Prevost, ten years his senior and the widow of a British army officer. The Burrs moved to New York City as soon as the British evacuated it. Four children were born: two sons, who died at birth; a daughter, who died in 1789; and Theodosia, the firstborn, who disappeared at sea in 1812.

Burr became noted as a superior attorney; he won many cases "by default." The city's other lawyers, including Alexander Hamilton, sought Burr as co-counsel in arduous litigations. People reported other traits: Burr seldom ventured opinions on public issues, he had difficulty in expressing his wishes or seeking favors, and he seldom joined groups—though groups joined him. Observers noted his unusual interest in the well-being of children. Mental health professionals indicate that the trauma of early parental death can lead to such behavior.

Life's Work

As a military hero and the heir of the Reverend Mr. Edwards and the Reverend Mr. Burr, Colonel Burr would be an asset to any of the political groups forming in New York, but he refused to join the factions led by Senator Philip Schuyler, Governor George Clinton, or Chancellor Robert Livingston. In 1784, a radical group convinced him to allow his name to be placed in nomination for the state assembly; he agreed and was elected. In February, 1785, he sponsored a bill to emancipate all those of "Negro, Mulatto, Indian and Mustee blood born in New York." The measure failed, but Burr continued to seek legislative means to end slavery. Burr was reelected but seems not to have served; he declined further nomination. Refusing to join any faction, Burr nevertheless developed friendly relations with Schuyler's son-in-law, Hamilton, and Livingston's brother, Edward. The Schuyler and Livingston factions supported the new Constitution, while Clinton opposed ratification. In 1789, after New York joined the Union, Clinton attempted to placate Burr by appointing him attorney general. Burr was an efficient official and before resigning prepared a series of recommendations to liberalize the state's laws.

In 1791, the Livingstons, angered by Hamilton's use of his friendship with President George Washington to secure favors for the Schuyler group, combined with the Clintons to prevent the reelection of Senator Schuyler. Burr was elected in his place. Outwardly, Burr and Hamilton remained friends, but Hamilton was determined to "destroy" Burr.

As senator, Burr became identified with the Thomas Jefferson group led by James Monroe in the Senate and James Madison in the House. Burr supported measures to make Senate sessions public and liberalize laws. Because of his stand on slavery, however, he was not fully trusted by the Jeffersonians. He praised the French Republic and objected to the presence of British forts on American soil; he favored funds to the military to protect Americans from Indian raids. After Monroe left the Senate, Burr was acknowledged as Jeffersonian spokesman in the Senate, and his name was unsuccessfully put forward for vice president in the 1796 campaign.

Following the death of his wife, Burr did not seek reelection. Returning to New York, he entered the legislature, where he was instrumental in passing a manumission law, securing the construction of public and private roads and canals, and in creating the Manhattan Company with its "notorious" bank. The Bank of the Manhattan Company, by providing venture capital, enabled New York City to replace Philadelphia and Boston as the preeminent American financial center. The bank also provided an alternative source of capital to the Bank of the United States, dominated by the Schuyler faction (or Federalists), which had used the bank to deny loans to Anti-Federalists.

As an attorney, Burr represented individuals being prosecuted under the Federalist-sponsored Alien and Sedition laws. Although never a member, he helped restructure the Tammany Society into a political organization. Despite his leadership role in the Anti-Federalist, or Democratic Republican, Party, Hamilton, in 1798, convinced Federalist governor John Jay to appoint Burr overseer of the state's defenses to prepare for war with France.

Burr blueprinted a plan which would have prevented a foreign fleet from entering New York Harbor. The legislature rejected most of the plan as too costly. Burr, however, was able to convince many Federalists, most of whom had considered the Anti-Federalists as too pro-French, to switch parties. He gathered a slate of candidates which would ensure that pro-Jeffersonians would be selected as presidential electors for the election of 1801. When, for the first time, the state elected an Anti-Federalist slate, the Jeffersonians agreed that Burr would be their vice presidential candidate.

Unfortunately, Burr and Jefferson received an equal vote for president; the House of Representatives would have to elect the president. The balloting started February 11, 1801. Burr received a majority of the votes, but, for him to be elected, nine states had to concur; Jefferson had a majority in eight states, Burr a majority in six, and two states split evenly. By February 16, the Federalists, having reached an understanding with Jefferson's spokesman, Samuel Smith, abandoned their opposition to Jefferson, who was elected president while Burr became vice president.

With the Senate evenly split between Federalists and Republicans, Burr's role as president of the Senate became crucial in securing passage of Jef-

fersonian legislation. Only when the Administration attempted to impose an embargo on trade with the black revolutionists of Haiti did Burr act in opposition. By 1804, however, Burr, realizing that Jefferson was grooming Madison as his successor, decided to seek the governorship of New York. Much to Hamilton's annoyance, the Federalists decided to support Burr. Tammany also endorsed Burr, but the Livingston and Clinton groups combined to nominate their own candidate. Burr carried New York City, Albany, and a few urban centers but was overwhelmed in rural areas.

After the defeat, Burr's supporters persuaded him to question Hamilton about some comments he allegedly had made. Despite the efforts of Hamilton's friends, Hamilton exacerbated the issue. He was fatally wounded in the resulting duel. Burr's enemies in New York and New Jersey (where the duel took place) attempted to arrest Burr, who fled to Philadelphia.

Burr returned to Washington, where as president of the Senate he frustrated another Administration attempt to place an embargo on trade with Haiti and presided over the unsuccessful attempt to impeach Judge Samuel Chase. Following an emotional farewell speech, Burr left the Senate.

Unable to return to New York or New Jersey because of the illegal murder indictments—dueling was legal in New Jersey, and New York had no jurisdiction in the matter—Burr, having secured the temporary presidential appointment of several of his friends to important posts in Louisiana Territory, took a trip down the Ohio and Mississippi rivers to New Orleans. He returned to Washington in the fall of 1805 and held a series of meetings with Jefferson, who, in January, 1806, sought and received Senate confirmation of the appointment of Burr's friends. Amid talk of war with Spain, Burr embarked on a second voyage down the rivers. Soon rumors began to circulate that Burr planned either to separate the Mississippi Valley from the rest of the country or to invade Spanish territory. All Burr would say was that he had purchased land along the Washita River and that he intended to populate the region with individuals capable of organizing a strike force in the event of war with Spain.

Burr's ally, General James Wilkinson, the highest-ranking officer in the army, governor of Louisiana, and a paid Spanish agent, suddenly declared that Burr was a traitor. After a series of trials along the Mississippi in which he was found innocent, Burr was captured by troops and dragged to Richmond, Virginia, to stand trial for treason. Burr acted as his own attorney, although he was assisted by some of the best legal minds in the country. Chief Justice John Marshall acted as circuit judge. The trial became a landmark, because it defined the constitutional meaning of treason, clarified who had the right to declare martial law, and established the right of a defendant to subpoena the president. Burr was found not guilty. The government then charged him with committing a misdemeanor. He was found not guilty. When the government ordered that he stand trial on the same charges in Ohio, he fled to Europe.

In England he was welcomed by Jeremy Bentham and William Godwin, the widower of Mary Wollstonecraft, whose feminist views Burr shared. Burr attempted to convince the British government to help liberate Latin America. He also tried to persuade those Spaniards who were resisting the French occupation of their country to adopt the liberal constitution developed by Bentham. He failed in both attempts. He left England for Germany, Sweden, and France. In Paris he sought the aid of Napoleon in removing all European colonies from the Western Hemisphere. Again he failed.

He returned to New York in 1812; he learned that his only grandchild had died and that his daughter's ship had disappeared at sea. Burr remained in New York—the murder indictments had been quashed, but the treason charges would not be dropped until 1816. He resumed his legal practice and maintained a low profile. His private and legal papers, however, indicate that he was still active in politics. He corresponded with South American revolutionists and was offered a post in their army. He maintained his friendship with Andrew Jackson and Martin Van Buren, the latter serving as co-counsel on several cases. Toward the end of his life, he became interested in bringing German settlers to Texas and attempted to establish contact with Texan revolutionists.

Burr suffered a minor stroke in June, 1830, but that did not prevent him from either continuing his work or, on July 1, 1833, marrying Eliza Jumel, a wealthy widow twenty years his junior. A year later, Mrs. Burr sued for divorce, charging that Burr had taken some of her money for the Texas project. After a sordid trial—the legal grounds for divorce being adultery—the divorce was granted July 14, 1836, to become effective September 14. Since Burr died on that day, Mrs. Burr decided that she did not want the divorce.

Summary

In some ways, Burr represented the America that was to be rather than the America that was. He opposed slavery and favored the education of blacks; he was a feminist who believed that women should be educated to the same degree as males and that women should be able to divorce men who abused them; he opposed property qualifications for voting and did everything possible to void or circumvent the laws. He encouraged government support for commerce and industry; to protect American commerce and independence, he favored the military and naval establishment. He advocated the annexation of Florida and Texas and the United States' support for the liberation of Latin America. In his legal work, he insisted that the burden of proof rested with the prosecution and challenged the validity of circumstantial evidence; he demanded that courts follow the rules of evidence.

The contested election of 1801, the killing of Hamilton, and the treason trials made Burr a political pariah. Many of his friends would publicly shun him but privately seek his advice. Most of the legislation he proposed as attorney general became law; Tammany Hall became a model for democratic urban political machines; the Bank of the Manhattan Company blueprinted a policy that was to become normal in the 1980's and Martin Van Buren secretly called upon his expertise during the War of 1812. People would follow Burr's ideas as long as they could omit his name.

Bibliography

Burr, Aaron. *The Papers of Aaron Burr.* Edited by Mary-Jo Kline. 27 reels. New York: Microfilm Corporation of America, 1978. The basis for all current scholarly research. All known and available documents to and from Burr are included, as are all existing legal papers. Where the original document has disappeared, printed versions are included. At times a typed transcription of the manuscript is appended. Includes not only all archival documents but also documents from private collectors and family collections that have never been used.

———. *Political Correspondence and Public Papers of Aaron Burr.* Edited by Mary-Jo Kline. 2 vols. Princeton, N.J.: Princeton University Press, 1983. Using selections from the microfilm edition of Burr's papers, the editor has grouped well-edited and well-annotated papers into topical sections, which are introduced by superb long historical essays. While recognizing Burr's personality faults, it presents a positive view of his role.

Daniels, Jonathan. *Ordeal of Ambition: Jefferson, Hamilton, Burr.* New York: Doubleday, 1970. An excellent popular political biography of Burr, Jefferson, and Hamilton, in which the author is rather impartial.

Davis, Matthew Livingston, ed. *Memoirs of Aaron Burr.* 2 vols. New York: Harper, 1836. A political ally of Burr, Davis used Burr's papers to write a defense of his actions prior to 1809. Liberties were taken with the documents.

———. *The Private Journal of Aaron Burr.* 2 vols. New York: Harper, 1836. A continuation of the memoirs, covering the period 1809-1836. The basis of the work is the journal kept by Burr while in Europe, letters written to his daughter and son-in-law, and letters from various individuals interested in Latin American affairs. The journal, written in abbreviated English, French, German, Swedish, and Latin, is quite salacious and shocked Davis, who sanitized it for publication. The original manuscript was sold to William K. Bixby, who decoded and translated it as *The Private Journal* (published by Genesse Press in 1903).

Geissler, Suzanne. *Jonathan Edwards to Aaron Burr, Jr.: From the Great Awakening to Democratic Politics.* New York: Edwin Mellin Press, 1981. Using unpublished documents, the author traces the development of a democratic ideology. An excellent defense of Burr's position.

Hammond, Jabez D. *The History of Political Parties in the State of New York.* 2 vols. Cooperstown, N.Y.: Phinney, 1845. Well written, this is still the best work describing the conflict among the supporters of Burr, Hamilton, Clinton, and Livingston.

Lomask, Milton. *Aaron Burr: The Years from Princeton to Vice President, 1756-1805.* New York: Farrar, Straus, 1979.

———. *Aaron Burr: The Conspiracy and Years of Exile, 1804-1836.* New York: Farrar, Straus, 1982. A popular biography. The first volume repeats much that had been previously written. The second volume, however, benefited from the publication of the microfilm edition of the Burr papers and presents some positive new insights.

Parmet, Herbert S., and Marie B. Hecht. *Aaron Burr: Portrait of an Ambitious Man.* New York: Macmillan, 1967. Making extensive use of documents in various archives, the authors have presented a well-written, scholarly, but unflattering biography.

Rogow, Arnold A. *A Fatal Friendship: Alexander Hamilton and Aaron Burr.* New York: Hill and Wang, 1998. Short biographies of Hamilton and Burr provide a basis for discussion of the manner in which their paths crossed politically and the effects of the gossip they spread about each other. Viewed by critics as an "all-aspects" overview of this historic episode.

Sanford, Bruce W. "No Contest: The Trumped-Up Conflict between Freedom of the Press and the Right to a Fair Trial." *Media Studies Journal* 12, no. 1 (Winter 1998). Examines how the balance between freedom of the press and the right to a fair trial have been in conflict as far back as Burr's 1807 prosecution for treason.

Syrett, Harold C., and Jean G. Cooke, eds. *Interview in Weehawken: The Burr-Hamilton Duel as*

Told in Original Documents. Middletown, Conn.: Wesleyan University Press, 1960. A complete collection of all the letters, memoranda, editorials, and testimony leading up to and following the Burr-Hamilton duel.

J. Lee Shneidman

SIR RICHARD FRANCIS BURTON

Born: March 19, 1821; Torquay, Devonshire, England

Died: October 20, 1890; Trieste, Italy

Areas of Achievement: Exploration, scholarship, and diplomacy

Contribution: Burton was a British explorer and Orientalist who explored in Asia, Africa, and South America. He was famous as an author of travel books and many literary translations, including *The Arabian Nights' Entertainments.*

Early Life

Richard Francis Burton was born on March 19, 1821, in Torquay, Devonshire. He was the eldest son of Mary Baker and Colonel Joseph Netterton Burton, an Irish officer who retired from an undistinguished military career in 1821. His parents moved to Tours, France, where Burton acquired a fluency in European languages while accompanying his parents on their frequent travels on the Continent. After an inconsistent early education, including a brief stay at a private school in Richmond, Burton returned to the Continent, where his adolescence consisted of an unruly, undisciplined lifestyle. He attended Trinity College, Oxford, from 1840 to 1842, but he was dismissed for an ambivalent attitude and disobedience. Fellow students at Oxford called him "Ruffian Dick."

Having developed an interest in Oriental languages while at Trinity College, Burton enlisted in 1842 as an officer in the East India Company Army. He was sent to Gujarat and then to the Sind, where he lived among the Moslems for seven years while learning several Eastern languages, including Hindi and Arabic. Burton served briefly as an intelligence officer under Sir Charles Napier, the British Commander during the Indian Wars (1842-1849). He often performed intelligence missions which entailed going to the native bazaars in disguise and bringing back reports, which were generally excellent. On Napier's orders in 1845, Burton, with his usual thoroughness, undertook an investigation of the influence of homosexual brothels on British soldiers, and his detailed study led to their destruction. Unfortunately, a jealous officer later used the report in an effort to destroy Burton's military career. Although exonerated, Burton, suffering from cholera, was sent back to England on extended sick leave in 1849.

Burton lived with his family in Boulogne for the next three years while writing three books about his Indian experiences. At the age of thirty, Burton was an imposing figure. Almost six feet tall, with piercing eyes and a dark complexion, he looked like an Arab. While in France, he continued his study of Oriental languages (during a lifetime of travel, he would eventually master more than forty languages and dialects) and completed plans for his first great adventure, a visit to Arabia.

Life's Work

Burton had always wanted to visit the Moslem shrines in Mecca. In 1853, the Royal Geographic Society helped him obtain a leave from the army, and Burton traveled by caravan from Cairo to the sacred city of Mecca disguised as an Afghan doctor. Using four languages and performing all the ceremonies and rituals of a devout Moslem, he penetrated the holiest shrines of Islam. Instead of returning to England to write of his experiences,

Burton traveled to the equally forbidden Moslem city of Harar in Abyssinia. In 1854, he became the first European to visit Harar without being executed. He later wrote *Personal Narrative of a Pilgrimage to El-Medinah and Meccah* (1855-1856), which was not only a great adventure story but also a commentary on Moslem culture, and *First Footsteps in Africa* (1856), which described his adventures in Harar.

While in Africa, Burton met John Hanning Speke, also an East India Company officer. After his visit to Harar, the two officers led an expedition into Somaliland. Their camp was unexpectedly attacked by Somali warriors near Berbera. One member of the expedition was killed, and Speke was seriously wounded. Burton suffered a spear-wound in the jaw and was forced to return to England to recover.

In July, 1855, Burton volunteered for the Crimean War and trained the Turkish Bashi-Bazouk Irregular Cavalry while serving as chief of staff to General William F. Beatson. Despite his efforts, Burton saw no action at the front, and when Beatson left the army, Burton also resigned and returned to England in October, 1855.

In London, Burton again met Speke, who had also served in the Crimea, and described his plan to form an expedition to find the source of the Nile River. Speke had for a long time shared this goal, and when Burton asked him to join the expedition, Speke readily agreed. Since Burton had secured a grant of a thousand pounds from the Foreign Office and had obtained the patronage of the Royal Geographic Society, he was the leader of the expedition, with Speke as second in command. Their charge was to ascertain the limits of the Sea of Ujiji, which had been described by East African missionaries, to determine the exportable goods of the interior and to study the ethnography of the tribes. They were also instructed to discover the source of the Nile and the location of the legendary, but nonexistent, Mountains of the Moon. Organizational ability was not one of Burton's great talents, and they wasted nearly six months planning and exploring the coastal areas near Zanzibar before hurriedly recruiting porters and moving into the interior.

On July 1, 1857, Burton and Speke departed from Bagamoyo and followed the traditional trade route to Kazeh, the site of modern Tabora. They reached Kazeh on November 7 and spent nearly a month reorganizing the expedition. They set out for Ujiji on December 5 with the knowledge gained from Swahili-speaking merchants that the Sea of Ujiji was actually three lakes—Nyasa, Tanganyika, and Victoria. Both Burton and Speke suffered remittent bouts of fever during this part of the journey. On February 13, 1858, Burton became the first European in modern times to see Lake Tanganyika. Speke was bitterly disappointed because he had contracted ophthalmia and could see nothing but a glare. Frustrated because their health precluded an exploration of Lake Tanganyika and running low of supplies, they started back to the coast on May 26. By this time, a growing strain in their relationship had turned to open animosity. While Burton recovered from malaria at Kazeh, Speke decided to examine the more northern Lake Victoria, which he reached on August 3. Although unable to explore the massive lake, he was convinced that Victoria was the source of the Nile. Burton, a much more literate geographer, refused to accept Speke's theory, which led to more quarrels and their eventual estrangement. Speke quickly returned to England, where he was feted and given command of a new expedition by Sir Roderick Murchison, President of the Royal Geographic Society. Burton, when he finally arrived, was ignored and denied financing for a new expedition. He wrote *Lake Regions of Central Africa* (1860), a highly acclaimed book which attacked Speke's theory and exacerbated their public feud.

In 1860, Burton unexpectedly sailed for the United States, where he traveled by stagecoach to Salt Lake City to visit the Mormon capital. In *City of the Saints* (1861), he compassionately described the Mormon Church, its leadership, and its controversial practice of polygamy. After returning to England, Burton married Isabel Arundell on January 22, 1861. She was the daughter of an aristocratic Catholic family, and Burton had been courting her since 1856.

A turning point came in Burton's life in 1861, when he left the Indian army to accept a consular service appointment to Fernando Po on the unhealthy West African coast. During the next three years, he explored Dahomey, the Bight of Benin and Biafra, the Cameroons, and the Gold Coast. He used these experiences to write five anthropological books about the tribes of that region.

Burton returned to London in September, 1864, and was scheduled to debate Speke about his second expedition and the claim that Lake Victoria was truly the source of the Nile. After an introductory meeting, Speke died of a self-inflicted shotgun wound in a questionable hunting accident. Although most scholars agreed with Burton's theory, the source of the Nile remained unknown until 1876, when Henry Morton Stanley proved that Speke's intuition had been correct. Shortly after Speke's death in 1864, a bitterly disappointed Burton was given a consulate position at Santos, Brazil, where he continued his writing and explored the interior of South America. He quickly developed an aversion to Santos and began drinking heavily.

In 1869, after several pleas from his wife, Burton was transferred to Damascus but was recalled in 1871 when he and Isabel became involved in local affairs which offended several Moslem leaders. Burton argued that his actions had been misrepresented, and his conduct was finally approved by a Foreign Office review. After some months, he reluctantly accepted the consulate appointment to Trieste, but he believed that his diplomatic career was ruined. Trieste was Burton's last appointment, and he used the position to travel and to write and translate an astounding number of books. In February, 1886, Burton was remembered for his service to the Crown when Queen Victoria made him a Knight Commander of St. Michael and St. George. Burton accepted the knighthood in the hope that it would lead to a better appointment, but he was never formally invested.

Burton's last years were spent in completing his monumental translation of *The Arabian Nights' Entertainments* (1885-1888), more correctly called *The Thousand Nights and a Night*. He had suffered from the gout since 1883, and his health began to deteriorate noticeably. After two minor heart seizures, Burton died of a heart attack in Trieste on October 20, 1890. His body was returned to England and buried at the Roman Catholic cemetery at Mortlake, Surrey, in a white marble mausoleum sculptured in the form of an Arabian tent. After his death, his wife destroyed his forty-year assemblage of diaries, notes, and journals, including the revised edition of *The Perfumed Garden of the Cheikh Nefzaoui* (1886), on which he was working when he died. The significance of that loss to biographers, historians, and anthropologists is immeasurable.

Summary

Sir Richard Francis Burton's adventurousness, curiosity, linguistic skills, and writing talent make a summary of his contributions almost impossible to believe. He was a Renaissance man: soldier, diplomat, explorer, ethnologist, archaeologist, translator, and poet. He was also competent as a botanist, zoologist, geologist, swordsman, artist, and physician. His greatest claim to fame, however, was in the field of exploration. He possessed the same passion for geographical study that produced great British African explorers such as Speke, Stanley, David Livingstone, Samuel Baker, and others. Unlike his fellow explorers, Burton was a scholar, who described much more than his expeditions. In carefully footnoted and annotated books, he described tribes, customs, religions, climate, geography, and countless other topics. He wrote forty-three volumes on his explorations and travels, two volumes of poetry, and more than a hundred articles, and he translated twenty-eight volumes from other languages.

Burton's translations of Oriental erotica, including the *Kama Sutra of Vatsyayana* (1883), *The Perfumed Garden of Cheikh Nefzaoui*, and the unexpurgated "Arabian Nights" tales, earned for him greater literary fame and financial rewards than his heavily documented works on exploration, swordsmanship, falconry, religion, gorillas, and archaeological ruins.

In the field of human sexual behavior, Burton anticipated the psychological insights of Sigmund Freud and Havelock Ellis. Burton has been recognized by modern scholars as one of the pioneers in anthropology. Unfortunately, many of Burton's scientific achievements were overshadowed by his adventures in Mecca and Harar, his expeditions to Africa, and his public anger over the cant and hypocrisy of Victorian prudery. He approached all challenges with enthusiasm, earnestness, dedicated scholarship, and courage. Burton's adventurous life and difficult disposition dominated the books that he wrote, but he lived according to his personal creed that he preferred honor to honors.

Bibliography

Assad, Thomas J. *Three Victorian Travellers: Burton, Blunt, Doughty*. London: Routledge, 1964. An interpretive character study. Concentrates almost exclusively on Burton's preoccupation with Arabia and the Moslem world.

Brodie, Fawn M. *The Devil Drives: A Life of Sir Richard Burton*. London: Eyre and Spottiswoode, and New York: Norton, 1967. A highly respected psychoanalytic biography which argues that Burton was "devil-driven" as an explorer-adventurer.

Farwell, Byron. *Burton: A Biography of Sir Richard Francis Burton*. London: Longman, and

New York: Holt Rinehart, 1964. The best biography of Burton. Objective, straightforward, and engagingly written.

Hastings, Michael. *Sir Richard Burton: A Biography.* London: Hodder and Stoughton, and New York: Coward, McCann, 1978. A popular biography. While it lacks documentation, it does provide some information lacking in earlier biographies.

Lovell, Mary. *A Rage To Live: A Biography of Richard and Isabel Burton.* London: Little Brown, and New York: Norton, 1998. The author uses previously unavailable sources to produce a joint biography that illuminates this couple, at odds with Victorian society.

Moorehead, Alan. *The White Nile.* Rev. ed. London: Hamilton, and New York: Harper, 1971. A marvelous and powerfully written account of the quest for the source of the Nile. Excellent integration of Burton's role in the exploration of East Africa.

Mountfield, David. *A History of African Exploration.* London and New York: Hamlyn, 1976. A well-illustrated coverage of African exploration. The sections on East Africa and Burton's expeditions are excellent.

Rawling, Gerald. "Ruffian Dick." *British History Illustrated* 5 (February/March 1979): 6-18. Brief, colorful coverage of Burton's controversial life. Excellent description of Burton's African explorations.

Rice, Edward. *Captain Sir Richard Francis Burton.* New York: Scribner, 1990. Rice creates an action-filled biography based on extensive research and offering some unorthodox opinions of Burton.

Phillip E. Koerper

SIR THOMAS FOWELL BUXTON

Born: April 1, 1786; Castle Hedingham, Essex, England

Died: February 19, 1845; Northrepps Hall, Norfolk, England

Areas of Achievement: Social reform and abolitionism

Contribution: Buxton was for a long time active in a variety of humanitarian causes, including prison reform and charitable relief, but he is best known for his sustained efforts to bring about the abolition of slavery.

Early Life

Thomas Fowell Buxton was born on April 1, 1786, in Castle Hedingham, Essex. He was the eldest son of Thomas Fowell Buxton of Earl's Colne, Essex, and Anna, daughter of Osgood Hanbury of Holfield Grange, Essex. The Hanburys and their relations, the Gurneys, as well as many within their circle, were Quakers. Although the young Thomas was brought up in the Church of England, an affiliation he retained throughout his life, evangelical and Quaker influences upon him were strong. Because he was only six years old when his father died, his mother's role was accentuated.

He was sent to school in Kingston when only four and a half years old, but sickness caused his removal to the school of Dr. Charles Burney of Greenwich. He left school at the age of fifteen without having distinguished himself academically. In 1801 he first visited the home of the Gurneys at Earlham Hall on the outskirts of Norwich. The eleven youngsters, children of John Gurney, were his distant cousins, owing to the marriage of his aunt, Rachel Hanbury, to Richard Gurney, their uncle. With one of them, Hannah, the young "Fowell," as he was now called, fell instantly in love. Through the association with the Gurneys the Quaker influence upon him was strengthened, and he also acquired a desire to give up what he now saw as idleness and to apply himself studiously to continuing his education. In 1802 he prepared himself for college, and in October, 1803, he entered Trinity College, Dublin. Upon passing his examinations, mostly with distinction, he received the university gold medal. On May 7, 1807, Buxton married Hannah Gurney.

At the age of twenty-one, Buxton's was an imposing figure: six feet, four inches tall and broadchested, with the physique of an outdoor sportsman. His fondness for hunting and shooting remained with him longer than his splendid build. His first child, Priscilla, was born in February, 1808, and shortly after, through the good offices of his uncles, Sampson and Osgood Hanbury, he joined the brewery firm of Truman, Hanbury, and Company. In 1811 he became a partner and worked long hours to reform the company's methods and bookkeeping. These improvements ensured that he would throughout the rest of his life have a comfortable income, affording him the leisure to pursue those philanthropic causes that had already begun to interest him.

Life's Work

From the early years of his employment with the brewery firm, Buxton took an active part in charitable enterprises in the district of Spitalfields, where the brewery was. This district was a center for silk-weaving, a trade that suffered numerous vicissitudes, as during the depression of 1816, when starvation was widespread. Buxton's first important public speech, at the Mansion House in 1816, raised more than forty-three thousand pounds for the relief of the poor of the area. This speech first brought Buxton to the attention of the famous reformer William Wilberforce, who had been largely instrumental in outlawing the slave trade in Great Britain in 1807.

Although this connection would later be of the utmost importance in Buxton's career, for the time being a far greater influence upon him was his sister-in-law, Elizabeth (née Gurney) Fry and her circle, whose chief interest lay in prison reform. After his Mansion House speech, Buxton went through Newton jail, and this as well as other visitations resulted in his publication in 1818 of a volume titled *An Inquiry Whether Crime and Misery Are Produced or Prevented by Our Present System of Prison Discipline.* This work went through five editions within a year and led to the founding of the Society for the Reformation of Prison Discipline. Buxton's zeal for prison reform also seems to have brought him to political awareness. He decided that his best chance for effecting changes would be as a Member of Parliament.

He stood for election in 1818 as candidate for Weymouth. Against all odds, despite the fact that he would not stoop to the electioneering methods then in vogue, he won. Thus he began his long parliamentary career, representing Weymouth for almost two decades, until he lost the election of 1837. Early in this career he served on two parliamentary select committees inquiring into capital punishment, a penalty he opposed, except for murder. In 1820 he supported Sir James Mackintosh's motion to abolish the death penalty for forgery, which was then but one of the many offenses so punished.

That same year brought great personal tragedy, for his eldest son died, followed by three of his daughters. After this loss he moved from his Hampstead house to Cromer Hall in Norfolk, in the district of his wife's family. He soon returned to Parliament, however, and participated in bills concerning prisons and education, and inquiries into the Hindu practice of suttee and the slave trade. Increasingly, Wilberforce noticed Buxton with approval. Finally, on May 24, 1821, that great abolitionist wrote Buxton to ask for his help in the struggle to end slavery and, in the event that he himself should become unable to pursue the cause, to ask that Buxton would carry on the effort. Wilberforce's request for help was reinforced by the dying prayer of Buxton's sister-in-law, Priscilla Gurney, on behalf of the slaves.

So began a reorientation of Buxton's parliamentary efforts. He was an active member of the African Institution. Besides Wilberforce, he worked with figures such as Zachary Macauley, Dr. Stephen Lushington, and the third Baron Suffield. The Anti-Slavery Society was formed in 1823, with the purpose of collecting evidence and spreading information. On May 15, 1823, Buxton brought before the House of Commons a resolution for the gradual abolition of slavery throughout the British Empire, on the grounds that that institution violated the principles contained in the British constitution and the Christian faith. The foreign secretary, George Canning, moved amendments that vitiated the real thrust of Buxton's resolution by adopting a process of "amelioration" of the condition of slaves. Accordingly, the British government issued a circular to its colonial governors recommending certain reforms with regard to slaves. In essence, the West Indian planters denounced the advice to the governors as an attack upon their rights.

While Buxton thus did not meet with success in the House of Commons, it was clear that extraparliamentary opposition to slavery was growing, and that the popular if unenfranchised voice was becoming increasingly a factor in parliamentary poli-

tics. Reform was in the air. Although evangelicist and Quaker sections of the public may not have been beloved by Members of Parliament, they usually were not disbelieved. Their petitions carried weight. One of them, said to have seventy-two thousand signatures, Buxton presented to Parliament in 1826, with a demand for better treatment for West Indian slaves. Parliament, he said, would have to enact reform measures, since the colonial governments would not. Furthermore, the petitioners wanted to end the system by which sugar produced by slave labor was subsidized by the British government. In other words, they raised the issue of free trade. Increasingly, the aims of the reformers were finding endorsement in the attitudes of the rank and file as well as the educated mind. Slavery was becoming abhorrent to the British conscience.

In 1829, Parliament voted to allow Catholic emancipation; in other words, Catholics could now hold civil and military office on equal terms with Anglicans. The death of King George IV in the following year required a general election, which in the existing climate of affairs almost ensured a movement in the general direction of reform. In April of 1831, Buxton, impatient with the government's failure to act on the slavery issue, brought forward in Parliament a resolution for the abolition of slavery. His initiative failed because the reforming efforts of Parliament were then devoted to the House of Commons itself. When the Reform Act of 1832 finally became law, he and his supporters could hope that abolition would become reality.

So as to forestall the motion Buxton intended, the government promised in 1833 that it would introduce a bill to abolish slavery. The legislation the government proposed was a compromise, allowing compensation to slave owners and an apprenticeship period before slaves would receive complete freedom. The bill passed Parliament just after the death of Wilberforce and received the king's assent on August 28, 1833. It would go into effect on August 1, 1834.

After his triumph on abolition of slavery, Buxton hoped to use that momentum to gain protection for the native Africans of the Cape Colony against "vagrancy" laws and other discriminatory acts. In 1835 he pressed for and obtained a select committee of the House of Commons to consider the state of the aborigines in the British Empire. His report on the aborigines, frequently referred to as the Buxton Report, became public in 1837. It called for sweeping protections for aboriginal rights, particularly with regard to native lands and customs. The spirit of this report animated the Treaty of Waitangi with the Maori of New Zealand in 1840, and there is little question that compliance with the treaty would have prevented the Maori Wars. In South Africa the report contributed to the Great Trek of the Boers or Afrikaners, and the terrible divisiveness that ensued. The report was a high-flown idealistic statement that could not be made operational.

Buxton's attention was now riveted upon the slave issue. In 1839 and 1840 he published two volumes, *The African Slave Trade* and its sequel, *The Remedy*. He recommended a larger naval patrol in West African waters, treaties with native chiefs to stop the slave trade, the purchase of Fernando Po as a headquarters, an expedition up the Niger River to make more treaties with native chiefs and to establish a model farm, and the forming of a company for introducing agriculture and commerce into Africa. For these purposes the Society for the Extinction of the Slave Trade and the Civilisation of Africa was established. Buxton's influence induced the British government to dispatch a Niger expedition that proved a failure and cost many lives.

In 1839 Buxton was suffering from ill health, so he toured abroad as a change of pace. He could not resist, however, turning his journey to valuable advantage by investigating the crimes of banditti and the state of Roman jails.

He had lost his parliamentary seat in 1837. After his return to England he resumed private life, broken only by the queen's granting him a baronetcy in 1840. He devoted himself to the cultivation of his estates and to land improvement. His essay on the management of his estates won the gold medal of the Royal Agricultural Society in 1845.

By the spring of 1843, his health was failing, and he died on February 19, 1845, at Northrepps Hall, Norfolk. Admirers raised a monument to him in Westminster Abbey.

Summary
Sir Thomas Fowell Buxton's life was one of almost constant toil for humanitarian goals. He wanted to save life and improve conditions of life. To an unusual degree his idealistic efforts were crowned with success, for he saw in his lifetime penal and judicial reform and, above all, the abolition of sla-very throughout the British dominions. His account of how to end the African slave trade was vague and unrealistic in its optimistic vision, and the Niger expedition to end the slave trade which those writings inspired ended in fiasco. Nevertheless, Buxton was in large measure responsible for bringing to an end an institution that had tyrannized an entire race. That his health was gravely affected by his emotional response to the failed expedition attests his identification with and fervent support of a lifelong cause.

Bibliography
Buxton, Sir Thomas Fowell. *The African Slave Trade and Its Remedy.* London: Murray, and New York: Benedict, 1840. This volume contains the two books that Buxton first published in 1839 and 1840. The first part contains many statistics on the extent of the slave trade, and the second part demonstrates Buxton's vision of a civilized and Christianized Africa.

———. *Memoirs of Sir Thomas Fowell Buxton.* Edited by Charles Buxton. London: Murray, 1848; Philadelphia: Longstreth, 1949. The principal source for knowledge of Buxton's private life as well as much of his public life.

Gallagher, John. "Fowell Buxton and the New African Policy." *Cambridge Historical Journal* 10 (1950): 36-58. Discusses the plans for the Niger expedition.

Great Britain, Parliament. *Report of the Select Committee on Aborigines (British Settlements) with Minutes of Evidence, Appendix, and Index.* 2 vols. Capetown, South Africa: Struik, 1966. This important document shows what Buxton considered the best ways to protect aboriginal rights.

Harlow, Vincent, and Frederick Madden, eds. *British Colonial Developments, 1774-1834.* Oxford: Clarendon Press, 1953. A series of important colonial documents, including a letter from Buxton.

Mottram, Ralph H. *Buxton the Liberator.* London and New York: Hutchinson, 1946. Dated and slim, but draws heavily from the published memoirs.

Pugh, Patricia M. *Calendar of the Papers of Sir Thomas Fowell Buxton, 1786-1845.* London: Swift, 1980. An important reference tool.

Mary B. Wickwire

LORD BYRON

George Gordon

Born: January 22, 1788; London, England
Died: April 19, 1824; Missolonghi, Greece
Area of Achievement: Literature
Contribution: Not only did Byron write satirical and lyrical poetry of the highest order, but also his life seemed, to many of his contemporaries, to be the embodiment of the revolutionary spirit of Romanticism. His figure of the "Byronic hero" became vastly influential in nineteenth century European culture.

Early Life

George Gordon was born in London on January 22, 1788. He had an aristocratic heritage on both sides of the family. On his father's side, the Byrons had long been known for their eccentricity, and Byron's father, Captain John Byron, led a wild and reckless life, squandering the family wealth. He died when the poet was three, having separated from his wife the previous year. The poet's mother, Catherine Gordon of Gight, was descended from one of the most notable families in Scotland.

Until 1798, the young Byron lived with his mother in Aberdeen, Scotland, but on the death of his great uncle, the notorious "Wicked Lord," he became the sixth Baron Byron of Rochdale, and he and his mother moved to Newstead Abbey in England, the traditional family seat. Byron was schooled at Harrow and Cambridge, where the personality which would entrance so many soon became apparent: generous and openhearted, ambitious and idealistic, self-willed, but with an almost feminine quality of softness and sentimentality.

Byron also had the advantage of being strikingly handsome; his fellow poet Samuel Taylor Coleridge remarked, "so beautiful a countenance I scarcely ever saw . . . his eyes the open portals of the sun—things of light, and for light." Byron's classic, almost Grecian beauty was flawed only by a deformed right foot, which embarrassed him throughout his life, and a tendency to become overweight, which he combated by strict dieting and exercise.

His literary career was launched when, after privately printing two volumes of verse anonymously, he published *Hours of Idleness* (1807) and a highly successful satire about contemporary writers, *English Bards, and Scotch Reviewers* (1809), which went through four editions in three years. In 1809, he took his seat in the House of Lords, and for a number of years he anticipated a career as a statesman.

In spite of Byron's early success, however, his restless spirit was seeking to escape from the increasingly dissolute life he was living in London. He always sought new experiences and felt strongly the lure of foreign climes. In July, 1809, he embarked on a tour of Europe with his lifelong friend John Cam Hobhouse. They visited Portugal, Spain, Sardinia, Sicily, Malta, Albania, and Greece, which was then under Turkish rule, and later traveled to Ephesus and Constantinople. Athens in particular made a deep impression on Byron, and his two years of traveling gave him a cosmopolitan outlook which shaped his future life and attitudes. He always preferred the spontaneity and freedom of life in the Mediterranean lands to what he saw as the restraint and hypocrisy of English upper-class society. His travels also gave him a virtually inexhaustible supply of literary material. It was from his experiences on this first European tour that he wrote the first two cantos of *Childe Harold's Pilgrimage*, and it was the publication of this work in 1812 which first brought him widespread fame.

Life's Work

With the overwhelming success of *Childe Harold's Pilgrimage*, Byron became celebrated in the social circles of fashionable upper-class London. Women in particular were fascinated by the handsome, sensitive, and apparently melancholy poet of noble birth; his romantic wanderings in Greece made him mysteriously attractive. For his part, Byron was always ready to cultivate women friends and lovers. He could not, he said, exist without some object of attachment, and he always felt more at ease in the company of women. In particular, he became involved with the impulsive and unstable Lady Caroline Lamb, and for several months during 1812 they carried on an indiscreet, passionate, and tempestuous affair.

Byron's fame, popularity, and literary reputation continued to grow between the years of 1812 and 1815, following the publication of his "Oriental" verse tales: *The Giaour* (1813), *The Bride of Aby-*

dos (1813), *The Corsair* (1814), which sold an un-precedented ten thousand copies on the day of publication, and *Lara* (1814). Each of these romances contained the famous figure of the "Byronic hero," a restless and moody wanderer, an outcast from society, who possessed a lofty disdain for conventional values and for the common run of mankind.

Byron's personal life during this period remained tempestuous. In part to free himself from the now unwelcome and frequently absurd and vindictive attentions of Caroline Lamb, he entered into a marriage with Annabella Millbanke, an intelligent, serious-minded young woman who was in every way the opposite of Caroline. The marriage, however, proved short-lived and disastrous. Byron, worried by financial difficulties, drank heavily and went into wild rages. Annabella, pregnant with their child, could not cope with his erratic behavior and was also deeply shocked by her discovery of Byron's incestuous relationship with Augusta, his half sister. The brother and sister had been brought up separately but had spent time together during 1813, and Byron always felt at ease in Augusta's supportive and undemanding company. Annabella convinced herself that Byron was insane, and they separated in January, 1816, exactly one year after their marriage.

During 1816, Byron's fortunes in England began to decline. Rumors regarding the nature of his liaison with Augusta were widespread, and he found himself a social outcast. In April he left England, never to return. Traveling to Switzerland, he met in Geneva another poet in exile, the young Percy Bysshe Shelley. It was the beginning of a famous friendship. Shelley was accompanied by his future wife Mary Godwin and Claire Claremont, a young girl who had forced her attentions on Byron in London and who was now pregnant with Byron's child.

During his four-month stay in Geneva, Byron wrote more stanzas of *Childe Harold's Pilgrimage* as well as two of his most popular and accomplished works, the dramatic monologue *The Prisoner of Chillon* (1816), which was inspired by his own visit to the castle at Chillon, and the drama *Manfred* (1817), Byron's version of the Faust legend.

By October, 1816, Byron and his friend Hobhouse had moved on to Italy, visiting Milan and Rome (his impressions of which formed the core of the fourth canto of *Childe Harold's Pilgrimage*) and settling in Venice. Italy was to be Byron's home for seven years. Having sold Newstead Abbey, he was able to clear his debts and enjoy a com-fortable income, and his years in Italy were to be some of the most productive of his life. In the fall of 1817, he wrote the light satire *Beppo: A Venetian Story* (1818), which in form and tone served as a prelude to his masterpiece, the mock-heroic epic *Don Juan* (1819-1824, 1826), which he began in July, 1818. He was to continue working on it intermittently for the next five years; the *ottava rima* verse form which he adopted was ideally suited to the easy, colloquial style which came naturally to him and in which he was best able to express himself. The poem had a controversial impact in England. Byron's publisher called it "outrageously shocking," and many readers were offended by its bawdiness. During this period Byron also wrote a masterful satire directed toward his fellow poet Robert Southey, *The Vision of Judgment* (1822).

In Italy Byron continued to indulge his sensual and romantic nature, entering into numerous love affairs with local women. In particular, he formed a liaison with the nineteen-year-old Countess Teresa Guiccioli, who had recently married a man forty years her senior. Byron became her *cavalier servante*, or sanctioned lover. It was to be his last passionate affair.

Through his involvement with Teresa's nationalistic family, the Gambas, Byron became involved in the movement to free northern Italy from Austrian rule. He became a member of the Carboneria, a secret revolutionary society, and was regarded by the Austrian authorities as a dangerous subversive. When the Gambas were forced to move to Pisa in 1821, Byron went with them, where he was reunited with Shelley and his friends, and they were joined by the colorful adventurer Edward John Trelawny, and the writer Leigh Hunt and his family. The "Pisan circle" dissolved in 1822, when the Gambas were expelled from the state of Tuscany, and Shelley was drowned. Byron, still with Teresa, moved on to Genoa, his fourth and last residence in Italy.

Byron was becoming bored and dissatisfied with the directionless drift of his life and longed for active involvement in a great cause. By 1823 he had decided to travel once more to Greece, in order to aid the Greeks in their war of independence against the Turks. He made large amounts of money available to the Greeks, and on July 15, with his small group of friends and servants, he sailed to the island of Cephalonia, one of the Ionian islands under British protection. There he assessed the political situation, before sailing for Missolonghi on the Greek mainland in November,

where he was greeted enthusiastically by the local population. In Missolonghi he kept five hundred Albanian warriors under his pay, and he planned to lead an assault on the Turkish garrison at Lepanto. The planned action never materialized, however, and as the months passed, Byron felt increasingly depressed at the apparent failure of his mission. He had not succeeded in bringing together the quarreling Greek factions; he could not even trust his own soldiers; and his health, already weakened by years of excessive dieting, was deteriorating. On April 10, he contracted a fever, and he died nine days later. There was mourning throughout Greece for the loss of the English lord who had embraced their cause as his own, and the news of his death, according to the *London Magazine* in August, 1824, "came upon London like an earthquake."

Summary

Byron's name will forever be associated with the cause of Greek freedom. Not only his efforts in life but also the wave of feeling which swept through Greece at his death helped to galvanize and unite the Greek people. To this day, Byron is a national hero in Greece; almost every town has a street named for him, and his statue stands at Missolonghi.

His literary achievements are many. Johann Wolfgang von Goethe called him "the greatest genius of our century," and the Italian nationalist leader Giuseppe Mazzini truly said that Byron "led the genius of Britain on a pilgrimage throughout all Europe." Byron's work, and the myth surrounding his name, became a pervasive influence throughout nineteenth century European culture. He has never belonged to England alone, nor did he ever wish to belong solely to the country of his birth. *Childe Harold's Pilgrimage*, for example, was translated forty-one times and appeared in ten different languages in the nineteenth century. In France, novelist Honoré de Balzac, painter Eugène Delacroix, and composer Hector Berlioz were inspired by Byron's work. In Russia, novelist Fyodor Dostoevski, poet Alexander Pushkin, and composer Pyotr Ilich Tchaikovsky all felt Byron's spell. Throughout Europe, countless minor writers, now forgotten, took up Byronic attitudes and adopted Byronic themes. In his poetry and his life, Byron seemed to embody the restless and rebellious spirit of the Romantic age. The mysterious and aloof "Byronic hero," impatient of convention and scorning established authority, endorsed the kind of self-assertive individualism that the age found attractive.

Although in the late twentieth century Byron's standing as a poet is lower than that of fellow Romantic poets such as William Wordsworth, Shelley, and John Keats, *Don Juan* stands untouched as the most amusing long poem in the English language, and many of Byron's short lyrics stand comparison with the best.

Bibliography

Byron, George Gordon, Lord. *Byron*. Edited by Jerome J. McGann. Oxford and New York: Oxford University Press, 1986. The most comprehensive one-volume edition of Byron's poetry and prose. Includes complete text of *Childe Harold's Pilgrimage* and *Don Juan*, as well as other poems and plays, and also includes selections from Byron's incomparable letters.

———. *Byron's Letters and Journals*. Edited by Leslie A. Marchand, 12 vols. Cambridge, Mass.: Belknap Press of Harvard University Press, 1973-1982. Byron's letters were always witty, irreverent, and highly entertaining, written quickly and without inhibitions. They mirror his many-sided personality and the charm of his conversation.

Glass, Loren. "Blood and Affection: The Poetics of Incest in 'Manfred' and 'Parisina.'" *Studies in Romanticism* 34, no. 2 (Summer 1995). Discusses the relationship between incest and the poet's imagination in Byron's "Manfred" and "Parisina."

Jump, John D. *Byron*. London and Boston: Routledge, 1972. Intelligent and circumspect introduction to Byron's life and works. Emphasizes the social and historical context of his work and the cultural and intellectual tradition in which he stands.

Longford, Elizabeth. *The Life of Byron*. Boston: Little Brown, 1976; as *Byron*, London: Hutchinson, 1976. Concise, slightly romanticized, but factually accurate biography.

Marchand, Leslie A. *Byron: A Portrait*. New York: Knopf, 1970; London: Murray, 1971. The best one-volume biography, condensed from Marchand's own three-volume biography of Byron (1957). Well documented, judicious, and highly readable.

Parker, Derek. *Byron and His World*. London: Thames and Hudson, 1968; New York: Viking Press, 1969. Concise, attractively presented pictorial life, with illustrations of Byron, his associates, and the places associated with his name.

Quennell, Peter. *Byron in Italy.* London: Collins, and New York: Viking Press, 1941. Detailed study of Byron's career in Italy, from 1816 to 1823. Also attempts to give an account of the Romantic movement, as a cultural force which exercised a major influence on the nineteenth century.

Rutherford, Andrew, ed. *Lord Byron: The Critical Heritage.* London: Routledge, 1995. Critique and analysis of the works of Byron in essays by noted scholars.

Bryan Aubrey

FRANCES XAVIER CABRINI

Born: July 15, 1850; Sant' Angelo Lodigiano, Lombardy, Italy

Died: December 22, 1917; Chicago, Illinois

Areas of Achievement: Religion and social reform

Contribution: Founder of a religious community dedicated to helping the poor, Mother Cabrini contributed to missions among Italian immigrants to America, eventually establishing convents, schools, and charitable orphanages all over the world.

Early Life

Frances Xavier Cabrini was the last of thirteen children born of Augustino and Stella (Oldini) Cabrini. She was baptized Maria Francesca, at which time miraculous evidence of her piety was said to have appeared in the form of white doves which flitted about the house on that day. Her family was well-known for its dedication to the Roman Catholic church, and one of her uncles, Luigi Oldini, was a priest and foreign missionary. Luigi taught her games associated with missionary work which helped to mold young Frances into a surprisingly serious and pious young girl.

By the time Frances was twelve, she began taking an annual oath of virginity, which she declared permanent at the age of eighteen. She attended a private normal school under the direction of the Daughters of the Sacred Heart of Arluno, where her sister Rosa was preceptress. Frances graduated in 1870. In September of that same year, the united Kingdom of Italy was established after the Papal States capitulated and acknowledged the sovereignty of Savoyard forces. The birth of a united Italy resulted in a severe curb on the traditional authority of the Roman Catholic church over schools, hospitals, and charitable enterprises.

In 1872, Frances fell victim to a smallpox epidemic while caring for the sick. While she was still recovering, she began teaching at the school of Vidardo, where she found her ability to teach Christian doctrine firmly repressed by secularizing laws. Unsatisfied with her limited opportunities to serve the Catholic church in this role, she petitioned in 1874 to become one of the Daughters of the Sacred Heart. Her petition was denied on the basis of her fragile health, but her zeal was noted by Father Antonio Serrati, who appointed her to supervise an orphanage in Codogno.

Three years later, in 1877, Frances founded a new convent, called the Institute of the Missionary Sisters of the Sacred Heart. Her foundation grew rapidly; in 1888, her society received an official decree of commendation. Mother Frances Xavier, as she then became known, led the sisters in founding orphanages and schools all over Italy. Pope Leo XIII commended her work and called her "a woman of marvelous intuition and of great sanctity."

Life's Work

Mother Frances Cabrini also expressed a strong desire to begin a foreign mission, preferably in China. Pope Leo XIII instead decided to send her to the United States, an area which was becoming a great concern among Vatican leaders. More than one million Italian immigrants were flooding into the United States between 1880 and 1902. These new arrivals crowded into makeshift tenements located in teeming neighborhoods in large American cities. They worked long and grueling hours for pitiful wages under the control of Italian *padrones*, agents who organized labor gangs to work in exchange for paying for their passage across the Atlantic, and American sweatshop owners. Practically all of these Italian émigrés considered themselves to be Roman Catholics, but their religious practices, if they engaged in any at all, consisted of an informal jumbling of local traditions from back home and family superstitions that bore little resemblance to official Catholic teachings.

By the 1880's, the Vatican was beginning to take an intense interest in the plight of Italian Americans. With the support of Pope Leo XIII, Giovanni Battista Scalabrini began a concentrated endeavor to minister to the spiritual and physical needs of these uprooted people. A Scalabrinian mission was sent to New York. As part of this ministerial program, the Catholic church would encourage female religious orders to assist Italian American Communities by providing staff for local orphanages and schools.

Cabrini was sent to New York to fulfill plans for an Italian orphanage for girls proposed by Countess Mary Reid DiCesnola. The countess' proposal to fund a Catholic charity was common in a day when the intellectual and social elite were expected to engage in at least a token attempt to alleviate the suffering of the illiterate and unwashed masses. Consequently, the countess designed an orphanage to provide young girls with basic schooling as well

as training in fine needlework and fine laundry-work, all skills which would be useful to the countess' society friends, where the girls were expected to practice their crafts.

When Scalabrini and the pope suggested that Mother Cabrini go to New York, Cabrini was given the impression that her charitable work would be performed under the supervision of Archbishop Michael Corrigan of New York, and that preparations had already been made for the arrival of the sisters. Cabrini arrived in New York on March 31, 1889, only to find that her superiors in Italy had been gravely misinformed. No accommodations for the sisters had been secured; in fact, Corrigan had written to Cabrini shortly before her departure from Italy suggesting that she delay her journey, but the letter had arrived too late.

Corrigan greeted Cabrini coolly and suggested that the sisters return to Italy immediately. Cabrini stoutly refused. Corrigan finally agreed to allow the nuns to stay if they would establish an Italian school on the lower East Side of the city. He quickly came to loggerheads with the countess over this issue. The countess wanted the sisters to serve as inexpensive labor for her orphanage and suggested that they support themselves by seeking outside employment. In the end, the countess was forced to yield to the archbishop and turn control of the orphanage, along with all money previously collected, over to Mother Cabrini. The orphanage opened on April 21, 1889.

Growing tension between the countess and the archbishop convinced Mother Cabrini of the necessity of acquiring another site for the orphanage. By June, 1890, she had raised sufficient funds to purchase a Jesuit novitiate which became the new site of Sacred Heart Orphan Asylum and a novitiate for the Missionary Sisters of the Sacred Heart. Cabrini also became more closely involved in the projects begun by the Scalabrinian missionaries in New York, including a proposal to build an Italian hospital, for which Cabrini and her sisters solicited the funds. Columbus Hospital was incorporated on May 18, 1891.

Not content to rest on her laurels, the dynamic Mother Cabrini left her New York projects in he hands of other sisters and traveled to Nicaragua in September, 1891, where she founded a house and school. From there she opened a school for Italian children in New Orleans, where she remained until recalled to New York to settle a dispute between the Scalabrinian priests and her nuns.

She returned to New York in April of 1892, where she found the Columbus Hospital in dire financial straits. The leader of the Scalabrinian mission, the Reverend Felice Morelli, had pushed the mission deeply into debt by borrowing money at exorbitant interest to purchase buildings and land. Morelli was unable to pay the debt on the hospital, which was threatened with public auction to satisfy his creditors. In Mother Cabrini's absence, Morelli had attempted to shift the debt onto the shoulders of the sisters. Cabrini decided to disassociate her order from the original hospital and, with a grant of $550 from Archbishop Corrigan and some wealthy Italians, she opened a new Columbus Hospital in two rented apartments. The new hospital was expanded in 1894.

The work of the Missionary Sisters of the Sacred Heart continued to grow after Corrigan's death in 1902 to include more schools and orphanages. The sisters also visited hospitals and almshouses, tombs and prisons. Quietly but persistently, the small and frail Frances Cabrini cultivated the support of bishop after bishop throughout the United States and around the world. She founded orphanages and schools in Denver, Los Angeles, Chicago, Seattle, and Philadelphia, as well as in such far-off locations as Buenos Aires, Paris, Madrid, London, and Brazil. She also founded several modern charitable hospitals in New York, Chicago, and Seattle.

Following a brief illness, Mother Cabrini died on December 22, 1917, at Columbus Hospital in Chicago. At her death, she was mother-general to some four thousand nuns and had founded seventy charitable institutions the world over. Her funeral was officiated by Archbishop (later Cardinal) Mundelein and her remains were laid to rest in New York. Soon after her death, her associates, led by Cardinal Mundelein, promoted her cause before the pope and the archdioceses of New York and Chicago. She was beatified by the Roman Catholic church on November 13, 1938, after the rule which required fifty years to elapse before the beatification process could be initiated was waived for her case. She became the first American to achieve this honor.

Summary

Frances Xavier Cabrini brought increased unity to the Italian community in New York through her charitable efforts. Her highest goal in her mission work was to strengthen the ties between the Italian immigrants and the Roman Catholic church. Although she was often frustrated in her failure to wipe out "the worldly spirit" that she felt all around her, she contributed greatly to the growth of popular faith in the Italian community in New York City and in cities throughout the United States. Her worldwide missions also established charitable organizations to help those living in less affluent parts of the world.

Mother Cabrini achieved a worldwide reputation for her religious zeal, her diplomatic skill, and her talents as a businesswoman. She fought valiantly to create a role for Catholic women in foreign missionary work. When reminded by a male colleague that missionaries historically had always been men, Cabrini is said to have replied, "If the mission of announcing the Lord's resurrection to his apostles had been entrusted to Mary Magdalene, it would seem a very good thing to confide to other women an evangelizing mission." Contemporaries often referred to her as "a great man" or "a statesman" for want of a better term. Pope Pius XI considered her name "equal to a poem—a poem of activity, a poem of intelligence, a poem above all of wonderful charity." Through her zeal and her intrepid determination, Mother Cabrini helped to establish a vital role for Catholic women in the area of foreign missions and to increase their visibility within the Roman Catholic church.

Bibliography

Borden, Lucille Papin. *Francesca Cabrini: Without Staff or Scrip.* New York: Macmillan, 1945. An older biography meant for popular audiences, this work is extremely sympathetic to Cabrini and focuses primarily on her role as head of the Missionary Sisters of the Sacred Heart.

Di Donato, Pietro. *Immigrant Saint: The Life of Mother Cabrini.* New York: McGraw-Hill, 1960. This modern, scholarly biography of Cabrini gives the best background information on the period in which she lived. It uses archives of the Vatican, as well as materials from the Congregation of Propaganda Fide, which have been opened recently by Pope John Paul II.

DiGiovanni, Stephen Michael. "Mother Cabrini: Early Years in New York." *Catholic Historical Review* 77, no. 1 (January 1, 1991): 56-77. This is the most comprehensive account of the circumstances that led to Mother Cabrini's dispatch to New York and of her early work with the Italian population there. DiGiovanni sets Cabrini's work in the context of the political developments within the Roman Catholic leadership both in Rome and in New York in the 1880's.

Martindale, Cyril C. *Mother Francesca Saverio Cabrini, Foundress of the Missionary Sisters of the Sacred Heart.* London: Burns and Oates, and New York: Benziger, 1931. Based on biographical materials collected by the Institute of the Missionary Sisters of the Sacred Heart, this brief treatment of Mother Cabrini was compiled as part of the campaign by her colleagues and friends to convene a hearing for Cabrini's beatification.

Maynard, Theodore. *Too Small a World: The Life of Francesca Cabrini.* Milwaukee: Bruce, 1945; London: Guifford, 1947. An uncritical and simple biography, this book concentrates on Mother Cabrini's role as a worldwide ambassador for the Roman Catholic church. It is the best source for study of Cabrini's work outside the United States.

Kimberly K. Estep

CALAMITY JANE

Born: May 1, 1852 (?); Princeton, Missouri (?)
Died: August 1, 1903; Terry, South Dakota
Areas of Achievement: Exploration and military affairs
Contribution: Independent and determined to live as she chose in a man's world, Calamity Jane became famous, legendary, and exemplary of the almost mythical character of the American West.

Early Life

Calamity Jane was born, according to her seven-page autobiography, in Princeton, Missouri, and was christened Martha Cannary (or Canary). Despite her having written her life's story, having been photographed many times, and having had many witnesses to her activities, her early life, like her later life, is greatly lacking in valid documentation and is shrouded in tall tales and accounts of fictive deeds. There is no official evidence that she was born in Missouri instead of Illinois or Iowa, that "Jane" was either a middle name or an early nickname, or that 1852 was her birth year, and not, as some biographical accounts have claimed, 1847, 1848, or 1853. One biographer, Clarence Paine, cites an official census that places an Illinois-born M. J. Conarray—age sixteen and living with an Abigail Conarray—in Marion Township, Missouri, in 1860. If M. J. Conarray is M(artha) J(ane) Cannary, the birth date of Calamity Jane would have to be 1844. Her mother may have been Abigail Conarray or the Charlotte Canarry who was married to a young farm-bred idler named Bob. Also, her father may have been either a heavy drinker named John Cannary or a Baptist minister named B. W. Coombs. The written statements about her early life are so variable that one must consider her own statements, however ill-informed and exaggerated they may be, to be practicable.

In her autobiography, Calamity Jane claims to have had two brothers and three sisters. Again by her account, the family moved from Princeton, Missouri, to Virginia City, Montana, in 1865. She developed her skills as a horse rider and markswoman in her teens. Her mother, she writes, died in 1866, followed by her father in the following year, after having moved his family to Salt Lake City. From Utah, Calamity Jane and, presumably, her siblings, moved on to the Wyoming Territory.

The autobiography becomes demonstrably fanciful at this point. Flouting historical accuracy, the writer claims that she joined "General Custer as a scout at Fort Russell . . . in 1870, and started for Arizona for the Indian Campaign." Scholar Roberta Beed Sollid points out, however, that "Custer never was at Fort D. A. Russell" and that Custer "never in his lifetime set foot inside the bounds of Arizona, much less fought in the Indian campaigns there." Calamity Jane dates her donning the uniform of a soldier and getting "to be perfectly at home in men's clothes" to this period. During her year of activity in Arizona (1870-1871) at the age of nineteen, whatever the actual circumstances, Calamity Jane is seen to have perfected her skills with horses and firearms and to have matured.

Life's Work

Men's clothing was in accord with the masculine cast of Calamity Jane's physique and features. The photographs of her make this clear. Those that can be authenticated show her to be plain featured and stocky with a somewhat plump oval face, high cheekbones, and a long, prominent nose. Photographs of a trim, handsome, square-jawed younger woman, one in the buckskin trappings of an armed scout and one in full feminine finery, almost seem to be a different person but are generally accepted as the young Calamity Jane; at least they are consistent with verified photographs of Calamity Jane by the grave of James Butler "Wild Bill" Hickok and laid out in her coffin, in which her aged and gaunt face may recall a youthful angularity.

The striking photograph of the buckskin-clad female scout fits Calamity Jane's purported military activities in Wyoming from 1872 to 1876. This is the period during which, in her account, she was named Calamity Jane by a grateful Captain Egan, whom she, on horseback, had rescued from American Indians. There are numerous explanations of how she gained her epithetic name, most having to do with her being either the source or the carrier of calamity and many reflecting her hard-driving activities, coarse language, heavy drinking, rough attire, and constant gun wielding. The epithet is also associated with her devoted care of a little girl who was terminally ill with a contagious disease, against which contagions he took no preventive measures for herself. The most that can be said about her acquisition of the epithet with any approximation to historical accuracy is that it occurred during the very early 1870's and that it was well known by the time she had moved to Deadwood City, South Dakota.

In 1876 she became a friend of James Butler "Wild Bill" Hickok at Fort Laramie, Wyoming, and accompanied him to Deadwood City, South Dakota, in June of that year. It was here, Hickok's death within two months of their arrival notwithstanding, that the legends of Wild Bill Hickok and Calamity Jane took root, the former as gambler and gunfighter, the latter as a gun-carrying virago. The personal relationship of the two cannot be established beyond mutual regard and possible friendship. It is certain that they were never joined in wedlock, although this became part of the legend.

There were other marriages attributed to Calamity Jane. She is said to have married a railroad man named Steers in Rawlins, Wyoming, in 1874 and, in the following year, a Sergeant Frank Siechrist, whom she supposedly accompanied in disguise on an infantry escort for mineralogists who were to determine the extent of a gold find in the Black Hills of South Dakota. Sollid lists a total of twelve variously reported husbands, with three of whom Calamity Jane was supposed to have had one child each; with Clinton Burke, her husband of actual record and the only one she acknowledges in her autobiography, she is said to have had one daughter, as she herself claims, and possibly a second.

Her livelihood in Deadwood was gained chiefly by prostitution, although her claim, not without some basis, was that it was gained as a Pony Express rider "between Deadwood and Custer, a distance of fifty miles." Her distress when Wild Bill Hickok was shot in the back by Jack McCall in the Nuttall and Mann saloon on August 2, 1876, was very likely genuine, but not to the extent, as she claims, of her confronting McCall with a meat cleaver. McCall had, in fact, been arrested within an hour; a local court subsequently acquitted him, honoring the allegation that Hickok had murdered McCall's brother in Kansas and, as Duncan Aikman surmises, probably "relieved to be rid of the peril of Mr. Hickok's presence."

Continuing her involvement with construction crews and military units, Calamity Jane was active in South Dakota, Wyoming, and Montana after Hickok's death. In recounting her activities, she

embellished them, as was the custom of miners, soldiers, and gamblers, and she came, perhaps, to believe some of the tales herself, as they ultimately found their way into her autobiography.

History accommodates her, however, in recording her noble ministrations to the smallpox victims of Deadwood during the plague of 1878. Heedless of contagion and sincerely devoted to attending and comforting those stricken, Calamity Jane lived through her finest hour. Oddly, she makes no mention of it in her autobiography. Sollid cites three reliable commentators on this episode—Estelline Bennett (*Old Deadwood Days*, 1935), William Elsey Connelley (*Wild Bill and His Era*, 1933), and Lewis Crawford (*Rekindling Camp Fires*, 1926). Each attests her humanitarian efforts, although Connelley dates the plague a year late and Crawford says that this was when "the people gave her the name 'Calamity Jane.'" Sollid cites two other sources who wrongly date the christening of "Calamity Jane" to this year (1878).

During the years after 1877, Calamity Jane became the subject of Wild West data and fiction. Horatio N. Maguire's book *The Coming of Empire*

(1878) included an engraving of "Miss Martha Canary, the Female Scout." Pulp fiction, five-cent pocket library weeklies, and, later, dime novels were to follow as Calamity Jane became part of the colorful gallery that included Deadwood Dick, Wild Bill Hickok, Buffalo Bill, Belle Starr, Billy the Kid, and others. Her notoriety ranged from that of selfless nursing and charitable activism to prostitution, drunkenness, and imprisonment. That she did serve time in jail is documented: Cheyenne, Wyoming, in 1876; Miles City, Montana, in 1883; Rawlins, Wyoming, in 1885; Laramie, Wyoming, in 1890; and Livingston and Billings, Montana, in 1902 (the year before her death).

Capitalizing on her notoriety, Calamity Jane made public appearances on stage. She writes that her "first engagement began at the Palace Museum, Minneapolis, January 20, 1896, under Kohl and Middleton's management." She does not mention joining William Frederick Cody in his Buffalo Bill's Wild West show, although in various of her letters she claims to have been part of his exposition (this would be during the years 1893-1895). Her itinerary in 1896 is said to have extended to Chicago and New York. Her appearance in the Pan-American Exposition at Buffalo, New York, in 1901 was not a success, owing primarily to her alcoholism. Buffalo Bill Cody himself nurtured the legend that he paid her fare as far as Chicago when she returned to the Midwest.

Calamity Jane's health failed after the terminus of her show-business efforts. In the year of her death, she asked that she be buried next to Wild Bill Hickok. She died in Terry, South Dakota, and was interred about eight miles northeast of Deadwood in Mount Moriah Cemetery next to Hickok in accordance with her request.

Summary

There is evidence, varying in degree from slight to strong, that Calamity Jane was a markswoman, scout, soldier, Pony Express rider, prospector, layabout, prostitute, humanitarian, entertainer, author, and contributor in all of these contexts to the legends of the American Wild West.

Fictional accounts of her exploits have appeared in various printed narratives. Meanwhile, the factual biography of Calamity Jane is emerging in the scholarly research and writings of investigators such as Roberta Beed Sollid, Elizabeth Stevenson, and James D. McLaird. In film, Calamity Jane has been represented as an attractive, frequently glamorous heroine of the West, as played by Jean Arthur in *The Plainsman* (1936), Yvonne de Carlo in *Calamity Jane and Sam Bass* (1949), Doris Day in the musical *Calamity Jane* (1953), Jane Hamilton in the television movie *Calamity Jane* (1985), Anjelica Huston in the television miniseries *Buffalo Girls* (1994), and Ellen Barkin in *Wild Bill* (1995). Barkin's portrayal is closest to the Calamity Jane of fact and legend; dressed like the Calamity Jane photographed in the trappings of a scout, she achieves verisimilitude as a lean, attractive, coarse, sexually active, and capable virago.

Bibliography

Aikman, Duncan. *Calamity Jane and the Lady Wildcats*. New York: Holt, 1927. This is a standard, entertaining story of the life and attributed deeds of Calamity Jane. Her short autobiography is included in the appendix.

Lackmann, Ron. *Women of the Western Frontier in Fact, Fiction, and Film*. Jefferson, N.C.: McFarland, 1997. This volume includes a brief but informative biography of Calamity Jane with a summary of fictional works and films based upon her character and legend. Also included are eight very good photographs.

McLaird, James D. "Calamity Jane: The Life and the Legend." *South Dakota History* 24 (Spring 1994): 1-18. This scholarly investigation focuses on Calamity Jane's last year of life.

Mumey, Nolie. *Calamity Jane: 1852-1903*. Denver: Range Press, 1950. This collection of documents and photographs includes a facsimile of her autobiography, newspaper reports, and a diary falsely ascribed to Calamity Jane.

Robinson, Gillian. *The Slow Reign of Calamity Jane*. Kingston, Ontario: Quarry Press, 1994. This is a long, free-verse poem in which Calamity Jane recounts paying Jack McCall to kill Wild Bill Hickok, her marriage to Charlie [Burke], and her status as a "free woman."

Sollid, Roberta Beed. *Calamity Jane: A Study in Historical Criticism*. Helena: Montana Historical Society Press, 1951. Sollid's accurate, well-researched study prunes the excesses of the legend. The book includes the autobiography, excellent photographs (including one of Calamity Jane in her coffin), and a good bibliography (added by John Hakola).

Stevenson, Elizabeth. "Who Was Calamity Jane? A Speculation." In *Figures in a Western Land-*

scape: Men and Women of the Northern Rockies. Baltimore: Johns Hopkins University Press, 1994. Stevenson outlines a factual approach to the life of Calamity Jane based on rejection of the romanticized legend. The book incorporates authentic information from the private papers of William Lull.

Roy Arthur Swanson

JOHN C. CALHOUN

Born: March 18, 1782; Abbeville District, South
   Carolina
Died: March 31, 1850; Washington, D.C.
Areas of Achievement: Government and politics
Contribution: In addition to wielding great influence in national politics for four decades, Calhoun wrote incisively on the problem of protecting minority rights against majority rule in a democracy.

Early Life

John C. Calhoun was born on March 18, 1782. His birthplace was a settlement on the Savannah River in South Carolina, near the modern Abbeville. Of Scotch-Irish ancestry, Calhoun's forebears had made their way from Pennsylvania to Bath County, Virginia, then had been forced to migrate to South Carolina by the turmoil of the French and Indian War (1754-1760). The Up Country—as the western part of South Carolina is called—was a wild, untamed region, as evidenced by the murder of Calhoun's grandmother by marauding Cherokees in 1760. Calhoun's father, Patrick, was the youngest of four brothers who tenaciously carved out lives in the wilderness surrounding "Calhoun's Settlement." Patrick's first wife having died, he married Martha Caldwell, with whom he produced a daughter and four sons; the next-to-youngest child was named John Caldwell, after one of Martha's brothers.

Calhoun spent his youth on the family farm working in the fields with his father's slaves. Patrick's death in 1796 left John with a future seemingly bound by the needs of the farm and responsibilities to his family. Yet upon the urging of an older brother, he enrolled in Yale College in 1802 and was graduated with honors in 1804.

After Yale, Calhoun studied law at Tapping Reeve's Litchfield (Connecticut) Academy. During the two-year regimen at Litchfield, he developed habits in logic and discipline that would be his trademark in later years. Yet he also discovered that the prospect of being an attorney bored him. A stint in Henry De Saussure's Charleston law office and, shortly thereafter, his opening a successful practice of his own near Abbeville did not enliven his interest. He soon left the profession to become a prosperous planter and to follow his consuming interest in politics.

This career change was made possible by his marriage, in 1811, to his second cousin, Floride Bonneau Calhoun. The marriage brought Calhoun property which, when added to his, allowed him financial independence. Although Floride was ten years his junior, they were quite happy, and the marriage produced nine children. Calhoun would eventually establish residence at a plantation he built near his birthplace. He named it "Fort Hill" because the site once had been a garrison against Indian attack.

By the time of his marriage, Calhoun had developed those traits that would distinguish him for the remainder of his life. Physically imposing, standing over six feet tall, lanky, and with a rather hawk-like face, he was craggily handsome. As the years wore away at him, ceaseless labor and care combined with checkered health to render the stern countenance fixed in the minds of students by the photograph taken by Matthew Brady around 1848. In it, Calhoun, nearing sixty, sits with a face that is lined, hollow, and unsmiling, yet lit by an arresting and wild stare. Perhaps this face was merely a mirror of his lifelong personality. Even as a boy, he was overly serious, and he seems to have always conducted relationships outside his family with the same cold logic he applied to his political theories. Anything but outgoing, Calhoun commanded respect but seldom inspired affection. Associates sometimes referred to him as the "cast iron man," describing a man who, while not unfriendly, nevertheless remained ever aloof and hence, on a personal level, essentially alone and friendless.

Life's Work

Calhoun entered state politics in 1807 and, after one term in the South Carolina legislature, won election to the United States House of Representatives in 1810. There he joined the ranks of the War Hawks, that group of influential congressmen (Speaker of the House Henry Clay was the most conspicuous of their number) who were intent upon war with Great Britain to protect American maritime rights.

During the War of 1812, Calhoun steadfastly supported all measures to bolster the nation's failing defenses. When the Treaty of Ghent ended the war in 1814, he remained convinced that it was only a truce before the renewal of the conflict. Beginning in 1816, he urged the adoption of a national program to prepare for another wave of British aggression. He supported a protective tariff, a national bank, an improved transportation system through federally financed internal improvements, and a large standing army. His nationalism won for him both praise and a place in James Monroe's cabinet as secretary of war in 1817. Seeking to correct the many flaws made apparent by the poor showing of American forces in the recent war with Britain, Calhoun initiated numerous improvements for the army. These included the establishment of new departments, especially those of commissary, quartermaster, and surgeon general. Well suited to the administrative demands of the War Department, he filled the post during Monroe's two terms with a flair for innovative management.

Calhoun adroitly remained aloof from the angry political turmoil that marked the end of the Era of Good Feelings and the beginning of the formation of a new national party system. Elected to the vice presidency in 1824 and 1828, he thus served in the administrations of both John Quincy Adams and Andrew Jackson, despite the bitter feud between the two. At the end of the 1820's, it appeared that he would succeed Andrew Jackson as president with Jackson's blessing, but the nullification controversy in South Carolina irrevocably estranged them and nearly ruined Calhoun's political career.

In spite of his earlier advocacy of the protective tariff, he became convinced that steadily increasing its duties financially victimized Southern agriculturalists for the benefit of Northern industrialists. When he wrote "South Carolina Exposition and Protest" in 1828, which stated his theory of Nullification, it marked a significant turning point in his political career. Because he still hoped to attain the presidency, he kept secret his authorship of the doctrine. By turns, however, he was rapidly transformed from an American nationalist into a Southern sectionalist. Elaborating upon Thomas Jefferson's ideas in the Kentucky Resolutions of 1798, Calhoun declared that a state could nullify a federal law it deemed unconstitutional or harmful to its interests by refusing to enforce the statute within its borders. Essentially then, Nullification was a device whereby a minority could protect itself against the harmful will of the majority.

When South Carolina attempted to apply his theory by nullifying the Tariff of 1832, it brought the nation to the brink of civil war. Dismissing Nullification as illegal, Jackson threatened to invade South Carolina to enforce federal law, and when it was revealed that Calhoun was the doctrine's father, Jackson branded him a subversive. In disgrace with the Administration, Calhoun resigned the vice presidency, his national reputation in shambles. Yet the governor of South Carolina promptly appointed him to the Senate, and there he worked feverishly with Henry Clay to draft a compromise tariff that helped to diminish the immediate crisis.

After the Nullification controversy, Calhoun dropped all vestiges of his earlier nationalism and became the champion of Southern planter interests in particular and Southern rights in general. In the process, he earned the admiration of many Southerners, and in South Carolina he came to exert virtually total control over a political system which only occasionally was not a reflection of his will. His towering reputation and talent made him a fixture in the Senate, wherein he increasingly focused his intellectual and political energies on combatting what he perceived as Northern assaults upon the Southern way of life. Even his brief absence from the Senate—to serve as John Tyler's secretary of state from 1844 to 1845—was marked by his sectionalism: He successfully managed the annexation of Texas into the Union as a slave state.

As a strident antislavery movement grew in the North, Calhoun countered that slavery was a positive good. He opposed the Mexican War (which most of his Southern colleagues supported) because he feared that Northerners would try to exclude slavery from Western territories gained in the conflict. When his fears proved true, he was ultimately persuaded that Northern restriction of slavery in the territories was a preliminary step toward the thorough abolition of the institution in the South as well. The result, he thought, would be economic and social chaos, avoidable only by the South's secession from the Union.

His apprehension over both abolitionism and secession compelled him in his final months to attempt the unification of the South into an implacable front threatening secession. By so menacing the Union he hoped to frighten the North into concessions on the slavery question. Therein lay the safety of the South and the Union as well. His plan was unsuccessful, and as the nation reeled ominously toward disruption under the compounded sectional crises of 1850, he appeared before the Senate on March 4, 1850, almost for the last time. So ill that a colleague had to read his speech, Calhoun sat glowering from his chair as the chamber

and crowded galleries heard his dire prediction that Northern agitation over the slavery issue would inevitably destroy the Union. His warning, unhappily prophetic, went unheeded. As the nation strained toward yet another compromise, his shattered health forced him to his deathbed. He died on March 31, 1850, in his Washington quarters. His last words were "The South . . . the poor South."

Summary

John C. Calhoun ranks as one of the most innovative political theorists in American history. Beginning with his complex arguments to justify Nullification, he ever afterward sought legal and logical means whereby to protect minority rights against the overriding and insensible will of the majority. His fears over the diminishing influence of the South in national councils drove him, in 1843, to begin drafting proposals for significant innovations in American constitutional government. The notion of the concurrent majority became central to his thesis in both *A Disquisition on Government* (1851) and *A Discourse on the Constitution of the United States* (1851).

In these works, Calhoun declared that the nation was composed of not only sections and states but also communities, each of these last possessing a unique character and interests different from the rest. The problem lay in the fact that any one community might be significantly smaller in relation to the others. The great danger in a democracy thoroughly wedded to majority rule, he insisted, was that a combination of larger communities could unjustly impose its will on any such minority through sheer force of numbers, ignoring the rights and privileges of the injured community. The resulting tyranny of the majority would be the very antithesis of the American ideal of government.

In order to avoid this result, he proposed that each unique community, regardless of its size, be given an equal voice in matters affecting the whole nation. A majority obtained under this arrangement would not reflect merely numerical strength, but would assure a general concurrence from all sectors of the society. In short, a concurrent majority would protect the rights of any minority. To reinforce the method further, he proposed instituting a dual presidency, one executive from each major section, each to have a veto on national measures.

Neither *A Discourse on the Constitution of the United States* nor *A Disquisition on Government* was completed when he died—indeed, his involvement in the sectional controversy of 1850 and his labors on these manuscripts combined to destroy his health—but they were published posthumously in 1851. They were lauded at the time by many Southerners and scorned by many Northerners. Calhoun's theories were complicated and made more so by the occasionally obscure prose of the former work. The latter work was often simply misunderstood. As the nation stumbled toward the disruption he had predicted, and after it had suffered the terrible Civil War, he was dismissed as both an ugly prophet of secession and a major cause of the catastrophe that followed.

Undoubtedly, before the Civil War he influenced in some degree the thinking of virtually every Southerner and, it might be argued, a significant number of Northerners. Yet subsequent scholarship has been unable to reach a consensus about Calhoun and the real meaning of the theories he produced. Cited as a major contributor to the outbreak of the Civil War, he also has been praised for tirelessly searching for ways to avoid it. Branded as little more than a sophisticated opportunist, always seeking his own advancement, he also has been eulogized as a careful statesman, aloof from the ordinary concerns of office and election. Labeled a stultifying obstructionist of the majority will, he also has been hailed as an innovative protector of minority rights.

In spite of the diversity of interpretation, one certainty emerges. For all of his imagination and mental agility, Calhoun never escaped the boundaries of his time and place. He bent his considerable talents to protecting and even extending the institution of slavery, a mockery of the ideals of liberty and, even in his time, disgraced by the considered judgment of mankind. Possessed of boundless vision, he yet remained blind to the fundamental evil of slavery and thus was at once a great man and a tragic figure.

Bibliography

Bartlett, Irving H. *John C. Calhoun: A Biography.* New York: Norton, 1993. Comprehensive account of Calhoun, his tenure as vice president under two administrations, his time in the House and Senate, and the value that a study of his philosophy has in the contemporary world.

Calhoun, John C. *The Papers of John C. Calhoun.* Edited by Frank M. Meriwether, Edwin W. Hemphill, and Clyde N. Wilson. 16 vols. Columbia: University of South Carolina Press, 1959-1985. An ambitious project consisting of Calhoun's papers from 1801 to 1843, with skillful editorial comment integrated throughout.

Capers, Gerald M. *John C. Calhoun, Opportunist: A Reappraisal.* Gainesville: University of Florida Press, 1960. A revisionist biography which argues that self-interest was the primary motive for all of Calhoun's actions. Marred by a polemical tone, but valuable as a counterweight to uncritical biographers.

Coit, Margaret L. *John C. Calhoun: An American Portrait.* Boston: Houghton Mifflin, and London: Eyre and Spottiswoode, 1950. Pulitzer Prize-winning biography that offers an extraordinarily favorable view of its subject. Coit lauds the agrarian ideal and praises Calhoun as its defender who resisted the evils of an industrial society. The most humanized depiction of Calhoun, but frequently overly sympathetic.

———, ed. *John C. Calhoun.* Englewood Cliffs, N.J.: Prentice-Hall, 1970. A brief compilation consisting of selections from Calhoun's writings, contemporary observations about him, and scholarly interpretations regarding his political theories. A good introductory survey of the diversity of modern scholarly opinion concerning those theories.

Freehling, William. *Prelude to Civil War: The Nullification Controversy in South Carolina, 1816-1836.* New York: Harper, 1966. An excellent work on the great crisis that marked Calhoun's shift from nationalism to sectionalism. Includes a good description of his reluctant participation in the event and provides a penetrating analysis of the real significance of Nullification.

Hamilton, Holman. *Prologue to Conflict: The Crisis and Compromise of 1850.* Lexington: University of Kentucky Press, 1964. An indispensable study of the complex problems afflicting the nation at the time of Calhoun's death. His significant part in the drama is competently portrayed and explained.

Lindsey, David. *Andrew Jackson and John C. Calhoun.* Woodbury, N.Y.: Barron's Educational Series, 1973. Dual biography of these major figures that is surprisingly thorough, given its brevity. Offers a good introduction to Jackson and Calhoun and is marked by measured judgments supported by broad research.

Safford, John L. "John C. Calhoun, Lani Guinier, and Minority Rights." *Political Science and Politics* 28, no. 2 (June 1995). The author argues that the concept of minority veto originated with Calhoun's political philosophy and compares Calhoun's views with those of political scientist Vakan Kuic.

Spain, August O. *The Political Theory of John C. Calhoun.* New York: Bookman, 1951. A learned and well-researched exposition of the origin, development, and maturation of Calhoun's theories on government, but flawed by Spain's defense of Calhoun's racial attitudes.

Wiltse, Charles M. *John C. Calhoun, Nationalist, 1782-1828.* Indianapolis: Bobbs-Merrill, 1944.

———. *John C. Calhoun, Nullifier, 1829-1839.* Indianapolis: Bobbs-Merrill Co., 1949.

———. *John C. Calhoun, Sectionalist, 1839-1850.* Indianapolis: Bobbs-Merrill, 1951. Grounded in decades of research and loaded with a wealth of detail, these three works (this and the two previous entries) comprise an almost definitive biography. Especially good in placing Calhoun in perspective with the social, economic, and political forces of the early nineteenth century, but somewhat imbalanced by an overly sympathetic view of Calhoun and his ideas while hypercritical of his adversaries.

David S. Heidler

JEAN-JACQUES-RÉGIS DE CAMBACÉRÈS

Born: October 18, 1753; Montpellier, France
Died: March 8, 1824; Paris, France
Areas of Achievement: Law and government
Contribution: Cambacérès served France as a skilled jurist, an able legislator, and a prudent administrator during the revolutionary period. As second consul to Napoleon I, he effected a new civil code, controlled the media, and served as a moderating influence on the emperor. Without personal political ambitions, he dedicated himself to maintaining Napoleon's power and to serving his country.

Early Life

Jean-Jacques-Régis de Cambacérès was born in Montpellier, France, on October 18, 1753, one of eleven children of Jean-Antoine and Marie-Rose (née Vassal) Cambacérès. The Cambacérès family was a distinguished one, long active in politics. Cambacérès' father served as Mayor of Montpellier, and Cambacérès was destined for a career in law. He attended the Collège d'Aix, rather than the one at Montpellier, which was judged not good enough for the young Cambacérès. A bright and diligent scholar, he excelled and developed a reputation for exactitude and a painstaking devotion to detail—these traits were to stand him in good stead later when he was helping to draft the civil code for France.

By 1769, he was practicing law in Montpellier, where he later (in 1774) became councillor of the local fiscal court (*Cour des comptes et des aides*). In 1771, he renounced his estate, a political move in keeping with the tenor of the times; Cambacérès was adept at gauging political barometers. His father had suffered some financial reverses, and Cambacérès had attempted to restore the family's financial position. He was ultimately to become a very rich man through his services to Napoleon. Because of his growing legal reputation, he was elected in 1789 president of the criminal tribunal at Hérault, and when the states-general were convened that year he was chosen as the nobility's second representative for the Montpellier district. When Montpellier was judged to be entitled to only one representative from the nobility, he returned from Paris. That political setback did not daunt Cambacérès, who in 1790 helped found the Société des Amis de la Constitution et de l'Égalité at Montpellier.

Because of his political activity and legal reputation, he was elected in 1792 to the National Convention. A political moderate, he attempted to steer a middle course and avoid the impending excesses of the leftists, but the trial of King Louis XVI eventually forced him to take a stand, qualified as it was. After losing the fight to have the convention judged not competent to try the king, he did find the king guilty, but he recommended that the king's execution be effected only if France were invaded.

Cambacérès' "moderation" was politically dangerous, and he attempted to divert suspicion by absorbing himself in legislative and judicial matters. He submitted in 1793 a plan, containing 695 articles, for a civil code, but though the code reflected the politics of the times, it was not revolutionary enough for the convention; a shorter version, with only 297 articles, was rejected as well. When the convention became more moderate, after Robespierre's downfall in 1794, Cambacérès emerged as one of its leaders, serving as president of the convention and later as president of the Committee for Public Safety. In that role, he helped conclude the peace treaties of 1795 with Prussia and Spain. He also called for a general amnesty and attempted to prevent vindictive behavior and new persecutions. When the convention was dissolved, he became a member of the Council of Five Hundred, but the Directory which came to power regarded his moderation with suspicion. His third draft of the civil code was also rejected, and he retired from his position as president of the Council and returned to practicing law.

Life's Work

Cambacérès returned to the government, serving as minister of justice, in June, 1799, just prior to the *coup d'état* of the Eighteenth Brumaire, which overthrew the Directory and established the consulate. Although he took no active part in the revolution, Cambacérès played a typically discreet role in assisting Napoleon and Emmanuel Sieyès with the coup. In recognition of his help and of his acknowledged legal prowess, Napoleon, who was named first consul in December, 1799, named Cambacérès second consul. (Charles François Lebrun, a sixty-year-old Norman with financial experience and more conservative views than Cambacérès, was named third consul.)

Although as second consul he was theoretically second in command to Napoleon, Cambacérès had no political ambitions of his own and directed his considerable abilities and energies to furthering Napoleon's interests. Cambacérès succeeded, through negotiating with selected ministers and reducing the size of the legislative body and the Tribunate, in reducing the number of influential opponents of Napoleon and engineered the assemblies' 1802 election of Napoleon as consul for life. Cambacérès' strategy effectively brought an end to representative government in France, and Napoleon was free to enact the long-desired civil code and to become emperor only two years later. Napoleon's ascension resulted in a promotion for the loyal Cambacérès, who became arch-chancellor of the empire, presiding in the emperor's frequent absence over the senate.

Although Napoleon held all the real power, Cambacérès was the emperor's trusted adviser and confidant, a bureaucrat who worked diligently to help Napoleon retain control of France. As his voluminous papers indicate, Cambacérès was in constant communication with Napoleon, even when the emperor was on one of his numerous military campaigns. One of Cambacérès' primary functions was to serve as an unofficial minister of propaganda for Napoleon, who recognized the value of the press. Cambacérès not only reviewed political articles and decided the fates of individual generals but also inserted articles in selected journals. He also was involved in ordering that books be written on selected topics, and in 1806 he printed the fictitious *Ms. trouvé dans le cabinet du roi de Prusse à Berlin*, a book about the partition of Poland. Though he was primarily concerned with domestic affairs, he did oversee the publication and distribution of maps of battles and campaigns. Even the discussions of the Council of State were edited by Cambacérès before they were subsequently printed in the *Moniteur*, the government's journal. This control was extended in 1811, when a special decree gave Cambacérès control over the telegraph linking Paris to major European cities—he effectively determined what messages would be transmitted.

In addition to managing the news, Cambacérès was active in the elaborate patronage system Napoleon and he devised in order to create a new supportive nobility to replace the old nobility. Since titles were not attached to land or to family but were granted by the state for service, people were encouraged to serve the state and to remain loyal to the new empire.

Cambacérès served not only as Napoleon's second in command but also as his personal legal adviser, though Napoleon's personal affairs certainly impinged upon his public political life. When the emperor wanted his marriage to Joséphine nullified, Cambacérès handled the intricate and delicate negotiations.

During his Napoleonic years, Cambacérès exercised considerable power over the media, the government, and the legal system, which he helped create. He also served as a moderating influence on Napoleon. Yet his most important attempted interventions—to save the life of the Duc d'Enghien and to forestall the military campaigns of 1812-1813—were futile.

When Napoleon abdicated and the Bourbons were restored to power in 1814, Cambacérès survived and even endorsed the return of the monarchy, the current stabilizing force in France. When Napoleon returned to power the following year, Cambacérès was persuaded to resume his pre-Restoration duties, this time to direct the Ministry of Justice and preside over the Chamber of Peers, though he had undoubtedly had reservations about the likelihood of Napoleon's continued success. The Hundred Days did, indeed, end with Napoleon's defeat at Waterloo; upon Louis XVIII's final restoration to power, however, Cambacérès was not as fortunate as he had been before. He was exiled and moved to Belgium. Although he was permitted in 1818 to return to France and to regain his civil and political rights, he did not again hold public office. Six years later he died in Paris.

Summary

As the titular head of the French government during Napoleon's frequent, extensive absences, Jean-Jacques-Régis de Cambacérès theoretically had a considerable amount of power. In fact, some historians have maintained that he governed France while Napoleon was away. As his own voluminous correspondence to the emperor indicates, Cambacérès was essentially an adviser and the administrator of Napoleon's policies, though he certainly had a hand in drafting key legislation and in coordinating and supervising the various codes that were implemented during Napoleon's reign.

Because Napoleon would not or could not delegate authority, the power to decide significant events was his alone; yet that centralized authority caused delays in dealing with governmental affairs and produced administrators unwilling to take the initiative and assume responsibility. Napoleon's grand schemes, including the reform of the codes, required implementation by an administrator who could handle detail, however trivial. Cambacérès, the legal technician, was the consummate lawyer, equally at home in administrative, legal, and financial matters. He also discharged some military tasks for Napoleon. Though he did not serve on the commission Napoleon appointed in 1800 to prepare a new draft of the civil code, Cambacérès' previous three drafts and his ideas found their way into the civil code adopted in 1804.

Cambacérès was a political survivor, an administrator, and a legislator who steered a middle course between extremes in the hope of serving in a stable, efficient French government. His moderation, his vacillation, and his desire to please all parties have made him as suspect to contemporary historians as he was to his political colleagues on the far Left. During his political career he was a Republican, an anti-Terrorist, a regicide, a Jacobin, an enthusiast, and a sometime supporter of Napoleon and the Bourbons—in short, whatever was expedient and consonant with his advocacy of a stable government.

Given his aversion to political chaos and corruption, which were rampant from 1795 to 1799, his support of Napoleon seems almost inevitable. He seems to have been attracted by Napoleon's authoritarianism and expediency and his desire to effect needed change. Although Cambacérès may have been more inclined to authoritarianism than Napoleon, his actions were as moderate as his views, and while he counseled Napoleon, he seems not to have urged his views with any vigor. Richard Boulind, who has studied Cambacérès' ties to Napoleon, sees Cambacérès' homosexuality as the key to their productive working relationship. In a classic case of alter egos, Cambacérès, possessed with "feminine" tact, reflectiveness, and precaution, balances and is attracted to the "masculine" Napoleon, who is assertive and decisive. Regardless of how this working relationship is seen, there is no question about Cambacérès' having been the ideal statesman to complement Napoleon and his dreams for France.

Bibliography

Bergeron, Louis. *France Under Napoleon*. Princeton, N.J.: Princeton University Press, 1981. Part of Bergeron's book concerns the patronage system instituted under Napoleon's rule. Bergeron explains the system, examines Cambacérès' role, and shows how the system benefited both the recipients and Napoleon. Details of Cambacérès' social and financial ascent are provided.

Boulind, Richard. *Cambacérès and the Bonapartes*. New York: Kraus, 1976. Boulind includes the unpublished papers of Cambacérès, both letters to Napoleon and papers on the personal and dynastic interests of Napoleon. The introductions to both parts provide the most extensive discussion in English of Cambacérès. Boulind provides a brief biography and a psychological reading of the relationship between Cambacérès and Napoleon.

Cronin, Vincent. *Napoleon Bonaparte: An Intimate Biography*. New York: Morrow, 1972. As the title suggests, Cronin's book mingles history with anecdotes and personal details. He is helpful in providing a comparison and contrast between Napoleon and Cambacérès and in detailing the degree to which Cambacérès advanced Napoleon's cause.

Holtman, Robert B. *Napoleonic Propaganda*. Baton Rouge: Louisiana State University Press, 1950. Holtman examines the means by which Napoleon and Cambacérès managed the news during Napoleon's rule. According to Holtman, Cambacérès was the primary agent of control—news releases, the telegraph, fabricated books, and the like.

Marquart, Robert. "The Fortunes of Cambacérès." *Revue de l'Institut Napoléon* 127 (1973): 43-52. Marquart provides a thorough discussion of Cambacérès' acquisition of an immense fortune through prudent management and imperial generosity. Marquart's findings attest to the social and financial rise of a class that replaced the old nobility.

Thompson, J. M. *Napoleon Bonaparte: His Rise and Fall*. Oxford; Blackwell, and New York: Oxford University Press, 1952. Thompson's book is particularly helpful in its discussion of Cambacérès' role in obtaining Napoleon's canonical divorce from Joséphine. Thompson details Cambacérès' painstaking preparation of the case and sees the divorce as evidence of the deterioration of Napoleon's character under stress.

Thomas L. Erskine

ALEXANDER CAMPBELL

Born: September 12, 1788; Balleymena, County Antrim, Ireland

Died: March 4, 1866; Bethany, West Virginia

Areas of Achievement: Religion and theology

Contribution: Campbell became a leader in a movement that attempted to restore the original structure of the Christian church of the first century, helping spawn both the Disciples of Christ and the Churches of Christ in the process.

Early Life

The son of Thomas Campbell and Jane Corneigle Campbell, Alexander Campbell grew up in Ireland in a highly religious household that emphasized study of the Bible. When he was young, Campbell preferred the outdoors to academics and spiritual reflection but eventually developed a phenomenal memory and overcame his loathing of study. Around age sixteen, Campbell accepted the teaching of Christianity and began to fulfill his father's and his own dream of becoming a preacher. He read moral philosophy and church history. Although a Presbyterian, Campbell was especially impressed by the ideas of independent ministers such as John Walker and James Alexander Haldane, who suggested that creeds and denominational structures were made by humans.

These early encounters, augmented by his own reading of scripture and history, led Campbell to believe that the existing arrangement of Christian churches into various denominations was contrary to divine teaching and was the source of disunity. If the biblical principles of church membership, worship, and organization alone were the basis for church polity and practice, then a genuine unity among Christian people would be possible.

During this time, Thomas emigrated to the United States and eventually invited the rest of his large family to join him there. Circumstances permitted Campbell to attend the University of Glasgow for one year before moving to Pennsylvania in 1809. At Glasgow, Campbell was formally exposed to a set of assumptions called Scottish Common Sense Realism, according to which the human mind possessed the capacity to interpret right from wrong and could, therefore, determine which religious doctrines were true and which were false. Further, this approach to knowledge was inductive, so that one ascertained the great principles from religion by examining specific

moral, ethical, and scriptural issues before drawing any general conclusions.

After joining his father in the United States, Campbell helped establish the Christian Association of Washington in 1809. The association was actually an independent church whose principles were articulated in a document called the Declaration and Address. Its purpose was to spread the Campbells' ideas about Christian Union and approaches to studying the Bible. The Campbells' creed and mode of divining appropriate Christian practices was "where the scriptures speak, we speak; where they are silent, we are silent." They hoped that these ideas would spread and that the divisive denominational labels of other Christian faiths would disappear and cause churches to restore the original organization and practice of Christianity of the first century, as depicted in the New Testament book of Acts. Campbell devoted the remainder of his long life to the realization of this cause.

Life's Work

Campbell's physical traits made him suitable to confront the labyrinth of Christian ideas in the moral landscape of the antebellum United States. He was tall, perhaps six feet, with powerful shoulders that he had developed by doing farm labor as a youth. He moved with vigor and grace. His face was of fair complexion and somewhat irregular in shape. A long, thin nose gave it some symmetry, but it was his cheerful expression that gave it order. He possessed remarkable powers of concentration, great personal discipline, and skill as a speaker.

Campbell began to proclaim his ideas as a travelling preacher in 1810. He began to preach regularly at the Brush Run Church in Pennsylvania, which was organized along Campbell's principles. During this period, he became convinced that full immersion was the only appropriate mode of baptism, and he and his new wife, Margaret Brown, were baptized in 1811. He later came to conclude that baptism was not merely an ordinance or a symbol but actually part of the process of salvation and that immersion of the body was necessary for the remission of one's sins. This moved Campbell quite far from his Presbyterian roots and from the beliefs of many American Protestants and Catholics.

Campbell established the Buffalo Seminary at Bethany, Virginia (now in West Virginia), in 1818 to train young ministers and spread his own reli-

gious ideas. Students from the surrounding countryside boarded with Campbell, and he instructed them in the morning and evening, leaving much of the day free for farming, from which Campbell drew his living. He operated the seminary for several years.

In addition to teaching and preaching, Campbell spread his ideas in a series of well-attended debates with a variety of people. In the nineteenth century, debates were a form of outdoor theater that extended for hours in front of an always raucous and sometimes attentive audience. In 1820, he debated John Walker, a Presbyterian, on the subject of baptism. Campbell held that in New Testament times infants were not baptized, that immersion was the only mode for baptism, and that baptism was necessary for the forgiveness of sins.

In 1823, Campbell debated W. L. McCalla in Washington, Kentucky, again on the subject of baptism. Like many of the public exchanges and discourses of the nineteenth century, this one was eventually published. Campbell explained that salvation came through faith but baptism was a formal and necessary part of the process of faith. In 1829,

Campbell debated Robert Dale Owen, a Utopian Socialist who had recently established a model community in Indiana. Owen was a skeptic who asserted that religion was a fruit of human ignorance. Campbell held forth for what he believed was the truth of religion as revealed in the Bible. At the conclusion of the debate, which about twelve hundred people attended, Campbell asked for all those who favored the spread of Christianity to move to one side. All but three in the audience did so. This debate elevated Campbell's standing from that of an obscure frontier preacher to that of a well-known controversialist.

In 1837, Campbell debated Bishop John B. Purcell. The real issues of debate pitted Catholicism against American Protestantism, which was itself doctrinally divided. Unlike his other debates, Campbell did not emerge a clear winner, but both he and Purcell conducted themselves with equanimity so that the stature of both men was elevated in the public eye. In 1843, Campbell debated N. L. Rice, a Presbyterian. Henry Clay, an imminent politician, moderated the debate. Campbell and Rice argued about baptism, the Holy Spirit, and religious creeds, with Campbell holding that the scriptures plainly described and defined these terms. He believed that by looking at them in context, one could inductively arrive at the truth.

Campbell also busied himself for over forty years as an editor. In 1823, he founded the *Christian Baptist*, a religious periodical through which he attacked ideas and practices in American Christianity that he found contrary to scripture. In 1830, he ended the *Christian Baptist* and began a periodical called the *Millennial Harbinger*. Like many Americans, Campbell was fascinated with the idea of the Second Coming of Christ. Soon, however, the publication became the major medium for spreading Campbell's ideas about the Bible, baptism, and church organization. Campbell's list of subscribers for his publications was so large that the town of Bethany was given a post office and Campbell was made postmaster.

Although Campbell, like most ministers, typically eschewed formal involvement in politics and public issues, he did allow himself to be elected to serve as a delegate to the Constitutional Convention in Virginia in 1829-1830. The major issue confronting the convention involved political apportionment and whether all people—including slaves—should be counted while determining legislative districts. If slaves were included, the Tidewater region of Virginia would continue to have significantly greater political clout. Campbell and other upcountry constituents preferred to only count white people.

In the course of his service, Campbell debated John Randolph of Roanoke, Virginia, on the practical effects and morality of slavery. Campbell believed that slavery not only impoverished the slaves but also elevated the planter above the mass of laboring white people. Although he, like many white Christians, believed that the Bible did not condemn slavery per se, he believed that it specifically condemned many of the abuses of power and people perpetrated by white slave owners. Therefore, he worked for laws providing for the emancipation of slavery and spoke out against the abuses in the practice of the system. Although not an abolitionist in the manner of William Lloyd Garrison, he was increasingly antislavery in his opinions.

Ironically, however, Campbell's greatest achievement ran counter to his stated goal of effecting Christian unity. He, in the end, helped to found a sect called the Disciples of Christ. Initially a Presbyterian, Campbell broke with that denomination because he did not believe in infant baptism but in the immersion of those old enough to respond to the teachings of Jesus as contained in the New Testament. He then affiliated with the Baptists, but they did not find his emphasis on baptism for the remission of sins acceptable. Thus, he founded a loose association of like-minded people that he preferred to call the Disciples of Christ. Their goal was not to become a denomination—although that is what eventually happened—but to work with other groups of other people who also hoped to reform American Christianity and improve American society by restoring the fundamentals of New Testament doctrine and practice. Some of these people used the term "Christians" to describe themselves, and the Christians and the Disciples of Christ worked closely together, especially in the upper Ohio River Valley.

The Restoration Movement—nineteenth century efforts to effect Christian unity by adhering to the primitive teachings of the Christians of the first century—did not achieve its goal. Campbell's Disciples of Christ became just another denomination, which itself fractured over issues raised by the American Civil War and questions of biblical interpretation. Many southern and literalist members

termed themselves Churches of Christ, while more northern and less legalist brethren adhered to the name Disciples of Christ.

Campbell continued his labors to win adherents to his ideas and create a basis for Christian unity. In 1840, he established Bethany College in Bethany, which has been in continuous operation since that time. He traveled throughout the eastern half of the United States raising money for its endowment. His excursions even took him to Canada, France, and Great Britain. He also taught courses at the college in inductive biblical interpretation and moral philosophy.

In 1865, Campbell's health broke. He was bedridden for a time, after which he slowly regained the energy to continue his ministerial labors. He recovered enough in December, 1865, to deliver what is commonly called his "last discourse," which was based upon a fresh reading of Ephesians I. However, he caught a cold and was bedridden again through early 1866. He died on March 4 of that year.

Summary

Despite his failure to effect Christian unity, Campbell nonetheless played a major role in the vigorous religious climate of antebellum America, which has been described as a "spiritual hothouse." His views on scriptural interpretation blended well with the democratic ethos prominent in the United States. By virtue of possessing a human brain, one could ferret out truth in both the Constitution and the Bible. Moreover, the Disciples of Christ continued to function more than one century after he founded the denomination.

Bibliography

Garrett, Leroy. *The Stone-Campbell Movement.* Joplin, Mo.: College Press, 1981. This is the most accessible history of the restoration movement and appraises Campbell's role in it.

Hughes, Richard T., ed. *The American Quest for the Primitive Church.* Urbana: University of Illinois Press, 1988. An excellent anthology of secular historical scholarship that places Campbell's restoration movement in historical context.

Richardson, Robert. *Memoirs of Alexander Campbell . . .* 2 vols. Phildelphia: Lippincott, 1868-1870. The basic source of Campbell's life by a longtime ministerial associate. Includes some of Campbell's own writings.

Seale, James M., ed. *Lectures in Honor of the Alexander Campbell Bicentennial, 1788-1988.* Nashville, Tenn.: Disciples of Christ Historical Society, 1988. Contains scholarly appraisals of Campbell's life and work and their meaning for subsequent U.S. history.

West, Earl Irvin. *The Search for the Ancient Order.* 3 vols. Nashville, Tenn.: Gospel Advocate Company, 1974. This larger work looks at the successes and failures of Campbell's attempt to forge a truly national Christian unity movement.

E. R. Crowther

GEORGE CANNING

Born: April 11, 1770; London, England

Died: August 8, 1827; Chiswick, England

Area of Achievement: Government

Contribution: By placing British power behind the national independence movements in Latin America and Greece, Canning helped further Great Britain's own economic and political interests and weakened the forces of reaction in Europe.

Early Life

George Canning was born April 11, 1770, in London, England. His father, who had the same name, came from an English family that had taken a manor in Londonderry, Ireland. The family had disinherited the elder George Canning, however, because of his misadventures, including his marriage to Mary Annie Costello, a beautiful but impoverished woman. The castoff son died on the first birthday of the younger George Canning. The widowed mother, desperate for a living, took up acting, a career then especially disdained by the more genteel. She married an actor named Reddish, who had a very unsavory reputation. Stratford Canning, a London banker and brother of the deceased father, ended the family's isolation from the outcast son's offspring. He took the young George Canning, then eight years old, into his home and provided for his education. The boy's grandfather provided him with an estate worth two hundred pounds annually.

At Eton and Oxford, Canning's knack for composition, prose, oratory, and witty expression soon became apparent. Along with other Etonians, he published the *Microcosm*, a journal that gave him an opportunity to develop further the witty style that he would later use to lampoon his political opponents. Canning would always be remembered as an acid-tongued rhetorician whose clever phrases could devastate an enemy. His opponents have so maligned his character that it is difficult to form a proper estimate of the man, but it is certainly true that self-effacing humility was not one of his virtues. Very early in his career he displayed overweening ambition and arrogance. His obsession with seizing power so offended his contemporaries that sometimes his career would go into temporary eclipse. Yet his rhetorical abilities were so impressive and his self-confidence so strong, that even with a legion of enemies he could not permanently be denied leadership. Canning had an abundance of energy and a capacity for hard work. Despite his flair for seeking the limelight, he was capable of spending long hours at work in government positions which brought him little attention or glamour. He also had a reputation for being a master of political intrigue. Portraits of Canning reveal a rather round face, a balding head with curly locks at each side, and eyes that suggest intensity and confidence.

In 1791, after completing three years at Christ Church, Oxford, Canning entered Lincoln Inn to begin the study of law. Politics quickly attracted the young scholar, and leading Whigs, such as Charles James Fox, saw in the oratorical skills of Canning a shining new star for the party. Canning's early dislike for the aristocracy and his initial inclination toward French revolutionary ideas drew him toward the Whigs at first. His Whig tendencies subsided quickly, however, as the revolution became a movement aiming to spread its excesses beyond France to the rest of the Continent. On the other hand, perhaps his perception that prospects for a rapid rise to political power were more favorable with the Tories motivated his decision to switch to that party. In 1793, it was as a Tory and a staunch supporter of Prime Minister William Pitt that Canning entered the House of Commons for Newton, Isle of Wight. His marriage to the wealthy Joan Scott on July 8, 1800, would give Canning the independence and financial security to pursue his political career without distraction. The marriage also produced four children.

Life's Work

Pitt gave Canning the post of undersecretary of foreign affairs in 1796, and he served until 1799. During this time, he contributed to the *Anti-Jacobin*, a weekly journal dedicated to ridiculing English and French revolutionaries. From 1799 to 1800, Canning served as a member of the board of commissioners governing India. In 1800, he began a brief term as paymaster of the forces but left that office the next year, when Pitt resigned as prime minister. Canning spent the next few years as a member of the opposition, but in 1804, when Pitt returned to power, Canning became treasurer of the navy.

Canning did not receive a cabinet position until 1807, a year after Pitt died, when he received the important post of foreign secretary under the administration of the Duke of Portland. Canning displayed an ability to act with decision in his new office. Aware of a secret French plan to seize the Danish navy, Canning dispatched a force of twenty-seven ships of the line to attack Copenhagen and seize the Danish navy. British sailors manned the captured Danish warships and sailed them back to England. Canning's decisiveness weakened the French effort, but since Copenhagen had not willingly surrendered its forces, Canning endured the abuse of foreign powers as well as the condemnation of the opposition party in England. A dispute with Viscount Castlereagh, Secretary of War, produced even more suspicion of Canning. The foreign secretary had approved of the peninsular campaign against French power in Spain, but he disagreed with Castlereagh's manner of conducting the operation. Canning had no patience with those he considered inferior to himself, and he was restless in his quest for command. He tried without success to persuade the Duke of Portland, the prime minister, to remove Castlereagh. Finally, Canning gave up his purge effort and resigned on September 9, 1809. Shortly afterward, the secretary of war learned of Canning's plot against him and challenged him to a duel. Canning suffered a slight injury to his thigh.

During the years from 1809 to 1822, Canning held no major office but continued to serve as a Member of Parliament. Beginning in 1812, he represented Liverpool. In 1814, he became the ambassador to Portugal and two years later became a member of the board of control for India. Canning gave up his position in the government in 1820 because of his disapproval of the treatment of Queen Caroline, whose husband, George IV, had just become monarch. Caroline had been living in Europe for many years, and the new monarch tried to prevent her return to England or her recognition as queen. Failing this, George tried unsuccessfully to win his freedom in a divorce trial before the House of Lords. To protest his government's support of King George IV in the dispute, Canning resigned in December, 1820.

From 1822 to 1827, Canning finally achieved the pinnacle of power he had so long sought. He was nominated Governor-General of India on March 27, 1822, but resigned this post before embarking for India. Castlereagh's suicide opened the path to be foreign secretary. Despite the king's hesitation, he approved Canning for both the secretaryship and the leadership of the House of Commons. Canning would be at the helm for the next five years.

The new foreign secretary continued and extended Castlereagh's policy of using England's influence to weaken the reactionary forces of the four major monarchies in Europe: Austria, Russia, France, and Spain. Since the Congress of Vienna (1815), these powers had concerted their efforts to repress liberal, constitutional, republican, and nationalistic movements in Europe. They had attained a measure of success under the leadership of Austrian prince Klemens von Metternich. In 1823, French forces entered Spain to shore up the rule of Ferdinand VII against revolutionary challengers. The fear that France, with the encouragement of other reactionary countries, might undertake the restoration of the recently independent Latin American republics to a colonial status under Spain spurred Canning to propose to President James Monroe that the United States join England in supporting the independent republics. Canning's suggestion intrigued Secretary of State John Quincy Adams, who encouraged the president to state unilaterally a policy that has come to be known as the Monroe Doctrine. Adams thought it would be unseemly for the United States to appear to be a cockboat following in the wake of the British man-of-war. The United States warned Europe to surrender any aspirations for recolonizing Latin America. It was George Canning who proposed the warning, however, and it was the power of the British navy that would enforce the prohibition. Great Britain hoped to protect its recently gained trading privileges with the former Spanish colonies. Thus, in 1825, Canning took the further step of granting recognition to the independent republics.

In the last years of his secretaryship, Canning put England's diplomatic power behind the Greek struggle for independence from Turkey. He also helped the Portuguese repel a threatened Spanish takeover (1826-1827). On February 17, 1827, Lord Liverpool's sudden paralysis removed him from office, and Canning became prime minister. Sir Robert Peel and other leading ministers resigned because of their disagreement with Canning's Roman Catholic policies. Canning supported removal of Catholic civil disabilities. The difficulty of forming a government without his former allies and the strain of keeping his beleaguered government in control took a heavy physical toll, and Canning died on August 8, 1827, having served less than half a year as prime minister.

Summary

George Canning's famous remark, "I called the New World into existence to redress the balance of the Old," summarizes his most important achievement in foreign affairs. The position taken by England nullified in advance any dreams of reinstituting European monarchical control over Latin America. The defeat of the "Holy Alliance," a term used to describe the joint efforts to repress nationalistic efforts, can in part be attributed to Canning. No longer could Austria, Russia, Spain, and France hope by means of "congresses" to squelch revolutionary tendencies.

Canning's support of national movements in Europe itself was also significant. No other individual outside Greece had more to do with Greek independence. Canning was not carried away with romantic mysticism in his support for Greece against Turkey; he said that he would not go into battle for "Aristides or Saint Paul." Nevertheless, public opinion in Great Britain strongly supported the Greek struggle for independence from the Turkish empire, and the death of Lord Byron in his attempt to aid the cause did stir the imagination of the English public. Canning's concern was more political. He did not wish to see Russia impose its own solution. Czar Alexander proposed establishing three separate partially independent Greek states. Supposedly, the Greeks would still have a tie to the Turkish empire, but the situation would provide Russia a chance to exert influence in the new states. Canning's negotiations with the Russians led to the Treaty of London of July, 1827. Russia, France, and England then undertook to make Greece autonomous, with only nominal control by Turkey. The three allies promised to take military action to force Turkish troops out of Greece. Canning did not live to see the Battle of Navarino in October of 1827, but his policies prepared the way for the destruction of Egyptian and Turkish naval forces at Navarino and the consummation of the Greek struggle for independence.

Bibliography

Bagot, Josceline. *George Canning and His Friends*. 2 vols. London: Murray, and New York: Dutton, 1909. Contains many letters not available to earlier biographers. Many of the letters display Canning's distinctive wit. Included are not only letters to and from Canning but also references to him in the letters of third parties.

Edgecombe, Rodney Stenning. " 'Little Dorrit' and Canning's 'New Morality.' " *Modern Philology* 95, no. 4 (May 1998). Proposes that Canning's 1797 attack on the opponents of William Pitt the Younger influenced Charles Dickens' "Little Dorrit."

Hinde, Wendy. *George Canning*. London: Collins, 1973; New York: St. Martin's Press, 1974. A well-written, scholarly account that ably blends the political and the personal life. Hinde views Canning as a victim of his own arrogance and stubbornness, a man whose own actions kept him in the twilight for long periods yet who was one of the ablest and most brilliant political leaders of his time.

Lee, Stephen M. " 'A new language in Politicks': George Canning and the Idea of Opposition, 1801-1807." *The Journal of the Historical Association* 83, no. 271 (July 1998). A study of the arguments used by Canning in justification of his opposition to Henry Addington's ministry in Great Britain.

Marshall, Dorothy. *The Rise of George Canning*. London and New York: Longman, 1938. A carefully researched study of Canning's early career. It is concerned primarily with the formation of his character and views and does not cover the last decades of his life, when he held power.

Rolo, P. J. V. *George Canning*. London: Macmillan, 1965. Rolo's book contains three parts. In the first section, Rolo deals with the man himself. He believes that personality played an especially significant role in Canning's career. In the second section, Rolo provides a consecutive account of Canning's political record. In the third, he evaluates Canning as a statesman. He concludes that the man was not exceptional in dealing with domestic matters but argues that he ranks with Otto von Bismarck in his brilliant handling of foreign policy.

Stapleton, Augustus Grenville. *Political Life of Canning, 1822-1827*. 3 vols. London: Longman, 1831. The author was Canning's private secretary and wrote in part to clear the man's memory from "aspersions" of his enemies. Despite bias and lack of access to documents as yet unavailable, it is an important work.

Temperley, Harold. *The Foreign Policy of Canning, 1822-1827*. London: Bell, 1925. A very carefully researched and laudatory study of Canning's record as foreign secretary from 1822 to 1827, written by one of the early biographers of Canning. This book places Canning's later years in the context of European diplomacy.

Richard L. Niswonger

ANTONIO CANOVA

Born: November 1, 1757; Possagno, near Venice
Died: October 13, 1822; Venice
Area of Achievement: Art
Contribution: Canova fixed the ideal style in neoclassical sculpture for generations. His works were considered the standard of international artistic excellence in his day and his name and opinion held great authority.

Early Life

Antonio Canova was born on November 1, 1757, in Possagno, to Angela and Pietro Canova. In 1761, at age twenty-six, Pietro, a stonemason, died. In 1762, Angela remarried and moved to a village west of Possagno, leaving young Antonio in the care of Pasino Canova, his paternal grandfather, who was also a stonemason. In 1768, Antonio was apprenticed to Giuseppe Bernardi, known as Torretti, in nearby Pagnano. He received his first formal lessons in this active studio which manufactured garden sculpture. There, Canova would have absorbed proficiency in handling stone, in efficient delegation to specialized assistants of the various mechanical steps in the production process, and in the administration of the technical and financial aspects of a studio.

In autumn of 1768, Torretti took the young Canova to his other studio in Venice. For the first time Canova was able to study Greco-Roman sculpture in private Venetian collections. He also studied the collections of plaster casts in the palace of Filippo Farsetti and frequented the academy. In 1770, Senator Giovanni Falier, who had shown an interest in Canova's work, commissioned two baskets of fruit in stone and two life-size figures.

Encouraged, Canova left Torretti's studio and in 1775 established his own studio in the cloister of Santo Stefano in Venice. At this time he won second place in a competition organized by the Venice Academy. Having achieved a reputation for portraiture, he carved the naturalistic life-size marble *Daedalus and Icarus* (1779), his first truly original work, for the procurator Pietro Vittor Pisani. Exhibited at the annual Venetian art fair of the Ascension, it was a great public and financial success. With this money Canova left for Rome October 9, 1779.

On November 4, 1779, via Bologna and Florence, Canova arrived in Rome. He was received by the Venetian ambassador Girolamo Zulian, who provided him with a studio in the embassy palace. There he was able to study private and public collections and the sculpture of Roman churches. The young Canova also benefitted from his acquaintance with the most advanced artists and critics of the age.

Life's Work

In the winter of 1780, Canova visited Naples, where he saw great collections of antiquities. Back in Rome, he exhibited a plaster cast of his *Daedalus and Icarus* to the influential artist and archaeologist Gavin Hamilton, who recognized his talent. Hamilton advised Canova on the direction his style should take and was instrumental in turning him from the Baroque to the revolutionary neoclassical style first propagated by the German archaeologist and historian Johann Joachim Winckelmann. The young sculptor became determined to study antique style thoroughly.

Winckelmann's aesthetic revolution carried an enormous moral charge. He condemned the excesses of the Baroque as not only offensive to sensibility but also injurious to rationality, man's highest faculty. He favored the pure Greek art with its noble simplicity and calm grandeur over the corrupt Roman art.

In 1781, Ambassador Zulian commissioned the marble *Theseus and the Minotaur*. This gave Canova the chance of proving himself in the new style. He accepted the advice of men he had grown to respect, restrained his natural inclination toward liveliness, and altered his style in accordance with the new doctrine of tranquil grandeur.

In 1783, the Venetian Giovanni Volpato, to whose daughter Canova had been briefly engaged, attained for Canova the commission for the monumental *Tomb of Pope Clement XIV* (1783-1787). Here he purifies the Baroque elements represented by such funerary monuments as Gianlorenzo Bernini's *Tomb of Pope Urban VIII* by replacing Bernini's lavish allegorical approach with figures in noble, body-clinging draperies, their restraint and pose reinforcing the clean severity of the entire composition. The figures do not interact but appear to be juxtaposed, an arrangement which heightens the quiet solemnity. At the unveiling of this piece in 1787, Canova's international reputation was established. The immediate, enormous success made him the most celebrated sculptor of his time.

Canova's work on the tomb of Clement XIV was so intense that, as a result of his constant running

of the drill which had to be pressed against the stone with his chest, he suffered severe deformation of the ribs. This injury was connected to the cause of his death. Canova's output would vary between two stylistic extremes: powerful, life-size monuments and intimate figures of an erotic nature. Works such as the tender *Cupid and Psyche* (1787-1793) were calculated to give greatest satisfaction when contemplated in a private manner.

Canova's sculpture combined the purity of white marble and the simplicity of antique forms with the softness of execution. His mature works were so successful because the references to the ancients were always clear. Their sensuality was often heightened by the working of the marble and by the definite sense of line and silhouette. Except for a few works, Canova's productions are of a translucent delicacy.

Canova's human figures display his knowledge of formalized anatomy. He did not try to portray the body realistically. Part of the appeal of such pieces as *Hebe* (1796) is the intricate, undulating lines which abstract the forms, aided by the unnatural whiteness of the marble, and thus negate realism. Canova's movement toward abstraction was evident by the ease with which his works translated into outline engraving without losing total effect.

With the rise of Napoleon I, circumstances in France changed for sculpture. Neoclassicism, because it assumed a political position of patriotism and social progress, was the ideal style for propagandizing the very meaning of the Empire. Canova's popularity generated commissions from Napoleon and his family. In most of these pieces he sought to depict the dynasty as successors to their imagined imperial Roman ancestors.

The period from 1800 to 1814 was extremely productive for Canova. Two of his greatest masterpieces, *Pauline Borghese as Venus Victorious* (1804-1808) and the *Tomb of Archduchess Maria Christina* (1805-1809), were produced during this period. The tomb deliberately detaches itself from the church, focuses the viewer's attention exclusively on itself, and remains stoically silent about the possible meaning or resolution of death. It is strangely lacking in both instruction and celebration. The participants do not face the observers; they simply participate in the endless procession to the grave. The portrait of Pauline Borghese is an ideal image where the elements of classicism, technical virtuosity, and a submerged sensuality are joined in a subtly evocative whole. This cool yet voluptuous figure shows the wide range of sexuality which Canova's outline style can express. With these two works, Canova reached the peak of his career; unlike most artists he managed to stay there for the rest of his life.

In his later life, Canova traveled extensively between Venice, Rome, Vienna, Paris, and London. His reputation for neutrality, for his dedication to basic ethical causes as well as his reputation as an artist, made Canova the ideal papal agent at the Congress of Paris in 1815. The Papal States won back most of their vast artistic treasures through Canova's shrewd diplomatic tactics. From Paris he traveled to London, where he saw the Elgin marbles. There he quickly realized that most of the works on which he had based his style had been Roman copies, and he identified the copies as affected, exaggerated, and conventional. His advanced age, however, prevented any further change in his artistic direction.

Very little is known about Canova's intimate life. Although he experienced enduring hurt over his father's early death and his mother's abandonment, there appeared to be a detachment from conventional personal affections or passions. Yet throughout his life Canova was a modest, kind, and generous man, especially to young and struggling artists and to his half brother, who seemed not to deserve his generosity. In 1820, the first sharp symptoms of his fatal illness appeared and undermined his strength as he continued to work. Scarcely able to eat, suffering from severe abdominal pain, he died on October 13, 1822. He was buried in the new Tempio, the church which he built for Possagno, his native town.

Summary

Antonio Canova's achievement was to remain the ideal exemplar for academic sculptors throughout most of the nineteenth century. He worked in enough genres to provide a variety of imitable forms. His superficially simple antique style was pure and graceful without overemphatic voluptuousness. It was repeated all over Europe and America but with an intensification of hardness and dryness which became too evident in the studio repetitions and other copies of his art.

Canova was the one man who actually made sculpture in accordance with Winckelmann's theories. The lack of high-quality sculpture in the classical manner after Canova's death resulted from following those theories which deadened more talents than they inspired since imitation soon became mechanical. Eventually it was the entire neoclassical style within which Canova worked, with all of its moral and political overtones, that was completely rejected.

Because of the highly polished purity of Canova's marble forms and their intentional connections with the masterpieces of antiquity, he has received negative criticism from modern critics who favored the sketch over the finished work and who condemned imitation as the enemy of spontaneity. Late nineteenth century criticism condemned his sensuality and his idealization of nature. The twentieth century turned against him for precisely opposite reasons: He was considered too blandly realistic and too lacking in sensual fervor.

During Canova's lifetime and well after his death, however, his excellence was not questioned. The success of his style entailed its spread in the form of originals, copies by assistants, and engravings which he himself commissioned.

The greatest following of Canova's style was in France. His own style was partly formed from French ideas as a result of his friendship with the antiquarian Quatremère de Quincy. Their exchange of letters over many years enlightened Canova with a program of classical aesthetics. The Frenchman made subject suggestions and gave encouragement and approval. Canova even tried tinting some of his statues according to ancient practice as suggested by Quatremère's researches.

Canova was highly influential among such contemporary French artists as the sculptors Antoine Chaudet and Joseph Chinard and the painters Anne-Louis Girodet, François Gérard, Pierre Guérin, and J. A. D. Ingres. These painters were inspired by his delicately linear representations of the nude. Many of Girodet's works adapt Canova's figures to paint. Ingres' *Bather of Valpinçon* (1808) was influenced by Canova's *Venus Italica* (1804-1812).

Canova's popularity in England is evidenced by the large number of his works in English collections. The sculptor and draftsman John Flaxman, who obtained at least one commission from Canova, was strongly influenced by his style.

Canova's significance, in part a result of his diplomatic activities, passed beyond the boundaries of the art world and made him a figure accessible to a broad public. With the exception of Peter Paul Rubens, no other artist had ever been able to ingratiate himself and his art to so many European courts during his lifetime.

Bibliography

Boime, Albert. *Art in an Age of Revolution, 1750-1800.* Vol. 1, *A Social History of Modern Art.* Chicago: University of Chicago Press, 1987. A brief treatment of Canova's career and the significant political implications of his art in the light of events at the end of the eighteenth century.

Clark, Anthony M. *The Age of Canova.* Providence: Rhode Island School of Design, 1957. An appreciative evaluation of Canova's work in this brief catalog for the exposition of his work held in the Museum of Rhode Island School of Design, fall 1957.

Honour, Hugh. *Canova's Theseus and the Minotaur.* London: Victoria and Albert Museum, 1969. An excellent, in-depth, and scholarly essay explaining the complete evolution of this, the first neoclassical piece of sculpture by the artist. Bibliography, detailed notes, black-and-white reproductions.

Honour, Hugh, et al. *The Age of Neoclassicism.* London: Arts Council of Great Britain, 1972. A comprehensive catalog for the fourteenth exhibition of the Council of Europe housed in the Royal Academy and Victoria and Albert Museum, fall 1972. Includes eleven essays on seminal aspects of neoclassical culture, ideas, and specific art forms; bibliographical outline for each artist; historical sketch of each artwork; plates.

Johns, Christopher M. S. "Portrait Mythology: Antonio Canova's Portraits of the Bonapartes." *Eighteenth-Century Studies* 28, no. 1 (Fall 1994). Discusses Canova's portrait treatment of the Bonaparte's in the early 1800s and its departure from the traditional politically undercurrents in Rococo style.

Licht, Fred. *Canova.* Photographs by David Finn. New York: Abbeville Press, 1983. This elaborate and handsome volume, the only major recent work in English, presents Canova's sculpture by means of photographic and textual interpretation. More than three hundred color and black-and-white photographs sensitively convey both the grandeur and delicacy of Canova's sculpture. Contains detailed analyses on individual works. Epilogue, notes, chronology, and an excellent bibliography.

Pavanello, Giuseppe, and Giandomenico Romanelli, eds. *Antonio Canova.* Venice: Marsilio, 1992. Stunning volume published to coincide with a 1992 exhibit of Canova's work in Venice. Includes excellent photography and essays by several scholars on the subject.

Praz, Mario. *On Neoclassicism*. Translated by Angus Davidson. London: Thames and Hudson, and Chicago: Northwestern University Press, 1969. Chapter 6 is an analytical review of the predominantly adverse criticism accompanied by a reassessment of Canova's art within the larger context of the aesthetics of neoclassicism.

John A. Calabrese

DON CARLOS

Born: March 29, 1788; Aranjuez, Spain

Died: March 10, 1855; Trieste, Austrian Empire (now Italy)

Areas of Achievement: Government and politics; and military affairs

Contribution: Don Carlos was the first of the Carlist claimants to the throne of Spain. His life was dedicated to disputing the right of his niece, Doña Isabel, to Spain's throne and upholding the principles, laws, and institutions of the Old Regime.

Early Life

Carlos María Isidro de Borbón was the second surviving son of Charles IV and Louisa María Isidro, king and queen of Spain. In 1808, with the help of French troops, Don Carlos' older brother became Ferdinand VII, king of Spain. Later that year, however, the royal family was ordered to Bayonne where Don Carlos, his brother, and his uncle, Don Antonio, were held captive and conducted to Valençay in central France, where they lived under house arrest until 1814. Ferdinand was persuaded to abdicate the throne in favor of Napoleon's brother, Joseph Bonaparte; however, Don Carlos, who was supposed to succeed his brother to the throne if the latter left no male heirs, refused to renounce his right to the throne, saying that he would rather be dead than betray his obligation to the Spanish people.

After his return to Spain in 1814, Don Carlos lived as a prince in Madrid. In September, 1816, he married Princess María Francesca de Asís de Braganza, daughter of King John VI of Portugal and sister of the wife (Queen Isabel) of Ferdinand VII. A loving brother and a loyal subject of Ferdinand VII, Don Carlos was rewarded with a few formal offices but with no substantial role in government. In June, 1814, Ferdinand VII made him a colonel of the Carabineros Reales, Spain's royal cavalry corps, and two months later named him captain general and commander in chief of the army. Ferdinand VII also allowed him to preside over the Council of State and the Council of War.

Don Carlos was always known for his devout Catholicism and unswerving belief in a traditional Spain in which the monarch governed absolutely. In 1820, when soldiers supposed to go to America rioted in favor of reinstating the liberal constitution of 1812, Don Carlos, as head of the Council of State, declared that it was necessary to oppose their demand with all possible force. Nevertheless, a revolutionary government during the Liberal Triennium (1820-1823) expelled the royal family from Madrid and made them go to Seville, where they were deprived of their rights and accused of treason. The royal family was then garrisoned in Cádiz, only to be rescued by French intervention, which put down the revolution in 1823. Once the royal family was free, the royalists deliberately set out to destroy the liberals. The most extreme royalists were the *apostólicos* (Apostolics), who believed in the infallible righteousness of the Catholic Church and the legitimacy of a monarchy that would represent its interest. When Ferdinand VII, under international pressure, refused to sanction the worst excesses in the persecution of liberals, the royalists began to look to Don Carlos as their true leader.

Life's Work

If Don Carlos had been inclined to lead an insurrection against Ferdinand VII, the *apostólicos* would have risen against the king. Don Carlos refused to betray his brother, but his Portuguese wife and her older sister, María Teresa, the princess of Beira, had fewer scruples and actively intrigued with the *apostólicos*. In March, 1833, the princess of Beira, who happened to be in Madrid for the wedding of her son, Don Sebastian, was advised to leave for Portugal, and Don Carlos and his wife were authorized to accompany her. In April, the king asked Don Carlos, still in Portugal, to swear allegiance to his daughter Isabel, who had been born on October 10, 1830. In his letter of reply, Don Carlos refused to give up his claim to the throne unless Ferdinand would also bear a son.

Legal complexities exacerbated the disagreement over the right to succession. In 1789, the Cortes (Spain's parliament) had approved the Pragmatic Sanction on the right to succession. Charles IV, not wishing to promulgate the new law, published a revised Spanish legal code in 1805 in which the 1789 law was not mentioned but the semi-Salic law of Philip V, dating back to 1713, was. The older law stated that succession to the throne was to consist of male children of the king and his male descendants; females could reign in their own right only when no such males existed. Each brother had solid arguments in his favor. Ferdinand VII could argue that the 1789 law only

needed promulgation and that the right of female succession had been in force in Spain for centuries before 1713. Don Carlos could counter that the Pragmatic Sanction had lapsed during the long interval between its approval by the Cortes and its promulgation on March 29, 1830; moreover, Don Carlos was born in 1788 and thus could argue that the 1789 law, even if valid, did not apply to him.

The death of Ferdinand VII on September 29, 1833, unleashed the forces behind the First Carlist War, or the Seven Years' War (1833-1840). The queen regent, María Cristina of Bourbon-Two Sicilies, indicated that she would favor the liberals if they supported her daughter's claim to the throne. She also ordered Don Carlos to Italy, but he refused to leave the Iberian Peninsula and tried to slip back into Spain, where his supporters were uprising and proclaiming him Carlos V. Failing to cross the heavily patrolled border, he helped Dom Miguel, a pretender to the Portuguese throne, who promised to reciprocate later in Spain.

The dynastic quarrels and the struggle between absolutism and liberalism in the Iberian Peninsula could not fail to arouse the interest of the rest of Europe. The old Holy Alliance of Russia, Prussia, and Austria was sympathetic to Don Carlos but held back material assistance. On the other hand, the government of Isabel received the support of the Quadruple Alliance (England, France, Portugal, Spain), which was formed on April 22, 1834, to support liberal constitutional government in Western Europe by driving Don Carlos and Dom Miguel out of the Iberian Peninsula. Dom Miguel had to renounce his claim to the Portuguese throne and was expelled to Genoa. On June 1, 1834, Don Carlos was allowed to leave for England, where he refused to renounce his rights to the throne in exchange for an annual pension. He slipped away under disguise to France, which he crossed to finally join his loyal junta and troops in Navarre in July, 1834. His wife, Doña María Francesca, remained in England and died of fever on September 4.

Although the uprisings in favor of Don Carlos were scattered throughout Spain and he enjoyed considerable sympathy in rural areas, the heart of his support was the Basque provinces, Navarre, Catalonia, and the mountainous area of the Maestrazgo. The Carlists could win battles from one end of Spain to another, with the exceptions of all-important Madrid and the twice-sieged Bilbao, but they could maintain control only in the countryside and small towns of the northeast. One of Don Carlos' tactical problems was his hesitation to close decisively on strategic targets, especially Madrid, because he erroneously expected that the masses would take up arms and fight for his cause. Some historians believe that the princess of Beira unintentionally created more problems for Don Carlos after their marriage in 1838. Very much in the camp of the *apostólicos*, this strong-willed woman alienated Don Carlos' more moderate supporters.

The end of Don Carlos' hopes to win the crown came with the signing of the Convention of Vergara on August 31, 1839, when General Rafael Maroto of the Carlist northern army agreed to accept the conditions for peace offered by Captain-General Baldomero Espartero, the leader of Spain's army. Don Carlos bitterly remarked that Maroto had sold out God, king, country, and *fueros* (rights and privileges of certain groups) for military rank and foreign gold. No longer able to hold out in the Basque provinces, Don Carlos and thousands of troops sought refuge in France on September 14. Don Carlos was arrested attempting to slip back into Spain across the eastern Pyrenees to join Ramón Cabrera and his Carlist army, which continued to fight until July,

1840. Don Carlos and his family were sent to Bourges, France, where they lived under house arrest until he abdicated in favor of his oldest son, Carlos Luis, on May 18, 1845, and took on the title of the count of Molina. That year Don Carlos established residence in Trieste, where he and his wife established a Spanish royal court in exile that became a gathering place for European traditionalists. In his final years, Don Carlos was frail and semi-invalid; he died, after receiving his last rites, on March 10, 1855, comforted by his second wife, the princess of Beira, and his second son, Don Fernando. He is buried in the San Guisto Cathedral of Trieste.

Summary

To the very end, Don Carlos refused to acknowledge Queen Isabel II or accept the new liberal order, which recognized the sovereignty and will of the people. Carlists defended the dynastic claims of Don Carlos and his descendants for well over one hundred years. Carlism never prevailed in restoring an absolutist monarchy, reestablishing a traditional Spain, or regaining all the privileges and properties that the Catholic Church once had in Spain. However, Carlism has had a decided impact on Spanish life. The Second Carlist War (1846-1848) was centered in Catalonia and was spurred on by Carlos Luis (Carlos VI). Carlos Luis' second son, Don Carlos (Carlos VII), led the Third Carlist War (1872-1876). Carlism was an important force on the nationalist side in Spain's Civil War of 1936-1939, although Franco's victorious Falange and the Carlists soon parted company.

Today, Carlists have no intention of starting a war to establish a Carlist monarchy. King Juan Carlos I is, on his father's side, a descendant of King Alfonso XIII of Spain and Queen Victoria of England. On his mother's side, he is related to Don Carlos de Borbón. The two dynastic branches—those of Isabel II and the Carlist pretenders—that were separated upon the death of Ferdinand VII in 1833 have come together again in Juan Carlos, who remains a popular monarch and a symbol of national unity. However, Carlists continue to argue for the reestablishment of a traditional Spain in which there would be Catholic unity, strong regional rights to counter centralism, and a corpora-tive Cortes in which the traditional estates of the clergy, aristocrats, and other interest groups would be represented. They would prefer a monarch who would pledge to uphold the customs, principles, and laws of traditional Spain. Above all else, they remain implacable enemies of liberalism.

Bibliography

Blinkhorn, Martin. *Carlism and Crisis in Spain, 1931-1939*. Cambridge and New York: Cambridge University Press, 1975. The first chapter provides a review of Carlism up until 1931. The rest of the book is a study of Carlism's role in the fall of Spain's Second Republic and the rise of political extremism and Franco's Falange. Includes illustrations, maps, and bibliography.

Clarke, H. Butler. *Modern Spain: 1815-1898*. Cambridge: Cambridge University Press, 1906; New York: AMS Press, 1969. Clarke treats all the major figures and critical turning points of Spain in the nineteenth century. The book contains many details forgotten in more recent studies of the period and includes a map and a bibliography.

Holt, Edgar. *The Carlist Wars in Spain*. London: Putnam, and Chester Springs, Pa.: Dufour Editions, 1967. This even-handed analysis of the three Carlist Wars has an epilogue covering events up to 1965 and includes illustrations, a map, and a bibliography.

Wilhelmsen, Alexandra. "Antonio Aparisi y Guijarro: A Nineteenth-Century Carlist Apologist for a Sacral Society in Spain." In *Saints, Sovereigns and Scholars*, edited by R. A. Herrera, James Lehrberger, and M. E. Bradford. New York: Lang, 1993. This is a good review of what the *apostólicos* wanted and the effects they have had on Spanish life. Includes bibliography.

_____. "Maria Teresa of Braganza." In *Mediterranean Studies* 6. Kirksville, Missouri: Thomas Jefferson University Press, 1996. The Princess of Beira, Don Carlos' second wife, had a major influence over him even before their marriage. This article, which includes illustrations and a bibliography, is particularly good for details on Don Carlos' later life.

Steven L. Driever

THOMAS CARLYLE

Born: December 4, 1795; Ecclefachan, Dumfriesshire, Scotland
Died: February 5, 1881; London, England
Areas of Achievement: Historiography and literature
Contribution: As the most eminent man of letters in the Victorian age, Carlyle thundered against what he saw as the materialism and moral decadence of the age. The uniqueness of his vivid and emphatic style, and his ability to re-create the flavor and feeling of historical events, have earned for him a place among the masters of English prose.

Early Life

Thomas Carlyle was born in the Scottish village of Ecclefachan on December 4, 1795. His father was a stonemason who later became a small farmer, and Thomas was the eldest child of a large, close-knit family. The influence of his early upbringing, in an atmosphere of stern piety and moral rectitude, was to remain with him all of his life.

Carlyle was educated at the local Annan Academy, as a preparation for his entry into Edinburgh University in November, 1809, at the age of thirteen. He was an able student, reading widely in English literature and excelling in the study of mathematics. He also developed the habit of supplementing his formal studies with long periods of solitary reading. In 1814, he became a tutor of mathematics at Annan School, and in the following year accepted a teaching post at Kirkcaldy. Carlyle disliked teaching, however, and resigned his position in 1818. With no clear vocation (he rejected the career which was expected of him, in the Church), he faced an uncertain future. For several difficult and frustrating years, during which he often complained of ill health, he survived by private tutoring and translating.

In 1819, he began his study of German philosophy and literature, and in 1820 his first-published work, a series of anonymous biographical essays, appeared in the *Edinburgh Encyclopaedia.* These were followed by his biography of the German poet Johann von Schiller, which appeared in the *London Magazine* in 1823, and a translation of Johann Wolfgang von Goethe's *Wilhelm Meisters Wanderjahre* (1821). In 1826, he married Jane Welsh, an intelligent and talented young woman who came from a respected and fairly prosperous family in Haddington, which was a short distance from Edinburgh. They had first met five years previously; Carlyle, nearly six feet tall, with thick brown hair, intense blue eyes, and a strong jaw, had cut an impressive and unusual figure.

By 1827 Carlyle had become a regular contributor to the prestigious *Edinburgh Review,* and the groundwork for his major achievements of the next thirty years had been laid. The world would soon hear from this strong-willed, self-reliant, and hardworking Scotsman, a man who in his personal life could be sarcastic, irritable, and impatient, but who also possessed great kindness, loyalty, and a capacity for close and enduring friendships.

Life's Work

From 1828 to 1834, the Carlyles lived at the farm of Craigenputtoch in Dumfriesshire, Scotland. It was here that Carlyle wrote his first major work, *Sartor Resartus.* Although the manuscript was completed by 1831, Carlyle was initially unable to find a publisher. It was eventually published in magazine form in London in 1833-1834, and the first book edition appeared in the United States in 1836, through the help of Ralph Waldo Emerson.

Sartor Resartus remains the most widely read of Carlyle's works and contains the essence of the philosophy which he espoused throughout his life. It is an extraordinary combination of novel—including strong autobiographical elements—and essay, written in Carlyle's characteristic exclamatory, oratorical style, full of imagery and metaphor, a style so distinct that it came to be known as "Carlylese." The central idea of *Sartor Resartus* is that man must learn to distinguish between external appearances and true reality. Because everything in the time and space world is an emblem, or reflection, of an internal, spiritual condition, it is necessary to perceive the workings of spiritual laws in material forms and events. Carlyle calls this "Natural Supernaturalism," and he develops the argument in terms of an extended metaphor of clothing. Outer appearances are like clothing; they obscure the essential reality which is hidden within them.

In 1834, the Carlyles moved to Chelsea, London, and in the following year Carlyle commenced work on his history of the French Revolution. Disaster struck when the entire manuscript of the first volume was inadvertently used by a maid to light the fire (an act for which Carlyle's friend John Stu-

Pamphlets (1850). In all these publications Carlyle sternly opposed what he saw as the rampant materialism of the age, which was leading people further and further into moral and spiritual decay. He did not support the growth of democracy and called for a strong leader, a hero, who would rule according to nature's laws, as a representative of the divine spirit which is immanent in all things. Individuals must also reform themselves and bring duty, work, order, and self-discipline into their lives, as well as an awareness of the spiritual dimension of their lives and actions. With this philosophy, vigorously espoused, Carlyle emerged as the great prophet of mid-Victorian England, at a time when many people feared that social unrest would soon lead to violent revolution.

His standing as the most prominent man of letters in England well established, Carlyle continued to produce major works. His edition of the letters and speeches of Oliver Cromwell was published in 1845, and his biography of John Sterling in 1851—a book which remains one of his most readable and popular works. In 1854, Carlyle began his study of the eighteenth century Prussian leader Frederick the Great, a task which was to take him twelve years to complete. The first two volumes were ready by 1858, and volumes five and six by 1865. The effort involved had been prodigious and painful; Carlyle had never regarded writing as an easy or pleasurable task (although he tended to feel even more miserable when he was not working), and *The History of Friedrich II of Prussia, Called Frederick the Great* turned out to be the hardest labor of all.

The compensations, however, were many. He was now the world-famous "Sage of Chelsea," at the center of the most brilliant literary circle of the day. Carlyle was a brilliant conversationalist. Although his talk was often a near monologue, the monologue was usually so compelling that others were happy to absorb it silently.

Carlyle's major achievements were now behind him, but honors continued to come his way. In 1865, he was appointed Lord Rector of Edinburgh University, and his public speech of acceptance early the following year was received with wild enthusiasm by the university students. Only three weeks later, however, his wife, Jane, died, following many years of ill-health. Although the marriage had not been a smooth one, it had endured for forty years, and Carlyle was plunged into deep grief over his loss. He immediately wrote out his

art Mill, to whom Carlyle had lent the manuscript, accepted responsibility). Only a few fragments survived. Yet Carlyle, undaunted, rewrote the entire manuscript, and *The French Revolution* was published in three volumes in 1837. The vivid and dramatic narrative, in which the description of events took on the quality of eyewitness reports, was an immediate success.

Now with an established reputation as a historian and man of letters, Carlyle began to accumulate a wide circle of friends and acquaintances drawn from the leading literary figures of the day. These included not only his contemporaries such as Robert Southey but also younger men such as Robert Browning; Alfred, Lord Tennyson; Charles Dickens; William Makepeace Thackeray; Edward Fitzgerald; and the philosopher John Stuart Mill. In later years John Ruskin became a close friend.

In the next few years, Carlyle wrote a number of influential essays on contemporary political and social issues, such as *Chartism* (1839); *Past and Present* (1843), which was his response to the crisis of high unemployment and the poverty of industrial workers; and the controversial *Latter-Day* memories of her early years, as well as reminiscences of other friends such as Edward Irving and Francis Jeffrey. These essays were published posthumously as *Reminiscences* (1881). With the reminiscences, Carlyle's literary work was virtually complete.

In 1874, he received the Prussian Order of Merit, but the following year he declined a baronetcy offered to him by Prime Minister Benjamin Disraeli. He died on February 5, 1881, two months after his eighty-fifth birthday. Immediately after his death, he was universally hailed as one of the great men of the Victorian age, the *Saturday Review* calling him "the greatest writer of his time . . . a living teacher . . . a prophet."

Summary

Thomas Carlyle lived during a time of rapid and bewildering social change. Great Britain had yet to come to terms with the massive changes which were occurring as a result of industrialization. There had been a huge drift of the population from the land to the cities, resulting in the creation of a new working class, who lived in poverty, cut off from their former stable foundations of life.

Carlyle, acutely aware of the crisis, responded to the urgent problem of social organization with vigor, eloquence, and prophetic fire. He spoke out against the dehumanizing effects of the machine age, and against what he saw as increasing chaos and disorder. He did not share the fashionable belief in "progress" and "prosperity" ("Progress whither? . . . prosperity in what?"), and what others saw as the growth of "freedom" Carlyle viewed as the destruction of authority. Yet he did not merely advocate a return to established traditions—traditions, like clothes, wear out and must be replaced. Authority, he believed, must be held by the wise, who understand nature's laws and the workings of the divine will. The hero-leader must achieve *entsagen* or *Selbsttodtung* (renunciation of self); otherwise, the power he holds is usurped, not genuine.

Carlyle's prophetic and inspirational message, as well as the power and force of his prose, is well conveyed by some of the final words of his essay "Characteristics" (1831): ". . . behind each one of us, lie Six Thousand Years of human effort, human conquest: before us is the boundless Time, with its as yet uncreated and unconquered Continents and Eldorados, which we, even we, have to conquer, to create; and from the bosom of Eternity there shine for us celestial guiding stars."

Bibliography

Campbell, Ian. *Thomas Carlyle*. London: Hamilton, and New York: Scribner, 1974. Fair-minded, and despite its brevity, illuminating on many issues concerning both the man and his thought.

Carlyle, Thomas. *A Carlyle Reader: Selections from the Writings of Thomas Carlyle*. Edited by G. B. Tennyson. New York: Modern Library, 1969; Cambridge: Cambridge University Press, 1984. The best one-volume selection from Carlyle's voluminous works. Representative texts from all periods and types of his writing, including his letters and journal, and the complete text of *Sartor Resartus*.

Collis, John Stewart. *The Carlyles: A Biography of Thomas and Jane Carlyle*. London: Sidgwick and Jackson, 1971; New York: Dodd, Mead, 1973. Centers on the Carlyles' marriage.

Froude, James Anthony. *Froude's Life of Carlyle*. Abridged and edited by John Clubbe. London: Murray, and Columbus: Ohio State University Press, 1979. Condensation (largely through the omission of Carlyle's letters) of Froude's superb four-volume biography, *Thomas Carlyle* (1882-1884), which created a furious controversy when first published. Froude was Carlyle's close friend and appointed biographer. His biography contained revelations of Carlyle's stormy relations with his wife, which did not show Carlyle in the best of lights.

Kaplan, Fred. *Thomas Carlyle: A Biography*. Cambridge: Cambridge University Press, and Ithaca, N.Y.: Cornell University Press, 1983. The standard biography, replacing Froude. A mass of detail, including some previously unpublished material, welded into a comprehensive and readable study.

Rosenberg, Philip. *The Seventh Hero: Thomas Carlyle and the Theory of Radical Activism*. Cambridge, Mass.: Harvard University Press, 1974. Deals with Carlyle's writings during the fifteen productive years that ended with *Past and Present*. Shows Carlyle struggling with problems that still confront political and social thinkers today.

Trela, D. J., and Rodger L. Tarr, eds. *The Critical Response to Thomas Carlyle's Major Works*. Westport, Conn.: Greenwood Press, 1997. Impressive volume including some of the best critiques (some previously unavailable) of Carlyle's major works covering both early and mature levels of comment.

Vanden Bossche, Chris R. *Carlyle and the Search for Authority.* Columbus: Ohio State University Press, 1991. Study of Carlyle's development based on an exhaustive knowledge of the available literature.

Waring, Walter W. *Thomas Carlyle.* Boston: Twayne, 1978. Concise and straightforward introduction to Carlyle's thought.

Bryan Aubrey

ANDREW CARNEGIE

Born: November 25, 1835; Dunfermline, Scotland
Died: August 11, 1919; Lenox, Massachusetts
Areas of Achievement: Steel manufacturing and philanthropy
Contribution: One of the wealthiest men in the world at the time of his retirement from business in 1901, Carnegie achieved great fame for his business success and for his many benefactions, which became the chief interest of his later years.

Early Life

Andrew Carnegie was born November 25, 1835, in Dunfermline, Scotland. His father, William Carnegie, a prosperous handloom weaver at the time of Andrew's birth, was unable to compete with the new technology of steam looms and fell into poverty as Andrew grew older. Andrew's mother, Margaret Morrison Carnegie, proved under these circumstances to be the bulwark of the family. Ambitious for her two sons, Andrew and younger brother Thomas, she organized a move to the United States in 1848.

They settled in Allegheny, Pennsylvania, where they had relatives and attempted to rebuild the family's fortunes. Although William Carnegie was never again a success, the family got by through hard work and timely assistance from the Pittsburgh area's close-knit Scottish community. Working long, hard hours in factories, Andrew improved his skills, learning double-entry bookkeeping in night school, and in barely a year left factory work to become a telegraph messenger in 1849, an operator in 1851, and in 1853, secretary and personal telegrapher to Tom Scott, superintendent of the Pennsylvania Railroad's western division.

Life's Work

Carnegie remained with the Pennsylvania Railroad for a dozen years, acquiring managerial skills and a sharp insight into the economic principles of the capitalist economy, and forming close personal relationships with several entrepreneurs who were to prove instrumental in his own success. Scott, who delegated increasing responsibility to the resourceful Carnegie, became vice president in 1859; he then named Carnegie superintendent of the western division, perhaps the most challenging position of its kind with any railroad in the United States. The demands of the Civil War would vastly increase his responsibilities, but Carnegie proved equal to

them. At Scott's behest, he organized the movement of Union troops into beleaguered Washington in April, 1861, restored regular rail service between Washington and the north, and stayed in the capital for some months as Scott's assistant in charge of railroads and telegraph services. (Scott had been appointed assistant secretary of war with special responsibility for railroads.) Carnegie then returned to Pittsburgh to resume his duties with the Pennsylvania Railroad.

Carnegie was already losing interest in a salaried position. On a tip from Scott, he had purchased six hundred dollars' worth of stock in the Adams Express Company in 1856. The first dividend check he received was a revelation, and legend has it that Carnegie, thrilled to realize that he could earn money without physical toil, exclaimed, "Here's the goose that lays the golden eggs." More investments followed: in the Woodruff Sleeping Car Company, the Columbia Oil Company, and the Keystone Bridge Company, in which Carnegie held a one-fifth interest, enough to make him the dominant shareholder.

By 1863, Carnegie was earning more than forty thousand dollars annually from his investments, several times his salary, and left the Pennsylvania Railroad at the end of the Civil War to devote more of his time to the management of Keystone and to the Union Iron Mills, which was a principal supplier of Keystone. Carnegie left the operating decisions to experts in bridge construction, while concentrating on sales and finances. With Keystone, he secured contracts to sell materials to such projects as the Eads Bridge at St. Louis, the Ohio River bridges at Cincinnati and Point Pleasant, West Virginia, and the Brooklyn Bridge.

Carnegie's involvement in finance required that he travel often to Europe, and his life-style changed. Always interested in the world of ideas, he never allowed his lack of formal education to keep him from broadening his knowledge. He read extensively and cultivated friendships in Europe and in New York City, to which he moved with his mother in 1867. A bachelor throughout these years, Carnegie enjoyed the companionship of women and led an active social life. He also actively sought the company of intellectuals and eventually would count among his friends the British statesman William Gladstone and literary figures such as Matthew Arnold, Richard Watson Gilder, John Morley, Herbert Spencer, and Mark

Twain. A man of much personal charm, the small-statured Carnegie—he stood but five feet, three inches tall—was equally at ease discussing ideas with the learned and business with financiers or potential customers.

Carnegie was still not content with his lot in life, for he believed that he had become too involved in financial speculation and wished instead to turn to manufacturing, which he considered a more constructive and respectable pursuit. His familiarity with the needs of railroads made him believe that there were large profits to be made in steel, for improved rails would be needed in immense quantities. In 1872, he organized a partnership, drawing on Pittsburgh business acquaintances of long duration to establish Carnegie, McCandless and Company to manufacture steel by the Bessemer process. After several reorganizations involving many different combinations of partners over the years, this firm would become known as Carnegie Steel Company, Limited, in 1892. By 1874, the gigantic new Edgar Thomson Works was under construction, its development supervised by Alexander Holley, the foremost American expert on the Bessemer process, and its operations turned over to Bill Jones, who brought in top-notch department heads from other companies. Characteristically, Carnegie turned over the day-to-day operations to experts such as Jones, while he concentrated on sales and finances, employing the efficient cost-based management techniques learned in the railroad business.

Always alert to technological improvements that would lower the cost of production and lead to increased sales and profits, within a decade, Carnegie introduced to his plants the open-hearth steel production process. Carnegie's business philosophy led him to expand and diversify. In the mid-1880's, his organization acquired the massive Homestead Works and developed a major new market by selling steel structural members to the elevated railways and skyscrapers which were beginning to appear in major American cities.

In 1880, Carnegie met Louise Whitfield, the twenty-three-year-old daughter of a prominent New York merchant. Louise endured the tribulations of a relationship troubled by Carnegie's frequent and extended business travel. Moreover, he initially refused to marry, out of deference to his mother's wishes. The two were finally married in 1887, less than a year after the death of Carnegie's mother. The couple had one daughter.

At the time of his marriage, Carnegie was a millionaire several times over. The 1890's brought more prosperity, as well as some of Carnegie's greatest disappointments. The prosperity came in substantial measure from Carnegie's faith in the continued growth of the American economy and the business acumen of Henry Clay Frick. Chairman of the company since 1889, Frick conducted an aggressive campaign of expansion and cost-cutting which led to one of the bitterest episodes in American labor history, the Homestead Strike of 1892. During this period, Carnegie remained in virtual seclusion in Scotland, giving Frick authority to handle negotiations with the Amalgamated Association of Iron and Steel Workers. The labor-management strife led to intense press criticism of Carnegie in both England and the United States and, along with other issues, precipitated a split between Carnegie and Frick.

Carnegie, who held an interest of more than fifty percent in the firm, resumed a more active role in company affairs, forcing Frick out as chief operating executive at the end of 1894 and leading the business to its most profitable years. The key was Carnegie's success in increasing the firm's share of the market during the depression of the 1890's, acquiring ownership of more of its basic raw materials, its own railroads and its fleet of ore-carrying ships, and its modernizing facilities. Carnegie Steel's annual profits grew eight hundred percent between 1895 and 1900. In Charles Schwab, a brilliant executive totally loyal to Carnegie, the company at last had a worthy successor to Frick.

At the end of the 1890's, new troubles arose from competitors. On the one hand, Carnegie relished a fight; on the other hand, he was willing to sell out, provided the price was right. It was—nearly $500,000,000, of which Carnegie's share was $300,000,000 in five percent first-mortgage bonds in the successor company, United States Steel. The investment banker J. P. Morgan, who had handled the transaction, said that Carnegie was "the richest man in the world." While a similar claim has been made for Carnegie's contemporary, John D. Rockefeller, there is no doubt that Carnegie had built one of the most formidable business enterprises of the nineteenth century; Carnegie Steel produced more than the combined output of the entire steel industry of Great Britain.

Carnegie devoted his remaining years to philanthropy. It was, however, philanthropy with a difference. In Carnegie's hands, philanthropy, a term

which he disliked, itself became big business. In two articles published in 1886, Carnegie, a widely published author, had called for an understanding of the needs of the working man and for the acceptance of unions. The bitterness of the Homestead Strike had inevitably made Carnegie appear a hypocrite, and Carnegie was determined to demonstrate to the world that he was not insensitive to the needs of the less privileged. In an essay entitled "Wealth," first published in 1889 and often reprinted as "The Gospel of Wealth," he had set forth the essentials of his views on charitable giving. He held that the man of means should spend his fortune during his own lifetime in ways that would advance society. The millionaire, he argued, was but a trustee who should approach philanthropy scientifically and endow institutions such as universities, public libraries, and recreational areas for the masses.

On a relatively small scale, he had begun to dispense grants at the end of the 1880's, increasing the number and size of his benefactions as the years passed. In retirement, Carnegie had the time to systematize his giving. While he did provide some money for medical facilities, his usual response to a request for support from a hospital or medical school was to say "That is Mr. Rockefeller's specialty." The great bulk of Carnegie's support went to libraries and the support of education. He ultimately provided more than fifty million dollars to establish twenty-eight hundred public libraries, the vast majority in the United States and Great Britain. Carnegie ordinarily provided funds for the building only, for he expected the communities concerned to provide the revenues needed for books and maintenance. Fond of the limelight, Carnegie often appeared at the dedication of his libraries.

He also gave large amounts of money to Edinburgh University and three other universities in Scotland, and he established the Carnegie Institute of Technology in Pittsburgh (later the Carnegie-Mellon University) and the Carnegie Institution in Washington, D. C., which subsidized basic research in several disciplines. Another substantial sum went to the Carnegie Foundation for the Advancement of Teaching. Ostensibly a pension plan for college faculty, in practice the foundation did much to set standards that raised the quality of higher education in the United States. The largest sum of all, $125,000,000, was used in 1911 to endow the Carnegie Corporation of New York, which had the mission of advancing knowledge through the promotion of schools, libraries, research, and publication. Carnegie dispensed still more money to causes designed to promote international peace, while he spent various amounts on such diverse items as church organs; the Hero Fund, which recognizes valorous deeds performed in everyday life; New York City's Carnegie Hall; and pensions for the widows of United States presidents and for tenant farmers on his Scottish estate, Skibo Castle.

During his lifetime, he had succeeded in giving away slightly more than $350,000,000, utilizing the Carnegie Corporation as his principal means of organizing the distribution of his fortune. Its establishment indicated Carnegie's recognition that it was impossible for a single individual as wealthy as he to supervise personally the administration and meaningful use of his own fortune, the tenet he had advocated in "The Gospel of Wealth." After his death at his summer home in Lenox, Massachusetts, in 1919, his will revealed that there were but thirty million dollars left to distribute; he had already made provisions for his wife and daughter. Praise for his generosity in the press was widespread.

Summary

Andrew Carnegie was a man of contradictions. Despite having little formal education himself, he had a great respect for knowledge, writing books and essays on several topics, reading widely, and making it possible for countless others to read through the thousands of libraries he established. A ruthless businessman, he made platitudinous statements about the dignity of labor but denied many workers that dignity through the practices of his company, a denial which culminated in the Homestead Strike. Yet, as a businessman, he must be remembered as an outstanding success, for, in three separate fields, he showed mastery. His first triumph was with the Pennsylvania Railroad, in whose employ he rose from secretary to one of its most responsible executives at a time when railroads were at the forefront of establishing patterns of modern business management. His next and greatest triumph was in building the giant Carnegie Steel Company. Finally, the practices that had served him so well in the business world enabled him to organize philanthropy on an almost unprecedented scale, as he spent his fortune generously and, on the whole, wisely. To many, he symbolized widely shared values in American culture: generosity combined with the success ethic.

Bibliography

Bridge, James Howard. *The Inside History of the Carnegie Steel Company.* New York: Aldine, and London: Limpus, Baker, 1903. Written by a man who assisted Carnegie in some of his writing endeavors. The author knew not only Carnegie but also most of his key associates. Tends to see the management controversies of the 1890's from Frick's perspective.

Carnegie, Andrew. *The Autobiography of Andrew Carnegie.* Boston: Houghton Mifflin, and London: Constable, 1920. Published the year after Carnegie's death, this book contains a wealth of interesting information but tends to be self-serving.

———. *Triumphant Democracy: Or, Fifty Years' March of the Republic.* New York: Scribner, and London: Sampson, Low, Marston, 1886. Carnegie wrote several books, even more essays, and still more letters that appeared in newspapers under his name. This book and "The Gospel of Wealth" are perhaps his best-known works. Makes clear his ardent faith in capitalism, democracy, and opportunity.

Hendrick, Burton J. *The Life of Andrew Carnegie.* 2 vols. New York: Doubleday, 1932; London: Heinemann, 1933. Written in a vigorous style by a man who had a chance to talk with Carnegie's widow and many of his business associates.

Hendrick, Burton J., and Daniel Henderson. *Louise Whitfield Carnegie.* New York: Hastings House, 1950. Begun by Carnegie's first major biographer and completed by Henderson. Sympathetic but only marginally concerned with Carnegie the businessman.

Hessen, Robert. *Steel Titan: The Life of Charles M. Schwab.* New York: Oxford University Press, 1975. The best study of any of the hard-driving executives who did so much to put Carnegie Steel at the top of American industry. The first half of this biography deals with Schwab's early life and his years with Carnegie. The latter part discusses Schwab's own considerable success after he left United States Steel.

Hogan, William T. *Economic History of the Iron and Steel Industry in the United States.* 5 vols. Lexington, Mass.: Heath, 1971. The first two volumes of this five-volume work provide invaluable work on the steel industry during the years in which Carnegie was its dominant personality.

Livesay, Harold C. *Andrew Carnegie and the Rise of Big Business.* Edited by Oscar Handlin. Boston: Little Brown, 1975. Brief but invaluable biography that places Carnegie's business accomplishments in the context of developments in nineteenth century business management.

Martin, Robert S., ed. *Carnegie Denied: Communities Rejecting Carnegie Library Construction Grants, 1898-1925.* Westport, Conn.: Greenwood Press, 1993. Examines the reasons why some towns that were granted funds for Carnegie libraries later opted to turn them down. Although this choice is historically believed to be linked to Carnegie's reputation as a "robber baron," Martin provides a deeper analysis.

McHugh, Jeanne. *Alexander Holley and the Makers of Steel.* Baltimore: Johns Hopkins University Press, 1980. Biography of the man generally considered to be the foremost American expert in the Bessemer process. Attempts to place its subject in the context of the late nineteenth century technological revolution in steelmaking.

Swetnam, George. *Andrew Carnegie.* Boston: Twayne, 1980. While Carnegie will always be remembered as an industrialist and philanthropist, he became an author even earlier. This valuable, brief book examines his interest in writing and his best-known works.

Van Slyck, Abigail A. *Free to All: Carnegie Libraries and American Culture, 1890-1920.* Chicago: University of Chicago Press, 1995. The author delves into the positive and negative history of the Carnegie Libraries.

Wall, Joseph Frazier. *Andrew Carnegie.* New York: Oxford University Press, 1970. More than a thousand pages in length, this is the definitive biography of Carnegie and is likely to remain so for many years.

Lloyd J. Graybar

LEWIS CARROLL

Born: January 27, 1832; Daresbury, Cheshire, England

Died: January 14, 1898; Guildford, Surrey, England

Areas of Achievement: Literature, mathematics, and photography

Contribution: Lewis Carroll wrote stories and poems that fundamentally changed and enlivened children's literature. He also pioneered children's photography and published books that advanced the fields of logic and mathematics.

Early Life

Lewis Carroll was the pen name of Charles Lutwidge Dodgson, who was born in Daresbury, Cheshire, England, on January 27, 1832. His father, Charles Dodgson, had given up his fellowship and lectureship in mathematics at Christ Church, Oxford University, to marry Frances Jane Lutwidge in 1827. Carroll was the first son of their eleven children. The family lived in Daresbury, where Carroll's father was parish curate, until 1843. Carroll showed an early talent for mathematics, cultivated by his father, and comic verse. Growing up in a close-knit upper-middle-class family, living in a secluded village, and deeply influenced by a stern but doting father, Carroll found childhood a time of innocent exploration and wonder, a view that colored his later literary works.

In 1844 Carroll attended a grammar school in Yorkshire, and in 1846 he went on to Rugby, one of England's leading private schools. Instructors at both schools helped him develop his mathematical and literary talents, but he disliked boarding away from his family. At Rugby the often harsh discipline administered by older students especially repelled him. For the rest of his life he disliked boys. At home on vacations, he helped his father teach in the local school, was a leader in games (many of which he invented), and wrote poetry and stories for magazines that he issued to amuse family and friends. These early poems were usually parodies of moralistic verse common in the early nineteenth century, and he explored several themes that appeared in his mature writing: violence, dreams and nightmares, family relationships, and the child's view of a bewildering adult world.

Carroll was a brilliant student. He won a scholarship to Christ Church, his father's alma mater. Like his father, he won a first in mathematics, the highest scholastic distinction for an undergraduate, and was awarded a fellowship even before he earned his bachelor of arts degree in 1854. The fellowship provided him a yearly stipend and rooms at Christ Church for life. He was appointed a lecturer in mathematics in 1855 and took vows as an Anglican deacon in 1861, becoming the Reverend C. L. Dodgson. From then on he dressed in black clerical clothes almost exclusively. A stammer made him shy of public speaking, and his clean-shaven boyish features, thick dark hair, and retiring manner made him seem ethereal to some contemporaries.

Using his birth name, Dodgson began to attract attention as a comic poet soon after earning his degree by publishing in newspapers and magazines some of the poems that he later incorporated into his children's books. In 1856 he published his first work under the name Lewis Carroll, an anagram of the latinized form of his first two names. The same year, he met Alice Pleasance Liddell, the daughter of Christ Church's dean, and took up photography. These interests—literature, photography, and Alice—blended to produce the most creative period of his life during the next twenty years.

Life's Work

Carroll remained a fellow at Christ Church for the rest of his life. He never married; in fact, the terms of his fellowship forbade it. He devoted himself to tutoring, lecturing, and performing religious and administrative duties at the college, but such work could not use up his creative energy, and he also pursued social and cultural interests outside his academic work.

Carroll was fastidious and almost obsessive with details, and he loved gadgets. Photography was ideally suited to him. At the time he took it up in 1856, it was a cumbersome art with bulky equipment. The photographer had to smear a glass plate with a colloid and dip it into silver nitrate, insert the plate into the camera, expose it for as much as a minute, and then develop the plate in a darkroom. During the exposure the subject had to stay perfectly still. Carroll soon mastered the techniques and tested his skill on architectural subjects and celebrities. Among those he photographed were the poet laureate Alfred, Lord Tennyson; the poet-painter Dante Gabriel Rossetti; and Queen Victoria's youngest son, Prince Leopold.

Photography was a means for Carroll to enter intellectual society and make friends. He soon ingratiated himself with parents by photographing their children. Although he occasionally photographed boys, he preferred girls. He believed that girls of about ten to fourteen years of age epitomized innocent beauty. Carroll told the girls stories or posed riddles of his own invention to put them at ease, dressed them in romantic costumes, and carefully posed them. Sometimes he photographed them nude. In all cases he first obtained the mother's permission and arranged for chaperonage. As well as photographing girls, he regularly sought their company, taking them to plays and museums and entertaining them at dinner parties. Deeply religious, conservative, and rigidly correct in his Victorian-era manners, he behaved with propriety; nonetheless, modern literary critics have speculated that Carroll's interest in girls came from suppressed pedophilia.

His favorite was Alice Liddell. On July 4, 1862, Carroll and his friend Robinson Duckworth took Alice and two of her sisters on a boating trip up the Thames River for a picnic. To entertain them on the return journey, he told them a tale, making it up as he rowed the boat. This became the nucleus of *Alice's Adventures in Wonderland* (1865), which became an international best-seller. In the story, the fictional Alice falls asleep and dreams of a bewildering array of eccentric characters in the form of animals such as the White Rabbit and March Hare, people such as the Mad Hatter, and playing cards. The blending of fantasy, puns, games, nonsense poetry, and adventure story appealed to both children and adults. Even if comically presented, its themes—violence and punishment, growth, obedience, education and games, correct behavior, and the development of identity—nevertheless addressed the world from a child's point of view.

The sequel, *Through the Looking-Glass and What Alice Found There*, followed in 1871. Again, Alice falls asleep. This time she dreams of crawling through a mirror and becoming a pawn in a mammoth chess game. As she advances across the chessboard countryside to be crowned a queen, she meets some of Carroll's most beloved characters, such as the twins Tweedledee and Tweedledum and the White Knight, and hears more nonsense verse, including his most celebrated poem, "Jabberwocky." Many of the same themes appear, and the narrative emphasizes logical absurdities as the basis of humor as well as word play and bi-zarre behavior. Though not as successful as the first book, *Through the Looking-Glass and What Alice Found There* still sold well and brought praise from reviewers.

In 1876 Carroll published *The Hunting of the Snark*, his last masterpiece of nonsense literature. The puns of the subtitle—*An Agony in Eight Fits* (a struggle in eight chapters)—hint that it parodies epic poetry. Indeed, the story's quest for a mythical beast, the snark, by a brave band is a typical epic plot, but little else in the poem makes rational sense. Narrative jumps, eerie illogic, and the tension of supernatural peril give it a nightmarish quality. The poem attracted dedicated fans, especially among intellectuals, but it was not a popular success.

Carroll wrote other books of poetry, short stories, and games, including *Phantasmagoria* (1869), *Rhyme? and Reason?* (1883), *A Tangled Tale* (1885), and *Three Sunsets and Other Poems* (published posthumously in 1898). His last book-length prose tale for children came out in two parts: *Silvie and Bruno* (1889) and *Silvie and Bruno Concluded* (1893). It contains some of his best comic verse, but the story is convoluted and at times sermonizing. It had few admirers. Additionally, Carroll wrote articles and pamphlets on social problems and university affairs and left behind more than 92,000 letters.

As Dodgson, he earned a modest reputation during his lifetime as a mathematician. He was best known for clarifying the works of the classical Greek geometer Euclid in *Euclid and his Modern Rivals* (1879) and *Curiosa Mathematica, Part I* (1888) and for expositions of logical analysis such as *The Game of Logic* (1887) and *Symbolic Logic*, (1896). He also published writings on number theory, and his work on voting theory was pioneering.

Carroll died of complications from a bronchial infection on January 14, 1898, while staying at his sisters' house in Guildford, Surrey. Because his health had always been excellent, the sudden death surprised and saddened his readers, colleagues, and friends. Although Carroll could be prickly and prudish, he was famous for his kindness, having supported his sisters and helped friends through financial straits.

Summary

Lewis Carroll's biographers claim that he is second only to William Shakespeare as the most quoted

English author. Certainly, the Alice books were widely popular, supporting almost continuous republication in many media. A musical called *Alice in Wonderland*, based on *Alice's Adventures in Wonderland*, was staged in 1886 with Carroll's help, and the first of sixteen motion picture versions appeared in 1903. The story has been told in cartoons, coloring books, pop-up books, audio cassettes, and audio-visual teaching guides. It was translated into at least seventy languages.

Before the Alice books, children's literature aimed to teach correct behavior and practical knowledge rather than entertain. Carroll mocked the moralism of this style to the delight of his young readers and gave them a character who embodied their point of view. His approach was revolutionary, and it inspired many imitators. Moreover, Carroll was among the first children's authors make a girl the main character.

Almost immediately, intellectuals and artists began adapting the skewed logic and naïveté in his stories, poems, and photographs for purposes that spanned the variety of modern culture. For example, scientists employed his logic to explain the theories of relativity and quantum mechanics, surrealist painters borrowed his images, politicians quoted him, songwriters echoed his phrasing, psychoanalysts found archetypes and pathology in his characters, and philosophers pondered his elusive remarks on existence and reality. Many features of the Alice stories entered popular culture as well and became familiar even to people who never read the books, including the image of Alice at the Mad Hatter's tea party, such coinages as "chortle" and "galumphing," and such phrases as "off with his head!" and "curiouser and curiouser."

Bibliography

Carroll, Lewis. *The Annotated Alice*. Introduction and notes by Martin Gardner. New York: Potter, and London: Blond, 1960.

_____. *The Annotated Snark*. Introduction and notes by Martin Gardner. New York: Simon and Schuster, 1962. These two books have abundant marginal notes that explain references in the Alice tales and *The Hunting of the Snark* to Carroll's life, events and controversies in Victorian England, and mathematics. They also reproduce the original illustrations.

Cohen, Morton N. *Lewis Carroll: A Biography*. New York: Knopf, and London: Macmillan, 1995. Cohen argues that Carroll rigidly conformed to Victorian Christian morality but that beneath his conservatism raged a painful incompleteness in his life, which he palliated through chaste friendships with girls and young women. His attempts to amuse them inspired his most beloved books. Carroll's photographs and drawings accompany the text.

Collingwood, Stuart Dodgson. *The Life and Letters of Lewis Carroll*. London: Nelson, 1898; New York: Century, 1899. As Carroll's nephew, Collingwood had firsthand knowledge of his uncle's life. The biography is accordingly full of anecdotes. The letters quoted in the text often exemplify Carroll's dexterity with humor.

Guiliano, Edward. *Lewis Carroll Observed*. New York: Potter, 1976. This handsome, large-format book contains many drawings and photographs by Carroll, illustrations of his tales, and clips from early films. The text comprises fifteen essays about the children's books, photography, Carroll's style of humor and reputation, logic, and film versions of the Alice stories.

Thomas, Donald. *Lewis Carroll: A Portrait with Background*. London: Murray, 1996. Thomas surmises the formative influences on Carroll's personality and intellect as he describes Victorian England. An invaluable guide for readers who want to understand how manners and ideas changed during Carroll's lifetime.

Roger Smith

KIT CARSON

Born: December 24, 1809; Madison County, Kentucky

Died: May 23, 1868; Fort Lyon, Colorado

Areas of Achievement: Western exploration, Indian relations, and the military

Contribution: As trapper, guide, Indian agent, and soldier, Carson helped open the American West to settlement. His frontier adventures continue to impress those fascinated by the West's romantic era.

Early Life

Christopher "Kit" Carson was born into a large Kentucky family on the day before Christmas, 1809. Of Scotch-Irish heritage, Lindsey Carson fought in the American Revolution and fathered five children before his first wife died in 1793. Three years later, he married Kit's mother, Rebecca Robinson. The second marriage yielded ten more children, Christopher being the sixth. Before he was two years old, the family moved to Missouri, settling in Howard County. A falling tree limb killed his father when Kit was only nine years old. At fourteen, he was apprenticed to a saddler in Franklin. Kit received little formal schooling and remained illiterate most of his life (many years later, he did learn to write his name). Instead, he earned an education in the American wilderness from men tutored in frontier ways.

Before long, the young apprentice found the saddle trade "distasteful" and vowed to flee his fate at the first chance. Longing to visit new lands, he decided to join the first party headed for the Rocky Mountains. With his master's apparent connivance, Carson ran away in August, 1826, following a wagon train bound for Santa Fe, New Mexico. Taos then became Carson's adopted home, where he always returned after his long journeys.

From 1827 to 1829, Carson served as a cook, drove a wagon to El Paso, Texas, interpreted Spanish, and worked for a copper mine near the Gila River. In August, 1829, he joined Ewing Young's trapping party bound for California. Although not the first trapping venture to cross the continent, the Young expedition provided Carson with invaluable experience and helped shape his life. After trapping beaver along several Arizona streams, the party moved on to California, trapped in the San Joaquin and Sacramento valleys, and finally returned to Taos in April, 1831. Carson once again joined an experienced trapper's expedition, this time that of Thomas Fitzpatrick, known to Indians as "Broken Hand." Fitzpatrick's men headed north to trap in the central Rockies. For the next ten years, Carson roamed the American interior, hunting and trapping in much of present-day Colorado, Wyoming, Utah, Idaho, and Montana.

Carson immediately established a reputation as a reliable trapper and a man useful in a fight. Although later known for his wise counsel, at this point in his life he craved action and adventure. Experience taught him the value of caution; though excitable, he remained firm and determined in dangerous situations. Carson admitted that his most fearful moment came when two angry grizzly bears forced him up a tree. In 1835, an insufferable French trapper goaded him into a celebrated duel at point-blank range—so close, in fact, that Carson's face received powder burns. Wounded in the arm, the Frenchman gave Carson no more trouble.

Carson and his fellow trappers often fought Indians, particularly the Blackfeet, who struggled with the whites over hunting grounds and supplies of valuable horses. In 1835, a Blackfoot warrior wounded Carson in the shoulder, his most serious injury. Early in life, Carson decided that Indians could not be trusted; subsequent clashes confirmed his view that wayward Indians must be severely chastised. Still, he had no special hatred for Native Americans; he respected and understood them well enough to take two native women as his wives (although the second union ended in divorce).

In the Rockies, Carson traveled with many noted mountain men, including Jim Bridger, "Old Bill" Williams, Richard Owens, and Alexis Godey. Trappers lived a rigorous yet unrestrained life, no sooner trading their beaver pelts than setting off again for the mountains. By 1840, overtrapping brought their days to an end, but not before they began to pacify the frontier. Just over thirty years of age, Carson was left with an uncertain future.

In 1836, Carson acquired an Arapaho wife, Waanibe (or Singing Grass). She bore him two daughters but died sometime in 1840-1841. For a wandering trapper, Carson was considerate of his Indian wife; her death meant that he had to care for two young daughters. In 1842, he decided to leave one daughter with Missouri relatives. Returning westward, he met John C. Frémont on a Missouri

River steamer. This chance meeting proved a turning point in Carson's life.

Despite his fame as a mountain man and Indian fighter, Carson was barely average in height and spoke in a soft, nearly feminine voice. He nevertheless immediately impressed army explorer John C. Frémont, who described the frontiersman in his memoirs as "broad-shouldered and deep-chested, with a clear steady blue eye and frank speech and address; quiet and unassuming." Others agreed that Carson was a man of rare character: honest, dependable, fierce under fire, and modest. Younger than many experienced trappers, he became their equal and then won greater fame as Frémont's guide.

Life's Work

In 1842, John C. Frémont was directed by the United States Army to survey the Oregon route as far as South Pass in Wyoming. Known to be reliable, Carson had traveled the mountains extensively, and thus Frémont hired him as guide and hunter at one hundred dollars a month. Eventually, the two men developed great respect for each other, and their friendship proved of lasting benefit to both. Frémont later swore that "Carson and truth are one."

Beginning in June, 1842, Carson guided the main party along the Platte River to Fort Laramie. There rumors of Indian reprisals against white travelers compelled Carson to make an oral last will, a trapper custom. Frémont persisted, and the party safely crossed the Rockies. Carson assisted the explorer in planting the American flag atop one of the Wind River peaks, then accompanied him in a rubber raft down the Platte on the return trip. The party escaped injury in an otherwise costly accident; then Carson took his leave at Fort Laramie. In January, 1843, he returned to Taos to marry his third wife, Josefa Jaramillo, who eventually bore him seven children.

Carson again served as guide (along with Thomas Fitzpatrick) for Frémont's second expedition of 1843-1844 to Oregon and California. Crossing the Rockies, Frémont and Carson examined the Great Salt Lake in a rubber boat, then continued to the British posts in the Oregon country. Frémont next struck southward to explore the Great Basin, finally deciding to enter California across the high Sierra Nevada in the dead of winter. From a Sierra pass, Carson caught a glimpse of the California Coast Range which he had first seen as a member of the Young party fifteen years earlier. After much hardship, he helped guide Frémont to the familiar Sacramento Valley.

The party encountered further trouble returning on the old Spanish Trail. A band of Indians robbed a Mexican family of their horses and then killed most of the family. Carson and Alexis Godey volunteered to pursue the marauders, expecting others to do the same. When none did, the two guides tracked the offenders for fifty miles and alone attacked the camp of thirty braves. The Indians were caught off guard and fled. Carson and Godey returned with two scalps and most of the horses, earning Frémont's everlasting praise. Later, another man was killed by Indians, but the addition of famed trapper and guide Joseph R. Walker helped the party to reach Bent's Fort on the Arkansas River without further injury in July, 1844.

The publication of Frémont's reports of his first two expeditions in 1843 and 1845 brought Carson to the attention of an American nation eager to create heroes of its drive to the West. In his first report, for example, Frémont wrote that "mounted on a fine horse, without a saddle, and scouring bareheaded over the prairies, Kit was one of the finest pictures of a horseman I have ever seen." Such descriptions created a frontier legend that helped Carson earn further fame in the service of his nation.

Along with Richard Owens, Carson started a farm in New Mexico but gladly sold their assets at a loss in August, 1845, to serve on Frémont's third expedition. The party crossed the Rockies and again investigated the Great Salt Lake. Frémont decided to strike straight across the desert to the West, sending Carson and an advance party on a forced march to locate water and grass. Crossing the Great Basin and then the Sierra again in winter, the party arrived in California amid growing turmoil between Mexico and the United States. In March, 1846, Mexican authorities ordered Frémont's army of American frontiersmen to leave the province. After a show of defiance, Frémont did pass northward into Oregon. On the route, Carson joined much of the party in attacking an Indian village, leaving more than a hundred dead in their wake. He believed this "butchery" justified as a deterrent to attacks on American settlers. The same night, a messenger from Washington arrived; Klamath Indians surprised Frémont's camp, killing three of the party. Carson was angered at the death of his friends, and he led the men in exacting vengeance on a nearby Indian village. In a subsequent encounter with the Klamath, quick action by Frémont and James Sagundai, one of Frémont's Indian auxiliaries, spared Carson's life.

Frémont had received messages that induced him to return to California to lead a revolt of American settlers in June, 1846. Although not authorized by the United States government, Frémont's actions earned for him more national acclaim and raised his guide's renown as well. Carson served in the volunteer California Battalion, assisting in the occupation of San Diego and Los Angeles. Apparently at Frémont's direction, Carson's men executed three Mexican prisoners in retaliation for the killing of two Americans. Carson avoided mentioning this grim episode in his memoirs. With California apparently pacified, Frémont sent Carson east in September, carrying news of the conquest to Washington, D.C.

Crossing New Mexico, Carson encountered General Stephen Watts Kearny commanding a force of United States dragoons. With great reluctance, the famous guide agreed to lead the general to California. Arriving in December, 1846, the small American army clashed with determined Californians at San Pasqual. Riding in an advance party, Carson barely escaped death when his horse tumbled and his gun was broken. Many of the soldiers were killed, and Kearny was wounded. The command urgently needed help, so Carson, Navy Lieutenant Edward F. Beale, and a Delaware Indian crept away at night and ran barefoot to San Diego. Despite the hardship and heroism of their actions, a relief force had already been dispatched to rescue Kearny. Carson was again present to see Los Angeles occupied by American forces.

In 1847 and 1848, Carson traveled twice across the continent carrying government dispatches. In the spring of 1848, George Brewerton accompanied Carson from California to New Mexico. The young lieutenant later wrote of his ride with the famous scout. Carson arrived in the East with early news of the California gold strike. At the capital, he and Jessie Benton Frémont urged President James K. Polk to assist her husband in a dispute over authority with General Kearny. Carson had another meeting with the president and was appointed first lieutenant in the United States Army. The Senate, however, refused to confirm the nomination, because of hostility toward the Frémont family. Informed of the rebuff, Carson nevertheless fulfilled his duty in carrying dispatches overland to California. Late in 1848, he returned to private life.

Carson did not accompany Frémont on his ill-fated final expeditions, but he did succor the exhausted explorer in Taos after his fourth expedition

had ended in disaster in the San Juan Mountains. For the next several years, Carson engaged in various pursuits, often aiding government parties. In 1849, he guided soldiers seeking to rescue Mrs. James White and her child, who had been taken by Apache. Carson was saddened when the commander hesitated to follow his instructions; the Indians killed the mother and escaped with the child. In 1853, he took part in a great drive of sheep to California. Early in 1854, he began a new career as an Indian agent, primarily for the Ute.

From his office in Taos, Carson distributed government supplies to the Ute and took part in numerous efforts to pacify other tribes. In 1855, he helped government troops defeat hostile bands in battles at Saguache and Ponca Pass in Colorado. Despite the handicap of illiteracy, Carson proved an effective Indian agent. His facility with Spanish and many Indian languages offset his inability to read and write. Moreover, he knew and respected Indian customs. His hope was to see Indians removed from harmful contact with whites, where they could learn to provide their own support. Sometime in 1856, he dictated his memoirs, probably to his secretary. In 1860, a fall from his horse left Carson in declining health.

Until June, 1861, Carson continued in his post as Indian agent. Then the Civil War came to New Mexico Territory, bringing him a new career as military leader. Born a Kentuckian, Carson sided with the Union, helping to erect a United States flag in Taos after secession sympathizers raised the Confederate banner. He was commissioned a colonel in a New Mexico volunteer regiment. In February, 1862, his troops engaged invading Confederates at Valverde, New Mexico. Later action forced the rebels to withdraw.

For the remainder of the war, Carson sought to pacify several Southwestern Indian tribes. Most notable was his 1863-1864 campaign against the Navajo, a large and proud nation. Following the orders of General James H. Carleton, he fought essentially a scorched-earth campaign, destroying crops and seizing livestock. His efforts to force the Navajo to surrender earned for him the name "The Rope Thrower." In January, 1864, his troops drove the Navajo from their Canyon de Chelly stronghold. Relatively few were killed in the conflict; cold and starvation forced the defeated people to move to the Bosque Redondo, a remote reservation. Hundreds of Navajo died on the journey, however, because of inadequate provisions. Carson had not been responsible for the harsh policy and urged that more food be provided. His campaign helped settle the government reservation system, but in 1868 the Navajo were allowed to return to their tribal lands.

Carson's largest battle took place at Adobe Walls along the Canadian River in Texas. In November, 1864, he led more than three hundred troops (and seventy-five Ute and Apache) against a large force of Kiowa and Comanche. His troops destroyed an Indian village before perhaps as many as three thousand Indians forced him to withdraw. Carson was not beaten; his caution and experience prevented a potential disaster similar to General George A. Custer's defeat. Carson's foray inaugurated a long campaign to pacify the Kiowa and Comanche. In March, 1865, he was breveted brigadier general of United States Volunteers for his valuable service in New Mexico.

In 1866, Carson commanded Fort Garland in Colorado. The next year, he resigned his military position and was appointed superintendent of Indian affairs for the Colorado Territory. In poor health, he accompanied several Ute chiefs on a tour of Eastern cities, hoping to negotiate a favorable trea-

ty. He also visited his old friends the Frémonts and sought medical help. On his return to Fort Lyon, Colorado, his wife died after giving birth to another child. A month later, on May 23, 1868, the famous scout succumbed to death from an aortic aneurysm. Buried initially at Boggsville, Colorado, both Carsons were later moved to Taos, New Mexico, their beloved home. A river, a mountain pass, and the capital city of Nevada bear the Carson name.

Summary

Kit Carson was an ideal representative of the American frontiersman. Unlettered but resourceful, he and his fellow mountain men lived a brief, romantic existence before decline of the beaver population brought their way of life to an end. Forced to become guides, traders, or Indian agents, former trappers continued to facilitate the West's settlement, but in roles subordinate to the more powerful agents of American expansion. As Frémont's guide, Carson surpassed all the mountain men and emerged as a legendary figure of the American frontier. At the same time, his judgment and experience contributed to the success of Frémont's ventures. Through such former trappers as Carson, geographical knowledge of the West passed into the hands of army explorers such as Frémont. As an Indian agent, Carson sought to end Indian-white conflict, while his Civil War service helped protect the Southwest from Confederate attack and Indian unrest.

Carson's adventures require little embellishment, yet writers created a fictional Kit Carson, familiar to most Americans as a loyal army scout and Indian slayer. An early example of the Western hero, the Carson figure linked earlier Eastern woodsmen (such as Daniel Boone) to the Indian fighter of the Western mountains and plains. Barely civilized himself in these fictional accounts, the famous scout assisted in the spread of American civilization to barren Western lands. More than most legendary heroes, however, the historical Kit Carson approaches his fictional reputation. Several brutal encounters with Indians and Mexicans mar his otherwise impressive career. Carson was nevertheless a man of simple courage and devotion to duty. He remains an American character deserving regard.

Bibliography

Brewerton, George D. "A Ride with Kit Carson." *Harper's Magazine* 7 (August 1853): 307-334.

This is one of the few accounts of Carson written by a man who knew and rode with the famous guide.

Canfield, J. Douglas. "Kit Carson, John C. Fremont, Manifest Destiny, and the Indians: or, Oliver North abets Lawrence of Arabia." *American Indian Culture and Research Journal* 21, no. 1 (Winter 1998). Discusses changes in the historical views of two "Western heroes," Carson and Fremont. Focuses on Carson's reputation as a racist as a result of the Navajo battles of 1863 and 1864.

Carter, Harvey Lewis. *"Dear Old Kit": The Historical Christopher Carson*. Norman: University of Oklahoma Press, 1968; London: University of Oklahoma Press, 1990. This authoritative work provides a richly annotated edition of Carson's memoirs, virtually the only source of information for his life to 1856. Includes a survey of works on Carson and assesses his character and later life.

Estergreen, M. Morgan. *Kit Carson: A Portrait in Courage*. Norman: University of Oklahoma Press, 1962. Inaccurate in some respects, this helpful account is based partly on Carson family memories.

Frémont, John C. *The Expeditions of John Charles Frémont*. Edited by Donald Jackson and Mary Lee Spence. 3 vols. Urbana: University of Illinois Press, 1970-1984. The widely read reports of John C. Frémont's first two expeditions (in volume 1) made Carson a national hero.

Gordon-McCutchan, R. C. "Revising the Revisionists: Manifesto of the Realist Western Historians." *Journal of the West* 33, no. 2 (July 1994). Compares the views of Kit Carson as "Indian killer vs. Indian fighter," held by revisionist and realist Western historians, respectively.

Guild, Thelma S., and Harvey L. Carter. *Kit Carson: A Pattern for Heroes*. Lincoln: University of Nebraska Press, 1984. Readable and generally reliable, this biography is based primarily on Carson's memoirs.

Kelly, Lawrence C., ed. *Navajo Roundup: Selected Correspondence of Kit Carson's Expedition Against the Navajo, 1863-1865*. Boulder, Colo.: Pruett, 1970. Generally favorable to Carson, this source contains many valuable documents covering his Navajo campaign.

Sabin, Edwin Legrand. *Kit Carson Days*. Rev. ed. New York: Press of the Pioneers, 1935; London: University of Nebraska Press, 1995. Dated and flawed in parts, this standard biography is still useful for Carson's later career. Includes his agent and military reports.

Trafzer, Clifford E. *The Kit Carson Campaign: The Last Great Navajo War*. Norman: University of Oklahoma Press, 1982; London: University of Oklahoma Press, 1990. This work examines Carson's 1863-1864 campaign from the Navajo perspective.

Vernon L. Volpe

MARY CASSATT

Born: May 22, 1844; Allegheny City, Pennsylvania
Died: June 14, 1926; Château de Beaufresne,
  France
Area of Achievement: Art
Contribution: Using Impressionist techniques to
  create vivid, unsentimental portraits, Cassatt became America's foremost woman painter at a
  time when the art world was regarded as an exclusively male domain.

Early Life

Mary Stevenson Cassatt was the second daughter
and fourth child of Robert and Katherine Johnson
Cassatt. Robert Cassatt earned a comfortable income from stock trading and real estate. In 1849,
the family moved to Philadelphia, but in 1851, they
left for an extended stay in Europe.

The Cassatts first lived in Paris, but in 1853 they
moved to Germany, where the eldest son, Alexander, could study engineering, and another son,
Robert, could receive medical attention. In 1855,
Robert died and was buried in Darmstadt; many
years later, Mary Cassatt would have his body
moved to be interred with others of the family at
her French château.

The family returned to the United States in 1855,
settling first in the Pennsylvania countryside and
then back in Philadelphia, where Mary enrolled, in
1861, at the Pennsylvania Academy of Fine Arts.
During her four years at the academy she received
a solid, if uninspiring, education in artistic fundamentals. Students began with drawings from casts
of statues, progressed to live models, and completed their training by making oil copies of paintings.
The faults of this process were that the instructors
were competent but undistinguished, and the paintings available for students were mediocre. At this
time there were no major collections of art in the
United States. Cassatt realized that to become an
artist she needed exposure to the best in art, so she
decided she must go to Europe.

In 1865, it was unheard of for a young woman to
become a professional artist, and shocking for her
to leave family and embark alone on a tour of Europe. Yet these were precisely the goals which Cassatt determined to achieve. There was considerable
opposition from her family, to both her desire for an
artistic career and the European visit, but she convinced them to accept her plans. This determination

was characteristic of Cassatt, and its lifelong nature
could be seen in her appearance. She was tall, thin,
with fine but strong features and blue-gray eyes. Direct and forceful, she expressed her beliefs and
opinions without reserve or regard for the sensibilities of others. Extremely energetic, she could work
from dawn until the light faded but was able to put
her paintings aside to care for her family; she herself never married. Such was the young woman
who sailed for Europe in 1866, anticipating the first
steps in her real artistic apprenticeship.

Life's Work

In Paris, Cassatt enrolled in the École des Beaux
Arts and studied briefly with a fashionable society
painter. Soon she left to study independently, mainly visiting museums and galleries and copying
their paintings.

In 1867, the Paris World's Fair was held. Outside
the official exhibitions, the painters Gustave Courbet and Édouard Manet held a private show. Unlike
conventional painters, Courbet and Manet chose
subjects which were contemporary rather than
classical and portrayed them with vivid, unsparing
realism, precise in observation and presentation.
Cassatt was deeply influenced; Manet had the most
important impact on her work prior to her association with Edgar Degas.

During the Franco-Prussian War of 1870, Cassatt returned to Philadelphia, but in 1871 she was
back in Europe, spending eight months in Parma,
Italy, where she made an extensive study of the
painter Antonio Allegri da Correggio. The result
can be seen in her work, chiefly in her depictions
of children, which owed much to Correggio's
paintings of Madonna and Child. She visited
Spain, where she was particularly impressed by Diego Rodriguez de Silva Velázquez and El Greco.
She also visited the Netherlands, where the paintings of Peter Paul Rubens, with his outstanding
flesh tints and mastery of the human form, made a
profound contribution to her style.

In 1873, Cassatt decided to settle permanently in
Paris. Given the artistic ferment of the French capital and its central role in art, at the time it was the
only natural place for a serious artist. In 1872, a
painting of hers, signed "Mary Stevenson," had
been accepted by the Paris Salon. She continued to
submit work to the Salon for several years but grew

increasingly disenchanted with the Salon's arbitrary and restrictive standards. One of her paintings was rejected because the background was too light; with a darkened background the painting was resubmitted and accepted.

Decisions such as this were one reason Cassatt ceased exhibiting in the Salon after 1877. The most important reason, however, was her discovery of the Impressionist movement and her association with Edgar Degas. The first Impressionist show was held in 1874, with works by such artists as Degas and Manet. The exhibition was fiercely attacked by traditional critics, but Cassatt perceived immediately the breakthrough which had been made. The Impressionist group contained widely diverse artists, who shared a common preoccupation with light—how to capture it, how to set it down on canvas. Their use of light and color was the key element in the movement, and after Cassatt viewed their work, light and color became essential in her work as well.

Degas had seen her work and admired it, and in 1877, they met. At forty-three, he was ten years older, an established artist known for his paintings and his sharp, often cutting remarks. The two had a stormy but productive relationship that lasted forty years. Although some have speculated on a romantic liaison between the two, it appears likely that their friendship, while close, was mainly professional. They had bitter arguments, over painting, politics, or personalities, but they always reconciled, usually at Cassatt's initiative. Degas was certainly the most important influence on Cassatt's artistic career.

Degas asked her to join the 1877 exhibition of the Impressionists. "I accepted with joy," she later said. "Now I could work with absolute independence without considering the opinion of a jury. I had already recognized who were my true masters. I admired Manet, Courbet, and Degas. I took leave of conventional art. I began to live."

Cassatt's relationship with Degas reinforced her natural strengths. They both chose contemporary subjects, preferring the human figure rather than landscapes, and both insisted on the importance of drawing and line. It was through Degas that Cassatt came to know the Japanese prints which had been introduced to France in the 1850's. From these she developed a simple, strong style that emphasized unusual angles of vision (from above, from the side, with the main figure only partially in view), a flattening of perspective, and the use of contrasting areas of pattern. Some of her best pieces were aquatints inspired by the Japanese prints.

By 1880, Cassatt was an acknowledged member of the Impressionist movement and exhibited regularly in their shows; she was the only American painter ever to do so. Urged on by Degas, she branched into pastels and prints, showing great promise in both.

Her father, mother, and sister Lydia joined her in Paris in 1877; nursing them through a series of illnesses often deprived her of painting time. In 1880, her brother Alexander and his family came to live with the Cassatts. Inspired by her nieces and nephews, Mary began her paintings of mother and child, the theme with which she is most popularly associated.

The 1890's were Mary Cassatt's most creative and productive period. In addition to her paintings and pastels, it was then that she produced the series of aquatints inspired by Japanese wood prints, which she exhibited in her first one-woman show of 1891.

Back in the United States, her fame grew slowly. An exhibit of the Impressionists in 1886 included three of her works, and her paintings were shown in Philadelphia, Boston, New York, and other cities. By 1891, she was well-known enough to receive a commission for a mural on the theme of "modern woman" at the Chicago World's Fair. She painted the canvas, her largest work, at the Château de Beaufresne, which she had recently purchased. Still, full recognition in her homeland lagged; her first one-woman show in New York (1895) had a lackluster reception, and she was not fully appreciated until after her death. In France, however, Cassatt was well-known. Her second one-woman show, held in Paris in 1893, was a large one: ninety-eight works, consisting of oils, pastels, and graphics. Her exhibition was well received by the public and the critics. Other shows were equally acclaimed, and she was quickly recognized as a major artist. In 1904, she was awarded the Legion of Honor.

In addition to being a creative artist, Cassatt was extremely important in bringing artwork to the United States. In 1873, she met Louisine Elder, who shared her interest in art. In 1901, Cassatt went on an extended European purchasing tour with Elder and Elder's husband, the wealthy banker H. O. Havemeyer. Over the next decade Cassatt advised them on a large number of purchases. Thanks to her perceptive eye and knowledgeable advice, the Havemeyers bought many Impressionist works and many important earlier paintings, such as El Greco's *View of Toledo* and his *Assumption of the Virgin*—the two most notable works of that artist to be found outside Spain. In 1929, the Havemeyer Collection went to the New York Metropolitan Museum of Art, forming the foundation of a national treasure.

After 1900, Mary Cassatt's work declined in quantity and, to some extent, in quality. Partly this was a result of her extensive work in collecting, but primarily her artistic decline was caused by family problems and failing eyesight. Her sister Lydia had died at an early age; in 1895, her mother died after a long illness, during which Cassatt was occupied as her nurse. The death of her favorite brother, Alexander, in 1906 was another severe blow, and five years later, after a tour of Egypt, her brother Gardner fell seriously ill and died in Paris. For a time, Mary Cassatt suffered from what she, and others, termed a "breakdown." It was not until 1912 that she began to work again.

When she did, it was in pastels, mainly because her failing eyesight did not allow the precision of prints or oils. Bothered by cataracts, she submitted to treatments and operations, none of which restored her sight; by 1913 her work was ended. She spent World War I removed from her beloved Château de Beaufresne because it was close to the battle lines.

In 1917, her friend and fellow professional, Degas, died. He had been the last link with the work and success of earlier years. She returned to her château in 1920 and remained there for the rest of her life. Nearly blind, she could not work but entertained young artists, mostly Americans, with her fiercely held, forcefully delivered views on art. She died at the Château de Beaufresne on June 14, 1926.

Summary

"I am not willing to admit that a woman can draw that well," Degas said upon viewing a work by Cassatt. This remark of an exceptional artist, who was Cassatt's closest friend and influence, reveals the obstacles facing a woman artist in the latter half of the nineteenth century. It is proof of Cassatt's determination and talent that she was accepted during her lifetime as one of the premier artists of the day; significantly, Degas purchased the very picture which inspired his comment.

Cassatt's contributions to art came in two phases: her own creations and her work in collecting. As an adviser to wealthy Americans such as H. O. Havemeyer and the banker James Stillman, Cassatt helped build some of the truly outstanding art collections of this century and brought priceless treasures to American museums. Cassatt made certain that no American art student would again face her early dilemma of living in a country which possessed no great artistic works. Such collections were important to Cassatt, because she firmly believed that the only way of learning to paint was to see, and copy, great paintings.

The energy that went into building collections was energy lost to her own work. She was also burdened with caring for her family, and she was increasingly troubled with eye problems. Cassatt, therefore, had a relatively limited production as an artist: about 225 prints and 617 oils and pastels, many of them studies rather than finished works.

It is the excellence of her work, rather than its quantity, which assures her undeniable achievement. In her chosen subjects, mothers and children, and the female form, she achieved a powerful, accurate, and original vision that rejected traditional sentiment and convention. She brought together the emphasis on light stressed by the Impressionists, the new angles of vision revealed by photography and Japanese prints, and the clarity and directness demanded by all great painters. Mary Cassatt blended these qualities together through her own honesty, efforts, and genius, producing a body of work that is among the most important in modern art.

Bibliography

Breeskin, Adelyn. *Mary Cassatt: A Catalogue Raissoné of the Oils, Pastels, Watercolors and Drawings*. Washington, D.C.: Smithsonian Institution Press, 1970. Contains a short but highly informative biography of Cassatt's life and career. The notes that accompany the illustrations are excellent and provide the reader with a solid guide to Cassatt's development as an artist.

Boone, Elizabeth. "Bullfights and Balconies: Flirtation and Majismo in Mary Cassatt's Spanish Paintings of 1872-73." *American Art* 9, no. 1 (Spring 1995). Explores Cassatt's use of flirtation and majismo in her paintings completed in Spain and argues that this theme represents the artist's escape from Victorian mores.

Bullard, E. John. *Mary Cassatt: Oils and Pastels.* New York: Watson-Guptill, 1972; Oxford; Phaidon Press, 1976. The introductory sketch of Cassatt's life is excellent, and the commentary on the pictures is first-rate. Cassatt believed that the only way to learn painting was to copy great works; the best way to study her is to look at her works.

Carson, Julia. *Mary Cassatt*. New York: McKay, 1966. A fine introductory biography, geared toward the younger reader.

Cassatt, Mary. *Cassatt and Her Circle: Selected Letters*. Edited by Nancy Mowll Mathews. New York: Abbeville Press, 1984. A generous collection of letters by Cassatt and her associates. More of interest to the specialist than the general student.

Hale, Nancy. *Mary Cassatt*. New York: Doubleday, 1975. This biography is generally good on facts and relationships but occasionally strays into confusing speculation about Cassatt's thoughts and motives.

Mathews, Nancy M. *Mary Cassatt: A Life*. New York: Villard Press, 1994. This study of Cassatt's life focuses on her life in France, her conflicts with the American and Parisian avant-garde, and provides fresh insight into her personal life.

McKown, Robin. *The World of Mary Cassatt*. New York: Crowell, 1972. A wide-ranging view of Cassatt's development as an artist; the work assumes that the reader already has a fair understanding of the period under discussion. Contains an excellent bibliography.

Sweet, Frederick. *Miss Mary Cassatt: Impressionist from Pennsylvania*. Norman: University of Oklahoma Press, 1966. This biography has good sources—Sweet was one of the first authors with wide access to letters of Cassatt and her associates—and excellent documentation. The approach, however, is uncritical and nonanalytical.

Michael Witkoski

VISCOUNT CASTLEREAGH

Robert Stewart

Born: June 18, 1769; Dublin, Ireland
Died: August 12, 1822; Cray Farm, North Cray, Kent, England
Areas of Achievement: Diplomacy, government, and politics
Contribution: Castlereagh's political skills helped pass the Act of Union between Great Britain and Ireland, thus creating the United Kingdom. His role in the peace negotiations following the Napoleonic Wars helped ensure a just and long-lasting peace.

Early Life

Robert Stewart was born in his grandfather's house in Dublin on June 18, 1769. His mother, Lady Frances Seymour-Conway, was the daughter of the Earl of Hertford, Lord Lieutenant of Ireland in 1765. She died in 1770. His father, Robert Stewart, came from a landed Presbyterian Ulster family. The little boy's elder brother died the year he was born. He was the only surviving son of his father's first marriage. Baptized a Presbyterian, Stewart was brought up as an Anglican so as to avoid any obstacles to a political career. At the time, not only Roman Catholics but also non-Anglican Protestants lacked first-class citizenship.

Until he was eight years old, Stewart lived with his paternal grandparents. Then he attended the Royal School at Armagh, from which an early letter (October 6, 1777) assured his family that he was still a loyal "American," by which he meant a supporter of the American revolutionaries, as both his father's and his stepmother's families were. He then joined his father's household at Mount Stewart, County Down, and transferred to a nearby school. His father's second wife was the daughter of the British Lord Chancellor Camden, a formidable figure in English Whig circles, who took a great interest in his step-grandson's future. Camden persuaded Stewart's father to send him to Cambridge, and he duly matriculated at St. John's College in 1786. Until then, he had taken pleasure in the usual pursuits of the gentry—riding, sailing, dancing—and had shown no particular academic aptitude. At Cambridge, he was not impressed by the intellectual life and never took his degree.

Meanwhile, with the general election of 1790 looming, Stewart's father was determined to reassert the family's political influence in Down and to avenge his own electoral defeat in 1784 by putting up his son for a county seat in the Irish House of Commons. At enormous expense (some said sixty thousand pounds), Stewart was successful. He had not been quite twenty-one when he declared his candidacy, standing as an Independent Reformer. His father had accepted an Irish peerage so that both father and son would attend the new Irish Parliament, one as peer, the other as M.P.

Three points about Stewart's next few years are especially important. First, he went abroad, to Spa in 1791 and to Brussels in 1792. His acumen in assessing the impact of the French Revolution was quickly apparent. He told the refugees at Spa that there was no hope of restoring the France of 1789; at the same time, he foretold the collapse of the revolutionary paper currency, the assignats. Stewart's departure from the Whig principles of Charles James Fox dates from this time, as does Lord Camden's advice to him before his maiden speech in the Dublin Parliament. Camden explained that although his family tradition and election platform opposed the unreformed character of the Irish executive, which was responsible to the British cabinet, Stewart could all the same indicate his sympathy with William Pitt the Younger, prime minister in Great Britain. He could and did.

Second, in 1794, the tall, slim, and handsome M.P. married the Lady Amelia (Emily) Hobart, daughter and only child of the Earl of Buckinghamshire's second marriage. This match reinforced the aristocratic English connections already begun with his mother's family and continued with his stepmother's. Third, he combined the tenure of his seat in the Irish House of Commons with election to a seat in the House of Commons of Great Britain. He first sat for Tregony, Cornwall, and later for Orford, Suffolk, until, in 1797, his acceptance of office in Ireland obliged him to give up any British seat. When he returned to Westminster it would be as M.P. in that new entity, the United Kingdom of Great Britain and Ireland, which he did so much to create.

By this time, Stewart's admiration for Pitt and distrust of the French Revolution cut him off from his earliest political supporters in Ireland, many of whom continued to support the French Revolution and to hope that war between England and France would force England to make further concessions to Ireland as had happened during the American Revolutionary War. Stewart, however (now Viscount Castlereagh), had already voted with Pitt to suspend habeas corpus in England. While shuttling between Dublin and Westminster, he supported the measures to limit civil liberties in both countries. He had moved away from his early Irish Whig reform principles and joined the Pittite supporters of an act of union, amalgamating the kingdoms of Great Britain and Ireland.

Life's Work

Castlereagh's appointment as Keeper of the Privy Seal in Ireland obliged him to resign his seat in the British Parliament, and at that time, 1797, he was reelected for his Irish seat at County Down. Already, Castlereagh had played a role as officer in the yeomanry, distinct from Pitt's militia, which had been raised as an alternative to the suspect Irish Volunteers. Informers betrayed the leadership of the United Irishmen, which had begun to link Ulster Presbyterians with southern Roman Catholics in a revolutionary organization, and Castlereagh participated in a preemptive strike at its leadership in Ulster in 1797. This success undoubtedly limited the scale of the Ulster rebellion in 1798. By that time, Castlereagh had become acting Chief Secretary of Ireland, during the illness and absence of Thomas Pelham (Lord Pelham and later second Earl of Chichester). He was the right-hand man of the Lord Lieutenant, chief resident executive of Ireland. His calm resourcefulness during the rebellion recommended him to the new Lord Lieutenant, Lord Cornwallis, who arrived after the suppression of the rebellion in the south at the Battle of Vinegar Hill, June 21, 1798. Cornwallis strongly supported Castlereagh as permanent replacement to Pelham as chief secretary in November, 1798.

Meanwhile, the last French effort to intervene failed. In 1796, General Hoche had been unable to make a landing at Bantry Bay. Another force under General Humbert, ill-coordinated with the local Irish rebellion, landed in August and surrendered in September, 1798. Had Napoleon Bonaparte sailed for Ireland rather than for Egypt, the outcome might have been different. As it was, Cas-

tlereagh's problem was one of conciliation. He embraced Cornwallis' amnesty for past rebels, though it infuriated ardent Protestant members of Orange Societies, thirsting for revenge. Castlereagh began serious correspondence with Pitt about a union of Ireland with Great Britain as a long-term solution to the problem of the relations of the two kingdoms.

Castlereagh had no confidence in a policy of concessions to Roman Catholics in the narrow context of a quasi-autonomous Ireland. The religious problem could be addressed only after Ireland merged with the larger entity of a single united kingdom. For almost two years (1799-1800), Castlereagh devoted himself to the job of persuading the Irish Parliament to abolish itself and to accept representation by one hundred M.P.'s at a new House of Commons at Westminster. These means of persuasion harked back to those used at the unification of Scotland with England in 1707: bribery, compensation for the loss of "property" in control over boroughs, new peerages, and promotions within the peerage. The idea that a borough "owner" was entitled to monetary compensation was current. Pitt had used it in his own abortive plan to reform the British House of Commons. Castlereagh's task was to distribute some one and a quarter million pounds so as to guarantee majority votes in the Irish Parliament. Because most of the borough "owners" were Irish peers, they received most of the money.

Just as the whole Scottish peerage was not absorbed into the House of Lords of Great Britain, so the Irish peerage was to elect twenty-eight of its number to join the House of Lords of the United Kingdom. Yet Scottish peers were elected at every general election; the Irish representative peers were to be elected for life. Therefore, Irish peers not elected as representative peers were to be eligible for election to the new House of Commons. Castlereagh was not affected, as his courtesy title left him eligible anyway. He did not succeed his father as an Irish peer until 1821 (by then the title had become Marquis of Londonderry). Others, such as Viscount Palmerston, were to find an Irish peerage compatible with not being an elected Irish representative peer.

The Act of Union with Ireland went into effect January 1, 1801, and by the time Castlereagh attended the new House of Commons, he had resigned as chief secretary. George III obstinately refused to accept ending the barriers to Roman Catholics being elected to the House of Commons and to their holding office. No precise pledge had been made by Pitt or Castlereagh, but Pitt's cabinet had been favorable and Castlereagh hopeful. Indeed, Castlereagh hoped that with political union accomplished, the Roman Catholics would receive not only equal civil rights but also relief from tithes paid to support the Anglican Church in Ireland. He hoped that the state would increase funds for the education of both Roman Catholic and non-Anglican Protestant clergy in Ireland. None of these measures passed in his lifetime. The immediate result of the royal opposition was the resignation of Pitt with many cabinet colleagues and the departure of both Cornwallis and Castlereagh from their Irish posts. On arriving at Westminster, Castlereagh sat near Pitt on the government back benches, while Henry Addington succeeded Pitt as prime minister. Castlereagh believed that if Pitt had not been so tired and ill he might have dealt with the king more effectively.

Castlereagh had no intention of joining the opposition, however, and in fact accepted office as president of the Board of Control (India) under Addington in 1802. He had to mediate between East India Company directors in London and the governor-general in India, which required tactful management of prickly personalities. When Pitt returned as prime minister, he kept Castlereagh as president and made him secretary for war in July, 1805. Though Castlereagh lost both offices the next year, after Pitt's death, he alone of the cabinet had sat with Pitt in the House of Commons, sharing with him the negotiations with Czar Alexander I in 1805, the basis for Castlereagh's own foreign policy in 1815.

Back at the War Office in 1807, Castlereagh improved the recruitment procedure and developed the militia for home defense. The disastrous military failure at Walcheren led him to resign in 1809. Rivalry with George Canning preceded his resignation. Castlereagh challenged Canning, and their duel was fought September 21, 1809. On the second firing, he wounded Canning. Contemporaries thought the duel unnecessary as well as undesirable. Certainly it revealed the emotions churning behind Castlereagh's mask of cold indifference to public opinion. His view was that Canning's intrigues to oust him from office justified the duel and his insistence on a second shot. Castlereagh returned to office as foreign secretary in 1812 and, when Prime Minister Spencer Perceval was assassinated on May 11, 1812, as leader of the House of Commons under the premiership of Lord Liverpool. He held both positions until his death ten years later.

Castlereagh now revealed on a grander scale the qualities already exhibited as chief secretary in Ireland. Industry, method, and application won a greater acceptance if not acclaim. Castlereagh never equaled Pitt's Biscayan roll in oratory or Canning's memorable eloquence. Similarly, his French, while fluent, was so far from idiomatic as to reduce sophisticates such as the Princess Lieven to fits of laughter. The House of Commons listened to him carefully for his substance, not his style.

As Pitt's heir, Castlereagh promoted allied unity first of all. If he made little headway in 1813, he was eventually successful with the treaty of Chaumont, March 9, 1814, which not only bound the allies to continue the war against Napoleon but also committed them to work together for twenty years afterward to secure the peace. Pitt's blueprint for postwar Europe had included an enlarged Netherlands, backed by Prussia, and an enlarged Piedmont, backed by Austria. The czar had agreed with

Pitt that the war was against Napoleon, not against the French people. Therefore, a generous peace was most likely to stabilize postwar France. In 1805, neither Pitt nor Alexander I was committed to a restoration of the Bourbons, but both wished to establish something like a concert of Europe to avert future wars.

Castlereagh achieved most of the British objectives in the first peace of Paris, May 30, 1814. France was left with her 1792 borders and no indemnity. He was criticized for allowing France a five-year delay in abolishing the slave trade, though this was certainly congruent with the basic policy of a lenient peace, to assist the restored Bourbon monarchy as arranged by Talleyrand. At the Congress of Vienna, Castlereagh's most daring initiative came when he organized a secret alliance of Austria, France, and England against Prussian demands. There was little that Castlereagh could do about the Russian occupation of Poland, but the Prussians were forced to back down and accept a compromise over Saxony. Napoleon's return, ousting Louis XVIII from his throne, brought a new crisis. Again, Castlereagh was calm and persevering. He defeated those in Parliament who were ready to patch up a peace with Napoleon and, after Waterloo, outmaneuvered those who were now determined to have a punitive peace. France was reduced to the frontiers of 1790 and had to pay an indemnity and accept an occupation force. The Bourbons were restored, however, and Wellington supported Castlereagh for this comparatively lenient peace. Castlereagh's crowning diplomatic achievement was winning parliamentary support for the Quadruple Alliance, accepted in England as of February 20, 1816. The agreement bound the allies to maintain the peace and to meet together periodically: the concert of Europe, or congress system, idea.

The first of the congresses, held at Aix-la-Chapelle in 1818, saw the completion of arrangements for payment of the indemnity, an end to the occupation, and the acceptance of France as a peacekeeping partner in what now became the Quintuple Alliance. Thereafter, difficulties posed by revolutions in Spain and Italy made Castlereagh more reluctant than Prince Metternich to support a policy of military intervention. At Troppau in 1820, the English sent only an observer, and they did the same at Laibach in 1821. Castlereagh was drawing a distinction between deterring aggressors bent on destroying the international balance of power worked out in 1815 and intervening in the internal politics of states as Metternich and the czar were more inclined to do. Castlereagh met Metternich for the last time in October 1821, in Hanover. They understood that their main objective, peace, was the same, even if their tactics differed.

At home, Castlereagh suffered great unpopularity for the repressive measures which he was responsible for steering through the House of Commons. It is fair to say that, like his mentor Pitt, he continued to support repression long after the evidence of clear and present danger had passed away. It is curious that he was singled out far more than his colleagues Lord Liverpool and Lord Sidmouth (as Addington had become) for the ferocious attacks by critics. Perhaps he drew more fire because he was so visible as Leader of the House, perhaps because his lofty disdain enraged more opponents.

By 1822, Castlereagh's labors had worn him out. Observers feared for his sanity after the end of the parliamentary session. Wellington insisted that his doctor accompany him to his country retreat in Kent. There, on August 12, 1822, he committed suicide by cutting his throat. He was certainly deranged. It is less clear that his principal delusion was fear of blackmail for a homosexual offense in which he had been entrapped. Wellington dismissed this as sheer delusion. Psychohistorians might ask why that particular delusion. His widow insisted on burial in Westminster Abbey, and the hostile mob followed him there, jeering and hooting. Some obituaries were outright jubilant. Yet a dispassionate assessment would award him high marks both for his farsighted views respecting the conciliation of Roman Catholics in Ireland and for his enlightened commitment to European peace through periodic conferences.

Summary

There seems little doubt that without the blocking of Roman Catholic emancipation by the Crown, the history of the United Kingdom would have been happier; it is at least possible that the Irish problem in the form confronting Sir Robert Peel and later William Ewart Gladstone might have vanished. Viscount Castlereagh's vision at least offered that possibility. In foreign affairs, Castlereagh could not have hoped to hold the line precisely where he had drawn it in 1820, even if he had lived. His death certainly accelerated the collapse of his policy as Metternich turned to reliance on Russia, and Canning, Castlereagh's successor, abandoned the commitment to Europe. Most contemporary English criticism was shortsighted or simply unfair. For example, Castlereagh never had anything to do with the "Holy Alliance," that strange vision of Czar Alexander. Castlereagh's vision of some means to anticipate and deter the menace of future Napoleons long survived the details of his diplomacy. Not surprisingly, in 1919, when another great peace conference was to be held, the Foreign Office went back to the records of Castlereagh's peacemaking to guide the English delegation at Versailles.

Bibliography

Bartlett, Christopher J. *Castlereagh*. London: Macmillan, and New York: Scribner, 1966. The author discounts H. Montgomery Hyde's conversion to the blackmail delusion as the proximate cause for the suicide. Contains a good bibliography.

Hyde, H. Montgomery. *The Rise of Lord Castlereagh*. London: Macmillan, 1933. This is the fullest treatment of the early years. Hyde rejects the blackmail story out of hand.

————. *The Strange Death of Lord Castlereagh*. London: Heinemann, 1959. Here Hyde reverses himself completely concerning the suicide without giving any cogent reasons for the reversal.

Leigh, Ione. *Castlereagh*. London: Collins, 1951. Until Bartlett's study this was the best short biography, and it is better organized.

Webster, Charles K. *The Congress of Vienna*. London and New York: Oxford University Press, 1919. This was used by the British delegates at Versailles.

————. *The Foreign Policy of Castlereagh, 1812-1815*. London: Bell, 1925. The first volume of a magisterial study which, while not uncritical, rescues Castlereagh from the more ridiculous charges made against him.

————. *The Foreign Policy of Castlereagh, 1815-1822*. London: Bell, 1925. Sequel to the preceding volume.

Barry McGill

GEORGE CATLIN

Born: July 26, 1796; Wilkes-Barre, Pennsylvania
Died: December 23, 1872; Jersey City, New Jersey
Areas of Achievement: American Indian art and ethnology
Contribution: Catlin provided some of the earliest paintings showing the culture of the upper Missouri River Valley Indians, and his books include much significant ethnological material about tribal ceremonies.

Early Life

George Catlin was born July 26, 1796, in Wilkes-Barre, Pennsylvania. The fifth of fourteen children born to Polly Sutton and Putnam Catlin, he achieved the most fame. Polly, his mother, had been born on the Pennsylvania frontier and as a child had been captured by the Indians during the 1778 "Wyoming Massacre." His Connecticut-born father, Putnam Catlin, served as a fife major during the American Revolution. After the war, Putnam studied law, moved to Wilkes-Barre, and married Polly Sutton. The Catlins hoped that young George would become a lawyer also, and in 1817, they sent the twenty-one-year-old back to Connecticut to study.

His training completed, in less than two years he returned home with reasonable skills but little enthusiasm for the law. Rather, he wanted to become a portrait painter, and even during court proceedings he sketched scenes and people in the room. Sometime between 1821 and 1823, he quit his law practice and moved to Philadelphia, where he set out on his life's work. A handsome young man of no more than five feet nine inches, he had a deep scar on his left cheek, black hair, blue eyes, and a medium complexion. He was a friendly, outgoing person, who made friends easily and usually kept them for life. These attributes enabled him to penetrate the artistic society in Philadelphia, and by early 1824, he became a member of the Pennsylvania Academy, the literary and artistic group in that city.

Soon he had enough commissions for miniatures and portraits, and financial security seemed at hand, yet Catlin was restless and dissatisfied. A visiting group of Indian leaders who were in the East to negotiate with the government caught his attention. They seemed natural and dignified compared to his city acquaintances, and Catlin decided to paint them and record their customs. Before he could do so, he continued to do portraits and to make friends with wealthy and prominent people to finance his later western travels. While in Albany, New York, working on a portrait of Governor De Witt Clinton, Catlin met Clara Bartless Gregory, and on May 20, 1828, the two were married. Between portrait assignments, Catlin traveled to nearby reservations to paint Indian leaders, and he did several portraits of the noted Seneca leader Red Jacket. Despite his marriage, his continuing restlessness overcame him, and in early 1830, Catlin set out for St. Louis to begin what was to be his life's work: painting, observing, and describing the western Indians.

Life's Work

In St. Louis, Catlin met the famous explorer William Clark, who was then superintendent for Indian affairs for the tribes beyond the Mississippi. Clark knew the western tribes as well as anyone and proved to be very helpful. He answered Catlin's questions and invited him to paint portraits of the Indians who came to the city to confer with him. During the summer of 1830, Catlin accompanied Clark to Prairie du Chien, Wisconsin, to observe a treaty council meeting there, and later that same year, they visited Indians encamped along the Kansas River. In late 1830, Catlin traveled to Fort Leavenworth to observe and paint tribes there, while the next spring, he accompanied an Indian agent up the Missouri River to what is now Omaha, to visit other villages. By the end of 1831, the artist had observed, met, and painted Indians from perhaps fifteen distinct tribes, and he had acquired artifacts from many of them in addition to his sketches and portraits.

Still, Catlin wanted to observe villages and tribes that were farther removed from white society. His chance came in March, 1832, when he set off up the Missouri River on the American Fur Company steamboat *Yellowstone*, traveling upstream to Fort Union, at the mouth of the Yellowstone River in western North Dakota. Catlin worked as rapidly as possible, painting as many as five or six pictures a day. From Fort Union, Catlin and two trappers went back down the Missouri in a small skiff. Along the way, they halted at the Mandan villages in central North Dakota, where Catlin drew detailed pictures of the Mandan Okeepa Ceremony. Five years later, a smallpox epidemic virtually destroyed this tribe; his data, as a result, constitute almost the only information about the ceremony that survived.

Two years later, Catlin accompanied an army expedition west onto the southern plains. Catlin also traveled north to Fort Snelling at what is now Minneapolis-St. Paul to paint villagers there. In 1836, he decided to visit the famous Pipe Stone Quarry in southwestern Minnesota, the site from which the Sioux obtained the red stone which they used for their pipes. Despite the Indians' efforts to discourage them, Catlin and several companions traveled to the quarry, where he made sketches and gathered samples of the stone. A geologist later named the mineral Catlinite in his honor. By this time, Catlin had executed approximately six hundred paintings and sketches of Indians, as well as collecting artifacts that varied from a Crow tepee to beads and feather headdresses. He had taken copious notes which he would later transcribe and publish along with his drawings.

By 1837, he had moved this collection east, and late that year, he began exhibiting his paintings and artifacts, or Indian Gallery, as he called the collection. The exhibit drew large crowds, and he soon took it to Washington, Philadelphia, and Boston. Catlin, however, proved to be an inept businessman. He hoped to sell his material to the United States government and worked for some years to interest Congress in buying it. When it became apparent that the government had little serious interest in Indian materials, a disappointed Catlin set sail for England. He arrived there in 1839, and again exhibited before large and enthusiastic crowds. In 1841, he published the first of his several books about the Indians. Always short of money, by 1845 he moved to Paris, where he was asked to exhibit the paintings at the Louvre.

Catlin's years in France were among the most unhappy of his life. On the edge of bankruptcy, and with little chance of getting back to the United States, he became discouraged at the news that Congress voted repeatedly not to buy his paintings. Then, in July, 1845, his wife, Clara, died of pneumonia, and a year later his three-year-old son George died as well. His wife's family arranged for his three daughters to return to the United States, but Catlin remained mired in debt and unable to leave Paris. In 1852, Joseph Harrison, a wealthy American, bought Catlin's paintings and took them back to Philadelphia, leaving the artist more or less free from debt. With little more than determination, he began to paint new copies of his original Indian Gallery dur-

ing the 1850's. He also made several trips to South America and to the west coast of North America. In 1870, he returned to the United States and was reunited with his daughters. Catlin died in 1872, believing that his country had spurned his life's work and that the Indian Gallery had been lost.

Ironically, had Congress bought the paintings in the 1840's, they would not have survived the Smithsonian fire. As it was, when Catlin's exhibit of his cartoon collection failed in New York in 1870, Joseph Henry of the Smithsonian invited the artist to display them in Washington.

Summary

George Catlin stands out as a man with single-minded purpose: to preserve knowledge of the western Indians, their dress and customs, for all Americans. This goal took him west, where he painted Indians from dozens of tribes. As art, his work does not rank as great. He was largely self-taught, and he often painted hurriedly and under crude conditions. When he had time, he used a style similar to that which he had employed as a Philadelphia portrait painter. Often he sketched quickly, focusing on a person's face and barely sketching in the remainder of the body. Regardless of the style, Catlin's work is considered among the most accurate and unadorned in depicting Native Americans. Hundreds of his paintings have survived, and he did succeed in preserving knowledge of Indian life.

In addition to his paintings, Catlin kept knowledge of the Indians alive in other ways. As a showman and exhibitor, he exposed thousands of Americans to Indian scenes and artifacts during the mid-nineteenth century. Of more significance, his writings provide valuable ethnological data for knowledge of the tribal societies that he visited. His more significant books include *Letters and Notes on the Manners, Customs and Conditions of the North American Indians* (1841), *Catlin's North American Indian Portfolio* (1844), *Life Amongst the Indians* (1861), and *Last Rambles Amongst the Indians of the Rocky Mountains and the Andes* (1867). In addition to these, Catlin published catalogs of his exhibits and many articles for newspapers in the United States. Throughout his career, he labored to bring knowledge of the Indians to white society. For artists and ethnologists, his legacy is rich.

Bibliography

Catlin, George. *Episodes from Life Among the Indians and Last Rambles.* Edited by Marvin C.

Ross. Norman: University of Oklahoma Press, 1959. Includes selections from Catlin's first and last books about his experiences with Indians. This well-edited collection includes more than 150 photographs of Catlin's paintings.

———. *Letters and Notes on the Manners, Customs and Conditions of the North American Indians.* 2 vols. London: Bogue, 1841; Mineola, N.Y.: Dover, 1973. This is a clearly reprinted edition of Catlin's most significant ethnological writing, done only a few years after he left the West.

Ewers, John C. *Artists of the Old West.* New York: Doubleday, 1965. Ewers is probably the most knowledgeable student of Catlin's contributions to ethnology, and he discusses those in his chapter on Catlin.

Haberly, Loyd. *Pursuit of the Horizon: A Life of George Catlin, Painter and Recorder of the American Indian.* New York: Macmillan, 1948. A full-length popular biography of Catlin that gives a balanced treatment of his long life, including his years in Europe. It has neither notes nor bibliography but is based on solid research.

Hassrick, Royal B. *The George Catlin Book of American Indians.* New York: Watson-Guptill, 1977. This volume, featuring both color and black-and-white plates, reproduces a generous selection of Catlin's paintings. It briefly discusses his life, art, and writings, but its value lies chiefly in the illustrations.

Haverstock, Mary Sayre. *Indian Gallery: The Story of George Catlin.* New York: Four Winds Press, 1973. This popular biography focuses primarily on Catlin's pre-1839 activities. The last four decades of his life are compressed into a mere fifty pages.

McCracken, Harold. *George Catlin and the Old Frontier.* New York: Dial Press, 1959. The result of thorough research, this well-written biography focuses almost entirely on Catlin's life to 1839; it devotes only two of twenty-two chapters to his career between 1839 and 1872.

Roehm, Marjorie Catlin. *The Letters of George Catlin and His Family: A Chronicle of the American West.* Berkeley: University of California Press, 1966. Based on several hundred Catlin family letters used for the first time, this book combines the author's narrative with extensive selections from family correspondence. Half of the book considers Catlin's activities after he left the country. The use of family papers gives an immediacy to the story.

Stevenson, Winona. "Beggars, Chickabobbooags, and Prisons: Paxoche (Ioway) Views of English Society, 1844-45." *American Indian Culture and Research Journal* 17, no. 4 (Fall 1993). The author reconstructs Catlin's published work concerning the views of English society held by the Paxoche people. Provides insight into the views of Native Americans on issues such as keeping animals in zoos, the homeless, and Christianity.

Taylor, Colin F. *Catlin's O-kee-pa: Mandan Culture and Ceremonial: The George Catlin O-kee-pa Manuscript in the British Museum.* Wyk, Germany: Verlag Amerikanistik, 1996. Previously felt to be too sexually explicit, Taylor reproduces the unabridged manuscript of Carlin's account of the O-kee-pa ceremonial of the Mandan people of the upper Missouri. Contains many illustrations, maps, and reproductions of original watercolors never before seen.

Roger L. Nichols

COUNT CAVOUR

Born: August 10, 1810; Turin, French Empire
Died: June 6, 1861; Turin, Italy
Areas of Achievement: Politics and government
Contribution: As prime minister between 1852 and 1861, Cavour gave Piedmont the economic and diplomatic leadership of Italy and played a key role in the country's political unification. He is generally regarded as the founder of modern Italy.

Early Life

Count Camillo Benso di Cavour was born in Turin on August 10, 1810. His mother, née Adèle de Sellon, came from a line of wealthy Huguenots who had been expelled from France by Louis XIV and had settled in Geneva. His father, the Marquis Michele Benso di Cavour, was the head of an ancient noble family, a businessman and administrator who rose to high office in the reactionary regime of Restoration Piedmont. Cavour soon rejected this world. As a second son, he was expected to make his living in the army, but, while attending Turin's Royal Military Academy, he was frequently punished for rebelling against military routines. He was graduated in 1826 and served in the army for five years, while formulating increasingly liberal political views. After the Revolution of 1830, in which Charles X of France was overthrown, Cavour was put under surveillance by Piedmontese authorities as a dangerous radical. In November, 1831, he resigned his commission.

Cavour was eager for a political career, but his ambitions remained blocked by Piedmont's autocratic government for the next sixteen years. Instead, he engaged in various economic activities, supervising family estates, investing in new factories, banks, and railway companies, and speculating profitably in government securities and foreign exchange. He also devoted himself to the study of political and economic developments in Great Britain and France, visiting both countries periodically and acquiring a deep admiration for the ideas of Jeremy Bentham and the practices of François Guizot and Sir Robert Peel.

By the mid-1830's, he had become an advocate of the *juste milieu*, or middle way, which he thought would obviate the dangers posed by the extremes of reaction and revolution. Specifically, he recommended a parliamentary government controlled by an educated, wealthy elite which would promote so-cial progress by means of gradual, rational reform. Thus, after briefly espousing radical opinions in his youth, Cavour adopted a liberal-conservative stance which he maintained for the rest of his life.

Life's Work

Cavour's political opportunity finally arrived as a result of King Charles Albert's reluctant reforms during the revolutionary atmosphere of the late 1840's. In 1847, Cavour was one of the founders and the editor of a moderate liberal newspaper, *Il Risorgimento*. In 1848, he served on the commission which established a restricted parliamentary franchise similar to his own ideal and, in June, was elected to the Chamber of Deputies.

Initially, Cavour's chances of rapid political advancement must have appeared slim, for he had neither parliamentary allies nor a commanding personal presence. He was short and stocky, with a round face, thinning, reddish hair, a scanty beard, and spectacles, and was more familiar with the French language than Italian, which he spoke imperfectly and unattractively. Yet he proved an engaging character, self-confident, down-to-earth, humorous, and conscientious, with the somewhat racy image of an incorrigible gambler, a lifelong bachelor, and a womanizer. More important, he was a highly skilled politician, well versed in parliamentary practice, and an extremely penetrating, logical speaker. He quickly won the allegiance of conservatives by backing Massimo d'Azeglio's center-right government and of leftists by supporting the Siccardi laws against ecclesiastical privileges. It thus came as no surprise when he was appointed minister of marine, commerce, and agriculture in October, 1850, added the Finance Ministry six months later, and became the dominant figure in the government. He was able to seize complete power in 1852, when Azeglio resigned in protest at the senate's rejection of a civil-marriage bill. Cavour was a rationalist who generally sympathized with attempts to reduce the Church's authority, but on this occasion he agreed to King Victor Emmanuel II's demand that the bill be abandoned and was appointed prime minister on November 4.

In the early years of his premiership, Cavour concentrated on domestic affairs, attempting to convert backward Piedmont into the most progressive and powerful country in Italy. Accordingly, he resisted royal attempts to subvert parliament's constitutional supremacy, resumed the attack on the Church by dissolving half of the monasteries in 1855, and increased military expenditure. In addition, he terminated Piedmont's dependence on costly loans from the Rothschilds' Paris bank and promoted economic growth by expanding bank credit, financing the development of mines, railways, and utilities, and maintaining tariff agreements that he had negotiated earlier as finance minister. As a result, Piedmont became the only liberal, reforming state in the peninsula and the acknowledged leader of the Italian national cause.

Cavour's important contribution to that cause was a tribute to his remarkable flexibility and opportunism. At heart a Piedmontese nationalist, he was concerned to further the interests of his native state. To do so, he invariably opposed revolutionary efforts by republicans such as Giuseppe Garibaldi and Giuseppe Mazzini but otherwise was prepared to modify tactics and objectives in the light of experience and circumstances. In the 1840's, he expected the Italians themselves to expel Austria and create a Turin-based, northern kingdom to the exclusion of the central and southern parts of Italy. Austria's easy victories over Piedmont in 1849, however, convinced him that little could be achieved without foreign aid and he carefully avoided hostilities until the Crimean War. Before its outbreak, Cavour was reluctant to meet British and French requests for help and only did so in 1855 in order to foil Victor Emmanuel's plan to replace him with a more warlike minister. Nevertheless, participation in the war proved a boon.

On the one hand, the army's creditable performance increased Piedmont's prestige in Italy. On the other, at the Congress of Paris in 1856 Cavour raised the Italian question in an international forum for the first time and learned that Napoleon III was sympathetic to the idea of a moderately powerful, independent kingdom in northern Italy. Subsequently, he maintained contact with the emperor and, in 1858, negotiated the secret Pact of Plombières, committing France to send military assistance in return for territorial concessions if Cavour engineered a crisis in which Austria appeared the aggressor. He was able to do so in April, 1859, largely because of Austria's foolish ultimatum demanding unilateral demobilization by Piedmont. During the resultant war, however, stiff Austrian resistance led Napoleon to withdraw after two narrow victories and negotiate the Armistice of Vil-

lafranca with Emperor Francis Joseph. Cavour, who was not invited to the talks, was bitterly disappointed at the peace terms, which obliged Austria to cede only Lombardy and ordered the restoration to the central Italian duchies of absolutist rulers who had been ousted during the war and replaced by Piedmontese sympathizers. On learning that Victor Emmanuel had accepted the terms, he angrily resigned on July 11, 1859.

In the last two years of his life, a series of unexpected developments enabled Cavour to achieve goals he had previously dismissed as impracticable. While he was out of office, the faltering alliance with the French was replaced by British support. Foreign Minister Lord John Russell criticized the Villafranca agreement as unworkable, insisting that Italians be allowed to determine their own future, and pressured Victor Emmanuel into reinstating Cavour in January, 1860. On his return, he was thus fully confident that Piedmont's control would soon be extended into central Italy. In March, after he had guaranteed Napoleon's acquiescence by ceding Nice and Savoy to France, plebiscites were held in Modena,

Parma, Romagna, and Tuscany, whose subjects voted overwhelmingly for annexation. At this juncture, Cavour looked for a lengthy period of peace in which the new territories could be consolidated, but his hopes were rudely shattered by Garibaldi's startling conquest of Sicily and Naples between May and September, 1860. Desperate to prevent Italian leadership's falling into popular, democratic hands, he first convinced Napoleon that his purpose was to protect the pope from advancing revolutionaries and then boldly sent the army south. Having taken Umbria and the Marche, the central and eastern parts of the Papal States, it entered Naples, where Garibaldi relinquished authority to Victor Emmanuel in late October. Subsequently, the people of Naples, the Marche, and Umbria voted for annexation by Piedmont. In January, 1861, elections were held for a national parliament which, on March 17, gave the Italian crown to Victor Emmanuel. Tragically, Cavour was unable to enjoy the fruits of his triumph, for soon afterward he contracted a fever, probably malaria, and died on June 6, 1861.

Summary

Count Cavour's achievements fully justify his reputation as one of the most successful statesmen in modern European history. In a mere eight years, he made Piedmont the leading Italian state and, with a rare combination of diplomatic skill, opportunism, and military daring, unified most of the peninsula. When he died, the only remaining independent territories were Venetia and Rome, which were added in 1866 and 1870, respectively. Yet Cavour's legacy was by no means untarnished. Essentially, the process of unification entailed the imposition on all Italy of Piedmont's political system, which gave power to the largely anticlerical upper middle class. In conjunction with Cavour's seizure of papal territory, the extension of the political system contributed to the rift that was to divide church and state for the remainder of the century. It also aroused intense hostility among the thousands who had fought or voted for annexation expecting democracy, and aggravated the serious class and regional conflicts that racked Italian society. Equally detrimental were Cavour's methods of controlling parliament, such as tampering with elections, invalidating unfavorable returns, and disarming opposition by giving office to its moderate elements. The latter practice underlay the *connubio* (marriage), which united Cavour's moderate conserva-

tive deputies and Urbano Rattazzi's center-left group from 1852 to 1857, when leftist electoral losses facilitated a return to the Right.

Such expedients enabled Cavour to establish a virtual dictatorship, unfettered by king, cabinet, or parliament. Whether he viewed them as temporary, emergency measures is unclear because he died so soon after the prolonged national crisis ended. After 1861, the imitation of these measures by less talented politicians produced many of the features which characterized later Italian politics, including a tendency to tolerate autocratic power, the absence of cabinet responsibility, and reliance on fluctuating centrist coalitions which survived only by avoiding controversial issues. Thus, Cavour can be viewed as the founder not only of the Italian state but also of traditions responsible for its chronic political weakness.

Bibliography

Coppa, Frank J. *Camillo di Cavour.* New York: Twayne, 1973. A brief, well-written biography by an American Catholic scholar, focusing on aspects of Cavour's career not normally stressed. Particularly useful for church-state relations and diplomacy prior to Plombières. Contains a detailed bibliography with some omissions.

Hearder, Harry. *Cavour.* 2d ed. London: Historical Association, 1985; New York: Longman, 1994. An updated version of a 1972 pamphlet. Provides an excellent introduction, with sections on Cavour's life, opinions, and achievements and a well-balanced assessment of his contribution to Italian history. Contains a useful, short bibliography.

———. "Clarendon, Cavour, and the Intervention of Sardinia in the Crimean War, 1853-1855." *The International History Review* 18, no. 4 (November, 1996). Discusses the influence of George Villiers and Sir James Hudson on Count Cavour's decision to enter the Crimean War.

Mack Smith, Denis. *Cavour.* London: Weidenfeld and Nicolson, and New York: Knopf, 1985. A fully documented, lucid biography, containing much fresh information and new insights. Good on all aspects of Cavour's life but particularly economic policies and the development of his character. Contains a useful bibliographical note. Essential reading.

———. *Cavour and Garibaldi, 1860: A Study in Political Conflict.* Cambridge: Cambridge University Press, 1954; New York: Kraus, 1968. A seminal work based on newly released archival material. Brilliantly clarifies the complex events of 1860, demonstrating the conflicts between Italian leaders and undermining traditional myths about Cavour. The 1985 reissue includes the author's reflections on the controversy generated by the original edition.

Whyte, A. J. *The Early Life and Letters of Cavour, 1810-1848.* London: Oxford University Press, 1925; Wetsport, Conn.: Greenwood Press, 1976. A scholarly account of Cavour's life before his entry into parliament, making extensive use of his correspondence. Offers useful insights into his character and his preparations for a political career.

—. *The Political Life and Letters of Cavour, 1848-1861.* London: Oxford University Press, 1930; Wetsport, Conn.: Greenwood Press, 1975. The sequel to the above entry, with similar qualities. Deals with Cavour's political career, emphasizing his diplomatic activities.

Ian Duffy

SIR GEORGE CAYLEY

Born: December 27, 1773; Scarborough, York-shire, England

Died: December 15, 1857; Brompton, Yorkshire, England

Areas of Achievement: Aeronautics, invention, and social reform

Contribution: Cayley was the first to conceive and publish the modern idea of the airplane: namely, the concept that an airplane should consist of one or more fixed wings, a fuselage, and a tail. Moreover, he was the first to carry out a serious program of aeronautical research.

Early Life

Sir George Cayley was born on December 27, 1773, in a house named Paradise, in Scarborough, England. His mother, Isabella Seton Cayley, was a member of a well-known Scottish family descended from Robert Bruce. His father, Sir Thomas Cayley, was descended from the Norman invaders of England in 1066. Because of the chronic ill health of his father, Cayley's parents spent much time abroad, and Cayley's early days were spent at the family house at Helmsley, where he enjoyed much freedom. There, he acquired an early interest in mechanical devices, and he was frequently to be found at the village watchmaker. After the death of his grandfather (also Sir George Cayley), the major and extensive family estate at Brompton passed quickly to his father, who lived for only another eighteen months, and then to George Cayley. By the year 1792, Sir George Cayley had become the sixth baronet at Brompton Hall—at the early age of nineteen. He was to spend the rest of his life as a moderately well-to-do Yorkshire country squire.

As was not unusual in the eighteenth century, Cayley had virtually no formal education. There is some evidence that he went to school briefly in York, but his main education stemmed from two powerful and influential tutors: George Walker, a mathematician of high reputation, Fellow of the Royal Society and a man of extensive intellect; and George Morgan, a Unitarian minister, scientist, and lecturer on electricity. Both tutors were freethinkers, and they had a major impact on the wide breadth of education and open-mindedness acquired by Cayley during the first twenty-five years of his life. Cayley never lost his enthusiasm for knowledge and invention; by the early 1800's he was recognized and sought-after as one of En-gland's leading scholars in matters of science, technology, and social ethics.

Struck by the beauty and intelligence of his first tutor's daughter, Sarah Walker, Cayley fell deeply in love in 1792, the same year in which he acquired the family estate at Brompton. Three years later they were married; their marriage was to last for sixty-two years, ended only by Cayley's death in 1857.

Cayley's contributions to aeronautics also began in his early life. At the age of nineteen, he designed and flew a simple helicopter-like model made of wood and feathers and powered by a string-and-bow mechanism. This was the leading edge of a virtual outpouring of aeronautical thought, research, and invention to follow for the next eighteen years.

Life's Work

The concept of the modern airplane—namely, that of a machine with fixed wings, fuselage, and horizontal and vertical tail—was first advanced by Cayley in 1799. This concept was a marked departure from all previous aeronautical thinking, which was focused on machines called ornithopters, characterized by flapping wings for both lift and propulsion—an idea fostered from the Greek and Roman ages in an attempt to emulate bird flight directly. Cayley's idea was ingenious. It involved the separation of the mechanisms for producing lift and thrust: A fixed wing, inclined to the airflow would produce the lift, and a separate mechanism using either flappers or an airscrew driven by an internal combustion engine would provide the propulsion. In 1799, Cayley etched a picture of his airplane concept on a small silver disk (about the size of an American quarter); this disk is the first rendering of the modern airplane, and it is now displayed with distinction at the British Science Museum in South Kensington, London.

In 1804, Cayley designed and successfully flew a hand-launched glider made of wood and cloth, incorporating his fixed-wing, fuselage, and tail concept. It was the first modern configuration airplane to fly in history. During the first decade of the nineteenth century, Cayley carried out numerous aeronautical experiments, the results of which were published in a momentous "triple paper" titled "On Aerial Navigation," which appeared in three issues of *Nicholson's Journal of Natural Philosophy, Chemistry, and the Arts* (November, 1809; February, 1810; and March, 1810). In this paper, Cayley published many "firsts" in the technical development of aeronautics. He was, for example, the first to use a whirling arm for obtaining aerodynamic data on the lift and drag force exerted on winglike shapes; the first to realize that lift is obtained from the combination of low pressure on the top surface of the wing and high pressure on the bottom surface; the first to recognize that a cambered (curved) airfoil shape produces more lift than a straight, flat surface; the first to realize that a dihedral angle (wings bent upward slightly from the center section) achieves lateral (rolling) stability for the airplane; and the first to obtain research results on aeronautical streamlining to reduce drag. This triple paper by Cayley is of such aeronautical and historical significance that it was reprinted by the Royal Aeronautical Society in 1876, 1910, and 1955; by the American journal *The Aeronautical Annual* in 1895; by two French journals in 1877 and 1912; and, as appendices, in two definitive books on Cayley, one by J. Laurence Pritchard (1961) and the other by Charles H. Gibbs-Smith (1962).

In concert with his aeronautical interests, Cayley carried out extensive works on the design of internal combustion engines. He recognized that existing steam engines, with their huge external boilers, were much too heavy in relation to their power output to be of any practical application to airplanes. To improve on this situation, Cayley invented the hot-air engine in 1799 and spent the next fifty-eight years of his life trying to perfect the idea, along with a host of other mechanical designers of that day. The invention of the successful gas-fueled engine in France in the mid-1800's finally superseded Cayley's hot-air engine.

For reasons not totally understood, Cayley directed his aeronautical interest to lighter-than-air balloons and airships during the period from 1810 to 1843, making contributions to the understanding of such devices and inventing several designs for steerable airships. Then, from 1843 until his death in 1857, he returned to the airplane, designing and testing several full-scale aircraft. One was a machine with triple wings (a triplane) and human-actuated flappers for propulsion; in 1849 this machine made a floating flight off the ground, carrying a ten-year-old boy for several yards down a hill at Brompton. Another was a single-wing (monoplane) glider, which in 1853 flew across a small valley (no longer than five hundred yards) with Cayley's coachman aboard as an un-

willing passenger. (At the end of this flight, the coachman was quoted as saying, "Please, Sir George, I wish to give notice. I was hired to drive and not to fly.")

Although Cayley's standing in history is based on his aeronautical contributions, this broadly educated and liberal-thinking man accomplished much more during his long life of eighty-four years. Of particular note is his invention in 1825 of the tracted land vehicle, a vehicle that was the forerunner of the Caterpillar tractor and the military tanks of the twentieth century. In 1847, he invented an artificial hand. This artificial limb was a breakthrough in such devices, replacing the simple hook which had been in use for centuries. Cayley's interests were purely humane; he expected and received virtually no financial compensation for this invention.

Other nonaeronautical accomplishments by Cayley are, to list only a few, concern for parliamentary reform, leading to a publication on that subject in 1818; election to the chair of the powerful Whig Club at York in 1820; his work as a Member of Parliament for Scarborough (starting in 1832); his founding of the Polytechnic Institution in Regent Street, London, in 1839, for scientific and technical exhibitions and education (now the Regent Street Polytechnic, an institution for continuing education); and his inventions to promote railway safety (again, he was driven by a genuine concern for improving the lot of mankind, especially that of the poor). His social conscience was never more in evidence than in his efforts to help unemployed laborers from the York area in 1842; he wrote an appeal for help in the newspapers and contributed a large sum of his own money (although he was not a rich man) to help relieve the social and economic distress in the area.

A portrait of Sir George Cayley hangs in the National Portrait Gallery in London; it was painted when he was sixty-eight years old. It shows a still-handsome man with a soft, kindly, and scholarly countenance. It is no surprise that Cayley was well liked and respected by his family as a father and husband, by his friends as a kind, thoughtful, and humorous country squire, and by his scientific and technical colleagues as one of the most innovative, knowledgeable, and well-read people in England at the time. When Cayley died, peacefully at Brompton Hall on December 15, 1857, many members of social and scientific England strongly felt his loss, as evidenced by numerous obituaries and statements at that time.

Summary

It is well known that Orville and Wilbur Wright accomplished the first successful, heavier-than-air, powered, manned flight, on December 17, 1903. If Sir George Cayley had been alive at that moment, he would have been the first to applaud the accomplishment, because it is clear from his writings that he took for granted the eventual successful development of the airplane. Contrary to much popular belief, however, the Wright brothers did *not* invent the concept of the airplane; instead, they invented the world's first successful, working airplane. The concept of the modern airplane is Cayley's, and his alone. All modern historians of aviation agree to this, and indeed even the Wright brothers gave credit to Cayley in this regard.

It is interesting to note that credit to Cayley for his aeronautical contributions faded during the last half of the nineteenth century, in spite of his numerous publications in the field. Many would-be inventors in aviation either repeated some of Cayley's work or used his ideas without knowing the source, mainly because of their ignorance of the literature. Historical research in the twentieth century, however, clearly gives Cayley his rightful place in history as the grandparent of modern aviation. He established, in total, all the essential ideas of powered heavier-than-air flight, even including the invention of a lightweight, wire-braced wheel for an undercarriage—a wheel which was to be utilized as the bicycle wheel when that vehicle was invented, in the late 1880's. Perhaps no better accolade for Cayley can be given than that voiced by the French historian Alphonse Berget in 1909, who wrote: "It is necessary to inscribe the name of Sir George Cayley in letters of gold on the first page of the aeroplane's history."

Bibliography

Anderson, John D., Jr. *Introduction to Flight*. 3d ed. New York: McGraw-Hill, 1989. Molds the elementary technical aspects of the airplane with extensive historical notes, including a lengthy discussion of Cayley's technical contributions.

Gibbs-Smith, Charles H. *Aviation: An Historical Survey from Its Origins to the End of World War II*. 2d ed. London: Her Majesty's Stationery Office, 1985. A balanced survey of the historical development of aviation, including Cayley's work. This is a good book from which to obtain an overall perspective of Cayley's contributions in comparison with the complete picture of aeronautical development.

―――. *Sir George Cayley, 1773-1857*. London: Her Majesty's Stationery Office, 1968. An excellent pamphlet printed for the Science Museum, with a concise presentation of Cayley as the man and the inventor.

―――. *Sir George Cayley's Aeronautics, 1796-1855*. London: Her Majesty's Stationery Office, 1962. A thorough and definitive historical presentation of Cayley's technical contributions, along with insightful commentary on Cayley's work. A must for any serious student of Cayley's life and contributions.

Pritchard, J. Laurence. *Sir George Cayley: The Inventor of the Aeroplane*. London: Parrish, 1961. This is the definitive biography of Sir George Cayley. This is also a must for any student of George Cayley's life.

John D. Anderson, Jr.

PAUL CÉZANNE

Born: January 19, 1839; Aix-en-Provence, France
Died: October 22, 1906; Aix-en-Provence, France
Area of Achievement: Art
Contribution: Cézanne's innovative and brilliant style challenged the conventions of nineteenth century art and had a major influence on twentieth century cubists and abstract artists.

Early Life

Paul Cézanne was born at Aix-en-Provence, a town in the south of France, not far from Marseilles and the Mediterranean. His father's family came from the Italian Alpine village Cesana (hence the surname) in the seventeenth century and had a history of minor business activities. Louis-Auguste, Paul's father, started out as a hat maker, at which he was a success, and eventually became a banker in Aix. He lived with Anne-Élisabeth-Honorine Aubert for several years before marrying her in 1844, and Paul was one of their children born before they were married. The family was financially secure, and Paul was educated locally. Interested in art, he took some instruction at the local École des Beaux Arts. One of his closest friends then, and in later life, was Émile Zola, who was to become one of France's greatest men of letters.

Cézanne's enthusiasm for art was tolerated by his father, but he was expected to make a career in the law. He was a good student and entered the University of Aix-en-Provence to study law, but after passing his first-year exams, he asked his father if he might join his friend Zola, who had gone to Paris to make his way as a journalist. Cézanne wanted to study at the prestigious Académie des Beaux-Arts in Paris. His father allowed him to quit school in late 1859, but he kept him in Aix until April, 1861, when he took him to Paris to study as an artist. Cézanne was refused entrance to the school and joined the Académie Suisse, a studio in which young artists banded together to work with live models. He was virtually untrained and his work showed little promise. Often difficult and inclined to be morose and withdrawn, he was often unhappy with himself and his work. His father supported him, but not generously. In September he gave up, returned to Aix, and joined the family bank.

Life's Work

Cézanne's self-portraits reveal a thick-set, hard-mouthed peasant glaring out of the canvas, and if there is one thing that marks him as a man and as an artist it is his weighty, determined stubbornness which the paintings suggest. Once back in Aix, he began to draw again and to take some classes locally. In 1862, his father gave in once again and allowed him to return to Paris, and he began to associate with a group of young artists whose work had been rejected by the conservative power structure of artists, critics, and teachers who controlled the Académie des Beaux-Arts and the annual Salon, an exhibition of supposedly the best art being produced in France. Camille Pissarro became his closest friend, but he also came to know Édouard Manet, Auguste Renoir, and Claude Monet, all, in one way or another, out of step with established standards of taste in the art world.

This group of painters would ultimately be called the "Impressionists," a name which was originally imposed on them with contempt because of their insistence on a new, looser, lighter style of painting in which they attempted to catch the transitory nature of visual experience. There was considerable difference in their individual contributions to the movement, and it can be argued that Manet, whose work was sometimes accepted by the Salon, was on the fringe of the group. The artist most clearly not quite an Impressionist was Cézanne. After attempting to get his work accepted by the Salon and being pointedly rejected, he joined the Impressionists in exhibitions outside official circles, and he continued to exhibit with them for several years, and, like them, he was to be ridiculed and neglected.

In the late 1860's, he established a relationship with the model Marie-Hortense Fiquet, who was often a subject of his paintings; they had a child, Paul, in 1872. Like his father, Cézanne did not wed his mistress for several years. He sold practically nothing, was still dependent upon his father, and often disappeared for months at a time. In 1877, he exhibited for the last time with the Impressionists and was so derided for his work that he simply gave up public exhibitions.

His early work was often awkward, his colors muddy, his themes uninviting. Rape, murder, or other emotionally excessive subjects seemed to mirror personal problems with which he was attempting to deal in his art. There is much piling on of paint with the palette knife, and a sense of great power not quite successfully expressed. In the

Self-portrait by Cézanne

1870's, he was closest to being something of an Impressionist. He spent a considerable amount of time with Pissarro, who was something of a teacher-father to him, and began to paint less morbid subjects, his colors becoming brighter, and his draftsmanship more sophisticated. He was still tonally serious, and he never quite gave way to the looser, feathery style of the Impressionists. Where the Impressionists attempted to record the evanescence of experience, its constant change, he chose to seek its basic structures, painting the planes, the conjunctions, the solidity of objects. By 1880, he had finally developed a style all his own, entirely different from that of any other painter, incorporating the "open air" freshness of Impressionism to the austere monumentality of painters such as Nicolas Poussin and Gustave Courbet. In a sense, he invented himself.

Cézanne went his own way, almost forgotten, spending most of his time around Aix, painting landscapes, still lifes, and portraits very slowly, painstakingly, in planes of color placed sometimes at seemingly perverse angles, eschewing line for mass, teasing volume, depth, relationships out of small dabs of color, knowing that colors laid flatly side by side suggest depth or protrusion to the human eye. At close range it resembles a jigsaw puzzle.

Cézanne seemed to reject the idea that a painting was supposed to be an accurate rendering of reality. His paintings start with reality, but ultimately are independent of it: They are aesthetic experiences with their own internal logic. He often subverted the commonly held idea that paintings represent one point of view. He deliberately tipped one end of a table, while the other end was left perfectly flat. He represented his subjects from more than one point of view in ways which are often subtle shifts of perspective. What looks simply like bad draftsmanship was, in fact, deliberate distortion, which creates rhythms, associations, patterns transcending normal representational painting.

This experimental urge is absorbed in a tender solemnity of tone which suggests that the paintings, however simple in subject, have a haunting metaphysical weight, often reminiscent of the same deep stillness in the work of Jean-Baptiste-Siméon Chardin. The subject, ultimately, is less important than the experience of its aesthetic presence. He painted more than sixty studies of Mont Sainte-Victoire, a rather unimposing mountain which can be seen on the horizon just across the road from his last studio on the Chemin des Lauves on the outskirts of Aix. The paintings are all quite magnificent, all disturbingly alike factually and aesthetically different, often quite clearly presaging the cubist attempt to turn reality into design.

In the late 1890's, he began to receive some public recognition, and a group of young artists became aware of the fact that he was not only a formidable painter, but also that he had broken new ground in how one might think about art.

Cézanne worked doggedly, never entirely satisfied, avoided by most because of his notorious irascibility, completely committed to his work. He was beginning to get the attention he had deserved, but seemed not to need it. Watercolors became more important than ever to him, proving his long-held theory that there was no such thing as line and modeling; there were only contrasts. His oils are gloriously rich in his later years, and his work kept exploring the old themes, a few apples, a jug, the old hill, bits and pieces that can still be seen on the tables in the studio as he left it. He suffered from diabetes, but continued to work. He caught a cold while painting on October 15, 1906, but he was painting the next morning. He died a week later.

Summary

It is generally accepted that Paul Cézanne is one of the greatest artists in the history of painting. His own work as a colorist and as an exponent of an entirely original style in both the oil and the watercolor might be sufficient proof of this judgment, but he was much more than simply a superlative practitioner. For all of his rough provincialism, he was a theorist who not only put his theories into practice but also showed the way for the entirely new art of the twentieth century. It is difficult to think how that art might have gone had Cézanne not provided it with three singularly important clues.

His own work—beginning so unpromisingly, slowly accumulating form and individuality, absorbing the influences of the past and that of his contemporaries, especially the struggling Impressionists, blossoming into one of the most singularly distinctive styles in the history of painting—proved that there was always room for making art new if ambition, will, and talent could hold out against indifference, neglect, and derision.

His decision not to become a follower of Impressionism, to be a second-class artist, but to use it to go forward into his own realm of expression allowed him to discover one of the most important secrets behind one of the major movements of twentieth century painting: that just as light is always on the move across the landscape, so is the eye. Therefore, the point of view need not be fixed in a painting but can express that movement in the single canvas. This insight was the key needed to trigger the cubist movement in modern art.

Perhaps even more important, he proved that art need not necessarily be an accurate representation of what the eye sees. Styles had changed through the centuries, as had theories about how the artist was to represent reality. Cézanne argued for the proposition (and put it into action in his art) that the work of art might start in nature but need not simply reflect it. It could transcend reality; it could be abstract.

He had said it best: "The eye is not enough, reflection is needed." And he had illustrated it best in paintings which at one and the same time could convey the aesthetic illusion of depth and the sense of flat design consistent with the nature of the medium. His one-man show of 1895, organized by his old friend Pissarro, started him on his way to the reputation he deserved. In 1907, a memorial showing of fifty-six paintings was displayed in Paris at the Salon which so long before had turned him away. From that moment onward, he was to be seen as the most influential painter of the century.

Bibliography

Callen, Anthea. *Techniques of the Impressionists.* London: New Burlington Books, and Secaucus, N.J.: Chartwell, 1982. So much of understanding Cézanne is dependent upon a recognition of the central concern of the artist and his Impressionist friends for technique. This book analyzes individual paintings by artists prior to the Impressionist period and during the period of Impressionist activity. Two Cézanne paintings are carefully discussed.

Cézanne, Paul. *Paul Cézanne.* Edited by Ellen H. Johnson. Paulton, Britsol: Purnell, 1967; New York: Funk and Wagnalls, 1978. Book 18 of the Great Artists series. Contains a short, informed article by Johnson, which is mindful of the general audience. Large reproductions of several paintings, accompanied by short, but sensible notes.

Harris, Nathaniel. *The Art of Cézanne.* New York: Excalibur Books, 1982; London: Chancellor, 1996. A short, inexpensive, but generously illustrated discussion of the artist's life and his painting.

Lewis, Wyndham. *Wyndham Lewis on Art: Collected Writings, 1914-1956.* London: Thames and Hudson, and New York: Funk and Wagnalls, 1969. Lewis was a great admirer of Cézanne, about whom he speaks with the cogency of a practitioner of the same trade.

Morris, Robert. "Cézanne's Mountains." *Critical Inquiry* 24, no. 3 (Spring 1998). Analysis of Cézanne's paintings of Mont Sainte-Victoire, which were completed near the end of his life.

Rewald, John. *Paul Cézanne: A Biography.* New York: Simon and Schuster, 1948; London: Thames and Hudson, 1986. Based on the correspondence of the painter and his friends, this biography has a homey intimacy and easy charm.

———. *Paul Cézanne: The Watercolours, a Catalogue Raisonné.* London: Thames and Hudson, and New York: Graphic Society Books, 1984. The watercolors have often been ignored, but they are not only first-class art in their own right but also provide another way of understanding the artist's obsession with technique and that peculiar way in which he achieves dimensional effects by juxtaposing slabs of pure color.

Turner, Norman. "Cézanne, Wagner, Modulation." *Journal of Aesthetics and Art Criticism* 56, no. 4 (Fall 1998). Examines the use of modulation in the works of Cézanne and Wagner.

Charles Pullen

EDWIN CHADWICK

Born: January 24, 1800; Longsight, near Manchester, England

Died: July 6, 1890; East Sheen, Surrey, England

Areas of Achievement: Social and administrative reform

Contribution: The most active and determined of Jeremy Bentham's disciples, Chadwick sought to reform British government with utilitarian rigor and efficiency, in the hope of making it responsive to the massive social problems created by industrialization and urbanization.

Early Life

Edwin Chadwick was born January 24, 1800, in Longsight, near Manchester, England. His grandfather Andrew, a friend of John Wesley, was a major figure in the establishment of the first Methodist Sunday schools in Lancashire. Edwin's father, James, was an unsuccessful businessman who, inspired by the French Revolution and the ideas of Thomas Paine, became a radical journalist. Edwin's childhood was rendered difficult through his father's financial straits and his mother's early death. Yet he received a sound education at local schools and from private tutors. He moved to London in 1810 when his father assumed an editorial post there. In 1818, he embarked upon his legal education by entering an attorney's office as an apprentice. In 1823, having raised his sights to the more prestigious profession of barrister, he entered the Middle Temple to begin seven years of residence and study.

There was little formal structure to legal education in this period, leaving Chadwick with ample opportunity to explore the exciting and turbulent life of the capital. His residence, Lyon's Inn, was in the midst of London, close not only to the law courts and lawyers' offices but also to the medical schools, hospitals, and the very center of government itself—the Houses of Parliament. Eager, curious, and resolute, Chadwick explored every corner of his new world, from the corridors of power in Westminster to the most appalling and wretched slums of east London. He was also quick to strike up acquaintances, many of whom became lifelong friends and colleagues. The intersecting spheres in which he moved and studied in the late 1820's— law, medicine, politics, and administration—were to shape the course and define the content of his career as a reformer.

Among Chadwick's first and most enduring contacts from these years were medical men such as Thomas Southwood Smith and Neill Arnott, who belonged to the group of intellectuals and reformers known as the Philosophical Radicals. Followers of Jeremy Bentham, they shared his disdain for existing institutions and longed to reform political and legal structures along Utilitarian lines. Finding the tone and style of this iconoclastic set exactly to his taste, Chadwick quickly became a fixture of the Benthamite circle. He began to attract the notice of the more eminent Philosophical Radicals such as Francis Place, Joseph Hume, and John Stuart Mill. In 1830, he was introduced to Bentham himself and was invited by the eccentric and reclusive old sage to become his private secretary. This was a signal honor and opened the prospect of Chadwick becoming Bentham's intellectual heir. Indeed, when Bentham died in 1832, he left his library to Chadwick, along with a promise of a comfortable annuity in return for Chadwick devoting his life to carrying out Bentham's literary projects. Chadwick declined this bequest, for he had already embarked on a more ambitious public career.

Life's Work

Although he would be called to the bar in 1830, Chadwick would never practice law. Possessed of energy, wide-ranging interests, and considerable writing ability, he was at first inclined to pursue a career in journalism. His first article, on life insurance, appeared in 1828 in the major organ of the Philosophical Radicals, *The Westminster Review.* It was followed in 1829 and 1830 by articles on medical charities in France and on preventive police in the short-lived radical journal *The London Review.* These latter articles brought Chadwick to the attention not only of Bentham but also of certain influential political economists such as Nassau William Senior and to reform-minded Whigs such as Henry Brougham. It was through them that Chadwick was soon to be propelled into government service as an investigator and analyst of social problems and as a designer of new administrative structures to solve them.

The victory of the Whigs in the turbulent election of 1830 provided Chadwick with his opportunity. Beyond their commitment to parliamentary reform, many members of the aristocratic Whig cabinet believed that it was necessary to devise solutions to social and economic problems such as child labor in factories and the abuses of the poor law system. Since some cabinet ministers had been exposed to the principles of political economy as well as to Benthamism, they naturally turned to economists and Philosophical Radicals to undertake the inquiries and write the official reports that would serve as the basis of remedial legislation. In 1832, Chadwick was brought in as an expert investigator on two new royal commissions—on the poor laws and on child labor in the factories. Shortly thereafter, he abandoned his journalistic career by resigning as subeditor of the radical newspaper, *The Examiner.* For the next twenty-two years, with one brief but important foray into private enterprise, he was to be a hard-driving, innovative, and controversial civil servant.

With Chadwick taking a dominant part on both royal commissions, the Benthamite character of the inquiries was enhanced. Yet Bentham's insistence that the superiority of expert investigation derived in part from its impartiality was not borne out. Far from being impartial, Chadwick commenced his inquiries with his mind largely made up as to the nature and extent of the abuses as well as the necessary remedial measures. He was quite willing to ignore or even suppress evidence contrary to his opinions. Furthermore, he crafted his reforms in terms of both political expediency and the advancement of his own career.

The clamor to reform the poor law system proceeded from a widespread perception that poor relief policies were overly indulgent, resulting in higher rates (local taxes), population growth, the breakdown of labor discipline, and the loss of social cohesion. Some followers of the gloomy doctrines of Thomas Malthus claimed that catastrophe could be averted only by the total abolition of the poor laws. Chadwick, however, followed Bentham in his insistence that a public relief system could be safely maintained if it was rigorously overhauled and infused with deterrent strategies.

The major recommendations of the report of the royal commission on the poor laws, written largely by Chadwick and issued in 1834, were the principle of less eligibility and the use of the workhouse test. The former embodied the concept that the condition of the pauper receiving public relief should be less eligible (less desirable) than that of the lowest paid independent laborer. The workhouse test was designed to put this concept into

practice. The harsh regimen of the new workhouses would act as a test of destitution for the able-bodied and would ensure that any laborer who did subject himself to the discipline, hard work, and monotonous diet of the new workhouses would seize the first opportunity to take even the lowest-paid job on the outside. The spirit, if not the complete letter of these recommendations, was enacted by Parliament in 1834 as the Poor Law Amendment Act, or New Poor Law.

For his prominent part in forging the workhouse system, Chadwick provoked the wrath of the poor and their defenders. Simultaneously, he was incurring unpopularity for his part in the royal commission on child labor in the factories. The government had appointed this royal commission after a humanitarian-dominated parliamentary investigation (the Sadler Committee) had recommended abolition of all factory labor for children. Chadwick's commission was widely viewed in the factory districts as a device to negate the Sadler Committee, and its proceedings were picketed and disrupted. Nevertheless, the commission took much evidence, including medical testimony about the effects of factory labor on children. Chadwick's Factory Report of 1833 and the ensuing Factory Act abolished all labor for children under the age of nine and limited it to eight hours per day for those aged nine to thirteen.

Chadwick deeply resented the public abuse that was loaded on him because of his key role in these two measures. He also suspected, with some reason, that the government found it convenient to have him as the scapegoat for unpopular policies. Furthermore, he believed both the New Poor Law and the Factory Act to be in the poor's best interest. The Poor Law restored the dividing line between honest, respectable labor and the condition of pauperism, a line that had become blurred before 1834, with consequent demoralization of the poor. The Factory Act, even if the protection afforded did not go as far as the misguided Sadler bill, had an all-important enforcement mechanism in the form of the factory inspectors. This Benthamite device of an inspectorate would ensure that protection of the young was real and enforceable, not a set of pious wishes.

Although Chadwick believed that the government had mangled both pieces of legislation, he looked forward eagerly to implementing the New Poor Law. Anticipating an appointment to the new Poor Law Commission, he was bitterly disappointed when the three positions were filled by time-honored methods of aristocratic patronage. He reluctantly accepted the post of secretary to the Commission, with the promise that he would be a virtual "fourth commissioner." His thirteen-year tenure in this post would be deeply frustrating. Resented by his superiors, whom he considered incompetent, he was unable to prevent what he considered a gross maladministration of the new law, characterized by a fitful and very partial application of the workhouse test.

In spite of these frustrations, Chadwick persuaded the cabinet to let him undertake investigations into other areas of needed reform such as police and public health. Both inquiries were in part an outgrowth of his poor law work. Attacks by angry laborers on the new workhouses had convinced him of the need for a rural constabulary, while the evidence of a close correlation between sickness and poverty pointed him toward sanitary reform. Named to a royal commission on rural police in 1836, he conducted lengthy investigations and published his report in 1839. The ensuing Rural Constabulary Act was a keen disappointment, however, since it did not embody his recommendation of a centralized police system along Benthamite lines. Instead, control of the new county forces was entrusted to the unpaid rural magistracy, dominated by peers, squires, and clergy—the same elements that controlled many of the local poor law boards of guardians.

The sanitary investigation was ostensibly conducted by the Poor Law Commission, but in fact it was done entirely by Chadwick. Published under his name in 1842 as *The Report on the Sanitary Condition of the Labouring Population*, it is Chadwick's greatest work. Deploying a formidable array of statistics and expert medical testimony, he made a compelling case for the connection between sickness and poverty. He also demonstrated that much if not most sickness was a result of the appalling overcrowding and lack of sanitation in the towns. Chadwick called for dramatic government action to provide fresh water and create radically new sewer systems using small-bore earthenware pipes so that urban refuse could be efficiently removed before a deadly "miasma" (believed to be the predisposing cause of most illness) could form.

The 1840's witnessed a major public health movement throughout England, and Chadwick was one of its most determined proponents. Believing himself to be the virtual inventor of the "sanitary idea," he was increasingly impatient with those reformers who refused to accept him as the movement's leader. Some of them in turn found Chadwick arrogant, irascible, and wedded to unproven engineering solutions to the public health crisis. He was further irritated by the unwillingness of the government (controlled by the Conservative party since the 1841 general election) to act. Cabinet ministers fobbed him off with vague promises and kept him occupied with further inquiries. The most notable of these was the investigation into the appalling state of the cemeteries of London, which resulted in Chadwick's notable *Interment Report* of 1843. Yet once again the government refused to adopt the necessary remedial legislation.

Despairing of government action, Chadwick sought sanitary reform as well as riches by launching the Towns Improvement Company in 1844. The company was a joint stock enterprise designed to provide a range of urban services, including water supply, drainage, and sewers on contract to municipalities at home and abroad. With typical Chadwickian thoroughness, it also included a plan to sell the "sewer manure" to nearby farms. Ingenious though it doubtless was and reflective of his peculiar passion for efficiency, it failed to attract sufficient investment and expired in 1846. During these two years Chadwick was obsessed by the scheme and bent every effort, including the manipulation of related official inquiries, to push enabling legislation through Parliament that would have conferred signal advantages on his own company.

Driven by the failure of his company back to a career of official service, he was heartened by the return of the Whigs to office in 1846. Since they were disposed to accept some kind of sanitary legislation, his prospect of securing a post in the new executive board seemed bright. He first had to contend with a crisis in the Poor Law Commission when a local case of abuse of paupers in a workhouse became a national scandal. The ensuing inquiry into the abuses at Andover (where the workhouse was located) pitted Chadwick against his superiors in a barrage of lurid charges and countercharges. Drawing fully upon his powerful combative instincts and skillfully mobilizing public opinion, he gained the upper hand. The case ended with the commissioners as well as Chadwick deprived of their posts in a major poor law reorganization. Chadwick, however, managed to force the government into promising him a public health post in return for his refraining from any further embarrassing disclosures on poor law administration.

With the passage of the Public Health Act of 1848, Chadwick at last tasted real executive authority. While he considered the statute defective in its coercive powers over recalcitrant local authorities, he set to work vigorously with his colleague on the General Board of Health, Lord Shaftesbury, to reform England's sanitary institutions. Between 1848 and 1854, Chadwick made the board as well as the Metropolitan Commission of Sewers powerful instruments of sanitary reform. Using his limited coercive powers to the full, he compelled many reluctant municipalities to appoint local boards and begin the process of draining, sewering, and providing fresh water. He also made numerous enemies by his dictatorial and dogmatic manner, especially in London, where the powerful entrenched metropolitan vestries joined leading civil engineers in opposing Chadwick's nostrums. This proved to be the undoing of both Chadwick and the General Board of Health. The hue and cry against his overbearing manner and the flaws in some of his engineering nostrums finally reached Parliament. In 1854, Chadwick was stripped of his post, and the general board was reorganized and placed under the control of one of his leading critics. It was to be his last paid government position.

In spite of this repudiation by Parliament, Chadwick continued to be a dynamic force in the public health movement for the remaining thirty-six years of his life. Indeed, his many publications as well as his active participation in groups such as the Social Science Association made him a revered elder statesman of the sanitary movement. He also continued his interest in other reforms, including his pet scheme of "half-time education" (half the school day to academic subjects, the other half to military drill and physical exercise). He failed repeatedly to win a seat in Parliament, but another lifelong ambition was at last realized in 1889, when he received a knighthood. Sir Edwin Chadwick died a year later at his home in East Sheen, Surrey, leaving the considerable sum of forty-seven thousand pounds, most of it in trust to provide an annual prize to the local sanitary authority showing the greatest reduction of the death rate.

Summary

Edwin Chadwick's influence on British government and society was considerable. He possessed, as John Stuart Mill put it, "one of the organizing and contriving minds of the time." His passion for efficiency and comprehensiveness knew no bounds. Building on the legacy of Jeremy Bentham's *Constitutional Code* (1830), he labored to create a rationally structured government providing an array of social services while it simultaneously deterred crime and pauperism through an efficient national police and a deterrent workhouse system. He hated waste in all of its forms and believed that all members of society could be rendered efficient and productive by a vigorous, enlightened government. He drove himself incredibly hard throughout his life, taking few holidays and little time off.

Chadwick considered the legislation that resulted from his inquiries to be a series of half-measures, the result of the laziness and ignorance of government ministers and the opposition of vested interests. He seemed not to appreciate that part of the opposition was to his abrasive personality. His dictatorial manner and humorlessness, coupled with a tendency to deviousness, made for him and for his measures many enemies. Furthermore, the rigid ideology he embraced was hostile both to the aristocratic laxness of the established order and to the emerging democratic system. As *The Economist* put it after his fall from power in 1854: "He is essentially a despot and a bureaucrat. He thinks people ought to be well governed, but does not believe in the possibility of their governing themselves well." Clearly, what were sometimes described as his "Prussian" tendencies were out of step with the values of most Victorians, but this makes his many achievements all the more remarkable. His dogged persistence led to a number of key reforms, and he is rightly viewed as an intrepid early pioneer in the making of the British Welfare State.

Bibliography

Brundage, Anthony. *The Making of the New Poor Law: The Politics of Inquiry, Enactment, and Implementation, 1832-1839*. London: Hutchinson, and New Brunswick, N.J.: Rutgers University Press, 1978. Detailed account of the politics of one of Chadwick's key reforms, showing how the act was shaped more by the aristocracy and gentry than by Benthamite principles, in spite of Chadwick's determination and sometimes devious methods.

Finer, S. E. *The Life and Times of Sir Edwin Chadwick*. London: Methuen, 1952; New York: Barnes and Noble, 1970. A full and very readable biography with a tendency to ignore some of

Chadwick's more questionable tactics. While noting Chadwick's personality quirks and his punitive ideas on the poor laws, treats him as the embattled hero of an attempt to overcome vested interests and indifferent political leaders.

Hamlin, Christopher. "Could You Starve to Death in England in 1839? The Chadwick-Farr Controversy and the Loss of the 'Social' in Public Health." *American Journal of Public Health* 85, no. 6 (June 1995). Discusses a controversy between Chadwick and William Farr involving whether or not starvation was a cause of death in England of the 1830s. Their conflict set the stage for the separation of medicine and social medicine.

Henriques, Ursula. *Before the Welfare State: Social Administration in Early Industrial Britain*. London and New York: Longman, 1979. A judicious, well-balanced treatment of all aspects of governmental reform during Chadwick's ascendancy, noting his contributions but also stressing the complexities of each reform.

Lewis, R. A. *Edwin Chadwick and the Public Health Movement, 1832-1854*. London: Longman, 1952; New York: Kelley, 1970. Skillful analysis of Chadwick's active involvement in the public health movement and his emergence as one of the principal leaders of the sanitary movement. Like Finer, however, Lewis is inclined to turn a blind eye to some of Chadwick's less admirable methods.

MacDonagh, Oliver. *Early Victorian Government, 1830-1870*. London: Weidenfeld and Nicolson, and New York: Holmes and Meier, 1977. A useful survey of the major areas of government growth and reform, similar to the book by Henriques in its sense of balance and avoidance of ascribing too much influence to Chadwick or to Benthamism generally.

Mixon, Franklin G. "Congressional Term Limitations: Chadwickian Policy as an Antecedent to Modern Ideas." *American Journal of Economics and Sociology* 55, no. 2 (April 1996). Examines Chadwick's early writings as a precursor to contemporary ideas on term limits for legislators.

Roberts, David. *Victorian Origins of the British Welfare State*. New Haven, Conn.: Yale University Press, 1960. An important study of nineteenth century reforms in the poor laws, factory acts, public health, police, education, and other areas, noting the influence of paternalism on the reforms as well as the powerful opposition to centralization. Good biographical detail on Chadwick and the other key officials of the period.

Anthony Brundage

JOSEPH CHAMBERLAIN

Born: July 8, 1836; London, England

Died: July 2, 1914; Highbury, Birmingham, England

Areas of Achievement: Government and politics

Contribution: An influential Victorian politician, Chamberlain supported the British Empire and a strong economic union between its members.

Early Life

Joseph Chamberlain, perhaps the most important Victorian statesman who never became prime minister, was born the son of a Unitarian shoemaker in London on July 8, 1836. He received his early education in London at one of the most famous of the dissenting academies, University College School. After graduation he planned to attend University College, but his father opposed "that godless school." In addition, his father refused to educate Chamberlain any more than he would be able to afford for his younger sons, and instead offered Chamberlain two hundred pounds to enter the ministry, which was refused.

At age eighteen Chamberlain was sent from London to Birmingham to represent his father's interests in a family woodscrew-manufacturing firm which had been influenced by an American invention for screw manufacturing displayed at the Crystal Palace Exhibit of 1851. In Birmingham, Chamberlain prospered, retiring with a comfortable income after twenty successful years in business. Machine technology had made him rich and he now turned his attention to social engineering. Chamberlain's first foray into the political world involved his election to the Birmingham school board in 1870. Chamberlain strongly stressed the principle that education should be universal, compulsory, and free. His efforts on behalf of educational reform led him to higher office, first as city councillor, later as mayor.

Life's Work

While mayor of Birmingham, Chamberlain established a reputation as a radical; he endeavored in particular to improve housing conditions and public education. Encouraged by his local political successes, in 1876 he entered Parliament as a Liberal member from Birmingham. Birmingham, one of the large industrial towns to benefit from the Reform Bill of 1867, was allotted three seats in the House of Commons, and all three were dominated by the Liberal Party.

By close association in the House with Sir Charles Dilke, Chamberlain was able to rise in party prominence until the 1880 elections, when he was invited by Prime Minister William Gladstone to serve in his cabinet as president of the Board of Trade. Although still a virtual newcomer after only four years in the Commons, Chamberlain benefited from a disagreement between Gladstone and Dilke on the choice of a government post. Dilke had contacted Gladstone about cabinet posts for himself and his friend Chamberlain. "I also think that we are far more powerful together than separated," claimed Dilke; Gladstone's compromise was to give a minor cabinet job to Chamberlain and the undersecretaryship to Dilke.

Although Chamberlain held radical views on questions of social reform, he was traditional in his sense of maintaining and expanding the British Empire. When Gladstone introduced an Irish home rule (political autonomy) bill in 1886, Chamberlain chose to resign from the cabinet rather than support the government's policy. "I can never consent to regard Ireland as a separate people," he claimed, "with the inherent rights of an absolutely independent community." Chamberlain then founded the National Liberal Federation, which he hoped would become a national party in opposition to the Gladstonian Liberals; instead, his dissenting effort forged an influential role for himself in an ultimate union with the Conservative Party.

In 1895, the Marquess of Salisbury formed a coalition government, a combination of traditional Conservatives and the followers of Chamberlain, called Liberal Unionists. Chamberlain could have named practically any cabinet position for himself but chose the Colonial Office as the agency with which to propel himself into national prominence for the next decade. For Chamberlain, the Colonial Office allowed him to fulfill an imperial vision he had long relished: "I said again I should prefer the Colonies—in the hope of furthering closer union between them and the United Kingdom." While colonial secretary he maintained two objectives: cementing the ties between Great Britain and the colonies, and increasing the trade within the Empire. The passive imperialism of the 1870's had been replaced in the 1890's with pride in Great Britain's imperial possessions and a belief that Great Britain was becoming a world state, with her colonies an extension of herself. The word "imperialism" had come to defend proudly Great Britain's civilizing mission along with the British system of peace and good government.

To help spread the concept of good government and preservation of peace, Chamberlain favored an imperial *Zollverein*, a union of freely trading partners within the Empire. He thought that a commercial union would give an opportunity to call together representatives from various parts of the Empire—a gathering which could lead to the creation of an imperial council, one step along the way toward an imperial federal parliament. An opportunity arose in 1897, the year of Queen Victoria's Diamond Jubilee celebrating her sixty-year reign; representatives from throughout the Empire had gathered in London to mark the occasion. An informal conference with the colonial representatives was arranged, with Chamberlain presiding, but sentiments were mixed as to whether there was a need for an imperial parliament. The best Chamberlain could solicit was an agreement for periodic conferences for the discussion of "matters of common interest." The subsequent colonial conferences became, therefore, the means by which colonial views came to be aired collectively. Those views, however, were never united.

Of all Chamberlain's imperial activities, he is most closely associated with those in South Africa. South Africa was to serve as a proving ground for the Victorian mission of progress. Such lofty ideals, however, were quickly cast aside when gold and diamonds were discovered there in the 1870's. Chamberlain's policies in South Africa were influenced by the interests of Cecil Rhodes and his fellow mining magnates, who had practically overwhelmed the two small agrarian states of the Transvaal and the Orange Free State. Both were sparsely populated with Boer farmers descended from Dutch settlers, but had been inundated with outsiders (Uitlanders) who poured into the mining areas during the gold and diamond rush. Rhodes, having made a tremendous fortune, became convinced that all South Africa should come under British control. Resistance by the Boers persuaded Rhodes and his friends that the only solution to this dilemma was a military one. As a result, they hatched a half-baked scheme for the invasion of the Boer Republics, which led to the ill-fated Jameson Raid of 1895-1896. Chamberlain seems to have had knowledge of the plan, as he informed the prime minister on December 26, 1895, that there would probably be an uprising in the Boer

Republics within the next several days. During the subsequent debate in the Commons over responsibility for the raid, Chamberlain asserted that all parties other than Leander Starr Jameson were "equally ignorant" of the plans for the raid, and a parliamentary investigation cleared Chamberlain of any complicity. Following the raid, the Boer Republics began a frantic arms build-up which better prepared them for the war that began with Great Britain in 1899.

Scholars have debated the role of Chamberlain in fomenting the resultant Anglo-Boer War of 1899-1902. Although he was exonerated by the House of Commons for complicity in the Jameson Raid, modern scholars have proved his strong interest in the need for British annexation of the Boer Republics and exposed his gift to Rhodes of a free hand in the attempted Jameson takeover. Before the war there was no strong public demand for war, but Chamberlain, increasingly influential in the Salisbury government, was able to win support from several members of the cabinet for strong ultimatums sent to the Boer Republics—ultimatums which could only be rejected by the Boers.

Following the war, in 1903 Chamberlain resigned from the Conservative-Unionist government over the question of whether tariff barriers for the members of the Empire should be reduced, thus creating an imperial customs union. He spent the remainder of his public life campaigning for his plan of "imperial preference," which would create a commercial union to solidify the Empire. In a speech in Birmingham on May 15, 1903, he made his formal declaration for imperial preference. This speech has been described as a turning point in Edwardian politics. The issue threatened to divide not only the cabinet but also the country and the Empire.

Chamberlain began a whistle-stop tour in the autumn of 1903 to take his imperial preference plan to the people. His speeches were tailored to meet the interest of each audience, discussing mining in Cardiff, agriculture in the provinces, and industry in Birmingham. In several by-elections in December, 1903, the success of his efforts was demonstrated. Even Chamberlain commented on how impressive were the effects of his speeches in winning over two opposition seats to the side of the government. A powerful Tariff Reform League was established and headquartered in his home bastion of Birmingham. In spite of the growing influence of Chamberlain within the Unionist cabinet and the increasing monies spent on his crusade, Chamberlain's hold on the country declined by early 1904, and he was never again able to ride such a political crest. The tariff reform campaign failed to persuade the British masses.

In addition to winning over the country, Chamberlain also had to deal with a deteriorating relationship with Lord Salisbury's successor as prime minister, his nephew Arthur James Balfour. Balfour, far more philosophically conservative than Chamberlain, had to be won over to preferential tariffs and active social reform. By 1905, however, elections had to be called, and the coalition government of Chamberlain and Balfour was voted out of office by the Liberal Party.

In the short term Chamberlain won a personal victory over Balfour. In the long run, however, Chamberlain failed entirely in his imperial and tariff schemes. On July 10, 1906, he delivered an exhausting speech at Bingly Hall, Birmingham. The next day, after returning to London for a Tariff Commission meeting, he felt "a wreck." On the evening of the eleventh he collapsed with a stroke which paralyzed his right side. Chamberlain would never again actively participate in politics. He was confined to a wheelchair until he died suddenly in Birmingham in July, 1914.

Summary

Joseph Chamberlain possessed great gifts of personality, oratory, and intellect. During his career he was an overwhelming success as businessman, mayor, House of Commons member, and cabinet member. At various times he almost captured the leadership of both the Liberal and Conservative parties. He also almost brought about a colonial policy that would unite the Empire economically. Ultimately, however, he failed. His failures have been blamed on a variety of causes. He was known to be excessively impulsive. "Pushful Joe," as he was sometimes called, with his monocle in place, his orchid in his lapel, and his ostentatious home in Birmingham, was considered by a still strongly aristocratic political world to be "just a tradesman" over-reaching his station.

On the other hand, there are perhaps more subtle accomplishments to the career of Joseph Chamberlain. Beginning with his political origins in Birmingham he was able to recognize the coming influence of the newly enfranchised masses. He was able to construct a political machine in Birmingham that expanded to a national scale during his early days in Parliament, and his organizational tactics were used by both Liberals and Conservatives, as well as much later, by the Labour Party. His business background also gave Chamberlain increased sensitivity to Great Britain's industrial decline toward the end of the nineteenth century; he was far more in touch with business realities, for example, than either Salisbury or Balfour. Perhaps one reason for the failure of his dream of imperial preference was the too favorable position it provided for Great Britain; the colonies would gain little while Great Britain would benefit greatly.

There was one additional significant gift for Great Britain left by Joseph Chamberlain. His two sons were major figures in British political affairs well into the twentieth century. The elder son, Austen (1863-1937), held high cabinet office, was offered the prime ministry twice, and, in 1925, was awarded the Nobel Peace Prize for his work on the Locarno peace pact. The younger son, Neville (1869-1940), held cabinet rank and was prime minister from 1937 to 1940. Joseph Chamberlain, therefore, founded a brief political dynasty unique in British history.

Bibliography

Chamberlain, Joseph L. *Mr. Chamberlain's*

Speeches. Edited by C. W. Boyd. London: Constable, and Boston: Houghton Mifflin, 1914. A collection in two volumes of some of the most representative of Chamberlain's speeches.

————. *A Political Memoir, 1880-1892*. Edited by C. H. D. Howard. London: Batchworth Press, 1953; Westport, Conn.: Greenwood Press, 1975. An autobiographical fragment that unfortunately stops just at the climax of Chamberlain's career. This account deals primarily with the making of a politician.

Drus, Ethel. "A Report on the Papers of Joseph Chamberlain Relating to the Jameson Raid and the Inquiry." *Bulletin of the Institute of Historical Research* 25 (1952). One of several studies of the role of Chamberlain in the Jameson Raid. Although a parliamentary commission exonerated Chamberlain of playing any part, scholars such as Drus have been far more critical.

Fraser, Peter. *Joseph Chamberlain*. London: Cassell, 1966; South Brunswick, N.J.: Barnes, 1967. Until recently, this was the standard biography. Although it is still quite reliable for general information, it does not contain the most recent interpretations.

Garvin, J. L., and Julian Amery. *Life of Joseph Chamberlain*. 6 vols. London: Macmillan, 1934-1969. This massive "official" biography runs to six thick volumes. It is quite sympathetic to Chamberlain and reproduces numerous letters and documents.

Jay, Richard. *Joseph Chamberlain: A Political Study*. Oxford: Clarendon Press, and New York: Oxford University Press, 1981. Perhaps the best interpretive study. This account incorporates the most recent scholarship and tries to set Chamberlain in his times.

Judd, Denis. *Radical Joe: A Life of Joseph Chamberlain*. London: Hamilton, 1977. One of the newer interpretive works. This biography provides a serviceable survey, although it fails to be entirely convincing in some of its attempts at breaking new ground.

Loughlin, James. "Joseph Chamberlain, English Nationalism and the Ulster Question." *Journal of the Historical Association* 77, no. 250 (June 1992). The author evaluates Chamberlain's career with emphasis on the personal qualities that affected his decisions.

Newton, Scott, and Dilwyn Porter. *Joseph Chamberlain, 1836-1914: A Bibliography*. Westport, Conn.: Greenwood Press, 1994. An excellent introduction for historians and researchers interested in Chamberlain and his career. A must for academic libraries.

Tyler, J. E. *The Struggle for Imperial Unity*. London and New York: Longman, 1938. A work that stresses the economic background of the imperial preference battle from the time before Chamberlain became involved until he was fully committed to the fray.

Newell D. Boyd

CHANG CHIH-TUNG

Born: September 2, 1837; Nan-p'i, Chihli, China
Died: October 4, 1909; Peking, Chihli, China
Areas of Achievement: Government and education
Contribution: Chang Chih-tung was a leading scholar-official in China during the last half-century of the Ch'ing Dynasty. His educational, military, and economic reforms contributed greatly to the survival of China's last imperial dynasty.

Early Life

Chang Chih-tung came from a gentry family of modest means. His father, Chang Ying, provided him with a rigorous classical education, and Chih-tung responded with diligence and precocity. At age thirteen, he passed the prefectural exam, becoming a *sheng-yüan*. At fifteen, Chih-tung, in competition with almost ten thousand scholars, led the list of about one hundred who received the *chü-jen* degree in Chihli Province.

He delayed taking the metropolitan exam, deterred in part by his father's death in 1855. In 1863, however, he passed the Peking exam, becoming a *chin-shih* degree-holder and member of China's upper gentry. His palace examination, though somewhat controversial, apparently pleased Tz'u-hsi, the empress dowager, who appointed him to the Hanlin Academy in Peking.

From 1867 to 1881, Chang Chih-tung alternated between provincial posts in education in Hupeh and Szechwan, and positions at the Hanlin Academy. At the capital, he associated with a group of conservative Confucian scholars who called themselves the Ch'ing-liu, or purists. The Ch'ing-liu demanded that China adopt a militant stand against foreign encroachment and characterized the policies of moderating as constituting cowardly appeasement. Chang was no better than any of the purists, however, in his constant efforts to please Tz'u-hsi. He condoned her decision, in 1875, to defy Confucian tradition by breaking the normal line of succession and securing the throne for her nephew, Emperor Kuang-hsü. When a censor, Wu K'o-tu, committed suicide in 1879 to protest Tz'u-hsi's policies, Chang wrote a lengthy memorial criticizing Wu and justifying the empress dowager's actions.

Chang's memorials were usually less sycophantic and usually concerned foreign policy. He and the purists called for military action against Russia over the I-li and against France over the status of Annam. In the first instance, their bellicose postur-

ing appeared to be effective, and Russia agreed to replace the earlier Treaty of Livadia (October, 1789) with the less favorable Treaty of St. Petersburg (February, 1881). Unfortunately, the purists, encouraged by their apparent success in I-li, prodded the throne into applying the same kind of threatening approach to France, which precipitated the Sino-French War (1883-1885). The fighting resulted in France's destruction of the Chinese fleet and shipyards at Foochow, and China reluctantly agreed to the unfavorable terms of the Li-Fournier Agreement (May, 1884).

Most of the purists were discredited for having pushed China into a losing war, and Chang might have suffered a similar fate. Fortunately for him, he had already embarked upon a more substantive career than that of warmonger. The bitter experience of witnessing China's ignominy during the Sino-French fiasco had radically altered Chang's perspectives on the West and on change, and he had become an energetic reformer.

Life's Work

Earlier, while still basking in the success at I-li, Chang received several rapid promotions and became Governor of Shansi Province in 1881. As governor, Chang initiated numerous industrial and educational projects to help reduce the deplorable economic conditions in Shansi. In 1884, during the Sino-French hostilities, the throne appointed Chang Viceroy of Liangkwang (Kwangtung and Kwangsi). At the conclusion of the war, the throne not only criticized Chang for his earlier bellicosity but also praised him for having undertaken several positive measures, including the defense of Kwangtung. Chang began to adopt the ideas of Feng Kuei-fen, who in the early 1860's had popularized the concept of *tzu-ch'iang*, or self-strengthening.

To Chang, strengthening China required the adoption of Western technology. He was, however, deeply concerned with the relationship between modernization and Westernization—the dilemma facing all Chinese reformers. His interest was not to alter China in a radical way but rather to save it by entertaining certain modifications. Thus, he insisted upon preserving Confucianism as the central core of Chinese culture. To this end, Chang promoted the slogan *Chung-hsueh wei t'i, Hsi-hsueh wei yung*, or "Chinese studies as the foundation, Western studies for their practicality." This signi-

fied that modernization should not entail Westernization, because Chinese values were superior to those of the West.

Among Chang's many proposals was the construction of a railway line between Peking and Hankow. The throne appointed Chang Viceroy of Hunan-Hupeh in 1889, with instructions to oversee this project. Having earlier constructed a foundry in Kwangtung, Chang also undertook to establish the Han-Yeh-P'ing Iron and Steel works in Han-yang. Though small and wiry, Chang was apparently tireless in his efforts to seek funds for these and other projects. His zeal, however, did not mean that he understood either the mechanics or the financial underpinnings of successful industrialization. When it became evident that he could not obtain the necessary capital for either of these projects, he turned them over to private corporations.

During the Sino-Japanese War of 1894-1895, when the Viceroy of the Anhwei-Kiangsu-Kiangsi area, Liu K'un-i, was commanding troops, Chang took over at Nanking on an interim basis. In his efforts to prepare China for continued war, Chang undertook the creation of a self-strengthening army, with German advisers and foreign weapons. Chang turned over this modern force to Liu upon the latter's return to Nanking, but he re-created essentially the same type of units on his resumption of the viceroyalty post at Han-yang.

During 1895-1898, Chang associated with many young zealous reformers, who ultimately became involved in the famous Hundred Days Reform during the summer of 1898. Prior to this abortive movement, Chang published his famous *Ch'üan Hsüeh P'ien* (exhortation to study). The reformers, reading their own convictions into this work, construed it as a rallying platform. For his part, Chang, who had originally financed and sponsored many of the reformers, became alarmed by their misrepresentation of his ideas. He also disliked their leader, K'ang Yü-wei for his constant representation of Confucius as a radical reformer. As the reformers moved toward constitutional monarchy, Chang, who distrusted participatory democracy, began to distance himself from them. When Tz'u-hsi's coup ended the Hundred Days Reform, Chang was one of the first to call for the severe punishment of the reform leaders. He even refused to join Liu K'un-i in memorializing the throne against the threatened deposition of the young emperor. Chang emerged from this movement the object of suspicion and hatred, both by court conservatives and young re-

formers. Whatever remaining ties existed between Chang and the new reformers ended in 1900, when Chang arrested and executed twenty conspirators who had been plotting the overthrow of Tz'u-hsi.

During the Boxer Rebellion (1899-1900), Chang joined a few other provincial leaders in guaranteeing the safety and property of foreigners in southern China. While he complied with orders from the court to send troops to the north, he kept his strongest units at home and sent untrained recruits to the capital. At the conclusion of the Boxer Rebellion, he and other moderate provincial officials requested that foreign powers not hold Tz'u-hsi accountable for Boxer outrages. Chang thus consolidated his position at the court and also endeared himself to many foreigners in China. He eventually made use of his ties to British representatives, asking them repeatedly to intercede on his behalf at the imperial court.

With the deaths of Li Hung-chang and Liu K'un-i, in 1901 and 1902, respectively, Chang became China's senior statesman. Among many reform activities, he spearheaded a commission to study the future of the civil service examination system. Calling at first for their gradual abolition, Chang suddenly suggested an immediate end to the exams and the creation of a national Confucian school system. Tz'u-hsi complied with alacrity and on September 2, 1905, abolished the examination system, ending what was probably the most salient feature of China's Confucian imperial system.

In the summer of 1907, Chang came to the capital as a grand secretary, but the court also made him a grand councillor and directed him to head the Ministry of Education. By this time, however, he was beset both by infirmity and considerable doubts about the Ch'ing Dynasty's ability to survive. The death of Tz'u-hsi in November, 1908, did little to improve his outlook. Chang had come to accept the idea of a constitutional monarchy but was frustrated by what he construed as moral decay in China. On October 4, 1909, the same day he submitted a memorial eulogizing Tz'u-hsi, he died, surrounded by friends and family.

Summary

An educational innovator who founded dozens of academies and modern schools and an initiator of numerous industrial and communications ventures, Chang Chih-tung unquestionably helped to arrest the continued decline of the Ch'ing Dynasty. Yet he embodied both the best and worst features of

China's traditional elite class. Honest to a fault, Chang died a relatively poor man. Yet his loyalty to a dynasty led him to tolerate the venality and corruption of Tz'u-hsi, the empress dowager. He understood that China was weak and needed reform, but he also remained firmly convinced that China's traditional value system should remain virtually intact. In essence, he failed to grasp the relationship between technological modernity and the sociocultural foundations that were necessary for such modernization. His formulas for self-strengthening proved to be bankrupt rationalizations that failed to acknowledge inherent weaknesses in China's cultural tradition itself. His occasional opportunism was a reflection of the corrupt state of the Ch'ing Dynasty, and, in the end, most of his projects served only to retard the process of dynastic deterioration. Chang could neither save the dynasty nor conserve the Confucian tradition that he cherished. He died a famous and respected man but ultimately was a failed leader of a country that had become weaker during his own lifetime. Although he did not bear the principal responsibility for this decline, the empress dowager, the Ch'ing Dynasty, and, in large measure, the unaltered Confucian tradition that he supported, all contributed to China's decay.

Bibliography

Ayers, William. *Chang Chih-tung and Educational Reform in China*. Cambridge, Mass.: Harvard University Press, 1971. Although concentrating on Chang's role as an educational reformer, this well-documented work can serve as a biography of his life as well.

Bays, Daniel H. *China Enters the Twentieth Century: Chang Chih-tung and the Issues of a New Age, 1895-1909*. Ann Arbor: University of Michigan Press, 1978. A thorough and analytical account of Chang's career during the last fifteen years of his life.

Cohen, Paul A., and John E. Schrecker, eds. *Reform in Nineteenth-Century China*. Cambridge, Mass., and London: Harvard University Press, 1976. Numerous articles discuss Chang's association with the Ch'ing-Liu reformers and his other activities. Most of the articles provide an excellent background for a study of Chang.

Eastman, Lloyd E. *Throne and Mandarins: China's Search for a Policy During the Sino-French Controversy, 1880-1885*. Cambridge, Mass.: Harvard University Press, 1967. An excellent review of this period, with much discussion of Chang and the purists.

Hummel, Arthur W., ed. *Eminent Chinese of the Ch'ing Period (1644-1912)*. 2 vols. Washington, D.C.: Government Printing Office, 1943-1944. Volume 1 contains a fairly detailed biography of Chang which is still accurate and useful.

Levenson, Joseph R. *Confucian China and Its Modern Fate*. 3 vols. London: Routledge, and Berkeley: University of California Press, 1958-1965. In volume 1, the author discusses the conflict between continuity and change during the Ch'ing Dynasty. Referring frequently to Chang, the author gives a superb analysis of the dilemma facing Confucian reformers.

Powell, Ralph L. *The Rise of Chinese Military Power, 1895-1912*. Princeton, N.J.: Princeton University Press, 1955. Offers substantial coverage of Chang's military reforms and his efforts involving the self-strengthening army.

Wright, Mary C. *The Last Stand of Chinese Conservatism: The T'ung-Chih Restoration, 1862-1874*. Stanford, Calif.: Stanford University Press, 1957. Although concentrating on the period prior to Chang's prominence, this classic is essential to understanding the struggle between conservatism and modernization in the late Ch'ing Dynasty. The author frequently refers to Chang's ideas and actions.

Hilel B. Salomon

WILLIAM ELLERY CHANNING

Born: April 7, 1780; Newport, Rhode Island
Died: October 2, 1842; Bennington, Vermont
Area of Achievement: Religion
Contribution: Channing led the attack by Unitarian clergy on New England Congregationalism and helped establish the basis for modern liberal Christianity.

Early Life

William Ellery Channing was born in British-occupied Newport toward the end of the Revolutionary War, one of ten children of William and Lucy (née Ellery) Channing. Young Channing was the grandson of a signer of the Declaration of Independence on the paternal side, and of perhaps the richest merchant in Newport on the maternal side. The boy attended school in Newport until the age of twelve, at which point he was sent to New London, Connecticut, to prepare for Harvard. He began his collegiate studies at Harvard in 1794 and spent four happy years there. During his Harvard years, young Channing had an adolescent religious experience, and the event convinced him to seek a career in the clergy. He was a popular student, and at the end of his stay at Harvard, the class of 1798 elected him as their graduating speaker.

Upon graduation, Channing went south to Richmond, Virginia, to take a post as a tutor to the socially prominent Randolph family. The young New Englander felt ill at ease in Richmond's heady atmosphere of dancing, drinking, and Deism, and for the most part he shunned society and read books. Alone in his study, Channing again had a conversion experience, and his letters of 1800 demonstrate the intensity of his encounter and his belief that faith alone provided the basis of Christian belief. He returned to Newport in 1800 and struck up a friendship with the local minister, Samuel Hopkins, who had once been a follower of the great Jonathan Edwards. Hopkins had shed some of his earlier adherence to the rigid Calvinist notions of predestination, and in turn his thinking influenced Channing. In December, 1801, Channing returned to Harvard as a divinity student, and upon his ordination in 1803, he was called to the ministry of the well-to-do Federal Street Church in Boston, a post he held until his death four decades later.

Channing postponed marriage until 1814, when he wed his cousin Ruth Gibbs. The couple had four children over the next six years, but only two survived infancy. Channing himself suffered from ill health throughout his adult life. He was a small man, only five feet tall, and weighed little more than a hundred pounds. Portraits painted of him each decade after his coming to Federal Street show a once handsome man with a face growing ever thinner and more pinched. Yet if his frame was unprepossessing, his voice more than made up for any deficiency in stature. By all accounts, Channing was one of the finest religious speakers in nineteenth century America.

Life's Work

William Ellery Channing's name has come down in history in connection with the famous "Unitarian Controversy" in early nineteenth century New England. Few of his contemporaries at divinity school might have predicted that the quiet, intense Channing would someday lead a revolt of rationalist Christians against the remnants of the Congregational church established by the Puritans in the 1630's. The controversy first became public in 1805 when Harvard appointed a known Unitarian, Henry Ware, to a chair in theology. The name "Unitarian" implied a host of beliefs at the time, not simply the contention that the deity was single and unfragmented, as opposed to the more traditional "Trinitarian" concept of God as Father, Son, and Holy Ghost. Many clergymen opposed to Ware publicly protested the appointment, and after failing to get Ware dismissed, the recalcitrants in 1809 established their own rival school of theology at Andover.

The years between 1805 and 1820 saw bitter intellectual and personal struggles between the Harvard and Andover wings of New England Congregationalism. The vituperation of the controversy seems out of proportion to the actual differences between the two camps, but it is worth remembering that the split came at a time of general religious fervor in the nation, a period known as the Second Great Awakening, and a time when toleration was difficult to practice. Beyond the nominal difference between Unitarianism and Trinitarianism over the nature of God, Unitarians differed from traditional New England Calvinists in disputing the total depravity of man. Men such as Channing believed that human beings were a mixture of good and bad and that part of the clergy's job was to encourage the former and discourage the latter. Unitarians also had doubts about the Calvinist doctrine of predestination, or the notion that God had already determined the fate of all human beings and that mortal actions on earth could have no influence on the divine. Moreover, Channing and other Unitarians refused to believe the old Congregationalist doctrine that mankind on earth could be divided into the "elect" (those who knew their salvation) and all the rest. Unitarians, under Channing's leadership, came to believe that salvation was within all men's power but that people needed careful religious instruction in order to avoid the many falsehoods and errors inherent in the various denominations of Christianity.

Channing kept a low profile during the most heated years of the Unitarian Controversy, between 1809 and 1815. He emerged as a Unitarian leader only in 1819 with a deliberately crafted public address that served as a counterblast to the Andover wing. Indeed, his address was so compelling and succinct that the split in Congregationalism became permanent. After Channing's 1819 "Baltimore Sermon," Unitarianism and Trinitarian Congregationalism went their separate ways.

The location for his grand theological pronouncement was a bit unusual. Instead of Boston, Channing chose the southern city of Baltimore as the setting, and the ordination of a Harvard-trained minister named Jared Sparks as the occasion. Sparks had been called to the pulpit of the newly established First Independent Church of Baltimore, an outpost as far south as any that Unitarianism had established.

Channing took as his text for his Baltimore Sermon a verse from 1 Thessalonians: "Prove all things; hold fast to that which is good." The audience was filled with a host of Unitarian ministers, and Channing sought to summarize for them his belief that rationalism should be the core of Unitarian religious practice. He told the ordination assembly that as Christians they needed to affirm that the Bible was, in part, God's revelation to mankind but also, in part, man's imperfect attempt to understand God. Channing emphasized that the Old Testament was full of errors and superstitions and that Christians should concentrate on the teachings of Jesus. The job of the Unitarian minister, he went on, was to separate the divine in the Bible from the mundane by use of reason and scholarship, all for the benefit of the congregation. This required a sound education in many fields for the would-be clergyman, from knowledge of the ancient lan-

guages to a familiarity with modern science. More than any other Unitarian leader, Channing sought to push the clergy into seeing its role as primarily one of scholar-teacher.

Channing also used the occasion of Sparks's ordination in Baltimore to pull together the separately articulated but as yet uncollected strands of Unitarian doctrine. He insisted that the notion of a Trinity was a logical absurdity and maintained as well that the doctrine of Original Sin mocked God by ascribing base motives to Him such as jealousy and rage. From these two assumptions, Channing went on to reason that the purpose of Christ was to perform an errand for the superior God by sending a message that mankind was forgiven its sins. Moreover, Channing proposed that Christ had only partly completed his mission, which, fully understood, involved transforming mankind into a species marked by complete love and goodness.

The Baltimore Sermon of 1819 circulated widely in print and made its author famous on both sides of the Atlantic. In the early 1820's, Channing and his family journeyed to England and the Continent, where he was received by many leading intellectuals, including William Wordsworth and Samuel Taylor Coleridge. He continued to speak out forcefully against the Trinitarian Congregationalists (many of whom called him an infidel), and in 1825, he helped establish the American Unitarian Association, thereby officially ratifying the schism in the Church that John Winthrop and John Cotton had created in 1630.

Though honored as a leader while still a comparatively young man, Channing had a less than happy tenure at Federal Street Church in the years after 1819, particularly in his last decade. He faced two great challenges, one moral and one intellectual, that troubled him until his death. The first was the problem of slavery in America. Channing knew of Southern slavery from his Richmond days, but a visit to the West Indian island of St. Croix in 1831 upset him deeply. He saw directly the hard lot of black slaves on the sugar plantations, and he returned to Boston just as the abolitionist movement began organizing in that city. American abolitionism in the 1830's was highly unpopular, in large part because its backers were thought to favor interracial marriage. Boston and other cities were wracked by anti-abolitionist mob violence, and while Channing condemned the mob, he also earned the scorn of the abolitionists for not wholeheartedly endorsing their cause. Only in his "Duty of the Free States," written in 1842 just before his death, did he come to see slavery as a manifestation of evil so great that forceful means would be required to overcome it. Until that time, Channing had hoped that Christian appeals to the conscience of the Southern slaveholder would work to end the institution without violence.

The other great challenge to Channing and the new Unitarian Association was from within: the intellectual challenge of the Transcendentalists. The sources of Transcendentalism are complex, found partly in European Romanticism, partly in the reflected enthusiasm of Jacksonian America, but in any event, its notions of the primacy of sensation, intuition, and nature posed a direct challenge to the rationalist approach to Christianity. Channing died before his former student Ralph Waldo Emerson would call Boston Unitarianism "corpse-cold," but even by 1842, Channing could see that Unitarianism was not satisfying the spiritual needs of many its adherents.

Summary

By devising a rational Christianity still reliant on faith, Channing reached an optimistic end similar to that proposed by a contemporary New England "Universalist" preacher named Hosea Ballou, who interpreted the Crucifixion as the sign that all sinners everywhere and forever had been pardoned in advance and that salvation would be "universal." In their own ways, the rationalist Channing and the Universalist Ballou built the basis for an American liberal Christianity that offered hope without resorting to threats of hellfire and brimstone. Indeed, after the Civil War, Unitarians and Universalists saw their common interests and, after many fits and starts, eventually effected a merger in the twentieth century.

Channing also took liberal Christianity in the direction of social reform. His stress on the goodness of man and the possibility of moral instruction got him involved in many of the reform movements of Jacksonian America. He was an active temperance enthusiast, supported the emerging antiwar movement, and advocated an extensive system of public education. Channing communicated many of these concerns to the public, first in sermons at Federal Street and then in pamphlets written for a wider audience. At the same time, Channing served as mentor to many of the young writers and thinkers in Boston, men such as Ralph Waldo Emerson, Henry Wadsworth Longfellow, and Robert Lowell. Channing's 1830 pamphlet *Remarks on American Literature* was a direct call for American writers to create a new, national, and republican literature that was divorced from the monarchical and anti-democratic British literature then in fashion. The call was taken up in the great flowering of New England culture in the last decades before the Civil War. Like any good teacher, then, Channing should be remembered as much for the students he helped tutor as for the ideas he advanced himself.

Bibliography

Channing, William Ellery. *The Works of William E. Channing.* 6 vols. Boston: Munroe, and London: Chapman, 1848. The chief virtue of Channing's papers is that they allow one to gauge the breadth of his interests. Here is a clergyman involved in an extraordinary range of religious and secular matters.

Delbanco, Andrew. *William Ellery Channing: An Essay on the Liberal Spirit in America.* Cambridge, Mass.: Harvard University Press, 1981. This work is concerned mostly with placing Channing in the context of American thought in the early nineteenth century. Especially good at discussing the intellectual origins of Unitarianism as a reaction against Calvinism.

Edgell, David D. *William Ellery Channing: An Intellectual Portrait*. Boston: Beacon Press, 1955. The first modern biography of Channing. Seeks to understand him as the synthesizer of rational Christianity.

Mendelsohn, Jack. *Channing the Reluctant Radical: A Biography*. Boston: Little Brown, 1971. Mendelsohn gives considerable detail about Channing's personal and family life. A sympathetic account of liberal Christianity then and now.

Robinson, David. *The Unitarians and the Universalists*. Westport, Conn.: Greenwood Press, 1985. Strong on the Unitarian Controversy and its aftermath, this work also considers Channing's response to the Transcendentalist challenge.

Wright, Conrad, ed. *A Stream of Light*. Boston: Unitarian Universalist Association, 1975. A series of essays commemorating the establishment of an official Unitarian church. The chapter by Charles Forman is helpful in giving Channing's place in the Unitarian Controversy.

————. *Three Prophets of Religious Liberalism: Channing, Emerson, Parker*. Boston: Beacon Press, 1961. This handy volume contains Channing's Baltimore Sermon, as well as a helpful introduction to American Unitarianism.

James W. Oberly

CHARLES XIV JOHN

Jean-Baptiste-Jules Bernadotte

Born: January 26, 1763; Pau, France
Died: March 8, 1844; Stockholm, Sweden
Areas of Achievement: Politics and the military
Contribution: Charles XIV lived virtually two distinct lives. He was first a soldier in the French army with strong republican convictions, and then the conservative King of Sweden.

Early Life

On January 26, 1763, Jean-Baptiste-Jules Bernadotte was born at Pau in the southern province of Gascony. The son of Henri, an attorney, and Jeanne, he was reared in a typical provincial bourgeois manner. He abandoned his law education after the death of his father in 1780 and joined the army. An intelligent young man, with a better education than the French army was accustomed to, he rose through the ranks. On the eve of the French Revolution, he held the rank of sergeant major, the highest noncommissioned position in the army. When the Revolution opened the ranks of the officer corps to men of ability, Bernadotte was among the first to benefit. He was commissioned a second lieutenant in November, 1791.

Soon after France went to war with Russia and Austria in April, 1792, he was promoted to captain. He first saw combat at the head of a company in 1793. Promotions came quickly for able officers in those crucial years of the French Republic, and Bernadotte was catapulted in one year, 1794, from captain to general of division. Campaigning in Belgium and on the Rhine, he earned the reputation of a competent and careful division commander. He took an active part in the campaigns of 1795 and 1796. Then in February, 1797, Bernadotte was sent to Italy with reinforcements for Napoleon I. This was the first time that he served under the future Emperor of the French. As was the case with the other generals of division in the army of Italy, Bernadotte was senior in time served but with the same rank as Napoleon and resented the fact that he had to serve under an officer who had never commanded a division in combat until he was given the army of Italy in 1796. Bernadotte was also six years older than the twenty-seven-year-old aristocrat from Corsica and had much more combat experience. Yet Napoleon had already won stun-

ning victories over the Austrians at Castiglione, Arcola, and Rivoli before Bernadotte had arrived and had established somewhat of a reputation. The newcomer from the Rhine had no choice but to take orders. He played a waiting game.

Life's Work

Bernadotte had spent all of his adult life as a soldier until 1798. In that year, he was appointed by the government of the Directory to be ambassador to Austria. His stay in Vienna was brief, as a lack of social graces combined with strong republican beliefs caused him to be quite unacceptable in the heart of aristocratic Europe. Returning to Paris after only a few months in Vienna, he met and quickly married Désirée Clary. In 1795, Napoleon had unsuccessfully sought her hand in marriage after his brother Joseph had married Désirée's sister Julie. As a result of his marriage, Bernadotte became a part of the extended Bonaparte family. Despite this relationship, he was seldom on good terms with the man who would rule France for fifteen years. When Napoleon went to Egypt in 1798, Bernadotte remained in Paris, and in July of the following year he was appointed minister of war by the Directory. It was his strong republican views that won for him this position, but he did not work well with the directors, and within a few months he was relieved of the office. When Napoleon returned to France and took part in the *coup d'état* of Brumaire, Bernadotte refused to have any part in the overthrow of the government. He sat on the sidelines while Napoleon made himself master of France with the title of first consul.

To ingratiate the staunch republican, Napoleon named Bernadotte councillor of state in January, 1800. Despite the fact that he remained a republican, he accepted the prestigious position and gave tacit support to the new regime. He was also given a command in the army, and between 1800 and 1804 he served in the west of France and in northern Europe. It seems to have been during the first decade of the nineteenth century that Bernadotte was transformed from a republican into a monarchist. Napoleon showered him with wealth, titles, honors, and decorations, which he could never have gained under a republic. Yet if the emperor was able to buy his loyalty and support, he was not able to purchase his affection. Bernadotte never came to like Napoleon.

In 1805, when war again broke out with Austria and Russia, Bernadotte commanded the I Corps of the Grand Army. At the Battle of Austerlitz, he held the left flank and supported Marshal Nicolas Jean de Dieu Soult's decisive attack against the center of the Russian line. His corps fought well, and he contributed to this, perhaps Napoleon's finest, victory. The following year, Bernadotte was made Prince of Ponte-Corvo. By the end of the summer of 1806, France was again at war with a Continental power. This time it was Prussia and the campaign was in southeast Germany. Unlike at Austerlitz, however, Bernadotte and his I Corps sat idly in between the Battles of Jean and Auerstadt on October 16. He was strongly criticized by Napoleon and the army for not marching to the aid of Marshal Louis N. Davout, who fought and defeated a Prussian army at Auerstadt that was more than twice the size of his III Corps. Although the emperor threatened to court-martial Bernadotte for his lack of initiative, no action was taken against him, and the I Corps, rested and unscarred, led the pursuit of the devastated Prussian army. Bernadotte received the surrender of the city of Lübeck and then marched east to support the main army. He was not at the Battle of the Eylau in February, 1807, but he was wounded in action at Spanden in June of the same year, shortly before the campaign came to a victorious conclusion with the defeat of the Russian army at Friedland. Upon his recovery from his wound, he was named Governor of Hamburg, Bremen, and Lübeck.

During the two years he spent in northern Germany he had various dealings with Serden, which had held territory on the south Baltic coast. The renewal of hostilities with Austria in the spring of 1809 brought Bernadotte back into Central Europe at the head of the IX Corps. Following the victory at Eckmuhl and a setback at Aspern-Essling, Napoleon engaged the Austrian army at Wagram on July 5. Bernadotte's Saxon Corps held the left center of the French line. When the Austrians attacked the French left, the Saxons broke and fled to the rear. Despite Bernadotte's efforts, it was necessary to fill the gap created by redeploying Marshal André Masséna's IV Corps. Napoleon was furious with Bernadotte. He accused him of losing the battle, which the French eventually won, and of cowardliness in the face of the enemy. Bernadotte was ordered to leave the army in disgrace and to retire to Paris.

The year 1810 was a pivotal one for Bernadotte. In 1809, the Swedish king, Gustavus IV Adolphus, was forced into exile, and his uncle was put on the throne with the title of Charles XIII. With the death of Charles XIII's adopted son, the Swedish Parliament elected Bernadotte crown prince. Having formally changed his name—he was now Charles John—and his religion, he left France with Napoleon's blessing, landing in Sweden on October 20, 1810. As crown prince, Charles John did not become involved with domestic affairs, but he did play an active role in foreign policy. He realized that Sweden's interests lay in cooperation with Russia and England, not France. Therefore, in 1813 he encouraged the Swedes to declare war on France in order to acquire Norway, owned by Denmark, as compensation for the loss of Finland, which had been taken by the Russians in 1809. Charles John led a Swedish army of twenty thousand men into Germany to fight against France. He defeated Marshal Nicolas Charles Oudinot at Gross-Beeren on August 23, 1813, and arrived at Leipzig on the last day of the three-day battle to witness the defeat of Napoleon. He played a minor role in the campaign of 1814 that forced the French emperor to abdicate in April of that year. He seems to have grasped at the hope of becoming King of France but was never seriously considered by the French. Most Frenchmen, and in particular those in the army, considered him to be a traitor.

Returning to Sweden, Charles John played no part in the campaign of the Hundred Days when Napoleon returned in 1815. Yet Sweden did receive Norway as a reward for having joined the grand alliance against France in 1813. When Charles XIII died in 1818, the once-strong republican was crowned Charles XIV, King of Sweden. His twenty-six-year reign was not particularly eventful. He had been put on the throne by the grace of Parliament, and he did not overstep the limitations placed on the Crown. He became progressively more conservative, and in the later years of his reign clashed with the reform-minded Parliament. Charles John died at Stockholm on March 8, 1844, and was succeeded by his son Oscar I.

Summary

As Charles XIV John, King of Sweden, the man born Jean-Baptiste-Jules Bernadotte found an improbable fulfillment of his ambitions. If his story sounds like something out of the pages of Alexandre Dumas, the reality was considerably less romantic. The reign of Charles XIV John came at a time in Sweden's history when power was decisively shifting from the throne to Parliament; this period was the foundation of modern Swedish democracy. Still, if Charles's role was sharply circumscribed, his years on the throne were peaceful and prosperous ones for Sweden, and history has labeled him as a good king.

Bibliography

Barton, Dunbar Plunket. *Bernadotte: The First Phase, 1763-1799; Bernadotte and Napoleon, 1799-1810; Bernadotte, Prince and King, 1810-1844.* London: Murray, and New York: Scribner, 1914, 1921, 1925. Taken together, these three volumes still represent the definitive work on Charles John. They provide a detailed account of his long and active life with numerous quotations from his correspondence. See also the abridged one-volume edition of Barton's work, entitled *The Amazing Career of Bernadotte* (1929), which is much more widely available then the multivolume study.

Heathcote, T. A. "'Serjent Belle-Jambe': Bernadotte." In *Napoleon's Marshals*, edited by David G. Chandler. London: Weidenfeld and Nicolson, and New York: Macmillan, 1987. A very good twenty-two-page chapter in an excellent study of the marshals of the Napoleonic Empire. The emphasis is on Charles John's early years and his career in the French army. There is virtually nothing on him as King of Sweden.

Muriel, John St. Clair. *Sergeant Belle-Jambe: The Life of Marshal Bernadotte.* London and New York: Rich and Cowan, 1943. This readable account, favorable toward its central figure, concentrates on Charles John's military career during the Napoleonic years. The study is primarily concerned with military affairs and tends to minimize the political and administrative aspects of Bernadotte's life.

Scott, Franklin D. *Bernadotte and the Fall of Napoleon.* Cambridge, Mass.: Harvard University Press, 1935. This is a scholarly study of Charles John's role in the removal of Napoleon from the throne of France in 1814. Although it covers only a brief period of the life of Charles John, it provides a good understanding of the man and his ambitions and motivations.

Wencker-Wildbery, Friedrich. *Bernadotte: A Biography.* London: Jarrolds, 1936. Written in a popular style with many undocumented quotes, this is a very readable account of the life of Charles John. It also contains a number of good pictures of him and his family into the twentieth century. Although it is reasonably accurate, it is not a scholarly work.

John G. Gallaher

SALMON P. CHASE

Born: January 13, 1808; Cornish, New Hampshire
Died: May 7, 1873; New York, New York
Areas of Achievement: Civil rights, law, and politics
Contribution: As an attorney, politician, and constitutional theorist, Chase contributed to the abolition of slavery. During the 1850's, he served as a United States senator and as governor of Ohio, and he participated in the formation of the Republican Party. He was later appointed secretary of the treasury and was Chief Justice of the Supreme Court.

Early Life

Salmon P. Chase was born in Cornish, New Hampshire, in 1808. His father, Ithamar Chase, whose family had come to America during the 1640's, was a farmer who held minor local offices and occasionally served in the state legislature. His mother, Janette Ralston, was the daughter of Scottish immigrants who became prominent landowners in Keene, New Hampshire. Ithamar died when the younger Chase was eight, so the boy spent his youth living with various friends and relatives, including his uncle, Philander Chase, the bishop of the Episcopal Church in Ohio. In 1821, Chase entered Cincinnati College, where his uncle Philander was president. Philander's influence on his nephew was profound. For the rest of his life, Chase would be extremely pious. His later commitment to the abolition of slavery would be as much religious as political. By 1823, Chase had returned to New Hampshire, where he briefly taught school before entering Dartmouth College. In 1826 he was graduated eighth in his class, a member of Phi Beta Kappa. Chase then moved to Washington, D.C., where he taught school before beginning law studies under William Wirt in 1827. In December, 1829, he was admitted to the bar.

In 1830, the athletic, tall, vigorous, and ambitious Chase settled in Cincinnati, where he practiced law and took an active role in civic affairs. Between 1831 and 1833, he published historical essays in *The North American Review*, anonymous editorials in Ohio newspapers, and a three-volume, comprehensive compilation of Ohio's laws, *The Statutes of Ohio* (1833-1835). Chase was neither brilliant nor eloquent in court, but he was hardworking, careful, and scholarly. These traits brought him a comfortable and growing commercial practice which, by 1835, included such clients as the Bank of the United States and the Lafayette Bank of Ohio. By 1845, his firm of Chase and Ball earned an estimated ten thousand dollars a year—an extraordinarily large sum for the era. In 1834, Chase married his first wife, who died in 1835. Two other marriages (in 1839 and 1846) would also end with the death of his wives. Of his six daughters only two, Katherine Chase Sprauge and Jeanette Chase Hoyt, survived to adulthood.

Life's Work

Chase's national career had four phases: abolitionist lawyer; United States senator and governor of Ohio; secretary of the treasury; and Chief Justice of the United States.

From 1830 to 1849, Chase lived in Cincinnati, where his law firm flourished. In addition to this profitable practice, Chase offered free legal services to abolitionists, fugitive slaves, and free blacks. In 1836, mobs destroyed the office of Cincinnati's antislavery newspaper, the *Philanthropist*, and threatened the life of its editor, James G. Birney. Also threatened was Chase's brother-in-law, Dr. Isaac Colby. Through this incident, Chase became an attorney for the antislavery cause. Chase was initially attracted to the abolitionist movement because he abhorred the mob violence and disrespect for law directed against it. He evolved into a passionate and articulate supporter of the cause. In 1836, he won a damage suit against members of the mob, recovering some money for Birney to rebuild the office of the *Philanthropist*. A year later, Chase unsuccessfully defended the freedom of a fugitive slave, Matilda, who had been harbored by Birney. Birney was then convicted for helping Matilda, but Chase won a reversal on appeal.

By 1841, Chase was a leading antislavery attorney in Ohio. Chase rejected the anticonstitutionalism of William Lloyd Garrison and instead developed a constitutional theory consistent with opposition to slavery. In 1843 and 1848, he was the chief author of the platform of the national Free Soil Party. Besides his Free Soil political activities, Chase defended numerous fugitive slaves and their white and black allies. In the 1840's, Chase corresponded with antislavery lawyers throughout the Midwest, convincing them to take cases that he had no time to handle and advising them on legal strategies. Chase lost his most famous fugitive slave case, *Jones v. Van Zandt* (1847), but his printed Supreme Court brief, titled "Reclamation of Fugitives from Service," added to his growing national reputation as the "attorney general for fugitive slaves."

In 1849, a small group of Free Soilers held the balance of power in the Ohio legislature. Guided in part by Chase, these political abolitionists secured two victories: They negotiated the repeal of most of Ohio's racially restrictive "black code," and they secured the election of Chase to the United States Senate.

In the Senate, Chase failed in his attempt to create a "Free Democracy" made up of antislavery Democrats such as himself. Effectively separated from all parties, he remained one of the most uncompromising Senate opponents of slavery, constantly challenging Southerners and their Northern allies. As a politician, Chase was somewhat ponderous, pompous, and self-righteous. While he was not a great debater, his carefully written speeches read well on the stump and in the Senate. In 1850, Chase was one of the leading opponents of the Fugitive Slave Law and other proslavery aspects of the Compromise of that year. While in the Senate, Chase continued to develop his antislavery constitutional analysis, arguing that the Fifth Amendment made slavery unconstitutional wherever the federal government had jurisdiction. This led to his concept of "freedom national, slavery sectional," which became a rallying cry for the Republican Party, especially after the Dred Scott decision (1857). Chase also laid out the theoretical basis for the Republican Party's slogan of 1856: Free Soil, Free Labor, Free Speech, Free Men. In 1854, Chase emerged as a leader of the opposition to the Kansas-Nebraska Act and in the process once again tried to organize a party of "Independent Democrats." No "Independent Democracy" emerged in 1854, but by 1855 a broader coalition of Free Soilers, Northern Democrats, and Whigs had united into an "Anti-Nebraska Party," which soon became the Republican Party. Chase was instrumental in the founding of this new political organization in Ohio. In 1855, he became one of the first Republican governors in the nation by defeating candidates from both the Whig and Democratic parties. In 1857, he was reelected governor of Ohio.

As governor, Chase helped create the Republican Party in Ohio and the nation. In part because of his cold personality, however, he was unable to unify the state party behind his own presidential ambitions; in both 1856 and 1860, he was unsuccessful in gaining the Republican nomination for

that office. While governor, Chase opposed the extradition of fugitive slaves but was unable to prevent the removal of the slave Margaret Garner, who killed her own daughter to prevent the child's return to slavery. After the rescue of an alleged fugitive slave near Oberlin, however, Chase gave support to the rescuers and appeared willing to confront federal authorities. In another case, Chase prevented the extradition of a free black accused of helping slaves to escape from Kentucky. This ultimately led to the Supreme Court decision in *Kentucky v. Dennison* (1861), in which Chief Justice Roger B. Taney chastised Ohio for its antislavery activities but refused actually to order the return of the accused fugitive. Throughout his governorship, Chase tried to walk a fine line between actual defiance of federal law and the Constitution, and his thoroughgoing opposition to slavery and the Fugitive Slave Law. When not sparring with the federal government, Governor Chase directed his energies to reorganizing the Ohio militia, which would ultimately be a major asset to the Union during the Civil War.

In 1860, Governor Chase failed to obtain the Republican presidential nomination. He was, however, elected to the United States Senate in the fall of that year. During the secession crisis, he served as a "peace commissioner" from Ohio, where he opposed any extension of slavery into the territories but also disclaimed any intention of interfering with slavery where it already existed. In March, he had barely taken his seat in the Senate when President Lincoln appointed him secretary of the treasury.

In his new office, Chase faced the formidable task of financing the Civil War. With the aid of financier Jay Cooke, Chase was able to market government bonds, thus providing a constant flow of capital into the national treasury. Chase's initiatives led to the establishment of a national banking system in 1863 with a system of currency backed by federal bonds and securities. Because the Treasury Department was also responsible for confiscated and abandoned property from the Confederacy, Chase was able to take an active role in the dismantling of slavery.

Chase, the most radical abolitionist in Lincoln's original cabinet, used his office to chip away at slavery in the period before the Emancipation Proclamation (1862). He supported generals who used their power to undermine or destroy the institution, as long as they did not overtly go beyond administration policy. Under Chase's protégé, Edward L. Pierce, the first steps toward educating ex-slaves for life as free men and women took place in 1862 on the sea islands of South Carolina. Chase encouraged dedicated abolitionists to run this "rehearsal for reconstruction." In the Cabinet, Chase argued for an early end to slavery itself. Chase strongly supported the Emancipation Proclamation, even though he believed that it did not go far enough. Chase's personal piety led him to convince Lincoln to ask for the "gracious favor of Almighty God" at the end of the proclamation.

Throughout his tenure as secretary of the treasury, Chase's relationship with Lincoln was strained. He had serious policy disagreements with Lincoln, especially on such issues as emancipation and black rights. Chase was far ahead of his president on these matters. In addition, Chase wanted Lincoln's job: Chase had his eye on the White House in 1856 and 1860. He thought that after a single term Lincoln would step aside, and he could step forward. Chase's feuding with Secretary of State William H. Seward and his persistent campaigning for the Republican presidential nomination in 1864 made it increasingly difficult for him to remain in the Cabinet. In June, 1864, a conflict over the appointment of a subordinate led Chase to offer his resignation. This was the fourth or fifth time he had done so. Much to his surprise, Lincoln accepted the resignation and Chase was out of the Cabinet.

In spite of his disagreements with Lincoln, Chase ultimately campaigned actively for the Republican ticket throughout the fall of 1864. After his reelection, Lincoln appointed Chase to replace the late Roger B. Taney as Chief Justice of the United States. Chase was a logical choice. He had been an eminent attorney and had developed the most coherent antislavery legal-constitutional arguments of the antebellum period. He was sympathetic to emancipation and the other war policies of the Lincoln Administration.

Rather than marking a fitting end to his lifetime of public service, however, Chase's years in the Supreme Court were an anticlimax if not an embarrassment. Chase joined a Court that was deeply divided between antislavery Lincoln appointees and proslavery holdovers from the prewar years. During Reconstruction, the court was asked to decide on questions which were at the heart of the political crisis of the period. The Court's answer, and Chase's leadership, were mixed.

Chase presided over the impeachment of Andrew Johnson with fairness and skill. He earned the respect of most of the Senate, and of much of the nation. This might have been the capstone of his career. Chase still had his eye on the presidency, however, and he used his newfound prestige to campaign for the office. Chase's hunger for the White House led him to repudiate his previous support for black suffrage, in hopes of getting the Democratic nomination. He failed in this effort and in the process lost support from moderates as well as former abolitionists.

When he appointed Chase, Lincoln told a friend "we wish for a Chief Justice who will sustain what has been done in regard to emancipation and the legal tenders." Had Lincoln lived, he would have been disappointed by Chase on the latter issue. In *Hepburn v. Griswold* (1870) and in the Legal Tender cases (1871), Chase voted to void the financial system that he had set up as the secretary of the treasury. The chief justice was severely criticized for this.

On black rights, Chase's record was more consistent. Despite his willingness to oppose black suffrage in order to gain the presidential nomination in 1868, Chase was a genuine supporter of black rights. In the Slaughterhouse cases (1873), Chase vigorously dissented, arguing that the majority opinion undermined the rights of the freedmen. In other Reconstruction decisions, Chase generally supported Congress over the president or the states. The one major exception was the loyalty oaths, which Chase opposed from the bench. In his most important Reconstruction decision, *Texas v. White* (1868), Chase upheld the basic theory of Congressional Reconstruction in an opinion that was sensitive to the political realities of the era. Chase also upheld the power of Congress to limit Supreme Court jurisdiction in the postwar South in *Ex parte McCardle* (1868). In *Ex parte Milligan* (1866), however, he denied the right of the executive branch to abolish civilian courts in those states which remained within the Union.

Summary

Few men in American history have held so many important governmental positions. Chase's contributions to the antislavery movement and the Republican Party were critical. His defense of fugitive slaves and abolitionists was unmatched by other lawyers of his age; his development of a coherent antislavery constitutional theory helped pave the way for Lincoln's victory in 1860 and the ultimate abolition of slavery. As secretary of the treasury, Chase was a valuable and hardworking member of Lincoln's cabinet. Besides organizing the financing of the war effort, Chase helped develop Reconstruction policy. In the early years of the war, he also helped Lincoln manage the War Department, which was being incompetently and corruptly run by Secretary of War Simon Cameron.

As chief justice, Chase was a disappointment. He was unable to assert the authority and leadership that he had displayed in his other public positions. His opinions were never as sharp as his prewar speeches had been. Moreover, his positions, so clear and consistent in the antebellum period, were sometimes vague on the bench. His grasping for the presidency reflected poorly on him and on the office he held. Nevertheless, Chase guided the Supreme Court through the impeachment crisis with dignity. He also avoided running afoul of Congress at a time when that branch might have seriously damaged the Supreme Court, had Chase and his brethren opposed Congressional Reconstruction policies. Similarly, Chase left the bench on a high note, vigorously asserting the rights of the freedmen in the Slaughterhouse cases, at a time when a majority of the Supreme Court and the nation were rejecting any commitment to racial equality.

Bibliography

Blue, Frederick J. *Salmon P. Chase: A Life in Politics.* Kent, Ohio: Kent State University Press, 1987.

Chase, Salmon Portland. *Inside Lincoln's Cabinet: The Civil War Diaries of Salmon P. Chase.* Edited by David H. Donald. New York: Longman, 1954. Chase kept a detailed diary while in the cabinet. This carefully edited edition offers great insight into Chase and his role in the cabinet. Part of the diary is also available, along with many Chase letters, in volume 2 of the *Annual Report of the American Historical Association for the Year 1902*, published by the United States Government Printing Office in 1903.

Foner, Eric. *Free Soil, Free Labor, Free Men: The Ideology of the Republican Party Before the Civil War.* New York: Oxford University Press, 1970; London: Oxford University Press, 1971. Contains an important chapter on Chase's con-

stitutional theory and its relationship to Republican ideology. Throughout this book, Chase is a major figure.

Hart, Albert Bushnell. *Salmon Portland Chase.* Boston: Houghton Mifflin, 1899. Although dated, this volume remains the best available biography of Chase. The book is relatively weak on his judicial career, but it is an excellent introduction to his abolitionist efforts and political career.

Hyman, Harold M., and William M. Wiecek. *Equal Justice Under Law: Constitutional Development, 1835-1875.* New York: Harper, 1982. Covers the developments in constitutional and legal thought during Chase's career.

Kutler, Stanley I. *Judicial Power and Reconstruction Politics.* Chicago: University of Chicago Press, 1968. Best short introduction to the problems of the Supreme Court under Chase.

Maizlish, Stephen E. "Salmon P. Chase: The Roots of Ambition and the Origins of Reform." *Journal of the Early Republic* 18, no. 4 (Spring 1998). Examines Chase's life, the trials he faced, and how they shaped his career and beliefs regarding the defense of the rights of slaves.

Niven, John. *Salmon P. Chase: A Study in Paradox.* New York: Oxford University Press, 1995. A biography of Chase that emphasizes his most significant case—the attempted impeachment of President Andrew Jackson.

Schuckers, Jacob W. *The Life and Public Services of Salmon Portland Chase.* New York: Appleton, 1874. Written by one of Chase's protégés, this book presents an overly heroic portrait of its subject but is nevertheless useful, particularly for the many Chase letters and speeches that it reprints.

Warden, Robert. *An Account of the Private Life and Public Services of Salmon Portland Chase.* Cincinnati, Ohio: Wilstach, Baldwin, 1874. Much like the Schuckers biography, this volume is useful but uncritical.

Wiecek, William M. *The Sources of Antislavery Constitutionalism in America, 1760-1848.* Ithaca, N.Y.: Cornell University Press, 1977. Places Chase's antislavery theories and legal arguments in the context of other abolitionist constitutional theorists.

Paul Finkelman

CHATEAUBRIAND

Born: September 4, 1768; Saint-Malo, France
Died: July 4, 1848; Paris, France
Area of Achievement: Literature
Contribution: The father of French Romanticism, Chateaubriand popularized the melancholy hero and deeply influenced many other nineteenth and twentieth century writers.

Early Life

The youngest of ten children, François-August-René de Chateaubriand was born at Saint-Malo, France, on September 4, 1768. His father, René-Auguste de Chateaubriand, had become rich as a shipowner and merchant sailor; with his wealth, he had purchased the château of Combourg. There the young Chateaubriand spent a lonely childhood, wandering the woods with his sister Lucile, four years his senior, who early recognized and fostered her brother's genius. Already as an adolescent he revealed himself as a dreamer. He later recalled that when he spoke with Lucile about the world, "it was the world that we carried within us," that of the imagination.

His father initially intended for Chateaubriand to pursue a naval career. To this end the youth attended the College of Dol, near Combourg, and then the Jesuit college of Rennes. Having rejected the sea, Chateaubriand next went to the College of Dinan to study for the priesthood but soon abandoned this field as well. An older brother, Jean-Baptiste, who was living in Paris and moving in court circles, then secured for him a military commission; Chateaubriand was to remark that both he and Napoleon I began their careers as sublieutenants. He was also to observe that he spent fifteen years as a soldier before devoting fifteen to writing and another fifteen to politics.

Actually, his military career was considerably briefer. When his father died in September, 1786, Chateaubriand left the army, returned to Combourg, and, in 1789, joined his brother at the French capital. An unintentional witness to the fall of the Bastille and the increasingly violent French Revolution that ensued, in July, 1791, Chateaubriand sailed to America to find true liberty, fraternity, and equality.

On the banks of the Ohio, he chanced upon a newspaper report of the flight of Louis XVI. He hastened back to France to fight for the monarchy.

Lacking funds sufficient to join the émigré army, he married the rich and acerbic Céleste Buisson de la Vigne. Wounded and left for dead at the siege of Thionville, he managed to escape to England, where he made a living as a tutor and translator.

Life's Work

In the evenings, he also began to produce original works. Among the earliest of these is his "Lettre sur l'art du dessin dans les paysages" (1795; letter on the art of landscape painting), a significant contribution to the Romantic movement. From the Renaissance through the eighteenth century, artistic theory emphasized the importance of learning technique through imitation of past masterpieces. Chateaubriand recognized the importance of technical skill, but he argued that the painter must first immerse himself in nature and respond to it emotionally, then attempt to recapture these feelings in his work. The artist should faithfully record what he has observed—Chateaubriand had studied bota-

ny before going to America so that he would recognize and understand what he was seeing—but landscape painting should seek not photographic realism but rather the ideal. One sees here a number of concepts that recur in writings on Romantic literary theory.

Just as Chateaubriand's observations on landscape painting challenged the neoclassical aesthetic, so this *Essai sur les révolutions* (1797; *An Historical, Political, Moral Essay on Revolutions*, 1815) rejected the political attitude of the Enlightenment. Intended as the first volume of a detailed study of revolutions, it devotes relatively little attention to the one then engulfing Europe. Yet it does comment on events in France, denying the idea of progress and perfectibility, seeing the French Revolution as only one of an ongoing series of upheavals that left people no freer or happier than they were before.

The next year he apparently began to change his mind about religion, though he would never allow his devotion to Catholicism to interfere with his pleasures. He began work on *Le Génie du Christianisme* (1799, 1800, 1802; *The Genius of Christianity*, 1802), a spirited defense of traditional belief. Again he was rejecting the views of the eighteenth century philosophers, and, by couching his arguments in aesthetic and emotional terms, he was allying himself once more with the Romantics.

Some portions of this work were published in England, but Chateaubriand was still revising the manuscript when he returned to France in May, 1800. Seeking literary fame and needing money, he detached from *The Genius of Christianity* a novella intended to illustrate how religion improves literature; this piece he published separately in 1801. *Atala* (English translation, 1802), the first work by a European to use the American wilderness and the Indian as central features, told of the love of Atala for the Indian Chactas. Unwilling to betray the vow of chastity made to her dying mother, and unable to overcome her passion for her lover, Atala poisons herself. Here, as in *René* (1802; English translation, 1813), Chateaubriand portrayed the melancholy Byronic hero well before George Gordon, Lord Byron, himself, did so. The dreamlike landscapes that mirror the inhabitants' moods and at the same time seem to control their actions, the emphasis on emotion, the descriptions that use the senses (as when each blade of grass emits a different note) are devices that would influence succeeding generations of writers.

The popularity of *Atala* was matched, if not surpassed, by that of its parent work when it appeared in France the next year. The timing of its publication could not have been more fortunate for the author: On April 8, 1802, Napoleon concluded the Concordat, restoring Catholicism as the official religion of France; *The Genius of Christianity* appeared six days later.

Encouraged by the book's success and by recommendations from Chateaubriand's current mistress, Pauline de Beaumont, Napoleon appointed the author to the post of secretary to the French embassy in Rome (1803). Chateaubriand soon sought, and obtained, another assignment, that of chargé d'affaires to the puppet state of Valais. Yet before he could settle his affairs in Paris, he learned of Napoleon's kidnapping and execution of the Bourbon Duke of Enghien, an act meant to warn the Royalists against any attempted coup. Chateaubriand resigned his office and broke with the French ruler.

Using Royalist funds, he bought the newspaper *Mercure de France* and, on July 4, 1807, published a harsh attack on the dictator. Napoleon retaliated by forcing him to sell the paper, though at a profit sufficient to allow Chateaubriand to acquire a country house outside Paris, where he completed *Les Martyres* (1809; *The Martyrs*, 1812), another tale of doomed love. The heroine, Cymodocéa, is modeled on Natalie de Noailles, who had succeeded Pauline de Beaumont as Chateaubriand's mistress. Throughout his life, he would attract France's most beautiful and clever women, earning for himself the title "the enchanter." Short, stocky, broad-shouldered, and pale, he had a leonine head that compensated for any physical flaw, flashing gray eyes, and wild brown hair that gave him an aura of romance.

Set in the reign of Diocletian, *The Martyrs* presents a thinly veiled attack on Napoleon by comparing the French emperor to the Roman. Having arrested the pope and, therefore, having been excommunicated, Napoleon chose to ignore the criticism and sought to renew his friendship with the leading French Catholic author of the day. He arranged Chateaubriand's appointment to the prestigious Académie Française, but the writer's acceptance speech, so harsh that Napoleon censored it, showed that reconciliation was impossible.

In 1814, Chateaubriand wrote an even sterner indictment of the French ruler. "What have you done, not with a hundred thousand, but with five million Frenchmen . . . our relatives, our friends, our brothers?" he asked in *De Buonaparte et des Bourbons* (1814; *On Buonaparte and the Bourbons*, 1814). Again Chateaubriand's timing was perfect: The piece appeared on the day the allied troops entered Paris, and the newly crowned Louis XVIII claimed that the publication was worth 100,000 soldiers.

Yet Chateaubriand's relationship with the Bourbons was uneasy. On June 4, 1814, Louis issued a charter that reaffirmed individual rights and sought to establish a constitutional monarchy along English lines, with ministerial responsibility to the legislative majority rather than to the king. Within two years, though, Chateaubriand was disillusioned. In his memoirs he was to write, "Descending from Bonaparte and the Empire to those who followed them, is like falling from . . . the summit of a mountain into an abyss." While supporting the freedoms won since 1789, Chateaubriand claimed that the king's ministers did not share the views of the majority of Frenchmen and were thus betraying the Charter of 1814.

On February 13, 1820, the Duc de Berry, son of the future Charles X, was assassinated at the opera. In his newspaper *Le Conservateur*, Chateaubriand wrote, "The hand that struck the blow does not bear the greatest guilt; they that have murdered the Duc de Berry are those that have been introducing democratic laws into the Monarchy for the last four years." The government of Elie Decazes fell, and its successor named Chateaubriand minister of state and envoy to Berlin. He did not remain in Prussia long before returning to Paris to devote himself to Juliette Récamier, Claire de Duras, and Delphine de Custine. In January, 1822, he again went abroad, this time as ambassador to the Court of St. James, where his chef, Montmireil, immortalized his name among many who never would read *René* or *Atala* by naming a thickly cut beefsteak for the diplomat. Chateaubriand left London in September to represent France at the Congress of Verona, and on December 28, 1822, he was named minister of foreign affairs. He was to claim that in this office he succeeded in doing what Napoleon had not—conquering Spain. A popular revolution had dethroned Ferdinand VII, and Chateaubriand persuaded France to intervene and restore the king to his throne.

In June, 1824, Chateaubriand was himself deposed, losing his ministerial position, though in 1827 he returned to a government post as ambassador to Rome. When Charles X named the conservative Jules de Polignac as chief minister, Chateaubriand resigned. As Chateaubriand feared,

Polignac proved to be the downfall of the Bourbon monarchy; in 1830, the Orléans Louis-Philippe assumed the throne after a short revolution. Despite his treatment by the Bourbons, Chateaubriand refused to take the oath of allegiance to the new king, preferring to renounce his titles of peer and minister of state together with the salary they carried.

By then, he no longer needed this stipend, for he had been paid 550,000 francs for the rights to the collected works, and he received another 156,000 francs and a life pension for his memoirs, which appeared posthumously. Chateaubriand's last years were dedicated to the completion of this autobiography and to Juliette Récamier, who was with him when he died in Paris on July 4, 1848. At his request, he was buried in a simple tomb on the rock of Grand Bé off the coast of Saint-Malo.

Summary

In 1831, when the Gothic church of Saint-Germain l'Auxerrois faced demolition, Chateaubriand played an important role in its preservation, though he remarked that too many such buildings were appearing in the literature of the day. That writers were filling their pages with descriptions of Gothic cathedrals was, however, in large part attributable to Chateaubriand himself. Théophile Gautier claimed that *The Genius of Christianity* restored the popularity of Gothic architecture, just as *Les Natchez* (1826; *The Natchez*, 1827) unlocked the natural sublime and *René* invented the modern melancholy hero. Chateaubriand was an idol to a generation of French Romantics—the young Alphonse de Lamartine waited outside Chateaubriand's house for two days to catch a glimpse of the man—and later authors such as Gustave Flaubert and Charles Baudelaire were equally influenced by his works.

The first writer to appreciate the literary potential of the American frontier, Chateaubriand placed within that setting the brooding hero that Byron would popularize a decade later. The poet of sadness, night, suffering, and ennui, he gave the world the character who searches for a self he will never find. He also taught the French how to read their own classics. He was among the first to recognize the tragic sense that underlies much of Molière's comedy and the sadness and dreamlike qualities of Jean de La Fontaine, Blaise Pascal, and Jean Racine.

Honoré de Balzac wanted to be a literary Napoleon; Chateaubriand hoped to be a political Napoleon as well. He lacked the talent and temperament necessary to rival his fellow sublieutenant in the field or in the cabinet, but in the study he reigned supreme. As Bonaparte remarked, "Chateaubriand has received the sacred fire from Nature; his works bear witness to it. His style is not that of Racine but that of the prophet."

Bibliography

Evans, Joan. *Chateaubriand: A Biography*. London and New York: Macmillan, 1939. Relies primarily on Chateaubriand's autobiography but corrects and supplements this work with other accounts. Readable, with many fine vignettes but little analysis.

Hilt, Douglas. "Chateaubriand and Napolean." *History Today* 23 (December 1973): 831-837. Traces Chateaubriand's political career under Napoleon and the author's subsequent portrayal of Napoleon in his memoirs.

Irlam, Shaun. "Gerrymandered Geographies: Exoticism in Thomson and Chateaubriand." *MLN* 108, no. 5 (December, 1993). Irlam analyzes the use of exotic locales in the works of Chateaubriand and James Thomson as mirrors of national consciousness.

Maurois, André. *Chateaubriand: Poet, Statesman, Lover*. Translated by Vera Fraser. New York and London: Harper, 1938. Drawing heavily on Chateaubriand's own writing, Maurois artfully weaves his subject's own words into a readable narrative.

Painter, George D. *Chateaubriand: A Biography*. London: Chatto and Windus, and New York: Knopf, 1977. A projected three-volume work, when complete it will be the definitive biography. Painter offers an extensively detailed account; the first volume traces the life from 1768 to 1793.

Porter, Charles Allan. *Chateaubriand: Composition, Imagination, and Poetry*. Saratoga, Calif.: Anma Libri, 1978. A stylistic analysis of Chateaubriand's major works. Like many of Chateaubriand's contemporaries, Porter sees discontinuities of time and space in the prose. Porter finds in these disjunctions a modern attempt to engage the reader in the creative process.

Sieburg, Friedrich. *Chateaubriand*. Translated by Violet M. MacDonald. London: Allen and Unwin, 1961; New York: St. Martin's Press, 1962. Concentrates on biography rather than literary analysis. Argues that "Chateaubriand's ambition and his desire for action were . . . forever undermining the foundations of his existence" and that his life is a tissue of contradictions.

Weil, Kari. "Romantic Exile and the Melancholia of Identification." *Journal of Feminist Cultural Studies* 7, no. 2 (Summer 1995). Discusses the effects of geographic exile on expatriates as depicted in Chateaubriand's "René" and Mme. de Duras' "Ourika."

Joseph Rosenblum

ANTON CHEKHOV

Born: January 29, 1860; Taganrog, in the Crimea, Russia

Died: July 15, 1904; Badenweiler, Germany

Areas of Achievement: Literature, theater, and drama

Contribution: Although Chekhov had a significant impact on the creation of modern drama with his four major plays, his most important influence has been on the development of the modern short story. With his numerous lyrical stories, Chekhov liberated the short story in particular from its adherence to the parable form and fiction in general from the tedium of the realistic novel.

Early Life

Anton Chekhov was born on January 29, 1860, in a small port town on the Sea of Azov in the Crimea. His grandfather was a former slave who bought his own freedom. In what is perhaps the best-known remark Chekhov ever made about his life, he said he felt the necessity to "squeeze the slave" out of himself. Chekhov's father, Pavel Egorovich, owned a small general store in which Chekhov worked as a child. When Chekhov was sixteen, however, his father had to declare bankruptcy and escape his creditors by going to Moscow. Chekhov's mother, along with the two youngest children, followed soon after. Chekhov stayed behind as a tutor to the son of one of his mother's former boarders.

After living in poverty and fending for himself for three years, Chekhov was graduated from high school in Taganrog and went to Moscow to enter medical school at Moscow University. Because his father had a low-paying job outside town and was only home on Sundays and holidays, Chekhov had to assume the role of head of his family's household and find work. Having shown an early interest in writing while he was a child in Taganrog, he sought to supplement his family's meager income by contributing anecdotes and stories to humorous magazines, especially at the urging of his elder brother Aleksander, who was already earning a small income by publishing in such magazines. At first Chekhov had little success with his writing efforts, but in March, 1880, his first story was published in the humor journal *Strekoza* (dragonfly). Chekhov later called this the beginning of his literary career.

Life's Work

In 1882, Chekhov became a regular contributor of jokes and anecdotes to a weekly St. Petersburg magazine, *Oskolki* (fragments), edited by Nikolai A. Leikin. He submitted a large number of short pieces to the journal, many under various pseudonyms. By 1884, he had published more than two hundred short pieces, but when his first collection, *Skazki Melpomeny* (1884; *Tales of Melpomene*, 1916-1923), was published, he included only twenty of them. Also in 1884, Chekhov finished his degree and began practicing medicine. By the following year, when he went to St. Petersburg, he found, much to his surprise (because he did not consider his work significant), that he was quite well known as a writer there.

Chekhov's increasing desire to write more serious fiction, however, made him chafe against the restrictions of the humor magazines, as well as against Leiken's insistence that he stick to jokes. Thus, when Aleksey S. Suvorin, the owner of the influential newspaper *Novoye vremya* (new times), asked Chekhov to contribute more substantial stories to his newspaper, Chekhov was pleased to comply. During 1886 and 1887, Chekhov wrote a large number of stories and short pieces for Suvorin, including some of his best-known stories. His second collection, *Pystrye rasskazy* (motley stories), was published in 1886, and a third, *V sumerkakh* (in the twilight), was published in 1887.

Still, Chekhov was not personally satisfied with his work, believing it to be ephemeral. Moreover, in 1886, he began to suspect that he had tuberculosis, although he refused to have another doctor give him an examination. In this spirit of anxiety about his health and dissatisfaction with his work, Chekhov left on a trip to his hometown in the Crimea to visit friends and relatives. This trip seemed to rejuvenate him, for several important stories of the provincial life of the people he encountered resulted from it. Perhaps the most important result of the journey, however, was his lyrical story "Step'" ("The Steppe," 1915), which was published in a highly reputable literary monthly in 1888. Following the story's publication, Chekhov was given the Pushkin Prize for literature by the Academy of Sciences. Even Chekhov himself could no longer doubt that his work had more than ephemeral value.

Also in 1888, Chekhov turned to writing plays, beginning with *Leshy* (1889; *The Wood Demon*, 1925), which was so poorly received that he quit writing serious drama until 1895. This failure, along with a general sense of malaise, what Chek-

hov called a stagnation in his soul, was the cause of his decision to take a most treacherous journey to the penal colony on Sakhalin Island in the Northern Pacific to learn about the living conditions of the prison inmates. Taking extraordinary means to study the geography and history of the island, he embarked on April 21, 1890, and arrived on July 11. Chekhov spent three months on the island and did enough research on the inmates, he said, for "three dissertations." Although *Ostrov Sakhalin* (1893; the Island of Sakhalin) was the formal result of the trip, more lasting fictional results are such stories as "V sylke" (1892; "In Exile," 1912) and "V ovrage" (1900; in the ravine).

On his return to Moscow, Chekhov once again had the urge to travel, this time to Europe. He found Vienna, Venice, Rome, and Florence overwhelming in the beauty of their art and landscapes. On his return, Chekhov purchased a country estate about fifty miles outside Moscow in Melikhovo, where he became a country gentleman and landowner and wrote many of his most famous stories, such as "Chorny monakh" (1892; "The Black Monk," 1903), "Palata No. 6" (1892; ward no. six),

"Student" (1894; the student), "Muzhiki" (1897; peasants), and "Dom s mezoninom" (1896; the house with an attic).

In 1895, Chekhov began writing plays again, working on *Chayka* (*The Seagull*, 1909), which was first staged at St. Petersburg in October, 1896, but, partly because of the nature of the production, was an abysmal failure. Once again, Chekhov swore never to write plays. Shortly thereafter, his health worsened and he began to hemorrhage from the lungs. After entering a clinic, he was officially diagnosed as having tuberculosis and was advised to spend the winter months in a warm climate; he soon left for Nice, France. While Chekhov was in France, the Moscow Art Theater asked for permission to stage *The Seagull*. Although Chekhov first refused, he later agreed and went to Moscow to meet the cast. Among them was Olga Knipper, whom Chekhov would marry a few years later.

Chekhov's ill health again forced him to leave Moscow, this time for Yalta, where he had a house built. On December 17, 1898, *The Seagull* opened and was a tremendous success. Thus encouraged, Chekhov rewrote his first failure, *The Wood Demon*, and renamed it *Dyadya Vanya* (*Uncle Vanya*, 1914), which the Moscow Art Theater staged in 1899. The following year, when the troupe began a tour of the Crimea with both *The Seagull* and *Uncle Vanya* among their repertoire, Chekhov was at last able to see his two plays on the stage. He was also able to spend more time with Olga Knipper. Soon after, Chekhov finished his third play, *Tri sestry* (1901; *Three Sisters*, 1920). He and Olga Knipper were married on May 25, 1901.

In 1902, Chekhov's health took another turn for the worse; it is a tribute to his determination and genius that during this year he worked on his final play, *Vishnyovy sad* (*The Cherry Orchard*, 1908), and completed it in October. It was scheduled to premier on January 29, 1904, on his forty-fourth birthday; it was also presented in celebration of his twenty-five years as a writer. When Chekhov arrived at the theater after the third act, much to his embarrassment, he was honored with speeches and applause.

Chekhov went back to Yalta for the rest of the winter; on his return trip to Moscow in the spring, his health became worse. On June 4, he and his wife went to Berlin to see a specialist; from there, they went to Badenweiler, a spa in Germany. Chekhov died early in the morning on July 15, 1904. His body was shipped back to Moscow, where he was buried by his father.

Summary

Anton Chekhov was one of the most influential literary artists at the close of the nineteenth century to usher in the era of modernism in narrative fiction, particularly in short fiction. When his stories were first made widely available in English in the famous Constance Garnett translations between 1916 and 1923, they were termed sketches or slices of life, lacking in all the elements that constituted the short-story form. Critics soon began to realize, however, that Chekhov's freedom from the prevailing conventions of social realism and formalized plot indicated the beginnings of a modern kind of narrative, which combined the specific detail of realism with the poetic lyricism of Romanticism.

Chekhov's most significant contributions to the short-story form, contributions which have influenced modern writers such as Ernest Hemingway and Raymond Carver, include the following: the presentation of character as a lyrical or psychological mood rather than as a two-dimensional symbol or as a realistic personality; the conception of a story as a lyrical sketch rather than as a highly plotted tale; and the assumption of reality as basically impressionistic and as a function of narrative perspective or point of view. The final result of these innovations has been the modernist and postmodernist view of reality as a fictional construct.

With Chekhov, the short story took on a new respectability and began to be understood as the most appropriate narrative form to reflect the modern temperament. Today, most critics agree that there can be no understanding of the short story as a genre without an understanding of Chekhov's contribution to the form.

Bibliography

Baehr, Stephen L. "The Locomotive and the Giant: Power in Chekov's 'Anna on the Neck.' " *Slavic and East European Journal* 39, no. 1 (Spring 1995). Examines the metaphors used by Chekov for sexual power in "Anna on the Neck," his study of a dominated woman who uses her feminine guile to her advantage.

Clyman, Toby, ed. *A Chekhov Companion.* Westport, Conn.: Greenwood Press, 1985. A collection of critical essays, especially commissioned for this volume, on all aspects of Chekhov's life, art, and career. Some of the most important critics of Chekhov's work are represented here in essays on his major themes, his dramatic technique, his narrative technique, and his influence on modern drama and on the modern short story.

Hahn, Beverly. *Chekhov: A Study of Major Stories and Plays.* London and New York: Cambridge University Press, 1977. Hahn focuses on *The Cherry Orchard* as the principal Chekhov play with which to introduce his dramatic technique, although she does discuss the earlier plays as well. This study is particularly notable for its study of Chekhov's relationship with Tolstoy and of his depiction of women in his plays.

Hingley, Ronald. *Chekhov: A Biographical and Critical Study.* Rev. ed. London: Unwin, and New York: Barnes and Noble, 1966. Hingley provides a general introduction to the life and work of Chekhov, focusing on both Chekhov's language and his relationship to the social issues significant in Russia during that time.

———. *A New Life of Anton Chekhov.* London: Oxford University Press, and New York: Knopf, 1976. A more detailed and more thoroughly biographical study than Hingley's earlier work, this biography makes use of many documentary materials not previously available, particularly eight volumes of Chekhov's letters. It also focuses more on the mysterious subject of Chekhov's relationships with women than do previous studies.

Kirk, Irina. *Anton Chekhov.* Boston: Twayne, 1981. A general introduction to the life and art of Chekhov, focusing primarily on Chekhov's stories as being the embodiment of the search for a philosophy of life and the search for love and home. Although most of the book focuses on discussions of the stories, one final chapter analyzes the plays.

Pitcher, Harvey. *The Chekhov Play: A New Interpretation.* London: Chatto and Windus, and New York: Barnes and Noble, 1973. A detailed discussion of the four Chekhov plays in the light of several premises Pitcher establishes about their basic nature: for example, that they focus primarily on the emotional side of life, that they follow a certain structural formula, that they follow the ensemble approach of the Moscow Art Theater, and that the language of the characters is dominated by a feeling of informality.

Pritchett, V. S. *Chekhov: A Spirit Set Free.* London: Hodder and Stoughton, and New York: Random House, 1988. This study by a master of the short story is neither straight biography nor literary criticism but rather a leisurely mixture of the two, with an emphasis on the latter. Pritchett discusses many of Chekhov's stories in detail and attempts to distill the essential qualities of his art.

Winner, Thomas. *Chekhov and His Prose.* New York: Holt Rinehart, 1966. A chronological study of Chekhov's development as a story writer, from his beginnings as a writer of humorist anecdotes, to his experimentation with his impressionistic style, through his final concern with the Russian social scene.

Charles E. May

LYDIA MARIA CHILD

Born: February 11, 1802; Medford, Massachusetts
Died: October 20, 1880; Wayland, Massachusetts
Areas of Achievement: Literature, abolitionism, and social reform
Contribution: Child was one of America's first successful women writers and editors, combining popular writing with a lifetime's dedication to the causes of racial equality and general public enlightenment.

Early Life

Lydia Maria Child, born Lydia Maria Francis in Medford, Massachusetts, on February 11, 1802, wished when young that her father had paid as much attention to her as he did to her older brother, Convers. Maria, as she preferred to be called, envied her brother's inquisitive spirit and her father's willingness to encourage it. Throughout her life, her choices would reflect the strength of mind and heart that she so early learned from having to act on her own.

Maria's father, David Convers Francis, a prosperous baker, had little time for his strong-minded daughter. When his wife, Susannah (Rand) Francis, died, he sent twelve-year-old Maria to live with a married sister in Norridgewock, Maine. By age fifteen, Maria was already reading the works of John Milton, Homer, and Sir Walter Scott and was beginning to show the literary interests that were soon to make her famous. At eighteen, she opened a private academy, which had become well established when next she decided to join her brother Convers, now a Unitarian minister, and his wife in Watertown, Massachusetts, just outside Boston. There, her literary career began to flower.

Francis' first novel, *Hobomok* (1824), was an instant success. This romance, involving an Indian male and a white female, reflected her childhood talks in Maine with local Abamake Indians and foreshadowed her lifelong opposition to the United States government's Indian policies. *Hobomok* also hinted at Maria's radical social views, since the plot featured an interracial marriage. A second work, *The Rebels: Or, Boston Before the Revolution* (1825), also sold well, and in 1826 she began publishing the *Juvenile Miscellany*, America's first periodical created exclusively for children. All the while, Francis continued to teach in the private academy which she had founded in Watertown. Her childhood dream of being as independent as her brother was rapidly becoming a reality.

Her popular writing soon brought her notice in Boston's aristocratic literary circles, where she became known for her charm and intelligence, though she was not regarded as a natural "beauty." By 1827, she had been successfully courted by David Lee Child, a dashing figure eight years her senior, who had diplomatic experience in Europe and who aspired to become a politician. They were married on October 19, 1828, and settled in Boston, where David, for a meager salary, edited a political newspaper. To augment family income, Child published yet another successful book, *The Frugal Housewife* (1829), which passed on to readers the methods she was learning for running a household at low cost. (One cake recipe, however, did call for twenty-eight eggs and three pounds of butter.) The volume, which sold widely in both Europe and the United States, brought the Childs much-needed income, for from the start David Child did poorly in his career. His newspaper attacks on Andrew Jackson for forcibly removing the Cherokee Indians from their land in Georgia after the discovery of gold there made him unpopular, as did his sudden decision to become a vigorous opponent of slavery.

Child, however, agreed with her husband's radical views. While he editorialized, she wrote a history of the Indians in her own region, *The First Settlers of New England* (1829); she soon became an abolitionist as well. In 1831, she encountered William Lloyd Garrison, the most militant of New England's antislavery leaders, and was immediately converted to his cause. Yet once she had embraced this controversial new reform, her popularity as a writer vanished. Patrons snubbed her, and publishers refused her work. Her lucrative career was at an end. "Hardly ever was there a costlier sacrifice," remarked Wendell Phillips, a close friend of Child and another leading Bostonian abolitionist. "Fame and social position [were] in her grasp. But confronted suddenly by the alternatives—gagged life or total wreck—she never hesitated." In 1832, Child had irrevocably committed herself to emancipating the slaves and to seeking social justice. From then on, her brief enjoyment of fame was transformed into a lifetime of struggle against the formidable challenges of poverty and unpopularity.

Life's Work

In 1833, Child published her views on slavery, *An Appeal in Favor of That Class of Americans Called Africans*, a highly influential work which guaranteed her banishment from Boston's literary circles and sealed her public commitment to a career as a social reformer. The work persuaded Charles Sumner, Wendell Phillips, Thomas Wentworth Higgins, and others to examine the slavery question, particularly because Child presented her case in such a logical fashion. (In all of her radical publications, Child seldom made use of overemotional rhetoric.) In calm tones, she denounced racial prejudice, called for equal education and employment opportunities for blacks, demanded an immediate abolition of slavery, and called for the repeal of all segregation laws, including those prohibiting racial intermarriage. Several other abolitionist publications soon followed, and the sales of her other books dwindled in proportion. Even another romantic novel, *Philothea* (1836), set in ancient Greece, failed to sell.

In the place of popularity came mobs of enraged citizens, anxious to purge the North of dangerous radicals such as Child. The famous Boston mob of 1835 specifically aimed at suppressing the Boston Female Anti-Slavery Society of which Child had become a leading member. By 1840, she had secured prominence in antislavery circles, becoming a close associate of Henry B. Chapman and Maria Weston Chapman and of Ellis Gilman Loring and Louise Gilman Loring, as well as of Phillips, Garrison, and other Bostonians who provided leadership for the American Anti-Slavery Society. In 1840, she was named to the executive committee of that society, and in 1841, Child moved to New York City to edit its official weekly newspaper, *The National Anti-Slavery Standard*.

When Child left for New York, David Lee Child remained behind in Massachusetts, nearly destitute but committed to the goal of producing sugar from beets, hoping to develop free-labor alternatives to slave-grown cane sugar from the South. In 1837, he and Child purchased a ramshackle farm in Northampton, Massachusetts, where for three years they had struggled to eke out a living. The need for additional income explained much of Child's reason for assuming the editorship of *The National Anti-Slavery Standard* and for temporarily leaving her husband. While the paper's readership grew substantially under her direction, she found the day-to-day work demoralizing and the endless controversies with her abolitionist colleagues distracting. When she resigned in 1843, her husband (now disengaged from the sugar beet business), briefly replaced her before moving on to Washington, D.C., to lobby at an uncertain salary for antislavery causes. In the meanwhile, Child remained in New York. The patterns of extended separation between her and her husband that would be repeated over the years had now become established. Though each would always profess and show deep love for the other, David's inability to secure a rewarding career had caused their marriage to fracture partially. The couple would always remain childless.

Alone in New York City, Child succeeded somewhat in reestablishing her literary career. Her popular *Letters from New York* (1843) gave readers vivid pictures of all aspects of life in the nation's major metropolis. Some of her scenes depicted the grinding poverty of New York's slums, the injustices endured by the black community, and the degradation suffered by its unskilled workers. She also investigated prison conditions and the bistros and bawdy houses of the notorious Five Points District. She passed no smug judgments on the social outcasts she encountered, writing, "They excite in me more of compassion than dislike." God alone knew, in her opinion, "whether I should not have been as they are, with the same neglected childhood, the same vicious examples, the same overpowering temptation of want and misery." Such insights soon led her to publish *Fact and Fiction: A Collection of Stories* (1846), a book describing the plight of New York's prostitutes.

Though *Letters from New York* proved a popular success, and though Child contributed frequently to other literary periodicals, by 1849 she and her husband continued to face destitution. Still lacking a stable income, David returned to his spouse, and in 1850 both moved to Weymouth, Massachusetts, to take up farming on land furnished at no cost by their Boston friends, the Lorings. By 1852, however, penniless and exhausted, they moved again, this time into a house in Wayland, Massachusetts, owned by Child's father (now in his eighties). There, Child tended to both her husband's and her father's needs, until the latter died, in 1856. During this arduous period of domestic labor, she somehow continued to write a history of Western religion, *The Progress of Religious Ideas* (1855), in three volumes, which few purchased. Her next work, *Autumnal Leaves* (1857), a set of inspirational selections for those facing old age, suggested that, at age fifty-five, Child, too, believed her career to be ending. Indeed, she had written little about social questions since leaving New York City, though she participated in antislavery gatherings in Boston in the 1850's.

John Brown's 1859 raid on Harper's Ferry changed this state of affairs. "Before this affair," she wrote, "I thought I was growing old and drowsy, but now I am as strong as an eagle." She defended Brown's effort at violent emancipation in numerous pamphlets and letters that circulated all over New England. Her offer to nurse the injured Brown as he awaited execution provoked a widely read exchange of letters between Child and the wife of Virginia Senator James M. Mason. By mid-1863, as the Civil War raged, Child had moved fully into the forefront of the struggle against slavery, a struggle she continued by demanding full black equality once the war ended. In 1865, she published *The Freedmen's Book* at her own expense, a compilation of writings of successful blacks for the instruction of newly emancipated slaves. In the im-

mediate postwar period, she pressed the Republican Party to legislate racial equality through the Fourteenth and Fifteenth amendments and supported the impeachment of President Andrew Johnson.

By 1868, however, Child was clearly feeling her age. She rarely traveled from Wayland, where she and her husband, now crippled from arthritis, began living in near seclusion. In that year, she published her last important reform statement, *An Appeal for the Indians*, recalling her first humanitarian efforts nearly forty years earlier. In 1874, when David Lee Child died, Child felt even less reason to engage the outside world. She became intensely reclusive, developing an interest in spiritualism. Few noticed when her last set of essays, *Aspirations of the World*, was published in 1878. When she died in Wayland at age seventy-eight, the few surviving abolitionist crusaders attended; John Greenleaf Whittier rendered a poem, "Within the Gate," and Wendell Phillips delivered the oration.

Summary

Lydia Maria Child embodied the idealism and reform spirit that lay behind the great crusade against slavery. Her most enduring work, *An Appeal in Favor of That Class of Americans Called Africans*, is recognized as a classic expression of the abolitionist's version of a racially just and egalitarian society. Her many-sided interests, her noteworthy sense of humor, her suspicion of self-righteous rhetoric, moreover, disproved the stereotype of the abolitionists as a collection of narrow-minded fanatics and eccentrics. Further, her long association with the cause of black equality illustrated the depth and sincerity of the abolitionist's commitment.

Child's literary career and her long struggle for self-sufficiency also suggest the limits and possibilities of female emancipation in the pre-Civil War years. Clearly, her novels and other writings mark her as a pathfinder in the area of women's literature. Yet she wrote often about the virtues of housework and cheerful obedience to the demands of husband and children. Her lifelong struggle to maintain not only herself but also her husband testifies to the tremendous burdens faced in the nineteenth century by "independent-minded" women who still believed in the primary importance of these domestic roles.

Bibliography

Baer, Helen G. *The Heart Is Like Heaven: The Life of Lydia Maria Child*. Philadelphia: University of Pennsylvania Press, 1964. A good modern biography of Child, based on primary research and a grasp of the scholarly literature then available on the antislavery movement.

Child, Lydia Maria. *An Appeal in Favor of That Class of Americans Called Africans*. Boston: Allen and Ticknor, 1833. Her classic abolitionist exposition of doctrines and arguments. Conveys the full range of Child's opinions on slavery, race equality, and racial prejudice, while standing as a fine example of her expository style as a reformer.

———. *Letters from New-York*. New York: Francis, and London: Bentley, 1843.

———. *Letters from New York: Second Series*. New York: Francis, 1845. Child's reports on poverty and luxury in America's largest city give vivid glimpses of her social convictions. Other parts show her facility as an art critic, theatergoer, and fashion commentator. The best introduction to Child's "popular" writings.

———. *Philothea: A Romance*. Boston: Otis Broaders, 1836. Typifies Child's literary romanticism. Set in ancient Greece, the plot features proslavery and antislavery themes but also incorporates a dramatic love story and much melodrama. Since it tried to appeal to both reformers and the general reading public, this romance reveals in one work most of Child's intentions as a fiction writer.

Karcher, Carolyn L. *The First Woman in the Republic: A Cultural Biography of Lydia Maria Child*. Durham, N.C.: Duke University Press, 1994. An admirable account of the life and work of Child, which places her work in a contemporary context where nineteenth and twentieth century feminist issues are seen to be similar.

Meltzer, Milton. *Tongue of Flame: The Life of Lydia Maria Child*. New York: Crowell, 1965. The best popular biography of Child, written by an experienced historian and based on primary research. Presents Child's personality in especially vivid terms while giving a compact, readable summary of her public and private lives.

Stewart, James Brewer. *Holy Warriors: The Abolitionists and American Slavery*. Rev. ed. New York: Hill and Wang, 1996. This brief synthesis of the history of the abolitionist crusade gives attention to principal figures and events that bore on Child's career. This work traces the development of antislavery from its origins in the eighteenth century until the end of Reconstruction.

Thomas, John L. *The Liberator, William Lloyd Garrison: A Biography*. Boston: Little Brown, 1963. This major biography of Boston's leading abolitionist conveys an excellent sense of the culture, people, and movements with which Child was intimately associated. A major scholarly study of the person who most permanently influenced Child's views on social reform.

James Brewer Stewart

FRÉDÉRIC CHOPIN

Born: March 1, 1810; Zelazowa Wola, Poland
Died: October 17, 1849; Paris, France
Area of Achievement: Music
Contribution: Chopin achieved eminence in two usually distinct areas of music: as a performer and as a composer. He became the foremost pianist of his time, despite the fact that his delicate style and unwillingness to perform in public placed him outside contemporary fashion and practice. His eminence as a composer is equally startling, for unlike every other composer of comparable stature, Chopin devoted himself almost exclusively to keyboard music. Against what some have perceived as the narrowness of his interests, one may posit the brilliance and diversity of his compositions.

Early Life

Frédéric Chopin was born in the Polish village of Zelazowa Wola, located thirty-four miles from the then-provincial city of Warsaw. His mother, Justyna, was the well-educated daughter of an impoverished, upper-class family. His father, Nicholas, a Frenchman by birth, was employed as a tutor by another and more well-to-do branch of that same family, the Skarbeks. Shortly after Frédéric's birth, the family moved to Warsaw, where Nicholas eventually secured a position as a teacher of French at the Lyceum. Impressed by the playing of his mother and older sister, Ludwika, Chopin began to play the piano at the age of four or five. At six he was already composing and taking lessons from Wojciech Zwyny. His first published work, the Polonaise in G Minor, appeared when he was only seven, and he made his first public appearance the following year (1818) at a charity concert. Soon afterward, he played before Poland's Grand Duke Konstantine and in 1825 was selected to demonstrate the aeolomelodicon before Czar Alexander I. While still a student at the Lyceum (1823-1826), Chopin began taking lessons from Josef Elsner, director of the Warsaw Conservatory. Elsner proved an especially fortunate choice; himself inclined toward the Romanticism that Chopin would perfect, he was willing to bend his own strict academic standards to accommodate his student's evident genius. While under Elsner's tutelage, Chopin composed his first major work, a set of variations on Wolfgang Amadeus Mozart's "La ci darem" from *Don Giovanni* (1787), which evidenced a surprising originality and maturity. The trip he made to Berlin in 1828 seems to have whetted his appetite for travel and, more important, for a wider musical world than Warsaw could then provide, and so, after having their request for a travel scholarship rejected by the government, his parents financed his 1829 trip to Vienna themselves. There with the help of a letter of introduction from Elsner, Chopin secured a publisher for his Mozart variations and, as part of his agreement with the publisher, Tobias Haslinger, gave a free concert in order to advertise his work. In fact, Chopin gave two concerts while in Vienna, both of which were successful. His audience was surprised by the lightness of his touch and delighted by his technical skills and use of Polish materials. Upon his return to Warsaw, he fell in love with Konstantia Gladkowska and continued to be well received by Polish audiences. Chopin grew restive, however, and on November 2, 1830, he again journeyed to Vienna, this time accompanied by his close friend, Tytus Wojciechkowski. News of the Polish revolt against the Russians reached them later that month. Wojciechkowski immediately returned to Poland. Chopin, at the urging of his family, remained in Vienna, where he expected to repeat his earlier success. In this he was mistaken. The few concerts he gave attracted little attention and even less cash. After eight months he left Vienna for Paris, learning en route that the revolt had failed and Warsaw had fallen.

Life's Work

Until his death nineteen years later, Paris was to be Chopin's home. The city was then the center of European culture, and thanks to a Viennese friend, Chopin quickly gained entrance to its cultural life. Just as important, Paris was also home to a large number of Polish émigrés, including Adam Mickiewicz, an exile, a poet, and a patriot. Unlike Mickiewicz, Chopin could return to Poland but chose not to do so. Although sensitive to the plight of his countrymen and even supportive of many of them, Chopin was not an activist; nor are his works nationalist in the same sense or to the same degree that Mickiewicz's poems and plays clearly are. Himself half French, Chopin quickly adapted to his new home, largely because it received him so warmly. His first concert on February 26, 1832, attended by Franz Liszt and Felix Mendelssohn, was

a decided success, and in the autumn of that year he was invited to play for the Rothschilds. Having gained entry into the highest level of Parisian society, Chopin quickly became the most fashionable and highest paid piano teacher in the city. Financially secure, he could afford to give up the public concert hall performances he disliked so much and which were so ill-suited to both the character of his music and the delicacy of his playing. His immense and financially rewarding success in the salons of Paris, however, extracted its own price. By the 1830's, an important shift had occurred in the world of music. Aristocratic patrons of the arts, especially music, had begun to play a less significant role, while the mass audience was beginning to exert a far greater influence than ever before. Liszt's style of music and playing was well suited to this new audience; Chopin's was not. The aristocratic salons of Paris therefore played a most important role in nurturing Chopin's genius, but not without limiting or at least misunderstanding it as well, for what the Rothschilds and others prized was not Chopin's compositions but his playing, his imitations, and his improvisations in particular.

Three years after his introduction into this world, there began a sequence of events that was to have a profound effect on Chopin's life and art. Chopin met and fell in love with Maria Wodzinska in 1835, but when he proposed marriage, the family, having heard the rumors of the composer's poor health, refused to give their consent. Disappointed, Chopin paid a short visit to England and within the year had begun his famous liaison with Amandine-Aurore-Lucile Dupin, or George Sand, as she is better known. It was Sand who made the first overtures (in 1836), and these Chopin refused, disturbed by her evident masculinity. Yet in 1837 he became as passionately drawn to her as she was to him. Over the next nine years, he would transform that passion into some of his greatest music. (Over the same period, Sand's passion would undergo a quite different change in the direction of maternal devotion.) At Sand's suggestion, they spent the winter of 1838-1839 on the Island of Majorca. Poor food and even worse weather, coupled with the islanders' fear of contagion caused by Chopin's tubercular condition as well as their distaste for this evidently immoral bohemian household, made composing difficult and the worsening of Chopin's health inevitable. They returned to the mainland in February, but the seriousness of Chopin's condition (he had begun to hemorrhage) forced them to delay their arrival at Sand's country home in Nohant until June. Located 180 miles south of the French capital, Nohant was well suited to Chopin's needs. Sensitive to noise and other distractions, and physically weak, Chopin always found it difficult to write while in Paris, and so the summers he spent at Nohant (1839, 1841-1849) proved to be especially rewarding. Even as his art advanced, the relationship with Sand deteriorated into recriminations and finally separation, first as her passion cooled and then as the result of plots hatched by her two grown children.

Chopin's physical decline, which had begun on Majorca and which had worsened upon his learning of his father's death (May 3, 1844), advanced more precipitously following his estrangement from Sand. On February 16, 1848, he gave his first public concert in ten years; it was also the last one he would ever give in Paris. A second concert had been planned but had to be canceled when revolution broke out in the city's streets. The revolution of 1848 put an end not only to the French monarchy but to Chopin's patronage as well. Out of necessity, he accepted an invitation from Jane

Stirling, a wealthy former pupil, to visit Great Britain. After spending much of the year traveling and performing in London and Scotland, Chopin returned to Paris in late 1848, too weak either to write or to teach. Generously supported by the Stirlings and comforted by his sister, he continued to decline. His death occurred on October 17, 1849, but preparations were so elaborate that the funeral had to be delayed nearly two weeks. Some three thousand mourners were in attendance as the funeral march from his Sonata in B Minor and (at Chopin's own request) Mozart's *Requiem* were played. Chopin was buried in Paris, and his heart was interred in Warsaw.

Summary

For Frédéric Chopin, playing and composing were integrally related. A brilliant if unusual performer, he preferred to be judged chiefly as a composer, and it was to this end that he increasingly devoted himself from the late 1830's onward. Chopin gave no public concerts from 1838 until 1848; in fact, he gave only thirty public performances during his entire career. Yet as Derek Melville has noted, "Curiously enough, the less he played in public, the more legendary he became." Unfortunately, the acclaim he received as early as 1837 as Europe's greatest pianist overshadowed his work as a composer. Even after his death, Chopin's compositions have rarely been given the credit they are due. That he wrote almost exclusively for the piano has been misunderstood as a major limitation, one that has barred him from the ranks of greatness. While his contribution to harmonic development has been acknowledged, critics have tended to slight his overall achievement.

The narrow range of that achievement is not a sign of weakness, however, but of a strength comparable to what his near contemporary, the novelist Jane Austen, managed to achieve on her "inch of ivory." To defend Chopin's breadth is impossible, and to defend his sense of musical structure along conventional lines is fruitless. This is not to say that he was, as often accused, inattentive to form or unable "to develop his materials on a large scale." Chopin's great strength lies not in his adherence to the conventions but in his innovations, including his use of a "departure and return pattern" in many of his works and his experimentation with organic form in a number of his later ones. When he felt the need, he was more than willing to learn and to adopt traditional techniques, such as counterpoint, which he began to study in earnest only in the 1840's. The very real narrowness of range of Chopin's oeuvre needs, therefore, to be reevaluated. As a performer, Chopin was physically too frail to compete with his contemporaries in terms of virtuosity and dramatic effects, and as a result both as performer and as composer he chose, or was perhaps forced, to explore and exploit the subtleties of his playing, his music, and his medium, the piano, in compositions and performances far better suited to the intimacy of the salon than to the impersonal space of the concert hall. Moreover, although he wrote almost exclusively for the piano, he did so with incredible variety: waltzes, nocturnes, preludes, études, scherzos, polonaises, and mazurkas, with the emphasis clearly on the solo piano (139 of his 167 compositions). In his desire to make the piano imitate the human voice, Chopin utterly transformed keyboard music and keyboard technique. One needs to realize that in Chopin's age, the piano was essentially a new instrument. The introduction of leather-bound hammers, for example, made possible the production of much softer tones than in previous times. Although it was John Field and J. N. Hummel who first began to compose music adapted to this new instrument and sound, it was Chopin who came to exploit the piano so masterfully.

Legend often portrays Chopin as at best a melancholy Romantic and at worst a pampered high society narcissist. Fact portrays a quite different figure, fashionable in his dress and fastidious in his conduct, sickly and shy, less proud than committed to his art, and not so much a recluse as an introvert. The facts are perhaps too few to draw as complete a portrait as one might like. For this reason one may turn to the music to distinguish more definitely the character of the man from the qualities of his music: passionate yet introspective; emotional but never sentimental; delicate and refined; expressive yet restrained; as much concerned with perfection as with originality. In many respects, he is the very embodiment of Romanticism, yet he is a strange avatar of the Romantic movement, for his music was clearly influenced by the classical style of Johann Sebastian Bach and Mozart at least as much as it was by the Italian opera of his own age. Chopin's influence on others has, however, been far greater than anyone's on him: on the keyboard music of Liszt, Arnold Schönberg, and others, and on the use of national—especially folk—materials by Antonín Dvořák, Manuel de Falla, Pyotr Ilich Tchaikovsky, and others. Chopin stands as the first and perhaps the most important of the modern composers who have become aware that the breadth, grandeur, and order that were both possible and inevitable in the classical period may no longer be advisable even if they are technically still possible. Narrowness, or specialization, Chopin proved, has its own possibilities and its own frontiers.

Bibliography

Abraham, Gerald. *Chopin's Musical Style*. London and New York: Oxford University Press, 1939. A brief but important study of the "unfolding and maturing of Chopin's musical style," intended chiefly, but by no means exclusively, for performers and students of harmony. Abraham distinguishes three significant periods of development (1822-1831, 1831-1840, and 1841-1849) but fails to discuss the problems of chronology within each period. Nor does he consider the origins of Chopin's style. Nevertheless, long considered the standard work on the subject.

Chopin, Fryderyk. *Chopin's Letters*. Edited by Henryk Opienski. Translated by E. L. Voynich. New York: Knopf, 1931. Although it has been largely superseded by later editions, Opienski's work is noteworthy both for its relative extensiveness (given the time it was published) and for the excellence of Voynich's translations from the original Polish and French. The dating of many items is, however, incorrect.

———. *Selected Correspondence of Fryderyk Chopin*. Edited and translated by Arthur Hedley. London: Heinemann, 1962; New York: McGraw-Hill, 1963. This volume is abridged from Chopin's correspondence, collected and edited by Bronislaw Edward Sydow. Although less exhaustive than Sydow's volume of nearly eight hundred items, Hedley's book does add appreciably to the slimmer Opienski work. Yet Hedley not only omits pieces included in Sydow but also abridges a number of items. Even so, this is an indispensable volume; the eleven-page appendix concerning the history and inauthenticity of the erotic "Chopin-Potocka Letters" is especially interesting.

Hedley, Arthur. *Chopin*. London: Dent, 1947; New York: Pellegrini and Cudahy, 1949. Especially noteworthy because Hedley's *Chopin* does not merely summarize previous scholarship. Recognizing the inadequacy of the standard English-language study, Frederick Niecks' *Fredrick Chopin* (1888), Hedley has examined materials at first hand and many for the first time. He devotes somewhat more than half of his authoritative study to Chopin's biography and the remainder to discussions of Chopin as performer, as teacher, and as composer and of Chopin's works according to type.

Huneker, James. *Chopin: The Man and His Music*. New York: Scribner, 1900; London: Reeves, 1903. Trained as a pianist, Huneker was the foremost American music critic at the time he wrote this study. Enthusiastic and knowledgeable, he devotes the first third of this book to biographical analysis, the import of which is clearly evident in his chapter titles "The Artist" and "Poet and Psychologist." The remaining chapters deal with each of the various kinds of musical compositions Chopin wrote.

Kallberg, Jeffrey. *Chopin at the Boundaries: Sex, History, and Musical Genre*. Cambridge, Mass.: Harvard University Press, 1996. Kalberg examines the complexities of Chopin's life with emphasis on his questionable sexual identity and its intersection with his chosen musical genres.

Melville, Derek. *Chopin*. London: Bingley, and Hamden, Conn.: Linnet, 1977. Part of the Concertgoer's Companion series, Melville's book includes a surprising amount of material in its very few (108) pages. Besides going unnecessarily far in his efforts to undermine the credibility of George Sand's remarks about Chopin, Melville's writing is balanced and especially well informed. His lengthy annotated bibliography of works in English about Chopin and his music (pp. 62-78) is particularly useful.

Rink, John. *Chopin: The Piano Concertos*. Cambridge: Cambridge University Press, 1997. A handbook on Chopin's E minor and F minor piano concertos, including their development, his performance of them, and his use of them as a teaching tool. Also includes analysis of the third concerto, the Allegro de concert.

Robert A. Morace

KATE CHOPIN

Born: February 8, 1851; St. Louis, Missouri
Died: August 22, 1904; St. Louis, Missouri
Area of Achievement: Literature
Contribution: Author of the early feminist novel *The Awakening*, Kate Chopin created works that showcased the Louisiana bayou country and often featured women struggling against society's restrictions.

Early Life

Katherine O'Flaherty was born February 8, 1851, in St. Louis. Her father was an Irish merchant and her mother was the daughter of an old French family. Chopin's early fluency with French and English, and her roots in two different cultures, were important throughout her life.

Kate's father, Thomas O'Flaherty, was killed in a train accident in 1855 (the imagined effect on her mother was later depicted in "The Story of an Hour"). Kate lived her preteen years in a female-centered household. Her sophisticated grandmother had a great impact on Kate, encouraging her to reject hypocrisy, to love music and storytelling, and to indulge in unconventional behavior. Kate's formal education began at Sacred Heart Academy, a Catholic school devoted to creating good wives and mothers, while also teaching independent thinking. Kate's readings included fairy tales, *The Pilgrim's Progress*, old-fashioned romances, and contemporary popular novels by women.

The Civil War meant that Kate spent much time at home; she saw the war's violence at first hand. After Kate returned to the academy, her English teacher encouraged her to write. Kate kept a "commonplace book" from 1867-1870, where she recorded observations on her reading and studies. At the age of eighteen, Kate was known as one of St. Louis' prettiest and most popular belles. Her diary, however, reveals that she was torn between social pressures—to attend dances, flirt, and be agreeable—and her passion for voracious reading of authors such as Victor Hugo, Dante, Molière, Jane Austen, and Henry Wadsworth Longfellow. In an age known for producing restless women, Kate also seemed to want something more.

When she was twenty, Kate married Oscar Chopin, a twenty-six-year-old businessman of cosmopolitan background. In their first ten years of marriage, Kate gave birth to five sons and a daughter. Motherhood's joys and demands, as well as societal restraints on women, are important themes in her fiction. During these years, Kate and the children lived three seasons in New Orleans and spent long summers at the Creole resort Grande Isle.

In 1879, Oscar Chopin's money-lending business was in deep trouble. The family moved to Cloutierville, Louisiana, where Oscar ran a general store. Kate Chopin's sophisticated behavior and dress inspired gossip in the small, closely knit town. Her husband, worn down by financial worries, died in 1882, leaving Kate with debts of some $12,000 and six children to rear alone. She decided to manage Oscar's businesses herself. During this time she was romantically linked with Albert Sampite, a handsome and unhappily married man. In 1884, Kate left Cloutierville and Sampite to return to St. Louis, where she lived with her mother.

Her mother's death the following year left Kate devastated; a physician friend suggested that she write for solace—and for much-needed money. Kate's writings at the time indicate that she sometimes longed for the security of marriage, but also recognized that the deaths of the two people closest to her gave her independence unavailable to other women. She later characterized this period as a time of "growth."

Life's Work

These sudden deaths and her own unconventional ideas demanded that Kate Chopin make her own way. She started her first short story in 1888, and became a published author in 1889 when her poem "If It Might Be" appeared in the journal *America*. Her stories and sketches from this early period show that she questioned traditional romance. "Wiser Than a God" depicts a woman who chooses a career as pianist over marriage. Other stories portray a suffragist and a professional woman who try to determine their own lives. Chopin's friends during this period included "New Women"—single working women, suffragists, and intellectuals—who doubtless influenced her previously private questioning of women's role in society.

At Fault (1890), Chopin's first novel, focuses on a woman who renounces her lover after she learns he is divorced. The conflict between morality and sexual attraction is a major theme, and the novel is ahead of its time in depicting an alcoholic woman, the lover's estranged wife. This novel suggests that environment is a greater influence on behavior than

heredity—an unpopular idea in the 1890's. *At Fault* was praised for its local color and believable characters, but was attacked by literary moralists, who disliked its subject matter and language. Because one publisher had rejected the novel and Chopin was impatient for publication, she paid to have it printed and distributed.

Chopin also wrote children's stories that appeared in national magazines. Her stature as author began to grow. In her adult stories, she persisted in writing about taboo subjects: "Mrs. Mobry's Reason" (1893), repeatedly rejected, concerned venereal disease; "The Coming and Going of Liza Jane" (1892) focuses on a woman who, longing for a more glamorous life, leaves her husband. Chopin's output from this period is oddly split between formula writing of predictable morality tales and stories of individuals' conflicts with society.

Throughout her career, Chopin gained inspiration from her time in Louisiana. Much of her fiction was set there: she valued its dreamy, less structured and more sensual atmosphere. Chopin was pigeonholed as a regional writer, but badly wanted to reach a national audience. She tried

hard to place her collection of Creole stories and finally succeeded. *Bayou Folk* (1894) collected mostly Cane River country stories. Praised for its exotic and bewitching subjects and atmosphere, the collection solidified Chopin's reputation as a local colorist.

The 1890's were a time of achievement for Chopin. *Bayou Folk*'s success led to more short story publications in national magazines and to regional celebrity. "The Story of an Hour" (1894) recounts the ironic reversal in emotion—from grief to joy—of a woman who mistakenly believes she has been widowed. It is one of Chopin's most powerful—and controversial—stories, and it anticipates *The Awakening* in its depiction of a repressive marriage.

In St. Louis, Chopin held salons where the city's cultural elite could play cards, listen to music, and argue about philosophy and literature. Chopin translated contemporary French writer Guy de Maupassant's tales, and was greatly influenced by his writing. Maupassant was thought to be immoral; his satires, like Chopin's mature fiction, focus on betrayal of ideals, questioning of traditional values, sex, and depression.

Through the mid-1890's, Chopin wrote mainstream fiction, but continued to address more daring subjects such as aging, obsessive love, extrasensory perception, and gambling. *A Night in Acadie* (1897), Chopin's second short story collection, focused on the Cane River country she knew so well. Women characters, some repressed and others rebelling, were prominent. This collection was generally well received, though some reviewers disliked its coarseness—a muted charge that would become a roar with the publication of *The Awakening* in 1899.

The Awakening features a strong female protagonist. After twenty-nine years "asleep" to life's possibilities, Edna Pontellier awakens to the need to find her identity. Like her creator, Edna sometimes feels as if she lives a double life: one that conforms and one that questions. Edna's attraction to both sides is illustrated in her friendships with the conventional "mother-woman" Adele Ratignolle and the eccentric pianist Mademoiselle Reisz.

Edna grows up desiring unattainable men. Believing that she is renouncing the world of illusion, she marries a man for whom she has only fondness and no passion, and settles into motherhood. In a series of small incidents at Grand Isle, however, Edna's rebellion against her rigid role is shown:

her unexpected emotional response to Mlle Reisz's concert; her exultation on learning to swim; her desire for Robert Lebrun, a young man with whom she is in sympathy; and her defiance of her husband's wishes.

Edna disproves Victorian ideas about women's moral superiority through her open longing for Robert and her affair with the roguish Alcée Arobin; she moves into her own house and tries to attain fulfillment through painting and an unconventional social life. For a time she behaves solely in accordance with her desires. Eventually Adele summons Edna to her bedside and implores her to think of her children. Edna realizes that she cannot give her children honor and good reputation without sacrificing her independence, her sensuality, and her newfound enjoyment of life. Ironically, freedom means that a "solitary soul" (the novel's original title) will be isolated from society and from sensual experience. Because of her husband's death and her own strength, Chopin was able to escape rigid social convention to an extent. Edna, unable to compromise her desires with her duties, commits suicide.

The Awakening became Chopin's major literary achievement; it was also far in advance of its time. One of the earliest American novels to question marriage as an institution, Edna's discontent and her various attempts to find fulfillment caused a scandal. The novel was attacked as immoral and as unfit for reading. Critics praised the beauty and power of the novel's style and setting, its careful pacing, and its subtly drawn characters, but many questioned Edna's (and Chopin's) morality. Like Norwegian playwright Henrik Ibsen's *A Doll's House*, *The Awakening*'s realistic portrayal of a woman's desire to find her identity outraged many.

Chopin was hurt by the negative reaction to the novel, though she published a tongue-in-cheek "retraction" apologizing for Mrs. Pontellier making such a mess of things and ensuring her own damnation. Chopin's career slowed markedly after 1899. She continued to write poetry and reviews, but published little until her death in 1904. At that time Chopin was eulogized chiefly as a regional writer of note; little was said of *The Awakening* until decades later.

Summary

Kate Chopin's reputation as a writer initially faded soon after her death. After the initial sensation when the novel first appeared in 1899 and in a 1906 reprinting, *The Awakening* was out of print for half a century. By the late 1960's, however, Norwegian writer Per Seyersted rediscovered Chopin and edited *The Complete Works* and a critical biography in 1969. Chopin's reputation blossomed, and her novel is considered a classic, taught in university literature and women's studies courses. Largely through the attention of scholars and critics, Chopin's work has enjoyed a renaissance. Her writing beautifully illustrates a variety of feminist concerns: the clash between individual freedom and social duty; the stifling quality of unequal marriage; the hypocrisy of the sexual double standard; women's desire for creativity and independence. Her characters are utterly believable: complex, thoughtful, and intelligent.

The Awakening is a fine example of the rehabilitation of a "disappeared" writer. Considered out of step with its times, it is a powerfully written novel by a writer whose work had been safely categorized as regional and domestic; these reasons explain its fading from public view. Like several other women's novels enjoying renewed attention as American classics (African American writer Zora Neale Hurston's *Their Eyes Were Watching God* and New Yorker writer Dorothy Parker's cynical comedies, for example), *The Awakening* is being reevaluated by critics and readers. It is a startlingly radical and honest book, which deservedly stands as a classic.

Bibliography

Chopin, Kate. *The Awakening: An Authoritative Text, Contexts, Criticism.* Edited by Margaret Culley. 2d ed. New York: Norton, 1994. The novel's complete text, including helpful explanatory footnotes that help explain its context. Contains excerpts from writers contemporary with Chopin as well as a sampling of reviews from the novel's first publication to its rediscovery in the 1960's.

————. *The Complete Works of Kate Chopin.* Edited by Per Seyersted. Baton Rouge: Louisiana State University Press, 1969. Reprints Chopin's work, including unpublished and uncollected stories, sketches, essays, and poetry. Valuable for the overview these writings give of Chopin's evolution as a writer.

Rankin, Daniel. *Kate Chopin and Her Creole Stories.* Philadelphia: University of Pennsylvania Press, 1932. An early biography that relies on interviews with Chopin's friends and relatives and Chopin's manuscripts and journals. Examines Chopin primarily as writer of unique and rich Creole stories; reprints some stories and sketches.

Seyersted, Per. *Kate Chopin: A Critical Biography.* Baton Rouge: Louisiana State University Press, 1969. A reexamination of Chopin's life and career, using previously unavailable materials. Examines her importance as a writer of realism and her ambitious and assertive life; links Chopin's experience and her work.

Showalter, Elaine. *Sister's Choice: Traditions and Change in American Women's Writing.* Oxford: Clarendon Press, and New York: Oxford University Press, 1991. Showalter discusses the links between and development of women writers and feminist literary theory in the postcolonial period. The author concentrates on three classics, including *The Awakening,* and follows the development of themes in these works.

Simons, Karen. "Kate Chopin on the Nature of Things." *Mississippi Quarterly* 51, no. 2 (Spring 1998). Examines and expands the usual interpretations of Chopin's *The Awakening* beyond the standard references to gender versus self.

Toth, Emily. *Kate Chopin.* New York: Morrow, 1990; London: Century, 1991. A detailed and fascinating critical biography; gives much valuable information on Chopin's childhood and passionate, secretive life. Shows relationships and influences in Chopin's life and effects on her writing. Includes thorough bibliography of Chopin's writings and criticism of her work, a chronology, and exhaustive footnotes.

Wheeler, Otis. "The Five Awakenings of Edna Pontellier." *Southern Review* XI (January 1975): 118-128. Focuses on Edna's rejection of "angel in the house" and "scarlet woman" roles; traces Edna's development through her awakenings about personhood, true love, sex, biology, and despair. A useful psychological study of Chopin's most complex character.

Ziff, Larzer. *The American 1890s: Life and Times of a Lost Generation.* New York: Viking Press, 1966; London: Chatto and Windus, 1967. Examines the decade when Chopin flourished as a writer. Ziff puts in context the two impulses of American society—conformity versus individuality—and criticizes the literature of the decade as overly optimistic and unrealistic.

Michelle L. Jones

HENRI CHRISTOPHE

Born: October 6, 1767; Island of Grenada, British West Indies

Died: October 8, 1820; Sans Souci palace, Haiti

Areas of Achievement: Government and politics

Contribution: Christophe was one of the three great black leaders of the Haitian Revolution. With the removal of Toussaint-Louverture to France and the assassination of Jean-Jacques Dessalines, he was chosen president of the Haitian Republic in 1806.

Early Life

Henri Christophe, who was known as the "Civilizer," was born on the island of Grenada four years after the island was ceded to Britain by France in accord with the Treaty of Paris. For political reasons, Christophe was always imprecise about his family background, but it seems probable that one of his parents was not of pure African descent (his own complexion was not black but a deep red-brown) and that he was born free. Even as a child it is said that he was flinty, argumentative, and unbendable. Before he was ten years old, his father sent him to sea as a cabin boy to the French skipper of a coasting vessel, who in turn found him too much of a handful and sold him to a Saint-Dominican sugar planter named Badêche. He set the small boy to work as a helper in his own kitchen and, after getting reports of his neatness and energy, decided to train him as a cook.

Badêche employed Christophe at the Couronne, a hostelry that he owned, but here again Christophe's initial stay was short. He went off at the age of eleven with a regiment that a French officer raised from mulattos and free blacks to aid the insurgent American colonists. He was slightly wounded at the siege of Savannah and subsequently sailed back to Haiti. Within ten years of his return to the Couronne, he was in effect managing the hotel. For several years, Christophe apparently stayed clear of the violent turmoil that plagued Haiti after 1789. However, in 1794, at the age of 27, he joined Toussaint-Louverture's forces and began his fight for the independence of Haiti as a sergeant.

Life's Work

In 1796, having already ascended to the rank of major, Christophe distinguished himself in a campaign against mulatto commanders and became a colonel. In 1801, when civil war erupted between the mulattos who held the south and the blacks under Toussaint-Louverture, Christophe again distinguished himself and was promoted to brigadier. After Toussaint-Louverture secured absolute domination over the island with the defeat of the Spanish in Santo Domingo, Christophe was given divisional jurisdiction in a system of military administration that divided the island into districts run by senior military personnel.

With a French attempt to restore dominion over Haiti in 1802, Toussaint-Louverture and his generals, Jean-Jacques Dessalines and Henry Christophe (his admiration for everything English prompted him to begin to sign his first name with a *y* rather than the French *i*), were beaten back. After running low on food supplies, Christophe suspended hostilities and was given a command in the French army with 1,500 of his regular troops. The surrender and imprisonment of Toussaint-Louverture followed soon after.

As the French forces became weakened with illness, French commander Charles Leclerc was increasingly forced to depend on the black and the mulatto generals, particularly in the face of a revolt as word spread of impending restoration of slavery. As French atrocities against blacks and mulattos increased, Christophe joined the rebels. With the black and mulatto generals united under Dessalines, the French forces were finally defeated. Under Dessalines, Haiti was declared independent on January 1, 1804. The country was divided into four districts, and Christophe was appointed the general in command of the north. When Dessalines invaded Santo Domingo in 1804, Christophe led the invasion force in the north and quickly overcame French and Spanish troops.

Dessalines was killed in 1806 during an attempt to quell an uprising of generals in the south. Christophe was declared provisional leader, but a constitutional assembly, controlled by mulatto generals, drafted a republican constitution that provided President Christophe with very little power. In response, Christophe led his black forces from the north toward Port-au-Prince, the capital. After some initial success, Christophe was forced to retreat back to the north, where he set up a separate state. The country remained divided for thirteen years, and, in 1811, Christophe declared himself king.

Christophe had many reasons for turning Haiti into a kingdom. Vanity was not the least of them, but neither was it the greatest. A king was still a man of power and splendor, not yet an antique oddity. The title gave him an advantage over Alexandre Pétion—the president in the south—in the eyes of the people of both regions, who had been brought up to honor kings. Christophe also expected his declaration to raise Haiti in the estimation of the white world, were French emperor Napoleon Bonaparte was still setting up kingdoms for his relations. It was a valuable reinforcement of his authority in domestic affairs, now that he was about to turn to his long-contemplated but equally long-delayed reforms at home. As king of the blacks, he would have a greater chance to lead his people to equality with white people.

Since Christophe could neither read nor write more than his signature, he imported English teachers to staff the schools that he opened. His organization of the north rested on a combination of benevolent qualities (with certain military despotism) and a nobility that he created and cultivated. Under this system, estates, now in government hands, were given to loyal supporters and the wealthy on five-year leases. Labor was organized along militaristic lines with a heavy emphasis on hard work and discipline. The workers got one-quarter of the income of the plantations and were also given small plots of land to provide for their personal needs. The system was economically successful, allowing Christophe to raise revenue equaling that of the immediate pre-revolutionary period during which Saint Domingue was France's richest colony. However, the system was rooted—like all monarchies—in firm class divisions and rested on a labor force with few civil and political rights.

The laissez-faire system of the south under Pétion enticed many from the north. Hostilities with the south intensified Christophe's dislike and distrust of the mulatto population. He began to persecute them. His own people began to distrust him, and he in turn began to distrust everybody. He ordered the construction of the Citadelle, a fortress conceived in fear and built at an untold cost of toil, tears, and blood. The fortress characterized the tyrant into which Christophe had grown. The end came when Christophe, suffering from a paralytic stroke, was deserted by his army and most of his courtiers. In 1820, he is said to have shot himself at his palace of Sans Souci, after which the queen and one faithful courtier dragged his body up the pre-cipitous trail to the Citadelle. Unable to find tools or sufficient men to dig a grave, they buried his body in a heap of quicklime.

Summary
Under the triumphant republic, Henri Christophe's reputation was denigrated, his name and monuments erased. In 1847, however, he was at last lifted from the bed of lime and given a proper burial in a simple concrete tomb on the Citadelle's Place d'Armes. Even then he was not allowed to rest in peace. While seeking the treasure that legend said Christophe had hidden in the fortress, someone broke into the tomb; finding nothing, the thief took a finger bone as a souvenir. Others followed, until the walls of the Citadelle that had been constructed to protect the king continued to stand guard over nothing at all.

Bibliography
Beard, John R. *The Life of Toussaint L'Overture*. London: Ingram, Cooke, 1853; Westport, Conn.: Negro University Press, 1970. Beard covers the history of the independence movement under Toussaint-Louverture's leadership. Contains a chapter on Christophe.

Cole, Herbert. *Christophe: King of Haiti*. London: Eyre and Spottiswoode, and New York: Viking Press, 1967. Cole's book remains the best biographical scholarship on Christophe. Contains photographs and illustrations of him and his kingdom.

James, C. L. R. *The Black Jacobins*. 2d ed. New York: Vintage, 1963; London: Allison and Busby, 1980. This book provides a very complete biography of Toussaint-Louverture, Dessalines, and Christophe and gives details of their personal relationship and their political agendas. Includes an appendix with a table of events.

Moran, Charles. *Black Triumvirate*. New York: Exposition Press, 1957. This biography of Toussaint-Louverture, Dessalines, and Christophe focuses on the political aspect of their lives and work. Includes photographs, illustrations, and an appendix with a chronology of events.

Syme, Ronald. *Toussaint: The Black Liberator*. New York: Morrow, 1971. Syme's book includes a section on Christophe and an extensive bibliography.

Juana Goergen

CARL VON CLAUSEWITZ

Born: June 1, 1780; Burg, near Magdeburg, Prussia
Died: November 16, 1831; Breslau, Silesia
Areas of Achievement: The military and philosophy
Contribution: Clausewitz played an important role in Prussian military and political history during the Napoleonic Wars. He is best known, however, as the leading philosopher of war. His most famous work, *On War*, has been characterized as "not simply the greatest, but the only great book about war."

Early Life

Carl von Clausewitz was born into a Prussian family that, despite its pretensions to nobility, was in fact of middle-class origins. The elder Clausewitz had obtained a commission in the army of Frederick the Great but was forcibly retired during Frederick's purge of nonnoble officers after the Seven Years' War. Clausewitz seems, however, to have believed in the family's claim to noble status; on the basis of his own achievements, Clausewitz had his claim confirmed by the King of Prussia in 1827.

The ambiguity of Clausewitz's social position may be a key to understanding his life and personality, although it does not appear to have blocked his advancement. He tended, as his correspondence and comments by contemporaries reveal, to feel and to be treated like an outsider. Sensitive, shy, and bookish by nature, he could also be passionate in his politics, his love for his wife, and his longing for military glory. Slim and rather handsome, he frequently displayed coolness and physical courage in battle. His keen analytical intelligence was accompanied by a certain intellectual arrogance. These qualities may account for the fact that, although he rose to high rank in the Prussian service, he served always as a staff officer rather than as a commander.

Clausewitz entered the Prussian army as a cadet at the age of twelve; he first saw combat, against revolutionary France, at thirteen. After 1795, he spent five years in the rather dreary garrison town of Neuruppin. There, he applied himself energetically to his own education, a project in which he was so successful that he was able to gain admission to the new War College in Berlin in 1801. With this appointment, his rise to prominence had begun.

Life's Work

The director of the War College was Gerhard Johann von Scharnhorst, who was to become Clausewitz's mentor and a key figure in the Prussian state during the upheavals of the Napoleonic Wars. Many of Clausewitz's basic historical, political, and military views derived from the influence of Scharnhorst and other Prussian military reformers.

Clausewitz was graduated first in his class in 1803 and was rewarded with the position of military adjutant to the young Prince August. The same year, he met and fell in love with his future wife, the Countess Marie von Brühl. Yet the ambiguity of his social background and his poverty posed problems. Marie's family would resist this poor match for seven years, until Clausewitz's rapid promotion undermined their objections to a marriage.

Prussia had remained at peace with France since 1795 but, alarmed at the devastating French victories over Austria and Russia in 1805, mobilized for war in 1806. Clausewitz and most other Prussian officers anticipated the struggle with confidence, but the timing was poor and the nation was ill-prepared. The Prussian forces were shattered in humiliating defeats at Jena and Auerstedt. Both

Clausewitz and Prince August were captured. The experience was both shocking and enlightening for Clausewitz. When he returned from internment in 1808, he joined Scharnhorst and the other members of the reform movement in helping to restructure both Prussian society and the army, in preparation for what Clausewitz believed to be an inevitable new struggle with the hated French. His enthusiasm was not, however, shared by the king, who was more concerned with maintaining his position in the much-reduced Prussian state. Clausewitz's disillusionment reached a peak when Prussia, allied with France, provided an army corps to Napoleon I to assist in the 1812 invasion of Russia. Along with about thirty other officers, Clausewitz resigned from Prussian service and accepted a commission in the Russian army. He fought at the bloody Battle of Borodino and witnessed the disastrous French retreat from Moscow. He then played a role, the importance of which is disputed, in negotiating the defection of the Prussian corps from the French army.

None of this won for him any affection in the court at Berlin, where he was referred to on at least one occasion as "Louse-witz." The eventual entry of Prussia into the anti-Napoleon coalition nevertheless led, after some delay, to his reinstatement in the Prussian army. Clausewitz participated in many key events of the "War of Liberation," but bad luck and the lingering resentment of the king prevented him from obtaining any significant command.

In 1818, Clausewitz was promoted to general and became administrative head of the War College. This position offered him little scope to test his educational theories or to influence national policy. Perhaps because of the conservative reaction in Prussia after 1819, as a result of which many of the liberal reforms of the war years were weakened or rescinded, Clausewitz spent his abundant leisure time quietly, writing studies of Napoleonic campaigns and preparing the theoretical work that eventually became his magnum opus, *Vom Kriege* (1832-1834; *On War*, 1873).

Clausewitz saw war as essentially a creative activity: Victory goes not to the general who has learned the rules but to the general who makes them. Therefore, military theory must not attempt to prescribe a general's actions but should aim instead at educating his judgment so that, on the battlefield, he will be able to weigh all the factors that apply in his own unique situation. Clausewitz was scornful of military dilettantes such as Adam Hein-

rich Dietrich von Bülow, who tried to reduce the art of war to a mathematical equation. The strategist, like the artist, will make use of science, but the end result in both cases will be something quite different from the predictable, repeatable results of an experiment in physics. This outlook surely stemmed from Clausewitz's own experience of the overthrow of traditional armies by the radically new forces of the French Revolution.

Clausewitz's approach contrasts with that of his initially more influential contemporary, the Swiss theorist Antoine-Henri de Jomini. Where Jomini saw fixed values, Clausewitz looked for variable quantities. Where Jomini worried about physical forces, Clausewitz discussed the effects of morale and psychological factors. Where Jomini prescribed unilateral action, Clausewitz showed that war is the continuous interaction of opposites. Where Jomini sought to achieve certainty on the battlefield, Clausewitz stressed uncertainty, chance, suffering, confusion, exhaustion, and fear, factors that added to what he called the "friction" of war.

The most famous and often-quoted line from *On War*, possibly the only line ever read by most quoters of Clausewitz, is that "War is the continuation of politics by other means." His point was that war is not in any way a sphere separate from politics and that military operations must always serve a rational political end. The crux of the problem is that neither soldiers nor statesmen are infallible, even within their own areas of competence, and Clausewitz's dictum will work only if the generals and the politicians understand one another's limitations.

Clausewitz returned to active field duty in 1830, when revolutions in Paris and Poland seemed to presage a new general European war. Before leaving, he sealed his manuscripts with the warning, "Should the work be interrupted by my death, then what is found can only be called a mass of conceptions not brought into form . . . open to endless misconceptions." Although war was averted, Clausewitz remained in the east, organizing a sanitary cordon to stop the spread of a cholera epidemic from Poland. He returned home to Breslau in 1831, seemingly healthy, but contracted the deadly disease and died the same day. He was fifty-one years old. Despite his note of warning, his fiercely loyal wife continued his work. It was she who edited and published *On War*, the first volumes of which appeared in 1832.

Summary

Although Carl von Clausewitz wrote a considerable amount of history, particularly campaign studies, he is read almost exclusively for the military philosophy contained in *On War*. This book was received with the respect its famous author deserved but remained in obscurity until cited by Helmuth Karl Bernhard von Moltke as the key to his victories over Austria in 1866 and France in 1870-1871. It then became a virtual military cult object. *On War* has gradually assumed a status as the preeminent philosophical examination of war and military theory.

Unfortunately, many later interpreters have twisted Clausewitz's argument—and even altered the text—concerning the relationship of war and political policy, with the intent of winning greater independence for military leaders. Colmar von der Goltz, writing in 1883, reconciled these two seemingly irreconcilable ideas by saying that "war serves the ends of politics best by a complete defeat of the enemy," even though this formulation directly contradicted the lessons of Prussia's greatest military-political successes, that is, the victorious wars against Austria and France.

Although Clausewitz is often supposed to have been the "apostle of total war," in fact, this is merely the unfortunate by-product of his quasi-Hegelian analytical method, which led him to begin with a discussion of war as an "absolute," an ideal. Clausewitz was writing in the years before nuclear weapons, but his abstract discussion of absolute war seems now to be prophetic of today's balance of terror. There is even a group of modern strategic theorists who have been called the "neo-Clausewitzians," including such prominent nuclear strategists as Henry Kissinger and Herman Kahn. Clausewitz, however, recognized that war could be either total or limited and that in reality no war would be a perfect example of either.

That *On War* or its misinterpretation actually led to the debacle of World War I, as some have charged, is dubious. Few generals of this war ever read this notoriously difficult book. Furthermore, as Clausewitz himself recognized, war changes over time; societies fight the wars for which they are physically, socially, and psychologically equipped. The nature of war in any given environment is determined by Clausewitz's trinity of government policy, the capabilities of the army, and the attitudes of the population.

If Clausewitz's work is understood as descriptive in nature, it can be a useful tool for military analysis. If, instead, the reader tries to use it prescriptively, as Clausewitz feared might happen, he will constantly be misled by his own cultural preconceptions and by the tendency to see war in its ideal, absolute form, rather than in the disorderly form in which it actually exists. To see in Clausewitz's rather matter-of-fact description of war as "a continuation of policy" a justification for resorting to arms is to miss the point of his argument; no leader who truly grasps Clausewitz's description of the role of chance in war is likely to take the gamble lightly.

Bibliography

Aron, Raymond. *Clausewitz: Philosopher of War*. Translated by Christine Booker and Norman Stone. London: Routledge, 1983; Englewood Cliffs, N.J.: Prentice-Hall, 1985. Although not a good translation from the French, this book contains a useful biography of Clausewitz, a subtle analysis of his ideas, and an account of the scholarly controversies which they have spawned.

Clausewitz, Carl von. *On War*. Edited and translated by Michael Howard and Peter Paret. Princeton, N.J.: Princeton University Press, 1976; London: David Campbell, 1993. The best of three English translations of Clausewitz's major theoretical work. The volume also contains essays on Clausewitz by each of the editors as well as a guide to reading by Bernard Brodie, a prominent American strategic analyst.

Gallie, W. B. *Philosophers of Peace and War: Kant, Clausewitz, Marx, Engels, and Tolstoy*. Cambridge and New York: Cambridge University Press, 1978. Treats Clausewitz's theories in their philosophical and military contexts.

Gat, Azar. "Clausewitz and the Marxists: Yet Another Look." *Journal of Contemporary History* 27, no. 2 (April 1992). The author argues that Clausewitz did not so much influence Marx and Engels as he was simply a product of a similar environment.

Handel, Michael I., ed. *Clausewitz and Modern Strategy*. London: Frank Cass, 1986. A collection of essays discussing Clausewitz, his theories, and his influence on the military strategies followed by various nations, including Germany, France, and Italy.

Paret, Peter. "Clausewitz." In *Makers of Modern Strategy: From Machiavelli to the Nuclear Age*, edited by Peter Paret and Gordon A. Craig. Princeton, N.J.: Princeton University Press, and Oxford: Clarendon Press, 1986. A short essay on

Clausewitz in an excellent anthology of essays on other strategic thinkers.

———. *Clausewitz and the State: The Man, His Theories, and His Times*. Princeton, N.J.: Princeton University Press, and Oxford: Clarendon Press, 1976. The most sophisticated biography of Clausewitz.

Roxborough, Ian. "Clausewitz and the Sociology of War." *British Journal of Sociology* 45, no. 4 (December 1994). An overview of Clausewitz's assessment of the interface between society and the military with respect to their approaches to the waging of war.

Christopher Bassford

HENRY CLAY

Born: April 12, 1777; Hanover County, Virginia
Died: June 29, 1852; Washington, D.C.
Areas of Achievement: Government and politics
Contribution: Clay was a dominant figure in American politics during the first half of the nineteenth century. His American System and his efforts to bring compromise in the controversy over slavery helped ease the growing tensions within the Union.

Early Life

Henry Clay was born April 12, 1777, on a farm near Richmond. His parents, the Reverend John Clay, a Baptist minister, and Elizabeth Hudson Clay, were of English descent and reasonably prosperous, though certainly not wealthy. His father died when Henry was four, but his mother was remarried within a year to Captain Henry Watkins, who maintained the family's financial status. Henry received a few years of schooling and developed remarkable penmanship, a skill which served him well when his stepfather moved the family in 1792. Only fifteen, Clay stayed in Richmond to work for the Clerk of the High Court of Chancery. In 1793, Clay was hired by the famous lawyer George Wythe as a part-time secretary. Almost seventy, Wythe was a leader of Virginia's bar and had enjoyed a distinguished career as teacher of law and classics. Under Wythe's tutelage, Clay studied the law and, a few years later, left his clerk's position to study under Robert Brooke, former governor and later attorney general of Virginia. In November, 1797, Clay passed his bar examination.

Like other ambitious Virginians, the young attorney moved to Kentucky, where confusion over land claims created a lawyer's paradise. At twenty, Clay was over six feet tall, thin, and walked with a shambling gait. His face, capable of creating considerable impact with a change of expression, was capped by hair so light as to be almost prematurely white. His eyes were small, gray, and piercing, his nose prominent, and from his large mouth issued his most valuable asset: his voice. Coupled with an emotional temperament, this voice, suited for an actor, made him a formidable opponent in frontier courts, where persuasion was frequently more important than legal knowledge.

The stage for Clay's legal theatrics was Lexington, Kentucky, a village on its way to becoming the "Athens of the West." Though appearing in frail health, Clay demonstrated his skill in local debates and was admitted to the Kentucky bar on March 20, 1798. Before a successful legal career made him a local legend, the budding jurist married Lucretia Hart, daughter of the influential merchant Thomas Hart. The marriage not only connected Clay with an important local family but also provided him with a patient, loving wife, who bore him eleven children. By 1800, Henry Clay was a member of Lexington's establishment.

Life's Work

Clay's debut as a radical Jeffersonian came when he spoke for a liberalization of the state's constitution and made speeches attacking the Alien and Sedition acts. He supported Jefferson in 1800 and, in 1803, won election to the Kentucky legislature. There he demonstrated his talent as a parliamentary tactician and also flirted with disaster by becoming counsel for Aaron Burr, who was charged with an alleged conspiracy to invade Mexico. Unaware of the extent of Burr's activities, Clay successfully defended Burr in Kentucky's courts, but later, as the import of Burr's schemes became apparent, Clay repudiated his dangerous client.

While acting as counsel for Burr, Clay was selected to fill an unexpired term in the United States Senate. Apparently no one paid any attention to the fact that he was a few months short of the required age. This brief performance in Washington, D.C., began a lifelong crusade for a national program based on internal improvements at federal expense and a protective tariff. Such measures were joined by an expansionistic, anti-British foreign policy. Clay's jingoism increased when he moved to the House of Representatives and became its Speaker. There, along with other "war hawks," Clay helped push the nation into the War of 1812. When the struggle did not bring victory, Clay found himself a member of the American delegation sent to Ghent, Belgium, to negotiate an end to the war he had helped to create. In spite of the negative reaction of John Quincy Adams, head of the delegation, who objected to Clay's Western habits of drinking, swearing, and gambling, the Kentuckian proved an able diplomat.

In the postwar years, Clay became a chief proponent of American nationalism and envisioned a truly united country tied together by bonds of economic interest as well as a common ideology. The government's role in his American System was to promote harmony through economic development. Key to his system was a new national bank. Suspicious of the first Bank of the United States, Clay had helped to block its recharter in 1811, but financial confusion during the war convinced him that a centralized financial system was imperative. From this time until the end of of his career, Clay's name would be associated with the idea of a national bank.

His legislative success made it seem that Clay's elevation to the White House was only a matter of time. His successful solution to the slavery controversy further encouraged his supporters. In 1819, Missouri applied for admission as a slave state. Hostility on both sides of the question threatened to divide the Union. Though a slave owner himself, Clay had moral reservations about slavery and supported gradual emancipation coupled with colonization. In fact, Clay had been a founder of the American Colonization Society in 1816. In his mind, however, the abolition of slavery was of less importance than the preservation of the Union. In the House, he helped frame the famous Missouri Compromise, which brought in Maine as a free state to balance Missouri and divided the rest of the Louisiana Territory. Though many politicians were involved, the compromise was seen as Clay's handiwork.

Clay's popularity did not immediately convert into political success. Clay was unhappy with the Monroe Administration. The president selected a New Englander, John Quincy Adams, as secretary of state, a post that Clay had expected. Sectional harmony had been purchased at the cost of alienating Kentucky's "Hotspur." Clay frequently criticized the Administration's lack of support for the Latin American revolutions, a stand which made him popular in South America. His persistence was rewarded with Monroe's famous declaration in 1823, but from Clay's perspective it was too little, too late. Most important, however, his quibbling with the Monroe Administration obscured a serious threat to his political future: Jacksonian democracy.

Since 1800, the nation had been dominated by Jefferson's party, but, in 1824, four prominent leaders, Clay, Andrew Jackson, William H. Crawford, and John Quincy Adams, entered the contest for president. Almost everyone underestimated the military hero, Jackson. When the final votes were in, no candidate had a majority, but Jackson won a plurality. Shocked and disappointed, Clay came in fourth and was thus eliminated from consideration

by the House. When Clay announced his support for Adams, which in effect made Adams president, Jackson was furious. Suspicions of underhanded dealing seemed confirmed when Clay was appointed secretary of state. This supposedly "corrupt bargain" provided a rallying cry for Jacksonians in the next election. While there is no evidence of prior arrangement, Jackson's complaint reveals an important difference between him and his rivals. Adams, Crawford, and Clay were all part of the leadership in Washington. Jackson, while a national military hero, had never been part of the Washington establishment. There was simply not enough room at the top, and Jackson became a lightning rod attracting those in politics and society who felt left out. Moreover, Democrats, taking advantage of extended suffrage, directed their appeal toward the common man even though Jackson and his allies were hardly common men.

Clay's new role in foreign affairs turned out be of little political value. The real drama was taking place internally, where followers of Jackson made a wreck of Adams' administration. The president was no match for the new kind of politician. Adams' style of leadership suited an earlier age; politics now stressed personality. Cold, aloof, and even arrogant, the president introduced a program designed to improve his constituents. Jacksonians were content to direct their appeal to the lowest common denominator. In 1828, Jackson's presidential victory changed American politics forever.

With Jackson and his minions ensconced in the White House, the anti-Jacksonian opposition began to fall apart. By mid-1829, however, Clay's Kentucky estate had become the center of another presidential campaign, and, in late 1831, its master once again returned to the Senate and was quickly nominated for president by a national Republican convention. The ensuing struggle revolved around the second Bank of the United States. Motivated by partisan concerns, the bank's supporters pushed for recharter before it was necessary. Clay believed that the effort would place Jackson in an untenable position. He was wrong. Jackson reacted quickly by vetoing the recharter bill and destroying the bank by removing government deposits. Jackson's policies did cause defections among his supporters, but his enemies miscalculated the impact on the electorate. As ignorant of banking practices as their president, voters sympathized with Jackson's struggle, and the result was a smashing defeat of Clay's presidential aspirations.

There was no time for recriminations. As dust from the election settled, a South Carolina convention passed an Ordinance of Nullification against the tariffs of 1828 and 1832. The power to act rested with the president. Supposedly in favor of states' rights and less than enthusiastic about a tariff, Jackson, as usual, surprised everyone. Standing firmly for national supremacy, he asked Congress to pass the so-called Force Bill, granting the executive special authority in the crisis. Congress began to scramble for a compromise that would avert a military confrontation between South Carolina and the federal government. At center stage was Henry Clay. His compromise tariff gave South Carolina an excuse to back down without losing face. Once again, Clay had been instrumental in saving the Union.

In Jackson's second term, a new opposition party was created by a single idea: hatred of Andrew Jackson. It reached into British history for a name signifying resistance to tyranny: Whig. Its program was dominated by Clay's American System coupled with a bias against executive power, but it also adopted attitudes toward political opportunism pioneered by Jacksonians. To Clay's disappointment, the new party was too fragmented to unite around a single candidate in 1836. Hoping to throw the election into the House, the Whigs selected three sectional candidates to face Jackson's successor, Martin Van Buren. The strategy failed; Van Buren won. Whig frustration vanished when, a few months into the new administration, the country was rocked by an economic depression. Clay, secure in the Senate, was in an excellent position for the election of 1840, but his fellow Whigs were unsure. With his legions of enemies, Clay's name could unite Jacksonians as nothing else could. As a result, the party's convention turned away from its real leader and chose William Henry Harrison. Inwardly furious, Clay publicly supported the Harrison ticket.

The Whigs won, at last, by turning the tables on their enemies. Harrison was a military hero, and the campaign which elected him avoided serious political discussion. Still, most Whigs viewed the victory as a chance to reverse the tide in favor of Clay's American System. They soon realized that they were mistaken. Harrison's death a few months after inauguration brought to the White House a man who did not share Whig ideals. John Tyler had been nominated for vice president to ensure the loyalty of Southern Whigs. When Congress passed the Whig legislative agenda, Tyler promptly vetoed the most significant measure, a bill creating a na-

tional bank. The result was chaos. Most of the Cabinet resigned, and Tyler governed without party backing.

Tyler's defection left Clay the unchallenged leader of his party, and the presidency, in 1844, seemed his. Once again, however, fate intervened. Pressure for annexation of Texas had been growing. Clay, like other established leaders, feared Texas would rekindle the slavery controversy. Though generally an expansionist, he came out against annexation, expecting that a similar stand by the likely Democratic nominee, Van Buren, would remove the touchy question. After Clay's nomination, the Democrats repudiated Van Buren and nominated the ardent annexationist James K. Polk of Tennessee. As the campaign progressed, Texas captured the public imagination, and Polk's narrow victory was probably the bitterest defeat of Clay's career.

In such circumstances most men would have welcomed retirement, but Clay's unquenchable love of political combat made it impossible. Moreover, the country needed him. As feared, Texas brought with it the Mexican War and reopened debate over slavery. Clay hoped for the Whig presidential nomination in 1848, but for the last time his party betrayed him. Concerned about his age and poor health, the Whigs nominated another military hero, Zachary Taylor.

Bitter but unbowed, Clay played one last role on the American political stage. Unsophisticated in politics, newly elected President Taylor only exacerbated the conflict over slavery. When California applied for admission as a free state with the Administration's blessing, the country once again faced disunion. As always, the Senator from Kentucky stood in the way of a complete rupture within the Union. In spite of frail health, he framed a series of measures that became the famous Compromise of 1850. Working in the brutally hot Washington, D.C., summer until his health broke, Clay turned over the leadership of the compromisers to a younger colleague, Stephen Douglas of Illinois, and watched from the sidelines as Douglas pushed through the final legislation. This desperate attempt at sectional peace had only a brief life, but Henry Clay did not live to see it collapse. He died in Washington, D.C., the scene of so many of his triumphs, on June 29, 1852, two years before his last compromise unraveled.

Summary

Throughout his long career, Clay's programs and personality were always controversial. To supporters, he was the best that American politics had to offer, and they often regarded him with near adulation. To enemies, he represented America at its worst, and they hated him with unbridled passion. Like most politicians, some of his positions changed with time and circumstance, but one element remained consistent—his vision of national purpose. Clay saw his country as the hope of mankind. He genuinely believed the republican system to be superior and looked forward to its spread. In a sense, his American System was designed to further this aim by making America stronger. The Union could continue to exist, Clay believed, only if the states would work for mutual benefit. The cement which would glue the nation together was a cooperative economic system managed by the common government.

Clay's vision was a short-run failure. During his own time, the American System was submerged under the rising tide of Jacksonian democracy and the new style of politics it spawned. Only eight years after Clay's death the country he loved was embroiled in the civil war that his many compromises had sought to avert. Like so many of his generation, Clay had been unable to face the moral dilemma created by slavery, which could not be compromised away. In the long run, however, Clay's vision was a success. The country that emerged from the Civil War was much closer to Clay's America than to Jackson's.

Bibliography

Eaton, Clement. *Henry Clay and the Art of American Politics*. Boston: Little Brown, and London: Scott Foresman, 1957. A concise biographical treatment in "The Library of American Biography," edited by Oscar Handlin. Concentrating on Clay's political career, it follows the evolution of Clay from an advocate of Western interests to a true nationalist.

Howe, Daniel Walker. *The Political Culture of American Whigs*. Chicago: University of Chicago Press, 1979; London: University of Chicago Press, 1980. A thoughtful analysis of Whig ideology. Clay is a central figure, and the book contains valuable insights into the source of Whiggery.

Jasinski, James. "The Forms and Limits of Prudence in Henry Clay's (1850) Defense of the Compromise Measures." *Quarterly Journal of Speech* 81, no. 4 (November 1995). Jasinski discusses and analyzes Clay's rhetorical performance during the Compromise debate of 1850.

Mayo, Benard. *Henry Clay: Spokesman of the New West*. Boston: Houghton Mifflin, 1937. The classic, scholarly biography of Clay. A colorful, well-written account which deals with Clay's private as well as public life. The treatment of Clay's early life in Kentucky is particularly valuable.

Poage, George Rawlings. *Henry Clay and the Whig Party*. Chapel Hill: University of North Carolina Press, 1936. A biographical treatment which concentrates on Clay's role in the founding and development of the Whig Party. The work is well documented but somewhat dated.

Remini, Robert V. *Henry Clay: Statesman for the Union*. New York and London: Norton, 1991. Remini recreates Clay as he has Andrew Jackson in the past. A passionate biography grounded in excellent sources, the author breathes new life into his subject.

Sargent, Epes. *The Life and Public Services of Henry Clay Down to 1848*. Buffalo, N.Y.: Derby, Orton, and Mulligan, 1853. Completed soon after Clay's death as a memorial to the leader of

American Whiggery. Biased and dated, but still an excellent example of the pro-Clay biographies written during his era.

Van Deusen, Glyndon G. *The Life of Henry Clay.* Boston: Little Brown, 1937. A somewhat critical biography of Clay. Well researched and written, the study provides balance when compared with the usual attitude of Clay's biographers.

David Warren Bowen

GROVER CLEVELAND

Born: March 18, 1837; Caldwell, New Jersey
Died: June 24, 1908; Princeton, New Jersey
Areas of Achievement: Government and politics
Contribution: Cleveland, who was both the twenty-second and the twenty-fourth president of the United States, brought great strength of character and inestimable political courage to the United States during years of political turmoil and economic crisis.

Early Life

Steven Grover Cleveland was the fifth of nine children born to Richard Falley and Ann Neal Cleveland. His father, a graduate of Yale University, was a minister who moved his growing family from Caldwell, New Jersey, to Fayetteville, New York (where Grover spent most of his youth), Clinton, New York, and thence to Holland Patent, New York. The Cleveland family, staunchly middle-class, was influenced by their Puritan heritage, their Presbyterian faith, and their belief in hard work. Young Grover had few intellectual, cultural, or academic interests, preferring instead the outdoor life and fishing. When his father died in 1853, Grover found it necessary to work and help support his family. After teaching for one year as an assistant at the New York Institute for the Blind, he decided that his fortune and future lay to the West.

Cleveland followed the westward path, however, no further than the booming town of Buffalo, New York. There, Cleveland worked for and lived with his uncle, Lewis P. Allen, a wealthy cattle farmer, helping to keep the record books for the farm. After a year, he decided to read law and joined the office of Henry W. Rogers, Dennis Bowen, and Sherman Rogers as a clerk. By 1856, young Cleveland was completely self-supporting. In that year, also, he determined to join the Democratic Party—not a typical choice but one which reflected the party affiliation of the law office in which he worked and his own opinion that the Republican presidential nominee, John C. Frémont, was too radical. Cleveland began to work for the Democratic Party, attending meetings and working in the wards. At the age of twenty-five, he was elected ward supervisor and the same year served a brief appointment as assistant district attorney.

Cleveland's years in Buffalo served as preparation for his meteoric rise to national fame. There he astounded his colleagues with his capacity for long hours, attention to tedious detail, powers of concentration, and phenomenal physical energy. He showed little flair or imagination or awareness of either a cultural world or a world much beyond the boundaries of Buffalo. Cleveland, a bachelor, associated in his spare time with the other young men of the town, hunting, fishing, and enjoying an occasional beer in the local saloons. He was a large, round-faced man, with sandy hair and brilliant blue eyes. His girth led his nieces and nephews to call him "Uncle Jumbo"; his size represented considerable strength, however, rather than excess fat.

Cleveland was a staunch Unionist, a war Democratic, but when the Civil War broke out, he felt no particular inclination to fight. He provided the major support for his mother and two sisters, and, when drafted in 1863, he hired a substitute soldier, as permitted by law. In 1870, Cleveland was elected sheriff of Erie County, a position attractive in part because of the regular income it provided. While sheriff, Cleveland himself pulled the lever to hang two convicts, believing that it was wrong to require of others that which he was not willing to do himself. This incident provided further evidence of the absolute integrity which was an integral part of Cleveland's character. After one term as sheriff, Cleveland resumed his practice of law.

For the next ten years, Cleveland was a diligent and respected member of the bar in the expanding city of Buffalo (its population grew from 42,000 in 1850 to 155,000 in 1880). He was a contented plodder, satisfied with his place in the world and admired for his common sense. With its larger size, however, Buffalo government and politics became more corrupt, and when the Republicans nominated a "ring" candidate for mayor in 1881, the Democrats looked for an honest alternative. Attracted to Cleveland by his integrity (though, as a political novice, he was not the party's first choice), the Democrats persuaded him to run. At the age of forty-four, Cleveland was sworn in as mayor of Buffalo in 1882. His attacks on corruption and his courage in defying political bosses quickly gained for him a statewide reputation.

Life's Work

Luck played a part in Cleveland's career. The New York Democratic Party was badly divided over the power of Tammany Hall. The same moral outrage of the people who had elected Cleveland mayor of

Buffalo made him an attractive candidate for governor of New York. Once again, the Republicans nominated a machine politician and the Democrats looked for a reformer. The big, bluff man from Buffalo caught the party's attention, was nominated, and in 1882 was elected governor of New York. Cleveland's administration was notable for its honesty, openness, strong values, good appointments, and courage in quarreling with John Kelly, the leader of Tammany Hall.

Once again, luck played a role in Cleveland's career, for the national Democratic Party was seeking a reformer, especially after the Republicans nominated James G. Blaine, a politician tainted with corruption since the Ulysses S. Grant Administration, for President of the United States. The opposition of Tammany Hall to Cleveland's nomination merely endeared his candidacy to other Democrats across the country, and in 1884 he received the Democratic nomination for president. As in his races for mayor and for governor, the major issue was corruption, and Cleveland's strength was his unquestioned honesty and integrity.

The campaign of 1884, however, soon collapsed into mudslinging. Blaine was increasingly identified with corruption in government, while the Republicans countercharged that Cleveland had fathered an illegitimate child. In reaction to the rhyme "Ma! Ma! Where's my pa? Gone to the White House, Ha! Ha! Ha!" Cleveland responded only, "Tell the truth." The truth appeared to be that Cleveland had acted honorably in a relationship with Mrs. Maria Halprin, and his courage and honesty once again impressed itself upon his countrymen. Cleveland made only four speeches during the campaign, while Blaine traveled more widely. A turning point came in the closing days of the campaign, when the Reverend Mr. Samuel D. Burchard, who accompanied Blaine, charged that the Democrats were the party of "Rum, Romanism, and Rebellion." This influenced a heavy turnout among the Irish Catholic voters of New York City, and by a narrow margin Cleveland became America's first Democratic president since 1856.

Cleveland was admirably suited to the needs of the United States in 1885. He headed a government which endeavored to correct the abuses of the past and establish honesty and efficiency in the administration of government. Cleveland appointed an excellent cabinet, including the Southern wing of the party once again. The major issues of his first administration were civil service reform, the role of silver currency, and a reduction of the tariff. He successfully expanded the Civil Service Act and moved toward a more professional government bureaucracy. In connection with the many patronage bills which flowed through Congress, Cleveland vetoed more than three hundred measures in his first administration (compared to 132 vetoes by the previous twenty-one presidents). He opposed the free-silver faction in the party, supporting instead a sound money policy based on gold. He was forced to retreat on the tariff issue in the face of Congressional opposition.

His administration was also noteworthy for the passage of the Dawes Act, which encouraged the Americanization of the Indians. Additionally, the Interstate Commerce Act was adopted under and signed by Cleveland. There was a greater awareness of labor unrest as well, provoked by the Haymarket Square Riot in Chicago in 1886, which left several persons dead and reawakened a fear of organized labor. For the public, however, the most memorable part of Cleveland's first administration was his marriage in 1886 to Miss Frances Folsom, the twenty-two-year-old daughter of his former law partner (Cleveland was the first president to be married in a White House ceremony). The public was delighted with the romance, and, indeed, the marriage was a remarkably happy one.

As the election of 1888 approached, the Republicans began to gather funds and support to regain control of the national government. To oppose Cleveland, they nominated Benjamin Harrison, who vigorously campaigned against Cleveland and especially against tariff reform. Cleveland once again won a majority of the popular vote, but this time he narrowly lost the electoral vote to Harrison. Cleveland took his family to New York City, where he resumed the practice of law and where his first child (known to the country as "Baby Ruth") was born.

As discontent with the extravagant policies of Harrison grew, the Democrats turned once again to Cleveland in 1892. Again opposed by the New York Tammany Hall machine, Cleveland nevertheless was nominated on the first ballot. With his usual courage, he endorsed the gold standard in the face of strong party support for free silver. He was reelected president and returned to Washington (where his daughter Esther became the first child born in the White House) on the eve of the great Panic of 1893. Once again, the country needed a man of courage and honesty and was fortunate to

have the leadership of Cleveland—who possessed these qualities in great abundance, along with a certain stubbornness and a lack of vision.

Before attending to the economic problems of the nation, Cleveland had to attend to a problem of his own—a malignant growth was discovered in the roof of his mouth. Fearing that public knowledge of his illness would fuel the panic, Cleveland chose to undergo a secret operation on board a borrowed yacht. The operation was successful, and not for twenty-five years did the full truth of that cruise emerge. Meanwhile, the debate over free silver was spurred on by the economic crisis. Cleveland continued to stand firm for a solid currency. He called a successful special session of Congress to repeal the Sherman Silver Purchase Act, which Cleveland believed contributed to the continuing economic decline. Unable to obtain adequate tariff reform, Cleveland continued nevertheless to protest the high tariff as also contributing to the Panic.

In an effort to avert the constant drain of gold from the United States Treasury, Cleveland agreed to a sale of government bonds handled by J. P. Morgan. Although a financial success, this apparent "sell-out" to the interests of big business hurt Cleveland and his party, already badly divided over the question of free silver. Similarly, his action in sending federal troops to help put down the Pullman workers' strike (1894) and his hostility to the unemployed workers who marched to Washington, D.C., as Coxey's Army, convinced the working-class supporters of the Democratic Party that Cleveland had abandoned them in favor of the rich.

In the area of foreign policy, Cleveland opposed imperialism, refusing to bring the treaty for Hawaiian annexation before the Senate. He maintained strict neutrality in the Cuban revolt, though encouraging Spain to moderate her treatment of the Cuban people. In the border dispute between British Guiana and Venezuela, Cleveland encouraged arbitration. He supported the Monroe Doctrine and appeared ready to risk war with Great Britain if a peaceful settlement was not reached. Once again, Cleveland acted strongly and courageously and won both the respect of and stronger ties with Great Britain as a result.

Silver continued to be the simplistic, single answer for those in and out of the Democratic Party who sought relief from the Panic. As the election of 1896 approached, it was clear that Cleveland had lost much of his party's support. Once again, Cleveland stood with courage for his principles and

against free silver; this time, courage without compromise proved fatal. Although he had no desire for a third term, the Democratic convention repudiated him thoroughly in their platform. With William Jennings Bryan as their candidate and free silver as their issue, the Democrats' repudiation was silently returned by Cleveland, who found his private sympathy with the Republicans in the election. He was satisfied with the election of William McKinley, though it must have hurt to notice that Bryan, in losing, received almost a million votes more than Cleveland had received in his 1892 victory.

After the inauguration of McKinley, Cleveland and his family planned to retire to private life. Because of the children, Cleveland and his wife preferred an area less crowded than New York City and chose to settle in Princeton, New Jersey. There, Cleveland mellowed and enjoyed to the fullest his children and his community. He became deeply involved in the life of Princeton University, where he received an honorary degree and in 1901 was named a trustee. There, the eldest of his five children (his daughter Ruth) died in 1904, leaving a great void in her father's life. There also Cleveland knew, liked, and quarreled with the next Democrat to be elected president, Woodrow Wilson. There, also, Cleveland died, in June, 1908.

Summary

Grover Cleveland was admirably suited to his time. His disciplined life made him more comfortable as a supporter of the status quo than as a reformer, and his courage and conscience made him strong in actions he believed best for the interests of the United States. It was Cleveland's misfortune sometimes to be wrong in his judgment of what was best; the rigid strength of character which held him firm before the winds of pressure from special interests held him equally firm against compromise when it would, perhaps, have been wise. Nevertheless, Cleveland brought conscience, courage, and honesty to the White House at a time when those qualities had often been lacking. He provided an image—backed up by reality—of the integrity and leadership which America needed. He worked long hours, bringing his legal intellect to the consideration of all sides of a problem before making a rational decision about the wisest course to follow. Once that decision was made, he did not depart from it.

Though Cleveland was wildly unpopular in 1896, especially among the Bryan faction of Democrats, it was always his position and never his character which came under attack. In later years, he emerged with much greater popularity, and Americans, Democrats and Republicans alike, honored him for his courage and his honesty. The nation had come to realize the value of his leadership and to believe that the economic stability which had eventually prevailed would not have been possible without his strong opposition to free silver. Cleveland was a good man in an age in which goodness was not often cherished. The verse of James Russell Lowell perhaps best memorializes his contribution to America:

We, who look on with critic eyesExempt from action's crucial test,Human ourselves, at least are wiseIn honoring one who did his best.

Bibliography

Cleveland, Grover. *Letters of Grover Cleveland: 1850-1908*. Edited by Allan Nevins. Boston: Houghton Mifflin, 1933. Useful for insight into Cleveland's mind and the reasons for his decisions. Includes some delightful letters of a more personal nature as well.

———. *Presidential Problems*. New York: Century, 1904. Writings of the president after leaving office. Clear and comprehensive but not particularly insightful, which is generally true of the many books and articles Cleveland wrote in his retirement.

Ford, Henry Jones. *The Cleveland Era: A Chronicle of the New Order in Politics*. New Haven, Conn.: Yale University Press, 1919. One of a series of books on American history. Concise, without much interpretation.

Heinze, Andrew R. "The Morality of Reservation: Western Lands in the Cleveland Period, 1885-1897." Journal of the West 31, no. 3 (July 1992). Focuses on Cleveland's views on land ownership and the period's demand for a Western policy.

Hollingsworth, Joseph Rogers. *The Whirligig of Politics: The Democracy of Cleveland and Bryan*. Chicago: University of Chicago Press, 1963. Excellent coverage of political events from 1892 to 1904. A readable account, especially helpful on the antagonisms within the Democratic Party and the silver issue. Strong analysis of the election of 1896.

Merrill, Horace Samuel. *Bourbon Leader*. Boston: Little Brown, 1957. Excellent analysis, again largely political, of Cleveland and the Democratic Party both nationally and in New York.

Nevins, Allan: *Grover Cleveland: A Study in Courage*. New York: Dodd, Mead, 1932. Indispensable Pulitzer Prize-winning biography. The definitive study of Cleveland and his political career, covering all the details as well as offering a broad analysis of Cleveland's career. Wonderfully readable style.

Taylor, John M. "Grover Cleveland and the Rebel Banners." Civil War Times Illustrated 32, no. 4 (September-October 1993). Examines the controversy created by Cleveland's decision to return Confederate flags to their home states.

Welch, Richard E., Jr. *The Presidencies of Grover Cleveland*. Lawrence: University Press of Kansas, 1988.

Carlanna L. Hendrick

DEWITT CLINTON

Born: March 2, 1769; Little Britain, New York
Died: February 11, 1828; Albany, New York
Areas of Achievement: Government and politics
Contribution: Clinton controlled New York State for his faction of the Republican Party, advocating both social stability and an active role for government. He was an unsuccessful presidential candidate and fought the emerging power of Martin Van Buren. His best-known project is the Erie Canal, concrete and practical, like his approach to politics, and exemplifying a proper resolution of several types of problems in a growing nation.

Early Life

DeWitt Clinton was born in Little Britain, Ulster (later Orange) County, New York colony, on March 2, 1769. His ancestors, Englishmen who were transplanted to Ireland, had immigrated to America in 1729, settling in New York in 1731, where DeWitt's father, James, was born. James, married to Mary DeWitt, of Dutch ancestry, had been a major general in the Revolution; his brigade had received the British colors at Yorktown. DeWitt was educated at the grammar school of the Reverend Mr. John Moffat and then studied for two years at the Kingston Academy, the best in the state. Two years later, in 1786, having emphasized courses in natural philosophy and mathematics, he was graduated from Columbia College at the head of his class. After studying law with Samuel Jones, Jr., he was admitted to the bar in 1790 but did not often practice; his legal training aided him in land transactions and in his growing involvement in politics.

Clinton's uncle, George Clinton, was the first governor of New York and the creator of a powerful political machine; thus, Clinton was accustomed to a political environment. In the *New York Journal* in November, 1787, Clinton published a series of letters from "A Countryman," opposing ratification of the proposed constitution; he attended sessions of the New York ratifying convention at Poughkeepsie and wrote a report from the Anti-Federalist position. He became his uncle's private secretary and shortly thereafter also secretary of the board of regents and of the board of fortification. While early involved in politics, he did not engage in politicking at the lower levels of party workers; this fact may explain his inability to deal with the mechanics and compromises of factional and party maneuvering.

Clinton was an impressive man, six feet tall and often referred to as "Magnus Apollo." His high forehead, large square face and firm features, and dark eyes gave the impression of strength and determination. He married Maria Franklin, daughter of an important Quaker merchant, who brought him four thousand pounds and landed property, on February 13, 1796. They had ten children, of whom four sons and three daughters were still living when Maria Clinton died in 1818. At the time of his marriage, Clinton was not active in politics, as the Republicans had succumbed to the greater political strength of the Hamiltonians (Federalists); Governor George Clinton retired in 1795, and the Federalists elected John Jay to the office. Clinton would undoubtedly have become a scientist of note had not opportunity and environment joined to bring him back into politics. Defeated for the state assembly in 1796, he was elected in 1797, and in 1798 won a four-year term in the state senate.

In 1801, the assembly elected Clinton as one of the four senators who, with the governor, constituted the council of appointment. This body controlled nearly fifteen thousand civil and military appointments and was therefore deeply entwined with the complex politics of both state and nation, still in flux in the early constitutional period, and with a two-party system not yet fully developed. The policy and partisan balances of state and national governments were also still unclear, and the tensions between executives and legislatures stemming from Revolutionary politics were institutionalized in the new constitution and exacerbated when different parties controlled the two branches. With its large number of presidential electors, the state of New York was vital, under the influence of Aaron Burr, in the "Revolution of 1800," which brought the Republicans to national power. State politics, however, were characterized by factions among the Republicans; Burr did not attempt to control the state, and the influential Livingston family, politically neglected by the Federalists, gave its support to the popular Clinton group. Clinton emerged as the state's Republican political leader.

The relative powers of the governor and council had not been completely clarified in the 1777 constitution, and consequently a bitter argument developed, ending in an appointment stalemate. Clinton at this time was young, energetic, and ambitious;

than the older one of personal and local factions within the state alone).

On February 19, 1802, Clinton was appointed to a vacant seat in the United States Senate. During the next two sessions, he opposed a Federalist proposal to seize New Orleans from Spain over the issue of the right of deposit and supported the proposed Twelfth Amendment. The Senate at this time tended to be overshadowed by the House, however, and Clinton's personal and party interests were in New York. Late in 1803, Clinton resigned from the Senate to accept appointment (from Governor George Clinton and the council) as mayor of New York City. This was an important office, and its fifteen-thousand-dollar annual income was also welcome to Clinton, whose finances were frequently in disorder.

Life's Work

For the remainder of his career, Clinton acted in the state, rather than in the national, political arena. From 1803 to 1815 (except for 1807-1808 and 1810-1811), he was mayor of New York. At the beginning of his political career, in the assembly, he had been concerned with sanitation laws, debt reform, abolition, and the encouragement of steam navigation and agriculture. As mayor, he organized the Public School Society and aided the New York Orphan Asylum and the New York Hospital. In 1806, he supported the removal of political disabilities from Roman Catholics. As required of a mayor, he attended fires, helped to calm mobs, and inspected markets and docks. With a $100,000 defense appropriation, he supervised construction of fortifications on Governor's Island and elsewhere in the city. He took a firm stand against British impressment and blockade attempts off New York City. He supported a plan for city development and presided in the mayor's court. During his tenure as mayor, he served also as state senator (1806-1811) and lieutenant governor (1811-1813).

Dominating New York politics, Clinton assured the nomination of Morgan Lewis as governor in 1804. Thereafter, the Burr wing lost power in the party and Clinton broke with the Livingstonians, succeeding in having his choice, Daniel D. Tompkins, elected governor. Although basically a Republican, Clinton not only often attracted the support of Federalists but also was frequently in opposition to the Virginia Dynasty and to New York's Tammany Society. The Tammany "Martling-Men" or "Bucktails" viewed him as a politi-

his integrity and self-confidence and his ability to attract political loyalty were major advantages, balancing his ineffectiveness in handling people and in developing compromises. He was not a political theorist, always preferring the concrete and the practical, but his ideas were clear concerning the proper approach of the victorious Republicans to the offices of government. Opposing the Federalists' exclusion of Republicans from office, Clinton maintained that Republicans must be appointed in order that appointive positions might correspond to the verdict of the elections. To accomplish this, it was necessary to remove Federalists from most if not all major offices and from a sufficient number of minor ones to equalize the parties. As a dominant council member, Clinton took the lead in removing most of the governor's power over appointments and in implementing the appointment of Republicans. Rather than being the origin of the "spoils system," as many historians have suggested, this policy was simply more active in accommodating the appointive positions rather closely to the elective ones under the new political conditions of a developing national two-party system (rather cal heretic and a cunning dealer in political offices and influence.

Federalist leaders in 1812 strongly favored Clinton as a presidential candidate, and the New York Republican legislature nominated him; his position on the War of 1812 was, however, equivocal. Had he received Pennsylvania's twenty-five electoral votes, Clinton, rather than James Madison, would have been president. (Soon afterward, on December 22, 1812, Clinton's father died.) Following his defeat, Clinton turned his energies to the development of "Clintonianism," a political position rather than a party, opposed to party labels and organization, seeking a wide base of support in the state. Clintonian Republicans saw an intellectual and benevolent elite, opposing "Jacobinical" chance, factions, and mobs, urban vice, and crime; yet they considered governmental power as derived from the people as a whole and to be used to meet their needs. An urban politician, hoping to make New York a cultural center to rival Boston and Philadelphia, Clinton was sufficiently Jeffersonian to develop a strong rural bias in his programs; the canal project was designed to stimulate both commercial prosperity and a westward movement, thereby reducing poverty and violence and averting the development of an urban proletariat and demagoguery. Clinton was ambivalent about both urban centers and government itself; appealing to both Federalists and Republicans, operating outside the increasingly delimited national party boundaries, Clinton emphasized the work of private societies to accomplish the necessary expansion of knowledge and the provision of facilities for "the people" in general.

Clinton's involvement in voluntary societies was by no means merely a personal and private activity but was closely associated with his political life. He belonged to several dozen societies, was active in most, and held offices in many. He was a member of several agricultural societies, the New York Bible Society, the American Bible Society, foreign and domestic scientific societies (natural history, geology, biology), the American Antiquarian Society, the Western Museum Society, the American Academy of Arts and Sciences, the American Philosophical Society, the New York Military Society, the New York Historical Society, and the Education Society of the Presbyterian Church. He was a prominent Mason; in 1814, he was cofounder and president of the Literary and Philosophical Society, presenting a book-length paper on American natural history; in 1816, he was able to get one large

building to gather all the cultural societies in New York under one roof. His defeat in 1812 reduced his political power; he lost renomination for lieutenant governor and in 1815 lost the mayoralty as well. Yet he was rebuilding his support: His brother-in-law, Ambrose Spencer, was influential in President James Monroe's administration, he continued to attract Federalist as well as Republican voters, and the canal project was very popular.

As early as 1810, Clinton had been one of the commissioners planning a state canal between the Hudson River and the Great Lakes. The War of 1812 delayed the project, but by 1816 Clinton was actively promoting it; he was on the commission responsible for planning the canals between the Hudson, Lake Erie, and Lake Champlain. When Governor Tompkins resigned in 1817 to become vice president, Clinton was nominated (by a state convention including both Federalists and Republicans) and won by a landslide over Tammany's Peter B. Porter. Thereafter, however, President Monroe directed the majority of the federal patronage in New York not to the Clintonians but to their minority opposition, Martin Van Buren's Tammany Bucktail faction. Monroe's encouragement of intraparty strife was intended to avert a successful bid by Clinton in the 1820 presidential election; Monroe also believed that Clinton's associates in Congress were intensifying the Missouri crisis in order to reorganize national parties along sectional lines, a development which he considered a threat to the nation. Although Clinton won the gubernatorial election in 1820, the New York Republican Party schism was permanent: The Bucktails controlled the legislature and therefore the state patronage as well (through the council of appointment). At this point, Clinton attacked Monroe for having interfered in the state election process, a states' rights stand which could evoke support from both parties. In order to affect the 1821 state constitutional convention, Clinton had to prove his charges, which he did by submitting bulky documents, in a green cover, to the assembly. His "Green Bag Message" set off a debate over the permissible extent of political activity on the part of federal officials.

The Administration's hostility having prevented him from consolidating his political position, Clinton decided not to seek a third gubernatorial term in 1822. Van Buren was therefore able to develop his control and establish the "Albany Regency," which controlled New York State politics for a long time thereafter. (Tammany Hall was to benefit also from the flood of Irish voters resulting from the constitutional amendment Clinton had supported, eliminating the property requirement for voting.) The regency's removal of Clinton from the canal commission in 1824 provoked a reaction which helped the "People's" party elect him governor in November of that year. It was therefore as the state's executive that he participated in the 1825 celebrations opening both the Erie and Champlain canals.

Clinton declined the post of minister to England offered to him by President John Quincy Adams. In 1827, an Ohio convention nominated him as a presidential candidate, but he would have had little chance: He had a states' rights stand, there was a strong Anti-Masonic movement, and the issues of patronage and party organization continued to alienate support from the Clintonian group. On February 11, 1828, Clinton died suddenly. He was survived by his second wife, Catharine Jones, daughter of a New York physician, whom he had married on May 8, 1819; the New York legislature voted to appropriate ten thousand dollars for his minor children, as Clinton had left debts. His chief association in the public mind was with one of his most cherished projects, the great Erie Canal.

Summary

DeWitt Clinton, at the outset of his political career, was associated with the great national political figures of the time, the young postrevolutionary leaders who were to dominate national politics until the Civil War. He was always to be involved in the complex and bitter partisanship of the early nineteenth century, pitting state, sectional, and national interests against one another, swirling in a confusion of intrastate and intraparty factions. In contrast to his political contemporaries such as James Monroe, John C. Calhoun, John Quincy Adams, Henry Clay, Martin Van Buren, and Andrew Jackson, Clinton's primary political service was to be in his state rather than at the national level. Yet as a dominant politician in New York State, Clinton was necessarily a factor in national politics, and he shared the presidential aspirations of his colleagues: The electoral votes of only one state kept him from the presidency in 1812, and he remained a real political threat to the Virginia Dynasty.

As a politician, Clinton was a figure of ambiguities and contradictions. His preferences and policies placed him from time to time in all the varying political denominations; an elitist with a power base in one state only, he could never have developed a party organization around his own national leadership. He was never able in the mechanics of politics, and his personality, reserved and cold, did not attract supporters. Despite these shortcomings, he was usually admired and respected for his governmental abilities and positive programs. He supported states' rights yet viewed government as the necessary agency for developing programs to ensure general prosperity, balance and order in society, economic expansion and opportunities. His version of an earlier "country ideology" led him to numerous local agricultural societies, to the Society for the Promotion of Agriculture, Arts, and Manufactures, and to the canal project. At the same time, he was concerned with urban problems, advocating, for example, the inexpensive Lancasterian educational system and supporting the establishment of Emma Willard's academy at Troy; from 1805 until his death, he was president of the New York Free School Society. His concept of the role of government frequently gained for him Federalist support, yet he had begun in politics as a Republican. Conflicts with the Virginia Dynasty and Tammany Hall meant that he could never control the Democratic Republican Party, despite his support of Jackson, yet to play a prominent part among the National Republicans, he would have had to cooperate with John Quincy Adams, whom he disliked. A patrician elite providing leadership for the independent yeomanry was an idea belonging more to the eighteenth century than to the nineteenth, but Clinton was somewhat ahead of his time in his concept of government as a meliorative agency in society.

Closely connected to Clinton's emphasis on learned and benevolent societies was his own work in the sciences. In the undifferentiated field of early nineteenth century science, professionals and amateurs studied and worked over a wide range. Contemporaries (including the eminent scientists David Hosack, Samuel Latham Mitchill, and Constantine S. Rafinesque) considered Clinton a great naturalist, and he was responsible for the discovery of a type of American indigenous wheat and of the archaeological remains of prehistoric Indian tribes in New York. No theorist, he nevertheless agreed with the intellectual radicals of the day in accepting the concept of biological extinction as opposed to the consensus view of a static "chain of being." He played a major role as a patron and promoter of science, primarily through the voluntary societies and whatever governmental aid he could provide, as in the establishment of the New York Institution for the Promotion of the Arts and Sciences.

Not a Renaissance man, not a scientific theorist, not the founder of a new political alliance, long a state governor but never president, Clinton enjoyed a fruitful career of public service. Less of a national figure in historical perspective than his fellow senators were to be, he has been less well-known than they, to later times. The Erie Canal, one of his favorite projects, has enjoyed greater publicity than the man who helped to develop it in the context of wide programs for public improvement. Although Clinton may have taken a narrower view of public policies than his contemporaries, he nevertheless worked to acquire political support for his programs from a wide range of intrastate interests and areas, a political condition which, if operating at the national level, might have helped avert the increasing political polarization obvious even before the Missouri crisis. Although he died at a relatively young age, he had probably already accomplished nearly all that would have been possible for him in the social and political conditions of his time.

Bibliography

Bobbé, Dorothie De Bear. *De Witt Clinton.* New York: Minton, Balch, 1933. Written in the early 1930's, this is the only full-length biography since James Renwick's in the early 1840's. A rather uncritical admiration.

Cornog, Evan. "American Antiquity." *American Scholar* 67, no. 4 (Autumn 1998). Focuses on Clinton's contributions to the American cultural heritage, including his views on American versus European intellectual life.

Fish, Carl Russell. *The Civil Service and the Patronage.* Cambridge, Mass.: Harvard University Press, 1904; London: Oxford University Press, 1910. A general history of the subject. A clear and concise summary, with references to Clinton.

Hanyan, Craig R. "De Witt Clinton and Partisanship: The Development of Clintonianism from 1811 to 1820." *New-York Historical Society Quarterly* 56, no. 2 (1972): 108-131. Clear analysis of the political developments and programs, and intraparty factionalism in the state. Based chiefly on primary sources.

Harris, Jonathan. "De Witt Clinton as Naturalist." *New-York Historical Society Quarterly* 56, no. 4 (1972): 264-284. Examines Clinton as a scientist and concludes that his contributions were more as a promoter of science. Includes 1825 portrait of Clinton by George Catlin.

Hopkins, Vivian C. "The Empire State—DeWitt Clinton's Laboratory." *New-York Historical Society Quarterly* 59, no. 1 (1975): 6-44. Has higher opinion of Clinton as a scientist than in the Harris article.

McBain, Howard Lee. *De Witt Clinton and the Origin of the Spoils System in New York.* New York: Columbia University Press, 1907. Volume 28, number 1 in "Studies in History, Economics and Public Law," edited by the faculty of political science at Columbia University. This book is based largely on previously unused primary documents. Insightful study of developing party politics in the early national period and Clinton's role.

Nadler, Solomon. "The Green Bag: James Monroe and the Fall of DeWitt Clinton." *New York Historical Society Quarterly* 59, no. 3 (1975): 202-255. Good examination of national and state politics and issues of the 1810's and 1820's and Clinton's position.

Marsha Kass Marks

WILLIAM COBBETT

Born: March 9, 1763; Farnham, Surrey, England
Died: June 18, 1835; Normandy Farm, near Guildford, Surrey, England
Areas of Achievement: Journalism and politics
Contribution: Cobbett, "the Poor Man's Friend," was the leading radical journalist of his day and was among the more prolific writers in English history. For thirty-three years (1802-1835), *The Political Register* led the popular attack on privilege and corruption in English government.

Early Life

William Cobbett was born on March 9, 1763, into the "Old England" of the picture books. His father, George Cobbett, was a farmer and publican in the quiet Surrey village of Farnham, forty miles southwest of London. His mother figures little in Cobbett's fragmentary memoirs. Apart from his father's tutelage, Cobbett had no formal education. His childhood was given completely to traditional rural pursuits: riding, hunting, visiting fairs, or working in the fields, gathering in crops that in his later recollection were always rich and bountiful. Over the whole scene of his remembered youth there hangs a golden glow that determined the peculiarly retrospective nature of his radicalism. Whatever else he became, Cobbett was first to last a farmer. To preserve the rural virtues in the new industrial age was his sustaining political purpose.

Yet for all his love of it, the English countryside could not long contain Cobbett. At age fourteen, he went on a whim to London, where he happened on a copy of Jonathan Swift's *A Tale of a Tub* (1704). Swift produced in him "a sort of birth of the intellect." He learned from *A Tale of a Tub* the power of prose satire and political common sense. After a few more restless years on the farm, Cobbett returned to London as a legal clerk in Gray's Inn. He "sighed for a sight of the world," however, and in 1784 enlisted in the army. His public career began five years later, when, upon return from his posting in Nova Scotia, he published his first pamphlet, *The Soldier's Friend* (1792), exposing the corruption of the officer class and expressing the grievances of the common infantryman.

After his marriage to Ann Reid in 1792 and a brief sojourn in revolutionary France, Cobbett went to America. From his father, he had "imbibed principles of republicanism" and was thus "ambitious to become a citizen of a free state." Yet the United States brought out the English patriot in Cobbett. In a series of polemical pamphlets, he denounced Jeffersonian Democrats (he was only slightly more approving of the Anglophilic Federalists), French revolutionaries, Thomas Paine ("mad Tom"), Jean-Jacques Rousseau, and anyone else who indulged "this eternal cant about *virtue* and *liberty*." Cobbett spent eight years in the United States, first in Wilmington, then in New York, teaching English, becoming a self-taught authority on English grammar, and acquiring a reputation on both sides of the Atlantic as a determined defender of the English government. Indeed, upon his return to London in 1800, Cobbett was offered control of one of the two government newspapers, but he declined it, preferring, he said, to remain independent. On January 16, 1802, he brought out the first issue of *The Political Register*, destined to make him, as Hazlitt later remarked, "a fourth estate in the politics of the country."

Life's Work

Initially in *The Political Register*, Cobbett simply carried on his patriotic diatribe against democratic reformers at home and abroad. With a subscription list headed by the Prince of Wales, he published in twelve volumes his American writings, dedicating the lot to the founder of a "Loyal Association against Republicans and Levellers." Slowly, however, he began to realize that the England he defended was not the England he had long imagined, was not the England of his idyllic youth. Living in London, he became aware of the extent of corruption in high places, of the essential injustice of England's system of taxation, of the whole body of pensioners and placemen that lived, so it soon seemed to him, at the crippling expense of the honest provincial laborer. In 1803, Cobbett reread Paine, whose diagnosis of the English financial system he now found astute. When nothing came of his several proposals for fiscal and military reform, when in fact he found himself under the suspicious scrutiny of the very Tory government he had so long professed to support, Cobbett committed himself to the necessity of parliamentary reform. He undertook to publish verbatim transcripts of parliamentary debates (since 1812 known as *Hansards Parliamentary Debates*) in order to strengthen the principle of public accountability. He wrote a popular *Parliamentary History of England* (1804-1812), in which he traced the decline of democratic institutions since 1066. By 1806, this erstwhile anti-Jacobin had embraced the French and American revolutions and was intervening in constituency by-elections on behalf of "we, the people."

Physically, Cobbett was well suited to the life of public agitation that he now undertook. At six feet, one inch, he dwarfed most of his contemporaries. His voice was strong and deliberate, his countenance hale and portly. In dress, complexion, and manner, he was the perfect representation of what he always wished to be—an English gentleman farmer. He was supremely confident, even in the face of repeated disappointment, of his own ability to alter the course of his nation's history. Indeed, he was justified in his belief: By 1818, circulation of *The Political Register* had risen to more than fifty thousand copies a week. Avoiding theoretical abstraction, relying instead on perfected rhythms of everyday English and the powerfully distilled prejudices of ordinary people, Cobbett achieved a unique relationship with his readers.

He became the voice of his own audience and thus represented a potentially explosive force in domestic politics.

Cobbett's first run-in with the government came in 1810, when he was convicted of sedition for having satirically exposed the practice of military flogging. For the next two years, he edited *The Political Register* from a comfortable cell in Newgate Prison, where he also wrote his well-known monetarist treatise, *Paper Against Gold* (1815); he was not alone in finding the innovation of paper currency responsible for much of England's economic distress. Upon his release in 1812, Cobbett affirmed his radicalism by repudiating the war against France, which had been fought, he now thought, in the interests not of the people but of autocracy and corruption. At the same time, he began to interest himself in the plight of industrial workers. He blamed the cotton masters—seigneurs of the twist, he called them—for the social crises attendant upon industrialization, and he recommended working-class enfranchisement as the only remedy for the recent outbreak of industrial violence: the Luddite Riots. Indeed, in spite of all of his agrarian predilections, in the years after the war Cobbett became the leading public spokesman for the rights of industrial labor. He advocated controlled agitation rather than sporadic violence, but the authorities could not appreciate the distinction. When in 1817 the government suspended habeas corpus as part of its ongoing suppression of popular discontent, Cobbett fled to the United States. There, he lost much of his direct influence over political events in England. He returned in 1819, having written three more books and bringing with him the now sanctified bones of Thomas Paine, to find a radical movement that had gone on without him and did not seem to need him. He regained prominence in 1820 as a champion of Queen Caroline, whose husband, the degenerate George IV, was attempting to renounce her. He stood twice unsuccessfully for Parliament, first at Coventry and then at Preston, and wrote a series of highly personal radical advice books: *The Farmer's Friend* (1822), *The Poor Man's Friend* (1826), *Advice to Young Men* (1829). In all these, and in the pages of *The Political Register* (which he had continued to produce even from the United States), Cobbett propounded upon his now familiar themes: agricultural distress, industrial exploitation, governmental corruption, and aristocratic profligacy. In 1830, in the midst of the rural "Swing Riots," he was again tried for sedition, but this time he acquitted himself to the government's grave discomfiture. After the reform of Parliament in 1832, he was finally returned, at age sixty-nine, for the industrial borough of Oldham. He spent three years in the Commons championing the cause of factory reform and resisting the introduction of the infamous Poor Law Amendment Act of 1834. He died on June 18, 1835, at home on his farm near Guildford.

Summary

Much has been made of William Cobbett's "conversion" from Toryism to radicalism. Indeed, historians frequently resort to the awkward formula "Tory Radical" to describe the oddly nostalgic progressivism that Cobbett represented. Yet if one thinks of him essentially as a populist, the conversion looms less large and the emotive consistency of his politics begins to emerge. In his youth, Cobbett defended an England of self-subsisting yeoman farmers that in fact existed only in his imagination. Once aware of that, he turned not so much radical as angry, in a desperate effort to restore what he perceived as lost democratic liberties. His enemies were the oligarchs, plutocrats, speculators, and sinecurists whose privileged grasp was strangling the decent, hardworking men and women of England. He was no political theorist, no Socialist, no revolutionary. He was simply a journalist, inspired to political activism by a populist faith in the rightness of common people.

Politically, his influence passed quickly. Industrialization proceeded apace in England, independent farming went into precipitous decline, and universal manhood suffrage was, at his death, still the better part of a century away. Yet Cobbett's style lingered. Simplicity, truthfulness, and directness in writing was the creed he passed on to well-known masters of the political essay such as George Orwell. *Rural Rides* (1830), Cobbett's volume of ruminations on the state of the English countryside, and country, in the 1820's, is an acknowledged, though neglected, classic of English prose. Through *The Political Register*, Cobbett established the tradition in England of independent journalism. As an editorial critic of established elites, he has never been matched.

Bibliography

Chesterton, G. K. *William Cobbett*. London: Hodder and Stoughton, and New York: Dodd, Mead, 1926. More revealing of Chesterton perhaps than Cobbett, but a pungent and brilliantly written testament to Cobbett's hold over the English political imagination in the early twentieth century.

Cobbett, William. *The Opinions of William Cobbett*. Edited by G. D. H. Cole and Margaret Cole. London: Cobbett, 1944. A useful and representative sample of Cobbett's writing, all of which, but for *Rural Rides, Cottage Economy* (1822), *The English Gardener* (1828), and *Advice to Young Men*, is out of print.

Cole, G. D. H. *The Life of William Cobbett*. London: Collins, 1924; Westport, Conn.: Greenwood Press, 1971. The once-definitive biography by a figure significant to British labor history in his own right. Still invaluable for a sense of what Cobbett meant to English Socialists a century after his death.

Green, Daniel. *Great Cobbett: The Noblest Agitator*. London: Hodder and Staughton, 1983; New York: Oxford University Press, 1985. A highly approving biography by a latter-day Cobbettite. Concentrates deliberately, and, again, approvingly, on Cobbett's "Tory" phase, but prefers to stress the "populist" theme.

Nattrass, Leonora. *William Cobbett: The Politics of Style*. New York and Cambridge: Cambridge University Press, 1995. A study of William Cobbett as a literary stylist who appeared to be a sympathetic reformer but who elicited radical public reactions.

Sambrook, James. *William Cobbett*. London and Boston: Routledge, 1973. Written for the publishers' Authors Guides series; combines an alternative critical reading of Cobbett with rare literary appreciation.

Spater, George. *William Cobbett: The Poor Man's Friend*. 2 vols. Cambridge and New York: Cambridge University Press, 1982. The most recent definitive biography of Cobbett. Great detail and able handling.

Spence, Peter. *The Birth of Romantic Radicalism: War, Popular Politics, and English Radical Reformism, 1800-1815*. Aldershot, Hampshire: Scolar Press, and Brookfield, Vt.: Ashgate, 1996. Spence takes a comprehensive look at Romanticism, its development and failings with emphasis on the interface between politics, public opinion, internal reform, and international issues.

Thompson, E. P. *The Making of the English Working Class*. London: Gollancz, and New York: Vintage, 1963. Only passingly about Cobbett, Thompson's work offers a broad sense of the popular movement in which he was involved. Contains an invaluable discussion of Cobbett's relationship to the emergent working-class consciousness in England.

Williams, Raymond. *Cobbett*. Oxford and New York: Oxford University Press, 1983. A brief but dense volume in the Oxford Past Masters series by a highly learned literary and cultural critic. Passes quickly over Cobbett's life to a deft discussion of themes and issues.

Stewart A. Weaver

RICHARD COBDEN

Born: June 3, 1804; Heyshott, Sussex, England
Died: April 2, 1865; London, England
Areas of Achievement: Politics and trade policy
Contribution: Cobden was the undoubted champion of free trade in Victorian Britain and a well-known figure in the Manchester school of economic thought. With the Anti-Corn Law League, Cobden led the fight for repeal of the corn and provision laws in 1846. He negotiated the Cobden-Chevalier Treaty with France in 1860.

Early Life

Richard Cobden was born in the tiny hamlet of Heyshott, near Midhurst in western Sussex, on June 3, 1804. He was the fourth of eleven children of William Cobden and his wife, née Millicent Amber. Cobden's father was descended from a long line of Sussex yeoman farmers, but he was forced to sell his land in the agricultural crisis at the conclusion of the Napoleonic Wars. This experience was undoubtedly traumatic for the young Richard Cobden, for he was unable to speak about it as an adult. Relatives took charge of the Cobden children, and Millicent Cobden's brother-in-law, a London merchant, sent the ten-year-old boy to an appallingly harsh school in Yorkshire which he was forced to endure for five years. In 1819, young Cobden became a clerk in his uncle's warehouse. He had an abiding desire to understand the affairs of the world and hoped that by self-education he could improve his situation. To the dismay of his guardians he taught himself French and devoted his spare time to "book learning."

The youthful Cobden was quite a romantic figure in appearance. His alert face was clean-shaven and dominated by his dark hair and eyes; it revealed the sincerity and curiosity which were the hallmarks of his character. Cobden was imbued with what he himself characterized as a "Bonapartian" feeling that any obstacle could be overcome if confronted with sufficient energy. His confidence was considerable. Contemporaries found Cobden to be intelligent, engaging, and above all practical. He showed interest in theoretical principles, such as the phrenological conceptions of George Combe or the political economy of Adam Smith, but his practical sense grounded him in the actualities of the present. Cobden preferred to deal with specific issues rather than with abstractions; perhaps that is why he was a superb organizer.

Beginning in 1825, Cobden worked as a commercial traveler for his uncle, taking orders on his route for muslins and calicoes and collecting accounts. He learned the workings of the calico trade, and with two friends Cobden determined to set up his own business in 1828. The three raised one thousand pounds, most of it borrowed, and made arrangements with a Manchester calico printer, Fort Brothers and Company, for selling goods on commission. By 1831, the partners were successful enough to lease their own factory at Sabden and expand their trade. Within a year, Cobden was a wealthy man and took up residence in Manchester, where he was soon a prominent citizen and active in the borough incorporation movement.

Financially secure for the moment, Cobden traveled extensively. He went to France and Switzerland. He visited the United States in 1835 and on a lengthy Mediterranean tour visited Greece, Egypt, and Turkey the following year. His visit to Germany in 1838 convinced him of the potential political and economic value of the recently organized customs union of German states, the Zollverein.

Life's Work

Travel played a considerable role in shaping Cobden's views. He entered public life with the publication of *England, Ireland, and America* (1835) under the pseudonym "A Manchester Manufacturer." The pamphlet advocated free trade, nonintervention in foreign affairs, and substantial domestic reforms, and recognized the potential of the United States as a formidable competitor. The following year, Cobden published *Russia and the Eastern Question* (1836), in which he urged Great Britain to abandon balance of power and foreign intervention as principles of her foreign policy and to recognize the primacy of commercial interests. Such views came to be called "Cobdenism" in foreign policy.

Cobden became involved in the Manchester Anti-Corn Law Association in late 1838 and was instrumental in transforming it into the National Anti-Corn Law League. The League agitated virtually without interruption for the next seven years for the total and immediate repeal of those laws which restricted by high import duties the importation of foreign cereal grains (corn) to Great Britain.

526

With John Bright and others, Cobden organized local anti-Corn Law associations, stumped the country for free trade, lobbied Parliament, and helped the League organize its electoral activities. The League sent out lecturers, collected signatures on petitions, held mass meetings, and published its own newspapers, tracts, pamphlets, and books. Cobden was at the center of all this activity.

At first the League concentrated upon what Cobden called "enlightenment of the public mind" on the issue of free trade and upon petitioning, but after 1842 the League increasingly focused upon enrollment of new members, fund-raising by means of subscriptions, and registration of electors to take the campaign for repeal to the hustings. League agitations created the political climate that made repeal of the Corn Laws irresistible to Sir Robert Peel in early 1846, as the effects of the potato famine in Ireland made immediate relief imperative. The prime minister himself acknowledged in the House of Commons that no one had done more to achieve repeal of the Corn Laws than had Richard Cobden.

At Stockport in 1837, Cobden stood for election to Parliament on a broad radical platform which included free trade, suffrage extension, and the secret ballot. He narrowly lost that poll, but with League help he was successfully returned for that constituency in 1841. In Parliament Cobden was noted for his earnestness and command of factual detail, but it was at public meetings of the League that he was most effective. He was a very persuasive public speaker, invariably choosing apt illustrations and presenting his arguments in a fashion which carried the listener to the understanding which he intended. He was always certain of his facts and ready to meet any objection.

Between 1838 and 1846, Cobden devoted nearly all of his attention to League activity, though he married a Welsh schoolmate of his sister, Catherine Anne Williams, in May of 1840. His business, left in the less than capable hands of his brother Frederick, failed, and Cobden's League friends had to raise a subscription of eighty thousand pounds to relieve his embarrassment and provide him an income. His investments in the Illinois Central Railway showed little return, and a second subscription of forty thousand pounds was raised in 1860.

In 1847, Cobden was returned again for Stockport and by the numerous electors of the West Riding of Yorkshire. Cobden chose to sit for the county and represented that constituency in Parliament for a decade. While a Member of Parliament

for the West Riding, Cobden worked for international arbitration, financial reform, and arms reductions. He attended several Peace Congresses and carried on a lively correspondence with all manner of reformers and Radicals. He opposed the Ecclesiastical Titles Bill in 1851 and supported removal of Jewish disabilities.

Cobden was a consistent supporter of education; he believed that suffrage extension and national education must go hand in hand. Though an Anglican, he had supported the Maynooth Grant to supply public funds to a Roman Catholic seminary in Ireland in 1845 on the grounds that it would educate the teachers of millions of Irishmen. This was the only occasion on which Cobden and his friend and ally, John Bright, differed in the House of Commons in nearly a quarter of a century of public life.

Cobden resented what he perceived as aristocratic control of diplomacy and the military and believed that only landlords benefited from armed conflict and the preparations for it. In a series of pamphlets, *1793 and 1853, in Three Letters* (1853), *How Wars Are Got Up in India* (1854), and *What Next? And Next?* (1856), Cobden warned of the dangers of what he termed "Palmerstonism" in foreign policy. He opposed the conduct of the Crimean War and was among several proponents of "Cobdenism" to be defeated in the general elections of 1857. This defeat, combined with the recent loss of his son to scarlet fever, Mrs. Cobden's melancholia, and the temporary disability and exhaustion of his friend Bright caused him to retire from public life for a time. Cobden traveled to the United States once again, where he was astonished at the progress that had been made in two decades.

Cobden returned to Parliament in 1859 as Member of Parliament for Rochdale. He twice declined offers to join the cabinet, but in 1860 on a volunteer mission he successfully negotiated significant reciprocal tariff reductions with France for the Palmerston Government. The Cobden-Chevalier Treaty stimulated trade and industry in both nations and improved the strained relations between them as well. For this effort Cobden was offered a baronetcy, but he declined the offer.

Cobden continued to differ with Palmerston over defense issues in the 1860's. As an opponent of slavery he expressed support for the federal government in the American Civil War. He differed with Palmerston on the issue of whether Great Britain should oppose Prussia and Austria in the Danish War, and on this occasion nonintervention carried the day.

Cobden fell ill in the autumn of 1864 and died in London from the complications of bronchitis on April 2, 1865. He was buried in the churchyard at Lavington in Sussex. Within a year of Cobden's death, some of his old Anti-Corn Law League friends founded the Cobden Club as a memorial to the "Apostle of Free Trade" and as a way to advance his principles. The club took "Free Trade—Peace—Goodwill Among Nations" as its motto and promoted Cobden's internationalism and economic principles into the next century.

Summary

Richard Cobden was a middle-class manufacturer and Member of Parliament who advocated free trade, nonintervention in foreign affairs, and a variety of Radical political reforms, including suffrage extension and the secret ballot. He saw repeal of the Corn Laws as the keystone in the arch of "aristocratic misrule" and was the best known lecturer and organizer of the Anti-Corn Law League. He opposed monopoly in all of its forms, economic and political, and advocated the laissez-faire doctrines associated with the Manchester school of economic thought and nineteenth century Liberalism. A free-trade Radical, Cobden believed that adoption of a new commercial policy would bring unprecedented economic growth and political progress.

Bibliography

Cobden, Richard. *The Political Writings of Richard Cobden.* 2 vols. London: William Ridgway, and New York: Appleton, 1867. A complete collection of Cobden's pamphlets.

———. *Speeches of Richard Cobden, Esq., M. P., Delivered During 1849.* London: James Gilbert, 1849; New York: Kraus, 1970. A series of speeches revised by Cobden himself for publication on the subjects of peace, retrenchment, colonial reform, and other subjects.

———. *Speeches on Questions of Public Policy by Richard Cobden, M. P.* Edited by John Bright and J. E. T. Rogers. 2 vols. London: Unwin, 1870. A fine collection of Cobden's speeches in Parliament, on the hustings, for the League, and at public meetings. Topically organized.

Dawson, William Harbutt. *Richard Cobden and Foreign Policy.* London: Allen and Unwin, 1926; New York: Frank-Maurice, 1927. An examination of Cobden's views on nonintervention, international peace and arbitration, and arms expenditure, with particular reference to the international problems of the 1920's. Makes considerable use of excerpts from Cobden's speeches and correspondence.

Edsall, Nicholas. *Richard Cobden: Independent Radical.* Cambridge, Mass.: Harvard University Press, 1986. Credits Cobden with a major role in defining radical Liberalism and reasserts the significance of his thought. Especially good for the post-repeal period.

Gowing, Richard. *Richard Cobden.* London and New York: Cassell, 1890. A very brief popular biography in the World's Workers series. Concentrates on the period to 1846 and views Cobden's life as a watershed in modern history.

Hinde, Wendy. *Richard Cobden: A Victorian Outsider.* New Haven, Conn.: Yale University Press, 1987. A sympathetic biography which portrays Cobden the man as well as the public figure. Makes extensive use of Cobden's letters and papers. Illustrated.

McCord, Norman. *The Anti-Corn-Law League, 1838-1846.* 2d ed. London: Allen and Unwin, 1968; Brookfield, Vt.: Gregg Revivals, 1993. An excellent and thoroughly scholarly study, which concentrates upon the organizational structure and institutional activities of the League. Outlines the League's methods of proselytization and propaganda, its modes of fund-raising, and its electoral and parliamentary tactics. Makes good use of League papers and those of its most prominent members.

Morley, John. *Life of Richard Cobden*. 2 vols. London: Chapman and Hall, 1879. A lengthy and rather detailed nineteenth century biography by a prominent Liberal quite sympathetic to Cobden. Still the place for the serious student to begin. Dated but quite readable and very useful for its lengthy extracts from Cobden's correspondence. Chronological in organization and narrative in style. No index but has an extensive table of contents.

Read, Donald. *Cobden and Bright: A Victorian Political Partnership*. London: Arnold, 1967; New York: St. Martin's Press, 1962. An excellent comparative study of the two best-known free-trade Radicals. Drawn from a wide reading of manuscript sources. Read argues that Bright's Radicalism has been overplayed, that Cobden's views were not always identical with Bright's, and that it was Cobden, and not his Quaker friend, who was the more thoroughgoing democratic Radical.

Taylor, Miles. *The European Diaries of Richard Cobden 1846-1849*. Aldershot, Hampshire: Scolar Press, and Brookfield, Vt.: Ashgate, 1994. This volume includes previously unpublished diaries from Cobden's tour of the continent, which began in 1846. These diaries record his observations of European conditions and are the basis for the development of his belief that peaceful economic cooperation is the only way to lasting international stability.

Richard Francis Spall, Jr.

WILLIAM FREDERICK CODY

Buffalo Bill

Born: February 26, 1846; Scott County, Iowa
Died: January 10, 1917; Denver, Colorado
Areas of Achievement: Scouting and showmanship
Contribution: Capitalizing on the legends created about his prowess as a plainsman, Cody popularized the American West through his Wild West show, which brought the sights of the last frontier to eastern America and to Europe.

Early Life

William Cody was born in Iowa but grew up on the Kansas plains. His father, a staunch abolitionist, was pursued and attacked more than once by proslavery fanatics in the Kansas territory, and on several occasions only the young Cody's daring saved his father's life. When his father succumbed to illness in 1857, Cody sought work with what would become the firm of Russell, Majors, and Waddell, who hired him as a cattle driver and later as a Pony Express rider and stagecoach driver. By age twenty, the young man, grown to six feet and sporting shoulder-length, wavy hair and a goatee, had achieved his reputation among plainsmen as a daring scout and buffalo hunter, working for the army and for the railroads. His brief stint in the Union Army during the Civil War brought him no distinction but did provide the opportunity for him to meet and woo Louisa Frederici in St. Louis. They were married in 1866, and Cody took his bride back to Kansas, to share his life on the plains.

Cody's work as a scout and buffalo hunter led to several important encounters that secured his future fame. A dime novelist, traveling the West in search of new material, was introduced to Cody and from that meeting took away ideas for future novels. During the next four decades, more than two hundred novels about "Buffalo Bill" appeared. Eastern America soon was familiar with Cody's exploits as a buffalo hunter (extravagant claims put his total kill for a single day into the thousands) and as an Indian fighter, slayer of chiefs Tall Bull and Yellow Knife.

Cody's skill as a hunter for the railroads, the source of the legends which earned for him the sobriquet "Buffalo Bill," led to other career-enhancing engagements. He was called upon to lead several hunting expeditions for celebrities, including the Grand Duke Alexis of Russia, and a group of wealthy New York businessmen. Some of the latter invited Cody to visit in New York, and from that visit his career as America's premier showman was launched.

Life's Work

When Cody went to New York City in 1872, he was merely accepting the invitation of the East Coast magnates whom he had entertained on a buffalo hunt. Once there, his reputation having preceded him, he found that he was a minor toast of the town. One evening's entertainment included a trip to the theater to see a play, *Buffalo Bill, the King of Border Men* (1871). Cody was captivated by the attention given to him by the audience in the theater, and to his stage character. E. Z. C. Judson, who as novelist Ned Buntline had done much to build Cody's legend, encouraged him to take up the stage part himself. Reluctant at first, Cody finally gave in, and Judson then quickly wrote and produced *The Scouts of the Plains* (1872). While the show was extremely confusing and without dramatic merit, and Cody was stiff in his role, the play was a box-office success, and for several years, Cody appeared in a number of stage dramas. Through this endeavor, he met Nate Salsbury, who was to manage his later efforts with the Wild West show. Salsbury, along with publicist and lifelong friend John Burke, would remain one of Cody's staunchest supporters when that show brought pressures to bear on the flamboyant and somewhat irresponsible Cody.

For several years, Cody alternated his acting career with real-life work as a scout and mediator in the last of the Indian Wars. Then, in 1883, he helped form a traveling troupe which would bring the western plains to the cities and towns of the East and Midwest. Buffalo Bill's Wild West show toured for the next three decades, making stops in virtually every city of significance in the United States.

The troupe for Cody's show consisted of Indians whom Cody recruited from tribes that had been sent to reservations; plainsmen who had driven stagecoaches, herded cattle, or fought some of the same Indians with whom they now toured; and hundreds of horses, cattle, and buffalo. In the early years, Cody was the main attraction, performing feats with his rifle and introducing the cast in their grand parade at each location. He was joined at various times by other legendary figures such as Chief Sitting Bull, the victor of Little Big Horn, and trick-shot artist Annie Oakley. Cody managed to secure for his show the original Deadwood Stage, and the exciting chase that led to its rescue from marauders became a highlight of the performance.

The show played at such diverse locations as the World Cotton Exposition in New Orleans in 1884 and the World's Columbian Exposition in Chicago in 1893. Cody and some of his cast were invited to the Vatican in 1889. Queen Victoria attended a performance in 1887, and the Prince of Wales, later Edward V, saw the show on more than one occasion. New Yorkers saw the show performed in Madison Square Garden; the residents of Paris and Barcelona also witnessed the feats of Cody's performers. Well into the new century, Cody moved with his collection of people, animals, and paraphernalia, collecting huge receipts from people whose appetite for the West seemed insatiable.

Showmanship took its toll on Cody, however, and brought out the worst as well as the best in his character. Always a hard drinker, he was sometimes so drunk while on tour that colleagues feared that he would not be able to perform. A generous man by nature, he often squandered huge sums of money on projects in which unscrupulous entrepreneurs or well-intentioned but ill-fated friends encouraged him to invest.

Cody found himself caught up in the fast life, and his relationship with his wife, never strong, deteriorated. For years, he had been accustomed to leave behind Louisa and his children, first for duty with the army, then for his career onstage and with the Wild West show. Other women pursued him; certainly he pursued some of them. His relationship with Louisa reached its low point in 1904, when Cody sued for divorce, claiming that Louisa had tried to poison him at Christmas in 1900, and that he could no longer live with her. At the divorce trial, Cody's affair with an actress and other improprieties were made public, Louisa was able to generate substantial public sympathy, and the suit was dismissed. After a period of estrangement, the two were reunited, and Cody managed to live amicably with Louisa in his later years.

The Wild West show's prosperity, especially during the first decades of its life, allowed Cody to obtain significant real estate holdings in the West, most notably in the North Platte, Nebraska,

area, and in Wyoming. He was also instrumental in founding the town in Wyoming which bears his name. Often, he would retire to one of these places during the off-season, to relax and renew ties with the land which he helped portray to the rest of the world.

Running a business such as the Wild West show entailed certain risks. On one trip down the Mississippi River, a steamboat crash cost Cody half of his livestock. On one of the early tours in Europe, his Indians began to get homesick and to desert the show. Disease took a major portion of his livestock in another year. Competition became fierce at times, and especially after the death of Salsbury in 1902, Cody found himself going more and more in debt to keep the show running. Eventually, he found it necessary to accept offers from outsiders to finance his operation. In 1913, the show was seized by agents to pay creditors.

The last years of Cody's life were not pleasant. He tried his hand at the new motion-picture industry, convincing the aged General Nelson Miles to assist him in producing a documentary of the famous Battle of Wounded Knee. The film was not a commercial success. Other schemes, including a mining venture, were similarly unsuccessful. Meanwhile, Harry Tammen, an unscrupulous editor of the *Denver Post*, managed to loan Cody sufficient capital for his ventures so that Cody soon found himself unable to reach a settlement and break his contract with Tammen. As a result, Tammen was able to force Cody to tour with the Sells-Floto Circus in 1914 and to restrict his activities further by limiting his salary and expense account.

By 1916, Cody was suffering the infirmities of old age. In the winter of 1916, he traveled to Denver to stay with his sister. There, on January 10, 1917, he died in her home. Despite his wishes to be buried in Wyoming, he was laid to rest atop Lookout Mountain, outside Denver.

Summary

As a frontiersman, scout, and hunter, Cody would have achieved a place in American history without the fame that his Wild West show provided him. Even when the exaggerations about his exploits are stripped away, his accomplishments in helping to settle the West were substantial: He helped bring to a successful close several skirmishes and one major uprising in the Indian Wars; he participated as the youngest member of the celebrated Pony Express team; he kept the railroads moving across the country by providing meat for the construction crews.

Cody's Wild West show did more than his real-life exploits on the frontier to bring to the civilized world of the eastern United States and to the countries of Europe a sense of the life of the American West. He was a symbol of that land: handsome, brash, generous, free-living, unafraid of any danger. Carrying on the tradition of the showman established by the legendary Phineas T. Barnum, Cody barnstormed across two continents, sharing the sense of excitement that had characterized the West in its infancy and adolescence. While he toured, the West matured, and the frontier that Cody dramatized in his shows was disappearing. Nevertheless, the thrills Cody and his fellow performers generated in countless youngsters lived on for years after his death. Cody's legacy continues in the games of "Cowboys and Indians" which endure, long after the last buffalo and the last Indian were confined to reservations within a West that has become homogeneous with the rest of the United States.

Bibliography

Burke, John. *Buffalo Bill: The Noblest Whiteskin.* New York: Putnam, 1973; London: Cassell, 1974. A popular biography, providing sufficient details about Cody's early life on the frontier but concentrating on the years Buffalo Bill spent as an actor and showman in the eastern United States and in Europe. Informal style, highly readable.

Cody, William F. *Story of the Wild West and Camp-Fire Chats.* Philadelphia: Historical Publishing Co., 1888. Contains accounts of various plainsmen and one of Cody's several autobiographies. Since many details of Cody's early life are drawn from this autobiography, it is important for scholars; additionally, its informal style and tendency toward exaggeration mark it as typical of popular literature about the West written during the late nineteenth century.

Croft-Cooke, Rupert, and W. S. Meadmore. *Buffalo Bill: The Legend, the Man of Action, the Showman.* London: Sidgwick and Jackson, 1952. A brief account of Cody's life, relying heavily on Cody's autobiography for details of the early life. Contains an interesting introductory chapter on the impact that the Wild West show had in England.

Cvancara, Miroslav, and Cvancara, Frank. "Buffalo Bill." *Wild West* 9, no. 4 (December 1996). A profile of Cody that includes his buffalo hunting career, his time in show business, and his performance in Paris in 1889.

Havighurst, Walter. *Annie Oakley of the Wild West.* New York: Macmillan, 1954; London: Hale, 1955. Life story of one of the star attractions in the Wild West show; provides much information about Cody and others who traveled with him.

Hine, Robert V. *The American West: An Interpretive History.* 2d ed. Boston: Little Brown, 1984. Provides excellent background about the American West; discusses Cody as the foremost American hero.

Russell, Don F. *The Lives and Legends of Buffalo Bill.* Norman: University of Oklahoma Press, 1960. A well-researched, scholarly biography that goes far in separating the legend from the facts about Cody's life.

Wickstrom, Gordon M. "Buffalo Bill the Actor." *Journal of the West* 34, no. 1 (January 1995). Discusses Cody's career as a scout who found his acting abilities useful in the field.

Yost, Nellie S. *Buffalo Bill: His Family, Friends, Fame, Failures, and Fortunes.* Chicago: Sage,

1979. A carefully researched biography, relying heavily on records from the nineteenth century and on interviews with people who knew Cody or his family and friends. Debunks many legends and establishes a historical basis for many others.

Laurence W. Mazzeno

FERDINAND JULIUS COHN

Born: January 24, 1828; Breslau, Lower Silesia
Died: June 25, 1898; Breslau, Lower Silesia
Areas of Achievement: Botany and biology
Contribution: Cohn is considered one of the founders of modern bacteriology. As a botanist, he contributed to understanding the evolutionary position of many microscopic plantlike organisms by elucidating their life histories.

Early Life

The eldest of three sons of a poor Jewish merchant, Issak Cohn, Ferdinand Julius Cohn was born in the Breslau ghetto. He was a precocious child who, it is said, was able to read at the age of two and enter school at the age of four. At the age of seven he began higher school at the *Gymnasium* of St. Maria Magdelina, and he began attending the University of Breslau at the age of fourteen. Influenced at the university by professors Heinrich Goeppert and Christian Nees von Esenbeck, he became interested in botany. Because of the rules against Jews receiving advanced degrees at Breslau, he could not be granted one there. Thus, in 1846, he moved to the more liberal University of Berlin, from which, a year later, he obtained a doctorate in botany. At Berlin, he was influenced by several professors, especially Christian Ehrenberg in microscopy and Johannes Müller in physiology. He was in Berlin during the uprisings of 1848, with which he sympathized but in which he did not actively participate. Returning the next year to Breslau at the age of twenty-one, he became a privatdocent at the university, working under Professor Jan Evangelista Purkinje in his Institute of Physiology. There he began his work on the microscopic aspects of living organisms, at that time a new area of biological investigation, particularly because of the newly proposed cell theory of Theodor Schwann and Matthias Schleiden. In 1859, he became an extraordinary professor at the university, and in 1867, he married Pauline Reichenbach. The remainder of his professional career was spent at the University of Breslau, where he became an ordinary professor in 1872.

Life's Work

Cohn's interests were in microscopic organisms, both plant and animal, which he used to try to understand their relationships with higher groups of organisms and to understand their development and physiology. At first, he studied various microscopic algae, and, especially using the unicellular *Protococcus pluvialis*, he concluded that these organisms had a regular life cycle and various developmental phases including sexuality, and that the cellular substance was similar in all cells, both plant and animal. The latter conclusion led him to call the cell substance protoplasm, the name Hugo von Mohl had used for that in plant cells, rather than the term sarcode, which had been used by Felix Dujardin for animal cell substance. Cohn is best known for his studies of bacteria. He believed that these organisms were more plantlike than animallike. He showed that they had stable characteristics of form which varied within certain limits, allowing them to be given firm generic names and, at least, provisional specific names. His hesitation about specific names was based on his knowledge that sometimes those of the same form had different fermentative properties. He recognized six genera of bacteria based on their shapes: micrococcus (ball-shaped); bacterium (short rods); bacillus

(straight threadlike); vibrio (wavy-shaped); and spirochete (long, flexible spirals). The genera were placed into four larger groups: spaerobacteria for the round ones; microbacteria for the rod-shaped ones; desmobacteria for the longer rod- and thread-shaped ones; and spirobacteria for the wavy or spiral-shaped ones. Because of his clear presentation of the information about the characteristics of bacteria, their cultivation, and their physiology, Cohn helped found the modern science of bacteriology.

Cohn was involved in some of the most important aspects of the developing field of microbiology. He undertook to understand why some bacteria in hay infusions were able to withstand high temperatures. He was able to show that certain bacilli were able to form heat-resistant endospores. This discovery came at a time to help Louis Pasteur, and later John Tyndall, substantiate the attack on the idea of spontaneous generation of microorganisms. Because he was the major Germanic worker with bacteria, and because he had been trying to prove the importance of bacteria in causing diseases, the then-young Robert Koch wrote to Cohn asking if he could come and demonstrate his evidence for the bacterial cause of anthrax. Koch visited Breslau for three days and convinced Cohn and others at Breslau that he had definite proof that *Bacillus anthracis* was the sole cause of the disease. Cohn was very impressed with Koch's ability, supported his research program, and published his paper on anthrax in 1876, in the journal *Beitrage zur Biologie der Pflanzen* (contributions to the biology of plants), which Cohn had established in 1872 and used to publish many of his own findings.

Work in botany and the popularization of biology also occupied Cohn's time. From 1856 to 1886, he served as secretary of the botanical section of the Schlesische Gesellschaft für Vaterländische Cultur (Silesian society for the culture of the fatherland), in which capacity he organized and edited a multivolume work on the cryptogamic flora of Silesia. Cohn wrote a popular work on bacteria, *Über Bacterien, die kleinsten lebenden Wesen* (1872; *Bacteria, the Smallest of Living Organisms*, 1881), and one on plants, *Die Pflanze* (1882; the plant). In this way, and by articles and lectures, he helped to interest the general public and students in biological subjects. In 1866, he was able to establish an Institute of Plant Physiology at the University of Breslau, the first of its kind in the world, thus fulfilling a long-held dream. He made studies of tissues in plants that were involved with rapid movements which he believed to be similar to animal muscle tissue.

Summary

Ferdinand Julius Cohn is historically important as a major figure in the foundation of modern microbiology, and as a sponsor of Robert Koch in his important studies of disease-causing bacteria. Cohn placed microscopic organisms, particularly algae, fungi, and bacteria, which he considered to be plants, into a Darwinian evolutionary framework. By elucidating their life cycles, and when possible their sexuality, he furthered biological understanding. He recognized the importance of protoplasm as the universal living substance of cells. An important educator, he popularized botany and bacteriology by his writings and lectures.

Bibliography

Brock, Thomas D., ed. *Milestones in Microbiology.* Englewood Cliffs, N.J., and London: Prentice-Hall, 1961. Two of Cohn's important papers—with some deletions—in English translation are given: "Studies on the Biology of the Bacilli," concerned with the survival of spores of some bacteria after boiling, and "Studies on Bacteria," describing some of the problems in classifying bacteria and considering them best related to the fungi. Comments accompany the papers indicating their historical importance.

Bulloch, William. *The History of Bacteriology.* London and New York: Oxford University Press, 1938. Cohn's work is considered in the context of the history of bacteriology. His studies on the survival of bacteria after sterilization of their media are considered, as are his ideas about bacterial classification.

Cohn, Ferdinand. *Bacteria, the Smallest of Living Organisms.* Translated by Charles S. Dolley, with an introduction by Morris C. Leikind. Rochester, N.Y.: Phinney, 1881. Originally published in German by Cohn in 1872, this introduction to bacteriology was written for the general reader. It gives a brief history of the knowledge of bacteria and presents a summary of what Cohn and others knew and thought about bacteria. The reprint in the Johns Hopkins University Press book (1939) contains a short biography and the original complete bibliography of Cohn's writings.

Geison, Gerald L. "Ferdinand Julius Cohn." In *Dictionary of Scientific Biography*, edited by

Charles Coulston Gillispie, vol. 3. New York: Scribner, 1971. This scholarly biography of Cohn is the only substantial one in English. In addition to providing basic biographical information, it stresses Cohn's importance in the development of microbiology and botany. Provides a detailed bibliography.

Lechevalier, Hubert A., and Morris Solotorovsky. *Three Centuries of Microbiology.* New York: McGraw-Hill, 1965. Cohn's place in the development of bacteriology is considered briefly. The authors stress Cohn's studies of spontaneous generation of microorganisms in relation to Pasteur's work and the relationship between his work and Koch's bacterial studies.

Talbott, John H. *A Biographical History of Medicine: Excerpts and Essays on the Men and Their Work.* New York: Grune and Stratton, 1970. A brief biographical sketch of Cohn, with a composite drawing, stresses his contributions to botany. It includes a long quotation from the English translation of his book, *Bacteria, the Smallest of Living Organisms*, which emphasizes the importance of bacteria as disease organisms and as possible extraterrestrial initiators of life on Earth.

Emanuel D. Rudolph

SAMUEL TAYLOR COLERIDGE

Born: October 21, 1772; Ottery St. Mary, Devonshire, England

Died: July 25, 1834; Highgate, London, England

Areas of Achievement: Literature and theology

Contribution: Coleridge wrote several of the finest lyric poems in the English language and is considered one of the most brilliant of literary critics. As a speculative religious thinker, he had a seminal influence on many of the great minds of the nineteenth century.

Early Life

Samuel Taylor Coleridge was born on October 21, 1772, in the town of Ottery St. Mary, in Devonshire. He was the youngest of ten children born to Ann Bowden, the second wife of Coleridge's father, John Coleridge, a clergyman and schoolmaster. Coleridge was an intellectually precocious child, with an early love of books and study. He was particularly enthralled by *The Arabian Nights' Entertainments* (c. 1450), which he read at the age of five.

In 1782, one year after the death of his father, Coleridge was enrolled in the Christ's Hospital Grammar School in London. He was a superior student and a voracious reader, devouring everything from classics to theology, philosophy, and medical books. In 1791, when he was almost twenty years old, this sometimes untidily dressed young man with dark penetrating eyes, a fine forehead, and long black, flowing hair, received a scholarship to Jesus College, Cambridge, where he continued to read extremely widely. He also gained a reputation as an enthusiastic and spellbinding talker, and his gregarious, generous, and sensitive nature won for him many friends. In spite of this, however, he tended to be dissatisfied with himself, annoyed by what he described as his own indolence. He was also beginning to experience the ill health which dogged him throughout his life.

In 1794, Coleridge became friends with fellow student Robert Southey, who was two years his junior and also destined to be a poet of distinction. Together they planned to emigrate to the United States and set up an ideal community in Pennsylvania on the banks of the Susquehanna. Coleridge was excited by the proposed venture, which he called "Pantisocracy" (meaning "equal government for all"). The plan came to nothing, but through it Coleridge became engaged to Sarah Fricker, one of several members of the Fricker family who were involved in the scheme. Coleridge married her in October, 1795; she was later to bear him four children.

Having left Cambridge without taking a degree, Coleridge and his new bride moved to the village of Nether Stowey, near Bristol, where they rented a small cottage. The marriage was not destined to be a happy one; nevertheless, Coleridge was on the threshold of several productive and creative years, in which he was to write all the poems which were to make him famous.

Life's Work

Coleridge's first major poem, "The Eolian Harp," dates from his period at Nether Stowey. During this time, he also gave public lectures on political topics, preached as a Unitarian, and started a short-lived journal called *The Watchman.*

In 1797, following a visit by William Wordsworth to Nether Stowey, one of the most famous friendships in literary history began. Coleridge relished the acceptance and encouragement he received from Wordsworth and his sister Dorothy, and he believed that he had discovered a receptive audience for his wide-ranging ideas and speculations. Wordsworth, for his part, found his conception of his own poetic task defined more clearly through his conversations with Coleridge. Coleridge, however, always generous in his admiration of others, felt inferior (although unjustifiably so) to a man of Wordsworth's talents.

In January, 1798, Coleridge's financial problems were eased when he received a lifetime annuity of £150 from his friends Josiah and Tom Wedgwood. The security this provided, together with his almost daily contact with the Wordsworths, who were now living at nearby Alfoxden, stimulated Coleridge to a year of brilliant achievement. In February, he wrote the fine lyric poem "Frost at Midnight" and completed *Christabel* (which would be published in 1816). The next month, he finished *The Rime of the Ancient Mariner*, probably the greatest of all of his poems. "Kubla Khan," a visionary dream-poem of extraordinary power and beauty, followed in May. In September, *The Rime of the Ancient Mariner* was published in a joint collection with Wordsworth entitled *Lyrical Ballads.*

In the same month, Coleridge and Wordsworth traveled to Germany. Coleridge remained there, learning the language and studying German metaphysics, until July, 1799. On his return, he met and fell in love with Sarah Hutchinson, the sister of Wordsworth's wife, Mary, and in 1800 he and his wife followed the Wordsworths to live in the Lake District in the northwest of England.

Coleridge was now to enter a dark period of his life, a decade of gloom, failure, guilt, and despair. He was to write only a few more outstanding poems, notably "Dejection: An Ode" and "To William Wordsworth." His physical health deteriorated alarmingly, aggravated by mental anxieties; his distress is readily apparent from his poem "The Pains of Sleep." He took to opium—a drug which was frequently prescribed for medical reasons at the time—and soon became dependent on it. He could not settle down to important work. Although he had many projects in mind, he was unable to persevere with them. The greater the task he set himself, the more paralyzed he became, and he constantly lamented his inability to concentrate on one project at a time.

In an attempt to improve his health, Coleridge left England in 1804 for a two-year stay in Malta, but on his return in 1806 his condition had not improved. He formally separated from his wife, and by 1808, after a nomadic year, he went to live with the Wordsworths in the Lake District village of Grasmere. There, he managed to launch a new periodical, *The Friend*, which kept going for twenty-seven issues. In 1810, however, came a serious, indirect quarrel with Wordsworth, when a friend passed on to Coleridge some critical remarks that Wordsworth had made regarding his self-destructive way of life. The breach took many years to heal.

The next few years of Coleridge's life were increasingly desperate. He was consuming larger quantities of opium than ever before (although he tried hard to break his addiction), and he wrote of his guilt and the complete paralysis of his will. At one point, he even wished to be admitted to a private lunatic asylum.

In late 1811, however, Coleridge roused himself sufficiently to give a successful series of lectures on William Shakespeare and John Milton, which established his reputation as a literary critic of genius. During this period, he also produced three excellent short critical works, collectively titled "On the Principles of Genial Criticism Concerning the Fine Arts" (1814), as well as *Biographia Literaria: Or, Biographical Sketches of My Literary Life and Opinions*, written in 1815 and published in 1817.

The latter is notable for Coleridge's assessment of Wordsworth's poetry and for his own critical theories, particularly those dealing with the creative function of the imagination.

In 1816 came a rescue. James Gillman, a physician from Highgate, London, who was captivated by the power of Coleridge's mind, took him into his house and cared for him. Initially it was intended as a temporary measure, but Coleridge was to live at Highgate with Gillman and his wife for the remaining eighteen years of his life. During these years, he gained a new lease on life. He gave more lectures on Shakespeare and other topics and also wrote the religious works which were to have such a strong impact on nineteenth century thought. These include the three lay sermons published as *The Statesman's Manual* (1816), *Aids to Reflection* (1825), *On the Constitution of the Church and State, According to the Idea of Each* (1830), and the posthumously published *Confessions of an Inquiring Spirit* (1840). His projected magnum opus, which was to synthesize all branches of existing knowledge into one coherent, all-embracing philosophy of nature, was never written.

During the later years, a social circle formed itself around the "Sage of Highgate"; many people were drawn to the compelling flow of Coleridge's conversation, which ran its course, as it had always done, like a mighty, meandering river.

When Coleridge died, on July 25, 1834, worn out at the age of sixty-one, his friends were quick to pay tribute to him. Wordsworth declared him to be the most "wonderful" man he had ever known, and Coleridge's lifelong friend Charles Lamb said, "never saw I his likeness, nor probably the world can see again."

Summary

Samuel Taylor Coleridge's literary criticism and theory has remained influential for more than a century and a half, and although his greatness as a poet rests on only a handful of poems, his honored place in the history of English literature is unlikely ever to be challenged. His best poems are highly original; he had a marked gift, particularly noticeable in *The Rime of the Ancient Mariner* and *Christabel*, for evoking an atmosphere of the strange and the supernatural. In his "conversation poems," as they have come to be known (such as "Frost at Midnight" and "Dejection: An Ode"), he invented what is sometimes called the Greater Romantic lyric: a meditative lyric which features an isolated speaker interacting with his natural environment, resolving a problem or deepening an understanding, before the poem rounds back on itself to give a sense of resolution and wholeness.

Coleridge's philosophical thought was central to the English Romantic movement. Highly eclectic but rooted in Neoplatonism and German idealism, his mind was dominated by a search for unity. Coleridge opposed the mechanistic philosophy, with its tendency to fragment knowledge into separate compartments, with an organicism which viewed everything in connection with everything else, "the one life within us and abroad," as he put it in "The Eolian Harp." The "one life" could be realized through the power of the imagination, the creative aspect of the mind, which could overcome the ultimately false division between subject and object. Coleridge's later work is characterized by an attempt to reconcile this "dynamic philosophy" with orthodox Christianity.

Coleridge's later religious writings elaborated an unusual, subjective approach to Christian belief, analyzed the relation between reason (including the scientific method) and faith, and discussed the Bible's claim to authority and the role of the Church in national life. All these issues became central to Victorian religious inquiry.

Given the range of Coleridge's achievement, it is not surprising that the Victorian philosopher John Stuart Mill called him "one of the great seminal minds of England," to whom the Victorian age was indebted not only for "the greater part of the important ideas which have been thrown into circulation among its thinking men but for a revolution in its general modes of thought and investigation."

Bibliography

Barfield, Owen. *What Coleridge Thought*. Middletown, Conn.: Wesleyan University Press, 1971; London: Oxford University Press, 1972. One of the clearest and most penetrating brief expositions of Coleridge's thought.

Bate, Walter Jackson. *Coleridge*. New York: Macmillan, 1968; London: Weidenfeld and Nicolson, 1969. Sound and balanced introduction to Coleridge's life and work by a leading literary critic and scholar.

Chambers, E. K. *Samuel Taylor Coleridge: A Biographical Study*. Oxford: Clarendon Press, 1938; Westport, Conn.: Greenwood Press, 1978. Factually accurate, but spoiled by a censorious tone and lack of sympathy for its subject.

Coburn, Kathleen, ed. *Coleridge: A Collection of Critical Essays*. Englewood Cliffs, N.J.: Prentice-Hall, 1967. Distinguished literary critics present the range and brilliance of Coleridge's achievement in poetry and literary criticism.

Coleridge, Samuel Taylor. *The Portable Coleridge*. Edited by I. A. Richards. New York: Viking Press, 1950. One-volume selection from Coleridge's voluminous works. Includes poems, letters, notebooks, literary criticism (including long extracts from *Biographia Literaria*), and sections of *The Statesman's Manual* and *Aids to Reflection*.

————. *Samuel Taylor Coleridge: Selected Letters*. Edited by H. J. Jackson. Oxford and New York: Oxford University Press, 1985. Extensively annotated edition, which includes letters from every phase of Coleridge's career. Reveals his myriad-minded self as he ranges over everything from poetry to science and chronicles his tormented inner life.

Ford, Jennifer. *Coleridge on Dreaming: Romanticism, Dreams, and the Medical Imagination*. Cambridge and New York: Cambridge University Press, 1998. Examines Coleridge's views on dreams and the debates on the subject among the philosophers, scientists, and poets of the Romantic period.

Hanson, Lawrence. *The Life of S. T. Coleridge: The Early Years*. London: Allen and Unwin, 1938; New York: Oxford University Press, 1939. Sympathetic, sometimes even rhapsodic, account of Coleridge's life up to June 1800.

Hewitt, Regina. *The Possibilities of Society: Wordsworth, Coleridge, and Sociological Viewpoint of English Romanticism*. Albany: State University of New York Press, 1997. Hewitt challenges many standard assumptions in the areas of literature and sociology, providing an original approach to rethinking our visions of Romantic poetry.

Willey, Basil. *S. T. Coleridge*. New York: Norton, 1971; London: Chatto and Windus, 1972. Traces Coleridge's intellectual and spiritual autobiography, from his early Unitarianism to the Christian orthodoxy of his later years.

Bryan Aubrey

SAMUEL COLT

Born: July 19, 1814; Hartford, Connecticut
Died: January 10, 1862; Hartford, Connecticut
Areas of Achievement: Invention and technology
Contribution: Colt developed the revolving pistol and the revolving rifle and pioneered the mass production of guns with interchangeable parts. Colt firearms played a significant role in nineteenth century U.S. history and also provided a key link in the transformation of weapons of war.

Early Life

Samuel Colt was born in Hartford, Connecticut, one of eight children of Christopher and Sarah Caldwell Colt. Christopher was in the manufacturing business in Connecticut and Massachusetts. Samuel's grandfather, Major Caldwell, was in the shipping and banking business and was one of the wealthiest men in Hartford. Major Caldwell, who had fought in the Revolutionary War, expressed strong opinions on military matters and weaponry and strongly influenced young Colt.

During his early school years, Colt performed poorly in subjects such as reading, writing, and arithmetic until his mother, to whom Colt was very close, impressed upon him that such disciplines were a means to better understand the workings of guns and the process of explosions. Colt's mother died when he was seven, but two years later his father married Olivia Sargent, who continued to support Colt's inquisitive nature.

Throughout those formative early years, Colt's increasing fascination with firearms and explosives led him to develop an interest in the natural sciences: physics, chemistry, and electricity. A series of experiments with firearms and gun powder culminated in Colt's development of a way to ignite an underwater charge of gun powder with an electrical spark. On July 4, 1829, at the age of fifteen, Colt successfully ignited an underwater mine with an electrical charge in a Ware, Massachusetts, pond in front of a crowd of people that included Elisha Root, a fellow inventor who would come to play a central role in Colt's future success in the manufacture of guns.

In August, 1830, at the age of sixteen, Colt signed on the brig *Carlo* as a seaman and headed for India. He occupied his off-duty hours whittling models of ships and firearms—most significantly, models of double-barreled handguns. Colt was in-

tent on developing a more practical revolving handgun. However, he found that a revolving handgun with multiple barrels was impractical, so he concentrated on designing a more practical repeating handgun with a single barrel and a revolving spindle. The solution was a result of his observations of the workings of the ship's wheel. As the wheel was turned to navigate the ship, a clutch aligned the spokes and locked the wheel in position to maintain the ship's course; the clutch was then released to change course. In February, 1836, Colt secured the patent to a repeating handgun with a revolving and locking cylinder whose bullet chambers came in line with the single barrel by pulling the hammer back to the cocked position.

Life's Work

Colt sought financial backing from his father to develop some working steel models of his handgun, but initial test firings of the models proved unsuccessful, and his father stopped financial support. Convinced that his repeating revolver was destined for success, Colt funded the enterprise by traveling around the United States and Canada using the stage name "Doctor Coult" and giving public demonstrations of nitrous oxide (laughing gas). The years Colt spent on the road raising capital also allowed him time to refine his design models and to have steel models produced and tested.

The manufacture of Colt firearms began in 1836 following Colt's travels abroad to secure patents in England, France, and Prussia; his first U.S. patent was granted on February 25. The Patent Arms Manufacturing Company of Paterson, New Jersey, produced five- and six-shot revolvers, revolving rifles, carbines, shotguns, and a few muskets—all referred to by the public as Colts—using the armory method of mass production, which was characterized by the use of a factory system, the specialization of labor, the use of precision tools and gauges, and the production of weapons with interchangeable parts that could be taken from one gun and used in another gun of the same model. Thus, damaged gun parts from one model could be replaced using spare parts from similar models. Prior to the introduction of the armory method of production, guns were laboriously crafted one at a time. Colt believed that the mass production of guns could best be produced by machinery.

Although the Patent Arms Manufacturing Company experienced financial failure in 1841, a number of significant events in the development and adoption of Colt firearms transpired during the six year of its existence. Colt guns manufactured in Paterson proved to be successful in tests and demonstrations for the government in Washington, D.C., but bureaucratic government officials were unable or unwilling to accept the advanced revolving design and dynamics of the weapons. In addition, the national financial climate was unsettled. Therefore, Colt was unable to land a government contract. Undaunted, he believed that contracts for his weapons would come through increasing demonstrations, advertising, and placing his guns in the hands of active fighting men. During these financially lean years without the resources of an armory, Colt turned his attention away from guns and devoted his energies toward the successful development of waterproof ammunition and the successful development of underwater mines designed for harbor defenses. In addition, his association with Samuel F. B. Morse led to the development of the telegraph.

Colt's belief in himself and his revolving guns eventually paid off. He experienced his first success at placing his weapons in war conditions during the Second Seminole War, which raged in Florida from 1835 through 1842. Although the Seminole Indians had a tactical edge in fighting in the Florida Everglades and possessed rifles as good as the U.S. soldiers, Colt's repeating pistols and rifles were soon recognized as the weapons of choice by the Second Dragoons and played a key role in the conflict. The success of Colt's guns did not go unnoticed by military practitioners outside of Florida. The ever-increasing influx of white settlers into Native American territory in Texas and the emerging conflict between the Republic of Texas and Mexico played significant roles in the evolution of Colt firearms and their adoption by men at war.

In 1844, U.S. dragoon forces and Texas Rangers armed with Colt firearms, some obtained from the Texas Navy, began confronting Native Americans as white settlers pushed west. In 1846, when the Mexican War began, Captain Samuel H. Walker of the U.S. Army met with Colt, and the two collaborated on the design of a new, more powerful revolver to replace the Paterson six-shooter. The newly designed "Walker" met with immediate success, and the U.S. Ordinance placed an order for a one thousand of the new six-shooters. Colt suddenly found himself back in the gun business but with-

out an armory. To meet the increasing demand for his weapons, Colt contracted with Eli Whitney, Jr. (son of the inventor of the cotton gin), to produce Colt guns at his Whitneyville, Connecticut, arms and cotton gin manufacturing facility.

In 1848, when Colts were no longer contracted for production at the Whitneyville armory, Colt built a small armory in Hartford, Connecticut, with the multitalented mechanic and inventor Elisha Root serving as its superintendent. The refinement of the armory production process and the continuing development of a wide range of sophisticated revolving guns produced at the Hartford armory led to the adoption of Colts for official use by Wells Fargo Express messengers and by the U.S. Navy during Matthew Perry's visit to Japan in 1852.

In response to an increasing demand for his pistols and rifles, Colt established an armory in London, England. Upon returning to the United States, he built the Armsmear factory located at South Meadows in Hartford, Connecticut, which was to become the largest private armory in the world upon its completion in 1855. The years of production of Colt guns at Whitneyville, the first Hartford armory, London, and Armsmear led to the continued development and refinement of pocket pistols, belt pistols, holster pistols, repeating rifles, sporting rifles, and shotguns for hunters, as well as special Colt models for military personnel and law-enforcement officers throughout the United States.

Colt was nearly forty-two when he married Elizabeth Hart Jarvis in 1856. Immediately following their wedding, they traveled to Europe and were entertained by European heads of state. They returned to the United States in 1857. As rumblings of an imminent civil war echoed throughout the country, Colt was burdened by the idea that the guns he had manufactured and sold to Texas would become instruments of war that fellow Americans from the North and South would use against each other. Colt showed sympathy toward the South prior to the Civil War; however, once the war between the states broke out, he devoted all of his arms manufacturing resources to production for Union forces. The Colt revolver was the revolver of choice by the Northern Army, and it became the practice of many Northern cavalrymen to carry two Colts in their belts and two Colts on their saddles. Nearly 40,000 revolvers, 100,000 muskets, and 7,000 rifles were supplied to the Union troops by the Colt armories.

Summary

Samuel Colt died on January 10, 1862, at the age of forty-eight. At his death, it was said of him that "Abe Lincoln may have freed all men, but Sam Colt made them equal." Colt will be remembered for his invention of the Colt revolver, which revolutionized methods of warfare and provided the critical link in the development of arms from the muzzle-loading musket to the magazine rifles and machine guns of the twentieth century. In addition, Colt developed and refined the armory method of weapons production, and the famed Colt revolver became one of the first products of American manufacture available around the world.

Bibliography

Edwards, William B. *The Story of Colt's Revolver.* Harrisburg, Pa.: Stackpole, 1953. Edwards' book provides a detailed biography of Colt. Includes illustrations.

Hosley, Walter. *Colt: The Making of an American Legend.* Amherst: University of Massachusetts Press, 1996. Hosley's voluminous, large-format biography places Colt in social and historical contexts. The book contains numerous illustrations.

Hounshell, David A. *From the American System to Mass Production, 1800-1932: The Development of Manufacturing Technology in the United States.* Baltimore: Johns Hopkins University Press, 1984. This is an overview of the rise of mass production in the United States.

Mitchell, James L. *Colt, a Collection of Letters and Photographs about the Man, the Arms, the Company.* Harrisburg, Pa.: Stackpole, 1959. As the title implies, Mitchell uses personal correspondence and photographs to trace the development of Colt's inventions and company.

Hugh J. Phillips

AUGUSTE COMTE

Born: January 19, 1798; Montpellier, France

Died: September 5, 1857; Paris, France

Areas of Achievement: Philosophy, sociology, historiography, and religion

Contribution: One of the greatest systematic thinkers of nineteenth century France, Comte was the father of positivism, a philosophy which saw the evolution of new ideas as the shaping force in history and regarded the empirical method of science as the only valid basis of knowledge. Comte sought to extend the method of science to the study of man, coining the word "sociology." His later thought took a Romantic swing, emphasizing the primacy of the feelings, glorifying religion in a secular guise, and proposing a highly regulated social order.

Early Life

Isidore-Auguste-Marie-François-Xavier Comte, the eldest of four children, was born in the French university town of Montpellier on January 19, 1798. His father, Louis-Auguste Comte, was a tax official, a man of strict habits and narrow interests; his mother, Félicité-Rosalie Boyer, twelve years older than her husband, was a warm, emotional person who devoted her life to her children. Both parents were devout Catholics and royalists.

Young Comte was nearsighted and small—his head and trunk seemed too large for his limbs. He had an extraordinary memory, however, and proved to be a brilliant student in the local lycée, winning prizes in Latin and mathematics, on occasion substituting for his teacher. At the age of fifteen, he was admitted to the prestigious École Polytechnique in Paris. There his diligence and acuteness led his awed classmates to nickname him "the philosopher." Napoleon I had given this school, like Comte's lycé, a military tone and discipline. Yet Comte, who at age fourteen had already rebelled against the religion of his parents by becoming an atheist, was one of the most unruly students at the school. Comte was a prominent spokesman for the students when they supported Napoleon during his futile attempt to regain control of France in 1815. Later, Comte was judged by authorities a ringleader of a student effort to oust an unpopular professor, a conflict so heated that it served as a pretext for temporarily closing the school. He was sent home and was placed under police surveillance.

In 1817, Comte returned to Paris, studying independently and tutoring students in mathematics to support himself. The possibility of an offer to teach in a new American polytechnical school led Comte to immerse himself in the writings of Thomas Paine and Benjamin Franklin, but the project was not funded. Comte therefore became secretary to the exuberant social philosopher Henri Saint-Simon, borrowing the broad outlines of many of his own later doctrines while writing essays and articles which appeared under Saint-Simon's name. Comte served Saint-Simon for seven years, but was uncomfortable with the religious bent of Saint-Simon's late writings and believed that his social theory needed a more systematic theoretical foundation. A critical preface by Saint-Simon to an essay Comte published under his own name precipitated the end of the relationship in 1824.

By then, the headstrong Comte had dropped his first name, Isidore, in favor of Auguste; had fathered an illegitimate daughter, who would die at the age of nine, by an Italian woman; and was living with Caroline Massin, herself the offspring of an unmarried provincial actress, whom he had known for three years and would marry in 1825. He praised her kindness, grace, wit, and cheerful disposition; she had been sold by her debauched mother to a young lawyer when in her mid-teens and was by this time a registered prostitute. It was partly to help her get her name off of police rolls that he agreed to the marriage. Their union was marred by his seeming indifference to their straitened economic circumstances and her occasional disappearances. A final separation came in 1842. Nevertheless, she had provided needed support through the difficult period when he produced his most important work, the six-volume *Cours de philosophie positive* (1830-1842; course on positive philosophy). The most important part of this support came shortly after he had begun the series of seventy-two lectures out of which this book grew, when he had a nervous breakdown so severe that he was incapacitated for more than a year (1826-1827), was judged incurably insane by one physician, and attempted suicide.

Life's Work

Comte wanted to be a philosopher-prophet, like Francis Bacon, Nicolas Condorcet, or his mentor Saint-Simon. Living in an era scarred by deep so-

cial antagonisms and warring ideologies, he dreamed of creating a persuasive philosophical synthesis which could restore both spiritual and social order to European society. Such solid intellectual underpinning was lacking, he believed, in Saint-Simon's thought. Comte reasoned that if the method of science could be extended to every aspect of life, the intellectual unity which had characterized medieval Europe could be restored on a more lasting basis, and unity of thought would bring social order.

Comte interpreted the rise of science and its extension to the study of man in the context of a general theory of human intellectual development he borrowed, via Saint-Simon, from the eighteenth century economist and statesman Jacques Turgot. The "law of the three stages" held that as positive knowledge of nature gradually replaces earlier tendencies to attribute much in life to unseen powers, thought moves from a theological to a metaphysical stage, replacing imagined divinities with nonobservable abstractions. Yet they too fall to skepticism, and a scientific or positive outlook triumphs. For Comte, this concept constituted a general theo-

ry of history, accounting for institutional as well as intellectual development. Thus, he held that theological societies have military political systems; metaphysical societies have a juristic social organization; and positivist societies will have an industrial polity. A positivist approach to phenomena came first in the simple sciences, such as astronomy and physics, while metaphysical or even theological modes of thought linger where phenomena are more complex. Since sciences dealing with the latter must rest on the foundation of more general, simpler ones, of necessity new positive sciences emerged in the following order: mathematics, astronomy, physics, chemistry, biology, and sociology. Although the later volumes of the book contain many prescriptive judgments about the future needs of society which now would not be termed scientific, *Cours de philosophie positive* was a tour de force, a landmark in both philosophy and the historical study of science.

With its publication and the growth of his reputation, Comte secured academic posts at the Institut Laville and the École Polytechnique. His outspoken criticisms of some academicians at the school led to the rejection of his candidacy for a chair there. He retaliated by appealing to European public opinion through a bitter attack on his opponents in the preface of the last volume of *Cours de philosophie positive*, an action which brought his final break with Caroline and cost him his positions. His financial difficulties led admirers in both France and England (including John Stuart Mill, later a critic) to raise funds on his behalf.

Comte lived modestly in his last years. The most significant episode in this period was a passionate emotional relationship with a beautiful but unhappy and ill young woman, Clotilde de Vaux. He had known her only a year and a half when she died in the spring of 1846 from tuberculosis. Yet her memory absorbed him through his remaining years. He dedicated his late work to her, including a second monumental book, the four-volume *Système de politique positive* (1851-1854; *System of Positive Polity*, 1875-1877). He declared that it was she who had taught him the importance of feelings.

System of Positive Polity is a work which prophesies in great detail the future of Western society. Its vision is in part a realization of the plan of Comte's youth, but it reveals a remarkable shift in emphasis from reason and scientific understanding to the emotions. He had come to regard as futile his earlier dream of achieving intellectual unity through science. Now he made men's wants, that is, morality, the foundation for intellectual unity in positivism. The emphasis in this work had been presaged in his *Considerations sur le pouvoir spirituel* (1826; considerations on spiritual power), in which he wrote that the Catholic church, shorn of its supernaturalism, might provide an ideal structural model for positivist society. It was probably Comte's intense feelings for de Vaux that brought this hitherto inveterate rationalist to emphasize the heart above intelligence and knowledge, and to prescribe a cult of womanhood as the emotional center of his secular religion.

The object of worship in this system, which T. H. Huxley dubbed Catholicism minus Christianity, was humanity itself, past, present, and future. Scientist-priests were to control both religion and education, positivist in content, which would be the foundation of the new social order. Actual political power, Comte declared, would rest with bankers and industrialists, whom economic developments were already thrusting to the fore. They would, however, operate under the spiritual guidance of the priests. The new industrial working class, its morals strengthened by religion and examples of feminine virtue, would accept the dominion of the industrialists but also give full backing to the priests. The latter, as shapers of powerful public opinion, would ensure that the workers's interests were safeguarded.

Thus, Comte, who earlier had declared the intellect his lord, now saw the feelings, not reason, as the key to social unity. He contended that man has a benevolent instinct—coining the word "altruism" to describe it—but that it is weak unless nurtured by good institutions. This need provided Comte a rationale for dictating the features of his positivist utopia in obsessive detail, from career paths to private devotions, from indissoluble marriage and perpetual widowhood to the particular heroes of human progress who were to be honored on each day of the (thirteen-month) positivist calendar.

Summary

Like many in his age, including his German contemporary Georg Wilhelm Friedrich Hegel (whose complex philosophy paralleled Auguste Comte's in remarkable ways), Comte was a visionary, a self-proclaimed prophet for the ages who believed that he had unveiled profound truths with sweeping social implications. As was true of most other utopian visionaries, his concrete predictions were off the mark. Thus, while many were dazzled by the younger Comte's brilliance as an interpreter of the evolution of science and defender of its method in all realms of thought, the impact of his later writings was quite limited. Whereas a number of intellectuals, including Hippolyte-Adolphe Taine, Ernest Renan, and the logical positivists of the twentieth century, inherited his skepticism about nonempirical thinking, his religion of humanity was essentially stillborn, even though it championed the Humanism made popular by the Enlightenment. In emphasizing the limits of reason and the importance of emotions, he was at one with the Romantic movement, as were many other major writers of the nineteenth century. His sympathy for medieval institutions, if not medieval belief, was also widely shared by other intellectuals of his time, particularly in literature and art—it was the period of Walter Scott and Gothic revival, the period when the works of Dante (whom Comte much admired) were finally translated into English. Yet Comte's humorless preoccupation with order and perfection was not well suited to winning for him a broad and enthusiastic following. He antagonized onetime supporters such as Mill with his obsession with ordering—down to the level of minute details of thought and feeling, artistic creation, and religious devotion—the life of positivist society, for which he planned to be the high priest. His indifference to democracy and individual freedom separated him from the liberals of his day. His interest in old forms without old content alienated conservatives, and he had no interest in the growing nationalism which was to provide yet another basis for ideology in the decades which followed him. Yet, curiously, his thought had an affinity to a modern development for which he could have had little sympathy. In his obsession with uniformity and order, his vision of a society which sought to control every facet of man's intellectual and emotional life for social ends dictated by a small elite group, he was a precursor of the totalitarian movements of the twentieth century.

Bibliography

Comte, Auguste. *A General View of Positivism.* Translated by J. H. Bridges. London: Trubner, 1865; New York: Speller, 1957. This book, written during the ferment of the Revolution of 1848 and published shortly after Comte founded the Positivist Society, is an excellent introduction to his later social philosophy. It relates his ideas to contemporaneous social developments.

Gould, F. J. *Auguste Comte*. London: Watts, 1920. This biography, though brief, provides a balanced survey of Comte's life and thought. It gives more attention than does the Sokoloff volume to those who comprised his intellectual circle and treats his ideas more fully. The curious positivist calendar is appended.

Lévy-Bruhl, Lucien. *The Philosophy of Auguste Comte*. Translated by Kathleen de Beaumont-Klein. London: Sonnenschein, and New York: Putnam, 1903. A thorough and sympathetic treatment of Comte's thought by a highly regarded French scholar. Takes issue with Mill's contention that there are serious discrepancies between Comte's early and later writings.

Manuel, Frank. *The Prophets of Paris*. Cambridge, Mass.: Harvard University Press, 1962. This survey of a number of important French social philosophers devotes an illuminating chapter to Comte. The study provides a good perspective from which to assess Comte in relation to his intellectual milieu. Seen in the company of other visionaries, his detailed prescriptions are somewhat less puzzling.

Mill, John Stuart. *Auguste Comte and Positivism*. London: Trubner, 1865; Ann Arbor: University of Michigan Press, 1961. This critical assessment of Comte's ideas remains one of the most important books by an English author on Comte. Highly critical of Comte's later writings, it slights the elements of continuity they share with the rest of his work.

Pickering, Mary. *Auguste Comte: An Intellectual Biography*. Cambridge and New York: Cambridge University Press, 1993. In the first of two planned volumes, Pickering presents an intellectual biography of Comte, the founder of Positivism, by reevaluating his early career, his problems with mental illness, poverty, and strained relationships.

Scharff, Robert C. *Comte after Positivism*. Cambridge and New York: Cambridge University Press, 1995. Scharff has created the only systematic reconsideration of Comte currently available and argues that his Positivism has significant contemporary relevance.

Sokoloff, Boris. *The "Mad" Philosopher, Auguste Comte*. New York: Vantage Press, 1961. A brief, readable biography which summarizes Comte's chief ideas while treating more fully the biographical context within which they developed. Gives more attention to his youth and his relationship with women than to his ties to other intellectuals.

R. Craig Philips

JOHN CONSTABLE

Born: June 11, 1776; East Bergholt, Suffolk, England

Died: March 31, 1837; London, England

Area of Achievement: Art

Contribution: Constable combined a passion for nature with his conception of an ideal rural England to create some of the most evocative, poetic landscapes of all time.

Early Life

John Constable was born in East Bergholt, Suffolk, on June 11, 1776, the fourth of the six children of Golding Constable and Ann Watts. Like Rembrandt's father, Golding Constable was a miller, owner of water mills at Flatford and Dedham and two windmills at East Bergholt. He also shipped grain, imported coal, and served on the commission which oversaw shipping on the River Stout. In 1774, he had moved from Flatford to East Bergholt, a mile away, to live the life of a country squire in a newly built mansion.

Young Constable went to schools in Lavenham and Dedham, but his preoccupation with painting from an early age made him an inattentive pupil. Golding Constable had originally intended his second son—John's older brother was mentally handicapped—to become a clergyman, but when the boy proved to be no scholar, it was decided that he should go into milling. Although Constable eventually worked in his father's mills for only a year, he boasted, as an adult, of his broad, sensitive miller's thumb, which enabled him to judge a sample of flour by sifting it between his thumb and forefinger.

Constable's interest in art found considerable encouragement. He was friends with John Dunthorne, an East Bergholt plumber, glazier, and amateur painter. The two often went sketching together. Constable's mother approved of his ambitions and arranged for him to be introduced to Sir George Beaumont, an amateur painter, collector of paintings, and patron of the arts, whose mother lived at Dedham. Beaumont introduced the aspiring artist to landscapes by such painters as Lorrain Claude and Thomas Girtin, allowed Constable to copy his pictures, and kept him up to date on the latest aesthetic debates. In 1796, Constable, while visiting his uncle in Edmonton, met John Thomas Smith, who was working as a drawing master there. Smith encouraged Constable to find the subjects for his landscapes in domestic scenes and taught him to paint what actually appeared rather than invent figures.

When Golding Constable forced his son to work in his countinghouse in 1797, Constable wrote: "I see plainly that it will be my lot to walk through life in a path contrary to that in which my inclination would lead me." He continued painting, and in 1799 he met a final major influence, Joseph Farington, a pupil of landscape painter Richard Wilson. Farington had him copy the old masters, especially Jacob van Ruysdael, who had influenced Thomas Gainsborough, Constable's fellow painter of Suffolk landscapes.

That same year, Constable finally began devoting his full energies to art, enrolling in the Royal Academy Schools in London, where he was to study until 1811. His early landscapes were considered clumsy, and too often, under the pressure of criticism, he subverted his individuality to make his paintings resemble the work of other artists. He painted well enough, however, to receive his first considerable commission, *Old Hall, East Bergholt,* in 1801.

Life's Work

In 1802, Constable turned down the post of drawing master at a military academy in High Wycombe. He wrote John Dunthorne that if he had accepted the position, "it would have been a death blow to all my prospects of perfection in the Art I love." That same year, he exhibited his first painting at the Royal Academy and bought a studio in East Bergholt, near his parents' house. By 1803, he was convinced that he could produce paintings that "shall be valuable to posterity."

Since Constable felt compelled to prove to his family that he could make a living as an artist, he began producing life-size portraits in the mornings at East Bergholt, beginning in 1804, while devoting his afternoons to landscapes. The artist described landscape as his "mistress": "'tis to her I look for fame, and all that the warmth of imagination renders dear to man." He continued painting portraits for years, and the work he did for hire also included painting the altarpiece for Brantham Church, repairing and copying paintings for Lord Dysart of Helmingham Hall, and painting the background for a portrait by another artist. As late as 1828, he painted a mermaid for an inn sign in Warwickshire.

Constable was breaking new ground by devoting his serious art to the scenery of East Anglia. During this period, the Lake District, North Wales, Scotland, and the Peak District were fashionable for painters; the Stour Valley was not. Constable wanted to paint that into which he had insight, and he thoroughly understood the history, botany, and agriculture of the Stour Valley. Constable's family found his subjects to be too ordinary and suggested that he paint more dramatic scenery. Such pressure may have resulted in a tour of the Lake District in 1806 which produced six landscapes exhibited at the Royal Academy over the following two years. Golding Constable was unimpressed by his son's progress and considered him to be "pursuing a shadow." Yet the painter's father continued to finance his career. Family income supported Constable throughout his life.

Constable, a plain man with a sloping forehead and a beak of a nose, fell in love with Maria Bicknell in 1810. Her father was solicitor to the Admiralty, and her grandfather, the Reverend Dr. Durand Rhudde, was rector of East Bergholt. The wealthy Dr. Rhudde opposed his granddaughter's marriage plans since Constable refused to abandon art and earn a respectable living, and perhaps because of the artist's friendship with Dunthorne, reputedly an atheist. The Bicknell family gave in to the rector's wishes since Maria was expected to inherit his fortune. Her parents forbade Maria to meet with Constable, but the two continued to correspond. In 1811, Constable failed to appease Dr. Rhudde with a watercolor of his church.

Constable discovered another important inspiration for his landscapes in 1811, when he first visited Salisbury. Constable had met the Bishop of Salisbury in 1798, when John Fisher was rector of Langham, and now met the bishop's nephew, Archdeacon John Fisher, who was to become his closest friend. The younger Fisher was a substitute for the enlightened public Constable hoped for but never found. Through his friendship with Fisher, Constable came to feel the same affection for Salisbury as he had for the Stour Valley. He exhibited *Salisbury: Morning* at the Royal Academy in 1812.

Despite showing numerous paintings at the Academy, Constable displayed few signs of becoming a professional painter, though he sold paintings for the first time in 1814. His mother's death the next year was a blow, for she had always sympathized

with his ambitions, even though she believed he would have more success as a portrait painter.

Golding Constable died in 1816, and since his son's share of the estate placed the artist in a better financial situation, the Bicknells agreed to allow their daughter's marriage. As the wedding day approached, however, Constable began worrying about having less time for his painting and wanted to postpone the ceremony. John Fisher soothed his friend's fears and married the couple at the church of St. Martin-in-the-Fields in London on October 2, 1816. The Constables spent part of their honeymoon with Fisher and his wife at their vicarage in Osmington, Dorsetshire. Maria's father eventually grew to approve of Constable, and her grandfather relented enough to leave her four thousand pounds. The Constables lived in Hampstead for most of their marriage, and the painter spent his last extended period in East Anglia in the summer of 1817. The first of the couple's seven children was born at the end of that year.

The White Horse, the first of Constable's large paintings of a canal scene on the Stour, was well received when exhibited at the Royal Academy in 1819. Though this success led to his election as an associate member of the Academy, Constable's full acceptance by this institution which determined what was officially art in England was not to come for several years. John Fisher purchased *The White Horse* and was to buy many more Constable paintings. The artist wrote his friend in 1820, "I should almost faint . . . when I am standing before my large canvases was I not cheered and encouraged by your friendship and approbation." He also confided to Fisher that he feared, for his family's sake, that he would never be a popular artist but must be reconciled to pleasing himself.

Living in Hampstead, Constable felt isolated from his aesthetic roots. "The Londoners with all their ingenuity as artists," he wrote in 1821, "know nothing of the feeling of a country life (the essence of Landscape)—any more than a hackney coach horse knows of pasture." This sense of isolation, together with the Royal Academy's indifference to a man it considered a pretentious amateur obsessed by rural scenery and the lack of economic rewards, led to Constable's seeing himself as an outsider in the art world. Regarding his failure to be elected to the Academy in 1822 he wrote, "I have nothing to help me but my stark naked merit, and although that (as I am told) far exceeds all the other candidates—it is not heavy enough."

Constable's best-known work, *The Hay Wain* (given its name by Fisher), was shown at the Royal Academy in 1821 and later at the British Institution. This painting, *View on the Stour near Dedham*, and *View on Hampstead Heath* were exhibited in Paris in 1824 and were immensely popular. They were acclaimed by French artists, especially Eugène Delacroix, and were awarded a gold medal by Charles X. This success encouraged French art students to show more interest in landscapes.

When Constable began selling his works to the Paris dealers John Arrowsmith and Claude Schroth in 1824, he was finally making money. A disagreement with Arrowsmith the next year, however, ended their relationship, and Schroth went out of business soon afterward. Constable's relative lack of success was as much the result of his personality as of his unfashionableness in English art circles. He had a reputation for being difficult with patrons, for being coarse and slanderous about his fellow artists. He is reported to have been a malicious gossip and was disliked by many for his sarcasm. In addition, he referred to his paintings as his "children" and was unwilling to part with art he considered successful. He wrote that he loved such paintings too well "to expose them to the taunts of the ignorant."

Constable's financial problems were solved unexpectedly in 1827 by the death of his father-in-law, who left a larger fortune than had been anticipated. This burden lifted, Constable wrote, "I shall stand before a 6 foot canvas with a mind at ease (thank God)."

This ease of mind, however, was short-lived. Worn out by childbearing— the last was born in January, 1828—Maria Constable, who had for years suffered from tuberculosis, died November 23, 1828, at forty-one. Constable was devastated by her death, and his landscapes began to become lonelier, more distanced; he increasingly saw nature as unstable. His mourning of Maria can be seen in *Hadleigh Castle. The Mouth of the Thames—morning after a stormy night* (1829). The aftermath of a storm, the ruined castle, and a lonely shepherd reflect his mental state, his sadness at the impermanence of human endeavor.

Constable was at last elected to the Royal Academy in 1829 but by only a single vote. Sir Thomas Lawrence, president of the Academy, told him that he was lucky to have been elected at all, since several painters of historical subjects—considered superior to landscape artists—had also been under consideration. Fisher called his friend's election, "the triumph of real Art over spurious Art . . . of patient moral integrity over bare chicanery." The very next year, the Academy's hanging committee, of which Constable was a member, rejected his *Watermeadows at Salisbury* as a "nasty green thing."

After exhibiting the unusually large number of eight paintings at the Royal Academy in 1832, Constable began to work less because of rheumatism. He also experienced more sadness as both John Fisher and John Dunthorne, who had become his assistant, died. Constable called his friendship with Fisher "the pride—the honour—and grand stimulus of my life."

Constable died, probably of angina, on March 31, 1837. While working on *Arundel Mill and Castle* three days before, he is reported to have said, "It is neither too warm nor too cold, too light nor too dark, and this constitutes everything in a picture."

Summary

John Constable's closest friend in his final years was the American painter C. R. Leslie, who published a biography of the artist in 1843, despite his belief that the English public would be indifferent to his subject. Although Constable labored under the shadows of his fellow landscapists Thomas Gainsborough and J. M. W. Turner, his genius was occasionally recognized during his lifetime. Critic Robert Hunt referred to him as the quintessentially English painter in 1823, and *The Times*, in 1827, called him "unquestionably the first landscape painter of the day."

Throughout his career, Constable was discouraged by his lack of recognition, though he occasionally agreed with critics that his landscapes were not as finished as they might have been. His work was not appreciated, according to Constable, because it "flatters nobody by *imitation*, it courts nobody by *smoothness*, it tickles nobody by *petiteness*, it is without either *fal de lal* or *fiddle de dee*, how then can I hope to be popular?" He was confident, however, that his art would eventually be recognized. While painting *Trees Near Hampstead Church* in 1821, he commented that the painting would one day be worth as much as the field it depicted.

Constable's reputation increased slowly after his death, but it did not begin to assume its present status until 1888, when one of his daughters gave nearly one hundred paintings and three hundred drawings to the Victoria and Albert Museum.

These paintings, unseen by the public for half a century, could then be appreciated because of similar work done in the interim, especially by the French Impressionists. By this time, however, these artists had forgotten how Constable had influenced their mentors in the 1820's.

Constable's landscapes reflect what Leslie called a "peculiarly social" view of nature, since he painted scenes abounding in human associations. His paintings are full of cottages, farmhouses, churches, boats, wagons, and human figures, almost always in motion, engaged in some worthwhile activity. The interrelatedness of man and nature reflects the artist's view of an ordered, moral world. The inseparability of man and nature in Constable's art has led many to see his work as the equivalent of the Romantic poetry of William Wordsworth. The power of his paintings comes in part from their being reminiscences of places to which Constable was emotionally attached. Such qualities help engender in his art a timeless, rugged beauty more impressive now than during his own time, since this ordered world exists only in his landscapes.

Bibliography

Brighton, C. R. "John Constable's Anomaly." *The British Journal of Aesthetics* 34, no. 1 (January 1994). Discusses a Constable technique that created an anomaly for the theory of "chiaroscuro."

Constable, John. *John Constable's Correspondence.* Edited by R. B. Beckett, 6 vols. London: H. M. S.O., 1962-1976. Main source of biographical information about the painter. These volumes include substantial explanatory material.

Cormack, Malcolm. *Constable.* Cambridge and New York: Cambridge University Press, 1986. This critical biography emphasizes Constable's part in the Romantic movement and his scientific attitude toward landscape, particularly in relation to weather. Beautifully illustrated.

Fleming-Williams, Ian, and Leslie Parris. *The Discovery of Constable.* London: Hamilton, and New York: Holmes and Meier, 1984. Explains Constable's gradual rise to fame in the century following his death. Examines the role of his descendants in the reappraisal of his work. Also looks at his forgers and imitators.

Gadney, Reg. *Constable and His World.* New York: Norton, and London: Thames and Hudson, 1976. Brief overview of Constable's life and career; for general readers.

Leslie, C. R. *Memoirs of the Life of John Constable, R.A.* Edited by J. H. Mayne. 3d ed. London: Phaidon Press, 1995. Biography by the artist's close friend, first published in 1843. Based primarily upon Constable's substantial correspondence.

Peacock, Carlos. *John Constable: The Man and His Work.* Rev. ed. London: Baker, and Greenwich, N.Y.: New York Graphic Society, 1971. This three-part study looks at Constable's life, Romanticism, and the artist's relation to the sea. Discusses his influence on French painting.

Reynolds, Graham. *Constable: The Natural Painter.* London: Cory, Adams, and MacKay, and New York: McGraw-Hill, 1965. Analysis of Constable's work interwoven with biographical information in study by the then-keeper of the Constable collection at the Victoria and Albert Museum.

———. *The Early Paintings and Drawings of John Constable.* 2 vols. New Haven, Conn.: Yale University Press, 1996. Reynolds has selected fresh contexts for his biographical portrait, which place Constable clearly within his period.

Rosenthal, Michael. *Constable.* London and New York: Thames and Hudson, 1987. Covers the highlights of Constable's life while providing an overview of his work. Emphasizes the social, political, and moral context of Constable's art.

Michael Adams

JAY COOKE

Born: August 10, 1821; Sandusky, Ohio
Died: February 18, 1905; Ogontz, Pennsylvania
Area of Achievement: Banking
Contribution: Cooke was the foremost investment banker during the mid-nineteenth century and pioneered new ways of mobilizing the savings of Americans for productive ends.

Early Life

Jay Cooke, born August 10, 1821, was the third son of Eleutheros and Martha Cooke. The family had relocated in several moves from New England to the Lake Erie settlement of Sandusky. Eleutheros was an ardent Whig politician and served in Congress for a term when Jay was a young boy. The family atmosphere was devoutly Protestant. Jay attended public school in Sandusky until the age of fourteen, when he ended his formal education and took a job as a clerk in a general store. After a year at work, Jay left Ohio for St. Louis, staying there a year, until the commercial disruption following the Panic of 1837 caused him to return to Sandusky. Still only sixteen, Jay left Sandusky in the spring of 1838 for Philadelphia, where he obtained work with his brother-in-law's canal transport company. The firm failed shortly after Jay's arrival in the city, and he returned once more to Sandusky, staying only a few months, until he was lured back to Philadelphia with a job offer from the banker E. W. Clark. From 1839 to 1857, Cooke worked in the Clark banking house, first as an office boy; soon, because of his head for figures and nose for profits, he became a partner at the age of twenty-one.

An early photograph taken of Cooke in the 1840's shows a young man of modest stature, clear eyes, and somber nature. He looks as if he were trying to look older than he was. This fits the character of the man: earnest, sober, deeply religious, and a family man. Jay took his older brothers Henry and Pitt into partnership when each needed money and supported them throughout numerous misadventures for most of their lives. He started his own family shortly after his 1844 marriage to Dorothea Allen, and the couple had eight children, though not all survived childhood. The Cookes did not entertain extensively, keeping the Episcopal Church at the center of their lives.

As a partner at E. W. Clark and Co., Cooke practiced mercantile banking as it existed before the Civil War. The profits of the firm came from dealing in "domestic exchange," that is, banknotes from various parts of the country that the firm discounted according to risk. The nation in those days had no official government currency except metallic money, so the paper medium of daily exchange was provided by private bankers. With the banknotes of so many banks in circulation, the banker had to judge shrewdly the worth of the paper that purported to be "good as gold." The firm also loaned money for short periods of time to Philadelphia merchants and engaged in the commodity trade. As he prospered at E. W. Clark and Co. in the 1850's, Cooke began to invest his own money in a number of outside ventures. These included a daring land speculation in Iowa and Minnesota that originated as a project to give work to his bankrupt brother Pitt. Cooke sent Pitt west to the Iowa prairies to obtain land from the government at prices below $1.25 an acre, with careful guidance about how to resell it to incoming farmers at three and four dollars an acre. The speculation made so much money that Pitt paid his debts and Cooke became even more wealthy. Growing restless as a junior partner at E. W. Clark and Co., he left the firm in 1857 and devoted his attention to private investing, particularly in railroads, for the next few years. He decided to reenter the banking business on the eve of the American Civil War and opened Jay Cooke and Co. on January 1, 1861.

Life's Work

Abraham Lincoln took office to find the Treasury nearly empty, and with the firing on Fort Sumter, he faced a greater challenge in raising money than in raising volunteers. Wars are expensive to fight, and governments can finance them either by taxation, borrowing, or printing paper money. The rebel government in Richmond chose the last option and, by the end of the war, had an inflation rate of five thousand percent. The Union government of Lincoln chose to borrow to pay for the war, a better strategy, but one that worked only because of the efforts of Jay Cooke.

The traditional method of government finance was to offer government bonds at competitive auction to private bankers. This practice worked well enough in peacetime, but in 1861, many bankers were unsure whether the Union would survive to pay the debt. Secretary of the Treasury, Salmon P. Chase, insisted on selling the bonds at par (one

hundred cents on the dollar), but most bankers considered them to be too risky at that price. The Treasury and the nation muddled through 1861, unable to raise enough money but uncertain of any other way of doing business. Cooke, however, had an idea about how to raise hundreds of millions for the war effort. Through his older brother Henry, a Washington journalist, Cooke approached Secretary Chase and offered to be the government's sales agent for government bonds. For a small fee, Cooke promised to sell all the bonds that the government could issue. He based this confident assertion on his earlier experience as the fiscal agent for the State of Pennsylvania in selling a bond issue of three million dollars. He had simply marketed the bonds directly to the public at par, bypassing other investment bankers.

As the war turned against the Union in the summer of 1862, Chase became more receptive to Cooke's idea, if only out of desperation. In October, the secretary appointed Jay Cooke and Co. sole agent to sell fifty million dollars of government bonds at six percent interest. The bonds were due in twenty years, but the government could re-

deem them in five, hence the popular name of the debt was "5-20's." Cooke promised to sell a million dollars a day of 5-20's and took a fee of one half of one percent, on the first ten million dollars worth sold, and three eighths of one percent on the remainder. Cooke faced two challenges in selling the debt. First, he had to build a distribution network of retail sales agents to sell the bonds, and second, he had to convince the public to buy them. In each case, he was spectacularly successful. Cooke appointed twenty-five hundred subagents to sell bonds throughout the Union and by using the telegraph, effectively coordinated the efforts of this sales team. A heavy use of newspaper advertising and handbills worked to convince the public of the patriotic necessity of buying government bonds. Any Northern newspaper of 1863 was likely to carry a prominent ad placed by Cooke urging citizens to buy bonds. The sales campaign began in earnest in February, 1863, and by the end of June, Cooke had marketed more than $175,000,000 in 5-20's. Over the next seven months, until the loan was oversubscribed by late January, 1864, he sold more than $325,000,000. After paying advertising costs, office expenses, and commissions to the subagents, Cooke was left with a commission of perhaps one sixteenth of one percent of the sales. He did not get rich selling the bonds; rather, he earned something even greater, the title Financier of the Union.

The government bond business made Jay Cooke and Co. the best-known banking house in the United States, and this when Cooke was still in his early forties. In 1865, he repeated his earlier coup in helping the government to finance a new issue of bonds, the so-called 7-30's. This loan drive was even more extensive and more successful than the 1863 issue of 5-20's. From January, 1865, through the end of July of that year, Cooke managed to sell more than $800,000,000 worth of new government bonds. The sales force was more than double that of the earlier sale, and for the 7-30's, Cooke even had itinerant salesmen follow the progress of the Union Army in the South to sell the Union public debt to the conquered rebels.

For several years after the war, Jay Cooke and Co. engaged in further government debt financings. By 1869, the government finance business had wound down and opportunities for profit appeared elsewhere. Cooke had some antebellum experience in railroad finance, and it was in this direction that he took his firm in 1869. That year, he agreed to be the banker and agent for the Northern

Pacific Railway Company, a line projected to link Lake Superior with Puget Sound on the Pacific. The nation had just completed one transcontinental railroad in the Union Pacific-Central Pacific, linking Omaha to San Francisco, but the Northern Pacific promised to be the largest construction project in American history. Cooke was attracted to the Northern Pacific for a number of reasons. He had speculated in Minnesota lands in the 1850's and believed in the future of the Northwest. He renewed his land speculation near the tiny settlement of Duluth in 1866, and when he visited the place in 1868, he saw it as the next Chicago, a mighty future metropolis handling the produce of the American West. Early in 1869, Cooke sold bonds for the Lake Superior and Mississippi Railroad, linking Duluth to St. Paul, and the success of that venture convinced the investor to take on the Northern Pacific's tasks of raising capital to build the two-thousand-mile railroad.

The original financing plan intended for the Northern Pacific to build westward in anticipation of the traffic along the line. This, together with land sales from its magnificent fifty-million acre land grant from Congress, would finance further construction, operations, and debt service. This plan proved too optimistic, since there was almost no white settlement along the route. Cooke managed to raise five million dollars for construction in 1870, but only with great difficulty. His efforts to interest European bankers and investors failed, as they thought the Northern Pacific too risky.

In 1871, Cooke began a public campaign to sell $100,000,000 in Northern Pacific bonds at 7.3 percent interest, the goal of the drive being to raise enough money from small investors to complete the road. Cooke used the same techniques he had learned in selling government bonds during the war: a nationwide network of subagents and hundreds of thousands of dollars spent on advertising. Indeed, Cooke made the Northern Pacific bond-selling slogan, "Safe! Profitable! Permanent!" ubiquitous in the country in 1871 and 1872. The results, however, were disappointing. Cooke only sold about sixteen million dollars worth of bonds in 1871 and 1872. The investing public judged the Northern Pacific too risky an enterprise, despite the high interest rate offered and the reputation for reliability that Cooke brought as the railroad's banker.

Gradually, Cooke crossed the line between banker and promoter of the Northern Pacific. The railroad repeatedly overdrew its account with Cooke's

bank and showed signs of mismanagement. The road's problem was that in its first few years, it had substantial expenses and little revenue. The Cooke banking houses in Philadelphia, New York, Washington, and London became overextended in Northern Pacific affairs by 1872, and when a tightening of the money market in 1873 pressed banks in general, Jay Cooke and Co. was forced to close its doors: It no longer had sufficient reserves to pay the demands of its depositors. The shock of the failure of the leading private bank in the United States caused a panic on Wall Street and ushered in the worst business recession Americans had experienced to that date.

Cooke declared bankruptcy in 1873, and lost most of the multimillion dollar fortune he had accumulated. He spent the next several years satisfying his creditors and by 1880, he resumed business as an investor in Western mining ventures. He made a second fortune before his death but preferred to live a quiet life as an old man devoted to family and church. He died in Ogontz, Pennsylvania, in 1905.

Summary

Jay Cooke performed three great services in his adult life as a banker. First, he earned the title Financier of the Union because he came to the rescue of an empty Treasury at a critical time in the Civil War. Had Cooke not successfully sold the 5-20's to the public in 1863, the Treasury would have probably had to resort to extensive printing of paper money, much as the Confederates did. The result would have been ruinous inflation and perhaps a different outcome to the war.

Second, even though Cooke failed in his endeavor to make the Northern Pacific a money-maker in the early 1870's, he did succeed in getting the road launched, and his vision of the Northwest as a great grain-, timber-, and coal-producing region of free and prosperous Americans did come true. Despite his 1873 bankruptcy, Cooke lived long enough to see his idea of the Northwest emerge as emigrants from eastern America and immigrants from Europe poured into the region. While Duluth never became the next Chicago, it developed into the greatest inland grain, coal, and iron port in North America, and the citizens of that city gratefully remembered Jay Cooke's part in their rise.

Third, Cooke helped change the nature of investment banking. Prior to his financing the Civil War debt, private banking consisted of discounting notes and short-term loans from bankers to merchants. The savings of average Americans were not tapped in any way except through a handful of small savings-and-loan associations. Cooke changed that by reaching out to hundreds of thousands of Americans in the war and appealing for their small holdings to support the cause. In the century following, Wall Street would devote increasing amounts of time and effort to attracting the savings of the individual investor. Without Cooke's innovation, the great financial undertakings of the day could not have taken place. Without the savings of millions of people, the government debt and the great industrial projects, such as the railroads, could not have been funded.

Bibliography

Cooke, Jay et al. "Guide to the Lands of the Northern Pacific Railroad in Minnesota." In *The Fruits of Land Speculation*, edited by Paul Wallace Gates. New York: Arno Press, 1979. This pamphlet amply demonstrates Cooke's talent as a promoter. It explains the route of the Northern Pacific and the advantages of moving to the country west of Duluth.

Hammond, Bray. *Sovereignty and an Empty Purse: Banks and Politics in the Civil War*. Princeton, N.J.: Princeton University Press, 1970. This book examines how the Treasury found itself in desperate condition in 1861, and how it mobilized itself to raise the necessary funds to prosecute the war. The author treats at length Cooke's relationship to the Treasury.

Larson, Henrietta M. *Jay Cooke: Private Banker*. Cambridge, Mass.: Harvard University Press, 1936. This is the standard biography of Cooke, concentrating on his banking career from the 1840's through the 1873 failure. Among biographies of businessmen, this is one of the most outstanding.

Minnigerode, Meade. *Certain Rich Men*. New York and London: Putnam, 1927. This book consists of biographies of wealthy Americans of the late nineteenth century. The contrast between Cooke and some of his less scrupulous colleagues is noteworthy.

Oberholtzer, Ellis Paxton. *Jay Cooke: Financier of the Civil War*. Philadelphia: Jacobs, 1907. Oberholtzer was the first to make use of the magnificent Jay Cooke Papers manuscript collection at the Historical Society of Pennsylvania. There is considerable emphasis on the private side of Cooke's life.

Trescott, Paul B. *Financing American Enterprise: The Story of Commercial Banking*. New York: Harper, 1963. This book has a good chapter on American railroad finance and puts the Northern Pacific episode in perspective.

James W. Oberly

WILLIAM FOTHERGILL COOKE AND CHARLES WHEATSTONE

William Fothergill Cooke

Born: May 4, 1806; Ealing, Middlesex, England
Died: June 25, 1879; Fearnham, Surrey, England
Area of Achievement: Telegraphy

Contribution: From the joining of Cooke's entrepreneurial skills and Wheatstone's scientific knowledge came the world's first commercial telegraph network.

Charles Wheatstone

Born: February, 1802; Gloucester, England
Died: October 19, 1875; Paris, France
Areas of Achievement: Telegraphy, electrical engineering, and physics

Contribution: In addition to his pioneering telegraph work with Cooke, Wheatstone made valuable contributions to later developments in telegraph as well as dynamo technology, electrical engineering, and the physics of sound, light, and electricity.

Early Lives

William Fothergill Cooke was born May 4, 1806, near Ealing, Middlesex, England. His father, Dr. William Cooke, was a surgeon, then professor of anatomy at Durham College (later Durham University). After the customary classical studies at Durham, Cooke attended the University of Edinburgh, renowned for its medical school. The young man seemed destined to enter his father's profession, while his brother, the Reverend Thomas Fothergill Cooke of the Church of England, chose the cloth. At the age of twenty, though, Cooke quit his studies and entered the army of India as an ensign (January 8, 1826). Yet army life, particularly in mutinous India, was capable of providing ample firsthand anatomical experience.

In 1836, after ten years of service, Cooke resigned his commission, hoping to return to medical studies in the classroom. He attended lectures on anatomy and physiology in Paris and learned to model anatomical sections in wax. He was rather skilled at wax modeling and prepared a number of models for his father's anatomy classes. Late in 1836, Cooke attended some lectures at the Anatomical Institute of Heidelberg, where he saw Professor Georg Wilhelm Muncke demonstrate an electric telegraph. Muncke had published numerous articles on electricity and had received the telegraph from another German scientist.

Excited by the idea of commercializing Muncke's demonstration apparatus, Cooke built a telegraph of his own during the next month, partly at Heidelberg and partly at Frankfurt. Upon returning to England,

he obtained a conditional arrangement with the Liverpool and Manchester Railway Company to test his device in Liverpool's Lime Street tunnel. In early 1837, Cooke showed his telegraph to Dr. Peter Mark Roget, credited with discovering the persistence of vision, and Michael Faraday, perhaps the greatest English scientist of his day and the author of an important extended study of electrical phenomena. Upon their recommendation, he visited Professor Wheatstone.

Charles Wheatstone was born February, 1802, in Gloucester, England, the son of William Wheatstone, who made a living making and selling musical instruments. Charles was educated in a private school in Gloucester and early showed an aptitude for physics and mathematics. His family was of more modest means than that of Cooke, and Wheatstone had to learn a trade and earn a living. After an apprenticeship at an uncle's music shop, Wheatstone and his brother William began making and selling musical instruments in London in 1821.

Wheatstone was enthusiastic about the wave theory of light and believed that a wave model would also explain acoustical phenomena. While helping to run the music shop, he began experimenting in acoustics and cleverly combined his scientific interests with the commercial need to advertise the shop. Wheatstone exhibited his first invention, which he called an "enchanted lyre," at the music shop to attract public attention and business. He also wrote a paper that explained how the instrument worked and that used his wave theory of sound. The paper appeared in an English scientific

Charles Wheatstone

journal in 1823 and was soon translated and republished in French and German. Wheatstone's scientific career had begun.

The ability to combine the scientific and the practical marked that career. For example, over the following decades, as he continued his work on acoustics, Wheatstone published several scientific articles and reaped practical financial reward from those studies with his invention of the concertina, which he patented in 1829. In 1834, in recognition of his important scientific work, he became professor of experimental physics at King's College, London. Wheatstone had become part of the London scientific establishment.

His scientific curiosity and interest in wave explanations of phenomena drew him deeper into the physics of light and electricity and into closer relationships with the prominent scientists of the day. On one occasion, he built an instrument for Faraday to measure the velocity of electricity. Wheatstone attempted to measure the velocity of light with it. As electricity fascinated him more and more, he began to wonder whether electricity could be used as a means of communication.

Wheatstone obtained permission from the London and Birmingham Railway to conduct an experiment with an electric telegraph along their tracks. In a note appended to an account of a German telegraph, published in the *Magazine of Popular Science* on March 1, 1837, the editor mentioned that Wheatstone, the previous June, had given a lecture at King's College in which he proposed using the instrument he had built for Faraday as a kind of electric telegraph. At that point, William Cooke introduced himself to Wheatstone.

Lives' Work

The two men tested Cooke's telegraph in Wheatstone's laboratory over a wire some four and a half miles long: It failed. Instead of a signaling mechanism using electromagnets, Cooke suggested galvanometers, instruments which measured current by the deflection of a needle. That, however, had been Wheatstone's idea. The two men realized that each had something to contribute and decided on a partnership. In May, 1837, they jointly applied for a patent for a galvanometer, or, as it was called, a needle telegraph. The patent was granted on June 10, 1837, but only in November, 1837, did they formalize their partnership with an agreement. Cooke became their business manager, for which he received a certain percentage of the profits, and the remainder was to be divided equally between the two.

The first Cooke-Wheatstone telegraph began operating on July 25, 1837, between Euston Square (the terminus of the London and Birmingham railway) and Camden on a railroad line built on an inclined plane. The instruments required five needles and five line wires to transmit and receive, although the deflections of only two needles were required to form signals. As a result, for every mile of line, five miles of wire had to be strung.

Wheatstone largely returned to his scientific work. In 1837, he began publishing his "Contributions to the Physiology of Vision" and invented the stereoscope in 1838, which he described at a meeting of the British Association for the Advancement of Science. Meanwhile, Cooke sought to commercialize the Cooke-Wheatstone telegraph. In April, 1838, he signed an agreement with the Great Western Railway for a line between Paddington and West Drayton (completed on July 9, 1839). Full of confidence in the newly founded telegraph business, Cooke was married to Louisa Wheatley on June 5, 1838. Cooke's mother disapproved of the marriage, and Cooke received very few letters from her afterward.

In early 1840, Cooke sold another line, this time to the London and Blackwall Railway (completed July, 1840). As telegraph sales increased, Cooke and Wheatstone sought to simplify their system, especially the number of line wires required. On the Blackwall line in 1841, Cooke and Wheatstone initiated the use of the earth return in their telegraph circuits, a practice invented by the Alsatian scientist Carl Auguste Steinheil. The earth return saved wire by having current pass through the ground. In 1842, they patented a version of their telegraph that had only two indicating needles and required a single line wire. An 1845 version operated with one needle that was deflected to the right or left. The Cooke-Wheatstone needle instruments were a great success; in 1885, there were about fifteen thousand in use in Great Britain.

As one railroad company after another bought a telegraph line, Cooke sought to expand the market for them. In 1842, he advertised in the *Railway Times* and invited engineers and "other parties" to look at their telegraph "adapted for mines, coal pits, docks, &c." One 1842 announcement even claimed the patronage of the queen and Prince Albert. Moreover, for one shilling, the public could see the telegraph function at either Paddington or Slough station. On September 1, 1846, the South Eastern Railway Company, which then had a telegraph line 132 miles long—the longest in the world at the time—permitted messages of twenty words to be sent for one and a half pence per mile with a five-shilling minimum charge. Despite the great expense, the era of public use of the telegraph had begun.

In 1845, Cooke and Wheatstone sold their telegraph business to the newly founded Electric Telegraph Company, whose head was John Lewis Ricardo, a Member of Parliament and the nephew of the famed political economist David Ricardo. Cooke was one of the four other company directors. After obtaining an act of Parliament in 1846, the company greatly expanded the number of lines and, by 1847, had built twenty lines covering 1,250 miles and connecting 253 stations with nearly four hundred instruments. An 1849 contract with the Post Office to run telegraph lines from the General Post Office to most of the large towns in England and Scotland further ensured the company's future. Messages of twenty words or less on these lines went for one pence the first fifty miles. In 1849, the company transmitted the first message directly between London and Manchester.

In contrast with the enormous success of the telegraph, relations between Cooke and Wheatstone were hardly friendly. Cooke wanted commercial success, as well as at least a part of the scientific glory. He objected to being seen as merely Wheatstone's sleeping partner. Their relationship became especially strained in 1840. The telegraph appeared bound for success, and Wheatstone, independent of Cooke, invented a large number of new instruments: a so-called dial telegraph, which received messages by pointing to letters arranged along the edge of a dial; a printing telegraph, which printed messages in alphabetical characters on a strip of paper; a magnetoelectric telegraph, which required no batteries; an electric clock; and a "chronoscope," an instrument for measuring durations of small intervals of time (one seventy-three thousandth of a second).

These inventions heaped press attention on Wheatstone as an inventor, without placing Cooke in the limelight. Angry letters were sent back and forth between Cooke and Wheatstone. Overtaken by jealousy, Cooke demanded, and Wheatstone insisted upon, arbitration of the question "Who invented the telegraph?" The arbitrators were Marc Isambard Brunel, engineer, acting for Cooke, and John Frederick Daniell, Professor of Chemistry at King's College, Wheatstone's colleague and friend. On April 27, 1841, they made their decision: Cooke had played the role of the entrepreneur and Wheatstone that of the scientist, leaving unanswered any question about the invention of the telegraph.

Cooke's discontent was not Wheatstone's only problem. On November 26, 1840, he read a paper before the Royal Society of London describing his electric clock. Alexander Bain, a mechanic employed by Wheatstone between August and December, 1840, accused Wheatstone of having stolen from him the idea of the electric clock and, in a later series of allegations, the printing telegraph as well. Wheatstone's electric clock, however, was an adaptation of his magnetoelectric telegraph, patented before Bain's tenure with Wheatstone.

After Cooke assumed his position on the board of the Electric Telegraph Company in 1845, telegraph business continued to consume his time and energy, and he stopped filing for telegraph patents. During the 1850's, Cooke's jealousy resurfaced and spilled out into a pamphlet war with Wheatstone. In 1865, emotionally and financially spent, he moved to the country, purchased a quarry, and obtained the first of several patents for inventions relating to stone mining. When Cooke was knighted in 1869, he was in such financial straits that he had to depend upon money raised by relatives and a Civil List pension.

In contrast, Wheatstone prospered. An April, 1843, agreement between Cooke and Wheatstone had paved the way for selling their joint patents to the Electric Telegraph Company, but also reserved solely to Wheatstone the rights to underwater and private telegraphy. Private telegraph lines were owned or leased by individuals or companies and usually connected distant offices or offices and warehouses. Created in 1860, the Universal Private Telegraph Company used Wheatstone's dial instrument and was worth more than £180,000 when purchased by the Post Office.

Wheatstone had planned a telegraph line across the English Channel to France as early as 1840 and played a role in the laying of the Atlantic telegraph cable. In 1859, the Board of Trade selected him as a committeeman to investigate underwater cables, and in 1864 he was a member of the scientific committee appointed to advise the Atlantic Telegraph Company as to the manufacture, laying, and working of the 1865 and 1866 cables.

In 1868, Wheatstone invented a form of automatic telegraph that used patterns of holes punched in paper tape to transmit. The Wheatstone automatic operated at a rate higher than most instruments then used in Great Britain or elsewhere and therefore saved money. It was particularly helpful on high traffic lines such as those carrying press reports. When the Post Office took over all domestic telegraphs starting in 1869-1870, it sought ways to bring down operating costs. Though only four circuits had been using the Wheatstone automatic in 1870, two years later fifteen additional lines were using it. When Wheatstone died in 1875, there were 140 automatics in use in Great Britain alone. Although Wheatstone had received twelve thousand pounds for his automatic patent in 1870, it was so useful that the government agreed, in 1872, to pay an additional nine thousand pounds in six annual installments.

In addition to his numerous telegraph inventions and research into optics, acoustics, and electricity, Wheatstone contributed in no little way to the invention of the dynamo. His lasting fame among electrical engineers rests upon a portion of a speech that he delivered in 1843 before the Royal Society of London, of which he became a member in 1836. The paper described various methods for determining electrical voltage, amperage, and resistance. His means for determining an unknown resistance has since become known as the Wheatstone bridge method and continues to be a standard practice in electrical engineering.

Summary

After some early attempts with semaphore, the electric telegraph provided the Industrial Revolution with its communications revolution. Neither Cooke nor Wheatstone invented the electromagnetic telegraph. More important, however, they turned it into a practical technology and, of equal importance, were the first to understand and exploit the telegraph's commercial value. Consequently, and despite the bitterness and anger that marked the eight years (1837-1845) of their collaboration, Cooke and Wheatstone laid the foundation for the establishment of Great Britain's and the world's first telecommunications network.

Significantly, their major customers were railroad companies. As long as trains ran on a single set of rails, they would have to travel slowly so as not to collide. Canals would remain the major commercial transport. The Cooke-Wheatstone telegraph allowed trains to signal one another, thereby lessening the likelihood of accidents and providing a means for sending assistance to the scene of an accident in a timely fashion. This marriage of rail and telegraph meant that trains could move goods faster and safer, resulting in larger profits for the railroad companies. This marriage also furnished the means for tying local producers and consumers together into regional economic units and, eventually, into national markets by the end of the nineteenth century.

Bibliography

Clark, Latimer. "Sir William Fothergill Cooke." *Journal of the Society of Telegraph Engineers* 8 (1879): 361-397. Detailed, though incomplete, accounting of the early years of the Cooke-Wheatstone partnership. While it favors Cooke and the materials published in the 1850's, it also draws upon family material that is no longer available.

Cooke, William Fothergill. *The Electric Telegraph: Was It Invented by Professor Wheatstone?* 2 vols. London: Smith, 1857. This two-volume work contains Cooke's 1854 pamphlet of the same title (which sets forth his claim to being the true inventor of the telegraph while attacking Wheatstone for falsely making the same claim for himself); Wheatstone's reply of 1855; and Cooke's response to Wheatstone's counterattack (published separately in 1856). The second half is of more historical interest and is a reproduction of the 1841 arbitration papers and drawings.

————. *Extracts from the Private Letters of the Late Sir William Fothergill Cooke, 1836-1839, Relating to the Invention and Development of the Electric Telegraph.* Edited by F. H. Webb. London and New York: Spon, 1895. This collection is for those who cannot see the letters at London's Institution of Electrical Engineers, although the selections have been made to cast Cooke in a favorable light.

————. *Telegraphic Railways.* London: Simpkin, Marshall, 1842. Sets forth Cooke's notions about the value of the telegraph for railroads: safety, economy, and efficiency. Contains the idea of using telegraph for what has become known as the block system of railroad signaling.

Hubbard, Geoffrey. *Cooke and Wheatstone and the Invention of the Electric Telegraph.* London: Routledge, 1965; New York: Kelley, 1968. A careful attempt to determine what Cooke and Wheatstone accomplished during their eight-year partnership. Based upon the manuscript letters of Cooke in the collections of the Institution of Electrical Engineers and the manuscript papers of Wheatstone at King's College, London. In the light of the lack of any historically respectable accounting of the early history of the telegraph, this book is a must.

Jeans, William T. *Lives of the Electricians.* London: Whittaker, 1887. Pages 105-230 are an account of Wheatstone's various accomplishments that heavily favors the scientist over Cooke.

Kemp, Martin. "Wheatstone's Waves: The Nineteenth-Century Creative Genius Sir Charles Wheatstone Invented a Wave Machine and Other 'Philosophical Toys' that Had a Serious Purpose in Demonstrating the Laws of Physics." *Nature* 394, no. 6691 (July 23, 1998). Discusses Wheatstone's wave machine, invented in the early 1840's, and his Phonic Kaleidoscope.

Wheatstone, Charles. *A Reply to Mr. Cooke's Pamphlet.* London: Taylor and Francis, 1855. Wheatstone's point-by-point rebuttal of Cooke's pamphlet.

————. *The Scientific Papers of Sir Charles Wheatstone.* London: Taylor and Francis, 1879. Available in microprint in the Landmarks of Science series. New York: Readex Microprint, 1973. Contains virtually all of Wheatstone's published scientific works.

Whitaker, Robert J. "The Wheatstone Kaleidophone." *American Journal of Physics* 61, no. 8 (August, 1993). Discusses Wheatstone's kaleidophone and the related apparatus for curve tracing.

Andrew J. Butrica

JAMES FENIMORE COOPER

Born: September 15, 1789; Burlington, New Jersey

Died: September 14, 1851; Cooperstown, New York

Area of Achievement: Literature

Contribution: Cooper pioneered the historical novel based on American themes and characters. He also wrote the first sea novel. In his fiction and nonfiction, he proved himself an astute social critic of the excesses of democracy.

Early Life

The eleventh child of William Cooper and Elizabeth Fenimore Cooper, James Cooper—he was to add the Fenimore in 1826—was born in Burlington, New Jersey, on September 15, 1789. When Cooper was thirteen months old, the family left the urban Burlington for the wilderness at the southern shore of Ostego Lake. Here William Cooper built Ostego Hall and developed the surrounding area as Cooperstown. This frontier village would serve as the model of Templeton in *The Pioneers* (1823), as the novelist's father would become the aristocratic Judge Temple in that novel and Ostego Lake turn into Lake Glimmerglass. By the time the Coopers settled in New York, the Indians had departed; Cooper's Indians derive from books, not personal knowledge. The wilderness remained, though, and figured prominently in many of his novels.

Cooperstown soon established a local academy, which Cooper attended before going to Albany to study under the Reverend William Ellison. In 1803, Cooper entered Yale. At the age of thirteen, he was more interested in pranks than studies. After blowing up a classmate's door with gunpowder, Cooper was expelled.

The following year, he was sent to sea aboard the *Stirling*, where he encountered a series of adventures he would later use in his nautical novels. Off the coast of Portugal, the ship was pursued by pirates. Entering British waters, they found themselves no safer. With the Napoleonic Wars raging, Britain was impressing American seamen into its navy; the *Stirling* was boarded and several sailors removed.

Cooper returned safely to the United States, where he was eligible for a commission as midshipman in the navy. His first assignment was to a ship in dry dock in New York; his second was to a ship still under construction on Lake Ontario. Eager to see active service in open water, he maneuvered to secure a berth aboard the *Wasp*, an eighteen-gun sloop. Again, though, he was disappointed, for the commanding officer was so impressed with the midshipman that he made him his recruiting officer, a post that required Cooper to remain onshore. Despite this series of disappointments, Cooper had learned much about ships, and this knowledge found its way into both his fiction and his nonfiction.

In December, 1809, Cooper's father died; in May, 1810, Cooper therefore requested a twelve-month furlough to attend to family business. This business included wooing Susan Augusta DeLancey, daughter of a country squire. On January 1, 1811, the two were married.

Cooper had promised Susan that he would surrender his commission in the navy, so he turned his attention to earning a living as a gentleman farmer and speculator. Between 1813 and 1819, his six siblings died, making him heir to his father's extensive land holdings but also leaving him responsible for his brothers' dependents and debts. As he struggled with these various financial difficulties, a happy accident changed the course of his life and of American letters as well.

Life's Work

In 1820, the Coopers were living in Scarsdale. Among the popular recreations of the family was reading aloud. One day, Cooper began Jane Austen's *Persuasion* (1818). After a few pages, Cooper threw the book down in disgust and announced, "I could write you a better book than that myself." Since Cooper disliked any writing, even letters, his wife expressed her incredulity and challenged him to make good his boast. The result was *Precaution* (1820).

In itself, this first book is not noteworthy, for the work is a novel of manners typical of female British writers of the period. *Precaution* is important, though, because it launched Cooper's literary career. He next turned his attention to an American theme, though he found the writing difficult. As he wrote to Andrew Thompson Goodrich, "The task of making American manners and American scenes interesting to an American reader is an arduous one—I am unable to say whether I shall succeed or not." The popular response to *The Spy*

(1821) resolved any doubts. The book quickly went through three editions and was adapted for the New York stage; a French translation appeared within a year. Critical appraisals were equally favorable: The *North American Review* called Cooper "the first who deserved the appellation of a distinguished American novel writer."

The novel was based on the actual life of a spy who served under John Jay during the American Revolution. Harvey Birch's wanderings between the British and American lines in Westchester County allowed Cooper to depict the landscape and manners of New York. The book is American in more than setting, though. Unlike the heroes of British fiction, Birch is an outsider, who, despite heroism and integrity, is never integrated into society.

With his next novel, *The Pioneers*, Cooper struck an even more responsive chord. The book sold some three thousand copies on the day of publication and introduced a character as enduring as Robinson Crusoe. Natty Bumppo, the pioneer, is a mythic figure whose image was to descend through the dime novels of Erastus F. Beadle to the Lone Ranger (whose companionship with Tonto mirrors Bumppo's relationship with the Indian Chingachgook) and similar television and film heroes. In this self-reliant frontiersman, Cooper produced an archetypal American and a microcosm of the nation moving ever westward.

The Pioneers was the first of five novels collectively known as the Leatherstocking Tales, which together trace Bumppo's life from his youth (*The Deerslayer*, 1841) in the 1740's to his death on the Great Plains in 1804 (*The Prairie*, 1827). Not only did Cooper create the mythic pioneer in these works but also he painted a mythic frontier that was to reappear in the histories of Francis Parkman and Frederick Jackson Turner. This frontier is majestic and overwhelming. Armies enter the wilderness to emerge as tattered remnants. The small forts are dwarfed by their harsh, rugged surroundings.

In this setting, Cooper plays out the conflict between savage Indians and the forces of white civilization. Cooper's novels thus serve as an apology for the displacement of the American Indians, many of whom, like the Iroquois and Sioux, are portrayed as too evil to deserve survival. Not all of Cooper's Indians are bad; he incorporates the myth of the noble savage into his descriptions of the Delaware and the Pawnee tribes. These good Indians, though, are doomed by their very virtues, which render them easy prey to less scrupulous members of both the white and red races. Further, despite their nobility, they remain savage.

Though Cooper's frontier novels justify the conquest of the West, they also recognize the tragic consequences. The Indians are displaced, but so are the pioneers. Natty Bumppo's life is a series of migrations westward, because he brings a civilization that cannot tolerate his ways. Nor is Cooper unaware of the beauty of this wilderness vanishing beneath the ax of civilization. When Judith Hunter in *The Deerslayer* asks Bumppo where his love is, he replies,

> She's in the forest, Judith—hanging from the boughs of the trees, in a soft rain—in the dew on the open grass . . . and in all the other glorious gifts that come from God's Providence.

Cooper's next novel also broke new ground. At a dinner party in New York City, Cooper's companions of the Bread and Cheese Club were praising Sir Walter Scott's *The Pirate* (1822) for its realism. Scott, unlike Cooper, had never been to sea; Cooper quickly demonstrated numerous flaws in the work. When challenged to do better, Cooper responded with *The Pilot* (1824). Though Cooper is best remembered as a writer of the frontier, he was to produce eleven nautical novels, all replete with precise detail; later writers of the sea, among them Herman Melville and Joseph Conrad, praised Cooper's efforts in this area. Set, like *The Spy*, during the American Revolution, *The Pilot* was also successful.

Cooper's popularity led to his appointment to the committee that welcomed the Marquis de Lafayette when he returned to the United States in 1824. In that year, too, Columbia University recognized his achievements by awarding him an honorary master of arts degree.

The Last of the Mohicans (1826), another of the Leatherstocking Tales, further enhanced his reputation. In 1826, on the eve of his departure for Europe, Cooper was feted by the Bread and Cheese Club. Among those present were De Witt Clinton, governor of New York; General Winfield Scott; Charles King, later to be president of Columbia University; and James Kent, former chancellor and chief justice of New York. In one toast, King placed Cooper on the same level as Sir Walter Scott; in another, Kent called Cooper "the genius which has rendered our native soil classic ground, and given to our early history the enchantment of fiction."

Cooper went to Europe nominally as American consul to Lyon, but his real intent was to see Europe and to arrange for the publication of his novels abroad. While in Europe, Cooper was urged by Lafayette to dispel certain misconceptions about the United States. The result was *Notions of the Americans* (1828), a glowing account of his native land. At Lafayette's prompting, he also involved himself in a pamphlet war between French monarchists and republicans.

Despite his defense of democracy, Cooper's reputation was declining in the United States. He was criticized for intervening in the political affairs of France, and his European novels—*The Bravo* (1831), *The Heidenmauer* (1832), and *The Headsman* (1833)—were not well received back home. By the time he returned to the United States on November 5, 1833, he was no longer the hero he had been seven years earlier. Nor was he pleased with what he regarded as the excesses of democracy that had accompanied the presidency of Andrew Jackson. In *A Letter to His Countrymen* (1834), Cooper began a series of criticisms of the United States, and he announced his retirement as a novelist.

He was to return to fiction in 1838, but he was not idle during the intervening years, publishing a series of travel books and a social satire on both England and the United States, *The Monikins* (1835). In his European novels, Cooper had warned his countrymen to beware of oligarchies and not to sacrifice their freedoms to powerful commercial interests. Now that he was home, he saw greater danger to the Republic from the lower, rather than the upper, classes. *The American Democrat* (1838) offers Cooper's clearest vision of the United States, where "acts of tyranny can only proceed from the publick. The publick, then, is to be watched in this country, as, in other countries, kings and aristocrats are to be watched." He still believed in democracy as the best form of government, but his ideal democracy was Jeffersonian, not Jacksonian. Merit should have the chance to succeed regardless of pedigree, but the natural aristocrat should govern. While people should enjoy equality under the law, social distinctions should remain.

The American Democrat aroused little controversy, but the two novels issued that year to incorporate its ideas received harsh treatment: *Homeward Bound* and *Home as Found* were sharply attacked in the press. Cooper's aristocratic appearance did not help his popularity, either. In Mathew Brady's photograph he looks like a stern autocrat, with high forehead, penetrating gaze, Roman nose, and firm chin.

As the new decade began, Cooper briefly regained his popularity when he produced the last two of the Leatherstocking Tales, *The Pathfinder* (1840) and *The Deerslayer*. His next two novels, *The Two Admirals* (1842) and *The Wing-and-Wing* (1842), also mark a return to his earliest writing, in this case the sea adventure.

He could not keep away from controversy for very long, though. In 1839, the Antirent War began in New York, as tenants insisted on owning their land instead of renting it. Cooper's sympathies were with the landowners, and the Littlepage novels—*Satanstoe* (1845), *The Chainbearer* (1845), and *The Redskins* (1846)—justify their position. Cooper was as disgusted with the politicians as with the tenants, and in his preface to *The Redskins*, he wrote that if the government could not curb the antirent faction, the sooner that government was abolished, the better.

Cooper's next novel, *The Crater* (1847), allowed him to achieve that wish, at least in fiction. An island arises in the South Pacific, and at first its government is a perfect Jeffersonian democracy. With the arrival of lawyers, journalists, and Fundamentalist preachers—all of whom Cooper regarded as the bane of American life—this ideal is corrupted. As if in divine retribution, the island then sinks back into the ocean.

Despite Cooper's long-standing feud with his countrymen, after his death at Cooperstown on September 14, 1851, Washington Irving arranged a memorial tribute for him in New York City. William Cullen Bryant delivered the eulogy, Daniel Webster attended, and leading literary figures sent tributes. Whatever the editorialists and general public thought of him, these men recognized the great contribution that Cooper had made to American letters.

Summary

In *Notions of the Americans*, Cooper complained that the United States did not offer material for a national literature. In his thirty-two novels, though, Cooper gave the lie to this statement. He proved that the United States did offer the fabric for the romancer and dramatist to create a truly American literature.

Cooper's novels are American not only because of their setting but also because of their characters: pioneers, Indians, slaves, and the hero who is an outsider, shunning and shunned by society. The themes, too, are native; even when they criticize contemporary society they do so from the perspective of the ideals of the Founding Fathers.

Cooper, however, did not simply create American novels; he also created an audience for them. Early in the nineteenth century, Sidney Smith had asked in *The Edinburgh Review*, "Who reads an American book?" He might have asked, too, "Who publishes an American book?" Cooper's own publisher, Carey of Philadelphia, had issued only two American novels before 1820. Between 1830 and 1840, it published 142. Other publishers in this country followed suit, and abroad Cooper's novels were printed in more than thirty cities.

As such works as *The History of the Navy of the United States of America* (1839) demonstrate, Cooper knew history and could present it well. His historical novels are not so much history, though, as myth. They established the prevailing image of the Indian as treacherous foe or doomed noble savage. They created the fiction of the empty wilderness waiting for the white man to settle it and so fueled the imagination of those who sought to fulfill America's manifest destiny to rule from sea to sea. Drawing on the already existing stories about Daniel Boone, Cooper provided in Natty Bumppo the American hero, whom Henry Nash Smith in *Virgin Land* (1957) calls "the most important symbol of the national experience of adventure across the continent."

Quintessentially American, Cooper nevertheless saw the dangers of rampant democracy. His social criticism was not popular, but it established a literary mode that, like his frontier and nautical novels, influenced later writers. William Dean Howells, Frank Norris, and Sinclair Lewis are but three who followed in this mode. Like his most famous creation, then, Cooper was indeed a pathfinder and pioneer.

Bibliography

Boynton, Henry Walcott. *James Fenimore Cooper.* New York: Century, 1931. Focuses on Cooper the man rather than Cooper the writer. Boynton notes Cooper's faults but tends to gloss over them or explain them away.

Franklin, Wayne. *The New World of James Fenimore Cooper.* Chicago: University of Chicago Press, 1982. Through a close reading of five of Cooper's novels—*The Pioneers, The Wept of Wish-ton-Wish* (1829), *Wyandotté* (1843), *The Crater* (1847), and *The Last of the Mohicans*—Franklin examines Cooper's attitude toward the frontier. Maintains that for Cooper, the wilderness begins as a place of hope and promise but ends as the source of tragedy.

McWilliams, John P. *Political Justice in a Republic: James Fenimore Cooper's America.* Berkeley: University of California Press, 1972. Argues that Cooper remained a dedicated republican all of his life. McWilliams shows that while Cooper's views are consistent, American society changed dramatically between 1820 and 1850 and hence produced a darkening vision of the fiction.

Railton, Stephen. *Fenimore Cooper: A Study in His Life and Imagination.* Princeton, N.J.: Princeton University Press, 1978. A psychological approach to Cooper's life. Railton sees Cooper as dominated by his father and reads the life and fiction in the light of an Oedipal complex.

Rosenberg, Bruce A. *The Neutral Ground: The Andre Affair and the Background of Cooper's "The Spy."* Westport, Conn.: Greenwood Press, 1994. Rosenberg argues that the capture and execution of spy John Andre in 1780 served as the basis for Cooper's second novel, *The Spy.*

Rosenwald, Lawrence. "*The Last of the Mohicans* and the Languages of America." *College English* 60, no. 1 (January 1998). The author considers Cooper's portrayal of Native American language in *Last of the Mohicans.*

Spiller, Robert Ernest. *Fenimore Cooper: Critic of His Times.* New York: Balch, 1931. Concentrates on Cooper's social views and sees him as a writer who sought to analyze and express as well as criticize the United States of his day.

Walker, Warren S. *James Fenimore Cooper: An Introduction and Interpretation.* New York: Barnes and Noble, 1962. A biography organized around the various themes in Cooper's writing—the frontier, the sea, American democracy. A concluding chapter reviews critical response to Cooper from 1820 to the middle of the twentieth century.

Waples, Dorothy. *The Whig Myth of James Fenimore Cooper.* New Haven, Conn.: Yale University Press, and London: Oxford University Press, 1938. Claims that many of the attacks on Cooper during his lifetime came from Whigs who distorted his character. Stresses Cooper's political views.

Joseph Rosenblum

GUSTAVE COURBET

Born: June 10, 1819; Ornans, France

Died: December 31, 1877; La Tour-de-Peilz, Switzerland

Area of Achievement: Art

Contribution: Courbet contributed to the formation of modern art by liberating subject matter and style from academic dogma. The most profound aspects of his contribution are the influences his works have had upon the subsequent analysis of realism.

Early Life

Gustave Courbet was born at Ornans, a town in the scenic Loue River valley of Franche-Comté in eastern France. There, his father, Eléonor Régis Stanislaus Courbet, was a prosperous landowner, whose ancestral home was in the neighboring village of Flagey. Gustave's mother, Suzanne Sylvie Oudot, came from a similar economic background of landed proprietors in Ornans. It was in the Ornans home of his grandfather, Jean-Antoine Oudot, a veteran of the French Revolution, that Gustave was born.

Courbet's early life and studies prior to his 1839 arrival in Paris at age twenty had provided him with valuable skills. The young artist's tutelage under Père Beau at Ornans followed his first years of school in 1831 at the *petit seminaire*. It was there that Courbet began to paint from nature. Subsequently, while attending the Collège Royal at Besançon (after autumn, 1837), Maître Flajoulot's emphasis on painting from the live model added another aspect of current artistic training to Courbet's abilities.

During this period, Courbet acquired a deep and lasting appreciation for the cultural heritage and rugged beauty of his native Franche-Comté. This region did not formally become a part of France until 1678 because of a long and complex history of geographical and political factors. The tradition of independence emanating from his native province played an important role in the formation of Courbet's character and notably influenced his attitudes toward formal training and academies.

In Paris, Courbet studied briefly with a minor painter. A greater source of inspiration was discovered at the Louvre, where Courbet diligently copied Dutch, Flemish, Venetian, and Spanish masters. Also significant were the friends he established in Paris: Alexandre Schanne, who became a character

in Henri Murger's *Scènes de la vie de bohème* (1847-1849), the painter François Bonvin, and later, the writers Charles Baudelaire and Champfleury.

The decade of the 1840's proved to be a very important one for Courbet, in which his prodigious talent and originality became recognized. His first salon successes were *Self-Portrait with a Black Dog* (1844) and *The Guitarist* (1845). The artist's handsome features and vigorous physicality are evident in other numerous self-portraits of this period. With *After Dinner at Ornans* (1849), for which he received a gold medal at the Salon of 1849, Courbet had developed an artistic formula for elevating and monumentalizing common subjects that led to his first truly revolutionary works: *The Stonebreakers* (1849) and *The Burial at Ornans* (1849).

Life's Work

The Revolution of 1848 had occurred during the first crucial decade of Courbet's mature formation. Growing discontent with the failure of Louis-Phil-

ippe's government to incorporate democratic reform or acknowledge socialist ideas had led to this uprising which had a direct impact on Courbet's art. Courbet emerged as a pictorial advocate of a new, more democratic aesthetic. *The Stonebreakers*, which appeared at the Salon of 1850-1851, depicted a young boy and an old man laboring side by side to repair a road. Courbet was, in fact, depicting a form of public service (*corvée*) that was customary in rural France; yet the Parisian audience found his large-scale, unidealized figures to be offensive, and even threatening, as they harbored connotations of peasant uprising or violence. Courbet's realist manifesto, *The Burial at Ornans*, also exhibited at the Salon of 1850-1851, recorded a funeral in his native town. Again, Parisians were provoked by a scene which did not depict a known historical event or idealize its characters. Courbet had glorified the idea that the peasantry and rural bourgeoisie were worthy of the serious artistic treatment usually reserved for aristocratic subject matter and concerns. Courbet's works thus threatened established Parisian social and aesthetic values.

Courbet had entered the decade of the 1850's as an artist with strong political associations, which were subsequently incorporated into his total philosophy, as is evident in a statement from the period: "I am not only a socialist, but a democrat and a republican; in short, I am in favor of the whole revolution, and above all I am a realist."

The ability of an artwork to shock its viewers was used by Courbet in major salon submissions from this time onward to draw attention to his name and artistic message. Courbet was thus a subject of great controversy; yet, whether in praise or criticism, there was widespread acknowledgment of the impact of his style. Two works, *Young Ladies of the Village* (1851) and *The Bathers* (1853), demonstrate how Courbet's art had begun to interact with salon criticism. The first painting portrayed his three sisters in a rural setting bestowing a charitable gift upon a young shepherdess. Even Courbet was surprised when the honest depiction was mocked for its ugliness, as he had thought it dignified, even gracious. Courbet decidedly responded in the Salon of 1853 by creating a depiction of woman that was more truly a mockery of the sort his critics espoused. *The Bathers* depicted two very corpulent and egotistical women decadently bathing in the pool of a wooded glade. The very decadence of the women became his prime focus. Thus, a new aspect

of Courbet's works developed, which may be termed the painted caricature.

By the mid-1850's, Courbet had entered into politics of a different kind which formalized his new conception of the artist's role as activist and showman. Partly in reaction to the amount of negative criticism that he inevitably generated, and partly out of his own entrepreneurial desire to make his painting more profitable, he established his own exhibition independent of the combined Salon and World Exhibition of 1855. For this occasion, he conceived of a large canvas, *The Painter's Studio: A Real Allegory of Seven Years of My Artistic Life* (1854-1855), in which Courbet depicts himself in the act of painting. He paints amid two groups, one composed of supportive patrons and the other composed of a puzzling assemblage of diverse characters and types that Courbet claimed to have seen in his travels. This huge work has had numerous interpretations and remains problematic, yet quite clearly it is an essential revelation of Courbet, as he sees himself in the process of creating, which is quite necessarily an act and role that he revolutionized.

Also beginning around 1855, Courbet envisioned a serial approach for his art, thus incorporating past works with future endeavors to create entire cycles of related paintings which would compare and contrast different aspects of society. The idea is said to have come from the novels of Honoré de Balzac; its relevance is exemplified in Courbet's works between the years 1855 and 1866.

In 1861, Courbet began to experience a strange mixture of acclaim and adversity. His *Fighting Stags* (1861) was widely admired, and there was even rumor of an official state purchase and Courbet's decoration with the highest honors. Yet, in the end, he only received a second-class medal—a great affront to an artist who had painted what many considered to be the best work in the salon.

This blow caused Courbet to break forever with the praised and accepted aesthetics of his time, as dictated by the salon. His reaction was deliberately to insult taste and sensibility in his salon submissions of 1863, 1864, and 1868. Yet, in the intervening year 1866, he reversed this trend and awed the critics with a new and fantasy-inspired image, *Woman with a Parrot*. Again, there was rumor of governmental purchase and Courbet's decoration. It did not come and was clearly meant to reprimand Courbet's past condemnation of accepted taste. A final reconciliation with the salon came in 1870, when he submitted two beautiful seascapes painted at Étretat in 1869, *The Stormy Sea* and *Cliffs at Étretat After the Storm*. Finally, the critics were filled with enthusiasm. Courbet had become a popular and briefly unproblematic artist.

Courbet's subsequent nomination for the Legion of Honor in June, 1870, caused a sensation; however, the painter held firm to his socialist principles and declined the award. With the outbreak of the Franco-Prussian War in July, Courbet was elected chairman of the arts commission, responsible for the protection of artworks in and around Paris. The duties of this position ultimately cast political overtones upon Courbet as the leader of a large and active group.

Courbet was transformed into a political scapegoat and held responsible for the destruction of the Vendôme Column. The subsequent trials, imprisonment, and exorbitant fines threatened to ruin Courbet and ultimately forced his exile to Switzerland, where he died four years later, a celebrated, but saddened, artist.

Summary

Throughout his life, Gustave Courbet maintained a spirit of Fourierist political optimism. Though his paintings were often conceived to provoke confrontation, he nevertheless believed that through a liberated artistic manifesto man could ultimately derive a philosophy of social harmony. These ideas had become formalized in Courbet's early maturity and were perpetuated by the artist's relations with his greatest patron, Alfred Bruyas, and with the social philosopher Pierre-Joseph Proudhon. Through their encouragement and support, Courbet was able to assess his role and the nature of his art: "To know in order to be able to create, that was my idea. To be in a position to translate the customs, the ideas, the appearance of my epoch, according to my own estimation; to be not only a painter, but a man as well; in short, to create living art—this is my goal." Courbet had set these ideas down in paint as early as 1849 with *The Burial at Ornans*. That the message of Courbet's art was clear to his contemporaries is demonstrated by the 1851 commentary of Paul Sabatier:

Since the shipwreck of the *Medusa*, . . . nothing as original has been made among us. The clothes, the heads, have a solidity, a variety of tone and a firmness of drawing that is half Venetian, half Spanish; it is close to Zurbarán and to Titian. . . . It was not an easy thing to give dignity . . . to all these modern clothes. . . .

Courbet's late seascapes and somber still lifes are unique pictorial expressions. They represent his most poetic statements, in which the sheer physicality of paint invigorates the expressive power of the work. Courbet's influence on modern art is documented by subsequent generations of avant-garde artists who studied and even collected his works, notably Puvis de Chavannes, Henri Matisse, André Dunoyer de Segonzac, and Pablo Picasso.

Bibliography

Chu, Petra ten Doesschate, ed. *Courbet in Perspective*. Englewood Cliffs, N.J.: Prentice-Hall, 1977. Part of the Artists in Perspective series. Art historical essays from the nineteenth and twentieth centuries. A very useful gathering and translation of important contemporary accounts of Courbet's life and art, including contextual and stylistic essays.

Clark, Timothy J. *Image of the People: Gustave Courbet and the 1848 Revolution*. London: Thames and Hudson, and Princeton, N.J.: Princeton University Press, 1982. The most detailed analysis of Courbet's life and art between 1848 and 1851. Clark's approach, which is both Marxist and structuralist, sheds light on the social and political situations of the Second Republic and the simultaneous developments in Courbet's art—which became strikingly appropriate pictorial representations of these underlying social tensions.

Courbet, Gustave. *Letters of Gustave Courbet*. Ed. and trans. by Petra ten Doesschate Chu. Chicago: University of Chicago Press, 1992. Monumental compilation of all of Courbet's letters (over 600), some of which were previously unpublished and untranslated. Opens a new understanding of Courbet's creativity and place in nineteenth century France.

Faunce, Sarah, and Linda Nochlin. *Courbet Reconsidered*. New Haven, Conn., and London: Yale University Press, 1988. A comprehensive, well-illustrated exhibition catalog composed of six essays and 101 entries. Topics addressed are critical and historical summary of Courbet's oeuvre, reinterpretation of *The Painter's Studio*, gender studies in Courbet, contextual art history, and America's response to Courbet.

Lindsay, Jack. *Gustave Courbet: His Life and Art*. London: Jupiter, and New York: Harper, 1973. A comprehensive biography which incorporates most of the literature available at the time of publication. Includes eighty-nine black-and-white illustrations and an extensive bibliography.

Mack, Gerstle. *Gustave Courbet.* London: Hart-Davis, and New York: Knopf, 1951. The first monograph in English, which is primarily based on the first substantial French biography and its nineteenth century sources by Georges Riat, *Gustave Courbet peintre* (1906).

Nochlin, Linda. *Gustave Courbet: A Study of Style and Society.* New York: Garland, 1976. A sophisticated analysis of the origins of Courbet's style by one of the foremost authorities on the artist. Select bibliography and 121 black-and-white illustrations.

Przyblyski, Jeannene M. "Courbet, the Commune, and the Meanings of Still Life in 1871." *Art Journal* 55, no. 2 (Summer 1996). Discussion of Courbet's still life, "Still Life: Apples, Pears, and Primroses on a Table," and its depiction of class identity.

Rubin, James Henry. *Realism and Social Vision in Courbet and Proudhon.* Princeton, N.J.: Princeton University Press, 1980. Rubin considers Courbet's art, particularly *The Painter's Studio*, in relation to the theories of Proudhon, a contemporary and acquaintance of Courbet, to compare and contrast the doctrines of both enigmatic figures.

Toussaint, Hélène, et al. *Gustave Courbet, 1819-1877.* London: Arts Council of Great Britain, 1977. The largest retrospective of Courbet's work in the twentieth century. The catalog is a well-illustrated and scholarly monograph, with new interpretive breakthroughs made possible by sophisticated laboratory analysis at the Louvre. Essays include an introduction by Alan Bowness, an authoritative biography by Marie-Thérèse de Forges, and catalog entries and reinterpretive analysis of *The Painter's Studio* by Hélène Toussaint.

Claudette R. Mainzer

STEPHEN CRANE

Born: November 1, 1871; Newark, New Jersey
Died: June 5, 1900; Badenweiler, Germany
Area of Achievement: Literature
Contribution: Crane is best remembered for his war novel, *The Red Badge of Courage* (1895); he also wrote estimable poetry and more than a dozen other novels and collections of stories.

Early Life

Stephen Crane, the youngest son of a youngest son, was the last of fourteen children born to the Reverend Jonathan Townley Crane and his wife, Mary Peck. Crane's father was a presiding elder of the Newark, New Jersey, district of the Methodist Church (1868-1872) when Stephen was born and served in a similar capacity in the Elizabeth, New Jersey, district of the church from 1872 until 1876. Because Methodist clergymen were subject to frequent transfer, the young Stephen was moved from Newark to Paterson, New Jersey, before he was old enough to attend school and to Port Jervis, New York, shortly before he began school. His *The Third Violet* (1897) and *Whilomville Stories* (1900) are set in villages modeled after Port Jervis.

Crane's father died in 1880, when the boy was eight years old, and, in 1883, Stephen and his mother moved to Asbury Park, New Jersey, a seaside resort some sixty miles from New York City, to be near the Methodist camp community of Ocean Grove, a town adjacent to Asbury Park, which Jonathan Crane had been instrumental in establishing. Stephen's brother Townley already ran a press bureau in Asbury Park, and soon their sister Agnes moved there to teach in the public schools.

As Stephen strayed from the religious teachings of the Methodist Church, his mother became concerned about his spiritual welfare, and, in 1885, she sent him to Pennington Seminary, some ten miles from both Trenton and Princeton, in the hope that he would receive a solid academic background and would simultaneously grow closer to the Church. Crane's father had been principal of Pennington Seminary for the decade from 1848 to 1858, and his mother had spent the first ten years of her marriage at Pennington.

Stephen, a handsome, dark-haired youth with a prominent nose, sensuous lips, and deep, dark eyes, rankled under Pennington's strong religious emphasis. In 1888, he enrolled in the Hudson River Institute in Claverack, New York, a coeducational institution with a military emphasis for its male students. It was perhaps during this period that Crane became extremely interested in war.

During the summers, Crane assisted his brother in his news bureau, learning something about journalism as he went about his work. He entered Lafayette College in 1890 to study engineering, but failed in his work there and left after the Christmas holiday to attend Syracuse University, where he played baseball, managed the baseball team, and worked on the school newspaper. He was not a strong student, and he left school in 1891 to seek his fortune in New York City. His mother died on December 7 of that year.

Stephen, who had met and established a friendship with Hamlin Garland in the summer of 1891, tried to make his living as a newspaperman, but he was not initially successful in this work. In 1892, however, the serial publication of seven of his "Sullivan County Sketches" gave him the encouragement he needed to pursue a literary career diligently.

Life's Work

Buoyed up by seeing his work in print, Crane, in 1893, paid for a private printing of *Maggie: A Girl of the Streets* (1893), a book gleaned from his experience of living in New York City's Bowery during the preceding two years. This early work, highly shocking in its time because it views with sympathy a girl who becomes pregnant out of wedlock and shows the hypocrisy of her lower-class family's morality, was first published under the pseudonym Johnston Smith.

Maggie was unabashedly naturalistic, somewhat in the tradition of Émile Zola. Despite William Dean Howells's attempts to get the book distributed, it sold hardly any copies in its original edition. In 1896, however, Crane revised it, cutting out much of its offensive profanity, omitting some of its graphic description, and regularizing the grammar and punctuation. His reputation had by this time been established with the publication, the preceding October, of *The Red Badge of Courage*, a book that grew out of Crane's fascination with war, battles, and men in combat. *Maggie*, although it still was deemed shocking to delicate sensibilities, was more favorably received in 1896 than it had been three years earlier.

The Red Badge of Courage existed in some form in 1894, when it was published abridged in newspapers by the Bacheller Syndicate. *George's Mother* (1896) appeared two years later, and in its use of realistic detail it goes far beyond that of William Dean Howells, who had become Crane's friend.

With the publication of both *The Black Riders and Other Lines* and *The Red Badge of Courage* in 1895, Crane became an overnight celebrity. In March of that year, he also went to Mexico for the first time, and the trip made a substantial impression upon him. With the appearance of *George's Mother, Maggie, The Little Regiment and Other Episodes of the American Civil War* (1896), and *The Third Violet*, it was quite apparent that Crane, still only twenty-five years old, was on the way to becoming one of the leading literary figures in the United States. If readers complained because he wrote about subjects that depressed them, they could not reasonably contend that the conditions about which he wrote did not exist or that he wrote badly about them.

Although Crane was fascinated by war and by 1896 had written much about the subject, he had never known the battlefield, and he was keenly aware of this lack in his experience. Therefore, when the Bacheller Syndicate offered to send him as a correspondent to join the insurgents who were fighting against Spanish rule in Cuba, Crane enthusiastically accepted the assignment. He went first to Jacksonville, Florida, to wait for a ship, the *Commodore*, to be outfitted for the short trip to Cuba. Arriving in Jacksonville in November, he met Cora Stewart, who owned a brothel and nightclub, the Hotel de Dream.

It took until December 31 for the *Commodore* to be ready to sail, and by that time Crane and Stewart, who already had a husband, had fallen in love. Nevertheless, Crane sailed for Cuba as planned. The ship, however, got only several miles down the St. John's River before it ran aground. Crane and some of his shipmates were forced to put to sea in a small, flimsy lifeboat before the *Commodore* capsized with some loss of life.

It was fifty-four hours before Crane and his companions were able to ride the heavy surf to shore at Daytona. One of his companions was drowned as they came to shore. From his frightening experience in the lifeboat, Crane wrote what is probably his best known and most artistically confident short story, "The Open Boat." The shipwreck scuttled, for the time, Crane's plans to go to Cuba. Instead, he and

Stewart sailed for Greece in late March, both of them to report on Greece's war with Turkey.

In mid-1897, Crane and Stewart, who was six years older than he, went to England, where he wrote some of his most memorable short stories, including "The Monster," "Death and the Child," and his much anthologized "The Bride Comes to Yellow Sky." He introduced Cora Stewart as his wife, although the two had never been married because she was not free to do so. It was at this time that Crane met Joseph Conrad and became his close friend.

After Crane's collection *The Open Boat and Other Tales of Adventure* (1898) was published, the author returned to the United States to join the armed forces in the Spanish-American War, which the United States had just entered. He was, however, rejected for military service and instead went to Cuba as a war correspondent for Joseph Pulitzer. He was fearless in combat situations, but his health began to fail. He did some work in Puerto Rico and in Cuba for the Hearst newspapers, but in 1899, the year in which *War Is Kind* (1899), *Active Service* (1899), and *The Monster and Other Stories* (1899) were published, he returned to England, this time to live in the stately Brede Place in Sussex. While celebrating Christmas, Crane had a massive hemorrhage brought on by tuberculosis.

In the spring of 1900, the year in which *Whilomville Stories* and *Wounds in the Rain* were published, Crane's health declined, and in May, he and Cora, accompanied by a retinue consisting of their butler, maids, nurses, and a doctor, went to Badenweiler in Germany's Black Forest, hoping that the climate would benefit the ailing writer's health. There Crane died on June 5. Three of his works, *Great Battles of the World* (1901), *Last Words* (1902), and *The O'Ruddy* (1903), were published shortly after his death.

Summary

Dead at twenty-eight, Stephen Crane had just begun to come into his own as a writer. His early work, particularly the original version of *Maggie*, reflected his passionate interest in reform and his understanding of the problems of the poor, but much of this early book was seriously flawed, largely because Crane had not yet mastered the basic mechanics of expression.

Yet with *The Red Badge of Courage*, which stands as one of America's acknowledged classics, Crane demonstrated that he was getting a firm grip on his art. The classic naturalism of *Maggie* and of *George's Mother*, the conventional realism of *The Red Badge of Courage* and of *The Little Regiment and Other Episodes of the American Civil War*, and the impressionistic symbolism of *The Black Riders* suggest the great versatility of which Crane was capable.

Both in his insistence on living an action-packed life, often quite close to the edge, and in his accuracy and economy of description, Crane reminds one of Ernest Hemingway, along whose lines he might have developed had he lived a normal life span.

Bibliography

Bruccoli, Matthew J. *Stephen Crane, 1871-1971*. Columbia: Department of English, University of South Carolina, 1971. Extremely valuable bibliography, although not easily accessible.

Cady, Edwin H. *Stephen Crane*. Rev. ed. Boston: Twayne, 1980. This updating of Cady's 1962 edition is carefully researched and well reported. It is a standard critical biography of Crane. Its updated bibliography is useful.

Colvert, James B. *Stephen Crane*. New York: Harcourt Brace, 1984. This biography, aimed specifically at the nonspecialist, is highly readable and is enhanced by numerous illustrations. Its bibliography is limited but well selected. The author's research is impeccable.

Gibson, Donald B. *The Fiction of Stephen Crane*. Carbondale: Southern Illinois University Press, 1968. This study, although badly dated, is valuable in suggesting the sources of much of Crane's fiction and in establishing some of Crane's literary relationships.

Gullason, Thomas A., ed. *Stephen Crane's Career: Perspectives and Evaluations*. New York: New York University Press, 1972. The contributors to this book consider Crane in the light of his times and his background. They trace sources of his stories, review Crane research, consider Crane's short fiction quite thoroughly, and present some of Cora Stewart's original writing.

Johnson, Claudia D. *Understanding the Red Badge of Courage: A Student Casebook to Issues, Sources and Historical Documents*. Westport, Conn.: Greenwood Press, 1998. Johnson examines historical documents (some published never before), related readings, and commentary designed to enhance the reader's understanding of the themes and context of the Civil War classic, *The Red Badge of Courage*.

Katz, Joseph, ed. *Stephen Crane in Transition: Centenary Essays*. DeKalb: Northern Illinois University Press, 1972. The nine essays in this centenary edition that commemorates Crane's birth consider the novels, the stories, Crane's journalistic career, his literary style, and his radical use of language. The introduction is astute, and the afterword gives a fine overview of resources for study.

Nagel, James. *Stephen Crane and Literary Impressionism*. University Park: Pennsylvania State University Press, 1980. Nagel sees Crane in a new light that suggests his remarkable versatility. The book has especially strong insights into *The Black Riders*.

Solomon, Eric. *Stephen Crane: From Parody to Realism*. Cambridge, Mass.: Harvard University Press, 1966. A penetrating study that shows Stephen Crane's remarkably swift development as a writer who found his metier in realism despite his sallies into naturalism and impressionism.

Stallman, Robert W. *Stephen Crane: A Critical Bibliography*. Ames: Iowa State University Press, 1972. This book is now somewhat dated; it is still useful to scholars, however, and is more easily available generally than Matthew J. Bruccoli's splendid bibliography, which was completed the year before Stallman's.

Wertheim, Stanley. *A Stephen Crane Encyclopedia*. Westport, Conn.: Greenwood Press, 1997. An excellent reference volume providing a complete view of Crane's short but creative life. Includes a chronology, bibliography, hundreds of entries about his friends and family, places he lived, and more.

Wolford, Chester L., Jr. *The Anger of Stephen Crane*. Lincoln: University of Nebraska Press, 1983. Walford considers Crane a semiliterate genius and presents his work as a repudiation of the epic tradition and of conventional religion. Although the book is not always convincing, it is engaging and original in its approach.

R. Baird Shuman

CRAZY HORSE

Tashunca-uitko

Born: 1842?; Black Hills of South Dakota
Died: September 5, 1877; Fort Robinson, Nebraska
Area of Achievement: Native American leadership
Contribution: Crazy Horse, the greatest of the Sioux chiefs, led his people in a valiant but futile struggle against domination by the white man and white culture. He fought to the last to hold his native land for the Indian people.

Early Life

Little is known of Tashunca-uitko's early life; even the date of his birth and the identity of his mother are somewhat uncertain. He was probably born in a Sioux camp along Rapid Creek in the Black Hills during the winter of 1841-1842. Most scholars believe that his mother was a Brule Sioux, the sister of Spotted Tail, a famous Brule chief. His father, also called Crazy Horse, was a highly respected Oglala Sioux holy man. Tashunca-uitko was apparently a curious and solitary child. His hair and his complexion were so fair that he was often mistaken for a captive white child by soldiers and settlers. He was first known as "Light-Haired Boy" and also as "Curly." At the age of ten, he became the protégé of Hump, a young Minneconjou Sioux warrior.

When he was about twelve, Curly killed his first buffalo and rode a newly captured wild horse; to honor his exploits, his people renamed him "His Horse Looking." One event in Crazy Horse's youth seems to have had a particularly powerful impact on the course of his life. When he was about fourteen, His Horse Looking witnessed the senseless murder of Chief Conquering Bear by the troops of Second Lieutenant J. L. Gratton and the subsequent slaughter of Gratton's command by the Sioux. Troubled by what he had seen, His Horse Looking went out alone, hobbled his horse, and lay down on a high hill to await a vision. On the third day, weakened by hunger, thirst, and exposure, the boy had a powerful mystical experience which revealed to him that the world in which men lived was only a shadow of the real world. To enter the real world, one had to dream. When he was in that world, everything seemed to dance or float—his horse danced as if it were wild or crazy. In this first crucial vision, His Horse Looking had seen a warrior mounted on his (His Horse Looking's) horse; the warrior had no scalps, wore no paint, was naked except for a breech cloth; he had a small, smooth stone behind one ear. Bullets and arrows could not touch him; the rider's own people crowded around him, trying to stop his dancing horse, but he rode on. The people were lost in a storm; the rider became a part of the storm with a lightning bolt on his cheek and hail spots on his body. The storm faded, and a small red-tailed hawk flew close over the rider; again the people tried to hold the rider back, but still he rode on. By the time he revealed this vision a few years later, His Horse Looking had already gained a reputation for great bravery and daring. His father and Chips, another holy man, made him a medicine bundle and gave him a red-tailed hawk feather and a smooth stone to wear.

When he went into battle thereafter, he wore a small lightning streak on his cheek, hail spots on his body, a breech cloth, a small stone, and a single feather; he did not take scalps. He was never seriously wounded in battle. His Horse Looking's father, in order to honor his son's achievements, bestowed his own name, Crazy Horse, upon the young man (he then took the name Worm) and asserted to his people that the Sioux had a new Crazy Horse, a great warrior with powerful medicine.

The Grattan debacle had one immediate effect other than the vision: It resulted in brutal reprisals by the Bluecoats. On September 3, 1855, shortly after Crazy Horse had experienced the vision, General W. S. Harney attacked the Brule camp in which Crazy Horse was living with Spotted Tail's people. The soldiers killed more than one hundred Indians (most of them women and children), took many prisoners, and captured most of the Sioux horses. Crazy Horse escaped injury and capture but was left with an abiding hatred of the whites. Since the major white invasion of the West did not begin until after the Civil War, Crazy Horse spent his youth living in the traditional ways: moving with the seasons, hunting, and warring with the other plains Indians.

Life's Work

The solitary boy grew into a strange man who, according to Black Elk, would go about the village without noticing people or saying anything. . . . All the Lakotas (Sioux) liked to dance and sing; but he never joined a dance, and they say nobody heard him sing. . . . He was a small man among the Lakotas and he was slender and had a thin face and his eyes looked through things and he always seemed to be thinking hard about something. He never wanted many things for himself, and did not have many ponies like a chief. They say that when game was scarce and the people were hungry, he would not eat at all. He was a queer man. Maybe he was always part way into that world of his vision.

Crazy Horse and the Oglala north of the Platte River lived in relative freedom from the white man's interference until 1864. From the early 1860's, however, there was ever-increasing pressure from white settlers and traders on the United States government to guarantee the safety of people moving along the Oregon and Santa Fe trails and to open the Bozeman Road which ran through the Sioux country.

The military began preparations early in 1865 to invade the Powder River Indian country; General Patrick E. Connor announced that the Indians north of the Platte "must be hunted like wolves." Thus began what came to be known as Red Cloud's War, named for the Sioux chief who led the Sioux and Cheyenne warriors. General Connor's punitive expedition in 1865 was a failure, as were subsequent efforts to force the free Indians to sign a treaty. In 1866, General Henry B. Carrington fortified and opened the Bozeman Road through Sioux territory. By 1868, having been outsmarted, frustrated, and beaten again and again by Red Cloud's warriors, the United States forces conceded defeat, abandoned the forts, closed the Bozeman Road, and granted the Black Hills and the Powder River country to the Indians forever.

Crazy Horse rose to prominence as a daring and astute leader during the years of Red Cloud's War. He was chosen by the Oglala chiefs to be a "shirt-wearer" or protector of the people. All the other young men chosen were the sons of chiefs; he alone was selected solely on the basis of his accomplishments. Crazy Horse played a central role in the most famous encounter of this war. On December 21, 1866, exposing himself repeatedly to great danger, he decoyed a troop of eighty-one of Colonel Carrington's men, commanded by Captain William J. Fetterman, into a trap outside Fort Phil Kearny. All the soldiers were killed.

Red Cloud's War ended in November, 1868, when the chief signed a treaty which acknowledged that the Powder River and Big Horn country were Indian land into which the white man could not come without permission. The treaty also indicated that the Indians were to live on a reservation on the west side of the Missouri River. Red Cloud and his followers moved onto a reservation, but Crazy Horse and many others refused to sign or to leave their lands for a reservation; Crazy Horse never signed a treaty.

As early as 1870, driven by reports of gold in the Black Hills, many whites began to venture illegally into Indian territory. Surveyors for the Northern Pacific Railroad protected by United States troops also invaded the Black Hills in order to chart the course of their railway through Indian land. Crazy Horse, who became the war chief of the Oglala after Red Cloud moved onto the reservation, led numerous successful raids against the survey parties and finally drove them from his lands. The surveyors returned in 1873; this time they were protected by a formidable body of troops commanded by Lieutenant Colonel George Armstrong Custer. In spite of a series of sharp attacks, Crazy Horse was unable to defeat Custer, and the surveyors finished their task. In 1874, Custer was back in Indian territory; he led an expedition of twelve hundred men purportedly to gather military and scientific information. He reported that the hills were filled with gold "from the roots on down"; the fate of the Indians and their sacred hills was sealed. Not even the military genius of their war chief, their skill and bravery, and their clear title to the land could save them from the greed and power of the white men.

During the years between the signing of the 1868 treaty and the full-scale invasion of Indian lands in 1876, Crazy Horse apparently fell in love with a Sioux woman named Black Buffalo Woman, but she was taken from him through deceit and married another man, No Water. Crazy Horse and Black Buffalo Woman maintained their attachment to each other over a period of years, causing some divisiveness among the Sioux and resulting in the near-fatal shooting of Crazy Horse by No Water. Crazy Horse eventually married an Oglala named Tasina Sapewin (Black Shawl) who bore him a daughter. He named the child They Are Afraid of Her, and when she died a few years later, he was stricken with grief.

Because of the reports concerning the great mineral wealth of the Black Hills, the United

States government began to try to force all the Indians to move onto reservations. On February 7, 1876, the War Department ordered General Philip Sheridan to commence operations against the Sioux living off of reservations. The first conflict in this deadly campaign occurred March 17, when General George Crook's advance column under Colonel Joseph J. Reynolds attacked a peaceful camp of Northern Cheyennes and Oglala Sioux who were on their way from the Red Cloud Agency to their hunting grounds. The survivors fled to Crazy Horse's camp.

Crazy Horse took them in, gave them food and shelter, and promised them that "we are going to fight the white man again." Crazy Horse's chance came in June, when a Cheyenne hunting party sighted a column of Bluecoats camped in the valley of the Rosebud River. Crazy Horse had studied the soldiers' ways of fighting for years, and he was prepared for this battle. General Crook and his pony soldiers were no match for the Sioux and Cheyenne guided by Crazy Horse. Crook retreated under cover of darkness to his base camp on Goose Creek.

After the Battle of Rosebud (June 17), the Indians moved west to the valley of the Greasy Grass (Little Big Horn) River. Blackfoot, Hunkpapa, Sans Arc, Minneconjous, Brule, and Oglala Sioux were there, as well as the Cheyenne—perhaps as many as fifteen thousand Indians, including five thousand warriors. The soldiers had originally planned a three-pronged campaign to ensnare and destroy the Indians. Crook's withdrawal, however, forced General Alfred Terry to revise the plan. On June 22, he ordered Colonel John Gibbon to go back to the Bighorn River and to march south along it to the Little Big Horn River. Custer and the Seventh Cavalry were to go along the Rosebud parallel to Gibbon and catch the Indians in between. General Terry, with the remaining forces, would trail them and provide whatever support was necessary. General Terry expected that Gibbon and Custer would converge and engage the enemy on June 26.

General Custer and his troops arrived on June 25, and Custer elected to attack the Indian encampment without waiting for Gibbon's column. His rash decision was fatal to him and to the Seventh Cavalry. The Sioux and Cheyenne, led by Crazy Horse and Gall, Sitting Bull's lieutenant, crushed Custer; more than 250 soldiers died. Perhaps Crazy Horse and Gall could have defeated the troops of Gibbon and Terry as well, but they were not committed to an all-out war, as were the whites, and they had had enough killing, so they moved on, leaving the soldiers to bury their dead.

The Battle of the Little Big Horn is recognized as a great moment in the history of the Sioux nation, but it also proved to be a sad one, for it confirmed the United States government's conviction that in spite of the Treaty of 1868, the free Indians must be either confined to a reservation or annihilated. In the brutal days which were to follow, Crazy Horse clearly emerged as the single most important spiritual and military leader of the Sioux.

The government's response was swift: On August 15, a new law was enacted which required the Indians to give up all rights to the Powder River country and the Black Hills. Red Cloud and Spotted Tail succumbed to what they took to be inevitable and signed documents acknowledging that they accepted the new law. Sitting Bull and Gall fought against the forces of General Crook and Colonel Nelson Miles during the remainder of 1876 but decided to take their people to Canada in the spring of 1877. Crazy Horse alone resolved to stay on his own lands in the sacred Black Hills.

General Crook led an enormous army of infantry, cavalry, and artillery from the south through the Powder River country in pursuit of Crazy Horse, and Colonel Miles led his army from the north, looking for the Oglala war chief. Crazy Horse was forced to move his village from one place to another in order to avoid the Bluecoats. He had little ammunition or food, the winter was bitterly cold, and his people were weary. In December, he approached Colonel Miles's outpost and sent a small party of chiefs and warriors with a flag of truce to find out what the colonel's intentions were. The party was attacked as it approached the outpost; only three Sioux survived. Miles's brutal intentions were made quite clear, and Crazy Horse was forced to flee again.

Colonel Miles caught up with the Sioux on January 8, 1877, at Battle Butte; in spite of his lack of ammunition and the weakened condition of his warriors, Crazy Horse was able, through bravery and superior tactics, to defeat Miles. Crazy Horse and his band escaped through the Wolf Mountains to the familiar country of the Little Powder River. The soldiers decided to cease their military operations until spring, but they redoubled their efforts to persuade the Indians to surrender. Numerous emissaries were sent throughout the northern lands with pack trains of food and gifts to tempt the suffering Sioux and Cheyenne into coming in to the security of the agencies. Many small bands yielded to these entreaties, but Crazy Horse only listened politely and sent the messengers home. His fame and his symbolic value to the Indians grew daily; the longer he resisted, the more important he became to the thousands of Indians now confined to reservations. When Spotted Tail himself came to entice them to give up, Crazy Horse went off alone into the deep snows of the mountains in order to give his people the freedom to decide their own fate. Most chose to stay with their leader, but Spotted Tail did convince Big Foot to bring his Minneconjous in when spring came.

In April, General Crook sent Red Cloud to plead with Crazy Horse and to promise him that if he surrendered, the Sioux would be given a reservation in the Powder River country, where they could live and hunt in peace. At last, Crazy Horse gave in; the suffering of his people was so great, the prospects of renewed conflict with Crook and Miles so grim, and the promise of a Powder River reservation so tempting that he led his band to the Red Cloud Agency, arriving in an almost triumphal procession witnessed by thousands on May 5, 1877. Predictably, Crazy Horse did not like living at the agency, and General Crook did not make good on his promise of a Powder River reservation. Black Shawl died, and Crazy Horse married Nellie Larrabee, the daughter of a trader. The more restive Crazy Horse became, the more concerned the government became, and the more vulnerable the chief was to the plots of his enemies. Wild rumors that Crazy Horse planned to escape or to murder General Crook circulated. The government officials decided that it would be best to arrest and confine the war chief. On September 4, 1877, eight companies of cavalry and four hundred Indians, led by Red Cloud, left Fort Robinson to arrest Crazy Horse and deliver him to the fort. Crazy Horse attempted to flee but was overtaken and agreed to go and talk with Crook. When it became clear to him that he was not being taken to a conference but to prison, Crazy Horse drew his knife and tried to escape. He was restrained by Little Big Man and other followers of Red Cloud, and Private William Gentles bayoneted him. He died in the early hours of September 5; his father, Worm, was at his side. Crazy Horse's parents were allowed to take the body; they rode into the hills and buried their son in a place known only to them.

Later that fall, the Sioux were forced to begin a journey eastward to the Missouri River and a new reservation/prison. Among the thousands of Indians were Crazy Horse's Oglala. After approximately seventy-five miles of travel, the Oglala, two thousand strong, broke from the line and raced for Canada and freedom. The small cavalry contingent could only watch as these Sioux fled to join Sitting Bull—manifesting, in their refusal to submit to the white man, the spirit of Crazy Horse.

Summary

Crazy Horse, like numerous other Indian patriots, was a martyr to the westward expansion of the United States, to the unity and technological superiority of the white culture, to its assumed racial and cultural superiority, and to the greed of white Americans. He also seems to have been a truly exceptional and admirable man; he was the greatest warrior and general of a people to whom war was a way of life. He provided a powerful example of integrity and independence for the Indians during a very difficult period of their history; he never attended a peace council with the whites, never signed a treaty, never even considered giving up his lands: "One does not sell the earth upon which the people walk." Furthermore, he seems to have been a basically selfless man who was genuinely devoted to the greater good of his people, to protecting his native land and his traditional way of life. To quote Black Elk:

> He was brave and good and wise. He never wanted anything but to save his people, and he fought the Wasichus (the whites) only when they came to kill us in our own country. . . . They could not kill him in battle. They had to lie to him and kill him that way.

When Crazy Horse was born, the Sioux were a strong, proud, and free people; they were skilled horsemen and masters of war and hunting. The rhythms of their lives were the rhythms of the seasons and of the game they hunted. They venerated nature and cherished individual freedom and achievement. When Crazy Horse died, the Sioux were still proud, but they were no longer truly strong or free. Freedom, independence, and cultural integrity were realities for Crazy Horse in his youth, but particularly after the tragic battle at Wounded Knee in December, 1890, freedom and independence and integrity as a people have only been dreams for the Sioux—dreams in which the legend and spirit of Crazy Horse, fierce, intelligent, indomitable, continue to play a vital part, as is evidenced by Peter Matthiessen's choice of a title for his angry and eloquent 1983 study of the contemporary struggles of the Sioux: *In the Spirit of Crazy Horse*.

Bibliography

Andrist, Ralph K. *The Long Death: The Last Days of the Plains Indians*. New York: Macmillan, 1964; London: Macmillan, 1969. The story of the military conquest of the plains Indians, the Sioux as well as others. A vivid, meticulous, and well-written survey. Excellent maps.

Brininstool, E. A. "Chief Crazy Horse: His Career and Death." *Nebraska History* 12, no. 1 (1929). Scholarly source of basic biographical information.

Brown, Dee. *Bury My Heart at Wounded Knee: An Indian History of the American West*. New York: Holt Rinehart, and London: Barrie and Jenkins, 1971. A revisionist history of the West from 1860 to 1890 from an Indian point of view. Crucial to a full understanding of American history and the destruction of the culture and civilization of the American Indian. Crazy Horse's story is one of many.

Connell, Evan S. *Son of the Morning Star: Custer and the Little Bighorn*. San Francisco: North Point Press, 1984; London: Pavilion, 1985. An intelligent and thorough reconstruction of what might have happened and why at the Little Big Horn on June 25, 1876. A fascinating study of the major participants in that historic battle. Focus is on Custer.

Gilbert, James N. "The Death of Crazy Horse: A Contemporary Examination of the Homicidal Events of 5 September 1877." *Journal of the West* 32, no. 1 (January 1993). Discussion of the circumstances surrounding the death of Crazy Horse, which occurred at the hand of an army private the day after his surrender.

Hinman, Eleanor. "Oglala Sources on the Life of Crazy Horse." *Nebraska History* 57, no. 1 (1976). Interviews with Oglala Indians who witnessed various events in the life of Crazy Horse. Provides particularly interesting insights into his conduct in battle, his feud with No Water, and his death.

Josephy, Alvin M., Jr. *The Patriot Chiefs: A Chronicle of American Indian Resistance*. New York: Viking Press, 1958. The life stories of outstanding Indian leaders, including Crazy Horse, Tecumseh, and Chief Joseph. A good brief biography. Places Crazy Horse's struggle in the context of the heroic and tragic resistance of Indians throughout North America to the white man.

McMurtry, Larry. *Crazy Horse*. New York: Viking, 1999. McMurtry departs from previous biographies and creates a dignified portrait of Crazy Horse, what he meant to his people, and what he means to subsequent Sioux generations.

Neihardt, John G. *Black Elk Speaks*. Lincoln: University of Nebraska Press, 1961; London: Barrie and Jenkins, 1972. A fascinating document which contains the life story of an Oglala holy man as told by himself. He was a member of Crazy Horse's tribe, was present at the Little Big Horn as well as at Fort Robinson when Crazy Horse was killed. Invaluable insights into the Sioux culture and way of life.

Olson, James C. *Red Cloud and the Sioux Problem*. Lincoln: University of Nebraska Press, 1965. Well-documented appraisal of Indian affairs in the Western plains in the 1860's and the 1870's. Thorough account of relations between the Sioux and the federal government. Judicious treatment of contending leaders.

Sandoz, Mari. *Crazy Horse: The Strange Man of the Oglalas*. New York: Knopf, 1941. A comprehensive and authoritative biography in which the author attempts to tell not only the chief's story but also that of his people and culture. Told from Crazy Horse's point of view.

Vaughn, Jesse W. *Indian Fights: New Facts on Seven Encounters*. Norman: University of Oklahoma Press, 1966. A flawed study of seven significant battles that occurred between 1864 and 1877 in Wyoming and Montana. Vaughn's accounts of the Fetterman Massacre and Major Reno's part in the Battle of the Little Big Horn are quite useful.

Hal Holladay

DAVID CROCKETT

Born: August 17, 1786; Greene County, Tennessee
Died: March 6, 1836; the Alamo, San Antonio, Texas
Areas of Achievement: Exploration, government and politics, literature, and military affairs
Contribution: Crockett, a congressman from western Tennessee and the author of a best-selling autobiography, became the most celebrated backwoodsman in the United States. His death at the battle of the Alamo turned him into one of America's legendary frontier heroes.

Early Life

David Crockett grew up in the poverty-stricken frontier regions of eastern Tennessee, where his father operated a tavern. His formal education was limited to a six-month period during which he worked two days per week for the village schoolmaster in return for board and four days of schooling. Crockett's manuscript letters prove that he learned basic literacy in the one hundred or so days he attended school, although his spelling was always erratic and his grasp of grammatical rules was uncertain. On August 14, 1806, shortly before his twentieth birthday, he married Mary Finley, with whom he had three children. Crockett moved to central and then west Tennessee in search of better land, supporting his family through subsistence farming and his skill as a hunter.

When the Creek Indian War broke out in 1813, Crockett enlisted and served as a scout until March of 1815, during which time he was promoted to sergeant. Crockett's duties took him south into Alabama and eventually to Pensacola, Florida. The army was poorly supplied and constantly short of food; Crockett spent much time hunting to help feed his companions. He observed with some bitterness the effect of his lack of social rank when the commander of his regiment ignored his warning that an Indian attack was imminent but acted immediately when an officer reported the same information the next day.

Shortly after Crockett's return from the war, his first wife died. Within one year he had remarried. His new wife, Elizabeth Patton, was a widow with two young children of her own, as well as a substantial inheritance of cash and slaves. Her funds enabled Crockett to move to Lawrence County and set up a gristmill and a distillery in the spring of 1817.

For a while he seemed to prosper, but his businesses did not succeed. In 1831 he had to sell some slaves in order to reduce his debts. Crockett was appointed a justice of the peace by the state of Tennessee in November, 1817. The next year his neighbors elected him colonel of the fifty-seventh regiment of militia in Lawrence County. In 1821 he was elected to the state legislature and was reelected in 1823. He failed to win his bid for Congress in 1825, but in 1827 he went to Washington, D.C., for the first of his three terms in the House of Representatives.

Life's Work

Crockett's tall tales and backwoods humor entertained and attracted the press, which covered his activities, real or imaginary, in detail and spread his fame across the country. Many of the reports were intentional exaggerations, such as claiming that his reputation as a hunter had spread so wide among the animals that when he aimed his rifle at a treed raccoon the animal meekly climbed down and surrendered, or that while traveling to the 1829 session of Congress he had waded into the Ohio River and towed a disabled steamboat back to shore. He was reputed to have shot forty-seven bears in one month and was said to ride alligators for exercise. When Crockett supported President Andrew Jackson, the Whig papers sneered at him as an example of an uncivilized westerner and alleged that he drank the water from his finger bowl at a White House dinner. After Crockett broke with Jackson, the Whig papers began to compliment him while the Jacksonian press, which had praised his rustic wisdom and virtue, began to attack him.

As much as he enjoyed his celebrity status and was willing to perform the part of the ignorant but shrewd backwoodsman, Crockett took seriously his work as a congressman. He was frustrated by his lack of success in advancing the interests of his subsistence farming constituents. In the state legislature, he had championed the cause of the western Tennessee squatters against the eastern Tennessee landholding aristocrats. In Congress he broke with the Jackson forces when they failed to support his Tennessee Vacant Land Bill, which would have allowed those living on and improving federal lands in western Tennessee to secure title to the land. When Crockett opposed Jackson's Indian Removal Bill in 1830 and also proposed using federal funds to aid poor American Indians living in his district, the break with Jackson was complete. Jacksonian opposition led to Crockett's loss in the 1831 election; however, he succeeded in winning a third term in 1833.

After his break with the Jacksonians, Crockett wrote an autobiography with the assistance of Thomas Chilton, a Kentucky congressman who lived in the same Washington, D.C., boarding house as Crockett. Crockett freely acknowledged Chilton's help and informed his publisher that Chilton was entitled to half the royalties from the work. The book was a campaign autobiography intended to help Crockett's bid for reelection. Like Benjamin Franklin's autobiography, a copy of which Crockett owned, the work described the rise of a self-made man who overcame hardships to achieve greatness. Crockett's voice and language dominated the book, which was a fairly accurate account of his life except for some exaggerations about his military career in the Creek Indian War and his prowess as a hunter. Crockett described several battles during which he was not present. The work portrayed a humorous braggart and backwoods trickster who rose to national prominence as a congressman. The language of the autobiography faithfully reproduced Southwestern frontier idioms, and the book included some of the first printed examples of frontier humor. For example, when Crockett returned from an extended hunting trip to discover that his companions had reported him dead, he remarked, "I know'd this was a whapper of a lie, as soon as I heard it."

Narrative of the Life of David Crockett of the State of Tennessee appeared in 1834 and was an immediate success. Within one year, it went through seven editions, including one in London, England, and twelve new printings were released in 1835. Encouraged by the success of the autobiography, Crockett permitted the Whigs to publish, under his name, two books attacking the Jacksonians. *An Account of Colonel Crockett's Tour to the North and Down East* (1835) described the reception of Crockett's speeches attacking Jackson during his tour of Whig cities in the North. *The Life of Martin Van Buren* (1835) was a vitriolic satire of the Jacksonian candidate for president in 1836. Crockett wrote neither book, and they failed to attract the public.

The autobiography's success as a literary work did little to advance Crockett's political career. He reacted bitterly when he lost a hotly contested election for his House seat in August, 1835. He told his

constituents that they could go to hell and that he was going to Texas. On November 1, Crockett and several of his friends left for Texas, where American settlers had revolted against Mexico. He hoped to find fertile land where he and his family could rebuild their fortunes and perhaps revive his political career in the new republic. Crockett was welcomed wherever he went in Texas, and in January, 1836, he took an oath of allegiance to the provisional government of Texas that entitled him to vote and run for office during the pending constitutional convention. He then joined the rebel army and moved south to San Antonio in early February.

The president of Mexico, General Antonio López de Santa Anna, determined to crush the Texan rebellion, arrived at San Antonio with some 2,400 troops. The Texan defenders, numbering 183, barricaded themselves in an old mission building, the Alamo, where they held out from February 23 to March 6. Santa Anna had ordered his men to take no prisoners, and none of the defenders survived. Crockett's active role and bravery during the siege is attested in all authentic accounts. However, the legendary scene in which Crockett, out of ammunition and using his broken rifle as a club, dies surrounded by the bodies of a dozen Mexicans he has shot is mythical. Documentary evidence shows that Crockett, along with a half-dozen other defenders, was captured after resistance ceased and brought before Santa Anna, who angrily ordered him executed.

Summary

The process of turning David Crockett, eccentric backwoods congressman, into Davy Crockett, legendary superhero, began while Crockett was still alive. His colorful personality had made him one of the best-known politicians of the 1830's. Even before his death, exaggerated stories about him, some based on tall tales he loved to tell to amused Washington reporters and congressmen, had begun to circulate. Many were included in a work that Crockett repudiated, although it was published under his name: *Sketches and Eccentricities of Colonel David Crockett of West Tennessee* (1833). The work contained incidents that appeared to be based on Crockett's anecdotes.

Crockett's heroic death elevated him to mythological status. Crockett's publisher immediately commissioned Richard Penn Smith to write a fictional diary of Crockett's activities in Texas called *Col. Crockett's Exploits and Adventures in Texas, Written by Himself* (1836). Only the first two chapters, which were based on letters Crockett wrote to his publishers, are authentic. The fifty Crockett almanacs printed between 1835 and 1856 completed the transformation of Crockett into an American legend. These pamphlets, along with the usual calendars, weather predictions, domestic hints, and farming suggestions, included improbable Crockett hunting stories and endowed him with superhuman powers. Crockett is credited with saving the earth one winter when the entire planet froze: Crockett thawed the earth's axis with hot bear grease and kicked it loose again. Another tale claimed that he deflected Halley's comet from a collision course by climbing the Allegheny Mountains and twisting the tail off the comet.

Davy Crockett also figured as a fantastically successful hunter in six nineteenth century dime novels. A play that ran for over two thousand performances between 1874 and 1896 portrayed him as a handsome frontiersman whose gentlemanly conduct won the love of a wealthy neighbor's daughter. The most influential presentation of the legendary figure was Walt Disney's 1955 television production and film, *Davy Crockett, King of the Wild Frontier*, which used many of the legends that had grown up over the years to portray him as an ideal frontiersman and martyr of the Alamo. The production set off an enormous fad: Every young boy seemed to need a coonskin hat and fringed Crockett-style jacket so they could copy their hero. Crockett had become an icon of American heroism, and historians who wrote about the factual Crockett were assailed for subverting the image of this truly American hero.

Bibliography

Crockett, David. *Narrative of the Life of David Crockett of the State of Tennessee*. A facsimile edition with annotations and an introduction by James A. Shackford and Stanley J. Folmsbee. Knoxville: University of Tennessee Press, 1973. The insightful annotations make this the most useful version of Crockett's autobiography.

Derr, Mark. *The Frontiersman: The Real Life and the Many Legends of Davy Crockett*. New York: Morrow, 1993. Derr supplies an informative and entertaining narrative of Crockett's life.

Hauck, Richard Boyd. *Crockett: A Bio-Bibliography*. Westport, Conn.: Greenwood Press, 1982. This book contains an excellent biography of Crockett and an analysis of the style and content of his writings.

Kilgore, Dan. *How Did Davy Die?* College Station: Texas A&M University Press, 1978. Kilgore provides a careful analysis of the evidence concerning the way Crockett died.

Lofaro, Michael A., ed. *Davy Crockett: The Man, The Legend, The Legacy, 1786-1986*. Knoxville: University of Tennessee Press, 1985. This volume deals mostly with the legends about Crockett, from the early almanacs to Disney's television version.

Lofaro, Michael, and Joe Cummings, eds. *Crockett at Two Hundred: New Perspective on the Man and the Myth*. Knoxville: University of Tennessee Press, 1985. This book contains ten scholarly articles on Crockett's life, death, and writings, along with an extensive bibliography.

Shackford, James Atkins. *David Crockett: The Man and the Legend*. Edited by John B. Shackford. Chapel Hill: University of North Carolina Press, 1956. This is the definitive scholarly biography of Crockett, although it needs to be brought up to date by Kilgore's book on Crockett's death.

Milton Berman

CALEB CUSHING

Born: January 17, 1800; Salisbury, Massachusetts
Died: January 2, 1879; Newburyport, Massachusetts
Areas of Achievement: Diplomacy, government and politics, and law
Contribution: Cushing enhanced the power and status of the attorney general's office through his legal opinions, writings on the historical development and function of that cabinet post, and recommendations for reform of the federal judiciary.

Early Life

Caleb Cushing was the firstborn and only surviving son of John Newmarch Cushing, a merchant and shipowner, and Lydia Dow. A duty to serve his country came from his grandfather namesake, Judge Caleb Cushing, a representative in the Massachusetts General Court for twenty-seven years, and his uncle, Benjamin Cushing, who had fought in the American Revolution. His father's shipping trade with India influenced Cushing's promotion of U.S. trade to Asian markets.

Cushing received a bachelor's degree from Harvard in 1817. He then entered Harvard Law School and served a three-year apprenticeship under Ebenezer Moseley in Newburyport before being admitted to the bar in 1822. In November, 1824, he advanced his legal career by marrying Caroline Elizabeth Wilder, the daughter of a Massachusetts Supreme Court justice. The couple had no children, and Cushing never remarried after his wife's death in August, 1832.

Ambitious, intelligent, and tireless, Cushing quickly became a prominent resident of Essex County, Massachusetts, through his legal and literary accomplishments. By 1826, he was arguing cases before the Supreme Judicial Court of Massachusetts and had been commissioned a justice of the peace. In addition, Cushing received much acclaim for his articles on law, nature, history, philosophy, and science that were published in the *North American Review, U.S. Literary Gazette, Annual Register, Boston Monthly Magazine,* and *Boston Lyceum.* He also gained notice for his translation of French jurist Robert-Joseph Pothier's *Supplément au Traité du contrat de louage: ou, Traité des contrats de louage maritimes* (1764; *A Treatise on Maritime Contracts of Letting to Hire,* 1821), his discussion of the tariff in

A Summary of Practical Principles of Political Economy (1826), and his historical scholarship in *The History and Present State of the Town of Newburyport* (1826).

Influenced by Federalism's strong roots in Essex County and modelling himself after statesmen-scholars Edward Everett and Daniel Webster, Cushing entered politics in 1824 as a supporter of John Quincy Adams. He won election as a representative to the Massachusetts General Court and two years later became a state senator. In 1826, Cushing sought the North Essex District Congressional seat. He lost the contest to pro-Andrew Jackson candidate John Varnum in a campaign marked by excessive mud-slinging, which influenced Cushing's opposition to abolitionism. After serving three more terms in the general court, Cushing was elected to the House of Representatives in 1834 as a member of the anti-Jackson Whig Party.

Life's Work

Cushing served four consecutive terms in Congress (1835-1843). A staunch Whig during the first three terms, Cushing supported his party's economic programs—a protective tariff, internal improvements, reestablishment of the national bank, and distribution of proceeds from the sale of public lands among the states. He distinguished himself by leading Whig opposition against the financial policies of presidents Jackson and Martin Van Buren, particularly the Independent Treasury Bill. Furthermore, he resisted Southern efforts to suppress the reading of antislavery petitions in Congress (the "gag rule"). As a member of the House Committee on Foreign Affairs, Cushing's Anglophobia and ardent support for U.S. territorial and commercial expansion became quite evident. He demanded Britain's withdrawal from the disputed Aroostook Valley in northern Maine and urged an end to the agreement with Britain to jointly occupy the Oregon territory. Cushing also supported the annexation of Texas to check British interests there. Finally, he promoted trade with China to challenge British supremacy in the Pacific.

Cushing's dislike of Senator Henry Clay and his preference for territorial expansion advocated by the Democratic Party led him to abandon the Whigs. He supported William Henry Harrison rather than Clay as the party's standard-bearer in the presidential election of 1840. Following Harrison's death in April, 1841, Clay pushed his economic program in an unsuccessful attempt to catapult himself into the White House in 1844. Cushing defended President John Tyler's vetoes of Clay's national bank and tariff bills as consistent with Tyler's Southern states' rights principles. He thus became the leading member of the president's "Corporal's Guard," a small group of staunch Tyler Whigs in the House of Representatives. Irate Whigs rejected Cushing's assertion that he had opposed Clay on patriotic grounds and ignored him throughout the remainder of the Twenty-seventh Congress. Cushing decided not to seek a fifth congressional term after learning that his support of Tyler had been unpopular with many of his constituents and that Massachusetts Whigs had already declared their intention to support Clay in the next presidential contest. Tyler repaid Cushing for his loyalty by nominating him for secretary of the treasury in March, 1843. The Senate, however, rejected the appointment three times in one evening as both Democrats and Whigs questioned Cushing's political convictions.

Despite this embarrassment, Tyler remained determined to reward Cushing for his loyalty. In May, 1843, Tyler took advantage of a congressional recess to appoint Cushing envoy extraordinary and minister plenipotentiary to China with instructions to negotiate a commercial treaty. In July, 1844, Cushing concluded the Treaty of Wanghia, the first Sino-American trade agreement. The treaty increased U.S. trade with China by opening Canton, Amoy, Fuzhou, Ningbo, and Shanghai to U.S. merchants. It also granted the United States most-favored-nation trade status with China, established commercial and tariff regulations, and included the principle of extraterritoriality.

After returning from China, Cushing associated himself with Southern Democrats. He became more adamant in demanding the annexation of Texas and supported the acquisition of Cuba. His aversion to abolitionism increased as he accepted the states' rights defense of slavery. One of the few Northern politicians to support the Mexican War, Cushing organized the First Massachusetts Volunteer Regiment with his own money. Known for his discipline and strict adherence to regulations, he attained the rank of brigadier general but did not participate in any battles. Massachusetts Democrats nonetheless recognized Cushing's military service by nominating him for governor in 1847 and 1848, but he lost both elections. In 1851, Cushing became mayor of Newburyport. The following year he was appointed associate justice of the Supreme Judicial Court of Massachusetts. There Cushing won the respect of his colleagues with his fairness and legal brilliance. In 1852, Cushing, a delegate to the National Democratic Convention, helped manage the party's nomination of Franklin Pierce as a compromise candidate for president. After winning the election, Pierce appointed Cushing attorney general of the United States.

As the first full-time attorney general, Cushing enhanced the prestige and influence of the office. At the request of Secretary of State William L. Marcy, Cushing assumed responsibility for judicial appointments, extradition cases, pardons, and official correspondence between department heads. His study of the function of the attorney generalship became the standard description of the office. His official opinions clarified jurisdiction between federal and state power and defined the administration of executive power. Finally, despite his failed effort to reform the federal judiciary and organize a law department, his recommendations shaped the creation of the Department of Justice in 1870.

Cushing's advancement of the Pierce administration's pro-Southern domestic and foreign policies, however, overshadowed his accomplishments as attorney general. He advocated the strict enforcement of the Fugitive Slave Law, discouraged any union between Democrats and Free-Soilers (a third party that advocated free homesteads, free speech, and a higher tariff), and favored the Kansas-Nebraska Act (1854) and proslavery territorial legislature in Kansas. Furthermore, Cushing aggravated the slavery debate by supporting the Gadsden Purchase (the 1853 purchase of a strip of Mexican land by the United States) and endorsing the Ostend Manifesto, which advocated the purchase of Cuba from Spain.

Cushing's love for the Union led him to join the Republican Party during the secession crisis of 1860-1861. While he expected the South to defend slavery at all costs and had supported Southern extremists in nominating John Breckinridge for president in 1860, Cushing deemed secession illegal and deserted Southern Democrats once South Carolina left the Union. He supported President Abraham Lincoln against General George B. McClellen in the presidential election of 1864. Cushing later strengthened his standing within the Republican Party by assisting Senator Charles Sumner and Congressman Thaddeus Stevens in writing the Fourteenth Amendment.

After the American Civil War, presidents Andrew Johnson and Ulysses S. Grant benefitted from Cushing's legal and diplomatic reputation and skill. Under Johnson, Cushing chaired a commission that revised and codified the statutes of the United States. In 1868, Cushing continued a lifelong commitment to expanding U.S. commerce by negotiating a treaty with Colombia for a canal across the Isthmus of Panama. Three years later, Grant appointed Cushing counsel for the United States before the Geneva Tribunal of Arbitration on the Alabama Claims. Cushing's knowledge of international law, linguistic skill, persistence, and patriotism helped his government secure a $15,500,000 settlement.

Despite these achievements, Cushing's allegiance to the Republican Party continued to be questioned. When Grant nominated him as chief justice of the United States in 1873, Republicans uncovered a letter from Cushing to Jefferson Davis written in March, 1861, recommending a former clerk in the Ordinance Department in Washington, D.C., for a job in the Confederacy. This attack on Cushing's loyalty to the Union forced him to withdraw his name from consideration for the post. He then served as minister to Spain from 1874 to 1877.

Summary

Cushing's tenure as attorney general and his diplomatic success in China, Colombia, Spain, and Geneva, Switzerland, would rank him as a prominent figure in nineteenth century U.S. politics had he not supported the states' rights defense of slavery during the 1840's and 1850's. While not an apologist for slavery, Cushing's blind attachment to rational, legalistic procedure prevented him from understanding the moral dilemma of slavery addressed by abolitionists. Although he recognized the political threat that slavery posed to the Union, his overemphasis in applying reason to politics led him to embrace policies (territorial expansion, states' rights, and enforcement of federal law) that exasperated the slavery debate. Cushing's support of these policies and the use of force to maintain the Union led to two major political shifts during his public career that left him vulnerable to charges of being a political opportunist. This criticism cost him the ultimate achievement of his legal training, chief justice of the United States, and a place alongside his mentors Edward Everett and Daniel Webster as an eminent statesman-scholar in U.S. history.

Bibliography

Belohlavek, John M. "Race, Progress, and Destiny: Caleb Cushing and the Quest for American Empire." In *Manifest Destiny and Empire: American Antebellum Expansionism*, edited by Sam W. Haynes and Christopher Morris. College Station: Texas A&M University Press, 1977. Cushing's arrogant and aggressive application of Social Darwinism in promoting U.S. expansion before the American Civil War is addressed through an examination of his writings and speeches on U.S. nationality. Contains valuable notes.

Dennett, Tyler. *Americans in Eastern Asia: A Critical Study of United States' Policy in the Far East in the Nineteenth Century*. New York: Macmillan, 1922. Includes five chapters covering the foundations of U.S. policy in Asia during the first four decades of the nineteenth century, preparations for the Cushing mission to China, and the negotiation of the Treaty of Wanghia. Comprehensive bibliography.

Donahue, William J. "The Cushing Mission." *Modern Asian Studies* 16 (April 1982): 193-216. Donahue praises Cushing as an "able diplomat" for the commercial success of his mission to China but recognizes that throughout the nineteenth century the United States followed Britain's lead in acquiring trade concessions from China. Includes extensive notes and an abbreviated version of the Treaty of Wanghia.

Fuess, Claude M. *The Life of Caleb Cushing.* 2 vols. New York: Harcourt Brace, 1923. Fuess defends Cushing's political shifts by presenting him as a man of honest convictions, moral courage, and principle who helped preserve the Union and defend the nation's honor as a member of Congress, attorney general, and a diplomat. Based on exhaustive use of the Caleb Cushing Papers, it is the most complete biography on Cushing.

Hodgson, Sister M. Michael Catherine. *Caleb Cushing: Attorney General of the United States, 1853-1857.* Washington, D.C.: Catholic University of America Press, 1955. This study focuses on Cushing's efforts to strengthen the office of attorney general as well as his influence on the foreign policy of the Pierce administration. Includes appendices and a bibliographical note.

Nichols, Roy Franklin. *Franklin Pierce: Young Hickory of the Granite Hills.* Rev. ed. Philadelphia: University of Pennsylvania Press, 1958. Nichols criticizes Cushing as Pierce's worst cabinet appointment because of his lack of political principles and common sense. Discusses Cushing's role in helping Pierce secure the Democratic party presidential nomination in 1852 and his strong voice in the cabinet on both domestic and foreign affairs. Extensive notes and bibliography.

Dean Fafoutis

GEORGE A. CUSTER

Born: December 5, 1839; New Rumley, Ohio

Died: June 25, 1876; Little Big Horn River, Montana Territory

Area of Achievement: The military

Contribution: Although greatly obscured by the events surrounding his death at the Battle of the Little Big Horn, Custer's illustrious Civil War exploits made him one of the nation's most respected military figures and a national idol. After the war, his expeditions into the Yellowstone region and the Black Hills earned for him renown as an explorer and compiler of scientific information.

Early Life

George Armstrong Custer was born December 5, 1839, in New Rumley, Ohio. In 1849, his father sent him to live with the boy's married half-sister, Lydia Reed, in Monroe, Michigan. The elder Custer wanted his favorite son to acquire the best possible education, and he had been assured by his daughter that the private "Young Men's Academy" in Monroe would benefit George.

At the age of sixteen, "Autie," as his family affectionately nicknamed him, returned to his parents' home and began a career as a schoolteacher. Always devoted to his family, Custer faithfully presented his mother his monthly salary of twenty dollars as a token of his appreciation of their sacrifices to enable him to become educated.

Like many young men who had been swept up in the thrilling accounts of the Mexican War, Custer nurtured his boyhood love for the military and was determined to make it his profession. In 1857, Custer entered West Point, but during his four years at the Academy his academic record and numerous demerits placed him near the bottom of his class. "My career as a cadet," he recounted in his "War Memoirs" (1876), "had but little to commend it to the study of those who came after me, unless as an example to be carefully avoided." What became known as "Custer's luck" prevailed, however, and in early summer, 1861, the Union Army, desperate for officers, took Custer's entire class, and three days before the first Battle of Bull Run, Second Lieutenant Custer reported to the Army of the Potomac.

Life's Work

Serving as aide-de-camp to Generals George Brinton McClellan, Philip Kearny, and Alfred Pleason-ton, Custer's enthusiasm, bravery, and dedication to duty earned for him rapid promotion to the rank of captain. While under Pleasonton, the chief of the Union cavalry, Custer gained a reputation for zeal, sound tactics, and active participation in combat. Consequently, upon Pleasonton's recommendation, on June 29, 1863, Custer, at the age of twenty-three, was made brevet brigadier general in command of the Michigan Cavalry Brigade.

As a general, Custer's initial distinction was his attire. In an attempt to achieve a look of maturity, the sad-eyed youth grew a mustache and allowed his sandy blond locks to drape nearly to his shoulders. To adorn his wiry five-foot, ten-inch, 165-pound frame, the army's youngest general chose rather foppish clothing. Unlike his more conservative fellow officers, Custer wore a broad-billed hat, blue velvet coat with a wide sailor collar, red silk tie, gold insignia tie clasp, white gloves, and loose trousers tucked inside high riding boots.

Any doubts as to the well-dressed cavalier's leadership qualities vanished quickly, as his junior

officers marveled at his acts of bravado. Custer enjoyed the thrill of battle and led his men into the fray, waving either his hat or sword, and exhorting them to charge with a shrill "Come on, you Wolverines!" Unlike many Union commanders, Custer gave his troops all the credit for his victories, while shouldering all blame in defeat. This gave "Old Curly," as his men dubbed him, the reputation of being a "soldiers' general," and by the end of the war Custer ranked behind only Ulysses S. Grant, William Tecumseh Sherman, and Philip Sheridan as a beloved savior of the Union.

His combat record was outstanding, and his victories over J. E. B. Stuart's forces at Gettysburg and Yellow Tavern were instrumental in the ultimate triumph of the North. To honor his achievements, Custer, who had risen to the rank of brevet major general in 1864 and had accepted Robert E. Lee's symbolic white towel of surrender, was permitted to witness Lee's official surrender in the McLean House at Appomattox. General Sheridan then purchased the table upon which the document had been signed and presented it to Custer's wife, Elizabeth, with the notation: "There is scarcely an individual in our service who has contributed more to bring about this desirable result than your very gallant husband."

Custer's war record was sufficient to warrant his place as an American military hero. Custer differed from many of his fellow generals, however, in that he felt himself too young to retire on his laurels and had no desire to enter politics. Therefore, he remained in his chosen profession and was sent West.

In May, 1865, he was dispatched to Texas to help destroy the remnants of General Edmund Kirby-Smith's rebel forces, and the following year he was ordered to Washington, D.C., to testify before a congressional committee on conditions in Texas and western Louisiana. In 1866, he reverted to his regular army rank of captain and returned to Monroe. The remainder of that year was spent writing his memoirs and accompanying President Andrew Johnson on his campaign "Swing Around the Circle."

In late 1866, Custer was promoted to lieutenant colonel and assigned to Fort Riley, Kansas, to head the newly formed Seventh Cavalry. The next year, he participated in General Winfield S. Hancock's campaign against the Sioux and Cheyenne. During this expedition, Custer and his men broke through a virtual siege of Fort Wallace and rescued the garrison. Finding the post ravaged by cholera, he took part of his command on a two-hundred-mile trek to

Fort Harker to obtain medical supplies for Fort Wallace. He sent the medicine back with a junior officer, while he obtained permission from the commanding general at Fort Harker to return to Fort Riley to visit Elizabeth. Following the disastrous campaign, Hancock told Congress that he had been undermined by actions of his subordinates, especially Custer, and demanded that the offending junior officer be court-martialed for deserting his command. Despite saving Fort Wallace from attack and disease and having authorization for his absence, Custer was found guilty and suspended, without pay, for one year.

In September, 1868, Generals Sherman and Sheridan had Custer reinstated to lead the Seventh Cavalry on another campaign. Sheridan told Custer: "I rely on you in everything, and shall send you on this expedition without orders, leaving you to act entirely on your own judgment." This faith was rewarded, as a surprise dawn attack on an encampment of hostile Cheyenne along the Washita River resulted in one of the military's most successful Indian battles. Custer seized large quantities of ponies, blankets, weapons, and food, but found himself criticized in the Eastern press because during the daylong fighting fifty-three Indian women and children were slain.

Four years of relative inactivity ended in 1873, when Custer was named second in command for General David Stanley's fifteen-hundred-man force assigned to guard the Northern Pacific Railroad Company survey party. During this service in the Yellowstone region, Custer enhanced his reputation as an Indian fighter by defeating a war party of three hundred Sioux, while sustaining only one casualty among his ninety men.

In July, 1874, Sheridan again called upon Custer, whom he said was "the only man who never failed me," this time to lead an expedition into the Black Hills of the Dakotas. Sheridan feared that if the Sioux went to war, they would use their sacred territory in that area as a refuge. Since the Black Hills had never been explored by whites, Custer was instructed to take more than one thousand men, including soldiers, geologists, paleontologists, zoologists, botanists, and photographers, to reconnoiter the region. Custer sent back voluminous data on scientific discoveries, but the public was most interested in his finding of gold and other precious minerals. Soon a rush of miners flooded onto land reserved by treaty for the Sioux.

Ironically, Custer's downfall was his successful Black Hills expedition. As the Sioux joined with the

Northern Cheyenne to repel the white trespassers, the federal government embarked upon a military campaign intended to celebrate the nation's centennial by ridding the Plains of all Indian resistance to white expansion. A coordinated three-prong attack, under the leadership of Generals Alfred Terry, George Crook, and John Gibbon, was to converge on the suspected main Indian encampment along the Little Big Horn River in the Montana Territory. Custer, commanding the only cavalry in the expedition, was sent ahead by Terry to scout the area, and he arrived at the Little Big Horn late on June 24, 1876, two days before the scheduled rendezvous. On the morning of June 25, fearing that his force had been seen and that the enemy would flee before the vise could close around them, Custer decided to launch an attack. Splitting his forces for a pincer movement, as he had done successfully in the past, Custer found himself facing between three thousand and five thousand warriors, nearly three times the number Sheridan had predicted. Cut off from all assistance, Custer and the remainder of his 225 men staved off two charges before succumbing to the superior numbers and weaponry of the Indians.

Summary

Articulate and intelligent, Custer exemplified the nineteenth century career officer by making the motto "duty, honor, country" a way of life. Although his best friends at West Point were Southerners, Custer fought against them because he believed their cause was traitorous. Personally sympathetic to the plight of Indians being driven from their land, he fought against them because his government ordered him to do so. Insubordination was intolerable to Custer, and he believed that orders, no matter how personally offensive, had to be obeyed. Contrary to allegations, Custer did not attack a day early because he sought glory, but rather because his orders from Terry permitted him to act upon his own best judgment.

In death, Custer achieved the ultimate goal of the campaign. National outrage demanded vengeance, and, to avoid possible annihilation, the Indian forces disbanded. Even defeat could not dim Custer's fame in the eyes of his adoring country.

Bibliography

Carroll, John M. *Custer in the Civil War: His Unfinished Memoirs.* Edited by John M. Carroll. San Rafael, Calif.: Presidio Press, 1977. A compilation of documents relating to Custer's Civil War career, followed by a reprinting of the seven chapters of the general's unfinished "War Memoirs," first published in *Galaxy Magazine* in 1876. These chapters, although self-centered, are significant because they represent the final works in Custer's prolific literary career.

Connell, Evan S. *Son of the Morning Star: Custer and the Little Bighorn.* San Francisco: North Point Press, 1984; London: Pavilion, 1985. A thoroughly researched examination of the personalities of Custer, government officials, and Indian leaders. A skillful blend of biography and history of the Plains Indian Wars.

Custer, Elizabeth. *Boots and Saddles: Or, Life in Dakota with General Custer.* London and New York: Harper, 1885. Recounts the travels of "Libbie" with her husband from the spring of 1873 through what she calls "Our Life's Last Chapter." An adoring wife, Mrs. Custer dedicated her life to the glorification of her husband. This book, like her *Tenting on the Plains* and *Following the Guidon,* is in her husband's memory and, for that reason, must be read with scrutiny.

Custer, George A. *My Life on the Plains.* Edited by Milo Quaife. New York: Citadel Press, 1962. Originally written as a two-year series of articles for *Galaxy Magazine,* this first appeared in book form in 1874. It offers a self-serving account of Custer's activities from 1867 through 1869. This edition offers the best introductory material and a faithful reprinting of the original.

Frost, Lawrence A. *The Custer Album.* Seattle: Superior Publishing, 1964. Former curator of the Custer Room of the Monroe County (Michigan) Museum, Frost is one of the foremost experts on his hometown hero. The text is completely sympathetic to Custer, but even those who do not share that view will be fascinated by the wealth of photographs of Custer and his family.

Graham, William A. *The Custer Myth: A Source Book of Custerania.* Harrisburg, Pa.: Stackpole, 1953. An encyclopedia of events concerning Custer's last battle. Graham spent much of his life obtaining interviews with Indian and white participants of the Little Big Horn. Essential for anyone seriously interested in Custer.

Jackson, Donald Dean. *Custer's Gold: The United States Cavalry Expedition of 1874.* New Haven, Conn.: Yale University Press, 1966. A brief, scholarly account of the Black Hills expedition and its impact on both Indians and westward expansion.

Kreyche, Gerald F. "The Two Faces of George Armstrong Custer." *USA Today* 122, no. 2588 (May 1994). Discusses Custer as a controversial figure unfairly criticized after the massacre at Little Bighorn.

Monaghan, Jay. *Custer: The Life of General George Armstrong Custer.* Boston: Little Brown, 1959. Perhaps the most balanced biography of Custer. Well-researched and written in a flowing narrative, the book is sympathetic to Custer, but Monaghan resists the temptation to gloss over the general's flaws.

Van de Water, Frederic F. *Glory-Hunter: A Life of General Custer.* Indianapolis: Bobbs-Merrill, 1934. As the title indicates, this is a hostile biography, written to counter the image set forth by Mrs. Custer's works. Custer is portrayed as a selfish, vain glory-seeker, willing to risk his men's lives to achieve fame. Still considered by many "Custer haters" as a classic, this book should be read with Frost's or Monaghan's to gain a more accurate picture of Custer.

Wert, Jeffry D. *Custer: The Controversial Life of George Armstrong Custer.* New York: Simon and Schuster, 1996. An accurate account of Custer's life based on previous works and newly identified sources.

Bruce A. Rubenstein

GEORGES CUVIER

Born: August 23, 1769; Montbéliard, Württemberg
Died: May 13, 1832; Paris, France
Area of Achievement: Biology
Contribution: Cuvier was an anatomist who greatly extended the classification system of Linnaeus by dividing living organisms and the fossil record into phyla. He was also an antievolutionist, who adapted the theory that organic changes in the world were shaped by a series of catastrophes.

Early Life

Georges Léopold Chrétien Frédéric Dagobert Cuvier was the son of a retired French officer. His father had married late in life and had moved to Montbéliard. Montbéliard had been part of French Burgundy but came under the control of the Duke of Württemberg. The region kept the French language but adopted Lutheranism. His family had originally wanted young Cuvier to become a Lutheran minister, but he was denied a scholarship to theology school. In 1784, he found a patron in the wife of the governor of the city and was able to attend Caroline University, near Stuttgart. Although his initial studies were in legal and administrative areas, Cuvier befriended the zoology lecturer Karl Kielmayer, who taught him comparative anatomy and the intricacies of dissection. Cuvier was a short man with bright blue eyes and thick red hair. His weight increased throughout his life, with the result that he eventually was given the nickname "Mammoth."

Cuvier completed his studies in 1788, and for the next six years he served as a private tutor to a noble Protestant family in Normandy. During this time, the French Revolution was occurring, and, while many dramatic and far-reaching events were taking place in Paris, Cuvier lived his life quietly in the countryside. There he continued his dissection of various ocean organisms and recorded his work. An acquaintance suggested to Cuvier that he send his unpublished papers to Étienne Geoffroy Saint-Hilaire. Invited by Geoffroy to be his assistant at the Museum of Natural History, Cuvier went to Paris in 1795 and launched his career in science.

Life's Work

Once he settled in Paris, Cuvier's career progressed rapidly through the combination of his scientific accomplishments, his teaching abilities, and his administrative acumen. As a result of the dissections he performed in Normandy, he presented a paper in which he demonstrated that the classification of invertebrate animals into insects and worms could be reclassified into mollusks, crustaceans, insects, worms, echinoderms, and zoophytes. With his keen eye for detail and his ability to classify organisms accurately, he was appointed both professor of zoology and assistant professor of animal anatomy. For the rest of his life, promotions and honors came to him almost without pause. In 1800, he succeeded the eminent anatomist Louis Daubenton as a professor at the Collège de France and was given the responsibility of organizing the science departments of several lower schools. In 1808, Napoleon I made him university counselor, and he provided leadership in organizing the new Sorbonne in Paris. With the restoration of the monarchy in 1814, Cuvier continued to offer his services. Beginning in 1819, he chaired the Council of State in the Interior Department. He was made a baron in that same year, was elevated to the Legion of Honor in 1824, and became a Peer of France in 1831.

Cuvier's scientific accomplishments were the direct result of his position at the Museum of Natural History. The French government was committed to the creation of an internationally recognized research institution. Upon Cuvier's arrival, he immediately arranged to increase the anatomy collection. By 1804, he had increased this collection to three thousand items and by 1832 to more than thirteen thousand items. Without leaving Paris, Cuvier could dissect and prepare the anatomy of his organisms and create his classification systems for birds and fish. In fact little progress had been made before Cuvier in the classification of invertebrates. They were all thrown into a single catchall group called worms. In 1795, when Cuvier first arrived in Paris, he divided these into six new classes. By 1812, he was able to classify all animals into four phyla: vertebrates, mollusks, articulates, and radiates. Within these phyla, Cuvier discovered a number of new classes, orders, and families. Some of these had been grouped with others, and many were simply overlooked.

Cuvier's method of classification was a departure from the earlier Linnaean system, in which an organism had a number of independent and arbitrary characteristics. Taking a cue from Comte de Buffon, who treated organisms as a whole entity, Cuvier expanded this idea into the correlation of

parts. Since all the functions of an organism are dependent on one another, the anatomical parts are also integrated in the organism. Through one well-preserved bone, it is possible to determine the class, order, genus, and in many cases the species of the animal. The application of this method not only produced rapid advances in the study of comparative anatomy but also was expanded to fossil remains. As early as 1804, Cuvier had tried to reconstruct the shape of the muscles of an extinct animal from the imprint left on the bones. The final step was to imagine a skin on this extinct animal, and it was resurrected.

Cuvier's contributions to anatomy and paleontology could have placed him among the earliest of the evolutionists. He found that several geological strata contained organisms peculiar to them. He also possessed ample evidence of extinction, since he examined the remains of an extinct elephant that differed significantly from any known living species. In addition, his knowledge of comparative anatomy was unequaled until the publication of Charles Darwin's theory of evolution. Cuvier, however, rejected all evolutionary explanations of his

discoveries. One possible explanation for this position can be found in his belief that nature was an immense network that had remained fixed in place since the Creation. After 1812, he admitted that creation must have taken place over several stages, and he adapted Charles Bonnet's theory of catastrophism, which postulated that the world was totally flooded on several occasions. After each flood, life was created again, hence the various strata and different organic remains.

Although Cuvier was a devout Christian, his opposition to evolution could have originated from his intellectual makeup rather than from his religious beliefs. A review of his extensive writings shows that religious doctrines rarely entered his scientific work. Possibly, Cuvier rejected the notion of evolution because he did not see a chain of organisms that evolved from simple to more complex functions. His network was not a continuous one moving from a series of related species, but rather a discontinuous one in which each species was complete in itself, and the parts worked in total harmony. Also, the geological record of his time was limited and supported the conclusion that organic forms from one stratum could not be found in a later one. Later, when Cuvier found a similar organic form in several strata, he modified his catastrophe theory toward local events such as earthquakes, volcanic action, and mountain building.

Whatever Cuvier's reasons were for rejecting a theory of evolution, he became engaged in a famous academic conflict, beginning in 1802, that was to last until his death in 1832. The conflict involved his former friends Geoffroy and Jean-Baptiste de Lamarck. The conflict produced secret investigations on the religious beliefs of Lamarck and Geoffroy. Mummified animals were brought back from Egypt to demonstrate the transformation of species. In a further episode, Cuvier had erroneously classified an extinct crocodile, an event which brought Geoffroy to the attack. While this battle was vigorously fought among the combatants and their disciples, the press and political groups also entered the fray to champion their own views. Despite his power and prestige, Cuvier was unable to prevail in this dispute. As Cuvier lay dying, Sir Charles Lyell published his work on geology, which produced crucial evidence for Darwin's theory of evolution.

Summary

Georges Cuvier lived and worked in a world that was undergoing rapid change. The French Revolution dramatically altered European society and culture. Cuvier moved adroitly through a dangerously revolutionary Paris, rose to prominence under the empire of Napoleon, and maintained his administrative positions through the restoration of the monarchy and its fall in the July Revolution of 1830. He was a Protestant in a predominantly Catholic country, and he was a poor man who acquired wealth and titles. Even without his scientific contributions, his activities would rate a minor place in the history of France. He was a man who had extensive interests; indeed his personal library included more than nineteen thousand books covering history, law, and natural sciences. He absorbed this material and committed it to memory. With this knowledge, he completed a vast amount of work as secretary of the National Institute, and under Napoleon he shaped and changed the university system of France.

It was not a narrowness of vision which kept Cuvier from arriving at a theory of evolution or considering the merits of such an idea. He possessed a grand and ordered view of nature, along with an intricate knowledge of the anatomical parts of hundreds of species. For him, each organic form was already perfect, with not one evolving into greater complexity. Perhaps he understood too much to see the simple mechanism of change built into the individuals of a species. Without his discoveries in anatomy, paleontology, and the theory of correlation of parts, however, many others would have had to duplicate this work before the theory of evolution could have been developed.

Bibliography

Bourdier, Franck. "Geoffroy Saint-Hilaire Versus Cuvier: The Campaign for Paleontological Evolution (1825-39)." In *Toward a History of Geology*, edited by Cecil J. Schneer. Cambridge, Mass.: MIT Press, 1969. Covers the acrimonious conflict between Cuvier and Geoffroy through the differences in their temperaments and careers. The author's sympathies lie with Geoffroy, and he cites him as one of the great precursors to Darwin. Reviews some new sources of information to make his case.

Coleman, William R. *Georges Cuvier, Zoologist: A Study in the History of Evolutionary Theory.* Cambridge, Mass.: Harvard University Press, 1964. Covers Cuvier's zoological and anatomical work in detail. Several sections are too complex for the general reader, but the information on Cuvier's methodology and classification is valuable. Suggests that Cuvier's rejection of evolution is less influenced by his religious attitudes than by his intellectual makeup.

Eiseley, Loren. *Darwin's Century: Evolution and the Men Who Discovered It.* New York: Doubleday, 1958; London: Gollancz, 1959. Presents Cuvier as a crucial predecessor to Darwin in the story of evolution. The sections on Cuvier are scattered in several parts of the text. Written in a simple style with ample information on Cuvier. An excellent overview of the history of evolutionary theory.

Gould, Stephen Jay, and Rosamund Purcell. "Revealing Legs." *Science* 34, no. 4 (July-August 1994). Discusses scientific theories that are later disproved by facts including Cuvier's work with certain fossils.

Mayr, Ernst. *The Growth of Biological Thought: Diversity, Evolution, and Inheritance.* Cambridge, Mass., and London: Harvard University Press, 1982. Mayr is the recognized authority on Darwin and the history of biological evolution. In each of the major sections of this work there are sections on Cuvier and his contributions to the world of biological ideas. The material can be difficult at times, but the treatment is definitive.

Nordenskiöld, Eric. *The History of Biology.* New York: Tudor, and Londo: Knopf, 1928. Chapter 2 of part 3 covers Cuvier's life and career. The topics include comparative anatomy, correlation of parts theory, paleontology, catastrophe theory, and the controversy with Geoffrey. Dated but competent.

Rudwick, Martin J. *Georges Cuvier and Fossil Bones and Geological Catastrophes.* Chicago: University of Chicago Press, 1997. Rudwick presents the first modern translation of Cuvier's writings on fossils, linking them with his own narrative and comments to produce a credible introduction to Cuvier's work.

Victor W. Chen

JACQUES DAGUERRE

Born: November 18, 1787; Cormeilles, near Paris, France
Died: July 10, 1851; Bry-sur-Marne, France
Areas of Achievement: Invention and technology
Contribution: Daguerre's greatest renown rests upon his contribution to the technology of photography. He achieved the earliest fixed-image photograph developed from a latent image. The process discovered by him produced a photograph on a polished iodized silver plate that was patented as the "daguerreotype."

Early Life

Jacques Daguerre's formal education in the schools of Orléans was brief and poor because of the distractions of the French Revolution. Fortunately, he revealed a gift for drawing early in his childhood, which, in some measure, offset the quality of his education. Daguerre was apprenticed by his father to a draftsman. Though the training in detailed exactitude was later to prove beneficial, it was Daguerre's wish to study painting. In 1804, his father allowed him to go to Paris for that purpose. He was apprenticed to the chief stage designer at the Paris Opera, with whom he lived and worked for three years.

At the end of this apprenticeship, Daguerre took employment with Pierre Prévost, a painter who had achieved a certain celebrity with his panoramas. These were representations akin to those currently called cycloramas. The viewer was situated at the center of a cylindrical painting of very large dimensions, comprising a single expansive view. Such paintings must be executed with scrupulous attention to accuracy of scale and fidelity to perspective. Once more, his experience in draftsmanship served him well. In 1810, one week before his twenty-third birthday, Daguerre married twenty-year-old Louise Georgina Smith, sister of a fellow employee at the Prévost studio. He continued his association with Prévost for six years after his marriage, starting an independent career only in 1816.

Daguerre quickly distinguished himself as a set designer, where an ability to achieve delightful illusions and exotic effects came fully into play. Until 1821, he was engaged in designing sets for some of the best-known theaters in Paris, and in 1819 the Académie Royale de Musique enlisted his widely acclaimed talents. For two years, he was one of the chief designers for the Académie.

Life's Work

During 1821 and 1822, Daguerre devoted much time and effort to the development of a new technique for creating scenes of very convincing realism that he called the "diorama." This new form of illusion was developed by Daguerre in conjunction with another former associate from Prévost's studio, Charles-Marie Bouton.

The diorama was clearly the product of a series of incremental advances on previous techniques for creating visual illusion. The most recent, the diaphanorama, was itself a departure from the panorama. Franz Niklaus König, the creator of the diaphanorama, was Swiss by birth and was also an experienced set designer.

König's effects were produced by painting with watercolors on transparent papers, the backs of which he subsequently oiled to increase their translucence. Displayed at a distance in darkened rooms, the paintings were illuminated by controlled, reflected light played on the back as well as the front, the relative intensity of the light being adjustable in minute transitions. It is a virtual certainty that Daguerre witnessed a display of König's ingenuity when the latter traveled to Paris in 1821 and that his own diorama was actually a refinement of the basic concept devised by König.

Daguerre and Bouton bought land and constructed a specially designed structure. An enormous building was necessary because of the very large paintings involved and the distance to be maintained between the paintings and the viewers. The "picture rooms"—there were two—lay at the end of corridors which were arranged like spokes radiating from the circular viewing salon, widening as they moved away from the audience. Viewers sat or stood in a darkened, circular, revolvable salon that was positioned in such a way that they could look down only one of the two corridors, at the end of which was the scene.

After all the effects of the first scene had been rehearsed, the gallery faded into darkness, and the salon was imperceptibly made to revolve to the position from which the second gallery could be brought into view by the gradual introduction of light upon the second scene. Illumination was achieved by light introduced through windows, controlled by shutterlike devices, sometimes colored by filters and conducted to the desired surfaces by reflection. The structure itself and the inge-

nious system of illumination were so central to the scheme that they were independently patented.

The paintings, which were periodically changed so that audiences could return to see a new set of scenes, were executed upon both sides of a white calico fabric, optimally translucent and prepared with sizing. The pigment was suspended in a turpentine vehicle and applied to the fabric in as thin a coat as would achieve the effect without causing complete opacity. The painting was then shaded with translucent colors. By illuminating the painting first on one side and then the other and by using lights of various colors, parts of the composition were made to disappear, while others seemed to advance. It was possible in this manner to present a before-and-after history of a scene, for example, a peaceful Swiss valley that fell victim to an enormous landslide. By using several painted cloths in echelon with the lighting such that the viewer could see through one, two, or more of them simultaneously, it was possible to achieve an astonishing degree of three-dimensional realism as well as to give the illusion of transitory atmospheric effects.

The diorama was received with enthusiasm, and Daguerre was made a Chevalier of the Legion of Honor in 1824; however, the enterprise appears never to have been much of a financial success. In March of 1839, a fire destroyed the Paris Diorama, which, because of the highly combustible materials it contained, was a constant danger.

By that time, Daguerre had brought to fruition his work on a means of fixing an image made upon a light-sensitive surface in a camera obscura. A man of his time, Daguerre was motivated not only by an interest in the accurate study of proportion and perspective but also by a desire for celebrity and wealth. Possibly this drive to distinguish himself explains why he periodically made claims to successes that proved to be false or that were only subsequently achieved.

Sometime during the year 1826, Daguerre learned of the work being done on heliography by Nicéphore Niépce. Niépce, in 1826, had produced the world's first photograph. Using a pewter plate coated with bitumen of Judea (asphaltum) and placed at the back of a camera obscura, he achieved an image of a scene from the second story of his country home. The process, however, required an exposure time of eight hours. Upon learning of this shortcoming in the exposure process, Daguerre at

once approached Niépce by letter. By misrepresenting the extent of his own success, Daguerre drew a reluctant Niépce into a partnership. Having failed to secure any return on his own developments, Niépce on December 14, 1829, signed an agreement with Daguerre, who said that he had a strategy by which Niépce could profit from his discoveries. The partnership was entitled "Niépce-Daguerre," and by its terms Daguerre was obliged to "improve" a process of which Niépce was named "inventor." Daguerre was also to contribute a camera of an improved design, which he claimed to have developed and which would substantially reduce the exposure time. The camera, in the form described by Daguerre, did not exist. Daguerre, however, was twenty-two years younger than the senior partner, and Niépce hoped to enjoy the fruits of the great capacity for hard work and the unflagging optimism that characterized his new partner.

Daguerre learned from Niépce that it was not necessary to expose a plate until the image became visible on its surface; a faint or even completely invisible image could be brought out (developed) by chemical processes. Daguerre also seems to have learned from his partner that iodine could be used as the photosensitive coating to receive the image.

Niépce died in great poverty in 1833, before the partnership yielded any advantage to him. His son and legatee, Isidore, succeeded him as Daguerre's partner. At that time, the original problems remained unsolved: Images using iodine were negative, the exposure time remained seven to eight hours, and no means had been found to prevent the image from deterioration in light.

Daguerre, however, began to make critical discoveries after the death of Niépce. First, he made the discovery (evidently by the purest chance) that iodized silvered plates could be used as the surface upon which to secure light images in the camera. Then, sometime in 1837, he found (also quite by chance) that mercury vapors would precipitate out on the light-affected portions of an iodized silver surface. These two critical discoveries are credited entirely to Daguerre in spite of his haphazard methods. The great advantage in them was the production of a positive image at a substantial reduction in the exposure time, though he had not as yet discovered any means of making the image thus obtained permanent.

On May 9, 1835, Daguerre secured a modification of the partnership agreement. Isidore reluctantly signed, and Daguerre soon announced publicly that he had discovered a means of fixing permanently the images that he was securing. In fact, it was not until two years later, in May of 1837, that he made such a discovery.

Over the strong objections of Isidore, terms of the partnership were again revised. The names in the partnership were reversed, and it was made clear that Daguerre had pressed beyond mere improvement of someone else's discovery. Isidore was told that the new process (mercury development) reduced exposure time to four minutes. In truth, it still required twenty to thirty minutes of exposure to secure an image, which was still too long to make portraiture a practical possibility.

An effort to finance further development of the process through a public subscription failed in 1839. In March, the diorama was consumed in a spectacular fire. Daguerre was fifty-one, and his fortunes seemed to have hit a low point. He and Niépce decided to realize what they could by offering the process to the French government. They revealed the method to François Arago, a member of the Chamber of Deputies as well as president of the Academy of Sciences. Arago then secured the government's acceptance. Daguerre was made an Officer of the Legion of Honor, and both he and Niépce were given comfortable life pensions. The French government at once donated the process to the world at large.

Within months, a flood of developments vastly improved the quality and practicality of daguerreotypy. Among the more important of these were the use of thiosulfate as a fixative; a lens that corrected Daguerre's original mirror image; the introduction of the tripod and leather bellows, which made the camera more easily portable; and the discovery of bromoiodide and iodine bromochloride to increase significantly the sensitivity of plates, which, coupled with improved cameras, reduced exposure time to between 90 and 120 seconds for good-quality results.

Daguerre, much lionized for his discoveries, retired to a country estate at Bry-sur-Marne, where he died quite suddenly on July 10, 1851, at the age of sixty-three. The surviving daguerreotypes taken of their eponymous creator reveal a gentleman of ample but not excessive girth, a very round face still crowned by a full complement of curly, salt-and-pepper hair, a full mustache, and a look of fixed determination about the hooded eyes.

Summary

During an age when an individual's worth was considered to be the precise equivalent of his wealth and the self-made man was the social ideal, Jacques Daguerre, by hard work and seriousness of purpose, built upon native talents rather than education or social privilege to become both wealthy and famous. In the creation of the diorama, he produced not merely the most exciting optical illusion prior to motion pictures but also techniques that are still used in stage settings for the ballet and the opera to achieve mysterious or transitional effects.

Daguerre turned his attention to the emerging technology of photography when the diorama provided recognition but no appreciable wealth. Though the extent of his indebtedness to Niépce remains unresolved, it is certain that it was his own efforts that resulted in the first fixed-image photograph developed from a latent image. It is, therefore, equally certain that the foundation for the art in its present state was laid by Daguerre.

Bibliography

Bisbee, A. *The History and Practice of Daguerreotyping*. Dayton, Ohio: Clafting, 1853. An early and very clear description of the process used by Daguerre. This little book was written for the American public at the crest of the enthusiasm over the technology.

Eder, Josef Maria. *History of Photography*. Translated by Edward Epstean. New York: Columbia University Press, 1945. This book is annoyingly chauvinistic but sound in its scholarship. It is technically more informed than the Gernsheim work. Eder always thought that the critical discoveries were those of Niépce and evidently thought Daguerre not above taking credit for discoveries not, in fact, his own.

Gernsheim, Helmut, and Alison Gernsheim. *L. J. M. Daguerre: The History of the Diorama and the Daguerreotype*. Rev. Ed. New York: Dover, 1968. The only biography devoted to Daguerre's life and work. This study includes plates of the earliest efforts at photography and the two best daguerreotypes of Daguerre.

Rinhart, Floyd, and Marion Rinhart. *The American Daguerreotype*. Athens: University of Georgia Press, 1981. This book, which includes a number of photographs of original daguerreotype equipment and some beautiful examples of the art, includes a brief account of its development.

Werge, John. *The Evolution of Photography.* London: Piper and Carter, 1890; New York: Arno Press, 1973. Werge emphasizes the haphazard nature of Daguerre's research and recounts in detail stories that emphasize the utter happenstance by which the critical discoveries were made.

John Knox Stevens

GOTTLIEB DAIMLER

Born: March 17, 1834; Schorndorf (near Stuttgart), Württemberg

Died: March 6, 1900; Cannstatt, Germany

Areas of Achievement: Engineering, invention, and technology

Contribution: Daimler, as much as any one man, was the inventor of the first high-speed motor; because of his carburetion process and his development of light engine weight his motor became adaptable to driving both motor cars and aircraft.

Early Life

The second son of a master baker, Gottlieb Daimler was born in Schorndorf, Württemberg, on March 17, 1834. Daimler was relatively well educated. He attended public school, followed by two years of Latin school. One of young Daimler's closest friends was the son of a master gunsmith, under whose tutelage he apprenticed himself for three years until he produced a piece of work that qualified him as a journeyman. His work entailed precise drawings, which Daimler particularly loved and carried into later life with his depictions of plants and animals.

Journeyman status meant further training en route to mastery. Gottlieb went to work in Alsace, designing machine tools. Recognizing his educational deficiencies, particularly in mathematics, he soon applied his earned savings for two additional years of formal training, this time at the Stuttgart Polytechnic. While in Stuttgart, he came in contact with some of developing Germany's leading engineers such as Ferdinand von Steinbus. Steinbus, who had been instrumental in the industrial development of Württemberg, subsidized Daimler's further training in France and England, where he worked variously as a mechanic, foreman, and manager before returning to Württemberg as the manager of Bruderhaus of Rentlingen's—a highly esteemed firm of machine builders.

While at Bruderhaus, Daimler met Wilhelm Maybach, whose career he helped to shape and with whom he would later collaborate. Maybach, a remarkable young man twelve years Daimler's junior, had already demonstrated his manual skills and his grasp of mathematics, physics, and mechanical drawing. In 1868, when Daimler assumed the management of one of Karlsruhe's leading machine shops, he brought Maybach into his drawing office.

As the by-then-unified Germany rapidly industrialized under Otto von Bismarck and opportunities for skilled men blossomed, Daimler accepted a position with the firm of Otto and Langen in Deutz. Nikolaus August Otto and Eugen Langen furthered the practical design and production of an internal-combustion engine. Beginning in the 1860's, Étienne Lenoir made several hundred marketable gas (not gasoline) fired internal-combustion engines employed in machine shops and for pumping water. To Lenoir's impressive, if commercially unsuccessful work, Otto and Langen added the development, largely because of Daimler, of the first four-cycle engine, which in its operations is still the basis of most gasoline engines.

Life's Work

In his late forties, Daimler decided to leave his employers' Deutz plant and establish a plant for himself at Cannstatt in 1882. With him went Wilhelm Maybach, by then a masterful machine builder. Daimler's objective was to develop a practical, high-speed, gasoline-driven motor that would be adaptable to vehicle locomotion. By the beginning of the 1880's, Daimler's new four-stroke machines achieved between 150 and 180 revolutions per minute. At 250 revolutions per minute, however, there were problems with ignition and with the proper metering and timing of admixtures of gasoline and air. Daimler had resolved this problem in mechanical terms while working for Otto and Langen by introducing a flame carried in a special slide valve. This commercial result was Daimler's high-speed motor, capable of nine hundred revolutions per minute. Thirty thousand of these motors were sold internationally within the first decade of its development.

The problem that Daimler set out to resolve when he left Otto and Langen's remarkably inventive works had to do with the uses to which his inventions were put amid bitter international patent battles. Most of the Otto and Langen (or so-called Deutz) motors were sold to perform stationary functions. After years of losses and borrowing, Otto and Langen, to survive, addressed the available market for their product—customers who required stationary engines requisite to the needs of small workshops and mines. The production of moving vehicles, not only on the ground but also in the air, however, was what Daimler had in view.

Gottlieb Daimler with his Daimler-Wagen in 1886

At his Cannstatt workshop, he had by 1884 developed a high-speed gasoline engine in which the fuel for the combustion chambers was metered by a wick carburetor and ignited by an electric spark. It was a vertical engine which would soon be built in sizes from one-half to twenty-five horsepower with one, two, and four cylinders and eventually ran at six hundred revolutions per minute. Daimler claimed that he had created the basis for an entirely new industry.

He tested his new motor on a wooden cycle, which he drove in the garden of his Cannstatt home in November, 1885, and then on a boat, the first to be powered by a gasoline engine, both tests proving successful. By the following year, he had produced the four-wheeled Daimler carriage, which soon began making its appearance in Cannstatt and nearby Stuttgart. Its top speed was about six kilometers per hour. Daimler's motor, with improvements constantly insisted upon by Maybach, was swiftly patented. Maybach, meanwhile, urged Daimler to join his motor and chassis to form a sin-

gle machine unit. Since Daimler was excited by prospects of mass-producing his vehicles as well as by turning a profit, he soon acquiesced and built a four-wheeled, gasoline-driven carriage that really was an automobile.

While late nineteenth century Germany furnished a marvelous environment for invention and technological innovation, and as a consequence had become one of the world's foremost industrial powers, Daimler's automobile did not become popular in that country. It remained for the French to lend the notoriety to Daimler's car that was essential to its popularity.

On July 1, 1894, the first international automobile race, along the one-hundred-kilometer Paris-Rouen road, was held. The winner was a Daimler machine that reached unprecedented speeds of up to 110 kilometers per hour. With world attention on the race, Daimler received eighty thousand francs in prize money. It was manifest at a practical level that the automobile was no longer a rich man's toy. The race had justified the previous formation of the

Daimler Motoren-Gesellschaft in Cannstatt on January 28, 1890, a concern which became one of the world's great producers of automobiles.

Daimler and Maybach came to be driven less by pure technical considerations than by demands from prospective customers to increase the power of their automobiles from nine horsepower to thirty and forty horsepower. Under these immediate pressures, Daimler by 1900 developed and produced the first modern automobile, judged by power and appearance. Its name was "Mercédès."

Daimler did not live to enjoy the success of the first Mercedes after 1900. His health had been declining, and he was unable to bear the pressures under which he had worked for more than forty years. He died on March 6, 1900, in Cannstatt.

Summary

A brilliant technician and industrial entrepreneur, Gottlieb Daimler resolved the major problems that had plagued, and had thus retarded, the progress of men who had sought to design and produce automotive vehicles. His competence and technical skill exercised in the development of an efficient carburetor and a lightweight, gasoline-driven engine were responsible for the emergence of the world's first true automobile, the ultimate expression of which was the Mercedes. His vision was extraordinary as was demonstrated in 1897 by his recommendations to German authorities that they entertain plans for the creation of a motor-driven airship.

Daimler, like so many nineteenth century men of achievement, combined an extraordinary capacity for hard work with keen powers of observation and exceptional farsightedness. Daimler had spoken to his ultimate objectives while still a young man, and he never deviated from them.

Bibliography

Burstall, Aubrey F. *A History of Mechanical Engineering*. New York: Pitman, and London: Faber, 1963. Chapters 7 and 8, although they spend little time on Daimler, place him in context. Excellent schematic illustrations of the Otto engine and Daimler's 1897 gasoline engine. Directed to intelligent lay readers, it is richly illustrated. Contains reference footnotes, bibliographies, and an index.

Clerk, Dugald. *The Gas, Oil, and Petrol Engine*. 2 vols. London and New York: Longman, 1909. Few other works so extensively trace the evolution of these varied engines and the problems that had to be resolved to render them effective. Volume 2 is particularly pertinent in regard to Daimler's achievements. While the work is old, it remains authoritative and is quite readable. Contains illustrations, bibliographical notations, and a useful index.

Field, D. C. "Internal Combustion Engines." In *The Late Nineteenth Century, c. 1850 to c. 1920.* Vol. 5 in *A History of Technology*, edited by Charles Singer, E. J. Holmyard, A. R. Hall, and Trevor Williams. Oxford: Clarendon Press, 1958. Clearly and authoritatively written for a general readership, this essay places Daimler's major contributions in context. There are many precise illustrations. Good select bibliographies follow this (and other) chapters, and there is a useful index for the entire volume.

Hill, Frank Ernest. *The Automobile: How It Came, Grew, and Changed Our Lives*. New York: Dodd, Mead, 1967. Intended primarily for high school readers rather than for college or university students. The early chapters, while somewhat simplistic compared to works cited above, nevertheless afford a sound general picture of Daimler's work. Includes photographs and an index.

Rae, John B. "The Internal Combustion Engine on Wheels." In *Technology in the Twentieth Century*. Vol. 2 in *Technology in Western Civilization*, edited by Melvin Kranzburg and Carroll Pursell. New York: Oxford University Press, 1967. Written by specialists for a general readership. Rae's chapter helps place the work of Daimler and other early automotive pioneers in an evolutionary context. Contains an extensive bibliography and an extensive index.

Rolt, Lionel Thomas C. *Great Engineers*. London: Bell, 1962; New York: St. Martin's Press, 1963. The only work in English that affords personal details on the life of Daimler and those with whom he worked and competed. Rolt, a British engineer, established himself as a fine, readable historian of engineers, precise and accurate without being pedantic. Contains a useful index.

Clifton K. Yearley

FIRST MARQUESS OF DALHOUSIE
James Andrew Broun Ramsay

Born: April 22, 1812; Dalhousie Castle, Midlothian, Scotland

Died: December 19, 1860; Dalhousie Castle, Midlothian, Scotland

Area of Achievement: Government

Contribution: Dalhousie's greatest accomplishment was the creation of a communications system linking all of India.

Early Life

James Andrew Broun Ramsay was born April 22, 1812, in the family seat at Dalhousie Castle in Scotland, the last of three brothers. His father, George, the ninth Earl of Dalhousie, served with distinction during the Peninsular War from 1812 to 1814, and from 1819 to 1828, he was captain-general and governor-in-chief of Canada. Christina, his mother, was the heiress of Charles Broun of Colstoun.

In 1816, the ninth earl became lieutenant-governor of Nova Scotia, and Ramsay accompanied his father and mother to their new home. In 1817, the Ramsay's learned that James's middle brother, Charles, had died of the measles. Further sadness struck in 1832, when Ramsay's elder brother died of rheumatism. Ramsay now became the heir to the title.

Ramsay received his early education from a private tutor, but in 1825, he entered Harrow. For the next two years, Ramsay was an energetic if not devoted student, occupying his time in playing cards, smoking, and drinking. These activities led to his withdrawal from the school at the end of 1827. In 1829, he entered Oxford, from which he received his B.A. in 1833.

Early in his life, Ramsay showed a predilection for introspection. In 1824, at the age of twelve, he began a diary which he continued until the end of his official career. Already, the sensitivity on which his contemporaries were later to remark was evident, as was a hint of melancholy. His physical appearance, along with this sensitivity, at first suggested weakness, for he was both short and small. His profile showed his true strength, however, in the aquiline nose, straight brows, and firm mouth. Ramsay's melancholic temperament did show itself with time, spurred by the death of his two brothers, the paralytic stroke suffered by his father in 1832 and his death in 1838, the death the following year of his mother, and the untimely death of his wife in 1853.

In the mid-1830's, Ramsay entered public life, standing as a Conservative candidate for the city of Edinburgh, where he was defeated. In 1836, he married Lady Susan Hay, the daughter of the Marquis of Tweeddale, a political ally. Standing for election again in 1837, this time in Haddingtonshire, he was successful, but he was forced to give up his seat on his accession to the earldom at his father's death in 1838.

Life's Work

In the House of Lords, Dalhousie gained confidence under the eye of the Duke of Wellington, whose personal regard for the ninth earl was immense. Sir Robert Peel appointed him to his first government position, vice president of the Board of Trade, in 1843. In this capacity, Dalhousie concerned himself with the burgeoning railway system in Great Britain. His abilities were recognized by the leaders of both parties, and in 1847, Lord John Russell appointed him governor-general of the British possessions in India.

Dalhousie immediately faced the problems created by the Second Sikh War. The question of the annexation of the Punjab was instrumental in setting Dalhousie's policy of British expansionism for the rest of his term in office. Following the defeat of the Sikh army at Guzarat, Dalhousie decided that the British would rule the Punjab directly, rather than through a local prince, and on March 29, 1849, he declared the Punjab a British province. This move established a precedent, which was often invoked in subsequent years.

Dalhousie also took steps to abolish rituals and traditions fundamental to Indian society. The practice of suttee was suppressed and the right of Hindu widows to remarry established, as were the rights of converts from Hinduism. In addition, Dalhousie advanced a plan for a system of education that would extend throughout India, and he drew India together by erecting telegraph lines, building railroads, instituting a cheap postal service, and completing the Great Trunk Road that connected Peshawar, Bombay, Calcutta, and Delhi.

In the 1850's, Dalhousie's policy of outright annexation of territory proceeded apace. Upon the cessation of hostilities in the Second Burmese War in 1851, Dalhousie proclaimed Lower Burma a

British province under the same guidelines as the Punjab. The province of Oudh also was annexed because of "misgovernment" on the part of its rulers. At the same time, Dalhousie declared that the traditional practice by which a childless rajah adopted an heir would no longer be recognized by the government. Any territory without a legitimate heir would automatically come under direct British rule. Nagpur, Jhansi, and Sattara fell to British control in this manner. The annexation policies of Dalhousie contributed greatly to the general anti-British feeling in India. The suppression of both Hindu and Muslim traditions, especially his refusal to recognize the right of adopted sons to carry on royal lines, created a backlash against his policies. At the same time that Dalhousie was attempting to build what he considered a better society, Indians were preparing to reaffirm and, if necessary, reassert by force their age-old customs. The rumor that new cartridges for the use of the sepoys in the Indian Army in 1857 were greased with pig and cow fat was the trigger. The Indian Mutiny followed and Dalhousie was ordered back to Great Britain.

Dalhousie's health had suffered greatly while he was in India. His wife had died unexpectedly in 1853, and his habit of overwork drained his energies. The disappointment and anguish of the mutiny diminished his strength further and he went directly to Dalhousie Castle on arrival in Great Britain. He died there on December 19, 1860. He was survived by his two daughters.

Summary

First Marquess of Dalhousie's reputation has suffered much from studies blaming him for the onset of the Sepoy Mutiny. While these works are not wrong in assuming that Dalhousie was largely unaware of the tremendous tensions developing in India through the 1850's, many of the preconditions for rebellion existed prior to Dalhousie's regime.

Dalhousie must also be considered as the architect of modern geographical India. The building of roads and telegraph systems as well as the beginning of railroad construction date from his tenure as governor-general and rank among his most cherished accomplishments. Although subsequent rulers developed this web of communication and transportation further, Dalhousie set out its parameters and planned its expansion. Nevertheless, Dalhousie was also an archetype of the British colonial administrator. His educational reforms aimed not at creating schools in which natives might become literate but rather institutions in which future clerks and minor officials could learn English and join in administering the Empire. His decision to put aside the inheritance rights of adopted sons of native princes spread direct rule by the British throughout India. In short, Dalhousie demonstrated his belief that Western, and specifically English, ways were inherently superior to those of India, and he set about, piece by piece, undermining all Indian customs he deemed either barbaric or detrimental to the proper workings of the Empire.

Finally, Dalhousie was extraordinarily conscientious and hardworking. A day's work was not over until his desk was clear. While this heavy load almost certainly contributed to his early death, colonial affairs proceeded more smoothly during his tenure in India than they ever had before, primarily as a result of Dalhousie's intelligence and attention to detail. Dalhousie set an example for colonial administrators of every nation.

Bibliography

Lee-Warner, Sir William. *The Life of the Marquis of Dalhousie K.T.* 2 vols. London and New York: Macmillan, 1904. Although outdated in style and interpretation, Lee-Warner's work remains the most comprehensive biography of Dalhousie. Lee-Warner had access to all of Dalhousie's private papers and was himself stationed in India.

Lloyd, T.O. *The British Empire, 1558-1983.* 2d ed. Oxford and New York: Oxford University Press, 1996. A general account of Great Britain's imperial expansion and decline. Allows comparison of Indian policies generally, and Dalhousie's specifically, with other territories and times.

Mason, Philip. *The Men Who Ruled India.* London: Cape, and New York: St. Martin's Press, 1954. A study covering the period from 1600 to 1947. Mason's work provides valuable material about the middle-level bureaucrats who carried out and often opposed Dalhousie's policies.

Moore, R.J. *Sir Charles Wood's Indian Policy, 1853-66.* Manchester: Manchester University Press, 1966. Provides an account of Indian policy from the point of view of the home government. Moore admits that Dalhousie must shoulder some of the blame for the Sepoy Mutiny but that his later years in office more than made up for his early stumbles. Valuable for its perspective of Dalhousie's policies.

John Phillips

JOHN DALTON

Born: September 6, 1766; Eaglesfield, Cumberland, England
Died: July 27, 1844; Manchester, England
Areas of Achievement: Physics, chemistry, and meteorology
Contribution: Dalton was the founder of the modern atomic theory.

Early Life

John Dalton, born September 6, 1766, in Eaglesfield, Cumberland, was the second son of Joseph Dalton, a poor weaver, and Deborah Greenup, a woman of vigor and intelligence. His parents came from old Quaker stock, and they had six children, three of whom, Jonathan, John, and Mary, lived to maturity. John was deeply influenced by his mother's tenacity and frugality. The Society of Friends, which formed a strong social fabric in west Cumberland, was another powerful influence. The Cumberland Quakers emphasized both general education and particular training in natural philosophy, and this provided a favorable environment for John's development as a scientist.

Dalton made rapid progress under John Fletcher in the village school, and he quickly attracted the attention of Elihu Robinson, a prominent Quaker naturalist who became Dalton's patron and lifelong friend. Because of the poverty of his family, Dalton was forced to work for a time as a farm laborer, but in 1781 he was liberated from this way of life by an invitation to replace his elder brother as assistant at Kendal, a boarding school some forty miles from Eaglesfield. The school, newly built by Quakers, had a well-stocked library that contained Sir Isaac Newton's *Philosophiae Naturalis Principia Mathematica* (1687; *Mathematical Principals of Natural Philosophy*, 1729) as well as works of both British and Continental natural philosophers. As at Eaglesfield, so at Kendal, Dalton was fortunate in forming an important friendship. In this case, his patron and friend was the blind natural philosopher John Gough. Under Gough's tutelage, Dalton made rapid progress in mathematics, meteorology, and botany. In imitation of his master, Dalton started in 1787 keeping a daily meteorological record, a practice he continued until the day of his death.

At Kendal, Dalton began giving a series of public lectures in physics and astronomy. As a teacher, he was clear and orderly, though rather colorless.

In physical appearance, he was a tall, gaunt, and awkward man with a prominent chin and nose, and he dressed in the Quaker fashion: knee breeches, gray stockings, and buckled shoes. Though modestly successful at Kendal, he became restless and sought a different profession. He made inquiries about studying medicine at Edinburgh, but he met with discouraging replies. Eventually, Dalton accepted a position as professor of mathematics and natural philosophy in Manchester. He was pleased with this appointment because, in addition to mathematics and natural philosophy, he was allowed to teach chemistry.

In 1800, encouraged by his success in Manchester, Dalton decided to resign his position and open his own "mathematical academy," where he would offer courses in mathematics, experimental philosophy, and chemistry. This endeavor prospered, and within two years Dalton had enough students to provide him with a modest income. Private teaching on this scale would occupy and support him for the rest of his days.

Life's Work

Dalton was deeply influenced by the British tradition of popular Newtonianism, a way of visualizing the world through the internal makeup of matter and the operation of short-range forces. As shown so well by Newton, these forces could be described mathematically. Besides his interest in theoretical Newtonian physics, Dalton was involved with more practical concerns—constructing barometers, thermometers, rain gauges, and hygrometers. Dalton produced essays on trade winds, proposed a theory of the aurora borealis, and advanced a theory of rain. His meteorological investigations led him to question how the gases of the air were held together: Were they chemically united or were they physically mixed together in the air just as sand and stones were in the earth? He concluded that gases, composed of particles, were physically mixed together, and this led him to deduce that in a mixture of gases at the same temperature, every gas acts independently (Dalton's law of partial pressures). It is ironic that in trying to provide a proof for his physical ideas, Dalton discovered the chemical atomic theory. What started as an interest in meteorology ended up as a new approach to chemistry.

To support his theory of mixed gases, Dalton experimented on the proportions of the different gases in the atmosphere. It was this investigation which accidentally raised the whole question of the solubility of gases in water. In 1802, he read a paper to the Manchester Literary and Philosophical Society in which he proposed that carbon dioxide gas (which he called "carbonic acid" gas) was held in water, not by chemical attractive forces but by the pressure of the gas on the surface, forcing it into the pores of the water. This explanation provoked William Henry, Dalton's close friend, to begin a series of experiments to discover the order of attractions of gases for water. He eventually found that, at a certain temperature, the volume of a gas taken up by a given volume of water is directly proportional to the pressure of the gas (Henry's law). Dalton was quick to see the relevance of Henry's results to his own ideas. He saw the absorption of gases by water as a purely mechanical effect. He realized that the greatest difficulty with the mechanical theory of gas-water solubility came from different gases obeying different laws. Why does water not admit into its bulk every kind of gas in the same way? Dalton answered this question by saying that gases whose particles were lightest were least absorbable and those with greater weight were more absorbable. Therefore it is clear that Dalton's important decision to investigate the relative weights of atoms arose from his attempt to find experimental support for his theory of mixed gases. The paper which he wrote on this subject in 1803 closed with the very first list of what would come to be called atomic weights.

Dalton's method of calculating the relative weights of atoms was quite simple. Following the postulates of his theory of mixed gases, he assumed that when two elements come together in a chemical reaction, they do so in the simplest possible way (the rule of greatest simplicity). For example, Dalton knew that water was a compound of oxygen and hydrogen. He reasoned that if water was the only compound of these two elements that could be obtained (and it was at the time), then water must be a binary combination of one hydrogen atom and one oxygen atom (HO). Dalton also gave rules for deciding on formulas when there were two or more compounds of two elements. Armed with this mechanical view of combining atoms, it was easy for Dalton to argue from the experimental knowledge that, in forming nine ounces of water, eight ounces of oxygen combined with one ounce

of hydrogen to the statement that the relative weights of their atoms were as eight to one.

When he published his table of atomic weights in a Manchester journal, his theory, for the most part, provoked little reaction. It is true that Humphry Davy at the Royal Institution rejected Dalton's ideas as speculations that were more ingenious than important. Despite this lack of enthusiasm, Dalton continued to develop his theory, and in 1804 he worked out the formulas for different hydrocarbons. By 1807, he was spreading the news of his system of chemical philosophy (the first part of which was published in 1808, the second part in 1810). With this publication, the chemical atomic theory was launched. Unfortunately, the theory was the climax of Dalton's scientific creativity, and although he did much work in several scientific fields for the next twenty-five years, the main thrust of his work was in providing atomic weights for known chemical compounds, a problem that would plague chemists for the next fifty years.

Dalton's scientific studies were nourished by the Manchester Literary and Philosophical Society. This group gave him encouragement, an audience, and recognition. In contrast, the Royal Society was dilatory in making him a member, which they did in 1822 at the urging of some of Dalton's friends. In 1831, Dalton helped to found the British Association for the Advancement of Science, and he chaired several of its committees. His activity in these scientific societies was halted in 1837 by two severe paralytic attacks, which left him an invalid for the remaining years of his life.

Dalton lived according to regular and rigid habits. He never married, but he was deeply attached to several relatives and associates, in particular, Jonathan, his brother, and Peter Clare, his closest friend. In his later years, Dalton was admired by his countrymen, and after he died on July 27, 1844, he was given a civic funeral with full honors. His body lay in state in the Manchester Town Hall for four days while more than forty thousand people filed past his coffin. This response to his death was an indication of his scientific achievements and a manifestation of the love for him felt by the inhabitants of the city where he spent his happiest years.

Summary

John Dalton sometimes used the word "atom" in the sense of the smallest particle with a particular nature. If the atom were divided any further, it would lose its distinguishing chemical characteristics. Dalton also began, however, to think of atoms in the more radical sense of indivisible particles. With this usage, he provided a new and enormously fruitful model of matter for chemistry, because he was able to develop a way of determining atomic weights.

In his *New System of Chemical Philosophy* (1808, 1810), Dalton emphasized that chemical analysis is only the separating of ultimate particles, and synthesis is only the uniting of these particles. God created these elementary particles, and they cannot be changed. All the atoms of a particular element are alike, but the atoms of different elements differ. Though the atoms cannot be changed, they can be combined. Water, Dalton wrote, is composed of molecules formed by the union of a single particle of oxygen to a single ultimate particle of hydrogen.

Many chemists were unwilling to adopt Dalton's chemical atoms. Others used the atomic theory in a pragmatic way, for it helped to make sense of their observations in the laboratory, but they could not grasp its philosophical basis. Some scientists continued to object to atoms well into the twentieth century. They were a minority, however, and a characteristic theme of nineteenth century chemistry was the triumphant march of Dalton's ideas.

Bibliography

Cardwell, D. S. L., ed. *John Dalton and the Progress of Science.* Manchester: Manchester University Press, and New York: Barnes and Noble, 1968. A valuable record of the conference held in Manchester in 1966 to celebrate the bicentennial of Dalton's birth. It contains articles by scholars on various aspects of Dalton's achievement. The focus is on the intellectual background to the chemical atomic theory.

Greenaway, Frank. *John Dalton and the Atom.* London: Heinemann, and Ithaca, N.Y.: Cornell University Press, 1966. This book, intended for general audiences, explores the reasons that Dalton's atomic theory had greater impact on the scientific world than other similar theories produced before his time. Greenaway also investigates Dalton's work in other fields, such as his discovery of color blindness.

Hunt, David M., et al. "The Chemistry of John Dalton's Color Blindness." *Science* 267, no. 5200 (February 17, 1995). Discussion of a contemporary examination of Dalton's eyes which were preserved after his death. Analysis of DNA clarifies the type of color blindness that Dalton had and the physiologic reasons for it.

Patterson, Elizabeth C. *John Dalton and the Atomic Theory: The Biography of a Natural Philosopher.* New York: Doubleday, 1970. Patterson's study developed out of the fusion of two of her interests: early nineteenth century science and autodidacts, or self-taught persons. The book was part of the Science Study series for high school students, and it provides an analysis of Dalton and his work for the young student or layman.

Roscoe, H. E., and A. Harden. *New View of the Origin of Dalton's Atomic Theory: A Contribution to Chemical History, Together with Letters and Documents Concerning the Life and Labour of John Dalton, Now for the First Time Published from the Manuscript.* London and New York: Macmillan, 1896. Most of Dalton's manuscripts were destroyed in World War II, but important extracts from Dalton's notebooks have been preserved in this book. For example, it contains selections from Dalton's notebooks during the crucial years from 1802 to 1808. The reprint includes an introduction by Arnold Thackray.

Smyth, A. L. *John Dalton, 1766-1844: A Bibliography of Works by and about Him with an Annotated List of His Surviving Apparatus and Personal Effects.* 2d ed. Manchester: Manchester Literacy and Philosophical Publications, 1997; Aldershot, Hampshire, and Brookfield, Vt.: Ashgate, 1998. This revised bibliography contains 50 percent more entries than the 1966 edition and includes letters, extensive annotations, and many illustrations.

Thackray, Arnold. *Atoms and Powers: An Essay on Newtonian Matter-Theory and the Development of Chemistry.* Cambridge, Mass.: Harvard University Press, 1970. This book provides an excellent treatment of the background by means of which Dalton's ideas were developed. It traces the development of chemistry from Newton to the radical break with Newtonian chemistry engineered by Dalton.

————. *John Dalton: Critical Assessments of His Life and Science.* Cambridge, Mass.: Harvard University Press, 1972. Thackray is a leading scholar on Dalton, and in this book, which relies on new documentation, he situates Dalton in the social and cultural context of the Industrial Revolution. He also uses Dalton to exemplify certain aspects of scientific change.

Robert J. Paradowski

CHARLES DARWIN

Born: February 12, 1809; Shrewsbury, Shropshire,
England
Died: April 19, 1882; Downe, Kent, England
Areas of Achievement: Biology and natural history
Contribution: Darwin's theory of evolution
through natural selection, which he set forth in
On the Origin of Species, revolutionized biology
by providing a scientific explanation for the ori-
gin and development of living forms.

Early Life

Charles Robert Darwin was born on February 12,
1809, in Shrewsbury, the fifth of six children. His
mother, Susannah, the daughter of famed potter Josiah Wedgwood, died when he was eight, leaving
him in the care of his elder sisters. His father, Robert Waring Darwin, was a robust and genial country doctor with a wide practice. In 1818, young
Darwin entered Dr. Butler's Shrewsbury School,
where he learned some classics but little else. At
home he was a quiet, docile child, with an interest
in solitary walks and collecting coins and minerals.

In 1825, Darwin was sent to Edinburgh to study
medicine, since his family hoped he would enter
his father's profession. He proved to be a poor student, showing little interest in anatomy and disliking the crude operations performed without anes-
thetics. When he left Shrewsbury, his father
rebuked him, saying, "You care for nothing but
shooting, dogs, and rat-catching, and you will be a
disgrace to yourself and all your family."

As a last resort, the young Darwin was sent to
Christ's College, Cambridge, to prepare for the
ministry, a profession for which he felt no more enthusiasm than he did for medicine, and he soon fell
in among the sporting set. Though not a distinguished student, Darwin took an interest in natural
science and was influenced by Alexander von
Humboldt's *Personal Narrative of Travels to the
Equinoctial Regions of the New Continent During
the Years 1799-1804* (1814-1829) and Charles Lyell's *Principles of Geology* (1830-1833). He met
John Stevens Henslow, a botany professor who encouraged his interest in natural history and helped
to secure for him a position as naturalist aboard
HMS *Beagle*, soon to depart on a five-year scientific expedition around the world. The *Beagle*
sailed from Devonport on December 31, 1831.
Darwin's experiences during the voyage from 1831

to 1836 were instrumental in shaping his theory of
evolution.

The voyage of the *Beagle* took Darwin along the
coast of South America, where twenty-nine months
were spent charting the waters off the Pacific coast.
Darwin explored the Andes and the pampas and
kept detailed journals in which he carefully observed differences among the South American flora
and fauna, particularly on the Galapagos Islands,
where he found a remarkable divergence among the
same species from different islands. Before he began his voyage, he had no reason to doubt the im-
mutability of species, but from his firsthand experiences he gradually began to doubt the creationist
view of life. He would later draw upon these extensive field observations to formulate his theory of
natural selection. Darwin was able to draw together
from his travels vast amounts of scientific evidence
to buttress his arguments against scientific and religious challenges. When he returned to England on
October 2, 1836, he was an accomplished naturalist,
collector, and geologist with a new view of the natural history of life.

After his return to London, Darwin settled in an
apartment and began a detailed study of coral
reefs. He became secretary to the Geological Society and a member of the Royal Society. He married
his first cousin, Emma Wedgwood, in January,
1839. Because his health was poor, the couple settled outside London, in Kent. Here, despite his infirmities, Darwin did his most important work. A
thin man, about six feet tall, Darwin walked with a
stoop that made him appear shorter, especially as
his illness worsened later in life.

Life's Work

At Downe House in Kent, Darwin worked for the
next twenty years on his journals from the *Beagle*
trip, gathering information to support his theory of
evolution through natural selection. In 1837, Darwin
had begun his first notebook on the "species question." A chance reading of Thomas Robert Malthus'
*An Essay on the Principle of Population as It Affects
the Future Improvement of Society* (1798) in 1838
introduced him to the idea of the struggle for existence, which Darwin thought applied better to plants
and animals than to humans, who can expand their
food supply artificially. Darwin had returned from
his voyage with many unanswered questions. Why

were the finches and tortoises different on each of the Galapagos Islands, even though the habitats were not that different? Why were similar creatures, such as the ostrich and the rhea, found on separate continents? Why did some of the South American fossils of extinct mammals resemble the skeletons of some living creatures? The species question fascinated him, and gradually Darwin formulated a theory of the mutability and descent of living forms, although he was still unsure about the mechanisms of adaptation and change.

Two preliminary sketches of 1842 and 1844 presented Darwin's theory of evolution in rudimentary form, but he was determined to amass as much detail as possible to support his deductions. He turned to the work of animal breeders and horticulturalists for evidence of artificial selection among domesticated species. His preliminary work might have continued indefinitely if he had not received on June 18, 1854, an essay from Alfred Russel Wallace, a field naturalist in the Malay archipelago, outlining a theory of evolution and natural selection similar to his own. Darwin immediately wrote to his friends, Sir Charles Lyell and Joseph Hooker, explaining his dilemma and including an abstract of his own theory of evolution. Lyell and Hooker proposed that in order to avoid the question of precedence, the two papers should be presented simultaneously. Both were read before a meeting of the Linnean Society in Dublin on July 1, 1858, and were published together in the society's journal that year.

Darwin then began writing an abstract of his theory, which he entitled *On the Origin of Species*. All 1,250 copies sold out on the first day of publication in London on November 24, 1859. Darwin argued that since all species produce more offspring than can possibly survive, and since species populations remain relatively constant, there must be some mechanism working in nature to eliminate the unfit. Variations are randomly introduced in nature, some of which will permit a species to adapt better to its environment. These advantageous adaptations are passed on to the offspring, giving them an advantage for survival. Darwin did not understand the genetic mechanism by which offspring inherit adaptations. It would take another seventy years before the forgotten work of the Austrian geneticist Gregor Mendel was rediscovered and Sir Ronald Fisher integrated the theories of Darwinian selection and Mendelian genetics.

A quiet and retiring man, Darwin was surrounded by a storm of controversy after the publication of *On the Origin of Species*. Objection came both from orthodox clergy and unconvinced scientists. At Oxford in 1860, there was a famous debate on evolution between Thomas H. Huxley and Bishop Samuel Wilberforce, in which Huxley answered the creationist arguments against evolution and silenced the religious critics. For the rest of his life, Darwin worked at home on orchid- and pigeon-breeding experiments and successive editions of *On the Origin of Species*, as well as further studies on plant and animal domestication, climbing plants, cross-fertilization, orchids, the expression of emotions, and his famous *The Descent of Man and Selection in Relation to Sex* (1871). His wife, Emma, nursed him during his bouts of illness, whose origin is uncertain. She also reared their ten children, seven of whom survived to adulthood, three to become distinguished scientists and members of the Royal Society. In his later years, Darwin regretted the loss of his appreciation for poetry and music, complaining that his mind had become a "machine for grinding general laws out of large collections of facts." Still, he maintained a wide correspondence and enjoyed entertaining close friends and occasional visitors at home. He died on April 19, 1882, at Downe House in Kent, and was buried with full honors in the scientists' corner at Westminster Abbey, next to Sir Isaac Newton.

Summary

Perhaps more profoundly than any other single work, Charles Darwin's *On the Origin of Species* shaped the development of modern biology and, more broadly, the modern view of human nature. No longer was it possible to accept uncritically the biblical view of creation, with the implied special place of man in the divine order. Man became a creature among creatures, with a traceable evolution and descent from earlier hominoid forms. Darwin's ideas exerted a wide cultural influence, with a popular version of "the survival of the fittest" diffusing into the politics, literature, and sociology of the age, especially through Herbert Spencer's "social Darwinism." Unfortunately, Darwin's ideas were often mistakenly used to justify racism, discrimination, and repressive laissez-faire economic practices. Though Darwin drifted toward agnosticism and did not believe in a divinely sanctioned morality, neither did he condone a world of amoral violence and brute struggle for domination. He believed that human morality was the product of man's social and cultural evolution and that it did confer survival benefits. A gentle man who abhorred violence and cruelty, he would have been horrified at the political and social misapplications of Darwinian principles. Nevertheless, Darwin was not a Victorian liberal and accepted many of the unenlightened views of his age concerning "primitive" cultures.

During his lifetime, Darwin faced formidable challenges to his evolutionary theory, first from the scientist Fleeming Jenkin, who argued that fortuitous adaptations would be "swamped" and disappear in larger populations, and later from Lord Kelvin, who mistakenly questioned Darwin's estimate of the geological age of the earth on the basis of the laws of thermodynamics. These challenges led Darwin to revise *On the Origin of Species* extensively in successive editions and to back away from some of his earlier claims about the long timespan needed for slow, evolutionary changes to take place. In order to accommodate Lord Kelvin's shortened estimate of the earth's age, Darwin moved toward a neo-Lamarckian position concerning the inheritance of acquired characteristics. Darwin had no way of knowing that Mendel's discoveries in genetics would have answered many of his doubts about the sources of variation and the mechanisms of inheritance.

Darwin has had an immeasurable influence on the development of modern biology, ecology, morphology, embryology, and paleontology. His theory of evolution established a natural history of the earth and enabled humans to see themselves for the first time as part of the natural order of life. A lively debate continues among scientists about revisionist theories of evolution, including Stephen Jay Gould's notion of "punctuated equilibria," or sudden and dramatic evolutionary changes followed by long periods of relative stability. While they disagree about details, however, modern biologists agree that neo-evolutionary theory remains the only viable scientific explanation for the diversity of life on earth.

Bibliography

Alter, Stephen G. *Darwinism and the Linguistic Image: Language, Race, and Natural Theology in the Nineteenth Century.* Baltimore, Md.: Johns Hopkins University Press, 1999. Examination and analysis of the arguments used in nineteenth-century Darwinian debates. Of particular interest to scholars and students is the controversy over Darwin's *The Origin of Species.*

Brackman, Arnold. *A Delicate Arrangement: The Strange Case of Charles Darwin and Charles Russel Wallace.* New York: Times Books, 1980. Brachman argues that Darwin and his friends conspired to deny Wallace credit for having first discovered the theory of biological evolution.

Clark, Ronald W. *The Survival of Charles Darwin: A Biography of a Man and an Idea.* New York: Random House, 1984; London: Weidenfeld and Nicolson, 1985. A study of Darwin's life and work, concentrating on the genesis of evolutionary theory and its development after Darwin's death.

Colp, Ralph, Jr. *To Be an Invalid: The Illness of Charles Darwin.* Chicago: University of Chicago Press, 1977. A detailed study of the various theories about what caused Darwin's chronic, debilitating illness after the *Beagle* voyage.

Darwin, Charles. *Charles Darwin's Letters: A Selection, 1825-1859.* Frederick Burkhardt, ed. Cambridge and New York: Cambridge University Press, 1996. An unusual selection of letters that outline Darwin's life through daily experiences from his early days to the publication of *The Origin of Species.*

————. *The Autobiography of Charles Darwin, 1809-1882.* Edited by Nora Barlow. New York: Harcourt Brace, and London: Collins, 1958. A new edition of Darwin's autobiography, edited by his granddaughter, with the original omissions restored.

De Beer, Sir Gavin. *Charles Darwin: A Scientific Biography.* New York: Doubleday, 1965. The standard authorized biography of Darwin by an English scientist who enjoyed full access to the Darwin Papers at Cambridge University.

Eiseley, Loren. *Darwin's Century: Evolution and the Men Who Discovered It.* New York: Doubleday, 1958; London: Gollancz, 1959. A rigorous intellectual history of the concept of evolution and its antecedents, from Darwin's precursors through the publication of *On the Origin of Species* and its reception.

Irvine, William. *Apes, Angels, and Victorians: The Story of Darwin, Huxley, and Evolution.* New York: McGraw-Hill, 1955; London: Readers Union, 1956. A detailed cultural study of Darwinism and its impact on the Victorian mind.

Sears, Paul B. *Charles Darwin: The Naturalist as a Cultural Force.* New York: Scribner, 1950. A succinct study of Darwin's contribution to modern thought.

Andrew J. Angyal

JACQUES-LOUIS DAVID

Born: August 30, 1748; Paris, France
Died: December 29, 1825; Brussels, Belgium
Area of Achievement: Art
Contribution: David was the founder of nineteenth century neoclassicism. His participation in the political events of his time directed not only the course of his own art but that of European painting as well.

Early Life

Jacques-Louis David's birth on August 30, 1748, coincided with the beginning of many profound political, social, and aesthetic changes in France. He was born in Paris into the merchant-and-artisan middle class, although his grandmother was the cousin of François Boucher, first painter to the king. During his early schooling, David was by all accounts an indifferent student who preferred drawing to any of his other studies. In 1764, at the age of sixteen, having declared his firm resolve to become a painter, David sought the help of Boucher. Although no longer accepting students himself, Boucher saw promise in the young David and advised that he study with Joseph Vien, a professor at the Royal Academy of Painting and Sculpture. Vien was, according to Boucher, a good painter and teacher, but somewhat cold. He advocated a return to classical antiquity as a source of moral as well as artistic inspiration; his own work, however, consisted mostly of superficial borrowings of classical motifs that lacked understanding of the true meaning of the classical spirit.

After two years in Vien's studio, David entered the academy as a student. In the light of his subsequent actions against the academy, it is important to note that at this time David did not question the academy's control over the arts in France. Accepting the academy's hierarchy of categories in painting, he aspired to the highest—that of history painting—and was determined to win the coveted Prix de Rome, which would allow him three years of study at the academy's branch in Rome and almost certainly guarantee his eventual membership in the academy. As an academician, eligible for the best royal commissions and allowed to exhibit his work at the Salon, he would be assured of a successful career.

After three unsuccessful attempts to win the Prix de Rome, David contemplated suicide. Even though he finally won the competition in 1774 with his *Antiochus and Stratonice*, he now harbored a bitter resentment of the academy's earlier rejections of his work, never forgiving the academicians for their failure to recognize the talent he was certain he possessed. In fact, his style at this time was fragmented, reflecting the many currents in French painting in the early 1770's—he painted classical themes with something of Vien's sense of theatricality and exaggerated dramatic effect, while his use of light and brushwork came from the rococo tradition.

While studying in Italy from 1778 to 1780, David was influenced by Greco-Roman classicism, the masters of the High Renaissance, and the early Baroque works of Caravaggio and the Carracci family. He went to Rome determined not to be seduced by classical antiquity, believing it to be lifeless and static. After studying classical sculpture and the Pompeian frescoes, however, he realized that he had based his work on a false principle. He sensed that he would have to repudiate everything he had once thought about art. The qualities of virtue, austerity, and moral strength which he saw in ancient classical art reinforced his own desires for simplicity and strength. His work soon began to evidence the characteristics that would mark his mature style: solidity of drawing, clarity of form and narrative structure, and a Caravaggesque realism of light and texture.

Life's Work

David's first public acclaim came with the exhibition of twelve paintings in the Salon of 1781, the most popular of which was *Belisarius*—the story of false accusation and unjust punishment in a past age, which viewers equated with a contemporary general falsely accused and executed for treason. In the next few years, David's reputation increased—he was praised by the encyclopedist Denis Diderot for his creation of a noble, didactic art, and he attained academy membership.

David's involvement with the political events of his day began with *The Oath of the Horatii* of 1785. This painting, with its theme of self-sacrifice for a noble cause, was perceived by viewers as a pictorial call to arms for the revolutionary sentiments rapidly gaining momentum in France. Just as he had done in *Belisarius*, David created a parallel between contemporary events and ancient history with this theme of the three Horatii who, united by a strict patriotic discipline of body and soul, swear an oath to fight to the death for their country, while the tragic personal loss which always accompanies heroic military feats is evidenced by the group of mourning wives and children who witness the oath. Then, with the exhibition of *The Death of Socrates* in 1787 and *Brutus Receiving the Bodies of His Sons* in 1789—both of which portray the same message of self-sacrifice for a greater good—David's reputation as a prophet of the Revolution was firmly established in the minds of the French public.

David, now a fervent Jacobin and friend of Robespierre, took a more active role in revolutionary events after the fall of the Bastille. He became the director of all revolutionary festivals. He was elected as a deputy to the National Convention, during which time he voted for the execution of the king in 1793, signed hundreds of arrest warrants during the Reign of Terror, and proposed the creation of national museums that he also helped to organize. In 1790, he had avenged himself upon the academicians by organizing other dissident artists into the Commune des Arts, and, in 1793, he persuaded the convention to abolish the academy, replacing it with a jury to supervise the awarding of Salon prizes. As the principal juror, David had become the virtual dictator of the arts in France. Always a reformer, he freed French art from some of the old academic constraints while he led the way toward a new academicism.

David's political activities continued to give direction to his painting. The prophet of the Revolution became the chronicler of the historic events of the present. His works of this period range from *The Oath of the Tennis Court* (1791)—commemorating the deputies of the Third Estate's writing of a new constitution—to his apotheosis of such slain republican heroes as Jean-Paul Marat, Vicomte Paul François Barras, and Paul Michel Lepeletier.

Political involvement, however, almost cost David his life. After the execution of Robespierre in 1794, David was arrested and, although his enemies demanded his death, he was imprisoned instead. An amnesty in 1795 set him free. While in prison, David—having vowed at his trial that he would henceforth attach himself to principles and not to men—began planning his next great classical painting, *The Battle of the Romans and Sabines* (1794-1799), a work which restored his artistic reputation.

His determination to avoid political involvements was quickly forgotten when, in 1797, he ac-

quired a new patron and hero, Napoleon Bonaparte—then first consul and later Emperor of France. David became his court painter, documenting all the military splendor and pageantry of Napoleon's reign in portraits, in depictions of Napoleon leading his armies to victory, and finally in the coronation itself. David, who had earlier used history and mythology to refer to contemporary events, now turned contemporary events into new historical myths. His neoclassicism influenced everything from painting and sculpture to fashion and furniture design, and some of his most important works date from this period.

Unfortunately, David's political activities again proved to be his undoing. Napoleon's abdication and the First Bourbon Restoration of 1814 found David stubbornly maintaining his allegiance to the emperor, believing perhaps that his international reputation as an artist would protect him. During the Hundred Days, in fact, he met with Napoleon, who made him a Commander of the Legion of Honor, and he rashly signed the *Acte additionnel* (1815), again repudiating the rule of the Bourbon Kings of France. The Second Restoration, however, saw the enactment of a law banishing all who had signed the *Acte additionnel*, and David, at the age of sixty-seven, went into exile in Brussels.

Despite some attempts at reprisal by his enemies in France, David's last years in Brussels were happy and productive. Sale of his works brought him financial security, and he enjoyed a position of prominence within the artistic community. He painted continually, concentrating on portraits and mythological subjects such as *Cupid and Psyche* (1817) and *Telemachus and Eucharis* (1818)—themes which were less dangerous, perhaps, than the real or legendary histories of Greece and Rome which had served him so well during the politically active years of the Revolution, the Republic, and the Empire. He died peacefully at his home in Brussels on December 29, 1825, at the age of seventy-seven.

Summary

Jacques-Louis David's art, like his personality, was extremely complex. Friends described him as intense and dogmatic, sensitive and spartan—an assessment of character substantiated by the severe, doctrinaire classicism of his prerevolutionary works, all of which are remarkable for their stoicism and their sense of emotion held in check by icy control. David eventually realized that the success of these heroically ethical creations—which had proclaimed a new aesthetic and moral order—could not be repeated indefinitely, even by him. In 1808, he declared that the direction he had set for art was too severe to please for very long in France.

A different facet of David's personality was reflected in his attempt to separate artistic activity from the demands of morality by concentrating on purely aesthetic problems in *The Battle of the Romans and Sabines*—a work in which he modified the severity of his Roman classicism for a more Greek and abstract refinement. In his paintings of contemporary events during the Napoleonic era and in many of his portraits, David proved himself an acute observer of nature and a realist.

As the different goals and interests embodied in later nineteenth century movements such as Romanticism and Impressionism led artists to turn away from classicism, David's principles and his art were shunned, and his reputation went into an eclipse that lasted until 1913. At that time, an exhibition in Paris prompted an interest in his work which has continued to grow, and today he is acknowledged as the true founder of nineteenth century European neoclassicism.

Bibliography

Brookner, Anita. *Jacques-Louis David*. New York: Harper, and London: Chatto and Windus, 1980. One of the most complete biographies, this book contains important documentation, never before published in English, of David's artistic sources and his political activities. Also contains an extensive catalog of paintings and drawings, although most plates are monochrome.

Crow, Thomas. *Emulation: Making Artists for Revolutionary France*. New Haven, Conn.: Yale University Press, 1995. Art historian Thomas Crow examines five painters from Revolutionary France including David and four of his pupils—Drouais, Girodet, Gerard, and Gros and the relationships among them.

French Painting, 1774-1830: The Age of Revolution. Detroit: Wayne State University Press, 1975. Catalog of a French-American exhibition of paintings from the age of revolution. Excellent essays by foremost Davidian scholars discuss the artistic disunity of the era and analyze David's contribution to mainstream trends. Includes brief biographies of all exhibitors.

Friedlaender, Walter. *David to Delacroix*. Translated by Robert Goldwater. Cambridge, Mass.: Harvard University Press, 1952. Emphasizes the historical structure of French painting by studying the sources of various stylistic and intellectual currents of the period. Discusses classicism and other trends in David's art and the transformation of his principles by his followers.

Johnson, Dorothy. *Jacques-Louis David: The Art of Metamorphosis*. Princeton, N.J.: Princeton University Press, 1993. A collection of essays on David's artistic development and creativity. Johnson's study centers on David's writings on a number of subjects and highlights the intellectual content of his work.

Nanteuil, Luc de. *Jacques-Louis David*. New York: Abrams, 1985; London: Thames and Hudson, 1990. Detailed account of David's development from early styles through mature styles. Clear, concise discussion of political events which shaped his thinking. Excellent color plates of most significant works, with analysis of the formalistic elements of each.

Rosenblum, Robert, and H. W. Janson. *Nineteenth Century Art*. New York: Abrams, 1984. Contains a perceptive analysis of David's style through the Napoleonic era, contrasting his use of classical sources to that of his contemporaries, and also relates his political allegiances to his painting. Continues with detailed accounts of David's followers and their efforts to maintain the neoclassical style in spite of the growth of Romanticism.

LouAnn Faris Culley

JEFFERSON DAVIS

Born: June 3, 1808; Christian County, Kentucky
Died: December 6, 1889; New Orleans, Louisiana
Areas of Achievement: Government and politics
Contribution: Davis served his country ably as senator and secretary of war; his commitment to the South led him to accept the presidency of the Confederacy and attempt to preserve Southern independence against bitter opposition and overwhelming odds. Reviled or idealized as a symbol of the Confederacy, Davis' consistency of principle and unflagging efforts balance out the fact that he was not well fitted for the demands of the times and the position.

Early Life

In the turbulent decades of the early 1700's, a son of Welsh immigrants moved his family from Philadelphia to the Georgia area; Evan Davis' son Samuel, as reward for his services as a Revolutionary guerrilla captain, was granted land near Augusta. He was chosen county clerk and in 1783 married Jane Cook. Continuing the family pattern, Samuel migrated often; in 1792 he moved to Kentucky, where his tenth and last child, Jefferson (Finis) Davis, was born at Fairview in Christian (later Todd) County, on June 3, 1808. By 1811, the family was living in Louisiana but later moved to Wilkinson County, Mississippi Territory. In these frontier areas, owners worked in the fields with their slaves; Samuel Davis was able to give only a single slave to each of his children when they married. His eldest son, however, Joseph Emory Davis, demonstrated in his life the "flush times" and upward mobility of the Lower South: He became a lawyer, the wealthy owner of a great plantation, and a "father" to his youngest brother.

In his youth, Jefferson Davis spent two years at the Roman Catholic St. Thomas' College in Kentucky and then attended local schools near home; in 1821, he studied classics at Transylvania University in Lexington, Kentucky. Just after his father's death, late in 1824, he entered West Point Military Academy. He was over six feet tall, slender, an active, high-spirited young man, with brown hair and deep-set gray-blue eyes, a high forehead and cheekbones, and an aquiline nose and square jaw. In 1828, twenty-third out of a class of thirty-three, he was graduated as a second lieutenant. For the next seven years he was on frontier duty at the dangerous and lonely posts in Wiscon-

sin and Illinois, acquitting himself well and with initiative; in 1832, he briefly guarded the captive chief Black Hawk. In 1833, at Fort Crawford, Wisconsin, he met Sarah Knox Taylor, daughter of the commandant, Colonel Zachary Taylor; despite the latter's objections, they were married June 17, 1835, at her aunt's home in Kentucky.

Despite Davis' conviction of his aptitude for the military, he resigned his commission; Joseph gave the young couple an adjoining new plantation, Brierfield, and fourteen slaves on credit. As neither was acclimatized, they left for the Louisiana plantation of a Davis sister, but they both contracted malaria, and Knox Davis died on September 15, 1835. A grieving Davis, convalescing in Havana and New York, spent some time also in a senatorial boardinghouse in Washington, D.C., but soon returned to Brierfield. For the next eight years he led a solitary and reclusive life, reading extensively in literature, history, and the classics and associating primarily with his brother. During this period he developed the basic system of Brierfield, which was almost an ideal plantation: benevolent master, slaves trained and working according to their abilities and making many decisions concerning their labor and earnings, and Davis' personal slave James Pemberton as overseer with a practically free hand. During these years Davis developed his attachments, both theoretical and personal, to the soil, the South, and the new aristocratic society of the Lower South. His identification was completed and symbolized by his marriage on February 26, 1845, to Varina Anne Banks Howell; she was half his age, a black-haired beauty of Natchez high society, with a classical education and a vivacious temperament. Throughout her life, "Winnie" Davis was high-strung, demonstrative, and emotionally turbulent, a determined woman who fought fiercely for those she loved and who was not always either tactful or forgiving.

By this stage of his life, Davis' personality had been formed. Despite his military experience and life as a planter, he had never really had to fight for place and position; he was more of a theoretician than a realist. He was affectionate with family and friends, essentially humorless, coldly logical, with a deep-rooted egotism and a sense of his own merit; he was never able to believe that others' criticism or disagreement could be sincere or impersonal. Committed firmly to aristocracy and slavery, state sovereignty and states' rights (under the Constitution and within the American nation), always a Democrat, Davis moved into politics. In 1843, he lost an election for the state legislature to a well-known Whig; in 1844 he was a Polk elector. In 1845, he was elected to the United States House of Representatives.

Davis entered into marriage in February, 1845, and entered Congress in December; in June, 1846, on the outbreak of the Mexican War, he resigned from the House to become colonel of the volunteer mounted First Mississippi Rifles. He trained his regiment and equipped his men with the new percussion rifles, and under Major General Zachary Taylor it participated creditably in the victory at Monterrey. When, in the following February, General Antónío Lopez de Santa Anna led fifteen thousand men across two hundred miles of desert to confront Taylor's five thousand at Buena Vista, Davis' Mississippi Rifles fought off a Mexican division in an action (the famous V-formation) that may have been decisive for the American victory. Davis led the regiment despite a wound in the foot that kept him on crutches for two years and in intermittent pain for the next decade. This episode gained for Davis a popular reputation as a military hero and reinforced his already ineradicable conviction of his own military capability.

After Buena Vista, with Taylor's influence waning and the regiment's enlistment expiring, Davis again resigned a military commission, and in December, 1847, was appointed to a vacancy in the Senate. An expansionist, he supported President Polk on the Mexican Cession, even suggesting American acquisition of Yucatan; although he acquiesced in extending the Missouri Compromise line to the Pacific, he asserted that there was no constitutional power to prohibit slave property in any territory. The complex politics associated with the Compromise of 1850 included several Southern groupings: Unionists, radical states' righters (in favor of immediate secession), Southern "nationalists" (or "cooperationists," anticipating possible later secession by the South as a whole). When his fellow Mississippi senator Henry S. Foote ran for governor on a Union ticket (a coalition of Whigs and some Democrats), Davis was persuaded to resign from the Senate (in September, 1851) and oppose him on the Democratic ticket; Davis lost by a thousand votes. Political defeat was offset by the birth of the Davis' first child, Samuel Emerson, on July 30, 1852.

Having aided in the campaign to elect Franklin Pierce, Davis was appointed secretary of war in March of 1853. Ironically, these four years were to be the most congenial and productive of his life. He was in good health and spirits; "Winnie" Davis was a charming and vivacious hostess and the Davis house was the social center of official Washington circles. There was a growing family: Although Samuel died on June 30, 1854, Margaret Howell (Maggie or Pollie) was born on February 25, 1855, and Jefferson, Jr., on January 16, 1857. As secretary of war, Davis supported the concept (developed by John C. Calhoun during his tenure of the office) of an expansible army; infantry units were issued the new percussion-cap muzzle-loading rifles and Minié balls; infantry tactics were made somewhat more flexible; West Point officers were encouraged to study in Europe and to develop military theory; and the regrettable system of army departments was strengthened. Davis urged the use of camels in the Southwest, but the experiment failed. Davis was unable to influence the Administration on the issues of the *Black Warrior* seizure and the Ostend Manifesto, but as a Southern expansionist he enthusiastically organized a research expedition to the Southwest to provide data which led to the Gadsden Purchase.

The end of Davis' term in the cabinet was soon followed by his election to the Senate; he took his seat in March, 1857. Another son, Joseph Evan, was born on April 18, 1859. Davis' time as senator would have been the peak and epilogue of his political career, had it not been prologue to suffering and defeat. Nearly fifty, he was gaunt and neurotic; he suffered from dyspepsia and neuralgia and lost the sight of his left eye. He was an effective orator, aided by the obvious intensity of his convictions, and he strongly supported the South's interests in the increasingly bitter sectional confrontations of the 1850's. Within the Democratic Party, he fought the popular sovereignty position of Stephen A. Douglas and worked to prevent the latter's nomination as Democratic candidate in 1860.

Abraham Lincoln's election and nonnegotiable stand against expansion of slavery into the territories convinced Davis of the necessity and inevitability of secession; on January 21, 1861, upon learning of Mississippi's secession, he resigned from the Senate. Like few others at the time, Davis expected war, probably anticipating a command position; he was indeed appointed major general of Mississippi's troops. The Montgomery convention,

which established a provisional government, however, needed a president more acceptable to the moderates (or earlier "cooperationists") and early in February, 1861, elected Jefferson Davis.

Life's Work

Davis was elected president of the Confederate States of America, for the constitutional six-year term, on October 6, 1861; on December 16, William (Billy) Howell was born. Davis was inaugurated in the official Confederate capital of Richmond, Virginia, on February 22, 1862. On March 6, 1861, the Confederate Congress had authorized a hundred thousand volunteers for a twelve-month enlistment, but even after Fort Sumter, Davis did not move to ensure an adequate munitions supply or a financial base (for example, the use of cotton supplies to secure paper currency). The emphasis on protecting the capital at Richmond effectively divided the Eastern and Western Confederacy; Davis retained the system of military departments, their heads responsible directly to him, and therefore eliminated the possibility of unified strategy or well-coordinated action. His military strategy was only to defend, meeting Union forces wherever they might move. He failed to understand that the military situation, as well as the political situation, was a revolutionary one; he could not come to grips with the conditions and concepts of this first modern war. It is true that few at that time fully comprehended its implications; Lincoln, Ulysses S. Grant, and William Sherman were probably the only ones who realized its necessities.

Davis' long-standing quarrel with Joseph E. Johnston stemmed from the latter's failure to be ranked highest of the five Confederate full generals. Late in the war, Davis removed Johnston from command in Georgia at a critical point: General John Bell Hood's loss of Atlanta aided in Lincoln's reelection and continued Northern support of the war. Public and congressional opinion did not influence Davis: He refused to remove General Braxton Bragg despite that officer's ineffectiveness in battle, and when forced to remove Judah P. Benjamin as secretary of war, he "promoted" him to secretary of state. Davis spent too much time in battle areas; he neglected the West and refused to authorize the transfer of troops across the boundaries of military departments to areas where they were needed. Even after Antietam, he could not see that only a major offensive held any hope of victory and independence; instead, he insisted on scattering garrisons

and attempting to hold every inch of territory. Robert E. Lee's offensive into Pennsylvania came too late and could not thereafter be repeated.

Close control of military policy overshadowed all other considerations in Davis' administration, although all policy in fact concerned the pursuit of the war. Davis' commitment to a "Southern nation" provoked opposition, from "fire-eaters" such as Robert Barnwell Rhett and William L. Yancey, states' righters such as Governors Joseph E. Brown of Georgia and Zebulon B. Vance of North Carolina, and Vice President Alexander H. Stephens. The influential *Richmond Examiner* and *Charleston Mercury* regularly opposed Davis' policies; his imperious approach and inability to handle the political situation gave rise to vague but frightening rumors that he was a despot who at any moment might take over the entire government and even use the army to control the people. The tension between sovereign states and an embryo national government in wartime can be seen in most of the controversial issues: general conscription was denounced as unconstitutional, attempts to suspend the writ of habeas corpus were deemed tyrannical. The "rich man's war and poor man's fight" continued with increasing military setbacks and declining supplies and morale.

During the last winter of the war, Davis remained strangely optimistic. He had always had strong faith; in May of 1862 he had joined St. Paul's (Episcopal) Church. Although devastated by the death of Joseph, who fell from a balcony on April 30, 1864, he was consoled by the birth of Varina Anne (Winnie) on June 27, 1864. He urged a draft of forty thousand slaves (to be freed after victory); he sent an agent to offer Great Britain an emancipation program in return for recognition and military alliance. Peace movements, projects to remove Emperor Maximilian from Mexico, the Hampton Roads conference: Davis would consider no compromising of Southern independence (just as Lincoln was committed absolutely to the Union). He seemed to believe that at the last moment the South might yet be saved, perhaps by one great battle led by General Lee and by himself that would sweep the Union armies from the field.

Having evacuated his family, Davis, along with several associates, left Richmond on April 3, 1865, still committed to continuing the war. News of Appomattox convinced the party to head southward; a cabinet meeting in Greensboro, North Carolina, agreed that General Johnston should ask for terms.

At Charlotte, twelve days later, the group recognized Confederate defeat and dispersed, Davis moving south into Georgia to rejoin his family and attempt to leave the country. On May 10, the Fourth Michigan Cavalry came upon them at Irwinville, Georgia; Davis' brief attempt to slip away in a hastily snatched-up rain cape belonging to his wife gave rise to the story that he had tried to disguise himself as a woman to evade capture.

For the next two years, Davis remained a state prisoner in a damp casemate cell in Fortress Monroe. He was once put forcibly in irons for five days, with a lamp burning continually and the guard marching regularly outside, without adequate clothing or books, and suffering from erysipelas. His fortitude, faith, and kindliness impressed the doctors assigned to him, and finally he was placed in more comfortable quarters in the fortress, his family (which had been kept in Savannah) permitted to join him and friends permitted to visit him. On May 4, 1867, he was arraigned on a charge of treason in the federal district court in Richmond and released on bail supplied by ten men, among them Horace Greeley and abolitionist Gerrit Smith. Thereafter, he and his family traveled at various times to Canada, Cuba, New Orleans, Vicksburg, and Davis Bend, as well as to Europe. He was never brought to trial, as the complex constitutional issues surrounding secession remained too controversial and politically incendiary (especially during the Reconstruction period) to be aired in connection with the former president of the defeated Confederacy. His case was dropped on December 5, 1868.

During the remaining years of his life, Davis experienced a series of business failures, several unprofitable European trips, and a gradual recovery of his health. Maggie became Mrs. J. Addison Hayes and settled in Memphis, but Billy died of diphtheria in 1872, and the remaining son, Jefferson, Jr., having failed at Virginia Military Institute, died of yellow fever in 1878. Davis was able to salvage only part of the value of his old plantation in 1878. A friend of Varina, the widowed Mrs. Sarah A. E. Dorsey, gave him a cottage in which to work, on her plantation "Beauvoir," near Biloxi, on the Mississippi Gulf coast. Varina was finally reconciled to this cooperation, and to Davis' inheritance of the estate in 1879, and aided him in his writing of the two-volume *Rise and Fall of the Confederate Government* (1881), primarily a justification of the constitutionality of secession. In the South, Davis

was largely "rehabilitated," being often invited to make speeches and dedicate memorials (including one near his birthplace). His youngest, Winnie, the "Daughter of the Confederacy," was assailed for wishing to marry a New York lawyer, grandson of an abolitionist, and died in 1898 at thirty-three, still single and grieving.

Despite financial problems, Davis, as he had done previously, continued to support both Howell and Davis relatives and several poor children and to entertain a variety of visitors. In 1889, he fell ill with bronchitis in New Orleans, Louisiana, and died there on December 6; he was buried there but, on May 31, 1893, reinterred in Richmond. He had steadfastly refused to ask for a federal pardon, even in order to be elected senator from Mississippi, averring that he had committed no legal offense. On October 17, 1978, a unanimous joint resolution of Congress restored his citizenship.

The year after Davis' death, his widow wrote her two-volume *Memoir* (1890); living in New York, she kept his reputation alive, with the help of Joseph Pulitzer and the Confederate "expatriates" in the North. She died in New York on October 16, 1906, at the age of eighty, and was given a military funeral in Richmond.

Summary

Jefferson Davis was poorly suited for the task of political leadership of the Confederacy at its birth. He had a strong will and iron self-discipline, willing to drive himself relentlessly despite failing health and personal troubles, but he could neither deal effectively with political personalities nor catch the public imagination and gain popular support. In a revolutionary situation he was a conservative and a legalist. Satisfied as to the right of secession and the constitutional basis of state sovereignty, he regarded Northern opposition as motivated only by jealousy, greed, and aggression; yet committed to the ideal of the Southern nation, he could not tolerate independent action by state governments or opposition to policies (such as drafting slaves) that the Confederate government believed were necessary to the war effort. He shared with many the delusion that cotton was king and that economic pressures would lead quickly to European aid and victory; he therefore agreed to policies that resulted in the Confederacy's economic isolation. Free to act out his lifelong perception of himself as master strategist and commanding general, Davis kept tight control over all military aspects, never freeing even Lee from it completely, and refusing sound advice at crucial moments. Up to the end of the war, Davis never believed that defeat was possible; he thought that one more major campaign would turn the tide.

Davis' policy was passive-defensive; he always expected European aid even though he was informed of the actual situation. Politically naive, he apportioned cabinet appointments evenly among the states, thereby making bad choices and alienating the powerful radical secessionists. He dominated his cabinet, so that its able members could not act effectively, yet did not urge his cautious treasury secretary, C. G. Memminger, to be as financially audacious as necessary for real accomplishment. He himself frequently functioned as secretary of war, a position he would have preferred to the presidency or to any other except that of commanding general. He understood neither the proper role of the executive nor the exigencies of strategy, and in attempting to be both president and general, he failed to fulfill either function well.

A nationalist facing sovereign states, a logical theoretician dealing with volatile personalities and political realities, an egotist who could see only the goal but who could not believe that his political opponents also strove for ideals, a leader in revolutionary times who could not rally popular support for great sacrifices: Davis was more of a debit than a credit entry in the Confederacy's account. Yet his dedication was total and his efforts unrelenting, and in the aftermath of defeat, Davis enjoyed more popular admiration than at any other time in his life. He had been a great senator and a great secretary of war. He had never sought public office, but accepted it as a duty. He attracted intense loyalty and admiration as well as provoking bitter enmity, and with all his failings, it is impossible to imagine that any other man in the Confederacy could have done better in those circumstances. Surviving personal tragedies and the loss of an independent South, Davis died unshaken in his beliefs and conscious of his own rectitude and unswerving loyalties, in his own mind fully justified and fulfilled.

Bibliography

Beringer, Richard E. "Jefferson Davis's Pursuit of Ambition: The Attractive Features of Alternative Decisions." *Civil War History* 38, no. 1 (March, 1992). Discusses the effect of cognitive dissonance (psychological state created when one attempts to make inconsistent ideas appear consistent) on Davis's ability to make decisions and how this ultimately assisted in the fall of the South.

Davis, Jefferson. *Jefferson Davis: Private Letters, 1823-1889.* Edited by Hudson Strode. New York: Harcourt Brace, 1966. Very effectively edited, providing practically a condensed biography. As with the three-volume biography, strongly biased, placing even more emphasis than Strode's work on personalities.

Davis, Varina. *Jefferson Davis, Ex-President of the Confederate States of America: A Memoir by His Wife.* 2 vols. New York: Belford, 1890. A laudatory account, more than sixteen hundred pages; includes long quotations from Davis' speeches and correspondence as well as biographical information dictated by Davis shortly before his death and valuable information from participants in events. Apart from Davis' obvious bias, the book is detailed and usually reliable.

Dodd, William Edward. *Jefferson Davis.* Philadelphia: Jacobs, 1907. Written by a professor at Randolph-Macon College, the book reflects nineteenth century biases of time and place: contented slaves, good masters, Anglo-Saxon civilization. Dodd attempts to balance his own commitment to the United States with strong attachment to the rightness of Davis and the South on the constitutional issues and the "War Between the States."

Sanders, Charles W., Jr. "Jefferson Davis and the Hampton Roads Peace Conference: 'To secure peace to the two countries.'" *Journal of Southern History* 63, no. 4 (November, 1997). Discusses the differing opinions as to Davis' reasons for holding the Hampton Roads peace conference in 1865.

Strode, Hudson. *Jefferson Davis: American Patriot, 1808-1861.* New York: Harcourt Brace, 1955.

———. *Jefferson Davis: Confederate President.* New York: Harcourt Brace, 1959.

———. *Jefferson Davis, Tragic Hero: The Last Twenty-five Years, 1864-1889.* New York: Harcourt Brace, 1964. This detailed, three-volume biography by a professor of creative writing is the result of painstaking research, based on both secondary sources and primary documents including a thousand previously unavailable personal letters. Neither scholarly nor analytical; detailed narrative and quotations replace the historian's generalizations. Pro-Davis with a pro-

Southern, secessionist bias; often reads more as special pleading than as careful interpretation.

Tate, Allen. *Jefferson Davis*. New York: Putnam, 1969. A very brief account by one of the Nashville "Agrarians." Emotional and often contradictory defense of Davis as representative of the stable agrarian Southern society facing the aggression of the new industrial North; simultaneously blames Davis for the Confederate defeat.

Warren, Robert Penn. *Jefferson Davis Gets His Citizenship Back*. Lexington: University Press of Kentucky, 1980. Very brief, almost a memoir of the author's boyhood in the early twentieth century South, by a master writer. Effective evocation of the war and the man.

Wiley, Bell Irvin. *Confederate Women*. Westport, Conn.: Greenwood Press, 1975. Relatively brief but informative work, based on primary sources. Excellent portrayal of the lives, ideas, and influence of Virginia Clay-Clopton, Mary Boykin Chesnut, and Varina Davis.

Marsha Kass Marks

SIR HUMPHRY DAVY

Born: December 17, 1778; Penzance, Cornwall, England

Died: May 29, 1829; Geneva, Switzerland

Areas of Achievement: Chemistry, invention, and philosophy

Contribution: As a philosopher of science, brilliant chemist, and president of the Royal Society, Davy advanced the cause of science as few men had before him. He identified the chemical elements barium, chlorine, magnesium, potassium, sodium, and strontium; pioneered anesthesiology with his experiments with nitrous oxide; invented the Davy lamp to save miners from the perils of explosions; made significant contributions to the application of science for the betterment of society in fields such as agricultural chemistry and tanning; and wrote widely read books on philosophy, flyfishing, and travel.

Early Life

Humphry Davy, born on December 17, 1778, in the remote town of Penzance in Cornwall, England, was the eldest of five children. Grace Millet Davy, his mother, was an orphaned child of a middle-class family. Robert Davy, his father, was a woodcarver who was of yeoman stock. He was an industrious, though not very successful businessman, who tried farming and who speculated in tin mining.

For the eighteenth century an unusual amount of detail is available on the future scientist's childhood. He was an active, healthy, and precocious child, who walked at nine months and spoke fluently at two years of age. This sweet, affectionate child was the family favorite. Even before he could read, which was at age five, he was reciting from *The Pilgrim's Progress.* At six, he went to school, which was a disappointment. Years later, he wrote, that "learning is naturally a true pleasure," but that even the best school he went to made it painful. Davy considered it fortunate that his teachers generally left him alone and declared that "what I am I made myself." Though he left a grant to the school in his will, it was on the condition that the children be given a day off every year.

Robert Davy died in 1794, saddling his widow with a large debt as a result of his mining adventures. She supported her family by opening a millinery store until she received a small inheritance in 1799.

The twin crises of Humphry's childhood were the move of his family to a farm when he was six and the death of his father when he was fifteen. For the sake of his education, young Humphry lived in Penzance with the old surgeon and apothecary (pharmacist), who had reared his orphaned mother, and only saw his family on weekends. The lonely boy suffered from nightmares and sleepwalking and was terrified by ghost stories and tales of the French Revolution. He learned to amuse and frighten other boys by telling stories of faraway places based mainly on *The Arabian Nights' Entertainments.* He also loved to hunt and to fish and became passionately devoted to nature.

The death of his father changed Davy's life. He was determined to help his mother, by making something of himself. He set himself an extraordinarily ambitious program of self-study and actually accomplished much of his plan. Though soon apprenticed to a surgeon and apothecary, he was determined to prove his genius. Shortly after reading his first chemistry book, he wrote an article on heat and light that so impressed Dr. Thomas Beddoes of Clifton that nineteen-year-old Davy was invited to become superintendent to the Pneumatic Institution, where Beddoes was experimenting with the use of gases in medical treatment. Typically, the remainder of his five-year indentureship was waived as he took a crucial step toward scientific fame.

In his several years in Clifton, Davy carried out some extremely dangerous and important experiments with nitrous oxide (laughing gas). His friends William Coleridge, Peter Roget, and Robert Southey were among the guinea pigs for his experiments. The most dangerous ones he saved for himself. The laughing gas experiments almost killed him and may have caused long-term damage to his health. He recommended that the gas be applied as an anesthesia for certain surgical procedures. Unfortunately, it would be half a century before nitrous oxide would be used to save lives in that way.

Davy's attention turned to the area of electrochemistry, which was made possible by the invention of the voltaic pile. He used electrical power to conduct experiments, isolate elements, and invent the carbon arc. In 1801, Davy was appointed lecturer at the Royal Institution and was made professor of chemistry the following year. This "boy wonder" had achieved the amazing feat of gaining a professorship five years after reading his first

chemistry book. His previous plan of studying medicine at the University of Edinburgh and the idea of becoming a physician seems to have gradually fallen by the wayside.

Portraits and descriptions of Davy reveal that he was of medium height with a slight build, hazel eyes, and an aquiline nose. He had a lifelong boyish quality that caused him to appear younger than his years. He was lively and enthusiastic in manner and sometimes careless in his dress. The intensity of his eyes and the power of his intellect were remarked upon by his contemporaries.

Davy brought an amazing amount of energy to his scientific endeavors and typically made most of his discoveries in a short period of time as he sought proof for his intuitive flashes of insight. He was not the stereotypical prodding type of scientist who generalized only after examining all the facts. He was a passionate and poetic man. As he aged, however, his tendency toward irritability, mood swings, and vanity increased. Coleridge's fear, expressed when Davy was age twenty-five, that he would succumb to the vice of "ambition into vanity," was justified by both the snobbery and the nar-

cissistic self-involvement that became apparent after his knighthood and marriage in 1812.

Life's Work

Davy's life was devoted to the understanding and popularization of nature. At the Royal Institution, he threw himself into laboratory research, lecturing, and editing. He gave courses on subjects such as applied chemistry, galvinism, "pneumatic chemistry," and tanning. Unlike many scientists, he considered his public lectures to be of great importance and carefully rehearsed them.

He attained celebrity status, since as many as a thousand people flocked to hear his extraordinary mixture of chemistry, latest research findings, poetry, and philosophy. They listened raptly to subjects as mundane as the chemical composition of organic fertilizers. His yearly Bakerian Lecturers to the Royal Society, from 1807 to 1812, brought him international fame. The Napoleon Prize was awarded to him by the Institute of France. In 1813, while England was still at war with France, he traveled to Paris to receive this award.

Davy, who was always eager to tackle the problems of applied science, almost had his career cut short in 1807 when he contracted a severe case of malaria while trying to save the inmates of Newgate Prison, who were being decimated by this dreaded disease. His popularity was reflected in the public issuance of hourly bulletins as to his health. His close scrape with death and slow recovery did not cure him of risk-taking for the sake of science. Years later, he was almost blinded by an explosive that he knew to be extraordinarily dangerous. He also took some risks by going down into the coal mines to find a safe way of lighting those dangerous shafts. The result was the Davy lamp, on which he refused to take a patent, that made possible a great increase in coal production. Though pride of invention was also claimed for George Stephenson and Dr. William Clanny, much to Davy's chagrin, the coal mine owners recognized the priority of his invention by giving him an extremely expensive gift. The outcomes of some other projects, specifically unrolling the ancient Herculaneum papyri in Italy, protecting the copper sheathing on the Admiralty's ships, and ventilating the House of Lords, were not as successful. One of his greatest discoveries was of the chemist Michael Faraday.

Davy was knighted in 1812, and immediately thereafter he married a rich, intellectual widow named Jane (Kerr) Apneece. The marriage that began with high hopes soon became unhappy. The couple fought publicly and were informally separated as much as they were together. There were no children.

Davy was elected to the presidency of the Royal Society in 1820. He began his tenure with great expectations of major scientific achievements. He hoped to achieve the conversion of the British Museum into a research institution and hoped, too, to obtain far more financial support from the government for his projects. He was unsuccessful in these endeavors, as well as in inspiring most of his fellow scientists to greater efforts. Before long, Davy would be caricatured as one of the "humbugs of the age." In fact, he was uncomfortable in his administrative role and thought to escape it by foreign travel. Though his health deteriorated severely in 1825, Davy continued to travel, experiment, and write—his emphasis being on philosophical books such as *Salmonia: Or, Days of Fly Fishing* (1828) and *Consolations in Travel: Or, The Last Days of a Philosopher* (1830). He died on May 29, 1829, in Geneva.

Summary

Sir Humphry Davy was a scientist of considerable achievement whose reputation was greater in his own lifetime than subsequently. His nitrous oxide experiments, invention of the safety lamp, isolation of a half dozen chemical elements, and improvements in tanning earned for him his reputation. In addition, he wrote the textbook on agricultural chemistry that would be used for more than a generation. His poetry, which does not read well to the twentieth century ear, was of sufficient quality to warrant the praise of Coleridge and Southey.

Yet Davy's greatest achievement was as an advocate and popularizer of the scientific investigation of nature. The British, first in competition with and then in victory over the French, were eager to know the composition of the world that they dominated. Davy is an example par excellence of the self-made men who built the institutions of British greatness.

Bibliography

Davy, Sir Humphry. *The Collected Works of Sir Humphry Davy*. Edited by John Davy. 9 vols. London: Smith, Elder, 1839-1840; New York: Johnson Reprint, 1972. Volume 1 of this nine-volume set is a biography of Davy's famous brother. This very useful collection is far from definitive, since many sources were ignored and others were selected from rather than printed in their entirety.

Elovitz, Paul H. "The Childhood Origins of Sir Humphry Davy's Preoccupation with Science, Magic, and Death." In *Psychology and History*, edited by Jerrold Atlas. New York: Long Island University Press, 1986. The author draws on his dual training in history and psychoanalysis to offer an explanation for Davy's total devotion to the service of "Mother Nature." He provides psychological explanations for Davy's failure as president of the Royal Society, his physical collapse in 1825, and his disquieting belief in extraterrestrial communication and magic.

———. "Psychohistorical Dreamwork: A New Methodology Applied to a Dream of Sir Humphry Davy." In *The Variety of Dream Experience*, edited by Montague Ullman and Claire Limmer. New York: Continuum Publishing Co., 1987. Davy was an unusually active dreamer who relied on dreams for insight and inspiration. He wrote an entire book on the basis of one of his dreams. Elovitz created a new method for biographers to use dreams to understand their subjects better.

Forgan, Sophie, ed. *Science and the Sons of Genius: Studies on Humphry Davy*. London: Science Reviews, 1980. These seven papers are the results of the Davy Bicentenary Symposium held in honor of the famous chemist at the Royal Institution. The authors examined his scientific procedures, policies, personality, and literary productions.

Fullmer, June Z. "Davy's Priority in the Iodine Dispute: Further Documentary Evidence." *Ambix*, March, 1975: 39-51. The author was trained as a chemist before devoting herself to the history of science and becoming the most outstanding contemporary authority on Davy. This is one of more than a dozen articles that she has published on many different aspects of his career and life. In this case she examines his goals during the period he was traveling in France in 1813. Though Napoleon had given this Englishman a guarantee of safe passage and prize, he was still under intellectual assault in the land of the enemy. An informative and interesting article.

Kendall, James P. *Humphry Davy: "Pilot" of Penzance*. London: Faber, and New York: Roy, 1954. This is one of a large number of Davy biographies, some in foreign languages, written for younger audiences. Writing for adolescents,

Kendall classifies Davy as a "Romantic" and avoids the pious platitudes of the Samuel Smiles type of biography. Unfortunately, he relies too heavily on the caricatured, often inaccurate biographies by John Davy and J. A. Paris.

Knight, David. *Humphry Davy: Science and Power.* Reprint. Oxford and Cambridge, Mass.: Blackwell, 1992. A well written and entertaining biography of Davy based largely on analysis of his poetry and informal writings.

Miller, David P. "Between Hostile Camps: Sir Humphry Davy's Presidency of the Royal Society of London, 1820-1827." *The British Journal for the History of Science* 16 (March, 1983): 1-47. Davy's presidency of the Royal Society began with high hopes which were soon dashed at the time ill health forced his resignation in 1827. Davy was seen by many as a failed leader. The author traces the struggles of competing groups within the British scientific establishment.

Thoman, Charles, J. "Sir Humphry Davy and Frankenstein." *Journal of Chemical Education* 75, no. 4 (April, 1998). Argues that Mary Shelley most likely based her novel *Frankenstein* on Davy's experiments with cadavers and electric current.

Treneer, Anne. *The Mecurial Chemist: A Life of Sir Humphry Davy.* London: Methuen, 1963. This excellent life of Davy stresses his Cornish origins, affiliation with the Romantic poets, and nonscientific activities. It is well written and recommended for the nonscientific reader.

Paul H. Elovitz

FERENC DEÁK

Born: October 17, 1803; Söjtör, Zala County,
  Hungary
Died: January 28, 1876; Pest, Hungary
Areas of Achievement: Government and politics
Contribution: Deák's persuasive and undaunting
  efforts brought about Hungary's most important
  compromise, the *Ausgleich.* He also led the liberals in the passage of much needed social reforms and was one of Hungary's greatest
  codifiers of progressive laws that brought Hungary out of feudalism.

Early Life

Ferenc Deák, Sr., a third-generation nobleman, followed the family tradition of increasing wealth and
power through marriage. In the 1780's, he married
Erzsébet Sibrik of Szarvaskend, the daughter of the
deputy sheriff of Gyor County. On October 17,
1803, their youngest of six children, Ferenc Deák,
Jr., was born. Several days later, Erzsébet died of
complications from childbirth. Consequently, her
husband rejected his infant son and sent him to an
uncle, József Deák. The family soon moved to Ke-
hida, where Ferenc Deák, Sr., died on January 25,
1808. At that time, young Ferenc's elder brother,
Antal, became his legal guardian.

Ferenc was tutored by a Franciscan until 1808.
At that time, he started his formal education by attending elementary school at church schools in
Köszeg, Keszthely, and Pápa. In 1817, Ferenc was
graduated from the *Gymnasium* in Nagykanizsa
and then began his studies at the Royal Law Academy in Gyor, where he excelled in German, Latin,
and constitutional law and history.

Ferenc's future career and his thought processes
were influenced by two major factors. First, he witnessed legislative resistance to royal decrees by local assemblies. Ferenc was maturing in an intense
atmosphere of revolution and opposition to the
Habsburg regime. In 1821, he attended, against
royal mandate, the Assembly of Gyor and witnessed its refusal to execute what it considered to
be an unconstitutional royal decree. Then, he saw
similar defiance in Zala County, when that assembly resisted the absolutism of the Metternich system. Zala County led the opposition against Austrian absolutism and Antal Deák led Zala County.
The second major factor influencing Ferenc was
the leadership of his brother. Antal advocated that

loyalty to the dynasty should not prevent resistance
to despotism and that local assemblies had a responsibility to resist any unconstitutional ordinanc-
es. He was well known throughout Hungary, and
Ferenc was inspired by him.

In December, 1821, Ferenc was graduated from
the Academy, and Zala County declared him legally of age. His first act was to emancipate his former
wet nurse, symbolic of his future work in abolishing feudalism and in obtaining rights for all Hungarians. In November, 1822, Ferenc arrived in Pest
and passed the bar examination with distinction on
December 19, 1823. While in Pest, Hungary's cultural center, he came into contact with numerous
cultural organizations. The most important of these
was the *Auróra* circle, through which he developed
lasting friendships with several liberal statesmen,
politicians, and poets, many of whom greatly contributed to his intellectual development.

Ferenc began his public service at the county
level by holding several unpaid positions. His first
was given to him as a gesture of recognition for
Antal's hard work. On December 13, 1824, Ferenc
was elected notary to the County Commission for
Orphans. He also held the position of county magistrate and was elected deputy high sheriff surrogate; however, he never took the latter post. When
the national legislative body, the diet, convened in
Pozsony in 1832, Antal represented Zala County as
deputy. In January, 1833, he resigned and recommended Ferenc to replace him. On April 15, 1833,
Ferenc was subsequently elected to a seat in the
Lower House. With this position, his county service ended. His career as a national political figure
began at this time and would influence Hungarian
and Austrian history for the next forty-three years.

Life's Work

The 1830's and 1840's were critical years for Hungary. Plague, peasant revolts, and economic depression were widespread, and Hungary had a feudal constitution. Deák's experience at the county
level enabled him to understand legal procedure
and alerted him to Hungary's social, economic, and
political problems. Thus, he joined the reform-
minded liberals, led by Baron Miklós Wesselényi.

In 1836, Deák introduced his first legislative
measure, calling for the emancipation of the serfs.
When Ferdinand I vetoed the measure, Deák called

an unofficial session of the diet. As a result of this episode, Deák was acknowledged as the leader of the liberals in the Lower House.

On May 2, 1836, Deák returned to Zala County to report on the proceedings of the diet. He also proposed a program of reforms, which was printed and published by the assembly and sent to other counties without royal approval. The Crown reprimanded the assembly and ordered all copies to be collected. The assembly rejected the reprimand, and Deák became the symbol of Hungarian progressive ideas. In appreciation for his legislative leadership, he was elected an honorary member of the Academy of Sciences on November 21, 1839.

Deák successfully concluded his first compromise during the Diet of 1839-1840. Many liberal leaders had been arrested in 1836, and Deák had offered his services as mediator; however, the Crown was unwilling to compromise. He then warned that if the Crown did not respect Hungarian laws and rights, Hungary would employ passive resistance and defiance. Thus, on June 6, 1839, when Ferdinand summoned the diet, Deák recommended that they not discuss any royal proposals until all grievances were resolved. He met privately with an agent of the Crown in March, 1840, and achieved a compromise to the satisfaction of the liberals.

Deák entered the 1840's with hopes for a legal revolution that would transform Hungary from a feudal to a modern state through peaceful legislation. At the 1841 diet, he proposed drastic changes in the judiciary, but his legislative attempts all met with failure. Deák became apathetic and inactive; his aloofness began to compromise his influence. At this time, Lajos Kossuth assumed the leadership of the liberals. In 1846, Deák reluctantly helped write the Liberal Party platform, which called for universal reforms. This work promoted the unification of Hungary's first opposition party.

By August, 1847, Deák temporarily left Hungary, allegedly under doctor's orders. He was short and stocky, with great physical strength, but he was prone to sickness. In reality, however, he did not believe the liberals could achieve their goals at this time because of the stubbornness of the Crown. He realized the only course for Hungary was violence and revolution—actions which were against his values.

When the last feudal diet (1847-1848) was summoned, Kossuth sent a list of grievances (written by Deák) to Ferdinand I. By 1848, much of the empire was in revolt. Faced with chaos, Ferdinand consented to the list of demands and granted Hungary independence. The first elected parliament met in July, 1848, and passed a series of reforms known as the April Laws, ending feudalism and introducing a liberal form of government. Deák led the new Lower House and achieved the greatest social reforms of his legislative career. He was named Minister of Justice and succeeded in having his earlier judicial reform measures (of 1841) passed as the Press Act in 1848.

On September 11, 1848, Austria invaded Hungary. Deák abandoned his office, the ministry was in chaos, and counterrevolution began. On December 2, 1848, Ferdinand abdicated in favor of his nephew Francis Joseph I. Hungary considered the new ruler a usurper because he did not swear the required oath of loyalty to the Hungarian constitution. On April 14, 1849, the parliament deposed the Habsburg dynasty. Consequently, Francis Joseph ordered a massive assault on Hungary.

By August, 1849, the Hungarian revolution ended. Hungary was partitioned and placed under a repressive regime for many years. Most of the revolutionary leaders were either executed or exiled.

Deák appeared before a military tribunal on December 14, 1849, and was interrogated for five months. Finally, he was released, as he had not supported the deposition of the royal dynasty.

From 1850 to 1859, Deák offered passive resistance to the Crown. In 1854, he sold the family estate and permanently moved to the Hotel Angol Királyné in Pest. At this time, he became the director of the Hungarian Academy of Sciences. His passive resistance ended in December, 1860, when he was granted an audience with Francis Joseph. The two men immediately developed a mutual trust and respect for each other. Deák was honest, always spoke frankly, and was open-minded. He accepted Francis Joseph's offer to participate in the Lord Chief Justice's Conference (January 23 to March 3, 1861) aimed at reconciling Hungary's civil and criminal court procedures with Austria's system. On February 27, however, the Crown announced its intention to reduce Hungary to a province. Deák left the conference angrily, believing that revolution was Hungary's only hope of remaining autonomous.

He again became inflexible in his attitude toward the empire. In 1861, the Crown summoned the first diet in twelve years. This time, Deák represented Pest. Dissension among the liberals gave rise to two new political parties: the Party of Petition led by Deák and the Party of Resolution led by Count László Teleki. After Teleki committed suicide, Deák assumed the position of the leading statesman in Hungary.

With hostilities again developing, the Crown adopted more oppressive measures. Deák recommended a policy of passive defense to parliament, which was adjourned by the Crown on August 22, 1861. On November 5, 1861, Hungary became a province of the empire. From this position, Deák enjoyed his greatest level of prestige. He began to lay the foundations for a compromise. He anonymously wrote an article in *Pesti Naplo* entitled "Easter Article," followed by a series of similar articles. Through this vehicle he offered a solution to the volatile situation between Hungary and the dynasty. Deák knew that the time was right for compromise; Austria was nearly bankrupt and the empire's collapse was imminent.

Negotiations began and a new parliament was summoned in September, 1865. Deák's party won a majority of the seats. Deák began to shape Hungary's history and proved himself to be a practitioner of realpolitik. He did not create movements or ideas; he merely took advantage of situations, planned the right strategies, and knew how to manipulate the political forces that existed. For the first time in his long career, Deák exercised his very forceful and persuasive leadership ability. On December 20, 1865, the Deák Party Club was established to organize campaign strategies. Deák developed goals to be achieved and principles to be followed. He demanded discipline but never used force or humiliation to obtain his objectives.

On June 17, 1867, Austria went to war with Prussia. Deák now pushed for compromise. He met for a second time with Francis Joseph, and they agreed upon the *Ausgleich*, the Compromise of 1867. It provided for the following: the creation of the state of Austria-Hungary with a dual monarchy in the person of the emperor; the restoration of the Hungarian constitution of 1848; the separation of parliamentary bodies—the Hungarian Parliament would meet in Budapest and the Austrian parliament in Vienna; the joint administration of military and foreign affairs by delegates from the two parliaments and three joint ministers (foreign affairs, war, and finance); and the renewal of terms of the *Ausgleich* every ten years. There was some opposition to the *Ausgleich*, especially from Kossuth. Yet most Austrians and Hungarians rejoiced in the settlement, as it resolved a thirty-year-old conflict and provided stability for the empire (which lasted until World War I).

Deák also proposed a series of acts which created a new Hungary. The two most important were the Croatian-Hungarian Compromise and the Equality of the Nationalities Act. He finally saw fulfilled a lifetime of efforts to obtain and protect the rights of all people. Furthermore, Deák wanted Hungary to become a true democracy. After the *Ausgleich*, however, his party began to splinter, and his health deteriorated.

By 1871, Deák's era was coming to an end. His influence also began to wane, and he experienced legislative defeats. His last political act created the Parliamentary Liberal Party in 1873, with Kálmán Tisza as head, but liberalism was also beginning to decline. Deák's last speech was delivered to parliament on June 28, 1873. It was very reflective of his first presentation made forty years earlier in that his main emphasis was placed on the need for progressive legislation and liberalism.

In 1875, Deák was elected for the last time to parliament, but he was never seated. On January 28, 1876, he died in his hotel suite in Pest. The parliament, in his memory, commissioned a statue of him to be placed in front of the Academy of Sciences building in Budapest.

Summary

Ironically, while Ferenc Deák was the author of the greatest compromise in Hungarian history, he was very uncompromising on moral, constitutional, and social issues. He believed firmly in the Christian ideals of the brotherhood of all men and the stern morality of the ancient Hebrews. He emulated the Romans in their respect for the law and admired the Hellenistic culture for its love of beauty. These ideals were the basis for his moral standards and behavior.

His commitment to certain values became apparent when, on his second day as a freshman member of the diet, he broke with tradition and asked for the floor. It was here that he demonstrated for the first time his excellent oratorical skills and took the first step in his long journey toward making laws more humane and liberal.

Deák gained almost immediate recognition as a reformer. He spent the greater part of his life working toward creating a more liberal government in Hungary. He strove to remove the last remnants of feudalism and to achieve equality for all citizens through peaceful legislation. He strongly believed that law was the backbone of society. He therefore advocated changing unjust laws—not violating them. He worked earnestly at strengthening and modernizing the judiciary.

Deák was a man before his time. This was proved in his first legal case, which illustrated his basic philosophy. The case involved József Babics, a man charged with highway robbery, murder, and several lesser offenses. Deák admitted his client's guilt but not fault. The defense rested on the premise that society was responsible for Babics' actions because it had not provided him with an education and values. Deák lost the case, but he argued against capital punishment and for societal responsibility.

Deák's life's ambition was to achieve a true self-government for Hungary and to obtain the passage of liberal laws. He did not consider the *Ausgleich* the climax of his career. Instead, he viewed it as a necessary interruption to his real task, the completion of the work that the liberals had begun in Hungary during the Reform Era of the 1830's and 1840's. He attempted to create a truly democratic government and society; he sin-cerely cared about the deprived masses and sought reform in their name.

Bibliography

Jászi, Oscar. *The Dissolution of the Habsburg Monarchy.* Chicago: University of Chicago Press, 1929. This work contains an excellent bibliographical section for research on the Habsburgs, Austria, and Eastern Europe. Many of the works included, however, are in German. Describes Deák's political career from the 1830's through 1867 and his role in the Compromise of 1867.

Kann, Robert A. *The Multinational Empire: Nationalism and National Reform in the Habsburg Monarchy, 1848-1918.* 2 vols. New York: Columbia University Press, 1950. This work contains background information on the Austrian Empire. Addresses Deák's leadership ability and his drive for fair treatment of minorities. Volume 1 contains 444 pages with somewhat more emphasis on Deák's role in the government than the 423 pages of volume 2. Each volume contains an introduction and a notes section, and volume 2 has a selected bibliography and index.

Király, Béla K. *Ferenc Deák.* Boston: Twayne, 1975; London: University Press of America, 1987. An excellent although somewhat biased biography containing a chronology of the Deák family from 1665, when the family was ennobled, to Ferenc's death in 1876. Stresses Ferenc's devotion to his political career and also contains a thorough discussion of his private life. The 243 pages include notes, references, bibliographical sections, and an index.

May, Arthur J. *The Hapsburg Monarchy, 1867-1914.* Cambridge, Mass.: Harvard University Press, 1951. This work contains a notes section, a bibliography, and an index, and emphasizes Deák's work on the Compromise of 1867 and his role as the leader of the moderates. Also discusses his other political contributions, including his influence after the Compromise of 1867. The 532 pages emphasize Deák's great negotiating skills, needed to placate the various minority groups in Hungary. Contains quotes taken from Deák's correspondences and speeches.

Murad, Anatol. *Franz Joseph I of Austria and His Empire.* New York: Twayne, 1968. A standard biography of Franz Joseph, with an index, genealogical chart, and chronology from 1830 to

1916. Also contains a selected bibliography. Emphasizes details about the circumstances under which the Compromise of 1867 was agreed upon and Deák's role in obtaining Franz Joseph's approval as well as the relationship between Deák and such important revolutionaries as Count Gyula Andrássy.

Victoria Reynolds

ALFRED DEAKIN

Born: August 3, 1856; Melbourne, Victoria, Australia

Died: October 7, 1919; Melbourne, Victoria, Australia

Areas of Achievement: Government and politics

Contribution: After serving a ten-year apprenticeship in Victoria's legislative assembly from 1880, Deakin spent the next decade working toward the federation of the Australian colonies. One of the primary founders of the Commonwealth of Australia, he served three times as prime minister, dominating the government during its first, formative decade.

Early Life

Alfred Deakin was born on August 3, 1856, at Melbourne in the colony of Victoria. His Welsh-born mother, née Sarah Bill, and his father, William Deakin, an English salesclerk, arrived in South Australia from England in December, 1849. After following the gold rush to Victoria (1851), they eventually settled in the Melbourne suburb of Collingwood, where their second child, Alfred, was born.

Educated primarily at the Melbourne Church of England Grammar School, as a young adult Alfred Deakin attended lectures in law at the University of Melbourne at night. His father's income as accountant with a big coaching company being modest, Deakin supported himself, partly by teaching, while qualifying for the bar and pursuing a deep and continuing interest in mysticism, religion, and psychic phenomena (in 1878 serving as president of the Victorian Association of Spiritualists) and a love of literature and writing. These interests introduced him to his true vocation and to his future wife.

Through David Syme, the powerful proprietor of the Melbourne *Age*, to whose newspaper he became a regular contributor, Deakin entered a political career, almost by chance. When the incumbent of the seat of West Bourke died during a constitutional crisis, Syme pushed Deakin forward, and in July, 1880, he took his place in Victoria's legislative assembly with the governing Liberal Party, an alliance of farming, manufacturing, and labor interests. His talents as a conciliator soon became evident: He helped to secure the Council Reform Act of 1881 and by 1883 was minister in a coalition government of Liberals and Conservatives.

Deakin was a tall, handsome man, fully bearded with dark hair and eyes and a rich voice which he used effectively as an outstanding orator and debater. On April 3, 1882, he married Pattie (christened Elizabeth Martha Anne) Browne, the daughter of a wealthy distiller and spiritualist; she had once been Deakin's pupil at the Progressive Lyceum, a spiritualist Sunday school conducted on American lines. The first of their three children, all girls, was born the following year.

At thirty, Deakin became leader of the Liberal Party and so, with Conservative Duncan Gillies, joint leader of the government. He headed the Victorian delegation to the Colonial Conference of 1887 in London, making his mark in an outspoken attack on the Colonial Office. His speech foreshadowed the federation of the Australian colonies, an objective to which he was to devote much of his time after the fall of the coalition government in October, 1890.

Life's Work

Alfred Deakin's experience as a conciliator and a leader in the Victorian parliament served him well from the time he supported the proposal put by Sir Henry Parkes, the great federationist from New South Wales, that a national Australian convention be held in Sydney in 1891, until the inauguration of the Commonwealth of Australia ten years later, and beyond.

After the drafting at the 1891 convention of a constitution modeled chiefly on the British North America Act and the United States Constitution, nothing much happened for a time. Deakin resumed the practice of law and attended parliamentary sessions, resisting suggestions that he again take a leadership role. During 1897 and 1898, however, the Federal Convention met at Adelaide, Sydney, and Melbourne under the leadership of Edmund Barton of New South Wales (Parkes having died). The only member of the Victorian delegation who had also taken part in the 1891 convention, Deakin again took on the role of arbitrator while a new constitution bill was being framed. The next step was to present it to the people in referenda to be held in all the colonies. Determined to gain its adoption in Victoria, where strong forces appeared to be rallying in opposition, Deakin campaigned vigorously. His historic speech at Bendigo on March 15, 1898, at the annual conference of the influential Australian Natives Association, is regarded as one of his greatest, winning over Syme and impressing reluctant members of government. Victoria voted overwhelmingly (100,520 to 21,099) for the bill.

In 1900, Deakin went to London as part of an Australian delegation headed by Barton. Agreement on the constitution finally having been reached in Victoria, Tasmania, New South Wales, South Australia, and Queensland (Western Australia had not yet held a referendum), the Australian colonies had been requested to be represented while the act constituting the Commonwealth of Australia was being passed by the British parliament.

Barton became the first prime minister of Australia the following year, with Deakin's full support. The cabinet, established on lines proposed by Deakin, included his friend and ally as attorney general. Early legislation included a uniform tariff and the exclusion of non-European immigrants (the "white Australia" policy). On the passing of the Judiciary Act of 1903, setting up the High Court of Australia, Barton retired and was appointed one of the three justices. At forty-seven, "Affable" Alfred, the member for Ballarat (Victoria), became prime minister and minister for external affairs on September 24, 1903.

At this time, three parties were represented in the parliament: Deakin and the Liberal-Protectionists; Labor, led by John C. Watson; and the Free Traders, whose leader was Sir George Reid, former premier of New South Wales and a reluctant federationist. Barton had received Labor's support, and Deakin also felt more comfortable working with Watson than with Reid.

In April, 1904, a dispute over an arbitration bill started a game of musical chairs. Deakin went out of office and Watson came in, with William M. Hughes as his minister for external affairs. Within a matter of months it was Reid's turn. Deakin started his second term, which was considered a productive ministry, on July 15, 1905, although after the 1906 elections his party was the smallest of the three. Usually, therefore, only measures supported by all—such as the introduction of old-age pensions—were likely to be accepted.

Foreign affairs and defense were areas of great concern to Deakin from the time of the 1887 Colonial Conference—at which he raised the issue of French involvement in the New Hebrides. The Naval Agreement made then did not please him, nor did the revised agreement of 1902, under which

Australia paid a subsidy to the imperial government toward the cost of maintaining the Australian Station of the Royal Navy. He foresaw Australian seamen becoming members of a squadron under local control, manning Australian-owned ships and with their wages being paid by Australia. His defense bill foreshadowed this, as well as universal military service and a military college, but in November, 1908, his government fell before the bill could become law.

Labor's second term (under Andrew Fisher) was almost as brief as its first. On June 2, 1909, Deakin was sworn in for his third term, this time as head of what was called the Fusion Ministry, an alliance of groups opposed to Labor. Deakin's personal reputation suffered from this decision to work with some of his hitherto political opponents, however, and in April, 1910, Labor won a decisive victory in both houses. His domination of Parliament had ended.

Deakin had no personal fortune. His income came mainly from what he earned as lawyer, journalist, and parliamentarian. From the 1890's onward, the family spent the summer holidays at Point Lonsdale, a small settlement near Melbourne on

Port Phillip Bay, where Deakin would read, write, and swim. Abstemious and family-minded, Deakin was accompanied by his wife and baby daughter to California in 1884, and in 1900 his wife Pattie, his beloved sister Kate, and his three daughters (Ivy, Stella, and Vera) went with him to London. Pattie also (rather reluctantly) traveled with him to London for the Colonial Conference of 1907.

Like many brilliant, hardworking men, Deakin found relaxing difficult; he also suffered from insomnia. His health began to deteriorate after he entered the Commonwealth parliament, and from 1907 on, memory lapses caused him increasing distress. Deakin was a very private person, and his innermost thoughts were revealed only to his diary and notebooks, in which he also recorded hundreds of prayers. He retired from Parliament in January, 1913, broken in health, which was never restored despite visits to medical specialists in London and New York. He died on October 7, 1919.

Summary

Of his time in the Victorian parliament, Alfred Deakin liked to recall that he introduced pioneering social legislation (the Factories and Shop Act of 1885) regulating factory working conditions. A greater and more personal achievement, however, when he was the minister of water supply, was the Irrigation Act (1886). This came out of a commission on droughts which he chaired and which resulted in water rights being transferred to the Crown to avoid ownership disputes similar to those prevalent in the United States. *Irrigation in Western America* (1885) reports the findings of a visit to the United States during which he met the Canadian-born Chaffey brothers, irrigation experts whom he later enticed to Victoria to establish a settlement at Mildura modeled on theirs at Ontario, California.

A consummate politician, Deakin's support was sought by men of all political factions, yet when he acted independently he took full responsibility and was even, at times, ruthless. As the minister in charge, in 1890 he called out the police and troops during a time of strikes and industrial unrest in Victoria. He did not hesitate when Labor was no longer prepared to give him unconditional support to make an arrangement with the Free Traders and then to drop them if they did not fulfill their commitments. Many of his policies were endorsed or adopted because they were appropriate for the times. One of his last official acts as

prime minister was to place an order for three vessels for the Australian Navy, thus contributing greatly to Australia's readiness in 1914 when World War I began.

Alfred Deakin was also a sensitive man, more interested in intellectual and philosophical pursuits than many of his countrymen. He saw Australia, Canada, New Zealand, and South Africa remaining in the British Empire as equal partners with Great Britain, their interests being one and the same. More than once he referred to himself as an "Independent Australian Briton." Although an imperialist, Deakin declined offers of honors and knighthoods and lived simply, preferring to walk or ride a bicycle from his house in South Yarra to Parliament House, which until 1927 was in Melbourne. His fine intellect and political achievements won respect at home and abroad. Theodore Roosevelt, who ordered the "Great White Fleet" (sixteen American battleships showing the flag around the world) to call at Australian ports in 1908 at Deakin's personal request, wrote in 1912, "He is one of the statesmen for whom I have long cherished a very sincere and real admiration." A university in Victoria bears his name.

Bibliography

Deakin, Alfred. *The Federal Story: The Inner History of the Federal Cause.* Melbourne: Melbourne University Press, 1963. First published with some omissions in 1944, this is a valuable primary document on events leading to federation. Includes an introduction by J. A. La Nauze.

———. *Federated Australia: Selections from Letters to the "Morning Post," 1900-1910.* Edited by J. A. La Nauze. Melbourne: Melbourne University Press, 1968. From 1900 until 1914, Deakin, identified only as "Australian Correspondent," wrote regularly on Australian affairs for the London *Morning Post.* His letters provide an excellent firsthand account of events during the Commonwealth's first decade.

Gabay, Al. *The Mystic Life of Alfred Deakin.* Cambridge and New York: Cambridge University Press, 1992. Gabay examines the spiritual life of Deakin and his poetry and mysticism.

La Nauze, J. A. *Alfred Deakin: A Biography.* 2 vols. Melbourne: Melbourne University Press, and New York: Cambridge University Press, 1965. A scholarly study, with references and bibliography, written by a protégé of biographer Sir Walter Murdoch (see below).

Meaney, Neville. *The Search for Security in the Pacific, 1901-1914*. Sydney: Sydney University Press, 1976. An original, well-documented study of Australia's development of an independent national defense and foreign policy which places into perspective Deakin's contribution as a key policymaker.

Murdoch, Walter. *Alfred Deakin: A Sketch*. London: Constable, 1923. Written with complete family cooperation, this is an affectionate but still relevant biography by a university professor who knew him.

Royce, Josiah. "Impressions of Australia." *Scribner's Magazine* 9 (January, 1891): 75-87. Includes a valuable description of a meeting in 1888 in Australia with Deakin by the American philosopher, then, like Deakin, in his early thirties.

Souter, Gavin. *Lion and Kangaroo: Australia, 1901-1919, The Rise of a Nation*. Sydney: William Collins, 1976. A well-written and entertaining account of the early years of the Commonwealth of Australia and the milieu which Deakin adorned.

Annette Potts
E. Daniel Potts

STEPHEN DECATUR

Born: January 5, 1779; Sinepuxent, Maryland
Died: March 22, 1820; Bladensburg, Maryland
Area of Achievement: Military affairs
Contribution: Decatur was the most colorful and successful open-sea naval commander and hero of the Barbary Wars and the War of 1812.

Early Life

Stephen Decatur's father, Stephen, was a seafaring man who earned his living as a merchant ship captain and, during the American Revolution, as a privateer. Decatur was a sickly child during his early years. At the age of eight, suffering from a prolonged and severe cough, he accompanied his father on a voyage to the French port of Bordeaux. His malady, probably whooping cough, disappeared.

Because his father was at sea much of the time, Decatur was raised in Philadelphia, Pennsylvania, by his mother, Ann, who sent him to the Episcopal Academy and later to the University of Pennsylvania in the hope that he would become either a clergyman or a scholar. However, despite his health problems and his mother's wishes, Decatur craved the active over the contemplative life. As a young man, he was 5 feet 10 inches in height, possessed a muscular build, and had a handsome countenance with an aquiline nose.

Decatur first worked as a clerk in 1796 for Gurney and Smith, a Philadelphia shipping company, but after the United States Navy was established on April 30, 1798, and a naval war had commenced with France, Decatur, through his father's influence, secured a midshipman place on the newly constructed ship, the *United States*. Built in Philadelphia, this forty-four gun frigate was familiar to Decatur. Its captain, John Barry, was both a friend and professional colleague of Decatur's father.

The reasons for Decatur's determination to join the Navy are unclear. Perhaps it was the lure of adventure presented by the new United States Navy and the war with France, or perhaps he wanted to follow his father's nautical footsteps. A more murky reason was the apparent result of Decatur's attack upon a prostitute who had solicited him. He struck her with a blow that was powerful enough to kill her. To avoid a prison sentence for their client, Decatur's lawyers assured the court that Decatur would join the Navy.

Life's Work

Decatur's first real taste of glory occurred in 1804 during the Barbary Wars, when, as captain of the schooner *Enterprise* in Commodore Edward Preble's Mediterranean squadron, he captured a Barbary slave ship, the *Mastico*. Renamed the *Intrepid*, it was 60 feet in length with a 12-foot beam. A scheme was devised to burn the former U.S. frigate *Philadelphia*, which had run aground and been captured by the Tripolitans. Decatur chose a crew of seventy-four volunteers who would sail the *Intrepid* into Tripoli Harbor under the guise of a Barbary ship seeking repairs from a recent storm. The Americans were to board, burn, and escape, leaving the *Philadelphia* in ashes. It was a daring plan well suited to Decatur's adventuresome temperament.

Although delayed for one week because of severe weather, the attack, when executed at dusk on February 16, 1804, was a huge success. Decatur's crew sailed within a few yards of the *Philadelphia* before they were found out. They quickly overcame the defenders, many of whom feared for their lives and jumped overboard. During the next thirty minutes, twenty Tripolitans were killed, combustibles were laid and ignited, the attackers returned to the *Intrepid*, and the *Philadelphia* was engulfed in flames. During all of this, only one of Decatur's sailors was wounded. Burning the *Philadelphia* assured Decatur's role as a hero. He was promoted to captain at the age of twenty-five, the youngest American naval officer to attain that rank. Lord Horatio Nelson called the attack "the most bold and daring act of the age." President Thomas Jefferson presented Decatur with a sword and words of praise.

Later that same year, Decatur's brother, James, was killed by the commander of a Tripolitan gunboat, who shot James when he was boarding the already surrendered vessel. Along with ten others, Decatur tracked down the commander and killed him after some brutal hand-to-hand fighting. During the melee, Decatur's life was saved by a sailor who intentionally absorbed a blow that would have killed Decatur.

At the conclusion of the Tripolitan phase of the Barbary Wars, Decatur returned home, where he broke with his former fiancée and met and married Susan Wheeler, the daughter of the mayor of Norfolk, Virginia. She was a popular and beautiful young woman who had already rejected advances

Decatur (center) stuggles with Algerian pirates

made by Vice President Aaron Burr and Jerome Bonaparte.

Decatur served in various naval positions during the six years from 1806 to 1812. In 1807 he served on the court martial panel that suspended Captain James Barron, Decatur's erstwhile friend and former tutor, from the navy for five years because of his behavior as captain of the *Chesapeake*. Barron was found guilty for failing to adequately prepare his ship for action against the British ship the *Leopard* and thereby humiliating the United States Navy by demonstrating its inability to prevent the seizure of four British navy deserters, three of whom were Americans impressed earlier by the British. Another more personal reason for the deterioration and ultimately fatal culmination of Decatur's and Barron's relationship was the latter's implied criticism of Decatur's attraction to Susan Wheeler when Decatur already had a fiancée in Philadelphia. Decatur thought that it was none of Barron's concern.

When Britain and the United States went to war in 1812, the still young United States Navy consisted of just sixteen warships. Decatur was captain of one of them, the familiar *United States*. Sailing alone between the Azores and Madeira, he sighted the *Macedonian*, a British frigate. The U.S. ship was larger and now carried fifty-four 24-pound guns, compared to the *Macedonian*'s forty-nine 18 pounders. Ironically, this very encounter had been discussed prior to the war by Decatur and Captain John Carden, commander of the *Macedonian*. Despite the heavier gun advantage of the *United States*, Carden had argued that his ship would prevail because its crew was more experienced and because the *Macedonian* was a more maneuverable vessel.

As it turned out, even though Carden had the wind advantage, he failed to recognize the *United States* and instead assumed it was a smaller frigate with guns of lesser range and shot than his own. Carden's tactics played into Decatur's hands by allowing Decatur to press his advantage of more guns and greater destructive shot. Carden surrendered the *Macedonian* after losing one-third of his three-hundred-man crew in a two-hour fight, while seven were killed and five wounded aboard the *United States*. Decatur's reputation as a hero reached its summit. The government also awarded him thirty thousand dollars in prize money. Decatur's achievements during the remainder of the war were a good deal less dramatic, although his status as a genuine American hero remained high.

By tightening their blockade along the Atlantic coast, the British were able to prevent most ships from entering and sailing from U.S. ports. On January 14-15, 1815, unaware that the war had ended three weeks earlier, Decatur attempted to liberate his ship, the *President*, by escaping from New York Harbor. Heavy winds caused the ship to run aground for two hours and compelled Decatur to make a fifty-mile run along the Long Island coast. Four British warships chased him, and, although the frigate *Endymion* had to retire because of battle damage, the remaining British ships forced his surrender. British losses were less than half of the twenty-four Americans killed and the fifty-five who were wounded. Despite the defeat, Decatur maintained his status as a hero. A naval court of inquiry not only exonerated him but also determined that the surrender of the *President* was an American victory.

Two months after the Treaty of Ghent, which ended the War of 1812, the United States was at war again, this time with Algiers. Decatur, now a commodore (at that time the highest rank in the United States Navy), assembled a squadron of ten ships, including three frigates, one of which was the *Macedonian*. After capturing the Algerine flagship and killing the grand admiral of the Algerine fleet, Decatur's entire squadron sailed into Algiers Harbor. A treaty favorable to the United States was the result. Additional concessions were later made by Tunis as well. Decatur was the principal negotiator in both cases.

After returning home, Decatur was appointed to the three-member Board of Naval Commissioners. The Decaturs (they had no children) moved to Washington, D.C., where Decatur continued to contribute to naval affairs.

Decatur died as he had lived: defending his honor. The cashiered Barron returned to the United States from Denmark in 1818 and unsuccessfully applied for reinstatement in the U.S. Navy. Barron blamed the Board of Naval Commissioners and Decatur in particular. He initiated a correspondence with Decatur that ended when Barron challenged Decatur to a duel. They met at Bladensburg, Maryland, on March 22, 1820. Although Decatur, an excellent pistol marksman, aimed to wound his opponent, Barron aimed to kill—and succeeded. Shot in the groin, Decatur died twelve hours later. Congress adjourned to attend Decatur's funeral, naval officers wore crepe for thirty days, guns on ships at Washington and Norfolk fired at thirty-minute intervals, and numerous eulogies were presented by people of all ranks and classes. President James Monroe and his cabinet marched in the funeral procession.

Barron was finally reinstated in 1824. He was given command of the Philadelphia Navy Yard and later the Norfolk Navy Yard. He died in 1851 at the age of eighty-three.

Summary

Decatur's contributions to the United States were revered a great deal more during his lifetime than by subsequent generations of Americans. Although no naval history of the post-Revolutionary War period would be complete without devoting considerable attention to Decatur, his heroic accomplishments, impressive as they were, made a limited impact on naval policy and strategy. Early nineteenth century Americans needed a hero to help represent and justify their nation's brief history and its full membership among contemporary nations. Decatur was the right person at the right place at the right time. Perhaps his dedication to his country was best expressed by a toast he made at a dinner held in his honor in 1816: "Our Country! In her intercourse with foreign nations, may she always be in the right, but our country right or wrong."

Bibliography

Anthony, Irvin. *Decatur*. New York and London: Scribner, 1931. Anthony's book is subjective but remains one of the few book-length biographies of Decatur. Includes much personal detail.

Blassingame, Wyatt. *Stephen Decatur: Fighting Sailor*. Champaign, Ill.: Garrard, 1964. This volume is suitable for early elementary students.

Dunne, W. M. P. "Pistols and Honor: The James Barron-Stephen Decatur Conflict, 1798-1807." *The American Neptune* 50 (Fall, 1990): 245-259. Dunne provides an account of the early relationship of Decatur and Barron, including events leading to their enmity.

Guttridge, Leonard F., and Jay D. Smith. *The Commodores*. New York: Harper, 1969; London: Davies, 1970. This volume includes pithy accounts of Decatur and Barron, along with other high-ranking naval officers. Especially valuable for the Bladensburg duel.

Lewis, Charles Lee. *The Romantic Decatur*. Philadelphia: University of Pennsylvania Press, and London: Oxford University Press, 1937. This is the standard book-length biography of Decatur. For the most part, Lewis remains objective throughout the book.

Schroeder, John H. "Stephen Decatur: Heroic Ideal of the Young Navy." In *Command Under Sail: Makers of the American Naval Tradition*, edited by James C. Bradford. Annapolis, Md.: United States Naval Institute, 1985. Most of this overview of Decatur's naval career is supported by primary sources.

Tucker, Glenn. *Dawn Like Thunder: The Barbary Wars and the Birth of the U.S. Navy*. Indianapolis, Ind.: Bobbs-Merrill, 1963. Tucher details Decatur's participation in the Barbary Wars.

John Quinn Imholte

RICHARD DEDEKIND

Born: October 6, 1831; Brunswick
Died: February 12, 1916; Brunswick, Germany
Area of Achievement: Mathematics
Contribution: Dedekind gave a new definition to the concept of irrational numbers, based exclusively on arithmetic principles. He helped clarify the notions of infinity and continuity and contributed to the establishment of rigorous theoretical foundations for mathematics.

Early Life

Julius Wilhelm Richard Dedekind was one of four children born to a well-established professional family in Brunswick. His father was a professor of jurisprudence at the local Collegium Carolinum, and his mother was a professor's daughter. In school, Dedekind was primarily interested in physics and chemistry, but when he enrolled in the Collegium Carolinum, it was as a student of mathematics. From a résumé, written somewhat later and in Latin, it is clear that this change was based on his dissatisfaction with the lack of rigor in the natural sciences.

In 1850, Dedekind was matriculated at the University of Göttingen, where he followed various courses in mathematics (studying under Carl Friedrich Gauss), astronomy, and experimental physics. In 1852, Dedekind presented his doctoral dissertation, which, in the opinion of Gauss, showed promise. At that time, the standard of mathematics at Göttingen was not very high, and Dedekind spent the following two years studying privately and preparing himself to become a first-class mathematician. No doubt his friendship with the brilliant Georg Friedrich Bernhard Riemann, at Göttingen at the same time, was also a positive influence. In fact, Dedekind attended Riemann's lectures even after he himself qualified as a university lecturer in 1854. When Gauss died in 1855, Peter Gustav Lejeune Dirichlet, previously professor in Berlin, succeeded him. Dedekind described Dirichlet's arrival in Göttingen as a life-changing event. Dedekind not only attended Dirichlet's lectures but also became a personal friend of the new professor.

Life's Work

In 1858, the Federal Institute of Technology in Zurich, Switzerland, appointed Dedekind as professor of mathematics on Dirichlet's recommendation. Riemann also applied for the post but his work was considered too abstract. Dedekind stayed in Zurich until 1862 and then accepted an invitation from his old college in Brunswick, which had become a polytechnic by then. While in Zurich, Dedekind taught differential and integral calculus and was disturbed by having to use concepts that had never been properly defined. In particular, he wrote: "Differential calculus deals with continuous magnitude, and yet an explanation of this continuity is nowhere given." He also deplored accepting without proof the belief that an increasing infinite sequence with an upper bound converges to a limit. He was dissatisfied that the notions of limit and continuity were based solely on geometrical intuition. On November 24, 1858, Dedekind succeeded in securing "a real definition of the essence of continuity." He waited until 1872 to publish this definition in book form, with the title *Stetigkeit und Irrationale Zahlen* ("Continuity and Irrational Numbers," translated in *Essays on the Theory of Numbers*, 1901).

Dedekind's problem was essentially that of irrational numbers, known already to the ancient Greeks. Rational numbers are dense in the sense that between any two rational numbers there is always another rational number, although there are infinitely many gaps between them. These gaps can be thought of as irrational numbers, and, before Dedekind began his work, they were characterized by infinite, nonrecurring decimal fractions. Dedekind devised a method, using "cuts," to define irrational numbers in terms of the rationals. If rational numbers are divided into two sets such that every number in the first set is smaller than every number in the second set, this partition defines one and only one real number. Should there be a largest or smallest number in one of the sets, the Dedekind cut corresponds to that rational number, while an irrational number is defined if neither set has a smallest or largest member. A Dedekind cut can be imagined as severing a straight line composed of only rational numbers into two parts. Rational and irrational numbers together form the set of real numbers, and this set can now be made to correspond to all the points of a straight line. With this method, Dedekind not only managed to define irrational numbers in terms of rationals without recourse to geometry but also showed that a line, and by implication three-dimensional space, is complete, containing no holes. Furthermore, Dedekind upheld his philosophical principles, according to which numbers do not exist in a Platonic sense but are free creations of the human mind.

Closely connected to this work was the introduction of the concept of "ideals." Dedekind edited and published Dirichlet's lectures on number theory after the death of the latter. Dedekind can, in fact, be considered the author of the book, since Dirichlet left only an outline plan for publication, and that was already based on Dedekind's notes. In the tenth supplement to the second edition of this influential book, Dedekind developed the theory of ideals, following to a certain extent a line Ernst Eduard Kummer had already taken. Dedekind, however, went far beyond Kummer, avoided his mistakes, and made the theory more exact.

Ideals are an extension and generalization of the common number concept. According to the fundamental theory of arithmetic, ordinary integers either are prime numbers or can be uniquely factorized into primes. Unique factorization is a useful feature but does not generally apply to all algebraic integers in a given algebraic number field, algebraic numbers being defined as the roots of polynominal equations with integer coefficients. With the introduction of ideals, unique factorization can be restored. Dedekind subsequently revised and further developed this theory. In an important paper coauthored by Heinrich Weber, the analogy between algebraic numbers and algebraic functions was demonstrated with the help of ideals.

In *Was sind und was sollen die Zahlen?* (1888; "The Nature and Meaning of Numbers," translated in *Essays on the Theory of Numbers*, 1901), Dedekind utilized the concept of what he called systems, which later became known as sets, and developed logical theories of original and cardinal numbers and of mathematical induction. In addition to contributing papers to mathematical journals, Dedekind coedited Riemann's collected works and supplied a biography of Riemann.

Dedekind stayed at Brunswick until his death and became a director of the polytechnic between 1872 and 1875. It seems that Dedekind was not offered the posts he would have accepted, while he refused the posts, most notably the one at Halle, that he was offered. Dedekind never married but lived with one of his sisters until her death in 1914. Although he lived in relative isolation, he was never a recluse. He was an excellent musician: He played the cello as a young man and the piano in later life. His portraits show a fine-featured man with thoughtful eyes; his character was described as modest, mild, and somewhat shy.

Summary

Although Richard Dedekind was a corresponding member of several academies and an honorary doctor of several universities, he never received the recognition he so fully deserved. It can be seen that his work was one of the most influential in shaping twentieth century mathematics. He is one of only thirty-one mathematicians meriting an individual entry in *Iwanami Sugaku Ziten* (1954; *Encyclopedic Dictionary of Mathematics*, 1977), in which he is described as a pioneer of abstract algebra. Transcending pure calculation, Dedekind made an attempt to find theoretical foundations to concepts used in algebraic number theory and in infinitesimal calculus. He defined and thereby created new mathematical structures that generalize the notions of number and serve as examples for further generalization.

Dedekind met Georg Cantor on a holiday in Switzerland and became his friend and also, at times, his frequent correspondent. Cantor submitted his theories to Dedekind for comment and criticism, and Dedekind was one of the first to support set theory in the face of hostility by other mathematicians. Independently of Cantor, he also utilized the concept of the actual, or concrete, infinite—a concept that was then regarded as taboo because there existed no theoretical foundation for its existence. Dedekind's work assisted in finding just such a foundation.

Bibliography

Bell, Eric T. "Arithmetic the Second." In *Men of Mathematics*. New York: Simon and Schuster, and London: Gollancz, 1937. This short chapter in a well-known collective biography of mathematicians discusses the life and work of Kummer and Dedekind. Bell makes a good attempt to explain the abstract and often difficult concepts that are necessary for the understanding and appreciation of Dedekind's work.

Dauben, J. W. *Georg Cantor: His Mathematics and Philosophy of the Infinite*. Cambridge, Mass.: Harvard University Press, 1979. Not a biography of Cantor, but a study of the emergence of a new mathematical theory. Dedekind's life, his work, and his influence on Cantor are featured extensively, but these references are dispersed throughout the book. Readers whose main interest is in Dedekind can rely on the well-constructed index and the twenty-four-page bibliography.

Dedekind, Richard. *Theory of Algebraic Integers.* Introduction and translation by John Stillwell. Cambridge and New York: Cambridge University Press, 1996. Full translation of Dedekind's memoir, *Sur la Theorie des Nombres Entiers Algebriques.* Discusses the mathematician's development of algebraic theories.

Edwards, Harold M. "Dedekind's Invention of Ideals." *The Bulletin of the London Mathematical Society* 15 (1983): 8-17. Traces the influences on Dedekind's set theoretic approach mainly to Dirichlet but also to Kummer and Riemann. Évariste Galois' influence was limited and resulted in steering Dedekind toward conceptual thinking as opposed to mere calculating. Dedekind went beyond Dirichlet, and against the accepted classical doctrine, by using completed infinites. The author stresses the innovative nature of Dedekind's theories and the analogy between cuts and ideals.

————. "The Genesis of Ideal Theory." *Archive for History of Exact Sciences* 23 (1980): 321-378. Analyzes Kummer's, Leopold Kronecker's, and Dedekind's versions of the theory of ideal factorization of algebraic integers. The author advances the thesis that as Dedekind revised the theory several times to match his philosophical principles, it did not improve from the mathematical point of view, and the first formulation remained the best.

Fowler, David. "Dedekind's Theorem: Square Root of 2 x Square Root of 3 = Square Root of 6." *The American Mathematical Monthly* 99, no. 8 (October, 1992). Analysis of Dedekind's belief that the proof of theorems is based on the definition of addition.

Gillies, D. A. *Frege, Dedekind, and Peano on the Foundations of Arithmetic.* Assen, the Netherlands: Van Gorcum, 1982. A short paperback with an adequate index and a list of references. Investigates the relationship between logic and arithmetic in the work of the three men. Gillies regards Dedekind as fundamentally a logician and compares him to Gottlob Frege, who denied that a set was a logical notion, and to Giuseppe Peano, who thought that arithmetic could not be reduced to logic.

Grattan-Guinness, I. "The Rediscovery of the Cantor-Dedekind Correspondence." *Jahresbericht der Deutschen Mathematiker Vereinigung* 76 (1974): 104-139. Recounts what happened to Dedekind's side of the correspondence, which seemed to have disappeared after the publication of the mathematical extracts in 1937. Ninety-eight items are listed, including notes, drafts, and letters to Ferdinand Georg Frobenius and Weber in addition to the Cantor-Dedekind correspondence. Contains extracts from the letters in German, with connecting text in English. The reader gains some insight into why Dedekind refused the position offered to him at Halle.

Jourdain, Philip E. B. "Richard Dedekind (1833-1916)." *The Monist* 26 (1916): 415-427. Obituary article with long extracts from the English translation of Dedekind's works. Contains virtually no biographical details, but gives a clear explanation of the Dedekind cuts and mentions the connection between what Dedekind called systems and set theory introduced by Cantor. Ideals are not discussed. The importance of finding rigorous foundations to arithmetic is stressed.

Judit Brody

EDGAR DEGAS

Born: July 19, 1834; Paris, France
Died: September 27, 1917; Paris, France
Area of Achievement: Art
Contribution: Degas was one of the great figural painters and draftsmen of the nineteenth century. His work combined a deep understanding of tradition with a commitment to innovative portrayals of modern life. His artistic independence was asserted in his role as one of the leading figures of the Impressionistic exhibitions of 1874-1886.

Early Life

Edgar Degas was born into a comfortable, upper-bourgeois Parisian family in 1834. His father managed the local branch of the family bank, headquartered in Naples, and his mother was the daughter of a cotton broker in New Orleans. The family's social connections in France, Italy, and the United States would play an important role in shaping Edgar's life and character. Frequent visits to the Louvre, as well as to the homes of friends who had substantial private collections, were regarded as an essential part of the boy's upbringing. Edgar attended the prestigious Lycée Louis-le-Grand in Paris, where he received his first instruction in drawing. Upon graduation in 1853, he briefly studied law but soon turned his attention wholeheartedly to a career in art.

Degas' early artistic training consisted of two stages: the period 1853-1856, spent mostly in Paris, and the period 1856-1859, dominated by two lengthy sojourns in Italy. In Paris, Degas studied under Louis Lamothe, a follower of the disciplined classicism of Jean-Auguste-Dominique Ingres. Working independently, Degas devoted much time to copying paintings in the Louvre and prints in the Bibliothèque Nationale. In 1855, he enrolled in the École des Beaux Arts. Instead of completing his formal studies and competing for the coveted Prix de Rome, however, he decided to go to Italy on his own. In Naples and Florence, where he visited relatives, and in Rome, where he stayed at the French Academy, Degas' devotion to the art of the past was expanded and deepened. At the same time, his contact with other young French artists studying in Italy, such as Gustave Moreau, helped turn his attention to the more recent achievements of artists such as Eugène Delacroix.

Apart from many copies and sketches, the most important works produced by Degas during these early years were portraits of family members. The crowning achievement of these early portraits was *The Bellelli Family*, a large painting of his Florentine relatives begun in Italy in 1858 and completed several years later in Paris. In its technical mastery and psychological sensitivity, this painting announced the beginning of a major career.

Life's Work

The emergence of Degas' artistic personality during the 1860's was characteristically complex. Soon after his return from Italy, he established a studio in Paris and began to work on a series of large history paintings. Although inspired in part by the classical tradition, Degas' historical scenes tended to recast tradition through a disarming straightforwardness of treatment. The last of this group of pictures, *Scene of War in the Middle Ages*, was shown at the Salon of 1865 as Degas' first major publicly exhibited work. Ironically, that marked the beginning of Degas' public career and the end of his interest in history painting. The following year, he exhibited *The Steeplechase*, and in 1868 he showed *Mlle Fiocre in the Ballet "La Source."* The themes of the racetrack and the ballet proclaimed the artist's new commitment to the subject matter of contemporary life. This commitment would be a decisive factor in determining the subsequent course of his career.

Degas' interest in contemporary subjects was inspired and shared by a growing circle of progressive artists and writers with whom he began associating during these years. By around 1862, he had met Édouard Manet, leader of a new generation of artists devoted to painting modern life, and Edmund Duranty, a naturalist writer and critic who would become a champion of Degas' art during the 1870's. Through the frequent gatherings of artists at the Café Guerbois, Degas became familiar with Claude Monet, Auguste Renoir, and other young artists who would eventually form the core of the Impressionist group. His keen, perceptive intellect and brusque humor soon established Degas' prominence within the group. Although his role would develop into one of dedicated leadership, he would always maintain a degree of the aloofness of an outsider. An intriguing glimpse of this complex personality is provided in the *Self-Portrait* of about 1863, in which confidence, irony, and self-consciousness seem to coexist behind a façade of bourgeois elegance.

Self-portrait of Degas

The 1870's were both a climax and a turning point in Degas' career. His paintings of familiar urban entertainments such as the ballet achieved full maturity, and his circle of colleagues finally banded together and organized a series of independent exhibitions. At the same time, however, he experienced some unexpected setbacks. The Franco-Prussian War of 1870-1871 found him serving in the artillery, and at this time he began to have problems with his eyesight. His financial security was seriously compromised as a result of the failure of the family bank following his father's death in 1874. Degas' commitment to the risky venture of the independent exhibitions from the first show in 1874 until the last one in 1886 is all the more impressive in the face of these circumstances.

Degas' accomplishments as an artist during the 1870's were an extraordinary combination of fully realized maturity and restless experimentation. The ballet scenes were a dominant theme, beginning with such works as *The Orchestra of the Opera* (c. 1870) and *The Dance Class* (1871), which established the performance hall and the rehearsal studio as the two realms of Degas' exploration of the dance. His portraits achieved new complexity and psychological depth, as exemplified by the group of paintings of his New Orleans relatives, done when the artist visited them in 1872-1873, and by various portrayals of friends and colleagues such as the portrait of Duranty of 1879. Several new themes were introduced or given greater prominence during the years of the Impressionist exhibitions, including the café and the café-concert, milliners, laundresses, and prostitutes. Along with these diverse themes, an increasing attention to varied techniques such as pastel, lithography, monotype, and sculpture contributed to the rich complexity of Degas' mature art.

The most decisive changes in Degas' later work were introduced in the years around 1880. The interest in sculpture was bold, experimental, and largely private. The subjects of the sculptures, especially dancers and bathers, paralleled the themes of his paintings at a time when pastel was increasingly replacing oil as his principal pictorial medium. The rich textures and glowing colors of the pastel bathers of the 1880's and 1890's represent the grand culmination of Degas' career. Seven such pictures were shown at the last Impressionist exhibit in 1886, including the famous *Woman Bathing in a Shallow Tub*. By presenting the nude in unconventionally natural poses seen from unexpected angles in realistic surroundings, these works revitalized tradition through an emphasis on the immediacy of experience and the ingenuity of artistic innovation.

Degas' late work was hampered by failing eyesight, although flashes of brilliance continued to appear until he finally had to stop painting entirely around 1908. He was able to turn his attention to collecting because of the rising prices he was receiving for his works, but for the most part the last years leading up to his death in 1917 were characterized by a frustrating inactivity and isolation.

Summary

Edgar Degas' artistic contribution can be summarized in terms of his complex relation to Impressionism. As a leading figure behind the Impressionist exhibitions, Degas made a historic commitment to artistic independence which would help set the stage for the development of modern art. His dedication to subjects drawn from modern life and to bold technical and stylistic innovation are aspects of his art which played an integral role within the group. On the other hand, he was persistently somewhat of an outsider whose attitudes and alliances increasingly factionalized the group. He particularly opposed the label Impressionist (he preferred "Independents") and its associations with a spontaneous, directly naturalistic art. Although his art was committed to contemporary subjects and steeped in observation and experience, Degas was never entirely a naturalist. In contrast to Monet, who rejected tradition and painted directly before his subjects in nature, Degas executed his works in the studio and relied heavily on calculation, imagination, and memory of earlier works of art. His artistic repertoire expanded from an early love of Ingres and the classics to include such nontraditional sources as Japanese prints and photography, but throughout his career Degas' art remained informed by other art as much as by nature. Even his favorite themes, such as the theater and the ballet, reveal an antinaturalistic orientation in which the artificiality of costume, pose, and stage set are celebrated. By studying the richness of life in a variety of such artificial contexts, Degas was creating an art dedicated to the modern city. By advancing the importance of direct experience and innovation in art without discarding the lessons of tradition, he was both contributing to the emergence of modernism and transcending it.

Bibliography

Adriani, Götz. *Degas: Pastels, Oil Sketches, Drawings*. Translated by Alexander Lieven. London: Thames and Hudson, and New York: Abbeville Press, 1985. The English translation of the catalog was produced in conjunction with the 1984 exhibition in Tübingen and Berlin. Includes a scholarly introductory essay, a well-documented catalog, and excellent illustrations.

Boggs, Jean Sutherland. *Degas at the Races*. Washington D.C.: National Gallery of Arts, 1998. Study of Degas' consuming interest in horses, jockeys, and racing and its place in his work. Over 120 paintings, drawings, prints, sculptures, and pastels. Catalogs the 1998 exhibit of Degas' work at the National Galley of Art in Washington, D.C.

—————. *Portraits by Degas*. Berkeley: University of California Press, 1962. A classic study of an important, but often neglected aspect of Degas' art. The portraits are presented as being central to Degas' career. Careful analyses of sitters and their relations to the artist and his paintings are included.

Browse, Lillian. *Degas Dancers*. London: Faber, and New York: Studio, 1949. An early investigation of Degas' art from a thematic perspective, focusing on his most popular theme but presenting it in a more scholarly, interpretive context.

Degas, Hilaire Germain Edgar. *Degas: The Complete Etchings, Lithographs, and Monotypes*. Text by Jean Adhémar and François Cachin. Translated by Jane Brenton. London: Thames and Hudson, and New York: Viking Press, 1974. A thoroughly illustrated and documented catalog of Degas' prints, with brief, informative introductory essays.

—————. *Letters*. Edited by Marcel Guérin. Translated by Marguerite Kay. Oxford: Cassirer, 1947. The English translation of the standard edition of the artist's letters. Provides important personal insights into his art, thought, and character.

—————. *The Notebooks of Edgar Degas*. Edited by Theodore Reff. 2 vols. Oxford: Clarendon Press, 1976. A carefully documented and annotated catalog of Degas' thirty-seven notebooks in the Bibliothèque Nationale in Paris. An indispensable publication on the artist's sources, development, and creative processes.

Halévy, Daniel. *My Friend Degas*. Translated by Mina Curtiss. Middletown, Conn.: Wesleyan University Press, 1964; London: Hart-Davis, 1966. A personal account of Degas during his later years, based on the journal Halévy began keeping in 1888 and continuing through the artist's death.

Kendall, Richard. *Degas and the Little Dancer*. New Haven, Conn.: Yale University Press, 1998. This is the first full-length study of Degas' sculpture, "Little Dancer Aged Fourteen." Kendall provides new information on this, the basis of twentieth-century sculpture. Catalogs the 1998 exhibit at the Joslyn Art Museum in Omaha, Nebr.

McMullen, Roy. *Degas: His Life, Times, and Work*. Boston: Houghton Mifflin, 1984; London: Secker and Warburg, 1985. A comprehensive biography that is both scholarly and readable. Although considerable attention is given to major works, the emphasis throughout is on the artist's life and character. The best general biography in English.

Reff, Theodore, ed. *Degas: The Artist's Mind*. London: Thames and Hudson, and New York: Harper, 1976. A collection of essays on various aspects of Degas' art. Most of the essays are revised versions of articles originally published in scholarly journals. A selection of important motifs, sources, and techniques are considered with a goal of better understanding Degas' artistic thought.

Dennis Costanzo

EUGÈNE DELACROIX

Born: April 26, 1798; Charenton-Saint-Maurice, France

Died: August 13, 1863; Paris, France

Area of Achievement: Art

Contribution: Delacroix, a powerful colorist, became the most important figure in the development of the Romantic painting movement in France in the nineteenth century. A prolific artist, he sought to stir viewers deeply by appealing to their senses even though he chose to explore the dark side of their human emotions.

Early Life

Eugène Delacroix was born in a Paris suburb called Charenton-Saint-Maurice. His father, Charles, a schoolteacher, rose to become minister of foreign affairs in 1795 under the revolutionary regime and French ambassador to the Netherlands some eighteen months later. His wife, Victoire Oeben, descended from a distinguished family of royal cabinetmakers. Controversy surrounds Eugène's paternity. Some scholars maintain that his biological father was Talleyrand, one of Europe's most brilliant statesmen, to whom the artist is said to have borne a striking resemblance.

While in Marseilles, as a result of an administrative appointment for his father, Charles, the young Eugène exhibited a precocious talent for piano and violin. His legal father died in late 1805, and Eugène's mother moved the family back to Paris and enrolled Eugène at the Lycée Imperial, one of the best schools in the capital. There Delacroix excelled in Latin, Greek, and drawing. He also furthered his drawing skills by copying prints in the manner of the English caricaturist James Gillray, a practice which shaped a career-long habit of seeking expressions of character and animated gestures. When not yet eleven, Eugène had a fateful experience—a visit to the Louvre on one of his free days. The sight of such pictorial variety, scale, and technical mastery caused him to decide upon a painting career.

When Delacroix was seventeen, his career goal was aided by an introduction to Pierre-Narcisse Guerin, a successful painter and follower of Jacques-Louis David, head of the neoclassical movement in art and practically an art dictator under Napoleon I. In Guerin's atelier, Delacroix drew rigorously, learning human anatomy from classical references. He enjoyed working on large historical compositions involving faraway battles. While there he met Théodore Géricault, once a Guerin pupil. The young Delacroix felt an immediate kinship with Géricault's ideas of infusing French art with sensuousness plus an insistence upon spontaneity. Unfortunately, Delacroix was forced to withdraw from Guerin's atelier after only six months, probably because he could not afford the cost of tuition.

In 1816, Delacroix enrolled at the École des Beaux Arts. Orthodoxy ruled at this government-patronized school where all students progressed in basically the same manner. The primary methodology, like that for Guerin's classroom, was the study of classical form through seemingly endless copying of antique imagery from plaster casts, sculpture busts, coins, and, finally, male and female models. Delacroix was responsive to such instruction, but concurrently he searched for flexibility of expression and, on his own, explored the print-making mediums of etching and engraving as well as the new print form lithography.

Delacroix's growing need for emotional release was soon met by the emergence of a friendship with Géricault. The timing could not have been more propitious, as the slightly older Géricault was embarking on a sensational large work, *The Raft of the Medusa* (1819). Its subject, chosen to embarrass the restored monarchy of France with the hope of possibly becoming a success by scandal, depicts the moment of the initial sighting of the above-mentioned raft by a passing ship on the Atlantic horizon. The raft contained a dozen or so men who had survived twelve days adrift, their two ropes connected to lifeboats having been mysteriously cut within a day of abandoning the stranded and broken frigate *Medusa*. The ship had been on its way to Senegal with about four hundred passengers before running aground off the West African coast, thanks to an incompetent captain. Delacroix posed for the seminude figure lying face down near the edge of the raft in the central foreground. Though *The Raft of the Medusa* was overpoweringly raw, it proved to be the emotional elixir Delacroix was seeking. He may have been marked by its example, for his best paintings subsequently dealt with cruelty and death.

As with other artists falling under the perplexing umbrella of Romanticism, Delacroix's appearance and manner could be misleading. By age twenty, his aristocratic lineage was evident in his stiff posture and finely etched features. Fashion-conscious, he was one of the first to introduce the English-cut suit to Parisians, and to many people Delacroix was a pretentious dandy. Yet some historians suggest that the artist's elegant attire and fine manners were used to mock France's increasingly industrialized society, which he thought was crassly hopeful in its newfound material prosperity.

Delacroix also had a withdrawn and pessimistic nature, which he cultivated further by emulating the melancholic pathos in Dante's poetry and the works of George Gordon, Lord Byron. By contrast, the painter's work Delacroix most admired from the past was that of Peter Paul Rubens, whose high-keyed colors and dramatic action enthralled him. Yet it was Lord Byron who became a personal hero with a personality profile containing passion, bravery, elegance, melancholy, a love of freedom, and pessimism.

Life's Work

Desiring a successful career in painting, which in his day meant salon acceptance, Delacroix began a salon entry in 1821, one that would ideally attract critical reviews but not a storm of controversy. Touched by reading *The Inferno* from Dante's *The Divine Comedy*, he selected an episode from Canto VIII. Known by various titles, for example, *Dante and Virgil Crossing the Styx* and *The Bark of Dante*, the 1822 painting simulated the emotional potential and large scale of Géricault's *The Raft of the Medusa*, still fresh in Delacroix's memory. Unfortunately, polite taste, long accustomed to contained forms, polished technique, and clarity of color and values, was not ready for the ambiguous spaces and murky tones of Delacroix's painting.

Yet something more troublesome than salon taste marked Delacroix's subsequent career, namely the fact that many of his best paintings depicted injury, frenzy, and killing. He did not need to wait long for those types of thematic opportunities. In 1822, as many as twenty thousand Greeks on the island of Chios in the eastern Mediterranean were killed by invading Turks. Delacroix seized the chance to compose a potentially sensational work riding the crest of public interest in the war. Called *The Massacre at Chios* ("and the massacre of painting" by some of his contemporaries), it would seem to have been intended as a history set piece, except that the artist was basically apolitical.

A chance encounter with three landscape paintings by English Romantic painter John Constable at a Paris picture gallery may ultimately have been as important to Delacroix's subject and stylistic development as the gruesome massacre imagery. The artist noticed the application of color in bright flecks and dabs. Then he tested Constable's choppy, unblended color strokes and found, as did Constable, that a viewer's eyes mix the colors. The effects are not as crucial as Delacroix's intentions, which was not fidelity to atmospheric conditions but a contribution to a depressing mood combining murder and eroticism. From that point onward, color and a more vigorous painting method played a larger role in his art.

The Massacre at Chios shocked conservatives but enraptured youthful artists. It also stimulated Delacroix to explore more themes of death with erotic overtones. In fact, an immediate exploration of that sort was his entry for the 1827 Salon. Known as *The Death of Sardanapolus*, it was inspired by a Lord Byron play based upon the suicide of an Assyrian prince whom Byron named Sardanapolus. That world-weary aesthete choreographed his own conflagration as a final work of art.

Through Byron, Delacroix illustrated the sickening preparations for the prince's funerary pyre, during which Sardanapolus watches without remorse as his favorite wives, horses, and dogs are killed in front of him by his officers.

The Death of Sardanapolus suffered disapproval by the press, and the French government refused to purchase it. Delacroix was warned by the head of the Academy of Fine Arts to refrain from painting any more like it for a long time lest he become ineligible for state commissions. Luckily for the artist, new officials, eager to overthrow the tastes of their predecessors, came to power in the aftermath of the July Revolution of 1830. Delacroix was soon in their good graces, and one of his few political paintings, *Liberty Leading the People*, was finished by late 1830. This painting became a much-copied icon of revolutionary propaganda, with versions appearing often as posters well into the twentieth century. It was born of a public uprising in Paris that Delacroix witnessed but in which he did not participate because, even here, he had little faith in the proletariat.

In *Liberty Leading the People*, a ragged army surges forward, stumbling over a barricade of paving stones, debris, and fallen comrades. They are led by a solidly built, resolute, young bare-breasted woman (Liberty), who holds a musket in her left hand and raises the flag of France with her right hand. The conflict stemmed from unresolved grievances of the Revolution in 1789 plus retrogressive decrees in July of 1830 by King Charles X, which dissolved the Chamber of Deputies, suspended freedom of the press, and overturned the voting rights of the merchant class and the new industrialists. Delacroix seemed to express perfectly the collective sentiment of the Parisians in revolt, perhaps even the universal will of ordinary citizens to revolt against intolerable conditions. Yet those were not his intentions. Nevertheless, the artist valued most the French flag defiantly raised by the spirit of Liberty, which was returned to the north tower of Notre Dame on July 28, 1832, and is visible at the extreme right of the composition.

The year 1832 was a turning point in Delacroix's development, for at that time he accepted an invitation to accompany Count Charles de Mornay on a goodwill trip to Morocco. The artist was asked to record picturesque events of a treaty-exploring journey which followed the recent French takeover of neighboring Algeria. In North Africa, Delacroix hoped to find brilliant colors, sensuality, and ferocity. Instead, he observed civility, dignity, simple life-styles, and a sense of unbroken traditions. From the first day ashore, he began to fill sketchbooks with drawings, watercolor vignettes, written notes on color, and descriptive details of his discoveries such as bright robes, exotic women, and non-European types of buildings. A short trip to Algiers was just as fruitful, for, once there, he realized a fantasy of long standing—entry into a harem. Two years after completing his North African trip, Delacroix produced an enchanting work drawn from that rare experience, *Algerian Women in Their Quarters*. In it, reverie and sensuality are fused and suspended.

The diaries and sketchbooks Delacroix filled sustained his art until his death in 1863. Equally remarkable is the fact that, despite the time lapse between the 1834 watercolor studies and the paintings derived from them, the latter did not lack freshness. The most popular works best typify Delacroix's taste for violence and cruelty: *The Lion Hunt* (1861) and *Arabs Skirmishing in the Mountains* (1862). For almost three decades, beginning in the 1830's, Delacroix was also involved with commissions sponsored by the government for major public buildings. There were church commissions, too. Altogether, they were exactly the type of employment to which most artists aspired at the time. Noteworthy contracts included wall and ceiling compositions at the National Assembly-Paris, the Luxembourg Palace (1845-1846), the Apollo Gallery at the Louvre (1850-1851), and the Church of Saint-Sulpice (1856-1861). Delacroix's last years were marked by failing health while he worked on these large projects. He died in 1863 in Paris after willing nearly six thousand works to public sale.

Summary

Eugène Delacroix became the leading figure of the Romantic movement of painting in France and did so without trying. Actually, he may not have seen himself as a leader of anything. Like a number of major figures in art during his life, he was an enigma fraught with contradictions. For example, his thematic preferences ran quickly to scenes of high drama on the seas and depictions of fierce animal combat. Ironically, it was the gentle *Algerian Women in Their Quarters* which was later much admired, copied, and assimilated by artists of such stature as Pierre Renoir, Paul Cézanne, Henri Matisse, and Pablo Picasso.

Delacroix's output was phenomenal, including 850 paintings, hundreds of watercolors, about sixty sketchbooks, many lithographs, thousands of drawings, a three-volume journal, and the beginnings of a dictionary of the fine arts. Furthermore, Delacroix, so full of energy, so prolific in his career, so strong-willed, seemingly had little faith in civilization. His pessimism, which was at first cultivated as a badge of distinction, eventually enveloped him like an unwelcomed, unshakable cloak. He is remembered as a rich colorist who painted dark themes. Delacroix died in 1863. By then Romanticism had been eclipsed by Édouard Manet's unvarnished naturalism in the 1863 Salon, which would lead to the emergence of the next major painting movement, Impressionism.

Bibliography

Delacroix, Eugène. *The Journal of Eugène Delacroix.* Translated by Walter Pach. London: Cape, 1938; New York: Crown, 1948. The first English translation of the artist's private thoughts recorded intermittently from 1822 to 1832 and from 1847 to 1863. Perhaps the most relished are entries of his impressions of a six-month trip to North Africa in 1832. Delacroix's intentions toward his own art will be appreciated by those seeking to understand his state of mind when at work on key paintings.

Hannoosh, Michelle. *Painting and The Journal of Eugene Delacroix.* Princeton, N.J.: Princeton University Press, 1995. Examines Delacroix as a writer and artist. The author analyzes four of Delacroix's narratives on his public decorations showing that his writing is central not only to his artistic creativity, but to his opinions on life issues.

Huyghe, René. *Delacroix.* London: Thames and Hudson, and New York: Abrams, 1963. One of the best monographs on Delacroix to appear in English. Huyghe skillfully weaves quotations from the artist's journal and statements from Delacroix's contemporaries with his own observations. Illustrations of key paintings are analyzed diagrammatically, stressing the compositional structure in Delacroix's aesthetics. Important themes or works in series are suitably illustrated in black and white as preparatory drawings, multiple painted versions, and lithographs.

Jobert, Barthelemy. *Delacroix.* Paris: Gallimard, 1997; Princeton, N.J.: Princeton University Press, 1998. Published in conjunction with the bicentenary of Delacroix's birth, Jobert creates a visually compelling tribute that examines the artist and the man.

Johnson, Lee. *The Paintings of Eugène Delacroix: A Critical Catalogue, 1816-1831.* 2 vols. Oxford: Clarendon Press, 1981. A publication of major importance. The first attempt at a complete compilation of Delacroix's paintings since the basic effort of Alfred Robaut in 1885. Johnson covers the artist's formative period and his early salon successes. He airs new data regarding problems of dating paintings, presents paintings absent in Robaut's books, offers new biographical information on several of Delacroix's portrait subjects, and relates pertinent drawings to their respective paintings.

Le Bris, Michel. *Romantics and Romanticism.* New York: Rizzoli, 1981. An intriguing and well-illustrated study of Romanticism as an international movement with roots in literature and folklore. By stressing themes and contextual tendencies, the book separates itself from watered-down profiles and superficial catalogs. Nineteenth century Romantic tendencies aptly explored include the appetite for death and pessimism, the desire to experience non-Western cultures, the yearning for lost worlds, and phantoms and the deadly sublime.

Prideaux, Tom. *The World of Delacroix.* New York: Time-Life Books, 1966. A cultural-historical approach is used in this offering. Places Delacroix's art within the artistic and historical currents of his time. Prideaux weaves biography, politics and revolution, the painter's craft, and pedagogical issues into an engaging and lively text. A common thread of encounter in Delacroix's art is explored and found to be the result of a fertile imagination impelled toward invention and daring.

Trapp, Frank A. *The Attainment of Delacroix.* Baltimore: Johns Hopkins University Press, 1970. An ambitious monograph which addresses the artist's major works in dutiful fashion. The author's primary interests lie in Delacroix's paintings from literary sources and in themes from past history and current events. The last two chapters, which are entitled "Theory and Practice" and "Delacroix and His Critics," are perhaps the most welcome. The black-and-white illustrations are uneven in quality.

Tom Dewey II

LÉO DELIBES

Born: February 21, 1836; Saint-Germain-du-Val, France
Died: January 16, 1891; Paris, France
Area of Achievement: Music
Contribution: Delibes contributed significantly, as a composer, to the French ballet and opera of the nineteenth century.

Early Life

Clément-Philibert-Léo Delibes was born into a family which, on the maternal side, evinced musical talent. His grandmother was an opera singer, and his uncle, Antoine Édouard Batiste, was a noted organist and held important posts at the churches of Saint-Nicholas-des-Champs and at Saint Eustache. Clémence, Delibes' mother, was herself a musician, while his father, Philibert, worked as a civil servant in the postal service.

When Leo was eleven years old, his father died. His mother, who had provided her son with the fundamentals of music, moved the household to Paris. At this point, young Léo entered the Paris Conservatory and, in 1850, was awarded a *premier prix* in solfège. This skill in sight singing stood the future composer in good stead when he later turned his attention to opera. During his tenure at the conservatory, Delibes acquired skill as an organist through his study with François Benoist, a winner of the Prix de Rome in 1815 and a composer of ballets and operas, the two genres in which his pupil was eventually to make his mark. More important, Delibes studied composition with Adolphe-Charles Adam, a master of the opéra-comique (that is, *Le Postillon de Longjumeau*, 1836) and creator of such popular ballets as *Giselle* (1841) and *Le Corsaire* (1856). Adam, a pupil of François-Adrien Boïeldieu, became not only a mentor but also a partial father figure to his student.

Delibes' other musical enterprise as a youth included experience as a chorister at the Madeleine Cathedral and, on April 16, 1849, in the premiere of Giacomo Meyerbeer's *Le Prophète* at the Opéra. With the help of Adam, several professional positions were proffered him in 1853, and he thus found himself toiling as an accompanist at the Théâtre-Lyrique and as an organist at the Church of Saint Pierre de Chaillot. Despite his affinity for the organ (he worked as an organist steadily until 1871), Delibes developed an attraction for the the-

ater. With the exception of a brief interlude as a critic (1858) for the *Gaulois hebdomadaire*, for which he wrote under the pen name Eloi Delbès, this attraction was cemented as early as 1856. In that year, his first stage work, *Deux sous de charbon*, was produced at Hervé's Folies-Nouvelles and received a favorable reception.

Life's Work

Delibes found the light opera, or operetta, to be a genre well suited to his talent and inclination. Over the next fourteen years, he provided some dozen such entertainments, a few of which were staged at Jacques Offenbach's theater, the Bouffes-Parisiens. Among them was the enormously popular *Deux Vieilles Gardes*. In his role as chorus master at the Théâtre-Lyrique, the young creator arranged the vocal score of Charles Gounod's *Faust* (1859) and worked also on two other major staples of the French operatic repertory, *Les Pêcheurs de perles* (1863) by Georges Bizet and *Les Troyens à Carthage* (1863) by Hector Berlioz. By 1864, in his role as chorus master at the Opéra, Delibes capitalized on the opportunities which presented themselves to him. His early successes were enlarged upon and solidified with the performance on November 12, 1866, at the Opéra, of the ballet *La Source: Ou, Naila*, on which he collaborated with the established Austrian-born composer, Ludwig Minkus. Delibes' contribution to the music for scenes 2 and 3 has been adjudged superior to Minkus' contribution to scenes 1 and 4. A year later, with a divertissement for a revival of *Le Corsaire* by Adam, *Valse: Ou, Pas des Fleurs*, the composer had created for himself a considerable following. An opera bouffe entitled *La Cour du roi Pétaud*, produced on April 24, 1869, at Variétés, proved to be his final work in this genre.

The single most acclaimed composition by Delibes, the ballet *Coppélia: Ou, La Fille aux yeux d'émail*, was mounted on May 2, 1870, at the Opéra. The first ballet to use symphonic music throughout and to unify the dance and music into a homogeneity heretofore absent in this art form, *Coppélia* is based on Ernst Theodor Hoffman's story "Der Sandmann" (1816; "The Sandman," 1844). Set in two acts and three scenes, the work opens with a prelude; after the atmosphere has been created, there follow twenty musical numbers, the last of which comprises eight individual sections. The story line, which will be familiar to those who know Jacques Offenbach's *Les Contes d'Hoffmann* (1880), centers on the mechanical doll Coppélia, whose lifelike presence impels Franz, a young man who has become infatuated with her, to pursue her to the consternation of his fiancée, Swanhilda. Dr. Coppelius, the eccentric toymaker and magician who created the automaton, loves her as a daughter. When "the girl with the enamel eyes" is proved to be merely a toy, the lovers unite in marriage. It is at this juncture that number 20 of the score, "Festival of the Bell," with its eight sumptuous pieces featuring various uses of the bell, brings the ballet to a scintillating close. Assorted national dances such as the mazurka number 3, *Thème slave varié* number 6, the czardas number 7, and the bolero number 16 coupled with orchestral brilliance and coloration, contribute to the opulence of the composition.

In 1871, Delibes made the decisions to marry Léontine Estelle Denain and to devote himself entirely to composition; the latter determination caused him to refrain from time-consuming activity as an organist and chorus master. *Le Roi l'a dit*, Delibes' first major operatic opus, was produced on May 24, 1873, at the Opéra-Comique. Its immediate success in Paris resulted in a performance in Antwerp (August 18, 1873) and, during the next year, performances in Vienna, Karlsruhe, and Prague. Returning to the ballet, the musician produced a second masterpiece in this genre with *Sylvia: Ou, La Nymphe de Diane;* it was premiered on June 14, 1876, at the Opéra. The story, based on Torquato Tasso's *Aminta* (1573), deals with Sylvia, a nymph of Diana, and her love affair with the shepherd Aminta. Interest and contrast are created by the involvement in the story of Diana, Eros, and Orion. Stylistically, this work differs from *Coppélia;* indeed, the political climate in France was also different. *Coppélia* was a creature of the Second Empire, a period in which Paris was the pleasure capital of the world. *Sylvia*, on the other hand, with its stylized mythology, came at a time when France, now a republic, retained strong memories of the Franco-Prussian War and the internal upheavals of the commune. The orchestral scoring in *Sylvia* reveals immediately a more serious emotionality of expression; there are, in addition, traces of Wagnerian influence. Distinguished musicians, among them Peter Ilich Tchaikovsky, who probably

heard *Coppélia* during his several trips to Paris in the 1870's, were exposed to *Sylvia* in Vienna.

Now riding the crest of a triumphant wave, Delibes produced his three-act *drame lyrique, Jean de Nivelle*, on March 8, 1880, at the Opéra-Comique. It was very successful and received one hundred performances until January 6, 1881, at this theater. During the period 1880-1882, it was also performed in Stockholm, Budapest, Copenhagen, Vienna, Geneva, St. Petersburg, and Brussels. Oddly, after its revival at the Gaîté-Lyrique on October 5, 1908, it has fallen into oblivion.

Perhaps feeling a need to supplement his reputation as a composer with academic respectability, Delibes took a position as professor of composition at the Paris Conservatory in 1881, this despite admitted weaknesses in fugal and contrapuntal technique. Yet another side of this artist's talent emerges in the *Le Roi s'amuse, six airs de danse dans le style ancien*, written for a revival of Victor Hugo's *Le Roi s'amuse* (1832; *The King's Fool*, 1842), performed on November 22, 1882, at the Comédie-Française. Here, he reveals a distinct rapport for seventeenth century French classicism.

The three-act opera *Lakmé* premiered on April 14, 1883, at the Opéra-Comique. The exoticism of this work (the setting is India) in which the female lead, Lakmé, is the daughter of the Brahmin priest Nilakantha, has attracted audiences up to modern times. In this nineteenth century story, the British officer Gérald is in love with the heroine, much to her father's displeasure; indeed, the priest vows to kill the English suitor. When, however, Lakmé realizes that Gérald is torn between his duty and his love for her, she eases his burden by committing suicide. Of all its many excellences, the coloratura showstopper, the "Bell Song," remains a tour de force. From 1883 until his death, no other major work was completed by the composer, although an incomplete opera, *Kassya*, was produced on March 24, 1893, at the Opéra-Comique. Jules Massenet provided the orchestration but did not add the overture that Delibes did not live to compose.

Summary

Léo Delibes was described by French composer Henri-Charles Merechal as "restless, fidgety, slightly befuddled, correcting and excusing himself, lavishing praise, careful not to hurt anyone's feelings, shrewd, adroit, very lively, a sharp critic." This characterization aptly depicts those traits which most strongly affected the ballet master's creative path. The early works, notably the operettas, are always cited for their facile technique, their light and airy manner, and their elegance and wit. There is no plumbing of depths, no attempt at profundity. Delibes' operettas represent skillful treatment of a genre then in vogue and one which reached an apex of popularity in the hands of Offenbach, who, as a matter of interest, collaborated with Delibes on *Les Musiciens de l'orchèstre* (1861) and at whose theater Delibes produced nine of his light operas. Even at the height of his own fame, Delibes took time to complete Offenbach's *Belle Lurette* (1880) and *Mamzelle Moucheron* (1881).

As he matured, Delibes absorbed a variety of influences. Eclecticism as a *modus operandi* seems to have enabled the musician to create strikingly appealing dance numbers in *Coppélia* and *Sylvia*. In addition to the graceful turns of phrase, the orchestration reveals a genuine gift for originality. The use of alto saxophone in the barcarolle of *Sylvia* is a masterful stroke and one of the earliest efforts to make this instrument a viable member of the orchestra. The "Pizzicati" from the same ballet has been emulated by later composers. The oriental atmosphere in *Kassya* is skillfully wrought and is a portent of the direction in which Delibes was moving at his death.

Because his reputation had been solidified as a consequence of his stage works, there is a tendency to pay little heed to Delibes' many choruses, songs, piano pieces, and religious music such as the *Messe brève* for two equal voices with organ and string quartet, the *Ave maris stelle* for two voices, and the *Ave verum* for two voices. There is no uniformity of opinion with regard to Delibes' historical place. It is significant, however, that in his own lifetime he was elected a member of the Institut de France (1884). Delibes was viewed by the establishment as one worthy to carry on the French traditions deemed meritorious.

Because as a genre ballet has not attained the status of symphonic music, chamber music, or piano music, Delibes' position in the pantheon of musical celebrities has suffered, and because he was not a prolific composer, the total number of his works that survive in today's repertory is less than one dozen. Those who have seen or heard his best creations, however, have experienced an enchantment that lives long in the memory.

Bibliography

Cronin, Charles P. D., et al. "Theodore Pavie's 'Les babouches du Brahmane' and the Story of Delibes's 'Lakme.' " *The Opera Quarterly* 12, no. 4 (Summer 1996). Argues that Delibes' "Lakme" was inspired by Theodore Pavie's story "Les babouches du Brahmans," as opposed to Loti's "Rarahu, ou Le mariage de Loti," as is historically assumed.

Curtiss, Mina. *Bizet and His World.* New York: Knopf, 1958; London: Secker and Warburg, 1959. Contains useful and insightful information about the relationship between Delibes and Bizet.

Downes, Olin. *The Lure of Music: Depicting the Human Side of Great Composers, with Stories of Their Inspired Creations.* New York: Harper, 1918; London: Harper, 1922. Contains an excellent essay on Delibes and his music, and takes the position that Delibes' ballets are far more than a potpourri of uninspired dance pieces.

Macdonald, Hugh. "(Clément Philibert) Léo Delibes." In *The New Grove Dictionary of Music and Musicians*, edited by Stanley Sadie, vol. 5. London: Macmillan, 1980. Probably the finest English-language reference article on Delibes. Includes a comprehensive list of works.

Studwell, William E. *Adolphe Adam and Léo Delibes: A Guide to Research.* New York: Garland, 1987. The heart of the section dealing with Delibes is a comprehensive annotated bibliography arranged topically and alphabetically. There is a valuable summary of Delibes' life and work, a discussion of the composer's relationship to his more illustrious contemporaries, and a commentary on the historical role of Delibes and his music's place in history. The bibliography includes four published writings of Delibes.

Van Vechten, Carl. "Back to Delibes." *Musical Quarterly* 8 (October, 1922). Perusing an old copy of *Coppélia*, Van Vechten credits the composer with revolutionizing the ballet by introducing a symphonic approach to the orchestration and by infusing his scores with melodic grace.

David Z. Kushner

FOURTEENTH EARL OF DERBY
Edward George Geoffrey Smith Stanley

Born: March 29, 1799; Knowsley Park, Lancashire, England

Died: October 23, 1869; Knowsley Park, Lancashire, England

Areas of Achievement: Politics and government

Contribution: One of the leading British politicians at a time when Great Britain was at the height of its economic and political power, Derby oversaw the relatively peaceful democratic reform of his country.

Early Life

Edward George Geoffrey Smith Stanley, the fourteenth Earl of Derby, was born on March 29, 1799, at Knowsley Park in Lancashire, into one of the greatest and oldest aristocratic families in Great Britain. The Stanleys had been ennobled in the fifteenth century and the first Earl of Derby was created by Henry VII as a reward for abandoning Richard III. This was not the last time that the Stanleys would change their political allegiance dramatically. So great was their preeminence in the north of England that the Earls of Derby were virtually uncrowned kings of Lancashire.

Young Edward Stanley was educated at Eton and Christ Church, Oxford. As the Stanley heir, a brilliant political future was predicted for him. In March, 1822, he was first elected to the House of Commons as a moderate Whig for Stockport, in his native Lancashire, a borough which his father had represented. His first session in Parliament established his reputation as a fine speaker. Over the years, Stanley's brilliance as a slashing parliamentary debater was of major importance in bringing him political leadership, which even wealth and title could not guarantee. Perhaps the most significant development during his maiden session was personal. He was married in May, 1825, to Emma, the second daughter of Edward Wilbraham, later Lord Skelmerdale. In July, 1826, she gave birth to a son, Edward Henry Stanley, who would carry on the family tradition of political leadership as the fifteenth earl. Just before his son's birth, in June, Stanley was elected for Preston which, unlike Stockbridge, was a popular borough, with a substantial electorate. One of the borough's two seats was usually held by a nominee of the Stanleys, and Stanley easily defeated the popular Tory journalist William Cobbett. In April, 1827, he accepted his first ministerial position, undersecretary for the colonies in George Canning's moderate Tory government, only leaving office when an ultra-Tory government came in (January, 1828).

Life's Work

Stanley's rise to the highest ranks of politics began when, after a long period of Tory dominance, the Whigs returned to power in July, 1830, under the second Earl Grey. Stanley was offered the post of secretary for Ireland, a thankless but important task because, following Daniel O'Connell's leadership, a revived Irish nationalism was stirring. Stanley's satisfaction at being offered this challenging post was chastened by an electoral setback. Ministers at this time, on appointment, were obliged to resign their seats and stand for reelection. When Stanley did so in August, 1830, a time of enthusiasm for reform, he was defeated by the radical candidate Henry "Orator" Hunt, and a safe seat had to be found for him before he could take up his responsibilities in July. A seat was found in Windsor in February, 1831. While Stanley generally acquitted himself well as Irish secretary, his personal relationship with O'Connell was extremely bitter. At one point he challenged the Irish leader to a duel, though nothing came of it.

The principal business of the Grey ministry was to deal with the demands for electoral reform. There had been virtually no redrawing of the boundaries of election districts for two centuries, though there had been much population growth and, more recently, movement of people as industrialization began to urbanize the country. As a result, virtually unpopulated areas had representation—"pocket" or "rotten" boroughs, such as Stanley's own first seat—while the newly grown cities were underrepresented or completely unrepresented. Property qualifications for voting also excluded from political participation substantial numbers of prosperous literate citizens. The remedy for these complaints was electoral reform, which finally passed into law after some grave difficulties, in June, 1832. Stanley had a leading role as one of the managers of the legislation's successful passage through the house, though he had begun as a rather skeptical supporter of reform.

He was hardly a believer in pure democracy, and his personal attitude is best exemplified by his suspicion that the secret ballot (not yet adopted at this time) would be used principally to conceal electoral fraud.

In December, 1832, following the elevation of his father to the peerage in his own right, as Lord Stanley of Bickerstaffe, he was elected to his father's seat as member for North Lancashire, which he held for the balance of his service in Commons. Then, in October, 1834, on the death of Stanley's grandfather (the twelfth earl), Edward Stanley became known by the courtesy title Lord Stanley, though still a commoner.

In March, 1833, Stanley changed office and became secretary for war and the colonies, and it became his responsibility to steer through the Commons a bill for the abolition of slavery in the British Empire. Despite his success, and the growth of his reputation, Stanley was displeased with his colleagues on the Irish issue, most particularly with Lord John Russell. Stanley was adamant that nothing should be done which might lead to depriving the Irish church of its privileged position. The state church in Ireland had more income than it could employ for ecclesiastical purposes. Russell pressed for the government to appropriate these funds for secular purposes. In protest, in May, 1834, Stanley led his followers, including three other cabinet ministers, out of the Whig Party and into opposition. O'Connell promptly dubbed them sarcastically "the Derby Dillies." While reluctant, at first, to make more than a tactical alliance with the Tories under Sir Robert Peel, and declining to enter the first Peel ministry, eventually, in July, 1835, Stanley cast his lot with them. He was quickly accepted as one of the principal Tory leaders, second only to Peel. By 1841, Stanley had joined the Carleton Club, making permanent his adherence to the Tories. Peel, forming his second ministry, that year offered Stanley the Colonial Office, which he accepted. As a result of Stanley's objections, a relatively new Tory member, Benjamin Disraeli, was kept from a place. Stanley thought him a scoundrel.

In October, 1844, accepting a peerage as Lord Stanley of Bickerstaffe, probably because of growing differences with Peel, Stanley gave up his place in the Commons. At the time, Peel's ministry was confronted with a growing demand for free trade, ending the protection of British agriculture by the Corn Laws. While many Tory landlords believed that this would ruin them, the rest of the Tory Party, and about a third of the Tory M.P.'s, following Peel, conceded that free trade was necessary. The party split sharply, and Stanley, though not an ardent protectionist, led the Tory backbenchers out of the government and into opposition. Together with his sporting friend Lord George Bentinck, who was as passionately devoted to horse racing and breeding as Stanley himself, Stanley provided the natural leadership of the anti-Peelite Tories. Bentinck brought in his train the unlikely figure of Disraeli, hardly a rural Tory but useful in the Commons as an effective speaker. When Bentinck died unexpectedly in 1848, Stanley found himself linked with Disraeli in an enduring political partnership which, not many years before, would have been thought impossible.

Peel died suddenly in 1850, which added to the continuing political instability. Leaderless, his followers gradually drifted toward the emerging Liberal group within the Whig Party. Liberalism was beginning to divide the Whigs as free trade had split the Tories, but the process was a slower and less dramatic one. In the meantime, Stanley's protectionist Tory Party, though the largest group in Parliament, was not numerous enough to form a ministry on its own. Despite Disraeli's urgings, Stanley declined to abandon protectionism, at least until public opinion had been tested on the issue by a general election. The Tory rejection of free trade isolated them, making it difficult, if not impossible, to join any governing coalition.

In February, 1851, when the government fell, Stanley failed to organize a ministry. In June of that year, his father died, and he succeeded to the earldom. The following February, Lord Derby, as he now was, finally became prime minister, with Disraeli as his Chancellor of the Exchequer. The rest of the government (which included his son at the Foreign Office) was so young, inexperienced, or insignificant that it was dubbed contemptuously the "who, who ministry." The government was crippled from the start and never possessed the strength to carry on effectively. Derby clung to power, without a majority, until the end of the year. The succeeding government, Lord Aberdeen's coalition of Whigs and Peelites, lasted until it blundered unprepared into the Crimean War. Once again, in 1855, Derby was offered the opportunity to form a government. Despite much grumbling from his followers, again, he was reluctant to accept responsibility without any prospect of success. When he finally managed to form his second ministry in February, 1858, on the fall of Lord Palmerston's ministry, he had little success and was succeeded by Palmerston's returning to office in June, 1859.

A central difficulty for Derby was that, in addition to his own antipathy to the Whig leader Russell, Palmerston declined service in any government which included Derby. Palmerston's breezy popularity, in Parliament and the country, made him virtually indispensable in all the coalitions of the midcentury. Derby's problems with forming a government were thus nearly impossible to surmount, despite the impatience of his party to enter a government coalition.

When the American Civil War interrupted the supply of raw cotton to British mills (many of which were in Lancashire), Derby played a leading role in organizing voluntary relief. Eventually supplies of cotton from the empire ended the "cotton famine" and its devastating unemployment.

After Palmerston's death in 1865, the way was open and Derby succeeded, in June, 1866, in organizing his third ministry with Disraeli as his chancellor and Leader of the House. Derby found widespread demand for electoral reform and a larger measure of democracy. Rather than leave the issue to the Whigs and Liberals, the Tories stole their program and passed the Reform Bill of 1867, which dramatically enlarged the electorate. Derby, carrying the bill through the Lords, conceded frankly that the new course, however necessary, was a leap in the dark. Derby's last ministry, like its predecessors, was too weakly based to survive for long. Derby, now close to seventy, in poor health, much troubled by gout, resigned in February, 1868. He went home to Lancashire in the summer of 1869 and died, after a lingering illness, on October 23, 1869.

Summary

The fourteenth Earl of Derby's career in politics spanned half a century. Though almost from the first he was near the pinnacle of power and a brilliant success was expected for him, it was thirty years before he led a government. In the end, his record was one of disappointment and frustration. All three of his ministries were relatively short-lived; the first two accomplished little and in the third the lion's share of the credit for its singular accomplishment, the passage of the Reform Bill, went to Disraeli. Derby played a leading role in passing three of the century's most important pieces of legislation: the abolition of slavery and the two reform acts. It is a curious achievement and legacy for a highly aristocratic and intensely conservative politician that he had a central role in laying the foundation of modern democracy in Great Britain. Derby was not a democrat, or even a political reformer, as a matter of conviction. His goal was to preserve the existing social order, church, and empire. The concessions made to democracy were, in his own eyes, a statesmanlike gamble, which he had the necessary self-assurance to make, in order to preserve as much as possible of the world he knew.

Despite his important achievements, Derby has been seen essentially as a failure. Peel and Disraeli have overshadowed him in the annals of his party. His contemporaries feared his sharp tongue and regarded him as unstable because he had twice broken with his leadership. He had the bad luck to lead the Tories at the nadir of their fortunes, when they were politically isolated and impotent, for which he received much of the blame. Even his frustrated Tory followers, though they respected him, tended to view him as an aloof, remote figure, not as much interested in political success as in horse racing, shooting partridges, and winning at whist. It is undeniable that Derby was, in his personal habits, a country squire, though on a vast scale. The pose of the amateur politician, indifferent to power, however, masked, in classic Victorian fashion, a more complicated figure, a classical scholar who translated Homer and, above all, a shrewd lifelong professional politician who tried to cope with a society changing in unprecedented fashion and with extraordinary velocity. Modern historians, whether fairly or not, have tended to follow the Victorian judgment. On the crowded stage of Victorian statemanship, despite his accomplishments, he is seen as a supporting player.

Bibliography

Blake, Robert. *Disraeli*. London: Eyre and Spottiswoode, 1966; New York: St. Martin's Press, 1967. The standard life of Derby's great lieutenant and successor.

Conacher, J. B. *The Peelites and the Party System*. Newton Abbott: David and Charles, 1972. A careful political study of 1846-1852. Together with his work on the Aberdeen government and Gash's work, Conacher's book comprises a detailed study of the critical decade following the repeal of the Corn Laws when both parties, Whig and Tory, were deconstructed and new ones created out of their pieces.

Gash, Norman. *Sir Robert Peel: The Life of Sir Robert Peel After 1830*. London: Longman, and Totowa, N.J.: Rowman and Littlefield, 1972. The second of two volumes covering the whole of Peel's career. Whether as Derby's collaborator or antagonist, he was the dominant figure in British politics from the first reform bill to his death.

Jones, Wilbur D. *Lord Derby and Victorian Conservatism*. Athens: University of Georgia Press, 1954; Oxford: Blackwell, 1956. The standard modern work on Derby. Covers the whole career but the value is limited because its author did not have access to the Derby papers.

Prest, John. *Lord John Russell*. London: Macmillan, and Columbia: University of South Carolina Press, 1972. The political career of Derby's contemporary and lifelong rival.

Southgate, Donald. *The Most English Minister: Politics and Policies of Palmerston*. London: Macmillan, and New York: St. Martin's Press, 1966. A study of the dominant political figure between 1850 and 1865.

Stewart, Robert McKenzie. *The Politics of Protection: Lord Derby and the Protectionist Party, 1841-1852*. London: Cambridge University Press, 1971. A sympathetic treatment of the critical political decade, based on the Derby manuscripts. Stewart's more recent work *The Foundations of the Conservative Party, 1830-1867* (New York: Longman, 1978) is a careful and well-documented overview of party politics.

S. J. Stearns

GEORGE DEWEY

Born: December 26, 1837; Montpelier, Vermont
Died: January 16, 1917; Washington, D.C.
Area of Achievement: Naval service
Contribution: Dewey defeated the Spanish in the Battle of Manila Bay on May 1, 1898, and subsequently served as senior officer of the navy until his death.

Early Life

George Dewey was born December 26, 1837, in Montpelier, Vermont, the son of Julius Y. Dewey, a physician, and Mary Perrin Dewey. His mother died when he was five, but he seems to have had a happy childhood anyway, full of high spirits and practical jokes. He enjoyed a very close relationship with his father. After attending a military school in Norwich, Vermont, Dewey sought appointment to the United States Military Academy; because there were no vacancies at West Point, however, he went to the United States Naval Academy instead, graduating in 1858, fifth in a class of fifteen.

Promoted to lieutenant just as the Civil War began, he served with distinction in the blockading fleet and especially on the Mississippi, where his courage and resourcefulness earned for him positions of considerable responsibility, despite his youth. It was also on the Mississippi that he came to admire the daring Admiral David G. Farragut, later famous for the immortal, although perhaps apocryphal, words "Damn the torpedoes! Full speed ahead!" More than thirty years later, Dewey would have reason to ponder these words.

Dewey reached the rank of lieutenant commander by the war's end; then, like other career officers, he had to settle down to the dull circumstances of the peacetime navy. On October 27, 1867, he married Susan B. Goodwin, daughter of a New Hampshire governor. She died in 1872, after the birth of their son, George Goodwin Dewey. The bereaved husband remained a bachelor for the next twenty-seven years—and a very eligible one he was: trim, sporting a glorious mustache, and handsome even into advanced middle age. He was also fairly well-to-do by virtue of his holding shares in his father's life insurance company.

Life's Work

The post-Civil War navy had too many officers for its shrinking and obsolete fleet, yet Dewey managed by seniority and competence to gain his share

of promotions and even more: commander in 1872, captain in 1884, and commodore in 1896. He spent fewer of these years at sea than is the norm, preferring duty in Washington, D.C. There he became head of the Bureau of Equipment in 1889 and president of the Board of Inspection and Survey in 1895. He sometimes used these positions to encourage naval progress, but he was too senior—and too devoted to intraservice harmony—to identify fully with the younger, reform-minded officers of that era. Like many other senior officers, he cultivated political connections instead. One of his friends, Assistant Secretary of the Navy Theodore Roosevelt, along with a Vermont senator, arranged for his appointment as commodore of the United States Asiatic Squadron in 1897.

Dewey was not an advocate of imperialism, but he knew that the Philippines in general, and the Spanish fleet in Manila Bay in particular, would be likely American targets should there be war with Spain. When that war began in April of 1898, his squadron was already well advanced in its prepara-

tions for combat. With the declarations of war, Dewey's ships were suddenly deprived of the services of Hong Kong and all other neutral ports, and they had none of their own. He could perhaps have violated Chinese neutrality by using a port on her coast—and the impotent Chinese government would not have been able to stop him—but that would have been no more than a temporary expedient. Hence, his squadron either had to steam out of the Far East or conquer a base for itself in Manila Bay. Leaving was unthinkable: Apart from the psychological and diplomatic consequences of departing without a fight, the United States could hardly abandon its interests in Asia; nor could it allow Spain to keep the Philippines, valuable as they would be as bargaining chips at the peace table—or as the site of a permanent American base in the Far East to assist in the expansion of American interests there.

Flying his flag in the magnificent light cruiser *Olympia*, Dewey led five other ships out of Hong Kong on his way to battle. Spain's Admiral Patricio Montojo awaited him in Manila Bay with seven ships, but they were smaller and less well armed than Dewey's, and with fewer well-trained crews. Some of his ships were in wretched condition. Spanish weakness afloat could in theory be offset by some other factors: If Montojo could disperse his ships, he might be able to harass American commercial shipping indefinitely, or the Spanish could shelter their ships under the guns of Manila and sow mines in Dewey's path. Yet none of these options came to anything: The Spanish ships could not scatter without exposing Manila to bombardment; Manila's coast artillery was inadequate; and the Spaniards lacked insulated wire with which to arm their mines. Thus, the gloomy Montojo fully expected to go down fighting for honor's sake alone, even giving up the slight protection of Manila's guns so as to spare the civil population an enemy bombardment.

The Americans could not have been fully aware of the extent of Spanish weakness. Although the United States consul in Manila had indicated Montojo's dilemma, his information might not have been complete; it was, in any case, many days old by the time Dewey set sail. The Spaniards might yet score heavily with lucky hits from their guns or with the few makeshift mines they had managed to sow, thereby making an American victory, if it could be achieved, either incomplete or dreadfully Pyrrhic. Dewey himself, on the other hand, had

nothing but contempt for the Spanish defenses. He was more than willing to "damn the torpedoes," that is, the mines. His final words on the subject were perhaps not as stirring as Admiral Farragut's, but just as decisive: "Mines or no mines, I'm leading the squadron in myself." When his ships got in range of Montojo's, he gave his soon-to-be famous order to the captain of the *Olympia*: "You may fire when you are ready, Gridley." The result was the total destruction of Montojo's squadron in the Battle of Manila Bay, May 1, 1898; there were no American combat fatalities. Dewey subsequently maintained a blockade of Manila and cooperated with the newly arrived United States Army so as to force the city's surrender.

Two long-term international problems arose during the Manila Bay campaign. One was America's relationship with the anti-Spanish Filipino insurrectionists. Their leader, Emiliano Aguinaldo, claimed that Dewey had promised freedom for the Philippines in return for the insurgents' help in defeating the Spaniards on land. Dewey denied agreeing to anything but a purely military alliance, with no commitments regarding the future of the islands. Given his—and Aguinaldo's—political naïveté, it is perhaps likely that they had genuinely misunderstood each other. In any case, their disagreement was a minor milestone on the road to war between the United States and the Filipino rebels.

Dewey's other political problem during the blockade concerned the attitude of Germany. The kaiser's Asiatic fleet visited Manila Bay and openly displayed its sympathy for the Spaniards. Americans wondered if the Germans wanted the islands for themselves. It is true that the Germans sometimes behaved as if the rules of blockade simply did not apply to them, and their ships far outclassed Dewey's. Fortunately, the matter was resolved, but Dewey, and many other Americans, carried away from this experience a lingering suspicion of Germany's intentions all over the world.

In 1899, Dewey returned to the United States, where he was lionized to an incredible degree. There were Dewey hats, cigarettes, canes, songs, and even paperweights. Congress elevated him to the rank of admiral of the Navy, making him the senior officer of the two armed services, with the right to remain on active duty for life. In 1900, he was appointed head of the Navy Department's General Board, and in 1903, he became the chairman of the Joint Army-Navy Board.

Meanwhile, there had been a Dewey-for-president boom, looking toward the election of 1900. Disliking public adulation, Dewey nevertheless allowed himself to be talked into running; his candidacy soon fell flat, however, mostly because of his own political ineptitude. For one thing, his cause was damaged by his comment about how easy the job of president would be. For another, his political ideas were few and ill-considered: He declared himself a Democrat, yet he despised the radical wing of that party; although he had originally wanted nothing in the Philippines but a coaling station, he nevertheless officially associated himself with the Republican president's decision to seek the annexation of the entire archipelago.

Dewey's second marriage, on November 9, 1899, also worked to his political disadvantage. He was the nation's darling, and for him to marry at all was bound to arouse popular jealousy; his choice of bride made the situation all the worse: She was Mildred McLean Hazen, a wealthy widow with the image of a snob. Worse yet, she was a Protestant who had turned Catholic, apparently for no better reason than to please the best social circles in Austria, where she had once happened to live. Anti-Catholics in the United States therefore claimed that she might someday donate Admiral Dewey's house to the Catholic Church—a house which had been purchased for him by subscription by the people of a grateful nation. It was all very silly, but the fuss engendered by his marriage nevertheless contributed to the collapse of Dewey's political hopes, such as they were, and he eventually withdrew from the presidential race. (His wife later turned Protestant again.)

Dewey's service as senior officer of the navy showed him to be a conscientious but uninspired leader. He sought compromise, no matter what the cost, to prevent arguments within his beloved navy. He tried to please both sides in the controversy between the partisans of Admiral William T. Sampson and those of Admiral Winfield S. Schley concerning the latter's role in the Caribbean phase of the Spanish-American War; but his efforts along these lines led only to an obvious self-contradiction. In another matter, he supported the young reformers who wanted to establish a general staff within the Navy Department, yet he turned against them when their tactics offended his sense of propriety. He wanted the navy to have modern battleships, yet he refused to make full public use of his prestige in order to acquire them because he dis-liked arguing with naval conservatives. Like many others, he suspected that the next war for the United States would be with Germany, but in this case he carelessly allowed his opinion to become public knowledge, thereby embarrassing his country.

Old age and arteriosclerosis finally took their toll on him, especially after a slight stroke in 1913. He died in Washington, D. C., on January 16, 1917.

Summary

Dewey's career from 1865 to 1897 was only somewhat more lustrous than those of many other officers. He was resourceful and courageous enough, in 1898, to make his ships ready and then to seize the opportunity for glory in Manila Bay, yet the praises and promotion that followed were all out of proportion to his achievement. Sampson and Schley, after all, had commanded more and more heavily armed ships than Dewey had ever possessed, and in a more important theater of war, the Caribbean; moreover, they defeated a Spanish fleet that was stronger than Montojo's. Dewey, it is true, had displayed a certain phlegmatic panache; clearly, however, what made him so much greater than Sampson and Schley in the public's eye was the mere fact that his triumph came at the very beginning of the war, before anyone else's victory could claim the headlines.

Nor did his postwar career provide much justification for his elevation to the highest of ranks. His judgments in the realm of politics were often ludicrous, and even in strictly naval matters they were sometimes flawed, largely because of his obsession with intraservice harmony. Perhaps Dewey's most important contribution after 1898 was his support for the modernization of the battle fleet, but even in this case he was simply on the side of an irresistible trend, and halfheartedly at that. Avoiding conflict within the navy came at the cost of a more forceful and forward-looking role as his department's most senior admiral.

Bibliography

Cosmas, Graham A. *An Army for Empire: The United States Army in the Spanish-American War.* Columbia: University of Missouri Press, 1971. Despite its title, this book sheds much light on all aspects of the Spanish-American War. It is very scholarly, but also readable.

Graves, Ralph. "When a Victory Really Gave Us a New World Order." *Smithsonian* 22, no. 12 (March, 1992). Discusses the 1898 Battle of Manila Bay, a three-hour skirmish that destroyed the Spanish fleet, made the United States a world power, and Dewey a hero.

Herrick, Walter R., Jr. *The American Naval Revolution*. Baton Rouge: Louisiana State University Press, 1966. Another scholarly and well-written book. Herrick covers the political events that led to the building of the United States' modern fleet during the 1890's; this was the program that gave Dewey the qualitative edge he enjoyed in Manila Bay.

Karsten, Peter. *The Naval Aristocracy: The Golden Age of Annapolis and the Emergence of Modern American Navalism*. New York: Free Press, 1972. This is an important book that re-examines the naval officer corps of the late nineteenth century, including the generation of reformers whose projects Dewey sometimes endorsed.

Kirby, John. "Fire when Ready!" *All Hands,* no. 972 (May, 1998). Provides a detailed account of the Battle of Manila Bay.

O'Toole, G. J. A. *The Spanish War: An American Epic, 1898*. New York: Norton, 1984. A very enjoyable popular account.

Potter, E. B., and Chester W. Nimitz, eds. *Sea Power: A Naval History*. Englewood Cliffs, N.J.: Prentice-Hall, 1960. This is the standard textbook on all naval history, used, for example, at the United States Naval Academy. The editors are, respectively, an eminent naval historian and a great World War II admiral.

Spector, Ronald. *Admiral of the New Empire*. Baton Rouge: Louisiana State University Press, 1974. This is the only modern biography of Dewey; fortunately it is a magnificent, albeit brief, account. The author is a very prominent scholar as well as a good stylist. The brevity of his book is a result in part of a lack of existing source material.

Sprout, Harold M., and Margaret Sprout. *The Rise of American Naval Power*. Princeton, N.J.: Princeton University Press, 1939. An older but highly respected survey of American naval history.

Karl G. Larew

MELVIL DEWEY

Born: December 10, 1851; Adams Center, New York

Died: December 26, 1931; Lake Placid Club South, Florida

Areas of Achievement: Education

Contribution: Dewey was the single most original and effective American educator in developing modern library organization and the professional training of librarians.

Early Life

Melvil Dewey (he shortened his first name from Melville) grew up in rural upstate New York. Descended from one of the original English settlers in America, Dewey's family was comfortable but not wealthy; their income was based on small properties and business operations. During the first half of the nineteenth century, upstate New York was a center of intense Protestant evangelical zeal and movements for social reform. Reflecting this fervor, Dewey's youthful diaries recorded the beginning of his dedication to reform and concentrated work.

In 1870 Dewey chose to enroll in Amherst College in Massachusetts because it had an innovative curriculum that included physical education. Because of a life-threatening sickness during his youth, Dewey was concerned about maintaining his physical health. Another concern became the use of his time with maximum efficiency. The young man was tall and dark-haired with strong features, especially a prominent chin. Although only an average student, he did nonetheless distinguish himself in mathematics.

It was as a student employee in the Amherst College library that Dewey accomplished the first of a series of historic contributions he would make to librarianship. At that time, books in libraries were arranged by fixed location on shelves. The books were not arranged in relation to each other based on their contents but rather by their placement on a particular shelf in a bookcase. Dewey considered such a system ineffective. In 1873, as a junior, he devised a method for arranging books and other library materials based on subject matter using a system of whole and decimal numbers.

Life's Work

Upon graduation in 1874, Dewey became head of the Amherst library. He proceeded to apply and refine his decimal classification system, which, in its fundamental principles, is much the same today as it was then. In 1876 he published the first edition of his book on classifying library materials. It became the bible for library cataloging and is now known as the decimal classification and relative index. It was in its twenty-first edition as of 1996. The classification method became known as the Dewey decimal classification (DDC) system and was adopted in later decades by libraries in the United States and throughout the world.

Also in 1876, after meeting and corresponding with some of the leading librarians of the time, Dewey was the key person in organizing the American Library Association (ALA). Its first meeting occurred in Philadelphia, Pennsylvania, and Dewey was elected secretary. He also became managing editor of the association's official publication, the *Library Journal*. In 1878 Dewey married Annie Godfrey, librarian of Wellesley College. They had one son, Godfrey, born in 1887.

Improvements in libraries were only one of several reform movements that engaged Dewey. He was also instrumental in organizing associations for the use of the metric system in the United States and the reform of English spelling. After resigning from Amherst College in 1875, he began a series of businesses for selling supplies, equipment, and publications related to his reform interests. All of these interests had the common goal of using time more efficiently.

In 1883 Dewey was appointed head of the library of Columbia College (now University) in New York City. He quickly moved to reorganize and consolidate its library collection and supervised the construction of a new building. Because of the need for trained personnel for his expanding library work, Dewey established the first library school for the professional training of librarians in 1887, thereby establishing the modern profession of librarianship. This school, however, proved to be a bone of contention to the college administration. Dewey believed that librarianship was a field highly appropriate for "college-bred" women. Columbia, however, did not at the time admit women students. In opposition to this policy, Dewey enrolled women in the inaugural classes of his School of Library Economy. The ensuing controversy caused him to leave the college the following year.

In 1889 he became the state librarian of New York and moved to Albany. In addition, he was made secretary to the board of regents for the University of the State of New York. The latter was not an educational institution but a government agency that supervised educational institutions. He moved his library school with him, renaming it the New York State Library School. As state librarian, Dewey initiated many innovations and presided over extensive growth. He determined that the library should collect not only books but also visual and audio materials. To expand access to materials, he established traveling libraries in book wagons (modern bookmobiles) and began statewide extension services. In addition, he established special services and collections for the blind, for women, for children, and for medicine. Dewey's position as secretary to the regents had a political dimension that often led him to display a confrontational manner. He entered into conflict with other state officials concerning increased funding for public libraries, extension education, and certification of educational institutions. The bitterness of one of these conflicts forced him to resign as secretary in 1899. He nevertheless remained state librarian.

Dewey and his wife had long dreamed of establishing a recreational club in an area of natural beauty that would foster healthy recreation and cultural improvement. They selected Lake Placid, just north of Albany in the Adirondack Mountains, as the site of this club. The club, formulated in 1893, was meant to congregate the social peers of the Deweys, that is, upper-middle-class Protestant white people of Anglo-Saxon descent. To foster a wholesome atmosphere, the club prohibited or regulated smoking, drinking, gambling, and certain dancing. Furthermore, it prohibited the admission of African Americans and Jews. The latter, a growing ethnic group of rising influence in New York, challenged this prohibition in 1904. They questioned why a state official being paid by taxpayers that included Jews should be allowed to conduct such an exclusionary policy. Because of mounting criticism and controversy, Dewey presented his resignation as state librarian the following year.

Beginning in 1906, Dewey concentrated his attention almost exclusively on development of the Lake Placid Club. Transferring his residence there, Dewey expanded and elaborated its comforts and offerings so that in the following decades it became one of the largest and most famous resorts in

the world and the pioneer for winter sports activities. The club hosted the Winter Olympics in 1932.

In 1922 Dewey's wife died, and he remarried in 1924. During this decade, comments about intimate relations that Dewey attempted to impose on female colleagues and employees became increasingly open. A former stenographer threatened a lawsuit. In 1926 Dewey began spending his winters in Florida, where he devised the idea of establishing a club resort similar to the one in New York and created Lake Placid South. In 1931, he died in the midst of this endeavor just after his eightieth birthday.

Summary

With exceptional energy and commitment to a range of educational reforms, Dewey was the single most important influence on the development of the profession of librarianship and the modern organization of libraries. Through his library schools, he created the core of professionals who developed and managed the exceptional infrastructure of libraries in the United States and who influenced the development of librarianship throughout the world.

His reforming efforts for metric measure and English spelling were not as successful as those for improved libraries. The nonlibrary movements had to struggle against deeply ingrained patterns of behavior and long-standing interests. The library movement, however, was an innovation without entrenched interests to oppose it. Moreover, it had the winds of time behind its sails. There was intense public interest in and support for improved and expanded educational opportunities, which offered the chance for the rapidly increasing U.S. population to obtain access to the goods and services of an expanding American economy and society. Libraries and librarians were considered vital elements in the educational process.

During Dewey's lifetime, public and college libraries in the United States increased rapidly in number. Steel magnate and philanthropist Andrew Carnegie was responsible at this time for building more than one thousand public libraries throughout the small towns and big cities of the United States. The energy and resolution of Dewey's commitments, however, frequently found him conflicted and overextended. Although known for his efficiency and for having accumulated a small personal fortune, he became mired in situations beyond his limits in terms of time and money. Moreover, in contradiction to the moral and cultural ideals he preached, he would later be judged for serious racist and sexist behavior.

Bibliography

Dawe, Grosvenor. *Melvil Dewey: Seer, Inspirer, Doer, 1851-1931.* Lake Placid, N.Y.: Lake Placid Club, 1932. This biography was published immediately after Dewey's death by the winter sports resort center that he founded and nurtured to world renown. Uncritical and full of high praise, the work is divided into three parts: early development, professional achievements, and a compilation of important writings. The work is extensively illustrated with photographs.

Rider, Fremont. *Melvil Dewey.* Chicago: American Library Association, 1944. The chapters of this slender volume each outline the contributions Dewey made in his various fields of endeavor. While highly praiseworthy of the founder of the ALA, it frankly confronts some of his personality difficulties.

Stevenson, Gordon, and Judith Kramer-Greene, eds. *Melvil Dewey: The Man and the Classification.* Albany, N.Y.: Forest Press, 1983. This work, published by a press founded by Dewey, is a compilation of presentations from a seminar in 1981 sponsored by the New York State Library commemorating the fiftieth anniversary of Dewey's death. Examining Dewey and his legacy from various perspectives, the articles deal with reminiscences about him, his evangelical zeal and ideals, and his work for the development and organizing of the library profession.

Vann, Sarah K., ed. *Melvil Dewey: His Enduring Presence in Librarianship.* Littleton, Colo.: Libraries Unlimited, 1978. The first fifty pages of this work provide a capsule life of Dewey. The remaining two hundred pages are a selection of Dewey's writings on librarianship, libraries, the ALA, education, cataloging, classification, and the future. It also includes a list of his publications.

Wiegand, Wayne A. *A Biography of Melvil Dewey: Irrepressible Reformer.* Chicago: American Library Association, 1996. This book by a noted library history scholar is among the most detailed, frank, and readable works on the life of Dewey. Through extensive archival research, Wiegand demonstrates the origins and methods of Dewey's thought and activities. Because of its candor and thoroughness, the book escapes an older mold among librarians of canonizing Dewey and stands as a singular contribution to understanding the complexities and contradictions of the man.

Edward A. Riedinger

CHARLES DICKENS

Born: February 7, 1812; Portsmouth, Hampshire, England

Died: June 9, 1870; Gad's Hill, Rochester, Kent, England

Area of Achievement: Literature

Contribution: The most popular novelist of his time, Dickens created a fictional world that reflects the social and technological changes of the Victorian era.

Early Life

Charles John Huffam Dickens was born at Portsmouth, England, on February 7, 1812, the second of eight children. His father, John Dickens, a clerk in the Naval Pay Office, was always hard-pressed to support his family. Because his father's work made it necessary for him to travel, Dickens spent his youth in several different places, including London and Chatham. When he was only twelve years old, his father's financial difficulty made it necessary for the young Dickens to work in a shoeblacking warehouse while his father was placed in a debtor's prison at Marshalsea—an event that was to have a powerful influence on Dickens throughout his life. Oliver Twist's experience in the workhouse is one of the best-known results of what Dickens considered to be an act of desertion by his parents.

After his father was released from prison, Dickens was sent to school at an academy in London, where he was a good student. When he was fifteen, he worked as a solicitor's clerk in law offices and two years later became a shorthand reporter of parliamentary proceedings and a free-lance reporter in the courts. In 1829, he fell in love with Maria Beadnell, the daughter of a banker, but broke with her in 1833. At age twenty-one, he began publishing his *Sketches by Boz* and joined the *Morning Chronicle* as a reporter. His first collection of *Sketches by Boz* appeared in 1836, the same year he began a series of sketches titled *Pickwick Papers* (1836-1837). Also in 1836, he married Catherine Hogarth, the daughter of a journalist. As *Pickwick Papers* became a striking popular success in serial publication, the Dickens phenomenon began, and Dickens was on his way to becoming the most powerful and widely read author in nineteenth century England.

Life's Work

With Dickens' sudden fame came offers of more literary work. He began editing a new monthly magazine for which he contracted to write another serial story, which he called *Oliver Twist* (1837-1839) and which began to appear while *Pickwick Papers* was still running. Thus, Dickens started the breakneck speed of writing which was to characterize the energy of his work throughout his life. While *Oliver Twist* was still running in serial form, Dickens also began publishing *Nicholas Nickleby*, another great success, first in serial form (1838) and then as a book (1839). Immediately thereafter, he began the serialization of *The Old Curiosity Shop* (1840-1841) in a weekly publication, followed soon after by *Barnaby Rudge: A Tale of the Riots of '80* (1841).

Dickens paused from his writing between 1836 and 1841 to travel in the United States, the result of which was *American Notes* (1842) and, more important, the serialization of *Martin Chuzzlewit* (1843-1844), outraging many American readers with its caricature of life in the United States. During the Christmas season of 1843, Dickens achieved one of his most memorable successes with *A Christmas Carol*, which gave the world the character of Ebenezer Scrooge. The poor circulation of *Martin Chuzzlewit* was cause enough for Dickens to cease his writing once again for an extended visit to the Continent. Yet the poor reception of *A Christmas Carol* was not enough to prevent Dickens from publishing two more Christmas stories—*The Chimes* (1845) and *A Cricket on the Hearth* (1845).

Returning from Italy in 1845, Dickens began editing a new daily newspaper, *The Daily News*, but resigned from that job after only three weeks. He began instead the serialization of *Dombey and Son* (1846-1848), only to begin the serialization of *David Copperfield* (1849-1850) the following year. During this time, Dickens began working with amateur theatricals as an actor and a director, mostly to benefit literature and the arts. He then began editing the periodical *Household Words* and writing what many call his most ambitious work, *Bleak House*, in 1852, which ran for a year and a half.

In 1854, *Hard Times* was published serially in order to boost the failing circulation of *Household Words*, and soon thereafter, Dickens began serialization of *Little Dorrit* (1855-1857). At this time, Dickens purchased a home at Gad's Hill, on the road between London and Dover, but his home life was not to be that of country tranquillity. In

1858, he separated from his wife amid much bad publicity.

Also in 1858, Dickens began another major aspect of his professional life—a series of public readings from his own work. Although he published *A Tale of Two Cities* in 1859, the public readings in London did not abate. In 1860, he began writing *Great Expectations* (1860-1861) to increase the circulation of a new weekly, *All the Year Round*. London readings continued through 1863, when he went to Paris for another series of readings there. Although he was experiencing poor health, Dickens wrote *Our Mutual Friend* (1864-1866) and performed public readings in London until 1868, when he made his last trip to the United States for a tour of readings which brought him much money but which taxed his already failing health.

When Dickens returned to England after several months in the United States, he took up readings again in London, Scotland, and Ireland, in addition to beginning his last work (which he did not live to finish), *The Mystery of Edwin Drood* (1870). In 1870, on June 8, after working all day, Dickens suffered a stroke while at his Gad's Hill home and died the next day. He was buried in Westminster Abbey.

Summary

As any account of his life makes clear, what most characterizes Charles Dickens is the amount of work he produced and the fact that all of it was originally written for serial publication—a demanding way to publish. To keep up with the demand, Dickens was writing constantly. Although audiences followed Dickens' work as closely as they follow television soap operas today, identifying with his characters as if they were real people and eagerly awaiting each new installment, the fact that Dickens had to keep writing continuously to meet the demands of serialization has made many academic critics scorn his work as popular melodrama catering to the tastes of the masses.

Yet the widespread popularity of Dickens, which continues unabated into the late twentieth century, cannot be accounted for so simply. In spite of the fact that Dickens cranked out novel after novel, as if he were a one-man literary factory, he impresses even skeptics as a masterful storyteller and a genius at characterization.

Many critics have tried to account for what might be called the mystery of Dickens: his amazing aptitude for visualizing scenes in concrete detail, his ability to control and develop highly elaborate plots, and most of all, his puzzling method of creating characters that, even as they are obviously caricatures, seem somehow more real in their fictionality than most realistic characters are. Simply to name such characters as Mr. Pickwick, Scrooge, Fagin, and Mr. Micawber is to conjure up images that are destined to remain memorable.

The fact that Dickens' novels have been so easily adapted to film has added to the almost hallucinatory way with which his works are imprinted on the mind of twentieth century readers and viewers. Such scenes as Oliver in the workhouse asking for more gruel, Sydney Carton on the scaffold in *A Tale of Two Cities*, saying what a far, far better thing he does, and Miss Havisham in her decayed wedding dress in *Great Expectations*, have become part of the mind and memory of millions of Dickens' admirers.

Dickens drew his inspiration primarily from three sources. First, much of his writing is autobiographical. One can see the deserted, poverty-stricken child in Oliver Twist, the aspiring young writer in David Copperfield, and the misguided young man in Pip. Second, Dickens wrote about the many social and technological elements of Victorian society. *Bleak House* is a compendium of Dickens' knowledge about the complexities of the law courts, just as *Martin Chuzzlewit* is a satiric overview of Victorian (and American) social absurdities. In such works as *Hard Times*, Dickens focused on the deficiencies of Utilitarian philosophy of the period, and in *Little Dorrit*, he turned his attention to the bureaucracy of the business world. Finally, Dickens' fiction developed out of the same source from which all fiction ultimately springs, that is, the many conventions of fiction itself. In spite of the fact that Dickens was not highly educated, he was well-read, especially in the wellspring works of storytelling and character-making such as *The Arabian Nights' Entertainments*, Murasaki Shikibu's *The Tale of Genji*, and Miguel de Cervantes' *Don Quixote de la Mancha* (1605, 1615), as well as the masterworks of the novel's beginning in the eighteenth century, such as Daniel Defoe's *Robinson Crusoe* (1719), Henry Fielding's *Tom Jones* (1749), and Tobias Smollett's *Roderick Random* (1748). Thus, in spite of the fact that Dickens' characters seem so very real when the reader remembers them, they seem real precisely because they are so artificial; that is, they are pure fictional creations who can exist only in Dickens' imaginative world.

The number of Dickens' admirers seems to grow each year. Such adaptations of Dickens' work as the highly popular musical version of *Oliver Twist*, the ambitious (day-long) and masterful Royal Shakespeare Company's stage presentation of *Nicholas Nickleby*, and the yearly tradition of countless presentations of *A Christmas Carol*, introduce new readers to Dickens' works over and over again. There is little doubt that he will continue to be the most popular and influential spokesman of Victorian England, for, in the minds of the majority, Victorian England is Dickens' England.

Bibliography

Ayres, Brenda. *Dissenting Women in Dickens' Novels: The Subversion of Domestic Ideology.* Westport, Conn.: Greenwood Press, 1998. The author argues that Dickens' novels actually subvert Victorian ideology with respect to women.

Coolidge, Archibald C., Jr. *Charles Dickens as Serial Novelist.* Ames: Iowa State University Press, 1967. A helpful study of a very important aspect of Dickens' work: The fact that his writing first appeared in serialization had a great influence on the nature of his narrative.

Fielding, K. J. *Charles Dickens: A Critical Introduction.* 2d ed. London: Longmans, and Boston: Houghton Mifflin, 1965. One of the best brief studies of both the life and work of Dickens.

Forster, John. *The Life of Charles Dickens.* London: Chapman and Hall, 1872-1874; New York: Oxford University Press, 1879. The first authoritative biography, in three volumes (two in the revised edition), written by a friend and literary adviser of Dickens, and valuable for the many factual details and anecdotes which it includes.

House, Humphrey. *The Dickens World.* 2d ed. Oxford and New York: Oxford University Press, 1960. An important book which helped to initiate the revival of the study of Dickens as a serious novelist; focuses on Victorian social issues in Dickens' work.

Johnson, Edgar. *Charles Dickens: His Tragedy and Triumph.* 2 vols. New York: Simon and Schuster, 1952; London: Gollancz, 1953. The definitive biography; also contains much very good criticism of Dickens' work.

Kaplan, Fred. *Dickens: A Biography.* New York: Morrow, and London: Hodder and Stoughton, 1988. Acclaimed biography of Dickens, whose life in many ways mirrored those of his characters. Kaplan uses unpublished and abandoned sources to create a three-dimensional portrait of Dickens' life including his passions, unhappy marriage, and complicated family life.

Leavis, F. R., and Q. D. Leavis. *Dickens the Novelist.* London: Chatto and Windus, 1970; New York: Pantheon, 1971. Focuses on the novels from *Dombey and Son* through *Great Expectations;* excellent criticism by two highly respected British critics.

Marcus, Steven. *Dickens: From Pickwick to Dombey.* London: Chatto and Windus, and New York: Basic Books, 1965. A study of Dickens' early work, focusing on Victorian cultural life; a stimulating study by a well-known critic of Victorian literature and life.

Miller, J. Hillis. *Charles Dickens: The World of His Novels.* Cambridge, Mass.: Harvard University Press, and London: Oxford University Press, 1958. A stimulating study of the creative universe fashioned by Dickens, by one of America's best-known and most controversial critics.

Nelson, Harland S. *Charles Dickens.* Boston: Twayne, 1981. Not the usual introductory survey, this study focuses on the way Dickens wrote and published and how the basic elements of his novels engage the reader.

Wilson, Angus. *The World of Charles Dickens.* London: Secker and Warburg, and New York: Viking Press, 1970. Perhaps the best single-volume study of Dickens' life as well as his work as a popular novelist.

Charles E. May

EMILY DICKINSON

Born: December 10, 1830; Amherst, Massachusetts

Died: May 15, 1886; Amherst, Massachusetts

Area of Achievement: Poetry

Contribution: Dickinson, living a reclusive social life, led an inner life of intense, imaginative creativity that made her one of America's greatest poets.

Early Life

The sparse facts of Emily Elizabeth Dickinson's external life can be summarized in a few sentences: She was born in the town of Amherst, Massachusetts, on December 10, 1830, spent her entire life in her family home, and died in it on May 15, 1886. She was graduated from Amherst Academy in 1847, then attended nearby Mount Holyoke Female Seminary for one year. She traveled occasionally to Springfield and twice to Boston. In 1854, she and her family visited Washington and Philadelphia. She never married and had no romantic relationships. Yet her interior life was so intense that a distinguished twentieth century poet and critic, Allen Tate, could write, "All pity for Miss Dickinson's 'starved life' is misdirected. Her life was one of the richest and deepest ever lived on this continent." It is a life which has proved a perplexing puzzle to many critics and biographers.

What led to Dickinson's monastic seclusion from society? Was it forced on her by a possessive, despotic father? Was it self-willed by her timid temperament, by rejected love, or by her neurotic need for utmost privacy while she pursued the muse of poetry? Speculation abounds, certainty eludes; nothing is simple and direct about her behavior. Perhaps the opening lines of her poem #1129 are self-revealing:

> Tell all the Truth but tell it slant—
> Success in Circuit lies
> Too bright for our infirm Delight
> The Truth's superb surprise

When Dickinson was born, Amherst was a farming village of four to five hundred families, with a cultural tradition of Puritanism and a devotion to education as well as devoutness. The Dickinsons were prominent in public and collegiate activities. Samuel Fowler Dickinson, Emily's grandfather, founded Amherst College in 1821 to train preachers, teachers, and missionaries. Edward Dickinson (1813-1874), Emily's father, was the eldest of nine children. He became a successful attorney and, at age thirty-two, was named treasurer of Amherst College, a position he kept for thirty-eight years. He served three terms in the Massachusetts legislature and one term as a member of Congress. Even political opponents respected him as forthright, courageous, diligent, solemn, intelligent, and reliable; he was the incarnation of responsibility and rectitude. In a letter to her brother, Dickinson mocked him (and her mother): "Father and Mother sit in state in the sitting-room perusing such papers, only, as they are well assured, have nothing carnal in them."

Emily's mother, Emily Norcross (1804-1882), was born in Monson, Massachusetts, twenty miles south of Amherst. Her father was a well-to-do farmer who sent his daughter to a reputable boarding school, where she behaved conventionally, preparing herself for the respectable, rational marriage that ensued after Edward Dickinson had courted her politely and passionlessly. The mother has received adverse treatment from most of Dickinson's biographers because of several statements the daughter wrote to her confidant, Colonel Thomas Wentworth Higginson (1823-1911):

> My Mother does not care for thought.
> I never had a mother. I suppose a mother is one to whom you hurry when you are troubled.
> I always ran Home to Awe when a child, if anything befell me. He was an awful Mother, but I liked him better than none.

Richard Sewall indicates in his magisterial two-volume *The Life of Emily Dickinson* (1974) that Emily's acerbic remarks should not be taken at their surface meaning in the light of the poet's continued preference for remaining in the familial home. To be sure, Dickinson's mother read meagerly and had a mediocre mind, but she was a tenderhearted, loving person who committed herself wholly to her family and to the household's management. While she never understood her daughter's complex nature, she also never intruded on Dickinson's inner life.

Dickinson's brother Austin (1829-1895) was closest to her in disposition. Personable, sensitive, empathic, and sociable, he became an attorney, joined his father's practice, and succeeded him as Amherst's treasurer in 1873. He shared his sister's wit, taste in books, and love of nature; his vitality was a tonic for her. He married one of her schoolmates, Susan Gilbert, vivacious, worldly, and articulate.

Dickinson and her sister-in-law, living next door to each other, were in each other's homes frequently during the first years of this marriage. Dickinson had a near-obsessive concern for her immediate family and greatly desired to make of her sister-in-law a true sister in spirit. She sent Sue nearly three hundred of her poems over the years—more than to anyone else. Yet a satisfyingly soulful friendship never quite materialized. To be sure, Sue's parties did keep Dickinson in at least limited circulation in her early twenties. The two women exchanged books and letters, with Dickinson occasionally seeking Sue's criticism of her poems. Dickinson, always fond of children, was particularly delighted with her nephew Gilbert; tragically, he died of typhoid fever at the age of eight; Dickinson's letter of condolence called him "Dawn and Meridian in one."

Yet the two women's paths ineluctably diverged. Sue had a husband and, eventually, three children and was an extroverted social climber. For unknown reasons, Dickinson and Sue quarreled in 1854, and Dickinson wrote her the only dismissive letter in her correspondence: "You can go or stay." They resumed their friendship, but it proved turbulent, as did Sue's and Austin's marriage. In 1866, Sue betrayed Emily's confidence by sending her poem "A Narrow Fellow in the Grass" to the *Springfield Republican*, which mutilated it by changing its punctuation. "It was robbed of me," Dickinson bitterly complained.

With her natural sister Lavinia (1833-1899), Dickinson bonded intimately all her life. Like her older sister, Lavinia remained a spinster, remained at home, and outlived her family. Dickinson and Lavinia were devotedly protective of each other. The younger sister was relatively uncomplicated, steady in temperament, pretty, and outgoing. Their only quasi-serious difference centered on Vinnie's love of cats, contrasted to Dickinson's care for birds. It was Lavinia who organized the first large-scale publication of Dickinson's poems after her death.

Outside her family circle, Dickinson had only a few friends, but they mattered greatly to her—she called them her "estate" and cultivated them intensely. While still in her teens, she established a

pattern that was to recur throughout her life: She sought to attach herself to an older man who would be her confidant and mentor or, to use her terms, "preceptor" or "master." These pilots would, she hoped, teach her something of the qualities which she knew she lacked: knowledge of the outer world, firm opinions and principles, sociability, and intellectual stability.

Dickinson's first candidate was Benjamin Newton (1821-1853), only nine years her senior, who was a law student in her father's office from 1847 to 1849. He served her in the roles of intellectual companion, guide in aesthetic and spiritual spheres, and older brother. He introduced her to Ralph Waldo Emerson's poetry, encouraged her to write her own, but died of consumption in his thirty-third year, before she became a serious poet. Her letters to him are not extant, but in a letter she wrote Higginson in 1862, she probably refers to Newton when she mentions a "friend who taught me Immortality—but venturing too near, himself— he never returned—."

Dickinson's first mature friendship was with Samuel Bowles (1834-1878), who inherited his father's *Springfield Republican* and made it one of the most admired newspapers in the United States. Bowles had a penetrating mind, warmth, wit, dynamic energy, strongly liberal convictions, and an engaging, vibrant personality. Extensively seasoned by travel, he knew virtually every important public leader and was a marvelous guest and companion. He, and sometimes his wife with him, became regular visitors in both Edward and Austin Dickinson's homes from 1858 onward. Thirty-five of Dickinson's letters to Bowles survive, and they show her deep attachment to—perhaps even love for—him, even though she knew that he was out of her reach in every way—just as her poetry was out of his, since his taste in literature was wholly conventional. In April, 1862, Bowles left for a long European stay. Shortly thereafter, Emily wrote him, "I have the errand from my heart—I might forget to tell it. Would you please come home?" Then, in a second letter, "[I]t is a suffering to have a sea . . . between your soul and you." That November, the returned Bowles called at Amherst. Dickinson chose to remain in her room, sending him a note instead of encountering him.

Life's Work

The turning point in Dickinson's career as a poet, and hence in her life, came in her late twenties. Before 1858, her writing consisted of letters and desultory, sentimental verses; thereafter, particularly from 1858 to 1863, poetry became her primary activity. As far as scholars can ascertain, she wrote one hundred in 1859, sixty-five in 1860, at least eighty in 1861, and in 1862—her *annus mirabilis*—perhaps as many as 366, of a prosodic skill far superior to her previous achievement. What caused such a flood of creativity? Most—but not all—biographers attribute it to her unfulfilled love for the Reverend Mr. Charles Wadsworth (1814-1882).

Dickinson and Lavinia visited their father in Washington, D.C., during April, 1854, when he was serving his congressional term. On their return trip, they stopped over in Philadelphia as guests of a friend from school days and heard Wadsworth preach in the Arch Street Presbyterian Church, whose pastor he was from 1850 to April, 1862. Married and middle-aged, of rocklike rectitude, shy and reserved, Wadsworth nevertheless made an indelible impression as a "Man of sorrow" on Dickinson. He was generally regarded as second only to Henry Ward Beecher among the pulpit orators of his time. A contemporary newspaper profile described him in these terms:

> His person is slender, and his dark eyes, hair and complexion have decidedly a Jewish cast. The elements of his popularity are somewhat like those of the gifted Summerfield—a sweet touching voice, warmth of manner, and lively imagination. But Wadsworth's style, it is said, is vastly bolder, his fancy more vivid, and his action more violent.

It is presumed that Dickinson must have talked with Wadsworth during her Philadelphia visit. Few other facts are known: He called on her in Amherst in the spring of 1860, and again in the summer of 1880. She requested his and his children's pictures from his closest friend. In April, 1862, Wadsworth moved to San Francisco, becoming minister to the Calvary Presbyterian Society. Dickinson found this departure traumatic: She used "Calvary" ten times in poems of 1862 and 1863; she spoke of herself as "Empress of Calvary," and began one 1863 poem with the words, "Where Thou art—that is Home/ Cashmere or Calvary—the Same . . ./ So I may come." With probable reference to her inner "Calvary" drama of loss and renunciation, she began at this time to dress entirely in white. By 1870, and until his death, Wadsworth was back in Philadelphia in another pastorate, but the anguished crisis he had caused her had ended by then.

After Dickinson's death, three long love letters were found in draft form among her papers, in her handwriting of the late 1850's and early 1860's. They address a "Master," and have therefore come to be called the "Master Letters." Their tone is urgent, their style, nervous and staccato. In the second of them, "Daisy" tells her "Master": "I want to see you more—Sir—than all I wish for in this world—and the wish—altered a little—will be my only one—for the skies." She invites him to come to Amherst and pledges not to disappoint him. Yet the final letter shows the agony of a rejected lover, amounting to an almost incoherent cry of despair. For whom were these letters intended? Thomas Johnson and most other biographers designate Wadsworth. Richard Sewall, however, argues for Bowles, on the internal evidence that some of the images in the unsent letters parallel images in poems that Dickinson did send Bowles.

In 1861, Dickinson composed the most openly erotic of her poems, #249, with the sea the element in which the speaker moors herself:

Wild Nights—Wild Nights!
Were I with thee Wild Nights should be
Our luxury!
Futile—the Winds—
To a Heart in port—
Done with the Compass—
Done with the Chart!
Rowing in Eden—
Ah, the Sea!
Might I but moor—Tonight
—In Thee!

Is this poem derived from autobiographical experience—or, at least, intense longing for such experience—or is the first-person perspective no more than that of the poem's persona or speaker? Again, Dickinsonians divide on this question.

On April 15, 1862, having liked an article by Thomas Wentworth Higginson, Dickinson sent him four of her poems and a diffident note, asking him if he thought her verses were "alive" and "breathed." Trained as a minister, Higginson had held a Unitarian pulpit in Newburyport, Massachusetts, then resigned it to devote himself to social reforms, chief of which was abolitionism. He had made a reputation as a representative, influential mid-century literary critic, with particular interest in the work of female writers. The four poems Dickinson mailed him were among her best to date; in his evaluative replies, however, he showed an obtuse misunderstanding of them, as well as of her subsequent submissions, which were to total one hundred.

Dickinson undoubtedly felt a strong need for another "preceptor"—Wadsworth had just departed for San Francisco—and especially for a literary rather than romantic confidant. Higginson was to prove her "safest friend" for the remainder of her life. A warm, courteous, sympathetic man, he regarded her with mystified admiration. After their correspondence had been under way for several months, he asked her to send him a photograph. Her response was, "I had no portrait, now, but am small, like the Wren, and my Hair is bold, like the Chestnut Bur, and my eyes, like the Sherry in the Glass, that the Guest leaves." After Higginson had met her eight years later, he confirmed this self-portrait and added to it that Dickinson was a "plain, shy little person, the face without a single good feature."

Dickinson's poetry, unfortunately for both of them, was simply beyond Higginson's grasp. He immediately and consistently advised her not to seek its publication because it was "not strong enough." His critical judgments were invariably fatuous,

showing deaf ears and blind eyes to her original language, syntax, meter, and rhyme. She resigned herself to his recommendation against publication but gently yet firmly ignored his strictures concerning her poems' construction. Thomas Johnson summarizes the relationship as "one of the most eventful, and at the same time elusive and insubstantial friendships in the annals of American literature."

In the late 1870's, nearing her fiftieth year, Dickinson fell in love with Otis Phillips Lord (1812-1884). He was a distinguished lawyer who, from 1875 to 1882, served as an associate justice of the Massachusetts Supreme Court. He answered Dickinson's constant need for a settled, senior friend-tutor, intellectually gifted and personally impressive; he became her last "preceptor." She had first known Judge Lord when he had called on Edward Dickinson; like her father, he was vigorous, conscientious, commanding, and highly disciplined. Their affection developed after December, 1877, when Lord's wife died. Fifteen of her letters to him survive and indicate that, over the objection of his nieces, Lord apparently offered to marry her. With her father and Bowles now dead and her mother an invalid requiring many hours of her time each week, Dickinson found considerable solace in their correspondence. Yet she also knew that her reclusive life was too rigidly established for her to adapt to the major changes that marriage would require of her.

On April 1, 1882, Wadsworth, the man she had called "my closest earthly friend," died. On May 1 of that year, Lord suffered a stroke; on May 14, Dickinson wrote him a fervent letter of joy at his (temporary) recovery, assuring him of her "rapture" at his reprieve from impending death; on October 5 came news of her beloved nephew Gilbert's death; on November 14, her mother finally died, after years of serious illness. It is not surprising that Dickinson then underwent a "nervous prostration" that impaired her faculties for many weeks.

After an 1864 visit to Boston for eye treatment, Dickinson did not leave Amherst for the remainder of her life. Her withdrawal from society became gradually more marked. By 1870, she did not venture beyond her house and garden, preferring to socialize by sending brief letters, some of them accompanied by poems, flowers, or fruit. She retreated upstairs when most visitors came to call, sometimes lurking on an upper landing or around corners. While strangers regarded her eccentricities as unnatural, her friends and family accepted them as the price of her retreat into the intensity of her poetry. Perhaps her most self-revealing poem is #303, whose first stanza declares,

> The Soul selects her own Society—
> Then—shuts the Door—
> To her divine Majority—
> Present no more—!

Emily Dickinson died of nephritis on May 15, 1886.

Summary

Emily Dickinson's nearly eighteen hundred poems, only seven of which saw print during her lifetime, constitute her "Letter to the World" (#441), her real life. They establish her, along with Walt Whitman, as one of this nation's two most seminal poets. Her sharp intellectual wit, her playfulness, and her love of ambiguity, paradox, and irony liken her poetry to the seventeenth century metaphysical achievements of England's John Donne and George Herbert and New England's Edward Taylor. Yet her language and rhythm are often uniquely individual, with a tumultuous rhetoric that sharply probes homely details for universal essence. She is a writer who defies boundaries and labels, standing alone as a contemporary not only of Herman Melville and Nathaniel Hawthorne but also, in the poetic sense, of T. S. Eliot, W. H. Auden, Robert Frost, Robert Lowell, and Sylvia Plath. Her work ranks with the most original in poetic history.

Bibliography

Dickinson, Emily. *The Complete Poems of Emily Dickinson*. Edited by Thomas H. Johnson. Boston: Little Brown, 1960; London: Faber, 1970. The text of the three-volume edition with the variant readings omitted.

———. *The Letters of Emily Dickinson*. Edited by Thomas H. Johnson and Theodora Ward. 3 vols. Cambridge, Mass.: Harvard University Press, 1958. The definitive editions of Dickinson's poetry and letters. They have been arranged in the most accurate chronological order possible and numbered. In 1890, the first collection of Dickinson's poems was brought out by Mabel Loomis Todd and Higginson, with two more volumes in 1891 and 1896, all in disorderly, random selections, with gross editorial violations of the poet's spelling and syntax. Johnson has therefore done an invaluable service to American literary scholarship by taking Dickinson's jottings, scribbles, and semifinal drafts and sorting them out. Even so, his choices of alternative language have sometimes been questioned by other Dickinson specialists.

———. *The Poems of Emily Dickinson*. Edited by Thomas H. Johnson. 3 vols. Cambridge, Mass.: Harvard University Press, 1955. "Including variant readings critically compared with all known manuscripts."

Johnson, Thomas H. *Emily Dickinson: An Interpretive Biography*. New York: Atheneum, 1955. A gracefully written, authoritative critical biography by the dean of contemporary Dickinson scholars. It is the first that discusses in detail Higginson's significance in Dickinson's life and career.

Sewall, Richard B. *The Life of Emily Dickinson*. 2 vols. New York: Farrar, Straus, 1974; London: Faber, 1976. By far the most comprehensive Dickinson interpretive biography. Sewall devotes his first volume to Dickinson's family, his second to her friends, and intertwines her life with both circles with great tact, sympathetic understanding, and impressive learning. The prose is clear and often eloquent. One of the most admirable modern literary biographies.

———, ed. *Emily Dickinson: A Collection of Critical Essays*. Englewood Cliffs, N.J.: Prentice-Hall, 1963. A rich and diverse collection of critical essays, displaying an almost bewildering range of interpretive views. Such important critics and scholars as Charles Anderson, R. P. Blackmur, John Crowe Ransom, Allen Tate, and George Whicher are represented.

Gerhard Brand

RUDOLF DIESEL

Born: March 18, 1858; Paris, France
Died: September 29, 1913; at sea, in the English
Channel
Areas of Achievement: Invention and technology
Contribution: Diesel invented the diesel engine.
His invention has found many applications—in
automobiles, trucks, ships, and submarines, and
for generating electricity.

Early Life

Born to Bavarian parents residing in Paris, Rudolf
Diesel was exposed at an early age to the mechanical arts, both in his father's leather-goods shop and
at the nearby Conservatoire des Arts et Métiers.
The Diesel family fled to London in September,
1870, in the face of growing anti-German sentiment during the Franco-Prussian War. After eight
weeks there, his father, realizing there were too
many mouths to feed, sent twelve-year-old Rudolf
to Augsburg, Bavaria, to live with an uncle.

Diesel's uncle enrolled him in a county trade
school, where Diesel decided, at the age of fourteen, to become an engineer. At the trade school,
he studied mathematics, physics, mechanical drawing, and modern languages. It was there also that
Diesel realized that his life's ambitions would
come true only through hard work and a mastery of
science. In the summer of 1875, Diesel advanced
to the next level of education in the German system
by enrolling, on a scholarship, in the new Technische Hochschule in Munich.

At the Technische Hochschule, Diesel heard the
lectures of Professor Carl von Linde on the subject
of heat engines. He was particularly struck by the
low efficiency of the steam engine and began to
think about ways to improve that efficiency. The
firm grounding in thermodynamics which he received from Linde's lectures later formed his approach to the problem of designing a better engine.
In December, 1879, Diesel passed his final exams
at the Technische Hochschule with honors and began his career as an engineer.

Life's Work

Linde, who had so impressed Diesel in school, became his first employer. Diesel took a job as the
Paris representative of the refrigeration machinery
business Linde had founded. By working with heat
engines and heat pumps, Diesel gained experience

with the subject which most interested him: thermodynamics.

For ten years, Diesel worked in his spare time on
various heat engines, including a solar-powered air
engine. A heat engine produces work by heating a
working fluid; the fluid then expands and exerts
pressure on a moving part, usually a piston. Like
many of his contemporaries, Diesel investigated
the use of ammonia, ether, and carbon dioxide as
substitutes for steam as the working medium in a
heat engine. He tried to build an ammonia engine
but found ammonia too difficult to handle (even
small leaks proved hazardous to the health of nearby workers). He then turned to air as a working
medium for two reasons: It was abundant and the
oxygen in air could support combustion, thus eliminating the need for a separate firebox.

Having thoroughly studied thermodynamics, Diesel understood the Carnot cycle and attempted to apply it to his new heat engine, in the belief that it
would improve the engine's thermal efficiency. First
published in 1824 by the French engineer Nicolas-Leonard-Sadi Carnot, the Carnot cycle describes the
ideal heat engine of maximum thermal efficiency
and consists of four phases: isothermal (constant
temperature) combustion, adiabatic (no loss or gain
of heat) expansion, isothermal compression, and
adiabatic compression to the initial state. In order to
realize the highest possible efficiency, Carnot noted,
the heat to be converted into work must be added at
the highest temperature of the cycle, and it must not
raise the temperature of the cycle.

The difficulty of adding heat (through combustion) while maintaining a constant temperature did
not daunt Diesel; he felt confident that he could design such an engine—an ideal Carnot engine. His
solution was to heat the air by compressing it with
a piston inside a cylinder. At the top of the stroke,
the air temperature would be at a maximum. He
would then add a small amount of fuel, which the
high air temperature would ignite. The heat produced by combustion would then be offset by the
tendency of the air temperature to drop as the piston moved down and the air expanded, thus producing isothermal combustion. While theoretically
correct, this idea met with many practical difficulties, the most formidable being that the engine had
to work at extremely high pressures in order to
achieve maximum efficiency.

In Diesel's 1892 patent application for his engine, he listed isothermal combustion as the essence of his invention. A year later, Diesel published *Theorie und Konstruktion eines rationellen Wärmemotors zum Ersatz der Dampfmaschinen und der heute bekannten Verbrennungsmotoren* (1893; *Theory and Construction of a Rational Heat Motor*, 1894), in which he fully described his ideas and supported them with calculations and drawings. This book was important to Diesel as a way of promoting his ideas and thus gaining financial backing. With the endorsement of some of Europe's leading thinkers in thermodynamics, Diesel gained the support of two industrial giants: Krupp and Maschinenfabrik Augsburg. Under the agreement that he reached with these firms, Diesel received a good salary and the use of their facilities. Despite this boost, it would take him four years of hard work to begin to realize his dream of a more efficient engine.

In the process of writing his book, Diesel realized that the ideal engine he had envisioned would be almost impossible to build because of the high air pressures required by the theory, which were well beyond the practice of the day. Thus, he began, in 1893, to scale down his ideas and to settle for good, but less-than-ideal, efficiencies. Even with the changes in his theoretical goals, building a working engine proved to be a challenge. His first experimental engine, tested in late 1893, exploded upon ignition of the fuel. His second engine ran under its own power for a minute, but only at idling speed. Not until 1897 did a prototype run smoothly, but it had neither the reliability nor the economy to be a marketable engine. Furthermore, it operated at a thermal efficiency far below what Diesel had originally set out to achieve.

Despite the remaining problems, Diesel announced in June, 1897, at a meeting of the Society of German Engineers that his engine was ready to be sold. The resulting fiasco almost ruined Diesel financially, brought him to the brink of a nervous breakdown, and gave his engine a bad name. Continued refinement of the engine over the next five years, however, restored the diesel engine's reputation. It eventually gained a respectable share of the market, as the number of engines being sold every year increased steadily. By 1908, when Diesel's basic patent expired, the diesel engine was firmly established as an important type of power plant.

By 1912, doubts were being raised as to Diesel's role in the invention of the engine which bore his name. By some accounts, men other than Diesel—those who had taken his highly theoretical ideas and produced a working engine—deserved credit for the diesel engine. Those same critics saw Diesel as little more than a promoter. Diesel had always been high-strung (he was prone to migraines when under extreme stress) so it is not surprising that these criticisms stung him sharply. When he heard, in 1912, that a history of the diesel engine was being written, he countered with his own history, "Die Entstehung des Dieselmotors" (he published a book of the same title the following year). In November, 1912, he presented this paper at a professional meeting of engineers, at which two professors attacked him, pointing out that the diesel engine bore little resemblance to his original concept. At the same time Diesel was suffering these attacks upon his integrity, he was also suffering financial setbacks; bad investments had taken a heavy toll, despite good income from various sources. On the night of September 29, 1913, Rudolf Diesel disappeared from a steamer while crossing the English Channel. His son later identified the effects taken from a body at the mouth of the Schelde River as those of his father. The death was ruled a suicide.

Summary

The diesel engine of today bears little resemblance to Rudolf Diesel's original rational engine, but one is still quite justified in calling him the inventor. Few inventions spring from their creator's mind without the need to refine and improve them, and Diesel's brainchild was no exception. Significantly, Diesel kept a hand in his engine's development throughout the lengthy development period. Furthermore, today's engine retains three essential features of Diesel's original concept. First, all diesel engines are high-compression engines which use air as the working medium. Second, fuel is still injected into the cylinder at the end of the compression stroke. Third, it is still the heat of the compressed air which ignites the fuel.

Diesel engine production grew dramatically after Diesel's death. It is difficult to estimate the number of diesel engines in service, but the fact that millions are built each year throughout the world helps put their importance in perspective. The diesel engine's high thermal efficiency and the low cost of diesel fuel combine to make it an extremely economical engine. As a result, diesel engines have found a growing number of applications such as submarines, ships, locomotives, heavy road and off-road vehicles, passenger cars, and electric generating plants. These engines aptly carry the name of the man who worked so hard to make them a reality.

Bibliography

Burke, James. "Connections." *Scientific American* 277, no. 6 (December, 1997). Examines scientific achievements of several inventors including Diesel.

Bryant, Lynwood. "The Development of the Diesel Engine." *Technology and Culture* 17 (July, 1976): 432-446. A carefully documented case study of the nature of invention, development, and innovation. Contains a brief but useful discussion of the claims against Diesel in 1912. Highlights the many difficulties Diesel encountered in developing his engine and the many modifications to his original idea. Contains footnotes.

———. "Rudolf Diesel and His Rational Engine." *Scientific American* 221 (August, 1969): 108-117. A careful examination of the intellectual evolution of the diesel engine. Well illustrated and written for the layman, the article explains each step in Diesel's progress toward the diesel engine of today. Contains an especially useful section, with graphs and illustrations, of the Carnot cycle—Diesel's starting point.

Diesel, Eugen. "Rudolf Diesel." In *From Engines to Autos: Five Pioneers in Engine Development and Their Contributions to the Automotive Industry*, by Eugen Diesel, Gustav Goldbeck, and Friedrich Schilderberger. Chicago: Regnery, 1960. Written by Diesel's son, this is, nevertheless, a reasonably objective account of Diesel's life and work. Details of engine development follow a concise, ten-page summary of his early life. Suffers from a lack of documentation, but is notable for the insights it provides into Diesel's personality.

Grosser, Morton. *Diesel: The Man and the Engine*. New York: Atheneum, 1978; Newton Abbott: David and Charles, 1980. A very readable account of the development of the diesel engine from Diesel's original idea through the date of the book's publication. Generally dependable in technical details. Contains a glossary and a list of books for further reading, as well as photographs and illustrations.

Nitske, W. Robert, and Charles Morrow Wilson. *Rudolf Diesel: Pioneer of the Age of Power*. Norman: University of Oklahoma Press, 1965. Biography with two chapters at the end on the diesel engine in the modern world. Not totally reliable. Written mostly from secondary sources and without footnotes; as such, it offers little new information about Rudolf Diesel or his engine.

Brian J. Nichelson

BENJAMIN DISRAELI

Born: December 21, 1804; London, England
Died: April 19, 1881; London, England
Areas of Achievement: Government, politics, and
literature
Contribution: Disraeli overcame social and political
prejudice in nineteenth century Great Britain to
become leader of the Conservative Party, served
twice as prime minister, and formulated a "Tory
Radicalism" distinctively free from the prevalent
Whig-Liberal philosophy of Utilitarianism.

Early Life

Benjamin Disraeli was born in London on December 21, 1804, the oldest son of Isaac D'Israeli, an antiquarian, literary scholar, and writer, and his wife,
Maria Basevi. The child was the namesake and
grandson of Benjamin D'Israeli, an Italian-Jewish
immigrant and successful businessman. Isaac's dispute with the synagogue of Bevis Marks led to the
four D'Israeli children's baptism as Christians in
1817, a step which later made it possible for Disraeli
to have a career in the House of Commons, from
which Jews were excluded until 1858. Benjamin's
family relations with his father and older sister Sarah were especially close. The younger generation
simplified the family name by dropping the apostro-
phe. As a youngster, Benjamin attended school at
Blackheath near London and Higham Hall at Ep-
ping Forest. In 1821, Benjamin—now a man of medium height, slender build, and pale, aquiline features, with a high forehead, black, wavy hair, and an
intellectual countenance—began legal training in
the office of a London solicitor.

Bored with the law and hoping to attain fame and
fortune quickly, Disraeli in 1824 plunged into
stock-market speculation, lost money beyond his
resources, and was forced to borrow at interest rates
so ruinous that his debts became too great for him
to pay until he was past middle age. In 1825, Disraeli organized a political and literary newspaper,
The Representative, which quickly foundered amid
more debts and the ill feeling of such influential associates as John Murray and John Gibson Lockhart.
In an anonymous *roman à clef, Vivian Grey* (1826-
1827), Disraeli caricatured these and other figures
in the world of literature and politics, gaining notoriety, but at some cost to his reputation.

From 1827 to 1830, Disraeli retreated into minor
writings and ill health, producing *The Young Duke*
(1831), a hack novel "delightfully adapted to the

most corrupt taste," to help finance a sixteen-
month (1830-1831) trip to Europe, the Mediterranean, the Balkans, the Levant, Palestine, and
Egypt. This experience of the atmosphere and reality of "the East" was an influence on his later novels and perhaps on his statecraft. The year 1832
found him frequently invited to London parties as
both a foppishly dressed raconteur on exotic lands
and an author of the amusing "society" novels
which were his main, if insufficient, source of income. During Disraeli's travels the long dominance of the Tories had ended, and the new Whig
government's proposals for extending voting rights
to more of the middle class were nearing enactment as the Reform Bill of 1832. Disraeli decided
to seek a seat in the House of Commons to participate in this new political era.

Life's Work

Disraeli made three unsuccessful attempts at parliamentary election as a Radical, a role which
gave him maximum independence but no significant financial or political support. In 1835, he
joined the Tory Party and, after contesting a hopeless seat, was in 1837 elected as the junior member for Maidstone. His first speech in the House
of Commons was howled down by Irish and Whig
members, but he soon established himself as an
effective speaker among the Tory-Conservative
opposition led by Sir Robert Peel. In 1839, Disraeli abandoned his previous well-publicized love
affairs and married Mrs. Mary Anne Wyndham
Lewis, a widow possessed of a generous income
for life from the estate of her first husband. She
was twelve years older than Disraeli and noticeably tactless in her conversation, but affectionate
and admiring in her nature. The union was largely
one of mutual devotion until her death from cancer in 1872.

Disraeli was given no part in the Conservative
administration which Peel formed after the election
of 1841. He lacked influence and did not represent
any large interest. Peel had his pick of older Tories,
close political associates, important ex-Whigs such
as Edward Stanley (later the fourteenth Earl of
Derby), and rising young men of promise such as
William Ewart Gladstone. There was no compelling reason for him to include in the ministry an
outsider of conspicuously independent views and
noticeably restless ambition, and indeed there was

no prospect that Peel would ever want Disraeli as a colleague in government.

Disraeli's rejection by Peel prolonged the former's leisure for developing further his own political ideas. In the pamphlet of 1833 "What Is He?" he had presented himself as both a Radical and a Tory, and in his "Vindication of the English Constitution" in 1835, he pointed out that the Utilitarian maxim of "the greatest good for the greatest number" depended very much on who judged what was good. The history of political change in England had been termed "progress" by the bourgeoisie, which gained wealth and power through the changes, and by 1832, with the Reform Bill's redistribution of seats, the Whig merchants and manufacturers had begun to overbalance the parliamentary representation of Tory landlords. Peel's new "Conservatism" appeared to accept the proposition that the Whigs were entitled to determine who had the right to vote and that henceforth the Conservatives could promise only to preserve the status-quo interests of the "middle class." Disraeli argued that since the aristocratic principle had collapsed, the Tory Party should now appeal to the democratic principle of government.

The Young England movement of George Smythe, Lord John Manners, Alexander Baillie Cochrane, and Henry Hope provided for a time Disraeli's only House of Commons allies, and his best-known political novels reflected this connection in *Coningsby: Or, The New Generation* (1844) and *Sybil: Or, The Two Nations* (1845). These novels gave a realistic picture of the distress of the poor and criticized the indifference of Peel and his Conservatives to these victims of the Industrial Revolution and the Whigs' New Poor Law of 1834. Disraeli's argument, clearly, was for a Tory economic and social policy to meet the plight of the people, and for a radical departure from the laissez-faire doctrines of Manchester economics embraced by the Whigs.

Disraeli's opportunity to challenge Peel's leadership came with the latter's 1846 proposal to repeal the Corn Laws. This abolition of the protective tariff on grain and conversion to free trade would not afford any quick relief for the immediate Irish famine resulting from the 1845 potato blight, and the cabinet had already split over what the "backwoods" Tories saw as a betrayal of British farm interests mostly beneficial to British factory owners. A party revolt of some magnitude was inevitable, but Disraeli acted on his own in leading off the de-

bate for the protectionists, scathingly recounting the inconsistencies of Peel's political record and pouring scorn on his appeals for party loyalty. Having already charged that Peel "found the Whigs bathing and walked off with their clothes," Disraeli now termed him a "burglar" of other men's ideas and denounced "this huckstering tyranny of the Treasury bench . . . these political pedlars that bought their party in the cheapest market and sold us in the dearest." No other spokesman for the landed Tories could equal Disraeli for the brilliant invective which now expressed the feelings of a majority of the Tory Party.

Repeal of the Corn Laws passed with Whig votes, but the Conservative Party, divided and defeated on an Irish "coercion bill," was split between the Peelites (including the first Marquess of Aberdeen and Gladstone) and the more numerous protectionists, headed by Edward Stanley, soon fourteenth Earl of Derby, with Disraeli gradually winning acceptance as protectionist leader in the House of Commons. When, in 1852, Lord Derby was asked to form a minority government, he and Disraeli revived the "Conservative" label for the party. Their efforts to reconcile Peel's followers (Peel died in 1850), however, were unsuccessful. Disraeli served as Leader of the Commons and Chancellor of the Exchequer for the 1852 government. His budget and the administration were doomed by the opposing coalition even before Gladstone, in the budget debate, made the bitter personal attack on Disraeli which began the open hostility of these two political rivals.

The coalition of Whigs, Liberals, and Radicals split in 1858 over Lord Palmerston's foreign policy, and Derby and Disraeli again headed a minority government, from 1858 to 1859. This time they succeeded in passing the Removal of Jewish Disabilities (1858), hitherto blocked by the House of Lords. Disraeli proposed in 1859 an extension of the vote based on profession, government or bank savings, government pensions, or residential qualifications. This was defeated by the Whigs, Liberals, and Radicals as they reunited to restore Palmerston to office.

In 1866, Derby and Disraeli formed a third minority government after Lord John Russell and Gladstone were defeated on a franchise bill. The Tories introduced their own franchise reform bill in 1867. Disraeli made extension of voting rights in the boroughs according to residence qualifications the main thrust of the bill and accepted several Radical amendments, while persuading the House to reject Gladstone's attempt to control the terms of the bill, describing him as "a candidate for power" who "has had his innings." Despite the coalition majority, Disraeli's bill passed. Lord Derby retired in 1868, and Disraeli became prime minister, a fulfillment which he described in the sardonic expression, "at last I have climbed to the top of the greasy pole." In the 1868 election, however, Gladstone made disestablishing the Anglican church in Ireland the issue on which he gained enough votes from the "Celtic fringe" in Ireland, Scotland, and Wales to give the Liberals a majority.

From 1868 to 1874, Disraeli fought off challenges to his leadership, rebuilt party organization and finance, sustained a personal loss in his wife's death on December 15, 1872, and also expanded his political creed to include more emphasis on pride in the British Empire. The popular notion, however, then and since, of Disraeli as an imperialist and Gladstone as a "Little Englander" more accurately described their speeches than their policies in office. The Gladstone ministry meanwhile outlived the early years of its reforms, had no remedy for the hard times following 1872, and justified Disraeli's description of the Treasury bench as "a row of exhausted volcanoes." The election of 1874 gave the Tories a majority in the Commons, and Disraeli finally became prime minister of a workable government.

In his administration of 1874 to 1880, Disraeli promoted "social reform" in terms of the working and living conditions of the laboring class. The Artisans' and Laborers' Dwelling Act of 1875 was a pioneering step in the field of slum clearance and public housing, while the 1875 Public Health Act began a systematic and codified approach to this problem. The Factory Acts of 1874 and 1878 applied the same systematic approach to work safety regulations and also gave trade unions organizing, bargaining, and picketing rights, the so-called Magna Carta of Labor. The Merchant Shipping Act of 1876 owed more to Samuel Plimsoll than to the political leaders, but Disraeli gave government support to this reform of marine safety and insurance. This broad social welfare approach to industrial problems was very different in form from the rural society ideas of *Coningsby* and *Sybil*, but the principle of Tory reforms to help the working poor was essentially the same.

In foreign and colonial affairs, Disraeli conducted a generally successful policy. His 1875 purchase from the Khedive of Egypt of about forty-five per

cent of the shares in the Suez Canal was a bargain investment for Great Britain financially, an important improvement of the British route to India and the Orient, and a significant expansion of British military, economic, and political presence in the Middle East for the next eighty years. The creation of a new title for the queen, "Empress of India," in 1876, was a more debatable accomplishment, and Disraeli's attempt in 1876 to conserve his failing health by becoming Earl of Beaconsfield naturally weakened his influence in the Commons.

The 1878 Congress of Berlin on Balkan problems raised by the Bulgarian Revolt of 1876 and the Russo-Turkish War of 1877-1878 saw Disraeli successfully combining British, Turkish, Austrian, and Italian interests and policies to check the expansion of Russian influence in Southeastern Europe. Upon his triumphant return to London, Disraeli described the Berlin settlement as "peace with honor." The last years of Disraeli's ministry were, however, clouded by military problems in Afghanistan and Zululand and by the Depression of 1873, which still gripped Great Britain. In the general election of 1880, the disorganized Conservative Party was defeated. For almost a year, Disraeli continued as the active leader of the Tory opposition to Gladstone's second administration, but in March of 1881, his health began to fail rapidly. He died on April 19, 1881, at his London house, and was buried beside his wife at their Hughenden estate.

Summary

The legacy of Benjamin Disraeli was in great part the courage and determined perseverance of his career from outsider to prime minister and in some part the romantic extravagance and wit with which he dramatized his own legend. His writings, however, and his later legislation established a rationale and a record of rejecting a status-quo conservatism limited to accepting only past changes, and the later leaders of his party have accepted Disraeli's teaching that only by continuing to propose basic changes to meet the needs of the whole nation can Toryism succeed as a political faith.

Bibliography

Blake, Robert. *Disraeli*. London: Eyre and Spottiswoode, 1966; New York: St. Martin's Press, 1967. Accepted as the most useful one-volume biography available, this work skillfully incorporates the scholarship of Monypenny and Buckle (below), adds several matters which they omitted, and makes good use of letters which came to light between 1920 and 1967. In the area of politics, the book is comprehensive; Lord Blake's account is readable and enjoyable as well as scholarly.

Bradford, Sarah. *Disraeli*. London: Weidenfeld and Nicolson, 1982; New York: Stein and Day, 1983. An important supplement to Monypenny and Buckle and to Blake. Easily the best account and analysis so far of Disraeli's personal life. The author draws on previously unpublished letters which show Disraeli and Mary Anne in several "storms" in the first decade of their generally happy marriage; on the whole, the book gives a good sense of the emotional side of Disraeli's character. The best source on his private life.

Disraeli, Benjamin. *Benjamin Disraeli: Letters*. Edited by J. A. Gunn et al. Toronto: University of Toronto Press, 1982. A major and ongoing international enterprise, the Disraeli Project aims at a virtually complete edition of Disraeli's letters. Earlier collections of Disraeli's letters have been well mined by Monypenny and Buckle and by Blake.

Eldridge, C. C. *England's Mission*. London: Macmillan, 1973; Chapel Hill: University of North Carolina Press, 1974. The author reviews several historians' arguments about nineteenth century British imperialism and offers his own analysis of "the Empire of Disraeli's Dreams." Well documented.

Feuchtwanger, E. J. *Disraeli, Democracy, and the Tory Party*. Oxford: Clarendon Press, 1968. Only election and party organization buffs will fully appreciate this detailed and scholarly work. The appendices include a useful "glossary" of the secondary figures involved in Tory Party organization from 1867 to 1885.

Jerman, B. R. *The Young Disraeli*. Princeton, N.J.: Princeton University Press, 1960. Brief, general, scholarly, and readable. Covers the period to 1837.

Levine, Richard A. *Benjamin Disraeli*. New York: Twayne, 1968. A useful and appreciative evaluation of Disraeli's place in literature.

Monypenny, William Flavelle, and George Earl Buckle. *The Life of Benjamin Disraeli, Earl of Beaconsfield*. 6 vols. London and New York: Macmillan, 1910-1920. Volumes 1 and 2 were written by Monypenny, and after his death the work was completed by Buckle. This work, although dated in some respects, remains the definitive and indispensable biography for scholars or serious readers, or for reference purposes. Much of the work consists of extensive quotations from Disraeli's writings, letters, and speeches. The authors let their subject speak for himself, and Disraeli's rhetoric has a personality which communicates the man to the reader with a force for which ordinary biography is no substitute.

Richmond, Charles, and Paul Smith, eds. *Disraeli, the Fashioning of Self*. New York: Cambridge University Press, 1998. A collection of essays by historians, psychiatrists, and experts in literature that combine to profile the "self-made" Disraeli. Topics include his educational background, politics, and more.

Smith, Paul. *Disraeli: A Brief Life*. Cambridge and New York: Cambridge University Press, 1996. A brief study of Disraeli offering significant reappraisal of his personality and career.

K. Fred Gillum

DOROTHEA DIX

Born: April 4, 1802; Hampden, Maine (then part of Massachusetts)
Died: July 17, 1887; Trenton, New Jersey
Area of Achievement: Social reform
Contribution: A crusader for the rights of the mentally ill, Dix devoted her life to establishing psychiatric hospitals to provide proper care for those with mental and emotional problems.

Early Life

Dorothea Lynde Dix had a difficult childhood. Her father married, by his family's standards, below his station. Since married students were not accepted at Harvard, where he was studying at the time, he was sent to manage family holdings in Maine—nothing less than the frontier in the early nineteenth century. Never a financial success, he did win some notice as a traveling Methodist preacher and a writer of tracts. Thus, Dorothea was often without her father, and unfortunately, her mother was often too ill to give her the attention that young children require.

Dorothea's happiest memories of her solitary childhood revolved around visits to her paternal grandparents in Boston. Her grandfather, a successful if curmudgeonly physician, and grandmother provided a warm welcome. Dorothea's first exposure to public service came from watching her grandfather practice medicine. She had few playmates her own age and was four years older than her nearest sibling. At least one biographer believes that isolation from children and involvement with adults led to a high degree of self-interest and blocked the development of personal emotional commitment. In any case, she never married, and most, though not all, of her friendships were with people involved in her charitable endeavors.

At about twelve, unhappy at home, she began to live permanently with her then-widowed grandmother. To her dismay, her grandmother insisted on both academic and social discipline, and Dorothea's sense of rejection was actually worsened. After two years, she was sent off to live with a great-aunt, where she finally found a congenial home. Although still a teenager, she was allowed to open a school for small children, which she ran successfully for three years before returning to Boston. Two years later, in 1821, she opened a school for girls. Education for women was unusual—public schools accepted girls only for the few months when many boys were out for agricultural labor—and even more unusual was Dix's insistence on including natural science in the curriculum. Dorothea Dix proved to be a gifted teacher, and she seemed to have found her life's work. In a gesture that was a harbinger of her future, she added a program for poor girls who otherwise had no opportunity for schooling.

Ill health—apparently tuberculosis—and the collapse of a romance with her cousin resulted in a new direction for Dix. While recovering her strength in the mid-1820's, she became interested in Unitarianism and the ideas of William Ellery Channing. This Christian sect's emphasis on the goodness of humanity and the obligation to serve it would inspire her for the rest of her life. A new attempt to run a school, however, led to her complete collapse in 1836 and her doctor's orders never to teach again.

Life's Work

While recuperating, Dorothea Dix visited England. During her two-year stay with the William Rathbone family, she met a variety of intellectuals and reformers. When she returned to the United States, she found that the deaths of her mother and grandmother had left her financially independent. She spent several years seeking some focus for her life. Then, in 1841, she was asked to teach Sunday School for women at the East Cambridge Jail. She found the innocent and guilty, young and old, sane and insane crowded into the same miserable, unheated facility. Those regarded as insane were often chained or otherwise restrained. Her discussions with humanitarians such as George Emerson, who would become a longtime friend, led her to understand that conditions in East Cambridge Jail were, if anything, better than those in most jails. There was virtually no distinction made between mental illness and retardation, and in the entire country there were only about 2,500 beds specifically for those with emotional problems. Dix quickly had a sense that she had come upon something important that needed doing.

Dix's first move was to demand and get heat for the insane in the East Cambridge Jail. Then, after talking with other reformers, including Samuel Howe and Charles Sumner (later a radical Republican leader during Reconstruction), she began a survey of facilities for the insane in Massachusetts. Although the McLean Psychiatric Hospital was relatively progressive, most of the mentally ill were kept in local poorhouses, workhouses, and jails. She visited every one. Conditions were horrendous. Patients were often locked in dirty stalls, sometimes for years, and many were chained to the floor. Many were virtually naked, and physical restraint was virtually universal. She also found time to discuss treatment with the best doctors, finding that much more humane treatment was being successfully used in leading hospitals in Europe and a few in the United States. More common in America were strong sedatives to induce quiescence and the application of shocks, such as surprise dousings with ice water, to bring individuals back to reality.

After eighteen months, Dix prepared a petition to the Massachusetts legislature. The petition stated psychiatric facilities should provide for physical health and comfort (she would later expand this to prisons) and seek, with kindness and support, to cure diseased minds. When it was published, this document at first produced embarrassment and denial and then attacks upon the author. Her friends—Howe, Sumner, and others—rushed to defend her. She had her first victory when a bill providing for more and better accommodations for the mentally ill was passed. Her career was beginning to take shape.

Her initial investigations had occasionally taken Dix outside Massachusetts, where she found conditions to be generally worse than in her home state. From the mid-1840's to the mid-1850's, she traveled many thousands of miles around the United States and Canada, finding and exposing the suffering of the indigent insane. Although she did not travel to the far West (she did work in Texas), Dix visited almost every one of the thirty-one states of that era. She developed an investigative technique in which, by means of simple persistence and will, she forced her way into every facility where the insane were kept. There followed dramatic revelations of suffering and abuse that shamed all but the most hardened and/or fiscally conservative. Finally, she launched a petition to the legislature for the necessary funds and regulations to ensure improved care. She found the inevitable compromises necessary in any political campaign frustrating, but she settled for whatever state legislatures would fund and began again.

Results varied. New Jersey and Pennsylvania established state psychiatric hospitals as a result of her efforts. New York, however, rejected her call for six hospitals and only expanded the beds avail-

able in an existing facility. In 1845, with the help of Horace Mann and George Emerson, Dix expanded her efforts to prison reform and published a manual on that subject. Proper care for the mentally ill, however, remained her main focus.

From 1845 to 1846, Dix worked in Kentucky, Tennessee, Louisiana, Alabama, Georgia, and Arkansas, and she was working her way up the Mississippi when, in September, she collapsed in Columbus, Ohio. By December, she was sufficiently recovered to resume traveling, and in January, 1847, she presented a petition to the Illinois legislature, which resulted in the passage of a bill creating a psychiatric hospital. Later that year and in the following year, she had similar successes in Tennessee and North Carolina. Her fame was growing enormously, as were the respect and love with which Americans regarded her. One of the greatest marks of the latter came in 1863, when Confederate troops invading Pennsylvania stopped a train on which Dix was riding. A North Carolina officer recognized her, and the train was released to continue on its way. Not even the passions of Civil War could change people's feelings about Dorothea Dix.

Despite local successes—between 1844 and 1854 she persuaded eleven states to open hospitals—Dix recognized by the late 1840's that only a national effort would resolve the problems of the insane. No more than one-fourth of those needing care got it. She began to push for a federal effort, suggesting that 5 million acres of public land be committed to set up a fund to provide care for insane, epileptic, and mentally impaired Americans. A bill to this effect was introduced in Congress in 1848. Dix was provided with a small office in Washington from which to lobby. Questions about cost and constitutionality blocked the various versions of the bill until 1854, when, to her joy, it passed both houses. Her exultation was brief, however, for President Franklin Pierce vetoed the bill on the grounds that Congress had no authority to make such grants outside the District of Columbia. It was the final blow—the effort was abandoned.

Exhausted and ill, Dix planned to renew efforts in individual states, but friends and doctors persuaded her to rest. She visited friends in England, and within two weeks she was involved in efforts to reform psychiatric care there. She went so far as to go personally to the home secretary, Sir George Grey, to argue for improvements in Scotland. Before she left, a Royal Commission to investigate the problem was in the works. She also helped to sustain a reform effort in the Channel Islands before touring the Continent, where she visited hospitals, asylums, and jails, exposing problems and demanding change. The force of her personality seems to have made her irresistible; even Pope Pius IX was forced to initiate improvements in the Vatican's handling of the mentally ill.

Her return to the United States in 1856 brought a large number of requests for aid. She was soon traveling again, seeking various reforms and funding. In the winter of 1859 alone, she asked state legislatures for a third of a million dollars, and in 1860, she got large appropriations for hospitals in South Carolina and Tennessee. The outbreak of the Civil War brought reform work to a halt, and Dix promptly volunteered her services. Appointed superintendent of United States Army Nurses, she spent four years of very hard work developing the Medical Bureau from a service set up for an army of ten thousand to one that could handle more than that many casualties from one battle. Unfortunately, she was too straitlaced at age sixty to cope with the rough-and-tumble style of the military. Her New England Puritanism showed in her tendency to think that an army doctor who had had a few drinks should be dishonorably discharged. Although her work in ensuring the provision of nurses and medical supplies at the beginning of the war was of great importance, in 1863 her authority was quietly reduced, to her bitter disappointment. After the war, Dix spent another fifteen years traveling as the advocate of the insane. Worn out in 1881, she retired to the hospital (the first created by her efforts) in Trenton, New Jersey, where she lived until her death in 1887.

Summary

Dorothea Dix's importance can be seen from simple statistics. In 1843, the United States had thirteen institutions for the mentally ill; in 1880, it had 123. Of the latter, 75 were state-owned, and Dix had been a key factor in the founding of 32 of them. She had also been able to get a number of training schools for the retarded established, and specialized training for psychiatric nurses had begun.

More important, the lives of many unfortunate people had been made easier thanks to her efforts. The idea that the insane, even if poor, deserved humane care and treatment intended to help them recover had been established in the United States. Dix's efforts began a process that has continued throughout the twentieth century and has left the United States a world leader in the treatment of mental illness.

Bibliography

Brown, Thomas J. *Dorothea Dix: New England Reformer.* Cambridge, Mass.: Harvard University Press, 1998. This study of Dix provides new insight into her passions and methods.

Dain, Norman. *Concepts of Insanity in the United States, 1789-1865.* New Brunswick, N.J.: Rutgers University Press, 1964. A useful description of attitudes and problems that Dix had to confront during her career.

Dix, Dorothea. *On Behalf of the Insane Poor: Selected Reports.* New York: Arno Press, 1971. A valuable source of Dix's ideas and opinions expressed in her own words. Her eloquence and passion shine through.

Gollaher, David. *Voice for the Mad: A Life of Dorothea Dix.* New York: Free Press, 1995. A balanced biography highlighting Dix's strengths and weaknesses, her efforts in the area of legislative reform, and her second career as head of the Civil War nurses.

Marshall, Helen. *Dorothea Dix: Forgotten Samaritan*. Chapel Hill: University of North Carolina Press, 1937. Although it is sometimes overly sympathetic to its subject, this is a solid and well-written biography.

Snyder, Charles M., ed. *The Lady and the President: The Letters of Dorothea Dix and Millard Fillmore*. Lexington: University Press of Kentucky, 1965. Provides interesting insights into one period of the life of Dorothea Dix.

Tiffany, Francis. *Life of Dorothea Lynde Dix*. Boston: Houghton Mifflin, 1890. Although it is dated and overly kind to Dix, this biography is reasonably good for its era.

Tuke, Daniel. *The Insane in the United States and Canada*. London: Lewis, 1885; New York: Arno Press, 1973. This contemporary description of the problems Dix tried to solve gives a valuable perspective of the situation. It is very useful for modern students trying to achieve an understanding of her work.

Wilson, Dorothy Clarke. *Stranger and Traveler: The Story of Dorothea Dix, American Reformer*. Boston: Little Brown, 1975. This relatively superficial biography emphasizes Dix's role as a woman who achieved much against great odds. A bibliography and many illustrations are included.

Fred R. van Hartesveldt

GAETANO DONIZETTI

Born: November 29, 1797; Bergamo, Cisalpine Republic
Died: April 8, 1848; Bergamo, Austrian Empire
Area of Achievement: Music
Contribution: Donizetti was the most prolific composer of Italian operas in the first half of the nineteenth century. Though his work are uneven in quality, he was, at his best, the greatest and most vital exponent of Italian Romanticism before Giuseppe Verdi.

Early Life

Gaetano Donizetti was the fifth of six children born to Andrea and Domenica Nava Donizetti. He was born in a basement apartment, where, according to his later recollection, "no glimmer of light ever penetrated." His father, who discouraged him from pursuing a career as a composer, followed no particular trade; after 1808, he earned a miserable existence as the janitor of the local pawnshop.

In 1806, a free music school was established in Bergamo under the direction of Johann Simon Mayr. The eight-year-old Donizetti was one of the first students to enroll in the institution which would later bear his name (Istituto Musicale Gaetano Donizetti), and he continued his studies there until 1814. Donizetti's extraordinary fluency in composition in later years was a result at least in part of the rigorous training of Mayr, himself a successful composer of Italian operas.

At Mayr's urging, Donizetti went to Bologna to study counterpoint and fugue at the Liceo Filarmonico, then perhaps the most distinguished music school in Italy. His master in Bologna was the highly erudite Padre Mattei, who had formerly taught Gioacchino Rossini. Though Mattei did not inspire affection, Donizetti applied himself vigorously to the study of the contrapuntal forms; sixty-one exercises in his hand survive in manuscript.

Donizetti returned to Bergamo in 1817. Working with that facility and ease which was to mark his entire career, Donizetti composed four operas during a period of four years and a large body of non-operatic works. In the latter category, Donizetti composed eighteen string quartets; though modest, these works have a certain vernal charm. Donizetti was also forced at this time to devote considerable energy to the avoidance of military service. With the help of a woman who admired his talent,

Donizetti was able to purchase an exemption in 1818.

Donizetti had by this time matured into a well-favored young man. His passport of 1821 describes him as tall and slender, with blue eyes and chestnut hair; associates found him to be handsome, generous, and charming. As a young man, Donizetti was high-spirited; later, personal tragedies caused a melancholia to descend upon him.

Life's Work

Donizetti's career as a composer of opera was firmly launched in 1822, with the success of a serious opera in Rome. Donizetti was next offered a commission by the Teatro Nuovo in Naples. Then the most robust operatic center in Italy, Naples had been dominated musically by Rossini since 1815. Donizetti's first offering to the Neapolitan public, the semiserious opera *La zingara* (1822) was an immense success. For the next several years, Donizetti made Naples the base of his activities;

like all successful opera composers of his day, however, he was forced to travel frequently.

Though none of the operas before *Anna Bolena* (1830) has maintained a place in the active repertory, Donizetti was stunningly productive during the fifteen-year span from 1822 to 1837. Donizetti completed forty-nine operas in this remarkably fertile period. All the subgenres of Italian opera are represented in the canon of Donizetti's works: opera buffa (comic opera), opera seria (serious opera), and opera semiseria.

Donizetti relied largely on the formal conventions of Italian opera as established by Rossini. Most of the scenes in Donizettian opera are reducible ultimately to an opening recitative (rapid declamation of text) and a section in a brisk tempo (*tempo d'attacco*), in which the dramatic situation is presented; a slow reflective aria; an interruption of mood in a faster tempo (*tempo di mezzo*); and a brisk concluding section replete with vocal fireworks (*cabaletta*). This formula could be applied to ensembles as well as to solo scenes; in the former case, the brilliant concluding passage was called the *stretto*. Yet Donizetti deployed the basic pattern in an infinite variety of ways; moreover, in his intuitive understanding of its dramatic potential, he surpassed Rossini. Donizetti was not an inventive harmonist, and his scoring sometimes consisted of the simplest accompaniment patterns repeated shamelessly; yet in dramatic pacing, in the creation of adrenaline-charged melodies, and in sheer élan, he had few peers.

Though earlier works had given ample indications of a strong talent, Donizetti did not reach artistic maturity until the composition of *Anna Bolena*. This work marks the ascendancy of the full-blooded Romantic melodrama in Italian opera. *Anna Bolena* is one of four Donizettian operas based on Tudor history. Donizetti created a score of great power and emotional sincerity. The work also marks the beginning of a preoccupation on the part of Italian composers with libretti which depict fallible women, in this case Anne Boleyn, in pitiable circumstances. In the moving final scene, in which Boleyn is alternately delirious and lucid before her execution, Donizetti offers a foretaste of the famous "mad scene" from his later opera *Lucia di Lammermoor* (1835).

Anna Bolena brought Donizetti international acclaim, and it probably marked the peak of his personal fortunes as well. Donizetti had been married, in 1828, to Virginia Vasselli. By all ac-

counts, the union was a happy one. In the 1830's, however, three children born to them died in infancy, and in 1837, Virginia died of cholera. Donizetti never fully recovered from these losses, though he remained artistically productive for several years after Virginia's death.

The years between 1830 and 1837 constituted the zenith of Donizetti's career as a composer of Italian opera. In a series of striking works, including *Parisina* (1833), *Lucrezia Borgia* (1833), *Marino Faliero* (1835), *Lucia di Lammermoor*, and *Roberto Devereux* (1837), Donizetti solidified his achievement in the genre of the *melodramma* and also composed a comic opera of enduring charm in *L'elisir d'amore* (1832; *The Elixir of Love*). *Lucrezia Borgia*, an adaptation of Victor Hugo's play by Felice Romani, is a lurid drama steeped in violence and touching upon incest; in its sensationalism and explosiveness, Donizetti's setting adumbrates the *Verismo* opera school of the end of the century. Donizetti also happened upon a new musical texture for the setting of conversation in this work: The characters Rustighello and Astolfo chat in recitative in act 1, while a portentous motive sings in the orchestra (a device often credited to Verdi). *Marino Faliero*, with text supplied by Emanuele Bidera based indirectly on Lord Byron, prefigures Verdi's *I due Foscari* (1844), and *Simon Boccanegra* (1857) in its Venetian local color and its liberal political undercurrents. *Roberto Devereux* is the last of Donizetti's forays into Tudor history; his musical portrait of Elizabeth I in this work is one of his finest.

Lucia di Lammermoor has proved to be Donizetti's most durable work. It was his first collaboration with the distinguished librettist Salvatore Cammarano, and their joint effort is regarded by many as the touchstone of the entire bel canto repertory (as the works of Rossini, Vincenzo Bellini, Donizetti, and their contemporaries are collectively known).

In the final phase of his compositional career from 1838 to 1845, Donizetti was drawn into the orb of Parisian grand opera. He composed four operas to French texts for the stages of Paris; of these, the comic *La fille du régiment* (1840; *The Daughter of the Regiment*) and the serious *La favorite* (1840) became repertory staples. Donizetti's greatest achievement in the category of Italian opera buffa was also written for a foreign commission: His comic masterpiece *Don Pasquale* (1843) was written for the Théâtre Italien in Paris. Two serious operas with Italian texts, *Linda di Chamounix* (1842) and *Maria di Rohan* (1843), were commissioned by a Viennese theater.

Donizetti's life was rapidly approaching its own tragic denouement. In 1844, Donizetti began to show unmistakable symptoms of the last stages of syphilis. His condition deteriorated to the point where institutionalization was required in 1846. In 1848, Donizetti's died in Bergamo.

Summary

It was Gaetano Donizetti's misfortune to be the middle child in the family of nineteenth century Italian opera composers, preceded and followed by the more towering figures of Rossini and Verdi. Donizetti's primitive orchestrations and predictable melodic formulas were seen as tokens of his inferiority. A later generation of scholars has by contrast marveled at the professional standard Donizetti maintained given the conditions under which he worked. More detailed knowledge of his works has also bred increased respect; many effects associated with Verdi (or known through Sir Arthur Sullivan's parodies) have been found to be the products of Donizetti's imagination.

Appreciation of Donizetti's contribution has also been retarded by a lack of understanding of the subgenre in which he did his finest work, the *melodramma*. Modern critics have realized that the *melodramma* should not be judged according to the dramaturgical standards of a later generation. Texts which struck later generations as ludicrous were understood by Donizetti and his colleagues to be mere verbal semaphores reinforcing the profound emotional content of the music. Donizetti's role in the creation of the *melodramma* earns for him an honored place in the company of Victor Hugo, Hector Berlioz, and the other innovators who dismantled the edifice of artistic classicism.

Bibliography

Ashbrook, William. *Donizetti and His Operas.* Cambridge: Cambridge University Press, 1982; New York: Cambridge University Press, 1983. The definitive work in English on Donizetti. Part 1 offers biographical information; part 2 provides analytic comment on all the operas. Appendices supply synopses and information about Donizetti's librettists.

Ashbrook, William, and Julian Budden. "Gaetano Donizetti." In *The New Grove Masters of Italian Opera.* London: Macmillan, and New York: Norton, 1983. Concise account of Donizetti's life and valuable analytic commentary by two first-rate scholars of Italian opera. Contains the most accurate catalog of Donizetti's works available.

Glasow, E. Thomas. "Quarter Notes." (Editorial) *The Opera Quarterly* 14, no. 3 (Spring 1998). Discusses Donizetti's prolific career and the criticism he sustained for producing "superficial" works.

Gossett, Philip. *"Anna Bolena" and the Artistic Maturity of Gaetano Donizetti.* Oxford: Clarendon Press, and New York: Oxford University Press, 1985. Detailed discussion of *Anna Bolena*, the watershed work in Donizetti's career. Gossett offers a revisionist view of Donizetti's achievement.

Gossett, Philip and E. Thomas Glasow. "Donizetti: European Composer." *The Opera Quarterly* 14, no. 3 (Spring 1998). Profile of Donizetti focusing on his time in Paris.

Tomlinson, Gary. "Italian Romanticism and Italian Opera: An Essay in Their Affinities." *19th Century Music* 10, no. 1 (1986). Useful essay suggesting that Donizetti was in the aesthetic vanguard of his day.

Weinstock, Herbert. *Donizetti and the World of Opera in Italy, Paris, and Vienna in the First Half of the Nineteenth Century.* London: Methuen, and New York: Pantheon, 1963. Full-length study of Donizetti's life aimed at a popular audience. Slightly out of date given the increase in scholarly interest in Donizetti, but highly readable.

Steven W. Shrader

FYODOR DOSTOEVSKI

Born: November 11, 1821; Moscow, Russia
Died: February 9, 1881; St. Petersburg, Russia
Area of Achievement: Literature
Contribution: One of the world's greatest novelists, Dostoevski summoned to imaginative life areas of psychological, political, and aesthetic experience which have significantly shaped the modern sensibility.

Early Life

Fyodor Dostoevski is one of only two great nineteenth century Russian writers—Anton Chekhov is the other—who failed, unlike Alexander Pushkin, Nikolai Gogol, Ivan Turgenev, Leo Tolstoy, and others, to be born into the landed gentry. Whereas aristocrats such as Turgenev and Tolstoy depicted settled traditions of culture and fixed moral-social norms, Dostoevski spent his early years in an atmosphere which prepared him to treat the moral consequences of flux and change, and dramatize the breakup of the traditional forms of Russian society. His father, Mikhail Andreevich, derived from the lowly class of the nonmonastic clergy, succeeded in rising to the status of civil servant by becoming a military doctor and then became a surgeon attached to a hospital for the poor on the outskirts of Moscow. His mother, Marya Feodorovna, née Nechaev, was a merchant's daughter, meek, kind, gentle, pious—obviously the inspiration for most of Dostoevski's fictive heroines. The elder Dostoevski was not the repulsively dissolute prototype of Feodor Karamazov that many early biographies describe. He was, however, while devoted to his family, extremely strict, mistrustful, irritable, and easily depressed. The son was to acknowledge in later life his inheritance, from his father, of oversensitive nerves and uncontrollable explosions of temper. In addition, Dostoevski suffered from epilepsy, a condition which also ran in his family.

Fyodor was the second child and second son in the family. In 1838, the elder Dostoevski sent his sons to St. Petersburg's Academy of Engineers, determined to push them into secure careers despite their preference for literary achievement. In February, 1839, the father suffered a partial stroke when Fyodor failed to be promoted during his freshman year; in early June, 1839, Dostoevski's father died. All biographers assumed until modern times that he had been murdered on his small country estate by peasants outraged by his severity toward them. Jo-

seph Frank, however, in *Dostoevsky: The Seeds of Revolt, 1821-1849* (1976), the first volume of his monumental biography of Dostoevski, shows that important new evidence points to the probability of the elder Dostoevski's dying of an apoplectic stroke rather than at the hands of killers. Nevertheless, Dostoevski all of his life believed that his father had been murdered and therefore assumed a heavy burden of parricidal guilt, for the peasants who—so he imagined—had killed his father were merely enacting an impulse which he had surely felt.

In August, 1843, Dostoevski was graduated from the academy and placed on duty in the drafting department of the St. Petersburg Engineering Command. He neglected his work, preferring to read widely among French and German Romantic authors. By far the deepest influence, however, was that of Gogol. In 1844, Dostoevski resigned from the army, published a translation of Honoré de Balzac's *Eugénie Grandet* (1833; English translation, 1859), and began to work on his first novel, which was published in January, 1846, as *Bednye lyudi* (*Poor Folk*, 1887).

This is a poignant story of frustrated love, told in the form of letters passed between a poor government clerk and an equally poor girl who lives near him. Dostoevski's insight into the tortures of humiliated sensibility constitutes his major departure from what is otherwise a Gogol-like protest against the upper class's condescension to the lower. The most influential literary critic of the 1840's, Vissarion Belinsky, hailed the book as Russia's first important social novel.

Belinsky was less enthusiastic about Dostoevski's second novel, *Dvoynik* (*The Double*, 1917), which also appeared in 1846. Gogol's fiction again served as the model, particularly "Nos" ("The Nose") and "Zapiski sumasshedshego" ("Diary of a Madman"). Dostoevski's protagonist, Golyadkin, a middle-ranking bureaucrat, is driven by inner demons. His unquenchable thirst for self-worth and dignity causes him to distort reality and create for himself a world that will mirror his self-conflicts. Golyadkin's split personality disintegrates into two independent entities: A double appears who confronts him with his worst faults, both reflecting the suppressed wishes of his subconscious and objectifying his accompanying guilt feelings. While Dostoevski erred in failing to establish a moral perspective from which the reader could evaluate

Golyadkin either straightforwardly or ironically, he did succeed in hauntingly portraying, for the first time, the kind of obsessive, divided self that was to dominate his later, greater fiction.

Life's Work

Dostoevski's darkest decade began the night of April 22-23, 1849, when he was taken into police custody in St. Petersburg as a member of a circle headed by Mikhail Butashevich-Petrashevsky. A czarist court of inquiry concluded that fifteen of the accused, including Dostoevski, had been guilty of subversion and conspiracy. On December 22, 1849, the prisoners were taken to a public square and lined up before a firing squad. By prearrangement, literally in the last seconds before their expected execution, an aide-de-camp to the czar commuted their punishment to four years of hard prison labor and four additional years of military service as privates—both in Siberia. From this moment onward, the secular, progressive, idealistic influences from such writers as Friedrich Schiller, Victor Hugo, and George Sand, which had determined Dostoevski's previous philosophy, receded before the onrush of a spiritual vitality that overwhelmed him as a revelation. Always a believing Christian, he strove for the rest of his life to emphasize an ethic of expiation, forgiveness, and all-embracing love, based on a conviction of the imminence of the Day of Judgment and the Final Reckoning.

Some scholars interpret Dostoevski's consequent right-wing conservatism and mistrust of human nature as a psychic-emotive transformation caused by his disillusioning prison camp experiences. Joseph Frank takes a more acute view: Dostoevski came to regard each downtrodden convict as potentially capable of love and compassion but focused on the Russian peasant, regarding persons outside the Slavic culture and Orthodox faith as historically and religiously outcast. He became a fervent Slavophile, insisting that religious and cultural isolation from Western materialism had enabled the Russian people to avoid what he regarded as Europe's demoralization and decadence.

The Dostoevski who returned to St. Petersburg in mid-December, 1859, had matured enormously as a result of having confronted mortality, discovered the egotistic drives dominating his fellow convicts, and undergone a conversion crisis. In 1864, he published a novelette, *Zapiski iz podpolya* (*Notes from the Underground*, 1918), written primarily as a satirical parody of the views expressed in Nikolay Chernyshevsky's didactic novel *Chto delat'?* (1863; *What Is to Be Done?*, c. 1863), which affirmed rational egotism as the panacea for all human problems. Not at all, says the Underground Man. He is a malicious, brilliantly paradoxical skeptic who challenges the validity of reason and of rational solutions. He insists that, above all, man is determined to follow his often foolish, perverse, and even absurd will. Against the Enlightenment premises of utilitarianism, order, and good sense, the Undergroundling opposes chaos, self-destruction, cruelty, and caprice. This work is now generally recognized as the central text in Dostoevski's canon, the prologue to his greatest novels. The problem he would now confront is how to preserve human freedom from nihilism, how to restrain its destructive implications.

Raskolnikov, the protagonist of *Prestupleniye i nakazaniye* (1866; *Crime and Punishment*, 1886), is another Underground Man, despising ordinary people and conventional morality. He commits murder to test his theory that an extraordinary person is beyond good and evil. He then suffers harrowing isolation and self-disgust. Only his growing love for the sacrificial Sonia will open him slowly to processes of compassion, remorse, and regeneration. Yet Raskolnikov's self-will continues to battle his surrender to selfless Christian atonement until his Creator finally nudges him into God's camp.

In *Idiot* (1868; *The Idiot*, 1887), Dostoevski presents a Christlike man, Prince Myshkin, yet shows all of his saintly virtues mocked by the world. Myshkin is innocent and gentle, a good-natured sufferer of insults who becomes involved in the whirlpool of others' egotistic drives; is broken by their pride, lust, avarice, and vanity; and ends back in the world of idiocy from which he had emerged. The love and sympathy he brings to the world only fans more intensely its flames of hate, resentment, and self-will.

Besy (1871-1872; *The Possessed*, 1913) is Dostoevski's bitterest and most reactionary novel. He bases his plot on a notorious historic episode: A Moscow student was murdered in 1869 by a group of Nihilists who followed Mikhail Bakunin's terrorist doctrines. Dostoevski fills this work with crimes, fires, debasements, and other forms of social and psychological chaos. The political drama centers on the Nihilistic leader Peter Verkhovensky, a cynical, slippery, vicious, and monstrously criminal man. Dostoevski also pursues a metaphysical drama at whose center stands his most enigmatic character, Nikolai Stavrogin, who is attracted equally to good and evil and is full of mystery, power, pride, and boredom. He dominates all events while remaining passive and aloof. He liberates himself from any fixed image by confounding everyone's expectations. He is a fallen angel, a Satan, who succeeds, unlike Raskolnikov, in destroying others without scruple or passion. His suicide is his only logical act.

Dostoevski's last novel, *Bratya Karamazovy* (1879-1880; *The Brothers Karamazov*, 1912), sums up his leading themes and ideas. Here Dostoevski tries for no less than a dramatization of the nature of humanity, caught in the conflicting claims of man's desire for sainthood, symbolized by the youngest brother, Alyosha; for sensuality, embodied by the lust-driven middle brother, Dmitry; and for intellectual achievement, exemplified by the eldest brother, Ivan. The last, a brilliant rationalist, organizes a revolt against a God-ordered universe in his powerful "Legend of the Grand Inquisitor," which denounces a world tormented with senseless, undeserved suffering. In the legend, Dostoevski, through Ivan, depicts man as weak, slavish, and self-deceptive, willing to renounce freedom and dreams of salvation in exchange for economic security and autocratic guidance. Like Raskolnikov and Stavrogin, Ivan believes that everything is permissible, including the murder of his depraved father. The counterarguments are mounted by the Elder Zossima and his disciple, Alyosha: "All are responsible for all." They preach and practice meekness, humility, compassion, and Christian commitment. Whether Dostoevski succeeds in refuting Ivan's skeptical secularism in this novel is questionable; most critics believe that he fails. He planned a sequel, with Alyosha as the dominant character, but died of a pulmonary hemorrhage in 1881, before he could write it.

Summary

Perhaps Fyodor Dostoevski's greatest literary achievement was to marry the novel of ideas to the novel of mystery and crime, thereby creating a philosophical novel-drama, or metaphysical thriller. To be sure, he has glaring faults: His construction and style are often congested; his tone tends to be feverish; his language has sometimes unnerving changes of pace and rhythm; his pathos can become bathos; he crowds his fiction with more characters, incidents, and ideas than most readers can reasonably absorb; and he can burden his plots with irrelevant excursions and pronouncements. Yet his vision, grasp, and skill in dramatizing the complexities and contradictions of man's nature exceed those of any other novelist. His psychology is amazingly modern in its emphasis on the irrational nature of man, on the human psyche as far subtler and more paradoxical than previous writers realized. He anticipates many of the findings of contemporary depth psychology in his awareness of the personality's duality, of the roles played by unconscious drives, and of the symbolic function of dreams. His is a creative process that grasps intuitively not only the outline but also the philosophical implications of events. His characters are wholly absorbed by their thoughts and emotions: They live as they think and feel, translating their ideas and passions into entirely appropriate actions. Dostoevski's hypnotic art, filled with a fury that sometimes verges on hysteria, prepares readers for the ideological and moral struggles that have characterized the twentieth century.

Bibliography

Dostoevsky, Fyodor. *The Brothers Karamazov.* Edited by Ralph Matlaw. Translated by Constance Garnett. New York: Norton, 1976. Includes relevant letters by Dostoevski and a dozen critical essays which suggest a diversity of approaches to the text: thematic, stylistic, mythological, structural, and religious.

―――. *Crime and Punishment.* Edited by George Gibian. Translated by Jessie Coulson. Rev. ed. New York: Norton, 1975. This valuable edition has extracts from Dostoevski's letters and notebooks and more than a score of outstanding critical essays representing distinguished Russian, Italian, and German as well as American scholarship; eight were not previously translated into English.

Frank, Joseph. *Dostoevsky: The Seeds of Revolt, 1821-1849.* London: Robson, and Princeton, N.J.: Princeton University Press, 1976.

―――. *Dostoevsky: The Years of Ordeal, 1850-1859.* London: Robson, and Princeton, N.J.: Princeton University Press, 1983.

―――. *Dostoevsky: The Stir of Liberation, 1860-1865.* Princeton, N.J.: Princeton University Press, 1986; London: Robson, 1987.

―――. *Dostoevsky: The Miraculous Years, 1865-1871.* Princeton, N. J.: Princeton University Press, and London: Robson, 1995. Frank is engaged in one of the most ambitious and illuminating literary projects of the late twentieth century: a five-volume study of Dostoevski's life and career. Since Frank specializes in intellectual history, his study subordinates the melodramatic personal struggles that have dominated most biographies. Instead, he stresses the sociocultural context in which his subject lived and wrote, taking particular care to analyze the great contemporaneous issues in which Dostoevski participated. Indispensable.

Freud, Sigmund. "Dostoevsky and Parricide." In *Dostoevsky: A Collection of Critical Essays*, edited by René Wellek. Englewood Cliffs, N.J.: Prentice-Hall, 1962. Freud's famous essay traces Dostoevski's epilepsy and gambling mania to what the great psychoanalyst regards as his Oedipus complex and links the parricidal theme of *The Brothers Karamazov* and Dostoevski's trauma suffered after his father's death to his masochistic need for self-punishment to atone for his unconscious drive to kill his father. Though based on flawed historical sources, it remains a striking application of depth psychology to literature.

Mochulsky, K. V. *Dostoevsky: His Life and Work*. Translated with an introduction by Michael A. Minihan. Princeton, N.J.: Princeton University Press, 1967. Commonly regarded as the best one-volume interpretation of Dostoevski. Mochulsky has a particularly brilliant analysis of *Crime and Punishment* as a five-act tragedy with a prologue and epilogue.

Gerhard Brand

STEPHEN A. DOUGLAS

Born: April 23, 1813; Brandon, Vermont
Died: June 3, 1861; Chicago, Illinois
Areas of Achievement: Government and politics
Contribution: Endowed with a vision of nationalism, Douglas worked to develop the United States internally and to preserve the Union.

Early Life

Born on April 23, 1813, in Brandon, Vermont, Stephen A. Douglas spent his early life in Vermont and western New York State. His father died when Douglas was only two months old, and he lived on a farm with his widowed mother until he was fifteen. At that point, he set off for Middlebury, Vermont, to see "what I could do for myself in the wide world among strangers." He apprenticed himself to a cabinetmaker, but a dispute developed and he returned home after eight months. His mother remarried in late 1830, moved with her new husband to his home in western New York near Canandaigua, and Douglas accompanied them.

His early schooling in Vermont had been of the sketchy common-school variety, but in New York he entered the Canandaigua Academy, where he boarded and studied. There, he began to read law as well as study the classics, until he left school on January 1, 1833, to devote himself to full-time legal study. Early interested in politics, and particularly that of Andrew Jackson, Douglas associated himself for six months with the law office of Walter and Levi Hubbell, prominent local Jacksonians. New York State requirements for admission to the bar being very stringent—four years of classical studies and three of legal—Douglas decided to move. He was a young man in a hurry, and in June, 1833 (at twenty years of age), he moved west to seek his fortune.

He went first to Cleveland, Ohio, before finally settling further west in Illinois. Douglas taught school briefly in Winchester, Illinois, and then decided to apply for his law certificate. Requirements for admission to the bar were far easier to satisfy on the frontier than they were in the settled East, and in March, 1834, Douglas was examined by Illinois Supreme Court Justice Samuel D. Lockwood and received his license to practice. At age twenty-one, he had a vocation as a licensed attorney and could pursue his real love, which was politics. Douglas was not physically imposing, standing only five feet, four inches, with a head too large for his body, but he possessed tremendous energy. He would later receive such nicknames as the "Little Giant" and "a steam engine in britches."

Douglas' rise up the political ladder was meteoric. In 1835, he was elected state's attorney for the Morgan (Illinois) Circuit, and his political career was launched. He held a series of elective and appointive offices at the state level and was elected to the United States House of Representatives for the first time in 1843, at age thirty. He held that position until he resigned in 1847, having been elected to the United States Senate, a post he held until his death in 1861 at age forty-eight.

Life's Work

Douglas' life work was clearly political in nature. He had a vision of America as a great nation, and he wanted to use the political system to make his dream of "an ocean bound republic" a reality. He was willing to do whatever was necessary to develop and expand the United States and to preserve what was sacred to him, the Union. He expended enormous amounts of energy on his dream of developing the West by working to organize the Western territories and by urging the construction of a transcontinental railroad to bind the nation together.

Two of the highlights of Douglas' career in the Senate involved the Compromise of 1850 and the Kansas-Nebraska Act of 1854. There is a certain irony in the fact that the former was thought to have saved the Union while the latter destroyed it. Upon the acquisition of a vast amount of territory in the Mexican War, the nation was on the verge of disunion in 1849-1850 over the question of whether slavery should be allowed to expand into the area of the Mexican concession. It was Douglas, taking over from an ailing Henry Clay, who put together the package which has come to be called the Compromise of 1850. That compromise, which required months of intense political maneuvering, included such items as California's entry into the Union as a free state, the organization of New Mexico and Utah as territories without restriction on slavery, a stronger fugitive slave law, the abolition of the slave trade in the District of Columbia, and the settlement of the Texas Bond issue. That this legislation was passed is a testimony to Douglas' ability to put together what appeared to be impossible voting coalitions.

With that compromise widely acclaimed as the "final settlement" of the nation's problems, Douglas sought but failed to get the Democratic nomination for the presidency in 1852. It went instead to Franklin Pierce, who defeated General Winfield Scott in the general election and who is regarded in retrospect as one of the weakest American presidents. Pierce, fearing Douglas' unconcealed political ambitions, excluded him from the inner circle of presidential power, and that exclusion compounded the great despair into which Douglas was plunged following the death of his first wife in January, 1853. His wife was the former Martha Martin of North Carolina, and her short life ended from the complications of childbirth. In an effort to overcome his grief, Douglas left the United States for a tour of Europe in the spring of 1853, and when he returned for the opening of the Thirty-third Congress that fall, he was out of touch with political developments in this country.

In the preceding session of Congress, Douglas' Senate Committee on Territories had reported a bill to organize Nebraska Territory with no mention of slavery. By the time he returned from Europe, the political dynamics had changed, and the pressure mounted to organize two territories and to include a section dealing directly with the slavery question. Kansas-Nebraska lay wholly within the area acquired by the Louisiana Purchase in 1803, where slavery had been forbidden by the Missouri Compromise of 1820. Convinced that it was crucial to the national interest to get these territories organized as quickly as possible, and firmly believing that the slavery question was a phony issue, Douglas rewrote his organization bill. The new version called for two territories, Kansas and Nebraska, and included a sentence which stated that the 36°30' section of the Missouri Compromise was inoperative as it had been "superseded by the principles of the legislation" passed in 1850, which had made no reference to slavery. Such a statement was consistent with Douglas' long-standing belief in popular sovereignty, the idea that the people of a given territory should determine for themselves the institutions they would establish.

When the bill passed after months of the most hostile infighting in the United States Congress, and the president signed it into law in May, 1854, a storm of protest swept over the United States the likes of which had not been seen before and has not

been seen since. The Kansas-Nebraska Bill split the Democratic Party and occasioned the rise of the Republican Party as the vehicle for antislavery sentiment. Douglas had misjudged the growing moral concern over slavery, and the nation was aflame; the flame would not be extinguished for more than a decade of controversy and bloody war. The situation was so critical as to make impossible an effective concentration by the government on other issues deserving of attention. The man who in 1850 and 1853 wanted to avoid the slavery issue and sought to consolidate and unify the United States became an instrument of its division.

His association with the Kansas-Nebraska Bill and his consistent failure to perceive the moral nature of the slavery question would haunt the rest of Douglas' abbreviated political career. It would frustrate his efforts to secure his party's nomination for the presidency in 1856 and would cost him dearly in the momentous election in 1860 which Abraham Lincoln won. In between, in 1858, Douglas defeated the Republican Lincoln for the United States Senate from Illinois, but that was a small victory in the overall scheme of national life.

Summary

If ever a man represented the best and the worst of his times, it was Stephen A. Douglas. He was born in 1813 as the nation moved into an intensely nationalistic period; he lived through the Jacksonian period with its turbulent trends toward democracy; he died just as his beloved Union came apart in the Civil War. Douglas was devoted to the concept of democracy, but it was a democracy limited to white adult males. Given his view (widely held at the time) that blacks were inferior beings, he saw no reason to be concerned about their civil rights—they simply had none. His political career was shaped by his love for the Union and by his desire to see the United States grow and expand, for he was truly a great nationalist. He thought in terms of the West and of the nation as a whole and did not constrict himself to a North-South view.

Douglas was, perhaps, the most talented politician of his generation, but his moral blindness, while understandable, was his tragic flaw. He alone among his contemporaries might have had the capacity and the vigor to deal with sectionalism and prevent the Civil War, but his fatal flaw kept him from the presidency. Once the war broke out, Douglas threw his support to his Republican rival Abraham Lincoln and in an attempt to rally northern Democrats to the cause of Union he said, "We must fight for our country and forget our differences."

Beset by a variety of infirmities at the age of forty-eight, Douglas hovered near death in early June, 1861. On June 3, 1861, with his beloved second wife Adele by his bed, he died. His last spoken words, passed through Adele as advice for his young sons, suggest Douglas' ultimate concern as a politician: "Tell them to obey the laws and support the Constitution of the United States."

Bibliography

Capers, Gerald M. *Stephen A. Douglas: Defender of the Union*. Boston: Little Brown, 1959. As the title suggests, this volume is generally pro-Douglas and forgives his moral blindness. It is fairly brief and is well written.

Hamilton, Holman. *Prologue to Conflict: The Crisis and Compromise of 1850*. Lexington: University of Kentucky Press, 1964. A valuable work and one which was a pioneering effort in quantitative history. Hamilton uses statistics to analyze voting patterns and to clarify the way Douglas put the compromise together. The writing is excellent, as one might expect from a former newspaper man. Hamilton was the first historian to give Douglas the credit he deserved.

Huston, James L. "Democracy by Scripture versus Democracy by Process: A Reflection on Stephen A. Douglas and Popular Sovereignty." *Civil War History* 43, no. 3 (September, 1997). Discussion of the controversy between the ministers of the 1850s and Senator Douglas with respect to the definition of democracy.

Johannsen, Robert W. *The Frontier, the Union, and Stephen A. Douglas*. Urbana: University of Illinois Press, 1989.

————. *Stephen A. Douglas*. New York: Oxford University Press, 1973. This volume is the definitive work on Douglas. Johannsen is meticulous in his research, fair in his assessment, and thorough in his coverage.

Nichols, Roy Frank. *The Democratic Machine: 1850-1854*. New York: Columbia University Press, 1923. While Nichols' book is dated, it is still worth reading. The author probably knew more about the politics of the 1850's than any single individual.

Potter, David M. *The Impending Crisis: 1848-1861*. New York: Harper, 1976. This major interpretation puts Douglas' political activity in the context of his times and provides many insights into his character.

Terill, Robert E., and David Zarefsky. "Consistency and Change in the Rhetoric of Stephen A. Douglas." *The Southern Communication Journal* 62, no. 3 (Spring 1997). Examination of texts from Douglas's public career and the contradictory aspects of his personality.

Charles J. Bussey

FREDERICK DOUGLASS

Born: February, 1817?; Tuckahoe, Talbot County, Maryland

Died: February 20, 1895; Washington, D.C.

Areas of Achievement: Civil rights and social reform

Contribution: Douglass' lifelong concerns were with freedom and human rights for all people. He articulated these concerns most specifically for black Americans and women.

Early Life

Frederick Douglass was born a slave in Tuckahoe, Talbot County, Maryland, and originally was named Frederick Augustus Washington Bailey. He was of mixed African, white, and Indian ancestry, but other than that, he knew little of his family background or even his exact date of birth. Douglass believed that he was born in February, 1817, yet subsequent research indicates that he may have been born a year later in February, 1818. Douglass never knew his father or anything about him except that he was a white man, possibly his master. Douglass' mother was Harriet Bailey, the daughter of Betsey and Isaac Bailey. Frederick, his mother, and his grandparents were the property of a Captain Aaron Anthony.

In his early years, Frederick experienced many aspects of the institution of slavery. Anthony engaged in the practice of hiring out slaves, and Douglass' mother and her four sisters were among the slaves Anthony hired out to work off the plantation. Consequently, Douglass seldom saw his mother and never really knew her. The first seven years of his life were spent with his grandmother, Betsey Bailey, not because she was his grandmother but because as an elderly woman too old for field work she had been assigned the duty of caring for young children on the plantation.

The boy loved his grandmother very much, and it was extremely painful for him when, at the age of seven, he was forced by his master to move to his main residence, a twelve-mile separation from Betsey. It was there, at Anthony's main residence, that Douglass received his initiation into the realities of slavery. The years with his grandmother had been relatively carefree and filled with love. Soon, he began to witness and to experience personally the brutalities of slavery. In 1825, however, Douglass' personal situation temporarily improved when Anthony sent him to Baltimore as a companion for young Tommy Auld, a family friend. Douglass spent seven years with the Aulds as a houseboy and later as a laborer in the Baltimore shipyards. The death of Anthony caused Douglass to be transferred to the country as a field hand and to the ownership of Anthony's son-in-law. Early in 1834, his new owner hired him out to Edward Covey, a farmer who also acted as a professional slave-breaker. This began the most brutal period of Douglass' life as a slave.

After months of being whipped weekly, Douglass fought a two-hour battle with Covey that ended in a standoff, and the beatings stopped. Douglass' owner next hired him out to a milder planter, but Douglass' victory over Covey had sealed his determination to be free. In 1836, Douglass and five other slaves planned an escape but were detected. Douglass was jailed and expected to be sold out of state, but the Aulds reprieved him and brought him back to Baltimore, where he first served as an apprentice and then worked as a ship caulker. However improved Douglass' situation might be in Baltimore, it was still slavery, and he was determined to be a free man. On September 3, 1838, Douglass borrowed the legal papers and a suit of clothes of a free black sailor and boarded a train for New York.

In New York, he was joined by Anna Murray, a free black woman with whom he had fallen in love in Baltimore. Douglass and Anna were married in New York on September 15, 1838, and almost immediately moved further north to New Bedford, Massachusetts, where there were fewer slave catchers hunting fugitives such as Douglass. It was also to elude slave catchers that Douglass changed his last name. He had long abandoned his middle names of Augustus Washington; he now dropped the surname Bailey and became Frederick Douglass. The move and the name change proved to be far more than symbolic; unknown to Douglass, he was about to launch on his life's work in a direction he had never anticipated.

Life's Work

New Bedford was a shipping town, and Douglass had expected to work as a ship caulker; however, race prejudice prevented his working in the shipyards and he had to earn a living doing any manual labor available: sawing wood, shoveling coal,

sweeping chimneys, and so on. Anna worked as a domestic when she was not caring for their growing family. Anna bore Douglass five children: Rosetta, Lewis, Charles, Frederick, Jr., and Annie. Unexpectedly, the abolition movement of the 1830's, 1840's, and 1850's changed both Douglass' immediate situation and his whole future.

Within a few months of his escape to the North, Douglass chanced on a copy of William Lloyd Garrison's abolitionist newspaper, *The Liberator*. *The Liberator* so moved Douglass that, in spite of his poverty, he became a subscriber. Then, on August 9, 1841, less than three years after his escape, Douglass and Garrison met. This and subsequent meetings led to Garrison offering Douglass an annual salary of $450 to lecture for the abolitionist movement. Douglass was so convinced that he would not succeed as a lecturer that he accepted only a three-month appointment. In fact, he had begun his life's work.

Scholars have debated whether Douglass' greatest accomplishments were as an orator or a writer; both his speaking and his writing stemmed from his involvement with the abolition movement, and both were to be his primary activities for the remainder of his life.

From the beginning, Douglass was a powerful, effective orator. He had a deep, powerful voice which could hold his audiences transfixed. Moreover, Douglass was an impressive figure of a man. He had a handsome face, bronze skin, a leonine head, a muscular body, and was more than six feet in height. He stood with dignity and spoke eloquently and distinctly. Indeed, his bearing and speech caused critics to charge that Douglass had never been a slave; he did not conform to the stereotypic view of a slave's demeanor and address. Even Douglass' allies in the abolition movement urged him to act more as the public expected. Douglass refused; instead, he wrote his autobiography to prove his identity and thus began his career as a writer. *Narrative of the Life of Frederick Douglass: An American Slave* (1845) remains his most famous and widely read book. It was an instant success. Yet in the narrative, Douglass had revealed his identity as Frederick Bailey, as well as the identity of his owners, making himself more vulnerable than ever to slave catchers. Anna was legally free, and because of her their children were free also, but Douglass was legally still a slave. To avoid capture, he went to England, where he remained for two years.

In England, Douglass was immensely successful as a lecturer and returned to the United States, in 1847, with enough money to purchase his freedom. By end of the year, he was legally a free man. Also in 1847, Douglass moved to Rochester, New York, and began publication of his own newspaper, *North Star*. While editing *North Star*, Douglass continued to lecture and to write. In 1855, he published an expanded autobiography, *My Bondage and My Freedom;* he also published numerous lectures, articles, and even a short story, "The Heroic Slave" in 1853. Much later in life, he published his third, and most complete, autobiography, *Life and Times of Frederick Douglass (1881)*.

In all of his writings and speeches, Douglass' major concerns were civil rights and human freedom. As a person born in slavery, and as a black man living in a racially prejudiced society, Douglass' most immediate and direct concerns were to end slavery, racial prejudice, and discrimination. Yet he always insisted that there was little difference between one form of oppression and another. He proved the depth of his convictions in his championing of the women's rights movement at the same time he was immersed in his abolitionist activities. In fact, Douglass was the only man to participate actively in the Seneca Falls Convention which launched the women's rights movement in the United States in 1848. Moreover, his commitment was lasting; on the day of his death, in 1895, Douglass had returned only a few hours earlier from addressing a women's rights meeting in Washington, D.C.

By the 1850's, Douglass was active in politics. He also knew and counseled with John Brown and was sufficiently implicated in Brown's Harpers Ferry raid to leave the country temporarily after Brown's capture and arrest. From the beginning of the Civil War, Douglass urged President Abraham Lincoln not only to save the Union but also to use the war as the means to end slavery. Douglass also urged black men to volunteer and the president to accept them as soldiers in the Union armies. By the end of the Civil War, Douglass was the most prominent spokesman for black Americans in the country. With the end of the war and the advent of Reconstruction, Douglass' work seemed to have reached fruition. By 1875, with the passage of the Civil Rights Act of that year, not only had slavery been ended and the Constitution amended but also the laws of the land had guaranteed black Americans their freedom, their citizenship, and the same rights as all other citizens. Yet the victories were short-lived. The racism, both of North and of South, that had dominated the antebellum era triumphed again in the 1880's and 1890's. According to the Constitution, black Americans remained equal, but it was a paper equality. In fact, prejudice and discrimination became the order of the day across the whole United States.

For Douglass personally, the years following the Civil War contained a number of successes. He was financially solvent. He served in a number of governmental capacities: secretary of the Santo Domingo Commission, marshal and recorder of deeds in the District of Columbia, and United States minister to Haiti. For twenty-five years, he was a trustee on the board of Howard University. Nevertheless, these personal successes could not alleviate Douglass' bitter disappointment over the turn of public events, and he never ceased to fight. He continued to write, to lecture, and even began another newspaper, *New National Era*.

Summary

Frederick Douglass' career and his personal life were all the more remarkable when one considers the times in which he lived. His life was an example of the human will triumphing over adversity. Born into slavery, by law a piece of chattel, surrounded by poverty and illiteracy, he became one of America's greatest orators, an accomplished writer and editor, and for more than fifty years he was the most persistent and articulate voice in America speaking for civil rights, freedom, and human dignity regardless of race or sex. Douglass, more than any other individual, insisted that the ideals of the Declaration of Independence must be extended to all Americans.

Douglass' personal life reflected the principles for which he fought publicly. He always insisted that race should be irrelevant: Humanity was what mattered, not race, and not sex. In 1882, Anna Murray Douglass died after more than forty years of marriage to Frederick, and in 1884, Douglass married Helen Pitts, a white woman who had been his secretary. The marriage caused a storm of controversy and criticism from blacks, whites, and Douglass' own family. Yet for Douglass there was no issue: It was the irrelevance of race again. His own comment on the criticism was that he had married from his mother's people the first time and his father's, the second.

Douglass is most frequently thought of as a spokesman for black Americans and sometimes remembered as a champion of women's rights as well. Up to a point, this is accurate enough; Douglass was indeed a spokesman for black Americans and a champion of women's rights, because in his own lifetime these were among the most oppressed of America's people. Douglass' concern, however, was for all humanity, and his message, for all time.

Bibliography

Chesebrough, David B. *Frederick Douglass: Oratory from Slavery.* Westport, Conn.: Greenwood Press, 1998. Analysis of Douglass' oratory skills and techniques. Beginning with a biographical sketch, the author moves to Douglas's techniques and finally presents three speeches from different periods in his career.

Douglass, Frederick. *The Narrative and Selected Writings.* Edited by Michael Meyer. New York: Modern Library, 1984. In addition to being a readily accessible, complete edition of *Narrative of the Life of Frederick Douglass,* this book includes excerpts from Douglass' two later autobiographies and twenty selected writings by Douglass on various topics which are not easily obtainable.

———. *Narrative of the Life of Frederick Douglass: An American Slave.* Boston: Anti-Slavery Office, 1845; London: Somers and Isaac, 1847. The work covers Douglass' life up to 1845; it was his first book and remains the most widely read of his three autobiographies.

———. *My Bondage and My Freedom.* New York: Miller, Orton and Mulligan, 1855. This is the least read of Douglass' autobiographies.

———. *Life and Times of Frederick Douglass.* Hartford, Conn.: Park, 1881; London: Christian Age Office, 1882. The 1892 reprint is the most commonly reproduced and the most complete of the three autobiographies.

Factor, Robert L. *The Black Response to America: Men, Ideals, and Organization from Frederick Douglass to the NAACP.* Reading, Mass.: Addison-Wesley, 1970. Factor offers an interesting theoretical interpretation of Douglass as a black spokesman and informative comparison of Douglass with other black spokesmen and leaders.

Foner, Philip. *Frederick Douglass.* New York: Citadel Press, 1964. A thorough biography, unfortunately out of print, but available in libraries.

Huggins, Nathan Irvin. *Slave and Citizen: The Life of Frederick Douglass.* Boston: Little Brown, 1980. Brief and readable life of Douglass.

Lawson, Bill E., and Frank M. Kirkland. *Frederick Douglass: A Critical Reader.* Malden, Mass.: Blackwell, 1999. Essays by fifteen leading American philosophers who revisit Douglas and the place his work has in contemporary social and political thought.

Meier, August. *Negro Thought in America: 1880-1915.* Ann Arbor: University of Michigan Press, 1963. Meier offers a good account of the varieties of thought among black Americans for the period covered and suggests an intriguing, plausible thesis regarding shifts of opinion in the black community. Although the era dealt with by Meier covers only the last fifteen years of Douglass' life, it is still worth reading the book for insight into Douglass and especially for any comparison or contrast of Douglass with later black spokesmen such as Booker T. Washington and W. E. B. Du Bois.

Quarles, Benjamin. *Frederick Douglass.* Washington, D.C.: Associated Publishers, 1948. This is an easily available, thorough biography.

D. Harland Hagler

SIR ARTHUR CONAN DOYLE

Born: May 22, 1859; Edinburgh, Scotland
Died: July 7, 1930; Crowborough, Sussex, England
Area of Achievement: Literature
Contribution: Doyle created one of the first and most popular and long-lived of fictional detectives: Sherlock Holmes.

Early Life

Sir Arthur Conan Doyle was born into an artistic Catholic family and grew up in Edinburgh, Scotland, a Protestant stronghold. His grandfather and his uncle were illustrators; Richard, his uncle, gained fame drawing for *Punch*. Doyle's father, Charles, became clerk of the Board of Works in Edinburgh, but he also drew. He illustrated the first edition of his son's *A Study in Scarlet* (1887), the first tale of Sherlock Holmes. Charles suffered from mental illness and alcoholism and was institutionalized from 1879 until his death in 1893. Doyle's mother, Mary Foley, was an Irish Catholic. She reared seven children, of whom Arthur was the fourth. Ever a practical woman, she oversaw Doyle's education, sending him to Jesuit schools at Stoneyhurst and at Feldkirch, Austria, despite the family's comparative poverty. She later encouraged him to study medicine at the University of Edinburgh. They remained close until her death in 1921.

Doyle grew into a large and sturdy man, over six feet tall. Photographs show him square-headed and mustached, with a direct, self-confident gaze. A fine athlete, he was welcomed on cricket and soccer teams well into his middle years.

Having started medical study in 1877, Doyle began his writing career soon after. He published his first story, "The Mystery of Sasassa Valley," in 1879. At the university, he met two professors who became models for his most famous literary creations: Dr. Joseph Bell, the inspiration for Sherlock Holmes, and William Rutherford, the prototype for Professor Challenger of *The Lost World* (1912). Before finishing his bachelor of medicine, Doyle sought adventure, signing on as surgeon for an arctic whaling cruise in 1880. After taking his degree in 1881, he tried a second cruise, this time to Africa.

Doyle practiced medicine in Plymouth, then in Southsea, a suburb of Portsmouth, and finally in London, but he was never notably successful. Upon completing his M.D. in 1885, he married Louise Hawkins. Within the first year of their marriage, Doyle wrote two novels but failed to publish them, though he continued to publish magazine pieces.

A decisive moment in his career came in 1886, when he finished *A Study in Scarlet*, his first Sherlock Holmes adventure. The tale appeared in *Beeton's Christmas Annual*, where it attracted enough attention to warrant a separate edition in 1888.

As he entered fully into his writing career, Doyle seemed to be a man of balanced opposites: a lapsed Catholic who still respected the faith, a man of science turning to a profession in the arts, a man of reason already attracted to the Spiritualist movement, a man of physical strength and activity who also loved scholarship, a man who dreamed of producing great historical literature in the vein of Sir Walter Scott yet who was about to achieve greatness writing what he considered potboilers for a new popular magazine.

Life's Work

To an extent, Doyle captured this balance of opposites in Sherlock Holmes and Dr. Watson. In Holmes, the powers of reason are developed at the expense of the emotions. He solves crimes by keen observation, building hypotheses based on established facts, and testing those hypotheses. Watson, though quite competent, is a more ordinary man, a doctor who eventually marries and lives a prosaic life, except when with Holmes on a case. Then his life blossoms into adventure. Holmes is a creative genius, using a "scientific method" in an artistic manner to produce masterpieces of detection. Watson turns these masterpieces into what Holmes often describes as trivial romances, more entertaining than instructive.

Though Doyle proceeded to write what he considered great historical novels, some of which were quite well received, the public showed more interest in Holmes. At the request of *Lippincott's Magazine*, Doyle produced *The Sign of Four* (1890). Giving up his medical practice in 1891, he turned to writing for his living. He then wrote a series of Holmes stories for *The Strand*, beginning with "A Scandal in Bohemia." These were so popular that the editors asked for more. Before he had finished twelve—collected in *The Adventures of Sherlock Holmes* (1892)—he was tired of his characters and told his mother he intended to kill Holmes in the last one. She recommended against this course.

When *The Strand* asked for more Holmes stories in 1892, Doyle tried to put them off, as he had when they asked for the second six in 1891. Then he had asked the "ridiculous" price of fifty pounds, which *The Strand* gladly paid. This time he asked for one thousand pounds per story, and again, *The Strand* was eager. Eventually collected as *The Memoirs of Sherlock Holmes* (1894), this series ended with "The Final Problem," in which Holmes dies, falling down the Swiss Reichenbach Falls in the grip of Moriarty, "the Napoleon of crime."

Having taken Louise to Switzerland after discovering her tuberculosis, Doyle was away from London when *The Strand* readers learned of Holmes's death. Nevertheless, he heard in no uncertain terms the sorrow and anger of Holmes's fans. Still, he published no more Holmes stories until *The Hound of the Baskervilles* (1902).

Between 1892 and 1901, Doyle continued writing popular stories for *The Strand*, the best about Etienne Gerard, a comic soldier in Napoleon's army. He also made a successful reading tour of the United States, sailed up the Nile with Louise, and visited the Sudan as a war correspondent. Having been convinced that the climate of Surrey was good for tuberculosis patients, Doyle and Louise settled there in 1896. In 1897, Doyle met and fell in love with Jean Leckie, then twenty-four. With typical loyalty and honor, Doyle maintained a platonic relationship with her until after Louise's death. He married Jean in 1907. They had three children: Denis (1909), Adrian (1910), and Lena Jean (1912).

Before the outbreak of the Boer War in 1899, Doyle published story collections, novels, poetry, and drama. When the war began, he was turned down for combat because of his age, but he served under terrible conditions and without pay as a medical officer. His experiences in the war led to two books. In the second, *The War in South Africa: Its Causes and Conduct* (1902), he defended the British role in the war. For this service, he was knighted in 1902.

After running unsuccessfully for Parliament in 1900, Doyle visited Dartmoor. There, he heard legends that became the inspiration for *The Hound of the Baskervilles*. In this most famous Holmes story, Watson and Holmes solve the murder of a country gentleman and save the life of his heir, both of whom are beset by a "hell hound," supposedly the product of an ancestral curse.

While this novel was appearing in *The Strand*, William Gillette's play, *Sherlock Holmes* (1899), opened successfully in London, and the demand for more Holmes stories increased. American and British publishers offered Doyle approximately seventy-five hundred dollars per story to write more. He began a new series with "The Adventure of the Empty House," in which Holmes returns after three years of hiding from surviving members of Moriarty's gang, for he had not really fallen with Moriarty over the falls. This series was collected in *The Return of Sherlock Holmes* (1905).

Doyle continued to produce Holmes stories sporadically for the rest of his life. *The Valley of Fear* (1915) recounts an encounter with agents of Moriarty. *His Last Bow* (1917) collects stories that had appeared in *The Strand* between 1893 and 1917. *The Case-Book of Sherlock Holmes* (1927) collects stories from 1921 to 1927. Doyle's last Holmes story was "The Adventure of Schoscombe Old Place."

Though his popularity and subsequent fame have rested mainly upon the Holmes tales, Doyle was reluctant to see these as his enduring achievements. Energetic, inquisitive, and ambitious, he sought to influence public opinion in many ways. In 1906, he ran for Parliament, again unsuccessfully. After Louise's death, he took humanitarian interest in English legal reform and in Belgian policy in the Congo. He spoke out on political issues such as Irish home rule, participated in an Anglo-German auto race, traveled widely in Europe and America, and was a war correspondent during World War I.

In 1916, Doyle became convinced that he had received a spirit message and proceeded to become a leader of the Spiritualist movement. He wrote several books on Spiritualism, including *The History of Spiritualism* (1926), a study that has been praised despite the prejudices of its author. He also came to believe in fairies and wrote about them. He gave generous financial support to research into the paranormal, especially communication with the dead. His friendship with Harry Houdini came to an end because Houdini exposed so many fraudulent claims.

The best-remembered creation from the last third of his life is another character, Professor Challenger, the hero of *The Lost World* (the novel which provided the basis for the classic film, *King Kong*, 1933). Challenger is a passionate scientist, eager to explore unknown worlds. Like Holmes, Challenger eventually became a film hero as well as appearing in several successful novels and stories, but he never approached the popularity of Holmes.

Doyle fell ill with heart disease in 1929 and died in 1930 at his home, Windlesham, where he was buried.

Summary

Sir Arthur Conan Doyle's biographers all characterize him as a late Victorian type. Throughout his life, he remained confident in the soundness of his own moral vision and in the basic goodness of British morality. As a public personage, he repeatedly took the lead, both in praising British principles and in criticizing particular policies. He is credited with helping to modernize British defense between the Boer War and World War I, especially the defensive gear of common soldiers. He twice played detective himself, investigating cases of people unjustly condemned to prison. One of these, the Edalji case (1906), contributed to establishing a court of criminal appeal in 1907. Even his support of Spiritualism was a public crusade to effect the spiritual transformation of a nation he feared was in decline.

While his public services were many, including credit for introducing skiing to the Alps, Doyle will continue to be remembered mainly for the Sherlock Holmes stories. Holmes and Watson are indelible fixtures of Western culture, encountered in virtually every popular medium. These stories have influenced every important writer in the detective genre, from traditionalists such as Agatha Christie, Dorothy Sayers, and Ellery Queen, to "hard-boiled" writers such as Raymond Chandler, Ross MacDonald, and P. D. James.

Bibliography

Carr, John Dickson. *The Life of Sir Arthur Conan Doyle*. London: Murray, and New York: Harper, 1949. Written with the help of Adrian Doyle, this biography draws on primary sources unavailable to subsequent biographers but avoids some problematic sides of his life.

Cox, Don Richard. *Arthur Conan Doyle*. New York: Ungar, 1985. Cox describes and discusses virtually all of Doyle's writing, with chapters on historical fiction, Sherlock Holmes, other genres, and the nonfiction. A portrait of Doyle as revealed in his writing.

Edwards, Owen Dudley. *The Quest for Sherlock Holmes*. Totowa, N.J.: Barnes and Noble, 1983; London: Penguin, 1984. Concentrating on the years before *A Study in Scarlet*, Edwards uses records from Edinburgh and Doyle's schools to examine parental and educational influences.

Higham, Charles. *The Adventures of Conan Doyle*. London: Macmillan, and New York: Norton, 1976. Combining biography and a critical review of Doyle's fiction, Higham consults uncollected materials such as Doyle's letters to the London *Times*. Gives special attention to the relationship between Doyle, Louise, and Jean Leckie.

Huntington, Tom. "The Man Who Believed in Fairies: For Sir Arthur Conan Doyle, Creator of Sherlock Holmes, the Proof was in the Pictures." *Smithsonian* 28, no. 6 (September, 1997). Discussion of Doyle's belief in communication with the dead, perceptions of others, and how his reputation was affected by his support of the famous Cottingley fairy photographs.

Kestner, Joseph A. *Sherlock's Men: Masculinity, Conan Doyle and Cultural History*. Aldershot, Hampshire, and Brookfield, Vt.: Ashgate, 1997. Overview of the male stereotype in Doyle's Sherlock Holmes stories, the way models of masculinity are documented therein, and how popular fiction influences cultural paradigms.

Nordon, Pierre. *Conan Doyle: A Biography.* Translated by Frances Partridge. New York: Holt Rinehart, 1966. This objective and scholarly biography focuses on relationships between Doyle's public life and his writing, with special attention to his interest in Spiritualism.

Shreffler, Philip A., ed. *The Baker Street Reader.* Westport, Conn.: Greenwood Press, 1984. A collection of critical material on Doyle's detective stories, this book helpfully places Doyle's work in the traditions of detective fiction and explores the reasons for its popularity.

Terry Heller

JAMES BUCHANAN DUKE

Born: December 23, 1856; Durham, North Carolina
Died: October 10, 1925; New York, New York
Area of Achievement: Business
Contribution: From modest beginnings, Duke organized and built up the largest conglomerate of tobacco companies in the nation, comprising the American Tobacco Company and its subsidiaries; he also founded power and textile companies and established the Duke Endowment in support of Duke University as well as other educational and charitable institutions.

Early Life

James Buchanan Duke was born on December 23, 1856, in a six-room farmhouse near Durham, North Carolina. He was the youngest in the family: There were two half brothers from his father's first marriage, and a brother and a sister had also preceded James. In 1858, his mother, Artelia Roney Duke, died from typhoid fever, which also claimed his older half brother. His father, Washington Duke, owned about three hundred acres of land, on which he grew corn, wheat, oats, and some tobacco. During the Civil War, he served for two years with the Confederate artillery; in 1865, Union soldiers looted his farm and left behind little but leaf tobacco. Immediately thereafter, however, demand for tobacco mounted, and prices rose; between 1866 and 1872, the Duke family's production increased from 15,000 to 125,000 pounds. James took part in the planting and preparation of their crop. His early education took place in local schools. Evidently he learned quickly, but preferred mathematics to the humanities. In 1872, he enrolled in the New Garden Academy, near Greensboro, North Carolina; quite abruptly, he gave up his courses there and left for the Eastman Business College in Poughkeepsie, New York, where he studied bookkeeping and accounting.

By 1874, Washington Duke felt sufficiently confident in the industry's future that he sold his farm and bought a tobacco factory in downtown Durham. Although he originally intended to go into business on his own, James Duke accepted with alacrity his father's offer that made him, and his brother Benjamin Duke, one-third partners in the new concern. Leaving correspondence and other official functions to the others, James Buchanan Duke kept their financial records and devised nu-

merous means by which to economize on the operations of their tobacco firm.

Somewhat daunting in bearing if not precisely handsome, as he entered manhood Duke gave an impression of strength and energy. He was six feet, two inches tall and powerfully built; his features were distinguished by a broad brow, a straight, thick nose, and piercing blue eyes. His lank red hair, parted at the side, showed a tendency to thinness in his later photographs. He spoke in a gentle drawl; often among others he would remain silent for protracted periods, and then hold forth at some length on matters of concern to him.

Life's Work

Although the Dukes seemed overwhelmed by their competitors, notably the massive Durham Bull Company in their native city, they began to advertise on local billboards. They also began to promote cigarettes, which hitherto had not sold well but were peculiarly suited to the bright tobacco leaf that was grown in abundance across parts of North Carolina and Virginia. They launched promotional campaigns in many states; they obtained permission from a touring French actress to use her picture in the company's cigarette advertisements. The Dukes also readily adopted another innovation: In 1884, they had the newly invented Bonsack cigarette-rolling machine installed in their plant. While it was sometimes inclined to clog during use, this device could produce more than two hundred cigarettes a minute, or about fifty times as many as an expert artisan working by hand.

Sensing that a national market might exist for the company's cigarettes, in 1884 Duke moved to a small apartment in New York City and opened an office there. After two years, this branch was also turning a profit, in part because of Duke's meticulous familiarity with all aspects of the tobacco trade, and in part as a result of his flamboyant innovations in advertising. The company offered complimentary cigarette packs to immigrants coming into New York harbor; it sponsored sporting events; it issued coupons, enclosed in its cigarette cartons, which could be redeemed for cash. Billboards, posters, and advertisements in newspapers and magazines promoted the various brands the company offered. By 1889, of some 2.1 billion cigarettes produced in the United States, about 940 million had come from the factories of W. Duke and Sons. Its sales were well over $4 million, of which $400,000 was profit.

After prolonged and tortuous negotiations, Duke persuaded the presidents of four other leading tobacco concerns to form the American Tobacco Company; to win over his erstwhile rivals, Duke obtained a contract with the Bonsack company restricting sales of their rolling machines to the new trust. As president, Duke expanded upon his promotional methods: New coupon schemes were devised, and pictures of attractive women in tights were issued in packs of some of the company's brands. Moreover, the trust's vast resources allowed it to absorb smaller concerns, many of which were bought up outright or controlled through subsidiaries or holding companies. Duke also turned on the few powerful corporations that had remained independent. The Durham Bull Company was taken over, and the trust acquired a controlling interest in the Liggett and Myers Company and the R. J. Reynolds Company. By 1900, the American Tobacco Company accounted for 92.7 percent of American cigarette production and 59.2 percent of the nation's output of pipe tobacco. By 1901, James B. Duke added the American Cigar Company to this business empire, and became its president; with this stroke, one-sixth of the country's cigar trade came under his control.

With annual sales of about $125 million, the American Tobacco Company was in a position to determine prices and wages as it saw fit. During the Spanish-American War of 1898, Congress had imposed a surtax on tobacco, and repealed it three years later; Duke's trust held their cigarette prices at the previous levels and kept the balance as profits. Competitive bidding for tobacco was curtailed; prices to farmers were held as low as three cents per pound, spawning organized violent outbreaks by "night riders" operating in Kentucky and Tennessee. Foreign markets were also exploited. The trust acquired subsidiaries in Australia and New Zealand; in 1895, it obtained several Canadian firms. In 1901, a two-thirds interest was obtained in one of the leading German cigarette dealers. It also opened offices in Japan and built factories in China to accommodate the demand for its products. Seeking to reduce competition in international markets, in 1902 the American Tobacco Company reached agreement with representatives of the Imperial Tobacco Company, which delimited the areas where each company could do business. The

British-American Tobacco Company was formed, with assets of about thirty million dollars and an established network in the British Empire; Duke became its president.

In the course of his work, Duke had occasionally seen Mrs. Lillian McCredy, a divorced woman with a dubious reputation. In 1904, after some years of intermittent and rather surreptitious courtship, they were married in a small private ceremony. It was a troubled and tempestuous union; after ten months, Duke claimed that his wife had been unfaithful and sued for divorce. In a sensational trial, he offered the evidence of company detectives and intercepted messages from his wife's paramour. In 1906, the court found in Duke's favor. He was later introduced to Mrs. Nanaline Holt Inman, the widow of a cotton merchant from Atlanta. Duke was captivated by her expressive, classical features. She responded to his attentions, and in 1907 they were married in a small church in Brooklyn. Their daughter and only child, Doris, was born in 1912; during his later years, Duke displayed a pronounced fondness for her.

Shortly before his second marriage, Duke was confronted with the most serious challenge of his business career. The American Tobacco Company, which was estimated to control eighty percent of all tobacco production in the United States, was brought to court in antitrust litigation by the Department of Justice. In 1908, Duke himself was required to testify. A federal court found that the American Tobacco Company had indeed operated in restraint of trade. The Supreme Court upheld this ruling, and in 1911 the defendants were ordered to dissolve the trust. Accordingly, snuff and cigar companies were cut loose. R. J. Reynolds and Liggett and Myers were severed from the American Tobacco Company, which after reorganization held perhaps two-fifths of its previous assets.

Already Duke had diversified his business interests, and after the antitrust suits he turned with redoubled attention to concerns in his native region. In 1905 he had provided support for hydroelectric works along the Catawba River, which flows through the western portions of North and South Carolina. Between 1907 and 1925, eleven plants were built for the Southern Power Company, which in 1924 was rechristened the Duke Power Company. In short order, Duke also came to own textile mills that used the electricity his plants supplied. Against the advice of others in the business, Duke also underwrote the construction of a hydroelectric complex along the Saguenay River in Upper Quebec, and in time this venture became profitable.

Over the years, the Duke family contributed in increasing amounts to Trinity College, a small Methodist institution in North Carolina; in 1892 a subvention from Washington Duke supported work on a campus in Durham. James Buchanan Duke, though possessing only a limited formal education, increasingly had come to believe that institutions of higher learning held out the best hopes for widespread social progress. In 1918, he became one of Trinity's trustees. In collaboration with the college's president, William P. Few, plans were devised for a series of gothic buildings, including a magnificent chapel and tower. Duke personally supervised the selection of the local stone that was used; he took great interest in plans for a new medical center. In all, Duke contributed nineteen million dollars to the college, of which eight million dollars were offered when Few agreed to change its name to Duke University. (There is no substance to stories that previously Duke had made similar, unsuccessful, offers to Princeton, Yale, or other universities.) During the year before he died, Duke composed a will establishing the Duke endowment, which in all comprised about eighty million dollars in securities and at that time was the largest permanent foundation of its sort in the nation. In addition to providing continuing support for Duke University, it also left substantial sums for other colleges, hospitals, orphanages, and Methodist churches in North Carolina. Much of the remainder of his estate was left to Duke's wife Nanaline and their daughter Doris. Duke himself suffered from pernicious anemia; after his health declined for several months he died, rather suddenly, on October 10, 1925, at his home in New York. Ultimately, he was buried in the chapel of the university to which he had given his name.

Summary

Duke was an accomplished businessman; it was said that for years he would work twelve hours a day in his office, and then visit tobacco stores to learn more about the retail trade. He was able to capitalize upon three major developments: He realized early the potential popularity of cigarettes; he utilized advertising nearly to the limit of its effectiveness; in an age in which manifold business combinations became possible, he proved to be a shrewd, hard-bitten bargainer able to form and direct massive industrial organizations to his own advantage. Even when antitrust proceedings compelled its reorganization, Duke was able to retain control of more parts of his original company than his opponents had thought possible. His persistent exploitation of the opportunities that existed in his day, in the tobacco industry and in power and textiles, indicated the combination of business sense and ruthlessness which accompanied his rise. His philanthropic endeavors, which have left lasting monuments to the Duke family fortune in his native state, were inspired by his own notions of social betterment. Although he owned several magnificent houses, and in his later years enjoyed the pleasures his wealth could buy, Duke seemed intent on achieving recognition that, as he expressed it to the university's president, would last for a thousand years. Driven by personal imperatives to achieve business supremacy, and then to provide philanthropic support for an institution and an endowment bearing his name, Duke left an enduring legacy which attests the curious and complementary duality of his ambitions.

Bibliography

Cunningham, Bill. *On Bended Knees: The Night Rider Story.* Nashville, Tenn.: McClanahan, 1983. Vivid though awkwardly written history of the armed bands that arose to resist farmers' collaboration with the American Tobacco Company. Despite its somewhat melodramatic tone, this work reflects extensive research.

Durden, Robert F. *The Dukes of Durham: 1865-1929.* Durham, N.C.: Duke University Press, 1975. Sound scholarly study which uses a number of manuscript collections at Duke University. Avoiding extremes of adulation or debunking, this work considers both the business activities and the philanthropic concerns of the family; particular attention is paid to their support for educational institutions.

Jenkins, John Wilber. *James B. Duke: Master Builder.* New York: Doran, 1927. Admiring biography which ascribes Duke's success to business acumen and hard work; his marketing innovations are credited, but relatively little is said about the personal or corporate conflicts that affected his life and work. The last chapters provide a sympathetic overview of his philanthropic activities.

Kroll, Harry Harrison. *Riders in the Night.* Philadelphia: University of Pennsylvania Press, 1965. Although brisk and informal, this work on conflict in the tobacco-growing regions of Kentucky and Tennessee is well informed and steeped in local color. While evoking the plight of the farmers, the author does not explicitly take sides in the confrontations he discusses.

Porter, Earl W. *Trinity and Duke, 1892-1924: Foundations of Duke University.* Durham, N.C.: Duke University Press, 1964. The most complete work on the creation of Duke University, this study traces its formative years as Trinity College and considers the involvement of educators and administrators in securing support from the Duke family.

Tilley, Nannie May. *The Bright-Tobacco Industry: 1860-1929.* Chapel Hill: University of North Carolina Press, 1948. Massive treatment of the subject which is important for the general context of Duke's business activities. Both the technical and the economic aspects of tobacco marketing during this period are discussed in great detail.

Winkler, John K. *Tobacco Tycoon: The Story of James Buchanan Duke.* New York: Random House, 1942. Detailed biography which is somewhat derogatory in tone, and which relies heavily upon earlier works, such as that of Jenkins. Provocative in its treatment of the more scandalous periods of Duke's life, such as his divorce and his reaction to antitrust litigation.

J. R. Broadus

ALEXANDRE DUMAS, *père*

Born: July 24, 1802; Villers-Cotterêts, France
Died: December 5, 1870; Puys, France
Areas of Achievement: Literature, theater, and drama
Contribution: Dumas was a major playwright who helped to revolutionize French drama and theater. He was one of the best historical novelists, publishing more than two hundred novels.

Early Life

Alexandre Dumas is usually designated *père* to distinguish him from his father and son of the same name. The son, known as *fils*, was also an important writer of drama and of fiction. Dumas' father was an impoverished, disillusioned general in Napoleon's Egyptian campaign. His prowess and exploits were models for the character Porthos and for many incidents in Dumas' works.

Dumas was born in the village of Villers-Cotterêts on July 24, 1802. His boyhood was spent there and in neighboring villages (Soissons and Crépy, for example). Early influences were his father, poachers with whom he lived and hunted in the nearby forest, and the sight of Napoleon I en route to and from Waterloo. An early visit to Paris brought him into contact with his father's friends, all field marshals under Napoleon. Dumas' early learning was limited to reading and penmanship, later enhanced only slightly by attendance at Abbé Grégoire's village day school. Literary influences were a production of William Shakespeare's *Hamlet* and reading the works of Friedrich Schiller, Johann Wolfgang von Goethe, Sir Walter Scott, and Lord Byron. At the age of fifteen, he was a clerk in a solicitor's office. At the age of eighteen, he met and collaborated on three vaudevilles with Adolphe de Leuven, a young Swedish aristocrat, who awakened him to drama. At this time he became a clerk to M. Lefèvre at Crépy.

In late 1822, following Leuven's return to Paris to attempt to stage the plays, Dumas and a fellow clerk went to Paris alternating walking and riding the clerk's horse, poaching game en route to barter for lodgings. At Paris, Dumas saw the Théâtre Française, met the famous actor François-Joseph Talma, attended a play, and received a touch on the forehead for luck; Leuven had been instrumental in arranging the meeting. Returning home, Dumas quit his job, pooled his assets, and re-embarked for Paris, this time in a coach.

Life's Work

After a series of successes and failures, Dumas became a major writer in several genres. His literary reputation rests primarily on his novels, his plays, his memoirs, and his many travel books, in which he recorded his experiences in as well as his impressions of Italy, Spain, Switzerland, Russia, Germany, the south of France, and Egypt.

From 1823 to 1844, although he published some fiction and other works, Dumas was primarily a playwright. His early success resulted partly from the acquaintances he made and partly from good luck. His first job at Paris was as a copyist for the Duke of Orléans, the future King Louis-Philippe, in whose palace was housed an important theater, the Comédie-Française. On attending the Théâtre Française, Dumas met the famous writer-theater critic Charles Nodier. Leading actresses often found Dumas attractive, and some were among his mistresses; Talma and other leading actors became his lifelong friends. Political figures, including the Marquess de Lafayette and Giuseppe Garibaldi, were his close associates and his commanders in two wars.

He found his dramatic calling with *Christine* (1830). Seeing a bas-relief depicting an assassination ordered by Queen Christina of Sweden, he studied the incident in a borrowed book. Collaborating with Leuven (the first of many collaborators for Dumas), he wrote the five-act verse drama in 1829. Through Nodier's influence, the play was accepted for staging, though such was delayed until the following year. Another historical drama, *Henri III et sa cour* (1829; *Catherine of Cleves*, 1831) was produced first. This work is historically significant because Dumas for the first time applied the methods of Sir Walter Scott to drama. A third important serious drama, *Antony*, was to appear in 1831 (English translation, 1904).

When the Revolution of 1830 began, Dumas began his career as a soldier, following duty and his current mistress to Villers-Cotterêts and Soissons and leading insurgents to victory at his birthplace. At Soissons, he and two students stormed and took an arsenal, recovering powder kegs in the face of a garrison. Disillusioned that his commander and friend Lafayette allowed Louis-Philippe to be chosen king and spurning minor posts offered him, he resigned from the new king's employ. The next year, his first child was born by Belle Krebsamer, another mistress.

Events of interest during 1832 and 1833 included a dispute over billing for *La Tour de Nesle*, which was a rewriting by Dumas of an inferior play by Frédéric Gaillardet, the latter being given first billing, and M. Three Stars (Dumas) second; after the latter was given top billing, Gaillardet went to court and also challenged Dumas to a duel. About the same time, Dumas inadvertently discovered the cure for cholera when he mistakenly took undiluted ether. During Mardi Gras, Dumas gave an extended dinner party to which important artists, writers, actors, and actresses were invited. Drawing on his boyhood acquaintances, the poachers, and bartering the excess of game for other provisions, Dumas did the cooking and fed more than one hundred guests.

Dumas returned to the theater to stage *Antony* and his most popular serious drama, *La Tour de Nesle* (1832; English translation, 1906). In 1841, he turned to comedy, staging two of his three best that year, *Mademoiselle de Belle-lsle* (1839; *Gabrielle de Belle Isle*, 1842) and *Un Mariage sous Louis XV* (1841; *A Marriage of Convenience*, 1899). The third was staged in 1843; later, in 1855, it was selected as a command performance by Queen Victoria upon hers and Prince Albert's visit to Paris.

Though Dumas had published fiction earlier and drama later, the real shift to fiction came in 1842, with the publication of his first great historical novel, *Le Chevalier d'Harmental* (1842; English translation, 1856). The following years saw the publication of his most popular, though not regarded as his best, novels, *Les Trois Mousquetaires* (1844; *The Three Musketeers*, 1846), *Le Comte de Monte-Cristo* (1844-1845; *The Count of Monte-Cristo*, 1846), and *La Tulipe Noire* (1850; *The Black Tulip*, 1851).

Dumas' recognized best novels are not always as well known. *Le Vicomte de Bragelonne* (1848-1850; English translation, 1857), perhaps the most popular of these, is the sequel to *Vingt Ans après* (1845; *Twenty Years After*, 1846) and *The Three Musketeers*, forming with them a trilogy. As noted in the publishing dates, Dumas, like Charles Dickens, often issued his novels in serial form in journals. The following are also among his best works in this genre of historical fiction, *Les Quarante-cinq* (1848; *The Forty-five Guardsmen*, 1847), *Ange Pitou* (1853; *Taking the Bastille*, 1847), *Black* (1860; *Black: The Story of a Dog*, 1895), and *Conscience l'Innocent* (1852; *Conscience*, 1905).

In January of 1860, Dumas met Garibaldi and traveled with a letter from him. Dumas purchased a schooner, *The Emma*, sailing the Mediterranean with friends. Eventually, he joined Garibaldi's campaign with the same spectacular success he and his father had previously enjoyed in Egypt and France. In freeing Naples from the Bourbons, he avenged his father of the imprisonment and torture he had suffered at their hands. In Palermo, Dumas was popular as a writer and a hero until the political climate changed: Garibaldi, like Napoleon and Lafayette before him, swerved from complete dedication to republicanism. After supporting and later criticizing Garibaldi publicly, Dumas returned to Paris.

Having been regarded as the most important playwright and now the most famous novelist in France, the aging Dumas found his luck failing him. Having made a fortune and having wasted it through his lavish lifestyle and his unbridled generosity, he worked furiously trying to save his palatial estate and his tarnished reputation. As his method had always been to work with collaborators who supplied ideas and minor works, or who provided details and basic plots, to which Dumas gave his touch of literary genius, he was now faced with accusations and even suits charging him with plagiarism. Posterity has vindicated Dumas, since none of his collaborators has achieved anything of note unaided by him. His prolific productions came to be expanded by his need for money: He published novels in serials; he wrote accounts of his many travels (regarded as among the best travel literature); and he wrote and published *Mes Mémoires* (1852; *My Memoirs*, 1907-1909), sharing numerous details of his own experiences and observations as well as information about the people he had known, who numbered among them the most famous of his day. Eventually, after further travel, he lingered and died in bed at his son's estate in Puys.

Summary

In writing about Alexandre Dumas, *père*, one is overwhelmed not only by the amount that he wrote (estimates run from seven hundred to more than one thousand volumes) but also by the great volume of information, often of much interest, about the man, his family, and his famous acquaintances. He, like his characters, was lavish, demonstrative, flamboyant, wealthy, and generous, as well as quarrelsome and forgiving. A quadroon, he was descended from paternal grandparents of the lower aristocracy and of West Indian black ancestry. His physical appearance changed from slender and military to portly with a large overhanging belly. He had fuzzy hair, thick lips, and blue eyes. His tastes in clothing were extravagant. After being rebuked for presenting his mistress Ida Ferrier to the king, he was boxed into an unwanted marriage, which, as was his wont, he graciously accepted. He would have publicly acknowledged all three of his illegitimate children, but the mother of his younger daughter refused to permit this. His friend Victor Hugo lacked his fame but surpassed him in poetic ability. The two share credit for revolutionizing the theater of France.

Bibliography

Bell, A. Craig. *Alexandre Dumas: A Biography and a Study.* London: Cassell, 1950; Folcroft, Pa.: Folcroft Library Editions, 1979. Attempts to vindicate the genius of Dumas in the light of hostile critics, flippant biographers, and neglectful literary historians. Lists authentic and spurious works and provides an index.

Castelar, Emilio. "Alexandre Dumas." In *The Life of Lord Byron, and Other Sketches.* Translated by Mrs. Arthur Arnold. London: Tinsley, 1875; New York: Harper, 1876. A chapter of rhythmic prose on Dumas in a collection composed of a lengthy life of Lord Byron and brief treatments of Dumas, Hugo, and three lesser-known writers.

Dumas, Alexandre. *An Autobiography-Anthology Including the Best of Dumas.* Edited by Guy Endore. New York: Doubleday, 1962. As the title suggests, included are excerpts from Dumas' own works, from *My Memoirs*, travel books, prose fiction, and others, interspersed with introductory comments by the editor, providing a running commentary on the life, writing career, and particular works.

——. *The Road to Monte Cristo: A Condensation from the Memoirs of Alexandre Dumas.* Translated by Jules Eckert Goodman. New York: Scribner, 1956. Goodman finds in the more than three thousand pages of the six volumes of the memoirs two types of material: much matter of lesser importance, since Dumas was paid by the line in his later years, and, interspersed among this matter, much that makes up an exciting and intriguing autobiography of Dumas for thirty years.

Foote-Greenwell, Victoria. "The Life and Resurrection of Alexandre Dumas." *Smithsonian* 27, no. 4 (July, 1996). Discusses Dumas' life and the problems he experienced as the grandson of a Haitian slave.

Grenier, Cynthia. "Dumas, the Prodigious: A Profile of Alexandre Dumas." *World and I* 13, no. 6 (June, 1998). Profile of Dumas, his techniques, and his novels' renderings of French history.

Maurois, André. *Alexandre Dumas: A Great Life in Brief.* Translated by Jack Palmer White. London: Hutchinson, 1955; New York: Knopf, 1964. For the first reader of the life of Dumas, provides the basic facts in readable and limited fashion. Maurois is one of the recognized authorities on Dumas.

——. *The Titans: A Three-Generation Biography of the Dumas.* Translated by Gerard Hopkins. New York: Harper, 1957. Emphasis in the first of ten parts is devoted to Dumas and his young son. Parts 2 through 6 focus on Dumas, *père*, 7 and 8 on *père* and *fils*, 9 and 10 on *fils*. The same work was published in England under the title *Three Musketeers*.

George W. Van Devender

JEAN-HENRI DUNANT

Born: May 8, 1828; Geneva, Switzerland
Died: October, 30, 1910; Heiden, Switzerland
Area of Achievement: Social reform
Contribution: Dunant is considered both the father of the International Red Cross and the co-founder of the World's Young Men's Christian Association.

Early Life

The eldest of five children, Jean-Henri Dunant was born in Geneva, Switzerland, at a time when there was great concern for a variety of humanitarian issues. His father, Jean-Jacques Dunant, was a prominent businessman who held a position in the Office of Guardianships and Trusteeships, where he was charged with the welfare of prisoners and their families. His mother, Antoinette Colladon, nurtured his religious convictions and liberal humanitarian concerns. Dunant's interest in social issues was fostered early. At the age of six, an encounter with chained convicts so moved him that he vowed someday to help them. At thirteen, he was admitted to Geneva College.

At eighteen, Dunant became active in the League of Alms, a Christian organization whose members sought to aid Geneva's underprivileged, ill, and imprisoned, and he soon assumed a leadership role. In 1855, Dunant proposed international guidelines for a federation of young men's Christian associations.

During that same period (1853-1859), Dunant was trying to earn his living in the banking profession. In the course of his work, he was sent to Algeria to manage the bank's interests, and there he succeeded in convincing many wealthy and influential Genevans and French to invest in the mills at Mons-Djémila. He sought additional land and water concessions from the French government but was unable to gain his ends. Undaunted, in the spring of 1859 Dunant set out to bring his ideas for Algeria to the French emperor Napoleon III, who was then on a campaign in Italy. Dunant followed the advancing French troops through northern Italy. Although he never met the emperor, his trip would set in motion a series of events that would forever change the way conflicts would be waged.

Life's Work

On June 24, 1859, in pursuit of the emperor, Dunant arrived in the town of Castiglione. All that day, only a few miles to the west, 150,000 French and Allied forces and 170,000 Austrian troops were waging one of the bloodiest conflicts of the nineteenth century, the Battle of Solferino.

Although it is not clear whether Dunant ever saw the fighting, he did see the casualties, estimated at forty thousand. He was so moved by the carnage and suffering that he spent the next eight days treating the wounded, seeking doctors, and procuring necessary medical supplies and food for the wounded of both sides. To the hundreds of wounded Dunant helped, the slender, handsome, dark-haired man in white became their symbol of hope. These eight days would serve as the focus for the remainder of Dunant's life.

Returning to Geneva, Dunant continued his business ventures but remained haunted by Solferino. In November, 1862, Dunant published *Un Souvenir de Solferino* (*A Memory of Solferino*, 1939), describing the plight of the wounded and proposing an organization of trained volunteers to aid them. Copies of the book were sent to influential people across Europe. Response to his book was pro-

found. Gustave Moynier, a Geneva lawyer, recommended that a special committee be organized to promote Dunant's plans on an international scale. That permanent international committee consisted of Dunant, Moynier, Guillaume-Henri Dufour, Louis Appia, and Theodore Maunoir. The committee proposed an international conference to be convened in Geneva on October 26. During the summer of 1863, Dunant traveled throughout Europe, artfully convincing government after government to send representatives to the Geneva meeting. This conference was followed in August, 1864, by a second, officially sponsored by the Swiss government. The product of this second conference was an international treaty, the first of the Geneva Conventions, which served as the foundation for the International Red Cross and set guidelines for the treatment and status of the wounded during wars.

Dunant's role in the conference was insignificant. His strengths were in his ideas and in dealing with people on an individual basis. Some sources suggest that Dunant did not even attend the meetings of the second conference, but such accounts appear unfounded. As the conference came to a close, Dunant had to turn his attention to his own financial problems. Since his visit to Solferino, he had not paid enough attention to his Algerian investments.

Dunant's only hope for his ailing Mons-Djémila ventures was to get concessions from the French government. Yet even a meeting with the emperor in 1865 proved futile. In 1867, a rapid chain of events would lead Dunant to bankruptcy. In the early 1860's, Geneva had been hailing Dunant as one of its greatest sons, but after 1867, as the Calvinistic principles of the time dictated for the crime of bankruptcy, Genevans turned their backs on Dunant. Under these same rigid principles, he could never return to Geneva. In addition, under extreme pressure from Moynier, from whom he had become alienated, on August 25, 1867, Dunant was forced to resign from the international committee.

The period 1867-1887 was one of steady decline for Dunant, as he became an exile wandering about Europe. There were times when he was able to afford neither housing nor regular meals, and he slept on park benches or in train stations. Yet he continued to work for a variety of causes, including a Jewish homeland in Palestine, a world library, and a broadening of the Geneva Conventions to include guidelines for conducting warfare at sea and for treatment of prisoners of war.

As his means for survival slowly ebbed and a variety of health problems sapped his vitality, his brother Pierre brought him home to Switzerland. For the last twenty-four years of his life, the small village of Heiden would be Dunant's home. Extreme bitterness and an intense paranoia made even the closest relationships difficult for Dunant.

In 1895, Dunant allowed a young Swiss journalist to interview him. Largely because of these published interviews, the world became aware that the founder of the Red Cross was still alive. Although virtually forgotten for nearly thirty years, he now received honors. The culmination of these occurred in 1901, when Dunant, along with Frédéric Passy, was awarded the first Nobel Prize in Peace. Dunant died on October 30, 1910. In accordance with the conditions of his exile, Dunant's ashes were buried in an unmarked grave in Zurich.

Summary

The life of Jean-Henri Dunant is one of profound irony. On one hand, he was an idealistic humanitarian, who changed the conduct of warfare forever and who must be credited with the saving of millions of lives. The International Red Cross, the Geneva Conventions, and the Young Men's Christian Association stand as monuments to his great vision. On the other, he was a tragic victim of his own weaknesses. He experienced the tributes of royalty and the pain of extreme poverty.

Nevertheless, Dunant was consistent in the belief that he could make a difference in the world. In 1906 and 1926, the Geneva Conventions were expanded to cover the victims of naval warfare and prisoners of war, respectively, causes that Dunant had championed since the late 1860's. For his many accomplishments, it is only fitting that each year the world celebrates May 8, his birthday, as World Red Cross Day.

Bibliography

Deming, Richard. *Heroes of the International Red Cross*. New York: Meredith Press, 1969. Chapter 1 provides a condensed biography of Dunant that emphasizes his role as father of the Red Cross.

Dunant, Jean-Henri. *A Memory of Solferino*. Washington, D.C.: American National Red Cross, 1959. A short, moving description of the Battle of Solferino, Dunant's role in the aftermath, and the genesis of the principles that would ultimately inspire formation of the International Red Cross.

Gagnebin, Bernard, and Marc Gazay. *Encounter with Henry Dunant*. Translated by Bernard C. Swift. Geneva: Georg Geneva, 1963. A short, readable account of Dunant's life, supplemented by photographs, paintings, maps, and photocopies of published and unpublished manuscripts.

Kübler, Arnold. "Dunant." In *The International Red Cross Committee in Geneva, 1863-1943*. Zurich: Corzett and Huber, 1943. A short account of the unique circumstance that led Dunant to found the Red Cross, focusing on his efforts during and after Solferino.

Libby, Violet Kelway. *Henry Dunant: Prophet of Peace*. New York: Pageant Press, 1964. A longer biography that focuses on how the evolution of the religious and business climate within Dunant's Geneva both provided an ideal atmosphere to foster his humanitarian concerns and severely punished him for his business failings. Includes a short list of other sources.

Peachment, Brian. *The Red Cross Story: The Life of Henry Dunant*. Oxford: Religious Education Press, and Elmsford, N.Y.: Pergamon Press, 1977. A brief account of Dunant's life, intended for the younger reader.

Rich, Josephine. *Jean Henri Dunant: Founder of the International Red Cross*. New York: Julian Messner, 1956. A biography that focuses particularly on Dunant's relationships with his family. Also emphasizes Henri's lifelong concern with social causes.

Rothkopf, Carol Z. *Jean Henri Dunant: Father of the Red Cross*. New York: Watts, 1969; London: Watts, 1971. Follows Dunant's life but focuses on how the principles behind the Red Cross are deeply rooted in history. Provides a modest secondary bibliography.

Ronald D. Tyler

PAUL LAURENCE DUNBAR

Born: June 27, 1872; Dayton, Ohio
Died: February 9, 1906; Dayton, Ohio
Area of Achievement: Literature
Contribution: Dunbar's writing is recognized as providing the most authentic representations of African American life in the United States during the late nineteenth and early twentieth centuries.

Early Life

Paul Laurence Dunbar's parents, Joshua and Matilda Murphy Dunbar, were slaves until the early or mid-1860's. Matilda had been married to another slave, Willis Murphy, with whom she had two sons, both born in slavery. Willis, who joined the Union army and was never heard from again, sent his wife and sons to Dayton, Ohio, where they remained, presuming Willis was dead.

Matilda, ever eager to learn, attended night school. She soon became literate and mastered enough mathematics to keep her own accounts. In 1871, Matilda married Joshua Dunbar, who was twenty years her senior. In the following year, their first child, Paul Laurence Dunbar, was born.

Joshua never tired of telling his young son about his exploits, about how he clandestinely learned to read and write when slaves were punished, sometimes even killed, for trying to achieve literacy. Joshua recounted to his fascinated son details about his escape from slavery with the help of abolitionists via the Underground Railroad and his subsequent enlistment in the Fifty-fifth Division of the Union army, where he achieved the rank of sergeant. The tales Joshua wove eventually found their way into Dunbar's writing, which his mother had encouraged from Dunbar's earliest days. When Joshua and Matilda's second child, Elizabeth, died before her first birthday, Matilda focused all her attention and centered all of her hopes upon Paul.

Meanwhile, Joshua, unable to find work despite being literate and having a spotless military record, began to drink, causing dissension in the household. To relieve tension, Matilda spun tales about plantation life, which helped create a basis for much of Dunbar's later writing. Matilda finally divorced Joshua, after which Joshua spent his remaining years in the Soldier's Retirement Home in Dayton, where Dunbar often visited him.

Dunbar, who was the only African American in his high school graduating class, was class president and class poet. While still in high school,

Dunbar published poetry in the *Dayton Herald* and worked as an editor for the *Dayton Tattler*. One of his fellow students was Orville Wright, who, along with his brother Wilbur, constructed and flew the first airplane. Dunbar and Orville remained good friends throughout their lifetimes.

Too poor to attend college, Dunbar discovered that Dayton offered few desirable jobs to African Americans at that time. He finally took a job as an elevator operator, which gave him time to write. He produced a number of stories and poems during this period, some of them written in the black-dialect style that first drew national attention to his writing.

Dunbar was invited to address the Western Association of Writers at its 1892 convention in Dayton. This initial appearance was arranged by Helen Truesdell, one of Dunbar's high school English teachers. At this meeting, Dunbar met James Newton Matthews, who wrote a letter praising Dunbar's writing. This letter was published in an Illinois newspaper and was subsequently reprinted in newspapers throughout the United States, bringing Dunbar considerable celebrity. James Whitcomb Riley read Matthews' letter and wrote an admiring letter to Dunbar. It was the encouragement the young poet received from Matthews and Riley that led him to collect his poems into the volume *Oak and Ivy* (1893). Printed at Dunbar's own expense, the poet quickly repaid the $125 printing costs by selling copies of the collection to people who rode his elevator.

Life's Work

The publication of *Oak and Ivy* changed the course of Dunbar's life. The collection contained many poems in standard English, which had been drilled into the young Dunbar by his mother. His "Ode to Ethiopia" remains among his most influential poems, recording as it does the accomplishments of African Americans and entreating them to have pride in their race. "Sympathy" focused on the dismal status of black people in American society. The poems that caught the attention of the white community, however, were the collection's dialect poems that presented vivid portraits of plantation life and ruminated on the feelings of both free and enslaved black people. Many members of the black community resented Dunbar's dialect poems, arguing that they presented black people as uneducated, illiterate buffoons much like the exaggerated black characters presented by the minstrels of that day. On the other hand, white readers, some of them prominent in literary circles, applauded the dialect poems while dismissing Dunbar's poems in standard English as derivative and ordinary.

The publication of *Oak and Ivy* brought Dunbar to the attention of a prosperous Toledo attorney, Charles A. Thatcher, who was sufficiently impressed by Dunbar's writing that he offered to pay the poet's expenses if he wished to attend Harvard University. Bent on promoting his career as a writer, however, Dunbar rejected Thatcher's generous offer. Thatcher, nevertheless, did what he could to advance Dunbar's career, as did Thatcher's friend, Toledo psychiatrist Henry A. Tobey, who helped Dunbar through many difficult periods by lending him money and promoting his books.

Thatcher and Tobey encouraged Dunbar to publish a second volume of verse, *Majors and Minors* (1895). The book was divided into two sections: "Majors," or poems in standard English, and "Minors," or dialect poems. The publication of this volume drew considerable praise from William Dean Howells, probably the most prominent man of letters in the United States at that time. Although Howells' criticism of Dunbar's poems in standard English was somewhat dismissive, he heaped praise upon the dialect poems, calling Dunbar "the first man of his color to study his race objectively." The authenticity that Howells found in the dialect poems stemmed directly from Dunbar's early exposure to the tales his father and mother spun for him as he was growing up.

The publication of *Majors and Minors* marked the emergence of Dunbar as a nationally significant literary figure. Through Thatcher and Tobey, he was accepted as a client by Major James B. Pond, a New York City literary agent who represented such illustrious authors as Mark Twain, Henry Ward Beecher, and Frederick Douglass, whom Dunbar had met in 1893 and to whom he was close until Douglass' death in 1895. Pond persuaded Dunbar to leave Dayton and move to New York, which Paul did in the summer of 1896. Pond arranged numerous engagements for Dunbar to speak and to read his poetry. More important, however, he introduced him to publishers who were eager to offer him contracts.

Finally, Dodd, Mead offered the poet a four-hundred-dollar advance against royalties (an astronomical advance for a poet to receive at that time) and a generous royalty arrangement. The book for which Dodd, Mead contracted, *Lyrics of Lowly Life* (1896), which essentially drew poems from his two earlier volumes, was a resounding success among white readers and clearly established Dunbar as the leading black poet of his day. The success of this book led to a six-month reading tour of England.

Dunbar realized that the move to New York had been wise. Meanwhile, he began a correspondence with Alice Ruth Moore, a writer and teacher with whom he had fallen in love. Alice's parents discouraged her from marrying a writer whose income was uncertain at best. In 1897, however, Dunbar received a clerkship at the Library of Congress, affording him the means to marry Alice. The two moved to Washington, D.C., where Dunbar published his first collection of short stories, *Folks from Dixie* (1898), whose incisive insights into racial prejudice were well received by liberal white audiences.

Critics dismissed Dunbar's first novel, *The Uncalled* (1898), based on Nathaniel Hawthorne's *The Scarlet Letter* (1850), as trite and unconvincing. The book received little popular acceptance. The following year, however, a new collection of his poems, *Lyrics of the Hearthside* (1899), redeemed his literary reputation.

Long plagued by lung and respiratory problems made worse by Washington's climate and by the dust from the books he constantly handled at the Library of Congress, Dunbar was forced to quit his job in 1898. He immediately undertook another lecture tour, but within a few months his health had deteriorated so badly that he had to move first to New York's Catskill Mountains and then to Colorado for long periods of rest.

In *The Strength of Gideon and Other Stories* (1900), which presented disturbing vignettes about black people during the days of slavery and emancipation that followed, Dunbar wrote passionately but without his usual humor about racial injustice. His next novel, *The Love of Landry* (1900), dealt with white characters and was generally unconvincing. His next novel, *The Fanatics* (1901), also focused on white characters and presented its minor black characters as caricatures. It was dismissed as an inconsequential work. Despite these setbacks, Dunbar was sufficiently esteemed to be an honored guest at the inauguration of President William McKinley in 1901.

Dunbar's last novel, *The Sport of Gods* (1902), was a strident protest novel focusing on a black servant falsely accused of theft who was vindicated only after serving time in prison and seeing his family disintegrate. It was followed by three more collections of poetry, bringing the total number of volumes of verse he produced in his lifetime to fourteen. Racked by illness, Dunbar controlled his pain by drinking. When Alice left him in 1902, Dunbar returned to Dayton, where he continued to write and from which he still made occasional speaking trips. His lungs destroyed by tuberculosis, he died in Dayton on February 9, 1906.

Summary

Paul Laurence Dunbar brought views of plantation life, slavery, and racial inequality to a white reading public and became an influential voice in the struggle of black citizens to obtain their rightful place in American society. Dunbar also established black dialect as a reputable and legitimate literary vehicle, even though many black readers in his day, including his own wife, considered it demeaning and much preferred the work he produced in standard English.

Bibliography

McKissack, Patricia C. *Paul Laurence Dunbar: A Poet to Remember.* Chicago: Children's Press, 1984. Directed toward an adolescent audience, this book provides an accurate and engaging overview of Dunbar's life and writing.

Martin, Jay, ed. *A Singer in the Dawn: Reinterpretations of Paul Laurence Dunbar.* New York: Dodd, Mead, 1972. Valuable contributions by scholars who participated in the Centenary Conference on Paul Laurence Dunbar at the University of California, Irvine, in 1972. Balanced and intellectually sound.

Redding, J. Saunders. *To Make a Poet Black.* Chapel Hill: University of North Carolina Press, 1939. This critical assessment by a major black author demonstrates the black bias against Dunbar's dialectal writing and the preference for his writing in standard English.

Revell, Peter. *Paul Laurence Dunbar.* Boston: Twayne, 1979. Following the usual format of Twayne's United States Authors Series, Revell presents a readable and accurate account of the author, his work, and his critical reception.

Wiggins, Lida Keck. *The Life and Works of Paul Laurence Dunbar.* New York: Dodd Mead, 1907. This profusely illustrated volume contains Dunbar's complete poetry and his best stories and anecdotes. It also includes William Dean Howells' introduction to *Lyrics of Lowly Life* and Wiggins' complete biography of the writer.

R. Baird Shuman

ELEUTHÈRE IRÉNÉE DU PONT

Born: June 24, 1771; Paris, France
Died: October 31, 1834; Philadelphia, Pennsylvania
Area of Achievement: Business
Contribution: Combining sharp business acumen with innovative technical methods and tenacious moral principles, Du Pont founded E. I. Du Pont de Nemours and Company, which became a powerful American empire.

Early Life

Eleuthère Irénée Du Pont was born on June 24, 1771, in Paris, France. He was named in honor of liberty and peace (after the Greek words for these ideals) at the insistence of his godfather, Turgot, who was also his father's benefactor. His father, Pierre Samuel Du Pont, served the corrupt French throne for many years and was rewarded with nobility. His mother, Nicole Charlotte Marie Le Dée, died when Irénée was fourteen years old. He also had an older brother, Victor, to whom he was very close. Irénée grew up at the family estate at Bois-des-Fosses, about sixty miles south of Paris.

Irénée spent all of his young life in the harsh and oppressive political atmosphere of France during the epochs of Louis XVI, of the revolutionary mobs whose favorite instrument was the guillotine, and finally of Napoleon Bonaparte. After the death of his mother, Irénée's life became closely interwoven with that of his politically active father. In 1788, when Irénée was seventeen years old, the popular rebellion took place. As the nation's ideology was more and more identified with the political Left, Pierre remained on the Right. He and the Marquis de Lafayette, with whom he shared the title of commander of the National Guard, founded the Société de 1789, an organization composed of the most conservative wing of the bourgeoisie, which favored a constitutional monarchy. Pierre and Irénée began to attack the Jacobins, the radical party of the petite bourgeoisie, from their newly acquired publishing house in Paris. On August 10, 1792, they led their sixty-man private guard to defend the king's palace from a Jacobinian assault that was demanding an end to the monarchy. During this period, at the age of twenty, Irénée married Sophie Madeleine Dalmas, with whom he had seven children during the course of their marriage.

After the uprising, Irénée served as apprentice to the chemist Antoine Lavoisier, the greatest scientist of his day and a close friend of his father. Lavoisier was the head of the French monarch's gunpowder mills, and it was there that Irénée learned the craft of gunpowder-making and acquired a precise sense of the scientific method. The revolution struck, however, and the king and Lavoisier were guillotined per the orders of Robespierre. Pierre was arrested shortly thereafter and would have also been guillotined had not the bourgeoisie, now convinced that their revolution was irreversible, asserted their control over the revolution by seizing power from the radicals. Robespierre was executed and Pierre was granted his freedom.

At this point, Irénée was making a precarious living operating the publishing house. The print shop, which was the main source of his income, had once been wrecked by the mob during a political uproar and there was no guarantee that the same thing might not happen again. His newspaper, *Le Républicain,* carried a revolutionary theme. Pierre's new newspaper, *L'Historien,* was a vehicle for reviving royalism and opposing Napoleon's appointment as commander-in-chief of the French forces in Italy. The bourgeoisie, however, struck and backed Napoleon's coup. Pierre and Irénée were imprisoned. With the help of a friend who was a member of the commission that prepared lists for deportation, Pierre regained their freedom under a plea of senility, but he had to pledge to leave France.

So it was that the Du Pont family set sail aboard the *American Eagle* and arrived on the shores of Newport, Rhode Island, on December 31, 1800. It was in the United States that Irénée's individuality, creativity, innovative spirit, and strong character began to emerge. His physical appearance—he was small in size, with a cleft chin, a long sharp nose, and weak lips—belied the strength and courage he later displayed as he built his empire. His ability to restrain his emotions and his instinctive caution in befriending anyone who was not family also contributed to the building and solidifying of his dynasty in years to come.

Life's Work

Du Pont found in the United States a political climate that was very different from that of France. Insistence on freedom had led to the Declaration of Independence and the American Revolution. The American economy encouraged initiative, and the door of advancement was open to all.

Gunpowder was a much-needed commodity on the American frontier. It was needed for protection from Indians and wild animals, to shoot game for meat and skins, and to help clear land to build new homes and roads. American powder makers during the Revolution had made some acceptable powder, although ninety percent had been bought from France. By 1800, explosions and British competition had put most of the domestic mills out of business.

Shortly after his arrival in the United States, Du Pont went to purchase some gunpowder for hunting. His expert eye recognized its poor quality and its inability to meet the urgent needs of the American frontier. This discovery sparked his ingenuity and his dream was born. On July 19, 1802, at the age of thirty-one, he purchased land on the Brandywine Creek near Wilmington, Delaware, on the site of what had been the first cotton mill in America. He had originally planned to call his plant Lavoisier Mills out of respect for his mentor. He reconsidered, however, and decided to name it Eleutherian Mills, in honor of freedom, as a happy portent to political refugees. In the spring of 1804, the first Du Pont gunpowder went on public sale.

Du Pont spent thirty-two years on the Brandywine Creek as president of E. I. Du Pont de Nemours and Company. Throughout these years, the shortage of liquid capital was a constant problem for him. Although his original investors had pledged funds to build and run the mills, they did not give the amount promised, and he was forced to raise the difference through notes. When the mills began to show a profit, the stockholders demanded the earnings in dividends instead of reinvesting a portion to increase production and sales as he wanted to do. Du Pont had the business acumen of a twentieth century entrepreneur, while his investors were stagnating in eighteenth century procedures. His way out of the impasse was to purchase their stock. They demanded exorbitant prices, so he signed more notes to meet them. In this way, he assured himself that only he and other family members would control the company, and by the time of his death, most of these notes had been paid off.

During his tenure with the company, Du Pont established the technical, methodological, and ethical principles to which the company still adheres. With regard to the technical and methodological aspects, Du Pont addressed the need to give careful attention to raw material preparation. Charcoal was made from willow trees because they always grew new branches and had an inexhaustible supply. Saltpeter was always thoroughly cleaned regardless of its state of cleanliness when it was received. Sulphur was always pure and clear in color. Du Pont also had the foresight to install a labor-saving device for kerneling powder. In times of prosperity as well as in times of adversity, Du Pont always sought out means to improve the quality of his product and improve his methods. This was the forerunner of the product and process improvement approach of modern industry. He even anticipated the modern principle of enlarging a company's income and usefulness through diversification. Du Pont provided one of the earliest examples of industrial integration by growing grain for the horses which transported the gunpowder in fields adjacent to the mills.

Du Pont was a man who abided by an exemplary code of ethics. The most salient example of this manifested itself during the tragedy which befell his mills in March, 1818. Explosions ruined much of the plant and killed forty men. At that time, there were no laws which committed the company to compensate the families of the victims, but Du Pont pensioned the widows, gave them homes, and took responsibility for the education and medical care of the children. He paid these costs and those of rebuilding the plant by renewing his notes and signing more. Another example of Du Pont's strong social and moral consciousness involved his principle that quality was a matter of pride, with which no compromise could be made. He constantly refused offers to manufacture inferior powder for shipping. He was once approached by the government of one of the states, which was irritated at a new federal tariff law and had threatened to resist its reinforcement by force of arms. Du Pont replied that he had no powder for such a purpose.

Du Pont's unyielding adherence to these principles brought him rewarding results. In 1804, during the first year of production, he made 44,907 pounds of gunpowder, which sold for $15,116.75. In 1805, both amounts had tripled. In 1808, an additional mill and new facilities accounted for the annual production of 300,000 pounds. In 1810, the profits exceeded thirty thousand dollars. In 1811, with a profit of forty-five thousand dollars, the Du Pont mills were the largest in the Western Hemisphere. The War of 1812 brought government orders totaling 750,000 pounds of gunpowder. Although this would appear to be a profitable assignment, the business realities proved to be the contrary. The company had to risk its cash and borrow heavily to extend the capacity of the mills. Du Pont purchased an adjoining property called the Hagley Estate, erected additional facilities, renamed it the Hagley Yards, and thereby completed the first major expansion in the company's history. By the time of his death on October 31, 1834, the output of corps of workmen, with constantly improving machinery and equipment, exceeded one million pounds. The Brandywine mills had become a major American enterprise.

Summary

Du Pont created much more than a family business; he bred a tradition which still endures. This tradition espoused his code of business honor which was inseparable from his code of personal honor. His guiding principle was that privilege was inextricably bound to duty, and this principle ruled his entire life. He had a sense of obligation to his customers which was a rarity in the business world of his time. He staked personal fortunes on many occasions in order to fulfill a pledge. His commitment to technological innovations and increased productivity never undermined his commitment to top-quality products. His foresight and ingenuity antedated his century in technological and moral consciousness. These precepts, which originated from the Brandywine mills, still guide the Du Pont Company. The Du Pont family empire is a global one which has expanded to include real estate, arms and defense industries, computers, communications, media, utilities, oil, food industries, banks, aviation, chemicals, rubber, insurance, and many other businesses.

When Du Pont came to the United States in 1800, he was a strange man in a strange country. Yet he recognized that the United States was a land of opportunity, and the Du Pont Company grew because the fledgling nation's needs, and free traditions, encouraged progress. America grew because people such as Du Pont contributed the seeds of growth that bloom in risk, courage, and innovation. He may have been forced to come to the United States, but he died as Delaware's most valuable citizen.

Generations of men and women contributed to the development of the Du Pont Company from a single gunpowder mill to a company which is international in scope and significance. The original Du Pont mills have been replaced by more modern and efficient buildings and procedures, but it is the spirit of Du Pont which remains and reigns: His code of business honor and his code of personal integrity, of privilege and duty, still pervade his business empire.

Bibliography

Dorian, Max. *The Du Ponts: From Gunpowder to Nylon*. Boston: Little Brown, 1961. Concentrates on the Du Pont genealogy and the way in which each family member contributed to the building of the empire. Stresses the role of Pierre Du Pont, his service to Louis XVI, his title of nobility, and the political connections which enabled him to migrate to America.

Dujarric de la Rivière, René. *E. I. Du Pont de Nemours: Élève de Lavoisier*. Paris: Librairie des Champs-Élysées, 1954. Focuses on the period of Du Pont's life during which he served as apprentice to Lavoisier, who taught him the craft of gunpowder-making. This expertise served him well in the United States, where he established the first gunpowder mill, which later evolved into the Du Pont dynasty.

Du Pont de Nemours, E. I., and Co. *Du Pont: The Autobiography of an American Enterprise*. Wilmington, Del.: Du Pont, 1952. The best book on Du Pont's life and ingenuity. Also explores the century and a half that followed the first gunpowder mill on the Brandywine in terms of the parallel development of the Du Pont Company and the United States.

Du Pont de Nemours, Pierre Samuel. *Irénée Bonfils*. Wilmington, Del.: Du Pont, 1947. Discusses the religious beliefs of the Du Pont family, which were somewhat redefined after the death of Du Pont's mother, who was a Catholic. The tone is one of tolerance toward other religions and a strong appeal is made for a united church.

Winkler, John K. *The Du Pont Dynasty*. New York: Reynal and Hitchcock, 1935. Explores the Du Pont family history from their early days in France to their early days in Delaware. It also details the advancements and expansion of the company from its inception.

Zilg, Gerard Colby. *Du Pont: Behind the Nylon Curtain*. Englewood Cliffs, N.J.: Prentice-Hall, 1974. Chronicles the life of the Du Pont family from France, their migration to America, the success of Du Pont's first gunpowder mill, and the expansion of the Du Pont dynasty.

Anne Laura Mattrella

FIRST EARL OF DURHAM
John George Lambton

Born: April 12, 1792; London, England

Died: July 28, 1840; Isle of Wight, England

Areas of Achievement: Politics and government

Contribution: Known as "Radical Jack" for his advanced ideas of parliamentary reform and later appointed Governor-General of Canada, Lord Durham wrote his famous *Report on the Affairs of British North America* in 1839. Because the report insisted upon British-style responsible government for the colony, it has been regarded as the charter document for the British Commonwealth of Nations.

Early Life

Though John George Lambton's father, William, died when the child was but five years old, he bequeathed to his son lively intelligence, fierce family pride, and dedication to liberal causes. At his guardian's insistence, John was not sent away to school in his youth but received private tutoring in math and science and later received his conventional education in Greek and Latin at Eton. Lambton was not a distinguished scholar and stubbornly resisted his guardian's plans for a university education, preferring instead a commission in the Tenth Hussars, a prestigious cavalry regiment. Equally headstrong in romance, Lambton eloped with Henrietta Cholmondeley in 1812. Finally declared "of age," he settled with his wife at Lambton Hall in Durham County and was elected to the House of Commons in 1813.

In the Commons, Lambton aligned himself with his father's old faction, the liberal wing of the Whig Party. As a new M.P., Lambton spoke occasionally for his causes and against the conservative Tory government. Just as he had begun to attract attention, he was struck by a personal tragedy which would become a recurrent nightmare. His young wife lay dead of tuberculosis—a disease that would later claim their three daughters and, eventually, Lambton himself. His health had been and remained precarious following any intellectual or physical exertion. His portraits reveal a handsome man, with dark curls and fine features. His was not a robust beauty, but he possessed enough aristocratic bearing to enforce his presence anywhere.

Lambton considered quitting public life at his wife's death, but his friend Henry Brougham (with whom he would eventually quarrel) persuaded him to resume his seat in the Commons. Marriage to Lady Louisa Grey on December 9, 1816, brought him more than great personal happiness; the marriage brought him into the inner councils of the Whig Party led by his father-in-law, Earl Grey. Grey saw stern integrity behind the young man's petulance and violent temper. As a result of his father-in-law's patronage and forbearance, Lambton was included in the Whig governments of the 1830's.

Life's Work

While his party was in opposition, Lambton's restless energy flitted from the development of the Davy's safety lantern for his coal miners to educational reform. He inspired acrimonious debate in Parliament and the press when he espoused two highly controversial issues of the decade: parliamentary and colonial reform. In 1821, Lambton introduced legislation to reapportion the seats in the House of Commons and extend the franchise. As a

bill without official support, it stood no real chance of passing, but the Tories used political trickery to ensure an especially humiliating defeat. His vindictive outburst when he learned of his bill's fate earned for Lambton further opprobrium. The press referred to him deprecatingly as "Radical Jack," "King Jog," "The Dictator," and "Robert le Diable."

Outside the Commons, Lambton gave his name and blessing to the New Zealand Company. Organized by Edward Gibbon Wakefield, it advocated and sponsored emigration. Colonies were not a popular cause in the 1820's; the loss of America was too fresh for men to appreciate new possibilities for the Empire. Most ambitious politicians would have shunned this as a dead issue and Wakefield, a former convict, as an "improper gentleman." Lambton courageously, if eccentrically, publicly approved of his ideas.

Though King William IV thoroughly despised Lambton and his causes, he created Lambton a Peer of the Realm, Lord Durham, in 1827. His peerage recognized generations of Lambton service to the state, but the Tory press speculated that Baron Durham (as he was then known) had been bribed away from his ideals. In the 1820's and 1830's, the press frequently suggested that Lambton would head a third political party comprising radicals, democrats, and popular demagogues. Those who knew him well, however, never doubted his loyalty to Earl Grey and to the Whig Party.

In 1830, the long Tory domination of government was broken, and Earl Grey became prime minister. He appointed Durham Lord Privy Seal and asked his son-in-law to head a committee to draw up a bill for parliamentary reform. No minutes were kept by the committee, so it is impossible to determine each man's contribution, but the bill they created was much like Durham's 1821 failure. The Whig bill proposed to abolish representation of "rotten" and "pocket" boroughs, shift their numbers to the new cities created by the Industrial Revolution, and extend the franchise to every male householder occupying premises worth ten pounds per annum. Though essentially moderate, the bill stirred passionate resistance by those who wished no change in the old, easily managed political system. It drew equally passionate support from those who wished to see the old oligarchical system dead. After a protracted struggle characterized by Tory intransigence, royal wavering, and Grey's resignation and return to power, the bill passed both houses and received the royal assent in

1832. Known as the Great Reform Bill, it did not bring mob rule to England as its critics feared but did allow the upper-middle classes the vote. Durham would not live to see the other reform bills of 1867 and 1884 which enfranchised most adult males, but his democratic spirit permeated them.

After a distinguished term as ambassador to the court at St. Petersburg (1835-1837), Durham returned home to honors and a great challenge. In 1838, Queen Victoria selected Durham to become a Knight of the Order of the Bath. He scarcely had time to savor his recognition before the new Whig prime minister, Lord Melbourne, requested his service. On March 31, 1838, Durham was commissioned Governor-General of Canada and Lord High Commissioner, delegated to study the causes of recent rebellions there. When Durham and his staff, including Wakefield, Charles Buller, and Thomas Turton, arrived in Canada, they discovered the coals of rebellion still smoldering. Despite the fact that Canada was divided into Lower Canada (largely French) and Upper Canada (largely British), the causes of rebellion in both provinces were the same. Rebels in both provinces resented the fact that legislation passed by their elected assemblies could be ignored or defeated by appointed councils. Government, therefore, was by oligarchy, not by popular will.

Durham's first official act was the Ordinance of July 28, 1838, which freed all but several leaders of the rebels; these eight leaders were exiled to the British colony of Bermuda. The ordinance was welcomed as a generous solution which quickened Canadian hopes for a fair resolution of their grievances. Durham and his staff then set about the laborious process of interviewing disgruntled citizens and studying past policies. In the midst of these efforts, Durham learned that the home government had disallowed his ordinance on technical grounds. His former friend Henry Brougham and others had been undermining his mission since his departure, criticizing its expense, his inclusion of Wakefield and Turton, both of whom had scandalous pasts, and his failure to communicate properly with the Colonial Office. Durham resigned his post, announcing his betrayal to the Canadian press. For this, the London *Times* titled him "Lord High Seditioner," and he returned to England in November under a cloud of suspicion and misunderstanding.

In January, 1839, Durham presented the Melbourne government with his *Report on the Affairs of British North America*. The "Durham Report," as it was popularly known, created a stir in Parliament and the press. Its most salient feature was an eloquent plea for the continuation of Great Britain's connection with Canada but within a new context. According to Durham, Great Britain could build this connection and avoid future rebellions only by granting responsible government to a single executive and legislature in a united Canada. Responsible government meant to Durham that in matters of domestic policy the executive would rule at the pleasure of a majority in the legislature which supported its program. In external or foreign affairs, the British Parliament would remain supreme. By uniting the two Canadas, Durham believed that the French population would become Anglicized, thereby producing racial harmony. Responsible government was the heart of the Durham Report, though it contains numerous appendices addressing other specific problems. The British government accepted the suggestion of union and passed a bill to that effect in the spring of 1840. Durham lived to see the bill passed but not long enough to see the evolution of responsible government. He died of tuberculosis on July 28, 1840.

Summary

Lord Durham was a man whose vision of change continuously outdistanced his contemporaries. While he maintained a respect for tradition, he recognized that only those traditions which retained their integrity deserved to survive. He believed deeply that parliamentary government was stable enough to endure change and flexible enough to serve maturing nations. He was a statesman who hated oligarchical control of peoples even though he was born to oligarchic status.

Durham's greatest contribution to English history rested in his *Report on the Affairs of British North America*. Though some of his analyses were wrong (the French-Canadian identity would not be extinguished, and the line between internal and external affairs of a colony was vague), Durham's insistence upon responsible government meant that Canada would have self-government in the same form as it existed in England. It would be Durham's son-in-law, Lord Elgin, who would, as Governor-General of Canada in 1848, first exercise the duties of a responsible executive. When Canada refined her constitution in the British North America Act of 1867, it would insist upon two principles—loyalty to the British Crown and responsible government. Canada led the way for what became the journey of dozens of nations from colony to self-governing dominion. Though Durham's vision may not have stretched that far into the future, his ideas have been the charter for the British Commonwealth of Nations.

Bibliography

Canadian Historical Review 20 (June, 1939). This entire issue is devoted to articles which commemorate the centenary of the report. The volume provides an excellent summary of the scholarship and interpretations of Durham's contribution to the idea of "dominion status."

Cooper, Leonard. *Radical Jack: The Life of John George Lambton*. London: Cresset Press, 1959. A popular biography filled with colorful anecdotes, but largely derivative from Chester New and Stuart Reid. Adds no new insight into the enigma of Durham's personality.

Durham, John George Lambton. *The Durham Report*. Edited by Sir Reginald Coupland. Oxford: Clarendon Press, 1945. The first abridgment with the intent to acquaint post-World War II generations about to embark on a new phase of Commonwealth with Durham's ideas. Excellent brief introduction elucidating the report's main features.

————. *Lord Durham's Report on the Affairs of British North America*. Edited by Sir Charles Lucas. 3 vols. Oxford: Clarendon Press, 1912; New York: Kelley, 1970. The finest, most complete edition of the report. Volume 1 contains some interpretive differences from the later standard biography by Chester New, volume 2 is a complete text of the report, and volume 3 provides a complete set of appendices.

New, Chester. *Lord Durham: A Biography of John George Lambton, First Earl of Durham*. Oxford: Clarendon Press, 1929. The standard scholarly biography, with an extensive bibliography of all pertinent works to date. New writes elegant prose and presents a balanced look at Durham's career—neither tipped toward hero worship and overemphasis of his accomplishments, nor hesitant to insist upon a restored appreciation for Durham's work.

Reid, Stuart J., ed. *Life and Letters of the First Earl of Durham, 1792-1840*. 2 vols. London and New York: Longmans, 1906. Reacting to other scholars' tendency to ignore Durham because his contemporaries underrated him, Reid makes the most extended case for his inclusion as a major figure in early nineteenth century affairs. Reid tends to be a bit breathlessly enthusiastic and slips into a moralizing tone on occasion, but his work succeeds in its purpose.

Rose, J. Holland, A. P. Newton, and E. A. Benians, eds. *The Cambridge History of the British Empire*. Cambridge: Cambridge University Press, and New York: Macmillan, 1929. This venerable series is useful for anyone who has need of a survey that goes beyond the superficial. Durham and his report are well covered in volume 2.

Kathryne S. McDorman

ANTONÍN DVOŘÁK

Born: September 8, 1841; Nelahozeves, Bohemia
Died: May 1, 1904; Prague, Bohemia
Area of Achievement: Music
Contribution: Dvořák was one of the most notable European composers of the nineteenth century. He became one of the chief creators of the Czech national style of music and also had a profound influence on the development of American music.

Early Life

Born into the family of a butcher-innkeeper in the small Bohemian village of Nelahozeves, Antonín Leopold Dvořák did not seem destined to a musical career. As was the case with other young men at that time, Antonín was expected to carry on the family business, which his father had inherited from his own father. In spite of these expectations, Antonín began to play the violin with his father, who performed with the village orchestra at various rustic festivals and ceremonies. The young Dvořák soon proved more capable than his father at the bow, and his musical promise attracted the notice of the local schoolmaster, a musician named Josef Spitz.

From Spitz, Dvořák learned the elements of the violin. In 1853, Dvořák was sent to his maternal uncle's house in Zlonice to continue his studies. There, under the tutelage of Antonín Liehmann, Dvořák gained familiarity with the viola, organ, and figured bass. Liehmann tutored the boy in modulation as well as extemporization, which he called "brambuliring." It was with Liehmann that Dvořák first came into contact with the German language, which, as Bohemia was then part of the Austrian Empire, was an important prerequisite to further study. In order to perfect his German, he was sent to live with a German family in the nearby village of České Kamenice.

In České Kamenice, Dvořák continued his musical progress under the choirmaster at St. Jakub's Church, for whom he frequently substituted at the organ. Liehmann's suggestion that the boy continue his musical studies at Prague was received unfavorably by Dvořák's father, who asserted that there was no money to finance such an undertaking. At Liehmann's insistence, however, Dvořák's childless uncle agreed to pay for the boy's schooling at the Organ Conservatory in Prague, which Dvořák entered in 1857. Dvořák's musical talents rapidly

developed at the conservatory under the guidance of such men as Josef Leopold Zvonař (voice), Josef Bohuslav Foerster (organ), and František Blažek (theory). Many of these men laid the initial foundations for the national style of Czech music.

During his days as a student, Dvořák found an extracurricular outlet for his creativity in the orchestra of the musical society Cecilia, in which he played viola. He participated in the weekly rehearsals of the society, which was at that time under the direction of Antonín Apt, an ardent admirer of Robert Schumann and Richard Wagner.

Life's Work

Dvořák's musical career began at the end of the Romantic era in Bohemia. After the cultural renaissance of the Czech nation, the *národní obrození*, during which time poets such as Jan Kollár, František Čelakovský, and, above all, Karel Hynek Mácha carved out a wide area of cultural autonomy for the Czech nation, it became common for poets, musicians, and artists to find inspiration for their

work in national hagiography and legend. In the 1860's, however, the vivid élan of Romanticism was slowing into the less revolutionary, nostalgic era of the Biedermeier. It is helpful to keep this literary distinction between Romantic and Biedermeier in mind when one speaks of the music of Dvořák. For, like the poet Karel Jaromir Erben, Dvořák, in this early period of his career, composed works suffused with languor and a certain *fin d'époque* melancholy. In addition to two symphonies which date from this period—the *Bells of Zlonice* in C minor and the Second Symphony in B flat major—the composer set Moravian poet Gustav Pfleger's "Cypress Trees" to music as a song cycle.

When the Czech National Opera opened in 1862, the members of the Cecilia society's orchestra formed its backbone. The contemporary atmosphere inspired Dvořák to compose his first venture for the musical stage: *Alfred* (1938), based on the lyric epic poem by Vítězslav Hálek. This work, however, was never produced onstage. Its overture was published in 1912—eight years after the composer's death—and is noted for its technical finesse.

Much of Dvořák's work predating 1870 was destroyed by the composer himself. In 1872, he took a curious journey back to the period of literary Romanticism in Bohemia. It was in this year that he set to music a few songs from the Ossian-like "Old Czech" forgeries of Václav Hanka—the *Rukopis královédvorský* and *Rukopis zelenohorský*. Like the literary works themselves, Dvořák's adaptations of the *Rukopisy* achieved some measure of fame beyond the borders of Bohemia. In 1879, they were published in German and English translation.

In 1873, Dvořák turned to a mode of composition which was to reward him with much musical success—the composition of quartets. One of the most beautiful of these works—written in this year of Dvořák's marriage to his former student Anna Čermáková—is the String Quartet in F minor, Op. 9. A growing sense of self-confidence, spawned perhaps by conjugal satisfaction, inspired Dvořák to resign from the National Opera and take a post in St. Vojtěch's Church. Then came the Symphony in D minor, Op. 13, which, however, was to lie dormant for a full twenty years.

The lure of the opera continued to be strong, and the year 1874 brought the composer's return to the operatic stage with the adapted puppet show *King and Collier*. The work was an immediate success, and Dvořák was hailed as a promising representa-tive of a revivified Slavic music. Dvořák followed this event with another quartet, this time in A minor. The composer's career began to take off in earnest after these successes. In 1875, he was awarded a generous stipend from the Austrian government for his musical achievements; on the award's selection committee was Johannes Brahms, later to become Dvořák's lifelong friend. More chamber pieces and another collection of folk songs (the *Moravian Duets*) followed, as did the Symphony in F, Op. 24, which was to add greatly to the composer's renown abroad.

Personal tragedy struck the composer at the zenith of this fecund period. In 1876, while Dvořák was at work on another opera (*Wanda*, based on an ancient Polish legend), his daughter became sick and died. This painful occurrence inspired the composer to create one of his greatest musical works, the *Stabat mater*. This work made Dvořák's name famous in Great Britain, where he conducted the work himself to rave reviews in 1884.

Dvořák's steady, conquering march on the musical world was continued with his *Slavonic Dances*. Curiously enough, critics initally looked upon these works with coolness, as they were commissioned by the German music publishing firm of Simrock. Yet time has proven the great value of these sterling compositions, and the critics were soon silenced by voices such as Hans Richter's, who praised Dvořák's "God-given talent" after hearing the earlier *Symphonic Variations for Orchestra* (1877).

Dvořák consolidated his leading position among composers of the Czech national school during these years with the composition of various pieces of music deeply imbued with patriotic feeling. Such works are the *Hussite Overture* (1883), which contains as a theme the famous Hussite hymn "Ktož jste Boží bojovníci" ("You Who Art the Warriors of God"), and the tone poem suite *Ze Šumavy (From the Bohemian Forest)*. Of special interest to the adept of comparative arts is Dvořák's chorale adaptation of Erben's Bürgeresque ballad *Svatební košile (The Spectre's Bride)*.

About this time, Dvořák's fame began to burgeon in the Anglo-Saxon countries. In England, for example, his *Stabat mater* was hailed as "one of the finest works of our times" by a musical critic, when it was performed for the eight hundredth anniversary of Worcester Cathedral under the baton of the composer himself. For the next few years, Dvořák was to divide his time between the British

Isles and his native Bohemia, where he had just acquired a peaceful, rustic cottage as a quiet retreat for composition. His Symphony in G, Op. 88, although dedicated to the Imperial Bohemian Academy for the Fine Arts, has become known as the "English Symphony," as it was published uncharacteristically in London. His popularity in England is attested by the Birmingham Festival's invitation to set John Henry Newman's *Dream of Gerontius* to music for the year 1891. The composer opted instead for something less literary: the *Requiem Mass*, Op. 89. This work was again received favorably when performed at the festival yet did not win for the composer the same high accolades as the seemingly unsurpassable *Stabat mater*.

Dvořák soon put the pen aside for conservatory instruction. In 1891, he accepted the chair of composition at the Prague Conservatory and embarked on a teaching career that was to last for five years and carry him across the ocean. Only one year after his appointment to the Prague professorship, he was granted a leave of absence by the institution to undertake similar duties at the New York Conservatory for what was at that time a generous salary.

The composer was to remain in America until 1896. From this stay in New York came what is perhaps his most recognizable work to the American ear, the Symphony in E minor, Op. 95, known popularly as *From the New World*. As George Gershwin was to do in the next century, Dvořák infused new blood into the musical scene by incorporating heretofore exotic musical elements—of Indian, African, and American flavor—into his strong European musical heritage. This last great work of his had enormous consequences for American symphonic music. Karel Hoffmeister goes so far as to suggest—with some justification—that Dvořák's impact on American music can be compared to that of George Frideric Handel on the music of England.

Dvořák returned from America to the hero's welcome which had greeted him constantly in these last few years of artistic grandeur. As his stay on American soil seemed to have affected his composition by introducing new motifs and styles in his European background, so his return to Bohemia reawakened his Slavic muse. Among his greatest successes from this last period of his life are the symphonic poems he composed, based on Erben's highly popular collection of folk-styled ballads entitled *Kytice* (*The Wreathe*) and his final great opera *Rusalka* (*The Water-Nymph*).

Dvořák's last effort in this field, the opera *Armida*, built around Jaroslav Vrchlický's libretto, ended in fiasco. It seems strange that the brilliant career of such an artist should end in failure, yet this is indeed what happened. Falling ill toward the end of March, 1904, the composer died on May 1. As a sign of the great esteem in which the Czech people held the composer, Dvořák was laid to rest on the grounds of the royal castle of Vyšehrad in Prague on May 5, 1904.

Summary

Antonín Dvořák is lauded as one of the greatest composers of the modern era. A technical genius whose absolute devotion to music gave birth to unforgettable symphonies, operas, and chamber works, Dvořák influenced and was highly regarded in his own day by colleagues such as Brahms and Richter. As pedagogue, he left his unique mark upon musicians such as Oskar Nedbal, who came under his tutelage at conservatories in Prague and New York. Yet Dvořák is most widely known as the one composer who, more than anyone else in the late nineteenth century, popularized Slavic themes and musical styles to European and American audiences unaccustomed to the fertile region of East and Central Europe. In this, Dvořák can be compared to Frédéric Chopin, who preceded him in the early part of the century.

Dvořák is also remembered as a musical innovator who introduced American rhythms to the older traditions of Europe. He is unique in modern musical history as a composer who has had a profound effect on at least two, if not three (counting Germany), musical cultures—that of Bohemia and the United States—and deserves to be held in honor by the American, as well as the Czech, public as an illustrious founder of a musical culture which might have developed in a radically different fashion had he not participated in its nurturing.

Bibliography

Beckerman, Michael, ed. *Dvorak and His World*. Princeton, N.J.: Princeton University Press, 1993. A collection of essays and sources such as letters, reviews, and criticism of Dvorak's work, this book argues for critical reassessment.

Boruch, Marianne. "Worlds Old and New." *Iowa Review* 27, no. 3 (Winter 1997). Reflections on Dvorak, the development of the "New World Symphony" and the similarities in his approach to that of Walt Whitman.

Clapham, John. *Dvořák*. Newton Abbott: David and Charles, and New York: Norton, 1979. Clapham's biography contains a wealth of information concerning the composer's life and compositions. Particularly valuable to the student who is interested in Dvořák's American years and his British successes. Some illustrative musical annotation, a "Catalogue of Compositions," a generous bibliography, and a helpful "Chronicle of Events" make this biography an excellent and easy-to-use reference tool. Black-and-white photographs.

Fischl, Viktor, ed. *Antonín Dvořák: His Achievement*. London: Drummond, 1943; Westport, Conn.: Greenwood Press, 1970. This book is a helpful and enlightening collection of essays written by critics such as Edwin Evans, Thomas Dunhill, and Harriet Cohen. Topics discussed in the eleven papers cover every aspect of the composer's creative oeuvre, from his orchestral works and opera to his chamber music and sacral creations. An excellent text for both initiate and musically refined student because it presents Dvořák's life and compositional heritage in well-written, logically arranged sections.

Hoffmeister, Karel. *Antonín Dvořák*. Edited and translated by Rosa Newmarch. London: Bodley Head, 1928; Westport, Conn.: Greenwood Press, 1970. This is a well-constructed biography, divided into two main sections. The first introduces the composer as a person and the second proceeds to a detailed discussion of his works, with generous snippets of musical notation which exemplify and reinforce the critical commentary. The reader, however, should be aware of a few minor miscues which detract from an otherwise excellent work. Hoffmeister at one point refers to a period in the composer's life as being quite "stormy and stressful," thus creating a misleading reference to the German literary period *Sturm und Drang* (late eighteenth century). Also, the author suggests that the Czech national revival began in the mid-nineteenth century, when it actually began as early as 1785.

Moore, Douglas. *A Guide to Musical Styles: From Madrigal to Modern Music*. Rev. ed. New York: Norton, 1962. Although not totally devoted to Dvořák, Moore's book is a concise, excellent introduction to the European musical heritage, with generous commentary on composers and musical styles which had a profound influence on Dvořák. Aids greatly in the understanding of the composer and his place in and significance for music. Generous musical annotation assists the adept in aurally experiencing the main points of the author's dialogue, while his easy style and helpful definitions make this book an indispensable tool for both beginning and advanced students of musical history.

Schonzeler, Hans-Hubert. *Dvořák*. London: Boyers, and New York: Scribner, 1984. A contemporary, more in-depth biography of the composer than Hoffmeister's work. Many excerpts from the composer's own letters and writings make this work an especially interesting study. The book for those who wish to come to know Dvořák as a person rather than a composer. Contains sixty-seven well-chosen black-and-white photographs.

Charles Kraszewski

JAMES BUCHANAN EADS

Born: May 23, 1820; Lawrenceberg, Indiana
Died: March 8, 1887; Nassau, New Providence Island, Bahamas
Areas of Achievement: Business, invention, and engineering
Contribution: Eads revolutionized long-span bridge construction; the Eads Bridge, spanning the Mississippi River at St. Louis, is the only such structure bearing an engineer's name. He was a highly successful capitalist and an inventor of note, with more than fifty patents credited to him.

Early Life

James Buchanan Eads was born on May 23, 1820, in Lawrenceburg, Indiana, an Ohio River town. His family was of moderate means, moving in search of better fortune to Cincinnati, Ohio, then to Louisville, Kentucky. As a result of economic difficulties, between the ages of nine and thirteen Eads had only minimal formal education. Nevertheless, by the time he was eleven years old, Eads, working from observations made during family moves on steamers, had already constructed a small steam engine and models of sawmills, fire engines, steamboats, and electrotype machines.

In Louisville, Eads's father experienced serious business reverses, so at only thirteen Eads traveled to St. Louis, working passage on a river steamer and seeking employment. After suffering hardships, Eads found well-paying work in a St. Louis mercantile establishment. Recognizing Eads's abilities, an employer opened his library (reportedly one of the Mississippi Valley's finest) to him, and Eads used it intensively to study civil engineering, mechanics, and machinery. When he was nineteen, his family moved to Dubuque, Iowa, where young Eads signed as second clerk aboard the river steamer *Knickerbocker*, which operated between Dubuque and Cincinnati. In the next few years, having risen to purser, he served aboard several Mississippi steamers and became intimately acquainted with the navigational characteristics of the river with which his life became intimately linked.

Life's Work

In 1842, now an attractive, industrious, tactful, ingenious, and personable man, Eads placed his savings into copartnership with Case and Nelson, a firm of St. Louis boat builders, in order to help the company to expand into the salvage of river wrecks.

Hundreds of steamers were lost annually during the mid-nineteenth century because of boiler explosions, contact with bars or snags, and other accidents, and millions of dollars were lost to river pirates and to the unpredictabilities of the river itself. As a consequence, Eads and his partners extended their salvage operations the length of the Mississippi and to the Gulf countries of Central America, profiting greatly. Nevertheless, Eads sold his shares and established the first glass manufactury west of the Mississippi, an equally profitable enterprise.

Drawing upon his vast experience with the Mississippi and its tributaries, Eads founded his own salvage company in 1847. His success lay in his design and construction of a series of "submarines," diving bells raised and lowered by derricks and supplied with compressed air, which revolutionized salvage work. Not only were sunken cargoes recovered, but also vessels themselves could be refloated. His final salvage boat, bought from the American government and redesigned, was the largest, most powerful of its type ever built. Eads was so successful with his diving bells and snag boats that in 1856-1857 he proposed a federal contract to clear obstructions and maintain free navigation of the Mississippi and other Western rivers over subsequent years. His proposal was defeated, however, chiefly by the opposition of Senators Judah P. Benjamin of Louisiana and Jefferson Davis of Mississippi, the former to serve in several capacities Davis' Confederate Cabinet. Thwarted, but already wealthy, at the age of thirty-seven Eads retired with his second wife to the comfort of a St. Louis suburb, ostensibly to recover from his latest bout with tuberculosis

Yet the most significant phases of his career lay ahead. Edward Bates, a friend of the Eads family who had entered Abraham Lincoln's cabinet as attorney general, alerted Eads to the possible need for his services as secession of the South threatened in 1860; the Administration was anxious to preserve free navigation of the Mississippi. Shortly after war erupted in 1861, Eads won federal contracts for construction of seven six-hundred-ton armored steamers to be ready for action in sixty-five days. Greatly handicapped by his illness, Eads still assembled men and materials from ten states and from the mills of half a dozen cities, successfully completing his first delivery in forty-five days. Within one hundred days he designed and con-

structed an aggregate of five thousand tons of military shipping. These vessels contributed to Union victories at Forts Henry and Donelson and at Island No. 10, thereby opening the northern Mississippi. Indeed, at the time of these victories, Eads actually owned the vessels, having paid for them with his own funds (he had not yet been reimbursed by Washington). Before 1865, Eads built fourteen heavily armored gunboats, four mortar boats, and seven armored transports, all delivered on time and to specifications. Furthermore, his revolving gun turrets later became standard. For this and other inventions, Eads was elected a Fellow of the American Academy for the Advancement of Science. Devoid of engineering training, Eads had amply demonstrated not only a mastery of novel shipbuilding but also a profound knowledge of iron and steel potentials. Combined with his grasp of the Mississippi's peculiarities, his ingenuity, tenacity, high civic esteem, and organizational abilities, he was brilliantly equipped for his next enterprise: bridging the Mississippi at St. Louis.

With canal-building and the era of the river steamer waning, railway expansion dominated the postwar period. From 1865 until Eads' death in 1887, railway mileage increased from about forty thousand to more than 200,000 miles. Concurrently, need for bridges (hitherto of wooden or iron truss constructions) of long spans and heavy bearing capacities became imperative. Proposals for a St. Louis span had been made earlier than 1867 by Charles Ellet, Jr., as well as by John Augustus Roebling, engineers of distinction, but Eads's plan won the vital approval of the St. Louis business community and of the city's officials.

For his unprecedented scheme, Eads employed unprecedented means. Aware of his own weaknesses, he created a superb staff: Charles Shaler Smith joined him as chief engineering consultant; two other able men were chosen as assistant engineers; and the chancellor of Washington University served as mathematical consultant. With Bessemer steel then available, Eads selected steel as his basic construction material. This ran against the advice of many engineers; indeed, the British Board of Trade banned the use of steel for bridges until years later. Moreover, Eads helped transform Bessemer steel into chrome steel, that choice alone altering subsequent major bridge construction, in which special steels came to supersede iron. Foundations created special problems. Eads knew the Mississippi, and by treading its bottom in his diving bell he confirmed that three or more feet of sand and silt moved along the river bed at speed of flow. Winter ice jams and the necessity of keeping navigational channels open further complicated planning. The pneumatic caissons devised for foundation work were not new in principle but they had seldom been tested and never on the scale or at the depths required to reach bedrock: 123 feet below the mean water level on the Illinois side and eighty-six feet at St. Louis. Moreover, these iron-shod timber caissons were seventy-five feet in diameter and designed to sink under their own weight as work progressed. Consequently, several lives were lost, others frequently endangered and cases of "bends" from depths and pressures were numerous.

Double-decked for trains and for normal traffic, the bridge featured unique arches that had been cantilevered into position, the central sections coming last. Moreover, the three arched spans were of unprecedented length: 1,560 feet overall. Notwithstanding distinguished assistance, Eads designed and oversaw, as his engineers testified, every one-eighth of an inch of the structure, and his aesthetic sense produced a masterwork of great beauty, one still in service. It was completed in 1874, just as the nation's first and longest industrial depression struck. Bondholders foreclosed on the bridge's mortgage. Eads's own bank proved to be one of the great financial disasters of the day. By 1877, the financier and speculator Jay Gould assumed control of the bridge.

Eads, however, swiftly recovered from this crash. By 1875 he had begun overriding congressional opposition to a $5,250,000 contract for permanently clearing major bars at the mouth of the Mississippi and extending its South Pass jetties into deep Gulf waters. Again through ingenuity developed after study of European river jetties, Eads designed an inexpensive "mattress" construction, successfully completing the job and recouping his fortune. Indeed, he offered seventy-five million dollars of his own money if Congress would charter his company for construction of a ship-railway across the Mexican isthmus at Tehuantepec, thereby bringing the Pacific twelve hundred miles nearer to the Mississippi than Ferdinand de Lesseps' ongoing Panama project. Even as Congress moved to accept his proposal, however, Eads's health failed. He died on March 8, 1887, in Nassau, the Bahamas.

Summary

Either as a great capitalist or as a great engineer, Eads would have enjoyed distinction. Essentially filling the ideal of the American self-made man, he combined both roles, distinguishing himself in both. He revolutionized the salvage business with his inventions, notably with his design of steam-driven centrifugal pumps and his diving bells. He revolutionized bridge construction with his arch designs and, above all, with his introduction of steel for such structures. He resolved through financial, political, and engineering inventiveness and skill the freeing of the river around which so much of his life revolved. In 1884, he became the first American recipient of the Albert Medal from the British Royal Society of Arts. Further, of the eighty-nine persons elected to the Hall of Fame for Great Americans, Eads (elected in 1920) was the sole engineer or architect chosen during the institution's first sixty years of existence.

Bibliography

Condit, Carl W. *American Building: Materials and Techniques from the Beginning of the Colonial Settlements to the Present.* 2d ed. Chicago: University of Chicago Press, 1982. Sweeping and expert analysis. Chapter 12, "Long-Span Bridges in Iron and Steel," treats Eads in proper technical context.

Kouwenhoven, John A. "The Designing of the Eads Bridge." *Technology and Culture* 23 (1982): 535-568. Scholarly work in a widely available, learned journal.

———. "James Buchanan Eads: The Engineer as Entrepreneur." In *Technology in America: A History of Individuals and Ideas*, edited by Carroll W. Pursell, Jr. Cambridge, Mass.: MIT Press, 1981. Chapter 8 on Eads is excellent; scholarly and well written.

Scott, Quinta, and Howard S. Miller. *The Eads Bridge: Photographic Essay.* New York: Columbia University Press, 1979. The fullest description of the bridge; less useful for the general context of Eads's other activities.

Woodward, Calvin M. *A History of the St. Louis Bridge: Containing a Full Account of Every Step in Its Construction and Erection.* St. Louis: Janes, 1881. This account of the building of the Eads Bridge is old but is the most exhaustive.

Yager, Rosemary. *James Buchanan Eads: Master of the Great River.* New York: Van Nostrand Reinhold, 1968. Interesting overview of Eads's life and activities, but not the final word on Eads's work.

Clifton K. Yearley
Kerrie L. MacPherson

THOMAS EAKINS

Born: July 25, 1844; Philadelphia, Pennsylvania
Died: June 25, 1916; Philadelphia, Pennsylvania
Area of Achievement: Art
Contribution: Eakins produced a handful of major paintings which were to add to the reputation of the United States as a center of art independent of Europe. He was also an important influence on art education in the United States.

Early Life

Thomas Eakins was born in Philadelphia on July 25, 1844, and was to die in the family home in that city in 1916. Eakins' father, Benjamin Eakins, of Scottish-Irish parentage, was a writing master in the Philadelphia school system, and Thomas had early ambitions to follow his father into that work. His mother was of English and Dutch descent. It was a close, middle-class family with a modest private income which was to help support Eakins throughout his life, since his teaching and painting did not always do so. He was particularly close to his three sisters, and they often appear in his paintings.

He evidenced early talents in draftsmanship and drawing and was to study them formally from high school onward, but he also had strengths in science, mathematics, and languages. Eakins was to use his knowledge of science and mathematics extensively in the preparation of his more complicated paintings.

Eakins studied at the Pennsylvania Academy of Fine Arts in Philadelphia, from 1861 to 1866. Drawing from casts of fine antique sculpture was the center of the technical studies at the school, and to Eakins' dissatisfaction, little drawing was done from live models. He supplemented his work by enrolling in anatomy classes at Jefferson Medical College, where he was allowed to watch surgeons operating, and where he began a practice which he admitted he disliked, but which he considered essential to the student artist—the study of anatomy—by taking part in dissection classes. By the end of his time at the academy, he had done very little painting. In September, 1866, he left for France in order to study in Paris.

He entered the conservative École des Beaux-Arts, choosing to study under the painter Jean-Leon Gerome, who was himself somewhat conservative and old-fashioned, but who gave Eakins a thorough grounding in drawing, with emphasis on the use of live models. Eakins again added anato-

my classes to his studies, and when he started to paint seriously in his second year, he took a studio where he could work alone while continuing his instruction under Gerome. His correspondence evidences little interest in what was going on about him in Paris, although it was a time of considerable ferment in the art world, and the early work of the painters who were to become the Impressionists was being shown and discussed. At the end of his three years in Paris, he toured the galleries of Spain, showing particular enthusiasm for the technique and realistic subject matter of José Ribera and Diego Velázquez. On July 4, 1870, he returned to Philadelphia, where he was to live and work for the remainder of his life.

Life's Work

There had been indications of a fully formed skill in a few of Eakins' paintings in the late 1860's, and that maturity was soon confirmed in his work in the 1870's. A solid and stocky young man (he can be seen hovering in the middle-background of some of his paintings) with an active interest in rowing and hunting, he brought the world of his athletic pleasures into his paintings, and he is best known for a group of stunningly forceful studies of rowers which exemplify the American love of high athletic skill and outdoor life. *John Biglin in a Single Scull* (1873) and *Max Schmitt in a Single Scull* (1871) are the most popular examples of these intense, imploded moments of athletic focus, in which the subjects, patently modest, convey an aesthetic rightness, a kind of metaphysical truth about life which connects them with the earlier tradition of American paintings celebrating the rugged men working the rivers of America.

This paean to personal skill is explored again in his pictures of surgeons at work, musicians at play, and prizefighters in action. Eakins was, however, to run into trouble with the public, who found his paintings of surgeons at work in the operating theaters too gruesome and bloody, and his paintings of male and female nudes were often considered too crudely unblinkered. He could, on the other hand, be quietly tender in his paintings of musicians, particularly in his studies of his sisters.

As a result, he established a reputation as one of the foremost realists of the latter half of the nineteenth century, but he did not sell many pictures. In his later years, he turned more and more to por-

Thomas Eakins (center) consults with a colleague and a pupil.

traits, generally using friends and acquaintances as subjects, and he rarely was commissioned to do so. He showed little inclination to idealize his portraits. Rather, he tended to catch his sitters in the introspective moment, and he was often successful in getting something of their character on the canvas. His later portraits often went further and revealed physical and emotional vulnerabilities which did not always please his subjects.

It is possible to think of him as a portraitist from beginning to end with the athletes and men of action showing the best of prime human endeavor, and some of the latter sitters revealing the cruel, inexorable nature of time passing. Yet it is those early pictures of sportsmen which are, quite rightly, best remembered.

This mixed reputation that he developed as a painter, of being enormously talented but a bit crude, carried over into his parallel career as an art teacher and administrator. In 1876, he joined the Pennsylvania Academy of Fine Arts as their instructor in the life classes; gradually he became so important to the school's work that in 1882 he became the director. As he did in his own painting, he put heavy emphasis upon drawing from life, not because he did not appreciate the greatness of ancient sculpture but because he saw the naked human form as the best subject for the young artist. He also urged his students to take anatomy classes with medical students. Over the years, opposition built up, inside the school and outside, over his insistence that students, male and female, should draw from life. In 1886, his exposure of a male model, completely nude, before a class of female students caused such an avalanche of protest that he was asked to resign. He took a large group of male students with him, and they formed the Art Students League of Philadelphia with Eakins as the sole, unpaid instructor. The school lasted for six years but foundered eventually for financial reasons. Eakins continued to teach in art schools as a guest lecturer, but his insistence on using nude models often got him into trouble, and by mid-life, he ceased to teach.

He had a continuing interest in sculpture and left a few pieces which show considerable skill, but the later years were in the main confined to doing portraits, with occasional returns to his studies of athletes and nudes.

Summary

Eakins made a double contribution to American culture. As an educator, he championed, to his own detriment, the need to repudiate the sometimes prurient sexual morality of the late nineteenth century in favor of an intelligent acceptance of the human body as the basis for study in art colleges. His fight, often played out in public, made it easier for such artistic and educational freedoms to become a common aspect of American art instruction.

He was also the first prominent art teacher to bring science into the classroom and studio. His personal use of, and instruction in the preparation of mathematically precise preliminary studies, his use of scale models, and particularly his pioneering use of photography were to become commonly applied tools.

Despite his training in France and his admiration for Spanish painters, he was peculiarly American. His choice of subjects and his refusal to idealize them are examples of his solid, down-to-earth approach to art. Other painters romanticized the portrait; Eakins used it to record reality, however uncomplimentary. He has been called antiartistic, but he proved that art could be made out of life as it was seen. His refusal to compromise for profit and popularity is an example of his American forthrightness, and his affection for science, for mathematics, for photography, for sport, for high professional endeavor may also be seen as marks of his American character.

Possessed of abundant painterly skills, he often seems too skeptically stolid to make use of them, but at his best, particularly in his sporting pictures, he can make the simple moment accumulate a splendor which links him with painters such as Paul Cézanne and Jean-Baptiste-Siméon Chardin. At those moments of pastoral innocence, the paintings achieve a poetic density which transcends and glorifies the simplicity of the mundane act of living. Then, he is at his best—and his most American.

Bibliography

Goodrich, Lloyd. *Thomas Eakins*. Cambridge, Mass.: Harvard University Press, 1982. An updated look at Eakins, including interviews with Eakins' widow, students, and sitters. Good bibliography of articles on Eakins.

———. *Thomas Eakins: His Life and Work*. New York: Whitney Museum of American Art, 1933. A major study combining critical biography and catalog in which the reviving reputation of the artist is assessed in conjunction with the neglect which followed his death.

———. *Thomas Eakins: Retrospective Exhibition*. New York: Whitney Museum of American Art, 1970. A paperback monograph, prepared for the major retrospective show at the Whitney Museum of American Art by the scholar most involved with putting Eakins into the mainstream of American art. Good, with numerous reproductions and an excellent short essay.

Hendricks, Gordon. *The Life and Work of Thomas Eakins*. New York: Grossman, 1974. An obsessively detailed study, provocative in its assumptions.

Johns, Elizabeth. *Thomas Eakins: The Heroism of Modern Life*. Princeton, N.J.: Princeton University Press, 1983. An interesting study of specific subjects painted by Eakins, putting them into the context of how other artists have used the same subjects.

Porter, Fairfield. *Thomas Eakins*. New York: Braziller, 1959. An edition of "The Great American Artists" series, this inexpensive paperback includes a generous selection of his paintings, some in color, and a short, sensible critical comment upon Eakins' life and career.

Siegl, Theodor. *The Thomas Eakins Collection*. Philadelphia: Philadelphia Museum of Art, 1978. A careful assessment of Eakins' individuality as a painter and a sympathetic consideration of his personality.

Charles H. Pullen

WYATT EARP

Born: March 19, 1848; Monmouth, Illinois
Died: January 13, 1929; Los Angeles, California
Area of Achievement: Law
Contribution: Earp, a lawman in the early cow-towns of the Old West, established a reputation that made him an American legend. To some, he epitomized revenge; to others, he was an American hero.

Early Life

Wyatt Berry Stapp Earp, named after his father's company commander during the Mexican-American War, was born in 1848, the third son to Nicholas and Virginia Earp. As an early settler of Monmouth, Illinois (1843), Nicholas provided law and order in the community. His father's principles would impact Earp throughout the rest of his life. Nicholas, a restless farmer, saw the opportunity of abundant farmland in Pella, Iowa. In 1850, he moved his wife, his daughter Martha, and his four sons, Newton (Nicholas's son from a previous marriage), James, Virgil, and Wyatt (age two). Newton, James, and Virgil fought for the Union during the Civil War. In 1863, in the middle of the Civil War, the Earp family, which now included three more children (Morgan, Warren, and Adelia), moved again, this time to San Bernardino, California, where lush fields and prospering cities promised wealth.

On the wagon train traveling westward to California, Earp learned to handle a gun, shoot, hunt, scout, and, most important, stay cool in pressure situations. All of these skills would aid Earp in his brief but famous career as a frontier marshal. However, at the young age of sixteen, Earp was still very uncertain as to what he wanted to do. It was not until he reached California that he determined that farming was not for him. Instead, he began driving stage coaches across the deserts of California and Arizona. Though short-lived, the experience enhanced Earp's frontier skills.

In 1868, Earp's family returned to Iowa, then quickly moved to the small town of Lamar, Missouri. It was there that Earp married Urilla Sutherland in January, 1870. Just two months later, he was appointed as the constable of Lamar, a job that he found much more enjoyable than farming for his father. Earp seemed to have everything in order. Suddenly, however, his world came crashing down around him. Before their first wedding anniversary, Urilla suddenly died. The cause of her death remains a mystery. Speculation has ranged from complications while giving birth to a stillborn baby to typhoid. It has been suggested that the Sutherlands blamed Earp for Urilla's death and engaged him and his brothers in a fight. Some biographers believe that Earp left his job and the town of Lamar because of the bitterness and the grief he felt over the death of his wife, but not before allegedly embezzling twenty dollars from the town. Charges were filed, but nothing ever came of it.

After leaving town, Earp headed to the Indian Territory, where the federal government charged him with stealing horses. However, he jumped bail and headed to Kansas. He was able to evade the law by blending into the West as a Kansas buffalo hunter. His reputation as a lawman eventually began in the rough-and-tumble cowtowns of Kansas.

Life's Work

After he spent a few years buffalo hunting, Earp sought his livelihood in the cowtowns of Kansas. As legend has it, Earp was forced into law enforcement in Ellsworth, Kansas, and found it to his liking. From there Earp moved to Wichita, Kansas, where he spent three years breaking up fights, dealing with drunken cowboys, and defending the city. In 1876, during an election for the town marshal, Earp physically attacked the opposing marshal for remarks made against his family. He was immediately fired. However, having heard of Earp's success with some of the ruffians of Wichita, the mayor of Dodge City immediately called upon him to come to what had become one of the wildest and wickedest cowtowns in the West. Even though Earp thought he would be the marshal of Dodge, he was given the deputy marshal's job and became chief enforcer. He only stayed in Dodge for one season before, according to legend, he went to Deadwood, South Dakota, for the fall and winter. There he cut and sold firewood while learning to gamble. Thereafter, gambling became an added source of income for Earp. During the next cattle season, Earp returned to Dodge City but not to his job. Instead, he spent the next year bounty hunting fugitives from Dodge throughout Kansas, the Indian Territory, and Texas. It was during an excursion to Fort Griffin, Texas, in 1877 that he met his life-long friend Doc Holliday, a noted gambler, gunman, and killer. This friendship would always cast a dark shadow on Earp's reputation.

In 1878, Earp returned to Dodge and was hired back as a deputy and began his career with noted lawman Bat Masterson. Earp and Masterson were credited with taming Dodge. Earp was effective at keeping order without resorting to gunplay, which was precisely what the saloon keepers, merchants, and bankers who ran Western boomtowns wanted. By the time he left Dodge in 1879, he had established himself as the top lawman in the West. Some would argue that he attained this reputation through intimidation and excessive force, while others would say that he epitomized law enforcement with a cool temper and nerves of steel. Earp had tamed the Wild West of Kansas, no doubt with help from a progressive railroad that essentially killed the cattle trade and a temperance movement that restricted alcohol.

Meanwhile, Virgil, Earp's brother, had heard of a silver strike in the small mining camp of Tombstone, Arizona. He wrote to Earp to come and make his fortune. In December of 1879, Earp arrived in Arizona with Celia Ann "Mattie" Blaylock, his common-law wife whom he had met while in Dodge but had never married. Along with Earp and

Mattie came Earp's brother James and James's family. Virgil and Morgan arrived shortly after.

Earp was soon back into law enforcement when he was named deputy sheriff of Pima County. Virgil had been named U.S. deputy marshal of the same region. The Earp bothers conflicted with some of the surrounding ranchers, cowboys, and suspected villains. The term "cowboy" had taken on a negative connotation by this time and referred to thieves, robbers, cutthroats, and lawless citizens. The Clantons and McLaurys, two families that have been perceived as lawless cowboys in history books, clashed with the Earps, who tried to reestablish the laws that had grown lax. The cowboys claimed that the Earps were simply taking advantage of their position. These confrontations eventually blew up in a shootout near the O.K. Corral on October 26, 1881. By that time, Earp and Morgan had been made special deputies under Virgil. According to most accounts, the Earps sought a peaceful resolution to threats that Ike Clanton had made. The incident placed Billy and Ike Clanton, Frank and Billy McLaury, and Billy Claiborne near the O.K. Corral. Speculation still circles as to whether these men were waiting to ambush the Earps or were just riding out of town. Whatever their intentions, their plans were severely changed when Virgil, Earp, Morgan, and Holliday, who had been deputized for the occasion, met them on Fremont Street. Again, legend varies as to who fired first, but after the shootout, Billy Clanton and both McLaurys lay dead. Virgil, Morgan, and Holliday were wounded. To this day it is debated whether the shootout was a cold-blooded murder by men who hid behind their badges or justified law enforcement for violence against innocent citizens of Tombstone.

Earp and Holliday stood trial for the shootout. They eventually were acquitted, but the Earps suffered much criticism from the local papers and citizenry. Attention to the trial added to the incident's infamy. In retaliation for the shootout, an assassination attempt was made on Virgil. He survived, but at the cost of losing the use of his right arm. Next, Earp's favorite brother, Morgan, was assassinated. It was not until Earp tried to move the rest of his family west and another assassination attempt was made that Earp responded with lethal vengeance by killing one of the assailants. This controversial act was seen by some as murder and by others as justified vengeance. Earp's lethal crusade continued until he felt that he had accounted for all of the men who had killed his brother. After killing two more men, Earp and his posse fled to Colorado to escape indictment.

Earp stayed in Colorado expecting a pardon that never came. It was not until late 1882 that he joined Virgil in San Francisco, California. Meanwhile, Mattie, who had returned to California with Earp's family, returned to Tombstone after realizing that Earp was not coming for her. She committed suicide in 1887. During that time, Earp rekindled a romance with Sadie Marcus that had begun in Tombstone. For forty-seven years, Sadie and Earp remained with each other, gambling, mining, working in saloons, and moving from boomtown to boomtown in the American West. Earp died in 1929 in Los Angeles, California, a few months before his eighty-first birthday.

Summary

Wyatt Earp's career as frontier marshal, only a small portion of his eighty years, was the reason for his notoriety. The saga of a brave frontier lawman fighting for justice has captured the hearts of Americans. His initial biography was released in the dreary days of depression, prohibition, and gangster activity. Because of public perceptions of police who are less than effective or consumed by corruption and a court system that fails to adequately punish criminals, Americans continue to seek someone who will supersede the law to preserve order. Wyatt Earp stands as a powerful symbol of just such a lawman.

Bibliography

Banks, Leo. "Wyatt Earp." *Arizona Highways* 70 (July 1994): 4-13. This short but detailed article covers the chronology of Earp's life and his appeal to American society.

Bartholomew, Ed. *Wyatt Earp, The Man and The Myth.* Toyahvale, Tex.: Frontier Book Company, 1963. This is one of the earliest books that attempts to account for errors in the Earp story by substantiating events with factual information.

Brooks, David. "Wyatt Usurped." *The National Interest* 37 (Fall 1994): 66-70. Brooks's brief historic overview of Earp argues that motion pictures have perpetuated a western myth that has become representative of America.

Lake, Stuart. *Wyatt Earp, Frontier Marshall.* Boston: Houghton Mifflin, 1931. Lake's biography was supposedly written with the help of Earp himself. This interesting but fantastic book is important because it has become one of the major sources of the Earp myth.

Peterson, Roger. "Wyatt Earp. Man Versus Myth." *American History* 29 (August 1994): 54-61. This magazine article provides a brief history of Earp and discusses how his legend began and how it may have been corrupted.

Tefertiller, Casey. *Wyatt Earp, The Life Behind The Legend.* New York: Wiley, 1997. Tefertiller's book is an excellent source for explaining the myth of Earp and why it has been misunderstood.

Tonya Huber

MARY BAKER EDDY

Born: July 16, 1821; Bow, New Hampshire
Died: December 3, 1910; Chestnut Hill, Massachusetts
Area of Achievement: Religion
Contribution: A deeply religious thinker, Mary Baker Eddy established the Church of Christ, Scientist—the first church movement to be founded in the United States by a woman.

Early Life

The youngest of six children, Mary Morse Baker was born in 1821 on her parents' farm in the township of Bow, New Hampshire. Her father, Mark Baker, was a respected farmer whose deep interest in theology prompted him to engage in serious religious debates with his neighbors. Mary's mother, Abigail Ambrose Baker, had grown up as the daughter of a prominent deacon of the Congregational church in nearby Pembroke and was known for her tender solicitude toward her family and neighbors. Both parents were devout members of the Congregational church; Mary was nurtured in their Calvinist faith and joined the church herself at the age of twelve.

As a young girl, Mary began her formal education in 1826. An intelligent, highly sensitive child, Mary suffered from ill health that frequently kept her at home. She became a diligent reader and an avid writer of poetry. Mary received individual instruction from her second brother, Albert, who served as a schoolmaster at Mary's school when he was twenty. Her brother's instruction provided Mary with an education well in advance of that commonly available to young women of the period, and she was introduced to the rudiments of Greek, Latin, and Hebrew as well as contemporary works of literature and philosophy.

In December of 1843, Mary Baker was married to Major George Washington Glover, a successful builder with business interests in the Carolinas. The newlyweds eventually settled in Wilmington, North Carolina. By June of 1844, George Glover's investments in building supplies for a project in Haiti were lost, and he was stricken with yellow fever. He died on June 27, forcing his pregnant and impoverished widow to return to her parents' home. Despite her dangerously poor health, Mary gave birth in September to a healthy son, whom she named George in honor of his late father. When

Abigail Baker died in 1849, however, her daughter's grief and precarious health made further care for the boisterous young George Glover even more difficult. Mark Baker's second marriage less than one year later forced Mary and her son to leave the Baker house. Mary went to stay with her sister Abigail Tilton, but George Glover was placed in the care of Mary's former nurse. Mary was devastated by her separation from her son, but her family insisted that reuniting the two would further strain Mary's tenuous health.

In 1853, Mary was married to Dr. Daniel Patterson, a dentist who promised to provide a home for her and her son. That promise was never fulfilled, however, and Patterson's failings as a husband became increasingly evident. Mary's son moved with his foster parents to the West; they later told him that his mother had died. Mary's new husband was often absent in the course of his itinerant practice, and the couple found lodgings in various communities in New Hampshire. In the spring of 1862, while on commission to deliver state funds to

Union sympathizers in the South, Patterson was taken prisoner by Confederate forces.

Barely able to care for herself, Mary sought relief from her persistent ill health at an institute in New Hampshire that promoted hydropathy, or the water cure. Finding little improvement during her visit, she traveled to Portland, Maine, to visit Phineas P. Quimby, a clock maker who had developed a reputation as a magnetic healer and hypnotist. After her first treatment at his office, Mary experienced a marked improvement in her health. In her enthusiasm to learn more about the methods Quimby used, she sought to reconcile Quimby's ideas with the spiritually based biblical healings with which she was so familiar.

Reunited with her husband in December of 1862 after his escape from prison, Mary returned to New Hampshire, where she experienced relapses of ill health. She sought relief by visiting Quimby at various times but could not discover a permanent cure for her illnesses. After Quimby's death in early January of 1866, Mary was seriously injured when she fell on an icy pavement in Lynn, Massachusetts, on February 1. Taken to a nearby house, she eventually regained consciousness sufficiently to convince her doctor and friends to move her to her lodgings in nearby Swampscott, where she was given little hope of recovery from the injuries to her head and spine. Visited by a clergyman on the Sunday after her accident, she asked to be left alone with her Bible. Turning to the ninth chapter of Matthew, she read the account of Jesus' healing of the man sick of the palsy (paralysis). Upon reading the story, she felt a profound change come over her and found that she was fully recovered from her injuries. Rising from her bed to dress and then greet the friends who waited outside her door, Mary astonished them with the rapidity and completeness of her healing, one that she credited to the power of God alone.

Life's Work

During the decade from 1866 to 1876, Mary Patterson's outward life seemed little improved, yet her conviction that she could discover the source of her healing experience inspired her to continue her study of the Bible. Her husband deserted her soon after her healing; they were divorced in 1873, and she resumed using the surname Glover.

Although her financial situation was precarious and she was still separated from her son, Mary realized that, at the age of forty-five, she was healthier than she had ever been in her entire life. For three years after her recovery, she dedicated herself solely to searching the Bible for answers to her questions regarding spiritual healing, withdrawing from social pursuits and her temperance movement activities in order to record the revelations she was gaining through her studies. She lived frugally in a series of boarding houses, began sharing her notes and interpretations of Bible passages with individuals who seemed receptive to her new ideas, and occasionally offered instruction in her healing methods in exchange for the cost of her room and board. A group of committed students eventually began to gather around her. In October of 1875, she managed to publish the first edition of her work, entitled *Science and Health*, with the financial assistance of some of her students.

It was in March of 1876 that Asa Gilbert Eddy, a native of Vermont who was ten years her junior and worked in Massachusetts as a salesman for the Singer Sewing Machine Company, became one of Mary's students. Asa Eddy, better known as Gilbert, became a successful healer. At a time when many of her most talented students were challenging her authority and attempting to undermine her teachings, Mary came to rely on Gilbert Eddy's sound judgment and his steady support of her leadership. The two were married on January 1, 1877.

Around this time, Mary Baker Eddy began revising *Science and Health*, adding five new chapters. This two-volume second edition was so rife with typographical errors that only the second volume was circulated. During this time, Eddy began to lecture weekly at the Baptist Tabernacle in Boston. The success of her public sermons led her to make a motion at a meeting of her students in 1879 that they organize a church; it was called the Church of Christ, Scientist. In Eddy's own words, the purpose of this church was "to commemorate the word and works of our Master, which should reinstate primitive Christianity and its lost element of healing." The new church was incorporated under a state charter, and Eddy was designated its president and appointed its first pastor. By the winter of 1879, Eddy and her husband had moved to rooms in Boston to be nearer to the growing church. She continued to teach new adult students about Christian Science, and the church established a Sunday school for the instruction of children in 1880. That same year, Eddy published the first of her many pamphlets: a sermon entitled *Christian Healing*. In an effort to give a more solid legal foundation to her classes, Eddy applied for a state charter in order to incorporate the Massachusetts Metaphysical College, a school dedicated to furthering the spread of her healing method by ensuring that students received unadulterated instruction directly from her.

Earlier, Mary Baker Eddy had begun revising and expanding *Science and Health* once again. The third edition of *Science and Health*, which appeared in 1881, was the first accurate edition of her writings to incorporate part of the treatise she used to instruct students in her classes. This publishing enterprise brought Eddy into contact with one of the leading printers of her day: John Wilson of the University Press in Cambridge, Massachusetts. Prospects for selling all one thousand copies of the third edition were not promising, but Wilson was convinced that Eddy would be able to finance the printing of her book through its sales. By 1882, the book had gone back to print for two additional editions of one thousand copies each.

Other publishing activities began. In April of 1883, Eddy published the first issue of *The Journal of Christian Science*. Originally a bimonthly periodical with articles designed to explore issues of interest to both newcomers and longtime students of Eddy's religion, the *Journal* was expanded to become a monthly publication and was one of the first authorized organs of the Christian Science church. A sixth edition of *Science and Health* appeared in 1883; it was the first to contain Eddy's "Key to the Scriptures," a section initially consisting of a glossary with her metaphysical interpretations of biblical terms and concepts. By 1885, nine additional printings were made, bringing the total number of copies in circulation during the book's first ten years to 15,000.

The years following the publication of the sixth edition of *Science and Health* were prosperous ones, with many new students working to spread Christian Science and its healing practice throughout the United States. Nevertheless, several events occurred in the period from 1889 to 1892 that radically altered the structure and direction of the Christian Science church. Schisms among her students and the burdens resulting from those who increasingly relied on her personal leadership in all matters led Eddy to close her college at the height of its popularity and resign her post as pastor of the Boston church. Services continued to be conducted in Christian Science churches, but students voted to adjourn the activities of the National Christian Scientist Association for three years beginning in 1890. Withdrawing to a new home in Concord, New Hampshire, Eddy commenced work on a major revision of *Science and Health* to be published as the fiftieth edition in 1891.

September 23, 1892, marked the establishment of Eddy's newly reorganized church: the First Church of Christ, Scientist, in Boston, Massachusetts, also known as The Mother Church. She consulted with attorneys familiar with Massachusetts statutes in order to find a legal means to incorporate her church that would place its corporate government on a solid basis without encouraging undue attachment to her personal authority. The new charter provided a powerful centralized structure in the form of a five-member Board of Directors responsible for management of the church's affairs; it also fostered the practice of democratic self-government already established in the branch churches outside of Boston that were affiliated with the growing church movement. All members of these branches were invited to apply for concurrent membership in The Mother Church. Eddy was henceforth designated as the Discoverer and Founder of Christian Science. To her mind, this title expressed the scientific aspect of her work— emphasizing her role in formulating and articulating its religious teachings in much the same way that scientific laws and principles are formulated and articulated, but not created, by those who discover them.

In October of 1893, the building of the new church edifice was begun in Boston's Back Bay area, with the cornerstone of the church laid in May of 1894 and the first service held on December 30, 1894. Eddy took the unusual step of ordaining the Bible and *Science and Health*, rather than human ministers, as pastors of the church. When she published the *Manual of The Mother Church* in 1895, setting forth the rules by which the church was to be governed, she made provisions in its bylaws for the election of lay readers who would read texts from the Bible and from *Science and Health* relating to twenty-six topics she set forth. These texts were selected by a special committee; the resulting lesson sermons were studied daily by individual members and were read Sundays at Christian Science church services throughout the world. These changes were instituted by Eddy in order to avoid the adulteration of her teachings through personal preaching. In this way, she believed that the healing message contained in the Bible and in her book would speak directly to all who attended her church without the injection of personal opinion or conflicting interpretations.

In 1898, Eddy established a Board of Education to provide for the formal instruction of students in Christian Science by those who were approved to serve as teachers. She also established a Board of Lectureship to which practitioners (ordained healers within the church) and teachers of Christian Science were appointed. These lecturers were responsible for preparing and delivering public lectures on Christian Science in order to introduce and clarify its teachings to those unfamiliar with the religion. The Christian Science Publishing Society was created through a deed of trust and was charged with the responsibility for publishing and distributing *Science and Health* and Eddy's other books as well as *The Christian Science Journal* and the newly founded periodical, *The Christian Science Weekly* (renamed *The Christian Science Sentinel* in 1899). In 1902, Eddy completed work on her final major revision of *Science and Health*; it was the 226th edition of the book known as the Christian Science textbook.

Although she enjoyed the relative peace and seclusion of her New Hampshire estate, known as Pleasant View, Eddy faced bitter personal attacks in the popular press during early 1900's that threatened to undermine her church. These articles reflected the sensational "yellow journalism" of the period. Few pieces were more damaging than those published by Joseph Pulitzer, whose *New York World* newspaper claimed that Eddy was near death from cancer and that her alleged fortune of $15 million was being wrested from her control. Refusing to meet with Pulitzer's reporters, Eddy granted audience to representatives of several other leading newspapers and press associations. After answering three brief questions concerning her health, Eddy gave evidence of her well-being by departing to take her daily carriage ride.

Despite Eddy's efforts to disprove the rumors concerning her health, her son George was approached by the publishers of the *New York World* and was encouraged, on the basis of the paper's erroneous accounts of his mother's welfare, to begin legal proceedings to determine Eddy's mental competence and ability to conduct business affairs connected with her church. Although funded by Pulitzer's newspaper fortune, this lawsuit ultimately collapsed after a panel appointed to determine Eddy's competence held a one-hour interview and

established that she was in full possession of her mental faculties.

Refusing to back down in the face of these personal attacks, Eddy was prompted to establish a trust for her property in order to preserve its orderly transfer to the church after her death. More important, Eddy was impelled to launch an enormous new undertaking: She directed the Trustees of the Publishing Society to establish a daily newspaper to be known as *The Christian Science Monitor*, which began publication in 1908. By bringing national and international events into clearer focus for its readers, *The Christian Science Monitor* would fulfill Eddy's vision of its purpose: to combat the apathy, indifference, and despair that were common responses to world affairs through its spiritually enlightened, problem-solving journalism.

Having witnessed the fruition of her long-cherished hopes, Eddy died quietly in her sleep on December 3, 1910.

Summary

Regardless of one's perspective on the validity of her religious beliefs, Mary Baker Eddy clearly led a remarkable life—one full of extraordinary success despite the prejudices that confronted her as a woman attempting to establish a spiritually minded religious movement during an age of rampant materialism. Novelist and humorist Mark Twain, who was one of Eddy's most outspoken critics, once remarked that she was "probably the most daring and masterful woman who has appeared on earth for centuries." A pragmatic and capable administrator who inspired her followers by her example of single-minded dedication, Eddy was equally comfortable in her role as a religious thinker—one who refused to compromise her conscience "to suit the general drift of thought" and was convinced of the importance of maintaining the intellectual and spiritual purity of her writings. Her church remains an active presence in the United States and throughout the world, and her book *Science and Health* was recognized by the Women's National Book Association in 1992 as one of seventy-five important works by "women whose words have changed the world."

Bibliography

Gill, Gillian. *Mary Baker Eddy.* Reading, Mass.: Perseus, 1998. Biography of Eddy based on Gill's examination of Christian Science church archives. Eddy is finally presented as a three-dimensional figure, powerful and significant in her contributions.

Gottschalk, Stephen. *The Emergence of Christian Science in American Religious Life.* Berkeley: University of California Press, 1973. Although its examination of Christian Science from the perspective of intellectual history may make it less easily accessible to general readers, this work sets forth the distinctive contributions Christian Science has made to American theology and culture.

Knee, Stuart E. *Christian Science in the Age of Mary Baker Eddy.* Westport, Conn.: Greenwood Press, 1994. An interesting look at Christian Science in the historical context of the close of the Civil War.

Orcutt, William Dana. *Mary Baker Eddy and Her Books.* Boston: Christian Science Publishing Society, 1950. Written by a distinguished bookmaker who worked closely with Eddy from 1897 to 1910 and helped design the oversize subscription edition of *Science and Health* that was released in 1941, this memoir provides an intriguing window on Eddy's career as an author.

Peel, Robert. *Mary Baker Eddy: The Years of Discovery.* New York: Holt Rinehart, 1966.

———. *Mary Baker Eddy: The Years of Trial.* New York: Holt Rinehart, 1971.

———. *Mary Baker Eddy: The Years of Authority.* New York: Holt Rinehart, 1977. Written by a Harvard-educated scholar who had unprecedented access to church archival materials, this monumental three-volume biography remains the definitive work on Eddy's life. Although Peel was himself a Christian Scientist, his work gives evidence of his conscientious effort to provide "a straightforward, factual account free from either apologetics or polemics."

Thomas, Robert David. *"With Bleeding Footsteps": Mary Baker Eddy's Path to Religious Leadership.* New York: Knopf, 1994. Trained in the theories of psychoanalysis, Thomas brings this psychological perspective to bear on his study of Eddy's character and behavior. Despite his serious, scholarly approach, Thomas fails to provide a complete assessment of Eddy's significance as a religious leader and seems to fall short of bringing his subject fully alive. Nevertheless, this biography is useful as one of the few fair-minded studies of Eddy to have appeared since Peel's three-volume work, cited above.

Wendy Sacket

Josephson, Matthew. *Edison: A Biography.* London: Eyre and Spottiswoode, and New York: McGraw-Hill, 1959. An excellent full-scale biography of Edison which treats his professional and personal life in detail. Contains cogent discussions of Edison's inventions, innovations, and relationships with financial figures such as Jay Gould and J. P. Morgan.

Passer, Harold C. *The Electrical Manufacturers, 1875-1900.* Cambridge, Mass.: Harvard University Press, 1953. Passer treats Edison as a pioneer inventor-entrepreneur and places his work in the context of the economic changes of late nineteenth century America. An excellent and often-cited work.

Phillips, Ray. *Edison's Kinetoscope and Its Films: A History to 1896.* Westport, Conn.: Greenwood Press, and London: Flick Books, 1997. Examination of Edison's invention of the Kinetoscope including a detailed explanation of its operation and descriptions of the "parlors" where films were shown. An index includes information on Edison's films made between 1892 and 1896.

Harry J. Eisenman

CHARLES WILLIAM ELIOT

Born: March 20, 1834; Boston, Massachusetts
Died: August 22, 1926; Northeast Harbor, Mount
  Desert, Maine
Area of Achievement: Education
Contribution: Combining administrative skill with
  a readiness to undertake novel and irregular ven-
  tures, Eliot transformed the structure and func-
  tion of higher education in the United States.

Early Life

Charles William Eliot was born on March 20,
1834, in Boston, Massachusetts. The only son of
Mary Lyman and Samuel Atkins Eliot, who were
both from prominent New England families,
Charles attended the Boston Latin Grammar
School.

Upon graduation from Boston Latin, he entered
his father's alma mater, Harvard College, in 1849.
He became especially interested in mathematics
and science and profited greatly from his study
with a number of notable professors, among whom
were Louis Agassiz, Asa Gray, and Josiah Parsons
Cooke. It was under Cooke, in fact, that the young
Eliot was given the then unique opportunity for an
undergraduate student to conduct laboratory and
field work in science.

Eliot graduated in 1853, among the top three students in his class of eighty-eight, and the following
year became a tutor in mathematics at Harvard. In
1858 he married his first wife, Ellen Derby Peabody, and in that same year he received a five-year
appointment as assistant professor of mathematics
and chemistry. While in this position, he introduced a number of curricular innovations at Harvard, including the first written examination and
placing a greater emphasis on laboratory exercises
as a learning tool.

Failing to secure promotion at the end of his five-
year appointment as assistant professor, Eliot left
Harvard in 1863 and even considered abandoning
the teaching profession. The governor of Massachusetts offered him an appointment as lieutenant colonel of cavalry in the state's militia, but poor eyesight and family financial reverses forced Eliot to
decline the offer. Instead, he embarked upon the
first of two voyages to Europe for the purpose of
further study. During his first trip abroad, Eliot was
appointed to the faculty of the newly founded Massachusetts Institute of Technology, where he began

teaching upon his return from Europe in September,
1865. Eliot gave four years of distinguished service
to that institution. He not only organized the chemistry department in collaboration with Francis Storer but also collaborated with him in writing the Eliot and Storer manuals of chemical analysis, the first
textbooks to feature laboratory and experimental
work along with theoretical principles.

Eliot's study of European education while
abroad and his experiences as a teacher at Harvard
and MIT convinced him that American colleges
and high schools were inadequate for the needs of
individual students and American society. His
thoughts about secondary and higher education
were presented in two notable articles on "the new
education," which appeared in the *Atlantic Monthly* early in 1869 and were widely read and quoted.
These articles brought him to the attention of Harvard's Board of Overseers, which was seeking a
new president for the school. Despite initial opposition to his election by some board members, Eliot
was inaugurated as the twenty-second president of
Harvard on October 19, 1869.

Life's Work

Photographs of the beardless, bespectacled middle-
aged Eliot show a profile befitting that of a late
nineteenth century college president: a receding
hairline, firmly set chin, and mutton-chop sideburns. His presidency marked a new era at Harvard. Under Eliot's leadership, Harvard's faculty
grew from sixty to six hundred and its endowment
increased from a mere two and one-half million
dollars to more than twenty million. He restructured Harvard into a university, concentrating all
undergraduate studies in the college and building
around it semiautonomous professional schools
and research facilities. In 1872, he developed graduate M.A. and Ph.D. programs, followed in 1890
by the establishment of a Graduate School of Arts
and Sciences. In the schools of medicine, law, and
divinity, he formalized entrance requirements,
courses of study, and written examinations. He assisted reformers who were interested in providing
higher education for women, which led to the
founding in 1894 of Radcliffe College.

Among Eliot's policies affecting Harvard, none
was more fundamental than the improvement of
faculty working conditions. He raised faculty sala-

ries and introduced a liberal system of retirement pensions which Harvard maintained independently until 1906, when the Carnegie Foundation made provisions for this purpose. His introduction of the sabbatical year as well as French and German exchange professorships provided faculty with greater opportunities for contact with European scholars and greater leisure for research.

The most radical and far-reaching innovation introduced during Eliot's administration was the elective principle. This reform grew out of Eliot's conviction that college students needed more freedom in selecting courses so that they might acquire self-reliance, discover their own hidden talents, rise to a higher level of attainment in their chosen fields, and demonstrate a greater interest in their studies. Eliot also believed that modern subjects such as English, French, German, history, economics, and especially the natural and physical sciences should have equal rank with Latin, Greek, and mathematics in the college curriculum.

Gradually under Eliot's leadership, Harvard adopted the elective principle. In 1872, all course restrictions for seniors were abolished. Seven years later, all junior course restrictions were abolished. In 1884 sophomore course restrictions came to an end, and the following year those for freshmen were greatly reduced. By 1897, the required course of study at Harvard had been reduced to a year of freshman rhetoric.

Eliot's influence was felt in other areas of college life. The long-standing rule requiring student attendance at chapel was abolished, and participation in all religious activities was made voluntary. Eliot demonstrated a keen interest in athletic policy, too. He established a general athletic committee, composed of alumni, undergraduates, faculty, and administrators. In addition, Eliot played an important role in the introduction of stricter eligibility requirements for college athletes at Harvard and other American colleges.

Although higher educational reform occupied most of his energies, Eliot used his position to influence primary and secondary schools as well. His numerous published articles and addresses covered a wide range of subjects. He argued for better training and greater security of teachers and for improved sanitary conditions in schools; he supported Progressive Era educators' efforts to improve schooling; and he emphasized the need for teachers and schools to train the senses, the body, and the imagination of the student. At the same time, he

raised and diversified admissions requirements at Harvard to exert pressure upon schools to improve the quality of their instruction.

After Eliot resigned from the presidency of Harvard in 1909, he continued to participate in a wide range of activities. As a member of Harvard's Board of Overseers, Eliot maintained an interest in campus affairs. He was influential in shaping the policies of the General Education Board, the Rockefeller Foundation, and the Carnegie Foundation for the Advancement of Teaching. Eliot devoted the remainder of his time to writing, speech-making, and correspondence. Fully active until the last year of his life, he died at Northeast Harbor, Mount Desert, Maine, on August 22, 1926.

Summary

In countless ways, Eliot exerted a powerful influence upon the development of higher education in the United States. During his long and productive career, the university emerged as a preeminent force in Americans' lives. It became the primary service organization which made possible the function of many other institutions in society. The university not only brought coherence and uniformity to the training of individuals for professional careers but also provided a formal structure for the techniques Americans employed in thinking about every level of human existence.

Eliot was able to accomplish so much because, to an extraordinary degree, his own outlook mirrored the hopes and fears of many other late nineteenth century Americans. Eliot's contribution to change in higher education made a difference in American history at a crucial moment, when aspiring middle-class individuals were struggling to define new career patterns, establish new institutions, pursue new occupations, and forge a new self-identity. The university was basic to this struggle; it became a central institution in a competitive, status-conscious society. Eliot played a key role in this process by giving vitality to the American college at a time when its remoteness from society imperiled the whole structure of higher education in the United States.

Bibliography

Bledstein, Burton J. *The Culture of Professionalism: The Middle Class and the Development of Higher Education in America.* New York: Norton, 1976. The best single book about the activities and ideology of Eliot and other leaders of late nineteenth century American higher education. Although somewhat overcritical, offers a needed corrective to other accounts.

Carnes, Mark C. "And to Think That it Happened on Mt. Auburn Street: Dr. James, Harvard, and the Making of Manhood." *Reviews in American History* 25, no. 4 (December 1997). Examines the fixation on masculinity at Harvard University during the Eliot's tenure as its President.

Eliot, Charles W. *Charles W. Eliot and Popular Education.* Edited by Edward A. Krug. New York: Teachers College Press, 1961. This short anthology includes nine of Eliot's articles, addresses, and reports on education in the United States during the late nineteenth century and early twentieth century. It also contains a lengthy introduction which discusses and analyzes his contribution to the educational reform movement.

———. *Educational Reform: Essays and Addresses.* New York: Century, 1898. Contains some of Eliot's early essays and addresses. Provides readers with a sample of his thinking on American education's problems and their solutions.

———. *A Late Harvest: Miscellaneous Papers Written Between Eighty and Ninety.* Boston: Atlantic Monthly Press, 1924. This volume contains typical products of Eliot's thought during the last years of his life. In addition to a brief autobiographical piece, it includes papers on a wide range of subjects. Of particular note is a partial bibliography of Eliot's publications from 1914 to 1924.

Hawkins, Hugh. *Between Harvard and America: The Educational Leadership of Charles W. Eliot.* New York: Oxford University Press, 1972. The best single book on Eliot's tenure as president of Harvard. It analyzes his efforts to make the university ideal a reality in the changing, sometimes hostile social environment of late nineteenth century and early twentieth century America.

James, Henry. *Charles W. Eliot, President of Harvard University, 1869-1909.* 2 vols. London: Constable, and Boston: Houghton Mifflin, 1930. Marred by its uncritical perspective, this nevertheless well-written, highly detailed biography of Eliot remains indispensable; all subsequent studies of Eliot's life have drawn on it.

Rudolph, Frederick. *The American College and University: A History.* New York: Knopf, 1962. Provides a rich analysis of Eliot's early years as president and reformer at Harvard. Generally balanced and well researched, it provides a clear, objective account of the elective system's revolutionary impact on higher education in the United States.

Tyack, David B. *The One Best System: A History of American Urban Education.* Cambridge, Mass.: Harvard University Press, 1974. This highly readable, well-documented study only briefly discusses Eliot's activities on behalf of public schooling, but it provides a detailed account of the social milieu in which he worked and shaped his ideas about education.

Veysey, Laurence R. *The Emergence of the American University.* Chicago: University of Chicago Press, 1965. A massive study that includes more references to Eliot than to any other person. Valuable chiefly for its background information and incisive analysis of the social and intellectual context within which late nineteenth century American higher educational reform proceeded.

Monroe H. Little, Jr.

GEORGE ELIOT
Mary Ann Evans

Born: November 22, 1819; Chilvers Coton, Warwickshire, England

Died: December 22, 1880; London, England

Area of Achievement: Literature

Contribution: Because of her philosophical profundity and her mastery of fictional technique, Eliot won a reputation as one of the world's great novelists and helped establish the novel as an appropriate vehicle for the serious exploration of ideas.

Early Life

The woman who wrote her novels under the pseudonym George Eliot was born Mary Ann Evans on November 22, 1819, on Arbury Farm, near Coventry in the rich farming district of central England. Her father, a man with an almost legendary reputation for integrity and competence, worked as an estate agent, or general overseer, on the extensive lands of the aristocratic Newdigate family. Her upbringing in the evangelical traditions of the Church of England gave her strong moral convictions that remained with her all of her life and formed the basic moral imperatives of her fiction.

When Evans was twenty-two, she and her father, who had retired from active work, moved to a house just outside Coventry. Evans' closest friends in Coventry were Charles and Cara Bray and Cara's sister Sara Hennell. Like many others who took part in the intellectual and religious ferment of early Victorian England, the Brays questioned the validity of Christian theology, although they had no serious reservations about the value of Christian moral teachings. Contact with them reinforced the doubts about her evangelical religion which Evans had already begun to entertain. In 1844, she began translating *Das Leben Jesu* by the German theologian David Friedrich Strauss, which she published two years later under the title *The Life of Jesus, Critically Examined.* Her work on Strauss further undermined her Christian orthodoxy.

Shortly after her father's death in 1849, Mary Ann Evans, who was now spelling her name Marian, became associated with John Chapman, editor of the *Westminster Review,* a prestigious intellectual quarterly whose first editor had been John Stuart Mill. Although the social customs of Victorian England made it impossible for a woman to bear the title of editor of an important journal of opinion addressed largely to a male audience, Evans exercised primary editorial responsibility for the *Westminster Review.* She not only solicited and selected articles and planned the content of the issues, but she wrote many reviews. ("Reviews" in Victorian intellectual journals were really independent essays that might run to fifteen or twenty pages in length.) Although shy and retiring by nature (her shyness may have been reinforced by her lack of physical beauty—she had a prominent nose and rather heavy features), Evans was at the center of intellectual life in Victorian England.

Among the many people with whom Evans became acquainted at this time was George Henry Lewes. One of the most versatile of the Victorian intellectuals, Lewes was a biologist, novelist, drama critic, biographer of Goethe, and author of a history of philosophy. Lewes's wife, Agnes, was openly adulterous, but Lewes had accepted her extramarital affairs and registered her illegitimate children as his own. When Lewes and Evans fell

in love, there seemed to be no way that Lewes could divorce Agnes. Not only was divorce in Victorian England expensive and legally complex, but the usual grounds of divorce, adultery, had been eliminated by Lewes's generous acceptance of Agnes' illegitimate children. After deciding that they could hurt only themselves by a common-law marriage, Marian Evans and George Henry Lewes agreed to live together as husband and wife. In July, 1854, they began a honeymoon trip to Germany; Marian wrote to tell her friends of this relationship and to ask that they henceforth address her as Marian Lewes.

Life's Work

Her common-law marriage with Lewes initiated the most productive period in Evans' life. Lewes provided her with the emotional support she needed and encouraged her when she decided to try her hand at writing fiction. Because of the scandal which was associated with her relationship with Lewes and because she did not want to compromise her reputation as a translator and a reviewer, Evans wrote under a pen name; she selected "George Eliot." Lewes protected her anonymity and carried on all negotiations with publishers.

George Eliot's first published fiction was "The Sad Fortunes of the Reverend Amos Barton," which appeared in the issue of *Blackwood's Magazine* that came out on New Year's Day, 1857. With two other short works of fiction which also appeared in *Blackwood's Magazine*—"Mr. Gilfil's Love-Story" and "Janet's Repentance"—it was reprinted in book form in *Scenes of Clerical Life* in 1858. Her first major work of fiction was *Adam Bede*, published by Blackwood's in 1859. *Adam Bede* was a popular and critical success, and "George Eliot" was hailed as an important new talent. Among the principal writers of the time, Charles Dickens was one of the few who suspected that *Adam Bede* had been written by a woman.

In chapter 17 of *Adam Bede*, Eliot makes one of the most important statements of the creed of the realistic novelist. Art, she says, should always remind us of the world's "common coarse people, who have no picturesque sentimental wretchedness"; the artist should be "ready to give the loving pains of a life to the faithful representing of commonplace things." Moreover, the novelist's purpose is not only to achieve the kind of accuracy of representation one finds in Dutch painting but also to ensure that a "fibre of sympathy" ties the au-

thor—and, by implication, the reader—to the "vulgar citizen" with whom one is in contact in everyday life so that, as she says, "my heart should swell with loving admiration of some trait of gentle goodness in the faulty people who sit at the same hearth with me." The aim of the novelist, then, is not only to depict life accurately, but also to enlarge the reader's human sympathies.

George Eliot's second novel, *The Mill on the Floss* (1860), is her most autobiographical work, nostalgically recalling her own childhood with her brother Isaac Evans in her depiction of Maggie and Tom Tulliver. The novel also embodies, in the adult character of Maggie, the moral issues that Eliot was to explore again and again in her fiction: the dangers of self-indulgence and self-deception, often associated with some inappropriate sexual relationship, and the need for self-sacrifice and the renunciation of egotistical desires. *The Mill on the Floss* was followed in 1861 by *Silas Marner*, which is perhaps the most familiar of all of her novels. Her shortest major work, it suggests more directly than her other novels the way in which human relationships based on Christian morality provide the support that in previous ages might have been afforded by the institutional church. *Romola* (1863), a historical novel set in Renaissance Florence, is Eliot's only novel which does not have an English setting. The historical novel was a genre which enjoyed considerable prestige at the time, and Eliot's research into the historical background of the novel was both exhaustive and exhausting. Yet the novel, which was published in the *Cornhill Magazine*, then edited by William Makepeace Thackeray, was not a popular success. In order to compensate Thackeray for the comparative failure of *Romola*, Eliot gave him, without charge, a short story for publication in the *Cornhill Magazine*.

In her next fiction, *Felix Holt, Radical* (1866), Eliot returned to an English setting and to her previous publisher, Blackwood's. *Felix Holt, Radical*, perhaps Eliot's least-read novel, has a plot marred by excessive reliance on obscure coincidences, but also contains some of her most profound psychological analysis. Her next work, *The Spanish Gypsy* (1868), is a blank verse tragedy, another genre that enjoyed considerable prestige in Victorian England. Eliot's literary gifts did not, however, include the ability to write good poetry, and *The Spanish Gypsy*, in spite of some commercial success, must be rated as her least effective major work.

Eliot's first three novels have a warmth and humor that has charmed her readers. Her works of the mid-1860's show an advance in psychological complexity and philosophical depth, but often lack the seeming spontaneity of her early novels. All of her talents as a novelist, however, have their greatest expression in her next novel, *Middlemarch* (1871-1872), which is one of the supreme achievements of English fiction. A novel with dozens of deeply studied characters, *Middlemarch* examines the limitations and opportunities of life in a provincial English town in the early 1830's. Eliot's final novel, *Daniel Deronda* (1876), combines some of her most profound psychological analysis with a plot that anticipates the Zionist movement to establish a national homeland for the Jews in Palestine.

When *Daniel Deronda* was published, Eliot was widely regarded as the greatest living English novelist. Her literary achievement, the more liberal moral code of the late Victorian period, and the obvious respectability of her life with Lewes had largely dissipated the scandal once associated with their common-law marriage, and she and Lewes were received in the highest literary and social circles. Both, however, were afflicted with ill health, and on November 30, 1878, Lewes died at the age of sixty-one. Devastated by the loss of the man who had given her so much companionship and encouragement for more than twenty years, Eliot turned for support to John Cross, a young man who had been their close friend for several years. On May 6, 1880, she and Cross were married, but their marriage was to be a short one, for on December 22, 1880, Eliot died.

Summary

George Eliot was approaching forty when she embarked on the career as a novelist for which she is known today. Her previous work as a translator of theological and philosophical treatises, her experience as the virtual editor of one of the leading intellectual quarterlies of the day, her authorship of many extensive essay reviews, and her friendship with leading Victorian thinkers had given her a depth of knowledge unmatched by any previous novelist. As her standing as an intellectual was widely recognized in her own day, Eliot probably did more than anyone else to change the view that the novel could only be regarded as popular entertainment and to win recognition for this genre as a vehicle for the serious examination of ideas. Like other great novelists, she expanded both the range and the technical resources of the novel. Whereas previous novelists had, in general, emphasized the external events in the lives of their characters, Eliot emphasized their thoughts and feelings. In her novels, her characters' psychological response to an event is almost always more significant than the event itself. The expansion of the subject matter of fiction often requires new techniques of novel writing; Eliot's examination of her characters' mind and emotions is frequently presented through elaborate patterns of imagery which allow her to express the subtleties and complexities of their emotional and ethical dilemmas.

Eliot is not generally considered a feminist, but what she accomplished in her career unquestionably did much to enhance the status of women. Other women—for example, Jane Austen and Charlotte Brontë—had achieved critical or popular success as novelists, but Eliot's recognition as the greatest living English novelist was an unprecedented achievement for a woman.

Although Eliot wrote primarily of English subjects, she was highly regarded in the United States as well. Her defense of realism in chapter 17 of *Adam Bede* was echoed on both sides of the Atlantic, and she was a major influence on some of America's most important novelists, among them William Dean Howells and Henry James.

Bibliography

Haight, Gordon S. *George Eliot: A Biography*. Oxford: Clarendon Press, and New York: Oxford University Press, 1968. A careful and thorough biography by one of the leading Eliot scholars, this book avoids interpreting Eliot's personality beyond elaborating on a statement by Charles Bray that "she was not fitted to stand alone." It is the most reliable source for detailed factual information about Eliot.

―――. *George Eliot and John Chapman, with Chapman's Diaries*. New Haven, Conn., and London: Yale University Press, 1940. A detailed study of Eliot's work on the *Westminster Review* and of her personal relationship with John Chapman. Includes transcripts of Chapman's diaries.

Kitchel, Anna. *George Lewes and George Eliot*. New York: John Day, 1933. A standard work on Lewes as well as a useful study of the most important relationship in Eliot's life, this biography gives a good picture of Eliot's emotional and intellectual development.

Laski, Marghanita. *George Eliot and Her World.* London: Thames and Hudson, 1973; New York: Scribner, 1978. A richly illustrated short biography. Less sympathetic to Lewes than most biographers, Laski tends to support the conjecture, mentioned in other biographies as well, that Eliot's marriage to Cross soon after Lewes's death may have been prompted by her discovery of evidence that her common-law husband had been guilty of infidelity.

Redinger, Ruby. *George Eliot: The Emergent Self.* New York: Knopf, 1975; London: Bodley Head, 1976. An interesting and often persuasive attempt to explore the interplay of events and personality traits that contributed to the development of Eliot as a writer. Redinger emphasizes the psychological damage caused by Eliot's father's insistence on evangelical orthodoxy and by her brother's cruel rejection of her when she associated herself with Lewes.

Rignall, John, ed. *George Eliot and Europe.* Aldershot, Hampshire, and Brookfield, Vt.: Scolar Press, 1997. A collection of essays by participants in a 1995 conference held to examine Eliot's place in the literature of Europe. Treatments include biography, critique, and comparisons with emphasis on her work rather than public perceptions.

Robertson, Linda K. *The Power of Knowledge: George Eliot and Education.* New York: Lang, 1997. Discusses Eliot's opinions on education as based on analysis of her essays, fiction, and letters.

Sprague, Rosemary. *George Eliot: A Biography.* Philadelphia: Chilton, 1968. A well-written biography with a considerable appeal for the general reader. It includes critical comments on Eliot's novels.

Willey, Basil. *Nineteenth Century Studies.* London: Chatto and Windus, and New York: Columbia University Press, 1949. A classic study of the impact of German theology and "higher criticism" on Eliot's early evangelicalism. Of special interest are the chapters "George Eliot: Hennell, Strauss and Feuerbach" and "George Eliot, Conclusion."

Erwin Hester

RALPH WALDO EMERSON

Born: May 25, 1803; Boston, Massachusetts
Died: April 27, 1882; Concord, Massachusetts
Area of Achievement: Literature
Contribution: Emerson was a spokesman for a peculiarly American culture. His writings contributed to that culture and encouraged others to add still further to it.

Early Life

The fourth child of Unitarian minister William Emerson and Ruth Haskins Emerson, Ralph Waldo Emerson was born in Boston, Massachusetts, on May 25, 1803. His father's death in 1811 left the family poor, and his mother had to maintain a boardinghouse to support the family of six young children.

Despite this poverty, Emerson's education was not neglected. He attended the prestigious Boston Latin School (1812-1817) and in 1821 was graduated from Harvard. Even when he was an undergraduate, his interest in philosophy and writing was evident. In 1820, he won second prize in the Bowdoin competition for his essay "The Character of Socrates," and the following year, he won the prize again with "The Present State of Ethical Philosophy." In these pieces he demonstrated his preference for the present over the past, praising the modern Scottish Common Sense philosophers more highly than Aristotle and Socrates.

This preference derived largely from his belief that the modern philosophers offered more guidance in how to live. Despite the mysticism that informs much of Emerson's writing, he remained concerned with daily life. Thus, his purpose in *Representative Men* (1850) was to draw from the lives of great men some lessons for everyday behavior, and in the 1850's he gave a series of lectures collected under the title *The Conduct of Life* (1860).

After graduation from Harvard, Emerson taught school for his brother William before entering Harvard Divinity School in 1825. In 1826, he delivered his first sermon in Waltham, Massachusetts; typically, it dealt with the conduct of life. Emerson warned that because prayers are always answered, people must be careful to pray for the right things. One sees here another strain that runs through Emerson's writings, the optimistic view that one gets what one seeks.

Three years later, in 1829, Emerson was ordained as minister of Boston's Second Church, once the Puritan bastion of Increase and Cotton Mather. In the course of his maiden sermon there, he spoke of the spiritual value of the commonplace. He reminded his audience that parables explain divine truths through homey allusions and noted that if Jesus were to address a nineteenth century congregation, he "would appeal to those arts and objects by which we are surrounded; to the printing-press and the loom, to the phenomena of steam and of gas." Again one finds this love of the commonplace as a persistent theme throughout his work. As he states in *Nature* (1836), "The meal in the firkin; the milk in the pan; the ballad in the street; the news of the boat" all embody universal truths.

In the same year that Emerson became minister of the Second Church, he married Ellen Louisa Tucker. Her death from tuberculosis in 1831 triggered an emotional and psychological crisis in Emerson, already troubled by elements of Unitarianism. In October, 1832, he resigned his ministry, claiming that he could not accept the church's view of communion, and in December he embarked for a year in Europe. Here he met a number of his literary heroes, including Samuel Taylor Coleridge, William Wordsworth, and Thomas Carlyle. He was less impressed with these men—Carlyle excepted—than he was with the Jardin des Plantes in Paris. At the French botanical garden he felt "moved by strange sympathies. I say I will listen to this invitation. I will be a naturalist."

Returning to Boston in 1833, Emerson soon began the first of numerous lecture series that would take him across the country many times during his life. From the lectern he would peer at his audience with his intense blue eyes. Tall and thin, habitually wearing an enigmatic smile, he possessed an angelic quality that contributed to his popularity as a speaker. The subject of his first lectures was science, a topic to which he often returned. His literary debut came, however, not from a scientific but from a philosophical examination of the physical world.

Life's Work

In 1835, Emerson married Lydia Jackson (rechristened Lidian by Emerson), and the couple moved to Concord, where Emerson lived the rest of his life. The next year Waldo, the first of their four children,

was born. In 1836, too, Emerson published a small pamphlet called *Nature*. Condemning the age for looking to the past instead of the present, he reminded his readers that "the sun shines to-day also." To create a contemporary poetry and philosophy, all that was necessary was to place oneself in harmony with nature. Then "swine, spiders, snakes, pests, madhouses, prisons, enemies" will yield to "beautiful faces, warm hearts, wise discourse, and heroic acts . . . until evil is no more seen. . . . Build therefore your own world."

The volume was not popular: It sold only fifteen hundred copies in America in the eight years following its publication, and a second edition was not published until 1849. It served, though, as the rallying cry for the Transcendentalist movement. In literature this group looked to Carlyle and Johann Wolfgang von Goethe; indeed, Emerson arranged for the publication of Carlyle's first book, *Sartor Resartus* (1836), in the United States some years before it found a publisher in England. In philosophy the Transcendentalists followed Immanuel Kant in believing that man can transcend sensory experience (hence the movement's name); they thus rejected the view of John Locke, who maintained that all knowledge comes from and is rooted in the senses. In religion it rejected miracles and emphasized instead the Bible's ethical teachings.

Addressing the Phi Beta Kappa Society at Harvard on August 31, 1837, Emerson returned to his theme in "The American Scholar." He warned against the tyranny of received opinion, particularly as it appeared in books: "Meek young men grow up in libraries, believing it their duty to accept the views, which Cicero, which Locke, which Bacon have given," but "Cicero, Locke, and Bacon were only young men in libraries, when they wrote these books." The American scholar should, therefore, read the book of nature. He should do so confidently, believing that in him "is the law of all nature, . . . the whole of Reason."

Thus guided by his own insight and revelation rather than by outdated cultures, the scholar would lead others to a union with the spiritual source of life. This enlightened individual was to be American as well as scholarly, for the nature he was to take as his mentor was that of the New World rather than the Old.

In 1838, Emerson presented the controversial "Divinity School Address." To his audience of intellectual, rational Unitarians he preached the doctrine of constant revelation and called each of his listeners "a newborn bard of the Holy Ghost." Once more he was urging the rejection of the past—in this case historical Christianity—in favor of the present and trust in personal feelings rather than doctrine and dogma. His criticism of what he saw as the cold lifelessness of Unitarianism so shocked his listeners that he was barred from Harvard for almost three decades.

Such a reaction, though, was what Emerson was seeking; he wanted to shock what he saw as a complacent nation into regeneration through an appreciation of the present. "What is man for but to be a Reformer," he wrote. First person was to reform, that is remake, himself; hence, Emerson took little interest in political parties or the many Utopian experiments—some started by members of the Transcendental Club—of the 1840's. When enough individuals reformed themselves, society would necessarily be improved.

Among those who shared Emerson's vision were a number of neighbors: Bronson Alcott, Ellery Channing, Margaret Fuller, Elizabeth Peabody, Jones Very, and Henry David Thoreau. From 1840 to 1844, this group published *The Dial*, a quarterly magazine rich in literature that expressed the Emersonian vision. Emerson frequently contributed to the journal, and for the magazine's last two years he was its editor also.

His new philosophy spread well beyond Concord. In his journal in 1839, Emerson recorded that "a number of young and adult persons are at this moment the subject of a revolution [and] have silently given in their several adherence to a new hope."

In 1841, he published *Essays*, which includes what is probably Emerson's most famous piece, "Self-Reliance." The themes of the essays were by now familiar, but the expression was forcefully aphoristic. Attacking contemporary religion, education, politics, art, and literature for their adherence to tradition, he declared, "Whoso would be a man must be a nonconformist." In 1844 appeared *Essays: Second Series*, with its call for an American poet who would sing of "our logrolling, our stumps, . . . our fisheries, our Negroes, and Indians, . . . the northern trade, the southern planting, the western clearing, Oregon, and Texas." The American poet would not care for "meters, but meter-making argument."

Emerson attempted to fill this role himself. His aunt Mary Moody had encouraged his youthful efforts in this area, and at the age of ten he had begun a poetic romance, "The History of Fortus." His early efforts had earned for him the role of class poet when he was graduated from Harvard in 1821. *Poems* (1847) suggests, however, that he lacked the ability or inclination to follow his own advice. The poems often remain tied to meter and rhyme rather than the rhythms of natural speech. In "Days," one of his more successful pieces, he described himself as sitting in his "pleached garden" and forgetting his "morning wishes." In "The Poet" he lamented, "I miss the grand design." Shortly before his second marriage, he had written to Lidian that though he saw himself as a poet, he knew he was one "of a low class, whose singing . . . is very husky." Some poems, though, like "The Snow Storm," reveal the power and beauty of nature through language that is fresh and immediate. Others, such as "Brahma" and "The Sphinx" (Emerson's favorite), use symbols well to convey spiritual messages and suggest the correspondence among man, nature, and the spiritual world that is one of the tenets of Transcendentalism.

In the next decade, Emerson published three important works based on his lectures: *Representative Men* (1850), *English Traits* (1856), and *The Conduct of Life* (1860). His lectures were not always well attended, even though he was in great demand. One course of lectures in Chicago brought only thirty-seven dollars; another audience in Illinois quickly left when it found a lecture lacking in humor.

The books that emerged from these lectures are more sober than his earlier writings. His youthful idealism is tempered by a darker sense of reality. In "Fate," the first chapter of *The Conduct of Life*, he recognizes the tyrannies of life and notes that man is subject to limitations. In the concluding essay of the book, he reaffirms liberty and urges again, "Speak as you think, be what you are," but he concedes, too, the power of illusion to deceive and mislead.

After the Civil War, Emerson published two more collections of his essays, *Society and Solitude* (1870) and *Letters and Social Aims* (1876), this second with the help of James Elliot Cabot. Much of the contents of these books is drawn from lectures and journal entries written decades earlier.

Although he was reusing old ideas, his popularity continued to grow. In 1867, he was invited to deliver the Phi Beta Kappa address again at Harvard; the previous year the school had indicated its for-

giveness for the "Divinity School Address" by awarding Emerson an honorary doctorate. When he returned from a trip to Europe and the Middle East in 1873, the church bells of Concord rang to welcome him back, and the townspeople turned out in force to greet him.

Emerson recognized, however, that his powers were declining. As he wrote in "Terminus," "It is time to be old/ To take in sail/ . . . Fancy departs." John Muir saw him in California in 1871 and was amazed at the physical transformation, one mirrored by his fading mental abilities as his aphasia worsened. After John Burroughs attended a lecture by Emerson in 1872, he described the address as "pitiful." When Emerson attended the funeral of his neighbor Henry Wadsworth Longfellow in March, 1882, he could not remember the famous poet's name. A few weeks later, on April 27, 1882, Emerson died of pneumonia and was buried near his leading disciple, Thoreau.

Summary

Emerson said that Goethe was the cow from which the rest drew their milk. The same may be said of Emerson himself. Walt Whitman derived his poetic inspiration from "The Poet," as Whitman acknowledged by sending a copy of the first edition of *Leaves of Grass* (1855) to Concord. Emerson was among the few contemporary readers of the book to recognize its genius. Thoreau, though an independent thinker, also took much from Emerson. In "Self-Reliance," Emerson had written, "In the pleasing contrite wood-life which God allows me, let me record day by day my honest thoughts without prospect or retrospect. . . . My book should smell of pines and resound with the hum of insects." Here is a summary of *Walden* (1854). Emerson's emphasis on the miraculous within the quotidian may even have influenced William Dean Howells and other American realists later in the century.

As an advocate of literary nationalism, of a truly American culture, he urged his countrymen to look about them and celebrate their own surroundings. His was not the only voice calling for an intellectual and cultural independence to mirror the country's political autonomy, but it was an important and influential one. Oliver Wendell Holmes, Sr., referred to "The American Scholar" as "our intellectual Declaration of Independence."

In calling for a Renaissance rooted in the present of the New World rather than the past of the Old, Emerson was paradoxically joining the mainstream of the American spirit. Like John Winthrop in his sermon aboard the *Arbella* in 1630, he was advocating a new spirit for a new land.

Like his Puritan forerunners, too, Emerson stressed spiritual rather than material salvation. Having grown up poor, he harbored no illusions about poverty. He knew that "to be rich is to have a ticket of admission to the masterworks and chief men of every race." Because of such statements, H. L. Mencken said that Emerson would have made a fine Rotarian. This misreading of Emerson ignores the view that he expressed near the end of his life: "Our real estate is that amount of thought which we have." For Benjamin Franklin, the American Dream meant the opportunity to earn money. For Emerson, as for the Puritans, it meant the opportunity to live in harmony with oneself, to save not one's pennies but one's soul. Emerson's lectures and essays forcefully articulate a vision of America that has continued to inform American thought and writing.

Bibliography

Allen, Gay Wilson. *Waldo Emerson: A Biography.* New York: Viking Press, 1981; London: Penguin, 1982. The definitive biography of Emerson, at once scholarly and readable. Allen is concerned with the personal as well as the public side of his subject. He also shows the evolution of Emerson's ideas by citing the stages of their development in journal entries, letters, lectures, essays, and poems.

Bode, Carl, ed. *Ralph Waldo Emerson: A Profile.* New York: Hill and Wang, 1969. How did Emerson's contemporaries view him? How has that view changed since his death? Bode offers a selection of biographical sketches by friends and scholars. Some of the earlier pieces are not readily available elsewhere.

Cadava, Eduardo. *Emerson and the Climates of History.* Stanford, Calif.: Stanford University Press, 1997. A study of Emerson's use of the weather as metaphor for historical and political issues of his day. The author argues that Emerson's writings are not, as historically maintained, a flight from history, but rather a reassessment of history in terms of questions of representation.

Engstrom, Sallee. *The Infinitude of the Private Man: Emerson's Presence in Western New York, 1851-1861.* New York: Lang, 1997. Engstrom investigates Emerson's lectures of 1851-1861 and the reform movements of the time.

Leary, Lewis Gaston. *Ralph Waldo Emerson: An Interpretive Essay.* Boston: Twayne, 1980. Offers an intellectual biography with a thematic arrangement. The focus is on understanding Emerson's ideas and their relationship to his life.

McAleer, John J. *Ralph Waldo Emerson: Days of Encounter.* Boston: Little Brown, 1984. Each of the eighty short chapters treats a stage in Emerson's growth as a person, thinker, or writer. Much of the book deals with actual encounters between Emerson and his contemporaries to illustrate their mutual influence.

Matthiessen, Francis Otto. *American Renaissance: Art and Expression in the Age of Emerson and Whitman.* London and New York: Oxford University Press, 1941. Investigates the intellectual climate that produced so much significant American literature between 1850 and 1855. Focus is on literary criticism of the works themselves. Appropriately, Matthiessen begins with Emerson and explores all of his major works, not simply his publications in the early 1850's.

Miller, Perry. "From Edwards to Emerson." In *Errand into the Wilderness*, 184-203. Cambridge, Mass.: Belknap Press of Harvard University Press, 1956. An insightful essay exploring Emerson's intellectual debt to the Puritans at the same time that it shows the radical newness of Emerson's ideas.

Rusk, Ralph Leslie. *The Life of Ralph Waldo Emerson.* New York: Scribner, 1949. Rusk's was a pioneering study, the most detailed biography of Emerson up to that time and still useful for its meticulous detail. Rusk carefully examined unpublished material to present an authoritative picture of Emerson's life. Concentrates more on the man than on his ideas.

Joseph Rosenblum

FRIEDRICH ENGELS

Born: November 28, 1820; Barmen, Prussia

Died: August 5, 1895; London, England

Areas of Achievement: Social reform, government, and politics

Contribution: In partnership with Karl Marx, Engels analyzed the origins and nature of industrial capitalist society and worked to bring about the overthrow of that society by a working-class revolution.

Early Life

Friedrich Engels was born into the social class whose domination he later strove to overturn. His father, Friedrich, owned one of the principal cotton mills in the Wupper Valley, in the Rhineland territory that Prussia had taken over in 1815 after the Napoleonic Wars. It was assumed that young Friedrich, the first of nine children, would enter the family business, and university education was considered unnecessary for a business career; Friedrich left grammar school in 1837 without taking the final examinations, having shown strong academic skills, particularly in languages. His literary inclinations, he believed, could be pursued without academic credentials; indeed, he became impressively self-educated.

By 1838, when he began a sort of businessman's apprenticeship in the export business of a family friend in Bremen, Engels had already broken away from the strong Pietist fundamentalist Protestantism of his family and of Barmen. His letters also included sarcastic attacks on the Prussian king, Friedrich Wilhelm IV, calling him oppressive and stupid. His taste in philosophy favored D. F. Strauss and the Young Hegelians, in literature, Heinrich Heine and the Young German movement. Engels had defined himself as an alienated young man, but the newspaper articles that he wrote from Bremen were generally amusing, mocking rather than vehement in tone, though Engels did attack both capitalists and Pietists.

Engels returned to Barmen in 1841, and later that year went to Berlin to do his military service as a one-year volunteer in the Prussian artillery. His military duties, which he often avoided, were so undemanding that he was able to attend lectures at the university, associate with enthusiastic young radicals, and write copiously on political and philosophical issues. In October, 1842, his military

service completed, he visited Cologne and the offices of the *Rheinische Zeitung*, whose editor, Moses Hess, claimed credit for converting Engels from generic revolutionary to communist.

From November, 1842, to August, 1844, Engels was in England, working in the Manchester branch of his father's firm and preparing his vivid attack on industrial capitalism, *Die Lage der arbeitende Klasse in England* (1845; *The Condition of the Working Class in England in 1844*, 1887). In Paris, on the way home from England, Engels met Karl Marx, beginning a partnership that lasted till Marx's death. The two had met, coolly, in November, 1842. Now Engels' firsthand acquaintance with industrial society impressed Marx, who was beginning to interest himself in economic issues. The university-educated Marx, two years older than Engels, was profound, while Engels was quick; Marx mapped out huge projects that remained unfinished, and Engels responded to the needs of the moment. Together they attempted to change the world.

Life's Work

Marx and Engels defined their differences from other socialists of the day in their first collaborative writings and joined in organizing various revolutionary groups in Brussels, Paris, and London. One of these, the Communist League, aspired to be an international organization of the revolutionary working class, under the slogan "Workers of the World, unite!" Engels drafted this group's program and Marx revised it into *Manifest der Kommunistischen Partei* (1848; *The Communist Manifesto*, 1850). Although this program of a weak organization had little effect in 1848, it combined philosophy and economic history into a powerful prophecy that the course of history would soon make it possible to eliminate class rule and inaugurate true human freedom. The successes of the Industrial Revolution, carried out by the middle classes, were creating the conditions for a workers' revolution. Despite its dated denunciations of ephemeral leftist rivals, *The Communist Manifesto* remains the central expression of Marxism's ideas and style.

Revolution broke out in Paris in February, 1848, followed by upheavals elsewhere. Liberalism and nationalism were the issues of the day, not communism. Engels and Marx devoted their efforts to the *Neue Rheinische Zeitung*, published in Cologne, which advocated the unification of Germany as a democratic republic, ignoring for the moment the eventual goal of abolishing capitalism. Engels wrote caustically on the deliberations of the Frankfurt Assembly as that body failed to unite Germany, and he discussed revolution-related military campaigns in Hungary, Italy, and elsewhere. The authorities suspended the paper's publication in September and October, and Engels fled, taking an extended walking tour in France and returning to Cologne in January, 1849. He replaced Marx as editor-in-chief in April and May. In early May, uprisings occurred in several German areas, including Engels' hometown. He left Cologne to take part, but order was soon restored; he went back to Cologne, but the government, recovering its sense of initiative, shut down the *Neue Rheinische Zeitung* for good.

As revolutionary hopes faded everywhere in Europe, the Prussian king declined the invitation of the Frankfurt Assembly to serve as ruler of a new united Germany; only two small states supported the defiant, obviously doomed call to unite the country as a republic. Engels joined the volunteer corps, led by August Willich, as the revolutionary diehards held out for more than a month against overwhelming Prussian and other forces; he was among the last to cross into Switzerland. His sole experience of revolutionary combat showed the limitations of slogans and zeal against military organization.

Engels sailed from Genoa to London, already the refuge of Marx and many other revolutionary refugees. Debates on tactics and organization soon led to a split between the "party of the *Neue Rheinische Zeitung*," who argued that a real revolution would depend on years of preparation, education, and economic development, and those (including Engels' former commander Willich and other officers) who wished to revive the revolution by immediate conspiratorial and military action. As on several other occasions, Marx and Engels opposed more impatient revolutionaries. One consequence of this émigré discord (1850-1851) was that Engels took up the study of military science, to contest the opposing faction's monopoly on military expertise.

Bowing to economic necessity, Engels went to work at his father's company in Manchester. After his father's death in 1860, he became a partner in the firm, selling out his interest in 1869. His income from the textile mill, and later from successful investments, supported an official address where he met his business contacts, and a home where he lived with Mary Burns, a factory worker whom he had met during his visit to England in 1842-1844. It also furnished the chief, and often the only, source of support for the Marx family in London.

Until he was able to move to London in 1869, Engels corresponded daily with Marx. He wrote articles, often under Marx's name, for sale. When Eugen Dühring came forward with a rival socialist philosophy, Engels replied with *Herrn Eugen Dührings Umwälzung der Wissenschaft* (1877-1878; *Herr Eugen Dühring's Revolution in Science*, 1934), following Dühring into natural philosophy as well as politics. The work and an excerpt from it, *Die Entwicklung des Sozialismus von der Utopie zur Wissenschaft* (1882; *Socialism: Utopian and Scientific*, 1892), are Engels' best-known works, standing alongside *The Communist Manifesto* as summaries of Marxist thought, and sometimes accused of leading subsequent Marxists into simplistic materialist determinism. His foray into anthropology, *Der Ursprung der Familie, des Privateigentums und des Staats* (1884; *The Origin of the Family, Private Property, and the State*, 1902), has attracted some attention from feminist scholars. At great cost to his eyesight, Engels worked through vast quantities of overlapping, ill-organized drafts in Marx's wretched handwriting to produce volumes 2 and 3 of Marx's *Das Kapital* (1885, 1894; *Capital: A Critique of Political Economy*, 1907, 1908, best known as *Das Kapital*).

Described as military in bearing and nicknamed "General" by Marx's daughters after writing his brilliant articles on the Franco-Prussian War, Engels made a specialty of military science. In addition to writing about wars and crises as bread-and-butter journalism, he studied war as a phenomenon which might improve or diminish the prospects of revolution. Some capitalist states were more regressive and obnoxious than others, and Engels and Marx were never indifferent to the wars of their lifetimes. The most important fruit of Engels' military studies was his conclusion, after the Austro-Prussian War of 1866, that all the great powers would have to adopt the Prussian-style universal-service army. That meant that there was hope for the revolution, despite the folly of insurrection against an intact army; a socialist electoral majority would be reflected by a majority in the ranks, and the army would vanish as a counterrevolutionary instrument.

After Marx's death in 1883, Engels found himself in the role of interpreter of Marx's theories and as leader of the movement. He dispensed encouragement and advice to the younger socialists and presided over splendid parties in celebration of holidays and socialist election victories. His companion Mary Burns had died in 1863, succeeded in Engels' household by her sister Lizzie, whom Engels married on her deathbed in 1878. Engels presided at the Zurich Conference of the Second International in 1893, the grand old man of a growing, confident, worldwide movement. When Engels died of throat cancer in 1895, his ashes were scattered in the sea off Beachy Head.

Summary

Friedrich Engels' name usually appears preceded by "Marx and." He was indeed important, not apart from Marx, but as a full partner in the creation of Marxism. In addition to providing Marx's material needs, protecting Marx's scholarly labors from interruption, and furnishing his friend vital psychological support for forty years, Engels brought to Marxism a quick intelligence and an acquaintance with the real world of capitalism. Involved in conceiving and elaborating all the varied aspects of Marxism and predominant in the crucial area of revolutionary tactics, Engels played an indispensable part in creating Marxism as an intellectual system and as a political and social movement.

Bibliography

Berger, Martin. *Engels, Armies and Revolution: The Revolutionary Tactics of Classical Marxism.* Hamden, Conn.: Archon Books, 1977. Emphasizes Engels' thought on war and military institutions as a key to Marxist views on international relations and the timing and tactics of revolution.

Henderson, W. O. *The Life of Friedrich Engels.* 2 vols. London: Cass, 1976. A detailed study, strongest on Engels' business life in England.

Hunt, Richard N. *The Political Ideas of Marx and Engels.* 2 vols. London: Macmillan, and Pittsburgh: University of Pittsburgh Press, 1974-1984. A standard account. Differentiates Marx and Engels from both Leninist and Social Democratic varieties of Marxism.

Labica, Georges. "Engels and Marxist Philosophy." *Science and Society* 62, no. 1 (Spring 1998). An analysis of the philosophies of Engels and Marx.

Lichtheim, George. *Marxism: An Historical and Critical Study.* 2d ed. London: Routledge, and New York: Praeger, 1965. An unusually coherent account of Marxism, placing Engels in context.

McLellan, David. *Friedrich Engels.* New York: Viking Press, 1978. A concise (120-page) introduction in the Modern Masters series, a by-product of the author's major Marx biography.

Marcus, Steven. *Engels, Manchester, and the Working Class.* London: Weidenfeld and Nicolson, and New York: Random House, 1974. A perceptive study of Engels' *The Condition of the Working Class in England in 1844* as a literary work.

Mayer, Gustav. *Friedrich Engels: A Biography.* Translated by Gilbert Highet and Helen Highet. London: Chapman and Hall, and New York: Knopf, 1936. A condensation of the great two-volume German original (1934). Still a sound treatment.

Wilson, Edmund. *To the Finland Station: A Study in the Writing and Acting of History.* Garden City, N.Y.: Doubleday, 1940. A classic popular account of the development of Marxism. Contains a good sketch of the Marx-Engels relationship.

Wood, Ellen Meiksins. "The 'Communist Manifesto' after 150 Years." *Monthly Review* 50, no. 1 (May 1998). The author argues that Marx and Engels' book *The Communist Manifesto* is often over-complicated by scholars and critics when it is simply a public statement of a political agenda.

Martin Berger

LOUIS FAIDHERBE

Born: June 3, 1818; Lille, France
Died: September 29, 1889; Paris, France
Areas of Achievement: Colonial administration and the military
Contribution: Faidherbe, through war and diplomacy, laid the foundation of France's West African empire. He stemmed the Muslim military advance in West Africa but respected Islam. He improved Senegal economically, socially, and culturally. His generalship retrieved France's honor in the Franco-German War.

Early Life

Louis Léon César Faidherbe was born at Lille, France. His father, a moderately successful merchant, suffered imprisonment under Napoleon I. Louis studied at the Universities of Lille and Douai, the École Polytechnique, and the École d'Application. In 1842, he became a lieutenant in the Engineering Corps. In Algeria, where he was stationed from 1843 to 1846 and again from 1849 to 1852, Faidherbe embraced French imperialism and became adept in warfare. He showed ingenuity in designing and supervising a fort's construction in newly occupied Bou-Saada, where he commanded for two years. While in Algeria, Faidherbe experienced an intellectual awakening. He learned Arabic and read Ibn-Khaldūn's history of the Berbers. He developed respect for Arabo-Berber culture and for Islam. Nevertheless, he supported French conquest, whatever the tactics, because it benefited the so-called barbaric peoples.

In Guadeloupe, where he was stationed in 1848 and 1849, Faidherbe turned to republicanism and negrophilism, yet he did not allow these views to interfere with promoting French interests and his own career. The engineering detachment's reduction in Guadeloupe led to his recall and another stint in Algeria. In 1852, Faidherbe became subdirector of engineers in Senegal. He participated in seizing Podor and constructing its fort, attacking Diman's capital, and reinforcing Bakel's defenses in 1854. He wrote "Les Berbères" and began learning Wolof, Pular, and Sarakolé from his Sarakolé wife. He became interested in exploring the Niger River. Admiring Faidherbe's activities, major Bordeaux firms doing business with Senegal recommended him for Senegal's governorship.

Life's Work

Faidherbe served two terms as Governor of Senegal, 1854-1861 and 1863-1865. Determined to erect a stable *Pax Francia*, he instituted an aggressive policy of conquest and expansion of trade. He took decisive steps to advance eastward from St. Louis through the Senegal River valley and the vast Sudan region to Lake Chad. He even dreamed of a French African empire stretching from the Atlantic Ocean to the Red Sea. He sought to create a firm basis for its future development culturally as well as politically and economically.

Militarily, Faidherbe first sought to protect the gum trade along the Senegal River and to quell the Moorish Trarzas, who were raiding and opposing the Wolof peasants living along the river's south bank. In February, 1855, Faidherbe ordered his forces to expel Trarza clans from Walo. War ensued with Walo, whose leadership rebuffed Faidherbe's plan to "liberate" them; in April, Faidherbe had to fight the principal Trarza warrior clans. By the end of 1855, he had overcome Walo, which became the first sub-Saharan state dismembered and annexed by France. In 1858, having employed divide-and-conquer tactics, Faidherbe made treaties with the Trarzas of southern Mauretania. The Trarzas agreed to respect French traders and to commute the controversial "customs" charges into a fixed export duty of 3 percent.

Faidherbe's endeavor to end all African control over French navigation along the Senegal River, particularly the toll at Saldé-Tébékout in central Futa-Toro, brought greater hostilities. Conflict erupted with the traditional leaders of Futa-Toro and with the Tukolor Muslim reformer and state builder al-Hājj Umar Tal. In 1858-1859, Faidherbe forced the confederation of Futa-Toro to make peace with France on French terms. Faidherbe divided the confederation into four client states of France.

Faidherbe's greatest adversary, Umar, was the charismatic leader of the Tijaniyya fraternity in West Africa. Before Faidherbe's governorship, Umar had attacked the French because of their prohibiting the firearms trade in the Senegal valley. Faidherbe resisted Umar's thrust along the Senegal. In July, 1857, Faidherbe gallantly led a small force with fixed bayonets in relieving Médine from Umar's three-month siege. In 1860, Faidherbe negotiated a demarcation line along the Bafing River with Umar's emissary and provisionally agreed to

send his own envoy to discuss future relations with Umar. Faidherbe hoped that, in return for political support and supplies of firearms, Umar would permit France to enact a line of fortified trading posts from Senegal to a base for navigation on the Niger. With Umar's cooperation, Faidherbe envisioned pushing French trade and influence downstream and averting the monopoly which Great Britain, through traders in the delta, threatened to establish over the Niger. Returning as governor in 1863, Faidherbe sent Lieutenant Eugène Mage to contact Umar. Eventually Mage negotiated a treaty with Umar's successor, Ahmadu Tal, wherein Ahmadu renounced holy war against France and permitted French trade and exploration in his territories, while France allowed him to buy goods in St. Louis. While fighting Umar, Faidherbe's forces gutted the principal villages of Buoye, Kaméra, and Guidimakha, after which Faidherbe made treaties with new client rulers in each state.

As early as 1859, Faidherbe had also turned his attention to the kingdom of Cayor. His aim was to prevent its warriors' interference in the collection of peanuts by peasants and to open a trail with three small forts placed along it and a telegraph line to link St. Louis to Dakar and Gorée via the coastal route. Faidherbe first tried peaceful means but, rebuffed by Damel Biraima, he used force. When Biraima died, Faidherbe claimed that Biraima had agreed on his deathbed to France's demands. Biraima's successor, Macodu, would not recognize the treaty. Faidherbe declared war and sought to replace Macodu with Madiodio. Thereupon Lat Dior progressed in seizing power. Faidherbe's replacement, Governor Jean Jauréguiberry, allowed Lat Dior to expel Madiodio and become ruler. In his second governorship, Faidherbe moved to restore Madiodio, who ceded more territory to France. As disorder still prevailed in Cayor, Faidherbe retired Madiodio and annexed the remainder of Cayor in 1865.

Faidherbe's military successes owed much to his personal touch. In 1857, he organized the Senegalese Riflemen. He created two battalions of volunteers recruited as much as possible from the free population of Senegambia. The first recruits were paid relatively well; they served short, two-year terms, wore special, colorful uniforms, were allowed a looser discipline than that of European troops, and received traditional food. Faidherbe labored in numerous ways in Senegal. He founded a school for the sons of chiefs, and lay schools for Muslims. He established scholarships for primary education in St. Louis and secondary education in France. He built small technical schools at Dakar. He opened a museum and a newspaper at St. Louis. Faidherbe founded the Bank of Senegal, laid out St. Louis afresh as befitted a capital city, promoted the export of groundnuts, made valuable and detailed studies of the indigenous people, and founded Dakar.

After the conclusion of his second term as Governor of Senegal, Faidherbe returned to Algeria, where he spent the years from 1865 to 1870. In addition to his military duties, he gave considerable time to writing during this period. In December, 1870, Faidherbe became Commander in Chief of the Army of the North in the Franco-Prussian War. Despite fever and exhaustion, he commanded superbly in the Battles of Pont Noyelles, Bapaume, and St. Quentin. A confirmed republican, Faidherbe in 1871 declined election to the National Assembly because of its reactionary character. In 1879, he accepted election to the Senate. In 1880, he became Grand Chancellor of the Legion of Honor. He continued his writing until his death, in 1889. After a public funeral in Paris, he was buried in Lille.

Summary

Louis Faidherbe stood center stage in modern French imperialism. He initiated firm French control of the Senegal valley, which became the springboard for further expansion in West Africa. By opening the trade of Senegal, he provided the means for reaching the Niger Basin. His plan for railroad construction eventually materialized. His proposal, rejected by his superiors, for France and Great Britain, and France and Portugal mutually to arrange exchange of territories in West Africa would have created the French Gambia valley. Faidherbe grappled firmly but humanely with Islam in West Africa. He used war and diplomacy to stop the westward push of the great Al-Hājj Umar Tal. Faidherbe's policy of opposing Christian proselytism of Muslims caused a lasting prestigious francophile Muslim community and tradition in Senegal.

Faidherbe further affected West Africa. In Senegal, his governorship distinguished priorities and allocated limited resources. Faidherbe started new public works and aided the peasants. His policies of non-French settlement and restricted assimilation into French citizenship became models for French West Africa. Faidherbe accomplished still more. He reorganized the Legion of Honor and reformed its educational work. He wrote extensively on ancient Egypt, Carthage, Numidia, the Franco-Prussian War, West Africa, and army reorganization. His scholarship gained for him election to the Academy of Inscriptions and Belles-Lettres.

Bibliography

Abun-Nasr, Jamil M. *The Tijaniyya: A Sufi Order in the Modern World.* London and New York: Oxford University Press, 1965. An excellent, impartial treatment of the movement led by Faidherbe's major foe, Umar. Clear analysis of the reasons for the clash between Faidherbe and Umar, the warfare between the French and Umarians, and the negotiations bringing peace. A fine map, footnotes, a bibliography, and an index.

Barrows, Leland C. "Faidherbe and Senegal: A Critical Discussion." *African Studies Review* 19 (April 1976). A scholarly and detailed study of Faidherbe's governorship of Senegal. Presents the background for his work. Critical of Faidherbe's so-called radicalism, especially his stand on slavery and his ambiguity in defining the positions of blacks and mulattoes. Stresses Faidherbe's militarism as his chief contribution to the creation of French West Africa.

Cohen, William B. *Rulers of Empire: The French Colonial Service in Africa.* Stanford, Calif.: Hoover Institution Press, 1971. Cohen emphasizes Faidherbe's founding of a workable administrative organization in West Africa, which remained unchanged and, indeed, lasted with few modifications until the very end of the French occupation. Extensive endnotes and a bibliography. Contains a map, illustrations, and tables.

Hargreaves, John D. *Prelude to the Partition of West Africa.* London: Macmillan, and New York: St. Martin's Press, 1963. Pinpoints Faidherbe's faith in the possibilities of penetrating the Sudan by the upper Senegal route and his freedom from strong anti-Muslim prejudice achieved during service in Algeria. Good on Anglo-French relations in West Africa. Contains a useful annotated bibliography, an index, and maps.

Howard, Michael. *The Franco-Prussian War: The German Invasion of France, 1870-1871.* London: Hart-Davis, and New York: Macmillan, 1961. Shows that Faidherbe's object was not to defeat the enemy but to pin down the greatest possible number of Germans and, by attacks, to facilitate Paris' relief. Seventeen maps, a select bibliography, and an adequate index.

Kanya-Forstner, A. S. *The Conquest of the Western Sudan: A Study in French Military Imperialism.* Cambridge: Cambridge University Press, 1969. Underlines Faidherbe's vigor and his envisioning the future French African empire most clearly. Notes the declining fortunes of Senegal following his departure in 1865 but the revival of his Niger plan after 1876. Contains valuable footnotes, a bibliography, an index, and two maps.

Klein, Martin A. *Islam and Imperialism in Senegal: Sine-Saloum, 1847-1914.* Stanford, Calif.: Stanford University Press, 1968. Stresses Faidherbe's laying the foundation of France's West African empire in spite of the skepticism of France's government and its reluctance to sanction an aggressive policy. Recognizes Faidherbe's imagination. A first-rate consideration of Faidherbe's relations with the Senegambian rulers. Notes Faidherbe's compromise with slavery but his enlightened outlook toward Islam. Very good maps, charts, and lists of African rulers and French officials. Splendid glossary, notes, and bibliography.

Robinson, David. *The Holy War of Umar Tal: The Western Sudan in the Mid-Nineteenth Century.* Oxford: Clarendon Press, and New York: Oxford University Press, 1985. A reliable account of Faidherbe's encounter with Umar. Shows Faidherbe's ingenuity: use of intelligence reports and manufacturing his own propaganda to counter the appeal of Umar's holy war. Contains an excellent map, with tables, notes, and a bibliography.

Singer, Barnett. "A New Model Imperialist in French West Africa." *Historian* 56, no. 1 (Autumn 1993). Profile of Faidherbe's life with emphasis on his role in the creation of French West Africa.

Erving E. Beauregard

MICHAEL FARADAY

Born: September 22, 1791; Newington, Surrey, England

Died: August 25, 1867; Hampton Court, Surrey, England

Areas of Achievement: Physics and chemistry

Contribution: Considered by many as the greatest British physicist of the nineteenth century, Faraday's discoveries in electromagnetism were fundamental to the development of field physics. His inventions of the dynamo and electric motor provided the basis for modern electrical industry.

Early Life

Michael Faraday was the third of four children born to James Faraday, a Yorkshire blacksmith, and Margaret Hastwell, the daughter of Yorkshire farmers. Both were of Irish descent. Shortly before his birth, the family moved to Newington, near London, in search of better opportunities. James Faraday's health deteriorated, limiting his ability to work, and the family had only the bare necessities for survival. Young Faraday's education consisted of the rudiments of reading, writing, and arithmetic. The family belonged to the small religious sect of Sandemanians, which emphasized the Bible as the sole and sufficient guide for each individual, and Faraday was a devoted, lifelong member.

In 1804, Faraday was an errand boy for George Riebau, a London bookseller and bookbinder. His seven-year apprenticeship produced an extraordinary manual dexterity, a skill characteristic of his experimental researches. He also read omnivorously, from *The Arabian Nights' Entertainments* to the *Encyclopaedia Britannica*. The latter's article on electricity awakened him to a new world, as did Jane Marcet's *Conversations on Chemistry* (1806), a book which converted him in his teenage years into a passionate student of science. With his apprenticeship nearing an end in 1812, it was not likely that Faraday would be anything but a bookbinder. A customer's gift of tickets to a series of lectures by Humphry Davy at the Royal Institution changed his life. Davy was a scientist of international stature and a brilliant lecturer, largely responsible for the success of the Royal Institution, a center both for research and for the dissemination of science to a general audience.

Faraday, enthralled by the lectures, desperately wanted to become a scientist. When Davy became temporarily blinded in a laboratory explosion, a customer at Riebau's bookshop recommended Faraday to him as secretary for a few days because of Faraday's fine penmanship. Faraday subsequently bound in the bookshop his neatly written lecture notes with his own illustrations and sent the volume to Davy asking for a job. Davy had nothing for him at the time. Suddenly, in 1813, however, Davy fired his laboratory assistant for brawling, and the twenty-one-year-old Faraday became his assistant.

In that same year, Davy married a rich widow and set out on a grand tour of Europe, including visits to the major scientific centers to meet the most distinguished Continental scientists. Faraday went along to assist Davy in his research. The tour was a remarkable experience; the young man had never been more than a few miles from London. His letters home were full of amazement over meeting renowned scientists during the eighteen-month tour. On his return to England, the Royal Institution appointed Faraday superintendent of apparatus. Now in his early twenties, he possessed a robust intelligence, considerable scientific knowledge, and the good fortune to be at the Royal Institution.

All Faraday's contemporaries described him as kind, gentle, and simple in manner. Serenity and calm marked his life and countenance; no scientist has been referred to more as humble or saintly. These attributes stemmed from his Sandemanian faith, with its stress on love and community. He had an unquestioning belief in God as creator and sustainer of the universe and saw himself as merely the instrument by which the divine truths of nature were exposed. His faith and his science meshed completely.

Otherworldly, Faraday had a contempt for money-making and trade, and he rejected all honors which raised him above others. He refused both knighthood and the presidency of the Royal Society. In 1821, he married a fellow Sandemanian, Sarah Barnard. The marriage was childless but most happy. She lavished her maternal feelings on the nieces who lived with them and on her husband. United by a deep, enduring love, secure in their faith, the tone of the household (they lived in rooms provided in the Royal Institution) was one of gaiety, and domestic life was completely satisfactory.

Life's Work

Faraday was a late bloomer with no important discovery until he was more than thirty. He lacked familiarity with mathematics, the language of physics, and remained outside the mathematical tradition of universities and of Continental physics. From 1815 to 1820, he earned a modest reputation as an analytical chemist, publishing several papers on subjects suggested by Davy. These were the years of his scientific apprenticeship.

In 1820, the Danish physicist Hans Christian Oersted discovered the magnetic effect of the electric current. This discovery of electromagnetism caused a sensation and provoked both an explosion of research and much confusion. In 1821, the editor of a journal asked Faraday to review the experiments and interpretations and present a coherent account of electromagnetism. Faraday's genius now became evident, for he demonstrated that there were no attractions or repulsions involved in the phenomenon; instead, a force in the conductor made a magnetic needle move around it in a circle. He also devised an instrument to illustrate the process, producing the first conversion of electrical into mechanical energy. He had discovered electromagnetic rotation, and as a by-product, he had invented the electric motor.

Faraday did not follow up this major discovery with anything comparable until 1831, although his chemical researches continued to be fruitful, notably the 1825 discovery of benzene, which he isolated from an oil that separated from illuminating gas. He also conducted a lengthy project for the Royal Society on the improvement of optical glass used in lenses. It ended with no apparent useful results, but he did prepare a heavy lead borosilicate glass which later proved indispensable to his electromagnetic work.

In 1825, the Royal Institution promoted Faraday to director of the laboratory. Faraday instituted the Friday Evening Discourses, which soon became one of the most famous series of lectures on the progress of science, serving to educate the English upper class in science and to influence those in government and education. In 1826, he began the Christmas Courses of Lectures for Juvenile Audiences, which further extended the appeal of the institution. His lectures, based on a careful study of oratory, were full of grace and earnestness, and exercised a magic on hearers. He was at his best with children: a sense of drama and wonder unfolded, and they reacted with enthusiasm to the marvels of his experiments. Two of his courses for juveniles were published as *The Chemical History of a Candle* (1861) and *The Various Forces of Nature*

(1860). They have remained in print as classics of scientific literature.

In 1831, Faraday made his most famous discovery, reversing Oersted's experiment by converting magnetism into electricity. He used the Royal Institution's thick iron ring as an electromagnet, winding insulated wire on one side with a secondary winding on the other side. With a battery linked to one winding and a galvanometer to the other, he closed the battery circuit and the galvanometer needle moved. He had induced another electric current through the medium of the iron ring's expanding magnetic force. He called his discovery electromagnetic induction and elaborated a conception of curved magnetic lines of force to account for the phenomenon.

Over the next several weeks, Faraday devised variations and extensions of the phenomenon, the most famous one being the invention of the dynamo. He converted mechanical motion into electricity by turning a copper disc between the poles of a horseshoe magnet, thereby producing continuous flowing electricity. From this discovery came the whole of the electric-power industry. Faraday realized that he had a possible source of cheap electricity, but he was too immersed in discovery to pursue the practical application.

In 1833, Faraday made his most monumental contribution to chemistry. A study of the relationship between electricity and chemical action disclosed the two laws of electrochemistry. He then devised a beautiful, elegant theory of electrochemical decomposition which involved no poles, no action at a distance, no central forces. Faraday's theory, totally at odds with the thinking of his contemporaries, demanded a new language for electrochemistry. In 1834, in collaboration with the classical scholar, William Whewell, he invented the vocabulary of electrode, anode, cathode, anion, cation, electrolysis, and electrolyte, the word electrode meaning not a pole or terminal but only the path taken by electricity. Faraday's stupendous labors of the 1830's were too much for him, however, and in 1838, he suffered a serious mental breakdown. So bad was his condition that he could not work for five years.

In 1845, William Thomson (Lord Kelvin) suggested to Faraday some experiments with polarized light which might reveal a relation between light and electricity. This stimulated Faraday into intense experimentation. He had no success until he tried a stronger force, an electromagnet, and passed

a polarized light beam through the magnetic field. At first unsuccessful, he remembered his heavy borosilicate glass from the 1820's. Placing it between the poles of the magnet, he sent the light beam through the glass and the plane of polarization rotated; he had discovered the effect of magnetic force on light (magneto-optical rotation).

The fact that the magnetic force acted through the medium of glass suggested to Faraday a study of how substances react in a magnetic field. This study revealed the class of diamagnetics. Faraday listed more than fifty substances which reacted to magnets not by aligning themselves along the lines of magnetic force (paramagnetics) but by setting themselves across the lines of force, a finding that attracted more attention from scientists than any of his other discoveries.

In the 1850's, Faraday's theorizing led to the idea that a conductor or magnet causes stresses in its surroundings, a force field. The energy of action lay in the medium, not in the conductor or magnet. He came to envision the universe as criss-crossed by a network of lines of force, and he suggested that they could vibrate and thereby transmit the transverse waves of which light consists. (The notion of the electromagnetic theory of light first appeared in an 1846 Royal Institution lecture.) His speculations had no place for Newtonian central forces acting in straight lines between bodies, or for any kind of polarity. All were banished for a field theory in which magnets and conductors were habitations of bundles of lines of force which were continuous curves in, through, and around bodies.

Faraday's mental faculties gradually deteriorated after 1855. Concern for his health reached Prince Albert; at his request, Queen Victoria in 1858 placed a home near Hampton Court at Faraday's disposal for the rest of his life. There, he sank into senility until his death in 1867. Like his life, his funeral was simple and private.

Summary

Michael Faraday was an unusual scientist. He never knew the language of mathematics. To compensate, he had an intuitive sense of how things must be, and he organized his thoughts in visual, pictorial terms. He imagined lines of force stretching and curving through the space near magnets and conductors. In this way, he mastered the phenomena. His vision of reality was incomprehensible to a scientific world preoccupied with the Newtonian paradigm. Only when James Clerk Maxwell showed how Faraday's ideas could be treated rigorously and mathematically did the lines-of-force conception in the guise of field equations become an integral part of modern physics.

Faraday coupled his inventive thinking with an unmatched experimental ability. His ingenuity disclosed a host of fundamental physical phenomena. One of those phenomena, his seemingly humble discovery of the dynamo, became the symbol of the new age of electricity, with its incalculable effects on society and daily life.

Bibliography

Agassi, Joseph. *Faraday as a Natural Philosopher.* Chicago: University of Chicago Press, 1971. Faraday's biographers stressed his experimental contributions, downplaying his speculations until historians of science rediscovered him as a daring natural philosopher. This work is a product of that rediscovery.

Cantor, Geoffrey. *Michael Faraday: Sandemanian and Scientist, A Study of Science and Religion in the Nineteenth Century.* New York: St. Martin's Press, 1991. The first detailed account of Faraday's public and private life that shows how all facets of his life were closely linked to his Sandemanism, the doctrine of a small, strict sect of fundamentalist Christians.

Crowther, James G. "Michael Faraday." In *British Scientists of the Nineteenth Century.* London: Routledge, 1935. A fine study; very perceptive concerning Faraday's insights, contributions, and personality.

Ihde, Aaron. "Michael Faraday." In *Great Chemists*, edited by Eduard Farber. New York: Interscience, 1961. An excellent discussion of Faraday's contributions to chemistry.

James, Frank A. J. L., "The Tales of Benjamin Abbott: A Source for the Early Life of Michael Faraday. *British Journal for the History of Science* 25, no. 85 (June 1992). Discusses the close friendship between Faraday and Benjamin Abbott. Most records of Faraday's early life are a result of this friendship, the letters between them, and Abbott's personal notes.

Jones, Henry Bence. *Life and Letters of Faraday.* 2 vols. London: Longman, and Philadelphia: Lippincott, 1870. A collection of letters to and from Faraday and excerpts from diaries with a biography written by a close friend and colleague at the Royal Institution.

Kendall, James. *Michael Faraday, Man of Simplicity*. London: Faber, and New York: Roy, 1955. A popular biography with simple handling of difficult subject matter in a way understandable to the general reader.

Thompson, Silvanus P. *Michael Faraday, His Life and Work*. London and New York: Cassell, 1898. The author depicts Faraday from the point of view of an expert electrical engineer to whom Faraday's experimental discoveries outweigh his field theory.

Tyndall, John. *Faraday as a Discoverer*. London: Longman, and New York: Appleton, 1868. The first biography of Faraday, written by his successor at the Royal Institution. Essential reading, for it reveals what friends of Faraday thought of him and his physical theories. A lucid discussion of his vast basic contributions to science.

Williams, L. Pearce. *Michael Faraday: A Biography*. London: Chapman and Hall, and New York: Basic Books, 1965. Indispensable. The first major appraisal by a historian of science. Lively, readable, comprehensive, and based on painstaking scholarship, Williams' work traces the full context of Faraday's contributions and his genius as both a daring theorist and experimentalist.

Albert Costa

DAVID G. FARRAGUT

Born: July 5, 1801; Campbell's Station, Tennessee
Died: August 14, 1870; Portsmouth, New Hampshire
Area of Achievement: The naval service
Contribution: The first admiral in the United States Navy, Farragut is most noted for his victory over Confederate forces in the Battle of Mobile Bay.

Early Life

The son of George Farragut and the former Elizabeth Shine, David Glasgow Farragut was born James Glasgow Farragut at the site of Campbell's Station, near Knoxville, Tennessee, on July 5, 1801. His mother was a native of Dobbs County, North Carolina, while his father was an immigrant of Spanish ancestry from the British (later French) island of Minorca. George Farragut served as both an army and then a naval officer during the American Revolution, then moved his family to Tennessee and again westward.

In Louisiana after 1807, George Farragut was a sailing master in the navy who, the following year, suffered the loss of his wife to yellow fever at their home on the shore of Lake Pontchartrain. Since he did not expect to remarry and thought that he could no longer give proper care and attention to his children, the elder Farragut arranged for his son's adoption by his friend, Commander David Porter. Porter was the commandant of the naval station at New Orleans.

Porter took his adopted son with him to Washington in 1809, and there and at his later home in Chester, Pennsylvania, he gave him better schooling than he had hitherto known. He also introduced him to Paul Hamilton, Secretary of the Navy, who promised him a commission as a midshipman. This was issued December 17, 1810, although Farragut was only nine years of age. From 1811 through 1815, Farragut served under Porter aboard the frigate *Essex*, saw action in the Atlantic and the Pacific in the War of 1812, and even had the brief opportunity at the age of twelve to command a captured prize ship, the *Barclay*. Although finally made a prisoner of war after an unsuccessful battle with the British ship *Phoebe*, the thrill of this early service and the pride he took in his adoptive father's growing reputation caused Farragut, upon release in 1814, to change his name legally to David. This was also

the name of his foster brother, David Dixon Porter; the two maintained a healthy rivalry and friendship down through the years.

At home, in Chester, Farragut added to his education. He then served briefly apart from Porter following a paroled prisoner of war exchange, and concluded the war aboard the brig *Spark*. With never a thought toward a civilian occupation, Farragut immediately took service aboard a ship-of-the-line, the *Independence*, which sailed to the Mediterranean Sea to back up Commodore Stephen Decatur's squadron against the Barbary pirates in what was called the Algerine War. After this he served aboard a similar ship, the *Washington*, until he was afforded the opportunity to study under the American consul at Tunis, Charles Folsom. In addition to diplomacy, polite manners, and foreign languages, he was able to develop an understanding of English literature and mathematics. He was a bright young man, though impressive only in demeanor as he was five feet, six and a half inches tall and of average build. With his formal education complete late in 1818, Farragut embarked upon his naval career in earnest.

Life's Work

Duty was undertaken aboard the *Franklin* and the *Shark*, and while aboard the latter brig, Farragut was recommended for promotion to the rank of lieutenant at the unusually young age of eighteen. Recalled to Norfolk, Virginia, he was ordered to sea again in the sloop-of-war *John Adams*; in 1823 he volunteered for duty aboard the *Greyhound* when he heard that this ship was to be placed under the command of Captain Porter's brother, Lieutenant John Porter, and that the captain himself was to command the squadron of which it was a part. The squadron was prepared to fight pirates in the Caribbean Sea, and this was especially welcome duty to Farragut, who had come to detest piracy.

Confiscating the booty of numerous pirates and burning their ships, the "Mosquito Fleet," as the squadron was known, did effective service over the next two years. British forces then arrived to finish the job, and piracy was virtually eliminated as a common practice in Caribbean waters. An incident which occurred in the town of Foxardo, Puerto Rico, however, while he was in command of the squadron, led to Commodore Porter's court-martial and resignation from the navy. In later years he would serve his country as a diplomat.

After six months' service in the Caribbean in 1823, Farragut returned to Norfolk to marry a young woman he had met there. On September 24, 1823, Susan C. Marchant became his wife.

With formal promotion to lieutenant in 1825, Farragut was ordered once again to active duty aboard the frigate *Brandywine*, which carried the celebrated old hero of that Revolutionary battle, the Marquis de Lafayette, back to France. When he returned to the United States, Farragut found his wife suffering greatly from neuralgia. Despite a convalescence at New Haven, Connecticut, she continued to decline from the disease until her death on December 27, 1840.

While in New Haven, Farragut had come to attend lectures at Yale and reflect on the lack of educational opportunities available to young boys aboard ships. Upon returning to Norfolk, he organized a school for "ship's boys," said to be the first of its kind.

From 1828 to 1829, from 1833 to 1834, and again from 1841 to 1843, Farragut served in the South Atlantic waters off South America. He rose from first lieutenant (executive officer) of the sloop-of-war *Vandalia* to captain of the schooner *Boxer*. Several years of shore duty were then followed by orders to Pensacola, Florida, in 1838, where he was placed in command of the sloop-of-war *Erie* and given duty off Vera Cruz, Mexico. He was then advanced to the rank of commander in 1841.

Returning to Norfolk early in 1843, Farragut met and married Virginia Loyall, a native of that community, on December 26, 1843. They would have one child, a son, Loyall, born in 1844. As war with Mexico approached, Farragut anxiously requested duty off Vera Cruz and pressed his ideas for an attack on its fort, Castle San Juan de Ulloa, upon George Bancroft, Secretary of the Navy. His over-zealousness in doing so, however, delayed his being given a proper command. Finally, in February, 1847, almost a year after the war got under way, he was given the sloop-of-war *Saratoga* and sent to the port. By that time, however, Vera Cruz had already been captured by army forces under General Winfield Scott. Nothing came of his service in this war except frustration, a bout with yellow fever, bitterness, and ill feelings.

Assignment to the Norfolk Navy Yard followed the Mexican War in 1848. Posted in California in 1854, Farragut was responsible for the establish-

ment of the soon-to-be-important navy yard at Mare Island. In 1855, he was promoted to the rank of captain. Returning to the east three years later, he was named to command a new steamship, the wooden sloop-of-war *Brooklyn*. From 1858 to 1860, he remained her captain, assigned primarily to the Gulf of Mexico.

With the election of Abraham Lincoln, the secession of Southern states began in late 1860. As his native state of Tennessee and adopted state of Virginia threatened to follow others and join the Confederacy, Farragut had the same mixed feelings which struck Scott and other Southern unionists; like them, however, he professed his loyalty and stood by the same colors he had served so long.

The war's beginning, on April 12, 1861, with the firing upon Fort Sumter, was formalized by Lincoln's call for seventy-five thousand volunteers and establishment of a naval blockade of the Confederate coast. Farragut took his family out of Norfolk and established a home for them at Hastings, New York. On December 21, 1861, Farragut met the assistant secretary of the navy, Gustavus Vasa Fox, and received from him orders to take command of the Western Gulf Blockading Squadron, gather all available vessels, and proceed to capture New Orleans. Farragut designated the steam sloop-of-war *Hartford* his flagship and departed Hampton Roads in February, 1862, for Ship Island in the Gulf. Seventeen vessels, mostly gunboats, were brought in and sailed up the Mississippi; on April 18, 1862, Farragut, as his orders directed, set his mortar boats to work bombarding Fort Jackson. The fort, however, was too strong to be reduced in this manner, and so Farragut took it upon himself to run past this fort, and Fort St. Philip upstream, at night. After 2:00 A.M. on August 24, the run was successfully completed, Confederate vessels sent against them were destroyed, and New Orleans was taken through the instrument of Benjamin Butler's army. Farragut then passed Vicksburg on June 28. Instantly he became a national hero and was promoted to rear admiral on July 16, 1862. He added little to his fame with further actions on the Mississippi, which was soon in the capable hands of David Dixon Porter.

In August, the admiral made his headquarters in the evacuated harbor of Pensacola. His blockade of the Gulf Coast was now complete save for the fortified Confederate port of Mobile. This was a hornets' nest of blockade runners and Farragut's last objective. Receiving added ships and support from Secretary of the Navy Gideon Welles, he took a fleet of nineteen ships into Mobile Bay on August 5, 1864, past the Confederate batteries of Fort Morgan and through a mine field. When his lead ship, the *Brooklyn*, hesitated upon spotting the mines, and the monitor *Tecumseh* was sunk by one (then called a "torpedo"), Farragut ordered his flagship to take the lead and not to slow down. "Damn the torpedoes!" he said, and ordered the *Hartford* ahead at full speed. Successful at moving by the fort and through the mine field, Farragut's fleet defeated all Confederate vessels easily except for the *Tennessee*, a ram which held out through a desperate battle until it had suffered so badly that it surrendered at last. Soon Fort Morgan was in Union hands and the Confederate coast was closed.

As his health, ravaged by many tropical diseases, was declining, Farragut was recalled to New York in November, 1864. There he became a communicant of the Episcopal Church. A month later, as of Christmas, he was promoted as the first to hold the rank of vice admiral of the navy. The people of New York claimed him as a citizen of their city and bestowed a gift of fifty thousand dollars upon him as the war drew to a close.

On July 25, 1866, Congress created the new rank of admiral for him. He served aboard the flagship *Franklin* in command of the European Squadron, returning to New York in 1868. He then traveled to California the following year, but suffered a heart attack on the return via Chicago. Taken by steamship to be the guest of an admiral at the Portsmouth, New Hampshire, naval yard, Farragut died there on August 14, 1870.

Summary

David Farragut is regarded by many twentieth century historians as an ideal example of the nineteenth century career naval officer. Despite numerous disappointments while in uniform, his adoptive father's court-martial, and his roots in the South, Farragut remained constant in his allegiance to the United States Navy and the government it represents. His patriotism, coolness and courage under fire, thorough preparation, and belief in education are part of the heritage he and others like him left for later generations of naval officers.

His career of fifty-nine years in the service of his country has been equaled by very few men. What is more, it was a career featuring promotion as the first American to hold the rank of admiral, and it was crowned with the glory of the preeminent naval victory of the Civil War—the Battle of Mobile Bay. Had his health been better at the war's close, and had he been so inclined, virtually no appointive or elective office would have been beyond his reach.

As it was, he died, like Lincoln, near the peak of his fame and at the high tide of his fortunes. His passing was not so dramatic, but neither was much of his life. It was simply a life of dedicated service.

Bibliography

Barnes, James. *David G. Farragut*. London: Kegan Paul, and Boston: Small, Maynard, 1899. This book is a passable turn-of-the-century substitute for the Mahon book written by a then-popular biographer.

Duffy, James P. *Lincoln's Admiral: The Civil War Campaigns of David Farragut*. New York: Wiley, 1997. Duffy offers new insight into the life of the United States' first full admiral. Based on source materials made available in the last twenty years.

Farragut, Loyall. *The Life of David Glasgow Farragut: First Admiral of the United States Navy, Embodying His Journal and Letters*. New York:

Appleton, 1879. The author, Farragut's only child, has written a hagiography greatly improved by his use of Farragut's letters and journal.

Latham, Jean L. *Anchor's Aweigh: The Story of David Glasgow Farragut*. New York: Harper, 1968. The best of the modern juvenile works on Farragut, this book is well illustrated and contains useful maps.

Lewis, Charles Lee. *David Glasgow Farragut*. 2 vols. Annapolis, Md.: United States Naval Institute, 1941-1943. The author of several excellent books on naval officers has here produced the most scholarly biography available, one enriched by original research.

Mahan, A. T. *Admiral Farragut*. New York: Appleton, and London: Sampson Low, 1892. A classic work on the subject written by another famous admiral, this biography nevertheless is dated and deemed unnecessarily laudatory.

Nash, Howard P., Jr. *A Naval History of the Civil War*. Cranbury, N.J.: Barnes, and London: Yoseloff, 1972. Concise and to the point, this is an outstanding one-volume history of the naval struggle between the North and the South. Many references are made to Farragut.

Spears, John R. *David G. Farragut*. Philadelphia: Jacobs, 1905. Essentially an early juvenile biography written by a prolific author of nautical adventures, this book has some unique insights to share with the reader. It is also remarkably well illustrated with maps and charts.

Joseph E. Suppiger

DAME MILLICENT GARRETT FAWCETT

Born: June 11, 1847; Aldeburgh, Suffolk, England
Died: August 5, 1929; London, England
Areas of Achievement: Women's rights and social reform
Contribution: Mrs. Fawcett was a leader in advancing the causes of women's suffrage, education, and social reform. She also worked to end the double standard in the grounds for divorce, to improve women's rights of guardianship over their children, and to open the legal profession to women. From 1897 to 1919, she was president of the nonviolent National Union of Women's Suffrage Societies.

Early Life

Millicent Garrett Fawcett was the fifth daughter of ten children of Newson Garrett, a self-made wealthy corn and coal merchant and shipowner, and Louisa Dunnell. Millicent's mother was deeply religious and had less influence on her than her father. Millicent attended a school run by the aunt of the poet Robert Browning at Blackheath until she was fifteen. An apocryphal story recounted by Ray Strachey in her history of women's suffrage, *The Cause* (1928), tells how one night, after Millicent, her sister Elizabeth, and their friend Emily Davis had discussed what each might accomplish, Emily responded as follows: "I must devote myself to securing higher education, while you open the medical profession to women. After these things are done, we must see about getting the vote. . . . You are younger than we are Milli, so you must attend to that." They all succeeded.

In 1864, Elizabeth met Henry Fawcett, a blind professor of political economy at Cambridge. He proposed to her but was spurned. In the meantime, Millicent frequently visited Louise, the oldest of the Garrett sisters, in London. Louise, like Elizabeth, was a feminist. In 1865 she took Millicent to hear a speech on women's rights by John Stuart Mill. There Millicent, who was eighteen, also met Fawcett, a disciple of John Stuart Mill. Eighteen months later, in April, 1867, over the objections of Elizabeth, who saw his modest income and his blindness as obstacles, they were married. A year later, Philippa, their only child, was born.

Life's Work

In 1865, Henry Fawcett entered Parliament as the Member from Brighton. A Liberal free-trader, his feminism was derived from his opposition to government regulation. Mrs. Fawcett acted as his secretary and soon added to her education. He encouraged her to submit articles to journals such as *Macmillan's Magazine* in 1868 and to write *Political Economy for Beginners* in 1870. It provided, in simplified form, the economic gospel of Mill, heavily salted with self-help and individualism. It was an immediate success and went to ten editions. Together, the Fawcetts wrote *Essays and Lectures in Political Subjects* in 1872. At that time, Mrs. Fawcett's views on self-help were extreme. She even opposed free education because, as a result, a father otherwise prone to alcoholism might instead strive to provide an education for his children.

Henry Fawcett supported Mill's effort to give women the vote in 1867, favoring a bill that included not only widows and spinsters (who had become heads of households) but also married women. In 1884, as postmaster general in Gladstone's cabinet, he clashed with the prime minister's opposition to including women in the 1884 Franchise Reform Act. He also opposed legislation in 1874 regulating the labor of women in the textile industry. Unfortunately, Henry Fawcett died in 1884 from pleurisy.

Before his death, Mrs. Fawcett published a successful novel, *Janet Doncaster* (1875). It was slow-moving, with little action, and was mainly a temperance tract. Her second novel, published under a pseudonym so that she could see if it could stand on its own merits, was not as successful.

A widow at the age of thirty-seven, Mrs. Fawcett intensified her interest in the cause of women's rights. Even while she had written about economic topics in the 1870's, she had continued her interest in the cause of women's suffrage. In July, 1867, she had become a member of the first regular Women's Suffrage Committee in London and had made her first speech in Manchester in 1868. Now, in the 1880's and 1890's, she became active in two related causes of interest to women: the Contagious Diseases Acts controversy and the Henry Cust case. When the Contagious Diseases Acts controversy had first emerged as an issue in the 1860's, Mrs. Fawcett had refused to become involved for fear that it might split the suffrage movement. The acts aimed to protect members of the armed forces from venereal diseases by requiring the compulsory examination of suspected prostitutes. Both feminists and moralists opposed the acts for seeming to accept prostitution while discriminating against women by forcing them to submit to involuntary medical examination. The appearance of William Thomas Stead's articles on white slavery in the *Pall Mall Gazette* came in 1885, shortly after Mrs. Fawcett's husband's death. It provided her with a cause she could support in her husband's memory and on behalf of women's rights. She became a leader in the Vigilance Society, which was formed to repeal the acts and protect the virtue of young women. Later, in 1927, she wrote a biography of Josephine Butler, its leader.

Mrs. Fawcett waged another moral crusade in 1894, over Henry Cust, a Conservative M.P. from Manchester. Cust had seduced and made pregnant a young girl whom he subsequently abandoned; he then proposed marriage to another woman. When the girl wrote Cust a letter begging him to marry her, he flaunted its contents to some friends. As a Vigilance Society member, Mrs. Fawcett launched a campaign that finally succeeded in forcing Cust to abandon his candidacy and marry the girl whom he had seduced. Unfortunately, Mrs. Fawcett continued attacks on Cust until her friends had to restrain her zeal because of the damage it was doing to the cause of women's suffrage.

As a women's rights advocate, Mrs. Fawcett argued for equal grounds for divorce and improvement in the rights of women as guardians of children. She was a staunch defender of the family; her championing of the rights of women did not extend to supporting sexual freedom. Even her daughter Philippa contributed to the cause of women's equality when, in 1890, she proved superior to the senior wrangler (the Cambridge honors graduate in mathematics) on the mathematical tripos list.

Throughout the 1880's, Mrs. Fawcett tried to remain aloof from party commitment. The 1867 Reform Act had given the right to vote to all male borough householders who personally paid rates or rented lodgings at more than ten pounds a year. The 1884 Reform Act extended these provisions to the rural areas of Great Britain. The strenuous efforts by Liberal Party managers to exclude women householders from the Reform Bill of 1884 made Mrs. Fawcett reject an invitation to join the Council of the Women's Liberal Federation, and finally in 1887, as a nationalist, she abandoned her husband's party to join the Liberal Unionists over the issue of home rule. She broke with it in 1903 because of her commitment to free trade. Throughout

her life, she remained committed to liberal principles and evolutionary politics but not economic reform. She championed the right of women to work in the mining industry. In 1898, she opposed attempts to prohibit women working with phosphorus. Her opposition was based on feminist and libertarian grounds.

The 1890's witnessed some gains and some reversals in the women's suffrage movement. In order to understand the irregular progress of the women's suffrage movement in Great Britain and the obstacles facing Mrs. Fawcett, it must be realized that even opponents of women's suffrage believed that all rate payers ought to vote in local municipal elections, if not for Members of Parliament. In 1869, the Municipal Franchise Act had enfranchised women taxpayers, although the courts later ruled that this included only single women. Married women with taxpayers, however, could vote for school boards in 1870, poor law boards in 1875, county councils in 1888, and parish and district councils in 1894. Moderate women suffragists could look to the past with some satisfaction as a precedent for a gradual strategy.

In 1887, Lydia Becker, the leader of the Manchester Women's Suffrage Society and editor of the *Women's Suffrage Journal*, died. In April, 1892, Sir Arthur Rollitt's private member's bill to enfranchise widows and spinsters who already had the right to vote failed by a mere twenty-three votes. Between 1890 and 1897, the number of women's suffrage societies dwindled from one thousand to fewer than two hundred. Finally, in 1897, a committee met in Westminster Town Hall and elected Mrs. Fawcett president of a new umbrella organization, the National Union of Women's Suffrage Societies (NUWSS). It was composed of independent societies in all parts of the nation and proposed to gain the same terms for suffrage as were currently or might eventually be granted to men. A petition drive netted more than a quarter million signatures, and more than 140 meetings were held. Mrs. Fawcett was busy speaking, lobbying individual members of Parliament, and organizing parades in all parts of the country. By 1906, the majority of NUWSS members were supporters of the Liberal Party, and the majority of Liberal M.P.'s elected in the 1906 landslide had individually pledged themselves to the women's cause.

Before 1906, however, the center stage of political concern was occupied by the Boer War, which had begun in 1899, and Mrs. Fawcett was sent in July, 1901, to South Africa as a leader of an all-woman commission to investigate the conditions in British concentration camps exposed by Emily Hobhouse.

Throughout her life, Mrs. Fawcett was a nationalist and imperialist, and while her report was on the whole sympathetic to government goals, her criticisms entitle her to be considered the "Florence Nightingale" of the Boer War. Her recommendations were implemented by Viscount Milner, and within a year the camp mortality rate fell below that of Glasgow, although not before more than twenty-five thousand had died from measles and typhoid epidemics.

The suffrage cause therefore languished between 1899 and 1905, when the Women's Social and Political Union (WSPU) was founded. At first its militancy was welcomed by Mrs. Fawcett for the discussion it drew to the issue, but as eccentricity turned to violence she strongly condemned the use of physical violence in propaganda in 1908. She had earlier supported Ann Cobden Sanderson, who had been imprisoned, and her sister Elizabeth, who was a WSPU member for three years. In 1910, a temporary truce between the WSPU and NUWSS was reached and a joint parade and demonstration were staged.

The NUWSS during this period received heavy financial support from Mrs. Fawcett. She donated more than one hundred pounds to it, and by 1900 organizers received salaries totaling one thousand pounds and included six workingwomen. Until May, 1912, Mrs. Fawcett supported a policy which endorsed individual M.P.'s rather than parties to secure suffrage, but at that time she accepted the decision of the NUWSS to support Labour Party candidates because it had become the only party to support women's suffrage. It was in essence a declaration of war on the Liberal Party, given her opposition to socialism and support of self-help.

When the outbreak of World War I was imminent, the NUWSS held a large peace meeting in London, on August 4, but after the declaration of war, Mrs. Fawcett and most of the membership of the NUWSS called upon women to sustain the vital forces of the nation. In 1915, she defeated an attempt by pacifists to alter NUWSS policy. When the problem of adjusting the franchise to accommodate servicemen arose near the end of 1915 and the question of women's suffrage was raised, she reinitiated private lobbying efforts. Later, as compulsory service legislation in February, 1917, rekindled interest in change of suffrage, Mrs. Fawcett supported a limited measure of women's suffrage and was encouraged when David Lloyd George replaced H. H. Asquith, whom she no longer trusted. In June, 1917, the measure passed the House of Commons, and in January, the House of Lords. In gratitude, Mrs. Fawcett broke her former attitude of nonpartisanship and became an outspoken supporter of Lloyd George and the coalition government. It was at the celebration of the suffrage victory in 1918 that the suffrage hymn utilizing William Blake's poem *Jerusalem* was set to music by Sir Hubert Parry.

After World War I, the granting of family allowances, which was supported by Eleanor Rathbone, caused a split in the NUWSS. Mrs. Fawcett was convinced that allowances would destroy family life and were still another example of creeping socialism. As a consequence, she resigned from the National Union of Societies for Equal Citizenship (the new name for the NUWSS). Even so, she continued to support efforts to open the legal profession to women and to grant equal franchise to women under thirty years of age. The latter was achieved in 1928 while she was in Palestine. In 1929, she died of pneumonia.

Summary

Dame Millicent Garrett Fawcett was not flashy or charismatic. She epitomized the type of woman voter who supporters of women's suffrage believed would exercise the privilege responsibly: She was dignified and reliable, conciliatory yet determined. Though she disliked making speeches, her efforts were well prepared and logical; her delivery was clear and spiced with her keen sense of humor. Though lacking the beauty of the Pankhurst family, Mrs. Fawcett was an attractive woman, with a serene face, radiant complexion, and shiny brown hair. She was a hard worker and never employed a secretary. Her hobby was listening to music. While she championed women's rights, she never believed in war between the sexes. As the *Daily Telegraph's* obituary read, "The name of militants . . . are sometimes quoted as the leaders to victory, but in reality it was the woman of sweet reasonableness, womanly manner, quiet dress and cultured style who did more than any other in the cause of emancipation."

Bibliography

Banks, Olive. *Faces of Feminism: A Study of a Social Movement.* Oxford; Martin Robertson, and New York: St. Martin's Press, 1981. Best balanced, overall treatment of the subject. It covers more than suffrage, treating family, legal, and economic subjects.

Fawcett, Henry, and Millicent Garrett Fawcett. *Essays and Lectures on Social and Political Subjects.* London: Macmillan, 1872. Contains four essays by Henry Fawcett and eight by Millicent Garrett Fawcett that show the influence of John Stuart Mill and opposition to overprotective legislation that might retard women's independence and their ability to compete in society.

Fawcett, Millicent Garrett. *What I Remember.* London: Unwin, 1924; New York: Putnam, 1925. Typically understates Mrs. Fawcett's role but evidences the methodical planning and organization that characterized her leadership.

———. *The Women's Victory and After: Personal Reminiscences.* London: Sidgwick and Jackson, 1920. Interesting on the war years and the role of Lloyd George in achieving the partial attainment of women's suffrage.

Fawcett, Millicent Garrett, T. C. Jack, and E. C. Jack. *Women's Suffrage: A Short History of a Great Movement.* London: People's Books, and New York: Dodge, 1912. Written during the period of WSPU militancy, this book shows Mrs. Fawcett's faith in democracy within the ranks of the movement.

Liddington, Jill, and Jill Norris. *One Hand Tied Behind Us: The Rise of the Women's Suffrage Movement.* London: Virago, 1983. Lively, balanced, incisive treatment with a good bibliography, this volume is mainly a study of the left-wing, nonmilitant, anti-WSPU women's suffrage movement in Lancashire.

Oakley, Ann. "Millicent Garrett Fawcett: Duty and Determination." In *Feminist Theorists,* edited by Dale Spender. New York: Random House, and London: Women's Press, 1983. Fails to allow for historical perspective at times and understand the ideological stance of mid-Victorian liberalism. Interestingly, Oakley is one of few modern feminists to have studied Mrs. Fawcett.

Pugh, Martin. *Women's Suffrage in Britain, 1867-1929.* London: Historical Association, 1980. A good historiographic survey which analyzes succinctly the relationship between the Edwardian period and wartime suffrage for franchise reform.

Rover, Constance. *Women's Suffrage and Party Politics in Britain, 1866-1914.* London: Routledge, 1967. A lively account of the political aspects of women's suffrage and narratives of the cabinet-WSPU battle.

Stephen, Leslie. *The Life of Henry Fawcett.* London: Smith Elder, 1885; New York: Putnam, 1886. Details Fawcett's views on women's suffrage and feminism and is valuable for understanding why his wife did not become an antimale crusader.

Strachey, Ray. *Millicent Garrett Fawcett.* London: Murray, 1931. Written by her close friend of many years, this work is bland and uncontroversial. It views Mrs. Fawcett and NUWSS as part of a development broader even than the women's movement.

Norbert C. Soldon

GUSTAV THEODOR FECHNER

Born: April 19, 1801; Gross-Särchen, Prussia
Died: November 18, 1887; Leipzig, Germany
Areas of Achievement: Philosophy and physics
Contribution: Fechner is widely regarded as the founder of psychophysics, or the science of the mind-body relation, and as a pioneer in experimental psychology. His most important contributions are a number of quantitative methods for measuring absolute and differential thresholds that are still employed by psychologists to study sensitivity to stimulation.

Early Life

Gustav Theodor Fechner was born in the village of Gross-Särchen, near Halle in southeastern Germany, the second of five children of Samuel Traugott Fechner and Johanna Dorothea Fischer Fechner. His father was a progressive Lutheran preacher, who is said to have astounded the local villagers by mounting a lightning rod on the church tower and by adopting the unorthodox practice of preaching without a wig. Although he died when Gustav was only five years old, already the young Fechner was infused with his father's fierce intellectual independence and his passion for the human spirit.

Fechner attended the *Gymnasium* at Soran, near Dresden, and was matriculated in medicine at the University of Leipzig in 1817. He was not a model student, opting to read on his own rather than attend lectures. During this period, Fechner became disenchanted with establishment views: He professed atheism and was never able to complete the doctorate which would have entitled him to practice medicine. His studies were not a waste of time, however, since he began composing satires on medicine and the materialism which flourished in Germany during this period. Some fourteen satirical works were published by Fechner under the pseudonym "Dr. Mises" between 1821 and 1876.

In 1824, Fechner began to lecture on physics and mathematics at the University of Leipzig without any remuneration. Translating scientific treatises from French into German (about a dozen volumes in six years), although onerous work, helped him to make a living. He managed to publish numerous scientific papers during this period, and a particularly important paper on quantitative measurements of direct currents finally secured for him an appointment with a substantial salary as professor of physics in 1834.

This period marked the happiest time in Fechner's life. The year before his appointment, he had married Clara Volkmann, the sister of a colleague at the university. The security of a permanent position and marital bliss did nothing to dampen his enthusiasm for hard work; an enviable social life was simply incorporated into his already cramped schedule. Evenings at the local symphony conducted by Felix Mendelssohn were regular events to which, on occasion, the Fechners were accompanied by Robert and Clara Schumann, his niece by marriage.

Fechner's idyllic life was shattered in 1839 by an illness that forced him to resign his position at the university. At first, he experienced partial blindness caused by gazing at the sun through colored glasses as part of a series of experiments on colors and afterimages; depression, severe headaches, and loss of appetite soon followed. For three years, Fechner sheltered himself in a darkened room, and his promising career seemed to be over. One day, however, he wandered into his garden and removed the bandages that had adorned his eyes since the onset of his illness. He reported that his vision not only was restored but also was more powerful than before because he could now experience the souls of flowers. After the initial trauma of restored eyesight faded, Fechner recovered with a revitalized religious consciousness. It was this newfound awareness of the importance of the human spirit that marked the beginning of Fechner's mature period.

Life's Work

The focal point of Fechner's work was a deep-seated antipathy toward materialism, or the view that nothing exists except for matter and its modifications. His first volley against materialism was the enigmatic *Nanna: Oder, Über das Seelenleben der Pflanzen* (1848; Nanna, or the soul life of plants), which advanced the notion that even plants have a mental life. Three years later, his *Zend-Avesta: Oder, Über die Dinge des Himmels und des Jenseits* (1851; *Zend-Avesta: On the Things of Heaven and the Hereafter*, 1882) proclaimed a new gospel based on the notion that the entire material universe is consciously animated and alive in every particular. The phenomenal world explored by physics, Fechner asserted, is merely the form in which inner experiences appear to one another. Since consciousness and the physical world are coeternal aspects of the same reality, materialism (or what Fechner referred to as the "night view") must be repudiated because it examines the universe in only one of its aspects.

More pertinent, Fechner submitted that his alternative "day view" dissolves the traditional problem of the mind-body relation. There is no need to worry about how the physical is converted into the mental, because mind and body are not distinct kinds of things. All that one needs is to display the functional relationship between consciousness and its physical manifestations. Since it was uncontested that physical qualities could be measured, Fechner discerned that he would have to specify a means for measuring mental properties if the scientific establishment was to be convinced that his alternative program represented a legitimate contender to materialism.

The German physiologist Ernst Heinrich Weber had submitted in 1846 that a difference between two stimuli (or an addition to or subtraction from one or the other stimulus) is always perceived as equal if its ratio to the stimulus remains the same, regardless of how the absolute size changes. If a change of one unit from five can be detected, Weber's result specifies that so can a change of ten from fifty, of one hundred from five hundred, and the like. On the morning of October 22, 1850, Fechner discovered what he regarded as the fundamental relation between the mental and the physical world. Where Weber's result was restricted to external stimulation, Fechner posited a general mathematical relationship between stimulus and sensation, such that for every increase in stimulation there is a corresponding increase in sensation. This functional relationship is now known as the Weber-Fechner law. It asserts that the psychological sensation produced by a stimulus is proportional to the logarithm of the external stimulation.

Although Fechner's law represents a development of Weber's work, he did not rely on Weber's substantive result. Indeed, it was Fechner who realized that his psychophysical principle corresponded to Weber's result and gave it the name Weber's law. Perhaps he was overly generous. Weber's result conflicts with low stimulus intensities. By incorporating the activity of the subject's sensory system into the equation, Fechner was able to overcome this difficulty.

Fechner's law is a genuine psychophysical law in the sense that it relates mental phenomena to external stimulation. Comparing it with Sir Isaac

Newton's law of gravitation, Fechner laid out his ambitious program for a science of the functional relations of mind and body in his classic work, *Elemente der Psychophysik* (1860; *Elements of Psychophysics*, 1966). Along with his method for measuring the relationship between psychological and physical phenomena, Fechner refined three methods—the method of barely noticeable differences, the method of right and wrong cases, and the method of average error—for measuring thresholds, or the point at which a stimulus (or a stimulus difference) becomes noticeable or disappears. These techniques for measuring sense discrimination are still prominent in psychological research. Fechner also established the mathematical expressions of these methods and contributed to the literature a series of classical experiments on human sensitivity to external stimulation.

Fechner's program for a psychophysics attracted few converts. Vocal opponents, such as William James, the eminent American philosopher and psychologist, objected that mental properties are not quantifiable. Fechner sought to measure sensations by measuring their stimuli, but he furnished no independent evidence for the presupposition that it is sensations that are measured. This objection was significant granted that there was good reason to suppose that sensations cannot be measured. Sensations are not additive; a larger sensation is not simply a sum of smaller sensations. Anything that is not additive, Fechner's opponents declared, cannot be measured. What he had measured, rather, was observer response to stimulation; Fechner had produced an account of sensitivity and so had confused the sensation with the excitation of the subject.

These and related objections led to the downfall of psychophysics. Although Fechner's ideas were examined by Hermann von Helmholtz, Ernst Mach, and other scientists who were interested in related subjects, Fechner's attempt to place the mental on a par with the physical was dismissed as pure whimsy. The failure of Fechner's program, however, does not diminish his importance as a philosopher. Fechner's methods for measuring sensitivity were assimilated into the basis of empirical psychology. Since Fechner's methods presume that chance is a characteristic of physical systems, Fechner achieved a measure of victory over materialism. If he was right, mental phenomena could not be straightforwardly reduced to matter and its modifications.

Although Fechner continued to contribute to the literature on psychophysics, he turned to other matters late in his life. An interest in aesthetics proved to be a rather natural development of his interest in stimulation and his long-standing affection for the arts. The culmination of his work on the study of beauty was *Vorschule der Aesthetik* (1876; introduction to aesthetics), which argued that aesthetics is the study of the objects that produce aesthetic experiences. This work proved to be seminal in the history of experimental aesthetics.

Summary

Gustav Theodor Fechner was a man of great erudition—not only was he a physicist and a philosopher but also he was the author of a detailed theological theory, a poet, and a satirist. What united his diverse pursuits was a struggle to reconcile the empirical rigor of the exact sciences with a spiritual conception of the universe. Although Fechner's attempt to place consciousness on a par with the physical was rejected by the scientific community, his vision helped to lay the foundations for the emerging science of empirical psychology.

Fechner's greatest contributions, the functional proportion between sensation and stimulus and his numerous techniques for measuring psychological response to stimulation, do not compare favorably with the concept of universal gravitation. Fechner's philosophy of nature as consciously animated and alive in every particular was rejected by the scientific community, and so his contributions did not revolutionize science. Yet without his techniques for measuring psychological variables, the science of empirical psychology would not have reached maturity.

Bibliography

Boring, Edwin G. *A History of Experimental Psychology*. 2d ed. New York: Appleton, 1950. A comprehensive account of the emergence of experimental psychology. Although Boring credits Fechner with laying the foundations for empirical psychology, he contends that it was merely an unexpected by-product of Fechner's philosophical interests.

Fechner, Gustav Theodor. *Elements of Psychophysics*. Translated with a foreword by Helmut E. Adler. New York: Holt Rinehart, 1966. The author's introduction provides an overview of the problem concerning the mind-body relation and an outline of his program for a science of psychophysics. The translator's foreword places Fechner's contributions in their nineteenth century historical context.

James, William. *The Principles of Psychology*. London: Macmillan, and New York: Holt, 1890. Contains a faithful presentation of Fechner's contributions and a searching critique of his philosophical outlook. Perhaps the best indicator of why psychophysics fell into disfavor.

Savage, C. Wade. *The Measurement of Sensation: A Critique of Perceptual Psychophysics*. Berkeley: University of California Press, 1970. A thorough discussion of the central philosophical issues in the measurement of sensation. The excellent bibliography is a useful guide to the wealth of literature on this topic.

Snodgrass, Joan Gay. "Psychophysics." In *Experimental Sensory Psychology*, edited by Bertram Scharf. Glenview, Ill.: Scott, Foresman, 1975. A concise introduction to the history of psychophysical theory and its methods. For the technically minded reader, the analysis of the relationship between Weber's result and Fechner's psychophysical law helps to illustrate Fechner's contributions to the measurement of sensation.

Brian S. Baigrie

MARSHALL FIELD

Born: August 18, 1834; near Conway, Massachusetts

Died: January 16, 1906; New York, New York

Areas of Achievement: Retailing and philanthropy

Contribution: Founder of Marshall Field and Company, which became the largest wholesale and retail dry-goods store in the world, Field introduced many retailing concepts that set the standard for modern merchandising.

Early Life

Marshall Field was born near the town of Conway, Massachusetts, on August 18, 1834, to John and Fidelia (née Nash) Field. His family had lived in Massachusetts since 1629, when his ancestor Zechariah Field had come over from England. Although his father was a farmer, the agrarian life did not appeal to young Marshall. Instead, he left home at the age of seventeen and took a job in a dry-goods store owned by Deacon Davis in Pittsfield, Massachusetts. He worked there for five years, but, even though Davis offered him a partnership in the business, Field had other plans. He saw the West as the site of his future, as the place where huge fortunes could be made by those ambitious and talented enough to take advantage of the tremendous opportunities caused by its rapid development and population growth. Accordingly, he left New England in 1856 and moved to the rude and dirty, but potentially thriving, city of Chicago, Illinois.

Field arrived in Chicago with little money and secured a job as a clerk with Cooley, Wadsworth and Company, the largest wholesale dry-goods firm in the city at the time. His starting salary was four hundred dollars a year and, as an indication of his future business sense, he managed to save half of this amount by living and sleeping in the store. A small, handsome young man with a serious and polite demeanor and a large handlebar mustache, Field also displayed a true flair for the dry-goods business and a unique appeal to and concern for the customer. As a result, he rapidly advanced through the hierarchy of the firm. Within a year of his arrival in Chicago, he was made a traveling salesman for the company, and in 1861 he became general manger of the Chicago store. His rapid rise culminated in 1862 when he was invited to be a full partner in the company, which changed its name to Cooley, Farwell and Company. In 1864, when the

financial wizard Levi Z. Leiter joined as a new partner, Field finally had his name added to the company's title, Farwell, Field and Company. Impressed by the entrepreneurial and financial skill of Field and Leiter, the millionaire Potter S. Palmer offered to sell them his retail and wholesale dry-goods business in 1865. The two men jumped at the chance and, with money borrowed from Palmer himself, they formed the new firm of Field, Palmer, and Leiter. Palmer dropped completely out of the business two years later in order to concentrate exclusively on his hotel interests, leaving Field and Leiter in sole control of the growing firm. In only eight years, and by the age of thirty, Marshall Field had risen from a lowly clerk to the co-owner of one of the largest dry-goods operations in Chicago.

Life's Work

After Palmer retired from the firm in 1867, Field invited his two younger brothers, Henry and Joseph Field, to join as partners, thus consolidating his control of the business at Leiter's expense. Nevertheless, Leiter remained a partner until he sold his interest to Field in 1881, after which the business assumed the name Marshall Field and Company. Wholesale and retail sales, which had stood at approximately ten million dollars annually at the time of Palmer's withdrawal, climbed to nearly thirty-five million dollars by the early 1890's and had surpassed sixty-eight million dollars by the time of Field's death in 1906. Not even such catastrophes as the Chicago fire of 1871 (which completely destroyed his retail store and wholesale warehouse), the financial panic of 1873 (which ruined many Chicago merchants), or another fire in 1877 in his main retail outlet at the corner of State and Washington streets significantly slowed this pattern of expansion. As an example of this powerful drive to succeed, Field led Chicago in its recovery from the 1871 fire by establishing a temporary store in a horse barn at State and Twentieth streets only two weeks after the flames had died out.

At first, the wholesale aspect of the business interested Field more than the retail side. As time went on, however, and Field realized the immense profit potential of quality retailing, he devoted more and more of his energy to it, to the exclusion of the wholesale part of the firm. In 1873, the retail branch was physically separated from the whole-

sale branch with the opening of a new store at State and Washington streets. A program of continual expansion followed, culminating in the creation of the magnificent, cityblock-square entrepôt in 1912, six years after Field's death. This massive structure still stands and serves as the flagship store of the Field Company as well as a familiar landmark in the heart of downtown Chicago.

Field was not a merchandising innovator, but he was very adept at adopting the newest methods in retailing that had been pioneered by others. His store plainly marked the price on all goods, so that the customer knew exactly what the cost of an item was when he or she first looked at it. He established resident buyers in England, France, and Germany in order to ensure his store a steady supply of quality foreign-made goods and frequently made it a practice to become the exclusive agent of popular products in Chicago—thus making sure that if customers wanted a certain product, they had to come to Fields to buy it. His reputation for honesty and courtesy was legendary, and he is credited with coining the motto The Customer Is Always Right. He also was among the first to adopt what is now the accepted practice in retailing marketing: He purchased products at wholesale for cash before there was any real customer demand for them and then, through advertising and attractive window displays, created that demand. This practice allowed Field to undersell his numerous competitors, who waited for demand to materialize before placing an order with a manufacturer, thus paying a higher wholesale price for the time. Marshall Field and Company was also the first retail outlet in the Midwest to employ window displays, to offer such personal services as gift-wrapping to customers, to establish a "bargain basement," and to open a restaurant within the store.

Field recognized ability when he saw it and often promoted talented managers to partners in his firm as a reward for their dedicated service. Former employees such as Harlow N. Higinbotham, Harry Gordon Selfridge, and John Shedd all became millionaires as a result of this practice. Once they had earned their fortunes as Field's partners, however, he then frequently proceeded to buy out their interest in the company in order to provide room for younger up-and-comers. The achievement of the American Dream was a real possibility for those who worked for Marshall Field, as long as they demonstrated the ambition, imagination, and ability he admired.

The American Dream was certainly good to Marshall Field as well. By the time of his death, he had amassed a fortune of $120,000,000. He did not waste this wealth on ostentatious display, as did so many other self-made millionaires of his era. Although he did build himself a grand mansion on Chicago's prestigious Prairie Avenue (constructed in 1873, at a cost of $100,000, by Richard Morris Hunt, the famous architect who had designed the fabulous palaces of William Vanderbilt and John Jacob Astor in New York), he otherwise lived a rather simple life dominated by his devotion to his work. He preferred to walk to his office and frequently ridiculed the pretensions of the wealthy. For example, when he was informed that a clerk was dating his daughter, he responded, "Thank God, there is no disgrace in being a clerk."

Field was not a prolific philanthropist, but when he did give, he made his gift count. After he first arrived in Chicago, he became active in such diverse organizations as the Chicago Relief and Aid Society, the Young Men's Christian Association, the Chicago Historical Association, the Art Institute, and the Civic Federation. Yet, as the years went by, business concerns monopolized an increasing portion of his time, and he let his membership in most of these organizations lapse. The year 1889 saw the rejuvenation of his charitable generosity. In that year he donated a ten-acre parcel of land, valued at $125,000, to serve as the site of the new University of Chicago. He later supplemented that gift with a $100,000 endowment to the school. In 1891, he gave $50,000 worth of land to the Chicago Home for Incurables, and, in 1893, he gave $1,000,000 to create the Columbian Museum at the Chicago World's Fair. A provision in his will for a further $8,000,000 allowed this museum to construct a permanent building on Chicago's Lake Shore Drive and to enlarge its collection. In appreciation of his support, the institution took the name the Field Museum of Natural History; it remains one of the best museums of its type in the United States.

Field's personal life contained a large share of tragedy. His first wife, Nannie Scott (they were married in January, 1863), left him in the late 1880's and took up permanent residence in France. After she died in 1896, he secretly courted Mrs. Delia Spencer Caton and married her shortly after her husband's death in 1905. Then, in November, 1905, his only son, Marshall Field, Jr., accidently shot and killed himself while preparing for a hunting trip. This last blow proved to be too much for the elderly multimillionaire. He came down with pneumonia in late December, 1905, and died on January 16, 1906. The bulk of his huge estate was left in trust to his two grandsons, Henry Field and Marshall Field III. The latter would become the founder and first publisher of the *Chicago Sun-Times*.

Summary

Marshall Field embodied those characteristics of ambition, business sense, hard work, and simplicity that Americans of his era valued so highly. The fact that a New England dry-goods clerk could become one of the wealthiest men in the United States suggested that success was within the grasp of anyone willing to work hard enough. Although there were thousands of failed clerks for every Marshall Field, Field nevertheless served as a shining example for every ambitious young man who entered the business world.

His impact on the American retail trade was equally striking. Although not an innovator himself, Field was willing to gamble on the innovations of others. He thus introduced many ideas first pioneered on the East Coast to Chicago and made his store the most progressive in the city throughout the nineteenth and early twentieth centuries. His emphasis on fairness and "the customer is always right" also won for him millions of loyal customers. As a result, in Chicago the name Marshall Field is still associated with honesty, courtesy, and high-quality merchandise at a fair price.

Finally, Field also had a profound influence on the history and institutions of the city of Chicago. Without his generosity, it is doubtful that the University of Chicago and the Field Museum of Natural History would exist. The prosperous State Street business district grew up around his State and Washington store and thus owes its life to Field's initial decision to locate there in 1873. His descendants, notably Marshall Field III, would play prominent roles in local politics and the press. Finally, several generations of Chicagoans have grown up with fond memories of Christmas trips to Field's to talk to Santa Claus, to gaze at the gigantic Christmas tree towering from the center of the Walnut Room, and to be dazzled by those magical Christmas window displays. Christmas and Field's go hand in hand in the hearts of Chicagoans and in the memories of ex-Chicagoans. Perhaps it is this feeling that represents Marshall Field's most profound gift to his beloved adopted city.

Bibliography

Cromie, Robert. *The Great Chicago Fire*. New York: McGraw-Hill, 1958. A detailed account of the holocaust that destroyed a good portion of the city in 1871. Also provides an informative description of Field's efforts to get both his business and the city back on their feet again after the fire.

Drury, John. *Old Chicago Houses*. Chicago: Rand McNally, 1941. Includes drawings, photographs, and an accurate description of Field's mansion on Prairie Avenue.

Pierce, Bessie Louise. *A History of Chicago*. Vol. 3, *The Rise of a Modern City, 1871-1893*. New York: Knopf, 1956. An excruciatingly minute history of the city during the late nineteenth century which includes numerous, and often colorful, anecdotes on the life, business, and contributions of Field.

Twyman, Robert W. *Marshall Field and Company, 1852-1906*. Philadelphia: University of Pennsylvania Press, 1954. Based on the author's doctoral dissertation, the book provides an excellent, although occasionally dry, analysis of the rise of Field's retailing empire.

Wagenknecht, Edward C. *Chicago*. Norman: University of Oklahoma Press, 1964. A brief, rather impressionistic, portrait of the history of the city that also presents a spotty but productive investigation of Field's influence during the late nineteenth century.

Wendt, Lloyd, and Herman Kogan. *Give the Lady What She Wants*. Chicago: Rand McNally, 1952. An exciting and well-written history of Marshall Field and Company up until 1950.

———. *Chicago: A Pictorial History*. New York: Bonanza Books, 1958. Although brief on text, this visual history contains photographs of Field, his stores, and his mansion.

Christopher E. Guthrie

STEPHEN J. FIELD

Born: November 4, 1816; Haddam, Connecticut
Died: April 9, 1899; Washington, D.C.
Area of Achievement: Constitutional law
Contribution: In the last quarter of the nineteenth century, Justice Field's brilliant and ingenious legal opinions protected the United States' entrepreneurs from what they perceived to be the destructive power of popular government.

Early Life

Stephen Johnson Field was the sixth child of nine (seven boys and two girls) born to David and Submit Field. His father was an austere Congregational minister. His mother, whose Puritan father had given her the name "Submit" as an expression of Christian virtue, imbued her son with an independence of mind and motives which graphically demonstrated that she had been misnamed. Field's earliest education was the product of his parents' unchangeable convictions. "Our whole domestic life," wrote his brother, "received its tone from this unaffected piety of our parents, who taught their children to lie down and rise up in that fear of the Lord, which is the beginning of wisdom." At thirteen, Field's hearthside education ended when he accompanied his older sister and her husband to Greece, where they were to establish a school for young women. Two and a half years later, Field returned to Massachusetts with a less provincial view of the world and a determination to enroll at Williams College. In 1833, he entered Williams and was graduated valedictorian four years later.

Faced with the problem of choosing a vocation at the age of twenty-one, Field joined his brother's law firm in New York City. In 1841, he passed the New York bar. After ten years of service in the family law firm, however, he was anxious to set off on his own; with his brother's encouragement, he moved to San Francisco to try his luck at gold mining and lawyering. In California, it soon became apparent that he was a better lawyer than a miner. San Francisco was much too expensive for his meager purse, however, so he made his way up the Sacramento River to the frontier town of Marysville. In Marysville, he had the good fortune of rendering legal services to General John Augustus Sutter, on whose land gold had been discovered in 1849. With Sutter's help, he was elected the *alcalde* (the Mexican equivalent to the justice of the

peace) of the Marysville township. A year later, with the installation of the newly drafted California constitution, he exchanged his position of *alcalde* for a seat in the legislature. In 1853, he ran for the California senate but was defeated by two votes and, with the defeat, never again sought a political position in the state.

The next six years were devoted to establishing a successful law practice and becoming financially independent. Indeed, by 1857 he had acquired enough influence with the rich and powerful people in California to be nominated and appointed to the state supreme court.

A few years later, as a result of his brilliantly reasoned and orderly *laissez-faire* legal opinions, he became the chief justice of the court. In 1863, although a Democrat, Field was appointed by the Republican President Abraham Lincoln to the United States Supreme Court.

Life's Work

Field's judicial activities covered more than forty years, thirty-four of which were on the federal bench, and during which time he wrote more than one thousand opinions. It was not the number of opinions but rather their quality which was to become his national legacy, a legacy in defense of the entrepreneurial class that was to last for more than half a century. Often he was the minority voice in his own court, yet long after majority decisions had lost their influence and had grown silent, his opinions directed the course of law in the United States.

Field's appearance, when he sat on the Supreme Court bench, was reported by some to be reminiscent of that of a Hebrew prophet. He was, in fact, short and stout, with a rounded body and an oval face covered with a white flowing beard that curled around the back of his neck and ears; yet this profusion of hair was wholly missing from the top of his head.

It is not difficult to find the foundations for Field's arguments in his religious training as a child. It was the inexorable propositions of the Bible that solidified his moral convictions and were later to mold his notions of natural and inalienable rights. As a mature judge, he found easy the transition from the God of the Bible to the Creator of inalienable rights. These autonomous, God-given rights became the bedrock conviction of nineteenth

century American judicial conservatism. In his earliest opinions, Field was hard put to find precedent for his inalienable rights arguments. While the Declaration of Independence mentioned inalienable rights, the Constitution itself, which was the primary document for legal decisions, had nothing to say about such rights. With the drafting of the Fourteenth Amendment, however, Field finally had a federal document wholly adequate to his legal mission.

The critical passage in the Fourteenth Amendment read:

> No state shall make or enforce any law which shall abridge the privileges or immunities of citizens of the United States; nor shall any state deprive any person of life, liberty, or property without due process of law; nor deny to any person within its jurisdiction the equal protection of the laws.

In later years, the "due process" and "equal protection of the laws" clauses were to become the most quoted words in the amendment, but for Field the "shall [not] abridge the privileges or immunities" clause was exactly the terminology he

was looking for to secure his doctrine of inalienable rights.

In his earliest opinions, Field consistently applied the "privileges or immunities" clause to those cases in which individuals were seeking redress from the intrusion of government into their private lives. Eventually, however, as his influence and leadership in the Court grew, so also did his more collective definition of inalienable rights grow.

Soon he transposed and expanded his doctrine so as to accommodate the concept of citizen to include "citizens in the aggregate." Ostensibly, he argued that natural or inalienable constitutional rights applied to groups *qua* groups, and specifically to corporations. Business institutions and corporations had the same rights of protection from the invidious usurpation of privileges as did the individual citizen. This transposition from private to public rights was dramatically exhibited in a series of landmark opinions he wrote between 1865 and 1885. The earliest of these opinions was concerned with the abridgment of rights that individuals suffer at the hands of majoritarian legislation; but by 1875 he was applying the rationale he had employed in private rights cases to corporate business and industry.

For example, in 1865 there was a series of cases commonly described as "test-oath" cases that came before the Court. *Cummings v. Missouri* was one such case. In this case, the state of Missouri had required those seeking public office to declare under oath that they had not been disloyal to the United States or to the state of Missouri. This was divisive legislation since, in this border state, roughly half the population's sympathies lay with the South during the Civil War. It was legislation clearly intended to punish those who had backed the wrong side. As a consequence, anyone refusing to take this oath was to be prohibited access to various public stations and privileges. For example, they could not vote, hold public office, teach, preach, practice law, or administer public trusts.

Field was unequivocally opposed to test-oath restrictions. He argued that the requirement was punitive and in no manner tested the fitness or unfitness of citizens. Such a law, he continued, was *ex post facto*, intended to punish people without trial for past allegiances—punishment, in fact, for behavior that at the time committed was not a prosecutorial offense. Field joined a majority of the Court in striking down this legislation on the grounds that it was an abrogation of a citizen's inalienable right not to be subjected to sanctions for an act performed before the institution of a statute.

A second set of so-called due process cases was known as the "Chinese immigration" laws. Soon after the gold rush of 1849, enterprising shipping merchants began importing Chinese workers into California to do the menial labor brought on by the rapid industrial growth. In order to complete the transcontinental railroad, greater and greater numbers of Chinese were brought into California, and by 1869 government authorities were devising ways to limit the influx of these immigrants into the state. They enacted a series of laws that were unabashedly discriminatory. The Supreme Court had the task of determining the constitutionality of these laws. One law, for example, declared in the most general terms that "undesirable" Chinese were forbidden entry into the port of San Francisco, leaving the definition of undesirable up to city officials. Undesirables might mean prostitutes, or the poor, or unbonded workers. Another particularly pernicious law required that imprisoned Chinese men have their hair shorn, even though the cutting off of their plaited hair (*queue*) was for them an act of religious degradation. Again, there was a law requiring those Chinese wishing to establish a laundry business to obtain in writing the support of at least twelve taxpayers in the same city block. This was obviously a law intended to restrain the trade of the Chinese. In almost all these cases, Field argued that these laws accomplished nothing worthwhile and were merely acts of "hostility and spitefulness," clearly intended to deprive the Chinese of their natural and inalienable rights.

By 1870, Field was ready to transfer his inalienable rights doctrine from individuals to corporations and to expand his definition of persons to include "bodies of persons with a common interest." One of the earliest constitutional cases in which he argued in this fashion was *Hepburn v. Griswald*. *Hepburn v. Griswald* was a "legal-tender" or "greenback" case. Greenbacks referred to paper money, and many people had no confidence in paper money, particularly in its inflated state immediately after the Civil War. Despite private protest, however, the government insisted on paying its postwar debts with paper currency; creditors of the government regarded this practice as unstable because the government could print currency as it was needed, thus making it less and less valuable. For this reason, creditors began demanding payment *special basis*, that is, in gold and silver. In most of these legal-tender cases the Court majority supported the right of the government to pay its debts in greenbacks. Field, however, at times single-handedly, supported the creditors' right not to be required to accept these highly fluctuating, unstable paper notes. These creditors, he argued, had the right to payment special basis: They had the right to assess the worth of the payment, once it could be shown that the debtor had agreed to the value of the original contract. Legal-tender cases were clear evidence of Field's defense of his inalienable rights doctrine applied not only to aggrieved individuals but also to aggrieved groups of individuals, specifically, to corporations and industry.

Some of Field's most noteworthy "corporate citizen" arguments revolve around a series of cases pertaining to the country's railroads, and particularly to the railroad interests of some of Field's most influential California friends, men with controlling interests in Midwestern and far-Western railroads (Leland Stanford, Collis P. Huntington, Charles Crocker, and Mark Hopkins). In the 1840's and 1850's, in order to stimulate the growth of railroad building across the continent, Congress had provided railroad companies with enormous financial subsidies, tax exemptions, and outright land donations. As a result, these companies grew at an unbounded pace with powerfully unfair economic advantage over other commercial institutions. This advantage grew even larger during the next two decades because the railroads were able to escape the country's rising tax burden. The railroads also demonstrated an arrogance indicative of their power. They charged exorbitant and discriminatory rates, undercut their competitors, and refused to service the communities that they judged antirailroad. In due course, legislators, with popular support, began to introduce initiatives whose express purpose was to reduce the power and influence of these companies. In an effort to regain years of lost tax revenue, for example, the California Constitutional Convention of 1878 introduced a provision that would levy a tax against these companies' vast housing and equipment holdings. It was clear to everyone that this legislative maneuver was discriminatory since most of the inventory held by railroads was mortgaged inventory, and mortgage holdings were tax-exempt for private citizens in California.

The railroads refused to pay what they perceived as an inequitable tax and brought the disputed provision before the Supreme Court in 1882 (*San Mateo v. Southern Pacific*). This case gave Field an unambiguous opportunity to defend his "corporate citizen" argument once again. The Fourteenth Amendment, he declared, is intended to protect corporations in the same manner that individual citizens are protected. "Due process" requires that railroads, despite their vast wealth and holdings, are entitled to the same provisions of justice afforded the humblest citizen. Congress, he argued, fully intended that corporate interests receive "equal protection of the laws," and those lawyers who argued that this amendment was intended solely for black Americans were interpreting the amendment much too narrowly.

Field had considerable personal charm and was known as an enjoyable party guest. Yet he was also intensely disliked by many—with good reason, for he had some very unlikable character traits. He was a constant public moralizer, insatiably ambitious, at times vindictive, and not above making ethical compromises. Two of his brothers, David Dudley Field and Cyrus Field, became powerful, influential industrialists, and Stephen Field was accused, and not without some provocation, of tailoring his legal judgments to fit his brothers' financial interests. Off the bench, Stephen Field was intimate with Stanford, Huntington, J. P. Morgan, Jay Gould, and other wealthy industrialists, and on one occasion he even attended a private dinner party with them the night before he was to hear legal arguments in his court against their business holdings.

Stephen Field's tenure on the Supreme Court was longer than that of any justice who had gone before. He finally stepped down as a result of failing health at age eighty-two. While his devotion to individual rights was not always steadfast (he later ruled against private citizens such as women, laborers, and even the Chinese), his commitment to the interests of corporations and business never faltered. He died in Washington, D. C., on a cold, gray day in April, 1899, with the wealthy and powerful in government and business close at hand. There was also his wife, Sue Virginia, to whom he had been devoted for more than forty years.

Summary

Stephen Field's significant contribution to American society was unquestionably his brilliant legal opinions in defense of private rights. This defense was consistently sustained in support of private over public jurisdictions, opposition to loyalty oaths, opinions against the government's "legal tender" arguments, and his antislavery sympathies manifested in the "Chinese immigration" decisions. This fearless independence of mind set the direction of the Court for many years.

Bibliography

Black, Chauncey F. *Some Account of the Work of Stephen J. Field.* New York: Smith, 1881. This book is a systematic collection of Field's legal opinions. It includes his work as a member of the California supreme court as well as his decisions on the United States Supreme Court. There is a long introduction by John Norton Pomeroy, who was a law professor at the University of California during Field's lifetime. The introduction is of high scholarly quality but overly favorable to Field. One must, however, expect this from a volume put together by Field's political and legal friends during his lifetime.

Field, Stephen J. *California Alcalde.* Oakland, Calif.: Biobooks, 1950. This is Field's personal record of his reasons for coming to California, how he became the administrative judge of Marysville and eventually ran for the newly formed California legislature. There is also a description of his stormy struggle to obtain various political and judicial appointments, culminating in an appointment to the California supreme court.

————. *Personal Reminiscences of Early Days in California.* New York: Da Capo Press, 1968. Field produces, in lively fashion, personal sketches of his early days in California, his first few days in San Francisco, his success and good luck in Marysville, his legislative years, and his membership on the California supreme court. Also included is his version of what he describes as an attempt to assassinate him by former chief justice of the California supreme court, David S. Terry, in 1889.

McCloskey, Robert Green. *American Conservatism in the Age of Enterprise.* Cambridge, Mass.: Harvard University Press, 1951. This is provocative, albeit unsympathetic analysis of Field's legal influences in the post-Civil War era. McCloskey attempts to show a conceptual line of influence, from the Social Darwinism of William Graham Sumner through the legal conservatism of Field to the entrepreneurial, *laissez-faire* ideology of the capitalist Andrew Carnegie. McCloskey argues that Sumner and Field produced the moral and legal foundation for American capitalism.

Swisher, Carl Brent. *Stephen J. Field: Craftsman of Law*. Washington, D.C.: Brookings Institution, 1930. This is the best account of Field's career. It offers a rich record of his early years, his appointment as a Democrat from California to the United States Supreme Court by the Republican President Abraham Lincoln, and his political aspirations to be the Democratic nominee for president in 1880. Field had a dramatic and strenuous career, and Swisher's book covers it with literary skill.

Warren, Charles. *The Supreme Court in United States History*. 2 vols. Rev. ed. Boston: Little Brown, 1926. This two-volume work is one of the greatest treatments of American constitutional history available. The fact that it was published in 1926 is irrelevant. In volume 2, chapters 30-34, Warren offers a concise record of the constitutional period between 1863-1888, the period during which Field's legal decisions so indelibly influenced the bench. Readers may find Warren's style excessively juridical, but the work is an invaluable account of Field's and other justices' supporting and dissenting opinions.

Donald Burrill

MILLARD FILLMORE

Born: January 7, 1800; Summerhill, New York
Died: March 8, 1874; Buffalo, New York
Areas of Achievement: Government and politics
Contribution: In 1850, President Fillmore pushed for legislation designed to resolve a deadlock between Northern and Southern states over the admission of California to the Union and extension of slavery into new territories. Fillmore's support of the compromise legislation cost him the Whig presidential nomination in 1852; it also may have postponed the Civil War for a decade.

Early Life

Millard Fillmore was born January 7, 1800, in a log cabin on the farm in Locke township, New York, that his father, Nathaniel, and his uncle Calvin had purchased in 1799. Nathaniel and his wife, Phoebe Millard Fillmore, had come to the western frontier from Vermont, prompted by the prospect of more fertile land in the Military Tract set aside by New York State after the American Revolution in order to pay bonuses to veterans. In time, there were nine children in the Fillmore family; Millard was the second child and first son.

In 1815, Millard Fillmore was apprenticed to a wool carder and cloth-dresser at New Hope, near the farm in Niles, New York, that Nathaniel Fillmore had leased after title to the property in Locke proved invalid. He attended the district school in New Hope, teaching there and in Buffalo schools after 1818, and there he met his future wife Abigail Powers. Fillmore spent the years between this first acquaintance and their marriage, on February 5, 1826, establishing himself as a lawyer. He studied law from 1820 under Judge Walter Wood in Montville, New York, and in 1822 began work as a clerk in the Buffalo, New York, law firm of Asa Rice and Joseph Clary. Even though he had not completed the usual seven-year period of study, Fillmore was admitted to practice before the Court of Common Pleas and opened his own law practice in East Aurora, New York, in 1823. He moved to Buffalo in 1830 and in time went into law partnership with Nathan K. Hall and Solomon G. Haven.

Fillmore's appearance and public manner marked him for a career in politics. Just under six feet tall, he had broad shoulders, an erect carriage, and bright blue eyes. His hair was thick and yellow, but by middle age it had turned snowy white. His voice was deep and masculine. Never an orator like Daniel Webster or Edward Everett, both of whom served him as secretary of state, Fillmore struck juries and audiences as carefully prepared, sincere, and unaffected. An associate of Thurlow Weed in formation of the Anti-Masonic Party, he was elected three times to the New York State Assembly (1829-1831). Fillmore's chief accomplishment in the legislature was authorship of a law eliminating the imprisonment of debtors and providing for a bankruptcy law. Characteristic of his mature political style was the careful balancing of individual and business interests that this legislation achieved.

Life's Work

Since the chief impetus behind the formation of the Anti-Masonic Party was reelection of John Quincy Adams and defeat of Andrew Jackson in the election of 1828, the party lost strength when Jackson was elected, although it retained local influence chiefly in New York, Pennsylvania, and New England. Fillmore was elected to the House of Representatives as an Anti-Mason (1833-1835), but he followed Thurlow Weed into the newly formed Whig party in 1834. Subsequently, he was sent to Congress as a Whig (1837-1843) after William Henry Harrison was elected president in 1840. Fillmore served as chairman of the House Ways and Means Committee, and in that position he engineered congressional approval of protective tariff legislation in 1842.

Mentioned as a senatorial or vice presidential candidate prior to the 1844 election, Fillmore accepted Weed's advice—perhaps intended to keep the vice presidential prospects of William H. Seward alive—that he run for governor of New York. He was defeated by the popular Democrat Silas Wright but came back in 1847 to win election as New York's comptroller. Fillmore and Seward were both favorite son prospects for the Whig vice presidential nomination in 1848. The presidential candidates were Henry Clay, General Winfield Scott, and General Zachary Taylor. When the convention chose Taylor, and some delegates objected to Abbott Lawrence of Massachusetts as his running mate, the antislavery Clay delegates put their votes behind Fillmore and assured him the vice presidential slot. He was not assured of influence within the Taylor Administration itself when, having won the election, the new president took office in 1849. William H. Seward, Weed's ally and the newly elected senator for New York, worked to minimize Fillmore's influence on the new president. Unable to control party patronage in his home state, Fillmore was limited chiefly to his constitutional duty of presiding over the debates of the United States Senate.

California had petitioned for admission to the Union. There were thirty states at the time, fifteen slave and fifteen free, and California would tip the balance in the debate over slavery. The same issue complicated discussion of territorial governments for Utah and New Mexico, acquired at the end of the Mexican War, and an outstanding Texas-New Mexico border dispute. Abolitionists and Free-Soilers campaigned to limit the expansion of slavery into new states and territories, even trying to prohibit the slave trade in the District of Columbia, while Southern political leaders argued for the extension of slavery and for more vigorous enforcement of laws requiring the capture and return of fugitive slaves.

Senator Henry Clay, the support of whose delegates at the Whig convention of 1848 had assured Fillmore the vice presidential nomination, proposed an omnibus package of compromise legislation to deal with these issues. President Taylor, though a slaveholder from Louisiana, indicated that he would veto the bill if it extended slavery into the territories gained from Mexico. He also claimed he would use federal troops to resolve the Texas-New Mexico boundary dispute. Initially, Fillmore supported Taylor's position on Clay's omnibus bill, but, in 1850, he advised the president that he would vote to accept the package if required to cast a tiebreaking vote in the Senate. Fillmore never had to cast that vote. Taylor became ill after attending ceremonies at the Washington Monument on July 4, and died on July 9, 1850, making Millard Fillmore the thirteenth President of the United States.

After taking the oath of office and accepting the resignations of Taylor's entire cabinet, Fillmore moved to occupy a pro-Union political position. He appointed Daniel Webster as secretary of state and John Crittenden as attorney general, and he filled the rest of the cabinet with equally moderate men. Fillmore repeatedly insisted that slavery was morally repugnant to him, but he also said that he intended to be the president of the entire United States. He was prepared to make compromises in

the interest of national unity. When Senator Stephen A. Douglas, a Democrat, took over Senate management of Clay's stalled "omnibus bill," Fillmore indicated his willingness to sign the provisions of the omnibus as separate pieces of legislation. Between September 9, and September 20, 1850, he signed five measures designed to hammer out a compromise between Northern and Southern interests. California was admitted as a free state; Utah and New Mexico were given territorial status, with the citizens eventually to determine the status of slavery there; and Texas was compensated for the loss of territory in the adjustment of its border with New Mexico. Fillmore also signed a tougher law dealing with fugitive slaves and another prohibiting the slave trade, but not slavery itself, in the District of Columbia.

This reversal of Taylor's position achieved a political solution to a conflict threatening to erupt into military action. Fillmore had to send troops into South Carolina to deal with threats of secession and threatened to use them in the North to enforce the Fugitive Slave Act before there was general acceptance of these measures. While moderate men of all political parties supported Fillmore's position, both the Southern and New England factions of his own Whig party blamed him for those parts of the compromise package of which they disapproved. Therefore, Fillmore did not get the Whig presidential nomination in 1852 and retired to Buffalo in 1853, turning over the powers of the office to the Democrat Franklin Pierce.

In the face of the virtual dissolution of the Whigs as a national political party, Fillmore accepted the presidential nomination of the American, or Know-Nothing, Party in 1856. He attempted to distance himself from the proslavery, anti-Catholic, nativist principles of the party and to run his campaign on the Unionist basis he had advocated while president. The strategy did not work. In a three-way race against Democrat James Buchanan and Republican John C. Frémont, Fillmore came in a poor third.

With the election of Buchanan in 1856, Fillmore's national political career came to an end. Abigail Powers Fillmore died in Washington, District of Columbia, on March 30, 1853, only a few weeks after her husband had left the White House. On February 10, 1858, Fillmore married Caroline Carmichael McIntosh, a widow, in Albany, New York. He died in Buffalo, New York on March 8, 1874; Caroline McIntosh Fillmore died there on August 11, 1881.

Summary

During the Civil War and in the years following, the popular press depicted Millard Fillmore as a Southern sympathizer. He supported the candidacy of General George B. McClellen in 1864, and he also expressed approval of Andrew Johnson's efforts to achieve reconciliation with the South at the war's end. Properly speaking, Fillmore's positions were not so much pro-Southern as conservative, exactly as they had been when he accepted the compromise legislation of 1850 in the name of preserving the Union. His role in passage of that legislation was the central achievement of his term as president.

Fillmore's initiatives in foreign policy were modest, but they too reflected his unwillingness to adopt extreme positions. Fillmore resisted moves to annex Cuba and Nicaragua; he expressed disapproval of Austria's handling of the Hungarian uprising led by Lajos Kossuth, and he blocked French attempts to make the Hawaiian Islands a protectorate. Fillmore's administration moved to normalize relations with Mexico and opened negotiations to build a canal connecting the Atlantic and Pacific oceans through Nicaragua. He sent Commodore Matthew Perry on his mission to open the ports of Japan to merchant ships of the United States.

Like Taylor, Pierce, and Buchanan, Fillmore's reputation has been affected by the failure of nineteenth century American politics to avert the Civil War. The administration of each of these presidents struggled to control the forces that led to military conflict. The legislation passed in 1850 was the most significant attempt to defuse the sectional conflict, and Millard Fillmore's role in its passage is his chief claim to historical importance.

Bibliography

Barre, W. L. *The Life and Public Services of Millard Fillmore.* Buffalo, N.Y.: Wanzer, McKim, 1856. Barre's book provides an undocumented contemporary account of Fillmore's life and tenure as president.

Crane, Angus E. "Millard Fillmore and the Mormons." *Journal of the West* 34, no. 1 (January 1995). Despite his differences with the Mormons, Millard Fillmore appointed Brigham Young as governor of Utah, demonstrating his recognition of the needs of this oppressed community.

Fillmore, Millard. *Millard Fillmore Papers.* Edited by Frank H. Severance. 2 vols. Buffalo, N.Y.: Buffalo Historical Society, 1907. These volumes contain the only printed collection of Fillmore's public papers.

Forness, Norman O. "The Seward-Fillmore Feud and the U.S. Patent Office." *Historian* 54, no. 2 (Winter 1992). The Seward-Fillmore feud over the slavery issue is symbolic of the divisions that plagued the Whig party and threw the Patent Office into crisis.

Goodman, Mark. *High Hopes: The Rise and Decline of Buffalo, New York.* Albany: State University of New York Press, 1983. While Goodman's book deals with Fillmore only in passing, it contains a fascinating account of local reactions to his 1856 campaign as the presidential nominee of the American, or Know-Nothing, Party.

Holt, Michael F. *The Political Crisis of the 1850's.* New York: Wiley, 1978. Holt argues that disintegration of the Whig-Democrat two-party structure was a cause and not an effect of the political crisis of the 1850's.

Potter, David M. *The Impending Crisis, 1848-1861.* Edited by Don E. Fehrenbacher. New York: Harper, 1976. This excellent history of the period places the various conflicts Fillmore dealt with squarely within the ideological framework of Manifest Destiny.

Rayback, Robert J. *Millard Fillmore: Biography of a President*. Buffalo, N.Y.: Henry Stewart, 1959. The book explains the complex factors that drew Fillmore into the Anti-Masonic Whig and American parties and the effects of these associations on his political career.

Schelin, Robert C. "A Whig's Final Quest: Fillmore and the Know-Nothings." *Niagara Frontier* 26, no. 1 (1979): 1-11. Schelin focuses on Fillmore's 1856 campaign for president against the background of Whig decline and Know-Nothing appeals to prejudice.

Smith, Elbert B. *The Presidencies of Zachary Taylor and Millard Fillmore*. Lawrence: University Press of Kansas, 1988.

Snyder, Charles M., ed. *The Lady and the President: The Letters of Dorothea Dix and Millard Fillmore*. Lexington: University Press of Kentucky, 1965. The correspondence of Fillmore and Dix, the chief nineteenth century American advocate for reform in the treatment of the mentally ill; gives insight into Fillmore's personality as well as his actions as a public official and political candidate.

Robert C. Petersen

GUSTAVE FLAUBERT

Born: December 12, 1821; Rouen, France
Died: May 8, 1880; Croisset, France
Area of Achievement: Literature
Contribution: The most influential European novelist of the nineteenth century, Flaubert, who is most famous for his masterpiece *Madame Bovary*, is regarded as the leader of the realist school of French literature.

Early Life

Born in Rouen, Gustave Flaubert was the son of Achille Cléophas Flaubert, a noted surgeon and professor of medicine, and Caroline (Fleuriot) Flaubert, a woman from a distinguished provincial family. As a child Flaubert was high-strung, delicate, and precocious. He developed a love of literature early.

In his adolescence, Flaubert became attracted to the Romantic movement. Consequently he declared a hatred for bourgeois values and a passionate devotion to art; he maintained these attitudes throughout his life. They were strengthened through his youthful friendship with Alfred Le Poittevin, a young philosopher, whose pessimistic outlook affected Flaubert deeply. Another formative influence was his father's practice and teaching of medicine, which led him to value the discipline, intelligence, and clinical eye of the surgeon and helped shape his own approach to his literary materials.

In 1836, at the age of fifteen, Flaubert met Élisa Schlésinger, a married woman eleven years his senior, and succumbed to a devastating romantic passion for her which was destined to remain unrequited and to serve in his mind as an ideal which was never to be reached in his subsequent relationships with women.

Flaubert was sent to Paris in the autumn of 1842 to study law, a profession which did not attract him. He was committed to literature but reluctant to publish his work and susceptible to episodes of serious depression. In January, 1844, he gave up the study of the law upon suffering a nervous breakdown that was then diagnosed, probably erroneously, as epilepsy. Following a yearlong recuperation, he began to devote his time and energy to literary creation and to turn away from his earlier romantic subjectivism.

Flaubert's father died in January, 1846, leaving him an inheritance which enabled him to pursue his literary career full-time. His sister Caroline

died the following March, leaving an infant daughter. Flaubert and his mother adopted the child and began living at their estate at Croisset, near Rouen, where he spent most of the remainder of his life. In July, 1846, Flaubert met the poet Louise Colet in Paris, and began a tempestuous, intermittent affair with her that ended ten years later, in 1856.

In 1847, Flaubert went on a walking tour through Brittany with his writer friend Maxime Du Camp and wrote about the tour in *Par les champs et par les grèves* (with Du Camp; *Over Strand and Field*, 1904), which was published posthumously (1885). At this time, he was also engaged in writing the first version of *La Tentation de Saint Antoine* (1874; *The Temptation of Saint Anthony*, 1895), begun in 1846. Although he expended much energy and care on the manuscript, his friends found it florid and rhetorical and advised him to burn it. Disheartened, he set it aside and set out with Du Camp in November, 1849, on travels through Egypt, Palestine, Syria, Turkey, Greece, and Italy. Upon his return to Croisset in the summer of 1851, he was preparing to begin a very different kind of novel.

Life's Work

Flaubert spent the next five years of his life hard at work on *Madame Bovary* (1857; English translation, 1886). In the first two months of 1857, the French government brought Flaubert to trial, charging him with writing an immoral work, but he was acquitted and *Madame Bovary* won widespread success.

In the writing of *Madame Bovary*, Flaubert found himself, both as a man and as an artist. The novel relates dispassionately the story of a young provincial girl whose incurably romantic notions about life and passion lead her to adultery, financial ruin, and suicide. Her yearnings are of a kind with which Flaubert himself had been all too familiar, as is evidenced in his famous remark, "Madame Bovary, c'est moi" (Madame Bovary is myself). In projecting his own temperament upon this fictional character and subjecting it to relentlessly objective scrutiny, Flaubert was working to exorcise inner weaknesses that had bedeviled him all of his life.

Flaubert's painstaking care with the observation of concrete facts and psychological details in *Madame Bovary* and his constant concern to present his materials impersonally constituted a revolution

in the art of the novel and earned for him recognition as the leader of a new realist school of literature. This designation is misleading, however, and, in fact, somewhat ironic. Flaubert himself detested it, commenting, "People think I am in love with reality, though I hate it; for it is out of hatred of realism that I undertook the writing of this novel."

It is important to note the prevailing idealism in Flaubert's temperament and art. He saw art as an escape from life's ugliness; the paradox of *Madame Bovary* is that it takes a story that is essentially sordid and commonplace and transforms it into a vessel of beauty. The medium of this transformation is Flaubert's language: Through his ideas about and use of this medium, he has come to epitomize the dedicated literary artist. He refused to rush his art, and would spend hours in anguish searching for the right word or phrase to express his vision.

From *Madame Bovary* Flaubert turned to the subject of ancient Carthage; in 1862, he published *Salammbô* (English translation, 1886), a minutely researched novel whose fictitious narrative is set against the actual historical background of the 240-237 B.C. uprising of the mercenaries against Carthage. *Salammbô* was a popular success, but, to Flaubert's disappointment, it failed to win approval from the critics.

After writing three unsuccessful plays, Flaubert took up for extensive revision the manuscript of *L'Éducation sentimentale* (1869; *A Sentimental Education*, 1898). The novel, which Flaubert called a "moral history of the men of my generation," is set in Paris in the 1840's, and fictionalizes Flaubert's personal experiences within the panoramic and solidly realized historical context of France under the July Monarchy. Flaubert considered this novel his masterpiece, but the reviews were very unfavorable and the reading public unsympathetic.

Other troubles also plagued Flaubert in his last years. He was beset by financial problems after sacrificing his own fortune in 1875 to save his niece's husband from bankruptcy. He was, nevertheless, highly respected by other writers and generous in his advice to young authors, including Guy de Maupassant—who became his disciple—as well as Émile Zola and Alphonse Daudet. He formed friendships with the novelists Ivan Turgenev and George Sand.

Flaubert's last novel, which he left unfinished, was *Bouvard et Pécuchet* (1881; English transla-

tion, 1896). He interrupted his work on this long novel in 1875-1877 to write *Trois Contes* (1877; *Three Tales*, 1903), three stories that display the range and diversity of Flaubert's art and received immediate recognition. *Bouvard et Pécuchet* is a portrayal of human folly and frailty, specifically in its modern manifestation as an uncritical confusion of science and truth.

Flaubert died at home in Croisset after suffering a stroke on May 8, 1880. He was buried in Rouen.

Summary

Gustave Flaubert greatly influenced the development of the modern novel. In the historical context of French literature, his work forms a bridge between romanticism and realism, and his art arises out of the conflict within his mind and temperament between these two tendencies. *Madame Bovary* has been called the first modern novel and is widely hailed as one of the greatest works of fiction ever written.

Although he was a kindhearted man and a loyal friend, Flaubert's vision of life in his fiction was tragic and pessimistic. It epitomizes for many a quintessentially modern outlook. His ironic stance; his understanding of solitude, ennui, suffering, and loss; his dissatisfaction with materialistic and empty bourgeois values and the pursuit of ideal beauty; and his fascination with the destructive force of time and the preserving power of memory are attitudes that are found in the works of many writers of the late nineteenth and twentieth centuries. His understanding of human psychology was precise and deep. Flaubert's painstaking devotion to style and form raised the status of the novel to a form of high art and made him a model of the literary artist for subsequent generations of writers and readers.

Bibliography

Addison, Claire. *Where Flaubert Lies: Chronology, Mythology and History.* Cambridge and New York: Cambridge University Press, 1996. The author argues that the "errors" in the chronologies in Flaubert's works are not errors at all, but rather intentional, and evidence of the influence of personal mysticism in his work. Addison also discusses how Flaubert weaves his family life and historical events into his characters' lives, emphasizing the interplay between life and an artist's work.

Bart, Benjamin F. *Flaubert.* Syracuse, N.Y.: Syracuse University Press, 1967. This lengthy and comprehensive critical biography makes copious use of Flaubert's letters, private papers, and drafts for his novels to present a detailed account of his life, of his aesthetic, and his ideas about prose fiction.

Brombert, Victor. *The Novels of Flaubert: A Study of Themes and Techniques*. Princeton, N.J.: Princeton University Press, 1966. A thorough study of the texture, structure, patterns, and themes in Flaubert's fiction, stressing the nonrealistic and autobiographical aspects of his art. Brombert argues that Flaubert is essentially a tragic novelist.

Buck, Stratton. *Gustave Flaubert*. New York: Twayne, 1966. A comprehensive and authoritative introduction, for students and general readers, to Flaubert's novels and correspondence. Buck traces the evolution and composition of each of Flaubert's novels, describes their nature and contents, and assesses their artistic importance.

Constable, E. L. "Critical Departures: 'Salammbo' Orientalism." *MLN* 111, no. 4 (September, 1996). Although Flaubert's "Salammbo" does not fall within the nineteenth century criteria for Orientalist text, when it is read as a critique of the literary trends of the period, the techniques and exaggerations are more understandable.

Culler, Jonathan. *Flaubert: The Uses of Uncertainty*. London: Elek, and Ithaca, N.Y.: Cornell University Press, 1974. A sophisticated study, with a critical approach influenced by structuralism. Culler addresses Flaubert's early writings in sequence, demonstrating in them predominant themes, especially human stupidity and irony, in the later novels, which he then treats at length together. Culler concludes by discussing Flaubert's writings in terms of their value and sources of interest for modern readers.

Flaubert, Gustave. *The Letters of Gustave Flaubert*. Selected, edited, and translated by Francis Steegmuller. 2 vols. Cambridge, Mass.: Harvard University Press, 1980-1982. Flaubert's letters are crucial to an understanding of his personality, life, and works. This edition, which includes authoritative notes, appendices, indexes, and illustrations, presents Flaubert's letters from 1830 through 1880.

Nadeau, Maurice. *The Greatness of Flaubert*. Translated by Barbara Bray. London: Alcove Press, and New York: Library Press, 1972. A general introduction to Flaubert's life and career by the editor of the author's complete works. Nadeau stresses Flaubert's lifelong and never fully realized quest, as he became an artist, for a coherent sense of his own identity. Nadeau characterizes Flaubert's work as a body of "social, philosophical, and moral criticism."

Spencer, Philip H. *Flaubert: A Biography*. London: Faber, and New York: Grove Press, 1952. A sensible and highly readable narrative that provides a vivid introduction to Flaubert's life. Spencer views Flaubert in terms of an interrelated set of conflicts between self and society, idealism and disillusionment, beauty and ugliness, and escapism and commitment, and explores these conflicts as they manifest themselves in his life and motivate him as an artist.

Starkie, Enid. *Flaubert: The Making of the Master*. London: Weidenfeld and Nicolson, and New York: Atheneum, 1967. Starkie draws previously unused materials from manuscripts, notes, and letters in this comprehensive and well-documented critical biography of Flaubert through 1857, concluding with a study of *Madame Bovary*, its antecedents, its publication and censorship trial, and Flaubert's aesthetic doctrine. Includes illustrations, bibliography, notes, and index.

———. *Flaubert, the Master: A Critical and Biographical Study, 1856-1880*. London: Weidenfeld and Nicolson, andNew York: Atheneum, 1971. In this, the sequel volume to her *Flaubert: The Making of the Master* (1967), Starkie presents a sympathetic and thorough analysis of Flaubert's life and art after the publication of *Madame Bovary*. She argues that Flaubert's later works represent the fundamental aspects of his genius. Includes illustrations, bibliography, notes, and index.

Vargas Llosa, Mario. *The Perpetual Orgy: Flaubert and Madame Bovary*. Translated by Helen Lane. New York: Farrar, Straus, 1986; London: Faber, 1987. A thoroughgoing study of Flaubert's art in *Madame Bovary* by the celebrated Peruvian novelist. Vargas Llosa begins by charting vividly his particular experiences with this novel. He then addresses in depth the biographical, historical, and geographical origins of *Madame Bovary*, and analyzes important recurring themes and innovative techniques.

Eileen Tess Tyler

EDWIN FORREST

Born: March 9, 1806; Philadelphia, Pennsylvania
Died: December 12, 1872; Philadelphia, Pennsylvania
Area of Achievement: Theater
Contribution: Despite early obstacles, Forrest became the first great American actor, the first to gain international acclaim.

Early Life

Both by temperament and circumstance, Edwin Forrest typified the rough, self-reliant individualism of the early nineteenth century pioneer. Though he was born into a comfortable middle-class environment, his choice of an acting career compelled him to leave the security of his home and to learn his craft in some of the wildest places amid some of the wildest men in the country.

His father, a bank clerk, died when Forrest was thirteen but had already made plans for him to enter the safe, prestigious career of the ministry. The boy's remarkable memory, gift for mimicry, and already distinctive voice, however, were better suited to the playhouse than the pulpit. At ten, he was a member of an amateur theatrical troupe, playing female roles. Tradition suggests that he was shrieked and laughed at on the stage, but this early failure only cemented his determination to act.

By his early teens, Forrest had held a number of jobs, including one as an apprentice printer. In the meantime, he was studying, reading, running his own juvenile acting company, and performing his first recitations in a neighbor's old barn.

Forrest's early commitment to the stage was abetted by the fortuitousness of geography, for Philadelphia, his native city, was a vital cultural hub, a theatrical center whose playhouses were among the oldest, liveliest, and most important in the country. It seems likely that the young actor enjoyed easy access to the many plays both produced and published in Philadelphia, as well as ample opportunity to study the styles and techniques of many actors in a variety of roles.

What is certain is that one of his youthful recitations so impressed several well-to-do citizens that they supported him in his studies for the next few years. Incredibly, Forrest made his professional debut at the Walnut Street Theatre in Philadelphia on November 27, 1820, playing Young Norval, a popular juvenile lead in John Home's *Douglas* (1756).

The part was perfect for him, requiring an amount of physical action which allowed him to show his grace and agility, and declamatory speech which showed to advantage his already impressive timbral voice. His success was unqualified; Forrest was only fourteen.

Life's Work

Though he performed in several plays over the next few months, Forrest was convinced that he had to break the image of a juvenile actor and gain broader experience. To do this, he decided to travel west, across the Allegheny Mountains, where he would have more freedom to learn the profession, to experiment, to grow. Thus, in 1821, having been engaged by the theatrical company of Collins and Jones, Forrest embarked on a career as a strolling player for eight dollars a week.

By October, 1822, he was in Pittsburgh, once again playing Young Norval, developing the rugged physique and booming voice that were to become the crucial ingredients in his acting style. A few months later, he and his fellow strollers sailed a flatboat down the Ohio, stopping at Lexington, Kentucky, for several performances, and then traveling overland by covered wagon to Cincinnati, opening there in February, 1823.

The experience gained in these Western cities was decisive in shaping Forrest's career. He learned the importance of holding an audience under exacting and restrictive conditions—theaters with poor lighting, a paucity of props and scenery, and a change of bill nightly. Each member of the small troupe was expected to play a variety of parts: the dramatic lead in one play, the clown in the other, the dancer in the encore or afterpiece.

In 1823, the troupe went bankrupt and Forrest was out of a job. Broke, he stayed on in Cincinnati, living with a theatrical family who admired his work. He spent the next few months in poverty, reading the works of William Shakespeare.

Finally, he accepted an offer to play in New Orleans, a key city in the Southern and Western circuit. By the winter of 1824, just short of his eighteenth birthday, Forrest opened there in a Restoration tragedy, but his leisure time in that city was spent carousing with James Bowie (who gave the young man one of his famous knives), with a roustabout steamboat captain, and with "domesticated" Indian chiefs and other frontier types. Such figures comported with his robust, hot-tempered, and impulsive spirit, complementing his basically unrefined education.

Throughout the spring of 1825, Forrest played a variety of roles in New Orleans, including Iago in Shakespeare's *Othello, the Moor of Venice* (1604) and the title role in John Howard Payne's *Brutus: Or, the Fall of Tarquin* (1818), one of his most popular portrayals. His persistence was finally rewarded. The following year, he obtained an engagement in Albany, New York, playing with Edmund Kean, the famous British actor. Shortly thereafter, he arrived in New York City, still poor but rich in experience and in a deepened understanding of his craft.

The turning point of his career was this New York debut. Opening at the Bowery Theater in November, 1826, playing Othello, he brought to the role all the experience his life on the road and in the Western playhouses had given him. He was a brilliant success. At the age of twenty, Edwin Forrest had conquered the American stage. His New York triumph was the beginning of a reputation that was to last for the next thirty years. In less than a year, he became the most famous and highest paid American actor of the period, advancing from a salary of twenty-eight dollars a week in 1826 to two hundred dollars per night in 1827-1828 to five hundred dollars per night in the late 1830's.

At this point in his career, Forrest dedicated himself to the production of American plays. To encourage the development of a national drama and, shrewdly, to find just those plays in which he could use his tall, powerfully built body to advantage, Forrest sponsored a yearly competition to attract the best work. Among the many plays submitted, two in particular became important contributions to American dramatic literature of the nineteenth century. *The Gladiator* (1831), by Robert Montgomery Bird, and *Metamora: Or, the Last of the Wampanoags* (1829), by John A. Stone, were significant examples of the history play and the play on Indian themes, respectively. Both were well suited to Forrest's gifts, containing sonorous, orotund poetry which displayed his powerful voice and quick, physical action which demonstrated his athletic prowess. Both supplied him with his most famous and popular roles to the end of his career.

Twice during the 1830's he went to England, becoming the first great American actor appearing on the London stage. With nationalistic zeal, he

Actor Edwin Forrest in costume

opened his London engagement with *The Gladiator*, playing the role of Spartacus. In England, he met Catherine Sinclair, an actress, marrying her in 1837, at the peak of his fame. It was eventually an unhappy relationship. Often rash, jealous, and increasingly petulant, Forrest sued her for divorce in 1850. The trial was nasty and scandalous, becoming more notorious by Forrest's frequent exercises in public self-justification. Though the episode did little damage to his career as an actor, it did reveal the weaker side of his character as a man.

Even before this public squabbling about his domestic life, however, Forrest's role in one of the most infamous events in the history of the American theater gave further proof of a truculence that characterized much of his professional life. For years, Forrest was the chief American rival of William Macready, the noted British actor; the two were barely civil to each other. When Forrest was hissed on opening night in his second London tour of 1845, he bluntly attributed the heckling to a Macready faction, and when, in turn,

Macready played in America and Forrest bitterly denounced him in the press, the feud took on a nationalistic, patriotic hue. On the night of May 7, 1848, supporters of Forrest stormed the Astor Place Opera House in New York City, where Macready was playing. Before the police broke up the riot, some thirty people had been killed. This so-called Astor Place Riot was the beginning of Forrest's decline.

His decline was assured, as well, by his body. Riddled with gout and arthritis, he was by the 1850's in great pain; his imposing, muscular frame, which had been in large measure responsible for his success, now became an impediment to his active, robust acting style. His retirement was imminent.

Trying to recapture his past glories, Forrest accepted an invitation to visit California. He played Cardinal Richelieu, a favorite role, but the audience saw only a gouty, ill-tempered old actor, and a month later, the play closed.

California having been for him a failure, Forrest returned to Philadelphia, now taking any engagement, anywhere, that would keep him going. At this point in his career, just before the Civil War, he was living on his reputation, but it was steadily eroding as younger actors such as Edwin Booth began to eclipse him.

By the late 1860's, he was in virtual, enforced retirement, living alone in his gloomy Philadelphia mansion. Few engagements were left him. His last performance was as Richelieu in Boston, April, 1872. A few public readings closed his career, though he never stopped exercising, trying to keep his failing body in shape. On the morning of December 12, while pursuing rigorous exercise, Edwin Forrest sustained a massive stroke and was found dead later that day. In his will, he had made a provision for the establishment of a home for aged actors, but his estranged wife and an army of lawyers dismembered the will, and the provision died with Forrest.

Summary

Edwin Forrest's rise to fame and fortune was a phenomenon characteristic of the period in American history when the country was just beginning to recognize its nationalistic aspirations and to realize its political identity. The country was ready to take a native cultural hero to its heart, especially one who could compete favorably with the British and with the rest of Europe. For the American theater, Forrest came along at the right time. He had a physical dynamism that projected an image of strength, agility, and forthrightness, those traits which Americans most cherished. Critical opinion of his ability has varied, ranging from William Winter's famous remark about Forrest's being "a vast animal bewildered by a grain of genius" to more recent studies which appraise Forrest's contributions from the vantage point of history and his influence on generations of later actors.

Forrest was intensely patriotic, and his efforts to promote the American drama at a time when English drama and English actors held preference on the stage constituted a pioneering achievement from a man who had the strengths—and the moral weaknesses—of the pioneer spirit.

Bibliography

Barrett, Lawrence. *Edwin Forrest*. Boston: Osgood, 1881. A fine early biography. Written less than a decade after Forrest's death, the book is valuable as an accurate and brief account by a contemporary fellow actor. The style is often laden with Victorian circumlocutions and overripe delicacies, but the assessment of Forrest that emerges is largely sympathetic and well balanced.

Csida, Joseph, and June Bundy. *American Entertainment: A Unique History of Popular Show Business*. New York: Watson-Guptill, 1978. A largely pictorial panorama of American theatrical history, with reproductions of playbills, posters, and advertisements, as well as portraits of famous actors and actresses. The book contains a lively assessment of Forrest's character and acting ability by fellow actor John W. Blaisdell. Also treats the theatrical milieu of the Forrest era.

Hughes, Glenn Arthur. *A History of the American Theatre: 1700-1950*. New York: French, 1951. Discusses, sometimes too sketchily, the theatrical times, customs, and personalities during Forrest's rise. A good overview rather than a specific treatment.

Moses, Montrose J., and John Mason Brown, eds. *The American Theatre as Seen by Its Critics: 1752-1934*. New York: Norton, 1934. Contains William Winter's famous critique of what he called Forrest's "ranting" style. Winter dismissed Forrest as an actor who lacked intellectual depth but possessed a "puissant animal splendour." An important anti-Forrest assessment.

Wilson, C. B. *A History of American Acting*. Bloomington: Indiana University Press, 1966. Provides an incisive account of Forrest's acting style, emphasizing the influence of Edmund Kean; rich in detail and quite readable. Most of the more important critics are cited.

Edward Fiorelli

WILLIAM EDWARD FORSTER

Born: July 11, 1818; Bradpole, Dorsetshire

Died: April 5, 1886; London, England

Areas of Achievement: Education, politics, and government

Contribution: Forster was most famous for reform in education. He was an "advanced" Liberal, responsible for the Education Act of 1870, the Ballot Act of 1872, and advancement of other Radical causes. He was less revered for his policy of coercion in Ireland.

Early Life

William Edward Forster grew up in a prominent Quaker family but was expelled from the Society of Friends in 1850 when he married Jane Martha, the eldest daughter of Dr. Thomas Arnold of Rugby School. His parents, William and Anna Buxton Forster, were Quaker missionaries. His father died on an antislavery mission in Tennessee in the United States in 1854. All William's formal education was in Quaker schools of Bristol and Tottenham. He traveled in Ireland as a representative of the Friends' Relief Fund during the famine. After his marriage, he joined the Church of England, and he became a successful woolens manufacturer. A model employer, Forster was known as the "working-man's friend" and "Lond Forster." He was in sympathy with the goals of Chartism and was acquainted with Robert Owen, Thomas Cooper, the Reverend Frederick Denison Maurice, Thomas and Jane Carlyle, Richard Cobden, and John Bright. Between 1861 and 1886, Forster represented Bradford in the House of Commons. Forster remained childless, but he adopted four orphans of his wife's brother, one of whom, H. O. Arnold-Forster, became a cabinet minister.

Life's Work

Other nicknames given to Forster were "Education Forster," "Buckshot Forster," and the "English Robespierre"—not all were terms of endearment. These names reflect phases of his career: Early in his parliamentary career, on the occasion of the death of Lord Palmerston, he was made Undersecretary for the Colonies, launching his national political career and representing a continuing interest for the rest of his life. He became a privy councillor in 1868.

During William Ewart Gladstone's government of the late 1860's and early 1870's, Forster became the equivalent of minister of education. His title was Vice President of the Committee of Council on Education. He formulated and guided through Parliament the Education Act of 1870, which provided for the first national system of elementary education for England and Wales. There were later provisions for Ireland and Scotland, as well as universally obligatory and free education provisions. The Forster Education Act did lay the foundation for a comprehensive centralized system of education, and it introduced changes in the concept of the child and the child's place in society and the community.

Like most other legislation, the bill underwent a process of political compromise. Most controversy centered on the "religious difficulty," concerns of Roman Catholics, Anglicans, and Nonconformists, the latter being especially determined to prevent monopolistic domination by the Church of England, the established religion. The "conscience clause," the denominational system, and "the Cowper-Temple amendment" excluding the teaching of catechisms all entered into the conflicts. The resulting act pleased no one and especially displeased the Nonconformists and some powerful Radicals, notably Joseph Chamberlain. (Indeed, Gladstone later blamed his defeat of 1874 on the Education Act.) The act provided for a "dual system" of elementary education: side-by-side and separate voluntary schools and local authority schools. Local school boards, elected by secret ballot and under national oversight, were established. They were empowered to provide education for all.

Forster is credited for this unprecedented achievement, but it came at a price. His constituents at Bradford were among those disappointed with the act and censured him. Perhaps more significant, Forster, in effect, was passed over for party leadership. In 1875 Gladstone "retired" for the first time. (He would return to the prime ministership twice.) In the political manipulating within the Liberal Party, Joseph Chamberlain and the powerful Nonconformists made sure that the choice for his replacement was Lord Hartington and not Forster.

Forster's obituary in *The Times* included an observation by a contemporary: "The invective of both [extremes] of irreconcilables was mercilessly poured out upon Mr. Forster." A modern analysis of educational provisions in England during the nineteenth century by Philip Gardner laments the demise of many viable and effective working-class private schools, "the people's schools," displaced by the state system.

With "great tactical ability" during the parliamentary sessions of 1871 and 1872, Forster guided the famous secret Ballot Act of 1872 through both houses. Debates were especially lengthy. Moving on to other reforms, he participated in such causes as antislavery, arbitration, and working men's interests; he was pro-North during the American Civil War and anti-Russian in international affairs. It was Forster's persistent questioning, in 1876, which elicited Prime Minister Benjamin Disraeli's disastrous attempt to explain the Bulgarian atrocities, the murdering of Christians by Turkish authorities. Forster, a former Quaker who obviously was moving toward the political and religious center, was an enthusiastic "volunteer," a kind of national guard or militia leader.

Gladstone resumed his leadership of the Liberal Party and was returned to office as prime minister in 1880. Forster wanted the Colonial Office but received instead the Chief Secretaryship for Ireland, a most challenging position at a time when the Irish leader, Charles Stewart Parnell, and his Land League were establishing positions of enormous power within and outside Ireland. Forster determined to suppress crime and violence in Ireland. He formulated and had passed, again despite extraordinary parliamentary obstruction, the Irish Coercion Bill of 1881, which provided for suspension of habeas corpus and arrest of suspects without trial. The bill was ruthlessly enforced, gaining for Forster the sobriquets "Buckshot Forster" and the "English Robespierre." In fact, the bill was counterproductive: Violence increased. It was later determined that several assassination plots were aimed at Forster. In the meantime, Gladstone and the cabinet sought alternative policies. Parnell, in a Dublin prison himself, was secretly approached. Negotiation and promises of conciliation led to an agreement, the Kilmainham (prison) Treaty of May, 1882. Forster mistrusted Parnell, objected, and announced his resignation. Four days later, his successor, Lord Frederick Cavendish, and another Irish official were brutally murdered in Phoenix Park, Dublin.

Forster continued to maintain special interest in colonial matters. He went to great lengths, including personal tours of the area, to become an expert on the Eastern Question (concerning British affairs in Egypt). He increasingly opposed Gladstone, voting for censure of the government in the sensational case of Charles "Chinese" Gordon and the Khartoum disaster (1885). Forster opposed home rule for Ireland. Shortly before his death, he became the first head of the Imperial Federation League, an imperialist pressure group.

While still a Quaker, Forster wrote his first work, an apology for the leader of the Society of Friends, William Penn, in response to a critique by the historian Thomas Babington Macaulay. Subsequently, he contributed to the *Leader, Westminster Review*, and *Edinburgh Review* on issues associated with his causes such as right to work, distress in colonial areas, and opposition to slavery. In 1875 he was elected Lord Rector of the University of Aberdeen. There is a revealing exchange between Gladstone and Forster's biographer, Thomas Wemyss Reid, editor of the *Leeds Mercury*, in the periodical *Nineteenth Century*, in 1888. Gladstone summarized the career and contributions of Forster, pointing out that Forster had often stood up for his convictions even when it brought conflict with close friends: "By political creed a Radical, he dissented from the first article of Radicalism . . . , the maintenance of the Church Establishment in England."

Forster's funeral was held in Westminster Abbey, and he was buried at Burley-in-Wharfedale. His portrait, by H. T. Wells, hangs in the National Portrait Gallery in London, and a statue stands on the banks of the Thames near the location of the London School Board building. His widow died in 1890.

Summary

The nicknames given to this Quaker turned Anglican statesman illustrate trends of his career and his political development: "Lond" was an affectionate appellation for a sensitive employer, "Education" signifies his most important contribution, and "Buckshot" indicates his unfortunate and coercive policies as Irish minister toward the end of his life.

William Edward Forster was a brilliant and successful politician and parliamentarian. He was particularly persuasive in debate and particularly effective in manipulating votes. Repeatedly he sacrificed personal political advancement and special interests in colonial-imperial matters to lead controversial and essential reforms. He was the quintessential Victorian reformer.

Bibliography

Armytage, W. H. "The 1870 Education Act." *British Journal of Educational Studies* 18 (June 1970): 121-133. A detailed account of the formative education legislation, describing the areas of dispute and compromise, such as election of boards, the conscience clause, and permissive compulsion. There is a chronology of the legislative process; more than two hundred members spoke in the debates.

Gardner, Philip. *The Lost Elementary Schools of Victorian England*. London and Dover, N.H.: Croom Helm, 1984. A modern revisionist critique of Forster's Education Act. There existed in nineteenth century England a viable system of traditional, working-class, private schools, an "alternative educational culture." Some schools were linked to Chartism and Owenism. They were practical and purposeful, and they had contributed to a relatively high literacy rate. Gardner laments their demise, as they were bureaucratically replaced after 1870.

Middleton, Nigel. "The Education Act of 1870 as the Start of the Modern Concept of the Child." *British Journal of Educational Studies* 18 (June 1970): 166-179. Forster's act brought neither free nor compulsory education, but it was quite significant because it introduced fundamental changes: a new type of society which radically altered the place and the concept of the child.

Murphy, James. *Church, State, and Schools in Britain, 1800-1970*. London: Routledge, 1971. A chapter is devoted to the impact of the Education Act of 1870 on the church-state and interdenominational controversies in Great Britain during the past two centuries. Good at sorting out the complexities associated with the denominations, radicals, Nonconformists, Anglicans, pressure groups, and other activists.

Reid, Thomas Wemyss. *Life of the Right Honourable William Edward Forster*. 2 vols. London: Chapman and Hall, 1888; New York: Kelley, 1970. The standard biography by a close friend, editor of the *Leeds Mercury* and a political supporter—Forster's apologist. Reprinted, twice, in 1970.

Roper, Henry. "W. E. Forster's Memorandum of 21 October 1869: A Re-examination." *British Journal of Educational Studies* 21 (February 1973): 64-75. An intriguing and speculative thesis based on new research. Roper claims there were two drafts by Forster outlining the education bill. Gladstone insisted on alterations. The omitted sections related to the two most controversial issues: religion and attendance. Contends that the original version would have forestalled basic objections by critics.

Eugene L. Rasor

CHARLOTTE FORTEN

Born: August 17, 1837; Philadelphia, Pennsylvania

Died: July 22, 1914; Washington, D.C.

Areas of Achievement: Education, literature, and civil rights

Contribution: Charlotte Forten, an African American educator, author, and abolitionist, spent her life furthering the cause of fellow African Americans.

Early Life

Charlotte Lottie Forten was born on August 17, 1837, in Philadelphia, Pennsylvania. Representing the fourth generation of Fortens born free in the United States, she was the only child of Robert Bridges Forten, and his first wife, Mary Virginia Woods Forten. Acknowledged as the most prominent and wealthy free black family in America, the Fortens avidly pursued reform, equality, and the abolition of slavery. Mary Virginia Woods Forten died when Charlotte was three. After her mother's death, Charlotte grew up under the tutelage of her aunts and other relatives.

The ideals and influences of Charlotte's family shaped the rest of her life. Her grandfather, James Forten, Sr., petitioned the United States Congress in 1800 to end the African American slave trade, establish guidelines to abolish slavery, and provide legislation that would weaken the Fugitive Slave Act of 1793. Congress denied the petition with a vote of eighty-five to one. Forten and his friends were not easily discouraged as they continued their pursuit for equality. Forten actively criticized legislation that would ban free blacks from Pennsylvania and the Colonizationists' efforts to move free blacks to Africa. James Forten, Sr., believed that blacks in the United States were entitled to the country's resources and equal protection under the law. Similarly, Charlotte Forten's father, her aunts, and her uncles played vital roles in the abolitionist movement. The family also supported women's rights.

Surrounded by the most prominent intellectuals of the era, Charlotte knew the importance of scholarly achievement. Robert Forten arranged for his daughter to have private tutors until she could have an excellent public education in Salem, Massachusetts. At the age of sixteen in 1854, she moved to Salem, where she prepared herself for a teaching career. Determined to please her father, Charlotte applied herself to her studies. Residing with prominent black abolitionist Charles Lenox Remond and his wife in Salem, Charlotte acquainted herself with William Lloyd Garrison, Wendell Phillips, John Whittier, Abigail and Stephen Foster, and many other notable figures of the time. She thrived in her intellectual duties at the Higginson Grammar School. In 1855, she entered Salem Normal School and was graduated in 1856. Gaining a reputation as a local poet, she often submitted poems for publication. One of her poems, written in praise of William Lloyd Garrison, was published in the *Liberator* magazine in March, 1855.

Life's Work

After graduation, Charlotte Forten began teaching and continued studying in her free time. She practiced French, German, and Latin and studied European and Classical history. She also enjoyed literature, including the works of her contemporaries.

The pursuit of knowledge became Forten's primary interest. As a deeply religious person, she believed that God intended her to uplift and educate the people of her race. Her self-sacrificing nature made it difficult for Forten to appreciate herself and the contributions she made. She was aware of the racial hostility around her and sometimes allowed it to influence her self-image, in spite of compliments on her appearance, her manners, and her intelligence. Furthermore, her father's move to Canada in 1853 left her somewhat estranged from her immediate family.

During her stay in Salem, Forten began the first of her series of five journals in which she discussed all aspects of her life including family, politics, education, and important leaders of the time. In 1856, she accepted a teaching position at Epes Grammar School in Salem. Soon, however, she had to return to Philadelphia after suffering from a respiratory illness and severe headaches. By July of 1857, she was back at Epes, only to resign in March, 1858, because of her recurrent health problems.

Again Charlotte returned home where she rested and taught privately. The extra time allowed her to write poetry and essays for publication. In May of 1858, her poem entitled "Flowers" was published in *Christian Recorder* magazine. In June of that year, her essay "Glimpses of New England" appeared in the *National Anti-Slavery Standard*. "The

Two Voices" and "The Wind Among the Poplars" were printed in 1859. In January of 1860, "The Slave Girl's Prayer" was published in the *National Anti-Slavery Standard*.

Forten regained her health sufficiently to return to Salem in September of 1859, to accept a teaching post at the Higginson Grammar School. During the next spring, however, she again fell ill. While battling to regain her health, she taught briefly in a school for black children. She visited John Whittier upon her return to Salem in the summer of 1862. During this visit Whittier proposed that Forten could further the cause of her people if she went to teach the contraband slaves in the South.

On October 22, 1862, Charlotte Forten sailed to Port Royal, South Carolina. Stationed on St. Helena Island, she secured a position as a teacher among the slaves. With a fond regard for her students, she sought to prepare them for life as freed men and women. Her primary task included teaching the fundamentals of a formal education to contraband children of all ages. Forten taught reading, writing, spelling, history, and math. She emphasized the importance of proper moral and social behavior to the older blacks. She leaned toward assimilation, believing that blacks would find it difficult to interact with society if they remained culturally different.

Charlotte also met with prominent whites during her stay on St. Helena. As the first black teacher among the slaves, she had to face the reactions of white teachers and Union soldiers. Usually she was politely received, and people associated with her even more when abolitionist friends and acquaintances arrived. Among some of her close friends were Colonel Thomas Wentworth Higginson, who commanded the First South Carolina Volunteers, and Colonel Robert Gould Shaw, commander of the all-black Fifty-fourth Massachusetts regiment. Forten also had a very close friendship with Dr. Seth Rogers, a white surgeon in Higginson's First South Carolina Volunteers.

Charlotte's friendships and the teaching she accomplished made her stay on St. Helena a rewarding one; eventually, however, her health failed her once again. Her declining health and news of her father's death from typhoid fever on April 25, 1864, convinced Forten to move back to the North permanently. Although she still suffered from poor health, she accepted a position as secretary of the Teachers Committee of the New England Branch of the Freedmen's Union Commission in October of 1865. She continued to further her own education by studying and translating French literature. Her translation of *Madame Thérèse: Or, The Volunteers of '92*, a novel by Emile Erckmann and Alexandre Chatrain, was published by Scribner in 1869. Charlotte's role as secretary of the Teachers Committee required her to act as a liaison between teachers in the South who taught former slaves, and the people in the North who sent financial and material support. In October of 1871, she resigned from that position to teach at the Shaw Memorial School in Charleston, South Carolina. Forten then moved to Washington, D.C., where she taught in a black preparatory high school from 1872 to 1873. She left that position and accepted a job in the Fourth Auditor's Office of the United States Treasury Department as a first-class clerk. Although poor health continued to frustrate her, she continued to work in Washington, D.C.

Charlotte Forten married Francis Grimké on December 19, 1878. The Princeton-trained minister was twelve years her junior; he was described as intelligent, noble, and morally upright. The couple had one daughter who died in infancy. Charlotte and Francis Grimké worked hard to dispel discrimination in society. They attacked racial oppression in numerous essays and sermons. In 1885, they moved to Florida, where Francis Grimké accepted the pastorate at Laura Street Presbyterian Church. After four years they returned to Washington, D.C., and continued missionary work.

Although Charlotte Forten Grimké combined her efforts with those of her husband, she did not abandon her interest in writing poetry and essays. Several poems from that period include "A June Song" (1885), "Charlotte Corday" (1885), "At Newport" (1888); some essays that survive are "On Mr. Savage's Sermon: 'The Problem of the Hour'" (1885), and "One Phase of the Race Question" (1885). Evidently essays and poetry remained an important facet of her life. Throughout her life she continued writing her journals, of which there are five, titled by number, date, and the locations of her residence.

She spent her last years surrounded by family and friends. Her home was enlivened socially and intellectually with well-known political activists. She also enjoyed a close relationship with her niece Angelina Grimké, who lived in Washington, D.C., with the Grimkés. In spite of her illnesses, Charlotte lived a full, happy life. She died on July 22, 1914, in her home at the age of seventy-six.

Summary

Charlotte Forten did not complete one monumental task for which she is well known. Instead, she worked diligently to help others. In spite of frequent illnesses and insecurities, she willingly dedicated her time and energies to further the cause of her oppressed race. As a woman, Charlotte Forten far exceeded the intellectual expectations of the time. She tirelessly pursued knowledge and shared it with others. As a poet and writer, she voiced her opinions and interests to the American public. It was her philanthropic deeds, however, that she performed in the name of her race. As a free black woman, she tirelessly sought liberation, equality, and education for her people.

In an era when the white society oppressed the black, Charlotte stood out as a person who tried to correct injustices. Her quiet demeanor belied the active mind and spirit that were revealed by her pen. Her unassuming personality and eagerness to please led her in a life of service to others. The quiet dignity of Charlotte Forten and her lifelong efforts made her one of America's notable women and an inspiration to all Americans.

Bibliography

Barker-Benfield, G. J., and Catherine Clinton. *Portraits of American Women: From Settlement to the Present*. New York: St. Martin's Press, 1991; London: Oxford University Press, 1998. This publication is a combined volume presenting biographies of American women, arranged according to historical eras. Each biography discusses the impact each woman made on her contemporaries. The book is amply illustrated.

Braxton, Joanne M. "Charlotte Forten Grimké and the Search for a Public Voice." In *The Private Self: Theory and Practice of Women's Autobiographical Writings*. Edited by Shari Benstock. London: Routledge, and Chapel Hill: University of North Carolina Press, 1988. An analysis of Forten's complete journals, based on archival research and a personal appreciation of the journals. The author maintains that, as a young woman, Forten used her journal as a means to try out different poetic voices.

"Charlotte Forten." *Blacfax* 8, no. 35 (Winter 1998). Short profile of Forten. Provides historical information on her parents, her work, and her death in 1914.

Forten, Charlotte L. *The Journals of Charlotte Forten Grimké*. Edited by Brenda Stevenson. New York: Oxford University Press, 1988. This volume comprises the five journals written by Charlotte Forten. They provide insight into the politics and people of the abolitionist era. The editor provides an introduction and notes for each journal, as well as a chronology and brief biographies of people mentioned.

McPherson, James M. *The Struggle for Equality: Abolitionists and the Negro in the Civil War and Reconstruction*. Princeton, N.J.: Princeton University Press, 1964. A complete and thorough analysis of the abolitionists, including Forten, and the roles they played during and after the Civil War. Includes a bibliographic essay describing the manuscripts, correspondence, publications, and archives used.

Quarles, Benjamin. *Black Abolitionists*. New York: Oxford University Press, 1969; London: Oxford University Press, 1970. Providing the reader with a thorough background of the African American abolitionists, the author covers the early efforts of black preachers and writers to the antislavery underground; the book also describes the organizational efforts of later abolitionists. This volume includes detailed bibliographic notes separated by chapter.

Wildemuth, Susan. "A Teacher Who Made a Difference." *Cobblestone* 19, no. 2 (February 1998). Profile of Forten, and her background and participation in the Port Royal Experiment to educate former slaves.

Dover C. Watkins
Elisabeth A. Cawthon

STEPHEN COLLINS FOSTER

Born: July 4, 1826; Lawrenceville, Pennsylvania
Died: January 13, 1864; New York, New York
Area of Achievement: Music
Contribution: Working within the most popular, sometimes vulgar, style of the day, Foster wrote works of unaffected simplicity and melodic beauty that became among the finest representatives of the American folk song.

Early Life

In one of history's notable coincidences, Stephen Collins Foster, "America's troubadour," was born precisely fifty years after the signing of the Declaration of Independence, on the same day also as the deaths of Thomas Jefferson and John Adams. The ninth child of William and Eliza Collins, "Stephy," as he was sometimes called, was the baby of the family, nurtured in a warm and loving environment. His father, one of the pioneers in the establishment of Pittsburgh as a thriving "Western" city, was a middle-class businessman, would-be entrepreneur, and minor public official whose fortunes were always tottering between solvency and indigence, a condition that would carry over into Stephen's own later life.

Tutored first by his older sisters, he was educated at a number of private academies in and around Pittsburgh and in Towanda in northern Pennsylvania. Gentle, sensitive, and often pensive, he was never the scholar, and he chafed under the discipline of academic life. His only real interest was in music, a subject that he studied on his own and for which he early showed a rare ability. Even his father, who wished a business career for his youngest son, could not help but observe the boy's "strange talent." Family anecdotes describe the seven-year-old boy as picking up a flute for the first time and in a few minutes playing "Hail Columbia" and of his teaching himself to play the piano. Sent to Jefferson College in Canonsburg, Pennsylvania, Foster dropped out after a week, homesick, and returned to his family in the summer of 1841.

For the next few years, Foster lived at home, visiting relatives with his mother and occasionally attending theatrical events and concerts with his favorite brother, Morrison, his first official biographer. During this tranquil period, Foster became increasingly absorbed in his music. In December, 1844, he published his first composition,

the music to a poem, "Open Thy Lattice, Love." Derivative and harmonically awkward, the song was a creditable piece of work for a boy of sixteen and already bore the naturalness, the spontaneity that was to be its composer's trademark.

Life's Work

Home life was thus somehow a catalyst to Foster's inspiration. Even after the publication of his first song, Foster continued living with his family despite efforts on their part to find him some employment. "Stephy" was always the dreamer, though the only photograph of him, taken years later when he had become famous, shows a strong face, with prominent brow, large, dark eyes, and full, almost pouting lips.

In 1845, Foster joined the Knights of S.T., a club of young men who met twice weekly at the Foster home. The members wrote verses and sang popular songs of the day. Membership in this club was probably crucial in determining Foster's career, for it provided the young composer with both a ready audience for his work and a further source of inspiration. Through the club, he came into contact with examples of the minstrel song, or, as it was then called, the "Ethiopian" melody.

Additionally, the minstrel show was just coming into its prime as a popular American form of entertainment. Pittsburgh, in fact, had, in the fall of 1830, been the scene of one of the earliest minstrel shows when a twenty-two-year-old Thomas "Daddy" Rice, the father of American minstrelsy, first put on blackface and cavorted on the stage as Jim Crow, a good-humored, illiterate black man. Whether Foster had seen this first performance is uncertain, but it is clear that by the 1840's he had become friends with Daddy Rice and had submitted to him a number of pieces in the minstrel style, which Rice politely refused.

Foster kept composing, however, and the Knights kept singing his songs "in almost every parlor in Pittsburgh," so that by 1847 Foster's songs were being circulated largely from singer to singer, a fact which explains their success as authentic creations of a basically oral folk culture rather than as products of a formal musical tradition. Emerging from this oral culture was the first of his great songs. "Oh! Susanna," a nonsense song in the American minstrel manner, was first sung in

Andrews' Eagle Ice Cream Saloon in Pittsburgh in September, 1847, though it was not published until the following year.

"Oh! Susanna" made Foster famous, not only because minstrel companies all over the country appropriated it and publishers and other songwriters altered and rearranged it, but also because thousands of pioneers carried the song along with their hopes to the gold fields of California.

Curiously, Foster was at first somewhat blasé about payment for his early work. In a letter dated 1849, for example, he mentions that he gave manuscript copies of "Oh! Susanna" to "several persons" before submitting a copy to W. C. Peters for publication. Scores of pirated editions of this and later songs point out the laxity in those days with regard to copyrights, but it is clear also that Foster at first regarded songwriting as a questionable occupation for a gentleman. That he was at least partially embarrassed by or indifferent to fame as a songwriter is evident in the fact that he gave permission to the famous minstrel impresario Edwin P. Christy to perform and publish his "Old Folks at Home"—popularly known as "Swanee River"—as Christy's own. In return, Foster was paid fifteen dollars and was encouraged to submit further work.

His association with Christy, in fact, was crucial to Foster's career. The Christy Minstrels were among the most popular theatrical troupes before the Civil War, and Foster's connection with Christy assured him of both a steady income and a ready market. Christy's Minstrels performed all over the country, transmitting Foster's songs orally months before they were ever published.

The early 1850's were Foster's most prolific period and the happiest of his life. In July, 1850, he had married Jane McDowell, daughter of an eminent Pittsburgh physician who had treated Charles Dickens on his stopover in Pittsburgh during his famous American tour in the 1840's.

Always close to his family, Foster took his young wife to live with his parents, and once again the surroundings of familial love and contentment fueled his creative powers. Often locking himself in his study for hours—a labor which belied the spontaneity of the finished compositions—he produced dozens of his best songs during the next two or three years, securing Firth and Pond of New York as his principal publisher. During this period, Foster composed "Camptown Races" (1850), "Ring de Banjo" (1851), "Old Folks at Home" (1851), "Massa's in de Cold, Cold Ground" (1852), "My Old Kentucky

Home" (1853), "Jeanie with the Light Brown Hair" (1854)—inspired by his wife—and "Come Where My Love Lies Dreaming" (1855), all masterpieces which have never lost popular appeal and which have secured for their composer a preeminent place in nineteenth century American music.

The year 1855 marked a turning point in Foster's life and career. At the peak of his fame and at the height of his creative powers, Foster could now command unusual prerogatives from his publishers, one of which was to prove disastrous. He was temperamentally unfit for the plodding routine of the businessman, but songwriting was a joy, and he soon convinced himself that he could live comfortably on his *potential* as a composer. In effect, Foster pawned his future for a secure present. He developed the practice of drawing advances from his publishers, selling outright all future royalties from his published songs. As soon as a song was printed, he would calculate its future value and sell its royalties.

Living thus beyond his means, and having to write songs to live, Foster composed over the next few years scores of works, most of which were markedly inferior to his early material. "Come

Where My Love Lies Dreaming" was written in 1855, but not until 1860, with "Old Black Joe," did he write a song with the powerful simplicity of his best work. In between were temperance songs and sentimental ballads, the spontaneous gaiety of his minstrel style all but gone. Not unexpectedly, Foster was experiencing domestic problems as well. His relationship with Jane became strained, and on several occasions the couple separated because of Foster's inability to support her.

By the advent of the Civil War in 1860, Foster had moved to New York City to be nearer his publishers. From this time on, he became a sort of song factory, churning out to order virtual potboilers for a public eager to hear anything new from him. Deeper in debt, he produced work that was facile, commercial, and dull: saccharine hymns, topical comic pieces, patriotic war songs, and the usual sentimental ballads of mother, home, and sloe-eyed love. Little of this work is of any importance in the canon of Foster's songs. It represents, rather, a pitiful decline in the composer's art and fortunes.

Eventually, Foster received less and less for his work—work which he must have sensed was inferior to his earlier compositions. He began drinking heavily, getting steadily weaker and falling into states of depression. Poor and in ill health, Foster was taken to Bellevue Hospital in January, 1864, where he died three days later. Found in his pockets were a few scraps of paper and a few coins totaling thirty-eight cents. In March of that year, a last great song was published from among his final papers. Called "Beautiful Dreamer," it was a final return to the gentle lyricism and honesty of his greatest work.

Summary

It is ironic that the man whose music is richly evocative of the Old South never traveled below the Mason-Dixon line. Such irony suggests the most telling characteristic of Foster as a composer—his instinctive, unschooled, spontaneous lyricism. Foster was a self-taught composer whose lack of formal, technical knowledge of the rules of composition hampered the success of his instrumental pieces, his dozen or so attempts to write "serious" music. For simple, unaffected melody, however—for "parlor" songs sung by respectable, middle-class folks—Foster's songs are unsurpassed among the works of nineteenth century composers.

Though at first reluctant, Foster steadfastly held to his commitment to become the best of the "Ethi-opian" melodists. He produced songs that in effect reformed the American minstrel style. His best work bore none of the vulgarity common to the minstrel show; there was no coarseness, no crudity even in his nonsense and comic songs. His work reveals the honest, homespun simplicity that was the strength of the oral folk tradition.

Bibliography

Foster, Morrison. *My Brother Stephen.* Indianapolis, Ind.: Hollenbeck Press, 1932. A brief account of the composer's life, particularly his relationship with his family. Not totally objective, it ignores much of the less flattering aspects of Foster's life and character but does provide, as the earliest biography, some important information about his music.

Howard, John Tasker. *Stephen Foster: America's Troubadour.* New York: Crowell, 1934. The definitive biography, well researched and unbiased. Drawing almost too minutely on private collections of Foster material, including family papers, Howard recounts Foster's schooling, travel, relationships, and financial habits. A thorough appendix includes a complete list of Foster's compositions.

Milligan, Harold Vincent. *Stephen Collins Foster: A Biography of America's Folk-Song Composer.* New York: Schirmir, 1920. The first objective biography. Pays particular attention to Foster's early life and to what its author perceives as a major drawback to Foster's cultivation of serious musical taste. Also treats Foster's final days and his undramatic death.

" 'Oh! Susanna': Oral Transmission and Tune Transformation." *Journal of the American Musicological Society* 47, no. 1 (Spring 1994). A history of Foster's standard, "Oh! Susanna," changes in it when performed by minstrels, and its publications.

Walters, Raymond. *Stephen Foster, Youth's Golden Gleam: A Sketch of His Life and Background in Cincinnati, 1846-1850.* Princeton, N.J., and London: Princeton University Press, 1936. Treats a period of Foster's life while the composer was a bookkeeper for his brother, Dunning. Suggests that the Cincinnati waterfront, with its wharves and its black music, was a profound influence on Foster's creative achievements. Both Howard and Milligan also discuss this period, though both regard it as somewhat "sketchy."

Wittke, Carl. *Tambo and Bones*. Durham, N.C.: Duke University Press, 1930. An accurate and entertaining history of the American minstrel show, the book provides a clear perspective through which to appreciate Foster's success and his contribution to American music.

Edward Fiorelli

CHARLES FOURIER

Born: April 7, 1772; Besançon, France
Died: October 10, 1837; Paris, France
Areas of Achievement: Social reform and social science
Contribution: Fourier was one of the founding fathers of nineteenth century Utopian socialism. Although the few experiments in building a model community based upon his theories proved short-lived, Fourier's writings have continued to attract interest.

Early Life

François-Marie-Charles Fourrier (he stopped using the second *r* apparently when he was eighteen) was born on April 7, 1772, at Besançon, France, a town near the Swiss border, the fifth child and only son of a prosperous cloth merchant. In 1781, his father died, leaving him a substantial inheritance. He attended the local Collège de Besançon, where he received a solid if uninspiring classical education. His ambition appears to have been to study military engineering at the École de Génie Militaire, but he lacked the noble status requisite for admission. He was apprenticed to a cloth merchant around 1790, first at Rouen, then at Lyons. He was ill-suited for, and unhappy in, the world of business.

Fourier was involved in the savagely suppressed 1793 counterrevolutionary uprising in Lyons against the Convention (central government). As a result, he was imprisoned and narrowly escaped execution. In 1794, he was called for military service; he was discharged two years later. Although the details remain unclear, he lost the bulk of his inheritance. He thereafter worked as a traveling salesman and then as an unlicensed broker. He also began writing short articles and poems, which appeared in the Lyons newspapers starting in 1801. He set forth an outline of his developing ideas in two papers written in late 1803, "Harmonie universelle" and "Lettre au Grand-Juge." In 1808, he published—anonymously and with a false place of publication to protect himself against prosecution by the authorities—his first major work, *Théorie des quatre mouvements and des destinées générales* (*The Social Destiny of Man: Or, Theory of the Four Movements*, 1857). In 1812, Fourier's mother died, leaving him a modest lifetime annuity. The money allowed him to devote himself full-time to elaborating his ideas in a projected *Grand*

Traité (great treatise). Although he never finished this great treatise he did publish in 1822 his two-volume *Traité de l'association domestique-agricole* (later retitled *Théorie de l'unité universelle*; *Social Science: The Theory of Universal Unity*, 185?). A briefer and more accessible statement of his position would appear in his *Le Nouveau Monde industriel et sociétaire: Ou, Invention du procédé d'industrie attrayante et naturelle distribuée en series passionées* (1829).

Fourier never married, appears to have had no lasting romantic attachment, and lived most of his life in cheap lodging houses and hotels. He was a deeply neurotic personality—what the French call a *maniaque* (crank). There is even evidence that he seriously thought himself to be the son of God. As he grew older, he became increasingly paranoid about his supposed persecution by his enemies. His jealousy of rival would-be saviors of humanity resulted in an 1831 pamphlet, *Pièges et charlatanisme des deux sectes Saint-Simon et Owen, qui promettent l'association et le progrès* (traps and charlatanism of the Saint-Simonian and Owen sects, who promise association and progress). The last of his major writings to be published during his lifetime was the two-volume *La Fausse Industrie morcelée, répugnante, mensongère, et l'antidote, l'industrie naturelle, combinée, attrayante, veridique, donnant quadruple produit et perfection extrème en tous qualités* (1835-1836). A manuscript entitled *Le Nouveau Monde amoureux*—written around 1817-1818 and demonstrating the central place in his thinking of his vision of a sexual revolution—was not published until 1967.

Life's Work

Fourier's starting point was his repudiation of the eighteenth century philosophes, who had enthroned reason as mankind's guide. He dismissed reason as a weak force compared to the passions, or instinctual drives. He postulated the existence of twelve fundamental human passions. These in turn fell into three major categories. There were the so-called luxurious passions (the desires of the five senses of sight, hearing, taste, smell, and touch); the four group, or affective, passions (ambition, friendship, love, and family feeling or parenthood); and the serial, or distributive, passions (the "cabalist" desire for intrigue, the "butterfly" yearning for

variety, and the "composite," or desire for the simultaneous satisfaction of more than a single passion). Fourier held that since all the passions were created by God, they were naturally good and harmonious. Thus, they should be allowed the freest and fullest expression. He preached that mankind had achieved sufficient mastery over the forces of the natural world to make possible the satisfaction of all human wants.

The trouble was that in capitalist society—which Fourier in his sixteen-stage scheme of human history termed civilization—most people found their passions repressed or, even worse, so distorted as to become vices. What was required was a new social order that would channel the passions in salutary directions. His ideal world—which he called Harmony—was a paradise of sensuous enjoyments: a continuous round of eating, drinking, and lovemaking. The prerequisite for its attainment was a properly designed community, or phalanx, which would constitute the basic social unit. Each phalanx would consist of sixteen hundred to two thousand persons. This number would allow inclusion within the phalanx of the full range of different individual personality types and thus of potential combinations of passions. There were, he calculated, no more than 810 fundamentally different varieties of men and the same number for women. The perfect society required that each type interact with all other types.

All the members of the phalanx would live in one large building, known as the phalanstery. He even specified the architectural design: a building about six stories high, consisting of a long main body and two wings with inner courtyards and a parade ground immediately in front. Almost always, individuals would not engage in their occupations or pastimes alone or as part of a haphazard gathering, but rather as members of scientifically arranged groupings. Individuals with the same interests would voluntarily form a small group, and groups with like occupations would similarly combine naturally into what he termed a series. This organizational scheme would give full scope simultaneously to the cooperative and competitive impulses, because each group would consist of volunteers passionately devoted to the purpose of the group and the different groups would vie with one another to win the praise of the other members of the phalanx.

Boredom would be eliminated because of frequent changes in jobs and sex partners. Phalanx members would work at any given task typically only one hour per day, with two hours as the maximum. Leadership would be similarly rotated depending upon the activity. Most important, phalanx members would join only those groups and series that attracted them. Within each group, they would perform only that part of the work that appealed to them. Thus, for example, the would-be Nero would find an outlet for his bloodthirsty tastes by working as a butcher. This matching of job with personality was the fundamental difference between Civilization and Harmony. "In the former," Fourier explained, "a man or a woman performs twenty different functions belonging to a single kind of work. In the latter a man performs a single function in twenty kinds of work, and he chooses the function which he likes while rejecting the other nineteen."

Fourier did not propose to abolish private property. He allowed differential rewards for those with superior creative abilities and, accordingly, differences in the degree of pleasures according to resources. Even the poorest in the phalanx would lead much richer and more pleasurable lives than was attainable by even the richest in the existing society. As for who would do society's so-called dirty jobs, he had a simple answer: children. "God," he explained, "gave children these strange tastes to provide for the execution of various repulsive tasks. If manure has to be spread over a field, youths will find it a repugnant job but groups of children will devote themselves to it with greater zeal than to clean work."

A revolutionary educational policy was at the heart of Fourier's system. Whereas civilized education repressed the faculties of the child, the new education that he envisaged would be aimed at developing all the child's physical and intellectual faculties, especially the capacities for pleasure and enjoyment. He most antagonized contemporary opinion—and dismayed even many of his disciples—by his advocacy of free love. He was convinced that the amorous desires of most people were polygamous. He thus attacked the family as the number-one example of an unnatural institution, stifling both men and women. Marriage in contemporary society, he charged, was "pure brutality, a casual pairing off provoked by the domestic bond without any illusion of mind or heart."

From 1822 on—except for a brief return to Lyons in 1825—Fourier lived in Paris. He was constantly appealing to would-be patrons to finance the establishment of an experimental phalanx to provide scientific proof of the correctness of his theories. Every day on the stroke of twelve noon, he would return to his lodgings to await the arrival of the hoped-for benefactor. He was the target of frequent newspaper ridicule, but he attracted a small but loyal band of disciples. In 1832, the first Fourierist journal, *Le Phalanstère*, was launched; the same year witnessed the first attempt to establish a model phalanx at Condé-sur-Vesgre. From 1833 on, Fourier suffered from worsening intestinal problems that sapped his health. For the last year of his life, he was an invalid confined to his apartment. On the morning of October 10, 1837, the building concierge found him dead, kneeling by his bed dressed in his frock coat.

Summary

Charles Fourier himself constitutes a fascinating psychological problem, given the contrast between his free-ranging, sensual imagination and the crabbed drabness of his personal life. Much of his writing is simply incoherent—rambling, repetitive, and filled with invented pseudoscientific jargon. He goes into flights of fantasy—such as his portrayal of the planets copulating, his prophecy of the oceans turning into lemonade, his vision of the pests of man, such as fleas, rats, crocodiles, and lions, becoming transformed into more pleasant species, anti-fleas, anti-rats, anti-crocodiles, and anti-lions—that raise questions about his sanity. Yet his vision of a freer, happier, and more harmonious social order to replace the poverty, misery, and conflict of early industrial society exerted a strong attraction upon his sensitive-minded contemporaries, ranging from the young Fyodor Dostoevski to the New England Transcendentalists assembled at Brook Farm.

Although all the attempts to establish a model phalanx proved failures, Fourier has received renewed attention as the prophet of what have become the animating values for much of Western society—liberation of the senses from the repressions of middle-class life, exaltation of the instincts, and an all-pervading impulse toward self-gratification. He has attracted perhaps most interest as the precursor of the sexual revolution because of his calls for freedom from sexual taboos, his attacks on the barrenness of the marriage relationship, and his implicit assumption that there was no such thing as a sexual norm. He anticipated Sigmund Freud in key respects, particularly in his recognition of the importance of the sexual drive and the mechanisms for its repression and sublimation.

Fourier's direct contribution to these later developments was minor, if not nil. Yet he was a more astute reader of human nature—and thus of the future—than the eighteenth century philosophes whom he so strongly attacked.

Bibliography

Altman, Elizabeth C. "The Philosophical Bases of Feminism: The Feminist Doctrines of the Saint-Simonians and Charles Fourier." *Philosophical Forum* 7 (Spring/Summer 1974): 277-293. A laudatory examination of Fourier's advanced (at least from a present-day feminist perspective) ideas concerning the stifling effects of middle-class marriage upon women and his egalitarian views about the role of women in the phalanx.

Beecher, Jonathan. *Charles Fourier: The Visionary and His World*. Berkeley: University of California Press, 1986. An impressive piece of research into the extant published and manuscript materials on Fourier, this work should remain for the foreseeable future the definitive biography. The book is divided into three major parts: Part 1 details Fourier's life up to 1822; part 2 is an in-depth explication of his ideas; and part 3 traces his efforts to publicize and implement his program.

Fourier, Charles. *The Utopian Vision of Charles Fourier: Selected Texts on Work, Love, and Passionate Attraction*. Edited and translated by Jonathan Beecher and Richard Bienvenu. Boston: Beacon Press, 1971; London: Cape, 1972. As the subtitle indicates, the book contains English translations of selections from Fourier's writings. The editor-translators have avoided the temptation of pruning the nonsense and even gibberish with which Fourier filled so many of his pages; students without a knowledge of French thus can get at least a taste of Fourier's style. The seventy-five-page introduction provides an excellent, relatively brief introduction to Fourier's thinking.

Guarneri, Carl J. *The Utopian Alternative: Fourierism in Nineteenth-Century America*. Ithaca, N.Y.: Cornell University Press, 1991; London: Cornell University Press, 1994. Winner of the 1992 Society of Historians of the Early American Republic Book Award. Wonderful narrative following the Fourierist movement in the United States from its birth in the trials of the 1830s through its demise after the Civil War.

Manuel, Frank E. *The Prophets of Paris*. Cambridge, Mass.: Harvard University Press, 1962.

The author has written a perceptive account of five late eighteenth/early nineteenth century French prophets of a transformed social order—Anne-Robert-Jacques Turgot, Marquis de Condorcet, Comte de Saint-Simon, and Auguste Comte, along with Fourier. Manuel explains the similarities and differences in their ideas. He gives a sympathetic appraisal of Fourier as Freud's precursor in his psychological insights.

Poster, Mark, ed. *Harmonian Man: Selected Writings of Charles Fourier*. New York: Doubleday, 1971. Although Poster's introduction is short, the volume offers a handy selection of translated excerpts from Fourier's writings. Approximately half of the selections are nineteenth century translations, mostly by Arthur Brisbane. The rest—including excerpts from *Le Nouveau Monde amoureux*—were translated for this volume by Susan Ann Hanson.

Prendergast, Christopher. "Utopia." *New Left Review*, no. 225 (September-October 1997). Discusses Fourier's work involving human happiness and utopias.

Riasanovsky, Nicholas V. *The Teaching of Charles Fourier*. Berkeley: University of California Press, 1969. A lucidly written, comprehensive, and systematic analysis of the major themes in Fourier's thinking that should be the starting point for any serious examination of his ideas. An admirer of Fourier, Riasanovsky makes him appear too sensible and perhaps too modern by downplaying the fantastic and bizarre elements in his writings.

Spencer, M. C. *Charles Fourier*. Boston: Twayne, 1981. The volume includes a brief biographical sketch along with a summary of the major points in Fourier's thinking. Yet Spencer's own interest lies on the aesthetic side, and he has suggestive comments about Fourier's influence on French literature from Charles Baudelaire to the Surrealists.

John Braeman

JOSEPH FOURIER

Born: March 21, 1768; Auxerre, France
Died: May 16, 1830; Paris, France
Areas of Achievement: Mathematics and physics
Contribution: In deriving and solving equations representing the flow of heat in bodies, Fourier developed analytical methods which proved to be useful in the fields of pure mathematics, applied mathematics, and theoretical physics.

Early Life

Jean-Baptiste-Joseph Fourier, twelfth child of master tailor Joseph and ninth child of Édmie, became an orphan at the age of nine. He was placed in the local Royal Military School run by the Benedictine Order and soon demonstrated his passion for mathematics. Fourier and many biographers after him attribute the onset of his lifelong poor health to his habit of staying up late, reading mathematical texts in the empty classrooms of the school. He completed his studies in Paris. He was denied entry into the military and decided to enter the Church and teach mathematics.

Fourier remained at the Benedictine Abbey of St. Benoit-sur-Loire from 1787 to 1789, occupied with teaching and frustrated that he had little time for mathematical research. Whether he left Paris because of the impending revolution or because he did not want to take his vows is uncertain. He returned to Auxerre and from 1789 to 1794 served as professor and taught a variety of subjects at the Royal Military School. The school was run by the Congregation of St. Maur, the only religious order excluded from the post-revolutionary decree confiscating the property of religious orders.

Fourier became involved in local politics in 1793 and was drawn deep into the whirlpool as internal unrest and external military threats turned the committees on which he served into agents of the Terror. Fourier made the mistake of defending a group of men who turned out to be enemies of Robespierre. He was arrested and very nearly guillotined, spared only by the death of Robespierre. He became a student at the short-lived École Normale, mainly to have the opportunity to go to Paris and meet Pierre-Simon Laplace, Joseph-Louis Lagrange, and Gaspard Monge, the foremost mathematicians in France. In 1795, the École Polytechnique was opened, and Fourier was invited to join the faculty, but he was arrested once again, this time by the extreme reactionaries who hated him for his role in the Terror, even though he did much to moderate the excesses of the Terror in Auxerre. As with many other aspects of Fourier's life during the Revolution, the exact reason for his release is unknown. In any case, he was released and occupied himself with teaching and administrative duties at the École Polytechnique.

In 1798, Fourier was chosen to be part of Napoleon I's expedition to Egypt. Fourier was elected permanent secretary of the newly formed Institute of Egypt, held a succession of administrative and diplomatic posts in the French expedition, and conducted some mathematical research. Upon his return to France in 1801, Fourier was named by Napoleon to be the prefect of Isère, one of the eighty-four newly formed divisions of France. It is during his prefecture that Fourier began his life's work.

Life's Work

Fourier's work in the development of an analytical theory of heat diffusion dates from the early 1800's, when he was in his early thirties, and after he had distinguished himself in administration of scientific and political institutions in Egypt. He had demonstrated a talent and passion for mathematics early, but he had not yet made significant contributions to the field. It was during whatever time he could spare from his administrative duties as prefect that he made his lasting contribution to physics and mathematics.

Fourier remained at Grenoble until Napoleon's downfall in 1814. He turned a poorly managed department into a well-managed one in a short time. It is not clear why Fourier began to study the diffusion of heat, but in 1804 he began with a rather mathematically abstract derivation of heat flow in a metal plate. He conducted numerous experiments in an attempt to establish the laws regulating the flow of heat. He expanded the scope of problems addressed, polished the mathematical formalism, and infused physical concepts into the derivation of the equations which expressed heat flow. He presented in 1807 a long paper to the French Academy of Sciences, but opposition from Laplace and others prevented its publication. At issue was a fundamental disagreement over mathematical rigor and the underlying physical concepts.

Laplace's first objection was that Fourier's methods were not mathematically rigorous. Fourier claimed that any function could be represented by an infinite trigonometric series—a sum of an infinite number of sine and cosine functions each with a determinable coefficient. Such series were instrumental in Fourier's formulation and solution of the problems of the diffusion of heat. Only later were Fourier's methods shown to be strictly rigorous mathematically. The second objection concerned the method of derivation. Laplace preferred to explain phenomena by the action of central forces acting between particles of matter. Fourier, while not denying the correctness or the usefulness of that approach, took a different approach. Heat, for Fourier, was the flow of a substance and not some relation between atoms and their motions. He attempted, successfully, to account for the phenomenon of heat diffusion through mathematical analysis. His paper of 1807 languished in the archives of the Academy of Sciences, unpublished.

As a result of his work in Egypt and his position as permanent secretary of the Institute of Egypt, Fourier edited and wrote the historical introduction to the *Description de l'Égypte* (1809-1828; description of Egypt). He worked on this project from around 1802 until 1810.

A prize was offered in 1810 by the Academy of Sciences on the subject of heat diffusion, and Fourier slightly revised and expanded his 1807 paper to include discussion of diffusion in infinite bodies and terrestrial and radiant heat. Fourier won the prize, but he had faced no serious competition. The jury criticized the paper in much the same way as the 1807 paper had been criticized, and again Fourier's work was not published. Eventually, after years of prodding, the work was published in 1815.

Fourier was probably not very happy being virtually exiled from Paris, the scientific capital of France. He seemed destined to live out his days in Grenoble. With Napoleon's abdication in April, 1814, Fourier provisionally retained his job as prefect during the transfer of power to Louis XVIII. He also managed to alter the route Napoleon took from Paris to exile in Elba, bypassing Grenoble, in order to avoid a confrontation between himself and Napoleon. Upon Napoleon's return in March, 1815, Fourier prepared the defenses of the town and made a diplomatic retreat to Lyons. Fourier returned before completing the journey upon learning that Napoleon had made him prefect of the Rhône department. He was dismissed before Napoleon fell once again.

Fourier's scientific work began again after 1815. One of his former pupils was now a prefect and appointed Fourier director of the Bureau of Statistics for the Seine department, which included Paris. He now had a modest income and few demands on his time. Fourier was named to the Academy of Sciences in 1817. During the next five years, he actively participated in the affairs of the Academy, sitting on commissions, writing reports, and conducting his own research. His administrative duties increased in 1822, when he was elected to the powerful position of permanent secretary of the mathematical section of the Academy. His *Théorie analytique de la chaleur* (1822; *The Analytical Theory of Heat*, 1878) differs only slightly from his 1810 essay. The papers he wrote in his later years contained little that was new. He led a satisfying academic life in his last years, but his health began to deteriorate. His rheumatism had returned, he had trouble breathing, and he was very sensitive to cold. Fourier died from a heart attack in May, 1830.

Summary

The core of Joseph Fourier's scientific work is *The Analytical Theory of Heat*. This work is basically a textbook describing the application of theorems from pure mathematics applied to the problem of the diffusion of heat in bodies. Fourier was able to express the distribution of heat inside of and on the surface of a variety of bodies, both at equilibrium and when the distribution was changing because of heat loss or gain.

He significantly influenced three different fields: pure mathematics, applied mathematics, and theoretical physics. In pure mathematics, Fourier's most lasting influence has been the definition of a mathematical function. He realized that any mathematical function can be represented by a trigonometric series, no matter how difficult to manipulate the function may appear. Some scholars single out this concept as the stepping stone to the work of pure mathematicians later in the century, which resulted in the modern definition of a function. Additional influences are that of a clarification of a notational issue involving integral calculus and properties of infinite trigonometric series.

Applied mathematics has been influenced to a great extent by Fourier's use of trigonometric series and techniques of integration. The class of problems that Fourier series and Fourier integrals can solve extends far beyond diffusion of heat. His methods form the foundation of applied mathematics techniques taught to undergraduates. Some mathematicians before him had used trigonometric series in the solutions of problems, but the clarity, scope, and rigor that he brought to the field was significant.

His influence in theoretical physics is more subdued, perhaps because of the completeness of his results. There was little room for others to extend the physical aspects of Fourier's work—his results did not need extending. Other branches of physics appear to have been influenced by his approach, and a direct influence on the issue of determining the age of the earth by calculating its heat loss has been documented.

Bibliography

Bell, Eric T. *The Development of Mathematics*. 2d ed. New York and London: McGraw-Hill, 1945. Presents a narrative history of the decisive epochs in the development of mathematics without becoming overly technical. Chapter 13 is where the most references to Fourier may be found.

Fourier, Joseph. *The Analytical Theory of Heat*. Translated by Alexander Freeman. Cambridge: Cambridge University Press, and New York: Stechert, 1878. Fourier's preliminary discourse to his most famous work explains in very clear terms what he is attempting in the work. Devoid of technical matters, this book offers the reader a glimpse of why Fourier has achieved the status he has.

Fox, Robert. "The Rise and Fall of Laplacian Physics." *Historical Studies in the Physical Sciences* 4 (1974): 89-136. This paper presents a description of the research program of Laplace, which dominated French science at one of its most successful periods, from 1805 to 1815. Fourier led the revolt against this program.

Friedman, Robert Marc. "The Creation of a New Science: Joseph Fourier's Analytical Theory of Heat." *Historical Studies in the Physical Sciences* 8 (1977): 73-100. This paper concentrates on conceptual and physical issues rather than the mathematical aspects stressed in most older works. Also discusses how Fourier's philosophy of science compared to that of his contemporaries.

Gonzalez-Velasco, Enrique A. "Connections in Mathematical Analysis: The Case of Fourier Series." *American Mathematical Monthly* 99, no. 5 (May 1992). Looks at the influence of Fourier's study of heat loss and heat conservation on the creation of new concepts, methods, and formulas for convergence, functions, integration, set theory, and uniform convergence.

Grattan-Guinness, Ivor, with J. R. Ravetz. *Joseph Fourier, 1768-1830: A Survey of His Life and Work, Based on a Critical Edition of his Monograph on the Propagation of Heat, Presented to the Institute de France in 1807*. Cambridge, Mass.: MIT Press, 1972. Intertwines a close study of Fourier's life and work with a critical edition of his 1807 monograph. The 1807 monograph is in French, but everything else is in English. Contains a bibliography of Fourier's writings, a list of translations of his works, and a secondary bibliography.

Herivel, John. *Joseph Fourier: The Man and the Physicist*. Oxford: Clarendon Press, 1975. While this work does not claim to be the definitive biography of Fourier, it goes much further than any other work written in English. Although the book is almost devoid of technical detail, the prospective reader would benefit from a knowledge of the history of France from 1789 to 1830.

Roger Sensenbaugh

LYDIA FOLGER FOWLER

Born: May 5, 1822; Nantucket, Massachusetts
Died: January 26, 1879; London, England
Areas of Achievement: Medicine and women's rights
Contribution: The first woman to become a professor at an American medical school, Fowler became a well-known lecturer on physiology, temperance, and women's rights during the years in which the medical field gradually opened to the entry of women.

Early Life

Lydia Folger, the daughter of Gideon and Eunice Macy Folger, was born on May 5, 1822, on the small island of Nantucket off the coast of Massachusetts. Her father, who had spent various periods in his life as a mechanic, a farmer, a candle maker, a ship owner, and even a sometime politician, was a direct descendant of Peter Folger, who had arrived on Nantucket in 1663 as one of the earliest settlers of the island. The Folger clan, which also includes Benjamin Franklin, can be traced back to English nobility in the person of the Earl of Shrewsbury.

Another well-known relative of Lydia Folger Fowler was her distant cousin Maria Mitchell, who grew up in Nantucket as a contemporary of Fowler's and who would one day become a professor of astronomy at Vassar College. In fact, it was through Maria Mitchell's father, a popular teacher in the community, that Fowler gained a consuming interest in her studies, particularly in math and science. Additionally supported by an uncle who fancied himself an amateur astronomer, Lydia Folger Fowler felt a special devotion to the field in which her cousin Maria would find such distinction. All in all, Fowler's early education, with its inclusion of subjects generally thought of as unsuitable for women students, appears to have been quite extensive when compared to that of other women of the era.

One possible explanation for this circumstance is the distinctive character of the community in Nantucket. For the most part, the men of Nantucket worked in seafaring trades—trades that demanded that they leave the island for weeks and months at a time. Such necessities helped to form an atmosphere of independence and self-reliance among the women of the island, who were often forced to run the affairs of the community while the men were away. Lucretia Mott, one of the early leaders of the women's rights movement and a native of Nantucket, is a good example of the kind of attitudes fostered there. Add to this the fact that the island at this time was inhabited primarily by Quakers, who were defined by an openness to social reform and a devotion to the ideal of equality, and one can begin to imagine more clearly the environment from which Lydia Folger Fowler emerged.

Life's Work

Lydia Folger left Nantucket in 1838 to study for a year in Norton, Massachusetts, at the Wheaton Seminary, where she would later spend two years (1842-1844) as a teacher. This stint ended with her marriage, on September 19, 1844, to Lorenzo Niles Fowler. They would have but one child together, a daughter named Jessie Allen, born in 1856.

Lorenzo Fowler was at this time one of the most well-known and vocal proponents of the budding science of phrenology. He and his brother Orson had been exposed to phrenological theories during the 1830's while they were both studying at Amherst College in preparation for a life in the ministry. Convinced of the tenants of this new science, the brothers became two of its most famous adherents by embarking on numerous lecture tours and even establishing the publishing house of Fowlers and Wells in 1842 in order to become the publishers of the *American Phrenological Journal*. Beginning in 1845, Lydia Folger Fowler accompanied her husband during the journeys to his speaking engagements, and later, in 1847, she began to give lectures of her own at the opening of each congregation. These lectures covered such topics as anatomy, physiology, and hygiene, and formed the basis for the two books Fowler would publish in 1847 through the auspices of her husband's publishing operation. *Familiar Lessons on Physiology* and *Familiar Lessons on Phrenology* (to be followed in 1848 by a third volume, *Familiar Lessons in Astronomy*) appeared as books intended for young readers and enjoyed some sales success.

Heartened by her successes as a lecturer and author, Lydia Folger Fowler decided to pursue a medical degree and enrolled at Central Medical College in November, 1849. Located first in Syracuse, New York, and later moving to Rochester in 1850, Central was the first medical school to make a regular policy of admitting women. The school even included a so-called "Female Department," of which Fowler served as principal during her second term of study. Although there was this emphasis on Central's campus and though there were several other women who joined her entering class, Lydia Folger Fowler was the lone female graduate in June of 1850, making her only the second woman ever, after Elizabeth Blackwell, to receive a medical degree in the United States.

Fowler was soon to gain a first of her own. After she had worked briefly as a "demonstrator of anatomy" to students at Central, Fowler was promoted in 1851 to the position of professor of midwifery and diseases of women and children, thereby becoming the first woman professor at an American medical college. The professorship was not long-lived, however, because Central Medical College merged with a rival institution in 1852 and Fowler left to practice privately in New York City. While in New York, Fowler resumed teaching, and in 1854, she began a series of private medical lectures for women at Metropolitan Medical College, a physiopathic school that existed between 1852 and 1862. Fowler also succeeded in publishing three articles in the pages of Metropolitan College's alternative medical journal. These articles were entitled "Medical Progression," "Female Medical Education," and "Suggestions to Female Medical Students." These articles argued the necessity of women physicians, noting that women needing medical care were often precluded by their modesty from seeking help from the heretofore exclusively male profession.

The early 1850's also witnessed Fowler's increased politicization, as she became involved in several causes for reform. Twice she served as secretary to national women's rights conventions (1852 and 1853), and once she was a delegate to a meeting of the state Daughters of Temperance (1852). In February of 1853, Fowler presided over a women's temperance meeting in New York City, during which she utilized her well-honed skills at public speaking. In addition to supporting these reform movements, Fowler continued to give public lectures on the topics of physiology and hygiene. She remained in New York City until 1860, when she left with her husband as he embarked on a speaking tour of Europe. After spending the year studying and working in Paris and London, Fowler returned to New York in 1861. In 1862, she became an instructor in midwifery at the New York

Hygeio-Therapeutic College. The next year, Lorenzo Fowler left the publishing house, and he and Lydia Fowler moved to London, where they would spend the rest of their days.

While in London, Lydia Folger Fowler chose not to practice medicine but continued to remain extremely active within the temperance movement, becoming an honorary secretary of the Woman's British Temperance Society. This period also allowed Folger the leisure to focus on her writing. *Nora: The Lost and the Redeemed*, a temperance novel that earlier had been serialized in America, appeared in book form in 1863. A series of Folger's lectures on child care was published in 1865 as *The Pet of the Household and How to Save It*. Finally, in 1870, a book of poems entitled *Heart Melodies* became Folger's last published work. Lydia Folger Fowler died in London of pleuropneumonia on January 26, 1879.

Summary

Lydia Folger Fowler's list of accomplishments easily leads one to see her as an inspiring symbol of women's determination to break down the social and institutional barriers that excluded them from the study and practice of medicine. That she made such great strides and enjoyed so much success at Central Medical College, becoming the second American woman to receive a medical degree and the first to become a professor in an American medical school, secures forever Fowler's place among the early pioneers of women's rights within the medical field. To stress her symbolic importance, however, is to misrepresent the true nature of her influence upon the other women of her era. Lydia Folger Fowler's efforts were of a much more practical kind. During her many extended tours of public lectures, Fowler addressed wide and varied audiences, meeting and speaking with countless admirers and skeptics. It was during these moments, when she brought her message and personal example so immediately to those in attendance, that Lydia Folger Fowler had her greatest impact. No other woman physician of the moment could claim to have influenced so many people in so direct and intimate a manner. While it is true that much of Fowler's lecturing was done in connection with the thoroughly debunked science of phrenology and that she continually found herself working in alternative or marginal situations, this does not seem so surprising if one considers the hostility she must have felt emanating from a medical institution that sensed that its days as a closed fraternity were numbered.

Bibliography

Hume, Ruth Fox. *Great Women of Medicine*. New York: Random House, 1964. Fowler is mentioned as an able practitioner though a graduate of an eclectic college. The portrayals of the six women in the book—Elizabeth Blackwell, Florence Nightingale, Elizabeth Garrett Anderson, Sophia Jex-Blake, Mary Putnam Jacobi, and Marie Curie—provide the reader with a good introduction to the medical profession in the 1800's.

Lopate, Carol. *Women in Medicine*. Baltimore: Johns Hopkins University Press, 1968. In the first chapter, Lopate gives good background concerning the entrance of American women into the medical profession. She explains the importance of eclectic schools such as the one Lydia Folger Fowler attended in offering women entrance.

Morantz-Sanchez, Regina Markell. *Sympathy and Science: Women Physicians in American Medicine*. New York: Oxford University Press, 1985. The best discussion of Lydia Folger Fowler appears in this comprehensive history of women in American medicine. Morantz-Sanchez explores the role of feminism in this history as well as the unique contributions women made to the field of medicine.

Walsh, Mary Roth. *"Doctors Wanted: No Women Need Apply"*: *Sexual Barriers in the Medical Profession, 1835-1975*. New Haven, Conn.: Yale University Press, 1977; London: Yale University Press, 1979. In this work, Lydia Folger Fowler is mentioned on the first page as the first American woman to be graduated from an American medical college. This book is an excellent study of the barriers women faced in entering the medical profession in the United States as well as a good overview of the progress of medicine in the nineteenth century, helping to put Fowler in perspective.

Wilson, Dorothy Clarke. *Lone Woman: The Story of Elizabeth Blackwell, the First Woman Doctor*. London: Hodder and Stoughton, and Boston: Little Brown, 1970. Wilson shows how Elizabeth Blackwell's achievement led to the adoption of a coeducational policy by the Rochester Eclectic College of Medicine. Fowler was the first woman graduate of Rochester and thereby benefited from Blackwell's endeavor.

Bonnie Ford

ANATOLE FRANCE

Born: April 16, 1844; Paris, France
Died: October 12, 1924; Saint-Cyr-sur-Loire, France
Area of Achievement: Literature
Contribution: Anatole France's reclusive devotion to books turned to militancy in the wake of the Dreyfus affair, and he used his satirical skills thereafter to campaign against intolerance and social injustice. He was awarded the Nobel Prize in Literature in 1921.

Early Life

Anatole François Thibault was the son of François Noël Thibault, a devoutly Roman Catholic and politically conservative bookseller. Anatole grew to adolescence surrounded by the cultural heritage of France and quickly acquired a keen appreciation of its worth. To begin with, he took aboard his father's religious and political beliefs in a meekly obedient fashion, with the result that his childhood was untroubled by conflict. He remembered it as a comfortable and happy time that he revisited nostalgically throughout his writing life, evoking aspects of it in *Le Livre de mon ami* (1885; *My Friend's Book*, 1913), *Pierre Nozière* (1899; English translation, 1916), *Le Petit Pierre* (1919; *Little Pierre*, 1920) and his final novel, *Le Vie en fleur* (1922; *The Bloom of Life*, 1923). A portrait painted when he was six shows him with a serious expression, a Cupid's-bow mouth and a narrow chin (which he was to conceal throughout adult life with a luxuriant beard and mustache).

The young Anatole became a devoted scholar, although he left the Collège Stanislas in 1862 without qualifications for reasons that his biographers have been unable to clarify. He refused to take over his father's business—which the elder Thibault then liquidated—and set out to make a living from his pen using the pseudonym Anatole France. He began to frequent the salon of the Parnassian poet Charles Leconte de Lisle in 1867 but supported himself in the field of academic journalism, which was unusually lucrative in nineteenth century France by virtue of the rapid postrevolutionary establishment of universal literacy and an attendant hunger for education. His subjects ranged from such writers of ancient Greece and Rome as Lucius Apuleius and Terence to such contemporaries as Paul Bourget and Émile Zola. The classical philos-

ophy of Epicurus and the social upheavals of revolutionary France became particularly fascinating for Anatole. The Catholic faith and Monarchist sympathies that Anatole had inherited from his father were ameliorated by polite Epicurean skepticism and an idealistic commitment to liberty, equality, and fraternity.

Early manhood proved to be a more troubling period of his life. A passionate infatuation with Élise Devoyod in 1865-1866 was unreciprocated. He married Marie-Valérie Guérin de Sauville in 1877, but the marriage was disrupted by a hectic love affair with a married woman, Léontine Arman de Caillavet, which turned his gradual retreat from moral orthodoxy into a headlong rush in the late 1880's. His marriage was dissolved in 1893, shortly before his involvement with the celebrated case of Alfred Dreyfus—a Jewish army officer wrongly convicted of selling military secrets—presented his newfound radicalism a cause that he could pursue in the public arena.

Life's Work

France's first full-length work, issued in 1868, was a study of the poet Alfred de Vigny. He published a poetry collection of his own in 1873 and a poetic drama, *Les Noces corinthiennes*, in 1876, but the latter was not performed until he had become famous; it was first produced at the Odéon in 1902. His first book of prose, *Jocasta et le chat maigre* (1879; *Jocasta and the Famished Cat*, 1912), consisted of two novellas, but his breakthrough to popular success was *Le Crime de Sylvestre Bonnard* (1881; *The Crime of Sylvestre Bonnard*, 1890), a novel about an unworldly booklover's struggle to cope with the vicissitudes of everyday life. This was followed in 1883 by the long, moralistic fairy tale "L'Abeille," variously known in English as "Honey-Bee," "Bee" and "The Kingdom of the Dwarfs," which became the longest item in the story collection *Balthasar* (1889; English translation, 1909).

France wrote two novels dramatizing his feelings for Léontine Arman de Caillavet. The first, written while he was still married, was *Thaïs* (1890; English translation, 1891), based on a legend that he had already recapitulated in a poem written in 1867. Paphnuce, a hermit living in the same locale as Saint Anthony (whose oft-illustrated temptations had been vividly described in an ex-

travagant novel by Gustave Flaubert), persuades a famous Alexandrian courtesan to repent her wicked ways and become a nun but is then driven mad by the erotic feelings she has awakened in him. The second novel, set in the city of Florence, which he and Madame Arman de Caillavet visited while touring Italy in the wake of his divorce, was the infinitely more relaxed and sentimental love story *Le Lys rouge* (1894; *The Red Lily*, 1898).

The resentment against Christian asceticism embodied in *Thaïs* was further extended in the stories in *L'Étui de nacre* (1892; *Tales from a Mother of Pearl Casket*, 1896), which opens with the notorious "Le procurateur de Judea" ("The Procurator of Judea"), in which an aged Pontius Pilate, reminiscing about old times, reveals that he has no memory whatsoever of his brief encounter with Christ, although he remembers Mary Magdalene very well. The collection also includes further ironic pastiches of the legends of the saints in the same vein as *Thaïs*. The trend continued in *Le Puits de Sainte-Claire* (1895; *The Well of Santa Clara*, 1909), which included a fine tale of a satyr saint that summarized France's arguments about the tragedy of the Church's rejection of the pagan heritage and the novella "L'humaine tragédie" ("The Human Tragedy"), in which a medieval holy man discovers that the Church has become the enemy of true Christian ideals and that the rebellious spirit of its traditional enemy—Satan—better embraces the traditional ideals of hope and charity.

Other works elaborating France's new spirit of dissent included the Rabelaisian satire *La Rôtisserie de la Reine Pédauque* (1893; *At the Sign of the Reine Pédauque*, 1912) and *Les Opinions de M. Jérome Coignard* (1893; *The Opinions of Jerome Coignard*, 1913), but his work changed direction markedly in 1897 when he began a four-volume series of novels set in contemporary France. This consisted of *L'Orme du mail* (1897; *The Elm Tree on the Mall*, 1910), *Le Mannequin d'osier* (1897; *The Wicker Work Woman*, 1910), *L'Anneau d'améthyste* (1899; *The Amethyst Ring*, 1919), and the semiautobiographical *Monsieur Bergeret à Paris* (1901; *Monsieur Bergeret in Paris*, 1922). The last book features a hero whose decision to remain aloof from politics is overturned by outrage at the refusal of the French military authorities to admit that Captain Dreyfus had been wrongly convicted and at the consequent continuation of Dreyfus' imprisonment on Devil's Island. France's own sense of outrage broadened to include other social injustices, some of which were scathingly chronicled in the sarcastic tales collected in *Crainquebille, Putois, Riquet et plusieurs autres récits profitables* (1904; *Crainquebille, Putois, Riquet and Other Profitable Tales*, 1915). The Dreyfus affair formed the basis for the final sequence of his hugely successful satire *L'Île des pingouins* (1908; *Penguin Island*, 1914), in which a population of accidentally baptized penguins reproduce all the errors and follies of human social evolution.

France offered more earnest accounts of his philosophical development in his reconstruction of debates in *Le Jardin d'Épicure* (1894; *The Garden of Epicurus*, 1908) and a novel examining the difficulties of predicting the future, *Sur le pierre blanche* (1905; *The White Stone*, 1909), whose attempted description of a future Marxist utopia reflected the author's increasing attachment to socialism. He eventually joined the Communist Party, but only briefly; he found its narrow faith as stultifying as the one he had deserted in adolescence. He always preferred to develop his ideas satirically and relatively light-heartedly, as in *Contes de Jacques Tournebroche* (1908; *The Merrie Tales of Jacques Tournebroche*, 1910), which contained stories in the same slightly bawdy mock-medieval vein as Honoré de Balzac's *Droll Tales*, and *Les Sept Femmes de la Barbe-Bleue et autres contes merveilleux* (1909; *The Seven Wives of Bluebeard and Other Marvellous Tales*, 1920), a collection of ironic fairy tales that concludes with a long exercise in moral symbolism in which emissaries of an unhappy king search in vain for the shirt of a happy man with which to redeem the king's melancholy spirit. France had been much troubled himself by the controversial remarriage of his divorced daughter Suzanne in 1908; he refused to speak to her thereafter, and the estrangement continued until her death in the 1918 Spanish flu epidemic.

The ultimate satirical product of France's conversion to radicalism was his literary masterpiece, *La Révolte des anges* (1914; *The Revolt of the Angels*, 1914), written on the eve of World War I. The story tells how a guardian angel is converted to free thought by *De rerum natura* (Lucretius' summary of Epicurean philosophy) and sends out a new call to arms to the fallen angels, most of whom have become teachers and artists. He offers the commanding role to Satan, who is working as a humble gardener and who politely declines on the grounds that liberation from divine tyranny must be won within the hearts and minds of men, not on the field of battle. The carefully considered rejection of violent means was carried forward from *Les Dieux ont soif* (1912; *The Gods Are Athirst*, 1913), his heartfelt historical novel analyzing the French Revolution of 1789 and the consequent Reign of Terror. He had turned to that subject in the wake of the death, in 1910, of his longtime companion Madame Arman de Caillavet. He did marry again in 1920, and in 1921 he received the Nobel Prize in Literature at the age of seventy-six. He was still working despite his age, and his last few published works, although slight, showed that he had lost none of his clarity of mind.

Summary

Despite his Nobel Prize, Anatole France's international reputation has always suffered somewhat from the fact that he does not fit into either of the literary categories currently regarded as the most prestigious. His early adventures in poetry were undistinguished, and the bare handful of realistic novels that he produced are very obviously novels of ideas rather than novels of character. His best work is in the tradition of Voltairean *contes philosphiques*, which never won much acclaim outside France and petered out even within its native land. He remains, however, one of the finest contributors to the later days of that tradition (and a very significant influence on James Branch Cabell, the one writer who tried hard to import it into the United States). France's greatest virtues—his painstaking erudition and the dispassionate coolness of his intelligence and wit—are sometimes held against him by critics who prefer more intimate narratives and more intricate plots, but they are rare virtues that ought to be accounted more precious than they often are. *The Revolt of the Angels* remains the classic work of the tradition of "literary Satanism" that sprang from William Blake's observation that the author of *Paradise Lost*, John Milton, had been "of the devil's party without knowing it." Such literature raises the important question of whether the commandments of a jealous God are really the best basis for human morality.

Bibliography

George, W. L. *Anatole France*. London: Nisbet, and New York: Holt, 1915. This was the first study of France in English. Written shortly after publication of *The Revolt of the Angels*, it deftly summarizes his career from that viewpoint.

Jefferson, A. C. *Anatole France: The Politics of Skepticism*. New Brunswick, N.J.: Rutgers University Press, 1965. A careful analysis of France's philosophical progress, his involvement in contemporary issues, and the position he eventually adopted.

Levy, D. W. *Techniques of Irony in Anatole France: Essay on "Les Sept Femmes de la Barbe-Bleue."* Chapel Hill: University of North Carolina Press, 1978. A minute dissection of a key exemplar of France's satirical method.

Sachs, M. *France: The Short Stories*. London: Arnold, 1974. A comprehensive survey of France's short fiction, offering a useful account of work that is sometimes neglected in more conventional studies that tend to place the novels in the foreground.

Virtanen, R. *Anatole France*. New York: Twayne, 1968. A useful general survey of the author's life and work.

Brian Stableford

FRANCIS JOSEPH I

Born: August 18, 1830; Schönbrunn Palace, near
Vienna, Austria
Died: November 21, 1916; Schönbrunn Palace,
near Vienna, Austria
Area of Achievement: Government
Contribution: The reign of Francis Joseph I was
one of the longest in European history. Ascending the throne at the age of eighteen, he eventually became the living symbol of an imperial ideal
of government doomed to vanish at his death,
which occurred near the end of World War I.

Early Life

The person who had the most profound effect upon
the character of Francis Joseph was his mother,
Princess Sophie of Bavaria. This younger daughter
of Maximilian I married Charles Francis, the second son of Emperor Francis I, in 1824, and, until
the birth of her first son, she devoted her time to
mastering the bewildering etiquette of the Austrian
court as well as the maze of imperial politics.

The heir to the throne, Archduke Ferdinand, was
mentally handicapped and suffered from epilepsy.
It was expected that the crown would pass to Sophie's retiring and irresolute husband. Since she was
already regarded as the best political mind in the
family, few had any doubts about who would govern the empire. Metternich, the man who had re-
drawn the map of Europe in 1815, dashed Sophie's
hopes by arranging a marriage for the hapless Ferdinand and persuading the emperor that his heir
was capable of ruling Austria. In 1835, Francis
died and Ferdinand ascended the throne.

Archduke Charles Francis was a loving and devoted father to his children, but their mother was in
charge. Although young Francis had been given a
household of his own at birth, his mother totally
controlled his upbringing. Slowly, the charming
prince began to evolve into a devout and gallant
young gentleman. Although he was not a scholar,
Francis was a conscientious student, but his real
love was military science. At the age of thirteen, he
was appointed a colonel of dragoons and began to
train seriously for a career as a soldier. The handsome, graceful youth proved an instant favorite
who fit easily into the carefree world of Vienna in
the last years before the Revolution of 1848.

The events that shook the foundations of the empire between March and December of 1848 provided the opportunity for which the Archduchess
Sophie had long waited. With Metternich a fugitive
in England, she easily persuaded her husband to renounce his claim to the throne in favor of their eldest son. On December 2, 1848, Emperor Ferdinand gladly abdicated in favor of his nephew, who
assumed the name Francis Joseph in memory of
Joseph II, the great reforming emperor of the late
eighteenth century. As the imperial family journeyed from Vienna, however, it was the new em-
press-mother who was busily charting the course
of the new reign, not the young emperor.

Life's Work

During the first three years of his reign Francis Joseph demonstrated his hostility to liberalism and
constitutional government by methodically revok-
ing most of the changes which had been made by
the revolutionaries. Even freedom of the press was
denied lest criticism of the regime become too
widespread. With the confidence of youth, the emperor sought to fashion a centralized absolutism in
which all power and responsibility would reside in
him. While a number of worthy administrative reforms were made to implement this policy, he totally ignored the potent force of nationalism. When
the Hungarians under Lajos Kossuth resisted, their
fledgling republic was crushed by troops sent from
Russia by Czar Nicholas I, who was delighted to
further the cause of reaction.

When a Hungarian patriot tried unsuccessfully to
assassinate Francis Joseph in February, 1853, the
young sovereign's sense of mission only deepened.
He believed that he had been sent to revive the de-
funct Holy Roman Empire in partnership with a revitalized Roman Catholic church. Apart from this
rather grand scheme, his foreign policy was rather
erratic and unimpressive.

Against his mother's wishes Francis Joseph married his sixteen-year-old cousin, Elizabeth of Bavaria, on April 24, 1854. Unfortunately for the young
couple, Sophie decided to mold her niece into her
image of an empress. Elizabeth was equally determined to resist, and the struggle of these two
strong-willed women eventually led to an estrangement between Francis Joseph and his wife. Sophie
then assumed the responsibility for rearing her three
grandchildren while their mother frequented fashionable spas, seeking to restore her health.

At the moment his personal happiness began to vanish, the emperor was forced to face the loss of all of his Italian possessions except Venetia. The combined armies of France and Piedmont-Savoy defeated the Austrians at Solferino on June 24, 1859. This bloody battle and the peace terms arranged at Villafranca the next month forced Francis Joseph to make some drastic changes in the way in which the empire was governed.

The liberals, whom the emperor had rejected at the beginning of his reign, were now wooed with the creation of an imperial parliament, whose membership was effectively restricted to the moneyed classes. The Hungarians, Poles, and Czechs refused to cooperate, but Francis Joseph proceeded with his plan for a largely German legislature. Having lost most of his Italian possessions, the emperor turned his attention to regional affairs. His dream of an Austrian-led central Europe brought Francis Joseph unwittingly into conflict with Otto von Bismarck.

In 1864, Bismarck lured the Austrians into a war against Denmark to prevent the incorporation of the largely German duchies of Schleswig and Holstein into that kingdom. The war lasted barely six months, and with its end the control of Schleswig passed to Prussia and the control of Holstein to Austria. While he diplomatically isolated Austria, Bismarck began a war of nerves over the administration of Holstein. Goaded beyond endurance, Austria went to war against Prussia in June, 1866. On July 2, 1866, the Prussians and their allies won a decisive victory at Königgrätz. Francis Joseph was forced to acquiesce to the absorption of most of northern and central Germany into the Prussian dominated North German Confederation. There were repeated calls for the emperor's abdication in favor of his younger brother Maximilian. The final humiliation was the seizure by Italy of Venetia with the blessing of Prussia.

To prevent the complete disintegration of the empire, Francis Joseph agreed to the Compromise of 1867, which created an independent Hungary within a dual monarchy. As Emperor of Austria and King of Hungary, he presided over a government which shared control of foreign affairs, armed forces, and finances between Vienna and Budapest. Shortly after his coronation in Hungary in June, 1867, Francis Joseph learned of the death of Maximilian before a firing squad in Mexico. For three years Maximilian had been emperor of that turbulent country with the support of the French, but the desertion of his allies left him at the mercy of his rebellious subjects.

The death of his brother was the first of a series of personal tragedies which haunted the remaining years of Francis Joseph's life. When Sophie died in 1873, the possible reconciliation between her son and daughter-in-law did not take place; instead, the gulf that separated them grew wider. Although intelligent and liberal in his political outlook, Crown Prince Rudolf did not display the same dedication to duty which his father prized, nor was his personal life exemplary. When Rudolf and his mistress committed suicide in January, 1889, the very foundations of the empire were shaken. The empress never recovered from her son's death, and her wanderings became more aimless until she died at the hands of an assassin in Geneva in September, 1898.

Francis Joseph's last years were marred by the murder of his nephew and heir, Franz Ferdinand, at Sarajevo in June, 1914, and by World War I. A man of peace, he would have preferred to spend his last days with his grandchildren. Instead, he died like a good soldier immersed in war-related work on November 21, 1916.

Summary

The rapid disintegration of the Austro-Hungarian Empire in the last months of the war surprised a number of experts. It had survived so many crises since the end of the Napoleonic era, including revolution and the constantly disruptive force of nationalism, that it seemed eternal. Francis Joseph I was the force that held together the diverse elements that composed his empire. The ideas which he brought to the throne were those of his mother, Metternich, and Felix Schwarzenberg, his first prime minister. As he matured, these youthful ideas were modified or discarded. Personal tragedy tempered his nature and endeared him to his people.

It may well be that he perceived the incurable weaknesses in his empire long before they became apparent to others, but with a tenacity born of adversity he devoted his life to preserving the rather antiquated structure. With age and infirmity, he was forced to curtail his public duties and leave the cares of state to lesser men. By then he was already a legend, almost a national icon. He was the one element that held the Austro-Hungarian Empire together, and when he died, it died with him.

Bibliography

Bagger, Eugene S. *Francis Joseph, Emperor of Austria-King of Hungary.* London and New York: Putnam, 1927. This standard biography, while almost contemporary with its subject, remains a work of solid and reliable scholarship. The author tends to avoid an in-depth analysis of private and personal matters in favor of a strict historical narrative. It should be read as background to other later works.

Crankshaw, Edward. *The Fall of the House of Habsburg*. London: Longman, and New York: Viking Press, 1963. The bulk of this work is devoted to the reign of Francis Joseph and the collapse of the Austro-Hungarian Empire after his death. Well-written and well-documented. Contains a useful bibliography.

McGuigan, Dorothy Gies. *The Habsburgs*. London: Lane, and New York: Doubleday, 1966. Although a general history of the Habsburg Dynasty, one-quarter of this work is devoted to Francis Joseph. The notes and bibliography are extremely valuable. Useful for its sensitivity to the forces that destroyed the empire and to the destiny that trapped the last Habsburgs.

Marek, George R. *The Eagles Die: Franz Joseph, Elisabeth, and Their Austria*. New York: Harper, 1974; London: Hart-Davis, 1975. The rather complicated, yet tragic relationship between Francis Joseph and his wife is the theme of this work. The men and women who influenced their lives are carefully profiled. The portrait of the emperor is particularly sensitive and complete.

May, Arthur J. *The Hapsburg Monarchy, 1867-1914*. Cambridge, Mass.: Harvard University Press, 1951. The primary focus of this work is the period from the Compromise of 1867 to the outbreak of World War I. A work of depth and scholarship. The chapter notes are particularly valuable.

Wandruszka, Adam. *The House of Habsburg: Six Hundred Years of a European Dynasty*. Translated by Cathleen Epstein and Hans Epstein. New York: Doubleday, and London: Sidgwick and Jackson, 1964. Gives a valuable overview of the entire dynasty with a brief but incisive treatment of Francis Joseph. The genealogical charts are particularly useful.

Clifton W. Potter, Jr.

CÉSAR FRANCK

Born: December 10, 1822; Liège, Belgium
Died: November 8, 1890; Paris, France
Area of Achievement: Music
Contribution: Franck's mastery of the principles of orchestration and the harmonic theories of the nineteenth century made him the acknowledged leader of French music of the era and one of the world's great composers.

Early Life

César Auguste Franck was the firstborn son of a minor bank official who had come from Aix to settle in Liège in 1817 and had married a German woman in 1820. Nicholas-Joseph, the father, was an ambitious, frustrated man. Himself a lover of music and amateur musician, he curried the favor of the writers and artists of Liège and transferred his thwarted ambition for fame and fortune onto César, who early displayed musical ability. Nicholas-Joseph arranged a strict schedule for the boy, forcing him to rigorous study of the piano and composition. By the time César was eight years old, the elder Franck enrolled him at the local conservatory, where his musical aptitude gained for him the notice of his teachers.

In 1835, when Franck was thirteen, his father sent him to Paris to study counterpoint and harmony under the most notable music masters of the day. Eager to succeed through the merits of his son, Nicholas-Joseph arranged a number of public concerts at which his young son performed as a prodigy, along with such established musicians as Franz Liszt. At these concerts, Franck played some of his own compositions. Though competent, they were undistinguished.

Realizing that a foreigner had very little chance to make his way into the musical establishment of Paris, Nicholas-Joseph became a naturalized French citizen and won for Franck the right to enroll in the prestigious Paris Conservatory in 1837. Franck's talents were so extraordinary that by the end of the first year he had taken a special first prize for playing a difficult piano piece, astonishing his examiners by transposing the work into another key while sight reading.

For four years the young Franck pursued his studies, especially of the organ, an instrument which was to be a crucial factor in his career. Then—probably at his father's perverse insistence—Franck resigned from the conservatory in 1842. His father had arranged a series of weekly concerts to be held in his own home and Franck obligingly performed, playing some of his own pieces—fantasias, adaptations of tunes from popular light operas, and other theatrical music. He also composed a set of four piano trios (1843), works which brought him some serious attention, but by and large the music of this concert period was more attuned to public taste and personal profit than to serious artistic concerns.

Gradually, Franck grew restive under the despotism of his father. Though he had made a number of artistic friendships through his father's contrivances—people such as Franz Liszt and Hector Berlioz—Franck bridled under his father's overbearing control, which forced him to produce the kind of music which the old man thought would advance his son's, and his own, career.

One such composition was *Ruth* (1846), an oratorio composed from earlier musical jottings. Based on the Old Testament story of Ruth and Boaz, the work comprised fifteen numbers, and when first performed drew a number of serious reviews. Critics noted its simplicity, its almost childlike directness, and though the work was a failure it remains the first major achievement of the composer, one that he would come back to and revise some thirty years later.

Meanwhile, Franck had met and fallen in love with one of his piano pupils, Félicité Saillot-Desmousseaux, whose parents were actors in the Comédie Française. Franck married Saillot in February, 1848. The marriage signaled a formal break with his father; Franck was now on his own.

Retiring from public music, Franck began making his living primarily as a teacher, as accompanist at a conservatory in Orléans and, significantly, as organist at the Church of Saint-Jean-Saint-François-au-Marais and, more important, at the Church of Sainte-Clotilde. These were key events in his artistic career. The modern organ of Franck's time, especially the wonderful instrument at Sainte-Clotilde, was capable of producing a wide range of tones and orchestral coloring and presented Franck with the opportunity of developing a musical technique based on this symphonic capability. For the rest of his life Franck was to dedicate himself to the mastery of the organ, though his duties as church organist kept him, for almost two decades, from creating any music more significant than improvisational pieces and routine liturgical works. Thus, from the late 1840's to the beginning of the Franco-Prussian War in 1870, Franck lived and worked in virtual obscurity.

Life's Work

In retrospect, this obscurity was a period of creative gestation during which Franck worked out his musical ideas. *Six Pièces* (1862) were short, improvisational experiments filled with a majestic tonality and a melodiousness which were to characterize his later masterpieces. Liszt, who was one of Franck's earliest and most important friends, regarded these pieces as worthy of comparison to those of Johann Sebastian Bach.

Meanwhile, the contacts he had made during a thirty-year career as musician, teacher, and minor composer began to bear fruit. Liszt had been playing Franck's 1843 trios in Germany and had gained for the composer some small measure of fame. Additionally, Franck's mastery of the organ now brought him into contact with French musicians who specialized in that instrument. The Franco-Prussian War raised French nationalistic sentiment, so that by late 1871 a group of French composers and musicians organized the National Society of Music. Its purpose was to promote, through concerts, the music of French composers. At fifty, Franck was the oldest in the group, but he was to become one of its most important artists.

The years immediately after Franck's fiftieth birthday were central in his career as a composer. He was appointed professor of the organ at the conservatory in 1872, and though the position did little for him financially it did establish his preeminence and brought his music more serious attention. Parts of his oratorio *Ruth*, which had lain in comparative neglect since the late 1840's, were given fresh performances. Amid such renewed interest in his music, Franck determined to compose an ambitious work.

The work was *Rédemption* (1873), which Franck conceived as a symphonic poem for orchestra and voice. The text is in three parts. Part 1 tells of man's paganism and his expectations of the coming of Christ. Part 2 records man's Christian joy through the centuries, and part 3 laments the Fall of Man and contemplates a second redemption through prayer.

Though the obvious religiosity of the subject deeply appealed to the composer, the work was a resounding failure, not only because of poor copies of the orchestration and bad conducting but also because the piece lacked dramatic tension. Nevertheless, *Rédemption* is important in the Franck canon as a transitional work, particularly the section of symphonic interlude, bearing characteristics of harmony and tonality that distinguish the best of Franck's music.

Despite this setback, however, Franck continued his duties as teacher, establishing a profound influence on the younger generation of French composers and musicians who embraced his ideas of harmony and the relationship of chords and keys. One of his pupils, Vincent d'Indy, a composer in his own right and one of Franck's first biographers, records his famous impression of Franck at the organ, his flowing white hair and whiskers setting off his dark, piercing eyes.

In 1874, Franck first heard the prelude to Richard Wagner's *Tristan und Isolde* and was reassured about his own harmonic techniques. The following year, Franck composed *Les Éolides*, first performed in Paris in 1876. A major orchestral work, this symphonic poem is the first composition which fully integrates structure and tonality, combining lyrical delicacy with structural grace. *Les Éolides* introduced the last phase of Franck's achievement. The work ushered in a period of creative efflorescence that continued unabated until the composer's death some fifteen years later. At the age of fifty-three, when most composers had already completed most of their best work, Franck was just beginning to produce his masterpieces.

Les Béatitudes was completed in 1879 and published the following year. A large-scale oratorio based on Christ's Sermon on the Mount, the work is impressive in its structural integrity and its use of certain keys to denote psychological states. Also in 1879, Franck astonished the musical world with one of his greatest works, *Quintet in F Minor for Piano and Strings*. Filled with dramatic energy and passion, it still retains a formal structure that provides a balance and cohesiveness, making the quintet among the composer's most popular works. Still another oratorio, *Rebecca*, appeared the following year, but it was the two symphonic poems, *Le Chasseur maudit* (1882) and *Les Djinns* (1884), and the *Variations symphoniques* (1885) that finally established Franck as one of France's greatest composers. These works are characterized by a lush harmony within a tightly structured cyclical form, a technique of restating themes and chords as a principle of musical organization.

The awarding of the Legion of Honor to Franck in 1885 was a tribute no less to his achievement as a composer as to his standing as a professor and his character as a man. Such official recognition was thus the culmination of the public's belated acknowledgment. With the *Sonata in A Major for Violin and Piano* (1886), he produced a masterpiece of chamber music—concise, eloquent, and finely structured. It is one of his most popular compositions.

At the height of his creative powers, Franck climaxed his career as a composer in the production of his only symphony, the magnificent *Symphony in D Minor*. For sheer expressiveness, controlled by classical form, and as an example of chromatic richness and harmonic beauty, the symphony ranks as the composer's crowning work. Though it earned for him a mixed reception at its first performance—some of the criticism leveled particularly at the use of the English horn in the first movement—the symphony has never lost its appeal. It is regarded by many as one of the great symphonies of the world.

The *String Quartet in D Major* (1889), his last major composition, is also one of his best. Typical of his greatest work, the quartet is masterfully structured, melodically rich, a superb example of the cyclical form at its most subtle and concise.

In October, 1890, still involved in several projects, Franck caught cold. By November, his condition worsened. Pleurisy developed and he died on November 8.

Summary

Among great composers, César Franck was the least prolific. He contributed only one symphony to the orchestral repertory and only three major works in chamber music. Yet the quality of these compositions assures for Franck a place as the foremost composer of absolute—that is, nonprogrammatic—music in France during the nineteenth century.

Though he wrote numerous choral works throughout his career, his genius was not as a composer for the voice. His oratorios, while creditable, lack the texture of harmonic fullness, even the drama, of his orchestral scores. His opera *Hulda*, written hastily between 1884 and 1886, was never produced during Franck's lifetime; another, "Ghiselle" was never completed. Neither is of any consequence.

Yet in his symphonic poems, his chamber music, and his symphony, Franck led the way among all French composers of the nineteenth century. In a period when French music was dominated by theatrical forms, especially the opera and operetta, Franck looked back to the classical forms of Bach and Ludwig van Beethoven and created works of forceful and melodic character. As a teacher, Franck influenced a generation of French composers who carried their master's dedication to well-designed harmonic structure into the twentieth century.

Bibliography

Davies, Laurence. *César Franck and His Circle.* London: Barrie and Jenkins, and Boston: Houghton Mifflin, 1970. A classic study not only of Franck but also of his influence on the lives and works of his pupils and musical descendants. Such composers as Ernest Chausson, Henri Duparc, and Vincent d'Indy brought to their music the principles of their master, who must thus be considered a precursor of modern music.

Demuth, Norman. *César Franck.* London: Dobson, and New York: Philosophical Library, 1949. A musical study of the composer with copious examples of notation and scoring. Suggests that Franck was a pioneer in the creation of the symphonic poem. A good biography, though rather technical for the lay reader.

Indy, Vincent d'. *César Franck.* Translated by Rosa Newmarch. London: Lane, 1909; New York: Lane, 1910. An important early biography, representing the biased view of one of Franck's pupils. Himself a composer, d'Indy writes reverently of Franck and his music, glorifying the composer in tones amounting almost to deification. Assessments aside, historical details are accurate.

Klopcic, Rok. "Franckly Speaking." *Strad* 108, no. 1289 (September 1997). Examines Franck's sonata for violin and piano.

Jackson, Francis. "Changing Fashions." *Choir and Organ* 2, no. 3 (June 1994). Discusses Franck's compositions for the church, his style, and guidelines for organists.

Ulrich, Homer. *Chamber Music.* 2d ed. New York: Columbia University Press, 1966. A good, brief examination of Franck's chamber works, noting particularly their cyclical form. A basic knowledge of musical composition would help the lay reader to appreciate fully Franck's structural methods.

———. *Symphonic Music, Its Evolution Since the Renaissance.* New York: Columbia University Press, 1952. Views Franck as a late Romanticist and notes his mastery of the cyclical form, with several examples of notation. Interesting reference to Franck's skill as master organist and the effect of such on his orchestral writing.

Vallas, Léon. *César Franck*. Translated by Hubert Foss. London: Harrap, and New York: Oxford University Press, 1951. The avowed purpose of this study is to demythologize the life and work of Franck as established by d'Indy and others. Though accurate, it devotes as much space to Franck's choral music as to his more important orchestral works and is thus somewhat too detailed.

Edward Fiorelli

GOTTLOB FREGE

Born: November 8, 1848; Wismar
Died: July 26, 1925; Bad Kleinen, Germany
Area of Achievement: Mathematics
Contribution: Frege is the founder of modern symbolic logic and the creator of the first system of notations and quantifiers of modern logic.

Early Life

Friedrich Ludwig Gottlob Frege was the son of the principal of a private, girls' high school. While Frege was in high school in Wismar, his father died. Frege was devoted to his mother, who was a teacher and later principal of the girls' school. He may have had a brother, Arnold Frege, who was born in Wismar in 1852. Nothing further is known about Frege until he entered the university at the age of twenty-one. From 1869 to 1871, he attended the University of Jena and proceeded to the University of Göttingen, where he took courses in mathematics, physics, chemistry, and philosophy. By 1873, Frege had completed his thesis and had received his doctorate from the university. Frege returned to the University of Jena and applied for an unsalaried position. His mother wrote to the university that she would support him until he acquired regular employment. In 1874, as a result of publication of his dissertation on mathematical functions, he was placed on the staff of the university. He spent the rest of his life at Jena, where he investigated the foundations of mathematics and produced seminal works in logic.

Frege's early years at Jena were probably the happiest period in his life. He was highly regarded by the faculty and attracted some of the best students in mathematics. During these years, he taught an extra load as he assumed the courses of a professor who had become ill. He also worked on a volume on logic and mathematics. Frege's lectures were thoughtful and clearly organized, and were greatly appreciated by his students. Much of Frege's personal life, however, was beset by tragedies. Not only did his father die while he was a young man but also his children died young, as did his wife. He dedicated twenty-five years to developing a formal system, in which all of mathematics could be derived from logic, only to learn that a fatal paradox destroyed the system. During his life, he received little formal recognition of his monumental work and, with his death in 1925, passed virtually unnoticed by the academic world.

Life's Work

Frege's first major work in logic was published in 1879. Although this was a short book of only eighty-eight pages, it has remained one of the most important single works ever written in the field. *Begriffsschrift: Eine der Arithmetischen Nachgebildete Formelsprache des reinen Denkens* (conceptual treatise: a formula language, modeled upon that of arithmetic, for pure thought) presented for the first time a formal system of modern logic. He created a system of formal symbols that could be used more regularly than ordinary language for the purposes of deductive logic. Frege was by no means the first person to use symbols as representations of words, since Aristotle had used this device and was followed by others throughout the history of deductive logic.

Earlier logicians, however, had thought that in order to make a judgment on the validity of sentences, a distinction was necessary between subject and predicate. For the purposes of rhetoric, there is a difference between the statements "The North defeated the South in the Civil War" and "The South was defeated by the North in the Civil War." For Frege, however, the content of both sentences conveyed the same concept and hence must be given the same judgment. In this work, Frege achieved the ideal of nineteenth century mathematics: that if proofs were completely formal and no intuition was required to judge the correctness of the proofs, then there could be complete certainty that these proofs were the result of explicitly stated assumptions. During this period, Frege began to use universal quantifiers in his logic, which cover statements that contain "some" or "every." Consequently, it was now possible to cover a range of objects rather than a single object in a statement.

In 1884, Frege published *Die Grundlagen der Arithmetik* (*The Foundations of Arithmetic*, 1950), which followed his attempt to apply similar principles to arithmetic as his earlier application to logic. In this work, he first reviewed the works of his predecessors and then raised a number of fundamental questions on the nature of numbers and arithmetic truth. This work was more philosophical than mathematical. Throughout the work, Frege enunciated three basic positions concerning the world of philosophical logic: Mental images of a word as perceived by the speaker are irrelevant to the meaning of a word in a sentence in terms of its truth or falsity. The word "grass" in the sentence "the grass is green" does not depend on the mental image of "grass" but on the way in which the word is used in the sentence. Thus the meaning of a word was found in its usage. A second idea was that words only have meaning in the context of a sentence. Rather than depending on the precise definition of a word, the sentence determined the truth-value of the word. If "all grubs are green," then it is possible to understand this sentence without necessarily knowing anything about "grubs." Also, it is possible to make a judgment about a sentence that contains "blue grubs" as false, since "all grubs are green." His third idea deals with the distinction between concepts and objects. This distinction raises serious questions concerning the nature of proper names, identity, universals, and predicates, all of which were historically troublesome philosophical and linguistic problems.

After the publication of *The Foundations of Arithmetic* Frege became known not only as a logician and a mathematician but also as a linguistic philosopher. While the notion of proper name is important for his system of logic, it also extends far beyond those concerns. There had existed an extended debate as to whether numbers such as "1,2,3, . . ." or directions such as "north" were proper names. Frege argued that it was not appropriate to determine what can be known about these words and then see if they can be classified as objects. Rather, like his theory of meaning, in which the meaning of a word is determined by its use in a sentence, if numbers are used as objects they are proper names.

His insistence on the usage of words extended to the problem of universals. According to tradition, something which can be named is a particular, while a universal is predicated of a particular. For example, "red rose" is composed of a universal "red" and a particular "rose." Question arose as to whether universals existed in the sense that the "red" of the "red rose" existed independently of the "rose." Frege had suggested that universals are used as proper names in such sentences as "The rose is red."

Between 1893 and 1903, Frege published two volumes of his unfinished work *Grundgesetze der Arithmetik* (the basic laws of arithmetic). These volumes contained both his greatest contribution to philosophy and logic and the greatest weaknesses of his logical system. Frege made a distinction between sense and reference, in that words frequently had the same reference, but may imply a different sense. Words such as "lad," "boy," and "youth" all have the same reference or meaning, but not in the same sense. As a result, two statements may be logically identical, yet have a different sense. Hence, $2 + 2 = 4$ involves two proper names of a number, namely "$2 + 2$" and "4," but are used in different senses. Extending this idea to a logical system, the meaning or reference of the proper names and the truth-value of the sentence depend only on the reference of the object and not its sense. Thus, a sentence such as "The boy wore a hat" is identical to the sentence "The lad wore a hat." Since the logical truth-value of a sentence depends on the meaning of the sentence, the inclusion of a sentence without any meaning within a complex statement means that the entire statement lacks any truth-value. This proved to be a problem that Frege could not resolve and became a roadblock to his later work.

A further problem which existed in *Grundgesetze der Arithmetik*, which was written as a formal system of logic including the use of terms, symbols, and derived proofs, was the theory of classes. Frege wanted to use logic to derive the entire structure of mathematics to include all real numbers. To achieve this, Frege included, as part of his axioms, a primitive theory of sets or classes. While the second volume of *Grundgesetze der Arithmetik* was being prepared for publication, he received a letter from Bertrand Russell describing a contradiction that became known as the Russell Paradox. This paradox, sometimes known as the Stranger Loop, asks, Is "the class of all classes that are not members of itself" a member of itself or not? For example, the "class of all dogs" is not a dog; the "class of all animals" is not an animal. If the class of all classes is a member of itself, then it is one of those classes that are not members of themselves. Yet if it is not a member of itself, then it must be a member of all classes that are members of themselves, and the loop goes on forever. Frege replaced the class axiom with a modified and weaker axiom, but his formal system was weakened, and he never completed the third volume of the work.

Between 1904 and 1917, Frege added few contributions to his earlier works. During these years, he attempted to work through those contradictions which arose in his attempt to derive all of mathematics from logic. By 1918, he had begun to write a new book on logic, but he completed only three chapters. In 1923, he seemed to have broken through his intellectual dilemma and no longer believed that it was possible to create a foundation of mathematics based on logic. He began work in a new direction, beginning with geometry, but completed little of this work before his death.

Summary

In *Begriffsschrift*, Gottlob Frege created the first comprehensive system of formal logic since the ancient Greeks. He provided some of the foundations of modern logic with the formulation of the principles of noncontradiction and excluded middle. Equally important, Frege introduced the use of quantifiers to bind variables, which distinguished modern symbolic logic from earlier systems.

Frege's works were never widely read or appreciated. His system of symbols and functions were forbidding even to the best minds in mathematics. Russell, however, made a careful study of Frege and was clearly influenced by his system of logic. Also, Ludwig Wittgenstein incorporated a number of Frege's linguistic ideas, such as the use of ordinary language, into his works. Frege's distinction between sense and reference later generated a renewed interest in his work, and a number of important philosophical and linguistic studies are based on his original research.

Bibliography

Bynum, Terrell W. Introduction to *Conceptual Notation*, by Gottlob Frege. Oxford: Clarendon Press, 1972. An eighty-page introduction to the logic of Frege. While sections of the text on the logic are not suited for the general reader, the introductory text is clear, concise, and highly accessible. The significant works by Frege are outlined in simple terms, and the commentary is useful.

Carl, Wolfgang. *Frege's Theory of Sense and Reference: Its Origins and Scope.* Cambridge and New York: Cambridge University Press, 1994. Wolfgang discusses Frege's philosophy in a new and systematic way.

Currie, Gregory. *Frege: An Introduction to His Philosophy.* Brighton: Harvester Press, and Totowa, N.J.: Barnes and Noble, 1982. Discusses all the major developments in Frege's thought from a background chapter to the *Begriffsschrift*, theory of numbers, philosophical logic and methods, basic law, and the fatal paradox. Some parts of this text are accessible to the general reader; other parts require a deeper understanding of philosophical issues.

Dummett, Michael A. E. *Frege: Philosophy of Language.* 2d ed. London: Duckworth, and Cambridge, Mass.: Harvard University Press, 1973. One of the leading authorities on the philosophy of Frege. The advantage of this text over others is that Dummett is in part responsible for the idea that Frege is a linguistic philosopher. Somewhat difficult but good introduction to Frege.

Grossmann, Reinhardt. *Reflections on Frege's Philosophy.* Evanston, Ill.: Northwestern University Press, 1969. Delineates three major areas of Frege's thoughts as found in *Begriffsschrift* and *The Foundations of Arithmetic*, and describes the distinction between meaning, sense, and reference. Within these areas the author writes an exposition on a few selected problems which are of current interest.

Hill, Claire O. *Rethinking Identity and Metaphysics: The Foundations of Analytic Philosophy.* New Haven, Conn.: Yale University Press, 1997. The author provides a reassessment of the bases of twentieth century analytic philosophy through examination of the writings of Frege, Bertrand Russell, and Willard Quine. Hill's conclusions show how the lack of clarity inherent in the abstract issue of identity has implications for solid subjects such as medical ethics.

Kneale, William, and Martha Kneale. *The Development of Logic.* Oxford: Clarendon Press, 1962. Three chapters in this work are very useful. Chapter 7 covers Frege and his contemporaries, Frege's criticism of his predecessors, and Frege's definition of natural numbers. Chapter 8 covers Frege's three major works and outlines his contributions to the world of logic. Chapter 9 covers formal developments in logic after Frege and reveals his pivotal position in the development of modern symbolic logic.

Victor W. Chen

JOHN C. FRÉMONT

Born: January 21, 1813; Savannah, Georgia
Died: July 13, 1890; New York, New York
Areas of Achievement: Exploration and politics
Contribution: John C. Frémont's exploits as an explorer helped to propel the American people westward toward Oregon and California. When the continental nation he helped to create was faced with civil war, he fought to maintain the Union and end slavery.

Early Life

When John Charles Frémont was born on January 21, 1813 in Savannah, Georgia, his parents were not married. In 1811, Ann Beverly Whiting had left her elderly husband John Pryor to run away with Charles Frémon, a young French emigrant who taught dancing and French. For several years the struggling Frémon family traveled the South, but after the father died they settled in Charleston, South Carolina, where John Charles grew to maturity.

At age fourteen, Frémont clerked in the law office of John W. Mitchell, who soon sent the young man to Dr. John Roberton's academy. In 1829, Frémont entered the junior class of the College of Charleston. Showing promise, he nevertheless fell behind in his studies from a lack of diligence as well as the distraction of a young love. In 1831, the faculty reluctantly dismissed him for "incorrigible negligence," three months short of his graduation.

In 1833, saved from obscurity by Joel Poinsett, former minister to Mexico, Frémont taught mathematics on the USS *Natchez* on a South American cruise and then earned an appointment in 1835 as professor of mathematics in the navy. He nevertheless declined this position to join Captain William G. Williams in surveying part of a proposed railroad route from Charleston to Cincinnati. This first assignment earned for him a second as Williams' assistant in 1836-1837, surveying the lands of the Cherokee Indians in Georgia. Frémont showed little concern for the forced removal of the Cherokees across the Mississippi, but he did discover a longing to pursue a life in unexplored lands.

With the help of Secretary of War Poinsett, Frémont was assigned in 1838 to assist Joseph Nicolas Nicollet, a respected French scientist mapping the region between the Mississippi and Missouri rivers. He was commissioned a second lieutenant in the United States Topographical Corps and from Nicollet received valuable experience in frontier survival, as well as rigorous training in mapmaking and scientific observation. As Nicollet's protégé, Frémont stood ready to replace the gravely ill scientist on future missions.

Bright and inquisitive, Frémont already possessed the knowledge of surveying, mathematics, and natural sciences, as well as the impulsiveness, that would shape his later career. Bearded and slightly but sturdily built, he was able to endure great physical and personal hardships. His dark hair, olive skin, and piercing blue eyes attracted the friendship and affection of men and women alike. In 1841, he won the lifelong admiration and love of the young and talented Jessie Benton, acquiring not only a bride but also another powerful benefactor in her father, Senator Thomas Hart Benton of Missouri.

Life's Work

Frémont received his first independent assignment in 1841 to survey the Des Moines River region. On his return, he secretly married Jessie, soon benefitting from his family connection with Senator Benton: Advocates of American expansion, led by Benton, were eager to encourage emigration to the Oregon country, and Frémont was thus given command of his first western expedition, assigned to examine part of the trail to Oregon while gathering information useful to emigrants and the government.

In Missouri, Frémont enlisted Kit Carson as his guide and set off from the Kansas River in June, 1842. Following the Platte to the Sweetwater River, he went on to cross the Rocky Mountains at South Pass in Wyoming, later describing the route as no more difficult than the ascent up Capitol Hill. He then explored the headwaters of the Green River in the Wind River Range, unfurling an American flag atop one of its loftiest peaks. Returning, Frémont led six men in a collapsible boat down the Platte. When the current became swift and dangerous, he rashly decided to run the rapids, resulting in an accident that destroyed much of his equipment and part of the expedition's records.

Frémont's second expedition of 1843-1844 was more ambitious. With a large, well-equipped party (including an unauthorized howitzer cannon), he was to complete his survey of the overland trail all the way to Oregon. Setting off in May, the explorer first sought a new pass through the Colorado mountains but soon rejoined the Oregon Trail. Crossing at South Pass, he pushed on to the British forts in the Oregon country, finally reaching Fort Vancouver on the Columbia. On this expedition, Frémont made the first scientific investigation of the Great Salt Lake; his reports inspired Brigham Young to lead his Mormon followers to settle there and make the region bloom, as Frémont had predicted.

From Oregon, Frémont embarked on a perilous journey southward, exploring and naming the Great Basin and then attempting a risky winter crossing of the Sierra Nevada into California, successfully leading his men to Sutter's Fort in the Sacramento Valley. Inspired in part by American interest in the Mexican province of California, Frémont's adventures intensified American passions to possess this valuable Pacific prize. Returning via the old Spanish Trail, Utah Lake, and Bent's Fort on the Arkansas River, Frémont emerged in August, 1844, a national celebrity.

With Jessie's valuable help, Frémont prepared reports of his first and second expeditions that captured the excitement and promise of the new land. Congress ordered the reports published for public distribution, providing emigrants a guide for western travel. The popular reports helped to dispel the notion that the Plains region was an arid wasteland, showed the Oregon Trail passable, and praised the fertile valleys of Oregon and California.

With a well-armed party of sixty men, the brevet captain's third expedition would place him in California just as relations with Mexico worsened. Starting in June, 1845, the party followed the Arkansas and then crossed the central Colorado Rockies. Frémont paused to examine further the Great Salt Lake, then led his party across the desert to the west. While the main party followed a safer route, Frémont led a smaller group directly across the Great Basin and then attempted another winter crossing of the Sierra. Encountering less difficulty than on the previous trip, he arrived once again at Sutter's Fort, eager to play a role in California's future.

Frémont's formidable force earned the suspicion of Mexican officials, who ordered the party to leave the province. Although war with Mexico was months away, Frémont defied the order, raised the American flag, and prepared for a confrontation. When none developed, he slowly moved toward Oregon but retraced his steps after

the arrival of a messenger from Washington. Marine Lieutenant Archibald Gillespie had carried important dispatches to Consul Thomas O. Larkin at Monterey, directing him to conciliate the native Californians to accept American rule. Gillespie repeated these instructions to Frémont and relayed news of trouble with Mexico. Frémont misinterpreted the government's instructions to mean that he should return to California and act to protect American interests there. After a bloody clash with Indians, he returned to the Sacramento Valley, assuming command of the "Bear Flag" revolt of American settlers in June, 1846.

Frémont's actions secured northern California for the United States, but were contrary to the government's wishes to win the province peacefully with the aid of its citizens. Once hostilities with Mexico began, American naval forces seized the ports of Monterey and San Francisco in July, 1846. Frémont's frontiersmen and settlers then formed the "California Battalion" to assist Commodore Robert F. Stockton in securing southern California. San Diego and Los Angeles were quickly occupied, but a revolt by Californians forced the Americans to retake the south. Assembling a large force in the north, Frémont arrived too late to join in the battle for Los Angeles, but he did accept (without authority) the Californians' surrender at Cahuenga.

In January, 1847, Stockton appointed Frémont governor of California. This position embroiled the current lieutenant colonel in a bitter dispute over proper authority between the Commodore and General Stephen Watts Kearny, who had arrived from Santa Fe only to be bloodied by Californians at San Pasqual. As governor in Los Angeles, Frémont recognized Commodore Stockton's authority while unwisely resisting General Kearny's commands, resulting in his arrest and return east virtually a prisoner. In a celebrated court-martial defense, he won public sympathy, but in January, 1848, was found guilty of mutiny, disobedience, and conduct prejudicial to military order. He was sentenced to dismissal from the service. President James K. Polk disallowed the mutiny conviction but upheld the lesser charges while suspending the punishment. Frémont spurned Polk's gesture and resigned his commission instead, ending his career as an explorer for the United States Army.

To regain his injured honor, Frémont organized a privately funded fourth expedition in late 1848. Intended to locate suitable passes for a central railroad route to the Pacific, the expedition attempted

a midwinter passage of the severe San Juan Mountains in southern Colorado. Disregarding the advice of mountain men and perhaps misled by his guide "Old Bill" Williams, Frémont plunged into the snowy mountains, only to find disaster. Cold and starvation eventually took the lives of ten of his thirty-three men, while a few survivors may have resorted to cannibalism. Frémont withdrew to Taos, New Mexico, sending a relief party to his surviving men. With a smaller party, he pushed on to California by the Gila River route, arriving in early 1849.

Frémont's fortunes revived once more as gold had just been discovered in California. In 1847, he had directed Consul Larkin to buy a tract of land near San Francisco; instead Larkin had secured a large grant in the interior. At first apparently worthless, the Mariposa grant yielded immense wealth in gold and became the Frémonts' California home. Then in December, 1849, Frémont was selected one of California's first United States senators, serving a short term from 1850 to 1851 as an antislavery Democrat.

Not chosen to lead one of the five government parties surveying the best route for a Pacific railroad, Frémont in late 1853 undertook his fifth and final expedition to prove the superiority of a central route. On this venture, Frémont found less hardship in attempting another winter crossing of the Colorado mountains. Crossing into Utah, however, his men were again on the brink of starvation, whereupon he swore them not to resort to cannibalism. The party was finally saved in February, 1854, when it arrived at a Mormon settlement in Parowan. The route was not adopted for the Pacific railroad.

As tension grew between North and South, Frémont emerged as a candidate for president in 1856, first for the Democratic party and then for the newly organized Republican party. Hostile to slavery, he favored the Republican position, opposing slavery's westward expansion, and in June, 1856, accepted the first presidential nomination of the young party. In the general election he faced both Democrat James Buchanan and the candidate of the Know-Nothing Party, Millard Fillmore. The "Pathfinder" made few campaign utterances, but his illegitimate origins and false campaign charges that he was a Catholic virtually overshadowed his opposition to the spread of slavery to Kansas. While he carried eleven free states, lack of campaign organization and money in critical states such as Pennsylvania and Indiana probably cost

him the election. Perhaps Frémont was not the best man to lead his nation in time of crisis, but his popularity helped to establish the Republican party and thus contributed to the election of Abraham Lincoln four years later.

After his disappointing defeat, Frémont temporarily retired to private life, absorbed in developing the Mariposa, by now encumbered with debt. When the Civil War erupted in April, 1861, he was in Europe on business. Born a Southerner, he did not hesitate to support the Union in its greatest crisis. On his own authority he purchased arms and ammunition for the Union in England and France, and then returned home to accept an appointment as a major general commanding the Western Department based in St. Louis.

Beginning in July, 1861, Frémont's challenging task was to pacify the divided state of Missouri while raising an army to undertake an offensive down the Mississippi. He received little support from Washington, and his duties were overwhelming. While he reinforced the strategic Illinois town of Cairo, he did not act quickly enough to aid Nathaniel Lyon, who was defeated and killed at Wilson's Creek on August 10. Charges of favoritism and corruption in government contracts haunted Frémont's command, but most controversial was his sudden order of August 30 declaring martial law in Missouri, threatening to shoot captured guerrillas, and freeing the slaves of rebel masters.

While antislavery advocates praised Frémont's emancipation edict, Lincoln feared its effect on the border states and directed him to modify the order. The general stubbornly refused to heed Lincoln, forcing the president to reverse the measure publicly. With Frémont's command assaulted by powerful political enemies, Jessie went east to present his case, but her stormy interview with Lincoln did more harm than good. As Frémont sought to lead his troops to victory in southwestern Missouri, Lincoln removed him from command of the Western Department in November, 1861.

Outcry over Frémont's removal induced Lincoln to appoint him in March, 1862, to command the newly formed Mountain Department, designed to capture an important railroad at Knoxville, Tennessee. Abandoning this effort, Frémont was also outmarched by Stonewall Jackson in the Virginia Valley Campaign of 1862. At the battle of Cross Keys on June 8, Frémont proved ineffective against Confederate troops, and when Lincoln added Frémont's force to the command of John Pope, Frémont asked to be relieved. In 1864, Frémont was nominated to the presidency by some Democrats and radical Republicans dissatisfied with Lincoln. At first accepting the nomination, he soon feared a Democratic victory and withdrew from the race, helping to ensure Lincoln's reelection.

As the war came to an end, Frémont lost much of his wealth as well as control of his beloved Mariposa. His ambitions turned to railroad finance, as he still hoped to realize his dream of a Pacific railroad. He became involved with unscrupulous business associates, however, squandering the remainder of his fortune and a good portion of his reputation when the Southwest Pacific failed in 1867 and the Memphis & El Paso did so in 1870.

From 1878 to 1883, Frémont served as governor of Arizona Territory. With Jessie's help he wrote his memoirs, published in 1887. Belated gratitude from his nation came in April, 1890, when he was restored to his rank as major general and placed on the retired list with pay. Death came in New York in July, 1890, from a sudden attack of peritonitis.

Summary

Frémont's exploits as an explorer exemplified the restless energy and unbounded ambition of mid-nineteenth century America. Proud and self-reliant, Americans resented restraints and the rulings of authority. Frémont's career also reflected the lack of discipline and wisdom born of experience that led the young and sometimes careless American people into such tragedies as the brutal treatment of American Indians, the war on Mexico, and the spilling of brothers' blood in the Civil War. Like his nation, Frémont climbed heights of adventure and opportunity, but also found failure, conflict, and injustice.

Frémont never claimed to be a "Pathfinder"; his mapping expeditions usually followed paths already worn by fur traders and early emigrants. Yet his romantic journeys spurred American expansion to the Pacific, his reports encouraging western emigration while providing travelers with useful information. Frémont's mapping and scientific work rivaled that of earlier explorers, improving knowledge of the vast interior region from the Rockies to the Sierra, while helping to clarify the true natures of the Continental Divide and the Great Basin.

As politician, soldier, and financier, Frémont found less glory. His unauthorized actions in the California revolt remain controversial, while his service during the Civil War provoked charges of political opportunism and military ineffectiveness.

His mining and railroad schemes typified the boom period of American industrial expansion, but left him almost destitute. His death in 1890 coincided with the end of the romantic age of the American West, where he left his name and his mark.

Bibliography

Allen, John Logan. "Division of the Waters: Changing Concepts of the Continental Divide, 1804-44." *Journal of Historical Geography* 4 (October 1978): 357-370. This article helps to clarify Frémont's contributions to geographical knowledge of the American interior.

Canfield, J. Douglas. "Kit Carson, John C. Frémont, Manifest Destiny, and the Indians: or, Oliver North Abets Lawrence of Arabia." *American Indian Culture and Research Journal* 21, no. 1 (Winter 1998). Discusses changes in the historical views of two "Western heroes," Carson and Frémont.

Dellenbaugh, Frederick S. *Frémont and '49*. New York and London: Putnam, 1914. An old but detailed account primarily of Frémont's expeditions. The author traces the explorer's routes and includes several useful maps.

Egan, Ferol. *Frémont: Explorer for a Restless Nation*. New York: Doubleday, 1977. By focusing on Frémont's career to 1854, this work praises his accomplishments more than most.

Frémont, John Charles. *Memoirs of My Life*. Chicago: Belford, Clarke, 1887. Frémont's own memoirs are the only source for much of the available information on his personal life as well as his career. An intended second volume was not published.

Goodwin, Cardinal L. *John Charles Frémont: An Explanation of His Career*. Stanford, Calif.: Stanford University Press, and London: Oxford University Press, 1930. This is perhaps the most critical account of Frémont's life. It views the explorer as a "drifter" who entered into corrupt financial dealings.

Harlow, Neal. *California Conquered: War and Peace on the Pacific, 1846-1850*. Berkeley: University of California Press, 1982. Much of this work examines Frémont's controversial role in the California conquest. It also discusses his dispute with Kearny and subsequent arrest.

Jackson, Donald, and Mary Lee Spence, eds. *The Expeditions of John Charles Frémont*. 3 vols. Champaign: University of Illinois Press, 1970-1984. This multivolume collection of documents is an invaluable source of information for Frémont's expeditions. It includes his reports, important correspondence, and the record of his court-martial.

Nevins, Allan. *Frémont: Pathmarker of the West.* 2 vols. New York: Ungar, 1961. Perhaps the best study of Frémont, this work by a famous American historian portrays the explorer as a flawed hero of American expansion.

Rolle, Andrew. "Exploring an Explorer: Psychohistory and John Charles Frémont." *Pacific Historical Review* 51 (May 1982): 145-163. This article presents an interesting if speculative psychological interpretation of Frémont's often erratic career.

Volpe, Vernon L. "The Frémonts and Emancipation in Missouri." *Historian* 56, no. 2 (Winter 1994): 339-355. Argues that Fremont deserves more historical recognition for his efforts at social reform, in particular for his order to free slaves held by rebel Missourians which predated that of Lincoln's proclamation.

Vernon L. Volpe

FRIEDRICH FROEBEL

Born: April 21, 1782; Oberweissbach, Thuringia

Died: June 21, 1852; Marienthal, Thuringia

Area of Achievement: Education

Contribution: Froebel founded the first kindergarten. He believed in the underlying unity in nature, for him God, and emphasized that schools should provide pleasant surroundings, encourage self-activity, and offer physical training for children.

Early Life

The unhappiness of Friedrich Wilhelm August Froebel's childhood affected his entire life. Born on April 21, 1782, to Johann Jakob and Eleonore Friderica Froebel, Friedrich was left motherless when he was nine months old. His father, a Lutheran pastor, was aloof and pompous. Upon his second marriage, he lost interest in Friedrich, who was still too young for school. After Johann's wife bore their child, Friedrich was treated like an interloper. His stepmother addressed him in the formal third person rather than in the familiar second person normally used with children.

The father considered his son stupid and rebellious. He conveyed these feelings to Friedrich, who developed a sense of personal unworthiness. When Friedrich began school, his father insisted that he attend the girls' school, making Friedrich feel more unusual than he already considered himself.

When he was ten, Friedrich was sent to live with a kindly uncle in Stadt Ilm, remaining there for five years. On his return home, however, the antagonisms that plagued his earlier days resurfaced, so his father apprenticed him to a woodcutter at Neuhof, the former home of educational reformer Johann Heinrich Pestalozzi, where he stayed for two years.

At seventeen, Friedrich visited his brother, a medical student at the University of Jena. Although he was ill-prepared for the university, Froebel attended elementary lectures in philosophy, the sciences, and mathematics until he was jailed by the university for indebtedness. After his father reluctantly posted his bail, Froebel drifted for five years. After a flirtation with architecture, he turned to tutoring, and found that he loved teaching.

In 1805, Froebel made his first short visit to Yverdon, where Pestalozzi had just established his experimental school. After a brief stay in Frankfurt, he returned to Yverdon to spend four years as an assistant to Pestalozzi. He perceived that Pestalozzi's approach failed both to interconnect the subjects being taught and to give much attention to the students' spiritual connection with the universe. These reservations spurred Froebel into formulating his own philosophy of education.

Life's Work

When Froebel completed his four-year stay at Yverdon in 1810, he returned to Frankfurt as a tutor. He soon decided, however, that he had a dual destiny. On the one hand, he saw himself as a potential educational reformer. On the other, he was trying to find a unity in nature, an explanation of the mysteries of existence. Accordingly, he was enrolled in the University of Göttingen in 1811, first studying ancient languages in his search for the underlying unity in existence. He then turned his attention to mathematics, the sciences, and philosophy, subjects to which he had been exposed at Jena.

In 1812, Froebel moved to the University of Berlin to study crystallography; his interest in this subject was awakened by an essay he had written on the symbolism of spheres the preceding year at Göttingen. By 1813, he was assistant curator at the university's museum of mineralogy. He continued his research in crystals, viewing them always as symbols of an underlying unity.

Although Froebel was offered a teaching position at the University of Berlin in 1816, he believed that his greatest contribution could be made by opening a school. In that year, in a humble cottage not far from Pestalozzi's Neuhof, he founded the Allegemeine Deutsche Erziehungsanstalt (universal German institute of education). The student body consisted of five of Froebel's nephews. His declared purpose was to teach people how to be free, something that he himself was still in the process of learning.

By 1817, the school had grown. Froebel moved it to more imposing quarters in nearby Keilhau. He was soon joined by Wilhelm Middendorff and Heinrich Langethal, friends he had made in 1813 during his brief service in the military. The school almost foundered in 1818 after Froebel's marriage to Wilhelmine Hoffmeister aroused contention in the closely knit school community. The origins of the discord are perhaps attributable to homosexual overtones, overt or covert, in Froebel's relationship with Middendorff and Langethal. One of Froebel's

brothers rescued the school with both funds and a new approach to running its business. The school's enrollment rose to sixty.

As the enterprise succeeded, Froebel became increasingly absolutist, autocratic, and tyrannical. Students began to rebel against him, and word reached public officials that all was not well at the institution. An official investigation cleared the school of the charges against it, but the damage had been done. By 1820, Froebel's influence was minimal, although he was associated with the school until 1831. From the Keilhau experience Froebel wrote *Die Menschenerziehung* (1826; *The Education of Man*, 1885), which details his philosophy of teaching children to age ten.

Essentially, the book is guided more by intuition than reason. It is based on nothing resembling scientific method. Froebel's stated aim is to help his students unlock what is inside them and to find a harmony between their inner selves and the external world, which to Froebel is the entire universe. The approach is mystical and shows Froebel as a deeply religious man who, presuming a divine origin for the universe, proceeds to suggest ways to bring human beings into a balance with that divine, creating force. As Froebel searched for absolutes, his search made him increasingly absolutist.

Froebel believed that everything, no matter how small, has a purpose. His scheme of education was to lead people to discover that purpose. He agreed with Pestalozzi's belief that, because the universe is constantly changing, nothing in life is static. This reasoning led him quite naturally to a dynamic *Weltanschauung*. For Froebel, people are themselves an inherent part of all activity. They can be guided by skillful teachers, but real teaching proceeds only from self-activity. Froebel's conception of human development is not one in which infancy, childhood, youth, and maturity are separate entities, but one in which these stages are entities evolving into subsequent stages of which they are forever parts. Such speculation suggests the taxonomies of such educational theorists as Benjamin S. Bloom and Lawrence Kohlberg and also presages Sigmund Freud.

Froebel, like Jean-Jacques Rousseau, presumed that children are inherently good. He thought that evil resulted from bad education. He considered the ideal educational institution to be the earliest one—the family—at whose heart, he believed, is the mother as chief teacher of the young. Froebel's own education lacked the fundamental ingredient of effective learning—a mother who both loved and taught. Froebel virtually deified mothers, and in so doing, moved in the direction of what was to be his greatest educational contribution, the kindergarten—literally a garden whose blossoms are children. Froebel was rationalizing guilt feelings about what he perceived as his own evil when he wrote that wickedness proceeds from a mother's neglect of her young child.

Froebel left Keilhau in 1831 and went to Switzerland, where he opened a school; he opened a second at Lucerne. Soon, however, he was forced to disband these schools, partly because Lucerne's Catholic populace was suspicious of him and partly because his nephews, his former students at Keilhau, bore him great animosity and did everything they could to discredit him. By 1833, Froebel had developed a plan for the education of Bern's poor, but he had yet to find his real vocation.

In 1835, Froebel was appointed director of the orphanage at Burgdorf, the site of some of Pestalozzi's pre-Yverdon teaching, and he operated the orphanage according to Pestalozzi's methods, training teachers at the orphanage and teaching the children. At Burgdorf, Froebel began to concentrate on the education of young children and especially of those normally considered too young for school. He left Burgdorf in 1836 to go to Berlin, where he studied nursery schools.

In 1837, at the age of fifty-five, Froebel established a school in Blankenburg, not far from Keilhau, for the training of very young children. He called it a *Kleinkinderbeschäftigungsanstalt* (an institution for the occupation of small children), but in 1840 he changed the name to the less cumbersome, more familiar kindergarten. In this school, he instituted his method of teaching through gifts and occupations. Children received, over a period of time, ten boxes of gifts, objects from which they could learn, and they also were assigned ten occupations, activities that would result in their creating gifts.

Part of Froebel's technique was to devise games to interest and actively involve children both physically and mentally. He recorded these techniques in *Die Pädagogik des Kindergartens* (1862; *Friedrich Froebel's Pedagogics of the Kindergarten: Or, His Ideas Concerning the Play and Playthings of the Child*, 1895), published posthumously. His most successful book of that period was *Mutter- und Kose-lieder* (1844; *Mother-Play and Nursery Songs*, 1878), a book containing fifty original songs and finger plays that would help mothers interact with their infants. This book attracted an enthusiastic following.

Successful though Froebel's first kindergarten was in many respects, it fell into debt by 1844, and he had to disband it. People expressed great fears about kindergartens, worrying about the political and religious philosophies to which very young, impressionable children were exposed in Froebel's institution, which enrolled students from ages one through seven. By 1851, the Prussian government had banned kindergartens as threats to society. Meanwhile, Froebel's influential nephews worked hard to discredit him.

On June 21, 1852, a year after he married Luisa Leven, his second wife, who was thirty years his junior, Froebel died at Marienthal, his kindergartens banned in Prussia until 1860.

Summary

Friedrich Froebel's experimental school, the kindergarten, has affected education and society significantly. Froebel had vigorous supporters, among them his widow and the Baroness Berthe von Marenholtz-Bülow, both of whom traveled widely to disseminate his ideas. Indeed, Charles Dickens wrote a favorable account of a kindergarten he had seen.

Mrs. Carl Schurz and her sister, both trained by Froebel, imported the kindergarten to the United States in 1855, establishing a German-language kindergarten in Watertown, Wisconsin. Elizabeth Peabody established the first English-language kindergarten in the United States in Boston in 1860.

The term *kindergarten* has survived in the United States, although it now frequently designates that single year before a child enters the primary grades. The kindergarten as Froebel perceived it now exists in the United States as the preschool, attended by infants of several weeks to children of four or five.

Bibliography

Bock, Gordon. "Twice around the Block." *Old House Journal* 26, no. 5 (September-October 1998). Short presentation of information on Froebel Blocks and Lincoln Logs, children's construction toys.

Downs, Robert B. *Friedrich Froebel*. Boston: Twayne, 1978. An accurate, brief overview of Froebel. Solid presentation of facts, although generally short on analysis. The book serves the basic purpose for which it is intended, that of informing the reading public and college undergraduates.

Froebel, Friedrich. *Autobiography of Friedrich Froebel*. Translated and annotated by Emilie Michaelis and H. Keatley Moore. Syracuse, N.Y.: Bardeen, 1889; London: Sonnenschein, 1903. Froebel's only autobiographical record exists in two long letters, one written to the Duke of Meiningen in 1827, the other to Karl Krause in 1828. These letters, well translated and accurate, along with Johann Barop's notes on the Froebel community, comprise this useful volume. Helpful for biographical details.

Kilpatrick, William H. *Froebel's Kindergarten Principles Critically Examined*. New York: Macmillan, 1916. Despite its age, an indispensable book for Froebel scholarship because it describes how the intractability of the International Kindergartners Association, founded in 1892, eventually clashed with Granville Stanley Hall's more scientifically devised psychological approach to early childhood education. An accurate, objective assessment of an important topic.

Lawrence, Evelyn, ed. *Friedrich Froebel and English Education*. London: University of London

Press, 1952; New York: Philosophical Library, 1953. Six British educators discuss Froebel's influence on the schools of Great Britain and on education in general. A balanced view of Froebel's contributions outside Germany.

Marenholtz-Bülow, Berthe von. *Reminiscences of Friedrich Froebel*. Translated by Mary Mann. Boston: Lee and Shepard, 1895. This book by one of Froebel's former students and staunchest supporters provides important details about his later years, during which he was implementing his concept of the kindergarten.

R. Baird Shuman

MARGARET FULLER

Born: May 23, 1810; Cambridgeport, Massachusetts

Died: July 19, 1850; at sea near Fire Island, New York

Areas of Achievement: Journalism and social reform

Contribution: A pioneering feminist far ahead of her time, Margaret Fuller was a perceptive literary and social critic, and America's first woman foreign journalist.

Early Life

Sarah Margaret Fuller was born on May 23, 1810, in Cambridgeport, Massachusetts, the first of the nine children of Timothy Fuller and Margaret Crane Fuller. Her father, a prominent figure in Massachusetts politics, was a graduate of Harvard College and the absolute authority in his household. Keenly disappointed that his first child was a girl, Timothy Fuller nevertheless determined to educate her according to the classical curriculum of the day—an experience usually afforded only to boys.

Even as a small child, Margaret was directed by her father in a rigorous schedule of study. She learned both English and Latin grammar and, before she was ten years old, read Vergil, Ovid, and Horace as well as Shakespeare. At age fourteen, Margaret went briefly to Miss Prescott's School in Groton but soon returned home to immerse herself again in study. Although Margaret was intellectually developed far beyond her years, the girl's intensity caused trouble in friendships, a pattern that continued throughout her life. Margaret was also uncomfortable with her physical appearance. Therefore, she decided to cultivate her intellect, spending fifteen-hour days reading literature and philosophy in four languages, breaking only for a few hours of music and walking each day.

By the late 1820's, Margaret was forming strong friendships with Harvard students such as James Freeman Clarke and Frederic Henry Hedge, many of whom would later become involved, as she did, with the Transcendentalist movement. She was becoming known in intellectual society in Cambridge and at Harvard as a formidable conversationalist. The same determination that brought her such success, however, also brought criticism. Margaret tended toward sarcasm, offending even close friends in intellectual discussions, and the great de-mands that she placed upon herself she also placed upon others.

In 1833, Timothy Fuller moved his family to a farm in Groton. Margaret taught her younger siblings and, when her mother's health declined, took over the household. She continued to read, particularly German literature and philosophy, but her life at that time was a strain. Early in 1835, Margaret fell seriously ill, then recovered; in October of that year, her father died.

At this turning point, Margaret's future seemed uncertain and difficult. She had planned a European trip to expand her horizons but had to cancel it in order to support the family. After a three-week visit at the home of Ralph Waldo Emerson (a Transcendentalist and a literary figure) in Concord, she decided to take a teaching position at Bronson Alcott's experimental Temple School in Boston. In 1837, Margaret accepted a teaching position in Hiram Fuller's (no relation) Greene Street School in Providence, Rhode Island.

During her two years in Providence, Fuller also continued her scholarly work—often at the expense of her health—translating Johann P. Eckermann's *Conversation with Goethe*, for example, and publishing poems and international literature reviews in a liberal, Unitarian journal edited by James Freeman Clarke. In addition, she wrote her first piece of important criticism, which was published a year later in the first issue of the Transcendentalist publication the *Dial*. Although Margaret was a successful teacher, she missed the intellectual stimulation of Boston, so in 1839 she moved back to Jamaica Plain, a Boston suburb, where she was joined by her mother and younger siblings.

Life's Work

When Margaret Fuller moved back to Boston, her involvement with Transcendentalism (which began when she met Emerson in 1836) increased. As a movement, Transcendentalism focused around a common perspective on religion and philosophy rather than any particular doctrine, and intellectuals met regularly for discussion about the nature of freedom and spirit. In 1840, Fuller became the first editor of the Transcendentalist literary quarterly the *Dial*. She also wrote much of the copy and kept the periodical alive—almost single-handedly—until she resigned her editorship two years later.

Fuller supported herself during this time by conducting "Conversations," highly successful weekly discussions attended by the society women of Boston. Fuller believed that women were not taught how to think, and she determined to remedy this with discussions of topics from Greek mythology to ethics to women's rights. Through these "Conversations," which continued until she moved to New York in 1844, Fuller became known as a powerful speaker and intellectual critic. During this time, she was also involved with Brook Farm, a Transcendentalist experiment in the nature of ideal community that began in 1841 (she did not actually live there).

Fuller was frequently Emerson's houseguest in Concord. She said of Emerson, "From him I first learned what is meant by the inward life." They had a strong friendship, and through their discussions, both were able to develop their knowledge and appreciation of literature. The friendship was complex, however, and Fuller and Emerson were not always comfortable in each other's presence, much less with each other's ideas.

During this period, Fuller traveled outside the boundaries of New England. Her journey to the Midwest is recorded in Fuller's first book, *Summer on the Lake* (1843), in which she investigated the relationship between nature and society, focusing on people and social manners. While conducting research for this book, Fuller became the first woman to receive permission to enter the library at Harvard University. The book also brought Fuller to the attention of Horace Greeley, editor of the *New York Tribune*. He invited her to become the newspaper's literary critic, and—against the advice of friends such as Emerson—Fuller accepted. In December, 1844, she moved to New York, leaving the constraints of family and friends behind, to become the first female member of the working press in the United States.

Horace Greeley said that Fuller was, in some respects, the greatest woman America had yet known, and he gave her almost a free hand with her writing. Fuller's style became more solid, and her thinking deepened even further as she wrote regularly on major authors and ideas of her time. While at the *Tribune*, Fuller also became concerned about public education and social conditions. She visited prisons, poorhouses, and asylums, and her front-page articles about them moved people's feelings and laid the foundation for reforms.

In 1845, Greeley published Fuller's *Women in the Nineteenth Century*, the first American book-length discussion of equal rights for men and women. The book became a public sensation and made Fuller's name known throughout the English-speaking world. A classic in American feminist literature, it combined the spiritual focus of a transcendental vision with the need for practical action and was influential in the Seneca Falls conference on women's rights in 1848. In 1846, Fuller published *Papers on Literature and Art*, a compilation of her critical reviews which set a high standard for American literary criticism.

The strain of writing on deadline made Fuller's chronic headaches worse, however, and she was also trying to recover from a broken romance. In August, 1846, Greeley commissioned her as America's first foreign correspondent, and she visited first England, then France, and finally Rome, in April, 1847. Everywhere she went, Fuller met with major figures of the time and sent dispatches back to the *Tribune*. Fuller was disturbed by the misery that she saw around her, particularly that of working-class women. More and more, life—not art—became her preoccupation, and Fuller's articles on the common worker appeared prominently in the *Tribune*.

In the summer of 1847, Fuller made an extended tour of Italy. She was drawn into the Italian struggle for independence, and in the course of her travels she met Giovanni Angelo Ossoli, a young Italian count who was committed to the liberal cause. Ossoli and Fuller became lovers and, it seems, planned for a life together. Because Ossoli would have been disowned by his aristocratic family for marrying a non-Italian and a non-Catholic, however, the marriage was delayed for more than a year.

Ossoli and Fuller spent the winter of 1848 involved in the Republican struggle in Rome. Fuller continued to send detailed articles about the revolution to the *Tribune*, but she kept her relationship with Ossoli a secret for a long time, even from family and friends in America. Fuller was expecting a child, so she moved to Rieti, outside Rome, where she gave birth to a son, Angelo, on September 5, 1848. Fuller stayed with the child until April, then left him with a nurse and returned to Ossoli and the fighting in Rome, where she directed an emergency hospital and ran supplies to her husband's fighting unit. When the Italian liberals were finally defeated in July, 1849, Ossoli and Fuller were forced to leave Rome. They took Angelo and fled to Florence, where Fuller wrote what she thought was the most important work she had done to date: a history of the Italian Revolution.

Fuller wanted to publish the manuscript in the United States, so the family set sail for New York City on May 17, 1850, despite Fuller's deep foreboding about the journey. Difficulties started soon after they set sail: The ship's captain died of smallpox; then Angelo became sick with the disease, and he almost died. On July 17, just after land was sighted, a storm came up and the inexperienced captain ran the ship aground near Fire Island, New York. Whenever the storm abated, people tried to swim to shore, only a few hundred feet away, but Fuller resigned herself to death and refused to leave the ship. She eventually allowed a sailor to try to save the baby, but Fuller and her husband stayed on board as the ship was pulled apart by the sea. Angelo's body finally washed ashore, but Fuller, Ossoli, and Fuller's manuscript were never found.

Summary

Those who remember Margaret Fuller most often do so within the context of her association with New England Transcendentalism, but her most significant contributions were in the areas of literary criticism and social reform. Despite the fact that her own writing style was inconsistent, Fuller is nevertheless considered to be one of the two real literary critics of the nineteenth century, along with Edgar Allan Poe. She developed a theory of criticism that combined perspectives of realism and romanticism, and she held to high standards that did not fluctuate with the prevailing winds of the times.

Fuller was also a pioneering journalist and perceptive social critic on both the national and the international level. In *Tribune* columns, her commentary on public education and social conditions looked deeply into American values. She visited and wrote about Sing Sing and Blackwell's Island prisons, for example, which led to the establishment of the first halfway house for newly released female convicts. Her dispatches from Europe—especially her account of the Italian revolution—helped Americans grow in their understanding of the world around them.

Although Fuller did find fulfillment as a wife and mother, her powerful character was not circumscribed by these traditional female roles. In her behavior, Fuller questioned economic, social, and political assumptions about women; in her writing, she propagated her belief in equality through. Her major work, *Women in the Nineteenth Century* (1845), is generally considered to be the first important feminist work by an American woman.

Fuller fascinated the readers of her day and challenged their ideas about what a woman could and should be. More than a century later, her argument that people should be able to express themselves as individuals, not simply as representatives of their gender, continues to offer insights into the unlimited potential of human nature.

Bibliography

Allen, Margaret Vanderhaar. *The Achievement of Margaret Fuller.* University Park: Pennsylvania State University Press, 1979. This biography presents probably the most strikingly feminist perspective on Fuller's life and work. Allen concludes that Fuller was easily the equal of Emerson and Thoreau.

Blanchard, Paula. *Margaret Fuller: From Transcendentalism to Revolution.* New York: Delacorte Press, 1978. This biography is written from a clearly feminist perspective, though with a more subtle voice than Margaret Allen's. It has helped to make Fuller more accessible to the general reading public.

Capper, Charles. *Margaret Fuller: An American Romantic Life: The Private Years.* New York and Oxford: Oxford University Press, 1992. The first of a two-part biography, this stunning narrative is the first to deal comprehensively with Fuller's identity as a female intellectual, the primary issue in her life. Based on sources, many of which have never before been used, this volume covers her early years and her beginnings as an American prophet/critic.

Chevigny, Bell Gale, comp. *The Woman and the Myth: Margaret Fuller's Life and Writings.* Old Westbury, N.Y.: Feminist Press, 1976. The major study changed Fuller scholarship in the mid-1970's and is essential reading for anyone who is seriously interested in Fuller.

Edwards, Julia. *Women of the World: The Great Foreign Correspondents.* Boston: Houghton Mifflin, 1988. This work presents a lively and vivid account of Fuller's activities in Europe and quotes liberally from her communiques to the *Tribune.* It gives a real sense of Fuller within the context of the times.

James, Laurie. *Why Margaret Fuller Ossoli Is Forgotten.* New York: Golden Heritage Press, 1988. James, an actress, has done extensive research in preparing her original one-person drama about Fuller, which has toured internationally. In this sixty-five-page book, James presents her thesis that Fuller has been buried in history because the authors of her "definitive" biography *Memoirs of Margaret Fuller Ossoli* (1852) intentionally misrepresented her life and works. James builds quite a case against Ralph Waldo Emerson, William Henry Channing, and James Freeman Clarke. She elaborates further in her *Men, Women, and Margaret Fuller* (1990).

————, ed. *The Wit and Wisdom of Margaret Fuller Ossoli.* New York: Golden Heritage Press, 1988. This selection of quotations is organized around topics such as "love," "equality," "revolution," "toys," and "faith and soul." Fuller's astute, often wry observations have not gone out of date, and the reader can get a real taste of Fuller from this small book. It also includes a list of Fuller's major achievements and a bibliography.

Myerson, Joel, comp. *Critical Essays on Margaret Fuller.* Boston: Hall, 1980. These articles represent Fuller criticism from 1840 to the date of this publication. As Myerson observes, it is obvious that from the start, critics were more interested in Fuller's personality than in her work. The fifty-three mostly short selections make interesting reading.

Myerson, Joel, ed. *Margaret Fuller: An Annotated Bibliography Criticism, 1983-1995.* Westport, Conn.: Greenwood Press, 1998. Often neglected in the past by the scholarly community, studies of Fuller have grown in number recently. Myerson cites several hundred scholarly studies on Fuller published between 1983 and 1995 (with annotations) and includes a comprehensive index and entries for over one hundred works about the author.

Watson, David. *Margaret Fuller: An American Romantic.* Oxford: Berg, and New York: St. Martin's Press, 1988. This is a useful account of Fuller's life, work, and reputation. Watson examines Fuller's roles as romantic, feminist, and socialist, suggesting that she deserves to be taken seriously as a contributor to historically important bodies of thought. Of particular interest is Watson's examination of modern feminist Fuller scholarship. He concludes that modern attempts to "rescue" Fuller do not always escape the myopic traps to which they are opposed. Includes a chronology, an index, and a bibliography.

Jean C. Fulton

ROBERT FULTON

Born: November 14, 1765; Little Britain Township, Pennsylvania

Died: February 24, 1815; New York, New York

Areas of Achievement: Engineering and invention

Contribution: Fulton built the first profitable steamboat, established the traditions that distinguished American steamboats for the remainder of the century, and laid the groundwork for future submarine and torpedo warfare.

Early Life

At the beginning of 1765, Robert Fulton, a successful tailor and leading citizen of Lancaster, Pennsylvania, sold most of his possessions and borrowed money in order to purchase a large farm, thirty miles to the south in Little Britain Township. There, on November 14, 1765, his first son, Robert Fulton, Jr., was born. Nothing else went well for the inexperienced farmer. Six years later, the elder Fulton returned to Lancaster, a bankrupt and dispirited man. He died in 1774, leaving his wife and six children without means of support other than the charity of relatives. Thus, at the age of nine, Robert Fulton learned the meaning of failure and poverty. For the remainder of his life, he struggled to achieve financial success and social status.

With the outbreak of the American Revolution, Lancaster changed from a small, isolated agricultural community to a bustling military and economic center. The population swelled with refugees, soldiers on the march, military prisoners and gunsmiths. As young Fulton's curiosity attracted him to the new inhabitants, his quick intelligence and enthusiasm induced strangers to give time to the dark, handsome boy. Fulton spent an increasing amount of time with the gunsmiths, for whom he made mechanical drawings and painted signs. Perhaps he was having too good a time: His mother apprenticed him to a Philadelphia jeweler.

Little is known about Fulton's Philadelphia years. His master was a former London jeweler named Jeremiah Andrews. Fulton's talent at drawing and painting prepared him to produce miniature portraits on ivory lockets. By 1785, Fulton was listed in a city directory as a "miniature painter." The following year saw Fulton struck with two burdens that characterized the remainder of his life. He borrowed money to help his mother and sisters purchase another farm. At the same time, Fulton was ill with respiratory ailments. Despite his debts, the young man borrowed money and took the waters at Bath, a spa in northern Virginia favored by the upper class. There, Fulton recovered his health and doubtlessly heard about the steamboat experiments of a local man named James Rumsey. Upon his return to Philadelphia, Fulton found another steamboat pioneer, John Fitch, running his strange vessel across the Delaware River. At this time, however, Fulton displayed no interest in steam engines. He was a painter who desired to improve his skills and status. That meant that he, like other American painters before and since, had to work in Great Britain. Thus, in the summer of 1787, Fulton sailed for England. He would be absent from the United States for the next thirteen years.

Thanks to a letter of introduction, Fulton settled in London as a student of Benjamin West, an American painter popular with Britain's upper class. Fulton was not a gifted painter: He was, however, very successful at cultivating wealthy friends and patrons. Thus, Fulton managed to survive for several years as a painter. By the early 1790's, Fulton turned toward machines and canals. He devoted considerable time to studying canals and, in 1796, wrote *Treatise on the Improvement of Canal Navigation.* Many of his ideas were quite dated, but the volume was distinguished by its format. Fulton demonstrated details with excellent drawings, attempted to base designs upon mathematical calculations, and focused all canal features toward the concept of an inexpensive and national transportation system. The book established Fulton as a canal engineer.

Life's Work

With France and Great Britain at war in the mid-1790's, the patents of citizens of one nation were freely copied by the citizens of the other nation. Fulton believed that his canal ideas were valuable and ought to be patented in France. He arrived in France in 1797 and soon abandoned canals. After all, that nation had been building canals for more than a century and had little use for experts who lacked experience. Anyway, Fulton already had a new patron and a new mechanical passion.

Benjamin West had given Fulton an introduction to Joel Barlow, a Yale graduate who was making much money by running American ships through the British blockade and into French ports. Barlow and his wife, Ruth, welcomed Fulton into their Paris residence. The three lived together for the next seven years. The educated Barlow tutored Fulton in science and mathematics, and it was probably Barlow who introduced Fulton to the subject of submarine warfare. Barlow had been at Yale when another student, Robert Bushnell, designed *Turtle*, a submarine that had engaged in unsuccessful attacks upon British warships during the American Revolution. Bushnell, living in seclusion in Georgia, had sent Thomas Jefferson a detailed description of his submarine efforts, and the latter made the material available to Barlow. By the end of 1797, Fulton was working on submarines.

Within three years, Fulton completed a submarine, and in late 1800, he launched several unsuccessful attacks against British warships off French ports. His submarine *Nautilus* was an enlarged and refined version of the craft that Bushnell had built more than twenty years before. The method of attack was similar: The submarine carried a mine (called a torpedo by Fulton) to the enemy vessel. If the intended victim moved, it was safe from the slow, awkward submarine. Nor could the hand-cranked *Nautilus* overcome contrary tides or currents. In one attempt, however, Fulton and his crew of two remained submerged for more than six hours. That record was unequaled until the late nineteenth century. Fulton reached the obvious conclusion that *Nautilus* was inadequate as a weapon; he dismantled the submarine—perhaps to protect its secrets from imitators and its weaknesses from critics.

While still trying to collect funds from the French government for past submarine activities and future proposals, Fulton opened negotiations with British agents. In exchange for a substantial monthly payment, Fulton agreed to develop plans for small rowboats to tow torpedoes against French ships. In the midst of this scheme, Robert Fulton found a new patron.

Robert R. Livingston was one of the wealthiest men in America. Since helping to draft the Declaration of Independence, he had been active in public service. In 1801, Livingston became the American minister to the French government. For the past three years, the wealthy New Yorker had tried to promote steam navigation. While his brother-in-law, John Stevens, had set up a machine shop in New Jersey to conduct steamboat experiments, Livingston had secured a monopoly to steam navigation on New York waters. The two men, howev-

er, were not suited as partners. Hence Robert Fulton, the engineer anxious to win fame and fortune, and Livingston satisfied each other's needs. They became partners.

Fulton first studied the design of earlier steamboats and their engines. Next, he built models to test his own designs. Finally, in 1803, he placed a British engine aboard a craft of his own design, but the vessel moved too slowly. Fulton then left France, telling Livingston that he would return within two weeks. Fulton remained in England for two years working on his favorite project, undersea warfare. Fulton finally left England and sailed for New York.

The tall, handsome man who landed in America after nearly twenty years abroad was often mistaken for a foreign aristocrat. The boy from Lancaster had come a long way. Robert Fulton wasted no time: In the remarkably brief space of eight months, Fulton assembled the first steamboat to earn money for its owners. Fulton hired one of the best builders, Charles Brown, to construct the hull. The boat was supposed to have been designed in accordance with Fulton's study of water and wind resistance. Still, the vessel looked like an enlarged

British canal boat. The engine was the best that could be bought, a Boulton and Watt from England. After a brief trial run, Fulton informed Livingston that the vessel was ready.

On August 17, 1807, *The North River Steamboat* left New York City with forty passengers, mostly apprehensive relatives of Livingston. On its way up the Hudson River to Albany, the vessel stopped at Livingston's river estate, Clermont, the origin of the steamboat's unofficial but popular name, *Clermont*. Only a few passengers ventured aboard the steamboat for its first commercial run several weeks later. Public acceptance of the vessel increased, however, as it maintained a regular schedule. By the time river transportation closed for the winter, Livingston was earning a small but steady return on his investment.

During the winter of 1807-1808, Fulton rebuilt the steamboat with more comfortable accommodations. Because the vessel lacked sails to roll her about and voyaged on the relatively smooth waters of the Hudson River (locally called the North River), Fulton could install furniture that a sailing vessel could not accommodate. In the remaining seven years of his life, Fulton completed twenty more steamboats, each with fancier fittings than its predecessor. Thus, Fulton established the tradition of steamboat luxury. This tradition distinguished steam vessels from sailing vessels and attracted passengers.

In January, 1808, Fulton married Harriet Livingston, the beautiful niece of Robert Livingston. Once again, Fulton was working on torpedoes. In 1810, he published *Torpedo War and Submarine Explosions*, the first "do-it-yourself" book on that subject. Besides an expanding transportation system, a growing family, and torpedo work, Fulton was spending much time defending the steamboat monopoly that Livingston had pushed through the legislature years earlier. Other builders saw no more reason for a steamboat monopoly than one for sailing ships. Further, New Jersey citizens resented the Livingston-Fulton claim that New York's waters extended to the Jersey shore. The lawsuits dragged on for years.

When the War of 1812 began, Fulton concentrated on naval weapons. In marked contrast with his numerous letters and public demonstrations that characterized his earlier work in France and England, Fulton now worked in secret. He built a semisubmersible vessel to tow torpedoes against British warships off New London, Connecticut. A

storm washed the vessel ashore, and the British later blew it up. Fulton's major work during the war was *Demologes*, a steam-driven battery. With its heavy cannon and thick sides, people (including British officers) expected the warship to destroy British blockaders near New York. Yet on February 24, 1815, shortly before the vessel was finished and just as news of peace reached the United States, Robert Fulton died. Exhausted by rushing the steam battery toward completion, by court actions over the steamboat monopoly, and by overexposure to a cold winter, he was too weak to resist another bout with respiratory problems.

Summary

The achievement of Robert Fulton was in developing a commercially successful steamboat. Other men may vie for the honor of inventing the steamboat, but their work failed to alter marine transportation. Robert Fulton and *The North River Steamboat* ended the dependence of ships upon the wind. Moreover, whereas travel had always involved varying degrees of hardship, Fulton developed the concept of voyaging in comfort. Finally, in an age suspicious of change, Fulton introduced the modern practice of continual product development.

It is ironic that Fulton's fame in steamboats came so easily when compared with the brief time involved. That he succeeded in steam navigation was because of his willingness to build upon the work of others, to cooperate with financial backers, and to follow a logical pattern. Research, conceptualization, scale models, and mathematical calculations distinguished his work method. As a result of Fulton's efforts, the vision of steamboat pioneers became a reality.

In turn, Fulton's pioneering work in submarines and torpedoes had to wait upon further advances in technology. Yet his vision of undersea warfare fascinated contemporaries and inspired people throughout the nineteenth century. Fulton's ideas were employed with some success by the Confederacy during the Civil War, and Jules Verne named his imaginary submarine after Fulton's *Nautilus*. The United States Navy completed Fulton's *Demologes*, the world's first steam warship, renamed it *Fulton*, and then left the vessel to rot.

Robert Fulton belonged to a select group of Americans. Along with Francis Cabot Lowell and Eli Whitney, Fulton introduced technology to American society and laid the foundation for the nation to become the industrial leader of the world.

Bibliography

Chapelle, Howard I. *Fulton's Steam Battery: Blockship and Catamaran.* Washington, D.C.: Smithsonian Institution Press, 1964. Most detailed account of the steam battery based upon plans located in Denmark in 1960. Although the author is best known for his many books on American sailing vessels, he devoted the same care and expertise to collecting and analyzing the plans of steamships. Using copies of the steam battery's plans that were located in Danish archives, the author has produced the lost detailed account of Robert Fulton's last work.

Flexner, James T. *Steamboats Come True: American Inventors in Action.* New York: Viking Press, 1944. An excellent account of steamboat pioneers before Fulton.

Fulton, Robert. *Torpedo War and Submarine Explosions.* New York: Elliot, 1810. Fulton's descriptions of underwater warfare not only guided the efforts of Americans who attempted to attack British warships during the War of 1812 but also became required reading for British officers aboard those same ships.

Hutcheon, Wallace, Jr. *Robert Fulton: Pioneer of Undersea Warfare.* Annapolis, Md.: Naval Institute Press, 1981. The best account of Fulton's underwater work. Draws on many different sources for its information.

Morgan, John S. *Robert Fulton.* New York: Mason/Charter, 1977. A good overview of Fulton's life and work. The author provides the reader with a clear and well-written summary of Fulton's life and work. This book meets the needs of the general reader.

Philip, Cynthia O. *Robert Fulton.* New York: Watts, 1985. This well-researched biography is particularly good for its thoughtful analysis of Fulton's character and behavior. The author's conclusions about the relationship between Fulton and the Barlows are not accepted by all scholars.

Taylor, George R. *The Transportation Revolution: 1815-1850.* New York: Holt Rinehart, 1951. This standard history examines the role of the steamboat in the expansion of the American economy and society during the first half of the nineteenth century.

Joseph A. Goldenbergs

JAMES GADSDEN

Born: May 15, 1788; Charleston, South Carolina

Died: December 26, 1858; Charleston, South Carolina

Areas of Achievement: Business and industry, diplomacy, engineering, and military affairs

Contribution: Though Gadsden was an accomplished soldier, engineer, and railroad executive, his lasting fame came as the United States' minister to Mexico in the mid-1850's. While in Mexico City, he negotiated the Gadsden Purchase, the U.S. acquisition of a strip of territory that became the southern portions of Arizona and New Mexico.

Early Life

James Gadsden was born into one of South Carolina's most reputable families. The source of this prominence came from his paternal grandfather, Christopher Gadsden, who owned several stores, a commercial wharf, and a plantation. He also served in the South Carolina Assembly and organized Charleston's resistance to the Stamp Act in 1765. Ten years later, Christopher acted as a delegate to the Continental Congress and eventually served as a Revolutionary War general.

Christopher's son, Philip, lived in the shadow of his famous father. Philip entered his family's mercantile business and stayed in Charleston his entire life. He married Catherine Edwards, whose father was also a local businessman and Revolutionary War patriot. Desirous of a large family, the couple managed sixteen offspring. Philip, a devout member of the Protestant Episcopal Church, taught his children, through mild discipline, about Christian moral principles. He also gave his sons the best formal education. They were sent to a well-known preparatory school, the Associated Academy of Charleston, and then shipped to Connecticut for a classical education at Yale.

In 1803, when Philip's third son, James, reached Connecticut, he was welcomed by his two older brothers, C. E. and John. Away from home for the first time, young Gadsden found comfort in the companionship of his siblings. There were also new friendships, including one with John C. Calhoun, a fellow South Carolinian. Within a few decades, Calhoun would become a national political figure exerting great influence on James. It is possible that in later years the pious Philip was most proud of his eldest son C. E., who pursued the ministry and became a Protestant bishop. His son John emerged as a U.S. District Attorney but died at a relatively young age. The path of the younger James often appeared uncertain, and in the end, more closely resembled the diverse pursuits of his grandfather, General Christopher Gadsden.

Life's Work

James Gadsden graduated from Yale in 1806 and returned to Charleston. The recent death of his grandfather led him to enter the family's mercantile business. After several years, he grew restless and prayed for new opportunities. His prayers were answered in 1812 with the outbreak of war between the United States and Great Britain. With the help of his congressman, he was commissioned a second lieutenant in the U.S. Army and trained in the Army Corps of Engineers. Military service changed his life forever.

Gadsden's military career lasted ten years. Early in the war he helped prepare for the invasion of Canada and saw action in several major battles. He was later dispatched to New York to build defenses in Brooklyn and Harlem Heights. In 1815 Gadsden transferred to New Orleans, Louisiana, to assist General Andrew Jackson in the construction of fortifications along the Gulf of Mexico and the southwestern frontier. The flamboyant Jackson took the young lieutenant under his wing, making him his personal aide-de-camp. President James Madison asked Gadsden, who was already the chief engineer of the New Orleans district by 1816, to evaluate all regional defense posts. The next year, Gadsden accompanied Jackson in a campaign against the Seminole Indians of Spanish Florida. Jackson, on his own initiative, captured several Spanish garrisons, which soon led to the acquisition of Florida by the United States.

Gadsden had distinguished himself in the Seminole War; as a result, he was promoted to captain and placed in charge of all construction works in the Gulf of Mexico frontier. Several years later he received two of the Army's most senior administrative positions. In October, 1820, he was appointed inspector general of Jackson's Southern Division with the rank of colonel. In 1822, at the request of Secretary of War John Calhoun, President James Monroe appointed him adjutant general of the entire army. His appointment was opposed, however, by many politicians who disliked Monroe and Calhoun; ultimately, the Senate forced Gadsden out of office.

In late 1822 Gadsden returned to Charleston to resume his business career. However, Calhoun once again intervened by asking his friend to negotiate a treaty with the Seminoles. Gadsden consented, moved to Florida, and did not return to South Carolina for sixteen years. In September, 1823, he signed the Treaty of Fort Moultrie, which effectively relocated the Seminole Indians from central to southern Florida. Afterward, he agreed to survey the boundaries of the new reservation. In 1824, he received appointment to Florida's first legislative council, accepted a federal contract to survey a major roadway in the territory, and married Suzanna Gibbes Horte.

After his marriage, Gadsden tried to establish roots as a planter near Tallahassee, Florida, but, bored with the slow pace of plantation life, he set his sights on politics. He attempted to associate himself with the legend of war hero Jackson and relied on the general's friends for political support. Between 1825 and 1837, he campaigned five times, all unsuccessfully, to become the territory's delegate to the U.S. Congress. During this time he declined several federal job offers and finally settled for a position as Florida's assistant engineer. His primary activities focused on improving the territory's transportation network with new roadways, canals, and railroads. This brought him into frequent contact with local Seminole Indians. In 1832 he became involved in new treaty negotiations to move the Seminoles west. When President Andrew Jackson dispatched the army to remove the American Indians, the natives resisted, starting the seven-year Seminole War. Gadsden served in various administrative capacities during the war, but by 1839 he had grown disillusioned and moved to the safety and stability of South Carolina.

Gadsden quickly immersed himself in Charleston's business community. He had brought from Florida new ideas for increasing commercial activity in the port city and the entire South. Several years earlier he had recognized the potential of coordinated railroad networks for Florida's economic development. For that purpose he had advocated a southern rail line from New Orleans to the Atlantic coast. He promoted this vision in Charleston but on an increasingly large scale. In 1840 Gadsden was elected president of the new Louisville, Cincinnati, and Charleston Railroad and remained in that position for ten years while the company was reorganized as the South Carolina Railroad Company. Throughout the 1840's, he actively promoted the idea of a southern transcontinental railroad stretching from Charleston to San Diego, California.

Plans for a transcontinental railroad had political ramifications. Northerners also wanted the economic benefits of a national railroad and had proposed a northern line running through Chicago, Illinois, to San Francisco, California. Moreover, they feared that a southern route would expand slavery to the southwestern territories. Such fears were well founded. Gadsden, for example, owned more than one hundred slaves and supported the practice of slavery in the West. In fact, he wanted to use slave labor to build the new railroad. As slavery became an increasingly controversial issue in the 1850's, he joined his friend Calhoun in the secessionist movement that ultimately led to the Civil War. However, it was diplomacy, not rebellion, that brought him lasting fame.

Through the influence of Secretary of War Jefferson Davis, a fellow Southerner, Gadsden was appointed U.S. minister to Mexico in May, 1853. He hoped to resolve various disputes between the United States and Mexico that had arisen since the 1848 Treaty of Guadalupe Hidalgo. Most important was the demarcation of a border separating the two nations that allowed adequate land for a southern transcontinental railroad. In December, 1853, after months of negotiation, Mexican dictator Antonio López de Santa Anna signed a treaty to sell land (45,535 square miles) in northern Mexico to the United States for fifteen million dollars. The U.S. diplomat proceeded to Washington, D.C., and presented the treaty for ratification.

Congressional approval of the Gadsden Purchase did not come easily. The Senate, like much of the country, was divided over the issue of slavery in the Western territories. Many Northerners were not inclined to buy Mexican land likely to benefit Southern slave owners. When some senators revised the treaty by radically decreasing the size and price of the land purchase, it failed to attract enough votes for passage. Finally, a new compromise was reached and ratified on April 25, 1854. In its final version, the treaty stated that the United States would buy 29,640 square miles of land for ten million dollars and that certain protections would be given to U.S. railroad investments in Mexico. Gadsden returned to Mexico City and received de Santa Anna's approval of the revisions. He remained the U.S. minister to Mexico until October, 1856. After retiring to South Carolina, his health declined rapidly. He died the day after Christmas, 1858, at the age of seventy-one.

Summary

Like his paternal grandfather, James Gadsden lived a remarkable life and participated in many important currents in antebellum U.S. history. As a soldier, engineer, and negotiator, he played a central role in the development of Florida and the Old Southwest. Consequently, several military installations, towns, and counties in the southeastern United States have been named in his honor. The significance of Gadsden's life, however, transcends regional importance.

From a national perspective, Gadsden's activities often signaled the progress and problems associated with U.S. territorial expansion. At the time of his birth, the nation consisted of only the original thirteen states, but the country expanded rapidly south and west. A dozen years after the Louisiana Purchase, he joined Andrew Jackson's conquest of Florida at the expense of native people and a European power. In the spirit of manifest destiny, Gadsden also welcomed the annexation of Texas and other territories farther west, especially after the United States defeated Mexico in war. During this time he became one of the nation's leading proponents of a transcontinental railroad. An ardent Southern Democrat who favored free trade and the expansion of slavery, his motivations for a southern rail line were economic and political. As the U.S. envoy to Mexico, Gadsden enthusiastically acquired land crucial to the construction of a southern railroad extending from the Atlantic to the Pacific. Although this railroad was not realized in his lifetime, the ratification of the Gadsden Purchase represented one of the last major sectional compromises before the Civil War and signaled the end of the United States' contiguous expansion on the continent.

Bibliography

Blassingame, Wyatt. *The First Book of American Expansion.* New York: Watts, 1965. This elementary book describes the Gadsden Purchase within the context of the territorial expansion of the United States from the Louisiana Purchase to the annexation of Hawaii.

Clary, David A., and Joseph W. A. Whitehorne. *The Inspector General of the U.S. Army, 1777-1903.* Washington, D.C.: Center of Military History, 1987. Contains brief discussions of Gadsden's career as inspector general of the Southern Division and as adjutant general. It is a detailed source for understanding the U.S. Army's early development and administration.

Garber, Paul N. *The Gadsden Treaty.* Philadelphia: Press of the University of Pennsylvania, 1923. For many decades this book has served as the standard account of the Gadsden Treaty. It remains the most descriptive book and provides considerable background on James Gadsden.

Godbold, E. Stanly. *Christopher Gadsden and the American Revolution.* Knoxville: University of Tennessee Press, 1982. This is a full-length biography of Gadsden's influential grandfather. Aside from analyzing Christopher's role in the American Revolution, the book is an excellent source that describes the Gadsden family and antebellum life in South Carolina.

Jeffrey J. Matthews

ALBERT GALLATIN

Born: January 29, 1761; Geneva, Switzerland
Died: August 12, 1849; Astoria, New York
Areas of Achievement: Banking, government and politics, and science
Contribution: Drawing upon the social philosophy of the French Enlightenment, Gallatin contributed, as secretary of the treasury to the administrations of Presidents Thomas Jefferson and James Madison, to the fiscal stability of the new nation and, as the first president of the American Ethnological Society, to the development of American anthropology.

Early Life

Abraham Alfonse Albert Gallatin was born January 29, 1761, in Geneva, Switzerland. Both his mother, née Sophie Albertine Rolaz, and his father, Jean Gallatin, died when Albert was an infant, so his care was entrusted to a distant relative of his mother, Mlle Catherine Pictet. The Gallatin family, part of the Geneva aristocracy and supplier of lords and councillors to the city-state, saw to it that young Gallatin was provided an excellent education. Despite access to the rich cultural heritage of his family, who counted Voltaire as a close friend, and a fine education at the academy, from which he was graduated in 1779, Gallatin resisted the aristocratic trappings of his family and identified with a growing number of students who supported Jean-Jacques Rousseau's Romantic call of "back to nature."

When his grandmother successfully gained for Gallatin an appointment as lieutenant colonel in the army of her friend Frederich, the Langrave of Hesse, then preparing to fight as mercenaries for England against the American Colonies, Gallatin rebelled and with a friend fled Geneva at the age of eighteen for America. He arrived in Massachusetts in 1780 and, without much money, set off for the frontier of Maine. After spending a year there, he returned to Boston, where he eked out a living as a tutor teaching French to students at Harvard College. Finding the atmosphere in Boston too cold for his tastes, Gallatin moved to the back country of Pennsylvania in 1782. Through business dealings, he acquired land in the region and, as a good Romantic, settled down to devote his life to farming. At one point, Gallatin hoped to establish a Swiss colony on the American frontier, but these plans came to nothing. Gallatin was successful as

neither farmer nor land speculator. Personal tragedy also touched him when his wife of a few months, Sophia Allegre, whom he had met in Richmond, Virginia, died at his farm, Friendship Hill. Despondent, Gallatin contemplated returning to Geneva, but an inability to sell his farm and the fighting in Geneva triggered by the French Revolution caused him to remain in America.

His intelligence and gregariousness led him to politics, first in Pennsylvania as a member of the Harrisburg conference of 1788, which met to consider ways in which the United States Constitution could be strengthened, and then as a member of the convention that met in 1789-1790 to revise the Pennsylvania constitution. In 1790, he was elected representative of Fayette County to the Pennsylvania state legislature.

Life's Work

Gallatin had three careers: politics, business, and science. Although he believed that his investigations in science, rather than his work in government, would cause his name to be remembered in history, the reverse, ironically, proved to be the case. Western Pennsylvania elected Gallatin twice to the state legislature, and then he was elected by the legislature to the Senate of the United States. There, his eligibility was challenged because he had not been a citizen for nine years. Removed from the Senate, Gallatin returned to Pennsylvania, taking his new bride Hannah, daughter of Commodore James Nicholson of New York. His stay in Pennsylvania proved short, for in 1794 the voters of western Pennsylvania sent him to the House of Representatives, in which he served three terms. A Republican, Gallatin defended the farming interests of western Pennsylvania; at the same time, his grasp of international law and public finance and his reasoning ability and cogent arguments made him a valuable legislator at a critical time in America's early history.

In May of 1801, Thomas Jefferson appointed Gallatin secretary of the treasury. Gallatin held this post through Jefferson's two administrations and through part of James Madison's first administration. Accusations that his financial policies hindered American efforts to fight the British in the War of 1812 prompted Gallatin to leave the treasury in 1813 and accept an appointment as a special envoy to Russia, which had offered to mediate

the conflict between Great Britain and the United States. Great Britain, however, refused to accept mediation and, thus, frustrated Gallatin's mission. Rather than returning to the treasury, as Madison expected, Gallatin chose to remain in Europe in diplomatic service. So began Gallatin's career as diplomat.

Along with John Quincy Adams and Henry Clay, Gallatin drew up the Treaty of Ghent, which ended the War of 1812. With the work on the treaty concluded, Gallatin, Adams, and Clay traveled to England and negotiated a commercial treaty with the British. On his return to the United States, Gallatin accepted the post of minister to France, which he held from 1816 to 1832. Upon his return from France, he intended to retire from government service and to devote the rest of life to being a gentleman farmer at Friendship Hill, but, although Gallatin was increasingly upset with the emphasis on gain in American politics, he allowed his name to be put forward for vice president. Henry Clay's ultimate acceptance of the nomination allowed Gallatin happily to withdraw his name. Life at Friendship Hill proved boring for the Gallatins

after seven years in Paris, and so Gallatin once again accepted diplomatic assignment, his last, in 1826, as minister to England.

The America to which Gallatin returned in 1827 seemed foreign to him. The robust activity of Jacksonian America seemed to make a shambles of the Jeffersonian idealism to which Gallatin subscribed. So disorienting did the new United States seem to him that he seriously considered leaving the country and returning with his family to Geneva. Although he did not return to Europe, he did retire from government service, beginning a new career in business.

Gallatin moved to New York City, where John Jacob Astor urged him to accept the presidency of Astor's new National Bank. In this position, which Gallatin held from 1831 to 1839, he not only wrote on fiscal reform in articles such as *Considerations on the Currency and Banking System of the United States* (1831) but also protested slavery, the annexation of Texas by the United States, and the war with Mexico. In addition, he found time to indulge his interests in ethnology and, especially, linguistics.

While Gallatin had been living in Paris, he had made the acquaintance of the famous German scientist Alexander von Humboldt. Gallatin's knowledge of several European languages and his interest in linguistics complemented Humboldt's study of linguistics and American Indian languages. Humboldt prevailed upon Gallatin to write on Indian languages, and thus, even before Gallatin left public service, he had begun his scientific career. His first major publication in this field was *A Synopsis of the Indian Tribes Within the United States East of the Rocky Mountains and in the British and Russian Possessions in North America* (1836), followed by *Notes on the Semi-Civilized Nations of Mexico, Yucatan, and Central America* (1845) and *Indians of North-west America* (1848). Besides writing in the field of ethnology, Gallatin served as president of the American Ethnological Society, an organization he helped to found in 1842.

Summary

Although sometimes indulging in Romantic notions, Gallatin was first and foremost a gentleman of the Enlightenment. With his superb forensic skills and his ability to remain calm under personal attack, Gallatin proved a consummate politician, negotiator, and diplomat. His brilliance of mind led Jefferson to rely on Gallatin not only to oversee national finance but also to proofread his speeches and act as personal confidant. As secretary of the treasury and disbursing agent, Gallatin assumed a major role in promoting the exploration of the West and settlement of the Western frontier.

Governed by an Enlightenment philosophy that emphasized idealism and humanism in politics, learning, and society, Gallatin became uncomfortable with the raw commercialism of Jacksonian America, which seemed to him to promote only the base side of human potential. By the time of his death, Gallatin was out of step with his time: an Enlightenment figure in Jacksonian America. Yet for many he remained the Enlightenment conscience of America's idealistic beginnings.

Bibliography

Adams, Henry. *The Life of Albert Gallatin*. Philadelphia and London: Lippincott, 1880. Still a classic account of Gallatin's life. Henry Adams, the grandson of John Adams, provides an intimate glimpse into Gallatin's life and values and places both in the context of Gallatin's European experience and a rapidly developing American society.

Allen, John Logan. *Passage Through the Garden: Lewis and Clark and the Image of the American Northwest*. Urbana and London: University of Illinois Press, 1975. Logan's work discusses Gallatin's economic contribution as secretary of the treasury and his intellectual contribution to the exploration of the West.

Balinky, Alexander. *Albert Gallatin: Fiscal Theories and Policies*. New Brunswick, N.J.: Rutgers University Press, 1958. An extensive study of Gallatin's theories and policies on public finance.

Bieder, Robert E. *Science Encounters the Indian, 1820-1880: The Early Years of American Ethnology*. Norman: University of Oklahoma Press, 1986. Contains a chapter on Gallatin, his study of American Indians, and his place in the early development of American ethnology.

Gallatin, James. *The Diary of James Gallatin, Secretary to Albert Gallatin, a Great Peace Maker, 1813-1827*. Edited by Count Gallatin. New York: Scribner, 1926. A highly intimate and entertaining account of Gallatin's years in Paris and London, written by his son, who served as Gallatin's secretary.

Kuppenheimer, L. B. *Albert Gallatin's Vision of Democratic Stability: An Interpretive Profile*. Westport, Conn.: Praeger, 1996. The author builds a profile of Gallatin based on analysis of the intellectual climate in Europe that influenced his philosophical and political perspectives.

Smelser, Marshall. *The Democratic Republic: 1801-1815*. Edited by Henry S. Commager and Richard B. Morris. New American Nations Series. New York: Harper, 1968. Mentions Gallatin in the larger context of the growth of the American republic.

Walters, Raymond, Jr. *Albert Gallatin: Jeffersonian Financier and Diplomat*. New York: Macmillan, 1957. Walters differs from Balinky in emphasizing Gallatin's Jeffersonian ties and diplomatic career.

White, Leonard D. *The Jeffersonians: A Study in Administrative History, 1801-1829*. New York: Macmillan, 1951. Now dated but still useful in its consideration of Gallatin's administration of the treasury.

Robert E. Bieder

ÈVARISTE GALOIS

Born: October 25, 1811; Bourg-la-Reine, near Paris, France
Died: May 31, 1832; Paris, France
Area of Achievement: Mathematics
Contribution: Galois produced, with the aid of group theory, a definitive answer to the problem of the solvability of algebraic equations, a problem that had preoccupied mathematicians since the eighteenth century. Consequently, he laid one of the foundations of modern algebra.

Early Life

Èvariste Galois' father, Nicolas-Gabriel Galois, was a friendly and witty liberal thinker who headed a school that accommodated about sixty boarders. Elected mayor of Bourg-la-Reine during the Hundred Days after Napoleon's escape from Elba, he retained office under the second Restoration. Galois' mother, Adelaïde-Marie Demante, was from a long line of jurists and had received a more traditional education. She had a headstrong and eccentric personality. Having taken control of her son's early education, she attempted to implant in him, along with the elements of classical culture, strict religious principles as well as respect for a stoic morality. Influenced by his father's imagination and liberalism, the eccentricity of his mother, and the affection of his elder sister Nathalie-Théodore, Galois seems to have had a childhood that was both happy and studious.

Galois continued his studies at the Collège Louis-le-Grand in Paris, entering in October, 1823. He found it difficult to adjust to the harsh discipline imposed by the school during the Restoration at the orders of the political authorities and the Church, and, although a brilliant student, he was rebellious. In the early months of 1827, he attended the first-year preparatory mathematics courses taught by H. J. Vernier; this first exposure to mathematics was a revelation for him. He rapidly became bored with the elementary nature of this instruction and with the inadequacies of some of his textbooks and began reading the original works themselves.

After appreciating the difficulty of Adrien-Marie Legendre's geometry, Galois acquired a solid background from the major works of Joseph-Louis Lagrange. During the next two years, he attended Vernier's second-year preparatory mathematics courses, then the more advanced ones of L. P. E.

Richard, who was the first to recognize Galois' superiority in mathematics. With this perceptive teacher, Galois excelled in his studies, even though he was already devoting much more of his time to his personal work than to his classwork. In 1828, he began to study some then-recent works on the theory of equations, on number theory, and on the theory of elliptic functions.

This was the time period in which Galois' first memoir appeared. Published in March, 1829, in the *Annales de mathématiques pures et appliquées* (annals of pure and applied mathematics), it demonstrated and clarified a result of Lagrange concerning continuous fractions. While it revealed a certain astuteness, it did not demonstrate exceptional talent.

Life's Work

In 1828, by his own admission Galois falsely believed—as Henrik Abel had eight years earlier—that he had solved the general fifth-degree equation. Quickly enlightened, he resumed with a new approach the study of the theory of equations, a subject which he pursued until he elucidated the general problem with the aid of group theory. The results he obtained in May, 1829, were sent to the Academy of Sciences by a particularly competent judge, Augustin-Louis Cauchy. Fate was to frustrate these brilliant beginnings, however, and to leave a lasting impression on the personality of the young mathematician.

First, at the beginning of July, his father, a man who had been persecuted for his liberal beliefs, committed suicide. A month later, Galois failed the entrance examination for the École Polytechnique, because he refused to use the expository method suggested by the examiner. Barred from entering the school which attracted him because of its scientific prestige and liberal tradition, he took the entrance examination for the École Normale Supérieure (then called the École Préparatoire), which trained future secondary school teachers. He entered the institution in November, 1829.

At this time he learned of Abel's death and, at the same time, that Abel's last published memoir contained several original results that Galois himself had presented as original in his memoir to the Academy. Cauchy, assigned to supervise Galois' work, advised his student to revise his memoir, taking into account Abel's research and new results. Galois wrote a new text that he submitted to the Academy in February, 1830, that he hoped would win for him the grand prix in mathematics. Unfortunately, this memoir was lost upon the death of Joseph Fourier, who had been appointed to study it. Eliminated from the competition, Galois believed himself to be the object of a new persecution by both the representatives of institutional science and society in general. His manuscripts preserve a partial record of the revision of this memoir of February, 1830.

In June, 1830, Galois published in *Bulletin des sciences mathématiques* (bulletin of mathematical sciences) a short note on the resolution of numerical equations, as well as a much more significant article, "Sur la théorie des nombres" (on number theory). That this same issue contained original works by Cauchy and Siméon-Denis Poisson sufficiently confirms the reputation that Galois had already acquired. The July Revolution of 1830, however, was to initiate a drastic change in his career.

Galois became politicized. Before returning for a second year to the Ècole Normale Supérieure in November, 1830, he had already developed friendships with several republican leaders. Even less able to tolerate his school's strict discipline than before, he published a violent article against its director in an opposition journal. For this action he was expelled on December 8, 1830.

Left alone, Galois devoted most of his time to political propaganda. He participated in the riots and demonstrations then agitating Paris and was even arrested (but was eventually acquitted). Meanwhile, to a limited degree, he continued his mathematical research. His last two publications were a short note on analysis in the *Bulletin des sciences mathématiques* of December, 1830, and "Lettre sur l'enseignement des sciences" (letter on the teaching of the sciences), which appeared on January 2, 1831, in the *Gazette des écoles*. On January 13, he began to teach a public course on advanced algebra in which he planned to present his own discoveries; this project appears not to have been successful. On January 17, 1831, Galois presented the Academy a new version of his memoir, hastily written at Poisson's request. Unfortunately, in Poisson's report of July 4, 1831, on this, Galois' most important piece of work, Poisson suggested that a portion of the results could be found in several posthumous writings of Abel and that the rest was incomprehensible. Such a judgment, the pro-

found injustice of which would become apparent in the future, only encouraged Galois' rebellion.

Arrested again during a republican demonstration on July 14, 1831, and imprisoned, Galois nevertheless continued his mathematical research, revised his memoir on equations, and worked on the applications of his theory and on elliptic functions. After the announcement of a cholera epidemic on March 16, 1832, he was transferred to a nursing home, where he resumed his investigations, wrote several essays on the philosophy of science, and became immersed in a love affair which ended unhappily. Galois sank into a deep depression.

Provoked into a duel under unclear circumstances following this breakup, Galois sensed that he was near death. On May 29, he wrote desperate letters to his republican friends, hastily sorted his papers, and addressed to his friend Auguste Chevalier—but intended for Carl Friedrich Gauss and Carl Gustav Jacob Jacobi—a testamentary letter, a tragic document in which he attempted to outline the principal results that he had attained. On May 30, fatally wounded by an unknown opponent, he was hospitalized; he died the following day, not even twenty-one years of age.

Summary

Èvariste Galois' work seems not to have been fully appreciated by anyone during his lifetime. Cauchy, who would have been able to understand its significance, left France in September, 1830, having seen only its initial outlines. In addition, the few fragments published during his lifetime did not give an overall view of his achievement and, in particular, did not provide a means of judging the exceptional interest of the results regarding the theory of equations rejected by Poisson. Also, the publication of the famous testamentary letter does not appear to have attracted the attention it deserved.

It was not until September, 1843, that Joseph Liouville, who prepared Galois' manuscripts for publication, announced officially that the young mathematician had effectively solved the problem, already investigated by Abel, of deciding whether an irreducible first-degree equation is solvable with the use of radicals. Although announced and prepared for the end of 1843, the memoir of 1831 did not appear until the October/November, 1846, issue of the *Journal de mathématiques pures et appliquées*, when it was published with a fragment on the primitive equations solvable by radicals.

Beginning with Liouville's edition, which appeared in book form in 1897, Galois' work became progressively known to mathematicians and subsequently exerted a profound influence on the development of modern mathematics. Also important, although they came too late to contribute to the advancement of mathematics, are the previously unpublished texts that appeared later.

While he formulated more precisely essential ideas that were already being investigated, Galois also introduced others that, once stated, played an important role in the genesis of modern algebra. Furthermore, he boldly generalized certain classic methods in other fields and succeeded in providing a complete solution and a generalization of problems by systematically drawing upon group theory—one of the most important structural concepts which unified the multiplicity of algebras in the nineteenth century.

Bibliography

Bell, Eric T. *Men of Mathematics*. London: Gollancz, and New York: Simon and Schuster, 1937. Historical account of the major figures in mathematics from the Greeks to Giorg Cantor, written in an interesting if at times exaggerated style. In a relatively brief chapter, "Genius and Stupidity," Bell describes the life and work of Galois in a tone that both worships and scorns the young mathematician and mixes fact with legend in his discussion.

Boyer, Carl B. *A History of Mathematics*. 2d ed. New York: Wiley, 1989. In this standard and very reputable history of mathematics, Boyer devotes a brief section to Galois. Galois is described as the individual who most contributed to the vital discovery of the group concept. The author also assesses Galois' impact on future generations of mathematicians. Includes charts, an extensive bibliography, and exercises for the student.

Infeld, Leopold. *Whom the Gods Love: The Story of Èvariste Galois*. New York: Whittlesey House, 1948. This biography takes great license with the facts (many of which are unknown) of Galois' life and creates an interesting, if fictional, account. The author, maintaining that biography always mixes truth and fiction, puts Galois' life in the historical context of nineteenth century France by creating scenes and dialogues that might have occurred. Contains a bibliography.

Kline, Morris. *Mathematical Thought from Ancient Times to Modern Times*. New York: Oxford University Press, 1972. In this voluminous work, the author surveys the major mathematical creators and developments through the first few decades of the twentieth century. The emphasis is on the leading mathematical themes rather than on the men. The brief section on Galois gives some biographical information and discusses the mathematician's work in finite fields, group theory, and the theory of equations.

Rolfe, Patricia. "Novel Look at Numbers." *Bulletin with Newsweek* 116, no. 6095 (October 28, 1997). Profiles Galois and Australian novelist Tom Petsinis who modeled his book, *The French Mathematician,* on the life of Galois.

Struik, Dirk J. *A Concise History of Mathematics*. Vol. 2, *The Seventeenth Century-Nineteenth Century*. 4th ed. New York: Dover, 1987. In this book devoted to a concise overview of the major figures and trends in mathematics during the time period covered, a brief section is devoted to Galois. The author spends approximately equal time discussing Galois' life and major achievements, and views the mathematician both as a product of his times and as a unique genius.

Genevieve Slomski

FRANCIS GALTON

Born: February 16, 1822; Birmingham, near Sparkbrook, England

Died: January 17, 1911; Haslemere, Surrey, England

Areas of Achievement: Statistics, genetics, and eugenics

Contribution: Galton was responsible for developing modern statistical methods and laid the foundation for modern psychology and for the eugenics movement.

Early Life

Francis Galton was born at Birmingham, England, on February 16, 1822, to Samuel Tertius Galton and Violetta Darwin Galton, the daughter of Erasmus Darwin. Thus, Galton and Charles Darwin were cousins.

Galton's early education was provided by his sister Adele, who was his elder by twelve years. She took a special interest in Francis' education. Before Francis enrolled in school for formal education, Adele had already taught him to read English, Greek, and Latin and had taught him simple arithmetic. In 1836, at the age of fourteen, Galton was enrolled in King Edward's school in Birmingham, where the curriculum was primarily Latin and Greek. In *Memories of My Life* (1908), Galton wrote that while at the school he craved "an abundance of good English reading, well-taught mathematics, and solid science."

After attending King Edward's School for two years, Galton became a pupil at the Birmingham General Hospital to prepare for a career in medicine. For a young boy of sixteen, he was immediately given a position of much responsibility in the dispensary. He prepared infusions, decoctions, tinctures, and extracts. In *Memories of My Life*, his early medical experiences are emotionally described. Galton's inquisitiveness led him to sample the various medicines in the dispensary, stopping when croton oil, with its emetic effects, temporarily cured his investigative tendencies. In 1839, he continued his formal theoretical medical training at King's College, London.

In 1840, Galton left medical study at King's College and enrolled at Cambridge (Trinity College) to study mathematics. A nervous breakdown forced him to miss a term and abandon his plans to receive honors in mathematics. Instead, he finished studies for a medical degree. Galton's stay at Trinity College proved to be very influential as he met, socialized with, and was stimulated by many prominent educators.

Undoubtedly inspired by Charles Darwin's *The Voyage of the Beagle* (1839), Galton had a propensity for travel, of which his first taste came during the summer of 1840. In *Memories of My Life*, Galton said, "in the Spring of 1840 a passion for travel seized me as if I had been a migratory bird." The "passion" took him to various countries on the Continent.

In 1844, after the death of his father, who left him independently wealthy, Galton "abandoned all thought of becoming a physician." With no apparent sense of vocation, he traveled for several years.

Life's Work

Having abandoned his medical studies and being independently wealthy, Galton resumed his interest in traveling, climbing, and mountaineering. He

traveled to Egypt and Spain in 1845 and under the aegis of the Royal Geographical Society visited Southeast Africa from 1850 to 1852. His travels won for him the gold medal of the Royal Geographical Society and established his position in the scientific world. His account of his travels to Southeast Africa was published in 1853 as *Tropical South Africa*. He published in 1855 *Art of Travel*, which became the most popular of all publications of the Royal Geographical Society. Galton eventually became editor of the *Proceedings of the Royal Geographical Society*. His work for the Royal Geographical Society secured his election as a fellow of the Royal Society in 1856.

Through his association with the Royal Geographical Society, Galton became a member of the Managing Committee of the Kew Observatory in 1858. His work at the observatory included the establishment of a means for standardizing sextants and other angular instruments and verifying the accuracy of thermometers. He also developed a photographic method used to record readings from a barometer, discovered anticyclones, took part in the construction of weather charts for publication in daily newspapers, and made several minor inventions. He became chairman of the observatory in 1889 and held that post until 1901.

In the 1860's, while still at Cambridge, Galton noticed that academic talent ran in families, and he became very interested in heredity, especially of human characteristics. This interest was sparked by Darwin's *On the Origin of Species* (1859). Galton stated in *Memories of My Life* that *On the Origin of Species* "made a marked epoch in my own mental development."

Galton first outlined his ideas on human heredity in the June and August, 1865, issues of *Macmillan* magazine in an article titled "Hereditary Talent and Character" but elaborated on them and developed them more fully in a book, published in 1869 and titled *Hereditary Genius: An Inquiry into Its Laws and Consequences*. Galton's purpose as stated in the introduction of the book was to show "that a man's natural abilities are derived from inheritance, under exactly the same limitations as are the forms and physical features of the whole organic world." In the book, he describes his method based on the normal distribution of classifying people by ability. He outlines the kinships of judges, statesmen, scientists, poets, and so on. His conclusions about the power of heredity are clear: "I object to pretensions of natural equality. The experiences of

the nursery, the school, the community, and of the professional careers, are a chain of proofs to the contrary." Galton believed that human intelligence and behavior were under the same influences as any physical trait. Thus, he concluded that if one can breed horses with "peculiar powers of running . . . so it would be quite practicable to produce a highly gifted race of men by judicious marriages during several consecutive generations." Galton, believing that "heredity was a far more powerful agent in human development than nurture," decided to explore "the range of human faculty . . . in order to ascertain the degree to which heredity might . . . modify the human race."

Galton realized that the development and spread of his ideas on heredity were hampered by a lack of knowledge of a hereditary mechanism. In 1871, he succeeded in establishing cross-circulation between two breeds of rabbits in an effort to study Darwin's gemmule theory of inheritance. Neither breed was altered by the experiment, casting doubt on a gemmulelike theory. In later studies, Galton came very close to discovering the principles of the continuity of the germ plasm and corroborating Gregor Mendel's principle of segregation.

Galton's own theory of inheritance was a biometrical one. "The laws of heredity are concerned only with deviations from the median. . . . It supposes all variability are a result of different and equally probable combinations of a multitude of small independent causes." This work led to his development of the correlation coefficient.

In 1872, Alphonse de Candolle published a response to *Hereditary Genius: An Inquiry into Its Laws and Consequences*, in which de Candolle concluded that environment and not heredity was more important in determining mental character. In an effort to determine the relative importance of nature and nurture, Galton sent questionnaires to 180 selected fellows of the Royal Society. The questionnaires inquired about parents, physique, comparable success of relatives, energy, memory, mechanical aptitude, religious beliefs, and origin of the interest in science. The results of the questionnaires formed the foundation for *English Men of Science* (1874). Although one could interpret Galton's results in favor of an environmental influence, he said "the results of the inquiry showed how largely the aptitude for science was an inborn and not an acquired gift, and therefore apt to be hereditary."

Galton, realizing the wealth of information on the nature/nurture debate to be gained from the study of twins, located and questioned several pairs of twins. The results, which supported Galton's suspicions about the power of heredity, were published in the *Journal of the Anthropological Institute* in 1875 and 1876. Galton concluded:

The impression that all this evidence leaves on the mind is one of some wonder whether nurture can do anything at all. There is no escape from the conclusion that nature prevails enormously over nurture when the differences of nurture do not exceed what is commonly to be found among persons of the same rank of society and in the same country.

In his continuing quest to obtain hereditary data on humans, Galton published the *Record of Family Faculties* in 1884. The *Record of Family Faculties* was a list of questions about topics ranging from mental powers to temperament. Prizes were awarded to those who provided the most complete answers. The information from the questionnaires was used for *Natural Inheritance*, published in 1889. Galton's interest in human characteristics provided the stimulus for the opening in 1885 of an anthropometric laboratory at the South Kensington Museum, where data on height, weight, sight, hearing, and so on, were collected. The laboratory remained open for eight years. His studies at the laboratory on children's ability to remember number and letter spans were noticed by Alfred Binet and incorporated into Binet's intelligence test. One emphasis of the laboratory was in the use of fingerprints as a means of identification, a technique pioneered by Galton. *Finger-Prints* was published in 1893.

In Galton's attempts to discover the mechanisms involved with hereditary phenomena, he studied, as suggested by Darwin, inheritance in sweet peas. The results of the sweet-pea experiments and subsequent studies on humans showed a direct correlation between parent and offspring for the various characteristics he studied. The studies directly led to the discovery of the correlation coefficient and the concept of regression. Many of his results were published in *Natural Inheritance*, the publication of which led to the formation of the biometric school of heredity, a direct rival of the Mendelian school. Galton's work on the inheritance of human characteristics secured his election as president of the Anthropological Society in 1885. Six years later, Galton helped launch *Biometrika*, of which he became a consulting editor. The journal was intended as a forum for the publication of biological studies of a statistical nature.

Galton is best known for his work in eugenics, an interest that directly evolved from his work on the inheritance of human characteristics. In *Inquiries into the Human Faculty and Its Development* (1883), he defined eugenics as

the science of improving stock which is by no means confined to questions of judicious mating but which, especially in the case of man, takes cognizance of all influences that tend in however remote a degree to give the more suitable races or strains of blood a better chance of prevailing speedily over the less suitable than they otherwise would have had.

Galton's conviction that intelligence and virtually all other behavioral characteristics were inherited led him to believe that social ills could be cured by controlling the reproduction of undesirables (negative eugenics) and encouraging the breeding of superior individuals (positive eugenics) to the end of breeding a better race. It was clear to Galton that the breeding of criminals, the insane, the feebleminded, and paupers should be limited, by compulsory means if necessary. In the Huxley Lecture delivered in 1900, Galton stated that doing so "would abolish a source of suffering and misery for a future generation. . . ." Again, his ideas attracted little attention.

In May, 1904, Galton lectured before the Sociological Society. In that lecture, he defined eugenics as "the science which deals with all influences that improve the inborn qualities of a race; also with those that develop them to the utmost advantage." He continued, "What Nature does blindly, slowly, and ruthlessly man may do providently, quickly and kindly."

Late in 1904, Galton gave the University of London five hundred pounds per year for three years to set up a eugenics laboratory. Galton acted as superintendent. Monies were also given for a research fellow and a research assistant. The laboratory was called the Eugenics Record Office; the lab's official definition of eugenics was "the study of the agencies under social control that may improve or impair the social qualities of future generations either physically or mentally." The Eugenics Education Society was founded three years later, and Galton was appointed honorary president.

Galton was knighted in 1909. He died on January 17, 1911, in Haslemere, Surrey, England. On his death, he bequeathed forty-five thousand pounds to the University of London to endow a Chair of Eugenics.

Summary

Francis Galton's work had a profound impact on scientific research. His development of the correlation coefficient and the concept of regression marked the dawn of the statistical era of scientific inquiry and revolutionized the way scientists analyze their experimental results.

Work on the inheritance of psychological characteristics, the use of twin studies, and the use and development of statistical methods made Galton the father of modern psychology. Galton is best known for his work in eugenics. He was convinced that heredity was the most important factor in determining psychological characteristics. There is little doubt that he was influenced by Darwin's theory of natural selection. Galton saw that Darwin's theory easily applied to man and that the process of natural selection could be accelerated by human intervention. At first, his eugenic proposals attracted little attention and few followers.

After the rediscovery of Mendel's law in 1900, Galton's eugenic ideas began to take hold. His ideas spread throughout Europe and to the Americas and quickly found influence in the United States. The eugenics movement was seen as a large-scale social-hygiene program aimed at curing social ills. In the United States, the movement culminated with the passing in 1924 of an immigration restriction law. The rise of Nazism clearly demonstrated how eugenics could be misused by those in authority. Adolf Hitler delivered the final death knell to eugenics as an organized movement.

Bibliography

Burbridge, David. "Galton's 100: An Exploration of Francis Galton's Imagery Studies." *British Journal for the History of Science* 27, no. 95 (December 1994). Examination of Galton's studies of mental image and the scientific climate at the time.

Forrest, D. W. *Francis Galton: The Life and Work of a Victorian Genius*. London: Elek, and New York: Taplinger, 1974. The only modern biography of Galton. It contains many letters written to family members and colleagues.

Galton, David J., and Clare J. Galton. "Francis Galton: And Eugenics Today." *Journal of Medical Ethics* 24, no. 2 (April 1998). Discusses the issue of eugenics including its abuse in the United States and Germany and its implications for the future.

Galton, Francis. *Memories of My Life*. London: Methuen, 1908; New York: Dutton, 1900. An account of Galton's personal and scientific life from his own perspective. There are some errors which have probably resulted from Galton's failing memory.

Haller, Mark. *Eugenics: Hereditarian Attitudes in American Thought*. New Brunswick, N.J.: Rutgers University Press, 1963. An excellent account of the origin and development of the eugenics movement in both Great Britain and the United States.

Porter, Theodore M. *The Rise of Statistical Thinking, 1820-1900*. Princeton, N.J.: Princeton University Press, 1986. An excellent study of the development of statistical thinking among nineteenth century social scientists, biologists, and physicists; includes extensive discussion of Galton. The author is a historian, and his account demands very little mathematical background.

Stigler, Stephen M. *The History of Statistics: The Measurement of Uncertainty Before 1900*. Cambridge, Mass.: Harvard University Press, 1986. A magisterial history of statistics, from its origins in the seventeenth century to the full-fledged development of statistical methods at the beginning of the twentieth century. In contrast to Porter (see above), Stigler writes for the mathematically knowledgeable reader, and his engagingly written book is dense with equations, formulas, and statistical tables. Includes a biographical sketch of Galton and thorough discussion of his probability machine. Illustrated.

Charles Vigue

LÉON GAMBETTA

Born: April 2, 1838; Cahors, near Toulouse, France

Died: December 31, 1882; near Paris, France

Areas of Achievement: Government and politics

Contribution: Gambetta, one of the most vocal critics of the Second Empire of Napoleon III in the 1860's, became the virtual dictator of France in 1870 during the resistance to the Prussian invasion. He was one of the most prominent and the most popular republican politicians of the period.

Early Life

Léon Gambetta was born in 1838 in Cahors, in southern France. His Italian grandfather had moved his family to the region in 1818, and the Gambettas became shopkeepers. In 1837, Gambetta's father, Joseph, married Marie Magdeleine Massabie, the daughter of a local chemist; Gambetta's family, on both sides, might best be described as lower-middle-class. Gambetta's father wished him to follow in the family business, but in 1857 Gambetta went to Paris to study law. He had long been an opponent of the Second Empire of Napoleon III, and in the 1860's he began to write and speak against the regime. He made his mark during that decade in his defense of various individuals accused of political crimes against the Empire. In 1869, he was elected to the French Legislative Assembly, representing the southern city of Marseilles though he had also been victorious in the working-class Parisian district of Belleville. Though young, he was already a recognized leader of the opposition.

Throughout his life, Gambetta suffered from various medical problems, including the loss of an eye as a child. He was of less than average height and put on substantial weight as a young man, but his long hair and his pronounced nose gave him a dramatic appearance, especially in profile. This imposing physical presence was complemented by a charismatic rhetorical style.

Life's Work

In 1870, France and Prussia went to war as a result of Otto von Bismarck's Machiavellian diplomatic machinations. The French public demanded war, and although Napoleon III's own inclinations were toward peace, he led France against its enemy from across the Rhine. This action proved disastrous. Napoleon was captured and soon abdicated,

French armies were defeated, and in Paris on September 4, 1870, the former regime was replaced by a republic and a government of national defense was established. The new government was composed primarily of those elected to represent the various Parisian districts in the previous year's election. Gambetta, who had been elected from Belleville, became minister of the interior. As Prussian troops approached Paris, it was decided to establish another governmental presence in Tours, and soon the decision was made to reinforce the Tours government with Gambetta, the youngest member of the cabinet. In Tours, he became minister of war as well as minister of the interior and became the most powerful individual in France.

Earlier, Gambetta had joined with a number of his fellow republicans to warn against the war with Prussia, but, unlike some of his republican allies, Gambetta was no pacifist. He fervently believed in France and was willing to resort to arms to save France and the republic. In Tours, Gambetta faced what he considered internal treason as well as foreign invasion; the result was that by the end of the year Gambetta had become in effect dictator of France. Some of his critics had their doubts.

Although impressively assembled, the French troops were no match for the Prussians. Gambetta wished to continue the war, but as the winter elapsed the opinion of the French public turned toward peace. Eventually, Gambetta was forced to give way, and he resigned on February 6, 1871. He had both saved France's honor and left a residue of considerable controversy.

In the elections to the National Assembly which followed, Gambetta was victorious in ten different constituencies but chose to represent a department in Alsace, fated to be lost, along with Lorraine, to Germany as a result of the peace. When the treaty was accepted, Gambetta resigned in protest, the cause of the lost provinces remaining of paramount concern to Gambetta and to France. In the following months, Gambetta attempted to recover his damaged health, and in July he was again elected to the assembly, choosing to represent working-class Belleville.

In the years which followed, Gambetta's prestige and influence remained widespread. Fully committed to the ideals of the republic, he initially demanded that the assembly be quickly dissolved and a new one elected with the clear objective of producing a republican constitution. He feared, along with many other republicans, that the existing assembly was too monarchist in sentiment, intent on restoring either the house of Bourbon or that of Orléans. He particularly feared a Napoleonic revival. Gambetta was also concerned about the power of the Church. Sympathetic to the positivism of Auguste Comte, he had few orthodox religious feelings. His animosity toward the Church was based less on its claims to spiritual truth than on its institutional influences on French society, particularly in education.

In time, Gambetta began to believe that the assembly could in itself become safely republican and that there might be no need to call a new constituent assembly. That required compromise on his part, particularly in his acceptance of a senate, which many conservatives demanded as a curb on the democratically elected Chamber of Deputies. Accepting a senate not chosen directly by the voters, he argued that democratic reforms could be made in the future, but his willingness to compromise gained for him a reputation as an opportunist.

The future of the republic remained problematical during the early 1870's. In 1875, the assembly adopted, by a narrow vote, a method to choose the eventual successor to the President of France, the conservative Marshal MacMahon, thus transforming the provisional republic into a more permanent one. There was no formal constitution, merely the acceptance of a series of laws which established the powers of the president, a Senate, and a Chamber of Deputies.

Gambetta, as he had earlier, pushed for Republican Union, the name of his bloc in the Chamber of Deputies, but there were more radical republicans to the Left and more conservative republicans to the Right. While no socialist, Gambetta did believe in the right of labor to organize and the necessity for some government regulation of business. Unlike many of his fellow republicans on both the Right and the Left, Gambetta, the nationalist, believed in the need for a strong government, both internally and externally. In 1876, he was chosen head of the important Budget Committee of the Chamber of Deputies. In early 1879, he became president of the chamber, a position of considerable prestige but which compromised Gambetta's political leadership. Many argued that the president of the chamber should remain above the party fray, but it was difficult for Gambetta to distance himself. Soon some claimed that Gambetta was wielding hidden power.

Many predicted that Gambetta would soon become premier and form his own government, but MacMahon's successor, the conservative republican Jules Grevy, refused to summon Gambetta, a longtime rival, until November, 1881.

Only then did Gambetta form his long-awaited Grand Ministry. There were great expectations, but, for both personal and political reasons, Gambetta was unable to fulfill his ideal of republican unity. Many of the most prominent of his republican colleagues refused to join his government, and he was forced to rely upon his own often young and untried supporters. He himself often acted too imperiously when several years earlier he might have been more accommodating. In attempting to strengthen the central government, he alienated various local interests; in advocating railroad regulation, he caused consternation among some conservative republican businessmen. He took the Foreign Affairs ministry himself and was particularly concerned to ally France with England in Egypt.

The issue which caused his downfall was an issue with which he was long associated. Gambetta, in order to create a stronger unity among republicans, had long urged that deputies should be selected not from individual districts but collectively representing larger areas. For once, Gambetta's opportunism failed him, and the legislature, elected by individual districts, was unwilling to adopt a different system, especially so early in its term of office. Also, many were suspicious of Gambetta's possible dictatorial bent, and when he lost a key vote in the chamber, his government resigned after only seventy-four days.

Summary

Léon Gambetta was only forty-three years old when he resigned. His health had long been poor, and after resigning he took time away from politics to recover his strength. When he returned, he took up the cause of military reform. Gambetta's reputation ever since 1870 had been connected to the fortunes of the military, and many accused him of being too adventurous, particularly in his desire to regain Alsace and Lorraine. Gambetta was conscious of those accusations, and while he never forgot the lost provinces he remained hopeful that someday Germany might be willing to exchange them for overseas territory. Unlike many of his countrymen, Gambetta was interested in colonial development, both in Africa and in Southeast Asia. A colonial empire would add to France's strength;

in addition, colonies might someday be traded for Alsace and Lorraine.

On November 27, 1882, while handling a revolver, Gambetta accidentally shot himself in the hand. The wound, itself minor, became infected. Gambetta gradually weakened, dying on the last day of the year. He was given a state funeral, and his body, at his father's demand, was buried in Nice. In 1920, with the return of Alsace and Lorraine after World War I, Gambetta's heart was placed in the Pantheon in Paris, coinciding with the golden jubilee of the Third French Republic, the republic to which he had been so committed.

An oft-expressed criticism of Gambetta was that he was too closely tied to the working classes of Belleville and that they would ensure that his words and actions would remain too radical for the moderate inclinations of most French voters. Yet he did not see himself as representing only the working classes. He did speak of the "new social strata" which would come to power under the republic, but for Gambetta that controversial phase referred not to the working classes exclusively but rather to the majority of the French population, including the middle classes, which, he argued, had been excluded from power under the kings and emperors of France's past. Gambetta was always more a political than an economic radical, committed to majority political rule instead of advancing the claims of particular economic classes. In that he was a nineteenth century liberal, not a Marxist. Still, his opponents accused him of revolutionary radicalism.

Léon Gambetta's career had been full of paradoxes: a half-Italian who personified French patriotism; a moderate republican who in the eyes of many epitomized revolutionary radicalism; a pragmatic politician accused of being both an ideologue and an opportunist; a representative of the proletariat, or the middle classes, who wished to become dictator. When he died, some argued that he was still posed between Left and Right, and it is impossible to say in which direction he might have turned. What can be said is that he dominated French politics from 1870 until his death in 1882 as did no one else of that time.

Bibliography

Brogan, D. W. *France Under the Republic: The Development of Modern France (1870-1939)*. New York and London: Harper, 1940. Brogan's elegantly written study of the Third Republic is considered one of the classic historical accounts of the subject. Gambetta plays a significant role in the first part of the work, sometimes published separately under the title *From the Fall of the Empire to the Dreyfus Affair*.

Bury, J. P. T. *Gambetta and the Making of the Third Republic*. London: Longman, 1973. The author is the major English biographer of Gambetta. In *Gambetta and the National Defense* (1970), he analyzed Gambetta's role during the Prussian invasion of France in 1870-1871. Here he carries the story of Gambetta and the Third Republic through 1877.

———. *Gambetta's Final Years: "The Era of Difficulties," 1877-1882*. London: Longman, 1936; New York: Longman, 1982. Bury concludes his exhaustive study of Gambetta. The author is sympathetic toward his subject, finding Gambetta to be perhaps the crucial figure in the founding of the Third Republic. Bury is not uncritical, however, suggesting that in his later years Gambetta's judgment was corrupted by his power and popularity.

Deschanel, Paul. *Gambetta*. London: Heinemann, and New York: Dodd, Mead, 1920. Written by a later President of the Third Republic. Well written and sympathetic to the subject. Less a scholarly work than an interpretation of Gambetta's contributions to later French history.

Horne, Alistair. *The Fall of Paris: The Siege of the Commune, 1870-71*. London: Macmillan, 1965; New York: St. Martin's Press, 1966. The author is a specialist in modern French history. Horne presents a very readable story of the aftermath of the Franco-Prussian War, in which Gambetta plays a central role.

Lehning, James R. "Gossiping about Gambetta: Contested Memories in the Early Third Republic." *French Historical Studies* 18, no. 1 (Spring 1993). Analysis of republicanism in the French Third Republic and a discussion concerning the circumstances of Gambetta's death in 1883.

Mayeur, Jean-Marie, and Madeleine Reberioux. *The Third Republic from Its Origins to the Great War, 1871-1914*. Cambridge and New York: Cambridge University Press, 1984. This valuable work is more analytical and more structured than Brogan's work, which was published a generation earlier. Gambetta plays a major role in the early chapters.

Stannard, Harold. *Gambetta and the Foundation of the Third Republic*. London: Methuen, and Boston: Small Maynard, 1921. Like Deschanel's, this study of Gambetta was also written soon after Germany's defeat in World War I. In contrast to Deschanel, however, Stannard is not French, and although he admires Gambetta, Stannard is more critical. Suggests that regardless of Gambetta's own motives, some of his statements and actions did seem to imply, to others, the turn toward dictatorship.

Eugene S. Larson

JAMES A. GARFIELD

Born: November 19, 1831; Orange Township, Ohio
Died: September 19, 1881; Elberon, New Jersey
Areas of Achievement: Government and politics
Contribution: During his almost two decades, first as congressman, then briefly as president, Garfield played a key role in every issue of national importance. As party leader, he helped resolve the factionalism within the Republican Party and enabled the Republicans to lead the United States into the twentieth century.

Early Life

James Abram Garfield was born in a log cabin on November 19, 1831, to Abram and Eliza Garfield, members of the Disciples of Christ church. Abram died in 1833, thus leaving Eliza a widow, the sole provider for her family.

Next to hunting, reading was young Garfield's greatest interest. He liked history and fiction, especially stories of the American Revolution and stories of the sea. At the age of sixteen, Garfield went to Cleveland, where he was shocked and disappointed by a drunken captain to whom he had applied for work. On that same day, August 16, 1848, Garfield secured a job as driver with his cousin on a canal boat that carried goods between Cleveland and Pittsburgh. After six weeks of working on the canal, Garfield became quite ill and returned home. During his recuperation, his mother and Samuel Bates, a schoolteacher, convinced Garfield of the importance of education.

Garfield enrolled and studied at Geauga Academy in Chester, where he became the academy's prize Latin student. Originally, Garfield planned to spend the winter months at the academy and the spring and summers on the canal, but after he absorbed himself in his studies, he decided to forget the canal life.

In the fall of 1851, Garfield enrolled in the newly established Western Reserve Eclectic Institute at Hiram, Ohio, where he plunged into his studies with a fierce determination to excel. Garfield's popularity and prominence at the Western Reserve Eclectic Institute were based on his scholastic ability as well as his physical prowess. His commanding physical appearance—he stood almost six feet tall, with broad shoulders and a massive head topped by a shock of unruly tawny hair—and his ability to outrun and outwrestle his schoolmates instilled automatic respect. This, combined with his serious demeanor, which gave an impression of quiet dignity, and his unaffected friendliness contributed to Garfield's popularity. Enjoying success as a debater, Garfield discovered that he possessed the ability to sway an audience, and the oratorical techniques which he learned during this period prepared him to become one of the most effective political speakers of his time.

In 1853, Garfield began preaching at neighboring churches. The following year, having completed his studies at the Eclectic Institute, he enrolled in Williams College. There, he was elected president of two major campus organizations—the Philogian Society, a literary society, and the Equitable Fraternity, an organization designed to combat the influence of the Greek fraternities. In addition, in spite of his Campbellite beliefs, Garfield was elected president of the Mills Theological Society, a Calvinist organization. He was also elected editor of the *Williams Quarterly*, a pioneer college journal of exceptional quality, to which he contributed extensively. Indeed, Garfield never lost an election at Williams College, nor any election in which he was a candidate for the rest of his life. On August 7, 1856, he was graduated from Williams College with honors in a ceremony that included his delivering an oration on the conflict between matter and spirit.

Life's Work

As an inspiring and electrifying evangelist, Garfield preached continually during the last of the series of so-called Great Awakenings—periodic religious revivals that had begun in the Colonial era. In 1857, at the age of twenty-six, Garfield was elected president of Western Reserve Eclectic Institute, defeating his former teacher, the institute's oldest and most distinguished faculty member. As president, Garfield made the Eclectic Institute the educational center of the region, changing a sectarian academy into an institution that welcomed students of all denominations.

He believed the curriculum should reflect the trends of the time and serve as a medium through which students could prepare for successful living. He sponsored teacher-training workshops and seminars on teaching methods and school administration, and he prepared a series of lectures on Ameri-

can history, a subject which had not been included in the curricula of American colleges.

Garfield did not confine himself to administrative duties; he taught a full load of classes in a style designed to encourage students to think independently. Garfield's kindness and immense vitality, his readiness to praise, his deep concern for the overall welfare of his students, his enthusiasm, his ability to introduce his students to the meaning of education and the high ideals of life, and his participation with them in the extracurricular activities, especially athletic events, inspired great loyalty. The Eclectic Institute prospered under Garfield's leadership. On November 11, 1858, Garfield married Lucretia Rudolph, daughter of Zeb Rudolph, a pioneer Hiram Disciple and one of the school's most prominent trustees.

On August 23, 1859, based on his prominent background and popularity, the Republican Party of the Twenty-sixth Ohio Senatorial District nominated him for the state senate, a seat he handily won, October 11, 1859. This feat ultimately led him to the center stage of the national political arena. Garfield distinguished himself on a number of

key issues, especially those pertaining to slavery and the impending crisis—the Civil War. He stood strong against slavery and, shedding his pacifism, believed that war was the best solution to the problem of slavery. When the war began, he took an active role in raising troops, influencing the governor of his state to appoint him lieutenant colonel in the Twenty-fourth Ohio Infantry; later, he was put in charge of the Forty-second Ohio Volunteer Infantry as a full colonel. Learning about Garfield's commission, the young men of Hiram, who held Garfield in the highest esteem, enthusiastically joined the Forty-second Ohio Volunteer Infantry to follow and fight with their hero.

At the outset of Garfield's military service, General Don Carlos Buell assigned him command of the Eighteenth Brigade and gave him the responsibility of planning the campaign to drive the Confederate army out of eastern Kentucky. In spite of the fact that Garfield had no military education or military experience, he accepted the task, presenting a plan which Buell accepted. Under Garfield's leadership, the Confederate forces were driven out of Kentucky.

Assuming control of the administration of eastern Kentucky, Garfield pursued a policy of reconciliation. Promoted to brigadier general, he served outstandingly as chief of staff under General William S. Rosecrans, commander of the Army of the Cumberland. Garfield reached the peak of his military career in the Chattanooga campaign, fighting in one of the epic battles of military history, the Battle of Chickamauga. Garfield's outstanding achievements in the Kentucky campaign led his friends and the Republican Party of the Nineteenth Congressional District to nominate him as their representative to Congress, September 2, 1862. While still in the army carrying out his military duties and without participating in the campaign, he won the right to represent the Nineteenth District by an impressive victory, in the congressional election of October, 1862.

Beginning with the election of 1862, Garfield easily won nine consecutive terms, splendidly serving the people of the Nineteenth District for the next eighteen years as chairman of the Military Affairs Committee (in which capacity he was the first to introduce a bill that proposed an ROTC program for the colleges), chairman of the Banking and Currency Committee, and chairman of the powerful and prestigious Appropriations Committee.

When the Democratic Party won a majority of the seats in the House of Representatives in the congressional election of 1874, Garfield assumed the leadership of the Republican minority in the House. Having lost his chairmanships, he skillfully and relentlessly spoke out against the policies of the Democratic Party. As a member of a bipartisan committee selected to investigate the 1876 presidential election in the state of Louisiana, Garfield submitted a thorough report based on data presented to him by the election board and interviews he held with those who participated in the election and those denied participation, especially voters who were terrorized by white secret societies such as the Ku Klux Klan, the Knights of the White Camellia, and the Rifle Clubs. His report helped influence the election board to nullify Samuel Tilden's majority, and Rutherford B. Hayes was granted the electoral votes of Louisiana.

The 1876 election ended in an intense controversy involving the returns of Florida, Louisiana, and South Carolina. This situation produced a political stalemate that set the stage for a potential crisis that might have led the opposing parties back to the battlefields in a new civil war. Garfield served as a member of a special Electoral Commission to elect the president and participated in the historic conference that led to the compromise between the leaders of the Republican Party and the Southern Democrats. These actions resolved the impending crisis, and Hayes became the nineteenth president of the United States.

On March 29, 1879, Garfield established himself as the outstanding leader of the Republican Party when he delivered one of the most dynamic speeches in the history of Congress. The Democrats' dogged advocacy of the principle of states' rights motivated Garfield to present his greatest speech—a speech that upheld the principle of federalism and inspired the Republicans to quit squabbling and act together as a strong united party. This speech influenced his state's legislature to elect him to serve in the United States Senate, and ultimately led to his nomination and election as President of the United States.

In 1880, Garfield was elected to serve as a delegate to the Seventh National Nominating Convention of the Republican Party, which met in Chicago. He came to the convention without any intention of seeking the nomination, but because of his great popularity, he was considered a darkhorse candidate. On the thirty-sixth ballot, the deadlocked delegates chose Garfield, hoping that he could unify the party. In a move that displeased a large number of Republicans, but as a means of placating the highly disappointed Stalwarts, who had supported Ulysses S. Grant for a third term, the imperious political boss of the New York Republican Party, Chester Alan Arthur, was selected as the party's candidate for vice president.

In November, Garfield's ability to control the various factions of his party and brilliantly manage his campaign, resulted in his winning the presidency in the closest presidential election of the century. In view of the fact that he did nothing either before or during the convention to obtain his party's nomination (he strongly opposed the effort that culminated in his nomination) and the fact that his party had all but self-destructed since the assassination of President Abraham Lincoln, Garfield achieved a magnificent victory.

On July 2, 1881, only a few months after his inauguration, Garfield was shot by a crazed office-seeker, Charles Guiteau. He died on September 19, 1881.

Summary

Garfield's election to the presidency was the crowning achievement of a spectacular and glorious career that began as the driver of a towboat on the Ohio Erie Canal. His was a classic American success story, brought to a tragically premature end.

The legacy of Garfield's brief term suggests what he might have accomplished had he lived to complete it. He laid the foundation for the development of a more independent and vigorous presidency that proved vital for a nation destined to become one of the most powerful nations in the world. The Pendleton Act of 1883, which led to the end of the spoils system in the federal government, was the logical conclusion of his efforts.

Bibliography

Booraem, Hendrik. *The Road to Respectability: James A. Garfield and His World, 1844-1852.* Lewisburg, Pa.: Bucknell University Press, 1988.

Brisbin, James S. *From the Tow-Path to the White House: The Early Life and Public Career of James A. Garfield.* Philadelphia: Hubbard, 1880. A flattering campaign biography, written in a romantic style shortly after Garfield's nomination. Although hurriedly written, Brisbin's work vividly recounts the story of a leader who exemplified fundamental American values. Includes illustrations.

Caldwell, Robert G. *James A. Garfield, Party Chieftain*. New York: Dodd, Mead, 1934. An exhaustive scholarly chronicle of the life of Garfield that, in effect, summarizes American political history from 1861 to 1881. Includes an excellent bibliography.

Clark, James C. *The Murder of James A. Garfield: The President's Last Days and the Trial and Execution of his Assassin*. Jefferson, N.C.: McFarland, 1993. An objective treatment of the subject in an enjoyable narrative style. Clark profiles Garfield's killer, Charles Guiteau, and covers the assassination plot, the medical care given to Garfield afterwards, the president's funeral, and the trial and execution of Guiteau.

Doenecke, Justus D. *The Presidencies of James A. Garfield and Chester A. Arthur*. Lawrence: University Press of Kansas, 1981. This is one of the volumes of the American Presidency Series, intended to present historians and the general public with interesting, scholarly assessments of the various presidential administrations. Includes excellent notes and bibliographical essays.

Hinsdale, Mary L., ed. *Garfield-Hinsdale Letters: Correspondence Between James Abram Garfield and Burke Aaron Hinsdale*. Ann Arbor: University of Michigan Press, 1949. The correspondence between James A. Garfield and his lifelong friend, Burke A. Hinsdale, a former pupil of Garfield, superintendent of Cleveland's Public School System, outstanding teacher at the University of Michigan, and president of Hiram College. The letters between Garfield and Hinsdale discuss the various issues that confronted America between 1857 and 1881, as well as the most popular books of the period; they also reveal the writers in their lighter moods. Their correspondence, which began when Hinsdale was nineteen and continued until Garfield's death, provides graphic self-portraits of Garfield and Hinsdale, and is a significant resource for scholars of Garfield.

Leech, Margaret, and Harry J. Brown. *The Garfield Orbit*. New York: Harper, 1978. An absorbing story of the life of Garfield, showing him as a man of complex and contradictory character, in whom ambition and desire warred with firm principle. The book reveals more of the man and less of the vital issues that he confronted. Includes a Garfield genealogy; a selection of Garfield's letters; notes and references; sixty-three illustrations, mainly photographs and sketches; and maps of the Western Reserve and the military campaigns of Garfield during the Civil War.

Riddle, Albert G. *The Life, Character and Public Services of James A. Garfield*. Cleveland, Ohio: Williams, 1880. This is a classic biography of Garfield that covers the period from his birth to his nomination as the standard-bearer of the Republican Party.

Smith, Theodore Clark. *The Life and Letters of James Abram Garfield*. 2 vols. New Haven, Conn.: Yale University Press, 1925. Smith's biographical study is principally based on Garfield's own words contained in his letters, journals, school and college notes, speeches, and memorabilia. The author's masterful selection and arrangement of the materials produces the effect of Garfield himself interpreting his life.

James D. Lockett

GIUSEPPE GARIBALDI

Born: July 4, 1807; Nice, France
Died: June 2, 1882; Caprera, Italy
Area of Achievement: The military
Contribution: Hero of the Risorgimento, Garibaldi inspired Italy to unite under the leadership of Victor Emanuel of Piedmont and Sardinia. His victory over Naples was the key achievement in bringing about a unified Italy and capped a life devoted to wars of liberation.

Early Life

Giuseppe Garibaldi was born in Nice on July 4, 1807, the son and grandson of sailors. Nice was, in 1807, a French town, but it was ceded to the Kingdom of Sardinia and Piedmont in 1815. Garibaldi is said to have learned to speak and read Italian from a priest, who also taught him the history of Italy and filled him with an enthusiasm for his country. His youth was marked by numerous events, some difficult to distinguish from the legends that naturally arise around a charismatic figure. One such story describes an escape with friends from school at age fourteen, including the seizure of a sailboat and embarkation in it for Constantinople. Garibaldi's disinclination toward disciplined intellectual activity induced him to leave school at an early age and to embark upon a career as a seaman, and he first pursued a sailor's life working on cargo ships in trade with the eastern Mediterranean and Black Sea.

On one of his voyages, a shipmate informed him of an organization inspired by the Italian nationalist leader Giuseppe Mazzini, Young Italy, pledged to the cause of liberating Italy from foreigners. By 1834 an ardent member of the society, Garibaldi participated in a plot to seize a ship in the port of Genoa; the plot was discovered and Garibaldi fled to Marseilles, where he learned from an Italian newspaper that he had been condemned to death.

From Marseilles, Garibaldi sailed for South America, reaching Rio de Janeiro. Brazil and the republic Rio Grande do Sul were at war. Talking to some prisoners, Garibaldi quickly resolved to help the small state in its war, and the rest of his twelve years on the continent were spent fighting for Rio Grande in its war with Brazil and for Uruguay in its war with Argentina. He fought primarily at sea as a pirate, attacking Brazilian shipping until 1843, when he formed an Italian legion, whose "uniform" consisted of red shirts (from a happy oppor-

tunity to buy at a good price shirts otherwise destined for workers in slaughterhouses). During this time, he carried off (1839) and later married Anna Maria Ribeiro da Silva, who shared his exploits and glory until her death in 1849.

In South America, Garibaldi practiced and mastered the techniques of guerrilla fighting that were to serve him in Italy. He also learned how to command and inspire men. In later life, he was criticized for being a rather lax disciplinarian, but it may be said in his defense that comradeship is perhaps better than strict discipline at inspiring a volunteer guerrilla army. Surely he gained more experience in military matters than any other Italian of his generation.

His greatest battles were perhaps fought toward the end of his South American exile, in behalf of Uruguay. His victory at Sant'Antonio in 1846 won for him fame in Italy, where a sword of honor was inscribed for him. In 1847, commanding the defense of the capital, Montevideo, he met Alexandre Dumas, *père*, whose life of Garibaldi added adventures to an already adventuresome life.

Life's Work

Early in 1848, news reached Garibaldi of the revolutions taking place in Europe, and, together with his wife and children and many members of his Italian legion, he set sail for Italy, intending to participate in the war for independence against Austria. In Italy, his offers to fight were rebuffed first by Pope Pius IX, then by King Charles of Piedmont-Sardinia. Garibaldi and his men fought for Charles anyway and engaged in several bloody fights at Como, Varese, and Laveno. His troops were finally scattered, and Garibaldi retired into Switzerland. Soon afterward, he made his way to his childhood home of Nice, where he and his wife enjoyed a few months of domestic life.

The intense fervor to unify Italy, still seen as a visionary and quixotic dream by all but the most ardent followers of Mazzini, stirred Garibaldi to go to Rome when, with the pope in flight, an opportunity presented itself in late 1848. There he tried to organize Rome's independence, but, when the French planned to reinstate the pope as head of the government, Garibaldi fought against the French siege of the city. Although victory was highly unlikely, Garibaldi, his men, and indeed the

people of Rome fought gallantly for nearly three months, ringing the bells of the city at the approach of the French and erecting barricades in the streets to prevent or delay their entrance. Eager not to fall into the hands of French and papal supporters, Garibaldi and about four thousand of his men began a retreat across Campagna to the Adriatic. The enemy pursued him hotly, and Garibaldi was compelled to hasten his retreat. He managed to escape, but at the cost of his dear wife, who died from the exertions.

A fugitive again, unwelcomed by the King of Piedmont-Sardinia, hunted by the Austrians, Garibaldi left his children with his parents in Nice and went to live and work on Staten Island, New York. He soon returned to sea and became the commander of a Peruvian sailing vessel. Learning in 1853 of the death of his mother and the repeal of the order banishing him from Italy, he returned to Nice. In 1856, he bought a parcel of land on the island of Caprera, between Sardinia and Corsica, and planned to retire. In 1859, when the war of France and Sardinia against Austria broke out, King Victor Emanuel of Piedmont-Sardinia and his minister Count Cavour invited Garibaldi to form an army and fight with them. He formed the Cacciatori delle Alpi and achieved notable success by guerrilla maneuvers in the Tirol region of the Alps.

In May, 1860, Garibaldi set sail for Sicily with about one thousand volunteers, later to be celebrated in Italian history as the mythical *Mille*, who made the Italian peninsula into a modern nation. His aim was ostensibly to aid an insurgent revolt against Sicily's master, Naples. Garibaldi landed at Marsala amid artillery fire from several Neapolitan frigates and at once met with success. With additional volunteers constantly joining his ranks, he defeated the Neapolitan army at Calatafimi and marched toward Palermo, the largest and most important city in Sicily. The city was well fortified with Neapolitan soldiers, but, after several feints, Garibaldi entered the city in the dawn of May 26 and had the city in his control by mid-morning. Additional volunteers kept coming from all Sicily to join him, and the Neapolitan troops withdrew. He declared himself dictator and established provisional governments throughout the island. Taking advantage of his victories, he hastened across the Strait of Messina and charged through Calabria to Naples, which he entered on September 7, 1860. As "Dictator of the Two Sicilies" he fought a battle against a Neapolitan army

in October. By then, his army had increased to thirty thousand, the largest number of men Garibaldi had ever commanded, and it held the line victoriously at the Volturno River.

Plebiscites conducted throughout the southern peninsula and in Sicily gave Garibaldi the authority to present these lands to Victor Emanuel. When the king arrived in November, Garibaldi met him ceremoniously, but when the king and his court—perhaps anxious about some of Garibaldi's radical and revolutionary ideas, perhaps envious of Garibaldi's enormous popularity—would not grant him powers over these newly added lands, Garibaldi retired to his home in Caprera. His retirement was short-lived. In April, 1861, he was elected to the Chamber of Deputies, where he opposed Cavour and the king. He also caused embarrassment when in July, 1862, he appealed to Hungary to revolt against Austria. When some of his officers were arrested, Garibaldi threatened to attack Rome. Slipping through a blockade of Napoleon III, he landed in Italy and, with more than two thousand of his followers, fought a battle near Aspromonte. Garibaldi was badly wounded and imprisoned but was soon released and returned to Caprera. Though he had seemed to be independent, it became clear that he was working with the king to effect Rome's accession to the kingdom. Between 1867 and 1871, Garibaldi participated in two more campaigns, another unsuccessful expedition to the Papal States and an attempt to help France in its war with Prussia. He then retired to his home in Caprera, wrote his memoirs, and tried to overcome the infirmities of age and of a body scarred with thirty battle wounds. He died in 1882.

Summary

Few in their own lifetimes enjoyed as much repute as did Giuseppe Garibaldi. Abraham Lincoln invited him to take a command at the beginning of the Civil War; unhappy with Lincoln's refusal to take a stronger stand against slavery, however, Garibaldi refused. When in 1864 Garibaldi went to England, he was received by thousands of well-wishers. The peoples of the world recognized in Garibaldi a man sincere in his love of freedom, a man selfless in his devotion to his cause, a man absolutely incorruptible. Because he was uncompromisingly idealistic, he was an inspiration to his people; indeed, more than Mazzini, Cavour, or even Victor Emanuel himself, Garibaldi represented the spirit of Italian unification.

Garibaldi's military successes were perhaps also a manifestation of his character and most particularly of his courage. What academy-trained military man would have ventured the risks he did and against such overwhelming odds? Indeed, the very riskiness of his adventures often secured their success, for surprise was easier to achieve when the hazards seemed overwhelming. Garibaldi stands as one of the great patriots of all time, a "hero of two worlds" and for all times. If he was at times over-credulous and naïve, such may be attributed to his good heart, the same good heart which was the source of his heroic splendor.

Bibliography

Garibaldi, Giuseppe. *Autobiography of Giuseppe Garibaldi.* Translated by A. Werner, with a supplement by Jessie White Mario. London: Smith and Innes, 1889; New York: Fertig, 1971. A two-volume translation of Garibaldi's memoirs, certainly the starting place for serious study of Garibaldi. The supplement provides insights by one of the subject's friends.

Hibbert, Christopher. *Garibaldi and His Enemies: The Clash of Arms and Personalities in the Making of Italy.* London: Longman, 1965; Boston: Little Brown, 1966. Deliberately not a social history. The subtitle suggests its focus: the person-alities and events out of which came the Risorgimento. A less flattering biography than older accounts.

Mack Smith, Denis. *Garibaldi: A Great Life in Brief.* New York: Knopf, 1956. A readable biography, providing a portrait of Garibaldi as more a passionate than an intellectual figure.

———, ed. *Garibaldi.* London: Hutchinson, 1957; Englewood Cliffs, N.J.: Prentice-Hall, 1969. A biography put together from original documents, here all conveniently translated into English.

Ridley, Jasper. *Garibaldi.* London: Constable, 1974; New York: Viking Press, 1976. A highly detailed and massive biography, perhaps relying too much on secondary sources for Italian history, but vivid in its portrayal of Garibaldi as a personality.

Trevelyan, G. M. *Garibaldi's Defence of the Roman Republic (1848-9).* London and New York: Longman, 1907.

———. *Garibaldi and the Thousand (May, 1860).* London and New York: Longman, 1909.

———. *Garibaldi and the Making of Italy (June-November, 1860).* London and New York: Longman, 1911. For many years the most widely read books about Garibaldi in the English-speaking world. Notable for their romantic portrait of Garibaldi as hero.

James A. Arieti

WILLIAM LLOYD GARRISON

Born: December 10, 1805; Newburyport, Massachusetts

Died: May 24, 1879; New York, New York

Areas of Achievement: Abolitionism and antebellum reform

Contribution: A crucial figure in the demise of American slavery and the coming of the Civil War, Garrison combined Protestant Evangelicalism, Jeffersonian liberalism, and Quaker humanism into a radical antislavery doctrine that called for the immediate end of the institution of slavery.

Early Life

In his 1913 biography of William Lloyd Garrison, John Jay Chapman described his subject's emergence as a radical abolitionist in 1830 as a streaking, white-hot meteorite crashing into the middle of Boston Commons. Little in Garrison's background, however, foretold of his career as a professional reformer and as the father of the radical antislavery movement. His parents, Abijah and Frances (Fanny) Maria Lloyd Garrison, had once lived simply and obscurely in wealthy Newburyport, Massachusetts. By the summer of 1808, however, President Thomas Jefferson's embargo had nearly destroyed New England's merchant marine, inflicting immense suffering upon lower middle-class sailing masters such as Abijah. That same summer, the Garrisons' five-year-old daughter died from an accidental poisoning. Abijah Garrison could not withstand the pressure and grief of this period. He took to heavy drinking and then deserted his struggling family of three. The childhood of young William Lloyd was then an even greater ordeal, and he often had to beg for food from the homes of Newburyport's wealthy residents.

In 1815, Lloyd, as he was called, was apprenticed to a Maryland shoemaker, but the young boy simply lacked the physical strength to do the work. In 1817, Lloyd found himself back in Newburyport, alone and apprenticed to a cabinetmaker. That work also proved unsuitable. When he was thirteen, his luck began to change when he secured an apprenticeship with the editor of the Newburyport *Herald.* Lloyd feared another failure, but within weeks he displayed remarkable skill and speed. The editor quickly made him shop foreman. Garrison had found his life's work.

After mastering the mechanics of the trade, Lloyd was eager to print his own writing. Like Benjamin Franklin a century before, he submitted editorials under a pseudonym (Garrison used "An Old Bachelor") which his boss liked and published. "An Old Bachelor" gained much attention, even from conservative political leaders. In 1826, with a loan from his former employer, Garrison purchased his own newspaper, which he immediately named the *Free Press.* Seeking respectability and entrance into the ruling elite of Massachusetts, Garrison advocated the conservative politics and social ideas of the Federalist Party. The *Free Press* became bellicose in its political stands, denouncing everything that smacked of Jeffersonian democracy. During his brief tenure at the paper, Garrison discovered the poet John Greenleaf Whittier, published his first poetry, and also made some oblique criticisms of the institution of slavery, but he revealed nothing that gave the slightest indication of what lay only four years in the future.

Following this relatively conservative initiation into his journalistic career, Garrison became more and more strident in his style and radical in the

opinions he voiced in editorials, to the extent that he lost subscribers, defaulted on his loan, and lost his paper. In 1828, he drifted to the *National Philanthropist*, a temperance paper, and attacked dancing, theatergoing, dueling, and gambling. The fiery editor denounced war and began to display a more thoroughgoing disdain for the institution of slavery by decrying a South Carolina law outlawing black education. Garrison soon repeated his familiar pattern and within six months found himself without a job. He managed to secure a position at the *Journal of the Times* in Bennington, Vermont, and there railed at intemperance and advanced his ideas concerning peace and gradual emancipation.

In 1829, Garrison had become radicalized on the issue of slavery, about one year after reading Benjamin Lundy's newspaper, the *Genius of Universal Emancipation*. Garrison had met Lundy, a Quaker abolitionist, in 1828 and had adopted his views on the gradual emancipation of American slaves. On July 4, 1829, again unemployed, Garrison delivered his first antislavery speech, indicting the North for its racism and declaring that gradual emancipation was the only possible way to end slavery. Then, after reading the works of black Americans such as David Walker and English abolitionists such as James Cropper, Garrison decided to dedicate his life to ending what he viewed as the greatest abomination in American history. He went to work for Lundy and moved back to Baltimore, Maryland, where he coedited the *Genius of Universal Emancipation*.

Before the end of 1829, Garrison had abandoned gradual emancipation—Lundy had not—and called for the immediate end of slavery. He lashed out against slaveholders and even against New Englanders who countenanced the institution. On April 17, 1830, he was confined to a Baltimore jail for criminal libel against a New England merchant. Word of Garrison's imprisonment circulated throughout the North and eventually reached the ears of the wealthy New York merchants and reformers, Arthur and Lewis Tappan. They bailed Garrison out of jail and paid his fines. He wandered back to Boston and decided to set up a new paper there.

On October 16, 1830, Garrison advertised a series of public lectures on the subject of slavery and the American Colonization Society. The ACS, established in 1817, claimed to oppose slavery and favored black uplift and the evangelization of Africa, but Garrison sought to expose it as a tool of the slaveocrats who actually perpetuated slavery. At the October lectures, Garrison denounced the ACS as a racist organization that intended to expel free black Americans if they refused to leave voluntarily. Boston's liberal and conservative clergy alike reacted to the lectures with disgust. Other thinkers, such as Samuel Joseph May, a renegade Unitarian minister and reformer, Bronson Alcott, a Transcendentalist educator and May's brother-in-law, and Samuel E. Sewall, May's cousin, became captivated by Garrison's moral vigor and earnestness. They instantly converted to radical abolitionism and pledged to aid the young editor. Emergence of the *Liberator* the following year established Garrison as the leader of the radical antislavery movement.

Life's Work

William Lloyd Garrison stood about five feet, six inches tall. His slender, almost fragile frame supported a massive bald head, and his powerful blue eyes were framed by tiny, steel, oval-shaped spectacles. Although relentless on the lecture platform, in private Garrison comported himself with great dignity and grace. Like many reformers, he married late. While lecturing in Providence, Rhode Island, in 1829, he met Helen Benson, the daughter of the Quaker philanthropist, George Benson. Timid in the presence of women and lacking a stable career, Garrison initiated a long courtship, finally marrying Helen on September 4, 1834.

On January 1, 1831, Garrison published the first issue of the *Liberator*. It angered Northerners as irrational and incendiary and struck fear in slaveholders as an uncompromising condemnation. Garrison, as a pacifist, eschewed violent rebellion, but his strident language—something entirely new in the long history of American antislavery thought—inaugurated a new era in American history. He denounced slavery as sin, called upon all true Christians immediately to abandon it no matter what the cost to the Union, and blasted those who thought slavery might be gradually abandoned. What, gradually stop sin? Tell a man to rescue his wife from a rapist gradually? Garrison thundered. Why complain of the severity of my language, he cried, when so unutterable an evil abounded. Ignoring his critics, Garrison lashed out: "I *will be* as harsh as truth, and as uncompromising as justice. . . . I will not excuse—I will not retreat a single inch—AND I WILL BE HEARD."

Garrison's antislavery appeal fused the evangelical fervor of the Second Great Awakening, which had begun in the 1790's, with the long-standing

Quaker opposition to slavery. He had tapped an essential root of American thought, and if he could convince Americans that slavery was, in fact, sin, then they would have to accept his second proposition that it be immediately abandoned. Southerners understandably recoiled from his rhetoric, but they were horrified when, eight months after appearance of the *Liberator*, Nat Turner turned Virginia inside out by fomenting a slave rebellion and killing dozens of whites, including women and children. Southerners connected the two events, blamed Garrison for the killings, put a price on his head, and demanded that Massachusetts suppress the newspaper and its editor.

In January, 1832, Garrison and twelve men—antislavery apostles—founded the New England Anti-Slavery Society. In June, he published his influential *Thoughts on African Colonization* (1832), and, for the next three years, Garrison and his associates dedicated themselves to destroying the credibility of the American Colonization Society. He helped found the American Anti-Slavery Society on December 4, 1833. Between 1833 and 1840, two hundred Auxiliaries of the American Anti-Slavery Society were organized from Massachusetts to Michigan with about 200,000 members. They sent antislavery agents throughout the North to whip up controversy and support for the cause.

The growth of radical antislavery thought caused great consternation. Between 1830 and 1840, abolitionists suffered from personal and physical abuse. Rocks, bricks, and the contents of outhouses were thrown at them. They were denounced as anarchists who would destroy the Union if it suited their whim. In 1836, Southern states requested Governor Edward Everett of Massachusetts to suppress Garrison and his friends. On November 7, 1837, Illinois abolitionist editor Elijah P. Lovejoy was assassinated by a rampaging mob determined to destroy his newspaper, the *Alton Observer*. The attacks on abolitionists and the murder of Lovejoy sparked unprecedented sympathy for the antislavery advocates, who could now justifiably claim that abolitionism and a defense of a free press and free speech were inseparable.

To Garrison, abolitionism was only the most important of a collection of reforms, from women's rights to temperance, connected by a liberal Christian faith in a benevolent God and the rejection of all forms of force and violence. In 1836, Garrison learned of two extraordinary women from Charleston, South Carolina. Sarah and Angelina Grimké,

born into a slaveholding family, had rejected their home and human bondage, converted to Quakerism, and moved north. In 1837, Garrison arranged a speaking tour for them in New England. Huge crowds turned out for the sisters, who risked their reputations to ignore the social restrictions against women speaking in public. Indeed, during the course of their tour, the Grimkés became ardent exponents of women's rights, having seen how prominent clergymen denounced their violation of women's restricted sphere. Garrison supported the sisters and opened up the Massachusetts Anti-Slavery Society to women, urging his conservative colleagues to do the same.

Garrison's support for women's rights brought howls of protest from other abolitionists, who urged him to avoid "extraneous" issues and stick to antislavery work. He refused to compromise and answered his critics by becoming even more radical. At the September, 1838, meeting of the American Peace Society, Garrison, May, and Henry C. Wright, a radical Garrisonian, attempted to gain the society's acceptance of nonresistance thought. They wanted to outlaw as utterly unchristian all forms of war, force, and violence, even denying one's right to defend oneself. When faced with an attacker, according to nonresistance thought, one could only respond with Christian meekness and manifestations of love. Garrison, May, and Wright all claimed that they had personally disarmed robbers or criminals with love. Conservatives refused to accept the new doctrine or to permit women to participate in their society, and they left the meeting. In response, Garrison and his friends formed the New England Nonresistance Society to spread what they saw as true Christian principles.

Garrison's extreme ideas fractured his own Massachusetts Anti-Slavery Society in 1839 and the American Anti-Slavery Society in 1840. Although the antislavery movement seemed to be crumbling, Garrison responded in typical fashion. While many of the best young male abolitionists avoided Garrison's organizations and went into politics, Garrison damned the political system. In 1842, he advocated the dissolution of the Union. The nation had become so corrupt, so dominated by slave power that no hope existed for slavery's end so long as the South remained in the Union. Although his critics argued that no hope for the end of slavery existed if the South left the Union, Garrison ignored them. In 1843, the *Liberator* adopted its most radical stand yet. The "compact which exists between the North and the South is 'a covenant with death, and an agreement with hell'—involving both parties in atrocious criminality; and should be immediately annulled." Beginning March 17, 1843, Garrison placed the slogan "NO UNION WITH SLAVE-HOLDERS!" on the masthead of his newspaper, where it remained until the Civil War.

Split over women's rights and nonresistance ideas, the antislavery movement nearly ended by the mid-1840's. Little money flowed in and few Americans could accept disunionism, no matter how much they hated slavery. Passage of the Fugitive Slave Act in 1850 boosted the American Anti-Slavery Society's prospects, since most Northerners came to hate the law as an infringement of constitutionally protected rights. As the nation moved toward civil war during the 1850's, Garrison increased his attacks on slavery, the Constituion, and the Union. With the firing on Fort Sumter in April, 1861, however, he supported Abraham Lincoln and the Union cause. Although many of his associates thought the South ought to leave the Union peacefully, Garrison saw the war as perhaps the only opportunity to end slavery, even if it did violate his peace principles. He thus supported the Lincoln Administration's war policy, all the while urging the president to abolish slavery. When Lincoln signed the Emancipation Proclamation in 1863, Garrison was ecstatic, and when the nation adopted the Thirteenth Amendment, abolishing slavery, in 1865, he felt vindicated. Believing his life's purpose fulfilled, Garrison retired from activism, though he continued to support the Republican Party and causes such as temperance and women's rights. He died in New York City on May 24, 1879.

Summary

Although Garrison harbored some racial prejudice, he was a pioneer of racial justice. He argued that racism and slavery worked hand-in-hand and that Northern prejudice and Southern intransigence shared equally in the responsibility for perpetuating slavery. Garrison's message of racial justice and abolitionism threatened the nation's class system, which exploited free Northern blacks as well as Southern slaves and endangered the tenuous bonds that had kept the Union together since the formation of the Constitution. Public reaction to Garrison did not change until passage of the Emancipation Proclamation in 1863. Before the war's end, he became a prophetic figure to Americans. The Boston mobs that tried to lynch him in 1834

raised statues to him in 1865. Modern historians have recognized Garrison's indispensable role in the ending of American slavery and have hailed him for his simple claim that the Declaration of Independence ought to speak for everyone, black and white, male and female.

Bibliography

Browne, Stephen H. "Textual Style and Radical Critique in William Lloyd Garrison's 'Thoughts on African Colonization'." *Communication Studies* 47, no. 3 (Fall 1996). Examines Garrison's "Thoughts on African Colonization" as an example of how textual styles can influence reform movements.

Chapman, John Jay. *William Lloyd Garrison*. 2d ed. Boston: Atlantic Monthly Press, 1921. A sympathetic early biography by the son of one of Garrison's associates.

Friedman, Lawrence J. *Gregarious Saints: Self and Community in American Abolitionism, 1830-1870*. Cambridge and New York: Cambridge University Press, 1982. Representative of the best modern studies of the abolitionist movement. Gives an inside look at the subtle distinctions the reformers made on a variety of topics related to voting, the Constitution, and how distinct groups of reformers sprang up around charismatic figures such as Garrison, Gerrit Smith, or the Tappan brothers.

Garrison, William Lloyd. *The Letters of William Lloyd Garrison*. Edited by Walter M. Merrill and Louis Ruchames. 6 vols. Cambridge, Mass.: Harvard University Press, 1971-1981. The best way for the student to become acquainted with Garrison is to read the activist's own work. These are copiously annotated personal and public letters that fully display the thinking and the sometimes idiosyncratic personality of the *Liberator*'s chief editor.

Kraditor, Alieen S. *Means and Ends in American Abolitionism: Garrison and His Critics on Strategy and Tactics, 1834-1850*. New York: Pantheon Books, 1969. Far and away the best book on Garrison's movement and thought. Kraditor fully explores the controversy of the "woman question" and argues convincingly that, in order for Garrison to gain acceptance of a minimum of antislavery thought, he had to remain more radical than the nation and many of his antislavery brethren.

Mayer, Henry. *All on Fire: William Lloyd Garrison and the Abolition of Slavery*. New York: St. Martin's Press, 1998. A revisionist biography centering on Garrison's intellectual life and the activist stands he took. Dry style; recommended only for academic libraries.

Merrill, Walter M. *Against Wind and Tide: A Biography of William Lloyd Garrison.* Cambridge, Mass.: Harvard University Press, 1963. A thorough and often critical examination of the abolitionist's career. The text emphasizes Garrison's personality, which could be extremely abrasive and unforgiving. The author recognizes, however, that it took an abrasive personality to challenge the foundations of American society.

Perry, Lewis. *Radical Abolitionism: Anarchy and the Government of God in Antislavery Thought.* Ithaca, N.Y.: Cornell University Press, 1973. The most sophisticated treatment of antislavery thought, concentrating on Garrison and his non-resistance colleagues. Perry examines the origins of Garrison's thinking and connects it to wider trends in Western Christian thought.

Stewart, James B. *Holy Warriors: The Abolitionists and American Slavery.* New York: Hill and Wang, 1976. A good, readable survey of the antislavery movement, emphasizing Garrison's role and the religious nature of the movement that stemmed from the influence of the Second Great Awakening.

Thomas, John L. *The Liberator: William Lloyd Garrison, A Biography.* Boston: Little Brown, 1963. The best study of Garrison; it appreciates his central role in the movement but remains critical of his tactics and personality. Thoroughly researched, and more detailed than Merrill's biography.

Donald Yacovone

PAUL GAUGUIN

Born: June 7, 1848; Paris, France
Died: May 8, 1903; Atuana, Marquesas Islands
Area of Achievement: Art
Contribution: Gauguin epitomized a rejection of nineteenth century realism and its final phase, Impressionism, in favor of a new approach to painting based on primitive art; a simplification of lines, colors, and forms; and a suppression of detail, all intended to enhance the intellectual-emotional impact of a work of art. His program amounted in fact to a deliberate overthrow of the primacy of the optical sensation that had dictated all art since the Renaissance and is therefore the single most revolutionary thought introduced by a nineteenth century artist.

Early Life

An extraordinary childhood and youth preceded Paul Gauguin's entry into the bourgeois world of business and finance. His parents, Clovis and Aline, active in liberal circles, felt forced to flee Paris (after the *coup d'état* of Napoleon III in 1851) and to seek refuge in Peru, where Aline's uncle, Don Piot Tristán y Moscoso, who would soon adopt her as his daughter, lived a life of leisure and luxury. Clovis died during the ocean voyage, but Aline, with children Marie and Paul, arrived in Lima to remain there for four years. Although only a small child during his stay in Lima, Gauguin was never to forget that country. Indeed, his persistent longing for the faraway and exotic no doubt had its roots in his rich, unencumbered childhood years in Peru.

Mother and children returned to France in 1855, and Paul spent the next seven years as a solitary, morose, and withdrawn schoolboy who learned "to hate hypocrisy, false virtues, tale-bearing, and to beware of everything that was contrary to my instincts, my heart, and my reason." In his seventeenth year, he hired on as a seaman on a ship sailing to South America, beginning a career that would keep him at sea for six years, part of that time as an enlisted man in the French navy.

Aline, who died at age forty-two in 1865, had appointed a business friend as guardian to her children, and it was through him that Gauguin in 1871 became a stockbroker, sufficiently successful to offer marriage to a Danish woman, Mette Sophie Gad, in 1873. In his financial career, he met Émile

Schuffenecker, a Sunday painter who convinced Gauguin to take up the same hobby; his interest in art, together with a reasonable affluence that enabled him to become an art patron, brought him into contact with Camille Pissarro, the paterfamilias of the Impressionist group, whose influence is readily detected in Gauguin's early, still-hesitant paintings. In 1883, by now the father of five children, he resigned as a stockbroker to devote all of his energy to the arts.

Life's Work

Gauguin's first official entry into the art world took place in 1876, when he exhibited a canvas in the Impressionist style at the annual Parisian Salon. From 1879 until 1886, he showed in the last five exhibits of the Impressionists. Shortly thereafter, with his family settled in Copenhagen, he set out for Central America, working for a time on the construction site of the Panama Canal, then stopping in Martinique, where he produced his first canvas depicting a tropical paradise, a view of the Bay of Saint-Pierre, still in the Impressionist spirit, yet with a color vibrancy that reflects his emotional reaction to the subject.

Back in France in 1888, he took up residence in Pont-Aven, Brittany. "I love Brittany," he said in a letter to Schuffenecker. "I find here the wild and the primitive. When my clogs ring out on its granite soil, I hear the low, flat, powerful note I seek in painting." Joining him in Pont-Aven were Émile Bernard and Louis Anquetin, young experimental painters whose ideas were close to Gauguin's. All three felt moved by the rich colors of medieval enamelwork and cloisonné, and favored reducing visual phenomena to abstract lines and flat colors, a pictorial method clearly employed by Japanese printmakers, whose works were then much in vogue. Gauguin's Brittany paintings, such as *The Vision After the Sermon* (1888), must be seen as an affirmation of these ideas, with its use of receding planes of flat primary colors enclosed by angular, dark lines and dramatized by a drastic perspective. The result is an overall effect far removed from any visual reality. This intense concentration on the visual and emotional totality of the subject rather than on its separate components, the synthetic view, would characterize the majority of Gauguin's paintings. The landscape and people of French

Polynesia, where he spent most of his creative life, tended to mellow his temperament and turn his pictures into vibrantly colorful, sinewy linear, often mysteriously muted paeans to primitive nature. On his return to Paris from Pont-Aven in the summer of 1888, he met Vincent van Gogh, and that fall joined van Gogh in Arles in the Midi of France. In spite of turbulent conflicts during the three months they spent together, the Arles experience left its positive impact on both artists, as seen in canvases of closely related subjects produced during their joint outings in the fertile Provençal countryside.

In 1889, during the World's Fair in Paris, Gauguin and his friends from the artist colony in Pont-Aven arranged a private exhibit of one hundred of their works in an Italian bistro within the fairground, Café Volpini. Hardly taken seriously by the public at that time, the Volpini Exhibit is today considered one of the milestones in nineteenth cen-

tury art. While the exhibitors called themselves "Impressionists" and "Synthetists" they had clearly abandoned the gracefully textured, retinally oriented approach of Claude Monet, Pierre-Auguste Renoir, and Pissarro. Instead, they presented pictures with large patches of contrasting colors separated by dark lines, minimal emphasis on depth and perspective, and, in Gauguin's case, a steady procession of peasants at their melancholy tasks or in worshipful contemplation.

During his stay in Brittany, and more so after his return to Paris in 1890, Gauguin continually toyed with the idea of settling in a more exotic part of the world, preferably with fellow painters in a new "Barbizon" of primitive nature, but if necessary he would go alone. Prior to his departure for Tahiti in the spring of 1891, his Paris friends—and by now there were many of them, artists, writers, government officials—eased his transition, helping him with an auction of his works, which brought a substantial amount of money, and arranging a farewell banquet presided over by Stéphane Mallarmé, the avant-garde poet.

During the two years of his first stay in Tahiti, Gauguin produced some of his most stunning canvases depicting the landscape, the people, and a civilization of beauty and innocence in the process of vanishing. A Tahitian landscape with a village surrounded by wildly exotic, swirling trees, backed up by mountains in sharp, receding planes and surmounted by white clouds against a cerulean sky, is reminiscent of his landscapes in Brittany, except that the dark, angular lines separating the color surfaces in the Brittany scenes have yielded to softer, more undulant patterns in this new, exotic setting. Similarly, his depiction of people of Tahiti, though in form and color resembling his efforts in Brittany, has something new and mysterious in it, close-up views mostly of women, singly or in clusters, with guarded, secretive mien and in hushed poses of ritual solemnity. "Always this haunting silence," Gauguin wrote in a letter to his wife. "I understand why these individuals can rest seated for hours and days without saying a word and look at the sky with melancholy."

Despite his enchantment with the Polynesian ambience, however, he felt confined and out of touch with the art world. Besides, he was financially destitute, incapable of providing for his daily bread. He decided to return to France and succeeded in finding a lender to advance his travel expenses. In the early fall of 1893, he was back in Paris with his Tahitian paintings, preparing for an exhibit and hoping for wide acceptance. His display of more than forty canvases generated few sales, and even his presentation to the French state of the magnificent *Ia Orana Maria* (1891; we hail thee, Mary) was rejected. A few close supporters, Edgar Degas and Mallarmé among them, helped Gauguin—Degas by making a purchase and Mallarmé by praising the Tahitian works.

Such signs of approval, however, were scarce, and Gauguin soon regretted his return to the insensitive, overcivilized world he had once abandoned. An unfortunate altercation during a visit to Brittany left him hospitalized and maimed, and an encounter with a Parisian prostitute resulted in syphilis. All of this resulted in a life of creative stagnation and physical agony, and as soon as he was able to move about he began to prepare for his second and final journey to Tahiti. A major sale of his paintings and belongings was arranged to finance the venture, and, planning to issue a catalog of the items on view, he asked a new acquaintance, the dramatist August Strindberg, to write a preface. In a long and detailed letter, Strindberg enumerated the reasons for his refusal to do so. Yet it appears that he understood Gauguin's creative impulse, sensed its depth. Gauguin, detecting a positive note in Strindberg's rejection, printed the letter as the preface. The sale, however, was a failure. In fact, in a letter to his wife, he records a detailed account showing a net loss of 464 francs. Nevertheless, with the assistance of several picture dealers and a guarantee that they would market his subsequent works, he was able to raise a sum sufficient for the voyage and his immediate subsequent needs; he left France in June of 1895, never to return.

In his second Tahitian period, Gauguin produced one hundred paintings, more than four hundred prints, and numerous pieces of sculpted wood. In addition, he wrote hundreds of letters, an intriguing journal, and reworked text and illustrations in his *Noa Noa* (English translation, 1919), published in France in 1900.

During his first stay, his works, like his visual reactions to life in Brittany, had reflected the primal quality of the Tahitian landscape, the natural innocence of a people still close to the beginnings of time, and the legendary quality of Tahitian spirituality. Thus, desiring to share his experiences with the art audience at home, he had attempted to serve as a messenger from a remote world and a civilization still unspoiled yet inevitably doomed. In his second stay, he found these subtle links with the past already severely eroded through Western colonization. His works from this final period are therefore more introspective and deliberately ponderous. Typical of this approach is his monumental masterpiece *Where Do We Come From? What Are We? Where Are We Going?* (1897-1898), "designed to embody a total philosophy of life, civilization, and sexuality." As in early Renaissance altar panels, it is a work whose imagery transcends time and place, a composite of ritual episodes moving from the outer perimeter toward a central, all-embracing Godhead. A significant and influential aspect of his last Tahitian stay is found in a series of tropical woodblocks carved and hand printed in 1898-1899. Viewed in sequence as in a frieze, they seem to constitute a summary of his visual and spiritual experiences in the land and society he had adopted.

Gauguin never denied his admiration for certain other artists of the nineteenth century, and among his last works are paintings reminiscent of Eugène Delacroix's epochal depictions of women of Morocco, nudes and horses clearly indebted to Degas, and still-lifes of fruits and flowers echoing those of van Gogh painted in Arles.

Still on his easel at the time of his death was his final work, *Breton Village Covered by Snow*. Painted in feverish, death-conscious agony, it is a profoundly melancholy dream evoking the beginnings of a career devoted to a futile search for an earthly paradise.

Summary

Paul Gauguin was the first nineteenth century artist to move away from naturalism to a world of visual dreams inspired by the primitive magic of the medieval past and intensified by a direct exposure to societies less marred by Western civilization. From childhood experiences in Latin America and a turbulent youth at sea and in the Caribbean, he was irresistibly drawn to the untamed and the exotic, finding part of it in a Brittany still steeped in its past and more in the faraway islands of the South Seas. With their purity of line and surface, vibrancy of color, and subtle evocation of the human condition in a tenuous state of innocence, his paintings opened up entirely new vistas in the world of the arts, through the depiction of rare and exotic subject matter. They also paved the way for equally bold strivings among artists of future generations. "I wanted to establish the right to dare everything. My capacity was not capable of great results, but the machine is none the less launched. The public owes me nothing . . . but the painters who today profit from this liberty owe me something."

Bibliography

Andersen, Wayne. *Gauguin's Paradise Lost*. New York: Viking Press, 1971; London: Secker and Warburg, 1972. An American scholar's attempt at reaching an understanding of the artist's psychological development through a parallel probing of his works and writings.

Brettell, Richard, et al. *The Art of Paul Gauguin*. An exhibit catalog prepared by Richard Brettell, François Cachin, Claire Freches-Thory, and Charles F. Stuckey, with assistance from Peter Zegers. Washington, D.C.: National Gallery of Art, 1988. Numerous catalogs have been issued in conjunction with many exhibits of Gauguin's works mounted worldwide. The exhibit jointly sponsored by the National Gallery and the Art Institute of Chicago was accompanied by a catalog so comprehensive, so authoritative, and so richly illustrated that it supersedes all previous efforts in that direction. Drawn from collections in North and South America, Europe, and Asia, the exhibit included 280 separate items, nearly all described in terse but excellent articles.

Danielsson, Bengt. *Gauguin in the South Seas*. Translated by Reginald Spink. London: Allen and Unwin, and New York: Doubleday, 1965. A Swedish anthropologist and explorer, the author is the only Gauguin biographer intimately familiar with the artist's Tahitian people, their mores, and their land, and he succeeds in conveying to the reader the artist's enchantment and frustrations as he pursues his dream. In a series of photographs inspired by Gauguin's paintings, Danielsson shows both the continuity and the disruption of the civilization the artist depicts.

Gauguin, Paul. *The Intimate Journals of Paul Gauguin*. Translated by Van Wyck Brooks, with a preface by Émile Gauguin. London: Heinemann, 1931. The original manuscript, finished in 1903, has the title *Avant et après* and was published in facsimile editions in 1913 and 1953. The English edition was endorsed by Gauguin's son, who in his preface says, "These journals are the spontaneous expression of the same free, fearless, sensitive spirit that speaks in the canvases of Paul Gauguin."

————. *Paul Gauguin: Letters to His Wife and Friends*. Edited by Maurice Mallinge. Translated by Henry F. Stenning. London: Saturn Press, 1946; Cleveland: World Publishing, 1949. This collection sheds much light on the strained relationship between the artist and his estranged wife, Mette Gad, who at the time of Gauguin's first stay in Brittany returned with their five children to her childhood home in Copenhagen. Characterized by Gauguin's continual quest for understanding and her pervasive bitterness, the letters also contain much information on his creative activities.

Gauguin, Pola. *My Father, Paul Gauguin*. Translated by Arthur G. Chater. London: Cassell, and New York: Knopf, 1937. Written by Gauguin's youngest son, an artist and art historian who lived in Norway, this biography draws much of its information from family letters and documents whose content up to that time had been unavailable to the public. Remarkably dispassionate in its narration, it tends to counterbalance the relentless bitterness of Gauguin's wife.

Gray, Christopher. *Sculpture and Ceramics of Paul Gauguin.* Baltimore: Johns Hopkins University Press, 1963. Gray's volume spans Gauguin's entire career and shows how his early efforts in ceramics foreshadowed the three-dimensional works produced in Tahiti. An appendix twice the size of the principal text contains a detailed catalog of the artist's known works in these media.

Pincus, William H. *The Problem of Gauguin's Therapist: Language, Madness and Therapy.* Aldershot, Hampshire, and Brookfield, Vt.: Avebury, 1994. The author argues that the mental health field is, in fact, a socializing force designed to mold patients to society's standards and uses Gauguin to highlight psychology's shortcomings in its efforts to deal with conflict between the individual and society.

Rewald, John. *Post-Impressionism: From Van Gogh to Gauguin.* 3d ed. London: Secker and Warburg, and New York: Museum of Modern Art, 1979. This magnificently illustrated work by a principal authority in late nineteenth century European painting presents the total fabric of the Post-Impressionist movement in which van Gogh and Gauguin occupied centerstage, with many others playing supporting roles.

Sweetman, David. *Paul Gauguin: A Complete Life.* New York: Simon and Schuster, and London: Hodder and Stoughton, 1995. In the best Gauguin biography yet published, Sweetman unearths facts and presents them in an original way. Attention is paid to the importance of Gauguin's early life in Peru and its effect on his self-image, his relationships with unconventional women, and more.

Reidar Dittmann

CARL FRIEDRICH GAUSS

Born: April 30, 1777; Brunswick, Germany
Died: February 23, 1855; Göttingen, Lower Saxony
Areas of Achievement: Mathematics, astronomy, and physics
Contribution: Gauss, one of the greatest scientific thinkers of all time, often ranked with Archimedes and Isaac Newton, made significant contributions in many branches of science. Perhaps his greatest achievement was that he arrived at the two most revolutionary mathematical ideas of the nineteenth century, non-Euclidean geometry and noncommutative algebra.

Early Life

Carl Friedrich Gauss was born into a family of town workers who were struggling to achieve lower-middle-class status. Without assistance, Gauss learned to calculate before he could talk; he also taught himself to read. At the age of three, he corrected an error in his father's wage calculations. In his first arithmetic class, at the age of eight, he astonished his teacher by instantly solving a word problem which involved finding the sum of the first hundred integers. Fortunately, his teacher had the insight to furnish the child with books and encourage his intellectual development.

When he was eleven, Gauss studied with Martin Bartels, then an assistant in the school and later a teacher of Nikolay Ivanovich Lobachevsky at Kazan. Gauss's father was persuaded to allow his son to enter the *Gymnasium* in 1788. At the *Gymnasium*, Gauss made rapid progress in all subjects, especially in classics and mathematics, largely on his own. E. A. W. Zimmermann, then professor at the local Collegium Carolinum and later privy councillor to the Duke of Brunswick, encouraged Gauss; in 1792, Duke Carl Wilhelm Ferdinand began the stipend that would assure Gauss's independence.

When Gauss entered the Brunswick Collegium Carolinum in 1792, he possessed a scientific and classical education far beyond his years. He was acquainted with elementary geometry, algebra, and analysis (often having discovered important theorems before reaching them in his books), but he also possessed much arithmetical information and number-theoretic insights. His lifelong pattern of research had become established: Extensive empirical investigation led to conjectures, and new insights guided further experiment and observation.

By such methods, he had already discovered Johann Elert Bode's law of planetary distances, the binomial theorem for rational exponents, and the arithmetic-geometric mean.

During his three years at the Collegium, among other things, Gauss formulated the principle of least squares. Before entering the University of Göttingen in 1795, he had rediscovered the law of quadratic reciprocity, related the arithmetic-geometric mean to infinite series expansions, and conjectured the prime number theorem (first proved by Jacques-Salomon Hadamard in 1896).

While he was in Brunswick, most mathematical classics had been unavailable to him. At Göttingen, however, he devoured masterworks and back issues of journals and often found that his discoveries were not new. Attracted more by the brilliant classicist Christian Gottlob Heyne than by the mediocre mathematician A. G. Kästner, Gauss planned to be a philologist, but in 1796 he made a dramatic discovery that marked him as a mathematician. As a result of a systematic investigation of the cyclotomic equation (whose solution has the geometric counterpart of dividing a circle into equal arcs), Gauss declared that the regular seventeen-sided polygon was constructible by ruler and compasses, the first advance on this subject in two thousand years.

The logical aspect of Gauss's method matured at Göttingen. While he adopted the spirit of Greek rigor, it was without the classical geometric form; Gauss, rather, thought numerically and algebraically, in the manner of Leonhard Euler. By the age of twenty, Gauss was conducting large-scale empirical investigations and rigorous theoretical constructions, and during the years from 1796 to 1800 mathematical ideas came so quickly that Gauss could hardly write them down.

Life's Work

In 1798, Gauss returned to Brunswick, and the next year, with the first of his four proofs of the fundamental theorem of algebra, earned a doctorate from the University of Helmstedt. In 1801, the creativity of the previous years was reflected in two extraordinary achievements, the *Disquisitiones arithmeticae* (1801; *Arithmetical Inquiries*, 1966) and the calculation of the orbit of the newly discovered planet Ceres.

Although number theory was developed from the earliest times, in the late eighteenth century it consisted of a large collection of isolated results. In *Arithmetical Inquisitions*, Gauss systematically summarized previous work, solved some of the most difficult outstanding questions, and formulated concepts and questions that established the pattern of research for a century. The work almost instantly won for Gauss recognition by mathematicians, although readership was small.

In January, 1801, Giuseppi Piazzi had briefly discovered but lost track of a new planet he had observed, and during the rest of that year astronomers unsuccessfully attempted to relocate it. Gauss decided to pursue the matter. Applying both a more accurate orbit theory and improved numerical methods, he accomplished the task by December. Ceres was soon found in the predicted position. This feat of locating a distant, tiny planet from apparently insufficient information was astonishing, especially since Gauss did not reveal his methods. Along with *Arithmetical Inquisitions*, it established his reputation as a first-rate mathematical and scientific genius.

The decade of these achievements (1801-1810) was decisive for Gauss. Scientifically it was a period of exploiting ideas accumulated from the previous decade, and it ended with a work in which Gauss systematically developed his methods of orbit calculation, including a theory of and use of least squares. Professionally this decade was one of transition from mathematician to astronomer and physical scientist. Gauss accepted the post of director of the Göttingen Observatory in 1807.

This decade also provided Gauss with his one period of personal happiness. In 1805, he married Johanna Osthoff, with whom he had a son and a daughter. She created a happy family life around him. When she died in 1809, Gauss was plunged into a loneliness from which he never fully recovered. Less than a year later, he married Minna Waldeck, his deceased wife's best friend. Although she bore him two sons and a daughter, she was unhealthy and very often unhappy. Gauss did not achieve a peaceful home life until his youngest daughter, Therese, assumed management of the household after her mother's death in 1831 and became his companion for the last twenty-four years of his life.

In his first years as director of the Göttingen Observatory, Gauss experienced a second burst of ideas and publications in various fields of mathematics and matured his conception of non-Euclidean geometry. Yet astronomical tasks soon dominated Gauss's life.

By 1817, Gauss moved toward geodesy, which was to be his preoccupation for the next eight years. The invention of the heliotrope, an instrument for reflecting the sun's rays in a measured direction, was an early by-product of fieldwork. The invention was motivated by dissatisfaction with the existing methods of observing distant points by using lamps or powder flares at night. In spite of failures and dissatisfactions, the period of geodesic investigation was one of the most scientifically creative of Gauss's long career. The difficulties of mapping the terrestrial ellipsoid on a sphere and plane led him, in 1816, to formulate and solve in outline the general problem of mapping one surface on another so that the two were "similar in their smallest parts." In 1822, the chance of winning a prize offered by the Copenhagen Academy motivated him to write these ideas in a paper that won for him first place and was published in 1825.

Surveying problems also inspired Gauss to develop his ideas on least squares and more general problems of what is now called mathematical statistics. His most significant contribution during this period, and his last breakthrough in a major new direction of mathematical research, was *Disquisitiones generales circa superficies curvas* (1828; *General Investigations of Curved Surfaces*, 1902), which was the result of three decades of geodesic investigations and which drew upon more than a century of work on differential geometry.

After the mid-1820's, Gauss, feeling harassed and overworked and suffering from asthma and heart disease, turned to investigations in physics. Gauss accepted an offer from Alexander von Humboldt to come to Berlin to work. An incentive was his meeting in Berlin with Wilhelm Eduard Weber, a young and brilliant experimental physicist with whom Gauss would eventually collaborate on many significant discoveries. They were also to organize a worldwide network of magnetic observatories and to publish extensively on magnetic force. From the early 1840's, the intensity of Gauss's activity gradually decreased. Increasingly bedridden as a result of heart disease, he died in his sleep in late February, 1855.

Summary

Carl Friedrich Gauss's impact as a scientist falls far short of his reputation. His inventions were usually minor improvements of temporary importance. In theoretical astronomy, he perfected classical methods in orbit calculation but otherwise made only fairly routine observations. His personal involvement in calculating orbits saved others work but was of little long-lasting scientific importance. His work in geodesy was influential only in its mathematical by-products. Furthermore, his collaboration with Weber led to only two achievements of significant impact: The use of absolute units set a pattern that became standard, and the worldwide network of magnetic observatories established a precedent for international scientific cooperation. Also, his work in physics may have been of the highest quality, but it seems to have had little influence.

In the area of mathematics, however, his influence was powerful. Carl Gustav Jacobi and Henrik Abel testified that their work on elliptic functions was triggered by a hint in the *Arithmetical Inquisitions*. Évariste Galois, on the eve of his death, asked that his rough notes be sent to Gauss. Thus, in mathematics, in spite of delays, Gauss reached and inspired countless mathematicians. Although he was more of a systematizer and solver of old problems than a creator of new paths, the very completeness of his results laid the basis for new departures—especially in number theory, differential geometry, and statistics.

Bibliography

Bell, Eric T. *Men of Mathematics*. London: Gollancz, and New York: Simon and Schuster, 1937. Historical account of the major figures in mathematics from the Greeks to Giorg Cantor, written in an interesting, if at times exaggerated, style. In a lengthy chapter devoted to Gauss titled "The Prince of Mathematicians," Bell describes the life and work of Gauss, focusing almost exclusively on the mathematical contributions. No bibliography.

Boyer, Carl B. *A History of Mathematics*. 2d ed. New York: Wiley, 1989. In "The Time of Gauss and Cauchy," chapter 23 of this standard history of mathematics, Boyer very briefly discusses biographical details of Gauss's life before summarizing the proofs of Gauss's major theorems. Boyer also discusses Gauss's work in the context of the leading contemporary figures in mathematics of the day. Includes charts, an extensive bibliography, and student exercises.

Buhler, W. K. *Gauss: A Biographical Study*. New York: Springer-Verlag, 1981. The author's purpose is not to write a definitive life history but to select from Gauss's life and work those aspects which are interesting and comprehensible to a lay reader. Contains quotations from Gauss's writings, illustrations, a bibliography, lengthy footnotes, appendices on his collected works, a useful survey of the secondary literature, and an index to Gauss's works.

Dunnington, Guy Waldo. *Carl Friedrich Gauss, Titan of Science: A Study of His Life and Work*. New York: Exposition Press, 1955. Gauss and the times in which he lived are depicted to reveal the man as well as the scientist. Contains the largest bibliography yet published and includes appendices on honors and diplomas, children, genealogy, a chronology, books borrowed at college, courses taught, and views and opinions.

Epple, Moritz. "Orbits of Asteroids, a Braid, and the First Link Invariant." *Mathematical Intelligencer* 20, no. 1 (Winter 1998). Detailed examination of Gauss's formula connecting the geometry of magnitude with that of position.

Turnbull, H. W. *The Great Mathematicians*. 4th ed. London: Methuen, and New York: New York University Press, 1962. Useful as a quick reference guide to the lives and works of the major figures in mathematics from the Greeks to the twentieth century.

Genevieve Slomski

JOSEPH-LOUIS GAY-LUSSAC

Born: December 6, 1778; Saint-Léonard-de-Noblat, France
Died: May 9, 1850; Paris, France
Areas of Achievement: Chemistry and physics
Contribution: A preeminent scientist of his generation, Gay-Lussac helped prepare the way, through his discoveries in chemistry and physics, for the modern atomic-molecular theory of matter. His investigations of gases led to the law describing how they react with each other in simple proportions by volume, and his chemical investigations led to the discovery of a new element, boron, and to the development of new techniques in qualitative and quantitative analysis.

Early Life

Joseph-Louis Gay was born on December 6, 1778, at Saint-Léonard-de-Noblat, a small market town in west central France. He was the eldest son of five children of Antoine Gay, a lawyer and public prosecutor, who, to distinguish himself from others called Gay, later changed his surname to Gay-Lussac, after the family property in the nearby hamlet of Lussac. Joseph-Louis used this expanded name throughout his life. His early education from a priest and his comfortable social and economic position were ended by the Revolution of 1789, and in the turbulent years that followed, his teacher fled the country, and his father was arrested.

With the fall of Robespierre in 1794, the Revolution took a more moderate direction, and Gay-Lussac's father was freed. Antoine Gay-Lussac was then able to send Joseph-Louis to Paris to continue his education at religious boarding schools. His father expected him to study law, but Gay-Lussac became increasingly interested in mathematics and science. His excellent record in mathematics gave him the opportunity to enter the École Polytechnique, then a young but already prestigious revolutionary institution for the training of civil and military engineers. Gay-Lussac completed his studies there with distinction, and he was graduated in November, 1800. He then entered the École des Ponts et Chaussées. He saw engineering not as a career but as a position to fall back on if he did not succeed in pure science.

During these years of study, Gay-Lussac came under the wing of Claude Louis Berthollet, a distinguished chemist and former companion to Na-poleon I in Egypt. In his triple role as teacher, father-substitute, and patron, Berthollet became the most important influence on Gay-Lussac's life. Some of Gay-Lussac's greatest early work was done at Berthollet's country house at Arcueil, where important scientists would gather and where the Society of Arcueil was later formed. Gay-Lussac continued his studies at the École des Ponts et Chaussées, but his relationship with the school grew more nominal as he spent more and more time on scientific research at Arcueil.

Life's Work

Gay-Lussac's initial research was of considerable importance both because of its permanent scientific value and because it marked his successful initiation into a career of pure science. In 1802, after painstaking measurements, he showed that many different gases expand equally over the temperature range from 0 to +100 degrees Celsius. Despite the thoroughness of his studies and the significance of his results, Gay-Lussac is not generally credited with the discovery of the quantitative law of the thermal expansion of gases. Some chemists recalled that Jacques Charles, a French physicist, had found in 1787 that certain gases expanded equally, but Charles had also found that other gases, those that dissolved in water, had different rates of expansion. Since Charles never published his work and since he did not completely understand the phenomenon of thermal expansion, many scholars believe that justice demands that this discovery should be known as Gay-Lussac's law.

Gases were central to another of Gay-Lussac's early research projects. In the early nineteenth century, scientists debated whether the percentage of nitrogen, oxygen, and other gases was different in the upper and lower atmosphere. A similar diversity of opinion existed about the behavior of a magnet at low and high altitudes. To resolve these differences, Gay-Lussac and Jean-Baptiste Biot, a young colleague, made a daring ascent from Paris in a hydrogen-filled balloon on August 24, 1804. By observing oscillations of a magnetic needle, they concluded that the intensity of the earth's magnetism was constant up to four thousand meters, but they did not have time to collect samples of air. Therefore, to answer the question about the atmosphere's composition, Gay-Lussac made a solo balloon ascent over Paris on September 16, 1804. He reached a height of more than seven thousand meters, an altitude record that would remain unmatched for a half century. He discovered that the temperature of the atmosphere decreased by one degree Celsius for every 174-meter increase in elevation. When he analyzed the air samples that he had collected, he found that the composition of air was the same at seven thousand meters as it was at sea level (his technique was not sensitive enough to detect the differences that were later found).

Shortly after the balloon flights, Gay-Lussac began to collaborate with Alexander von Humboldt, a Prussian nobleman, world traveler, and scientist. Gay-Lussac had just received an appointment to a junior post at the École Polytechnique when he met Humboldt, who was interested in his analysis of the atmosphere. Humboldt and Gay-Lussac agreed to collaborate in a series of experiments on atmospheric gases. Their research led to a precise determination of the relative proportions with which hydrogen and oxygen combine to form water: almost exactly two hundred parts to one hundred parts by volume. Though they were not the first to discover this 2:1 ratio (Henry Cavendish had noted it in 1784), the experiment convinced Gay-Lussac that scientists should study the reactions of gases by volume instead of by weight.

Because of the fruitfulness of their collaboration, Gay-Lussac wanted to accompany Humboldt on a European tour he was planning, to make a systematic survey of magnetic intensities. Gay-Lussac was granted a leave of absence from the École Polytechnique, and in March, 1805, he and Humboldt embarked on a year of travel through Italy, Switzerland, and Germany. Through their tour, Gay-Lussac made many contacts with important physicists and chemists such as Alessandro Volta, the inventor of the electric battery. A tangible result of his European travels was a paper on terrestrial magnetism. Because of this and other studies, he was elected in 1806 to the National Institute (the revolutionary replacement for the Royal Academy of Sciences). Although this was a major step in Gay-Lussac's career, his base of operations remained the École Polytechnique and Arcueil.

In 1807, Gay-Lussac completed a series of experiments to see if there was a general relationship between the specific heat of a gas and its density. Specific heat is a measure of a substance's capacity to attract its own particular quantity of heat. For example, mercury has less capacity for heat than water; that is, mercury requires a smaller quantity of heat than does water to raise its temperature by the same number of degrees. Gay-Lussac knew that the compression of gases was accompanied by the evolution of heat and their expansion by the absorption of heat, but he wanted to find the relationship between the absorbed and evolved heat. Through an ingenious series of experiments, he discovered that the heat lost by expansion was equal to the heat gained by compression, a result significant in the history of physics, particularly for the law of the conservation of energy.

Although Gay-Lussac had studied the 2:1 chemical combination of hydrogen and oxygen in 1805, he did not generalize his results until 1808, when he again became interested in gas reactions. At that time, he began his long collaboration with Louis Jacques Thenard, a peasant's son who had risen from laboratory boy to Polytechnique professor. In one of their early experiments, they heated a mixture of calcium fluoride and boric acid in an iron tube. Instead of getting the expected fluorine, they obtained fluoric acid (now called boron trifluoride), a gas which, on coming into contact with air, produced dense white fumes that reminded them of those produced by muriatic acid (now called hydrogen chloride) and ammonia. In fact, they found that boron trifluoride and ammonia reacted in a 1:1 ratio by volume, just as hydrogen chloride and ammonia did. With these and other examples from his own experiments, along with results reported by others in various papers, Gay-Lussac felt secure enough to state that all gases combine in simple volumetric proportions. He announced this law, now known as Gay-Lussac's law of combining volumes, at a meeting of the Société Philomatique in Paris on December 31, 1808. This law would later be used to teach students about the evidence for the atomic theory, but at the time of its proposal Gay-Lussac rejected John Dalton's atomic theory.

Despite Gay-Lussac's important research at the École Polytechnique and Arcueil, his career was stalled. During the years 1808 and 1809, his friends tried to lobby on his behalf for a position commensurate with his accomplishments. The death of Antoine Fourcroy in 1809 provided the opportunity for which Gay-Lussac's friends had been waiting, and on February 17, 1810, Gay-Lussac became Fourcroy's successor to the chemistry chair at the École Polytechnique. Another reason for this activity on Gay-Lussac's behalf was his impending marriage to Geneviève-Marie-Joseph

Riot, to whom he was married in May, 1809. The marriage was a happy one, eventually producing five children.

During the time that Gay-Lussac's friends were trying to find him a position, Gay-Lussac and Thenard were doing important work on the alkali metals. These soft metals with great chemical reactivity had recently been isolated by Humphry Davy, the great English chemist who would become Gay-Lussac's competitor in many discoveries. Davy had used the giant voltaic batteries at the Royal Institution to discover sodium and potassium. Because of the rivalry between Great Britain and France, Napoleon ordered the construction of an even larger collection of batteries at the École Polytechnique, and he urged Gay-Lussac and Thenard to do experiments with this voltaic pile. Ironically, they actually found that they could ignore electrolysis and use chemical means to produce large quantities of sodium and potassium. Davy's electrical method had liberated only tiny amounts of the new metals, whereas Gay-Lussac and Thenard's method of fusing potassium and sodium salts with iron filings at high temperatures produced great amounts of sodium and potassium more cheaply.

Gay-Lussac and Davy were both interested in isolating the element contained in boric acid. On June 21, 1808, Gay-Lussac and Thenard heated boric acid with potassium in a copper tube, producing a mixture of products, one of which was the new element. Their first published claim to the discovery of boron was in November, a month before Davy submitted a similar claim to the Royal Society. They delayed publishing their discovery because they wanted not only to decompose boric acid but also to recompose it.

After their work on boron, Gay-Lussac and Thenard examined oxymuriatic acid. At the beginning of the nineteenth century, chlorine was called oxymuriatic acid because chemists thought that it was a compound of oxygen and muriatic acid. This belief was based on its preparation by heating muriatic (now called hydrochloric) acid with a substance such as manganese dioxide with its abundance of oxygen. Gay-Lussac and Thenard were therefore astonished when they passed oxymuriatic acid gas over red-hot charcoal and the oxygen which was supposedly in the acid refused to combine with the charcoal. This led them to doubt that the gas contained oxygen and to suggest that it might be an element. Historians of chemistry usually report that Davy first recognized the elementa-

ry nature of chlorine, because in Gay-Lussac and Thenard's report in the 1809 volume of the Arcueil Memoires, which was known to Davy, they conservatively stated that their experiments caused them to doubt the existence of oxygen in oxymuriatic acid, whereas Davy in 1810 unambiguously stated that it was an element, for which he proposed the name chlorine.

In addition to the misconception about chlorine, chemists of the time were also grappling with a faulty theory of acids since Antoine Lavoisier had earlier proposed that all acids contained oxygen. Until Gay-Lussac's research on iodine in 1814 and on prussic acid in 1815, he had accepted Lavoisier's theory of acidity. Gay-Lussac's discovery and investigation of hydriodic acid reopened the question for him, and he concluded that hydrogen, not oxygen, was necessary to convert iodine to an acid. He clearly stated that hydrogen played the same role for one class of substances that oxygen did for another. He introduced the concept and name "hydracid" for the first class, and his studies of hydrogen chloride, hydrogen iodide, and hydrogen fluoride prepared the way for a new theory of acids.

Gay-Lussac's early work was based on the recognition, common among chemists since the eighteenth century, that each substance possessed a unique chemical composition that could be represented by a unique formula. During the 1820's, Gay-Lussac and other chemists discovered pairs of compounds, each member of which had the same number of the same atoms but with quite distinct properties. Gay-Lussac straightforwardly interpreted this phenomenon, called isomerism, as a result of the different atomic arrangements in the two substances. This idea, that different structures result in different chemical properties, would become an extremely important theme in the history of modern chemistry.

During the final decades of Gay-Lussac's career, he turned his attention more and more to applied science. The economic needs created by his growing family caused him to do more industrial research, where the financial rewards were greater than in theoretical work. Particularly noteworthy was his development of a superior method of assaying silver using a standard solution of common salt. This precise method, which he developed after he became Chief Assayer to the Mint in 1829, is still used.

In 1832, Gay-Lussac accepted a distinguished position at the Museum of Natural History. In his last years, he worked so hard to provide for his family that he produced little theoretical work, but he continued to reap honors for his brilliant early discoveries. In 1839, he became a Peer of France, even though his election was accepted reluctantly by those who thought that he worked too much with his hands to be a gentleman. He had a brief political career in the 1830's, after which he held a number of advisory positions, where he used his technical knowledge to suggest improvements in such industrial chemical processes as the production of gunpowder and oxalic acid. He died in Paris on May 9, 1850, lamenting his departure from the world just when science was becoming interesting.

Summary

The quest for laws dominated Joseph-Louis Gay-Lussac's scientific life. He believed that if a scientist lacked this desire, then the laws of nature would escape his attention. His most important discovery was the law of combining volumes, which helped pave the way for the modern atomic-molecular theory of matter.

Gay-Lussac managed to pass relatively unscathed through three political revolutions. Nevertheless, his life reflected the social and political
changes taking place around him. His education occurred largely in schools founded or modified by the Revolution. Berthollet and the Society of Arcueil, the shapers of Gay-Lussac as a scientist, owed much to the patronage of Napoleon. During the 1830's and 1840's, under Louis-Philippe, Gay-Lussac became a conservative member of the professional class or upper bourgeoisie. Through all these changes he continued to be a French patriot. This chauvinism surfaced in his scientific controversies with the British chemists Humphry Davy and John Dalton.

Just as his political life was a curious blend of liberalism and conservatism, so too was his scientific life. In his early career, devoted to pure science, he made so many important discoveries in so many areas that no one in post-Napoleonic France could teach chemistry without frequent references to his work. During the Restoration, however, he made few contributions to pure science, and he seemed to many young scientists to represent an enervating conservatism. For example, he adhered to the caloric theory of heat (heat as a substance) rather than embracing what most scientists saw as the superior kinetic theory (heat as motion). Despite these weaknesses in his later career, Gay-Lussac's place in the history of science is secure. His achievements in chemistry, physics, meteorology, and geology led him to become a central figure in the French scientific establishment, and he was influential in shaping such institutions as the École Polytechnique and the Museum of Natural History. His facility in applying chemistry to practical problems set an example that had wide repercussions later in the century. He also had great influence internationally—he emerges as a key figure of European science in the first third of the nineteenth century.

Bibliography

Crosland, Maurice. *Gay-Lussac, Scientist and Bourgeois.* Cambridge and New York: Cambridge University Press, 1978. Crosland takes a thematic rather than a strictly chronological approach to the life and work of Gay-Lussac. He relates Gay-Lussac both to the history of science and to contemporary social and political history. His account, which is refreshingly frank in dealing with issues of scientific rivalry and academic politics, is intended for historians of science as well as for social and economic historians, but because Crosland explains the science of the times so well, his work should be accessible to a wider audience.

————. *The Society of Arcueil: A View of French Science at the Time of Napoleon I.* London: Heinemann, and Cambridge, Mass.: Harvard University Press, 1967. This book contains an important account of the social context of Gay-Lussac's early work. Crosland also uses Arcueil to make some good general points about the nature of patronage and about French science.

Ihde, Aaron J. *The Development of Modern Chemistry.* New York: Harper, 1964. Ihde, who taught the history of chemistry for many years at the University of Wisconsin, emphasizes the period from the eighteenth to the twentieth century. His approach is more encyclopedic than analytic, but descriptive enough so that it is readable by high school and college chemistry students. Contains an extensive annotated bibliography.

Laing, Michael. "Lavoisier Preempted Gay-Lussac by 20 years!" *Journal of Chemical Education* 75, no. 2 (February 1998). Discusses the experiments of Gay-Lussac and Lavoisier involving the creation of water molecules.

Scott, Wilson L. *The Conflict Between Atomism and Conservation Theory, 1644-1860.* London: Macdonald, and New York: Elsevier, 1970. Scott focuses on the conflict between groups of scientists over the issue of whether force (later called energy) is conserved when one hard body strikes another. This debate had important implications for the atomic theory, and Gay-Lussac's ideas and experiments were integral to it. The book is based on extensive research, but because the author can tell a story and explain scientific concepts clearly, his account is accessible to readers without any special scientific knowledge.

Szabadvary, Ferenc. *History of Analytical Chemistry.* Oxford and New York: Pergamon Press, 1966. This book, first published in Hungarian in 1960, is a detailed account of the historical development of analytical chemistry. Gay-Lussac's contributions to qualitative and quantitative, gravimetric and volumetric analyses are extensively discussed. The book is based largely on original sources and is intended for the reader with some knowledge of chemistry.

Robert J. Paradowski

GEORGE IV

Born: August 12, 1762; St. James' Palace, London, England

Died: June 26, 1830; Windsor Castle, Windsor, England

Areas of Achievement: Politics and government

Contribution: Through his incompetence and disreputable personal behavior, King George IV eroded traditional British respect for and reliance upon the monarchy as a viable, governing institution. Inadvertently, he thus strengthened the powers of Parliament and weakened those of the British king.

Early Life

George Augustus Frederick—the eventual George IV, King of Great Britain—was the first child of George III (who reigned from 1760 to 1820) and Queen Charlotte Sophia, the former Princess of Mecklenburg-Strelitz. As heir to the throne of one of the world's great powers, George received the finest education possible, in accordance with the standards of the eighteenth century. Beginning at the age of five, he was privately tutored under a disciplined regimen, learning the classics, English, and the rudiments of French, German, and Italian. He would eventually achieve fluency in French. At the age of thirteen, the rigor of George's education was intensified by order of his father, the king. His tutors added history, religion, ethics, law, government, mathematics, and the natural sciences to his studies, while in his spare time he learned to play the cello, fence, box, sing, and appreciate the fine arts. Music, sculpture, and painting would remain lifelong interests.

As a child, George was universally popular with his teachers, family, the court, and friends. He was variously described as amiable, affectionate, cheerful, and intelligent, while he achieved a reputation as an enthusiastic and responsive pupil. He already possessed that wit and charm for which he would later become both famous and notorious. Altogether, George's early years were as promising as any enjoyed by a Prince of Wales (the traditional title bestowed by the English upon the heir to the throne).

The future king's difficulties began in his late teens, when he developed an obsessive desire for heavy drinking and womanizing. In these endeavors, he was assisted by numerous roguish companions, an excellent physique, and irresistible handsomeness. Soon, his drunken escapades, numerous love affairs, and casual sexual liaisons became well-known to the British public. His heavy spending, supported by the taxpayers, and his constant philandering cost him the esteem and affection of the nation. He never fully recovered from the playboy image he earned as the Prince of Wales.

George's behavior also cost him the respect and trust of his father. King George III regularly excluded the prince from consultation on the affairs of state, while begging him to mend his ways. Relations between father and son became especially strained when, during the 1780's, the prince gradually began to align himself with the opposition Whig Party. The Whigs generally favored liberal causes, such as Catholic emancipation, political reform, and the curtailment of the king's prerogatives. Carlton House, the prince's residence in London, became the meeting place for Whig politicians and intriguers. The Whigs' opponents, the Tory Party, could remain in power, however, as long as George III reigned. The king nevertheless deeply resented the prince's collusion in attacks upon his political favorites, the Tories.

Public disapproval of George III swelled during the so-called Regency Crisis of 1788-1789. The king suffered from a rare, hereditary metabolic disorder known as porphyria, whose effects upon the central nervous system caused extreme pain and sometimes insanity. When George III endured a particularly acute attack of the disease in late 1788, the prince and the Whigs scrambled to establish George IV as Prince Regent with unrestricted powers. George III's sudden recovery in early 1789 caused much embarrassment for the prince and disappointment for the Whigs. The British people, who dearly loved George III, long remembered and resented the eagerness with which the prince hastened to supplant his father.

A new source of friction between the king and his son emerged after 1792, when Great Britain became involved in war with revolutionary France. The prince desired an important, active military command similar to those possessed by his younger brothers. George III refused to comply with his son's request, citing the need for the prince to prepare himself for the kingship, as well as the foolishness of exposing to combat the heir to the throne. The young George's vanity was wounded by this denial of the opportunity to participate in

The coronation of George IV

the military glory which others garnered. The quarrel between father and son lasted for almost two decades, as the war with France continued almost without respite until 1815.

George's romantic life assumed some stability after 1785, when he married Mrs. Maria Anne Weld Fitzherbert (née Smythe), a wealthy widow who had been married twice before. The wedding ceremony and the prince's relationship to his new wife were loosely guarded secrets, however, because the marriage was contracted without the king's permission and Mrs. Fitzherbert was a Roman Catholic, both violations of British law. Despite bitter quarrels and prolonged separations, the couple remained devoted to each other until 1809, when they mutually agreed to end their relationship. The prince's love for Mrs. Fitzherbert had not stopped his philandering entirely, merely slowing him down—the most important factor in the deterioration of their relations.

Although the king was much distressed by persistent rumors of George's wedding, the illegality of the union with Mrs. Fitzherbert permitted a royal marriage. Burdened by stupendous debts and faced with the need to produce an heir to the throne, George married Princess Caroline Amelia Elizabeth of Brunswick in 1795, casting a covetous eye upon her dowry and income. This union was to become a marriage in name only, as George conceived an instant distaste for his bride. Sexual relations between the couple ceased after the birth of their only child, Princess Charlotte, in 1796. An informal separation was also arranged in that year, George claiming to be revolted by his wife's vulgar behavior and conversation.

In late 1810, George III, slowed by blindness and old age, was struck once again by an acute attack of porphyria and lapsed into an insanity from which he never recovered. For a few months, the nation awaited the possibility of the king's restoration to health. Discouraged by the doctors' poor prognoses, Parliament voted to establish Prince George as Regent with full royal powers, a position he assumed on February 5, 1811.

Life's Work

The Whigs greeted George's regency with high expectations. With the pro-Tory George III out of the way, they anticipated an invitation from his son to form a new government. Unfortunately for them, the prince's political attitudes had gradually changed markedly over the preceding decade. Like many Europeans, he had been appalled by the violence, the excesses, and the aggressiveness of revolutionary France. He was no longer the enthusiastic supporter of liberal causes which he had once been. Moreover, George admired the doggedness with which the Tories were pursuing the war against Napoleon. By the end of 1812, it was clear to the Whigs that the prince would retain the Tories in power.

By then it was equally clear that George was not a well man. The illness which afflicted him bore symptoms very similar to those exhibited by his father. It is probable that the prince also suffered from porphyria, although not in the acute form which caused George III's insanity. The prince's health problems would contribute to his indecisiveness and ineffectiveness as a political leader in the years ahead.

In 1815, following the Battle of Waterloo, Great Britain emerged victorious from the long war with France. The nation which the prince regent viewed in its hour of triumph was considerably different from that of his youth. Rapid commercial and economic growth, coupled with advancing industrialization, was causing much social dislocation and distress. The influence of the French Revolution aroused many Englishmen to favor further democratization of British politics. Discontent was expressed through riots (the Peterloo Massacre), assassination plots (the Cato Street Conspiracy), and vociferous demands for political reform. During the next fifteen years, George aligned himself with conservative Tories in defense of the status quo. The death in 1817 of Princess Charlotte, whose liberal views were well-known, caused the Whigs to despair of ever achieving their political program.

On January 29, 1820, George III died, and his son became king in his own right. The first crisis of George IV's reign occurred when he attempted to exclude Princess Caroline from enjoying the prerogatives and benefits of being queen. George's legal maneuverings caused Caroline to return to England from the Continent, where she had been residing since 1814. The populace greeted her arrival with great acclaim, perceiving her as the hapless, innocent victim of George's infidelities and cruelties. Caroline's popularity was an accurate gauge of the dislike of ordinary Englishmen for George and the Tory government. The king was outraged by Caroline's courting of the populace and caused a divorce bill on the grounds of adultery to be introduced in the House of Lords in August of 1820.

Caroline's extramarital affairs had been known to George and his advisers since the early 1800's. In 1806, a special Commission of Enquiry had established that she had probably engaged in several illicit affairs since her marriage to George. To the information gathered by this committee—known as the "Delicate Investigation"—there had been added massive, new evidence of Caroline's riotous living and immoral life on the Continent after 1814. This new investigating body, the Milan Commission, depicted Caroline as romantically involved with an Italian nobleman, appearing seminude in public on several occasions, and openly boasting of her numerous sexual liaisons. Confronted by overwhelming evidence, the Lords voted in favor of the divorce bill, but only marginally.

The public response, moreover, was intimidating. Mobs, some of them egged on by the Whig opposition, protested against the queen's conviction. The ministers, prominent Tory politicians, and even George himself were booed and heckled when they appeared in public. The Whigs seemed determined to use this opportunity to bring the ministry down. In the face of potentially violent disturbances, George's advisers suggested that he quietly withdraw the divorce bill from further consideration by the House of Commons. This he did, but only with great reluctance. George was relieved from further mortifying embarrassment by the queen's behavior when she died suddenly in 1821. The incident had graphically demonstrated to the Tories the extent of their unpopularity, and, consequently, slow progress toward Tory liberalization began.

Nevertheless, despite the urgent need for change, reform proceeded at a snail's pace under the Tory administrations of the 1820's. George proved to be even more conservative than his ministers, opposing reformist ideas and initiatives and espousing a strong royal prerogative. Initially, he resisted the liberalization of British foreign policy under Foreign Secretary George Canning (who served from 1822 to 1827), whereby Great Britain withdrew unqualified support for the suppression of revolutionary movements and subsequently recognized the independence of Latin America from Spain. As George's esteem and affection for Canning replaced an earlier hatred, the foreign secretary's ideas became more attractive to him. George's later acceptance of Canning's policy demonstrated a serious defect in the king's use of the royal prerogatives: To a great extent, he was easily swayed by his personal feelings toward individual ministers and politicians.

The king's resistance to the Tories' one substantial piece of reformist legislation, the Roman Catholic Relief Act of 1829, was more typical of his stubbornness and reactionary political attitudes. Only after months of obstructive behavior—including threats to abdicate or veto the bill—did he finally relent in the face of a tactful lobbying effort by his most esteemed friends and advisers, led by the Duke of Wellington. George's strong opposition to Catholic emancipation was all the more incredible in the light of the potentially revolutionary situation in Ireland.

In spite of occasional fits of assertiveness, George's royal style was characterized more often by indecisiveness and deliberate inattention to his duties. Ministers frequently had to hound him for weeks to secure his signature on important documents. As he had been wont to do in his youth, he dissipated his time in heavy drinking and social events. The greater part of his positive energies was devoted to the refurbishing of Windsor Castle and Buckingham Palace in unsurpassed opulence at great expense to the British public. In his final years, George's social activities were curtailed by obesity, gout, and arteriosclerosis. These debilitating conditions made him an invalid during the waning months of his life. He died on June 26, 1830, from a ruptured blood vessel in the stomach region.

Summary

George IV was one of the more incompetent and ineffective monarchs of Great Britain. His alcoholism, sexual promiscuity, financial extravagance, and general irresponsibility made him extremely unpopular with most segments of British society, and hampered his abilities to govern the nation in the aggressive style forged by his father, George III. During his regency and reign, the royal prerogatives were further eroded through lack of intelligent and consistent use. In this way, George inadvertently contributed to the strengthening of parliamentary institutions and the concomitant deterioration of royal power in Great Britain.

Bibliography

Cowie, Leonard W. *Hanoverian England, 1714-1837*. London: Bell, and New York: Humanities Press, 1967. A brief but comprehensive account of Great Britain under the Hanoverian dynasty.

Gash, Norman. *Lord Liverpool: The Life and Political Career of Robert Banks Jenkinson, Second Earl of Liverpool, 1770-1828*. London: Weidenfeld and Nicolson, and Cambridge, Mass.: Harvard University Press, 1984. Much more than a simple biography, Gash's work provides a brief introduction to English politics in the era of George IV. Liverpool was prime minister from 1812 to 1827 and was much detested, but he was indispensable to George IV.

Hibbert, Christopher. *George IV: Prince of Wales, 1762-1811*. New York: Harper, and London: Longman, 1972. The finest of the modern biographies of George. Comprehensive in its scope and based upon extensive research in archival sources. Fair-minded and judicious in its evaluations.

———. *George IV: Regent and King, 1811-1830*. London: Allen Lane, and New York: Harper, 1973. Continues the story begun in the author's above-cited work.

Leslie, Doris. *The Great Corinthian: A Portrait of the Prince Regent*. London: Eyre and Spottiswoode, and New York: Oxford University Press, 1952. A well-written, colorful narrative of George's life before 1821. Describes the pageantry and beauty of aristocratic life in Regency England. Distressingly short on that political and character analysis necessary to an understanding of George IV.

Machin, G. I. T. *The Catholic Question in English Politics, 1820 to 1830*. Oxford: Clarendon Press, 1964. Scholarly background to the Roman Catholic Relief Act of 1829. Places the question of Ireland and Catholic emancipation clearly in the context of politics during the reign of George IV.

Richardson, Joanna. *George IV: A Portrait*. London: Sidgwick and Jackson, 1966; as *George the Magnificent: A Portrait of King George IV,* New York: Harcourt Brace, 1966. A short biography of George, attempting to rehabilitate his character by neglecting the political and private sides of his life. Places great stress on George's role as a patron of scholars, writers, architects, and artists.

Michael S. Fitzgerald

HENRY GEORGE

Born: September 2, 1839; Philadelphia, Pennsylvania

Died: October 29, 1897; New York, New York

Area of Achievement: Social and economic reform

Contribution: George's writings and lectures on land, labor, and economic policies expressed a popular radicalism that challenged established economic doctrines and dominant political practices, exercising a profound influence for reform both in the United States and abroad.

Early Life

An oldest son, Henry George was born into a large, devoutly Episcopalian family on September 2, 1839, in Philadelphia, Pennsylvania, close to Independence Hall, a source of lifelong inspiration to him. His father, Richard Samuel Henry George, was a sea captain's son whose once prosperous resources were depleted prior to his death. Accordingly, throughout his life Richard earned a steady, but modest, income working variously as a schoolteacher, a dealer in religious books, and for a longer period as a clerk in Philadelphia's United States Customs House—a Democratic Party political appointment. Catharine Vallance, Henry's mother, was as devout as her husband; also a former schoolteacher, she bore nine children and was proud of her descent from a close friend of Benjamin Franklin. Overall, the George household was warmly Christian and modestly comfortable. Henry George remained attached to his family all of his life.

Though receiving some primary instruction at home, the young George's formal education was brief. What there was of it failed to impress him. At six, he entered a small private school, and at nine moved on to Philadelphia's famed Episcopal Academy but performed poorly and withdrew. He was subsequently coached for admission to the city's esteemed public high school—this tutoring, he later believed, providing his best educational experience. Once enrolled, however, he quit almost immediately, thus ending his formal education at thirteen. When fully mature, he was to praise only vocational or practical learning, but in his early years there were other cultural advantages which derived from his regular use of the libraries of the Franklin Institute, the American Philosophical Society, and a small, convivial literary society.

Regardless of his formal deficiencies, they were never a handicap. Largely self-taught, reflective, ambitious, and combative, with a romantic sense of individuality and a slowly acquired ability to concentrate his energies, George would eventually meet many of the Western world's best-educated, most learned, and most politically important figures, either directly or by debating them; at such times, George was equal to his discussion partners or debating adversaries in maintaining his own faith—and, almost without exception, he gained the respect of these men.

Two sets of events brought Henry George to youthful independence and helped pave a path toward his life's work. In 1855, through family connections, he sailed as foremast boy on a sixteen-month voyage from New York to Melbourne and Calcutta. Returning to Philadelphia, he secured a job from which he rose to journeyman typesetter, a skill which carried a number of his famous contemporaries into journalism or writing. In the depressed economy of 1857, however, his friends and relatives were already living on the Pacific Coast, and he determined to join them. With an offer for a job in his pocket, he thus started his journey west. Again, thanks to parental persuasions, he sailed as an ordinary seaman on a government lighthouse vessel, which, upon arrival in San Francisco, he deserted. He would remain in the new and bustling state of California from 1858 to 1880.

Life's Work

Initially there was an unsteady quality to George's California days, especially during the Civil War. Like many, he caught "gold fever" and explored northward as far as British Columbia. He weighed rice, served as a foreman, dabbled in journalism, joined in the operation of a San Francisco newspaper, and even abandoned the Democratic Party for California's liberal brand of Republicanism, at least through the Grant Administrations. Such ventures or allegiances, however, were either short-lived or failures. Consequently, along with many young Eastern emigrants during the 1860's, he suffered economic hardships, at one point verging on desperation. Nevertheless, he was establishing mature foundations.

In 1861, George married Annie Fox, a Catholic orphaned by a broken British colonial marriage, and they started a family of their own. Moreover, in

March, 1865, by his own account, he determined to devote his life to writing, exploring social issues through the economic contrasts and conflicts that appeared so stark in California. Between 1866 and 1879, he pursued this course as editor variously of eight San Francisco, Oakland, and Sacramento newspapers. Editorially he advocated (and sometimes joined) movements toward free trade and public ownership and regulation of railroads, the telegraph, and municipal utilities. He sought revisions in the state's land policies, as well as revisions in national land policy under the Morrill Act, thus encouraging more equitable land distribution both in California and in the nation.

Generally George favored trade unionism, the eight-hour day, and strikes as a last resort. He believed that high wages, leading to a greater respect for labor, would help lead to an economy of abundance. Favoring competition, he staunchly opposed its excesses or monopolies in any form. Similarly, on the then hotly debated "currency question," he proposed an end to credit manipulations by bankers and by government and a gradual restoration of wartime greenbacks (inflated currency) to equivalency in gold: a gradual return to a hard-money policy. Distressed by the cornering of California lands by a handful of speculators and wealthy individuals and anxious to see the state continue as a utopia for the common man, he urged restrictions on immigration, particularly Chinese immigration. The issues with which he dealt were current ones, engaging wide popular attention and commentary by American and British political economists of whom George was aware and whom he acknowledged, but his faith, common sense, keen personal observations, and experienced reflections lent special force to his writings.

His editorials and lectures brought George notoriety. It was two books specifically, however, that won for him national and even international recognition. In 1871, he published *Our Land and Land Policy, National and State* (really a 130-page pamphlet) in San Francisco. In it he argued that public lands should be made more available to ordinary homesteaders (eighty-acre or forty-acre allotments rather than 160-acre allotments); that existing enormous landholdings should be divested and their future restricted chiefly through the fairest and most collectible of all taxes: a tax on land. Barring the rapid drift toward land monopolies and a reopening of accessibility, he predicted revolutions in Europe and America which would begin among

the dispossessed peoples of their growing and spreading urban areas. Thus spoke the frail, bald, but bearded, mustachioed, flashing-eyed Prophet of San Francisco, a man by then inspiring pragmatic land reform movements.

Then, in 1879, George published *Progress and Poverty: An Inquiry into the Causes of Industrial Depressions, and of Increase of Want with Increase of Wealth—The Remedy*. Injustices were explicit in the subtitle. The remedy was nationalization of land and imposition of one single tax (later The Single Tax). Land values, George argued, as personal knowledge of stark contrasts between extraordinary wealth and dire need in San Francisco and New York convinced him, were communal, societal creations inherent in the scarcity of land. Pressures of population, production necessities, or monopolistic urges thus raised land and rental values and depressed wages. The mere possession of land often made millionaires of nonproducers or noncontributors to human welfare. A tax, therefore, on such socially created rents would allow government to redistribute such gains to alleviate want and enhance community life. George was no socialist. Indeed, since the basis of local revenues was a general property tax and since George abhorred centralization over local responsibilities, he expected local governments to fulfill these necessary functions.

Progress and Poverty earned for George international fame even greater than the fame he was enjoying at home. In 1880, he moved to New York City, there to write, lecture, and carry his message abroad. He was active among reformers, land restoration leaguers, and labor and economic circles in England and Ireland in 1882 and again in England and Scotland (with particular success in the latter) in 1884. By the end of the 1880's, he had been active on the Continent as well as in Australia. In fact, he had, with some justice, come to believe that *Progress and Poverty* was the most influential work of its kind since Adam Smith's *The Wealth of Nations* (1776). Even Karl Marx, while critical, regarded George's work as a significant assault upon economic orthodoxy.

Inevitably George's prominence brought him into the political forum. After the Civil War and Reconstruction era, he had returned to the Democratic Party, though not uncritically. While many reformers championed him for the nation's and for New York State's highest political offices, he either avoided selection or lost the votes. In fact, it was the politics of New York City that claimed him. His prolabor positions were well-known. So too were his urban progressive reforms: an end to bossism, municipal ownership of utilities, and the secret ballot, among others. His idea for a single tax and his other economic proposals, such as free trade and antipoverty activities, also had wide currency. Attuned to rural dissents, he was recognized also for his awareness that the future of America lay with the consciences of its growing urban citizenry. Nominated by New York's Central Labor Union for the mayoralty in 1886, he lost in a hotly disputed three-way race. Afterward, he continued with his mission, writing and lecturing, until he tried once more to become New York's mayor in 1897 as the candidate of The Democracy of Thomas Jefferson. Indefatigable to the end, but exhausted from campaigning, he died on October 29, 1897.

Summary

No American reformer loomed larger in his generation nationally and internationally than Henry George. *Progress and Poverty* was widely translated and received a degree of attention that few other books ever have; it was in its time far more influential than the first volume of Karl Marx's *Das Kapital* (1867). George's idealism and devotion to democracy, though professional economists found his Single Tax idea flawed, did more to shake economic thinking by directing it to profound social and related political problems than anyone else's. In a narrow economic sense, he came close to developing the idea of marginal productivity. More practically, his ideas linked land questions with taxation and helped spawn tax reforms that were placed in effect not only in parts of the United States but also in Canada and Australia. If George represented popular radicalism, his roots were natively American, drawing from the best of the Jeffersonian and Jacksonian traditions. He was firmly procapitalist and a believer in fair competition. Despite flirtations with socialism, he had little regard for any type of governmental centralization. Rather, the somewhat utopian visions of democracy in which he placed his faith emphasized local government and local responsibilities. Finally, as he carried his ideas into the heart of the world's greatest city, his forceful Christianity influenced most major reformers of the Progressive era that followed his death.

Bibliography

Barker, Charles Albro. *Henry George*. New York: Oxford University Press, 1955. The richest, most exhaustively researched, perhaps definitive biography. Coverage is meticulously chronological, but Barker makes his own careful evaluations of George's development and ideas, both in the context of his time and in historical perspective.

Borcherdin, Thomas E., et al. "Henry George: Precursor to Public Choice Analysis." *American Journal of Economics and Sociology* 57, no. 2 (April 1998). Compares contemporary interest in "public choice analysis" with George's recognition of public market efficiencies.

De Mille, Anna George. *Henry George: Citizen of the World*. Edited by Don C. Shoemaker. Chapel Hill: University of North Carolina Press, 1950. George's daughter concentrates upon her father as a family man and devotes more attention to her mother's role than is to be found in any other work.

Dorfman, Joseph. *The Economic Mind in American Civilization*. Vol. 3. New York: Viking Press, 1959. Chapter 6 places George, with depth and excellence, in a context of the economic history of Popular Radicalism between 1865 and 1918.

Geiger, George Raymond. *The Philosophy of Henry George*. New York: Macmillan, 1933. A close, if pedantic and somewhat ahistorical analysis. Stresses George's pragmatism.

George, Henry, Jr. *The Life of Henry George*. London: Heinemann, 1900; New York: Doubleday, 1905. Much material later incorporated in George, Jr.'s *The Complete Works of Henry George*. 10 vols. New York: Fels Fund Library Edition, 1906-1911. An associate of his father from his adolescence onward, George, Jr., later a congressman, faithfully reflects paternal decisions and ideas in this memoir.

Nock, Albert Jay. *Henry George*. New York: Morrow, 1939. A brilliant analysis of George's character and mind.

Seligman, Edwin R. A. *Essays in Taxation*. 10th ed. New York: Macmillan, 1925. Still readily available, this work by America's foremost authority on taxation concludes that on political, social, economic, and moral grounds, the Single Tax was a mistake. Yet Seligman freely acknowledges its great usefulness in drawing attention to abuses of medieval land systems abroad, to inequities in the general property tax in the United States, and to unjust privilege.

Schwartzman, Jack. "The Death of Henry George: Scholar or Statesman?" *American Journal of Economics and Sociology* 56, no. 4 (October 1997). Discusses George's drive and dedication during his last months of life, which was when he attempted to complete his book on political economy while running for mayor of Greater New York.

Thomas, John L. "Utopia for an Urban Age: Henry George, Henry Demarest Lloyd, Edward Bellamy." *Perspectives in American History* 6 (1974): 135-166. A lucid comparison of George's utopian strains with those of two famous contemporaries.

Clifton K. Yearley
Kerrie L. MacPherson

THÉODORE GÉRICAULT

Born: September 26, 1791; Rouen, France
Died: January 26, 1824; Paris, France
Area of Achievement: Art
Contribution: Géricault helped to move French art away from neoclassicism, which was dominant between the revolutionary and Napoleonic eras, into new, more modern directions. Nineteenth century Romantic and realistic painters alike claimed to have been inspired by his work.

Early Life

Jean-Louis-André-Théodore Géricault was a descendant of a respectable Norman line. His father, Georges-Nicolas Géricault, a prosperous lawyer and later businessman, was forty-eight at the birth of his only child. His mother, Louise-Jeanne-Marie (née Caruel), had turned thirty-nine.

The Géricaults moved to Paris around 1796. Théodore soon entered boarding school and in 1806 commenced study at the Lycée Impérial, an academy known for its fine, classical education. Only an average student, he nevertheless showed artistic talent. Théodore also was fortunate to have been taught by Pierre Bouillon, winner of the 1797 Grand Prix de Rome. Géricault later competed for this government-sponsored award, which carried with it art study in Italy.

The death of his mother in 1808 caused Théodore to reconsider his circumstances. It also brought him closer to home: Théodore decided that he had had enough of academic training and decided to live with Georges-Nicolas. Furthermore, his mother's large estate and his father's business interests allowed the young man to devote himself wholly to art, without concern for finances. One obstacle remained: Georges-Nicolas objected to Théodore's career pursuit. With moral support from his maternal uncle, Jean-Baptiste Caruel, the younger Géricault allegedly went to work but actually entered the studio of Carle Vernet. Thus, Géricault eased his way into art.

Life's Work

According to the professional codes of the day, enrollment in a master's studio was the first of manly steps toward status as a painter. Géricault's affinity for Vernet, primarily an equestrian artist, appears logical: One of Géricault's first actions after the death of his mother had been to buy a horse.

As a teacher, Vernet ran a very loose studio, providing his own atmosphere and personal warmth but little artistic direction. Géricault nevertheless maintained a lifelong enthusiasm for both riding and equestrian art. The early twentieth century Parisian critic Louis Dimier ventured, "Only when it came to horses did he paint to perfection." This verdict is open to much scrutiny. It may be more accurate to say that Géricault took equestrian painting from a rather stodgy, still form and gave it life, placing the animals in motion and illustrating their diverse work and sporting roles. To do that, he frequently employed gouache or watercolor washes with brown ink or pencil on beige paper. Yet the artist used oils for his larger, more ambitious works.

After spending roughly two years in Vernet's studio, Géricault may have felt the need for a more rigorous, professional approach. He then became affiliated with Pierre Guérin, a painter who had attained considerable renown in his day and owed inspiration to the revered Jacques-Louis David. A method instructor, Guérin required his students—Eugène Delacroix also was one of them—to paint antiquarian and heavenly subjects. Géricault, however, asserted his individuality. During a particular session, he first began to copy, then radically alter, the composition of his master's work. When queried by a perturbed Guérin, the younger artist allegedly responded, "I had taken it into my head to inject some energy into it, and you can imagine how that turned out." Géricault stayed with the classical painter for only eleven months, into 1811. He then studied independently, frequenting the Louvre. Most authorities admit that the young artist was influenced by the warm colors, brush techniques, and lifelike images of Peter-Paul Rubens, Titian, and the Italian masters.

If scholars disagree on Géricault's style, perhaps this stems from the fact that contemporary French society underwent many changes very quickly—from the turbulent Revolution to the Napoleonic conquests to the restoration of the Bourbon monarchy. Some of the democratic ideals advocated during the Revolution, for example, harked back to classical Greece and Rome; hence, the philosophical commitment and tremendous popularity of the neoclassicist David. Napoleon I, on the other hand, sought to ennoble his own image and contributions. In 1810, the emperor identified two thematic classifications—historic and current—by which

the government-sponsored Salon was to judge its art competition. Napoleon also brought to Paris cultural riches from his far-flung conquered lands, rendering the Louvre a truly eclectic treasure chest. Thus, Géricault benefited from a much broader exposure than did, for example, David.

If influences were widening, the attainment of status followed an established track. Géricault therefore enrolled in the École des Beaux Arts and, because of his affiliation, began to enter competitions. Certainly the largest and best known of these, the Salon, accepted his *Charging Chasseur* for its 1812 exhibition. Géricault's work depicted a mounted officer of the Imperial Guard, poised for action. Although executed quickly, it won critical acclaim, more so, in fact, than any of Géricault's subsequent Salon showings. The *Charging Chasseur*—with its warm colors and effective sense of light and motion—also emphasized the artist's interest in military subjects.

Two years later, the Salon displayed both the *Charging Chasseur* and a new creation, the *Wounded Cuirassier* (1814). Reception this time proved to be rather poor. The less buoyant tone of the *Wounded Cuirassier* followed Napoleon's military losses, but the critical ambivalence also may be attributed to stylistic factors and disappointment over the painting's failure to fulfill expectations.

In 1816, Géricault vied for the top award: the Prix de Rome. When he did not capture the honors, he decided to finance his own studies in Italy. Personal as well as art-related reasons motivated him: Géricault had become involved with Alexandrine-Modeste de Saint-Martin Caruel, his uncle's young wife. Perhaps the painter was depressed over this relationship, or maybe he sought foreign refuge before the family became embroiled in a full-fledged scandal. His affair with Alexandrine, continuing after his return from Italy, never proved to be happy, although it produced one son, Georges-Hippolyte, in 1818.

Géricault's Italian odyssey lasted for a year, during which time he became entranced with the work of Michelangelo and other masters. The youthful painter also witnessed a uniquely Roman event, the riderless horse race of Barberi, which meshed his artistic and equestrian interests. Although Géricault rendered many sketches of this intended life-size project, it remained unfinished. Most authorities agree that the tall, slender, handsome painter—with his curly reddish-blond hair and deep-set eyes—was suffering from a lack of confidence.

The artistic grandeur of Rome possibly aggravated his perceived inadequacies.

Returning to France in September, 1817, Géricault resumed his friendship with Horace Vernet, the son of his former teacher and an artist in his own right. It was under Vernet's influence that Géricault first produced lithographs, again using military subjects as a theme. Unfortunately, the works hardly sold. Knowing of Géricault's financial independence, his art publisher even advised him to seek another career.

Disappointed over the lithographs and with his child on the way, Géricault spent eighteen intensive months preparing the most important work of his life, *The Raft of the Medusa* (1818-1819), which was based on a controversial contemporary event. A government frigate, the *Medusa*, sank off the coast of Africa, largely because of the incompetence of its captain, who owed his commission to political patronage. The errant officer also retained the most serviceable lifeboats for himself and his friends, forcing the rest of the passengers to construct a raft from the sinking ship's parts. Of the 149 people stranded aboard the improvised vessel, only fifteen survived. Cannibalism, among other horrors, had occurred.

Géricault tackled his project in the manner of a chronicler: He interviewed the survivors and went to local hospitals and morgues to observe the dead and dying. Intensely committed to a realistic portrayal, he prepared numerous sketches. A model, possibly commenting on this frenetic process, said, "Monsieur Géricault had to have complete silence, nobody dared speak or move near him; the least thing disturbed him."

The dramatic, monumental masterpiece—measuring sixteen by twenty-four feet—appeared in the Salon of 1819 but bore the brunt of debate. Disparate factions blamed one another for the circumstances that ultimately determined the *Medusa*'s fate, and many argued about Géricault's political interpretations. Writing in typically partisan journals, art critics also viewed the painting harshly. Its dark tones and frank depiction of human torment also worked against it. Still, the Salon awarded Géricault a medal for his labor of love. One judge even commissioned him to do another painting. Fatigued from the intensive preparation and controversial aftermath of *The Raft of the Medusa*, however, Géricault transferred the proposed assignment to his friend Delacroix. French art circles may have been divided in their assessment of

The Raft of the Medusa, but in 1820 an English gallery owner invited Géricault to show his work in London, where it was praised. The painting subsequently traveled to Dublin.

Géricault returned to Paris in December, 1821. The following year, a friend who specialized in mental disorders commissioned the artist to paint portraits of ten psychiatric patients; five of these portraits survive. Notwithstanding the radical changes in psychiatry, the series deserves respect for its realistic approach: a study of men and women with problems rather than the subhumans popularly perceived during the early nineteenth century.

A normal existence, and therefore painting, would become increasingly difficult for Géricault toward the end of his life. In 1822, he suffered two falls while horseback riding. Undaunted, he continued to pursue his favorite sport and also to sketch more advanced versions of *African Slave Trade* (1823) and *Liberation of the Prisoners of the Spanish Inquisition* (1823). Both of these paintings took an enlightened view; the second was critical of the restored Bourbon monarchy.

Géricault never allowed his wounds to heal properly. By 1823, the riding injuries caused his spine to deteriorate. Doctors operated several times but ultimately failed to save him. Géricault died on January 26, 1824, at the age of thirty-two.

Summary

The three paintings that Théodore Géricault exhibited during his lifetime currently hang in the Louvre, testimony to his endurance as an artist. When his studio was cleared for sale ten months after his death, many works surfaced, far more than had been known to exist.

Géricault likely doubted his compositional and drawing skills and, therefore, sketched numerous life studies before proceeding with a master painting. Once confident of his ability to portray people and events realistically, he added the motion, lighting effects, and drama which often characterize him as a Romantic. If experts disagree on Géricault's style, they also ponder his social consciousness. The artist, in his later years, expanded his repertoire from military and equestrian themes to controversial political subjects and studies of the downtrodden. During his British tenure, for example, he sketched a public hanging, a paralytic woman, and an impoverished man. Géricault nevertheless became increasingly enamored of the relatively highbrow, distinctly English, equestrian crowd.

The artist's premature death left his life open to speculation and, occasionally, legend. Yet, from 1824 through much of the twentieth century, various patrons of the arts—collectors, gallery owners, scholars, and museum directors—have shown consistent interest in what now appear to be his prodigious efforts.

Bibliography

Athanassoglou-Kallmyer, Nina. "Géricault's Severed Heads and Limbs: The Politics and Aesthetics of the Scaffold." *Art Bulletin* 74, no. 4 (December 1992). Discusses several of Géricault's works depicting severed heads and limbs and their interpretation as public statements of the need for political and artistic rejuvenation.

Canaday, John. *The Lives of the Painters.* Vol. 3, *Neoclassic to Post-Impressionist.* New York: Norton, and London: Thames and Hudson, 1969. A chapter describing the classic-Romantic schism in France contains a short synopsis of Géricault's life and creative output. The painter appears as a prominent force, whose work embodied a number of nineteenth century trends.

Eitner, Lorenz. *Géricault.* Los Angeles: Los Angeles County Museum of Art, 1971. Text accompanies this catalog of 125 paintings (plates) displayed during a 1971 exhibition. The introductory chapter mostly discusses the posthumous fame and changing perceptions of Géricault's art. Also includes a ten-page timeline and a table of exhibitions and literature.

_____. *Géricault: His Life and Work.* Ithaca, N.Y.: Cornell University Press, and London: Orbis, 1982. Fusing biography and art history, nearly four hundred pages yield a comprehensive study of Géricault. Extremely useful for assessing the creative process: how his original ideas and subject matter changed during the course of a painting. Contains many color and black-and-white plates.

Grunchec, Philippe. *Géricault's Horses: Drawings and Watercolors.* New York: Vendome Press, 1984; London: Sotheby's, 1985. Although more than an equestrian artist, Géricault elevated the genre to new heights and broadened its dimensions. This book examines horse painting as the primary nexus between the master's career and outside life. Contains a bibliography, a chronology of exhibitions, and numerous plates, most of which are in color.

————. *Master Drawings by Géricault.* Washington, D.C.: International Exhibitions Foundation, 1985. Heavily illustrated with reproductions of Géricault's sketches, this work seeks to demonstrate his stylistic and thematic tendencies. Text also discusses friends and other artists who influenced him, as well as the posthumous dispersal of his art. Contains a timeline and a well-annotated list of paintings.

Lethève, Jacques. *Daily Life of French Artists in the Nineteenth Century.* Translated by Hilary E. Paddon. New York: Praeger, 1968; London: Allen and Unwin, 1972. The book offers insights into how artists lived, executed and marketed their work, and gained recognition. Students of Géricault will find several interesting details and quotations, but the most important contribution is an understanding of the institutions (such as the Salon) which made an impact upon his professional career. Contains notes, a bibliography, and illustrations.

Whitney, Wheelock, and Theodore Géricault. *Géricault in Italy.* New Haven, Conn.: Yale University Press, 1997. Whitney creates a detailed account of Géricault's year in Italy (1817) with emphasis on the works produced during this time and the influence the trip had on his later career.

Lynn C. Kronzek

GERONIMO

Goyathlay

Born: c. 1827; near modern Clifton, Arizona
Died: February 17, 1909; Fort Sill, Oklahoma
Area of Achievement: Native American leadership
Contribution: For two decades the most feared and vilified individual in the Southwest, Geronimo, in his old age, became a freak attraction at fairs and expositions. His maligned and misunderstood career epitomized the troubles of a withering Apache culture struggling to survive in a hostile modern world.

Early Life

While the precise date and location of his birth are not known, Geronimo most likely was born around 1827 near the head of the Gila River in a part of the Southwest then controlled by Mexico. Named Goyathlay (One Who Yawns) by his Behonkohe parents, the legendary Apache warrior later came to be called Geronimo—a name taken from the sound which terrified Mexican soldiers allegedly cried when calling on Saint Jerome to protect them from his relentless charge.

Geronimo's early life, like that of other Apache youth, was filled with complex religious ritual and ceremony. From the placing of amulets on his cradle to guard him against early death to the ceremonial putting on of the first moccasins, Geronimo's relatives prepared their infant for Apache life, teaching him the origin myths of his people and the legends of supernatural beings and benevolent mountain spirits that hid in the caverns of their homeland. Through ritual observances and instruction, Geronimo learned about Usen, a remote and nebulous god who, though unconcerned with petty quarrels among men, was the Life Giver and provider for his people. "When Usen created the Apaches," Geronimo later asserted, "he also created their homes in the West. He gave to them such grain, fruits, and game as they needed to eat. . . . He gave to them a climate and all they needed for clothing and shelter was at hand." Geronimo's religious heritage taught him to be self-sufficient, to love and revere his mountain homeland, and never to betray a promise made with oath and ceremony.

Geronimo grew into adulthood during a brief period of peace, a rare interlude that interrupted the chronic wars between the Apache and Mexican peoples. Even in times of peace, however, Apache culture placed a priority on the skills of warfare. Through parental instruction and childhood games, Geronimo learned how to hunt, hide, track, and shoot—necessary survival skills in an economy based upon game, wild fruits, and booty taken from neighboring peoples.

Geronimo also heard the often repeated stories of conquests of his heroic grandfather Mahko, an Apache chief renowned for his great size, strength, and valor in battle. Like his grandfather, Geronimo had unusual physical prowess and courage. Tall and slender, strong and quick, Geronimo proved at an early age to be a good provider for his mother, whom he supported following his father's premature death, and later for his bride, Alope, whom he acquired from her father for "a herd of ponies" stolen most likely from unsuspecting Mexican victims. By his early twenties, Geronimo (still called Goyathlay) was a member of the council of warriors, a proven booty taker, a husband, and a father of three.

Life's Work

In 1850, a band of Mexican scalp hunters raided an Apache camp while the warriors were away. During the ensuing massacre, Geronimo's mother, wife, and three children were slain. Shortly after this tragedy, Geronimo had a religious experience that figured prominently in his subsequent life. As he later reported the incident, while in a trancelike state, a voice called his name four times (the magic number among the Apache) and then informed him, "No gun can ever kill you. I will take the bullets from the guns of the Mexicans, so they will have nothing but powder. And I will guide your arrows." After receiving this gift of power, Geronimo's vengeance against Mexicans was equaled by his confidence that harm would not come his way.

While still unknown to most Americans, during the 1850's, Geronimo rose among the ranks of the Apache warriors. A participant in numerous raids into Mexico, Geronimo fought bravely under the Apache chief Cochise. Although wounded on several occasions, Geronimo remained convinced that no bullet could kill him. It was during this period that he changed his name from Goyathlay to Geronimo.

War between the United States government and the Apache first erupted in 1861 following a kidnaping-charge incident involving Cochise. The war

lingered for nearly a dozen years until Cochise and General O. O. Howard signed a truce. According to the terms of the agreement, the mountain homeland of the Chiricahua (one of the tribes which made up the Apache and Geronimo's tribe) was set aside as a reservation, on which the Chiricahua promised to remain.

Following Cochise's death in 1874, the United States attempted to relocate the Chiricahua to the San Carlos Agency in the parched bottomlands of the Gila River. Although some Apache accepted relocation, Geronimo led a small band off the reservation into the Sierra Madre range in Mexico. From this base, Geronimo's warriors conducted raids into the United States, hitting wagon trains and ranches for the supplies needed for survival.

In 1877, for the first and only time in his life, Geronimo was captured by John Clum of the United States Army. After spending some time in a guardhouse in San Carlos, Geronimo was released, being told not to leave the reservation. Within a year, however, he was again in Mexico. While a fugitive, he was blamed in the American press for virtually all crimes committed by Apache "renegades" of the reservation.

Upon the promise of protection, Geronimo voluntarily returned to the San Carlos Agency in 1879. This time, he remained two years until an unfortunate incident involving the death of Nochay-del-klinne, a popular Apache religious prophet, triggered another escape into the Sierra Madre. In 1882, Geronimo daringly attempted a raid into Arizona to rescue the remainder of his people on the reservation and to secure for himself reinforcements for his forces hiding in Mexico. This campaign, which resulted in the forced abduction of many unwilling Apache women and children, brought heavy losses to his band and nearly cost Geronimo his life. The newspaper coverage of the campaign also made Geronimo America's most despised and feared villain.

In May, 1883, General George Crook of the United States Army crossed into Mexico in search of Geronimo. Not wanting war, Geronimo sent word to Crook of his willingness to return to the reservation if his people were guaranteed just treatment. Crook consented, and Geronimo persuaded his band to retire to San Carlos.

Geronimo, however, never adjusted to life on the reservation. Troubled by newspaper headlines demanding his execution and resentful of reservation rules (in particular, the prohibition against alcohol-ic drink), Geronimo in the spring of 1885 planned a final breakaway from the San Carlos Agency. With his typical ingenuity, Geronimo led his 144 followers off the reservation. Cutting telegraph lines behind him, he eluded the cavalry and crossed into Mexico, finding sanctuary in his old Sierra Madre refuge. Although pursued by an army of five thousand regulars and five hundred Apache scouts, Geronimo avoided capture until September, 1886, when he voluntarily surrendered to General Nelson Miles. (He had agreed to a surrender to General George Crook in March but had escaped his troops.)

Rejoicing that the Apache wars were over, the army loaded Geronimo and his tribesmen on railroad cars and shipped them first to Fort Pickens in Florida and then to the Mount Vernon Barracks in Alabama. Unaccustomed to the warm, humid climate, so unlike the high, dry country of their birth, thousands of the Apache captives died of tuberculosis and other diseases. In 1894, after the government rejected another appeal to allow their return to Arizona, the Kiowa and Comanche offered their former Apache foes a part of their reservation near Fort Sill, Oklahoma.

Geronimo spent the remainder of his life on the Oklahoma reservation. Adapting quickly to the white man's economic system, the aged Apache warrior survived by growing watermelons and selling his now infamous signature to curious autograph seekers. While the government technically still viewed him as a prisoner of war, the army permitted Geronimo to attend, under guard, the international fairs and expositions at Buffalo, Omaha, and St. Louis. In 1905, Theodore Roosevelt even invited him to Washington, D.C., to attend the inaugural presidential parade. Wherever Geronimo went, he attracted great crowds and made handsome profits by selling autographs, buttons, hats, and photographs of himself.

In February, 1909, while returning home from selling bows and arrows in nearby Lawton, Oklahoma, an inebriated Geronimo fell from his horse into a creek bed. For several hours, Geronimo's body lay exposed. Three days later, the Apache octogenarian died of pneumonia. As promised, no bullet ever killed him.

Summary

The Industrial Age of the late nineteenth century altered the life patterns of American farmers and entrepreneurs, women and laborers. No groups, however, were more affected by the forces of modernization than were the Native American Indians. Geronimo's tragic career as warrior and prisoner epitomized the inevitable demise of an ancient Apache culture trapped in a web of white man's history.

While a stubbornly independent and uncompromising warrior, Geronimo symbolized to countless Americans the treacherous savagery of a vicious race that could not be trusted. Highly conscious of his wrath and unrelenting hatred, the American public never knew the deeply religious family man who yearned to abide in his mountain homeland.

During his last twenty-three years of captivity, the legend of Geronimo grew, even as the public's hatred of the once-powerful Apache mellowed into admiration. Always a good provider, Geronimo established for himself a profitable business by peddling souvenirs and performing stunts at Wild West shows. A living artifact of a world that no longer existed, Geronimo became the comic image of the tamed American Indian finally brought into white man's civilization.

Bibliography

Adams, Alexander B. *Geronimo: A Biography*. New York: Putnam, 1971; London: New English Library, 1973. A well-researched history of the Apache wars that contains much material on Mangas Coloradas, Cochise, and other warriors as well as Geronimo. Replete with documentation of the connivances, blunders, and savagery that characterized the removal of the Apache from their homelands, this biography exposes the limitations of General Nelson Miles and the inexperience of the white leadership in Indian affairs.

Betzinez, Jason, with Wilbur Sturtevant Nye. *I Fought with Geronimo*. Harrisburg, Pa.: Stackpole, 1959. Another firsthand narrative account of the Apache wars written by the son of Geronimo's first cousin. Includes stories told more than half a century after the event. An entertaining primary source, but it must be used with caution.

Brown, Dee. "Geronimo." *American History Illustrated* 15 (May 1980): 12-21; 15 (July 1980): 31-45. The best article-length introduction to the life of Geronimo. A lively and sympathetic overview of the career of this clever Apache warrior.

Clum, Woodworth. *Apache Agent: The Story of John P. Clum*. Boston: Houghton Mifflin, 1936. A story of the only man who ever captured Geronimo. Written from the notes of John Clum, a man who hated Geronimo with a passion. Biased yet entertaining account.

Davis, Britton. *The Truth About Geronimo*. New Haven, Conn.: Yale University Press, and London: Oxford University Press, 1929. An entertaining narrative filled with humorous and thrilling incidents written by an author who spent three years in the United States Army attempting to locate and capture this Apache warrior.

Debo, Angie. *Geronimo: The Man, His Time, His Place*. Norman: University of Oklahoma Press, 1976; London: Pimlico, 1993. The best of the many Geronimo biographies. Carefully researched and documented, this balanced account portrays Geronimo neither as villain nor as hero, but as a maligned and misunderstood individual trapped in an increasingly hostile environment. Highly recommended.

Faulk, Odie B. *The Geronimo Campaign*. New York: Oxford University Press, 1969. A reassessment of the military campaign that ended with the surrender of Geronimo in 1886. Includes much information collected by the son of Lieutenant Charles B. Gatewood, who arranged the surrender and was one of the few white men Geronimo trusted.

Geronimo. *Geronimo: His Own Story*. Edited by S. M. Barrett and Frederick Turner. New York: Duffield, 1906; London: Cooper, 1975. The personal autobiography dictated by Geronimo to Barrett in 1905. A chronicle of Geronimo's grievances, in particular against the Mexican nationals. Includes informative sections on Apache religion, methods in dealing with crimes, ceremonies, festivals, and appreciation of nature.

Lieder, Michael, and Jake Page. *Wild Justice: The People of Geronimo vs. the United States*. New York: Random House, 1997. Fascinating book by a writer/attorney team, which covers the thirty years of work by the Indian Claims Commission, including the Apaches' incarceration in Florida, Alabama, and Oklahoma as war prisoners. The authors conclude that the commission used methods that precluded fair evaluation of the harm sustained by Native American cultures.

Roberts, David. "Geronimo." *National Geographic* 182, no. 4 (October 1992). Detailed profile of Geronimo.

Terry D. Bilhartz

JAMES GIBBONS

Born: July 23, 1834; Baltimore, Maryland
Died: March 24, 1921; Baltimore, Maryland
Area of Achievement: Religion
Contribution: As the most influential American archbishop of the late nineteenth century, Gibbons helped establish Catholicism as an important and vital religion in modern American society.

Early Life

James Gibbons was born July 23, 1834, in Baltimore, Maryland, the eldest son in a family of five children. His parents, Thomas Gibbons and Bridget (Walsh) Gibbons, were Irish immigrants. When James was three, his family returned to Ireland because of his father's poor health. They resettled in New Orleans in 1853, six years after his father's death.

Upon his return to the United States, Gibbons worked as a clerk in a grocery store for two years. In 1855, he entered Saint Charles College, Ellicott City, Maryland. He moved on to Saint Mary's Seminary in his native Baltimore in 1857 and was ordained a priest of the Roman Catholic Church on June 30, 1861.

Throughout the Civil War, Gibbons pastored various congregations in the Chesapeake Bay area. In addition, he served as a volunteer chaplain at Forts McHenry and Marshall. His dedicated service earned for him much public admiration, and he was one of only three Catholic priests invited to pay their respects when the body of the assassinated President Abraham Lincoln passed through Baltimore.

Following the war, Gibbons' influence in the Catholic Church rapidly increased. In 1865, he was appointed secretary to the archbishop of Baltimore. A year later, he became assistant chancellor for that archdiocese. Gibbons was consecrated as bishop of North Carolina in 1868 and in the following year attended the Vatican I Council in Rome as the youngest bishop among the more than seven hundred in attendance. In 1872, Gibbons assumed the duties of the vacant Richmond see in addition to retaining his responsibilities in North Carolina. Despite the extraordinary demands on his time, he wrote his best-known work, *The Faith of Our Fathers* (1877), in 1876. This extremely popular book, written for the general public, presented an explanation and defense of Catholicism.

Photographs of Gibbons reveal an individual of slight but well-defined physical features, with a calm and peaceful demeanor. His unassuming appearance did not indicate the acumen and depth of the spiritual resources that enabled him to provide decisive leadership to the Catholic Church in America during the most volatile period in its history.

Life's Work

In 1877, at the age of forty-three, Gibbons became the ninth archbishop of Baltimore—a position he would hold until his death in 1921. The oldest archdiocese in the United States, it was also the most prestigious. Such a position made Gibbons the unofficial leader of American Catholics.

Gibbons was a highly effective administrator and spiritual leader, although he did not gain national attention until he presided over the Third Plenary Council in Baltimore in 1884. The council brought together American bishops and archbishops to enact legislation on doctrine, ecclesiastical governance, and parochial education. A major accomplishment of the council was the establishment of Catholic University in Washington, D. C. There, Gibbons provided distinguished leadership as both its first chancellor and its principal advocate.

Gibbons' work at the Third Plenary Council was highly acclaimed. He had diplomatically avoided many controversial social issues that would bitterly divide conservative and liberal Catholics throughout the remainder of the nineteenth century. His efforts prompted Pope Leo XIII to make Gibbons a cardinal in 1886. With this rapid rise to national prominence, Gibbons was thrust into the role of resolving a number of social issues. With the aid of his principal allies, Archbishop John Ireland and Bishop John J. Keane, Gibbons faced the pressing problems of organized labor and immigration.

Because of the deplorable working conditions of late nineteenth century America—for example, twelve-hour workdays and inadequate wages—the Knights of Labor was formed in 1869 to establish various labor unions. Its goals were primarily to limit working hours, improve working conditions, and increase wages. Since labor organizers were routinely fired by their employers, however, the membership and activities of the Knights of Labor became secretive. The pope had declared that membership in an organization requiring secret

oaths and activities was incompatible with the Catholic faith. For this reason, as well as fear of Socialist tendencies, conservative Catholic leaders opposed the Knights of Labor. In 1884, Cardinal Elzéar Taschereau of Quebec obtained a ruling from the Vatican forbidding Catholics to belong to the labor organization. Conservatives argued that the ruling included the United States as well.

Gibbons fought for the laborers. He maintained that the prohibition applied only to Quebec and that it would be wrong for the Catholic Church to oppose the American labor movement. Although Gibbons and his liberal allies admired the achievements of capitalism, they believed that adequate wages, improved working conditions, and shorter working hours were demanded by the principles of Christian charity and justice. Furthermore, Gibbons warned that condemnation of the Knights of Labor would create an unnecessary conflict of conscience for Catholic laborers. A Catholic would be forced to choose between a union and the Church. Since the goals of the labor movement were just, Gibbons argued, opposition was uncalled for.

Gibbons backed a series of strikes in 1886 and a year later presented the pope with a lengthy document defending the Knights of Labor. In 1888, the Vatican removed its ban on the organization. This reversal represented a major victory for Gibbons and set a precedent for strong Catholic support of labor reform in the following years.

The great wave of immigration in the nineteenth century created a second pressing issue for Gibbons. During this time, the Catholic population in the United States increased from three million in 1860 to more than twelve million by 1895. This rapid growth inspired strong anti-Catholic sentiments within American society, as seen in the formation of such organizations as the Know-Nothing Party (1854) and the American Protective Association (1887). These groups claimed that Catholic teachings opposed democracy and the separation of Church and State, and they feared that priests would instruct their parishioners on how to vote based on orders from the Vatican. American society, they declared, was being attacked from an outside religious force.

Although such claims bore minimal influence on public opinion, they did create problems concerning how Catholics viewed their participation in American life. These attacks emphasized the ethnic differences that already existed among Catholics. For example, German Catholics tended to be rural, Midwestern, and conservative, whereas Irish Catholics tended to be urban, Eastern, and liberal. In response to these tensions, conservative Catholics began viewing American society as largely Protestant and hostile. They maintained that Catholics should not accommodate themselves to the larger culture but should preserve their religious and ethnic identity through traditional beliefs and customs.

Gibbons fought both the anti-Catholic claims and the conservative position. He countered that Catholicism was not opposed to democracy and could flourish in a nation where Church and State were legally separated. He believed that Catholics could, and must, simultaneously be good citizens and faithful members of the Church. As a liberal, he argued that Catholics must adapt to the American situation rather than preserve their traditional beliefs and ethnic customs. Catholics should be assimilated into American society by actively participating in its social, political, and educational institutions.

The liberal position that Gibbons advocated was popularly titled "Americanism." It was loudly condemned as heretical by its opponents and acclaimed as progressive by its supporters. The debate, however, was not decisive, since in 1895 Pope Leo XIII both praised the liberty of the Catholic Church in the United States and questioned whether the separation of Church and State was the most desirable situation. Although Gibbons had not won a clear victory, he clearly set the pattern for full Catholic participation in an increasingly pluralistic American society.

Summary

The lengthy career of this distinguished religious leader reflected the changing, often turbulent, character of American society at the close of the nineteenth century and beginning of the twentieth century. Gibbons' concern over labor and immigration reflected the problems of a nation that was simultaneously becoming prosperous and ethnically diverse. He brought a strong religious and moral commitment to the pressing political, economic, and social issues of his day.

Gibbons' range of interests was quite broad. He was routinely consulted on Church-State issues and provided advice to a variety of political leaders. Often invited to preach in Protestant churches, he worked toward improving relations between different religions and participated in the World Parliament of Religions in Chicago in 1893. The patriotism of Gibbons was unparalleled as he helped establish the National Catholic War Council at the United States' entry into World War I in 1917. His tireless will helped not only Catholics but all Americans as well to define the national character at a crucial time in history.

Bibliography

Browne, Henry J. *The Catholic Church and the Knights of Labor*. Washington, D.C.: Catholic University of America Press, 1949. An in-depth examination of the Knights of Labor controversy within the Catholic Church. Particular attention is directed toward the role Gibbons played in changing his Church's position on the labor organization.

Cross, Robert D. *The Emergence of Liberal Catholicism in America*. Cambridge, Mass.: Harvard University Press, 1958. A comprehensive overview of the various controversies between conservative and liberal Catholics in late nineteenth and early twentieth century America.

Dolan, Jay P. *The Immigrant Church*. Baltimore: Johns Hopkins University Press, 1975. Although this book concentrates on issues that divided German and Irish Catholics living in New York City in the mid-nineteenth century, it provides a good framework for understanding the various ethnic and immigrant issues that Gibbons and the Church faced.

Ellis, John Tracy. *American Catholicism*. 2d ed. Chicago: University of Chicago Press, 1969. An excellent concise introduction to the history of Catholicism in the United States.

Fohlen, Claude. "American Catholics and the Separation of Church and State in France." *Catholic Historical Review* 80, no. 4 (October 1994). Discussion of the negative U.S. reaction to France's decision to separate church and state in 1905. Oddly, Gibbons led the American resistance, despite identical separations on the United States' part years before.

Gibbons, James Cardinal. *A Retrospect of Fifty Years*. Baltimore: Murphy, 1916. An autobiographical recounting of the major events that shaped the author's career.

McAvoy, Thomas T. *The Great Crisis in American Catholic History, 1895-1900*. Chicago: Regnery, 1957. An extensive and excellent inquiry into the Americanism controversy.

————, ed. *Roman Catholicism and the American Way of Life*. Notre Dame, Ind.: University of Notre Dame Press, 1960. A series of essays written by both Catholics and Protestants that review and evaluate the role of Catholicism in early twentieth century American society.

Marty, Martin E. *Pilgrims in Their Own Land*. Boston: Little Brown, 1984. Reviews the history of various religions in the United States. The chapter "Adapting to America" provides a concise and helpful framework for understanding the immigration and labor issues of the late nineteenth century.

Ryan, James Emmett. "Sentimental Catechism: Archbishop James Gibbons, Pass-Print Culture, and American Literary History." *Religion and American Culture* 7, no. 1 (Winter 1997). Focuses on Gibbons' catechism, "The Faith of our Fathers: Being a Plain Exposition of the Church Founded by our Lord Jesus Christ," and its use of nineteenth century American sentimentalism to convey European ideas of religious devotionalism.

Brent Waters

JOSIAH WILLARD GIBBS

Born: February 11, 1839; New Haven, Connecticut
Died: April 28, 1903; New Haven, Connecticut
Areas of Achievement: Physical chemistry and theoretical physics
Contribution: Gibbs established the theoretical basis for modern physical chemistry by quantifying the second law of thermodynamics and developing heterogeneous thermodynamics. This and other work earned for him recognition as the greatest American scientist of the nineteenth century.

Early Life

Josiah Willard Gibbs, later known usually as J. Willard Gibbs (to distinguish him from his father, who bore the same name), was the fourth child—the only son among five children—of J. W. Gibbs, professor of sacred literature at Yale College Theological Seminary, and Mary Anna Van Cleve Gibbs. Born in New Haven, Connecticut, Gibbs would live all of his life in that city, leaving only to take one trip abroad, dying in the very house in which he had grown up.

Well educated in private schools, Gibbs was graduated from Yale College in 1858, receiving prizes in Latin and mathematics. In 1863, he took his Ph.D. in engineering at Yale—one of the first such degrees in the United States; his dissertation was entitled *On the Form of the Teeth of Wheels in Spur Gearing.* For the next three years he tutored at Yale in Latin and natural philosophy, working on several practical inventions and obtaining a patent for one of them, an improved railway brake. The foregoing points to a not inconsiderable practical element in the chiefly theoretical scientist that Gibbs would become.

In 1866, Gibbs embarked on a journey to Europe, where he attended lectures by the best-known mathematicians and physicists of that era, spending a year each at the Universities of Paris, Berlin, and Heidelberg. What he learned at these schools would form the basis for his later theoretical work. His parents having died, and two of his sisters as well, he traveled with his remaining sisters, Anna and Julia, the latter returning home early to marry Addison Van Name, later Librarian of Connecticut Academy, in 1867.

Upon his return to New Haven in 1869, Gibbs began work at once on his great theoretical undertaking, which he would not complete until 1878.

He lived in the Van Name household, as did his sister Anna; neither he nor she was ever married. In 1871, he was appointed professor of mathematical physics at Yale—the first such chair in the United States—but without salary. He was obliged to live for nine years on his not very considerable inherited income. When The Johns Hopkins University, aware of the significance of his work, offered him a position at a good salary, Yale decided to offer Gibbs two-thirds of what Johns Hopkins would pay; it was enough for Gibbs.

In 1873, he published his first paper, "Graphical Methods in the Thermodynamics of Fluids," which clarified the concept of entropy, introduced in 1850 by Rudolf Clausius. The genius of this insight was immediately recognized by James Clerk Maxwell in England, to whom Gibbs had sent a copy of the paper. The work was published, however, in a relatively obscure journal, *The Transactions of the Connecticut Academy of Arts and Sciences,* where almost all of Gibbs's subsequent writings would appear. In addition, his style was so terse, austere, and condensed as to be unreadable to all but a few readers who were already well acquainted with his underlying assumptions. Consequently, for most of his life Gibbs would remain largely unknown, especially in the United States, except among a small circle of his scientific colleagues.

This undeserved obscurity never seemed to trouble Gibbs. By all accounts, he was a genuinely unassuming and unpretentious man, tolerant, kind, approachable, and seemingly unconscious of his intellectual eminence. He was by no means gregarious and probably more than a little aloof; he had few really close friends, though he kept up a large correspondence. He attended church regularly. Physically, he was of slight build and owed a certain frailty in health to a severe case of scarlet fever in childhood. Yet he was strong enough to ride and was known as a good horseman. Photographs of him reveal a handsome but somewhat stern man with a well-trimmed, short beard. The photographic image leaves an apt impression of what he was in life: a gentleman, a professor, and a scientist of unimpeachable integrity.

Life's Work

Gibbs published yet another paper in 1873, "A Method of Geometrical Representation of the

a "young investigator, having discovered an entirely new branch of science, gave in a single contribution an exhaustive treatment of it which foreshadowed the development of theoretical chemistry for a quarter of a century." Gibbs's was thus an achievement almost unparalleled in the history of science. Ostwald predicted that the result of Gibbs's work would determine the form and content of chemistry for a century to come—and he was right. A French scientist compared Gibbs, in his importance to chemistry, with Antoine Lavoisier. It should be mentioned that the editors of *The Transactions of the Connecticut Academy of Arts and Sciences* published Gibbs's work on faith alone as they were not able to understand it completely; they obtained the money for publishing the long treatise through private subscription.

Of special importance in Gibbs's work is its sophisticated mathematics. It is therefore not possible to summarize his discoveries in a brief article. There are two features, however, that must be noted. First, Gibbs succeeded in precisely formulating the second law of thermodynamics, which states that the spontaneous flow of heat from hot to cold bodies is reversible only with the expenditure of mechanical or other nonthermal energy. Consequently, entropy (S), equal to heat (Q) divided by temperature change (T), must continually be increasing. Prior to Gibbs, thermodynamics simply did not exist as a science.

Second, Gibbs derived from his more complex heterogeneous thermodynamics the "phase rule," which shows the relationship between the degrees of freedom (F) of a thermodynamic system and the number of components (C) and the number of phases (P), so that $F = C + 2 - P$. He showed how these relationships could be expressed graphically, in three dimensions. Often phase-rule diagrams proved to be the only practical key to the solution of hitherto insoluble problems concerning the mixing of components so that they would remain in equilibrium and not separate out and destroy the mixture. The phase rule helped make it possible to calculate in advance the temperature, pressure, and concentration required for stability—thus eliminating months and possibly years of tedious trial-and-error experiments. This would have important application in industry as well as in the laboratory.

Thermodynamic Properties of Substances by Means of Surfaces." In 1876, the first 140 pages of his major work appeared (again in *Transactions*), the final 180 pages finally being published by that journal in 1878; both parts bore the title, "On the Equilibrium of Heterogeneous Substances." This work, of the utmost importance to science, never appeared in book form in English in Gibbs's lifetime. Its significance was appreciated by Maxwell, who incorporated some of its findings into his own books, but he unfortunately died in 1879. Continental Europeans perceived the general importance of Gibbs's discoveries, but had real difficulty reading Gibbs's text. (Gibbs himself rejected all suggestions that he rewrite his treatise as a readable book.) Hermann Helmholtz and Max Planck both duplicated some of Gibbs's work, simply because they did not know of it. A German translation of it, by the great scientist Wilhelm Ostwald, appeared only in 1892. French translations of various sections of the treatise were published in 1899 and 1903. Meanwhile, scientists came to perceive—in the words of physics professor Paul Epstein—that

Interestingly, after Gibbs's one major treatise on thermodynamics, he never wrote another important paper on the subject. He had said the last word, and he knew it. He did not, however, remain idle. Between 1883 and 1889, he published five papers on the electromagnetic theory of light. This work, too, was well received.

Meanwhile, he had begun to receive a certain amount of more or less perfunctory recognition at home: He was elected to the National Academy of Sciences in 1879 and to the American Academy of Arts and Sciences in 1880; in 1880 he received the Rumford Medal from the latter; in 1885 he was elected a vice president of the American Association for the Advancement of Science.

In the period between 1889 and 1902, Gibbs lectured on the subject of statistical mechanics but published almost nothing on the topic except for a brief abstract. This would be his major work during the final portion of his life; it would require about the same gestation period as did his investigation of thermodynamics. Simultaneously, however, he was lecturing and publishing papers on vector analysis and multiple algebra; the theory of dyadics which appeared in these works is regarded as his most important published contribution to pure mathematics. A book based on his lectures, *Gibbs' Vector Analysis*, was edited and published by a student, E. B. Wilson, in 1901.

That year, Gibbs was awarded the Copley Medal by the Royal Society of London for being the first to apply the second law of thermodynamics to the exhaustive discussion of the relation between chemical, electrical, and thermal energy and the capacity for external work. This was the highest honor for scientists prior to the founding of the Nobel Prize.

In 1902, Gibbs's final important work was published under the title *Elementary Principles in Statistical Mechanics Developed with Special Reference to the Rational Foundation of Thermodynamics*. In this brilliant study, Gibbs was as far ahead of his time as he had been with his first major treatise. The later work has been called "a monument in the history of physics which marks the separation between the nineteenth and twentieth centuries." Gibbs's perception of the role played by probability in physical events made his last work a true precursor to quantum mechanics, which did not develop fully until the 1920's.

During the year following the publication of his final gift to the world, Gibbs suffered from several minor ailments. One of these resulted in a sudden and acute attack from an intestinal obstruction, which led to Gibbs's untimely death on April 28, 1903.

Summary

Gibbs's contribution to American society occurred chiefly after his death. It is regrettable that few Americans had the capacity to recognize his achievements while he was alive, but it seems pointless to try to fix the blame for this. On the one hand, he himself declined to make his papers more accessible by revising them for a wider readership. On the other, physical chemistry was only beginning to develop in the United States. Few professors of either chemistry or physics had the background that would have enabled them to understand Gibbs's work; there were no grand figures such as Rudolf Clausius, James Clerk Maxwell, William Thomson (Baron Kelvin), or Wilhelm Ostwald in America to welcome the new young genius personally.

In addition, the chemical industry in the United States was conservative in the matter of adopting new methods derived chiefly from theory, while at the same time it was caught up in the chaos of a greatly expanding industrialism. There was virtually no one available to examine the implications for the chemical industry of Gibbs's new phase rule. Gradually, however, as the industry turned more and more to synthesizing new compounds and developing metal alloys, there came a demand for precisely the sort of tool that Gibbs long before had provided. The phase rule had an early application in alloys of iron and carbon to produce different types of steel. Another application involved the industrial synthesis of ammonia from nitrogen and hydrogen, and of nitric acid from ammonia. While most of these applications were first worked out in Europe, American industry finally learned how to reap the benefits of bringing theory to bear on practical processes. It finally came to recognize what it owed to Gibbs.

The United States thus reaped the practical benefits of Gibbs's work; it also had the honor of claiming as its own one of the world's greatest theoretical scientists.

Bibliography

Bumstead, H. A. "Josiah Willard Gibbs." In *The Collected Works of J. Willard Gibbs*, edited by H. A. Bumstead. 2 vols. New Haven, Conn.: Yale University Press, 1948. With portrait. Reprinted, with some additions, from the *American Journal of Science* 4 (September, 1903). Also in a previous edition of *The Collected Works*, edited by W. R. Longley and R. G. Van Name. New York: Longman, 1928. Written by a former student who knew Gibbs well, this basic source for all other biographies includes a useful list of Gibbs's publications in chronological order.

Crowther, J. G. "Josiah Willard Gibbs." In *Famous American Men of Science*, edited by J. G. Crowther. New York: Norton, and London: Secker and Warburg, 1937. Two portraits, brief bibliography. Excellent psychological speculation about Gibbs's family and his social and academic life.

Deltete, Robert J., and David L. Thorsell. "Josiah Willard Gibbs and Wilhelm Ostwald: A Contrast in Scientific Style." *Journal of Chemical Education* 73, no. 4 (April 1996). Examines the teaching styles and personalities of Gibbs and chemist Wilhelm Ostwald.

Jaffe, Bernard. "J. Willard Gibbs (1839-1903): America in the New World of Chemistry." In *Men of Science in America: The Role of Science in the Growth of Our Country*. New York: Simon and Schuster, 1944. Excellent discussion of American reception (or lack of it) of Gibbs, and the consequences for American society. Good explanation of phase rule and its application in industry.

Kraus, Charles A. "Josiah Willard Gibbs." In *Great Chemists*, edited by Eduard Farber. New York: Interscience, 1961. Portrait. Good discussion of experimental work and of phase rule.

Rukeyser, Muriel. *Willard Gibbs*. New York: Doubleday, 1942. Portrait. Long text, reads almost like a novel, but offers good background detail that places Gibbs squarely within the context of the American culture of his time.

Seeger, Raymond John. *J. Willard Gibbs: American Mathematical Physicist Par Excellence*. Oxford and New York: Pergamon Press, 1974. Places greatest emphasis on details of mathematics and science. Includes useful chronology of life and work with a short bibliography.

Wheeler, Lynde Phelps. *Josiah Willard Gibbs: The History of a Great Mind*. Rev. ed. New Haven, Conn.: Yale University Press, 1962. The authorized biography. Same as revised edition of 1952 except for the addition of a foreword by A. Whitney Griswold; the two revised editions, unlike the first edition of 1951, contain an appendix summarizing newly discovered family correspondence. Wheeler was a student of Gibbs in the 1890's, and his account is comprehensive but rather genteel. Includes several portraits, a genealogical chart, a catalog of Gibbs's scientific correspondence, and an excellent bibliography of articles and books about Gibbs. Also includes text of Gibbs's first paper.

Donald M. Fiene

W. S. GILBERT AND SIR ARTHUR SULLIVAN

W. S. Gilbert

Born: November 18, 1836; London, England
Died: May 29, 1911; Grim's Dyke, Harrow Weald, Middlesex, England
Areas of Achievement: Music and theater
Contribution: In his collaborations with Sullivan, Gilbert forged a truly British character for light opera, in the process establishing operetta as a major dramatic subgenre and extending its boundaries to include melodrama, satire, and serious drama.

Early Lives

Born to William Gilbert, a sometime naval surgeon who became a prolific if not a talented novelist and playwright, and Anne Morris Gilbert, a doctor's daughter who is remarkable only for the apparent lack of effect she had on her son's life, William Schwenck Gilbert was the eldest of five children, and the only male child. When a toddler, he was kidnapped at Naples and held for ransom. His abductors demanded and received the princely sum of twenty-five pounds for their trouble, and it is possible that this experience provided part of the impetus behind the plot of *The Pirates of Penzance: Or, The Slave of Duty* (1879), in which a dim-witted nurse mistakes pirate for pilot, thus beginning the complications that dog young Frederick's life.

More important than the kidnapping, though, was the influence the elder William Gilbert exerted over his son. The two were entirely alike in temperament: combative, active, confident to a fault. The father instilled in the son an almost unhealthy need to win and an overweening sense of his own worth. This arrogance was Gilbert's early undoing, for at the Western Grammar School and later at Ealing he was a lazy student, until he realized, with a shock, that he was falling behind other boys whose intellectual capabilities he scorned. He began to apply himself, and at sixteen he became head boy at Ealing, going on to enter King's College, London, in 1853, and taking his degree in 1857.

The next period in Gilbert's life looms large in its impact on his career as a dramatist. In 1855, he entered the Inner Temple to study law, and in 1857, the year he took his degree, he joined the militia, beginning twenty years of service there. Both his experiences at the bar and his military service provided grist for Gilbert's satirical mill, not only in his operettas, but in *The Bab Ballads* (1869) as

Sir Arthur Sullivan

Born: May 13, 1842; London, England
Died: November 22, 1900; London, England
Areas of Achievement: Music and theater
Contribution: One of the foremost British composers of the nineteenth century, Sullivan displayed an amazing range, from overtures and oratorios to operettas and hymns; he is primarily remembered for his collaborations with W. S. Gilbert.

well. At any rate, his desire for military service in the Crimea was thwarted when that war inconveniently ended, and his service at the bar, beginning in 1863, was only slightly more successful; he earned only seventy-five pounds in two years.

In the meantime, Gilbert passed the long quiet time in his law office by becoming involved in literary affairs. His first lyric, a translation of the laughing song from Daniel-François-Esprit Auber's *Manon Lescaut*, debuted in 1858, and in 1861 Gilbert began contributing to a new satiric magazine, *Fun*, which would become the principal rival of *Punch*, to which Gilbert also contributed in 1865. More important, he began his stage-writing career with *Dulcamara: Or, The Little Duck and the Great Quack* (1866), an operatic burlesque, the first of five that he would produce during the 1860's. That year also saw the publication of "The Yarn of the Nancy Bell" and in 1867 *The Bab Ballads* began to appear in *Fun*.

In August of 1867, Gilbert married Lucy Blois Turner, a military officer's daughter. A tall man with a military bearing, Gilbert cut a handsome figure. His short brown hair swept back from his broad forehead and, together with his long mutton-chop sideburns, framed a narrow face. A square chin combined with these other attributes to give him a stolid, formidable appearance which seemed to heighten his personal characteristics of stubbornness and feistiness. These characteristics served him well in his literary life, for he was so confident of his talent that he often went over editors' heads and persuaded the owners of journals to publish his material. For this reason, and because he displayed a genuine talent for satire and parody, his literary career began to flourish, and by 1869, when he first met Arthur Sullivan, he had already achieved considerable success.

Six years' Gilbert's junior, Arthur Seymour Sullivan was born May 13, 1842, the second child of Thomas and Mary Coghlan Sullivan. Thomas Sullivan was a poor military musician and band director who provided his sons with a very early introduction to music, to which Arthur immediately took. Before he was twelve, young Arthur had mastered practically every instrument in the band. Singing and composing were Arthur's fortes, and they gained for him entry to the Chapel Royal, even though, at twelve, he was three years beyond the maximum age for admission. There he won, at age fourteen, the first Mendelssohn scholarship, an award that allowed him, two years later, to pursue his studies in Leipzig, at the conservatorium founded there by Felix Mendelssohn himself.

Thus began almost three years of incredible success for such a young musician. If Sullivan had been a prodigy before, he was now a marvel whose compositions gained public performance along with those of far more renowned artists. Indeed, his String Quartet in D Minor was played twice in rapid succession, a rare honor at that time, and both times the piece was received well. In addition, he was accorded the privilege of conducting the orchestra in its performance of his overture to a poem by Thomas Moore, an unheard-of honor for a mere student. The one-year scholarship had been extended for a second year, and at the end of that time, Sullivan was invited to stay on for further study, tuition-free. His masters were reluctant to see him go. Finally he was forced by financial exigency to return to London, where he faced his future with some trepidation. After the triumph in Leipzig, Sullivan feared that the know-it-all London critics would be waiting to ambush him.

His worries were needless. His return to London in the spring of 1861 passed largely unnoticed. Like any young artist, he settled in for a period of struggle that, for him, would not last long. This short, olive-skinned, dark-eyed and curly-haired youth with an open and appealing manner was too talented to go unnoticed for long. An engaging young man, Sullivan soon attracted influential acquaintances, and by 1862 his *The Tempest* music debuted with the Crystal Palace orchestra, and public and critical acclaim followed. From that time Sullivan's reputation grew, and by 1866, his *anno mirabilis*, it soared. He was appointed professor of composition at the Royal Academy of Music. Later that year, his *In Memoriam*, a musical response to the death of his father, firmly established him as

the great hope of English music. He was twenty-four years old.

Lives' Work

As the 1860's progressed, Arthur Sullivan's reputation grew. He took on the specter of Georg Frideric Handel with *The Prodigal Son*, an oratorio, and in that year he was accorded an honor unprecedented in one so young: The queen requested a copy of his complete works. Sullivan, however, always eager to extend his range of accomplishment, began what would become his greatest achievement, the resurrection of light opera in Great Britain. His early collaborator was F. C. Burnand, with whom he wrote, among other productions, *The Contrabandistas* (1867) and *Cox and Box* (1867), works that bore a strongly Continental flavor reminiscent of Gioacchino Rossini and Charles-François Gounod. These two operettas achieved growing popularity, and the form was on its way.

Meanwhile, William Gilbert was achieving a measure of prominence as a drama critic who wrote parodic reviews for *Fun* and as a librettist in his own right, providing plays and librettos for German Reed's Royal Gallery of Illustration. At a rehearsal for one of these productions, the two men who would transform light opera into English operetta met, in 1869, but the meeting produced no immediate reaction. Sullivan was involved in a successful collaboration with Burnand, and Gilbert, at the time, was happy producing librettos for Frederic Clay and German Reed. Not until 1871 did Gilbert and Sullivan first collaborate, and then the product, *Thespis: Or, The Gods Grown Old*, was less than a triumph, for it closed within a month. That first stumbling effort was marked, nevertheless, by the kind of sensitive relationship between music and lyrics that would come to characterize Gilbert and Sullivan's work and, as a result of their leadership, the English operetta.

Four years passed, during which Sullivan displayed his versatility, attempting oratorios, hymns (among which is "Onward Christian Soldiers," 1874), and further involvements with both the serious and the comic stages. The awards and commissions rolled in, and he became universally recognized as the premier composer in Great Britain. Meanwhile, Gilbert was also achieving a large measure of success. His *Pygmalion and Galatea* (1871) earned for him forty thousand pounds, he continued to write serious dramas, and *The Bab Ballads* had also won for him separate recognition as a poet.

Both men were rich and famous before they experienced success together, but in 1875 events started to unfold that would firmly establish them as a team.

Gilbert had written a libretto based on a satiric mock trial that he had sketched for an 1868 issue of *Fun*. During a visit to Richard D'Oyly Carte, he found that that impresario was looking for a curtain raiser for Jacques Offenbach's *La Périchole*. Carte suggested that Gilbert write something that Arthur Sullivan could set to music, and the result, *Trial by Jury*, became not the curtain raiser but the main attraction. It opened March 25, 1875, and enjoyed a run of almost nine months. It was the first success for Gilbert and Sullivan, and their first teaming under the auspices of Carte. The success of this short operetta was a sign of things to come.

Though both men continued for a time to seek their separate fortunes, the team became famous in 1878 with the production of *H.M.S. Pinafore: Or, The Lass That Loved a Sailor*. Thus began a trying period of success for both. Together they completely reformed comic opera, moving operetta from the status of one-act light entertainment to full three-act main event, yet separately each man wished for a different kind of success. Gilbert longed to be taken seriously as a playwright, only giving up his dream in 1888, after the failure of *Brantinghame Hall*. Sullivan continued to think of himself as a serious composer, and he often chafed at what he believed was the disproportionate amount of attention the public paid to his operettas. The team became fabulously wealthy and famous as a result of their innovative efforts in operetta, yet both men felt stifled by that success, deprived of what each thought to be true destiny.

Despite their resentment of the operettas, the partners experienced one success after another. *The Pirates of Penzance*, their second full-blown operetta, led to American tours of both that operetta and *H.M.S. Pinafore*, and in 1881 the team debuted *Patience: Or, Bunthorne's Bride*, a spoof of the Aesthetic movement, which opened in April and moved in October into Carte's new theater, the Savoy, which was designed and built expressly for operetta. *Iolanthe* followed in 1882, *Princess Ida: Or, Castle Adamant* in 1884, *The Mikado: Or, The Town of Titipu* in 1885, *Ruddigore: Or, The Witch's Curse* in 1887, *The Yeoman of the Guard: Or, The Merryman and His Maid* in 1888, and *The Gondoliers: Or, The King of Barataria* in 1889. The collaboration had been fruitful indeed, but the two men were not without their problems. Always combative, Gilbert was

W.S. Gilbert

jealous of his fame, and he tended to bully the quieter Sullivan, who nevertheless believed that he, Sullivan, was the superior artist. The two fought often, several times breaking off their partnership, even during the periods of their greatest success. During the years from 1884 until 1890, Carte acted as referee, keeping the team together and smoothing over the affronts and slights, real and imagined. In 1890, however, Gilbert began a dispute that has become known as the carpet quarrel, an argument that ended in the dissolution of the partnership and in Gilbert's successful lawsuit against Carte.

The split lasted for three years, at which time Carte managed to bring Gilbert and Sullivan back together for *Utopia, Limited: Or, The Flowers of Progress* (1893) and *The Grand Duke: Or, The Statutory Duel* (1896), their last operetta. In 1900, Sullivan, always physically weak and troubled, from the 1870's onward, by serious recurrent kidney problems, contracted a cold which progressed into bronchitis. He refused to rest, and on November 21, his heart gave way. He died the next day. Gilbert also died of heart failure. On May 29, 1911, he rushed to the rescue of a woman who was drowning in a pond on his estate, Grim's Dyke, and the exertion proved to be too much for Gilbert's seventy-five-year-old heart.

Summary

During their long and tempestuous relationship, Gilbert and Sullivan accomplished much, both together and separately. Sullivan's musical accomplishments, though overshadowed by the operettas, resulted in a resurgence in serious British music, for his fame and fortune made music a more respectable profession. Sullivan and Burnand resurrected comic opera, establishing it as a financially successful theatrical form. Sullivan brought the art of writing musical scores to a new height, providing all of his collaborators with music that enhanced but never detracted from their words. His scores complemented the librettos, a relationship that led to both the establishment of the musical theater and the increasing use of music as theatrical accompaniment. Today's theater orchestras and film scores owe much to Sullivan's pioneering work in the Victorian theater.

Gilbert, too, made his individual contribution. His nonsense verse, *The Bab Ballads*, made a major contribution to the genre. His muse was more acerbic than that of Edward Lear or Lewis Carroll, and he reestablished satire as a major subject for popular poetry. This vein he pursued avidly in his librettos, in which he lampooned his own abortive careers of law, the military, and even poetry. He rolled back the restrictions that Victorian society had long placed on the theater, determinedly and often gleefully violating conventional propriety with such exuberance and with such a deft comic touch that audiences and censors alike laughed, and acceded. Gilbert may not have achieved his dearest goal, that of becoming a serious poet and playwright, but his verse, in the form of librettos, forced open the narrow parameters of the English stage, preparing the way for the giants of early twentieth century British drama.

Together, Gilbert and Sullivan almost single-handedly reinvented musical theater. Before them, operetta was lightly regarded. It had arisen in response to the Licensing Acts which, from 1739 through 1843, restricted plays with spoken dialogue to a limited number of theaters: In London, only Covent Garden and Drury Lane could produce actual drama. Operetta, in which the lines were sung, not spoken, combined with pantomime and tableau to form a program entertainment in houses such as German Reed's. It was Gilbert and Sullivan, however, who raised operetta to the stature of main attraction, ultimately propelling it to the point at which a full-length operetta was the only item on the evening's bill of entertainment. Their financial success brought actors, artists, money, and, more important, attention and respectability to the British stage, and their expansion of operetta from one-act play to full-length production laid the foundation for modern musical theater, most especially the modern musical.

Bibliography

Bradley, Ian, ed. *The Complete Annotated Gilbert and Sullivan*. New York: Oxford University Press, 1996. Contains the complete works of Gilbert and Sullivan (13 operas) with extensive annotations and commentary on the text and stage directions. This wonderful, informative volume describes the basis for each opera, identifies real people mentioned therein, and more.

Goldberg, Isaac. *The Story of Gilbert and Sullivan: Or, The "Compleat" Savoyard*. New York: Simon and Schuster, 1928; London: Murray, 1929. This volume presents a gossipy but detailed and fairly reliable account of the lives and careers of Gilbert and Sullivan, together and apart.

Helyar, James, ed. *Gilbert and Sullivan*. Lawrence: University of Kansas Press, 1972. A collection of essays covering much territory; includes essays by scholars who led the movement to reevaluate Gilbert and Sullivan's work.

Jones, John Bush. "Gilbert and Sullivan's Serious Satire: More Fact than Fancy." *Western Humanities Review* 21 (1967): 211-224. Bush deals in some depth with Gilbert's satire, which was often so scathing that Gilbert was declared *persona non grata* at court.

———. "Gilbertian Humor: Pulling Together a Definition." *Victorian Newsletter* 33 (Spring 1968): 28-31. Bush explains that Gilbert's humor is both more sophisticated and more satiric than most critics had thought.

———, ed. *W. S. Gilbert: A Century of Scholarship and Commentary*. New York: New York University Press, 1970. Spanning the century from 1868 to 1968, Jones's judiciously chosen collection provides a solid introduction to Gilbert's reputation through the years; the essay by Jane Stedman, in particular, is vital to an understanding of Gilbert's impact on the theater and the literary world of his day.

Moore, Frank L., ed. *The Handbook of Gilbert and Sullivan*. New York: Crowell, 1972. An encyclopedic fact book about the famous partnership and all the collaborative productions; the book does not go into depth, but it covers a wide range of material about the operettas and the D'Oyly Carte company.

Stedman, Jane W. *W. S. Gilbert: A Classic Victorian and His Theatre*. New York and Oxford: Oxford University Press, 1996. Well-written biography of Gilbert based on original sources and interviews with surviving contemporaries of the writer. Most accurate biography of Gilbert available.

William Condon

VINCENZO GIOBERTI

Born: April 5, 1801; Turin, Kingdom of Sardinia
Died: October 26, 1852; Paris, France
Areas of Achievement: Philosophy, religion, government, and politics
Contribution: Gioberti contributed the first comprehensive political program for the Risorgimento—the Italian national unification movement. He represented the progressive Catholic political tradition in nineteenth century Italy and sought to redefine the Church's political role in the process of creating the new Italian nation.

Early Life

Vincenzo Gioberti was born in Turin on April 5, 1801. He lost his father, Giuseppe, at an early age, and his mother, Marianna Capra—a learned and deeply religious woman—died on December 24, 1819. Gioberti received his education from a school run by a Catholic religious order—the Fathers of the Oratory, in Turin. Despite his ill health as a child, he studied diligently and demonstrated a particular interest in the writings of the Italian poet Vittorio Alfieri and the French philosopher Jean-Jacques Rousseau. Gioberti entered the religious order but apparently without much enthusiasm. In his studies for the priesthood, he became convinced of the need for religious reform and for the reconciliation between the Christian faith and modern science. After earning a theology degree in 1823, Gioberti joined the faculty of the theological college at the University of Turin. He was ordained a priest in 1825. The following year, he received an appointment as chaplain to the royal court of King Charles Felix of Piedmont-Sardinia.

Gioberti's service to the Savoy monarch in Turin did not alter his personal aversion to political authoritarianism. As a young man, he harbored the democratic and nationalist sentiments of many educated Italians in the early nineteenth century. The Italy of Gioberti's youth existed only as a "geographical expression"—an odd assortment of kingdoms, duchies, and principalities running the length of the Italian peninsula. Italians, inspired by the political ideas and events of the French Revolution, nurtured their aspirations for an independent, united Italy. The obstacles to unification were immense. Much of northern Italy was part of the Austrian Empire; Spanish royalty ruled southern Italy and Sicily; and the pope exercised sovereignty over a large part of the central region. Moreover, the European powers had agreed to maintain the status quo in Italy, even by military intervention if necessary. Many Italian nationalists, in their hopes for unification, looked to the strongest independent Italian state—Piedmont-Sardinia—for leadership. The conservative Savoy monarchs, however, had no desire to encourage political upheaval, nor did they wish to offend the Papacy or the European powers. Without the leadership of the Savoy monarchy or any other political authority, the task of Italian unification fell to a loosely connected network of secret patriotic societies. Gioberti's political activity began with his involvement with these conspiratorial organizations.

Life's Work

Gioberti first established contact with a secret society in 1828, when he traveled through northern Italy. During these travels (under the constant surveillance of the Austrian police), he also met with Giacomo Leopardi and Alessandro Manzoni, two leading nationalist writers. Later, he became acquainted with Young Italy, the republican society founded by Giuseppe Mazzini in 1831. He openly sympathized with Young Italy until Mazzini sponsored an unsuccessful insurrection in Piedmont in 1834.

Because of his preaching on civic and political matters, and his radical religious opinions, Gioberti was dismissed from the royal court in May, 1833. Shortly thereafter, he was arrested and imprisoned on the charge of advocating a republican form of government and distributing copies of Mazzini's newspaper *Young Italy* among Piedmontese soldiers. Given the choice between a lengthy prison sentence or exile, he left for France in September, 1833.

After a year in Paris without finding means for study or suitable employment, he accepted a teaching position at the Gaggia College in Brussels. There he began an intense period of writing. He published studies of aesthetics and the supernatural, a critique of Jesuit doctrines, and an introduction to philosophy. His most important work, *Del primato morale e civile degli italiani* (on the moral and civil primacy of the Italians), was published in two volumes in 1843.

In *Del primato morale e civile degli italiani,* Gioberti presented a far-ranging theological and historical justification for Italian independence and unity. He recounted Italy's past greatness as the center of the Roman Empire and Christian civilization. He reminded Italians of the moral and political legacy that they had bequeathed to the modern world, and he called on his country to resume its historic role as a leader among nations. In his program for a new Italy, he envisioned a federation of independent states, free from foreign rule, united under the aegis of a papal president, and protected by the strong military arm of the House of Savoy. Gioberti dismissed the idea of unification through a popular insurrection as dangerous and impractical. Instead, he looked to the rulers of each Italian state to demonstrate their patriotism and their political wisdom by enacting progressive reforms and joining the national federation on a voluntary basis. Gioberti's outline for Italian independence and unification included several practical suggestions: abolishing tariffs and duties; standardizing weights, measures, and currency; and other forms of economic cooperation.

With *Del primato morale e civile degli italiani*, Gioberti established his reputation as the leading theorist of Italian unification. The tedious, seven-hundred-page work was widely read and discussed, despite the ban on its circulation outside Piedmont. *Del primato morale e civile degli italiani* lifted the morale of Italian nationalists. Both King Charles Albert of Piedmont-Sardinia and Pope Pius IX came under its spell. Gioberti's program for unification inspired political moderates to action. Many nationalists in the upper classes feared the economic and social upheaval that might accompany unification. They were wary of any participation of the masses in the unification movement, and they found much assurance in Gioberti's idea of creating an Italian nation "from above."

Some Italian nationalists, even among the moderate element, were skeptical of Gioberti's proposals. He gave no indication of how to deal with Austria and its powerful army in northern Italy. His hopes for political cooperation among the rulers of the Italian states seemed hopelessly naïve. The most controversial point was the idea of a pope as president of a federation of Italian states. Gioberti's critics scoffed at the notion that the pope could have any positive role in Italian unification. Their criticism was well justified. The Papal States had a reputation unsurpassed in Europe for political oppression, corruption, and misrule. The Papacy stood as a defender of the old order and an obstacle to political progress. Many nationalists believed

that unification would be completed only when the pope surrendered civil authority over his territory and allowed Rome to become the capital of the new Italian nation. Yet when Pius became the new pontiff in 1846, the political climate in the Papal States changed markedly. The youthful, energetic ruler immediately instituted a series of democratic reforms within the Papal States, disbanded his mercenary army, and granted amnesty to political prisoners. His popularity grew throughout Italy, and he won support even among anticlerics. The explosion of revolutionary sentiment in 1848 eventually overtook the pontiff's program of reform, and Pius retreated behind a wall of intransigent conservatism. For a time, however, Gioberti's idea of a liberal pope seemed to be vindicated.

Gioberti's writing won for him national renown. He was recognized as the leader of the *Veri italiani* (true Italians), a circle of distinguished political moderates living in exile, and began corresponding with Charles Albert. The king, in turn, recognized his achievement by granting him an annual pension, which Gioberti donated to the church charity in Turin. While residing in Paris in 1846, he was elected to the Subalpine (Piedmontese) Parliament. He returned to Turin after almost fifteen years in exile, a celebrated figure in Italian political life. When he traveled through northern Italy, crowds greeted him as a national hero. In July, 1848, he was elected president of the Chamber of Deputies. In December, the king invited him to form a government.

Gioberti's tenure as prime minister was short and undistinguished. He lacked the requisite political skills and the ability to compromise. Somewhat vain and aloof, he refused to consult with his cabinet and advisers. His ineptness became apparent during a crisis in foreign affairs. An insurrection in Rome had driven the pope from the city. Gioberti sought ways to restore him to power before the European governments intervened. His attempts failed. The French army occupied the Papal States and ended the short-lived Roman Republic. The popular uprisings of 1848—particularly the one in Rome—left Pius frightened, embittered, and vindictive. He disavowed all progressive ideas and reforms, placed Gioberti's *Del primato morale e civile degli italiani* on the Index (list of works banned by the Church), and restored authoritarian rule to the Papal States.

Gioberti resigned in February, 1849, over the crisis in Tuscany. A popular uprising there had opened the way for unification with Piedmont. He refused to send troops to secure the region, and

Austrian forces eventually restored order. In the spring of 1849, he accepted the post of ambassador to France and remained in Paris until his death. His frustrating experience in Italian politics led him to write *Il rinnovamento civile d'Italia* (the civil renewal of Italy) in 1851. By this time, he had accepted the position of other political moderates that national unification was possible only under the auspices of the King of Piedmont-Sardinia. Gioberti died suddenly on October 26, 1852, leaving many of his writings unfinished.

Summary

In calling for papal leadership in Italy, Vincenzo Gioberti revived Guelphist politics—a tradition that dated from the Middle Ages, when the popes vied with the Holy Roman Emperors for political power in Europe. As a neo-Guelphist, he sought to restore papal authority as the moral and political arbiter of Christian nations. His critics dismissed this as a medieval solution to a modern problem, but some of Gioberti's ideas were validated by subsequent events. His belief that Italy needed to build a strong navy and acquire a colonial empire reflected foreign-policy goals followed by Italian governments until the end of World War II. The idea of making Italy "from above" was ultimately affirmed in the statesmanship of Count Cavour. For all of his assurances of the "moral and civil primacy of the Italians," Gioberti actually had little faith in the political maturity of his countrymen. He believed in paternalistic, Christian government—"everything for the people, nothing by the people." As he had envisioned, Italy was unified without the involvement of most Italians, but this lack of popular participation in the unification process ultimately proved a source of political weakness for the new Italian state.

Bibliography

Berkeley, C. F. H. *Italy in the Making*. Vol. 1. Cambridge: Cambridge University Press, 1932. This survey of Italian unification is a helpful source. The author, sympathetic to the Catholic church and the moderate political elements in the unification movement, deals at length with Gioberti's intellectual and political contributions.

Coppa, Frank J., ed. *Dictionary of Modern Italian History*. Westport, Conn.: Greenwood Press, 1985. Contains a brief biography of Gioberti taken from Italian sources.

Gioberti, Vincenzo. *Essay on the Beautiful*. Translated by Edward Thomas. London: Simpkin and Marshall, 1860. An English translation of one of Gioberti's several published works.

Grew, Raymond. *A Sterner Plan for Italian Unity: The Italian National Society in the Risorgimento*. Princeton, N.J.: Princeton University Press, 1963. Places Gioberti in the broader context of the moderate political tradition in the unification movement.

Haddock, Bruce. "Political Union Without Social Revolution: Vincenzo Gioberti's 'Primato.'" *Historical Journal* 41, no. 3 (September, 1998). Excellent attempt at rendering Gioberti's difficult *Del primato morale e civile degli italiani* (1843) readable through presentation in a context of reappraisal within the Catholic tradition spawned by nationalism.

Mack Smith, Denis. *The Making of Italy, 1796-1870*. London: Macmillan, and New York: Harper, 1968. A survey of the Italian unification movement, more balanced than Berkeley's history in its assessment of Gioberti and the political moderates.

Michael F. Hembree

WILLIAM EWART GLADSTONE

Born: December 29, 1809; Liverpool, England
Died: May 19, 1898; Hawarden, Flintshire, England
Areas of Achievement: Politics and government
Contribution: For more than half a century, Gladstone was a leading figure in the British Parliament, and he held a number of key cabinet positions, including prime minister, a post he filled four times between 1868 and 1895.

Early Life

William Ewart Gladstone, the fourth son of businessman John Gladstone, was born December 29, 1809, into a middle-class family that was on the rise socially and financially. The future prime minister's father had moved to the growing port city of Liverpool from his native Scotland, establishing his fortune in shipping, real estate, insurance, and commercial ventures that included trade in the slave-based industries in the West Indies. John Gladstone was elected to Parliament in 1827; he lived to see three of his sons seek similar office and to watch his most gifted son, William, rise meteorically in a variety of cabinet positions under the mentorship of Prime Minister Robert Peel.

Gladstone's upbringing was influenced decidedly by strong Christian principles, and though he moved gradually through a phase of rigorous commitment to the established Anglican Church to toleration for differences of form among worshippers, he was consistent in applying religious and moral touchstones to his personal and political life. Educated at Eton and then at Oxford, where he took a double first in classics and mathematics, the young Gladstone displayed his firm commitment to Tory principles while still an undergraduate. His speech at the Oxford Union so impressed a classmate, Lord Lincoln, that the latter convinced his father, the Duke of Newcastle, to support Gladstone for a seat in Parliament representing Newark, a borough which the duke controlled. Gladstone, who had difficulty deciding whether to seek a career in the Church or enter politics, agreed to stand for election and received Newark's nomination in 1832. As fate would have it, he entered Parliament in a session during which British history was changed: Under pressure from various groups throughout the country, the Parliament in that year passed the First Reform Bill, significantly enlarging the number of eligible voters and setting Great Britain on an inevitable course toward modern democracy.

At the same time that he was making a name for himself in politics, though, Gladstone was finding his social life a bit more perplexing. Though considered one of the handsomest young men in Parliament—tall with dark eyes and flowing brown locks—he suffered for half a decade the emotional paroxysms of youth in his pursuit of the opposite sex. After being rebuked by two women, each of whose hand he had ardently sought, he ultimately succeeded in winning the heart of Catherine Glynne, to whom he was married on July 25, 1839. Their union was to last a lifetime, and Mrs. Gladstone was to play a significant role in supporting her husband during his political career.

Life's Work

The man who is remembered as the leader of the Liberals in nineteenth century England entered politics as a Tory. Gladstone's remarkable ability as an orator and his capacity for work so impressed the Conservative leadership of the House of Commons that within two years he was offered a position in the cabinet, as Junior Lord of the Treasury (1834); within a year he had been elevated to Undersecretary for the Colonies. His busy schedule as a politician did not keep him from working at his first love, religious studies, and in 1838 he published *The State in Its Relations with the Church*, in which he supported the Church of England's privileged political status, a position he was later to repudiate.

In 1841, Gladstone accepted a position as vice president of the Board of Trade, not considered a choice position for a young politician on the rise, but one from which he was able to grow as a manager and financial expert. In 1843, he was elevated to president of the Board of Trade. During the 1840's, Gladstone began supporting measures that put distance between him and the leadership of the Tory Party, which now called itself the Conservative Party: tariff reform, state supervision of railroads, state subsidy for the Catholic Church in Ireland, the rights of minorities to hold seats in Parliament. When in 1845 Peel's government fell over the question of handling the famine in Ireland, Gladstone joined Peel in a move that broke apart the Conservative Party. In the new administration which Peel headed, Gladstone became Colonial

Secretary but lost his seat in Newark, since he no longer held favor with the conservative Duke of Newcastle. In 1847, he was returned to Parliament for Oxford, a seat he held until 1865, when his ever-advancing Liberalism made him unacceptable to that electorate.

Gladstone resigned his seat in Peel's government in 1846, over the issue of his support for the Catholic-controlled Maynooth College in Ireland. He remained a leading member of the Peelites, as the followers of Peel were called, distrustful of either the Liberals under Lord Palmerston or the Conservatives, whose leadership was passing to Benjamin Disraeli. In 1853, the Conservatives were turned out on a vote of no confidence following Disraeli's presentation of the 1852 budget. When Lord Aberdeen formed a coalition government, Gladstone joined the cabinet as Chancellor of the Exchequer. His 1853 budget was hailed as one of the most imaginative and comprehensive of the century, and secured his reputation as a financial wizard. He continued in this position until 1855 and returned to it for almost seven years, from 1859 to 1866. For a brief interlude when out of office, Gladstone served as Lord High Commissioner of the Ionian Islands in the Mediterranean, though his record there was not especially salutary.

As early as 1865, Gladstone was being touted as a candidate for prime minister. The call finally came to him in 1868, only months after he had succeeded Lord John Russell as head of the Liberal Party. In that year he formed the first, and by all assessments the most successful, of four administrations. He assumed the prime ministership with a primary goal of settling the political turmoil in Ireland, something that had haunted him for years. He saw his ascendancy to the head of government as a mission, and treated his work with religious fervor. Among his objectives were the disestablishment of the Anglican Church, a reversal of his earlier position of support for the political primacy of that religious body, and the resolution of problems between Irish tenants and their landlords, many of whom were absentee owners. His foreign policy was based on high-minded principles of mutual cooperation among nations and a belief that individual nations could operate on good faith with other countries—a policy that sometimes made Great Britain look foolish or weak within the international community. During this first administration, sweeping changes occurred in education in England, largely as a

result of the Education Act of 1870, although Gladstone had little interest in or influence on the outcome. He did, however, work to abolish religious tests at the universities.

After almost eight years, the Liberals were turned out of office in 1874. Gladstone, by then in his sixties, retired from the leadership of his party, though he retained his seat in Parliament. He turned his attention to classical studies, specifically to translations of Homer and extended commentary on the Greek writer, in which he sought to establish links between Homer and Christianity, a position scoffed at in his own day and discounted by later critics. He also wrote a series of tracts on religious issues.

Turkish atrocities in the Balkans in 1876 prompted Gladstone's return to an active role in politics. For the next four years, he argued vociferously in Parliament and throughout the country against Disraeli's conservative policies. In 1880, a barnstorming campaign on behalf of Liberal ideology swept his party back into office, and Gladstone once again became prime minister. This second administration lasted until 1885. These years were more tumultuous than those of the first administration, and Gladstone was forced to deal with the growing violence in Ireland and problems caused by British imperialism. On the home front, his growing association with Irish Nationalist Charles Stewart Parnell caused dissension within his own party and gave enemies a prominent target for political attacks. The murder of Gladstone's close friend and nephew-in-law Frederick Cavendish in Phoenix Park, Dublin, in May of 1882, escalated the difficulty, as he was forced to take sterner measures in dealing with the violence.

Abroad, British actions in the Middle East and North Africa caused additional difficulties for the prime minister. A major crisis in the Sudan in 1883 led to the massacre of a British garrison at Khartoum and the death of General Charles Gordon. Gladstone, who had hesitated to take strong action in the region for fear that it would lead Great Britain into yet another brush war, was blamed by the press and by the queen herself for Gordon's death. Ultimately, he was forced to deal with the problems in the area and to assume some responsibility for the deteriorating political system in Egypt, a country in which England had significant interest. The height of ignominy occurred for Gladstone in June, 1885, when his government, which had supported stronger home rule measures for Ireland,

was defeated on the issue of the budget by a coalition of Conservatives and Irish Nationalists.

Gladstone returned almost immediately to the prime ministership, and his third, short-lived administration was committed almost exclusively to one issue: home rule for Ireland. Only months after he began his crusade to give Ireland its own parliament and greater control over its own destiny, Gladstone saw his efforts dashed in Parliament in the summer of 1886, when the Home Rule Bill was defeated. Gladstone immediately resigned.

For the next six years, Gladstone worked as the leader of the opposition while the Conservatives held office. He continued to press for Irish home rule, working to hold his Liberal Party together as the Radical element within the organization gained strength. In 1892, he formed his fourth and last administration, once again championing Irish home rule. The pressures of leadership finally proved to be too much for a man in his eighties; Gladstone resigned in March, 1894. He spent the last four years of his life at Hawarden, the estate of his wife's family which he had helped preserve when the family was almost forced to sell it in the 1840's. He died May 19, 1898, and after an elaborate funeral ceremony was buried in Statesmen's Corner at Westminster Abbey.

Summary

William Ewart Gladstone's political career can be seen as the movement of a high-minded and deeply religious individual from conservative principles and High Church convictions to an eventual championship of individual rights and religious tolerance. Some have viewed it as a four-decade struggle against the other dominant figure in nineteenth century British politics, Conservative statesman Benjamin Disraeli. From whatever angle his life is observed, there is no doubt that Gladstone, never the pragmatist, believed deeply in the rightness of any cause he championed, and often sacrificed himself, his reputation, and his political party to ideals.

His liberalism bothered Queen Victoria; his manner in promoting it often offended her. The monarch who loved Disraeli frequently chastised Gladstone for his decisions and his behavior, but he always acted respectfully toward his sovereign. In spite of this stormy relationship, he was able to lead his country on the path toward democracy. Under his direction, and often only because of his strong hand, the British nation struggled—with remarkable success, in retrospect—with important human issues such as greater enfranchisement, improved working and living conditions for the lower classes, and greater concern for individual rights.

The force of his personality on British politics was recognized in his own time; in the later years of his life both friend and enemy alike took to calling him the "Grand Old Man," or "G.O.M." In a century that produced more than its share of giants in statesmanship, Gladstone has emerged as the dominant figure in British politics in the Victorian age.

Bibliography

Cecil, Algernon. "Mr. Gladstone." In *Queen Victoria and Her Prime Ministers*. London: Eyre and Spottiswoode, and New York: Oxford University Press, 1953. Assesses Gladstone's impact on Great Britain during his career as prime minister; reviews his relationship with the queen and with his colleagues in Parliament and in the cabinet. Focuses on Gladstone's efforts to pass the Irish Home Rule Bill.

Feuchtwanger, E. J. *Gladstone*. 2d ed. London: Macmillan, 1989. A detailed political biography, with extensive analysis of British politics, Gladstone's career in Parliament and the cabinet. Extensive treatment of Gladstone's years as prime minister. Contains a useful bibliography.

Hammond, John Lawrence. *Gladstone and the Irish Nation*. London and New York: Longman, 1938. A careful scholarly study of Gladstone's attempts to deal with the Irish nation and the question of Irish home rule, an issue that dominated his later administrations. Provides a wide-ranging look at both England and Ireland in the latter half of the nineteenth century.

Harrison, Robert T. *Gladstone's Imperialism in Egypt*. Westport, Conn.: Greenwood Press, 1995. A study of Gladstone's activities in Egypt in 1882 and their affect on that area of the world.

Knaplund, Paul. *Gladstone and Britain's Imperial Policy*. London: Allen and Unwin, and New York: Macmillan, 1927. Focuses attention on Gladstone's policies regarding the various colonies of the British Empire, which was the largest of all European empires in the nineteenth century. Gladstone had extensive impact on decisions regarding the colonies throughout his career, especially during his service as Secretary for the Colonies in Peel's cabinet, then later as prime minister.

———. *Gladstone's Foreign Policy*. New York: Harper, 1935; London: Cass, 1970. An assessment of Gladstone's views on foreign policy and a review of his actions in that area during his four terms as prime minister. Includes extensive analysis of his handling of crises in the Near East and Middle East.

Magnus, Philip. *Gladstone: A Biography.* London: Murray, and New York: Dutton, 1954. A full-scale biography that examines Gladstone's personal life, his political career, and his work in religious and literary studies. Presents a well-rounded portrait of this complex figure.

Marlow, Joyce. *The Oak and the Ivy: An Intimate Biography of William and Catherine Gladstone.* New York: Doubleday, 1977; as *Mr. and Mrs. Gladstone: An Intimate Biography,* London: Weidenfeld and Nicolson, 1977. A "dual biography" of Gladstone and his wife, focusing on the personal qualities of the statesman and on his personality and psychological makeup.

Matthew, H. C. *Gladstone, 1809-1898.* New York: Oxford University Press, and Oxford: Clarendon Press, 1995. Celebrated Gladstone scholar H. C. Matthew produces a concise biography of one of the most powerful men in British history. Topics include Gladstone's education, political career, and his public and private lives.

Morley, John. *The Life of William Ewart Gladstone.* 3 vols. London and New York: Macmillan, 1903. Written by a younger contemporary; contains much detail and includes extensive quotations from Gladstone's letters and diaries. Still a primary source for those wishing to understand the complexity of Gladstone's character and the magnitude of his achievements in politics and other fields.

Ponsonby, Lord. "William Ewart Gladstone." In *The Great Victorians,* edited by Harold John Massingham and Hugh Massingham. London: Nicholson and Watson, and New York: Doubleday, 1932. A brief character sketch that offers a good introduction to Gladstone's accomplishments, in a volume that provides similar sketches of his contemporaries, allowing readers to gain some idea of Gladstone's place in Victorian life.

Laurence W. Mazzeno

AUGUST VON GNEISENAU

Born: October 27, 1760; Schildau, Saxony
Died: August 23, 1831; Posen, Pomerania
Area of Achievement: The military
Contribution: As a Prussian field marshal and member of King Frederick William III's Military Reorganization Commission, Gneisenau fashioned the Prussian strategy that finally defeated Napoleon I in the campaigns of 1813 and 1814 and played a key role in reforming the Prussian army into the most professional military force in nineteenth century Europe. Gneisenau's organizational and operational reforms survive today as accepted elements in most of the world's armies.

Early Life

The scion of a noble but poor German military family, August von Gneisenau was born near Torgau, Saxony, during the Seven Years' War. His father, an artillery lieutenant in the Austrian army, abandoned him to friends who reared him in near poverty. A moneyed maternal grandfather subsequently assumed responsibility for the young orphan and entrusted his education to Jesuits. With the death of his benefactor, young Gneisenau inherited enough money to attend Erfurt University from 1777 to 1779. With his inheritance depleted, Gneisenau prematurely left the university, joined a local Austrian regiment as a cavalry subaltern, and fought against Prussia in the 1778 War of Bavarian Succession.

He subsequently joined the army of Bayreuth-Ansbach, a tiny principality that hired out its soldiers to the highest bidder. It was within this context that Gneisenau, now a lieutenant of chasseurs, traveled to North America in 1782 to fight as a British mercenary against the American colonists. He arrived too late to fight, but he came upon and embraced new concepts that would later define his role as a leading Prussian military reformer: the belief in a politically active citizenry and the use of open order tactics by civilian militias in warfare.

Gneisenau returned to Europe after one year and personally petitioned Frederick the Great to allow him to join the Prussian army. In 1786, he received a commission as a first lieutenant in the infantry. Although he did participate in the Polish campaign of 1793-1794, Gneisenau served for the next twenty years in different Silesian garrisons, where he immersed himself in military studies and further developed the unique blend of combat and staff skills for which he is rightfully famous.

Gneisenau was an undistinguished forty-six-year-old captain when war broke out between France and Prussia in 1806. On October 14, 1806, he commanded a company of infantry at the Battle of Jena and experienced at first hand Napoleon's annihilation of the once-invincible Frederican army. The defeat was a profound blow to Gneisenau, but even more devastating was the complete indifference shown by the Prussian middle class to the loss of the army. In fact, their perception of the army as a royal instrument promoting reactionary interests was in direct contrast to the nascent "people in arms" concept Gneisenau had seen in the Colonies.

Gneisenau adopted the citizen-soldier concept in his 1807 defense of Kolberg, a Pomeranian coastal town situated on the Baltic Sea and besieged by the French. Gneisenau's defense of Kolberg was the only successful Prussian military operation at the time and was directly attributable to his deliberate attempt to transform the local civilians from detached bystanders into active defenders who fought with the same spirit as his regular troops. Gneisenau's success earned for him the highly prized Pour le Mérite award, a promotion to lieutenant colonel, and the notoriety that laid the foundation for his major accomplishments.

Life's Work

Subsequent to the Prussian debacle at Jena-Auerstadt, King Frederick William III established the Military Reorganization Commission on July 25, 1807. Its charter was to review the army's performance and propose necessary reforms. Major General Gerhard von Scharnhorst, after rejecting a position as the director of an English artillery school, became chairman of the commission. Gneisenau, who saw himself as Scharnhorst's "Saint Peter," also became a member, as did two other protégés, Majors Karl Grolman and Herman von Boyen. Carl von Clausewitz, although never a full member of the commission, worked indirectly with it as Scharnhorst's aide. With royal sanction, these five military reformers would resurrect a new Prussian army from the ashes of the one previously destroyed by Napoleon. Gneisenau's influence was second only to Scharnhorst's; with the latter's premature death in 1813, he became the most prominent military reformer.

Gneisenau and his peers quickly ascribed the Prussian defeat to an outdated military and a reactionary society. The Frederican army that faced Napoleon relied on rigid tactics, brutal and unenlightened discipline, and overcentralized control. Common people, in turn, felt no sense of responsibility toward the state and greeted Prussian military failures with apathy. Gneisenau and the other reformers decided to reverse the situation, but they realized that to be competitive the Prussian army would have to revise its tactics, organization, and working relationship with civilians completely. A mere reorganization of the old-style army would not suffice.

Gneisenau also realized that the reformers needed to inspire a new loyalty to the state; they had to transform Prussian subjects into self-motivated citizens, inspired by patriotism and a belief in national honor. Yet Gneisenau believed that a people's army was impossible if Prussia did not change from a feudal society, dominated by landed Junkers, into a liberal, constitutional monarchy. In Gneisenau's estimation, neither a serf in hereditary bondage nor a member of the middle class restricted from local government or the officer corps would develop a devotion to the state in the absence of basic social and political rights. The regeneration of the Prussian military would occur only through the reformation of the state.

Gneisenau and the other commission members quickly introduced a number of enduring military reforms. In contrast to the murderous discipline of the past, an edict issued on August 3, 1805, introduced a humane system of rewards and punishments that deliberately limited corporal punishment. Humane treatment, the reformers hoped, would inspire soldiers to become self-motivated and thus develop a more enduring commitment to both the army and the state. Grolman, with the active support of Gneisenau, sponsored an August 6, 1808, decree that transformed the officer corps into a meritocracy, where members of the middle class could enter and succeed based on their demonstrated performance rather than on their family background.

A third innovation was the introduction of professional military education. By 1810, the Prussian army had reorganized all of its schools and introduced the prototype for the *Kriegsakademie*, the first modern war college. Those who attended the college received a liberal education that included,

for the first time, a systematic study of war. Thanks to Gneisenau and his fellow reformers, war was no longer for a brave dilettante but for cool professionals who subjected it to lifelong study.

Gneisenau also supported Baron Heinrich von Stein, the king's chief minister and a fellow reformer on the Military Reorganization Commission, who laid the foundation for a War Ministry responsible for directing, coordinating, and controlling the Prussian army. The nascent General Staff, organized within the General War Department of the War Ministry, would begin to flourish as the intellectual center of the German military under Helmuth von Moltke, the Elder.

Gneisenau's most cherished reforms, however, were the most imperfectly realized. He and the Military Reorganization Commission called for universal conscription as early as 1808, but Frederick William, who feared the destruction of the monarchy in a civil war between economic classes, balked at the idea of a nation in arms. It was only in 1814, when the defeat of Napoleon seemed possible, that Frederick William accepted national conscription. The principle survived, but Gneisenau did not see a lasting union of regular soldiers and militia into a military force crusading for freedom in Europe. The militia (*Landwehr*) enjoyed a brief, independent life but ultimately was subsumed under regular army control beginning in 1819.

Gneisenau worked hard for the above reforms and functioned as chief of the fortifications and engineering corps until Napoleon forced a powerless Frederick William to dismiss Stein and other reformers. In disgust, Gneisenau resigned and quietly undertook missions to Great Britain, Russia, and Sweden in order to muster support against France. His passionate humanism now focused on liberating Europe from Napoleon. When Prussia discarded its role as an unwilling satellite to France, Gneisenau returned to active service as Scharnhorst's *Ia*, or first general staff officer. When Scharnhorst died in June, 1813, Gneisenau became chief of the General Staff and served Marshal Gebhard von Blücher. In this capacity, Gneisenau planned the Prussian strategy for the major campaigns of 1813-1814, including the Battle of Leipzig.

During this phase of his career, Gneisenau introduced battlefield innovations that had a lasting influence. He was the first to make the chief of staff of a major command equal in responsibility with the commander. He believed that this arrangement would strengthen the General Staff system and establish spiritual unity between staff officers and combatants. He also developed the practice of issuing clear and comprehensive objectives while leaving room for the combat commander to exercise individual initiative and freedom of action. Gneisenau directly influenced Clausewitz's subsequent theory of war by insisting that the goal of an army was not to engage in maneuver warfare but to destroy enemy forces directly. Finally, he was an early practitioner of the battle of encirclement, later used with great success by Helmuth Karl Bernhard von Moltke and Alfred von Schlieffen. For these innovations and other successes, Frederick William ennobled Gneisenau in 1814.

Upon Napoleon's return from Elba in March, 1815, Gneisenau once again became Blücher's chief of staff. Each was good for the other: Gneisenau's powerful intellect and organizing skills tempered Blücher's mercurial personality and bulldog tenacity. It was Gneisenau, with prodding from Grolman, who at the Battle of Ligny decided not to retreat toward Prussia but north to Wavre, Belgium. Thus, when the Battle of Waterloo hung in the balance, the Prussians tipped it in

the Duke of Wellington's favor by attacking the French flank. The murderous pursuit of the French troops that followed was yet another example of Gneisenau's vigorous style of war.

With the final defeat of Napoleon, Gneisenau fell into disfavor. The absence of a common foe enabled the reactionary Junkers to reverse the more extreme changes he and the other reformers had introduced. Gneisenau subsequently resigned in 1816. He became governor of Berlin in 1818 and a field marshal in 1825. In 1831, during the Polish Revolution, he commanded the army of occupation on Prussia's eastern border. While on border duty, both he and Clausewitz, now his chief of staff, died of cholera.

Summary

As a reformer and combatant, August von Gneisenau had a lasting and widespread influence. He and the other Prussian reformers on the Military Reorganization Commission forever changed the character of modern armies. Following the Prussian example, rival powers introduced universal conscription and opened the officer corps to those with talent, regardless of their social background. They increasingly relied on nationalism rather than harsh discipline to motivate troops. They also formalized their military establishments by introducing war ministries, professional military education, and the General Staff system. Gneisenau was instrumental in developing and popularizing these innovations.

Yet he was bitterly disappointed in two respects. Prussia, rather than becoming a liberal constitutional monarchy, remained thoroughly autocratic. As a result, the army remained an isolated enclave of military technicians rather than a democratic institution manned by enlightened citizen soldiers who had a personal investment in supporting their government. Gneisenau overestimated the state's willingness to turn over a new leaf. Instead, the pattern for future Prussian jingoism was set.

As a combatant, Gneisenau believed that the army was the enemy's "center of gravity" and thus had to be destroyed. A vigorous pursuit was part of the process. Both concepts found expression in Clausewitz's *Vom Kriege* (1832-1834; *On War*, 1873), which later had an impact on German strategy and tactics (beginning in the Wars of German Unification). Given the influence of these combat techniques and his earlier organizational reforms, Gneisenau's sustained influence on modern military establishments is undeniable.

Bibliography

Britt, Albert Sidney. "Field Marshal August Neidhart von Gneisenau." In *The Consortium on Revolutionary Europe, 1750-1850: Proceedings, 1983*, edited by Clarence Davis. Gainesville: University of Florida Press, 1985. A basic treatment of Gneisenau's accomplishments that tries to prove that he was an outstanding example of ability improved by study.

Craig, Gordon. *The Politics of the Prussian Army, 1640-1945*. Oxford: Clarendon Press, 1955; New York: Oxford University Press, 1956. Craig's seminal work traces the role of the army in modern German history. Gneisenau and the reformers receive a sympathetic look for their attempts not only to resurrect an army but also to change a society.

Dupuy, Trevor Nevitt. *A Genius for War: The German Army and General Staff, 1807-1945*. Englewood Cliffs, N.J.: Prentice-Hall, and London: Macdonald, 1977. Dupuy performed statistical analyses of World War II battles and discovered that German combat effectiveness per man was better than for the Allies. He concludes that the Germans developed the ability to institutionalize military excellence. Analyzes how the Germans did this, beginning with Gneisenau and the reformers in 1807. The specific details on Gneisenau are valuable but limited.

Goerlitz, Walter. *History of the German General Staff, 1657-1945*. Translated by Brian Battershaw. London: Hollis and Carter, and New York: Praeger, 1953. This German historian traces the growing incompatibility between the German army and a society evolving toward a democratic-capitalistic system. Goerlitz identifies Gneisenau's zealotry as one reason that the reformers fell so quickly into disfavor. He also treats Gneisenau's impact as a combatant.

Ritter, Gerhard. *The Sword and the Scepter: The Problem of Militarism in Germany*. Translated by Heinz Norden. Coral Gables, Fla.: University of Miami Press, 1969; London: Allen Lane, 1973. As the title implies, this three-volume study analyzes the growth of German militarism from 1740 to the present. Gneisenau receives a factual review for reform efforts that unwittingly created the possibility for subsequent military adventurism.

Peter R. Faber

VINCENT VAN GOGH

Born: March 30, 1853; Zundert, the Netherlands
Died: July 29, 1890; Auvers-sur-Oise, France
Area of Achievement: Art
Contribution: During his brief artistic career, van Gogh gave expression to a passionate vision of nature and humanity. Following his death, his paintings came to be acknowledged by critics and the public as constituting one of the highest achievements of nineteenth century art.

Early Life

Vincent Willem van Gogh was born in Zundert, the Netherlands, on March 30, 1853. His father, the Reverend Theodorus van Gogh, was thirty-one years old at the time of Vincent's birth; his mother, Anna Cornelius Carbentus, was three years older than her husband. Among van Gogh's three sisters and two brothers, Vincent was to be close only to his brother Theodorus (called Theo), who was an important influence in his life. Vincent's family had been established for generations in the Dutch province of North Brabant, near the southern border with Belgium. Among his ancestors could be found preachers, craftsmen, and government officials, and his living relatives included several uncles prominent in business and government. Vincent's father, a Protestant minister, was a handsome man but not a gifted preacher. Working quietly in several rural parishes until his death at age sixty-two, he was able to provide for his family in a respectable but modest fashion.

Vincent enjoyed a happy childhood and was especially attached to the natural world; drawings he made as early as age eleven show a keen observation of plant life. His skill at drawing, which seems to have been fostered by his mother, does not foreshadow his later artistic genius, but it testifies to his capacity for solitary concentration. The recollection of Vincent's sister Elizabeth was that Vincent could be unapproachable and that he enjoyed solitude. Yet if he seems to have had a somewhat changeable personality as a boy, his education proceeded normally when he was sent at age twelve to a boarding school in the nearby village of Zevenbergen, from which he progressed to a state secondary school in the town of Tilburg. By age fifteen, he was well on the way to being a literate, if not yet sophisticated, young man.

After more than a year at home in Zundert, Vincent left in the summer of 1869 to work as a junior clerk in the branch of the French firm of Goupil and Sons in The Hague, a post for which his uncle Vincent, a partner in the firm, had recommended him. He enjoyed his work, found favor with his employers, and was transferred after four years to the London branch of the firm. Beginning with this period, there is a substantially continuous documentation both of Vincent's activities and of his emotional and intellectual experiences, for in August, 1872, he and Theo began a correspondence that was to last to the end of the artist's life.

In the summer of 1874, the first of several romantic disappointments struck van Gogh, when he declared his love for his landlady's daughter, Eugénie. Finding that she was engaged and had been playing upon his innocent devotion, he was cast into a despair, which he was unable to dispel during a three-month assignment to Goupil's Paris gallery. Returning to his London job in January, 1875, he once again failed to win Eugénie's love, and his distress, now colored by religious concerns, was intensified. In May he was permanently

transferred to Paris, where his spiritual preoccupations distracted him from his work and led to his dismissal from Goupil's in March, 1876.

Van Gogh returned to England the following month and took an unpaid position in Ramsgate as a teacher of French, German, and arithmetic. In July, he changed jobs again, teaching at a boys' school in Isleworth and preaching occasionally. The prospect of a religious vocation began to dominate his thoughts, but with his health failing he returned to his parents' home, which was now in Etten. Soon after, his uncle found him another job in a bookstore in the city of Dordrecht, but by May, 1877, van Gogh had determined to study for admission to the faculty of theology at the University in Amsterdam. For a little more than a year, he studied Greek and Latin with a congenial young Jewish scholar, Mendes da Costa, but in July, 1878, declaring his inability to learn these languages, he enrolled in a preparatory course for evangelists in Brussels. Falling to qualify for a regular parish, van Gogh was given a trial appointment as a missionary in the Borinage, a coal-mining district of Belgium, but the church authorities soon dismissed him for his unconventionally zealous behavior. Continuing his work alone, van Gogh seems to have gone through a period of extreme spiritual crisis, during which he began to draw the very people to whom he had been preaching. In the autumn of 1880, believing that his destiny was to be an artist, van Gogh left the Borinage for Brussels, seeking advice there from painters and attempting to improve his drawings.

During the following spring and summer, van Gogh was again in Etten, where a second disappointment in love occurred. At his parents' home he met a recently widowed first cousin, Kee Vos Stricker, and fell in love with her, but she fled to her parents when van Gogh declared his affection. In this affair, van Gogh's capacity for creating strained relationships with those closest to him had reached a new peak, and as a result he left again for The Hague, where he established a small studio in January, 1882, and lived with a prostitute, Clasina Hoornik, known as "Sien."

Life's Work

Through his employment at the Goupil establishments, van Gogh had been exposed to much art that was merely fashionable, but he had also seen the paintings of notable French and English painters such as Jean-François Millet, Thomas Gainsborough, and John Constable. In his own early work, however, he was guided less by artistic precedents than by a profound urge to render the life of laboring peasants and miners and to evoke compassion for the suffering of his fellowman. Van Gogh was, from the start, temperamentally incapable of following a commonplace path in his art, but he valued the advice of his fellow painters, including popular ones such as his cousin by marriage, Anton Mauve, from whom he received instruction in The Hague during the winter of 1881-1882. Perhaps for family considerations, van Gogh's uncle, Cornelius, also lent the struggling artist encouragement in 1882 by commissioning from him a series of drawings of city views, but it was Theo's regular allowance that kept van Gogh from abject poverty throughout his artistic career. Just as important, Theo gave moral support to his erratic and socially inept elder brother, becoming a spiritual as well as financial guardian. He was also the recipient of much of van Gogh's best work, as van Gogh did not sell a painting until the last year of his life.

Van Gogh's passionate devotion to his artistic self-education yielded solid results during his stay in The Hague; to the emotional conviction of his drawings he was able to add increasing fluency of form. His subjects, principally peasants and workers, are often shown in a wintry landscape that seems both accurately rendered and true to the artist's social vision. There is experimentation with materials, but it is always aimed at rendering a particular subject rather than at producing an attractive appearance.

In the summer of 1883, van Gogh began to work in earnest with oil paints and during the next two years, living again at home with his parents in the village of Nuenen, he produced dozens of canvases of the countryside and its people. The culmination of this work is a masterpiece, *The Potato Eaters*, completed in October of 1885. It is a canvas approximately three feet high and four feet wide, depicting a family of five peasants seated around a rough table, about to eat a meal of boiled potatoes. Each figure, including that of a girl whose face cannot be seen, is a distinct portrait of human dignity in the face of adversity. Darkly monochromatic and roughly textured, *The Potato Eaters* is an uncompromising study of the human condition and has none of the sentimentality that van Gogh sometimes found appealing in other artists and writers.

The year 1885 brought important new influences to van Gogh. In October, he saw old master paintings in the Rijksmuseum in Amsterdam and found special inspiration in the work of Rembrandt and Frans Hals. In late November, while studying briefly in Antwerp, he first saw Japanese prints, which were just beginning to be widely appreciated in Europe. The clarity and brilliance of the Japanese woodblock print, together with the freshness of van Gogh's seventeenth century Dutch predecessors, helped change his conception of light and color, which had been dominated by earth colors and dark tones. Early in 1886, this change was accelerated by his move to Paris, where the Impressionist painters were gaining recognition for their innovative style of rendering effects of light and color by applying brilliant, unblended pigments to their canvases. Van Gogh was soon associating with the Impressionists and befriending such artists as Camille Pissarro and Henri de Toulouse-Lautrec. Theo, as a representative of the new owners of Goupil's, was an agent for Impressionist paintings and fueled van Gogh's appreciation and understanding of them.

In the summer of 1886, Theo and Vincent took an apartment together in the Paris suburb of Montmartre. Despite the deep affection of the brothers for each other, their relationship was often strained almost to the breaking point; perhaps the remarkable progress of van Gogh's painting was Theo's reward for tolerating his volatile and inconsiderate brother. For van Gogh, however, the Paris years of 1886 and 1887 were a time of relative stability. He became acquainted with many personalities with valuable experiences and opinions to share. Among these were artists such as Émile Bernard, who later wrote perceptively about van Gogh, and the celebrated Julien Tanguy, an art-supply dealer who offered a haven—and quiet financial help—to many painters who were subsequently recognized as leading artists of their day. Van Gogh's 1887 portrait of "Père" Tanguy shows the quiet gentleman seated against a wall on which Japanese prints—which he also sold—are hung. In this celebrated work, van Gogh unites his affection for Tanguy and his reverence for Japanese art with a Postimpressionist technique likely borrowed from Paul Signac.

After a remarkable two years in Paris, van Gogh may have believed that he had exhausted the city's possibilities; in any case, the stress underlying his relationship with Theo could not continue indefinitely, and in February, 1888, he left Paris abruptly for the town of Arles, near the Mediterranean coast, arriving on February 20. The south of France

had then, as it has continued to have, rich associations for artists. In addition to the many reminders of classical Latin culture, the climate, light, and atmosphere could be powerful stimuli to creative work. In van Gogh's case, Arles and its environs was in some sense the cause of the astonishing outpouring of drawings and paintings that occurred between February, 1888, and May, 1890.

Ironically for an argumentative person such as van Gogh, he had been preoccupied by the idea of creating a brotherhood of artists, and his move to Arles was partly intended as a step in that direction. In the early months in Arles, he associated with several artist acquaintances, but more typically he formed friendships with local people such as the postman Joseph Roulin, whose portrait he painted many times. Yet in mid-October, van Gogh welcomed to his rooms in the "Yellow House" the stockbroker-turned-artist Paul Gauguin, another strong, even rebellious, personality with whom conflict might have been foreseen. Gauguin had traveled to Arles and was to be maintained there at Theo's expense in exchange for paintings. For a time, van Gogh and Gauguin valued their artistic relationship, but the domestic situation abruptly deteriorated, culminating—by Gauguin's account—in van Gogh's attack upon him with a razor blade. Before Gauguin could effect a departure from Arles, van Gogh had cut off part of his own earlobe, delivering it to the door of a local prostitute before returning, delirious and bleeding profusely, to his room at the Yellow House.

Following his recovery in the local hospital, van Gogh returned to the Yellow House on January 7 and began painting on the following day. The next month, he suffered hallucinations and was interned in a hospital cell for ten days, then released. By early May, he had agreed with Theo that he ought to enter an asylum in Saint-Rémy, several miles northeast of Arles, where he remained under the humane but ineffectual care of the asylum staff for slightly more than one year. A diagnosis of epilepsy, easily doubted but less easily supplanted by modern speculation, was made by the director, Dr. Peyron. Throughout his year at Saint-Rémy, van Gogh's condition varied enormously; sometimes he was not only calm and productive but also optimistic, and at other times he was uncommunicative and even suicidal. Remarkably, during his period of lucidity and physical well-being, he created many of his great masterpieces, including *The Starry Night* and a *Self-Portrait* of 1889. Like many of the works painted during his stay at Saint-Rémy, these canvases are characterized by vibrant color and the use of a sinuous line that make the surface of the painting seem to pulsate with energy. *The Starry Night*, along with another Saint-Rémy picture of irises, were included in a fall exhibition in Paris, where they attracted attention.

In January, 1890, the first article on van Gogh, and the only one published in his lifetime, appeared in *Mercure de France*. Entitled "The Isolated Ones: Vincent van Gogh," the article was the work of a perceptive young critic named G.-Albert Aurier, who had seen many of van Gogh's works at Theo's home. Aurier's observations were overwhelmingly enthusiastic, yet van Gogh wrote to Theo asking him to dissuade Aurier from writing any more about him. Although there was an element of modesty in this, it was more Vincent's accelerating exhaustion of spirit that caused him to be wary of acclaim. Events that buoyed his spirit, such as Theo's marriage and the birth of a nephew—also named Vincent Willem—could also have created new strains in his fragile mind.

Van Gogh left the asylum at Saint-Rémy on May 16, 1890, and traveled alone to Paris without incident, where he stayed four days with Theo and his family before traveling to nearby Auvers-sur-Oise to live under the supervision of Paul Gachet, an art-loving doctor of sixty-two. For several weeks, van Gogh carried on with his painting and even printed an etching using Gachet's press, but on July 27 he walked several hundred yards to a farm near Auvers and shot himself in the stomach. He managed to return to his room, and in the last thirty-six hours of his life he dozed, smoked his pipe, and spoke at length with Theo, who had been summoned from Paris. He died in the early morning hours of July 29, 1890. Only weeks later, Theo suffered a breakdown that seemed clearly connected to his grief over his brother's death, and on January 25, 1891, he died in Utrecht, the Netherlands.

Summary

Vincent van Gogh's tumultuous life is so well documented by his letters and the recollections of family, friends, and associates, that an unusual degree of study and speculation has been devoted to his personal circumstances and particularly to the tragedy of his illness. In this respect, van Gogh has become virtually an archetype of the modern artist—a man ill at ease with himself and society, and restless in the personal as well as the artistic sphere.

Van Gogh himself was well aware of the implications of his personality and his social situation, accepting his dependence upon his brother as well as his status as an outsider in order to pursue his art without compromise.

As compelling as van Gogh's story has been for critics and public alike, it is his paintings, and to a lesser extent his drawings, that are the cornerstone of his lasting significance. From the early drawings made during his ministry in the Borinage to the final paintings made in the weeks preceding his death in Auvers-sur-Oise, van Gogh's works are characterized by passionate sincerity. Yet as important as their psychological authenticity is their adventurous form. Starting in the early 1880's from a vigorous but rather insular style, he assimilated the heritage of Dutch painting, then went on to adapt the lessons of Impressionism to new and visionary purposes. Van Gogh's singular artistic triumph, differentiating him from his Postimpressionist colleagues such as Gauguin and Georges Seurat, was his ability to communicate both his visual experience of nature and his insight into man's social and spiritual condition.

Van Gogh, whose personal relationships were often catastrophic, saw his art as an act of love for humanity, and one avenue of psychological analysis views the fervor of his career as compensation for the emotional failures of his life. While there is doubtless some truth to this view, if taken too literally it can reduce the immense complexity of his life to a formula. Van Gogh was both highly intelligent and acutely self-aware, and it seems likely that even as he descended toward a tragic suicide, he was aware of the great, though painfully forged, achievement of his life as a painter.

Bibliography

Barr, Alfred H., Jr., ed. *Vincent van Gogh: With an Introduction and Notes Selected from the Letters of the Artist*. New York: Arno Press, 1966. This catalog to a 1935 exhibition of the artist's work at the Museum of Modern Art, New York, is joined to an annotated bibliography, originally published in 1942, of articles, books, and other materials on van Gogh.

Cabanne, Pierre. *Van Gogh*. London: Thames and Hudson, and Englewood Cliffs, N.J.: Prentice-Hall, 1963. Both the small format of this book and its somewhat breathless text frustrate the reader's wish to meet the artist, as much as possible, at first hand. Its efficiency is matched by its superficiality.

Gogh, Vincent van. *Complete Letters, with Reproductions of All Drawings in the Correspondence.* 3 vols. Greenwich, Conn.: New York Graphic Society, 1958. Van Gogh's letters rank among the finest literary artifacts in the sphere of visual art. Books of selected letters are useful but inevitably omit even items of general interest.

———. *Van Gogh: A Retrospective.* Edited by Susan Alyson Stein. New York: Macmillan, 1986. A magnificent collection of documentary material and excellent color plates, this large book also contains a lengthy chronology of the artist's life, which corrects a number of factual errors scattered throughout many earlier sources.

———. *Vincent van Gogh.* Text by Meyer Schapiro. New York: Abrams, 1950; London: Thames and Hudson, 1968. This volume, in a uniform series of artist monographs, contains a fine essay coupled with large color plates annotated on the facing page. The text is excellent as an introduction to the artist, but the plates do not reach the quality of modern reproductions.

———. *The Works of Vincent van Gogh: His Paintings and Drawings.* Text by J.-B. de la Faille. London: Weidenfeld and Nicolson, and New York: Morrow, 1970. A complete (so far as scholarship can ascertain) catalog of the artist's works, each one illustrated, follows an essay, "Van Gogh and the Words," by A. M. Hammacher, which provides a history of the appreciation of van Gogh's works by leading writers and critics.

Heinich, Nathalie. *The Glory of Van Gogh: An Anthropology of Admiration.* Translated by Paul L. Browne. Princeton, N.J.: Princeton University Press, 1996. Heinich examines the reasons for van Gogh's glorification as a cultural hero of the twentieth century, comparing this phenomenon with the manner in which saints rise in stature and are canonized.

Krauss, André. *Vincent van Gogh: Studies in the Social Aspects of His Work.* Atlantic Highlands, N.J.: Humanities Press International, 1987. This compact study is a doctoral dissertation investigating the issue of social messages in the painter's work. Though it is specialized, it is very readable.

Masheck, Joseph D, ed. *Van Gogh One Hundred.* Westport, Conn.: Greenwood Press, 1996. A collection of essays by noted van Gogh scholars on the one-hundredth anniversary of his death. Essays focus on the reasons for his popularity and his influence on twentieth century art.

Wallace, Robert. *The World of Van Gogh, 1853-1890.* New York: Time-Life, 1969. Aimed at a popular audience, the text of this well-illustrated book is reliable, though sketchy. A justifiable, and even valuable, limitation is that van Gogh is presented alongside his contemporaries Toulouse-Lautrec and Seurat.

C. S. McConnell

NIKOLAI GOGOL

Born: March 31, 1809; Sorochintsy, Ukraine, Russia

Died: March 4, 1852; Moscow, Russia

Area of Achievement: Literature

Contribution: Gogol made an important contribution to the development of modern comic fiction, particularly short fiction. By combining such disparate narrative elements as oral folklore and literary Romanticism, Gogol paved the way for such modernist writers as Franz Kafka.

Early Life

Nikolai Gogol was born on March 31, 1809, on his family's country estate in the Ukraine near the small town of Sorochintsy. A sickly child, he was so pampered and idolized by his mother when he was young that he developed an inflated opinion of himself. At the age of twelve, Gogol entered a boarding school in the city of Nezhin, where he stayed for seven years; however, probably because he was bored with the routine of the classroom, he was only an average student. He was, however, enthusiastic about literature and drama, actively taking part in school theatricals in every capacity, from stagehand to actor and director.

By all accounts, Gogol was a skinny, unattractive child with a bad complexion and a long nose; he was often called dwarfish by his schoolmates. Although there is no indication that he gave serious thought to a writing career while in school, Gogol did write one long poem during his adolescence entitled "Hans Küchelgarten" (1829), which he took to St. Petersburg with him after graduation in 1828 and published at his own expense. Yet, as most critics agree, the poem is highly imitative and immature; the derisive reception it received by the few reviewers who noticed it at all probably made Gogol decide to abandon poetry forever and focus instead on drama and prose, in which his talent for mixing traditional styles and genres could best be exhibited.

After his father's death, Gogol's mother was unable to manage the family estate profitably; as a result, Gogol found himself without funds and without prospects. Securing a position in the civil service to support himself, he began writing stories in his spare time about the Ukraine and submitting them to a St. Petersburg periodical. By gaining the attention of such influential Russian writers as Bar-

on Anton Delvig and Vasily Zhukovsky with these pieces, Gogol was introduced to the great Russian poet Alexander Pushkin, who admired Gogol's fiction. Gogol's early stories were published in two volumes in 1831 and 1832 as *Vechera na khutore bliz Dikanki* (*Evenings on a Farm Near Dikanka*, 1926), and they received an enthusiastic response from critics in Moscow and St. Petersburg; Gogol had thus arrived as an exciting new talent and was admitted to the highest literary circles.

Life's Work

The stories in *Evenings on a Farm Near Dikanka* introduce readers to Gogol's major stylistic innovation—the combining of the fanciful and earthy folklore of his native Ukraine with the literary and philosophic imagination of German Romanticism, about which he had learned in school. The hybrid generic form that resulted from the combination of fantastic events and realistic detail not only characterizes Gogol's short stories in particular but also typifies similar narrative experiments being conducted with the short prose form in the United States, Germany, and France; Gogol's experimentation with short prose fiction gives him a place in the creation of the short story equal in importance to Edgar Allan Poe, E. T. A. Hoffmann, and Prosper Mérimée.

In 1834, Gogol obtained a position as a history professor at the University of St. Petersburg and lectured there for a little more than a year; however, he was so bad at it that the administration gently compelled him to leave. Essays in art, history, and literature on which Gogol had been working while teaching appeared in 1835 under the title *Arabeski* (*Arabesques*, 1982). Although these essays were not distinguished in any way, the three new stories that appeared in the collection—"Portret" ("The Portrait"), "Nevsky Prospekti" ("Nevsky Prospect"), and "Zapiski sumasshedshego" ("Diary of a Madman")—are significant Gogol works. Along with "Nos" (1836; "The Nose") and "Shinel" (1839; "The Overcoat"), and often referred to as the Petersburg Cycle, these stories are his major contribution to the short story and the novella forms.

Of the three stories that appeared in *Arabesques*, "Diary of a Madman" is perhaps the best known. Drawing some of his ideas from the German Romantic writer Hoffmann, Gogol has his central

character, a minor government official, tell his own story of his hopeless infatuation with the daughter of the chief of his department. The story is an effective combination of social criticism, psychological analysis, and grotesque comedy, for, by intertwining the "mad" perception of the narrator with the supposedly "sane" perception of the bureaucratic world that surrounds the narrator, Gogol manages to underline the relativity of madness itself.

Gogol's story "The Nose" is perhaps second only to his masterpiece "The Overcoat" in its influence on subsequent fiction. The fantastic plot of the story begins when a St. Petersburg barber finds the nose of the assessor Major Kovalev, whom he shaves regularly, in his breakfast roll one morning. On the same morning, Kovalev wakes up to find a smooth, shiny place on his face where his nose used to be. When he goes to the police to have the case of the missing nose investigated, he is astonished to see his nose on the street wearing a gold-braided uniform. After finally recovering the nose, Kovalev tries unsuccessfully to stick it back on his face; finally, he wakes up one morning to find it back where it belongs. Although, like "Diary of a

Madman," the story is filled with ironic social criticism, what makes it so influential is the integration of this fantastic plot premise with the most straightforward style of narration. Like Kafka's twentieth century masterpiece *Die Verwandlung* (1915; *The Metamorphosis*, 1936), Gogol's "The Nose" only asks that the reader accept the initial incredible premise; all the rest follows in a strictly realistic fashion.

This combination of different realms of reality reaches a powerful culmination when Gogol unites it with two different literary styles in what all critics agree is his most nearly perfect work, "The Overcoat." The story of the poverty-stricken copyist with the absurd name of Akakii Akakiievich Bashmachkin is so well known that it has been said that most modernist Russian fiction springs from under Gogol's "overcoat." Once again, Gogol combines what seems to be social realism of everyday St. Petersburg life with the fantastic style of folklore. Indeed, most of the commentary that has been written on the story focuses on either its realistic nature or its fantastic style. Irish short-story writer Frank O'Connor has said that what makes the story so magnificent is Gogol's focus on the copyist and his emphasis on Akakii's implicit call for human brotherhood. On the other hand, in what is perhaps the best-known discussion of the story, Russian formalist critic Boris Eichenbaum claims that the genius of the story depends on the role played by the author's personal tone and the story's use of the oral conventions of Russian folktales.

Although Gogol published more ambitious works, at least in terms of scope, than these three short fictions, none of his later work surpasses them in narrative and stylistic control. Among Gogol's longer works, only one drama—*Revizor* (1836; *The Inspector General*, 1890)—and one novel— *Myortvye dushi* (part 1, 1842, part 2, 1855; *Dead Souls*, 1887)—remain as influential indicators of Gogol's genius. *The Inspector General*, although comic like his short fictions "The Nose" and "The Overcoat," is not fantastic like them. In fact, it has been called his most conventionally realistic work. Because of its satirical thrusts at government bureaucracy, the play was attacked, when it was first produced, by conservative critics as a slander on Russian government. Today it is remembered as one of Gogol's most emphatic social satires.

Many critics, more impressed with the broader scope of the novel than the more limited perfection of the short story, consider Gogol's novel *Dead*

Souls to be his undisputed masterpiece. Indeed, it is an ambitious work, taking Gogol six years to complete. Building on an idea given him by Pushkin—that dead souls, or serfs, are taken as live ones—Gogol creates the character Tchitchikov, who buys dead souls to bolster his own wealth. Boasting an unforgettable assembly of grotesque comic characterizations, *Dead Souls* is often called one of the great comic masterpieces of European literature.

During the last ten years of his life, after the publication of part 1 of *Dead Souls*, Gogol worked on part 2. All that remains, however, are the first four chapters and part of a final chapter. In 1845, he burned all the other manuscript pages of the novel he had been working on for four years. Before his death in March, 1852, he once again put a match to the work he had subsequently done on part 2. He died a little more than a week later.

Summary

Although Nikolai Gogol died when he was only forty-two, thus leaving a body of work that is relatively small—certainly nothing to rival the monumental output of such nineteenth century greats as Leo Tolstoy and Fyodor Dostoevski—his influence has loomed much larger than his output would suggest. Although he is generally remembered as a writer of biting social satire on Russian government bureaucracy and as a creator of comic types that rival those of Charles Dickens, it is his short fiction in particular that has had the most significant impact. Gogol is indeed a writer's writer, for short-story writers themselves are the ones who most recognize his greatness. From his countryman Ivan Turgenev to Irish short-story writer Frank O'Connor to American philosopher and fiction writer William H. Gass, Gogol has been recognized as a powerful nineteenth century innovator in the creation of that strange blend of fantasy and reality—the comic grotesque—that has come to be recognized as an essential element of modernism and post-modernism.

Bibliography

Driessen, F. C. *Gogol as a Short-Story Writer: A Study of His Technique of Composition*. Translated by Ian F. Finlay. The Hague: Mouton, 1965. A formalist study of Gogol's technique as a short-story writer. Focuses on anxiety as a major Gogol theme before analyzing selected stories, including "The Overcoat," which Driessen says represents an isolated attempt of Gogol to overcome his anxiety.

Erlich, Victor. *Gogol*. New Haven, Conn.: Yale University Press, 1969. A study of Gogol by an expert on Russian formalist criticism. Focuses on Gogol's technique and his most typical themes and images. More theoretical than practical in its approach to Gogol, the study contains numerous provocative ideas and concepts for understanding his genius.

Fanger, Donald L. *The Creation of Nikolai Gogol*. Cambridge, Mass.: Harvard University Press, 1979. An attempt to compensate for what the author calls the overabundance of eccentric views of Gogol in American criticism. Fanger outlines the Russian cultural context of Gogol's work and then examines his works to elucidate the progressive development of its basic underlying pattern.

Jenness, Rosemarie K. *Gogol's Aesthetics Compared to Major Elements of German Romanticism*. New York: Lang, 1995. The author argues that Gogol's beliefs on the creative process, the role of the poet, and the spirituality of art are in line with early German Romanticism.

Lindstrom, Thaïs S. *Nikolay Gogol*. New York: Twayne, 1974. A general introduction to Gogol's life and his art in chronological order. The focus is on Gogol's essential modernity and his creation of the comic grotesque. Includes a chronology of his life as well as a brief annotated bibliography of criticism.

Maguire, Robert A. *Exploring Gogol*. Stanford, Calif.: Stanford University Press, 1994. Fresh look at Gogol that presents his life and work as a whole through examination of the major texts set in a broad, intellectual context.

———, ed. *Gogol from the Twentieth Century: Eleven Essays*. Princeton, N.J.: Princeton University Press, 1974. Includes eleven essays on Gogol from the perspective of various twentieth century Russian critical approaches, including formalist, psychological, religious, sociological, and historical criticism. Includes a famous essay by Boris Eichenbaum, "How Gogol's 'Overcoat' Is Made."

Peace, Richard. *The Enigma of Gogol*. Cambridge and New York: Cambridge University Press, 1981. A study of Gogol's works from the point of view of their place in the Russian literary tradition, particularly focusing on the enigma of the scope of Gogol's influence on a realistic tradition in spite of his own grotesque rhetorical style.

Setchkarev, Vsevolod. *Gogol: His Life and Works*. Translated by Robert Kramer. London: Owen, and New York: New York University Press, 1965. A readable introduction to Gogol's life and art. This straightforward study does not pretend to break any new critical ground but rather summarizes previous criticism and analyzes Gogol's works both thematically and formally.

Charles E. May

SIR GEORGE GOLDIE

Born: May 20, 1846; Douglas, Isle of Man
Died: August 20, 1925; London, England
Area of Achievement: Colonial administration
Contribution: Employing his commercial skills and great administrative abilities, Goldie formed the Royal Niger Company and contributed immensely to the extension of British influence in Nigeria.

Early Life

Sir George Goldie was born George Dashwood Goldie Taubman in Douglas on the Isle of Man on May 20, 1846. (He changed his name to George Taubman Goldie in 1887, when he received his knighthood.) His father was a wealthy Manx merchant and landowner who was married twice. George Goldie, like his two brothers from his father's second marriage, entered the army and attended the Royal Military Academy at Woolwich for two years. Following graduation, the death of a wealthy relative left him financially independent, and Goldie journeyed to Egypt. While in Egypt and the Sudan, Goldie acquired a mistress, learned Arabic, and, most important, developed a deep interest in the Sudan area of West Africa. He studied intently Heinrich Barth's five-volume *Travels and Discoveries in North and Central Africa* (1857-1858).

Returning to England, Goldie failed to conform to the accepted norms of middle-class Victorian Britain. In 1870, he fell in love with the family governess, Mathilda Catherine Elliot, and the couple departed abruptly for France. There they were trapped by the siege of Paris during the latter phases of the Franco-Prussian War. Goldie returned to England in 1871 and married Mathilda the same year. They had one son and one daughter.

Goldie, at the mature age of thirty, still had no settled career, having already resigned his commission in the army. A thin, intense man with a large mustache and piercing eyes, Goldie impressed his contemporaries with his determination, pride, and quick temper. These personality traits, his atheism, and his scandalous background and marriage made it difficult for him to be accepted into polite Victorian society. Goldie was simply too unconventional and unpredictable to gain or to hold a position in government service or in politics. Like many of Great Britain's great empire builders, Goldie was to find fulfillment in the freer environment of the colonies.

Goldie's career opportunity came in 1875 through a member of his family. A sister-in-law's father, Captain Joseph Grove-Ross, was associated, largely unsuccessfully, to conduct commerce on the Niger River. The Taubman family, anxious to rid itself of an embarrassment, suggested Goldie as a man who could restore the company's prosperity. Still fascinated with Africa, Goldie took up the challenge and left for the Niger in 1876. Between his arrival in West Africa in 1876 and the revocation of the charter of his later Royal Niger Company in 1900, Goldie spent much of his time overseas. During these turbulent years, Goldie would remake the commercial structure of the Niger region and ultimately contribute to the annexation of what was later known as Nigeria.

Life's Work

On arriving on the Niger, Goldie quickly discerned the problems facing the English merchants seeking to trade in palm oil, a valuable lubricant for machinery and an important ingredient in fine soap. Powerful coastal African states, such as that of the Brassmen, were determined to protect their role as middlemen in this commerce and to prevent the European merchants from using the Niger River to trade directly with the palm-oil-producing regions farther to the north. Travel by steamer remained dangerous in the 1870's because of the absence of effective British protection. Furthermore, Goldie discovered that the intense rivalry among the large number of merchant companies conducting business on the Niger gave the African producers the opportunity to demand higher prices. Unless competition were restricted, Goldie feared, European profits would remain low and smaller companies such as his own would fail.

By 1879, Goldie had consolidated most of the European companies into the United African Company. Through his natural leadership abilities, he convinced his rivals of the benefits of establishing a monopoly which would restrict competition and lower the prices paid to the Africans for their palm oil. Goldie's problems were not, however, over. It was difficult to prevent new companies from being formed to challenge his United African Company. Also, by the early 1880's both the French and the Germans were beginning to show interest in the Niger, an area not yet claimed by any European government.

To counter these new threats, in 1882 Goldie formed the National African Company, and he attempted to obtain a royal charter from the British government giving him administrative control over the Niger region. The British government, still reluctant to extend its political responsibilities in West Africa, refused Goldie's request. The French annexation of Dahomey in 1883, however, and the German annexation of the Cameroons the following year strengthened Goldie's position. In 1884, he was given permission to make treaties with African chiefs. He also attended the Berlin Conference of 1884-1885, called by Germany to establish guidelines for African annexations, and he worked successfully to preserve British influence in the region and to ensure his control of navigation on the Niger River. Finally, in 1886, after almost two years of negotiation, he received a royal charter for his new Royal Niger Company. This charter gave Goldie administrative control of the lower Niger, over which Great Britain had belatedly established a protectorate in 1885. For his work in strengthening Great Britain's position in West Africa, Goldie received a knighthood in 1887.

Goldie's charter gave him the power to "protect" African states which had treaties with his company, to acquire new territory with the approval of the British government, and to levy taxes to pay for administrative costs. Goldie remained concerned, however, over the growing French influence in the Niger region. In 1894, he dispatched Captain Frederick Lugard to the Dahomey border to secure treaties with several African chiefs. These treaties forestalled French expansion from the west, but the two nations continued a rivalry in the north. It was not until 1898, after a major diplomatic crisis, that the British and French governments established by treaty the western and northern boundaries of what is now Nigeria. Goldie's territorial position was finally secure.

Goldie's last years in Nigeria also saw intense conflict with the powerful Muslim city-states in the north. In 1897, he waged war on the Emir of Nupe, who had engaged in slave trading in the territory of the Royal Niger Company. With only eight hundred men, Goldie defeated Nupe's army of fifteen thousand men, entered the capital, Bida, and deposed the emir. The state of Ilorin was also subdued by force. By 1899, Goldie's African work was largely over. Nigeria had been brought under British control at little expense to the British taxpayer, but the 1898 crisis with France illustrated the crucial importance of official British possession of Nigeria. Goldie's private company simply could not compete with a hostile foreign government. As a result, in 1899 the British Parliament revoked the charter of the Royal Niger Company and deprived it of its administrative powers. On January 1, 1900, Frederick Lugard became the new British High Commissioner for Northern Nigeria.

The revocation of the Royal Niger Company's charter ended Goldie's direct contact with Africa, although he remained interested in the empire and active in imperial affairs. He traveled widely and served as a member of a Royal Commission on the Boer War. In 1904, he visited Rhodesia to report on the status of the British South Africa Company. In his later life, he became involved in London politics and chaired the finance committee of the London County Council. Upon his death, on August 20, 1925, Goldie and his African work had largely faded from the public's consciousness.

Summary

In many ways, Sir George Goldie caught the spirit of imperial Great Britain in the late nineteenth century. His romantic view of Africa, which led him early in life to contemplate an east-west crossing of the Sudan, drew him to the so-called Dark Continent. Once in Africa, Goldie personified the private imperialist, using his business skills not only to make money but also to ensure British control of the most commercially valuable portion of West Africa. During much of his early career in Nigeria, a reluctant British government opposed an extension of its imperial responsibilities in such a remote area. Without Goldie's perseverance, Great Britain could easily have been squeezed out of the region by Germany and France. By maintaining a British commercial and administrative presence on the Niger in the 1870's and 1880's, Goldie retained for Great Britain the opportunity in the 1890's to consolidate its rule over the region. By 1900, after his company had lost its charter, Goldie was acknowledged "the Founder of Nigeria."

Goldie not only gave Nigeria its modern boundaries, but he also was instrumental in the development of British techniques of colonial administration. Largely because of financial necessity, he instituted a system of government whereby a few district officers ruled largely through the native chiefs, retaining much of the traditional African culture and law. Because of his desire to shun publicity and his decision to destroy his private papers, however, Goldie received little credit for this system of administration, which Lord Lugard later made famous as "Indirect Rule." It would be more than one hundred years after his death before Goldie would be rightfully recognized as one of the great British imperialists of the late nineteenth century.

Bibliography

Ajayi, J. F. A., and Michael Crowder, eds. *History of West Africa*. Vol. 2. 3d ed. London: Longman, 1985. Excellent study of West Africa from the early nineteenth century to 1960. Puts Goldie's work in perspective and highlights the role of the Royal Niger Company in the partition of West Africa.

Burns, A. C. *History of Nigeria*. 8th ed. London: Allen and Unwin, 1972. Written by a British official in Nigeria. Uncritical of Goldie's work in Nigeria but illustrative of Great Britain's view in the 1920's of its achievements.

Fage, J. D. "When the African Society Was Founded, Who Were the Africanists?" *African Affairs* 94, no. 376 (July, 1995). Profile of the Royal African Society, of which Goldie was a prominent member representing the economic community.

Flint, J. E. *Sir George Goldie and the Making of Nigeria*. London: Oxford University Press, 1960. The first and only complete study of Goldie's life and work. An excellent analysis of the methods by which he consolidated British influence in Nigeria. Weak on Goldie's private and personal life because of the destruction of his papers.

Geary, Sir William N. M. *Nigeria Under British Rule*. London: Methuen, 1927; New York: Barnes and Noble Books, 1965. Written by a former British colonial official. An early laudatory account of British administration in Nigeria which more than most accounts from this period praises the efforts of Goldie.

Hargreaves, John D. *West Africa Partitioned*. 2 vols. London: Macmillan, 1974; Madison: University of Wisconsin Press, 1985. Excellent study of the role of the Royal Niger Company in the diplomacy leading to the partition of Africa.

Perham, Margery. *Lugard: The Years of Adventure, 1858-1898*. Hamden, Conn.: Archon, 1956; London: Collins, 1960. The last section is an excellent discussion of Goldie's policies in Nigeria and his early relations with his friend and successor, Sir Frederick Lugard.

Wellesley, Dorothy. *Sir George Goldie: Founder of Nigeria*. Introduction by Stephen Gwynn. London: Macmillan, 1934; New York: Arno Press, 1977. The first lengthy study of Goldie. Written by a friend, it contains valuable information on Goldie's character and personality. An early, uncritical attempt to resurrect Goldie's central role in the creation of modern Nigeria.

Brian L. Blakeley

SAMUEL GOMPERS

Born: January 27, 1850; London, England
Died: December 13, 1924; San Antonio, Texas
Area of Achievement: The labor movement
Contribution: Gompers helped create the first successful national organization of trade unions in the United States, the American Federation of Labor (AFL), and he led the AFL almost continuously from its creation in 1886 to 1924.

Early Life

Samuel Gompers was the son of Dutch parents who had emigrated to London in 1844. Gompers' father was a cigar-maker, and the family lived in poverty. Samuel's total formal education consisted of attendance, from the ages of six to ten, at a free school provided by the Jewish community, plus some free evening classes. Samuel left school because of the family's poor financial condition, and, after a brief try at shoemaking, his father arranged for an apprenticeship as a cigar-maker. Gompers worked in this trade until he became a full-time union leader.

In 1863, the Gompers family followed relatives to the United States and settled in New York City. Gompers married Sophia Julian in 1867. Although they had many children, only five lived to reach adulthood. Sophia died in 1920, and Gompers remarried the next year. His second wife, Gertrude Neuschler, was thirty years younger than he, and the marriage was an unhappy one.

Gompers was Jewish by birth, but he did not practice his religion; nor did he exhibit any strong identification with other Jews. He had an attraction to fraternal orders, including the Foresters, the Odd Fellows, and the Masons. Gompers' father had been a union member in London, and father and son joined the Cigar-makers' Union in 1864. Gompers, however, was more involved with fraternal than with union activities until the early 1870's.

Hard times for skilled cigar-makers ultimately impelled Gompers into active involvement with the union. The introduction of a new tool, the mold, into the trade in 1869 simplified cigar-making and threatened the position of the skilled workers. The long depression of 1873-1877 made the situation worse. By 1872, Gompers had joined Adolph Strasser and Ferdinand Laurrell in trying to remake the faltering Cigar-makers' Union. In 1875, Gompers became president of a reorganized cigar-makers' local union in New York City. Gompers then helped elect Strasser as president of the national union in 1877. Together, they reconstructed the Cigar-makers' Union on the model of British trade unions. This meant high dues; financial benefits, such as a death allowance, sick pay, and out-of-work payments; and centralized control of strikes. From 1880 onward, Gompers held office in his local union, and, after 1886 and for the remainder of his life, in the national union.

In these early years, Gompers demonstrated the personal qualities that were to mark his later activities. He was pragmatic, indefatigable, honest, and totally devoted to the union cause, passing up many more lucrative job opportunities. Although short in stature and initially hampered by a stammer, Gompers became an accomplished speaker. Despite his meager formal education, he wrote extensively, including many articles as editor of the journal of the AFL. He gave his life to the labor movement, and he expected others to accept his leadership. Gompers rarely admitted a mistake or forgave an enemy.

Life's Work

As early as the 1870's, Gompers believed in the importance of a national organization to represent the trade unions of the country. Earlier efforts in the 1860's to create such an organization had failed. Gompers helped to form a weak federation of trade unions in 1881, and he was the leader, in 1886, in establishing a more powerful body, the AFL. He became its first president, and with the exception of 1894, he was reelected annually until his death. As president, Gompers developed his mature views on how the American labor movement should function, and he worked tirelessly to put them into practice.

Gompers believed that the labor movement must win acceptance by employers and the public as the representative of the workers' legitimate interests within the existing capitalist system. Any resort to violence or support of radicalism would lead to repression by the state. Thus, the labor movement must work within the law for goals understandable to most Americans: an improved standard of living, better opportunities for one's children, and security in one's old age.

Gompers was familiar with Socialist doctrine from his exposure to the movement in the 1870's. Although he retained certain elements of Marxism, particularly an intense belief in class as the determinant of political behavior, by 1880, he opposed the Socialists as being dangerous to the labor movement. He believed that the Socialists did not represent the views of most Americans on matters such as private property. Moreover, their demand for radical change threatened to stimulate repression. Since many workers were supporters of the two major political parties, the attempts of the Socialists to create an alliance between the trade unions and a radical third party were divisive. Gompers' struggles with the Socialists increased in intensity after 1890, and they were the major opposition to his leadership within the AFL.

For Gompers, legislation was not a major means for workers to win gains. Ultimately, this position flowed from his belief that politics was controlled by class interests. For Gompers, since the demands of workers would eventually conflict with the interests of other classes and since workers did not control the government and were unlikely to do so, political action would be dangerous for the labor movement. Gompers carried this idea to the point of opposing most labor legislation, because once the government intervened in the lives of workers, it would be more likely to do harm than good.

Rather than risk the danger of governmental intervention in labor matters, Gompers called upon workers to organize trade unions and to win their gains by this means. The trade union was the only institution in society fully under the control of the working class and responsive to its interests. This doctrine of voluntarism brought him into frequent conflict with social reformers, who pointed out that most workers were not members of trade unions. Strong opposition to Gompers' views also came from important elements within the labor movement—principally the weaker unions that saw little prospect of substantial immediate gains through their own efforts and who were therefore attracted to an alliance with middle-class reformers to secure labor legislation. This trend was most apparent during the two decades prior to World War I, known as the Progressive period.

On occasion, Gompers believed that political action might be necessary for limited objectives which were unachievable by trade-union action alone, or to protect the labor movement against as-

sault. An example of the latter was the campaign by the AFL, from 1906 to 1914, to win relief from the use of the Sherman Anti-Trust Act against the labor movement. In such a case, however, labor had to follow a policy of rewarding friends and punishing enemies, without reference to party. Gompers argued that this practice would counteract the allegiance of workers to the two major parties and avoid the permanent commitment to any political party that Gompers wanted to avoid.

Despite his foreign birth, Gompers led the AFL in its demand for a restriction of immigration. He undoubtedly expressed the views of most trade unionists, who feared that the newcomers would accept lower wages and that the arrival of vast numbers of both skilled and unskilled workers would create an additional pool of labor that employers could use to crush strikes or to operate new machinery. The AFL consistently supported immigration restriction, beginning in 1897.

Gompers initially favored the organization of all workers. He opposed the tendency in some trade unions to bar immigrants, blacks, women, or the less skilled, since by doing so a nonunion work force that could weaken the labor movement would be created. Yet Gompers eventually yielded on this point and left the issue to individual unions.

Gompers also increasingly favored the organization of workers by craft, rather than through unions representing all the workers in an industry. Gompers believed that the creation of industrial unions would produce conflict with the existing craft unions, thus weakening the labor movement. Moreover, he argued that the craft unions could effectively organize the less skilled workers. In the event, however, this did not occur—and as a consequence, the scope of the American labor movement was severely limited. It took a split in the AFL in the 1930's and the subsequent formation of the Congress of Industrial Organizations (CIO) to make industrial unionism a significant force in the United States.

Gompers consistently supported the peaceful settlement of international disputes until 1916, when he embraced the concept of preparedness. Gompers strongly supported the war effort once the United States entered World War I in 1917. This shift in attitude reflects several of his basic beliefs. First, he contended that the nation overwhelmingly supported preparedness and then the war, and it weakened the labor movement to oppose popular opinion. Second, Gompers viewed the issue with his usual pragmatism: He correctly believed that the administration of Woodrow Wilson would cooperate with the AFL to maximize production during the war. Yet the gains for the labor movement could not be sustained after the war, in the face of the severe Red scare of 1919 and the political and economic conservatism of the 1920's. By the time of Gompers' death in 1924, the AFL was only slightly larger than it had been prior to the war.

Summary

Samuel Gompers' views strongly influenced the character of the American labor movement until the appearance of the CIO in the 1930's. Gompers' leadership was a combination of experience, tenacity, hard work, and the web of personal contacts which he had built in the labor movement. He could only persuade and implore; he could not command. Because Gompers was elected annually by the votes of the larger craft unions in the AFL, he had to represent their interests. Yet Gompers was too strong a personality to stay with a labor movement that he could not support. The AFL was not exactly what Gompers might have wanted, but it did reflect many of his basic views. Thus, he was able to develop, defend, and lead the organization for more than four decades.

Bibliography

Dick, William M. *Labor and Socialism in America: The Gompers Era.* Port Washington, N.Y.: Kennikat Press, 1972; London: Kennikat Press, 1973. Traces Gompers' relations with the Socialists over the course of his career.

Fones-Wolf, Elizabeth and Ken Fones-Wolf. "Rank-and-File Rebellions and AFL Interference in the Affairs of National Unions: The Gompers Era." *Labor History* 35, no. 2 (Spring 1994). Study of the AFL in the early twentieth century and the changes brought about by Gompers.

Gompers, Samuel. *The Samuel Gompers Papers.* Vol. 1, *The Making of a Union Leader: 1850-86.* Edited by Stuart Kaufman. Urbana: University of Illinois Press, 1986. Excellent documentary history that covers Gompers' early life and career up to his accession to the presidency of the AFL. Other volumes to follow.

————. *Seventy Years of Life and Labor: An Autobiography.* 2 vols. New York: Dutton, 1925. Gompers' version of his life and times. Contains valuable information, but it must be used with care. Includes photographs.

Grob, Gerald. *Workers and Utopia: A Study of Ideological Conflict in the American Labor Movement, 1865-1900.* Chicago: Northwestern University Press, 1971. Examines Gompers' efforts to establish the AFL in competition with the Knights of Labor.

Livesay, Harold. *Samuel Gompers and Organized Labor in America.* Boston: Little Brown, 1978. Brief, interpretive, and readable study of Gompers.

Mandel, Bernard. *Samuel Gompers: A Biography.* Yellow Springs, Ohio: Antioch Press, 1963. Full-length biography that is rich in detail. Includes photographs.

McKillen, Elizabeth. *Chicago Labor and the Quest for a Democratic Diplomacy, 1914-1924.* Ithaca, N.Y.: Cornell University Press, 1995. Examination of the impact of the labor movement on U.S. foreign policy during World War I.

Reed, Louis. *The Labor Philosophy of Samuel Gompers.* New York: Columbia University Press, and London: King, 1930. Descriptive and analytical presentation of Gompers' views. The author sees a need for the AFL's type of unionism in the nineteenth century, but he believes that it became outdated in the twentieth century.

Taft, Philip. *The A.F. of L. in the Time of Gompers*. New York: Harper, 1957. Detailed account of the AFL; necessarily stresses Gompers' role. Generally supports the policies of the AFL and its leader.

Irwin Yellowitz

CHARLES GOODYEAR

Born: December 29, 1800; New Haven, Connecticut
Died: July 1, 1860; New York, New York
Area of Achievement: Invention
Contribution: Goodyear was the first man to vulcanize rubber, thereby rendering it usable for manufacturing numerous products.

Early Life

Charles Goodyear was born in New Haven, Connecticut, on December 29, 1800. He was the first child born to Amasa Goodyear and Cynthia Bateman Goodyear; their family later grew to include six children. Stephen Goodyear, an ancestor from London, had been one of a group of merchants who founded a colony in New Haven in 1638. Amasa Goodyear was also a merchant, selling hardware supplies to farmers, as well as an inventor. One of his patented farm tools was a hay pitchfork made from steel; it was a great improvement over the heavy cast-iron pitchforks that were used in the early 1800's.

Charles attended public schools in New Haven and Naugatuck, Connecticut, his father having moved the family in 1807 to a farm near Naugatuck to take advantage of a water-powered factory he had bought there. Charles helped his father, to whom he was a close companion, at both the factory and the farm. Contemporaries remembered him as a serious youth with a studious nature. An excellent Bible student, he considered being a minister, but when he finished public school at seventeen, he agreed with his father that he should enter the hardware business and was apprenticed, as a clerk, to a large Philadelphia hardware store run by the Rogers family.

Charles's tenure at the store was brief. He felt overworked, and his small, frail body soon wore out; ill health forced him to return to his father's house. Amasa Goodyear worked with his son as a business partner starting in 1826; together they sought to improve the farm tools of their era. During this time, in August of 1824, Charles married Clarissa Beecher, whose father was an innkeeper in Naugatuck.

Amasa Goodyear soon felt that his hardware sales were sufficiently good for him to open a branch store in Philadelphia. He sent his son to manage the new store; there the Goodyears sold only American-made goods, becoming the first United States hardware firm to eliminate British imports. Unfortunately, the young Goodyear's business sense was not acute. He often sold goods on credit, as did his father in Connecticut, and reached a point where his creditors became too numerous and he was deep in debt. Rather than declare bankruptcy (as the law allowed), he decided to pay off his debts gradually. When young Goodyear's creditors pressed for their money, he was put in debtor's prison for the first time. This was in 1830 in Philadelphia. Charles Goodyear would spend time in and out of debtor's prison for the next ten years.

During one of the times Goodyear was out of prison, in 1834, he traveled to New York to try to secure bank loans to pay his debts. He was caught in a harsh rainstorm on the streets of Manhatten and entered the Roxbury India Rubber Company to get dry. Inside the store, he noticed a life preserver made with a faulty valve. He purchased it, hoping to redesign the valve and impress the firm's owners. Perhaps they would pay him for his invention. Goodyear spent the next few weeks on this project, but when he returned to the Roxbury Company with a perfected valve, he was surprised to learn of the great difficulties the firm was having with rubber goods.

Rubber goods had been produced and marketed in the United States since 1830. The demand for these products was high, especially in New England, where residents wore rubber boots and raincoats. The gum rubber that was used to make these items, however, was a sticky substance that melted in the summer and froze in the winter. When Goodyear first contacted the Roxbury Company, it was closing down. Goodyear came away from this encounter with the idea of curing rubber so it could be used more readily for clothing, life preservers, and other goods.

Life's Work

When Charles Goodyear returned to his Philadelphia home in the summer of 1834, he began what would be a five-year period of experimenting to cure rubber. Because he was not trained in chemistry, his experiments were conducted on a trial-and-error basis. He worked in the kitchen of his small cottage, or in prison when he was confined there. He was fortunate in that gum rubber was inexpensive and plentiful. Goodyear had no tools, so he worked the rubber with his hands. He first mixed it with a variety of substances (one at a time) to see if he could eliminate its stickiness. The good properties of rubber that he wished to retain were its elasticity and flexibility, along with its strength. Among the items Goodyear mixed with rubber were sand, ink, castor oil, witch hazel, and even salt, pepper, and sugar.

When Goodyear tried a mixture of rubber, magnesia, and quicklime, he thought he had a successful type of rubber. It appeared smooth and flexible and was no longer sticky. He jubilantly announced his news of a discovery to the press. He even produced some small items from the mixture to display at two institute fairs in New York in 1835, the New York American Institute and the New York Mechanics' Institute. Although both fairs awarded Goodyear prize medals for his discovery, it soon proved to be a failure. This treated or "tanned" rubber, as he called it, was destroyed when any acid (even a very weak acid) came in contact with it.

Goodyear was not discouraged by this failure; rather, he continued to mix other substances with gum rubber to find a useful compound. So intent was he to promote his products that he would dress all in rubber.

The hardships Goodyear and his family endured while he worked to perfect rubber were many. They often had no shelter, at one point living in an abandoned rubber factory on Staten Island, or no food—neighbors reported seeing the Goodyear children digging in their gardens for half-ripe potatoes. They never had money; Goodyear sold furnishings and even his children's school books to purchase supplies.

The only way the family survived was by Goodyear's finding a series of financial backers for his experiments. Among the men who funded him were Ralph Steele of New Haven and later William de Forest, who had been a tutor to young Charles and later would become his brother-in-law. De Forest's total investment in Goodyear's work rose to almost fifty thousand dollars. Another pair of backers, William and Emery Ryder of New York, had to withdraw all their funds when the economic panic of 1837 ruined them financially.

On June 17, 1837, Goodyear had obtained a patent for a procedure to treat rubber that he called the "acid-gas process." The bankruptcy of the Ryder brothers shortly thereafter, however, gave Goodyear another setback—only a temporary one, however, for he soon met John Haskins in New York, who next helped him. Haskins was the

former owner of the Roxbury India Rubber Company; he still owned an empty factory in Roxbury, Massachusetts, and Goodyear and his family moved to nearby Woburn. Goodyear manufactured various rubber items using the acid-gas process; among the thin products he sold in 1838 were tablecloths and piano covers.

Goodyear had another meeting while he resided in Woburn. He became acquainted with Nathaniel Hayward, who had himself worked out a method of treating rubber. Hayward mixed gum rubber with sulphur and set the substance to dry in the sun; he called his process "solarization." Sharing their knowledge, Goodyear and Hayward began manufacturing what they believed to be permanent rubber products, no longer sticky and not likely to melt or freeze. As their reputation grew, the two men were awarded a United States government contract to produce 150 mailbags. After they had completed their order, they were disheartened to see that all the bags melted in the summer heat.

Ironically, although totally defeated (financially and publicly) by the mailbag disaster, Goodyear was very close to a successful curing of rubber. In the winter of early 1839, he accidentally dropped a piece of a ruined mailbag on the stove in his Woburn kitchen. He noticed that the sulphur-treated rubber did not melt, but charred as leather would when burned. Goodyear had worked long enough with rubber to realize he now had made a major breakthrough. The piece of charred rubber, when hung in the winter air overnight, also did not freeze.

The inventor still had a problem—no one, except his family, believed his new method was a success. Because of his past failures, the American press and any financial backers considered Goodyear a disturbed man who would never make a genuine discovery. It would be five more years before Charles Goodyear could slowly perfect his new treatment of rubber and have it patented on June 15, 1844. By that time, samples of Goodyear's new rubber had reached England, where one inventor, Thomas Hancock, had copied Goodyear's process. Hancock successfully obtained a British patent on this method of treating rubber, which he called "vulcanization," after the Roman god of fire, Vulcan.

Goodyear, however, did hold the American patent on vulcanization. When his countrymen began to realize that Goodyear finally had a truly usable product, he began to earn money. Royalties were paid to Goodyear by each company using his process to manufacture rubber goods in the United States.

Even after his great success with vulcanization, Charles Goodyear continued to spend large sums of money experimenting with rubber. After 1844, he concentrated on devising new rubber products. He also spent large sums of money promoting his products, especially in Europe. In 1855, Goodyear had built two elaborate exhibits abroad. In England, at the Crystal Palace Exhibition, he built a three-room Vulcanite Court completely furnished in rubber, at a cost of thirty thousand dollars. In France, at the Exposition Universelle in Paris, he constructed a similar exhibit for fifty thousand dollars. These expenditures, along with other debts, explain why Goodyear never became wealthy from his discovery of vulcanization.

Goodyear's wife Clarissa died in England in 1853, worn out by their lives of hardship and poverty; only six of their twelve children had survived to adulthood. Goodyear himself had always been a frail man, but in his final years he looked very old (although only in his fifties), and he had such severe gout and neuralgia that he could walk only with crutches for his last six years. He collapsed

and died in New York City on July 1, 1860, on the way to see his gravely ill daughter in New Haven.

Summary

It is ironic that Charles Goodyear's experiments with rubber aided Americans and all mankind so greatly and his family hardly at all. He was able to renew his patent on vulcanized rubber during his lifetime, but his heirs were refused renewals. The Goodyear Rubber Company, organized decades after his death, merely used his name to promote their rubber tires; the company was founded by strangers.

The rubber tire, so vital to modern transportation, is considered one of the most important outcomes of Goodyear's invention, as well as many other products essential to a life of good quality: in medicine, telecommunications, electronics—indeed, virtually every modern industry. It is difficult to imagine what daily life would be like without the availability of vulcanized rubber.

Bibliography

Beals, Carleton. *Our Yankee Heritage: New England's Contribution to American Civilization.* New York: McKay, 1955. Beals titles his chapter on Goodyear "Black Magic." In it, he emphasizes the inventor's personal life as well as his experimentation. This essay contains many details on Goodyear's family life not found in other sources. Beals also provides an analysis of Goodyear's character traits.

Chamberlain, John. *The Enterprising Americans: A Business History of the United States.* New York: Harper, 1963. Originally a series in *Fortune* magazine on famous American businessmen. In his lively and engaging account of Goodyear, the author places emphasis on the inventor's Yankee ingenuity. Includes a bibliography.

Fuller, Edmund. *Tinkers and Genius: The Story of Yankee Inventors.* New York: Hastings House, 1955. One book in a series called "The American Procession." The area on which Fuller focuses is New England and the mid-Atlantic states, from which many early inventors originated. The experiments made by Goodyear are explained simply but accurately and clearly; Fuller also shows Goodyear the man. Includes bibliography.

Gies, Joseph, and Frances Gies. *The Ingenious Yankees.* New York: Crowell, 1976. The authors focus on how America's Yankee inventors helped transform a farming country into a powerful technological nation. A biographical sketch of Goodyear is included, as well as an extensive bibliography.

Patterson, John C. *America's Greatest Inventors.* New York: Crowell, 1943. The author covers fully the lives and careers of eighteen inventors, including Goodyear. He includes interesting facts concerning Goodyear's work and personal difficulties, motivations, and thoughts.

Thompson, Holland. *The Age of Invention: A Chronicle of Mechanical Conquest.* New Haven, Conn.: Yale University Press, 1921. One volume in a series devoted to American life, history, and progress. It has a good-sized bibliography, as well as photographs and illustrations. Vivid descriptive passages of Goodyear at work are provided in the narrative of his life and work. Also details the workings of Goodyear's various experiments.

Trebilcock, B. "The India Rubber Man." *Yankee* (September 1989). Profile of Goodyear's life and career.

Wilson, Mitchell. *American Science and Invention: A Pictorial History.* New York: Simon and Schuster, 1954. A large volume which relies on period illustrations and photographs to describe the course of American invention. Concise and accurate on Goodyear's life as well as his discovery, with descriptions of how his experiments progressed. Also interesting on Goodyear's personal character.

Patricia E. Sweeney

CHARLES GEORGE GORDON

Born: January 28, 1833; Woolwich Common, England

Died: January 26, 1885; Khartoum, the Sudan

Area of Achievement: The military

Contribution: All the associations one might make with a man of the British Empire during the Victorian age—soldier, statesman, and adventurer—were forcefully expressed in the life of Charles Gordon.

Early Life

Charles George Gordon was born on January 28, 1833, in Kemp Terrace, Woolwich Common, England. He was the fourth son of eleven children born to Henry William Gordon and Elizabeth Enderby. His mother, for whom he had a very special affection, came from a rather prosperous merchant family, and his father was an officer in the Royal Artillery. His grandfather and great-grandfather had served in the military—the latter having fought with General James Wolfe at Quebec. It was hardly surprising, therefore, when young Gordon decided to follow in the steps of his paternal ancestors and chose to pursue his own career in the military.

At the age of fifteen, Gordon entered Woolwich Academy, where he soon became better known for his volatile temper and impetuous pranks than for his scholarly achievements. When he was graduated in 1852 as a sublieutenant in the Royal Engineers, he was posted first to Chatham and then to Pembroke. His first combat experience came in early 1855 in the Crimea, where he quickly established a reputation for bravery and almost reckless courage. He was cited for special distinction by his own government, received the French Legion of Honor, and won the friendship and admiration of future field marshal Garnet Wolseley.

Life's Work

After the war, Gordon spent almost two years in Bessarabia and Armenia surveying and mapping the new boundaries created by the 1856 Treaty of Paris. Following his return to England, he was promoted to captain and made adjutant at the headquarters of the Royal Engineers at Chatham. At age twenty-five, Gordon was described by those who knew him best as a man who was absolutely fearless, who possessed boundless energy, and who had a great capacity to adapt and survive under the most trying circumstances. His courage, energy,

and durability were attributes which would serve him well in the future. He was of average height—approximately five feet, nine inches—with brown curly hair, a small mustache, and a thin beard which served to accentuate a noticeably square jaw. Undoubtedly, Gordon's most striking physical feature was his vivid blue eyes, which, according to Wolseley, "seemed to court something while at the same time they searched the inner soul." Whatever the eyes may have disclosed about Gordon, they revealed to him a world cast in infinite shades of gray, for he was color-blind.

Gordon left his post at Chatham in July, 1860, when he was ordered to China, where the third in a series of trade wars between the British and the Chinese had been raging for almost two years. He arrived in Hong Kong in September, only two months before the conflict came to an end, and was subsequently assigned to the Tientsin area. In early 1863, he received permission from the British government to enter the service of the Chinese emperor, whose forces were attempting to crush the Taiping rebels. Assuming command of a rather modest force known pretentiously as the Ever Victorious Army, Gordon won a series of brilliant victories over the rebels and gave substance to what had earlier been an empty title. His campaigns in China made him at once a hero and a legend. The small rattan cane which he always carried into battle became known as the "Wand of Victory," and he would forever more be known as "Chinese Gordon."

When he returned to England in early 1865, Gordon received a grand reception from the British public but found himself almost ignored by the War Office. In fact, for the next ten years, he received assignments which hardly matched his demonstrated military abilities. He spent almost six years as Royal Engineer in command at Gravesend and later served for three years as Governor of Equatoria, where he waged a partially successful campaign to end the slave trade there.

Gordon had little more success with the slavers in the Sudan, where he served as governor-general from January, 1877, to January, 1880. During those three years, however, Gordon grew to love the Sudanese people and they to revere him. Appropriately enough, it would be in defense of the Sudan and its people that he would wage his last campaign in 1884-1885. In the years which intervened, the government once again seemed unable to find a place for him. He served briefly as secretary to Lord Ripon, Viceroy of India, returned to China in the summer of 1881, and in the spring of 1882, having been promoted to the rank of major general, went to South Africa to help bring the war with the Basuto to an end.

Gordon returned to England in the fall of 1882 for a brief visit, and in January, 1883, he traveled to Palestine, where he remained in virtual seclusion for almost a year. He both relished and needed this time, for though he was a public figure, Gordon remained throughout his life a very private individual. He once confided while in Cairo, following his appointment as Governor-General of the Sudan, that "the idea of dinner in Cairo makes me quail. I do not exaggerate when I say that ten minutes per diem is sufficient for all my meals and there is no greater happiness to me than when they are finished." Gordon was also a deeply religious man, though he never joined the Church or belonged to any particular sect. In his mind, "Catholic and Protestant are but soldiers in different regiments of Christ's army. . . ." He believed that the Bible was directly inspired by the Holy Spirit, and much of his time in Palestine was spent attempting to locate the exact site of the Crucifixion, the tomb of Christ, and the Garden of Eden. This proved to be a time for self-examination as well, and Gordon determined that he would make his life more "Christ-like."

Gordon decided while in Palestine that he would resign his commission and enter the service of Leopold II of Belgium for duty in the Congo. These plans changed, however, when he learned that Mohammed Ahmed—the self-proclaimed Mahdi or "Expected One"—had called for a Holy War in the Sudan and was marching on the capital of Khartoum. Though opinion in London was by no means unanimous, circumstances seemed to dictate that Gordon was the most logical choice to send to Khartoum. According to Lord Elton, a Gordon biographer, the harried government of William Ewart Gladstone found quite attractive the idea of sending "out the solitary, heroic figure, cane in hand, into the maelstrom of the Sudan."

Gordon left for Khartoum in January, 1884, under rather vague orders which required him to evacuate the city and report on the situation in the country. After reaching Khartoum, however, he attempted to hold the city hoping thereby to compel the government to send sufficient forces to crush the Mahdi. Sir Evelyn Baring, British Minister

Resident in Cairo, had earlier expressed some reservations about sending Gordon into the Sudan when he advised the Gladstone government that "a man who habitually consults the prophet Isaiah when he is in difficulties is not apt to obey the orders of any one." Whatever his reasons, Gordon did not evacuate the city, and Gladstone, though ultimately pressured into sending a relief force to Khartoum, did so too late. The city fell on January 26, 1885, and among those who perished defending it was General Charles Gordon.

Summary

It is difficult to imagine how Charles George Gordon might have been remembered had it not been for his heroic, if tragic, defense of Khartoum. History affords numerous examples, and this may be one, where an untimely death has intervened to save a deserving reputation and career from the ignominy of passing into history as an obscure and soon-forgotten footnote. Gordon will never endure that fate, though it is equally unlikely that he will enjoy the status of greatness accorded to one such as the first Duke of Marlborough or the Duke of

Wellington. He would appear to be more of the ilk of T. E. Lawrence or Orde Wingate—both of whom combined eccentricity with a certain genius much like that of Gordon himself.

Save for the Crimean War, imperial interests dominated British foreign policy during the latter half of the nineteenth century, and it was from the vast stage provided by the empire itself that Gordon won wide acclaim from an appreciative British public. His exploits inspired little such enthusiasm among members of Great Britain's political leadership, who, despite Gordon's demonstrated gifts as an officer of exceptional ability, a natural leader, and a progressive administrator, never felt comfortable with him.

Gordon was the embodiment of many of the values which dominated the Victorian age and may have considered himself to be, as he has been described, the epitome of the Christian warrior. Whether, at Khartoum, he died in defense of his empire or his faith is a question only he could have answered. To those who mourned him, it made little difference. Their emotions were best expressed in the words of Alfred, Lord Tennyson, whose epitaph for Gordon in Westminster Abbey reads:

Warrior of God, man's friend, not here below,but somewhere dead far in the waste SoudanThou livest in all hearts, for all men knowThis earth hath borne no simpler, nobler man.

Bibliography

Blunt, Wilfrid Scawen. *Gordon at Khartoum*. London: Swift, 1911; New York: Knopf, 1923. A contemporary of Gordon, Blunt was initially critical of the general. He later developed a more favorable appreciation of Gordon and his work, as reflected in this book.

Buchan, John A. *Gordon at Khartoum*. London: Davies, 1934. A sympathetic treatment of Gordon which focuses on his last days at Khartoum. Buchan assesses the tragedy of Khartoum in terms of general British policy and gives some insight into the personalities who shaped that policy.

Chenevix, Charles Trench. *The Road to Khartoum*. New York: Norton, 1979. The passage of time provides the historian with perspective and usually new sources of information. Chenevix uses both to good advantage in this well-researched and balanced treatment of Gordon and the empire he served.

Elton, Godfrey. *Gordon of Khartoum*. New York: Knopf, 1954. A well-written biography which scarcely conceals the author's great admiration for his subject. Elton does not overlook Gordon's many shortcomings, but neither does he dwell on them.

Forbes, Archibald. *Chinese Gordon: A Succinct Record of His Life*. New York: Funk and Wagnalls, and London: Routledge, 1884. This very descriptive account of Gordon's life was written before his death in the Sudan and provides, therefore, a rather incomplete analysis of his career.

Gordon, Charles George. *The Journals of Major-General C. G. Gordon, C.B. at Khartoum*. Edited by Egmont A. Hake. London: Kegan Paul, and Boston: Houghton Mifflin, 1885. Although these journals cover only the period between September 10 and December 14, 1884, they provide the best insight into Gordon's mind during his last days at Khartoum.

Hanson, Lawrence. *Chinese Gordon: The Story of a Hero*. New York: Funk and Wagnalls, 1954. An interesting, if somewhat superficial, treatment of Gordon which accords him the status of hero despite his personal faults.

Johnson, Douglas H. "In Search of Gordon's Head." *TLS*, no. 4713 (July 30, 1993). Short piece on Gordon's mysterious death at Khartoum, including the official version and various other versions of the story.

Strachey, Lytton. "The End of General Gordon." In *Eminent Victorians*. New York: Harcourt Brace, and London: Chatto and Windus, 1918. A controversial and critical treatment of Gordon which has been excoriated by the general's more ardent defenders—particularly Lord Elton.

Kirk Ford, Jr.

CHARLES GOUNOD

Born: June 18, 1818; Paris, France
Died: October 18, 1893; St. Cloud, France
Area of Achievement: Music
Contribution: Because of his great popularity and stylistic influence on the next generation of composers, Gounod is often considered to be the central figure in French music in the third quarter of the nineteenth century.

Early Life

Charles-François Gounod's father, Nicolas-François Gounod, was a gifted painter and winner of a Second Prix de Rome in 1783; his mother, Victoire Lemachois, a pianist, gave her son his early musical instruction. After completing his academic studies at the Lycée Saint-Louis, Charles Gounod received private musical training from composer-theorist Antoine Reicha; in 1836, when Gounod entered the Paris Conservatoire, he studied with such professors as Jacques Halévy (counterpoint), Jean-François Le Sueur (composition), and Pierre Zimmermann (piano). The extent of his musical education before entering the Paris Conservatoire, coupled with his exceptional talent, led him to win a Second Prix de Rome in 1837 and the Grand Prix de Rome two years later.

On December 5, 1839, Gounod left Paris for Rome; it was during his years in Rome that he met several women who played a significant role in his musical development. Felix Mendelssohn's married sister, Fanny Hensel, an accomplished pianist, introduced Gounod to the music of her brother, the music of Johann Sebastian Bach and Ludwig van Beethoven, as well as to the works of Johann Wolfgang von Goethe. Pauline Garcia was the sister of Maria Felicia Garcia Malibran, a singer who had been much admired by the young French artistic world before her death in 1836 at the age of twenty-eight. Pauline, besides being an excellent singer with a unique mezzo-soprano voice, was also married to Louis Viardot, director of the Théâtre-Italien and a valuable ally for a young composer. Yet another important influence in Gounod's life was the Dominican Friar Père Lacordaire. Lacordaire's sermons, which caused a great stir in Rome between the years 1838 and 1841, also impressed the young Gounod, whose sensibilities were constantly engaged in a battle between the sacred and the profane.

In the fall of 1842, Gounod left Rome for Vienna, where he received commissions for two masses, which were performed at the Karlskirche on November 2 (a requiem) and on March 25, 1843. During his stay in Vienna, Gounod had an opportunity to hear the Gewandhaus orchestra, probably the best orchestra in Europe at the time. Fortunate among French musicians of his generation, Gounod became acquainted with music, past and present, that was neither operatic nor within the French tradition.

After his return to Paris, Gounod became organist of the Missions Étrangères. Yet he soon found himself in conflict with congregations who viewed the music of Bach and Giovanni Palestrina, music which Gounod greatly admired, as strange and unattractive. At this time in his life, Gounod's inclinations as well as his work led him to frequent ecclesiastical circles. Undoubtedly, this fact, combined with the influence of Lacordaire's sermons, inspired his decision to study for the priesthood. Although he took courses at St. Sulpice be-

tween 1846 and 1848, Gounod later referred to this interest in the priesthood as but a passing fancy.

Life's Work

The music that Gounod wrote immediately after his ecclesiastical studies was still intended for the Church. When he discontinued his studies at St. Sulpice, however, he soon turned to the field cultivated by most French composers of his day, the opera. In fact, it was Pauline Viardot who persuaded him to write his first opera, *Sapho* (1851), by promising to sing the title role. Although Hector Berlioz praised the music, and another critic detected in it the influence of Christoph Gluck, the work was generally considered a failure.

Since her performance as Fides in *Le Prophète* in 1849, Pauline Viardot had been one of the favorite artists of Giacomo Meyerbeer, whose reputation in Paris was at its zenith. It is therefore not surprising that Gounod's next opera, *La Nonne sanglante* (1854), based on Matthew Lewis' *The Monk*, should have been crafted in the Meyerbeer tradition. Yet this opera also proved to be a failure. In the meantime, however, Gounod had written music for the choruses of François Ponsard's drama *Ulysse*, performed at the Comédie Française in 1852, and these earned for him an appointment as conductor of the largest male choir in Paris, L'Orphéon de la Ville de Paris. At this time he married Anna, the daughter of Pierre Zimmermann, who from 1820 to 1848 had been chief professor of the piano at the Paris Conservatoire.

During the decade 1855-1865, Gounod was at the height of his musical powers. In the area of church music, in which he had already succeeded, the *Messe solennelle de Sainte Cécile*, first performed on November 22, 1855, was a masterpiece in an ornate style which had come to replace the austere style in which he composed his early masses.

In 1858, Gounod began his association with the Théâtre-Lyrique, a theater founded in 1851 and dedicated to the performance of musico-dramatic works. Of the seven stage works that Gounod wrote between 1855 and 1865, five were first performed at the Théâtre-Lyrique; it is these five operas for which he is remembered more than a century later. Two of these are small-scale, lighthearted works in which his refined craftsmanship and unpretentious lyrical abilities were joined to well-known stories: Molière's play adapted by Jules Barbier and Michel Carré in *Le Médecin malgré lui* (1858) and the same adapters' version of

the classical myth in *Philémon et Baucis* (1860). In these, Gounod finally discarded his Meyerbeerian pretensions and cultivated his own unique brand of wit and lyricism. The same librettists wrote for him not only the comic opera *La Colombe* (1860) but also the far more important *Faust* (1859), the work by which the composer first became famous with the general public. The success of *Faust* had already opened the doors of the opera to Gounod. Yet it was only when he returned to the Théâtre-Lyrique and to the singer Marie Miolhan-Carvalho, who had sung the role of Marguerite in *Faust*, that Gounod scored two more major successes. The first was *Mireille* (1864), based on Frédéric Mistral's Provençal poem *Mirèio*, which had appeared in 1859. The second was the opera *Roméo et Juliette* (1867).

A disruption in Gounod's career as well as his private life came during the Franco-Prussian War of 1870-1871. On September 13, 1870, he and his family took refuge with English friends outside London. Although he was offered the directorship of the Conservatoire in June, 1871, it was not until June, 1874, that he returned to Paris.

While he never stopped writing occasional motets and cantatas for church use, he had written no mass since 1855; his major energies had been devoted to the opera. Even now it was an opera in which he eventually decided to incorporate for the first time his new musical ideals, which included writing music of tranquillity and feeling, music which transported the listener outside the realm of everyday life. While completing his opera *Polyeucte* (1878) in England, Gounod recognized the popularity of choral music in that country and was anxious to exploit both his own status as the composer of *Faust* and his experience as a choral conductor. Thus, when the Royal Albert Hall Choral Society was formed in 1871, Gounod became its first conductor. During this period in his life, Gounod was high in the royal favor (*Faust* was Queen Victoria's favorite opera) and was glad to indulge the demand for sentimental ballads popular in mid-Victorian England. He had already written the notorious *Bethléem* and *Jésus de Nazareth* in the mid-1850's; the *Méditation sur le prélude de S. Bach* (1852), from which come the endless arrangements of *Ave Maria*, was composed in 1852.

Gounod gave up all the advantages of his position in England, however, when, in February, 1871, he met Georgina Weldon, an amateur singer separated from her husband and well connected socially. Weldon sang the solo part in Gounod's patriotic cantata *Gallia* (1871) at the reopening of the Conservatoire and again at the Opéra-Comique that summer. When she returned to London in 1871, she took Gounod with her. He was installed in Tavistock House, Bloomsbury, which Weldon had taken for her projected National Training School of Music. Gounod was quite seriously ill at the time and responded with growing hysteria to the hectic life in which he found himself at the school. Yet, in spite of these conditions, he managed to write most of *Polyeucte*, the incidental music to Jules Barbier's *Jeanne d'Arc* (1873), a requiem, ten psalms and anthems, twelve choruses, and three songs and short pieces. Yet his social position was rapidly deteriorating. He was soon to enrage not only his own son, Jean, but also the English court as well when Weldon attempted to blackmail Queen Victoria into giving Gounod royal support for the Tavistock Academy and reinstatement in the Royal Albert Hall Choral Society after his falling out with the director.

For many reasons, then, Gounod's years in England seem to mark the end of his fruitfulness as a composer. As his ideals became loftier and his ideas more profound, his art became increasingly repetitive and platitudinous. The simplicity at which Gounod aimed in *Polyeucte* and *La Rédemption* (1882) disintegrated more and more into banality. Between 1882 and 1885, *La Rédemption* was performed all over Europe, including Vienna and Rome. Yet while it was immensely popular, it was sharply attacked by the critics. *Polyeucte* fared little better.

It was not until June, 1874, that Gounod finally returned to France after a frightening cerebral attack during which he lay unconscious for long periods of time. With failing eyes but much determination, he struggled to complete his last piece of music, a requiem for his grandson Maurice, who had died prematurely. While reading through the manuscript, Gounod lapsed into a coma and died two days later, on October 18, 1893.

Summary

In England, Charles Gounod had a strong and long-lasting influence on choral music, especially in the ecclesiastical and oratorio spheres, where *La Rédemption* occupied a prominent position in the 1880's. Like Giacomo Puccini and Richard Strauss a generation later, both Gounod and Mendelssohn expressed with skill and dignity the hopes and dreams of the contemporary bourgeoisie. The combination in *Faust* of tender sentiment and power of musical characterization with clean and imaginative craftsmanship made a deep impression on Peter Ilich Tchaikovsky, who owed almost as much to Gounod as to Georges Bizet and Léo Delibes.

Only a generation after Gounod's death, François Poulenc and Georges Auric were proclaiming as characteristically French the virtues of *Le Médecin malgré lui, La Colombe*, and *Philémon et Baucis* in their reaction against the music of Richard Wagner. All three works were revived by Sergei Diagilev in January, 1924. At the same time, a number of Gounod's songs were also revived; they have remained in the French repertory ever since. It was Gounod's belief that France was the country of "precision, neatness, and taste," and it is as a master of these qualities that he is best remembered.

Bibliography

Ashbrook, William. "An Article by Gounod: 'Composers as Conductors.' " *Opera Quarterly* 12, no. 4 (Summer 1996). Examines the prohibition in nineteenth century France against composers conducting their own works. The author argues that the official reasons cited can easily be reduced to prejudice and a desire to protect the conductors' rights.

Cooper, Martin. *French Music: From the Death of Berlioz to the Death of Fauré*. London and New York: Oxford University Press, 1951. Provides a historical perspective on French music and includes a brief section on Gounod. Offers a succinct overview of the composer's life. Contains a bibliography and a table of events listing the major composers and other artists (and their principal works) during the years 1870-1925.

Crichton, Ronald. "Old Sweet Song: with 'Faust,' Gounod Confirmed His Position as a Leading French Melodist." *Opera News* 61, no. 14 (April 5, 1997). Examines several Gounod compositions, in particular, "Faust," which has enjoyed renewed contemporary interest.

Gounod, Charles-François. *Memoirs of an Artist*. Translated by Annette E. Crocker. Chicago: Rand McNally, 1895. Gounod's intriguing but sentimental autobiography, spanning the years from his childhood to the writing of *Faust*.

Harding, James. *Gounod*. London: Allen and Unwin, and New York: Stein and Day, 1973. This informative biography discusses Gounod as a man of contradictions and extremes, demonstrating how the elements at war within his personality were reflected in his music. Assesses the impact of Gounod's music on later composers. Bibliography and appendix.

Hervey, Arthur. *Masters of French Music*. New York: Scribner, and London: Osgood, 1894. This work contains a lengthy chapter devoted to Gounod. The author also focuses his discussion on Gounod's *Faust*, especially on the themes of love and religion in the work.

Tiersot, Julien. "Charles Gounod: A Centennial Tribute." *Musical Quarterly* 6 (July 1918): 409-439. Tiersot examines the work and career of Gounod, as well as the man. Attempts to assess more objectively Gounod's contribution to French music.

Genevieve Slomski

WILLIAM GILBERT GRACE

Born: July 18, 1848; Downend, Gloucestershire,
England
Died: October 23, 1915; Eltham, Kent, England
Area of Achievement: Sports
Contribution: Grace's brilliance as a player, coupled with his immense personal popularity, consolidated cricket's position as England's national
game. He became a symbol of the manly com-
petitiveness which Victorians regarded as an essential element in the British character.

Early Life

William Gilbert Grace was born July 18, 1848, at
Downend, a village a few miles from Bristol. He
came from a cricketing family: His father, Henry
M. Grace, a doctor, was captain of a local team,
and his mother, Martha Pocock, was also devoted
to the game. Both parents coached Grace and his
brothers (two of whom also became famous players), and there was constant practicing in the orchard next to their house, with the family's dogs
helping with the fielding.

Grace received a few years of education at private schools in nearby villages, but cricket always
meant more to him than his studies. He was good
enough to play in adult matches at the age of ten,
and at fourteen, he made more than fifty runs
against the Somerset County XI, also distinguishing himself as a bowler in the same match. He
played against the All-England XI (a powerful
team of itinerant professionals) in that same year.
By 1864, he was well enough known to be selected
for major matches outside the Bristol area, and he
made his first big score, 170 runs, at the Oval
ground in London. Two years later, an even bigger
innings, 224 not out for the Rest of England
against Surrey, confirmed his reputation as the finest English batsman of his day.

A large man—six feet, two inches tall and powerfully built—Grace was a superb all-round athlete. He excelled in all aspects of cricket. Besides
being the greatest of English batsmen, he was also
a fine bowler—fast in his youth, later turning to deceptive slow spin bowling—and a brilliant fielder
with a magnificent throwing arm and huge hands
that made breathtaking catches at point-blank
range. As a young man, he regularly competed at
athletics meetings, once being given temporary
leave from an important cricket match at Lord's

ground to run in a 440-yard hurdles race, which he
duly won, at the Crystal Palace track. As a teenager, he was clean-shaven, but in his twenties he grew
the massive black beard that made him instantly
recognizable wherever he went.

Life's Work

Grace did more than anyone else to transform
cricket from the relatively primitive stage that it
had reached when he burst on the scene into something close to its modern form. Until the 1860's,
cricket had been dominated for many years by two
professional touring clubs—the All England XI
and the United England XI—which played exhibition games against local teams. By the mid-1860's,
however, county clubs containing a mixture of amateurs ("Gentlemen") and professionals ("Players") were growing in both strength and popularity. In 1873, the County Championship, a league of
nine teams (by the end of Grace's career the number had grown to sixteen), was formed to meet the

971

public appetite for more competitive cricket. Increased opportunities for leisure activities for both the middle and working classes, improved communications following the development of the railway, and widespread newspaper publicity combined to make cricket an extremely popular spectator sport.

Grace dominated the County Championship in its early years as no player since his time has ever done. His brilliant batting and astute leadership enabled his county, Gloucestershire, to win the championship four times in the first eight seasons. Year after year, he headed the national batting averages, sometimes with an average more than double that of his nearest rival, making light of the rough and physically dangerous conditions of many of the grounds on which he played. Before this time, an individual score of more than one hundred was almost unheard-of; Grace made it commonplace, occasionally going on to score a double or even a triple century. Crowds flocked to see him, the county clubs prospered financially, and no benefit game for a needy professional was complete without him.

Although Grace's career flowered before the beginning of regular international cricket, he played a major role in promoting the game's popularity in other countries. He was one of a team which toured the United States and Canada in 1872, he took part in two tours of Australia, and, when the regular series between England and Australia began in the 1880's, he was an automatic first choice for the England team. By then, he was devoting a bit less time to the game. In 1873, he married Agnes Nicholls Day, and during the next few years, he qualified as a doctor at Bristol Medical School and two London hospitals, St. Bartholemew's and Westminster. Yet he still captained England in five series against Australia, winning four of them, and continued to represent his country until he was past fifty. Many of his greatest triumphs occurred in the annual exhibition matches between the Gentlemen and the Players (the amateurs against the professionals). Before 1864, the Players had won twenty-two of the previous twenty-five games; from 1867, the Gentlemen were victorious in seventeen of the next twenty-five, several of which Grace won almost single-handedly.

Grace's dominance was founded on two things: technical mastery and power of personality. His contribution to batting technique was thus described by the great Indian batsman, K. S. Ranjitsinghi:

> He revolutionized batting. He turned it from an accomplishment into a science. . . . What W. G. did was to unite in his mighty self all the good points of all the good players, and to make utility the criterion of style. He founded the modern theory of batting.

Great physical strength, superb coordination, high technical skill, immense powers of concentration, and a certain ruthlessness: That was the formula that made "W.G." (as he was known to legions of admirers) and led one despairing opponent to declare that he ought to be made to play with a smaller bat.

Assessments of Grace's personality are more ambiguous. The crowds adored him, and those who knew him well thought him a genial, straightforward person, with a genuinely kind heart. Yet from some of the stories told about him it may seem surprising that he was a folk hero to followers of a game in which fair play and good sportsmanship were (and are) prized above all else. His high-pitched voice (another curious feature of so huge a man) was often raised in arguments with umpires, and he was said to "talk out" opposing batsmen by methods that certainly bordered on the unfair. He never actually went outside the laws, but an old professional once observed that it was wonderful what he could do inside them.

For someone who was ostensibly not paid for playing, Grace also made much money from cricket. There was always a clear distinction between the working-class amateur who played for money and the upper-class amateur who played for the love of the game, but the middle-class Grace seems to have been exempt from this. He always received lavish expenses, and after he began to practice medicine in Bristol in 1879 (with a substitute on call when Grace was away playing cricket), he was the recipient of several generously subscribed testimonial funds, the biggest of them after his spectacularly successful 1895 season. A malicious cartoon by Sir Max Beerbohm depicts the great "amateur" receiving a handsome check, with the funeral of one of his patients in the background. Yet the patients do not seem to have complained; when available, Grace was devoted to their welfare, and they could bask in the reflected glory of being treated, at least occasionally, by England's most famous sportsman.

The year 1895 was Grace's "golden summer," in which, at the age of forty-seven, he completely recovered his old form and broke yet more batting records. That season was a brief interruption, however, in a slow and inevitable decline. In 1899, he lost his place on the England team (he had put on so much weight that he could no longer field effectively), and during the same year he broke with Gloucestershire to run his own team, London County, which played a few seasons of exhibition matches. He still appeared in the Gentlemen-Players matches until 1904, played his last first-class match at the age of fifty-eight, and turned out in local club games at Eltham, where he was then living, until 1914. Before the end of his first-class career, he had taken up golf and bowls, achieving some prominence in the latter sport: He was President of the English Bowling Association in 1903 and captained the national team for two seasons.

Grace's later years were darkened first by the deaths of his daughter in 1898 and his eldest son in 1905, and then by the outbreak of World War I. A patriotic Englishman, Grace wrote to *The Sportsman* newspaper in August, 1914, urging younger cricketers to volunteer, but soon he was mourning the slaughter of many of them in the carnage of Flanders. He seems to have lost the vitality and zest for life that had been so marked a feature of his character, and after a stroke, he died at Eltham on October 23, 1915.

Summary

William Gilbert Grace was one of the most famous Englishmen of the Victorian Age. His great black-bearded figure, with cricket cap perched over his forehead, was known to millions, more familiar from cartoons in *Punch* and the sporting press than even the most celebrated statesman or military hero. He captured the public imagination and epitomized the spirit of vigorous, good-natured competition that, its adherents liked to think, was at the heart of the Victorian value system. Cricket was becoming a major ingredient in the cult of "muscular Christianity" instilled into generations of English school-boys; Grace provided the hero figure necessary for that cult's success.

Grace was also a powerful symbol of national unity. Cricket already differed from other sports in that working-class professionals played alongside aristocratic amateurs, although the latter naturally controlled the organization of the game. Grace was undeniably middle-class, but he became immensely popular among people of all classes: Admiration for his heroic deeds was something in which everyone could share. He thus contributed to a sense of English identity transcending class divisions, and indirectly promoted the growing spirit of patriotic nationalism on which mass support for British imperialism was built. Grace created modern cricket, but he also stood high in the ranks of Victorian heroes.

Bibliography

Altham, Harry Suntees, and E. W. Swanton. *A History of Cricket.* 2 vols. London: Allen and Unwin, 1926. A fine, detailed account of cricket history. Altham's volume is in three parts, the middle one being appropriately entitled "The Age of Grace."

Arlott, John, ed. *The Oxford Companion to World Sports and Games.* London and New York: Oxford University Press, 1975. Contains a good, short description of cricket and its history, with illustrations and also a brief entry on Grace.

Craig, Simon. "Amazing Grace." *In Britain* 8, no. 7 (July 1998). Profile of Grace's life and career.

Darwin, Bernard. *W.G. Grace.* London: Duckworth, 1934. Darwin was primarily an expert on golf but also wrote extensively on cricket. This is a short but elegantly written biography, lively and interesting, maintaining a clear narrative line, with lavish illustrations. The best written of the numerous Grace biographies.

Davis, H.W.C., and J.R.H. Weaver, eds. *Dictionary of National Biography: Supplement, 1912-1921.* London and New York: Oxford University Press, 1927. The entry on Grace sets out the essential facts of his life, apart from being rather weak on his later years. Also rather uncritical, ignoring the questions about Grace's amateur status and the charges that he sometimes bent the rules.

Grace, W.G. *Cricket.* Bristol: Arrowsmith, 1891. Partly autobiographical, partly a history of cricket, with comments on the players Grace knew and the issues confronting the game around 1890. Contains statistics of Grace's career until that year as well as many interesting anecdotes.

Menke, Frank G., ed. *The Encyclopedia of Sports.* 6th ed. New York: Doubleday, 1977. Contains a very brief description and history of cricket, useful as an introduction for the uninitiated. Grace is mentioned, but his full significance is not made clear.

Thomson, Arthur Alexander. *The Great Cricketer.* 2d ed. London: Hutchinson, 1968. A competent and thorough narrative of Grace's career, followed by chapters summarizing his achievements as cricketer, doctor, and "eminent Victorian." Useful for personal details as well as for the explanation of cricket; Thomson makes some effort to place Grace in historical context.

David Underdown

ULYSSES S. GRANT

Born: April 27, 1822; Point Pleasant, Ohio
Died: July 23, 1885; Mount McGregor, New York
Areas of Achievement: Government and military affairs
Contribution: Grant became the preeminent general of the Civil War, demonstrating the persistence and strategic genius that brought about the victory of the North.

Early Life

Ulysses S. Grant, born Hiram Ulysses Grant on April 27, 1822, in Point Pleasant, Ohio, was the eldest child of Jesse Root Grant and Hannah Simpson Grant. His father had known poverty in his youth, but at the time of his first son's birth, he had established a prosperous tannery business. In 1823, Jesse moved his business to Georgetown, Ohio, where Grant spent his boyhood. He received his preliminary education at Georgetown, at Maysville Seminary in Maysville, Kentucky, and at the Presbyterian Academy, Ripley, Ohio. He did not show special promise as a student and lived a rather ordinary boyhood. His most outstanding gift turned out to be a special talent with horses, enabling him to manage the most fractious horse. He also developed a strong dislike for work at the tannery and a lifelong fondness for farming.

Jesse Grant secured an appointment for his son to the United States Military Academy at West Point in 1839. His son did not want to go but bowed to parental authority. Concerned about the initials on his trunk, "H.U.G.," he decided to change his name to Ulysses Hiram Grant. Arriving at West Point, Grant had his first skirmish with military bureaucracy. His congressman, evidently confusing Grant with his brother Simpson, had appointed him as Ulysses S. Grant. The army insisted that Ulysses S. Grant, not Ulysses H. or Hiram Ulysses, had been appointed, and eventually Grant surrendered. Grant wrote to a congressman in 1864: "In answer to your letter of a few days ago asking what 'S' stands for in my name I can only state *nothing*."

He was graduated in the middle of his class in 1843. While at West Point, he developed a fondness for novels and showed a special talent for mathematics. Appointed a brevet second lieutenant in the Fourth United States Infantry, Grant served with distinction in the Mexican War (1846-1848). He fought in the battles of Palo Alto, Resaca de la Palma, and Monterrey under the command of Zachary Taylor, "Old Rough and Ready." Taylor impressed Grant with his informal attire and lack of military pretension, a style which Grant later adopted. He participated in all major battles leading to the capture of Mexico City and won brevet promotion to first lieutenant for bravery at Molino Del Rey and to captain for his behavior at Chapultepec. Although he fought with distinction, Grant believed that the Mexican War was unjust and later said that he should have resigned his commission rather than participate.

Grant married Julia Dent, the daughter of a St. Louis slaveholding family, on August 22, 1848. He had been introduced to his future wife in 1843, by her brother, a West Point classmate, while stationed at Jefferson Barracks, Missouri. The Mexican War, however, interrupted their romance. The Grants had four children, Frederick Dent, Ulysses S. Jr., Ellen Wrenshall, and Jesse Root, Jr. A devoted husband and father, Grant centered his life on his family. Indeed, the many surviving letters to his wife during absences caused by a military career provide the most poignant insights into the man.

Ordered to the Pacific Coast in 1852 with his regiment, Grant could not afford to take his wife and children. He grew despondent without his family, decided to resign his commission in 1854, and returned to live on his wife's family land near St. Louis to take up farming. For the remainder of Grant's life, rumors that he had been forced to resign on account of heavy drinking followed him. The next seven years were difficult for Grant. His attempt at farming did not work out, and he tried other occupations without real success. Finally, in 1860, he moved his family to Galena, Illinois, to work as a clerk in a leather-goods store owned by his father and operated by his two younger brothers.

Grant had never been a strident, political man. His father had been an antislavery advocate, yet Grant married into a slaveholding family. At one time, he owned a slave but gave him his freedom in 1858 at a time when Grant sorely needed money. His wife retained ownership of slaves throughout the Civil War. When news of the firing on Fort Sumter reached Galena, Grant believed that he had an obligation to support the Union. Because of his military experience, he assisted in organizing and escorting a volunteer company to Springfield, Illinois, where he stayed on to assist Governor Richard Yates in mustering in and organizing volunteer troops. Eventual-

ly, Yates appointed Grant colonel of the Twenty-first Illinois Volunteers, a disorganized and undisciplined unit. Grant quickly worked the regiment into shape, marched it to Missouri, and learned much about commanding volunteer soldiers.

Life's Work

On August 7, 1861, President Abraham Lincoln appointed Grant brigadier general, and Grant established headquarters at Cairo, Illinois, an important staging area for Union movement farther south. On September 6, he occupied Paducah, Kentucky, near the strategic confluence of the Tennessee, Cumberland, and Ohio rivers. Grant's first battle followed shortly. He attacked Confederate forces at Belmont, Missouri, with mixed results. He lost control of his troops after initial success and had to retreat when Confederate reinforcements arrived.

Grant gained national prominence in February, 1862, when authorized to operate against Fort Donelson and Fort Henry, guarding the Cumberland and Tennessee rivers, obvious highways into the Confederate heartland. He moved his small army in conjunction with naval forces and captured Fort Henry on February 6 and immediately moved overland against Fort Donelson, twelve miles away. The Confederates attempted to escape encirclement on February 15 in a brief, but bloody, battle. On February 16, the Confederate commander asked Grant for surrender terms. His response brought him fame: "No terms except an unconditional and immediate surrender can be accepted." The Confederates surrendered on Grant's terms, and Lincoln rewarded him for the first significant Union victory with promotion to major general.

Grant's next major engagement, the battle of Shiloh, April 6-7, left him under a cloud. Surprised by Rebel forces, Grant suffered heavy losses but managed to rally his army on the first day. The second day, General Grant counterattacked and drove the Confederates from the field. This bloody engagement cast a long shadow, and Grant faced newspaper criticism, with rumors of his heavy drinking appearing in the press. Major General Henry W. Halleck arrived on the scene to take command of Grant's forces, placing him in a subordinate position with little to do. Grant considered leaving the army. He retained his humor, however, writing to his wife, "We are all well and me as sober as a deacon no matter what is said to the contrary." Halleck, however, was called to Washington to act as general in chief, and Grant resumed command. Although many had criticized Grant, Lincoln refused to relieve a fighting general, thus setting the stage for Grant's finest campaign.

Confederate control of the Mississippi River rested on extensive fortifications at Vicksburg, Mississippi, effectively barring Midwestern commerce. In the fall and spring of 1862-1863, Grant made a number of attempts against this bastion. The overland campaign through northern Mississippi came to grief when Confederate forces destroyed his supply base at Holly Springs, Mississippi, on December 20, 1862. Grant then decided to move down the Mississippi to attack the city. Ultimately, Grant bypassed the city, marching his army down the west bank of the river. At night, he sent steamboats past the batteries to assist in crossing the river from Louisiana into Mississippi. The general then launched a lightning campaign into the interior of the state to destroy Confederate communications before turning back against Vicksburg. Thoroughly confusing his opposition, he won five separate battles and besieged the city on May 19. On July 4, 1863, Grant accepted the surrender of his second Confederate army.

After a brief respite, Grant was given command of all Union forces in the West on October 18 and charged with rescuing Union forces besieged in Chattanooga, Tennessee. In a three-day battle (November 23-25), Grant smashed the Confederate forces and drove them back into Georgia.

In March, 1864, Lincoln promoted Grant to lieutenant general and gave him command of all Union armies. Grant left Halleck at Washington as chief of staff to tend to routine matters and established the beginning of a modern military command system. He stayed in the field with the Army of the Potomac, commanded by Major General George G. Meade. Grant made Union armies work in tandem for the first time. Using the telegraph, he managed troop movements across the country, keeping pressure on the Confederacy at all points. The two major efforts consisted of Major General William T. Sherman, moving against Atlanta, and Meade attacking Confederate forces in Virginia, commanded by the South's finest general, Robert E. Lee.

The final campaign opened in May, 1864, with the battle of the Wilderness (May 5-6). After a series of bloody engagements, Grant maneuvered Lee into Petersburg, Virginia, where siege operations commenced on June 16. While Grant held Lee at Petersburg, Sherman proceeded to gut the South, capturing Atlanta in September, then marching across Georgia and capturing Savannah in December. Grant then planned for Sherman to march his army up through the Carolinas into Virginia. On March 29, 1865, Grant launched his final campaign. He smashed Confederate lines at Petersburg, then tenaciously pressured the retreating Confederates, and accepted Lee's surrender at Appomattox Court House on April 9. Grant's magnanimous surrender terms attest to his humanity and sensitivity. Seventeen days later, the last major Confederate force surrendered to Sherman and the Civil War ended.

Lincoln's assassination on April 14 deeply affected Grant, but he believed that President Andrew Johnson would be able to reestablish the Union on an equitable basis. Grant busied himself with the reorganization of the army, threatening French forces operating in Mexico, marshaling forces to fight Indians, and seeking to avoid political questions. Yet he could not avoid the growing antagonism between Johnson and the radical Republicans. Increasing doubts about Johnson's Reconstruction policy brought the two men into conflict. In the face of growing Southern persecution of blacks, Grant came to believe that blacks had to be protected by the federal government. In 1868, the breach between Johnson and Grant became public, and Grant believed that it was his duty to accept the Republican nomination for president.

A reluctant candidate, Grant easily defeated his Democratic opponent. His military background, however, had left him with a distaste for the hurly-burly of politics, and his two-term presidency (March 4, 1869, to March 4, 1877) had many problems. Already convinced of the need to protect blacks, Grant sought in vain to advance Civil Rights for them. With the Force Acts (1870-1871), he succeeded in breaking up the first Ku Klux Klan, but by 1876, conservative Southerners had regained control and reasserted their dominance.

In foreign policy, Grant did much to normalize relations with Great Britain with the Treaty of Washington in May, 1871, which settled the *Alabama* claims arising out of the Civil War. His stubbornness and persistence, which had served him so well in war, however, proved to be an embarrassment in his unsuccessful attempts to annex Santo Domingo.

Grant made a number of unfortunate appointments to federal office, and official corruption even reached into the White House with the Whiskey Ring Scandal. Although Grant was not personally involved, these scandals tainted his second term. Plagued by corruption and politics, Grant resisted attempts to draft him for a third term in 1876.

After the presidency, Grant made a two-year journey around the world, indulging a passion for travel developed early in his life. This triumphant tour brought him worldwide renown. Restless after returning to the United States, he unsuccessfully sought a third term in 1880. He then moved to New York City to pursue business interests in connection with his son, Ulysses S. Grant, Jr., and became a silent partner in Grant and Ward. Ferdinand Ward turned out to be a swindler, and in 1884, Grant found himself penniless.

To support his family, Grant decided to write his memoirs. At about the same time, Grant learned that he had contracted cancer of the throat. He completed the manuscript only days before his death, on July 23, 1885. This work has become a literary classic and is recognized as one of the best military memoirs ever written.

Summary

Grant's boyhood had been ordinary, showing nothing of the extraordinary man he would become. He had not sought a military career and did not like things military. He detested military parades, disliked military dress, and rarely carried a weapon. He left the army in 1854 and suffered through seven years of disappointment. The outbreak of Civil War, for all its national trauma, rescued Grant from a life of obscurity.

This seemingly common man turned out to have a genius for war unmatched by his contemporaries. Grant perhaps had an advantage in that he had time to learn gradually the art of war. Grant made mistakes, learned from them, and never repeated them. He grew into the responsibilities of higher command. He also understood volunteer soldiers and their motivations for fighting.

Grant's military writings are extraordinary. His instructions are clear, brief, and to the point. Subordinates made mistakes, but not because of ambiguity of instruction. Grant became the finest general that the Civil War produced, indeed, the greatest American military figure of the nineteenth century.

The Grant presidency had many shortcomings. Not a politician, Grant never really understood presidential power and its uses. In this sense, he was a nineteenth century man: He believed that Congress decided policy and the president executed it. Had Grant viewed the presidency in the same manner that he perceived military command, his two terms might have been far different.

Grant returned to wartime form in the fight to complete his memoirs. This literary classic is really a gift to the ages as he again demonstrated that he was truly an extraordinary American.

Bibliography

Arnold, James R. *Grant Wins the War: Decision at Vicksburg*. New York: Wiley, 1997. Arnold focuses on the impact of Grant's victory at Vicksburg and the battle's effective elimination of the South as a threat.

Catton, Bruce. *Grant Moves South*. Boston: Little Brown, 1960. This biography of Grant, covering his early Civil War career, is thoroughly researched and superbly written.

———. *Grant Takes Command*. London: Dent, and Boston: Little Brown, 1969. Catton continues his brilliant work, taking Grant from Chattanooga to Appomattox.

Garland, Hamlin. *Ulysses S. Grant: His Life and Character*. New York: Doubleday, 1898. This nineteenth century biography of Grant is among the best written. It is especially valuable because the author interviewed a number of Grant contemporaries.

Grant, Ulysses S. *The Papers of Ulysses S. Grant*. Edited by John Y. Simon. Carbondale: Southern Illinois University Press, 1967- . Fourteen volumes of this comprehensive series have been published, following Grant through April 30, 1865. This work makes it possible to evaluate Grant's career using documentary sources and demonstrates that Grant's literary flair in his memoirs was not a fluke.

———. *Personal Memoirs of U.S. Grant*. 2 vols. New York: Webster, 1885-1886; London: Constable, 1995. These volumes are magnificent from both a literary and a historical perspective. Grant's assessment of his life through the Civil War is powerful, compelling, and amazingly accurate.

Hesseltine, William B. *Ulysses S. Grant: Politician*. New York: Dodd, Mead, 1935. This highly critical account of Grant's presidency reflects the historical scholarship of the 1930's.

Lewis, Lloyd. *Captain Sam Grant*. Boston: Little Brown, 1950. This beautifully written biography examines Grant's life up to the Civil War. Catton takes over where Lewis left off.

McFeely, William S. *Grant: A Biography*. New York: Norton, 1981. A well-written biography that uses modern standards to judge Grant harshly, emphasizing what Grant should have done to protect black civil rights during Reconstruction.

Porter, Horace. *Campaigning with Grant*. New York: Century, 1897. Written by a Grant staff officer, this account is excellent for a personal view of Grant during the last eighteen months of the war.

Young, John Russell. *Around the World with General Grant*. 2 vols. New York: American News Company, 1879. Although there is considerable padding in these volumes, they have real significance because of the author's numerous interviews with Grant.

David L. Wilson

ASA GRAY

Born: November 18, 1810; Sauquoit, New York
Died: January 30, 1888; Cambridge, Massachusetts
Area of Achievement: Science
Contribution: The leading botanical taxonomist in nineteenth century United States and the founder of the discipline of plant geography, Gray was the first advocate of Darwinian evolution in the United States.

Early Life

The son of Moses Gray, a tanner, and Roxana Howard Gray (New Englanders who had migrated to upstate New York after the Revolutionary War), Asa Gray was born on November 18, 1810, in Sauquoit, New York. Educated at local schools and academies, Gray entered the College of Physicians and Surgeons of the Western District of New York in 1826. Alternating attendance at the lectures at the medical school with apprenticeship with practicing physicians, Gray received his medical degree in January, 1831.

Slight, short, and clean-shaven until his middle age, Gray was physically agile and appeared ever-youthful. This physical agility was matched by his mental quickness. Complementing these traits was a self-assuredness which led him to abandon medical practice in 1832 to follow his dream of becoming a botanist.

Life's Work

Gray's interest in botany had been sparked by James Hadley, one of the faculty at the College of Physicians and Surgeons, but his real mentor was John Torrey, one of the outstanding American botanists. After a tryout in 1832, Torrey hired Gray the following year to collect specimens for him. Ultimately, Gray moved into the Torrey home and became Torrey's collaborator on his *Flora of North America* (1838-1843).

Finding employment as a scientist in the 1830's was not easy. For the first few years after he rejected a medical career, Gray supported himself through part-time teaching and library jobs. In 1836, he was selected as botanist on the United States Exploring Expedition but resigned the position in 1838, before the expedition ever sailed, disgusted by the delays which had plagued the venture. Instead, he became professor of botany (the first such professorship in the United States) at the University of Michigan, spending the next year in Europe purchasing books and equipment for the university. The university's financial problems resulted, however, in the suspension of his salary in 1840, before he had ever taught a class. Not until April, 1842, with his appointment as Fisher Professor of Natural History at Harvard University, with responsibility for teaching botany and maintaining the botanical gardens, did Gray obtain a stable and permanent institutional home. He remained at Harvard (which also indirectly supplied him with his wife, Jane Lathrop Loring, the daughter of a leading Boston lawyer who was a member of the Harvard Corporation) for the rest of his life.

Manifest Destiny helped shape the contours of Gray's scientific career: Overseas exploration and domestic reconnaissance and surveying during the two decades before the Civil War had resulted in a huge flow eastward of botanical specimens gathered by army engineers, naval explorers, and collectors accompanying the expeditions. Gray spent most of his professional life worrying about the nomenclature and taxonomy of these plants. Through either

his own research or the coordination of the activities of other botanists, he was responsible for the description of flora gathered from Japan to Mexico.

By the 1850's, Gray was clearly the leading botanist in the United States. He was the cement that held together a huge network of amateur collectors. His publications included the *Manual of the Botany of the Northern United States* (1848) and extremely popular textbooks for college, high school, and elementary school students. A frequent visitor to Europe, he was well-known in international scientific circles.

The opportunity for Gray's greatest contribution to science came about because of his international reputation, but his connection with this flow of specimens enabled him to exploit fully the opportunity. Charles Darwin had written him in April, 1855, inquiring about the geographical distribution of Alpine plants in the United States. In response, Gray produced a statistical analysis of the flora of the northern United States, drawing on his wide knowledge of the botany of the Northern Hemisphere. This in turn encouraged Darwin in 1857 to let Gray in on his great secret—the theory of evolution.

At this point, Gray had in hand an extensive collection from Japan, gathered by Charles Wright during the North Pacific Exploring Expedition, as well as smaller collections from Matthew C. Perry's expedition, which opened up Japan. Gray discerned that the flora of Japan was much more similar to that of eastern North America than western North America or Europe. He rejected the possibility of separate creation and, applying Darwin's ideas, proposed instead that the similarities reflect the evolution of the flora from common ancestry under similar conditions. A single flora, Gray theorized, had stretched round the earth before the Ice Age; changing geological conditions resulted in the differences in Northern Hemispheric flora.

This public endorsement of Darwin in early 1859, the first in the United States, was followed by many others. Gray quickly became the leading American spokesman for Darwin's theory, and he negotiated the American publishing contract for *On the Origin of Species by Means of Natural Selection* (1859). Moreover, the review of this work in the *American Journal of Science*, the leading American scientific journal of the day, was written by Gray. Time and again he debated the leading anti-evolutionist in the American scientific community, the Swiss-born Louis Agassiz, director of Harvard's Museum of Comparative Zoology. In 1860, in a series of articles in *The Atlantic Monthly*, Gray defended Darwin from critics who charged that the theory of evolution was hostile to religion, taking a position on the compatibility of Darwinian evolution with theism which the author of the theory himself was unable ultimately to accept.

After his retirement from teaching in 1873, Gray continued his research and field trips. He spent six triumphant months in Europe in 1887, returning to the United States in October. A month later, he was taken ill and died in his home in Cambridge on January 30, 1888. He left behind the Harvard Botanic Garden, the Gray Herbarium, and a generation of botanists and collectors for whom he had provided training, guidance, and assistance.

Summary

Asa Gray was fortunate to be a botanist in the United States at a time when the expansionist drive of the nation resulted in its soldiers and sailors crisscrossing the North American continent and the Pacific Ocean. Describing the botanical fruits of these exploring and surveying expeditions was Gray's lifelong work. His skill helped set American botany on a par with its European counterparts. Prodded by Charles Darwin, he asked some important questions about plant distribution which led to the development of a new scientific field and further evidence for the evolutionary thought of Darwin.

Gray's greatest impact on American society, however, was as the defender of Darwin's theory of evolution. Gray, a member of the First Congregation Church of Cambridge, understood that if evolution was to be accepted by the deeply religious American scientific community of the mid-nineteenth century, it would have to be reconciled with a belief in the existence of God. Gray believed that Darwin's theory, whatever its scientific merits, had to be defended from accusations of atheism. His solution was to suggest that the Creator intervened by limiting or directing variations. Darwin could not accept such an interpretation, however, and Gray's vision died with him. If Darwin had made another choice, the intellectual, cultural, and philosophical history of the West might have taken a course much different from that which it subsequently followed.

Bibliography

Croce, Jerome. "Probalistic Darwinism: Louis Agassiz *v.* Asa Gray on Science, Religion, and Certainty." *Journal of Religious History* 22, no.

1 (February 1998). Discusses the views held by Louis Agassiz and Gray on Darwinism and its interface with Christianity.

Dupree, A. Hunter. *Asa Gray: 1810-1888.* Cambridge, Mass.: Belknap Press of Harvard University Press, 1968. The standard biography, well documented, interpretive, and accurate. Views Gray within the context of the social and intellectual history of the United States.

Eyde, Richard H. "Expedition Botany: The Making of a New Profession." In *Magnificent Voyagers: The U.S. Exploring Expedition, 1838-1842*, edited by Herman J. Viola and Carolyn Margolis, 25-41. Washington, D.C.: Smithsonian Institution Press, 1985. Discusses the problems surrounding the botanical activities of the expedition.

Glattstein, Judy. "My American Cousin." *American Gardener* 76, no. 3 (May-June 1997). Describes Gray's discovery of similar plant species in the United States and Japan and the significant theories that resulted from it.

Goetzmann, William H. *Exploration and Empire: The Explorer and the Scientist in the Winning of the American West.* New York: Knopf, 1966. A well-researched history of American exploration in the nineteenth century and the scientific discoveries which were its by-product. Although Gray is mentioned only briefly, this book describes the context of much of his scientific efforts.

Gray, Asa. *Darwiniana.* Edited by A. Hunter Dupree. Cambridge, Mass.: Belknap Press of Harvard University Press, 1963. A collection of Gray's essays on evolution, first published in 1876. Essential for understanding Gray's attempt to reconcile evolution and religion.

————. *The Letters of Asa Gray.* Edited by Jane Loring Gray. 2 vols. Boston: Houghton Mifflin, and London: Macmillan, 1893. This collection, edited by Gray's widow, includes Gray's autobiography.

Loewenberg, Bert James. "The Reaction of American Scientists to Darwinism." *American Historical Review* 38 (1933): 687-701. Dated, but still useful. Focuses on three representative figures: Gray, Agassiz, and James Dwight Dana, who was an example of those scientists who initially rejected evolution but eventually changed their position.

Lurie, Edward. *Louis Agassiz: A Life in Science.* Chicago: University of Chicago Press, 1960. The essential biography of Darwin's chief American scientific opponent.

Rodgers, Andrew Denny, III. *American Botany, 1873-1892: Decades of Transition.* Princeton, N.J.: Princeton University Press, and London: Oxford University Press, 1914. Discusses the evolution of American botany from a descriptive to an experimental science and Gray's role in that transition.

————. *John Torrey: A Story of North American Botany.* Princeton, N.J.: Princeton University Press, and London: Oxford University Press, 1942. A scholarly, although somewhat dated biography of Gray's mentor. Provides an excellent account of Torrey's scientific accomplishments and his role in developing American botany.

Marc Rothenberg

HORACE GREELEY

Born: February 3, 1811; Amherst, New Hampshire
Died: November 29, 1872; New York, New York
Areas of Achievement: Journalism and social reform
Contribution: A daring journalist and lecturer, Greeley engaged himself personally with a wide range of social issues—labor rights, abolitionism, territorial expansion, women's rights, and political reform—and his paper, the *New York Tribune*, became a medium for the best thought of his time.

Early Life

Horace Greeley's ancestors were among the founding families of New England, having arrived in 1640. The third of seven children of Zaccheus and Mary (Woodburn) Greeley, he was a frail boy, uncoordinated, with a very large head on a small frame. His mother was very protective of him, keeping him close as he was physically weak. She held great influence on him, and she urged him to read and study rather than risk injury in the rough-and-tumble world of children. Greeley could read at an early age, and with his delicate manners he became a favorite of teachers in Bedford, whose trustees were also impressed with the boy's brilliance. Some influential citizens even offered to underwrite Greeley at Phillips Academy in nearby Exeter. His parents declined the offer, as hard times seemed continually to press them to move from farm to farm, from Connecticut to Massachusetts and on to Westhaven, Vermont, all before Horace was ten years old. He continued with his self-education, aided and watched over by his mother. His ungainly appearance and odd wardrobe of baggy short trousers and a coat topped by equally odd slouching hats and caps did little to mitigate the impression made by the high-pitched, whining voice that came from his large, moonlike head. Youngsters called him "the ghost," and he became a subject for their merriment. Throughout his life he lacked social polish and a sense of dress.

At fifteen, Greeley was apprenticed to a small newspaper, the *Northern Spectator* of East Poultney, Vermont; there, he learned the rudiments of what was to become his life's work. He joined the local debating society, and, with his intense and serious attention to public affairs, he became a respected member of the community. The paper folded, however, and Greeley joined his family, which had moved to the Pennsylvania-New York border

village of Erie, where his father had again taken up farming. There he helped with the farm and gained printing jobs in Erie, Jamestown, and Lodi, all towns in New York State. The struggle for existence, let alone success, in the dismal marginal area depressed him, and in 1831, with ten dollars, he set out on foot for New York City.

Life's Work

Finding employment in New York was difficult, but Greeley was willing to take on a job that no other printer would do: set up print for an edition of the New Testament with Greek references and supplementary notes on each book. This job, which strained Greeley's already weak eyesight, brought him to the attention of other printers. He began work on William Leggett's *Evening Post*, from which he was fired because he did not fit the model of "decent-looking men in the office." Greeley, however, was able to save some money and form a partnership with Francis Vinton Story, and later, Jonas Winchester. They did job-printing as well as printing *Bank Note Reporter* (1832) and the *Constitutionalist* (1832), which dealt with popular lottery printing. They attempted a penny paper called the *Morning Post* using patronage investment by H. D. Shepard and supply credit from George Bruce, but a general lack of business acumen caused the venture to fail. With the failure of the penny daily, Greeley turned to putting out a successful weekly, the *New-Yorker*, which, coupled with his other publications, made the partnership now called Greeley and Company a success in journalism although not in the cash box. The habit of newspapers to extend credit rather than work on a cash basis was not to be changed until James Gordon Bennett's *Herald* demanded it in the 1840's. Greeley's weekly was nonpartisan in politics, stimulating, well written, and well edited. Greeley also made extra money by selling his writing to other papers, such as the *Daily Whig*.

In 1836, Greeley married Mary Youngs Cheney, formerly of Cornwall, Connecticut, then a teacher in North Carolina. They had first met while virtual inmates of Sylvester Graham's boardinghouse; Cheney was a devoted follower of the Grahamite cause, while Greeley was simply a teetotaling vegetarian satisfying his curiosity about Graham's unique regimen for healthy living. They were an odd match. She was plain, dogmatic, humorless,

supercilious, and uncommunicative; he was compassionate, outgoing, and egalitarian. From the first day of their marriage, on July 5, 1836, they did not get along.

As a matter of personal conscience, Greeley was never inclined to pyramid debt, and this contributed to the failure of his weekly. In addition, nonpartisanship was never Greeley's strong suit. Opinionated, he found advocacy-journalism more to his liking; therefore, he was more than willing to accommodate the proposition of Whig boss Thurlow Weed of Albany, New York, to put out a New York paper favoring the party. The result was the *Jeffersonian*, which brought Greeley a guaranteed salary of one thousand dollars per year and proved a success. More important, Greeley was mixing in state and national political circles. In 1840, the Whigs encouraged Greeley to publish another weekly, called the *Log Cabin*; because it had a guaranteed subscription list among the party faithful, the journal was an immediate success. Greeley edited the *Log Cabin* as well as his struggling *New-Yorker* until, on April 10, 1841, he combined the two publications using three thousand dollars, of which one-third was his cash, one-third was in supplies, and one-third was borrowed from James Coggeshall. The result was his *New York Tribune*. He had built a personal following through the political papers, and he now sought to capitalize on his name recognition.

As a conservative Whig daily, the *New York Tribune* was carefully structured, with sober news stories, minimal sensationalism, and a strong editorial section. Greeley turned over the business affairs to another partner, Thomas McElrath, while he concentrated on the journalism. Unlike Bennett, who was both a newsman and a businessman, Greeley was a man to whom opinions came first. His work was like an ongoing feature article. His Puritan background encouraged him to seek redress for the social wrongs that he saw everywhere. His belief in the rectitude of his moral cause made him impregnable to criticism. The common denominator linking many of his positions was his advocacy of the downtrodden and the oppressed. He strongly opposed the death penalty, which he saw as a violation of life and also a violence done by society against the weakest elements, who did not have the wherewithal to defend themselves; he led the fight for the rights of women and laboring classes, took up the cause of temperance as early as 1824, and championed the farming classes and frontier devel-

opment. That he would join the cause against slavery was inevitable.

Both wage slavery and chattel slavery were regarded by Greeley as outrages against humanity, and he admonished the press to be as "sensitive to oppression and degradation in the next street as if they were practiced in Brazil or Japan." Greeley, however, was an economic nationalist where foreign trade was concerned, pushing for protective tariffs. In the matter of women's rights, he was not in favor of suffrage, but he championed virtually every other plea by the burgeoning women's movement of the mid-nineteenth century. These causes, which promoted confidence in the people, brought enormous success to the *New York Tribune*, both critical and financial. Despite his success, Greeley was always financially hard-pressed. He never held controlling interest in the paper and was indifferent to that fact until his last years. By then it was too late, as the brilliant talents that he had recruited and cultivated had acquired dominant interest. His intuitive sense of talent brought the iconoclastic Margaret Fuller to the paper and even to live in his home for a time. Charles A. Dana joined Greeley in 1847 and was followed by Bayard Taylor in the following year. George Ripley, in 1849, was given a free hand to develop the literary department. In a continual struggle with the *Herald* for circulation and dominance, the *New York Tribune* vigorously pursued talent to make the paper a complete publication. In the 1850's came James S. Pike as Washington correspondent and editorial writer, F. J. Ottarson as city editor, W. H. Fry as music editor, Solon Robinson as agricultural editor, and then Fry and Richard Hildreth as byline reporters. The quality and intensity of the paper's political reporting, though uneven, was unequaled in the Civil War years. The newspaper's circulation under Greeley grew enormously, reaching well over a quarter million per week. This number is incredible in that the paper attracted subscribers only in areas outside the South.

The paper took strong positions on virtually every topic. Though this might have doomed other newspapers, the compelling intelligence of Greeley and his staff kept the *New York Tribune* in the forefront. At first reserved in judgment, Greeley gained confidence as his paper matured. He opposed the Mexican War, supported the Wilmot Proviso limiting slavery, and reluctantly supported Zachary Taylor. Greeley was an avid abolitionist and, in 1850, during the course of the debate on the Compromise of 1850, he stated that rather than have slavery on free soil he would "let the Union be a thousand times shivered." The Kansas-Nebraska Act infuriated him. He inveighed against its supporters and called upon antislavery forces to arm themselves and ensure that Kansas be without slavery. Greeley considered himself an astute politician, but when he fell out with his influential friends William H. Seward and Thurlow Weed, he destroyed his chances for political success. He broke from Seward as a result of a dispute over the status of slavery in Kansas and from Weed because of the latter's refusal to support him for governor of New York. Greeley had been a member of the House of Representatives for a brief three months in 1848-1849, and he enjoyed the excitement of political action. He failed reelection in 1850, however, and even failed in his attempt to gain the lieutenant governorship of New York in 1854. Greeley wanted Seward's Senate seat in 1861 and attempted to gain nomination to the Senate again in 1863, but he was thwarted by Weed's forces. He also failed to gain candidacy for the House in both 1868 and 1870 as well as the office of state comptroller in 1869. The Weed-controlled state machine was determined to force Greeley out of political life forever in retaliation for his attack on Seward's presidential candidacy in 1860 in favor of Abraham Lincoln.

At the onset of the Civil War, Greeley was very inconsistent. At first he was vehement in opposition to slavery, secession, and concessions on the expansion of slavery, but, shortly after, he suggested that secession might be allowed if a majority of Southerners wished it. In a return to his earlier position, Greeley's paper took up the cry of "Forward to Richmond" in an article by Charles Dana that was often attributed to Greeley and which committed him to join the crusade. He allied himself with the Radical Republicans Thaddeus Stevens, Charles Sumner, and Salmon P. Chase and opposed all attempts by Lincoln to conciliate the South. His paper supported the John C. Frémont emancipation in Missouri and followed with an article, "The Prayer of Twenty Millions," on August 20, 1862, which attacked the Administration on Confiscation Act manipulation, which favored Southern slaveholders. He rejoiced at the passage of the Emancipation Proclamation. Greeley worked to undercut Lincoln in 1864 by suggesting a new candidate, but by September of that year his paper endorsed Lincoln's reelection. He had, in the interim, suggested that to save the nation from ruin a one-year armistice be declared during which the blockade would be lifted and each side would hold on to what it had gained. As a result of that suggestion, his judgment was questioned; his influence waned even more with his pronouncements on Reconstruction. He advocated full equality of the freedmen while at the same time calling for a general amnesty for Southerners. At a time when most politicians were "waving the bloody shirt," he signed the bail bond of Jefferson Davis in Richmond on May 13, 1867, and pushed for his freedom. Greeley's reputation and his paper's circulation both suffered. He supported the nomination of General Ulysses S. Grant but after two years turned against him. He committed himself to defeating Grant in 1872, determined to use both himself and his paper to develop an independent party. He feared the destruction of his paper, which by now was held by as many as twenty interests.

When the desperate Democrats made an alliance with liberal Republicans, Greeley was itching to become a presidential candidate. With enemies in all camps, he took up the crusade, which exhausted him physically and emotionally. He was pilloried by cartoonists, who mocked his odd build, his floppy hats and strange white duster fluttering in the wind as he waddled, and the chin whiskers circling his face. By October, it was clear that there was little prospect for victory or even a good showing. In the election, he carried only six border and Southern states, suffering the worst defeat of any presidential candidate to that time.

Greeley's wife, who had been ailing for years, died on October 30, 1872, five days before the disastrous election. His love for this irascible woman was enduring, and he felt totally alone. They had seen the death of five of their seven children, and now there were only the daughters Ida and Gabrielle to stand with him. He attempted to return to the *New York Tribune*, but it, too, rejected him and humiliated him. His mind snapped, and he was institutionalized in the home of Dr. George S. Choate of Pleasantville, New York, where he died on November 29. The death of this great public man was noted throughout the nation. After a monumental funeral, he was buried in Greenwood Cemetery. He was remembered by his printer union friends with a bust over his grave and other statues.

Summary

Horace Greeley was forever a child prodigy, a passionate friend of mankind, one who understood the uses of money but who held no commitment to either gaining it or keeping it, and one who was possessed of and by ideas and by any and all who harbored them. Politically, he was a vain naïf caught in a cynical world. He was a man who wanted greatness for his nation and for its people. He had a compelling need to communicate his ideas, and he attracted to his paper people who themselves had something to say. He loved to explain things to a nation that was moving too quickly to do its own thinking.

Whether the issue was corruption in politics, the plight of women, love and marriage, crime, the burdens of the laboring classes, or the complexities of socialism, Greeley had something to say about it in a way that the common man could understand. The people were his true family, and his *New York Tribune*, his lectures, his books, and his essays were the instruments by which he instructed this family.

Bibliography

Baehr, Harry, Jr. *The New York Tribune Since the Civil War.* New York: Dodd, Mead, 1936. A useful book, especially the first section, which has some good illustrations of personalities associated with Greeley.

Commons, John Rogers. "Horace Greeley and the Working Class Origins of the Republican Party." *Political Science Quarterly* 24 (September 1909): 468-488. Provides insight into Greeley's approach to broadening the base of the party and his appeal to the laboring classes in nineteenth century America.

Dean, Bradley P. "Henry D. Thoreau and Horace Greeley Exchange Letters on the 'Spontaneous Generation of Plants.' " *New England Quarterly* 66, no. 4 (December 1993). Discussion of letters between Henry David Thoreau and Greeley that indicate a difference of opinion on the spontaneous generation of plants.

Greeley, Horace. *The American Conflict: A History of the Great Rebellion in the United States of America, 1860-'65.* 2 vols. Hartford, Conn.: Case, 1864-1866. This is an involved personal overview of the events leading to the Civil War, and the war itself, by a less than disinterested observer who nevertheless maintained a reasonable objectivity.

————. *An Overland Journey from New York to San Francisco in the Summer of 1859.* New York: Saxton Barker, 1860; London: Macdonald, 1965. This, along with Greeley's other works, gives a sense of the charm and intelligence of the man.

————. *Recollections of a Busy Life.* New York: Ford, 1869. This book should be read by anyone who wants to know Greeley. He was such a public man that even academics presume to know him without reading what is an unsung but truly remarkable autobiography.

Hale, William Harlan. *Horace Greeley: Voice of the People.* New York: Harper, 1950. A book that shows Greeley's intuitive understanding of the issues of his time.

Horner, Harlan Hoyt. *Lincoln and Greeley.* Urbana: University of Illinois Press, 1953. An examination of the curious relationship between Lincoln and the often presumptuous Greeley on issues of war and peace.

Isely, Jeter Allen. *Horace Greeley and the Republican Party, 1853-61: A Study of the "New York Tribune."* Princeton, N.J.: Princeton University Press, 1947. This work is necessary to an understanding of the making of the Republican Party and the exploitation of the Greeley paper toward that end.

Seitz, Don C. *Horace Greeley: Founder of the "New York Tribune."* Indianapolis: Bobbs-Merrill, 1926. Seitz provides a journalistic biography of Greeley with some very useful information on the editor's family life.

Schulze, Suzanne. *Horace Greeley: A Bio-Bibliography.* New York: Greenwood Press, 1992. Excellent reference source. Includes a chronology and biographical sketch, annotated entries on Greeley's works and on works about Greeley, and author and subject indexes.

Van Deusen, Glyndon G. *Horace Greeley: Nineteenth Century Crusader.* Philadelphia: University of Pennsylvania Press, 1953. This is the standard biography. Balanced, readable, well-documented; includes a general bibliography, "bibliography by chapter," and illustrations (a number of which are cartoonists' caricatures of Greeley).

Jack J. Cardoso

THOMAS HILL GREEN

Born: April 7, 1836; Birkin, Yorkshire, England
Died: March 26, 1882; Oxford, England
Areas of Achievement: Philosophy and education
Contribution: Green was both a theorist and a reformer who established the Idealist school of philosophy at Oxford, contributed political ideas that facilitated the movement away from Liberalism, and was a powerful advocate of educational reform.

Early Life

Thomas Hill Green was the youngest of four children, born on April 7, 1836, into a family with extensive clerical affiliations. His mother died when he was one year old, and his father, the Reverend Valentine Green, assumed full responsibility for his youngest child, educating him until he was fourteen. The personality traits Green displayed during early childhood did not augur well for the future—he was shy, awkward, and indolent—and, indeed, these characteristics occasionally asserted themselves during his later life. At fourteen, Green was sent to Rugby, a public school that enjoyed some fame as a result of its recent leadership by Dr. Thomas Arnold, the father of poet and critic Matthew Arnold. Green appears to have been a willful student, choosing to do well only when his interest was aroused by the subject matter. While compounding his indolence with rebelliousness, Green did assert himself in translating a passage from John Milton's *Areopagitica* (1644) and won a prize. On graduation, Green entered Balliol College at Oxford and began an association that lasted the rest of his life. That association did not begin auspiciously, because Green retained the same independence in pursuing his own interests and the same indolence that characterized his earlier life. Typical of his Oxford days was his fulfillment of the requirement that an essay be turned in every Friday. One of his friends remarked that Green's essay was usually submitted on Saturday, but it was also the best essay submitted.

Green chose to stand apart from most of his fellow undergraduates. His strong sense of personal purpose and commitment to social equality made him interested in the working class and the poor. His reputation as a political and religious radical kept him out of the mainstream of undergraduate life; most of Oxford was not ready to accept a serious undergraduate whose politics were directed toward practical rather than romantic ends, and his view that law and morality are the sole result of man's reason rather than natural law or innate rights undercut the foundation of popular Liberalism as it existed in Oxford during his student days. Green's appearance may have led his peers to make assumptions about his personality. Green had thick black hair, a pale complexion, and brown eyes that were deep-set and thus gave the impression of seriousness.

Green was undecided about a career: The Church attracted him, but his unorthodox ideas led him to conclude that ordination in the Unitarian Church was the only honest possibility available to him; he also considered journalism a possibility. The problem was solved for him by the offer of a one-year appointment teaching ancient and modern history at Balliol, and by the end of the year he was elected to be a Fellow of Balliol College. During the subsequent eighteen years, Green assumed ever-greater responsibilities for running Balliol. He also accepted a broad range of responsibilities dealing with social and political reform outside the university.

Life's Work

The work of historian Thomas Carlyle and two summer visits to Germany in 1862 and 1863 made Green reject the philosophy of John Stuart Mill, which was very popular at that time. Instead, Green's philosophical thinking was shaped by Aristotle and the Germans George Wilhelm Friedrich Hegel and Immanuel Kant. Like Kant, Green objected to the proposition of David Hume that knowledge was gathered by the impressions of the senses (that is, that knowledge was empirical) and to the notion that one should make choices based on the ability of the choice to give one happiness or to help one avoid pain, thus making morality and ethics a matter of calculating the alternatives. Green argued that information gathered by the senses was connected in the mind by a "consciousness" or a "spiritual principle" that actively participated in creating knowledge. "Consciousness" also allowed one to establish and obey moral rules higher than the pursuit of happiness or the avoidance of pain. The mere pursuit of happiness does not explain man's pursuit of excellence, observance of duty, concept of a higher and lower self, or willingness to sacrifice oneself in so many varied ways. There was a spiritual principle ultimately underlying everything that could be realized through the practical activities of man. For Green, then, it was imperative for a person to make decisions based on whether the action would further his own development or that of others. Self-development and social development were the fundamental goals in Green's system of thought. That emphasis marks the distinction between social reformers who believe that social problems can be solved by reforming the system and those who, like Green, consider the solution to social problems to lie in correcting the defects of individuals.

Green's metaphysics complemented his longstanding interest in social problems, and since his arrival at Oxford as an undergraduate, he had been active in various enterprises designed to help the working class. In December, 1864, he received an appointment to the Royal Commission on Middle Class Schools, headed by Lord Taunton. Many objections to popular education had prevented its introduction. Some opposed it as too expensive and a burden to taxpayers. Others opposed it on religious grounds as not offering instruction in their religion; there was serious disagreement between members of the Church of England and Dissenters as to the religion that should be taught. As a member of the Royal Commission and afterward, Green put forward arguments that advocated popular education as both expedient and morally desirable. Green proposed expanding and improving the secondary schools, reforming the existing universities, and creating new universities throughout the country. The benefits from his scheme were numerous. Social barriers would be broken down. Members of different social classes would be at ease with one another because they would become familiar with one another. Although Green normally favored improvements through the voluntary association of interested parties, education was an exception. The task was so large that it was beyond the capacity of voluntary associations; only the state could create and run a successful system of education. Furthermore, the voluntary principle would not be effective because some could not afford to pay for education; others were too mired in ignorance to want education for their children. Thus, while Green preferred voluntarism whenever possible, education was central to the self-development that would make social equality and justice possible, and state action was necessary.

The result of the Taunton Commission's work was the Elementary Education Act of 1870. From Green's point of view, this was a sorry compromise that commissioned the Education Department of the government to determine whether a district ought to have state schools. School boards were to be created in districts where they did not exist, but these authorities would have no jurisdiction over existing voluntary schools, which could not be given state aid. Green proposed a scheme of interlocking schools that would permit intelligence to be recognized and forwarded through the highest level appropriate to the child's ability. All children were to be educated to the age of thirteen; those destined for business might stay until fifteen or sixteen, and others would remain in school until eighteen, when they would go to a university. That was, indeed, a radical proposal. According to Green, universities would be occupied by real scholars instead of those who were merely economically advantaged. Green believed that his system of education would produce civil servants who represented the best minds in society and who were committed to the pursuit of the betterment of all. The very basis of the state would be changed by educational reform.

Green remained active as a champion of educational reform throughout the remainder of his short life. He became active in the National Education League, formed to promote reforms that would make school attendance compulsory and to support schools in places that lacked adequate financial support. Green also was active at the community level. In 1874, he was elected to the school board in Oxford (the following year, he was elected to the Oxford town council), led a movement to establish a grammar school in Oxford, established a scholarship for boys from Oxford, and served on the governing board of King Edward's School in Birmingham. At the university, Green extended efforts to make Oxford more accessible to poorer students; he also supported the extension movement, which offered Oxford's services to working men, and worked to create new universities. He died in Oxford on March 26, 1882.

Summary

Thomas Hill Green's diverse achievements have caused him to be considered by subsequent generations for his individual achievements. He is considered an important figure in the introduction of German Idealist philosophy into Great Britain. His political theory, which redefined freedom, not as the legal possibilities open to a person, but as access to the possibilities for self-development that are available to the person, in fact, was, for a time, considered a necessary assumption for state intervention, and Green is considered by some to be one of the forebears of the welfare state. In the long run, however, the position that Green delineated regarding the place of education in society is his most significant legacy. Green proposed that education be provided to all children and that it be based on the abilities of the student rather than membership in a social class. Each individual would get the access necessary to allow him to realize his all-important self-development. Society would be reshaped by a government composed of the subsequent meritocracy, becoming more egalitarian. Omitting the Idealist emphasis on the importance of self-development, these practical issues have been at the heart of English educational social policy since Green first addressed them in the 1860's. Considered together, Green's separate achievements mark him as one of the most important intellectuals who helped shape the transition from the nineteenth to the twentieth century.

Bibliography

Barker, Ernest. *Political Thought in England from Herbert Spencer to the Present Day.* London: Williams and Norgate, and New York: Holt, 1915. This is a classic study in the Home University Library series. Barker's chapter "The Idealist School—T. H. Green" is an excellent brief interpretation of Green's thought, although it should be read in conjunction with Clark.

Bevir, Mark. "Welfarism, Socialism and Religion: On T. H. Green and Others." *Review of Politics* 55, no. 4 (Fall 1993). A study of the views of Green and other political philosophers on the impact of loss of religious faith on the creation of welfare and socialism.

Cacoullos, Ann R. *Thomas Hill Green: Philosopher of Rights.* New York: Twayne, 1974. This work has the advantage of being more concise than that by Richter, but it lacks his clarity and appreciation of the larger context of Green's work.

Clark, Peter. *Liberals and Social Democrats.* Cambridge and New York: Cambridge University Press, 1978. Clark has written an excellent survey of political thought that questions the notion that Green was one of the forefathers of the welfare state.

Green, Thomas Hill. *The Works of Thomas Hill Green.* Edited by R. I. Nettleship. 3 vols. London: Longman, 1885-1888; New York: Longman, 1889-1890. This collection contains almost all of Green's works, except for his *Prolegomena to Ethics*, edited by A. C. Bradley and first published in 1883. The first two volumes are devoted to Green's philosophical works. Volume 3 contains a memoir which Nettleship assembled from Green's speeches and personal papers. The same volume includes Green's writings on education and religious essays.

Milne, A. J. M. *The Social Philosophy of English Idealism.* London: Allen and Unwin, 1962. Milne examines the influence of Kant and Hegel on Green's thought.

Richter, Melvin. *The Politics of Conscience: T.H. Green and His Times.* Cambridge, Mass: Harvard University Press, and London: Weidenfeld and Nicolson, 1964. Richter's study is unusually good as a biographical sketch, a survey of Green's intellectual context, and an analysis of the content and meaning of Green's thought. It is unquestionably the best single volume about Green.

Rodman, John R., ed. *The Political Theory of T. H. Green: Selected Writings.* New York: Appleton, 1964. Rodman gives an accessible, insightful, and convenient introduction to Green's political thought, as well as reprinting Green's essays "Liberal Legislation and Freedom of Contract," "The Senses of Freedom," and "The Principles of Political Obligation."

Ward, Mrs. Humphry. *Robert Elsmere.* London: Macmillan, and New York: Hart, 1888. Mrs. Ward, a friend of Green, wrote a novel that includes a character (Mr. Grey) who is modeled on Green. Indeed, Mrs. Ward dedicated this novel to Green and put portions of his work into the mouth of her character.

Weinstein, David. "Between Kantianism and Consequentialism in T. H. Green's Moral Philosophy." *Political Studies* 41, no. 4 (December 1993). A detailed account of Green's views on utilitarianism, his own moral theories and a comparison with J. S. Mill's version of utilitarianism.

Glenn O. Nichols

FRANCIS GREENWAY

Born: November 20, 1777; Mangotsfield, England
Died: September 26, 1837; East Maitland, Australia
Area of Achievement: Architecture
Contribution: Although surrounded by controversy, Greenway attempted to legitimate and regulate building practices in Australia during the period when it was regarded as a penal colony. More important, however, he gave to the early buildings aesthetically unique designs combining both beauty and practicality.

Early Life

Not much is known of Francis Howard Greenway's early life. He was born on November 20, 1777, in the parish of Mangotsfield, England, the fourth son of Francis Greenway and Ann Webb. His birthright links him with a two-hundred-year tradition of Greenways who were involved in stonemasonry, architecture, and construction in the Bristol area. Thus, his choice of occupation comes as no surprise. There is an indication that Greenway was educated in England and afterward was employed by and became the protégé of the famous architect John Nash, with whom he began to build both a minor reputation and career. In 1800, Greenway exhibited two architectural drawings at the Royal Academy, and he later designed the "market house," the Chapel Library, the Clifton Club, and the restoration of the Thornbury Castle.

In 1804, he married a woman whose identity is established by her first name only, Mary, by whom he probably had three or four children. A self-portrait pictures Greenway as a "fair and ruddy" man of approximately five feet, six inches, with auburn hair, hazel eyes, and a prominent nose. Accounts of Greenway's personality vary. His friends and admirers saw him as an extremely moral and practical man with a genius and passion for art and beauty. His enemies viewed him as a haughty and volatile man with grandiose ideas about his talents and abilities. His later actions seem to bear out both viewpoints.

Shortly after his marriage, Greenway went into business with his two brothers, Olive Greenway and John Tripp Greenway, offering the following services advertised in the *Bristol Gazette* in 1805: "All orders for marble monuments, Chimney Pieces, and every kind of ornamental stone work shall be carefully attended to, and executed in the most

artist-like manner." It appears that for the next four years, the business ran smoothly until April, 1809, when legal questions were raised regarding both the family business and some of its present and past contracts. One month later, the word bankruptcy appeared in the paper, and Greenway's career became jeopardized. As a result, the Greenways' possessions were put up for auction in order to satisfy their creditors. The precise reasons for the legal actions and subsequent bankruptcy have been lost in local legend and unclear newspaper reports regarding a long-standing issue of water rights in and around Bath (where construction of buildings for the use of visitors who wanted to take advantage of the healing waters was common). Greenway tried to show how he had been fooled by speculators and false promises, but his attempt proved fruitless.

Despite this setback, Greenway was still working as an architect in 1810, but another tragedy was in the making. Problems arose regarding a contract that Greenway had made with Colonel Richard Doolan, for whom he was doing some work. Greenway swore that the colonel had authorized an additional £250 for some extra work Greenway had provided. Unfortunately, the contract was lost and the colonel denied the charge. Greenway eventually produced the lost contract. In the court proceedings that followed, it was proved that Greenway had forged the contract, and Greenway was held at Newgate prison for sentencing. Three months later, in March of 1812, Greenway found himself in the dock at the Bristol Assizes. He pleaded guilty to the charges and was sentenced to death by hanging. Fortunately, he still had some influential friends, and they managed to get his sentence reduced first to lifelong exile in Australia (which was then a penal colony) and later to transportation to this colony for a term of fourteen years.

Life's Work

On February 7, 1814, Greenway arrived in Sydney, Australia, a colony made up largely of convicts with a population numbering about twelve thousand. There he found an architect's dream: a large, sprawling city with scattered houses and buildings showing little sign of any plan, direction, or beauty. Even more amazing to Greenway was the fact that there was little to distinguish private buildings from public or government buildings. The opportunities were immediately apparent to Greenway, and although in his mind he began construction on the future buildings of Sydney, it took him five months to reach Governor Luchlan Macquarie, who had his own visions of a new city.

Greenway assumed not only that the governor would put him to work but also that, as an architect, he would have complete freedom to do as he pleased. The governor, however, even in his desperate need for an architect, had plans of his own and asked Greenway to produce copies of a new courthouse and town hall from a book of previously constructed buildings. Greenway took immediate offense and instead sent to the governor a portfolio of his architectural drawings and a letter dated July, 1814, letting Macquarie know that for an artist merely to copy another's work is a "rather painful" undertaking. There is no record of the governor's reaction, but a few days later Greenway sent a letter of apology and a drawing of the buildings just as Macquarie had requested. The governor accepted the architect's apology, gave permission for Greenway's wife and family to join him, and unwittingly became Greenway's benefactor.

It would be quite some time before Greenway would become the "sole designer" of the colony, for the governor was cautious. For the next year or more, rather than fulfilling his role as an architect (despite the fact that he opened a private practice in December, 1814), Greenway acted as a surveyor of the public buildings already in progress. In these reports, Greenway not only cited the aesthetic and structural flaws he found but also made outraged statements against fraudulent contracts, the waste of materials and labor, and the inhumane treatment of the workers. The governor, whose entire building budget had already been used with very little to show for it, must have been grateful for Greenway's reports, for in March, 1816, Greenway found himself appointed acting government architect and assistant engineer for Australia. Along with this position went a house, rations for him and his family, a convict servant, a horse, and a salary of three shillings per day plus the promise of traveling expenses.

It seemed as if Greenway, a convicted exile, had indeed come a long way. Yet, he was not satisfied. He believed that his destiny to bring to the world, in this case Australia, the physical and spiritual merits of art and architecture was being hampered. He wanted to offer mankind the combination of "beauty, strength and convenience," and he wanted to do this through his idealistic and grand architec-

tural visions. Greenway found that such far-reaching and idealistic ambitions did not fit in with the concerns of the building contractors and suppliers with whom he had to deal. Thus, he continued to keep a close watch on what he saw as unethical building practices and continued to expose fraud, low-quality work, poor structural designs, substandard building materials, and ill-trained workers. In the process he made himself a number of enemies.

Macquarie, however, remained his friend, and between the two of them plans began to emerge for a new Australia. One of the first buildings attributed solely to Greenway was more a monument to the governor's and Greenway's artistic visions than a needed public facility. This building was the Macquarie Tower and Light House, for which the foundation stone was laid on July 11, 1816. This first building not only marked the beginning of a continuous building program for the cities of Sydney, Liverpool, Windsor, and Parramatta but also initiated a series of arguments, legal battles, and personal and professional setbacks that were to plague Greenway for the rest of his life.

Between the years 1816 and 1819, however, Greenway managed to break ground on a number of different projects—buildings which were considered superior to anything previously constructed in Australia. Among some of Greenway's most successful, although controversial, buildings were structures such as Fort Macquarie, the Military Barracks at Sydney, the Female Orphan School at Parramatta, the Liverpool Hospital, and the Government House. Yet while no one could question his artistic talents, and despite the fact that he fought to upgrade the quality of both the structures and the skills of the contractors, many of Greenway's own buildings became the subject of disputes, delays, structural flaws, or overcosts. Nevertheless, thanks to his friendship with Macquarie, he went ahead with his plans in the midst of controversies and arguments with private contractors. In fact, the governor saw fit to grant Greenway a conditional pardon in 1817, which was then made official in 1819, seven years before the end of his original sentence. He was, in effect, free to move into the higher social classes of Australia, a position to which he felt entitled.

Yet freedom, social status, and professional and economic success would not be enough to guard Greenway against his own propensity to make enemies. Also, many in England were becoming concerned that the original plan to keep Australia a penal colony was being diverted (a result, in large part, of Greenway's architectural plans). Thus, in 1822, with the removal of Governor Macquarie, Greenway's rocky rise to success received a troubling blow. In June, a letter from John Thomas Bigge, who had been sent in 1819 to Australia to survey and report on the troublesome progress being made in this so-called penal colony, recommended that the "Colonial Architect" (referring to Greenway) introduce a more "uniform and simple style of architecture" into the public and government buildings. Furthermore, Bigge recommended that a corps of engineers be appointed to oversee all future work in the colony.

It appears, however, that Greenway was unaware of Bigge's recommendations, for, as usual, he was embroiled in arguments and controversies. The most damaging of these ongoing controversies came to a head in 1822, when Greenway faced a libel suit, again over matters of lost contracts and promised payments. When he was denied the right of inquiry and appeal regarding the matter, he refused to continue his official work of "inspecting the progress of public works." This refusal, along with Bigge's earlier letter, produced the following results: "By direction of the Governor I am to acquaint you that from the present date your services to the Government will be dispensed with." Greenway received this letter on November 15, 1822, and for the second time in his life he was financially and professionally ruined.

Greenway, refusing to admit defeat, continued to live in the house Macquarie had appointed to him in 1814. Meanwhile, he tried in vain to appeal to the government for reimbursements of traveling expenses, compensation for work done by him at the "request" of his old friend and benefactor, and the usual "percentages" of revenues from buildings completed, as well as plans for future buildings. The amount he believed was due him came to £11,232. His petitions were continually denied, and for a third time in his life Greenway came under suspicion of document forgery, although he was never tried or convicted in this last matter. There also arose questions regarding Greenway's claim to eight hundred acres of land at Tarro in the Newcastle district. Again, documents proved faulty, causing Greenway additional anger and embarrassment, and he spent his last years writing letters and haranguing public officials. His efforts were in vain, however, for he died of unknown causes on September 26, 1837, impoverished and disgraced. A century later, a memorial tablet was erected on the North Porch of St. James's Church which reads: "In Memory of Francis Greenway Architect of This Church and of the Artisans and Labourers Who Erected It."

Summary

It is difficult to assess accurately Greenway's life and career. The legal controversies in which he was embroiled, coupled with the personal and professional conflicts that followed Greenway his entire life, cast shadows which cannot be easily dispelled. Yet Greenway's buildings speak for themselves; they are monuments to "beauty, strength and convenience" just as he had intended. He not only raised the standard of architectural design, but he also raised the standards of building construction and workmanship. Although clearly trained in the classical tradition of strict control of form and obviously influenced by the Georgian designs of Bristol in the early nineteenth century, Greenway managed to impose his own vision and imprint upon his designs, marking them as clearly the work of one talent, one man.

For all of his faults and failures, Greenway held firm to his passion for artistic beauty and its benefit to mankind. Australia, especially Sydney, owes much to Greenway's vision.

Bibliography

Ellis, M. H. *Francis Greenway: His Life and Times.* Sydney: Shepherd Press, 1949. Ellis has put together an exhaustive study of Greenway's life and times, as the title indicates. It is the only study of its kind and for this it is extremely valuable. It contains numerous references to and quotations from letters, documents, and papers, some of which were left behind by Greenway, others of which are official public documents and letters. While the chronology is sometimes difficult to follow, the material proves both interesting and enlightening.

Freeland, J. M. *Architecture in Australia: A History.* Melbourne: Cheshire, 1968. This is a fascinating account of Australia's history, from the late 1700's to the late 1960's. The pages dealing with Greenway, although not as specific as they could be, provide a good overview of the importance of his work in Australia's architectural growth. Freeland manages to highlight both the successes and failures of Greenway's career without being sidetracked by the turmoil that surrounded much of his life.

————. *The Making of a Profession*. Sydney: Angus and Robertson, 1971. Although Freeland's comments about Greenway barely cover three pages of this study, the information provided is interesting, for it places Greenway at the beginning of a new and rising tradition of architects in Australia.

Herman, Morton. *The Early Australian Architects and Their Work*. Sydney: Angus and Robertson, 1954. Herman's book is a very straightforward account of the beginnings of Australia's early architecture and architects. The material pertaining to Greenway provides a general overview of his career, referring only briefly to his personal life. It focuses primarily on Greenway's work and how it fits into the pattern of a new profession in a new land.

Deborah Charlie

SECOND EARL GREY

Born: March 13, 1764; Fallodon, Northumberland, England

Died: July 17, 1845; Howick, Northumberland, England

Areas of Achievement: Politics and government

Contribution: Grey recognized that parliamentary reform was necessary in order to maintain the ascendancy of the aristocracy in a rapidly changing English society. He led the government which passed the Reform Bill of 1832.

Early Life

Charles Grey was born on March 13, 1764, at Fallodon, the family's country house only a few miles from the sea in county Northumberland. His uncle was a baronet, whose nearby estate, Howick, Grey was later to occupy and then inherit. His father, Sir Charles Grey, had distinguished himself in military service, rose to the rank of general, and was made a peer in 1801. As the eldest surviving son (an older brother died no more than a few weeks after his birth), Charles Grey would succeed to his father's title and a seat in the House of Lords.

At the age of six, Grey was sent to a boarding school in Marylebone (London), where he spent three unhappy years until he arrived at Eton at age nine. During his eight years at Eton, Grey excelled in the largely classical curriculum, and in 1781, at the age of seventeen, he made the short journey to Trinity College, Cambridge. As was the case with many sons of the aristocracy and greater gentry, Grey did not take a degree. In 1784, he embarked on the Grand Tour, considered an essential part of the education of a young English aristocrat in the eighteenth century. He visited the south of France, Switzerland, and Italy. In 1786, during his last months on the Continent, Grey was elected a Member of Parliament for the county of Northumberland. He was to remain a county member until 1807, after which he was M.P. briefly for the pocket boroughs of Appleby and Tavistock.

In 1794, Grey married Mary Elizabeth Ponsonby, with whom he had fifteen children. While he developed a reputation in public life for being stiff and aloof, Grey's marriage was happy, his family life warm and affectionate. The contentment he found with his family would later account, at least in part, for his occasional tardiness in arriving for the parliamentary session, his absences for a ses-sion or more, or, once parliamentary business was completed, his prompt return to Howick, a four-day journey from London by coach in the late eighteenth and early nineteenth centuries.

Like many military families, Grey's had moderate Tory connections. Yet he affiliated himself with the Foxite Whigs. This association may well have been the result of personal friendships rather than political principle. In the 1780's, it would have been difficult to distinguish the Foxites from other aristocratic factions that claimed the Whig name and, thereby, connected themselves with the legacy of the Glorious Revolution, with which the Whigs had become identified. In the 1790's, however, the Foxites reinforced the association of Whiggery with liberty in general and with a number of specific liberal causes. Grey was instrumental in this development.

Life's Work

Grey earned a reputation as an excellent orator in an age when oratory was highly valued. After participating in the proceedings to impeach Warren Hastings, he gained special attention, even notoriety, for his role in founding the Society of the Friends of the People in April, 1792. The society was an organization of young men, most of them aristocrats like Grey, that supported the reform of Parliament. Decades later, Grey was embarrassed about his youthful ardor which, in these early years of the French Revolution, inspired him to organize the society. Yet from the outset, Grey and most of the Friends distinguished themselves from radicals. The very name, Friends of the People, signified an attitude of paternalism and benevolent condescension toward the lower orders. The Foxite Whigs with whom Grey associated remained an aristocratic party, and Grey considered aristocracy as the intermediary between the Crown, which might be inclined toward arbitrary power, and the people, whose liberties aristocrats were to defend. Grey was never a democrat, a designation he associated with varieties of radicalism, and always cherished his aristocratic connection. Nevertheless, among other aristocratic factions, proposals for parliamentary reform appeared as assaults on both aristocracy and monarchy, especially as the French Revolution entered its more radical phase. Consequently, Grey's motions for inquiries into the state of the representation in the 1790's and his proposal in 1797 for a reform of Parliament with triennial parliaments, a uniform property qualification for the suffrage, and abolition of rotten boroughs—parliamentary constituencies that had little or no population and were controlled by the owners of specific properties—were immediately rejected. The Friends of the People, however, succeeded in widening an already existing rift in the Whig opposition, enlisting the acquiescence if not the enthusiasm of Fox, and driving the more conservative Whigs to support William Pitt's government. In the 1790's, Grey also endorsed Fox's opposition to legislation considered to infringe on liberty—the suspension of habeas corpus (1794-1801), the Seditious Meetings Act (1795), and the Alien Bill (1799). After 1797, Grey joined the general Foxite withdrawal from parliamentary attendance for several sessions.

In 1806, Grey joined the cabinet as First Lord of the Admiralty in the Fox-Grenville coalition government. (He was then styled Lord Howick, a courtesy title resulting from his father's elevation to an earldom, but he remained in the House of Commons.) When Fox died in September, 1806, Grey succeeded him as secretary of state for foreign affairs and was generally acknowledged as leader of the Foxite Whigs. The ministry was dismissed by George III, technically on a matter concerning the appointment of Catholics as staff officers in the army, something which Grey thought an important gesture to conciliate Catholic Ireland. From their dismissal in 1807, the Whigs supported the right of Catholics to sit in Parliament.

In November, 1807, his father having died, Grey became the second Earl Grey. Twenty-three years were to elapse before he returned to government. During those years, he was generally considered to be the leader of the Whig Party, which in 1817 separated from the Grenvillites with whom they had co-operated in opposition since the dismissal of the Fox-Grenville government. Grey was so often removed from London and from Parliament, however, that he was little more than a titular leader, dispensing advice from afar. He frequently had to be coaxed by such friends as Lord Holland to take a more active part in politics. No longer enthusiastic about parliamentary reform, he often considered retirement. He was occasionally active, as in 1819, when he vigorously protested the Tory government's repressive Six Acts, and the following year, when he opposed George IV's divorce proceedings against Queen Caroline, thereby earning the king's

enmity and ensuring that he would never be called to cabinet office during the new reign. Other Whigs were drawn to join or to support George Canning's government in 1827 (Grey despised Canning), and when Wellington's government was compelled to pass a bill for Catholic Emancipation, the Whigs were deprived of the one issue that had unified them in opposition. Some Whigs, moreover, began to look for a new leader.

Several developments dramatically transformed the prospects of both the Whigs and Grey. George IV's death, his succession by William IV, and the elections of 1830 encouraged the Whigs in their organized opposition to Wellington's government. Wellington's subsequent intransigence on parliamentary reform resulted in his government's defeat (though, technically, it was defeated on another matter). Grey, at the age of sixty-six, was chosen by the king as his prime minister in November, 1830. It was understood that the government would be pledged to parliamentary reform.

Grey's government was a coalition, ministers being drawn from Whigs of Grey's generation, younger members of the party, Canningites, and Ultra-Tories. Of the thirteen men who formed the original Grey cabinet, nine were in the House of Lords and one was an Irish peer in the Commons. Three others were in the Commons, of whom one, the leader of the House, Lord Althorp, was heir to an earldom. Indeed, Grey's government was the most aristocratic of the century. A commitment to the ascendancy of the aristocracy and the preservation of existing institutions bound the cabinet together, along with the conviction that if an effective measure of parliamentary reform were not passed, the country would face the alternative of revolution. While the government was a coalition, its moving spirits were Whigs, and the committee of four ministers that Grey appointed to draft a reform bill—Lord Durham, Lord Duncannon, Lord John Russell, and Sir James Graham—had impeccable Whig credentials.

While the Reform Bill underwent numerous changes from its introduction in March, 1831, until its final passage in July, 1832, its central features remained the abolition of rotten boroughs, the addition of representation to hitherto neglected populous towns, and the extension of the franchise in the boroughs to all householders who either owned a house worth, or paid rent of, more than ten pounds yearly. When the government was defeated on an amendment in the House of

Commons, the subsequent election of April, 1831, ensured a lower house favorable to reform. When the House of Lords defeated the bill on its second reading in October, 1831, however, Grey and the cabinet were confronted with the problem of overcoming the resistance of the Lords while retaining the confidence of the king. Grey was a masterful politician during those years. His occasional threats to resign proved to be remarkably effective in stemming cabinet dissension. Moreover, the king's confidence was reposed in Grey personally rather than in the cabinet collectively. Retaining that confidence was crucial, all the more so since it became increasingly apparent that the only way to persuade the House of Lords to pass the bill was by resorting to a creation of peers by the king. Only with great reluctance did Grey eventually acquiesce in this alternative. It was his personal influence with King William which ultimately persuaded the monarch to consent to a creation, but only after the Duke of Wellington failed to form a coalition government in May, 1832. The Lords finally consented to the bill rather than witness a mass creation of peers.

The English Reform Bill of 1832 is one of the most significant acts of Parliament in British history. It was followed by bills for Ireland and Scotland. Grey's ministry also was responsible for other significant legislation, some of which it initiated, some of which it merely supervised. The Irish Church Reform Act of 1833 reduced the number of bishops in the Church of Ireland and eliminated the church cess, a tax paid by occupiers of land, mostly Catholic, to support the Protestant church. The Factory Act of 1833 was the first effective regulation of the conditions of factory labor. The abolition of slavery in the empire in 1833 complemented the abolition of the slave trade in 1807 by the Fox-Grenville ministry. Though it was passed after his resignation, the Poor Law Amendment Act was initiated when Grey was prime minister. Complementing its liberal record in domestic affairs, in foreign affairs Grey's government became associated with the defense of constitutionalism, especially in Belgium and Spain, against the reactionary policies of the eastern powers.

Grey's government came to an end in July, 1834. When Lord Althorp resigned as a result of an imbroglio involving secret dealings by other ministers with Daniel O'Connell concerning a renewal of an Irish Coercion Bill, Grey followed

him into retirement. Grey declined the king's proposal that he form a new government after the defeat of Peel's ministry in April, 1835. He spent his remaining years in tranquillity at Howick, where he died on July 17, 1845.

Summary

The second Earl Grey cherished his aristocratic connections and once observed that he had a predilection for old institutions. Both in his youthful days with the Friends of the People and during his premiership, he thought that parliamentary reform was necessary to preserve those institutions and the ascendancy of the aristocracy. He argued that reform was conservative. It was a concession to popular opinion that was necessary to maintain stability. He sincerely believed as prime minister that failure to implement a substantial reform of Parliament would result in a revolution which would destroy monarchy as well as aristocracy. One of his achievements, which few of his contemporaries could have managed, was to persuade the king that the alternative to reform was revolution; for without the king's support, however grudging, the Reform Bill could not have passed.

Grey never doubted the propriety of the aristocracy's ascendancy. Yet he recognized that to govern effectively, it had to retain the confidence of the people. He sometimes thought of reform legislation as a boon to be bestowed from above by an enlightened aristocracy, whose benevolence was to be properly acknowledged by a grateful populace. The deference of the people was a reflection of their proper subordination to their governors. While Grey recognized that the emerging middle classes had developed a new form of property which deserved representation in Parliament, he retained the idea that substantial landed property owners should direct the affairs of society for the benefit of all. Throughout his career, Grey scorned radicals and opposed any Whig connection with them, which, he thought, could only undermine the social order he sought to preserve. Committed to maintaining that order, he supported reform in order to preserve it.

Bibliography

Brock, Michael. *The Great Reform Act.* London: Hutchinson, 1973. This study considers the recent scholarship on the Reform Bill but accepts the established interpretation that it was a concession designed to maintain stability.

Davis, H. W. C. *The Age of Grey and Peel*. London: Oxford University Press, 1929; New York: Russell and Russell, 1964. An old but still valuable study of the Whigs and their values, especially good on the Whig suspicion of radicals. More critical of Grey than is G. M. Trevelyan (see below).

Derry, John. *Charles Earl Grey: Aristocratic Reformer*. Oxford and Cambridge, Mass.: Blackwell, 1992. Fresh and convincing interpretation of the character and achievements of Grey.

Kriegel, Abraham D. "The Irish Policy of Lord Grey's Government." *English Historical Review* 86 (January 1971): 22-45. Discusses the association of concession with coercion in the government's Irish policy and relates it to the Whigs' policy on parliamentary reform.

————. "Liberty and Whiggery in Early Nineteenth-Century England." *Journal of Modern History* 52 (June 1980): 253-278. Considers the Whig idea of liberty and its relationship to Whig legislation such as the Reform Bill.

Mitchell, Austin. *The Whigs in Opposition, 1815-1830*. Oxford: Clarendon Press, 1967. An excellent study of the Whig Party from the end of the Napoleonic Wars until the eve of Grey's government. Grey is portrayed as a reluctant leader during this period.

Roberts, Michael. *The Whig Party, 1807-1812*. London: Macmillan, 1939; New York: Barnes and Noble, 1965. Follows the intricate politics of the Whigs in opposition from the dismissal of the Fox-Grenville ministry until the establishment of George IV's regency in 1812.

Trevelyan, G. M. *Lord Grey of the Reform Bill*. London and New York: Longman, 1920. Not among Trevelyan's better studies, this old and dated biography is insufficiently critical but remains the only modern biography.

Abraham D. Kriegel

SIR GEORGE EDWARD GREY

Born: April 14, 1812; Lisbon, Portugal
Died: September 19, 1898; London, England
Area of Achievement: Government
Contribution: Grey, one of the great proconsuls of the British Empire, fused the arrogant, autocratic, decisive man of action with eclectic, radical, and democratic beliefs. He had a particularly profound influence on settlement, political developments, native policy, and ethnography, on three colonial frontiers: South Africa, South Australia, and, most important, New Zealand.

Early Life

George Edward Grey was born at Lisbon, Portugal, on April 14, 1812, the son of Lieutenant Colonel George Grey, who had been killed at the storming of Badajoz a few days before the birth of his son. Colonel Grey was a member of a family associated with the Earls of Stamford, and his wife, Elizabeth Vignoles, was an Anglo-Irish woman from County Westmeath whose evangelical religious fervor had a powerful influence on her young son. Grey was educated at Guildford Boarding School but ran away and was then tutored by the Reverend Richard Whately, late Archbishop of Dublin. He entered the Royal Military College, Sandhurst, in 1826 and as an ensign and lieutenant served in Ireland with the Eighty-third Regiment between 1830 and 1836. He was sickened by his experiences in Ireland, where he was employed in collecting tithe payments from the destitute and miserable peasantry in the interests of Anglo-Irish landlords and the Church of England. Until the end of his life, he advocated the emigration of the industrious poor from Great Britain to the new colonies of white settlement, Jeffersonian democracy on the American model, and radical measures designed to prevent the aggregation of land by a few large proprietors. Although he obtained an excellent report following a postgraduate course at Sandhurst in 1836 and was promoted to captain, he sold his commission and left the army.

In 1838, under the auspices of the Royal Geographical Society, Grey made two journeys of exploration, one to Shark Bay on the central coast and the other to Hanover Bay on the northwest fringe of Western Australia. Both expeditions found little land of economic importance and resulted in great hardships. Grey displayed exceptional bravery and endurance and was the first to find unique Aboriginal rock carvings, but his bushcraft was poor and he suffered a deep Aboriginal spear wound in the thigh, which gave him severe pain until his death. After recovering his health, Grey was made resident magistrate at King George Sound, and on November 2, 1839, he was married to Elizabeth Lucy, daughter of Sir Richard Spencer. The marriage was a most unhappy one. Their only son died in 1841, and, after domestic agonies, the couple was formally separated in 1860, although they were partly reconciled in 1896. Grey's solitary withdrawal and aloofness were reinforced by his tragic private life.

His star, however, was in the ascendant as his report on how to civilize native peoples attracted the favorable opinion of the Colonial Office. At only twenty-eight years of age, Grey was appointed governor of the struggling colony of South Australia in 1840.

Life's Work

Grey immediately stabilized the economy of South Australia by financial retrenchments which offended private interests dependent on the state. He brought order and uniformity to the public service, facilitated the profitable occupation of pastoral land rather than urban speculation, and was lucky in presiding over the discovery of copper and the successful development of wheat growing for export. He ruled alone and successfully by misrepresenting Adelaide opinion to London authority, and London instructions to Adelaide gentry, and he was politically dexterous and astute in dividing and governing South Australia. He was a skillful writer of reports and memoranda and was "as amiable in private life as he was cold and unscrupulous in public affairs." Grey's achievement in setting the infant Australian colony on the road to prosperity was nevertheless considerable, and he gained a deserved reputation as an imperial troubleshooter who could be relied upon to rescue infant British colonies from a wide range of teething problems.

In 1845, Grey was appointed governor of New Zealand, a colony beset by Maori-European confrontation, land disputes, and financial shortfalls. Here he gained his greatest triumph—a knighthood in 1848. Seizing military command, he ended the Bay of Islands rebellion of Kawiti and Hone Heke by capturing their *pah*, or fort, Ruapekapeka ("the bat's nest"), on a Sunday morning when the Maori defenders were at their devotions. By a variety of means he pacified the Maoris of the south, and he captured the savage chief Te Rauparaha, whom he detained without trial. He displayed his brilliant flair for being on the spot when successful military operations were being conducted, and, like a modern general, managed news, dispatches, and personnel with confidence and a talent for public relations. He was indifferent to money but, as William Pember Reeves suggests, greedy for credit. At this time he was a blue-eyed, quick, energetic young officer with a square jaw, a Roman nose, a firm yet mobile mouth, and a queer trick of half closing one eye when he looked at the person whom he was addressing.

Grey learned the Maori language and customs, and through flattery, force, and *mana* (prestige and "face") secured the adherence of Maoris on the fringes of the European frontier. While he built hospitals and schools and encouraged Maori agriculture and their absorption into the European economy, land sales proceeded apace. The lasting merit of his racial policies is still the subject of much dispute. Before he left New Zealand in 1853, he introduced a scheme of representative government, based on elected Provincial Assemblies and a national House of Representatives. This quasi-federal system later proved unworkable, although Grey, when he entered New Zealand politics as an elected member of Parliament, continued to uphold it.

Grey's first New Zealand governorship, like his South Australian tenure, was viewed as a great success. The mess created by his predecessors was dramatically rectified. His assessment of his own achievements was generally accepted in London, and he was transferred in 1854 to another trouble spot in the British Empire. He was made governor of Cape Colony and High Commissioner for South Africa and remained in that post until 1861. His task was to protect and pacify the northern Cape frontier against Kaffir unrest and to regulate the struggling white settlements. His formula, which he had developed as a result of his Australian Aboriginal and New Zealand Maori experiences, was applied on the frontier with the creation of a new buffer province of British Kaffraria.

Grey believed that while native customs were intrinsically interesting, they should be condemned as incompatible with European reason. As Christianity was a superior religion, all natives would eventually receive the Gospel, abandon supersti-tion, and adopt more European modes of life. Through European-sponsored magistrates, schools, hospitals, and farms, backed by a powerful army of white frontiersmen, the native peoples would become absorbed into the processes of colonization and development. Multiracial harmony, based on settler superiority and eventual amalgamation, would then inevitably follow. Grey's policies in South Africa, however, were disastrous for the blacks. He miscalculated the amount of agricultural land available, and charismatic prophets persuaded the Kaffirs to kill all of their cattle and cease planting corn. Devastation (1856-1857) resulted. The Kaffraria and Transkei populations were reduced by two-thirds. The chiefs were arrested and ruined, thirty thousand refugees were deported, and white farmers filled the vacuum. For the first time, Grey ran foul of the Colonial Office by his overspending and disobedience of orders not to attempt to federate Cape Colony, Natal, and Kaffraria with the Afrikaner Orange Free State. He was recalled by Sir Edward Bulwer-Lytton in 1859 but reinstated by the Duke of Newcastle with a warning to obey orders. Grey seldom did. He had the man-on-the-spot mentality and always took authoritarian command, believing that success in the end justified all devious means used to attain it.

In 1861, he was sent to New Zealand again at his own request to prevent further fighting between Maoris and white settlers over land. This time his regime was a mixed one of success, military gain, confusion, betrayal, and failure. For the first time he had to deal with an elected Parliament and a responsible Ministry. Grey played a lone, autocratic hand. He created policy and left his ministers to take the responsibility when things went wrong. He quarreled with the British general, Cameron, and pursued complicated and deceitful policies which, although militarily successful, resulted in major wars in the Waikato, West Coast, and Bay of Islands areas, the confiscation of hundreds of thousands of acres of Maori land, and the ruin of much of their society. He was sacked by the Colonial Office in 1868 for disobeying instructions. Sir George had retained British troops rather than sending them home, had increased expenditures, and was believed to have intensified the conflict by his forward military policy and huge land confiscations from the Maoris. His health broke, nervous problems appeared, his marriage disintegrated, and his self-control sometimes snapped. Increasingly isolated from his ministers and the Colonial Office, Grey was regarded as a dangerous, unscrupulous, and idiosyncratic autocrat. He retired to his retreat on Kawau Island in the Hauraki Gulf, where he devoted himself to literary, acclimatization, ethnographic, and scientific pursuits.

In 1874, Grey returned to politics, this time as the elected superintendent of Auckland Province. Two years later he became a member of the New Zealand House of Representatives and, between 1877 and 1879, led a radical ministry. His program of electoral reforms, the dismantling of big estates, labor regulation, and popular education was premature, but it was later carried out by Richard Seddon. Grey proved a secretive, unstable, and autocratic leader who could not hold his disorderly group of followers together.

Grey consistently advocated British annexation and New Zealand control of Pacific islands. New Caledonia, the New Hebrides, Tonga, Samoa, and Fiji were all part of his grand vision to make Auckland the great mercantile capital of the Southwest Pacific and New Zealand the country "ordained by Nature to be the future Queen of the Pacific." Grey opposed New Zealand's entering the Australian Federation on the grounds that only colored labor could properly develop that continent. A prophet to the last, he looked forward to a grand confederation of all the English-speaking peoples of the British Empire and the United States.

Grey again retreated to Kawau but, in 1894, precipitately left New Zealand for London, where the queen made him a privy councillor. He died of senile decay in London on September 19, 1898, and, a rare honor for an Empire man, was buried in St. Paul's Cathedral.

Summary

Sir George Edward Grey was a complex, enigmatic colonial administrator whose life spanned almost the entire reign of Queen Victoria. Grey decisively influenced events in three major British colonies—New Zealand, South Australia, and Cape Colony. He was a peculiar mixture of autocrat and democrat, a visionary and political manipulator. He is still capable of arousing controversy among historians, repeating in death the passions, hatreds, and adulation that he engendered in life. Grey was a man with a tremendous variety of talents—an able soldier, an intrepid explorer, a man of letters, a mature scientist, and a talented administrator—but he never attained the great reputation that his initial brilliance and creative powers might have been expected to produce.

His published collection of Maori legends, *Polynesian Mythology and Ancient Traditional History of the New Zealanders, as Furnished by Their Priests and Chiefs* (1855), is a classic, and his other writings on African, Aboriginal, and Maori languages are still of use to scholars. His generous donations of two magnificent libraries to the cities of Auckland and Cape Town are still remembered. Grey never accepted defeat. As his biographer James Rutherford comments, "He combined romantic idealism with a fierce determination to carry his ideas into immediate practice . . . he never altered what he once said." A man of immense physical and moral courage, his talents were flawed by his arrogance, disregard for orders, unscrupulous manipulation of evidence and events, and impetuosity. Above all, as his critics aver, he never had the supreme courage—the courage to recognize at critical times—that he was wrong. His virtues carried him through his halcyon days in Adelaide and Auckland, but as matters grew more complex, and he became more opportunistic and corrupted by office and his desire for a major place in imperial and democratic history, his judgment faltered. Contemporaries such as Seddon and Reeves saw much to admire in "good Governor Grey." He retained the affection of many of the Maori chiefs, although his native policies have come increasingly under critical scrutiny. His marriage was a disaster but he took great delight in children. He wanted to play all the major roles on several colonial stages, but, in the end, his audiences had departed and the applause had ceased.

Bibliography

Dalton, Brian John. *War and Politics in New Zealand, 1855-1870.* Sydney: Sydney University Press, 1967. Like Ian Wards's book, Dalton's study criticizes Grey's often insolent behavior as a statesman.

Grattan, Clinton Hartley. *The Southwest Pacific to 1900.* Ann Arbor: University of Michigan Press, 1963. A lively comparative account by an American historian setting Grey's actions within a Pacific context.

McLintock, Alexander H. *Crown Colony Government in New Zealand.* Wellington: Government Printer, 1958. The best work on the constitutional issues in the period before New Zealand was granted representative government in 1854. Grey's role is clearly delineated.

Pike, Douglas Henry. *Paradise of Dissent: South Australia, 1829-1857*. London and New York: Longman, 1957. The classic account of Grey's successful governorship when the infant colony of South Australia was transformed from a group of disheartened settlers and parasitic land sharks into a progressive agricultural settlement.

Rees, William Lee, and Lily Rees. *The Life and Times of Sir George Grey K.C.B.* 2 vols. London: Hutchinson, 1892. Rambling, highly flavored, and entertaining memoirs based on interviews and the selected and selective personal thoughts of Sir George Grey before he retired to die in England.

Reeves, William Pember. *The Long White Cloud: Ao Tea Roa*. 4th ed. London: Allen and Unwin, 1956. Chapter 12, "Good Governor Grey," is a brilliant pen portrait by a younger New Zealand radical that frankly illustrates the enigma and contradiction that was Grey.

Rutherford, James. *Sir George Grey: A Study in Colonial Government*. London: Cassell, 1961. The definitive life, based on a thorough mastery of a host of sources. While he has not solved some of the challenging puzzles of Grey's personal life and controversial public actions, Rutherford, an Empire historian, is essential reading.

Sinclair, Sir Keith. *The Origins of the Maori Wars*. Wellington: New Zealand University Press, 1957. The classic analysis of the New Zealand race wars, detailing Grey's ambiguous motives and authoritative role in both major episodes.

Wards, Ian. *The Shadow of the Land: A Study of British Policy and Racial Conflict in New Zealand, 1832-1852*. Wellington: Government Printer, 1968. Wards's book is a powerful indictment of Grey's character and, particularly, his policy toward native people. The author's thesis is declared on page 391 of his book, where he says that "Grey deliberately perverted his unquestionably great gifts in his own interests, and above all else he strove for personal success, and unimpeded exercise of authority. Self-interest corrupted his judgement, and the causes of whom he governed . . . took second place."

Wilson, Trevor G. *The Grey Government*. Auckland: Auckland University College, 1954. Critical, scholarly, and incisive, Professor Wilson takes a forensic look at a premature—and disastrous—radical New Zealand administration. Grey's shortcomings as a practical representative politician are clearly exposed.

Duncan Waterson

EDVARD GRIEG

Born: June 15, 1843; Bergen, Norway
Died: September 4, 1907; Bergen, Norway
Area of Achievement: Music
Contribution: Drawing on Norwegian folk culture for inspiration, Grieg created an original, distinctive music of Romantic nationalism that made him the foremost composer in Norway and the first Scandinavian composer to achieve world renown.

Early Life

Edvard Grieg was the fourth of five children born to Gesine Hagerup Grieg and Alexander Grieg. Edvard's mother was musically gifted and, having been reared in a prominent and prosperous family, had received the best musical training available in Bergen and Hamburg. She was in great demand as a pianist and throughout her life played an important role in the musical life of Bergen. She gave Edvard his first piano lessons when he was six. His father, Alexander, the son of a prosperous merchant, also took an active interest in music, playing piano duets with his wife and invariably attending concerts on his many business trips abroad. Even when his own financial position deteriorated, he selflessly supported Edvard's lengthy and expensive musical education. Grieg was undoubtedly fortunate to be born into a home where music was a part of everyday life, and to have cultivated, sympathetic, and even indulgent parents. In an autobiographical reminiscence, "My First Success" (1903), Grieg states that his early childhood years were deeply formative and that his later creativity would have been stifled if constraints had been placed too early upon his sensitive and imaginative nature. Not surprisingly, his temperament resulted in an increasing dislike of school: "School life was to me deeply unsympathetic; its materialism, harshness, and coldness were so contrary to my nature that I would think out the most incredible things to be quit of it even if only for a little while."

Although Edvard was fond of composing and improvising at the piano, he never thought of becoming an artist; he was certain that he would follow the path of numerous ancestors and become a minister. Yet, in the summer of 1858, the famous Norwegian violinist Ole Bull visited the Griegs and after hearing Edvard play persuaded Grieg's parents to send Edvard to the Leipzig Conservatory. Thus began for Grieg at age fifteen an experience that he always remembered with distaste. After overcoming his initial homesickness, he found the pedantic methods at the conservatory dry and uninspiring, even occasionally absurd, as when he was required to write a string quartet although he had received no instruction in the form and knew nothing of the technique of string instruments. He applied himself diligently to what he considered sterile exercises, but he was at best a mediocre student and left the conservatory nearly as ignorant as when he had entered it (an account of himself as a student that is curiously contradicted by the records which survive). At the bottom of Grieg's always-bitter reflections on his student days in Leipzig (1858-1862) was the conflict between his inherently lyrical-romantic nature and the German classicism which the conservatory required. He acknowledged that the quantity of music he was able to hear performed in Leipzig was important to his development, particularly the works of the Romantics Robert Schumann, Felix Mendelssohn, and Frédéric Chopin—compensation, he said, "for the instruction in the technique of composition which I did *not* get at the Conservatory." In 1862, he received his certificate and returned to Bergen, where he gave his first concert. In 1863, he took up residence in Copenhagen (then the cultural center of Denmark and Norway), where he met a number of musicians and artists: Hans Christian Andersen, some of whose poems Grieg had already set to music; author Benjamin Feddersen; singer Julius Stenberg; and Niels Gade, the leader of the Scandinavian Romantic school of music. He also met his cousin Nina Hagerup, a gifted singer who would, a few years later, become his wife. He had, however, not yet discovered his own distinctive musical personality.

Life's Work

In 1864, Grieg met the charismatic young composer and fiery champion of Norwegian nationalism Rikard Nordraak. While still a student in Berlin, Nordraak abandoned German music and literature and turned for inspiration to Norwegian sagas, folk tales, ballads, folk music, anecdotes, and history. He saw clearly what Grieg had only dimly felt: not only the sterility of German classicism but also the impossibility of using German Romanticism to create a new, distinctly Norwegian music. Prior to meeting Nordraak, Grieg had known little of Norway's folk culture. He had heard Ole Bull praise Norwegian folk music and had heard him play a few folk tunes, but Norwegian music had not been played in Grieg's home. In Copenhagen, he had met Gade, supposedly the leader of a new school of northern music, but whose compositions were actually heavily derivative of German Romanticism. Grieg's discovery of a rich native heritage was liberating and transforming. He at last felt able to link the best that was within him (his lyric-romantic nature) with the best that was in his native land—the untainted peasant culture with its long memory of an ancient past, its uninhibited expressions of both joy and sorrow, and its intense awareness of Norway's spectacular mountains, waterfalls, and fjords.

In 1865, Grieg, Nordraak, and Danish musicians C. F. E. Horneman and Gottfred Matthison-Hansen founded Euterpe, an organization to promote contemporary Scandinavian music. Although Euterpe flourished for only a short time, it was one indication of Grieg's orientation toward northern music. The early death of Nordraak from pulmonary tuberculosis in 1866 only strengthened Grieg's resolve to champion and create a truly national music, and Nordraak's death became the occasion for one of Grieg's most original and powerful compositions, *Sörgemarsch over Rikard Nordraak* (1866; funeral march in memory of Rikard Nordraak). In 1866, Grieg gave an overwhelmingly successful concert of Norwegian music in Christiania (modern Oslo), which established him as one of his country's foremost young musicians. He became a popular teacher and collaborated with critic Otto Winter-Hjelm to establish a Norwegian Academy of Music. In 1867, Grieg and Nina Hagerup were married, the same year his first book of *Lyriske smaastykker* Op. 12 (lyric pieces) for piano appeared, some of whose titles reflect a growing nationalism: *Norsk* (Norwegian), *Folkevise* (folktune), and *Faedrelandssang* (national song). In 1868, he composed his famous Piano Concerto in A Minor, the same year his only child, Alexandra, was born; she died thirteen months later. His discovery in 1869 of Ludvig Lindeman's collection of folk music was a further important impetus in his evolution toward a distinctively Norwegian style; it became a rich source of inspiration for the numerous tone poems he composed.

Partly because of the enthusiastic support he received from the famed Franz Liszt, Grieg obtained a

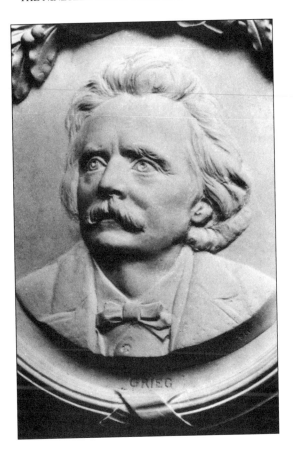

government grant to further his musical education by travel and study abroad. In 1870, he went to Rome, where he was gratified by Liszt's appreciation of his work, particularly of the recently completed Piano Concerto in A Minor. Grieg's prestige was further enhanced by his close association in the 1870's with Norway's most prominent dramatist-poets, Henrik Ibsen and Bjørnstjerne Bjørnson. He set many of Bjørnson's poems to music and collaborated with him to produce an opera, *Olav Trygvason* (a project which was never completed and which occasioned a long period of estrangement between the two artists). In 1874, Ibsen invited Grieg to compose music for a stage production of *Peer Gynt* (1867; English translation, 1892), which resulted in some of Grieg's best-known and most-loved compositions. Additionally, some of Ibsen's poems provided the inspiration for Grieg's highest achievements in song, his *Sex digte* Op. 25 (six songs). A government pension given to Grieg in 1874 freed him from his teaching responsibilities and allowed him to devote himself to composition. Still, Grieg continued to the very end of his life to give substantial amounts of time and energy to conducting and to concert tours (both at home and abroad), possibly as an escape from periods of non-productivity as composer but additionally to renew himself by contact with the centers of creative life abroad. Grieg's best remedy for artistic sterility, however, was to seek regeneration through contact with nature, particularly through Norway's spectacular scenery. In 1877, he moved to Lofthus in the Hardanger district, where he composed *Den bergtekne* Op. 32 (the mountain thrall), the String Quartet in G Minor Op. 27, *Albumblade* Op. 28 (album leaves), and *Improvisata over to norske folkeviser* Op. 29 (improvisations on two Norwegian folk songs). His love of "the great, melancholy Westland nature" caused him eventually to build a villa at Troldhaugen, overlooking the fjord a short distance from Bergen, even though the damp climate was not the best for the health problems that increasingly beset him in later life.

When the Griegs moved to Troldhaugen in 1885, they were moving into their first settled home, such had been the roving nature of their lives. Still, the final two decades of Grieg's life reveal the same restless life-style. As an internationally known composer-conductor-pianist, Grieg undertook numerous concert tours to England, Paris, Brussels, Germany, Sweden, Vienna, the Netherlands, and Warsaw. He met other famous musicians such as Johannes Brahms, Max Reger, Frederick Delius, and Peter Ilich Tchaikovsky. Kaiser William II invited Grieg aboard his yacht (moored in Bergen Harbor) to hear a program of Grieg's works performed by William's private orchestra. Despite increasing complaints about his failing powers and health, Grieg continued to be productive in composition, revising earlier compositions and creating new ones, including the important works for the piano, *Norske folkeviser* Op. 66 (1896; nineteen Norwegian folk tunes), and seven books of *Lyrische Stücke* (1901; lyric pieces). He also composed the last of his Norwegian songs and one of his most original works, *Haugtussa* Op. 67 (1895). *Slåtter* Op. 72 (1902-1903), published as a work for piano, was inspired by Hardanger violin tunes. His final composition was a choral work, Four Psalms Op. 74.

Many years earlier, while a student at Leipzig, Grieg had suffered an attack of pleurisy so severe that it had interrupted his studies and left him with a permanent health liability—a collapsed lung. Although his active life seemed to belie it (frequent walking trips through the mountains, exhausting concert tours, and great bursts of creativity), Grieg's health was always frail. During his last years, it deteriorated significantly. Still, in the last year of his life, he made a tour to Copenhagen, Munich, Berlin, and Kiel, sustaining himself largely through nervous energy and sheer will. Characteristically, Grieg was preparing to leave Norway for a concert tour of England when his doctor, realizing the gravity of Grieg's condition, insisted that Grieg go instead to the hospital in Bergen. He died there the next day, Grieg's funeral in Bergen, September 9, 1907, was an important national and international event, a final tribute to the eminence that Grieg attained as conductor, performer, and composer.

Summary

In assessing Edvard Grieg's contribution to music, typically two questions have been raised: How original an artist was he? and How major? Much that is attractive and uniquely expressive of the northern spirit in Grieg's mature style derives from Norwegian folk songs and dances: a bold use of dissonance reminiscent of the Hardanger fiddle; frequent use of second, seventh, and perfect as well as augmented fourth and fifth intervals; irregularities of rhythm and accent. Yet his music is far from being a transcription or adaptation of sources. Comparisons of Grieg's works with the sources of his inspiration reveal how thoroughly he assimilated their color and spirit and how he transformed them by his own romantic imagination. The result is a fresh, original music which is uniquely expressive of his country's spirit but which invariably bears the deep impress of Grieg's own musical gifts: his ability to express a wide range of emotions and ideas, and particularly his genius for idiosyncratic and impressionistic use of harmony.

The second question of Grieg's ranking among composers is more problematic. Although he attained a popularity such as few artists experience and achieved numerous distinctions (among them membership in the French Legion of Honor and honorary doctorates from Cambridge and Oxford), Grieg himself was ambivalent about his popularity and unimpressed by his many honors and awards. He was aware that his very popularity caused critics to view him with suspicion, lamenting that his "standing as an artist suffers thereby. . . . More fortunate are those artists who do not win so-called popularity while they are still living." Undoubtedly influenced by the prevailing critical standards that confounded greatness with bigness, Grieg was also dismayed by his inability to handle the so-called larger forms, such as oratorios, operas, and symphonies. Yet Wolfgang Amadeus Mozart, a great master of the larger forms, observed: "Our taste in Germany is for long things; BUT SHORT AND GOOD IS BETTER." Qualified critics today tend to view Grieg's songs and piano composition as his most substantial and distinctive achievement.

Bibliography

Abraham, Gerald, ed. *Grieg: A Symposium.* London: Drummond, 1948; Norman: University of Oklahoma Press, 1950. A collection of specialized critical essays that examines every aspect of Grieg's music. A bibliography (focused on the music rather than the man) contains few entries in English. Includes a chronological list of compositions and forty pages of musical examples.

Finck, Henry T. *Grieg and His Music.* London and New York: John Lane, 1909. Includes the author's visit with Grieg a few years before his death. An ardent supporter of Grieg, he offers an uncritical appraisal of Grieg's music and a warmly sympathetic account of his life. Contains numerous photographs, a bibliography, and a catalog of Grieg's compositions.

Grieg, Edvard. "My First Success." *Contemporary Review* (July 1905). Anecdotes and reminiscences of Grieg's childhood and three years spent at the Leipzig Conservatory. Provides insights into Grieg's character and a glimpse of the humorous and self-deprecating side of his personality.

Horton, John. *Grieg.* London: Dent, 1974; New York: Rowman and Littlefield, 1976. A succinct overview of Grieg's life and works. Contains an illuminating calendar of Grieg's life (correlated with the birth/death dates of contemporary musicians), an index identifying names important in any study of Grieg, a complete catalog of works, and an extensive bibliography. The survey of Grieg's life is concise and authoritative, the discussion of Grieg's music is scholarly but eminently readable.

Monrad-Johansen, David. *Edvard Grieg.* Translated by Madge Robertson. Princeton, N.J.: Princeton University Press, 1938. A full-length biography of Grieg by a well-known Norwegian composer who had access to documents and letters unavailable to other writers. A balanced and objective but enthusiastic appreciation of Grieg's work and life, especially of his significance for Norway. Contains a few photographs.

Steen-Nkleberg, Einar. *Onstage with Grieg: Interpreting His Piano Music.* Bloomington: Indiana University Press, 1997. Insight into the performance and background of Grieg's piano works by the composer's premier interpreter, Einar Steen-Nkleberg.

Sutcliffe, W. Dean. "Grieg's Fifth: The Linguistic Battleground of 'Klokkeklang.' " *Musical Quarterly* 80, no. 1 (Spring 1996). Detailed study and analysis of Greig's "Klokkeklang."

Karen A. Kildahl

JACOB AND WILHELM GRIMM

Jacob Ludwig Grimm

Born: January 4, 1785; Hanau, near Kassel, Hesse-Kassel (now Germany)

Died: September 20, 1863; Berlin, Prussia (now Germany)

Wilhelm Carl Grimm

Born: February 24, 1786; Hanau, near Kassel, Hesse-Kassel (now Germany)

Died: December 16, 1859; Berlin, Prussia (now Germany)

Areas of Achievement: Language and linguistics; and literature

Contributions: Remembered as the authors of probably the best-known book of fairy tales in the Western world, the Grimm brothers were two of the most noted philologists of the nineteenth century. They made significant contributions to linguistic theory, folklore, and the study of the German language and its literature.

Early Lives

Jacob and Wilhelm Grimm were born to a rather well-to-do family in a small village in what is now central Germany. Their father was a lawyer, judge, and public servant; however, he died suddenly at the age of forty-four, leaving his widow and his eleven-year-old son Jacob to take care of the other five children. Though times were financially difficult, Jacob and Wilhelm advanced academically, and by 1803 they were both studying law at the University of Marburg. Under the influence of a professor of legal history, the Grimm brothers became interested in the origins of the law and its growth and development in a cultural context. They also took up the study of philology (the investigations of ancient languages and texts) and began a serious inquiry into German folklore and linguistics. In 1825 Wilhelm married Dortchen Wild (who, along with other members of her family, provided the brothers with many of the folktales they would later use in their collections); Jacob never married.

In 1813, after the defeat of Napoleon Bonaparte, Jacob became a member of the local parliament. However, the local German princes regained their power, ending German reunification and democratization. The Grimm brothers took jobs as librarians and, from around 1815 to 1830, produced several books on German legends, legal history, and grammar. However, both brothers lost their librarianships and university teaching opportunities after failing to take loyalty oaths to the local monarchs. By 1840, however, their fortunes had changed, and

both were appointed professors at the University of Berlin, where they continued the work they had already begun on their massive *Deutsches Wörterbuch* (1854; German dictionary). Both became involved in politics again during the German revolution of 1848 and were elected to the local legislature, only to resign when the revolutionary movement collapsed.

Lives' Work

The work of the Grimm brothers cannot adequately be appreciated without some understanding of the intellectual and political climate of early nineteenth century Europe. By this time, most of the people and places of the world had been "discovered" by Westerners, though to be sure, much of the details still needed to be filled in. What European scholars at the time faced was a world of almost infinite variety in terms of cultural customs, races, languages, and religious beliefs. The task, then, was to try to put order into this apparent chaos: Why was the world so diverse? Why did people look so different? Why were there so many different languages? Previous answers, often based on biblical stories (such as the Tower of Babel to account for linguistic heterogeneity), were proving inadequate in light of new data coming in from ethnology, geology, and biology.

The American and French Revolutions had also called into question the notion of the monarch state, the role of the governor and the governed, and the nature of the political unit. Who should govern whom? What constitutes a "country"? Does every different group of language speakers deserve to be a separate nation? The work of the Grimm brothers was informed by all these questions.

In 1786 (the year of Wilhelm's birth), the British legal scholar and Asian specialist William Jones shocked the world by claiming that Sanskrit (the ancient holy language of India) was related to Greek and Latin, having "sprung from a common source which, perhaps, no longer exists." It had already been well known that many European languages shared a common ancestor in the past (for example, modern Romance languages such as French, Spanish, and Italian were derived from classical Roman Latin). What was startling about Jones's hypothesis was that he claimed that most of the languages of Europe were also connected to many other languages hitherto thought to be quite dissimilar. This supposed common parent language was termed "Proto Indo-European," and much of linguistic scholarship in the nineteenth century centered on trying to prove or disprove the Indo-European hypothesis. The Grimm brothers, particularly Jacob, made some important discoveries in this field and helped to establish the now commonly accepted view that the languages of today in the Indo-European family are actually all descendant from a common source.

The Indo-European hypothesis was one of the most critical issues of the nineteenth century. At stake were some of the deepest and strongest convictions held by Europeans: If linguistic affinity between Europe and India could be shown, notions of culture, race, and national identity would have to be reevaluated. Also, European scholars began to wonder just who these Indo-Europeans were, where they might have come from, and what some of their customs and beliefs might have been. It was an attempt to address some of these issues that prompted the Grimm brothers to begin their collection of fairy tales around 1806. They argued that the folktales they were finding had ancient Indo-European origins, and that the *Märchen* (magic fables or fairy tales) they were finding were survivals from old classical mythology. The characters in the folktales they gathered, then, were the modern remnants of old Teutonic gods and goddesses.

Also, the German *Volk* (people) in their folklore studies were always the primary focus for the Grimm brothers. In their time, the German-speaking people in northern and central Europe had not yet come together to form a nation-state. Thus, as

one translator put it, "from the beginning [the Grimm brothers'] principal concern was to uncover the etymological and linguistic truths that bound the German people together and were expressed in their laws and customs." In other words, people with a common tongue, a common mythology, and a common set of customs constituted a distinct culture or race deserving their own sovereignty; therefore, the Grimms sought to demonstrate the unity and origins of the Germans through their linguistic and folklore studies.

The Grimm brothers spent about forty years gathering their stories, though the first volume of their *Kinder- und Hausmärchen* (*German Popular Stories*, 1823-1826; best known as *Grimm's Fairy Tales*) was published in 1812 when the brothers were still in their mid-twenties. A second volume appeared in 1815. These first two books contained scholarly annotations and 156 stories, fables, legends and the like. These initial collections were not primarily intended as mere children's entertainment, but were to be read by educated lay adults and specialists who were interested in German folklore and culture. However, as time wore on, it became clear that children were as interested in these fairy tales as scholars. In 1819, the second (one-volume) edition appeared with 170 stories, and the annotations were purged and published separately. By the time of the final 1857 seventh edition, the collection contained 211 tales, now highly refined and revised. This is the version upon which most English translations are based, and it contains some of the most well-known stories in Western literature, including "Snow White," "Little Red Riding Hood," "Cinderella," "Sleeping Beauty," "The Frog Prince," "Hansel and Gretel," "Rapunzel," and "Rumpelstiltskin."

Contrary to popular belief, the Grimm brothers did not actually gather their stories from peasants in the field. Many informants were actually bourgeois friends or acquaintances who told stories to the Grimms at their leisure in their homes. Also, a number of stories were taken directly from earlier written sources, including a few Latin poems of the fourteenth century. In all cases, however, the Grimm brothers greatly expanded and edited the tales for dramatic and stylistic effect. Indirect speech was put into direct quotation, colorful language was embedded, and motivations of the characters were sometimes expanded upon or created. Chronologies were improved, and details that might detract from a story's flow were eliminated. The Grimm brothers, then, were interested in the literary quality of the tales as much as anything else. Also, as time went on and it became apparent that children were reading the stories as often as adults, pains were taken by the brothers to make them more palatable for young middle-class Christian German sensibilities. Sexual innuendo and coarse language were eliminated, and the Grimm brothers spent an increasing amount of effort emphasizing morals in their tales.

Summary

Jacob Grimm retired from his university post in 1848, as did Wilhelm in 1852. Throughout their lives, the brothers worked in consort and lived near or with each other. Jacob wrote twenty-one books during his lifetime, while Wilhelm wrote fourteen. They also produced eight books together. Jacob was noted for his linguistics work, while Wilhelm spent much of his energy as the primary editor and author of the fairy tales. When Wilhelm died in 1859, Jacob took the loss very hard but continued to carry on their work until his own death in 1863.

Each generation seems to have to reassess the Grimm brothers in the context of their own times.

By the 1870's, in Prussia and much of the rest of the German principalities, the Grimm tales had been incorporated into the school curriculum. Their popularity in the late twentieth century English-speaking world has been attested by the number of film adaptations that have been based on Grimm tales. There have been very few academic disciplines that have not had something to say about these fairy tales. Psychologists have searched them for universal archetypes and symbols of the human psyche and have sometimes seen commentaries being made on human development. Educators and philosophers draw attention to how the human morality play becomes manifested in these seemingly simple fables. Marxists point out how the Protestant work ethic and bourgeois values underlay most of the lessons found in the Grimm stories. Feminists argue that patriarchal notions of sex roles are reinforced by the Grimm brothers and sometimes even try to retell these fairy tales using their own vocabulary. Literary critics of all persuasions have analyzed them for tropes, stylistic features, and motifs of all kinds.

The Grimm brothers reinvented—or at least highly refined—a special genre: the literary folk tale. While the Grimms no doubt believed that their collection revealed the genius and essence of the German-speaking people, they also believed that their stories contained certain universal (or at least Western) truths that spoke to everyone from a culture or cultures long past. Yet they felt that the messages and wisdom they conveyed were still very much contemporary. In this sense, Grimm's fairy tales join some of the world's other great story collections—such as *The Arabian Nights' Entertainment* from the Middle East, *The Pañcatantra* from India, and *Aesop's Fables* from Greece—as exemplars and depositories of literary drama, human wisdom, and creativity, and as reflections of the human spirit. It is probably for these reasons that the stories are still read today and will likely be read for quite some time.

Bibliography

Grimm, Jacob, and Wilhelm Grimm. *The Complete Fairy Tales of the Brothers Grimm.* Edited and translated by Jack Zipes. New York: Bantam, 1987. This is perhaps the best of the many translations in English. The introduction is informative, and data is also given on the informants the Grimm brothers used in their research. Also included are thirty-two tales that the Grimms dropped from earlier editions, as well as eight variants showing how the Grimms edited and recreated tales as they were compiling their collection.

_____. *Complete Grimm's Fairy Tales*. Edited and translated by Padraic Colum. New York: Pantheon, 1972. This edition is famous for a fine thirty-page commentary by the renowned mythologist Joseph Campbell.

_____. *Grimm's Tales for Young and Old: The Complete Stories*. Edited and translated by Ralph Manheim. London: Gollancz, and New York: Anchor, 1977. Another standard translation.

Kamenetsky, Christa. *The Brothers Grimm and Their Critics: Folktales and the Quest for Meaning*. Athens: Ohio University Press, 1992. Kamenetsky provides a good literary and social analysis.

McGlathery, James. *Grimm's Fairy Tales: A History of Criticism of a Popular Classic*. Columbia, S.C.: Camden House, 1993. McGlathery traces the place of the Grimm tales in popular German and Western literature.

Peppard, Murry. *Paths Through the Forest. A Biography of the Brothers Grimm*. New York: Holt Rinehart, 1971. An approachable general biography.

Zipes, Jack. *The Brothers Grimm: From the Enchanted Forest to the Modern World*. New York: Routledge, 1988; London: Routledge, 1989. A good biography and criticism by one of the foremost Grimm translators.

James Stanlaw

SIR WILLIAM ROBERT GROVE

Born: July 11, 1811; Swansea, Glamorganshire, Wales

Died: August 1, 1896; London, England

Areas of Achievement: Invention, physics, and law

Contribution: Though trained as a lawyer, Grove invented the electric cell that bears his name. He also discovered and popularized the conservation of energy principle and helped to reform the Royal Society of London.

Early Life

William Robert Grove was born July 11, 1811, in Swansea, Wales, the only son of Anne Bevan and John Grove, magistrate and deputy lieutenant for Glamorganshire. After receiving instruction from private tutors, Grove attended Brasenose College, Oxford, graduating with a B.A. in 1832 and an M.A. in 1835. It appeared that he was fated to follow his father in the legal profession. He was admitted as a law student at Lincoln's Inn on November 11, 1831, and was called to the bar on November 23, 1835. On May 27, 1837, he married Emma Maria Powles, daughter of John Diston Powles of Summit House, Middlesex. They had two sons and four daughters.

Despite his preparation for a legal career, Grove had always been interested in science. In 1835, he appeared to suffer from bad health and turned from law to science, becoming a member of the Royal Institution in that same year. His scientific curiosity was drawn to the electric cell, invented by Alessandro Volta in 1800. As it evolved before 1835, the typical cell consisted of two pieces of different metals, called electrodes, placed in either one or two chemical solutions, called electrolytes. These cells were weak and provided current for only the shortest periods of time as a consequence of a phenomenon called polarization.

One of the first practical solutions to the problems of polarization was that of John Frederic Daniell, professor of chemistry at King's College, London. Unlike Grove, Daniell was a member of the Royal Society of London, which had awarded Daniell its prestigious Rumford Medal in 1832 for an improved pyrometer, an instrument for measuring very high temperatures. The Daniell cell, as it came to be called, brought its inventor another distinguished honor from the Royal Society, the Copley Medal, in 1837.

Starting in 1835, Grove experimented with different electrodes and electrolytes. In 1839, he hit upon the combination that became the standard form of his cell: a zinc electrode in dilute sulfuric acid and a platinum electrode in strong nitric acid. A porous membrane separated the two acids and eliminated polarization, the same means used in the Daniell cell. Grove's electrodes and electrolytes were different, however, and provided about twice the voltage of the Daniell cell and a current of up to ten amperes.

From a technical point of view, Grove had invented a superior cell. Yet it was not very practical. Platinum was very expensive. Worse, as the cell operated, the platinum and concentrated nitric acid reacted to create poisonous gas. The German chemist, Robert Bunsen, inventor of the laboratory burner of the same name, substituted an inexpensive carbon electrode for the platinum in 1841. This variation somewhat decreased the cell's voltage, but it doubled the current produced. The higher cost of nitric versus sulfuric acid made the Grove-Bunsen cell costlier per unit than the Daniell cell. In terms of voltage and amperage, however, the Grove-Bunsen cell provided significant savings over the Daniell cell and became the workhorse battery for applications requiring large currents, especially early forms of electrical lighting, long-distance telegraph lines, and the growing electroplating industry.

The invention of his cell immediately helped Grove's scientific career and brought him honor. On November 26, 1840, he was elected a Fellow of the Royal Society of London. The next year, he was appointed professor of experimental philosophy (physics) at the Royal Institution, a position he held until 1847. The only cloud on the horizon was Daniell, who accused Grove of having stolen his idea. Grove denied the charges in a series of letters published in the *Philosophical Magazine* in 1842 and early 1843. The subject of the dispute was the use of the porous membrane, which the French scientist Antoine César Becquerel had used as early as 1829. Despite the sharp language of their letters, the two men did not become bitter enemies.

Life's Work

Grove's scientific work did not end with the electric cell, which he continually improved. The focus of his later work was the same as that which had brought him to study the cell in the first place: an understanding of the relationship between electrical and chemical phenomena. Throughout 1839 and 1840, he published the results of his experiments in British, French, and German scientific journals.

In 1841, Grove published an article on a method for etching daguerreotype plates. The daguerreotype was the first photographic process and involved chemically fixing an image on a metallic plate. At that time, there was no process for reproducing a number of prints from a negative. Grove devised an electrochemical process that converted the daguerreotype plate into a reverse etching from which positive copies could be printed.

Grove was especially interested in the possibility of using gases rather than liquids as electrolytes in electric batteries. Into sealed test tubes of hydrogen and oxygen, he inserted platinum strips so that one end was in the gas and the other end rested in a dilute solution of sulfuric acid. Grove discovered that a current flowed from one platinum strip to the other. He published his findings in 1842 and called this device his "gaseous voltaic battery." Later, he used hydrogen and chlorine gas and increased the current produced.

Grove used his gas battery to decompose water into hydrogen and oxygen gas. He noted the electrical current created as a result of the chemical activity of the cell and the ability of that current to separate water chemically into hydrogen and oxygen. In short, it was a process of chemical and electrical energy conversions. As Grove wrote in 1842 in the *Philosophical Magazine*,

> This battery establishes that gases in combining and acquiring a liquid form evolve sufficient force to decompose a similar liquid and cause it to acquire a gaseous form. This is to my mind the most interesting effect of the battery; it exhibits such a beautiful instance of the correlation of natural forces.

The "correlation of natural forces" was the subject of his Royal Institution lecture given on January 19, 1842, on advances in the physical sciences since the institution's founding. He further developed the subject during his lectures that year. For Grove, the "correlation of natural forces" meant that the forces of nature, such as electricity, magnetism, heat, light, and chemical energy, could be converted into one another, could neither be created nor destroyed, and were manifestations of a sin-

gle force. It was a new idea that captured the excitement and built upon the discoveries of such contemporary scientists as Jöns Jakob Berzelius of Sweden, who attempted to explain all chemical reactions in terms of electricity, Hans Christian Oersted, the Dane who demonstrated the conversion of electricity into magnetism, and the Englishman Michael Faraday, who showed the production of magnetism from electricity.

The principle that Grove lectured about is fundamental to the modern understanding of the physical universe. Grove's single force that revealed itself as various physical forces such as electricity and light is now called energy. The "correlation of natural forces" is known as the conservation of energy, which was discovered simultaneously by a number of scientists. In addition to Grove, Faraday in England, Hermann Helmholtz (a physicist), and Justus von Liebig (a chemist) in Germany, to name a few, published articles and other works in the 1840's, setting forth the principle of energy conservation. The large number of laboratory experiments that illustrated transformations of one force into another, especially electrical and chemical ones, led Grove to give his lectures on the convertibility of physical forces. He also made reference to Samuel Taylor Coleridge, the English writer and proponent of German *Naturphilosophie*, a philosophical movement which had lead many in Germany to discover the conservation principle as well.

Grove's importance for the discovery of the conservation of energy was also his role as a science popularizer. Whereas others published their findings in the major scientific journals of the day, Grove first developed his ideas in the popular lectures he gave as professor of experimental philosophy at the Royal Institution in 1842. Over the next year, he refined these lectures and the Royal Institution published the kernel of Grove's ideas in 1846 as the fifty-two-page booklet *On the Correlation of Physical Forces: Being the Substance of a Course of Lectures Delivered in the London Institution, in the Year 1843.*

From this rather modest start, *On the Correlation of Physical Forces* grew in size from edition to edition and spread Grove's ideas throughout England as well as overseas. The second edition appeared in 1850 and was more than one hundred pages. The 1855 third edition was more than two hundred pages and was translated into French in 1856 and German in 1863. The fourth edition (1862) was nearly three hundred pages long and was republished in 1865 as the first American edition. The fifth edition (1867) was more than three hundred and the sixth edition (1874) almost five hundred pages.

In addition to popularizing scientific knowledge, Grove was highly interested in scientific institutions. He was an original member of the London Chemical Society and president of the British Association for the Advancement of Science in 1866. Elected a Fellow of the Royal Society of London in 1840, he was voted a member of the Council in 1845, a year when prominent members who wished to raise the society's standards were considering asking the government for a new charter. Grove joined the Charter Committee and played a significant role in realizing a number of reforms, such as the limitation of membership numbers, which were approved by the Council in 1847. Grove was also a member of the 1849 committee charged with reforming the process for awarding the society's important Royal Medal.

As a consequence of his reform efforts, Grove was proposed as a candidate to fill a vacant society secretary post in 1848, but lost because of fighting between representatives of the physical and life sciences. As late as 1870, he was considered as a candidate for president of the Royal Society and continued to play an active role in the society's life into the 1880's.

While maintaining an interest in the reform of the Royal Society and revising his book on the conservation of energy, Grove ceased to conduct experiments, perhaps because of his growing family (six children). He pursued a more financially rewarding career in law starting in 1853. In this, too, he excelled. In November, 1853, he became a member of the Queen's Court. Between 1862 and 1864, he combined his knowledge of science and law as a member of the Royal Commission on patent law.

Grove then distinguished himself as a judge in various courts. He became a judge in common pleas court on November 30, 1871; a justice of the high court, November 1, 1875; and member of the queen's bench division, December 16, 1880. He was knighted at Osborne, February 21, 1872. Grove retired from the bench in September, 1887, and wrote a number of odd philosophical works on the equilibrium of forces in nature before his death in 1896.

The high point of Grove's legal career was his defense of William Palmer, the Rugeley poisoner. Palmer had been dismissed from his apprenticeship with a Liverpool wholesale druggist for embezzlement. Apprenticed to a surgeon, he ran away after some misconduct. He eventually learned some medicine, became a member of the Royal College of Surgeons, and started a general practice. He then gave this up, was married, and devoted himself to horse racing as an owner and breeder. Palmer was also a gambler and ran up enormous debts.

On September 29, 1854, Palmer's wife died of "bilious cholera" and Palmer collected thirteen thousand pounds in life insurance. His brother Walter died suddenly and suspiciously the next year. Palmer did not receive any of the thirteen thousand pounds of insurance policies that he had on his brother. On December 15, 1855, Palmer was arrested and charged with poisoning his friend John Parsons Cook, a betting man. The multiple poisonings troubled the area's residents, who attributed a number of mysterious local deaths to the Rugeley poisoner, as Palmer came to be called. The case was therefore tried elsewhere, at the Old Bailey, on May 14, 1856. News of the trial and Palmer's poisoning of his wife, brother, and friend spread throughout England and Europe. Grove was Palmer's defense attorney. Palmer was found guilty and hanged at Stafford on June 14, 1856.

Summary

Although dynamos driven by steam and water turbines provide homes and industries with an enormous amount of electric power, the predecessor of these large-scale generating systems was the electric battery. The multitude of nineteenth century electrical applications that preceded the dynamo, such as electroplating, telegraphy, telephony, railroad signals, door bells, electric clocks, even electric motors and lights, depended upon the availability of a steady, inexpensive source of current. The batteries of the early decades of the nineteenth century were incapable of operating over extended periods because of polarization. The Daniell cell solved that problem inexpensively and set the stage for industrial use of the battery. Grove's cell provided an even higher voltage and amperage, both necessary for the increasingly larger-scale uses of the battery during the 1850's and 1860's. By 1870, the use of the Grove-Bunsen cell had grown to such an enormous extent, with many telegraph stations and electroplating plants each employing hundreds of them, that an alternative was sought: the dynamo.

As significant as the Grove-Bunsen cell was in the early development of electrical technology, Sir William Robert Grove's discovery of the conservation of energy has had more enduring impact. Energy conservation—the idea that energy is neither created nor destroyed—is fundamental to an understanding of the physical universe. While he was not its sole discoverer, Grove was an important popularizer of the concept at a time when amateurs could and did make major contributions to scientific knowledge. This, undoubtedly, more than any of his other work, was the basis for Grove's scientific reputation during his lifetime.

Far less known, however, are Grove's efforts to reform the Royal Society of London. The consequence of those reforms increasingly turned the society into an organization of professional scientists. Since then, the growing professionalization of science and scientists has also left its mark on education, funding, and a range of other activities. Today, science often entails team research, specialized training, and multibillion-dollar equipment. The gifted, curiosity-driven amateur, such as Grove, is the exception. Ironically, Grove's reforms have contributed to the creation of a world that would have excluded him.

Bibliography

Dunsheath, Percy. *A History of Electrical Power Engineering.* Cambridge, Mass.: MIT Press, 1962. Dunsheath places the invention of Grove's cell within the history of batteries as well as electrical engineering in general.

Grove, William Robert. *Address to the British Association for the Advancement of Science.* London: Longman, 1867. President of the British Association for the Advancement of Science in 1866, Grove delivered this speech on August 22, 1866, at the society's meeting in Nottingham. Its subject was Grove's favorite: the conservation of energy.

———. *On the Correlation of Physical Forces: Being the Substance of a Course of Lectures Delivered in the London Institution, in the Year 1843.* 6th ed. London: Longman, 1874. This volume provides Grove's arguments in favor of the conservation of energy. The first edition reproduces the original series of lectures at the Royal Institution. Later editions include revisions and new material. The sixth edition also contains reprints of many of Grove's early scientific papers.

Hall, Marie Boas. *All Scientists Now: The Royal Society in the Nineteenth Century.* Cambridge and New York: Cambridge University Press, 1984. Hall discusses Grove's role as a reformer of the Royal Society of London, though this work is mainly concerned with the evolution of the society from an amateur to a professional organization of scientists in the nineteenth century.

King, W. James. "The Development of Electrical Technology in the Nineteenth Century: 1. The Electrochemical Cell and the Electromagnet." *United States National Museum Bulletin* no. 228 (1962): 231-271. A look at Grove's contribution to the development of the battery.

Kuhn, Thomas S. "Energy Conservation as an Example of Simultaneous Discovery." In *Critical Problems in the History of Science,* edited by Marshall Clagett. Madison: University of Wisconsin Press, 1959. An important work for understanding the discovery of energy conservation by Grove and others. It underlines the role of laboratory experiments and German *Naturphilosophie.*

Morus, Iwan Rhys. "Correlation and Control: William Robert Grove and the Construction of a New Philosophy of Scientific Reform." *Studies in His-*

tory and Philosophy of Science 22, no. 4 (December 1991). Discussion of Grove's career and the importance of politics on science at the time.

Webb, K. R. "Sir William Robert Grove (1811-1896) and the Origins of the Fuel Cell." *Journal of the Royal Institute of Chemistry* 85 (1961): 291-293. A short article on what Grove called his "gaseous voltaic battery" and which led him to his understanding of the conservation of energy.

Andrew J. Butrica

SIR ROBERT ABBOTT HADFIELD

Born: November 28, 1858; Attercliffe, Sheffield, England

Died: September 30, 1940; Kingston, Surrey, England

Area of Achievement: Metallurgy

Contribution: Hadfield's discovery of manganese steel ushered in the age of alloy steels, which have proven to be essential to the development of modern industrial technology and weapons.

Early Life

The only son of Robert Hadfield and Marianne Abbott, Robert Abbott Hadfield was born November 28, 1858, in the village of Attercliffe, Sheffield. His father was the owner of Hadfield's Steel Foundry and one of England's pioneers in the manufacture of steel castings, an important step in the development of the English arms industry.

After studying at the Collegiate School in Sheffield, Hadfield chose to forgo further formal education at either Oxford or Cambridge, probably an early indication of his belief that learning by doing was superior to acquiring knowledge solely from books. Instead, in 1875 he briefly apprenticed with the local steel firm of Jonas and Colver. He also received private tuition in chemistry and established a personal laboratory in the basement of the family home. After only a few months at Jonas and Colver, Hadfield entered the family business, while at the same time initiating his systematic research into alloys. Combining a tremendous capacity for work with a very practical interest in the efficient organization of labor, Hadfield managed to be highly productive both as a businessman and as an experimental metallurgist.

Life's Work

It was during a visit to the Paris Exhibition in 1878 that Hadfield learned of the researches of the Terre Noire Company regarding the introduction of manganese into steel. They had discovered that adding up to three percent manganese hardened steel, but increasing the amount beyond that level left the steel extremely brittle. Hadfield decided to expand upon the French experiments by combining both manganese and silicon with steel in varying amounts.

Except for a break in the summer of 1882 to visit American steel-making facilities, especially those in Pittsburgh, Chicago, and Philadelphia, Hadfield worked on the first phase of his experiments on steel alloys for approximately four years. He increased the percentage of manganese considerably, ultimately discovering in late 1882 that twelve to fourteen percent manganese produced a steel alloy of novel properties, relatively soft, yet resistant to crushing and abrasion. He patented his discoveries in 1883-1884, while spending five additional years confirming his results. Not until 1887 did he publicly display his new product.

At age twenty-four, Hadfield had taken responsibility for the family firm because of his father's failing health. Upon the death of his father in 1888, he became chairman and managing director of Hadfield's Steel Foundry. Having discovered manganese steel was only the first step for a practical businessman. Hadfield still had to find commercial uses for it. He turned to the United States, which had impressed him greatly during his visit, as a potential market. (He would later turn to the Unites States for his bride, marrying Frances Belt Wickersham of Philadelphia in 1894). The first at-

tempted commercial application of manganese steel was railway car wheels, but the alloy proved unsatisfactory. Hadfield quickly learned, however, that it was superior to other metals for railway rails and switches. Other uses for the alloy were in ore-crushing machinery, paper-pulp beaters, and burglar-proof safes. The mining industry was revolutionized: Manganese steel dredge buckets could be twice as large and operate at much greater depths than their predecessors. The alloy also proved to be ideal for tank treads, steel helmets for soldiers, and other forms of modern military technology.

Another Hadfield discovery in the 1880's was a low-carbon silicon steel alloy. Although patented in 1883, silicon steel attracted little interest until the first decade of the twentieth century. Again, the United States provided the market. Silicon steel proved to be the solution to energy losses in alternating-current transformers, increasing the efficiency of the transformers from sixty-eight percent to ninety-nine percent.

Hadfield's metallurgical research generally followed a standard pattern. Having decided to investigate the influence of a given element on steel, he would create a large number of alloys, steadily increasing the proportion of the added element. Each alloy would be tested for its mechanical, electrical, and magnetic properties, with an eye for possible industrial applications. Later in his career, Hadfield would collaborate with physicists in his investigations, providing them with alloys for experiments, for example, on the effect of very low temperatures on metals. He also became extremely interested in the history of metals and encouraged archaeological research into the antiquity of iron.

Success as a metallurgist was complemented by success in business. During his lifetime, combining great energy, technical expertise, and enlightened labor policies, Hadfield turned the family firm into one of the world's largest steel foundries. In 1891, he introduced the eight-hour day into his firm, one of the earliest examples of this reform. Not surprisingly, such policies were rewarded by a loyal work force.

Photographs of the mature Hadfield show a high forehead, hooded eyes, and a full mustache. The impression is more of a scientist than a captain of industry. The elderly Hadfield looked much the same, except that the mustache had turned gray.

Hadfield won numerous honors. The Iron and Steel Institute awarded him its Bessemer Gold Medal in 1904. Knighted in 1908, he was made a baronet in 1917. He was elected a Fellow of the Royal Society of London in 1909, in recognition of his contributions to the field of metallurgy, and served as president of the Faraday Society from 1913 through 1920. In 1939, he was awarded the freedom of the city of Sheffield. In 1940, Hadfield died at home, on September 30.

Summary

Sir Robert Abbott Hadfield was an extremely important figure in the maturation of the British steel industry. When he entered the family firm, the Sheffield foundries were very traditional in their methods and their products. Trial and error was the system that governed the firms that had made Sheffield the world's leading steel-making center during the first half of the nineteenth century. There had been little or no interaction with the scientific community. Hadfield helped change that. Combining a systematic experimental approach, seemingly boundless energy, and an eye for the ever-increasing American market, he initiated the age of alloy steels. His genius did not lie in his methodology, which was essentially to interrogate nature slowly but surely, but in his rejection of his contemporaries' tendency to accept unproven assumptions about steel alloys rather than conduct tests and in his enthusiastic recognition of the potential of his discovery when others were indifferent. He saw the revolutionary possibilities when most steel makers did not. Once he proved the economic value of his experiments, however, others followed his example. The most significant of the later breakthroughs was the discovery of stainless steel by a fellow resident of Sheffield, Harry Brearley, in 1912.

Alloy steels have proven vital to the development of modern technology. In the United States in particular, the expansion of the railway system in the late nineteenth century and the progress of electrification in the early twentieth century were both dependent on Hadfield's discoveries. Indeed, so was the British military, which utilized the alloys for defensive purposes, such as steel helmets, and offensive purposes, such as armor-piercing shells. Hadfield's work, of clear benefit in many ways, helpful in the scientist's unraveling of the mysteries of metals, could also be applied in destructive ways. In that property it was not unique.

Bibliography

Carr, James C., and Walter Taplin. *A History of the British Steel Industry.* Cambridge, Mass.: Harvard University Press, and Oxford: Blackwell, 1962. A standard history for the period after the mid-nineteenth century which puts Hadfield's work in perspective.

Desch, C. H. "Robert Abbott Hadfield." *Obituary Notices of Fellows of the Royal Society* 3 (1940/1941): 647-664. Still the standard source for biographical information about Hadfield. Includes a bibliography of his scientific and technical publications.

Hadfield, Robert A. *Metallurgy and Its Influence on Modern Progress*. London: Chapman and Hall, 1925; New York: Van Nostrand, 1926. Presents Hadfield's own views on his work and its impact.

Smith, Cyril S. *A History of Metallography: The Development of Ideas on the Structure of Metals Before 1890*. Chicago: University of Chicago Press, 1960. Provides an extensive discussion of metallurgical theory and the state of knowledge prior to Hadfield's experiments.

Tweedale, Geoffrey. "Metallurgy and Technological Change: A Case Study of Sheffield Specialty Steel and America, 1830-1930." *Technology and Culture* 27 (April 1986): 189-222. Tweedale looks at the changing state of the Sheffield steel industry and the importance of the American market for the firms.

————. "Sir Robert Abbott Hadfield F.R.S. (1858-1940), and the Discovery of Manganese Steel." *Notes and Records of the Royal Society* 40 (November 1985): 63-73. An account of Hadfield's early experimental work based on an analysis of his diaries, notebooks, and letters.

Marc Rothenberg

ERNST HAECKEL

Born: February 16, 1834; Potsdam, Prussia
Died: August 9, 1919; Jena, Germany
Areas of Achievement: Biology, natural history, zoology, and philosophy
Contribution: Haeckel studied and classified many marine organisms, especially the radiolaria and the medusae. He is most noted for his refinement of Charles Darwin's theory of evolution, its extension to mankind and the origin of life, the refinement of the biogenetic law, and the development of monism as a religion.

Early Life

Ernst Heinrich Philipp August Haeckel was born in Potsdam, Prussia, on February 16, 1834, to Karl Haeckel and Charlotte Sethe Haeckel. Both the Haeckel and Sethe families contributed prominently to German history and intermarried on several occasions. In both families there were several prominent lawyers. Karl Haeckel was a state councillor.

Shorly after Ernst was born, his family moved to Meresburg. There, he attended school until he was eighteen. As a boy he had a great love of nature, which was fostered by his mother. He collected and classified many plants as a youth; his father occasionally gave him words of encouragement. He had a strong sense of independence and individuality, and even as a youth he was a compulsive worker.

In 1852, Ernst entered the University of Jena to work with Matthias Schleiden, a codeveloper of the cell theory. Schleiden taught him how to combine his interests in botany and philosophy. Not long after entering Jena, however, he became ill and had to return to Berlin to stay with his parents. He entered the University of Würzburg in the fall of 1852 to work with the botanist Alexander Braun. His father's persistence, however, made him turn his attention to medicine. While at Würzburg, he studied under Albert Kölliker, Franz Leydig, and Rudolf Virchow. At Würzburg, he developed an interest in embryology.

The philosophy at Würzburg, where learning through research was emphasized, was well suited for the young Haeckel. Natural phenomena were explained and studied through cause-and-effect relationships and allowed little opportunity for the intrusion of mysticism and the supernatural. These philosophies laid the foundation for Haeckel's future work.

Life's Work

During the summer of 1854, Haeckel had the opportunity to study comparative anatomy under Johannes Müller. Müller gave Haeckel permission to work in the museum. During that summer, Müller took the young Haeckel to sea, where he taught him how to study living marine organisms. Haeckel stayed the winter at Berlin and wrote his first essay under the great Müller. In the spring of 1885, Haeckel returned to Würzburg, where, under Kölliker's influence, he earned a medical degree in 1857 with a zoological/anatomical emphasis rather than a strictly medical one. Although Haeckel earned a medical degree, he seldom practiced medicine. This resulted from the fact that he spent most of his time studying marine animals and saw patients only from five to six A.M. During his first year of practice, he saw only three patients.

In the winter of 1859-1860, Haeckel studied the radiolaria collected off Messina. This project laid the foundation for his interest and future work in zoology. By the spring of 1860, he had discovered 144 new species of radiolaria. His work at Messina culminated in the publication of *Die Radiolarien* (*Report on the Radiolaria,* 1887) in 1862. This work was one of his finest and most influential, and it established his position as a zoologist. After a fifteen-year hiatus, he again pursued the study of radiolaria and published the second, third, and fourth parts of *Report on the Radiolaria* from 1887 to 1888. He eventually classified more than thirty-five hundred species of radiolaria.

In March, 1861, he was appointed private teacher at the University of Jena, and in 1862 he was appointed extraordinary professor of zoology at the Zoological Museum. In 1865, he became a professor at Jena. In August, 1862, he married his cousin, Anna Sethe. Anna died two years later at the age of twenty-nine. Stricken with grief over the loss of his beloved wife, he became a hermit and a compulsive worker, often surviving on only three to four hours of sleep each day. In 1867, he married Agnes Huschke.

In May, 1860, Haeckel read Charles Darwin's *On the Origin of Species* (1859). The book profoundly influenced Haeckel's intellectual development, and he became Germany's most devout supporter and popularizer of Darwinism. It has often been said that without Haeckel there would have been Darwin, but there would not have been Dar-

winism. Haeckel came to view evolution as the basis for the explanation of all nature.

Haeckel, whose faith was enfeebled by the study of comparative anatomy and physiology, was also profoundly influenced by his friend Johann Wolfgang von Goethe and became a believer in Goethe's God of Nature. Haeckel no longer believed in a Creator, since Darwin's theory permitted him to explain nature without divine influence. This enabled Haeckel to accept Darwinism better than Darwin. For Haeckel, it became possible to develop a philosophy of nature without having to interject God or a vital force. Haeckel's support of Darwinism made him the target of attack by his German colleagues, many of whom were doubters of Darwinian ideas. Haeckel first revealed his belief in Darwinism in *Report on the Radiolaria*. He acknowledges that in the radiolaria there are several transitional forms that connect the various groups and that they form "a fairly continuous chain of related forms," and he expresses his "belief in the mutability of species and the real genealogical relation of all organisms."

In an address to the Scientific Congress of 1863, eight years before Darwin published *The Descent of Man and Selection in Relation to Sex* (1871), Haeckel said that man must recognize his immediate ancestors in apelike mammals. He realized, however, that Darwin's theory may not be perfect and may need refinement. He especially realized that it explained neither the origin of the first living organism nor how man was connected to the genealogical tree. Haeckel thought that the first living organism was a single cell, a cell even more primitive than the eukaryotic cell. Not long afterward, the prokaryotic cell, a primitive cell without a nucleus, was described. After studying the brains and skulls of the primates, Haeckel produced a genealogical tree which showed the relationship of man to the other primates and to lower animals.

In the mid- 1860's, Haeckel began to study the medusae, a study which culminated in the publication of *Das System der Medusen* (*Report on the Deep-Sea Medusae*, 1882) in 1879. The treatise was a detailed description of the medusae. In the later 1860's, he studied the social aspects of the medusae.

Haeckel's greatest achievement was his *Generelle Morphologie der Organismen*, published in 1866. The monograph is considered a landmark and one of the most important scientific works of the latter half of the nineteenth century. In *Generelle*

Morphologie der Organismen, Haeckel clearly presented his reductionist philosophy. He reduced the cell to the laws of chemistry and physics, and through the influence of Darwin, raised the study of zoology to that of the physical sciences. He strengthened the laws of evolution, refined the biogenetic law, and presented a philosophy of life and a new story of its creation. In it, too, he described his early education as defective, perverse, and filled with errors. He lambasted the educational system that emphasized memory of dead material which interferes with normal intellectual development.

In *Generelle Morphologie der Organismen*, Haeckel presented two ideas, monism and the biogenetic law, which would occupy the rest of his life. The biogenetic law, which was originally proposed by Darwin, was refined and expanded by Haeckel. According to the biogenetic law, ontogeny recapitulates phylogeny, which means that during embryological development animals pass through developmental stages which represent adult stages from which the developing animal evolved. Haeckel viewed embryonic development of an individual animal as a brief and condensed recapitulation of its evolutionary history. Haeckel used the biogenetic law to strengthen his case for evolution. Although the law was eventually proved to be in error, it was accepted by many scientists and stimulated much discussion and research. In *Generelle Morphologie der Organismen*, he presented a genealogical tree with bacteria and single-celled organisms on the bottom. From the bacteria and single-celled organisms arose two branches: the animals and the plants.

In his search for a religion that did not rely on a vital force or a personal god, Haeckel developed monism, a scientific and philosophical doctrine which advocated nature as a substitute for religion. The basic principles of monism can be summarized as follows: Knowledge of the world is based on scientific knowledge acquired through human reason; the world is one great whole ruled by fixed laws; there is no vital force that controls the laws of nature; living organisms have developed by evolution through descent; nothing in the universe was created by a Creator; living organisms originated from nonliving matter; man and the apes are closely related and evolved from a common ancestor; God as a supreme being does not exist; and God is nature.

These outspoken and heretical ideas about God made Haeckel the target of attacks not only from the Church but also from his colleagues. Indeed, many of his colleagues called for his resignation as a professor, yet he stayed at Jena and raised it to the level of an intellectual metropolis. His reputation as a great scientist and thinker attracted many young, bright scientists to Jena.

Not being one to walk away from the battlefield and collapse under fire, Haeckel published *Natürliche Schöpfungsgeschichte* (*The History of Creation*, 1876) in 1868. This book was a condensation and a popularization on the ideas originally presented in *Generelle Morphologie der Organismen* and was written primarily for the layperson. In the book, Haeckel approached the problems of life through Darwinism. The book was attacked by theologians and by many scientists, but it became a best-seller in its time.

The History of Creation was followed by *Anthropogenie* (1874; *The Evolution of Man*, 1879), a survey of all that was learned in the nineteenth century about the history of mankind, and *Die Weltratsel* (1899; *The Riddle of the Universe at the Close of the Nineteenth Century*, 1900), an intentionally provocative and popular study of monism that was translated into more than a dozen languages.

In his many popular writings, Haeckel unleashed a relentless attack on the Church and the clergy, which he thought preyed on the gullibility of the ignorant masses in order to further their selfish aims. He was criticized for being outspoken against established, organized religion while ignoring what his critics regarded as more serious ills of his country. He answered these charges in *Die Lebenswunder* (*The Wonders of Life*, 1904).

Haeckel founded the phyletic museum at the University of Jena and the Ernst Haeckel Haus to house his collections, books, and letters. He retired from active teaching and research in 1909 at the age of seventy-five and died at Jena in 1919.

Summary

Ernst Haeckel was one of the greatest natural historians, zoologists, and philosophers of the nineteenth century. His descriptions of many marine organisms, especially of the radiolaria and the medusae, were monumental and unparalleled in the zoological sciences. He classified several thousand new species of plants and animals.

Moreover, Haeckel's knowledge of zoology provided him with a platform from which he launched an advocacy and popularization of the ideas of Darwin. He described evolution as "the most important advance that has been made in pure and applied science." He was quick to extend and develop Darwin's theory. He refined the biogenetic law and was one of the first to extend Darwin's ideas to the origin of life and mankind.

Haeckel's staunch support of Darwinism and his monistic philosophy alienated him from the clergy and from older scientists but attracted many younger scientists as disciples. Although he had many critics, more than five hundred university professors (many his critics) around the world contributed to the making of a marble bust of Haeckel, which was unveiled at the University of Jena in 1894. Haeckel's ideas influenced a generation.

Bibliography

Bölsche, Wilhelm. *Haeckel: His Life and Work*. Translated by Joseph McCabe. London: Unwin, and Philadelphia: Jacobs, 1906. This is the most extensive biography of Haeckel, and the only one to have been translated into English. It is an excellent account of Haeckel's work as a scientist and philosopher. Bölsche was one of Haeckel's students.

DeGrood, David H. *Haeckel's Theory of the Unity of Nature: A Monograph in the History of Philosophy*. Boston: Christopher, 1965. Originally written as a master's thesis, it was reprinted in 1982 by Gruner of Amsterdam. Summarizes Haeckel's monistic philosophy.

Haeckel, Ernst. *The Evolution of Man*. Translated by Joseph McCabe. London: Watts, and New York: Putnam, 1905. The first edition to be translated into English.

————. *The Riddle of the Universe*. Translated by Joseph McCabe. New York and London: Harper, 1900. This book offers a popularization of Haeckel's monistic philosophy "for thoughtful readers . . . who are united in an honest search for the truth."

Hanken, James. "Beauty Beyond Belief." *Natural History* 107, no. 10 (December 1998). Short profile of Haeckel that includes his work on biological evolution, its racist perspective, and his suspect methods.

Pennisi, Elizabeth. "Haeckel's Embryos: Fraud Rediscovered." *Science* 277, no. 5331 (September 5, 1997). Resurrects the discovery that a set of Haeckel's drawings fraudulently depicts the growth of several vertebrate embryos as similar.

Slosson, Edwin. *Major Prophets of To-day*. Boston: Little Brown, 1914. Contains a chapter summarizing the life of Haeckel as a scientist.

Charles L. Vigue

SARAH JOSEPHA HALE

Born: October 24, 1788; Newport, New Hampshire
Died: April 30, 1879; Philadelphia, Pennsylvania
Areas of Achievement: Literature and journalism
Contribution: The author of poetry, novels, plays, and cookbooks, as well as an important history of women, Hale is best known as the editor of *Godey's Lady's Book*, the most popular magazine in the United States before the Civil War. As editor of this women's magazine, Hale encouraged and supported women writers, and she advocated improved opportunities for women's education and work.

Early Life

Born October 24, 1788, on a farm outside Newport, New Hampshire, Sarah Josepha Buell was one of four children of Gordon and Martha Whittlesey Buell. Though opportunities for formal schooling for girls were limited at the time, Buell received a good education at home, and she credited her mother with inspiring her love of literature. Despite limited access to books, Buell read widely during her youth. By the time she was fifteen, for example, she had read all of William Shakespeare's works. Other favorites included the Bible, John Bunyan's *Pilgrim's Progress* (1678, 1684), and Ann Radcliffe's *The Mysteries of Udolpho* (1794). Buell also benefited from tutoring by her brother Horatio, who attended Dartmouth College. During Horatio's summer vacations at home, the two studied Latin, Greek, philosophy, English grammar, rhetoric, geography, and literature. Hale drew on her strong education when, at age eighteen, she opened a private school for children. She continued to teach until 1813, when she married David Hale, a lawyer in Newport.

During her marriage, Sarah Josepha Buell Hale continued her education. As she later recalled, she and her husband spent two hours each evening reading current literature and studying topics ranging from composition and French to science. During this period, Hale also worked on her own writing, publishing a few poems in local magazines.

Hale's life changed considerably when, in 1822, shortly before the birth of their fifth child, Hale's husband died suddenly. Concerned with providing for her family, Hale turned first to the millinery business, but she soon focused on becoming an author. Her first volume of poetry, *The Oblivion of*

Genius and Other Original Poems, appeared in 1823. After winning several literary prizes and becoming a regular contributor to magazines and gift annuals, Hale published her first novel, *Northwood: A Tale of New England,* in 1827. Though highlighting New England character traits, as the subtitle suggests, the novel focused on the contrasts between the North and South, including issues of race relations and slavery.

Life's Work

Soon after the publication of *Northwood,* Sarah Josepha Hale, at the age of thirty-nine, launched what to a great extent would become her life's work as a magazine editor. When a new periodical, the *Ladies' Magazine,* first appeared in January of 1828, Hale edited it from her home in Newport, but within a few months she moved to Boston, where the magazine was published. Though the *Ladies' Magazine* was not the first periodical intended for American women or edited by an American woman, it did differ considerably from earlier efforts, which often focused on fashion. Hale's *Ladies' Magazine* included fashion plates during part of its nine-year existence, but it was much more intellectual than previous women's magazines had been. Sketches of famous women were common features, and Hale's editorial columns often addressed issues of social reform, such as property rights for married women and the importance of women's education.

Publishing both poetry and fiction, the magazine also had a significant literary component, and Hale's support of American authors is particularly noteworthy. Whereas other magazine editors relied on anonymous material and reprinted British literature (generally without permission), Hale's magazine featured American authors, and she repeatedly encouraged her readers to recognize authorship as a legitimate profession. Therefore, she favored original submissions rather than reprints, encouraged attribution of authors, and supported the idea that authors should be paid for their work.

Throughout her editorship of the *Ladies' Magazine,* Hale continued her efforts as an author. Her own writings appeared frequently in the magazine, and some of them were published separately in book form. Her *Sketches of American Character* (1829) and *Traits of American Life* (1835) first appeared in the *Ladies' Magazine*. During this time, Hale also published two poetry collections, including *Poems for Our Children* (1830), which contained the poem "Mary's Lamb" (now famous as "Mary Had a Little Lamb").

Hale's career took an important turn in 1837, when after nine years of managing the *Ladies' Magazine*, Hale accepted a new position as editor of Louis Godey's *Lady's Book*, which Godey had founded in 1830 in Philadelphia. For the first several years, Hale edited the magazine from her home in Boston, but in 1841 she moved to Philadelphia. Even before the move, however, Hale carefully reformed the magazine, which initially lacked the intellectual and literary focus Hale had developed in the *Ladies' Magazine*. With Hale as editor, however, the *Lady's Book* (now often referred to by its later name, *Godey's Lady's Book*) became an important literary magazine for women. Though the magazine continued to publish the so-called "embellishments" for which Louis Godey had become famous (engravings, fashion plates, and so forth), Hale continued her earlier positions supporting American writers and improved opportunities for women's work and education. This combination of Godey's "embellishments" and Hale's literary and educational essays proved popular. By 1860, the magazine boasted 150,000 subscribers, making it the most popular U.S. magazine of its day.

With such a large audience, Hale was able to exert considerable influence on a number of social issues. Some of these, such as her efforts to preserve the Bunker Hill Monument and Mount Vernon, demonstrate her strong patriotic impulses. Many more of Hale's editorial campaigns were related to her belief in the power of what she and many of her contemporaries called "woman's sphere." Believing that women were innately more moral than men, Hale voiced strong support of women's charitable organizations, such as the Seaman's Aid Society, which tried to improve the lives of Boston's seamen and their families by founding schools, a library, a boarding house, and a clothing shop. Though Hale believed that the domestic space was part of women's sphere, she did not wish to confine women within the home. Quite the contrary, Hale encouraged women to extend their influence as widely as possible. Thus, for example, Hale voiced strong support for the founding of Vassar College (the first U.S. college for women), campaigned for women's medical colleges, and repeatedly called for women to take professional positions as teach-

ers and with the post office. Hale also took a particular interest in issues of women's health, arguing, for example, for women's physical education and denouncing tight corsets as unhealthy (a charge that was later fully substantiated). Though the *Lady's Book* sometimes prided itself on avoiding political topics, many of Hale's editorial campaigns had significant political implications. Her long-standing efforts to establish Thanksgiving as a national holiday, for example, were based on her belief during the antebellum period that if a nation shared a meal together once a year, it would be less likely to engage in civil war. Though Hale's ultimate goal of preventing civil war was, of course, unsuccessful, she did manage to convince President Lincoln to declare Thanksgiving a national holiday.

Throughout her editorship of the *Lady's Book*, Hale continued to publish her own work. In addition to contributing material to the *Lady's Book*, she published a number of poetry volumes and several short novels, and following the success of Harriet Beecher Stowe's *Uncle Tom's Cabin* in 1852, she issued a revised edition of *Northwood*. Hale also wrote a number of very popular cookbooks.

Hale's efforts as a writer were well regarded by her peers, and she was featured in many of the gift annuals and literary anthologies published before the Civil War. One of Hale's most ambitious projects as a writer was her 1853 *Woman's Record: Or, Sketches of All Distinguished Women from "The Beginning" till A.D. 1850*. This nine-hundred-page work presents biographical essays on more than two hundred women, with brief mentions of more than two thousand others.

After five decades as a magazine editor, Hale published her last column with the *Lady's Book* in December, 1877. She died on April 30, 1879, at the age of ninety and was buried in Philadelphia.

Summary

Though she was not the first woman magazine editor, Sarah Josepha Hale enjoyed a longer and more influential career than had any American woman before her. During her fifty-year editorial career, Hale made significant contributions to American literature and to women's issues. She published or reviewed the work of such writers as Edgar Allan Poe, James Fenimore Cooper, and Herman Melville. As editor of a popular women's magazine, Hale was able to support women writers, many of whom, such as Harriet Beecher Stowe and Lydia Sigourney, published their work in her magazines.

Through her editorial columns, Hale was also able to support other issues related to women. Although she did not advocate women's voting rights, she was a strong spokeswoman for property rights for married women, improved women's education, and increased opportunities for women's wage-earning work. Ultimately, one of Hale's most lasting contributions may have been in encouraging other women to pursue careers in publishing and periodicals. By proving that a women's literary magazine could be the nation's most popular periodical and by demonstrating that a woman could manage such a magazine, Hale undoubtedly helped to pave the way for later women editors, authors, and journalists.

Bibliography

Entrikin, Isabelle Webb. *Sarah Josepha Hale and "Godey's Lady's Book."* Lancaster, Pa.: Lancaster Press, 1946. A published dissertation, this work provides a good overview of Hale's editorial career and includes a bibliography of Hale's published works.

Finley, Ruth E. *The Lady of Godey's: Sarah Josepha Hale.* Philadelphia: Lippincott, 1931. The first full-length biography of Hale, this work provides a good overview of Hale's life, including her work as an author and editor and her support of issues such as national union and women's education.

Hoffman, Nicole Tonkovich. "*Legacy* Profile: Sarah Josepha Hale." *Legacy: A Journal of Nineteenth-Century American Women Writers* 7, no. 2 (Fall 1990): 47-55. This short sketch of Hale's life and career includes a selected bibliography as well as an excerpt from one of Hale's editorials.

Mott, Frank Luther. *A History of American Magazines, 1741-1850.* Vol. 1. New York and London: Appleton, 1930. Though subsequent studies show less bias against sentimental literature than evident here, this pivotal work includes a detailed sketch of *Godey's Lady's Book* and valuable information about the periodical industry.

Okker, Patricia. *Our Sister Editors: Sarah J. Hale and the Tradition of Nineteenth-Century American Women Editors.* Athens: University of Georgia Press, 1995. In addition to identifying more than six hundred women who edited periodicals in the nineteenth century, this work provides an in-depth analysis of Hale's editorial career, focusing specifically on her literary significance.

Rogers, Sherbrooke. *Sarah Josepha Hale: A New England Pioneer, 1788-1879.* Grantham, N.H.: Tompson and Rutter, 1985. Though it presents little new information, this biography is particularly suited to older adolescents.

Patricia Okker

SIR WILLIAM ROWAN HAMILTON

Born: August 3/4, 1805; Dublin, Ireland
Died: September 2, 1865; near Dublin, Ireland
Areas of Achievement: Mathematics, physics, and optics
Contribution: Hamilton, while questioning a commonly accepted three-dimensional concept of space on a plane, discovered quaternions and, in doing so, drastically altered the study of algebra, forcing the abandonment of the commutative law of multiplication that was dominant in his day and leading the way to new methods of vector analysis.

Early Life

William Rowan Hamilton was born exactly at midnight, a moment poised equally between August 3 and 4, 1805. His father, Archibald Hamilton, was away in the north at the time of his son's birth, carrying out his duties as agent to Archibald Rowan, a post he had held since 1800. Archibald Rowan, who was William Rowan Hamilton's godfather, had been in exile for eleven years. His agent, William's father, worked tirelessly to make possible Rowan's return to his estate at Killyleagh, an effort that resulted in Rowan's repatriation in 1806.

To help Rowan meet his expenses, Archibald Hamilton borrowed heavily at high interest rates. When these loans were called, Rowan failed to back Hamilton, who, in a year or two, had no alternative but to declare bankruptcy. By 1808, the family was sufficiently impoverished not to be able to provide for William, then three years old, and his sisters, Grace and Eliza, who had to be sent away to be cared for by relatives. The two girls presumably were sent to live with their father's sister, Sydney, and young William became the ward of his uncle, James Hamilton, a Church of England clergyman who ran the diocesan school at Trim, some forty miles to the northwest of Dublin in County Meath. William was to remain there until 1823, when he returned to Dublin as a student at Trinity College.

In retrospect, it appears to have been a stroke of good fortune that young William was forced by circumstance to live with his uncle, a man of considerable intellect. Before the boy was four years old, he was able to read English and showed a remarkable understanding of arithmetic. By the time he was five, William was able to translate from Latin, Greek, and Hebrew. He knew Greek and Latin authors well enough to recite from their works, and he was also able to recite passages from works by John Milton and John Dryden. He is said to have mastered fourteen languages by the time he was thirteen. Before he turned twelve, he had compiled a Syriac grammar, and two years later he was sufficiently fluent in Persian to compose a speech of welcome that was delivered to the Persian ambassador when he was a guest in Dublin.

Always advanced in mathematics, Hamilton was enormously exhilarated when he met the American mathematician Zerah Colburn in 1820. Colburn was able to perform complex mathematical computations quickly in his head, a skill that enticed the fifteen-year-old Hamilton. The youth had already read Sir Isaac Newton's *Philosophiae Naturalis Principia Mathematica* (1687) and Alexis-Claude Clairaut's *Elémens d'algèbre* (1746) by the time he met Colburn. The excitement generated by his meeting with Colburn led Hamilton in the following year to study the completed volumes of Pierre-Simon Laplace's five-volume *Traité de mécanique céleste* (1798-1825; *A Treatise of Celestial Mechanics*, 1829-1839).

Hamilton's detection of a flaw in Laplace's reasoning brought him to the attention of John Brinkley, a distinguished professor of astronomy at Trinity College who was then also president of the Royal Irish Academy. The following year, when he was seventeen, Hamilton sent a paper he had written on optics to Brinkley, who, upon reading the paper, declared to the Royal Academy that Hamilton was already the most important mathematician of his time.

Hamilton entered Trinity College in 1823. By 1825, he had completed his paper, "On Caustics," and submitted it to the Royal Academy, only to be rebuffed because the members of the Academy could not follow his often convoluted reasoning. Hamilton was awarded the *optime* in both classics and mathematics, the first Trinity College student to achieve this dual honor. While still an undergraduate, in 1827, he submitted his paper "Theory of Systems of Rays" to the Royal Academy, establishing with that paper a uniform method of solving all problems in the field of geometrical optics. The paper was of sufficient significance that before he had finished his undergraduate studies at Trinity College, the school's faculty elected William Rowan Hamilton to the Andrews professorship in astronomy, a post that established him as Royal As-

tronomer of Ireland and an examiner of graduate students in mathematics at Trinity College. He assumed that post immediately upon graduation.

Life's Work

The post to which the Trinity College faculty elected Hamilton carried with it a residence at the Dunsink Observatory, some five miles from Trinity College. In October, 1827, Hamilton moved into that residence and remained there for the rest of his life. Although he did not have a distinguished career as an astronomer, Hamilton had a large following of people who attended his lectures on astronomy because the range of his literary as well as his mathematical knowledge was sufficient to enliven his presentations.

Hamilton read encyclopedically and regularly wrote poetry, although his friend, the poet William Wordsworth, advised him that his lasting contributions would lie in mathematics rather than in poetry. In 1832, Hamilton published an important supplement to his paper on the theory of rays. This supplement was purely speculative, postulating a new theory about the refraction of light by biaxial crystals. Augustin Fresnel had already developed the theory of double refraction, but Hamilton took the theory an important step beyond where Fresnel had left it. He contended that in certain circumstances, one ray of incident light could be refracted into an infinite number of rays in a biaxial crystal and would be formed in such a way that a cone would then result. Humphrey Lloyd, following Hamilton's speculative lead, proved this theory of conical refraction within two months.

In 1833, after six years of living alone in his official residence, Hamilton—a man of average height and ruddy complexion—married Maria Bayley, whose father had been an Anglican rector in County Tipperary. Maria bore three children, two sons and a daughter. Not renowned for her domestic abilities, Maria presided over a somewhat chaotic household. Hamilton considered liquor a more reliable source of nourishment than anything Maria's cook could provide, and, through the years, he became a heavy drinker.

Hamilton's "On a General Method in Dynamics," published in 1835, brought together his work in optics and dynamics. He proposed a theory that showed the duality that exists between the components of momentum in a dynamic system and the coordinates that determine its position. In many ways, this work was some of Hamilton's most significant, although it took nearly a century for the development of research in quantum mechanics to demonstrate the brilliance and importance of Hamilton's theory.

Hamilton served as the major local organizer of the British Association for the Advancement of Science meeting in Dublin in 1835, an activity that led to his being knighted in the closing ceremonies of that event. In 1837, he ascended to the presidency of the Royal Irish Academy. In 1843, the Crown awarded him an annual life pension of two hundred pounds. During his final illness, Hamilton received word that he had been ranked first on the list of foreign associates of the National Academy of the United States.

The contribution for which Hamilton is best remembered is his discovery of quaternions. This discovery has fundamentally changed the way in which mathematicians deal with three-dimensional space. Hamilton had begun his extensive investigation into ordered paired numbers more than ten years before he made his monumental discovery of quaternions on October 16, 1843, when, during a walk along Dublin's Royal Canal, the answer to a question that had been haunting him for nearly a decade flashed almost supernaturally into his mind. So excited was he by this flash of insight that he carved the formula for his discovery, i2 = j2 = k2 = ijk = -1, into the Brougham Bridge.

Hamilton suddenly realized that in three-dimensional space, geometrical operations require not triplets, expressed as i, j, and k and representing space, as had been previously supposed, but rather that, because in three-dimensional space the orientation of the plane is variable, another element, a real term that represents time, must also be considered, resulting in quadruplets rather than triplets. One of the major consequences of this insight was its negation of the previously accepted commutative law of multiplication, which postulates (a b) = (b a).

Hamilton's work with quaternions, to which he devoted the last two decades of his life, was essential to the development of vector analysis. More recently, further important applications of his theory of quaternions have been instrumental in the description of elementary particles. Hamilton published his *Lectures on Quaternions* in 1853, and his influential *The Elements of Quaternions* appeared posthumously in 1866. William Rowan Hamilton died of gout on September 2, 1865, after a lingering illness.

Summary

Sir William Rowan Hamilton's name lives in both the history of mathematics and the histories of physics and optics. His pioneering work in vector analysis forced specialists in that field to abandon the theory of double refraction and to replace it with Hamilton's expanded theory of conical refraction. The work that led to these changes began while Hamilton was still an undergraduate at Trinity College and reached its culmination in the supplement to his "Theory of Systems of Rays" in 1832.

His next significant achievement posited a duality between the components of momentum in a dynamic system and the coordinates that determine its position, a theory that reduces the field of dynamics to a problem in the calculus of variations. This theory came to have considerable significance as the field of quantum mechanics developed.

By far Hamilton's most memorable contribution, however, was his discovery of quaternions, which forced mathematicians to break with the commutative law of multiplication. In its simplified form, termed vector analysis and adapted by J. Willard Gibbs from Hamilton's theory, Hamilton's theory of quaternions has been of great significance to modern mathematical physicists.

Bibliography

Aslaksen, Helmer. "Quaternionic Determinants." *Mathematical Intelligencer* 18, no. 3 (Summer 1996). A discussion of Sir Hamilton's discovery of quaternion matrices and the subsequent attempts at conclusive definition of them.

Bell, Eric Temple. *Development of Mathematics.* New York and London: McGraw-Hill, 1940. Bell relates Hamilton to some of the salient mathematical developments of his time. The coverage is sketchy and has been superseded by Thomas L. Hankins' biography.

————. *Men of Mathematics.* London: Gollancz, and New York: Simon and Schuster, 1937. Bell puts Hamilton in historical perspective. The chapter "An Irish Tragedy" focuses on Hamilton, but, although interesting, it is not factually dependable in all respects.

Graves, R. P. *Life of Sir William Rowan Hamilton.* 3 vols. London: Longman, 1882. The three enormous volumes of this set include extensive selections from Hamilton's correspondence, poetry, and miscellaneous writings, as well as extensive commentary. The work, remarkable in its time for its thoroughness, is badly dated and suffers from lack of selectivity.

Hamilton, William Rowan. *The Mathematical Papers of Sir William Rowan Hamilton.* 3 vols. Cambridge: Cambridge University Press, 1931-1967; New York: Cambridge University Press, 1960-1969. Volume 1, *Geometrical Optics* (1931), and volume 2, *Dynamics* (1940), are edited by A. W. Conway and J. L. Synge; volume 3, *Algebra* (1967), is edited by H. Halberstam and R. E. Ingram. Volumes 1 and 3 contain useful introductions. Omitted from the collection are Hamilton's *Lectures on Quaternions*, published in 1853 by Hodges and Smith, and *Elements of Quaternions*, published by Longman, in London in 1866. Yet these three volumes are superbly produced, and the highest standards of scholarship have been observed in their editing.

Hankins, Thomas L. *Sir William Rowan Hamilton.* Baltimore: Johns Hopkins University Press, 1980; London: Johns Hopkins University Press, 1981. Hankins' critical biography of Hamilton is the definitive work in the field. Meticulously documented, the book is written in such a lively style that it at times reads like a novel rather than like the eminently scholarly work that it is. The best book to date on Hamilton.

Synge, J. L. *Geometrical Optics: An Introduction to Hamilton's Method*. Cambridge: Cambridge University Press, 1937. Highly technical in nature, this book contains a brief but valuable preface. This book is for the specialist rather than the beginner.

R. Baird Shuman

MARCUS A. HANNA

Born: September 24, 1837; New Lisbon, Ohio
Died: February 15, 1904; Washington, D.C.
Areas of Achievement: Government and politics
Contribution: Hanna was the close political friend of William McKinley, helped him secure the presidency in 1896, and then served as an influential United States senator until his death.

Early Life

Marcus Alonzo Hanna was born September 24, 1837, in New Lisbon, Ohio. His father, Leonard Hanna, came from Scotch-Irish Quaker stock and was in the grocery business when he married Samantha Converse, a Vermont schoolteacher from Irish, English, and Huguenot stock. Hanna attended public schools in New Lisbon and, after 1852, in Cleveland, where his family had moved. He enrolled in Western Reserve College but was suspended in 1857 for faking programs to a school function. Going to work for his father's firm of Hanna, Garretson and Co., he took over his father's position by the early years of the Civil War. He served briefly as a volunteer in that conflict in 1864, and later married Charlotte Augusta Rhodes, on September 27, 1864. She was the daughter of a Cleveland dealer in iron and coal. By 1867, Hanna's business ventures had failed, and he became a partner in his father-in-law's firm of Rhodes and Company. From then on, Hanna was a success. In 1885, the coal and iron business was reorganized as M. A. Hanna and Company. He also had an interest in many aspects of the Cleveland economy. He owned an opera house, a local newspaper, several street railways, and a share of several banks. Hanna was a popular employer. "A man who won't meet his men half-way is a God-damn fool," he said in 1894, and he believed in high wages, the unity of capital and labor, and unions over strikes. By the time he was forty, Hanna was a capitalist of consequence in the Midwest, but it was his love for Republican politics in Ohio that made him a national figure.

Life's Work

Hanna began as a backstage fund-raiser for Republican candidates at the end of the 1870's; he played a large role in the campaign to make James A. Garfield president in 1880. He first identified himself with the national ambitions of Senator John Sherman during the ensuing decade and worked closely with Governor Joseph B. Foraker on Sherman's behalf. At the Republican National Convention in 1888, a dispute with Foraker over the Sherman candidacy ended the difficult alliance with the temperamental governor and started a feud that endured until 1904. Hanna then turned to the rising political fortunes of an Ohio congressman, William McKinley.

McKinley's friendship with Hanna was the dominant force in the latter's life for the next decade and a half. Cartoonists and critics after 1896 would depict a bloated, plutocratic Hanna as the manipulator of a pliable McKinley and thus create a popular image wholly divergent from the truth. In their political relationship, McKinley was the preeminent figure and Hanna was always the subordinate. The two men had met first in the 1870's but did not establish a working partnership until the years 1888 to 1892. McKinley relied on the fund-raising ability and the organization skills that Hanna supplied in his races for governor of Ohio in 1891 and 1893. For his part, Hanna accorded

McKinley an admiration that, in its early stages, verged on hero-worship.

McKinley's political fortunes prospered during the 1890's, a difficult time for the Democratic Party. After Benjamin Harrison failed to win reelection in 1892, the Ohio governor became a leading choice for the Republican nomination in 1896. Hanna helped McKinley through the embarrassing financial crisis in the Panic of 1893, when the governor became responsible for a friend's bad debts. By early 1895, the industrialist gave up his formal connection with his business interests to push McKinley's candidacy. Hanna set up a winter home in Georgia and began wooing Southern Republicans who would be convention delegates in 1896.

The nomination campaign for McKinley went smoothly in the first half of 1896, and a first-ballot victory came when the Republicans assembled in St. Louis in mid-June. Hanna's organizational abilities had helped McKinley gather the requisite delegate votes, but the candidate's popularity and advocacy of the protective tariff during the Depression made the task of his campaign manager an easy one. The two men also agreed on the currency plank of the Republican platform, which endorsed the gold standard in the face of the Democratic swing to the inflationary panacea of free silver.

Hanna and McKinley expected a relatively easy race until the Democrats selected the young and charismatic William Jennings Bryan, the champion of free silver, at their convention in July. As chairman of the Republican National Committee, Hanna supervised the raising of the party's financial war chest in the late summer. The eastern business community, frightened of Bryan, contributed between three and four million dollars to the party's coffers. Hanna then used these resources in what he called a "campaign of education." Setting up the major distribution point for campaign materials in Chicago, Hanna supervised the process that sent out more than one hundred million documents espousing the virtues of the tariff and sound money; an equal number of posters depicted McKinley as "the advance agent of prosperity" and promised to workers "a full dinner pail" if McKinley were elected. By October, the diversified Republican appeal and the strength of McKinley's campaign had overwhelmed the Democrats. Bryan's whistle-stop campaign had not made his inflationary message popular. He was, said Hanna, "talking Silver all the time and that's where we've got him." Hanna's strategy brought a resounding Republican victory in November, 1896.

As the new president formed his cabinet, he gave Hanna the opportunity to become postmaster general. Hanna's real ambition, however, was to be senator from Ohio. When John Sherman resigned his seat to accept the State Department portfolio, the governor of Ohio appointed Hanna to fill out the remainder of his senatorial term. There was much talk at the time that a nearly senile Sherman had been kicked upstairs to make way for Hanna. In fact, Sherman wanted the place in the Cabinet and accepted it voluntarily. Hanna was elected to a full term by the Ohio legislature early in 1898, after a close and bitter contest in which charges of bribery and other corrupt tactics were made against the Republican candidate. None of these allegations was proved, and Hanna took his seat in the Senate in January, 1897.

Hanna liked being in the Senate and the influence he enjoyed with his friend in the White House. He had a large voice in patronage decisions, especially in the South, and he was again important in the Republican campaign in the 1898 congressional elections. He advocated business consolidation into trusts, subsidies for the American merchant marine, and a canal across Central America. McKinley did not consult him as much on the large issues of foreign policy that grew out of the Spanish-American War. Initially, Hanna did not favor war with Spain over Cuba, but he accepted intervention when it came in April, 1898. By 1900, the president and the senator had drifted apart. McKinley did not like the stories that Hanna dominated him, and some time passed before Hanna was named to head the Republican reelection drive in 1900. The vice presidential nomination in that year went to the New York governor and war hero, Theodore Roosevelt. Hanna did not trust the flamboyant Roosevelt. "Don't you understand that there is just one life between this crazy man and the presidency if you force me to take Roosevelt?" he asked those who were pushing him. When McKinley refused to oppose the New Yorker, Hanna had no choice but to accept Roosevelt's selection.

In the campaign, the Republican organization functioned even more smoothly than it had in 1896 against Bryan, who was once again the Democratic standard-bearer. With McKinley sitting out the canvass as an incumbent, Hanna went out on the stump and proved second only to Roosevelt as a speaking attraction. Senator Richard F. Pettigrew of South Dakota, a silver Republican, had become a bitter enemy of Hanna, and they had clashed on the Senate floor. The Ohioan campaigned against Pettigrew in his home state and helped to deny him reelection. As McKinley's second term began, there was some talk of a Hanna candidacy for president in 1904.

McKinley's assassination in September, 1901, and Roosevelt's accession to the presidency shifted the political balance against Hanna. Much of his power over Republican patronage vanished when McKinley died. As the embodiment of corporate power in politics who was often depicted as a plutocrat in cartoons, Hanna would not have been a credible challenger to the young, popular, and forceful Roosevelt. Hanna knew this, and he never seriously entertained the prospect of disputing Roosevelt's hold on the Republican nomination in 1904. At the same time, he was reluctant to acknowledge the new president's preeminence too quickly. The resulting ambivalence placed Hanna in an awkward position during the last two years of his life. Friends in the conservative, probusiness wing of the Republican Party wanted him to be a candidate: That idea he resisted. Yet he could not bring himself to endorse Roosevelt wholeheartedly. The Hanna-Roosevelt relationship became tense.

Hanna and Roosevelt did cooperate fruitfully in the settlement of the anthracite coal strike of 1902. A believer in the essential harmony of capital and labor, Hanna became active in and eventually chaired the National Civic Federation, which sought the elusive goal of industrial peace through arbitration and conciliation. When the coal miners struck in 1902, for higher wages and shorter hours, Hanna tried to persuade the coal operators to negotiate with their men. He assisted Roosevelt's mediation efforts that finally brought a resolution of the dispute in October, 1902.

Within the Republican Party, Hanna remained the most plausible alternative to Roosevelt. His recommendation that the party should "stand pat" in the congressional elections of 1902 and make few concessions to reform contributed a phrase to the language of American politics and further endeared him to conservatives. Most of the talk about Hanna's hopes was illusory, as an episode in the spring of 1903 revealed. Hanna's old enemy, his senatorial colleague Foraker, asked that the Ohio Republican State Convention endorse Roosevelt for the presidency. When Hanna hesitated to agree, the president sent him a public message that "those who favor my administration and nomination" would support Foraker's idea "and those who do not will oppose them." Hanna performed a "back-action-double-spring feat" and gave in.

Hanna was reelected to the Senate in 1903, after a difficult contest against the Democratic mayor of Cleveland, Tom L. Johnson. Hanna's success revived talk of the White House, and Roosevelt prepared for a test of strength in the winter of 1904. Before it could come, however, Hanna fell ill with typhoid fever; he died in Washington, District of Columbia, on February 15, 1904. Hanna had three children: Mabel Hanna was retarded and caused her parents much anguish; Ruth Hanna McCormick was active in Republican politics; and her brother Dan Hanna pursued a business career.

Summary

Despite two sympathetic biographies, Hanna's reputation has never escaped the stereotypes that political opponents created during his lifetime. In fact, he was not the creator or mastermind of William McKinley but only a good friend and an efficient instrument who served the purposes of the twenty-fifth president. The Republicans won the presidential election of 1896 not because Hanna and his campaign organization bought votes or coerced industrial workers: With an appealing candidate, a divided opposition, and a popular program, Hanna used the money at his disposal to educate the electorate, not to manipulate it.

Hanna came to represent the power of big business in American politics. Part of that impression was deserved. He believed that size brought efficiency and a better standard of living. He also endorsed the protective tariff. At the same time, he thought that industrial workers should receive fair wages and a voice in the state of their working conditions. This view did not make him a New Dealer in the Gilded Age. It did reveal that his Republicanism had within it elements that explain why the GOP was the majority party of the nation between 1894 and 1929. As Theodore Roosevelt wrote of Hanna when he died: "No man had larger traits than Hanna. He was a big man in every way and as forceful a personality as we have seen in public life in our generation." That was a fitting epitaph for one of the most important politicians in the age of McKinley and Roosevelt.

Bibliography

Beer, Thomas. *Hanna*. New York: Knopf, 1929. Beer's father was a political associate of Hanna, and this biography is written from an admiring point of view. It contains many shrewd insights and is a pleasure to read.

Blum, John Morton. *The Republican Roosevelt.* Cambridge, Mass.: Harvard University Press, 1954. Blum's short study of Roosevelt has a chapter on the rivalry with Hanna from 1901 to 1904 that is important to understanding the senator's career.

Croly, Herbert. *Marcus Alonzo Hanna: His Life and Work.* New York: Macmillan, 1912. Croly had access to the Hanna papers and interviews with the senator's associates, and these documents are now at the Library of Congress in the Hanna-McCormick Family Papers. This is the best full biography of Hanna and is positive about his political achievements.

Gould, Lewis L. *The Presidency of William McKinley.* Lawrence: Regents Press of Kansas, 1980. Places Hanna's role in McKinley's career in the context of the presidency between 1897 and 1901. There are discussions of Hanna's appointment to the Senate, his part in the election of 1900, and his relation to the president.

Jones, Stanley L. *The Presidential Election of 1896.* Madison: University of Wisconsin Press, 1964. Jones provides the fullest treatment of Hanna's participation in the McKinley campaign. The book is richly documented and provides direction for further research into Hanna's political career.

Leech, Margaret. *In the Days of McKinley.* New York: Harper, 1950. Leech's is the most detailed study of McKinley as president, and there is much useful information about Hanna's dealings with the White House and the Administration.

Miller, Jay. "Marcus the Kingmaker." *Crain's Cleveland Business* 16, no. 49 (December 4, 1995). Profile of Hanna, a wealthy Cleveland businessman who was the first to use major fundraising as a campaign tactic for McKinley in 1896.

Morgan, H. Wayne. *William McKinley and His America.* Syracuse, N.Y.: Syracuse University Press, 1963. This is the best biography of McKinley, and Morgan offers a persuasive analysis of the Hanna-McKinley friendship as it affected his subject's life and political career.

Williams, R. Hal. *Years of Decision: American Politics in the 1890's.* New York: Wiley, 1978. Williams provides a penetrating look at the decade in which Hanna achieved national prominence. The book is essential for understanding why Hanna, McKinley, and the Republicans triumphed in this period.

Lewis L. Gould

KARL VON HARDENBERG

Born: May 31, 1750; Essenrode, Hanover

Died: November 26, 1822; Genoa, Kingdom of Sardinia

Areas of Achievement: Government, politics, and diplomacy

Contribution: Hardenberg played a leading role in the Prussian reform movement. He also directed the foreign policy of his country during the eventful years 1810-1822 and played a pivotal role in forming the coalition of powers that defeated Napoleon. He was the spokesman for Prussia at the Congress of Vienna in 1815, which determined the political fate of Europe for the next fifty years.

Early Life

Karl August von Hardenberg was born at Essenrode, Hanover, on May 31, 1750, to Christian and Charlotte von Hardenberg. His father, the scion of an old Hanoverian family, had a distinguished military career. Hardenberg's parents determined that he should pursue a career in government service, and they sent him to Göttingen University in 1766, to study law and political science. He also studied briefly at the University of Leipzig in 1768. He completed his studies in 1770, having returned to Göttingen. Upon graduation he entered the Hanoverian bureaucracy in the department of justice.

In 1775, Hardenberg made an unfortunate marriage to the Countess Juliana von Reventlow, after which Hardenberg was appointed as the Hanoverian minister to England. His wife became involved in a sordid affair with the Prince of Wales, which, when it became a public scandal in 1781, forced Hardenberg's recall from England and ultimately his resignation from service. Hardenberg managed to find a new post in the Brunswick bureaucracy in 1782, serving for more than a decade. His service in Brunswick was also terminated by a scandal when, after securing a divorce from Juliana, he married a divorcée. Leaving Brunswick in 1792, Hardenberg obtained a position in the Prussian bureaucracy as minister for several newly acquired provinces.

Life's Work

Hardenberg quickly displayed to his new monarch unusual ability in both internal administration and in foreign affairs. In domestic affairs, he was entrusted with the reorganization of the Prussian administrations of finance, justice, education, and transportation. In foreign affairs, Frederick William II made him plenipotentiary to conclude a territorial settlement with the revolutionary government of France in 1795. Through his adroit handling of the negotiations resulting in the Peace of Basel, Prussia actually emerged stronger than before, despite having fared poorly in the War of the First Coalition. Hardenberg continued to grow in favor, and in 1804 Frederick William III appointed him foreign minister of Prussia.

As minister for foreign affairs, Hardenberg openly advocated a policy of territorial aggrandizement, contending that the Prussian government should seize every opportunity to acquire new territory. He pursued a policy of peace with Napoleon and territorial expansion through negotiation. In 1806, however, Hardenberg's counsel was disregarded and Prussia allied with Russia in a new war against Napoleon.

The war ended disastrously for Prussia. The Prussian army was overwhelmingly defeated at the Battles of Jena and Auerstedt in 1806, and the Prussian monarch was forced to sign the Treaty of Tilsit in

1807. The treaty not only diminished Prussia territorially but also limited her autonomy. Part of the settlement at Tilsit was that Hardenberg, whom Napoleon distrusted, should retire from government service. Before leaving office, however, Hardenberg began the restructuring of the old administrative system, the first step in what has come to be known as the Prussian reform movement.

In 1807-1808, the reform movement was expanded by Freiherr vom Stein, who oversaw the emancipation of Prussian serfs and the extension of self-government to the municipalities of Prussia before being forced from office by Napoleon. Hardenberg remained in contact with Stein; during his forced retirement he produced his famous Riga Memorandum in 1808, which became the blueprint for the further reforms of Prussian institutions. The central thesis of the memorandum was that if the monarchical form of government was to survive in Prussia, the government must adopt many of the liberal institutions produced in France by the Revolution of 1789. Hardenberg's memorandum showed that he, like Stein, recognized that the forces of nationalism and democracy unleashed by the revolution in France would ultimately destroy the old order of Europe if they were not brought under control. He proposed that the Prussian government should introduce liberal reform from above to prevent revolution.

In 1810, Napoleon allowed Frederick William to recall Hardenberg to the Prussian government, this time as prime minister. His initial reforms aimed at making the tax structure of the kingdom more equitable and at simplifying tax collection. Hardenberg imposed a property tax on all citizens (the nobility had formerly been exempted), an excise tax on all areas, and a profit tax. Concurrently, most restrictions on trade and commerce were removed, and civic equality for Jews was established.

Hardenberg then took a hesitant step toward establishing a representative assembly to permit popular participation in the making of governmental policy. By convening an assembly of notables he hoped to create widespread enthusiasm for the further changes he intended to make. Unfortunately, the *junkers* (aristocratic landowners) opposed the idea of representative government and used their influence with Frederick William to thwart the hope of a national parliament. Nevertheless, Hardenberg was able to open admission of the officer corps and of the bureaucracy (formerly the exclusive preserves of the *junkers*) to all citizens.

From 1812 until his death, most of Hardenberg's attention was focused on foreign policy. In 1812, Napoleon forced Prussia to sign a military alliance in preparation for his planned invasion of Russia. When Napoleon's Russian campaign ended in a French debacle, Hardenberg saw the possibility of escaping the domination Napoleon had exercised over Prussia since 1806. Moving cautiously, Hardenberg engineered a military alliance in 1813 between Prussia and Russia, the Treaty of Kalisz. Ironically, Stein, in his new capacity as political adviser to Alexander I, was the Russian representative at Kalisz.

During the ensuing War of Liberation, a wave of patriotic enthusiasm swept through Prussia. After Napoleon's defeat at Leipzig in 1813 led to his withdrawal from the German states, Hardenberg went to Vienna to represent Prussia at the international congress whose purpose was to restructure Europe.

At Vienna, Hardenberg immediately came into conflict with Metternich, the Austrian representative. Metternich, an archconservative intent on reestablishing the old aristocratic order in Europe, opposed German unification in particular (Hardenberg's aim) and nationalism in general, which he saw as destructive to the interests of the multiracial Austrian Empire. The clash between Austria and Prussia over this and other matters at Vienna almost led to war and was instrumental in Napoleon's decision to return from his first exile and reclaim the throne of France.

After Waterloo, Hardenberg and Frederick William seemed to become more and more dominated by Metternich. They acquiesced to the creation of the Germanic confederation, a weakly unified government of largely independent small states. Hardenberg gave up his plan to introduce a constitution and a parliament in Prussia and signed the Holy Alliance, which obligated Prussia along with the other signatories to intervene militarily whenever a legitimate monarch anywhere in Europe was threatened by revolution. Nevertheless, domestic reform continued and considerable passion for unification and parliamentary government flourished, especially in Prussian universities.

After the assassination of a conservative newspaper editor by a young nationalist in 1819, Metternich convinced Hardenberg and Frederick William to adopt the Karlsbad Decrees, which ushered in a period of total reaction in the German states. The Prussian reform movement was ended. Hardenberg, completely under the spell of Metternich, continued to direct Prussian foreign policy until his death, in Genoa on November 26, 1822.

Summary

Karl von Hardenberg enjoyed considerable successes in domestic reform and diplomacy. Under his leadership, the principle of civic equality became firmly established in Prussia. Prussian Jews began to play leading roles in government, in the arts, and in education after 1812, as a result of Hardenberg's leadership in social reform. The bureaucracy and the army became more efficient because careers in those organizations were opened to all men of talent and promotions became based on merit rather than family. Hardenberg laid the foundation for the Prussian educational system to become the model and the envy of the rest of the world. Hardenberg was responsible for the establishment of a more equitable system of taxation and for the removal of many archaic restrictions on trade and commerce in Prussia.

Through his diplomacy, Hardenberg was instrumental in the defeat of Napoleon. His leadership in foreign affairs allowed the Prussian kingdom not only to survive the dangerous times of the Napoleonic Wars but also to emerge from the era larger and more powerful than it had been in 1780. For these accomplishments, Hardenberg is often recognized as being second in importance only to Otto von Bismarck among Prussian prime ministers. Despite these impressive accomplishments, Hardenberg is sometimes criticized for missing opportunities to accomplish much more. Yet Hardenberg's goals in foreign and domestic policy were to preserve the old order insofar as possible. He could not have led a movement that would have dismantled that order when the possibility existed of preserving most of it under the Metternichian system. In the final analysis, Hardenberg was an effective diplomat and an able administrator whose tenure as Prime Minister of Prussia was a decisive step toward the transformation of his country into a modern nation-state.

Bibliography

Holborn, Hajo. *A History of Modern Germany.* Vol. 2, *1648-1840.* New York: Knopf, 1964; London: Eyre and Spottiswoode, 1965. Contains several chapters on the reform movement and provides sketches of its most important leaders, including Hardenberg. Places the Prussian reform movement and the reformers in their proper perspective in German history.

Meinecke, Friedrich. *The Age of German Liberation, 1795-1815.* Translated by Peter Paret and Helmut Fischer. Berkeley: University of California Press, 1977. One of the best accounts of the period, Meinecke's book provides a good account of Hardenberg's life and work.

Schenk, H. G. *The Aftermath of the Napoleonic Wars: The Concert of Europe, an Experiment.* London: Kegan Paul, and New York: Oxford University Press, 1947. Perhaps the best account of the congress system implemented by Metternich after 1815. Hardenberg's role in diplomatic affairs during this era is amply and sympathetically treated.

Simon, Walter M. *The Failure of the Prussian Reform Movement, 1807-1819.* Ithaca, N.Y.: Cornell University Press, 1955. Simon is very critical of both the reforms and the reformers in Prussia, particularly Hardenberg. Simon argues that the failure of the reforms to establish a unified, parliamentary German state led directly to the development of the authoritarianism of the German Empire after 1871 and ultimately to the Third Reich.

Webster, C. K. *The Congress of Vienna.* London and New York: Oxford University Press, 1919. This older study of the Congress of Vienna is still the standard work on the subject.

Paul Madden

JAMES KEIR HARDIE

Born: August 15, 1856; Legrannock, Lanarkshire, Scotland

Died: September 26, 1915; Glasgow, Scotland

Areas of Achievement: Politics, government, and trade unionism

Contribution: Through agitation and enthusiasm, Hardie, more than any other person, helped inspire and organize both the Independent Labour Party and then the more broadly based Labour Party, which became one of Great Britain's two major parties after World War I.

Early Life

James Keir Hardie was born on August 15, 1856, in a small mining village in Lanarkshire, Scotland, the illegitimate child of a farm servant, Mary Keir. Keir later married David Hardie, an erratically employed ship's carpenter. They had a large family, and two of James's half brothers later became Labour Members of Parliament (M.P.'s). Constant moves and an unsteady income meant that the family circumstances were more like that of unskilled workers than of artisans. Young James was never apprenticed but began working odd jobs at age seven while in Glasgow. When the family moved back to the Lanarkshire coalfields, ten-year-old Hardie started working in the pits and continued working there until his early twenties. Already, Hardie's boldness, energy, and romanticism were apparent. Having been taught to read at home, he received his only formal education at a night school, improving his writing and learning shorthand. An avid reader, Hardie was enraptured with Robert Burns, both for his Scottish style and for his egalitarian ideas. Reared an agnostic, in his early twenties Hardie was converted to Christianity and joined the Evangelical Union Church, a less doctrinaire and a more evangelical and democratic denomination than the official Calvinist Presbyterian Church. Partially in reaction to his drunken stepfather, Hardie became a strong advocate of temperance. He thus reflected the late-Victorian pattern of self-help and self-control as a way to improve oneself.

In 1879, Hardie married Lillie Wilson, a simple patient woman with whom he had three children. She later kept their home in Cumnock (in Ayrshire, Scotland) when he resided in London. An active and passionate man, Hardie had brief affairs with several women. Hardie was stocky and of average height, but his unconventional dress and heavy beard would soon be the caricaturists' delight. His black beard turned gray by his late thirties, which reinforced his position as an "elder" pioneer in labor politics and his aura as a working-class folk hero.

Life's Work

Locally known as a public speaker on temperance, Hardie became involved in trade union activity in 1878, as a result of which he lost his job and never worked as a miner again. He soon became a local miners' union agent and then secretary of the struggling union in Ayrshire. His militant approach led to two humiliating strike defeats. He attempted but failed to create an effective Scottish Miner's National Federation.

Young, flamboyant, and well-known through his speaking, writing, and trade union activities, Hardie became active in Liberal politics. The Liberal Party was in flux: Its leader, William Ewart Gladstone, was becoming a champion of the masses, his

ministry was making both county and national government more democratic, most of its aristocratic element was leaving the party, and a radical wing was developing. Moreover, a few working-men were elected as Liberal M.P.'s (dubbed "Lib-Labs"). Yet Hardie was already evolving a political position of socialism or radical collectivism, advocating increased governmental involvement in society. Thus, it was unlikely that he would be selected as a Lib-Lab candidate when he formally sought the Liberal Party nomination in the 1888 Mid-Lanark parliamentary by-election. Rebuffed, he ran and lost badly as an independent, an experience which made him more distrustful of the Liberals.

At age thirty, by which time he was a Socialist, Hardie attended his first Trades Union Congress (TUC) and made incessant attacks on its cautious leaders. Although his views gained wider acceptance by the early 1890's as the more militant "new unionism" grew, he was still considered by the TUC establishment as a troublemaker. When in 1894 he was neither an active worker at his trade nor a full-time union official, he was barred under new standing orders from being a delegate to the TUC. By then, however, Hardie had persuaded the TUC to advocate the eight-hour day (1891) and nationalization of production, distribution, and exchange (1894).

In 1888, Hardie organized and served as secretary of the short-lived Scottish Labour Party, a loose coalition of various Scottish protest or labor organizations. In 1892, Hardie was elected M.P. for West Ham South in London's East End; he succeeded as an independent because of Liberal division there. Although he failed to nurture that constituency and was defeated in 1895, he cut a colorful figure in Parliament for those three intervening years. Disdaining the staid conventional dress of most M.P.'s, Hardie entered Parliament in yellow tweed trousers, a serge jacket, and a Sherlock Holmes-style deerstalker cap, all of which reflected his bohemian love of flashy clothes. While in the Commons, Hardie vehemently protested Parliament's recognition of a royal birth while it ignored a major Welsh mining disaster. Most significant, Hardie was the first to focus political attention on unemployment, which suddenly expanded in the early 1890's.

In 1893, while still in Parliament, Hardie was instrumental in founding the Independent Labour Party (ILP). Wanting it to become a broad-based party with significant electoral support, Hardie steered it carefully away from becoming branded merely a doctrinaire organization ("Independent" not "Socialist" was used in its title) and based it on existing local working-class or Socialist institutions. Serving as its first chairman (from 1894 to 1900, and later from 1913 to 1915), he then helped it become more centralized. Realizing that the ILP, however, was still only a small party based primarily in the north of England, Hardie championed the creation of the Labour Representation Committee (LRC, which became the Labour Party in 1906). It, too, was a coalition of organizations, Socialist ones (such as the ILP) as well as many non-Socialist trade unions. Hardie harnessed the financial and electoral support of trade unions to an effective and unified political party separate from the existing main parties.

The general election in 1900 caught the new LRC unprepared, but Hardie was returned to Parliament from the Welsh mining constituency of Merthyr Burghs and served until 1915. He benefited from friendly Liberal support, and in 1903 he agreed with the secret Liberal-Labour arrangement that in certain constituencies the two parties would not compete. That agreement helped Labour win twenty-nine seats in the 1906 election. By a one-vote margin, Hardie was elected Labour Party leader in the Commons (1906-1907). Although not considered a good leader, he did help achieve a reversal of the Taff Vale decision and a guarantee of civil immunity for unions on strike.

Hardie did not have the temperament to serve as spokesman for a consensus position within the party; he was the bold advocate of minority causes, be they Socialist or radical. He opposed the Boer War (1899-1902), supported the native populations in India and South Africa, and championed the suffragettes. The latter cause hurt him within the Labour movement, for Hardie supported Emmeline Pankhurst's Women's Social and Political Union and its extraparliamentary tactics and symbolic violence, as well as its emphasis on enfranchising primarily middle-class women.

Hardie was also an internationalist. He loved to travel, making trips to the United States, Canada, Europe, and elsewhere. With his appearance at the inaugural conference of the Second International (1889 in Paris), he became a fixture of international socialism. As with the ILP and the Labour Party, Hardie opposed doctrinaire attempts to exclude unorthodox Socialist organizations and to forbid cooperation of Socialist Parties with non-Socialist ones. An advocate of class solidarity (though not of class war), Hardie opposed the European drift toward World War I and tried in vain to convince the Second International to declare a general strike should a world war start. When all the major Socialist parties of Europe, as well as the British Labour Party, supported their governments' decisions for war, Hardie was crushed. After suffering from ill health, exhausted by his demanding schedule, Hardie died on September 26, 1915.

Summary

James Keir Hardie is the preeminent, first-generation Labour political figure. Agitator, propagandist, crusader, maverick—Hardie inspired two generations of Labour supporters. With little formal education, Hardie guided the creation of a Labour Party linking Socialist organizations (which contained some middle-class intellectuals) with the trade unions (mostly of non-Socialist skilled workers). A Scotsman residing in London representing a Welsh constituency for fifteen years, Hardie supported workers everywhere. At a time before radio and television, Hardie carried his message by rousing public speeches and by his newspaper columns throughout Great Britain, and his portrait became a fixture in many working-class homes.

Always vain and egotistical, Hardie did not work well with colleagues. Lax in financial matters and disliking details and procedures, he was never an effective administrator. He spoke and wrote passionately on issues, but he never tried to develop coherent programs for implementing socialism. He disdained theoretical analysis, and his socialism was emotional, rather than intellectual. Hardie's reputation as the erratic, sometimes irresponsible, flamboyant, pioneering Labour agitator, however, belies his other significant attributes.

He was practical and flexible. For Hardie, socialism was not only a future system but also a practical system to improve the lot of working people in his own day. He realized that the workers needed political representation, not as a minor adjunct of the Liberal Party but through their own party. He also realized that an effective party could not be created from the top, it must be based on existing local organizations. His range became increasingly wider and more effective: He had limited success with the ILP (1893) but achieved a significant victory with the LRC-Labour Party (1900), which finally included trade unions themselves. A romanticist (as well as an evangelical Christian who became also a spiritualist), Hardie never systematized his political views: He advocated a radical stress on personal liberties, governmental actions to improve conditions and eliminate unemployment, and future nationalizations. This broad political spectrum encouraged both Socialists and pragmatic trade unionists to participate in the Labour Party. His uncertainty as to whether this early party was a pressure group or a party seeking power furthered its broad-based appeal.

Within ten years of Hardie's death, Labour replaced the Liberals as one of Great Britain's two most important parties, even forming a government briefly in 1924. In the 1930's, the party became more precise in its programs and more determined to gain office to implement them, and it was successful following World War II. While the pioneering Hardie would seem out of place in the mid-twentieth century party, it was his persistence and organizational foresight which helped make that Labour Party possible.

Bibliography

Bealey, Frank, and Henry Pelling. *Labour and Politics, 1900-1906: A History of the Labour Representation Committee.* London: Macmillan, and New York: St. Martin's Press, 1958. A sequel to Henry Pelling's *Origin of the Labour Party*, this standard work well demonstrates Hardie's role in moving the LRC toward becoming an effective party by 1906. While stressing Labour's independence, Hardie worked carefully with the Liberal Party both on the national and local levels.

Brown, Kenneth D. *John Burns.* London: Royal Historical Society, 1977. Hardie's contemporary, sometime colleague, but usually bitter opponent, Burns moved from being a working-class Socialist agitator and organizer to a member of the prewar Liberal cabinet. This brief scholarly biography of Burns treats Hardie from his rival's perspective.

Howell, David. *British Workers and the Independent Labour Party, 1888-1906.* Manchester: Manchester University Press, and New York: St. Martin's Press, 1983. This is a masterful but complex treatment designed for specialists in the field. Howell brilliantly synthesizes his and many other researchers' work as he deftly examines local trade union and ILP branches as well as the national ILP center. This major work is a must for any sustained investigation of early labor politics.

Hughes, Emrys. *Keir Hardie*. London: Allen and Unwin, 1956. This is a laudatory biography written by Hardie's son-in-law and latter-day political disciple. Although uncritical and subjective, Hughes helps re-create the passions and the feuds of Hardie's life.

McLean, Iain. *Keir Hardie*. London: Allen Lane, and New York: St. Martin's Press, 1975. This excellent brief biography is favorable toward, but not uncritical of, its subject. It is the best introduction to Hardie, and it also explains background issues well for nonspecialist readers.

Morgan, Kenneth O. *Keir Hardie: Radical and Socialist*. London: Weidenfeld and Nicolson, 1975. This is the best comprehensive Hardie biography. Its generally favorable coverage fails to capture Hardie's flamboyance. It concludes with an excellent chapter relating Hardie's leg-acy on the party throughout the twentieth century.

Pelling, Henry. *The Origins of the Labour Party, 1880-1900*. London: Macmillan, and New York: St. Martin's Press, 1954. This standard, judicious appraisal focuses primarily on the function of Socialist organizations (and deliberately de-emphasizes trade unions) in establishing the Labour Party. Hardie's successes are recognized clearly in this treatment.

Reid, Fred. *Keir Hardie: The Making of a Socialist*. London: Croom Helm, 1978. Treating Hardie's early life through 1895, Reid focuses on his childhood, the fluid 1880's, and Hardie's establishing the ILP. Exhaustingly researched, it provides a deeper and more subtle understanding of Hardie's personality and his evolving political concepts.

Jerry H. Brookshire

THOMAS HARDY

Born: June 2, 1840; Higher Bockhampton, Dorset, England

Died: January 11, 1928; Dorchester, Dorset, England

Area of Achievement: Literature

Contribution: One of the great English novelists and poets of the late nineteenth century, Hardy is representative of the Victorian trauma of the loss of God and the search for a new order.

Early Life

Thomas Hardy was born in the hamlet of Higher Bockhampton on June 2, 1840. His father was a master mason, satisfied with his low social status and his rural surroundings. His mother, however, whom Hardy once called "a born bookworm," encouraged Hardy's education and urged him to raise his social standing. John Hicks, a Dorchester architect, took the boy on as a pupil at the age of sixteen. While in Hicks's office, Hardy met the well-known poet William Barnes, who became an important influence on his career. Another early influence was the classical scholar Horace Moule, an essayist and reviewer. Moule encouraged Hardy to read John Stuart Mill and the iconoclastic *Essays and Reviews* (1860) by Frederick Temple and others, both of which contributed to the undermining of Hardy's simple religious faith.

At age twenty-two, Hardy went to London to pursue his architectural training; by this time, however, he had also begun to write poetry and to entertain hopes of a literary career. In 1866, after reading Algernon Charles Swinburne's *Poems and Ballads: First Series* (1866), he began an intensive two-year period of writing poetry. He submitted many poems for publication during this time, but none was published, although many of these were published later, when he began writing poetry only.

After returning to Bockhampton in 1867, Hardy decided to try his hand at writing fiction. His first effort in this genre, "The Poor Man and the Lady," based on his perception of the difference between city and country life, received some favorable attention from publishers. After a discussion with novelist George Meredith, however, Hardy decided not to publish the work but, on Meredith's advice, to strike out in a new direction. In imitation of the detective fiction of Wilkie Collins, he thus wrote *Desperate Remedies* (1871). In spite of his success Hardy did not stay with the melodramatic novel

but instead took the advice of a reader who liked the rural scenes in his first work and wrote a pastoral idyll entitled *Under the Greenwood Tree* (1872). Although the book was well received by critics, its sales were poor. Yet Hardy had found his true subject—the rural English life of an imaginary area he called Wessex—and he was on his way to becoming a full-time writer. He began writing serials for periodicals, abandoned architecture, and launched himself on a career that was to last well into the twentieth century.

Life's Work

In 1874, Hardy married Emma Lavinia Gifford, a socially ambitious young woman who shared his interest in books. At about the same time, his first great novel, *Far from the Madding Crowd* (1874), appeared and received many favorable reviews. As a result, editors began asking for the works of Thomas Hardy. While living with his wife at Sturminster Newton in a small cottage, Hardy composed his next great novel, *The Return of the Native* (1878), and enjoyed what he later called the happiest years of his life. After a brief social life in London, Hardy returned to Dorset, had his home "Max Gate" built, and published the third of his five masterpieces, *The Mayor of Casterbridge* (1886). For the next several years, Hardy continued his writing, traveled with his wife, and read German philosophy.

By this time, Hardy himself was being seen as a philosophical novelist. What has been called his "philosophy," however, can be summed up in an early (1865) entry in his notebooks: "The world does not despise us; it only neglects us." The difference between Hardy and many nineteenth century artists who experienced a similar loss of faith is that while others such as William Wordsworth and Thomas Carlyle were able to achieve some measure of religious affirmation, Hardy never embraced a transcendent belief. He did not try to escape the isolation that his loss of faith created, although in all of his major novels and in most of his poetry, he continued to try to find some value in a world of accident, chance, and indifference. Indeed, all of Hardy's serious artistic work can be seen as variations on his one barren theme of the loss of God and the quest for a new value system.

Late in his life, Hardy said that he never really wanted to write novels and did so only out of eco-

nomic necessity. Indeed, many of his minor works are imitations of popular forms of the time. While he did imitate the detective novel or social comedy, however, when he wished to write a novel that more clearly reflected his own vision of man's situation in the world, he could find no adequate fictional model among the popular forms of the time. Thus, he returned to classical models such as the pastoral for *Far from the Madding Crowd* and *The Woodlanders* (1887), Greek tragedy for *The Mayor of Casterbridge* and *The Return of the Native*, and the epic for *Tess of the D'Urbervilles* (1891) and *Jude the Obscure* (1896).

Since these early genres were based on some sense of there being a God-ordered world, Hardy could not imitate them exactly but rather had to transform them into his own grotesque versions of pastoral, tragedy, and epic. As a result, in his pastorals nature is neither benevolent nor divinely ordered; in his tragedies, his heroes are not heroic because they defy the gods but precisely because there is no God; and in his epic works, his epic figures—Tess and Jude—are not heroes who represent the order of their society but rather are outcasts because neither their society nor indeed their universe has inherent value.

Thus, if Hardy is a philosophical novelist, as is often claimed, his philosophy is a simple and straightforward one—the world is an indifferent place and the heavens are empty of meaning and value. Although Hardy did not have a unified philosophical system, he was more committed to metaphysical issues than he was to the various social issues that preoccupied many novelists of the late nineteenth century. This is true in spite of the fact that the surface plot of *Tess of the D'Urbervilles* deals with the so-called marriage question in England and *Jude the Obscure* ostensibly deals with the problem of equal education.

Hardy's initial enthusiasm for his fourth important novel, *Tess of the D'Urbervilles*, was dampened when it was turned down by two editors before being accepted for serial publication by a third. The publication of this work brought hostile reaction and notoriety to Hardy—a notoriety that increased after the publication of his last great novel, *Jude the Obscure*. Hardy was both puzzled and cynical about these reactions to his last two novels for their iconoclastic views of sexuality, marriage, and class distinctions, but he was by then financially secure and decided to return to his first love, poetry.

In poetry, Hardy believed that his views could be presented in a less obvious and more distanced way. For the rest of his career, he wrote little else. His poems, of which he published well over a thousand, were very well received, and his experimental drama, *The Dynasts: A Drama of the Napoleonic Wars* (1903-1908), brought him even more respect, fame, and honor. The final years of Hardy's life were spoiled only by the death of his wife in 1912. Within four years, he married his secretary, Florence Dugdale, who cared for him in his old age. Hardy continued to write poetry regularly for the rest of his life; his final volume, *Winter Words* (1928), was being prepared for publication when he died on January 11, 1928. His death was mourned by all of England, and his ashes were placed in Westminster Abbey.

Summary

Thomas Hardy is second only to Charles Dickens as the most read and most discussed writer of the Victorian era. New books and articles appear on his life and work each year with no signs of abating. In terms of volume and diversity of work, Hardy is a towering literary figure with two highly respected careers—one as a novelist and one as a poet.

Interest in Hardy's work has followed two basic patterns. The first is philosophical, with many critics creating elaborate metaphysical structures which supposedly underlay his fiction. In the last two decades, however, interest has shifted to that aspect of Hardy's work which was most scorned before—his technical expertise and his experiments with many different genres. Only in the last few years has what once was termed his fictional clumsiness been reevaluated as sophisticated poetic technique. Furthermore, Hardy's career as a poet, which has always been under the shadow of his fiction, has been seen in a more positive light recently and has even been called by some critics the most significant and important part of his life's work.

Hardy was a curious blend of the old-fashioned and the modern. With a career that began in the Victorian era and did not conclude until after World War I, Hardy was contemporary with both the representative Victorian writer Matthew Arnold and the most frequently cited representative of the modern, T. S. Eliot. Many critics suggest that Hardy, more than any other writer, bridges the gulf between the Victorian sensibility and the modern era.

Although not a systematic philosophical thinker, Hardy was a great existential humanist. His hope for humanity was that man would realize that creeds and conventions which presupposed a God-oriented center of value were baseless. He hoped that man would loosen himself from religious dogma and become aware of his freedom to create his own value system. If only man would realize that all people were equally alone and without divine help, Hardy believed, he would realize also that it was the height of absurdity for such lost and isolated creatures to fight among themselves. The breakout of World War I was thus a crushing blow to whatever optimism Hardy held for modern man.

In his relentless vision of a world stripped of transcendence, Hardy is a distinctly modern novelist. As one critic has said of him, he not only directs one's attention back to the trauma of the loss of faith in the nineteenth century, he also leads one into the quest for renewed value that characterizes the modern era.

Bibliography

Beach, Joseph Warren. *The Technique of Thomas Hardy.* Chicago: University of Chicago Press, 1922. A classic, pioneering study which focused on Hardy's fictional technique rather than his philosophy.

Brady, Kristin. *The Short Stories of Thomas Hardy.* London: Macmillan, and New York: St. Martin's Press, 1982. A helpful study of an often-neglected part of Hardy's work, showing how his stories are a link between the old-fashioned tale and the modern short story.

Brooks, Jean R. *Thomas Hardy: The Poetic Structure.* Ithaca, N.Y.: Cornell University Press, and London: Elek, 1971. An excellent modern study which focuses on readings of the major works from the standpoint of linguistic patterns and poetic structure.

Carpenter, Richard. *Thomas Hardy.* New York: Twayne, 1964; London: Macmillan, 1976. More than an introductory overview, this study reveals the mythic structures that underlie much of Hardy's fiction.

Dean, Susan. *Hardy's Poetic Vision in "The Dynasts."* Princeton, N.J.: Princeton University Press, 1977. An interesting study of Hardy's experimental epic drama which proposes that the work is an objectification of the human mind.

Guerard, Albert J., Jr. *Thomas Hardy: The Novels and Stories.* Cambridge, Mass.: Harvard University Press, and London: Oxford University Press, 1949. One of the most important studies to stimulate the modern reevaluation of Hardy's work, this book did much to call attention to Hardy's antirealism and thus his similarity to such writers as Joseph Conrad and André Gide.

Hynes, Samuel. *The Pattern of Hardy's Poetry.* Chapel Hill: University of North Carolina Press, 1961. An important reevaluation of Hardy's poetry which did much to create a new interest in this neglected body of Hardy's work.

Kramer, Dale, ed. *The Cambridge Companion to Thomas Hardy.* Cambridge and New York: Cambridge University Press, 1999. A collection of essays providing an overview of Hardy's work, aesthetics, and the religious and philosophical climate of the late nineteenth century.

Miller, J. Hillis. *Thomas Hardy: Distance and Desire.* Cambridge, Mass.: Harvard University Press, and London: Oxford University Press, 1970. A stimulating, if often overly complex, study of Hardy's work from a contemporary phenomenological point of view.

Turner, Paul D. *The Life of Thomas Hardy: A Critical Biography.* Oxford and Malden, Mass.: Blackwell, 1998. This biography focuses on Hardy's life as a self-made man. Includes his self-education, personal trials, and use of personal experiences as a basis for his writing.

Weber, Carl J. *Hardy of Wessex: His Life and Literary Career.* New York: Columbia University Press, 1940; London: Routledge, 1965. A highly detailed biographical treatment of Hardy that is more valuable for the hard information it supplies about Hardy's life than it is for the somewhat old-fashioned and unenlightening criticism.

Charles E. May

WILLIAM RAINEY HARPER

Born: July 26, 1856; New Concord, Ohio
Died: January 10, 1906; Chicago, Illinois
Area of Achievement: Education
Contribution: President of the University of Chicago during its formative years, Harper was a major figure in the reshaping of American higher education.

Early Life

William Rainey Harper was born July 26, 1856, in New Concord, Ohio, the son of Samuel and Ellen Elizabeth (Rainey) Harper. His forebears on both sides were Scotch-Irish immigrants; his father was a small-town dry goods merchant. Intellectually precocious, Harper entered the preparatory school of the local Muskingum College at the age of eight, was graduated to the college itself at ten, and received his bachelor of arts degree in 1870. By that time, he had acquired sufficient fluency in Hebrew—the study of which became his lifelong passion—to deliver the salutatory oration at graduation in that language. For several years, he worked in his father's store while keeping up his study of languages. In 1872-1873, he taught Hebrew at Muskingum College. In September, 1873, he began graduate work at Yale. He received his Ph.D. in philology in 1875; his dissertation was titled "A Comparative Study of the Prepositions in Latin, Greek, Sanskrit, and Gothic." He served as principal of the Masonic College (in fact, a glorified high school) at Macon, Tennessee, from 1875 to 1876, and taught Greek and Latin in the preparatory department of Denison University in Granville, Ohio, from 1876 to 1878. Although his family background had been Presbyterian, he became a Baptist while at Denison.

In 1879, Harper moved to the Baptist Union Theological Seminary located in Morgan Park (a Chicago suburb) to teach Hebrew. In addition to earning a bachelor of divinity degree, Harper developed while at Morgan Park a set of correspondence courses in Hebrew, a series of Hebrew textbooks, and a summer course in Semitic languages and biblical studies that became the model for similar courses across the country. He was founder and editor of two journals: the *Hebrew Student* (renamed first the *Old and New Testament Studies* and then the *Biblical Scholar*) and *Hebraica* (which later became the *American Journal of Semitic Languages and Literatures*). In 1886, he went back to Yale as professor of Semitic languages in the Divinity School. Teaching at Yale, he gained a national reputation as a scholar, organizer, and editor. A major factor in his growing prominence was his association, dating from the summer of 1885, with the Chautauqua Institute; Harper's connection with the institute included the principalship of its college of liberal arts. In 1890, he was offered the presidency of the newly planned University of Chicago, to be established under Baptist auspices with major funding provided by the multimillionaire John D. Rockefeller. Before accepting, Harper laid down what he thought should be the guidelines for the institution. After the trustees accepted his proposal in December, 1890, Harper entered upon one of the most remarkably successful episodes in university-building in history. By the time the University of Chicago opened in the fall of 1892, he had recruited the nucleus of a topflight faculty; he would go on to make the university into one of the world's great academic centers.

Life's Work

Harper's first love was teaching; throughout his years as president of the University of Chicago, he continued his classroom work. Unlike most of his fellow academic empire-builders, he was a distinguished scholar in his own right. He was a major figure in the revival of Hebrew scholarship. In 1902, he published a detailed and exhaustive study, *The Priestly Element in the Old Testament*; three years later there appeared the companion *The Prophetic Element in the Old Testament* (1905) along with his monumental *Critical and Exegetical Commentary on Amos and Hosea* (1905). Although a professing, even devout, Christian, Harper was an adherent of the so-called higher criticism—that is, the application to the scriptural text of evidentiary tests drawn from philology and history. While affirming that the authors of the Bible were divinely inspired, he believed that their language reflected the linguistic, cultural, and religious context of their time. He accordingly insisted that critical scholarship would not undermine belief but rather would assist modern readers in understanding the real meaning of the Word of God as revealed through the Bible.

After becoming president of the University of Chicago, Harper continued for a time his association with Chautauqua and his journal editorships. He served on the Chicago Board of Education from 1896 to 1898, but the bulk of his energies was devoted to building his university. Along with a detailed conception of the University of Chicago, Harper had the advantage of starting from scratch and thus having neither hallowed traditions nor vested interests to overcome. He had the further advantage of finding in John D. Rockefeller a benefactor who kept his hands off university matters; Rockefeller rarely proffered advice even when asked. Harper could thus proceed with the plans he had outlined when accepting the presidency: the division of the year into four quarters with the summer quarter an integral part of the academic year, division of the undergraduate program whereby the first two years (the junior college) would be devoted to general education and the second two (the senior college) to more specialized study, faculty control of athletics, establishment of a university press, and structural organization of the institution along departmental lines. He was determined from the start that Chicago should not be simply an undergraduate college, but a center for graduate training and advanced research.

Probably the most distinctively innovative aspect of Harper's plans for the University of Chicago was its extension program. The inspiration came from Harper's messianic zeal to spread his own enthusiasm for learning; the model largely came from his association with Chautauqua, which had in turn based its program upon the example of the English university extension movement. Chicago's Division of University Extension had three major alternative programs of study. "Lecture-Study" involved traveling instructors giving a locally based series of lectures, one per week for six or twelve weeks; discussions with the instructor at the time of the lecture; and weekly written exercises based upon a printed syllabus. "Correspondence-Teaching" allowed students to pursue course work entirely via mail. Off-campus evening classes in the Chicago area provided classroom work for those who could not attend regular courses because of their jobs. Extension students could earn undergraduate and even graduate credit, but the larger aim was to bring culture to the uncultured. "If culture is not contagious," the *University Record* declared in 1903, "it should be . . . more or less infectious, and every person who is reaping some of the rewards of the earnest labors of scholarly men should see that something is done to bring others into touch with the same spirit."

Harper had his difficulties. One was the pressure to make the university into a Baptist institution in fact and not simply in name. The president and two-thirds of the trustees were required to be Baptists; the initial plans had envisaged compulsory chapel attendance for undergraduates. A man without much interest in theological debates, Harper parried questions from fundamentalist-minded Baptists about where he stood on the authority of the Bible with the equivocal answer that while the Bible was "in a very unique sense 'inspired,'" there was simultaneously present a "human element." He followed a similar balancing act regarding university policy. He exhorted the students to attend the voluntary religious services; he instituted strict moral supervision over undergraduate housing, activities, and publications; he even—to his eventual regret—acceded to sex segregation in the classroom for the first two undergraduate years. He successfully resisted, however, any screening of the faculty on the basis of religious belief. From the start, the faculty included a number of Jews; Jewish donors played an important part in supplementing the Rockefeller gifts.

Another difficulty faced by all university chief executives of the time was the pressure for conformity on political, social, and economic issues. The failure to renew in 1895 the contract of economist Edward W. Bemis, an outspoken critic of monopolies, led to widespread charges that the University of Chicago was under the thumb of Standard Oil. Yet the Bemis case was the exception—and his firing appears to have been attributable primarily to his personal shortcomings. Under Harper, Chicago gained the reputation of a bastion of academic freedom. "In the University of Chicago," he affirmed in his decennial report, "neither the Trustees nor the President . . . has at any time called an instructor to account for public utterances. . . . In no single case has a donor to the University called the attention of the Trustees to the teaching of any officer of the University as being distasteful or objectionable. Still further it is my opinion that no donor of money to a university . . . has any right . . . to interfere with the teaching. Neither an individual, nor the state, nor the church has the right to interfere with the search for truth, or with its promulgation when found."

Establishing a new university was an arduous task. The most serious problem was money. Harper's ambitions were constantly threatening to outrun the institution's financial resources, and the result was continuing friction between him and a dollar-conscious board of trustees. Harper successfully induced Rockefeller, however, to come up with additional funds at critical junctures. At a time when the average faculty salary ranged from fourteen hundred to fifteen hundred dollars annually, Chicago was paying as much as seven thousand dollars to department chairmen. Having such resources to work with gave Harper the leverage to build a distinguished faculty—often by raiding less generously endowed schools. The faculty during the first year included men who had achieved or were on their way to achieving leadership in their disciplines: Hermann E. von Holst in history, J. Laurence Laughlin in economics, Jacques Loeb in biology, Carl D. Buck in philology, and George Ellery Hale in astronomy. Later Harper brought in such future giants as historian J. Franklin Jameson, philosophers John Dewey and George Herbert Mead, economist Wesley C. Mitchell, Egyptologist James H. Breasted, and physicist Robert A. Millikan. Some would later depart Chicago—because, like Dewey, they became disappointed at failing to receive the financial support that they had been led

to expect or because, like Loeb, they received offers too generous to refuse. Most, however, imbued with Harper's vision for the university, would remain there for their full academic careers.

A man with a keen advertising sense, Harper engaged from the start in an active publicity campaign to attract students. A larger student population was seen as evidence of the university's prestige—and more tuition money added to its financial resources. Simultaneously, he pushed forward with an aggressive program of physical and institutional expansion. The Ogden Graduate School of Science was established in 1892 and within a few years was enrolling more than five hundred students doing graduate work. The Kent Chemical Laboratory was added in 1894, the Ryerson Physical Laboratory the same year, and the Hull Biological Quadrangle three years later. The Haskell Oriental Museum was completed in 1896. The Yerkes Astronomical Observatory, featuring one of the world's most advanced telescopes, was opened at Lake Geneva, in Wisconsin, in 1897. The College of Commerce and Politics (later renamed the School of Commerce and Administration) was organized in 1898, the School of Education in 1901, the Law School in 1902, and the School of Religious and Social Service in 1903-1904. The Decennial Celebration of 1901 was marked by the laying of the cornerstones of five new buildings along with the publication of a twenty-six-volume set of papers and monographs by faculty members. ("No series of scientific publications," Harper boasted, "so comprehensive in its scope and of so great a magnitude has ever been issued at any one time by any learned society or institution.") The broad range of programs offered by the University of Chicago led to its becoming popularly known as "Harper's Bazaar."

Harper exercised strong centralized control over the institution. Deans were his appointees; he retained final say on faculty appointments and promotions. He was deeply immersed in the details of even the physical plant—and the university's imposing and architecturally unified campus owes much to his fascination with systematic planning. Yet he largely eschewed the role of autocrat. He was willing to listen to others and profit from their advice; he even had a sense of humor. He was sufficiently flexible to abandon his own ideas when their implementation proved impracticable—for example, he abandoned the Greek requirement for the A.B. and agreed to make Hebrew optional in the divinity school. As John D. Rockefeller observed, "He knows how to yield when it is necessary in such a way that no sting or bitterness is left behind, and very few men in the world know how to do that." Although there was a short-lived faculty revolt in 1902, Harper ruled more by the force of his personality than by administrative fiat. After talking with Harper, an admirer recounted, one emerged "slightly dazed but tingling with the excitement of a new project, uplifted by a vision of ultimate possibilities, vibrant with a sense of power, for a brief moment feeling indomitable."

Harper had married Ella Paul, the daughter of the president of Muskingum College, on November 18, 1875. The couple had a daughter and three sons—one of whom, Samuel N. Harper, would become a member of the University of Chicago faculty in Russian history. A man of prodigious energy, Harper had the reputation of "a dynamo in trousers." For years, he went to bed at midnight and rose at dawn. Eventually overwork began to take its toll on even his robust constitution. "To the unthinking mind," he confessed in an address to students, "the man who occupies a high position . . . is an object of . . . envy. If the real facts were known, in almost every case it would be found that such a man is being crushed—literally crushed—by the weight of the burdens which he is compelled to carry." He admitted that "with each recurring year it has required greater effort on my part to undertake this kind of service." In 1904, he was found while undergoing an operation for appendicitis to have a cancerous infection that proved inoperable. X-ray treatment similarly proved ineffective. He died January 10, 1906, at only forty-nine years of age.

Summary

Harper's monument was the University of Chicago. He had succeeded in building within the brief span of a decade and a half one of the world's great institutions of learning. As of 1910, the university boasted the third largest total student enrollment in the country—behind Harvard and Columbia. Columbia was its only rival in the areas of graduate training and faculty research. At the same time, Harper had maintained a balance that kept in mind the separate needs of undergraduates. There were gaps in the record: Library facilities remained inadequate, the support available for research was uneven, and Harper himself was too prone to follow the model of the older, established universities on the East Coast. The most striking example of the latter was in regard to the law school, when he opted for the Harvard case-method approach rather than the more innovative ideas of political scientist Ernst Freund. Harper set the pattern for what became a long-term weakness in the university faculty appointment policy—too much emphasis upon bringing in established "stars" from outside while neglecting nascent talent within. His successors lacked his genius for combining organizational skills of the highest order with a larger educational vision. Nevertheless, the University of Chicago was firmly established as a major university. The first dean of the university's law school penned his fitting epitaph: "He had the mind and manners of a captain of industry, but he had the heart and soul of a scholar and a sage."

Bibliography

Goodspeed, Thomas Wakefield. *A History of the University of Chicago: The First Quarter-Century.* Chicago: University of Chicago Press, 1916. A detailed "bricks and mortar" account drawing upon the author's personal knowledge as a fundraiser and secretary of the board of trustees.

————. *William Rainey Harper: First President of the University of Chicago.* Chicago: University of Chicago Press, 1928. A hagiography by one of Harper's close associates. While Goodspeed did utilize archival materials, the work's major strength lies in the author's firsthand knowledge of the man and situation.

Gould, Joseph E. *The Chautauqua Movement: An Episode in the Continuing American Revolution.* New York: State University of New York Press, 1961. Deals extensively with Harper's association with Chautauqua and its relation to the University of Chicago extension program.

Nevins, Allan. *Study in Power: John D. Rockefeller, Industrialist and Philanthropist.* 2 vols. New York: Scribner, 1953. An excellent biography that relates the early history of the University of Chicago to Rockefeller's larger philanthropic activities.

Storr, Richard J. *Harper's University: The Beginnings.* Chicago: University of Chicago Press, 1966. The first volume (and only one published so far) of a planned multivolume history of the University of Chicago, this work is the most thoroughly researched and fullest account of the institution's founding and formative years.

Veysey, Laurence R. *The Emergence of the American University.* Chicago: University of Chicago

Press, 1965. An excellent and perceptive analysis of the transformation of American higher education in the late nineteenth and early twentieth centuries. Harper emerges as probably the most attractive of the empire-builders of his time.

John Braeman

JOEL CHANDLER HARRIS

Born: December 9, 1848; Eatonton, Georgia
Died: July 3, 1908; Atlanta, Georgia
Area of Achievement: Literature
Contribution: Harris was best known in his day for his collections of Uncle Remus tales, which were not created but recorded by him. When the American Academy of Arts and Letters was founded in 1905, Harris was elected to be one of the inaugural members. With the emergence of the Civil Rights movement, however, and with the portrayal of Uncle Remus as a man among cartoons in Walt Disney's movie *Song of the South*, the figure of Uncle Remus fell into some amount of literary and political disfavor. More recent studies of folklore have, however, established Harris' importance as a folklorist who collected authentic black folk tales.

Early Life

Born in Putnam County, Georgia, the illegitimate son of an Irish laborer who deserted the family just after his birth, Joel Chandler Harris spent a rather ordinary boyhood in rural Georgia. He was not very interested in school and seems to have preferred playing pranks to studying. In 1862, at age fourteen, Harris was given a job as a printer's devil by Addison Turner, an eccentric planter who published a rural weekly newspaper, *The Countryman*, on his nearby plantation. It is impossible to overestimate Turner's influence on young Harris, for in addition to allowing him to contribute pieces to the paper, Turner also encouraged him to read extensively in his private library and to roam around his thousand-acre plantation. It was here that Harris first heard the black folk narratives that were later to become the heart of the Uncle Remus stories. After working for Turner for four years, Harris held brief jobs at several newspapers around the South. In 1873 he married Esther LaRose and soon settled in Atlanta, where he lived until his death in 1908.

In 1876, Harris was hired to do editorial paragraphing for the Atlanta *Constitution*. Soon after his arrival, he was asked to take over a black-dialect column from a retiring writer, and, on October 26, 1876, his first sketch appeared, featuring the witty observations of an older black man. A month later the older black man was officially called "Uncle Remus," and a major new voice in American humor was born. Uncle Remus began as a rather thin, almost vaudevillian caricature of a black man

who supposedly dropped by the Atlanta *Constitution* office to offer practical comments, and some of Harris' own opinions, on corrupt politicians and lazy African Americans. The character grew, however, when Harris transferred the locale of the sketches to a plantation and incorporated tales he had heard in the slave quarters during his early days with Turner. In late 1880, Harris collected twenty-one "urban" and thirty-four "plantation" Uncle Remus sketches along with black songs, maxims, and proverbs in *Uncle Remus: His Songs and His Sayings*. The collection was an immediate success, and, much to Harris' astonishment and embarrassment, he was famous.

Life's Work

Uncle Remus: His Songs and His Sayings proved so popular that Harris went on to publish a half-dozen more Uncle Remus volumes in his lifetime. In 1881, Harris, who now had a steady and comfortable income, moved his family to a large farmhouse in Atlanta's West End, where he did most of his writing at night after returning home from work. His second collection, *Nights with Uncle Remus* (1883), is the most important and the one that most fully shows the fruits of his labor. In it, Uncle Remus is rounded out much more to become a complete character in his own right, and other characters on the plantation are introduced as storytellers, principally Daddy Jack, a character who speaks in a Sea Island dialect called "Gullah," and who Harris used to tell stories he perceived to be of a different cultural origin than the stories that Uncle Remus tells. As popular as these Uncle Remus collections were, Harris never considered that their merit was inherently literary. He always insisted that in them he was the "compiler" of a folklore and dialect that were fast disappearing in the South at the end of the nineteenth century. He was careful to include only the Uncle Remus tales that could be verified as authentic black oral narratives, and, with his usual diffidence, he minimized his own role in elevating them to artistic short fiction.

In *Mingo and Other Sketches in Black and White* (1884), Harris surprised his readers by temporarily moving away from the Uncle Remus formula. The collection was favorably reviewed, and Harris showed that his literary talents could be stretched to include what he considered to be more serious forms. The title story, "Mingo: A Sketch of Life in

Middle Georgia," is an admirable local-color portrayal of class conflicts. The central conflict is between two white families, the aristocratic Wornums and the poor-white Bivinses. Before the Civil War, the Wornums' daughter, Cordelia, had married the Bivinses' son, Henry Clay, much to the displeasure of the Wornum family, who promptly disinherited her. Henry Clay was killed in the war and Cordelia died shortly thereafter, leaving a daughter in the care of Mrs. Feratia Bivins, Henry's mother. Mrs. Wornum is overcome with grief after the death of the children and realizes that she has made a mistake in snubbing the Bivinses, but fiercely proud Feratia cannot forgive her. In a comic yet pathos-filled scene, Mrs. Wornum asks Feratia Bivins to let her see her granddaughter, whom she has never seen. Feratia coolly replies, "if I had as much politeness, ma'am, as I had cheers, I'd ast you to set down," and adamantly refuses to let Mrs. Wornum see the baby. The final wise commentary, however, comes from Mingo, a former Wornum slave who is loyal to his old master and acts as the surrogate father for the surviving child. It is the

black man's strength of character and endurance that promises reconciliation and social progress. Harris, a poor white by birth himself, is clearly antiaristocratic and sides with the underdog in times of changing social values, yet by applauding the virtues of loyalty and duty in the black, he comes very close to advocating a servile and passive acceptance, as some of his critics have charged.

Harris' *Free Joe and Other Georgian Sketches* (1887), and the frequently anthologized title story, "Free Joe and the Rest of the World," further illustrates his ambivalence on the "Negro question." In 1840, a slave-speculator named Major Frampton lost all his property except one slave, his body-servant Joe, to Judge Alfred Wellington in a famous card game. Frampton adjourned the game, went to the courthouse and gave Joe his freedom, and then blew his brains out. Joe, although freed, remains in town because his wife Lucinda is now the property of the Judge. All goes well for Joe until the Judge dies and his estate is transferred to the stern Spite Calderwood. Calderwood refuses to let Joe visit Lucinda. Joe's easy life comes to an end: The other slaves will have nothing to do with him, and he is an outcast from the white community, sleeping outside under a poplar tree. When Calderwood learns that in spite of his orders Lucinda has been sneaking out to meet Joe, he takes her to Macon and sells her; he even has his hounds kill Joe's dog. Joe, however, even when told the truth about Lucinda, seems incapable of understanding. Night after night he waits for his wife and his dog to return together in the moonlight, until one night he dies alone under the poplar tree, a smile on his face and humble to the last.

In "Free Joe and the Rest of the World," Harris achieves a balance between sentimentality and realistic portrayal in dramatizing the plight of the freeman in the antebellum South. Even though Joe is the humble, unassuming victim of white cruelty, his freedom also represents the vague, Gothic threat of social dissolution to the white community, who come to view him as "forever lurking on the outskirts of slavery, ready to sound a shrill and ghostly signal" of insurrection. Yet unlike Brer Rabbit, Joe is no ingenious trickster, and Harris obliquely hints that, all things considered, Joe may have been better off a slave since his freedom leaves him "shiftless" and incapable of fending for himself.

Of the six stories collected in *Balaam and His Master and Other Sketches and Stories* (1891), three are portraits of loyal black people and three treat the fate of a white man in a crumbling society. In this collection Harris again illustrates his favorite themes: the changing social values between blacks and whites, and the need for reconciliation through patience and understanding. "Balaam and His Master" is the story of the fiercely loyal manservant of young Berrien Cozart—the sensual, cruel, impetuous, and implacable son of a respected plantation family. As in many of Harris' aristocratic families, the older Cozart practices a benign paternalism toward his slaves, but his young son Berrien is nothing but a spoiled and dissolute gambler who abuses the privileges of his race. Yet despite his master's excesses, Balaam remains a constant and loyal valet, even to the point of participating in a scam to sell himself to a new master and then returning to Berrien. Berrien is finally arrested for murder, and Balaam breaks into the jail to be with him; but it is too late—Berrien is already dead. The story ends with Balaam loyally crouching over his dead master, who died with a smile as sweet as a "little child that nestles on his mother's breast." Even though Balaam is morally superior to his

white master, the message of the story is that loyalty and service are superior to social revolution.

In "Where's Duncan?"—another story in *Balaam and His Master and Other Sketches and Stories*—Harris gives a more apocalyptic version of the changing social values between blacks and whites. The story is narrated by old Isaiah Winchell, who meets a dark stranger named Willis Featherstone as he is hauling his cotton to market. As they camp for the evening, old Isaiah learns that Willis Featherstone is the mulatto son of a plantation owner who had educated him, grown to hate him, and then sold him. The next evening the group camps near the old Featherstone plantation, and a vampirelike mulatto woman comes to invite them to dinner at the "big house." Willis Featherstone, who seems to know the woman, enigmatically asks her "where's Duncan?" and she hysterically replies that old Featherstone has "sold my onliest boy." Later that evening, the camp is awakened by a commotion at the big house. Old Isaiah rushes up to see the house on fire, and through the window he glimpses the mulatto woman stabbing Old Featherstone and screaming "where's Duncan?" Willis Featherstone, say some of the observers, was inside enjoying the spectacle. The story ends with a Gothic scene of fiery retribution as the old plantation house burns and collapses, and old Isaiah still dreams of the smell of burning flesh. Violent confrontation is possible, Harris suggests, if white society continues to abuse the black.

In 1900, Harris quit his job at the newspaper so he could concentrate on writing full-time at his farmhouse. During his lifetime, he gained much attention from his book. He was admired by Mark Twain, and the two embarked upon a joint lecture tour. Harris was also invited to the White House in 1902 by President Theodore Roosevelt, who declared that Harris' books had been instrumental in repairing the rifts caused by the Civil War. In 1905, he and his son Julian began publishing a Southern literary magazine called *Uncle Remus's Magazine*, which achieved a circulation of 200,000 and became another huge success for the writer. Harris, however, was beginning to face recurrent illness in his old age, and the pressures of publishing a magazine did little to restore his health. He died at his home in 1908 after being diagnosed with cirrhosis of the liver.

Summary

As an editorialist, essayist, and humorist, Joel Chandler Harris was instrumental in trying to reconcile the tensions between North and South, black and white, left by the Civil War. Although he shared some of the racial prejudices of his time—one detects a paternalism for the black in much of the short fiction—he was a progressive conservative who, as one critic has said, "affirmed the integrity of all individuals, whether black or white; and he could not countenance unjust or inhumane actions by any member of the human race." In the 1870's and 1880's, his editorials in the Atlanta *Constitution* consistently argue against sectionalism, both literary and political, and in favor of a united country. Any literature, wrote Harris in 1879, takes its materials and flavor from "localism," yet "in literature, art, and society, whatever is truly Southern is likewise truly American; and the same may be said of what is truly Northern."

Bibliography

Baer, Florence E. *Sources and Analogues of the Uncle Remus Tales.* Helsinki: Academia Scientiarium Fennica, 1980. Essential to anyone trying to study the Brer Rabbit stories. For each tale, Baer gives a summary, the tale type number from *The Types of the Folk-tale* (1928), motif numbers from Stith Thompson's *Motif-Index of Folk Literature* (1955-1958), and a discussion of possible sources. She also includes an excellent essay discussing Harris' legitimacy as a collector of folktales.

Bickley, R. Bruce, ed. *Critical Essays on Joel Chandler Harris.* Boston: Hall, 1981. Traces the critical heritage about Harris, including contemporary reviews. Of particular importance is an article by Bernard Wolfe, which was printed in *Commentary* in 1949.

————. *Joel Chandler Harris.* Boston: Twayne, 1978. A full-length study, including chapters on the major as well as the later Uncle Remus tales, and Harris' other short fiction. Includes a brief, useful annotated bibliography.

Cousins, Paul. *Joel Chandler Harris: A Biography.* Baton Rouge: Louisiana State University Press, 1968. A biography that the author worked on intermittently for more than thirty years and that includes material from interviews with friends of Harris. Not a reliable source for critical evaluations of Harris' work.

Hemenway, Robert, ed. *Uncle Remus: His Songs and Sayings.* London and New York: Penguin, 1982. Hemenway's introduction is very clear and informative, one of the better all-around essays on the Brer Rabbit stories. Contains a brief bibliography.

Keenan, Hugh T. "Twisted Tales: Propaganda in the Tar-Baby Stories." *Southern Quarterly* 22 (Winter 1984): 54-69. This essay updates some arguments that Bernard Wolfe put forth in his *Commentary* article (included in R. Bruce Bickley's entry). Better researched than Wolfe's article and more even in tone.

Robert J. McNutt
(Revised by Thomas J. Cassidy)

BENJAMIN HARRISON

Born: August 20, 1833; North Bend, Ohio
Died: March 13, 1901; Indianapolis, Indiana
Areas of Achievement: Government and politics
Contribution: As the twenty-third president of the United States, Harrison gave the country an honest and straightforward administration devoted to Republican principles.

Early Life

Benjamin Harrison had notable ancestors: His great-grandfather was a signer of the Declaration of Independence; his grandfather was William Henry Harrison, ninth president of the United States; and his own father, John Scott Harrison, served in the United States House of Representatives.

The Harrison farm, known as The Point, was near Cincinnati. The family was a large one: Benjamin, the second child, had seven brothers and sisters, and two other children had the Harrisons as their guardians. Financial difficulties were not unusual, and the children learned the value of hard work and thrift. Benjamin spent much time with his grandmother at her home at North Bend, where he read widely in the excellent library gathered by his grandfather.

In 1847, Harrison went to Farmer's College in Cincinnati; two years later, he transferred to Miami University, where he met Carrie Scott, daughter of the Reverend Dr. John Scott, a professor. In 1853, a year after Harrison was graduated, he married Carrie; her father performed the ceremony.

The Harrisons settled at The Point while Benjamin studied law. He was admitted to the bar in 1854, and the couple moved to Indianapolis, where Harrison set up his law office. Difficult times faced the young couple initially, but Harrison's meticulous research, his command of the facts, and his ability to present those facts clearly and plainly soon won for him cases and respect. By 1855, Harrison was doing well, and he was drawn into politics.

An opponent of slavery, he was naturally attracted to the new Republican Party and was an avid supporter of John Charles Frémont in the 1856 election; this support was expressed so fiercely that it drew a rebuke from his father, who urged him to temper his language.

An extremely loyal party man throughout his life, Harrison became secretary to the Republican state central committee; this was to be his real entry into politics. His successes would be owed primarily to his steadfast devotion to the party's cause and the alliances he formed in its struggles.

Elected as reporter to the state supreme court in 1860, Harrison was torn between serving in that position and volunteering for the Union army. In 1862, he enlisted, and was given command of a regiment. He was a strict disciplinarian but was popular with his troops, since he took care to see that they were always well supplied.

Harrison was an able officer, cool and judicious in combat. During the Atlanta campaign, he fought well at the battle of Resaca and at Peachtree Creek; against a surprise Confederate attack, he helped save the Union army by holding a weak point in the line. By the war's end, he was a brigadier general; in politics, the veteran's vote was almost always his.

At the end of the war, Harrison looked much as he would for the remainder of his life. He was about five feet, six inches tall and stout. He wore a long, full beard, which, like his hair, was light brown and which turned silver as he aged. His

deeply blue eyes could be steely or warm, depending upon his mood. He had a fine voice, clear and penetrating; it was admirably suited to his manner of speaking, which was to stress the orderly arrangement of facts.

Life's Work

After the war, Harrison allied himself strongly with the section of the Republican Party which favored a radical reconstruction of the South, including voting rights for the freed blacks and harsh treatment of the defeated rebels. For a time, however, Harrison stuck to his law practice. It was not until 1872 that he took an active part in the political wars, campaigning successfully for Republican candidates.

In 1876, the Republican candidate for governor of Indiana abruptly quit the race when his associations with the corrupt Grant Administration were revealed. The party central committee hastily nominated Harrison, who was away on a fishing trip and had to be persuaded to run when he returned. He then mounted a vigorous campaign, promising government reform, supporting sound money, and waving the "bloody shirt" by accusing the Democrats of wartime treason. He covered the state and received much support from veterans but lost by five thousand votes. Still, he had greatly impressed party regulars. He increased this respect and won many supporters when he went on a speaking tour for presidential candidate Rutherford B. Hayes. Harrison spoke across the country, from New Jersey to Chicago, and established himself as a nationally recognized Republican leader.

In 1878, there occurred a tragic and bizarre incident. John Scott Harrison died in May. Leaving the cemetery, John Harrison, Benjamin's brother, noticed that the grave of a recently buried cousin had been disturbed. At that time, grave-robbing was commonly practiced by "resurrection men" who sold the bodies to medical schools. Fearing that this had happened, John Harrison and a sheriff visited the Ohio Medical College in Cincinnati. There they discovered the body, not of the cousin, but of John Scott Harrison, suspended in a pit in the school's basement.

Great public anger was aroused by what was called the Harrison Horror. After the father's reinterment, the cousin's body was located in Ann Arbor, a finding which revealed a widespread and regular traffic between medical schools and grave-robbers. Following this incident, reforms were en-

acted regulating the procurement of cadavers for medical studies.

Harrison was elected to the United States Senate in 1880. He sponsored extremely generous pensions for veterans and was a strong protectionist, favoring high tariffs. At the same time that he was voting to have the federal to have the federal government protect private industry, Harrison opposed flood control projects on the Mississippi, maintaining that the government had no constitutional right to assist individuals. In making such an argument, Harrison was following the essential Republican Party line, which strongly and unabashedly favored business, particularly big business. He never deviated from this line, disregarding the rise of labor and the growing emphasis on workers' rights.

In 1884, Harrison worked diligently for the Republican nominee, James G. Blaine, despite the charges of corruption that clung to the candidate. (Blaine sometimes closed his correspondence with the injunction, "Burn this letter.") In a close race, Blaine was defeated by Grover Cleveland after a Republican clergyman derided the Democrats as the party of "rum, Romanism and rebellion."

After the defeat, Harrison was in the vanguard of efforts to rebuild the Republican Party. In 1887, he was ousted from the Senate when the Democrats took control of the Indiana legislature (this was before the popular election of senators). That same year, President Cleveland launched a vigorous attack on the tariff, denouncing a protective system that allied the federal government and big business at the expense of the worker. This was a direct assault on the key Republican position and set the battle lines for the next campaign.

The Republicans had an issue but lacked a candidate, since Blaine declined to run and there was no other figure of national prominence in the party. Harrison, the dedicated and hardworking party man, won the nomination in 1888.

In the election, Harrison faced Grover Cleveland. The Republicans were well financed by business and trade associations, which naturally favored a high tariff to protect their interests. A dispute among Democrats in New York state proved decisive: Although Cleveland polled a ninety thousand popular-vote majority, he lost the electoral count by 233 to 168.

Personally honest and highly moral (he had considered the ministry as an alternative to law), Harrison was generally independent in selecting his cabinet. The one exception was his appointment of

Blaine as secretary of state. Actually, this appointment proved productive, since both were strong believers in closer ties with Central and South America. Their efforts led to a PanAmerican conference in 1889, during which representatives from most nations in the hemisphere toured the United States.

In line with his earlier efforts as a senator, Harrison pushed for increased veterans' pensions. He was also firmly in favor of protecting black voting rights in the South, moderate civil service reform, and limited use of silver in the currency—the last adopted to satisfy Republicans in the West, an area rich in the metal. The main struggle in Congress was over the tariff, which the Republicans wished to increase; they succeeded, raising customs duties an average of almost fifty percent. The tariff would once again prove to be a key issue in the presidential election.

The so-called Mafia incident in New Orleans arose in 1890. A policeman scheduled to testify on the activities of the alleged society was murdered; before he died, he named several Italians. After a long, tense trial, the accused men were acquitted. A mob stormed the jail and killed eleven Italian inmates who had not yet been released. Harrison denounced the event and offered his regrets to the Italian government but pointed out that the Constitution left considerable powers to the states; in this case, the federal government was unable to act. The incident was short-lived, but one major result was increased support for Harrison's call for a larger navy: During the brief war scare, observers noted that Italy had a much larger fleet of armored ships than did the United States.

In the election of 1892, Harrison faced, once again, the redoubtable Grover Cleveland. The election turned into a referendum on Republican policies, especially those regarding labor. The high tariff had protected the captains of industry but not the workers. Wages had been repeatedly cut, and many workers had been fired. Worse yet, a wave of antilabor violence swept the country. During a strike at the Homestead Plant of the Carnegie Steel Company, twenty men were killed in combat between locked-out workers and Pinkerton detectives. In July, a fight between striking miners and strikebreakers left thirty miners dead in Idaho; Harrison ordered in federal troops to restore order and keep the mines open. Another mine-related battle erupted in eastern Tennessee, where miners fought convicts who had been brought in to dig coal. The result of all this was a defection of thousands of voters from the Republicans to the Populist Party or to the Democrats.

Harrison did not campaign. His wife was gravely ill, and she died on October 25. Harrison was despondent, and seemed relieved when he lost the election. Following his presidential term, Harrison returned to the law but accepted only a few cases. He refused a chair at the University of Chicago, although he did give a series of lectures at Stanford, which later became the book, *Views of An Ex-President* (1901). He continued his extensive charitable contributions, especially for support of educating Southern blacks and for orphans.

In April, 1896, at age sixty-two, Harrison remarried; his bride was the widow Mary Lord Dimmick, daughter of his dead wife's sister. In February, 1897, they had a daughter; by his first wife Harrison had a son and a daughter.

With few exceptions, family life now occupied Harrison. In 1896, he firmly discouraged any talk of renomination, although he did campaign for the candidate William McKinley. In 1899, Harrison was retained by Venezuela in an arbitration case with Great Britain over disputed boundaries. In the course of a fifteen-month period, Harrison amassed three volumes of evidence, which he masterfully presented to the arbitration panel in Paris from June through October. Despite this, the panel decided in favor of Great Britain; it was later revealed that improper pressure from London had influenced the decision.

In March, 1901, Harrison caught a cold, which rapidly worsened and developed into pneumonia. On March 13, at his home in Indianapolis, he died.

Summary

Soon after his move into the White House, Harrison's private secretary had a talk with him. "I asked the President if he had ever seriously thought about being President. He said the thought had been with him many times when suggested by others, but he had never been possessed by it or had his life shaped by it."

This frank, disarming reply is characteristic of Harrison, and it reveals much about him and his administration. He was not driven by desire for office or inspired by a specific sense of mission. He seems to have regarded the the presidency as a duty to discharge faithfully and honestly but not a position through which to effect profound changes in American life. With few exceptions, he was probably quite satisfied with American life: The Union had been preserved, slavery ended, business was good, and public officials were becoming increasingly, if perhaps slowly, more honest.

Harrison was neither an innovator nor an experimenter. He clung closely to a narrow interpretation of the Constitution, one which limited the powers of the federal government and left private enterprise strictly alone. Exceptions were those activities which protected business: the tariff, a firm hand in labor disputes, and a strong currency. In this, he was in accord with the prevailing policy of his party and, indeed, of many in the country.

As a man, Harrison was honest, principled, and forthright. Personally, he was kind and generous, a charming, affectionate family man, and a devoted friend. Even his political foes admired and respected him. As president, he conducted himself within the constitutional limits he revered, and his term in office was like the man himself, solid and dependable.

Bibliography

Armbruster, Maxim. *The Presidents of the United States and Their Administrations.* 7th ed. New York: Horizon Press, 1982. Introductory sketch of Harrison and his times; good on the fundamental tenets of the Republican Party of the period.

Calhoun, Charles W. "Civil Religion and the Gilded Age Presidency: The Case of Benjamin Harrison." *Presidential Studies Quarterly* 23, no. 4 (Fall 1993). Discussion of Harrison's place as a president of the Gilded Age.

Graff, Henry, ed. *The Presidents: A Reference History.* 2d ed. New York: Scribner, and London: Simon and Schuster, 1984. A collection of articles by various historians. The essay on Harrison is an excellent short study of the man and his office, especially regarding foreign affairs. It is helpful to read also the biographies of other presidents contemporary with Harrison.

Harrison, Benjamin. *Public Papers and Addresses.* Washington, D.C.: Government Printing Office, 1893. Some of Harrison's official documents are of interest to the serious student of the period, especially those dealing with veterans' pensions and treatment of the South. Fortunately, his writing style was usually plain, simple, and direct.

———. *Speeches.* Compiled by Charles Hedges. New York: Lovell, Coryell, 1892. During his ca-
reer, Harrison had a reputation, at least among Republicans, of being an excellent orator. These examples demonstrate his clarity and suggest his forcefulness.

Malone, Dumas, ed. *Dictionary of American Biography.* Vol. 8, 331-335. New York: Scribner, 1932. For years the standard short biography of Harrison, this entry still presents a good overview of his life and career.

Nevins, Allan. *Grover Cleveland: A Study in Courage.* New York: Dodd, Mead, 1932. This work won for Nevins a Pulitzer Prize for American biography. It is an outstanding study of Cleveland and his times and provides much information relative to Harrison. The contrast between the two is considerable: Both were admirable individuals, but Cleveland was by far the better president.

Sievers, Harry J. *Benjamin Harrison: Hoosier Warrior, 1833-1865.* 2d ed. New York: University Publishers, 1960.

———. *Benjamin Harrison: Hoosier Statesman: From the Civil War to the White House, 1865-1888.* New York: University Publishers, 1959.

———. *Benjamin Harrison: Hoosier President: The White House and After, 1889-1901.* Indianapolis: Bobbs-Merrill, 1968. Together, these three volumes form the definitive modern biography of Harrison, one which is not likely to be improved upon or replaced soon. Sievers makes excellent use of the sources, including many of Harrison's papers and letters, and his biography is detailed but briskly paced.

Socolofsky, Homer Edward, and Allan B. Spetter. *The Presidency of Benjamin Harrison.* Lawrence: University Press of Kansas, and London: Eurospan, 1987.

Spetter, Allan. "Rev. Harry J. Sievers, S.J., the Arthur Jordan Foundation and the Biography of President Benjamin Harrison." *Presidential Studies Quarterly* 23, no. 3 (Summer 1993). Examination of the biography of Harrison produced by the Arthur Jordan Foundation including its cost, the time spent in its production, and its failure to achieve the balanced account of Harrison's presidency it sought to create.

Michael Witkoski

FREDERIC HARRISON

Born: October 18, 1831; London, England
Died: January 13, 1923; Bath, Somerset, England
Areas of Achievement: Social criticism and philosophy
Contribution: In his varied career as a professor of law, literary critic, and lecturer, Harrison was one of the staunchest advocates of the philosophy of positivism in mid-Victorian England.

Early Life

Frederic Harrison, born in London on October 18, 1831, was the son of Frederick Harrison, an architect turned stockbroker, and Jane (Brice) Harrison. The couple's firstborn had died in infancy; Frederic would become the eldest of the five sons who survived. The family, of some means, would often spend time in the English countryside. Frederic's mother taught him to appreciate history and French and Latin, while his father imparted a passion for the fine arts. Frederic's family life was characterized by stability and the loving concern of his parents and bordered on the aristocratic.

Before he was six, in 1837, Frederic witnessed the coronation of Queen Victoria. The family moved to Oxford Square, Hyde Park, in 1840, where Frederic attended the day school of Joseph King for two years, followed by enrollment in the sixth form (or grade) at King's College School, where he would remain until 1849. Because of the success of his earlier schooling, Frederic found himself in classes with boys several years older; though he played most sports and excelled as a student, for a time the others treated him condescendingly and nicknamed him "Fan."

The nickname vanished when Harrison was befriended by one of the older students, Charles Cookson, a passionate devotee of literature and the High Church movement. Associated with Edward Pusey, advocates sought to move the Anglican church closer to the Roman Catholic tradition. Harrison had been reared in the Anglican tradition of William Paley, with its emphasis on moral utilitarianism, but he would come to reject all forms of Christianity in favor of a new "Religion of Humanity." Harrison would teach that one's duty to mankind was paramount, not obeisance to a metaphysical deity. As part of his future positivist belief, Harrison's faith would rest in the essential goodness and progress of humanity. Yet what of individuals themselves, Harrison would wonder: Where should one's sympathies lie?

Revolutionary fervor was abroad on the Continent. With the publication of Karl Marx's *Manifest der Kommunistischen Partei* (1848; *The Communist Manifesto*, 1850), there were uprisings in Paris, Berlin, Vienna, and Rome; in England, bad harvests that same year brought a renewal of the working-class Chartist movement which sought parliamentary and electoral reforms. Harrison found himself sympathizing with the fall of the old regimes and with the demands of the working class; yet throughout his life he would struggle with the question of whether specific political action would ever usher in the universal positivist utopia.

Harrison was eighteen when he entered Wadham College in Oxford in 1849. He had come to detest the intense competition inherent in formal schooling in England, as well as professors who only "taught for the test." An exception was Richard Congreve, his history professor and the founder of the British positivist movement. Though, in later years, Harrison would lament Congreve's turn toward his own fanatical brand of positivism, Harrison applauded Congreve's presentation of history as the surging progress of humanity and not a list of names and dates and innumerable "periods."

Harrison was graduated from Wadham in 1853 but remained two more years as Librarian of the Union and as a tutor. Though still considering himself a Christian, Harrison was brought under the sway of the French positivist philosopher Auguste Comte, by a group of Oxford friends who called themselves "Mumbo-Jumbo" and who had already renounced the creeds of the Church. Harrison himself declined to take orders for a career in the Church and in 1855 began a study of law at Lincoln's Inn in London. In that same year, he met in Paris with Comte.

Harrison was the portrait of the active Victorian. An ardent mountaineer most of his life, he was physically rugged, with a large head, black hair, and fierce whiskers. Incurably optimistic (at least after his student days), he was at times pompous, quick-tempered, and irascible. He dressed to befit his class; punctuality was his hallmark. As one of his sons later observed, Harrison "liked time-tables, inventories, and everything that contributed towards the regular life, and he probably was the most consistently normal man who ever wrote books." He was a skilled debater and a personal friend of many of England's nineteenth century luminaries, including William E. Gladstone, Thomas Carlyle, and John Stuart Mill.

Life's Work

Harrison counted his meeting with Comte as the most significant of his life; his growing adherence to Comtian philosophy provided unity to a life full of many undertakings. Comte had rejected absolutist metaphysics as unproductive: Men had argued for thousands of years about God's existence and had come no closer to agreement. Instead, Comte proposed a philosophic system that was scientific, relative, and man-centered. As Harrison explained in two lectures given in 1920, three years before his death, the new system was scientific because it saw physical and social activity ordered by laws, but relative and man-centered because formulation of those laws depended on fallible human observation. Yet there was progress in man's understanding of the world. In ancient times, the world was explained in terms of myth; that gave way to the absolute generalizations of metaphysics, which led, in turn, to the scientific and relative positive philosophy of the nineteenth century. It was "positive" in the sense that it depended on substantive observations of the world (relative to man) and not on the manipulation of contentless abstractions. The sciences could be ordered by their complexity relative to man (with sociology, a term coined by Comte in 1837, the most complex), with each science having its own methodology. Thus ordered, the scientific enterprise becomes a powerful tool for progress (as heralded by the Industrial Revolution). Man's faith, then, turns from the worship of ill-defined abstractions to that of humanity itself, with one's highest goal the altruistic service to mankind.

Comte's was a grand vision, in many ways suited to the Victorian tones of optimistic progress amid the waning belief in the old verities preached by the Church, and yet it offered a renewed sense of the centrality of the family and the importance of personal morality. Positivism's appeal to Harrison was manifest with, as defined by Comte, its so-called Calendar of 558 names, from Homer to Moses, representing an overview of civilization, its library of 270 works divided into four categories as an organized scheme of general literature, and its emotional appeal in the worship of humanity.

Harrison did not want to promulgate merely a new sect; he was uneasy about partisan political involvement but believed that the lot of the working man had to be improved. Called to the bar in 1858, Harrison concentrated on the plight of those nations struggling for independence from imperialist regimes. He reported from Italy for the *Daily News* and *Morning Post* and believed that he won his countrymen to the Italian cause. In 1866, Harrison joined the Jamaica Committee to pressure the governor to lift the martial law imposed there, and he was on the Royal Commission on Trades Unions from 1867 to 1869. His work helped lay the foundation for future trade-union legislation.

Harrison married his cousin Ethel Harrison in 1870. Secure in his traditional marriage, he seemed never to waver from his new positive religion, to which he had converted Ethel. A decade earlier, Harrison had clarified his religious views in his reply to *Essays and Reviews* (1860), a series of articles, originating with the Broad Church or Liberal movement, which called for the redrawing of the boundaries of traditional Christian doctrines in the light of modern science (including Higher Criticism). Harrison, critical of the book, called the result "Neo-Christianity," an attempt to separate all religious feelings from matters of scientific fact. What was needed, he said, was a synthesis of the religious impulse in man with that of science, in the Religion of Humanity. (The future, for Harrison, belonged to positivism. Just as Christianity was no longer viable, so any idea of culture transforming the world, as advanced by Matthew Arnold, was simply wind.)

In the decade of the 1870's, Harrison saw Prussian imperialism at first hand in France as a correspondent for *The Times* of London. He joined the Chapel St. Group in 1870 under Congreve's leadership and in the mid-1870's worked for the disestablishment of the Church of England (though he did not succeed). He was appointed Professor of Jurisprudence, International and Constitutional Law by the Council of Legal Education in 1877, and lectured at Middle Temple Hall for twelve years thereafter.

Harrison reluctantly agreed to preside over a new positivist group which first met at Newton Hall in 1879. A year earlier, Congreve had broken with Comte and his successor in France, Pierre Lafitte, to develop further the ceremonial aspects of the Religion of Humanity; thus Newton Hall was founded to carry on the French tradition.

Harrison's only attempt to enter Parliament failed in the general election of 1886 and political activism gave way to his writing. Works on positivism as well as literary studies seemed to pour from his pen. He aided in the founding of the *Positivist Review* in 1893 (which died with his passing), journeyed to the United States for a series of lectures in 1901 (the year of Queen Victoria's death), and, succumbing to what he called a senile weakness, wrote a historical novel, *Theophano: The Crusade of the Tenth Century, a Romantic Monograph* (1904). He published two volumes of memoirs in 1911.

The Harrisons had four sons and one daughter. He died of heart failure on January 13, 1923, correcting proofs for a book of essays containing what was to be his last defense of positivism.

Summary

Frederic Harrison believed passionately in the family as the foundation for any scientifically ordered society of the future; education must begin in the home and women were to find their liberation in the care of the household. In criticizing John Stuart Mill's *Subjection of Women* (1869), Harrison affirmed that "nothing can be made right in sociology whilst society is regarded as made up of individuals instead of families." It was not the first time that theorists have envisioned a "new order" which is little but their own lives writ large and made universal.

Before his marriage, Harrison was a seeker, an activist. In the last half of his long life, he seemed to step back from the political fray for a longer view. He would be the librarian of the new positivist society, worshipping dutifully at the shrine of Humanity with a clear conscience, anticipating the social progress that was yet to come. His would be the genteel, the aristocratic role, in this most orderly revolution in history.

Yet positivism from the first was philosophically unsound. Despite his ardent defense of positivist faith, Harrison never saw that simply declaring metaphysical speculation off limits would never silence God; that Comte's absolute principles of historical progress were themselves metaphysical; and that the basic dualism between observation and man's conceptualizing of his findings made the positivist interpretation itself suspect.

Harrison's life and pursuits were quintessentially Victorian; he was the consummate amateur, always busy. Harrison the optimist lived to see one of his sons die in World War I, and, with positivism passing from the scene, he was regaled not for his advocacy but as the man who was the friend of the great men and women of the Victorian era; he was no longer the prophet, but the storyteller.

Bibliography

Harrison, Austin. *Frederic Harrison: Thoughts and Memories*. London: Heinemann, 1926; New York: Putnam, 1927. A valuable anecdotal view of Harrison by one of his sons. An impressionistic (not chronological) overview of Harrison's faith, character, and temperament. No substitute for a biography.

Harrison, Frederic. *Autobiographic Memoirs*. 2 vols. London: Macmillan, 1911; New York: AMS Press, 1977. Good source material on Harrison's early life, though less an autobiography (Harrison did not want to focus attention on himself) than a personal history of Victorian times. Volume 1 covers the years 1832-1870; volume 2, 1870-1910.

―――. *De Senectute: More Last Words*. London: Unwin, and New York: Appleton, 1923. Published posthumously, the book contains "A Philosophic Synthesis," two lectures given by Harrison in 1920 and his last published defense of positivism.

―――. *George Washington and Other American Addresses*. New York and London: Macmillan, 1901. In some of these addresses, Harrison struggled with the idea of democracy. How could the best minds surface in the United States if society treated everyone equally? Note also "Personal Reminiscences," a lecture given to Bryn Mawr Women's College in Pennsylvania, detailing Harrison's friendship with Comte, Charles Darwin, the novelist George Eliot, and many others.

―――. *The Meaning of History and Other Historical Pieces*. New York and London: Macmillan, 1894. In "The Use of History," Harrison advises his readers that knowledge of history is in large part knowledge of its great men; another chapter annotates some of the great books of history, and a third, "The Sacredness of Ancient Buildings," focuses on Harrison's love of architecture and expresses his view that buildings are living relics.

―――. *Tennyson, Ruskin, Mill, and Other Literary Estimates*. New York and London: Macmillan, 1899. Includes what amounts to almost a panegyric on Matthew Arnold (though it does reprise delicately some of Harrison's earlier criticism of Arnold's idea of Culture). This volume also contains a useful critique of Harrison's friend John Stuart Mill.

Himmelfarb, Gertrude. *Victorian Minds*. London: Weidenfeld and Nicolson, and New York: Knopf, 1968. A good introduction to the Victorian period through studies of some of its leading personalities: John Stuart Mill, Leslie Stephen, Walter Bagehot, and others. Harrison is scarcely mentioned, though he is characterized (in a list of Victorian paradoxes) as a religious libertarian with a Puritan morality.

Kent, Christopher. *Brains and Numbers: Elitism, Comtism, and Democracy in Mid-Victorian England*. Toronto: University of Toronto Press, 1978. A technical study of the politics of reform, especially as it is mirrored by Harrison's friend John Morley and by Harrison himself. Characterizes Harrison's political problem as that of reconciling government by an elite (which seemed logical to him) with the rising tide of democratic sentiment. Sets Comte into a middle-class context and clarifies his appeal. The book includes a large bibliography and makes reference to Harrison's personal papers.

Metraux, Guy S., and Francois Crouzet, eds. *The Nineteenth-Century World*. New York: New American Library, 1963. This work is especially interesting for Henri Gouhier's essay on "Auguste Comte's Philosophy of History," an essay generally sympathetic to Comte, crediting him with shrewdly understanding the impact of the Industrial Revolution.

Sullivan, Harry R. *Frederic Harrison*. Boston: Twayne, 1983. A valuable survey of Harrison's life and major concerns, with good bibliographic references. The chapters on positivism are clear enough; the two long chapters on Harrison's literary critiques seem valuable only to the antiquarian. A generally sympathetic nontechnical study.

Dan Barnett

WILLIAM HENRY HARRISON

Born: February 9, 1773; near Charles City, Virginia

Died: April 4, 1841; Washington, D.C.

Areas of Achievement: Government and military affairs

Contribution: Harrison became one of the nation's most glamorous military heroes because of his victory over the Indian forces of Tecumseh and the Prophet at the Battle of Tippecanoe in 1811. As a soldier and later governor of the Old Northwest Territory, he became identified with the ideas and desires of the West, eventually riding his military reputation into a brief tenure in the presidency.

Early Life

William Henry Harrison was born on February 9, 1773, at his family's famous Berkeley Plantation near Charles City in tidewater Virginia, the son of a Declaration of Independence signer. He attended Hampden-Sydney College and briefly studied medicine under the famous physician Benjamin Rush. Harrison entered the army in 1791, serving in the campaigns against the Indians in the Northwest Territory and eventually becoming a lieutenant and aide-de-camp to Anthony Wayne. After serving as a frontier army officer for seven years, in 1798 Harrison resigned his commission to accept appointment as secretary of the Northwest Territory. The following year, he was elected the territory's first delegate to Congress.

In Congress, Harrison was a spokesman for the West and was author of the Land Act of 1800, which provided for the disposition of public lands on more liberal terms than previously practiced. The same year, he was appointed governor of the newly created Indiana Territory, which included all of the original Northwest Territory except Ohio. His new job would require the talents of both the diplomat and the soldier, and with his tall and slender build, soldierly bearing, and amiable countenance, Harrison looked the part.

Life's Work

Harrison was given a nearly impossible charge. He was to win the friendship and trust of the Indians and protect them from the rapaciousness of white settlers, yet he was also urged to acquire for the government as much land as he could secure from the Western tribes. It appears that Harrison was genuinely concerned for the Indians: He ordered a campaign of inoculation to protect them from the scourge of smallpox and banned the sale of liquor to them. Nevertheless, he actively pursued the acquisition of Indian lands, and in 1809 negotiated a treaty with Indian leaders which transferred some 2,900,000 acres in the vicinity of the White and Wabash rivers to the United States. This cession brought the tension between red and white men in the Northwest to a boiling point and instigated the events upon which Harrison's fame and later career were founded.

In view of the uneasy relationship between the United States and Great Britain, many Americans assumed that the British had encouraged the "Indian troubles" of the interior. In reality, the growing hostility of the Western tribes was largely an indigenous reaction to the constant encroachments upon their lands by white settlers. Their frustrations finally reached a focus with the rise of two Shawnee half brothers, the chief Tecumseh and a one-eyed medicine man called the Prophet. The concept of a great Indian confederation was developed by Tecumseh, who argued that Indian lands were held in common by all the tribes and that the unanimous consent of those tribes was required if those lands were to be sold. The Prophet promoted a puritanical religious philosophy, and as his following grew, religion and politics gradually merged.

Harrison developed a healthy respect for the brothers' abilities and hoped to be able to find a way to placate them. Finally, however, in what must be considered an aggressive move, Harrison marched a force of about one thousand men north from his capital at Vincennes toward Indian lands in northwestern Indiana. Early on the morning of November 7, 1811, Harrison's encampment near an Indian settlement called Prophetstown in the vicinity of the confluence of the Tippecanoe and Wabash rivers suffered a surprise attack. The Indians who attacked Harrison were led, or at least inspired, by the Prophet; Tecumseh was in the South, organizing the tribes of that area. Harrison's forces beat back the attackers and later burned the Indian settlement.

Almost immediately there was controversy concerning the particulars of the Battle of Tippecanoe and Harrison's performance. Questions were asked about whether his troops were prepared for the Indian attack, why they had camped in a vulnerable position, whether Harrison or companion officers had actually commanded the defenses, whether Harri-

son's men were outnumbered. What, in fact, was the size of the attacking Indian force? In any case, Harrison, who was not a paragon of modesty, and his supporters immediately began to tell the story of a "Washington of the West" who represented the bravery and ambitions of Western Americans.

During the War of 1812 with Great Britain, Harrison served militarily in several positions, becoming supreme commander of the Army of the Northwest. He broke the power of the British and the Indians in the Northwest and southern Canada, his ultimate victory occurring in early October, 1813, at the Battle of the Thames. Although his reputation among the general public was apparently enhanced, his military performance once again met with controversy. In May, 1814, he resigned from the army and took up residence on a farm at North Bend, Ohio, on the banks of the Ohio River near Cincinnati.

At North Bend, Harrison worked at farming and undertook several unsuccessful commercial ventures, and the foundation for another aspect of his public image was established. Harrison's home at North Bend, a commodious dwelling of sixteen rooms, was built around the nucleus of a log cabin.

This humble kernel of his residence became one of the misrepresented symbols of "Old Tip's" 1840 presidential campaign. In 1816, Harrison resumed public life. He served successively as a congressman, senator, and United States minister to Colombia with competence but without distinction. In 1830, he returned to North Bend, where he seemed destined for a quiet life in retirement.

During the height of "Jacksonian Democracy" in the 1830's, there was a growing reaction against the alleged pretensions and aspirations of "King Andrew" Jackson. This contributed to the emergence of the Whig Party, made up of old National Republicans, former Anti-Masons, and various others who reacted strongly against Jackson or his policies. In 1836 the Whigs made their first run for the presidency against Jackson's chosen successor, Martin Van Buren. Harrison ran as the candidate of Western Whigs and showed some promise as a vote getter. As a result, he became a leading contender for the nomination in 1840.

By now widely known as "Old Tippecanoe," Harrison the military hero presented an obvious opportunity for the Whigs to borrow a page from the Democrats who had ridden "Old Hickory," Andrew Jackson, to great political success. The general's positions on key issues of the day were almost irrelevant, for he was to be nominated as a symbol of military glory and the development of the West. The Whigs wanted a candidate who would appeal to a broad range of voters and who was not too closely identified with the issues of the Jacksonian era. They did not offer a real platform, only a pledge to "correct the abuses" of the current administration. If the campaign were successful, the real decisions in a Harrison administration would be made by Whig leaders in Congress.

When, during the battle for the nomination, a Henry Clay partisan suggested that Harrison should be allowed to enjoy his log cabin and hard cider in peace, the tone and lasting fame of the campaign were established. A Baltimore newspaper said that if Harrison were given a barrel of hard cider and a pension, he would spend the remainder of his days in a log cabin studying moral philosophy. Whig strategists, recognizing a good thing when they heard it, created a winning campaign by portraying Harrison as a man of the people, a wise yet simple hero whose log cabin and hard cider were vastly preferable to the pretensions and trickery of "Old Kinderhook" Martin Van Buren. The Whigs waged the first modern presidential campaign, selling souvenirs, publishing and widely distributing campaign materials, flooding the country with speakers, and using songs, slogans, and verses, including the famous cry "Tippecanoe and Tyler too." Harrison made numerous speeches to large crowds and became the first presidential candidate to stump the country on his own behalf.

Inauguration day was chilly and rainy, and the new president caught a cold, which continued to nag him. Overburdened by the demands of his office, Harrison attempted to escape its pressures by concentrating on such minor details as the efficiency of operations in various government offices and even the purchase of supplies for the White House—leaving the weightier matters to Congress and his cabinet. The only major problem of his anticlimactic presidency, the Caroline Affair, was handled by his secretary of state.

On a cold March morning, the president went to purchase vegetables for the White House and suffered a chill which aggravated the cold he had contracted on inauguration day. The cold developed into pneumonia, and on April 4, 1841, Harrison died in the White House. He was carried back to North Bend for burial.

Summary

The fame of William Henry Harrison was somewhat out of proportion to the actual accomplishments of his life and career. He first became a major public figure through his victory in the Battle of Tippecanoe, a frontier conflict which was blown up to epic proportions by Harrison and his idolaters. There is even some doubt concerning the quality of Harrison's leadership in the battle, but it did establish him as a national hero who was particularly identified with the ideas and desires of the West. Many Americans believed that the battle was the product of British machinations among the Indians of the West, and the bad feelings generated became part of the package of Western grievances which helped trigger the War of 1812. Harrison later rode his military reputation and identification with the common man of the West into the presidency, but served only about a month and had virtually no direct impact on the office. The method of his election and the circumstances of his death, however, were of lasting importance. The 1840 campaign established a new style of presidential campaigning, and Harrison's death forced the nation for the first time to experience the elevation of a vice president to the Oval Office.

Bibliography

Burnett, Kevin. "Tippecanoe and Tyler Too." *Journal of the West* 31, no. 3 (July 1992). Discusses the contributions of Harrison to the Western frontier.

Cleaves, Freeman. *Old Tippecanoe: William Henry Harrison and His Times.* New York and London: Scribner, 1939. This is a full and detailed biography which contains a colorful account of the Battle of Tippecanoe and two chapters devoted to the campaign of 1840 and Harrison's presidency.

Curtis, James C. *The Fox at Bay: Martin Van Buren and the Presidency, 1837-1841.* Lexington: University Press of Kentucky, 1970. This study of the Van Buren presidency views the election of 1840 from the Democratic perspective.

Dangerfield, George. *The Era of Good Feelings.* New York: Harcourt Brace, 1952; London: Methuen, 1953. This Pulitzer- and Bancroft Prize-winning study contains an excellent chapter on the Battle of Tippecanoe, placing it in the general context of the War of 1812.

Goebel, Dorothy B. *William Henry Harrison: A Political Biography.* Indianapolis: Indiana Historical Bureau, 1926. This is a major, although dated, biography. Goebel is highly critical of Harrison's Indian policies as well as his military preparations before the Battle of Tippecanoe.

Green, James A. *William Henry Harrison: His Life and Times.* Richmond, Va.: Garrett and Massie, 1941. A laudatory popular account which inflates the Battle of Tippecanoe into one of the epic battles in American military history.

Gunderson, Robert G. *The Log-Cabin Campaign.* Lexington: University Press of Kentucky, 1957. This is a good narrative account of the election of 1840.

Peterson, Norma Lois. *The Presidencies of William Henry Harrison and John Tyler.* Lawrence: University Press of Kansas, 1989.

Stevens, Kenneth R. *William Henry Harrison: A Bibliography.* Westport, Conn.: Greenwood Press, 1998. Bibliography providing extensive sources on the life achievements of Harrison.

Tucker, Glenn. *Tecumseh: Vision of Glory.* Indianapolis, Ind.: Bobbs-Merrill, 1956. This is a fast-moving, colorfully written, and sympathetic biography which is especially critical of Harrison's efforts to embellish his own reputation.

James E. Fickle

NATHANIEL HAWTHORNE

Born: July 4, 1804; Salem, Massachusetts
Died: May 19, 1864; Plymouth, New Hampshire
Area of Achievement: Literature
Contribution: With a series of short stories and novels which bring to life New England's Puritan past, Hawthorne achieved one of the most distinguished literary careers of the nineteenth century.

Early Life

Nathaniel Hawthorne was born July 4, 1804, in Salem, Massachusetts. His great-great-grandfather, John Hathorne, was one of the three judges in the Salem witchcraft trials in 1692; his father, Nathaniel Hathorne, was a sea captain who died in Dutch Guinea when Nathaniel was four years old. Hawthorne added the "w" to his name when he was a young man. Hawthorne's mother, née Elizabeth Manning, came from a Massachusetts family prominent in business. Her brother, Robert Manning, was a well-known pomologist who assumed much of the responsibility for Hawthorne's care after the death of his father.

Hawthorne spent much of his adolescence in Raymond, Maine, where his Manning uncles owned property, and attended Bowdoin College in nearby Brunswick. He was a Bowdoin classmate of Henry Wadsworth Longfellow and Franklin Pierce (who would later become President of the United States). As a student, Hawthorne was adept in Latin and English, but was disciplined for gambling and faulty chapel attendance. He was a handsome young man of slender build, with dark hair and eyes. Although quiet, he had a reputation for conviviality and joining friends in clubs and outdoor sports.

Hawthorne took his degree in 1825—he stood eighteenth in a class of thirty-eight—and spent the next twelve years in Salem, where he read extensively and taught himself to write. The product of these twelve years was the indifferent novel *Fanshawe: A Tale* (1828) and more than forty stories and sketches, including such well-known pieces as "The Gentle Boy," "Roger Malvin's Burial," and "My Kinsman, Major Molineux." It was a rewarding apprenticeship in terms of his artistic accomplishment, and although it did not bring him much immediate fame or income, the publication of *Twice-Told Tales* in 1837 successfully launched his career.

In 1838, Hawthorne fell in love with Sophia Peabody of Boston, whom he married in 1842. During their courtship, he spent two years working at the Boston Custom House, and he joined the utopian community at Brook Farm for several months. Both of these experiences later proved fruitful for him as a writer. Hawthorne took his bride to live in the Old Manse in Concord, and there began a life as a happy and devoted husband and father of three children.

A second edition of *Twice-Told Tales* appeared in 1842, and in 1846, the year he left the Old Manse, Hawthorne published *Mosses from an Old Manse*. With these volumes, he began to receive high critical recognition. Edgar Allan Poe praised the second edition of *Twice-Told Tales* in a review that has become famous for its perceptive commentary on Hawthorne's "invention, creation, imagination, originality." When he left the Old Manse, Hawthorne was a mature artist, ready to write the novels for which he became famous.

Life's Work

With the help of influential friends, Hawthorne received in 1846 an appointment as surveyor of the Salem Custom House. He was dismissed from this position in 1849, a victim of the political spoils system, and then wrote his greatest work, *The Scarlet Letter* (1850). In the introduction to *The Scarlet Letter*, Hawthorne settled what he perceived as some old injustices at the customhouse and invented the fiction of having found his story in an old manuscript in the customhouse.

In *The Scarlet Letter*, Hawthorne develops his most powerful theme of the hardening of the heart in what he called the Unpardonable Sin. This theme, essentially an expansion of Saint Paul's admonition in I Corinthians 13 to practice charity, is dramatized in miniature in "Ethan Brand: A Chapter from an Abortive Romance" (1850). Ethan Brand has sought knowledge tirelessly, searching for the Unpardonable Sin, and when he learns that in his quest he has allowed his heart to atrophy, he realizes that he has found the answer in himself: The Unpardonable Sin is the cultivation of the intellect at the expense of one's humanity.

Thus, the Unpardonable Sin in *The Scarlet Letter* is not the very human adultery of Hester Prynne and the Reverend Arthur Dimmesdale, a sin that takes place before the novel opens and which re-

sults in Hester's scarlet letter "A" that she has to wear on her bosom, but the relentless, unforgiving persecution of Dimmesdale by Hester's cuckolded husband, Roger Chillingworth. Sadly, Chillingworth is a learned man to whom the implications of his uncharitable obsession with revenge are absolutely clear. The inescapable conflict between nature and civilization stands out tragically in *The Scarlet Letter*: Hester and Chillingworth are united in marriage, a civil institution, but it is a marriage without true feeling for Hester, whereas the passion between Hester and Dimmesdale is deep and natural yet adulterous and unsanctioned. The outcome is tragic for all three of them.

In *The House of the Seven Gables* (1851), Hawthorne returns to the Puritan past and works out another fable of the effects of sin, this time in the form of a hereditary curse. The story of the Pyncheons is a fable of guilt and expiation, of the impossibility of escaping the past. Hawthorne thought it a greater novel than *The Scarlet Letter*.

During his residence at the Old Manse in Concord, Hawthorne had formed close friendships with his Transcendentalist neighbors, Ralph Waldo Emerson, Henry David Thoreau, William Ellery Channing, and Bronson Alcott. (The Old Manse had been built by Emerson's grandfather.) Yet Hawthorne's sensibilities were too burdened by a sense of sin for him to accept the optimism and idealism expressed by these thinkers. Furthermore, his experience at Brook Farm had made him distrust the ideals expressed in the notion of intellectuals living together communally. In *The Blithedale Romance* (1852), he satirized many of the goals and values of Utopian thinkers. The novel is exceptionally acute in its perceptions of human psychology and is a measure of the distance between the student of Puritanism and the sin in the human heart and the Transcendentalists with their lofty vision of human possibilities.

Hawthorne also published in 1852 *The Life of Franklin Pierce*. This campaign biography of his Bowdoin classmate led to Hawthorne's appointment as United States consul in Liverpool, a post he held from 1853 to 1857. He left Liverpool to live in Italy for three years, an experience that culminated in *The Marble Faun* (1860). This novel made him one of the first American writers to treat the experiences of his countrymen in Europe, a theme developed by such later writers as Henry James, William Dean Howells, and Ernest Hemingway.

When he came home to the United States, Hawthorne bought a home in Concord, which he named The Wayside. After his death four years later while on a tour in Plymouth, New Hampshire, he was buried in Concord. By the time of his death he had earned a considerable reputation for his romances.

Summary

After the success of *The Scarlet Letter*, Hawthorne had lived for three years in Lenox, Massachusetts, in the Berkshire Mountains, and had there established a close friendship with his literary neighbor, Herman Melville. Melville had been one of the first to recognize Hawthorne's unique powers as a writer, and in a famous review—written anonymously—he had praised Hawthorne's "great power of blackness." Hawthorne's influence certainly became one of the influences on Melville's own masterpiece, *Moby Dick: Or, The Whale* (1851).

Melville was responding to Hawthorne's skill in portraying imaginatively the mysteries of the human spirit. Hawthorne's preferred approach to his fictions was through symbolism and allegory, a technique that locates his plots on the ambiguous dividing line between the real and the imaginary. Some critics, such as Poe and Henry James, faulted him for the indirectness of his method in such cloudy parables as "The Minister's Black Veil" and "Rappaccini's Daughter," and Hawthorne himself admitted that "I am not quite sure that I entirely comprehend my own meaning in some of these blasted allegories." His propensity for unfolding man's struggle with sin in these romances prompted Melville to comment on Hawthorne's "Calvinistic sense of Innate Depravity and Original Sin, from whose visitations, in some shape or other, no deeply thinking mind is always and wholly free." Another great writer, D. H. Lawrence, saw in Hawthorne a genius for perceiving the most "disagreeable" secrets in man's soul and presenting them in clever extended tropes and figures.

As an American writing in the nineteenth century, Hawthorne faced the problem of where to find his materials in a country short in a history of manners and morals. James Fenimore Cooper's solution was the frontier, Melville's the sea, and Poe's the psyche. For Hawthorne, the answer lay in the Puritan past and its theology rich in moral and spiritual complexity. When Young Goodman Brown goes into the dark forest and is hosted by the Devil to a Black Mass, he comes to know evil in his soul. When Robin searches for his kinsman, Major Molineux, in the nighttime town, he experiences his own introduction to the dark side of man's nature. In such stories of initiation and experience as these, Hawthorne shaped in fiction a superb body of moral philosophy that is unequaled in the dark stream of American literature.

Bibliography

Crews, Frederick C. *The Sins of the Fathers: Hawthorne's Psychological Themes*. New York: Oxford University Press, 1966; London: Oxford University Press, 1970. A sensitive analysis of the psychological implications of Hawthorne's fiction. Especially perceptive in its explication of Hawthorne's sense of the past. Suggestive chapter entitled "Hawthorne, Freud, and Literary Value."

Gable, Harvey L., Jr. *Liquid Fire: Transcendental Mysticism in the Romances of Nathaniel Hawthorne*. New York: Lang, 1998. Examination of Hawthorne's romances and his speculation on the nature of self.

Gerber, John C., ed. *Twentieth Century Interpretations of "The Scarlet Letter."* Englewood Cliffs, N.J.: Prentice-Hall, 1968. A useful collection of analyses of Hawthorne's masterpiece. Divided into essays on "Background," "Form," "Technique," and "Interpretations."

Gross, Seymour L., ed. *A "Scarlet Letter" Handbook*. San Francisco: Wadsworth Publishing, 1960. An especially useful work for beginning students, including an introduction, a generous collection of critical excerpts, topics and questions for discussion, and a selected bibliography of criticism.

Harding, Brian, ed. *Nathaniel Hawthorne: Critical Assessments*. 4 vols. Mountfield, East Sussex: Helm Information, 1995. An impressive collection of critical assessments covering Hawthorne's novels and short stories. A massive book that has 230 chapters in 1900 pages.

Hawthorne, Julian. *Hawthorne and His Circle*. New York and London: Harper, 1903. By Hawthorne's son. Rich source of intimate recollections.

Hawthorne, Nathaniel. *The American Notebooks*. Edited by Randall Stewart. New Haven, Conn.: Yale University Press, and London: Oxford University Press, 1932. The notebooks Hawthorne kept intermittently from 1837 to 1853. Excellently edited with discussions of Hawthorne's character types, his adaptations of the notebooks in his fiction, and his recurrent themes. Indispensable for all students of Hawthorne.

———. *The English Notebooks*. Edited by Randall Stewart. New York: Modern Language Association of America, and London: Oxford University Press, 1941. The notebooks Hawthorne kept while United States consul in Liverpool between 1853 and 1857.

Mellow, James R. *Nathaniel Hawthorne in His Times*. Boston: Houghton Mifflin, 1980. A detailed biography that portrays Hawthorne in relation to his contemporaries.

Newman, Lea Bertani Vozar. *A Reader's Guide to the Short Stories of Nathaniel Hawthorne*. Boston: Hall, 1979. Extremely helpful guide to the short stories, spelling out for each story its publication history, circumstances of composition, sources, influences, and relationship to other works by Hawthorne. Includes summaries of interpretations and criticism.

Stewart, Randall. *Nathaniel Hawthorne: A Biography*. New Haven, Conn.: Yale University Press, 1948. A skillful interpretation of Hawthorne by an excellent scholar. Very well written.

Frank Day

JOHN HAY

Born: October 8, 1838; Salem, Indiana
Died: July 1, 1905; Newbury, New Hampshire
Areas of Achievement: Diplomacy
Contribution: After a distinguished career as presidential assistant, poet, novelist, editor, and historian, Hay served as secretary of state from 1898 to 1905, implementing the foreign policy initiatives that resulted in the United States' rise to world power.

Early Life

John Milton Hay was born October 8, 1838, in Salem, Indiana, the fourth child of Dr. Charles and Helen Leonard Hay. Charles Hay, a country physician of Scottish and German lineage, was the grandson of Adam Hay, who emigrated from Germany to Virginia about 1750. Helen Leonard, born in Assonet, Massachusetts, had deep New England roots.

Shortly after John's birth, the Hay family moved to Warsaw, Illinois, where he began his education, studying first in the local public schools and then at a private academy in Pittsfield, Pike County. An excellent student and a voracious reader, he had completed six books of Vergil in Latin by the time he was twelve. In 1852, when he was fourteen, he enrolled at a Springfield college. Though barely more than a high school, the institution prepared him to enter Brown University as a sophomore three years later. Quickly establishing himself as a scholar, he was graduated near the top of his class in 1858. He also demonstrated a flair for rhyming that resulted in his election as class poet.

Although he was born and reared in the West, Hay's education at Brown gave him an appreciation for polished, sophisticated Eastern society. His trim, handsome features, and neat mustache, combined with his courtly manners, social charm, conversational wit, and appreciation for feminine beauty, marked him as a true gentleman. Accompanying these traits, however, were periodic rounds of melancholy that remained throughout his life.

Hay returned to Warsaw after graduating from Brown, but remained only briefly before moving back to Springfield, the state capital. In 1859, he joined the law office of his uncle, Milton Hay, and began preparing for a legal career. He also had the opportunity to observe the inner workings of state politics and to meet such figures as Stephen A. Douglas, Senator Lyman Trumbull, and Abraham Lincoln, whose law office was next door to Milton Hay's. After Lincoln's election as President of the United States in 1860, his secretary, John G. Nicolay, persuaded the president-elect that young John Hay would be valuable as an assistant secretary.

Hay remained with Lincoln until near the end of the Civil War, receiving callers, writing letters, smoothing the ruffled feathers of politicians and generals, and listening to the jokes, stories, and innermost concerns of the wartime president. In early 1864, Hay received an appointment as assistant adjutant general, with the rank of major, and was assigned to the White House as a military aide. Although not a military expert, Hay had a sensitivity for the political implications of military affairs that made him an invaluable asset in Lincoln's efforts to bring the war to a swift conclusion. Hay's association with Lincoln had a profound impact upon his career.

Life's Work

Hay's apprenticeship in diplomacy began in March, 1865, just before the end of the Civil War, when Secretary of State William H. Seward appointed him secretary to the American legation at Paris. There he enjoyed the social delights of diplomatic life at the Court of Napoleon III and composed verse that expressed his youthful democratic political ideas. He had little influence, however, in diplomatic matters. In mid-1867, after a brief furlough in the United States, he accepted an appointment as American chargé d'affaires in Vienna, Austria. With few serious diplomatic duties to perform, he traveled extensively, making tours of Poland and Turkey before his resignation in August, 1868. Ten months later, he became secretary of the American legation in Madrid, Spain, where he served until the summer of 1870.

After his initial round of diplomatic assignments, Hay embarked upon a remarkable literary career. In 1871, he published *Pike County Ballads and Other Pieces*, a collection of poems that celebrated life in Warsaw and the other Mississippi River towns of his youth. In *Castilian Days*, which appeared the same year, he reflected upon his travels in Spain. These books mirrored his early democratic optimism, established his reputation as a major literary figure, and led to friendships with authors such as Mark Twain, William Dean Howells, and Bret Harte. He also exercised his considerable talents as an editor for Whitelaw Reid's powerful *New York Tribune*.

Hay's writings acquired an increasingly conservative tone after his marriage in January, 1874, to Clara L. Stone, a daughter of Amassa Stone, a wealthy Cleveland industrialist and railroad builder. Already a gentleman by predisposition and education, Hay became an aristocrat by marriage. The extent of his change in attitude became fully apparent in 1884 with the publication of *The Bread-Winners*, a stinging attack against both labor unions and social mobility, and a defense of European-style class stratification. In the meantime, Hay had commenced an even more significant literary venture. In 1875, he and John Nicolay initiated their massive *Abraham Lincoln: A History*. By its completion in 1890, the project numbered ten volumes. Although it overly idealizes Lincoln, Nicolay and Hay's work remains a landmark study of the life of the sixteenth president.

While Hay devoted most of his energies between 1870 and 1897 to literary and historical pursuits, he never completely divorced himself from foreign policy concerns. From 1879 to 1881, he served as assistant secretary of state, learning much about the intricacies of foreign policy formulation. During the next fifteen years, he traveled extensively in Europe, acquiring a wealth of information and contacts that would be beneficial in future diplomatic endeavors.

Hay also maintained close ties with leading Republican politicians. When his friend William McKinley won the presidency in 1896, Hay received the appointment as ambassador to Great Britain. Convinced of the necessity of forging strong relations with the British, he used his considerable charm and tact to smooth friction created by the recent Venezuelan boundary dispute and the ongoing pelagic sealing controversy. When the Spanish-American War erupted in 1898, Hay's efforts ensured a stance of sympathetic neutrality on the part of England toward American intervention in Cuba.

In August, 1898, McKinley appointed Hay secretary of state. Although not an aggressive imperialist, Hay believed firmly that the United States should play a larger role in world affairs, and he worked vigorously throughout his tenure to accomplish that goal. During McKinley's administration, Hay focused much attention on affairs in Asia and the Pacific Ocean. In treaty negotiations to end the Spanish-American War, he supported the president's decision to acquire the Philippine Islands and then encouraged strong action to crush the in-

surrection led by Emilio Aguinaldo. Hay's most significant assertion of American influence in Asia was the famous Open Door notes, which sought assurances from the major powers that equal trading rights would be guaranteed within their spheres of interest. The following year, when the Boxer Rebellion triggered discussion of a partition of China by the European powers, Hay issued a second Open Door circular designed to preserve China's territorial integrity.

Hay also negotiated several treaties which paved the way for construction of the Panama Canal. In 1901, after the United States Senate rejected an earlier version, he concluded the Hay-Pauncefote Treaty with England, which abrogated the Clayton-Bulwer Treaty of 1850 and allowed the United States to construct and fortify an Isthmian canal. Two years later he negotiated the Hay-Herrán Treaty with Colombia, by which that nation was to allow the United States to build a canal across Panama. When Colombia refused to ratify the document, a convenient revolt erupted in Panama, and President Theodore Roosevelt promptly recognized its new government; Hay followed up by working out a treaty with

Philippe Bunau-Varilla in which Panama gave the United States rights to a Canal Zone through which a canal would be constructed.

One of the most persistent Anglo-American problems as the twentieth century dawned was a controversy over the location of the Canada-Alaska boundary. In January, 1903, after months of effort, Hay and British ambassador Michael Herbert signed a treaty which called for the establishment of a tribunal composed of six impartial judges, three representing each side, to resolve the matter. President Roosevelt generated new controversy when he appointed Senators Henry Cabot Lodge and George Turner to the tribunal, but the American position prevailed when the British jurist, in an effort to preserve Anglo-American harmony, rejected the views of his two Canadian colleagues and voted with the American representatives. Settlement of the Alaska boundary dispute was one of Hay's last major accomplishments. On July 1, 1905, after an extended illness, he died in Newbury, New Hampshire.

Summary

John Hay was a major literary and diplomatic figure whose life and works symbolize the momentous transformation of American society and the significant expansion of the nation's role in world affairs during the late nineteenth and early twentieth centuries. The dramatic shift in Hay's ideological perspective between the publication of *Pike County Ballads* and the appearance of *The Bread-Winners* suggests the growing uneasiness within the American upper class over labor unrest, immigration, political radicalism, and other perceived threats to the status quo. Yet Hay's high literary reputation and his ability to inspire trust and make friends also made it possible for him to gain the respect and friendship of those with whom he strenuously disagreed. Thus he retained the friendship of anti-imperialists such as Mark Twain and William Dean Howells, even when they opposed his conduct of American policy in the Philippines. When his reputation led to his election in 1904 as a charter member of the American Academy of Arts and Letters over such great writers as Henry Adams and Henry James, he rectified the error by arranging for their election on a later ballot.

Hay's accomplishments as secretary of state had lasting foreign policy implications. The Open Door notes undergirded American policy in Asia through World War II and beyond. The Panama Canal treaties and construction of the canal vastly expanded the nation's political and economic stake in Central America and the Caribbean region. The Hay-Herbert Treaty and the settlement of the Alaska boundary dispute contributed to a new era of Anglo-American friendship, which has been a foundation stone of twentieth century foreign policy. Finally, Hay's skill, dignity, and restraint as a negotiator helped to placate some of the ill-will created by Theodore Roosevelt's bellicosity in foreign policy matters. By the time of his death, Hay had participated fully in the emergence of the United States as a world power.

Bibliography

Beale, Howard K. *Theodore Roosevelt and the Rise of America to World Power.* Baltimore: Johns Hopkins University Press, 1956. John Hay is a central figure in this detailed, well-researched account of American expansion under Theodore Roosevelt. This volume is essential to understanding the values as well as the political and economic forces behind American imperialism.

Burlingame, Michael, ed. *Inside Lincoln's White House, The Complete Civil War Diary of John Hay.* Carbondale: Southern Illinois University Press, 1997. Acclaimed as the definitive edition of this previously published work, the diary is accurately produced here, where other editions were poorly edited and excluded important text due to Hay's handwriting.

Campbell, Charles S. *The Transformation of American Foreign Relations, 1865-1900.* New York: Harper, 1976. A well-written synthesis of scholarship on American foreign relations during the last thirty-five years of the nineteenth century. Excellent source of historical context for understanding foreign policy issues during the McKinley and Roosevelt administrations. Deals with Hay primarily in relation to the Open Door policy and Anglo-American relations.

Clymer, Kenton J. *John Hay: The Gentleman as Diplomat.* Ann Arbor: University of Michigan Press, 1975. A full-length treatment of Hay, this volume is especially useful for its explanation of his intellectual background and literary career. Although sympathetic to Hay, it is less satisfactory, on balance, in its discussion of his diplomatic service. Organized thematically, the volume is generally quite readable; the lack of a continuing chronology, however, sometimes makes it difficult to keep events in perspective.

Dennett, Tyler. *John Hay: From Poetry to Politics*. New York: Dodd, Mead, 1933. The best single biography of John Hay. Based upon extensive research into unpublished manuscripts, published works, and official documents. While sympathetic to Hay and his accomplishments, it also admits his defects and failures.

Dulles, Rhea Foster. "John Hay." In *An Uncertain Tradition: American Secretaries of State in the Twentieth Century.* Edited by Norman A. Graebner, 22-39. New York: McGraw-Hill, 1961. Summarizes Hay's major accomplishments as secretary of state. Pictures Hay as an implementor rather than as an initiator of policy whose ability to compromise and to accommodate were his major assets.

McCullough, David. *The Path Between the Seas: The Creation of the Panama Canal, 1870-1914.* New York: Simon and Schuster, 1977. A colorful, prizewinning study of the social, economic, political, and technological events surrounding construction of the Panama Canal. Based upon archival and manuscript sources from both sides of the Atlantic as well as interviews with surviving participants. Sympathetic to Hay in respect to his relationship with Roosevelt.

Thayer, William Roscoe. *Life and Letters of John Hay.* 2 vols. London: Constable, and Boston: Houghton Mifflin, 1915. A detailed account drawn heavily from Hay's personal letters, many of which are quoted at length or reprinted in their entirety. Although severely dated in interpretation, it remains a useful background source, especially on Hay's early life.

Zimmermann, Warren. "Jingoes, Goo-Goos, and the Rise of America's Empire." *Wilson Quarterly* 22, no. 2 (Spring 1998). Examines the five individuals who played prominent roles in the United States' entry into imperialism, including Hay.

Carl E. Kramer

FERDINAND VANDEVEER HAYDEN

Born: September 7, 1829; Westfield, Massachusetts

Died: December 22, 1887; Philadelphia, Pennsylvania

Areas of Achievement: Exploration and natural history

Contribution: Hayden organized and led scientific explorations throughout the Rocky Mountains in the 1860's and 1870's. The publicity surrounding his discoveries was a key factor in the creation of Yellowstone National Park, the first such park in the United States.

Early Life

Ferdinand Vandeveer Hayden was born in southwest Massachusetts in 1829. After his father's death, his mother sent him at age ten to live with an uncle on a farm near Rochester, New York. An ambitious young man, Hayden left the farm at age sixteen. He taught school for two years before walking to Oberlin College in Ohio; he gained entrance despite a lack of financial assistance and worked his way through to graduation. Hayden studied geology at the school and graduated in 1850. He then entered Albany Medical School, completed his doctor of medicine degree in 1853, and continued his study of geology and paleontology.

Instead of practicing medicine, Hayden traveled to the South Dakota Badlands with one of his professors to study geology. The trip promised adventure and began Hayden's lifelong obsession with the American West and its natural history. In the 1850's, he explored the area from the Missouri River to the Rockies, often alone, making geologic and scientific observations of the vast, uncharted regions. By 1860, having gained invaluable training and experience in exploration and science, he was ready to explore the legendary region of Yellowstone. However, the Civil War forced him to postpone these plans.

Hayden returned to medical practice during the war as a volunteer surgeon; he ended the war with the rank of lieutenant colonel. By 1865, he had become well known for his early explorations, and he gained additional experience and respect during the Civil War. After the war's end, he accepted an appointment as a professor of mineralogy and geology at the University of Pennsylvania. In 1866, he again returned west to the Dakota Badlands for further exploration and study. During the next sev-

eral years, he performed respected and well-received geological and topological surveys in Nebraska, Wyoming, and Colorado. In 1869, Hayden was asked to lead a series of surveys of the Rocky Mountains, which became one of the four great post-Civil War scientific explorations of the American West. His work was known as the United States Geological Survey of Territories.

Life's Work

Hayden assembled a group of experienced scientific professionals to accompany him on his surveys. Along with geologists, botanists, engineers, and topographers, he brought artists and photographers to sketch, paint, and photograph the wonders of the Rocky Mountains. These artists introduced the scenery of the Rocky Mountains to Americans and made the area a popular destination for farmers, settlers, and miners, who went to seek their fortunes. Such visual work helped to dramatize the beauty and wonders of the West for the American

people. Hayden's surveys, which were published as books with photographs, sold well.

Hayden began his reconnaissance of the Rocky Mountains with about one dozen men. Later his party would grow to include between twenty and thirty people, all professional scientists and hardy outdoorsmen. His *Third Annual Report* of 1869 detailed their explorations in New Mexico and Colorado and told of the great mineral wealth and possibilities for settlement in these areas. This report was highly successful, and the popularity of his explorations gained him support in Congress for continued surveys, this time in the northern Rocky Mountains. In the summer of 1870, Hayden and his party left for Wyoming. After yet another successful year and another popular annual report, he finally set out to explore the legendary Yellowstone and the magnificent Teton Mountains.

In 1871, Hayden led the first official government expedition into Yellowstone, one of the last truly unknown areas in the United States. Fur trappers and Native Americans had virtually avoided the area, finding easier game outside the rugged area. Rumors of the great geysers, hot springs, and spectacular waterfalls had persisted for decades. Such rumors, combined with Congress' desire to map the area and discover its possible fur and mineral wealth, helped spur Hayden's discoveries.

When Hayden and his men entered Yellowstone Valley, they found hundreds of bubbling hot springs that fed the streams that became tributaries of the Yellowstone River. Green pines and aspens covered the mountains, and the serene surface of Yellowstone Lake reflected the crystal blue sky. The meadows were covered with dark green grass and acres of multihued wildflowers. Mud pots and geysers dotted the valley. Mammoth Hot Springs, officially discovered by Hayden's survey, had dozens of springs with water ranging in color from pure white to bright yellow. In the morning, steam rose from the numerous vents in the earth and obscured the valley in a volcanic mist. Wildlife was abundant, and moose, beaver, deer, and grizzly bears could be seen everywhere. The party also stumbled across the Grand Canyon of the Yellowstone River and its two waterfalls. There seemed to be something unfinished and unearthly about the region. It was a wonder to behold, and the area fascinated Hayden. He wrote in awe of its stunning beauty. The survey left Yellowstone in late August, 1871, and returned east later that year.

Hayden's report on Yellowstone immediately grabbed the interest of the American people and Congress. A map of the region was published, the photos were reproduced, and Hayden wrote a number of articles for popular magazines such as *Scribners* to urge the nation to turn the rare wonders of Yellowstone into a protected park for all Americans. Congress unanimously passed such a bill, and on March 1, 1972, President Ulysses S. Grant signed the Yellowstone Park Bill, creating the first national park in the United States.

In 1872, Hayden returned to the northern Rockies, this time to the Grand Teton Mountains. Like Yellowstone, the Tetons were an area of natural grandeur with dense spruce forests, deep canyons, and cascading streams. Above it all towered the famed jagged mountain peaks, their glory reflected off pristine mountain lakes. The survey climbed many of the peaks, named streams and other natural landmarks, and collected information on the natural history of the Tetons. The party departed in early fall, before the first snows. From 1873 to 1876, the Hayden survey explored Colorado.

The four years that Hayden and his men spent in Colorado were just as exciting and rewarding as the previous years in the northern Rockies. They mapped the mountains, rivers, and drainage basins of the state, studied its geology and natural history, and gave names to many of the peaks. Hayden's men braved electrical storms, forest fires, blizzards, blistering heat, and wild animals. In 1873, the expedition discovered the legendary Mountain of the Holy Cross. This peak appeared to have a one-thousand-foot-tall cross of white snow blazed into its side. Photographs of this mountain were spectacularly popular and helped to further American interest in the recreational and developmental potential of Colorado. The next year, in 1874, a group of his men stumbled across ancient American Indian ruins in the southwest portion of the state. These cliff dwellings were a wonderful archaeological and historical find that helped gain further fame and public support for both Hayden and his wildly successful surveys.

The last two years of the survey were spent in Wyoming, Montana, and Idaho, where Hayden and his men continued their job of mapping the land and studying its geology and natural history. By 1878, Hayden's United States Geological Survey of the Territories had completed the task assigned to it. Hayden's work in the field continued until 1882, when locomotor ataxia forced him to begin to abandon the writing and exploration that he loved so greatly. Hayden died on December 22, 1887, in Philadelphia, Pennsylvania.

Summary

Ferdinand Hayden will be remembered for his twelve years of painstaking geological fieldwork in the American West. For eleven years, from 1867 to 1878, Hayden and his men explored, mapped, and studied areas in five states. His leadership of the United States Geological Survey of the Territories was superb, and his devotion to his task was unequalled. His survey not only discovered or publicized such natural wonders as Yellowstone and Grand Tetons but also found such legendary places as the Mountain of the Holy Cross and the ancient cliff dwellings of the American Southwest. His explorations and the subsequent publicity that accompanied them were crucial to securing the support of the American public for conservation of natural areas.

Hayden's Geological Survey of the Territories laid the foundation for much of American knowledge of the geology, zoology, and topography of the Rocky Mountains. Farmers, miners, and railroad companies used his maps and reports to help settle and conquer the American wilderness. His eleven years of fieldwork also proved to be a magnificent training ground for late nineteenth century American scientists, who became the leaders for the next generation. Hayden and his men demonstrated to a suspicious and uncertain American public that science was practical and important. With each new dramatic discovery, science became more accepted. Millions of Americans learned from his popular reports, viewed the pictures from his surveys, and visited museums that built upon information uncovered by his expeditions.

Hayden's most important accomplishment, however, was the establishment of Yellowstone National Park in 1872. It is quite possible that Yellowstone's incredible natural wonders would have been devastated by commercial development in the late nineteenth century. Hayden's efforts on behalf of the region's preservation, combined with photographs of the area's scenery reproduced for the public, forced Congress and President Grant to set aside Yellowstone for future generations. Today, more than fifty national parks preserve the greatest natural treasures in the United States.

Bibliography

Bartlett, Richard A. *Great Surveys of the American West*. Norman: University of Oklahoma Press, 1962. This is the best work on Hayden's actual surveys and contains four excellent, exciting chapters on his explorations. Bartlett's fine book places the surveys in their historical and political context and has an excellent bibliography.

Bruce, Robert. *The Launching of Modern American Science, 1846-1876*. New York: Knopf, 1987. Bruce's work puts Hayden's surveys in the context of post-Civil War expansionism and explains the beginnings of the American scientific community and the American quest for knowledge about the natural world.

Foster, Mike. *Strange Genius: The Life of Ferdinand Vandeveer Hayden*. New York: Rhinehart, 1995. This is the only modern full-length biography of Hayden. It covers Hayden's entire life in detail, with emphasis on his scientific explorations in the American West.

Goetzmann, William H. *Exploration and Empire: The Explorer and the Scientist in the Winning of the American West*. New York: Knopf, 1966. This Pulitzer Prize-winning book covers a century of exploration and conquest in the American West. It contains a fine, succinct chapter on Hayden's Survey.

_____. *New Lands, New Men: The Second Great Age of Discovery*. New York: Viking Press, 1986; London: Oxford University Press, 1987. This second book by Goetzmann details the scientific explorations of the nineteenth and twentieth centuries and shows the historical importance of Hayden, as well as the four other great surveys.

Jeff R. Bremer

RUTHERFORD B. HAYES

Born: October 4, 1822; Delaware, Ohio
Died: January 17, 1893; Fremont, Ohio
Areas of Achievement: Government and politics
Contribution: Though an ardent Radical Republican early in the Reconstruction era, Hayes moderated his views and as president ended that era by withdrawing military support for Republican state governments in the South. During his administration, Hayes also opposed inflation, defended the presidency from congressional attacks, and fought for civil service reform.

Early Life

The posthumous son of Rutherford Hayes, Rutherford Birchard Hayes was so weak that his mother, Sophia Birchard Hayes, did not expect him to survive. His parents, who were of old New England stock, had migrated to Ohio from Vermont in 1817, and, on his death, his father had left his mother a farm which she rented, some additional land, and a house in town, where she kept two lodgers. Her sorrow was deepened in January, 1825, when Hayes's older brother, a sturdy nine-year-old, drowned while ice skating, leaving only Hayes, a feeble two-year-old, and his four-year-old sister, Fanny. She was his constant companion, whom he adored and whose dolls he played with until he grew older and replaced them with toy soldiers. His understandably protective mother allowed him neither to do household chores nor to play games with boys until he was nine. A friendly, cheerful child, Hayes admired his mother's carefree, younger bachelor brother, Sardis Birchard, who left their household when Hayes was four but returned often for visits and paid for Hayes's education.

After Hayes's mother had taught him to read, spell, and write, he attended a private grade school and later was tutored by a local lawyer. When nearly fourteen, Hayes left home to attend Norwalk (Ohio) Academy, and the next year he attended Isaac Webb's Preparatory School in Middletown, Connecticut. In 1838, at sixteen, Hayes entered Kenyon College in Gambier, Ohio, and in 1842, he was graduated at the head of his class. After studying law for a year with a lawyer in Columbus, Ohio, Hayes entered Harvard Law School and received his bachelor of law degree in 1845.

Life's Work

From 1845 to 1849, Hayes practiced law in his Uncle Sardis' town of Upper Sandusky, Ohio, and was largely responsible for changing its name to Fremont. Anxious to be on his own in a challenging city, Hayes in January, 1850, opened an office in Cincinnati, Ohio, achieved prominence, and on December 30, 1852, married Lucy Ware Webb, a recent graduate of Wesleyan Female College. She was religious and a reformer with strong temperance and ardent abolitionist beliefs. In contrast, Hayes, a lifelong disciple of Ralph Waldo Emerson, never joined a church and before his marriage had shown little interest in organized reform. Beginning in September, 1853, however, he defended captured runaway slaves free of charge and soon helped found the Republican Party in Ohio. From 1858 to 1861, he held his first public office as Cincinnati's city solicitor. When the lower Southern states seceded (1860-1861), he was inclined to *"Let them go,"* but he was outraged when on April 12, 1861, their new Confederacy attacked Fort Sumter at Charleston, South Carolina. He organized half the Literary Club of Cincinnati into a drilling company of which he was captain, and on June 27, he was commissioned a major in the Twenty-third Ohio Volunteer Infantry. Hayes served throughout the war, was wounded four times, and emerged from the struggle a major general and a member-elect of Congress.

Serving from 1865 to 1867, Hayes consistently supported Radical Republican Reconstruction measures, but, as chairman of the Joint Committee on the Library, he worked hardest in developing the Library of Congress into a great institution. Unhappy in Congress, he resigned to run successfully for governor of Ohio and was reelected in 1869. His greatest achievements in his first two terms as governor (1868-1872) were Ohio's ratification of the Fifteenth Amendment and the establishment of Ohio State University. Returning to Cincinnati in early 1872, he loyally supported President Ulysses S. Grant for a second term and ran for Congress to help the ticket. Although Hayes lost, Grant won, and Hayes's services in a pivotal state placed him in line for a major appointment. When he was asked merely to be assistant treasurer at Cincinnati, he refused and retired from politics "definitely, absolutely, positively." With Lucy and their five children, he returned to Fremont to live with Uncle Sardis, who died in January, 1874, leaving Hayes the bulk of his estate.

The panic of 1873 reversed the Republican Party's fortunes, while the "corruptionists around Grant" tarnished its reputation in the eyes of Hayes and other respectable Republicans. By 1875, Ohio Republicans, anxious to save their state for their party, nominated a reluctant Hayes for a third term as governor. He won by a narrow margin and became a contender for the 1876 presidential nomination, which he also won because his rivals were either too corrupt, too ill, too radical, or too reformist. In contrast, Hayes was a fearless soldier, who was impeccably honest and from a crucial state, and, though both a Radical and a reformer, he was by nature moderate and conciliatory. To oppose him, the Democrats nominated Samuel J. Tilden, New York's reforming governor. They campaigned for white supremacy and the removal of the federal troops that upheld Republican regimes in the South and attacked the Grant Administration as corrupt. Republican orators warned voters not to let the rebels capture the federal government through a Democratic victory and promised that Hayes would reform the civil service.

When the election was over, both Republicans and Democrats disputed its result. Tilden had at least 250,000 more popular votes than Hayes, but Republicans, after some election night computations, claimed to have carried Florida, Louisiana, and South Carolina (states that Republicans, supported by federal troops, controlled, but which Tilden appeared to have won), giving Hayes 185 electoral votes and Tilden, 184. Republican-dominated returning boards reviewed the vote in those states, legally eliminating the entire vote in districts where they believed blacks were intimidated into not voting, and certified that Hayes had carried all three states. Charging the returning boards with fraud, Democrats certified that Tilden had carried those three states. To decide which electoral votes to count, the Democratic House of Representatives and the Republican Senate in January, 1877, agreed on the Electoral Count Act, creating the fifteen-member Electoral Commission, drawn from both houses of Congress and the Supreme Court and composed of seven Republicans, seven Democrats, and one independent. The independent, who was a Supreme Court justice, resigned to become a senator and was replaced on the commission by a Republican. By a strict eight to seven party vote,

the Electoral Commission decided the disputed election in favor of the Republicans and Hayes.

The commission failed to end the crisis. The electoral votes had to be counted in a joint session of Congress, and its angry Democratic majority obstructed the count with repeated adjournments. Some Southern Democrats, who had belonged to the pre-Civil War Whig party, while meeting with Republicans close to Hayes (who were also of Whig extraction), offered to cooperate in completing the count and suggested that they would desert their party to help Republicans organize the next House of Representatives (which the Democrats appeared to have won) and even join the Republican Party. In return, they wanted Hayes to withdraw the federal troops from Louisiana and South Carolina (the Florida Republican government had collapsed) and in effect complete the restoration of white supremacy governments in the South, to appoint to his cabinet one of their political persuasion to augment their strength with federal patronage, and a few of them pressed for a federal subsidy to construct the Texas and Pacific Railroad. There is no doubt that these negotiations took place, but how crucial they were in changing the Democratic votes that permitted completing the count is debated.

Hayes was inaugurated on schedule, becoming the nineteenth president of the United States. He appointed a Southern Democrat with a Whig background to his cabinet and in April, 1877, ended the Reconstruction era by removing the federal troops from South Carolina and Louisiana, after receiving assurances from their incoming Democrat regimes that they would observe the Fourteenth and Fifteenth amendments, granting civil and voting rights to blacks. The amendments were not faithfully observed, Southern Democrats neither helped Republicans organize the House nor joined their party, and Hayes ignored the Texas and Pacific Railroad.

Having disposed of the Southern question, Hayes moved on two fronts to reform the civil service. Since it suffered because political parties depended on government workers to finance and organize the nomination and election of candidates, Hayes ordered that civil servants not be assessed a portion of their salaries for political purposes and that they not manage "political organizations, caucuses, conventions, or election campaigns." He also determined to make the New York Customhouse, the largest federal office in the land, where

more than half the nation's revenue was collected, a showcase to prove that civil service reform was practical. That effort led to a spectacular but successful struggle with New York Senator Roscoe Conkling, who regarded the Customhouse as part of his political machine. Hayes's victory struck twin blows to promote reform and to restore executive power over appointments.

Despite enormous pressure to inflate the currency, Hayes was a consistent hard-money advocate. In February, 1878, he would not approve the mildly inflationary Bland-Allison Act (requiring the government monthly to purchase and coin two to four million dollars worth of silver), but Congress overrode his veto. In January, 1879, he was pleased when the Treasury Department began to pay gold for greenbacks (paper money issued during the Civil War without gold backing).

The Democrats challenged Hayes during the second half of his administration, when they controlled both houses of Congress. To necessary appropriation bills, they repeatedly attached riders that would repeal the federal election laws ("force bills") enforcing the Fourteenth and Fifteenth amendments, but Hayes consistently vetoed those bills. He argued that the federal government was justified in preventing intimidation and fraud in the election of its Congress and also that Congress, by attaching these riders, was trying to destroy the executive's constitutional right to veto legislation. Hayes won the battle of the riders; his vetoes rallied his party and the people outside the South to his side. Responding to political pressure, Congress passed the appropriations without the riders.

Returning prosperity and a united Republican Party bolstered Hayes's financial and political views and left him in a strong position, but he had vowed to serve only one term. He left office confident that his policies were instrumental in electing as his successor James A. Garfield, a fellow Ohio Republican.

In retirement, Hayes served effectively as a trustee of the Peabody Education Fund and as president of the Slater Fund, both dedicated to further the education of Southern blacks. He died in Fremont, Ohio, on January 17, 1893.

Summary

Hayes was a man of integrity, courage, and decision, but he was also a man of reason and moderation. He was an uncompromising defender of the Union and an opponent of inflation, but on other issues he was willing to compromise as he worked to achieve his goals. Although he was a reformer, he sought to convince people rather than coerce them. He had, for example, lectured in favor of temperance, but only after becoming president did he totally abstain from alcoholic beverages, and he opposed Prohibition legislation and one-issue political parties founded on temperance. His moderate, pragmatic, piecemeal approach often angered those who were impatient to right wrongs. Out of the entire government service, his administration instituted reform in only the Department of the Interior under Secretary Carl Schurz and the New York Customhouse and Post Office, but, in these showcases, reform succeeded and proved its practicality. Had it been universally applied, hostile administrators would have discredited civil service reform.

Hayes, who was in a no-win position, has been criticized for his Southern policy. With neither political support nor congressional appropriations, he could not reverse the policy of the preceding Grant Administration and reclaim Southern states by military force. From an impossible situation, he extracted promises from Southern Democrats to uphold Reconstruction amendments if he would remove the troops supporting powerless Republican governments. At the start, he naïvely believed that Southern Democrats would keep their word and thought that his policy would attract to his party respectable Southern whites who would not interfere with black civil rights. Even though his policy failed, given the bleak prospects for Southern blacks and Republicans in April, 1877, Hayes took the only feasible course by which their rights might have been protected.

Bibliography

Barnard, Harry. *Rutherford B. Hayes and His America*. Indianapolis: Bobbs-Merrill, 1954. An excellent psychological study that stresses Hayes's close relationship with his sister. In doing justice to Hayes's personal life, however, this biography underemphasizes his public life; less than half of the book is devoted to his election and presidency.

Davison, Kenneth E. *The Presidency of Rutherford B. Hayes*. Westport, Conn.: Greenwood Press, 1972. With its topical organization, this is a useful supplement to the Barnard biography.

Hayes, Rutherford B. *Diary and Letters of Rutherford Birchard Hayes: Nineteenth President of the United States*. Edited by Charles Richard Williams. 5 vols. Columbus: Ohio State Archaeological and Historical Society, 1922-1926. Hayes kept a diary most of his life (one of the few presidents to do so) but did go for weeks at times without an entry. To form a readable narrative, the editor has corrected spelling and grammatical lapses, has included letters, and has supplied introductions and transitions.

————. *Hayes, The Diary of a President, 1875-1881: Covering the Disputed Election, the End of Reconstruction, and the Beginning of Civil Service.* Edited by Harry T. Williams. New York: McKay, 1964. Virtually a facsimile edition of the diary, with the minor errors, gaps, deletions, and corrections made obvious.

Hoogenboom, Ari. *Outlawing the Spoils: A History of the Civil Service Reform Movement, 1865-1883.* Urbana: University of Illinois Press, 1961. The standard work on a major issue confronting the Hayes Administration, this study reflects the exasperation of the reformers with Hayes's moderate course.

Marcus, Robert D. "Lost and Found Department: A Gilded Age President." *Reviews in American History* 23, no. 4 (December 1995). The author critiques Ari Hoogenboom's "Rutherford B. Hayes: Warrior and President."

Paul, Ezra. "Congressional Relations and 'Public Relations' in the Administration of Rutherford B. Hayes." *Presidential Studies Quarterly* 28, no. 1 (Winter 1998). Paul's study of Hayes's presidency sheds light on presidential-legislative relations under difficult conditions.

Polakoff, Keith Ian. *The Politics of Inertia: The Election of 1876 and the End of Reconstruction.* Baton Rouge: Louisiana State University Press, 1973. This superb study of the disputed election argues that the negotiations between Southern Democrats and Hayes's friends had no effect on the settlement, that both parties were faction-ridden, that Hayes held the Republicans together better than Tilden held the Democrats together, and that in actuality Congress drifted into a settlement.

Unger, Irwin. *The Greenback Era: A Social and Political History of American Finance, 1865-1879.* Princeton, N.J.: Princeton University Press, 1964. In following the greenback issue in American politics to the resumption of specie payments under Hayes, Unger not only analyzes the complex forces favoring inflation but also explores the equally complex attitudes of people such as Hayes, for whom hard money was not an economic issue but an undebatable article of faith.

Williams, Charles Richard. *The Life of Rutherford Birchard Hayes: Nineteenth President of the United States.* 2 vols. Boston: Houghton Mifflin, 1914. This old-fashioned biography is uncritical of Hayes but is full of information on Hayes's public career that the Barnard study ignores and is also valuable for its quotation of letters and speeches that otherwise are unavailable in print.

Williams, T. Harry. *Hayes of the Twenty-Third: The Civil War Volunteer Officer.* New York: Knopf, 1965. An outstanding military historian follows Hayes throughout the Civil War as he rose from major to major general.

Woodward, C. Vann. *Reunion and Reaction: The Compromise of 1877 and the End of Reconstruction.* 2d ed. New York: Doubleday, 1956. This classic study of the disputed election, first published in 1951, argues that a crucial element in the compromise was a land grant for the Texas and Pacific Railroad, which Southern Democrats desired and Hayes's friends agreed to support but failed to deliver.

Ari Hoogenboom

GEORG WILHELM FRIEDRICH HEGEL

Born: August 27, 1770; Stuttgart, Württemberg
Died: November 14, 1831; Berlin, Prussia
Area of Achievement: Philosophy
Contribution: Hegel developed many theories of great philosophical importance that over the past century have influenced the social sciences, anthropology, sociology, psychology, history, and political theory. He believed that the mind is the ultimate reality and that philosophy can restore humanity to a state of harmony.

Early Life

Georg Wilhelm Friedrich Hegel was born into a Protestant middle-class family in Stuttgart, the eldest of three children. His father was a minor civil servant for the Duchy of Württemberg, and his family had roots in Austria. To escape persecution by the Austrian Catholics in the sixteenth century, his ancestors settled among the Lutheran Protestants of the German territories, which consisted of more than three hundred free cities, duchies, and states loosely united under the rule of Francis I of Austria. Though little is known about his mother, all accounts describe her as having been highly intelligent and unusually educated for a woman of that time. Hegel had the conventional schooling for his social class, entering German primary school in 1773, Latin school in 1775, and the Stuttgart *Gymnasium illustre* in 1780. Upon graduating from the *Gymnasium* (equivalent to high school) in 1788, he entered the famous seminary at the University of Tübingen to study philosophy and theology in preparation for the Protestant ministry. As a student, Hegel became friends with Friedrich Hölderlin, a Romantic poet, and Friedrich Schelling. He shared the top floor of the dormitory with Schelling, who became famous before Hegel as an Idealist philosopher. In 1790, Hegel received a master's degree in philosophy.

After passing his theological examinations at Tübingen in 1793, Hegel began many years of struggle to earn his living and establish himself as a philosopher. Instead of entering the ministry, he began working as a house tutor for a wealthy family in Bern, Switzerland. In 1797, he became a tutor in Frankfurt, continuing throughout this time to read, think, and write about philosophical questions, usually along radical lines. For example, he considered Jesus inferior to Socrates as a teacher of ethics, and he considered orthodox religion, be-cause of its reliance on external authority, an obstacle in restoring mankind to a life of harmony. Although Hegel always retained some of his skepticism toward orthodox religion, he later in life considered himself a Lutheran Christian. In 1798, he began to write on the philosophy of history and on the spirit of Christianity, major themes in his philosophical system. Upon his father's death in 1799, Hegel received a modest inheritance and was able to stop tutoring and join his friend Schelling at the University of Jena, in the state of Weimar.

Life's Work

Hegel's life's work as a teacher and philosopher began at Jena. From 1801 to 1807, Hegel taught as an unsalaried lecturer at the University of Jena, his first university position as a philosopher, for which he was paid by the students who attended class. While in Jena, Hegel cooperated with Schelling in editing the *Kritisches Journal der Philosophie*. He also published the *Differenz des Fichte'schen und Schelling'schen Systems der Philosophie* (1801; *The Difference Between Fichte's and Schelling's Philosophy*, 1977). During this time, Hegel began to lecture on metaphysics, logic, and natural law. In 1805, he was promoted to Ausserordentlicher Professor (Distinguished Professor) on the recommendation of the German Romantic poet Johann Wolfgang von Goethe. Hegel was very prolific, yet beginning in 1802 he announced each year a significant forthcoming book to his publisher without producing it.

These were momentous times. In 1789, just after Hegel's nineteenth birthday, the fall of the Bastille announced the French Revolution across Europe; in 1806, after putting an end to the thousand-year Austrian Empire, Napoleon I crushed the Prussian armies at the Battle of Jena. On October 13, 1806, Napoleon victoriously entered the walled city of Jena, an event that Hegel described to a friend as follows: "I saw the Emperor—that world-soul—riding out to reconnoiter the city; it is truly a wonderful sensation to see such an individual, concentrated here on a single point, astride a single horse, yet reaching across the world and ruling it. . . ."

October 13, 1806, was also the day that Hegel finished his book, long promised to his publisher, and sent the manuscript amid the confusion of war. The book was his early masterpiece, *Phänomenologie des Geistes* (1807; *The Phenomenology of Spirit,*

1931, also known as *The Phenomenology of Mind*). On October 20, the French army plundered Hegel's house, and his teaching position at the University of Jena came to an end. Hegel left for Bamberg in Bavaria, where he spent a year working as a newspaper editor. He then became headmaster and philosophy teacher at the *Gymnasium* in Nuremberg, where he worked successfully from 1808 until 1816.

The Phenomenology of Spirit, which exemplifies the young Hegel, was strongly influenced by German Romanticism. This movement provided a new and more complete way of perceiving the world and was developed by German philosophers and artists, such as Schelling and Hölderlin. German Romanticism stood in opposition to French rationalism and British empiricism, the two major philosophies of the seventeenth and eighteenth centuries dominated by reason and immediate sensory experience, respectively. German Romanticism had been influenced by the German philosopher Immanuel Kant, whose theory of knowledge synthesized rational and empirical elements. Kant argued that the laws of science, rather than being the source of rationality, were dependent on the human mind and its pure concepts, or categories, such as cause and effect. Kant believed that it is the mind which gives its laws to nature, and not the reverse.

Hegel's philosophical system expands upon this philosophy, which has reality depend on the rational mind for its perception. Hegel's absolute Idealism unites the totality of all concepts in the absolute mind or spirit, which he also referred to as the ultimate reality, or God. Hegel's metaphysics thus takes from German Romanticism the "inward path" to truth; the notion of nature as spirit, or the immanence of God within the universe; the quest for the totality of experience, both empirical and rational; and the desire for infinity.

Hegel argued that reality belongs to an absolute mind or a totality of conceptual truth, and that it consists of a rational structure characterized by a unity-amid-diversity. The purpose of metaphysics is to reveal the truth of this unified diversity. To this end, Hegel developed his highly influential theory of dialectic, a process involving three concepts: the thesis, the antithesis, and the synthesis. This dialectical process provides a way of transcending oppositions to a higher level of truth. Hegel argued that the dialectical triad, as the rhythm of reality, underlies all human knowledge and experience. Moreover, he defined the absolute mind as being the totality of concepts in a dialectical process. Yet Hegel believed that contradictions are never entirely overcome. Rather, the dialectic is both the essence of reality and the method for comprehending reality, which is always a unity-amid-diversity. Hegel's notion of conceptual truth, being immanent within the world, is time-bound rather than transcendental, despite his ambiguous reference to the absolute mind as God. Hegel's dialectic thus differs from that of Plato, which gives rise to timeless forms.

On the basis of his dialectic, Hegel begins *The Phenomenology of Spirit* by introducing his theory that the history of philosophy is a biography of the human spirit in its development over the course of centuries. The relationship between successive philosophies is one not of conflict but of organic growth and development. Hegel describes philosophy as a living and growing organism like the world itself. Each philosophy corresponds to the stage of a plant: the bud, the blossom, and the fruit. In addition to organicism, Hegel developed the metaphor of historicism, which holds that the understanding of any aspect of life is derived through its history, its evolution, and not through its static condition in the present. Hegel ends *The Phenomenology of Spirit* by arguing that the age of reason and philosophy must supersede the age of religious consciousness. He also argued that history evolves toward a specific goal, a state of freedom, and that the purpose of history is the unfolding of the truth of reason. Hegel's arguments on this topic are collected in his *Sämtliche Werke* (1927; translated in *Lectures on the Philosophy of History*, 1956).

During the time Hegel taught in Nuremberg, he published *Wissenschaft der Logik* (1812-1816; *Science of Logic*, 1929) and *Encyclopädie der Philosophischen im Grundrisse* (1817; *Encyclopedia of Philosophy*, 1959). Hegel regarded the latter as having a dialectical structure, with the opposites of thought and nature united in mind and society, and ultimately in the self-referential act of philosophical self-consciousness. In 1811, Hegel married Maria von Tucher of Nuremberg, and in 1816 his nine-year-old illegitimate son, Ludwig, joined the household. Also in 1816, Hegel became a professor at the University of Heidelberg and in 1817 for the first time taught aesthetics. By this time, his reputation was so well established that the Prussian minister of education invited him to accept the prestigious chair of philosophy at the University of Berlin, where Hegel taught from 1818 until his death during a cholera epidemic in 1831.

During this final period, the climax of his career, Hegel lectured for the first time on the philosophy of religion and the philosophy of history. He published one of the great works of genius of Western culture, *Grundlinien der Philosophie des Rechts* (1821; *Philosophy of Right*, 1875), which exemplifies the mature or late Hegel in contrast to the early Hegel seen in *The Phenomenology of Spirit*. Hegel argued in his moral philosophy that ethics, like the individual, has its source, course, and ultimate fulfillment in the nation-state, particularly the state of Germany. The nation-state is a manifestation of God, which Hegel defines not as a personal God but rather as the Absolute. This totality of truth manifests itself in stages to each of the key nations of history, culminating in Germany.

During the 1820's, Hegel toured Belgium and the Netherlands and also traveled to Vienna and Prague. In 1824, he interceded with the Prussian government to free his friend Victor Cousin, a French liberal philosopher. Hegel was not an eloquent lecturer, but after his death, a group of his students collated their lecture notes and published an edition of his works in eighteen volumes (1832-1840). Hegel's writing is notoriously difficult, both stylistically and conceptually.

Summary

Georg Wilhelm Friedrich Hegel's Idealist philosophy has been criticized for elevating the reality of concepts over the material aspects of reality, such as economics, environment, technology, and natural resources. Moreover, there seems to be a contradiction in Hegel's notion of the Absolute, in his definition of God as being externalized or existing in human consciousness. Finally, Hegel's philosophy of history has been criticized for masking a hidden defense for German nationalism, an aversion for democracy and individualism, and a fear of revolutionary change.

Nevertheless, Hegel has contributed many profound concepts to Western philosophy: the dialectical nature of thought, organicism and historicism, the concept of culture, the theory of ethics, and the theory of humanity's need for wholeness, in terms of both consciousness and social unification. Hegel believed that there are three important dialectical stages in ethical life responsible for social unity: the family, its antithesis in civil society, and their synthesis in the developed national state. As the French philosopher Maurice Merleau-Ponty says, "All the great philosophical ideas of the past century, the philosophies of Marx, Nietzsche, existentialism and psycho-analysis had their beginning in Hegel."

Although he supported Christianity, Hegel placed philosophy above religion. He believed that religion and art are different ways of understanding the absolute idea, but that philosophy is a better way because it allows one to comprehend the absolute conceptually, not in religious symbols, and thereby subsumes both religion and art. For Hegel, ethical ideals, such as the ideals of freedom, originate in the spiritual life of a society.

Bibliography

Butler, Clark. *G. W. F. Hegel.* Boston: Twayne, 1977. A comprehensive study of Hegel that aims not to be merely about Hegel but to communicate the essence of Hegelian philosophy to a wider public. Presenting Hegelianism in an abstract philosophical context, Butler strives to be accessible but not oversimplistic. Approaches Hegel from the cultural standpoint of the present. Contains a selected annotated bibliography and a chronology of Hegel's life.

Christensen, Darrel E., ed. *Hegel and the Philosophy of Religion: The Wofford Symposium.* The Hague: Martinus Nijhoff, 1970. Collection from the proceedings of the first conference of the Hegel Society of America. These excellent essays analyze many aspects of Hegel's philosophy of religion in relation to his historical context, his philosophical system, and the philosophies of Immanuel Kant, Friedrich Wilhelm Nietzsche, and Karl Marx. More appropriate for the advanced student.

Findlay, J. N. *Hegel: A Re-examination.* London: Allen and Unwin, and New York: Macmillan, 1958. Findlay is the one most responsible for reviving Hegel scholarship in the English-speaking world. Provides a close exposition of Hegel's system, paragraph-by-paragraph, and is especially good in its treatment of his logic and philosophy of nature.

Hegel, Georg Wilhelm Friedrich. *Hegel: The Essential Writings.* Edited by F. G. Weiss. New York: Harper, 1974. Contains an excellent introduction to Hegel's philosophy and also concise introductions to the different selections, which include *Encyclopedia of the Philosophical Sciences in Outline*, *The Phenomenology of Spirit*, and *Philosophy of Right*. Weiss also provides a useful annotated bibliography of primary and secondary texts. A popular text for introductory college philosophy.

Houlgate, Stephen, ed. *Hegel and the Philosophy of Nature*. Albany: State University of New York Press, 1998. New study of Hegel's philosophy of the natural world that concludes it is still significant despite nineteenth and twentieth century scientific developments.

Houlgate, Stephen. *The Hegel Reader*. Oxford and Malden, Mass.: Blackwell, 1998. The most comprehensive collection of Hegel's writings currently available in English, this volume includes an extensive bibliography listing the main German works, most of the available English translations, and several secondary readings.

Kojève, Alexandre. *Introduction to the Reading of Hegel: Lectures on the Phenomenology*. Edited by A. Bloom. Translated by J. H. Nichols. New York: Basic Books, 1969. Although he describes Hegel's thought as historicist and atheistic, Kojève has been instrumental in reviving Hegel's philosophy. Appropriate for beginning students;

makes lucid Hegel's influential theories in *The Phenomenology of Spirit*.

Lavine, T. Z. *From Socrates to Sartre: The Philosophic Quest*. New York: Bantam Books, 1984. A survey of six major Western philosophers, Hegel being the fourth and receiving a sixty-page condensed review. Lavine lucidly presents for the general public Hegel's life and work in relation to his intellectual and historical context, highlighting Hegel's influence on the theories of Marx. The book was aired as a Public Broadcasting Service television series.

Singer, Peter. *Hegel*. Oxford and New York: Oxford University Press, 1983. A clearly written, ninety-page book in the Past Masters series intended for readers with no background in philosophy. Singer provides a broad overview of Hegel's ideas and a summary of his major works. He also discusses Hegel's influence on Marx and the Young Hegelians. Contains a useful index.

William S. Haney II

HEINRICH HEINE

Born: December 13, 1797; Düsseldorf
Died: February 17, 1856; Paris, France
Area of Achievement: Literature
Contribution: Through his literary and journalistic works, Heine exposed the hypocrisy and oppressiveness of feudal society as it existed in many parts of Europe during the first half of the nineteenth century.

Early Life

Chaim Harry Heine was born in Düsseldorf, the economic and cultural capital of the German Rhineland, into a respected Jewish family. His father, Samson, was a moderately successful textile merchant, who had little influence on Heinrich's upbringing. Indeed, the boy was reared almost exclusively by his well-educated, rationalist mother, Betty, who instilled in him—as well as in his siblings Charlotte, Gustav, and Maximilian—a deep sense of justice and morality, on the one hand, and an aversion for anything deemed impractical (such as art, literature, and theater), on the other.

Despite his mother's efforts, Heine was eventually introduced to the arts and humanities—and also to Christian ideology—when he, at age ten, enrolled in the Jesuit school near his home. There, encouraged by his teachers, he began to develop his innate talent for writing, a talent upon which he hoped to build one day a viable literary career. His parents envisioned an entirely different future for him, however, and sent him to Hamburg in 1817 to begin an apprenticeship in business with his uncle Salomon Heine, a wealthy and influential banker, who was to become his longtime benefactor. Salomon attempted to transform his rather reluctant nephew into a true entrepreneur and even established a textile trading firm in the boy's name, but Salomon finally succumbed to the youth's wish to study law at the University of Bonn.

Once in Bonn, Heine did not pursue jurisprudence as he had originally planned, but instead took his course work in literature and history. Most noteworthy among his courses was a metrics seminar taught by the famed German Romanticist August Wilhelm von Schlegel, from whom he received valuable advice concerning the style and form of his early poetic attempts. After a year in Bonn, Heine transferred to the University of Göttingen to begin his legal studies in earnest, but involvement in a duel—strictly prohibited by university code—soon forced him to transfer again.

In 1821, he settled in Berlin, where he continued his education by electing courses in law and by visiting a series of lectures held by the renowned philosopher Georg Wilhelm Friedrich Hegel, a major proponent of the historical dialectic, of the history of ideas, and of personal and intellectual freedom. While in Berlin, Heine was befriended by Karl and Rahel Varnhagen von Ense, a liberal aristocrat and his outspoken Jewish wife, who were the focal points of a literary salon frequented by Hegel and other intellectual luminaries of the day. At the age of twenty-seven, Heine returned to Göttingen to complete his legal studies, earning his doctorate in 1825, a year significant in that it also marks his conversion to Christianity and thus to a way of life which could, in his estimation, promote him from a Jewish outsider to an active participant in European culture.

Life's Work

Heine's career as a writer—inspired by the events of his youth, which culminated in a series of travels to Poland, England, northern Germany, and the Harz Mountains during the 1820's—formally began in 1827, when he published his immensely popular *Buch der Lieder* (*Book of Songs*, 1856), which pairs such traditionally Romantic elements as idealism, melancholy, and sentimentality with a unique brand of satire and irony. This collection, containing poems written as early as 1819, has love or, more specifically, unrequited love as its central theme. It no doubt was influenced by Heine's unsuccessful attempt at wooing his cousin Amalie during his apprenticeship in Hamburg.

The year 1827 proved to be an eventful year for Heine. In addition to his *Book of Songs*, he published two volumes of *Reisebilder* (*Pictures of Travel*, 1855), describing his aforementioned trips and containing detailed commentaries on social and political ills, especially the oppression of Jews, blacks, and other minorities in many parts of Europe. *Pictures of Travel* brought Heine instant fame and notoriety—so much so, in fact, that Johann Friedrich von Cotta, the liberal-minded publisher of the great German masters Johann Wolfgang von Goethe and Friedrich Schiller, invited him to Munich early in 1827 to become coeditor of a new journal, *Politische Annalen* (political annals). Not particularly overjoyed by this offer because he had set his sights on a university appointment, Heine allowed himself a considerable amount of time to complete the journey to Munich from the north German city of Lüneburg, his home since 1825. Indeed, he made lengthy stops while en route, visiting the famous folklorists Jakob and Wilhelm Grimm in Kassel and Ludwig Börne, one of Germany's most controversial political writers, in Frankfurt. When he finally did arrive in Munich, he was only willing to commit himself to the *Politische Annalen* for a scant six months.

In the latter half of 1828, Heine left Bavaria and, following Goethe's example, traveled to northern Italy. His sojourn in this romantic area was cut short, however, by news of his father's death, upon which followed a rather abrupt return to Germany. Heine now settled with his grieving mother at the home of his Uncle Salomon in Hamburg. There, he put forth two additional volumes of *Pictures of Travel* (1830-1831), in which he primarily recounted his Italian travels. He also used these volumes to comment on the political situation in France, a na-

tion which had, in July, 1830, experienced a revolution, in the course of which the Bourbon Charles X was replaced by the more liberal "citizen-king," Louis-Philippe. So enthralled was Heine by this development that he proclaimed France the new "Promised Land" of the liberal cause and, in so doing, contrasted it with conservative Germany, still ruled by the oppressive proponents of the old feudal order.

In May, 1831, Heine, still subsidized by his Uncle Salomon, journeyed to Paris to experience the new wave of liberalism at first hand. There, he joined the ranks of the ultraliberal Saint-Simonians and, as a foreign correspondent for the *Allgemeine Zeitung* (city of Augsburg newspaper), attempted to acquaint Germans with the major tenets of French progressivism. Heine also attempted, in book form, to acquaint Germans with contemporary trends in French literature through the various volumes of his *Der Salon* (1834-1840; *The Salon*, 1893), which combine commentaries written in a distinctly conversational tone with a variety of original literary pieces, including the fragmentary novel *Der Rabbi von Bacherach* (1887; *The Rabbi of Bacherach*, 1891).

Heine was extremely popular in France. His extensive circle of admirers included such luminaries as Honoré de Balzac, Victor Hugo, George Sand, Hector Berlioz, and Frédéric Chopin. In his native Germany, however, where the archconservative Metternich government banned his works in 1835 because they allegedly represented an affront against "altar and throne," his circle of supporters was comparatively small. In fact, it was not until 1840, the year the ban was lifted, that it again became safe to appreciate Heine in Germany.

The year 1840 is significant in that it also marks the beginning of a very productive period in Heine's life, during which he resumed his reports for the *Allgemeine Zeitung* and began work on a wide variety of literary projects. These included the well-known mock epics *Atta Troll* (1847; English translation, 1876) and *Deutschland: Ein Wintermärchen* (1844; *Germany: A Winter's Tale*, 1892), both of which were directed against the hypocrisy and self-righteousness of the German bourgeoisie. In 1843, Heine interrupted his heavy work schedule for several months to travel to Hamburg, where he met with his mother as well as with his publishers at the firm of Hoffmann and Campe. Accompanying him on this journey was Mathilde (née Eugénie

Mirat), his Belgian-born wife of nearly two years. Shortly after he returned to Paris in 1844, his Uncle Salomon died, leaving Heine's economic future uncertain. His health also began to fail drastically, and in 1848, the year of the German revolution, his health deteriorated completely, leaving him a cripple, permanently confined to his bed.

Almost miraculously, Heine managed to remain lucid throughout the entire ordeal and, on his better days, even continued his writing. Using secretaries, he was able to produce a final great collection of poems in 1851, *Romanzero* (English translation, 1859).

After eight years of intense suffering, Heine—having readied many of his writings for publication in a collected works—died in February, 1856, at the age of fifty-eight. According to his wishes, he was buried in Paris' Montmartre Cemetery under a headstone bearing the simple yet significant inscription: "Here lies a German poet."

Summary

Heinrich Heine's fame is rooted primarily in his lyric poetry, which not only gave rise to some of the most beloved folk songs ever written in the German language but also appeared in countless foreign translations. On the basis of his early poetry, Heine is often classified as a major proponent of the Romantic tradition. In truth, however, he often criticized the Romantic movement for its idealism and its lack of social and political commitment. During the turbulent period preceding the Revolution of 1848, he called for a new German literature focusing on such pressing issues of the day as human rights, women's emancipation, and equal representation of the masses in national government. Indeed, Heine is still known as one of Germany's most outspoken champions of the liberal cause. His name is frequently associated with the progressive Saint-Simonians in France as well as with Young Germany, a prerevolutionary movement among liberal authors, of which Heine was generally regarded the spiritual leader.

Heine has often (and by no means incorrectly) been described as an anomaly, a literary outsider of sorts, who combines Judaism and Christianity, Romanticism and realism, rationality and imagination, and beautiful verses and the most biting forms of satire and irony in a single person. Yet it is Heine's uniqueness which has prompted such a lively interest in his life and works, an interest which has led to the formation of both a Heine Institute and a Heine Society in Düsseldorf and which has spawned countless scholarly publications throughout the world.

Bibliography

Atkins, H. G. *Heine*. London: Routledge, and New York: Dutton, 1929. A standard biography providing detailed information on Heine's life and work. Characterizes Heine as an unusually gifted poet but, at the same time, questions the validity of his political writings. Includes an excellent bibliography of secondary sources.

Brod, Max. *Heinrich Heine: The Artist in Revolt*. Translated by Joseph Witriol. New York: New York University Press, and London: Vallentine, 1957. A standard biography which frequently utilizes excerpts from Heine's works to shed light on important facts and events. Deals at length with Jewish-Gentile relationships and their bearing on Heine's life and career. Short but useful bibliography.

Browne, Lewis. *That Man Heine*. New York: Macmillan, 1927. This well-written, highly entertaining biography focuses on Heine's outsider status in terms of both literature and society. It characterizes his existence as a constant exile from the German feudal order. Bibliography centers on biographical references.

Butler, E. M. *Heinrich Heine: A Biography*. London: Hogarth Press, 1956; New York: Philosophical Library, 1957. This colorful account focuses on the Saint-Simonian influences on Heine, on his discovery of the Dionysian experience for German literature, and on his final years of great physical and emotional suffering spent in his "mattress grave."

Fejtö, François. *Heine: A Biography*. Translated by Mervyn Savill. London: Allan Wingate, 1946. A detailed account of Heine's life, aimed at identifying "the very essence of the man." Attempts to explain the personality capable of producing such a timeless and widely acclaimed work of art as the *Book of Songs*. Bibliography includes many sources on Heine's relationship to France.

Justis, Diana L. *The Feminine in Heine's Life and Oeuvre: Self and Other*. New York: Lang, 1997. Justis provides a comprehensive psychological analysis of Heine's attitude towards women.

Pawel, Ernst. *The Poet Dying: Heinrich Heine's Last Years in Paris*. New York: Farrar, Straus, and Giroux, 1995. A wonderfully written account of

Heine's final years spent in exile in Paris as a result of his attacks on German political oppression.

Rose, William. *The Early Love Poetry of Heinrich Heine: An Inquiry into Poetic Inspiration.* Oxford: Clarendon Press, 1962. In this excellent book, the author investigates—and seriously questions—the extent to which Heine's early love poetry can be viewed as an autobiographical confession.

Sammons, Jeffrey L. *Heinrich Heine: A Modern Biography.* Manchester: Carcanet New Press, and Princeton, N.J.: Princeton University Press, 1979. One of the most critical studies ever written on Heine's life and work. The poet emerges as a problematic individual, perpetually at odds with his surroundings. This biography is fully documented and avoids the subjectivity which pervades many early treatments of Heine's life. Contains an excellent discussion of Heine's reception in Germany as well as a useful bibliography.

Spencer, Hanna. *Heinrich Heine.* Boston: Twayne, 1982. This Twayne series book represents a brief introduction to Heine's life and works geared specifically to the beginning student of German literature. It includes a chronology of Heine's life, interpretations of his major works, and a select, annotated bibliography containing a large number of primary and secondary sources in English.

Dwight A. Klett

HERMANN VON HELMHOLTZ

Born: August 31, 1821; Potsdam, Prussia
Died: September 8, 1894; Berlin, Germany
Areas of Achievement: Physiology and physics
Contribution: Helmholtz contributed to the fields of energetics, physiological acoustics and optics, mathematics, hydrodynamics, and electrodynamics. His most important work was in establishing the principle of conservation of energy and in his experimental and theoretical studies of hearing and vision.

Early Life

Hermann Ludwig Ferdinand von Helmholtz was the eldest of four children born to Ferdinand and Caroline Penne Helmholtz. His mother was a descendant of William Penn. His father studied philology and philosophy at the University of Berlin and was a teacher at the Potsdam *Gymnasium*. He was a typical product of German Romanticism and Idealistic philosophy, with strong interests in music and art. These interests were passed on to his son, especially music, and became important aspects of his life and later work in physiological acoustics and optics.

Helmholtz was a sickly child, not entering the *Gymnasium* until the age of nine, but he advanced rapidly and was encouraged by his father to memorize the works of Johann Wolfgang von Goethe, Friedrich Schiller, and the Greek poet Homer. His interest soon turned to physics. In 1837, he received a scholarship to study medicine at the Friedrich Wilhelm Institute in Berlin, with the provision that he would serve for eight years as an army surgeon after completing his degree.

While in Berlin, Helmholtz supplemented his medical studies with many science courses at the University of Berlin and studied mathematics on his own. In 1841, he began research under the great physiologist Johannes Peter Müller, who followed the German tradition of vitalism in explaining the unique characteristics of living organisms. Helmholtz joined the circle of Müller's students, including Emil Du Bois-Reymond, Ernst Wilhelm von Brücke, and Carl Friedrich Wilhelm Ludwig, and they later became known as the Helmholtz school of physiology for their rejection of the nonphysical vital forces in favor of purely physical and chemical explanations of life processes.

Helmholtz completed his medical degree in 1842, with a dissertation showing that nerve fibers are connected to ganglion cells. After some further research on fermentation that seemed to support vitalism, he was appointed as army surgeon to the regiment at Potsdam. From that time on, he wrote at least one major paper every year except 1849, publishing more than two hundred articles and books before he died. In 1849, he was granted an early release from his military duty to accept an appointment as associate professor of physiology at Königsberg. Just before leaving Potsdam, he married Olga von Velten, the daughter of a physician, by whom he had two children.

Life's Work

Helmholtz began to make major contributions to science even during his five-year tour of duty in the army, when he had little free time or laboratory facilities. Pursuing the ideas of the chemist Justus von Liebig, he made a quantitative study with home-made apparatus of the effects produced by muscle contraction and showed that it is accompanied by chemical changes and heat production. With this experimental evidence for transformation of energy (or force, as he called it), he undertook to establish the general principle that energy remains constant in all processes, whether animate or inanimate.

Arguing from the impossibility of perpetual motion with surprising mathematical sophistication, he demonstated the principle of conservation of energy in its most general form and used it to refute vitalism. In 1847, "Über die Erhaltung der Kraft" ("On the Conservation of Force," 1853) was presented to the Physical Society in Berlin. The importance of this discovery led to fierce controversy over scientific priorities, but Helmholtz willingly shared the credit. Julius Robert von Mayer's prior announcement of this principle in 1842 was unknown to Helmholtz, whose work was much more detailed and comprehensive. James Prescott Joule is also given credit for this discovery for providing the first experimental verification.

After moving to his first academic post at Königsberg in 1849, Helmholtz began to try to measure the speed of nerve impulses, which Müller had considered too fast to be measured. This work led to the invention of the myograph for measuring short intervals from marks on a revolv-

ing drum. In 1851, he succeeded in measuring the speed along a frog's nerve by stimulating it at increasing distances from the muscle and found it to be surprisingly slow at about 30 meters per second. About the same time, he invented the ophthalmoscope, which brought him world fame in the field of medicine. This invention made it possible for the first time to view the inside of the living human eye, opening up the field of ophthalmology.

In 1855, Helmholtz became a professor of anatomy and physiology at Bonn. Continuing his work on sensory physiology, he published the first of three volumes of his massive *Handbuch der physiologischen Optik* (1856; *Treatise on Physiological Optics*, 1924). He also wrote several papers on acoustics. His interest in acoustics led to his first paper on theoretical physics in 1858, creating the mathematical foundations of hydrodynamics by finding vortex solutions. At this time he accepted a position as professor of physiology at Heidelberg.

After moving to Heidelberg in 1858, Helmholtz established the new Physiological Institute. At Bonn, his wife's health had started to deteriorate, and she died in 1859. During this stressful period,

he achieved his greatest success in acoustical research, formulating his resonance theory of hearing, which explains the detection of differing pitches through variations of progressively smaller resonators in the spiral cochlea of the inner ear. He also published analyses of vibrations in open-ended pipes and of the motion of violin strings. In 1861, he wed Anna von Mohl, by whom he had three more children. In 1862, he completed the first edition of his highly influential treatise *Die Lehre von den Tonempfindungen als physiologische Grundlage für die Theorie der Musik* (1863; *On the Sensations of Tone as a Physiological Basis for the Theory of Music*, 1875).

During this time, Helmholtz also continued his optical research, amending Thomas Young's theory of color vision to distinguish between spectral primaries and physiological primaries of greater saturation. The resulting Young-Helmholtz theory could then explain all color perception by proper mixtures of three physiological primaries and could be used to explain red color blindness as well. He incorporated these results in the second volume of *Treatise on Physiological Optics* and began work on the third volume, in which binocular vision and depth judgments were treated. This included a defense of empiricism against the nativist view that some aspects of perception are innate, leading to original work in non-Euclidean geometry. After the third volume was published in 1867, he believed that the field of physiology had grown beyond the scope of any one person, and he turned his attention almost exclusively to physics.

In 1871, Helmholtz accepted the prestigious chair of physics at Berlin after Gustav Robert Kirchhoff had turned it down. A new Physical Institute was established and he became the director, with his living quarters in the institute. He began his research in Berlin with a series of papers on electrodynamics, which brought James Clerk Maxwell's electromagnetic field theory to the attention of continental physicists. In Germany, the interaction between electric charges was explained by Wilhelm Eduard Weber's law of instantaneous action at a distance rather than action mediated by a field in an intervening ether. Helmholtz developed a more general action-at-a-distance theory but included Maxwell's field theory as a limiting case, allowing for wave propagation at the speed of light. This work inspired his former student Heinrich Rudolph Hertz to do experiments leading to the discovery of radio waves in 1887.

Returning to his early interest in energetics, Helmholtz began to investigate energy processes in galvanic cells and in electrochemical reactions. This led him to the idea that electricity consists of discrete charges, or atoms of electricity, and that chemical forces are electrical in nature. Research in thermochemistry resulted in the concept of free energy that determines the direction of chemical reactions. An analysis of solar energy led to an estimate of 25 million years as the amount of time since the formation of the planets; this estimate was far too conservative, however, because of the ignorance of nuclear processes. In the late 1880's, he formulated a theory for cloud formation and storm mechanics. One of his last great efforts was an unsuccessful attempt to derive all of mechanics, thermodynamics, and electrodynamics from Sir William Rowan Hamilton's principle of least action.

Helmholtz was elected Reactor of the University of Berlin for one year in 1877. He was granted hereditary nobility by Emperor William I in 1882. Helmholtz became the first president of the new Physical-Technical Institute in 1888, freeing him from teaching so he could spend more time in research. For several years, he had suffered from migraines and fits of depression, which only long vacations seemed to cure. In 1893, he traveled to the United States as a delegate of the German government to the Electrical Congress at Chicago. On his return voyage, he fell down the ship's stairs and injured his head. A year later, he suffered a cerebral hemorrhage, and, after two months of semiconsciousness, he died.

Summary

Hermann von Helmholtz was one of the leaders among German scientists who rebelled against the scientific romanticism of the first half of the nineteenth century. He successfully replaced vitalism with a rigorous physicochemical empiricism, but he also shared the goal of his predecessors in his desire to find unifying principles in nature. He succeeded in this goal with his elaboration of the principle of the conservation of energy. He demonstrated the interconnections among physiology, chemistry, medicine, and physics; he fell short, however, in his efforts to extend the principle of least action. Especially important were his three-color theory of vision, his resonance theory of hearing, and his invention of the ophthalmoscope.

Helmholtz also contributed to the transition of German universities from teaching academies to research institutions. The great laboratories he established at Heidelberg in physiology and at Berlin in physics placed Germany in the forefront of scientific research. Some of the most famous scientists at the end of the century had been his students, including Hertz, who discovered radio waves and the photoelectric effect, Max Planck, who introduced quantum theory, and the Americans Henry Augustus Rowland and Albert Abraham Michelson.

As a master and leader in biology, physics, and mathematics, he surpassed all others in the imposing theoretical and experimental treatises he produced, especially in sensory physiology. As perhaps the greatest scientist of the nineteenth century, he was the last scholar whose work embraced virtually all the sciences together with philosophy, mathematics, and the fine arts.

Bibliography

Boring, Edwin B. *Sensation and Perception in the History of Experimental Psychology.* New York and London: Appleton, 1942. This volume, dedicated to Helmholtz, is a comprehensive history of sensory physiology and psychology. Describes the work of Helmholtz in physiological optics and acoustics, its historical background, and later developments from his ideas.

Cahan, David, ed. *Hermann von Helmholtz and the Foundation of Nineteenth-Century Science.* Berkeley: University of California Press, 1993. A collection of fifteen essays focusing on the contributions of Helmholtz to the institutions, content, and goals of modern research science.

Elkana, Yehuda. *The Discovery of the Conservation of Energy.* Cambridge, Mass.: Harvard University Press, and London: Hutchinson, 1974. A history of the energy concept, including the physiological background and a chapter on the famous 1847 paper by Helmholtz on conservation of energy. Contains a bibliography and an appendix.

Helmholtz, Hermann von. *On the Sensations of Tone as a Physiological Basis for the Theory of Music.* Translated by Alexander Ellis. 3d ed. London and New York: Longman, 1895. An English translation of the fourth (and last) German edition (1877) of the great treatise on physiological acoustics. Includes a six-page introduction on the life of Helmholtz by Henry Margenau and a five-page bibliography of his major works with titles given in English translation.

Jungnickel, Christa, and Russell McCormmach. *Intellectual Mastery of Nature: Theoretical Physics from Ohm to Einstein.* Vol. 1, *The Torch of Mathematics, 1800-1870.* Chicago: University of Chicago Press, 1986. The first volume of this two-volume work on German science describes some of Helmholtz's physiological research. The second volume, *The Now Mighty Theoretical Physics, 1870-1925,* discusses his work in physics, especially in electrodynamics and energetics.

Königsberger, Leo. *Hermann von Helmholtz.* Translated by Frances Welby. New York: Dover, and Oxford: Clarendon Press, 1906. An abridged translation of the complete biography of Helmholtz in German published in 1906. The best source of information concerning his life and work, including discussions of his major publications.

Turner, R. Steven. *In the Eye's Mind: Vision and the Helmholtz-Hering Controversy.* Princeton, N.J.: Princeton University Press, 1994. Turner examines the actual controversy over human visual perception between Helmholtz and Ewald Hering and the broader issue of controversy's place in scientific development.

Warren, Richard, and Roslyn Warren. *Helmholtz on Perception: Its Physiology and Development.* New York: Wiley, 1968. Contains the English translations of six selections from lectures and articles by Helmholtz on sensory physiology. Includes a thirteen-page sketch of his life and work, a six-page evaluation of his work on sensory perceptions, and a five-page bibliography.

Joseph L. Spradley

JOSEPH HENRY

Born: December 17, 1797; Albany, New York
Died: May 13, 1878; Washington, D.C.
Area of Achievement: Science
Contribution: As the first secretary of the Smithsonian Institution, president of the National Academy of Sciences, and a leading experimental physicist, Henry was one of the most important molders of an American professional scientific community.

Early Life

The descendant of Scots who had immigrated to North America at the time of the Revolutionary War, Joseph Henry was born in Albany, New York, on December 17, 1797. His father, William Henry, was a cartman—a hauler and mover—of very modest financial circumstances, but his mother, née Ann Alexander, was from a more affluent family. Henry was brought up by an uncle in Galway, New York, and educated in the village school, learning arithmetic, reading, and writing (but very little about spelling, as his future letters would demonstrate). At age ten, he was working in a general store. The death of his father in 1811 and his uncle shortly thereafter led to his return to Albany, where he was apprenticed to a silversmith, but was attracted to the theater.

According to Henry's later recollection, the turning point in his life occurred in about 1815 when he read a popular introduction to the physical sciences, William Gregory's *Lectures on Experimental Philosophy, Astronomy and Chemistry* (1808), the first book he had ever read with attention. The questions that Gregory asked and answered about the way the natural world behaved piqued Henry's interest and led to his decision to devote his life to science.

The reality of his situation, however, was a lack of any training in science and the immediate need to earn a living. Henry worked as an actor, a schoolteacher, and a private tutor during the late teens and early twenties of the nineteenth century. Most important for his future, he attended the Albany Academy as an overage student between 1819 and 1822, his only formal education beyond the elementary level. His intelligence, capacity for hard work, ambition, and determination attracted the attention of the faculty of the academy and the scientific leaders of the community, leading to his election as a member of the Albany Lyceum of Natural History and its successor, the Albany Institute. He found work as a tutor and a surveyor until his appointment in September, 1826, as professor of mathematics and natural philosophy (physics) at the Albany Academy.

Life's Work

The Albany Academy was not the ideal place for an ambitious scientist. The teaching load was very heavy and much of it was on the elementary level, providing little intellectual stimulation. Research facilities were limited. Still, Henry's years on its faculty were very fruitful, marked by great creativity and insight. He initiated his lifelong research program of exploring the phenomena of and interrelationship of the so-called "imponderables"—electricity, magnetism, light, and heat—the major field of research in the physical sciences during the first half of the nineteenth century. During his Albany years, he developed his great electromagnet, created the telegraph, invented the first electric motor,

and discovered (independently of Michael Faraday) electromagnetic self-induction and mutual electromagnetic induction. The Henry of this phase, however, was a scientist who was not in control of his research program. Both of his major publications of this period were in response to European scientists announcing discoveries paralleling or anticipating Henry's research. In the case of the electromagnet, it was Gerrit Moll; in the case of induction, it was Faraday. He was always in danger of losing his claim of priority, of being ignored by the European community. He was not, however, ignored by his compatriots. His fame, especially for his great electromagnet, led to a professorship at the College of New Jersey (now Princeton University) in 1832, despite the lack of a college degree.

The man who arrived in Princeton in November, 1832, to teach natural philosophy was a mature family man. He had married Harriet Alexander, a first cousin, in 1830, and had a son by this time. Three daughters would follow.

Paintings and photographs of Henry show an oval visage and stocky build. He had brown hair, gray eyes, and a light complexion. As he aged he put on weight. At five feet, ten inches, he must have given the physical impression of solidity, which was also one of his significant mental traits.

Henry's chief characteristic, however, was his curiosity. No natural phenomenon was too trivial for observation or experimentation, whether it was snow melting on his porch, light changing color as it passed through a syrup, or water evaporating while being heated for shaving. This curiosity may explain why he often experimented in short, intense bursts with frequent shifts among topics. With all the unanswered questions to be examined, Henry had difficulty giving a single problem his undivided attention.

His years at Princeton were his most productive quantitatively. During this period, he examined lightning paths, discovered the concept of the transformer and the oscillational nature of the discharge of a capacitor, became the first individual to measure empirically the temperature difference between sunspots and the solar surface, and studied ultraviolet light—simply to point out the highlights.

These were also the years of his friendly interaction with Samuel F. B. Morse. Their first documented contact was in 1839, and subsequently Henry supplied Morse with technical advice and private and public support for his telegraph. By 1846, however, Henry was unhappy over what he perceived to be Morse's failure to give Henry proper credit for his contributions to the invention and development of a practical electromagnetic telegraph. Ultimately, the two men found themselves on opposite sides during the various court tests of Morse's telegraph patent in the 1850's.

By that time, Henry was in Washington, D. C. In December, 1846, he had accepted the position as secretary (director) of the newly established Smithsonian Institution. Although there had been tremendous confusion in Congress over the meaning of James Smithson's bequest to the United States to establish an institution for "the increase and diffusion of knowledge," there was no confusion in Henry's mind. The funds provided a unique opportunity to support research and scholarly publication, to encourage cooperation and international exchange. Henry defeated an effort to use the bequest to develop a national library and worked out an arrangement with Congress for the federal government to support the National Museum, which was under Smithsonian management, through appropriations. This left Henry relatively free to support research in a diversity of fields, including meteorology, botany, zoology, anthropology, and archaeology.

Administrative responsibilities did not leave much time, however, for personal scientific research. The acoustics of public buildings and investigations of fog-signals for the United States Light-House Board were the only major projects carried out by Henry during his years as secretary.

There were also the responsibilities that came from being a senior leader of the scientific community. During 1849-1850, Henry served as president of the American Association for the Advancement of Science. One of the original members of the National Academy of Sciences, he was elected its president in 1868 and served in that office until his death, turning the academy into an impartial supporter of research and the voice of the American scientific community. He was president of the Philosophical Society of Washington from 1871 until his death and chairman of the Light-House Board during the same period.

After decades of excellent health, Henry was struck by temporary paralysis in December, 1877. A victim of Bright's disease, Henry died in the Smithsonian Institution building on May 13, 1878.

Summary

When speaking of Henry, his contemporaries often compared him to Benjamin Franklin. The contributions to the understanding of electricity, the preeminence within the scientific community, and the international standing of the two men were all analogous. Like Franklin, too, Henry was to make contributions to his country which proved to be more far-reaching than his scientific discoveries; the reputation which he secured as an experimenter gave him the prestige and respect necessary for his success as a science administrator and leader. On behalf of his vision of science, Henry was able to call upon the support of intellectuals, community leaders, and politicians. Intensely patriotic, Henry viewed the shortcomings of the American scientific community with dismay. As secretary of the Smithsonian and president of various scientific organizations, he nurtured America's small community of research-minded men and women, asserted the primacy of basic research over applied, and fought to raise American science to international standards and gain European recognition of American achievements. He served as an articulate spokesman for the power, value, and necessity of basic scientific research, as well as a symbol of what Americans could accomplish in science.

Bibliography

Cochrane, Rexmond Canning. *The National Academy of Sciences: The First Hundred Years, 1863-1963*. Washington, D.C.: National Academy of Sciences, 1978. An official history of the academy based upon its archives. Discussion of Henry and his circle dominates the early chapters.

Coulson, Thomas. *Joseph Henry: His Life and Work*. Princeton, N.J.: Princeton University Press, 1950. The standard biography, now dated. Although marred by factual errors and a lack of understanding of Henry's milieu, it is still useful.

Hafertepe, Kenneth. *America's Castle: The Evolution of the Smithsonian Building and Its Institution, 1840-1878*. Washington, D.C.: Smithsonian Institution Press, 1984. An architectural historian discusses Henry's struggle to focus the resources of the Smithsonian on the support of original research and the role the Smithsonian Building played in thwarting his dreams. Especially valuable for its insights into the political struggles surrounding the Smithsonian.

Henry, Joseph. *The Papers of Joseph Henry*. Edited by Nathan Reingold et al. 5 vols. Washington, D.C.: Smithsonian Institution Press, 1972- . When complete, this will be a fifteen-volume collection of approximately six thousand letters, diary entries, laboratory notebook entries, and other manuscripts.

Hinsley, Curtis M., Jr. *Savages and Scientists: The Smithsonian Institution and the Development of American Anthropology, 1846-1910*. Washington, D.C.: Smithsonian Institution Press, 1981. An excellent integrative history of the rise and professionalization of a discipline. Provides a case study of Henry's role as a supporter of research.

Hughes, Patrick. "Keepers of the Flame." *Weatherwise* 50, no. 5 (October-November 1997). Report on the joint effort of the National Academy of Sciences, the American Philosophical Society, and the Smithsonian Institution to preserve the important contributions of Henry.

Mabee, Carleton. *The American Leonardo: A Life of Samuel F. B. Morse*. New York: Knopf, 1943. This work presents a nonpartisan, well-researched account of the telegraph controversy.

Millikan, Frank. "Joseph Henry's Grand Meteorological Crusade: The Story of the Scientist who Invented the National Weather Service, on the 200th Anniversary of His Birth." *Weatherwise* 50, no. 5 (October-November 1997). Profile of Henry, first director of the Smithsonian Institution and founder of the organization that would eventually become the National Weather Service.

Reingold, Nathan, and Marc Rothenberg. "The Exploring Expedition and the Smithsonian Institution." In *Magnificent Voyagers: The U.S. Exploring Expedition, 1838-1842*, edited by Herman J. Viola and Carolyn Margolis, 243-253. Washington, D.C.: Smithsonian Institution Press, 1985. Considers the creation of the National Museum at the Smithsonian in the context of the need for the federal government to find a home for its scientific collections.

Washburn, Wilcomb E. "Joseph Henry's Conception of the Purpose of the Smithsonian Institution." In *A Cabinet of Curiosities: Five Episodes in the Evolution of American Museums*, edited by Walter Muir Whitehill, 106-166. Charlottesville: University Press of Virginia, 1967. Although challenged by recent scholarship which considers the picture presented of Henry as too simplistic, this article offers what has become the standard interpretation of Henry's attitude toward the Smithsonian and especially the role of a museum in the Institution.

Marc Rothenberg

O. HENRY
William Sydney Porter

Born: September 11, 1862; Greensboro, North Carolina

Died: June 5, 1910; New York, New York

Area of Achievement: Literature

Contribution: William Sydney Porter advanced the state of American short stories and made his pen name of O. Henry synonymous with surprise endings. In a little more than one decade, he published more than two hundred stories in magazines and books, some of which are still well known one century later.

Early Life

The life of William Sydney Porter was much like the literature he wrote as O. Henry: a short story punctuated by unforeseen twists. His opening took place in the North Carolina mountain town of Greensboro, where he was born in the midst of the Civil War and grew up under the postwar occupation government.

His father, Algernon Sidney Porter, had a well-known drinking problem and no medical degree, but he was known as the best doctor in the county. His mother, Mary Jane Virginia Swaim, died of tuberculosis when Porter was only three years old. Porter and his older brother Shirley ("Shell") were mostly raised in their grandmother's boarding house by their Aunt Lina, a schoolteacher who encouraged Porter's love of books. By age ten, he was reading Charles Dickens and Sir Walter Scott. At fifteen he left school and became an apprentice pharmacist in his uncle's drugstore, just as his father had done. Four years later, he was a licensed pharmacist.

In March of 1882, Porter went to Texas with family friends, hoping that the Texas climate would help his persistent, racking cough. He spent two years on the Dull-Hall Ranch near Cotulla, where he lived as a sheltered guest in Dick Hall's home doing very little real ranch work. He sent some stories and letters to Greensboro, some of which appeared in the local newspaper.

In 1884, the Halls deposited Porter in Austin, the state capital. He worked briefly in a pharmacy and then part-time in a cigar store, but mostly he did little for two and one-half years but socialize, sing in a quartet and church choirs, and serenade women. Late in 1886, he was given a job as a real-estate bookkeeper. He learned this job quickly, but soon moved to a $100-per-month job as a draftsman in Hall's new Texas Land Office. Many of his later stories drew on the experiences of his four years there. In January, 1891, Hall had lost his gubernatorial bid, so his job as land commissioner and Porter's job as draftsman both ended. Within one month, however, Porter's friends got him a new job as a bank teller, also at $100 per month.

Meanwhile, Porter's serenading had been fruitful. A rather normal-looking but foppish man at a height of 5 feet 7 inches, with broad shoulders, blue eyes, chestnut brown hair, and a fashionable mustache, he eloped with young Athol Estes on July 1, 1887, less than three weeks after her graduation from high school. Athol apparently stimulated Porter into more frequent writing, as he sold some humorous items to the *Detroit Free Press* in 1887. On May 6, 1888, they had a son who died only hours after birth. This seems to have begun the decline in Athol's health that finally resulted in her death nine years later. On September 30, 1889, she bore their only other child, Margaret.

Life's Work

In March, 1894, Porter and a partner bought a struggling scandal sheet and its press and used it to publish humorous commentary and stories, many of them poking fun at the large German community of central Texas. They soon changed its name to *The Rolling Stone*, stimulating Austin through the next twelve months.

A crucial change in Porter's life began in December, 1894, when bank examiner F. B. Gray uncovered shortages in the accounts and charged him with embezzlement of bank funds. Porter left the bank to spend more time with *The Rolling Stone*, but it folded in April. In July, a grand jury refused to indict Porter, but Gray persisted.

In October, 1895, Porter accepted a new job writing for the *Houston Post*. In February, 1896, Gray succeeded in getting four indictments against him. Porter wrote his last *Houston Post* column on June 22. On July 6, he boarded a train heading up to Austin for his trial; after fifty miles he apparently got off and, hours later, boarded an eastbound train to seek anonymity in New Orleans, Louisiana. With his excellent command of Spanish, he decided that he could build a new life in Honduras, which had no extradition treaty with the United States, and that he could then send for his wife and daughter to join him there until the statute of limitations expired. Honduras was at that time a stereotypical banana republic but politically more stable than most of its neighbors. Once there, he mixed with the swindlers, bank presidents, confidence men, and other brigands who would later populate some of his stories. The pueblo of Trujillo, Honduras, later became Coralio, Anchuria, in his *Cabbages and Kings* (1904).

The flaw in Porter's Honduras plan was that Athol's tuberculosis was too serious to let her leave her mother's care. In January, 1897, he returned to Austin. He posted a new court bond and spent the next several months caring for his wife until, on July 25, she died. Porter stayed in Austin writing freelance articles and stories. He finally went to trial on February 15, 1898. The evidence seems to imply that Porter was innocent but unwilling to implicate others. However, the jury convicted him on three counts, and he was sentenced to the lightest possible term, five years in the Ohio State Penitentiary.

When he became prisoner 30664 on April 25, 1898, he showed the strains of the past two years, during which he had lost his young wife, his home, his job, and his good name. The good news, though, was that he was allowed to work in the night shift of the prison pharmacy, leaving him plenty of time to write stories. It was there that he was to really begin the writing career that brought his fame. The twist, however, was that the more famous he became, the more he feared that people would discover his imprisonment. He submitted his stories through friends in New Orleans and elsewhere.

A model prisoner, he was released from prison on July 24, 1901, and went to Pittsburgh, Pennsylvania, to stay with Athol's parents and his twelve-year-old daughter. He wrote some stories and newspaper features, but it was soon clear that he hated Pittsburgh. In April, 1902, he moved to New York City, which he was to call "Baghdad by the Subway." In New York, Porter's frequent drinking companion Bill Williams said he "drank as the Southern gentleman he was and carried his liquor as a gentleman does. I . . . never once saw him or heard of his being intoxicated." While Porter might not have gotten roaring drunk, he nonetheless drank whiskey steadily throughout his short life. In 1909 he began to fade from cirrhosis of the liver. He spent six months back in North Carolina in hopes that the healthier environment might help to cure his illness but eventually moved back to New York City.

Porter collapsed on June 2, 1910, and friends took him to the Polyclinic Hospital. As an attending nurse dimmed the light on the evening of June 4, Porter said, "Turn up the lights. I don't want to go home in the dark." Porter died the following day soon after sunrise.

It was apparently in the Travis County Jail as Porter awaited transportation to Ohio that his middle name migrated from the "Sidney" of his birth and of his father to the "Sydney" of his later years. An April, 1898, letter addressed him as "Mr. Sydney Porter," and prison records also used "Sydney." On the other hand, many theories purport to explain how he settled on his plebeian nom de plume. The first story published by "O. Henry" was also the first one he wrote in prison: "Whistling Dick's Christmas Stocking," which drew on his experiences in New Orleans and appeared in *McClure's Magazine* in December, 1899. In the December, 1901, *Ainslee's Magazine*, he used "Olivier Henry."

While Porter was awaiting trial after his wife's death, McClure's Syndicate bought "The Miracle of Lava Canyon" and published it months later under the name of W. S. Porter. A revision of that story later appeared as "An Afternoon Miracle." In all, Porter used twelve different names for his writing, and it was several years before he settled on using only O. Henry. Some say the name was abbreviated from the name of a French pharmacist, Etienne Ossian Henry. Porter told one writer that he picked "Henry" from a list of notables in the New Orleans society pages, then a friend suggested using a single initial, and he decided that "O is about the easiest written." An Ohio Board of Clemency chairman noted that the prison had employed a Captain Orrin Henry who had retired eleven years before Porter's incarceration but whose signature Porter could well have seen.

Porter's reason for using the pen name is clearer than its precise origin: He was embarrassed about his prison record and did his best to keep it a secret from friends and public alike.

Summary

Even after his death, the ending of Porter's life story took a characteristically ironic twist. Somehow, the Little Church Around the Corner had scheduled a wedding for 11:00 A.M. on June 7—the same time as Porter's funeral. The bridegroom's brother, trying to hide this omen from the bride, told the wedding party that another wedding was under way, so they spent the next hour in a nearby hotel while William S. Porter and O. Henry were eulogized in the church.

In the decade after his death, Americans bought nearly five million copies of his books, second only to Rudyard Kipling. They were translated into French, Spanish, German, Swedish, Danish, Norwegian, Russian, and Japanese. Ironically, this man's stories of the Western and urban life of America became even more popular in the new Soviet Union than in his own country. While American writers were using the Russian Anton Chekhov as their model, Russian writers were putting out O. Henry twist endings. In 1962, a Soviet postage stamp commemorated the one hundredth anniversary of Porter's birth, although his own country had never so honored him. His Christmas story "The Gift of the Magi" eventually became universally known to American schoolchildren, and one of his characters, the Cisco Kid, became a mainstay first to many radio listeners and then to a new generation of television viewers.

Bibliography

Current-Garcia, Eugene. *O. Henry (William Sydney Porter)*. Boston: Twayne, 1965. Summarizes O. Henry's life in one chapter, then focuses on the literary influences of his southern upbringing, Texas development, prison experiences, and New York life. Includes chronological summary, endnotes, extensive bibliography, and index.

Langford, Gerald. *Alias O. Henry: A Biography of William Sidney Porter*. New York: Macmillan, 1957. Covers O. Henry's entire life, with emphasis on his two marriages, his time in Houston, and the evidence in his embezzlement trial. Includes photographs, endnotes, index, and an extensive appendix about *The Rolling Stone*.

Nolan, Jeannette Cowert. *O. Henry: The Story of William Sydney Porter*. New York: Messner, 1943. Written as a juvenile novel with fictional dialogue. Includes line drawings, list of articles in periodicals, and index.

O'Connor, Richard. *O. Henry: The Legendary Life of William S. Porter*. New York: Doubleday, 1953. Covers O. Henry's entire life. Includes photographs and index.

Porter, Jenny Lind, and Trueman E. O'Quinn. *Time to Write: How William Sidney Porter Became O. Henry*. Austin, Tex.: Eakin Press, 1986. Emphasizes the life of O. Henry in Texas. Includes index and twelve short stories written while he was in federal prison in Columbus, Ohio, each with notes.

Watson, Bruce. "If His Life Were a Short Story, Who'd Ever Believe It?" *Smithsonian* 27 (January 1997): 92-102. Biography strewn with anecdotes and some literary criticism. Includes photographs.

Williams, William Washington. *The Quiet Lodger of Irving Place*. New York: Dutton, 1936. Firsthand account of Porter's life in New York written by a longtime friend and newspaper reporter with emphasis on the people and locations that inspired many O. Henry stories.

J. Edmund Rush

ALEKSANDR HERZEN

Born: April 6, 1812; Moscow, Russia
Died: January 21, 1870; Paris, France
Areas of Achievement: Social reform and literature
Contribution: As one of the "fathers" of the Russian intelligentsia, Herzen urged an increased pace of Westernization for Russia, yet harbored a Slavophile attraction for the village commune. From his offices in London, he edited the influential émigré newspaper *Kolokol* (the bell) from 1857 to 1866, thereby helping to shape the direction of Russian radical opinion.

Early Life

Aleksandr Herzen was the illegitimate son of Ivan Alekseyevich Yakovlev, of a distinguished aristocratic family, and of Louise Ivanovich Haag, a German daughter of a minor official from Württemberg. The name "Herzen" was given him by his father to indicate that he was the product of matters of the "heart," as was his elder and also illegitimate brother, Yegor Herzen.

In the family home on Arbat Street in Moscow, young Herzen was isolated from many children, but he developed a close friendship with Nikolay Ogaryov, with whom he developed a lifelong partnership. Attracted to the Romanticism of Friedrich Schiller, the two boys took an oath to avenge the five Decembrist rebels executed by Czar Nicholas I after the abortive uprising of 1825. Both entered the University of Moscow in 1829, and Herzen joined the department of natural sciences. At the university, he also acquired a deep interest in history, philosophy, and politics. His circle of friends included Ogaryov, Nikolai Satin, Vadim Passek, Nikolai Kh. Ketscher, and Anton Savich. These friends reflected a popular mystical bent for politics, and they avidly read the works of Friedrich Schelling and Saint-Simon, espousing the radical democracy of brotherly love, idealism, and even socialism. In 1834, following a critical remark about the czar which was reported to the police, Herzen was arrested, jailed for nearly a year, and exiled to Perm and Viatka.

Life's Work

In 1838, after three years in exile, he married Natalya Alexandrovna Zakharina in Vladimir, and the next year they had a son, Aleksandr, Herzen's only surviving male heir. The czar pardoned Herzen in 1839, and he entered state service in Novgorod,

partly to qualify for noble status and partly to acquire the rights of inheritance. His work caused him to travel often to St. Petersburg, where he quarreled with Vissarion Grigoryevich Belinsky over the ideas of Georg Wilhelm Friedrich Hegel. Ironically, Belinsky abandoned Hegelian thought shortly before Herzen's own conversion to that system. Herzen won the admiration of Belinsky, however, when he published two installments of his early memoirs, *Zapiski odnogo molodogo cheloveka* (1840-1841; notebooks of a certain young man).

In 1840, Herzen again ran afoul of the authorities and was arrested, only to be released owing to his wife's illness. It was about this time that he rejected his wife's religious inspiration for Hegel's more radical thought, blaming police harassment for his wife's new illness and the subsequent death of their second child. He abandoned the Idealism of Schelling for the realism of Hegel and a materialist worldview; hence, he was regarded as a Left-Hegelian. He wrote *Diletantizm v nauke* (1843; dilettantism and science), an essay reflecting his new radicalism. His newfound hostility toward religion and all officialdom caused difficulties with his wife.

From 1842 to 1846, Herzen formed a new circle of friends in Moscow, including Ketscher, Satin, Vasily Petrovich Botkin, E. F. Korsh, Timofei Granovski, Mikhail Shchepkin, and Konstantin Kavelin. Belinsky and his St. Petersburg friends were sometimes in attendance. Although an avowed admirer of Western socialist thought, Herzen was increasingly attracted to the Russian peasant and the commune, central to the thought of the Slavophile community. The Slavophile attraction to religion and disdain for the West kept Herzen from entering their circles. In 1845-1846, Herzen published *Pisma ob izuchenii prirody* (letters on the study of nature), which combined his interest in science and philosophy.

In 1846, Herzen inherited a substantial fortune from his father, including a Moscow house and 500,000 rubles. That same year, he left Russia, never to return. His wife, his three children, his valet, and two of his friends escorted him to the West. The year of his departure, he published a novel, *Kto vinovat?* (1845-1846; *Who Is to Blame?*, 1978), in which he paid his homage to George Sand and the women's movement. In Europe, Herzen read deeply the socialist literature of Louis Blanc, Charles Fourier, and Pierre-Joseph Proudhon. There followed *Pisma iz Frantsii i Italii* (1854; letters from France and Italy), *Vom andern Ufer* (1850; *From the Other Shore*, 1956), "Lettre à M. Jules Michelet" (1851), and "Lettre d'un Russe à Mazzini" (1849). These works reflected his pessimistic reactions to the revolutions in Europe two years earlier; he concluded that western institutions were fatally ill.

His commitments to socialism and atheism made life difficult for his wife, Natalya, whose own affair with the German poet Georg Herwegh led to a crisis in the marriage. Shortly after the couple's reconciliation in 1851, their deaf-mute son, Nicholas, and Herzen's own mother died in a boating accident in the Mediterranean Sea. On May 2, 1852, his wife died after giving birth to a stillborn child.

In 1852, Herzen left for England, where he lived for the next eleven years. There he worked on his *Byloe i Dumy* (1861-1867; *My Past and Thoughts: The Memoirs of Alexander Herzen*, 1924-1927). In London, Herzen also founded a journal, *Poliarnaia zvezda* (the polar star), which was founded in the year that Nicholas died and on the exact anniversary of the rebellion of the five Decembrists, whose pictures were in the first issue. He wrote a public letter to the new czar, Alexander II, giving him advice on the need for freedom for his people.

During these years, Herzen's home in London was a haven for Russian revolutionaries. There, Herzen carried on a vigorous dispute with his boyhood friend Mikhail Bakunin. With the visiting Ogaryov, he launched his newspaper *Kolokol*, (the bell). It was Ogaryov who suggested the title, reminiscent of the assembly bell of the Novgorodian republic which Grand Prince Ivan III removed, an action symbolically destroying the freedom of that community in the fifteenth century. The paper was extremely popular for eight years in Russia, where it was distributed bimonthly, despite the interference of the security police. Throughout this period, Herzen campaigned for the emancipation of the serfs, relief from government censorship, elimination of corporal punishment, and establishment of legal due process.

Despite his disappointment with the terms of the emancipation edict in 1861, Herzen's revolutionary radicalism was muted, since he began to doubt the efficacy of violence. Younger radicals were drifting to the more uncompromising positions of Nikolay Chernyshevsky, depicted often as the leader of the "sons" among the intelligentsia. Fearing loss of influence among the young radicals, Herzen was persuaded by Bakunin to support the Polish rebels in 1863, thereby risking the loss of many moderate

liberals in Russia. By then Herzen seemed to have resolved his ambivalence toward revolution and to have approved the new radical party, Land and Freedom. When the expected peasant uprisings failed to occur, Herzen was left without his former supporters.

Meanwhile, complications arose in his personal life. Ogaryov's wife, Natalya, arrived in London in 1856, and she and Herzen began an affair that resulted in a daughter, born in 1858, and in twin boys two years later. Strangely enough he and Ogaryov remained close friends. Four years later, the twins died of diphtheria in Paris. In 1865, Herzen moved his paper and journal to Geneva, but publication ceased two years later. When the radicals of Sergey Gennadiyevich Nechayev attempted to enlist Herzen's support in new conspiracies, he was wise enough to resist. Ogaryov, however, used his portion of the fund from *Kolokol* to aid the new movement in 1869. That year, Herzen first began to mention to Ogaryov his desire to return home, and he wrote to Bakunin expressing new reservations about violent revolt. On January 21, 1870, however, after a short illness, Herzen died in Paris. His remains were later removed to Nice.

Summary

Through *Kolokol* Aleksandr Herzen gave advice to czar and radical alike. Influenced by German philosophy and French socialism, he belonged to those educated Russians who looked upon their own nation as backward. As Herzen grew older, however, he strengthened his belief in the values of the Russian peasant and his unique village commune. He viewed the Russian peasant not as a backward and embarrassing example of Russian culture but as an exemplar of moral purity. Observing the seamier side of Western industrialism and capitalism, Herzen, like the Slavophiles, saw an opportunity to build socialism in Russia with the peasantry. By avoiding industrial capitalism, Russia could catch up with and even surpass Western Europe. The village commune offered a romantic alternative to, and an escape route from, the urban degradation that marked so many European cities of his day.

Unlike his younger colleagues, Herzen saw hope in political reform. He once addressed the czar as a true populist and a benevolent father. When the emancipation came for the serfs, he was disappointed by the terms of the edict but nevertheless recognized that the government had moved in a liberal direction and that further reforms were to be expected. He reproached those who refused to see anything positive in the state reform. To Herzen, they were more interested in revolution as an end in itself than they were in bettering society. To the younger radicals, however, Herzen was a haughty nobleman offering advice to his servants.

If Herzen typified the fathers, Chernyshevsky typified the sons. This split among the intelligentsia of the 1860's was best described by the writer Ivan Turgenev in his novel *Ottsy i deti* (1862; *Fathers and Sons*, 1867). How understandable that Leo Tolstoy the famed pacifist novelist deplored the decline of Herzen's influence since his influence was the last opportunity for radicalism to avoid terror and bloodshed. Yet his ambivalent attitude toward revolution enabled liberal, radicals, and Marxists to claim his support. What was not ambivalent was his constant defense of the dignity and freedom of the individual.

Bibliography

Acton, Edward. *Alexander Herzen and the Role of the Intellectual Revolutionary.* Cambridge and New York: Cambridge University Press, 1979. Stresses the era of 1847-1863, when Herzen struggled with the concept of revolution. The author's biographical approach shows the interaction between Herzen's personal life and his career.

Gershenzon, M. O. *A History of Young Russia.* Translated by James P. Scanlon. Irvine, Calif.: Schlacks, 1986. Although not a single chapter is devoted to Herzen, this paper edition remains a brilliant mine of ideas and information about him. The chapters on Ogaryov and others reveal different sides of Herzen.

Herzen, Aleksandr. *My Past and Thoughts: The Memoirs of Alexander Herzen.* Translated by Constance Garnett. London: Chatto and Windus, and New York: Knopf, 1924-1927. Still the best source not only for Herzen but also for all members of his circle. Beautifully translated and rendered enjoyable to read in a single volume.

Malia, Martin. *Alexander Herzen and the Birth of Russian Socialism, 1812-1855.* Cambridge, Mass.: Harvard University Press, 1961. The principal study of Herzen, treating his career up to the death of Nicholas. Malia seeks to explain why the basis for Russian socialism was laid in an era without an industrial working class.

Pomper, Philip. *The Russian Revolutionary Intelligentsia.* New York: Crowell, 1970. This short survey focuses on the principle that ideologies are as much traced to individual personalities as they are to ideas.

Ulam, Adam B. *In the Name of the People: Prophets and Conspirators in Prerevolutionary Russia.* New York: Viking Press, 1977. A fascinating account of nineteenth century radicals. Ulam sees the turning point in the conspiratorial caste of mind that was fashioned in the early 1860's.

Walicki, Andrzej. "Alexander Herzen's Russian Socialism." In *The Slavophile Controversy: History of the Conservative Utopia in Nineteenth Century Russian Thought.* Oxford: Clarendon Press, 1975; Notre Dame, Ind.: University of Notre Dame Press, 1989. Walicki describes how Herzen merged the utopias of the Slavophiles and the Western liberals. He shows Herzen's faith in the future of Russia despite his frequent bouts with disillusionment.

John D. Windhausen

THEODOR HERZL

Born: May 2, 1860; Pest, Hungary
Died: July 3, 1904; Edlach, Austria
Areas of Achievement: Diplomacy and journalism
Contribution: Often called the "father of modern Zionism," Herzl expounded on the need for a Jewish homeland and created an effective organizational framework for this political movement. His diplomatic missions to secure a Jewish state lent worldwide credibility to early Zionism.

Early Life

Theodor Herzl was born to a Jewish family which, like so many others of the era, displayed confused notions about its cultural heritage. His grandfather, Simon Loeb Herzl, adhered to traditional religious observance, while his two brothers converted to Christianity. A successful businessman and banker, Theodor's father, Jacob, hewed a middle line: He remained a culturally assimilated Jew. As the young Herzl approached his thirteenth year, his parents announced a "confirmation" rather than a "bar mitzvah." Thus, Theodor made the passage into Jewish manhood.

The city of Pest (which merged with Buda in 1872 to become Budapest) similarly polarized its residents into either the Hungarian or the German cultural camp. Nationalism was only beginning to stir Europe. With a respect for what she deemed the more refined and cosmopolitan culture, Jeannette Herzl inculcated in her son a love of German language and literature.

Herzl began his formal education at the age of six, attending a bilingual (German and Hungarian) parochial school, the Israelitische Normalhauptschule. In 1869, he moved to a municipal technical institute, where he could pursue his alleged proclivities for the sciences. During the course of four years, however, Herzl found himself only motivated by the humanities. He even initiated and presided over a literary society, an activity which foretold both his journalistic interests and his leadership drive. The anti-Semitic remarks of a teacher finally hastened Herzl's departure from the institute.

After these early educational experiments, the young Herzl at last entered the Evangelical Gymnasium, a nondenominational academy with a largely Jewish student body, which emphasized German culture and classical learning. He proved to be committed to his writing and, while still in secondary school, published a political article in the Viennese weekly, *Leben*, and book reviews for the *Pest Journal*. As Herzl neared graduation, his only sibling, an elder sister, Pauline, died of typhoid fever. The Herzls moved to Vienna one week later. Theodor returned to Budapest in June to complete his examinations, then entered the University of Vienna's law school.

Law school proved to be rather routine, except for one incident. Herzl joined Albia, a fraternity at the University of Vienna. When the organization endorsed a memorial rally—with strong anti-Semitic overtones—for the composer Richard Wagner, Herzl issued a vehement protest letter and offered his resignation. Albia responded by expelling him. Herzl received his law degree in 1884. He was admitted to the Vienna bar and subsequently worked for criminal and civil courts. A year after commencing his legal practice, he left law altogether, finally choosing a writer's life.

Perhaps Herzl most vigorously aspired to be a playwright. Though one of his works made it to the German-language stage in New York, critics generally judged his plays mediocre. He achieved far greater success writing *feuilletons*, observations of the various people, places, and characteristics defining late nineteenth century life. Summer travels, heavily subsidized by the elder Herzls, also yielded articles for the vaunted *Neue Freie Presse*. With his career advancing, Herzl married Julie Naschauer, an attractive young woman from a prosperous Jewish family. The union was to produce three children—and numerous difficulties. Thought to have had emotional problems, Julie probably also clashed with her domineering mother-in-law. Herzl's prolonged absences only exacerbated the situation.

Life's Work

Herzl, now married and in his thirties, received a professional assignment which, in its own way, was to change his life. October, 1891, brought a telegram from the Neue Freie Presse: The paper's editors wanted Herzl to serve as Paris correspondent. For the rest of his days, he remained affiliated with the journal. Herzl's locus, Paris, stood at the nucleus of late nineteenth century culture, and the writer developed from a feuilletonist into a journalist. With the trial of Captain Alfred Dreyfus, however, he also added a new element to his restless personality.

Dreyfus, a Jew, had been accused by the French government of treason. Perhaps the most egregious

aspect of the 1894 trial was the virulent, far-flung anti-Semitism which it invoked. True to journalistic ethics, Herzl did not debate Dreyfus' guilt or innocence; rather, he reported on the less-than-humane treatment meted out to the captain in this most civilized of Western European nations. As a result of the Dreyfus trial and a resurgence of anti-Semitism across the continent, Jewish issues emerged in Herzl's writings, thoughts, and most important, actions. Mid-1895 marked the initiation of his Zionist career.

Preparing for visits with millionaire Jewish philanthropists Baron Moritz Hirsch and members of the Rothschild family, Herzl crystallized and committed to paper his developing ideas about a Jewish state. The meetings did not go well. As some scholars note, the philanthropists dwelled on charity; Herzl instead pondered nationhood as a self-help mechanism for the Jewish people. The notes which Herzl prepared for these visits, however, subsequently appeared in a revised, printed form. *Der Judenstaat* (1896; *A Jewish State*, 1896) became both the inspiration of and the primer for a fledgling Zionist movement.

Herzl's booklet identified Jews as a people, rather than merely as a religious group. Moreover, it indicated that the absence of a homeland denied Jews the status enjoyed by other nations. Even those attracted to the more tolerant Western European countries, for example, could only assimilate and advance to a certain point before their increasing numbers and greater visibility would provoke anti-Semitism. Eastern European Jews lived in a constant state of racially based poverty and repression. Herzl concluded that statehood would "liberate the world by our freedom" and allow Jews—both individually and collectively—to realize higher goals.

These themes were not new, but Herzl added articulation and administrative structure to them. Small, loosely organized groups, *Hoveve Zion*, already had initiated isolated migrations to Palestine. Herzl argued, however, that without the existence of an autonomous state, a Jewish presence could easily kindle anti-Semitism. In order to advance nationhood, *A Jewish State* proposed a political/moral "Society of Jews" and a "Jewish Company," capable of conducting economic activities and land acquisition. Herzl suggested both Palestine and sparsely populated, fertile Argentina as possible sites for the homeland.

Reactions to *A Jewish State* varied. Comfortable Western European Jews believed that they had been granted adequate civil liberties and that Herzl's concept of nationhood might only raise anti-Semitic furor. Much to their discomfort, "Jewish unity" also linked them with their impoverished, ill-educated brethren in Russia and other countries. Yet Herzl did find an audience. His backers included intellectuals, students, and many Eastern European Jews for whom assimilation proved impossible and for whom misery was a way of life. With increasing fervor and occasional encouragement, he commenced publication of *Die Welt* (the world), the movement's premier communications vehicle. Supporters also urged their leader to organize a world conference in Basel, Switzerland. On August 29, 1897, the first Zionist Congress met, attracting 197 delegates. An organizational statement was adopted, membership goals and fees set, and a committee structure devised. A total of six Zionist conferences would convene during Herzl's lifetime. Each drew more delegates, media participation, and, sometimes, controversy.

In the interim, Herzl traveled through Europe, seeking diplomatic support for an automonous Jewish state. He financed his own trips, just as he underwrote the publication of *Die Welt*. The money came from his salary; by late 1895, the *Neue Freie Presse* had promoted him to literary editor. Journalistic renown may have opened diplomatic doors, but Herzl's demeanor won for him converts among heads of state. He was an impeccable dresser; his proud stance and trim profile added greatly to his five-foot, eight-inch frame. Yet the perfect manners and piercing, dark good looks belied ill health. Maintaining a demanding job, filling every spare minute with political activity, and balancing family finances with those of his organization slowly weakened an already ailing heart.

If Herzl was to grow weary by the failure actually to procure a Jewish homeland, his persistence lent Zionism global credibility. He eventually obtained audiences with the German kaiser Wilhelm II; Russian ministers Count Sergei Yulievich Witte and Vyacheslav Pleve; Pope Pius X; British ministers Neville Chamberlain, David Lloyd George, and Arthur James Balfour; Sultan Abdul Hamid II; and Italian king Victor Emanuel III. His approach was pragmatic: Sometimes he presented the Jewish state as a neutral, autonomous buffer in a region which would change radically after the inevitable collapse of the Ottoman Turkish Empire; on other occasions, he suggested that Zionism might help European countries alleviate "Jewish problems," anti-Semitic hatred, and the internal discord it evoked. Diplomatic efforts, however, were directed mainly at Turkey and England. The former was a rapidly deteriorating power, with a huge territory to administer and an equally large foreign debt. Turkey also held Palestine.

The Jewish Colonial Trust had been established by the second Zionist Congress for the purpose of generating funds to purchase land. Now Herzl sought an acquisition. He told the sultan that a sale of Palestine would boost the sagging Turkish economy. Furthermore, the Jewish settlers would bring new commerce to the empire and remain faithful to the Ottomans in the face of adversaries. However appealing the financial aid, Turkey refused to grant the Zionists a fair measure of autonomy. Negotiations broke in 1902.

Great Britain, on the other hand, had internal problems. With a reputation for political tolerance, it attracted Eastern European Jews fleeing repression. British leaders became concerned about limited jobs and other domestic issues; they sought to restrict Jewish immigration. While the debate proceeded, the British offered Herzl El Arish, in the Sinai peninsula, but irrigation and other problems barred the agreement. Then, in the wake of the Kishinev pogrom, which killed forty-five Jews and precipitated an outpouring of worldwide sympathy, the British suggested a Zionist charter for Uganda.

Herzl took the proposal to the sixth Zionist Congress in 1903. He explained that East Africa merely represented an interim step to Palestine. The congress voted, narrowly, to send a delegation to Uganda, but the powerful Russian delegation—fresh from the Kishinev pogrom—refused to accept anything resembling a territorial substitute and stormed out of the session. The Russian group presented Herzl with a leadership ultimatum several months later. Tremendously hurt, he nevertheless proved somewhat successful in ending the dispute. Herzl also continued on his diplomatic missions until halted by a severe heart attack in May, 1904. Ordered to rest, he became more sedentary but constantly accepted work and visits from his supporters. Pneumonia set in, further aggravating his heart condition. Herzl died on July 3, 1904, at the resort of Edlach, Austria. His remains were moved to the new State of Israel in 1949.

Summary

Theodor Herzl came to his mission relatively unaware of contemporary Zionist philosophy or Jewish issues in general. Yet he left many astute prophecies. Following the first Zionist Congress, he wrote, ". . . I founded the Jewish State. If I were to say this today, I would be met by universal laughter. In five years, perhaps, and certainly in fifty, everyone will see it." Israel came into being fifty years and three months after Herzl committed these visions to his diary. The connection, however, is far more direct. While the Uganda episode almost divided the fledgling Zionist movement and hastened Herzl's own death, it enabled him to establish relations with Lloyd George and Balfour, two British leaders responsible for the 1917 Balfour Declaration mandating Jewish settlement in Palestine.

Herzl's novel *Altneuland* (1902; *Old-new Land*, 1941) introduces the reader to a utopian state, circa 1923. The book describes conditions which were to inspire Israel's settlers: a desolate land transformed through agricultural technology; modern, gleaming cities; and a progressive social system. Most telling, however, the title page bears an inscription: "If you will it, it is no dream."

Bibliography

Bein, Alex. *Theodore Herzl*. Translated by Maurice Samuels. Philadelphia: Jewish Publication Society of America, 1941; London: East and West Library, 1957. This sympathetic general biography views Herzl as an exemplary, independent, and selfless leader whose Zionist organization strongly advanced democratic participation while abiding by an ordered structure. Contains a good bibliography, though many additional sources subsequently have been published.

Elon, Amos. *Herzl*. New York: Holt Rinehart, 1975; London: Weidenfeld and Nicolson, 1976. Drawing heavily on archival material made accessible since the release of Bien's work, this book presents Herzl, the sensitive journalist, sometime playwright, and driven activist, who infused a sense of drama into statecraft.

Herzl, Theodor. *Theodor Herzl: A Portrait for This Age*. Edited by Ludwig Lewisohn. Cleveland: World Publishing, 1955. The book uses Herzl's own writings to show the personal conflicts behind the Zionist leader. An interesting psychological study, employing historical analysis and assessment of the subject's literary career.

Kornberg, Jacques. *Theodor Herzl: From Assimilation to Zionism*. Bloomington: Indiana University Press, 1993. Intellectual biography of Herzl focusing on his personality and his development of Zionism as a means of coming to grips with his Jewish identity.

Laqueur, Walter. *A History of Zionism*. New York: Holt Rinehart, and London: Weidenfeld and Nicolson, 1972. Perhaps the most authoritative source on Zionism. Lacquer devotes fifty pages exclusively to Herzl. Excellent chronological overview of the subject's politics, diplomatic efforts, and organizational endeavors, with a fine summary of *A Jewish State*, his most influential work. The book includes a concise, useful bibliography, a glossary, and six maps.

Neumann, Emanuel. *Theodor Herzl: The Birth of Jewish Statesmanship*. New York: Herzl Press, 1960. Unfailingly sympathetic in its depiction of Herzl, this brief work proves most valuable when discussing the philosophical differences between the practical Zionists, seeking colonization or infiltration into Palestine, and the political Zionists, who focused their efforts on securing an independent, autonomous homeland. Contains a timetable.

Patai, Raphael, ed. *Herzl Year Book*. Vol. 3. New York: Herzl Press, 1958. Twenty-one scholars address little-known aspects of Herzl's life, gather reminiscences, argue the merits of his political and diplomatic involvements, and reflect upon his legacies. Part of a six-volume set, this collection is designed for those who want to research more specific Herzelian issues.

Robertson, Ritchie, and Edward Timms, eds. *Theodor Herzl and the Origins of Zionism*. Edinburgh: Edinburgh University Press, 1997. A collection of essays on Herzel, his influence as a journalist, his efforts to establish a national territory for Jews, and the manner in which his fiction reshaped Jewish identity.

Lynn C. Kronzek

WILD BILL HICKOK
James Butler Hickok

Born: May 27, 1837; Troy Grove, Illinois

Died: August 2, 1876; Deadwood, Dakota Territory (now South Dakota)

Areas of Achievement: Law and military affairs

Contribution: Hickok's prowess with a pistol made him one of the deadliest gunfighters in the American West and one of the most forceful and accomplished lawmen of the Kansas cattle towns. Hickok's exploits as a soldier, scout, gunfighter, and lawman made him one of the most recognized figures from the American frontier.

Early Life

James Butler Hickok was the fourth of six children born to William Alonzo and Polly Hickok. William moved his family to Troy Grove, Illinois, in 1836, where he opened the community's first general store. Known as the Green Mountain House, his business doubled as a way station on the Underground Railroad. Slavery deeply troubled William, and his boys regularly assisted their father in helping runaway slaves escape. William's business failed during the financial panic of 1837, forcing him to turn to farming.

As a young boy, James Hickok kept to himself, and many considered him a loner. Early in his life, he demonstrated a penchant for weaponry, and he acquired his first gun around the age of twelve. At every opportunity, young Hickok retreated into the woods to practice his marksmanship. When William died in 1852, his boys took over the family farm. Because of his prowess with a gun, James was given the responsibility of supplementing his family's diet. He spent much of his time prowling through the woods and fields, hunting deer and small game. He also earned extra income by killing wolves and collecting bounties on their pelts. By his late teenage years, Hickok was known as one of the best shots in La Salle County. His skill and dexterity with firearms would later serve him well as a frontier lawman and soldier.

Throughout Hickok's life, he had a tendency to never back down from a threat, and he regularly stood up for those who could not defend themselves. His first recorded altercation with another man occurred at the age of eighteen while he was working for the Illinois and Michigan Canal. Charles Hudson, a local camp bully, did not like

Hickok and, after exchanging some heated words, a fight broke out. As the pair exchanged blows and wrestled along the bank of the canal, the edge gave way, sending them into the water. Bystanders jumped into the water and pulled Hickok off Hudson, who lay motionless in the canal. Thinking that he had killed his adversary, the youthful Hickok fled the scene and retreated to the family farm. Shortly thereafter, Hickok, along with his brother Lorenzo, left home and headed west to Kansas.

Life's Work

Hickok arrived in Kansas in 1856 as a nineteen-year-old teenager and, except for brief trips east, spent his entire adult life in the American West. During his twenty years on the Great Plains, Hickok worked as a frontier scout, spy, soldier, teamster, showman, gunfighter, gambler, and lawman. He witnessed many of the important events associated with the development and settlement of the American West, and he personally participated in the Indian Wars, policed the cattle towns, and saw the decimation of the buffalo.

The man who would become one of the most recognized figures of the frontier era stood more than six feet tall. He had piercing grey-blue eyes that reportedly looked right through people. His long and curled auburn hair tumbled to his shoulders, and a drooping mustache hung over his lip. He sometimes dressed in the buckskin clothing of the plainsmen but later became more elegant, sporting a Prince Albert frock coat. Topping off Hickok's appearance were his ever-present guns, two Navy Colt revolvers tucked butts-forward into a red sash wrapped around his waist.

When the Hickok brothers arrived in Kansas in 1856, the territory was on the verge of civil war. Hickok briefly labored as a plowman in Johnson County, but when hostilities erupted over the issue of slavery along the Kansas-Missouri border, Hickok joined Jim Lane's Free-State Army of Kansas. Whether he saw battle is unknown, but legend claims that he became Lane's personal bodyguard.

After leaving Lane's Kansas militia in late 1857, Hickok took his first job in law enforcement as a constable for Monticello Township in Johnson County. He held this position for less than one year before he went to work for the transportation and

Army. During the war he served as a wagon master, scout, sharpshooter, and spy. He fought at the battles of Wilson's Creek and Pea Ridge. Hickok also spent time behind enemy lines, scouting enemy positions and intercepting Confederate orders and documents. It was during the Civil War that Hickok first gained notoriety. While in Independence, Missouri, Hickok, with his pistols in his hands, dispersed a mob that was threatening to lynch a man. It was from this incident that Hickok earned the name "Wild Bill." After breaking up the mob, a lady from the crowd yelled out, "Good for you, Wild Bill." The name stuck and from then on James Butler Hickok went by the name Wild Bill.

Hickok's Civil War service as a scout and an 1865 gunfight in which he killed Dave Tutt in Springfield, Missouri, enhanced the name of Wild Bill around Missouri and Kansas. In 1867, an article about Wild Bill in *Harper's New Monthly Magazine* made Hickok a household name and a national hero. The story, written by George Ward Nichols, greatly exaggerated Hickok's Civil War exploits and claimed that he killed ten men at the Rock Creek gunfight. Nichols' portrayal of Hickok influenced later writers who further embellished Hickok's law enforcement career by claiming that he had killed one hundred men in the line of duty. Hickok did not like his image as a "man-killer," but this portrait of him as a deadly gunman earned him respect, which made policing the rowdy cattle towns easier.

Although Hickok's career in law enforcement lasted only a few years, he gained notoriety as one of the best Western lawmen. From 1867 to 1870 he served as a deputy U.S. Marshal, chasing army deserters and stock thieves. In 1869 Ellis County, Kansas, elected Hickok sheriff. Hays City, the county seat, was an end-of-the-line railroad town full of gamblers, brawlers, soldiers, buffalo hunters, prostitutes, and gunmen. In three months service, he killed two men in gunfights and was largely credited with establishing law and order. After losing his re-election bid to his deputy sheriff, Hickok drifted around from place to place. On July 17, 1870, while back in Hays City, Hickok became involved in a drunken altercation with five soldiers from Fort Hays. In the fracas that ensued, Hickok shot two soldiers, killing one and seriously wounding the other.

Because of Hickok's reputation as a lawman and gunfighter, the Kansas cattle town of Abilene hired him as city marshal in 1871. Hickok largely succeeded in quelling disturbances by prohibiting

freighting outfit of Russell, Majors, and Waddell. For two years he drove wagons and stagecoaches on the Santa Fe Trail. While on one of these trips to Santa Fe, Hickok reportedly met Kit Carson, his boyhood hero. Little did Hickok know that within a few years his own status as a Western hero would equal or surpass that of Carson.

In 1861 Hickok was working at Rock Creek Station in southeastern Nebraska. It was here, on July 12, 1861, that Hickok fought his first gun battle. The incident grew out of an ongoing feud between a local bully named Dave McCanles and the station's manager. When McCanles, his son, James Woods, and James Gordon appeared at the station and threatened the manager and his wife, Hickok stepped in and shot elder McCanles, Woods, and Gordon. McCanles died almost instantly. Woods and Gordon, both wounded by Hickok, attempted to escape but were hunted down and dispatched by station employees. Nebraska authorities arrested Hickok and two others, but a jury determined that they had acted in self-defense.

After his acquittal, Hickok drifted into Kansas, where he enlisted as a civilian scout in the Union cowboys from carrying guns and keeping a close eye on the drinking and gambling establishments that they frequented. Hickok was involved in only one shooting during his stint in Abilene. On October 5, 1871, Hickok confronted Phil Coe and a number of Texans who had shot their revolvers at stray dogs. Sensing danger from the gun in Coe's hand, Hickok pulled out his revolvers. The two exchanged shots, but only Hickok's found their mark. In the heat of the conflict, Mike Williams, a friend of Hickok who was a special policeman for the Novelty Theater, came running to Hickok's assistance. Catching a glimpse of the fast-approaching Williams out of the corner of his eye and believing him to be a friend of the wounded Coe, Hickok fired two shots, killing Williams.

The death of Williams had a tremendous impact on Hickok. Shortly thereafter he retired from law enforcement and supposedly never again fired his pistols at anyone. After 1871 Hickok tried his hand at acting. He performed with several Wild West shows, including that of William Frederick "Buffalo Bill" Cody. Realizing that acting was not for him, Hickok returned to the Great Plains where, in March, 1876, he married Agnes Lake Thatcher, a former circus performer. Legend holds that Hickok also had a relationship with Martha "Calamity Jane" Cannary, but there is no basis for such a claim. In July, 1876, Hickok joined the gold rush to the Black Hills in the Dakota Territory hoping to strike it rich and return to his new wife. Hickok, however, seems to have known that his days were numbered. He regularly told his friends that Deadwood in the Dakota Territory might be his last camp. On August 2, 1876, Hickok's premonitions came true when Jack McCall shot him in the back of the head while he played poker in a local saloon. The cards held by Hickok—aces and eights—have come to be known as the "dead man's hand."

Summary

The historical life of James Butler Hickok is quite interesting but of little significance. He served his country bravely during the Civil War, scouted during the Plains Indian Wars, killed up to ten men in gunfights, and policed some of the rowdiest cattle towns in the West. Perhaps his role as a lawman made those wild and rollicking towns a safer place to live, but on a larger scale, his contributions to history and his impact on American society were minimal.

The legendary Wild Bill Hickok, however, is a much different story. He has had a tremendous impact on American culture. Hickok's life and his exploits—whether fact or fiction—have received attention in films, in dime novels, on television shows, and from serious historians. Places such as Deadwood, South Dakota; Abilene, Kansas; and Hays City, Kansas, consider Wild Bill as one of their own and continue to promote his name and his image as a colorful frontier figure. Hickok's life has captured the imagination of thousands of people, and he has gone down as one of the true heroes of the American frontier.

Bibliography

Dykstra, Robert S. *The Cattle Towns*. New York: Knopf, 1968. Analyzes the origins and development of the Kansas cattle towns of Abilene, Ellsworth, Wichita, Dodge City, and Caldwell. Although Hickok is not a central figure, this work is important to understanding the social world in which he worked as a lawman.

Miller, Nyle H., and Joseph W. Snell. *Great Gunfighters of the Kansas Cowtowns, 1867-1886*. Lincoln: University of Nebraska Press, 1967. Formerly published under the title *Why the West was Wild*, this book provides a documentary history of the violence associated with the Kansas cattle towns. Using excerpts from newspapers, diaries, letters, and public documents, this work examines the gun battles and exploits of twenty-one Western gunfighters, including Hickok.

Rosa, Joseph G. *They Called Him Wild Bill: The Life and Adventures of James Butler Hickok*. 2d ed. Norman: University of Oklahoma Press, 1974. The definitive Hickok biography. Probably the best work on any Western gunfighter and lawman.

_____. *The West of Wild Bill Hickok*. Norman: University of Oklahoma Press, 1982. A pictorial biography of Hickok and the people and places associated with his career. Almost every known photograph, drawing, and painting of him appears in this volume.

_____. *Wild Bill Hickok: The Man and His Myth*. Lawrence: University Press of Kansas, 1996. An examination of the many myths and legends surrounding Hickok's exploits in the American West. Addresses his reputation as a "man-killer" among other topics.

Mark R. Ellis

THOMAS WENTWORTH HIGGINSON

Born: December 22, 1823; Cambridge, Massachusetts

Died: May 9, 1911; Cambridge, Massachusetts

Areas of Achievement: Literature, military affairs, social reform, and women's rights

Contribution: Higginson wrote prolifically but is best known in the literary world as the discoverer of Emily Dickinson's poetry. He is notable for commanding a regiment of black enlisted men in the Civil War and for laboring in social causes such as the abolition of slavery and women's rights.

Early Life

Although the large family into which Thomas Wentworth Storrow Higginson was born in 1823 as the youngest child was not as wealthy as they had once been, there was never any doubt that he would be educated at Harvard. In 1823 Stephen Higginson, then serving as Harvard University steward, had retained a library of one thousand books from more prosperous days, and by the age of four Thomas was rummaging among them. The boy's grandfather and great-grandfather had been merchants and shipowners, and the former continued to live in style despite hard times. Thomas' mother, Louise, was descended from Appletons and Wentworths, both colonial New England families of note, but she had been orphaned early and had lodged with relatives.

Thus the young Thomas Higginson knew early that he came from a privileged family with concomitant civic and social responsibilities but one forced to come to terms with the limitations and impediments of relative poverty. These lessons would later help guide him in his multifaceted career. Because his bright sister Louisa numbered the brilliant Margaret Fuller among her friends, Higginson, the future champion of women's rights, also became aware that girls could not expect the Harvard education that young men of good families in his area could virtually take for granted. After five years in a "Dame School," the nine-year-old Higginson began to study the obligatory Latin grammar in a private school, where one of his friends was the future poet James Russell Lowell. The next year Higginson's father, who had been dismissed from his Harvard post several years earlier, died; in 1837, the thirteen-year-old boy entered Harvard as its youngest freshman.

His next decade began and ended there, with several short-lived jobs sandwiched between. As an undergraduate, Higginson absorbed Harvard's liberal intellectual atmosphere and took up one of its more extreme liberal positions: abolition. In the 1840's he began to write poetry and grew a beard, then a symbol of defiance of the established order. At length he settled on a career as a minister, earned an impressive record at the Divinity School, and graduated in 1847.

Life's Work

In 1847, after a long engagement, Higginson, buoyed by the prospect of a pastorate in Newburyport, Massachusetts, married Mary Channing. He also met and came to admire Lucy Stone, one of the pillars of the movement for women's rights, but his own advocacy of women and black Americans won him few friends among the prominent white males in his congregation, and after two years he was asked to leave.

Shaken by the rejection, Higginson did not seek another pastorate but for the next three years worked for various liberal causes. In 1852, however, he accepted an appointment as the first pastor of the newly organized Free Church in Worcester, Massachusetts, and found there a congregation receptive to his abolitionist views. Increasingly, he preferred action to sermonizing on behalf of his causes, and his activities turned disruptive and even violent. He accompanied Stone and Worcester reformer Abby Kelley Foster to the World's Temperance Convention in New York in 1853, and when the efforts of Higginson, Stone, and Susan B. Anthony to instill women's rights issues into the convention split the delegations, they formed their own "Half World's Convention." The following year, Higginson spearheaded an abortive rescue of a captured fugitive slave, Anthony Burns, in the course of which a policeman was killed. Those arrested and indicted for promoting a riot included Higginson, although he was never brought to trial. In the fall of 1856, he left his congregation to an assistant pastor and joined a group of Free-Soil activists in Kansas. Although he does not seem to have participated directly in violence there, this adventure acquainted him with the militant activities of John Brown, whom Higginson championed thereafter. One of Higginson's more peaceful efforts of the 1850's was performing the marriage ceremony of Lucy Stone and Henry Blackwell, brother of Elizabeth Blackwell, the nation's first female physician.

Higginson also wrote industriously during these years, including a considerable body of largely unsuccessful poetry and, more important, a series of essays on various topics in *The Atlantic Monthly.* The essay with the most far-reaching effects did not appear until early in 1862. Titled "A Letter to a Young Contributor," it inspired some of the most intriguing letters ever written by a literary person. After reading Higginson's essay of advice to young writers, a totally unknown poet in Amherst, Massachusetts, responded in April of 1862 with an idiosyncratic letter enclosing four of her poems. A correspondence developed between Higginson and Emily Dickinson, and he befriended and encouraged this strikingly unconventional poet. Because Higginson has been accused of shortcomings as a critic of Dickinson's poetry, it is well to note that he stands as the first professional man of letters to recognize her as (to use his phrase) "a wholly new and original poet." His letters to her have not survived, but hers to him make clear his importance to her. When she died in 1886 with her poems, nearly 1,800 of them, still in manuscript, Higginson coedited them with Mabel Todd, wife of an Amherst College professor. The volume that they produced in 1890, *The Poems of Emily Dickinson*, has suffered in comparison with the collection edited by Thomas H. Johnson more than a half century later, its most serious flaw being a tendency to "correct" not only her unusual punctuation but also, at times, her diction. It appears, however, that Todd, not Higginson, was mainly responsible for these editorial shortcomings.

The year that marked the beginning of the Higginson-Dickinson correspondence, 1862, also saw the beginning of Higginson's military career. In March of that year he decided to forego regular duties as a clergyman and began recruiting a Massachusetts regiment of volunteers for the war that had erupted between the North and the South the previous year. Before the regiment could join the conflict, Higginson, whose abolitionist sentiments had long been well known, was asked to command the First South Carolina Volunteers, a regiment made up of black Southern refugees. Higginson learned to admire the spirit and resourcefulness of the African American soldiers. Wounded in his regiment's unsuccessful attempt to cut the railroad between

Charleston, South Carolina, and Savannah, Georgia, in the summer of 1863, Higginson, who had attained the rank of colonel, was in and out of hospitals for the duration of the war.

Thereafter he wrote, lectured, and cared for his invalid wife. Along with Stone, Julia Ward Howe, and others, he organized the New England Woman Suffrage Association and contributed to its publication, *The Woman's Journal.* In 1870 he published *Army Life in a Black Regiment.* By this time his activities other than writing had slowed considerably. The abolition battle had been won, and though much remained to be done before anything like full civil rights would be extended to the freed slaves, the task would require the efforts of a new generation of reformers long after Higginson's death. The same pattern can be seen in the struggle for women's rights. In 1850, shortly after Elizabeth Blackwell obtained her medical degree, the first medical school for women opened in Philadelphia, Pennsylvania, and the states gradually began admitting women to the bar. Property rights for married women and free universal secondary education for all girls were other goals that the women's movement attained as the nineteenth century wore on. After about 1870, Higginson offered mainly moral support. For various reasons the suffrage movement lost momentum, and it was not until 1920 that the passage of the Nineteenth Amendment to the Constitution guaranteed women the right to vote.

In 1877 Higginson's first wife died; two years later he married Mary Thacher. His only two children, both daughters, were born in 1880 and 1881. Only one survived to adulthood. Poetry, both its composition and criticism, now engaged Higginson more than social reform. Between 1877 and 1904 he wrote all the poetry reviews for *The Nation*. His health, generally robust until about the age of sixty, declined. The women whose work he did so much to foster began to die. He spoke at funeral services for Dickinson in 1886 and Stone in 1893. Higginson's later books—a good example is *Cheerful Yesterdays* (1896)—reflect the mellowing of this once-fire-breathing liberal activist. When he died in 1911, few remembered the social activist of the 1850's and 1860's; instead, he was mainly regarded as a "grand old man of literature." However, in an appropriate gesture, the pallbearers at his funeral, a half century after the war in which he had accepted a command unprecedented in U.S. military history, were young black soldiers.

Summary

Because of their subject's versatility, the biographers of Thomas Wentworth Higginson do not agree about his most important achievement. To lovers of American literature, his relationship to Emily Dickinson, a great poet who once wrote him, "You have saved my life," stands out. Admirers of his activities on behalf of social justice cite his early championing of women's rights initiatives and his militant—and military—efforts to abolish forever the evil of slavery. He combined literary competence and bold activism to an unusual degree; he impresses both by his word and deeds in his attack on injustices in American society.

Both women and black Americans continued to suffer from the heavy weight of injustice. From the perspective of several generations later, it is obvious that their battles had scarcely begun and that Higginson was limited by his vision, which was the vision of a white American male born early in the nineteenth century into an old New England family. Nevertheless, he contributed mightily to a great wave of social reform in the third quarter of that century. It would require further bursts of reforming energy in the twentieth century to consolidate and extend the earlier advances that Thomas Wentworth Higginson helped bring about.

Bibliography

Edelstein, Tilden G. *Strange Enthusiasm: A Life of Thomas Wentworth Higginson*. New Haven, Conn., and London: Yale University Press, 1968. The best source of information concerning Higginson's literary activity, including not only a substantial discussion of his literary criticism but also the only sustained criticism of Higginson's little-known poetry.

Higginson, Thomas Wentworth. *Army Life in a Black Regiment*. Boston: Lee and Shepard, 1869. Higginson's own account of his experiences as a commander of a controversial regiment of black soldiers in the Civil War. His assessments of his troops, though displaying the prejudices characteristic of even the most liberal thinkers of his time, stand out as beacons of enlightenment in that time.

Meyer, Howard N. *Colonel of the Black Regiment: The Life of Thomas Wentworth Higginson*. New York: Norton, 1967. Emphasizes Higginson's military distinction as the commander of a regiment of Southern black fugitives, his interest in race relations, his early championing of Susan B. Anthony, and his later promotion of the women's suffrage movement.

Tuttleton, James W. *Thomas Wentworth Higginson*. Boston: Twayne, 1978. Stresses Higginson's unusual relationship with Emily Dickinson as his chief contribution to American literature but also portrays Higginson as an original writer who illuminated the place of the professional man of letters in nineteenth century America.

Wells, Anna Mary. *Dear Preceptor: The Life and Times of Thomas Wentworth Higginson*. Boston: Houghton Mifflin, 1963. The first of several biographies marking the resurgence of interest in Higginson in the 1960's. As the title suggests, the book highlights the Dickinson connection, but at the same time it is the most balanced and readable life of Higginson.

Robert P. Ellis

OCTAVIA HILL

Born: December 3, 1838; Wisbech, Cambridgeshire, England
Died: August 13, 1912; London, England
Area of Achievement: Social reform
Contribution: Hill sought to cope with the social consequences of slum housing by creating and managing a system of humane and personal contact between landlord and tenant. Concern with the urban environment also led her to preserve open spaces for public use, to fight against smoke pollution, and to assist in the establishment of the National Trust.

Early Life

Octavia Hill was the eighth of the ten daughters of James Hill and the third of five daughters of Caroline Southwood Smith, James Hill's third wife. She was born in 1838 at Wisbech, shortly before her father entered into bankruptcy and despondency, necessitating the division of the family. The children of the first two marriages were shipped off to maternal grandfathers, but the third Mrs. Hill, with the help of her father, Dr. Thomas Southwood Smith, an important sanitary reformer, managed to keep her five daughters together. So Hill grew up without brothers, while her weak and bewildered father hovered ineffectually in the background. Hill's mother was left with responsibility for the large contingent of daughters and Hill herself, obviously the most competent of the brood, rapidly became their recognized leader, as their mother necessarily busied herself with earning the cash required to keep the family going. Hill, then, functioning from an early age in an essentially all-female household, became accustomed to exercising leadership. This youthful experience, foreign to most Victorian women, was the source of her strength. Physically, Hill was short, in later life even dumpy, but her broad shoulders and massive head reinforced the power of her personality.

The family's unsettled finances resulted in frequent uprooting during Hill's childhood, and Hill lived in a succession of villages implanted in the fields on the outer fringes of London. Hill received no formal schooling but, mastering reading and writing before she was five, was educated by her mother, by interaction with her sisters, and through her own voracious reading. In consequence of her mother's connection with Frederick Denison Mau-

rice's Christian Socialist movement, Hill at age fourteen was put in charge of a workshop where Ragged School girls made toy furniture. She used her burgeoning artistic talents to design the furniture; she was also responsible for the management of the girls, some of them older than she, and for the operation's finances. From her experience at the workshop, Hill learned for the first time about living conditions for the poor in London. During the same period, she made the acquaintance of John Ruskin, the art critic, who visited the workshop and supplied advice on color. The connection with Ruskin led to lessons in art with Hill copying paintings at the public museums under Ruskin's direction. By 1862, the sisters had established a girls' school in Nottingham Place, Marylebone, in north-central London, where Hill shared in the teaching tasks.

Life's Work

In time, Ruskin became convinced that Hill did not have real artistic talent. While that realization was taking hold, Hill's experience in Marylebone turned her mind to serious consideration of the social problems arising from wretched inner-city housing. Ruskin and Hill, in a fruitful meeting of minds, determined to establish Hill as a landlord, purchasing a few working-class houses with Ruskin's money and utilizing Hill's managerial talent. Three houses, virtually slums, the first of many, were acquired in Paradise Place, Marylebone, in 1864. The plan was to improve the working-class tenants by improving their living environment. The houses were cleaned, repaired, and painted, and their surroundings were spruced up, all the work being done under Hill's close supervision and much of it at first by her personally. Tenants were assured that a certain percentage of their rent money would be spent on the buildings, on repairs if necessary, but on improvements if tenants cared for their own quarters in such a way as to obviate the need for repairs. It was hoped and expected that tenants in more pleasant houses would become themselves more civilized, more sober, and more productive members of society.

An important part of the scheme was to become acquainted with the tenants as individuals—to convert the weekly calls for the collection of rent into social occasions at which the rent collectors, first Hill in person, and later one of the many young ladies she mobilized to help in the work, would meet the tenant's family over tea, offer advice and friendship, and treat them as respected human beings. Tenants' parties and country outings conducted by Hill supplemented the rent collection visits as part of the effort to establish friendly guidance for the tenants. Tenants who fell behind on the rent were, after suitable grace periods, evicted. Hill was convinced that there was good in most people, but not in all. She was willing to abandon those who did not live by her rules, which she assumed were the rules of respectable society.

An annual report, entitled "Letters to My Fellow Workers," which Hill first issued in 1871, supplied a means of communication for Hill to her ever-widening circle of assistants and trainees. The work was not totally philanthropic. The houses were expected to produce a small income, both in order to protect the tenants from any feeling that they were relying on charity, and also to demonstrate to other landlords that money could be made from decently maintained dwellings. By the early 1880's, properties managed under the Hill system housed 378 families, or about two thousand individuals. These numbers increased substantially in the mid-1880's when she became the agent for the Ecclesiastical Commission's properties in south London. Even with the great expansion of her work, her interest always lay in the rehabilitation of small preexisting dwellings, not in the construction by charity or public money of vast new and, she thought, dehumanizing housing projects.

In 1877, by which time she was already well-known for her work in housing, Hill was forced to face unambiguously the choice between career and marriage which in a less obvious manner confronted many other Victorian women. In that year, she became engaged to Edward Bond, a colleague in housing work. Yet it soon became clear that Bond's widowed mother did not want to give up her son. For Hill, it was not an attractive proposition to abandon public activity for a role as a dutiful and reclusive wife in a household dominated by a mother-in-law. Hill chose to continue her career. The engagement was cancelled, but the strain of the decision led to a severe nervous breakdown. Hill withdrew from her work for two years to recuperate by traveling on the Continent with a new companion, Harriot Yorke, chosen by her friends to watch over her. Yorke stayed with Hill throughout the rest of Hill's life, being her chief-of-staff, best friend, and personal companion.

Hill's work with her tenants led directly to her second area of activity, her concern with issues of conservation and preservation encompassed at the time by the word "amenity." Swiss Cottage Fields, an undeveloped area where Hill had played as a child and where she often took her Marylebone tenants on outings, was in 1873 carved up into streets and house lots. In an unsuccessful fight against its urbanization, Hill was introduced to the Commons Preservation Society and became acquainted with its solicitor, Robert Hunter. Her connections with both were immensely important in her subsequent work.

Shortly after the failure at Swiss Cottage, one of Hill's sisters, Miranda, urged the establishment of a society to introduce beauty into the lives of the poor. Hill, seizing upon the idea, founded in 1875 the Kyrle Society, named for John Kyrle, who had, through his personal endeavors, as celebrated by Alexander Pope, beautified his own surroundings. Hill's new society sought to bring to the people of the London slums beauty in all of its forms: in small gardens and green spaces, in freshly cut wild flowers, in works of art liberated from intimidating museums, in bright paint splashed on dull gray walls, in great literature, in choral music. Hill sought in Kyrle, as in her housing activity, close personal involvement with the poor.

Of the greatest public importance was Kyrle's Open Spaces Division, which supplied the organizational structure enabling Hill to begin her efforts for the preservation of open spaces near London. Hill, working sometimes in coordination with the Commons Preservation Society, raised money to prevent building at Hilly Fields, Parliament Hill, Vauxhall Park, and other areas in the metropolis. In concert with the Metropolitan Public Gardens Association, Kyrle's Open Spaces Division acquired rights over disused burial grounds in central London, redesigning them as small open air sitting rooms for the neighborhood. Similar Kyrle Societies came into existence at Birmingham, Bristol, Nottingham, Leicester, and Liverpool.

In 1895, Hill and Hunter, reinforced by Canon Hardwicke Rawnsley, an acquaintance from early years in inner London social work, founded the best known of the Victorian environmental organizations, the National Trust. The trust was designed to protect buildings or areas of natural beauty or historic interest by buying or otherwise acquiring title to them. It focused originally on saving ancient monuments, medieval buildings, ocean cliffs, and pleasant south-of-England hilltops. Hill took no formal office in the National Trust but attended its committee meetings regularly, actively solicited and explored projected National Trust properties, and raised money through numerous contacts within her oft exploited personal network.

Hill's interest in housing also led her to become closely involved with the movement for smoke abatement. She organized a Smoke Abatement Exhibition during the winter of 1881-1882, where 116,000 people examined devices designed to burn fuel more cleanly and efficiently so as to reduce smoke while, incidentally, saving money. The exhibition's manifest success led to the establishment of the National Smoke Abatement Institution, which in turn inspired the foundation in 1898 of the Coal Smoke Abatement Society.

Indicative of Hill's reputation as an expert on social issues was her inclusion among the members of the Royal Commission on the Aged Poor, in 1893 and 1894, and on the Royal Commission on the Poor Laws, of 1905 to 1909. As an active proponent of the doctrine of the Charity Organization Society, with which she had worked since the late 1860's, Hill on both commissions supported the role of private initiative and the free economy as against suggestions for active state involvement, clashing against Beatrice Webb's socialistic views on the latter of the two commissions. Hill died on August 13, 1912, at the home on Marylebone Road, London, which she and Yorke had shared during the last twenty-one years of her life.

Summary

Octavia Hill was best known to her contemporaries for her work in housing, although her approach appears to later twentieth century observers as distastefully patronizing to the tenants. It has left no mark on housing policies of late twentieth century England. Hill's labor intensive system could offer shelter to only a minute percentage of the vast and increasing London lower classes. Hill herself pointed out in 1875 that the twenty-six thousand people housed through various philanthropic schemes in the preceding thirty years represented about six months' increase in London's population. It has been argued that the public attention which became focused on Hill's endeavors actually delayed any effective overall attack on the problem of housing of the London poor.

More significant for the future was Hill's lesser known work in conservation and preservation. Many London open spaces were protected from urban development by the fund-raising efforts of Hill and her Kyrle Society. Although Kyrle died with Hill, her well-publicized successes helped encourage other private groups and, eventually, the state, to pursue similar objectives. The National Trust survives and prospers as a major civilizing element in contemporary England. Concentrating on acquisition and preservation of many of the great English country houses and on protecting the remaining unspoiled segments of the English coastline, the National Trust has become the third largest landowner in England and one of the country's most visible voluntary agencies. Hill's work in smoke abatement encouraged establishment of the Coal Smoke Abatement Society in 1898. A lineal descendant of that society was active in passage of mid-twentieth century legislation which at long last effectively dealt with smoke pollution in Britain. When in the 1960's there came a great surge of interest in environmental protection, Hill's status as a significant and constructive environmental pioneer became recognized.

Bibliography

Bell, E. Moberly. *Octavia Hill*. London: Constable, 1942. The standard biography, although imprecise in documentation and generally uncritical.

Boyd, Nancy. *Three Victorian Women Who Changed Their World: Josephine Butler, Octavia Hill, Florence Nightingale*. London: Macmillan, and New York: Oxford University Press, 1982. Section 2 sketches Hill's career as an introduction to an examination of its religious and moral motivation.

Hill, William Thomson. *Octavia Hill: Pioneer of the National Trust and Housing Reformer*. London: Hutchinson, 1956. Readable and uncritical, goes beyond Bell primarily in reference to Hill's environmental work.

Maurice, C. Edmund. *Life of Octavia Hill as Told in Her Letters*. London: Macmillan, 1914. The authorized biography, by Hill's brother-in-law, based largely on her letters, many of which are quoted at length. Detailed, but reticent on personal matters.

Meyer, Karl E. "Octavia Hill's Green Mansions." *New York Times* 144, no. 50152 (August 13, 1995). Profile of Hill, her career, her work in environmental preservation, and her dedication to the working-class poor.

"Money versus Mentoring: Wisdom for Helping the Poor from One Century Ago." *American En-*

terprise 8, no. 1 (January-February 1997). Discusses the renewed interest in Hill's belief that poverty was as much a behavioral problem as it was a financial one.

Owen, David. *English Philanthropy, 1660-1960.* Cambridge, Mass.: Harvard University Press, 1964. Treats its massive topic with grace and penetrating insight. Owen describes Hill's work in housing and in open spaces preservation with understanding while fitting them into their wider contexts.

Ranlett, John. "'Checking Nature's Desecration': Late-Victorian Environmental Organization." *Victorian Studies* 26 (Winter 1983): 197-222. An overview of the organization of the late-Victorian environmental movement, emphasizing the network of personal connections which linked the various volunteer societies and identifying Hill's position in that network.

Wohl, Anthony S. *The Eternal Slum: Housing and Social Policy in Victorian London.* London: Arnold, and New York: Holmes and Meier, 1977. A comprehensive discussion of lower-class housing and of a variety of private and public efforts for its regulation and improvement. Wohl finds Hill's contribution important but not altogether admirable.

John Ranlett

HIROSHIGE

Born: 1797; Edo, Japan
Died: 1858; Edo, Japan
Area of Achievement: Art
Contribution: Hiroshige was one of the last masters of the *ukiyo-e* woodblock prints in Japan and was famed for his poetic landscapes.

Early Life

Andō Hiroshige was born Andō Tokutarō in 1797 in Edo (modern Tokyo). His father, Andō Gen'emon, was an official of the fire department attached to Edo Castle. Hiroshige's talent for drawing surfaced early; even as a child, he showed an interest in art. First he studied with Okajima Rinsai, a painter and also a fireman, who had been trained in the traditional Kano school of classical Chinese academic painting. Hiroshige's mother died when he was twelve years old and when his father resigned shortly thereafter, Hiroshige was obliged to assume the hereditary duties. Attempting to study with the popular Utagawa Toyokuni, he was turned down; persevering, he managed, however, when he was fourteen, to be accepted as a pupil of the less popular Utagawa Toyohiro.

The following year, he was allowed to use the name "Utagawa Hiroshige," a sign of his promise as an artist. Despite this honor, Hiroshige did not publish until 1818, when book illustrations with the signature Ichiyūsai Hiroshige appeared. When Hiroshige was thirty-one, his master died, but Hiroshige did not take over his name or his studio, as would have been customary for the best pupil to do. About this time, he called himself "Ichiyūsai," then dropped the first character and signed himself simply "Ryusai."

Art historians sometimes divide Hiroshige's artistic career into three stages. In his student days, from 1811 to 1830, he spent his time learning from his predecessors, working on the figure prints of actors and warriors, and, in his mid-twenties, on figure prints of beautiful women. Lessons with Ōoka Umpō taught Hiroshige the Chinese-influenced Nanga style of painting, with its use of calligraphy in depicting landscape. From the Shijō style of painting, Hiroshige learned the art of using ink washes in paintings for a softer effect. His master, Toyohiro, passed on the Western technique of the single-point perspective, which he himself had learned from his teacher, Toyoharu. Hiroshige's early, limited success came from his representation of flowers and birds, sometimes with his own accompanying poem. Prints of these are rarer than his landscapes and are much treasured.

Life's Work

Hiroshige's early work featured sketches of warriors, courtesans, actors, and other subjects typical of *ukiyo-e*, the art form which resulted from the political and geographical shift of power from Kyoto, the old capital, to Edo. By the time Hiroshige was born, Edo, a relatively new capital established by the Tokugawa Shogunate, had turned into a populous city with more than one million inhabitants. Because of the complexity of the caste system then prevailing, the change in the capital of the country led to a series of other complex artistic, social, and commercial changes which defined the art form Hiroshige was to master so successfully. The main patrons of the arts in the old capital of Kyoto, the wealthy merchants called *machischū,* refused to be lured by the economic possibilities offered by the new capital, leaving the path open for merchants of a lower class (*chōnin*) to profit from Edo's position as the commercial capital of Japan. Though now successful economically, the lower-class merchants still had no social clout. In search of entertainment, they would seek out the pleasure districts which sprang up outside the city limits and allowed members of different classes to mingle. This "floating world" was composed of the world of the highly trained and respected courtesans in the pleasure districts, and the art form which evolved to record their activities was the *ukiyo-e* woodblock print.

While the staple subject of the *ukiyo-e* print was the varying fashions in hair, dress, customs, and manners of the evanescent world of the pleasure districts, the landscapes of which Hiroshige became a skilled master had always been traditional in Japanese painting, if only as background for the figures in *ukiyo-e* prints.

In the second and most productive stage of his career, from about 1830 to 1844, Hiroshige left the competitive field of figure designs and concentrated on landscapes. His most famous and finest series seemed to be a result of a journey he took around 1832, directly connected to his family tenure. The shogun in Edo, the real seat of power, annually presented horses from his stables to the emperor, secluded in Kyoto. As a minor official of the Shogunate, Hiroshige joined the expedition so as to Kyoto to paint the ceremony of the presentation for the shogun. During the journey, he made several sketches of the Tōkaidō, as the main highway between Edo and Kyoto was called. These sketches were the basis of the first *Tōkaidō Gojūsantsugi* (fifty-three stations of the Tōkaidō), a collection of fifty-five scenes consisting of the fifty-three stations on the highway and one each in Kyoto and Nihonbashi, the beginning and ending of the road. Published separately at first, the complete series was issued as a set in 1834. It brought Hiroshige immediate and enduring fame and success. Over the course of the next twenty-five years, in response to popular demand, Hiroshige designed some twenty additional sets of these views of the Tōkaidō.

Hiroshige's prints were so popular that some of his designs had runs of ten thousand, and he was kept so busy producing a series of prints on Edo, the suburbs, Lake Biwa at Otsu, and Kyoto that he was seldom present to direct the reproduction of his designs. Greedy publishers were responsible for turning out very inferior copies of his designs in their haste to cash in on their popularity, and Hiroshige himself was not consistently good.

The first Tōkaidō series is considered the most original of his landscape series. What distinguished Hiroshige's vision of the highway were his personal and direct reactions to what he saw. Though inspired by the landscape, Hiroshige adapted freely; he changed the seasons or the time of day or added nonexistent features if his sense of composition required it. Unlike the famous Hokusai, Hiroshige was interested in the human drama around him, not merely in the possibility of the design. Thus, his prints are praised for their humorous point of view, their warmth and compassion, and their close observation of the changing atmospheric conditions, their poetic sensitivity to the relationship between man and nature. He is even referred to as master of rain, mist, snow, and wind.

In the third stage of his career, from around 1844 to his death in 1858, Hiroshige became more interested in depicting figures in his landscapes. He worked in collaboration with Utagawa Kunisada, a figure print designer, and Utagawa Kuniyoshi, a designer of historical prints, to produce another Tōkaidō series jointly. Kunisada added the figures to Hiroshige's landscapes; the two also produced several other series. *Meisho Edo Hyakkei* (1856-

1858; one hundred views of Edo), which Hiroshige produced at the age of sixty, is particularly remarkable for the interesting points of view and the placement of the figures in the landscape.

By this time, Commodore Matthew Perry and the U.S. fleet had intruded upon the closed Japanese society. Japan's opening its market to world trade brought the end of the feudal Tokugawa era and the way of life reflected in the *ukiyo-e* prints. With the passing of Hiroshige, who probably died in the great cholera epidemic in 1858, went the world he had recorded with such wit and warmth.

Because popular artists were not deemed worthy of official records, relatively little is known of Hiroshige's personal life. Such skimpy details as are known suggest a life of personal sorrows. Not only was Hiroshige orphaned as a teenager but also his family had to be rebuilt. He was married twice, once to Tatsu, the widow of a samurai, by whom he had one son, Nakajiro; his wife died in 1840, his son in 1845. Hiroshige's second wife, Yasu, was twenty years younger. His small government pension kept Hiroshige from starving, but he was hardly ever a wealthy man.

Despite these personal setbacks, Hiroshige was a fun-loving man who was enormously productive as an artist. It is estimated, for example, that Hiroshige designed eight thousand woodcuts and that more than forty publishers were involved in publishing his designs. He was also enormously popular in his day, once receiving a commission from thirty innkeepers who wanted prints of their winehouses to present as souvenirs to their guests.

Summary

The last major figure in the development of *ukiyo-e*, Hiroshige is inextricably linked with Hokusai in historical reputation. Hiroshige was the more melancholy, romantic, and poetic artist, but like most of the great Edo masters of the woodblock print who came from middle-class artisan families, his work, intended for and appealing primarily to bourgeois circles, was not considered fine art until Western artists, particularly the Impressionists, discovered and glorified the woodblock print. The prints of Hokusai and Hiroshige, the last of the masters, were at the time still readily obtainable. The roster of great Western artists influenced by them includes James Whistler, Paul Cézanne, Henri de Toulouse-Lautrec, Paul Gauguin, and Vincent van Gogh.

James Michener, while critizing Hiroshige for his weak designs, his undistinguished drawing, and his lack of focus, accords him the rare talent of an "honest, clean eye." Though many of the Hiroshige prints available are the late copies which do not convey his subtlety, he is probably the most accessible of the *ukiyo-e* artists because, in Michener's words, Hiroshige's inspired eye "can teach an entire nation, or even a substantial segment of the world, to see."

Bibliography

Addiss, Stephen, ed. *Tōkaidō, Adventures on the Road in Old Japan*. Lawrence, Kans.: Spencer Museum of Art, 1980. A collection of essays about the Tōkaidō, including chapters on Hiroshige's humor and his Tōkaidō prints in the context of traditional Japanese painting.

Andō, Hiroshige. *The Fifty-three Stages of Tōkaidō*. Edited by Ichitaro Kondo. English adaptation by Charles S. Terry. Tokyo, Japan: Nippon Express, 1960. A brief introduction to Hiroshige's most popular series. Each print is accompanied by text in English and Japanese.

———. *Hiroshige*. Edited by Walter Exner. London: Methuen, and New York: Crown, 1960. An oversized book, with large-print text and color plates throughout. Contains a general introduction to the life and work of Hiroshige, written by the son of the Viennese art dealer who collected Hiroshige's work.

Gayford, Martin. "Japanese Master." *Spectator* 279, no. 8818 (August 2, 1997). Catalog and commentary on the paintings in the exhibit, "Hiroshige: Images of Mist, Rain, Moon, and snow," at the Royal Academy in London. Includes a list of the items exhibited.

Lane, Richard. *Images from the Floating World: The Japanese Print*. Oxford: Oxford University Press, and New York: Putnam, 1978. Provides historical background, tracing the rise of *ukiyo-e* through the seventeenth and eighteenth centuries. Contains color photographs, a bibliography, an index, and an illustrated dictionary of *ukiyo-e*.

Michener, James A. *The Floating World*. London: Secker and Warburg, and New York: Random House, 1954. Traces the life and death of the art known as *ukiyo-e* through the individual artists who practiced it. Contains sixty-five prints, a chronological table, brief biographies, a bibliography, and an index.

Narazaki, Muneshige. *Studies in Nature: Hokusai-Hiroshige*. Translated by John Bester. Tokyo, Japan: Kodansha International, 1970. Focuses on the achievements of these two artists in the depiction of flowers and birds, with a brief introduction to the development of the genre.

Uspenskii, Mikhail. *One Hundred Views to Edo: Woodblock Prints by Ando Hiroshige*. Bournemouth, Dorset: Parkstone Press, 1997. Detailed examination of the history of Edo Japanese wood-block prints. Includes 118 prints with extensive commentary and discussion of Edo's influence on European art.

Whitford, Frank. *Japanese Prints and Western Painters*. London: Studio Vista, and New York: Macmillan, 1977. Discusses the influence of Japanese woodblock prints on European painting in the nineteenth century. Contains a chronology, a glossary, a bibliography, an index, and color plates.

Shakuntala Jayaswal

HOKUSAI

Born: 1760; Edo, Japan
Died: 1849; Japan
Area of Achievement: Art
Contribution: A versatile, productive artist, Hokusai was one of the last great masters of the woodblock print.

Early Life

Katsushika Hokusai, a man who changed his name several times during his lifetime, was born Kawamura Tokitarō in Edo (modern Tokyo) in 1760. His family was probably of peasant stock and poor. When he was around four, a prestigious artisan family, the Nakajima, adopted him without, however, making him an heir. Later, Hokusai's own son was made an adopted heir; because of these two events, there is some speculation that Hokusai may have been the son of a Nakajima concubine.

The variety of occupations that characterized Hokusai's later life started early. He probably worked as a clerk in a bookshop and from age fifteen was an apprentice to a woodblock engraver for three years. Then, in 1778, he started his studies with Katsukawa Shunshō, the leading *ukiyo-e* master. The next year, his first publications under the pen name Shunrō appeared. During the twelve years of his apprenticeship with the Shunshō school, Hokusai published in the genre most associated with the school: prints of Kabuki actors, as well as prints of wrestlers, historical landscapes, and illustrations for novels. Among the most prized of his early work are the *surimono*, the delicate, high-quality prints issued in limited quantities and used as greeting cards or announcements by a small group of aesthetes.

Hokusai probably married his first wife in his twenties and had several children. His subject matter changed accordingly. Prints of historical and landscape subjects predominated, as well as prints of children. In 1793, his master, Shunshō, died, and then his young wife. Hokusai left the Shunshō school and struck out on his own. He studied the styles and techniques of more than a dozen different masters and schools: He learned about brushwork from the Kano school, based on classical Chinese painting, about ink paintings from the work of Sesshū, an ancient master, about flower and bird painting from the Chinese Ming period, and about perspective from Western paintings.

Life's Work

In 1797, Hokusai remarried and took the name by which he is known today. This time has been referred to as the start of the golden age of his work, when his delicate prints of girls, his stylish love scenes, his greeting prints, and his colored book illustrations marked the achievement of his first great style. Yet Hokusai's life never became settled or smooth. Indeed, the last of many names Hokusai took toward the end of his life, Gakyō-rōjin (the old man mad about drawing), characterizes the romantic turbulence that made him, in Richard Lane's words, "the prototype of the single-minded artist, striving only to complete a given task."

When his eldest son, the one who had been adopted by the wealthy Nakajima family, died in 1812, Hokusai no longer received a stipend. Supremely indifferent to money, Hokusai had several jobs—as an errand boy, a bookseller, and a novelist; he also sold calendars, red peppers, and painted banners to have enough money to continue painting.

Hokusai publicly exploited his talent in every conceivable way, drawing from bottom to top, right to left, painting with a finger or an egg or a bottle. The publicity sometimes worked for him, once even attracting the attention of the court. Though he charged highly for his work, he was always poor. He is said to have paid his bills in uncounted packets of money when he had it. He moved frequently, not only when he owed rent but also when his homes became too dirty. His children led equally turbulent lives, eventually leaving their spouses and returning to live with him; his irresponsible grandson was the cause of much of his financial problems.

The prodigality of his personal life matched the eclecticism in his professional life. He changed his name whenever he changed his artistic interests and is said to have used anywhere from thirty to fifty different names. He also wrote poetry, novels, and humorous works, and was widely read in Chinese and Japanese literature.

Even his crowning achievements as a woodblock print artist were marred by the vastness of his interests. Not content to work methodically and selectively, Hokusai produced more than thirty thousand designs in his restless search and eagerness to experiment. Indeed, it was his ambition, perhaps his lack of discrimination, that marred Hokusai's reputation in the view of Japanese critics.

In 1830, and for several years afterward, however, Hokusai published the series that changed the conception of *ukiyo-e* painting and established him in the first rank of artists. *Fugaku sanjūrokkei* (thirty-six views of Mount Fuji) is among the best known of Japanese woodblock prints in the West and is one of the most accomplished of Hokusai's achievements. It was so popular that ten more prints were added, making a total of forty-six in this most famous of Hokusai's work. It has been surmised that the "thirty-six" was kept in the title partly as a literary allusion, for the number thirty-six referred to all the known poets of the Heian period, and partly to make the most of a best-selling series. Three prints in particular, *Mount Fuji at Dawn*, *Mount Fuji in Storm*, and *Fuji Under the Wave at Kanagawa*, with their distinctive bright blues, are perhaps the most recognized of any Japanese prints in the West.

When the success of Hokusai's own series led to the popularity of a younger artist, Hiroshige, and his *Tōkaidō Gojūsantsugi* (fifty-three stations of the *Tōkaidō*) in 1833, Hokusai tried to surpass himself, which he did with a three-volume picture book, *Fugaku hyakkei* (1834; one hundred views of Mount Fuji). It is safe to say that Hokusai's obsession with this beautiful mountain in Japan has made it one of the most recognizable natural features in art.

Summary

Hokusai's reputation has sometimes been as checkered as his own life. Always popular among the lower classes from which he came and from whose point of view he worked, he was initially hailed in the West as the greatest of Japanese artists. Collectors were so eager for his work that anything remotely connected with him was snapped up, with the result that much of his inferior work reached European and American museums. The excessive inflation resulted, naturally, in a correspondingly steep decline in his reputation, until he was considered to be only a minor figure.

Because he was so prolific, so eager to experiment, and admittedly, so undiscriminating, Hokusai, like Hiroshige, suffers a paradoxical fate. The work of these two artists is probably the most accessible and easily recognized of all Japanese artists in the West, with endless reproductions of their most famous works appearing as postcards, calendars, and other mass reproductions—a justifiable fate for craftsmen who worked in the mode designed for the common folk. Yet the true originality of their work remains accessible only to the few who can examine original copies of their work.

Unlike Hiroshige, however, whose fondness for food, drink, and companionship made him seem more ordinary, Hokusai fits the romantic ideal of the driven artist, who sought ceaselessly with his talent to penetrate the mystery of what he saw. Though he lived a long and productive life, he is said to have shouted on his deathbed that if heaven would grant him ten more years, or only five, he might still become a great artist. In his attempts to synthesize a variety of styles, including Western techniques, Hokusai did make his unique style of Japanese art easily accessible to Western audiences, and, by so doing, he influenced European artists and opened the world of Japanese art to outsiders. Charmed by the prints of these two late masters of *ukiyo-e*, Western painters and collectors sought out the older masters. For some, Hokusai's own output is flawed by his excess; for others, the best he accomplished is still superb.

Bibliography

Bowie, Theodore R. *The Drawings of Hokusai*. Bloomington: Indiana University Press, 1964. Concentrates on a discussion of Hokusai as a draftsman, with examples drawn from the familiar as well as the little-known drawings. Includes chapters on Hokusai's stylistic shifts, his method of working, and his teaching. Contains notes, a bibliography, and an index.

Fenollosa, Ernest Francisco. *Hokusai and His School*. Boston: Museum of Fine Arts, 1893. The author's introductory remarks in this exhibition catalog provide a brief but useful background of Japanese art and set the work of both Hokusai and the *ukiyo-e* school of art in its historical context.

Katsushika, Hokusai. *The Thirty-six Views of Mount Fuji*. Edited by Ichitaro Kondo and Charles S. Terry. Tokyo, Japan: Heibonsha, 1966. A companion volume to Hiroshige's *Tōkaidō Gojūsantsugi*. The English adaptation accompanying the reproductions provides a brief introduction to Hokusai's most famous series. Contains prints with texts in Japanese and English.

Lane, Richard. *Images from the Floating World: The Japanese Print*. Oxford: Oxford University Press, and New York: Putnam, 1976. Provides historical background, tracing the rise of *ukiyo-e* through the seventeenth and eighteenth centuries. Includes color photographs, a bibliography, an index, and an illustrated dictionary of *ukiyo-e*.

―――. *Hokusai, Life and Work*. New York: Dutton, and London: Barrie and Jenkins, 1989. Complete study of Hokusai owing his style in part to European influences.

Michener, James A. *The Floating World*. London: Secker and Warburg, and New York: Random House, 1954. Traces the life and death of the art known as *ukiyo-e* through the individual artists who practiced it. Includes sixty-five prints, a chronological table, brief biographies, a bibliography, and an index.

Morse, Peter. Hokusai, *One Hundred Poets*. New York: Braziller, 1989. A masterful work with superb color reproduction of the complete Hokusai drawings and wood-block prints for the Hundred Poets, which Hokusai started late in life and which was never published.

Narazaki, Muneshige. *Studies in Nature: Hokusai-Hiroshige*. Translated by John Bester. Tokyo: Kodansha International, 1970. Focuses on the achievements of these two artists in the depiction of flowers and birds, with a brief introduction to the development of the genre. Includes prints.

Whitford, Frank. *Japanese Prints and Western Painters*. London: Studio Vista, and New York: Macmillan, 1977. Discusses the influence of Japanese woodblock prints on European painting in the nineteenth century. Includes a chronology, a glossary, a bibliography, an index, and color plates.

Shakuntala Jayaswal

JOHN PHILIP HOLLAND

Born: February 29, 1840; Liscannor, County Clare, Ireland

Died: August 12, 1914; Newark, New Jersey

Areas of Achievement: Invention and technology

Contribution: Holland developed and manufactured the first submarine capable of traveling long distances under water.

Early Life

John Philip Holland was the second of four sons of John Holland and Mary Scanlon Holland. Although his father's living as a member of the British Coast Guard was secure, Holland witnessed the Irish famine years, an experience that left him with a lifelong anti-British resentment. Holland attended Saint MaCreehy's National School in Liscannor, where he learned English (the language of his home was Gaelic), and later went to the Christian Brothers secondary school at Ennistomy. After Holland's father died, the family moved to Limerick in 1853, where Holland entered the monastery school. On June 15, 1853, he took the initial vows, joining the Teaching Order of the Irish Christian Brothers. After a brief novitiate, he was sent to teach at the North Monastery in Cork, where he was significantly influenced by Brother James Dominick Burke, a talented science teacher credited with founding vocational education in Ireland.

In 1860, ill health interrupted Holland's teaching career for two years, during which time he first became interested in submarines and the mechanics of flight. He was subsequently assigned to a series of teaching positions at Maryborough (Portaloise), Enniscorty, Drogheda, and Dundalk. At Dundalk he experimented with a clockwork submarine model and prepared plans and sketches for a one-man iron submarine.

Holland's brother, who was deeply involved in recurrent nationalistic uprisings, was forced to leave Ireland with his mother in 1872. Shortly thereafter, on May 26, 1873, alone and in poor health, Holland withdrew from the Christian Brothers and followed his family to the United States.

Life's Work

Shortly after arriving in Boston, Massachusetts, in November, 1873, Holland slipped and fell on an icy street, suffering a broken leg and a slight concussion. While confined to his room during recovery, he completed another submarine design. For the next two years, however, Holland worked as a lay teacher in St. John's Parochial School in Paterson, New Jersey.

In February, 1875, perhaps urged by a pupil's father who was a friend of the secretary of the Navy, Holland sent his submarine plans to the Navy. Although his description of a fifteen-foot, treadle-driven, one-man boat was included in a lecture on submarines at the Naval Torpedo Station in Newport, Rhode Island, the Navy rejected his submarine as impractical. Undiscouraged, Holland continued brainstorming with an engineer named William Dunkerly.

In mid-1876, Holland's brother Michael introduced Holland to Jeremiah O'Donovan Rossa, a member of the Fenian Order, a secret society of Irish revolutionaries. Rossa then introduced Holland to Jerome Collins, founder of the Clan-na-Gael (the United Order), a Fenian "umbrella" group. Later in 1876, Holland met John Devoy, chairman of the Fenian Executive Committee, and John J. Breslin (alias James Collins). Convinced of the practi-

cality of Holland's submarine as a weapon against the British Navy, the Skirmishing Fund of the Clan-na-Gael allocated $5,000 to construct Holland's first full-scale submarine, the *Holland No. 1*. The 2.25-ton boat was launched on May 22, 1878, and promptly sank. The boat was easily raised and underwent several days of tinkering. On June 6, Holland successfully dived and cruised a short distance. After several more dives, the longest lasting for one hour, the *Holland No. 1* was dismantled and sunk. In the process, Holland demonstrated the need for a constant reserve buoyancy and a low, fixed center of gravity to ensure lateral and longitudinal stability. He also proved the superiority of hydroplanes located at the stern and the practicality of an internal combustion engine for propulsion.

The trustees of the Skirmishing Fund then ordered a larger boat that was fully armed and capable of breaking an enemy blockade. With this order, Holland's teaching career ended, and he embarked on his life's work as an inventor, engineer, and promoter. Supported by the Fenians, Holland designed a three-man, 31-foot operational submarine. He engaged the Delamater Iron Works of New York to build the vessel, and work began on May 3, 1879. In spite of the continual argument and skepticism of the workers and staff of the iron works, the boat was launched on May 1, 1881, at an estimated cost of about $60,000. While the submarine was under construction, Swedish, Russian, Italian, German, and Turkish observers visited the yard; the Turks subsequently offered Holland a contract for a boat of their own.

The 31-foot *Fenian Ram* displaced 19 tons and was driven by a Brayton internal combustion engine rated at about 15 to 17 horsepower. The surface speed was 9 knots, and Holland believed the ship's submerged speed was probably about the same. (This was not an unlikely assumption since the ship was hydrodynamically clean, and similarly shaped nuclear submarines are faster submerged than on the surface.) In tests between May and November, 1883, the *Fenian Ram* submerged to 60 feet for one full hour. Holland also built a third submarine, the 16-foot *Fenian Model*, for testing modifications of the basic design. While Holland worked, the Fenians fell into dissension, and one faction "stole" both submarines. They sank the *Fenian Model* on their way to New Haven, Connecticut, and were incapable of operating the *Fenian Ram* after their arrival. Holland severed his association with them.

Holland later met William W. Kimball of the United States Navy, who introduced him to Edmund L. Zalinski, an artillery expert. Both of these men furthered Holland's plans. Kimball unsuccessfully sought a naval position for Holland, so the inventor went to work for Zalinski's Pneumatic Gun Company. Kimball and Zalinski then organized the Nautilus Submarine Boat Company to build Holland's fourth submarine. The 50-foot *Zalinski Boat*, constructed at Fort Lafayette during 1884, had a steel-framed wooden hull. Its centralized control station was a major innovation: The depth gauges, levers operating the flood valves, diving plane controls, steering lever, and throttle were all accessible to the operator's platform below the conning tower. An unsuccessful attempt to design a modified camera lucida for underwater visibility proved that underwater steering by direct vision was impracticable. The submarine was badly damaged during launch and made only a few trial runs. It was dismantled, and the Nautilus Submarine Boat Company was liquidated in 1886.

On January 15, 1887, Holland married Margaret Foley of Paterson, New Jersey. They had five children: John, Robert Charles, Joseph Francis, Julia, and Marguerite. Two additional children, John P. and Mary Josephine, died in infancy.

During the next three years, Holland and Charles A. Morris, an engineer who had been converted to Holland's projects during construction of the *Fenian Ram*, entered two Navy competitions for contracts to build a submarine. Both times, 1888 and 1889, their plans won, but problems with the contractor and political maneuvering prevented construction. As a consequence, Holland occupied himself with developing designs for a flying machine and, to support himself, took a job with the Morris and Cummings Dredging Company on May 1, 1890. Finally, on March 3, 1893, Congress appropriated $200,000 to reopen the submarine competition. Holland and Morris, in association with Elihu B. Frost, a lawyer for the dredging company, organized the John P. Holland Torpedo Boat Company. Frost effectively dominated finances of the business as Holland's stockholdings were less than a controlling interest. All of Holland's patents, inventions, and devices became company property. The company submitted plans for the competition on June 4, 1893. After further political maneuvering, the John P. Holland Torpedo Boat Company finally received a $200,000 contract for construction of the *Plunger*.

In order to meet naval specifications, the 85-foot *Plunger* was powered with two triple-expansion steam engines generating 2,500 horsepower for surface operation and a 70-horsepower electric motor for submerged operation. Another steam engine drove a generator for the bank of storage batteries supplying current to the electric motor. Construction was plagued by the Navy's continual close supervision. Also, the steam powerplant was too bulky and generated excessive heat within the hull. As a consequence, Holland promoted construction of a sixth submarine of his own design, with Morris as his superintending engineer.

Construction began in the winter of 1896-1897, and the *Holland VI* was launched May 17, 1897. The first surface run was made February 5, 1898, and the first dive on March 11, 1898. The first successful submerged cruise, however, occurred on March 17, when Holland demonstrated the boat and its dynamite gun before a representative of the Navy Board of Auxiliary Vessels. Although performance specifications set out for the *Plunger* were met, the board called for further modifications and testing. After two years, acceptance trials were completed, and on April 10, 1900, the Navy bought the *Holland VI*. On August 2, 1900, the Navy ordered six more submarines. In addition, England, Japan, and Russia ordered either Holland submarines or plans for them.

Meanwhile, the John P. Holland Torpedo Boat Company was merged with the Electric Boat Company, and Frost and his associates effectively eliminated Holland and Morris from further influence in the company. Naval architects in the Electric Boat Company began building submarines with flat decks that carried guns and other impedimenta contrary to Holland's advocacy of hydrodynamically streamlined hulls.

Holland resigned from the Holland Torpedo Boat Company on March 28, 1904, and on May 18, 1905, organized the Holland Submarine Boat Company to build submarines of his own design. The Electric Boat Company, however, successfully blocked Holland's access to his earlier patents, and his financial backers withdrew. This ended his career as a submarine designer and builder. Despite periodic spells of poor health, he survived to age seventy-three before dying of pneumonia.

Summary

John Holland was not the first to build submarines: Cornelius van Drebbel attempted a submarine in 1620; during the American Revolution, David Bushnell's *Turtle* (1775) was the first submarine to attack an enemy ship; and during the Civil War, the Confederate *Hunley* (1864) was the first to sink an enemy ship. Holland's innovations, however, resulted in the first submarines capable of successfully attacking surface vessels and, most important, escaping intact thereafter. Other contemporaneous experimenters include the American J. H. L. Tuck and his *Peacemaker*; the Swedish manufacturer Thorsten Nordenfeldt, who described his first submarine in 1886 and subsequently built submarines for Greece and Turkey; the French, who built the *Gymnote*, the first submarine accepted by a major naval power 1888; and other builders active in England, Italy, and Spain. Holland's *Holland VI*, later called the USS *Holland* (SS-1), however, was the first submarine capable of naval warfare. His John P. Holland Torpedo Boat Company, when it merged into the Electric Boat Company, became the principal U.S. submarine builder. Only sixteen years after the USS *Holland* was commissioned, submarines became a major naval weapon during World War I.

Bibliography

Cable, Frank T. *The Birth and Development of the American Submarine*. New York and London: Harper, 1924. This book was written by one of Holland's close associates in the early development of the submarine.

Holbrook, S. H. *Lost Men of American History*. London and New York: Macmillan, 1946. This volume includes an easy-to-read account of Holland's career that will satisfy casual readers.

Morris, R. K. *John P. Holland, 1840-1914*. Annapolis, Md.: Naval Institute Press, 1984. Morris's comprehensive biography covers all aspects of Holland's life. The definitive but uncritical account may be too detailed for the average reader.

Potter, E. B. *The Naval Illustrated History of the United States Navy*. New York: Galahad, 1971. Potter discusses the development and the tactical and strategic significance of submarines. As the title suggests, the book includes illustrations of the *Holland* and later U.S. Navy submarines.

Rush, C. W., et al. *The Complete Book of Submarines*. Cleveland: World, 1958. The authors provide an illustrated history of submarines from their beginning through the nuclear age. The volume shows Holland's place among his contemporaries and evaluates his significance.

Ralph L. Langenheim, Jr.

OLIVER WENDELL HOLMES

Born: August 29, 1809; Cambridge, Massachusetts
Died: October 7, 1894; Boston, Massachusetts
Areas of Achievement: Literature and medicine
Contributions: Holmes was an American doctor and teacher of medicine who helped pioneer many new medical techniques, including the use of microscopes and anesthesia. He was also a poet and essayist whose writings were dominated by wit and inventiveness.

Early Life

Oliver Wendell Holmes was born into a kind of New England aristocracy that he later called the Brahmin caste. His home atmosphere was a mixture of solid Puritanism dictated by his father, Abiel Holmes, a Congregationalist minister, and more liberal thought contributed by his mother, Sarah Wendell, the daughter of a successful Boston merchant with high social connections. Holmes received his early education fairly uneventfully in Cambridge, Massachusetts, where his scholasticism was termed average and where he was frequently punished for talking and whispering. This small fact foreshadowed his adult role as one of the premier lecturers, conversationalists, and wits of his day.

Also significant from his childhood years was his fear of being visited by doctors. Of small, frail stature both as a child and as an adult, Holmes also suffered from asthma. The misery brought on by these early doctors' visits may partially account for his lifelong discomfort with private medical practice, attributed to an oversensitivity to the patients' suffering.

Central to his beliefs as an adult were his early childhood revolts against the Puritan religious orthodoxy prevalent in his home and community. Holmes's father, while educated in the strictest Calvinist traditions, was a compassionate man and an occasional writer of poetry who apparently had some difficulty enforcing many of the unforgiving orthodox doctrines among his family. Holmes primarily rebelled against such inhumane religious beliefs as original sin—the idea that even an unbaptized baby who dies in infancy is guilty and unforgiven because of the Fall of Man in the Garden of Eden.

At the age of fifteen, Holmes boarded at Andover School for one year in preparation for his entrance into Harvard. Holmes entered Harvard in 1825 and graduated with the celebrated class of 1829. Upon his graduation, Holmes was not sure what profession to adopt and studied law for one year. Discovering that law was not his calling, he later encouraged his eldest son, who succeeded brilliantly as a United States Supreme Court justice, to enter the profession. Holmes then entered medical school, where one of his first-year professors identified Holmes's true spark as a medical man. While at first repelled by hospital wards and operating rooms, in which the use of anesthesia was rare, Holmes quickly became fascinated by anatomy. After two years of medical studies in Boston, Massachusetts, Holmes finished his studies in Paris, France. His choice of medicine as his permanent profession was cemented by these two years in France, where he attended lectures by the greatest and most progressive medical minds of his time.

Life's Work

During the ten years after Holmes graduated from medical school (1836-1846), he set up private practice in Boston, got married, and fathered three children. Holmes's wife, Amelia Jackson, has been described as his ideal mate. She was industrious and devoted and managed Holmes's affairs in an efficient manner that allowed him to apply himself to his profession and varied interests.

It was also during this period that Holmes wrote the medical essays on which his honorable reputation as a medical researcher is based. The most valuable and famous essay was "The Contagiousness of Puerperal Fever." Puerperal fever was an infection of the lining of the uterus that afflicted and killed many new mothers. Holmes argued that the infection was actually carried from patient to patient unknowingly by the attending physicians. This idea was extremely unpopular among the medical community, and Holmes's paper was viciously attacked. However, Holmes's theory was indeed true, and the medical community eventually came to accept it. While Holmes did not originate the contagiousness theory, it is believed that his essay was instrumental in getting doctors to accept and treat the real cause. The essay was meticulously prepared and argued, and one can argue that it was the calm and professional manner in which Holmes handled his critics that actually gave force to his position. Holmes researched and published other influential medical papers, which were collected in his *Medical Essays, 1842-1882* (1863).

In 1847 Holmes became a professor of anatomy and physiology at Harvard Medical School, a position he held for thirty-five years. This vocation released Holmes from the suffering of the actual sickroom while satisfying his thirst for knowledge in his area of fascination, anatomy. Holmes, ever the wit and entertainer, also enjoyed the opportunity to inform and amuse his audience at the same time. The Harvard medical student's schedule at this time was grueling. Students were expected to sit for rigorous lectures from 9:00 A.M. to 2:00 P.M. daily, with no break for rest or refreshment. Holmes was specifically assigned the 1:00 P.M. lecture because of his outstanding ability to hold the exhausted students' attention. While he was very serious about presenting information clearly and simply, Holmes nevertheless interjected the occasional anecdote and pun. In addition to his fame as a medical essayist and professor, he lectured extensively outside the college venue and championed such advances in medicine as the use of stethoscopes, microscopes, and anesthesia.

Running parallel with Holmes's distinguished medical career were his accomplishments as a writer. Holmes often commented that he would rather be remembered as a poet than as any other thing. One of his most famous poems, "Old Ironsides," was penned in 1830 directly after his graduation from Harvard. Holmes had read in the newspaper that the Navy Department intended to destroy the *Constitution*, a historic warship nicknamed "Old Ironsides." Holmes quickly composed his poem and mailed it to a Boston newspaper, where the poem was printed. The popular reaction to the poem's plea not to "tear her tattered ensign down!" was so strong that the ship was preserved. The noble verses in "Old Ironsides" were no doubt partially the result of Holmes's love as a youth for Alexander Pope's poetical translations of Homer's heroic *Iliad* and *Odyssey*.

Holmes had dabbled in writing poems from his youth, but he was not proud of most of these early attempts. As a student at Harvard, he and his companions entertained themselves and others with light, humorous verses for assorted events. In 1836, after graduating from medical school, Holmes published his first collection of poetry called *Poems*. This volume contained "Old Ironsides" and "The Last Leaf," which rivals "Old Ironsides" in fame, largely because of his contemporary readers' reaction to it. Edgar Allan Poe wrote a copy of the poem in his own handwriting, and Abraham Lin-

coln quoted it from memory at a public event. Hundreds of readers less renowned have loved it.

Probably more significant than Holmes's serious poetical efforts were his poems that fell into the category of light verse. Such poems as "My Aunt" and "The Height of the Ridiculous" demonstrated the apt descriptions and humor that led many people to call upon Holmes to compose poems. For fifty years, he was invited to write poems for significant occasions around Boston by medical societies, universities, clubs, and other organizations. While light verse is often seen as casual and easy, it can be very demanding. Holmes was accommodating and prolific, and the quality of his poems is affirmed by their contemporary popularity as well as their survival. While literary critics largely agree that Holmes was not someone who possessed poetic genius, he is considered the master of a type of poetry that is clear, graceful, unsentimental, and often humorous.

In 1857, James Russell Lowell, a poet and social reformer, had been hired as the editor of a new literary magazine. Lowell insisted that Holmes be the magazine's first and regular contributor. Holmes originally declined the offer because he had written very little creative nonfiction before, and, at the age of forty-seven, he considered himself too old to be truly creative. Lowell persisted, and Holmes agreed to contribute, beginning by naming the new magazine *The Atlantic*. The nonfiction essays that Holmes composed serially for the magazine were eventually collected in *The Autocrat of the Breakfast-Table* (1858), which most critics agree established him as a genius.

The autocrat in Holmes's essays was an imaginary figure who lived in a boarding house and conversed with and about his imaginary fellow boarders around the breakfast table. While this structure that surrounds the essays is fiction, the thoughts and ideas expressed in the essays genuinely belong to Holmes. The essays are reflective, thought provoking, sophisticated, and humorous. They comment insightfully on Holmes's contemporaries and nineteenth century New England, as well as on human nature in general. These "conversations" of literature continued to appear in *The Atlantic*, and additional volumes were eventually published: *The Professor of the Breakfast-Table* (1860), *The Poet of the Breakfast-Table* (1872), and *Over the Teacups* (1891). *The Atlantic*'s longevity has largely been attributed to the popularity of Holmes's essay series.

Holmes also wrote three novels, *Elsie Venner* (1861), *The Guardian Angel* (1867), and *A Mortal Antipathy* (1885), which are not well respected for their literary technique. However, the novels are considered entertaining and influential because they pioneered the importance of the characters' psychology and hereditary traits in determining their actions and moral choices.

Summary

Oliver Wendell Holmes has come to be representative of the type of high-quality citizen that American society and culture can produce. Typically associated with the New England renaissance of his day, he exemplified the power and value of original thought tempered with a respectful conservatism and compassion. Possibly one of the most illustrative examples of Holmes's best characteristics was his famous attitude toward the controversial issue of allowing women into Harvard Medical School to be trained as doctors. Holmes was essentially a conservative product of his society who believed in the importance of good taste and structure. He originally voted against women's admission, arguing that women's basic natures made them the best nurses. Shortly thereafter, in a speech to a Harvard audience, he turned on his own argument and reasoned that if a woman wanted to work hard and help others as a doctor, she should be allowed to. This example was typical of Holmes's clear-headed logic coupled with the compassion for which he was well known.

Bibliography

Crothers, Samuel McChord. *Oliver Wendell Holmes: The Autocrat and His Fellow-Boarders, with Selected Poems*. Boston: Houghton Mifflin, 1909. Brief, very useful summation of the generally accepted attitudes about Holmes's personality and works. Includes all of Holmes's most famous poems.

Holmes, Oliver Wendell. *Oliver Wendell Holmes: Representative Selections*. Edited by S. I. Hayakawa and H. M. Jones. New York: American Book Company, 1939. The literary criticism of Holmes's work found in the introduction to this source is insightful and is often referred to by other critics and biographers.

Hoyt, Edwin P. *The Improper Bostonian, Dr. Oliver Wendell Holmes*. New York: Morrow, 1979. This well-researched and accessible book contains valuable and entertaining anecdotes.

Morse, John T. Jr. *Life and Letters of Oliver Wendell Holmes, Volumes I and II*. Boston: Houghton Mifflin, and London: Sampson Low, Marston, 1896. Considered the definitive Holmes biography, particularly valuable because the author knew Holmes and many of his contemporaries personally. Morse's colorful writing style is not unlike Holmes's own.

Tilton, Eleanor M. *Amiable Autocrat, A Biography of Dr. Oliver Wendell Holmes*. New York: Schuman, 1947. Extremely well documented, enjoyable biography with valuable critiques of Holmes's writing.

Valerie Snyder

FRIEDRICH VON HOLSTEIN

Born: April 24, 1837; Schwedt an der Oder, Pomerania

Died: May 8, 1909; Berlin, Germany

Area of Achievement: Diplomacy

Contribution: Holstein was a controversial chief adviser on German foreign policy from 1890 to 1906, sometimes blamed for German diplomatic isolation before World War I.

Early Life

An only child, Friedrich von Holstein passed a sickly and lonely boyhood on his family's estate or in their Berlin town house. His adolescence was spent with his parents and private tutors at European health resorts, where he became fluent in English, French, and Italian, before attending the University of Berlin. Physically unfit to follow the example of his father's army career, Holstein was briefly and unhappily in the Prussian government's legal division. Through the influence of a neighboring family friend, Otto von Bismarck, Holstein was admitted to the diplomatic service in 1860 and sent as attaché to the legation at St. Petersburg, where Bismarck was then Prussian minister.

In 1863, Holstein passed his foreign service examination and was assigned to Rio de Janeiro but was recalled to Berlin by his patron, Bismarck, who had become Prussian minister-president. In the Danish War of 1864, Holstein served as one of Bismarck's liaison officers to Prussian army headquarters and was later sent to London for the 1864-1865 Conference on the Danish Question.

An 1865-1867 sojourn in the United States began as a travel leave with the purpose of self-discovery, as his father's accidental death in 1863 had left Holstein without family but with some inherited wealth. Photographs of the young baron depict a slender man of medium height with conventionally bearded good looks but a somewhat wary expression. He combined adventures on the Western frontier with a vague assignment at the Washington legation. His friendship with the unconventional young wife of Senator Charles Sumner was later magnified by gossip into an improbable tale of scandalous romance. More prosaically, Holstein began, in the United States, an ultimately unprofitable business enterprise, which continued after his 1867 return to Germany, caused him to leave diplo-

matic service in 1868, and apparently consumed most or all of his inheritance.

When the Ems Telegram in July of 1870 foreshadowed the Franco-Prussian War, Holstein put himself at Bismarck's disposal and was sent to Italy as the chancellor's private agent to organize anti-French republican activists there in case King Victor Emmanuel II supported Napoleon III. During the 1871 Prussian siege of Paris, Holstein served as Bismarck's unofficial contact with Communard leaders in order to weaken the French government's position in the preliminary peace negotiations.

After the war, Holstein remained in France as chief secretary for Germany's Paris embassy, soon headed by the baron's new chief, Count Harry von Arnim, a political ambassador of great influence and aspirations. Arnim intrigued to overthrow the new French republic as a step toward himself replacing Bismarck as chancellor. His exposure led to sensational trials involving, among much else, purloined state documents. A courtroom charge that Holstein had taken the missing papers made headlines, and his subsequent vindication was not as widely remembered as the false but memorable accusation. Holstein entered the public mind as a man suspected.

Life's Work

In 1876, Holstein was promoted to the Berlin foreign office, where he spent the rest of his career. He became head of an information apparatus for whatever Bismarck needed to know as well as a conduit for some of what Bismarck decided to do. The baron gradually became a work-absorbed bureaucrat. Rustic in dress and slightly grotesque in the special glasses his eyes came to require, he avoided government social functions and lived simply in three small rooms in an unfashionably remote suburb, though sometimes hosting a few personal friends, generally at Borchardt's restaurant.

Occasionally rude to his superiors, jealous of his prerogatives though considerate of the clerical staff, and with no clear public role, Privy Councillor Baron Holstein seemed to be a consequential official, simply because he possessed important information. The possibilities for blackmail in the German society of the time were abundant, and speculation grew about the basis for Holstein's influence. The result was the Holstein legend, since discredited, of an intelligence chief with spies everywhere and a "poison cupboard" of secrets about those in high places—a dim-sighted but dangerous "mole." Bismarck, among many, fed the rumors, when he described "the man with the hyena eyes" as useful because "sometimes I must do evil things."

In the foreign policy field which was much, though not all, of his job, Holstein followed Bismarck's views almost entirely for about five years. By the mid-1880's, however, his own anti-Russian sentiments increasingly diverged from Bismarck's insistence on a "bridge to St. Petersburg." Like others in German politics, Holstein assumed that the 1888 accession of Kaiser William II would hasten the day of Bismarck's retirement. The baron's efforts to postpone the break while preserving his own position were at least made with the knowledge of both parties.

It is sometimes claimed that from Bismarck's dismissal by the kaiser in March of 1890 to Holstein's own resignation in April of 1906, Holstein was "the real master" of German foreign policy. This exaggerates Holstein's control and underrates the extent to which he was forced to yield to the judgment of his superiors, the impulses of the kaiser, and the pressures of the Navy League and the colonial enthusiasts. The chancellorship of Leo von Caprivi (1890-1894) was the administration most influenced by Holstein, especially in the 1890 decision to abandon the Russian reinsurance treaty in order to have a free hand for pursuing an alliance with England. Yet the generous territorial exchanges of Caprivi's treaties with England were merely seen by the British government and press as "trying to buy our friendship." England showed no interest in joining the Triple Alliance of Germany, Austria, and Italy.

Meanwhile, Russia used her diplomatic "free hand" for the Franco-Russian Alliance of 1893-1894, a blow to German security on two fronts, which caused wide criticism of the kaiser's new advisers, including Holstein. When Chlodwig von Hohenlohe succeeded Caprivi as chancellor, Holstein was often reduced to ineffective protests against the kaiser's insistence on the 1895 Triple Intervention, which alienated Japan, the needless Kruger Telegram of 1896, and the naval construction program begun by Alfred von Tirpitz in 1898.

Holstein's renewed attempts at an English alliance expired in fruitless negotiations between 1898 and 1901. The Anglo-French Entente Cordiale of 1904 was a heavy blow to Holstein's policy direc-

tion, but the Far Eastern War between Russia and Japan did give Germany some diplomatic opportunities. Holstein supported the kaiser's hope of attracting Russia and perhaps even France into an anti-British front. At the same time, Holstein pressed on Chancellor Bernhard von Bülow and the kaiser a policy of detaching England from the Entente Cordial by challenging French claims in Morocco. The kaiser's speech in Tangier escalated this move into a crisis, and a war between France and Germany seemed an imminent possibility. Holstein argued that Great Britain would not support a France whose Russian ally was temporarily helpless and that therefore France would back down. He urged going to the brink of war, but the responsibility for going over the brink was not one the kaiser wished to take. The Algeciras Conference of 1906 found Great Britain ready to support France, the United States unexpectedly pro-French, and Italy predictably neutral. That left the Austro-German alliance diplomatically isolated. Such a conspicuous failure of German diplomacy caused foreign office reverberations leading to Holstein's resignation on April 16, 1906.

Summary

Friedrich von Holstein was a career foreign officer who became an important foreign policy adviser following Bismarck's dismissal. As such, he never possessed the real authority of policy decisions because he had no political power base. On the whole, his advice was better than the inconsistent policies of his superiors. Holstein worked in the unfavorable atmosphere of an autocratic regime on the way to the scrap heap of history. The kaiser, with his frequent delusions of grandeur, was surrounded by irresponsible flatterers who isolated him from reality. Too outspoken and abrasive for such an entourage, Holstein tried to promote sensible policies by influencing the monarch's key advisers. Inevitably his efforts were gossiped about as part of the court circle intrigues, and, after the defeat of 1918, memoirs of the fallen regime often made Holstein the scapegoat for the diplomatic blunders leading to the lost war.

Holstein's papers and modern research have vindicated his character from the charges of base motives. Of the men in the kaiser's government, he was certainly above average in ability, patriotic dedication, honesty, and courage, and less given to malice or feline remarks. That comparison does not elevate him to a place among leading statesmen. His long apprenticeship under Bismarck did not qualify Holstein as a diplomatic sorcerer.

On balance, Holstein's record shows an impressive command of European and world problems; he foresaw more clearly than most the danger to Europe of the growing power of Russia. Unfortunately, he was unable to comprehend effectively "the other side of the hill." He lacked the penetration, vision, and intuitive human understanding of great statesmanship. If by that standard Holstein failed, so also did the Germany and Europe of his generation.

Bibliography

Bülow, Bernhard von. *Memoirs of Prince von Bülow*. Translated by F. A. Voigt. 2 vols. Boston: Little Brown, 1931-1932. References to Holstein are widely scattered but plentiful, negative, and frequently malicious. Bülow presents Holstein not as a masterful gray eminence but as incompetent, disagreeable, and emotionally unstable.

Gooch, George Peabody. *Studies in Modern History*. London and New York: Longman, 1931. This essay by a widely respected historian, revised from a 1923 article, had great influence in establishing the Holstein legend for a generation of students and presents a readable collection of anecdotes.

Haller, Johannes. *Philip Eulenburg: The Kaiser's Friend*. Translated by Ethel Colburn Mayne. 2 vols. New York: Knopf, and London: Secker and Warburg, 1930. Holstein's attempts to influence Wilhelm II through the kaiser's adviser are well presented. Haller's biography is a frame for Eulenburg's collection of expansive letters and recollections. An appendix gives Eulenburg's specific comments on Holstein.

Holstein, Friedrich von. *The Holstein Papers*. Edited by Norman Rich and M. H. Fisher. 4 vols. London: Cambridge University Press, 1955. These four volumes collect the relevant data on which much of Rich's biography is based. Volume 1 includes a useful introduction as well as Holstein's autobiographical sketches. Volume 2 contains Holstein's diaries and volume 3 contains his correspondence.

Hull, Isabel V. *The Entourage of Kaiser Wilhelm II, 1888-1918*. Cambridge and New York: Cambridge University Press, 1982. The kaiser and Eulenburg are at the center of this comprehensive account, but Holstein's relation to the group is established in this study, which includes a useful examination of some of the Holstein-Eulenburg letters from a different perspective.

Rich, Norman. *Friedrich von Holstein*. 2 vols. Cambridge and New York: Cambridge University Press, 1965. A long-awaited work, this is the only full-length biography of Holstein. The narrative follows Holstein's viewpoint, but objective judgment is maintained. A historical context of considerable detail makes the book especially useful to scholars of German and diplomatic history.

K. Fred Gillum

WINSLOW HOMER

Born: February 24, 1836; Boston, Massachusetts
Died: September 29, 1910; Prouts Neck, Maine
Area of Achievement: Art
Contribution: Homer was an American artist who was known for his luminous watercolors and powerful oils, especially those depicting the power, moods, beauty, and menace of the sea.

Early Life

Winslow Homer's first known work of art was a small drawing of a boy lying on the ground gazing into the distance, his head resting on his arm. Entitled *Adolescence* (1846), it displays the proficiency one would expect from a preteen who lacks training or apparent promise. The sketch would hardly be worth even a first glance were its author not known. Yet the young artist no doubt received much encouragement from his mother, a decent watercolorist of flowers and birds. Mrs. Henrietta Benson Homer was the mainstay of her family of three sons, keeping the home running even when her husband, Charles, sold his hardware business, invested in mining machinery, and traveled to California to become a Forty-niner, returning two years later, completely penniless.

Winslow was thirteen when his father left. At that time, the family was living in Cambridge, having moved there in 1842, when Winslow was ready for school. The Homer home was down the street from Harvard College, but Winslow was not to get much of a formal education; he probably did not even finish high school. He continued to draw, but when he was nineteen, his father had him apprenticed to the printmaking establishment of John Bufford, thereby launching his son's professional career. In the days before photocopy, there was a great demand for capable commercial artists to draw scenes and portraits for newspapers and magazines. Homer's first artistic assignment was a portfolio of seventeen lithographs of pictures of Puritans for inclusion in a genealogical register. Other graphics followed: more drawings for books, mostly portraits or scenes from nature; title pages for sheet music, bearing such engaging titles as "The Ratcatcher's Daughter" and "The Wheelbarrow Polka"; and even a political cartoon.

Bufford also required his apprentices to do their share of drudgery—shopkeeping, cleaning lithographers' stones, and the like, tasks that increased Winslow's sense of frustration and resentment. Be-

ing a regular employee of a firm such as Bufford's held little attraction for Homer, and as soon as he turned twenty-one and his apprenticeship was officially over, he left, vowing to be his own master.

He rented a studio and began to work on commission; most of his early assignments were done for *Ballou's Pictorial Drawing-Room Companion* (known as *Ballou's Pictorial*), an all-purpose newsmagazine designed to appeal to those who did not like to think too much about what they were reading. *Ballou's Pictorial* had an impressive circulation of 100,000. Homer did various genre pictures, portraits, street scenes, and advertisements, which all appeared in the publication as woodcuts, a medium that limited the use of curves and made it difficult for the artist to draw very fine lines to produce variations of gray. Consequently, the wood engraving turned everything into black and white and gave its figures a static, or posed, quality. Homer did not do his own woodblocks, this task being the job of special designers.

Homer's work for *Ballou's Pictorial* attracted the attention of the editors of the newly founded *Harper's Weekly* of New York City. His first drawing for them was followed by an eight-month hiatus; then commissions became more frequent, so much so that in 1859, Homer moved to New York to be closer to his major market. This move also brought him into a more stimulating artistic environment and prompted him, for the first and last time in his life, to take formal instruction in art. He enrolled in night classes at the National Academy of Design and also took some lessons from French painter Frédéric Rondel, who taught him the basics of oil painting, how to lay down color, use brushes, set his palette. Even so, Homer remained mostly self-taught.

Working for the illustrated weeklies was the chief way he earned his income for the next two decades. He rapidly became one of the leading artists of *Harper's Weekly*, and, when the Civil War began, *Harper's Weekly* wanted to put him on staff as an artist-correspondent to draw pictures of the fighting. Homer, however, always insistent on his independence, remained free-lance. He did go to the front though, following the Union armies in George B. McClellan's ill-fated Virginia Peninsular Campaign of 1862. Practically every week, *Harper's Weekly* ran at least one of his works. Most of these are not pictures of the fighting as such, but rather of the activities of soldiers in camp or on bivouac: in short, the military equivalent of the genre pictures that he was accustomed to doing. Even Homer's battle drawings rarely showed blood and gore, and the enemy was hardly ever seen. He soon became recognized as one of the best war artists, but as the conflict was reaching its climax, Homer increasingly avoided doing woodblock engravings in order to develop his talent in another and ultimately more satisfying and important direction.

Life's Work

Not until he was nearly thirty did Homer try his first painting in oils, using as a subject a sketch he had done the previous year, 1862, printed as an illustration in *Harper's Weekly. The Sharpshooter* shows a Union soldier sitting in a pine tree, sighting his gun at a target somewhere off the canvas. This work was followed by *Punishment for Intoxication* (1863) and *A Skirmish in the Wilderness* (1864), which were also taken from drawings he had made while he was with the army. The paintings were done in his New York studio and are surprising for being such good first attempts. His most famous painting of the war was *Prisoners from the Front*, also a studio piece, done in 1866, when the war was over. Only the uniforms and several muskets make the picture military; the composition is very basic: The six principal figures simply stand in a ragged line in the foreground in studio poses. The picture was so well received by the experts and the public that it ensured Homer's election to full membership in the National Academy.

That same year, Homer made his first trip to Europe, staying in Paris, where two of his paintings, including *Prisoners from the Front* were to be shown at the Exposition Universelle. The paintings he did while abroad were mostly portraits of women, including two engaging oils of farm girls with pitchforks. He returned home after ten months.

Then began a period of great artistic creativity. In the fourteen years between his return in 1867, and 1881, when he again left for Europe, he produced more than half of the works of his entire artistic career. His search for new subjects and scenes took him all over New England, through Pennsylvania and Virginia. He liked painting in the mountains: the Catskills, the Adirondacks, the White Mountains of New Hampshire; he liked painting the beaches: New England, along the New Jersey

shore. As he became more practiced in oils, he also began to develop his talent in watercolor, a medium he also taught himself to use. He exhibited with the American Watercolor Society for the first time in 1874. He also continued to produce drawings for woodcuts in *Harper's Weekly* and other magazines, to earn extra money, but abandoned this form altogether in 1875.

A favorite subject continued to be women, whom he showed partaking in all sorts of respectable middle-class activities: picking flowers, playing croquet, tossing hoops. Even if the task was gathering eggs or taking care of sick chickens, the subjects hardly seemed engaged in real physical labor. Homer also liked to depict the pleasures of youth: children playing games, wading, dreaming, sitting on fences, gathering clams. For these bucolically pretty pictures, he filled his palette with bright warm colors, exactly the sort of hues that would appeal to his bourgeois clients. Yet he also did paintings that were not so commercially motivated, and these must be judged among the best of the period. These come from his stay in Virginia, where he had an opportunity to observe the rural poverty of the blacks. He revealed these people with a compassion and sensitivity rare for a time when blacks were seen as objects of derision.

As Homer became more involved in his art, he seemed to relate less successfully to his fellowman and became more attached to his solitude. In 1881, he again left the United States for Europe, but this time he did not go to a large urban center, but rather to Cullercoats, a drab fishing village on the Eastern coast of England, near Tynemouth. There, surrounded by working-class people, he found the isolation he wanted, his loneliness reinforced by watching the dark, changing moods of the North Sea and studying its effect on those who relied on it for their livelihood. He painted storms and shipwrecks and fisherwomen watching the dark waters for the return of their men. It was in England that he did the visual research, the artistic counterpart of working in an archive, for canvases that he would complete when he returned home. His famous *The Herring Net* (1885) almost certainly had its origins in his experiences there.

He returned to New York in late 1882, but he could never readjust to the urban life he once knew. In England, he had discovered the kind of simplicity he was seeking in life and wanted to portray in his work. Therefore, in 1883, he decided to settle on the craggy coast of Maine, on a rough promontory jutting southward into Saco Bay, known as Prouts Neck, which had been purchased by his father. There Homer built a studio; there he would remain for the remainder of his life, leaving only occasionally on excursions to Canada, Florida, and Bermuda. He continued the course he had charted for himself while in England, painting his greatest masterpieces. In 1909, he painted his last picture, *Driftwood*, which is also one of his best. After he finished, he smeared his palette and hung it on the wall, never to take it down again. The following year, he died. He was seventy-four.

Summary

Winslow Homer was one of the greatest autodidacts of the nineteenth century. His consuming passion for his craft, his intense struggle to succeed, perhaps an overcompensation for his lack of formal training, constantly nurtured his compulsion to improve, and the older he became, the better he became. He had many opportunities to see the works of famous predecessors, but he avoided doing so, reluctant to damage his own instincts and compromise his powers of observation and sense of style. He visited museums in Paris and London, but more out of a sense of obligation than out of a search for inspiration. If he was impressed by the Elgin marbles in the British Museum, it was because they offered him confirmation and reinforcement, not contrast. Homer also made little contact with other living artists, neither those who painted in the standard academic vein, nor those more revolutionary, such as the Impressionists and their successors. Homer's art remained grounded in his own narrow, artistic universe. He became wedded to a basic classical compositional framework established during his career as an illustrator.

Had this remarkable man died at fifty, he would have left many pleasing canvases and watercolors—his Civil War woodcuts might be regarded as interesting period pieces, but not the stuff of greatness. A notable exception was the *The Carnival* (1877), one of his pictures of the Virginia blacks. Homer arranged his figures in his usual manner, marching them across the foreground in rough formation, but rarely had he used oil color more dramatically and skillfully. Also remarkable was his depiction of character. In showing the determination with which these people celebrated their holiday, he revealed their sense of hopelessness; in painting a scowl on the face of a barefoot girl, he

projected their life of penury. To this he added a touch of irony: The two youngest children are carrying tiny American flags.

Homer's true greatness lay ahead, revealed in the last twenty years of his life, a time when he became a virtual recluse. If an artist's character is truly revealed in his art, then Homer presents something of a problem. There is a sense of pessimism and terror in many of his seascape oils, but his watercolors are full of joie de vivre and hope. These are boldly presented, not picky in color or detail, and convey a sprightly immediacy which is alien to many of his morose canvases.

Homer's reputation, however, will always be based on his great marine paintings. Compositionally, they are hardly revolutionary. There is a certain theatricality about the manner in which he arranges his subjects, as if he were a director constantly blocking his scenes in stage center or just back of the footlights. Although he liked to work outdoors, in many of these oils it almost seems as if the turbulent waters had come into his studio to pose. The waves crashing against the rocks often have the same sculptural quality as the rocks themselves. Homer depicts movement not so much by composition, for example in the frenetic way of a work by Eugène Delacroix, but in the fluidity of his brush strokes and in his use of color.

In the flesh tones of the bearded sailor in *The Lookout—All's Well* (1896), Homer builds up his colors in thin layers, juxtaposing warm with cool, until one can almost see underneath the man's saltwater-toughened skin. The sun-and-surf-punished decking of the small sailboat in *The Gulf Stream* (1899) and the water surrounding the hapless craft are painted with the skill of Claude Monet at his best. Homer also has a fine sense of drama and understanding of theme. For example, in *The Wreck* (1896), Homer concentrated on a rescue operation rather than the disaster itself. In the foreground, in full-length black rubber coat, stands a gaunt, spectral walrus-mustached veteran, his right hand raised as a signal for help or in warning to onlookers to keep away. The man has obviously been through such tragedies many times before.

In depicting such moments, Homer makes one forget the individual elements of his art, just as hearing a great symphony makes one forget the individual notes. Yet only by mastering the fundamentals was Homer, like all great artists, able to transcend his medium and convey the true immensity of his talent.

Bibliography

Beam, Philip C. *Winslow Homer at Prout's Neck.* Boston: Little Brown, 1966. Beam concentrates on the last and greatest period of the artist's life. He seeks to enhance understanding of Homer's work through an evaluation of the internal evidence in his pictures and an understanding of his relation to other American and European art of his time.

Cikovsky, Nicolai, Jr., ed. *Winslow Homer.* New Haven, Conn.: Yale University Press, 1995. Cikovsky examines Homer's life. Winner of a Choice 1996 Outstanding Academic Book Award.

Downes, William Howe. *Life and Works of Winslow Homer.* Boston: Houghton Mifflin, 1911. This biography, published a year after Homer's death, was the first attempt to create a chronology of the subject's life. The author was awed by his responsibility, for he seems to have included every scrap of information he could find. Unfortunately, Homer himself was not too cooperative, once telling Downes that no part of his life was of much concern to the public: "Therefore I must decline to give you any particulars in regard to it."

Flexner, James Thomas. *The World of Winslow Homer, 1936-1910.* New York: Time, 1966. This study, from the Time-Life Library of Art series, gives a fine presentation of Homer in the context of the development of American art. Especially helpful are such special sections as Homer as a watercolorist and the description of two other contemporary giants, Thomas Eakins and Albert Ryder.

Goodrich, Lloyd. *Winslow Homer.* New York: Macmillan, 1944. An artistic biography rather than an account of Homer's personal life. The author treats his subject with understanding and insight, the product of careful and meticulous research. Includes a twenty-page reminiscence by one of Homer's friends, John Beatty.

————. *Winslow Homer.* New York: Macmillan, 1973. The catalog to accompany the Winslow Homer exhibition organized by the Whitney Museum of American Art. Most of the book features reproductions of the works on display; these are put in context by an intelligent essay on Homer's life and the important stages in his artistic development.

Hannaway, Patti. *Winslow Homer in the Tropics.* Richmond, Va.: Westover, 1973. The restricted scope of this book is part of a recent development to concentrate on one aspect of the artist's life, in this case his output of watercolors done while he was in Florida and in the Bahamas. The book is a catalog of the principal products of those visits. The illustrations are particularly good and are accompanied by a short background piece and artistic commentary.

Hendricks, Gordon. *The Life and Work of Winslow Homer.* New York: Abrams, 1979. This well-researched, sumptuously produced volume includes many excellent reproductions, supplemented by intelligent commentary and an exhaustive listing of the artist's works in public collections in the United States.

Hoopes, Donelson E. *Winslow Homer Watercolors.* New York: Watson-Guptill, and London: Barrie and Rockliff, 1969. Representative samples of Homer's work from 1878 to 1904. Intelligent analysis of Homer's color technique and sense of composition.

Hyman, Linda. *Winslow Homer: America's Old Master.* New York: Doubleday, 1973. Intended primarily for the young reader, for whom it provides a good introduction to Homer's art. It is written in a simple, informative style and relies more on quotations from Homer, from his friends and family, and from newspaper accounts than on romantic speculation or fictionalizing.

Luce, J. V. *Celebrating Homer's Landscapes: Troy and Ithaca Revisited.* New Haven, Conn.: Yale University Press, 1998. Luce, a Homeric text authority, tours the locales of the *Iliad* and the *Odyssey,* providing photographs of the venues and arguing (with liberal quotations) that Homer's descriptions are technically accurate as opposed to poetic musings.

Wm. Laird Kleine-Ahlbrandt

SAM HOUSTON

Born: March 2, 1793; Rockbridge County, Virginia
Died: July 26, 1863; Huntsville, Texas
Areas of Achievement: Government and politics
Contribution: Houston served as commanding general of the Texan army during the Texas Revolution. He later won election as president of the Republic of Texas, governor of the state of Texas, and United States senator.

Early Life

Samuel Houston (always called "Sam" both formally and informally) was born in Rockbridge County, Virginia, on March 2, 1793. His father, Samuel Houston, Sr., was a farmer and veteran of the American Revolution. His mother, née Elizabeth Paxton, came from pioneer stock. Young Sam was the fifth of six sons in a family which also included three daughters. He attended school intermittently until his father's death in 1807, when his formal education ended. The widow Houston moved her family to Marysville, Tennessee, where Sam spent the remainder of his youth. For a time, he worked in the village store, although this was not to his liking. In his teenage years, he sought escape and left home on several occasions to live with the Cherokee Indians. In total, he spent almost four years with them, mastering their language, customs, and culture. The Indians accepted him as one of their own, giving him the name "Raven." He eventually returned home to live with his family.

Young Houston joined the army during the War of 1812, serving with distinction at the Battle of Horseshoe Bend. His personal exploits attracted the attention of General Andrew Jackson, who promoted him to the rank of lieutenant. After leaving the military in 1818, Houston studied law and became a practicing attorney at Lebanon, Tennessee. A physically large man of greater than average height, he had a powerful build graced by curly dark hair and a pleasing countenance. Known for his gregarious personality and public speaking ability, he had a dramatic air about him which made him the center of attention and an individual of great personal popularity.

Life's Work

Houston's neighbors in Tennessee elected him a state militia officer in 1819. During 1823, he gave up the practice of law and entered politics, securing in that year election to the United States Congress as a representative. Houston quickly became a leader in the Tennessee Democratic Party. He also forged a lifelong personal friendship with Andrew Jackson. Houston became the governor of Tennessee in 1827 and looked forward to a promising career in that state. He married Eliza H. Allen, daughter of a prominent Tennessee family, on January 1, 1829. Within months, Houston's success turned to bitter failure because of problems with his bride. Although historians have never agreed on the specific causes, the marriage to Eliza lasted only a short time. She returned home to her parents (eventually securing a divorce) while Houston, with some despondency, resigned the governorship in the spring of 1829 and moved to Indian territory to start life anew. The Tennessee years became a closed chapter in his life.

Houston spent the following years among his boyhood friends, the Cherokee. He adopted Indian dress and customs, became a citizen of the Indian nation, and took a wife according to the dictates of Cherokee law. His Indian wife, Tiana, assisted him in operating a small trading post. In addition, he served as an advocate for the Cherokee in various matters before the United States government. By 1832, the wanderlust had again struck Houston, and he began visiting Texas, although he maintained residence in the Indian nation for a time. He first arrived in the Anglo areas of Mexican Texas as an Indian agent and a representative of investors who sought land in the province. The exact date which he moved to Texas is lost in obscurity, but, by late 1833, he was taking an active part in Texas affairs as a resident. In the process, he left his life with the Cherokee, including Tiana, forever in the past.

His removal to Texas came in the midst of growing revolutionary fervor on the part of Anglo residents unhappy with Mexican rule. Houston played an important role in events which resulted in the eventual break with Mexico. He served as presiding officer of the Convention of 1833, which wrote a proposed constitution for Texas, and attended the Consultation of 1835, which marked the start of the revolution. He signed the Texas Declaration of Independence from Mexico while serving as a delegate to the Convention of 1836. The revolutionary government of Texas appointed him commander in chief of the army with the rank of major general on March 4, 1836. Forever after, in spite of the other high offices he would hold in his career, Sam Houston preferred the title "General."

Taking command of the army at Gonzales shortly after the Alamo fell to Mexican troops commanded by Antonio Lopez de Santa Anna, General Houston led his forces eastward across Texas in a retreat known as the "Runaway Scrape." Potential disaster for the Texans turned to stunning victory when Houston and his men met Santa Anna's army, which had pursued them, at the Battle of San Jacinto on April 21, 1836. Santa Anna was captured, his army soundly defeated, and General Houston became the hero of the day.

With independence secured, Houston won election as president of the Republic of Texas on September 5, 1836. His term saw Texas' failure to enter the Union because of opposition in the United States Congress, attempts to deal with the Comanche Indians, and growing political factionalism in the republic. While president of the republic, Houston married Margaret M. Lea on May 8, 1840. They eventually had eight children, including Andrew Jackson Houston, who served a short period as United States senator from Texas during the 1930's.

Since the republic's constitution forbade a president from succeeding himself, Houston left office after one term. Mirabeau B. Lamar, with whom Houston had political differences, replaced him. Houston, however, won election to the republic's congress, where pro-Houston and anti-Houston parties soon became the active political factions of the fledgling nation. Houston's opponents objected to several of his policies, including his attempts to keep Austin from becoming the capital city; others believed that he had failed to work hard enough for statehood. Other critics no doubt found the general's large ego and some of his personal habits objectionable, especially his frequent and heavy drinking of whiskey. Whatever the reasons for controversy, Houston would be at the center of politically motivated strife and criticism for the rest of his public career.

His reelection to the presidency of the republic in 1841 came after a heated campaign with the Lamar faction. Houston attempted to undo some of the programs of his predecessor and was faced with additional problems, including a minor, abortive Mexican invasion of Texas in 1842. He was able to deal with all these efficiently, although not always with complete success. By the end of his second term, in 1844, the annexation of Texas by the United States had become a distinct possibility. Houston, however, wavered in the face of statehood for Texas,

sometimes giving the impression that he favored continuing the republic. It fell to his successor, Anson Jones, to have the distinction of serving as the last president of the Republic of Texas.

Along with Thomas J. Rusk, Houston became one of the United States senators representing Texas once statehood had been secured in 1845. He would continue to serve in that body until the eve of the Civil War. Houston continued his pre-Texas affiliation with the Democratic Party during his days in the Senate. He played a role in the debates over the Compromise of 1850, siding with Southern delegates while he lobbied for an acceptable settlement to the Texas boundary controversy. He had aspirations for the Democratic Party presidential nomination in 1848 and in 1852, but in both instances he failed to attract enough delegate votes to make a showing at the convention.

Houston's role as a leader in the Southern bloc of the Senate came to an end with his vote on the Kansas-Nebraska Bill of 1854. A strong advocate of the Union, he voted with Free-Soilers and Whigs against the bill. This placed him at odds with his Southern colleagues and many slaveholders in Texas, all of whom wanted the bill passed. By the mid-1850's, Houston became increasingly distanced from the Democratic Party when he embraced the Know-Nothing movement because of his strong commitment to the preservation of the Union. He attended Know-Nothing meetings and conventions. Texas Democrats denounced him for these activities. Houston ran for the governorship of Texas in 1857 but was defeated by Hardin Runnels. He remained in the Senate until the end of his term, in 1859, whereupon he returned to Texas. He ran once more against Runnels for governor in 1859, this time winning by a small margin.

His term as governor, which began in December of 1859, proved to be a time of turmoil for Texas and a period of deep personal anguish for Houston. The election of Abraham Lincoln resulted in the secession crisis and the formation of the Confederate States of America. Texas was a slave state, largely settled by persons of Southern heritage, and most Texans favored secession although some preferred to remain with the Union. Houston fell into the latter camp. His commitment to the Constitution and the Union was stronger than his desire to secede. As governor, Houston thus found himself out of step with most Texans and their political leaders. Houston refused to cooperate with the State Secession Convention which met in Austin.

When the convention adopted a secession ordinance, the governor took the position that Texas had returned legally to her former status as an independent republic. He therefore refused as governor to take an oath of allegiance to the Confederacy. The Secession Convention therefore declared the office of governor vacant and named Edward Clark to the position. Houston, refusing an offer of federal troops from President Lincoln, decided to accede to the convention's decision and relinquished his office. He retired to Huntsville, Texas, where he died on July 26, 1863.

Summary

Sam Houston played an important role in the Westward movement of the United States during the nineteenth century. As a frontiersman, military figure, and political leader, he assisted in the development of two states (Tennessee and Texas) from frontier outposts into settled areas. His greatest contributions came in Texas, where he led an army to victory, helped to organize a republic, and participated in its transition into a part of the United States. As a senator in the 1850's, he was one of the few Southern leaders to foresee the consequences of national political policies which would lead to the Civil War. Once the war came, he stood alone as the most prominent Texas Unionist willing to sacrifice his career for the preservation of the Union. It is fitting that the largest, most industrial city in Texas bears his name.

Bibliography

Bishop, Curtis Kent. *Lone Star: Sam Houston.* New York: Julian Messner, 1961. Written for young readers, the book provides a clear assessment of Houston's career and relates the major facts of his life in an easy-to-read narrative.

Friend, Llerena B. *Sam Houston: The Great Designer.* Austin: University of Texas Press, 1954. Best scholarly biography. Treats Houston's entire career with an emphasis on his impact on national events. It is based on extensive archival research and is the best starting place for a full-scale study of Houston and his time.

Gregory, Jack, and Rennard Strickland. *Sam Houston with the Cherokees, 1829-1833.* Austin: University of Texas Press, 1967; London: University of Texas Press, 1976. Develops in detail the story of Houston's Indian marriage to Tiana and his role as Cherokee advocate. It is based on solid research previously unconsidered by historians, thereby providing an exhaustive analysis of Houston's years among the Indians.

Houston, Samuel. *Autobiography of Sam Houston.* Edited by Donald Day and Harry Herbert Ullom. Norman: University of Oklahoma Press, 1954. Houston paints himself in the best possible light, but this edited version provides insight into the man and his era.

———. *The Writings of Sam Houston, 1813-1863.* Edited by Amelia Williams and Eugene C. Barker. 8 vols. Austin: University of Texas Press, 1938-1943. A comprehensive collection of most important letters and papers dealing with Houston's career. Contains most of the extant Houston letters.

James, Marquis. *The Raven: A Biography of Sam Houston.* Indianapolis: Bobbs-Merrill, and London: Hutchinson, 1929. Provides a readable narrative with a colorful style. Highlights Houston's role as friend and political associate of Andrew Jackson. Until the appearance of the above-noted study by Friend, this biography ranked as the most complete analysis of Houston.

Roberts, Marge Thornall. *The Personal Correspondence of Sam Houston, Vol. 1: 1839-1845.* Denton: University of North Texas Press, 1996. The first volume of Houston's private correspondence, mainly with his wife, provides a look at his recovery from depression and alcoholism and his views on issues and people.

Wisehart, Marion K. *Sam Houston: American Giant.* Washington, D.C.: Luce, 1962. A laudatory, popular biography, full of detail. Although not scholarly in nature, it is useful because it is based on the important biographies noted above. An excellent study for readers at the high school level.

Light Townsend Cummins

ELIAS HOWE

Born: July 9, 1819; Spencer, Massachusetts
Died: October 3, 1867; Brooklyn, New York
Area of Achievement: Invention
Contribution: Howe was the first American inventor to build a workable sewing machine and have it successfully patented.

Early Life

Elias Howe, Jr., was born on July 9, 1819, in Spencer, Massachusetts. He was one of eight children born to a poor farmer, Elias Howe, Sr., and his wife, Polly Bemis Howe. Among the Howe family, two of Elias, Sr.'s brothers were inventors. Elias, Sr., himself ran a gristmill and cut lumber, in addition to farming, to support his family.

When Elias, Jr., was six, he worked along with his brothers and sisters sewing wires on cards by hand at home. This piecework, for a local cotton mill, brought in some extra money to help the family. His other work as a boy included repairs to his parents' farmhouse. He showed great patience and determination in his painstaking tasks, often repairing the farm machinery—work he enjoyed. The young boy's life, however, was not all work. Regarded as easygoing and companionable, he had several good friends. He attended school during the winter but spent the other seasons at work on the farm.

By the time the boy was twelve, his father realized that he could no longer feed and clothe him, so he was hired out to work on a neighbor's farm. This arrangement lasted for about one year but had to end when Howe's frailties interfered with his heavy chores. The youngster had been born small and frail, and he never had the endurance and strength necessary for hard labor, a fact with which he had to contend all of his life. He was also congenitally lame.

In 1835, Howe moved to Lowell, Massachusetts, where he found work repairing cotton-mill machinery. Although he was still a young man, he was admired for his advanced skill with machinery. Unfortunately, the economic panic in 1837 forced the cotton mills in Lowell to close, and young Howe lost his job.

He next moved to Cambridge, Massachusetts, where he roomed with a cousin and worked as a foreman for a hemp-carding company; this job was boring and fatiguing, so Howe stayed for only part of a year. His next position was a fortu-

nate one for him. He worked as a repairman for Ari Davis of Boston, a skilled watchmaker, who also made precision instruments for seamen and for the scientists at Harvard University. Davis' shop attracted many inventors, and it was here that Howe got the idea to invent a sewing machine. One day in 1839, he heard the loud-voiced Davis tell a customer who was struggling to invent a knitting machine that the invention of a sewing machine would make a man rich.

On March 3, 1841, Howe married Elizabeth J. Ames of Boston. In a few years, the couple had three children to support. To help her husband, Mrs. Howe did hand-sewing for her neighbors. Many evenings, Howe watched her sew, pondering how a sewing machine would work. In part from his fascination with machinery and in part from his desire to escape poverty and support his family, Howe became obsessed with the idea of inventing a sewing machine.

Life's Work

Howe quit his job at Davis' shop and moved into the attic of Elias Howe, Sr.'s house—now in Cambridge. There in 1843, working diligently, Howe was beginning to put together his first version of a sewing machine when a fire destroyed the house. A friend, George Fisher, took an interest in Howe's invention and generously funded him five hundred dollars for the equipment he needed; Fisher also boarded the Howes in his home. From 1844 to 1845 (especially during the winter months), Howe worked at a feverish pace to complete a functioning sewing machine. He used no blueprints or sketches but worked from a mental design; he also used the trial-and-error method of putting his ideas into moving parts, often discarding pieces of the machine that had not worked to his satisfaction. One of his most serious challenges was the designing of the proper needle for his sewing machine; needles with holes at the head (as women use in hand sewing) did not work on the machine. Finally, Howe had a dream in which men were threatening to kill him with spears; he noticed that all the spears had holes near their points—this was his solution. Howe's machine sewed perfectly when he used such needles.

By April of 1845, Howe and his business partner Fisher had a machine which they could present to

the public. A demonstration was held at the Quincy Hall Clothing Manufactory, where Howe, operating his machine, sewed at least five times faster than the best women hand-sewers. The stitching produced by Howe's machine was also neater and stronger than that done by hand.

Howe's sewing machine did not impress Boston's clothiers as a useful item for them to purchase. A few factors affected the marketing of Howe's invention to American industry. First, it was expensive—about three hundred dollars. Second, the hand-sewers would have to be retrained to work by machine, and their employers feared that they would refuse (the workers knew that the sewing machines would soon take most of their jobs). Finally, the clothiers already had cheap labor in their women workers, so they saw no need to buy machinery to do the sewing. Howe was also at a disadvantage in that the United States did not yet have a strong communication network. If news of his machine had reached major clothing firms in New York City, he may have found buyers for his invention.

When Howe realized that there were no eager buyers for his machine in the United States, he sent

his brother Amasa Howe to London, England, to try to market it there. The British industries were more organized than the American ones at this time and were also more acquainted with manufacture by machine. In October of 1846, Amasa Howe sold his brother's sewing machine to William Thomas of London for 250 pounds in British money. Thomas was a maker of corsets, shoes, and umbrellas, and he was also a dishonest man. He obtained a British patent for the Howe machine in his own name, rather than in Howe's as he had promised. Thomas also made a verbal agreement with Amasa to pay Elias a royalty on each sewing machine Thomas sold—an agreement which he ignored.

Howe's profits from the first sale of his invention quickly went to pay his debts. He found himself in poverty again and so accepted an offer from Thomas (still seemingly a fair man) to move to London and build for him a stronger sewing machine (presumably to sew leather for shoes). Howe and his family moved to a poor section of London, and he worked for Thomas for fifteen dollars a week. At the end of eight months, Howe had created the desired machine, and Thomas, not too graciously, ordered Howe to work as a repairman in his factory. Howe felt insulted and left.

The year 1848 was an especially difficult one for Howe. First, he had to be separated from his family. Unable to support them, he sent them home to the United States, while he remained in England to build another sewing machine with the financial help of Charles Inglis, a relatively poor man himself. When this machine was finished, Howe sold it cheaply and also pawned his American patent papers on his first sewing machine (along with a working model), in order to buy ship passage back to the United States.

He landed in New York, where he found employment as a mechanic at a good wage, but he had held this job for only a few weeks when tragedy struck. His wife, having battled consumption for two years, was dying. Elias Howe, Sr., sent his son money to travel home to see Elizabeth before she died; his brother-in-law lent him a suit to wear to her funeral. Howe also learned that the few household goods he owned had been lost in a shipwreck on their passage from England. His father and neighbors helped him through this crisis, taking care of his children.

Ironically, at about this time, Howe learned of several American copies of his sewing machine, produced with total disregard to his United States' patent. Fortunately, Howe remained persistent, patenting his first sewing machine on September 10, 1846, even though he had to mortgage his father's farm for the money that he needed to travel to Washington, D. C., to receive that patent.

Howe's legal patent made a considerable difference in the outcome of his life's work. He now elicited the aid of George Bliss, who had bought the fifty percent business interest in Howe's invention from George Fisher. Bliss and Howe employed the lawyers necessary to wage long court suits against the makers of American sewing machines. Howe wished to win a royalty from these manufacturers for each sewing machine they had sold in the United States; as the patented inventor of the machine, he had this right.

One of Howe's opponents in court proved to be a determined man himself. Isaac M. Singer, wishing to retain the fortune he was making from selling Singer sewing machines, hired help to refute Howe's claim that he was the rightful inventor. Singer located Walter Hunt of New York State, who had built a model of a sewing machine earlier than had Howe. Singer lost his case, however, when it was shown in court that Hunt's rebuilt machine did not work and that Hunt had never patented it.

Howe, after battling in court from 1849 to 1854, was victorious and, instantly, a rich man. All of his American competitors who were manufacturing and selling machines had to pay royalties to him. Soon, his income was about four thousand dollars a week. Yet Howe was a generous man, sharing his new wealth with the friends and relatives who had helped him in his years of struggle. His one deep regret was that his wife had died before he gained his fortune. The humorous and fun-loving aspects of Howe's personality had left him at her tragic death.

Howe was, however, left with his dedication, which he used to good advantage in his remaining years. In 1865, in Bridgeport, Connecticut, he built a large, modern plant for the manufacture of sewing machines (later managed by his brother Amasa). Howe became a prominent and respected citizen of Bridgeport. When he volunteered to serve as a private in the Union Army during the Civil War (despite his age and infirmities) many young Bridgeport men were moved by his example and volunteered as well. Howe generously outfitted the entire Connecticut Seventeenth Regiment Volunteers, which he helped to organize; he even provided horses for the officers and paid the men when their army wages were delayed. Howe served

in a Union Army camp near Baltimore, Maryland, but was forced to leave when his chronic frailty made it impossible for him to continue his duties as the camp's postmaster.

While visiting at his daughter's home in Brooklyn, New York, in 1867, Howe contracted Bright's disease; he never recovered and died October 3, 1867. The large factory he had built in Bridgeport, Connecticut, passed on to his son, who managed it until a fire leveled it on July 26, 1883. In the following year, the city of Bridgeport, in gratitude, erected a statue of Elias Howe, Jr., in their Seaside Park. He stands, hat in one hand and cane in the other, overlooking Long Island Sound. His face is large and solid, with a prominent nose, soft eyes, and firmly set lips—the face of a determined Yankee inventor.

Summary

With his invention of the sewing machine, Howe made a contribution to American industry that profoundly affected Americans' lives. The hand-sewn garments that women laboriously made for their families were replaced by mass-produced clothing that sold at affordable prices. Howe's invention also moved the making of many clothing items including shoes, out of cottage industries and tailor shops and into manufacturing plants. The sewing machine became a reasonably priced, convenient piece of equipment that was also found in a large number of homes; there sewing became a creative task, rather than a painstaking necessity.

Howe also played an important role in another area of American industrial development. He, along with several successful sewing machine manufacturers, held a conference in Albany, New York, in 1856, with the purpose of avoiding further lawsuits. These manufacturers, known as the Combination, became the first American industrial group to form a patent pool; they shared one another's machine designs and improvements for a reasonable fee, rather than remaining rivals.

Howe's inventiveness, perseverance, and mechanical skill won for him many well-deserved honors in foreign nations, including a gold medal at the famed Paris Exhibition of 1867. His genius and Yankee know-how gained for this once poverty-stricken American the acclaim of a grateful nation and a grateful world.

Bibliography

Burlingame, Roger. *March of the Iron Men: A Social History of Union Through Invention.* New

York and London: Scribner, 1938. A fascinating book, well researched and well organized. As an interpreter of social history, Burlingame has strong opinions, which he defends admirably. Outstanding bibliography, chronology chart, and illustrations. Good at showing inventors' motives, including Howe's.

Chamberlain, John. *The Enterprising Americans: A Business History of the United States.* New York: Harper, 1963. Originally a series in *Fortune* magazine on famous American businessmen. Includes an extensive and helpful bibliography. Emphasis is on the wit and ingenuity of some Yankee inventors, including Howe. A lively and engaging style throughout. A good book for the high school student.

Gies, Joseph, and Frances Gies. *The Ingenious Yankees.* New York: Crowell, 1976. The authors focus on the way in which America's Yankee inventors helped transform an agricultural country into a powerful technological nation. Offers clarity of exposition in an interesting narrative format. A biographical sketch of Howe is included, as well as an extensive bibliography.

Iles, George. *Leading American Inventors.* New York: Holt, 1912. Iles offers a careful analysis of Howe's personality, focusing on the characteristics that caused Howe's success. Iles brings his subject to life for the reader. Some of the details of Howe's life covered here are not found elsewhere; a portrait of him is included.

Poole, Lynn, and Gray Poole. *Men Who Pioneered Inventions.* New York: Dodd, Mead, 1969. A book suitable for a young person, from the Makers of Our Modern World series. Less factual information in its chapter on Howe than in the other books listed here. The Pooles describe how the sewing machine affected American life.

Thompson, Holland. *The Age of Invention: A Chronicle of Mechanical Conquest.* New Haven, Conn.: Yale University Press, 1921. One volume in a series devoted to American life, history, and progress. It has an ample bibliography, as well as photographs and illustrations. Vivid descriptive passages of Howe at work (slightly fictionalized) are provided in a narrative account of his life and work. Also details the mechanics of Howe's sewing machine.

Wilson, Mitchell. *American Science and Invention: A Pictorial History.* New York: Simon and Schuster, 1954. A large volume which relies on period illustrations and photographs to describe the course of American invention. Concise and accurate on Howe's life as well as his inventing. Good descriptions of how his machine operated. Also interesting on Howe's character, including his mechanical skill.

Patricia E. Sweeney

JULIA WARD HOWE

Born: May 27, 1819; New York, New York
Died: October 17, 1910; Newport, Rhode Island
Areas of Achievement: Literature and social reform
Contribution: Howe composed the lyrics to the inspiring patriotic song "The Battle Hymn of the Republic" and was an active crusader for women's right to vote.

Early Life

On May 27, 1819, in New York City, Julia Ward was born to Samuel Ward and Julia Rush Cutler Ward. She was the couple's second daughter and the fourth of their seven children. Another Julia had previously been born to the Wards, only to die at age three. All the surviving Ward children enjoyed good relations with one another for most of their lives, especially the girls. Samuel Ward's ancestors had migrated to America from Gloucester, England, and settled in Rhode Island, a state which two Wards served as early governors. Samuel Ward himself was a partner in the prestigious Wall Street banking firm Prime, Ward, and King. Julia Cutler Ward, young Julia's mother, had been born in Boston but had relatives living in South Carolina, where her own mother had been a Southern belle. Among the Cutler ancestors was General Francis Marion, the celebrated "Swamp Fox" of the American Revolution.

Little Julia, or "Little Miss Ward," as her family called her, had an intelligent nature combined with a sometimes fiery temper. As an adolescent, she developed scholarly habits that would remain with her throughout her life. Her father saw to it that all of his daughters were well educated; their private tutor, Joseph Cogswell, had them follow the Harvard curriculum of the early 1800's. Julia was also tutored in the Romance languages and took lessons in voice and piano from an Italian master.

All these things Mr. Ward was able to provide because of his comfortable financial status. He had a roomy, well-decorated house built at the corner of Bond Street and Broadway; one section of this dwelling housed his private art gallery. Mr. Ward was also, however, a strict and deeply religious man; he did not like his daughters to attend the theater or to mix too freely in New York society. Indeed, he delayed their entrance into society formally for some time, much to Julia's disappointment.

Once Julia entered New York society, she was an instant favorite. She was a petite young woman, only five feet and one-quarter inch tall. She had bright blue eyes and red hair combined with a creamy white skin in a lovely, oval-shaped face. She began to attend New York parties with some regularity when her brother, Samuel Ward, Jr., married Emily Astor of the wealthy Astor family, in 1837.

Julia Ward faced two tragedies in her early life. Her mother died when she was five; she had been tubercular and died of a fever days after giving birth to her seventh child. Mr. Ward was devastated by the early death of his wife, who was only twenty-eight; he invited her intelligent, witty sister, Miss Eliza Cutler, to reside in his home and care for his children. Little Julia showed much of the wit for which her aunt was noted; she also liked to write poetry, as her mother had done.

Julia had recently turned twenty when her father died. At that time Edward Ward, an uncle, looked after the orphaned children and managed their finances. Julia was deeply upset by her father's death. Shortly after, in 1841, she journeyed to visit friends in Boston to try to end her depression. Among her Massachusetts acquaintances was Henry Wadsworth Longfellow, a longtime friend of her brother, Samuel. While in Boston, Julia accompanied Longfellow on a visit to the Perkins Institute for the Blind. There she met the school's director, a famous educator and reformer, Dr. Samuel Gridley Howe. Dr. Howe, also a physician, was a tall and handsome bachelor of forty. Julia, now twenty-two, was attracted to him. They first appeared publicly as a couple in 1842 at a farewell dinner given for Charles Dickens in Boston, and shortly thereafter, their engagement was announced. They were married on April 23, 1843, after what is recorded as a stormy courtship.

The transition from girlhood and a relatively happy life among the cultured society of New York to that of a wife, mother, and homemaker in the unfamiliar setting of Boston was not easy for Julia Ward Howe. In New York she had been a favorite child in the extended Ward family living on clannish Bond Street; she had a quick wit, a winning charm, and skill as a conversationalist—all of which endeared her to New York society on the whole. In Boston, however, the new Mrs. Howe was a stranger. Her husband's friends included such men as Horace Mann, an educator of the deaf, and Ralph Waldo Emerson, the Transcendentalist, and while she got along well with these men, Boston society as a group did not embrace her.

Some of Howe's own actions caused Bostonians to keep their distance from her in the early years of her marriage. She did not know how to entertain guests in her home, since she had had servants to do that in New York. She also became a controversial figure because of her gift for repartee, which she could at times direct sharply against people. Howe had always been high-spirited—meaning that she had a mind of her own and often spoke her opinions. These traits not only hurt her in Boston society, where women were demure and passive, but also caused trouble between her and Dr. Howe, especially during the 1850's.

Dr. Howe was attracted to his wife for her beauty and vitality, but he never reconciled himself to her independent spirit. One of the greatest sources of argument for the couple was her literary career. She had a volume of lyric poetry published anonymously in 1854 under the title *Passion Flowers*, and some of the pieces in it proved too passionate to meet with her husband's approval. Dr. Howe was infuriated when Julia Ward Howe (by rumor) became publicly known as the book's author. Dr. Howe did not approve of women working outside their homes, and this was especially true for his own wife, who had their six children to rear.

Life's Work

In the tense, unstable years before the Civil War, Dr. Howe did turn to Julia for literary assistance. He was an active abolitionist and edited a newspaper, *The Commonwealth*, to aid the cause. Julia Ward Howe wrote literary columns for this paper and reviewed books, plays, and concerts, and was also its proofreader. Also, during the late 1850's, Howe and her husband helped shelter fugitive slaves, who were fleeing to Canada and freedom, in their South Boston home.

When the Civil War broke out, Howe was frightened that the North would not win. She had hoped to do volunteer work to aid the army, but she was not as adept at bandage-rolling and knitting as were her women friends. Instead, she joined the women's auxiliary unit of the United States Sanitary Commission, of which Dr. Howe was a prominent member. This group worked for sanitary conditions for soldiers in camps and in hospitals; the organization was a forerunner of the American Red Cross.

It was on work for the American Sanitary Commission that Dr. and Mrs. Howe traveled to Washington, D. C., in November of 1861. Howe, her minister, and his wife were taken by carriage one morning to review the Union troops just outside the city. A sudden Confederate raid, however, forced them all to march back into Washington. During the slow ride, Howe and her companions sang "John Brown's Body" a popular tune of the day. Her friends in the carriage suggested that she write more meaningful lyrics for the song. At dawn the next morning, Howe arose from her bed in the Willard Hotel to write the poetry that would make the song beloved and famous. Howe wrote "The Battle Hymn of the Republic" on the stationery of the American Sanitary Commission on the morning of November 18, 1861, and in February of 1862, it was published in the *Atlantic Monthly*.

The hymn quickly became a favorite, probably because of its inspirational quality. Howe had written her finest poem for this hymn; her language was evocative of the Bible and indicative of patriotism. The men of the Union Army sang the new tune as a spur to fight on for freedom for all men in the bloody months of the Civil War. Howe was always proud to have written "The Battle Hymn of the Republic," for she felt it was her own contribution to the cause of justice for which the Union Army was struggling.

Yet Howe had a full and illustrious public career even after the war years. In 1868, she became a founding member of the New England Woman's Club, a group that advocated the improvement of woman's place in American society; she would serve as its president for forty years. A similar group on the national level was the Association for the Advancement of Women, which Howe helped begin in the mid-1870's; she would lead it as president from 1878 to 1888. Howe firmly espoused her beliefs that women had to be allowed the freedom of a complete education and admission into the professions; she also became an advocate of suffrage for women.

As an elderly man, Dr. Howe suffered increasingly from ill health. Howe nursed him in his final illness and was with him when he died of a stroke in January of 1876. In her widowhood, she became even more dedicated to the causes of women's suffrage and world peace. She traveled throughout the United States and Canada, inspiring women to form women's clubs and suffrage associations in their cities. She also helped found the Women's International Peace Association beginning in 1871 and attended conferences in Europe on its behalf. Howe, despite her long life, would not live to see

either of these two major causes reach fruition. She firmly believed, however, that the glory in her life had been in waging a noble battle for justice and peace for all men and women. She remained an active lecturer and essayist up to the last day of her life. Howe died in Newport, Rhode Island, at her summer home on October 17, 1910; she was ninety-one years old.

Summary

When Howe died, she was greatly mourned. She had been a popular lecturer and social reformer active in American life for several decades. While not all Americans agreed with her ideas, almost all admired her courage in living by her convictions. She was also much admired for her great vitality and sound intelligence, which she sustained for all of her ninety-one years.

Howe became a very familiar figure at the Boston State House, where she testified for many years before the state legislature on bills advocating women's and children's rights, world peace, female suffrage, and improvement of sanitation systems. In her earliest days as a public speaker, Howe had specialized in lectures on philosophers (her favorites were Immanuel Kant and Baruch Spinoza) and religion. After reading her essays to her friends in her home in the mid-1860's, she was asked to speak at area churches as well. On her first such lecture in her own Unitarian church in January of 1864, she wore a sedate black dress and placed a white lace cap on her head; this garment was to become her standard dress on lecture platforms in America and Europe.

At the time of her death, Howe had written four volumes of poetry, two plays (one of which was produced), a memoir of Dr. Samuel G. Howe, a fine biography of Margaret Fuller, and several books of essays reflecting her travel experiences, social views, and religious beliefs. Howe accomplished all this in an era when women were strongly discouraged from having public careers.

Bibliography

Bean, Judith Mattson. "Margaret Fuller on the Early Poetry of Julia Ward Howe: An Uncollected Letter." *ANQ* 7, no. 2 (April 1994). Discussion of a letter from Margaret Fuller to Howe concerning the poet's work. Includes the text of the letter and the reasons it was written.

Clifford, Deborah P. *Mine Eyes Have Seen the Glory: A Biography of Julia Ward Howe, 1819-1910*. Boston: Little Brown, 1979. A scholarly study with illustrations and a good bibliography. Clifford is the first modern author to write a life of Howe. She judges Howe's literary talents for the reader, demonstrating the brilliance of the lectures in comparison with the poetry. Interesting discussion of Howe's difficulties with her marriage.

Elliott, Maud H., and Laura E. Richards. *Julia Ward Howe: 1819-1910*. Boston: Houghton Mifflin, 1915. Howe's two daughters won a Pulitzer Prize for this excellent study of their mother. They relied on many of Howe's own letters to tell her fascinating story—her personal life as well as her public life is recounted in this lively narrative.

Hall, Florence Marion Howe. *Memories Grave and Gay*. New York and London: Harper, 1918. The eldest surviving daughter of Julia Ward Howe gives the reader an intimate portrait of her mother in her reminiscences. Hall includes chapters on the antislavery movement, the Civil War, and her mother's work on behalf of soldiers and women. She also pays tribute to her mother in closing this book.

———. *The Story of The Battle Hymn of the Republic*. New York and London: Harper, 1916. Howe's eldest daughter re-creates the scene of the writing of the patriotic hymn. She also details how the song was used on subsequent occasions and how its fame affected her mother. Hall also carefully recalls the turmoil, bitterness, anguish, and tragedy of the Civil War era that affected the hymn's reception.

Howe, Julia Ward. *Reminiscences: 1819-1899*. Boston: Houghton Mifflin, 1899. Howe, from the perspective of age eighty, here reminisces about many interesting and famous people she met in her life, including such luminaries as Dickens, Thomas Carlyle, Longfellow, and William Wordsworth. She also discusses her husband and their life together.

Howe, Maud. *The Eleventh Hour in the Life of Julia Ward Howe*. Boston: Little Brown, 1911. Howe's daughter wrote this small volume immediately after her mother's death to read to family friends. It gives insight into the old age of a remarkably spry and solidly intelligent woman who faced her final years with unusual vigor and courage. Emphasizes Howe's keen wit and her need to give of herself for worthy causes.

Ream, Debbie Williams. "Mine Eyes Have Seen the Glory." *American History Illustrated* 27, no. 6 (January-February 1993). Profile of Howe and her 1861 visit to the nation's capitol, torn by battle, which served as her inspiration for the work.

Tharp, Louise H. *Three Saints and a Sinner: Julia Ward Howe, Louisa, Annie, and Sam Ward*. Boston: Little Brown, 1956. A very well-researched book with a good bibliography. The author keeps the reader eager for more of her engrossing and well-paced narrative. She is good at presenting the essential interactions among the Ward siblings, as she places them in the social background of nineteenth century New York, Boston, and Europe.

Patricia E. Sweeney

SAMUEL GRIDLEY HOWE

Born: November 10, 1801; Boston, Massachusetts
Died: January 9, 1876; Boston, Massachusetts
Areas of Achievement: Education and philanthropy
Contribution: A universal reformer, Howe's greatest
contribution was to the education of the blind, the
deaf-blind, and the mentally retarded. His monumental efforts significantly enhanced social concern for the handicapped in the United States.

Early Life

Samuel Gridley Howe was born on November 10,
1801, the son of Joseph Howe and Patty Gridley
Howe, both of old New England stock. His father
was a cordage manufacturer and steadfast Jeffersonian Republican. A man of principle, as his son
was to be, he accepted government bonds in payment for purchases during the War of 1812 and
suffered serious financial losses. Samuel attended
Boston Latin School and was frequently harassed
for his father's politics. The only one of three
brothers to attend college, Samuel entered Brown,
rather than Federalist-dominated Harvard, in 1817.
Young Howe excelled at campus pranks, but his
academic performance was mediocre. As a Unitarian among Baptists, Howe once again learned to
appreciate the position of the underdog—a useful
trait for a future philanthropist.

Being graduated in 1821, Howe enrolled at Harvard Medical School and began to apply himself,
enjoying especially anatomy and dissection. After
commencement, however, he decided against a traditional practice. Stirred by the Greek War of Independence, a popular cause of the time, Howe left for
the Peloponnisos, arriving in early 1827. In Greece
he played many roles with distinction. As a physician, he served Greek forces on land and sea. As the
agent of American relief committees, he distributed
emergency rations, briefly returning to the United
States to raise additional funds. Once back in
Greece, he developed and ran sizable work relief
programs. For his exertions, Howe was knighted by
the Greek king as a Chevalier of the Order of the
Holy Savior. With the war all but over, Chev, as his
friends now called him, returned to Boston in April,
1831. Tall, dark, and handsome, not yet sporting the
beard of later years, Howe was a knight-errant seeking a new cause to uplift humanity.

Life's Work

As luck would have it, the projected New England

School for the Blind, incorporated in 1829, needed
a director in order to become a reality; the trustees
of the school offered Howe the job. Excited by the
challenge, he accepted immediately and sailed for
Europe to study current techniques for educating
the blind. Howe soon became convinced that European efforts were either too intellectual or too mechanical. A more balanced curriculum, he believed, including physical education and greater
encouragement of self-reliance, was required. After imprisonment in Prussia for assisting Polish
refugees, Howe returned to Boston in July, 1832.
That August, the first school for the blind in the
nation opened its doors with seven students and
three staff members.

As director, Howe tried to tailor the curriculum—reading, writing, mathematics, geography,
music, physical education, and manual training—
to the needs and abilities of the individual student.
He fashioned letters of twine and glued them to
cards for reading instruction; he invented an improved method of raised printing which significantly lowered costs of manufacture. (Braille was
not yet in use.) Howe trooped his students before
legislative committees and popular audiences to secure funds, went out into the country to recruit students, and traveled to other states to promote more
schools for the blind. As a result of his strenuous
activity, the school, renamed Perkins Institution,
soon required larger quarters.

In 1837, Howe heard of Laura Bridgman, an
eight-year-old who, at the age of two, had lost her
sight and hearing through scarlet fever. Howe,
who believed in phrenology and innate mental dispositions, was confident that the child could be
taught, despite near-universal opinion that the
deaf-blind were completely uneducable. He induced her parents to enroll Laura at Perkins. For
several tedious months, Howe tried to get her to
match raised words with physical objects and
make words of letters. Suddenly one day, Laura
understood that here was a way to communicate
her thoughts to other minds; her face "lighted up
with a human expression." This was the greatest
single moment in Howe's career. John Greenleaf
Whittier proclaimed that Howe was "the Cadmus
of the blind." Charles Dickens, who met Laura
Bridgman in 1842, lionized Howe's accomplishment in *American Notes* (1842). Howe soon became a world-renowned figure.

Howe's international stature certainly aided his election as a Whig to the Massachusetts house of representatives in November, 1842. Though only a freshman legislator, he chaired the committee on public charities. Working closely with Dorothea Lynde Dix, Howe personally wrote the bill reforming care of the mentally ill, which passed by overwhelming margins in March, 1843.

In April, 1843, Howe married Julia Ward, who was of a prominent New York family. Their marriage was frequently tempestuous; their personalities did not mesh well. Prideful, demanding, and eighteen years her senior, Howe never approved of Julia's literary aspirations. He normally placed his many reform interests ahead of his wife and his eventual family of six children.

After returning to work in September, 1844, after a European honeymoon, Howe immediately joined his friend Horace Mann, secretary of the state Board of Education, in a battle to reform the Boston grammar schools. In 1845, Howe turned to education of the mentally retarded, undertaking an extensive, two-year training program which he followed up with a comprehensive report to the legislature. Once again, the lawmakers followed his bidding and established in 1848 the Massachusetts School for the Idiotic and Feeble-Minded Youth, another first in American history. Howe served as superintendent of that institution as well as of Perkins until his death in 1876.

Although Howe disapproved of slavery, he remained aloof from agitation until the admission of Texas drew him into the fray. During the Mexican War, Howe became a Conscience Whig, running unsuccessfully for Congress in 1846; in 1851, he helped orchestrate the election of his close friend Charles Sumner to the United States Senate. In response to the Kansas-Nebraska Act, Howe moved toward radical abolitionism. In 1854, he was an organizer of both the New England Emigrant Aid Company and the Massachusetts Kansas Aid Committee, the latter formed to obtain guns for antislavery settlers. In January, 1857, John Brown visited Howe and other Boston supporters (the "Secret Six"), obtaining money from the committee and several token guns from Howe personally. In March, 1858, the group gave Brown additional funding to liberate slaves, a plan which culminated in the Harpers Ferry raid of October, 1859. When authorities uncovered Brown's correspondence, Howe fled, panic-stricken, to Canada on the flimsy pretext that he was promoting education of the

blind. Involvement of the nation's foremost humanitarian in Brown's scheme further unnerved the South and increased sectional tensions.

During the Civil War, Howe returned to less violent philanthropy. He helped to establish the United States Sanitary Commission in June, 1861, serving on its board for the duration. The commission made important recommendations for "preserving and restoring the health of the troops," which doubtless reduced fatalities. Howe was also a member of the three-man American Freedmen's Inquiry Commission set up in 1863 to investigate the condition of free blacks and make proposals for their future welfare. The commission laid the foundations for the later Freedmen's Bureau.

In 1863, Massachusetts Governor John Andrew named Howe chairman of the new Massachusetts Board of State Charities, created to coordinate eleemosynary institutions and programs. After the war, Howe, who strongly disagreed with the sign language system used at the American Asylum in Hartford, sought a charter for a school for the deaf which would teach finger spelling and articulation.

The legislature again complied, incorporating Clarke Institution at Northampton in 1867.

Although in declining health after the war, Howe embarked in 1871 on his last crusade. President Ulysses S. Grant, manipulated by speculators, favored annexing Santo Domingo. The Senate rejected the treaty, in part because of Charles Sumner's virulent opposition, but Grant named an investigative commission in hopes of recouping support. Despite his long friendship with Sumner, Howe agreed to serve and after a visit to the island became converted to annexation. Howe apparently had hopes of concluding his career as a territorial governor who in philosopher-king fashion would reform Santo Domingo into a tropical paradise. Such dreams were doomed by continuing Senate opposition.

After the disappointing conclusion of the Dominican affair, Howe's health steadily deteriorated. In constant pain and severely depressed, he collapsed on January 4, 1876, and died five days later. Several hours before the end, Laura Bridgman (symbolically on behalf of all those who had or would benefit from his tireless philanthropy) kissed the unconscious Howe farewell.

Summary

Samuel Gridley Howe lived in an optimistic age, in a city and state seething with the ferment of reform; not only was he in harmony with the spirit of his times, he was a symbol of the age as well. In those heady days, true heroism was seen by many as victory over social evil and human suffering. As the foremost philanthropist in the nation, Howe was, in the words of John Greenleaf Whittier, "The Hero."

A Whig in politics and a Unitarian in religion, Howe was a Yankee elitist who accepted the essential goodness of God and man and the inevitability of progress. A nineteenth century romantic, Howe rejected John Locke's concept of knowledge drawn solely from the five senses for belief in innate mental dispositions. This thinking as well as Howe's emphasis on self-reliance was clearly in line with that of his friend Theodore Parker and other Transcendentalists. Like many other Americans of the era, Howe was also strongly influenced by phrenology. This pseudoscience (which posited a body-mind unity) maintained that a balanced education, both intellectual and physical, could influence cerebral growth and skull dimensions. Howe's phrenological and vaguely Transcendentalist assumptions frequently guided his reform endeavors. His temporary obsession with the abolitionist movement in the 1850's was typical of most antebellum reformers.

Howe was involved in many causes, but his major impact on American society was in his efforts for the education of the handicapped. He firmly believed that most physically and mentally handicapped persons could become independent and productive citizens. His refusal to accept traditional prejudices concerning the capabilities of the blind, the deaf-blind, the deaf, and the retarded led him to found institutions and develop instructional strategies still important today. Howe's most enduring legacy may be his creation of a continuing public consciousness that handicaps can be surmounted, that, in the words of his life motto, Obstacles Are Things to Be Overcome.

Bibliography

Brooks, Van Wyck. *Flowering of New England, 1815-1865*. London: Dent, and New York: Dutton, 1936. A scholarly, readable description of the intellectual environment within which Howe thrived. Howe is not discussed in detail, but many of his acquaintances, including Theodore Parker, are.

Clifford, Deborah P. *Mine Eyes Have Seen the Glory: A Biography of Julia Ward Howe*. Boston: Little Brown, 1979. A well-researched biography quite favorable to Mrs. Howe. It sheds light on Howe's stormy marriage and the more disagreeable aspects of his personality. For Howe, reform did not include the liberation of married women.

Dickens, Charles. *American Notes for General Circulation*. London: Chapman and Hall, and New York: Wilson, 1842. Though frequently critical of things American, Dickens was extremely impressed by Howe's work. He quotes extensively from Howe's annual *Reports* to the Perkins trustees concerning the education of Laura Bridgman, a source not readily available to the interested reader.

Howe, Samuel. *Letters and Journals of Samuel Gridley Howe*. Edited by Laura E. Richards. 2 vols. Boston: Dana Estes, 1906; London: Lane, 1907. Collection contains excerpts from Howe's letters, journals, and annual *Reports*, connected by a running commentary. Unfortunately, the period to 1832 is accorded the same weight as the rest of Howe's life. Despite such unevenness, this is the closest thing to a printed collection of Howe's papers.

Lamson, Mary Swift. *Life and Education of Laura Dewey Bridgman, the Deaf, Dumb, and Blind Girl*. Boston: New England Publishing, and London: Trubner, 1878. Lamson was one of Laura's teachers. She quotes extensively from her own journal, those of other teachers, and from Howe's *Reports*. A very personal account, it reveals the difficulties of working with Howe.

Richards, Laura E. *Laura Bridgman: The Story of an Opened Door*. New York and London: Appleton, 1928. A full-length biography, written by Howe's daughter, who was Laura Bridgman's namesake. Strong on the relationship between Howe and Bridgman. Includes source materials not readily available.

Sanborn, Franklin Benjamin. *Dr. S. G. Howe: The Philanthropist*. New York: Funk and Wagnalls, 1891. The first scholarly biography, still worth consulting. The author, one of the Secret Six, is laudatory, but the book contains extensive, frequently revealing quotations from original sources. Strong on the antislavery days.

Schwartz, Harold. *Samuel Gridley Howe: Social Reformer, 1801-1876*. Cambridge, Mass.: Harvard University Press, 1956. The most recent scholarly treatment of Howe. Based on extensive research in the Howe manuscripts in Houghton Library at Harvard. Places Howe solidly in his intellectual and social milieu. Notes influence of phrenology. A very balanced work.

Parker Bradley Nutting

VICTOR HUGO

Born: February 26, 1802; Besançon, France
Died: May 22, 1885; Paris, France
Area of Achievement: Literature
Contribution: Hugo was one of the great authors of the nineteenth century, and by the force of his personality he became one of its great public figures, using his enormous popularity in the service of many political and social causes. His literary career, spanning six of the most turbulent decades in modern European history, encompassed poetry, drama, the novel, and nonfiction writing.

Early Life

Victor-Marie Hugo was born on February 26, 1802, in Besançon, France, the third son of Joseph Léopold Sigisbert Hugo and Sophie Trébuchet Hugo. At the time of their marriage in 1797, Joseph Hugo was a rising young Bonapartist soldier imbued with the ideals of the French Revolution; Sophie, the orphaned daughter of a Breton ship's captain, had been reared by an aunt of pronounced Royalist sympathies. Thus, in his earliest years, the two poles of contemporary French politics became factors in his life.

An early estrangement of Hugo's parents, the result of personal incompatibilities magnified by the dislocations of his father's military career, became permanent, and Victor and his brother Eugène went with their mother to live in Paris. Though Victor's childhood was touched by the color and the upheaval of the Napoleonic era, by the age of seven he was able to read and translate Latin, and by his tenth year his spotty education had been augmented by trips to Italy and Spain.

After 1814, Hugo's education proceeded along more orthodox lines, but it left him time to write verse and plays; at age twenty, financial and critical recognition of his talent enabled him to wed his childhood playmate, Adèle Foucher, a shy, pious young woman to whom he had pledged his love in the spring of 1819. An early novel, *Han d'Islande* (1823; *Hans of Iceland*, 1845), is the feverishly emotional product of Hugo's courtship of Adèle, but more significant for Hugo's development at this time were his contributions to the short-lived periodical *Muse française*, which shows a modification of his Royalist sympathies and a recognition that a poet should play a role in society. Hugo's ideas of literary form were evolving from a conservative classicism, which had won for him early

popularity, toward a forward-looking but less well-defined Romanticism. In 1826, a small book of poems, *Odes et ballades*, signaled the poet's embrace of Romanticism by substituting the inspiration of "pictures, dreams, scenes, narratives, superstitious legends, popular traditions" for the authority of literary convention.

Though of somewhat short stature, Hugo was a strikingly attractive man in youth as well as old age. With a high forehead and penetrating eyes, he seemed both austere and engaging, and he had a reputation as an excellent conversationalist. Few nineteenth century personalities were portrayed as often as Hugo was; contemporary drawings and photographs show him as an extraordinarily intense and commanding personality. As early as the 1820's, the poet's home had become a magnet for other young authors and artists. Newly married to an attractive wife, he was often host to an informal group of Romantic personalities which included his friend Charles-Augustin Sainte-Beuve, the painter Eugène Delacroix, and the sculptor David d'Angers. Known as the *cénacle*, or brotherhood, Hugo's circle became not only a source of mutual support for its youthful members, but also a font of the new movement in art, Romanticism. Its ideals can be gauged by reference to Hugo's *La Préface de Cromwell* (1827; English translation, 1896), which was celebrated as a manifesto of Romanticism. In this preface to his long play *Cromwell* (1827; English translation, 1896), Hugo contributes to the redefinition of the three unities of time, place, and action that lie at the heart of French classical literature. He calls for greater realism and freedom in dramatic production, stating that "all that is in nature belongs to art" and arguing for the union of the grotesque and the sublime in the work of literary art. *La Préface de Cromwell* has been called Hugo's masterpiece as a literary apprentice; it marks his liberation from the vestiges of eighteenth century ideas and heralds the beginning of a productive decade that brought his work into the mainstream of French culture.

Life's Work

The publication in 1829 of a book of poems, *Les Orientales* (*Les Orientales: Or, Eastern Lyrics*, 1879), placed Hugo at the head of the Romantic movement, a role which was confirmed with the appearance of his melodramatic five-act play *Her-*

nani (English translation, 1830) in February, 1830. *Hernani* was a popular sensation and brought much-needed income into the Hugo household, which was strained by nearly a decade of pregnancies and shaky finances. In fact, the artistic success Hugo enjoyed in these years had been invisibly pursued by Adèle's unhappiness and a growing, secretive love between her and Sainte-Beuve, who was as much a family friend as an artistic colleague. Hugo was deeply shaken by the failure of his imagined, ideal relationship with his wife and the treachery of his friend, but he responded to his misfortune by composing the poems issued in November, 1831, as *Les Feuilles d'automne*, a collection that far surpassed his earlier verses.

Hugo had signed a contract in 1828 to produce a novel, but the project was displaced by his many other projects and by the July Revolution of 1830, which Hugo and his liberal contemporaries embraced. In September, 1830, he set to work on this novel in earnest, and completed *Notre-Dame de Paris* (1831; *The Hunchback of Notre-Dame*, 1833) within six months. A descriptive tapestry of fifteenth century Paris, the novel embodies the author's extraordinary visual imagination and his affinity for art and architecture. Hugo had, by this time, shown a related capacity for drawing, and in the years to come his sketches often achieved a mastery of dramatic visual effect and characterization quite beyond his nominally amateur status as an artist.

The theater continued to attract Hugo's interest. In November, 1832, *Le Roi s'amuse* (1832; *The King Amuses Himself*, 1842) was banned by the government following its first performance; yet on November 8, 1838, he achieved another triumph with *Ruy Blas* (English translation, 1890), widely considered to be his best play. It was also his last success as a dramatist; after the failure of *Les Burgraves* (*The Burgraves*, 1896) in 1843, Hugo no longer wrote for the stage. By then, however, he had achieved one of his main objectives in courting public and critical acclaim in the theater: election to the Académie Française, an event which occurred on his fifth attempt, on January 7, 1841. Celebrated as a poet, dramatist, novelist, and critic, Hugo's role as a youthful, rebellious Romantic had been outgrown. Financially secure, perhaps emotionally battered but artistically more refined, he now pursued his career with determination but with no less passion than before.

Since 1833, Hugo had maintained a liaison with a beautiful actress, Juliette Drouet, who for twelve years followed a cloistered existence relieved only by six-week summer holidays with her lover. Notwithstanding the author's devotion to Juliette and his increasingly frequent love affairs with other adoring women, he was a devoted father to two sons and daughters. In 1843, Léopoldine, Hugo's favorite, perished in a boating accident with her husband of six months. His sons, Charles and François-Victor, died prematurely in their middle years, after sharing in many of their father's trials and successes; his daughter Adèle died in 1915, after a life darkened by madness.

In the 1840's, Hugo was something of an establishment figure in French letters. In April, 1845, he was raised to the peerage, becoming Viscount Hugo—a circumstance which in July saved him from almost certain prosecution on the complaint of the husband of one of his mistresses. After this perilous event, Hugo remained prudently quiet for several years, but in 1848, with France again in political turmoil, he sought to renew his political influence. Initially supporting France's "bourgeois king," Prince Louis-Napoleon, through the newspaper that he had founded with his sons, Hugo soon came to oppose his rule. His sons were imprisoned, and Hugo himself skirted arrest until it seemed absolutely necessary to leave France. He departed for Brussels on December 11, 1851, probably with the unstated tolerance of the authorities.

Hugo's nineteen-year absence from France, at first a necessity, later became a matter of principle, which conferred upon him the distinction of an exile of conscience. In comfortable circumstances, first in Jersey and, from 1855, in Guernsey, Hugo wrote great quantities of verse and prose, much of it concerned with social and political problems. His popularity as a writer continued to grow. Among the notable volumes of poetry in these years are *Les Châtiments* (1853), which includes satiric poems aimed at Louis-Napoleon, *La Légende des siècles* (1859-1883; *The Legend of the Centuries*, 1894), and a collection of earlier work, *Les Contemplations*, which earned for him enough money within months of its publication in April, 1856, to buy Hauteville House, where he surrounded himself with his family and admirers. Drouet lived within sight of the house, and by 1867 her relationship with Hugo was acknowledged even by Hugo's wife. Madame Hugo was to die in her husband's arms in Brussels the following year, during a family holiday.

Hugo's prodigious and best-known novel, *Les Misérables* (English translation, 1862), was pub-

lished in 1861. It weaves together many of the themes of earlier books and manuscripts as well as historical and autobiographical elements from the author's youth. It is a singular novel both in Hugo's career and in the whole of European literature—a sprawling, twelve-hundred-page narrative that overcomes its liabilities by sheer energy. Hugo seeks to show no less than ". . . the advance from evil to good, from injustice to justice, from falsity to truth, from darkness to daylight, from blind appetite to conscience, from decay to life, from bestiality to duty, from Hell to Heaven, from limbo to God," and thus the book is in some fashion a religious book. *Les Misérables* is centered upon an account of the pursuit of a convict, Jean Valjean, by the detective Javert. Valjean, released on parole after nineteen years of imprisonment for a trivial crime, experiences a transformation of character that is repeatedly challenged both by his conscience and by Javert's detection. Within a vast framework of historical events and human affairs, the two principal characters are shown locked in a social and existential combat that remains compelling even for modern readers who are not conversant with the novel's political context.

Hugo's attention never wandered far from the political scene, and in 1870, as a prosperous Germany threatened war with a weakened France, Hugo determined to return to his homeland to aid it in its crisis. He arrived on September 5 to a tumultuous welcome, but by then the military situation was desperate. Paris was soon under full siege and the population was approaching starvation—Hugo himself was said to have been sent bear, deer, and antelope meat from the zoo at the Jardin des Plantes. In late January, 1871, an armistice was concluded and elections called for a National Assembly to make peace with the Germans and to debate the terms of defeat. Hugo ran successfully for the Assembly and traveled to Bordeaux to participate in it, but the rancorous events of the following months soon outpaced the capacities of a seventy-year-old man, and he returned first to Paris and then to Brussels, where, amid much public controversy, the Belgian government expelled him. After a few months in Luxembourg, he returned to Paris, where he was defeated in the elections of January, 1872.

From 1872 until his death in 1885, Hugo lived alternately in Guernsey and in Paris. His last years saw the completion of a major novel of the French Revolution, *Quatre-vingt-treize* (1874; *Ninety-three*, 1874), and the revival of several of his major

theatrical works. *L'Art d'être grand-père* (1877), a book about Hugo's experiences with his two grandchildren, became a sentimental classic with the French public. During the Third Republic—the more liberal political regime which followed the turmoil of 1869-1872—Hugo came to be regarded as a patriarch, and the nation gave him almost limitless affection.

The beginning of Hugo's eightieth year was celebrated as a national holiday on February 26, 1881, with 600,000 admirers filing past the windows of his apartment on the Avenue Eylau, which was soon renamed Avenue Victor-Hugo. In late summer, he made up his will, in which he stated:

> God. The Soul. Responsibility. This threefold idea is sufficient for mankind. It has been sufficient for me. It is the true religion. I have lived in it. Truth, light, justice, conscience: it is God. . . . I leave forty thousand francs to the poor. And I wish to be taken to the cemetery in a pauper's hearse.

Hugo had suffered a very slight stroke three years earlier, but otherwise his health was remarkably good for a man of seventy-nine. During the next two years, he supervised the publication of the little of his work that remained unpublished, but his creative activity was at an end. Juliette Drouet, who for fifty years had been his devoted friend, died in May, 1883. Hugo lived on until May 22, 1885, when an attack of pneumonia claimed him at the age of eighty-three. His last words were "I see black light."

Summary

Victor Hugo had one of the broadest-ranging, most celebrated public careers of his time. He was a poet, dramatist, novelist, literary and social critic, journalist, politician, and social activist, and often pursued more than one of these roles at a time. Above all a man of feeling, Hugo turned from the ardent Royalism of his childhood and adolescence to an equally passionate Romanticism, in which his natural literary gifts reached their full potential. As a poet, he was a great musician of words, who brought increasingly refined ideas to his work. His legacy as a dramatist is not as great as in other literary forms, but he helped effect a transition from classicism to Romanticism, and he held contemporary audiences spellbound on more than one occasion.

The contributions made by Hugo to fiction were diverse and influential. Some novels, such as *The Hunchback of Notre-Dame*, are notable for their descriptive power; others, such as the early *Le Derni-*

er jour d'un condamné (1829; *The Last Day of a Condemned*, 1840), combine adventurous narrative devices with a profound concern for social justice. *Les Misérables*, despite its unwieldy length, combines much of what is best in Hugo's craft and his philosophy, and after a century is still read as a ˌiving masterpiece. Other books, suffering perhaps from the miscalculation that can attend unbounded productivity, embody his poetic craft more than his sense of narrative substance.

In his life as well as in his work, Hugo was a spokesman for the common man against the power of the state; his long association with the political Left, however, was more a matter of human compassion than of social theory. He had experienced a range of political regimes, which made him a shrewd political observer, but increasingly he applied his genius to projects which transcended the affairs of his own historical epoch, creating an imaginative world of mythic dimensions.

Bibliography

Brombert, Victor. *Victor Hugo and the Visionary Novel*. Cambridge, Mass.: Harvard University Press, 1984. The author of this sophisticated, scholarly study of Hugo's novels became a dedicated "Hugolian" in 1940 as a teenager, during the German Occupation. His method of analysis is to combine the resources of modernist formal criticism with an "intricate network of aesthetic, social, political, psychological, and ethical preoccupations." Twenty-seven remarkable drawings by Hugo are reproduced.

Frey, John A. *A Victor Hugo Encyclopedia*. Westport, Conn.: Greenwood Press, 1998. This reference volume begins with a biography covering Hugo's early years, his development as a writer, and his political exile. The bibliography that follows covers his works, themes, ideas, and characters.

Grant, Elliott M. *The Career of Victor Hugo*. Cambridge, Mass.: Harvard University Press, 1945. This scholarly but very readable book is principally a survey of Hugo's literary production, although it deals of necessity with the circumstances of his life.

Grant, Richard B. *The Perilous Quest: Image, Myth, and Prophecy in the Narratives of Victor Hugo*. Durham, N.C.: Duke University Press, 1968. The author, who is the son of Hugo scholar Elliott Grant, defines the essential motif of Hugo's narrative works as the myth of the heroic quest toward an ideal. Isolating his discussion as much as possible from biographical detail, he argues the view that the novels, the main plays, and narrative poems can be viewed as self-contained artistic unities.

Ionesco, Eugène. *Hugoliad: Or, The Grotesque and Tragic Life of Victor Hugo*. New York: Grove Press, 1987. This uncompleted work of Ionesco's youth—written in the 1930's in Romanian—is a sort of polemical antibiography, intended to dethrone its subject. The reader must take responsibility for separating fact from fiction, to say nothing of judging the aptness of the playwright's cheerless embellishments of anecdotal material. Postscript by Gelu Ionescu.

Maurois, André. *Olympio: The Life of Victor Hugo*. Translated by Gerard Hopkins. New York: Harper, 1956. Originally published in French in 1954. This is probably as close an approach as possible to an ideal one-volume biography dealing with both the life and the work of a monumental figure such as Hugo. Of the sparse illustrations, several are superb; the bibliography, principally of sources in French, provides a sense of Hugo's celebrity and influence, which persisted well into the twentieth century.

————. *Victor Hugo and His World*. London: Thames and Hudson, and New York: Viking Press, 1966. The 1956 English translation of Maurois' text noted above was edited to conform to the format of a series of illustrated books. The result is interesting and intelligible, but rather schematic. In compensation for the vast cuts in text, a chronology and dozens of well-annotated illustrations have been added.

Richardson, Joanna. *Victor Hugo*. London: Weidenfeld and Nicolson, and New York: St. Martin's Press, 1976. Richardson's aim was to produce a comprehensive account of Hugo's life and work in the context of her specialty, the study of nineteenth century European culture. Her book is complementary to Maurois' account of Hugo and is somewhat more efficient as well as being agreeably less literary in style. There is an excellent biography and reproductions of several classic Hugo family photographs.

Robb, Graham. *Victor Hugo*. New York: Norton, and London: Picador, 1997. Excellent biography recommended for all libraries.

C. S. McConnell

ALEXANDER VON HUMBOLDT

Born: September 14, 1769; Schloss Tegel, near
  Berlin, Prussia
Died: May 6, 1859; Berlin, Prussia
Areas of Achievement: Geography, meteorology,
  and plant geography
Contribution: Humboldt, a native of Germany, undertook a famous four-year expedition to the
  Americas. The outcome of this expedition was
  the new sciences of geography, plant geography,
  and meteorology. Humboldt insisted on seeing a
  geographical site as a whole including climate,
  elevation, and distribution of plants, animals, and
  natural resources. He was one of the founders of
  modern science and scientific methods.

Early Life

The Humboldt family was, at the time of Alexander von Humboldt's birth, not part of the ancient
Prussian nobility. The title had only been in the
family a few generations. Alexander's father, Major Alexander George von Humboldt, had fought in
the Seven Years' War in the Prussian army and later became adjutant to the Duke of Braunschweig.
Because he was not of the ancient Prussian elite,
Major Humboldt decided that his sons would not
become military men, but scientists and politicians.

Alexander was the younger of two brothers, both
destined to become famous scholars—albeit in different fields. His other brother, Wilhelm, was early
perceived to be the one with scholastic aptitude,
whereas Alexander did not seem very interested in
academic pursuits. He liked nature and spent much
of his childhood in the parks surrounding his childhood home, Schloss Tegel, near Berlin. He also
showed early talent for map drawing and reading,
and for drawing nature.

The two brothers were, from the earliest years,
inseparable and would remain so throughout their
lives. They were only two years apart, and at least
one biographer claims that the strong bonding between them compensated for some degree of parental neglect—especially of Alexander because of
his perceived lack of talent.

Alexander read one of Georg Forster's works on
the South Sea Islands while he was still quite
young, and a desire to see the tropics was born in
him. He fell in love with the dragon tree and
dreamed of seeing one in real life. He collected
plants, insects, birds' eggs, and rocks.

The two brothers were initially taught at home
by tutors, but eventually Wilhelm went to university, and Alexander followed. The brothers studied
at the University of Frankfurt an der Oder and later at the University of Göttingen. While Wilhelm
studied philology and philosophy, Alexander focused his studies on mineralogy.

From his earliest years, Alexander had planned
to undertake a major scientific journey. His studies
and pursuits were all focused on this goal. In 1792,
however, he was employed by the Prussian government as superintendent of mines. He worked in this
capacity until 1797, gaining valuable experience.
From 1797 to 1799, he prepared himself for his
great journey.

Life's Work

While still a child, Humboldt met the towering
spirit of his time, Johann Wolfgang von Goethe.
Later, in 1797, he spent three full months in the
company of the great poet and scientific theoreti-

cian. The exposure to Goethe and his ideas about nature and science became central to Humboldt. His life's work became the practical application of some of the key aspects of Goethe's theories: He saw the world as a *Naturganzes*, or natural whole. To the Romantic theory he added an emphasis on stringent empirical observation.

His theoretical and scientific baggage securely packed in his fine mind, Humboldt embarked from La Coruña in Spain on June 5, 1799, on his expedition to the Americas. His companion on the trip was the French botanist Aimé Bonpland. The two scientists had strong mutual respect and divided the work between them, Bonpland being primarily responsible for collecting and studying plants.

The expedition was to last four years, from 1799 to 1803. The first part was focused on the Orinoco River in Venezuela, where Humboldt first tested his holistic theory, or his "idea of the physical nature of the world." He was interested in correlating facts and observations rather than in individual facts. He studied the biology, geology, geophysics, archaeology, and meteorology of the areas through which he passed. The two companions traveled the entire length of the seventeen-hundred-mile-long Orinoco River on foot and by canoe. Interestingly, the hardships of this travel restored Humboldt's health. For his entire youth, he had been frail and sickly, and he emerged from his trip along the Orinoco River the very image of good health. Contemporaries describe him as a short, healthy-looking, robust, and powerfully built man.

The work describing the trip and Humboldt's findings did not appear until many years later. It was published in French, because the bulk of Humboldt's life after the trip was spent in Paris. The work was published in thirty-three volumes under the title *Voyage aux régions équinoctales du Nouveau Continent, fait en 1799, 1800, 1801, 1802, 1803, et 1804, par Al de Humboldt et A. Bonpland* (1805-1834; a historical description of the voyage to the tropical regions of the new continent made in 1799, 1800, 1801, 1802, 1803, and 1804, by Al. de Humboldt and A. Bonpland).

The eighteenth century was an age of grand voyages and explorations. Humboldt's expedition fits the pattern, but there was a difference: His voyage had infinitely more repercussions for the future of science than probably any other until Charles Darwin's famous voyage on the *Beagle* a half-century later. Humboldt had a program. He firmly believed that nature embodied an overarching idea and that

studying nature as a whole and overlooking no aspect, however apparently insignificant, would bring him closer to an understanding of the idea. Humboldt believed that there is a unity to the cosmos and to the world. He saw this not as a phylogenetic unity of evolution but as a Platonic, idealistic unity: He thought that for each type of animal or plant there was a prototype. Another aspect of this unity is the so-called compensation principle (also known as metamorphosis or transformation), which states that if an animal or plant is strongly developed in one aspect, it will be lacking in some other aspect. Thus, if the giraffe has a long neck, it must be less developed somewhere else. This type of thinking was typical for Goethe and his followers. While the static, idealistic aspects of Humboldt's theorizing have since been abandoned in favor of evolutionary ones, the idea of studying environments as integrated wholes and the emphasis on empirical observation are central to modern geography and ecology. Exactly those aspects of his work have earned for him the reputation as a founder of modern geography.

Humboldt and Bonpland proceeded to Mexico, Peru, and Cuba to conduct further studies. They not only continued their meticulous studies of ecosystems wherever they went but also took the time to study indigenous cultures, dabble in archaeology, and take a fresh look at the Spanish-speaking societies of the New World. One witness who encountered them in Quito, Ecuador, recounts that Humboldt, after a long day's work of studying plants, minerals, and soil types, would spend most of the night gazing at the stars.

Many rivers, mountains, and counties in the New World bear Humboldt's name, and the entire expedition was a great success. He returned to Europe in 1804, sailing from Philadelphia to Bordeaux. Humboldt lived in Paris, working on his life's project. When the work was complete and his inheritance spent, he accepted a job as chamberlain of the Prussian court and lived the rest of his life in Berlin. Yet he made one more substantial trip. At the request of the Russian czar, he visited the Urals, the Altai, and parts of China. The purpose of the trip was to give advice regarding the economic exploitation of the areas covered on the trip. The scientific outcome of Humboldt's last major trip was meager compared to his trip to the Americas, but it was a success in terms of its stated goals. Humboldt could indeed give lucrative advice and make predictions with regard to the mineralogical composition of the Urals. Humboldt lived to the age of eighty-nine and worked until the very end. He died on May 6, 1859, in Berlin.

Summary

Alexander von Humboldt represents the emergence of modern empirical science. He was a child of his times in that his theoretical ideas about the world were rooted in German Romanticism and in that he joined many of his contemporaries in exploring parts of the world that were comparatively new to Europeans. Yet he also broke the mold by combining his Romantic idealism with a hard-nosed empiricism that helped usher in the new age of technology and science.

Humboldt was amazingly eclectic. He studied plants, rocks, volcanoes, fauna, archaeology, and comparative religions, and he studied everything in minute detail. The thirty-three volumes that constitute Humboldt's testimony to future scientists contain not only a catalog of his physiognomic-typological primary forms of plants but also the painstakingly accurate descriptions of ecological systems that have made his scientific heirs name him the founder of not only geography but also the specialized field of plant geography and modern, systematic, and scientific meteorology.

Bibliography

Gendron, Val. *The Dragon Tree: A Life of Alexander, Baron von Humboldt.* New York: Longman, 1961. More than anything else a psychological portrait of Humboldt. The approach is Freudian and verges, from time to time, on hero-worship. Written entertainingly, with bits of dialogue between the protagonist and his friends and colleagues. Especially good description of Humboldt's early life and relationships to parents and brother.

Kellner, L. *Alexander von Humboldt.* London and New York: Oxford University Press, 1963. A solid, scholarly biography. Relates Humboldt's early life as it emerges from the record without Freudian or other interpretations. Excellent account of the two major expeditions and of their scientific import.

Kettenmann, Helmut. "Alexander von Humboldt and the Concept of Animal Electricity." *Trends in Neurosciences* 20, no. 6 (June 1997). Profile of Humboldt's work on electrophysiology.

Klencke, W. *Lives of the Brothers Humboldt: Alexander and William.* London: Ingram, Cooke, 1852; New York: Harper, 1854. Focuses on the role of the Humboldt brothers in the emergence of modern Germany. A political monument that contains a good description of Humboldt's early life and his education.

Meyer-Abich, Adolph. "Alexander von Humboldt and the Science of the Nineteenth Century." In *Biological Contributions: A Collection of Essays and Research Articles Dedicated to John Thomas Patterson on the Occasion of His Fiftieth Birthday.* Austin: University of Texas Press, 1959. A good exposition of eighteenth century scientific ideas and beliefs. Sets the intellectual stage for Humboldt's achievements, primarily by explaining Goethe's scientific views: the holism, the types, and the compensation principle. Explains Humboldt's law of plant geography, which states, among other things, that the same type of climate will foster the same types of flora and fauna. Gives a list of the nineteen plant types Humboldt established. Compares Humboldt's scientific theories to such later developments as mechanism and evolutionary theory.

————. "Humboldt's Exploration in the American Tropics." *Texas Quarterly* 1 (1958). Brief but very full description of Humboldt's life and major expeditions. The focus is on exploring the nature of Humboldt's achievement. Outlines Humboldt's education and gives a good picture of the intellectual community to which he belonged.

Sachs, Aaron. "Humboldt's Legacy and the Restoration of Science." *World Watch* 8, no. 2 (March-April 1995). Discusses Humboldt's influence on environmental issues, Charles Darwin, and Simón Bolívar.

Per Schelde

ENGELBERT HUMPERDINCK

Born: September 1, 1854; Siegburg, near Bonn, Prussia (now Germany)

Died: September 27, 1921; Neustrelitz, Germany

Area of Achievement: Music

Contribution: As the developer and chief exponent of the "fairy-tale" opera, Humperdinck became, for a brief time, the most important German opera composer after Richard Wagner. Although he was soon eclipsed by other composers, his music survives in one enduringly popular work.

Early Life

Engelbert Humperdinck was born in the small Rhineland city of Siegburg, where his father was a teacher. Family pressures destined Humperdinck for a career in architecture, but he evidenced an early interest in music and began to study it around the age of seven. By his early teens, he was composing and was active in a number of musical organizations. After overcoming parental opposition to a musical career, he studied at the Cologne Conservatory for four years. In 1876 he won Frankfurt's Mozart Prize, which allowed him to study further in Munich. Some early compositions were performed during this period that demonstrated the influence of Richard Wagner. After winning Berlin's Mendelssohn Prize in 1879, he was able to travel to Italy, where he met his idol Wagner, who was then vacationing in Naples. Impressed by the twenty-five-year-old Humperdinck's honesty and geniality, Wagner soon drew the young man into his circle.

In Bayreuth, Humperdinck became Wagner's right-hand man during preparations for the premiere of the opera *Parsifal* in 1882. As chief copyist of the score, Humperdinck was called upon to add some music of his own; part of his contribution was eventually dropped, but it is likely that significant portions of what he wrote, especially in the area of the orchestration, remained in the final version of Wagner's last opera. Humperdinck fulfilled numerous other responsibilities while working with Wagner. However, after winning the Meyerbeer Prize of Berlin in 1881, Humperdinck broke free in the autumn of 1882 to take up residence in Paris, France. Wagner tried to get his young disciple to join him in Venice at the Marcello Conservatory, but this arrangement failed, although Humperdinck did assist Wagner in preparing for the latter's final performance. When Humperdinck returned to Paris, he was followed by the news of his idol's death on February 13, 1883.

In the following years, Humperdinck travelled widely around Europe and the Mediterranean. After an unhappy spell of teaching in Barcelona, Spain, he took an appointment at his alma mater, the Cologne Conservatory, in 1887. He also became adviser to the important music publishing firm of Schott and an active music critic. Still close to the Wagner family, he gave private music lessons to the late master's son, Siegfried. Like Humperdinck himself, Siegfried had been expected to train as an architect; perhaps recalling his own escape, Humperdinck was influential in steering the young man toward a career of his own as conductor and composer.

Humperdinck had not given up his interests in composing. An orchestral humoresque that he wrote met with some success, and he had composed a steady number of songs for voice and piano as well as choral pieces. However, his dreams of writing opera had gone unrealized: Wagner's lingering influ-

ence weighed heavily on him, and he had failed to find the right material. It was only when Humperdinck moved to new teaching and journalistic duties in Frankfurt that his breakthrough came.

Life's Work

In the spring of 1891, Humperdinck's sister, Adelheid Wette, a literary dabbler, invited him to join in one of her private theatricals using her children's miniature theater. She had adapted one of the Brothers Grimm's fairy tales as a *Singspiel* (a spoken play with songs and musical numbers), and she asked him to provide appropriate musical settings. The finished production was presented at a party for family and friends a few weeks later. One of the guests was Hugo Wolf, whose compositions Humperdinck had supported through his publishing connections. Wolf thought this tiny theatrical piece should be made into a full-length opera. Wette set to work on an expanded libretto and, though the idea of performability by children persisted, the project grew into the opera *Hänsel und Gretel*.

Securing a performance for the new work proved to be difficult at first, but parallel productions—at Weimar on December 23, 1893, under Richard Strauss, and two weeks later at Munich under old Bayreuth colleague Hermann Levi—caused a sensation. Critics who had bemoaned the lapse in German opera after Wagner's death and who were alarmed at the inroads made by the new Italian verismo movement hailed Humperdinck's work as bringing new life to German lyric theater. The opera swept through Europe and travelled around the world, establishing a barely matched record of unbroken popularity.

In his fusion of complex Wagnerian style (sumptuous orchestral apparatus and modified use of leitmotif references) with a folksy simplicity of tone (the feeling of a folk song and the naïve subject matter of folktales), Humperdinck unintentionally created what he recognized as a new idiom, the *Märchenoper* or fairy-tale opera. He moved quickly to consolidate the new audience he had created for his music. Another collaboration with his sister, *Die sieben Geisslein* (the seven little goats) was well received in 1895, but it failed to capture any lasting public interest. Meanwhile, after reluctantly being drawn into writing incidental music for a play by a friend's daughter, *Königskinder* (the king's children), Humperdinck turned it into a melodrama—a form of drama with lines spoken over closely keyed music. He went further,

notating rhythms and pitches for the spoken words. It was an idea that anticipated the *Sprechgesang* (speech-song), which was soon to become part of the radical style of Arnold Schoenberg, but it proved too demanding for the performers in a doomed production that turned into a fiasco when it premiered in 1897.

After relocating to Berlin, Humperdinck returned to the fairy-tale idiom with *Dornröschen* (Thorn-Rosie), an adaptation of the Charles Perrault tale commonly known as "The Sleeping Beauty." This new confection of sumptuous Wagnerian orchestration and childish naïveté with spectacular stage effects was highly acclaimed at its Frankfurt premiere on November 12, 1902, but once again it could not win the same popularity as *Hänsel und Gretel* and slipped quickly into obscurity. A shift into comedy was attempted with *Die Heirat wider Willen* (the involuntary marriage), with a libretto by the composer's wife, based upon Alexandre Dumas's drama *Les Demoiselles de Saint-Cyr* (1843; *The Ladies of Saint-Cyr*, 1870). Despite a lavish premiere in April, 1905, and praises accorded its music, a weak libretto (with copious spoken dialogue) doomed the work to neglect.

Still committed to theatrical composition, Humperdinck produced a Nativity-play opera for children, *Bübschens Weihnachtstraum* (toddler's Christmas dream, 1906), and then turned to writing a series of highly praised incidental scores for productions (mostly by Max Reinhardt at the Deutsches Theater in Berlin) of plays by William Shakespeare, Aristophanes, and Maurice Maeterlinck. However, he felt bound to give the fairy-tale opera one more effort to prove that the success of *Hänsel und Gretel* had not been a one-time aberration. Returning to the *Königskinder* play, which had been an abortive melodrama, he decided to utilize his original idea and make it into a full-fledged opera by recasting the earlier text and overhauling his previous music. The premiere, arranged at the Metropolitan Opera House in New York, took place, after many delays, in December, 1910, in the same month as that of Giacomo Puccini's *La fanciulla del west* (the girl of the golden west). Puccini's opera, which went on to survive as a part of the working international repertoire, was coolly received at first, while Humperdinck's work (now long forgotten) was ecstatically acclaimed for its beautiful music and theatrical effects.

At a seeming pinnacle of success and fame, Humperdinck composed a pantomime opera called

Das Mirakel (the miracle). However, at its London premiere in December, 1911, Humperdinck suffered a physical breakdown that initiated a deterioration of his health that plagued him for the remaining decade of his life. He continued to travel and compose, producing two more operas (in 1914 and 1919) that achieved no success at all and writing in other vocal and instrumental forms as well. Still receiving international honors, he retired from his Berlin posts in 1920, only to die on September 27 of the following year at age sixty-seven.

Summary

Engelbert Humperdinck was not exclusively an operatic composer. Besides other vocal music, he produced one major orchestral work—the *Moorish Rhapsody* (1899)—three string quartets (1873, 1875, and 1920), and a quintet for piano and strings (1875). However, it was in the theater that he felt most at home and strove to make his mark.

It was already clear by the time of his death that Humperdinck's successes had mostly become ephemeral. His early champion, Richard Strauss, had stolen a march on him: After establishing his commanding position as a composer of German orchestral music, Strauss had then assumed true leadership in German opera with his scandalous and decadent *Salome* (1905) and the shocking and brutal *Elektra* (1909), followed by the mellow *Der Rosenkavalier* (1911). With his operatic initiative taken away, Humperdinck also found himself adrift in the larger musical world being shaken by Schoenberg, Igor Stravinsky, and Bela Bartók. The idiom of the fairy-tale opera, which satisfied German cultural appetites of the moment, was actually built upon the illusion that the traditions of Romanticism were still vehicles for continued growth. Wagner's "music of the future" had quickly become a stale reaction in its own turn, for the musical world was rapidly moving into radical experiments with alternatives that left Humperdinck's aesthetics far behind.

Some of Humperdinck's music is still heard, and, at least in German houses, *Königskinder* and even *Dornröschen* might occasionally be revived. However, Humperdinck has survived in the dubious status of a one-work composer. *Hänsel und Gretel*—whether in the original German or as translated into almost every Western language—has curiously escaped the eclipse of everything else Humperdinck created amid such optimism. Its appeal to children as well as adults has given it an almost unique role as an introductory opera, and it has become an unshakable staple of Christmas performances. It is also, quite simply, a score filled with gorgeous music—the first and only truly viable *Märchenoper*, but one that justly deserves its enduring popularity.

Bibliography

Bettelheim, Bruno. *The Uses of Enchantment: The Meaning and Importance of Fairy Tales*. New York: Knopf, and London: Thames and Hudson, 1976. This book contains analysis of the original fairy-tale form of the Hansel and Gretel story, which is still useful despite the decline in the author's reputation.

Irmen, Hans Josef. *Die Odyssee des Engelbert Humperdinck, ein biographische Dokumentation*. Siegburg: Druck Schmitt, 1974. This represents the best access to the sources on the composer's life.

_____, ed. *Engelbert Humperdinck: Briefe und Tagebücher*. Cologne: Volk, 1976. Along with Irmen's other book, this is the best source of information on Humperdinck.

Humperdinck, Wolfram. *Engelbert Humperdinck: Das Leben meines Vaters*. Frankfort-am-Main: Kramer, 1965. This is a German-language biography of Humperdinck.

John W. Barker

HUNG HSIU-CH'ÜAN

Born: January 1, 1814; Hua-hsien, Kwangtung, China

Died: June, 1864; Nanking, China

Areas of Achievement: Government, politics, and religion

Contribution: Hung created and led the first revolutionary movement to shake the traditional Chinese political system. His movement, the T'ai-p'ing Heavenly Kingdom, was a cataclysmic upheaval that greatly influenced both Sun Yat-sen and Mao Tse-tung.

Early Life

Hung Hsiu-ch'üan was born in a small village thirty miles from Canton, the great port of south China. He was the third son of a Hakka family, clannish, hard-working peasants who spoke a distinct dialect and were often discriminated against by the Han Chinese majority. He was later described as tall with a fair complexion and large, bright eyes. For young Chinese men, there was one sure way to climb in the ancient society: to pass the civil service examinations used to assign positions in the bureaucracy. The examinations were based upon the Confucian classic texts and demanded proficiency in the Chinese language with its tens of thousands of characters. Students often had wealthy families who could support them, since study had to begin early and usually did not culminate before a man's late twenties or early thirties. Although poor, Hung had unusual intelligence; many of his relatives, therefore, sacrificed to enable him to study. At the age of sixteen, he had to quit studying and work on his father's farm. The villagers thought so much of his talents that they hired him to teach their children, giving him an opportunity for part-time study.

Despite Hung's intelligence and ambition, part-time study was not enough. He repeatedly failed the first level of the examinations. In 1837, he collapsed in nervous exhaustion and was bedridden for some time. In this state, he had a series of religious visions combining traditional Chinese notions with themes derived from Western Christianity.

Earlier, China had been strong and self-reliant and had repelled the repeated attempts of Western diplomats, businessmen, and missionaries to gain entrance. Yet problems, above all overpopulation, mounted. China's last dynasty, the Ch'ing (1644-1912), were Manchus, formerly a fierce warrior people. They had grown corrupt and incompetent and were unable to stem China's accelerating decline. By the time Hung was born, many Westerners were in China though their activities were closely regulated. Western businessmen, primarily British, were selling increasing amounts of opium. Great Britain hoped both to defray the costs of controlling India, where the opium was grown, and to use opium profits to pay for British purchases of Chinese teas and silks. The numbers of Western missionaries also increased rapidly, and their access to Chinese society expanded.

The missionaries meant well and made a lasting contribution to Chinese society by improving education and social welfare; China, however, had never known a monotheistic religion, and the impact of Christian ideas upon the Chinese was unpredictable. Hung had cursorily examined some translations of missionary texts the year before his collapse. In his illness, Hung had visions that continued over some months. He believed that God was calling upon him to drive evil spirits and demons, represented by the Manchus, out of China.

Life's Work

Hung recovered and began to preach ideas that struck most listeners as very strange. It was a time of great turmoil, however, and friends and relatives began to listen to Hung; soon he was making converts. In 1844, he damaged local temples and drew the attention of the authorities, who strictly prohibited teachings outside the three religions of Taoism, Buddhism, and Confucianism. Hung and one of his first converts, Feng Yün-shan, left for the neighboring province, Kwangsi. Kwangsi was very poor and many of its inhabitants were racial minorities such as the Yao, Miao, and Chuang peoples. The Chuang were the most numerous Chinese minority and had often served as mercenaries in Chinese armies in the past. That winter, Hung went back to Kwangtung, leaving Feng, who had relatives among the numerous Hakka in Kwangsi, to stay and preach. In Kwangtung, Hung continued to preach and write, studying briefly in Canton with a noted American missionary, Issachar J. Roberts. In 1847, Hung returned to Kwangsi. Feng was a spellbinding speaker and had been very successful in winning converts, particularly among the Chuang and the Hakka.

China was in increasing turmoil. The Manchus had fought and decisively lost a war with Great Britain in 1840-1842. The ostensible cause of the war was the Chinese attempt to control the opium trade, but the real issue was foreign demands for greater freedom of action in China. The Opium War, as it was called, caused immense dislocation in south China. Kwangsi, already very poor, suffered from recurrent drought; banditry became widespread. Many peasants joined secret societies, traditional organizations that frequently became violently anti-government. The authorities created local militia, which easily became tools of local despots.

Hung's congregations, known as the Society of God Worshipers, became embroiled in local conflicts, and the authorities attempted to suppress them. Yet the combination of Hung's messianic fervor and of Feng's mystical appeals was irresistible in troubled Kwangsi. In 1850, the Society of God Worshipers won a battle at Chin-t'ien village, attracting new converts as well as the cooperation of the secret societies and pirate bands eager for plunder. In 1851, his forces swollen with tens of thousands of new followers, Hung declared the "T'ai-p'ing T'ien-kuo" (the T'ai-p'ing Heavenly Kingdom) as both a new Chinese dynasty and a new holy order on earth. The group repelled government counterattacks and moved north, into the Yangtze River valley, China's populous economic center. Disaffected peasants flocked to Hung's banner. From 1851 to 1853, victory followed victory, and the T'ai-p'ing established their capital at Nanking, a major city on the Yangtze River. Yet the government in Peking rallied, led by a new generation of Han Chinese more willing to adopt Western weapons and techniques than the traditional Manchu leadership had been.

A major question was the attitude of the Western powers, who had won many privileges following the Opium War. They now had access to many Chinese ports and were gaining control of import and customs duties, making trade much easier. They were dubious of Hung's religious ideas, which were based upon only a small portion of the Bible, particularly upon the mystical Book of Revelation. Some thought him insane. A decisive issue in the minds of many foreigners was that Hung absolutely prohibited the opium trade. After considerable debate, the Western powers decided to maintain a public posture of neutrality, but they encouraged private assistance to the Manchu regime and gave necessary financial support. Foreign adventurers,

such as the American Frederick Townsend Ward and the Englishman Major Charles George "Chinese" Gordon, formed units of Filipino and Western mercenaries, who fought for the government and trained Chinese soldiers.

Fighting was widespread and savage. Armies of hundreds of thousands marched and countermarched across central China. Prolonged sieges of large cities resulted in mass starvation. Enormous fleets clashed on China's many lakes and rivers. The peasants often found it impossible to farm, and famines resulted. It has been estimated that from 20 to 40 million Chinese died in these upheavals.

Feng died in battle in 1852, but Hung had many talented soldiers, some of whom were made "kings" in the T'ai-p'ing Heavenly Kingdom. The T'ai-p'ing could not, however, win over the Confucian bureaucracy, who were instrumental in governing local communities in China. The Confucians preferred the Manchus, who were a known quantity and themselves highly Confucian, to the alien ideas of the T'ai-p'ing, who held land in common and preached social leveling and the equality of the sexes.

In August of 1856, the T'ai-p'ing were split by a series of internal struggles in which several of the kings died. Other able generals arose, and the war seesawed; however, the T'ai-p'ing failed to deal with their internal problems. Without the help of the local Confucian gentry, they could not produce the necessary revenues to fight an increasingly modern war. The foreigners openly supported the government. In the late years of the T'ai-p'ing kingdom, Hung grew increasingly isolated and less and less realistic. He believed that God would ultimately protect the T'ai-p'ing Heavenly Kingdom, but the capital at Nanking fell on July 19, 1864. Hung had died in June, reportedly by his own hand.

Summary

Despite his ultimate failure, Hung Hsiu-ch'üan had great impact for a Chinese peasant. The odds against him were very great. In Chinese history, only one peasant had founded a new dynasty, and that had been more than five hundred years earlier. Hung's religious ideas inevitably were unconventional. He necessarily perceived Western Christianity through the veil of his own Chinese culture, which alienated contemporary Western observers. Some scholars have questioned his sanity.

As well as dreaming of a China divinely purified of the Manchus, Hung also dreamed of a China that would be a better place for common men and women, a strong China free of foreign influence, without opium, slavery, prostitution, and marked social inequality. His example influenced a later generation of revolutionaries, such as Sun Yat-sen, another Hakka peasant from Kwangtung, who helped to overthrow the Manchus, becoming the first President of Republican China in 1913. Hung also influenced the Communists led by Mao Tse-tung, who founded the People's Republic of China in 1949. The Chinese government and people revered Hung as the first Chinese revolutionary, a visionary who fought for a new and more equitable Chinese government.

Bibliography

Boardman, Eugene. *Christian Influence upon the Ideology of the Taiping Rebellion, 1851-1864.* Madison: University of Wisconsin Press, 1952. Many works on the T'ai-p'ing rebellion largely ignore Hung as an individual, but not Boardman's. This work brings together everything that is known about Hung and examines his beliefs in both the Chinese and Western Christian context of the period.

Hamberg, Theodore. *The Visions of Hung-Siutshuen, and Origin of the Kwangsi Insurrection.* San Francisco: Chinese Materials Center, 1975. This book was written during the T'ai-p'ing rebellion by a Western missionary who investigated Hung's background, particularly his exposure to Christian ideas, and his resulting religious beliefs.

Jen, Yu-wen. *The Taiping Revolutionary Movement.* New Haven, Conn., and London: Yale University Press, 1973. Most scholarly works on the T'ai-p'ing rebellion are primarily interested in the contemporary Chinese social scene or in the war or in T'ai-p'ing institutions. This work treats in detail the issue of Christian influences upon Hung's values and beliefs.

Kuhn, Philip A. "The Taiping Rebellion." In *The Cambridge History of China Late Ch'ing, 1800-1911,* edited by John K. Fairbank. Vol. 10, Cambridge and New York: Cambridge University Press, 1978. Kuhn is one of the foremost historians of the rebellion, and this is an excellent introductory essay to it and to China during that period. Several other essays in the volume also relate to the rebellion. Contains a bibliographic guide to sources in Asian and Western languages.

Michael, Franz, and Chung-li Chang. *The Taiping Rebellion: History and Documents.* 3 vols. Seattle: University of Washington Press, 1966-1971. The first volume of this massive work is a narrative history of the rebellion. The final two volumes are translations of important documents. The work is considered a standard history for research purposes.

Teng, Ssu-yü. *The Taiping Rebellion and the Western Powers.* Oxford: Clarendon Press, 1971. Teng is a leading historian in the field. This is an excellent study of the diplomatic context of the rebellion, particularly of the relations between the foreign powers and the Chinese court.

Jeffrey G. Barlow

WILLIAM HOLMAN HUNT

Born: April 2, 1827; London, England
Died: September 7, 1910; London, England
Area of Achievement: Art
Contribution: As a result of his activity in the Pre-Raphaelite Brotherhood and his artistic success outside the Royal Academy, Hunt exerted a broadening influence on British art, reforming ideas regarding lighting and color and bringing considerations of content back into primary importance in painting.

Early Life

William Holman Hunt, the eldest of seven Hunt children (two sons and five daughters), was born in Wood Street, Cheapside, London, on April 2, 1827. He was named for his maternal grandfather. Hunt's father, also named William Hunt, a warehouseman in the Cheapside district, took care to introduce his son to art and literature but did not encourage the boy's interest in art. Until the age of thirteen, Hunt attended private schools, and then he became an assistant to Richard Cobden, a calico printer and minor politician. Dissatisfied with these pursuits, young Hunt gained permission to study art in the evenings, which he proceeded to do in the studio of portrait painter Henry Rogers.

By 1843, Hunt had given up his commercial employment for the full-time study of art, working as a student at the British Museum three days a week and making copies at the National Gallery for two more. After failing his first attempt to gain admission to the Royal Academy schools, he was admitted as a probationer in 1844 and was promoted to full studentship the next year. There Hunt became fast friends with John Everett Millais, a painter two years Hunt's junior, but one who had already gained recognition for his great promise as a painter. Hunt also formed his first acquaintance with Dante Gabriel Rossetti, with whom, along with Millais, he would form the Pre-Raphaelite Brotherhood (PRB) some years later. Primarily, however, Hunt spent these years learning to paint, and he began exhibiting at the Academy in 1846, with a picture titled *Hark!*, which he followed the next year with *Dr. Rochecliffe Performing Divine Service in the Cottage of Joceline Jocliffe at Woodstock*, a scene from a novel by Sir Walter Scott.

In 1848, Hunt first won individual recognition with his *Flight of Madeline and Porphyro*, adapted from John Keats's poem *The Eve of St. Agnes* (1820). This painting attracted the attention of Rossetti, who thought it the year's best painting and who, as a result, pressed Hunt to allow him to work under Hunt in Hunt's studio in Fitzroy Square. Thus began both an artistic association and a close personal friendship that would last for nine years. Hunt introduced Rossetti to Millais, and in the fall of 1848 these three, flush with the enthusiasm of their early success, laid down the principles and formed the nucleus of the PRB.

Life's Work

Hunt, a tall man with striking blue eyes, a high forehead, brown hair, and a long, silky, red-golden beard, made two major contributions to the history of the fine arts in England. First, Hunt's position as cofounder of the PRB established him as a leader in the reformation of painting as an art form. With Hunt, Rossetti, and Millais in the lead, the PRB led a revolt against fashionable painting of the time,

which emphasized technical perfection at the expense of content. The Pre-Raphaelites vowed to express only important ideas; to paint directly from nature, disregarding the accepted rules of design and color, which had limited artists to a relatively narrow range of colors and lighting effects; and to paint events realistically, as they were likely to have happened, rather than in the idealized, highly refined manner of the day. These three tenets, together with the suspicion aroused by the presence of a secret brotherhood, led to a public outcry against the works of the PRB, but the group gained an able champion in 1851, when John Ruskin came to the defense of Hunt's *Valentine Rescuing Sylvia from Proteus*, inspired by William Shakespeare's *Two Gentlemen of Verona*. Ruskin defended what the Pre-Raphaelites were trying to do, and he explained, in the process, that their works were a logical and a positive reaction against some bad influences in English painting. Thus, from 1851 onward, Hunt's works, as well as those of his fellow Pre-Raphaelites, gained in acceptance and value. More important, however, their principles gained wider and wider acceptance, even though Hunt was perhaps the only Pre-Raphaelite artist to follow them rigorously throughout his career. These early works of the PRB paved the way for later artists such as Edward Burne-Jones and William Morris, and for such widely divergent movements as aestheticism and purism, in which idea assumed the ascendancy over style and realism and faithfulness to nature overrode established ideas of composition and design.

In addition to this perhaps purely aesthetic success, Hunt's personal success in making a living from the proceeds of his art and in doing so outside the Academy blazed a trail for artists who came after him and who also violated the accepted practices of their day. Beginning in the 1850's, Hunt began to make a very good living from his art, even though he showed fewer and fewer paintings at the Royal Academy and even though his work violated accepted standards of composition, color, and design. By 1854, Hunt's *The Light of the World*, a work still widely reproduced, sold for about five hundred pounds, a significant sum of money at that time; *The Scapegoat* sold for a similar amount in 1856. The best, however, was yet to come. In 1860, when Hunt finished *The Finding of the Saviour in the Temple*, he sold the painting for fifty-five hundred pounds, and *The Shadow of Death* brought twice that sum in 1871. These were unheard-of

prices for the time, and Hunt's ability to thrive outside the Royal Academy broke the stranglehold which that body had long exercised on the visual arts. Hunt had brought ideas back into art, and his paintings, most of which explored New Testament themes according to a typological scheme of symbolism, increased in value and popularity as their artist's methods were vindicated by the increasing public and critical acceptance his work gained.

Hunt's methods were intimately connected with the success of his painting. His attention to detail, one of the primary traits of Pre-Raphaelitism, resulted from his absolute dedication to accuracy. This principle made him something of a legend, for he insisted on painting on site whenever possible. Thus, his major religious works were painted in Palestine, and they display an immediateness that is missing from most painting of the era, which was done largely from the artist's often mistaken impression of what such a place must be like. More than this trademark of authenticity, Hunt's attention to detail reinforced his typological method, allowing him to exploit a single moment in his subject's existence to encapsulate that subject's entire import. In *The Shadow of Death*, for example, Christ, a young man working in his father's carpentry shop, stops in the late afternoon to stretch. Behind him, his outstretched arms cast a shadow on the wall, and the shadow falls on a tool rack in such a way that it produces an image of the Crucifixion. In the lower left of the painting kneels the Virgin Mary, who has been looking at the contents of a trunk which is still open before her and in which can be seen the gifts the Magi brought to the child Jesus. Yet Mary is no longer looking at the gifts; her attention has been drawn to the shadow behind her, and her position suggests alarm, as if she senses the significance of the shadow on the wall. This one moment, then, condenses a considerable expanse of biblical history, from David, a type of Christ, to the Crucifixion itself, and, through the reference to the twenty-third Psalm, to the Resurrection. After all, the verse alluded to in the title does celebrate being led through the valley of the shadow of death. Hunt's method, then, brings not only a remarkable number of physical details into his work but also an impressive density of ideas, so that the painting must literally be explored by the viewer, who is responsible for dealing with all the complex resonances of the allusions in the work. By means of this typological method, Hunt brought ideas back into British art, and this is perhaps his greatest contribution to painting.

Hunt's personal life, in the meantime, was almost as stormy as his artistic career. Upon returning from his first trip to the Holy Land and soon after he had finished *The Finding of the Saviour in the Temple*, Hunt paid a visit, in the company of his friend and fellow Pre-Raphaelite Thomas Woolner, to the Waugh household, where Woolner had long been courting Fanny Waugh, the favorite daughter of her overprotective father. In the end, she refused Woolner, for she had already become attracted to Hunt, whose attachment to Fanny was tempered by his fear of a scandal involving some indiscreet love letters he had earlier written to Annie Miller, a model who had been much admired among the Brotherhood. The attraction weathered this possible scandal and the initial disapproval of Fanny's father, and on December 28, 1865, the two were married. A disastrous honeymoon, delayed by Hunt's insistence on finishing several pictures, followed. When the couple set out for the Holy Land for a working honeymoon, Fanny was already seven months pregnant. At Marseilles, the ports were closed because of cholera, so the Hunts crossed into Italy via Switzerland, but to no avail, since the same conditions were in effect there. They settled in Florence, where the heat and the effort of sitting for her husband weakened Fanny so that she was unable, ultimately, to recover from the rigors of childbirth. On October 26, 1866, Cyril Benone Holman Hunt was born in Florence, and about two months later, on December 20, Fanny died.

Hunt returned to England, bringing Cyril, who had, in the meantime, been twice almost starved by fraudulent wet nurses. His return led to the discovery that Fanny's youngest sister, Edith, was and always had been in love with him, and whether she was so much like Fanny or he simply found her attractive in her own right, Hunt found himself in love with her. Their union was proscribed as incestuous by the Affinity Laws, she being Hunt's sister under the law, so the two decided, reluctantly, to resist their attraction, and Hunt left for another Eastern journey, on which he began *The Shadow of Death* and attempted to put Edith out of his mind. Upon his return, nothing had changed, and the two, after great struggle and vacillation, finally decided to marry, in spite of the laws forbidding their union. Both their families disowned and disinherited them, but in November of 1875 Edith Waugh married her brother-in-law in Neufchatel, Switzerland, nine years after Fanny's death. Their marriage would not be recognized in Great Britain un-

til 1907, when the Deceased Wife's Sister's Marriage Act received royal approval. Hunt and Edith remained devoted to each other, a happy couple for the rest of his life. He died in 1910, and she survived him by twenty years.

Summary

For the most part, William Holman Hunt's life is exemplified by his art. A stubborn perfectionist with an intense vision about what art should be and do, Hunt refused to compromise his ideas. His early works, largely misunderstood, did not sell, but rather than change his methods, in 1850 Hunt contemplated giving up art and becoming a farmer. Ruskin's intervention relieved Hunt's distress, and increasing acceptance led to greater influence on artists who surrounded or succeeded Hunt. Perhaps Hunt's greatest aesthetic contributions were in the areas of color, realism, and symbolism. Eschewing the limited color range and chiaroscuro effects of his day, Hunt painted in bright, natural colors, and the lighting in his paintings was as bright or as dark as the actual situation demanded. In addition, Hunt concentrated on painting a scene the way it really appeared rather than imposing an unnatural conventional design onto the subject. This emphasis on verisimilitude was reinforced by his views on color and lighting, so that his work represents a return to realism, a desertion of the highly stylized artificiality which, Hunt believed, had increasingly marred European painting from the time of Raphael onward. Most important, Hunt brought serious ideas back into painting. Reacting against the example of such painters as Edwin Landseer (1802-1873), technically accomplished but lacking in substance, Hunt brought content to the foreground of his art. Combining a heightened attention to detail with a pronounced typological symbolism, Hunt produced works which were meaningful in themselves and which made statements with relation to other texts as well, whether those other texts came from literature or the Bible. Thus, Hunt's greatest works are narrative in nature, informed by texts alluded to in the subject of the painting and, in turn, commented on in the painting itself. This dialogue between texts provides the vehicle for the painting's statement and for art's return to an active involvement in the larger context of its culture.

Bibliography

Bennett, Mary. *William Holman Hunt*. Liverpool: Walker Art Gallery, 1969. The catalog of the

Hunt exhibition, this work is indispensable to the serious study of Hunt's art.

Fredeman, William E. *Pre-Raphaelitism: A Bibliocritical Study.* Cambridge, Mass.: Harvard University Press, 1965. Provides a complete overview of Pre-Raphaelitism and a full listing of source material for further study. This book is crucial to any study of Pre-Raphaelitism.

Hilton, Timothy. *The Pre-Raphaelites.* London: Thames and Hudson, and New York: Oxford University Press, 1970. Lavishly illustrated general introduction to Pre-Raphaelite painting. This book is the only modern history of the Brotherhood to concentrate solely on painting, so it is particularly useful as a starting place to study Hunt.

Holman-Hunt, Diana. *My Grandfather, His Wives and Loves.* London: Hamilton, and New York: Norton, 1969. This rather luridly titled but quite readable account of Hunt's private life is also surprisingly well documented, as the author had access to family papers not generally available at the time.

Hunt, William Holman. *Pre-Raphaelitism and the Pre-Raphaelite Brotherhood.* 2 vols. 2d ed. London: Chapman and Hall, 1913; New York: Dutton, 1914. Hunt's account of his career and of the history of the PRB, this book is highly subjective and somewhat self-justifying, but an important primary source of information. The two editions are collated in Bennett's catalog of the 1969 Hunt exhibition.

King, Laura, and Therese Southgate. "William Holman Hunt." *Journal of the American Medi-cal Association* 277, no. 17 (May 7, 1997). Short profile of Hunt, his views on art, his marriage, and his portrait of his wife.

Landow, George P. *William Holman Hunt and Typological Symbolism.* New Haven, Conn., and London: Yale University Press, 1979. The definitive interpretation of Hunt's accomplishments in painting. Landow explains Hunt's typological method and provides detailed and highly insightful explications of Hunt's paintings and those of other Pre-Raphaelites, most notably Rossetti.

————. " 'Your Good Influence on Me': The Correspondence of John Ruskin and William Holman Hunt." *Bulletin of the John Rylands University Library of Manchester* 59 (1976-1977): 95-126, 376-396. This compilation of Ruskin's correspondence with Hunt provides vital insight into Hunt's artistic endeavors and into the long friendship between this artist and his champion.

Ribner, Jonathan P. "Our English Coasts, 1852: William Holman Hunt and Invasion Fear at Midcentury." *Art Journal* 55, no. 2 (Summer 1996). Discusses Hunt's 1852 painting of sheep grazing on a cliff overlooking the English Channel and its interpretation as a depiction of English fears of a French invasion.

Welland, D. S. R. *The Pre-Raphaelites in Literature and Art.* London: Harrap, and New York: Barnes and Noble, 1953. Besides a useful general introduction to Pre-Raphaelite art, the book contains selections from writings by and about Pre-Raphaelite artists, poets, and critics.

William Condon

THOMAS HENRY HUXLEY

Born: May 4, 1825; Ealing, Middlesex, England
Died: June 29, 1895; Eastbourne, East Sussex, England
Areas of Achievement: Science and philosophy
Contribution: The first and most influential defender of Charles Darwin's theory of evolution, Huxley forcefully articulated its implications in the fields of religion, philosophy, and ethics.

Early Life

Thomas Henry Huxley was born on May 4, 1825, in Ealing, Middlesex, England, a village not far from London. The seventh and youngest child of George and Rachel Huxley, he was reared in a family of limited means. Though his father had taught mathematics, Huxley had had only two years of formal education before the Ealing school closed and his father changed professions. At the age of ten, Huxley became responsible for his own education.

Ironically, the inquisitive and self-motivated boy probably learned more on his own, systematically working through his father's library, than he would have in the incompetent semipublic education system of early nineteenth century England. Demonstrating the drive that would characterize his later years, he taught himself both French and German in order to read such writers as Rene Descartes and Johann Wolfgang von Goethe in their native languages. He read widely both in the humanities and in the sciences, laying a foundation that would serve him in his later efforts to bridge the two disciplines.

In 1842, Huxley won a scholarship to study medicine at London University's Charing Cross Hospital. A swarthy, energetic young man, whose keen eyes betrayed a voracious intellectual appetite, he took full advantage of his first complete course of instruction, winning the university's Gold Medal in Anatomy and Physiology upon his graduation in 1845. A few months later, he discovered a cellular component of human hair that came to be known as "Huxley's layer."

The following year, Huxley joined the navy and was appointed assistant surgeon on HMS *Rattlesnake,* a surveying ship that began a four-year cruise of the South Pacific. Though he was not officially the ship's naturalist, he undertook a rigorous study of marine plankton that earned for him the reputation of a serious and gifted young scientist upon its publication in London. In 1851, a year fol-

lowing his return to London, he was elected a Fellow of the Royal Society of London for the Promotion of Natural Knowledge, England's most respected scientific institution. In 1852, he won the society's gold medal for his studies of invertebrate animals. In 1854, he resigned from the navy, hoping against the odds to secure a position that would allow him to do scientific research in London. That same year, his gamble paid off and he received two such appointments, one as professor of natural history and paleontology in the Royal School of Mines, and the other as curator of fossils in the Museum of Practical Geography. Combining the two modest salaries, he earned enough to send for his fiancée, Henrietta Anne Heathorn of Sydney, Australia. In 1855, the two were married.

In the years that followed, Huxley built his reputation not only as a rigorous scientist but also as a gifted public speaker. He became known as a spokesman for the sciences, never afraid to defend controversial findings from attacks by politicians and religious leaders. When Charles Darwin published his *On the Origin of Species* in 1859, these attributes brought Huxley to the forefront of the century's most heated debate.

Life's Work

Though Huxley eventually made much use of Darwin's study, demonstrating its implications in a wide number of fields, he had opposed all previous theories of evolution. His reviews of the versions of it put forward by Robert Chambers and Jean Baptiste Lamarck had been scathing. It was only upon reading Darwin's work, following the course of Darwin's logic and tallying his numerous observations, that Huxley could embrace the controversial idea. For his own part, Darwin had sought Huxley's approval before publishing the book. A shy, retiring man, Darwin lacked the stamina required to defend his work from the onslaught of vicious attacks it was sure to receive. In Huxley, Darwin found a respected and able supporter.

In a series of heated debates following the book's publication, Huxley championed Darwin's theory of evolution as the most successful framework yet proposed, within which to organize the known biological facts. What is more important, he fought to defend the broader principle that such controversies are better settled by examining the observable evidence than by appealing to unsupported scripture. In the most important of these debates, opposing the influential Bishop Samuel Wilberforce of Oxford, Huxley defiantly asserted his and his colleagues' intention to continue to test Darwin's theory, without regard to the clergy's attempts to discredit them.

From 1860 to 1863, Huxley began the first of a series of studies intended to carry out this intention, extensively comparing primate anatomies. In *On the Origin of Species*, Darwin had only hinted that the theory of evolution could be applied to humans. In Huxley's most important book, *Evidence as to Man's Place in Nature* (1863), the younger scientist demonstrated that humans bear a close enough resemblance to the great apes to be included in their taxonomical class. Though a number of scientists initially rejected his conclusions, Huxley, like Darwin, thoroughly documented his findings with an entire volume of observed phenomena. His observations were there to be checked, and eventually the majority in the scientific community was convinced. No longer considered separate from the animal kingdom, humans joined the class of primates.

Sensitive to the fears that such findings engendered, Huxley devoted a large part of his later years to issues raised by the new science in the fields of religion, morality, and philosophy. In a line of his thought that culminated in the book *Evolution and Ethics* (1893), he attempted to ease concerns that a moral education could not be taught without religion, describing ethics as one of the human species' special survival mechanisms. He argued that when people in a group treat one another ethically, each member conscious of the well-being of the others, the survival of the group (and thus of each individual) is made more secure. For this reason, he firmly believed that in the public schools a good moral education should accompany both a rigorous scientific education and a firm grounding in the humanities. As one of the founding members of the school board of London, he had a chance to put these views into practice.

Huxley also took it upon himself to promote the education of adults who, like himself, had never had the benefit of a primary or secondary education. In his very popular Workingman Lectures, he took the time to express complex scientific and philosophical concepts in language that people from all walks of life could understand. He emphasized that science itself is nothing more than obser-

vation and common sense, applied in a systematic fashion and stored in books.

When Huxley died on June 29, 1895, in Eastbourne, East Sussex, England, he had published a number of important books and countless influential articles, he had received honorary degrees from some of the finest universities both in Great Britain and in the United States, and he had been elected president of Great Britain's Royal Society. His life's work has been carried on impressively by his son Leonard Huxley, a biographer and man of letters, and by his grandsons Aldous Huxley, the novelist, Andrew Fielding Huxley, cowinner of the 1963 Nobel Prize in Medicine, and Julian Huxley, a leading biologist who served as the first director general of the United Nations Educational, Scientific and Cultural Organization (UNESCO).

Summary

Though in the general public the controversy surrounding evolution has not ended, in the scientific community the theory has, with rare exceptions, been universally accepted since Thomas Henry

Huxley's time. Had the theory been disproved, Darwin, Huxley, and the few other scientists who had fought initially for its acceptance would probably have been ridiculed out of their profession. Instead, evolution has survived to become the cornerstone of modern biology, and all who have benefited from the great strides in twentieth century medicine and disease control owe a debt to these courageous scientists.

In addition, Huxley in particular helped his contemporaries to see how helpful results could be obtained in any area of human thought, through the application of scientific inductive reasoning—beginning with the observed facts and working up toward the answers to the larger questions. This aspect of Huxley's thought has been missed by many of his opponents. For example, his opposition in religious circles considered him an atheist, but Huxley did not actually believe that there was enough evidence either to prove or to disprove the existence of God. To describe his own position, he coined the term "agnostic" defining it as one who is not afraid to admit when there are not enough observable facts to have a reliable opinion on a given topic. As he stated in 1868 in his essay "On the Physical Basis of Life":

> Why trouble ourselves about matters of which, however important they may be, we do know nothing, and can know nothing? We live in a world which is full of misery and ignorance, and the plain duty of each of us is to try to make the little corner he can influence somewhat less miserable and somewhat less ignorant than it was before he entered it.

Bibliography

Ashforth, Albert. *Thomas Henry Huxley.* New York: Twayne, 1969. A fairly recent examination of Huxley's thought, focusing on the decade that followed Huxley's years defending Darwin. Ashforth discusses Huxley's reexamination of Western beliefs and values in the wake of nineteenth century scientific breakthroughs.

Bibby, Cyril. *T. H. Huxley: Scientist: Humanist, Educator.* London: Watts, 1959; New York: Horizon Press, 1960. Excellent modern biography. Provides a vivid picture of Huxley in his many activities. Well documented with original research.

Clodd, Edward. *Thomas Henry Huxley.* New York: Dodd, Mead, 1902. Draws heavily on Leonard Huxley's biography of his father, but valuable for its early twentieth century critical perspective. Reprinted in 1977.

Desmond, Adrian. *Huxley: From Devil's Disciple to Evolution's High Priest.* Reading, Mass.: Addison Wesley, and London: Penguin, 1997. Explosive biography of Huxley, who some call the century's greatest prophet and whose life was a metaphor for the full range of changes between the Victorian and modern ages.

Huxley, Leonard. *The Life and Letters of Thomas Henry Huxley.* 2 vols. London: Macmillan, 1900; New York: Appleton, 1901. The biography most often used as a source for other biographies, though not in itself complete. Notably lacking in details of Huxley's individual essays, lectures, and addresses.

Huxley, Thomas H. *Collected Essays.* 9 vols. London and New York: Macmillan, 1893-1894. Huxley brought together this collection from among what he considered to be his most important miscellaneous essays and lectures. Focuses primarily upon the impact of science on other areas of human thought. Includes volumes titled *Science and Education, Science and the Hebrew Tradition,* and *Science and the Christian Tradition,* among others.

———. *Evolution and Ethics.* London and New York: Macmillan, 1893. One of Huxley's most important works, the culmination of much of his thought on this subject. In this book, Huxley explains why morality does not need to rest upon religion.

———. *Man's Place in Nature.* Ann Arbor: University of Michigan Press, 1959. Huxley's most important scientific study. He demonstrates how, according to the established rules of taxonomical classification, humans belong in the primate group with the great apes, monkeys, and lower primates. Exhaustive in its documentation.

———. *Scientific Memoirs.* Edited by E. Ray Lankester and Michael Forster. 5 vols. London: Macmillan, and New York: Appleton, 1898-1903. Huxley's most important scientific essays, collected after his death.

Peterson, Houston. *Huxley: Prophet of Science.* London and New York: Longman, 1932. A lengthy critical discussion of Huxley's life and accomplishments, focusing on the philosophical underpinnings of his work. Rich in biographical detail.

Keith Bowen

HENRIK IBSEN

Born: March 20, 1828; Skien, Norway
Died: May 23, 1906; Christiana, Norway
Areas of Achievement: Theater and drama
Contribution: Ibsen is one of the leading figures in modern drama. Moving beyond the melodramas of the nineteenth century, Ibsen created a drama of psychological realism. His dramas helped to create modern realistic theater.

Early Life

Henrik Ibsen was born on March 20, 1828, in Skien, Norway, the second child of Knud Ibsen, a well-to-do merchant, and his wife, Marchinen, née Altenburg. Ibsen's house, which faced the town square, was across from a church and a town hall that housed lunatics in its cellar. Early in life, Ibsen was faced with what he would later see as the symbol of spiritual freedom (the church spire) countered by the forces of confinement (the town hall). When his father went bankrupt and the family was forced to move to a small farm, Ibsen felt the pressures of being socially ostracized. Also, rumors that he was illegitimate haunted the young Ibsen.

Theater was one of Ibsen's outlets, and by the age of twelve Ibsen had seen six plays by Augustin-Eugène Scribe and had read Friedrich Schiller. As a child, Ibsen amused himself by staging puppet shows, magic acts, and ventriloquist's routines. In 1843, Ibsen went as an apothecary's apprentice to Grimstead, where he fathered an illegitimate child by a servant girl. This event would account for the themes of guilt, fear, and burdensome responsibility attached to sexual relationships in his works. At Grimstead, Ibsen absorbed himself in the realism of Charles Dickens, the biting satire of Voltaire, the explosive dramas of William Shakespeare, and the Romantic tragedies of Schiller. Also, he began to develop his skill as a social critic by writing lampoons and satires. In addition, he wrote poetry which ranged from introspective meditations to political propaganda, and he published *Catalina* (1850; *Catiline*, 1921), his first play. It focused on one of his favorite themes: the conflict between the lone individual and the forces of power. That same year, Ibsen moved to Christiana to study medicine, but he paid more attention to his literary pursuits and never finished his degree. His play *Kjæmpehøien* (1850; *Burial Mound*, 1912) was produced by the Christiana Theater. Ibsen continued to sharpen his

skill as a poet, ventured into political journalism, and wrote perceptive theatrical criticism. Active in leftist political movements, he barely escaped being arrested. From then on, Ibsen distanced himself from political activism.

In 1851, Ibsen became stage manager and playwright-in-residence at Ole Bull's Norwegian Theater in Bergen. Having received a travel grant, he toured Denmark and Germany to learn the latest developments in theater. Overworked, underpaid, and unable to produce innovative works, Ibsen left Bergen to become the artistic director of the Norwegian Theater in Christiana. This job was no less frustrating, however, and Ibsen was eventually driven to bouts of depression and alcoholism. Given a small travel grant and aided by friends, Ibsen finally left Norway for Italy. He was to spend the better part of his career in exile from family and country.

During Ibsen's career in Norwegian theater, he wrote nationalistic sagas and satirical comedies. His experience as a director taught him how to structure his dramas and how to make effective use of visual and poetic imagery. Although the dramas of this early period are full of bombast and mechanical contrivances, Ibsen was starting to formulate a new kind of drama.

Life's Work

Ibsen's career as a major world dramatist began in Rome. Exiled from a Norway whose narrow provincialism had stifled him, and infuriated over his country's refusal to aid Denmark, Ibsen created *Brand* (1866; English translation, 1891), a monumental poetic drama delving into the spiritual crisis of a romantic idealist. Ibsen had now gone beyond the aestheticism of his earlier nationalistic sagas to write a profound drama which would rouse his countrymen from their complacency and force them to face the great issues of life. Widely discussed and hotly debated, *Brand* became a bestseller and won for Ibsen a pension from his government. Ibsen countered *Brand* with another massive poetic drama, *Peer Gynt* (1867; English translation, 1892), the story of an opportunistic double-dealer who compromises his inner self to achieve material gains. These two dramas established Ibsen's reputation.

In 1868, Ibsen moved to Dresden. He was lionized by the king of Sweden and later represented

Norway at the opening of the Suez Canal. By 1869, Ibsen started to move in the direction of modern realistic drama. *De unges forbund* (1869; *The League of Youth*, 1890) focused on a contemporary setting, employed colloquial speech patterns, and satirized political chicanery. In *Kejeser og Galilœer* (1873; *Emperor and Galilean*, 1876), Ibsen created an epic tragedy in prose. In this drama, Ibsen tried to reconcile the Christian call for self-sacrifice with the pagan command to enjoy the pleasures of life to the fullest, thereby exposing the underlying dilemma of the late nineteenth century.

Ibsen now began to dissociate himself from political reform movements in favor of a spiritual revolution based on a radical individualism bordering on anarchy. Influenced by the Danish critic George Brandes and the realist director George II, Duke of Saxe-Meiningen, Ibsen shifted away from historical plays and poetic epics to concentrate on prose dramas set in contemporary Norway. Eventually, he also helped to give form and depth to the modern realistic problem play. In *Et dukkehjem* (1879; *A Doll's House*, 1880) and *Gengangere* (1881; *Ghosts*, 1885), Ibsen helped to shape the path of modern drama. Both plays treat contemporary issues, center on a small ensemble of characters, and take place in confined settings. They are crafted around tightly constructed plots which are based on the careful unraveling of past events. Their terse, choppy dialogue is loaded with double meanings, their decor is reflective of the moods and shifts of the characters, and their conflicts are intensely psychological. Both plays deal with women who are asked to sacrifice their duty to themselves in order to meet social obligations. Nora in *A Doll's House* leaves her husband and children, whereas Mrs. Alving in *Ghosts* settles for a loveless marriage, wreaking destruction on her entire family.

In these two dramas, Ibsen exploded both the form and content of the contrived, sentimental, and moralistic melodramas of his time and considered such taboo subjects as venereal disease, incest, and mercy killing. Ibsen even attacked the cherished institution of marriage. On the legitimate stage, his plays were banned or rewritten, but in the new avant-garde theaters of Europe, Ibsen's works became staples of the new repertory. Ibsen created plays that attacked bourgeois values at the same time as he elevated domestic drama to the status of high tragedy.

Soon Ibsen would go beyond social drama to probe the recesses of the unconscious in such plays as *Rosmersholm* (1886; English translation, 1889). Ibsen now began to show that an individual's repressed drives can bring about his or her destruction. In *Hedda Gabler* (1890; English translation, 1891), Ibsen combined realistic techniques with psychological drama. He dropped the standard exposition, eliminated long monologues, and created broken dialogue infused with underlying meanings. Hedda is a middle-class woman with no purpose in life. She tries to release her pent-up drives by controlling the destinies of the men around her. Failing in this, she shoots herself in the head.

After wandering back and forth between Italy and Germany, Ibsen returned to Norway a national hero. He was given the Grand Cross in Denmark, honored by royalty, and celebrated in torchlight parades. Frightened and fascinated by the new generation, Ibsen passed through a series of platonic affairs with young girls such as Émile Bardach, Helene Raff, and Hildur Andersen. The theme of a young girl beckoning an aging architect to create a masterpiece appears in the first of his final plays, *Bygmester Solness* (1892; *The Master Builder*, 1893). In these plays, Ibsen experiments with a form of mystic and visionary drama. Ibsen now focuses on the artist and his relationship to art. These short, narrowly focused dramas have a somber, poetic quality laden with symbolic overtones. Their claustrophobic, intense, and anxious mood of finality foreshadows the techniques of the modernist dramas of the twentieth century.

In 1901, Ibsen suffered the first of a series of strokes, which would eventually lead to his death on May 23, 1906. His last words were "On the contrary!"—an appropriate exit line for a man who celebrated the individual's right to define himself contrary to both the wishes of the establishment and the pressures of the crowd.

Summary

Henrik Ibsen was one of the first playwrights to create tragic dramas about ordinary people caught in the webs of fate and forced to choose between their self-fulfillment and their responsibility to others. Ibsen helped to create the modern psychological drama which probes the recesses of the unconscious. His scenic details, suggestive imagery, poetic symbols, and double-edged dialogue created a dramatic technique that would help to revolution-

ize the modern theater. His dramas depended on a subtle, truthful form of acting which inspired ensemble productions free from rhetoric, bombast, and posturing. Ibsen's plays challenged avant-garde directors such as André Antoiné, Otto Brahm, and Konstantin Stanislavsky. Ibsen also influenced a diverse group of dramatists. George Bernard Shaw saw him as the champion of the propaganda drama. Arthur Miller centered on Ibsen's social dramas, whereas Luigi Pirandello and Harold Pinter focused on Ibsen's existential pieces.

Ibsen defies classification. He sought to go beyond photographic realism, yet he shunned symbolism. He attacked the hypocrisy of social and political establishments but refused to attach himself to any liberal reform movements. He probed deeply into the problems of women but dissociated himself from feminist causes. Ibsen, the true existentialist, had his characters ask two questions which would become the focal questions of modern drama: Who am I? and How can I be true to myself?

Bibliography

Beyer, Edvard. *Ibsen: The Man and His Work.* Translated by Marie Wells. London: Souvenir Press, and New York: Taplinger, 1978. A biographical, critical study of Ibsen which relates Ibsen's works to cultural and political events in Norway at the same time as it establishes his place in world literature. Profusely illustrated with drawings, editorial cartoons, and production photographs. Contains a substantial bibliography of critical works in English.

Chamberlain, John S. *Ibsen: The Open Vision.* London: Athlone Press, 1982. Analyzes *Peer Gynt, Ghosts, The Wild Duck*, and *The Master Builder.* Uses significant plays from the major periods in Ibsen's career to show how Ibsen creates dramatic tension by pitting a variety of intellectual positions against one another without settling on a single resolution. Offers detailed analysis of seminal works.

Clurman, Harold. *Ibsen.* New York: Macmillan, 1977; London: Macmillan, 1978. A very readable introduction to Ibsen's plays, covering his early works as well as his major plays. A theatrical director, Clurman pays careful attention to production values. Places Ibsen in perspective with other major dramatists. The appendix provides director's notes for several plays.

Fjelde, Rolf, ed. *Ibsen: A Collection of Critical Essays.* Englewood Cliffs, N.J.: Prentice-Hall, 1965. A sampling of articles covering a wide variety of plays. Focuses on both Ibsen's major themes and his techniques. Contains a balanced sample of the works of important Ibsen scholars.

Goldman, Michael. *Ibsen: The Dramaturgy of Fear.* New York: Columbia University Press, 1999. The author takes a fresh approach to Ibsen's work, concentrating on dialog, stage sets, psychological motives, and plot to analyze the impact of his work on the audience and culture. Several plays are used as examples including *The Wild Duck, A Doll's House, The Master Builder,* and *Peer Gynt.*

Haugen, Einar. *Ibsen's Drama: Author to Audience.* Minneapolis: University of Minnesota Press, 1979. Uses current communication theories to demonstrate how Ibsen's work can be decoded by a modern audience. Highlights a variety of themes, styles, and production techniques. The appendix includes a chronology of Ibsen's life and brief plot summaries of his works. Also has a detailed bibliography of foreign and English sources, plus a checklist of Ibsen's works using Norwegian titles.

Hurt, James. *Catiline's Dream: An Essay on Ibsen's Plays.* Urbana: University of Illinois Press, 1972. Using the techniques of depth psychology, Hurt traces the mythic pattern of ascent, descent, and transformation throughout Ibsen's works. Focuses on recurring motifs, characters, and symbols.

Meyer, Michael. *Ibsen: A Biography.* New York: Doubleday, 1971; London: Penguin, 1974. A lengthy and exhaustive biography detailing Ibsen's personal and professional life. It not only documents Ibsen's development as a dramatist, his working methods, and his philosophical shifts but also gives a detailed account of the production history of his plays in Germany, France, and England.

Northam, John. *Ibsen: A Critical Study.* Cambridge: Cambridge University Press, 1973. Covers Ibsen's major work, concentrating on the evolution of Ibsen's later prose plays from the themes of his earlier poetic works. Pays careful attention to Ibsen's imagery.

Shepherd-Barr, Kirsten. *Ibsen and Early Modernist Theatre, 1890-1900.* Westport, Conn.: Greenwood Press, 1997. The author reconstructs Ibsen's role in the radical artistic movements of his day using well-researched references to writings such as letters, essays, reviews, and speeches. Excellent for upper-level undergraduate libraries.

Templeton, Joan. *Ibsen's Women.* Cambridge and New York: Cambridge University Press, 1997. Examination of the women in Ibsen's plays and their similarities to the women in his life. The author makes use of Ibsen's letters and personal papers as well as critiques of his texts to draw her conclusions.

Thomas, David. *Henrik Ibsen.* London: Macmillan, 1983; New York: Grove Press, 1984. An excellent, concise introduction to Ibsen's work. Thomas offers a brief biographical sketch and discusses literary and theatrical influences. Analyzes selected plays using a thematic approach that highlights the role of women in Ibsen's plays as well as his use of symbolism. Also gives a brief production history of major dramas and a review of critical works in English.

Paul Rosefeldt

II NAOSUKE

Born: November 29, 1815; Hikone, Japan
Died: March 24, 1860; Edo, Japan
Areas of Achievement: Statecraft, government, and politics
Contribution: Ii was a conservative but pragmatic defender of the Tokugawa family's rule (*bakufu*) in nineteenth century Japan. While he temporarily slowed the decline of the *bakufu*, his policies in the long run were ineffective in dealing with either the growing domestic hostility toward the shogun or the Western pressures open Japan to full participation in world trade and politics.

Early Life

Ii Naosuke was born into the very large family of the domain (*han*) lord (daimyo) of Hikone, in central Japan. As the fourteenth son, he had little prospect of a major political career, since hereditary succession determined domain leadership. Lacking favorable prospects within the domain's administration, he realistically could expect only that his father would secure his fortunes by arranging his adoption into a suitable family. A common practice in Japan, adoption was a principal means of solidifying a family's political and military ties to other important families. His limited expectations were further restricted by the death of his mother when he was only five years old. Her passing left him without an adult to argue that he might be uniquely suited to participate in domain administration. It was largely chance that ultimately saved Ii from sharing with many of his elder brothers this fate as an adoptee and provided him with the opportunity to play a leading role in the national politics and diplomacy of a Japan that faced grave crises.

There was little in Ii's upbringing that specifically prepared him to direct domain, much less national, policy in these tumultuous times. Reared with his younger brother in a small house by the castle moat, he trained until age seventeen in the traditional fashion of upper-class samurai. He studied poetry, religion (Zen Buddhism), the arts, and such traditional disciplines as tea ceremony. He also diligently practiced martial arts (fencing, archery, horsemanship, and gunnery) and studied strategy. As a young adult, the focus of his studies came to include discussion of current political and administrative matters. Among his acquaintances was Nagano Shuzen, who became a lifelong teacher, adviser, and friend.

Following custom, Ii's elder brother, Naoaki, became daimyo, succeeding their father in 1834. By this time, some of Ii's other brothers had died and the rest had been placed as adoptees in other prominent families. With the passage of time, it became clear that Naoaki would have no heirs, so Ii, in his early thirties, unexpectedly became the heir to the family headship. In 1850, when Naoaki died, Ii was installed as Daimyo of Hikone.

Life's Work

With his rise to daimyo status, Ii was thrust onto the national political stage for the first time. In part, Ii would make his mark by dint of his forceful personality and his willingness to become the leader of the political faction that defended the Tokugawa shogunate. He was also virtually guaranteed a measure of prominence solely by virtue of the fact that his family was one of the very few who could provide candidates for the very powerful office of great councilor (*tairō*), a post he would assume in 1858.

When Ii took on the responsibilities for domain administration, he also joined the ranks of the highest class of warriors and political figures in Japan, the daimyo. During the mid-nineteenth century, these men came to exert uncharacteristic influence on national policies and actions. Since the daimyo as a group were not formally incorporated into the *bakufu*'s policy-making organization, there was no effective means for resolving disputes among the factions that arose among them. During the preceding two hundred years, when Japan had faced no major foreign threat or internal crisis, this absence mattered little. The arrival of Europeans, who pressed Japan to open her ports to trade, sparked a controversy that the *bakufu* could not control. In this setting, some daimyo sought to challenge *bakufu* authority and Ii rose to defend that authority.

A key issue in disputes among daimyo factions was the question of how Japan should respond to Western entreaties to open its ports. Should Japan open its ports to trade with the West, and if so, under what conditions? Should Japan keep its traditional policy of trading only with the Dutch on a very limited basis? As early as 1846, the emperor, encouraged by those who sought a means to intrude on the traditional authority of the *bakufu*, urged the shogun to keep these "barbarians" out of Japan. (That was the first of several important efforts by this faction to use the emperor's antiforeign opinions as a means to compromise shogunal authority.) Others, especially the students of the so-called Dutch Studies (actually, studies of Western nations), were aware of the growing technological and military power of the West. Some of these men argued that Japan could benefit from contact with the West. All suspected that Japan would have a very difficult, if not impossible, time keeping Westerners at bay for very much longer.

Commodore Matthew C. Perry's arrival in Japanese waters in July of 1853 brought urgency to the debate. Accompanied by several large and powerful steamships, the Perry mission was intentionally designed to impress, even to intimidate, the Japanese. Yet, at the same time, Perry brought examples of Western technology designed to entice the Japanese to trade with the United States. Perry's visit was brief, but, before he left, he told the Japanese that he would return in a year to sign a treaty of friendship.

Perry's visit caused substantial consternation among the Japanese. The nation had not confronted a foreign crisis of this magnitude for two centuries. In order to develop a response to Perry that would enjoy the broadest possible support from domain lords, Abe Masahiro, the most important shogunal adviser, requested all the daimyo to submit their opinions on the matter. Abe's hopes of developing a consensus policy were dashed by the lack of agreement among the daimyo and the strident tone of many of those opposed to dealing further with Perry. Tokugawa Nariaki, who was to be the leading opponent of contact with the West, argued that Japan should refuse the American demands, strengthen the nation's defenses, and be prepared for war. Ii, who soon became the leading advocate for a more restrained and pragmatic approach, agreed that Japan should strengthen its defenses but went on to argue that minimum concessions should be granted to Perry in order to avoid war. His proposals included extending the trading privileges granted to the Dutch to other Westerners.

Despite the division of opinion among the domain lords, the shogunate did sign a treaty of friendship with Perry when he returned in 1854. This treaty was very limited in scope, but it contained one provision that would keep the foreign policy dispute alive for several years—a provision to negotiate a full-scale commercial treaty with the United States. Townsend Harris was sent to Japan as ambassador, with the specific charge of completing the commercial treaty. From the time of his arrival in 1856, Harris was beset by Japanese attempts to limit the performance of his ambassadorial duties. Among the Japanese, his presence and his mission were always a source of contention, even an object of violent attack. Abe attempted to deal evenhandedly with each side in the debate. Ii was appointed to guard the emperor and to protect him from the Western barbarians. Ii's antiforeign nemesis, Tokugawa Nariaki, was placed in charge of coastal defenses. In the end, attempts to be fair only provoked heated reactions from each faction.

Between late 1855 and Ii's death in 1860, however, Ii was able to engineer the appointment of a number of his supporters to high positions. Beginning with the appointment of Hotta Masayoshi to the rank of senior councillor, the pragmatic defenders of the Tokugawa rule gained preeminence in that most powerful advisory body. This development would have put Ii's supporters in control under normal circumstances, but Nariaki was able to open another arena of competition which, if successful, would allow him to gain direct control of the shogunate itself.

The key issue was who would become the next shogun. Among the antiforeign faction, the preferred candidate was Nariaki's son, Keiki. If Keiki were to become the heir and eventually the shogun, Nariaki and his followers could dominate the councillors, reform the shogunate, make efforts to keep the West at bay, and generally guide national policy. Ii and his allies naturally opposed this effort.

In early 1858, the domestic and foreign policy disputes between these two factions came to a head. Hotta presented the emperor with a commercial treaty (the Harris Treaty with the United States) for his approval. Usually, the emperor's consent was automatic, but by this time the antiforeign faction and other supporters of Keiki had been able to convince the emperor that signing the treaty was not in Japan's best interests. They convinced him to refuse to approve the treaty. Rebuffed and embarrassed, Hotta fell from power.

Now Ii was given a special opportunity: He was appointed to the position of great councillor in early June. This office was not a regular one in the Tokugawa administration. Someone was appointed to this position only in great crises, and the authority to act decisively accompanied the title. Ii's actions were forceful, even impolitic. By July, Ii determined to push ahead with the signing of the Harris Treaty. He also agreed to sign similar treaties with other Western nations. Determined to protect his political flank, he appointed his own candidate, the Daimyo of Kii, heir to the shogunate. He also filled as many offices with his supporters as opportunity and his authority to force resignations allowed.

Finally, to remove further threats to his authority from Nariaki and others, he began a purge of his opponents. By 1860, he placed Nariaki under house arrest. About seventy people were arrested in all; seven were sentenced to death, and a number of others were either given short-term imprisonment or sentenced to exile. He dismissed other officials who disagreed with him. This aggressive assault on Ii's opponents created an atmosphere of retribution. Although Ii sought to close the rift between the court and the *bakufu*, his opponents moved quickly to secure their own position at the imperial court. They created situations to embarrass Ii politically. Each of these efforts failed and frustration rose among Ii's enemies. His aggressive attempts to support his own position created new foes.

Finally, opposition to Ii peaked in the spring of 1860. As he approached the Sakurada Gate of Edo on March 24, his carriage was attacked by a band of dissatisfied warriors, allies of Nariaki. Ii was hauled from his carriage and beheaded on the spot.

Summary

With Ii Naosuke's death, the last major attempt to preserve the traditional Tokugawa political order ended. In the arena of foreign affairs, he had tried to preserve Japan's independence by bending to Western demands enough to keep Westerners from invading Japan. Domestically, Ii sought to protect the traditional authority of the shogun, and he refused to grant additional authority to the emperor or the domains.

All Ii's efforts failed to stem the crescendo of anti-*bakufu* criticism. Had Ii defended the *bakufu*'s prerogatives less vigorously, the Tokugawa shogunate ultimately might have been able to compromise effectively with its critics and Tokugawa rule might have continued for more than another decade. Contrary to his expectations, Ii's purges did not still the opposition but merely created more and deeper opposition to his policies. By 1868,
four domains led a direct military assault on the *bakufu* and established a new, fully centralized government, which set Japan on the road to international preeminence.

Bibliography

Alcock, Rutherford. *The Capital of the Tycoon: A Narrative of a Three Years' Residence in Japan.* 2 vols. New York: Harper, and London: Longman, 1863. A widely available account of life and politics in late Tokugawa Japan by a British diplomat.

Lee, Edwin Borden. *The Political Career of Ii Naosuke.* New York: Columbia University Press, 1960. Lee argues that Ii was a patriot who temporarily fought off those who sought to compromise the authority of the *bakufu* and who pragmatically dealt with the problems posed by Perry's arrival and the advent of the "unequal treaty" system.

McMaster, John. "Alcock and Harris: Foreign Diplomacy in *Bakumatsu* Japan." *Monumenta Nipponica* 22 (1967): 305-367. Diplomatic negotiations from the Western side, as seen by a British and an American ambassador. McMaster discusses the broader international context (economic and political) in which the negotiations took place and provides some sense of the military threat Japan faced.

Totman, Conrad. "From *Sakoku* to *Kaikoku*: The Transformation of Foreign-Policy Attitudes, 1853-1868." *Monumenta Nipponica* 35 (1980): 1-19. A general reassessment of Japanese attitudes toward intercourse with the West. Totman suggests that at first loyalists and defenders of the *bakufu* shared the same goal for Japanese foreign policy—keeping foreign contacts to a minimum—but that they disagreed over the means. The ultimate victory of internationalization was the result of a change in fundamental Japanese perceptions of what was good for Japan, not the result of the ascendancy of a favorably disposed faction over isolationists.

Webb, Herschel. *The Japanese Imperial Institution in the Tokugawa Period.* New York: Columbia University Press, 1968. Chapter 4, "The Throne in Politics," analyzes the increased use of the emperor by the anti-Tokugawa forces. Ii's conflict with the imperial loyalists is discussed.

Philip C. Brown

JEAN-AUGUSTE-DOMINIQUE INGRES

Born: August 29, 1780; Montauban, near Toulouse, France

Died: January 14, 1867; Paris, France

Area of Achievement: Art

Contribution: Ingres championed sound draftsmanship and inspiration from Greek civilization. His idealized figures and flawless surfaces set an unequaled standard in the first half of the nineteenth century. In elevating aesthetic form and personal expression above orthodoxy, Ingres inadvertently became one of the earliest examples of art for art's sake, a concept which became important for the later modern movements.

Early Life

Jean-August-Dominique Ingres was born into a family of modest means in Montauban in southern France. Ingres' father, Joseph, originally from nearby Toulouse, practiced painting, sculpture, and architecture, but without much notice. He encouraged his young son to study the arts in general and gave him lessons in drawing, voice, and violin. By the age of eleven, Ingres was taking instruction in art at the Museum-du-Midi, Toulouse, under Jean Briant, a landscape painter. Not long after that, he entered the Académie de Toulouse to study painting with Guillaume-Joseph Roques and sculpture from Jean-Pierre Vigan. During this period, Ingres did not neglect his music studies.

In 1797, when barely seventeen, Ingres left Toulouse with the son of his first instructor and traveled to Paris. Once there, Ingres was no doubt immediately recognizable as coming from the south of France, since he was short, round-faced, and had an olive complexion. Eventually, his stiff posture and deliberate walk suggested a slight arrogance. Ingres entered the studio of Jacques-Louis David, the greatest French talent of the time. This formal association lasted at least three years, wherein Ingres was thoroughly exposed to David's brand of neoclassicism in both topical works and commissioned portraits. Their approaches to eighteenth century classicism in art diverged when Ingres' studio apprenticeship ended. David subscribed to a type of painting activity whose content addressed contemporary issues and moral questions, as he hoped to influence political action. His figures and their settings, however, recalled the Greek republican era. Ingres, by

contrast, was generally apolitical and content to explore and alter classical form as a satisfying concept in itself.

In 1800, he competed unsuccessfully for a Prix de Rome. The following year, he earned the coveted award, only to wait five more years in Paris as a result of unfavorable political events in Rome. Nevertheless, Ingres did not languish. Provided with studio space and a modest stipend, he delved into the art of past eras, especially antiquity. Surprisingly, Ingres' classical education to that point was poor, including a near-total deficiency in Greek and Latin. He began to correct his shortcomings by accumulating a modest library, including Greek and Latin poetry and books whose illustrations attracted him because of their special qualities of line.

Ingres traveled to Rome in 1806 to begin his postponed official stay of four years, but remained at the École de Rome for an additional ten years. The sixteen-year period was productive and was marked by several large commissions from Napoleon I for the Quirinale Palace, paintings sent from Rome as submissions to the annual Paris Salon, and stunning portraits of the French colony in Rome, which were characterized by stylization and purity.

Serious financial constraints, however, developed with the fall of the French Empire, the withdrawal of many in the French colony, and Ingres' first marriage. Collectively, these factors led to Ingres' initiation of graphite portraits as a speculative enterprise. This time, the resident English population in Rome provided Ingres with the majority of models, a number of whom were set in family compositions using a vitalistic line and almost no modeling. Already evident in these works is his preference for refined and delicate contour lines verging on the precious.

Ingres spent the years 1820 to 1824 in Florence, gathering data for a religious commission. While there, he came upon the works of Italian primitives which were either unknown or disdained in official circles at the time. These paintings, and the refinement he found in those of the centuries-earlier School of Fountainbleau, surfaced as influences in several quasi-historical genre paintings of that time, such as *Roger Freeing Angelica* (1819), *The Death of Leonardo da Vinci in the Arms of Francis I* (c. 1819), and *The Vow of Louis XIII* (1824).

Life's Work

Ingres returned to Paris at the end of 1824 and opened a studio which welcomed both commissions and students. He received both quickly. The return was a triumph, and official recognition, which he courted, came quickly too. By 1825, Ingres was awarded the Legion of Honor after experiencing salon success the previous year with *The Vow of Louis XIII*. The next year, he received a major commission for a ceiling painting in the new extension of the Louvre. It was known as *The Apotheosis of Homer;* its format conception was unusual, since it was destined for a ceiling but painted as an upright easel picture since Ingres sought to avoid traditional Baroque foreshortening devices.

Though this painting was received without enthusiasm in the 1827 Salon, it was quite important to the artist as a defense of the classical tradition in art and, more acutely, as his participation in the neoclassical movement was threatened by the rise of the Romantic movement in painting. In *The Apotheosis of Homer*, Ingres assembled great men of the past and present, paying tribute to the ancient Greek poet Homer. In fact, it is a group portrait of fine arts luminaries most admired by Ingres, a catalog of his tastes, and, hence, his influences.

Ancient admirers of Homer occupy a raised forecourt in a handsome Ionic peripteral colonnaded temple. At the center of that assembly sits Homer, being crowned by a winged victory figure, enthroned atop a stone base. Seated respectfully below Homer are personifications of the *Iliad* and the *Odyssey*. More recent homage bearers occupy the steps and orchestra pit and include Dante, Raphael, Michelangelo, Nicolas Poussin, Jean Racine, William Shakespeare, Wolfgang Amadeus Mozart, and Joseph Haydn. The overall composition was derived from Raphael's *Parnassus* and confirms Ingres' clear debt to the High Renaissance master. Just as important, Ingres valued Raphael as the last of a line of Italian Renaissance primitives, including Fra Filippo Lippi, Sandro Botticelli, and Petro Perugino, in whose art he saw naïveté and mannered grace in contrast to artists after Raphael, in whom Ingres perceived decadence.

The artist's fear concerning the rise of Romanticism and the decline of classicism did not subside upon completion of *The Apotheosis of Homer*. Ingres immediately assessed the varied directions in his oeuvre and returned to ideas explored in his École de Rome period. One resulting desire was to reinstate academic studies of the nude to a position of official and critical acceptance, but the climate for that had passed. Ingres did the next best thing; he added figures and occasionally drama to early works and amplified projects once shelved. A brief examination of the artist's reworked themes easily establishes his intentions for the nude.

Prominent among the rethought paintings is *Oedipus Solving the Riddle of the Sphinx* (1808), an appealing study of a male nude in an acceptable antique pose with a respectably engaging myth as a foil for the artist's interest in human form. By 1827, it was enlarged and altered by the addition of a Theban in the background fleeing Oedipus' audacity in terror. The Theban's fright contrasts dramatically to the poise and concentration of Oedipus. The work was a salon success in 1827, but it typified a problem in European academic art of the time. Serious artists attached to the human form had to place their figures in historical, biblical, or mythological scenes lest the compositions be criticized as vulgar by salon juries. The attitude became entrenched, discouraging innovation while demanding technical excellence. Almost by default, it encouraged a glut of uninspired formula art. Fortunately, Ingres avoided academic mediocrity by building a career of fresh invention.

Even more of a testament to Ingres' faith in classicism was the ambitious work *Antiochus and Stratonice*, begun in 1807 and thoroughly transformed in the 1830's. The subject, originally told by Plutarch, was familiar to Ingres and his contemporaries in painting and theater during their student years in Paris and Rome. Ingres' second version illustrated the moment when a physician diagnosed the bedridden Antiochus' illness (by a racing pulse) as passion for his stepmother, Stratonice.

Ingres spent six years on the painting in Italy, where he had accepted the directorship of the École de Rome. The artist did so after being rejected by the Salon of 1834, vowing not to submit again. He researched the correct period setting, documented local color, constructed the convincing illusion of a three-dimensional interior with an air of gravity yet style, and tested forty-five times the gesture of Antiochus shielding himself from the near-fatal view of Stratonice. In 1840, the tenaciously constructed painting was shown privately in Paris at the Palais Royal, where it was a critical success, one which set the stage for Ingres' triumphant return to the capital city the next year.

Throughout his career, Ingres was obsessed with the potential of the female form for serene grace, especially the undraped female form. By the 1830's and 1840's, he was reworking single figures and groups devoted to sensuality. *The Bathing Woman*, a small half-torso study of 1807, and *The Valpincon Bather* of 1808 were the first of a long series of those expressions. In both pictures, the models are viewed discreetly, with turned heads and long, curved backs. A full-length, reclining nude also viewed from the back was used in 1814 for *The Grand Odalisque*, a statement of languid beauty and fantasized oriental exoticism, complete with feathers, silks, fur, jewelry, and incense.

In 1839, Ingres returned to the motif of the reposing nude in an oriental world. Entitled *Odalisque with the Slave*, the work benefited from a study of Persian miniatures and exotic bric-a-brac. Ingres' careerlong obsession with pliant female nudes culminated with *The Turkish Bath* of 1863, four years before the artist's death. The tondo-framed painting presents some two dozen nudes in a harem, bathing, lounging aimlessly, or admiring themselves.

There was at least one more vital aspect to Ingres' fascination with women, namely portraiture, especially of the rising middle class that dominated French society by the mid-1850's. As with the nudes, Ingres found helpful precedents in his own early work, for example, the 1805 portraits of Madame and Mademoiselle Rivière. Ingres' major portraits of the last phase of his career include the *Vicomtesse d'Haussonville* (1845), the *Baronne de Rothschild* (1848), two interpretations of Madame Moitessier in 1851 and 1856, and *Princess de Broglie* (1856). Collectively, the portraits project sensuality, a sense of power, the deceit of informality borrowed from David, and certainly the artist's love of flesh, hair, lush fabrics, patterns, and jewelry. These captivating women seem suitably dressed to receive visitors or to attend a ball.

When Ingres returned to Paris in 1841, he was immediately the honoree of a banquet with 426 guests presided over by the Marquis de Pastoret, plus a concert organized by the composer Hector Berlioz. More honors and commissions followed. One year before his death, Ingres bequeathed to the city of Montauban a collection of his own paintings and drawings, plus prints, books, Etruscan sarcophagi, Greek vases, and musical scores. In return, the city of his birth established the Musée Ingres in 1869 in his honor.

Summary

Jean-Auguste-Dominique Ingres reached a position of prestige and professional success enjoyed by few other artists active from the Renaissance through the nineteenth century. Yet his life and art were full of contradictions and paradoxes. For example, constantly acclaimed as the chief exponent of neoclassicism, he was actually one player in a larger heterogeneous artistic and literary community known as Romanticism. Furthermore, despite his adamant positions supporting classicism and academic techniques, his art could be just as arbitrary as that of his primary rival, Eugène Delacroix, leader of the Romantic movement in painting. Ingres, the neoclassicist, mastered historical genre painting, religious themes, and realistic portraiture. He managed to stay in official favor through the successive regimes of Napoleon I, the Bourbon Restoration, the Civil Wars of 1830 and 1848 and Napoleon III, though he detested change. Perhaps part of his genius is tied to his refusal to be locked into historical time. After all, he refused to change with the prevailing winds of art throughout his life.

The artist professed to copy nature, stressing drawing as the first commandment of high art, using live models, and emphasizing the contours of forms. Yet, as if he were blinded by an obsession for human form, his figures frequently had suspect proportions, extra vertebrae, and rubbery necks. To Ingres, distortions and a mannered anatomy were justified in the service of his uppermost aims: first, the expression of mankind's feelings and situations, second, the attempt to place hybrid people in an idealized nature at once divine and within the measure of contemporary existence.

Bibliography

Condon, Patricia, et al. *Ingres, in Pursuit of Perfection: The Art of J.-A.-D. Ingres.* Louisville, Ky.: J. B. Speed Art Museum, 1983. A superbly crafted and highly didactic exhibition catalog. Draws together many versions and studies of works unlikely to have been seen in the United States until this exhibit and publication. Illustrations are of excellent quality and satisfying in number. The thoughtful appendix summarizing the artist's ancient and contemporary themes, plus the exhaustive separate indexes listing the artist's works by subject, location, medium, date provenance, and exhibition, are extraordinary.

Cummings, Frederick J., et al. *French Painting, 1774-1830: The Age of Revolution.* Detroit, Mich.: Wayne State University Press, 1975. This 712-page book serves as a necessary aid in comprehending a blockbuster exhibition devoted to major and minor painters grouped under four historical periods: Louis XVI, Napoleon I, the Bourbon Restoration, and Napoleon III. Cummings and other authors weave events in art, politics, and intellectual thought and re-create the concept of period styles.

Ingres, Jean-Auguste-Dominique. *Ingres.* Text by Jon Whiteley. London: Oresko, 1977. A relatively brief but well-prepared and well-illustrated overview of the artist's major themes. Seventy carefully chosen works representing Ingres' lengthy career comprise the plate portion. Eight appear in acceptable color. Most valuable are the well-researched and easily read notes adjacent to the illustrations.

————. *Ingres.* Text by Georges Wildenstein. London and New York: Phaidon Press, 1954. Part of Phaidon's French Art series, this work contains a concise examination of the artist's natural gifts and the goals he set for them as well as a discussion of his techniques. The chronology of Ingres' life is lengthy and detailed. The plate section of two hundred images, including good details, is highlighted by six key works in color.

Ockman, Carol. *Ingres's Eroticized Bodies: Retracing the Serpentine Line.* New Haven, Conn.: Yale University Press, 1995. The first full-length presentation of the feminist, social, and historical aspects of Ingres' art through study of the distorted and erotic body forms in his works.

Picon, Gaëton. *Ingres: A Biographical and Critical Study.* Translated by Stuart Gilbert. 2d ed. New York: Rizzoli, 1980. A large-format, handsomely produced monograph. Easily understood by professionals outside the field of art. The selected bibliography is extensive. The chronologically thorough listing of Ingres' exhibitions up to 1980 will assist serious students.

Ribeiro, Aileen. *Ingres in Fashion: Representations of Dress and Appearance in Ingres's Images of Women.* New Haven, Conn.: Yale University Press, 1999. The first examination of the manner in which clothing, accessories, and fabrics are used in Ingres' portraits of women. Written by a recognized dress historian, the book details Ingres' portrayals of women from the idealized to the real. Includes over 150 illustrations.

Tom Dewey II

HENRY IRVING
John Henry Brodribb

Born: February 6, 1838; Keinton Mandeville, Somerset, England

Died: October 13, 1905; Bradford, Yorkshire, England

Area of Achievement: Theater

Contribution: Breaking with the conventions of acting and staging current in Victorian England, Irving introduced a more natural acting style, greater reliance on authentic texts, and more realistic production values for the staging of William Shakespeare's plays.

Early Life

The actor-manager known to Victorian England as Henry Irving, the only child of Samuel and Mary Behenna Brodribb, was born John Henry Brodribb at Keinton Mandeville, Somerset, on February 6, 1838. His father was a struggling shopkeeper, and Irving lived from the ages of four to eleven with his mother's sister Sarah and her husband, Isaac Penberthy, a mine manager, at Haseltown, Cornwall. In 1849, he joined his parents in London, where until 1851 he attended Dr. Pinches' City Commercial School. He entered the law firm of Patterson and Longman as a clerk, but in 1852, he became a clerk in a firm of East India merchants. Irving did not have his sights set on a business career. Ever since his school days, he had been attracted to the theater. Despite the opposition of his mother, a Methodist who objected to Irving's choice on religious grounds, his goal was a life on the stage.

There was no institution in Victorian England to provide young people with theatrical training, but Irving set out to prepare himself for a stage career. He took elocution lessons, studied acting privately with William Hoskins, and observed the performances of Samuel Phelps, London's leading Shakespearean actor. Irving turned down an offer to work with Phelps; in 1856, however, he joined the stock company of E. D. Davis, whom he had met through Hoskins, at the Lyceum Theatre in Sunderland. He gave his first public performance using the stage name Henry Irving in the role of the Duke of Orleans in Edward Bulwer-Lytton's *Richelieu: Or, The Conspiracy* on September 18, 1856. During the next ten years, Irving learned his craft in provincial theaters throughout Great Britain. He worked with R. H. Wyndham for two and a half years in Edinburgh, with Charles Calvert in Manchester for nearly five years, and briefly in Dublin, Glasgow, and Liverpool. There were occasional London engagements during these years, but Irving was still mastering his craft and did not make strongly favorable impressions on audiences.

He struggled to overcome a Cornish accent and to control the lurching gait that gave him "the Crab" as a nickname. In time, he gained mastery over his tall, spare figure, and Ellen Terry, his most famous leading lady, thought his thin, pale face with its large nose and piercing eyes attractive. Those who saw him perform in his maturity commented on Irving's ability to convey a series of emotions using only facial expressions. His eyes were often called mesmeric. In 1866, Irving joined a company at the St. James's Theatre and had his first taste of London success that November as the villainous Rawdon Scudamore in Dion Boucicault's *Hunted Down*. Work in the provinces and on tour, including an engagement in Paris, followed, however, and not until June, 1870, when he appeared as Digby Grant in James Albery's *Two Roses*, a play at the Vaudeville that ran until March, 1871, did Irving have another solid success in London.

When Irving married Florence O'Callaghan on July 15, 1869, he used the name Brodribb when taking out the license. His sons Henry and Lawrence, born in 1870 and 1871, used that name until, as adults, they joined their father in the theater. Irving and his wife stopped living together in 1872, and in 1879 they effected a legal separation.

Life's Work

Irving's break with his wife was prompted, it is said, by a disparaging remark that Florence made after his opening-night performance of *The Bells*. Adapted by Leopold Lewis from Émile Erckmann and Alexandre Chatrian's *The Polish Jew*, a vehicle for such famous French actors as Coquelin Aîné, *The Bells* was Irving's first solid success in London, running from November, 1871, to May, 1872, and it became a permanent fixture in the actor's repertoire. Indeed, Irving performed Mathias, the central character in *The Bells*, the evening before his death in 1905. He had achieved this success under the management of "Colonel" Hezekiah Bateman, an American who had taken over the Lyceum

Theatre in 1871 and hired Irving to play opposite his daughter Isabel. Audiences and critics liked the comparative realism of Irving's performance in *The Bells*, and with Bateman, he embarked on a series of melodramas that were popular successes. Irving played the title characters in the premiers of William Gorman Wills's *Charles I* (1872) and *Eugene Aram* (1873), and in September, 1873, he took on the role of the cardinal in Bulwer-Lytton's *Richelieu*. His performance earned favorable comparisons with the acting of Phelps and William Macready, the critics finding impressive Irving's attention to authentic costuming, telling stage movements, and psychological motivation.

The same qualities marked Irving's performances in a series of plays by Shakespeare, the first a production of *Hamlet* that ran two hundred nights following its opening on October 31, 1874. Irving went back to the original text of the play to construct an acting version that was tighter and more dramatic than the ones used by earlier performers. He invented new stage business, abandoning many of the conventions for staging the play, and presented a characterization of Hamlet decidedly more romantic than that of many of his Victorian contemporaries. Something of the sort happened every time Irving undertook a new production of a play by Shakespeare. By meticulous attention to detail, he gave audiences performances more unified in conception than other actors of his time. They were also productions that were more beautifully staged and lighted than those to which his audiences had been accustomed.

While working with the Batemans, Irving staged *Macbeth* in 1875, *Othello* in 1876, and *Richard III* in 1877. He came up with an entirely new text for the latter, rejecting the version by Colley Cibber that had prevailed since the eighteenth century. At the same time that he was working on these plays, Irving continued to add to his repertoire of non-Shakespearean kings. He appeared in 1876 as Philip II of Spain in Alfred, Lord Tennyson's *Queen Mary*, and in 1878, he performed the title role in Boucicault's *Louis XI*.

After "Colonel" Bateman's death, Irving took over the management of the Lyceum from his widow in 1878, and he marked the occasion with a revival of *Hamlet* with Ellen Terry as Ophelia. The association of Irving and Terry continued until 1902, both at the Lyceum and on tour in England and the United States. Irving continued to provide audiences with new readings of the plays of Shakespeare, as he did with a sympathetic characterization of Shylock in *The Merchant of Venice* in 1879, at the same time that he personally supervised every aspect of the staging of the plays in which Terry and he appeared. In time, the company at the Lyceum comprised more than six hundred actors, technicians, and staff. Irving installed Henry Loveday and Bram Stoker as his lieutenants in management; he commissioned costume and set designs from artists as famous as Edward Burne-Jones and music from Sir Arthur Sullivan. The quality of the lighting and special effects at the Lyceum were noted by many critics, and Irving's ability to handle crowd scenes, as in the very successful production of *Romeo and Juliet* in 1882, was a striking feature of his direction. While Ellen Terry was more successful as Juliet than Irving as Romeo, both were applauded in the roles of Beatrice and Benedick in the production of *Much Ado About Nothing* later the same year. Irving staged a brief run of Shakespeare's *Othello* in 1882 as well, alternating in the roles of Othello and Iago with the American actor Edwin Booth.

For most of the rest of his professional career, Irving was the acknowledged head of the British theater. From October, 1883, to March, 1884, he took his company to the United States, the first of eight commercially successful tours. He continued to mount productions of new plays, such as Wills's version of *Faust* that ran from December, 1885, to April, 1887, in which Irving played the role of Mephistopheles, and productions of Shakespeare, such as the 1888 staging of *Macbeth*, for which Terry wore a green dress covered with iridescent beetles. Irving's conception of Macbeth as unheroic, even neurotic, did not please all audiences; it was an interpretation decades ahead of its time. Nevertheless, Irving himself was increasingly a success with the upper and middle classes. He hosted lavish receptions on the stage of the Lyceum after important first nights or milestone performances of particular plays, receptions attended on occasion by the Prince of Wales. In April, 1889, Irving and Terry gave a command performance before Queen Victoria at Sandringham, enacting the entirety of *The Bells* and the trial scene from *The Merchant of Venice*. In 1893, there was a performance at Windsor Castle of Tennyson's *Becket*, itself a great commercial and critical success. Irving received a knighthood from the queen in 1895, the first actor to be so honored, and Her Majesty was pleased to bestow it.

The new productions of Shakespeare's plays that Irving mounted toward the end of his career, such as his *Henry VIII* and *King Lear* in 1892, were less successful than the run of Tennyson's *Becket* the following year. Having given *Henry VIII* so lavish a staging that it became more historical pageant than dramatic vehicle, Irving turned to a series of plays set in historical times. He played Corporal Gregory Brewster in Arthur Conan Doyle's *Waterloo* in 1894, Napoleon in 1897 in an adaptation of Victorien Sardou's *Madame Sans-Gêne* by Comyns Carr, and in 1898 the title role in his son Lawrence's *Peter the Great*. Irving had always given attention to costuming and stage sets, but with these plays, he was in danger of staging nothing but costume drama. In 1898, a fire destroyed the warehouse in which the Lyceum stored the settings for Irving's plays, and the ensuing financial crisis caused Irving to turn over the theater to others. Under these circumstances, in 1899 he mounted a production of Lawrence Irving's translation of Sardou's *Robespierre*, and in 1901 he did *Coriolanus*, his last new production of a Shakespeare play. Terry left the Irving company in 1902, and the new management of the Lyceum lost the lease on the building.

Nevertheless, Irving struggled to mount new productions. Tours in the British provinces and the United States offset the lack of financial success of his *Dante*, written by Victorien Sardou and produced in 1903 from a translation by his son Lawrence. In his final appearance in London, Irving revived Tennyson's *Becket*, and he was on tour with the play when he collapsed and died in Bradford on October 13, 1905.

Irving was buried in Westminster Abbey. It was the last in a series of public honors, including honorary degrees from universities in Dublin (1892), Cambridge (1898), and Glasgow (1899). The coffin was covered with a pall of laurel leaves. They turned gold in the light coming through the Abbey windows. Irving would have appreciated the theatricality of the effect.

Summary

Henry Irving was the leading British actor-manager of the Victorian period. He wanted the middle and upper classes to accept theatrical work as genuine art, and he knew that would occur only if the public saw actors as respectable members of society. Irving worked consciously for social acceptance for himself and other members of his profession. He also worked hard to succeed as an actor. By supervising every element in the plays he staged at the Lyceum, Irving achieved greater stylistic and dramatic unity than had his Victorian predecessors. Admittedly, many of the plays that he chose were sentimental and melodramatic. With the questionable exception of Tennyson, Irving worked with no first-rate contemporary dramatist. Both Henry Arthur Jones and Arthur Wing Pinero, successful as writers of an English drama more realistic than Irving usually selected, worked for a time in the Lyceum company, but Irving was comfortable with the romantic costume dramas of Sardou, Wills, and Carr. In his capacity as a drama critic, George Bernard Shaw argued that both Terry and Irving were wasted as actors in much of the material that they staged. He attempted, perhaps sincerely, to persuade both to appear in the sort of realistic play that he himself was starting to write.

Because so much of the quality of an actor's work lies in details of actual performances, it is hard to assess Irving's importance. Recordings of his voice exist, but contemporary reviews and memoirs are the chief evidence of the fact that Irving was a magnetic performer. The notes that he made for his productions of Shakespeare, however, do give a sense of Irving's originality. He sought, in every play in which he appeared, a unified characterization of the man he played. Like the Russian director Konstantin Stanislavsky, Irving saw each character as a unique human individual, and he looked constantly for the detail of phrasing, movement, or gesture that would convey that character's nature to an audience. While later actor-managers such as Herbert Beerbohm Tree and John Martin Harvey followed Irving's lead in staging lavish productions of Shakespeare, they did not focus the details of a production toward the single, central effect characteristic of Irving. In a sense, Irving's heir as stage director was Terry's son, Edward Gordon Craig, and not Beerbohm Tree or Harvey.

Irving's real legacy to the English theater may lie less in his own acting than in his scholarly approach to the production of Shakespeare and his sensitivity to production values. His acting would perhaps not seem realistic to a twentieth century audience. Less mannered and stagey than the styles of his predecessors, Irving's acting was romantic in its emphasis on the individuality of the character and in its intuitive, rather than intellectual, approach to a role.

Bibliography

Baker, Michael. *The Rise of the Victorian Actor.* London: Croom Helm, and Totowa, N.J.: Rowman and Littlefield, 1978. This study focuses on the development of acting as a profession in Victorian England.

Bingham, Madeleine. *Henry Irving: The Greatest Victorian Actor.* Foreword by John Gielgud. London: Allen and Unwin, and New York: Stein and Day, 1978. An excellent account of Irving's life, the book fails to provide enough analysis of his work as actor and theatrical manager.

Darbyshire, Alfred. *The Art of the Victorian Stage: Notes and Recollections.* London: Sherratt and Hughes, 1907; New York: Blom, 1969. This chatty and anecdotal memoir gives a theatrical associate's perspective on Irving.

Emeljanow, Victor. "Erasing the Spectator: Observations on Nineteenth Century Lighting." *Theatre History Studies* 18 (June 1998). Examines Henry Irving's experimentation and development of lighting techniques for the stage, which completely changed the period's concept of the theater.

Hughes, Alan. *Henry Irving, Shakespearean.* Cambridge and New York: Cambridge University Press, 1981. Using prompt books and production notes, Hughes gives an invaluable scene-by-scene reconstruction of Irving's Shakespearean productions.

Joseph, Bertram. *The Tragic Actor.* London: Routledge, and New York: Theatre Arts Book, 1959. By placing Irving in the context of male tragic actors from the age of Elizabeth I to that of Victoria, Joseph makes it clear how Irving developed out of a long stage tradition.

Rowell, George. *The Victorian Theatre: A Survey.* Oxford and New York: Oxford University Press, 1956. This book is especially useful in providing a sense of the technical and literary resources available to Irving at the start of his career as a stage manager.

Terry, Ellen, with additional chapters by Edith Craig and Christopher St. John. *Ellen Terry's Memoirs.* New York: Putnam, 1932; London: Gollancz, 1933. The first half of the volume, written by Terry herself and published as *The Story of My Life* in 1908, contains a detailed account of her association with Irving at the Lyceum.

Wagenknecht, Edward. *Merely Players.* Norman: University of Oklahoma Press, 1966. The chapter on Irving focuses on him as a performer, particularly in the romantic melodramas that sustained his career.

Robert C. Petersen

WASHINGTON IRVING

Born: April 3, 1783; New York, New York

Died: November 28, 1859; Tarrytown, New York

Areas of Achievement: Fiction, history, and diplomacy

Contribution: Washington Irving, America's first international literary success, was responsible for making American letters respectable in the nineteenth century.

Early Life

Washington Irving was born into the large family of William Irving and Sarah Sanders Irving on April 3, 1783, in New York City. His father was a merchant of Scottish background and stern disposition. His mother, on the other hand, the granddaughter of an English curate, was gentle and kind. Although Irving's father, a church deacon, tried to restrict his children from simple pleasures, Washington, named after the United States' first president, would slip away to wander throughout the then small town of New York City. The youngest of eleven children, Irving was frail as a child and had an undistinguished record as a student, being somewhat lazy as well as mischievous. He did read extensively the tales of adventure in his father's library, however, all of which influenced his writings later.

Irving began apprentice law studies in 1802 with Josiah Ogden Hoffmann. Also in that year, his brother Peter began publication of the *Morning Chronicle*, an Anti-Federalist newspaper which supported Aaron Burr, for which Irving began to contribute letter essays under the pseudonym "Jonathan Oldstyle, Gent." Although these early contributions were amateurish and imitative of essays in the British periodical *The Spectator*, they allowed Irving to experiment with various literary conventions and writing styles. Between 1804 and 1806, Irving traveled widely in England and throughout Europe, during which time he honed his powers of observation and strengthened his health. When he returned to the United States, he was admitted to law practice.

His real interest and talent, however, lay in his writing. In 1807, along with his brother William and James Kirke Paulding, Irving helped establish another periodical, *Salmagundi*, a satiric and lively send-up of whatever the three young men thought needed parodying. Although Irving's father died in 1807, most biographers agree that the greatest trag-

edy in the early part of his life was the death of Matilda Hoffman, his first great love and the woman whom he intended to marry. In 1809, Irving published his first major work, *A History of New York*, a burlesquely comic narrative in which he created the persona Diedrich Knickerbocker, who appears later as the teller of Irving's most famous stories, "The Legend of Sleepy Hollow" and "Rip Van Winkle." The book brought Irving his first taste of literary success, and in 1812 he became the anonymous editor of *Analectic Magazine*.

In May, 1815, Irving traveled to Liverpool, England, on behalf of the hardware business of which he was a partner with his brothers Peter and William. It was here that he discovered what poor financial condition the business was in and here also that he faced with his brothers the bankruptcy courts. Thus, it was not a burning love of literature that made Irving begin his writing career in earnest, but rather his desperate need to make a living. Irving stayed in Europe for the next seventeen years, finally returning to the United States in 1832, but only

after he had become the famous author of *The Sketch Book of Geoffrey Crayon, Gent.* (1819-1820).

Life's Work

A few months after the bankruptcy of his company, Irving began writing in earnest on the first installments of his series of tales and essays that were to become *The Sketch Book*. Sending them to his brother Ebenezer in the United States for publication, Irving wrote, characteristically, that his greatest desire was to make himself worthy of the goodwill of his countrymen. He did much toward achieving his goal by including in this first number perhaps the most memorable mythic figure in all of American literature, Rip Van Winkle. In the installments that followed, Irving almost single-handedly established the beginning of American literature. No American work of literature, and few works from any country, received the amount of praise heaped upon *The Sketch Book*. It was truly the first international literary sensation to come from the New World.

Irving's newfound success freed him and his brothers from their money worries and allowed Irving to indulge himself in his great love of travel. After several months in Paris, Irving returned to England to publish *Bracebridge Hall* (1822), which focused on the customs of England. Then he was off again, traveling through Europe until settling in Dresden for six months, after which he lived in Paris from August, 1823, until May, 1824. When he returned to London, he published the appropriately titled *Tales of a Traveller* (1824). This work was not well received by the critics, however, and caused Irving his first professional disappointment. His biographers call this an important transition period in Irving's literary development, a period during which he seems to have decided to cease writing the imaginative sketches that had brought him fame and to focus more on historical and biographical works.

After four months in southern France, Irving went to Spain with an American legation, thus beginning his career as an American diplomat and ambassador. The fruits of Irving's Spanish sojourn are *A History of the Life and Voyages of Christopher Columbus* (1828), *A Chronicle of the Conquest of Granada* (1829), *Voyages and Discoveries of the Companions of Columbus* (1831), and *The Alhambra* (1832), which included sketches and tales.

In 1829, Irving returned to London to become secretary of the American legation and thus began his diplomatic life in an even more formal way. In April, 1830, he was given a gold medal by the Royal Society of Literature for preeminent work in the field of literature, and in the following month he was presented an honorary doctor of letters degree from Oxford University. Thus, it was at the height of his professional career, some seventeen years after he left the United States, that he finally returned to his native country, having succeeded beyond his wildest dreams in earning the goodwill of his countrymen. He returned to great acclaim and public enthusiasm, much to his surprise, and had to refuse invitations from many cities for dinners and banquets in his honor. Still the wanderer, Irving began tours of the American West and South, keeping diaries of his travels from which he published *A Tour of the Prairies* in *The Crayon Miscellany* in 1835.

Also in 1835, Irving bought ten acres of land at Tarrytown, on which sat a Dutch stone house which he named Sunnyside and in which he took permanent residence. In the next six years, Irving published more historical and biographical works, including *Astoria* (1836), written at the request of John Jacob Astor; *The Adventures of Captain Bonneville, U.S.A.* (1837); and short biographies of Oliver Goldsmith and Margaret Davidson. During this period he was offered, and refused, the position of secretary of the navy and the nomination for mayor of New York City. In short, as his biographers have noted, Irving took it easy in the ten years after returning to the United States. Although portraits of Irving as a young man present him as a keen-eyed, dark-haired Byronic dandy with curling dark locks of hair, the more popular image of him can been seen in a later sketch in which he looks the part of a genial middle-class landowner, reclining in a rural setting with his faithful dog Ginger beside him.

He did not, however, refuse the offer made to him by President John Tyler in 1842 to become minister to Spain, a position he held until the end of 1845, at which time he made his final return to the United States to spend the last years of his life in the idyllic setting of Tarrytown, expanding his biography of Oliver Goldsmith, arranging for the publication of his collected works, and writing his multivolume *The Life of George Washington* (1855-1859). Irving died at his home at Sunnyside on the evening of November 28, 1859.

Summary

Washington Irving was America's first grand old man of letters, America's first internationally famous author, and the first American writer to make American literature a tangible reality. *The Sketch*

Book, although imitative of several genres such as the personal essay and the folktale which were popular in the nineteenth century, became a phenomenal success, unprecedented at the time. Irving had great influence not only on such British comic writers as Charles Dickens and William Makepeace Thackeray, but also on American writers such as Nathaniel Hawthorne, Herman Melville, and Edgar Allan Poe. Irving was successful in blending the eighteenth century essay style of the British writers Joseph Addison and Richard Steele with the Romantic folktale popular in Germany. In this way, Irving was instrumental in creating the short genre that Hawthorne and Poe would later deepen and develop and thus make America's major contribution to world literature.

Although Irving was a prolific writer and his works fill numerous volumes, and although he was widely read during his time, few people, other than students, read his work today, and they only read a small portion of his total output. Yet two of his creations, Rip Van Winkle and Ichabod Crane, have become mythic figures in American folklore, comparable to Paul Bunyan and Johnny Appleseed. Everyone is familiar with these memorable icons of a more leisurely and peaceful time in American culture. In such tales as "Rip Van Winkle" and "The Legend of Sleepy Hollow," Irving used the persona of Diedrich Knickerbocker to give new life to old tales and thus allow his readers to identify with his comic characters. Regardless of age, many men have longed for a draught of the magic brew that allowed Rip Van Winkle to sleep through all of his adult responsibilities to emerge unscathed into a second childhood.

Washington Irving is responsible for making American literature a significant force in world culture at a time when the United States was felt to be England's cultural inferior. The secret of Irving's success, in addition to combining the essay and the tale form to sow the seeds for a new literary genre, was his own unique voice—a leisurely and genial point of view that expressed kindness, good humor, hospitality, and warmth, or, in short, the ideal of something uniquely American.

Bibliography

Bowden, Mary Weatherspoon. *Washington Irving.* Boston: Twayne, 1981. An introductory critical study which focuses on the political forces that influenced Irving's work. Sketchy on biography but detailed on literary development.

Hedges, William L. *Washington Irving: An American Study, 1802-1832.* Baltimore: Johns Hopkins University Press, 1965. A sound and fully developed critical study which places Irving within his cultural milieu and examines the many literary genres which Irving mastered. Clarifies Irving's emphasis on dreams, fantasies, and symbolic fiction.

Hellman, George S. *Washington Irving, Esquire: Ambassador at Large from the New World to the Old.* New York: Knopf, 1925; London: Cape, 1929. An early informal biography which focuses on Irving's travels, his association with influential peers, and his role as a cultural ambassador for the United States.

Irving, Pierre M. *The Life and Letters of Washington Irving.* 4 vols. New York: Putnam, and London: Bentley, 1862-1864. Written by his nephew, this is the first biography of Irving. Although in its respectful treatment it is far from an objective account, it is valuable in its dependence on Irving's notebooks, letters, and journals.

Kime, Wayne R. *Pierre M. Irving and Washington Irving: A Collaboration in Life and Letters.* Waterloo, Ontario: Wilfrid Laurier University Press, 1977. A detailed account of the professional relationship between Irving and his nephew, the author of his first biography.

McLamore, Richard V. "Postcolonial Columbus: Washington Irving and 'The Conquest of Granada.' " *Nineteenth-Century Literature* 48, no. 1 (June 1993). Examines Irving's work, "The Conquest of Granada," its satirical treatment of the period's justification for the Granada conquest, and Irving's use of its characters to state his opposition to colonization through force.

Myers, Andrew B., ed. *A Century of Commentary on the Works of Washington Irving.* Tarrytown, N.Y.: Sleepy Hollow Restorations, 1976. A collection of essays on Irving by artists and critics from Irving's own time up to the mid-twentieth century. Some of the most important criticism on Irving can be found here.

Piacentino, Ed. "'Sleepy Hollow' Comes South: Washington Irving's Influence on Old Southwestern Humor." *Southern Literary Journal* 30, no. 1 (Fall 1997). Discusses Irving's use of the folklore of the Dutch in New York in his work and how such usage became a pattern employed by Southern frontier writers.

Roth, Martin. *Comedy and America: The Lost World of Washington Irving.* Port Washington, N.Y.:

Kennikat Press, 1976. A helpful study of the literary genres of burlesque and satire that Irving borrowed from and developed, especially in his first important work, *The History of New York*.

Williams, Stanley T. *The Life of Washington Irving*. 2 vols. London and New York: Oxford University Press, 1935. The authoritative biography of Irving, based on extensive research in original manuscripts of Irving's journals, notebooks, travel notes, and letters. The most complete and dependable study of Irving's life and career.

Charles E. May

ANDREW JACKSON

Born: March 15, 1767; Waxhaw area, South Carolina

Died: June 8, 1845; the Hermitage, near Nashville, Tennessee

Areas of Achievement: Government and military affairs

Contribution: Possessing the characteristics of the roughly hewn Western frontiersman as opposed to aristocratic propensities of the Eastern and Virginia "establishment," Jackson came to symbolize the common man in America and the rise of democracy.

Early Life

Andrew Jackson was born March 15, 1767, in the Waxhaw settlement of South Carolina. Jackson's family came from County Antrim, Ireland. His father, Andrew, arrived in America in 1765 and died shortly before his son, the future president, was born. Andrew's teenage years were "rough and tumble." Acquiring little formal education, Jackson made his way through early life by hand-to-mouth jobs, helping his two older brothers support their widowed mother.

During the revolutionary war, the British invaded Waxhaw, an event that shaped much of Jackson's subsequent life and career. His two brothers were killed, and his mother died of cholera while caring for prisoners of war. Jackson, taken prisoner by the British, was orphaned at the age of fourteen, a situation that taught him independence, both in action and in thought.

In 1784, Jackson went to Salisbury, North Carolina, apprenticed to the law firm of Spruce McKay. Within three years, he was admitted to the bar, and in 1788, Jackson made the decision to go west, to Nashville, Tennessee, to seek his fortune.

While Jackson pursued a legal career as a practicing attorney, superior court solicitor, and judge, he also ventured into other activities. He became an avid horse breeder and racer, as well as a plantation owner. Jackson had no formal military training, but he quickly earned a reputation as an Indian fighter, and it was undoubtedly his experience in this area that led to his election in 1802 as major general of the western Tennessee militia. In 1791, Jackson married Rachel Donelson Robards, who had, she thought, been recently divorced from Lewis Robards. The divorce decree had not been issued in Virginia at the time Andrew and Rachel were wed in Natchez, Mississippi. Three years later, when Jackson learned of the error, he and Rachel remarried, but this action did not stop enemies from slandering his wife in subsequent political campaigns.

Jackson was one of few serious duelists in American history (Aaron Burr was another), and his most famous confrontation was with Charles Dickinson, essentially over a problem that started with race horses. On the occasion, Jackson wore a borrowed coat that was too large for him. When Dickinson fired, he aimed for the heart, located, he thought, at the top of Jackson's coat pocket. Since the coat was too big, the top of the pocket was below Jackson's heart. Dickinson hit the target, but Jackson still stood. Dickinson exclaimed, "Great God, have I missed?" Jackson then fired at Dickinson, mortally wounding him. Dickinson lived for a time after being shot, and it was characteristic of Jackson not to allow anyone to tell Dickinson that he really had hit his opponent; he died thinking that he had missed. Jackson was seriously wounded in the duel, and he convalesced for several weeks.

Jackson was a tall, thin man, six feet one inch in height, usually weighing 150 pounds. His nose was straight and prominent, and his blue eyes blazed fiercely whenever he lost his temper, which was often. In the early years, his hair was reddish-brown; in old age, it was white. He had a firmly set chin and a high forehead. Paintings and daguerreotypes suggest a man accustomed to giving orders and having them obeyed.

Life's Work

Jackson became a nationally known figure during the War of 1812. Though he had been elected to his rank rather than earning it by training and experience, he soon proved to be a capable leader. He endeavored to neutralize the Creek Indians in Alabama, who periodically attacked white settlers. He accomplished this objective at the Battle of Horseshoe Bend. So tough and unremitting was he at this engagement that his soldiers began to call him Old Hickory. His greatest battle was against the British at New Orleans. Amazingly, there were some two thousand British casualties, and less than a dozen for the army of Westerners, blacks, and pirates that Jackson had put together. Although the war was essentially over before the battle took place—news traveled slowly before the advent of modern communications—Jackson became a national military hero, and there was talk in some quarters of running him for president of the United States.

After the war, in 1818, President James Monroe ordered Jackson and his army to Florida, to deal with Indian problems. While there, Jackson torched Pensacola and hanged two Englishmen whom he thought were in collusion with the Indians as they attacked settlers across the border in Alabama. Jackson's deeds in Florida caused diplomatic rifts with Spain and England, and he clearly had exceeded his orders, but his actions appealed to a pragmatic American public, and the general's popularity soared.

When Jackson became a presidential candidate in 1824, some believed that it was the office to which all of his previous activities pointed. If ever there was a "natural" for the presidency, his supporters argued, it was Andrew Jackson. His opponents feared that if Jackson were elected, there would be too much popular government; Jackson, they argued, might turn the Republic into a "Mobocracy." Worse yet, he had little experience with foreign policy, and his confrontational style might create one diplomatic crisis after another.

Jackson missed the presidency in 1824, although he received more electoral votes than anyone else. It was necessary to get a majority of electoral votes—more than all the other candidates combined. Since there was no majority in 1824, the election was decided by the House of Representatives, which selected John Quincy Adams; Jackson protested that Adams' victory was engineered by a "corrupt bargain" with Henry Clay, whom Adams appointed as secretary of state after Clay's supporters in the House ensured Adams' election. In 1828, however, there was no doubt that Jackson would defeat Adams. A political "revolution" had occurred in the four-year term. In 1824, four candidates amassed altogether less than a half million popular votes. In 1828, however, two candidates, Jackson and Adams, collected about 1,200,000, meaning that in four years 800,000 voters had been added to the polls—in large part the result of liberalized voting qualifications—and most of them voted for Jackson.

Jackson's great objective while in office was "executive supremacy." He reasoned: Who was the only government official universally elected to office? The answer was the president. Was it not rea-

sonable, then, that the president was the chief symbol of the American people? Further, if he were the chief symbol, should not the executive branch be as powerful, or more so, than the Congress or the Supreme Court? This concept of executive supremacy displeased numerous congressional leaders. Congress had dominated the federal government since the Revolution, out of a general distrust of administrative centralization. After all, Britain's King George III was a "typical" administrator. Jackson pursued executive supremacy in a number of ways. One was the patronage system, by which he appointed friends to office. His enemies referred to this policy as the "spoils system"; Jackson called it "rotation in office." The number of those displaced, however (about ten percent of the government workforce), was no greater than previous or future executive terms. Another procedure that strengthened Jackson's presidency, perhaps the most important, was the "county agent" system that Martin Van Buren created for the Democratic Party. The forerunners of what became known as "county chairmen," these agents enabled the Democrats to practice politics on a grassroots level, going door-to-door, as it were, to collect votes and support for the president.

A very important part of Jackson's drive for executive supremacy was the presidential veto. He used this constitutional device twelve times, more than all of his predecessors put together. Moreover, he made good use of the "pocket veto." (If a bill comes to the president less than ten days before Congress adjourns, he can "put it in his pocket" and not have to tell Congress why he disapproves of it. A "pocket veto" enhances presidential power by preventing Congress from reconsidering the bill, an action that caused presidential critics to call Jackson "King Andrew I.") Though he was not the first president to use the pocket veto—James Madison was first—Jackson made more extensive use of it than any of his predecessors.

Perhaps the most significant presidential veto in American history was Jackson's rejection, in 1832, of the recharter bill, a bill that would have rechartered the Bank of the United States. Among other things, Jackson argued that the executive had the power to judge the constitutionality of a bill brought before him. According to Jacksonian scholar Robert Remini, Jackson's veto on this bill caused an ascendancy of presidential power that did not abate until Richard M. Nixon's resignation in 1974.

In foreign affairs, Jackson conducted a lively policy which gained new respect for the United States from major European powers. He nurtured good relations with England by a conciliatory attitude on the Maine-Canada boundary question and promising to exempt many English goods from the harsh tariff of 1828 (the Tariff of Abominations). He even held out the prospect of lowering the tariff against the British through a treaty. His positive stance on boundary lines and the tariff helped reopen full West Indies trade with the British. While Jackson may have been an Anglophobe most of his life, it is nevertheless true that he gained concessions from the English that had been denied to his predecessor, the so-called Anglophile, Adams.

The United States almost went to war with its oldest and most loyal ally while Jackson was president. The United States presented France with a "spoliation" bill, going back to the depredations of American shipping during the Napoleonic Wars. When, for various reasons, the French government refused payments, Jackson's tone became strident. In a message to Congress, he said that a "collision" was possible between the two governments if the French remained obstinate. Ultimately, Britain in-

tervened and urged the French to settle the "American matter," because of mutual problems developing with Russia.

Though Jackson personally believed that Texas would one day be a part of the American Union, he did not push its annexation while in office, for he feared that the slavery question that Texas would engender would embarrass his chosen presidential successor, Van Buren. After Van Buren was safely elected, Jackson publicly supported the annexation of Texas, which took place in 1845, the year Jackson died.

While Jackson was president, reforms occurred on state levels. Numerous state constitutions were revised or rewritten, all with liberal trends. Women found it easier to prosecute abusive husbands and, increasingly, they could purchase property and dispose of it as they chose, without getting permission from their nearest male kin. Prison reforms began in some states, and insane people were treated for their illnesses rather than being thought to be possessed by the Devil. Public education systems started in several states, notably Massachusetts and New York. In all these reforms, suffrage ever widened, exemplifying the belief that political participation should be based on white manhood rather than property qualifications. Noted scholar Clinton Rossiter has shown that the Jacksonian presidency changed the base of American government from aristocracy to democracy without fundamentally altering its republican character.

After serving as president from 1829 to 1837, Jackson happily returned to the Hermitage. There, he continued as the father figure of his country, receiving dignitaries from around the world, and giving advice to those who followed him in the presidential office. He was especially pleased to see his protégé, James K. Polk, win the office in 1844 and become widely known as "Young Hickory." Jackson died at the Hermitage on June 8, 1845.

Summary

It is fair to say that Andrew Jackson was first and foremost a beneficiary of rising democratic spirits in America. When he attained power, he put his stamp upon events and promulgated additional steps toward democracy. He suggested some reforms, many of which were ultimately enacted. He wanted senators to be popularly elected, as were members of the House of Representatives. He wanted additional judges to take the heavy burden off the judicial system. He believed that the United

States Post Office should be reshaped into a semi-private organization. He suggested some reforms which were not enacted but were widely discussed. He believed that a president should serve for six years and then be ineligible for further election. He thought that the electoral college should either be abandoned or drastically reformed, because, in his opinion, it did not always reflect the will of the electorate.

It is widely held that Jacksonian America heralded the "positive state," where government dominates the private sector. Jackson's presidency is frequently cited as starting the trend toward federal centralization. Jackson's legacy is most visible in his personification of America's common man, even though he, himself, was hardly a "common" man. His was an age of entrepreneurship in which it was believed that government should not grant privileges to one group that it withholds from another. This thought has motivated many reform philosophies in the twentieth century, not the least of which was the Civil Rights movement. In this and other significant ways, Andrew Jackson has spoken to Americans of subsequent generations.

Bibliography

Feller, Daniel. *The Jacksonian Promise: America, 1815-1840.* Baltimore, Md.: Johns Hopkins University Press, 1995. The author offers a new view of the Jacksonian Era and argues that, contrary to prior accounts, Americans during this time were not as pessimistic about their futures as is often assumed.

Gatell, Frank Otto, and John M. McFaul, eds. *Jacksonian America, 1815-1840: New Society, Changing Politics.* Englewood Cliffs, N.J.: Prentice-Hall, 1970. This collection of essays ranges from politics to societal judgments and lifestyles. The essays vary in quality, but the overall result is a lucid explanation of the Jacksonian era.

Pessen, Edward. *Jacksonian America: Society, Personality, and Politics.* Rev. ed. Homewood, Ill.: Dorsey Press, 1978. The best summary of the Jacksonian experience is to be found in this book. With an emphasis on social and economic affairs, the author very clearly ties up all the various threads of the period.

Ratner, Lorman A. *Andrew Jackson and His Tennessee Lieutenants: A Study in Political Culture.* Westport, Conn.: Greenwood Press, 1997. Study of ten associates of Jackson, the political culture of the time, and how their rise from working-class roots affected their values and attitudes in a manner different from that advanced by many historians.

Remini, Robert V. *Andrew Jackson and the Bank War: A Study in the Growth of Presidential Power.* New York: Norton, 1967. In this book, Remini refers to the bank veto as the most significant presidential rejection in United States history, a culmination of Jackson's drive for executive supremacy. After the veto, presidential power grew considerably.

———. *The Election of Andrew Jackson.* Philadelphia: Lippincott, 1963. Discusses the change, between 1824 and 1828, in the number of eligible voters, and how this change benefited Andrew Jackson.

———. *Martin Van Buren and the Making of the Democratic Party.* New York: Columbia University Press, 1959. Explains in detail how Martin Van Buren founded the Democratic Party. Van Buren was a politician *par excellence*, who always seemed to thrive while he held lower offices. His presidency (1837-1841), however, was not very successful.

Rossiter, Clinton L. *The American Presidency.* Rev. ed. New York: American Library, and London: Hart-Davis, 1960. A work that explains the age-old practice of ranking the presidents, and of trying to determine what constitutes greatness in presidential terms. Jackson's presidency was a time of transition in American society, and the way he benefited from it, and then helped to propel it, gave his tenure the label of "great."

Carlton Jackson

HELEN HUNT JACKSON

Born: October 15, 1830; Amherst, Massachusetts
Died: August 12, 1885; San Francisco, California
Areas of Achievement: Literature and social reform
Contribution: Jackson received the first government commission on behalf of American Indians and fought vehemently for their civil rights and liberties.

Early Life

Helen Maria Fiske was born on October 15, 1830, to Nathan Wiley Fiske and Deborah Vinal Fiske. Nathan Fiske was a Congregational clergyman and a professor of philosophy and language at Amherst College who brought his children up under strict Calvinistic authority. Helen's mother Deborah was a quiet, demure woman whose influence on the young vivacious Helen was minimal. Indeed, Helen's father's only real influence occurred when he either punished her physically or derided her in front of her friends. Although her home in Amherst provided her with stability and a strict code of ethics, little affection or warmth was conveyed to the young and impressionable Helen. For friendship and companionship, Helen would turn to her friend Emily Dickinson, who lived down the road from her house. Helen's friendship with the reclusive Emily proved to be a sustaining relationship throughout her life.

Illness was a common feature of New England life in the middle of the nineteenth century. Deborah contracted tuberculosis and died a few months after Helen's twelfth birthday—the year was 1844. Helen had been a devoted daughter and had received all of her education from her mother up to that point. By the summer of 1846, Nathan had also contracted tuberculosis, but he was set on traveling to the Holy Land. Since the death of Deborah, Helen had been separated from her younger sister Ann and had been attending various seminaries. A year after leaving Amherst, Nathan died, and he was buried on Mount Zion. Helen was nearly fifteen when she was faced with being separated from her only sister and living in seminaries with virtual strangers.

These early years of personal hardship and grief were formative in how Helen lived her life and clearly forged many of her later moral and political values. Despite such hardship, Helen maintained her somewhat carefree and unstructured lifestyle.

From these early years as a young girl until she finally came to live in San Francisco, Helen remained true to her own ideals rather than those of other people. Corresponding with Emily Dickinson was the one unaltered joy that sustained her through many personal and family hardships.

From this period in her life until her death in San Francisco, Helen was a traveler whose trunks and cases seemed to be permanently packed. These formative years gave the young, headstrong Helen a yearning to travel and to experience new and different places, becoming a part of society wherever she found herself.

Life's Work

Although Helen Hunt Jackson's novel *Ramona* (1884) made a lasting contribution to American literature, her literary and political endeavors had a rather inauspicious beginning. After the death of her first husband, Lieutenant Edward Bissel Hunt, in 1863 and the tragic death of her nine-year-old

son two years later, Jackson turned to writing as a form of solace. (She became Helen Hunt Jackson when she later married William S. Jackson, a wealthy Quaker financier, in 1875.) Recognizing that she had an ability to write, she set out to become a well-known and respected writer. Helen undertook a life dedicated to writing. Articles, poems, sketches, and novels became her life-blood. Outwardly, at least, Helen Jackson remained vivacious and ebullient, seemingly undaunted by the tragic life that had been hers in only thirty-five years.

In the summer of 1865, Parke Godwin, the assistant publisher of the *New York Evening Post*, published Helen's poem "The Key to the Casket." This unexpected acceptance of her work inspired Helen to move to the writing community of Newport, Rhode Island. Thomas Wentworth Higginson, a respected writer and critic, soon became Helen's writing mentor, friend, and confidant. Newport allowed Helen the freedom to write even though woman writers were at that time far from being accepted. Because women writers were still an enigma, Jackson was forced to publish her works anonymously. Only when *Ramona* was published in 1884 did Jackson believe that her true identity was no longer an issue.

Because of the phenomenal success of *Ramona*, many people have the impression that Jackson was really only the author of a solitary novel. This could not be further from the truth. From her early years at Newport and continuously throughout her life, Jackson wrote in many different subject areas.

Jackson's early writing, however, reveals little of the passion and conviction that the cause of the American Indians would eventually evoke in her. The seed for her later and most famous writing was planted during a trip to California in May of 1872. After crossing the Platte River, Helen was given her first close-up experience of what Indians looked like and how they lived. This singular encounter caused Helen a certain degree of heartache as she witnessed for herself the abject poverty in which this disenfranchised people lived.

Bits of Travel appeared in 1870, and *Bits of Travel at Home* was finally published in 1878. During the period between writing these complementary pieces, Jackson's very successful "No Name" novels were hailed as drawing-room masterpieces. Jackson published *Mercy Philbrick's Choice* in 1876 and *Hetty's Strange History* in 1877. Up to this point in her writing career, Helen Hunt Jackson had published under the name H.H.

When *Century of Dishonor* appeared in 1881, Helen received all the criticism and vindictive press that was associated with writing about the plight of American Indians. Jackson's hope was that this laboriously researched work, which told the history of how badly the Indians had been treated, would spark some sympathy for them. In fact, the opposite proved to be the case. At her expense, she mailed a copy of *Century of Dishonor* to every congressman, again to little avail.

A woman who was no stranger to tragedy and who was relentless in pursuing what she believed to be right, Jackson continued to badger members of Congress. In particular, she focused on getting the attention of the secretary of the interior, Henry Teller, as well as appealing to Hiram Price, commissioner of Indian affairs. Both thought that Jackson was raising the controversial question of Indian land rights as a means of gaining publicity, but eventually the constant letter writing and appeals paid off. Jackson's singular efforts gained for her the position of special commissioner of Indian affairs in Southern California. This was a major breakthrough, particularly because Jackson was the first woman to hold such a government position.

Abbot Kinney was her choice for coagent and interpreter—a traveler and visionary like herself. They met while she was on an assignment for *Century* magazine in California. Two years after *Century of Dishonor* had been published, Jackson and Kinney began their travels of the Southern California missions. What had originally begun as a crusade to gain land rights for the Ponca Indians in Nebraska turned into a full-scale investigation into how mission Indians were being treated under government laws.

By now, Jackson had become very familiar with all of the missions in Southern California, and she undertook her commission with passion and zeal. Much of her traveling in Southern California in 1883 was done by carriage. With old stagecoach routes as their only means of traveling from one mission site to the next, Jackson and her troupe crisscrossed the sand plains and traversed the rugged mountains of the three most southerly counties of California.

Even though theirs was a fact-finding trip, Jackson's party continually came upon violations of Indian rights by white land settlers. Helen's passion for writing was now being used to record facts, figures, and names that she hoped would indict those early landowners.

To her dismay, Jackson's fifty-six-page report, which was appended to *Century of Dishonor*, created little stir. Perhaps the government hoped that the task would be more than one person could bear and that the society lady from New England would return to writing children's books and homilies. Realizing that the plight of the Indians was still in the balance, she took the advice of her close friend J. B. Gilder and began to write a novel.

When Gilder had first suggested that a novel might be the way to prick the conscience of a nation, Jackson balked at the immensity of such a project. Now, however, Jackson saw the need for such a book and was prepared to write her best. The many trips to California had steeped her in Indian culture and lifestyle. Despite the fact that *Ramona* forcefully portrays injustices toward the Indians, the novel quickly became a classic because it paints an exquisite, romantic portrait of mission life in old California.

Summary

Helen Hunt Jackson was a woman who took up the cause of a people that had little or no voice in society. Like many other pioneering women of the nineteenth century, she contributed greatly to both literature and social reform.

Jackson's untimely death meant that she did not see the full effect of her efforts, but other individuals and groups took up where Jackson's work and unfailing devotion to the Indian people left off. The Women's National Indian Association quickly recognized Jackson's contribution and hailed *Ramona* as a strong voice for Indian reform. Members of Congress, the commissioner of Indian affairs, members of various Christian organizations, and Indian reformers gathered at Lake Mohonk to discuss ways of dealing with Indian land rights. Many of the reforms that were later implemented by the government came directly as a result of these meetings. Jackson's message had little impact while she was alive, but soon after her death, groups and individuals were to carry that message throughout America.

While Jackson's contribution to the American Indian cause has etched her name in American history, her personality and life also attest this same vision. Ralph Waldo Emerson considered Jackson one of America's greatest poets. Such an accolade only draws attention to Jackson as a woman who was forced to live in anonymity for much of her literary life. Helen Hunt Jackson provided the leadership and courage that would inspire many more American women to turn their dreams into reality.

Bibliography

Banning, Evelyn. *Helen Hunt Jackson*. New York: Vanguard Press, 1973. Relying heavily on the work of Ruth Odell's 1939 biography, this work takes a painstaking look at Jackson's lesser writings. Indian rights are not a central theme, yet its scholarly approach makes this a useful reference.

Garner, Van H. *The Broken Ring: The Destruction of the California Indians*. Tucson, Ariz.: Westernlore Press, 1982. Thorough and well researched, this work covers the period from the 1840's to the 1980's. There are a number of useful entries concerning Jackson's specific dealings with various Indian tribes.

Jackson, Helen H. *The Indian Reform Letters of Helen Hunt Jackson, 1879-1885*. Edited by Valerie S. Mathes. Norman: University of Oklahoma Press, 1998. A collection of over 200 letters, most published here for the first time, that illustrate Jackson's passionate belief in Indian rights and involvement with Indian reform. The letters are divided into sections, which allow for study of particular periods and Indian groups separately.

Jackson, Helen Hunt. *A Century of Dishonor*. Boston: Roberts Brothers, 1885. A thorough and meticulously researched document that became the backbone of Indian land reform. Much of the book resembles a legal brief, yet it manages to communicate the passion of Jackson's quest for reform.

Mathes, Valerie Sherer. *Helen Hunt Jackson and Her Indian Reform Legacy*. Austin: University of Texas Press, 1990. The purpose of this work was to reestablish Jackson as a prominent author and reformer. With thoughtfulness and sound research, this work offers an excellent insight into American Indian history.

May, Antoinette. *Helen Hunt Jackson: A Lonely Voice of Conscience*. San Francisco: Chronicle Press, 1987. This is a complete bibliography of Helen Hunt Jackson's life from early childhood to her death. May's writing is based primarily on anecdotal sources, and she embellishes much of Jackson's life with an almost fictional style.

Polanich, Judith K. "Ramona's Baskets: Romance and Reality." *American Indian Culture and Re-*

search Journal 21, no. 3 (Summer 1997). Discusses Jackson's portrayal of basketry in "Ramona" and its impact on the buying habits of the Victorian populace, which led to a shrinking supply. This is an example of Jackson's promotion of Indian causes through her depictions of them as resourceful, creative people.

Richard G. Cormack

STONEWALL JACKSON

Born: January 21, 1824; Clarksburg, Virginia
Died: May 10, 1863; Guiney's Station, Virginia
Area of Achievement: The military
Contribution: The ablest and most renowned of Lee's lieutenants, Jackson led daring marches and employed do-or-die battle tactics which resulted in key victories by which the Confederacy was sustained during the first two years of the Civil War.

Early Life

Thomas Jonathan Jackson was born January 21, 1824, in Clarksburg, Virginia (in modern West Virginia), a hilly, heavily forested region sparsely populated by the Scotch-Irish settlers who were Jackson's forebears. Self-reliance was thrust upon the boy at an early age; the third of four children, he was orphaned by the age of seven. Taken in by an uncle, Cummins Jackson, he grew up in a farm environment in which he acquired numerous practical skills but very little schooling. Even as a teenager, however, Jackson clearly demonstrated the traits of physical courage, uncompromising moral integrity, and high ambition serviced by an iron will. Resolved to improve his lot by education, Jackson obtained an appointment to the United States Military Academy at West Point. The shambling young man from the hills cut a poor figure among the generally more sophisticated and better educated cadets. Yet, impervious to taunts, he earned the respect of his classmates by perseverance and phenomenal concentration, finishing seventeenth in a class of fifty-nine.

Shortly after he was graduated in 1846, Jackson was ordered to Mexico as a second lieutenant of artillery. He took part in the siege of Vera Cruz and distinguished himself in several battles during the advance on Mexico City in the summer of 1847. Jackson's courage and effectiveness brought admiration from his superiors and a rapid succession of promotions; by the end of the war, at the age of twenty-two, he had attained the rank of brevet major. A photograph taken of him at that time shows a man with a trim figure (Jackson stood about five feet, ten inches, and weighed about 150 pounds) and a pleasant, earnest face characterized chiefly by the firm set of the mouth and clear, deep-set eyes that gaze out solemnly beneath a prominent brow. (The flowing beard that would give Jackson

the appearance of an Old Testament prophet was to come later.)

Assigned to Fort Hamilton, New York, in 1848, Jackson entered the routine existence of a peacetime army garrison for the next two years. During this time, however, he became more and more deeply involved in religious pursuits. Jackson came to think of his rather frail health, with its persistent digestive disorders, as a visitation of Providence to lead him into more righteous ways. He was baptized, unsure whether he had been as a child, and from that time on, the course of his life was inseparable from his sense of consecration to the will of the Almighty.

Life's Work

In the spring of 1851, an instructor's position at the Virginia Military Institute, founded twelve years earlier on the model of West Point, became available. Jackson was nominated for it, and, bored with his work as a peacetime army officer, he resigned his commission and reported to Lexington in July, 1851, to take up the duties of a professor of natural philosophy (or, in modern terminology, general science) and artillery tactics for the next nine years.

Not by any account an inspiring teacher, Jackson nevertheless mastered topics in which he had no formal credentials, thereby earning at least the grudging respect of his students. Jackson also came to be regarded as something of an eccentric for his rigid ways and odd personal mannerisms—for example, his habit of frequently raising his left arm, ostensibly to improve circulation, and his silent grimace serving in place of a laugh—which would be remarked on by his troops during the Civil War and give color and distinction to the legend of "Old Jack."

Settled in his new life, Jackson turned his thoughts to marriage. Seeking a wife from the religious community of Lexington, in 1853 he married Eleanor Junkin, the daughter of the Reverend Dr. George Junkin. The union was tragically brief; Eleanor died the next year in childbirth. Two years later and after a summer tour of Europe that restored him from the lethargy of mourning, Jackson courted and married Mary Anna Morrison, the daughter of another clergyman, who would remain his devoted wife until his death and would eventually bear him a daughter.

Life for the Jacksons during the next three years was characterized by affection, tranquillity, and a mutual sense of religious purpose (Jackson was by now a deacon of the Presbyterian Church and maintained a Sunday school for black slaves). The impending events of the Civil War were to bring all that to an end. While not a champion of either slavery or secession, Jackson felt loyalty deeply rooted to his native soil, and when Virginia seceded from the Union, his course was clear.

In April, 1861, Jackson was commissioned a colonel in the newly formed Confederate army and took command at Harpers Ferry. Within three weeks, he distinguished himself by establishing strict military order for the rather undisciplined garrison of raw, untrained soldiers and by capturing a large number of Northern locomotives and freight cars for use by the Confederate army.

Some three months later, Jackson earned the sobriquet of "Stonewall" at the Battle of First Manassas (or Bull Run). In this opening major conflict of the war, an army of some thirty-five thousand Federal troops under General Irvin McDowell marched south from Washington to crush the rebellion. On July 21, after some preliminary fighting, McDowell made his main attack near Manassas Junction. As the defending Confederates fell back toward Jackson's brigade, which was holding the ridge above Bull Run, General Barnard E. Bee rallied his troops with the cry "Look yonder! There is Jackson and his brigade standing like a stone wall!" Later in the day, it was Jackson's brigade that broke the Union line with a furious bayonet charge, thus halting General McDowell's offensive and forcing a rethinking of strategy in Washington.

With a huge increase in the Union army, the new strategy called for a seaborne assault upon Richmond via the Jamestown Peninsula, led by George McClellan (a classmate of Jackson at West Point) and supported by a secondary force coming down the Shenandoah Valley under the command of Nathaniel Banks. Jackson, now a major general, correctly surmised that a diversion up the Shenandoah Valley would not only neutralize Banks but also threaten Washington and thus divert troops from McClellan's peninsular offensive. Beginning in March, 1862, Jackson led his troops in a succession of battles renowned in military history as the Valley Campaign. Utilizing the tactics of deception, rapid forced marches, and hit-and-run assaults and retreats, Jackson blunted the Federal advance down the Shenandoah Valley, alarmed Washington,

and consequently stalled McClellan's attack upon Richmond.

Jackson's victories continued to inspire the South and dismay the North during the year 1862. In August, Jackson played the pivotal role in defeating the new Union offensive led by General John Pope at the Second Battle of Manassas. In December, at the Battle of Fredericksburg, he and James Longstreet shared the responsibility for the Confederate victory over the forces of General Ambrose Burnside.

In the spring of 1863, the Union forces, under yet another commander, Joseph "Fighting Joe" Hooker, gathered for a massive offensive upon Richmond. Robert E. Lee, outnumbered two to one, decided to risk his defense on a hazardous division of his forces, with a corps led by Jackson, now a lieutenant general, tasked with flanking Hooker's army. On the evening of May 2, 1863, the unsuspecting Union Eleventh Corps was routed by Jackson's attack some four miles west of Chancellorsville. Darkness brought a lull to the fighting, during which Jackson and a small staff reconnoitered the battlefield to determine a route for a further Confederate advance. Returning to its own lines, however, Jackson's scouting party, in one of the great ironic moments of history, was mistaken for a Union cavalry patrol and fired upon. Hit by several musket balls, Jackson fell, his left arm shattered. Amputation failed to save his life, and on May 10, 1863, he succumbed to pneumonia. His last words uttered in a final, sublime moment of lucidity were, "Let us cross over the river and rest under the shade of the trees."

Summary

Jackson's death was a mortal blow to the Confederacy. In subsequent battles in the Eastern theater, the absence of his leadership was sorely missed; Lee was to remark later that if he had had Jackson at Gettysburg, he would have won that crucial battle. Beyond such speculation, however, there is no doubt that the loss of such an inspiring leader—by far the most popular commander on either side— seriously undermined Confederate morale.

Jackson's charismatic popularity was the product of both his brilliant generalship and his singular force of character. Merciless in driving his own troops and ruthless in pursuit of his enemy, he nevertheless was admired by both for his legendary courage, integrity, and lack of egoistical motive. Lee venerated his memory, referring to him as "the great and good Jackson."

Jackson's battles (in particular, the Valley Campaign) have been studied as models by successive generations of military students in the United States and Europe. Jackson understood and applied the principles of mass and maneuver as well as any commander in history, concentrating his forces at decisive points against numerically superior but more dispersed opponents. Beyond his significance as a tactical genius, however, "Stonewall" passed early into the realm of national epic, defining an ideal of valor for generations of American youths.

Bibliography

Chambers, Lenoir. *Stonewall Jackson*. 2 vols. New York: Morrow, 1959. The most comprehensive biography of Jackson to appear in the twentieth century, Chambers' two-volume work has supplanted that of Henderson (see below) as the definitive study. A lucid, graceful writer, Chambers brings admirable clarity and insight to his subject.

Churchill, Winston L. S. *The American Civil War.* New York: Dodd, Mead, 1958; London: Cassell, 1961. A reprint of the chapters on the American Civil War in Churchill's four-volume *A History of the English Speaking Peoples* (1956-1958). In any edition, Churchill's brief history of the Civil War is a masterpiece and focuses especially well on the significance of Jackson's role.

Clark, Champ. *Decoying the Yanks: Jackson's Valley Campaign.* Alexandria, Va.: Time-Life Books, 1984. As the title suggests, primarily a history of Jackson's Shenandoah Valley Campaign in the spring of 1862. Contains, however, a good short biography of Jackson in his early years as well. Lavishly illustrated with contemporary photographs, paintings, and drawings, the book gives a vivid account of the most spectacular achievement of Jackson's generalship.

Henderson, G. F. R. *Stonewall Jackson and the American Civil War.* 2 vols. London and New York: Longman, 1898. The classic biography of Jackson. Henderson's thoughtful, elegant study has gone through numerous editions and is still, after more than three-quarters of a century, a valuable resource cited in virtually every work on Jackson that has appeared since its publication.

Robertson, James I., Jr. *Stonewall Jackson: The Man, the Soldier, the Legend.* New York: Macmillan, and London: Prentice-Hall, 1997. The author examines Jackson's military career and his life during the war, arguing that many of the historical accounts are exaggerated or false.

Tate, Allen. *Stonewall Jackson, the Good Soldier.* New York: Minton, Balch, 1928; London: Cassell, 1930. Short biography for the general reader by a leading Southern man of letters. Tate's Confederate sympathies date the book but also provide an interesting partisan slant; he excoriates Jefferson Davis for not unleashing Jackson at decisive points that might have turned the tide for the Confederacy.

Vandiver, Frank. *Mighty Stonewall.* New York: McGraw-Hill, 1957. Comprehensive, well-balanced one-volume biography of Jackson by a respected Civil War historian. Vandiver's research is thorough, while his lively, anecdotal presentation brings to life the historical events for the reader.

Wheeler, Richard. *We Knew Stonewall Jackson.* New York: Crowell, 1977. Extremely useful, well-conceived book of excerpts from contemporary accounts of Jackson linked by the author's commentary. In effect, an economical, accurate, short biography in which the author's sources speak for themselves.

Charles Duncan

JAMĀL AL-DĪN AL-AFGHĀNĪ

Born: 1838-1839; Asadābād, Iran
Died: March 9, 1897; Istanbul, Ottoman Empirel
al-Dn al-Afghn
Areas of Achievement: Philosophy and politics
Contribution: Afghānī was the Pan-Islamist politician and teacher whose intense hatred of, and opposition to, British colonial policies focused the energies of Middle Eastern, Central Asian, and Indian Muslim intellectuals on the plight of the masses. His untiring quest for Muslim solidarity influenced Egypt's nationalist movement and Iran's constitutional and Islamic revolutions.

Early Life

Jamāl al-Dīn al-Afghānī as-Sayyid Muhammad Ibn-i Safdar al-Husain was born into a family of sayyids in the village of Asadābād, near Hamadan, Iran. He claimed, however, that he was born in the village of As'adābād, near Kabul, Afghanistan. Only a sketchy account of Afghānī's childhood can be pieced together from the information provided by his biographer, Mīrzā Lutfullāh Asadābādī. Contrary to his own assertion that he grew up in Afghanistan, Afghānīi was educated at home in Asadābād until age ten. He then attended school in Qazvīn and Tehran. During his teens, he studied theology and Islamic philosophy in Karbalā and An Najaf, centers of Shi'ite learning in Iraq.

In 1855, around the age of seventeen, Afghānī traveled to Büshehr, on the Persian Gulf, and from there to India. In India, he observed British imperialism at work. Indian Muslims were openly discriminated against in government appointments, religious institutions, and education. The Muslims' struggle against British tyranny left an indelible impression on the young Afghānī. He agreed with the Indians that the British intended to undermine and discredit Islam. From India, Afghānī journeyed to Mecca and then returned to the Shi'ite centers of learning in Iraq, where he had studied earlier. He remained in that area until 1865, when he traveled to Iran and, the following year, to Afghanistan.

Documented reports of Afghānī's early years date to 1866, when he was part of the entourage of Muhammad A'zam Khān, the military ruler of Qandahār under Dōst Muhammad Khān. When Dōst Muhammad died in 1863, his three sons fought among themselves for the rulership. Amīr Shīr 'Alī Khān, Dōst Muhammad's third son, assumed power in Kabul, pledging to modernize the nation. Shīr 'Alī's brothers, however, rebelled in Quandahār and ousted him in 1866. A'zam became king, and Afghānī entered Afghan politics with him as his close confidant. Afghānī reportedly drew up a national recovery plan that included provisions for a network of schools, a national newspaper, a centralized government, and a well-regulated communications system. In politics, he advised the king to ally himself with Russia against the British in neighboring India. A'zam's rule was short-lived. Shīr 'Alī returned in 1868, deposing Muhammad A'zam and expelling Afghānī—a foreigner who spoke Farsi with an Iranian accent. Afghānī's modernizing reforms, however, were retained.

Life's Work

Afghānī was a mullah with a strong constitution. He had a magnetic personality and a dogged determination, both of which he used competently to penetrate exclusive circles and promote his cause. He cherished secrecy at the expense of social norms. He wore a white turban, while calling himself a sayyid, and adamantly refused any association with women. He was quicktempered, quick of action, and quick to envisage a British plot at every turn.

Afghanistan afforded Afghānī a worthy education by supplementing his understanding of the dynamics of struggle against imperialism with a possible response. He came to realize that the Shi'i and Persian rational philosophy that had inspired him in India could rid the Muslim masses of ignorance and poverty, if it were enhanced with armed struggle and savage confrontation. If Afghans with bare hands could defeat Great Britain in the First Afghan War, he imagined what the impact of an Islamic army under a charismatic leader would be. Afghānī decided to inject himself into the growing confrontation between the Muslim East and the Christian West in Afghanistan.

The Muslim ruler charismatic enough to realize Afghānī's secret aspiration was Abdülaziz, an Ottoman sultan. In 1869, Afghānī traveled to Istanbul by way of Bombay and Cairo, expecting to be named confidant to the sultan. Turkish officials, busy with the *Tanzīmāt* reforms, appointed him instead to a lesser position on the Council of Education. While serving in this office, Afghānī began a series of inspiring lectures on reform. These lectures, tinged with anti-imperialist allusions and modernist tendencies, and imbued with Shi'ite rational philosophy, raised the ire of the Sunnī ulema (holy men) in Istanbul, who found the lectures heretical. The powerful ulema waited for an opportunity to embarrass Afghānī publicly. This opportunity came when Afghānī compared the ulema with a human craft. The ulema brought their wrath down upon him, the sultan, and the *Tanzīmāt*. To save the *Tanzīmāt*, Abdülaziz was forced to expel Afghānī from Turkey.

With hopes dashed, Afghānī accepted Riyadh Pasha's invitation and, in 1871, went to Egypt. There he continued to teach and to pursue his dream of a Pan-Islamic nation free from imperialist domination. In a series of provocative lectures, he grafted the example of Egypt's economic strangulation by European banks to medieval Islamic philosophy in order to foment revolt against Western exploitation. He also formed and led a Masonic lodge in Cairo, among whose members were counted such promising young leaders as Muhammad 'Abduh, a future leader of the Pan-Islamic movement.

Afghānī's activities in Egypt brought him in direct confrontation with Khedive Isma'il of Egypt and his suzerain, Sultan Abdülhamid II, as well as with European, particularly British, powers. Afghānī had placed Khedive Ismā'īl in a difficult position by openly condemning his financial mismanagement as the cause of Egypt's capitulation to European bankers. To ward off Afghānī's allegations, Ismā'īl blamed the foreign bankers, who, in turn, pressured the sultan to depose the Khedive, which the sultan did in 1879. Muhammed Tawfīq Pasha, Ismā'īl's son, expelled Afghānī from Egypt that same year. From Egypt, Afghānī traveled to Hyderabad, south of India, where, for two years, he offered seminars, gave public lectures, and wrote. "The Refutation of the Materialists" (1881) was written at this time. This essay affords a glimpse of Afghānī's growing interest in social consciousness, modernism, and rational thinking.

Writing within the Utopian tradition, Afghānī described his vision of the "Virtuous City," as a hierarchically structured society that functions on the principles of shame, trustworthiness, and truthfulness, and aspires to the ideals of intelligence, pride, and justice. Higher intelligence, Afghānī argued, leads to new capabilities and advanced civilizations; pride leads to competition and progress; and

justice leads to global peace and harmony among nations. Naturalists (*neicherīs*), Afghānī argued, intended to destroy the solidarity of the Virtuous City through division and sectarianism.

From Hyderabad, Afghānī traveled to London and, shortly thereafter, to Paris, where he engaged the French philosopher Ernest Renan in a debate on the position of scientific discovery in Islam. Then, in 1844, Afghānī began his most consequential activity—his collaboration with Muhammad 'Abduh on editing a revolutionary journal in Arabic, *al-'Urwat al-Wuthqā* (the firmest bond). This publication established Afghānī as the champion of Pan-Islamism, the movement rooted in the bitter memory of Abdülhamid's 1877 defeat in the Russo-Turkish War—whereby the *Tanzīmāt* reforms had been proved ineffective—and in the 1882 occupation of Egypt by Great Britain. *Al-'Urwat al-wuthqā* published articles by Afghānī and 'Abduh on diverse topics. The sultan was not impressed. Disappointed, Afghānī left for Russia. Waiting at Büshehr to collect his books, Afghānī received an invitation from Nāser od-Dīn Shāh, the sovereign in Tehran, who had read a translation of an essay from *al-'Urwat al-wuthqā*. When this brief interview did not go well, Afghānī resumed his trip.

In Russia, Afghānī continued his anti-British activities. He argued that, with his mobilization of Indian and Central Asian Muslims, Russians would easily drive the British out of the subcontinent. The Russians humored him, delaying his departure to irk the British. Afghānī's two-year visit in Russia gained for him a second royal invitation to Tehran. Iran of the 1890's was much like Egypt of the 1870's. It was plagued with financial mismanagement and hounded by foreign investors, who sought concessions on every resource. The shah, however, unlike the Khedive, ruled under the protection of divine right. He could sell Iran to whomever he pleased.

Afghānī arrived in Iran from St. Petersburg at a time when Iranians were growing increasingly alarmed by Nāser od-Dīn's doling out their country's resources. Afghānī himself had distributed leaflets condemning these concessions. Afghānī was not received by his host, who also denied Afghānī's claim that he had been commissioned in Munich to go to St. Petersburg and make amends on Iran's behalf. Worse yet, Afghānī was clandestinely informed of orders for his arrest. To save himself from the shah's wrath, he took sanctuary (*bast*) in the shrine of Shāh Abdul 'Azīm, south of

Tehran. From there, using clandestine methods and superb oratorical techniques, Afghānī attracted Iranians in droves to his fiery attacks on the shah's past antireformist actions, especially the murder of Mīrzā Taqī Khān, Amīr Kabīr.

Afghānī predicted that Iran would capitulate to British might, as Egypt had in 1882. He demanded that Iranian revenues be spent on the construction of a railroad, on education and hospitals, and on a viable army to thwart imperialism, rather than on the shah's pleasure trips to Europe. Iranians, he said, must be given the right to express their opinions in publications independent of the government. Iran must have a constitution, a parliament, and a house of justice. Above all, he emphasized, Iranians deserved a just king.

Nāser od-Dīn was approaching his fiftieth year of rule. Since Afghānī had been instrumental in the shah's recent humiliation as the first shah to revoke his own writ—the tobacco concession—and since this action had precipitated Iran's first foreign debt, the shah ordered the unruly mullah to be expelled. Ignoring the rules of sanctuary, the shah's guards invaded the holy shrine in 1892, placed Afghānī, half naked and in the middle of winter, on the bare back of a mule, and deported him. Afghānī went to London, where he reestablished ties with his lodge members and then traveled to Turkey at the invitation of the sultan. Rather than becoming the sultan's confidant and Pan-Islamist consultant as Afghānī had hoped, he became the sultan's prisoner.

From Turkey, Afghānī continued to foment revolt in Iran, using his devotees to carry out his behests. One such devotee was Mīrzā Rezā Kermānī, who, in 1896, was commissioned to murder Nāser od-Dīn. Mīrzā Rezā carried out his mission on the anniversary of the shah's fiftieth year of reign in the very sanctuary in which Afghānī had been humiliated a few years before. Afghānī died of cancer of the chin at the age of about sixty and was buried in a secret grave. In 1944, the government of Afghanistan claimed him as a citizen, and his supposed remains were transferred to and buried on the grounds of the University of Kabul under a respectful shrine.

Summary

Jamāl al-Dīn al-Afghānī was an Iranian by birth. His activities and the corpus of his writings reflect that. When visiting Europe, he affiliated himself with Afghanistan; when in Afghanistan, he associated himself with Ottoman Turkey and called himself "Istanbūlī," to gain the confidence of Sunni rulers and evade Iranian officials. There are several reasons that Afghānī failed in materializing his dream. First, he put too much trust in the goodwill of Muslim rulers and too little in the people of the Middle East. In ignoring the grassroots support for his Pan-Islamism, he violated the rules of his own Virtuous City, a violation that he regretfully acknowledged in a letter he wrote from prison before his death. Second, he used religion to achieve political aims, and, assuming that world rulers acted independently of one another, secretly groomed all for the same office—that of caliph. This policy backfired on him many times, finally costing him his life. Third, he annoyed rulers by lecturing them. Nāser od-Dīn dismissed him when Afghānī blatantly offered himself as a sword with which the shah could cripple the imperialists. The sultan was more gracious. Finally, Afghānī failed to distinguish between policy and personal disposition. He sought Queen Victoria's assistance against Nāser od-Dīn within a short time of the tobacco boycott against British interests in Iran, a boycott that he himself had helped bring to fruition.

Bibliography

Ahmad, Aziz. "Sayyid Ahmad Khān, Jamāl al-Dīn al-Afghānī and Muslim India." *Studia Islamica* 13 (1960): 55-78. An important source of information on Afghānī's involvement in Indian Muslim affairs. Compares Afghānī's advocacy of *jihad* and *khilāfat* to Sayyid Ahmad Khān's policy of capitulation to British rule. Ahmad believes that Afghānī and Sayyid Ahmad Khān differed only in political matters.

Algar, Hamid. *Religion and State in Iran, 1785-1906.* Berkeley: University of California Press, 1969. Provides the larger picture. Examines the life and works of Afghānī's colleagues and assesses Afghānī's contribution in the light of past philosophical and doctrinal efforts.

Hodgson, Marshall G. *The Venture of Islam.* Vol. 3, *The Gunpowder Empire and Modern Times.* Chicago: University of Chicago Press, 1974. Hodgson examines Afghānī's efforts in the context of an alliance among the Shi'i ulema, the *bazaaris*, and the intellectuals. Afghānī emerges as an opportunist in his calls for reform, emphasizing the political, religious, or social aspects depending on the weight each carried in a particular situation.

Keddie, Nikki R. *An Islamic Response to Imperialism: Political and Religious Writings of Sayyid*

Jamāl al-Dīn "al-Afghānī." Berkeley: University of California Press, 1968; London: University of California Press, 1983. A comprehensive study of Afghānī's life. Includes sample translations of his works as well as analytical notes on his worldview. Also includes a bibliography and a good index.

Kedourie, Elie. *Afghani and 'Abduh: An Essay on Religious Unbelief and Political Activism in Modern Islam.* London: Cass, and New York: Humanities Press, 1966. Kedourie discusses Afghānī's teachings from the point of view of his disciple, 'Abduh, and of circumstances that influenced those teachings. Kedourie's discussion of Mahdīsm, as expounded by both Afghānī and Muhammad Ahmad of Sudan, is noteworthy.

Kramer, Martin. *Islam Assembled: The Advent of the Muslim Congresses.* New York: Columbia University Press, 1986. The first two chapters deal with the genesis of the Pan-Islamic ideal and its challenge to authority. The contributions of Afghānī are discussed in the context of a rising tide of discontent among Muslims from Indonesia, Sumatra, and Central Asia to Daghistan and the Crimea, as these are reflected at the court of the Ottoman sultans.

Iraj Bashiri

HENRY JAMES

Born: April 15, 1843; New York, New York
Died: February 28, 1916; London, England
Area of Achievement: Literature
Contribution: James is one of the most preeminent and influential writers of the modern novel in America. Both his life and his work are closely related to the United States' emergence in the twentieth century as a major world power.

Early Life

Henry James was born April 15, 1843, at 21 Washington Place in New York City, son of a wealthy and distinguished American family tracing its roots to an immigrant ancestor, William James. This founder of the James family in America had come from Northern Ireland two generations before, just after the American Revolution, and had made a fortune in real estate in Albany, New York, then a small city greatly influenced by the Dutch. Henry James's father, Henry James, Sr., married Mary Robertson Walsh, originally from Northern Ireland, and together they produced five children: William, Henry, Garth (known as "Wilky"), Robertson, and Alice. Henry's brother William, one year older than he, was to become one of the most famous American philosophers and psychologists.

Henry's first memory later in life was as an infant on his mother's knee, viewing the column in the center of the Place Vendôme in Paris, an extraordinarily fitting memory for someone whose attraction for Europe was to be one of the most pronounced aspects of his life. Indeed, the first two years of his life were spent with his family in England and France.

From 1845 to 1855, James lived in the United States and was educated by various tutors and schools. During this time, he knew Ralph Waldo Emerson, Washington Irving, and William Makepeace Thackeray, the first in a long line of renowned writers and artists with whom he associated throughout his life in the United States and Great Britain and on the Continent. As it turned out, this decade was also to be the longest continuous residence in the United States for James. As a boy, he was shy and a great reader.

Back in Europe in 1855 with his family, to improve his "sensuous" appreciation, he returned to the United States in 1858, only to leave again in 1859 for a year in Germany and Switzerland. His father, who in adult life became a devotee of the philosophy and theology of the Swedish thinker Emanuel Swedenborg, was dissatisfied with most of the schools available in both the United States and Europe; he continually sought other avenues of cultural enrichment for his children, particularly exposure to British and European society and heritage.

Having returned to Newport, Rhode Island, in 1860, James was prevented from joining the Union army in the American Civil War, which began in 1861, by a back injury, though his two younger brothers did so. Instead, he went to Harvard Law School in 1862 and began to write and publish stories; he dropped out of law school after one year to pursue his writing career fulltime. In 1864, his family moved to Boston. His friend, William Dean Howells, soon to become an editor at the *Atlantic Monthly* magazine, was helpful to him, and James published several pieces in the prestigious magazine.

At age twenty-six, he traveled again to England and grew the beard and mustache that would mark his visage until the end of the century. He dined with the eminent art critic and social historian John Ruskin, visited cathedrals, and at last went to Italy, where he formed a permanent impression of how the past impinges on the present, a hallmark of his later writings.

After a brief return to the United States a year later, he spent the years 1872-1873 in Great Britain, Paris, and Rome (which he would revisit in 1874). His residence in Rome during these years gave impetus to the writing of *Roderick Hudson* (1876), published in the *Atlantic Monthly*, about an expatriate American sculptor whose life abroad works to destroy him; obviously, James wondered whether Europe's pull on him would do the same.

The fall of 1875 saw James in Paris, writing *The American* (1877), the story of an American businessman who is treated very badly in Parisian high society. James himself, though apparently welcomed at this time into exclusive literary and social circles in Paris, never felt fully accepted there. In 1877, at age thirty-four, James went to London, yearning to become fully integrated into English life, breaking down the barriers of being a mere observer and foreigner. He wrote *The Europeans* (1878), *Daisy Miller* (1879), and *The Portrait of a Lady* (1881) in quick succession, the second of which finally established his reputation.

Life's Work

James returned to the United States in 1881, though now resolved that his mission as a writer was to return to Europe; a notebook entry this same year reads, "My choice is the old world—my choice, my need, my life." An essay called "The Art of Fiction" (1884), written for *Longman's Magazine*, is a kind of literary manifesto inaugurating the "modern" novel, exemplified not only by the works of James but also by those of Marcel Proust, Virginia Woolf, and James Joyce. James's mother died in Boston in 1882 and his father soon thereafter. James went back to London, writing, "It is an anchorage in my life."

By the end of the 1880's, he had become a seasoned writer and a true expatriate, ready to enter his last, most mature phase as an artist, abandoning as his main subject the interrelationships of Europe and America and the impact of Europe upon Americans. Henceforward, his novels would have as their more major concern elucidating the inward states of mind in his characters. One already sees some of this new emphasis in *Portrait of a Lady*, whose main character, Isabel Archer, is married to Gilbert Osmond, an extreme narcissist with the potential for bringing much evil into people's lives. It is the American expatriates in this novel, not the Europeans, who are the source of most of the deception and intrigue. The work contains portraits of various types of Americans abroad, all drawn with deft skill and subtlety; England, Florence, and Rome form the settings, all brought to life in the kind of convincing detail that only someone intimately familiar with life in these places could accomplish.

The novels of the later 1880's, *The Bostonians* (1886), *The Princess Casamassima* (1886), and *The Tragic Muse* (1889), were less successful in many ways. James himself believed that *The Bostonians* was diffuse and that he had also failed to bring to life people and places in America sufficiently well, because of his having lost touch with the American scene. *The Princess Casamassima* depicts the poverty of London in the most vivid terms; although it touches upon the most sensitive of political and social issues, this novel is also a good example of one of James's basic premises at work: that novels are meant to be "pictures," not "moral or immoral," not sermons or treatises. Naturally, the work of Charles Dickens was a model here. *The Tragic Muse* has as its subject the total immersion of the artist into art with all the arduous sacrifice that entails; it un-

doubtedly reflected James's own state of mind at the time, since he, too, was poised on the edge of just such a total dedication of the rest of his life.

In 1896, James settled in England, finally moving into Lamb House at Rye, which would be his residence for his last and most intense productive period, the time when the legendary Henry James most familiar to contemporary readers came into full bloom. He found Sussex to be a suitable environment for this last prolonged stage of his life and work, steeped as it is in history still clearly visible, as had been the Europe of his experience. He grew attached to the coast and the sea and the ancient towns thereabouts. He could still travel to London with ease when moved to do so.

The middle period of his career culminated in the publication of *What Maisie Knew* (1897), the still-famous and widely read *The Turn of the Screw* (1898), and *The Awkward Age* (1899). Before proceeding into his final most successful stage as a novelist, however, he made a highly unsuccessful bid for fame in the theater in the early 1890's. He had written a play based on the novel *Daisy Miller*, but it was never produced. He adapted another novel, *The American*, for the stage, but its London run was not very long and the reviews were negative. After a number of other such attempts, he at last gave up, convinced that the theater was a vulgar medium, its audiences demanding the wrong things from writers.

In 1900, he shaved the familiar beard and mustache of his early career, perhaps as a symbol of his new inner resolve. His clean-shaven face and balding head would now take on the prominent well-known profile found in the John Singer Sargent portrait of him, painted much later in honor of his seventieth birthday, at the insistence of his friends; this famous painting now hangs in the National Portrait Gallery.

In 1904, after having lived twenty years abroad, James returned briefly to the United States and toured many regions and levels of society. He was in the end, however, quite dismayed with what he found and felt unable to identify with what America had become in his absence. Later, by the start of World War I, after his return to Rye, he was to conclude that the civilization of Europe that he had cherished so much was now dead. In truth, James's life, spent as it was between Great Britain and the United States for the most part, gave him a unique vantage point on the passing of an age. The more innocent and isolated America of his youth was transformed, just as were the traditional rigidities of society in the Old World.

There are three novels which critics generally cite as representing the apex of James's career: *The Wings of the Dove* (1902), *The Ambassadors* (1903), and *The Golden Bowl* (1904). They are among the most difficult of his works to read but also probably the most rewarding. All three are concerned with the idea that improving one's perception of one's own personality and character, and thereby learning to understand better the personalities and characters of others, is the true road to freedom and maturity for human beings.

In *The Wings of the Dove*, the New York heiress Milly Theale is the leading character, the "dove" of the story. Upon her death, Merton Densher, who has pursued her for her money, finally cannot accept it; he has become a morally better person through his contact with Milly. Milly Theale is by no means naïve, but her simple grace and wisdom transcend the sordid materialism and artificial artfulness of those around her. The setting is London high society, perhaps best represented by the manipulative and grasping, polished and beautiful Kate Croy. This is perhaps the first modern novel to focus so intently and intricately upon subjective experience, the inner life; indeed, it is a forerunner in many ways of such major modernist fiction as that of Proust, D. H. Lawrence, Woolf, and Joyce.

The Ambassadors, actually written before *The Wings of the Dove* but published after it, was considered by James to be his best work; most critics and readers have come to agree. It is about the American Lambert Strether and his delayed liberation from the clutches of the deadening ethos of American Puritanism. Strether becomes an appreciator of European culture and enlightenment and an expert in understanding the importance of leading a sensitive and aesthetically fulfilling life; Paris is for him the new world that saves him, and this city is the ultimate symbol for James, too, of the best kind of life.

The Golden Bowl is in form and content a true culmination of James's progression as a novelist. The symbol of the golden bowl, taken from Ecclesiastes, represents life and sensibility; it must be broken near the end of the story, just as the protagonist Maggie Verver's life must be reconstituted on a higher plane, one more spiritual and refined. James obviously hoped that the American upper crust would similarly be transformed. Maggie remains essentially American but also an inheritor of

the best of European culture, and she is triumphant in the end over both European and American evils and distractions from the high road in life.

The "New York edition" of his writings, *The Novels and Tales of Henry James*, was published in 1907-1909; he made revisions and wrote prefaces to these works, the prefaces being separately published in 1934 as *The Art of the Novel: Critical Prefaces*. In 1908, at the age of sixty-five, he once again suffered from what he called "black depression," a condition which he had last experienced fourteen years previously; this time it continued for a longer period. Harvard University granted him an honorary degree in 1911, which he accepted in memory of his famous brother William. In 1915, he became a naturalized British subject. In the same year, he suffered two strokes. James was given the Order of Merit by the king in early 1916, and shortly thereafter, he died, on February 28, 1916, and was cremated; his ashes were put in the family grave in Cambridge, Massachusetts. A memorial plaque was erected in his honor in Chelsea Old Church in London; it reads, "A resident of this parish who renounced a cherished citizenship to give his allegiance to England in the first year of the Great War." Near the end of his life, James wrote, "One's supreme relation . . . is one's relation to one's country." Despite his attraction to England and Europe, Henry James was an American; his life and work are dominated by his "relation" to his homeland.

Summary

The novels of Henry James are in marked contrast to most other literature written between the American Civil War and World War I, a whole epoch. His work is quite unlike the romanticism of O. Henry, the local color of Sarah Orne Jewett and Bret Harte, the realism of Howells and Mark Twain, or the naturalism of Stephen Crane, Frank Norris, and Jack London. James was intensely preoccupied with artistic technique, psychological verisimilitude, and the mores and manners of a highly sophisticated elite. In both style and subject matter, he was the inaugurator of the modern novel. His belief in the power of consciousness as the ultimate shaper of people's lives and his denial of the fixed givens of life as determinants of destiny can be seen in retrospect as very American. Just as the United States itself was preparing to enter the world scene as a major power during his lifetime, James's life and work looks outward, despite its concern with interior states and developed sensibilities, to America's new adult relationship to England and Europe in the twentieth century. Although it took some time after his death for Henry James's reputation and influence to reach their height, he has finally come to be regarded as one of the great American authors; indeed some would say the greatest.

Bibliography

Cargill, Oscar. *The Novels of Henry James*. New York: Macmillan, 1961. A very informative commentary by a famous critic of James's novels. In addition, there are handy references to biographical and critical studies. Cargill's criticism here is particularly useful because it summarizes and incorporates most of the outstanding scholarship on James (up to 1960).

Edel, Leon, ed. *Henry James: A Collection of Critical Essays*. Englewood Cliffs, N.J.: Prentice-Hall, 1963. Contains eighteen essays, published elsewhere previously, a selected bibliography, and a list of important dates in James's life. Probably the most readily available collection of critical essays on the works of James.

———. *Henry James: A Life*. New York: Harper, 1985; London: Collins, 1987. Derived from Edel's monumental five-volume biography, published between 1953 and 1972, but updated and revised. This is the definitive work. Edel's additions to this one-volume version are particularly helpful on the subject of James's sexuality and its relationship to his writings. Based on unpublished correspondence, diaries, and other resources. This noted biography provides a comprehensive treatment of every aspect of James's life and career.

Edel, Leon, and Dan H. Laurence. *A Bibliography of Henry James*. 3d ed. Oxford and New York: Clarendon Press, 1982. Includes sections on "Original Works," "Contributions to Books, including prefaces, introductions, translations, unauthorized and fugitive writings," "Published Letters," "Contributions to Periodicals," "Translations," and "Miscellanea."

Edgar, Pelham. *Henry James: Man and Author*. London: Richards, and Boston: Houghton Mifflin, 1927. Provides both a biographical overview and a critical analysis of James's major fiction and nonfiction. Treats matters such as James's craftsmanship, early style, use of dialogue. Extended discussions of *The Spoils of Poynton* (1897), "The Figure in the Carpet," and *What Maisie Knew*. Concludes that by the age of thirty, James had formed the final impressions of America influential in his later writings.

Matthiessen, F. O. *The James Family: Including Selections from the Writing of Henry James, Senior, William, Henry and Alice James*. New York: Knopf, 1948. An interesting view of Henry James's relationship with other members of his famous family, especially his brother William, the well-known philosopher and psychologist. This book is largely a collection of quotations. Contains short biographical introductions about the four James family members included. A postscript compares Henry and William.

Perry, Ralph Barton. *The Thought and Character of William James*. 2 vols. Boston: Little Brown, and London: Oxford University Press, 1935. Especially useful on relationship of Henry James to his brother William. Deals with their education, upbringing, and correspondence. Contains many quotations from Henry James's letters and autobiographical writings. Attention is devoted to James's European experience and his impressions of the United States.

Putt, Samuel G. *Henry James: A Reader's Guide.* Ithaca, N.Y.: Cornell University Press, and London: Thames and Hudson, 1966. Introduction by Arthur Mizener. Contains fifteen chapters systematically commenting on most of James's major and minor works, attempting to make them more accessible to the general reader. Although the introduction claims that this book is aimed at beginning readers, it is really more helpful to the slightly advanced student of James's works. Covers all twenty-two novels Stevens, Hugh. *Henry James and Sexuality.* Cambridge and New York: Cambridge University Press, 1998. Stevens offers new and original interpretations of Henry James' fiction and contends that it includes radical (for his time) sexual representations of incestuous desires, homosexual passions and masochistic fantasies.

Stevens, Hugh. *Henry James and Sexuality.* Cambridge and New York: Cambridge University Press, 1998. Stevens offers new and original interpretations of Henry James's fiction and contends that it includes radical (for his time) sexual representations of incestuous desires, homosexual passions, and masochistic fantasies.

Wagenknecht, Edward. *Eve and Henry James: Portraits of Women and Girls in His Fiction.* Norman: University of Oklahoma Press, 1978. A study of many, but not all, of James's female characters which discusses many sides of their personalities. Wagenknecht organizes his commentary by employing certain types, such as women as victors, women as losers, women as victims, women as femmes fatales, and certain qualities such as destiny, modernity, innocence, love, and honor.

Walker, Pierre A., ed. *Henry James on Culture: Collected Essays on Politics and the American Social Scene.* Lincoln: University of Nebraska Press, 1999. A collection of eighteen articles by James, which comprise some of the best in World War I literature. The pieces cover political and social issues of the era. Eight of the articles have never been published before in book form, and several others have been difficult to obtain or unavailable.

Thomas J. Elliott

WILLIAM JAMES

Born: January 11, 1842; New York, New York

Died: August 26, 1910; Chocorua, New Hampshire

Areas of Achievement: Psychology, religion, and philosophy

Contribution: Seeking to reconcile a deep commitment to scientific thought with man's emotional nature and longing for some kind of religious faith, James helped create and popularize the modern science of psychology and the uniquely American approach to philosophy called pragmatism.

Early Life

William James was born on January 11, 1842, the eldest son of Henry and Mary (Walsh) James. His parents, who were of Scotch and Scotch-Irish ancestry, had four other children and provided one of the most remarkable home environments on record. There is little doubt that his childhood as part of this unusual family was instrumental in creating William James, the psychologist and philosopher, just as it helped mold his bother Henry, the equally famous American novelist.

Henry James, Sr., was a restless, perhaps even tortured intellectual with a religious bent, able to pursue his own private quest for truth because of a small inheritance. His family naturally became part of his search, and conversation around the James's dining table was more like a philosophical seminar than typical family chatter. The children were encouraged to think and to question and even defend their ideas under the watchful eyes of their parents. Education was considered too important to be left to chance. Henry, Sr., moved his family from the United States to Europe and back again several times, enrolling his children in numerous schools in an attempt to find the perfect atmosphere for learning. This varied and unsettled experience gave both William and his brother Henry an excellent command of languages and the basics of a liberal education without providing in-depth knowledge in any particular area. The gypsylike introduction to the academic world and family debates did provide, however, a healthy respect for diversity and a tolerance for other opinions, including sometimes very strange ones, that marked William James throughout his life.

As a youth, James was of slight to medium build with blue eyes and a less-than-robust constitution. Gradually, the determination to overcome his ten-

dency toward physical and emotional illness became an important undercurrent in his celebrated attitude toward life. If by the force of will a sickly, neurotic youth could transform himself into a dynamic professor with an iron-gray beard, who seemed to his students perpetually engaged in productive thought, then others were also free to make such transformations. His mature outlook was open and optimistic, and his personality, dominated by humor and tolerance, made him almost impossible to dislike. His students treated him with near worship, and his many friends and acquaintances in the intellectual community of the world, even when they disagreed violently with his ideas, loved the man himself. Yet the surface of this congenial thinker hid a storm raging beneath.

Life as part of the James family had been challenging, but it had not produced happiness. As a young man, William James continually struggled with bouts of emotional illness that at times necessitated an almost total retreat from the active world. At the center of the problem was the inability to reconcile his growing commitment to the rationalistic, scientific outlook of his age with the deep religious faith of his father. The elder James, who had rejected established religion as a young man, had been introduced to the ideas of Emanuel Swedenborg when William was two years old. Though Henry James, Sr., was never able to become a strict follower of the Swedish theologian, he constructed his own system of belief that became a necessary spiritual consolation. His son could never accept his father's simplistic faith, yet he always respected it and sometimes seemed to long for the certainty it provided. He later paid homage to his father's ideas when he published some of the elder James's letters in *The Literary Remains of Henry James* (1885).

The inability to please his father even haunted James's choice of vocation. When William was eighteen, the family had moved to Newport, Rhode Island, where he could study art with William M. Hunt. His father had not been happy with this choice, but he was even less happy when his eldest son abandoned art a year later and entered the Lawrence Scientific School at Harvard University. This decision, however, was a significant turning point. Not only did it begin a lifelong connection between William James and Harvard but it also began the gradual development of his personality be-

yond the influence of his family. The process would be difficult and never complete, but it was well on its way when the young man gravitated almost naturally toward medical school at Harvard. His studies were interrupted for a year in order to accompany the famous anthropologist Louis Agassiz on an expedition to the Amazon, but James still received his M.D. in June, 1869.

Too unstable emotionally to begin a medical practice, he remained in a state of semi-invalidism until he was appointed instructor in physiology at Harvard, in 1872. Characteristically, James believed that the conquest of his emotional problem was made possible by a philosophical conversion. While in Europe during a phase of his medical education, he had been introduced to the ideas of the French philosopher Charles Renouvier, whose stress on free will helped James reject the paralyzing fear of determinism. James's struggle for personal independence would reach a climax of sorts with his marriage to Alice H. Gibbens of Cambridge, Massachusetts. By all accounts, the union was a happy one and eventually produced five children. More important, however, the establishment of his own family at the advanced age of thirty-six coincided with the beginning of his productive career.

Life's Work

In the same year as his marriage, James agreed to a contract with Henry Holt and Company for the publication of a textbook on psychology. The agreement was, in part, recognition of his growing influence in an area of study that was undergoing transformation from a kind of mental philosophy into a laboratory science. During his European travels James had been influenced by the experimental approach to psychology current in Germany, and he taught his first course in psychology in 1875. His approach was revolutionary. Rather than the vague, often theological, speculation that characterized psychology in American universities, James started with physiological psychology, stressing the relationship between body and mind, and insisted on a thoroughly empirical approach. He soon established one of the first laboratories dedicated to psychological research in the United States.

His proposed textbook on psychology took almost as long to mature as James himself had. Scheduled for publication in 1880, the book did not appear until 1890, as *The Principles of Psychology*. It was hardly a textbook; instead, James had produced a monumental two-volume study covering the entire field as it stood in 1890 and proposing numerous theories which would influence psychology for years to come. Yet the work was not the empirical tour de force that one might expect. In spite of his dedication to science, James never liked laboratory research, and his own contribution was more impressionistic and philosophical than scientific. Moreover, the enthusiastic reception of his work owed as much to literary eloquence as it did to sound research.

In fact, James had already tired of experimental psychology before *The Principles of Psychology* was ever published. Though he would continue to be influential in the field and engage in numerous scholarly debates, his primary interest had turned to philosophy. It was not as much a change of direction as it was a change of emphasis. Since youth, he had been interested in philosophical speculation, and he taught his first course in philosophy in 1879. Much of his psychological work had philosophical overtones, and he was appointed professor of philosophy at Harvard in 1885. He had also exhibited an unusual interest in psychic phenomena, infuriating many of his fellow psychologists with his tolerant attitude toward the claims of spiritualists, mediums, and such dubious ideas as telepathy. This tendency was not an indication that James actually accepted parapsychology without qualification. Instead, it was a continuation of his quest for a reconciliation between man's need for spiritual meaning and his commitment to rational inquiry. This problem became the core of his philosophical questioning for the last decade of the nineteenth century.

James had been thinking about the problem for most of his life and had published essays on the subject while writing *The Principles of Psychology*. He began to draw these ideas together with the publication of his collection of essays, *The Will to Believe and Other Essays in Popular Philosophy* (1897). He carried his ideas further when invited to give the Gifford Lectures on natural religion at the University of Edinburgh. Ill health prevented him from appearing until 1901-1902. These lectures, published under the title *The Varieties of Religious Experience* in 1902, are his most definitive attempt at reconciling his empirical scientific approach with religion and the spiritual world. While his conclusions would hardly please the most orthodox, they stand as a ringing defense of the "right" to believe beyond physical evidence and an important recognition of the limitations of science, which James believed had erected a new orthodoxy as limiting as the old.

The remainder of James's life would be dedicated to defining and explaining his approach to philosophy, which he generally called pragmatism. The term was borrowed from his friend and fellow student Charles S. Peirce. Though Peirce clearly meant something different from James with the concept, it was James who popularized the term and made it part of American philosophical tradition. Unfortunately or perhaps fortunately, depending on one's perspective, most of James's writing was directed toward a popular rather than a philosophical audience. As a result, many of the principles of pragmatism actually depend upon which pragmatist is responsible for the explanation. This vagueness, however, is probably inherent in the doctrine and is, at least partially, responsible for its widespread acceptance.

James's final philosophical position had been evolving throughout his life and rested on a concept of the human mind which he had explained in his famous *The Principles of Psychology*. In this sense, James always remained a psychologist, but he carried his psychological perspective into the world of metaphysics. Very early in his intellectual development, James had committed himself to what he called "radical empiricism," which was firmly in the tradition of David Hume and John Stuart Mill and against the dominant rationalism implicit in the most influential philosophical school of his era, German idealism. Idealism, James believed, led to a concept of the "absolute" which resulted in a deterministic universe, something which he could not accept. Yet materialism, the chief opponent of idealism, also leads to a deterministic universe. James sought the middle ground which, above all, would be useful to mankind.

Usefulness is perhaps the key to understanding James's version of pragmatism. The meaning of an idea can only be judged by the particular consequences which result from it. If an idea has no real consequences, then it is meaningless. When placed in the context of James's radical empiricism, which accepts reality as that which is experienced, this doctrine means that human motives play a key role in human beliefs. Such an approach would have its most radical impact on the philosophical conception of truth. To James, this hallowed term should not apply to some mysterious ontological reality. Instead, it should refer only to one's beliefs about the world. To be true an idea must refer to some particular thing and have "cash value," that is, satisfy the human purpose for which it was intended. It is important to remember that for James and most pragmatists, this does not mean simply practicality or what might be called pure subjectivism. Rather, truth should be tied to rigid empirical criteria and motivations designed to maximize human values.

James spent the balance of his life defending his ideas in numerous essays and lectures, most of which have been published in various collections. In his last years, he became the best-known philosopher in the English-speaking world, and his ideas were seen as America's answer to the sterile speculations of continental rationalism. To answer those who criticized his tendency toward popularization, James hoped to bring his theories together in a complete metaphysical argument. Unfortunately, the project was never completed. His less-than-robust health failed him, and he died at his country home in New Hampshire, on August 26, 1910.

Summary

Never the ivory-tower intellectual, James always tried to live his own philosophy. For him, philosophy could never be separated from the real needs of human beings, and the answers he sought, even in the rarefied atmosphere of metaphysics, must have use beyond the lecture halls of universities. This explains his own tendency to simplify his ideas which, while leading to philosophical sloppiness, made them available to men without the training or the inclination for abstract thinking. It also explains his commitment to contemporary causes, such as his opposition to imperialism during William McKinley's administration, his general opposition to war, and his defense of unpopular ideas such as faith healing. James was always concerned first and foremost with the real fate of human beings.

His philosophy would become one of the most important intellectual influences in American life, particularly in the twentieth century. Like his famous personality which made him so popular with friends and students, his ideas were essentially optimistic and positive. To him, the universe was pluralistic and capable of being understood. Man was not a passive victim of the cosmos but an active agent, whose role was essentially creative. While man might not be able to change the dictates of nature, he could change the conditions of his own environment.

Bibliography

Allen, Gay Wilson. *William James*. New York: Viking Press, 1967. A full-length biographical study based on the James family papers. The author argues that James's life should be understood as an attempt to overcome emotional problems based on his self-acknowledged neuroses. Provides an excellent account of James's early life.

Bjork, Daniel J. *The Compromised Scientist: William James and the Development of American Psychology*. New York: Columbia University Press, 1983. Concentrates on James as a founder of American psychology. The author is particularly interested in James's clashes with contemporary American psychologists and the development of the discipline as a field of professional inquiry.

Conkin, Paul K. *Puritans and Pragmatists: Eight Eminent American Thinkers*. New York: Dodd, Mead, 1968. One of the finest examples of American intellectual history. Places James within the context of the development of American thought from Jonathan Edwards to George Santayana.

Feinstein, Howard M. *Becoming William James*. Ithaca, N.Y.: Cornell University Press, 1984. A biographical treatment of James which concentrates on the first three decades of his life. The author focuses on the psychological influence of James's family and has a particularly interesting analysis of James as a frustrated artist.

Gale, Richard M. *The Divided Self of William James*. Cambridge and New York: Cambridge University Press, 1999. Gale's book has been described by critics as "a powerful new interpretation of the philosophy of William James." Offers insight for those interested in the histories of religion, ideas, and pragmatism.

Perry, Ralph Barton. *The Thought and Character of William James*. 2 vols. London: Oxford University Press, and Boston: Little Brown, 1935. A collection of the letters and writings of William James, with biographical commentary.

Putnam, Ruth A., ed. *The Cambridge Companion to William James*. Cambridge and New York; Cambridge University Press, 1997. A collection of essays presenting new interpretations of James. Topics include his pragmatic theory of truth, speculation on religious questions, and the moral and political controversies of his time.

Roth, J. K. *Freedom and the Moral Life*. Philadelphia: Westminster Press, 1969. Concentrates on the relationship of James's concept of pragmatism to ethics. The author is particularly interested in stressing the continued value of James's idea of moral behavior.

Wild, John D. *The Radical Empiricism of William James*. New York: Doubleday, 1969. Places James within the continuing empiricist tradition. Contains excellent though technical discussion of the relationship of pragmatism and phenomenology.

Wilshire, Bruce. *William James and Phenomenology*. Bloomington: Indiana University Press, 1968. Concentrates on phenomenological aspects of James's ideas. While the book is not for the philosophical novice, it provides an important insight into the relationship of philosophical theories in the twentieth century.

David Warren Bowen

JEAN JAURÈS

Born: September 3, 1859; Castres, France

Died: July 31, 1914; Paris, France

Areas of Achievement: Government and politics

Contribution: Through the use of his powerful oratorical skills and his philosophical studies, Jaurès became the founding father of French socialism and a leading international advocate for peace prior to World War I.

Early Life

On September 3, 1859, Auguste-Marie-Joseph-Jean Jaurès was born the first son of Jean-Henri Jules and his wife Marie-Adélaïde Barbaza, a family of traders and rural smallholders in Castres, France. Because of his family's lower-middle-class standing, Jaurès was not held to the strict rules of behavior set by the wealthier middle class. Instead, he was free to form his own opinions and could intermingle with the laboring classes of the region, which had been a largely agricultural area but was slowly developing some industry.

Jaurès first attended school at the pension Séjal, a small private establishment run by a priest. He enthusiastically participated in school and, in 1869, was admitted to the Collège de Castres with a scholarship. During his seven years at the school, Jaurès impressed many of his fellow students and teachers. In 1875, his impressive intellect was noticed by Inspector-General of Schools Nicolas-Félix Deltour, who was seeking to recruit young men to help boost the educational system in France. Through Deltour's assistance, Jaurès began his Parisian education at Sainte-Barbe in 1876 in preparation for his move in 1878 to the École Normale Supérieure, one of the most demanding and prestigious schools in the nation.

Jaurès' obvious love of learning allowed him to flourish at the École Normale Supérieure. He chose philosophy as his field of study, although he was attracted to both languages and history as well. In 1881, he participated in the aggregation, a series of oral and written examinations to determine who would receive the best teaching posts in France. He placed third and requested a post in philosophy at the Lycée d'Albi in order to be near his parents. When his father died in 1882 and his mother came to live with him, Jaurès decided to move to Toulouse, where he was offered a position in the Faculty of Letters at the University of Toulouse in 1883.

Because of his outstanding oratorical skill and his passion for republican politics, Jaurès was placed on the republican list for his region in the 1885 elections. He was the youngest deputy in the 1885-1889 parliament and soon became disillusioned with republicanism. His true political education began after his defeat in the elections of 1889 when he returned to the University of Toulouse and threw himself into studying various political ideas, particularly the socialist theories of Louis Blanc, Pierre-Joseph Proudhon, Ferdinand Lassalle, and Karl Marx. Gradually, he began to initiate closer contact with the urban working classes and to develop a fledgling socialist commitment.

Life's Work

For Jaurès, the Carmaux mining strike of 1892 was a critical turning point. He saw the struggle between the miners and their employers as an issue of human dignity, an attempt by the workers to free themselves. He championed their cause and was elected deputy for Carmaux in an 1892 bielection and then in the 1893 general election. Throughout the 1890's his oratorical skills and his socialist theories pushed him to the forefront of the socialist faction of parliament. He spoke on a variety of topics in the Chamber of Deputies, ranging from education to military affairs.

Although busy as a deputy and leader of the socialists, Jaurès continued to participate regularly in labor disputes and came to understand some of the strengths of working-class culture as well as the weakness of working-class collective organization. He firmly believed in the power of socialist politics rather than a dependency on the sudden strikes and calls to the barricades advocated by the syndicalist faction of the socialist movement. During the Fourth Congress of the Second International meeting in London in 1896, Jaurès attempted to unify the various factions by denying that anarchism constituted part of socialism (thus singling out an extremely divisive element of the Congress) and by supporting syndicalism as an important part of socialism. However, he continued to make it clear that working through standard government politics was the preferred and more effective path. Despite his eloquent speeches, he failed to make the distinction between anarchism and syndicalism apparent to all.

By 1897 Jaurès had become involved in the Dreyfus affair, in which a Jewish army officer was falsely accused of selling military secrets. Jaurès was consumed with a desire to see justice prevail. He believed that the future of the republic lay in how socialists reacted. For Jaurès, socialists had to defend the republic and fight for justice in this matter. Because the bourgeois parties were failing to uphold the banner of republican government, he concluded that the socialists must take it. Jaurès proceeded to rail against the government's actions in the Dreyfus case. His outspoken moves would serve to work against him in the coming year.

When Jaurès arrived back in his home region in the spring of 1898 to campaign for reelection, he found that his opponents had already begun campaigning against him. They denounced him as an enemy of religion and an agent of the Jews. The employers of Carmaux were determined to see Jaurès defeated at all costs. They broke up socialist meetings and prevented Jaurès from forming an audience for his speeches. When the May votes came in, Jaurès found himself defeated. Instead of turning away from the issues that had caused his defeat, he continued to involve himself in the Dreyfus affair. He also began editing the Paris daily *La Petite République* (the small republic) and writing the *Histoire socialiste de la Révolution française* (1901-1907; socialist history of the French Revolution).

During his time away from the Chamber of Deputies, Jaurès devoted himself to supporting a reformist socialist approach to government. He backed the entry of Alexandre Millerand, a socialist lawyer, into the bourgeois government of René Waldeck-Rousseau in 1899 despite opposition from many leading socialists, such as Jules Guesde and Édouard Vaillant, who felt that he was compromising too many socialist ideas in the process. Despite this opposition, Jaurès continued to defend his position, believing that it was necessary for the socialists to defend and consolidate the republic. Breaking with Guesde and Vaillant in 1902, he formed the Parti Socialiste Français and joined with the radicals to form a leftist bloc that won a victory in the 1902 elections. Among the victorious electors, Jaurès was appointed one of the vice presidents of the Chamber of Deputies.

By 1904 Jaurès' leftist bloc had begun to disintegrate from attacks both within and without. Simultaneously, his Parti Socialiste Français was also dying. Realizing that his compromises with the bourgeois parties had diluted his message, Jaurès began calling for socialist unity. He repaired his relationships with Guesde and especially Vaillant. He abandoned his reformist notions in favor of a more traditional socialist line, embracing the class nature of the socialist struggle as well as its revolutionary character. In April, 1905, under Jaurès' leadership, a pact of union was signed, and the Section Française de L'Internationale Ouvrière (SFIO), a new unified socialist party, was formed.

Jaurès emerged as the undisputed leader of the new party. He formulated policy on almost every subject but was particularly concerned with a desire for closer unity between the syndicalist socialists and the SFIO. He showed a great ability for political flexibility regarding the syndicalists and even developed a complex theory of the working class. Jaurès also made military reform a priority. In his work *L'Armée Nouvelle* (1911; *Democracy and Military Service*, 1972), he stated that socialists should not work to undermine the military. Instead, the military should be adjusted to the pattern of the French revolutionary armies of 1792-1795, which would bring back the national spirit of 1792 and promote social cohesion. This program ultimately proved unpopular.

Aside from his political and military reform interests, Jaurès was also concerned with the growing militarism of Europe in the years prior to World War I. He called for a political reconciliation between France and Germany and declared arbitration as the best method to resolve disputes. He made several trips to places such as Basel, Switzerland (1912), and Brussels, Belgium (1914), to make speeches in favor of peace. Many began to feel that he was the final barrier against the growing war fever of European governments. However, Jaurès' stance against war brought his downfall. On July 31, 1914, as Jaurès sat in a Paris café with a group of his colleagues with his back to a window, a right-wing fanatic named Raoul Villain, who thought Jaurès' pacifism would lead the nation astray, shot him twice. He died within minutes. His ashes were later moved to the Pantheon on November 23, 1924.

Summary

Without the powerful leadership and oratorical grace of Jean Jaurès, it is doubtful that the socialist movement would have been able to unify itself in the turmoil of the early twentieth century. Too many divisive issues worked against this outcome.

Jaurès was able to use his unique ability to compromise and speak to the hearts of the working classes to help bring about the necessary cohesion to achieve advances for the lower classes.

His humble beginnings at Castres allowed Jaurès to identify with the working classes, and the educational opportunities he was given permitted him to bring the issues of the working classes to the government. By immersing himself in the works of great philosophers, he was able to conceive his own vision for how the Socialist Party should be constructed and run. His was a flexible policy. It was his strong personality that held the party to a middle course between the paths of reformists and revolutionaries. As Daniel Halévy stated in 1905, "What, then, was this party? I will define it in a word: it was Jaurès. It was his reflection. He created it. He kept it together."

Bibliography

Goldberg, Harvey. *The Life of Jean Jaurès*. Madison: University of Wisconsin Press, 1962. The definitive biography of Jaurès. Traces the development of Jaurès' political ideas and his rise to the head of the French socialist movement. Includes a detailed bibliography and some photographs.

Jaurès, Jean. *Democracy and Military Service*. London: Simpkin Marshall, 1916; New York: Garland, 1972. An English translation of Jaurès' *L'Armée Nouvelle*, which details his ideas for the military and the importance of capturing a democratic spirit for the nation.

Pease, Margaret. *Jean Jaurès: Socialist and Humanitarian*. London: Headley, 1916; New York: Huebsch, 1917. Written shortly after Jaurès' death, this book includes an excellent introduction by former British Prime Minister James Ramsay MacDonald. A fairly succinct biography of Jaurès but somewhat weakened by its lack of a bibliography.

Rebérioux, Madeleine. "Party Practice and the Jaurèsian Vision: The SFIO (1905-1914)." In *Socialism in France: From Jaurès to Mitterand*, edited by Stuart Williams. London: Frances Pinter, and New York: St. Martin's Press, 1983. A short essay on the particulars of Jaurès' vision for the united Socialist Party. Also includes ideas for how to approach the study of Socialist Party politics at the beginning of the twentieth century.

Tuchman, Barbara W. "The Death of Jaurès." In *The Proud Towser: A Portrait of the World before the War, 1890-1914*. London: Hamilton, and New York: Macmillan, 1966. An essay in a collection devoted to the study of the period prior to World War I. Follows Jaurès' ideas leading up to World War I as well as the impact of his assassination on world events. Includes some photographs.

Michael R. Nichols

Born: October 23, 1773; Edinburgh, Scotland
Died: January 26, 1850; Edinburgh, Scotland
Areas of Achievement: Journalism and law
Contribution: As founder and editor of the *Edinburgh Review*, Jeffrey created a forceful instrument for critical analysis and the shaping of popular opinion.

Early Life

Francis Jeffrey was born October 23, 1773, in St. George's Square, Edinburgh. He was the son of George Jeffrey. His mother, Henrietta Louden, was loving and gentle but died when Francis was thirteen. His father, a moody and pessimistic man, served as deputy clerk for the Court of Session.

Jeffrey's education, shaped by his father's high Tory views, was conservative. He found his real education, however, among the bleakly beautiful hills of Scotland and the books of an uncle's library. In 1791, he spent a year at Queen's College, Oxford, but was miserable and returned to Edinburgh to study law.

At twenty, Jeffrey was shy, slight of build, and romantic. He was barely five feet in height; his oval face was intensely expressive and his black eyes gleamed. It was a face, a friend noted, that reflected "honesty, intelligence and kindly fire." Like many sensitive young men maturing during the opening years of a revolutionary era, Jeffrey saw himself as a poet and dramatist. Nevertheless, economic reality dictated his career, and he was admitted to the Scottish bar in 1794.

Despite his father's Tory views and the strong patronage system of Scottish politics, Jeffrey had already made the great political transition. In 1793, in a youthful essay on politics, he adopted a lofty intellectual allegiance to the Whig Party, a loyalty that he never relinquished. He paid the price of conversion for nearly a decade. In Tory Scotland, legal fees and political opportunities were virtually nonexistent for young Whigs.

Jeffrey was married in 1801 and established his bride in a flat in Buccleuch Place. His wife, Catherine Wilson, was a cousin, and marriage gave the young Jeffrey a stable, happy home life. Around the young couple, a coterie of promising talent gathered. Edinburgh, long a center of learning, was filled with good conversation and conviviality. In 1802, a group of young men, including Sydney Smith and Henry Brougham, met at Buccleuch Place, and Smith proposed that they found a review. Jeffrey and the others had apparently discussed the idea for some time, but the expense of such a project was formidable. Nevertheless, their enthusiasm conquered their hesitation. Thus, almost casually, was born the *Edinburgh Review*, one of the foremost journals of the modern era.

Life's Work

The first issues of the *Edinburgh Review* were hastily put together in a dreary printing office off Craig's Close by a committee of friends, none of whom could have predicted its enormous popularity. Almost immediately, however, the sales startled the young contributors. In an era when a few hundred copies counted as a good circulation, the *Edinburgh Review* achieved a circulation of twenty-five hundred within six months. Clearly, financial success would have to breed greater efficiency. Although the witty Sydney Smith had acted as self-appointed edi-

tor of the earliest issues, he had little organizational ability. Moreover, although he remained a popular and eloquent essayist, Smith lacked intellectual depth. Within a year of its establishment, Jeffrey was appointed the official editor of the review.

One of his first and most important decisions was to pay contributors. Not yet thirty, Jeffrey had struggled with near-poverty for years. He recognized that a successful journal was often doomed after an original success when bright young authors had to choose between art and earning a livelihood. His own meager law practice made his income of fifty pounds an issue particularly precious. Others in the circle, he knew, would drift away to the dazzle of London. Generous payment for articles would hold young talent and attract proven authors. It was a wise decision and would be widely copied by later publications.

More important, Jeffrey set out to make the *Edinburgh Review* interesting, provocative, and authoritative. Although journalism traced its roots back to the formidable diatribes and satire of Joseph Addison and Sir Richard Steele, it remained, like acting, a somewhat suspect profession. Jeffrey constantly worried about the possible harm to his reputation or legal career from his editorship. The challenge and the work proved, however, irresistible. Under his direction, the *Edinburgh Review* continued to present the strongest essays on important issues as well as the most critical reviews of books and art in Great Britain. As a result, its circulation continued to expand, and by 1814 it was being read by a phenomenal thirteen thousand people.

Much of the *Edinburgh Review*'s popularity resulted from Jeffrey's ability to persuade others to work with him creatively. Although the original articles proudly proclaimed devotion to Whig, or liberal, principles, Jeffrey steered a moderate course politically. As a result, the early years of publication attracted writers of the stature and popularity of Sir Walter Scott. Scott, a staunch Tory, not only wrote several articles but also encouraged friends such as Robert Southey to consider the review. Nevertheless, the times were chaotic and dangerous and journalistic partisanship all too common. Increasingly, the *Edinburgh Review* reflected the Whig interpretations of events. Although kind and diffident with his family and friends, Jeffrey was a tiger when it came to his convictions.

In 1808, Jeffrey wrote, with minor assistance from Brougham, the famous Cevallos article. It was a scathing attack upon the Iberian campaign and British governmental policies in Spain. Scott was so incensed that he dropped his subscription and encouraged the founding of a rival publication, the *Quarterly Review.* Nevertheless, Jeffrey continued to express his opposition to the Napoleonic Wars and to the later war with the United States in 1812. Equally unpopular was his courageous support for Catholic emancipation.

The tone of the review after the Cevallos article became more openly liberal, and Jeffrey took pride in the quality of the discussion and the spread of liberal philosophy. In 1832, when the Reform Bill passed, he believed strongly that the *Edinburgh Review* for three decades had prepared the public for the great change in politics.

Ironically, it was not Jeffrey's politically controversial opinions that endangered his life, but rather his equally passionate views of poetry. Jeffrey, although an outstanding editor, was not always a good judge of poetic quality. A product of the Scottish Enlightenment in training, he disliked intensely the early outpourings of the "Lake Poets." In the fifteenth issue of the review, he attacked Thomas Moore's *Epistles, Odes, and Other Poems* (1806). Jeffrey considered them immoral and depraved. An indignant Moore challenged Jeffrey to a duel in 1806.

In the end, the meeting of editor and poet proved more ludicrous than dangerous. Moore had hastily borrowed pistols from a friend who in turn had reported the affair to the famous Bow Street Runners. As the two men tried to "do or die" on the field of honor, the police intervened and hauled both of them off to court. When the diminutive Jeffrey and the lanky Moore were questioned, it turned out that Jeffrey had intentionally not even loaded his pistol. He was willing to die for his views but not kill for them. Lord Byron later erroneously imputed the unloaded pistol to Moore.

As a result of their tumultuous introduction and their ignominious visit to the police, the two men wound up close friends. Moore later published articles in the *Edinburgh Review* and in 1825 visited Jeffrey in Scotland.

While touched by the amusing and the occasionally absurd, Jeffrey's personal life had taken a tragic turn. Within a month in 1805, he lost his young wife and his favorite sister. His only child had died two years earlier. In late 1810, a French refugee family, related to the controversial parliamentarian John Wilkes, visited Jeffrey. On their voyage to the United States, they were accompanied by their niece Charlotte Wilkes. Jeffrey fell deeply in love but realized the depth of his feelings belatedly. By that time, Miss Wilkes had arrived in the United States. Despite the fact that he was thirty-seven years old and prone to seasickness, and despite the fact that the War of 1812 had begun, Jeffrey resolved, like a Scottish Lochinvar, to find Wilkes. Calling on friends to take over the review for the interim, Jeffrey set sail for New York. His daring won Wilkes's hand.

After their marriage in 1813, Jeffrey traveled in the United States and met with President James Madison and Secretary of State James Monroe. Even before the outbreak of the War of 1812, he had been highly critical of British foreign policy in North America, but he was conscientious in explaining British sentiments and official policies to Madison and Monroe. His genuine concern for the young nation expressed frequently in subsequent review articles did much to dissipate British ire following the war. In addition to his editorial work, Jeffrey carried on a growing legal practice. He developed a rapport with Edinburgh juries that, combined with a passion for detail, real charm, and kindness, won his clients' acquittal. By 1820, he was considered one of Scotland's finest criminal attorneys. In 1830, Whig victories enabled the party to recognize his years of service with an appointment as lord advocate.

Jeffrey's new position required him to enter Parliament in the rough-and-tumble elections of 1830-1832. Jeffrey was fifty-seven and in poor health. He soon found the seemingly endless committee meetings and innumerable details of the reform bills to be exhausting. In 1834, he retired from Parliament to accept a judgeship in the Court of Sessions, becoming, on June 7, 1834, Lord Jeffrey.

Gradually, his legal and political life diverted Jeffrey from the *Edinburgh Review*. In 1829, he resigned from the journal. MacVey Napier succeeded him as editor. Although he occasionally contributed articles to the review after his return from Parliament, his judicial work took up much of his time. In addition, his home near Edinburgh, Craigcrook, and its gardens became an absorbing interest. In his old age, he served as a mentor to younger authors such as Charles Dickens, whose novels he loved, and as a stylistic consultant to fellow Whigs such as Thomas Babington Macaulay, whose early volumes he proofread. He died on January 26, 1850, and was buried in the Dean cemetery near Edinburgh.

Summary

Lord Jeffrey's contributions as editor to the *Edinburgh Review* made him a unique force in early nineteenth century journalism. The review soon captured a popular readership by the courage of its espousal of often unpopular causes, its dissent from conventional wisdom, and its sophisticated, readable style.

Everything that went into the early review was crafted and polished by Jeffrey, sometimes to the anger or dismay of the contributor. His legal logic, vivid style, and intellect made him a great and feared critic, yet he was quick to see both sides of an issue, generous to political foes, and swift to detect and encourage talent. Although the *Edinburgh Review* under Jeffrey soon faced competition from journals as renowned as the *Quarterly Review* and *Blackwood's*, its influence was unrivaled in the early decades of the century. Jeffrey's passionate devotion to Liberal politics, combined with his love of literature, caused an unusual tension in analytical criticism. It created an entirely new tone in periodical literature, combining philosophical, political, and literary topics not only to entertain but also to educate a readership. Jeffrey had created in large measure a revolution in the scope and purpose of journalistic literature.

Bibliography

Carlyle, Thomas. *Reminiscences*. Edited by James Anthony Froude. 2 vols. London: Longman, and New York: Harper, 1881. Contains an excellent and penetrating sketch of Jeffrey, who admired Thomas and Jane Carlyle intensely. Carlyle gives a fine description of Jeffrey's appearance, character, and legal prowess in criminal cases.

Cockburn, Henry Thomas, Lord. *Life and Correspondence of Lord Jeffrey*. 2 vols. London: Longman, 1852; as *Life of Lord Jeffrey: With a Selection from His Correspondence*. Philadelphia: Lippincott, 1852. This voluminous work, written shortly after Jeffrey's death, is dated but still essential to any study of his career. The letters give a sense of Jeffrey's critical acumen.

Houghton, Walter Edwards, ed. *The Wellesley Index to Victorian Periodicals, 1824-1900*. Toronto: University of Toronto Press, 1966; London: Routeledge, 1987. An invaluable work on nineteenth century journals. It deals with the early years of the *Edinburgh Review* (1802-1823) in the context of the entire publication.

Jeffrey, Francis Jeffrey, Lord. *Contributions to the Edinburgh Review*. 4 vols. London: Longman, 1844; Philadelphia: Carey and Hart, 1846. A selection of essays that indicates the quality and scope of Jeffrey's work. It includes his famous essay on beauty which appeared in the *Encyclopædia Britannica*.

Reid, Stuart J. *The Life and Times of Sydney Smith*. London: Sampson Low, Marston, 1884; New York: Harper, 1885. Contains a discussion of the founding of the *Edinburgh Review* and the friendship between Smith and Jeffrey, as well as some useful correspondence.

E. Deanne Malpass

SARAH ORNE JEWETT

Born: September 3, 1849; South Berwick, Maine
Died: June 24, 1909; South Berwick, Maine
Area of Achievement: Literature
Contribution: Author of twenty books, Jewett was the most accomplished of the American writers associated with literary regionalism and a major force in the creation and development of an American women's literary tradition.

Early Life

The second of three sisters, Theodora Sarah Orne Jewett was born into an established and wealthy family in South Berwick, Maine, on September 3, 1849. Her grandfather, Captain Theodore Furber Jewett, had prospered in the West Indies trade in the early part of the century, leaving the family financially independent.

Although Sarah received her formal education at Miss Raynes's School and at Berwick Academy in South Berwick, much of her true education came from her father, a country doctor. She was her father's frequent companion on his house calls, especially when bouts of ill health kept her out of school. As they moved from house to house, he shared with her his close observations of the surrounding landscape as well as his thoughts on life and literature. Later, Sarah, by now an accomplished writer, would credit her father with pointing out to her that really great writers do not write *about* people and things, but describe them just as they are.

Young Sarah read widely in her parents' substantial library, and when, at the age of seventeen, she read Harriet Beecher Stowe's *The Pearl of Orr's Island* (1862), she found in Stowe's portrayal of scenes from Maine life a hint of the possibilities of the regionalist fiction in which Sarah herself would excel.

Sarah's first published story, "Jenny Garrow's Ghost," appeared in *The Flag of Our Union*, a Boston weekly, on January 18, 1868. The nineteen-year-old author, unwilling at this point that others should know of her literary activities, used the pen name "Alice Eliot." In December of the following year, after two polite rejections, the prestigious *Atlantic Monthly* published her story "Mr. Bruce," confirming Sarah's conviction that she was at least an apprentice writer.

She continued to write for the *Atlantic* and other publications. Finally, William Dean Howells, the novelist and editor, suggested to Sarah that she organize some of her sketches and short stories into a book. Sarah found this work painfully difficult, but the result, *Deephaven* (1877), marked her arrival at maturity as a writer.

Life's Work

The death of her father in 1878 was a difficult blow for Sarah Orne Jewett. Until his death, her relationship with him had been the most important of her life. Her closest adult emotional relationships were her friendships with women. The most important of these was with Annie Fields, whom Sarah met in the 1870's, when Annie was married to the publisher James T. Fields, Annie's senior by some seventeen years. After Fields's death in 1881, Sarah and Annie's friendship flowered into a "Boston marriage." The term denotes a virtually spousal—although not necessarily, or even usually, sexual—relationship between two women. Sarah and Annie lived together for part of each year, they traveled together, and, when physically separated, kept in touch by letter. To their friends, it became natural to think of them as a couple.

In the years following *Deephaven*, Sarah continued to develop as a writer. She enjoyed her greatest success in the sketches and short stories set in her native Maine. That her life as an adult involved long periods of residence in Boston and of foreign travel seemed to strengthen her imaginative possession of the Maine setting. Her own experience justified the advice she later gave the younger novelist Willa Cather, that to know the parish one must first know the world.

She was mastering a form that was very much her own: a short narrative devoid of plot in terms of dramatic event and linear structure. The form allows for patient observation of the gradual unfolding of human relationships and the interrelationship of the human and the natural in places Sarah had known since childhood. Many of her stories have a conversational quality: a speaker, usually a woman, moves, by what seems superficially like random association, toward a clarification of emotional, spiritual, or moral truth that is the heart of the story.

She had less success with the more conventional sort of novel. Most readers find *The Country Doctor* (1884) her most interesting work in the novel form because of its content, the relationship of Nan Prince and Doctor Leslie, with its intriguing autobiographical resonance, and Nan's determination to enter the medical profession, which was regarded by her contemporaries as a male preserve. Yet the novel achieves only limited dramatic power.

Still, Sarah continued to develop as a literary artist. Her progress was dramatically displayed in the collection *A White Heron and Other Stories*, published in 1886. The title story of the collection, perhaps Jewett's most famous short story, exemplifies its author's respect for the reader's share in the literary experience. She credited her father for pointing out to her the importance in fiction of leaving readers some work to do, rather than bullying them into a passive acceptance of predigested motives and meanings. In this story, indirection in presenting the moment of decision involves the reader centrally in the process of making meaning. This is an art based on process rather than product, on cooperation rather than conquest. Some readers have suggested that it is very much a woman's sort of art, although appreciation of this art is by no means denied to men. In this case, any attentive reader must admire the delicacy and force (the two easily coexist in Jewett's work) with which the author brings into play within the reader's active mind many of the themes central to her fiction. She includes meditations on innocence and experience, on continuity and change, on the city and the country, on nature and culture, on masculine and feminine, on the imagination's power to soar, and on the reaching of the mind toward an androgyny of the spirit that may obviate the need for the sexual union of man and woman. This is much to build on a moment in the life of a nine-year-old girl, but Jewett (who, in a letter written when she was forty-eight, stated that she always felt nine years old) makes it all work.

The collections of stories and sketches published in the decade following *A White Heron and Other Stories* contain much of Jewett's best work in these forms. By now a fully mature artist, she published in 1896 *The Country of the Pointed Firs*, generally regarded as her masterpiece and the finest work of literary regionalism produced by any American writer. Like *Deephaven*, the new book consisted of a sequence of related short narratives unified by setting, characters, and, most powerfully, by the development of the narrator's involvement in the fictional community of Dunnet Landing. An im-

portant part of this development is the narrator's relationship with Almira Todd, a native of Dunnet Landing and one of Jewett's greatest triumphs of characterization. Structurally similar to *Deephaven*, *The Country of the Pointed Firs* is, because of its formal control and thematic depth, a much richer work. Writing in 1925, Willa Cather suggested that the work stands with Hawthorne's *The Scarlet Letter* (1850) and Mark Twain's *The Adventures of Huckleberry Finn* (1884) as one of the three American literary works of its century likely to achieve immortality.

Jewett would publish only two more books in her lifetime, *The Queen's Twin and Other Stories* in 1899 and *The Tory Lover*, an attempt at a historical novel, in 1901. In 1901, she was awarded an honorary degree by Maine's Bowdoin College, an all-male institution. She was delighted, she said, to be the only sister of so many brothers. Then, in September, 1902, she suffered a severe spinal injury from which she would never fully recover. Writing fiction became increasingly difficult and, finally, impossible. On June 24, 1909, she died in the Jewett family home in South Berwick, Maine.

Summary

Sarah Orne Jewett was inspired by Plato's maxim that the noblest service that can be done for the people of a state is to acquaint them with one another. The regionalist's literary vocation is precisely to acquaint the people of the larger society—ultimately, perhaps, of the world—with the life of a single region, often one remote from any cosmopolitan center. This vocation was realized by Sarah Orne Jewett more fully than by any other American writer. The stature of *The Country of the Pointed Firs* has been recognized since its first publication. Although there is always the danger that this book will dominate Jewett's posthumous reputation to the extent of reducing her to the status of the "one-book author," the last quarter of the twentieth century has seen a resurgence of interest in the totality of her work. This resurgence has in part been fueled by feminist concerns. That Jewett was a woman who wrote most powerfully about women and whose deepest emotional relationships were with women lends her an undeniable interest. Yet her audience has never been limited to women.

Jewett enjoyed considerable critical recognition in her lifetime. Among the writers who came to be associated with the regionalist movement, she was quickly and widely recognized as preeminent, as was the value of her sort of realism, even if it was a qualified sort. Although she tended to keep the grimmest of realities at the margins of her fiction, she did not expel them completely. For some of her characters, life in the country of the pointed firs follows a pattern of frustration and despair. Certainly, Jewett leaves her readers in little doubt that economic decline is the fundamental condition within which her characters live out their lives.

Jewett was an inspiration to such younger writers as Kate Chopin and Willa Cather, the latter of whom dedicated to Jewett the novel *O Pioneers!* (1913) and in 1925 edited and introduced a collection of Jewett's best fiction. Although Edith Wharton claimed to reject Sarah Orne Jewett's influence, many critics who are familiar with both writers find that the truth of the matter is more complicated.

Her stories continue to be published separately and in anthologies. Her work has been translated into German, Japanese, Spanish, and French. Critical interest in Sarah Orne Jewett's work has never been higher. Narrow though her range may have been, her work within that range reveals clarity, compassion, and the courage of an artist who de-veloped the forms that her imagination demanded. What Willa Cather said of *The Country of the Pointed Firs* may be said of its author: She confronts time and change securely.

Bibliography

Blanchard, Paula. *Sarah Orne Jewett: Her World and Her Work.* Reading, Mass.: Addison Wesley Longman, 1994. In this study of New England life at the turn of the century, the author examines Jewett's friendships with several women, providing insight into her fiction.

Cary, Richard, ed. *Appreciation of Sarah Orne Jewett: Twenty-nine Interpretive Essays.* Waterville, Maine: Colby College Press, 1973. This selection of criticism published prior to 1973 reflects the critical formalism dominant at the time of the book's publication. Supplemented by Nagel's collection.

———. *Sarah Orne Jewett.* New York: Twayne, 1962. This book, the earliest full critical review of Jewett's work, analyzes her materials, methods, and forms, examining each work in relation to the long maturation of her genius. The organization is, for the most part, topical rather than chronological, and the case for Jewett as more than a one-book author is made convincingly.

Donovan, Josephine. *Sarah Orne Jewett.* New York: Ungar, 1980. The author explores the themes of city versus country and isolation versus community in Jewett's mature fiction and finds in *The Country of the Pointed Firs* the consummation of her thematic and formal concerns.

Howard, June, ed. *New Essays on "The Country of the Pointed Firs."* Cambridge and New York: Cambridge University Press, 1994. A collection of essays on Jewett's *The Country of the Pointed Firs,* offering analysis of the influence of race, nationalism and literary market forces on the piece itself.

Mobley, Marilyn Sanders. *Folk Roots and Mythic Wings in Sarah Orne Jewett and Toni Morrison.* Baton Rouge: Louisiana State University Press, 1991. A critical study that asserts the importance of myth and folklore in the work of two women of different races and generations who draw on the cultural roots of their people.

Nagel, Gwen L. *Critical Essays on Sarah Orne Jewett.* Boston: Hall, 1984. A collection that supplements Cary's *Appreciation* and reflects later tendencies in Jewett criticism, including feminist perspectives.

Roman, Margaret. *Sarah Orne Jewett: Reconstructing Gender.* Tuscaloosa: University of Alabama Press, 1992. Argues that Jewett consciously collapses gender dichotomies, dissolving binary oppositions of gender.

Sherman, Sarah Way. *Sarah Orne Jewett: An American Persephone.* Hanover, N.H.: University Press of New England, 1989. Explores the growth of Jewett's art out of nineteenth century American culture and the terms in which that culture defined womanhood.

Silverthorne, Elizabeth. *Sarah Orne Jewett: A Writer's Life.* Woodstock, N.Y.: Overlook Press, 1993. This biography emphasizes the relationships between its subject's life and work and places her clearly within the literary and cultural life of her time.

W. P. Kenney

ANDREW JOHNSON

Born: December 29, 1808; Raleigh, North Carolina
Died: July 31, 1875; near Carter Station, Tennessee
Areas of Achievement: Government and politics
Contribution: Johnson was a Tennessee politician, a Civil War military governor of Tennessee, a vice president of the United States, and the seventeenth president of the United States, from 1865 to 1869. His lenient Reconstruction policies toward the South embittered members of Congress and postponed unification of the embattled republic.

Early Life

Andrew Johnson was the son of Jacob and Mary (McDonough) Johnson, illiterate tavern servants in Raleigh, North Carolina, where Andrew was born in 1808 and grew up in dire poverty. In 1822, Andrew was apprenticed to a tailor, where he learned a trade and the rudiments of reading. In 1826, Johnson moved to Tennessee, opened a tailor's shop, and, shortly after his nineteenth birthday, married seventeen-year-old Eliza McCardle. Under Eliza's tutelage, Johnson learned writing and arithmetic and practiced his reading. While never well educated, Johnson always strove for intellectual self-improvement.

Johnson was successful as a tailor but spent most of his spare time involved in debating societies and political discussions. In 1829, Johnson was elected alderman in Greeneville, Tennessee. Two years later, he was elected mayor of the town. He reached the state legislature in 1835, and the United States Congress in 1842.

Life's Work

By 1842, Johnson had permanently abandoned tailoring for the full-time pursuit of politics. He was extremely ambitious and anxious to rise to the top of the political heap.

From 1842 to 1852, Johnson served in Congress with a singularly undistinguished record. His congressional career, which would set a pattern for the remainder of his life, was marked by his inability to compromise, his unwillingness to work with anyone who opposed him, and his use of extremely vicious language against those who disagreed with him. Quick-tempered, ill-mannered, and notorious for his verbal assaults on his enemies, Johnson was popular with poor and nonslaveholding whites. Although not an imposing figure, the five-foot, eight-inch Johnson was physically strong and a vigorous campaigner, who scored points with the "plebeians," as he called them, by attacking the rich. He viewed each electoral success as something more than a personal triumph; for Johnson, a victory at the polls was a victory for the common man over those with education and wealth. Throughout his political career, Johnson made the most of his humble origins and his status as a tradesman, portraying himself as "the little man," the representative of "the people," against the rich. His class hatred was profound. One contemporary asserted, with some truth, that "if Andy Johnson were a snake, he would hide in the grass and bite the heels of rich men's children." His opponents correctly called him a demagogue, but he was a successful one.

After the Whigs gerrymandered him out of his congressional district, Johnson successfully ran for governor in 1853 and again in 1855. While his personality and style precluded an effective administration, Johnson was able to push through legislation creating the first public-school system in Tennessee. As governor, the man who grew up illiterate did not forget his roots, even though he had become well-to-do, having acquired a fine house, four slaves, and assets in land and bonds.

In 1852 and 1856, Johnson sought the Democratic nomination for vice president. In 1857, Johnson entered the United States Senate, where he accomplished little. He sought a Senate seat as part of his unquenchable thirst for success and political power. He saw the Senate as a way of thrusting him onto the national scene. In 1860, he was the favorite son of Tennessee at the Democratic National Convention, but he again failed to find a spot on the ticket and dutifully supported John C. Breckinridge.

During the secession winter of 1860-1861, Johnson worked for sectional compromise, even though he opposed compromises on principle. At this point, Johnson became a contradictory figure, and something of a heroic one. As a slaveholding Democrat, Johnson staunchly favored states' rights, disliked the Republicans, and was a vicious Negrophobe who especially hated free blacks. Yet Johnson also believed, almost religiously, in the Constitution. He considered secession illegal, unconstitutional, and treasonous. Thus, in February, 1861, he successfully rallied Unionists in Tennessee to oppose secession. Johnson continued to oppose secession in the spring, often speaking while armed, in response to death threats. After the firing on Fort Sumter, sentiment shifted, and in June, Tennessee left the Union.

Unlike every other Southerner in Congress, Andrew Johnson did not leave the Union. Johnson remained in the Senate, where he successfully sponsored a resolution asserting that the purpose of the war was to preserve the Union and not to end slavery. Consistent with his class analysis, Johnson saw secession as a plot by rich slaveowners to destroy the nation. He told one Union general that he cared nothing for the slaves but that he was "fighting those traitorous artistocrats, their masters."

As the only man from a Confederate state to remain in Congress, Johnson was something of a hero in the North. In 1862, Abraham Lincoln appointed Johnson military governor of Tennessee. This period was Johnson's finest hour. As military governor, he was resolute, firm, and brave, risking his life and property for the Union. He understood the nature of a civil war, and like Ulysses S. Grant and William Tecumseh Sherman, was willing to accept its costs. Thus, when rebel forces surrounded Nashville, Johnson declared that he would burn the city before surrendering it. In 1863, Johnson called a state constitutional convention for the purpose of reconstructing Tennessee's government. While military governor, Johnson reported directly to Lincoln. This experience made Johnson believe in the efficacy of direct presidential control of Reconstruction.

In 1864, Johnson was with Lincoln on a Union Party ticket. As a Southern Unionist and a former Democrat, Johnson was seen as a man who could help bind the nation's wounds at the conclusion of the war. After the election, Johnson remained in Tennessee until February, 1865, when he was able to install a legally elected governor under a new Unionist state constitution. When he took the oath of office in March, Johnson was, unfortunately, drunk and gave a rambling and incoherent speech, glorifying his roots and declaring, "I'm a plebeian!" Although Johnson was not a drunkard and was, at the time of his inauguration, suffering from the aftereffects of typhoid fever, his performance was nevertheless shocking and disgraceful. Lincoln was mortified, Republican senators were humiliated, and few could argue when a Democratic newspaper called Johnson a "drunken clown." A group of senators, led by Charles Sumner, demanded his resignation. While Lincoln was less harsh,

he nevertheless did not meet with his vice president until the afternoon of April 14. Whether that meeting signaled an end to Johnson's isolation from the Administration is unknown. By that night, the question was moot. At ten o'clock that evening, Johnson was awakened with the news that President Lincoln had been shot. The next day Johnson became president.

Johnson's presidency was a failure. His relationship with Congress was disastrous. Ultimately, Johnson was impeached by the House, tried by the Senate, and avoided conviction by only one vote. Since a conviction required a two-thirds guilty vote of the Senate, Johnson's acquittal could hardly be considered a vindication; a large majority in Congress believed that he should be removed from office. The impeachment trial was the culmination of conflicts with Congress that were rooted in two intractable problems: the nature of political Reconstruction and the role of blacks in the post-Civil War South.

Although notorious for his harsh rule as a military governor, Johnson actually favored a mild Reconstruction policy. He was quick to offer pardons for most former Confederates. His amnesty proclamation of May 29, 1865, reinstated political rights for former rebels, except those with taxable property of more than twenty thousand dollars. Johnson believed that the war had been caused by the "aristocrats in the South," and that only they should be punished. Yet his proclamation held out hope for the Southern elite, because he also promised to grant individual pardons whenever the "peace and dignity" of the nation allowed it. In the next few months, Johnson presided over a steady stream of rich Southerners, asking for pardons. Johnson made the most of this opportunity to force the "aristocrats" to look up to a "plebeian," reveling in his power but also granting thousands of pardons. Instead of confiscating the property of former slaveowners and giving it to the former slaves, as radicals such as Thaddeus Stevens wished to do, Johnson was busy enfranchising the master class.

While giving much to the former enemies of the nation, Johnson offered little to Southern Unionists, especially the former slaves. Johnson was a thoroughgoing racist, even by the benighted standards of the 1860's. He supported emancipation, in part because it would undermine the power of the planter elite. Yet he opposed black suffrage or any government aid to the freedmen. This attitude was made clear in his proclamation re-creating self-govern-

ment in North Carolina. The proclamation, much to the disappointment of many Republicans, gave the state exclusive power to determine suffrage under the laws of North Carolina before secession: This meant that blacks could not vote. Johnson's policies indicated that he saw the Civil War as having accomplished nothing more than ending slavery and permanently preserving the Union. Otherwise, Johnson wanted to re-create the Union as it had been before the war, with a small federal government that could not interfere with states' rights, and no meaningful protections for former slaves.

Throughout 1865 and 1866, Johnson labored to have the Southern states readmitted into the Union as quickly as possible and with no requirements that they grant equality to former slaves. When the Southern states passed "black codes," severely restricting the movement and rights of free blacks, Johnson expressed only mild disapproval. Similarly, when Southerners elected former Confederate officials and generals to Congress, Johnson indicated only slight displeasure and took no action.

Congress, however, did act. In December, meeting for the first time since Lincoln's death, Congress refused to seat representatives from the former Confederate states. Congressional hearings on conditions in the South revealed the continuing oppression of the freedmen by whites and the need for radical changes in the society. In February, 1866, Congress extended the life of the Freedmen's Bureau, a War Department agency, headed by war hero General Oliver Otis Howard, which had been established the previous spring to help blacks and whites in the wake of the war. The bill passed with the unanimous support of the Republicans in Congress. To the surprise of the Republican majority, Johnson vetoed the bill, arguing that Congress lacked the power or the right to spend money to feed, educate, or find land for freed slaves. In his veto message, Johnson argued that his role as president required him to protect the interests of the South, which was not represented in Congress. Despite feelings of betrayal, Republicans in Congress were not fully united, and the Senate narrowly sustained the veto.

The successful veto of the Freedman's Bureau Bill led Johnson to believe that he controlled the Republican Party and that he could stop those who sought to enfranchise blacks, create racial equality in the nation, or reconstruct the South in any meaningful manner. This illusion of power led Johnson to a major blunder. Three days after the Freed-

man's Bureau veto, Johnson publicly blamed the war and the assassination of Lincoln on antislavery radicals. He specifically named Senator Charles Sumner, Congressman Thaddeus Stevens, and the abolitionist orator Wendell Phillips, asserting that these men, and other radicals, were traitors to the nation and the equivalent of Southern secessionists. This speech undermined support for Johnson in Congress and throughout the nation, support which he would never regain.

Johnson, however, did not fully comprehend the damage done by the Freedman's Bureau veto and his speech attacking radical Republicans and abolitionists. In another major miscalculation, he vetoed the Civil Rights Act of 1866, even though it was a moderate measure which made the freedmen citizens and guaranteed them "equal protection of the laws." Johnson believed that this law would interfere with states' rights and the ability of the states to regulate social policy. His veto also revealed Johnson's deep-seated racism. For the first time in American history, Congress overrode a presidential veto.

In May and July, whites killed or injured hundreds of blacks in Memphis and New Orleans. In both cities, indecisive action by federal troops failed to stop the white mobs. Many of the victims of the mob in Memphis were black Union veterans who had been recently mustered out of service. These riots helped convince the North that Southerners had not yet accepted blacks as freedmen, much less equals, and that Johnson was more sympathetic to former rebels than he was to former slaves and Union veterans.

Johnson's support for Southern recalcitrance was also clear in his reaction to the Fourteenth Amendment, which Congress sent to the states for ratification in June. Although the president has no right to veto an amendment, Johnson publicly opposed the amendment, which would guarantee blacks citizenship and other rights and also fundamentally change the nature of the Union. Unlike the overwhelming majority of the Congress, Johnson seemed to be unaware that the Civil War had changed constitutional, racial, and political relations in the nation. By the end of the year, seven former Confederate states, taking their cues from Johnson, rejected the new amendment. Meanwhile, in July, Congress enacted a new Freedmen's Bureau Bill, over Johnson's veto.

In the fall of 1866, Johnson campaigned against Republican candidates for Congress. The result was an overwhelming rejection of Johnson. More than two-thirds of both houses were not only Republicans but also hostile to Johnson and leaning toward the Progressive racial policies of Stevens, Sumner, and Senator Ben Wade of Ohio.

In January, 1867, Congress overrode Johnson's veto of a bill giving the vote to blacks living in Washington, D.C. Veto overrides soon became almost commonplace. In the spring, Johnson vetoed the first Reconstruction Act, which gave the vote to blacks in the South, excluded former Confederate leaders from office and voting, required new state constitutions in the South, and gave the military the power to enforce these laws. This was Congress' response to the Memphis and New Orleans riots, the blacks codes, and Southern opposition to the Fourteenth Amendment. By an overwhelming vote, Congress overrode this veto. Johnson then vetoed Nebraska's statehood because, among other reasons, the state's constitution allowed blacks to vote. Congress again overrode the veto. Congress also changed its meeting time from December to March, so that it could be in almost continuous session to watch over Johnson's activities.

In March, Congress specifically provided that all military orders from the president had to go through General Grant, and that Grant could not be assigned to a post outside Washington against his will. This law indicated that Congress placed more faith in the war hero Grant than in the president. This provision was part of a larger appropriations bill, which Johnson signed, despite his distaste for the provisions concerning Grant. Johnson then vetoed the Tenure of Office Act, but Congress overrode the veto. This law, which prevented Johnson from removing any Cabinet officers without the permission of Congress, reflected congressional fear that Johnson would remove Secretary of War Edwin Stanton, who was sympathetic to congressional goals.

In March, 1867, Congress overrode Johnson's veto of the Second Reconstruction Act. Meanwhile, the House investigated whether Johnson ought to be impeached. On June 3, the House investigating committee adjourned, with four members in favor of impeachment and five against. In July, Congress overrode Johnson's veto of the Third Reconstruction Act.

In May, Johnson interpreted the Reconstruction Acts in a narrow fashion, to allow most former Confederates to vote and ordered all generals to act accordingly. Both Secretary of War Stanton and

General Grant opposed this interpretation. When General Philip Sheridan, headquartered in New Orleans, asked Grant if he should obey Johnson's order, Grant replied that it was not a legal order, because it had not come from him, as specified in the legislation of March, 1867. When forced to choose, Grant chose to follow the laws of Congress and not the whims of President Johnson. The army followed Grant. It was not unlikely that in a confrontation, the people would follow the hero of Appomattox rather than an unelected president of doubtful abilities.

In July, 1867, Johnson attempted to remove Sheridan from his position as military commander of Texas and Louisiana and to remove Stanton from the cabinet. Sheridan had followed congressional intent in the Southwest by removing former Confederates from office, in opposition to Johnson's policies. Stanton was, by this time, openly in sympathy with Congress and thus openly hostile to Johnson. Johnson asked Grant to take Stanton's place. At first, Grant refused but then accepted an interim appointment, pending the return of Congress from its summer recess. Under the Tenure of Office Act, Stanton could not be removed until Congress returned to session and gave its approval.

Following the removal of Sheridan, Johnson also removed other generals who were sympathetic to Congress. In September, 1867, Johnson exacerbated the situation by issuing a pardon for all but a few hundred former Confederate politicians and generals. The pardons, and the removal of Sheridan and other generals, led to new calls for impeachment. In November, the House Judiciary Committee voted five to four in favor of impeachment, but the entire Congress rejected this recommendation.

On January 13, 1868, the Senate, acting under the Tenure of Office Act, refused to concur in the removal of Stanton as secretary of war. General Grant immediately turned the keys to the office over to Stanton and then reported to Johnson that he was no longer secretary of war. In the days that followed, Johnson accused Grant of betraying him and of being a liar. Public opinion sided with the general, not with Johnson.

On February 21, Johnson, ignoring the recommendations of most of his confidential advisers, attempted to replace Stanton with Lorenzo Thomas, a lackluster general. Stanton, however, refused to give up his office or even, physically, to leave the

War Department. The next day, the House of Representatives voted overwhelmingly to send a resolution for the impeachment of Johnson to the Committee on Reconstruction, chaired by the radical Congressman Thaddeus Stevens.

On February 24, the House, by an overwhelming vote, approved a resolution of impeachment. The next day, Congressman Thaddeus Stevens, a radical, and John Bingham, a moderate, entered the Senate, where they informed that body that Johnson had been impeached and that specific articles of impeachment would be forthcoming. On March 2, the House adopted nine separate articles of impeachment. On March 12, the Congress passed, over Johnson's veto, the Fourth Reconstruction Act. On March 13, the trial of Andrew Johnson began before the Senate, presided over by Chief Justice Salmon P. Chase. Postponements delayed the proceedings until March 30. Then, for more than a month, the Senate heard evidence and arguments on the constitutionality of the Tenure of Office Act and the legal requirements for impeachment. Finally, on May 19, the Senate voted thirty-five to nineteen in favor of conviction on one of the articles of impeachment. The same vote prevailed, on May 26, for the other articles. This was one vote short of the two-thirds majority needed to remove Johnson from office. A coalition of Democrats and conservative Republicans saved Johnson by the thinnest possible margin. Later that day, Stanton resigned his office.

Johnson served out the remainder of his term with a continuation of his lackluster style and predictable veto overrides. Despite his opposition, the Fourteenth Amendment was ratified while Johnson held office. The only thing on which Johnson and Congress seemed to agree was the appropriation of funds to purchase Alaska, which came in 1868, more than a year after the treaty with Russia had been approved.

Johnson sought the presidency in 1868, but neither party would have him. He retired to Tennessee, and in 1875, he was again elected to the Senate. Four months after taking office, he died of a stroke.

Summary

Historians and scholars have long debated whether Johnson should have been removed from office. The question often turns on a point of law. If impeachment is strictly for an illegal act, then perhaps Johnson was innocent, since it is generally agreed that the law he violated—the Tenure of Office Act—was itself unconstitutional. On the other hand, no court had yet declared the law unconstitutional, and until the Supreme Court makes a final determination, Congress has the right to determine constitutionality on its own. If impeachment is essentially a political process, then the grounds for Johnson's removal are stronger. He was an accidental president, out of step with the nation and lacking the support of either political party. He had consistently thwarted the will of Congress and the American people. His racist response to black freedom mocked the consequences of the Civil War and certainly prevented blacks from attaining equality and justice in its aftermath.

Whatever their opinion on how the impeachment trial should have ended, almost all observers agree that Johnson's presidency was a total failure. Few presidents were so ill-equipped to handle the job. Arrogant, mistrustful of anyone with an education, insecure, unwilling to compromise, pigheaded in his ideas, and a racist, Johnson left a legacy in the White House that took years to reverse; he left a legacy for black Americans that has still not been completely overcome.

Bibliography

Benedict, Michael Les. *The Impeachment and Trial of Andrew Johnson*. New York: Norton, 1973. The best available study of the impeachment. Concludes, with much supporting evidence, that the impeachment was justified and conviction would have been proper. Available in paperback.

Castel, Albert E. *The Presidency of Andrew Johnson*. Lawrence: Regents Press of Kansas, 1979. Modern study of Johnson as a president. Focuses almost entirely on his presidential career. Balanced and judicious.

Franklin, John Hope. *Reconstruction: After the Civil War*. 2d ed. Chicago: University of Chicago Press, 1994. Short, easily read introduction to the era of Reconstruction by one of the nation's most important scholars.

Litwack, Leon. *Been in the Storm So Long*. New York: Knopf, 1979; London: Athlone Press, 1980. Pulitzer Prize-winning history of blacks during the early part of Reconstruction, when Johnson was president. While not about Johnson, this book demonstrates the tragedy of Johnson's policies toward the former slaves. Wonderfully written and superbly documented, this book shows what Reconstruction was like from the perspective of the freedmen.

McCaslin, Richard B. *Andrew Johnson: A Bibliography.* Westport, Conn.: Greenwood Press, 1992. The first complete, logical, and organized bibliography of one of the United States' most controversial presidents including a short chronology; chapters on biographies, archival sources, Johnson's writings, and different periods in his life; a section on periodicals; and author and subject indexes.

McKitrick, Eric L., ed. *Andrew Johnson: A Profile.* New York: Hill and Wang, 1969. Contains ten essays by nine different historians. Each essay focuses on a different aspect of Johnson's career. Book begins with a short biography of Johnson. Some of the essays are dated in their interpretation, but others, particularly those on his prepresidential career, hold up well.

Sefton, James E. *Andrew Johnson and the Uses of Constitutional Power.* Boston: Little Brown, 1980. An excellent short biography. Balanced, with modern interpretations. Probably the best comprehensive coverage of Johnson's life available.

Treffousse, Han. *Andrew Johnson: A Biography.* New York: Norton, 1989. Biography of Johnson with emphasis on his succession to president after Lincoln's assassination and his failures during the Reconstruction, which led to his impeachment trial. Compassionate treatment of tragic times.

Paul Finkelman

SCOTT JOPLIN

Born: November 24, 1868; Bowie County, near Texarkana, Texas

Died: April 1, 1917; New York, New York

Area of Achievement: Music

Contribution: Despite humble origins, racial prejudices, and cultural barriers, Joplin became a respected piano player and a composer of ragtime music. Known as the "King of Ragtime," his most famous composition, "Maple Leaf Rag" (1899), was the first piece of sheet music to sell one million copies in the United States.

Early Life

Scott Joplin was born on November 24, 1868, in Bowie County near Texarkana, Texas. He was one of six children belonging to Giles and Florence Givens Joplin. Although they were a poor black family, music was an important part of their lives. Giles, a railroad worker and former slave, played the violin, and young Scott heard from him the waltzes, polkas, reels, and folk music that Giles had played for his former masters on the plantation. Scott's freeborn mother sang and played the banjo, while his brother Will played guitar and violin and another brother, Robert, sang baritone.

At age seven Joplin began showing an interest in the piano. Florence worked as a servant for several white families in Texarkana, and while she cleaned, Joplin played their pianos. Eventually, the family put together enough money to buy a used piano for him to play at home. By age eleven he was writing and playing his own music, and his talent was well known in the community. Several local residents took an interest in his musical talent and gave him free lessons. The most influential of these people was a German music teacher, fondly remembered, who taught Joplin technique, sight reading, and harmony and gave him the opportunity to learn classical and popular European music.

Joplin argued frequently with his father about finding a steady job or trade, and after the death of his mother, the teenager left Texarkana to make his living in music. He worked as an itinerant musician in brothels, saloons, gambling halls, and traveling shows in towns and cities from Texas to the Mississippi River. He heard a variety of music played by musicians and singers, including a syncopated "ragged" style of music later known as "ragtime." Arriving in St. Louis in 1885, he socialized with other piano players at John Turpin's Silver Dollar Saloon. Joplin found steady work as a piano player and entertainer in a variety of St. Louis establishments and in other surrounding towns and cities.

In 1893, like many other African American piano players, Joplin sought a job at the World Columbian Exposition in Chicago but found most of his work in the red-light district of the city. It was here that many people from around the nation were first exposed to ragtime music. Joplin then met a young piano player, Otis Saunders, who became a close friend and would be an important advisor during his future career. When the exposition closed, Joplin and Saunders returned to St. Louis; in 1894 they moved to Sedalia, Missouri.

Life's Work

Sedalia greatly influenced Joplin's career, and it was here that he began to compose and sell his piano compositions. He joined the locally popular Queen City Concert Band and attended the Smith

School of Music at the George R. Smith College for Negroes, where he learned fundamentals of harmony and composition. In 1895 he returned to St. Louis and began spending time at Turpin's ragtime headquarters, the Rosbud Cafe. Turpin, credited with the first published black American rag, "Harlem Rag" (1897), became an inspiration and friend to Joplin.

Upon his return to Sedalia, Joplin formed a vocalizing harmony group, the Texas Medley Quartette. His brothers Will and Robert were singers in the group, while Joplin sang and played the piano. They performed a variety of folk and popular songs as well as Joplin's new music. They became so popular in Sedalia and the surrounding area that they decided to join a vaudeville tour and traveled as far as Syracuse, New York, where Joplin found publishers for two of his Victorian parlor songs, "A Picture of Her Face" (1895) and "Please Say You Will" (1895). He also composed marches and waltzes, although none of these were in the ragtime style that would later make him famous.

A second tour ended in Joplin, Missouri, and the group disbanded. Joplin returned to Sedalia in 1897 to play in various bars, bordellos, and social clubs, especially the Maple Leaf Club, which as owned by Tony Williams. Acquaintances knew Joplin as a polite, quiet, and well-spoken man who wanted to be respected as a serious composer. He often received support and encouragement from the white community and businessmen.

Joplin continued to compose music in Sedalia. He sold his first ragtime composition, "Original Rag" (1899), to publisher Carl Hoffman of Kansas City, Kansas, after a Sedalia publisher, A. W. Perry and Son, rejected it. After rejections by another publisher, Hoffman and Perry and Son, Joplin sold his second and most important ragtime composition, "Maple Leaf Rag" (1899), to John Stark and Son of Sedalia for fifty dollars and a one-cent royalty. The composition was an immediate success and quickly sold thousands of copies. Ragtime music was already popular, but the "Maple Leaf Rag" became the standard for the genre. With the royalties he earned, Joplin could now afford to stop playing the piano for a living and concentrate on composing and teaching. "Maple Leaf Rag" also made John Stark a leading publisher in ragtime music. He moved his music store to St. Louis and made music publishing his full-time business.

In 1900 Joplin and his new bride, Belle Hayden, also moved to St. Louis. Stark and Son published

"Peacherine Rag" (1901), "The Easy Winner" (1901), "A Breeze From Alabama" (1902), and "The Entertainer" (1902). The Louisiana Purchase Exposition in St. Louis inspired Joplin to write a musical tribute to it called "The Cascades" (1904). During his career Joplin would use various other publishers for his many rags, waltzes, songs, and an instruction book, *School of Ragtime* (1908). He occasionally visited the old St. Louis clubs and saloons to stay in contact with fellow ragtime friends and composers such as Turpin, Louis Chauvin, and Sam Patterson. He also played the "Maple Leaf Rag" and other songs on request.

Two of Joplin's young Sedalia protégés were Arthur Marshall and Scott Hayden. Joplin's music influenced both of them, and they collaborated on several musical compositions. Joplin and Hayden produced "Sunflower Slow Drag" (1901), "Something Doing" (1911), "Felicity Rag" (1911), and "Kismet Rag" (1913). Joplin and Marshall collaborated on two compositions: "Swipsey Cake Walk" (1900) and "Lily Queen—A Ragtime Two-Step" (1907). Joplin continued to influence and help other composers of ragtime music, such as James Scott and Joseph Lamb, throughout his career.

In St. Louis, Joplin concentrated on his desire to compose serious classical music. He wrote *Ragtime Dance* (1902), a nine-page, twenty-minute folk ballet with dancers and singers, which Stark reluctantly published. Popular as a production in Sedalia, it was a failure as sheet music. Joplin then decided to compose a ragtime opera, *A Guest of Honor* (1903). It was performed once in a St. Louis rehearsal, but Joplin was unsuccessful in finding a backer or publisher for the opera, including Stark. Meanwhile, Joplin's personal life was not a success either. His wife was not interested in his musical career. After the death of their infant girl, Belle and Joplin separated; she died two years later.

Depressed and discouraged, Joplin moved to Chicago in 1906. He stayed a short time with his friend Marshall, but he wanted to move to New York City. Stark had already opened a new publishing store there in 1905 to compete with the Tin Pan Alley music firms. Joplin finally moved to New York in 1907, and from this base he traveled with vaudeville tours to supplement his income. In 1909 he married Lottie Stokes, a woman who was interested in and supportive of his career. They opened a boarding house, and Joplin continued composing and teaching violin and piano.

Despite his first failures to succeed as a more serious classical composer, Joplin began a three-act opera, *Treemonisha* (1911), that drew from his experiences growing up on the Texas-Arkansas state border during Reconstruction. Its theme dealt with African American society, superstitions, and the necessity of education to better their lives. Joplin became obsessed with this work, spending much of his time and income on it. Unable to find a publisher for *Treemonisha*, Joplin copyrighted and published it himself. He even financed a 1915 rehearsal in front of a select audience in Harlem's Lincoln Theater. Without scenery or costumes and with only Joplin playing the piano, the performance was a failure. *Treemonisha*'s rejection devastated him.

Although Joplin wrote many new compositions in New York, his health was deteriorating from the advanced stages of syphilis he had contracted earlier in life. He suffered from mood swings and an inability to concentrate. He even had difficulty playing the piano and speaking coherently. Finally, in the fall of 1916, Lottie admitted him to the Manhattan State Hospital on Ward's Island in the East River where he died on April 1, 1917, from dementia paralytica-cerebra. Lottie buried him in St. Michael's Cemetery on Long Island.

Summary

Ragtime was the first distinctive American music. While the height of its popularity lasted for only a short period, from 1896 to 1917, it was a forerunner and influence on other music, especially jazz. It came from the African music, plantation melodies, and folk songs played on banjos and fiddles. It offered exciting, bouncy, and infectious syncopations. Ragtime was not considered respectable by white and black middle- and upper-class society because musicians originally played it in the saloons, bordellos, and sporting clubs of the red-light districts. Despite its disreputable beginning, it eventually became very popular and was played by bands and orchestras, in theaters, and on parlor pianos of respectable homes.

Scott Joplin is credited with shaping this new music and influencing other composers and imitators with his sophisticated and classical style. John Stark termed Joplin's music "classic rag" to sell it as the best type of ragtime music. It combined black folk music and rhythms with nineteenth century European classical music. Joplin raised ragtime from improvised entertainment to his own smooth style of published music. He was serious and less flashy than many of his contemporaries and encouraged his students and performers not to hurry the tempo of his compositions.

Joplin wrote sixty-six published compositions and two operas. Many other unpublished works were lost in the years following Lottie Joplin's death. When Scott Joplin died, Stark wrote a brief obituary that stated, "Scott Joplin is dead. A homeless itinerant, he left his mark on American music."

Bibliography

Berlin, Edward A. *King of Ragtime: Scott Joplin and His Era*. New York: Oxford University Press, 1994. A comprehensive biography with attention to Joplin's music. Examines new information from archives and newspapers. Contains photographs, illustrations, alphabetical and chronological listings of Joplin's works, extensive notes, and bibliography.

Blesh, Rudi, and Harriet Janis. *They All Played Ragtime*. Rev. ed. New York: Oak, 1966. A history of ragtime music and a study of its composers and players. Uses extensive personal interviews and correspondence and includes illustrations, photographs, complete musical scores, and lists of ragtime compositions.

Curtis, Susan. *Dancing to a Black Man's Tune: A Life of Scott Joplin*. Columbia: University of Missouri Press, 1994. Scholarly biography with an interpretation of the communities and societies of Joplin's era. Contains extensive chapter notes and a bibliography.

Gammond, Peter. *Scott Joplin and the Ragtime Era*. London: Abacus, and New York: St. Martin's Press, 1975. A scholastic and historical look at ragtime and Joplin's works. Contains illustrations and photographs.

Jasen, David A., and Trebor Jay Tichenor. *Rags and Ragtime: A Musical History*. New York: Seabury Press, 1978. A history of ragtime and a description of the major ragtime composers and their pieces. Contains illustrations and photographs.

Waldo, Terry. *This Is Ragtime*. New York: Hawthorn, 1976. A history of ragtime music. Includes illustrations, photographs, bibliography, and a select discography.

Vivian L. Richardson

CHIEF JOSEPH
Heinmot Tooyalakekt

Born: c. 1840; Lapwai Preserve, Wallowa Valley, northeastern Oregon

Died: September 21, 1904; Colville Indian Reservation, Washington

Area of Achievement: Native American rights

Contribution: Leader of his people in the Nez Perce War of 1877, Chief Joseph attempted to retain for his people the freedoms enjoyed prior to white American interest in their lands.

Early Life

Chief Joseph (Heinmot Tooyalakekt in his native tongue, which translates as Thunder-Rolling-in-the-Mountains) was born to Old Joseph (Tuekakas) and Asenoth. He was baptized Ephraim on April 12, 1840, by the Reverend Mr. Henry H. Spalding, who maintained a Presbyterian mission at Lapwai in the heart of the Nez Perce's country. This area, which comprises parts of Idaho, Oregon, and Washington, contains some of the most desirable land in the United States. As such, white Americans desired the land upon which the Nez Perce and other bands of Indians lived. In 1855, the United States government greatly reduced the holdings of all tribes and bands in the northwestern United States in a series of treaties at the Council of Walla Walla, called by the governor of the Washington Territory, Isaac Stevens. In those treaties, the Neemeepoo (meaning the people) or Nez Perce (pronounced nez purse) agreed to what amounted to a fifty percent reduction of their territory. The Nez Perce were able to keep this much of their land because the whites were not yet interested in the wild and remote country of west-central Idaho and northwestern Oregon. The Nez Perce had been exposed to Christianity as early as 1820. The existence of Christian names indicates that many practiced that religion. Chief Joseph was, or was generally believed to have been, baptized and named Ephraim. It would fall to him, a kind and gentle man, to deal with the problems—initially encroachment and then expropriation—which threatened the lands of his fathers.

The troubles of the Nez Perce developed in 1861, when gold in quantity was discovered along the Orofino Creek, a tributary of the Clearwater. Old Joseph attempted to keep the prospectors from the land but finally accepted the inevitable and sought to supervise rather than prohibit the activity. This plan failed. Once the area had been opened, many whites entered. In violation of the agreements, and of the treaties of 1855, which prohibited such white encroachments, some whites turned to farming. The results were surprising. The government, rather than forcing the whites to leave, proposed an additional reduction of the Nez Perce lands. The federal government indicated that as much as seventy-five percent of the holdings should be made available for white settlement. Old Joseph refused; his refusal apparently split the Nez Perce peoples. Some of them agreed to the reduction. Aleiya, called Lawyer by the whites, signed the agreement which the Joseph faction of the Nez Perce would refer to as the thief treaty. Hereafter, the Nez Perce were divided into the treaty and nontreaty bands. Old Joseph refused to leave the Wallowa Valley, where his nontreaty Nez Perce bred and raised the Appaloosa horse.

Old Joseph died in 1871, and, at his parting, he reminded his eldest son, Heinmot Tooyalakekt, or Young Joseph, "always remember that your father never sold his country. You must stop your ears whenever you are asked to sign a treaty selling your home. . . . This country holds your father's bones. Never sell the bones of your father and your mother." Chief Joseph was as adamant in his refusal to sell or part with the land as had been his father, but he realized the power and inconstancy of the United States government. In 1873, President Ulysses S. Grant issued an executive order dividing the area that the whites were settling between the whites and the Nez Perce. In 1875, however, Grant opened the entire region to white settlement. In 1876, he sent a commission to see Chief Joseph. The decision had been made to offer Joseph's band of nontreaty Nez Perce land in the Oklahoma Indian Territory for all of their Idaho holdings.

What transpired as a result of this decision has been termed by Jacob P. Dunn, Jr., in *Massacres in the Mountains* (1886), "the meanest, most contemptible, least justifiable thing that the United States was ever guilty of. . . ." Chief Joseph refused the offer to move to Oklahoma. General Oliver Otis Howard arrived with orders to enforce the presidential decision. General Howard proposed a swift compliance with those orders. Joseph realized that his Nez Perce could not long stand against a government and an army determined to take their land

and move them. Accordingly, a council of chiefs, including Joseph's younger brother Ollokot (a fine warrior), White Bird, Looking Glass, and the Wallowa prophet, Toohoolhoolzote, reached the decision to go to Canada rather than to Oklahoma. General Howard, however, declared that "the soldiers will be there to drive you onto the reservation. . . ."

Life's Work

The Nez Perce War of 1877 is misnamed. It would be more appropriate to label it a chase. It is the story of Chief Joseph's attempt to lead his people to the safety of Canada, where the geography and the climate were more similar to the traditional lands than were those of Oklahoma. The United States Army, under orders to deliver the Nez Perce to the Indian Territory, would pursue Chief Joseph's band during the 111-day war/chase which eventually found Joseph winding over fourteen hundred miles through the mountains. His attempt to elude the military would fail because of nineteenth century technology rather than his lack of ability.

Hostilities began when a member of White Bird's band of Nez Perce, Wahlitits, wanting to avenge the death of his father at the hands of white men, and two other youths, killed four white men. Apparently, some whites were of the opinion that only a war would guarantee the removal of the Nez Perce from the land, and some of them had been trying for some time to provoke that war. The men killed by Wahlitits had been the first white men killed by Nez Perce in a generation.

Joseph's reaction to the killings was one of regret and the realization that only flight would preserve his people. General Howard's reaction was to move immediately not only against White Bird's people but also against all the nontreaty Nez Perce. The initial engagement on June 17, 1877, was between two troops of the First Cavalry (about ninety men) under Captains David Perry and Joel Trimble. The cavalry was accompanied by eleven civilian volunteers. One of those civilian volunteers fired at the Nez Perce truce team. This action led to a short, unplanned, disorganized fight during which the Nez Perce, under Ollokot, killed thirty-four cavalry. (Important also was the capture of sixty-three rifles and many pistols).

This initial defeat led Howard, fearing a general uprising of all Nez Perce—treaty and nontreaty alike—to call for reinforcements. Troops from all over the United States were quickly dispatched, including an infantry unit from Atlanta, Georgia, to

the Washington Territory. Joseph's strategy was to seek protection from the Bitterroot Mountain range, where traditional cavalry tactics would be neutralized. Leading his approximately five hundred women and children and 250 warriors, he moved over the Lolo Trail, crossed the Bitterroots, and then, hoping to avoid detection, moved southward to the vicinity of the Yellowstone National Park, which he crossed in August, 1877. Joseph then swung northward into present-day Montana, hoping to reach Canada undetected. Seeking the security of the Bearpaw Mountains, Joseph moved his people as quickly as the women and young could travel. They were not quick enough: The Bearpaws would be the location of the final encounter with the military.

Joseph was not a military strategist; Ollokot was. Joseph urged that they try to reach Canada. Ollokot, Toohoolhoolzote, Looking Glass, and other chiefs preferred to fight. Battles had been joined several times along the route. At the Clearwater (July 11), at Big Hole (August 9-10), at Camas Meadows (August 16), at Canyon Creek (September 13), and at Cows Creek (September 23), sharp engagements were fought. Each resulted in Joseph's band eluding capture but with irreplaceable losses. The military, meanwhile, was receiving reinforcements in large numbers. Especially important was the arrival of Colonel Nelson Miles with nearly six hundred men, including elements of the Second and Seventh cavalries.

About thirty miles from the Canadian border, the Nez Perce halted, believing that they had succeeded in eluding the army and had the time to rest. Joseph was wrong: The telegraph and the railroad had outflanked him. Colonel Miles caught the Nez Perce unprepared on September 30, on the rolling plains of the Bearpaw Mountains. Joseph's band, hopelessly outnumbered, held out until October 4. After a hastily convened, makeshift council, Joseph decided to surrender. On October 5, he rode to the headquarters of Miles and General Howard, who had arrived in force the day before, and handed his rifle to Howard, who, in turn, passed it to Colonel Miles—still in command of the operation. Joseph said, through translators,

> Tell General Howard I know his heart. What he told me before I have in my heart. I am tired of fighting. Our chiefs are killed. Looking Glass is dead. Toohoolhoolzote is dead. The old men are all dead. It is the young men who say yes or no. He who led the young men [Ollokot] is dead. It is cold and we have no blan-

kets. The little children are freezing to death. My people, some of them, have run away into the hills, and have no blankets, no food; no one knows where they are—perhaps freezing to death. I want time to look for my children and see how many I can find. Maybe I shall find them among the dead. Hear me, my chiefs. I am tired; my heart is sick and sad. From where the sun now stands I will fight no more forever.

Joseph's surrender, apparently, was based upon an assumption ("Tell General Howard I know his heart. What he told me before I have in my heart.") that the Nez Perce could return to the Lapwai. This was not to be. The Nez Perce were loaded onto boxcars and transported to the Oklahoma Indian Territory. In this new climate and country, many of the remaining Nez Perce died. Joseph repeatedly begged for permission to return to the northwestern hunting grounds. Partial success came in 1885, when Joseph was allowed to return with his people to the Colville Reservation in Washington. Thereafter, every attempt on Joseph's part to effect a return to the Lapwai was unsuccessful. Joseph died on September 21, 1904, on the Colville Indian Reservation.

Summary

Chief Joseph of the Nez Perce was a dignified leader of his people. A man who loved the land of his ancestors, he attempted to retain it. His defiance of the United States government was a gallant, almost successful, effort. His failure marked the end of the wars of the Northwest and was the last important Indian resistance except for the Battle at Wounded Knee Creek. The removal of the Nez Perce to reservations marked the end of freedom as the American Indians had known it. As Joseph said, "you might as well expect the rivers to run backward as that any man who was born free should be content when penned up and denied liberty. . . ."

Bibliography

Allard, William Albert. "Chief Joseph." *National Geographic* 151 (March 1977): 408-434. A well-illustrated, concise, balanced, readily available source.

Andrist, Ralph K. *The Long Death: The Last Days of the Plains Indians.* New York: Macmillian, 1964; London: Macmillan, 1969. Includes a well-written, sympathetic chapter on the Nez Perce. Especially valuable for detailing the reasons for the decision to go to Canada.

Beal, Merrill D. *"I Will Fight No More Forever": Chief Joseph and the Nez Perce War.* Seattle: University of Washington Press, 1963. A carefully written, well-illustrated account which gives special attention to the hostilities.

Brown, Dee. *Bury My Heart at Wounded Knee: An Indian History of the American West.* New York: Holt Rinehart, 1970; London: Barrie and Jenkins, 1971. A classic study of white-Indian relationships which must be read by the serious student. It contains an excellent account of Chief Joseph and his attempted flight to Canada. White motivation in the contest is perhaps overstated.

Chalmers, Harvey, II. *The Last Stand of the Nez Perce: Destruction of a People.* New York: Twayne, 1962. Contains a valuable glossary of characters and a balanced account of the hostilities.

Dunn, Jacob P., Jr., *Massacres of the Mountains: A History of the Indian Wars of the Far West.* New York: Harper, and London: Sampson Low, Marston, 1886. A chapter devoted to what Dunn argues was an injustice committed by the United States government. Many later sources rely upon his analysis.

Hong, K.E. "The Last Years of Chief Joseph." *Cobblestone* 11, no. 9 (September 1990). Examines Chief Joseph's fight to regain the Nez Perce homeland in the Wallowa Valley after their surrender to the U.S. government. Provides accounts of the relocations that occurred.

Howard, Oliver O. *My Life and Experience Among Our Hostile Indians.* Hartford, Conn.: Worthington, 1907. Need not be consulted except by those concerned with movement of military personnel.

Josephy, Alvin M., Jr. *The Patriot Chiefs: A Chronicle of American Indian Leadership.* New York: Viking Press, 1961; London: Eyre and Spottiswoode, 1962. One of the few sources that deals with Chief Joseph as an individual. The account of the war is excellent.

Miles, Nelson A. *Personal Recollections and Observances.* Chicago: Werner, 1896. The final days of the Nez Perce recounted by the officer in the field commanding the United States military. Unsympathetic toward Joseph's motivation.

Park, Edwards. "Big Hole: Still a Gaping Wound to the Nez Perce." *Smithsonian* 9 (May 1978): 92-99. Deals with a serious setback during the great chase of 1877.

Stevens, Mark. "Chief Joseph's Revenge." *New Yorker* 70, no. 24 (August 8, 1994). Profile of Chief Joseph including information on the persecution of the Nez Perce Indians.

Richard J. Amundson

JOSÉPHINE

Born: June 23, 1763; Trois-Îlets, Martinique
Died: May 29, 1814; Malmaison, France
Areas of Achievement: Government and politics
Contribution: Joséphine's life exemplified the chaos and unpredictability of the French Revolution and subsequent warfare. Popularly loved as "the good Joséphine," her social talents assisted Napoleon Bonaparte in creating stability and reconciliation among the various factions dividing the citizens of France.

Early Life

Marie-Josèphe-Rose Tascher de la Pagerie was born on the French Caribbean island of Martinique. She descended from the middle ranks of the French nobility who had emigrated to the colonies to make their fortunes growing sugar and was therefore Creole (born overseas but of French ancestry). Everyone called her Marie-Rose until she met Napoleon Bonaparte, who preferred "Joséphine." She attended a local convent school for four years during a privileged childhood. When she was sixteen, her family arranged her marriage to a wealthy and well-educated Frenchman named Viscount Alexandre de Beauharnais. In France she entered a sophisticated world where her lack of formal education disappointed her husband. The birth of their son Eugene (1781) and daughter Hortense (1783) did nothing to draw the couple together.

Soon the viscount demanded his freedom by falsely accusing Joséphine of infidelity and ordering her out of his house. She took refuge in a convent and complained to legal officials about his unreasonable behavior. The courts ordained a permanent separation and ordered Alexandre to pay modest alimony and child support. The separation left Marie-Rose in a precarious position in a society in which unattached women suffered serious disabilities: She had two preschool children, a small income, and no home. She had neither great beauty nor accomplishments; her one gift was charm, an aura of empathy and graciousness that won her loyal friends and sexual admirers. To support herself and her children, she became a woman of society, holding a salon where people of all political and social ranks fell under her spell and rendered her financial assistance.

Life's Work

The momentous events of the French Revolution engulfed and transformed Joséphine's life. Early in the Revolution, her estranged husband rose to political prominence by advocating moderate reforms. When war broke out in 1792, Alexandre commanded French forces along the Rhine and suffered serious defeats. Austrians and Prussians dedicated to restoring the Bourbons invaded France. The republican revolutionists organized the nation for victory and wielded the Reign of Terror against domestic opponents. Some radicals charged that General Beauharnais's military failures suggested treason; they arrested and imprisoned him and his wife from April to August, 1794. Alexandre was guillotined on fabricated charges and Joséphine, fearing imminent death, became emotionally unstable. She survived because moderate revolutionaries, the Thermidorians, overthrew the Terrorists and established a new government composed of a five-man executive called the Directory. Joséphine became the mistress of Director Paul Barras and indulged in the atmosphere of dissolution that followed the Reign of Terror.

In 1795 the widowed Joséphine met the man who dominated the remainder of her life, a twenty-six-year-old revolutionary general named Napoleon Bonaparte. He fell passionately in love with Joséphine and proposed marriage. She hesitated to make this commitment but agreed after learning that Napoleon had received an important command in northern Italy that could bring fame and fortune. Napoleon's mother and adult brothers opposed the marriage, calling Joséphine an old woman (over thirty) with no money. Despite family bickering, they married in a simple civil ceremony in March, 1796. Within a week Napoleon departed to command the French army in northern Italy.

Napoleon brilliantly defeated the forces of monarchy clustered on France's southeastern borders. He sent home money and hundreds of artworks to enrich the Directory and practically dictated the terms of peace in 1797. Only Joséphine defied Napoleon's will; he implored her to come to Italy, but she resisted. She dallied in Paris, continued her relationship with Barras, probably took a new lover, and made money through war profiteering. When she finally traveled to Napoleon's headquarters near Milan, Italy, she had aroused his deepest suspicions and jealousy. In Italy Joséphine first assumed important public functions; she presided over lavish official ceremonies and was treated almost as royalty. Once the couple returned to Paris, their small home became a site of pilgrimage for French patriots.

Popular myths immediately developed about Joséphine, celebrating her as "Our Lady of Victories" and "the good Joséphine," a symbol of good fortune and prosperity. She indulged her joy in shopping and collecting items as diverse as clothing, art, jewelry, and rare plants. Her extravagance did possess positive aspects: She was generous to a fault, patronized charities, and loved giving gifts. She never ignored a plea for help, however humble, and she was gracious to all. Furthermore, she did not meddle in politics or attempt to influence her husband's policies. These characteristics rendered Joséphine "good" in the eyes of public opinion in marked contrast to the "bad" Queen Marie Antoinette.

While Napoleon remained in France, Joséphine appeared as his loyal spouse and helpmate. However, when he led the French expedition to Egypt and remained away for seventeen months (1798-1799), she reverted to some of her previous bad habits and companions. Joséphine did begin to reform her behavior, but negative reports had quickly reached Napoleon. His secret return in autumn of 1799 surprised Joséphine, and she attempted to intercept him before her critical in-laws did. Napoleon greeted her with silence behind a locked bedroom door, but within a short time her copious weeping melted his heart and brought reconciliation.

Napoleon had far more on his mind than his wife's behavior. The Directory had suffered military losses and regularly canceled any unfavorable election results. A wide spectrum of political and business leaders assured Napoleon that they would support him if he would overthrow the Directors. His brothers Joseph and Lucien were well positioned to assist him, and Napoleon decided to act. Thus occurred the coup of Brumaire VIII in November of 1799 and creation of the Consulate, a three-man executive with Napoleon as First Consul. A major aim of the Consulate was to bring reconciliation among the political, religious, and social factions dividing the French people. Joséphine was an asset to this policy because she always had friends in all political and social camps. The Consulate ended the unseemly social behavior of the Directory; the First Consul and his wife moved into the Tuileries palace and virtually reestablished a court.

Napoleon and Joséphine frequently escaped the formality of the Tuileries by visiting their country estate, Malmaison, where they relaxed with their extended families and Joséphine unleashed her domestic talents. She redecorated the chateau extravagantly and began monumental gardening projects. She aspired to collect an example of every plant in France and introduce many new ones. She patronized botanists who studied and classified thousands of species. Malmaison became Joséphine's true home and was closely associated with popular perceptions of her.

Napoleon's ability to solve France's problems made him a target for royalist assassination attempts and made the need for an orderly transition of power in case of his death obvious. Joséphine worried for his safety and also for her own position should someone else assume power. She also feared that Napoleon, who had always wanted children, might divorce her and remarry in hopes of having them. She temporarily protected herself by arranging for her daughter Hortense to marry Napoleon's brother Louis in 1802. This couple produced three grandsons for Joséphine, uniting Bonaparte and Beauharnais lines; Napoleon seriously considered adopting the oldest child before he died in 1808.

The creation of the First Empire (May, 1804) intensified Joséphine's fears about succession and divorce. She invoked the sanction of the Roman Catholic Church against divorce by informing Pope Pius VII, who was visiting Paris for Napoleon's coronation ceremony, that her marriage had been civil only. At Papal urging, Napoleon and Joséphine quickly had a brief religious wedding.

The spectacular coronation ceremony reached its high point as Napoleon crowned Joséphine and himself. Their relationship had grown into an affectionate partnership; they often dined privately at the end of long days in which she sustained the elaborate public rituals of the court, freeing him to work on pressing matters. When Napoleon was away, Joséphine calmly continued the court routine and assured France that all was well. She remained essentially apolitical and unhesitatingly supported Napoleon's policies. Joséphine's concerns about war and politics lay with loved ones serving the First Empire. Eugene was an active soldier and viceroy of the Kingdom of Italy; his politically dictated marriage to a Bavarian princess had turned out happily. Hortense became a queen as Louis Bonaparte was named king of Holland, but her marriage disintegrated.

A combination of personal and political pressures led Napoleon to divorce Joséphine in 1809. For years he doubted he could father a child; in 1806 and 1810, however, affairs produced two sons who were undoubtedly his, the latter by the Polish countess Maria Walewska. Simultaneously, political pressure mounted for Napoleon to divorce Joséphine and improve France's international position by marrying into the Russian or Austrian ruling house. Napoleon informed Joséphine of his decision and requested her understanding. This time her tears could not dissuade him. Joséphine retained Napoleon's affection, the title of empress, possession of Malmaison, and a handsome income. In 1810 he married the Austrian archduchess Marie-Louise and, in 1811, rejoiced at the birth of his son Napoleon-Francis, king of Rome.

Joséphine's life changed greatly after divorce, but Joséphine herself did not. At heart she understood Napoleon's decision, and she contrived to visit and play with his sons by Countess Walewska and Marie-Louise. She lived at Malmaison and again gathered about her interesting people of all political persuasions. Although she entertained many royalists, she remained loyal to Napoleon. She lamented the reverses Napoleon met in Russia and the subsequent campaigns. She was fiercely proud that Eugene remained faithful to the emperor as others betrayed him. In the spring of 1814, the victorious allies swarmed over Paris and restored the Bourbon monarchy. The new regime allowed Joséphine to keep Malmaison and receive important visitors, including the Russian czar. Her children and grandchildren found refuge with sympathetic rulers abroad. However, the downfall of the First Empire seemed to overwhelm her, and her health failed. Perhaps it was coincidence, but within one month of Napoleon's exile to Elba (May 4, 1814), Joséphine died at Malmaison (May 29).

Summary

Joséphine was as loved in death as in life. Twenty thousand people paid their last respects, and a huge number of popular pamphlets praised her virtues. This outpouring was partly a measure of Napoleon's continued popularity and partly an expression of genuine regard. Massive changes swept France in her lifetime as the old feudal order collapsed and modern concepts of liberty, nationalism, and government arose. Joséphine transcended political divisions and softened the edges of Napoleon's authoritarian government as France entered a new age. Joséphine was beloved because she buffered the cruelties and harshness of her times and extended human sympathy in a society beset with turmoil.

Bibliography

Cole, Hubert. *Josephine*. London: Heinemann, and New York: Tower, 1962. Reliable, basic account of Joséphine's life. Contains a useful bibliography.

Epton, Nina Consuelo. *Josephine: The Empress and Her Children*. London: Weidenfeld and Nicolson, 1975; New York: Norton, 1976. Adequately surveys Joséphine's entire life and suggests that what little happiness she found came mostly from her relationships with Hortense and Eugene.

Knapton, Ernest John. *Empress Josephine*. Cambridge, Mass: Harvard University Press, 1963; London: Penguin, 1974. A carefully researched scholarly biography that dispels some often-repeated inaccuracies and gives abundant historical details that carefully place Joséphine in relation to contemporary events and personalities. The bibliography is exceptionally informative.

Seward, Desmond. *Napoleon's Family*. London: Weidenfeld and Nicolson, and New York: Viking Press, 1986. Joséphine's life after meeting Napoleon is woven throughout the complicated story of the Bonaparte and Beauharnais families; highlights family battles and hostility to Joséphine.

Vance, Marguerite. *The Empress Josephine: From Martinique to Malmaison*. New York: Dutton, 1956. Romanticized view emphasizing themes from her childhood that persisted in later life. The author maintains, perhaps unfairly, that Joséphine was her own worst enemy because she always insisted upon having her own way.

Wilson, Robert McNair. *The Empress Josephine, the Portrait of A Woman*. London: Eyre and Spottiswoode, 1952. A reliable account that emphasizes the personal rather than public side of her life. Includes a bibliography.

Sharon B. Watkins

BENITO JUÁREZ

Born: March 21, 1806; San Pablo Guelatao, Oaxaca, Mexico
Died: July 19, 1872; Mexico City, Mexico
Areas of Achievement: Government and politics
Contribution: The dominant figure of mid-nineteenth century Mexican politics, Juárez embodied a liberal vision of a democratic republican form of government, economic development and modernization, virulent anticlericalism, and mandatory public education. Although he was prevented from fully implementing his ambitious agenda by years of warfare against foreign intervention and his policies were anathema to many entrenched conservative elements in Mexico, especially the Catholic church, Juárez's reform program laid the groundwork for a modern Mexican nation.

Early Life

Benito Juárez was born in the small mountain hamlet of San Pablo Gueletao in the state of Oaxaca in southern Mexico in 1806. He was orphaned when his parents died before he reached the age of four. Reared by his uncle until the age of twelve in a remote Zapotec Indian community, Juárez's beginnings could not have been more humble. In 1818, he walked forty-one miles to the state capital, Oaxaca City, and found work and shelter in the home of a Franciscan lay brother who was a part-time bookbinder. Juárez worked in the bindery and helped with chores, and in return was given school tuition. Since he excelled in school, he was encouraged to enter the seminary. Juárez later changed his mind, however, and in 1829 chose a career in law, entering the Oaxaca Institute of Arts and Sciences. Two years later, he earned his lawyer's certificate, and that professional degree proved to be his passport to politics. The same year he was graduated from law school, he became an alderman in the city council and subsequently served as state legislator. His improved social and economic standing was reflected by his marriage in 1843 to Margarita Maza, the daughter of a prominent Oaxacan family.

Even as a successful young lawyer, Juárez always remembered his roots and did *pro bono publico* work for groups of impoverished peasant villagers. Convinced that major structural change was needed to make Mexico a more just society, Juárez decided to forgo his law practice and dedicate his career to public service.

When war erupted between Mexico and the United States in 1846, Juárez, who at the time was a deputy in the Mexican national congress, was recalled to his home in 1847 to serve an abbreviated term as interim governor. A year later, he was elected to a full term. Juárez proved to be a capable and honest governor, overseeing the construction of fifty rural schools, encouraging female attendance in the classroom, trimming the bloated state bureaucracy, facilitating economic development through the revitalization of an abandoned Pacific port, and making regular payments on the state debt. Moreover, the idealistic governor raised eyebrows around Mexico when he refused to offer his state as sanctuary to General Antonio López de Santa Anna, the powerful dictator (caudillo) who would serve as president on eleven separate occasions during the first thirty chaotic years of Mexican nationhood. Santa Anna never forgave Juárez for this slight, and, when he became president for the final time in 1853, he arrested Juárez, imprisoned him for several months, and then exiled him aboard a ship destined for New Orleans.

Life's Work

In New Orleans, Juárez made contact with a burgeoning expatriate community who represented the best and brightest of a new generation of young, idealistic Mexicans. These liberals, who called themselves *puros*, were committed to wholesale changes in the political system, to modernizing the nation's stagnant economy, and to creating a more equitable society for all Mexicans. These *puros* knew that Mexico had been racked by political instability, that Mexico had suffered a humiliating defeat at the hands of the United States, that corporate institutions such as the military and the Church had a viselike grip on Mexican society, and that a small politically powerful and economically wealthy elite dominated thousands of impoverished Indians and mestizos. Influenced by nineteenth century European liberal thought and enamored of the North American republican experiment, the *puros* composed a statement of principles in exile and secured arms and ammunition for regional caudillos in Mexico who opposed Santa Anna. Juárez was smuggled into Mexico and served as an aide to Juan Alvarez, the caudillo who spearheaded the Ayutla Rebellion. In 1855, the rebels drove Santa Anna from power for the last time.

When the new government was formed, Juárez was named secretary of justice. Juárez's cohorts were determined to see Mexico erase the vestiges of the past and emerge from chaos and anarchy. The *puros* focused on the Catholic church as being the single most regressive institution in Mexican society and sought to curtail its pervasive influence. The secretary of justice was intimately involved with the first of a series of reform laws that attacked corporate interests. There came a series of reform laws—which gave the era its name, *La Reforma*—and which systematically dismantled the power of the Catholic church in Mexico. The *Ley Lerdo* prohibited corporate institutions from owning or administering property not used in their daily operations. The Church, local and state governments, and corporate Indian villages could retain their churches, monasteries, meeting halls, jails, and schools, but other property had to be put up for sale at public auction, with the proceeds destined for federal coffers. In the first six months following the implementation of the law, twenty-three million pesos worth of property was auctioned, twenty million of which had belonged to the Church.

The reform laws were incorporated in a new constitution (1857). This document gave Mexico its first bill of rights, abolished slavery and titles of nobility, and created a unicameral congress to diminish executive power. Conservatives, especially the Church, unleashed a torrent of invective against the liberal document. Priests who did not publicly disavow the constitution were suspended by the hierarchy. While bureaucrats who refused to take the oath of allegiance lost their jobs, soldiers who did take the oath were not treated in Catholic hospitals and were denied the last rites.

The War of the Reform broke out in 1858, when conservatives attacked and captured Mexico City, dissolved the congress, and arrested Juárez, who had recently been elected chief justice of the supreme court—a position that placed him next in line for the presidency. When President Ignacio Comonfort proved unequal to the task of reconciliation, he resigned. Juárez then managed to escape from conservative hands and was promptly named president by his liberal supporters. For three years, the war raged as Juárez made his temporary headquarters in the port city of Veracruz.

After a bitter and protracted struggle, the liberals persevered and in 1861 Juárez entered Mexico City triumphant. The president decided to treat his enemies leniently and tendered a generous amnesty. More pressing problems faced Juárez, since he inherited a depleted treasury and a destitute army that had not been paid. Moreover, Mexico owed a considerable amount of money to European creditors, who now demanded repayment. Juárez, in an act of fiscal desperation, ordered a two-year suspension of payments on the foreign debt. Spain, England, and France, in an effort to prod Mexican repayment, agreed jointly to seize ports along the Mexican coast to collect their claims.

Napoleon III viewed the joint occupation of the port of Veracruz as a vehicle to further his expansionistic aims. Hoping to re-create the empire of his great-uncle, Napoleon I, and to take advantage of a debilitated United States engaged in its own civil war, Napoleon III ordered his army to leave the port of Veracruz and march on Mexico City. (When the Spanish and English learned of Napoleon's true intentions, they withdrew their forces.) After a stiff fight, the French army reached Mexico City, only to find that Juárez had already evacuated the capital and had taken his government with him, constantly moving across the desert of northern Mexico to escape capture.

Napoleon III attempted to legitimate his imperialistic actions when he persuaded a Habsburg archduke, Ferdinand Maximilian, to leave Austria and become the Emperor of Mexico (with the backing of the French army). Conservatives and the Church, which had just been defeated in the War of Reform, were delighted and welcomed Maximilian. Maximilian, with his wife Carlota, arrived in Mexico in 1864 and quickly found that Juárez's liberals were still a force to contend with and that the French had not successfully pacified the country.

Portraying the conflict as a nationalistic struggle to oust the foreign usurper, the president inspired his forces to conduct a guerrilla campaign against the French. Juárez also asked and received war matériel from the United States, especially after the defeat of the Confederacy in 1865. Secretary of State William Seward sent threatening messages to the French king, protesting that the occupation was a violation of the Monroe Doctrine and demanding that the French withdraw from the Western Hemisphere. In addition, the French troops grew weary of the Mexican campaign, and Napoleon appeared

to have lost interest as well. Concerned with Otto von Bismarck's aggressive foreign policy closer to home, Napoleon ordered his troops home in the spring of 1866. Soon thereafter, Maximilian's forces surrendered.

Maximilian was tried by court-martial, and the state asked for the death penalty. Despite intense pressure from the international community, Juárez stood by the sentence. After a devastating loss of territory to the United States and a nightmarish foreign interlude that cost more than fifty thousand Mexican lives, Juárez believed that Mexico had to make it clear that it would not countenance any more intervention. Maximilian was tried, convicted, and shot in 1867.

Most historians mark 1867 as the beginning of the modern Mexican nation. Juárez called for presidential elections and announced that he would run for an unprecedented third term. Since the first two terms were spent at war, most Mexicans believed that, under these extraordinary circumstances, the president was justified in seeking reelection. Moreover, given his back-to-back victories against the conservatives and Maximilian, Juárez's popularity was cresting.

His third term (1867-1871) was the first time the president had an opportunity to implement his liberal program in a peaceful atmosphere. The first order of business was to reconstruct Mexico's economy, which had been ravaged by nine years of war. To encourage foreigners to invest in Mexico, the president had to change the nation's image abroad. A rural police force was expanded to safeguard silver shipments and to protect highways from bandits. Mexico's first railroad from Mexico City to its chief port, Veracruz, was finally completed in 1872 by a British company with subsidies from Juárez's administration. Juárez also revised Mexico's antiquated tax and tarriff structures and sought to revitalize the mining sector to stimulate foreign investment further. Finally, Juárez appointed a commission to overhaul the national educational system. All of these policies collectively represented Juárez's vision for Mexico's future, and, although many were never fully implemented by his administration, they did put Mexico on the road to modernization.

One major problem that persisted throughout his third term was political unrest, especially at the regional and local level. Juárez spent much of his energies quieting one local uprising after another and found it necessary repeatedly to ask the congress to grant him extraordinary powers (martial law). Juárez's opponents believed that he had abused the constitutional principles he had fought so ardently to defend and that his rule was growing increasingly arbitrary and heavy-handed with time.

Despite the fact that his popularity had been falling for some time, Juárez decided to run for a fourth term in 1871. Two candidates, Sebastián Lerdo de Tejada (the brother of the author of the *Ley Lerdo*) and Porfirio Díaz, opposed him in the election. When no candidate received the requisite majority, according to the 1857 constitution, the congress would decide the outcome. The legislature, dominated by Juárez's supporters, elected him for a fourth term. Although Díaz revolted, federal forces quelled the rebellion. Soon after Díaz's defeat, however, Juárez suffered a coronary seizure and died on July 19, 1872.

Summary

Benito Juárez defined Mexican politics from 1855 to 1872. The fact that a full-blooded Zapotec Indian could become president of the nation demonstrated that Mexico had broken with its aristocratic past. The leader of an ambitious group of idealistic liberals, Juárez knew that the power of the Catholic church, the caudillos, and the army had to be diminished. Notwithstanding his more autocratic rule during his last years, especially his controversial decision to run for a fourth term, he remained true to his democratic principles.

Although Juárez is best known for his defeat of Maximilian and his anticlericalism, his greatest political legacy was his ambitious third term, which set the agenda for future presidential administrations. Juárez's successors, Lerdo de Tejada (1872-1876) and Díaz (1876-1911), faithfully followed his policies and programs. While some economic policies proved successful, the breaking up of village lands led to the expansion of the great estates or haciendas, and the destruction of semiautonomous Indian villages. Although Juárez's democratic principles were abused by Díaz during his long dictatorship, Díaz's policies and strategies for modernization bore the indelible stamp of Benito Juárez.

Bibliography

Bazant, Jan. *Alienation of Church Wealth in Mexico: Social and Economic Aspects of the Liberal Revolution, 1856-1857.* Cambridge: Cambridge University Press, 1971. A thorough analysis of the implications of the *Ley Lerdo* and its effects on church wealth in Mexico.

Berry, Charles R. *The Reform in Oaxaca, 1856-1876: A Microhistory of the Liberal Revolution.* Lincoln: University of Nebraska Press, 1981. A critical examination of how liberal policies were implemented in Juárez's home region, Oaxaca. Berry dispels certain myths about the land reform, arguing that it was not as thoroughgoing and disruptive as previously believed.

Gugliotta, B. "A First Lady's Courageous Voyage." *Americas* 44, no. 2 (March, 1992). Examination of the life of Juárez and his wife, Margarita. Discusses inequalities in Mexico in the areas of education and government, Juárez's commitment to social change and his years in exile in El Paso and New Orleans.

Hanna, Alfred J., and Kathryn A. Hanna. *Napoleon III and Mexico: American Triumph over Monarchy.* Chapel Hill: University of North Carolina Press, 1971. A fascinating account of the role of the United States in dislodging the French from Mexico. Utilizing Seward's diplomatic correspondence and other North American sources, the authors also investigate the moral and material help the American government gave Juárez against Maximilian and the French.

Isais, Juan M. "Mexico." *Christianity Today* 42, no. 13 (November 16, 1998). Discusses the restrictions placed on religion and Bible study in Mexico by Juárez in response to the Catholic Church's power.

Meyer, Michael C., and William L. Sherman. *The Course of Mexican History.* 6th ed. New York: Oxford University Press, 1999. The best single-volume text on Mexican history. The material on Juárez is concise, thorough, and up-to-date.

Perry, Laurens B. *Juárez and Díaz: Machine Politics in Mexico.* DeKalb: Northern Illinois University Press, 1978. The only critical account of Juárez's arbitrary rule during his third term. Perry treats not only Juárez's administration but also the succeeding presidencies of Lerdo and Díaz.

Roeder, Ralph. *Juárez and His Mexico.* 2 vols. New York: Viking Press, 1947. A biography in English of Juárez, this massive, dated work details in narrative fashion his life and work.

Allen Wells